THE NEW
OXFORD COMPANION TO
MUSIC

The New Oxford Companion to Music

General Editor
DENIS ARNOLD

VOLUME 2 · K–Z

Oxford   New York
OXFORD UNIVERSITY PRESS

Oxford University Press, Walton Street, Oxford OX2 6DP
London New York Toronto
Delhi Bombay Calcutta Madras Karachi
Kuala Lumpur Singapore Hong Kong Tokyo
Nairobi Dar es Salaam Cape Town
Melbourne Auckland
and associated companies in
Beirut Berlin Ibadan Mexico City Nicosia

Oxford is a trademark of Oxford University Press

© *Oxford University Press 1983*

Reprinted (twice) 1984

British Library Cataloguing in Publication Data
The New Oxford companion to music.
1. Music—Dictionaries
I. Arnold, Denis
780'.3'21 ML100
ISBN 0–19–311316–3

Printed in Great Britain by Thomson Litho Ltd,
East Kilbride, Scotland

ABBREVIATIONS AND SYMBOLS

Standard abbreviations are used for American states, English counties, months of the year, degrees, honours, and so on. The following abbreviations and symbols are also used:

Amer.	American	rev.	revised
b	born	Russ.	Russian
bapt.	baptized	S., St	Saint
bar.	baritone	sop.	soprano
c.	*circa* (about)	Sp.	Spanish
con.	contralto	ten.	tenor
Cz.	Czech	*	cross-reference to another article, in which the reader will find more information on the subject under discussion
d	died		
ed.	edited		
edn	edition		
Eng.	English	[ ]	in certain long entries, material enclosed by square brackets has been added editorially at the request of the author
fl.	*floruit* (flourished)		
Fr.	French		
Gk	Greek		
Ger.	German	Pitch	for indication of the pitch of a note, the following system has been adopted:
Hind.	Hindi		
It.	Italian		
Lat.	Latin		*c′* = Middle C
MS	manuscript		*c″*, *c‴*, etc. = the octaves above Middle C
nr	near		
Pol.	Polish		*c*, C, C′, etc. = the octaves below Middle C
Port.	Portuguese		

K

K. See *Kirkpatrick*; *Köchel*.

Kabalevsky, Dmitry (Borisovich) (*b* St Petersburg, 30 Dec. 1904). Soviet composer. In his youth he was destined for a career in mathematics and economics, but a flair for the arts in general encouraged him to devote himself to learning the piano. He also studied composition with Catoire and Myaskovsky at the Moscow Conservatory (1925–9), and from around this time began to produce his earliest important works, including his First Piano Concerto (1928), his First String Quartet (1928), his Three Blok Poems (1927), and his First Piano Sonatina (1930): this last was to herald an important facet of Kabalevsky's future writing, his music for young people, which included much piano music and a series of concertos for violin (1948), cello (1948–9), and piano (his Third Piano Concerto, 1952). He also became active as a writer on music from 1927 (a collection of his articles was published in Moscow in 1963), and was a key figure in the Union of Soviet Composers, established in 1932. During the 1930s he wrote his Second Piano Concerto (1936)—perhaps the most striking and invigorating of the three—and began to launch into writing for the theatre, both incidental music and opera. His first opera was the three-act *Colas Breugnon* (1938), in which his gifts for lyrical melody, transparent orchestration, and vivid choral writing combined to make an effective stage piece, though it attracted criticism (primarily on account of certain aspects of the libretto) and Kabalevsky revised the score for its revival in 1971. A poor libretto dogged his next opera, *V ogne* ('Into the Fire', 1942), and Kabalevsky eventually withdrew it, incorporating some of the music into *Sem'ya Tarasa* ('The Family of Taras', 1947, rev. 1950 and 1967). He composed one other opera, *Nikita Vershinin* (1955), and two lightweight operettas, *Vesna poyot* ('Spring Sings', 1957) and *Syostry* ('Sisters', 1967). In his later years Kabalevsky has devoted much attention to choral works and solo songs, though he has continued to contribute to the instrumental repertory such works as the deeply felt, but tough and cogent Cello Sonata (1962).

GEOFFREY NORRIS

Kabuki. A popular Japanese theatrical entertainment. See *Japanese Music*, 6.

Kadenz (Ger.). 1. 'Cadence'. 2. 'Cadenza'.

Kagel, Mauricio (Raúl) (*b* Buenos Aires, 24 Dec. 1931). Argentinian composer. He studied literature and philosophy at the University of Buenos Aires (1950–5) and took private music lessons. In 1955 he began organizing concerts at the university while working as a choral coach and conducting at the Teatro Colón. His works from this period, such as the String Sextet (1953, rev. 1957), show an awareness of advanced serial techniques and a willingness to experiment with electronics, as in his *Música para la torre* ('Tower Music', 1952). He was, therefore, equipped to join the international avant-garde when he moved to Cologne in 1957. However, he quickly showed a taste for the bizarre or absurd which distanced him from such colleagues as Stockhausen. Though he explored new sounds and new formal procedures in, for example, *Transición II* for pianist, percussionist, and tapes (1958–9) and *Sur scène* for speaker, mime, singer, and three instrumentalists (1958–60), he was also attracted by the theatrical potential of unusual performance situations. This he has exploited in many subsequent works for the concert hall, opera house, cinema, and radio. Often the intention is to question commonly accepted musical conventions, such as those of the repertory opera company in *Staatstheater* (1967–70). Kagel has appeared widely as a performer (with his own Cologne New Music Ensemble since 1961), lecturer, and teacher; in 1974 he was appointed

Mauricio Kagel

professor of music theatre at the Cologne Musikhochschule.   PAUL GRIFFITHS

FURTHER READING
Dieter Schnebel: *Das musikalische Theater des Mauricio Kagels* (Cologne, 1978).

Kagura-bue. The largest transverse flute of Japanese art music. See *Japanese Music*, 3*c*.

Kaisermarsch ('Emperor March'). Work by Wagner for unison male voices and orchestra, composed in 1871 to celebrate the German victory in the Franco-Prussian War (1870) and the election of Wilhelm I as German emperor.

Kaiserquartett. See *'Emperor' Quartet*.

Kaiser-Walzer ('Emperor Waltz'). Waltz, Op. 437, by Johann Strauss II, composed in 1888 in honour of Emperor Franz Josef. Schoenberg arranged it for chamber ensemble (1925).

Kakadu Variations. Beethoven's Variations for piano trio, Op. 121*a*, probably composed in 1803 and revised in 1816. The theme is Wenzel Müller's song 'Ich bin der Schneider Kakadu' from the musical play *Die Schwestern von Prag* ('The Sisters from Prague') (1794). *Kakadu* is German for 'cockatoo'.

Kalevala (from *Kaleva*: 'Finland'). Finnish epic songs from the Kalevala region of Finland, transmitted orally for several centuries. In 1835 Elias Lönnrot published an edition of 12,000 verses, and in 1949 a second edition of 23,000 verses in trochaic verse, unrhymed, divided into 50 cantos or runes. This has been translated into Swedish, German, English, and French. Several of Sibelius's works draw on the *Kalevala*, including *Kullervo*, *Pohjola's Daughter*, and *The Swan of Tuonela*.

Kalinnikov, Vasily (Sergeyevich) (*b* Voina, Oryol district, 13 Jan. 1866; *d* Yalta, 11 Jan. 1901). Russian composer. He came from a poor family, and in his youth his extreme poverty possibly sowed the seeds of the consumption which brought about his premature death. He studied music in Moscow, and in 1893 was appointed conductor of the Italian Opera. However, he had to resign on grounds of ill health, and he spent the rest of his short life in the warmer climate of the Crimea. Here he devoted himself to composition, making his name especially with his effective First Symphony (1894–5). He also composed a Second Symphony (1895–7), some stage music, chamber works, piano pieces, and songs. In his final years he was sustained by the generosity of friends—especially the critic Semyon Kruglikov (1851–1910)—and in 1900

Rakhmaninov, who had visited Kalinnikov in Yalta, persuaded Jurgenson to publish some of Kalinnikov's works, including the First Symphony.
   PERCY SCHOLES, rev. Geoffrey Norris

Kalkbrenner, Frédéric [Friedrich Wilhelm Michael] (*b* between Kassel and Berlin, Nov. 1785; *d* Enghien-les-Bains, nr Paris, 10 June 1849). French composer born in Germany. The son of a minor composer, he studied piano and composition in Paris before settling from 1814 to 1828 in London, where he was a fashionable teacher and performer. In 1824 he joined the piano firm of Pleyel in Paris. He was generally considered the finest pianist of his generation. He composed a great deal of music, mainly virtuoso pieces for the piano (including a sonata for the left hand), and invented an arm rest as an aid to avoid using arm action while developing an independent finger technique.
   DENIS ARNOLD

Kalliwoda, Johann Wenzel (*b* Prague, 21 Feb. 1801; *d* Karlsruhe, 3 Dec. 1866). Bohemian composer and violinist. He studied at the Prague Conservatory and then joined the orchestra of the Stavovské Theatre, where Weber was conductor. In 1821 he undertook a concert tour of Germany, Switzerland, and Holland, and in the following year became conductor to the Prince of Fürstenburg at Donaueschingen, remaining there for the rest of his life. Kalliwoda was a prolific composer: he wrote over 300 works, including seven symphonies, numerous concertos for various instruments including violin, oboe, and bassoon, a *Fantaisie sur les chants bohémiens* for violin and orchestra, and an opera *Blanda, oder Die silberne Birke*. His Three Duos for Violin, Op. 181, published in Paris, were very popular in their day. Kalliwoda's son Wilhelm (*b* Donaueschingen, 19 July 1827; *d* Karlsruhe, 8 Sept. 1893) was a pianist, conductor, and composer active at Karlsruhe from 1853.
   WENDY THOMPSON

Kálmán, Emmerich [Imre] (*b* Siófok, 24 Oct. 1882; *d* Paris, 30 Oct. 1953). Hungarian composer. He studied at the Budapest Academy of Music and had his symphonic scherzo *Saturnalia* (1904) performed by the Budapest Philharmonic Orchestra when he was only 22. His interests gradually centred on the theatre: in 1906 he wrote a musical comedy *Das Erbe von Pereszlény* and had his first real success with *Tatárjárás*, 1908, given as *Ein Herbstmanöver* in Vienna (1909) and later produced in New York and London. He became one of the leading figures in the golden age of Viennese operetta in the early 20th century, retaining in most of his

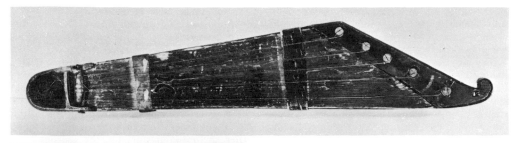

Kantele player in eastern Finland (1917); (above) the old five-string form of the instrument.

works—notably *Zigeunerprimas* (1912), *Die Csárdásfürstin* (the famous 'Gypsy Princess', 1915), and *Die Zirkusprinzessin* (1926)—a strongly Hungarian flavour that has contributed to their popularity. Kálmán was also active as a conductor in the 1930s, moved to Paris at the outbreak of the Second World War, and then settled in the USA, becoming an American citizen in 1942.   PETER GAMMOND

Kalmus, Alfred (August Uhlrich). See *Universal Edition.*

Kammer (Ger.). 'Chamber'; *Kammerduett,* 'chamber duet (i.e. for a room rather than a concert hall); *Kammerkantate,* 'chamber cantata'; *Kammerkonzert,* 'chamber concert' or 'chamber concerto'; *Kammermusik,* 'chamber music'; *Kammersymphonie,* 'chamber symphony' (for a small orchestra); *Kammerton,* 'chamber pitch' (see *Pitch,* 2).

Kammermusik ('Chamber Music'). Title

given by Hindemith to seven instrumental works composed between 1922 and 1927. No. 1 (1922) is for small orchestra, No. 2 (1924) is a piano concerto, No. 3 (1925) is a cello concerto, No. 4 (1925) is a violin concerto, No. 5 (1927) is a viola concerto, No. 6 (1927) is a viola d'amore concerto, and No. 7 (1927) is an organ concerto.

Kampuchea. See *South-East Asian Music.*

Kangen. Japanese orchestral music of the court. See *Japanese Music,* 5.

Kant (Russ., from Lat., *cantus*). Vocal composition, popular in Russia from the mid 17th century to around the mid 18th century. It originated in Poland and the Ukraine, and was introduced into Russia by the composer Vasily Titov (*c*.1650–*c*.1715). At first, Russian *kanty* were settings of religious texts, but later they tackled secular themes as well: during the 18th century the *kant* was the accepted vehicle for celebrating military victories, the accession or coronation of a tsar, and other important events. The genre is characterized by its simple three-part homophonic texture: generally the two upper voices move in thirds, while the third part provides a bass.   GEOFFREY NORRIS

Kant, Immanuel. See *Aesthetics of Music,* 3.

Kantele (? from Gk *kanōn,* a 'straight rod'). A traditional stringed instrument of Finland, also of the Baltic peoples of the USSR (named *kannel* etc.) and of neighbouring parts of Russia, here called 'wing' or 'bell' *gusli.* It has a wing-shaped soundbox 20″–28″ long, in old instruments hollowed out in pine from the back which remains open; modern designs, however, have built-up soundboxes. The kantele is played on the lap, with the long side furthest away and the tuning-pins to the left. From these the strings (now metal) converge fanwise to a transverse bar on the right. They number from five in old types to 14 to 30 in designs of the 20th century, mostly tuned diatonically.

The strings are today plucked and damped with the fingers individually. But the instrument was evolved for a quite different traditional technique. The right hand, with plectrum or finger-nails, strums to and fro, in long or short movements, across the strings where they lie close together (towards the right). The left-hand fingers and thumb lie over the strings where they are further apart (towards the left), ready to press upon and keep silent any strings not required by the melody at that instant; this allows a plectrum to be swept across all the strings giving a strong, resounding sound without accidentally playing an unwanted string which lies between two others. Players are very deft with this damping technique (compare *Lyre*), performing fast dance tunes and often harmonizing the melody in thirds.

The kantele has a place in the Finnish *Kalevala* saga corresponding to that of the 'harp' (i.e. lyre) in *Beowulf*. Various early forms of it have been found in Medieval sites in Poland and Russia (Novgorod), and something like it seems to have been known in the Byzantine empire to judge by a picture in an 11th-century manuscript.   ANTHONY BAINES

Kantional (Ger.). See *Cantional*.

Kantor [*Cantor*] (Ger.). The director of music at a German Protestant church and usually also of any choir school or similar institution attached to such a church. Bach, for example, was *Kantor* of the church and school of St Thomas's, Leipzig.

See also *Cantor*.

Kantorei [*Cantorei*] (Ger.). In the 15th and 16th centuries, a group of professional singers employed by a church or at a court.

Kapelle, Kapellmeister (Ger.). See *Chapel*.

Karelia. Overture and suite for orchestra, Opp. 10 and 11, by Sibelius, composed in 1893. Karelia is a province in southern Finland.

Karg-Elert, Sigfrid (*b* Oberndorf am Neckar, 21 Nov. 1877; *d* Leipzig, 9 Apr. 1933). German composer and organist. He studied at the Leipzig Conservatory under Reinecke and Jadassohn, and taught there from 1919. His creative output was enormous, but he is remembered only for his organ works, which themselves constitute a considerable body. Unusually among German composers of his time he was influenced by Debussyan harmony, and his organ pieces range from chorale improvisations to romantic impressions.   PAUL GRIFFITHS

Kassation (Ger.). See *Cassation*.

Kát'a Kabanová. Opera in three acts by Janáček; text by the composer, after Ostrovsky's drama *The Storm* (1859). Produced: Brno,

23 November 1921; London, Sadler's Wells, 10 April 1951; Cleveland, Ohio, 26 November 1957 (piano accompaniment only). Kát'a (sop.) is married to Tichon (ten.), whose mother Kabanicha (con.) hates her. She loves Boris (ten.), in spite of attempts to remain loyal to her husband, and meets him secretly outside her garden while her friend Varvara (sop.) meets the teacher Kudrjaš (ten.). During the storm, Kát'a confesses her guilt to her family and other sheltering passers-by; she escapes from Tichon's arms, and saying good-bye to Boris, throws herself into the Volga.

FURTHER READING
John Tyrrell, ed.: *Kát'a Kabanová*, Cambridge Opera Handbooks (Cambridge, 1981).

Katerina Izmaylova. See *Lady Macbeth of the Mtsensk District, The*.

Katuar, Georgy. See *Catoire, Georgy*.

Katzenmusik (Ger.). See *Charivari*.

Kazachok. A Cossack dance in quick duple time, often in the minor key. The speed increases as the dance progresses. Dargomïzhsky wrote a celebrated orchestral example, based on folk-tunes.

Kazoo. A popular instrument for changing the sound of the voice into something nasal and instrument-like: a version of the traditional comb-and-paper. It is normally a cigar-shaped metal tube with a paper or plastic membrane over a hole in one side, held in place by a screw-on metal cap. One hums strongly into the wider end, during which the hand can be flapped over the cup for warbling effects. Other names include 'zazah', 'zobo-flute', 'vocophone'. Corresponding instruments were formerly made with wood or cardboard tubes, or, in the 17th century, of metal with an onion-skin or bladder membrane (Fr.: *flûte eunuque*). Ethnologists often group such voice-disguisers under the French word *mirliton* and classify them under membranophones. The 'Danse des mirlitons' in Tchaikovsky's *The Nutcracker*, however, refers to panpipes.   ANTHONY BAINES

Kb. Abbreviation for *Kontrabass* (Ger.), 'double bass'.

Keel Row. English north-country folk-song. It originated in the Tyneside district, although it was first published in *A Collection of Favourite Scots Tunes* (Edinburgh, 1770). 'Keel' means a boat in the Newcastle dialogue, and the song refers to a girl's concern for her sailor sweet-heart, away on the sea. The tune resembles several English country dances, including one published in a collection of 1748. Its essentially melancholy nature appealed to Debussy, who used it as a basis for his *Gigues*, the first movement of his orchestral *Images* (1909-12).

Keen. See *Caoine*.

Keiser, Reinhard (*bapt.* Teuchern, nr Weissenfels, 12 Jan. 1674; *d* Hamburg, 12 Sept. 1739). German composer. He was the son of an organist and studied at St Thomas's, Leipzig, before becoming a musician at the Brunswick court. At least three of his operas were performed in Brunswick, and *c*.1696 his appointment as *Kapellmeister* in Hamburg gave him further opportunities to have his operas performed, at the famous Goosemarket Theatre. He became director, with Drüsicke, of the theatre in 1702, and between then and 1707 produced operas by Handel and Mattheson among others, as well as at least 17 of his own. In 1707 he had to give up the lease because of financial problems, but he continued to contribute to the repertory and by 1718 had composed 25 new operas. Between 1718 and *c*.1723 Keiser travelled abroad, taking appointments, briefly, at Stuttgart and Copenhagen, but returning twice to Hamburg for productions of his works. On his third return he decided to remain, and produced his last operas there before becoming *Kantor* at the cathedral (succeeding Mattheson) in 1728. Thereafter he seems to have concentrated almost exclusively on church music.

Keiser's popularity as an opera composer (he was much admired by his contemporaries, including the critic Scheibe and the composer Hasse) owed much to his sense of theatrical effect. He often expressed the characters most aptly, being a master of accompanied recitative. He also had a flair for Italian-style arias, allowing the singers to display their virtuosity. In his lifetime his most popular opera was probably *Störtebecker und Jödge Michaels* (Hamburg, 1701), but nowadays his music is rarely performed.   DENIS ARNOLD

Kellner, Johann Peter (*b* Gräfenroda, nr Weimar, 28 Sept. 1705; *d* Gräfenroda, 19 Apr. 1772). German organist who spent most of his life as *Kantor* in his birthplace. He met both Bach and Handel, and his music reflects their influence, especially Bach's. His son, **Johann Christoph Kellner** (*b* Gräfenroda, 15 Aug. 1736; *d* Kassel, 1803), a pupil of Benda, was organist and *Kantor* at Kassel.   DENIS ARNOLD

Kelly, Bryan (George) (*b* Oxford, 3 Jan. 1934). English composer. He studied with Herbert Howells and Gordon Jacob at the Royal College of Music (1951-5) and with Nadia Boulanger in Paris. In 1962 he was appointed professor of

theory and composition at the RCM. A versatile composer with traditional leanings, he has produced numerous educational and liturgical works—notably a Stabat Mater (1970)—as well as orchestral and chamber pieces of a light character.   PAUL GRIFFITHS

Kelly, Frederick Septimus (*b* Sydney, 29 May 1881; *d* Beaucourt-sur-Ancre, 13 Nov. 1916). Australian pianist and composer. He was educated at Eton and at Balliol College, Oxford. He then went to Germany to study piano, and returned to London in 1908 as a concert promoter. On the outbreak of the First World War he enlisted in the Navy, became a Lieutenant-Commander, and was killed in France at the age of 35. He left an Elegy for small orchestra written in 1915 in memory of his friend, the poet Rupert Brooke (1887-1915), a Serenade for flute and small orchestra, a Violin Sonata, and some piano pieces and several songs.   WENDY THOMPSON

Kelly, Michael (*b* Dublin, 25 Dec. 1762; *d* Margate, 9 Oct. 1826). Irish tenor, actor, and composer. He studied piano with Michael Arne and singing with several eminent Italian masters. In 1779 he went to Naples to further his studies, and from there went on to Vienna, where he stayed for four years, becoming a close friend of Mozart, and appearing in *Figaro* as Don Basilio and Don Curzio. On his return to England in 1787 he became principal tenor at Drury Lane Theatre until he retired from the stage in 1811. In 1793 he became stage manager of the King's Theatre, and from 1801 until he went bankrupt 10 years later he ran a music shop in Pall Mall and was involved in the wine trade.

Kelly wrote the music for 61 dramatic pieces, including *Blue Beard* (1798), *Cinderella* (1804), *The Forty Thieves* (1806), and *The Lady and the Devil* (1820). Sheridan, suspecting that some of Kelly's compositions borrowed material from foreign sources, suggested that the music shop should carry the inscription: 'Michael Kelly, Composer of Wines and Importer of Music'. Kelly's entertaining book of *Reminiscences* was published in 1826.   WENDY THOMPSON

Kennedy-Fraser, Marjorie (*b* Perth, 1 Oct. 1857; *d* Edinburgh, 22 Nov. 1930). Scottish folk-song collector and singer. She studied with her father, the singer David Kennedy, and in Paris. For many years she toured widely, giving lecture-recitals on various kinds of singing; she also made valuable collections of Hebridean folk-songs. Her autobiography is published as *A Life of Song* (London, 1929).   PAUL GRIFFITHS

Kerle, Jacobus de (*b* Ieper, 1531 or 1532;

d Prague, 7 Jan. 1591). South Netherlands composer. He was one of the leading composers of the Counter-Reformation. During his career he worked at Orvieto, Rome, Dillingen, Augsburg, and, from 1583 until his death, at the Imperial Court at Prague. His output, which includes masses, motets, and a cycle of hymns for the Church's year, conforms to the requirements of the Council of Trent in its economy, restraint, and emphasis upon the correct declamation of the text.   JOHN MILSOM

Kerll, Johann Kaspar (*b* Adorf, Saxony, 9 Apr. 1627; *d* Munich, 13 Feb. 1693). German organist and composer. His first employer, Archduke Leopold William at Vienna, sent him to Rome to study with Carissimi. In 1656 he was appointed *Kapellmeister* at the Bavarian court in Munich, and there he wrote a number of operas (including *L'Oronte* for the opening of the opera house) and ballets, apparently with some success. In 1673 he gave up his job, probably because of the current vogue for Italian musicians, and moved to Vienna, becoming court organist at St Stephen's Cathedral in 1674 and at the imperial court in 1677. His works include Masses (including the splendid *Missa a 3 chori*) and keyboard pieces, but his dramatic works are now lost. Handel appears to have thought enough of Kerll's music to 'borrow' from it; for example, the choruses 'Egypt was glad' from *Israel in Egypt* and 'Let all the angels' from *Messiah* both found their origins in keyboard canzonas by Kerll.   DENIS ARNOLD

Kern, Jerome (David) (*b* New York, 27 Jan. 1885; *d* New York, 11 Nov. 1945). American composer. After studying at the New York College of Music he entered the music business as a song-plugger in New York. He was sent by Charles Frohman to London, where he was employed in adding numbers to London shows to make them more suitable for eventual New York productions: his 'How'd you like to spoon with me', for example, was added to the show *The Earl and the Girl* in 1905. While in England he married a girl from Walton-on-Thames, in 1910.

Kern's first complete theatre score was *The Red Petticoat* (1911). By 1915 he had found an ideal partner in Guy Bolton, and two years later P. G. Wodehouse joined the team to produce a series of sophisticated new musical comedies that retained some of the lyrical qualities of the older operetta world but which also absorbed elements from ragtime and jazz. Kern was a pioneer in developing an entirely American idiom and launching the age of American dominance in the musical theatre, and as such was admired and followed by composers like George Gershwin and Richard Rodgers. His first big success was *Sally* (1920), but his classic came in 1927 when he joined forces with Oscar Hammerstein II to produce *Show Boat*. During the 1930s he wrote music for such shows as *Music in the Air* (1932) and *Roberta* (1933), which are remembered today for their excellent songs, like 'Smoke gets in your eyes' from *Roberta*. He found another creative outlet in Hollywood films, adding some fine songs to such musical productions as *Swing Time* (1936), *High, Wide, and Handsome* (1937), *Lady Be Good* (1941), *You Were Never Lovelier* (1942), and *Cover Girl* (1944). He was also commissioned to write the score for *Annie Get Your Gun*, but he died before he could begin work.   PETER GAMMOND

Ketèlbey, Albert W(illiam) [Vodorinski, Anton] (*b* Birmingham, 9 Aug. 1875; *d* Cowes, 26 Nov. 1959). English composer. He showed musical promise at an early age and at 11 composed a piano sonata which was performed at Worcester and earned the praise of Elgar. He won a scholarship to study composition at Trinity College, London, and at 16 was the organist of a church in Wimbledon. His proficiency on the piano, cello, clarinet, oboe, and horn helped to develop his career as composer and conductor, and at 22 he was musical director of the Vaudeville Theatre, and later of the Columbia Gramophone Company. His tuneful, sentimental compositions—like *In a Monastery Garden* (1915), *In a Persian Market* (1920), and *Sanctuary of the Heart* (1924)—were so successful that he was able to retire to the Isle of Wight in early middle age and concentrate entirely on composition. Some of his piano works were published under the pseudonym Anton Vodorinski.   PETER GAMMOND

Key. As a principle in musical composition, the adherence in any passsage to the material of one of the major or minor scales (see *Scale*, 3). This need not be a rigid adherence (since other notes may appear incidentally, without altering the sense of key), but a general one, with a recognition of the keynote of the scale in question as a principal, governing factor in its effect.

See also *Key signature*; *Harmony*; *Modulation*; *Tonality*.

Keyboard fingering. C. P. E. Bach was among the first teachers to examine the relationship between the shape of the hand and the disposition of the keyboard, and to treat this as the basis for a systematic approach to fingering. Wherever possible, he believed that the black keys should be played only by the three longest fingers, and that the thumb and little finger should be restricted to the white keys. Developing precepts suggested to him by his father, J. S. Bach, he defined the thumb as the 'principal' digit and as 'the key to all fingering'. In this way, he established the trend which ultimately led to the scale fingerings taught in present-day Tutors and easily consulted in scale-books for the piano. Under this system, a normal octave scale is divided into two groups, one of three notes, the other of four, representing two distinct hand positions. The main hurdle for the beginner is to connect these as imperceptibly as possible, to this end learning to pass the thumb under the long fingers, or the fingers over the thumb. In scales with sharps or flats, the change of hand position is made most comfortably where a long and short key occur contiguously (Ex. 1).

Ex. 1

The little finger is generally reserved for the highest note in the right hand or the lowest in the left, and the passing of the thumb under the little finger or the little finger over the thumb is avoided.

To a present-day performer, fingerings of this kind appear so natural and so well accommodated to the shape of the hand that it is difficult to imagine any other viable system. And indeed, if we bear in mind that the present arrangement of the keyboard with its keys on two levels had already come into existence by the beginning of the 15th century, we might well be forgiven for assuming that performers have always approached the art of keyboard fingering in the same way. On the contrary, however, for over two centuries after the appearance of the earliest extant teaching manual—Buchner's *Fundamentbuch* of *c*.1520 players employed a method of scale-fingering that differed radically from that of our own time.

It is important to observe that teachers throughout the ages have stressed the need for ease and comfort regardless of the fingering-system employed, an essential corollary of this being a relaxed hand position. As early as 1593, the Italian teacher, Girolamo Diruta, warned players against striking the keys; in all circumstances, the fingers were to be held close to the keyboard and the notes depressed in a gentle but controlled manner. According to Forkel, the small and light movements of J. S. Bach's fingers were scarcely noticeable, and his hands retained their neatly rounded shape 'even in the

most difficult passages'. Dussek, one of the leading early exponents of the English school of piano-playing, stated that the hands should rest gently on the surface of the keys and that the choice of fingering should never displace this quiet posture. All unnecessary movements of the hands, elbows, and arms were to be carefully avoided.

1. *Early Methods.* The major sources of the 16th and 17th centuries consistently recommend that extended scale passages should be played by pairs of fingers, for example by passing the third finger over the fourth when ascending with the right hand, or the third over the second when ascending with the left. This method was facilitated by the fact that early keyboards had a shallower touch and that the black keys reached further to the front than on modern instruments. When passing the third finger of the right hand over the fourth, Santa Maria (*Arte de tañer fantasia*, 1565) recommended that the former should be held rather higher, and that the latter should slide inwards towards the palm of the hand.

The choice of fingers for these paired groups was not arbitrary. Early keyboard fingerings were closely governed by musical accentuation, and many teachers required that 'good' (i.e. strong) fingers should be placed on 'good' (i.e. accented) beats. There were two independent schools of fingering: in the Italian tradition, represented by Diruta, the second and fourth were regarded as the strong fingers (Ex. 2a); whereas the fingerings included in the works of the English virginalists treat the third as the strong finger (Ex. 2b).

Ex. 2

(*a*)
Extract from Diruta: *Il transilvano*

[Good Bad G B G B G B G]

(*b*)
Extract from Bull: Prelude

[G B G B G B G B G]

The second mode of fingering reappears in a number of significant sources, notably in the prefatory instructions to Purcell's *Choice Collection of Lessons* (London, 1696) and in J. S. Bach's 'Applicatio' from the *Clavierbüchlein vor Wilhelm Friedemann Bach* (1720). Even in the second half of the 18th century, for the scales which contain an extended sequence of white keys, C. P. E. Bach put forward a number of alternative fingerings in which he often gives the paired method as the most practical. As late as 1782, Merbach, in his *Klavierschule für Kinder*, devised a special exercise introducing the beginner to the earlier technique (Ex. 3).

Ex. 3

Merbach

Today, such fingerings may appear unnecessarily complex, but they evidently caused little difficulty at the time. Türk, in his famous *Klavierschule* of 1789, recalled that W. F. Bach could play the most complicated figurations smoothly and with astounding speed merely by using the three middle fingers.

2. *The Evolution of Modern Scale Fingerings.* It would be wrong to assume that earlier musicians had neglected the thumbs completely. In 1565 in Spain, Santa Maria recommended their use for fast scalic passages (Ex. 4a), and the fingerings in many anthologies of English virginal music show frequent use of all five fingers (Ex. 4b).

Ex. 4

(a)

Santa Maria

(b)

John Bull, Prelude

But the real turning-point came with the vast expansion of the tonal system. As composers began writing pieces in more remote keys, patterns of fingering had to be reconceived to deal with them. C. P. E. Bach declared that it was his father who first devised a systematic approach to fingering which exploited the potential of the thumbs.

The so-called difficult keys at first brought wide divergences in fingering. Ex. 5, from François Couperin's *L'art de toucher le clavecin* of 1716, makes little attempt to secure a smooth connection of the two hand positions: the passing of the second finger over the fourth produces an inevitable jerk. C. P. E. Bach's suggestions are more sophisticated, but even he found himself in something of a dilemma.

Ex. 5

He worked from the basic principle that the left-hand thumb should always occur before a black key in an ascending scale, and for this reason considered his first, rather fussy, method to be more useful than his second, which has since become the norm.

Bach's influence was considerable. Even in England in the 1760s, a treatise by J. C. Heck purported to teach 'the rules and method of the celebrated Bach of Berlin'. In due course, however, the irregularities of his system were realized, and when J. C. F. Rellstab, a noted German publisher and composer, prepared a new and curtailed version of Bach's instructions in 1790, he corrected some of the most prominent weaknesses and dismissed Bach's unnatural fingerings in favour of our present methods. All the same, we know, for example, from Carl Czerny (who began his lessons with Beethoven in 1801) that even Beethoven's teaching-methods adhered closely to the format set out in Bach's *Versuch*. The following summary represents the most important aspects of his system.

1. When working out his fingering, the performer should always think ahead.
2. Save in certain chordal and octave passages, the thumbs should generally be avoided on the black keys.
3. The appropriate extension of the hand in broken chord figurations depends on the implied chord structure.
4. When playing two or more parts with one hand, the same finger may be used on adjacent notes (Ex. 6a).
5. To avoid an awkward hand position, it is sometimes necessary to omit one or more fingers in a scale passage (Ex. 6b).
6. To preserve a *legato* effect, fingers may sometimes be changed silently on a note (Ex. 6c).
7. A finger may slide from a black to a white key without impairing the smoothness of the passage (Ex. 6d).

Ex. 6

Extracts from C. P. E. Bach

8. Repeated notes generally presuppose a change of finger (Ex. 6e).

Since the middle of the 19th century, pianists have adopted a more flexible attitude towards the second of Bach's principles. In 1839, Henri Herz, the French virtuoso pianist, observed that it was no longer necessary to 'avoid placing the thumb or little finger on black notes', and in subsequent advanced schools of playing, pianists were encouraged to practise all scales with the conventional C major fingering.

3. *Fingering and Articulation*. One particular aspect of fingering—its relationship to articulation—has become an issue of considerable debate among recent performers and scholars. Should the player opt for the simplest fingering of any given passage, or should he be guided by the composer's articulation indications? On this vital issue, Muzio Clementi, often described as the founder of modern piano-playing, had absolutely no doubt. 'The effect, being of the highest importance', he wrote, 'is first consulted; the way to accomplish it is then devised, and that mode of fingering preferred which gives the best effect tho' not always the easiest to the performer.' This principle certainly appears to have been an essential consideration in earlier keyboard performance, though the extent of its application remains a rather moot point. Many believe, for example, that the paired fingerings of the 16th and 17th centuries imply a detached style and even an element of rhythmic inequality. It would certainly seem most easy to break the continuity at each shift of the hand (Ex. 7), though in this connection, we ought to bear in mind C. P. E. Bach's dictum that paired fingerings were often 'better suited for the attainment of unbroken continuity'.

Ex. 7

Other early fingerings, however, give clearer indication of the required articulation, and

provide valuable insight into performance ideals of the 17th and 18th centuries. (Ex. 8).

Ex. 8

(a)

Extract from Bull: Fantasia

(b)

Extract from Couperin: *L'art de toucher le clavecin*

(c)

Extract from Milchmeyer: *Die wahre Art das Pianoforte zu spielen* (1797)

During the early part of the 19th century, the growing preference for a mainly *legato* style encouraged teachers to place greater emphasis on simplicity of fingering. As a general principle, unnecessary changes of hand position were to be avoided, and, wherever possible, the fingers applied in their natural order. Charles Neate (a distinguished English pianist and friend of Beethoven) complained that it had become common practice among teachers to treat the art of fingering 'as though it were only to be the means of discovering the easiest way of executing notes or passages'. He argued that fingering 'ought to be the power of giving to music its true character and right expression', and for this reason, he (like Clementi) urged pianists to give careful consideration to the prescribed articulation before deciding on a suitable method of fingering.

4. *Fingering Indications*. Since the earliest stages of keyboard playing, various methods have been employed to indicate fingering. One of the most unusual, perhaps, is that found in

Alessandro Scarlatti's *Regole per cembalo*, where five different symbols are used to represent the five fingers. But in the majority of cases, numbers have proved a more viable means, and the only consistent discrepancy has been the numbering of the thumb. In early German sources, the thumb was generally represented by a cross or by the numeral 0, and the four fingers by 1, 2, 3, and 4. This method became common in England during the 18th century, and was subsequently described as the 'English' system, although in the earliest English sources (as also in Santa Maria's treatise of 1565 and the major publications of the French school) the normal procedure was to number the thumb 1 and the fingers 2 to 5. Curiously, in the 18th century, German musicians adopted this system, and more recently it became known as the 'continental' fingering. This method is now employed exclusively by all composers, teachers, and publishers.　　　　W. GLYN JENKINS

FURTHER READING
François Couperin: *L'art de toucher le clavecin* (Paris, 1716–17; modern edn with Fr., Ger., and Eng. texts ed. Anna Linde, Wiesbaden, 1933); C. P. E. Bach: *Versuch über die wahre Art das Clavier zu spielen* (Berlin, 1753–62; trans. into Eng. as *Essay on the True Art of Playing Keyboard Instruments* by William J. Mitchell, New York and London, 1949); Muzio Clementi: *Introduction to the Art of Playing on the Pianoforte* (London, 1801; facsimile reprint New York, 1974); Howard Ferguson: *Keyboard Interpretation from the 14th to the 19th Century* (London, 1975).

Key signature. A group of sharp or flat signs placed at the beginning of a composition (after the clef) or during a composition (normally after a double bar) to indicate the *key of the music that follows. By their positions on the staff the signs show which notes are to be consistently sharpened or flattened throughout, in all octaves, thus establishing the prevailing tonality of the music. Ex. 1 shows the 14 common key signatures, relating to all the available major and minor keys. Each signature indicates one of two keys: the white note represents the major key, the black the minor key with the same signature (the 'relative' minor, its keynote a minor third below the major).

Keynotes for the 'sharp' signatures rise a perfect fifth as each sharp is added, and the major keynote is always a semitone above the last sharp; keynotes for the 'flat' signatures fall a perfect fifth as each flat is added, and the major keynote is always a perfect fourth below the last flat (i.e. the same pitch as the penultimate flat). The order of sharps in the signature is also by rising fifths, the order of flats by falling fifths and equivalent to the order of sharps reversed.

Keys with six sharps (F♯ major and D♯ minor) are the *enharmonic equivalents of keys with six flats (G♭ major and E♭ minor); keys with seven sharps (C♯ major and A♯ minor) are the enharmonic equivalents of keys with five flats (D♭ major and B♭ minor). Composers use either signature according to convenience and familiarity, but 'key colour' may also play a part in their choice: for example, sharp keys are thought to suggest bright colours, flat keys sober ones (see *Colour and Music*).

Although the use of one flat as a key signature is found in the earliest staff notation (11th–12th centuries), the association of a prefatory signature with a particular tonality came only in the 18th century. The modal principles of Medieval music often resulted in 'partial' signatures, where different voice parts had different signatures, the lower ones often with one more flat than the upper ones. Sharps in signatures did not become common until the 17th century. Throughout the Renaissance and Baroque periods a wider range of keys was used than signatures suggest: pieces in minor keys were often written with one less flat and in major keys with one less sharp in the signature than is normal today, the 'missing' accidentals appearing regularly in the course of a piece where modern notation would include them in the key signature.

In the late 19th and 20th centuries chromaticism and atonality have contributed to the demise of the key signature's usefulness. At the same time, some composers have experimented with 'hybrid' signatures, including both sharps and flats, to draw attention to special features of tonality in their music.

See also *Accidental*; *Circle of fifths*; *Musica ficta*; *Notation, 2*; *Tonality*.

　　　　PERCY SCHOLES, rev. Judith Nagley

Khachaturian, Aram (Ilyich) (*b* Tiflis, now Tbilisi, 6 June 1903; *d* Moscow, 1 May 1978). Soviet composer. Although born in Georgia he

Ex. 1

was of Armenian descent. He studied in Moscow, at the Gnesin Institute of Music and then at the conservatory with Myaskovsky. His international reputation rests largely on the Piano Concerto (1936, introduced to England by Moura Lympany in 1940) and on the ballets *Gayane* (1942, from which comes the famous 'Sabre Dance') and *Spartak* ('Spartacus', 1954, revised 1968). But within the Soviet Union he is more widely regarded as one of the chief exponents of 20th-century Armenian 'nationalist' music, usually at his best in dramatic works, whether they be ballets, incidental music, or film scores, of which he wrote about 25, including *Vladimir Ilyich Lenin* (1948) and *Stalingradskaya bitva* ('The Battle of Stalingrad', 1949). These intensely patriotic films were

Khachaturian

made in the wake of the 1948 Zhdanov purges, when Khachaturian attracted criticism for some of his recent work, notably the Third Symphony (1947), written for the 30th anniversary of the October Revolution but marked not so much by musical substance as by spectacular celebratory effects (the symphony calls for a large orchestra, including organ and 15 extra trumpets). Later on, however, he achieved considerable success with a series of concert rhapsodies, for violin (1961–2), cello (1963), and piano (1965), which are characterized by vitality of rhythm, rich orchestration, and intoxicating,

highly spiced, and distinctive melody owing much to the inflections of Armenian folk music.

GEOFFREY NORRIS

FURTHER READING
Grigory Shneyerson: *Aram Khachaturyan* (Moscow, 1959).

Khrennikov, Tikhon (Nikolayevich) (*b* Elets, 10 June 1913). Soviet composer. He studied piano and composition in Moscow, graduating from Shebalin's composition class at the conservatory in 1936. He made his mark as a composer with his spirited First Piano Concerto (1932–3), which owes much to Prokofiev in its energy, rhythmic drive, and broad, lyrical sweep; his Second Piano Concerto (1971) and succinct Cello Concerto (1964) are written in much the same vein, though the music is tougher, more rhetorical in its gestures, and shows a liking for muscular melody and vivid orchestral colours. His orchestral works also include three symphonies and a Violin Concerto (1958–9), but most of his creative work has been done in the theatre. Of his several operas, *V buryu* ('Into the Storm', 1939, revised 1952) and *Mat'* ('Mother', 1957) have earned recognition as examples of 'song' operas in the tradition of *socialist realism, and *Into the Storm* is particularly notable in being the first Russian opera to feature Lenin as a character (though the first opera to assign him an actual singing role was Muradeli's *October* of 1961). Khrennikov has also written incidental music and some film scores, but his name is known especially in connection with his administrative work at the Union of Soviet Composers. In the shake-up of personnel during the 1948 Zhdanov purges Khrennikov emerged as the Union's secretary, and he has remained in this prominent and powerful post, through changing political climates, ever since.

GEOFFREY NORRIS

Kielflügel (Ger.). Harpsichord (from *Kiel*, 'quill', *Flügel*, 'wing'). The term alludes to the plucking mechanism and the over-all wing-shape of the instrument.

Kilpinen, Yrjö (Henrik) (*b* Helsinki, 4 Feb. 1892; *d* Helsinki, 2 May 1959). Finnish composer. He was largely self-taught and his output is predominantly for the voice. He wrote more than 600 songs to Finnish, Swedish, and German poetry. His best-known German settings are of Morgenstern (*Lieder um den Tod*, Op. 62) and possess remarkable concentration and atmosphere. His settings of both Swedish and Finnish poems are highly economical and strongly characterized. He is undoubtedly the greatest song composer that Scandinavia has produced since Grieg, and his style reflects something of his admiration for Hugo Wolf and even Musorgsky. His output also includes six piano sonatas, a cello sonata, and some choruses but no orchestral music. Few composers of the present century, however, succeed in conveying more powerfully both the spirit and the letter of a poem than he does.   ROBERT LAYTON

Kindermann, Johann Erasmus (*b* Nuremberg, 29 Mar. 1616; *d* Nuremberg, 14 Apr. 1655). German organist and composer. In *c*.1635 he was sent by the city council to study in Italy. He returned in 1636 and spent most of his remaining years there, from 1640 as organist at the Egidienkirche. His works include motets, cantatas, and dialogues (some of them showing Italian influence in the use of a continuo part and *concertato* writing), some beautiful chorale settings, and the *Harmonia organica* (1645), a collection of organ music including improvisatory preludes and fugal fantasias on chorale melodies.   DENIS ARNOLD

Kinderscenen ('Scenes from Childhood'). Thirteen pieces for solo piano, Op. 15, by Schumann, composed in 1838. The seventh piece is *Traumerei*.

Kinderstück (Ger.). 'Children's piece'.

Kindertotenlieder ('Songs of the Death of Children'). Song-cycle by Mahler to poems by Rückert. The five songs are for baritone or contralto and orchestra and were composed in 1901–1904.

King, William (*b* Winchester, 1624; *d* Oxford, 17 Nov. 1680). English composer. He was the son of the organist at Winchester Cathedral, George King, and was admitted to Magdalen College, Oxford, in October 1648. He graduated less than a year later, and spent the rest of his life at Oxford, from 1664 as organist of New College. He composed services, anthems, and a volume of *Poems of Mr. Cowley and others, composed into Songs and Ayres* (Oxford, 1668) for solo voice and continuo.   WENDY THOMPSON

King Arthur, or The British Worthy. Semi-opera in a prologue, five acts, and an epilogue by Purcell to a libretto by Dryden. It was first performed in London in 1691.

Kingdom, The. Oratorio, Op. 51, by Elgar to a text compiled by the composer from the Bible. It is for four soloists, chorus, and orchestra and was first performed in Birmingham in 1906. Elgar conceived it as a sequel to *The Apostles*.

'King of Prussia' Quartets. Name given to Mozart's last three string quartets: No. 21 in D major, K 575 (1789), No. 22 in B♭ major, K 589 (1790), and No. 23 in F major, K 590 (1790). They are so called because they were commissioned by Friedrich Wilhelm II of Prussia, himself a cellist (hence the prominent cello parts). He requested six quartets but only three were composed.

King Priam. Opera in three acts by Tippett; text by the composer, after Homer's *Iliad*. Produced: Coventry Cathedral, 29 May 1962; Karlsruhe, 26 January 1963. Priam (bass-bar.), supported by Hecuba (sop.), chooses the death of his baby son Paris, who (it is prophesied by the Old Man (bass)) will cause his father's death. But he is relieved to find, in the next scene, when out hunting, that the boy (sop.) has been spared; he and Hector (bar.) take him to Troy. Here Paris (ten.) and Hector quarrel; Paris fetches Helen (mezzo) from Sparta. In the last scene of the act, Hermes (ten.) arranges the Judgement of Paris; Aphrodite (i.e. Helen) is chosen.

In the war that ensues, Achilles (ten.) is sulking in his tent; the Trojans drive the Greeks back and fire their ships, but are weakened by Hector and Paris quarrelling. Patroclus (bar.) puts on Achilles' armour but is killed by Hector. The Trojans' rejoicing is interrupted by Achilles' war-cry.

The women reflect upon their role in the war. News of Hector's death at the hands of Achilles is brought to Priam. He goes to beg his son's body, and rouses Achilles' pity. He then withdraws into himself, and is killed before the altar by Achilles' son.

King Roger (*Król Roger*). Opera in three acts by Szymanowski to a libretto by J. Iwaszkiewicz and the composer. It was first performed in Warsaw in 1926.

Kinkeldey, Otto (*b* New York, 27 Nov. 1878; *d* Orange, NJ, 19 Sept. 1966). American musical scholar. He studied literature at New York University, then music with MacDowell at Columbia. In 1902 he went to study in Berlin and was for a time professor there, returning to America during the First World War to become at various times music librarian at the New York Public Library and Professor of Musicology (the first in the USA) at Cornell University. His book on 16th-century organ music is a classic (Leipzig, 1910), but his main achievement was to teach a whole generation of American scholars.   DENIS ARNOLD

Kinloch, William (*fl. c*.1600). Scottish composer of keyboard dances and variations. He was associated with the court of Mary Queen of Scots in the late 16th century.   JOHN MILSOM

Kirbye, George (*b* ? *c*.1565; *d* Bury St Edmunds, Oct. 1634). English composer. He spent much of his life in the household of Sir Robert Jermyn of Rushbrooke in Suffolk. His *First set of English madrigalls* (London, 1597) contains attractive works, mainly in a serious vein and with a style that owes much to Marenzio, and he contributed another madrigal, 'With angels face', to *The Triumphes of Oriana*. He was also a major contributor to Thomas East's psalter.

DENIS ARNOLD

Kirchencantate (Ger.). 'Church cantata'; see *Cantata*, 2.

Kirkpatrick. Abbreviation for the standard thematic catalogue of the keyboard sonatas of Domenico Scarlatti drawn up by the American musicologist Ralph Kirkpatrick (*b* 1911). There have been other attempts to catalogue Scarlatti's many sonatas, by Alessandro Longo (Naples, 1906–8) and by Giorgio Pestelli (Turin, 1967), but Kirkpatrick's is the one in common use. The sonatas are often referred to by Kirkpatrick number, usually further abbreviated to 'K' (but see *Köchel*).

Kirnberger, Johann Philipp (*bapt.* Saalfeld, nr Weimar, 24 Apr. 1721; *d* Berlin, 26–7 July 1783). German composer. After studying violin and harpsichord with various local teachers, in 1739 he became for a time a pupil of J. S. Bach. For about 10 years he took various posts at Leipzig and in Poland before joining the orchestra of Frederick the Great as a violinist in 1751. Seven years later he became music director to Princess Anna Amalia of Prussia, in whose service he remained until his death. A composer of little importance, he achieved more distinction as a theorist, his counterpoint method being especially useful. He also wrote a curious little pamphlet called *Methode Sonaten aus'm Ermel zu schüddeln* ('Method for tossing off sonatas', 1783), describing the process of making new sonatas from old.

DENIS ARNOLD

Kiss, The (*Hubička*). Opera in two acts by Smetana to a libretto by E. Krásnohorská after a story by K. Světlá. It was first performed in Prague in 1876.

Kissentanz (Ger.). 'Cushion dance'.

Kit (Fr.: *pochette*). Dancing master's fiddle of the mid 16th to the late 18th century, small and slim enough to fit into a case for carrying about

Dancing master with kit (1745), engraving by Le Bas after P. Canot.

in the tail-pocket of a frock-coat, and now a well-known object in museums. Kits were made in a variety of shapes, most typically like a truncheon, about 17″ long. Some of the prettiest of these are built up from ivory ribs. Others have a body in violin-shape, but are immediately distinguished from a miniature violin through the proportionately very much longer and broader neck. Even with this, the four strings of a kit are only about two-thirds the length of violin strings, and were no doubt tuned correspondingly higher. The bow, too, is normally shorter.

The instrument was primarily French, and it has been suggested that the 'violini piccoli alla francese' that appear briefly in Act 2 of Monteverdi's *Orfeo* may have been *pochettes*, then playing the parts an octave higher than written.

Kl. Abbreviation for *Klarinette* (Ger.), 'clarinet'.

Klagend, kläglich (Ger.). 'Lamenting'.

Klagende Lied, Das ('The Song of Sorrow'). Cantata by Mahler to his own text, for soprano, alto, and tenor soloists, chorus, and orchestra. It was composed in three parts: *Waldmärchen* ('Forest Legend'), *Der Spielmann* ('The Minstrel'), and *Hochzeitstück* ('Wedding Piece'). Mahler revised it (1892–3, 1898–9), omitting *Waldmärchen*.

Klang (Ger.). 'Sound', 'sonority'.

Klangfarbenmelodie (Ger.). 'Sound-colour-melody'. A term introduced by Schoenberg in 1911 for a 'melody' of timbre, in which the instrumentation of a piece is as important as the pitch and rhythm and has its own structural function. Schoenberg himself attempted this in the central movement of his Five Orchestral Pieces (1909), and the idea was taken up by Webern and by many composers after 1950.

Klar (Ger.). 'Clear', 'distinct'.

Klavierbüchlein ('Little Keyboard Book'). Title given by J. S. Bach to three of his collections of keyboard music. The first (1720) was for the instruction of his eldest son, Wilhelm Friedemann Bach; the second (1722–5) was a similar but smaller collection for his second wife, Anna Magdalena; and the third (1725) was a larger collection for his wife. The second and third are often referred to as the 'Anna Magdalena Books'.

Klavierstücke I-XI ('Piano Pieces I-XI'). Eleven piano pieces by Stockhausen. The first set, *Klavierstücke I-IV*, were written in 1952–3;

the second set, *V-X*, were composed in 1954–5, *IX* and *X* being revised in 1961; *Klavierstück XI* dates from 1956. They make considerable demands on the pianist, and the last of them is in 'open form': the performer chooses one of the 19 sections before him and selects his own tempo etc., following it with other permutations.

Klavierübung ('Keyboard Exercises'). J. S. Bach's title, taken from Kuhnau, for four sets of his keyboard works. The first (1731) contains the six partitas; the second (1735) contains the *Italian Concerto* and the Partita in B minor (or French Overture); the third (1739) is a book of organ works, including the 'St Anne' Fugue; and the fourth (1741–2) is the 'Goldberg' Variations.

Kleber, Leonhard (*b* Göppingen, *c*.1495; *d* Pforzheim, 4 Mar. 1556). German organist. He held posts at various churches in Germany, and from 1521 until his death was organist at Pforzheim. His works include some attractive song arrangements and improvisatory preludes for organ.   DENIS ARNOLD

Klein (Ger.). 'Small', or, of intervals, 'minor'.

Kleine Nachtmusik, Eine ('A Little Night Music'). Nocturne by Mozart, K 525, composed in 1787. It is scored for string quartet and double bass and is in four movements, but was originally in five (the first minuet was removed from the manuscript).

Kleine Orgelmesse ('Little Organ Mass'). Haydn's Mass No. 7 in B♭ major, composed in about 1775. Its full title is *Missa brevis Sancti Joannis de Deo*. See also *Grosse Orgelmesse*.

Kl. Fl. Abbreviation for *Kleine Flöte* (Ger.), the piccolo.

Klingen (Ger.). 'To sound'; *klingend*, 'resonant'.

Knaben Wunderhorn, Des ('Youth's Magic Horn'). Anthology of German folk poetry edited by Arnim and Brentano and published between 1805 and 1808. Several composers have set poems from it, including Strauss and, particularly, Mahler, who composed over 20 *Wunderhorn* songs for voice and piano or orchestra and who incorporated *Wunderhorn* songs into his Second, Third, and Fourth Symphonies.

Kneifend (Ger.). 'Plucking', the same as *Pizzicato*.

Knot Garden, The. Opera in three acts by Tippett; text by the composer. Produced:

London, Covent Garden, 2 December 1970;
Evanston, Ill., Northwestern University,
22 February 1974. The analyst Mangus (bar.)
has been invited by Faber (bar.) and Thea
(mezzo) to treat their ward Flora (sop.), but
perceives that the real trouble lies in the
marriage: Faber has grown too far outward,
Thea too far inward, and they no longer meet in
a true marriage. A homosexual couple arrive:
they are the Black writer Mel (bar.) and the
musician Dov (ten.). A further arrival is Denise
(sop.), Thea's sister and 'a dedicated freedom
fighter' who has suffered torture. Mangus con-
trives a series of devices to set their difficulties
to rights, including a charade based on *The
Tempest*; the stage devices include the revolving
of the symbolic knot garden of the title, in which
the characters play out their relationships.
Eventually Mel leaves with Denise, and Faber
and Thea find renewed marriage: Flora has
found adulthood and independence, and Dov
is left to set off upon a journey (recorded in
Tippett's *Songs for Dov*, which arose out of the
opera).

Knussen, (Stuart) **Oliver** (*b* Glasgow, 12 June
1952). English composer. He studied privately
in London with John Lambert and at Tanglewood with Gunther Schuller. His First
Symphony was performed by the London
Symphony Orchestra when he was 15, but since
then he has worked slowly in producing his
finely lyrical and well-crafted compositions,
keeping within the limits of mainstream van-
guardism. Among his works are two further
symphonies, a variety of vocal pieces, and music
for chamber ensemble.   PAUL GRIFFITHS

Köchel. Abbreviation for the standard thematic catalogue of the works of Mozart drawn
up by the Austrian musicologist Ludwig Köchel
(1800–77). The catalogue has been revised
several times, notably by Alfred Einstein for the
third edition (1937, often referred to as 'K-E')
and by Franz Geigling, Alexander Weinmann,
and Gerd Sievers for the sixth (1964, often
referred to as 'K6'). Mozart's works, especially
those without distinguishing title, are nearly
always referred to by Köchel number, usually
abbreviated to 'K' (but see *Kirkpatrick*).

Koczwara, František (Franz) [Kotzwara,
Francis] (*b* ?Prague, *c.*1750; *d* London, 2 Sept.
1791). Czech composer and instrumentalist.
Koczwara's origins are uncertain, but he was
one of the community of *émigré* musicians who
made an itinerant career in the orchestras of
Britain. As a performer his talents were catholic,
embracing a variety of wind and string instruments, the fortepiano and cittern. At the time of
his death his travels had brought him to the pit

of the King's Theatre as a double bass player.
His compositions comprise mainly chamber
music, including six string quartets and several
accompanied keyboard sonatas. Koczwara's
contemporary reputation, however, was secured
by his spectacularly successful programme
sonata *The Battle of Prague* for piano, cello,
and violin with drum ad lib, and later for solo
keyboard. This work, replete with a bevy of
appropriately militaristic effects, was sufficiently popular to run to some 40 editions and
to sire an army of comparably noisy offspring.
Koczwara's notoriety was further advanced by
the bizarre circumstances of his death: the
unsuccessful conclusion of an erotic experiment.   JAN SMACZNY

Kodály, Zoltán (*b* Kecskemét, Hungary,
16 Dec. 1882; *d* Budapest, 6 Mar. 1967). Hungarian composer. The son of a railway official
and enthusiastic amateur musician, Kodály
began to compose in his boyhood. In 1900 he
went to Budapest to study modern languages
at the university and composition, with Hans
Koessler, at the academy of music. He took his
D.Phil. in 1906, his thesis being on Hungarian
folk music, and from that time he began to
collaborate with his friend Bartók, both in
collecting folk-song and in pressing for a new
vitality in Hungarian musical life. Like Bartók
he was appointed to a professorship at the

Kodály

Budapest Academy in 1907, and he remained in the city for the rest of his life.

Kodály's early works, such as the Sonata for unaccompanied cello (1915), can be compared with Bartók's of the same period in their successful attempt to create a style on the basis of Hungarian folk music. However, Kodály was the more conservative musician; he did not share Bartók's penetration, and he was content to develop at a slower pace. His style changed little after he had established himself in Hungary and abroad with the *Psalmus hungaricus* for tenor, chorus, and orchestra (1923) and the witty, brilliant score for his opera *Háry János* (1926), from which he extracted a popular orchestral suite.

The experience of preparing the *Psalmus hungaricus*, which includes a boys' choir, led him to concern himself with musical education. He was instrumental in developing a school music curriculum which ensured that every child learned to sing at sight, and he wrote an enormous quantity of choral music and exercises for children and amateurs. In other fields he became much less prolific. All his important chamber works, including two quartets, were composed before 1920, and he wrote only a few orchestral pieces after *Háry János*. Of these few, the colourful and dynamic works founded in folk music—*Dances of Marosszék* (1930, after the piano version of 1927), *Dances of Galánta* (1933), and '*Peacock*' *Variations* (1938-9)—have proved more lasting than the more ambitious but long-winded Concerto for Orchestra (1939) and Symphony (1961).

PAUL GRIFFITHS

FURTHER READING
László Eősze: *Zoltán Kodály* (London, 1962); Percy M. Young: *Zoltán Kodály* (London, 1964).

Koechlin, Charles (Louis Eugène) (*b* Paris, 27 Nov. 1867; *d* le Canadel, Var, 31 Dec. 1950). French composer. He studied at the Paris Conservatoire with Massenet, Fauré, and others, and led an uneventful life, teaching, writing, and composing an enormous output of over 200 opus numbers. Little of his music has been published, but it is clear that he preserved a fastidious independence from prevailing trends: his symphonic poem *Les bandar-log* (1939-40), one of several works after Kipling, scornfully parodies the various schools of the time. His Viola Sonata (1902-15) is an early bitonal piece which might well have influenced his pupil Milhaud. Other works include the curious *Seven Stars' Symphony* (1933), where each movement is based on a screen personality.

PAUL GRIFFITHS

Koenig, Gottfried Michael (*b* Magdeburg, 5 Oct. 1926). He studied at the Brunswick Staatsmusikschule (1946-7), the North-West German Music Academy in Detmold (1947-50, composition with Günther Bialas), and the Cologne Musikhochschule (1953-4). After several years at the electronic music studio in Cologne (1954-64), where he assisted Stockhausen and others, he was appointed artistic director of the studio at Utrecht University. His output is small and consists mainly of tape works in which he has explored new means of sound generation, including since the mid-1960s the use of computers for such works as his *Projekt 1*, *CSP 1*, and *Projekt 2*.

PAUL GRIFFITHS

Kohaut, (Wenzel) **Josef** (Thomas) (*b* Saaz (now Žatec), Bohemia, 4 May 1738; *d* Paris, ? 1793). Bohemian composer and, according to Burney, an excellent trumpeter and lutenist. He deserted from his Austrian regiment and fled to Paris, where he became a successful composer of *opéras comiques*.

Kolb, Carlmann (*b* Kösslarn, nr Griesbach, Bavaria, Jan. 1703; *d* Munich, 15 Jan. 1765). German organist and composer. He spent most of his life at the Benedictine Abbey of Asbach, where he was ordained as a priest, and as a tutor to the family of the Count of Tattenbach-Reinstein in Munich. He wrote the *Certamen aonium* (Augsburg, 1733), a set of preludes, verses, and cadenzas in each of the church modes.

DENIS ARNOLD

Kolęda [*kolenda, colenda*]. A Christmas song; the Eastern European counterpart of the carol. There are many collections from the 16th, 17th, and 18th centuries.

Kol Nidrei [*Kol Nidre*] ('All Vows'). 1. Work for cello and orchestra by Bruch, composed in 1881. An Adagio on Hebrew melodies, it was also arranged for cello and piano.

2. Work, Op. 39, by Schoenberg for speaker, chorus, and orchestra, composed in 1938. It is a setting of the *Kol Nidre*, the opening prayer of the Jewish service on the evening of the Day of Atonement (Yom Kippur), which has tragic associations with the Spanish persecution of the Jews in the 17th century.

Kolomyka. A quick Polish dance in duple time, popular in the mountain districts.

Komabue. A transverse flute used in Japanese *komagaku* music. See *Japanese Music*, 3c.

Kombination (Ger.). 'Combination'. In organ music, applied to any mechanical device for preparing registrations.

König Stephan ('King Stephen'). Overture and incidental music, Op. 117, by Beethoven, composed in 1811. It was written for A. von Kotzebue's prologue given at the first night of the German theatre in Budapest (1812). See also *Ruinen von Athen, Die.*

Kontakte ('Contacts'). Work by Stockhausen for four-track tape alone and, in another version, with piano and percussion, composed in 1959-60. The tape was used in the music-theatre piece *Originale* (1961).

Kontrabass (Ger.). 'Double bass'.

Kontra-Punkte ('Counterpoints'). Work by Stockhausen for 10 instruments (flute, clarinet, bass clarinet, bassoon, trumpet, trombone, piano, harp, violin, and cello), composed in 1952

and revised in 1953. It is a revision of the orchestral work *Punkte* of 1952, itself revised in 1962, 1964, and 1966.

Kontretanz (Ger.). See *Country dance.*

Konzert (Ger.). 1. 'Concert'. 2. 'Concerto'.

Konzertmeister (Ger.). See *Concert-master.*

Konzertstück (Ger.). See *Concertino,* 2.

Kopřiva, Václav Jan (*b* Brloh, nr Citoliby, 8 Feb. 1708; *d* Citoliby, 7 June 1789). Czech composer. He worked at Citoliby, near Prague, for most of his life. His only surviving music is for the church. He had two sons, Jan Jáchym (1754-92) and Karel Blažej (1756-85), who also became musicians.

Korea

1. Introduction
2. History
3. Mode
4. Rhythm
5. Texture
6. Instruments
7. Ensembles
8. Court Music
9. Folk Music
10. Ritual Music

1. *Introduction.* The Korean peninsula extends southward from the mainland of north-east Asia and separates the Yellow Sea from the Sea of Japan. Korea existed as an independent kingdom until 1910 when it was annexed to Japan. After the Second World War, the country was divided into the Republic of Korea (South Korea) and the Democratic People's Republic of Korea (North Korea). In the following article, descriptions of musical practices before 1945 relate to the entire Korean peninsula, while descriptions of current practice refer to South Korea only, because of the paucity of information from the north.

Korean musical culture is a blend of Chinese elements with indigenous material. Traditionally, the Korean court repertory was divided into three parts: *aak* ('refined music', the Confucian ritual music), *tangak* ('Tang music', secular pieces of Chinese origin), and *hyangak* ('native music', secular pieces of Korean origin). In modern times, the *aak* and *tangak* portions of the repertory each contain only two pieces. Furthermore, the *tangak* pieces have been changed so radically that it is now difficult to distinguish them musically from pieces of Korean origin. The current practice is to recognize a basic distinction between the music of the court and aristocracy (*chŏngak*, 'correct music', or *aak*, a broader meaning of the term for the Confucian ritual music) and the music of the folk (*minsogak*, 'folk music').

2. *History.* By the 7th century (the beginning of the Unified Silla dynasty, 664-935), most of the major instruments of present-day Korean music were already in use. Since some of the music performed was borrowed from Tang China, the native Korean music, *hyangak*, was distinguished from *tangak* (Tang music). Two pieces in the surviving Korean repertory (*Sujech'ŏn, Tongdong*) presumably date from this period.

Under the next Korean dynasty (Koryŏ, 918-1392), Tang music was supplanted by Chinese music of the Sung dynasty, though it continued to be called Tang music in Korea. Two orchestral pieces (*Pohŏja, Nagyangch'un*) and one dance (*P'ogurak*) survive from this period. During this dynasty, two major instruments were introduced: the *haegŭm* (fiddle) and the *changgo* (hourglass drum). In 1116, the Sung emperor sent a gift of instruments and music for the Confucian ritual, the music of which is still performed. During the Chinese Yüan dynasty (13th and 14th centuries), large-scale import of Chinese music into Korea came to an end.

The Korean Yi dynasty (1392-1910) marked a series of important musical developments, particularly during the reign of King Sejong (1418-50). In 1430, the performance of the Confucian ritual music was revised. King Sejong himself is said to have arranged the four dance-suites which were subsequently recorded in his annals (1454), using a remarkably explicit

Ex. 1

Sŏgyŏng Pyŏlgok ('The Western Capital'), a 15th-century folk-song in a version suitable for a plucked chordophone. The percussion *ostinato* is given after the melody. The final bar is an instrumental refrain during which the voice would have rested.

(refrain)

Percussion *ostinato*

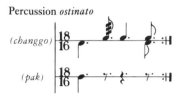

(changgo)

(pak)

musical notation. This score in Sejong's annals is the oldest surviving notation in Korea. One of the suites includes four complete settings of the epic poem, *Yong-bi-ŏ-ch'ŏn ka*, which Sejong had commissioned to be the first work written in the newly created Korean alphabet. Two of the other suites were subsequently rearranged to be used at the royal ancestral shrine ritual, where they are still performed, in much-altered form. In 1493, under King Sŏngjong, a major musical treatise, *Akhak Kwebŏm*, was compiled and printed. The surviving scores of the 15th and 16th centuries show that pentatonic scales and triple metres were as predominant in Korea then as they are now (Ex. 1).

During the middle of the Yi dynasty, foreign invasions led to a reduction in the previously grand scale of court music. The mensurally explicit notation of the 15th century was abandoned in favour of a system of tablature without mensuration. This system was in use at least until the early 19th century. Late in the Yi dynasty, two virtuoso folk traditions developed in south-western Korea, *p'ansori* and *sanjo*.

Korea was annexed by Japan in 1910, and the royal court, with its musical performances, came to an end. In 1951, the National Classical Music Institute was founded to preserve the court repertory. In the 20th century, contact with Western music has effected a tremendous increase in the composititon of new pieces and the refinement of a new system of mensural notation.

3. *Mode.* Two principal modes, both pentatonic, have been in use at least since the 15th century: *p'yŏngjo* (as in Ex. 1) and *kyemyŏnjo*. According to the treatise *Akhak Kwebŏm* these two modes were played in seven keys (EFGABCD), but this key-system was probably archaic in the 15th century. By 1600, the modes *p'yŏngjo* and *kyemyŏnjo* were played only in the keys of B♭ and E♭. The key of E♭ gradually came to be favoured over B♭, so that in the 20th century most of the court repertory is in E♭.

The notes of Korean modes are not conceived as static pitches. Certain notes are characteristically ornamented with *vibrato* or downward slides. Intervals are not rigidly fixed; performers occasionally make an interval wider or narrower for expressive purposes. Consequently, it is difficult to transcribe Korean music satisfactorily in Western staff notation.

4. *Rhythm.* Most Korean music is in triple metre. This readily distinguishes it from Chinese and Japanese music with their predominantly duple metres. Some slow, unmeasured music has no definite beat. Some ceremonial music has a definite beat but no regular metre (Ex. 2), and some music is in quintuple metre (Ex. 3*a*). The vocal genre *kagok* has a unique metre, 9/8 + 6/8 + 9/8. Duple metre is common only in folk music (see below, Ex. 6).

Ex. 2

An excerpt from *Nagyangch'un*, a ceremonial piece for court orchestra. The upper part is played by *taegŭm* (flute), *T'ang-p'iri* (oboe), fiddle, and (an octave lower) *ajaeng* (bowed zither); the lower part is played by the *p'yŏnjong* and the *p'yŏn'gyŏng* (bell- and stone-chimes).

○ = *puk* (barrel drum)   △ = *pak* (clappers)

Ex. 3

Two movements from the chamber version of *Yŏngsan Hoesang*: (a) opening of *Seryŏngsan* (third movement), (b) opening of *T'aryŏng* (eighth movement). Two of the seven melodic parts are given.

5. *Texture.* Ensemble music is heterophonic with each instrument playing an ornamented version of the tune. The same is true of a solo vocal part, when present. Generally wind parts are more ornamented than string parts (Ex. 3). In court music, where the parts are rigidly fixed, the performer is free to alter only small details of ornamentation. In folk music, each musician performs his own ornamented version of the tune.

6. *Instruments.* The *p'iri* is an oboe with eight finger-holes. The principal instrument of the court orchestra, it has a loud, brash sound, but is capable of great subtlety in dynamics and expressive *portamento*. The standard *p'iri* used in folk music and most court music is the *hyang-p'iri* ('native p'iri'). The *T'ang-p'iri* ('Tang or Chinese p'iri'), slightly different in shape and range, is used for those court orchestral pieces which are in the key of C. The *se-p'iri* ('thin p'iri') is identical to the *hyang-p'iri* but smaller in diameter (hence softer). It is used in court chamber music. The *hojŏk* (or *t'aep'yŏngso* or *nallari*) is a shawm with a conical wooden body, a metal bell, and a very small double reed. Its sound is so loud that it is played only outdoors, often with a wildly undulating *vibrato*.

The *taegŭm* is a large transverse bamboo flute with a thin reed membrane pasted over a hole next to the mouth-hole. The membrane adds to the tone quality a buzz which is most apparent when the *taegŭm* is played loudly in the upper register. The *tang-jŏk* (or *sogŭm*) is a small transverse flute (without a buzzing membrane). The *tanso* is a small notched vertical flute with a soft, sweet tone.

The *haegŭm* is a two-string fiddle played with a horse-hair bow. It has a muted, strongly nasal tone. The *ajaeng* is a large seven-string zither, with movable bridges, which is played with a rosined stick of forsythia wood. The wood rubbing against the strings produces a rasping sound. In Korea, the *haegŭm* and the *ajaeng* are customarily classed as wind instruments, presumably because they produce sustained sounds instead of the rapidly decaying sounds of the plucked strings.

The *kayagŭm* is a large 12-string zither with

Pl. 1. A sinawi ensemble with (left to right) *kayagŭm* (zither), *haegŭm* (fiddle), *taegŭm* (flute), *p'iri* (oboe), *changgo* (hourglass drum), *and ching* (gong).

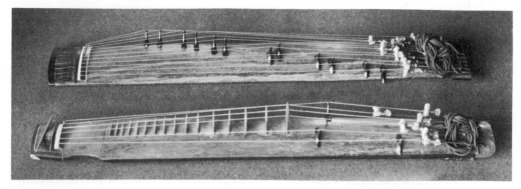

Pl. 2. The two plucked zithers, kayagŭm and kŏmun'go.

Pl. 3. Playing technique of the kŏmun'go (zither).

movable bridges. The strings are plucked with the fingers of the right hand while the left hand depresses the strings on the other side of the movable bridges, producing *vibrato, portamento,* and mordent-like ornaments. The *kayagŭm* is by far the most popular instrument among Korean amateurs. The *kŏmun'go,* a large six-string zither, has long been considered the noblest of Korean instruments. Of the six strings, I, V, and VI are supported by movable bridges, while II, III, and IV pass over a series of 16 frets. The melody is played exclusively on strings II and III; the other four strings function as drones (in present-day technique the drone strings are not plucked very frequently). The right hand plucks the strings with a pencil-sized bamboo stick, and the left hand depresses the melody strings on the frets. The *yanggŭm* is a dulcimer struck with a single beater. It is the only instrument to have entered the Korean instrumentarium during the Yi dynasty, and also the only Korean chordophone with strings of metal rather than of twisted silk fibre.

The *p'yŏnjong* is a set of 16 chromatically tuned bells, and the *p'yŏn'gyŏng* a matching set of L-shaped stone slabs pitched an octave higher. These magnificent instruments originated in ancient China, but survive only in Korea. The *p'yŏnjong* and the *p'yŏn'gyŏng* are always played together, in unison. The bells are all the same size and shape, as are the stones; the pitch of each bell or stone is determined by its thickness. The chromatic tuning allows the chimes to be played in all the keys called for by various Confucian rituals. Another chime, the *panghyang,* is a set of 16 chromatically tuned iron slabs; it is now rarely played.

The *changgo* (hourglass drum) is essential in most Korean ensembles. It is struck on the right head with a thin bamboo stick and on the left head with the palm. The *puk* (barrel drum) is struck on the right head with a thick wooden stick and on the left head with the palm. Two other barrel drums struck with soft-headed drumsticks are *chwago* (court orchestra) and *yonggo* (military band). Other percussion instruments include the *pak* (wooden clappers), the *ching* and the *kkwaenggwari* (large and small gongs), the *para* or *chabara* (cymbals), and the small hand-held wooden *mokt'ak* (slit-drum), used in Buddhist temples.

7. *Ensembles.* The basic ensemble of Korean music includes the *p'iri, taegŭm, haegŭm,* and *changgo* (oboe, flute, fiddle, and hourglass drum). The *samhyŏn yukkak* ensemble includes an additional *p'iri* and the *puk* (barrel drum). The court orchestra comprises the basic ensemble plus the *tang-jŏk* (small transverse flute) for the high treble part, the *ajaeng* (bowed zither) for the bass part, and the *chwago* (large barrel drum). In the court orchestra, the three melodic instruments, the *p'iri,* the *taegŭm,* and the *haegŭm,* are normally doubled. The director of the orchestra signals the beginning of a piece with a single stroke of the *pak* (clappers) and the end with three strokes. Some pieces include the *kŏmun'go* and the *kayagŭm* (plucked zithers) or the *p'yŏnjong* and the *p'yŏn'gyŏng* (bell- and stone-chimes), or both. The court chamber ensemble in its fullest form comprises the basic ensemble plus the *tanso* (vertical flute), the *kayagŭm* and *kŏmun'go* (plucked zithers), and

the *yanggŭm* (dulcimer). It is permissible, however, to play the chamber repertory with whatever selection of these instruments is available. None of the instruments is doubled.

The basic ensemble, with or without additional instruments, also accompanies shamanist rituals and various genres of folk music and dance. For the military band and for Buddhist instrumental music a very different ensemble, the *chorach'i*, is used. It includes the *hojŏk* (shawm), *nabal* or *nap'al* (horn), *nagak* or *sora* (conch shell), *chabara* (cymbals), *ching* (large gong), and *yonggo* (barrel drum). The shawm is the sole melodic instrument, and the horn and conch function as drones. Other special ensembles are used for the Confucian ritual and the farmer's band.

8. *Court Music.* Court music is performed primarily by instrumental ensembles. Most of the repertory dates from the 15th century or earlier, but the music has since undergone radical change. In mood, the music ranges from the grave and majestic *Sujech'ŏn*, the most revered piece in the repertory, to the lively and playful *T'aryŏng* (Ex. 3*b*). A considerable portion of the repertory is in expanded quintuple metres ($5 \times 6/8$ or $5 \times 3/8$) (Ex. 3*a*). Most of the pieces are now, or were at one time, used as dance accompaniments. The ceremonial pieces are distinctly different in character, with very slow tempo, minimal heterophony, and no regular metre (Ex. 2).

The backbone of the court chamber music repertory is a lengthy suite, the *Yŏngsan Hoesang*, from which various combinations of movements can be extracted (Ex. 3). This music was and is performed by amateurs as well as professional court musicians. The few court pieces for solo instruments all derive from ensemble pieces: a single instrument's part is played alone in elaborated form by the *taegŭm* (transverse flute), *tanso* (vertical flute), or *p'iri* (oboe). All of these pieces are unmeasured.

In addition to the chamber version of the *Yŏngsan Hoesang* suite (known as *Kŏmun'go Hoesang* or *Chunggwang*), there are versions for the *samhyŏn yukkak* ensemble (*Samhyŏn Yŏngsan Hoesang* or *P'yojŏng Manbang*) and for a larger wind and string ensemble (*P'yŏngjo Hoesang* or *Yuch'osin*). Each version is in a different mode. The various versions have either eight or nine movements, with a total duration of approximately 45 minutes; the first movement is very slow, and each succeeding movement is somewhat faster.

Three vocal genres were sung both within the court and outside it. *Kagok* is a lengthy song cycle with separate versions for male and female voices. The solo singer is accompanied by the chamber ensemble. As with *Yŏngsan hoesang*, parts of the cycle can be excerpted for performance. All the songs are cast in the same seven-part form, including an instrumental prelude and interlude.

Kasa is a repertory of 12 songs accompanied by flute and hourglass drum, with optional inclusion of the small oboe and the fiddle; most of the songs are strophic. *Sijo* is a style of singing the poetic form of the same name. The poems are sung to a small number of standard melodies. The singer is accompanied by the hourglass drum, with optional inclusion of the small oboe, flute, and fiddle. Each of these three genres has its own highly developed vocal technique, with particular attention paid to different types of *vibrato*. *Kasa* technique includes switching back and forth between normal voice and falsetto, by female as well as male singers (Ex. 4).

Ex. 4

Opening of the *kasa* 'Spring Sleep' (*Ch'unmyŏn-gok*) (accompanying instrumental parts omitted).

o = *falsetto*

Ex. 5

Refrain of *Kangwŏndo yŏkkŭm Arirang*, a song from the eastern region (transcription by Hahn Manyoung).

A - ri - rang, a - ri - rang, a - ra - ri - yo,_____

yŏl-lyŏt - ta - ga____ nog-a - ji - ni____ pom-i han ch'ŏl i - ra.____

9. *Folk Music*. In contrast to court music, folk music is primarily vocal and performed by soloists. Korean folk-song can be divided into four distinct regional groups, each of which has a characteristic mode: Seoul region (E F♯ A B C♯ = *p'yŏngjo*); eastern region (E G A C D = old *kyemŏnjo* in A); south-western region (*namdo*) (Ē A B C D); north-western region (*sŏdo*) (D Ē G Ā C). In each mode, three of the five notes are more important than the other two (underlined above) (Ex. 5); in some songs one or both of the subordinate notes may not appear at all. For the south-western and north-western regions, the note which receives the most prominent *vibrato* is indicated by a wavy line.

Two virtuoso folk genres derive from south-western Korea. *P'ansori* is a repertory of five tales, related in song and spoken narration by a single singer accompanied by the *puk* (barrel drum). A complete performance lasts from five to eight hours. The very demanding technique calls for a loud, hoarse vocal quality. *Sanjo* is a

Ex. 6

Excerpts from three different sections of *kayagŭm sanjo* (transcribed from Nonesuch H-72049).

kayagŭm

changgo

solo instrumental form comprising three or more sections in progressively faster tempos. The soloist is accompanied by the *changgo* (hourglass drum). Although *sanjo* was probably improvised at one time, it is now learned as a set piece in the style of one's teacher. It is most frequently played on the *kayagŭm* (12-string zither) (Ex. 6). *P'ansori* and *sanjo* are organized around the same set of *changdan* (rhythmic patterns), each of which has a particular tempo, metre, and drum *ostinato* (the *ostinato* may be varied at the drummer's discretion).

Sinawi is the shamanist instrumental music of south-western Korea in which each player improvises independently of the others—a striking contrast to the heterophony typical in Korean ensembles.

Nongak ('farmer's music') is played by a percussion band comprising *kkwaenggwari* (small gong—the principal lead instrument), *changgo* (hourglass drum), *yonggo* (barrel drum), and *ching* (large gong), with the optional inclusion of the *hojŏk* (shawm). The exciting rhythms of this ensemble serve as accompaniment to dancers wearing hats with long streamers which they set in motion by moving their heads. The music is traditionally associated with the transplanting and harvesting of rice.

10. *Ritual Music.* The semi-annual sacrifice to Confucius is accompanied by an ancient Chinese ensemble comprising bell- and stone-chimes, flutes (vertical, transverse, and globular), panpipes, zithers, and an array of percussion. Two orchestras play in alternation. The music has very slow, equal notes with upward slides performed by the winds at the end of each note. Buddhist ritual music includes several different styles of chanting, some of which are in the same mode as folk-song of the eastern region, and one of which, *chissori*, features remarkable choral slides as wide as an octave. Unfortunately, this music is now kept alive only by a minor sect with few monks. There is also a loud, robust instrumental music to accompany ritual dancing; similar music (*Tae-ch'wit'a* or *Muryŏng*) is played by the military band.

JONATHAN CONDIT

FURTHER READING
Sŏng Hyŏn, ed.: *Akhak Kwebŏm* [Book of Music] (Seoul, 1493, reprinted 1968); Song Bang-song: *An Annotated Bibliography of Korean Music* (Providence, 1971); Chang Sa-hun: *Glossary of Korean Music* (Seoul, 1972); *Survey of Korean Arts: Traditional Music*, ed. [Korean] National Academy of Arts (Seoul, 1974); Robert Provine: 'The Treatise on Ceremonial Music (1430) in the Annals of the Korean King Sejong', *Ethnomusicology*, xviii/1 (1974), pp. 1–30; Jonathan Condit: 'A Fifteenth-century Korean Score in Mensural Notation', *Musica asiatica*, ii (1979), pp. 1–87.

Korngold, Eric(h) Wolfgang (*b* Brno, 29 May 1897; *d* Hollywood, 29 Nov. 1957). American composer. He emerged very early as a composer: he was only 11 when his pantomime *Der Schneemann* was produced at the Vienna Hofoper. Among later successes was the sensational opera *Der tote Stadt* (1920). In 1935 he settled in Hollywood, where he applied his talents for ripe romanticism and stirring drama to the composition of film scores. His other works include two string quartets and a Violin Concerto (1946). PAUL GRIFFITHS

Kortholt (Eng., Ger.; Fr.: *courtaut*). One of the rarer Renaissance-period wind instruments with double reed, now in manufacture again (Fig. 1): a cylindrical bore leads down and up again through a round pillar of wood, the bore ending at a hole in the side near the top. The reed is blown through a reed-cap as on a *crumhorn. As with other cylindrical reed instruments of the time, no overblowing is possible; but the kortholt (made in two sizes) can give a compass of nearly two octaves since—in addition to the usual seven fingers and thumb—the other little finger, the other thumb, and also the middle joints of both index fingers (each covering a hole offset to the side, which allows the finger to remain covering its 'normal' hole at the same time; compare the *racket) are used. Kortholts make the usual reedy burbling sound of these narrow cylindrical-bore reed instruments, like a crumhorn but softer.

Its restoration is based on an instrument illustrated by Praetorius in *Syntagma musicum* (1619) for which the standing length would be

Fig. 1.

about 28″; Praetorius says that he had seen it but could not find much information about it. Nor is any original example known to exist, though there are four originals (in Vienna) of a closely similar type which Praetorius illustrates as a family of four under the name *Sordunen* (see *Instruments, Renaissance*, Fig. 1). They differ from the above kortholt in having no reed-cap, the reed evidently being taken directly in the mouth. The name occurs in Italy as *sordoni*, and again in a five-part pavan of *c*.1600 by Count Moritz of Hesse-Cassel; the instruments are here named along the top and form an interesting group—*fiauto* (recorder), *cornetto muto*, trombone, *sordano*, and viola da gamba. If they played the parts in this order, the *sordano*, on the tenor part (range *e–f′*), could have been the smallest of the family, an instrument about 9″ tall plus the reed.

How definitive was the difference between the reed-cap form (kortholt) and non-reed-cap form (*sordun*) we hardly know. The name 'sordun' refers to sound of muted quality, 'kortholt' on the other hand to an outward appearance which evidently reminded people of a 16th-century short-barrelled piece of artillery, in French *courtault* (It.: *cortaldo*; Eng.: *curtal*). In France the 'courtaut' as a wind instrument is illustrated (by Mersenne, 1636) as being of the non-reed-cap type. But nomenclature was anyway somewhat fluid: in Italy the instrument 'cortaldo' was, or could be, the racket, while in England 'curtal' denoted the dulcian, predecessor of the bassoon (see *Bassoon*, 4*a*).

ANTHONY BAINES

Koteletten Walzer (Ger.). See *Chopsticks*.

Koto. A Japanese 13-stringed zither. See *Japanese Music*, 3*b*.

Kotter, Hans (*b* Strasbourg, *c*.1485; *d* Berne, 1541). German organist and composer. He was a pupil of Paul Hofhaimer before moving to Fribourg as organist of St Nikolaus in 1514; there he turned Protestant and was expelled from the town. He spent his later years as a schoolmaster in Berne. Most of his works are included in a volume of keyboard music containing preludes, dances, and arrangements of vocal music by Hofhaimer, Isaac, and other composers.   DENIS ARNOLD

Koussevitzky, Serge [Kusevitsky, Sergey Alexandrovich] (*b* Vyshny-Volochok, 26 July 1874; *d* Boston, Mass., 4 June 1951). American conductor, composer, and double bass player of Russian birth. He studied the double bass at the Moscow Philharmonic School, played widely in Russia, and made his international débuts in Berlin (1903) and London (1907). In the fol-

lowing year he made his conducting début with the Berlin Philharmonic Orchestra. In 1909 he set up a publishing business (Éditions Russes de Musique) to help publicize new Russian music, and in 1914 bought up the firm of Gutheil for 300,000 rubles: Gutheil already had Rakhmaninov on his books, and Koussevitzky added such composers as Prokofiev, Stravinsky, and Skryabin for whose music he had particular enthusiasm. Koussevitzky emigrated from Russia after the 1917 Revolution, and attained yet higher fame as an orchestral conductor on being appointed to the Boston Symphony Orchestra (1924–49). In 1942, he created, as a memorial to his first wife, the Koussevitzky Music Foundation, which (among other activities) commissions works by composers on either side of the Atlantic. The work of the Foundation is continued by his second wife, Olga.

PERCY SCHOLES, rev.

Kovařovic, Karel (*b* Prague, 9 Dec. 1862; *d* Prague, 6 Dec. 1920). Czech composer, conductor, and accompanist. He studied the piano, harp, and clarinet at the Prague Conservatory, and composition with Fibich. In the 1880s, while he was harpist of the National Theatre orchestra, he was also in demand as a piano accompanist, playing regularly with the violinist Odříček and at a guest appearance in 1885 with Sarasate. Kovařovic gained experience as a *répétiteur* at Pivoda's vocal school in Prague, and as an operatic conductor at the Czech Theatre in Brno (1885–6). Up to 1900 he composed several effective stage works, most notably the operas *Psohlavci* ('The Dog Heads', 1897) and *Na starém bělidle* ('At the Old Bleaching House', 1901), and the ballet *Hašiš* (1884), each exploiting a rich lyrical vein often reminiscent of Dvořák. On his appointment as chief conductor of the Czech National Theatre in 1900 Kovařovic neglected composition to devote his energies to what has come to be regarded as his greatest achievement, the improvement of orchestral and vocal standards in the Theatre. In his time there he premièred operas by Dvořák, Foerster, Novák, and Ostrčil, and gave the first performance in Prague of Janáček's *Jenůfa* (1916). He was also responsible for reviving interest in 19th-century classics of the Czech repertory. Though he was not above making extensive changes to both the substance (Dvořák's *Dimitrij*) and the texture and orchestration (Janáček's *Jenůfa*) of a work, his performances remained a model for Czech operatic conductors for many years.   JAN SMACZNY

Kozeluch [Kotzeluch, Koželuh], **Leopold** (*b* Velvary, 26 June 1747; *d* Vienna, 7 May 1818). Czech composer, pianist, teacher, and publisher. Although baptized Jan Antonín, he later took the name Leopold to avoid confusion with his cousin, the composer and teacher Jan Antonín Kozeluch (1738–1814). His earliest musical training in Velvary was followed by tuition from his cousin in Prague and lessons with F. X. Dušek. After considerable success with theatre music in Prague, Kozeluch left in 1778 to explore the greater opportunities offered by the Austrian capital. Here, with remarkable industry and a certain ruthlessness, he forged a career as pianist, teacher, and composer; in 1785 he founded his own publishing house. His contacts with British publishers were especially good, and many of his works were issued in England at the same time as Vienna. Later, in common with Haydn and Beethoven, he made many folk-song settings for the Scottish publisher George Thomson. In 1792 Kozeluch succeeded his rival Mozart as *Kammer Kapellmeister* and *Hofmusik Compositor*, posts which occupied his time and energy until his death. Kozeluch was influential in diverting attention away from the harpsichord in favour of the fortepiano both as a teacher and a composer. His 49 sonatas and numerous solos were important in cultivating a style of writing suited to the fortepiano. The best of his early work reflected current Rococo and Classical trends, and later (Three Caprices for fortepiano *c.*1797) an anticipation of pre-Romantic styles is perceptible. Kozeluch was prolific in other genres producing symphonies, concertos, cantatas, songs, and a large number of accompanied keyboard sonatas (trios), but it was for his distinguished fortepiano music that he was considered, according to Ernst Ludwig Gerber's Tonkünstler-Lexicon (1790–2): 'without doubt . . . the most widely popular of all composers now living'.   JAN SMACZNY

Kraft (Ger.). 'Strength', 'vigour'; *kräftig*, 'strong', 'vigorous'.

Kraft, William (*b* Chicago, 6 Sept. 1923). American composer. He studied with Luening, Ussachevsky, and Cowell at Columbia University and with Orr at Cambridge. A professional percussionist, he has written numerous works with solo percussion parts as well as music for the theatre and cinema, including a concerto for four percussionists and orchestra (1964), a Piano Concerto (1972), and the orchestral works *Contextures: Riots Decade '60, I* (1968) and *II* (1974).   PAUL GRIFFITHS

Krakowiak [*krakoviak*] (Fr.: *cracovienne*). A lively Polish dance, named after the Kraków region. It is in quick duple time with syncopated rhythms and has been described as a simple type of *polonaise. It is danced by several couples, who strike their heels together, shout, and sing.

The *krakowiak* became very popular in the early 19th century, when the dancer Fanny Elssler introduced it to western Europe. Chopin's Op. 14, the Grand Concert Rondo for piano and orchestra, is a *krakowiak*.

Kraus, Joseph Martin (*b* Miltenberg am Main, nr Darmstadt, 20 June 1756; *d* Stockholm, 15 Dec. 1792). German musician who became conductor at the theatre in Stockholm and later *Kapellmeister* to Gustav III. He wrote several operas and a few by no means negligible symphonies.

Krebs. German family of musicians. **Johann Tobias Krebs** (*b* Heidelheim, Weimar, 7 July 1690; *d* Buttstädt, 11 Feb. 1762) was an organist and composer. He studied harpsichord with J. G. Walther and composition with Bach. Of his organ music, only a few pieces have survived.

His son, **Johann Ludwig Krebs** (*bapt.* Buttelstedt, Weimar, 12 Oct. 1713; *d* Altenburg, 1 Jan. 1780), was also an organist. He entered St Thomas's, Leipzig, and became one of Bach's best pupils; Bach jokingly referred to him as 'the best crayfish [Krebs] in the brook [Bach]'. In 1737 Krebs was appointed organist of the Marienkirche, Zwickau, and in 1744 organist to the Zeitz court. On Bach's death Krebs applied for his post as *Kantor* of St Thomas's, but another candidate was selected, and in 1755 he took the post of organist to the Altenburg court. He published some clavier suites, trio sonatas, and sonatas for harpsichord and one or two flutes, but most of his works (including a double concerto for harpsichords and his organ pieces) remained in manuscript. Some of his works are in the Baroque style of Bach's, but others are more forward-looking.   WENDY THOMPSON

Krebsgang (Ger.). 'Crab motion'; see *Retrograde*.

Kreis (Ger.). 'Circle', 'cycle'; *Liederkreis*, 'song cycle'.

Kreisler, Fritz (*b* Vienna, 2 Feb. 1875; *d* New York, 29 Jan. 1962). American violinist and composer of Austrian birth. Son of a distinguished doctor, he was an infant prodigy as a violinist, entering the Vienna Conservatory at the age of seven and winning the Premier Prix of the Paris Conservatoire when 12. He toured America in 1889, but returned to Vienna, where for a time he studied medicine and did his military service. He then resumed his career as a concert violinist in which he remained for the rest of his life, with the exception of a short period in the Austrian army in 1914, being wounded soon after his entry. A splendid interpreter of the standard classics, he composed some charming salon pieces, sometimes passing them off as arrangements of 'old masters', as well as the operetta *Apple Blossoms* (1919). Between the two World Wars he lived first in Berlin, then Paris. In 1939 he went to the USA, taking up American citizenship in the following year. DENIS ARNOLD

Kreisleriana. Work for solo piano, Op. 16, by Schumann, composed in 1838 and revised in 1850. It consists of eight fantasies and was dedicated to Chopin. The title refers to the character Kreisler in E. T. A. Hoffmann's stories.

Krenek[Křenek], Ernst (*b* Vienna, 23 Aug. 1900). American composer of Austrian birth. He studied with Franz Schreker in Vienna and Berlin (1916-23), during which period he wrote several works, including two symphonies, influenced by Bartók, Mahler, and his teacher. In 1924 he visited Paris and there was attracted to neoclassicism. He made a conscious return to Schubert in his song cycle *Reisebuch aus dem österreichischen Alpen* (1929) and to a lesser extent in his opera *Jonny spielt auf* (1925-6), whose contemporary setting and use of jazz brought it immense popularity. Krenek then began a study of serial methods, which he adopted in his opera *Karl V* (1930-3). In 1938 he moved to the USA, where he was professor at Vassar College (1939-42) and Hamline University (1942-7). Since the mid-1950s, influenced by the European avant-garde, he has used complex serial techniques, often in forms of geometrical precision. He is also author of the books *Music Here and Now* (New York, 1939, reprinted 1967); *Studies in Counterpoint, Based on Twelve-Tone Technique* (New York, 1940), *Johannes Ockeghem* (New York, 1953), and *Horizons Circled* (Berkeley, Los Angeles, and London, 1974). PAUL GRIFFITHS

Kreutzer, Conradin (*b* Messkirch, nr Baden, 22 Nov. 1780; *d* Riga, 14 Dec. 1849). German conductor and composer. He studied briefly with Haydn, and produced several successful operas in Vienna before embarking on a career as musical director to several of the smaller German courts. From 1822 he worked again in Vienna, first at the Kärntnertor-Theater and then at the Theater in der Josephstadt. His opera *Das Nachtlager von Granada* (performed 1834) is still occasionally heard. DENIS ARNOLD

Kreutzer, Rodolphe (*b* Versailles, 16 Nov. 1766; *d* Geneva, 6 Jan. 1831). French violinist and composer. He worked mainly in Paris, before the Revolution in the chapel of Louis XVI, and afterwards in that of Louis XVIII. During the Republic he worked for Napoleon and as professor of violin at the Institut National de Musique set up by the Revolutionaries; he remained there when it became the Conservatoire in 1795. He met Beethoven in Vienna while on a concert tour in 1798, but Beethoven's 'Kreutzer' Sonata was composed and dedicated to Kreutzer after he had returned to Paris, and he is thought never to have played it in public.

Kreutzer composed several violin *études* and wrote a useful *Méthode de violon* (Paris, 1803); he also composed several *opéras comiques* and other dramatic works for theatres in Paris, but they are scarcely known today. DENIS ARNOLD

'Kreutzer' Sonata. 1. Nickname of Beethoven's Violin Sonata in A, Op. 47, composed in 1802-3. It is so called because it was dedicated to Rodolphe Kreutzer, who is believed never to have played it.

2. Subtitle of Janáček's String Quartet No. 1, composed in 1923 and incorporating part of a scrapped piano trio of 1908-9. On the score Janáček wrote 'Inspired by L. N. Tolstoy's *Kreutzer-sonata*' (a novel published in 1890).

Kreuz (Ger.). 'Cross', i.e. the sharp sign (♯).

Kreuzflöte (Ger.). 'Transverse flute'.

Krieger. German family of rugmakers of which two members became well-known musicians. **Johann Philipp Krieger** (*b* Nuremberg, Feb. 1649; *d* Weissenfels, 6 Feb. 1725) showed talent as an organist at the age of eight. He studied in Copenhagen before entering the service of Margrave Christian Ernst of Bayreuth in *c*.1673; while in the Margrave's service he went to Italy for about two years. In 1677 he became organist at Halle, and moved with the court, as *Kapellmeister*, to Weissenfels in 1680. He was a prolific composer of sacred and secular music, including trio sonatas, suites (the *Lustige Feld-music* (1704) was modelled on Lully's ballet suites), and many cantatas to Latin and German texts. He also wrote operas, but only a few arias from them survive.

His younger brother, **Johann Krieger** (*bapt.* Nuremberg, 1 Jan. 1652; *d* Zittau, 18 July 1735), followed Johann Philipp to Bayreuth in 1672, serving as court organist there, and later to Halle; in 1680 he was appointed *Kapellmeister* at the Eisenberg court. His last 53 years were spent as organist and director of music at Zittau. He was less prolific as a composer than his brother, but his organ playing and music were much admired by Handel. DENIS ARNOLD

Krieger, Adam (*b* Driesen, nr Frankfurt an der Oder, 7 Jan. 1634; *d* Dresden, 30 June 1666). German composer. While studying in Leipzig he founded a musical society among the university students, for which he wrote some entertaining and attractive songs. In 1655 he became organist at the Nikolaikirche, Leipzig, and two years later applied for the post of *Kantor* at St Thomas's; he was not successful, and from 1658 until his death served as organist to the Elector of Saxony at Dresden. His songs, mostly for solo voice and continuo, were his most important works, and a collection was published in Leipzig in 1657; other songs survive in manuscript, including the beautiful *Adonis' Tod*.

DENIS ARNOLD

Křížkovský, (Karel) Pavel (*b* Holasovice, 9 Jan. 1820; *d* Brno, 8 May 1885). Czech choirmaster and composer. As a child he was discouraged from a musical career but received some basic training from the choirmaster of Neplachovice, and later as a chorister in Opava. He studied philosophy in Olomouc and finally Brno where he settled in 1843. Here Křížkovský founded a student choir and began to study composition. In 1848 he took holy orders in the Augustinian monastery where he also became choirmaster, in which capacity he influenced a generation of Moravian composers including Janáček and Vojáček. Křížkovský did much to expand Brno's musical life, promoting both the classics and Czech composers, but above all cultivating an interest in Moravian folk-song. His own enthusiasm had been encouraged by the folklorist František Sušil, a fellow teacher. As choirmaster of the Brno Beseda musical society he gave many concerts in Moravia and Bohemia, and in 1861 his performances and settings of folk-song and poetry attracted the favourable attention of Smetana. Křížkovský's exclusively vocal output embodied his aspirations for the country's music. While his church music made a modest contribution to the Cecilian Movement in Moravia, his secular choruses served as a stimulus and model for Smetana, Dvořák, Janáček, and a host of other composers. Ranging from simple folk-settings to original compositions embodying the contours and harmonic characteristics of Moravian folk music, Křížkovský's work helped mould a style of choral writing based on folk-song which formed an important part of his nation's musical revival.

JAN SMACZNY

Krommer, Franz [Kramář, Krommer-Kramář, František Vincenc] (*b* Kamenice u Třebíče, 27 Nov. 1795; *d* Vienna, 8 Jan. 1831). Czech composer and *Kapellmeister*. Although he studied the organ and the violin with his uncle, it would seem that Krommer was largely self-taught as a composer. He served as an organist in Turǎn for a few years before following the well-worn path to Vienna in 1785. After pursuing a career as *Kapellmeister* to various of

the Hungarian nobility and Duke Ignaz Fuchs in Vienna, he eventually succeeded his compatriot Leopold Kozeluch as the Emperor's *Kammer Kapellmeister* and *Hofmusik compositor* in 1818. Krommer's music, in particular his many quartets and quintets, were admired in Vienna and disseminated widely throughout Europe. He was held in high regard in England, France, and Italy receiving honorary memberships of the conservatories of Paris, Milan, and Vienna. His musical style faithfully reflected the changing tastes of his day, from Rococo to early Romantic, and though his contemporary reputation was founded mainly on his chamber music, in particular the string quartets of which he was considered a major exponent, interest today focuses on Krommer's solo wind concertos and occasional wind ensemble pieces.

JAN SMACZNY

Krumpholtz, Jean-Baptiste [Johann Baptist] (*b* Budenice, Bohemia, 3 May 1742; *d* Paris, 19 Feb. 1790). Bohemian harpist and composer. In 1773 he entered the chapel of Prince Nikolaus Esterházy in Vienna as a harpist and a composition pupil of Haydn. In 1777 he went to Paris, making his début at the Concert Spirituel with one of his own harp concertos. Krumpholtz was one of the first harpists to use harmonics and other devices designed to increase the range and facility of the instrument. Krumpholtz's works include sonatas, variations, and concertos (mainly for the harp), and two 'symphonies' for harp and orchestra.

His brother, **Wenzel Krumpholtz** (*b* ? Budenice, *c*.1750; *d* Vienna, 2 May 1817), was a violinist in the Esterházy chapel and, from 1796, in the court opera in Vienna. He was also a minor composer.

WENDY THOMPSON

Kuhlau, (Daniel) Friedrich (Rudolph) (*b* Uelzen, nr Hanover, 11 Sept. 1786; *d* Copenhagen, 12 Mar. 1832). Danish composer born in Germany. The son of a military bandsman, he became a pianist and teacher in Copenhagen, where he went in 1810 to avoid conscription in Napoleon's army. He composed a great deal of flute music and piano music, but also music for the Royal Theatre in Copenhagen, where he was chorus master from 1816 to 1817.

DENIS ARNOLD

Kuhnau, Johann (*b* Geising, Erzgebirge, 6 Apr. 1660; *d* Leipzig, 5 June 1722). German composer. He studied at Dresden, where he was a soprano in the Kreuzkirche, and then moved to Leipzig to study law. In 1684 he was appointed organist at St Thomas's, and in 1701 *Kantor*; he was also director of music at the university. (His successor in these posts was Bach.)

Kuhnau's surviving works include Latin motets and around 30 German sacred cantatas (several more survive without music). His keyboard music, which was published in Leipzig, includes the two volumes of *Neue Clavier-Übung* (1689, 1692), collections of suites and, in the later volume, the earliest sonata to be published in Germany; the *Frische Clavier Früchte* (1696), seven more sonatas; and a set of six programme sonatas, the *Musicalische Vorstellung einiger biblischer Historien* (the 'biblical' sonatas, 1700), illustrating in vivid musical terms scenes from the Bible such as 'The Fight between David and Goliath'. In 1700 he published a satirical novel, *Der musicalische Quack-Salber* ('The musical charlatan').

WENDY THOMPSON

Kuhreihen [*Kuhreigen*] (Ger.). See *Ranz des vaches*.

Kujawiak. A Polish dance in quick triple time, named after the region of Kujawy. It is a type of *mazurka.

Kullervo. Symphonic poem, Op. 7, by Sibelius for soprano, baritone, male chorus, and orchestra, composed in 1892. It is based on the *Kalevala*. The work was withdrawn after its first performance and not played again until 1958.

Kunst (Ger.). 'Art'; *Künstler*, 'artist'; *Kunst der Fuge*, see *Art of Fugue*; *Kunstlied*, 'art song' (folk-song is *Volkslied*).

Kunst der Fuge, Die. See *Art of Fugue, The*.

Kurrende [*Currende*] (Ger.). Term originating in the 16th century for the choirs of Latin schools in Germany which were composed of boys from impoverished families who earned their keep by singing at weddings, funerals, and civic occasions.

Kurz, kurze (Ger.). 'Short'.

Kusevitsky, Sergey. See *Koussevitzky, Serge*.

K.V. (followed by a number). Abbreviation for *Köchel-Verzeichnis*, the chronological list of Mozart's works published in 1862 by Ludwig von Köchel. Mozart's works are customarily referred to for purposes of identification by Köchel's numbering, preceded by the letters K.V., or just K.

Kyrie (Gk., 'Lord'). Part of the Ordinary of the Roman Catholic *Mass, sung between the Introit and the Gloria. Each of the three invocations, 'Kyrie eleison; Christe eleison; Kyrie eleison', is sung three times. (See also *Plainchant*, 2.) The Kyrie was retained in the Anglican liturgy as 'Lord have mercy; Christ have mercy; Lord have mercy' and appears in the Communion Service (see *Common Prayer, Book of*).

L

L. Abbreviation for *Links* (Ger.), 'left'; L.H., abbreviation for *linke Hand*, 'left hand'.

La, lah. The sixth degree of the scale in the *solmization system. In French and Italian usage *la* has become attached, on the fixed-doh principle, to the note A. See *Tonic Sol-fa*.

Lächelnd (Ger.). 'Smiling'.

Lâcher (Fr.). 'To loosen' (e.g. the snare of a side-drum).

Lachnith, Ludwig Wenzel (*b* Prague, 7 July 1746; *d* Paris, 3 Oct. 1820). Bohemian horn player and composer. In 1773 he appeared at the Concert Spirituel in Paris, where he settled permanently in 1781, having studied composition with Philidor. He wrote a great deal of instrumental music, but was best known for his pasticcio operas, such as *Les mystères d'Isis* (performed 1801), which is an 'adaptation' of Mozart's *Die Zauberflöte* incorporating music by Haydn and Mozart as well as his own.

WENDY THOMPSON

Lachrimae. Collection of 21 pieces by Dowland for five viols and lute, published in 1604. The full title is *Lachrimae, or Seaven Teares*, the 'seaven teares' being seven pavans entitled *Lachrimae*, each of which begins with the theme of Dowland's song 'Flow my Tears' followed by variations. The other 14 pieces are dances, such as galliards.

Lachrymae. Work for viola and piano, Op. 48, by Britten, 'reflections on a song of John Dowland'. It was composed in 1950 and arranged for viola and orchestra in 1976.

Lacrimoso, lagrimoso (It.). 'Lachrymose', 'tearful'.

Lady Macbeth of the Mtsensk District, The (Russ.: *Ledi Makbet Mtsenskovo uyezda*). Opera in four acts by Shostakovich; text by the composer and Alexander Preys, after Nikolay Leskov's story (1865). Produced: Leningrad, Maly Theatre, 22 January 1934; Moscow, Nemirovich-Danchenko Music Theatre, 24 January 1934; Cleveland, 31 January 1935 (semi-staged); London, Queen's Hall, 18 March 1936 (concert performance). At first *Lady Macbeth* was received with widespread critical acclaim in the Soviet Union. However, these were the early, uncertain days of *socialist realism, and, whereas the opera had initially been regarded as a model of socialist realist virtues, Stalin (who saw it in January 1936) reacted violently to the score's uncompromising gestures and (often) harsh dissonance, to the libretto's themes of lust and cruelty, and to the explicit scenes of sexual infidelity on stage. The opera was subsequently condemned in a notorious *Pravda* editorial entitled 'Chaos instead of Music' (*Sumbur vmesto muzyki*, 28 January 1936). It was withdrawn from the repertory, and remained proscribed throughout Stalin's lifetime. However, after Stalin's death (1953) and with the relaxing of official cultural attitudes, Shostakovich revised parts of the text and score, and the opera was given a second première, under its original subtitle *Katerina Izmaylova*, at the Stanislavsky-Nemirovich-Danchenko Music Theatre, Moscow, on 26 December 1962 (official date, 8 January 1963). Revived London, Covent Garden, in this revised version, 2 December 1963.

Katerina Izmaylova (sop.), married to a wealthy but dull merchant Zinovy (ten.), is tired of her life in the provincial Mtsensk district, and while her husband is away she has an affair with Sergey (ten.), a young employee on the estate. Her father-in-law Boris (bass), himself intending to seduce her, orders Sergey to be flogged when he discovers him descending from the window of Katerina's bedroom; in revenge Katerina kills Boris by sprinkling rat-poison on to the mushrooms he eats for supper. Zinovy returns unexpectedly and finds Katerina and Sergey together; Sergey kills him, and they hide the body in the cellar. The body is discovered during the festivities for the wedding of Katerina and Sergey; the couple are arrested and exiled to Siberia. Here Sergey rejects Katerina, and instead takes up with another convict, Sonetka (con.). Katerina, aware at last of Sergey's insincerity, drowns herself, pulling Sonetka with her. The opera ends with a chorus expressing the boredom and agony of the prison camp, just as it had begun with Katerina's lament at her own life of tedium and frustration.

FURTHER READING
Geoffrey Norris: 'The Operas', *Shostakovich: the Man and his Music*, ed. Christopher Norris (London, 1982), pp. 115–24.

Lady Nevell's Booke, My. See *My Ladye Nevells Booke*.

Lady of Shalott, The. Cantata by Phyllis Tate to Tennyson's poem. It is for tenor, viola, percussion, two pianos, and celesta, and was composed in 1956 for the tenth anniversary of the BBC Third Programme.

Lage (Ger.). 'Position'. 1. In string playing, *erste Lage*, *zweite Lage*, etc. refer to 'first position', 'second position'. 2. *Enge Lage*, *weite Lage*, 'close position', 'wide (open) position' (of chords). 3. *Hohe Lage*, *tiefe Lage*, 'high position', 'low position' (of voice-ranges).

Lai [*lay*] (Fr.). An extended song form of the 13th and 14th centuries featuring several stanzas of varying poetic structure each set to a different melody. The 13th-century *trouvère* repertory contains over 30 monophonic *lais*, including examples by Gille li Vinier, Thibault IV, and Ernoul le Vielle as well as anonymous authors, and these works exhibit considerable variety in number and length of stanzas em- ployed. The four *lais* in the early 14th-century *Roman de Fauvel* are more standardized in these respects, and form the immediate background to the *lais* of Guillaume de Machaut, which have been described by Richard Hoppin as 'one of the high points of medieval song'. With the increased notational accuracy of the *Ars Nova period, Machaut was able to take full command of the musical as well as the poetic aspect of his *lais*, and brought to his melodic writing a subtle variety and variation of pace which fully matches his virtuosic treatment of language. All but two of Machaut's 19 *lais* use the same over-all approach: there are 12 stanzas, the first and last of which have an identical poetic form and are thus set to the same music, this being transposed (usually a fifth higher) for the final statement. Each of the other stanzas employs a different poetic form, with varying rhyme schemes, lengths, and numbers of lines, and each is provided with its own music. Stanzas are divided into structurally identical halves or quarters, involving a double or fourfold statement of the melody provided (see Ex. 1).

Four of the *lais* depart from tradition in being

Ex. 1

Quadruple and double division of stanzas in Machaut: *Le lay mortel*

polyphonic, and Machaut uses several methods to achieve this. In *Le lay de confort* each stanza is written as a three-part canon, while monophonic and canonic stanzas alternate in *Le lay de la fontainne*. In *Le lay de consolation* both halves of each stanza have different music, these together forming a two-part texture, and the three-part writing of 'En demantant' is a result of the combination of each group of three stanzas. If his aim was to make the *lai* more acceptable within the growing fashion for polyphonic composition, Machaut was ultimately unsuccessful, for the *lai* was ignored by later French composers.   PETER DAVIES

Laisser (Fr.). 'To allow', 'to leave'. The expression *laisser vibrer* is a direction to a percussion player to let the sound 'ring on', i.e. not to damp it.

Lalande [Delalande], **Michel-Richard de** (*b* Paris, 15 Dec. 1657; *d* Versailles, 18 June 1726). French composer. He was a choirboy at St Germain-l'Auxerrois, Paris. At the age of 15, disappointed in his application to join Lully's orchestra, he is said to have sworn never to play his violin again. Certainly in the years after this he became primarily an organist, and although he was considered too young to be appointed *organiste du roy* he was chosen to teach the royal children. In 1683 Louis XIV intervened to ensure that Lalande was made one of the four *sous-maîtres* of the royal chapel and by 1714 he was in complete control. In 1684 he married Anne Rebel, one of the best singers at court and the sister of Jean-Féry Rebel. They had two daughters, both of whom also became singers, and the three women undoubtedly took part in the performances of some of his grand motets with elaborate soprano parts. The daughters died of smallpox in 1711 and Anne de Lalande died in 1722. In 1718 Lalande had taken over the less demanding position of *surintendant*, and in 1722 reverted to his previous position of one of four *sous-maîtres*. In the same year Louis XV made him a Chevalier of the Order of St Michel. He was buried at the church of Notre Dame de Versailles.

Lalande lacked the versatility of some of his contemporaries, but within his limits he was an extremely fine composer. His secular vocal music is of little importance, but his instrumental music survives in a number of versions under the title of 'Symphonies pour les soupers du Roy', and is more interesting. Some of the *symphonies* are taken from his dance music for *divertissements*, but there are several 'Caprices' and 'Caprices ou Fantaisies', imaginatively scored pieces in several movements, independent of dance rhythms. His greatest achievement, however, lies in his *grands motets*, mainly

Michel-Richard de Lalande, engraving after a portrait by Sanguine de Santerre.

Latin psalm settings of huge proportions, with solos, recitatives, and choruses. In these motets Lalande combines contrapuntal skill with a rich harmony, achieving an emotional power beyond that of Lully or Charpentier. They were favourites at Versailles and at the Concert Spirituel (several were given at the opening concert in 1725), and copies found throughout Europe indicate that they were probably the best-known French vocal music of the Baroque period.   DENIS ARNOLD

Lallouette, Jean François (*b* Paris, 1651; *d* Paris, 31 Aug. 1728). French composer. One of Lully's composition pupils, he became his assistant and provided **parties de remplissage* for some of his works. He was dismissed from this post for claiming to have written the best *airs* in Lully's *Isis*, and spent the year of 1678-9 in Turin, in the service of the Savoy court. On his return to Paris he was unsuccessful in trying to get an opera performed (Lully's privilege stood in his way) and in obtaining a post at the royal chapel. He seems to have left Paris again, returning only in 1700, as choirmaster of Notre Dame. His surviving music is mainly sacred (his opera is lost), including Masses, motets, and a *Miserere* (Paris, 1730).   DENIS ARNOLD

Lalo, (Victor Antoine) Edouard (*b* Lille, 27 Jan. 1823; *d* Paris, 22 Apr. 1892). French composer. He left home without an allowance (his father being opposed to a musical career) to study violin and composition at the Paris Conservatoire. For some years he composed drawing-room ballads, then chamber music. Then for 10 years, disgusted at the French public's lack of interest in music other than opera, he composed nothing, although he was active as the viola player of a string quartet. At 44 he tried his hand at an opera with no success. He then wrote a number of pieces for orchestra, including a Symphony in G minor (1885–6), using motto themes to link movements, and the ever-popular *Symphonie espagnole* (1875) for violin and orchestra. Eventually he wrote a successful opera *Le roi d' Ys* (1888) on a Breton legend and using some national folk material. His ballet *Namouna*, though criticized originally as too symphonic, was admired by Debussy, d'Indy, Dukas, and others, and influenced them a good deal. Deft orchestration was one of Lalo's strongest points. He left some excellent songs, mainly written for his wife. His son Pierre (1866–1943) was a well-known music critic. PERCY SCHOLES, rev.

Lambe, Walter (*b* 1450–1, *d* after 1499). English composer. He may have been born in Salisbury and have been a scholar at Eton College in 1467. His career was largely spent at St George's Chapel, Windsor, first as a singer and later as master of the choristers. Little of his music survives, but he was an important contributor to the *Eton Choirbook*, and some of his votive antiphons are of extraordinary length and complexity. JOHN MILSOM

Lambert, (Leonard) Constant (*b* London, 27 Aug. 1905; *d* London, 21 Aug. 1951). English composer. He studied with R. O. Morris and Vaughan Williams at the Royal College of Music, and while still a student gained a commission from Diaghilev for the ballet *Romeo and Juliet* (1926), a set of rococo dances gingered up in the manner of Stravinsky or Poulenc with harmonic modernisms and touches of jazz. He used a similar style in *The Rio Grande* for chorus and orchestra (1927), but other works, such as *Music for Orchestra* (1927) and the cantata *Summer's Last Will and Testament* (1935), are more overtly serious, though still marked by his imaginative flair and urbanity. His output remained relatively small, since he gave much of his energy to conducting and arranging for the ballet. In 1930 he was appointed musical director of the Sadler's Wells Ballet, and he wrote the scores for Ashton's *Pomona* (1926), *Horoscope* (1937), and *Tiresias* (1951). PAUL GRIFFITHS

FURTHER READING
Constant Lambert: *Music Ho!* (London, 1934, 3rd edn 1966); Richard Shead: *Constant Lambert* (London, 1973).

Lamellophone. A modern classification term for musical instruments with plucked flexible tongues (e.g. the musical box and the African *sansa*). See *Instruments, Classification of*.

Lament. 1. Specifically, music for bagpipes at Scottish clan funerals. 2. Any piece of music expressing grief, usually at the loss of a friend or a famous person. A well-known example in opera is Dido's lament 'When I am laid in earth' from Purcell's *Dido and Aeneas*. See also *Apothéose*; *Déploration*; *Dirge*; *Dump*; *Elegia*; *Epicedium*; *Lamento*; *Plainte*; *Planh*; *Threnody*; *Tombeau*.

Lamentations. Lamentations of the prophet Jeremiah, sung to plainchant melodies (or other settings such as the great ones by Tallis) in Roman Catholic churches in the week before Easter. The Greek word *Threni* is sometimes used.

'Lamentation' Symphony. Nickname of Haydn's Symphony No. 26 in D minor, composed in the late 1760s. It is so called because some of its themes resemble the plainsong melodies sung in Roman Catholic churches in the week before Easter. The symphony is also sometimes referred to as *Weihnachtssymphonie* ('Christmas Symphony') but the title has no apparent relevance.

Lamento (It.). In Italian opera of the Baroque period, a tragic aria, usually placed before the climax of the plot. A famous example is Monteverdi's *Lamento d'Arianna*.

Lamento d'Arianna ('Ariadne's Lament'). Only surviving music from Monteverdi's opera *L'Arianna* (1608). Monteverdi arranged it as a five-part madrigal *Lasciatemi morire* ('Leave me to Die'), published in Venice in 1623.

Lampugnani, Giovanni Battista (*b* Milan, 1706; *d* ? Milan, *c*.1786). Italian composer. He began a successful career as an opera composer in 1732 in his native city, soon obtaining commissions from theatres elsewhere in Italy. In 1743 he went to London, following Galuppi as composer to the King's Theatre in the Haymarket; he remained there until 1746, when he returned to Italy. His travels resumed in the 1750s with operas composed for Barcelona (1753) and London (1755), and he produced others for Italian theatres until 1769. From then onwards he seems to have been content to direct other men's works in Milan (he played second harpsichord in Mozart's *Mitridate* in 1770), ending his days at La Scala as *maestro al cembalo*. DENIS ARNOLD

Lancers. A square dance for eight or 16 couples (a simplified version of the *quadrille) which became popular in the mid 19th century. It was invented by Joseph Hart in 1819, and he published *Les Lanciers*, naming the five dances that made up the set 'La Rose', 'La Lodoïska', 'La Dorset', 'L'Étoile', and 'Les Lanciers'. The dance was further popularized by the Dublin dancing teacher John Duval, who greatly helped in putting it into general circulation.

PETER GAMMOND

Lancio (It.). 'Vigour'; *con lancio*, 'with vigour'.

Land der Berge. The Austrian national anthem. See under *Emperor's Hymn*.

Landi, Stefano (*b* Rome, 1586 or 1587; *d* Rome, 28 Oct. 1639). Italian composer and teacher. He was a boy soprano at the German College in Rome, and then became organist at S. Maria in Trastevere and, in 1611, a singer at the Oratory of Ss. Crocifisso. He left Rome to become *maestro di cappella* to the Bishop of Padua, but soon returned to become one of the favourite musicians of the Barberini family.

Landi was one of the most notable of the early school of Roman opera composers. His *La morte d'Orfeo* (performed 1619) is unusual for having comic characters, while *Il Sant'Alessio* (performed *c*.1632) is a grand spectacular opera, using big choruses and elaborate machines and scenery.

DENIS ARNOLD

Landini, Francesco (*b* Fiesole or Florence, *c*.1325; *d* Florence, 2 Sept. 1397). Italian composer. An attack of smallpox left him blind from childhood, but he became a skilled performer of keyboard instruments, especially the *organetto* or portative organ, and designed and built musical instruments; he also sang, wrote poetry, and possessed a keen academic mind with a deep knowledge of philosophy. Little is known of his early career, but he probably spent some time in Venice and elsewhere in northern Italy. In 1361 he was appointed organist at the monastery of S. Trinità in Florence, moving to

A page of music by Landini from a 15th-century manuscript. The illustration shows the composer playing a portative organ.

the church of S. Lorenzo in 1365; he is buried there, and the monument depicts him playing the portative organ.

Landini was the leading Italian composer of his day, and more music by him survives than by any other Italian composer of the 14th century, including some 140 *ballate* for two or three voices, 12 madrigals, and four incomplete motets. As these works embrace a wide variety of styles, drawing upon both French and Italian features, no definite chronology of the composer's artistic development can be made, although the works for three voices are probably mostly later than those for two. Landini's music is often noted for its fluid melodiousness and rhythmic grace, in contrast to the more angular style of his most talented French contemporary, Machaut.   JOHN MILSOM

Landini cadence. See *Cadence*, 1.

Ländler (Ger.). A rustic German and Austrian dance like a slow waltz, which originated in the Landel district of Austria (now Upper Austria). It was popular in the early 19th century: Mozart, Beethoven, and Schubert all wrote collections of *Ländler*. In its early form it was a hearty country dance, with stamping and clapping; the dancers sometimes sang or jodelled, while the typical instrumental accompaniment consisted of violin and double bass. A more refined version became popular in Vienna, and the dance soon began to resemble the *waltz, which eventually superseded it. The symphonies of Mahler and Bruckner use the characteristic rhythms and spirit of the dance, while Berg quoted a Ländler tune in his Violin Concerto, and in his opera *Wozzeck* (Act 2 Scene 4).

Ländlich (Ger.). 'Country-like', 'rustic'.

Land of Hope and Glory. Title of the finale of Elgar's *Coronation Ode* (1902) to words by A. C. Benson. It is for alto, chorus, and orchestra, and the tune is to a melody adapted from the trio section of Elgar's first *Pomp and Circumstance* march. It was also published as a separate song for alto and orchestra, with words different from those in the *Coronation Ode*, this being the version generally and communally sung.

Land of my Fathers (*Hen wlad fy nhadau*). Welsh national anthem by James James (1832–1902) to words by Evan James. It was composed in 1856 and first appeared in print in John Owain's *Gems of Welsh Melody* (1860).

Lang, Johann Georg (*b* Svojšín, 1722; *d* Ehrenbreitstein, nr Koblenz, 17 July 1798). German composer born in Bohemia. In 1746 he entered the service of the Prince-Bishop of Augsburg, remaining with him until he died. He was sent to study in Italy for three years before becoming, in 1758, the Prince's *Konzertmeister*. Ten years later he transferred to Ehrenbreitstein, retaining his position as *Konzertmeister*. He composed mainly instrumental music, some of which has been wrongly attributed to other composers, including Haydn and J. C. Bach.
                          WENDY THOMPSON

Langaus (Ger.). A late 18th-century Austrian dance, similar to the waltz or Ländler, which was banned by the police for its lack of restraint.

Langlais, Jean (François) (*b* La Fontenelle, 15 Feb. 1907). French composer. Blind from childhood, he studied at the Institut Nationale des Jeunes Aveugles (1917–30) and the Paris Conservatoire (1927–34), where his teachers included Marcel Dupré for the organ and Paul Dukas for composition. In 1945 he was appointed organist of Ste Clotilde, and he has also taught at the Institut (since 1931) and the Schola Cantorum (since 1961). Influenced by Messiaen, he has produced a large output of organ music, as well as various liturgical choral works.   PAUL GRIFFITHS

Langsam (Ger.). 'Slow'; *langsamer*, 'slower'.

Lanier, Emilia. See under *Bassano*.

Lanier, Nicholas (*b* Greenwich, Sept. 1588; *d* London, Feb. 1666). English composer. He was a member of a family of French descent which settled in England in the second half of the 16th century. His early years were spent in the service of the Cecil family and in 1616 he was appointed lutenist to the King's Musick. In 1617 he wrote some music in the new recitative style for Ben Jonson's masque *Lovers Made Men* (he also designed the scenery). On Charles I's accession he was made Master of the King's Musick, and was also sent to Italy to buy paintings on the king's behalf (Hampton Court contains some of the fruits of his labour). He was later made Master of the King's Miniatures, but the Civil War left him without a job, and he made his living trading in pictures and musical instruments abroad (his letters to Constantijn Huygens are a melancholy testament to his feelings at this time of 'exile'). On the Restoration he returned to his post as Master of the King's Musick.

Much of his music is now lost, but he wrote some of the earliest ayres in the declamatory style, and his recitative *Hero and Leander* shows a close knowledge of the Italian lament, helping to acclimatize operatic music in England. He was evidently a talented artist, and left a delightful self-portrait; Van Dyck also painted him. DENIS ARNOLD

Lanzentanz (Ger.). See *Pordon dantza*.

Laos. See *South-East Asian Music*.

Lappi, Pietro (*b* Florence, *c*.1575; *d* Brescia, 1630). Italian composer. He was *maestro di cappella* of S. Maria delle Grazie, Brescia, from *c*.1593 until his death. His music is all for use in the church, and includes Masses and motets, mainly in the polychoral Venetian manner but also in the smaller-scale *concertato* style, and some lively and attractive canzonas for instrumental ensemble. DENIS ARNOLD

Largamente (It.), **largement** (Fr.). 'Broadly', i.e. slow and dignified; *larguer* (Fr.), *larghezza* (It.), 'breadth'. See also *Largo*.

Larghetto (It.). Diminutive of **largo*—slow and dignified, but not as slow as *largo*.

Largo (It.). 'Broad', dignified in style; *largo di molto*, very slow and dignified. The term can also be used as the title of a movement or piece, e.g. Handel's famous aria 'Ombra mai fù' from his opera *Xerxes*, which is often performed in various instrumental versions as Handel's *Largo* (although Handel's aria was marked *larghetto*).

Largo appeared as a tempo marking at the beginning of the 17th century. Rousseau listed it in his dictionary (1767) as the slowest marking, but Purcell and his contemporaries evidently considered it to be midway between *adagio* and *allegro*.

Lark Ascending, The. Romance by Vaughan Williams for violin and orchestra inspired by the poem of that name by George Meredith (1828–1909). It was composed in 1914 and revised in 1920.

'Lark' Quartet (*Lerchenquartett*). Nickname of Haydn's String Quartet in D major, Op. 64 No. 5, composed in 1790. It is so called because of the soaring violin theme of its opening. The rhythm of the last movement has given rise to another, less frequently used nickname, the 'Hornpipe' Quartet.

La Rue, Pierre de (*b* ? Tournai, *c*.1460; *d* Courtrai, 20 Nov. 1518). Flemish composer. In 1483 he was a singer at Siena Cathedral, but by the end of the decade he had returned to the Netherlands, where he sang at 's Hertogenbosch Cathedral. He entered the service of the Archduke Maximilian at the Burgundian chapel in 1492, and when Maximilian became emperor La Rue remained as a member of the chapel

under Philip the Fair. In 1508 he became a singer in the chapel of Margaret of Austria, at Mechelen, and was evidently a great favourite. In 1514 he was in the private chapel of the Archduke Karl, and in 1516 became an abbot at Courtrai, where he died.

La Rue was one of the most celebrated Flemish composers of his day. His works have been hed up as models of the pure Netherlands style, devoid of Italian influence. Most of his 31 complete Mass cycles are based on a plainchant *cantus firmus*, but some are built on a secular melody (such as 'L'homme armé'), and the *Missa 'Ave sanctissima Maria'* is a parody Mass based on a six-voice motet which may also be by him. He also wrote about 30 motets, *Magnificat* settings, and Lamentations. Of his secular music about 30 charmingly wistful *chansons* survive, many of them in the lavishly illustrated *chansonniers* of Margaret of Austria. Most are for four voices. WENDY THOMPSON

Lasciare (It.). 'To leave', 'to allow'.

Laserna, Blas de (*bapt.* Corella, Navarre, 4 Feb. 1751; *d* Madrid, 8 Aug. 1816). Spanish composer. He worked in Madrid from the age of 23 until he retired in 1808. He was a champion of traditional Spanish dramatic music, writing about 700 *tonadillas*, 80 *sainetes*, and many other dramatic pieces. Nevertheless one of his most popular works was the Italianate *El majo y la italiana fingida* (1778). WENDY THOMPSON

Lass of Richmond Hill, The. Song by James Hook to words by L. McNally. It refers to Richmond, Yorkshire, not Surrey.

Lassu (Hung.). 'Slow'; see *Csárdás*.

Lassus, Orlande [Roland] **de** [Orlando di Lasso] (*b* Mons, *c*.1532; *d* Munich, 14 June 1594). Franco-Flemish composer. He was a choirboy at St Nicolas, Mons, and tradition has it that he was kidnapped three times for the beauty of his voice. At the age of 12 his parents allowed him to enter the service of Ferrante Gonzaga, and with him Lassus went to Paris, Mantua, Palermo, and Milan. When his voice broke he went to Naples in the service of a minor nobleman, and there he became a member of the Accademia de' Sereni, a literary and artistic circle. He then visited Rome as a guest of the influential Archbishop of Florence and obtained the important post of *maestro di cappella* at St John Lateran when he was only 21. Here he was again involved with a group of intellectuals, who were interested in modern ideas, including the use of chromaticism in music. He stayed in this post only briefly before being called home to visit his parents who were ill; they had both died by the time he arrived in Mons. In 1555 he was in Antwerp, and it was at this time that he began to publish his works, showing an extraordinary versatility in putting together a book of elegant madrigals for Antonio Gardane in Venice and a mixed set of madrigals, bawdy *villanelle* to Neapolitan dialect texts, French *chansons*, and Latin motets for Tylman Susato in Antwerp.

Lassus's reputation was well established by the publications of the 1550s, and in 1556 he was invited to become a singer at the Bavarian court of Duke Albrecht V in Munich. Within a few years he was head of the musical establishment, in the place of the then unfashionably Protestant Ludwig Daser; he held this position until his death. In 1558 he married Regina Wäckinger, the daughter of a court official, and resumed publishing his works on a massive scale, books of sacred and secular music appearing in Antwerp, Venice, Paris, Munich, and Frankfurt. In the early Munich years he proved himself a master of both the witty *chanson* and the more serious madrigal, giving in the madrigal a musical expression of the texts which few could equal, and not indulging in the less subtle word-painting which was soon to become fashionable. At this time he seems to have been very lively and cheerful, taking an active part in the celebrations for the royal wedding of Wilhelm V and Renée of Lorraine in 1568 as an actor in a traditional *commedia dell'arte*. He also travelled widely in search of singers and instrumentalists for the rapidly expanding musical establishment, to Flanders, Frankfurt, and especially northern Italy. He built up his *cappella* until it was the most famous musical centre in Europe, inspiring a host of young composers (including the Gabrielis) to study with him there.

Orlande de Lassus, woodcut from his 'Livre de chansons nouvelles' (1571).

Some of the church music of this time reflects this period of good fortune. The parody Masses on French *chansons*, for example, follow their models so closely that the secular words must often have sprung to mind. However, it was also about this time that the gloominess and intensity of Counter-Reformation ideas began to affect his music, most especially in his settings of the seven Penitential Psalms.

In 1579 economic circumstances and the accession of the new Duke, Wilhelm V, dictated a reduction in the *cappella*. Shortly after this Lassus was offered the post of *maestro* at the Saxon court at Dresden, but he refused it, partly because Albrecht had granted him an ample pension for life, but mainly because he was settled in Munich, with two town houses and one in the country. The effect of the new atmosphere is none the less noticeable in his music. The publications of the 1580s are largely concerned with church music, including settings from the Book of Job, the Penitential Psalms, and the Lamentations of the Prophet Jeremiah. His fifth book of madrigals (Nuremberg, 1585) sets verses by Petrarch on the passing of youth, and religious sonnets by Gabriel Fiamma. In 1585 he made a further visit to Italy, significantly making a pilgrimage to Loreto (the Lourdes of its time), and a couple of years later he dedicated a madrigal volume to the Munich court physician, who was growing increasingly worried by Lassus's mental state. By 1590 Lassus was suffering from melancholia, sometimes scarcely recognizing his wife, and was beset by thoughts of death. In 1594 he published a volume of six-part motets which the preface refers to as his swansong. Nevertheless, he accompanied his master to Regensburg in the same year, and was preparing for publication his cycle of religious madrigals, the *Lagrime di S. Pietro*, when he died. Of his four sons two, Ferdinand and Rudolph, became musicians and were in the service of the Bavarian court.

Lassus was acknowledged in his lifetime as one of the great masters of music. In 1604 a collected edition of his motets was published by his sons, and his church music, known from England to Poland, continued to be performed, especially in France, where his connection with the publishing house of Le Roy & Ballard had been very strong. Several more posthumous editions were published before about 1650, an unusual tribute to a composer's popularity at this period. Nevertheless, his music has not latterly received the attention it certainly deserves. The modern edition of his music is only now reaching completion, there is no really adequate biography in English, and gramophone recordings are relatively scarce. The reason for this lies partly in his expatriate life, in that no national body has been responsible for reviving his music. Another contributing factor may be the very versatility of his gifts; the 'canonization' of Palestrina probably owes much to the fact that his sacred music took up so much of his energies. Even so, Lassus's excellence in virtually all genres must receive its reward in due course. He is especially fine in the subtle expression of moods, in both church and secular music, and his *chansons* and *villanelle* can be seen as the equivalent of a great master's drawings or etchings, capturing the character of the grotesque or unusual in his fellow men.

DENIS ARNOLD

FURTHER READING
Jerome Roche: *Lassus* (London, 1982).

Last Post. British army bugle call. The First Post at 9.30 p.m. calls all men back to their barracks for roll call; the Last Post at 10 p.m. (formerly known as the 'Watch-setting') ends the day. By a natural and poetical association of ideas it has become the custom to sound the Last Post at all military funerals.

Last Rose of Summer, 'Tis the. Irish air, originally *Castle Hyde*, which became R. A.

Millikin's *The Groves of Blarney* (c.1790). Thomas Moore included it, to his own new words, in his *Irish Melodies* (1813). Beethoven set the air, Mendelssohn wrote a piano fantasia on it, and it is sung by a soprano in Act 2 of Flotow's *Martha*.

Last Sleep of the Virgin, The (*Le dernier sommeil de la Vierge*). Orchestral interlude from Massenet's oratorio *La Vierge* (1880), much favoured as an encore by Beecham and the RPO.

Latilla, Gaetano (*b* Bari, 12 Jan. 1711; *d* Naples, 15 Jan. 1788). Italian composer. He trained at the Conservatorio S. Maria di Loreto in Naples, and after initial successes there in the 1730s had operas produced throughout Europe. He spent over 15 years in Venice, from 1753 to 1766 in charge of the music at the Pietà, and from 1762 to c.1772 as assistant to Galuppi at St Mark's. He was one of the most popular composers of comic opera of his time and some of his works, with their attractive melodies and well-constructed finales, would repay revival.

DENIS ARNOLD

Latin America

1. Diversity of Traditions
2. Mexico and Central America
3. Spanish-speaking South America

4. Brazil
5. Caribbean Area

1. *Diversity of Traditions.* Latin America, with a population of over 340 million, stretches from Mexico and Cuba south to Cape Horn. In general, Latin American music can be said to blend (1) native Indian, (2) transported African, and (3) imported European elements. What gives each regional music its distinctive flavour is the relative strength of Indian, African, and European traditions in the mixture. The rural musics in highland areas of nations that still boast a large Indian population, such as Mexico, Guatemala, Peru, Bolivia, and Ecuador, integrate various aboriginal traits. These include 'tight' throat, 'out of tune' melodies, and ritualistic festive performances. Prominent 20th-century Mexican (Carlos Chávez, Candelario Huízar, Daniel Ayala), Guatemalan (Jesús and Ricardo Castillo), and Peruvian (Daniel Alomía Robles, Teodoro Valcárcel, Andrés Sas) composers have advantageously incorporated Indian and pseudo-Indian tunes in their works.

But, on the other hand, African influences now dominate both folk and art music in Caribbean island nations where before 1550 Blacks began replacing Indians in the labouring

force. So far as Spanish-speaking nations go, African influences have also strongly affected the folk music of coastal Mexico, Guatemala, Honduras, Panama, Venezuela, Colombia, Ecuador, and Peru. The marimbas of southern Mexico and Guatemala and the leg drums played by Blacks in coastal Colombia and Ecuador are generally conceded to be African derivatives. Even more strongly does Portuguese-speaking Brazil (which comprises half of South America in population and territory) testify to African influences and African intermixture. The works of the Brazilian mulattos José Joaquim Emerico Lôbo de Mesquita (c.1745-1805) and José Maurício Nunes Garcia (1767-1830) may not sound in any way idiomatically African. But certainly Brazilian *samba de roda* song repertories and Brazilian *maracatu* dance processions exemplify undeniable African traits persisting to the present day.

Apart from the relatively weak Indian element in Latin American music as a whole, and the stronger African component present in Caribbean and Brazilian areas, Latin American music everywhere and in every aspect betrays overwhelming indebtedness to European models. The many varieties of guitars that abound in the regional folk musics of Latin America are all adaptations of European models. Even the *charango*, a guitar backed with a dried armadillo shell that is popular in the Andes, had its predecessor in a double-string, five-course, discontinuously tuned guitar described in Mersenne's *Harmonie universelle* (Paris, 1636). The paired violins and trumpets that give Mexican *mariachi* music its characteristic flavour are completely European instruments— even though not played in a European manner. Apart from instruments, Latin rhythms and especially harmonies rely heavily on European models. The fast hemiola rhythms (6/8 alternating with 3/4) which lend vivacity to the *son jarocho* performed in the region of Veracruz, Mexico, with accompaniment of harps and guitars, are of Spanish derivation. Equally so are the hemiolas in the Peruvian *marinera* and Argentine *vidalita*.

Not only did Europe provide models for all the Latin American popular string instruments and for many of the most popular Latin American rhythmic clichés, but also Latin American folk music is prevailingly accompanied by European I–IV–V chordal harmony. The first printed example (1883) of the *joropo*, national dance of Venezuela, consists of 40 measures of D major violin or guitar music in 6/8, every bar being harmonized I–V. Such other folkloric favourites as the Mexican *jarabe*, the Colombian *bambuco*, and the Chilean *cueca* are all vigorous hemiola dances, cut up into four-bar phrases, and accompanied by I–IV–V chords.

2. *Mexico and Central America*. Long before Spaniards arrived, Mexican territory was the home of successive high civilizations. When *organum* was just coming to birth in Europe the Totonacs in the Veracruz region were already favouring quadruple and triple tube flutes made of clay that sounded four- and three-note chords. A protuberance at the necks of some archaic clay flutes dug up in Tabasco deflected the air through an 'oscillating air chamber' and gave them a reedy timbre. The Mayas with their delicate six-fingerhole flutes found in excavations of Jaina island were the Greeks of ancient Mexico. The Aztecs with their four-fingerhole flutes were the Romans. Between Mayas and Aztecs came the Toltecs who incised five holes on their human-bone flutes.

The Aztec sages taught that duality, maleness and femaleness, engendered the universe. In deference to the principle of engendering duality, the most important instruments of the Aztecs were the percussive two-toned wooden *teponaztli*, struck with two rubber-tipped mallets, and the upright cylindrical *huehuetl* tipped with jaguar skin which sounded two notes a fifth apart and which was played with two bare hands. These two percussion instruments, each sounding two pitches, joined to gladden the Aztec festivals that were celebrated with communal dances every 20 days. They also joined to solemnize such bloody ceremonies as those in 1502 when at Ahuitzotl's funeral '200 slaves were stretched on their backs over the same *teponaztli* that played the funeral music, and while on top of it their breasts were slashed open and their hearts extracted'.

Aztec musicians enjoyed high social prestige and exemption from tribute payments. Perfection of performance counted so heavily that *huehuetl* or *teponaztli* players who missed beats were immediately withdrawn from the playing ensemble to be executed by having their hearts cut out to propitiate Huitzilopochtli or any other deity being worshipped. Because the lengthy songs that they learned in the *calmécac* (training conservatory) comprised Aztec oral history, only musicians with prodigious memories remained in the profession.

The Aztecs immediately showed a voracious fondness not only for European instruments but also for European music in all its aspects. As early as 1556 the first music book printed in the New World appeared at Mexico City. Before 1600, 12 more music imprints were published at Mexico City for Indian consumption. By 1561 Indian instrumentalists were so rife that Philip

Fragment of a quadruple flute, Mexico, Aztec culture.

II issued in February of that year a *cedula* mandating against the 'present excessive number of musicians who consume their time playing trumpets, clarions, shawms, sackbuts, flutes, cornetts, dulzainas, fifes, viols, rebecs, and other kinds of instruments, in inordinate variety'. In 1565 Mexican ecclesiastical authorities petitioned the crown for 'a further abatement in the excessive number of Indian singers'.

Because the Indians, in addition to continuing to make their own instruments, almost at once learned to make clever imitations of European instruments, they were able as early as the mid 16th century to develop instrumental accompanying ensembles with unforeseen novel tone colour possibilities. They also began composing written music. According to Juan de Torquemada (1565-1624), 'their *villancicos*, their polyphonic music in four parts, certain masses and other liturgical works, all composed with adroitness, have been adjudged superior works of art when shown Spanish masters of composition'. Among Indian composers whose works have been published, Tomás Pascual (active at San Juan Ixcoi in Guatemala 1595-1635) and Juan Mathías (active at Oaxaca in Mexico at mid 17th century) prove Indian mastery in smaller forms. The greatest colonial genius identifiable as an Indian was, however, Don Juan de Lienas, active at Mexico City 1630-50, and composer of sublime *Salves*, Masses, and Lamentations. His *Missa super fa re ut fa sol la* for five voices and *Salve* for four voices have been published and recorded. Much of his music discovered in the 1970s is for double choirs.

The leading Spanish-born or Spanish-descended composers at Mexico City until 1800, all of whom left sizeable repertories, were Hernando Franco (chapelmaster of Mexico City Cathedral 1575-85), Antonio Rodríguez de Mata (1625-43), Luis Coronado (1643-8), Fabián Pérez Ximeno (1648-54), Francisco López Capillas (1654-74), José de Loaysa y Agurto (1676-88), Antonio de Salazar (1688-1715), and Manuel de Zumaya (1715-39). Both López Capillas and Zumaya were born at Mexico City. Zamaya, who died at Oaxaca in 1754, composed the first Mexican opera, *La Partenope*, 1711, to the same libretto of Silvio Stampiglia later used by Handel. Zumaya ranks as one of the paramount composers in New World annals. The master of charming melody, Ignacio Jerusalem (1749-69), born at Lecce, was the first native of Italy to direct Mexico City cathedral and theatre music simultaneously.

At Puebla, Mexico, the leading composers included Gaspar Fernandes of Portuguese birth (active as organist and cathedral chapelmaster, 1606-29) and his successor Juan Gutiérrez de Padilla (1629-64) born at Málaga. Fernandes left in autograph over 250 festal *chanzonetas* and *villancicos*, many of them highly spiced with Negro-dialect text and Negro-influenced rhythms. Padilla presided over Puebla music during its epoch of highest glory and bequeathed a large body of sumptuous double-choir music (including four Masses for eight voices). Padilla was, in addition, an excellent teacher who counted among his numerous fine pupils his successor, Juan García Céspedes.

After Independence, social and political unrest played havoc with music educational opportunities in Mexico as elsewhere in Spanish America. The roll of renowned 19th-century Mexican composers, all of whom made their reputations with operas—in their century the one sure passport to fame—ranged from Cenobio Paniagua (1812-82), Melesio Morales (1838-1908), Aniceto Ortego (1825-75), and Ricardo Castro (1864-1907), to Gustavo Emilio Campa (1863-1934). The Otomí Indian Juventino Rosas (1868-94) in 1891 wrote the world-famous waltz *Sobre las olas* ('Over the Waves') which even today remains one of the best-known Latin American pieces in existence. Next to the Mexican national anthem composed in 1854 by Jaime Nunó (1824-1908), the most famous song composed in Mexico during the 19th century was Narciso Serradell's *La golondrina* ('The Swallow', 1862), a farewell which distils the exquisite tears shed at the departure of a beloved friend.

The most widely known Mexican concert song of the 20th century is *Estrellita* ('Little Star') published in 1913 by Manuel María Ponce (1882-1948). Ponce's large works include the guitar *Concierto del sur* (1941) written for Andrés Segovia, a Romantic piano concerto, a violin concerto, and a symphonic triptych. The chief exponent of Indian themes and subjects in 20th-century Mexico was Carlos Chávez (1899-1978). Chávez's contemporaries and pupils include Silvestre Revueltas (1899-1940), whose symphonic poem *Sensemayá* (1938) crowned his œuvre, José Pablo Moncayo (1912-58), whose coruscating *Huapango* (1941) catches all the colourful gleam of folkloric dancing, and Blas Galindo Dimas (*b* 1910), who is a Huichol Indian. Rodolfo Halffter (*b* 1900) emigrated from Spain in 1940 to become teacher and prophet of a new generation not wedded to Mexican folklore or Aztec evocations. The younger composers Manuel Enríquez (*b* 1926), Héctor Quintanar (*b* 1936), Eduardo Mata (*b* 1942, better known as a conductor), and Mario Lavista (*b* 1943) eschew anything locally Mexican, and instead flow with prevalent international currents.

3. *Spanish-speaking South America (except the Caribbean coast)*. The favourite instruments of the Andean indigenes were *antaras* (panpipes) and *quena-quenas* (vertical flutes). Archaeological panpipes dug up along the Peruvian coast testify to a Nazca musical system that allowed for microtones in upper registers (the lowest note on Nazca clay panpipes never goes below violist's C). However, the Incas, who by 1492 had subdued South America from Quito south to the Maule River in Chile and east to what is now Sucre, favoured pentatonic melodies. The colour and number of drums counted as heavily in their ritual performances at their capital, 11,400′-high Cuzco, as did the timbre of the *qquepas* (trumpets) and *pincollos* (flutes) heard during ceremonies honouring either their Sun deity or their deceased rulers.

Before 1560 European music of the highest quality began being brought to Cuzco. Cristóbal de Morales's printed Masses (1544) were imported to the Inca capital only a decade after publication. Philippe Rogier and Philippe de Monte exemplify 16th-century Flemings, copies of whose polyphonic Masses still survive fragmentarily at Cuzco. The most distinguished composer in 16th-century South America was Gutierre Fernández Hidalgo, who successively directed the music at Bogotá (1584-6), Quito (1588-90), Cuzco (1591-7), and La Plata, present-day Sucre (1597-1620). Fernández Hidalgo equalled the best composers of his

Detail of a round clay vessel painted with a procession of Musicians, showing two panpipe players, Moche culture (c.100 BC-AD 800).

generation in Spain. His extant liturgical works, all of surpassing beauty and intensity, include *Salves*, *Magnificats*, and psalms. The first polyphonic composition published in the New World appeared at Lima in 1631. The text of this delightful marching song for mixed choir, *Hanacpachap cussicuinin*, is in Quecha, language of the Incas. Juan Pérez Bocanegra, who published it, spent most of his adult life at Cuzco.

The Spanish-descended composers at Lima, the capital of the vice-royalty of Peru—which was the richest dominion in the Spanish empire—included the erstwhile Portuguese royal chapel organist, Estacio de la Serna (active at Lima 1612-14), Cristóbal de Belsayaga (1622-30), Juan de Araujo (1670-6), and Tomás de Torrejón y Velasco (1676-1728). Araujo later emigrated to La Plata (Sucre), where he left a large legacy of sparkling *villancicos* composed during his directorship there, from 1680 to his death in 1712. Using a libretto written in 1660 by Pedro Calderón de la Barca, Torrejón y Velasco composed the earliest extant New World opera, *La púrpura de la rosa* ('The Purple of the Rose'), mounted at the vice-royal palace in Lima on 19 October 1701. After him, the chief composers were the native of Milan, Roque Ceruti (directed Lima cathedral music 1728-60); the native Peruvian who was a musical sentimentalist *par excellence*, José de Orejón y Aparicio (1760-5); and the peripatetic Bartolomé Massa from Novi Ligure, Italy, who in the latter half of the 18th-century conducted operas at both Buenos Aires and Lima.

Like other New World capitals wracked by revolutions and wars, Peru after 1821 lost its musical pre-eminence. José Bernardo Alzedo (1788-1878), composer of the Peruvian national anthem premièred in 1821, emigrated thereafter to Chile where he spent the best years of his life (1846-64) conducting Santiago de Chile cathedral music. Peruvian music in the 20th century benefited from the leadership of such European immigrants as the Belgian Andrés Sas (1900-67) and the German Rodolfo Holzmann (b 1910).

In 1717 Argentina welcomed a newly arrived Jesuit missionary from Italy, Domenico Zipoli (1688-1726). Because of the publication of his organ and harpsichord works at Rome in 1716 and at London c.1722 and 1725, Zipoli was the most internationally renowned of the numerous Jesuit musical missionaries sent to Argentina and Paraguay before 1767. Zipoli studied and laboured at Cordoba, seat of a university founded in 1613. Buenos Aires, capital of a vice-royalty established in 1776, came into its own during the 19th century as the centre of music publishing, opera, and concert life in Spanish South America. The present Teatro Colón (seats

3,950), opened in 1908, was preceded by the old Teatro Colón (1857-88), Teatro de la Ópera (1872), Teatro Nacional (1882), and other theatres showing Italian, French, and to a limited extent Argentinian operas. The most widely heralded South American composer of his generation, Alberto Evaristo Ginastera, born at Buenos Aires in 1916, made his international reputation with the operas *Don Rodrigo* (1964), *Bomarzo* (1967), and *Beatrix Cenci* (1971). Other prominent Argentinians who gained fame with operas include Francisco E. Hargreaves (1849-1900), Arturo Berutti (1862-1938), Eduardo García Mansilla (1866-1930), Constantino Gaito (1878-1945), and Juan José Castro (1895-1968).

On the other hand, Chilean 20th-century composers such as Enrique Soro (1884-1954), Alfonso Leng (1894-1974), Domingo Santa Cruz (*b* 1899), Alfonso Letelier Llona (*b* 1912), Juan A. Orrego-Salas (*b* 1919), and Gustavo Becerra Schmidt (*b* 1925) all eschewed opera, or any stage music for that matter. Chileans such as Samuel Claro-Valdés and Luis Merino Montero at the two universities in the capital made Santiago de Chile in 1982 the brightest centre for historical musicological research in South America. *Revista musical Chilena* founded in 1945 remains in 1982 the most significant and respected musicological periodical published in Latin America.

4. *Brazil.* The earliest extant dated piece of Brazilian music is a recitative and aria composed in 1759 by Caetano de Mello Jesus, chapel-master of Bahia Cathedral, and dedicated to a deputy of Pombal who founded an Academia dos Esquecidos (Academy of the Forgotten) that year at the then Brazilian capital. In 1763 the capital moved to Rio de Janeiro where the mulatto José Maurício Nunes Garcia, who was a priest, became chapelmaster of the cathedral in 1798. Garcia's rich surviving repertory of liturgical music in all genres evokes memories of the Europeans whom he idolized, Haydn and Mozart. None the less, he had his own rich vein of melody. His pupil, Francisco Manuel da Silva (1795-1865) composed the Brazilian national anthem in 1831.

During the Brazilian empire lasting from 1822 to 1889 (when Pedro II abdicated), Rio de Janeiro claimed the best library in South America, the most flourishing music publication industry in Latin America, concert seasons that attracted virtuosos such as Thalberg and Gottschalk, and above all a flourishing operatic life. António Carlos Gomes (1836-96), a protégé of Pedro II, composed two operas mounted at the Teatro Lirico Fluminense before he transferred to Milan, where eight of his operas were

produced between 1867 and 1891. *Il Guarany* (La Scala, 19 March 1870), the most successful of these, celebrated the love of a Brazilian Indian prince for a Portuguese governor's daughter. Travelling the world circuit it reached London's Covent Garden on 13 July 1872, St Petersburg on 12 February 1879, and New York on 3 November 1884.

Heitor Villa-Lobos (1887-1949) over-shadowed all other South Americans of his generation. Alone among Brazilians, he made a strong impact at Paris, where he lived on a subsidy from wealthy São Paulo backers (1923-5, and again in 1929). Aware of what was needed to impress European critics, he invented new musical forms (13 *Chôros*, eight *Bachianas Brasileiras*), highly spiced his middle-period chamber, choral, and symphonic works with tunes imitating popular Brazilian music, and posed as a descendant of an Indian tribe. His enormous output ran to 12 symphonies, six ballets, three operas, five piano concertos, and a correspondingly large production in all other traditional genres. Among renowned 20th-century composers, only Darius Milhaud perhaps exceeded him in quantitative output.

Other 20th-century Brazilians who necessarily suffer by comparison with him but who individually merit acclaim include Oscar Lorenzo Fernândez (1897-1948), Camargo Guarinieri (*b* 1907), Cláudio Santoro (*b* 1919), Édino Krieger (*b* 1928), and Marlos Nobre (*b* 1939). Brazil boasts a more flourishing popular music industry than any other South American nation, with contemporary stars of the first magnitude including Chico Buarque de Hollanda, Roberto Carlos [Braga], Jorge Ben, Milton Nascimento, Gal Costa, and at least two dozen others. Unlike Argentina, where the film celebrity Charles Gardel (1887-1935)—who reigned supreme and is still idolized as king of tango—was European-born, Brazil boasts male stars, Black and White, who are all natives of the country.

5. *Caribbean Area.* The immense wealth of her mainland colonies caused Spain to neglect her Caribbean outposts. Until Esteban Salas y Castro (1725-1803), Cuba lacked a first-rate composer. During the 19th century no Cuban dramatic composer impressed Europe until Gaspar Villate (1851-91) saw three of his operas mounted at Paris, The Hague, and Madrid. Eduardo Sánchez de Fuentes (1874-1944), Alejandro García Caturla (1906-40), and Amadeo Roldán (1900-39) typified right, centre, and left in Cuban music of their generation. Of these, Roldán, who wrote *Danza negra* (1928) and *Poema negro* (1930), took Cuba's Black heritage the most seriously, and therefore enjoys greatest prestige at Havana today. The expatriate

Ernesto Lecuona (1896–1963) in 1929 published the piano piece *Malagueña* and the song *Siboney*, both of which continue to rank among the best-known Latin American compositions of all time.

Jamaica's early composers included Samuel Felsted who published the oratorio *Jonah* at London in 1775. Sir Frederick Cowen (1852–1935) was born at Kingston, Jamaica. However, any art music traditions in Barbados, where a three-manual Father Smith organ was installed at Bridgetown in 1700, or on Guadeloupe where Joseph Boulogne, Chevalier de Saint Georges (1739–99), was born, or in any other former English, French, or Dutch possession, now take second place to the calypso, ska, and reggae, and other Black popular musical expressions born in those islands. (See also *West Indian Music*.)

Haiti (Saint-Domingue) during the last half of the 18th century witnessed a constant round of operas and other stage works by Gluck, Piccinni, Monsigny, Duni, Blaise, Rousseau, and their ilk. After Toussaint l'Ouverture and Henri Christophe, all such French stage traditions fled the island, to be replaced by a vigorous African-oriented musical culture emphasizing drums.

Curaçao's Mikvé Israël, erected in 1730–8, counts among the oldest continuously used synagogues in the Americas (organ installed in 1866) and Charles Maduro (1883–1947) of that faith ranks as the best-known composer born on the island. Paramaribo's Berachave-Shalom synagogue, five years younger than Mikvé Israël, has similarly continued a long-standing bastion of European musical culture in Surinam, where, however, the music that attracts visitors is dominated by drums and by the other African musical expressions of the economically disadvantaged.

As early as 19 December 1559, Juan Pérez Materano, resident at the Caribbean coastal port of Cartagena, gained a royal privilege to publish a treatise on polyphony and plainchant. Because of his erudition, his pupil Juan de Castellanos (1522–1607) called him a New World 'Josquin'. Pérez Materano also enjoyed great success using music to attract and convert numerous Blacks streaming into Cartagena as early as 1546.

At the head of Venezuelan musicians during that nation's period of colonial music glory stood the mulatto Juan Manuel Olivares (1760–97). His mulatto pupils included Juan José Landaeta (1780–1814), to whom is attributed the music of the Venezuelan national anthem, *Gloria al bravo pueblo*, Lino Gallardo (1773–1837), and at least another half-dozen reputable composers. Venezuela's renowned cathedral music director-composer, Cayetano Carreño (1774–1836), was the grandfather of the world-famous pianist Teresa Carreño (1853–1917).

José Ángel Lamas (1775–1814), who is generally considered the most gifted composer in Venezuelan music, gave his name to the national conservatory at Caracas. The best 19th-century Venezuelan composer, José Ángel Montero (1832–81), wrote the first opera by a native Venezuelan mounted in Caracas, *Virginia* (premièred 27 April 1872; revived at the Caracas Teatro Municipal, 28 February 1969.

ROBERT STEVENSON

FURTHER READING
Nicolas Slonimsky: *Music of Latin America* (New York, 1945, reprinted and enlarged 1972); Robert Stevenson: *Music in Mexico: a Historical Survey* (New York, 1952); R. Stevenson: *The Music of Peru* (Washington, DC, 1960); Gilbert Chase: *A Guide to the Music of Latin America* (Washington, DC, 1962); R. Stevenson: *Foundation of New World Opera* (Lima, 1973); R. Stevenson: *A Guide to Caribbean Music History* (Lima, 1975); R. Stevenson: *Latin American Colonial Music* (Washington, DC, 1975); Gerard Béhague: *Music in Latin America: an Introduction* (Englewood Cliffs, NJ, 1979).

Latin American Dance Music. The music of Latin America derives from three traditions: the music of the original Indian inhabitants, varying in character in different parts of the continent; the music of the Spanish and Portuguese conquerors and settlers; and the music of the Negro slaves brought in by the Europeans. Its strongest characteristics are rhythmical, arising in the first place from the ready supply of means for making percussion instruments: shells from the seashore, animals like the armadillo, gourds and hollowed tree trunks. The dominant solo instrument was the pipe or flute. The colonists brought the guitar and, contrary to some beliefs, the harp, which native musicians then constructed and played in highly individual styles. Later came the other European string and wind instruments. Only in a few remote jungles of the Amazon basin and the highlands of Ecuador is there now any chance of hearing any aboriginal music, the rest of South America now purveying fairly standardized forms with only residual regional characteristics.

The spread of popular Latin American music, first through South America and then abroad, happened slowly at first through the early travellers and then the visits of a few interested musicians. But, of course, it was the advent of the gramophone and radio which helped the music to make its sudden and powerful impact in the 20th century. The first Latin American musical form to make its mark in Europe was the *habanera from Cuba, followed much later by the more or less identical Argentine *tango, first publicized outside South

America in New York in 1911. Close on the heels of the tango came the *maxixe from Brazil, which proved too intricate a measure to attract Europeans and North Americans. An attempt to popularize the *samba in the 1920s was overshadowed by the continuing success of the tango. The 1930s became the decade of the Cuban *rumba, internationally popularized by Ernesto Lecuona, composer and leader of the first rumba band to gain wide recognition outside Cuba.

Instrumentally and vocally all these measures had considerable success, but their intricacies as dances mainly confined their use to the expert competitive circles of ballroom dancing. It was the more simplified dances of the 1940s, as exploited by Edmundo Ros, that really became popular with the general dancing public, with American swing overtones well mingled with the Latin American rhythms. The samba at last came into its own, pursued by the *mambo, the *calypso, and the cha cha cha (derived from the mambo). By the 1950s, with the advent of rock and roll, the general interest in Latin American music had already waned. But, as so often happens, the commercialized imitation had sparked an interest in the original music, and in the 1950s such artists as Dorita y Pepe began to sing authentic Latin American folk-songs. This led to a market for other folk musicians and authentic Latin American dance bands who played with a natural and deep understanding of the idiom. Today, even the early commercial pioneers have their nostalgic following, with names like Xavier Cugat, Tito Puente, Perez Prado, and Noro Morales now historically respectable. Similarly, the art of Carmen Miranda, who popularized the music in many Hollywood films, is now admired with scholarly objectivity.   PETER GAMMOND

Lauda Sion (Lat., 'Praise, O Sion'). One of the four *sequences allowed to remain in the liturgy of the Roman Catholic Church after the *Council of Trent (1542–63). It has its own traditional plainchant, but has also been set to music by composers, for example Palestrina, Mendelssohn (who used the plainchant, but in a degraded form), and Edmund Rubbra. The words were written by St Thomas Aquinas (c.1264) for the feast of Corpus Christi (on which they are still sung), at the request of Pope Urban IV.

Lauda spirituale (It., 'spiritual praise' (pl.: *laude*); the form *laude* (pl.: *laudi*) is also found). A type of sacred song, usually with Italian words though sometimes partly or wholly in Latin, cultivated in Italy from the 13th century to the 16th. Like the Spanish *cantiga and the English *carol, *laude* belong to the category of popular religious music sung by the laity, and never formed part of the formal worship of the Church. Their performance was fostered by guild-like fraternities of singers (called *laudesi*), which existed throughout Italy; *laude* were also popular within monastic communities, and were sometimes included in religious plays.

The earliest *laude* were penitential in tone; they were sung at times of warfare, plague, or other affliction, and were usually addressed to the Virgin or one of the saints, especially St Francis of Assisi. Later, verses of a more generally devotional or seasonal nature (concerning the Christmas story, the Passion, etc.) were also set. The poetry is homely and stereotyped in nature, and is rarely of any great literary distinction.

For its musical substance, the early *lauda* drew upon a wide variety of sources, its basic idiom owing much to folk and popular elements, but with the influence of plainchant and the songs of the *troubadours* also apparent. These *laude* were monophonic at first, with syllabic melodies moving largely by step, unsophisticated rhythms, and often including short refrains. During the 15th century, accompanying lines came to be improvised or composed around the original melody, most often in a note-against-note fashion, giving rise by the early 16th century to simple chordal works for four voices with an emphasis on the melody and bass, in a style not unlike that of the contemporary *frottola*. The market for *laude* was apparently large at this time, for the Venetian printer Petrucci published two collections. Although the *lauda* itself declined in importance later in the 16th century, some of its characteristic features were taken over in the music of the *rappresentazione sacra* and the early oratorio (see *Oratorio*, 1).   JOHN MILSOM

Laudesi (It.). See under *Lauda spirituale*.

Laudon [Loudon] Symphony. Haydn's Symphony No. 69 in C major, composed in the mid 1770s. Haydn approved the title of the symphony, which he dedicated to the Austrian field-marshal Ernst Gideon Freiherr von Loudon (1716–90).

Lauds. The second of the *Office Hours of the Roman Catholic Church.

Lauf (Ger., from *laufen*, 'to run'). A rapid passage; used particularly in connection with scales.

Laut (Ger.). 'Loud'.

Laute (Ger.). 'Lute'.

Lavolta, lavolte. See *Volta*.

Lawes, Henry (*b* Dinton, Wilts., 5 Jan. 1596; *d* London, 21 Oct. 1662). English composer, the elder brother of William Lawes. He was a Gentleman of Charles I's Chapel Royal from 1626, and five years later was appointed one of the king's musicians 'for the lutes and voices'. He wrote the music (only five songs survive) for Milton's masque of *Comus*, which was produced at Ludlow Castle on Michaelmas Night 1634, and to him Milton addressed his famous sonnet, 'To Mr. H. Lawes on his Aires':

> Harry, whose tuneful and well-measured song
> First taught our English music how to span
> Words with just note and accent . . .

He also became a fashionable teacher, and his first book of *Ayres and Dialogues* (1653) is dedicated to his earliest pupils, the daughters of the Earl of Bridgwater: in his preface he deplores the current taste for Italian music at the expense of that by English composers. At the Restoration he was reinstated in his court posts, and his anthem *Zadok the Priest* was performed at the coronation of Charles II.

Lawes was one of the most important songwriters of the 17th century. Over 400 of his songs survive, to verses by many contemporary poets including Carew, Suckling, and Lovelace, as well as Milton. The music he composed for the first and last acts of Davenant's opera *The Siege of Rhodes* (given at Rutland House in 1656) is now lost. WENDY THOMPSON

Lawes, William (*bapt.* Salisbury, 1 May 1602; *d* Chester, 24 Sept. 1645). English composer, the younger brother of Henry Lawes. He was a pupil of Coprario, and in 1635 joined his brother as a 'musician in ordinary for the lute and voices' at Charles I's court. He was a royalist, and followed his king on the campaigns of the Civil War; he was shot dead at the Battle of Chester, 'betrayed thereunto by his own adventuresness' (Fuller).

Unlike his brother, Lawes published nothing in his lifetime, but his music survives in manuscript and shows a mastery of a wide variety of styles. His viol music includes some fantasias which show the influence of the late Italian madrigal (he copied out works by Monteverdi and Marenzio) in their use of expressive, dissonant harmonies and in the awkward leaps of the melody lines, while his violin music consists of solo and trio sonatas after the more modern Italian style; they have virtuoso parts for the bass viol, on which Lawes was a well-known performer. He also wrote some attractive verse anthems and a considerable amount of music for masques, some of which shows a strong sense of

William Lawes, portrait (c.1625–50) by an unknown artist.

large-scale organization of the kind which Purcell was to explore in his theatre music.
DENIS ARNOLD

Lay clerk, Lay vicar. Alternative titles for a *vicar choral.

Layolle, Francesco de (*b* Florence, 4 Mar. 1492; *d* Lyons, *c.*1540). Italian composer and organist. He was a pupil of Bartolomeo degli Organi in Florence, and himself taught Benvenuto Cellini. He left Florence in 1518, and in 1521 moved to Lyons, where he was an associate of the publisher Jacques Moderne, editing and composing for him volumes of sacred music in the 1530s. He wrote Masses and motets, but most of his surviving music is secular, comprising *chansons*, canzonas, and madrigals. Andrea del Sarto depicted him in a fresco for the Florentine church of the Ss. Annunziata, and Jacopo da Pontormo painted his portrait, which now hangs in the Uffizi. DENIS ARNOLD

Leader. Principal first violin of an orchestra. See *Concert-master*.

Leading motif. See *Leitmotiv*.

Leading note. Seventh degree of the scale, a semitone below the tonic. It is so called because of its tendency to rise, or 'lead', to the tonic. In a minor key it is sometimes flattened in the descent, and is then called a 'flattened leading note'.

Lead, Kindly Light. Hymn of which the words were written by John Henry Newman (1801–90) after he had been ill in Sicily. The tune, *Lux benigna*, is by the organist the Revd

John Bacchus Dykes; it was first published under the name *St Oswald* in *Psalms and Hymns for the Church, School and Home* (1867, edited by D. T. Barry), and in an appendix (1868) to *Hymns Ancient and Modern*. Another tune, *Alberta*, by W. H. Harris, is printed in *Songs of Praise* (enlarged edn, 1931).

League of Composers. In 1923 American members of the *International Composers' Guild who were disenchanted with the group's avant-garde orientation founded the League of Composers in hopes of promoting a broader spectrum of contemporary music. To this end, the League commissioned new works from American and European composers, sponsored performances and radio broadcasts of contemporary music, and founded the quarterly *Modern Music* which ran from 1924 to 1947. Claire R. Reis was executive chairman of the League, 1923–48, followed by Aaron Copland, 1948–50. In 1954 the League of Composers merged with the *International Society for Contemporary Music (ISCM).   MARK TUCKER

Lebègue, Nicolas-Antoine (*b* Laon, *c*.1631; *d* Paris, 6 July 1702). French composer. He was the son of a miller-baker, and left Laon for Paris when he was in his 20s; there he may have studied with Chambonnières. In 1664 he was organist of St Merry and in 1678 was appointed one of four organists to the royal chapel. Much sought after as an adviser on organ building, he also had many pupils. In his later years he suffered first from a swindle which deprived him of his life savings, and then from a kidney stone, for which he had a successful operation at the age of 69. His harpsichord works helped to standardize the number and order of dances in the suite, and his organ works are delightful, especially the arrangements of popular *noëls*.
DENIS ARNOLD

Lebendig, lebhaft (Ger.). 'Lively'; *lebendiger*, 'livelier'.

Lebewohl, Das ('The Farewell'). Beethoven's title for his Piano Sonata No. 26 in E♭ Op. 81*a*. It is usually known as *Les Adieux*.

Le Cène, Michel-Charles. See *Roger, Estienne*.

Lechner, Leonhard (*b* South Tyrol, *c*.1553; *d* Stuttgart, 9 Sept. 1606). German composer. He was a pupil of Lassus at the Bavarian court in Munich, and later edited his works for publication. He would probably have stayed at the Bavarian court if he had not become a Protestant when he was about 18; instead he became an assistant teacher at the school of St Lorenz, Nuremberg, in *c*.1575. In 1583 he became *Kapellmeister* to Count Eitelfriedrich IV of Hohenzollern-Hechingen, but his religion again caused difficulties, and he eventually left to become a tenor at the Württemberg court. In 1595 he became *Kapellmeister* there and was in charge of a group of 48 musicians.

He was a prolific composer, and published many of his works in Nuremberg. They include motets and other sacred music, and several *Lieder*. His flood of publications came virtually to an end in 1595, but just before he died he wrote the *Deutsche Sprüche von Leben und Tod* ('German sayings on life and death'), an intense madrigalian cycle which made him a major figure in Baroque music. He also wrote a 'Lachrymae' pavan in homage to Dowland.
DENIS ARNOLD

Leclair, Jean-Marie (l'aîné) (*b* Lyons, 10 May 1697; *d* Paris, 22 Oct. 1764). French composer and violinist. The son of Antoine Leclair, a Lyons lacemaker and amateur cellist, Jean-Marie was one of eight children, six of whom became violinists. He intended to follow his father's profession, but in his early 20s was engaged as dancer and ballet-master at Turin. In 1723 he went to Paris, and that year his first book of violin sonatas was published there. From 1726 to 1728 he was again in Turin, where he studied the violin with J. B. Somis, meanwhile continuing to earn his living as a professional dancer. He then returned to Paris, where his talent as a virtuoso violinist led to numerous solo appearances at the Concert Spirituel. In 1733 Leclair entered the service of Louis XV,

Jean-Marie Leclair: engraving (1741) by J.-C. François after A. Loir.

but he continued to make extensive foreign tours, finally settling permanently in Paris in 1743. Shortly before his death he separated from his second wife and went to live in an insalubrious suburb of Paris. On the morning of 23 October 1764 he was found murdered on his own doorstep; his assassin was never traced, but the most likely suspect was his own nephew.

Leclair's works include four books of sonatas for violin and continuo (Paris, 1723–43); two of violin duets without continuo (Paris, 1730, c.1747); and several of trio sonatas. He also published books of *concerti grossi* (1737, 1745) and other chamber music, and his *tragédie lyrique*, *Scylla et Glaucus*, was performed in 1746. He was the founder of the French school of violin playing, renowned both for his musicianship and for his technical brilliance. His chamber and orchestral works represent a synthesis of the best elements from the French and Italian styles, while his opera, which has recently been revived, compares favourably with similar works by Rameau.   WENDY THOMPSON

Lecocq, Alexandre Charles (*b* Paris, 3 June 1832; *d* Paris, 24 Oct. 1918). French composer. He was physically handicapped from birth, but studied organ and composition at the Paris Conservatoire with Benoist and Halévy. In 1856 he took part in the composition competition sponsored by Offenbach, writing an operetta entitled *Le Docteur Miracle* to a libretto by Battu and Halévy, and won joint first prize with Bizet; neither of their respective works proved successful in performance. Undeterred, Lecocq continued to write light operas until he finally achieved success with *Fleur-de-thé* (1868) and *Les Jumeaux de Bergame* (1869). His most famous comic operas were *La fille de Madame Angot* (1872) and *Giroflé-Girofla* (1874).
                WENDY THOMPSON

Ledger lines [leger lines]. Short extra lines added below or above the stave to accommodate notes that are too low or too high to be placed on the stave itself.

Leer (Ger.). 'Empty'. The term is applied to the open strings of a violin etc.

LeFanu, Nicola (Frances) (*b* Wickham Bishops, Essex, 28 Apr. 1947). English composer. The daughter of the composer Elizabeth Maconchy, she studied at Oxford, in Italy with Petrassi, and in the United States. Her music is based on continuously evolving melodies which set out and explore areas of atonal harmony, and she has been specially successful in writing for solo voices, whether unaccompanied (e.g. *But Stars Remaining* for soprano, 1970), with instru-

mental ensemble (e.g. *The Same Day Dawns*, 1974), or in music-theatre pieces (*Antiworld*, 1972; *Dawnpath*, 1977).   PAUL GRIFFITHS

Legato [*legando*, *legabile*] (It., from *legare*, 'to tie', 'to bind'). A *legato* passage is one where the notes should be played smoothly and without noticeable breaks between them. This effect can be requested either by the use of a phrase mark over the passage in question, or by placing the word 'legato' at the beginning of the passage. The word *legatissimo*, always written out, is used where the *legato* effect is extreme. The opposite of *legato* is *staccato*.

Legatura (It.). 'Ligature'.

Legend (Fr.: *légende*; Ger.: *Legende*). A name given to short compositions of lyrical or epic character. Well-known examples are Dvořák's *Legends*, Op. 59, and Sibelius's four *Legends* for orchestra, Op. 22, which include the well-known *Swan of Tuonela*.

Legende von der Heiligen Elisabeth, Die ('The Legend of St Elizabeth'). Oratorio by Liszt to a text by O. Roquette, composed between 1857 and 1862. It is for soprano, alto, three baritones, bass, chorus, organ, and orchestra.

Léger, légère (Fr.). 'Light'; *légèreté*, 'lightness'; *légèrement*, 'lightly'.

Leger lines. See *Ledger lines*.

Leggero [*leggiero*], **leggeramente** (It.). 'Light', 'lightly'. 19th-century performance direction, usually meaning a light and detached style of playing in quick passages.

Leggiadro, leggiadretto (It.). 'Graceful'; *leggiadramente*, 'gracefully'.

Leggio (It., from *leggere*, 'to read'). 'Music desk'.

Legno (It.). 'Wood'; *col legno*, 'with the wood', a direction to string players to tap the strings with the wood of the bow, instead of playing with the hair; *bacchetta di legno*, 'wooden-headed drumstick'; *strumenti* (*stromenti*) *di legno*, 'wood(wind) instruments'.

Legrant, Guillaume (*fl.* 1418–56). French composer. He worked at the chapel of Pope Martin V from 1418 until at least 1421, and later at Rouen. His surviving works include *chansons* and Mass movements.   JOHN MILSOM

Legrenzi, Giovanni (*b* Clusone, nr Bergamo, Aug. 1626; *d* Venice, 27 May 1690). Italian composer. The son of a violinist, he became one of the organists at the principal church of Bergamo, S. Maria Maggiore, in 1645. He remained until 1656 when he was appointed director of music at the Accademia dello Spirito Santo in Ferrara. Here he began to compose opera. He stayed for about 11 years, but there follows a period of about 12 years when his whereabouts are not known for certain. In the early 1670s he moved to Venice where he was in charge of music at the Conservatory of the Mendicanti and, from 1685, *maestro di cappella* at St Mark's. His last years were clouded by illness.

Legrenzi wrote church music throughout his career and his motets for solo voice or small ensemble are especially attractive. His instrumental music took the form of sonatas, often for the trio ensemble of two melody instruments and continuo; in these works the contrasting sections begin to assume the character of individual movements. But his most distinguished work lies in the field of opera. His arias have easily memorable phrases based on dance rhythms and popular tunes, and he often guys the customary heroic plots with a distinctive sense of humour. His style influenced a whole generation of pupils, and both Bach and Handel knew his works.   DENIS ARNOLD

Lehár, Franz [Ferencz] (*b* Komárom, 30 Apr. 1870; *d* Ischl, 24 Oct. 1948). Austrian composer. He studied at the Prague Conservatory and began his career as a conductor of military bands (1894–9). In 1902 he turned to operetta with *Vienna Women*, and in 1905 established his dominance in the genre with *The Merry Widow*. Later works of this kind include *Gypsy Love* (1910), *The Land of Smiles* (1923), and *Frederica* (1928).   PAUL GRIFFITHS

Lehrstück (Ger.). 'Teaching piece'. A 20th-century musical work of a didactic, and often political, nature. Brecht and Hindemith wrote such pieces.

Leibowitz, René (*b* Warsaw, 17 Feb. 1913; *d* Paris, 29 Aug. 1972). French composer of Polish birth. He studied composition with Webern (1930–1) and Schoenberg (1932), and conducting with Pierre Monteux (1934–6). Having settled in France he worked as a conductor and teacher, introducing Boulez and others to serial methods in the mid-1940s. His output includes several operas, various concertos and other orchestral pieces, chamber and piano works, all in a 12-note style. He was also author of the books *Schoenberg and his School* (New York,

1948) and, with Jan Maguire, *Thinking for Orchestra* (New York, 1961).   PAUL GRIFFITHS

Leicht (Ger.). 1. 'Light', 'popular' (in style). 2. 'Easy', e.g. Matyás Seiber's *Leichted Tänze* ('easy dances') for piano duet. *Leichtigkeit*, (1) 'lightness'; (2) 'easiness'.

Leidenschaft (Ger.). 'Passion'; *leidenschaftlich*, 'passionately'.

Leigh, Walter (*b* London, 22 June 1905; *d* near Tobruk, Libya, 12 June 1942). English composer. He studied at Cambridge and at the Berlin Musikhochschule with Hindemith (1927–9), who had a decisive influence on his style. His compositions include the comic opera *The Jolly Roger* (1933), a concertino for harpsichord and strings, and various chamber pieces. He was killed in action.   PAUL GRIFFITHS

Leighton, Kenneth (*b* Wakefield, 2 Oct. 1929). English composer. He studied classics at Oxford University (1947–51) and composition in Rome with Petrassi (1951). From 1953 to 1956 he held a composing fellowship at Leeds University; since then he has taught at Edinburgh University, apart from a period back at Oxford (1968–70). His large output includes two symphonies, several concertos, and much church music, the style owing something to Bartók and Hindemith in its bold use of expanded diatonic and polytonal harmonies.   PAUL GRIFFITHS

Leighton, (Sir) William (*b*? Plash, Shropshire, *c*.1565; *d* London, July 1622). English editor and composer. Finding himself in ill repute and debt, he attempted to show 'the least part of my unfained and true repentance' by publishing a collection of penitential songs entitled *The Teares or Lamentacions of a Sorrowful Soule* (London, 1614), with works by himself, Bull, Byrd, Milton, Peerson, and others.
                    JOHN MILSOM

Leise (Ger.). 1. 'Soft', 'gentle'; *leiser*, 'more softly'. 2. Medieval devotional songs in the German language, perhaps called *Leise* because of their frequent use of the refrain 'Kyrie eleison', abbreviated to 'kirleis' or 'leis'. The oldest known example dates from the 9th century.

Leisten (Ger.). 'To perform'; *Leistung*, 'performance'.

Leitmotiv (Ger., 'leading motif'). A term coined by F. W. Jähns in a book on Weber (1871) to describe a musical motto or theme which recurs throughout a piece of music (usually an opera) to portray a person, object, emotion, etc. A better English equivalent than 'leading motif' would be 'representative motif'.

The technique of musical reminiscence has been used throughout the history of music in various guises, but the first composers to attempt a systematic use of *Leitmotive* were early German Romantics, especially Weber. In his *Singspiel, Der Freischütz* (1821), the diminished seventh chord signifies the sinister presence of Samiel; similarly, Oberon's three-note horn call in the eponymous opera (1826) recurs in different numbers throughout the work. The technique appears in its most highly developed and complex form in the operas of Wagner, although Wagner did not use the term himself, preferring to call the themes *Hauptmotiv, thematisches Motiv, Grundthema*, etc. In his operas, from *Der fliegende Holländer* onwards (but especially in the later works— the *Ring* cycle, *Tristan*, and *Parsifal*), each character or idea is associated with a musical theme or motto, for example Siegfried in the *Ring* by his famous horn call, while other motifs are attached to objects (the Rhine gold, Valhalla, etc.), emotional states (e.g. love's awakening), or concepts (e.g. redemption). Such motifs are woven into the musical fabric of the orchestra, and in some cases render the text almost superfluous.

The technique of *Leitmotiv* was used by some opera composers after Wagner, such as Humperdinck, Richard Strauss, Janáček, and Berg, whose *Lulu* uses a sophisticated system of character identification based on transformations of note-rows.

Similar devices to *Leitmotiv* are found in orchestral music, including Berlioz's *Idée fixe (used in his *Symphonie fantastique* to represent 'the beloved') and Liszt's metamorphosis of themes.   WENDY THOMPSON

Le Jeune, Claude (*b* Valenciennes, *c.*1530; *d* Paris, Sept. 1600). French priest and composer. In *c.*1580 he was master of the children at the court of the Duke of Anjou. Because of his Protestant sympathies he had to flee Paris in 1589, taking refuge in La Rochelle for a time, but later he was in the service of Henry IV. He was notable for his experiments in re-creating the music of the Greeks, using chromaticism and the principles of *musique mesureé; he was a member of Baïf's Académie. He also composed *chansons*, madrigals, and some church music— his metrical settings of the psalms were extensively used by Protestant churches during the 17th and 18th centuries.   DENIS ARNOLD

Lekeu, Guillaume (*b* nr Verviers, 20 Jan. 1870; *d* Angers, 21 Jan. 1894). Belgian composer. He first studied literary subjects, entering the

University of Paris in 1888, but in the following year he began studying composition privately with César Franck and continued until the latter's death in November 1890. He then received some tuition from d'Indy, who encouraged him to enter for the Belgian Prix de Rome in 1891, in which he received second prize, only to refuse it. By this time, he was composing fluently, and in the years until his death he produced several interesting chamber works including a piano sonata in the fugal style, a piano trio, and a violin sonata, which is still occasionally played. His music was highly thought of by almost all his French contemporaries, including Debussy, and by certain American critics. He died from typhoid after eating some contaminated sherbet.
                                DENIS ARNOLD

Lélio, ou Le retour à la vie ('Lélio, or The Return to Life'). Monodrama, Op. 14 *bis*, by Berlioz to his own text but with one number by A. Duboys after Goethe. It is for soloists, chorus, and orchestra, and was composed between 1830 and 1832 as a sequel to the *Symphonie fantastique*.

Leningrad Symphony. Subtitle of Shostakovich's Symphony No. 7 in C major, Op. 60, composed in 1941 during the German siege of Leningrad.

Claude Le Jeune, engraving from a collection of his 'Psalms of David' (Leiden, 1635).

Lennon, John (*b* Liverpool, 9 Oct. 1940; *d* New York, 8 Dec. 1980). English song-writer and pop singer. He was the son of a ship's steward. While studying at the Liverpool College of Art he became interested in music through the current skiffle craze and formed a group called The Quarrymen which included Paul McCartney and later George Harrison and Ringo Starr. The group changed its name to The Moondogs, The Rainbows, and The Silver Beatles until it finally became The Beatles in 1960. They built a local reputation at the Cavern Club in Liverpool, becoming more widely known after professional engagements in Hamburg. It was their work here that brought them to the attention of their future manager Brian Epstein and eventually led to a recording contract with Parlophone in 1962 which was the beginning of their overwhelming world-wide success and influence and the heights of Beatlemania in the 1960s. Amid the welter of pop bands and music in the new rock age, the work of The Beatles stood out as sophisticated and imaginative, reaching its heights in the album *Sergeant Pepper's Lonely Hearts Club Band*. Much of this was due to the original, sensitive, and often surrealistic songs that John Lennon wrote in partnership with his composer colleague Paul McCartney. Later he increasingly wrote and composed his own songs. The Beatles era ended with the breakup of the group in 1971. Lennon continued to write, including several books of verse, and by the end of the 1970s continued his recording career as a solo artist. In 1966 he had been awarded, with the rest of The Beatles, the MBE which he later returned as protest against British involvement in the Vietnam War; he became a figure-head of the pacifist movement. By the end of his career he had accumulated an estimated fortune of £100 million. The end of a meteoric career came when he was shot outside his New York home. For his songs see *The Beatles* and *McCartney*.

PETER GAMMOND

Lent (Fr.), **lento** (It.). 'Slow'; *lentando*, *lentato* (It.), 'slowing', 'slowed' (the same as *rallentando*); *lentement* (Fr.), *lentamente* (It.), 'slowly'; *lenteur* (Fr.), *lentezza* (It.), 'slowness'. *Lento* is one of the earliest tempo marks, appearing from the early 17th century. In French music of the mid-17th century onwards, *lentement* became one of the principal tempo marks.

Lentando (It.). See *Ralentir*, *rallentare*.

Leo, Leonardo (Ortensio Salvatore de) (*b* S. Vito degli Schiavi, now S. Vito dei Normanni, nr Brindisi, 5 Aug. 1694; *d* Naples, 31 Oct. 1744). Italian composer and teacher, one of the principal composers of the Neapolitan school. His parents were reasonably wealthy and he entered the Conservatorio S. Maria della Pieta dei Turchini, Naples, as a *convittore*, i.e. a fee-paying student. His master was Nicola Fago, and he made good enough progress to have an opera performed there when he was only 18. Soon after he became one of the organists at the royal chapel. He had a distinguished career in the service of the court, and from 1741 was director of the conservatory where he had studied; his last post was as *maestro di cappella* to the royal chapel. He married the daughter of a well-known opera singer and they had five children.

Leo left over 70 operas, including settings of Metastasio's librettos and comic operas after the manner of Pergolesi. In the revised version of his *Olimpiade* (performed 1737, rev. 1742-3) he added a role for the chorus—an innovation in the history of Neapolitan opera. He also wrote a great deal of church music, some with orchestral accompaniment but also some in the old contrapuntal *a cappella* style. Among his pupils were Jommelli and Piccinni.

DENIS ARNOLD

Leoncavallo, Ruggero (*b* Naples, 8 Mar. 1857; *d* Montecatini, 9 Aug. 1919). Italian composer. He was the son of a police official in Naples, and studied at the conservatory there, from which he graduated in 1876. He then went to study literature at Bologna University, attending the lectures of the famous poet Carducci, and becoming acquainted with Wagner's music. He started work on the libretto of an operatic trilogy on the Italian Renaissance, and composed an opera *Chatterton* to prepare himself, but failed to get this performed, an impresario decamping with the money Leoncavallo had put up. He then fell on bad times, working in Paris, London, and Egypt as a café pianist. He composed light songs (they are called 'sugary romances' by one commentator) for the Eldorado in Paris, and it was there that he met the famous baritone Maurel who introduced him to the leading publisher of Milan, Ricordi. Ricordi asked him to write a libretto for *Manon Lescaut* to be set by Puccini—who did not like it. Ricordi disapproved of *I Medici* (the first opera of the 'Renaissance' trilogy). Furious at his lack of success, Leoncavallo composed *I pagliacci*, the story based on one of his father's legal cases. This was published by Sonzogno (Ricordi's rival), performed in Milan under Toscanini in 1892, and was immediately successful. Designed originally in a single act, it suited Leoncavallo's talents by not demanding any extended continuous inspiration, allowing his short-breathed melodic ideas to express the violent emotions of theatrical characters who need not be seen in the round.

After this success, *I Medici* was performed in Milan in 1893: this was a failure. In this year it was announced that operas on Murger's *La bohème* were being composed by both Puccini (for Ricordi) and Leoncavallo (for Sonzogno). In the meantime *I Medici* was produced in Berlin to the delight of the Kaiser who commissioned an opera in praise of the Hohenzollerns. Leoncavallo's *La bohème* was performed in Venice in 1897, some months after Puccini's. At first both were successful, but Puccini's finally drove his rival's off the stage; and it is fair to say that although Leoncavallo's is an effective piece, it tends to melodrama rather than evokes the delicate, even humorous atmosphere of Puccini's.

Leoncavallo's next venture was a comedy, *Zazà*, an immediate success showing some signs of Massenet's influence. Thereafter his career was in decline. The Hohenzollern opera, *Der Roland von Berlin*, produced in 1904, was no good. He turned to operetta with *La jeunesse de Figaro* produced in the USA in 1906; *Malbrouck* (Rome, 1910); *Are you there?* (London, Prince of Wales Theatre, 1913). His final works included an opera *Edipo Re* (in an Italian version of Sophocles) and an operetta *A chi la giarrettiera?* ('Whose garter is this?'). He died of a heart attack. It is rare to see his lesser works even in Italy, but the judgements of today's Italian critics are harsh, seeing Leoncavallo just as an opportunist. Even so, *Pagliacci* is a minor masterpiece and reflects attitudes to life in the southern part of Italy.   DENIS ARNOLD

Léonin [Leoninus]. Composer active at the Cathedral of Notre Dame, Paris, probably between *c*.1160 and 1180. Léonin's name is known only from the writings of the anonymous English theorist known as Anonymous IV (*fl.c.*1270). He tells us that Léonin was 'optimus organista' ('the best composer [or singer] of **organum*'), and that he made a 'big book' ('magnus liber') of settings of Mass and Office chants used at Notre Dame.

The only surviving copies of music which might be by Léonin date from the mid 13th century; they give no composers' names, and, moreover, they contain music which is much later stylistically than anything Léonin is likely to have written. Probably Léonin contributed some of the earliest music in the manuscripts, some 60 to 80 years before the surviving copies

were made. Since Anonymous IV also implies that one of Léonin's successors, Pérotin, revised some of the earlier music, and since the surviving copies do indeed indicate a process of revision, it is impossible to be certain of exactly what Léonin composed; however, the following can be deduced with reasonable confidence.

Léonin's 'magnus liber' contained polyphonic settings of those portions of plainchant that were reserved for solo singers. The chants set were Vespers responsories, Mass Graduals, and Alleluias, and perhaps some processional antiphons. Only chants for the major festivals of the Church Year were set—between 40 and 50 compositions in all. Léonin probably took as a starting-point music like that in the Codex Calixtinus of *c*.1160 (see *Organum*, Ex. 2), where the chant is placed beneath a more florid upper voice, with its notes therefore frequently lengthened and sustained. Such a chant setting for two voices is known as *organum duplum*. Many of Léonin's settings appear to have been on a more extended scale than were previous chant settings, with an increased proportion of notes in the upper voice to those in the lower voice. Such music was probably not intended for performance in any regular rhythmic manner.

It is not clear whether Léonin's chant settings contained any sections in **discant* style, or whether these sections, very numerous in the surviving copies, are the work of later composers. Some of the simpler ones may date back to the earliest version of the 'magnus liber'. In them the chant is disposed in regular rhythm, moving in step with the upper voice. This occurs usually when there is a melismatic flourish in the original chant, as in Ex. 1. If such music really is by Léonin, then he probably played a part in the evolution of modal rhythm (see *Notation*, 3).

Léonin is also likely to have composed music in other popular forms of the time, such as the **conductus*, but no examples attributed to him are known.   DAVID HILEY

Leonore. Beethoven's intended title for his opera *Fidelio*, and the name of its heroine. The three overtures are known in English as *Leonora*.

Ex. 1

From *Alleluia Ascendens Christus*

Leopold I, Holy Roman Emperor (b Vienna, 9 June 1640; d Vienna, 5 May 1705). Leopold was crowned Emperor in 1658. In spite of a turbulent reign, during which Vienna was besieged by the Turks in 1683, he continued the Habsburg tradition of music patronage, expanding the *Hofkapelle* until it employed over 100 musicians, including performers and composers from Italy, and especially encouraging Italian opera; Cesti's *Il pomo d'oro* was commissioned for the celebrations surrounding his marriage to' Margherita of Spain in 1666 (but probably not performed until 1668). He was himself a more than competent composer, and many of his works were performed at court. They include ballet music, oratorios, and other sacred music, especially an impressive *Miserere* in G minor. DENIS ARNOLD

Lerchenquartett. See '*Lark*' *Quartet.*

Le Roux, Gaspard (*fl.* Paris, second half 17th century). French harpsichordist and composer. His attractive *Pièces de clavessin* (Paris, 1705) are important in the history of the suite, with pieces grouped together in the same key. He also arranged pieces for trio combinations, varied at will for wind or stringed instruments and harpsichord. DENIS ARNOLD

Le Roy, Adrian (b Montreuil-sur-mer, c.1520; d Paris, 1598). French music printer and publisher, lutenist, and composer. He was artistic director in the firm of Le Roy & *Ballard. Apart from his publishing activities he also composed (*chansons* and music for plucked string instruments), was a virtuoso lutenist, and wrote instruction books for lute etc. and a theoretical textbook. He was well connected, both socially and artistically, and his musical taste, expressed through the publications of his firm, helped to mould that of France as a whole during the late 16th century.

Les adieux. See '*Adieux*' *Sonata.*

L'Escurel, Jehan de (d Paris, 13 May 1304). French poet and composer. He appears to have been a cleric at Notre Dame Cathedral, Paris, and to have been hanged for debauchery. A small number of his monophonic *chansons* in the courtly tradition of the *trouvères* has survived; they show him to be, with Adam de la Halle, one of the most important precursors of Machaut. JOHN MILSOM

Lesto (It.). 'Agile', 'quick'; *lestamente*, 'agilely', 'quickly'.

Le Sueur, Jean-François (b Drucat-Plessiel, nr Abbeville, 15 Feb. 1760; d Paris, 6 Oct. 1837). French composer and writer on music. He attended schools at Amiens and Abbeville as a choirboy until 1776, and then worked as choirmaster in various French churches until his appointment in 1786 as choirmaster of Notre Dame, Paris. The novel methods he used there to attract congregations (introducing into the cathedral a full-size orchestra and singers from the Opéra) angered some of the clergy, and he left after only a year. He passed a few years in retirement and then, with the onset of the Revolution, turned to composing operas, in rivalry with Méhul and Cherubini. His *Paul et Virginie* (1794) and *Télémaque* (1796) were successful; in 1804 Napoleon appointed him to direct the Tuileries Chapel, which much enhanced his reputation, and his *Ossian ou Les bardes*, first given that year, achieved a major triumph. He taught at the newly formed Conservatoire from 1818, and after the closure of the chapel in 1830 turned to writing and philosophy: his ideas on music and aesthetics are set out in the influential four-volume *Exposé d'une musique* (1787).
PERCY SCHOLES, rev. Judith Nagley

Let's Make an Opera. 'Entertainment for young people', Op. 45, by Britten to a libretto by Eric Crozier. It is in two parts, the first being preparations by children and adults to put on an opera, and the second being *The Little Sweep*, the opera itself. A string quartet, piano duet, and percussion accompany the singers, and the audience participates in four of the songs. It was first given at Aldeburgh in 1949.

Letzt (Ger.). 'Last', 'final'.

Levare (It.). 'To lift', 'to take off'; *si levano i sordini*, 'the mutes are taken off'; *levate*, 'take off'.

Levet (? from It. *levata*, 'rising', 'getting up'). A trumpet call or musical strain to raise soldiers and others in the morning. On New Year's Day 1696, Judge Sewall of Boston, New England, recorded in his diary: 'One with a Trumpet sounds a Levet at our window just about break of day, bids me good morrow, and wishes health and happiness to attend me.'

Levezza (It.). 'Lightness'.

L.H. Abbreviation for left hand, *linke Hand* (Ger.).

L'homme armé. See *Homme armé, l'*.

Liaison (Fr.). 'Binding'. The term is used in three senses: (1) smooth performance (see *Legato*); (2) the slur that indicates such performance; (3) the *tie or bind.

Liberamente (It.). 'Freely', with regard to tempo, rhythm etc.

Liber usualis (Lat., 'The Book of Use'). A modern compendium of Latin chants and liturgical instructions which was used throughout the Roman Catholic Church until 1974. It conveniently combined the most essential features of four other books: the singers' book for the Mass and the daily Office Hours (i.e. the *gradual and *antiphoner), and the priests' books for the same two categories (i.e. the missal, now called the sacramentary, and the breviary). It excluded some historically important services, such as those for the weekdays in Lent, but included a few items originally from monastic usage not found in the other books, such as the Matins service for major feasts (Nativity, Maundy Thursday, Good Friday, Holy Saturday, Pentecost, Corpus Christi).

The words and chants found in the *Liber* can be divided into five main sections: those common to most Masses (the Mass Ordinary, pp. 11–111); those common to most Office hours (mostly chants for Psalms, pp. 112–316); those celebrating events in the life of Christ (the Proper of Time/Temporale, pp. 317–1110); those common to various categories of saints (the Common of Saints, pp. 1111–272); and those particular to specific saints' days (the Proper of Saints/Sanctorale, pp. 1303–762). Almost all of the chants have a number printed at their opening which indicates the church mode (there are eight altogether). In addition, antiphons have a pitch letter which warns the singer what the last note (termination) of the chant will be, so that it can be linked to an appropriate chant for the following psalm verse.

The *Liber usualis* was first compiled by the Benedictine monks of *Solesmes in 1896 (revised in 1903 and 1934; version with English rubrics, 1962). Their editions of liturgical books attempted to utilize the earliest surviving Medieval chant sources, but the Pope (Leo XIII) would not recognize them until 1901, and in fact the *Liber* never gained the status of an official Vatican liturgical book. For the musician it usefully preserves the pitch and form (if not the rhythm) of many Medieval chants and gives some idea of their liturgical context. The chants are studied either for their own sake or because they form the basis of many polyphonic compositions.   ANTHONY PRYER

Libitum. See *Ad libitum*.

Libraries. A library is far more than a mere collection of books, or, in our case, music. The very word 'library' seems to restrict our ideas as to the range of materials and services they offer. Indeed, the professional organization concerned has changed its name to the International Association of Music Libraries, Archives, and Documentation Centres on that account. The basic materials of a music library are scores and parts, books, and sound-recordings. These are made available for performance, study, and leisure. However, the history of music libraries shows how deceptively simple these two statements are.

1. *The History of Libraries.* The earliest collections of music are to be found in the form of manuscript plainsong antiphoners and polyphonic choir-books compiled for the day-to-day use in the great cathedrals and abbey churches. Yet because the music contained in them was in current use their survival once the music became obsolete was a matter of chance, helped to a large extent by the conservative nature of the Church and the ability to store unused material in an odd corner of their large buildings. The only musical books in the chapter library at that time would have been theoretical treatises. Needless to say, probably more has been lost than has survived. That performance material is ephemeral is even more evident from the survival rate of secular music. Only after 1500 does the printing of instrumental and secular vocal music result in the survival of a significantly increased amount, and even then not because it was specifically collected for preservation.

In England one of the earliest secular collections of music to have survived intact is that of the Music School of Oxford University, begun by the presentation of several sets of madrigal and motet part-books by the first Professor of Music, William Heather, in 1627. The Oxford Music School continued as a centre of performance throughout the 17th century, and this aspect gives its collection of both instrumental and vocal music particular importance. In 1885 it was transferred to the Bodleian Library, where it forms the basis of their extensive collections of research materials.

The 17th and 18th centuries saw the development of court orchestras and public opera houses. The archives of both types of institution have not been well documented. The importance of orchestral archives is underestimated and much material probably already lost. Opera-house archives are known to be valuable where they have survived, as those of the Opéra in Paris which are now part of the Bibliothèque Nationale. All too often these archives have been lost in the fires that destroyed the theatres.

Libraries for performance are often 'private', tend to specialize in one form of music, and have little care for what is not in the current repertory. Even today there are many collections belonging to string quartets, professional and amateur choirs and orchestras, chamber ensembles, and early music groups that will disappear when the group disbands. Some collections may be transferred to another library, others will be broken up and sold, some will be put in the rubbish bin, others will be left in the attic or cellar.

2. *Different Types of Library Today.* Public libraries, by their nature, also supply current needs, and discard the obsolete. Most of them have music in some form or other, and have access through inter-library loan schemes to the resources of other local libraries and to the music in the British Library Lending Division. The largest collections easily available are to be found in the public libraries of the great metropolitan centres of Birmingham, Edinburgh, Leeds, Liverpool, and Manchester. London has the Central Music Library, attached to Westminster Public Libraries, but serving all Londoners. Most public libraries also have local history sections which may contain archives relating to the musical activities and famous musicians of their area, such as the Holst collection in Cheltenham Public Library, or music by Charles Avison in Newcastle upon Tyne. Music colleges or 'conservatoires' generally have extensive collections of music in all genres, and often contain valuable bequests from former pupils. Both the Royal Academy of Music and the Royal College are particularly fortunate in this respect, and also have important antiquarian collections. The universities cater for the study of the history of music and the analysis of composition. Naturally their libraries concentrate on scores (rather than parts), literature, and sound-recordings for study, though the needs of performance within the university are not ignored. They also collect microforms, both film and fiche, of manuscripts and other primary sources which are an important help to musical research. Most universities also care for the preservation of the material considered valuable, and usually keep older music, printed before 1850 or so, separately.

The collection of music for preservation began in England in the 17th century following the destruction of so much church music during Cromwell's time. Starting with the collection, by copying into score from old part-books, and circulation of pre-Commonwealth church music by James Hawkins at Ely, Thomas Tudway in Cambridge, and others, the idea of collecting music became established. Both John Evelyn and Samuel Pepys included several volumes of music in their general libraries, but the first serious collectors of music alone were probably Thomas Britton and Henry Aldrich, Dean of Christchurch. Britton's collection, listed in Hawkins's *History*, was to some extent the practical library for his concerts and was sold after his death; Dean Aldrich's was the first extensive antiquarian collection, and survives complete at Christ Church, Oxford. The 18th and 19th centuries saw the formation and dispersal of many great collections, among them those of John Christoph Pepusch, Charles Burney, and Sir John Hawkins, the last sadly destroyed by fire. Several have survived through the foundation of libraries in institutions, such as Richard Fitzwilliam's in the Fitzwilliam Museum, Cambridge, and Sir Frederick Ouseley's at St Michael's College, Tenbury. After the foundation of the British Museum it too became a place for the receipt of complete collections, such as that of Paul Hirsch.

The development of the great national libraries curiously derives from two legal requirements, censorship and *copyright. Soon after the invention of printing the dangers to state authority were recognized, and control of presses imposed through licences to print. In France such licences were first introduced in 1537, and required the deposit of all publications in the King's Library. Music was regarded as ephemeral and presumably not preserved carefully for none survives from this source in the Bibliothèque Nationale until the 18th century. The earliest form of deposit in England was a private arrangement made between Thomas Bodley and the Stationers' Company in 1610 for the deposit in Oxford of all books issued by members of the Company, which meant all printers except the University Presses of Oxford and Cambridge. This arrangement, extended to include the Royal Library and Cambridge University Library, was subsequently made a legal requirement in the Licensing Act of 1662 which re-established state control of printing after the civil wars, and has continued to this day in the various Copyright Acts. The deposit of music was haphazard to say the least, and virtually none was received at the British Museum until the 1780s, and little attention paid to it there until the 1840s. Since then the continued receipt of British publications and the purchase and gift of foreign and antiquarian material gives us the magnificent collections that are now in the British Library Reference Division. National Libraries of course have a duty towards the music of their own nations, and today there is usually a library or group of libraries in each country with that state duty. Paris, Vienna, and Madrid have their national libraries, Copenhagen, Brussels, and

Stockholm their Royal Libraries, and America the Library of Congress. In Germany and Italy, both united only in the last century, the capitals of the constituent provinces contain important libraries deriving from the courts of former rulers.

The invention of the gramophone record (and more recently of tapes and cassettes) together with that of radio have had far-reaching effects on the musical world. The collection of discs and tapes, both commercially published and privately made, is already widespread. Indeed, in public libraries you are now more likely to find records and tapes than scores. However, as with scores, old and worn material tends to be discarded. Other institutional libraries are more likely to preserve recordings, though the technical problems for doing so are great: the records themselves are physically fragile, and the means of playing them become obsolete. Even now there are very few places where a piano-roll can be played, and there are even fewer phonographs for playing wax cylinders. New gramophones no longer play 78s, and how soon will it be before new types of sound-recording displace 33s? Nevertheless there is a growing interest in the sound-recordings of the past which will no doubt increase pressure on the relatively few archives of sound-recordings, the chief of these being the British Institute of Recorded Sound and the BBC Sound Archives. Many other countries have official national sound archives.

Another recent development has been the setting up in many countries of Music Information Centres for the promotion of new music of local composers. The United Kingdom has three of them: the Scottish Music Archive in Glasgow, the Welsh Music Archive in Cardiff, and the British Music Information Centre in London. Each of them has a library of scores and tapes of published and unpublished music supplied by the composers which are made available to musicians.

3. *Preparing to Use a Library*. These many different types of library contain enormous resources which the ordinary musician may find difficult to sort out. Finding musical sources is no easy task. For the earlier periods there is an excellent survey in *The New Grove Dictionary of Music and Musicians* under 'Sources'. For a wider range of printed and manuscript sources Robert Eitner's *Quellenlexicon* (Leipzig, 1900-4) used to be one's only recourse, but now it has been replaced by the International Inventory of Musical Sources (better known by its French acronym RISM), which has already published a catalogue giving locations for nearly all music printed before 1800, and has done several detailed catalogues of manuscripts of

early polyphonic music. It is now preparing a computer-based catalogue of manuscript music from the years 1600-1800. For the 19th century there are still few aids, though the new *Catalogue of Printed Music in the British Library to 1980* (London, 1980-), when complete, should be fairly good, at least for British publications! For the 20th century, in addition to the British Library catalogue, there is also the *Library of Congress Catalogs: Music* which have been published annually since 1943.

Finding the literature of music is possibly even more difficult than finding the music. RISM devotes two volumes to music literature up to 1800, but after that there is very little until the *Library of Congress Catalogs* from 1943 onwards (the new British Library Catalogue contains only music). Much important information is to be found in musical periodicals, which began towards the end of the 18th century. Imogen Fellinger's *Verzeichnis der Musikzeitschriften des 19. Jahrhunderts* gives locations for all 19th-century periodicals, and Tony Hodges's *British Union Catalogue of Music Periodicals* (in preparation) will include 20th-century periodicals held in British libraries. Since 1949 the *Music Index* has listed the contents of many periodicals, while the *Bibliographie des Musikschrifttums* has listed both books and articles since 1951. More important than these has been the establishment of the Répertoire Internationale de la Littérature Musicale whose *RILM Abstracts of Music Literature* have, since 1967, not only listed but also given brief abstracts of books, theses, and articles supported by a sophisticated subject index. It is now also available on-line through commercial computer information firms. These are just a few of the more important bibliographies that form the basis of the information service provided by the larger music libraries. Detailed lists of libraries are contained in *The New Grove*, and for a guide to many bibliographies, see Vincent Duckles's *Music Reference and Research Material* (3rd edn, New York, London, 1974).   RICHARD ANDREWES

Library of Congress. The Music Division of the Library of Congress in Washington, DC, was established in 1897. Its early development was shaped by the efforts of Oscar G. T. Sonneck, chief from 1902 to 1917, whose classification system (Music, Musical Literature, and Musical Theory or Teaching) was later adopted by many libraries. Successive chiefs (Engel, Strunk, Spivacke, Waters, Leavitt) have supervised acquisitions until today, at over 4,750,000 items, the Division's collection is one of the world's richest, particularly strong in American material, opera scores and librettos, pre-1800 books on music, and autograph scores and letters. Several foundations and funds established within the Division provide for commissions, acquisitions, concerts, recordings, and publications. Other departments of the Library important to musicians are the Archive of Folk Song and the Recorded Sound Section. NYM COOKE

Libretto (It., 'little book', from It. *libro*, 'book'). The name generally given to the book of the words of an opera. Though the earliest were some 8½" in height, the Italian diminutive was always used, and the term has been current in English since about the mid 18th century. The first libretto ever written was for Peri's *Dafne* at Florence in 1600; there have since been over 30,000. Early librettos usually began with a title-page succeeded by a preface in which the writer made obsequious dedication to his patron, and then by a few words addressed to the reader. The *argomento* (literally 'argument'), which also preceded the actual text in early librettos, was a summary of the events leading up to the action of the opera: these tended to increase in complexity, and even to take their place in the opera itself as a prologue (e.g. Verdi's *Il trovatore*). After the list of the characters in the opera came a catalogue of the

Frontispiece to the libretto (1793) of Mozart's 'Die Zauberflöte'.

scene changes, dances, perhaps also the scenic effects: this trait survives on to playbills of the English music theatre of the 19th century. Until about the end of the 18th century there would also be a *protesta*, in which the author affirmed his good Roman Catholic faith despite the opera's pagan references to *numi*, *fati*, etc.: this arose from the necessity of having the libretto approved in cities under Papal domination.

Essentially, a good libretto has always been a story, whether dramatic in origin or not, moulded to the needs of music drama. The sources of successful librettos have ranged from great dramatic masterpieces (*Othello* for Verdi) and great novels (*War and Peace* for Prokofiev) to sentimental novels (*Scènes de la vie de Bohème* for Puccini) and narrative poems (*Eugene Onegin* for Tchaikovsky), from heroic legend (most of Metastasio's librettos) to real-life incident (perhaps *Pagliacci*, Janáček's *Osud*), from metaphysics and questions of belief (*Parsifal*) to farce (most of Offenbach), from great painting (Hindemith's *Mathis der Maler*, Granados's *Goyescas*) to comic strip (Janáček's *Cunning Little Vixen*), from history or biography (*Rienzi*, and much French grand opera) to fairy tale (Russian opera in both categories). There are no rules of origin but a number of successful methods of their application, of which most composers have singled out conciseness and a capacity to depict human emotions in a dramatic context as prime but not exclusive virtues.

In the 17th and 18th centuries the established pattern of recitative, aria, and chorus made special demands on the librettist and determined the course of the action. The argument about the precedence of music or words has been raging ever since, and found operatic expression (if not resolution) in Strauss's *Capriccio*. Though conventions have naturally changed — with the virtues of formality and the contrasting virtues of freedom changing precedence — the vital element has remained dramatic potency as it charges a composer's imagination. Collaboration has not proved indispensable: Metastasio is the great example of a librettist, 27 of whose works did duty for 1,000 settings by 50 composers at least. At the other extreme, very fruitful results have come from the careful mutual planning of Quinault and Lully, Calzabigi and Gluck, Da Ponte and Mozart, Boito and Verdi, Gilbert and Sullivan, and Hofmannsthal and Strauss. Berlioz, Wagner, Charpentier, and Menotti are among the most successful of those composers who have preferred to shape their own librettos, which further suggests that any rules must follow rather than precede example.

The popularity of published librettos is as steady as ever, and many opera-lovers, if in lesser numbers outside Italy, still furnish themselves with copies both to study at home and to take to the performance. As candlegrease spots on the early specimens show, there is even an historical precedent for the now intolerable habit of trying to read the libretto with a light during the performance: in early days, with the audience expected to behave more informally and occasionally to consult its libretto to remind itself of the action on stage, these so-called *cereni* (from *cero*, a wax-candle) were on sale at the door for use during the performance. Librettos were also, however, published as part of a poet's collected works, in well-printed and handsomely bound editions. The translation of librettos became widespread during the development of national opera houses during the 19th century, and some works have been given in many different languages—*Lohengrin* in at least 22, *Rigoletto* in at least 21—and their librettos published. Gramophone companies now normally accompany complete opera sets with a full libretto (and, if necessary, translation), as well as synopses and notes, printing the original and the translation side by side, as was the normal practice at Covent Garden in Victorian times. Then, the libretto was still a natural part of a gentleman's equipment for the opera— palmy days when *Punch* imagined a young man saying:

> A pound, dear father, is the sum,
> That clears the opera wicket;
> Two lemon gloves, a lemon ice,
> Libretto, and your ticket.

JOHN WARRACK

FURTHER READING
Patrick Smith: *The Tenth Muse* (New York, 1970).

Licenza (It.). 'Licence', 'freedom'; *con alcuna licenza*, 'with some licence', i.e. freedom with regard to tempo and rhythm. The term was used in the 17th and 18th centuries to refer to a passage or cadenza improvised by the performer.

Lidholm, Ingvar (Natanael) (*b* Jönköping, 24 Feb. 1921). Swedish composer. He studied at the Royal College of Music in Stockholm (1940–6) and privately with Hilding Rosenberg and Mátyás Seiber (1954). He has held posts as conductor of the Örebro Orchestra (1947–56), head of chamber music for Swedish radio (1956–65), and teacher of composition at the Royal College (1965–   ). After an early neoclassical phase he entered the avant-garde mainstream with such works as *Ritornell* for orchestra (1955) and *Nausikaa ensam* for soprano, chorus, and orchestra (1963), showing a typically Scandinavian feeling for musical poetry.   PAUL GRIFFITHS

FURTHER READING
Bo Wallner: *Music of our Time in Scandinavia* (London, 1971).

Lidón, José (*b* Béjar, nr Salamanca, 1746; *d* Madrid, 11 Feb. 1827). Spanish composer. He was educated at the choir school of the royal chapel in Madrid, and in 1768 he was appointed fourth organist there, becoming *maestro de capilla* in 1805. In 1787 his *zarzuela*, *El baron de Illescas* (now lost), was staged in Madrid, and it was followed in 1791 by his Castilian drama *Glaura y Coriolano*. He also wrote sacred music, organ pieces, and some didactic works.

WENDY THOMPSON

Lié (Fr.). 'Bound', i.e. slurred, or tied.

Liebesliederwalzer ('Love-song Waltzes'). Eighteen waltzes, Op. 52, by Brahms for two pianos with soprano, alto, tenor, and bass soloists. The texts are from G. F. Daumer's *Polydora* and they were composed in 1868–9. A version was also published (Op. 52*a*) without the vocal parts. In 1874 Brahms composed 15 more, *Neue Liebesliederwalzer* (Op. 65), for the same forces (Op. 65*a* without voices).

Liebesmahl der Apostel, Das ('The Love Feast of the Apostles'). 'Biblical scene' by Wagner to his own text, composed in 1843. It is scored for male chorus and orchestra (which enters late in the work).

Liebestod ('Love-death'). Title generally applied to Isolda's final aria at the end of Act 3 of Wagner's opera *Tristan und Isolde* (or to the orchestral arrangement of it, often played as a concert piece with the Prelude to Act 1). Wagner himself applied the term to the love-duet in Act 2.

Liebesträume ('Love-dreams'). Three nocturnes for solo piano by Liszt (*c*.1850). They are transcriptions of his songs *Hohe Liebe*, *Gestorben war ich*, and *O Lieb, so lang du lieben kannst*, the third (in A♭) being the best known.

Liebesverbot, Das ('The Ban on Love'). Opera in two acts by Wagner to his own libretto after Shakespeare's *Measure for Measure*. It was first performed in Magdeburg in 1836.

Lied (Ger.). The accepted German word for 'song' since at least the 15th century; *Gesang*, also meaning 'song', is used less frequently (e.g. for *Meistergesang*, the song of the *Meistersinger*). The heyday of the *Lied* was the 19th century, and of the hundreds of composers who wrote thousands of songs, time has sifted out four—

Schubert, Schumann, Brahms, and Wolf—as the supreme masters of the genre.

1. *Before the 19th Century*. From the 15th century come three large song collections compiled in Germany: the *Lochamer Liederbuch* (*c*.1452–60), with 44 *Lieder* (i.e. German-texted songs), mostly monophonic, but including also nine pieces in two or three parts; the *Schedelsches Liederbuch* (1460s), with 128 pieces, 68 of which are polyphonic *Lieder*; and the *Glogauer Liederbuch* (*c*.1480), with 70 polyphonic *Lieder*, but many more pieces with French or Italian texts. The influence of composers from the Low Countries, France, and Italy on these late flowerings of vocal polyphony is strong, but the *Lochamer Liederbuch* contains an early example, the anonymous three-part 'Der Wald hat sich entlaubet', of an indigenous genre, the *Tenorlied*.

The composers of these 15th-century songs, where they are named at all, tend to be obscure, little-known figures, and it is only in the 16th

century that more important names begin to be regularly associated with German song: notably Hofhaimer, Finck, and Isaac (whose 'Innsbruck, ich muss dich lassen' is probably the best-known *Lied* from this period). The relative popularity of the *Lied* in the 16th century owed much to the advances made at the beginning of the century in the printing industry, particularly in Augsburg, Cologne, and Mainz. In the second half of the century, Lassus, Hans Leo Hassler, and Leonard Lechner can be seen as the last great masters of the tradition.

The solo *Lied* with continuo accompaniment, known as the *continuo Lied* or *Generalbass Lied*, began to supersede polyphonic song in Germany in the 1620s. In general, the music of the 17th- and 18th-century *Lied* was subservient to its text, and composers were much influenced by the theories of poets such as Martin Opitz (1597–1639), Caspar Ziegler (1621–90), Johann Gleim (1719–1803), and Johann Peter Uz (1720–96). *Lieder* by composers before Schubert—such as Heinrich

Autograph of the opening of Wolf's 'Alles endet, was entstehet' (dated 20 March 1897), from 'Drei Gedichte von Michelangelo'.

Albert and Adam Krieger in the 17th century, and J. A. P. Schulz, Christian Neefe, Reichardt, and Zelter (all based in Berlin) and J. R. Zumsteeg in the 18th—placed the emphasis on a syllabic and unpretentious vocal line, the keyboard part being indicated by the single-line figured bass, leaving the player free to interpret the accompaniment in his own way.

One important feature of many songs from the mid 18th century onwards was the adoption of a deliberately naïve or folk-like style, for example by J. A. Hiller in his songs for children and, especially, Schulz in his *Lieder im Volkston* (three collections: 1782, 1785, 1790). (See *Volkstümliches Lied*.)

2. *The 19th and 20th Centuries.* In at least some of Mozart's 40 or so songs a true 'accompaniment' was beginning to develop, and by Beethoven's time a full accompaniment was a standard feature. Since then the accompanist's role has run the risk of dominating the singer's. Most of Beethoven's over 80 songs are early works, his last important song collection, the *song-cycle *An die ferne Geliebte*, dating from 1816, by which time Schubert had scarcely begun.

Schubert wrote more than 600 songs, varying in size from a few bars to 20 or more pages. The vocal line may be anything from the simplest step movement in even rhythm to the virtuosity of *Der Hirt auf dem Felsen* (Müller; 1828), while the keyboard part could range from the static, almost non-existent accompaniment of Goethe's *Meeresstille* (1815) to the exacting *Erlkönig* (also Goethe; 1815). The moods embrace the folk-like *Heidenröslein* (Goethe; 1815), the cheerful, outdoor quality of 'Das Wandern' (from *Die schöne Müllerin*, Müller; 1823), the visionary *Lied eines Schiffers an die Dioskuren* (Mayrhofer; 1816), the evocative *Die Stadt* (Heine; 1828), and the ecstatic *Ganymed* (Goethe; 1817).

Other composers have a more limited range. Of Schumann's *c*.300 songs, about half were written in the year of his marriage, 1840; they include most of his best. The poet he found most congenial was Heine, and the song-cycle *Dichterliebe* (Op. 48, 1840) is perhaps the summit of his achievement as a *Lied* composer. Joseph von Eichendorff was another whose verse appealed to him: the chivalric fantasy of *Waldegespräch*, the eeriness of *Zwielicht*, the mysterious evocation of the distant past in *Auf einer Burg* (all from *Liederkreis*, Op. 39, 1840) struck responsive chords in Schumann's complex character. He was less at home in the frank pictorialism which Schubert (as in *Die Forelle*) found quite natural, and was at his best in suggesting shadowy, half-seen pictures and events; in such a song as *Mondnacht* (also from Op. 39) he paints for us a Whistlerian Nocturne.

Brahms was different again. More than half his total output was vocal, and included over 200 solo songs, drawing on a wide range of poets of very varied achievements. His music is a blend of sensuousness and scholasticism; seemingly suspicious of his first thoughts, he worked slowly over his compositions, or put them aside for long periods while they matured, like wine in casks. Songs with emotional outbursts such as *Von ewiger Liebe* (Hoffmann von Fallersleben; Op. 43, 1864) or *Liebestreu* (Robert Reinick; Op. 3, 1853) are most likely to be early; the best of his later songs, for example 'Immer leise wird mein Schlummer' (Hermann Lingg; Op. 105, 1886) or *Sapphische Ode* (Hans Schmidt; Op. 94, *c*.1884), have a serenity and poise which can only be described as 'autumnal'. But too much should not be made of this, and there are many middle-period songs—*An ein Veilchen* (Hölty; Op. 49, 1868); *An eine Äolsharfe* (Mörike; Op. 19, 1858); 'Wie bist du, meine Königin' (Daumer; Op. 32, 1864); *Regenlied* (Klaus Groth; Op. 59, 1873); to name but a few—that reveal a genial and relaxed mastery, with the demands of poetry and music finely balanced.

Hugo Wolf is the only one of these four whose reputation rests almost entirely on his songs, which his admirers cannot praise too highly. Unlike Brahms, whose music he despised, his 300 songs were composed rapidly, in a series of bursts of intense and frenzied activity, over a short period of about ten years. He found little to attract him in contemporary poets, preferring to draw on those of the past such as Goethe, Eduard Mörike, Eichendorff, and Emanuel Geibel and Paul Heyse (whose translations of yet earlier Italian and Spanish verse provided the material of his Italian and Spanish songbooks). His music is usually technically difficult, for both singer and pianist; some of his simpler pieces, for instance the popular *Fussreise*, are not always fully representative of his best, and one or two, such as *Verborgenheit*, are distinctly poor. *Das verlassene Mägdlein*, however, must be classed among his masterpieces. These three belong to the group of 53 Mörike songs, written in 1888—a collection which many people regard as the summit of his achievement. Of the *Spanisches Liederbuch*, written over the following two years, the first ten songs are grouped as a cycle on the Passion (called *Geistliche Lieder*): Christ's agony is mirrored in the self-torturing guilt of the human onlooker in music of writhing and dissonant chromaticism. The 51 Goethe settings are immensely varied, ranging from the exquisite *Anakreons Grab* and the amusing *Epiphanias* (both 1888) until in some, e.g. *Prometheus* (1889), the piano writing has burst the confines of the instrument, so that Wolf, with the example of Wagner before him (the Wesendonck songs, 1857-8), eventually turned to the orchestra. This was a practice followed more and more by Gustav Mahler in his song-cycles—e.g. *Kindertotenlieder* (Rückert; 1901-4) and *Lieder eines fahrenden Gesellen* (to Mahler's own poems, based on *Des Knaben Wunderhorn*; 1884)—and by others, until in the 20th century the *Lied* has all but parted company from its original small-scale format.

It is impossible to mention more than a handful of other *Lied* composers. Mendelssohn's *Auf Flügen des Gesangen* (Heine; c.1834) is typically graceful; its popularity has overshadowed several better songs, notably the excellent setting of a Goethe sonnet, *Die Liebende schreibt* (1831). The prolific Carl Loewe is at his best in his ballads, with *Erlkönig* (written at the same time as Schubert's) and *Edward* (1818) topping the list. Though much admired in his day, only a few of the 300 *Lieder* of Robert Franz have survived, but Liszt's songs display a real lyric gift, and deserve to be more widely known. Adolf Jensen (1837-79) is another all-but-forgotten composer of talent: his *In dem Schatten meiner Locken* compares favourably with Wolf's setting of the same poem (in the Spanish songbook).

Finally, there is Richard Strauss, a somewhat controversial figure. His 150 *Lieder*—extrovert, sometimes brash and even insensitive, but effectively written—stand at the opposite pole to those of his nervous, introvert, and at times over-sensitive contemporary, Wolf. He brought to the *Lied* a panache derived from opera which, some have objected, is foreign to the spirit of the *Lied*. But the range of the *Lied* has always been wider than the purist will admit. Strauss wrote his *Lieder* with the same zest he brought to all his work, and it is better to enjoy such masterpieces as *Ständchen* (Adolf Friedrich von Schack; Op. 17, c.1885), *Morgen* (John Henry Mackay; Op. 27, 1894), or the *Vier letzte Lieder* (Eichendorff and Hermann Hesse; 1948) with a clear conscience, leaving decisions as '*Lied* or not-*Lied*' to the pedantically minded.

LESLIE ORREY

FURTHER READING
Richard Capell: *Schubert's Songs* (London, 1928, rev. by Martin Cooper 1973); Eric Sams: *The Songs of Hugo Wolf* (London, 1961); R. T. Hinton: *Poetry and Song in the German Baroque* (Oxford, 1963); E. Sams: *The Songs of Robert Schumann* (London, 1969, rev. edn 1975); E. Sams: *Brahms Songs* (London, 1972); Anneliese-Landau: *The Lied: the Unfolding of its Style* (Washington, DC, 1980).

Lieder eines fahrenden Gesellen ('Songs of a Wayfaring Man'). Song-cycle by Mahler to his own poems, based on, or imitative of, *Des Knaben Wunderhorn*. The four songs are for baritone or mezzo-soprano and orchestra (or piano), and were composed between 1883 and 1885 and revised in the early 1890s. They are linked thematically with Mahler's First Symphony.

Liederkreis. General German term for song-cycle, first used by Beethoven to describe his *An die ferne Geliebte*. Schumann used it for two song-cycles for voice and piano—Op. 24, settings of nine poems by Heine, and Op. 39, settings of 12 poems by Eichendorff; both were composed in 1840.

Liedertafel (Ger.). 'Song table'. A name given to German male-voice singing societies which flourished in the nationalistic climate of the early 19th century. They were originally conceived as informal, convivial occasions at which members sat round a table with refreshments, but with the establishing of the more serious-minded Männergesangvereine (Male Song Societies) the aims became more artistic: around the middle of the century huge annual competitive festivals were held, notably the Lower Rhine Festivals (from 1817). *Orphéon is the French equivalent of the Liedertafel.

Lied ohne Worte ('Song Without Words'). Term introduced by Mendelssohn to describe pieces for piano solo in which a song-like melody progresses against an accompaniment. Mendelssohn published eight books of them, each containing six pieces: Book 1, Op. 19 (1830); Book 2, Op. 30 (1835); Book 3, Op. 38 (1837); Book 4, Op. 53 (1841); Book 5, Op. 62 (1844); Book 6, Op. 67 (1845); Book 7, Op. 85 (1850); Book 8, Op. 102 (c.1845). Most of the titles given to the pieces were not Mendelssohn's, the three *Auf einer Gondel* being exceptions. He also wrote a *Lied ohne Worte*, Op. 109, for cello and piano (c.1845).

Lied von der Erde, Das ('The Song of the Earth'). Song-cycle (symphony) by Mahler to poems, with his own additions, from Hans Bethge's *Die chinesische Flöte* (German versions of 8th-century Chinese poems). The six songs are for tenor and alto or baritone soloists and orchestra, and were composed in 1908-9.

Lieto (It.). 'Joyous'; *lietissimo*, 'most joyous'; *lietezza*, 'joy'.

Lieutenant Kijé (*Poruchik Kizhe*). Orchestral suite, Op. 60, by Prokofiev, composed in 1934. In five movements, it is derived from the music he wrote for the film of the same name, and it has an optional baritone part.

Lieve (It.). 1. 'Light'. 2. 'Easy'. *Lievezza, lievemente*, 1. 'lightness', 'lightly'; 2. 'easiness', 'easily'.

Life for the Tsar, A. See *Ivan Susanin*.

Ligature (from Lat. *ligare*, 'to bind'). A note form representing two or more notes. See *Notation*, 2, 3, 4, 6, 7.

Ligeti, Györy (Sándor) (*b* Diciosanmârtin, now Tîrnăveni, Transylvania, 28 May 1923). He studied with Ferenc Farkas and Sándor Veress at the Budapest Academy of Music, where in 1950 he was appointed lecturer in harmony, counterpoint, and analysis. Early works such as the First Quartet (1953–4) show him working away from the Hungarian folk-lore tradition and towards a 'micropolyphony' of clustered lines, but only after he had moved to the West in 1956 could he realize his conceptions fully. He settled in Cologne, where he worked at the electronic studio (*Artikulation* for tape, 1958) and began his first orchestral score, *Apparitions* (1958–9). The latter, together with *Atmosphères* for orchestra (1961) and the Requiem (1963–5), opened a quite new sound world of ominous, slowly evolving masses, while other works, notably *Aventures* for three singers and seven instrumentalists (1962), show a rare wit. In later works, such as the Double Concerto for flute, oboe, and orchestra (1972), Ligeti has reintroduced long melodic lines, though still enmeshed in ornate polyphony.

PAUL GRIFFITHS

FURTHER READING
Ove Nordwall: *Gÿorgy Ligeti: eine Monographie* (Mainz, 1971).

Light Cavalry (*Die leichte Kavallerie*). Operetta in two acts by Suppé to a libretto by C. Costa. It was first performed in Vienna in 1866, and its overture has subsequently become very popular.

Lighthouse, The. Opera in a prologue and one act by Peter Maxwell Davies to his own libretto. It was first performed in Edinburgh in 1980.

Lilburn, Douglas (Gordon) (*b* Wanganui, 2 Nov. 1915). New Zealand composer. He studied journalism and music at Canterbury University College (1934–6), but his success in winning the Percy Grainger prize for his *Forest* in 1936 established a career in music rather than literature. He studied with Vaughan Williams and R. O. Morris at the RCM, London (1937–40), winning the Cobbett Prize for his Phantasy String Quartet in 1939. In 1940 his *Aotearoa* Overture, performed at His Majesty's Theatre,

Ligeti

Haymarket, evoked the shimmer of light and sea of the New Zealand coast. His success in winning three out of four prizes in the New Zealand Centennial Music Competition established him immediately as New Zealand's most gifted composer to date.

On his return to New Zealand in 1940, after a brief spell on a farm, he essayed freelance composition and music criticism for the Christchurch *Press*, being stimulated by the young poets and painters surrounding Denis Glover and his Caxton Press. He began a collaboration with Ngaio Marsh and her university drama group, resulting in much effective theatre music, and his interludes for the poet Alan Curnow's *Landfall in Unknown Seas* (1942, to celebrate the tercentenary of the discovery of New Zealand by Tasman), for speaker and strings, developed the individual lyricism of the earlier *Aotearoa* in a poignant way. In 1947 he became a part-time lecturer at Victoria University of Wellington, and a special chair was created for him in 1970 as director and founder of the electronic music studio: this was the first such studio in the south Pacific, and its foundation followed Lilburn's visits to studios in Toronto and Europe while on leave in 1963. Since then the studio has had a seminal influence in training several generations of New Zealand composers.

Lilburn's music follows three distinct stages. In the first, he absorbed the influences of

Sibelius and Vaughan Williams to culminate in the broad sweep of his Second Symphony, in which the conflicting character of the New Zealand landscape arouses a deep response. In the second period he explored Stravinsky, contemporary Americans, notably Copland, as well as the Second Viennese School, to end in his acerbic single-movement, finely-crafted Third Symphony. His third period is almost entirely concerned with electronic music to which he has brought the qualities of emotional contrast and sensitivity to timbres so evident in his earlier works, accompanied by a strong sense of form and a renewed awareness of his Pacific environment. His electronic sound image to Alistair Campbell's masterly poem *The Return* (1965) initiated a series of works remarkable for their breadth and variety, from the jesting *Carousel* (1976) to the introspective brooding of *Three Inscapes* (1972) and the evocation of summer in *Of Time and Nostalgia* (1979). Lilburn has provided a touchstone for the now flourishing school of New Zealand composers. As composer in residence for several years in the late 1940s at the Cambridge Summer School of Music he influenced the younger generations. As a vigorous and forceful campaigner for composers' rights he contested proposed archaic copyright legislation in 1960; his other diverse activities include the establishment of the Waite-ata Press to publish editions of New Zealand composers and the formation of the Archive of New Zealand music at the Alexander Turnbull Library, Wellington. He has written much effective chamber music, including violin sonatas and a wind quintet. He believes music must reflect the ideals and aspirations of its own culture if it is to communicate fully in an international sense.　　　　　　　J. M. THOMSON

Lilliburlero. Tune of unknown origin which first appeared in print in 1686 in a book of 'lessons' for the recorder or flute, where it is styled 'Quickstep'. The following year it achieved popularity when sung to satirical verses, with the mock Irish word 'Lilliburlero' as a refrain, referring to the appointment to the Lord-Lieutenancy of Ireland of General Talbot, newly created Earl of Tyrconnel, whose name is mentioned several times. It has remained a song of the Orange party, sung to different words, as 'Protestant Boys'. In Purcell's *The Second Part of Musick's Hand-maid* (1687) for harpsichord it appears under the title 'A New Irish Tune'; Purcell also used it as a ground bass in his incidental music for the play *The Gordian Knot Unty'd* (1691).

Linke Hand (Ger., sometimes abbreviated to L.H.). 'Left hand'.

Linley. English family of musicians. **Thomas Linley (i)** (*b* Badminton, Gloucs., 17 Jan. 1733; *d* London, 19 Nov. 1795) settled in Bath in the mid 18th century, teaching singing and conducting local musical events. Later he moved to London, where he became one of the musical directors of Drury Lane Theatre. In 1775 he and his son, Thomas (ii), composed and compiled music for a performance of *The Duenna* by his son-in-law Richard Brinsley Sheridan, the famous playwright. He followed this success with over 20 more dramatic works composed between 1776 and 1797.

His eldest son, **Thomas Linley (ii)** (*b* Bath, 5 May 1756; *d* Grimsthorpe, Lincs., 5 Aug. 1778), was a talented violinist and composer. As a child he studied with Boyce. He was an exact contemporary of Mozart, whom he met in 1770 in Florence, where Linley was studying with Nardini. Burney, who also met him in Italy, reported that 'the Tourmasino (as he is called) and the little Mozart are talked of all over Italy as the most promising geniuses of their age'. Linley's own compositions included music for Shakespeare's *The Tempest* (performed 1777), an anthem with orchestra 'Let God Arise' (written for the 1773 Worcester Festival), an oratorio *The Song of Moses* (performed 1777), and a comic opera *The Cady of Bagdad* (performed 1778). His career was tragically cut short when he drowned while on holiday in Lincolnshire.

Thomas Linley (i) had five other musical children: his three daughters, Mary (1758–87), Maria (1763–84), and Elizabeth Ann (1754–92) were all singers (Elizabeth, the most celebrated for her beauty and accomplishment, married Sheridan in 1773), while of his sons Ozias Thurston (1765–1831) was an organist, and William (1771–1835) was a writer and composer who became joint manager with Sheridan of Drury Lane Theatre (1796–1800).

　　　　　　　WENDY THOMPSON

'Linz' Symphony. Nickname of Mozart's Symphony No. 36 in C major, K 425, composed in 1783. It is so called because it was composed and first performed in Linz.

Liquescent neumes. A form of neume used for singing certain consonants and dipthongs. See *Notation, 2*.

Lira da braccio, Lira da gamba. Two Italian bowed instruments of the 16th century and part of the 17th.

1. *Lira da braccio.* An instrument of much interest from the arrangement of its strings and method of playing. It is seen in pictures from

Lira da braccio, detail of a painting (1499) by Bartolommeo Montagna.

the 1490s onwards by Bellini, Raphael, and many others, and four or five instruments are preserved in collections. In build the lira basically resembles a violin or viola but has seven strings, two of which lie off the fingerboard, diverging from the rest on the bass side to sound their open notes only (see *Crwth*; *Fiddle*, 2). The tuning-pegs are in the front of a heart-shaped pegbox.

The tuning is shown in Ex. 1 as it is given at actual pitch in a later 16th-century addition to a lute manuscript in Pesaro: the first, second, third, and fifth strings are as on the violin, and the fourth is tuned an octave above the fifth. The sixth and seventh, off the fingerboard, sound octave Ds.

The short music examples in the Pesaro manuscript include the beginning of a *romanesca* (Ex. 2), written in a six-line tablature on the Italian system: top line = lowest string, here the seventh; where the first string is required, an extra line is added below the rest. The examples show how the lira was played in chords of from

three to six notes supporting the melody. The bridge thus needs a slightly curved top for it to be possible to bow the middle strings without touching the first and second, or the two at the side. The fourth and fifth strings are mostly fingered together in octaves, the higher note thickening the chords. The open sixth and seventh strings are likewise introduced together, to sound their octave Ds. Like the 13th-century fiddle, the lira was primarily for playing solo, in a contemplative mood, or for accompanying the player's voice, thus recalling Orpheus with his seven-string lyre, to which the name 'lira' here alludes. People would go round the streets singing to it, it was said.

The surviving liras vary greatly in size, having body lengths from 15″ to 20″—the latter (bigger than in the largest viola) being found in the earliest of the instruments, by Giovanni d'Andrea of Verona, dated 1511, preserved in Vienna; with a string length of 16″, it was probably tuned deeper than in Ex. 1 by about a fourth.

The lira offers the most illuminating evidence of advances in Renaissance 'fiddle' design prior to the violin family itself. One prominent visual feature is the two-lobed bottom outline, where the arcs of the two intersecting circles of the 'vesica' (so often an underlying factor in the geometrical design of stringed instruments) are allowed to meet in an inward-pointing peak instead of being connected in a way that produces a continuously rounded bottom outline as in the violin (see *Violin*, 3). This lobed shape is present in some other 16th-century Italian instruments, now with four strings but which may have been liras in their original state.

2. *Lira de gamba* (also 'arciviolata lira' or 'lirone'). A larger instrument with many more strings, held like a viol and fretted. It came later, about the 1570s. The finest specimen is in Vienna. It again had two off-fingerboard basses (or two pairs), tuned e.g. to low G (as a cello third string) and the G above. The other strings, from eight to 13, were tuned in various strange, partly cyclic or zigzagging ways, said to lend themselves to playing three- and four-part chords in any key. It could evidently be a useful continuo instrument and it remained in use in Italy through the first half of the 17th century.

ANTHONY BAINES

Ex. 1

Ex. 2

Lirico (It.). 'Lyric'.

Liscio, liscia (It.). 'Smooth'.

L'istesso (It.). 'The same'; *l'istesso tempo*, maintain the same speed as before. See also *Stesso*.

Liszt, Franz [Ferenc] (*b* Raiding, 22 Oct. 1811; *d* Bayreuth, 31 July 1886). Hungarian composer. In a long, full, and active career Liszt's varied nature manifested itself in many extreme ways. In the amorous Romantic sense he became an idol—'Lisztomania' was the term then coined— and he lived to become a legend as the white-haired abbé in his Roman cassock: a pious yet worldly old man who could still conjure up Mephisto at the keyboard. The evidence of his phenomenal pianistic powers lies in his scores and is echoed in the accounts of his many pupils. As composer he contributed to every genre of music except chamber music (only a few items) and theatrical works (only an early opera, *Don Sanche*, 1825). His most important piano works have always held the field; his pioneering of the symphonic poem, his mastery of transformation or 'metamorphosis' of themes, and his prominent place in the progressive musical tendencies of the time have been generally acknowledged. Outside the piano solo and concerto works, a handful of the orchestral pieces and his principal organ works have remained in the repertory.

1. *The Early Years.* His father was an employee on the Esterházy estates and an amateur musician. By the age of nine the boy's extraordinary pianistic talents earned him a financial award from several Hungarian aristocrats which enabled him to study in Vienna with Czerny and Salieri, and where he encountered Beethoven and Schubert. The family moved to Paris in 1823 and he continued studies with Paër and Reicha.

With ever-increasing concert appearances the child prodigy gained a great reputation and visited England three times before his father's sudden death in 1827. The next few years with his mother in Paris revealed four cardinal aspects of his nature: a mystical longing for the Catholic Church; an equally deep need for feminine attachments; a determination to expand piano technique (partly stimulated by Paganini's violin virtuosity and partly by the upsurge of interest in, improvements to, and love of the piano in contemporary society); and a Romantic, quasi-socialist desire to reform society through art. In this last he was spurred on by writers like Lamennais, Lamartine, Hugo, Heine, and Sand. The Saint-Simonist movement, the 1830 revolution, his association with

Piano recital by Liszt, frontispiece from Adam Brennglas, 'Berlin, wie es ist und—trinkt' (1842).

fellow composers such as Berlioz and Chopin and with artists such as Delacroix—all contributed to create in Liszt an artist of wide humanitarian and cosmopolitan idealism.

His vehicle was still the piano, but he now disdained the endless round of salons and soirées and eloped with a countess, Marie d'Agoult, first to Switzerland and later to Italy. She bore him three children, and he chronicled these years (1835–9) in a series of piano works which ultimately became the first two volumes of the *Années de pèlerinage* ('Years of Pilgrimage'). By the time of this liaison Liszt was regarded already as the greatest pianist the world had seen. Inevitably he returned to the concert platform, startling and delighting audiences with his solo 'recitals' (he was the first musician to give these) and from 1840 to 1847 touring every corner of Europe from Dublin to Moscow, from Spain to Turkey, being fêted at dazzling royal soirées and at villages where no railway was to be laid for years to come. This existence in its turn was to sicken him: his constant tours ruined his relationship with Marie and frustrated his inborn hopes as a composer. However, his finest works of the

1830s and 1840s were transcriptions, notably of Berlioz, Beethoven, and Schubert, as well as of Italian opera composers. In September 1847 Liszt abandoned his virtuoso career and thereafter earned nothing as a player. The few public appearances he made subsequently (and indeed many prior to 1847) were in aid of charity, and from that time no pupil parted with a fee in order to study with him.

2. *The Years of Maturity*. He settled in Weimar in 1848, having been appointed Kapellmeister Extraordinary to the ducal court. During 12 years there he created a centre for contemporary music, developed his conducting technique, and composed a vast body of music: 12 symphonic poems (the term was his own invention, and among his symphonic poems are *Les préludes*, 1848; *Orpheus*, 1853–4; and *Hamlet*, 1858), two symphonies, on Goethe's *Faust* (1854–7) and Dante's *Divine Comedy* (1855–6), two piano concertos (No. 1, 1849, rev. 1853 and 1856; No. 2, 1839, rev. 1849–61), *Totentanz* (1849, rev. 1853 and 1859) for piano and orchestra, many songs, and a host of solo piano works including the Sonata in B minor (1852–3), the

A page from the autograph MS of Liszt's Ballade No. 1 for piano.

Hungarian Rhapsodies (Nos. 1-15, 1846-51), the consolations, ballades, and polonaises, the final versions of the 'Dante Sonata' (1849), the *Études d'exécution transcendante* (1851), the *Grandes études d'après Paganini* (1851), two major works for organ—the Fantasy and Fugue on Meyerbeer's *Ad nos ad salutarem undam* (1850) and the *Prelude and Fugue on B-A-C-H* (1855, rev. 1870)—together with many transcriptions.

As conductor he championed artists dead and living: Beethoven, the lesser-known Schubert, Berlioz, Schumann, and, perhaps above all, Wagner—whom he helped with his purse, his baton, and his pen. He taught a new generation of pianists at Weimar, among them Hans von Bülow who, in 1857, married Liszt's daughter Cosima. Liszt's own companion throughout these years was the Princess Carolyne zu Sayn-Wittgenstein. His ideal of Weimar as a great centre for the amalgamation of the arts, old and new, literary, musical, and visual, failed to be realized for many reasons and his last few years there were darkened by a growing tide of resentment to his musical aims and by the death of his son.

His move to Rome in 1861 brought great spiritual satisfaction but little outward happiness: his hope of marriage to Carolyne (divorced from her Russian husband) was not to be fulfilled; one of his daughters died and his surviving child Cosima committed open adultery with Wagner; finally, Liszt's hope of becoming a vital force in the Roman Church's musical life fell on stony ground despite the personal friendship of Pope Pius IX. The great works of the Roman period are the two oratorios *St Elizabeth* (1857-62) and *Christus* (1862-7) together with liturgical, organ, and piano works, including the variations *Weinen, Klagen, Sorgen, Zagen* (1859) and the two St Francis *Légendes* (1863). Liszt took minor orders in the Church and lived partly in monastic seclusion.

Throughout his life Hungary, his homeland, inspired him. From 1869 he visited it every year for some months (establishing a music academy in Budapest) and spent most summers in Germany and winters in Italy. Thus, till his death a three-cornered progress (Rome-Weimar-Budapest, his 'Vie trifurquée') became his path. New female friends brought consolation and a reconciliation with Wagner and Cosima (who married in 1870) enabled him to display to the world his deep admiration for his new son-in-law. The most remarkable aspect of Liszt's last years is the legacy of his late compositions. In these works—mainly piano pieces, elegies, songs, one symphonic poem, and a number of choral works (including *Via Crucis*)—he was conscious of 'thrusting his lance far into the future'. Shortly after final visits to Paris and London he died at Bayreuth.

3. *Liszt's Music and Influence*. Liszt's contributions to the orchestral, piano, and organ repertories have long been acknowledged, but only in recent decades has due attention been given to other aspects of his output, notably the hundred or so choral works (especially his oratorios, psalms, Masses, and motets); a similar number of songs and recitations with instrumental accompaniment; and his transcriptions of other men's music (which account for about half the number of his works). The sacred choral works place Liszt at the forefront of Catholic church composers of the 19th century, and the best of the songs (mainly settings of French and German) give him no less a place among contemporary writers of *chansons* and *Lieder*. When recording and broadcasting removed the hitherto great value of the transcription, these works fell into disfavour, but Liszt's many such arrangements are the finest of their kind, both the 'straight' reproduction of a work in pianistic terms (as with the Beethoven symphonies) and the freer fantasy-types (as with the operatic paraphrases). Not only did he do the original composers a great service in these works, but in them he left a rich and rewarding heritage of music from the Baroque to that of his younger contemporaries for later generations of pianists and listeners—exploiting the orchestral and *cantabile* resources of the instrument in a unique way.

The music of the last 15 years anticipated many features of 20th-century styles. Liszt had always been a harmonic innovator and a free experimenter with form. In his late works he anticipates the whole-tone and pianistic-impressionistic techniques of Debussy, the atonality of Schoenberg, the sparse linear textures of Webern, and the Hungarian works of Bartók (although Liszt's 'Hungarian' works are mainly based on gypsy elements). His later admirers were as diverse as Busoni, who may be regarded as his spiritual heir, and Stravinsky, who praised Liszt the pioneer.

Perhaps the most generous and most cosmopolitan musical artist of his century, Liszt gave great encouragement to his younger colleagues, especially of the Nationalist schools: Albéniz, Grieg, Smetana, Borodin, MacDowell, Saint-Saëns, to name but a handful. As writer on music (partly aided by his female companions) and as editor of various editions he further promoted the music of others.

DEREK WATSON

FURTHER READING
Peter Raabe: *Franz Liszt: Leben und Schaffen* (Stuttgart, 1931, rev. edn 1968); Sacheverell Sitwell: *Liszt* (London, 1934, rev. edn 1966); Humphrey Searle: *The Music of Liszt* (London, 1954); Alan Walker, ed.: *Franz Liszt: the Man and his Music* (London, 1970); Derek Watson: *Liszt* (London, 1983).

Litany (Lat.: *litania*, *letania*, from Gk *litaneia*, 'prayer'). Form of prayer consisting of a series of petitions or biddings to God, the Virgin Mary, or the Saints, or the procession during which such supplications are made. The Roman Catholic litany consists of the Kyrie followed by several responses from the congregation, for example 'Mater Christi, ora pro nobis', and closes with the Agnus Dei.

The Anglican litany is a free translation by Thomas Cranmer of parts of the Latin litanies then in use in England; it was first issued in 1544 for use in the processions ordered by Henry VIII at a time when England was at war with France and Scotland. His Primer of the following year calls it the 'Common Prayer of Processions'. The structure, therefore, remained the same, with English responses such as 'Deliver us, O Lord' and 'Hear us, we beseech Thee'.

The most popular of all litanies, at least in Italy, was the *Litaniae laurentanae* ('Litany of Loreto') in honour of the Virgin Mary. It has attracted several polyphonic settings, by composers such as Victoria, Palestrina, and Lassus. Other litanies frequently chosen for polyphonic settings (but not before the mid-16th century) were the Litany of the Saints, the Litany of Jesus, and the Litany of the Blessed Sacrament.

Literes (Carrión), **Antonio** (*b* Artá, Majorca, June 1673; *d* Madrid, 18 Jan. 1747). One of the most important Spanish composers of the early 18th century. He was educated in the choir school of the royal chapel in Madrid, and in 1693 was appointed a bass viol player there. Together with José de Nebra he built up a new repertory of liturgical music for the chapel to replace that destroyed in a fire on Christmas Eve 1734. His own works include psalms, *Magnificat* settings, Masses, and three impor-

tant *zarzuelas*; they are mostly preserved in manuscript in various Spanish libraries.

WENDY THOMPSON

Lithography. See *Printing and Publishing of Music*, 2.

Lithophone (from Gk *lithos*, 'stone', *phōnē*, 'sound'). A term for percussion instruments made of stone, marble, etc. Some churches in Ethiopia are said to have a single slab, or a number of them, hanging outside the building to serve as church bells. China has known temple instruments of 16 L-shaped slabs, sometimes made of jade, and some dating back to the 2nd millennium BC. In Britain, there is a large 'rock harmonica' with basalt bars preserved in the museum at Keswick, Cumbria.

ANTHONY BAINES

Litolff, Henry (Charles) (*b* London, 7 Aug. 1818; *d* Bois-Colombes, 5 Aug. 1891). French pianist, music publisher, and composer. He learnt the piano with Moscheles in London and then went to Paris (1835) and, with the encouragement of Fétis, to Brussels (1839–41) to compose and pursue a solo career. In the 1840s and 1850s he gave concerts in Germany and the Netherlands, and in 1849 settled in Brunswick where through marriage he acquired the publishing firm of Gottfried Meyer, renamed it Henry Litolff's Verlag, and soon became an important figure in local musical life. His connections with Moscheles, Fétis, Berlioz, Liszt, and others contributed to its success, but it was chiefly later, under Theodor Litolff (1839–1912), Meyer's son whom Litolff adopted, that the firm gained a flourishing reputation as a publisher of piano music and teaching material, including notable collections

THE ROCK HARMONICON !

At Mr. Stanley's Rooms,
No. 21, OLD BOND STREET.

J. RICHARDSON'S THREE SONS

Will perform on the Instrument, at the above Rooms, daily, from Ten o'Clock until Seven.

Admission 1s. Children and Schools half price.

of the classics. Henry Litolff returned to Paris in 1858 and took up conducting and teaching. Meanwhile his compositions were fast accumulating: he wrote operas, choral and orchestral works, songs, and chamber music, but today he is remembered chiefly for his brilliant piano music, especially the *Concertos symphoniques* for piano and orchestra (No. 4 includes the famous 'Scherzo'). A colourful figure who was married four times, Litolff was much admired by his contemporaries, especially Liszt.

JUDITH NAGLEY

'Little Russian' Symphony. Nickname of Tchaikovsky's Symphony No. 2 in C major, Op. 17 (1872), so called because it uses folksongs from the Ukraine ('Little Russia').

Little Sweep, The. The second part of Britten's *Let's Make an Opera*.

Liturgical Drama. See *Church Drama*.

Liturgy. The officially authorized services of the Christian Churches. In the Roman Catholic Church these include the *Mass, the *Office, and the Sacramentals (i.e. the Burial Service, the Wedding Service, etc.). The liturgy does not, strictly speaking, include private devotions such as the saying of the rosary or prayers said in private meditations or retreats; neither does it include local processions, mystery plays, carols, and the like popularly associated with certain feastdays, especially in the Middle Ages. In the Roman Catholic Church the most recent analysis of the liturgy was set forth in the *Constitution on the Sacred Liturgy* of the Second Vatican Council (1962–5); only the Holy See can authorize changes in the liturgy. In the less centralized Anglican Church it is the General Synod of the Anglican Communion which authorizes such changes.

The chequered history of the Christian Church has led to many divergent theological viewpoints, liturgical practices, and chant forms and styles. Broadly speaking, six major liturgical factions are recognized; four belong to the Eastern Churches and two to the Western. The Eastern liturgies are: Syrian, Coptic, Byzantine, and Persian; and the Western ones: Hispano-Gallican and Franco-Roman. Each of these categories has several subdivisions. For example, the Byzantine group includes the Greek and Russian Orthodox Churches, the Coptic group the Churches of Egypt and Ethiopia, and the Hispano-Gallican group the Ambrosian, Mozarabic, and Celtic rites. Of most interest to the English-speaking world is the Franco-Roman group; it includes the Roman Catholic liturgy and its Reformed cousin Protestantism (further subdivided into Lutherans, Anglicans, Calvinists, etc.).

1. *The Eastern Liturgies*. The origins of the Eastern liturgical divisions lie in theological and political disputes, particularly those associated with the heresies of the 4th to 6th centuries. A central dispute concerned the manifestation of Christ as both Man and God. One faction, led by Nestorius (*d* 451), held that Christ had two juxtaposed natures (Nestorianism), whilst another, led by Cyril of Alexandria (*d* 444), said that He was one composite entity (Monophysitism). Things came to a head at the Council of Chalcedon (451), when the Nestorian view was partially upheld by Rome, Constantinople, and the Eastern Emperor Marcian. This caused a split with Christians in Egypt, Syria, and Armenia, who were all Monophysites. In the late 5th century the unrest in the Church began to worry the Eastern Emperor Zeno, and he reversed the Chalcedon edicts and adopted a compromise form of Monophysitism. This did not reconcile the earlier dissenters and it provided an opportunity for the Persian Church, which was trying to gain independence from the West, to break away into whole-hearted Nestorianism. So, from at least the 6th century there have been several independent Eastern liturgies.

In the case of the original Monophysite Christians (Syria, Armenia, and Egypt) the long years of separate development and their proximity to Oriental culture has produced a musical style rather removed from Western norms. For example, the chants of the Coptic churches show Arabic influence (the Arabs conquered Egypt in 641) in their ornaments and melody types, and in their modal system which is quite unlike the Gregorian system of modes. (The Persian Church also has a non-Gregorian modal system.) The early Coptic liturgical books have some rudimentary notation (a number are preserved in the John Rylands Library, Manchester), and some of their chants are accompanied by percussion instruments. In some respects the Syrian liturgy is closer to Western models in its use of a closely related modal system, its practice of performing psalms antiphonally, and so on. There is some difference of musical emphasis, however; for example, the Syrian liturgy provides no music for the so-called Little Hours of the Office (Prime, Terce, Sext, and None).

The city of Byzantium began its long period of contact with the West in AD 330, when it was renamed Constantinople by the Emperor Constantine. The Byzantine liturgy soon acquired some individual features written specially by St Basil (*d* 379), Bishop of Caesarea. St Basil's liturgy is still used for ten special services during the Orthodox Church Year. Other services are derived from a shorter liturgy prepared at Constantinople by John Chrysostom (*d* 404). St Basil was also important for encouraging Orthodox monasticism; after the 10th century a group of Greek monasteries on Mount Athos, near Salonika, became increasingly important for the development and perpetuation of the liturgy. The spread of the Byzantine liturgy to the Slavonic countries began *c*.860 when Rastislav, Prince of Moravia, requested missionaries. Two Greek brothers, Cyril and Methodius, were sent. They prepared an alphabet for the hitherto unwritten Slav language; the script was called Glagolitic (hence the title of a famous Mass setting by Janáček). In the second half of the 9th century the Slavonic ritual was adopted in Serbia, and in 927 the Bulgarians established an independent Church using the Slav language. Bulgarian influence also brought the Romanian Church into the Orthodox fold. The last major expansion came in 988 when Vladimir, the pagan prince of Kiev, accepted Orthodoxy for Russia. Liturgical books of Cyril and Methodius were brought to Kiev and in 1019 a bishop was appointed by Constantinople. After Constantinople fell to the Turks in 1453, Moscow became the leading Orthodox city. The Russian ruler, Ivan III, married Sophia Paleologue, niece of the last Byzantine emperor.

Many manuscripts of the Byzantine rite survive complete with chant. The liturgy was rather similar to Western rites, but it had many more hymns, the Credo was not sung, and there were other discrepancies. The modal system was almost identical to the Gregorian one, but it was integrated into the organization of the Byzantine Church Year, since each week was assigned a particular mode. The role of instruments in the Byzantine liturgy seems to have been limited, but the device of a vocal drone (*ison* singing) to accompany chant was a special feature from *c*.1400 onwards. The Russian Church is particularly taken with elaborate forms of ritual, and some aspects of the service are presented as a kind of liturgical drama. Examples include *Shestviye na oslyati* ('Procession on the Donkey' for Palm Sunday) and *Peshchnoye deystvo* ('Play of the Furnace', which tells the tale of the faithful children in the fiery furnace). This last item happens to be the only drama for which there is a surviving musical setting in the Byzantine rite. The 16th century saw the introduction of more elaborate chants, with many melismas, into the Russian rite. All of these features occur within the constraints of monophonic chant, known in Russia as the liturgy of the 'Old Believers'. In the 17th century polyphonic chanting was introduced and it has become a feature of the modern liturgy.

2. *The Western Liturgies*. Christianity took its early liturgical elements (psalms, scripture readings, prayers) from the Jewish religion. Following its origins in Palestine it was disseminated by the Apostles. They spoke Greek, and thus Greek became the liturgical language of Christianity for the first three centuries, even in Rome. After its acceptance as the state religion under Theodosius (379–95) the Latin language was gradually adopted, and the individual elements of at least the Mass became rapidly more fixed. The composition of the Office was still in disarray until the 6th century when St Benedict (*c*.480–*c*.547) organized Western monastic life. Perhaps the most famous liturgical administrator was Pope Gregory I (590–604); he appears to have played some part in organizing (rather than composing) some of the standard plainsongs which we now call Gregorian Chant (see *Plainchant*, 3). Furthermore, he encouraged the work of the professional papal choir—the *Schola Cantorum.

The transition from Greek to Latin as the liturgical language of the West was not instantaneous, neither was it ever really complete. There was a constant flow of Eastern clerics to positions of importance in the West. Eastern additions to the Western liturgy include the Kyrie eleison (these are Greek words), the Agnus Dei (introduced in the 7th century and translated into Latin), and numerous chants created after Greek models. Even today readings of the Solemn Papal Mass are given in Greek as well as Latin.

2a. *The Hispano-Gallican Liturgies*. We have seen that Greek was the original liturgical language of the Western Church. However, the language was hardly known in the north-west of Europe, and this probably played a part in the development of divergent liturgies there (Celtic and Gallican). In the case of the Hispanic and Ambrosian (Milanese) liturgies, on the other hand, the divergence was perhaps in part due to unusually direct links with the East. For example, St Augustine tells us that Ambrose (340–97), Bishop of Milan, introduced Eastern practices into Western liturgy—particularly a love of hymn singing, and the antiphonal performance of psalms. The liturgy of Milan is named after St Ambrose; much of its chant repertory survives, but the earliest sources are relatively late, dating from the 12th century. The Hispanic rite of Spain and Portugal (sometimes called the Mozarabic or Visigoth rite) was developed in Toledo, Seville, Saragossa, and Córdoba. It was used until the late 11th century when, as the Moors were gradually driven from northern Spain, the newly established monarchies imposed the Roman rite. Few of its authentically original chants survive. In the late

15th century Cardinal Ximenes designated a chapel in Toledo Cathedral in which the ancient liturgy would be preserved. Ximenes printed a version of the Hispanic rite in 1500, but by that time it was contaminated by Roman elements.

The Celtic liturgy originated in the monastic institutions founded in Ireland by St Patrick (d 461), who received his early training in Gaul. It was also used in Scotland, parts of England, and Brittany. During the 6th and 7th centuries it spread with Irish missionaries who moved eastwards across Europe establishing monasteries; the most famous was St Gall in Switzerland. The Celtic rite lacked a clear identity, as it borrowed freely from other liturgies. It did have a unique scheme for the use of psalms in its services, and hymn-singing played a major role. Only one or two Celtic melodies have survived, chiefly because they were transplanted to other liturgies (e.g. the hymn *Mediae noctis tempus est*). There is evidence that some Celtic chants were accompanied on the harp. The Gallican liturgy was observed in Frankish lands (which comprised much of presentday France and parts of Germany, Switzerland, and Italy) from the time of Clovis (d 511) until its fusion with elements of the Roman rite in the 8th century by Pepin and Charlemagne. No Gallican liturgical book with music survives, but certain elements of the rite have been retained elsewhere. The Roman Catholic liturgy, for example, derived the *Improperia (Reproaches of the Saviour on Good Friday) ultimately from the Gallican rite.

2b. The Franco-Roman Liturgies. The preeminence of the Roman rite in Western Europe began to emerge in the 7th and 8th centuries. The Celtic liturgy was gradually replaced in England after Pope Gregory I sent St Augustine to Canterbury in 596, and the change was officially recognized by the Synod of Whitby in 664. Also in the 7th century Romanized Anglo-Saxon monks such as St Boniface supplanted the Irish missionaries and their liturgy on the Continent. In Gaul the Gallican rite had many local variations, and it lacked important metropolitan centres to regulate its work. So, when Pepin (d 768) and Charlemagne (d 814) wished to strengthen the Frankish nation they imported the Roman rite in order to engender unity and gain support. Liturgical books were sent from Rome, but they contained only the great festal services celebrated by the Pope. Alcuin, an English monk and scholar, was given the task of completing some of the liturgical books; for this he drew upon local materials, so that the Roman liturgy came to incorporate Gallican elements. None of the books had notation and, in spite of several exchanges of singers between Gaul and Rome, there can be no doubt that variations crept into the chant. During the four centuries

following the death of Charlemagne the growth of the liturgy took place primarily on Franco-German soil. Simple congregational singing was replaced by ornate chants for soloists, and the standard chants were elaborated and augmented with *tropes, *sequences, and liturgical drama (see *Church Drama*, 1). The original Roman chant was (except for a few churches in Rome itself which adhered to the old chant) irreversibly transformed by its contact with the Frankish world, and the two cultures together gave us our Roman Catholic (or so-called Gregorian) Chant.

In the Middle Ages Catholicism was further subdivided into many local Uses with minor variations of liturgy. In England, there were the Uses of Hereford, York, Lincoln, and Salisbury (*Sarum Use), while France had the Uses of Paris, Lyons (still surviving today), and so on. Moreover, most of the monastic bodies had, and still have, their separate Uses, including the Carthusians, Cistercians, Carmelites, Dominicans, Gilbertines (an English order), and Premonstratensians. Curiously enough, the largest order—the Benedictines—did not have a separate Use, but adopted, with slight modifications, the Use of the locality in which their monastery was situated.

From the 13th century on, the increasing wealth and political involvement of the Church provoked a backlash. The founding of the Franciscan order devoted to poverty, the introduction of vernacular elements into the liturgy (translations of the Bible, the singing of carols, etc.), and open attacks on the Church by Wyclif (d 1384), Hus (d 1415), and others were portents of changes to come. Martin Luther (1483–1546) began his career as an Augustinian monk; he never did publish a definitive Lutheran rite, and the preface to his German Mass (1526) specifically requests that it should not be made a rigid law. Nonetheless, his suggested reforms were later taken up with less flexibility. Changes were fairly gradual in England, however. The First English Prayer Book of 1549 was not so far removed from the Sarum liturgy, but the final version of 1662 was a truly reformed liturgy (see *Common Prayer, Book of*).

3. *The Liturgy and Music.* An understanding of changing liturgical practices and chant variants can help to identify the provenance and context of polyphonic music. For example, much English Medieval Mass music appears anonymously in continental manuscripts, but can be identified by its use of specifically English tropes (e.g. the Kyrie *Deus Creator*) or chant variants. In the case of 16th-century music, an understanding of the differing liturgical practices of various Venetian churches is helping to pinpoint the original context of much of the music by

the Gabrielis. In the 18th century, although Germany and Austria shared many cultural, linguistic, and political features, Haydn and Mozart belonged firmly to the Austrian Catholic tradition in their church music, rather than to the German Lutheran—when the Austrian Emperor Joseph II enforced a papal ban on orchestral music in church in 1783, Haydn wrote no more church music for 13 years. In the next century, Brahms drew on the Lutheran tradition for his *German Requiem*, in using a vernacular text taken from the German Bible. As far as the Eastern liturgies are concerned, several composers have used their services and ceremonies as suitable material for art music. For example, Berlioz heard the Russian imperial chapel sing in 1847; he was deeply impressed, and even wrote his own settings of *Plain-chants de l'église grecque* (now lost). Glinka and Rakhmaninov have left several pieces for the Russian liturgy, and in the 20th century Stra-

vinsky not only wrote several small religious works with Slavonic texts (e.g. a setting of the Lord's Prayer), but also quoted a chant from the Russian liturgy in his ballet *The Wedding*.

Further information on different aspects of the liturgy and on later developments can be found under: *Antiphoner*; *Church Music*; *Common Prayer, Book of*; *Gradual, 1*; *Liber usualis*; *Plainchant*; *Reformation*; and the articles on different countries.   ANTHONY PRYER

Lituus. Originally an Etrusco-Roman ceremonial straight trumpet of bronze, long and narrow with an upturned hook-shaped bell recalling the crook-like staff of the augurs; a near-complete example (lacking the mouthpiece) is in the Vatican museum and many reproductions have been made from it. The European Celts had something like it, and a curious form with a bronze boar's head at the end is shown in works of art, held in a vertical

Capriccio from Locatelli's Violin Concerto No. 4, from 'L'arte del violino' (Amsterdam, 1733).

position for blowing; Greek lexicographers record the Celtic name *carnyx* (a word related to the Latin 'cornu' and 'horn'). See also *Ancient Greek Music*, 4, 7*b*.

In 18th-century German scores 'Litui' sometimes appears, apparently as a name for horns, as in J. S. Bach's Cantata BWV 118, composed for an open-air funeral. ANTHONY BAINES

Livret (Fr.). 'Little book', i.e. libretto.

Lo. Abbreviation for **loco*.

Lobgesang, ('Hymn of Praise'). Symphony-cantata, Op. 52, by Mendelssohn, his Symphony No. 2, composed in 1840. The last movement includes solo voices, chorus, and organ.

Lobo, Duarte (*b* Alcáçovas, ? 1565; *d* Lisbon, 24 Sept. 1646). Portuguese composer. His career was spent entirely in Portugal, first in Evora and later in Lisbon. He was an important teacher, as well as a celebrated composer of sacred music.

Locatelli, Pietro Antonio (*b* Bergamo, 3 Sept. 1695; *d* Amsterdam, 30 Mar. 1764). Italian composer and violinist. He went to Rome in 1711 and may have studied with Corelli and Valentini there. He was soon noted as a virtuoso violinist, and travelled a great deal in Italy and Germany, giving concerts in Venice, Munich, Berlin, and Kassel. In 1729 he moved to Amsterdam; there he continued to give concerts, entered the publishing business (assisting Michel-Charles Le Cène and acting as his own publisher), gave violin lessons, and from 1741 had an apparently thriving trade importing strings from Italy. He left an extensive collection of paintings and a substantial library.

Locatelli was one of the finest violinists of an age in which they abounded—Burney said that he 'had more hand, caprice and fancy than any violinist of his time'. That his technique must have been prodigious is evident from the solo parts of his concertos and sonatas, which make much use of high registers, double stopping, and the rapid alternation of open and stopped strings known as *bariolage*. His position as a composer falls between the Baroque style of Corelli and Vivaldi (both of whom influenced him considerably) and the Classical style of Tartini. The binary form of some of his sonata movements points forward to the development of sonata form, and his concertos give a substantial formal importance to the *ritornello* sections. The 12 concertos of *L'arte del violino* (Amsterdam, 1733) are given written-out cadenzas, or *capricci ad libitum*, which were later to be imitated by Paganini. Although he has been criticized for a lack of depth in his slow movements, Locatelli's music deserves to be valued for more than its technical skill.

DENIS ARNOLD

Locke, Matthew (*b* ? Devon, 1621–2; *d* London, Aug. 1677). English composer. He was trained as a choirboy at Exeter Cathedral, where his name is carved in the stone of the organ screen. There he established a firm friendship with Orlando Gibbons's son, Christopher, and probably met his future employer, the young Prince Charles (later Charles II), in 1644, when the royal family visited. Locke probably followed Charles into exile in the Low Countries later in the Civil War, but by 1651 he was again in England; during his period abroad he had become a Catholic convert.

Locke made his début as a composer for the stage with James Shirley's masque *Cupid and Death*, writing the music in collaboration with Christopher Gibbons, and in 1656 he was one of the composers involved in Davenant's opera *The Siege of Rhodes*. By the end of the decade he was associating regularly with eminent figures in London musical society, and at the Restoration he was chosen by Charles II as composer to the King, with responsibility also for the music for the royal wind and the royal band of violins. He was appointed organist to the new Queen, Catherine of Braganza, in 1662. As a Catholic, however, he could not join the Chapel Royal, and the favour shown him by the King, together with his quarrelsome nature, made him enemies among the Gentlemen of the Chapel Royal. By the end of the 1660s his favour with the King was also waning, Charles's tastes moving more and more towards the light, elegant French music of such composers as Cambert and Grabu, both resident in London. Locke continued to compose for the stage, however, and in 1674 was one of five composers invited to write music for Thomas Shadwell's adaptation of *The Tempest*. His successor as composer to the King was the young Henry Purcell, who wrote an ode on Locke's death, 'What hope for us remains now he is gone?'

In addition to his dramatic music, Locke was a notable composer of chamber music for strings. His extensive output includes several collections of dances, grouped in suites, entitled *Consort*, and scored for various combinations of treble and bass viols (or violins). His surviving sacred music consists of about 60 works, including over 30 anthems and various pieces to Latin texts. His anthems conform to the prevailing taste for substantial instrumental parts—the King loved instrumental music, but found vocal music boring. He also wrote a treatise, *Melothesia, or, Certain General Rules for Playing upon*

Mathew Locke, portrait (1662) attributed to Isaac Fuller.

a Continued-Bass (London, 1673), which contains preludes and dances for harpsichord and seven organ voluntaries as well as the earliest-known printed rules for realizing a figured bass.
WENDY THOMPSON

Loco (It.). 'Place'. Used after a sign indicating performance an octave higher or lower than written, reminding the performer that the effect of that sign is now cancelled. It is often encountered in the form *al loco*, 'at the place'.

Lodoïska. Opera in three acts by Cherubini to a libretto by C. F. Fillette-Loraux. It was first performed in Paris in 1791. It is also the subject of operas by Kreutzer (1791), Storace (1794), and Mayr (1796).

Loeillet. Flemish family of musicians. **Jean Baptiste Loeillet (i)** (*bapt*. Ghent, 18 Nov. 1680; *d* London, 19 July 1730) was the son of a barber-surgeon who died in 1685. Around 1705 he settled in London, where he changed his Christian name to John. From *c*.1707 to 1710 he made frequent appearances as oboist and flautist in the London opera orchestras, and from 1710 ran a series of highly profitable weekly concerts at his house in Hart Street, Covent Garden. Loeillet is credited with popularizing the side-blown flute in England. His works include nine suites of harpsichord *Lessons*, and trio and solo sonatas for recorder, flute, and oboe.

His uncle's son, **Jean Baptiste Loeillet (ii)** (*b* Ghent, June or July 1688; *d* Lyons, *c*.1720), entered the service of the Archbishop of Lyons,

where he remained until his early death. He composed some 48 sonatas for recorder and continuo (Amsterdam, 1710–17) in the style of Corelli; they were reprinted in London by Walsh & Hare. In his works he styled himself 'Loeillet of Ghent'.

His younger brother, **Jacques Loeillet** (*b* Ghent, July 1685; *d* Ghent, 28 Nov. 1748), worked for the Elector of Bavaria in the Netherlands and at Munich; later, he was a musician at the French court. His works include concertos for oboe and for flute, and sonatas for flute and continuo and for two solo flutes.
WENDY THOMPSON

Loesser, Frank (*b* New York, 29 June 1910; *d* New York, 28 July 1969). American songwriter. After leaving college he followed various occupations and, although from a very musical family, made his first steps into popular music as a lyric-writer, having his first lyric published in 1931. He worked as a writer for RKO pictures, and while serving in the army wrote songs for various army shows, including the official song of the infantry, 'Rodger Young'. At this time he wrote his first shows, starting in the revue field, before eventually writing his first complete Broadway musical, *Where's Charley?* (1948). His greatest success, *Guys and Dolls*, came in 1950, followed by *The Most Happy Fella* (1956), *Greenwillow* (1960), and *How To Succeed in Business Without Really Trying* (1961). From 1937 he wrote many songs for films, including the music for *Hans Christian Andersen* in 1952.
PETER GAMMOND

Loewe, Karl (*b* Lobejün, nr Halle, 30 Nov. 1796; *d* Kiel, 20 Apr. 1869). German composer. He received his early music education from his father, and went on to study music, theology, languages, and science at Halle University. In 1820 he was appointed teacher at the Stettin Gymnasium, living in Stettin for the rest of his life as composer, organist, conductor, and teacher. He visited London in 1847 and also travelled to Scandinavia and France. Loewe's substantial output includes six operas, two symphonies, choral music, and chamber and piano pieces, but he is best known for his songs with piano accompaniment (some 400 in all), in particular his ballads on poems by Herder and Goethe, among others. Among the best of his works in the genre are *Edward* (1818), *Erlkönig* (1818), *Elvershöh* (1825), *Der Zauberlehrling* (1832), *Die Glocken zu Speyer* (1837), *Prinz Eugen* (1844), *Archibald Douglas* (1857), and *Tom der Reimer* (1867).
WENDY THOMPSON

Log drum. This has been developed in the USA for modern percussion on the basis of an ancient Mexican species, the Aztec *teponatzli*, as a long wooden box with a thick vibrating tongue cut in the lid and struck with a rubber-ended beater. Sets giving contrasted pitches are said to be in use in some school percussion groups.

Logroscino, Nicola Bonifacio (*b* Bitonto, nr Bari, Oct. 1698; *d* ? Palermo, *c*.1765). Italian composer. He studied at the S. Maria di Loreto conservatory in Naples from 1714, but was expelled from his position as junior master in 1727. In 1728 he was in the service of the Bishop of Conza, but he returned to Naples in 1731. His last years were spent as a teacher in Palermo. Logroscino was a popular composer of *opere buffe*, but since only one such work survives complete, *Il governatore* (performed Naples, 1747), it is difficult to judge their quality.

DENIS ARNOLD

Lohengrin. Opera in three acts by Wagner; text by the composer, after the anonymous German epic. Produced: Weimar, Court Theatre, 28 August 1850; New York, Stadt Theater, 3 April 1871; London, Covent Garden, 8 May 1875. Originally intended for production in Dresden, the opera was rejected because of Wagner's revolutionary activities.

Liszt gave it, with an orchestra of only 38, in Wagner's absence in Switzerland; Wagner did not attend a performance until 1861 in Vienna.

King Henry the Fowler (bass), who has been visiting Antwerp to raise an army, holds court. He asks Frederick of Telramund (bar.) why the kingdom of Brabant is torn by strife. Telramund accuses his ward Elsa (sop.) of having murdered her young brother Gottfried in order to obtain the throne. Elsa describes a dream in which a knight in shining armour has come to defend her. The King's Herald (bar.) twice calls for a champion. A swan-drawn boat bearing a knight in shining armour arrives. The knight (Lohengrin, ten.) bids the swan farewell, and agrees to champion Elsa, offering her his hand in marriage on condition that she will never ask him his name or origin. Lohengrin defeats Telramund, generously sparing his life.

In the courtyard of the castle in Antwerp, Telramund, who has been banned as a traitor by the King, and his wife, Ortrud (sop.), are brooding on the state of events. Elsa appears on a balcony and sings a song to the night breezes. She descends, and Ortrud, offering her friendship, begins to sow distrust of Lohengrin in her mind. Dawn breaks, and processions form for the marriage of Elsa and Lohengrin. On the

Illustration by Theodor Pixis, based on the 1867 Munich production of Wagner's 'Lohengrin', with Heinrich Vogl (Lohengrin) and Mathilde Mallinger (Elsa).

steps of the Cathedral, Ortrud accuses Lohengrin of having defeated Telramund by evil means, and then Telramund repeats his wife's accusations. Elsa assures the knight that she trusts him; but the seeds of suspicion have taken root.

A brilliant orchestral prelude and the celebrated Wedding March open the scene, which is set in Elsa's bridal chamber. Elsa's happiness gives way to hysteria and she demands to know her husband's name. Telramund and four of his followers break into the room to attack Lohengrin, who immediately kills Telramund. He bids the nobles to bear the body to the King, and tells Elsa that he will reveal his secret to them all.

The scene changes to the banks of the Scheldt. The King and court assemble, and Lohengrin tells them that he has come from the Temple of the Holy Grail in Monsalvat; his father was Parsifal, and Lohengrin is his name. He bids Elsa a sad farewell, and then turns to greet the swan which has brought the boat for him. Ortrud rushes on and reveals that the swan is in reality Gottfried, Elsa's brother. Lohengrin falls on his knees and prays. The swan becomes Gottfried, and a white dove of the Grail flies down and draws the boat away.

Loin, lointain (Fr.). 'Distant', i.e. faint.

Lombardi alla prima crociata, I ('The Lombards at the First Crusade'). Opera in four acts by Verdi to a libretto by Solera after T. Grossi's poem (1826). It was first performed in Milan in 1843.

Lombardy style. See *Scotch snap*.

London College of Music. British music college, founded as a privately controlled institution in 1887 and at first devoted mainly to the musical education of amateurs. In 1939 the College was reincorporated as a public educational establishment. Courses now cater almost exclusively for full-time students preparing for a performing or teaching career; certain diplomas may be taken externally. The composer John McCabe was appointed Director in 1983.

Londonderry Air. Beautiful, anonymous Irish melody first printed in the Petrie collection of 1855. It is understood to be a genuine Irish folk-tune. It was given to Petrie by the folk-song collector Miss Jane Ross of Limavady who, with her sister, made a practice of noting down folk-tunes from the peasants who came to Limavady on market day.

The first words known to have been set to it were 'Would I were Erin's apple blossom o'er you' by Alfred Perceval Graves; the second setting was 'Emer's Farewell' by the same poet. The words now associated with it ('Danny Boy') are by F. E. Weatherly.

The melody has achieved world-wide popularity, and has been published in numerous arrangements for every conceivable vocal and instrumental combination. It even figures in some collections of hymn-tunes, and was used by Stanford in his First Irish Rhapsody. Parry described it as 'the most beautiful tune in the world'.

London Opera Centre. See *National Opera Studio*.

London Overture, A. Orchestral work by Ireland, composed in 1936. It was originally written for brass band in 1934, under the title *Comedy Overture*. One of the principal themes is said to have been inspired by a bus conductor's call of 'Piccadilly!'.

London Philharmonic Orchestra. British symphony orchestra, founded in 1932 by Sir Thomas Beecham as his answer to the BBC Symphony Orchestra. It gave its first concert at Queen's Hall, London, on 7 October 1932, and became a self-governing body in 1939. Sir Adrian Boult was Principal Conductor, 1950–7; subsequent conductors have been William Steinberg, John Pritchard, Bernard Haitink, and (from 1979) Sir Georg Solti.

'London' Symphonies. Haydn's last 12 symphonies, Nos. 93–104. They were composed between 1791 and 1795 for the impresario Salomon and were first performed in London during Haydn's visits in 1791–2 and 1794–5. The last of them, No. 104, is known as the 'London' Symphony (or 'Salomon' Symphony).

London Symphony, A. Symphony by Vaughan Williams, his second, but his first wholly orchestral one. It was composed 1912–13 and revised, substantially in 1920 and finally in 1933. Although it is not a programmatic work, it contains evocations of London life, such as Westminster chimes, a lavender-seller's cry, the jingle of hansom cabs, and the sounds of street musicians.

London Symphony Orchestra. British symphony orchestra, founded in 1904 by former members of Henry Wood's Queen's Hall Orchestra (they had resigned in protest at Wood's banning of the system of deputies, whereby a player would send a deputy to a concert while he took a more lucrative engagement elsewhere).

The first concert was at Queen's Hall, London, on 9 June 1904, conducted by Hans Richter, who remained Principal Conductor until 1911. Since the Second World War the orchestra's conductors have been Josef Krips, Pierre Monteux, Istvan Kertesz, André Previn, and (from 1979) Claudio Abbado.

Long. A note-value ( ) used in Medieval and Renaissance music. See *Notation*, 4–6.

Longueval, Antoine de (*fl.* 1503–22). French composer. He is recorded as having been at Ferrara in 1503, and he worked at the French royal chapel from 1507 until at least 1522, at first as a singer and later as choirmaster. His best-known work, a four-part Passion in motet style, was for many years ascribed to Obrecht.
JOHN MILSOM

Lontano ('In the Distance'). Orchestral work by Ligeti, composed in 1967.

López de Velasco, Sebastián (*b* Segovia, late 16th century; *d*? Madrid, *c.*1650). Spanish composer. In 1621 he was *maestro de capilla* to the Infanta Juana in the convent she had founded at Madrid. His surviving works appear in a *Libro de missas, motetes, salmos, magníficas y otras cosas* (Madrid, 1628).
WENDY THOMPSON

Lord's Prayer. See *Pater noster*.

Lorcley, Die. Unfinished opera in three acts by Mendelssohn to a libretto by E. Von Giebel. It is based on the German legend of the beautiful woman who sings on a mountain by the Rhine, luring sailors to death on the rocks below. The surviving fragments date from 1847; among them is an *Ave Maria*, sometimes performed in the concert hall. There are also operas on the subject by Lachner, Wallace, Bruch, Catalani, and others.

Lortzing, (Gustav) Albert (*b* Berlin, 23 Oct. 1801; *d* Berlin, 21 Jan. 1851). German composer. The son of a leather-merchant whose business deteriorated, he spent much of his early life on tour with his parents who became members of a troupe of travelling actors. He had little in the way of a formal musical education, but obtained a thorough knowledge of stagecraft which stood him in good stead when he turned to the composition of *Singspiele* in the 1820s. He was then engaged by various theatres, staying longest at Leipzig where some of his light operas had great success. His capacity for writing tunes in a simple quasi-folk-song style has ensured their continued popularity in Germany, especially

Zar und Zimmermann (1837), *Der Wildschütz* (1841)—notable for its scene in a billiard room— and *Der Waffenschmied* (1846). His one serious opera to have any success was *Undine* (1845), a charming score notable for its use of *Leitmotive* and some Mendelssohnian lightness of orchestration but for once lacking dramatic credibility. He moved to Vienna as Director of Music at the Theater an der Wien in 1846, but was not greatly liked by the critics. When his appointment was not renewed he tried to become Wagner's successor at Dresden but ended his days in charge of the music of a minor Berlin theatre, where he spent most of his time writing incidental music rather than opera. He died feeling neglected and in some financial straits.
DENIS ARNOLD

Los (Ger.). 'Loose', i.e. free in style.

Lost Chord, The. Song by Sullivan to a poem by Adelaide Anne Procter, composed in 1877 in sorrow at his brother's death. It is regarded as the archetypal Victorian drawing-room ballad.

Lotti, Antonio (*b c.*1667; *d* Venice, 5 Jan. 1740). Italian composer. His father was *Kapellmeister* at Hanover in the 1670s. In 1683 Antonio was studying in Venice with Legrenzi, and from 1689 he sang alto in the St Mark's choir. Soon after, he became one of the organists there, and finally *maestro di cappella* in 1736, a position he held until his death. In his day, Lotti was well known as an opera composer, but the little of his music that is performed today is sacred; most is in the *a cappella* style, in which Lotti shows himself capable of surprising expressiveness and power.
DENIS ARNOLD

Louise. *Roman musical* in four acts by Gustave Charpentier; text by the composer. Produced: Paris, Opéra-Comique, 2 February 1900; New York, Manhattan Opera, 3 January 1908; London, Covent Garden, 18 June 1909. Louise (sop.) is in love with Julien (ten.), but her parents (mezzo and bass) refuse to allow them to marry. They set up house together, but when Louise's mother comes to tell her that her father is seriously ill she returns home to help nurse him back to health. The parents refuse to allow Louise to rejoin Julien; she quarrels with her father and he throws her out of the house, accusing the city of Paris of destroying his home.

Louis Ferdinand, Prince of Prussia (*b* Friedrichsfelde, nr Berlin, 18 Nov. 1772; *d* Saalfeld, 13 Oct. 1806). The nephew of Frederick the Great, Louis Ferdinand showed early musical promise and, having proved himself on the

Lithograph poster for the first performance of Charpentier's 'Louise' (Opéra-Comique, Paris, 1900).

Lourd, lourde (Fr.). 'Heavy'; *lourdement*, 'heavily'; *lourdeur*, 'heaviness', 'weight'.

Loure (Fr.). 1. In the 16th and 17th centuries, a kind of bagpipe found in Normandy.

2. A dance popular in the late 17th and early 18th centuries. It resembles the *gigue, but the speed is slower. It is characteristically in moderate triple time, with dotted and syncopated rhythms. There is a loure in the prologue to Lully's opera *Alceste*, but the best-known example is by Bach, in his Fifth French Suite.

Louré (Fr.). 1. (It.: *portato*). In the playing of stringed instruments, a type of bowing, usually found in *cantabile* passages. Several notes are taken in a single bow-stroke, but slightly detached from one another and with separate bow pressure for each. It is indicated thus:

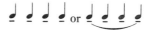

2. See under *Notes inégales*.

Lourié, Arthur (Vincent) (*b* St Petersburg, now Leningrad, 14 May 1892; *d* Princeton, NJ, 12 Oct. 1966). Russian, later American, composer. He studied at the St Petersburg Conservatory but disliked the formal teaching and turned to his own methods of composing, producing a number of experimental atonal vocal and piano pieces. In 1918 he was appointed commissar for music, but in 1922 he left for Berlin, where he was befriended by Busoni, and in 1924 arrived in Paris, where he first met Stravinsky, an acquaintance he was later to renew. He emigrated to the USA in 1941, taking American citizenship in 1947. Lourié was prolific, producing two operas, two symphonies, chamber music, piano pieces, songs, and a large number of sacred choral works which show some influence of the music of the Orthodox

battlefield by the age of 20, settled down to musical studies. He met Beethoven in Berlin in 1796, and the two evidently admired each other: Beethoven declared that Hummel's piano playing could not be compared with Louis Ferdinand's, and dedicated his Third Piano Concerto to the Prince. Louis Ferdinand had studied composition with Dussek, and in 1804 took him into his service as *Kapellmeister*. His works include piano trios and quartets, a piano quintet, and various other pieces of chamber music, mostly involving the piano. He was killed at the Battle of Saalfeld at the early age of 33.

WENDY THOMPSON

Costume designs by Isaak Rabinovich for Prokofiev's 'Love for Three Oranges' (Moscow, 1927).

Russian liturgy. In his later works he abandoned the atonality of his early years, preferring a modal style of writing, as typified in the *Sonata liturgica* (1928) for alto voices and chamber orchestra, and the *Concerto spirituale* (1929) for voices, solo piano, brass, double basses, and percussion.

JUDITH NAGLEY

Love for Three Oranges, The (*Lyubov k tryom apelsinam*). Opera in a prologue and four acts, Op. 33, by Prokofiev to his own libretto after Gozzi's play *Fiabe dell'amore delle tre melarance* (1761). It was first performed in Chicago in 1921. Prokofiev arranged an orchestral suite from the score (1919, revised 1924).

Love in a Village. Ballad opera ('pasticcio') in three acts by Arne to a libretto by Bickerstaffe. Arne composed 19 songs and collected and arranged the rest of the music, by 16 composers. It was first performed in London in 1762.

Love-potion, The. See *Elisir d'amore, L'*.

Lover and the Nightingale, The. See *Maja y el ruisenor, La*.

Love-song Waltzes. See *Liebesliederwalzer*.

Low Countries

1. Introduction
2. To 1500
3. The 16th Century
4. Religious Diversity
5. The 17th and 18th Centuries
6. To the Present Day

1. *Introduction.* For all its inexactitude as a geographical and political designation, the term 'Low Countries' is particularly useful in music history, suggesting as it does a region with a relatively unified cultural identity while avoiding the matter of its complex history of changing national boundaries. Only in the 19th century were the territories of Belgium, Luxembourg, and the Netherlands finally established in their present form, and it would be misleading to apply these names anachronistically to the Low Countries as they existed, for example, during the 15th and 16th centuries when much of the area, including the northernmost part of France, was governed first by the Dukes of Burgundy and later absorbed into the Holy Roman Empire. Because of this political instability through the centuries, no term exists which adequately describes the regional identity of composers and musicians emanating from the Low Countries from the Middle Ages to the present day; words such as 'Burgundian', 'Franco-Flemish', 'Netherlandish', 'Dutch', and 'Walloon' are loaded with specific geographic and temporal implications and need to be used with caution if their precise meanings are to be respected.

2. *To 1500.* Little as we know about the development of music-making in the Low Countries prior to the 14th century, it does seem likely that foreign influences played an important part in shaping its initial course. Books of plainchant from the region contain the more or less international repertory of Gregorian chant, although as in most other parts of Europe this gradually acquired a distinctive 'dialect' as local variants emerged and new chants were added, in particular hymns, sequences, and liturgical drama. Courtly song in the vernacular was also in widespread use by the 14th century, its development almost certainly stimulated by the *trouvère* tradition of northern France, and a small number of monophonic Netherlandish songs have come down to us with their music intact. There is little evidence of early polyphony in the Low Countries, the few motets which survive today again attesting to the influence of French models. If sources of actual music are scarce, however, documentary evidence suggests that music—and the arts in general—gradually won an important place in the civic life of the region as the textile trade brought increasing prosperity during the later Middle Ages; by the end of the 14th century, sophisticated music was being cultivated not only in churches and monastic communities but also by the nobility and wealthy educated class of the great weaving towns.

Although music has continued to occupy an important position in the cultural life of the Low Countries to the present day, there can be no doubt that the 14th and 15th centuries stand out as a true 'golden age'. During a period of almost 200 years the region nurtured an extraordinary dynasty of talented composers and musicians, the majority of them born and trained in the southern counties of Hainaut, Artois, Flanders, and Brabant—for which reason they are commonly described as being of 'Franco-Flemish' origin. While no simple reason can be offered for the initial rise of this movement, it is clear that choir schools, with their emphasis on theory and rigorous instruction, played an important part in maintaining a strong musical tradition. Equally significant was the acquisition of much of the Low Countries during the late 14th and 15th centuries by the Dukes of Burgundy. With their sumptuously elaborate style of courtly life and sophisticated tastes, the Dukes were liberal patrons of the arts and eagerly exploited the stock of native talent in their northern territories. Composers associated specifically with the Burgundian court during the 15th century include Tapissier, Binchois, Busnois, and Hayne van Ghizeghem.

As the reputation of Franco-Flemish composers strengthened, so the demand for composers trained in the region spread, and increasingly large numbers were attracted abroad. This tendency to migrate can be discerned as early as 1350, when the Liégeois composer Johannes Chiwagne—better known today as Ciconia—entered the circle of Pope Clement VI in Avignon, the first stage in a career which took him to most of the principal cities in northern Italy. Many others followed him: Dufay, for example, spent virtually all of his early career in Italy or the court of Savoy; Ockeghem worked almost exclusively for the French royal chapel; Josquin enjoyed the patronage of the Italian nobility for almost 40 years. Highly influential as they were abroad, however, experience of foreign styles played an equally important part in shaping the musical language of these composers, and ultimately of Franco-Flemish music in general. By the end of his career, Ciconia had absorbed many Italianate features into his essentially French style, while in the early years of the 15th century Dufay encountered—and thoroughly digested—the richly triadic, consonant music of Englishmen such as Power and Dunstable, imported to the Continent by the household chapels of the English nobility during their campaigns in France and northern Italy. Through this process of cultural cross-fertilization the music of Franco-Flemish composers gradually acquired a broadly cosmopolitan flavour which, together with its high level of craftsmanship, certainly helped to widen its international appeal.

Throughout the 15th and early 16th centuries, composers from the Low Countries, whatever their place of employment, were particularly recognized for their ability to write skilful, elegant counterpoint. At first the emphasis was on fluidity and expansiveness, heard to its best advantage in the works of Dufay, Binchois, and Ockeghem; but as the 15th century progressed, Franco-Flemish composers gradually established a new musical idiom in which audible unity rather than variety was the goal, achieved through the use of imitation and canon. In many cases compositions were also carefully planned to reflect geometric or arithmetic proportions or significant numbers from Christian theology in their design,

adding a mystical or symbolic dimension: music to stimulate not only the ear but also the intellect. As well as contributing significantly to the development of musical style throughout Europe, Franco-Flemish composers played a major part in the evolution of the three principal forms of the early Renaissance: Mass, motet, and *chanson*. Through their efforts isorhythm was gradually abandoned in favour of less rigid methods of incorporating plainchant into polyphony—free *cantus firmus*, for example, or paraphrase. They were the first to compose Masses based on secular models, whether single lines extracted from polyphonic *chansons* or the tunes of popular songs, and the first to write parody Masses. The *chanson*, though changing less rapidly, had by the end of the 15th century shed its Medieval exterior as the *formes fixes* were replaced by looser, less artificial verse, allowing scope for greater variety of musical setting. But above all it was the motet which attracted a spirit of exploration, particularly evident in the works of men such as Josquin and Isaac whose careers brought them into contact with Italian humanism. By rejecting the traditional backbone of a plainchant *cantus firmus* and concentrating entirely on the syntactical structure and word-rhythms of the text, their motets acquired a new declamatory, rhetorical manner—one of heightened naturalism—which has been valued in Western music ever since.

3. *The 16th Century.* By 1500 the works of composers from the Low Countries virtually dominated music-making throughout Europe. Although the ensuing century saw the emergence (or, in the cases of France and Italy, resurgence) of more obviously national schools of composition, all were heavily indebted to the Franco-Flemish idiom, accepting to a large extent the structural norm of a contrapuntal texture unified by imitation and sometimes canon. Even with this rise of native talent, however, the demand for musicians trained in the north was slow to wane, and many of the leading composers of the 16th century were *émigrés* of the Low Countries: Willaert in Venice; Cipriano de Rore in Parma and Venice; Vaet at the Habsburg court; Philippe de Monte variously in Naples, London, Vienna, and Prague; and, above all others, Lassus who, despite a career spent largely at Munich, was universally admired and widely influential.

None the less, the 16th century was essentially a period of decline in the Low Countries after its ascendency in the early Renaissance. A number of political and religious factors contributed to this downward course: the merging of the Duchy of Burgundy with the Kingdom of Spain and the Holy Roman Empire to form a single political unit under Charles V; a drop in economic prosperity throughout the region, resulting in a decline in the quality of education; above all, the divisive effect of religious dissension between Protestant sympathizers in the north and Catholics in the south. Although former standards were for a while upheld— by Clemens non Papa and the two principal imperial composers, Gombert and Crecquillon, for example—musical life in the Low Countries lost much of its former splendour and by the end of the 16th century appears peripheral beside the lively culture of Italy.

The rise of vernacular song in the Low Countries during the 16th century can be seen as evidence of a new spirit of regional identity, in contrast to the international outlook of the French-speaking Burgundian court. This trend can already be perceived in the output of Jacob Obrecht, one of the few late 15th-century composers associated with the area north of the Burgundian ambit and the first to write a substantial corpus of Dutch songs. In 1540 Symon Cock of Antwerp printed a collection of *Souterliedekens* (translations of the psalms into Dutch verse, set to popular or folk melodies); 11 years later the Antwerp publisher Tylman Susato issued the first of his *Musyck boexken* ('music booklets'), a series devoted to Flemish songs and dances and polyphonic arrangements of the *Souterliedekens* by Clemens non Papa and Gherardus Mes. Perhaps most patriotic of all in tone, however, was the *Neder-landtsche gedenck-*

Pl. 1. *Title-page of Kerle's 'Quatuor Missae' (Antwerp: Plantin, 1583).*

clanck of Adriaen Valerius, published post-humously in 1626, an historical account of the dispute between the Netherlands and Spain during the mid 16th century, illustrated by Dutch popular songs with lute and cittern accompaniment and including the present Dutch national anthem.

4. *Religious Diversity.* Following decades of conflict, the northern counties of the Low Countries, with their Protestant outlook, finally won a degree of political autonomy from the Catholic south through the establishment of the 'Republic of the Seven United Provinces' in 1588, a claim for independence fully realized only in 1648 with the signing of the Treaty of Westphalia at the end of the Thirty Years War. The new religion of the north followed Calvinist principles, Dutch translations of the Genevan Psalter having been adopted by the Church in 1568, although the original French texts of Marot and De Bèze were used locally, and set to polyphony by Sweelinck in a vast cycle published between 1604 and 1621. The use of the organ to accompany the singing of psalms was banned by the Dutch Reformed Church in 1572, a prohibition which remained in force until 1680 despite the eloquent arguments put forward by Constantijn Huygens, one of the leading musicians and intellectuals of the early 17th century. Instead, the organ was used as a solo instrument, playing before and after church services, at festivals, and in weekday recitals. Sweelinck's important output of keyboard works, written for the Oude Kerk in Amsterdam and one of the chief peaks in the tradition, was in fact composed to satisfy the requirements of the civic authorities rather than the Church. Later developments in organ music and the manufacture of organs can similarly be attributed to municipal pride and a state of rivalry between town councils.

In the southern Low Countries the sense of tradition was at first stronger. Under the rule of the Spanish Habsburgs Roman Catholicism remained the official religion, flirtation with Calvinism being discouraged by the threat of the Inquisition; only during 1566 was this state of repression temporarily relaxed, but quickly reinstated when the true extent of popular support for the Protestant faith became fully apparent. Soon after, the singing of metrical psalms again became an act of heresy and punishable by death. During this time the royal chapel at Brussels emerged as an important centre for Latin church music, especially in the early 17th century under the leadership of Géry de Ghersem (*c*.1573–1630), whose colleagues included two Catholic refugees from England, Peter Philips and John Bull, as well as the organist Peeter Cornet. As in the United Provinces, keyboard music flourished and the region became an important centre for the development of virginals and harpsichord manufacture, especially in the hands of the Ruckers family of Antwerp, whose activities can be traced back to 1579.

5. *The 17th and 18th Centuries.* The 17th and 18th centuries witnessed a further decline in the musical traditions of the Low Countries as foreign music—especially French and Italian—gradually saturated the market. Courtly patronage during these centuries was on the whole insubstantial, the impetus for musical activity lying with the Church and above all the bourgeoisie. Particularly important was the rise of *collegia musica* (amateur music societies devoted to the performance of vocal and instrumental works, often aided by professional civic musicians), which sprang up throughout the Low Countries during the early 17th century. Organ recitals remained common, while the popularity of another civic instrument, the carillon, also grew rapidly at this time. Local composers such as Jacob van Eyck of Utrecht—who is also remembered today for his works for solo recorder based on tunes popular in the Netherlands at this time—soon provided the basis of a repertory for the carillon which reached its peak in the virtuosic contrapuntal showpieces of the Louvain composer Matthias van den Gheyn. But if the carillon repertory of the Low Countries evinces a strong regional identity, the general trend was towards a more cosmopolitan style, discernible in the works of Constantijn Huygens, whose contact with Monteverdi in Venice assisted the introduction of the monodic style to the Netherlands. The presence of the Fiocco family (Pietro Antonio, *c*.1650-1714; Jean-Joseph, 1686-1746; and Joseph-Hector, 1703-41) at the royal court and chapel in Brussels from the 1680s to 1744 is symptomatic of the growing taste for Italian music, while the Amsterdam-based publishing firm of Estienne Roger and Le Cène, with its pioneering use of the engraving process, thrived on editions of works by Corelli, Vivaldi, Albinoni, and Locatelli (the last of these was a resident of Amsterdam from 1729 until his death 35 years later).

Pl. 2. Family Making Music, painting by J. M. Molenaer (c.1609-68); among the instruments are (left to right) ?virginals, cittern, violin, lute and cello.

Pl. 3. Title-page of Corelli's 'Sonate', Op. 5 (Amsterdam: Roger, c.1706), originally published in Rome (1700).

Ironically, two of the most talented composers born in the Low Countries during this period, Henry du Mont (1610-84) and Jean Baptiste Loeillet, worked exclusively abroad, in Paris and London respectively.

Opera was late to arrive in the Low Countries, although once established it quickly gained widespread popularity. Brussels and Amsterdam were the principal early centres, with productions dating from the early 1680s, but from the start their repertories were almost exclusively imported, primarily from France and Italy, and translations into Dutch or Flemish were rare. Few local composers turned their hands to opera, the one major exception, Grétry, writing largely for Parisian audiences, who regarded him as a leader of French comic opera. The early 18th century also saw the rise of public concerts, especially in Amsterdam and The Hague; here as in the theatre foreign music predominated, and the one major local composer of the period, Gossec, again left the region to work almost exclusively in Paris, where he became one of the most popular composers during the Revolution.

6. *To the Present Day*. In 1815, following the Napoleonic wars, north and south were brought together to form the 'United Kingdom of the Netherlands'; however, the union was dissolved in 1830, creating the kingdoms of Belgium and the Netherlands as they exist today. Foreign music continued to exert a strong influence throughout the Low Countries during the 19th century, although a certain degree of nationalist fervour can be detected in the works of Peter Benoit, who was instrumental in raising the standards of Flemish music to a more international level. At the Brussels Conservatory, founded in 1832, Fétis provided another form of leadership through his influential work as a teacher, critic, theorist, and musicologist. Important Belgian composers of the period were César Franck, Guillaume Lekeu, and the violinist-composers Henri Vieuxtemps and Eugène Ysaÿe. In the Netherlands the impact of German music was especially profound, evident in the works of Johannes Verhulst (1816-91), the leading Dutch composer of the mid 19th century, although several of his younger contemporaries aimed at a more self-consciously Dutch idiom, especially through the use of folk material. Musical life in Amsterdam acquired a new sense of focus with the inauguration of the Concertgebouw—one of the finest concert halls in northern Europe—in 1888, and the establishment of a permanent orchestra there in the same year.

During the 20th century the Low Countries have once again emerged as an important centre of European music. Among the most celebrated of recent Belgian composers have been Paul Gilson (1865-1942), Jean Absil, Marcel Poot (*b* 1901), Flor Peeters, Karel Goeyvaerts (*b* 1923), and Henri Pousseur, while in the Netherlands Willem Pijper, Henk Badings, and Ton de Leeuw (*b* 1926) have won widespread acclaim. There has been a revival of interest in both the organ and the carillon; in addition, the region has become a centre for music education, and has been especially active in the rediscovery of early music. In the Netherlands, ethnomusicology has attracted much scholarly attention, while the creation of the Donemus Foundation in 1947 has greatly assisted the promotion of Dutch music. The Holland Festival (centred on Amsterdam) and, in Belgium, the Flanders Festival, are now two of the outstanding events of the European cultural year, standing as eloquent testimony to the present healthy state of music in the Low Countries.

JOHN MILSOM

Lowe & Brydone. See *Printing and Publishing of Music*, 6.

Lower mordent. See under *Mordent*.

Lowland pipe. One of the Scottish bagpipes. See *Bagpipe*, 2.

Lübeck, Vincent (*b* Paddingbüttel, nr Bremen, 1654; *d* Hamburg, 9 Feb. 1740). German composer. He came from a family of organists who worked in north German churches in the 17th and 18th centuries, and was himself famous as an organist, spending most of his working life at St Nicolai, Hamburg. Although only nine organ works by him are known (preludes, toccatas, fugues, and chorale settings) he can be ranked with Buxtehude in importance. His Christmas cantata, *Wilkommen süsser Bräutigam*, is still popular in Germany.

DENIS ARNOLD

Lucia di Lammermoor. Opera in three acts by Donizetti; text by Cammarano, after Scott's novel *The Bride of Lammermoor* (1819). Produced: Naples, San Carlo, 26 September 1835; London, Her Majesty's, 5 April 1838; New Orleans, 28 December 1841. Lucy Ashton (sop.) is in love with Edgar Ravenswood (ten.), an enemy of her family. Her brother Henry (bar.) persuades her to marry Lord Arthur Bucklaw (ten.) by showing her a forged letter, supposedly written by Edgar. The wedding ceremony is interrupted by Edgar, who curses Lucy for betraying him. She goes mad, kills her newly-wed husband, and then dies. Edgar kills himself in grief.

Lucio Silla. Opera in three acts by Mozart to a libretto by G. da Gamerra. It was first performed in Milan in 1772. Anfossi (1774) and J. C. Bach (1774) also wrote operas on the subject.

Lucky Hand, The. See *Glückliche Hand*.

Ludford, Nicholas (*b* c.1485; *d* ? London, c.1557). English composer. He was a singer at the collegiate chapel of St Stephen, Westminster, until its dissolution by Henry VIII in 1547. His output included at least 17 Masses — more than by any other English composer — of which three are now lost and three survive incomplete. Seven of them form a unique cycle of Lady Masses for three voices, written in a manuscript which once belonged to Henry VIII and Catherine of Aragon. Like his more famous contemporary, John Taverner, Ludford wrote mostly in an idiom which emphasized abstract grandeur and exuberance of florid detail, rather than humanistic expressiveness or concision.

JOHN MILSOM

Ludus tonalis ('The Play of Notes'). Piano studies by Hindemith, composed in 1942. The set consists of a prelude, 12 fugues with 11 interludes, and a postlude (an inverted version of the prelude), being studies in counterpoint, tonal organization, and piano technique.

Luftig (Ger.). 'Airy'.

Luftpause (Ger.). 'Air-break', i.e. a pause for breath in wind playing or in singing, generally indicated by a $\lor$ mark above the stave. It has become the standard term for the traditional hesitation before the barline in Viennese waltz rhythms. See also *Atempause*.

Luisa Miller. Opera in three acts by Verdi; text by Cammarano, after Schiller's tragedy *Kabale und Liebe* (1784). Produced: Naples, San Carlo, 8 December 1849; Philadelphia, 27 October 1852; London, Her Majesty's Theatre, 3 June 1858. The opera, set in the Tyrol in the early 18th century, tells of the love of Luisa (sop.), daughter of an old soldier, Miller (bar.), for Rodolfo (ten.) son of Count Walter. Rodolfo is expected to marry Frederica (mezzo), Duchess of Ostheim, and when he refuses is imprisoned by his father. He also arrests Luisa's father and then gets his follower Wurm (bass) to make Luisa write a letter to Rodolfo saying she is in love with someone else. When Rodolfo is released from prison, he makes Luisa confess that she wrote the letter, and poisons both himself and Luisa. Before the poison takes effect, Luisa reveals to Rodolfo that Wurm forced her to write the letter, and Rodolfo kills him.

Lujon (from 'Lou' and 'John'). A modern American percussion instrument of six or more thin rectangular metal plates (usually aluminium), screwed by one edge to the tops of resonator boxes (or to a single box-like resonator) and struck with soft beaters to give softly booming sounds of different pitches, not necessarily tuned to definite notes. Berio includes it in *Circles* (1960). Electrical amplification is often used.

Lully, Jean-Baptiste [Lulli, Giovanni Battista] (*b* Florence, 28 Nov. 1632; *d* Paris, 22 Mar. 1687). French violinist, dancer, and composer of Italian origin.

Lully was the son of a miller, and during childhood was given only simple instruction in music, from a monk who taught him the guitar.

Lully, engraving by Bonnart.

Costume design by Bérain for Lully's ballet de cour 'Le triomphe de l'amour' (1681).

'The destruction of the palace of Armida', drawing by Bérain for the second edition (1713) of Lully's 'Armide', after the décor for the first production (1686).

He was taken to France in 1646 to serve as *garçon de chambre* and Italian teacher to Mlle de Montpensier. At her court in the Tuileries his musical talents soon attracted attention, and he became famous for his skill as a violinist. When Mlle de Montpensier was exiled from Paris Lully left her service, and in 1653 he was made *compositeur de la musique instrumentale* to Louis XIV, a position which involved writing music for the court ballets. He was admitted to the Vingt-quatre Violons, but found the band lacking in discipline and asked permission to set up his own Petits Violons of 16 players. Between 1656 and 1664 he trained this band until they were famous for their skill throughout Europe; by this time the larger group must have improved their own standard, as Lully allowed the two groups to combine for performances of court ballets.

In 1660 Lully's ballet *entrées* for Cavalli's *Xerxe* attracted more attention than the opera itself, and the following year Louis made him *surintendant de la musique de la chambre*. He became a naturalized French citizen, and a further mark of the royal favour, his appointment as *maître de musique* to the royal family, enabled him to marry the daughter of the composer Lambert. They had three sons, all of whom became musicians, and three daughters. Lully continued to compose many ballets, and in 1664 he wrote *entrées* for a revival of Corneille's *Oedipe* and his first *comédie-ballet* in partnership with Molière, a collaboration which

MS fragment of an unknown work, in Lully's hand.

was to culminate in 1670 with *Le bourgeois gentilhomme*, a minor masterpiece of witty music.

By the end of the 1660s the idea of opera was growing increasingly popular in Paris. In 1669 a privilege to establish opera academies in France was granted to Pierre Perrin, and despite Lully's initial scorn at the idea of large-scale dramatic works sung in French he was quick to take advantage of Perrin's fall from favour at court to buy his privilege in 1672. Soon after, and following some vicious intriguing, he was granted the right to compose and produce opera at the Académie Royale de Musique, a monopoly he held tenaciously for the rest of his life. The immediate result was France's first *tragédie lyrique*, *Cadmus et Hermione*, produced in 1673. The libretto was provided by Quinault, who also wrote texts for 10 other of Lully's *tragédies lyriques*, despite the composer's constant criticisms and cuts.

Lully was highly ambitious and capable of ruthless plotting against his rivals. As a result he made enemies, and only the royal favour saved him from prosecution for homosexual practices, although even Louis had occasion to reprimand him on this account in 1685. In the 1680s the court became more sober and restrained in its entertainments, and Lully turned his attention to church music. It was during a performance of his monumental *Te Deum* before the king in 1687 that Lully struck his foot with his conducting cane (it was his practice to keep time by striking it upon the floor), and later that year he died after the foot had turned gangrenous. He left a considerable fortune, including five houses in Paris, and the monopoly of the performing rights to his music. Because of his monopoly of the French operatic scene he also left a stultifyingly conservative musical tradition which was not completely broken for half a century.

Lully was not a great composer—it was only his position at the most powerful court in Europe that gave him his considerable influence. He may well have been the best orchestral trainer of his age, however, with his insistence on uniform bowing and exact rhythms, and his ability to please the French court with entertainments including a large element of dancing was remarkable. Having little or no experience of the aria-based operas of the Venetian theatre he stuck to earlier ideas of opera composition. His setting of the French language is faithful to its inflexions and rhythms, and although he uses short set pieces they do not break up the drama for purely musical purposes. He was a composer of pleasant dance music, and an impressive orchestrator, using a thick five-part texture. It is doubtful whether his dramatic works can be revived with much success until the art of 17th-century dancing has been effectively re-created, but his church music is well worth performing. The ceremonial solemnity of the grand motets, which effectively exploit the contrasting sonorities of solo and tutti groups, seems to find an exact musical equivalent to the grandeur of the palace at Versailles.   DENIS ARNOLD

FURTHER READING
James R. Anthony: *French Baroque Music from Beaujoyeulx to Rameau* (London, 1973, 2nd edn 1978).

Lumsdaine, David (*b* Sydney, 31 Oct. 1931). British composer. He studied at the New South Wales Conservatorium and at Sydney University, and then in London with Lennox Berkeley at the Royal Academy of Music and with Mátyás Seiber privately. In 1970 he was appointed lecturer in music at Durham University. His compositions, mostly for small ensembles, are in an avant-garde style marked by strong gestures and firmly directed argument; they include two ambitious pieces for soprano and instruments, *Annotations of Auschwitz* (1964) and *Easter Fresco* (1966).   PAUL GRIFFITHS

Lungo (It.). 'Long'; *lunga pausa*, 'long rest'.

Luogo (It.). The same as **loco.*

Luonnotar. Tone-poem, Op. 70, by Sibelius for soprano and orchestra, composed about 1910. It is a setting of words from the *Kalevala*, telling of the creation of the world.

Lupi, Johannes (*b* ? Cambrai, *c*.1506; *d* Cambrai, 20 Dec. 1539). Franco-Flemish composer. His career was spent mainly at Cambrai Cathedral, where he served as choirboy, singer, and, from 1527, choirmaster—a post from which he was almost dismissed on several occasions because of his lack of control over the choirboys. His surviving works include two Masses, motets, and *chansons;* they are notable for their high quality.   JOHN MILSOM

Lupo [de Almaliach]. Jewish family of string players, who came to England from Milan in 1540. Seven or possibly nine members of the family worked in the court string consort up to the outbreak of civil war in 1642; several of them were composers, but the only one whose music survives in quantity is Thomas Lupo (*b* ?7 Aug. 1571; *d c*.Dec. 1627). Although he was made composer to the royal violins in 1619, he appears mainly to have written viol fantasies in three to six parts.   PETER HOLMAN

Lusingando (It.). 'Flattering', i.e. to be played in a coaxing, intimate manner. Debussy misspelt the term 'lusigando'.

Lust (Ger.) 'Pleasure'; *lustig*, 'cheerful'; *Lustigkeit*, 'cheerfulness'; *Lustspiel*, 'comedy'.

Lustige Witwe, Die ('The Merry Widow'). Operetta in three acts by Lehár; text by Viktor Léon and Leo Stein, after Meilhac's comedy *L'attaché d'ambassade.* Produced: Vienna, Theater an der Wien, 30 December 1905; London, Daly's Theatre, 8 June 1907; New York, New Amsterdam Theatre, 21 October 1907. The gay, complicated plot deals with the attempts of Baron Mirko Zeta (bass) to obtain the Merry Widow Hanna Glawari's (sop.) fortune for his impoverished country of Pontevedria by getting his young compatriot Danilo (ten.) to marry her.

Lute

1. Description
2. History
3. Chitarrone, Theorbo
4. 'Lute' in a General Sense

1. *Description.* The lute (Fr.: *luth*; Ger.: *Laute*; It.: *liuto*; Sp.: *laùd*) is a plucked stringed instrument, with unmistakable large rounded back, and was one of the most important of European instruments for nearly four centuries from the later Middle Ages up to its demise in the latter part of the 18th century. With its enormous repertory, from *c*.1500, for solo lute or lute with voice, it has now come to be made and played again, as have the other kinds of lute that were developed principally for continuo playing (see below, 3).

Traditionally compared in shape to a sliced pear, the lute's rounded back is built up from thin strips of wood or 'ribs' (see below, 2*b*) and the soundboard is flat. The strings run to a bridge which is glued to the soundboard (as on a Spanish guitar). The soundhole is carved in intricate arabesque patterns in the soundboard itself and is called a 'rose' or 'knot'. The neck has a flat or slightly arched fingerboard and round this are tied gut frets, usually seven. The pegbox, containing the tuning-pins, is attached to the neck pointing backwards almost at right angles. The strings, originally gut, are generally in pairs (double courses: see *Stringed Instruments*, 3*c*), the highest-tuned, however, often being single.

2. *History*. In the course of its long history the lute changed greatly in ways that make accurate understanding of its true development difficult. There are many areas in our knowledge which still need clarification, and important discoveries are still being made.

(*a*) *To the 15th Century*. Precisely when and by what route the lute arrived in Europe is not certain. There had been instruments vaguely resembling lutes in ancient times (see below, 4), but the European lute derives both its form and its name from the Arab lute, *al 'ud*; the Arab penetration of Spain has left an 11th-century representation of it on an Arab coffer in Navarre. The earliest known occurrence of the name 'lute' in French is *c*.1270, when some other Arabic instrument names also first occur (see *Citole, Gittern*; *Rebec*). English references to a 'lutour' (the player) follow from late in the reign of Edward I (*d* 1307).

These early instruments probably had four double courses, often more than one rose (as the Arab lute still has), and no frets. They were played with a plectrum (again as the Arab instrument). Frets seem to have been added *c*.1400 and become increasingly used through the 15th century. The four courses were probably tuned in fourths around a central major third (the same intervals as the first four strings of a guitar), but during that century a fifth course was added to the treble side, giving a tuning (from treble to bass) fourth, fourth, third, fourth. (The actual pitch of the highest string is governed by the length of the instrument, so it is likely that the other courses were, in effect, lowered in pitch through the addition.) One at least of the lute's systems of tablature for writing the music was almost certainly first framed for this kind of instrument (see *Tablature*, 1).

Towards the end of the 15th century the plectrum was gradually abandoned in favour of the finger-tips, a development facilitating the playing of more complex polyphony. At much

the same time a sixth course was added on the bass side, giving the nominal tuning shown in Ex. 1. The lowest three courses were octave courses, one of the strings an octave higher to reinforce the upper harmonics in the tone.

Ex. 1

(*b*) *The 16th Century*. This six-course lute was the most common for the greater part of the 16th century, one of the most important periods in the lute's history, both on account of the perfection of the instrument itself and for the high quality of the solo repertory. Our earliest-surviving lutes are from the first half of the century, a number of them by makers who continued to be highly esteemed up to the 18th century, such as Laux Maler (*d* 1552) and Hans Frei, who both worked in Bologna. These instruments are all of a long slender shape, yet this is rarely seen in pictures of the time in which a more rounded form seems to be commoner. The probable explanation is that the long type has survived at the expense of the other because it came to be considered the more suitable for conversion to the types of lute which came into favour at later periods. None of these lutes from the first half of the century has survived in its original form, but we can get an idea of at least their original external appearance from pictures, and from a six-course lute made a little later, around 1580, by Georg Gerle of Innsbruck.

Pl. 1. Six-course lute, detail from 'The Virgin and Child with Saints' by Marco Marziale (fl. 1493-1507).

Pl. 2. Eight-course lute by Magno Dieffopruchar (Venice, 1609).

The instrument's subsequent development is closely allied to an increase in its downward range which, the instrument being strung entirely with gut strings, must have been initiated by developments in string-making. A seventh course, not common before the last quarter of the century, was tuned either a tone below the sixth, or a fourth below. Further courses were then added over a short space of time until 10 courses were in use not long after 1600, though the advent of each fresh type of lute did not render the earlier types obsolete, and the iconographical evidence occasionally shows even a six-course lute still in use after this period.

In the 1580s began a new style of lute-making which was to last some 50 years, leaving some of the most beautiful lutes to have survived. Previously lute backs seem to have been constructed mainly from hardwoods like maple or the fruitwoods, with nine or 11 ribs. But now we begin to find them with 13, 17, or 19 ribs of yew. The heartwood of yew is red, while the sapwood is white, and these instruments are so built that each rib is half one and half the other. Examples of such lutes are by Wendelio Venere, from the 1580s, and over the next 30 years the number of ribs was increased to 31, 37, and even 53, some made from such exotic woods as ebony and snakewood. It was also common for seven- and eight-course lutes to have a double first course, presumably through availability of thin gut strings of high quality.

Three excerpts from early lute music illus-trate the different kinds of tablature used in writing for the lute: German (Ex. 2), from Hans Judenkunig's *Utilis et compendiaria introductio*, *c.*1519; Italian (Ex. 3), from G. A. Casteliono's *Intabolatura de leuto*, 1536; and French (Ex. 4), from Robert Dowland's *A Varietie of Lute Lessons*, 1610.

Ex. 2

(c) *17th Century*. From around 1600 the pattern of development exhibits two distinct styles—in Italy, and in France and Northern Europe. Italian lutes show a logical continuation of the preceding development with ever more courses in the bass. With the difficulty of obtaining a good sound from these with plain gut strings, attempts were made at finding ways of increasing their length, and the system eventually most widely followed is that where the neck, instead of carrying a bent-back pegbox, is extended to bear a second pegbox at the end of the extension by which the bass strings can be some half as long again as the stopped strings. These lutes, in Italy termed 'liuto attiorbato', generally had seven stopped and seven long bass courses,

Ex. 3

many that survive being by Matteo Sellas of Venice.

In France and Northern Europe, instead of extending the range downwards while retaining the old tuning, different tunings were tried on the 10-course lute with a view to exploiting to a greater degree the natural resonances of the instrument. One type, 12-course, developed in Northern Europe, sought to overcome the problems of plain gut strings by keeping the bent-back pegbox for the first eight courses, followed by four courses on an extended head, each of them progressively slightly longer. We commonly see this 'double-headed' lute in Dutch genre paintings of the mid-century, and it is considered at length in Thomas Mace's *Musick's Monument* (London, 1676). In France it went out of fashion, to be superseded by a

Ex. 4

Ex. 5

return to 11 courses and a single pegbox, and one of the experimental tunings came to predominate: the so-called 'D minor' tuning (Ex. 5, the second course often single like the first) which remained with the lute for the rest of its active life.

This lute was widely cultivated in France throughout the century, and it was the repertory for it which had such a profound influence on the French 'clavecinistes' ('harpsichordists'). It is much to be regretted that we have no surviving 11-course lute of undoubted French provenance, since this music, perhaps more than any other, exploits the resonances and sonorities of the lute, and seems to rely heavily upon the qualities of the particular lute for much of its effect.

A number of representations of the period show the 11th course lying off the fingerboard and passing over an extension of the nut, and this, together with the so-called 'chanterelle rider' (a raised piece glued on to the pegbox to take the peg of the 11th string), leads us to conclude that the earliest 11-course lutes were conversions from 10-course instruments.

Towards the end of the 17th century the popularity of the lute declined in France, and we must move to Germany for the final episode in the lute's history. Composers in the German-speaking countries were much influenced by the French lutenists during the second half of the 17th century and the 11-course lute was adopted: German examples of it survive from well into the next century and music was published for it as late as 1747. At some time around or shortly after 1700 two further courses were added to the bass of the instrument. These were led to a structure added on the bass side of the pegbox which enabled them to be longer than the other courses by approximately one fret's length. It too is likely to have originated as a simple way of converting existing 11-course lutes: there are examples in manuscript music where the lower notes possible with the 13-course instrument have been added, as in the 'London MS' of works by Sylvius Leopold Weiss (d 1750), one of the first to write for the 13-course lute and among the greatest of lutenist-composers.

If the type of 13-course lute with the 'bass rider' addition to the pegbox were indeed originally a conversion from the 11-course, there was another form which was properly conceived as a 13-course lute. It involved the same principle as the 'liuto attiorbato' described above in which a number of courses (in this case

eight) lie over the fingerboard and can be stopped with the left hand, and a number of diapasons (in this case five) are taken to a second pegbox, by which they have about one-and-a-half times the length of the stopped strings. There is some difficulty concerning the origin of this fresh type and the date of the earliest true examples. It may have developed from a type of French theorbo (see below, 3), or the idea may have come from the 'angelica', a kind of lute with a harp-like tuning; it is unlikely that they were ever used as theorbos. This form of the 13-course lute represents the last major development of the instrument, which had all but disappeared by the end of the 18th century.

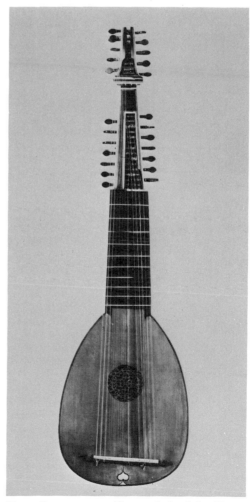

Pl. 3. Fourteen-course 'liuto attiorbato' by Matteo Sellas (Venice, 1637).

Pl. 4. Twelve-course 'double-headed' lute, painting 'The Music Lesson' by Frans van Mieris (1635–81).

3. *Chitarrone, Theorbo.* During the last quarter of the 16th century in Italy, musical style was passing through a period of great change. In accordance with the humanistic interpretation of the nature of Ancient Greek music, composers began to ascribe greater importance to the solo voice and dramatic rendering of the text. The development of the *basso *continuo* called for instruments capable of giving a strong but relatively simple harmonic support to the voice, with a particular emphasis on the bass line. Special types of lute were developed to provide for this.

The most important was the chitarrone or theorbo (Fr.: *théorbe*; It.: *tiorba*): whether these two names indicate distinct instruments or whether they are synonymous is as yet impossible to tell. The instrument was similar to the 'liuto attiorbato' already described, but considerably larger, both in terms of the stopped string-length and in the length-proportion of diapason string to stopped string. It generally had six or seven courses of stopped strings, single or double, and seven or eight single diapasons. It was strung throughout in gut, though one early 17th-century Italian source says that it was occasionally given metal strings.

The most important feature that distinguished the theorbo from all other types of lute was its large size in relation to pitch: the stopped strings were so long that it was impossible to tune the top course (and likewise usually the second) to its required pitch, so it had to be an octave lower. Ex. 6 gives the normal 'A' tuning for the theorbo; the string marked with an asterisk may also be tuned to give chromatic notes, F♯ or E♭. Notwithstanding this apparent inconvenience, the tone from the long thin strings and large body was so powerful and bright that the theorbo proved ideal support for the voice, and even in a small ensemble was able to provide the required harmonic and rhythmic foundation.

The backs of these theorbos seem most often to have been of the 'multi-ribbed' form which we have already noted in many of the contemporary lutes, while the use of very hard material

Ex. 6

like ebony and snakewood was not uncommon, presumably assisting that brightness of tone so important in these instruments.

Soon after the theorbo had become established in the musical life of Italy the specialist players began to develop a solo repertory which exploited the peculiarities of the tuning and possibilities accruing from its tone. But the large size rendered the theorbo unsuitable for rapid passage-work and its tuning made the playing of high-lying bass lines difficult, if not impossible. The instrument that could cope satisfactorily with such difficulties was the 'archlute' (Fr.: *archiluth*; It.: *arciliuto*), an ordinary lute with, generally, six stopped courses in normal lute tuning, but (usually) eight long single diapasons, thus sharing the characteristics of lute and theorbo. The proportions of the body to the lower neck were those of an ordinary lute, but the diapasons had the length associated with the theorbo. Obviously this instrument has some affinity with the 'liuto attiorbato', but it is worth noting the differences. The latter was usually smaller in over-all size and had seven double courses of stopped strings with, usually, seven double diapasons of about one-and-a-half times the length of the others. The archlute, on the other hand, had a longer stopped-string length and only six stopped courses, but eight single diapasons of at least twice the length of the stopped strings. There is some debate over when this 'archlute' form was developed, since many of the surviving examples seem to be conversions of earlier lutes, and the historical use of the names 'arciliuto' and 'liuto attiorbato' is also not precisely clear. What is certain is that the long-necked form was quite common as a continuo instrument by the second half of the 17th century and remained in use through much of the next.

There has been a great reawakening of interest in the lute and its music during the 20th century, beginning with the work of musicologists in their studies of the repertory. Later, a small number of people, including notable pioneers like Arnold Dolmetsch, began to play the lute and build modern replicas. For a time there was some confusion between the demands of a modern guitar-player's technique and those of the historical lute, but in more recent years great strides have been made, by both makers and players, in the understanding and cultivation of historical practice.

4. '*Lute*' *in a General Sense*. There exists a multitude of different instruments, especially across Asia (and reaching into eastern parts of Europe), which are described in Western literature under the heading 'lute' as the best available name we have for them. In current ethnological terminology (see *Instruments, Classification of*) the term is extended considerably further, but, this apart, a 'lute' may be understood as having some kind of bowl-shaped body, small or large, from a tortoiseshell to a fully ribbed construction in wood. A chief distinction is between a 'long lute' (meaning 'long-necked', as the *bouzouki) and a 'short lute' (relatively 'short-necked', as the lute itself). In either case the total length of the instrument may be anything from very long to quite small, the expressions 'short' and 'long' referring solely to the size of the neck in relation to that of the body.

(*a*) *Long Lutes*. These came first, going back to the second millennium BC in Mesopotamia, then Egypt, where several specimens have been found in tombs, with two or three gut strings over a long stick-like neck and skin belly. Descendants are nearly all fretted and many are strung with wire: thus the Greek bouzouki and tambora; the popular tamboritsa of the Slavonic Balkans; the *balalaika (with its unique triangular shape of soundbox); and numerous forms over Central Asia, where some take part in classical ensembles and others are played by singers and bards for their own accompaniment. Among Russian folk-song publications one whole book

Pl. 5. *Eleven-course 'French' lute played by Charles Mouton (1626–after 1692), portrait by François de Troy.*

is devoted to the repertory of a famous Kirgis bard with his 3′ long, three-string *komuz*, thrummed with a plectrum, the strings plucked as well, or rubbed with the hand, to mark 'programme' points in the recited epic. Further east is the Chinese *sanxian* and its derivative the popular Japanese *shamisen* of the theatre and the geisha, this with the belly traditionally of cat-skin, which may be forcefully struck along with the strings with the large wooden plectrum. Altogether, techniques vary greatly, from 'melody plus drone' with all strings struck at once, to single notes.

The Indian *sitār* is not strictly a long lute though influenced by former Persian instruments of that kind. In Greece the *laouto* manifests guitar influence on the older tambora. In Spain the present popular instrument called *laùd* is not a lute but something quite different (see *Bandora*, 5). The *banjo, with its stretched skin, also derives from the long lute in forms that may have reached West Africa from the Maghreb, where today, as the small and primitive *gnibri*, it is on sale in every Moroccan tourist shop.

In Europe the former *colascione* (Fr.: *colachon*) was a long lute adopted from the Turks in 15th-century Italy, and in Germany also, to play a small part in music. It came to vary much in shape and stringing, becoming in the 18th century something like a large mandolin. In its older form it is said still to be heard as a folk instrument around Naples.

(*b*) *Short Lute*. There are traces of such an instrument through later Antiquity; we do not know for certain which of the various Greek stringed instrument names described it (possibly *pandoura*). Subsequent forms are thought to go back to Central Asia in the early centuries AD, in a small, compact instrument, evolved perhaps as suitable in the life of horse nomads. Eastwards it grew in size to become the classic *piba* of China and *biwa* of Japan. Westwards it may or may not be directly ancestral to the Arab lute (celebrated in literature as the instrument of the *Arabian Nights*). The Arab lute is played with a short plectrum traditionally of an eagle quill. The sound is deep, and the tuning, in fourths, well suits the playing in step-wise

Pl. 6. Thirteen-course German Baroque lute by Leopold Widhalm (Nuremberg, 1755).

*Pl. 7. Chitarrone/theorbo by
Magno Dieffopruchar (Venice,
1608).*

melody, with rapid runs and often a quick
descent to the octave below, but few chords
other than an occasional fifth or fourth.

The *cobza*, prominent in Romanian folk
music, is also a short lute, unfretted, with four
double or triple courses of gut, strummed in
vigorous rhythms with a goose-quill plectrum in
accompaniment to the violin.

MICHAEL LOWE, ANTHONY BAINES

FURTHER READING
M. Prynne: 'The Fretted Instruments: I: the Lute',
Musical Instruments through the Ages, ed. A. Baines
(Harmondsworth, 1961); Gerald Hayes: 'Instruments
and Instrumental Notation: the Lute', *The Age of
Humanism, 1540–1630*, The New Oxford History of
Music, iv (London, 1968).

Lute Music in England. The most important
period of English lute music is the 16th and
early 17th centuries. Little is known of it in the
14th and 15th centuries, and after the 17th
century it is mainly insignificant. The history of
English lute music, then, properly begins during
Henry VIII's reign. The King was given a lute
by his father when he was seven, and is known
to have played well. We also know that Prince
Edward and Princess Mary played, having been
taught by Philip van Wilder. There is no
account of Elizabeth's skills upon the instrument, but an early miniature by Nicholas
Hilliard depicts her holding a lute. The English
repertory at this stage, however, was very small,
and Flemish and Italian lutenists dominated at
court. During the 1560s the influence of French
music was strong, and it remained so until the
1580s, when English musicians began to establish their own style. This coincided with an
assertive native keyboard style, lute music and
keyboard music often overlapping. Lute music
flourished especially between 1585 and 1630.
The increasing popularity of the lyra-viol and
string consorts, and the emergence of the
Baroque style, particularly the French, caused
the decline in English lute music during the
17th century. French lutenists were appointed
to the prestigious posts in England, Jacques
Gautier, for instance, receiving a position at
court in 1619. The *Mary Burwell Lute Tutor*,
which includes compositions by such masters as
Gautier and Vincent, shows the trend towards
the French Baroque in English music. Virtually
the last English lute music to be published was
contained in Thomas Mace's *Musick's Monument*
(1676), and here French influence is strong. The
occasional lute piece is found in the 18th century,
for example in Handel. There was an ineffectual
revival of lute music in the 19th century. Today
the genre receives a good deal of attention,

Queen Elizabeth I playing the lute, miniature by Hilliard.

although emphasis is clearly on playing rather than on composition.

1. *Sources.* The sources for English lute music, as for those for contemporary keyboard music, are mainly manuscripts. Four manuscripts in the University Library, Cambridge, best represent the solo lute music played between 1580 and 1615. The pieces range from very simple trifles to virtuoso masterpieces, by such distinguished composers as John Dowland, Daniel Bacheler, and Francis Cutting. Other notable manuscripts of the 'golden age' of lute

music are housed in various libraries and private collections. The so-called Wickhambrook manuscript (now kept at Yale University), a handsome book indeed, was probably compiled *c.*1590, being representative of the 'early' period. Lord Herbert of Cherbury's Lute Book (at the Fitzwilliam Museum, Cambridge), on the other hand, is a much later collection, probably put together *c.*1640.

There are very few printed books of lute music. William Barley's *New Booke of Tabliture* (1596) was the first publication wholly of English music. In addition to the lute, the orpharion and bandora are here specified, but there is no difference in the musical style, and the pieces are playable on any of the instruments. The last book, employing the old tuning, was Robert Dowland's *Varietie of Lute-lessons* (1610). This is an important publication, containing pieces by the most notable English and continental composers of the time. We also encounter one or two pieces printed in the books of ayres, for example John Dowland's galliard duet in his *First Booke* (1597), various pieces in Danyel's *Songs to the Lute* (1606), and Ford's *Musicke of Sundrie Kindes* (1607).

Both Barley and Dowland include instructions on lute playing: Barley incorporated Adrian Le Roy's rules from *A Briefe and Plaine Instruction* (1574); and Dowland printed his father's translation of Besardus's 'Necessarie Observations belonging to the *Lute* and Lute playing'. Characteristic of the Renaissance, composers were quick to theorize about their art. The translation of Robert Ballard's *An Exortation to All Kynde of Men How they shulde Lerne to Playe of the Lute* (1567) seems to have inspired the vogue in England.

Ex. 1

Ex. 2

2. *The Music*. The musical forms used for lute music are the same as those for the keyboard, namely fantasies, pavans, galliards, almains, 'light' pieces, and song arrangements. In the first, a 'point' is worked and developed contrapuntally. An impressive example is John Dowland's chromatic fantasy 'Forlorne Hope Fancye', which, as shown in Ex. 1, begins full of sadness.

One of the most famous Renaissance pieces was Dowland's 'Lachrimae' pavan, with its unforgettable opening phrase, given in Ex. 2.

This pavan was imitated by many composers, including Anthony Holborne in his 'Pauana Plorauit' (1599) and William Lawes; Byrd, Morley, Farnaby, Sweelinck, and others made keyboard arrangements of it. The galliard, a lively triple-time dance, was a popular form with composers for the lute. Almains were also not uncommon. 'Light' pieces included jigs, corantos, and other similar pieces generally in a lilting 6/8 rhythm. Several lute pieces are no more than songs without words, adapted from the books of ayres or from continental sources, notably the *chansons* of Lassus. Others are arrangements with variations of popular songs and ballad tunes. Among the best-known used are 'Fortune, my Foe', 'Goe from my window', and 'Walsingham'.

Music which incorporates the lute was common during the Renaissance, whether intended for the home, the court, or the theatre. Music for mixed consort—treble viol, flute, bass viol, lute, cittern, bandora—was an important kind. Lute composers edited such music, for example Thomas Morley, in his *First Booke of Consort Lessons* (1599), and Philip Rosseter, *Lessons for Consort* (1609). CHRISTOPHER WILSON

Lute-song. Peculiar to England is the lute-song or ayre of the late 16th and early 17th centuries. Although similar to the French *air de cour*, its inception, unlike that of its counterpart the English madrigal, was not dependent on continental influences. Indeed, manuscript sources show the independent and continued existence of the form in England from the 1560s. French elements are present in the ayre, but these are not specific—there are no direct borrowings. The genre is more closely related to the native and near contemporary *consort song, with its distinctive but not necessarily dominant solo vocal line which embodies the mood and form of the poem it sets. In the lute-song the vocal line is dominant; the bass assumes a harmonic function in contrast to the more polyphonic madrigal or consort song.

The period of the English lute-song can be accurately identified as 1597 to 1622, when the printed books appeared. These were all very nearly the same size and format, following John Dowland's example in *The First Booke of Songes or Ayres* (1597). Thus, minor differences in stylistic details notwithstanding, we can see a homogeneous movement confirmed, as it were, in the uniform manner in which it presented itself to the world.

The lute is the preferred accompanying instrument, although, as the title-pages of the printed books indicate, any chord-playing instrument will do. Indeed, Dowland published no songs specifically designated voice and lute. And in a third of the 600 or so songs published, alternative voice parts are given.

The lute-song, in contrast to the madrigal, is generally strophic and relatively short. The musical form arises out of the poetic form, but does not usually reproduce the inner details exactly. In most songs, continuity is largely dependent on sectional repetition, the commonest form being ABB. Campion, exceptionally, prefers to repeat the first strain also (AABB). The music of Dowland, Morley, and Danyel is more elaborate than the restrained style of Jones, Campion, and Rosseter. Yet, however insistently musical a composer wishes to be, vocal rhythms and a singing style prevail.

Lute-song composers were more discerning than madrigal composers in their choice of good texts. Campion is notable for setting his own verse; he was also set by other composers. Sir Philip Sidney, John Donne, and Fulke Greville are among the poets set. Moralizing and serious subjects contrast with amorous and light 'conceits'.

The lute-song lost its identity when the lute was replaced by the lyra-viol, and as the Baroque style displaced that of the Renaissance. Although a miniature form and comparatively short-lived, the lute-song has achieved a permanent place in England's finest musical heritage. CHRISTOPHER WILSON

Luther, Martin (*b* Eisleben, 10 Nov. 1483; *d* Eisleben, 18 Feb. 1546). German religious leader. He studied law at the University of Erfurt, but in 1505 turned instead to the Church, becoming an Augustinian monk. After visiting Italy, he became Professor of Theology at the University of Wittenberg, and it was there that he began his attacks on the Roman Catholic Church, nailing his 95 Theses to the door of the Schlosskirche in 1517, publishing documents against the papal authorities and their abuse of power, and finally appearing at the Diet of Worms (1521) as a final chance to recant and be restored to the Church. He refused, and over the following years began his work on reforming the Church. For his influence on music, see *Reformation*.

Luthier (Fr.). Originally a maker of stringed instruments in general (lutes, harps, viols, etc.), later implying a maker of instruments of the violin family in particular.

Lutosławski, Witold (*b* Warsaw, 25 Jan. 1913). Polish composer. He studied composition with Maliszewski, at first privately and later at the Warsaw Conservatory, where he also studied piano under Jerzy Lefeld (1932–6). During the Second World War he worked as a café pianist and also began his First Symphony (1941–7), a powerful and almost atonal work. The symphony was banned by the new communist government in Poland, and Lutosławski was obliged to create works of a lighter character, such as the Bartókian Concerto for Orchestra (1950–4). The lifting of artistic repression allowed Lutosławski to continue along the road of dense atonal counterpoint in his *Funeral Music* for strings (1954–8) and then to adopt limited aleatory procedures in *Jeux vénitiens* for small orchestra (1960–1). Subsequent works, which include the Second Symphony (1965–7) and other works for large orchestra, have combined fixed and loosely notated material in fine-spun harmonic developments. Lutosławski has also appeared widely since the mid-1950s as a teacher, lecturer, and conductor of his own music. PAUL GRIFFITHS

FURTHER READING
Bálint András Varga: *Lutosławski Profile* (London, 1976); Steven Stucky: *Lutosławski and his Music* (Cambridge, 1981).

Lutosławski

Lutyens, (Agnes) Elisabeth (*b* London, 6 July 1906; *d* Primrose Hill, London, 14 Apr. 1983). English composer. The daughter of the architect Sir Edwin Lutyens, she studied composition with Harold Darke at the Royal College of Music (1926–30). In 1931 she helped found the Macnaghten–Lemare Concerts, which offered a platform to young composers. Her first acknowledged works, such as the Chamber Concerto no. 1 (1939), were among the earliest serial pieces composed in England, and she kept abreast of younger contemporaries in most of her subsequent large output.

Most of her music, whether vocal or instrumental, was sparked off by literature, and she set an extraordinary range of texts, from Chaucer to Stevie Smith, from African poems to Flaubert letters, and from Japanese haiku to Wittgenstein, usually preferring a chorus or small ensemble of voices and instruments. Her many theatre works, though, usually employ her own words, whether the subject is ritual drama (*Isis and Osiris*, 1969–70) or an intimate play of contemporary mores (*Infidelio*, 1954).

PAUL GRIFFITHS

Luython, Carl (*b* Antwerp, *c*.1557; *d* Prague, Aug. 1620). Netherlands composer and organist. He was taken at an early age to serve as a choirboy at the imperial court chapel in Vienna, and became court organist and then composer there in succession to de Monte. He composed some attractive church and keyboard music, some of the latter written for a harpsichord with extra chromatic notes, which he owned. On the death of the Emperor Rudolf II he was dismissed and poverty forced him to sell this instrument, despite his long service at the court.

Luzzaschi, Luzzasco (*d* Ferrara, 10 Sept. 1607). Italian composer. He was a distinguished organist who worked at the d'Este court at Ferrara from the early 1560s until his death. He was also organist at Ferrara Cathedral and in charge of the music at the religious confraternity of the Accademia della Morte. He wrote many madrigals for five voices, and although his style is in the main unremarkable he was capable of startling chromatic harmonies (he was one of the few players of the famous *arcicembalo) and towards the end of his life declared that his ideas were close to those of Monteverdi's *seconda prattica* (see *Prima prattica, seconda prattica*). His most remarkable surviving music is the set of highly ornamented *Madrigali . . . a uno, e doi, e tre soprani* (Rome, 1601), written for the ensemble of women's voices for which Ferrara was famous. Most of his instrumental music has disappeared. Frescobaldi was one of his pupils.

DENIS ARNOLD

Lvov, Alexey (Fyodorovich) (*b* Reval, now Tallinn, Estonia, 5 June 1798; *d* nr Kovno, now Kaunas, Lithuania, 28 Dec. 1870). Russian composer and violinist. His father Fyodor Petrovich Lvov (1766–1836) was director of the Court Chapel Choir in St Petersburg, a post to which Alexey succeeded him in 1837. He had pursued a military career from 1818, and in 1834 was appointed adjutant to the tsar, who in 1833 invited Lvov to write the Russian national anthem, *Bozhe, tsarya khrani* ('God Save the Tsar'). Although he is known today chiefly for that one work, he also composed some delightful violin music (including 24 solo caprices, and a concerto, 1840), three operas, and some sacred choral works. He was also well known as a violin virtuoso, winning praise from Schumann and playing Mendelssohn's Violin Concerto at the Leipzig Gewandhaus in 1840, with Mendelssohn himself conducting.   GEOFFREY NORRIS

Lyadov, Anatoly (Konstantinovich) (*b* St Petersburg, 11 May 1855; *d* Polynovka, Novgorod District, 28 Aug. 1914). Russian composer. It is perhaps significant that he is known chiefly for failing to produce a score for Diaghilev's *The Firebird*, thus giving Stravinsky his first important opening in the theatre. In his working methods Lyadov was not specially disciplined: as a student he was expelled from Rimsky-Korsakov's composition class at the St Petersburg Conservatory because of absenteeism, and even as a mature composer he produced a relatively small number of works (though this was also due in part to his self-critical attitude). In his day Lyadov was valued both as a teacher (he taught Prokofiev and Myaskovsky) and as an establishment figure. He was one of the composers who gathered round the wealthy publisher Mitrofan Belyayev, and he acted as an adviser for Belyayev's publishing activities and for the Glinka Awards. Of his few orchestral works, *Baba-Yaga* (1904), the Eight Russian Folk-songs (1905), and *Volshebnoye ozero* ('The Enchanted Lake', 1909) have retained a precarious hold on the repertory, revealing as they do a certain tasteful lyricism and an ability for clear orchestration in the Rimsky-Korsakov vein.   GEOFFREY NORRIS

Lyapunov, Sergey (Mikhaylovich) (*b* Yaroslavl, 30 Nov. 1859; *d* Paris, 8 Nov. 1924). Russian composer and pianist. He studied at the Moscow Conservatory (counting Tchaikovsky and Taneyev among his composition teachers) and later moved to St Petersburg where he came under the influence of Balakirev. After the Revolution he emigrated to the West, and taught piano in Paris. Rimsky-Korsakov thought of him as a 'talented' composer, but he

was perhaps best known as a pianist. He composed much piano music, in which the influence of Liszt is paramount (notably in the *12 études d'exécution transcendante* Op. 11), and wrote many songs. It was natural that a pianist of his virtuosity should also write piano concertos (No. 1, 1890; No. 2, 1909), but these rarely reveal the tautness and generous gift for colour and scene-painting which mark the best of his vocal works and piano miniatures.
     GEOFFREY NORRIS

Lydian mode. The mode represented by the white notes of the piano beginning on F. See *Mode*, 2.

Lydian tetrachord. A tetrachord (scale of four notes) spanning an augmented fourth, as in the first four notes of the Lydian mode (see *Mode*, 2). Fauré wrote a song called 'Lydia', making poignant use of the Lydian tetrachord.

Lyre. 1. For the lyra glockenspiel, or bell lyra, see *Glockenspiel*, 4.
     2. The lyre, one of the great stringed instruments of Antiquity, took many forms, but always with the strings running to a crossbar or 'yoke' supported by two arms lying in the plane of the surface of the sound-box. The oldest lyres are Sumerian, then Egyptian. The Greeks in Homeric times had a four-stringed lyre, *phorminx*, on which warriors like Achilles, and professional bards like the blind Demodocus (Homer: *Odyssey*, viii) and probably Homer

Fig. 1. A player of the lyre 'tanbur', Northern Sudan (after Plumley). The strings are numbered by players as indicated.

Pl. 1. A lesson on the lira, Greek hydra (c.500 BC).

himself, accompanied their songs and epics and led the choral dance. From the 7th century BC the Greeks had two main types of lyre. One, the *lira* (Pl. 1), with a body formed from a tortoiseshell (see *Chelys*) or from wood in that shape, covered with skin, was the instrument of musical education and amateur enjoyment (the *barbitos* was a larger version of it prominent in Bacchic scenes of the late 5th century). The other, *kithara* (Pl. 2), was of wood, and was the instrument of professionals and the contests.

The strings were of gut and in number varied from seven to 11. No classical source describes their tuning. The names of the notes of the Greek musical scale were, however, derived from the sequence of the strings of the lyre, so offering clues as to their tuning but leaving much room for argument. Nor does any classical writer tell how the lyres were played. But it has been observed in modern times that in East Africa, from the Sudan and Ethiopia to Kenya—the only regions in the world where lyres are still regularly played—the instruments (Fig. 1) are in many respects identical with the Greek *lira* and are mostly played, accompanying the voice, in a very characteristic way that seems to be matched in Greek vase paintings. The right hand, with a plectrum, strums across the strings near the bridge where they lie close together. On the other side of the strings the left hand, passed through a strap which supports the instrument, extends the fingers fanwise along the strings ready to press (and thereby silence) such strings as are not required to sound during the plectrum stroke (compare the *kantele). Rapid figures can

be executed as well as chords (Ex. 1). The strings, now often of wire, are tuned in the general pentatonic pattern shown, with string No. 1 tuned the highest and No. 2 the lowest. Some of these lyres, however, are played with the two hands, more like a harp.

A simple form of six-stringed wooden lyre was the main stringed instrument of Germanic peoples through the migration period of the 5th to 7th centuries AD, and is almost certainly the 'harp' named in *Beowulf*. Remains of several have been found in Germany and England, in burials. One is the 'Sutton Hoo' lyre now in the British Museum, a small-sized example exhibited along with a modern reconstruction of the whole instrument. A descendant is the *crwth, a bowed instrument. See also *Instruments, Medieval*.

Other stringed instruments of the Greeks include the *psalterion* (see *Harp*, 10); the *pandoura* (see *Lute*, 4b); and the unidentified *epigoneion*, *magadis*, *pektis*, and *sambyke* (see S. Michaelides: *The Music of Ancient Greece: an Encyclopaedia*, 1978). See also *Ancient Greek Music*, 7a.

ANTHONY BAINES

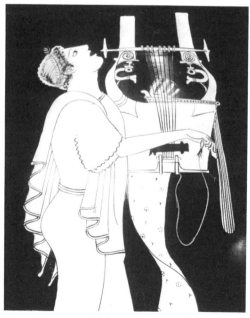

Pl. 2. Singer to the kithara at a contest, Greek amphora (c.490 BC).

Ex. 1

Lyric. 1. Strictly speaking, vocal performance accompanied by the lyre, but in fact broadened in meaning to denote any kind of accompanied vocal music, e.g. *drame lyrique* (Fr.), 'lyric drama', i.e. opera.

2. A short poem, i.e. not epic or narrative. Composers such as Grieg adapted this meaning to music, e.g. *Lyric Piece* (Ger.: *Lyrisches Stück*).

3. A vocal description, e.g. lyric tenor, lyric soprano, meaning somewhere between light and heavy vocal style.

4. The words of a song, especially used of popular 20th-century song.

Lyric Suite. 1. Orchestral work by Grieg, arranged from four of his six *Lyric Pieces* (Book 5), Op. 54. They are *Shepherd's Boy*, *Norwegian March*, *Nocturne*, and *March of the Dwarfs*, and they were orchestrated in 1904.

2. Work for string quartet by Berg, in six movements, composed in 1925-6. The second, third, and fourth movements were arranged for strings in 1928; the sixth movement also exists in a version with voice as a setting of S. George's translation of Baudelaire's *De profundis clamavi*. In 1977 the composer's annotated score of the *Lyric Suite* was discovered; it revealed that the work was inspired by Berg's love affair with Hanna Fuchs-Robettin, whose initials, combined with his own, provide the note row on which the music is based: B-F-A-B♭ (H-F-A-B in German notation). The suite also quotes from *Tristan und Isolde*, Zemlinsky's *Lyric Symphony*, and Berg's *Wozzeck*.

Lyrique (Fr.), **lyrisch** (Ger.). 'Lyrical'.

Lyrisches Stück (Ger.). See *Lyric*, 2.

M

Macbeth. 1. Opera in four acts by Verdi; text by Piave, after Shakespeare's tragedy (*c*.1605). Produced: Florence, Teatro della Pergola, 14 March 1847; New York, Niblo's Garden, 24 April 1850. For the Paris première (Théâtre-Lyrique, 19 April 1865) a new version was made by Verdi and Piave, which included the additions of Lady Macbeth's 'La luce langue', a new Exiles' Chorus, further choruses in Act 4, and a battle-fugue; Glyndebourne, 21 May 1938. A straightforward adaptation of Shakespeare's play, with Macbeth (bar.), Lady Macbeth (sop.), Banquo (bass), and Macduff (ten.).

2. Tone poem, Op. 23, by Richard Strauss, composed 1886–8 and revised 1889–90.

McCabe, John (*b* Huyton, Lancashire, 21 Apr. 1939). English composer. He studied at the Royal Manchester College of Music and at the Munich Music Academy. His compositions evince a concern to fuse and develop from the achievements of such mid-century figures as Bartók, Hindemith, and Hartmann, and he has proved a prolific composer in every genre from opera (*The Play of Mother Courage*, 1974, and *The Lion, the Witch, and the Wardrobe*, 1968) to keyboard music, his most successful works including *Notturni ed alba* for soprano and orchestra (1970), and the colourful symphonic poem *The Chagall Windows* (1974). He is also active as a pianist and writer on music (*Bartók Orchestral Music*, 1974; *Rachmaninov*, 1974), and is Director of the London College of Music.

PAUL GRIFFITHS

McCartney, (James) Paul (*b* Liverpool, 18 June 1942). English song-writer and pop musician. He was one of the original trio known as the Quarry Men who played skiffle style music in The Cavern club, Liverpool. In 1962 the trio, McCartney, John Lennon, and George Harrison, with the addition of Ringo Starr, became known as The Beatles and made their first recording—'Love me do' and 'PS I love you'. Under the management of Brian Epstein the group became one of the most popular of all time, achieving their first million-selling disc 'She loves you' in 1963; by 1970 three of their LP albums had sold over three million copies each. The songs which McCartney wrote in collaboration with John Lennon have been hailed as classics of the genre, with a lasting interest far beyond most 'pop' music, to be considered alongside the songs of Kern and Gershwin. Disagreement over the running of the company Apple led to the break-up of The Beatles in 1970, when each of the quartet went his own way, and McCartney formed the group Wings in 1971.

PETER GAMMOND

Macchina (It.). 'Machine', 'mechanism'; *macchina a venti*, 'wind machine'; *corno a macchina*, 'valve-horn' (see *Horn*); *tromba a macchina*, 'valve-trumpet' (see *Trumpet*).

MacDowell, Edward (Alexander) (*b* New York, 18 Dec. 1860; *d* New York, 23 Jan. 1908). American composer, pianist, and teacher. He received musical training as a boy, then moved with his mother to Europe in 1876 and lived there until his return to the USA 12 years later. A successful performance of his First Piano Concerto at Weimar in 1882 encouraged the young pianist to think of himself primarily as a composer. For the rest of his life he struggled to find time and energy to compose while making a living as a teacher and performer.

Settling in Boston in 1888, MacDowell taught privately and composed his two orchestral suites

Edward MacDowell

(No. 1, 1888–91, 1893; No. 2, 1891–5), as well as many works for piano. Public appearances as a pianist heightened his impact on American musical life. By 1896, when Columbia University named MacDowell its first professor of music, it did not seem an exaggeration to claim him, as the trustees did, 'the greatest musical genius America has produced.' His years at Columbia, however, proved frustrating. Throwing himself energetically into his new job, he found that it consumed almost all his time and that only in the summers could he compose seriously. A conflict with university authorities brought about his resignation in 1904. Soon afterward he showed signs of mental collapse, and he spent the last several years of his life in a state of childlike insanity.

To the public of his own day, expectantly awaiting the appearance of a 'great' American composer, MacDowell's music seemed more strikingly original than perhaps it does now. Nevertheless, works like *Woodland Sketches* for piano (1896, which include the well-known *To a Wild Rose*) blend diatonic melody with chromatically-tinged harmony, communicating a quality of restrained lushness and revealing MacDowell's distinctive, secure voice—a perfect exemplar of turn-of-the-century American Romanticism.   RICHARD CRAWFORD

McLeod, Jennifer (Helen) (*b* Wellington, 12 Nov. 1941). New Zealand composer. She graduated from Victoria University of Wellington in 1964, subsequently studying with Messiaen and Stockhausen (1964–6). Appointed a lecturer in music at Victoria University in 1967, she was later professor (1971–6). Her early works— *Cambridge Suite* (1962) and Little Symphony (1963)—revealed a strong talent, confirmed by her prize-winning *Piano Piece* (1965) and a chamber work *For Seven* (1965). Her theatre piece for children, based on the Maori creation myth, *Earth and Sky* (1967), galvanized the entire musical resources of the town of Masterton to make New Zealand musical history. Its successor, *Under the Sun* (1969–70), a music theatre piece for amateurs and children of Palmerston North, proved less creatively valid. She has written incidental music for plays, film scores, and a variety of songs and piano pieces. In 1976 she resigned her chair and became associated with the activities of the Divine Light Mission. In 1980 she trained as a stained-glass craftsman at Studio West Glass Company in Santa Monica, returning to New Zealand in 1981, where she has resumed composing. Her setting of 10 short poems written by herself, *Childhood* (1981), reaffirmed the spontaneity and zest at the heart of her music.

                                    J. M. THOMSON

Mace, Thomas (*b* 1612–13; *d* ? Cambridge, ? 1706). English composer and writer on music. He seems to have spent much of his life in Cambridge. Mace's best-known work is *Musick's Monument* (London, 1676), a dissertation on 'Practical Musick' of which part 1 deals with psalmody, part 2 with the lute and related instruments, and part 3 with 'The Generous Viol, in its Rightest Use'.

Machaut [Machault], **Guillaume de** (*b* ?Rheims, *c*.1300; *d* ?Rheims, 13 Apr. 1377). French composer and poet. He now appears as the most important French composer of the 14th century. Certainly he was influential in establishing polyphonic song in France, and his is the earliest-known complete setting of the Mass by a single composer. He took great care to preserve his complete works and they have survived more or less intact in six copies; this has undoubtedly favoured his reputation as compared with that of his near contemporary Philippe de Vitry. Altogether 141 of Machaut's works remain: they include 23 motets, 19 *lais*, 33 *virelais*, 21 *rondeaux*, 42 *ballades*, a Mass, and an instrumental hocket.

Machaut seems to have been brought up in Rheims. His earliest datable composition, the motet *Bone pastor Guillerme/Bone pastor qui pastores*, was probably written for the election of Guillaume de Trie as Archbishop of Rheims in 1324. In the same year Machaut received his first recorded appointment when he became Secretary to King John of Bohemia. He followed the king on military expeditions to Silesia, Bohemia, Poland, Prussia, and Lithuania. John of Bohemia was killed by the English at the Battle of Crécy in 1346. After John's death Machaut was employed by his daughter, Bonne, but he retained his connections with Rheims and was apparently based there for the rest of his life. His later patrons included King Charles of Navarre (for whom he wrote the poem *Le confort d'ami*), the Dauphin of France (who became King Charles V in 1364), Pierre I of Cyprus (Machaut tells of his exploits in *La prise d'Alexandrie*), and Jean Duc de Berry (for whom he wrote the poem *La fonteinne amoureuse* and from whose library a complete copy of Machaut's work survives). In later life Machaut acquired various ecclesiastical positions: he was canon both of St Quentin, whose patron saint is celebrated in the motet *Martyrum gemma latria/Diligenter/A Christo honoratus*, and of Rheims, where he lived his last days writing and supervising the copying of his works.

Machaut, although a cleric, wrote relatively little for the church. Only three of his 141 surviving works (the Notre Dame Mass and two of his Latin motets) have a specific place in the

Machaut, miniature depicting the composer visited by Nature and three of her children, Sense, Rhetoric, and Music.

church service. The Mass is the earliest setting for four voices. It has six movements (Kyrie, Gloria, Credo, Sanctus, Agnus, and Ite missa est); all except the Gloria and Credo are based on plainchant and some of the movements share common melodic material. Machaut's motets make full use of the new rhythms and more flexible notation developed in the 14th century; they are true examples of the *Ars Nova style, with many syncopations, small note values (the minim appears for the first time), and complex repetitions of the tenor part in diminished note values. A typical example is the motet *De bon espoir/Puisque la douce rousee/Speravi*, which is divided into two sections. The tenor tune is stated twice in each section but the two statements in the final section are twice the speed (half the note values) of those in the first. Another characteristic is the use of two French texts against the Latin tenor. This feature, and Machaut's preference for relatively few subdivisions within the main section, stands in contrast to earlier motets by de Vitry and others.

Machaut's most acclaimed achievement is in the realm of secular song. Almost all of his *virelais* and *lais* are monophonic, and his interest in these outmoded genres was somewhat unusual. However, his treatment of the polyphonic *ballades* and *rondeaux* was clearly innovatory: he greatly expanded the length of songs compared with earlier examples by Adam de la Halle and L'Escurel and introduced much more complex textures. Perhaps the most famous of his songs is the *rondeau, Ma fin est mon commencement*, in which the second voice sings the music of the first voice backwards. A more typical example is the *ballade, Nes que on porroit*, of which the opening of the top voice and tenor are shown in Ex. 1 (the contratenor is omitted). This shows a new, melismatic approach to polyphonic vocal writing, the fluid top part contrasting with the syncopated tenor. The example contains several of Machaut's melodic fingerprints: the fragment marked 'x' is found in almost a dozen other works and is transposed in several more, and the motif 'y' is one of Machaut's most characteristic melodic shapes. Incidentally, we are told in Machaut's autobiographical poem *Le voir dit* (c.1365) that he wrote this song for his lover Peronne, that it should be performed without ornamentation, and that it can be played on the organ or bagpipes.

Ex. 1 Machaut: *Nes que on porroit*

Nes   que on   por - roit

Soon after Machaut's death the poet Deschamps wrote a moving lament, *Armes, amours/ O flour des flours*, praising him as the 'master of all melody'. The lament was set to music by Franciscus Andrieu; he borrowed chords from the Gloria and Credo of Machaut's Mass to set the poignant words 'la mort Machaut'. Machaut was the last major figure to imitate the aristocratic poet–musicians of the 12th and 13th centuries by writing both monophonic songs and poems, and yet he also excelled in the new rhythmically varied style of polyphonic music which had been developed in Paris while he was still a young man. ANTHONY PRYER

FURTHER READING
Gilbert Reaney: *Machaut* (London, 1971).

Machicotage (Fr.). Extemporary ornamentation of plainchant by a soloist. The practice was common in France until the adoption of the Solesmes versions of plainchant early in the 20th century.

Machine à vent (Fr.). 'Wind machine'.

Mächtig (Ger.). 'Mighty', 'powerful'.

MacMillan, Kenneth (*b* Dunfermline, 11 Dec. 1929). British choreographer. He was resident choreographer with the Royal Ballet from 1965, director from 1970 to 1977, and since then has been principal choreographer. His ballets range from full-length narratives such as *Romeo and Juliet*, *Manon* (Massenet/ Lucas, 1974), *Mayerling* (Liszt/Lanchbery, 1978), and *Isadora* (Bennett, 1981) to studies in psychological relationships, and from the deep musical perception of *Song of the Earth* (Mahler, 1965) to the pleasurable ragtime diversion of *Elite Syncopations* (Joplin and others, 1974).
NOËL GOODWIN

Maconchy, Elizabeth (*b* Broxbourne, Hertfordshire, 19 Mar. 1907). English composer. She studied with Charles Wood and Vaughan Williams at the Royal College of Music (1923–9) and then in Prague. Her compositions include operas and a variety of concertante pieces, but she has seemed most at home in chamber music, and her cycle of ten string quartets, tautly argued in a somewhat Bartókian manner, is her outstanding contribution. The composer Nicola LeFanu is her daughter. PAUL GRIFFITHS

Macque, Giovanni de (*b* Valenciennes, *c*.1550; *d* Naples, Sept. 1614). Flemish composer and organist. After serving as a choirboy in the imperial chapel at Vienna he studied with Philippe de Monte. He then moved to Rome where, with Nanino and Marenzio among others, he was a member of the Compagnia dei Musici. In *c*.1585 he went to Naples and remained there for the rest of his life. His activities there included taking part in the music-making of the academy of Don Fabrizio Gesualdo, father of Carlo Gesualdo, and serving as organist at Santa Casa dell'Annunziata and the chapel of the Spanish Viceroy. He was also an important teacher, and his pupils included Luigi Rossi.

Macque's style of composition changed noticeably after he arrived in Naples. From having been relatively conservative in his music, he began to write madrigals, motets, *laude*, and *canzonette* in an advanced idiom, and his organ works from these years are full of chromatic harmonies and dissonances. DENIS ARNOLD

Madama Butterfly. Opera in two acts by Puccini; text by Giacosa and Illica, after Belasco's drama of the same name (1900). Produced: Milan, La Scala, 17 February 1904; Brescia, 28 May 1904 (new version); London, Covent Garden, 10 July 1905; Washington DC, 15 October 1906. Pinkerton (ten.), an American naval officer, falls in love with a Japanese geisha girl, Cio-Cio-San (sop.), known as Butterfly, and goes through a ceremony of marriage with her, despite the warnings of the American Consul, Sharpless (bar.). Pinkerton goes back to America, but Butterfly waits for his return with

Poster by Leopoldo Meincowicz for the first performance of Puccini's 'Madama Butterfly' (La Scala, Milan, 1904).

their child 'Trouble' and her servant Suzuki (mezzo). Pinkerton returns with his new American wife and learns that he has a son. The grief-stricken Butterfly kills herself.

Maderna, Bruno (*b* Venice, 21 Apr. 1920; *d* Darmstadt, 13 Nov. 1973). Italian composer. He studied composition and conducting at conservatories in Milan, Siena, and Rome, but the more significant influence on him was that of his private conducting teacher Hermann Scherchen. Still more important were his contacts with Stockhausen and Boulez, made in the early 1950s. He soon settled in Darmstadt, the Mecca of the international avant-garde, and there worked as composer, conductor, and teacher. In 1955 he assisted Luciano Berio in founding the electronic music studio in Milan. His works have a bigness characteristic of the man; they include various concertos, among them three for oboe, as well as *Hyperion* (1963–5), an aleatory theatre piece after Hölderlin. Among smaller compositions, his *Musica su due dimensioni* for flute, percussion, and tape (1952) was the first to combine live and electronic resources.   PAUL GRIFFITHS

Bruno Maderna

Madrigal

1. Introduction
2. The 14th-century Italian Madrigal
3. The Italian Madrigal in the 16th and Early 17th Centuries
4. The Madrigal Abroad
5. The Performance of Madrigals

1. *Introduction.* 'Madrigal' has been used as a term for two types of secular vocal music, one originating in the 14th century and not surviving much beyond *c.*1415, and the other, and better known, flourishing not only in Italy but also in most other European countries during the 16th and early 17th centuries. The two are not related in anything other than name. The origin of the word is a matter for dispute. Various derivations have been suggested—including *mandra* (Italian, 'flock'), which would imply a pastoral song—but the most likely is *matricale* (Italian, 'of the womb'), referring to the fact that madrigal texts are in the mother tongue, rather than in Latin.

2. *The 14th-century Italian Madrigal.* This earlier kind of madrigal did not adopt a more or less fixed form until the 1340s, some 20 years after its first appearance. From having a musical form which basically followed that of the verse, it settled into a standard length of two or three stanzas, each of three lines and each being set to the same music, the final stanza closing with a 'ritornello' of one or two lines, usually in a contrasting metre. The music is usually in

two, sometimes three, parts, and is highly melismatic, particularly in the upper voice. The rhythms are often lively, with frequent use of such techniques as canon and imitation. The most famous composers of the early madrigal were north Italians, such as Giovanni da Cascia, Gherardello da Firenze, and Jacopo da Bologna, but there are also some fine examples by Landini and Ciconia. Towards the end of the 14th century the madrigal yielded in popularity to the *ballata*— only 12 madrigals by Landini, for example, survive, compared to roughly 140 *ballate*. The early madrigal is characteristically bright and attractive, apt for virtuoso singing and playing.

3. *The Italian Madrigal in the 16th and Early 17th Centuries.* The 16th-century madrigal was based on a completely different principle: whereas the earlier madrigal followed a regular verse pattern, that of two centuries later tended to follow the meaning of the verse, with little attempt to establish a set formal structure. The earliest pieces of this kind to be called madrigals appear in a publication called *Madrigali de diversi musici* (Rome, 1530).

In the first years the madrigal was essentially a serious form, setting verse of a high quality, much of it the courtly love poetry of Petrarch, which was enjoying a new wave of popularity. Madrigals were composed mainly by the northern musicians who dominated the musical life of Italy at this time (see *Italy*, 3). The style is formed from a mixture of elements: the contrapuntal writing and smoothly flowing melodic lines of the motet; the more lively and rhythmic melodies and tendency towards harmonic thinking deriving from the **frottola*; and from the *chanson* short, memorable themes that made the music easy to perform by amateur musicians combined with the kind of programmatic writing that had made famous Janequin's 'La bataille de Marignan', with its imitations of horses' hooves, clashing of swords, and so on. The result is a work which puts a certain emphasis on tunefulness and singability, while using harmonic effects to underline a significant word or phrase, as in the following passage from Arcadelt's 'Il bianco e dolce cigno', where the word 'pian*gendo*' ('weeping') is aptly stressed by the sudden E♭ chord (Ex. 1).

These early madrigalists, such as Verdelot, Festa (both of whom contributed to the 1530 publication), Arcadelt, and Willaert, worked mainly in Venice and Rome. Their work gained increasing popularity through the 1530s and 1540s until, by the mid century, madrigals dominated secular music in Italy. There are signs of a growing sophistication in idiom, in particular with the use of quick *note nere* ('black notes', i.e. crotchets and quavers) to contrast with the 'white notes' (minims and semibreves) in which church music was written, which provided composers with a new resource for expressing verbal detail.

At about this time, a musician working at the court of the d'Este family in Ferrara, Nicola Vicentino, began experimenting with chromaticism, and *c*.1561 he built a keyboard instrument with keys to play extra chromatic notes (e.g. C♯ as well as D♭, A♯ as well as B♭). This 'arcicembalo' was not particularly successful (it was found impossible to keep it exactly in tune) and never achieved wide circulation, but chromaticism interested a number of composers, especially those who worked in or visited Ferrara, and soon madrigals using chromatic scales and the resulting new harmonies became quite common.

The master of these novel resources, and the most renowned composer of this mid-century period, was Cipriano de Rore, and it is no coincidence that he worked at Ferrara at just this time of experimentation and revolution. He chose poetry a little away from the elegant tradition of Petrarch, often with many more emotional words, and this allowed him to develop a more concentrated and intense musical style. Almost every significant word seems to suggest a corresponding image in sound. Minor keys and intervals express the sadder emotions, major ones joy; ascending notes symbolize such a word as 'heaven', low registers 'earth'. He uses dissonance to express pain or struggle, and places melismas on words which, although not suggesting programmatic expression, require emphasis. Jagged, difficult intervals are another means of emotional tone-painting, and the second section of his madrigal 'Mia benigna Fortuna' became a classic and much-imitated example of such music, because it opens with the 'forbidden' ascending major sixth (Ex. 2).

By the time of de Rore's death in 1565, the range of expression was widening rapidly, and over the next 15 years we can see the development of an 'avant-garde' movement, influenced to some extent by the Ferrara revolutionaries. One of its central figures was Luzzasco Luzzaschi, who worked in Ferrara and carried on the tradition established by de Rore, setting

Ex. 1

et io pian - gen - do   giun - go al fin   del vi - ver   mi - o.

et io pian - gen - do   giun - go al fin   del vi - ver   mi - o.

et io pian gen - do   giun - go al fin   del vi - ver___ mi - o.

et io pian - gen - do   giun - go al fin   del vi - ver   mi - o.

Ex. 2

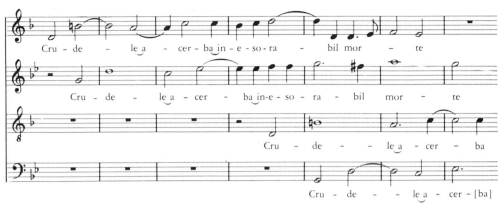

such verse as the famous passage 'Quivi sospiri' from Dante's *Inferno* with all the dramatic devices at his command.

At the same time, a more obviously pleasing type of madrigal was being composed in Venice, by Andrea Gabrieli among others, using only semi-serious verse and an idiom which became steadily more diatonic and more simply melodic. The verse set in this kind of madrigal is very often pastoral in nature, with plenty of rather pretty imagery about shepherds and shepherdesses tending their flocks, being pierced by Cupid's arrows, listening to the song of the nightingale, and so on. This gave rise to rather obvious musical depiction—even to the point of using notation that conveys meaning to the eye rather than to the ear, placing two semibreves side by side (o o) when the poem mentions the loved one's eyes, using black notation to convey the colour of her hair, and so on (see *Eye music*). By the 1580s this kind of imagery had become part of a highly artificial and playful idiom, pleasing to sing and apparently satisfying to those who insisted on a union of words and music without wanting anything too profound or difficult. The great master of the style was Luca Marenzio, working in Rome, whose early madrigal books (first published between 1580 and 1587) went through innumerable editions. His work is polished to a degree, able to take a somewhat emotional verse and set it to music which is never really extreme, but is nevertheless expressive and serious. At this stage, he is the classic master of the genre, balanced, and never neurotic or overwrought.

This pleasant 'Venetian' madrigal flourished until the end of the century, and gave rise to an offshoot, the *madrigal comedy, which went so far as to guy the serious style. But the really important developments were made by a group of composers who were dissatisfied with the current state of music, feeling that in spite of its obvious attempts to match the verse in mood and depth of feeling the result was no more deeply felt, and no less pretty in effect, than it had been before. So a new attempt at seriousness was made. Chromaticism was once again a resource to be used more fully, harmony was encouraged to be yet more dissonant, and the melody was increasingly based on speech rhythms, always allowing the words to be clearly heard. The verse chosen was still pastoral, but in place of the conventional images of natural objects, words with double meanings, often erotic in significance and intellectually passionate in much the same way as English metaphysical verse, became the norm. The result is often violent and neurotic in effect.

Marenzio adopted these techniques in his later years, but it was the younger men who saw its potential most clearly. Monteverdi, after writing a couple of madrigal books in the older manner, turned to the newer style in his mid 20s, probably influenced by Giaches de Wert, his senior at the court in Mantua and himself a pioneer in these novel means of expression. Monteverdi was especially interested in dissonance and angular melody, and some of the works in his fourth and fifth books of madrigals (1603, 1605) take these aspects as far as they could go within the limits of the genre. He was hotly attacked for this by some conservatives, but his work does enhance the emotional power of the idiom, mainly because of his unerring sense of musical proportion, which enables him to place just the right emphasis on each image of the verse, and to develop the musical material to its natural length. His work, though revolutionary, is rarely purely experimental.

This is less true of his contemporary Carlo Gesualdo, the last of the Ferrara composers (by marriage) to experiment with chromaticism. Much of his later work is indeed completely detached from the conventional resources of the madrigal: chromatic progressions completely destroy the sense of a stable mode or key, just as the sudden changes from relatively slow movement to a fast, freely-ornamented melody destroy the sense of a regular beat. Without words, this music would be totally incomprehensible; with them, however, it seems the natural expression of the double meanings in the verse.

By this time, yet another interpretation of Ancient Greek music was occupying the theoreticians. They established that any polyphonic genre was foreign to the Ancients, who had conveyed the emotions of the words by a form of heightened speech, rather than by musical organization. This theory, which was to lead to the development of *monody, destroyed the standard conception of the madrigal, and by *c*.1620 the genre had virtually died out in Italy, though the name continued to be used for some solo songs with keyboard accompaniment. Monteverdi and one or two others persevered with an ensemble madrigal which alternated accompanied duets and trios with *tutti* sections, but even this was abandoned by the mid 17th century. Thereafter in Italy, writing madrigals became a scholarly pursuit, and in the 18th century such a composer as Lotti or Bononcini might show his skill at counterpoint by writing a piece in the old madrigalian style.

4. *The Madrigal Abroad:* (*a*) *Germany and the Low Countries.* The vogue for madrigals (as opposed to indigenous forms such as the polyphonic *Lied*) outside Italy started quite early, mainly because of the employment of Italian or Italian-trained musicians at various courts north of the Alps. Lassus's stay in Rome (1552–4) introduced him to the madrigals of Arcadelt, Willaert, de Rore, etc., and he took the genre to Munich, where he worked from 1557 until his death. Similarly, Philippe de Monte visited Rome in the 1550s and again in the 1560s, and took the result of his experience with him when he went to work in Vienna in 1568. Lassus gathered a group of young Italians about him, and at first these musicians were very much in touch with the latest ideas, using chromaticism and modern methods of wordsetting. But by the 1570s they were beginning to fall behind, and in general the northern courts kept up only when they sent musicians to study abroad.

The southern Bavarians tended to go to Venice, and one notable composer, Hans Leo Hassler, studied with Andrea Gabrieli and wrote works very much in the Italian style. At the very end of the century, King Christian IV of Denmark started a tradition of sending young composers to study with Giovanni Gabrieli, and some of them, such as Hans Nielsen

(*c*.1580–*c*.1626) and Mogens Pedersøn (*c*.1583–1623), produced some fine modern madrigals, in the style of Monteverdi. The most distinguished of these northern composers, Heinrich Schütz, was sent by his master, the Elector of Saxony, on the same mission, and produced as his Op. 1 a book of extremist works, more advanced in some ways even than Monteverdi's, and full of lavishly-ornamented melody and strong, sustained dissonance.

(*b*) *England.* It was in England that the Italian madrigal was to have its greatest influence. Because of its break with the Papacy in 1534, England knew little continental music for several decades, and it was only in the late 1580s that the vogue for Italian music arrived (although a few manuscripts containing *chansons* and Italian madrigals did circulate before then). In 1588 Nicholas Yonge published the first anthology of madrigals—*Musica transalpina*. He provided English translations, an important incentive to composers who might otherwise have been put off composing madrigals because of the lack of suitable verse in English, and if the anthology was for the most part rather conservative, it did at least provide some up-to-date pieces by Marenzio. A second anthology, by Thomas Watson, called *Italian Madrigalls Englished*, came out two years later, and this consisted mainly of Marenzio's music. Thus the English composers who adopted the new fashion

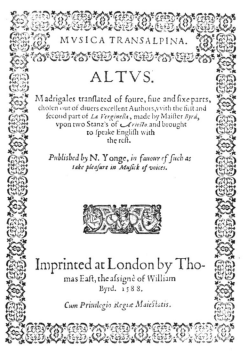

Title-page of the altus partbook of 'Musica transalpina' (1588), published by Nicholas Yonge.

began in much his style, setting pastoral verse to music that was pleasing to sing, full of memorable phrases, and always seeking out verbal images to 'paint'.

Thomas Morley was the master of this kind of music, rarely profound but always highly singable and expressing joyous emotions with rare zest. Morley's attitude set the tone of English madrigal writing, and most of his followers wrote well in the lighter vein. However, several turned also to more serious verse (though not often of the best quality), composing in the Italian style of the later 1580s. Weelkes explored chromaticism, and Wilbye and Ward dissonance, but there is nothing resembling the declamatory melody of the Italians, and no sign of the 'avant-garde' influence that could be found in Denmark or Germany. This explains why the English madrigal is, in fact, the most accessible and easy to perform, and why the tradition of madrigal singing persisted in England, even if only tenuously, throughout the 18th and 19th centuries and is still a popular pastime today. On the other hand, the composition of madrigals in England disappeared almost as suddenly as it arrived, and by c.1620 the fashion had died. There were some attempts to keep up with the Italians, in their use of keyboard-accompanied madrigals, but the Civil War effectively put a stop to that.

5. *The Performance of Madrigals.* The classic image of madrigal singing is that given by Thomas Morley in his *Plaine and Easie Introduction to Practicall Musicke* (1597), where he describes the plight of the Elizabethan gentleman out at a dinner party: 'Supper being ended and music books (according to the custom) being brought to the table, the mistress of the house presented me with a part earnestly requesting me to sing; but when, after many excuses, I protested unfeignedly that I could not, every one began to wonder; yea, some whispered to others demanding how I was brought up'. However, Morley was probably exaggerating the necessity for the well-educated man to be able to sing at sight (though some other books written at the time confirm his view), and it is important to realize that although amateur chamber music performance was important in England, it was far less so on the Continent. In Italy, madrigals were frequently composed for virtuosos to perform to their noble employers, and the court at Ferrara established a famous ensemble, with women's voices predominating. Other courts, including that at Mantua, imitated this ensemble, and there can be little doubt that in the last decades of the 16th century the Italian madrigal composer expected an appreciative audience for his works, and did not aim to please only the performer.

Nor were madrigals composed only for groups of solo voices. For banquets and for *intermedi* (given during the intervals of plays; see *Opera*, 2), choirs, with or without instruments, sang madrigals that had been especially written with such grand resources in mind. Some of the madrigals intended for wedding celebrations, by such composers as Marenzio and Giovanni Gabrieli, and perhaps even those by the English composers in Morley's collection *The Triumphes of Oriana* (1601), seem better suited to choral than to solo performance. All kinds of instruments were used to accompany the voices on these festive occasions: cornetts, trombones, shawms, and bassoons were common for open-air performance, while the rubric on the title-page of many English madrigal books 'apt for the viols and voices' indicates the support (or even occasional replacement?) of voices by strings on more intimate occasions. In the use of instruments, however, the principle seems to have been simply for the player to read the vocal part from the same part-book. There is no evidence that there was any conscious attempt at 'orchestration'—with, for example, trombones accompanying the loud *tutti* passages, and voices only for the quieter sections—in the way that has been attempted in some modern performances.

Thus, madrigal singing can be enjoyed simply as domestic music-making, or as something grander. The essential feature of a good performance is clarity of diction, with natural stresses; both the regular metric accents of later music (the original parts were, after all, unbarred) and, at the other extreme, heavy over-accentuation of syncopated notes must be avoided. *Vibrato* was used in the early 17th century, but as a consciously-applied ornament, and then only in solo songs. It is not merely unnecessary but a positive abomination in ensemble music, which gains immensely from a pure, clear sound. On the other hand, there must be no feeling that madrigals are 'quaint' or that they do not demand the full strength of the singer. The madrigal was the result of men striving to rouse the passions; it expressed many of the deepest emotions and must be treated with the seriousness that we accord to the *Lied* or the symphony.   DENIS ARNOLD

FURTHER READING
Edmund H. Fellowes: *The English Madrigal Composers* (London, 1921, 2nd edn 1948); Alfred Einstein: *The Italian Madrigal* (Princeton, 1949, rev. edn 1971); Joseph Kerman: *The Elizabethan Madrigal* (New York, 1962); Jerome Roche: *The Madrigal* (London, 1972).

Madrigal comedy. A short play set to music in the form of madrigals or similar vocal forms.

Perhaps the first such piece to use the title 'commedia musicale', and certainly the best known, was Orazio Vecchi's *L'Amfiparnaso* (1597).

Madrigali guerrieri ed amorosi ('Madrigals of Love and War'). Monteverdi's eighth book of madrigals, published in Venice in 1638. It contains 58 items, some instrumental, some for eight voices with two violins and continuo. Among them is the whole of *Il ballo delle ingrate*, and separate extracts from it, and the whole of *Il combattimento di Tancredi e Clorinda*, with extracts.

Madrileña (Sp.), **madrilène** (Fr.). A Spanish dance type originating in the province of Madrid.

Maestà, maestade (It.). 'Majesty', 'dignity'; *maestoso, maestevole*, 'majestic'; *maestevolmente, maestosamente*, 'majestically'.

Maestro (It.). 'Master', 'teacher'. The *maestro di cappella* (see *Chapel*) was the director of music at a court, church, or other musical establishment. Nowadays it means 'conductor'. The term implies high professional standing, and so notable conductors (of any nationality, not simply Italian) are addressed as 'maestro' as a mark of respect.

Magelone, Die schöne ('The Fair Magelone'). Fifteen songs (romances) for voice and piano, Op. 33, by Brahms, composed between 1861 and 1868. They are settings of extracts from the novel *Die schöne Magelone* by Ludwig Tieck (1773-1853).

Maggiore (It.). 'Major'.

Maggot. In Old English, a fanciful idea. In the 16th and 17th centuries it was used as a title for a pleasant piece of music, such as a dance, with the name of a person attached, e.g. 'My Lady Winwood's Maggot', and, on a less exalted level, 'Dick's Maggot'. In the 20th century, Maxwell Davies revived the word in his theatre piece *Miss Donnithorne's Maggot*.

Magnificat. *Canticle of the Virgin Mary in St Luke's Gospel, 'My soul doth magnify the Lord'. It is sung at Vespers in the Roman Catholic Church, and was taken over from that Office to be sung at Evensong in the Anglican Church (where it retains its Latin title). The *Magnificat* was the liturgical text set most frequently to polyphony between the 15th and the 17th centuries, by composers including Dunstable, Dufay, Binchois, Lassus, Palestrina, Monteverdi, Bach, and Schütz. Anglican com-posers often set the *Magnificat* and *Nunc dimittis* together, either on their own or as part of a Full Service.

Magnus liber organi ('Great book of organum'). Collection of two-voice plainsong settings for liturgical use, dating from the early Notre Dame period (c.1170). It has been attributed to Léonin and said to have been revised by Pérotin. The most important surviving work of the period, it is arranged for the church year in cycles of polyphonic settings of the Office and the Mass. Its title is taken from the 13th-century theorist Anonymous IV's description: 'Magnus liber organi de graduali et antifonario' ('The great book of organum for the gradual and antiphoner').

Mahagonny. See *Aufstieg und Fall der Stadt Mahagonny*.

Mahler, Gustav (*b* Kalište, Bohemia, 7 July 1860; *d* Vienna, 18 May 1911). Austrian composer and conductor. His 10 symphonies are among the finest monuments to the declining years of the Austro-German domination of European music and adumbrate developments which were to revolutionize the Viennese tradition in the works of Berg, Schoenberg, and Webern. In four of the symphonies he used the human voice and achieved a synthesis of song and symphonic form which, though not unique, has remained inimitable. He was a great conductor, especially of opera, his decade as director of the Vienna Court Opera being regarded as the zenith of that house's achievement.

1. *The Early Years*. Mahler was the second of 14 children born to a Jewish distillery owner, Bernhard Mahler, and his wife Marie. His parents were ill-matched in spite of their fertility, and he was an introspective child. Shortly after his birth, the family moved to Iglau (Jihlava). The bugles at the local barracks and the folk-songs sung to him by maidservants made an indelible impression. His father encouraged his obvious musical talent and in 1870 Mahler gave a piano recital in Iglau. The following year he was sent to school in Prague, where he was ill-treated and was fetched home in 1872. In 1875, on the advice of a farm manager who had heard him play, Mahler was taken to Vienna to play to Julius Epstein, piano professor at the conservatory. He was accepted as a student, but though successful in piano competitions at the conservatory, he abandoned playing in favour of composing. While in Vienna he attended lectures on philosophy at Vienna University and some of Bruckner's lectures. In the course of the next two years he worked as a teacher of piano and wrote the

libretto and music of his first major work, the dramatic cantata *Das klagende Lied*, which contains many of the individual features of his later style.

Mahler's career as a conductor began in operetta in 1880 at a small summer theatre at Bad Hall, Upper Austria. In 1883 he was appointed to a post at Olmütz (Olomouc). Already his exacting approach to his work was earning him notoriety among those singers who objected to the standards he imposed. His next appointment was at Kassel from 1883 to 1885. There he had a love affair with a singer, the unhappy end of which was sublimated in his song-cycle *Lieder eines fahrenden Gesellen* (1883–5, voice and piano, orchestrated 1891–3), for which he again wrote the texts. Themes from this work were also used in his First Symphony. Dissatisfied with Kassel, he moved to Prague for the 1885–6 season. There for the first time he conducted the Mozart and Wagner operas in which he was to excel. Prague was merely a marking-time operation before he took up the post of second conductor to Nikisch at Leipzig in 1886. There he conducted several Weber operas and was invited by the composer's grandson to 'complete' Weber's comic opera *Die drei Pintos* from the surviving sketches. This had a successful première in January 1888 and made Mahler famous. Mahler's next two operatic posts were of more significance. From 1888 to 1891 he reinvigorated the Royal Opera at Budapest. While there he conducted the first performance of his First Symphony (under the title Symphonic Poem) but it was not liked. At Hamburg in 1891 he encountered international singers for the first time and conducted up to 19 operas a month, including Wagner's *Tristan und Isolde*. In the summer of 1892 he made his only visit to London, where he conducted at Drury Lane and Covent Garden.

2. The Years of Maturity. From 1893 Mahler spent his summers at a retreat in the Salzkammergut (and later in Carinthia) where he devoted his time to composition. The Second and Third Symphonies were completed in the years 1893–6. The Second Symphony was performed complete in Berlin in 1895, Mahler's first real success as a composer. Among champions of his work at this time was Richard Strauss. In 1897, when the possibility of his appointment to the Vienna Court Opera arose, he fulfilled a necessary condition by being baptized as a Catholic. He was appointed director of the Opera in the autumn of 1897 and in 1898 conductor of the Vienna Philharmonic (an appointment which ended in 1901 after friction). Mahler's achievement in Vienna was his sensational raising of standards in all aspects of opera production, not only singing, but

Mahler

acting, lighting, and stage design. In 1902 he married Alma Schindler, a composer herself and daughter of an artist. Through her he became associated with the Sezession movement and, through the encouragement he gave them, he became the focal-point of the younger generation of composers such as Schoenberg, Berg, Webern, and Zemlinsky.

From 1899 to 1907 he composed his Symphonies Nos. 4, 5, 6, 7, and 8, and two big song-cycles. In 1907 the anti-semitic faction opposed to him secured his departure from the Opera. During this year his elder daughter, aged four, died from scarlet fever, and he was told that he had a malfunction of a heart valve. He left Europe for New York where he conducted at the Metropolitan Opera from 1908 to 1910, leaving when Toscanini arrived. From 1909 he was conductor of the New York Philharmonic Orchestra, where neither his strict standards of discipline, his concentration on unfamiliar works, nor his retouching of the orchestration of Beethoven's symphonies met with general approval. Each summer he returned to Europe, composing *Das Lied von der Erde* and the Ninth Symphony (1908–9), conducting his own works in major cities, and in 1910 supervising and conducting the first two performances at Munich of his enormous choral work, the Eighth Symphony. This was the crowning public triumph of his career. Back in New York for the 1910–11 season, he became seriously ill in February. He expressed a wish to return to

Vienna where his 50 years of life, lived at an incredible pitch of intense activity, ended in a clinic.

3. *Mahler's Style.* The importance of the influence of the folk-tale anthology *Des Knaben Wunderhorn* on Mahler's musical style cannot be exaggerated. The elements of satire, parody, and grotesquerie which are such a prominent feature derive from these tales and poems. Early audiences were repelled by Mahler's highly organized settings: the brilliance and clarity of the orchestration seemed to those accustomed to more conventional means to be at variance with the true nature of the material. Not only are the settings remarkable in themselves, they spilled over into Mahler's symphonic works. Thus, in the First Symphony, the funeral march is based on a parody of the children's round *Bruder Martin*; in the scherzo of the Second the song about St Anthony preaching to the fishes is quoted instrumentally, and the contralto sings the poem *Urlicht* as a prelude to the 'Resurrection' finale; in the Third, the children's vision of heaven *Es sungen drei Engel* is a principal motif, as is the song *Das himmlische Leben* which provides the last movement of the Fourth. Both the

Second and the Third Symphonies are on an enormous scale structurally, and their musical content is an extraordinary and convincing juxtaposition of military marches, fanfares, *Ländler*, and popular songs.

The Fifth, Sixth, and Seventh Symphonies are purely instrumental but are also linked with song-settings, in their cases the *Kindertotenlieder* (1901-4), the *Five Rückert Lieder* (1901-2), and the last two *Wunderhorn* settings, *Revelge* (1899) and *Der Tamboursg'sell* (1901). The Fifth may be defined as Mahler's 'Eroica', but the Sixth is his most tragic and classically formal symphony. It is also unusual in being concerned with one tonality, A minor, whereas in the other works a system of 'progressive tonality' is employed. The Seventh is a reversion to the earlier manner, but presented in a more sophisticated way. In these three central symphonies, a large orchestra is used economically, with passages of chamber music-like delicacy and refinement.

With the Eighth Symphony, Mahler again called upon the human voice. This, nicknamed the 'Symphony of a Thousand' because of the number of performers engaged at the Munich première, is in two parts, the first a gigantic

Autograph MS of Mahler's Ninth Symphony, a page from the first movement.

Bach-inspired polyphonic setting of the hymn *Veni Creator Spiritus*. The second half is a setting of the final scene of Goethe's *Faust*, a long movement in which elements of cantata, symphony, song-cycle, and even oratorio are merged. The result is undeniably impressive, but the song-symphony *Das Lied von der Erde*, its six movements based on the German translation of Chinese texts, is artistically more successful as an amalgam of the most potent aspects of Mahler's art. For his last two symphonies, the Ninth and Tenth, Mahler returned to wholly instrumental forces. Like *Das Lied von der Erde*, the Ninth is emotionally concerned with farewell, a reaction to the knowledge of his heart condition, but this aspect of the music can be over-stressed and sentimentalized. As a symphonic construction it shows Mahler looking ahead both harmonically and formally, for the opening slow movement is a novel structure in which a recurring crescendo governs the development—more properly fragmentation—of the material. The Tenth Symphony (1910-11), made available in a reconstruction by Deryck Cooke (1964, published 1976) of the short score, proves that Mahler had conquered the spiritual desolation implicit in the Ninth. His creative powers were undiminished: the first movement of the Tenth goes further along the path pioneered in the Ninth, and in the huge concluding movement he redevelops earlier themes in a way that transfigures them far beyond the normal recapitulatory process.   MICHAEL KENNEDY

FURTHER READING
Natalie Bauer-Lechner: *Recollections of Gustav Mahler* (Vienna, 1923; Eng. trans., ed. P. Franklin, London, 1980); A. Mahler, ed.: *Selected Letters of Gustav Mahler* (Berlin, 1924; Eng. trans., enlarged, ed. K. Martner, London, 1979); Bruno Walter: *Gustav Mahler* (Vienna, 1936; Eng. trans. 1937, 2nd edn 1941, reissued 1970); Alma Mahler: *Gustav Mahler: Memories and Letters* (Amsterdam, 1940; Eng. trans. 1964; rev. and enlarged, ed. D. Mitchell and K. Martner, London, 1975); D. Mitchell: *Gustav Mahler: the Early Years* (London, 1958, rev. edn 1980); D. Cooke: *Gustav Mahler: 1860-1911* (London, 1960, rev. and enlarged 1980); H.-L. de La Grange: *Mahler*, i (New York, 1973; London, 1974); D. Mitchell: *Gustav Mahler: the Wunderhorn Years* (London, 1975).

Maid of Pskov, The (*Pskovityanka*). Opera in four acts by Rimsky-Korsakov to his own libretto after L. A. Mey's play (1860). It was first performed in St Petersburg in 1873. Rimsky-Korsakov revised it in 1876-7 and again in 1891-2. The opera is also known by the title *Ivan the Terrible* following Diaghilev's 1909 Paris production.

Maid of the Mill, The. See *Schöne Müllerin, Die*.

Mailloche (Fr.). A kind of bass drum stick.

Main, mains (Fr.). 'Hand', 'hands'; *main droite* (sometimes abbreviated to M.D.), 'right hand'; *main gauche* (sometimes abbreviated to M.G.), 'left hand'; *deux mains*, 'both hands'; *quatre mains*, 'four hands', i.e. for keyboard duet.

Mainacht, Die ('May Night'). Song for voice and piano by Brahms, the second of his set of four, Op. 43 (1868). It is a setting of a poem by Ludwig Hölty.

Mainerio, Giorgio (*b* Parma, *c*.1535; *d* Aquileia, nr Venice, May 1582). Italian composer. He was *maestro di cappella* at Aquileia Cathedral in 1578. Of his surviving music, the most important is a volume of ensemble dance music entitled *Il primo libro de balli* (Venice, 1578) which was later reprinted by Phalèse in Antwerp.   DENIS ARNOLD

Maîtrise (Fr.). 'Choir school', usually attached to a cathedral. The word can also apply, by extension, to the body of choristers in a church choir or to their choirmaster.

Maja y el Ruisenor, La ('The Lover and the Nightingale'). No. 4 of Granados's *Goyescas* for piano. He later incorporated it as a song into scene 2 of his opera *Goyescas* and it is frequently heard as a separate concert aria with orchestra.

Majestätisch (Ger.), **majestueux, majestueuse** (Fr.). 'Majestic', 'majestically'.

Majeur (Fr.). 'Major'.

Major interval. See *Interval*.

Major scale. See *Scale*, 3.

Makropoulos Affair, The (*Věc Makropoulos*). Opera in three acts by Janáček; text by the composer, after Karel Čapek's drama (1922). Produced: Brno, 18 December 1926; London, Sadler's Wells, 12 February 1964; San Francisco, 19 November 1966. The famous singer Emilia Marty (sop.) intervenes in a lawsuit concerning some events of 300 years previously and shows first-hand knowledge of the case. She proves to be the victim of a process, invented at that time, for prolonging life, and to be unable to die until she finds the formula. Others, convinced of the truth of her story, are eager to share the secret; but for her, life has grown to be an intolerable burden, every pleasure hopelessly staled. In the end the formula is burnt, and she dies.

Mal (Ger.). 'Time'; *das erste Mal*, 'the first time'; *einmal*, 'once'; *zweimal*, 'twice'; etc.

Malaguena (Sp.). 1. A kind of *fandango from Málaga, in southern Spain. 2. An improvised Spanish song in free style and rhythm but based on a repetitive chordal accompaniment.

Malats, Joaquín (*b* Barcelona, 4 Mar. 1872; *d* Barcelona, Oct. 1912). Catalan pianist. From 1886 to 1888 he studied at the Municipal School of Music in Barcelona with J. B. Pujol, and subsequently at the Paris Conservatoire. He was a fine exponent of the piano works of his compatriot Albéniz: his own compositions included piano pieces and an orchestral work entitled *Impresiones de España* ('Impressions of Spain'). WENDY THOMPSON

Malaysia. See *South-East Asian Music.*

Malbrouck s'en va-t-en guerre. Eighteenth-century French nursery rhyme said to have been sung to the children of Louis XVI and Marie Antoinette. The tune is much the same, though rhythmically different, as that sung to 'For he's a jolly good fellow'. 'Malbrouck' probably does not refer, as is commonly thought, to the great Duke of Marlborough, as the name 'Malbrouck' is found in the Medieval *chansons de geste* and in other European literature. The song is referred to at the end of Beaumarchais' play *Le mariage de Figaro*.

Maldere, Pierre van (*b* Brussels, 16 Oct. 1729; *d* Brussels, 1 Nov. 1768). Flemish composer. In 1746 he was a violinist in the royal chapel at Brussels, and he seems to have remained in its service for most of his life, in spite of tours which took him to Dublin (where he directed the Philharmonic Concerts 1751-3), Paris, Vienna, and elsewhere in Europe. He was director of the Brussels Grand Théâtre from 1762 to 1767. A prolific composer, his symphonies especially were admired by Mozart and Haydn—indeed, several were attributed to Haydn in some sources. DENIS ARNOLD

Male alto. See *Alto voice.*

Malinconia, malinconico (It.). 'Melancholy'; *malinconoso, malinconioso*, 'in melancholy fashion'. Used by Beethoven to describe the introductory section of the fourth movement of his String Quartet in B♭ major, Op. 18, No. 6; the whole work acquired the nickname 'La malinconia'.

Malipiero, Gian Francesco (*b* Venice, 18 Mar. 1882; *d* Treviso, 1 Aug. 1973). Italian composer. He studied under Marco Enrico Bossi in Venice and Bologna, but also learned much from his independent work on early Italian music (he was later to produce a complete edition of Monteverdi among much other editorial work). Debussy, Stravinsky, and Casella were also important influences on his delicately worked music, and though his output was enormous and very uneven it does include distinctive masterpieces like the miniature operas *Sette canzoni* (1918-19), the fourth (1934) of his eight string quartets, and his First Violin Concerto (1932). PAUL GRIFFITHS

Malvezzi, Cristofano (*bapt.* Lucca, 28 June 1547; *d* Florence, 22 Jan. 1599). Italian composer. When his father left his post as organist of Lucca Cathedral in 1551 Cristofano accompanied him to Florence and spent the rest of his life there. He was in the service of the Medici, and in 1573 held the important joint position of *maestro di cappella* of S. Giovanni Battista and Florence Cathedral. He wrote keyboard *ricercari* and three volumes of madrigals, but is best known for his contribution to the *intermedi* performed as part of the celebrations surrounding the wedding of Ferdinando I and Christine of Lorraine in 1589.

DENIS ARNOLD

Mambo. A Cuban dance form developed in the 1930s and popularized by Perez Prado. It was shaped from the repetitive four-bar *nontuno* chorus of the *rumba, expanded into a complete form with a typical Latin American melodic line grafted on to the riffs of the 1930s jazz orchestra. Taken up by various jazz musicians and orchestras, the mambo was very popular in the late 1940s and early 1950s, and led the way to its less frenetic relative, the cha cha cha.

Mamelles de Tirésias, Les ('The Breasts of Tiresias'). Opera in two acts by Poulenc to a libretto by Apollinaire. It was first performed in Paris in 1947.

Ma mère l'oye ('Mother Goose'). Suite for two pianos by Ravel, based on fairy-tales by Péricault. Composed between 1908 and 1910, it is in five movements: *Pavane de la belle au bois dormant* ('Sleeping Beauty's Pavan'), *Petit poucet* ('Tom Thumb'), *Laideronnette, impératrice des pagodes* ('Empress of the Pagodas'), *Les entretiens de la belle et de la bête* ('Conversations of Beauty and the Beast'), and *Le jardin féerique* ('The Fairy Garden'). Ravel orchestrated the work and added a Prelude, *Danse de Rouet*, and four long interludes. It was performed as a ballet, to his own scenario, in Paris in 1912.

Man. 1. Abbreviation for *mano* (It.), 'hand'.

2. In German organ music, Man. I = Great (manual); Man. II = Swell; Man. III = Choir; Man. IV = Solo. This numeration is based on the order of importance. There is another, less commonly used, system based on the position of the manuals: I = Choir; II = Great; III = Swell; IV = Solo.

Mancando, mancante (It.). 'Giving way', in the sense of dying away.

Manche (Fr.). 'Neck' (of a violin etc.).

Manchega (Sp.). A lively type of *seguidilla danced in the former province of La Mancha, where Don Quixote came from.

Manchester School. A group of composers— Peter Maxwell Davies, Harrison Birtwistle, Alexander Goehr, and John Ogdon—who studied at the Royal Manchester College of Music and Manchester University under Richard Hall in the late 1950s.

Manchicourt, Pierre de (*b* Béthune, *c.*1510; *d* Madrid, 5 Oct. 1564). Franco-Flemish composer. In 1539 he was director of the choir at Tours Cathedral, and by 1545 was *maître de chapelle* at Tournai Cathedral. He also served as canon at Arras before moving to the Flemish chapel of Philip II in Madrid in 1559. His works include several Masses and motets, and over 50 *chansons* in both elegiac and satirical styles.

DENIS ARNOLD

Mancini, Francesco (*b* Naples, 16 Jan. 1672; *d* Naples, 22 Sept. 1737). Italian composer. He spent his life in and around Naples, where he was assistant musical director at the court from 1708 until Alessandro Scarlatti died in 1725, when Mancini succeeded him as director. He was also director of the Conservatorio di S. Maria di Loreto for 15 years from 1720. He was a popular opera composer, and his *Idaspe fedele* was the first opera to be performed entirely in Italian on the London stage (Haymarket, 1710). He also composed pleasant sonatas and concertos in a style deriving from Corelli's.

DENIS ARNOLD

Mandolin (often written in the Fr. way, *mandoline*). A lively stringed instrument played with a plectrum; today it is made in several different shapes, with a round or a flat back (see below, 1–3), but in all cases mounts four pairs of metal strings tuned as in the violin (E, A, D, G) and of about the same string-length and stopping intervals for the fingers. The mandolin is, like the violin, essentially a melody instrument and sustains the longer notes by a rapid *tremolando* with the plectrum (heart-shaped, of tortoise-shell or plastic), the double-stringing helping to produce two notes in rapid succession on each stroke (some electronic organs imitate the mandolin *tremolando* with ten or so note-repetitions per second).

1. *Neapolitan Mandolin* (round-back mandolin). This is the older form, with a deep rounded body (13″ long) built up in lute fashion with many ribs, most often of rosewood, though formerly also of maple or satinwood. The belly, very slightly convex, bends inwards at the level of the bridge at an angle of about 10 degrees. The low bridge is normally held in position by pressure of the strings, which are fastened at the foot of the body. The fingerboard has 17 frets (the tenth at the end of the body) taking the compass up to *a‴*.

2. *Flat-backed Mandolin or Portuguese Mandolin*. This is built of top, back, and sides, like a guitar. The pear-shaped outline is broader than in the preceding, but the volume of the internal air-space comes to much the same. Some of the prettiest designs have black and white 'barber's pole' inlay round the edge.

3. *American Mandolin*. This is also basically pear-shaped but most follow Gibson's arched-top model of early this century, with carved plates, round or *f*-shaped soundholes, and 'sunburst' finish (compare the 'cello-style' guitar; see *Guitar*, 4). Some designs have 'cut

Pl. 1. Neapolitan mandolin, from a catalogue of Theodor Stark (Markneukirchen, c.1900).

Pl. 2. (left) *American mandolin*, (right) *Portuguese mandolin.*

away' shoulders (giving a pointed appearance, as in many electric guitars) and then have 24 frets, reaching *e''''*. There are also electric mandolins with pick-ups and tone-controls.

4. *Mandolin Music.* The mandolin is most played in folk music, for which the flat-backed models (see above, 2 and 3) are generally preferred, being the easier to hold (especially if standing) and giving a brighter sound. Most of the prominent solo players of the last 60 years have used the American type, among them Dave Apollon in the 1930s and Bill Monroe, the 'Father of blue-grass'.

The abrupt sound of the mandolin, especially of the Neapolitan type, can be sufficiently penetrating to be effective in the symphony orchestra. It has been so used chiefly by composers working in Vienna during the first quarter of the 20th century, and not simply for associative effect (Italian serenades etc.), but as orchestral colour in its own right. Thus Mahler, at the end of *Das Lied von der Erde*, uses the mandolin for a few notes only, but with it expresses eternal resignation with unforgettable effect. Schoenberg (Serenade, Op. 24, and later *Moses und Aron*) and Webern (Five Pieces for Orchestra, Op. 10) also used the mandolin as an orchestral instrument, while Stravinsky used it to suggest Medieval minstrels (the galliard in *Agon*).

5. *History.* Back to the 15th century there had

been small instruments with lute-like bodies named in French 'mandore' and in Italian 'mandola' or 'pandurina'. They had four or five single gut strings tied to a fixed bridge and usually tuned in fourths and fifths. They became fairly popular in France during the 16th century, and some were made with flat backs. Mersenne (1636) mentioned the vivacity and 'aigu' of the sound, beside which a lute could hardly make itself heard. Tablature books appeared in France from 1578 but have not survived. The earliest extant collection seems to be in a German manuscript of *c.*1626, containing popular and dance airs with some simple chords, here for plucking; but a French work of 1629 is for playing with a quill, and Mersenne gives an extract from it, with a few chords at the end.

By the 18th century the mandola (or mandolino) was being made in Italy in numerous regional forms, with five or six pairs of gut strings played with a quill plectrum. Today they are usually described collectively as 'Milanese mandolin', and the mandolino which races all over the compass in Vivaldi's oratorio *Juditha triumphans* (also a concerto) and in Handel's *Alexander Balus* (with the harp to evoke Apollo's lyre) would have been of this kind.

The Neapolitan type dates from about 1750. Among its early makers the Vinaccia family of Naples made particularly beautiful instruments, strung with either gut or metal, the strings still tuned by plain pegs. The big difference, apart

Pl. 3. Milanese mandolins in the 18th century; painting of a domestic concert by Pietro Longhi (1702–85) (detail).

from the violin-tuning, is in the great depth of the body: in the previous types this roughly followed lute proportions, with the greatest depth typically equal to half the greatest width of the belly; but in the Neapolitan mandolin it far exceeds this through the addition of a very high rib (or two ribs) on each side (Fig. 1). This increases the air-space inside to strengthen emission of the lower frequencies and give the instrument its robust sound in the lower register. The resulting body shape somewhat brings to mind certain 'long lutes' (see *Lute*, 4a) of the Eastern Mediterranean like the Turkish *saz* (see also *Bouzouki*) from which indeed it may have been partly borrowed.

The two types of mandolin for some time continued in use together, which sometimes makes it difficult to know which was envisaged. The *cavatina* in Act 1 of Paisiello's *Il barbiere di Siviglia* and Mozart's famous serenade in *Don Giovanni* (today often played on the harp) are with little doubt for the Neapolitan, and so too

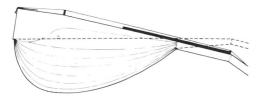

Fig. 1. Neapolitan mandolin, side view, with (in broken line) a Milanese mandolin for comparison.

are Beethoven's early sonatinas for mandolin and piano (Ex. 1). But some concertos, such as Hummel's (1799, written for an Italian soloist), are said to contain chords of up to six notes, pointing to the 'Milanese' variety.

Ex. 1

The Portuguese model, the earliest of the 'flat backs', must in this respect derive from the 'Portuguese guitar', i.e. the English guitar (see *Cittern*, 6) as used in Portugal since the late 18th century.

6. *Large Mandolins*. Tenor and bass mandolins are made for use in ensembles; they are named by analogy with the violin family: mandola, mandoloncello (or mando-cello), and mandolone. Mandolas (body length *c*.20″) were already made in the 18th century, and have some popularity today for accompanying folk music on other instruments, for instance in France. The entire set, with all sizes, came to be made for 'plectrum orchestras' of the late 19th century, one of the first to attract notice having been in Genoa in 1892, the programme including an arrangement of Hérold's *Zampa* overture.

ANTHONY BAINES

FURTHER READING
James Tyler: 'The Mandore in the 16th and 17th Centuries', *Early Music*, ix, 1 (January 1981), pp. 22–31; J. Tyler: 'The Italian Mandolin and Mandola', *Early Music*, ix, 4 (October 1981), pp. 438–46.

Manfred. 1.Incidental music by Schumann, Op. 115, for Byron's verse drama (1817), translated by K. A. Suckow. It consists of an overture and 15 items and was composed in 1848–9.

2. Symphony, Op. 58, by Tchaikovsky, after Byron. It is unnumbered and was composed in 1885.

Manfredini, Francesco (*bapt.* Pistoia, 22 June 1684; *d* Pistoia, 6 Oct. 1762). Italian violinist and composer. He played in the famous Bologna orchestra of S. Petronio until it was temporarily disbanded in 1696; he then spent some years in Ferrara before rejoining the orchestra in 1704. Between 1711 and 1727 he may have spent some years as *maestro di cappella* to the Monaco court, but his final post was in his native town, as *maestro* to the cathedral. His works include some attractive instrumental music, notably the Op. 3 set of concertos (1718), which ends with a Christmas *pastorale*—less inventive than Corelli's famous example, but of distinct charm.

DENIS ARNOLD

Manfredini, Vincenzo (*b* Pistoia, 22 Oct. 1737; *d* St Petersburg [now Leningrad], 16 Aug. 1799). Italian composer, the son of Francesco Manfredini. He went with his brother Giuseppe, a castrato, to Russia in 1758, and served there as *maestro di cappella* to the St Petersburg court; in 1762 he was appointed *maestro* of the Italian opera company there. He returned to Bologna in 1769 (succeeded by Galuppi in St Petersburg), but in 1798 was invited back to Russia, where he died the following year. He wrote a number of operas and a Requiem Mass for the Empress Elizabeth (1762) in Russia, but later devoted himself almost entirely to writing and teaching.   DENIS ARNOLD

Manica (It.). Shift of position in violin playing etc.

Manico (It.). The fingerboard of a stringed instrument.

Manieren (Ger.). 'Grace notes'.

Mann, Thomas. See *Novel, Music in the.*

Mannerism. Term usually used with reference to the visual arts, to describe the extravagance of certain 16th- and 17th-century painters, such as Giulio Romano, whose frescoes at Mantua are full of monsters and exaggeratedly emotional human beings, or Caravaggio, who was fond of extreme contrasts of light and shade to bring out the sinister or frightening aspects of a scene. The term has recently been applied to music, with less precision, to bridge a supposed gap between the Renaissance and the Baroque periods. It is quite apt when used to describe the works of the 16th-century 'avant-garde' madrigal composers such as Gesualdo (see *Madrigal*, 3) who in their attempts to depict words vividly used unusual harmonies and intervals, chromaticism, and so on, but it would be misleading to call the period *c.*1530-1630 'Mannerist', because much other music followed well-established traditions and is in no sense exaggerated.   DENIS ARNOLD

Mannheim school. Title given to a group of composers who worked at Mannheim in the 18th century. Their importance, shared to some extent with similar progressives in Vienna, Italy, and Bohemia, was in laying the foundations of the symphony as it was to be developed by Haydn and Mozart. The Mannheim orchestra was famous for its style of playing and for such 'special effects' as the so-called *Rakete* ('rocket'), a type of subject and figure that rises over a wide range of notes, usually in broken chords, sudden changes of dynamic, and extended passages of *crescendo*; to say that these effects had not been heard previously, however, is an exaggeration.

The principal composers of the Mannheim school were the Stamitz family, Holzbauer, Richter, and Cannabich. See also *Germany*, 5; *Orchestra*, 2; *Symphony*, 2.

Mano, mani (It.). 'Hand', 'hands'.

Manon. Opera in five acts by Massenet; text by Meilhac and Gille, after Prévost's novel *Manon Lescaut* (1731). Produced: Paris, Opéra-Comique, 19 January 1884; Liverpool, 17 January 1885; New York, Academy of Music, 23 December 1885. Massenet also wrote a sequel, *Le portrait de Manon* (1894). The Chevalier Des Grieux (ten.) falls in love with Manon (sop.), whom he meets as she stops at an inn in Amiens with her cousin Lescaut (bar.) on her way to a convent; the young lovers elope to Paris. De Brétigny (bar.), a friend of Lescaut, persuades Manon to go away with him. Des Grieux, in despair, decides to enter the priesthood, despite pleas from his father, the Count Des Grieux (bass). Manon comes and persuades Des Grieux to go off with her. At a gambling house Des Grieux is accused of cheating and Manon is arrested as a prostitute and condemned to transportation. Des Grieux bribes an officer for permission to speak to her and tries to persuade her to run away with him. She is too weak to do so and dies in his arms.

Manon Lescaut. Opera in four acts by Puccini; text by Giacosa, Illica, G. Ricordi, Praga, and Oliva, after Prévost's novel of the same name (1731). Produced: Teatro Regio, Turin, 1 February 1893; London, Covent Garden, 14 May 1894; Philadelphia, Grand Opera House, 29 August 1894. Des Grieux (ten.) falls in love with the young Manon (sop.) and they elope, thwarting the plans of the elderly roué Géronte (bass), who is planning to abduct her. Manon deserts Des Grieux and goes to live in splendour with Géronte, but the reappearance of Des Grieux awakens her former love. Géronte has her arrested and she is sentenced to be deported to Louisiana. Des Grieux persuades the captain of the ship to let him accompany her, and they are reunited in the desert near New Orleans, where she dies in his arms.

Mantra. Work by Stockhausen for two amplified, ring-modulated pianos with wood-block and crotales (played by the pianists), composed in 1969-70. The title is an Indian word for a mystical repetition ('a sound which makes one see'), and the whole score, which is conventionally written out, is based on one melodic formula.

Manualiter (Ger.). 'On the manuals', i.e. playing with the hands only.

Manzoni Requiem. Title sometimes given to Verdi's Requiem, which was composed in 1874 in memory of the Italian novelist and poet Alessandro Manzoni.

Maracas. Gourd rattles of Latin American dance music. The original form, as made by South American Indians and others, is of a gourd, with the pulp washed out and the seeds taken out, dried, and put back in the dried shell before affixing a wooden handle. Commercial types are of wood or plastic with lead-shot or suchlike inside (Fig. 1*a*). A pair of maracas, selected to give sounds of slightly different pitch, are shaken one in each hand in the characteristic eight-quaver rhythms of the rumba and other dances, using quick forward movements of the hands alternately. Many composers have since used maracas in their compositions, Boulez requiring up to three pairs differing in size to give higher and lower sounds.

Two other dance music rattles came in primarily with the Brazilian samba dance. The *chocolo* [*cholalho*] (Fig. 1*b*) is tubular, of bamboo or metal, about 15″ × 2″ in diameter with shot inside and closed at both ends, in some cases with parchment. Milhaud uses it in *Saudades do Brasil* (1920). Similar rattles are met also as European folk instruments, as in Sicily where, made of cardboard, they are used for quieting infants.

The *cabaza* (Fig. 1*c*) works on a different principle: a gourd is surrounded by beads threaded on a net which is struck and rustled with the hand. Some later *cabazas* have a metal canister instead of the gourd.

Vessel rattles of gourd, or of basketry, have played a prominent part in primitive music and ritual. In Europe, much louder kinds of rattle have generally predominated, though the vessel rattle, as a babies' rattle, is in Sicily alleged to

Fig. 1

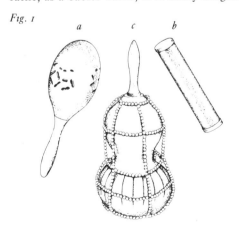

a   c   b

keep malignant spirits at a safe distance from the child. In the South American homelands of the maracas, too, Indian women will lull infants to sleep with a gourd rattle, strictly provided that it is not one in which the medicine man has put secret magic objects to heighten his and the instrument's powers.   ANTHONY BAINES

Marais, Marin (*b* Paris, 31 May 1656; *d* Paris, 15 Aug. 1728). French composer and player of the bass viol. He was a choirboy at St Germain-l'Auxerrois, and learnt to play the bass viol from the most important teacher of his day, Sainte-Colombe. He soon outclassed his master, and in 1676 entered the royal orchestra, later becoming a soloist and sharing the directorship of the Opéra orchestra with Collasse. In 1725 he retired from the royal service, to take up gardening, but he continued to teach a few pupils.

Marais studied composition with Lully, and wrote four extremely successful operas, including *Alcione* (1706), which became famous for its representation of a storm. Among his early chamber music is a collection of trios for upper instruments (Paris, 1692) which is in an old-fashioned, Lullyan style. His most important works, however, are the five sets of *Pièces de violes* (Paris, 1686-1725) written for his own instrument. These works for one to three bass viols and figured bass did for the viol what Couperin's *ordres* did for the keyboard, and include dances and descriptive pieces loosely organized into suites. A rather ghastly penchant for realism can be seen in *Le tableau de l'opération de la taille*, an evocation of an operation on a gall bladder which bears musical witness to Pepys's graphic description of the horrors of surgery at that time.

Marcando, marcato (It.). 'Marking', 'marked', i.e. emphasizing each note.

Marcello, Alessandro (*b* Venice, 1684; *d* Venice, 1750). Italian composer who also wrote poetry and painted. He held weekly concerts at his house in Venice, with Gasparini, Lotti, and Tartini among the regular visitors. He composed only a small number of works, of which the concertos are the best known, especially one in D minor for oboe which was transcribed for keyboard by Bach.   DENIS ARNOLD

Marcello, Benedetto (*b* Venice, July or Aug. 1686; *d* Brescia, 24 or 25 July, 1739). Italian composer, the younger brother of Alessandro Marcello. He was a considerable figure in Venetian public life, being Governor of Pola (Istria) and then Chamberlain at Brescia, where he died of consumption. He was more prolific than his brother and his works include several concertos and sonatas. His most famous compositions, published as *Estro poetico-armonico* (Venice, 1724-6), were settings of Italian paraphrases of the psalms in an *arioso* style. Nowadays he is better known for his delicious, if malicious, satire on the manners of the opera house, *Il teatro alla moda* (Venice, *c*.1720)—a book sometimes taken too seriously as a historical document.   DENIS ARNOLD

Marchand, Louis (*b* Lyons, 2 Feb. 1669; *d* Paris, 17 Feb. 1732). French composer and organist. He was an infant prodigy and before he moved to Paris held an appointment as organist at Nevers Cathedral at the age of 14. In Paris he had a distinguished career, entering the royal service *c*.1707 as *organiste du roi*, but his stormy character led to his dismissal, and in 1713 he made a long visit to Germany. It was in Dresden, in 1717, that a contest with Bach was planned for him, but Marchand left the court before Bach's arrival. He eventually returned to Paris and worked as organist at the Cordeliers there for the rest of his life. He was a well-known teacher, but although he charged high fees for his lessons he died in poverty.

Marchand's most important music is contained in five small volumes of organ pieces, and two suites for harpsichord; his music is notable not only for its contrapuntal skill but also for some interesting experimental harmonies.
                    DENIS ARNOLD

Marcha real ('royal march'). The second oldest national anthem, after 'God Save the Queen', chosen by Carlos III in 1770, and officially adopted by Spain in 1942. During the Spanish Republic (1931-6) a popular 19th-century patriotic song, the *Himno de riego*, was used as the national anthem.

Märchen (Ger.). 'Tales'; pieces of music with some suggestion of traditional or legendary forms.

Marching through Georgia. This American song commemorates General Sherman's famous Civil War march of 1864. The stirring, rhythmic verses and the swinging tune were both composed by Henry Clay Work (1832-84), a letterpress and music compositor by trade, who issued the song in print immediately. General Sherman himself is said to have disliked it.

Marcia (It.). 'March'; *alla marcia*, 'in march style'.

Marenzio, Luca (*b* Coccaglio, nr Brescia, *c*.1553; *d* Rome, 22 Aug. 1599). Italian composer. He was the third of seven children born to poor parents in a small Italian town. He may have been a choirboy at Brescia Cathedral before being taken up by Cardinal Cristoforo Madruzzo, who had a large establishment of musicians and actors in Rome in the 1570s. On Madruzzo's death in 1578 Marenzio stayed in Rome in the service of the powerful Cardinal Luigi d'Este. He travelled with him to Ferrara in 1580, and soon after this began to publish books of his madrigals. From having been known as a singer he soon became celebrated as the most popular madrigal composer of the time, a reputation which flourished until he began to develop a more serious manner in the mid 1580s. In 1586 Cardinal d'Este died, and in 1588 Marenzio entered the service of the Medici in Florence. He was involved in the celebrations surrounding the wedding of Ferdinando I and Christine of Lorraine in 1589, and composed the music for the second and third *intermedi* of *La pellegrina*. However, he returned to Rome later that year. In the 1590s he spent some years at the Polish court. He died soon after his return to Rome from Warsaw.

Marenzio's early madrigals, and the *villanelle* and *canzonette* which continued to be published throughout his life (not always by him), reveal his mastery of a singing style and his fondness for drawing attention to each detail of the pastoral verse he chose. The serious turn he began to take *c*.1585 reached a peak in the 1590s, when his style becomes much more advanced

Title-page of Marenzio's 'Il primo libro de madrigali a sei voci' (1584).

and difficult, and a preoccupation with death and decay shows in his choice of the more anguished and tormented verse of Petrarch and Guarini. The music is often jagged or chromatic in melody and dissonant in harmony, with sudden changes in mood—altogether unlike the smooth, sweet manner of his earlier work. These late madrigals were not appreciated in his lifetime, but the early works persisted in popularity throughout Europe. They were especially influential in England, where many were published in *Musica transalpina* and other collections, and where Wilbye, Weelkes, and many others imitated his style quite closely.

DENIS ARNOLD

FURTHER READING
Denis Arnold: *Marenzio* (London, 1965).

Marian antiphons. Name given to the antiphons of the Blessed Virgin Mary. See *Antiphon*.

Maria Stuarda. Opera in three acts by Donizetti to a libretto by G. Bardari based on Schiller's play. It was first performed in Naples, to an altered libretto by P. Salatino, in 1834, and first given in Donizetti's original form in Milan, in 1835.

Marienleben, Das ('The Life of Mary'). Songs by Hindemith for soprano and piano to texts by Rilke. The 15 settings were composed in 1922-3 and revised between 1936 and 1948. Hindemith orchestrated four of them in 1938 and two more in 1948.

Mariés de la tour Eiffel, Les ('The Newlyweds of the Eiffel Tower'). Ballet in one act by Auric, Honegger, Milhaud, Poulenc, and Tailleferre—five of Les *Six (excluding Durey)—to a libretto by Cocteau. It was choreographed by Börlin and first performed in Paris in 1921.

Marimba. Instrument similar to the xylophone but an octave deeper in compass (for compass diagram, see *Xylophone*, Fig. 1) and with wider wooden bars. Whereas a xylophone bar usually has a 'bite' hollowed on the underside at the centre, a marimba bar is thinned underneath for much of the length between the two supporting points, which considerably lowers the pitch in relation to length, helping to secure the deeper compass without bars of undue lengths while leaving sufficient weight at the ends to produce a full, clear sound, more mellow than the hard, dry quality of a xylophone. The sharps and naturals are on the same level, to suit playing with four beaters when required. For this the wrist is turned inwards, with two beaters crossed under the palm, their angle controlled by fingers and thumb.

The name 'marimba' is originally from Africa, where the instrument—in general classification 'xylophone'—is played together in ensembles, with expert and intricate polyphonic procedures. To the deep marimba sound is added a buzz from vibration of material from the cocoons of a large spider, gummed over openings in the gourds which form the resonators. Such instruments reappeared in Central America, evidently following the slave trade, and from these the well-known version was developed around 1910 in the USA, to become a popular instrument for variety soloists. An early model by Deagan, Chicago, was called 'marimbaphone', and this form of the name may be met in modern compositions. Today, it often figures as a major percussion tone-colour—a notable change since Percy Grainger, referring in 1929 to the marimba, vibraphone, and also dulcitone (see *Celesta*), complained of

the neglect of the exquisite 'tuneful percussion' instruments invented and perfected in America and elsewhere during the last thirty or forty years . . . Yet these same 'classicists'—who probably consider these mellow and delicate-toned instruments too 'lowbrow' to be admitted into the holy precincts of the symphony orchestra—endure without protest the everlasting thumping of kettledrums (which with brutal monotony wipes out all chord-clearness) in the Haydn-Mozart-Beethoven orchestrations.

Deagan, whom Grainger especially praises, also introduced a bass marimba, with a deep but short compass from *f* down to cello *C*, and available in various designs today. The resonators, like the bars, are wide, and the longest have to be turned up at the bottom to avoid raising the bars up to the level of the player's head. Heavy soft beaters are used.

ANTHONY BAINES

Marini, Biagio (*b* Brescia, *c*.1587; *d* Venice, 1663). Italian violinist and composer. In 1615 he joined the ensemble of St Mark's, Venice, as a violinist, and after returning to his home town as musical director of the Accademia degli Erranti he went to the court at Parma in 1621. He was one of the earliest Italian violin virtuosos to spend an appreciable time in Germany, passing the years between 1623 and 1649 at the Wittelsbach court in Neuburg an die Donau. On his return to Italy, he was successively *maestro di cappella* at S. Maria della Scala, Milan, director of the Accademia della Morte, Ferrara, and *maestro* at Vicenza Cathedral.

Marini's works include some of the most attractive early violin music and are important for their foreshadowing of the solo sonata. The *sinfonie* for three violins and continuo of the *Affetti musicali*, Op. 1 (Venice, 1617), are longer and more substantial than was usual at that time, and his Op. 22 (*per ogni sorte di strumento musicale diversi generi di sonate da chiesa, e da camera*) sets some of the sonatas into clearly marked separate sections. His writing for the violin is genuinely soloistic, using, for example, double and triple stopping and tremolo effects, the continuo acting simply as an accompanying part. His division of works into dance suites and more serious music is essentially the same as Corelli's distinction between *sonate da camera* and *sonate da chiesa*.   DENIS ARNOLD

Markiert (Ger.), **marqué** (Fr.). 'Marked'. 1. Clearly accented. 2. Brought out, for example a melody to be emphasized above an accompaniment.

Marlboro Music Festival. Every summer since 1950, groups of about 85 professional musicians have gathered at the campus of Marlboro College in southern Vermont to make music. In these eight-week sessions, hundreds of pieces are rehearsed by chamber ensembles of all sizes, and selected works are presented at weekly public concerts. Marlboro performances are more widely available through commercial recordings, tapes loaned to radio stations, and, since 1965, the 'Music from Marlboro' concert tours. From its inception the Festival has been directed by Rudolf Serkin.   NYM COOKE

Marsch (Ger.). 'March'.

Marschner, Heinrich (*b* Zittau, nr Dresden, 16 Aug. 1795; *d* Hanover, 14 Dec. 1861). German composer. He came from an artisan's family and became a musician after studying with Tomašek in Prague. After a period when a young man touring as a pianist and composer of songs, he was in the service of several minor noblemen before an opera *Heinrich IV und D'Aubigné* was produced successfully by Weber at Dresden. Thereafter he joined the staff of the Dresden theatre, subsequently becoming musical director at the Leipzig opera house where he produced two operas which made him famous. *Der Vampyr* (1828) was on a supernatural subject close to that of *Der Freischütz*, while *Der Templer und die Jüdin* (1829) provided some ideas for Wagner's *Lohengrin*. In 1830 he moved to Hanover where he remained until his retirement in 1859. There his most successful work was *Hans Heiling* (1833), a work still to be heard in Germany. His style has a mixture of simple songs in the *Singspiel* tradition with elaborate *concertante* finales which display a kind of *Leitmotiv* technique.   DENIS ARNOLD

Marseillaise, La. French national anthem, written and almost certainly composed by Rouget de Lisle as a sanguinary Revolutionary song in 1792. It was officially adopted in 1795 and has remained in use ever since, despite an attempt to replace it in the Second Empire of Napoleon III. The melody has often been quoted by other composers, for example by Schumann in his song 'Die beiden Grenadieren', Tchaikovsky in the 1812 Overture, and Debussy in *Feux d'artifice*.

Marson, George (*b* Worcester, *c*.1573; *d* Canterbury, 3 Feb. 1632). English organist and composer. He graduated B.Mus. from Trinity College, Cambridge, in 1598 and the following year became organist and choirmaster at Canterbury Cathedral. He was ordained in 1604. Marson contributed a fine five-part madrigal, 'The nymphs and shepherds danced lavoltas', to the *The Triumphes of Oriana*, and several pieces of his sacred music survive in manuscript.   WENDY THOMPSON

Marteau sans maître, Le ('The Hammer without a Master'). Work by Boulez for contralto, alto flute, guitar, vibraphone, xylorimba, percussion, and viola, to a text by René Char. It was composed between 1952 and 1954 and revised in 1957.

Martelé (Fr.). 'Hammered'. Type of bowing in string playing, in which the player is required to make a series of short, sharp bow-strokes, with the bow remaining in contact with the string. The point of the bow is normally used, unless *martelé au talon*, '... at the heel', is specified. See also *Détaché*.

Martellando, martellato (It.). 'Hammered', 'hammering'. The terms are normally used to mean **martelé*, i.e. in string playing, but they may also be applied to similar effect in piano playing, singing, or even, with Liszt, organ playing.

Martellement (Fr.). Seventeenth-century term for a **mordent*.

Martha, or Richmond Fair (*Martha, oder Der Markt zu Richmond*). Opera in four acts by Flotow to a libretto by F. W. Riese after V. de Saint-Georges's ballet-pantomime *Lady Henriette*, for which Flotow had composed some music. It was first performed in Vienna in 1847. *'Tis the Last Rose of Summer* is sung during the opera.

Martin, Frank (*b* Geneva, 15 Sept. 1890; *d* Naarden, 21 Nov. 1974). Swiss composer. The son of a Calvinist minister, he studied with Joseph Lauber and received encouragement from Ernest Ansermet but was mostly self-taught. He did military service during the First World War and then spent brief periods in

Frank Martin

Zurich, Rome, and Paris before returning to
Geneva to study eurhythmics at the Dalcroze
Institute (1925-7), where he remained as a
teacher of improvisation and rhythmic theory
until 1938. He adopted 12-note *serialism in his
First Piano Concerto (1933-4), one of the few
outside Schoenberg's circle to do so before the
Second World War. After the war he remained
in Europe to teach the method to a new
generation: now living in the Netherlands, he
commuted regularly to the Cologne Musikhochschule (1950-7), where his pupils included
Stockhausen.

Like many of his compatriots, Martin reflected in his art the twin cultural heritage of
Switzerland. The strongest Germanic influence
on him was not Schoenberg's (for despite its
serialism his music is predominantly tonal), but
Bach's. On the other hand, his sonorities often
suggest comparison with Debussy, Ravel, or
Roussel, and he generally used French texts and
titles. The result of this fusion is often a
distinctive combination of the ascetic and the
sensuous. His mature style was formed in *Le vin
herbé* (1938-41), a chamber oratorio on the
Tristan legend, and it changed little in the
works that followed. These include a bigger
oratorio, *Golgotha* (1945-8), various dramatic
works, and several concertos, of which the *Petite
symphonie concertante* for harp, harpsichord,
piano, and two string orchestras (1945) achieved
wide popularity.   PAUL GRIFFITHS

FURTHER READING
Frank Martin: *Responsabilité du compositeur* (Geneva,
1966); Bernhard Billeter: *Frank Martin* (Frauenfeld,
1970).

Martini, Giovanni Battista (Padre) (*b*
Bologna, 24 Apr. 1706; *d* Bologna, 4 Oct. 1784).
Italian writer on music and one of the most
influential theorists and teachers of the time.
Son of a string-player, he studied music at
Bologna, then entered the Franciscan order.
Apart from his novitiate, he spent all his life as
organist and *maestro* of the Bologna monastery
of his order. One of the earliest music historians,
he collected a vast range of music of the past
(most of it now forms the basis of the magnificent collection of the Civico Museo at Bologna),
and although his projected history was written
only to the 11th century (Bologna, 1761-81), he
was consulted by many, including J. C. Bach
and Mozart, about counterpoint in the 'old
style' of Palestrina. He refused the post of
maestro at St Peter's, Rome, preferring to stay in
his native city. He also composed much sacred
music and many instrumental and orchestral
works.   DENIS ARNOLD

Martini, Johann Paul Aegidius [known as
Martini 'il Tedesco'] (*b* Freystadt, nr Nuremberg, 31 Aug. 1741; *d* Paris, 10 Feb. 1816).
German composer who spent most of his life in
France. He went to Paris in 1764 and was
director of music to various members of the
nobility there, including the Prince of Condé.
He was nevertheless appointed an inspector of
the Paris Conservatoire during the revolutionary period, reverting to the service of the
Bourbons on their restoration. He wrote military music, operas, and some church music, but
is best remembered today for his song 'Plaisir
d'amour'.   DENIS ARNOLD

Martinů, Bohuslav (Jan) (*b* Polička, Bohemia,
8 Dec. 1890; *d* Liestal, Switzerland, 28 Aug.
1959). Czech composer. Born and brought up in
a small country town, he learned the violin and
began to compose while a boy. In 1906 the town
council sponsored him for further training at the
Prague Conservatory, but four years later he
was expelled for 'incorrigible negligence'. He
then earned his living by giving lessons and by
playing in the Czech Philharmonic Orchestra
until, in 1923, he left for Paris. There he took
private lessons with Roussel and lived humbly
for the next 17 years. He emigrated to America
in 1941 and spent his last few years in France
and Switzerland, since no appointment in
Czechoslovakia was forthcoming.

Martinů was an extremely prolific composer:
he left almost 400 works, ranging over every
musical genre. A large part of this output had
been produced before he went to Paris, but all
his important works date from after his studies
with Roussel, whose rhythmic propulsion,
soured tonality, and neoclassical forms left their
influence on his music. His six symphonies,

Martinů

many concertos, and numerous chamber pieces all exhibit the Roussel influence, modulated by the East European pathos of his own personality, for he remained a Czech composer despite his long exile. His operas, notably *Julietta* (1938), and large-scale vocal works, such as the *Field Mass* (1939) and *The Epic of Gilgamesh* (1954–5), were all composed to Czech texts. Other works, however, are more Parisian in manner, including the suite from the ballet *La revue de cuisine* (1927), with its tango and Charleston movements, as well as the orchestral pieces *Le jazz* and *Jazz-suite* (both 1928).

PAUL GRIFFITHS

FURTHER READING
Brian Large: *Martinů* (London, 1975).

Martín y Soler, Vicente (*b* Valencia, 2 May 1754; *d* St Petersburg, 11 Feb. 1806). Spanish composer. He studied music in Valencia, and then went to Madrid, where he began to write operas. In the late 1770s he was in Italy, but by 1785 he was living in Vienna, where he found himself competing with Mozart for the public ear. His opera *Una cosa rara* (performed 1786), to a libretto by Da Ponte, was a great success, and Mozart acknowledges this, ironically, by quoting from the first finale during the final act of *Don Giovanni*. In 1788 Martín y Soler was invited to St Petersburg by Catherine II, where he lived until 1790, and again from 1796 until his death. From 1790 until 1796 he was in London, where he worked at the King's Theatre and at the Salomon Opera Concerts. His music is primarily dramatic; as well as composing numerous operas, some to librettos by Metastasio, he produced some ballets for Italy and St Petersburg.

WENDY THOMPSON

Martucci, Giuseppe (*b* Capua, 6 Jan. 1856; *d* Naples, 1 June 1909). Italian composer. Son of a trombone player and bandmaster, he showed early talent as a pianist, entering the Naples Conservatory in 1867. After an early career as a concert pianist, he took to conducting, and he became one of the earliest champions of Wagner's music in Italy, directing the first Italian performance of *Tristan und Isolde* at Bologna in 1888. He was director of the music school there (1886–1902), giving many concerts of interesting music, and composing symphonies and concertos in the Germanic style. He spent the last seven years of his life as head of the Naples Conservatory.

DENIS ARNOLD

Martyrdom of St Magnus, The. Chamber opera in one act by Peter Maxwell Davies to his own libretto after George Mackay Brown's *Magnus*. It is for mezzo-soprano, tenor, two baritones, bass, and chamber ensemble and was first performed in 1977 in St Magnus Cathedral, Kirkwall, Orkney.

Martyre de Saint Sébastien, Le ('The Martyrdom of St Sebastian'). Incidental music by Debussy for a five-act mystery play by D'Annunzio. For soprano, two contraltos, chorus, and orchestra, it was composed in 1911; Debussy's friend André Caplet helped with the orchestration.

Marx, Joseph (Rupert Rudolf) (*b* Graz, 11 May 1882; *d* Graz, 3 Sept. 1964). Austrian composer. He studied with E. W. Degner at Graz University and in 1914 was appointed professor of theory and composition at the Vienna Music Academy, where he taught for much of his life. His works include a large number of songs in a style influenced by Wolf. No less traditionalist are his orchestral and chamber pieces (including three string quartets), though there are often touches of Debussyan harmony.

PAUL GRIFFITHS

Mary, Queen of Scots. 1. Opera in three acts by Thea Musgrave to her own libretto based on Amalia Elguera's play *Moray*. It was first performed in Edinburgh in 1977.
  2. Ballet by John McCabe, first performed in Glasgow in 1975.

Masaniello. Name usually given in Britain to Auber's five-act opera *La muette de Portici*

('The Dumb Girl of Portici'), to a libretto by Scribe and Delavigne. It was first performed in Paris in 1828. Its performance in Brussels in 1830 led to a Belgian revolt (the plot being based on a Neapolitan uprising against Spanish oppressors in 1647).

Mascagni, Pietro (*b* Livorno, 7 Dec. 1863; *d* Rome, 2 Aug. 1945). Italian composer. He was the son of a baker who would have liked him to become a lawyer, but an uncle arranged for him to study music and in 1882 he entered the Milan Conservatory where he studied with Ponchielli. He left after two years, and for the next few years he conducted a touring company giving operetta before marrying and settling in Cerignola in Puglia. He composed *Guglielmo Ratcliff* largely while on tour and then *Cavalleria rusticana*, this latter being entered by his wife in the competition held by the publisher Sonzogno for a one-act opera in 1888. It won, was produced in Rome in 1890, and had an immediate success, so that it was soon performed all over the world. Although it is today usually associated with Leoncavallo's *Pagliacci*, it is a better work than Leoncavallo's, with a genuine flair for popular melody approaching Italian folk-song, a rich orchestral sound, and real (as opposed to intellectually observed) passion.

Like Leoncavallo, he was never to have a similar success, but his other operas are by no means attempts at exploiting this 'realistic' vein. *L'amico Fritz* (1891), an undramatic piece set in Alsace, disappointed those who expected Mascagni to continue in the style of *Cavalleria rusticana*, and there were several flops before his

Mascagni

next success *Iris* (1899), a piece with a Japanese setting, which exploits exoticism several years before Puccini's *Madama Butterfly*. Sonzogno's attempt at a publicity stunt, whereby *Le maschere* was given a multiple première at seven theatres in 1901, had little effect; but it is interesting that this attempt to use the old *commedia dell'arte* pre-dates operas with the same idea by Busoni (*Arlecchino*, 1914-16) and Malipiero (several pieces, including *Tre commedie goldoniane*, 1920-2). His only later work which can be said to have achieved success is *Il piccolo Marat* (1921). Mascagni was a competent conductor of orchestral music as well as opera. When in 1929 Toscanini resigned from La Scala as a protest against Fascism, Mascagni took over certain of his duties and was thereafter tarred with the brush of being a supporter of Mussolini. He died in a shabby Roman hotel the year after that regime had perished, unhonoured and despised by Italian musicians in general: in which state his music has remained. As with Leoncavallo, it is difficult to see his lesser operas (though *Iris* is occasionally revived), and critics who study the scores complain of the 'stressing of the erotic to the exclusion of other feelings' and of 'vulgar melody'. But his operas are often based on original ideas and he had a better grasp of drama than Leoncavallo, so it may be that some would repay performance.   DENIS ARNOLD

Mascherata [*mascarata, mascherada*] (It.). 'Mascarade'. 1. An entertainment, popular in Florence in the Renaissance, in which masked performers mimed to musical accompaniment from carnival floats.

2. A kind of *villanella*, also related to street performances in the Carnival season; many such pieces were written by Lassus.

Maske. Old spelling of *masque. When found as the title of an instrumental piece, it probably implied that the piece was suitable for use in a masque.

Masnadieri, I ('The Robbers'). Opera in four acts by Verdi to a libretto by Maffei after Schiller's play *Die Räuber* (1781). It was first performed in London in 1847 (with Jenny Lind).

Mason, Daniel Gregory (*b* Brookline, Mass., 20 Nov. 1873; *d* Greenwich, Conn., 4 Dec. 1953). American composer. A grandson of the American musician Lowell Mason (1792-1872), he studied with Paine at Harvard and later with Chadwick and Percy Goetschius; he also had lessons with d'Indy in Paris in 1913. In 1909 he had been appointed to the staff at Columbia University, where he became professor of music

(1929–42). His works show an adaptation of European methods (ranging from Brahms to d'Indy) to American materials and subjects: his third and final symphony is subtitled 'A Lincoln Symphony', and he wrote a string quartet on Negro themes. He was also the author of many books on music.   PAUL GRIFFITHS

Mason, John (*d c.*1548). English cleric and composer. He may have worked at Eton before serving as *informator choristarum* at Magdalen College, Oxford, between 1508 and 1510; during this time he was awarded the Oxford B.Mus. After a brief period at the Chapel Royal, he held posts successively at Chichester and Hereford cathedrals, being appointed treasurer of the latter in 1545. Although surviving incomplete, his four known works—extended Latin antiphons for the Catholic rite —have received critical acclaim.   JOHN MILSOM

Masonic Music by Mozart. Mozart, a Freemason in a Vienna lodge, composed several works for masonic purposes, chief of which are: *Maurerische Trauermusik* ('Masonic Funeral Music'), K 477 (1785); the cantata *Die ihr des unermesslichen Weltalls Schöpfer ehrt*, K 619 (1791); the song *Lied zur Gesellenreise*, K 468 (1785); the cantata *Dir Seele des Weltalls*, K 429 (1785); the choruses *Ihr unsre neuen Leiter*, K 484 (1785), *Lasst uns mit geschlungnen Händen*, K 623a (1791), and *Laut verkünde unsre Freude*, K 623 (1791); the song *Lobegesang auf die feierliche Johannisloge*, K 148 (?1775–6); the cantata *Die Maurerfreude*, K 471 (1785); and the chorus *Zerfliesset heut', geliebte Brüder*, K 483 (1785).

Masque. A type of courtly entertainment used to celebrate special events in England during the 16th and 17th centuries. It consisted of dancing, speech, and song brought together in an allegorical 'device' in honour of the King or a prominent courtier. Nearly all masques were produced to celebrate a special occasion, such as a dynastic marriage, a state visit, or just the Christmas season. The masque differs from spoken drama or opera in that the action is carried forward by dance rather than by speech or song. The main characters, called 'masquers', were aristocratic amateurs who danced their roles, often led by a member of the royal family.

The masque had its origin in the 'disguisings' of Henry VIII's court, which were little more than evenings of social dancing clothed in flimsy allegory. Although a number of masque-like entertainments are known from the reign of Elizabeth, the masque proper came of age during the reign of James I. Many early Jacobean masques were the product of collaborations between such writers as Ben Jonson and

Inigo Jones's costume design for Queen Camilla, 'Masque of Queens'.

Thomas Campion, the architect and designer Inigo Jones, and composers such as Alfonso Ferrabosco (ii), John Coprario, and Robert Johnson. The best masques of this period, such as Campion's *Lord Hayes Masque* (1607) and Jonson's *Masque of Queens* (1609) and *Oberon* (1611), display a harmonious blend of their diverse elements that has never been surpassed. During the reign of Charles I the masque increased in length, complexity, magnificence, and cost with a new generation of collaborators, including the writers James Shirley and William Davenant and the composers William and Henry Lawes. During the 1630s masques like Shirley's *The Triumph of Peace* (1634) and Davenant's *Britannia triumphans* (1638) became a visible sign of the court absolutism and extravagance that contributed not a little to the Puritan revolution and to Charles I's downfall. The Banqueting House that still stands in Whitehall—built by Inigo Jones especially for the performance of masques—was chosen with a fitting sense of irony for Charles's execution in

King James I before the Whitehall Banqueting House, then under construction, portrait (c.1620) by Paul van Somer.

1649. As a court form, the masque barely survived the Civil War, though intimate masques continued to be performed in country houses and schools well into the Restoration period. The most important works of this type are undoubtedly Milton's *Comus* with music by Henry Lawes, produced at Ludlow in 1634 in honour of the Earl of Bridgewater, and Shirley's *Cupid and Death* with music by Christopher Gibbons and Matthew Locke, performed in London in 1653 and 1659. *Cupid and Death* is the only masque for which the music survives more or less complete.

It is often said that the masque is merely an imitation of the Italian *ballo* or the French *ballet de cour*. While it is true that the visual aspects of many masques are inspired by Italian Renaissance versions of classical antiquity, the other elements—dance, speech, and above all music—owe little or nothing to foreign models. Musical similarities between English masques and French ballets seem to be the product of similar circumstances rather than of direct contact.

Masque music was nearly always a collaboration between several composers and arrangers, partly because masques were frequently put together very quickly and partly because each element of the music—the songs, the dances, and the incidental instrumental music—was performed by a separate ensemble of royal musicians. The ensembles were spatially separated and normally never heard together, though Thomas Campion, notably in *Lord Hayes Masque*, experimented with polychoral effects in the Italian manner. Thus these three elements are best considered separately.

Masques were constructed around a series of formal dances or 'entries' performed at intervals during the entertainment. There were normally five of these, corresponding to some extent to the five acts of a spoken play. The central part of the masque consisted of three entries danced by the masquers to specially composed and choreographed music. A fourth entry, called the

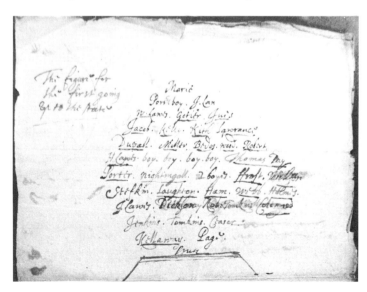

One of Whitelocke's stage plans for Shirley's 'Triumph of Peace' (1634), showing the positions of the soloists and choir.

'revels', consisted of social dances between the masquers and members of the audience. A fifth entry, or 'antimasque', was danced by professionals taking comic or grotesque characters such as *commedia dell'arte* figures, demons, witches, or even birds and animals. Dance music was normally provided by the court string orchestra, though antimasque dances were sometimes played by wind instruments. The main dances are usually written in the form of almans, with two repeated sections, though sometimes a third section in quick triple time was added. Their style is brisk and airy, with clear tonal harmonies. Antimasque dances express the grotesque and the comic by the sudden contrast of different tempos. Many of them are, in effect, patchworks made up from fragments of different dances.

The songs in Jacobean and Caroline masques were designed largely to introduce and comment on the dances. They were performed by singers of the royal music who appeared on stage in the guise of attendants or priests. Normally they accompanied themselves with lutes—hence the very large numbers of lutes sometimes mentioned in descriptions of masques. Masque songs tend to be very similar to ordinary songs of the period—indeed many of them are found in contemporary lute-song collections—though large ensembles and large halls tended to encourage a simple declamatory style which some scholars, rather unnecessarily, have seen as inspired by Italian monody. The masques of the 1630s show that composers like William Lawes were experimenting with long sequences of continuous solo and ensemble vocal music in an operatic manner. *Cupid and Death* develops this process still further, and was probably a prototype for Blow's all-sung masque *Venus and Adonis* (*c*.1682) and Purcell's *Dido and Aeneas* (1689).

Little can be said about the third musical element in English masques: the 'loud music' played by wind instruments which was used to cover the noise of stage machinery in scene changes. Unfortunately, none of it seems to have survived.   PETER HOLMAN

FURTHER READING
Edward J. Dent: *Foundations of English Opera: a Study of Musical Drama in England during the Seventeenth Century* (Cambridge, 1928, reprinted 1965).

Mass (Fr.: *messe*; Ger.: *Messe*; It.: *messa*; Lat.: *missa*). The principal service of the Roman Catholic Church. The following account refers to the full sung form of this Eucharistic service, known as High Mass, or *Missa solemnis*, as it was from *c*.1000 until the 1960s, when changes were made in the wake of the Second Vatican Council. A *Missa cantata*, or sung Mass, would have the same musical layout, but with fewer clergy and less ceremonial. Low Mass (*Missa lecta* or *Missa privata*) is celebrated without music, unless congregational hymns are sung.

1. *Structure of the Mass*. The various musical items belong either to the Ordinary, whose sections make up the musical entity normally referred to as a Mass and whose texts do not vary, or to the Proper, whose texts do vary according to the Church calendar. The following table sets out the sequence of events at High Mass; capital letters indicate the sections of the Ordinary and lower-case those of the Proper, while the portions intoned by the clergy are in parentheses (no mention is made of the various prayers recited silently).

Mass of the Catechumens
  Introit
  KYRIE
  GLORIA (except in Advent and Lent)
  (Collect)
  (Epistle)
  Gradual
  Alleluia (or, in penitential seasons, Tract)
  (Gospel)
  CREDO
Mass of the Faithful
  Offertory
  (Preface)
  SANCTUS/HOSANNA/BENEDICTUS/HOSANNA
  (*Pater noster*)
  AGNUS DEI
  Communion
  (Postcommunion)
  ITE MISSA EST (although strictly part of the Ordinary, this section is rarely set by composers)

It will be seen from the above that the sections of the Ordinary are widely separated, and that the effect of a continuous concert performance of a Mass written for liturgical use may be somewhat different from that envisaged by the composer.

2. *Medieval and Renaissance Masses*. The earliest notated music for the Mass, both Ordinary and Proper, is plainchant. There are 18 plainchant settings of the Kyrie, Gloria, Sanctus, Agnus Dei, and Ite missa est, each for a specific season or type of feast, and six separate Credo settings, most of which, in their present form, date from the 10th to 12th centuries, though some, including the well-known *Missa de angelis* and Credo III, are considerably later. The earliest polyphonic music for the Mass, such as the *organa* of Léonin and Pérotin, consists in fact of settings of the Proper, the Ordinary continuing to be chanted to plainchant, but in the 14th century this situation was reversed and,

perhaps for obvious practical reasons, composers increasingly turned their attention to the unvarying portions of the liturgy. Most of the 14th-century Mass music which survives consists of individual movements rather than complete settings of the Ordinary; in England this custom of setting single sections survived into the 15th century, with Dunstable and his contemporaries. The earliest complete polyphonic Mass known to survive is the so-called Tournai Mass (c.1300), which is probably the work of a number of composers. The first setting by a single composer is Machaut's *Messe de Nostre Dame*, a work of masterly craftsmanship from the later 14th century; the Kyrie, Sanctus, and Agnus Dei are based on plainchant and use contemporary techniques of isorhythm. The next surviving complete Mass settings date from the 15th century.

During the 15th and 16th centuries the polyphonic Mass was the largest and most important musical form in existence, and most Catholic composers—other than those who confined themselves entirely to secular music—concerned themselves with it to some extent. The Masses of many major composers such as Dufay, Ockeghem, Josquin, and Palestrina form an important part of their output, and the overall development of the polyphonic style can be clearly traced through the Masses of successive generations of composers up to the end of the 16th century.

The 15th century saw an increasing tendency not only towards the composition of complete Masses, but also towards giving these an overall unity, usually by the use of some kind of pre-existing material heard in all the movements; the majority of 16th-century Masses are based on existing music, and those that are not can often be recognized by such titles as *Missa quarti toni* or *Missa sine nomine*. Byrd's three Masses are of this type. The various kinds of pre-existing material may be summarized as follows:

(*a*) *Plainchant.* A small number of polyphonic Masses have each movement based on a different plainchant; a specific type of this is the *Missa de Beata Virgine*, examples of which are found in the work of Josquin and Morales, among others.

The majority of plainchant-based Masses are of the so-called *cantus firmus type, in which the same plainchant is used in each movement, appearing either in one voice only, usually the tenor, as in Josquin's *Missa Ave Maris stella*, or in all voices, as in his *Missa Pange lingua*.

(*b*) *Secular melodies.* Masses based on secular melodies are usually also of the *cantus firmus*

Pl. 1. Mass attended by François I and other members of the French court, woodcut from one of the seven volumes of Masses published by Attaingnant in 1532.

type; they are particularly characteristic of the 15th and earlier 16th centuries. Dufay's *Missa 'Se la face ay pale'* is an example of a Mass based on a melody from a *chanson* (his own), but melodies of unknown origin, possibly folktunes, were also used. The most commonly employed of these was the famous 'L'homme armé' melody. More than 30 'L'homme armé' Masses survive, by composers such as Dufay, Ockeghem, Obrecht, Josquin, de la Rue, Morales, and Palestrina. Several English composers utilized the 'Western Wynde' melody; Taverner's eponymous Mass (which, as was the custom at that time in England, has no Kyrie) is a remarkable *tour-de-force* of variation form. In a 'quodlibet' Mass, such as Isaac's *Missa carminum*, a selection of melodies is used.

(*c*) *Invented themes.* These might be drawn from the hexachord, or devised by applying *solmization syllables to the vowels in an appropriate phrase, as on Josquin's *Missa Hercules dux Ferrariae* (Ex. 1); they would then be used as *cantus firmi*.

Ex. 1

Derivation of the theme of *Missa Hercules dux Ferrariae* (as it appears in the Kyrie).

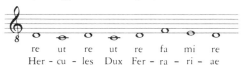

(*d*) *Complete pieces.* The type of Mass based on a complete polyphonic composition, whose material might be broken up and used in many different ways, with much or little alteration, has tended to be known as a 'parody Mass'. It became popular in the later 15th century, when the models were usually polyphonic *chansons*, as with Josquin's *Missa 'D'ung aultre amer'*, on a *chanson* by Ockeghem, but in the 16th century motets were more commonly used, as with Palestrina's *Missa Assumpta est Maria*, or Victoria's *Missa O quam gloriosum*, based on their own respective motets (though many of Lassus's Masses are still based on *chansons*). By the later 16th century this type of Mass was probably the most common; some three-quarters of Palestrina's Masses use parody technique.

The style of Mass composition was to some extent affected by the *Council of Trent, which insisted that the text must be clearly audible, so that composers such as Palestrina employed a more syllabic and declamatory style, and which brought to an end the overt use of secular pieces as models for Masses.

3. *The Baroque.* During the Baroque, the rise of opera as the main form of vocal music, and the development of larger-scale instrumental forms, caused Mass composition to lose its pre-eminent position, and few composers cultivated it with the assiduity of their predecessors. The stylistic changes of the early Baroque led to an increasing disparity between Masses written entirely in the traditional polyphonic manner (*stile antico*), whose principal concession to modernity was the use of the *basso continuo* and the gradual adoption of a wider harmonic vocabulary, and the Mass in modern style, with solo voices and instrumental *obbligati*, which eventually developed into the later Baroque and Classical orchestral Mass.

A further disparity between different types of Mass setting which grew up later in the Baroque period was that between the so-called *Missa solemnis* (the term being used in this instance not in its strict liturgical sense but purely with reference to the degree of musical elaboration involved), on an extended scale, with the longer sections divided into a number of movements, and requiring a large number of performers, and the *Missa brevis*, a more compact setting, with the words dispatched as expeditiously as possible, especially in the Gloria and Credo, and demanding much less extravagant resources.

Monteverdi's three Masses use the *stile antico* (that of 1610 is in fact a parody Mass based on the motet *In illo tempore* by Gombert), and his Roman contemporaries, such as Anerio and the Nanino brothers, also employed it extensively; increasing use was made of multiple separated choirs, with composers such as Benevoli producing Masses in 16 or more parts. This tradition was continued by later composers such as Carissimi (probably the last composer to write a Mass on 'L'homme armé'); Lotti, who produced both complete Masses and isolated Mass movements (such as the well-known *Crucifixus*); and Alessandro Scarlatti, eight of whose ten Masses are in the *stile antico*. Eighteenth-century composers such as Fux continued to cultivate the *stile antico* Mass, which was suitable for use on weekdays and at penitential seasons when large-scale orchestral Masses were neither practical nor appropriate, and in 19th-century Germany the *Cecilian Movement, which aimed at the reform of church music in the direction of greater plainness and simplicity redolent of a past age, helped to keep the tradition alive. Liszt's *Missa choralis* for choir and organ is one of the better-known examples of this type of Mass.

The only Mass music by Monteverdi in the modern style is the magnificent Gloria for seven voices and instruments, written in thanksgiving for the end of the Venetian plague of the 1630s. However, orchestral Masses (often omitting or greatly shortening the Sanctus and Agnus Dei, as was the Venetian custom) by his north-Italian contemporaries do survive, such as that of

Alessandro Grandi (1630), which uses soloists, chorus, and *obbligato* instruments. Cavalli's *Messa concertata* is in the same Venetian tradition, and exemplifies the mid-Baroque trend towards more extended Gloria and Credo settings and lyrical solo writing. A more massive, solidly polychoral type of Mass was cultivated by later 17th-century Bolognese composers, such as Colonna. The Italian style also spread to the German-speaking Catholic countries north of the Alps, and the festal Masses of composers such as Biber (who may be the author of the huge 53-part *Missa salisburgensis* formerly attributed to Benevoli) make much use of exciting instrumental colours, including high trumpets, and of the dialogue between solo voices and chorus that was to become characteristic of the 18th-century Viennese style. In France, Louis XIV's preference for Low Mass led to the cultivation of the motet as the main form of church music; only Charpentier, whose *Messe de minuit* is based on French Christmas songs and is thoroughly French in style, was greatly concerned with the Mass.

The so-called 'Neapolitan' or 'cantata' Mass style, which owed much to contemporary opera, and in which the text was divided into many short sections set as self-contained solo arias and choruses in a variety of styles (often including *stile antico*), had an important influence on 18th-century Mass composition. In particular it established the tradition of ending the Gloria and Credo with an extended Amen fugue. The well-known D major Gloria of Vivaldi (who wrote a number of Mass movements, but no complete settings) is of this type. The greatest example of this type of Mass is the Bach B minor Mass; its Kyrie and Gloria originally stood alone, as a Lutheran Mass (the Lutheran church retained these portions of the Mass in their

Pl. 2. Depiction of a musical performance (probably a Mass) in an 18th-century Catholic church, engraving by J. E. Mansfeld.

original languages, and four other such Masses by Bach survive), the remaining sections being added later.

4. *From the 18th Century to the Present Day*. The Viennese Mass of the 18th century combines operatic elements from the cantata Mass with features such as dialogue between soloists and chorus within the same movement, a characteristic choral style in which a homophonic but tuneful chorus part is accompanied by repeated figuration patterns for the violins, and, as the century progressed, a tendency to organize choral movements on principles similar to those developing in the symphony and concerto. The large-scale Masses of the first half of the century, by composers such as Fux, Caldara, and Reutter (the teacher of Haydn), still have Glorias and Credos divided into many movements, and make much use of the extended solo aria and a large orchestra; these elements are on the whole missing from the smaller-scale Masses intended for ordinary churches which were produced in great quantity at this time. These latter often look forward to Haydn, showing a talent for the integration of solo and tutti voices, and for unifying the longer sections with ingenious use of repeated material.

Thanks to the conditions of his work at Salzburg, many of Mozart's Masses are in the very compact *Missa brevis* form, as are some of Haydn's early ones—in some, such as Haydn's *Missa brevis S. Joannis de Deo*, the urge to set the Gloria and Credo as rapidly as possible causes each voice to sing a different set of words simultaneously. Mozart's unfinished C minor Mass is a late example of the cantata type, written by a great operatic composer, but the Gloria of the 'Coronation' Mass (K317) shows him organizing a choral movement in a symphonic manner. There is much use of such symphonic structures in Haydn's last six Masses, written between 1796 and 1802 for the Esterházy family; though some operatic elements still survive, the long sections are now divided into fewer movements and these are closely organized on a symphonic basis, with the soloists used as an ensemble rather than as individuals. There is careful attention to the setting of dramatic or emotive parts of the text, especially the 'Et incarnatus . . . crucifixus' passage in the Credo.

Beethoven's *Missa solemnis*, intended, though not completed in time, for the installation of Archduke Rudolf as Archbishop of Olmütz (now Olomouc) in 1820, is a natural successor to Haydn's late symphonic Masses and, like them, was considered suitable for liturgical use on a festal occasion. There are symphonic elements also in Schubert's large-scale Masses in E♭ and in A♭, and his use of solo voices,

almost always as a group, owes nothing to opera. His G major Mass, however, like those of contemporary Austrians such as Weber, is in a much simpler, even pastoral, vein.

Cherubini, whose eight surviving Masses were the first important corpus of Mass music by a French composer to appear for many years, also uses his solo voices as an ensemble, especially in the fine D minor Mass of 1811, in scale similar to Beethoven's *Missa solemnis*, but using the chorus for dramatic gestures in a way not explored by Viennese composers. His 1825 Mass, however, contains theatrical elements which point the way towards the distinction between concert Masses and those really intended for liturgical use which was to become more marked as the 19th century progressed. Rossini's *Petite messe solennelle* (with accompaniment for two pianos and harmonium instead of orchestra) is typical of the Italianate operatic Mass, mixing elaborate solo arias with contrapuntal, sometimes *stile antico*, choruses. Liszt's Mass for the coronation of the King of Hungary in 1867, intended for liturgical use, gives much of the thematic material to the orchestra, while Gounod, whose Masses were popular in Catholic churches in England as well as on the Continent, avoided florid solo writing and entrusted a greater part of the thematic material to the chorus. Bruckner, in his Masses with orchestra (such as the F minor), attempts to combine modern elements with characteristics of Renaissance polyphony and even plainchant.

Renaissance polyphony continued to exercise a strong influence on 20th-century composers of Masses, perhaps largely because of the *Motu proprio* (1903) of Pope Pius X, which emphasized that plainchant and polyphony were the true music of the Church and discouraged the use of orchestral Masses. Duruflé's *Missa cum jubilo* is a good example of a modern Mass setting very strongly influenced by plainchant, and Vaughan Williams's G minor Mass has strong affinities with Tudor polyphony. These, like Britten's *Missa brevis* for boys' voices, have a liturgical function, but though Stravinsky claimed that his Mass for chorus and wind instruments is liturgical in spirit, it is more usually heard in the concert hall.

The Latin Ordinary survives unaltered in the new form of Mass promulgated in 1970 by Pope Paul VI, so that where sung Latin celebrations still take place any appropriate setting from the past can still be used. Many ephemeral settings of the new vernacular texts, often requiring congregational participation, have been produced, but the new rites do not as yet seem to have stimulated the production of any very distinguished music.   ELIZABETH ROCHE

Massaino, Tiburtio (*b* Cremona, before 1550;

d Piacenza or Lodi, in or after 1609). Italian organist and composer. He worked at various courts and churches in northern Italy, Austria, and Germany in the late 16th and early 17th centuries. He composed a great deal of church music, but is best known today for his music for instrumental ensemble, which includes a canzona for 16 trombones and another for four violins and four lutes. DENIS ARNOLD

Massenet, Jules (Émile Frédéric) (*b* St Étienne, 12 May 1842; *d* Paris, 13 Aug. 1912). French composer. The son of an industrialist, he was first taught music by his mother, entering the Paris Conservatoire in 1851, specializing in piano. He won the Prix de Rome (largely on the recommendation of Berlioz) in 1862 and spent two years at the Villa Medici, followed by some time in Germany and Austro-Hungary. On his return to Paris, he married and kept himself and his wife by small commissions and playing percussion in the orchestra at the Opéra until his works began to make some headway. His earlier stage works were written for the Opéra-Comique but his first great success was a grand spectacular piece for the Opéra, *Le Roi de Lahore* (1877), which was soon known throughout Europe. Thereafter Massenet composed a stream of highly popular operas which made him one of the richest musicians of his time. *Hérodiade* (1881), *Manon* (1884), *Le Cid* (1885), *Werther* (1892), and *Thaïs* (1894) show his gifts at their best, being works of charm and theatrical

Massenet (1868)

effectiveness, even if, in some cases, they scarcely match the seriousness of the subjects which they treat. His later works were not quite as successful, probably because of the post-Wagnerian influences on French music, which made his music less fashionable, though it is noticeable that he was not content merely to follow his former paths exactly. *Le jongleur de Notre Dame* (1902), for example, had an all-male cast, in spite of Massenet's reputation for providing sensuous music for his heroines. Massenet was much honoured in his lifetime, being made the youngest member of the French Académie in 1879, eventually becoming its President. He taught in the Conservatoire, and had a number of distinguished pupils, including Reynaldo Hahn, Charles Koechlin, and Florent Schmitt. He died in Paris and was buried at the village of Égreville, where he had his country house. DENIS ARNOLD

Mässig (Ger.). 1. 'Moderate', 'moderately'; *mässiger*, 'more moderate'. The term is sometimes used as a tempo indication, meaning *andante*. 2. 'In the style of', e.g. *Marschmässig* ('in march style').

Massine, Léonide [Massin, Leonid Fyodorovich] (*b* Moscow, 8 Aug. 1895; *d* Weseke bei Borken, Westphalia, 15 Mar. 1979). Diaghilev's most important choreographer after Fokine. For the Ballets Russes he created *Parade*, *La boutique fantasque* (Rossini/Respighi, 1919), and *The Three-cornered Hat* (Falla, 1919); they are all still performed in his original choreography, as are some later works, including *Mam'zelle Angot* (Lecocq, 1943). His so-called 'symphonic ballets' *Choréartium* and *Les présages* (both 1934) have been lost to the repertory, but their controversial use of symphonies by Brahms and Tchaikovsky respectively led to a wider use of concert music in dance forms. NOËL GOODWIN

Mass of Christ the King. Work by Williamson for soprano, mezzo-soprano, tenor, and bass soloists, chorus, and orchestra. It was first performed in part at the Gloucester Festival in 1977, and in complete form in Westminster Cathedral in 1978.

Mass of Life, A (*Eine Messe des Lebens*). Work by Delius for soprano, alto, tenor, and bass soloists, chorus, and orchestra, to a German text selected by F. Cassirer from Nietzsche's *Also sprach Zarathustra*. It was composed in 1904–5 and the second part was first performed in 1908; the first complete performance (in English) was a year later. Delius also composed *Mitternachtslied* (1898, unpublished), a setting for baritone, male chorus, and orchestra of Zarathustra's Night-song.

Master of the King's (Queen's) Music. Since the first half of the 17th century, the title of the musician put in charge of the sovereign's private band of musicians. Nowadays the duties entail only the occasional composition of music for royal or state occasions, but previously the private band would accompany the King or Queen on their journeys. In the reign of Charles II the private band was developed into a string orchestra of 24 players in emulation of Louis XIV's *Vingt-quatre Violons. Holders of the title from 1625 to the present include Nicholas Lanier (1625–49, 1660–6), Louis Grabu (1666), Nicholas Staggins (1674), John Eccles (1700), Maurice Green (1735), William Boyce (1755), John Stanley (1779), William Parsons (1786), William Shield (1817), Christian Kramer (1829), Franz Cramer (1834), George Frederick Anderson (1848), William George Cusins (1870), Walter Parratt (1893), Edward Elgar (1924), Walford Davies (1934–41), Arnold Bax (1942–52), Arthur Bliss (1953), and Malcolm Williamson (1975).

Mastersingers. See *Meistersinger*.

Mastersingers of Nuremberg, The. See *Meistersinger von Nürnberg, Die*.

Matelotte (from Fr. *matelot*, 'sailor'). A Dutch sailors' dance, similar to the *hornpipe, performed in wooden shoes with the dancers' arms interlaced behind their backs.

Mathias, William (James) (*b* Whitland, Carmarthenshire, 1 Nov. 1934). Welsh composer. He studied at University College, Aberystwyth (1952–6) and with Lennox Berkeley at the Royal Academy of Music (1956–9). In 1959 he took a post at University College, Bangor, where in 1970 he was appointed professor of music. His large output includes contributions to the standard genres of orchestral and chamber music as well as a quantity of choral music. The style is diatonic, eclectic, and often vigorous, influenced by Bartók, Messiaen, Hindemith, and others.

PAUL GRIFFITHS

FURTHER READING
Malcolm Boyd: *William Mathias* (Cardiff, 1974).

Mathis der Maler ('Matthias the Painter'). Opera in seven scenes by Hindemith to his own libretto based on the life of Matthias Grünewald (*c*.1460–1530) and his altar-piece at Isenheim. It was composed between 1933 and 1935; the Nazis banned the German première in 1935 so it was first performed in Zurich in 1938. Hindemith wrote a symphony with the same title (1934), each of its three movements representing one of the panels from the Isenheim

altar-piece: 1. 'Engelkonzert' ('Angels' Concert'), 2. 'Grablegung' ('Burial'), 3. 'Versuchung des heiligen Antonius' ('Temptation of St Anthony').

Matin, Le; Midi, Le; Soir, Le ('Morning, Noon, Evening'). Haydn's Symphonies Nos. 6, 7, and 8, in D major, C major, and G major, probably composed in 1761. The last movement of *Le soir* is also known as 'La tempête' ('The storm'), the whole symphony sometimes being referred to as *Le soir et la tempête*.

Matins. The first of the *Office Hours of the Roman Catholic Church; also an alternative name for Morning Prayer in the Anglican Church (see *Common Prayer, Book of*).

Matrimonio segreto, Il ('The Secret Marriage'). Opera in two acts by Cimarosa to a libretto by G. Bertati after Colman and Garrick's comedy *The Clandestine Marriage* (1766). It was first performed in Vienna in 1792.

Matteis, Nicola (*b* ? Naples; *d* ? London, ? *c*.1707). Italian violinist and composer. He arrived in England *c*.1670, and in his *Diary* for 19 November 1674 Evelyn noted, 'I heard that stupendous violin, Signor Nicholao ... whom I never heard mortal man exceed on that instrument. He had a stroke so sweet, and made it speak like the voice of a man, and, when he pleased, like a concert of several instruments. He did wonders upon a note, and was an excellent composer.' Matteis's ability was also much praised by Roger North, according to whom Matteis became so wealthy and sought-after that he bought a grand house, and 'lived luxuriously, which brought diseases upon him of which he died'. Matteis's most interesting works are the 'ayres' for one or two violins and bass, including suites of dances and more serious, fugal pieces. In 1682 he published a treatise, *The False Consonances of Musick: Instructions for Playing a Thorough-Base upon the Guitarre*, and in 1696 and 1699 two volumes entitled *A Collection of New Songs*.

His son, **Nicholas Matteis** (*d* ? Shrewsbury, ? *c*.1749), was also a violinist. After a long period spent on the Continent, including about 37 years at the Habsburg court in Vienna, he returned to London, where he taught the violin and French, and, according to Burney, then settled in Shrewsbury. His works include violin sonatas which show the influence of Corelli.

WENDY THOMPSON

Matteo da Perugia (*d c*.1418). Italian composer, probably born in Perugia. Nothing is known about his life until 1402, when he was a singer at Milan Cathedral and moved into the service of Cardinal Petros Filargo di Candia (later chosen as Pope in an unsuccessful attempt to end the Schism); after the latter's death in 1410 Matteo may have worked for his rival, the antipope John XXIII, until finally returning to Milan a few years before his death. His surviving music comprises Mass movements and polyphonic songs in both French and Italian. Like that of Ciconia, his most important contemporary, Matteo's style blends French and Italian features; several works are especially advanced in their structural use of imitation, forward-looking harmonic language, and lack of rhythmic artifice.   JOHN MILSOM

Mattheson, Johann (b Hamburg, 28 Sept. 1681; d Hamburg, 17 Apr. 1764). German critic, theorist, and composer. He was the son of a tax collector, and showed a wide range of talents at an early age, embracing not only music, but also modern languages, law, and political science. From 1696 to 1705 he sang and conducted in the Hamburg opera company, which in 1699 produced his first opera, *Die Plejades*. In 1703 Handel arrived in Hamburg, and the two men instantly struck up a friendship, which was only temporarily marred when they quarrelled over which of them should play the harpsichord in a performance of Mattheson's *Cleopatra*. In the same year they were both invited to apply for the post of organist at Lübeck, in succession to Buxtehude; they turned the post down for the same reason: neither was prepared to marry Buxtehude's daughter, whose hand went with the position.

From 1706 to 1741 Mattheson was secretary to the English ambassador to Hamburg, Sir John Wick; from 1715 to 1728 he also served as *Kapellmeister* to Hamburg Cathedral, but increasing deafness forced him to give up the post. The rest of his life was occupied mainly with writing, and by the time he died at the age of 83 he had published several books which offer valuable information on the state of German music of the period, especially in Hamburg. The most important are *Das neu-eröffnete Orchestre* (1713), *Critica musica* (1722-5), *Der musicalische Patriot* (1728), and a collection of musical biographies, the *Grundlage einer Ehren-Pforte* (1740), which also contains his autobiography. His theoretical writings include treatises on the thoroughbass and the important *Der vollkommene Capellmeister* (1739). Unfortunately, few of Mattheson's musical works survived the bombing of Hamburg in the Second World War.   WENDY THOMPSON

Mattinata (It.). A morning song; similar to the French *aubade.

Mattins. See *Matins*.

Mauduit, Jacques (b Paris, 16 Sept. 1557; d Paris, 21 Aug. 1627). French composer. He was a student of philosophy and languages, and taught himself music. As well as holding the position of royal secretary, he was a member of Baïf's Académie (see *Musique mesurée*) and conductor and organizer of many concerts in Paris, including the St Cecilia's Day celebrations at Notre Dame and ballets and other royal entertainments. His works include a volume of *Chansonettes mesurées de Jean-Antoine Baïf* (Paris, 1586) and one of *Psaumes mesurées à l'antique* (published by Mersenne in his *Quaestiones celeberrimae in Genesim*; Paris, 1623).
                    DENIS ARNOLD

Maultrommel (Ger.). 'Jew's-harp'.

Maurerische Trauermusik ('Masonic Funeral Music'). Work by Mozart, K 477, composed in 1785. It is scored for two oboes, clarinet, three basset horns, double bassoon, two horns, and strings, and was written for the funeral of two Viennese Freemasons.

Má Vlast ('My Fatherland'). Cycle of six symphonic poems by Smetana, composed in the 1870s. They are: (1) *Vyšehrad* ('The High Citadel'); (2) *Vltava* (River Moldau); (3) *Šárka* (leader of the Bohemian Amazons); (4) *Z Českých luhů a hájů* ('From Bohemia's Woods and Fields'); (5) *Tábor* (stronghold of the Hussites); and (6) *Blaník* (Valhalla of the Hussite heroes, a mountain in south Bohemia).

Mavra. Opera in one act by Stravinsky to a libretto by Kochno after Pushkin's poem *The Little House in Kolomna*. It was first performed in Paris in 1922.

Maw, (John) Nicholas (b Grantham, Lincolnshire, 5 Nov. 1935). English composer. He studied with Paul Steinitz and Lennox Berkeley at the Royal Academy of Music (1955-8) and with Nadia Boulanger and Max Deutsch in Paris (1958-9). In his music he has joined with such contemporaries as Richard Rodney Bennett in mediating between tonality and serialism, though his rich harmonic manner, sometimes suggestive of Berg or Strauss, is individual. His small output includes a full-length comic opera, *The Rising of the Moon* (1969-70), and various vocal and orchestral pieces.
                    PAUL GRIFFITHS

Maxima (Lat.). 14th-century term for the duplex long, a note-value ◼ found in Medieval music. See *Notation*, 4.

Maxixe (Port.). A lively Brazilian dance in duple time, danced by couples. It was popular in Europe in the early 19th century, and reappeared c.1911–13 as a type of *tango, showing both Negro and Latin American influence.

Mayr, (Johannes) Simon (b Mendorf, Bavaria, 14 June 1763; d Bergamo, 2 Dec. 1845). German composer. The son of an organist, who taught him in his early years, Mayr studied at the Jesuit College and then at the university in Ingoldstadt. In 1787 he went to Bergamo, where a patron, Count Pesenti, paid for him to go to Venice in 1789. Mayr was successful there as a composer of oratorios and church music, but on the death of his patron in 1793 he turned to opera composition, having such a success with *Saffo* (performed 1794) that he became one of the most sought-after composers until the rise of Rossini 20 years later. His operas combine the Italian manner of the time with a more enterprising use of the orchestra learnt from the music of the German/Austrian school. In 1802 he returned to Bergamo as *maestro di cappella* of the principal church, remaining there until his death in spite of attractive offers from Napoleon to go to France. In his later years he became blind, and wrote mostly church music. He was Donizetti's teacher from 1806 to 1815.

DENIS ARNOLD

Mazeppa. 1. Piano pieces by Liszt, one composed in 1840, the other in 1851 (as the fourth of the *Études d'exécution transcendante*). Liszt also used the title for a symphonic poem (1851) after Hugo, basing the music on the piano study; it was orchestrated with Raff and revised in 1854.

2. Opera in three acts by Tchaikovsky to a libretto by V. Burenin, revised by the composer, after Pushkin's *Poltava*. It was first performed in Moscow in 1884. Mazeppa (1644–1709) was a Russian historical character.

Mazurka. A traditional Polish folk dance, named after the Mazurs, who lived in the plains around Warsaw. The name embraces several types of dance, including the *kujawiak* and the *oberek*. The mazurka spread to Germany in the mid 18th century, then to Paris, and was in Britain by 1830 and in the USA soon after. It is in moderate triple time, with dotted rhythms and a tendency to accentuate the weak beats. It is generally danced by couples in multiples of four, performing variations on a few basic steps and positions, often with much improvisation. In the 19th century, the male dancers were expected to click their spurs together, stamp their heels, and clap their hands.

Chopin wrote over 50 mazurkas for piano in a great variety of styles, often exhibiting a high degree of chromaticism. Some are in the style of the *kujawiak*, others, such as Op. 56 No. 2, in that of the *oberek*. Mazurkas occur in Glinka's *A Life for the Tsar* and in Musorgsky's *Boris Godunov*. The Polish composer Szymanowski wrote mazurkas for the piano.

The 'polka-mazurka', a combination of two dances, differs from the *polka in its triple rhythm, and from the mazurka in having an accent on the third beat of each bar.

Mc. For names beginning 'Mc', see under 'Mac'.

M.d. Abbreviation for *main droite* (Fr.), *mano destra* (It.), 'right hand'.

Meane [mean, mene]. In early English music, a term for the middle part of a three-part polyphonic work.

Measure. 1. In American usage, a term equivalent to the British term 'bar' when used to refer to a metrical unit in notation; for 'bar-line' the American usage is 'bar'. See *Bar*.

2. In early English usage, a general term meaning 'dance'; more specifically, in 16th- and 17th-century England a moderately slow and stately dance in duple time.

Mechanical Copyright Protection Society Ltd, The. See *Copyright*, 6.

Mechanical Musical Instruments

1. Introduction
2. The Barrel
3. Early Barrel Organs and Organ Clocks
4. Hand-turned Barrel Organs

5. Orchestrions
6. Barrel Pianos
7. Musical Boxes
8. Perforated Card and Paper-roll Systems

1. *Introduction.* It has been estimated that, prior to the development of the gramophone, street barrel organs of one kind or another were responsible for more than 85 per cent of the music heard by the average town-dweller in the 19th century. As late as 1920, 70 per cent of the 364,000 pianos manufactured in the USA were player-pianos, while great numbers of people in

Europe preserved no childhood recollection of instrumental music other than that provided by a musical box of some kind.

The mechanical dissemination of music can be said to have begun with inventors such as Apollonius of Perga (3rd century BC), who was credited with having devised such automata as singing birds, operated by a water-wheel which also pumped air into a whistle. But to reproduce actual music mechanically, some form of continuous rotary motion must be accurately converted into the momentary movements needed for sounding each note as required. The classic device for achieving this is the pinned cylinder, by which the functions of a musician's fingers and keyboard are taken over by a rotating 'barrel' armed with projections which trip levers to actuate the different notes. This is first described in a 9th-century Arabic treatise for an organ, worked by water power. By the late 14th century the barrel was being used for music with bells (see *Bells*, 6); then from the 16th century onwards in mechanical organs (barrel organs) and musical clocks; and next, from the late 18th century, in the Swiss musical box in which the pins of the cylinder act directly on flexible steel tongues to produce the sound. During the 19th century the pinned barrel became largely superseded by the punched card for fair organs, and then through the perforated paper roll through which air is drawn to move the playing keys pneumatically (player-pianos).

2. *The Barrel*. English barrel organs of the 18th and 19th centuries (see also below, 4) show most simply how this works. The cylindrical wooden barrel, which may be up to 3′ long, lies horizontally, turned by a handle which simultaneously works the bellows placed underneath. The barrel is first marked round its circumference with lines, one for each note and spaced at regular intervals in alignment with a row of metal levers mounted in a fixed frame to actuate the pallets which admit air to the pipes. Into these lines are inserted pins or bridges of flat brass wire, each placed to trip its corresponding lever at the correct moments as the barrel rotates. The pins give short notes, while bridges (bent strips) of various lengths sustain. Pl. 2 illustrates a stage in pinning a passage full of elaborate French ornament.

In most of these barrel organs, and in organ clocks, a single major scale suffices, although sometimes one or two accidentals are provided. More important is to provide for a change of tune. If not too long, one tune can immediately follow another. But normally the marked lines for the first tune are spaced out to leave room for pinning other tunes between. To change the tune the barrel is shifted a little along its axis to

Pl. 1. Barrel organ of c.1810 at Shelland Church, Suffolk.

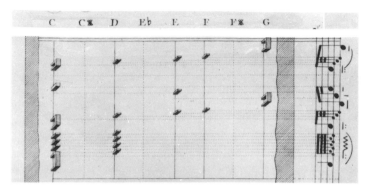

Pl. 2. Barrel-pinning (an example from Dom Bédos); the vertical lines mark the scale from C to G (dotted lines the black notes). On the right is a bar of music, and on the lines are the corresponding pins and (for the longer notes, here quaver or crotchet) the bridges.

bring a fresh set of pins in alignment with the actuating levers (a system already described in the 9th-century Arabic treatise mentioned above). Nine or more tunes are thus accommodated on the English barrels. Alternatively, the marked lines can spiral round the barrel, the axle of which then has a screw thread at one end so that while rotating it moves continuously in the opposite direction to the spirals and the tunes follow each other automatically. Most organs were supplied with at least three alternative barrels, stored in the bottom of the case. Domestic organs often add a percussion section of drum, cymbals, and triangle operated through extra pins in the barrel.

3. *Early Barrel Organs and Organ Clocks.* In the 16th and 17th centuries some mechanical organs were turned by water-wheel (described by Robert Fludd in 1618) and were set up in gardens in Italy and Austria. An early instance of a great musician providing music for such an instrument is Peter Philips, who arranged a madrigal by Striggio for the inventor Salomon de Caus—at least, this work appears in de Caus's book, *Les raisons des forces mouvantes* (1615), in which he describes his barrel organ worked by water power. Other organs were propelled by weight-driven clockwork, as with the famous combined keyboard-and-barrel organ-cum-carillon completed by Thomas Dallam in 1599 for incorporation into a great automaton clock which Elizabeth I sent to the Sultan of Turkey:

First the clock struck 22; then the chime of 16 bells went off and played a song of 4 parts. That being done, two personages which stood upon two corners of the second story, holding two silver trumpets in their hands, did lift them to their heads, and sounded a tantarra. Then the music went off, and the organ played a song of 5 parts twice over. In the top of the organ, being 16 foot high, did stand a holly bush full of blackbirds and thrushes, which at the end of the music did sing and shake their wings. (From Dallam's account.)

In Augsburg, a city famous for its organ clocks, the Bidermann family made barrel-operated virginals, and Rungger a combined organ-and-spinet with 16 pipes and 16 strings, all in a clock (1687). In London, in 1736, Charles Clay exhibited a clock which played its tunes on both bells and organ pipes, and Handel wrote and arranged for it a large number of pieces, mostly in two parts, but with occasional chords. Three clocks exist which play tunes written for them by Haydn between 1772 and 1793. Mozart's pieces written in 1790-1 (K 594, 608, 616) were 'for an *Orgelwerk* in an *Uhr*', or 'for a *Walze* ['cylinder'] in a small organ'.

4. *Hand-turned Barrel Organs.* These began at the end of the 17th century with 'bird organs' for teaching canaries to sing; they had about 13 high-pitched pipes and were small enough to place on the lap while sitting by the cage. (Their French name *serinette* (from *serin domestique*, 'canary') came later, in the 19th century, to denote instruments of harmonium or musical box types).

In England the barrel organ had a special place as a domestic instrument and also—a purely English development—in churches. The earliest date claimed for the latter is 1700, at Peak Forest, Derbyshire; the latest, 1879, at Ash Priors, Somerset. Altogether some 80 still existed in 1967 out of some 500 whose earlier existence in churches is recorded. One of the last to remain in regular weekly use was in the tiny church of Shelland, Suffolk. Organs of this kind were much appreciated and the very musical poet Mason, who was Precentor of the Cathedral of York from 1763 to 1797, in his *Essays, Historical and Critical, on English Church Music* (1795), says that he prefers 'the mechanical assistance of a Cylindrical or Barrel Organ to the fingers of the best parochial Organist'. The most frequent tunes on the barrels are 'Old 100th', 'Evening Hymn' (Tallis's Canon), 'Hanover' (Croft, often listed on the barrel as 'Old 104th'), and 'Portuguese Hymn' (*Adeste fideles*). Many barrels include a march, 'Rule, Britannia', or a piece from Handel, for use as a voluntary.

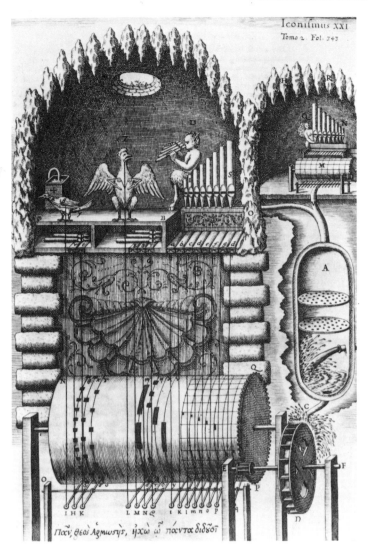

Iconismus XXI
Tomo 2. Fol. 343

Παν, θεοι Αρμωσης, ηχω ω παντα διδϐοῖ

Pl. 3. A water-driven barrel organ with automata, from Kircher's 'Musurgia universalis' (1650).

5. *Orchestrions* (mechanical orchestras). These were large barrel organs with pipes, reeds, and percussion for imitating an orchestra. They originated in Germany in the late 18th century, driven by weights. Some included automata playing instruments, notably the Panharmonicon made in Vienna by Leonard Maelzel (brother of the better-known J. N. Maelzel, inventor of the metronome). For this instrument Beethoven wrote *Wellingtons Sieg* (1813); it was J. N. Maelzel who suggested that the composer also scored the piece for orchestra, to raise money for the projected visit of all three— Beethoven, Maelzel, and the Panharmonicon— to London. The Maelzels finally settled in the USA, where they constructed in Boston

a set of musical automata, no less than 42 in number, which compose a complete orchestra, and execute several of the most difficult pieces of music in the most perfect manner: among others, the overtures to Don Juan, Giovanni [*sic*], Iphigenia, and La Vestale. Those which excite the most admiration and wonder are the violin-players, which execute their portion of the music precisely as if they were living performers— viz. by the motion of their fingers, etc. (*The Times*, October 1829.)

An especially notable orchestrion in the light of modern developments in musical composition was the Componium of the Dutch inventor D. N. Winkel in 1821, which could compose its own variations on a given theme. Now preserved in the museum of the Brussels Conservatoire, it has two barrels, each with the theme pinned on the far left. To the right are the pins for seven variations, in every case leaving two bars silent between every two which are pinned. Both barrels rotate continuously, and the missing bars of any one of the eight tunes of one barrel

Pl. 4. Bird organ (miniature barrel organ), engraving 'The Happy Canary' by R. Gaillard (1719-90).

can be substituted by bars from any of the eight on the other, the barrels being moved laterally under a clockwork 'computer'.

6. *Barrel Pianos*. These, turned by handle, began to be made in Italy in the late 18th century, at first small, then, from the 1880s, resembling an upright piano and placed on a two-wheeled cart. They were still made and played almost entirely by Italians until, after 1922, Mussolini, jealous for the dignity of his nation, recalled all Italians engaged in street music. Apart from these, a noted English maker of the early 19th century was John Hicks (London and Bristol), who made small portable models. Dr Busby, in his *Concert Room Anecdotes* (1825), describes among many new devices the 'Self-acting Pianoforte of Clementi, Collard & Co., on which while . . . the *piano* and *forte* passages are given with correctness and effect, the *forzandi* and *diminuendi* are produced by the slightest motion of the hand applied to a sliding ball at the side of the instrument'. Later there were barrel pianos driven by powerful clockwork motor for installation in dance halls and amuse-

Pl. 5. Orchestrion by M. Welte at the 1851 International Exhibition, engraving from 'The Illustrated London News' (20 September 1862).

Pl. 6. Swiss musical box, playing eight tunes.

ment arcades, along with automatic violins played with resined wheels. There is indeed hardly an instrument that has not been automated at some time—from harp and banjo to saxophone and concertina.

7. *Musical Boxes.* These produce their sound by plucking narrow tongues of specially tempered carbon steel, rigidly fixed at one end. They arose in the second half of the 18th century, devised by craftsman-watchmakers, first probably in the Jura region of Switzerland, the cradle of the musical box industry, though by 1850 it had moved to Geneva. Actuated by clockwork, the early movements had miniature pinned metal barrels or cylinders, small enough to be fitted into watches and snuff-boxes. The *Musical World* of 1837 reports the misadventure of a 'gentleman who had a snuff-box that played *Drops of Brandy* and *The glasses sparkle on the board*', and who, having it in his pocket in church, accidentally touched the spring. Since then there have been chairs which strike up a tune when sat upon, wine decanters which surprise a guest by offering him musical as well as liquid refreshment, and other fanciful devices of the kind from the Swiss designers and to be seen in the windows of tourist resorts. By 1810 there were also larger musical movements for fitting inside the bases of clocks, with cylinders up to 15″ long. From shortly afterwards, the tongues, originally made individually, were

made in the single comb-like assembly which has been familiar since in the Swiss musical box, with six to eight tunes on the cylinder. In most well-made musical boxes a tiny metal or feather damper is attached below each tongue, against which it is moved by the cylinder pin at the moment of plucking.

In 1886 Paul Lochmann in Leipzig, in conjunction with Ellis Parr in London, succeeded in replacing the musical box cylinder by a thin sheet-metal disc with punched projections on the underside. Thus came, a few years later, the Symphonion musical box, with easily interchangeable discs, manufactured in Leipzig. From there Gustave Brauchmann went to the USA where he set up the Regina Company in New Jersey. Some of the disc musical boxes were worked by clockwork, others by a handle. After 1912 musical boxes began to fall victim to the combined onslaught of the gramophone and the player-piano, though the Swiss musical box continues to be made by Reuge and others.

8. *Perforated Card and Paper-roll Systems: (a) Fair Organs.* In 1801 the Jacquard system of automatic control by perforated cardboard sheets was perfected for cloth-weaving looms. The first practical application to musical instruments was by the Parisian builder of fair and dance organs, Gavioli, when in 1892 he began to replace the barrels of his organs with a 'book' of perforated cardboard, folded zigzag, which, as it unfolds, is drawn by rubber-covered rollers

Pl. 7. Disc musical box, supplied with 20 discs.

across the key-frame of the organ. Spring-loaded metal levers rise whenever a hole appears, and are pushed down again as the hole passes on. Such organs were intended to be enjoyed visually as well as listened to, and were rich in ornament, colourfully painted; many acting on this principle are still playing in merry-go-rounds, their light-bulbs blazing, while the large street organs carefully preserved in Holland are now famous (two, however, still using barrels). To keep the music up to date, firms like Chiappa in London still make new books for fair or 'show' organs.

(*b*) *Organettes.* Organettes using free reeds (see *Reed*, 1), appeared around 1878, made by J. Carpentier in France, and John McTammany and Merritt Gally in the USA. They were first turned by handle, and eventually led to the 'orchestrelle' of the 1920s by the Aeolian Company. In 1897 came the pianola, developed by the American Edwin S. Votey, marketed by the Aeolian Company, and at first using a pneumatic machine which, pushed up in front of an ordinary piano, played on its keys with felt-covered wooden fingers. By 1901 it was incorporated into the piano itself, and such pianolas were made by Aeolian up to 1951. All the user has to do is to pedal with the bellows, which draw the air in through the holes in the paper roll, while operating speed and loudness controls with the hands, following the wavy indicator lines printed on the roll.

The next advance was to be able to record enough information on the roll to be able to re-create automatically and accurately an original performance given on another piano. The best-known models were Welte & Sons' 'Mignon' (German), and the Aeolian 'Duo-Art' and American Piano Co.'s 'Ampico'. Their special rolls contain all the necessary data for a delicate pneumatic computer to make the piano action impart exactly the right volume and intensity to each note. In a London performance of a Liszt Rhapsody, passages were performed alternately by the French pianist Cortot and by a Duo-Art roll as recorded by Cortot (the whole being so dovetailed that the effect was continuous). The critic Ernest Newman said that with closed eyes it was impossible to say which was which.

Composition direct for the player-piano (so ending the limitations inherent in composition for the mere ten fingers of the human hand) has been undertaken by Stravinsky (including an early version of *Les noces*), Malipiero, Hindemith, Casella, Goossens, Howells, and others. Chords of 30 or more notes can be used, and the high, middle, and bottom registers be sounded at once (Ex. 1).

Recently the digital control of pianos from specially encoded magnetic tape cassettes has made possible further developments. Until 1978 work had been restricted to the computer laboratory, but it is now possible to play an ordinary piano fitted with the necessary computer and tape interface and then have the piano replay the performance under the control of the tape. The first commercially available instrument operating on this principle is Superscope-Marantz's 'Pianocorder' introduced in the USA in 1978.

Ex. 1   Stravinsky: excerpt from *The Firebird* transcribed for player-piano

Médée ('Medea'). Opera in three acts by Cherubini to a libretto in French by F. B. Hoffmann after Euripides. It was first performed in Paris in 1797. Operas on the same subject have been written by several composers, including M.-A. Charpentier (1693), Benda (1775), Mayr (1813), and Milhaud (1938). There is also a ballet by Barber (1946).

Medesimo (It.). 'Same', e.g. *medesimo movimento*, 'the same speed'.

Medial cadence. See *Cadence*, 2.

Mediant. Third degree of the major or minor scale, so called because it lies midway between the tonic and the dominant.

Mediatio (Lat., 'mediation'). Subordinate cadence, occurring half-way through a verse in a psalm tone (see *Tonus*, 3).

Medieval. The concept of 'Medieval music' depends on an analysis of Western European cultural evolution which appears to have originated with Petrarch (1304-74). He saw the classical revival of his own day as a new dawn and the period since the eclipse of classical antiquity as a dark age from which one might be thankful to emerge. This was a literary revival, exemplified by the recovery and imitation of classical writings, and it was by no means the first of its kind; but it acquired a momentum which was to make it a permanent inspiration and to seem a genuine point of departure for the growth of the 'modern' world. In retrospect, however, the dawn seems to have been hailed somewhat prematurely, and in broad cultural terms, as exemplified by the arts of architecture, sculpture, and painting, as well as in the delayed impact of literary humanism, the main thrust of the classical revival belongs to the 15th century. As for music, in which a revival of this kind was an impossibility, the distinction between the Middle Ages and the Renaissance, if we are to insist on making it, can be identified only in terms of a profound change of direction capable of being seen in sufficiently close relation to that which overtook the other arts. By common consent such a change can indeed be recognized in the growth of a harmonic tonal sense during the 15th century, together with a loosening of formal rigidities and a new feeling for the relationship between words and notes. The earliest possible date for the end of the musical Middle Ages, if these criteria are adopted, is around 1420, the latest around 1500. Many writers have opted for 1450 as an appropriate compromise.

It is easier to define the beginnings of Medieval music, for they are coeval with the earliest substantial body of written music that we possess. The ability to write down music, never very widely cultivated in the Graeco-Roman world, was apparently lost in late antiquity. Ancient notation was alphabetical. When notation re-emerged in the 9th century it took the form of 'neumes', a system of signs which reflected the general contour of the melody but did not indicate its intervals or its rhythms with precision. When in the 11th century Medieval theorists devised an alphabetical notation which enabled them to define intervals exactly and concisely, they went on by means of the staff and its clef to harness the neumes to that system and hence to initiate the history of musical notation in the form in which we know it (see *Notation*, 2).

1. *The Music of the Church.* If we are to name one musical feature which runs like a thread through the whole Medieval period it must be the plainchant of the Roman Church. This does not mean that all Medieval music sounds like plainchant—far from it—but that plainchant was the one constant element to which all musicians, even those of the least cultural standing, could refer, a fundamental part of their experience and indeed of that of most people, for few would go through life without the regular (if not necessarily frequent) experience of sung liturgical worship. It is therefore a pervasive influence in much written music of the period, either by being used as a basic framework or *cantus firmus* in polyphonic composition, or by infiltrating its melodic style (as in much monophonic song and profane music). Even when not obviously present in these ways, it exerted a more general influence on the tonal language of music, and the theoretical discussion of such matters would have been impossible without a terminology derived from the plainchant theory of *modes. Indeed, even the tonal concepts of more recent times, such as those of the Baroque and Classical eras, are historically linked to the Medieval notions of *finalis* (the final note defining the tonality), of modes (reduced to major and minor), and of key (extended to embrace any degree of the chromatic scale). And although the Medieval plainchant tradition came to an end with the 16th-century Reformation and Counter-Reformation movements, it lived on in a corrupted form thereafter and enjoyed a genuine revival in the 19th century.

The origins of plainchant lie in the early history of the Western Church, for the term refers to the sung parts of the Latin church services, whatever form they took, up to the introduction of polyphony, and to most kinds of monophonic Latin liturgical song thereafter. We should bear in mind that Latin chant as we have it is the codification of a many-layered tissue of different forms and styles, in all probability having a multitude of origins, some directly from the Jewish liturgy, some from Eastern Christian sources, and others of purely Western origin. The Eastern Christian element, much modified, may have been predominant, as is evidenced by a variety of theoretical terms and liturgical texts borrowed from the East at different periods. The principal Eastern chant repertory was that known as Byzantine, the musical counterpart of the Greek-language Byzantine (or Constantinopolitan) Rite and one which can be deciphered from its own Medieval sources.

The Roman Rite and its chant did not immediately emerge as the unquestioned model for all Western Christendom. In Spain the Mozarabic Rite and chant (in two forms) survived until the 11th century; in northern Italy the Milanese or Ambrosian Rite and chant managed to experience its own 16th-century 'reform' and the 20th-century restoration of its Medieval tradition. But the native French (or 'Gallican') repertory suffered from the Carolingian attempt to impose the Roman Rite on the Frankish peoples, and virtually nothing of it has reached us in its original state. It was probably the Carolingian reform (named after Charles the Great or Charlemagne, reigned 768–814, from 800 as 'Emperor') which led to the attempt to fix the chant, hitherto a flexible and continuously evolving art, in writing. There is a good deal of evidence to suggest that the Romanization in France and Germany was by no means complete, and that the chant which survives in written form in Frankish sources from about 900 was not purely Roman but an amalgamation of Roman and Gallican (or Frankish) elements. This helps to explain its many divergences from the 'local' Roman tradition, which also survives. Paradoxically it was in its Frankish version that Roman chant finally emerged as triumphant, with the legend of its Gregorian origin attached to it (see *Plainchant*, 2–4).

For all its intended fixity, 'Gregorian' chant was immediately subjected to further expansion through *sequences, *tropes, and polyphonic elaboration. Sequences exemplified a form of melodic composition which was to become very characteristic of the Middle Ages, namely a series of phrases each heard twice. Sequences do in fact vary enormously in design but few of them lack this element altogether, and the principle was also applied to the melodic extension of other kinds of chant. Soon the sequence, like these others, was subjected to the device of 'prosing', the application of a syllable of text to each note of the melody. On this process, which gave rise to the technical term *prosa* and its diminutive *prosula*, a great deal of ingenuity was expended. A trope was an extension of an existing chant, composed in a similar style and with its words and its music already fitted together—though it too could be subjected to melodic extension followed by prosing. From these general ideas of liturgical expansion, rather than from the trope in any specific sense, were born the liturgical drama (see *Church Drama*) and the *conductus.

But it was the polyphonic elaboration of the chant which led to the most far-reaching developments. No one knows where the idea of part-music, based on an existing chant, came from. It is quite likely that the 10th-century monks who first drew attention to the possibility were drawing on their experience of secular music-making, always a probable inspiration for new departures in sacred music. The earliest practical source of church polyphony is an early 11th-century manuscript from Winchester, a tiny volume with an awe-inspiring quantity of music including 164 or so polyphonic parts to be added to existing plainchants. Unfortunately the music is written in unheighted neumes, which cannot be accurately deciphered, although some quite convincing reconstructions have been made.

The great age of plainchant composition had come to an end by 1200, but the device of polyphony ensured a healthy growth in the art, so drawing it apart from its Eastern cousins. In the 12th and 13th centuries, and above all in France, the strictly liturgical forms and the *conductus*, by this time the preserve of trained soloists, were given polyphonic settings of ever-increasing elaboration. The 13th century also produced the *motet, by far the strangest and most productive of the later Medieval forms. To a short fragment of plainchant, given in an artificially imposed rhythm and usually repeated, were added one or more upper parts, each with its own text (except for a small number of early examples with one text shared between two or three upper parts). This form might be given a liturgical application, in which case the added parts can be seen as a simultaneous application of the principle of troping; but the upper parts might very well be non-religious, even downright profane, or extend to the combination of a profane love-lyric and a song to the Virgin Mary. The aesthetics and the morality of this procedure have never been satisfactorily explained: it seems clear that the use of a plainchant tenor became a purely conventional convenience, but the combination of sacred and profane texts in the upper parts is harder to justify, even on the allegorical basis which is at the root of so much Medieval thought.

Many motet texts of the 13th and 14th centuries are satirical attacks on the vices of the clergy or ironical comments on political events, or neutral poems in praise of a city, a ruler, or musicians, rather than being profane in the amatory sense. In the end, the motet recovered an almost exclusively religious orientation, leading in the 15th century to more freely-composed types of sacred music and bequeathing its technical apparatus to the cyclic *Mass. In this form the movements of the Ordinary of the Mass were linked by common musical elements; and in its most fruitful manifestation, apparently an English invention, the movements were unified above all by a common *cantus firmus*, a plainchant chosen for liturgical or symbolic purposes and which, being proper to none of the texts of the Ordinary of the Mass itself, could appropriately serve as a musical basis for all of them. (By an ironic reversal, continental composers of the second half of the 15th century onwards as frequently used a secular *cantus firmus* as a sacred one, a procedure as hard to understand as that of the secular motet in earlier times.)

2. *Secular Music*. The emphasis on sacred music in this essay so far is understandable when we consider the monopoly of literacy enjoyed by the clergy in the early Middle Ages. Notation was invented in the monasteries, and it was not practised on any considerable scale outside the ecclesiastical sphere until the second half of the 13th century, when the earliest manuscripts of secular song (with a few exceptions) were produced. We also have to remember that even such notable later composers of secular polyphony as Machaut, Dufay, Binchois, and Busnois were clerics, and that many others were in the service of the Church as singers, organists, and choirmasters. The loosened rigour of ecclesiastical discipline in the 14th and 15th centuries enabled them to cultivate a type of song hitherto associated with the *troubadours*, *trouvères*, and *Minnesinger*, whose art was born of the tension between courtly and ecclesiastical society. If we go back still further we find nothing that is not of clerical origin. Such non-liturgical songs as survive are mostly political or semi-religious in character: *planctus* or laments on the deaths of Visigothic monarchs, a similar memorial to Charlemagne, and eschatological pieces, with fragments of classical verse and its Carolingian imitations, all in Latin and often with the familiar but undecipherable neumes. The six dramatic *planctus* of Peter Abelard, together with much other church drama and a good deal of composition in sequence and allied forms, fall into the same category. There are also collections of amatory lyrics, often mixed up with moral and political songs, all of an ecclesiastical provenance and again mostly in Latin. Many of these also have neumes, and several can be deciphered by comparison with later monophonic or polyphonic sources. This takes us from the 10th to the early 13th century, so far as the dates of the manuscripts are concerned: some of the poetry, certainly, is much older still. There are also a very few early poems in the vernacular languages which have come down to us, with music, in manuscripts of similar date.

In considering the regular written repertory of profane and other vernacular song, we are conscious of a closed, even a doomed, idiom. The *troubadours*, writing in their distinctive southern French dialect, cultivated an exclusive elaboration, both musical and verbal. From the involvement of their society with Manichean heresy came their virtual elimination as a result of the Albigensian crusade (1209). But they had passed on their aesthetic, not only to northern France but also to Germany, Italy, Spain, and England. The *trouvères* expanded the scope of the genre, cultivated a more natural style, and extended its social ambience. Their eventual adoption of popular refrain forms—used also for the sacred vernacular song of Italy and Spain—was the key to the future. Adam de la Halle was the first to write polyphonic *rondeaux* and *virelais*. Machaut and his successors enlarged these and, by adding the *ballade*, established the trio of late Medieval 'formes fixes'. The Italians of the 14th and early 15th centuries cultivated the *ballata* (a form of *virelai*) and two indigenous specialities, the *madrigal* and the *caccia*, the latter a type of canonic madrigal embodying a vividly descriptive text.

The written records of secular music cannot satisfy our curiosity as to the role of music in Medieval life. Even in the later Middle Ages, though there is plenty of music extant, it represents only the tip of an iceberg, the province of a courtly aristocracy at the pinnacle of a hierarchically ordered society. The further back we go, the less representative can the surviving material be said to be. Our picture must be rounded out by the evidence of historical literature, of song-texts, of musical theory, of the iconography of musical instruments, and by various hints and scraps of information which can sometimes lead to fragments of popular song, at least as to text and occasionally even as to music.

Clearly, much has been lost. At the outset of the period, in the early Anglo-Saxon poem *Widsith* (perhaps dating from the 7th century), we read of the travels of a *scop* and his companion, singing the deeds of dead kings and heroes at the courts of Germanic Europe. The heroic poetry of this world, epitomized by the Old English *Beowulf*, is as full as Homer of allusions to both travelling and resident minstrelsy. Elsewhere we learn of a polished art in

10th-century Frankish society; of the teaching of instruments to noble youths by Tuotilo of St Gall; of part-singing in Wales and Northumbria and of instrumental dexterity by Welsh and Irish musicians in the writings of the 12th-century archdeacon of St David's, Giraldus Cambrensis; and of the cultivation of secular music at all levels of society in the musical treatise of the otherwise unknown 13th-century Frenchman Johannes de Grocheo.

The process of adapting profane material to sacred purposes, a familiar one in the Middle Ages, has revealed a small body of tunes which would otherwise have remained hidden. A group of early sequences with instrumental or otherwise secular titles may belong to this category, while secular tenors and other parts buried in motets—even, in England, in otherwise purely religious motets—provide another example. A 'lai d'Aeliz', said to have been composed by an Irishman on his *rotte*, seems to have survived in the form of a double *contrafactum*, 'Flur de virginité' and the Latin 'Flos virginitatis'. The tune itself is extremely lively and bears the marks of improvised composition. The Medieval *carol, a secular dance-song in origin, was subjected extensively to sacred adaptation and gave rise in 15th-century England to a derivative polyphonic form which retains much of the freshness of popular music-making.

The role of music in entertainment is well illustrated by the long narrative poems known as *chansons de geste*, the musical form of which is known from their description by Johannes de Grocheo as well as from the analogous chantefable *Aucassin et Nicolete* (the music of which survives), by Adam de la Halle's pastoral play *Robin et Marion*, and by a body of lyrical *lais* which may well reflect the freedom of the original narrative form. The Breton origin of the latter is testified to by Chaucer and in the 14th-century English romance *Sir Orfeo*, itself an example of the reduction of the sung type to a standard spoken metrical pattern. This particular poem offers a vivid impression of courtly minstrelsy in Medieval England, a picture rounded out by the many references to music-making in such poems as *Sir Gawayne and the grene knight*, *Piers Plowman*, and those of Chaucer himself. The pleasant picture of Nicholas, the poor 'clerke of Oxenford', singing the popular (and well-preserved) 'Angelus ad virginem' to his 'gay sawtry' at night symbolizes the universality of the 'alternative' music-making traditions of Medieval Europe, the overwhelming preponderance in them of the bright, the colourful, and the joyous, and a staying-power which neither war, corruption, political instability, nor even the Black Death could reverse.　JOHN CALDWELL

FURTHER READING
Gustave Reese: *Music in the Middle Ages* (New York, 1940); Frank Harrison: *Music in Medieval Britain* (London, 1958, 4th edn 1980); Albert Seay: *Music in the Medieval World* (New Jersey, 1965); John Caldwell: *Medieval Music* (London, 1978); Richard Hoppin: *Medieval Music* (New York, 1978).

Medley (It.: *mescolanza*). 1. A term used by 16th-century composers, especially the Elizabethan virginal composers, for a piece which strings together several favourite tunes.

2. In the second half of the 18th century the term was applied to overtures that used well-known tunes; the first was published by Richard Charke in 1763. Later, such an overture would usually contain tunes from the work it preceded.

Medtner [Metner], **Nikolay** (Karlovich) (*b* Moscow, 5 Jan. 1880; *d* London, 13 Nov. 1951). Russian composer and pianist. He studied the piano at the Moscow Conservatory with, among others, Pavel Pabst (1854–97) and Vasily Safonov (1852–1918), graduating in 1900. After a career as a touring recitalist he settled in Moscow, teaching piano at the conservatory (1909–10, 1914–21) and also widening his activities as a composer. He wrote much piano music, songs, three piano concertos, and a little chamber music; but he did not show any interest in the orchestra or in opera. Brahms was a considerable influence on his piano music—at all events as to its general sentiment and its 'bigness' of style—but many of his works are also marked by a classical coolness and intellectual rigour. As a pianist he was highly regarded in Russia and abroad (he emigrated in 1921), settling in London in 1935. In his later years he received much support from the Maharajah of Mysore, under whose patronage he made a number of recordings.　PERCY SCHOLES, rev.

Megaphone. A precursor of the modern loud-hailer. A wide conical tube of metal or cardboard concentrates the energy of the voice in one direction. This was a familiar enough object in the past, mainly for speech, as at sea, though also for singing into, as in the 'vamp horns' of English country clergymen, used for leading the psalms as well as for giving out notices. Some of those preserved in museums reach 6' in length.

Mehr (Ger.). 'More'; *mehrstimmig*, 'more (than one) voice', i.e. polyphonic; *Mehrstimmigkeit*, 'polyphony'; *mehrere*, 'several'.

Méhul, Étienne-Nicolas (*b* Givet, Ardennes, 22 June 1763; *d* Paris, 18 Oct. 1817). French composer. The son of the head of the household to the Count of Montmorency, Méhul showed musical talent at an early age, becoming organist at the local Franciscan convent when he was

Méhul

about 10. After studying in nearby Monthermé he moved to Paris *c*.1778. There he became enamoured of Gluck's music, but in spite of some success with a setting of an *Ode sacrée* (now lost) by Rousseau given at the Concert Spirituel in 1782, his own fame came only in 1791 with *Cora*, the first of a long stream of operas. Méhul was most successful as a composer of *opéras comiques*, of which the best known today is probably *Joseph* (performed 1807), but he also composed a great deal of patriotic music during the Revolution, including a Mass probably intended for the coronation of Napoleon, but not performed on that occasion. He was one of the officials responsible for the curriculum at the Institut National de Musique (later the Paris Conservatoire). An innovator in the art of orchestration, he influenced Beethoven, Weber, Boieldieu, and Hérold, among others.   DENIS ARNOLD

Meistersinger (Ger., pl. *Meistersinger*). German amateur singers, largely artisans of the middle and lower classes. The *Meistersinger* flourished during the 15th, 16th, and 17th centuries, especially in the regions of Nuremberg and Strasbourg. The movement was organized within a system of guilds, which preserved strict codes of artistic rules and encouraged a spirit of competition. *Meistersinger* differed from the earlier *Minnesinger* not only in being of lower social status, but also in their preference for religious and narrative songs, often cast in *Bar* form, in which two musically identical phrases (called *Stollen*) are followed by a final section (the *Abgesang*). Several characters in Wagner's opera *Die Meistersinger von Nürnberg*, including the central figure, Hans Sachs (1494–1576), are modelled on actual members of the movement. See also *Minstrel*.   JOHN MILSOM

Meistersinger von Nürnberg, Die ('The Mastersingers of Nuremberg'). Opera in three acts by Wagner; text by the composer. Produced: Munich, 21 June 1868; London, Drury Lane, 30 May 1882; New York, Metropolitan, 4 January 1886.

In the Church of St Katherine in 16th-century Nuremberg, Walther von Stolzing (ten.) tries to attract the attention of Eva (sop.), daughter of the goldsmith Veit Pogner, who is with her nurse Magdalene (sop.). He learns that Eva will be betrothed next day to the winner of a singing contest held by the Guild of Mastersingers. Magdalene's admirer, the apprentice David (ten.), explains the rules to Walther. The Mastersingers gradually enter, led by Pogner (bass) and Beckmesser (bass-bar.), the small-minded town clerk who himself hopes to win Eva's hand. Hans Sachs (bass-bar.) the cobbler finally arrives, and the baker Fritz Kothner (bass) calls the roll. Pogner addresses the Masters and tells them of the contest. Walther is introduced as a candidate for the Guild; he is asked to tell of his background and training, and then invited to sing a trial song. Beckmesser is appointed marker, and enters a special box; Kothner reads the rules. Walther improvises a song about the spring and love, but soon Beckmesser's slate is full of the mistakes the knight has made. The meeting breaks up in disorder; only Sachs has seen something new and attractive in the song.

It is Midsummer Eve, and the apprentices are closing Sachs's shop. The cobbler himself sits under the elder tree and reflects on the events in the church. Eva makes her way from her house opposite Sachs's shop and questions him about the trial. Sachs, a widower, is himself half in love with Eva, but realizes that he is too old for her. He teases her and she rushes home in tears. Seeing the situation, Sachs resolves to help the young couple, who have met and planned to elope. Sachs prevents this by opening his window and letting light stream across the roadway. Beckmesser now arrives to serenade Eva. When Beckmesser protests at Sachs's hammering, he is told that his shoes will not be ready unless work continues. Sachs suggests he act as a marker, hammering each time Beckmesser makes a mistake. Beckmesser agrees, seeing a figure in the window above—it is really Magdalene in Eva's clothes. The serenade and hammering wake the neighbours and apprentices. Beckmesser receives a drubbing, and in the tumult Sachs prevents Eva and Walther from running off, and takes the latter into his

Hans Sachs and Beckmesser in a scene from Act 2 of Wieland Wagner's production of Wagner's 'Die Meistersinger'
(Bayreuth, 1958).

own house. The stage empties when the Night Watchman's horn sounds.

Sachs is musing over a large book. He does not hear the apologies proffered by David for his part in the riot. Left alone, he soliloquizes on the madness of the world, and the love of Walther and Eva. Walther comes to tell Sachs of a wonderful dream. Sachs writes this down, for it is a prize song—only the final stanza is lacking. While Sachs and Walther change into their festal robes, the aching Beckmesser enters. He sees the song and, believing it Sachs's, hastily pockets it. Sachs now returns and allows Beckmesser to keep the song. Eva appears, pretending that her shoes hurt, but really hoping to see Walther. While Sachs is attending to her shoe, Walther enters, and the sight of Eva inspires him to his final stanza. David and Magdalene are summoned, David is made a journeyman; the song is christened. All depart for the festal meadow. On the banks of the River Pegnitz the apprentices and guildsmen assemble. The apprentices dance with some girls. They are interrupted by the entrance of the Masters, who take their places on the stand. Sachs is acclaimed, and thanks the people. Beckmesser rises and makes a fiasco of the song. When the crowd laughs he accuses Sachs of having written it. Sachs disclaims authorship, but summons Walther to show how the song should be sung. Walther wins the prize and Eva's hand, but when Pogner moves to invest him with the insignia of the guild, he brushes

the chain aside, still smarting under his previous rejection. Sachs comes forward and persuades Walther to accept the honour, explaining the purpose of the Mastersingers in preserving the art of German song. Eva takes the wreath that she had placed on Walther's head and puts it on Sachs's amid the acclamations of the people.

Melisma (Gk, 'song'). Term used to describe a group of notes sung to one syllable of the text. It is used particularly to describe such passages in plainchant (see, for example, *Clausula*; *Jubilus*), where the contrast between syllabic and melismatic passages is an important stylistic feature. However, it is also appropriate to later music. Bach, for example, frequently used melismatic passages to emphasize such emotive words as 'wept' and 'scourged' in his Passions.

Thomas Ravenscroft called his 1611 collection of vocal pieces by the plural, *Melismata*.

Mellers, Wilfrid (Howard) (*b* Leamington, 26 Apr. 1914). English composer, educationalist, and writer. He studied English at Cambridge at a time when the critic F. R. Leavis was influential; his teachers in music included Egon Wellesz and Edmund Rubbra. He became known as a writer showing interest (like other disciples of Leavis) in the social background of the arts, and he was one of the first European critics to consider American music seriously. His most acclaimed scholarly work is a study of Couperin (London, 1950); but his writings also include the books *Music and Society* (London, 1946), *Romanticism and the 20th Century* (London, 1957), *Music in a New-Found Land* (London, 1964), *Harmonious Meeting* (London, 1965), *Caliban Reborn* (London, 1967), and *The Twilight of the Gods* (London, 1972). After a long period as an extra-mural teacher for Birmingham University and visiting professorships in the USA, Mellers became the foundation professor of music at York University, where he developed a remarkable department in which composition and intensive study of projects chosen largely by the students were strong elements. He has composed a great deal of music which reflects his eclectic tastes.

DENIS ARNOLD

Mellophone. See *Horn*, 8.

Melodica. See *Harmonica*, 5.

Melodic minor scale. See *Scale*, 3.

Mélodie (Fr.). The 19th-century French term for 'song', in fact the equivalent of the German *Lied*.

The term was probably first used by Hector Berlioz in his *Mélodies irlandaises* of 1829, and was no doubt suggested by Thomas Moore's books of *Irish Melodies*. French composers thereafter adopted the term to denote not a simple *air* but the more complex 'art song'.

The best-known *mélodie* writers are Fauré, Duparc, and Debussy. They chose verse from contemporary writers, including Victor Hugo, Verlaine, Baudelaire, and Leconte de Lisle, and also drew on older French writers such as Villon and Charles d'Orléans. In their sensitive handling of this poetry they were not alone, for most French composers have had a sure instinct for their own language, and the hundreds of *mélodies* by Louis Niedermeyer (1802-61), Berlioz, Gounod, Franck, Saint-Saëns, Bizet, Duparc, Fauré, Massenet, Debussy, Reynaldo Hahn (1875-1947), Ravel, and many others constitute a school of song composition second only to that of the *Lied*, most of which is all too little known in this country.

The *mélodie* derives from the *romance*, and while it could hardly escape being influenced by the *Lied* it was never engulfed by it. The vocal line maintained a suppleness directly dependent on the individuality of the French language, and the kind of poetry chosen for setting inspired piano accompaniments which supported the general mood of the poem rather than being specifically realistic or minutely illustrative. The frank onomatopoeia of Ravel's *Histoires naturelles* (1906), which scandalized the listeners who first heard it, is exceptional, although characteristic of its period.

The *mélodie* can hardly be discussed in isolation. The civilization of which France was so proud involved all the arts, and her composers were caught up in all the fashionable Symbolist, Impressionist, Fauvist, Cubist, and other movements. With this, too, came a revulsion against the complexities of German music. French music, reacting against the opulence of Wagner and Strauss, began to cultivate a spare, even ascetic, texture; the typical and traditional 'development' technique gave way to the concise, laconic music of Erik Satie and his followers. We can see this, for example, in some of Fauré's late *mélodies*, as in his cycle *Le jardin clos* (Van Lerberghe; 1914-15). Other composers, such as Emmanuel Chabrier, deliberately sought out poems that avoided romantic expressiveness and set them to music which defied classical 'good taste' by drawing inspiration from the Paris music halls. The instinct for satire (never far from French music) was carried further by the disillusionment consequent on the First World War; under Jean Cocteau's influence Poulenc, Honegger, and others continued to experiment with music which replaced traditional lyric values by the more impersonal styles from both Stravinsky and jazz.   LESLIE ORREY

Melodrama. A composition or section of a composition, usually dramatic, in which one or more actors recite with musical commentary. If for one actor, the term 'monodrama' may be used, if two, 'duodrama' (as in the duodramas of Georg Benda).

The form became popular in the second half of the 18th century. The first full-scale melodrama was Rousseau's *Pygmalion*, in which he tried 'to join the declamatory art with the art of music', alternating short spoken passages with instrumental music as a development of the *pantomime dialoguée*. On the whole French melodramas tended to interpolate brief self-contained numbers between speeches, whereas the Germans preferred a sense of musical continuity, even when interrupted by speech as well as accompanying it. Mozart, who admired Benda's *Ariadne auf Naxos*, planned a melodrama *Semiramis*, but does not seem to have progressed very far with it; he did use melodrama effectively in *Zaide*. Melodrama was cultivated for special uses in French *opéra-comique*, by Cherubini in *Les deux journées* and also by Méhul, Boieldieu, and others. The most successful examples of its power of heightening the dramatic tension are in the grave-digging scene in Beethoven's *Fidelio* and the Wolf's Glen scene in Weber's *Der Freischütz*. Beethoven also used melodrama in his incidental music, including that for *Egmont*; and Schubert, who included some in his operas, wrote a recitation with piano, 'Abschied von der Erde'. Weber wrote a complete concert melodrama, *Der erste Ton*, and for insertion in a play wrote a number in which speech moves in a controlled manner through speech–song into song; this technique is reflected in Gretchen's spinning song in Marschner's *Hans Heiling*.

Schumann and Liszt were among many 19th-century composers to write concert melodramas; and Berlioz made extended, if intermittent, use of it in *Lélio*. Both Verdi and Smetana included passages of melodrama in some of their operas; in Bohemian lands, it was particularly cultivated, and Fibich wrote a whole trilogy, *Hippodamia*. In the 20th century, it has been used by Schoenberg (in *A Survivor in Warsaw*, as well as in its form as speech–song), by Stravinsky (*The Soldier's Tale*), by Richard Strauss (a recitation with piano, *Enoch Arden*), by Honegger (*Jeanne d'Arc au bûcher*), and by Walton (*Façade*), among many others; and many opera composers have used it for particular effect at certain moments of their operas.

JOHN WARRACK

Melody. Melody is the result of the interaction of rhythm and pitch. Both the regular articulation of time (through heartbeat, breathing) and the capacity to produce and recognize variations in the frequency of sound are normal physiological characteristics of mankind. The functions that define melody overlap with those used to define human speech, so that both may be regarded as fundamental capacities of the species. Whereas speech is a form of communication, melody in all human cultures has been used typically as a form of emotional expression. It is suspected that this use of melody may be a capacity of other animals—a suspicion that arises inevitably when animals, be they birds or dolphins, produce organized sequences of varied pitch with no apparent communicating function or purpose.

In language, intonation is an important source of meaning. Many African and Asian languages depend on an intonational system much richer than those with Indo-European roots; for that reason, it is notoriously difficult for a European to learn, say, a modern Chinese dialect. The use of this kind of 'melodic' inflection to determine meaning in language is quite remarkable. Any reader of this text can unconsciously and accurately intone the phrase 'Jack and Jill went up

Ex. 1

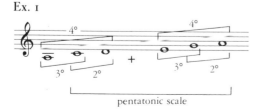

pentatonic scale

the hill' to convey quite different kinds of statement or question: for example, 'Jack and Jill went *up* the hill?' and 'Jack and Jill went up the *hill*?'. In music, just as in language, the way different qualities inhere in such a form of expression is complex. Musicians consider it to be so complex, and there are so many different types of melody from different cultures and ages, that melody is the least well-explained aspect of music theory.

The close empirical relationship between speech and melody suggests that melody may have had a long prehistory, especially in the sense that functional and ritual melody exists in all known 'primitive' societies on which our view of prehistory is modelled. It also seems that the physiological and acoustic condition of mankind provided a common source of melody. The most basic quality of a pitch succession is whether it ascends or descends. In the earliest music,

Ex. 2   Gregorian Chant

Glo - ri - a   in ex-cel-sis De - o.

Et   in ter - ra pax ho - mi - ni - bus

bo - nae vo - lun - ta - tis.

melodic descent is the outstanding quality, regardless of its provenance in one or another civilization. The most consistent intervallic characteristic of ancient melodic types is the fourth, subdivided by a third and a second. The slightly more elaborate vocabulary of superimposed fourths (lying with the octave) and their subdivisions provides a pentatonic scale, melodic material common to Chinese, Hebrew, American Indian, and many other ancient cultures of which we know (see Ex. 1).

It is important in the consideration not only of ancient music but also of the Western tradition to realize that the concept of scale is based on practice, rather than being the basis for practice. The complicated theory of modality in the Medieval period, for instance, was a response to a sophisticated, variable, and instinctive use of pitch by practising musicians (see *Mode*). The scale determines the kind of music made only in the sense that it becomes fixed in instrumental music. Thus the existence of five-string lyres some 3,000 years ago, as well as of wind instruments with certain possible fingerings and transpositional relationships to other

Ex. 3
Peri: *Euridice*

Ex. 4

instrumentss, suggests the fixed-pitch content of ancient melody on a pentatonic basis.

In the Western tradition, melody in the form of plainchant was the first aspect of music to be developed into an elaborate art form, before the last millennium of development of harmonic and rhythmic language. In the 5th and 6th centuries, a large repertory of plainchant was established, displaying a coherent melodic style. Ex. 2 illustrates some of these features: the mixture of melismatic and syllabic setting, the basically step-wise progression with expressive thirds and fourths which tend to be used at the beginning of a section, and, most important of all for the future of Western melody, the balance of ascent and descent around a focal pitch (in this case, the *finalis* E).

Since the first mature experiments in polyphony (the combination of melodically differentiated voices) around 1,000 years ago, monophony has played a relatively small part in our culture. In both sacred music and secular art music, Medieval and Renaissance composers thought in terms of contrapuntal equality (see *Counterpoint*). The melodic characteristics of one voice were like those of the others, although being able to invent florid melody to fit against a simpler *cantus firmus* was a highly-valued skill. At the beginning of the 17th century in Italy there was a major change in the attitude towards melody and its function. This stemmed from a desire to recapture, in secular music, the ancient prize of a true marriage of word and melody. The discovery of recitative spread rapidly. It exploited a melodic style closer to the inflection and rhythm of speech, sustained by a melodically sparse bass which carried the harmonic structure (see Ex. 3). The principle of a two-part texture, melody against bass with 'inner' parts providing homophonic or imitative richness, was the prevalent style of the Baroque and the fundamental nature of Classical and

Ex. 5

Ex. 6

Romantic music. A contrapuntal tradition continued within the new tonal language, exploited to some extent by all, but especially by Viennese composers, who continually returned to the study of J. S. Bach's counterpoint. These trends merged in the music of the early 20th century. Texture and colouring became so elaborate that Schoenberg had to notate for performers—and through them make clear to his listeners—just which part in a score carries the 'melody' at any point, with the indication H (for *Hauptstimme* or 'main part').

The characteristics of melody in tonal music make the traditional yardstick for the discussion of melody in general. Ex. 4 illustrates this. It shows that the second half of the clarinet melody which opens the third movement of Brahms's Symphony No. 1 repeats the first half upside down. It is an exact inversion, a procedure which became crucial in the melodic structure of serial music. Yet in plainchant, the melody of Western Christian church music which has endured nearly 2,000 years and has influenced the style of composers as culturally distant from each other as Machaut and Richard Strauss, inversion does not appear to be a significant feature.

Rhythmic articulation is another vital factor

in the nature of melody, and the difficulties of rhythmic theory and the problems of notation raise further complex issues. Musicologists have yet to uncover decisive evidence about the authentic rhythmic patterns of early Medieval liturgical melody, for which an adequate notation was not devised, nor indeed needed, at the time. Ethnomusicologists find that modern Western notation, of a kind which more or less adequately conveys to musicians the melodic intentions of the Brahms example within our living tradition, is barely adequate to capture the true or 'pertinent' melodic character of other cultures.

During most of the history of mankind, and still in many non-Western cultures, melody is itself synonymous with music. The combination of melodies in polyphony, one of the great artistic achievements of Medieval Europe, has produced the need for a more specialized explanation of melody in Western music. Melodic structure has to be described not only in terms of its overt linear properties, but also in terms of its harmonic implications. The English ballad 'Greensleeves' (Ex. 5*a*) demonstrates how pure melody nevertheless unfolds an harmonic progression (Ex. 5*b*).

In Classical music, this potential for har-

Ex. 7

Ex. 8

monic and contrapuntal implication in melody becomes a sophisticated source of musical unity. If we compare the melodies of the first and second minuets in the central movement of Mozart's Sonata in E♭ major, K 282 (Ex. 6a), it is clear that the different polyphonic implications of single-line melodies provide a common shape which contributes to the music's coherence (Ex. 6b: compare x and y in each case).

Similarly, the form of a melody is inherently tied to other properties of musical structure. Melodic patterns like ABA and AAB are perceived as structural, even as textural, patterns. Ex. 7a, in a simple AA pattern, may appear in

Ex. 9

Du näch - tig   to - des kranker Mond

an actual piece of music as AA′ when harmony and phrase-length vary the repetition (Ex. 7*b*), or even as AB when it is texturally obscured (Ex. 7*c*).

The extremes of structural relationship indicate the extremes of expressive range which have been exploited in the classical tradition. On the one hand, melody can be built almost exclusively from motivic 'cells', as in Ex. 8*a*. Here the figuration by three instrumental parts of a simple melodic line (Ex. 8*b*) produces one of the most memorable melodic inventions in the repertory—the opening of Beethoven's Symphony No. 5.

On the other hand, in an attempt to recapture the link between music and drama first investigated in the 17th century, Schoenberg paved the way for a new modern approach to melody. Ex. 9, from No. 7 of his *Pierrot lunaire*, shows the **Sprechstimme*, midway between recitation and song, relying on pitch relationships to guide the declamation of the voice, but specifically not 'singing' the notes, as Schoenberg's special notation here indicates. Schoenberg and Webern also investigated the idea of a **Klangfarbenmelodie* (or 'sound-colour melody'), in which variation of timbre substitutes for the variation of pitch which, as we have seen, underlies the whole history of melody.

Other composers, following the lead of, for example, Varèse's *Ionisation* (1931) for percussion, have experimented with music that avoids conventional melodic continuity. The rise of electronically-produced sound has barely affected this situation. Some composers seize on the opportunity to manipulate lines of sound in a way that bears little relation to the concept of melody. The synthesizer is in widespread use in popular music, however, to reproduce with new timbres the centuries-old melodic formulas of tonal music.

JONATHAN DUNSBY

Melusina, The Fair (*Die schöne Melusine*). Overture, Op. 32, by Mendelssohn, composed in 1833. It was inspired by Kreutzer's opera *Melusine*, to a libretto by Grillparzer based on the Romantic legend of the mermaid Melusina.

Membranophone. See *Instruments, Classification of*.

Mendelssohn(-Bartholdy), (Jakob Ludwig) **Felix** (*b* Hamburg, 3 Feb. 1809; *d* Leipzig, 4 Nov. 1847). German composer. His grandfather Moses was a distinguished philosopher and champion of Jewish emancipation. His father, Abraham, became a banker who was converted (adding the name Bartholdy, after some family property on the river Spree to distinguish the Christian branch). The family moved to Berlin in 1811 on the French occupation of Hamburg. Felix, second of three children, was given an extremely rigorous private education, beginning at 5 o'clock each morning, embracing languages, literature, drawing, and painting, as well as music. He showed talent at all of these, and it was comparatively late that he elected to make music his profession. He was given lessons by very distinguished teachers, including composition from Zelter, the director of the famous middle-class choral society, the Singakademie, which was much involved in the revival of Bach and Handel. Mendelssohn was composing quite fluently by his early teens,

Mendelssohn

being much influenced by Weber (whom he met), and by the age of 15 he had written several short, attractive symphonies for string orchestra. In 1825, on a visit to Paris with his father, he played to Cherubini who encouraged him to become a musician. Back in Berlin he composed his excellent String Octet (1825) and an opera *Die Hochzeit des Camacho* ('The Wedding of Camacho') which was given a single performance at the Berlin Schauspielhaus two years later. His Overture to *A Midsummer Night's Dream* (1826) was performed on the very same day (29 April 1827) in Stettin, but it was about this time that he became extremely interested in the music of Bach, and he gave the first 'modern' performance of the St Matthew Passion in 1829, an extraordinary feat for a man of 20.

This achievement caused some jealousy in Berlin, but his father had now carefully arranged the Grand Tour (or rather several) to complete his education, and later in 1829 he visited Britain, where his connections with Moscheles gave him the entrée to London musical life — he conducted his First Symphony in C minor (1824) at the Philharmonic Society — and after an extensive tour of Scotland, where he obtained ideas for the *Hebrides* overture (1830) and the 'Scottish' Symphony (No. 3, 1842), he hurt his leg in a road accident which kept him in London for two months. On a tour of Italy the following year he found less music of any substance (he was by this time inclined towards pan-German nationalism) although he was fascinated by the country and its antiquities. A commission from the Philharmonic Society of London stimulated the composition of the 'Italian' Symphony (No. 4, 1833) which he conducted there in 1833. He was now becoming sought after as a conductor, giving Handel's *Israel in Egypt* at the famous Lower Rhine Festival in Düsseldorf, after which he was offered a contract to direct the festival for three years.

Thereafter, his life was that of an extremely busy conductor for various institutions. Although he was not always tactful or patient in his dealings with orchestras and administrators, talent kept him in demand, not least because he was so interested in 'old' music, which he both edited and performed. As well as the Lower Rhine Festival, he briefly took on the directorship of the Düsseldorf orchestra and theatre (in the latter, his serious tastes proved too much for both public and management). He was appointed conductor of the Gewandhaus concerts at Leipzig in 1835, and here was at his happiest: he conducted the first performance of Schubert's 'Great' C major Symphony amongst much Beethoven and other classics. He was guest conductor at the Birmingham Festival in

1837, where he gave his oratorio *St Paul* (1836), which further secured his reputation in England. He was lured back to Berlin for a time by an offer to direct virtually a new conservatory, but arrangements for this proved unsatisfactory and he kept on his other engagements. His links with Leipzig were even strengthened when in 1843 the conservatory there opened under his directorship, with a very distinguished teaching staff (including Schumann).

This huge load naturally reduced time and energy to compose, and Mendelssohn's list of works shows a decline in quantity after *St Paul*. Small pieces such as the *Lieder ohne Worte* ('Songs without Words') for piano continued throughout his life, but larger-scale works became fewer. He composed a considerable amount of chamber music in the late 1830s. A choral symphony — 'Lobgesang' ('Hymn of Praise', No. 2), in the manner of Beethoven's Ninth but hardly with the substance — was produced in 1840 to commemorate the invention of printing; the 'Scottish' Symphony was finally completed in 1842, while his Berlin connections resulted in the royal commission of incidental music to Racine's *Athalie* (1845), Shakespeare's *A Midsummer Night's Dream* (1842), and Sophocles' *Oedipus at Colonos* (1845). But his second grand oratorio *Elijah*, planned as early as 1837, was finished and performed at the Birmingham Festival only in 1846. The Violin Concerto, finished in 1844, had taken nearly six years from conception.

The pace of his career was beginning to tell on his health in 1845, and although *Elijah* was splendidly received in England (Albert the Prince Consort sending him a most appreciative note), he found that to undertake six performances of it in England the following winter was too fatiguing. And on returning home he learned that his sister Fanny, to whom he had been very close, had died of a stroke aged only 41. A holiday in Scotland helped to revive him, but he seems to have suffered a similar condition and died after a short illness. He received almost a hero's obsequies: his body lay in state, and the train bringing his coffin to Berlin was greeted by mourners wishing to pay their respects at every station.

During his life and for some time afterwards, Mendelssohn was revered, his reputation receding only from the 1860s when Wagner's ascendancy among the intellectuals induced a patronizing attitude, partly encouraged by Wagner's antipathy and anti-Semitism (Mendelssohn's music was eventually proscribed by the Nazis). His wealthy background has been given as the cause of his superficiality, and he has been called a classic case of the youthful genius spoiled by success. Such simplistic theories about the relationship of life and work

Autograph MS of the opening of Mendelssohn's 'Song without Words', Op. 30 No. 1.

will not do. Mendelssohn did not have an easy life: he overworked from childhood to death. He did not compose easily: he was constantly revising works and they frequently took him a long period to complete. He admittedly was fortunate in his family life, his relationships with parents, sisters, wife, and children being excellent; no doubt also he enjoyed the admiration of royalty in Berlin and London. His professional relationships were often less satisfactory, especially those in Berlin where his early disappointment at not being appointed conductor of the Singakademie in 1832 always rankled. The successes and failures of his music stem more from the nature of the commissions and genres in which he wrote. In his correspondence (and in his competent and attractive sketches and watercolours) he revealed a gift for reacting to scenes; so too does his music, the best of it being in such works as the *Hebrides* overture and his mature symphonies. He was less interested in people or drama: consequently he wrote no successful operas, and his oratorios seem theatrical rather than dramatic, in spite of his good understanding of the nature of Handel's models. As a nimble pianist in the tradition of the players of light-touched pianos, he was good at *scherzando* music—as in the Octet and the *Midsummer Night's Dream* music. He was probably not a deeply devout man, yet his career as a choral conductor tended to provide incentives for religious music. At the last he did not decline from a high peak to profound depths: his later works include the Violin Concerto, and might well have included other fine pieces if time had permitted. It is best to take his achievement for what it is—that of a great but rather narrow composer—rather than grieve for what it is not.

DENIS ARNOLD

FURTHER READING
Philip Radcliffe: *Mendelssohn* (London, 1954, 2nd edn 1967).

Mendelssohn Scholarship. British musical scholarship founded shortly after Mendelssohn's death in 1847. The first holder was Arthur Sullivan, who won the prize in 1856. It was originally awarded to a young performer or composer, but is now reserved for composers. It is awarded every two years and the beneficiary may pursue his or her studies either at home or abroad.

Mennin [Mennini], Peter (*b* Erie, Pennsylvania, 17 May 1923). American composer. He studied composition with Norman Lockwood at the Oberlin Conservatory (1940–2) and with Bernard Rogers and Howard Hanson at the Eastman School (1943–7). In 1947 he began teaching at the Juilliard School, where in 1962 he was appointed president. His output includes eight symphonies and various other orchestral works in a solidly constructed, diatonic style.

PAUL GRIFFITHS

Menotti, Gian Carlo (*b* Cadegliano, 7 July 1911). American composer of Italian birth. He studied at the Milan Conservatory (1923–7) and then with Rosario Scalero at the Curtis Institute in Philadelphia (1928–33), where he taught from 1948 to 1955. In 1958 he founded the Festival of Two Worlds in Spoleto. Primarily an operatic composer, he achieved international attention in the years immediately after the Second World War with *The Medium* (1946), *The Telephone* (1947), and *The Consul* (1950), all of which show theatrical flair and an opportune use of music to heighten melodramatic situations. His television opera *Amahl and the Night Visitors* (1951) is gentler in its appeal, but such later works as *The Saint of Bleecker Street* (1954), *Maria Golovin* (1958), and *The Most Important Man in the World* (1970) show no lessening of dramatic incisiveness. Menotti has written the librettos for all his own operas and also for Samuel Barber's *Vanessa*.

PAUL GRIFFITHS

FURTHER READING
Robert Tricoire: *Gian Carlo Menotti* (Paris, 1966).

Mensural music, mensural notation. From the Latin *mensurata*, 'measured', i.e. with a specific rhythmic value. See *Notation*.

Mensurstrich (Ger.). The use of a line between the staves rather than through them, to mark off the bars. This is a method chosen by some editors of early music, in an attempt to avoid the emphatic and regular divisions of the bar-line and allow the music to be seen as relatively fluid, setting its own accents and metres within a looser constraint.

Binchois: 'Dueil angoisseus'

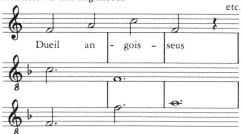

Menta, alla (It.). Improvised passage.

Mento. See *West Indian Music*, 3.

Menuet, menuett, menuetto. See *Minuet*.

Mephistowalzer ('Mephisto Waltzes'). Four works by Liszt, their title deriving from an abbreviation for 'Mephistopheles'. The first, originally for orchestra as the second (*Der Tanz in der Dorfschenke*) of *Two Episodes from Lenau's Faust*, was transcribed for piano solo and piano duet; the second was also originally for orchestra (1880–1) and transcribed for piano solo and piano duet. The third was composed for piano (1883) and orchestrated by Riesenauer; the fourth was also for piano (1885).

Mer, La ('The Sea'). Three symphonic sketches by Debussy, composed between 1903 and 1905. They are *De l'aube à midi sur la mer* ('From Dawn to Noon on the Sea'), *Jeux de vagues* ('Play of the Waves'), and *Dialogue du vent et de la mer* ('Dialogue of the Wind and the Sea').

Merbecke, John (*b* ? Windsor, *c*.1505–10; *d* *c*.1585). English composer. He was an organist and clerk at St George's Chapel, Windsor, in 1531, and in 1543 was condemned to be burnt as a heretic for his interest in Calvinism. He was reprieved by Henry VIII (maybe because of his musical abilities) and returned to his position at Windsor. He did not renounce his views, however, and continued to work on his concordance of the English Bible and a number of other controversial theological volumes, stating his position openly when Edward VI came to the throne in 1547.

Merbecke's musical importance lies in his publication of *The Booke of Common Praier Noted* (London, 1550), the first musical setting of services in the 1549 prayerbook. He adapted the plainsong of the Roman liturgy to the new English words, subtly rearranging the accentuation, and provided music himself in a similar style where necessary. The work's useful life must have been short, as after Mary's reign a newly prepared prayerbook superseded it. Merbecke's version was revived in the mid 19th century by the *Oxford Movement, which found his revival of plainsong in the Anglican use much to its taste.

PERCY SCHOLES, rev. Denis Arnold

Mercadante, Giuseppe (Saverio Raffaele) (*b* Altamura, nr Bari, Sept. 1795; *d* Naples, 17 Dec. 1870). Italian composer. An illegitimate child, he was sent to study in Naples at an early age, where he learned composition with Zingarelli and was encouraged by Rossini. His first opera was produced at San Carlo in 1819 and thereafter he wrote some 60 for all the major Italian opera houses. A stay in Paris in 1836 brought him into contact with Meyerbeer's works, and for a time he composed in a new, more dramatic style (as exemplified in his much praised *Il giuramento*) in which he was an important precursor of Verdi. From 1840 until his death he was director of the Naples Conservatory.   DENIS ARNOLD

Merrie England. Comic opera in two acts by German to a libretto by Basil Hood introducing Elizabeth I, Raleigh, and other Elizabethan characters. It was first performed in London in 1902.

Merry Widow, The. See *Lustige Witwe, Die*.

Merulo, Claudio (*b* Correggio, nr Reggio Emilia, 8 Apr. 1533; *d* Parma, 5 May 1604). Italian composer and organist. In 1556 he obtained the post of organist at Brescia Cathedral, and the following year was successful in a competition for a similar post at St Mark's, Venice, where he remained until 1584. He was a colleague of Andrea Gabrieli there, and they shared the duty of writing ceremonial music; Merulo composed some splendid motets, which were published in several collections (Venice, 1578–1605), as well as Masses, a substantial number of madrigals, and music for pastoral plays. He is best known for his organ music, especially the toccatas, which were known to Frescobaldi and Sweelinck and can be seen as the first in a line which was to lead to Bach's toccatas. In his last years he returned to Parma, where he was organist to the dukes and to their order of chivalry, the Steccata company. He was generally considered to be the finest organist of his day, and he was buried next to Cipriano de Rore in Parma Cathedral.   DENIS ARNOLD

Mescolanza (It.). 'Medley'.

Mesopotamian Music. See *Ancient Mesopotamian and Egyptian Music*.

Messa di voce (It.). 'Placing of the voice'. A Baroque vocal technique which is still used as a method of voice-training. It consists of a long-held note during which the tone swells to a climax, followed by a *diminuendo* to *pianissimo*. See also *Voice*, 9.

Messager, André (*b* Montluçon, 30 Dec. 1853; *d* Paris, 24 Feb. 1929). French composer. He studied in Paris with Saint-Saëns at the École Niedermeyer and in 1876 won an important prize with a symphony. He was then organist at various Paris churches and conducted in a number of theatres including the Folies Bergère. But from 1885 he became popular as the composer of excellent operettas, of which the best known today is *Véronique* (1898), and of ballet music, of which his *Les deux pigeons* was given at the Opéra in 1886. Around 1900 his energies turned more to conducting, including periods as musical director at the Opéra-Comique, the Opéra, and Covent Garden (he directed the first performance of Debussy's *Pelléas et Mélisande*), and in later years was much honoured.   DENIS ARNOLD

Messa per i defunti (It.). 'Mass for the Dead', i.e. *Requiem Mass.

Messe (Fr., Ger.). 'Mass'.

Messe des morts (Fr.). 'Mass for the Dead', i.e. *Requiem Mass.

Messiaen, Olivier (Eugène Prosper Charles) (*b* Avignon, 10 Dec. 1908). The leading French composer of the generation after Debussy and Ravel, he quickly developed a very distinctive musical style based on his '*modes of limited transposition', on a speculative interest in rhythm, and on his desire to expound in music the truths of the Catholic faith. Though these concerns have not been widely shared, he has had a determining influence on the avant-garde as the teacher of Boulez, Stockhausen, and others.

He studied at the Paris Conservatoire (1919–30), where his teachers included Paul Dukas, Maurice Emmanuel, and Marcel Dupré. In 1931 he was appointed organist of La Trinité, Paris, and in 1936 he began teaching at the École Normale de Musique and the Schola Cantorum. Works of this period include the first of several cycles on religious subjects: *L'ascension* for orchestra (1933) or organ (1934) and *La nativité du Seigneur* for organ (1935). In 1940 he was taken prisoner-of-war, and during his captivity he composed the *Quatuor pour la fin du temps* for clarinet, violin, cello, and piano (1941). On his release in 1942 he was appointed to the staff of the Paris Conservatoire, and the sequence of theological cycles continued with *Visions de l'Amen* for two pianos (1943) and *Vingt regards sur l'enfant Jésus* for piano (1944).

Major works of the later 1940s included a trilogy on the Tristan legend: *Harawi* (1945), a song-cycle to the composer's own texts invoking Peruvian mythology, the *Turangalîla-symphonie* (1946–8), a ten-movement work which exultantly combines all the features of his early style, and *Cinq rechants* for chorus (1949). This great outpouring was followed by a period of experiment with serial and numerical procedures in such works as the *Quatre études de rythme* for piano (1949–50) and the *Livre d'orgue* (1951).

Messiaen collecting bird-song.

Messiaen then began to capitalize on his long-standing interest in birdsong, which he transcribed more or less faithfully in *Réveil des oiseaux* for piano and orchestra (1953), *Oiseaux exotiques* for piano, wind, and percussion (1955-6), and the *Catalogue d'oiseaux* for piano (1956-8). The sweet modal harmonies of earlier works were now abandoned or much constrained, and the more jagged, brilliant style was continued in the abstract *Chronochromie* for orchestra (1960) as well as in three further works exploiting wind and percussion sonorities. *Sept haï-kaï* (1962), *Couleurs de la cité céleste* (1963) and *Et exspecto resurrectionem mortuorum* (1964). The oratorio *La Transfiguration de Notre Seigneur Jésus-Christ* (1965-9) offered a conspectus of Messiaen's whole development, to be followed by a similar summary in the orchestral sphere in *Des canyons aux étoiles* (1970-4). Messiaen then began work on his first opera, as yet uncompleted.   PAUL GRIFFITHS

FURTHER READING
Olivier Messiaen: *The Technique of My Musical Language* (Paris, 1950); Claude Samuel: *Entretiens avec Olivier Messiaen* (Paris, 1967, Eng. trans., 1976); Stuart Warmisley: *The Organ Music of Olivier Messiaen* (Paris, 1969); Robert Sherlaw Johnson: *Messiaen* (London, 1975); Roger Nichols: *Messiaen* (London, 1975).

Messiah. Oratorio by Handel to a text compiled by Charles Jennens from the Bible and the Prayer Book Psalter. It was first performed in Dublin in 1742. Handel revised the work and added to it for subsequent performances and in the 19th century it became customary to perform it with enormous forces.

Messing (Ger.). 'Brass'; *Messinginstrumente*, 'brass instruments'.

Mesto (It.). 'Mournful', 'sad'; *mestizia*, 'sadness'.

Mesure (Fr.). 1. 'Measure', i.e. bar. 2. Tempo, e.g. *à la mesure*, **a tempo*.

Metà (It.). 'Half'.

Metal blocks (Fr.: *blocs métaux*). See *Cowbell*, 2.

Metallophone. See *Instruments, Classification of*.

Metamorphosen. Study in C minor by Richard Strauss for 23 solo strings. It was composed in 1945 as a lament for the destruction of the German cultural world in which he had lived and it quotes from the funeral march of Beethoven's 'Eroica' Symphony.

Metastasio, Pietro [Trapassi, Antonio Domenico Bonaventura] (*b* Rome, 3 Jan. 1698; *d* Vienna, 12 Apr. 1782). Italian librettist. A grocer's son, he was taken up by a wealthy man of learning who taught him Latin and Greek. He took to writing dramas when aged 14, but his real career came only when on the death of his patron he went to Naples, where he was befriended by an opera singer La Romanina, who introduced him to Porpora and persuaded him to learn music. He wrote his first libretto *Didone abbandonata* for her (it was set by Sarrò). Thereafter his librettos were set by virtually all major composers including Gluck, Handel, Haydn, and Mozart. Set up to 60 times, every word of these librettos was known by the audiences of the day. He became court poet in Vienna in 1730, and having inherited money from his first patron, lived there in some comfort till his death.   DENIS ARNOLD

Meter. American spelling of **metre*.

Metner, Nikolay. See *Medtner, Nikolay*.

Metre. The pattern of regular pulses (and the arrangement of their constituent parts) by which a piece of poetry or music is measured in relation to its timespan. The prevailing metre of a piece of music is identified at the beginning (or wherever it changes) by a **time signature*, which indicates the number of beats in each bar and the note value of the beat itself.

Musical metre derives some of its terminology from poetic metre, its regular patterns of accented (strong) and unaccented (weak) beats in a bar being analogous to the patterns of long and short syllables in a foot of quantitative verse. The division of a line of poetry into feet is much like the division of a musical phrase into bars, but the conventional barring system of music divides the beats into groups each beginning with an accented beat, while conventional scansion systems in verse divide syllables into groups each beginning as the line begins, that is not allowing incomplete feet at the start of a line such as the incomplete bars permitted at the start of musical phrases (see Table 1, iambic and anapaestic examples).

Some common metrical patterns in both poetry and music are illustrated in the table below: a short syllable is indicated by the sign ⌣, a long syllable by the sign —; each example consists of two feet; and two possible musical interpretations are given in each case.

One notable direct application of poetic metre to music has been in connection with 13th-century rhythmic modes, a system of setting texts to music using the repetition of standard, simple rhythmic patterns (see *Notation*, 2). With a few special exceptions though (e.g. metrical *psalms, *musique mesurée*), composers setting poetry to music have not felt obliged to follow the poet's metrical scheme in detail: for example, they have not necessarily set iambic verse in triple metre and dactylic verse in duple, nor have they restricted themselves to one note per syllable (as any strict adherence to the scheme would prescribe). But composers have traditionally attempted to respect the text's accentuation by matching accented syllables to accented beats in the music, thus highlighting both rhythm and sense, often to the mutual benefit of both words and music.

For standard metres in hymn tunes, see *Hymns and Hymn-tunes*, 11; see also *Rhythm*; *Time signature*.

JUDITH NAGLEY

Metrical psalms. See *Hymns and Hymn Tunes*, 4, 5, 10, 11.

Metric modulation. Technique introduced by Elliott Carter, by which changing time-signatures effect a transition from one metre to another, just as a series of chords can effect a harmonic modulation from one key to another.

Metronome (Fr.: *métronome*; Ger.: *Taktmesser*; It.: *metronomo*). An apparatus for fixing tempos. Many different forms of such apparatus have been in use since the first (invented by Loulié in 1696, an instrument 6′ high). The commonest form now in use is the clockwork one of Johann Nepomuk Maelzel (1772–1838), for some time the friend of Beethoven, who took much interest in it. (Maelzel, however, seems to have stolen the principle from one Winkel.) This is the often-seen small pyramidal instrument, with a beating rod in front, and sometimes a bell that can be made to strike at every second, third, or fourth beat. From the use of this metronome came the practice of using the letters 'M.M.', as in 'M.M. ♩ = 100', i.e. Maelzel's Metronome set at 100 beats to a minute and each representing a crotchet.

About 1945 a pocket metronome, shaped like a watch, was introduced in Switzerland. Metronomes designed to synchronize irregular rhythms (three against five and the like), such as are found in much modern music, have also

TABLE 1

Metre	Poetry	Music
Iambic	⌣ — | ⌣ —	
Trochaic	— ⌣ | — ⌣	
Dactylic	— ⌣ ⌣ | — ⌣ ⌣	
Amphibrachic	⌣ — ⌣ | ⌣ — ⌣	
Anapaestic	⌣ ⌣ — | ⌣ ⌣ —	
Spondaic	— — | — —	
Tribrachic	⌣ ⌣ ⌣ | ⌣ ⌣ ⌣	

A selection of the metronomes available today.

been devised. Electric battery-operated models have recently come into common use.

Metronome marks, even when they originate with the composer and not merely some editor, are not to be understood as rigidly binding. Brahms said in a letter to Henschel: 'As far as my experience goes every composer who has given metronome marks has sooner or later withdrawn them.' Some of Schumann's marks are almost impossibly fast, suggesting that his own metronome was not in good order.

A watch of which one knows the tick-speed (generally five per second) can be quite conveniently used as a metronome. William Turner (*Sound Anatomized*, 1724) says that in what we now call *alla breve* time the crotchets are 'counted as fast as the regular motions of a watch'—which implies that all watches ticked alike in his day (as they now do not), and that all crotchets had the same value (as they now have not).

The metronome has been introduced into composition by Ligeti, who wrote a symphonic poem for 100 metronomes (1962), and Gordon Crosse (*Play Ground*, 1977), among others.

ANTHONY BAINES

Metropolitan Opera Company. America's oldest opera company in continuous existence. It opened in New York City in 1883, and has since become a national institution employing some 1,000 people, with a 26-week season (at Lincoln Center since 1966), an annual tour, weekly nation-wide radio broadcasts (since 1931), a 70,000-member Guild which publishes the magazine *Opera News*, a National Council which administers auditions throughout the USA, and an Opera Studio which brings performances by young singers to school-children in the eastern part of the country.

NYM COOKE

Mettere (It.), **mettre** (Fr.). 'To put'; *mettete il*

sordino (It.), *mettez les sourdines* (Fr.), 'put on the mute(s)'. In organ playing, *mettez* (Fr.) often means 'put (a stop) into action'.

Meyerbeer, Giacomo (*b* Berlin, 5 Sept. 1791; *d* Paris, 2 May 1864). German composer. Son of a wealthy Jewish banker, Jacob Liebmann Meyer Beer changed his name to Giacomo Meyerbeer on receiving a legacy from a rich relation called Meyer. He showed early promise as a pianist, playing Mozart's D minor concerto in public at the age of seven, and studied composition with Zelter and the Abbé Vogler. A magnificent score reader, he soon composed serious works including an oratorio and a biblical opera, but he thought of himself mainly as a pianist until, after his successful début and a failure of an opera in Vienna, Salieri advised him to go to Italy to acquaint himself with composing for the voice. He went to Venice, became enraptured with Rossini's music, and became a connoisseur of singers. He composed several operas in the Rossinian manner, all of them successful in Italy, but on his return to Berlin in 1823 he found this style despised by German critics to whom Weber's star was in the ascendant. However, Meyerbeer's next opera, *Il crociato*, was given with great acclaim in Venice in 1824 and two years later had a similar success in Paris, where he now settled. Dissatisfied with the Italian style, he met Scribe, the famous librettist, whose sure touch with the Parisian audience resulted in *Robert le diable*, a *grand opera taking up the manner of Spontini and Rossini's *William Tell* in its use of spectacular scenic effects and its brilliant orchestration. This made Meyerbeer the most famous and prosperous opera composer of the time, a fact confirmed by the even greater success of *Les Huguenots* (1836). Again this was less because of its musical qualities than its dramatic and scenic flair, which can only be compared with that of the Hollywood film epics of the 1930s.

Meyerbeer, drawing (1860) by Lehmann.

Nevertheless, the music is better than many of the later critics gave it credit for, being apt to express situation, if weak in memorable tunes.

An invitation to direct the Berlin Theatre after Spontini's departure in 1842 led to an unhappy period since he was an indifferent conductor and not really in tune with German taste. He eventually returned to Paris where *Le prophète* was given in 1849 and *L'étoile du nord* five years later. This slow output was caused by a perfectionism which made him constantly revise (he tried out various versions at orchestral rehearsals before deciding on the final one) and to insist on obtaining exactly the right cast. His last opera *L'africaine* was never put on in his lifetime for these reasons, being produced a year after his death. Virtually all his grand operas were immediately successful and brought him a fortune; but the early acclaim turned to adverse critical comment in later years, and he felt that a younger generation had taken over—as indeed it had. But the unkind essays of Wagner and others, especially in the anti-Semitic climate of the later 19th century, cannot obscure his tremendous influence, without which *Rienzi* (Wagner), Verdi's *Il trovatore*, *Don Carlos*, and *Aida*, and a host of French operas of the 1860s and 1870s would not have been written.

DENIS ARNOLD

Mezzo, mezza (It.). 'Half'; *mezza voce*, 'half voice', i.e. at half the vocal (or instrumental) power possible (not to be confused with **messa di voce*); *mezzoforte* (usually abbreviated to *mf*), 'half loud', i.e. not too loud; *mezzo-soprano*, see below.

Mezzo-soprano (It.). 'Half-soprano', i.e. a female voice (or artificial male voice) with a range midway between those of the contralto and the soprano, roughly *a–a″* (often *b″*). A high mezzo-soprano is often similar to a dramatic or *spinto* soprano and many roles can be sung by either. Several operatic roles written for sopranos are traditionally sung by and better suited to mezzos, e.g. Dorabella in *Così fan tutte*, Carmen, and Oktavian in *Der Rosenkavalier*. Occasionally a singer will describe herself as a mezzo-contralto, meaning a little lower in range than a mezzo.

Mf. Abbreviation for *mezzoforte*; see *Mezzo, mezza*.

M.g. Abbreviation for *main gauche* (Fr.), 'left hand'.

Mi, me. Third degree of the scale in the **solmization* system. In French and Italian the name has become attached, on the 'fixed-doh' principle, to the note E. See *Tonic Sol-fa*.

Michelangelo Buonarroti, Suite on Verses of. Songs, Op. 145, by Shostakovich for bass and piano, composed in 1974. Shostakovich made an orchestral version (Op. 145*a*) of the 11 songs in the same year.

Michelangelo Sonnets. See *Seven Sonnets of Michelangelo*.

Mico [Micho], Richard (*b* Taunton, *c*.1590; *d* London, Apr. 1661). English viol player and composer. His family was originally from France. Mico was in the service of the Petre household at Thorndon Hall, Essex, as teacher and player; his employers were Roman Catholic, and he became a convert to that faith. He wrote mainly consort music, including many fantasias, some pavans, and an *In nomine*. His music was praised by Christopher Simpson and Roger North. DENIS ARNOLD

Mi contra fa (Lat.). Part of a little rhyme alerting the singer against the awkward intervals, especially the tritone, that can occur when the two notes with the **solmization* syllables *mi* and *fa* come together. The full rhyme is *mi contra fa / diabolus est in musica* ('*mi* against *fa* is the devil in music'). See *Musica ficta*.

Microtone. Any interval smaller than a semitone. Such intervals have long been used in Asian musical cultures, but their use in Western art music is a phenomenon of the 20th century. Alois Hába and Julian Carrillo were among the prominent composers to introduce quartertones during the 1920s, while at the same time Harry Partch arrived at smaller intervals through his pursuit of just intonation. Microtonal music poses problems in performance, since it sometimes requires the construction of special instruments. In the electronic field, however, there are no limitations, though few composers have so far worked systematically with microtones in the tape medium.

PAUL GRIFFITHS

Middle Eastern Music. The Middle East stretches in a crescent from North Africa eastwards to the Soviet Republic of Uzbekistan. The written tradition of this vast region spans almost 13 centuries, and includes historical, theoretical, and poetical texts, many bearing on music. Since the beginning of the 20th century, ethnomusicological field-work has been conducted, and sound recordings (including early cylinders and 78 rpm discs) now supplement the older texts as sources of information. Ancient theory and modern practice often do not correspond, for example, intervals or modes described in a classical treatise may not occur in any known living tradition. Other intervals named in treatises do occur, but take one form in a town and another in the adjacent countryside. This somewhat perplexing evidence demonstrates the fact of musical change, even in these traditionally conservative Islamic societies.

Modern field-work has also revealed many different musical dialects throughout the Middle East, much to the disappointment of those who might wish to find uniformity, stemming from the original theoretical models. The *Oktoechos* (Byzantine principle of eight *modes) illustrates this point. These modal practices were always used in the eastern and Syriac language churches. According to the tradition, each Sunday of the church year has a prescribed mode for the performance of psalmody and chant. The cycle lasts eight weeks, beginning again on the ninth Sunday. The written theory is clear and indisputable; however, it is contradicted by practice. Certainly, on the first Sunday the first mode will always be used, but its interpretation varies from city to city. Thus there is not one '*Oktoechos* type', as described in the treatises, which is valid throughout the region. In reality there are many practices, some similar to and others vastly different from the written theory. What then is the significance of the original theoretical model? The scholar must acknowledge a multiplicity of dialects and explain their link to the theoretical source.

The Middle East has been a meeting point of peoples and cultures. It is heir to the ancient civilizations of Mesopotamia and Egypt, and with the expansion of Islam from the 7th century has embraced three great modern peoples: the Iranians, the Arabs, and the Turks. These three groups differ in many ways: the Ottoman Turks are etiquette-conscious and solemn in their search for meaning; the Iranians are introvert and meditative, verging on the esoteric; and the Arabs are typically abstract, yet have a firm grasp of practical problems. Nevertheless, a homogeneous musical culture has resulted. Among the Persians this is founded on a predominance of instrumental music; among the Arabs on the predominance of the voice; and among the Turks on a synthesis of the two. All three peoples favour the timbre, peculiar to the Middle East, resulting from orchestras of different instruments playing in unison. Another unifying musical feature is the rhythmic cycle, which can be in long periods (such as the 120/4 division, a cycle called 'the chain') where each value returns inexorably in regular intervals. The rhythm is determined by the beat of the percussion, be it dull or clear, heavy or light. This sophisticated practice incites the listener to reflect on the passing of time. (Iranian music of the 20th century has returned to simple, less esoteric rhythmic formulas in which 6/8 predominates.) Finally, the large forms of Middle Eastern music are, in the main, all based on the alternation of free sequences with improvised passages and fixed, measured melodic episodes. Such forms called *namhat* or *nouba* in North Africa, *waslé* in the Syro-Egyptian region, *fasil* in Turkey, *maqam* in Iraq, *mugam* in Azerbaijan, *dastgah* in Iran, and *shash-maqom* in Tajikistan and Uzbekistan. These compositions are vocal with instrumental accompaniment (or purely instrumental in Iran and Azerbaijan). They include either a soloist and an ensemble, or a choir with solo voices and an ensemble. Compositions are often anonymous, and have been constantly revised and corrected over the years by musicians whose names, in some instances, have been preserved. All these compositions use the great classical poetry in Arabic, Persian, Ottoman Turkish, Jagatai Turkish, and Azeri. These forms preserve the learned art of the prestigious courts of Damascus, Baghdad, Cordova, Istanbul, Ispahan, Samarkand, and Bukhara. Analysis of these forms reveals that they developed very slowly as new elements were successively juxtaposed to the older material. A striking example is the Syrian *waslé* (particularly as performed in the city of Aleppo). As convention dictates, the singer begins with a

Detail from the Khamsah Nizāmī (Persia, 1539-43), showing lute ('úd) player accompanied by a frame drum (daira).

qasīdah in classical Arabic (a monorhyme poem), then proceeds to a *mawal* (improvised form of four, five, or seven verses), which he must pronounce with a guttural accent—that of the nomads of the Syro-Iraqi desert (where the word *qalbi*, 'my heart', in classical Arabic is pronounced *galbi*). He concludes with a light piece, the *qadd*, which must be pronounced in the Aleppine dialect (where *qalbi*, 'my heart', is pronounced *albi*). This triple linguistic facility which any singer respectful of the tradition must master bears witness to a slow juxtaposition of three distinct historical periods, each of which has contributed to the modern *waslé* form of Aleppo.

The three cultural regions—Arabic, Persian, and Turkish—united by Islam, have bequeathed a harvest of manuscripts, many of which still await analysis. Many are in Arabic, the main lingua franca of the area. Adopted, then adapted, the Arabic script served as a basis for the writing of the Iranian and Turkish national languages, and later works on music. Conflicting claims have resulted, such as the nationality of the famous al-Farabi (the 'Alfarabius' of the Middle Ages) considered Arab by the Arabs, Iranian by the Persians, Turkish by the Ottomans.

The recognition of oral transmission has been the great revelation of recent years in these three cultures where writing has traditionally been regarded as an act of faith, forming the historical legacy. Increasing interest is being shown in the study of living music, and this research has brought to light many musical cultures hitherto overshadowed by the great classical written traditions. Since the 1950s studies have been made of Berber and Kabyle music (Morocco, Algeria), Hassaniya music (Mauritania), Kurdish (Turkey, Syria, Iraq, Iran), Baluchi (Iran), Cherkess (Syria, Jordan), Assyrian (Iraq, Syria), Laz (Turkey), Nubian (Egypt), and the scattered Armenian community. These studies may one day clarify the evolution of music in the Middle East and further field-work may shed light on ancient music of this region. These minorities, largely isolated from urban culture, developed independently. For example, they follow more or less the modal forms, which are the foundation of Arab, Persian, and Turkish music. However, they tune their instruments differently. Their long-necked lutes often have few frets, limiting the melodic range to tetrachords or pentachords, and rarely exploring the heptatonic system of most urban forms.

Minorities rarely perform in the music style of their immediate neighbours. Living in symbiosis with the Arab or Turkish world, a Kurdish musician will play his own Kurdish music even though his style may be called Turkish or Arab or Iranian. The melodies are harsh and dissonant, in contrast to the delicate classical styles.

Modern Arab musicology tends to be focused more on local origins, in studying the Arabian peninsula, than on an exchange with its two neighbours. Recent research has revealed in this region original musical practices different from pan-Arabic styles. Similarly, Turkish musicology is turning towards its cousins of the Asian plateau in a search for its origins, for example, the Qashqai nomads of Iran, the Azeri, Yürük, and Avşar nomads of Turkey, who all form part of the vast Turkish branch. A study of the individual musical styles is more significant than the formal cultural exchange between the three zones, suggesting a return to the ancient music of the classical courtly traditions. On the summits of Mount Taurus in Turkey the Yürük nomads practise an unusual form of polyphony which they play on a small *cura* (lute). They hold the instrument vertically between their legs, and pluck the strings high up on the neck with two or three fingers of both hands. This polyphonic style calls into question the classical conception of a homogeneity of cultural regions built on homophony and unison voices. At the extreme opposite, the pearl fishermen of Bahrain sing with an accentuated polyrhythm, a practice which contradicts the idea of rhythmic cycles, the spearhead of classical music. Another contradiction is found in the musical style of Kuwait, where a performance may begin with a set piece and proceed to improvised sections; this is the opposite of the classical norm, which dictates that the improvisatory section is performed first, and then followed by the set piece.

Iran was the only country not to return to sources, probably because of social problems, though given a similar situation its people might have spontaneously interested themselves in the music of the Tajik peoples (considered to be Iranians of old stock) or in Afghan music.

The Safavid dynasty (16th–17th centuries) was a troubled period, yielding little in the field of music. Music was opposed, fell into disgrace, and declined. When, at the beginning of the 20th century, some musicians attempted to save the art they injected into it new theoretical foundations derived from speculative thinking endemic in the Middle East at the end of the 19th century. Theoreticians such as the Lebanese Mikha'il Mushaga (1800–88), the Turk, Salahi Bey (1878–1945), the Egyptian, Mansur 'Awad (beginning of the 20th century), rethought the musical scale on the basis of the division of the octave into 24 equal parts, the unit of measurement of which is the quarter tone. In turn this concept was borrowed by the Iranian theoretician Ali Naqi Vaziri (*b* 1887) who tried to rescue an art which was but a vague survival of a past which had become incomprehensible. It was considered that at the end of the 19th century current practice was foundering in total anarchy, and that it could no longer serve as a tangible reference. The problem of the quarter tone became so anchored in the music of the Middle East in the minds of many that it was

taken for granted in any discussion. There was even a method for the lute ('ûd) using quarter tones but which was not based on any current practice. The quarter-tone theory has since been abandoned. Oral transmission—the living tradition—favours the three-quarter tone.

Two major preoccupations have dominated the musical scene of the Arab nations in recent years. First there is the desire to create a national music by amalgamating ethnic minority elements with mainstream urban and rural traditions, and including also certain borrowings such as harmony from the West. Thus there has emerged an Iraqi, Syrian, Jordanian, Libyan music, etc. Secondly, there is a desire to break from the past dominance of Ottoman music, and more recently from the melodramatic qualities of Egyptian music and the music of the Lebanon. The styles of two Lebanese singers, the Rahbanis, and the very famous voice of Feyruz have served to counterbalance a certain heaviness encountered so often in the Middle East, though they are closer to that taught in Western conservatories. A new situation has emerged, for each urban listener in whatever Arab state is confronted with a musical trilingualism: he knows the music of his own region; he is also familiar with Egyptian and Lebanese styles but is ignorant of anything being done in Turkey or Iran.

At the same time there are strong reactions to this situation. One has emerged in Morocco and is the product of an orchestral group of four musicians called Nass al-Ghiwâne. Another comes from an isolated endeavour by the famous Iraqi lutenist Munir Baschir, a diachronic proposition.

The Moroccan group, Nass al-Ghiwâne, in attempting both to break with Egyptian influences and to remain uninfluenced by the West could only draw on its own origins for its musical language. Coming from the Berber world, the group has been inspired by the music of the Gnawa. These were the descendants of Black slaves of Hausa, Bambara, or Peul origin who came from sub-Saharan Africa and settled long ago in Morocco, Algeria, and Tunisia, but who maintained their ethnic identity through time. Music features importantly in their culture. They have their own instruments, the most important being the *gumbri* lute which they accompany with metal castanets called *qaraqeb*. In a few years the ensemble made its mark on the Arab world. Its music is pentatonic, turning away from the essentially heptatonic classical tradition. The group has rapidly achieved success throughout North Africa with its emphasis on current indigenous practice rather than the rich culture of the past.

Nevertheless, regional polarization can only serve to heighten historical awareness, for the one cannot be separated from the other. Another example is the growth since 1979 of an Algerian musical movement called *Rai*. Beginning in the city of Oran and its environs, it rapidly spread throughout the country even jeopardizing the well-known and jealously preserved Andalusian style popular in the cities of Tlemcen, Constantine, and the capital, Algiers. *Rai* arose from the lowest classes of Oran. Its repertory belonged to the prostitutes of former times and is based on tetrachordal scales similar to those of psalmody. Its sad, despairing songs are sung in a guttural manner to the accompaniment of a *guesba* flute and the *derbuka*—the common goblet-shaped drum. Strangely enough, this hitherto little-known type approaches in its texture other styles encountered in the Syro-Lebanese coastal region called *'ataba*. This sudden eruption on the national scene of a purely local tradition encourages comparative work. The bringing together of two styles closely akin in their form and scales suggests historical exchanges between these two sections of the globe, both bordering the Mediterranean, which must go back to pre-Islamic times, possibly even Phoenician times.

The revolution of the Iraqi lutenist Munir Baschir supports this view. It breaks with the national fashionable trends which hybridized and distorted the great classical tradition and returns to the splendours of the Abbasid civilization and the élitist music of the palace. But the court music of Baghdad was devoted to singing—the chroniclers repeatedly confirm this. Munir Baschir's originality consists in developing a strictly instrumental and improvised repertory called *taqssim* which probably originated in the Ottoman capital and was mentioned by the famous theoretician Kantemiroglu (1673–1727). This was a short instrumental improvisation where the creator-interpreter displayed his mastery over the modes. The classical *taqssim* started with a strong mode, then moved to related modes, only to return to the first again. It was traditionally conceived as a short prelude creating the right mood in preparation for the singer. Munir Baschir broke new ground in instituting a recital entirely centred around the *taqssim* by developing improvisation in an unsuspected way and through a faultless instrumental technique, employing hitherto unsuspected resources of the *'ûd*. This includes the use of harmonics and a series of nuances unknown to Arab practice: diminuendo, sforzando, crescendo, etc. The traditional aesthetics of the *'ûd* were concentrated to a large part on resonantal effects. Finally, he has achieved—but here he is following the Ottoman school of lute-playing—the total mastery of the plectrum. In this field Arab musical thought is developing along the same lines as the great instrumental

rāga traditions of *India. However, Munir Baschir in attempting to understand a distant past, only succeeded in developing a 19th-century aesthetic.

The space-time relationship is certainly the main problem posed not only by the different types of music of the Middle East but by all orally transmitted music traditions. In the Middle East the problem is highlighted because of the availability of an abundance of historical writings.   CHRISTIAN POCHÉ

Midi, Le ('Noon'). Nickname of Haydn's Symphony No. 7 in C major, probably composed in 1761. See also *Matin, Le* ('Morning') and *Soir, Le* ('Evening').

Midsummer Marriage, The. Opera in three acts by Tippett; text by the composer. Produced. London, Covent Garden, 27 January 1955; Karlsruhe, 29 September 1973. The plot concerns the quest of two young people, Mark (ten) and Jenifer (sop.), for each other in marriage, which they cannot achieve until they have completely found themselves; they match with a secondary pair of lovers, the uncomplicated Bella (sop.) and Jack (ten.), in an acknowledged analogy with the couples of *The Magic Flute*. Jenifer's father is a businessman who resists their betrothal. The action is pitched between the practical and the mythical and magical, with mundane details (King Fisher and his secretary) acted out against the background of a timeless English midsummer with mysterious overtones (the presence of the seer Sosostris, and a group of Ancients). The action includes, centrally in the second Act, the Ritual Dances which illustrate conflict between the sexes in ballet terms. Eventually Mark and Jenifer achieve the fuller understanding that gives them the true condition for marriage.

Midsummer Night's Dream, A. Opera in three acts by Britten; text by the composer and Peter Pears, after Shakespeare's comedy (*c.* 1593–4). Produced: Aldeburgh, 11 June 1960; San Francisco, 10 October 1961. The plot follows Shakespeare closely, with the characters separated musically into three groups: the fairies Oberon (counter-ten.), Tytania (coloratura sop.), and Puck (speaking role, acrobat); the lovers Lysander (ten.), and Demetrius (bar.), initially both in love with Hermia (mezzo), who is in love with Lysander, and Helena (sop.), in love with Demetrius; and the rustics Bottom (bass-bar.), Quince (bass), Flute (ten.), Snug (bass), Snout (ten.), and Starveling (bar.). The high sounds of the fairies' voices (often associated by Britten with the exceptional or strange) are reinforced by the chorus of fairies, led by Cobweb, Peaseblossom, Mustardseed, and

Moth (trebles). The playlet of *Pyramus and Thisbe* in Act 3 parodies various devices of Romantic opera.

Mighty Handful. See *Five, The*.

Mignon. Opera in three acts by Ambroise Thomas to a libretto by J. Barbier and M. Carré based on Goethe's novel *Wilhelm Meisters Lehrjahre* (1795–6). It was first performed in Paris in 1866.

Migrant cantus firmus. See under *Cantus firmus*.

Mikado, The. Comic opera in two acts by Gilbert and Sullivan. Produced: London, Savoy Theatre, 14 March 1885; Chicago, 6 July 1885; Sydney, 14 October 1885; Vienna, Theater an der Wien, 2 March 1888. Set in Japan, this involves Nanki-Poo (ten.), son of the Mikado (bass), who has disguised himself as a wandering minstrel to avoid the attentions of the elderly Katisha (mezzo). At the Mikado's command, Ko-Ko (bar.), the Lord High Executioner, must behead someone within a month, and Nanki-Poo offers himself, on condition that he can marry Ko-Ko's ward Yum-Yum (sop.) A number of complications ensue, but all is resolved happily when Nanki-Poo reveals his true identity to his father, and Ko-Ko offers to marry the irate Katisha.

Mikrokosmos. 'Progressive pieces' for piano by Bartók, composed between 1926 and 1939. The 153 pieces were published in six volumes. Bartók arranged seven of them (Nos. 113, 69, 135, 123, 127, 145, 146) for two pianos. Seven (Nos. 102, 117, 137, 139, 142, 151, 153) were arranged for orchestra by Tibór Sérly, who also transcribed five (Nos. 102, 108, 116, 139, 142) for string quartet.

Milán, Luis de (*b* c.1500; fl. 1536–61). Spanish composer. All that is known of his life is that he was connected with the ducal court in Valencia. He was a virtuoso performer on the vihuela, and composed songs and solo music for his instrument. Most of his known music is contained in the didactic *Libro de música de vihuela de mano intitulado El maestro* (Valencia, 1536). His *romances* and *villancicos* have been compared to Dowland's lute ayres, and his fantasias are interesting not only for their technical brilliance but also for their early use of tempo indications and expressive rubato. Milán also wrote *El cortesano* (Valencia, 1561), a book modelled on Castiglione's *Il cortegiano* (1528) and dedicated to Philip II of Spain.   DENIS ARNOLD

Milanese chant. See *Plainchant, 2, 3*.

Milano, Francesco (Canova) da (*b* Monza, nr Milan, 18 Aug. 1497; *d* Milan, 15 Apr. 1543). Italian composer and the most famous lutenist of the 16th century. He was in the service of three popes (Leo X, Clement VII, and Paul III) in Rome before moving to Piacenza in the late 1520s. For a time around 1530 he may have been the organist of Milan Cathedral. He returned to Rome in 1535, working for two cardinals, Ippolito de' Medici and Alessandro Farnese, and for Pope Paul III, with whom he visited Nice in 1538. Milano composed a great deal of attractive music for the lute, most of it in the form of the *ricercar* or the fantasia, and made many arrangements of motets, madrigals, and *chansons*. His music was widely known, not only in Italy but also in France and England.

DENIS ARNOLD

Milhaud, Darius (*b* Aix-en-Provence, 4 Sept. 1892; *d* Geneva, 22 June 1974). French composer. He entered the Paris Conservatoire in 1909 and there studied with Gedalge and Widor; equally significant was his meeting at this time with the writer Paul Claudel (1868–1955). In 1913 he began to write music for Claudel's translation of the *Oresteia*, his setting of *Les Choéphores* (1915) being particularly remarkable for its use of speaking chorus with percussion, and for its introduction of polytonality, which was to remain a distinctive feature of Milhaud's style. He went as Claudel's secretary to Rio de Janeiro (1917–18) when the poet was appointed ambassador, and the two collaborated on a Brazilian ballet, *L'homme et son désir* (1918).

Back in Paris, Milhaud fell in with a group of young composers, including Poulenc and Honegger, who in 1920 were christened Les Six. The flippant, anti-conventional aesthetic of the group is reflected in several of his works from this period, notably the song-cycle *Machines agricoles* (1919), which sets extracts from a catalogue of agricultural machinery, and the ballet *Le boeuf sur le toit* (1919), in which he used Latin-American dance forms. Another exotic source was the jazz music which he heard in a Harlem night club, and which he put to use in his ballet *La création du monde* (1923). Milhaud did not, however, forget his own background as a Provençal and as a Jew. His small-scale opera *Les malheurs d'Orphée* (1925) translates the myth to the Camargue, and one of his most luminous and attractive orchestral scores is the *Suite provençale* (1936). As for the specifically Jewish works, they range from the song-cycle *Poèmes juifs* (1916) to the opera-oratorio *David* (1952), commissioned for performance in Israel.

From the 1920s onwards Milhaud wrote with astonishing fluency, his tally of works eventually reaching well over 400. Among them are 12

Milhaud

full-scale symphonies, a large number of concertos and other orchestral pieces, a body of chamber music which includes 18 quartets (nos. 14 and 15, curiously, may be played simultaneously as an octet), choral works and songs of all kinds, film scores and incidental music, and several big operas. *Christophe Colomb* (1930, text by Claudel) is the most ambitious of his operatic works, complex in its many-layered staging and grandly conceived in its choral and orchestral textures.

Milhaud spent the years 1940–7 in America, teaching at Mills College, California. On his return to France he was appointed professor of composition at the Paris Conservatoire, but he continued, despite persistent ill health, to travel regularly to the USA in order to teach at various institutions. He continued, also, to compose as prolifically as ever and to show, in almost everything he wrote, that Gallic lyricism to which his polytonality gave a personal piquancy.

PAUL GRIFFITHS

FURTHER READING
Darius Milhaud: *Notes without Music* (London, 1952); Christopher Palmer: *Milhaud* (London, 1976).

Milieu (Fr.). 'Middle'; *milieu de l'archet*, 'middle of the bow' etc.

Military. Nickname of Haydn's Symphony No. 100 in G major, composed in 1793-4. It is so called because of its use of 'military' instruments and a solo trumpet call in the second movement.

Military band and Corps of drums. Wind and percussion ensembles, not necessarily military, but equally civilian when organized by local societies, colleges, and schools. A band has woodwind and brass instruments together (though sometimes replaced by a *brass band); civilian bands now often prefer the name 'concert band' or 'wind orchestra'. A corps of drums may be of fifes and drums or bugles and drums; or a corps of pipes and drums (bagpipes).

Of bands, there were in Britain in 1980 36 Staff Bands (among them seven for the Guards Division and 16 for the Royal Armoured Corps); 48 Regimental Bands; 12 at the Junior Band training establishments; 24 Territorial Army Volunteer Reserve; and six for the Royal Air Force. Most of the infantry regiments also have a corps of drums, and this may combine with the band on a full parade.

Recruiting is the responsibility of the Director of Music or the Bandmaster concerned, each potential musician being auditioned before acceptance. The main schools of music in Britain are: the Royal Military School of Music, Kneller Hall; the Royal Artillery, Woolwich; the Junior Musicians' Wing of the Household Division, the Guards Depot, Pirbright; the Royal Armoured Corps, Bovington; the Royal Air Force School of Music, Uxbridge; and the Royal Marines School of Music at Deal.

In the USA, the leading bands include: The President's Band; West Point; US Marine Band; US Navy Band; and US Army Band.

For organizing civilian band festivals there are in Britain the National Concert and Military Bands Association, and the Corps of Drums Society. In the USA there are the Drum Corps Association and other societies.

1. *Bands.* A band usually has from 25 players up to as many as wished. In instrumentation it is basically like a symphony orchestra with the strings removed and the wind increased by extra clarinets and tubas (in British bands called 'basses') and by two or more saxophones. Thus, a band is able to play transcriptions of orchestral music, and on this its performing repertory, other than marches, has always very largely depended.

In Britain and the USA published editions for military band usually have parts for:

Flute and piccolo, oboe, E♭ clarinet

B♭ clarinets in three or four parts, mostly played by two or more players to each part: 'Solo', '1st', '2nd', and '3rd' (in USA these last three parts only)

Alto and bass clarinet: often in American editions, but in British seldom except in old editions which have no saxophones

Bassoons: one or two parts

Saxophones: in Britain, alto and tenor; in USA usually two altos, tenor, and baritone

Horns (French horns): two to four parts

Cornets (or trumpets): two parts; in USA often three

Trombones: three parts, the third for bass trombone

Euphonium (in USA 'baritone')

Basses: for instruments in E♭ and low B♭, the former playing the upper notes where the part is written in octaves. Often included is a special part for 'String bass' (double bass), an almost regular addition to a band when playing under cover

Percussion: side-drum; bass drum and cymbals; sometimes a part for timpani

Conductor: usually a 'short score' in up to four staves

Marches are printed on cards, to be clipped to a card-holder or 'lyre' attached to the instrument. The current tempos for the British army are stated as 116 paces per minute for a quick march and 65 for a slow.

The well-tried principles of transcribing orchestral music for a band lie basically in adapting the violin parts for clarinets, viola for the same or saxophone, cello for euphonium or tenor saxophone or bassoons, and then distributing the original wind parts among the other instruments (e.g. transferring important clarinet passages to cornet where possible). Harp parts can be a problem: Sousa took a harpist with him.

In Britain military bands are fewer than they were, not only through economies in the armed forces but also on the civilian wing through a lessening of interest among the young (which has, however, little affected the brass band). The Great Western Railway Military Band performing in Paddington Station in London every Saturday morning is a distant memory of the 1930s. There has been some revival in recent years; but it is in the USA that the amateur military band continues as ever to be a major institution, whether executing complicated and spectacular march routines at football matches or playing as a concert band. Extra parts may be written out for additional instruments (like contrabass clarinet) or players (like second and third flutes), making room for a greater number of musicians and so affording the overflow of competent wind-players in schools and colleges, denied through their sheer numbers a seat in the orchestra itself, an opportunity to play together and feel themselves part of a team.

European bands vary much in size. Small bands usually have clarinets and (less frequently in Germany) one or two saxophones, the rest being brass, the music laid out basically in a brass band manner. But some bands are very large, as a full *orchestre d'harmonie* in France, or enormous like some of the Italian municipal bands which include almost every species of wind instrument existing: saxophones from soprano to bass, flugel horns, bass trumpets, contrabass valved trombones, and even sarrusophones (as Beecham attempted in London with his wind orchestra of 1912). Opera selections are magnificently performed, the leading vocal parts entrusted usually to a solo cornet and a solo trombone.

2. *Corps of Drums*. For instruments employed, see *Bagpipe*, 2; *Bugle*; *Drum* (including 3); *Flute*, 9. Some of the civilian corps today use E♭ cavalry trumpets (see *Trumpet*, 4), often with bass trumpets, an octave deeper; or, mainly in Europe, the large circular French hunting horns (*trompes de chasse*, see *Hunting horn*). With them may be bell lyras (see *Glockenspiel*, 4) and other varied percussion. There has also been a trend, especially in the USA, to add more and more instruments, sometimes to include valved brass (so making virtually a kind of brass band) as well as percussion of every available type. In France this has long been done in an opposite way, i.e. adding bugles or *trompes de chasse* to an otherwise normal *fanfare* (brass band), the repertory then including published marches and other pieces in which the tunes can be played by, or at least partly by, such 'natural' brass instruments.

Quite distinct and of far older lineage are the Trumpets and Kettledrums of the Household Cavalry, heard either mounted or dismounted at state banquets and the like. France similarly has the Musique à Cheval de la Garde Républicaine, equally impressive with splendid historic dress and led by the powerful and imperturbable drum horse.

3. *History*. In the Middle Ages in Europe small bands of shawms and trumpets with a drummer would accompany royal armies on campaigns, following the rather older Saracen practice. Thereafter it became a matter of drum and fife for foot and trumpets and kettledrums for cavalry, until the mid 17th century, towards the end of the Thirty Years War (1618–48), when the Elector of Brandenburg formed infantry bands of three shawms with a bass dulcian (see *Bassoon*, 4a). Some years later (1663, it has been said) French royal regiments were allotted bands of the same size, using three oboes with bassoon, and this became the normal military band in England and Germany also, playing mainly marches but also, in Germany at any rate, small suites or *parthies* (partitas), providing music for the officers' mess wherever it might be. Horns began to be added in the 1720s and clarinets in the 1760s, bringing great enrichment to the *parthie* (or divertimento etc.), the finest examples of which were, however, written by Mozart and others for private civilian wind bands kept by Austrian and German aristocracy; here too began the band tradition of transcribing operatic music (see *Harmonie*). Further enlarge-

Pl. 1. Band of the Foot Guards (1753): 2 French horns, 2 bassoons, 4 oboes ('hoboys').

ment of bands came with the French Revolution. For the first time they were seen as a national institution and the Paris Conservatoire was set up largely to foster them. For a great national fête 100 players might be mustered to play marches and national hymns, nearly a third of the men being clarinettists.

After this, it was a question of incorporating the new brass instruments as they became available from 1810 onwards, first keyed and

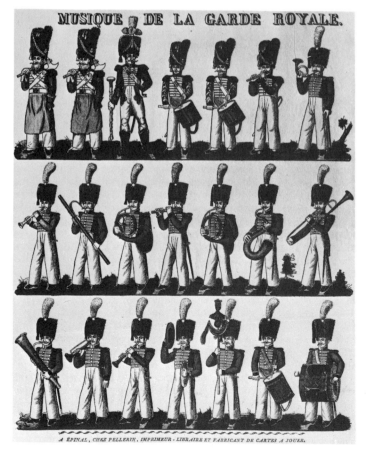

Pl. 2. Bandsmen of the French Garde Royale, after 1820. Among the instruments note especially: (top right) cornet ordinaire (see Post-horn, 2); (2nd row) two hand-horns (see Horn, 6c), *serpent and *trombone (this in a form with bell pointing to the rear; not all hand positions among the instruments are correctly drawn); (bottom row) serpent Forveille (see Serpent, 2), natural trumpet (short model) and on right, Jingling Johnny (see Turkish Music), caisse roulante (see Drum, 2c), and bass drum played with a switch in the left hand (see Drum, 4d).

then especially valved. In Britain the first band journal (i.e. serial publication of fresh items in band-parts) began in 1845 (Boosé's) and could almost be used today; likewise when the Royal School of Military Music (as it came to be called) was opened in 1857, the instrumentation taught was hardly different from now. Next, the great American band tradition got into full swing after the Civil War, its first renowned leader being Patrick Sarsfield Gilmore (1829-92), who had been a bandmaster in the US army during that war and toured Europe in 1878 with a band of 66 players. The next, John Philip Sousa (1854-1932), directed a band of the US marine corps from 1880, then resigned in 1892 to form his own band, which gave its first concert in Pittfield, New Jersey, in that year and toured the world in 1910-11.

In Britain an achievement of outstanding musical worth was the BBC's Wireless Military Band, which functioned from 1927 to 1943. Directed by Lieutenant B. Walton O'Donnell, it counted among its members many of the finest London orchestral players of the day, and its own arrangements of orchestral works were of exemplary quality, making full use of the varied range of tone-colours along with the highest professional standard of performance.

For the history of military music and of bands of all kinds past and present, a current periodical is *Band International*, the journal of the International Military Music Society.

4. *Beating the Retreat*. For this favourite ceremony there is no set pattern throughout. In the general sequence among British regiments, the band is formed up with the corps of drums behind, and on the order from the Drum Major they move off, countermarching up and down the barrack square to the slow march of the regiment. Then they break into quick time, led off by a five-pace roll or two three-pace rolls on the side-drum, for the band to play the regimental quick march or some other well-known quick march, the Corps of Drums alternating with their own marches. The Drum Major halts band and music for the Director of Music to come to the head of the band for performance of one or more of the short melodious pieces known as 'troops' (some in 3/4 time, like the favourite troop entitled 'Mayblossom'). After this interlude the Corps of Drums detaches itself under the Sergeant Drummer to sound the Retreat Call on the bugles (or in the cavalry, the trumpet), finally to rejoin the band for all to march off, most probably to the regimental march.

The origin is in Watch Setting: mounting the guard after sunset in days when army bands and regiments had only drum and fife to beat the Retreat. This was kept up later by the Guards regiments. After inspection of the picquet, the drummer played three rolls each accompanied by a different note on the fife, followed by a simple well-known tune (like 'The Ash Grove', 'Robin Adair', or some opera air), after the last note of which the Sergeant of the Guard hauled down the Union Jack.   ANTHONY BAINES

Mille, Agnes de (*b* New York, 1909). American choreographer. She successfully bridged commercial and non-commercial work, integrating specifically American themes into ballet with *Rodeo* (Copland, 1942) and *Fall River Legend* (Gould, 1948). She used classical technique as a springboard for integrating dance into musical theatre with *Oklahoma!* (1943), *Carousel* (1945), and other productions, and is the author of several stimulating books on dance.

NOËL GOODWIN

Millöcker, Carl (*b* Vienna, 29 Apr. 1842; *d* Baden, nr Vienna, 31 Dec. 1899). Austrian composer. He was one of the most successful composers of operettas, and spent his early years as a flautist in a Viennese theatre, then becoming a conductor and composer in Graz and Vienna. After the enormous success of *Der Bettelstudent* (1882), he gave up conducting and composed a stream of popular light operas in the tradition of Offenbach and Suppé.

DENIS ARNOLD

Milner, Anthony (Francis Dominic) (*b* Bristol, 13 May 1925). English composer. He studied at the Royal College of Music (1945-7) and had private composition lessons from Mátyás Seiber (1944-8). His output includes a variety of choral works, ranging from small-scale cantatas to the grandly conceived Second Symphony (1977-8); the style tends towards ecstatic lyricism and the subjects are often related to Catholic theology. Milner has also taught at Morley College (1946-62), the Royal College of Music (1961-   ), and King's College, London (1965-   ).   PAUL GRIFFITHS

Milton, John (*b* Stanton St John, nr Oxford, *c*.1563; *d* London, Mar. 1647). English amateur composer, and father of the poet. He was educated at Oxford and later became a member of the Scriveners' Company. He wrote anthems and consort music and contributed to Morley's *Triumphes of Oriana* and William Leighton's *Teares or Lamentacions of a Sorrowful Soule*.

JOHN MILSOM

Mime. A play in dumb show (i.e. using only gestures, not words), or an actor of such. Mime is an important constituent of ballet, and formed the basis of the 18th-century dramatic ballet, or *ballet d'action*, in which the dancers were expected to express emotions through gestures and facial expressions, as opposed to the stylized ritual of earlier court ballets, in which the dancers were often masked. Mime also played an important part in 18th-century Parisian fair theatres, when the monopoly of the Paris Opéra forbade singing in the fair entertainments. The connotation of farce, especially in pantomime, is, however, often present. A 'mimodrama' is a play (musical or otherwise) which is carried on in dumb show. The term has been used by composers: Roger-Ducasse described his *Orpheus* (1913) as a 'mimodrame'.

Minaccevole, minaccevolmente (It.). 'Menacing', 'menacingly' (also *minacciando*, *minaccioso*, *minacciosamente*).

Minder (Ger.). 'Less'.

Minim (♩). The half-note, i.e. a note half the value of the semibreve (whole note).

Minnesinger (Ger., pl. *Minnesinger*). German poet-musicians, often of aristocratic birth, of the 12th, 13th, and 14th centuries. Like the **trouvères* of northern France, the *Minnesinger* modelled their culture on that of the **troubadours*; their poetry reflects a social order of great refinement and education, dominated by a reverence for women, and generally expressed

in the language of courtly love. Although most of their verse was set to music, sung by the *Minnesinger* themselves and often accompanied by professional minstrels, few melodies have survived from the first two centuries of the movement's existence. Principal composers include Walther von der Vogelweide, Neidhart von Reuental (*d c.*1250), and Der Tannhäuser, whose works date from the 13th century; Oswald von Wolkenstein, one of the last of the *Minnesinger*, wrote a number of polyphonic songs as well as conventional monodies. See also *Meistersinger*; *Minstrel*.   JOHN MILSOM

Minor canon. In an English cathedral of the New Foundation, a clergyman whose duty is to intone the priest's part in the choral services (see also *Vicar choral*).

Minor interval. See *Interval*.

Minor scale. See *Scale*, 3.

Minstrel. In the early Middle Ages, a professional entertainer of any sort (story-teller, juggler, buffoon, acrobat, instrumentalist); later, a professional secular musician or poet-musician, either attached to a court or noble household, or a traveller.

'Minstrel', which had no specifically musical connotation before the end of the 13th century, serves as a useful portmanteau word for all types and nationalities of Medieval European secular musicians, who are documented as far back as *c.*900. The earliest of these on whom there is much information are the Celtic bards and epic poets, the Saxon gleemen, and the *joculatores* (Lat.), who were wandering entertainers with accomplishments that may have included playing an instrument; the French (*jongleur*), German (*Gaukler*), and English (juggler) cognates imply less dignity and suggest that *joculatores* were much involved in light entertainment, possibly including story-telling, conjuring, and juggling as well as music-making. As the Middle Ages progressed, so did the musician's image: a change in social status may have been marked by the introduction of the term 'ménestrier' (minstrel) as musicians were increasingly regarded as higher-class entertainers.

The art of *jongleurs* and minstrels transcended the boundaries between the countries of western Europe and Britain (encouraged by England's then close connections with France) and lasted several centuries. That of the **troubadours* and **trouvères* was much briefer—about 200 years, from the late 11th to the late 13th centuries—and much more localized, the *troubadours* being confined to the Provençal-

The Minnesinger Heinrich von Meissen ('Frauenlob') and musicians with (left to right) tabor, straight cornett, shawm, fiddles, and bagpipe, miniature from the Manessische Liederhandschrift (c.1320).

speaking areas of southern France, northern Spain, and northern Italy, and the *trouvères* to the French-speaking regions. Like the bards and epic poets (who seem anyway to have held a higher social position in Britain than their continental counterparts), *troubadours* and *trouvères* combined the roles and skills of poet, composer, singer, and instrumentalist and thereby earned a high place in society. Indeed, they included among their number many gifted members of the nobility, even kings (Thibaut IV of Navarre and Richard I of England, whose ancestry was partly Provençal). The terms 'troubadour' and 'trouvère' mean 'finder' (i.e. inventor), notably of verses and melodies; they left a vast legacy of courtly lyric poetry, though substantially less music, since the tradition of transmitting secular monophony was still largely oral.

The German counterparts of the *troubadours* and *trouvères* were the **Minnesinger*, who were approximately contemporary and likewise of noble rank. Like the *troubadours* they sang of heroism, love, and Nature, though their verse was perhaps more idealistic. Less of their music survives than of the *trouvères*, and that is mostly in late (and therefore less reliable) sources. The social structure and activities of the *Minnesinger* indirectly furnished the background for Wagner's *Tannhäuser*, and their poetry an early source for the Parsifal legend.

The rise of the craft guilds in 14th-century Germany prompted the formation of guilds of poet-musicians, the **Meistersinger*, who represented a middle-class continuation of the declining aristocratic *Minnesinger*. Unlike most earlier minstrels, they were not travellers but resident members of artisan guilds in cities such as Mainz, Augsburg, and Nuremberg, and as amateur poet-musicians they practised their art at weekly meetings and under strict academic regulations. The subject-matter of their earlier songs (*Meisterlieder*) was chiefly religious, but it was after the Reformation in the 16th century, when secular songs were admitted, that the movement achieved its most vigorous flowering. It was this period that attracted Wagner as a setting for *Die Meistersinger von Nürnberg*, which gives a generally helpful though somewhat romanticized idea of the activities of the Nuremberg guild.

In the 16th century, with the increasing institutionalization of music throughout Europe in both courtly and civic contexts, the role of the independent minstrel declined. Since then the term has been loosely and widely applied to many sorts of musician, ranging from the city **wait, the performer of **street music, and the **ballad singer of earlier days to the street busker and popular stage entertainer of modern times.

JUDITH NAGLEY

Minuet (Fr.: *menuet*; Ger.: *Menuett*; It.: *minuetto*). A stately French dance in triple metre (usually 3/4) which appeared as a social dance at the French court in the 1660s. Lully was the

Minuet danced at a state ball given in the covered riding-school of the Grand Stables at Versailles in 1745, after Cochin.

first composer to make extensive use of the minuet in stage works, both ballet and opera, and it then passed into the suite, where it was usually placed after the sarabande and followed by a *double* (a varied repeat with ornaments); this led eventually to the traditional arrangement of minuet–second minuet in contrasting style (*trio)–first minuet repeated.

The minuet was quickly taken up outside France and Italy, especially in England (where it became a popular ballroom dance and a regular component of the suite) and Germany (Pachelbel, Fischer, and Muffat wrote French-style minuets in their keyboard suites). Handel preferred the Italian variety, which was rather faster, in 3/8 or 6/8 metre, and some French composers of the period followed his example. Bach used both types in his keyboard partitas and suites, in all but one of his orchestral suites, and in his music for solo violin and cello.

In the Classical period, the minuet was adopted as a movement in the emerging forms of symphony, solo sonata, and string quartet. At first it acted as a finale (e.g. in the symphonies of Abel, J. C. Bach, Johann Stamitz, and Arne, the piano sonatas and trios of Haydn, and some Mozart concertos), but eventually the standard tripartite minuet and trio was adopted as the third movement of the four-movement plan of symphonies and quartets, generally designed to provide light relief between the slow movement and the finale. Some later examples introduce more complex techniques, such as canon (Mozart's Symphony No. 40 in G minor), and some treat the reprise of the minuet after the trio with elaborate embellishments.

From Beethoven onwards the traditional place of the minuet in symphonic and chamber music began to be taken over by the *scherzo. Beethoven still occasionally used the minuet (e.g. in the First and Eighth Symphonies), but in general the dance had little importance after 1800. It enjoyed a revival in the late 19th century, when French composers began to look to the past for inspiration (e.g. in Debussy's early *Suite bergamasque* for piano and in his *Petite suite* for piano duet; in Fauré's *Masques et bergamasques*; in Ravel's *Sonatine* and his *Menuet antique*; Satie's *Premier menuet*; and in Schoenberg's Serenade Op. 24 and his Piano Suite Op. 25). Vaughan Williams included a minuet in his 'masque for dancing', *Job*.

WENDY THOMPSON

'Minute' Waltz. Nickname of Chopin's Waltz in D♭, Op. 64 No. 1 (1846–7), for piano. It is so called on the assumption that it can be played in one minute—but that is only possible if it is played too fast.

Miracle. Nickname of Haydn's Symphony No. 96 in D major, composed in 1791. It is so called because it was said that at its first performance, in London in 1791, the audience rushed forward at the end to congratulate the composer, thereby miraculously escaping being injured by a chandelier that collapsed on their seats. The incident in fact occurred during Haydn's second visit to London, in 1795, after a performance of his Symphony No. 102—which thus deserves the nickname.

Miracle plays. See *Church Drama*, 2.

Miraculous Mandarin, The (*A csodálatos mandarin*). Pantomime in one act by Bartók to a scenario by Menyhért Lengyel. It was first performed in Cologne in 1926, but because of censorship, it was not performed in Budapest until 1946, the year after Bartók's death. Bartók arranged an orchestral suite from the score (1919, 1927).

Mirliton. See *Kazoo*.

Miroirs ('Mirrors'). Five piano pieces by Ravel, composed in 1904–5. They are *Noctuelles*, *Oiseaux tristes*, *Une barque sur l'océan*, *Alborado del gracioso*, and *La vallée des cloches*. Ravel orchestrated *Une barque sur l'océan* (1906, revised 1926) and *Alborado del gracioso* (1918).

Mirror canon. See *Canon*.

Mirror on which to Dwell, A. Song-cycle by Carter to poems by Elizabeth Bishop, composed in 1975. They are for soprano, piccolo, two flutes, oboe, cor anglais, clarinet, E♭ clarinet, bass clarinet, percussion, piano, violin, viola, cello, and double bass. The titles are *Anaphora*, *Argument*, *Sandpiper*, *Insomnia*, *View of the Capitol from the Library of Congress*, and *O Breath*.

Mise (Fr.). A 'placing'; *mise de voix*, the same as *messa di voce.

Missa (Lat.). 'Mass'. The *Missa brevis* is the 'short Mass', not so musically elaborate as to take a long time to perform and hence suitable for ordinary occasions as distinct from high ceremonial occasions on which a *Missa solemnis* would be performed. The *Missa solemnis* is the High, or 'solemn', Mass, performed by a priest with the assistance of deacon, subdeacon, and other ministers, together with a choir. Most of the texts are sung, the Proper, which changes according to the Church calendar, generally to plainchant, and the Ordinary, which remains the same, generally to a polyphonic setting (for the structure and history of the *Missa solemnis*, see *Mass*). The *Missa cantata* is practically the same as the *Missa solemnis* in that it is 'sung', but it is given with fewer clergy and less ceremonial. The *Missa lecta* ('read Mass'), or *Missa privata* ('private Mass'), is the Low Mass, performed by a priest and one clerk and celebrated without music except for hymns sung by the congregation.

Missa in tempore belli ('Mass in Time of War'). See *Paukenmesse*.

Missal (Lat.: *missale*). Book containing the chants, prayers, and lessons for Mass; see *Plainchant*, 5.

Missa Papae Marcelli ('Mass of Pope Marcellus'). Mass by Palestrina for six voices, published in his second book of Masses (1567). Pope Marcellus II established a commission to encourage the composition of polyphonic sacred music in which the words were intelligible. Legend has it that Palestrina composed this Mass for the commission (the Council of Trent), thereby 'saving church music'. There is no definite evidence that it was performed to the cardinals, and it may have been written some years earlier for Marcellus II, perhaps for his election as Pope (1555).

Missa super 'L'homme armé'. Work by Peter Maxwell Davies for speaker and ensemble to a Latin text and a passage from St Luke 22. It is a revision of an earlier work (composed in 1968) called *L'homme armé*, the name of the Medieval song on which it is based, and was first performed in 1971. See also *Homme armé, l'.*

Miss Donnithorne's Maggot. Theatre piece by Peter Maxwell Davies to a text by Randolph

Stow. It is scored for soprano and ensemble (including four metronomes, bosun's whistle, and chamois-leather rubbed on glass) and was first performed in 1974 in Adelaide, Australia.

Misura (It.). 'Measure', either in the sense of 'bar', or in the general sense of regular time; *alla misura* (It.), 'in strict time'; *senza misura*, 'without strict time', i.e. in free tempo; *misurato*, 'measured', i.e. strictly in time.

Mitridate, rè di Ponto ('Mitridates, King of Pontus'). Opera in three acts by Mozart to a libretto by V. A. Cigna-Santi after G. Parini and Racine. It was first performed in Milan in 1770.

Mitte (Ger.). 'Middle', e.g. *auf der Mitte des Bogens*, 'in the middle of the bow'.

Mixed cadence. See *Cadence*, 2.

Mixed voices. A term used in choral music to mean a combination of male and female voices, such as the standard choral combination of sopranos, altos, tenors, and basses (SATB).

Mixolydian mode. The mode represented by the white notes of the piano beginning on G. See *Mode*, 2.

M.M. See *Metronome*.

Mobile form. A kind of musical structure in which fragments may be differently assorted according to the performer's choice, so named by analogy with the mobiles of Alexander Calder. See also *Indeterminate music.*

Mock trumpet. See *Clarinet*, 4a.

Mode

1. Introduction
2. Mode and Scales or Melody Types in European Music
3. Folk Music and Non-European Cultures
4. Mode and Ethos

1. *Introduction.* In early Medieval theory the word *modus* was occasionally used to mean 'interval'—for example by Hucbald (*c*.840–930) and Guido of Arezzo (*c*.991–*c*.1033). This meaning survived in Ornithoparcus's *Musicae activae micrologus* (Leipzig, 1517) and was retained in John Dowland's translation of the same, *Of Moodes, or Intervals* (London, 1609). It is last found in the writings of Johann Heinrich Buttstedt (1666–1727).

There are two other meanings better known today: that of the rhythmic modes, found in the theory of rhythm of Medieval mensural music (see *Notation*, 3); and that of 'scale' or 'melody

type' (see below, 2). The latter covers a wide range of definition, from simple scales—arrangements of tones and semitones sometimes without any implication of a 'tonic' or main note—to a particular and typical melodic style or collection of motifs, perhaps with a definite 'tonic' and other notes in a hierarchy of importance—a meaning often found in discussions of non-European music, where melody types are widely employed in non-written musical traditions (see below, 3).

The adjective 'modal' is also commonly used today to denote music whose tonal design (if any) is not governed by the system of major and minor keys—very roughly speaking, comprising music written before the 18th century. Sometimes 'modal' is even used as an antithesis to 'tonal'. Section 2d therefore gives a brief discussion of these aspects of mode, although they might as easily be subsumed under the broad topic 'tonality'. The article concludes with a section on the ethical properties ascribed to modes.

2. *Mode and Scales or Melody Types in European Music: (a) To the 9th Century*. It was one of the most important tasks of late 8th- and early 9th-century Frankish musicians to construct a theoretical framework to accommodate the newly-created repertory of 'Gregorian' chant (see *Plainchant*, 3). This was not purely an intellectual enterprise, but also a practical necessity for the correct performance of chant, since it was important to ensure agreement on mode during the memorization of the huge chant repertory. A large part of the singers' duties consisted of the singing of psalm verses according to set formulas or 'tones' (see *Tonus*, 3). Each intonation was introduced and followed by an antiphon, and it was vital to use the tone which accorded best with the tonality of the antiphon. Thus there was effected a standardization of the chant repertory into eight modes, and correspondingly eight main psalm tones. It is perhaps not surprising, therefore, that the earliest evidence of the use of the modal system in plainchant should be found not in theoretical literature but in a tonary of the late 8th century, from St Riquier in north-eastern France, where chants to be sung at Mass are listed in order of their mode (later tonaries were more commonly restricted to Office antiphons).

It should be pointed out that the psalm tones themselves do not all cadence on the finals of their corresponding modes. In fact, each psalm tone is provided with several different cadences (or *differentiae*). This is because they are always succeeded by a repeat of an antiphon, and a smooth transition must be made from the end of the psalm verse back to the beginning of the antiphon. Tonaries may group chants not simply according to their mode, but also according to which *differentia* is most appropriate. Thus the antiphon *Qui me sanum fecit* (see *Antiphon*, Ex. 1) is classed as mode 1, first *differentia*, because the psalm it accompanies will be sung to the first psalm tone and will use the first cadence for that tone.

The names of the modes were as set out in Table 1.

The Greek names, like some other aspects of early Carolingian theory and practice, were borrowed from Byzantine chant; indeed, the system of eight modes itself is clearly based on the Byzantine *oktoechos*—a system of eight (*okto*) melody types (*echoi*).

The use of eight psalm tones, one for each mode, was not known in Old Roman chant, but was a Frankish innovation. There are several indications that the modal system was imposed upon a pre-existing body of chant—mainly the fact that a significant (albeit small) number of chants are not easily classified among the eight modes, usually because of a chromatic peculiarity of some sort, or because a chant cadencing in one mode will have inflexions characteristic of chants in another. Theorists—and tonaries—frequently disagree in their assignment of these chants to particular modes. Aurelian of Réomé's *Musica disciplina* (*c*.850) contains the following interesting statement, which also clearly connects the eight-mode system with the Byzantines (the status of the four added modes is dubious): 'A number of singing masters claimed that there

TABLE 1

1. 2.	*Protus*	*authenticus* *plagalis*	cadencing on D	D at bottom of range, range about an octave above D D in middle of range, range about a fifth either side of D
3. 4.	*Deuterus*	*authenticus* *plagalis*	cadencing on E	E at bottom of range, range about an octave above E E in middle of range, range about a fifth either side of E
5. 6.	*Tritus*	*authenticus* *plagalis*	cadencing on F	F at bottom of range, range about an octave above F F in middle of range, range about a fifth either side of F
7. 8.	*Tetrardus*	*authenticus* *plagalis*	cadencing on G	G at bottom of range, range about an octave above G G in middle of range, range about a fifth either side of G

were certain antiphons which could be accommodated to none of the formulas. Whereupon the Emperor Charlemagne ordered that four be added . . . And it was because the Greeks boasted of their skill in having acquired as many as eight modes that he decided to raise the number to 12.'

Although originating as a theoretical abstraction of a sort, the modal system as discussed so far fulfilled an important practical need. But 9th-century writers went beyond this, and sought to effect a *rapprochement* between the eight-mode system of plainchant and what was known of classical Greek theory, in particular its expression in Boethius's *De institutione musica* (early 6th century). Of course, Boethius's treatise is concerned chiefly with speculative discussion, for example of the arithmetical characteristics of intervals; it is not concerned with plainchant. He is most interesting for his provision of: (*a*) descriptions of the seven octave scales possible within the framework of a diatonic double-octave (i.e. the equivalent of octave scales on the white notes of the piano starting on A, B, C, D, E, F, and G); (*b*) the names Hypodorian (A), Hypophrygian (G), Hypolydian (F), Dorian (E), Phrygian (D), Lydian (C), and Mixolydian (B) for his seven octave scales; (*c*) the division of the diatonic double-octave into four *tetrachords (scales covering a perfect fourth) with the interval pattern semitone-tone-tone (i.e. two tetrachords for each octave, covering B-C-D-E and E-F-G-A); and (*d*) the use of the terms 'mode', 'tone', and 'trope', synonymously, to describe the seven scales.

Two 9th-century treatises, *De harmonica* by Hucbald of St Amand and the anonymous *Alia musica*, show a synthesis of these diverse elements. It is particularly interesting to see Hucbald using familiar passages of chant to exemplify points of Greek theory. He describes the tetrachord and the double-octave in the Greek (Boethian) manner, but then restructures the analysis by using a different interval pattern for his four tetrachords: tone-semitone-tone (i.e. two tetrachords for each octave, covering A-B-C-D and D-E-F-G). He singles out the tetrachord starting on D as consisting of the notes 'used in constructing the four modes or tropes. These are nowadays called "tones" and are the *Protus*, *Deuterus*, *Tritus*, and *Tetrardus* . . . These notes are called "finals" since everything that is sung ends among them.' Note that for Hucbald there are but four modes or tones, and that he uses the Byzantine-derived, rather than the classical Greek, names.

The author of *Alia musica*, on the other hand, took the Greek names and reassigned them among the existing eight church modes. This was the foundation of the modal system of the Medieval and Renaissance periods, and is set out in Ex. 1.

(*b*) *Later Chant Theorists.* As noted above, the modal classification of many chants was influenced at an early stage by their connection with psalm intonations, with the regular alternation of antiphon-psalm verse-repeat of antiphon. The Introit *Accipite* (see Ex. 2), for example, begins like a G mode (*Tetrardus*) piece, yet ends on E. Sometimes the melody was given the eighth psalm tone (i.e. that for the G mode), sometimes the fourth (that for the E mode), depending on whether the link with the beginning of the Introit was considered more important than the final cadence or not.

From the early 11th century, however, theorists rarely looked at anything other than the final note for determining the mode. This rational attitude is reflected in a widely-known treatise, the *Dialogus de musica* (written in northern Italy, *c*.1000): 'a tone or mode is a rule which distinguishes every chant in its final'. The *Dialogus* also cites ranges most often used in chants in each mode: Dorian, *c-e'*; Hypodorian, *a-bb'*; Phrygian, *d-e'*; Hypophrygian, *c-c'*; Lydian, *f-f'*; Hypolydian, *c-d'*; Mixolydian, *f-g'*; Hypomixolydian, *c-e'*.

Attempts were also made, in the *Dialogus* and in the writings of Guido of Arezzo, to provide a rational account of the choices of pitch for intermediate cadences in various chants. The German theorist John (writing *c*.1100; once known as John Cotton or John of Afflighem) pointed to the fact that the *tenor* (oft-repeated or 'held') notes of the various psalm tones also played an important role in other chants of the corresponding mode. His compatriots Berno and Hermannus Contractus of Reichenau went a stage further, and developed theories of important groups of notes (they called them 'species') spanning a fourth or a fifth— described, picturesquely, by Hermannus as the 'sedes troporum' (the 'seats of the tropes'; note the persistence of the alternative term for mode, not to be confused with the musical form described under *Trope*).

(*c*) *The Late Middle Ages and Renaissance.* Theoretical writing in the late Middle Ages was concerned more with polyphony than with monophony, and so it is not surprising to find that theorists of this period often composed their monophonic examples instead of searching through the chant repertory. Also, the freshly-composed examples could be made to fit more easily the new ideas developed by 14th- and 15th-century writers. There was clearly a strong desire to classify and compartmentalize in scholastic fashion. For instance, Marchettus of

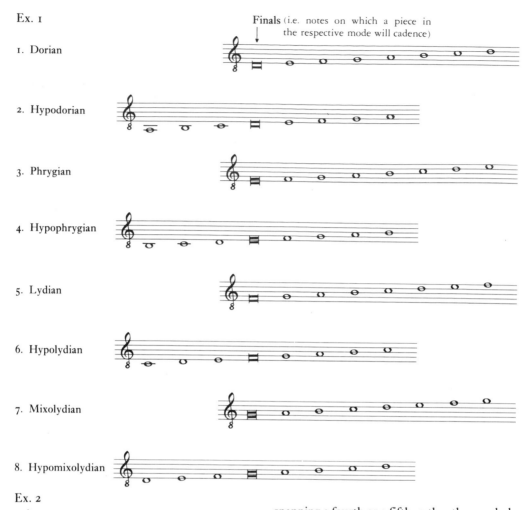

Ex. 1

Finals (i.e. notes on which a piece in the respective mode will cadence)

1. Dorian

2. Hypodorian

3. Phrygian

4. Hypophrygian

5. Lydian

6. Hypolydian

7. Mixolydian

8. Hypomixolydian

Ex. 2

Ac - ci - pi - te ju - cun - di - ta - tem

Padua's *Lucidarium* (*c*.1317) developed an interesting classification of the groups of notes discussed above as they were used within the various modes. He describes no fewer than six categories of note-groups: 'initial' (used at openings), 'terminal' (used at cadences), 'common' (the group found in both the authentic and the plagal form of a mode), 'proper' (the complementary group to the 'common', peculiar, or 'proper', to the authentic or plagal mode), 'composite' (joining 'common' to 'proper'), and finally 'commixed' (where a passage in one mode veers off into the characteristic progressions of another).

The insistence on these groups is partly a survival of Boethius's and later writers' tetrachord systems, but it also reflects the fact that melodies are commonly made from phrases spanning a fourth or a fifth, rather than a whole octave. The value of this sort of theoretical writing is that in it a sustained attempt is being made to understand what we would call the 'tonality' of music—what features, intervals, progressions, etc., are decisive in establishing mode.

Another point developed by Renaissance writers was that, since the use of Guido's F hexachord had led to B♭s being considered legitimate (see *Solmization*), the whole *Protus* or Dorian (D) mode could be transposed down a fifth, on to G. This is, in fact, what happened: very many pieces of secular and sacred Renaissance polyphony are notated with a B♭ key signature for all voices, although they could as easily have been written a fifth higher without any key signature. The fact that they were not may have something to do with the pitch standards of the time, or with a desire to avoid writing the extra sharps that would be necessary in the higher key. The use of a key signature of one flat (and occasionally of two flats) led to a reclassification of the modes. Tinctoris's *Liber de natura et proprietate tonorum* (1476) set out the modes as shown in Table 2.

It took some time for the application of modal theory to polyphonic composition to gain acceptance: in the late 13th century Johannes de Grocheo said they were mutually contradictory. Only in the late 15th century did theorists come to grips with the problems of defining the mode of polyphonic compositions. Tinctoris stated that the mode of the tenor voice determined that of the whole composition, but the top part seems to have been felt equally, or more, decisive. This fitted the common 16th-century disposition of parts in SATB, where the Superius had a range roughly an octave above the Tenor, and the Altus an octave above the Bassus.

It was dissatisfaction with the inability of the traditional eight-mode system to contain polyphonic procedures that prompted Heinrich Glarean, in *Dodecachordon* (Basle, 1547), to create a more comprehensive system. Perhaps acting on suggestions in the 11th-century German treatises he had read, he decided upon a 12-mode system. To the previous eight (see Ex. 1) he added the Aeolian (*a–a'*, with final on *a*), the Hypoaeolian (*e–e'*, with final on *a*), and the Ionian (*c–c'*), and the Hypoionian (*g–g'*), both with finals on *c*. He stated that the Ionian was the mode most commonly used in his time. Glarean drew upon extensive studies of Boethius and of classical Greek authors (such as Aristoxenus, only recently rediscovered and translated; see *Ancient Greek Music*, 6) to find names for his

new modes. For Ionian he also used the name Iastian; Hypomixolydian he also called Hyperiastian. Among modes mentioned by Glarean as conceivable, but not possible in practice, was the Hyperaeolian mode (*b–b'*, with final on *b*). In modern writing this is sometimes called the Locrian mode, but the name was not used in this sense by any Greek, Medieval, or Renaissance writer, although it is of classical Greek origin.

Glarean's system won a good deal of support, especially when the eminent theorist Gioseffo Zarlino adopted it in his *Istitutione harmoniche* (Venice, 1558). In a later edition Zarlino re-ordered the names and numbers of the 12 modes so that they followed the order of the hexachord: C–D–E–F–G–A. The gradual entry into circulation of more and more Greek texts spread confusion on this point. Medieval theorists since *Alia musica* called the D mode Dorian, but Boethius would have called the E one Dorian, and Zarlino now reassigned the name to the C mode. Late Renaissance theorists can be divided into three groups, according to whether they follow Glarean, Zarlino's later system, or a classical Greek model.

Little survived of modal theory in writings after 1650. Germany proved most conservative: Glarean is summarized as late as 1732, in J. G. Walther's *Musikalisches Lexicon*. This may partly have been because modal melodies of the 16th century and earlier were preserved in the Lutheran chorale repertory.

(*d*) *Mode and Tonality*. The term tonality is

TABLE 2

			Range	Final
♭ signature (*cantus mollis*)	*Protus*	mode 1 (Dorian)	*g g'*	*g*
		mode 2 (Hypodorian)	*d–d'*	*g*
	Deuterus	mode 3 (Phrygian)	*a–a'*	*a*
		mode 4 (Hypophrygian)	*e–e'*	*a*
	Tritus	mode 5 (Lydian)	*f–f'*	*f*
		mode 6 (Hypolydian)	*c–c'*	*f*
	(Note that the pitches of the F mode were retained, not transposed like the other modes—creating, in effect, the modern major key.)			
♭♭ signature (*cantus fictus*)	*Protus*	mode 1 (Dorian)	*c–c'*	*c*
		mode 2 (Hypodorian)	*g–g'*	*c'*
	Protus	mode 1 (Dorian)	*a–a'*	*a*
		mode 2 (Hypodorian)	*e–e'*	*a*
No signature (*cantus durus*)	*Tritus*	mode 5 (Lydian)	*c–c'*	*c*
		mode 6 (Hypolydian)	*g–g'*	*c'*
	(The literal transposition of the F mode would have involved F sharps, but Tinctoris did not stipulate them, once again creating, in effect, the modern major key.)			

here used in its broad sense of a system of relationships between pitches, having a 'tonic' and perhaps other important pitches. In this sense it seems legitimate to speak of the tonality of a piece of chant, as well as of its mode. And it is appropriate to characterize much of the Medieval writing about mode as an attempt to define the tonality of the chant repertory. For instance, when Guido of Arezzo says that notes within a phrase of chant should not be more than a fifth from the final of the phrase, while phrase beginnings and endings should not be more than a fifth from the final of the complete chant, he is setting tonal boundaries, displaying concern for the tonal integrity of a piece. The same thinking predictably recurs in writing on polyphony—in the 16th century, Gallus Dressler provided a table of pitches showing which notes were proper for cadences in each mode.

The main difference between chant and later 'tonal' music, however, is that there is little real possibility of a piece of chant containing more than one tonal centre. Recent research has shown that the chant repertory is dominated by pieces in an over-all pentatonic tonality, where the notes *e* and *b'* play a subsidiary role (cadences on, repetitions of, and leaps to and from these notes are avoided), and that the D, E, F, and G modes were subdivisions of this over-all tonal system. Its prevalence tends to exclude the possibility of contrast—some pieces do contain chromatically differentiated phrases, with *bb'* and *bᵇ'* both being used, but they are very rare. The only pieces where a 'modulation' can be said to take place is in some sequences, where the tonal centre may change during the course of the piece, usually by ascending a fifth (see *Sequence*, 2, Ex. 1). Here one has a strong impression of a 'progressive' tonality, one tonic being replaced by another.

One reason why chant is more or less incapable of suggesting modulation is its very restricted range. In Medieval polyphony the possibilities are still limited, yet there is evidence that composers of the 13th century were aware of tonal effect: the great *organa quadrupla* of Pérotin, swinging majestically from one pedal point to another, must lead one to speculate that the choice of sustained harmonies was calculated to produce tonal contrasts. More conclusively, some late 13th- and early 14th-century English compositions based on chant tenors actually alter, add to, or subtract from their plainchant bases in order to emphasize the tonic of the mode and its attendant consonances. And one piece of Parisian 13th-century polyphony, the two-voice *conductus, Hac in die rege nato*, begins and ends without a key signature, but moves through a long central section which is given a signature of two flats.

In spite of the obvious 'mode-consciousness' of Renaissance music theorists, it is clearly wrong to look in the music of that time for the cut and thrust of the tonal conflicts of later symphonic music. Although modulation was possible (several works, such as Josquin's 'Fortuna d'un gran tempo', modulate through a circle of fifths), it was not generally used to create opposing tonal centres as generating forces in the development of the composition, and it can safely be said that this was not done in the period when the eight-mode system held sway.

3. *Folk Music and Non-European Cultures.* Mode in Latin plainchant was basically a matter of pieces written within certain scales—scales without consecutive semitones and without intervals of more than a tone—and with more or less clearly defined tonic notes. The concurrence of melodic formulas, or melody types, characteristic of each mode was not a prime factor in modal theory, although it is undeniable that formula and mode do go together to a certain extent (see *Plainchant*, 6).

A rather different picture is presented by European folk-music traditions and by non-European musical cultures in general. Although one certainly finds music where the relative importance of melodic outline, motif, scale, and tonic note are roughly the same as in Latin chant, melody type and characteristic motif play a generally more important role in defining mode in these other musical traditions.

For instance, in English (and North-American) folk-song, one encounters the phenomenon of melodies which, though clearly at root identical, have different finals and move in different scales; through a process of oral transmission they have acquired slightly different tonal characteristics. The same tune may be found ending on D with no signature, or with one flat, or with one sharp, or ending on E, etc. The melody type is paramount; mode in the sense of scale and final is secondary. Such flexibility is extremely rare in plainchant, affecting only some hymns and other 'non-Gregorian' pieces. It may be characteristic of an oral tradition not bound to religious ritual and therefore not constrained by fidelity to tradition and authority. Interestingly, it is typical of the copies of *troubadour* and *trouvère* melodies that have come down to us.

Somewhere between the two extremes—that of dominant scale and final, and that of dominant melody type—lie some of the systems of Asian classical music, and, moreover, the middle-eastern Christian chant repertories (Byzantine, Syrian, etc.). In varying degrees, their 'modes' imply not so much scales as collections of characteristic motifs, phrases, and formulas peculiar to one mode and not found in the others.

There are many possible reasons why the various musical cultures have developed their own modal systems. The Arabic *maqām* and Indian *rāga* systems contain scores of different 'modes', each with its own motivic and intervallic identity; they are the product of a musical culture developed by solo, virtuoso, improvising vocalists and instrumentalists. Javanese gamelan and Japanese court gagaku, on the other hand, are composed ensemble music, where instruments of widely differing capabilities and character each play a part in enunciating and embellishing a central (or 'nuclear') theme. The modal categories (*paṭet* in Javanese, *chōshi* in Japanese) are few in number but capable of infinitely varied realization. Because there is little to distinguish these 'modes', apart from the scales in which they exist, it has become customary to think of them as scales, the opposite of Arabic or Indian melodies. But melodies in a different sense they remain; their scales are a convenient abstraction. They have a tonic, but no other predominant notes (e.g. no definite final). Such characteristics of non-Western musical cultures are not only interesting in their own right, but also suggest ways of understanding how Western plainchant and other music developed.

4. *Mode and Ethos.* One aspect of Western modal theory which recurs constantly, yet which seems to have no direct relevance to surviving music, is the expressive, ethical, or moral value attached to particular modes. Europe in the Middle Ages, through Boethius, inherited the idea that ethos and mode were associated, and also a number of illustrations of the supposed connection. (A favourite tale was that of a young man so aroused by a melody in the Phrygian mode that he was on the point of breaking into a young girl's room, when a change to the Hypophrygian mode restored him to a proper frame of mind.) Theorists did not always agree on the ethical character of a particular mode: for one the Hypolydian might be 'lacrymose', for another it was 'voluptuous'. Any student of chant or of Medieval and Renaissance polyphony will know how little the following descriptions, by Hermann Finck (1556), have to do with actual music: 'Mixolydian . . . resembles more Saturn . . . manifesting itself in stentorean voice and loud shouts, a terror to all'; while 'Hypomixolydian [is] not unlike an honest matron, who tries to mollify and sooth the wrath and agitation of the husband with pleasant discourse'.

Even less relevant were Medieval speculations relating the eight modes to celestial bodies, or likening authentic and plagal to male and female, as in the treatise of Johannes de Grocheo: 'Just as the masculine universally exceeds the female in skill and virtue, so it seems appropriate that the principal modes exceed their plagals in ascent'.

After the texts of classical Greek writers became available to musicians again in the 16th century, discussion of modal ethos became particularly vigorous. Yet the prevailing opinion of practising composers is probably accurately reflected in Claude Le Jeune's preface to his *Dodecacorde* (1598), a setting of 12 psalms, one in each of the modes (using Zarlino's order): '. . . two reasons have prevented me setting names alongside each mode: firstly, I wished to eschew the ostentation of learned words; and then, because of the dissension among the Ancients, and their diversities of opinions about such names, someone is required of more curious wit than I, who would prefer to be their disciple rather than their judge'.

It seems likely that the association of both name and ethos with particular modes in Ancient Greece was due to the fact that different tribes (e.g. the Phrygians) employed different melody types: the type became associated with the people, and took their name; and to it might be ascribed the fancied characteristics of the tribe ('excitable', 'vigorous', 'harmonious and well-ordered', etc.). Ideas of this sort could not be reconciled with the modal system of plainchant: hence the dichotomy evident in European theoretical writing. In this respect, Greek notions of mode were more akin to the Indian *rāga*s and their ethical properties—the Sanskrit word *rāga* means, literally, 'emotion', 'affect', or 'passion'.

DAVID HILEY

FURTHER READING
Willi Apel: *Gregorian Chant* (Bloomington, Ind., 1958, 3rd edn 1966).

Mode of limited transposition. A *mode which can be transposed only a limited number of times without duplicating itself. A simple case is the whole-tone mode, C–D–E–F♯–G♯–A♯. When transposed up a semitone, this produces a different form, C♯–D♯–F–G–A–B, but transposition by any other interval results in the duplication of one or other of these first forms. For example, if we take the mode up another semitone we arrive at D–E–F♯–G♯–A♯–C, which is equivalent to the original form. By contrast, the major mode, for example, is not a mode of limited transposition, since it has a different note content for each degree of the chromatic scale.

A mode will have the property of limited transposition if it contains a repeating unit. In the case of the whole-tone mode, of course, the repeating unit is simply the interval of a tone; other modes of limited transposition include those with repeating units of semitone–tone, or semitone–semitone–tone, etc. The term was introduced by Messiaen, who has used such modes in his music since the early 1930s and has made the most systematic study of them. However, they also appear earlier, in works by Debussy (particularly the whole-tone mode), Ravel, Liszt, Rimsky-Korsakov, and others.

PAUL GRIFFITHS

Moderato (It.), **modéré** (Fr.). 'Moderate', i.e. in moderate tempo; *moderatamente* (It.), *modérément* (Fr.), 'moderately'.

Moderne, Jacques (*b* Pinguente, Istria, *c*.1495–1500; *d* Lyons, *c*.1562). French music printer and publisher of Italian origin. In the 1520s he settled in Lyons, then an important cosmopolitan centre, and became a bookseller and printer of medical, religious, and other books. Between 1532 and 1552 he printed about 50 music books, adopting the diamond-shaped style of notes and single-impression technique of Pierre *Attaingnant, whose rival he remained for 15 years. The music he published covers a wide range (sacred and secular, vocal and instrumental), by local composers (e.g. Francesco de Layolle, who worked as his editor), those of the Parisian school (Sermisy, Janequin), and international figures (Gombert, Willaert, Arcadelt). Unlike Attaingnant, he was noted for publishing music by Italian, Spanish, and German composers. The popular dance arrangements by which he is known today were probably commissioned rather than compiled by him.

J. M. THOMSON

Modern Greek Music. Greece is remarkable for both the abundance and the variety of its traditional music. The music that can be heard there today has developed over many centuries and has been subject to multifarious historical and geographical influences. Whereas there is insufficient evidence to prove or disprove claims for the survival of elements of *Ancient Greek music, the influence of Byzantine ecclesiastical chant on secular music (and vice versa) is clearly discernible. In addition, different regions of Greece have been greatly influenced musically by their Turkish, Balkan, and Italian neighbours. Indeed, the musical diversity of Greek music is such that one is not confronted with a single musical tradition, but rather a whole series of distinctive musical traditions. Until recently the preservation of a rich musical culture has been assured by the continuation of age-old pastoral, agricultural, and maritime patterns of existence. Equally, the individuality of music in different regions has been protected by the country's mountainous terrain, its poor communications, and the isolation of communities from one another.

Since the end of the Second World War Greece has undergone enormous social and economic changes, the single most significant factor being the mass migration from the countryside to the towns (over half the total population now lives in the Athens–Piraeus area alone). None the less, musical traditions are being maintained to a degree that is striking, and music, dance, and song continue to play a central role in both urban and rural Greek life.

1. *Rural Traditional Music.* On the mainland the principal melodic instrument is the *klarino* (clarinet) which is usually accompanied by the *laouto* (long-necked lute) and sometimes the violin and *defi* (tambourine). In some regions, especially in the north, the *zournas* (shawm) is played—often in pairs with one *zournas* playing an underlying drone—to the accompaniment of the *daouli* (double-headed cylinder drum). Still in the north, the *daouli* is used to accompany the Thracian *lyra* (a pear-shaped fiddle played with underhand bowing), most notably in the ceremonies of the *Anastenarides* ('fire-walkers'). The *gaida* (bagpipe) is also popular and much esteemed in the north. Epirus, in the north-west, is renowned for its virtuoso clarinet players and especially for their performances of the instrumental *miroloyi* (lament). In addition, in some of the villages on the Albanian border polyphonic singing can be heard. In central and southern Greece heroic klephtic songs in free time are particularly popular. Most of these ballads celebrate the lives and exploits of brigands and freedom-fighters before and during the Greek War of Independence (1821–9). The Mani, a barren, inhospitable peninsula in the southern Peloponnese never fully subjugated by the Ottomans but riven with internal strife and blood feuding, is famous for its vocal laments.

In the Aegean islands the *lyra* (a pear-shaped fiddle similar to the Thracian *lyra*) is the most common melodic instrument. It is usually accompanied by the *laouto*. In some places the *lyra* has been replaced by the violin. The clarinet, the *tsambouna* (island bagpipe), and the *sandouri* (struck zither) are also to be found. (The *sandouri* and its brother instrument the *tsimbalo* are played on the mainland as well.) The music of the islands tends to be quicker in tempo and more lively than that of the mainland. In Crete and the Dodecanese, *mandinades* (improvised rhyming couplets) are popular and are sung in competition on festive occasions. The music of the Ionian islands is heavily influenced by Italian music. The guitar and the violin are the main instruments and the *kantada*

A Cretan wedding procession with lyra (left) *and laouto players.*

(romantic popular serenade) the characteristic form of song.

Rhythms other than the straightforward duple and triple times familiar in the West are very common all over Greece, Macedonia being particularly notable for rhythmic complexity. Open circular chain dances are found throughout the country, the *kalamatianos* (in seven time) and *syrtos* (in four time) being the most widespread types both on the mainland and in the islands. The *tsamikos* (in triple time) is common on the mainland only. In all these dances the leader performs improvised figures and acrobatic leaps while the other dancers give a basic, repetitive step. In the islands there are also couple dances such as the *sousta*, *ballos*, and *karsilamas* (also danced in Thrace). In every region of Greece dance and song are activities in which the whole community participates. Most villages have their own part-time instrumentalists; those that do not call musicians from neighbouring villages on special occasions. On the mainland many of the professional and semi-professional musicians are gypsies.

2. *Urban Traditional Music.* During the 19th century there appeared in the towns of Asia Minor and Greece a kind of oriental *café-chantant* called *café-aman*. The entertainers in these cafés included female singers and dancers, and the ensembles played instruments of the Ottoman classical ensemble such as the *ud*

(Arab lute), *kanun* (plucked zither), *zil* (finger cymbals), and *lyra* or violin. The music was *ala turka* (Turkish-style). These musical cafés were a familiar phenomenon in Greece before the turn of the century but became even more

A café-aman ensemble: Dimitrios Semsis (violin), *Agapios Tomboulis* (cümbüs, an ud-like instrument), *and Roza Eskenazi* (singer and defi player), *c.1930.*

numerous after 1922 when hundreds of thousands of refugees came to Greece following the disastrous Greek invasion of Asia Minor. Indeed, Asia Minor refugee musicians dominated the urban musical scene during the inter-war years.

Another form of urban traditional music with strong links with Asia Minor to flourish in Greece is the *rebetiko tragoudi* (*rebetiko* song). *Rebetiko* music and song first appeared in the low-life haunts of the Aegean seaports towards the end of the last century. The characteristic instrument of the *rebetiko* is the *bouzouki* (long-necked lute) and its smaller relations the *tzouras* and *baglamas*. The most popular dances in this milieu are the highly expressive solo *zeibekiko* (in nine time) and the *hasapiko*, a dance in duple time for two or three men. Since the *bouzouki* and *rebetiko* music were associated with the criminal underworld in general and the smoking of hashish in particular, they were frowned upon and even persecuted during the 1920s and 1930s. However, after the Second World War the audience for *rebetiko* music gradually broadened and the *bouzouki* and its repertory gained wide popularity among urban working-class Greeks. By the early 1950s the *bouzouki* had established itself as the urban popular instrument *par excellence* not only in Greece itself but also among the Greeks of the diaspora. Since the war the *rebetiko* has been influenced to some extent by Western music and instrumentation, but many *rebetiko*-type songs are still composed and the form remains extremely popular.

3. *Art and Popular Music*. Western art music did not gain a foothold in Greece until after the foundation of the independent Greek kingdom (1832). Efforts to promote interest in art music were almost entirely privately inspired and the growth of an audience for it slow. Touring European musicians—most of them Italian opera and operetta companies—came to Greece from the late 1830s onwards. However, 19th-century Greek composers of the 'Ionian School' such as Nikolaos Mantzaros (1795–1872; composer of the national anthem), Spyridon Xyndas (?1812–1896), and Pavlos Carrer (1829–96) were unable to rise above overwhelming Italian influences and failed to establish independent styles of their own. The Athens Conservatory was established in 1871 but promising musicians were still obliged to look outside Greece for musical education and experience. It was not until after the First World War that composers like Manolis Kalomiris (1883–1962) and Petro Petridis (1892–1978) proved Greece's ability to make a valuable and original contribution to Western music. Nikos Skalkottas, who studied under Schoenberg, is undoubtedly the foremost

avant-garde Greek composer of this period, although his large collection of works did not come to light until after his death in 1949. More recently another avant-garde composer, Yannis Xenakis, has won an international reputation for his electronic compositions.

Since the Second World War many of the younger Greek composers have sought inspiration in both rural and urban traditional music. Manos Hajidakis (*b* 1925) and Mikis Theodorakis (*b* 1925) have both used *rebetiko* melodies, rhythms, and instrumentation extensively in their music, the best-known examples being the film scores for *Never on Sunday* (Hajidakis) and *Zorba the Greek* (Theodorakis). Dionysis Savvopoulos (*b* 1944) and Yannis Markopoulos (*b* 1938) have used elements from the *rebetiko*, rural music, and Western pop music. One of the most promising young composers today is Christodoulos Halaris (*b* 1946) who has been making strikingly inventive use of traditional rural music and instrumentation.   RODERICK CONWAY MORRIS

FURTHER READING
T. Petridis: *Greek Dances* (Athens, 1975); F. Anoyanakis: *Greek Folk Musical Instruments* (Athens, 1979); R. Beaton: *Folk Poetry of Modern Greece* (Cambridge, 1980); R. Conway Morris: 'Greek Café Music', *Recorded Sound*, 80 (1980).

Modinha (Port.). A type of song, originating in Italian opera and other art (as opposed to folk) traditions. It became especially popular in Brazilian salons in the 19th century. The *modinha* was usually for solo voice and guitar and gradually came to be regarded as a folksong, retaining its sentimental character.

Modo (It.). 1. 'Manner'; *in modo di*, 'in the manner (style) of'. 2. 'Mode'.

Modulation. The contradiction of one key by the establishment of another. In the major-minor tonal system, a key may be either major or minor, with any of the 12 chromatic pitches as its tonic, so that 24 keys are available. According to the traditional view of tonal structure, a piece of music begins and ends in one key, but during its course it may modulate to one other key or to several others. Modulation may be diatonic, where the notes of the first key are not contradicted and only the harmonic disposition of the music suggests a new key (Ex. 1*a*); chromatic, where 'foreign' notes are introduced and must be contradicted in turn when the music returns to the original key (Ex. 1*b*: B♭ to B♮ to B♭); or enharmonic, where the actual note names and notation are contradicted by the new intervals formed in the modulation (Ex. 1*c*: note the augmented fourth and the diminished fifth marked *). An important aspect of the harmonic theory which explains modulation is the 'pivot' chord (see, for example, the chord marked ** in Ex. 1*b*) which is common to both the old and the new key. More remote modulations reduce the possibility of pivot chords. As Ex. 1*d* illustrates, the keys from and to which the progression in Ex. 1*c* modulates have no common triad: at opposite extremes of the *circle of fifths, they are as remote from each other as is possible.

Ex. 1

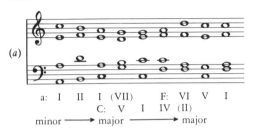

(a)

a: I II I (VII) F: VI V I
C: V I IV (II)
minor → major → major

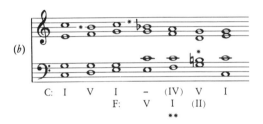

(b)

C: I V I – (IV) V I
F: V I (II)
**

(c)

C: I V I
F#: II I V I

(d)

C major   F# major

Both Schoenberg and Schenker realized, at a time when many composers were writing music either not ending in the original key or not establishing a sense of key at the beginning, that the concept of modulation is not an ideal explanation of tonal structure (see *Tonality*). 'Thus, tonality can be suspended, to be sure. But if it is present, then modulations are digressions from the principal tone, scarcely different in essence from any chord that is other than the tonic. They are just episodes of a large cadence . . .' (Schoenberg: *Theory of Harmony*, 1911). Schoenberg's theory of harmonic regions and Schenker's theory of diminution of the 'fundamental structure' (see *Analysis*, 3) have largely supplanted the traditional concept of modulation.   JONATHAN DUNSBY

Modus lascivus (Lat.). Medieval name for the Ionian mode. See *Mode*.

Moeran, E(rnest) J(ohn) (*b* Heston, Middlesex, 31 Dec. 1894; *d* nr Kenmare, Co. Kerry, 1 Dec. 1950). English composer of mixed Irish-Norfolk parentage. He owed much in his music to the stimulus of the landscapes of Ireland and East Anglia, and to the Norfolk folk-songs he collected. He studied at the Royal College of Music (1913-14) and then, after war service, had private tuition from John Ireland (1920-3), who had a powerful influence on his early style. Also impressed by Delius at this time, he spent the next few years writing mainly songs and trying to find his own voice; the fine *Seven Poems of James Joyce* (1929) marked the end of this period. In 1930 he retired to the Cotswolds, where he wrote his Symphony in G minor (1934-7), followed by concertos for violin (1942) and cello (1945), all these suggesting a poetic Anglo-Irish follower of Sibelius.
PAUL GRIFFITHS

Möglich (Ger.). 'Possible'; *so rasch wie möglich*, 'as quick as possible'.

Moins (Fr.). 'Less'.

Moitié (Fr.). 'Half'.

Moldau. See *Má Vlast*.

Molinaro, Simone (*b* ? Genoa, *c*.1565; *d* Genoa, 1615). Italian composer. He was *maestro di cappella* of Genoa Cathedral from at least 1602. As well as Masses and motets written for use in the cathedral, he wrote two books of lute music, which include dance movements and fantasias showing an unusually good grasp of lute technique. He published an edition of Gesualdo's madrigals in score rather than the usual part-book format, so that their remarkable harmony could be studied.   DENIS ARNOLD

Moll (Ger.). 'Minor', in the sense of key, e.g. *A moll*, 'A minor', *Moll Ton* (*Tonart*), 'minor key'.

Molle, mollemente (It.). 'Gentle', 'gently'.

Molter, Johann Melchior (*b* Tiefenort, nr Eisenach, 10 Feb. 1696; *d* Karlsruhe, 12 Jan. 1765). German composer. He served at the Karlsruhe court of the Margrave of Baden-Durlach, and in 1721 became *Kapellmeister* there. He spent the rest of his life there, except for nine years spent as *Kapellmeister* at Eisenach. His output was extensive, and his surviving instrumental works include over 170 symphonies, 14 overtures, 44 concertos, and sonatas, all written for a wide variety of instruments.

WENDY THOMPSON

Molto (It.). 'Much', 'very'; *molto allegro*, 'very quickly'; *moltissimo*, 'extremely'.

Momente ('Moments'). Work by Stockhausen for soprano, four choral groups, four trumpets, four trombones, two electric organs, and three percussionists, composed 1961–4. The texts are from the Song of Songs, Malinowski's *The Sexual Life of Savages*, onomatopoeic words, letters, and other sources. In 'open form', the work is a series of 'moments' of which some need not be performed. Stockhausen made two expanded versions, in 1964 and 1972.

Moment musical (Fr.). 'Musical moment'. The title given to Schubert's set of six piano pieces, Op. 94, of *c*.1828, which fall into the category of character pieces. The term was subsequently used by other composers to describe short piano pieces of a romantic nature.

Mompou, Federico (*b* Barcelona, 16 Apr. 1893). Catalan composer. He studied at the Conservatorio del Liceo in Barcelona and privately in Paris (1911–13) with Isidore Philipp and Ferdinand Motte-Lacroix for piano and with Marcel Rousseau for harmony and composition. Between 1921 and 1941 he lived again in Paris, returning then to Barcelona. His output consists for the most part of songs and short piano pieces in a delicate Spanish style comparable with that of the earlier Falla.

PAUL GRIFFITHS

Monckton, (John) Lionel (Alexander) (*b* London, 18 Dec. 1861; *d* London, 15 Feb. 1924). English composer. Son of Sir John Monckton, clerk of the City of London, he was educated at Charterhouse and Oxford where he acted and wrote for the Oxford University Dramatic Society. He was intended for a career in law and was called to the Bar in 1885. His first professional commission was to write a song for the show *Cinder Ellen* in 1891. Although he was a very successful writer, he was a retiring person who avoided the limelight, although his marriage to one of the idols of the Edwardian stage, Gertie Millar, did not make this too easy. He was music critic of the *Daily Telegraph* for many years. His most lasting scores, with many of them written for his wife, were *The Shop Girl* (1894), *The Circus Girl* (1896), *A Runaway Girl* (1898), *The Messenger Boy* (1900), *The Toreador*

(1901), *Kitty Grey* (1901), *A Country Girl* (1902), *The Orchid* (1903), *The Cingalee* (1904), *The Spring Chicken* (1905), *The Girls of Gottenburg* (1907), *The Arcadians* (1909), *Our Miss Gibbs* (1909), *The Quaker Girl* (1910), and *Bric-a-Brac* (1915), among others. Many of these were written in collaboration with Howard Talbot or Ivan Caryll.

PETER GAMMOND

Mondo della luna, Il ('The World on the Moon'). Opera in three acts by Haydn to a libretto by Goldoni. It was first performed at Eszterháza in 1777. Goldoni's libretto had previously been set by Galuppi, Paisiello, Piccinni, and others.

Mondonville, Jean-Joseph Cassanéa de (*bapt*. Narbonne, 25 Dec. 1711; *d* Belleville, nr Paris, 8 Oct. 1772). French violinist and composer. One of a musical family, he moved to Paris *c* 1733 where, after a short time in Lille, he lived all his life, renowned for his violin playing. For the Concert Spirituel he composed *grands motets* in a traditional style, but his violin sonatas were innovative, especially in their use of harmonics. He was a champion of the French in the Querelle des *Bouffons, and one of his operas, *Titon et l'Aurore* (performed 1753), was held up as an examplar of the French style as opposed to the Italian. He also wrote some extremely attractive *Pièces de clavecin avec voix ou violon* (Paris, 1748), in which, despite the title, all three parts are nearly always essential to the music.

DENIS ARNOLD

Monferrina (It.). A country dance in 6/8 time from the Piedmont region of northern Italy. It became popular in England around 1800, and many examples appear in printed dance collections of the time.

Monn, Matthias Georg (*b* Vienna, 9 Apr. 1717; *d* Vienna, 3 Oct. 1750). Austrian composer. As a boy he sang in the Klosterneuburg monastery, and some time after 1738 he was appointed organist at the newly-built Karlskirche in Vienna. He was an important member of the mid-18th-century school of instrumental composers, and played a significant part in the development of symphonic style. One of his 21 symphonies is the first we know of to have four movements with the minuet placed third (1740), although his others all have a three-movement structure; he also wrote seven harpsichord concertos and one for cello, which has imaginative and idiomatic writing for the solo instrument.

DENIS ARNOLD

Monochord. A string (wire or gut) stretched over a long narrow wooden soundbox with a calibrated rule under the string. Since the time of Pythagoras in the 6th century BC it has served for comparing the pitch-ratios of musical intervals, by moving a bridge under the string and noting its positions on the calibrated rule beneath. Its use as described by Boethius (*d* AD *c*.524) was taken over by Medieval theorists, in whose works the monochord and its divisions are constantly cited. It was also found useful for tuning organ pipes and bells, remaining so in use for many centuries and serving many other scientific and instrument-making purposes. It is sounded either by plucking the string or by bowing it.   ANTHONY BAINES

Monocordo (It.). In string playing, the performance of a piece or passage on one string only. Paganini was a celebrated exponent of the technique.

Monodrama (It.). A *melodrama for one speaker only.

Monody (from Gk *monōidos*, 'singing alone'). 1. The same as *monophony. 2. More specifically, a modern term for the solo song with *continuo accompaniment that was developed in reaction to the complicated polyphony of the 16th century, and in imitation of the music of the Ancient Greeks, by members of the Florentine *camerata* towards the end of the 16th century. The prime exponent of monodic song was Giulio Caccini, and his collection of solo arias and madrigals *Le nuove musiche* (1601-2) marks the beginning of its popularity and of a decline in polyphonic song (see *Song*, 4). Monody, in the form of a recitative-like melodic line over a continuo part, also played a large part in the early operas, especially in the hands of Caccini, with his lyrical attempts to 'move the understanding', and of Jacopo Peri, who aimed at 'an intermediate course lying between the slow and suspended movements of song and the swift and rapid movements of speech'. See also *Stile rappresentativo*.

Monophony. A term used to describe music consisting of only one melodic line, with no accompaniment or other voice parts (e.g. plainchant, unaccompanied solo song), as opposed to *polyphony and *homophony (each having several voice parts).

Monothematic. A term used to describe a composition or movement based on only one main theme. The term is sometimes used in connection with movements in *sonata form, in which two themes, or subjects, are usually introduced in the exposition; some composers of the Classical period, however, particularly Haydn, would base the second subject on thematic material taken from the first subject.

Monotoning. See *Intoning*.

Monsigny, Pierre-Alexandre (*b* Fauquembergues, nr St Omer, 17 Oct. 1729; *d* Paris, 14 Jan. 1817). French composer. Born into a noble family, he held several official positions in Paris before his connection with the Duke of Orléans afforded him an opportunity to take up composing. In association with the librettist Michel-Jean Sedaine, he enjoyed success in Paris from about 1760 to 1777 as a composer of comic operas at about the time when Philidor and Grétry were achieving great popularity. Though he never attained their facility in composition, or a comparable originality, he took great concern over matching his music to the text and had a gift for attractive melody. The social and political implications of his *Le roy et le fermier* (1762), based, unusually, on an English subject, added a new, extra-musical element to the traditions of *opéra comique*. In his 50s Monsigny suddenly gave up composing, for unknown reasons, and lived for 20 years or so in obscurity and some poverty, until his works enjoyed a revival in the early years of the 19th century.

PERCY SCHOLES, rev. Judith Nagley

Monte, Philippe de (*b* Mechlin, now Mechelen, 1521; *d* Prague, 4 July 1603). Flemish composer. From 1542 to 1551 he was in Italy, teaching the children of a noble family in Naples. By 1554 he was in Rome, and that year visited Antwerp before travelling to England, where he was a member of the private chapel of Philip II of Spain, husband of Mary Tudor;

Philippe de Monte

there he met Thomas Byrd, and he later corresponded with William, sending him a copy of his motet *Super flumina Babylonis* in 1583. He left England in 1555, and after a few more years in Italy was appointed court *Kapellmeister* to Maximilian II in 1568, remaining in the imperial service for the rest of his life and moving between Vienna and Prague, the favourite court of Maximilian's successor, Rudolf II. Having been brought up to write in the madrigal style of the post-Willaert generation, he felt increasingly cut off from later developments, and in his latter years made a conscious effort to modernize; but he was really best at the balanced classical manner of his youth. He also wrote a wide range of church music, including parody Masses and motets in a polyphonic style distinctly less smooth in melody than Palestrina's. An educated man who spoke and wrote five languages, he was buried in St Jakub, Prague.

DENIS ARNOLD

Montéclair, Michel Pignolet de (*bapt.* Andelot, Haute-Marne, 4 Dec. 1667; *d* Aumont, 22 Sept. 1737). French composer. He was born Michel Pignolet, adding the name of a fortress near his home only after he arrived in Paris in 1687; he had previously served as a choirboy at Langres Cathedral. In his early 20s he entered the service of the Prince de Vaudémont and visited Italy with him, but by 1699 he was back in Paris as a double-bass player in the *petit choeur* of the Opéra; he was one of the first to bring that instrument from Italy to France. He retained this position until his death, combining his duties as a performer with teaching and running a music shop.

Montéclair's dramatic works include a *tragédie lyrique*, *Jephté*, in which the free treatment of the biblical text caused it to be condemned by the Archbishop of Paris (thus probably ensuring its success), and a number of highly dramatic French and Italian cantatas. One of his theoretical works, the *Principes de musique* (Paris, 1736), includes a useful section on French ornaments of the time. DENIS ARNOLD

Monteverdi, Claudio (Giovanni Antonio) (*b* Cremona, 15 May 1567; *d* Venice, 29 Nov. 1643). Italian composer. Although Monteverdi was generally considered in the 19th and early 20th centuries to have been a revolutionary, responsible for the decline of the old polyphonic style developed since the Middle Ages and reaching its peak in the music of Palestrina, it is now clear that he was only part of a more general movement in this direction. But if many other composers participated in the new genre of opera and in the new style of accompanied melody known as monody, it was Monteverdi

who appreciated most fully what could be accomplished by these means. The basis of his work lay in the belief that music must 'move the whole man', that it must express man's deepest feelings, and even his lightest songs have some inner significance; this belief led to his other cardinal tenet—that the music must match the words it sets. To these ends he felt that musical 'rules', or conventions, were expendable if the demands of the art-work as a whole required it. His earlier music was written in the form of madrigals, which are essentially small-scale explorations of mood, and his skill in combining two or more contrasting emotions, moulding them into an integrated and satisfying unit, was to make him a supreme composer of operas. His later works explore the expression of human emotion in such a way that his characters become as vividly alive as they are in the works of Shakespeare, Mozart, Verdi, or any other great dramatist.

1. Cremona and Mantua. Monteverdi was the son of a barber-surgeon. He studied music with the *maestro di cappella* of Cremona Cathedral, Marc'Antonio Ingegneri, and was evidently a precocious pupil, publishing several books of sacred and secular music when he was still in his teens. This early period culminated in two madrigal books published by one of the most famous of Venetian printers in 1587 and 1590; they contain some extremely attractive works and are more modern in approach than Ingegneri's, perhaps as a result of studying the madrigals of Marenzio and other composers popular in the 1580s. However, as yet Monteverdi's aim appears to be to charm rather than to express passion, and this can be seen at its best in his well-known setting of Tasso's poem 'Ecco mormorar l'onde'.

It is not known exactly when he left his home town, but he entered the service of the Duke of Mantua *c.*1592 as a string player. In Mantua he was immediately thrown into contact with some of the finest musicians of the time. The most influential for him seems to have been the Flemish composer Giaches de Wert, the crux of whose style was that music must exactly match the mood of the verse, and must also attempt to set the words with a sense of their natural declamation. Monteverdi's next book of madrigals (Venice, 1592) shows all the hallmarks of de Wert's style, not always well digested but certainly representing a complete change of direction. The melody is angular, the harmony increasingly dissonant, the mood tense to the point of neurosis. Guarini is the favoured poet, and every nuance of the verse is expressed in the music, sometimes to the detriment of the overall balance.

Monteverdi, portrait by Bernardo Strozzi.

This new atmosphere seems to have caused some upset in Monteverdi's hitherto fluent productivity, and although he went on composing he published little for the next 11 years. In 1595 he accompanied Duke Vincenzo on an expedition to Hungary, and four years later to Flanders; that year he married a singer, Claudia Cattaneo, by whom he had three children, one of whom died in infancy. He had been passed over when the post of *maestro di cappella* became vacant on the death of de Wert in 1596, and felt bitter about this, but in 1602 he was appointed to that position at the very reasonable age of 35. In 1603 and 1605 he published two more books of madrigals. Both contain masterpieces, and although the aim is still to follow the meaning of the verse in great detail the musical problems of thematic development and proportion are solved. Dissonances are more severe, the melody sometimes still more irregular, but the effect is more varied in emotion, less neurotic, and if Guarini's eroticism stimulates a sensual musical style, there is also lightness and humour in Monteverdi's mature madrigals. His assimilation of these advanced musical means, especially the use of intense and prolonged dissonance, provoked attacks from more conservative composers and theorists, and Monteverdi became a kind of figure-head of the 'avant garde'. The attacks of a Bolognese theorist, Giovanni Maria Artusi, singled him out and provoked him to reply with an important aesthetic statement on the nature of his art; he disclaimed the role of a revolutionary, saying that he was only the fol-

lower of a tradition which had been developing for the last 50 years or more, and distinguished between two 'practices', as he called them, new and old, neither intrinsically having more merit than the other (see *Prima prattica, seconda prattica*).

If these madrigals gave him a reputation which extended well beyond northern Italy, it was his first opera that finally established him as a composer of large-scale music, rather than an exquisite miniaturist. Monteverdi may have attended some performances of the earliest operas by the Florentine composers Peri and Caccini, and he had certainly already written some stage music. In *Orfeo* (performed Mantua, 1607) he showed that he had a much broader conception of the new genre than had his predecessors, combining the opulence of the late Renaissance *intermedio* with the essential simplicity of the pastoral tale told in recitative which was the ideal of the Florentines. His recitative is more expressive, varying from something quite melodious to a fast-moving narration, in which individual words and phrases are expressed by astringent harmonies. He shaped whole acts into a coherent pattern rather than merely assembling them from small units. Most of all, he shows a flair for matching the climaxes in the action with musical climaxes, using dissonance, the singer's virtuosity, or instrumental sonorities to create the sense of heightened emotion.

A few months after the production of *Orfeo* Monteverdi suffered the loss of his wife and retired in a state of deep depression to his father's home at Cremona. However, he was summoned back to Mantua almost immediately to compose a new opera as part of the celebrations surrounding the marriage of the Gonzaga heir, Francesco, to Margaret of Savoy. Monteverdi returned unwillingly but composed not only an opera, *L'Arianna*, but also a ballet, *Il ballo delle ingrate*, and music for a play. A further tragedy occurred when *L'Arianna* was in rehearsal, for the singer playing the title role, a young girl who had been living in Monteverdi's house, possibly as a pupil of his wife, died of smallpox. Nevertheless, the part was recast and the opera finally produced in August 1608. It was an enormous success. The score has been lost, apart from the famous *Lamento d'Arianna* which survives in several versions and can be considered the first great operatic *scena*.

After this effort Monteverdi returned again to Cremona in a condition of collapse which seems to have lasted for some time. He was ordered back to Mantua in November and refused to go. He eventually returned, but thereafter hated the Gonzaga court, which he maintained had under-valued and under-paid

The room in the Ducal Palace, Mantua, where it is thought that Monteverdi's 'Orfeo' was first performed.

him. He does not, however, appear to have been unproductive, though the music he wrote in the next year or so reflects his depression. He arranged the *Lamento* as a five-voiced madrigal, and wrote a madrigalian threnody on the death of the young singer Caterina Martinelli (the *Sestina*, published later in the Sixth Book of Madrigals) which represents a peak of dissonant, anguished music in this style. In a more vigorous vein he wrote some church music, including a Mass in the old style and the famous music for Vespers on feasts of the Blessed Virgin Mary. If the Mass was a remarkable achievement, a deliberate attempt to show that the polyphonic idiom was still viable, the Vespers music is still more so, a veritable compendium of the different kinds of modern church music— grand psalm settings in the Venetian manner, virtuoso music for solo singers, instrumental music used for interludes in the service, and even an attempt to use up-to-date operatic music to set the emotional words of the *Magnificat*. But while this music is as 'advanced' as possible, Monteverdi makes it clear that it is for him merely an extension of the old tradition by using plainsong tunes as thematic material for the psalms and *Magnificat* settings. Above all, this is music to impress the listener with the power of the Church and its Maker.

The volume containing this music was published in 1610 and dedicated to Pope Paul V, Monteverdi visiting Rome apparently to present it in person. He may also have been seeking a new post in order to leave Mantua, but nothing came of this. We know nothing of his life for the next two years until in July 1612 Francesco Gonzaga succeeded his father and suddenly dismissed Monteverdi from his service, for reasons which are unknown today. Without a job Monteverdi returned to his father's house with his two sons, remaining there for about a year. Then the *maestro di cappella* of St Mark's, Venice, died, and after an audition of some of his music Monteverdi was invited to take his place. He took up his appointment in the autumn of 1613.

2. *Venice*. Monteverdi had been appointed largely because the musical establishment at St Mark's was in need of an experienced director after some years of decline, and because the last Venetian composer of distinction, Giovanni Gabrieli, had recently died. Although not primarily a church musician Monteverdi took his duties extremely seriously, and within a few years had completely revitalized the music, hiring new assistants (including Cavalli and Grandi), writing much church music himself,

and insisting on daily choral services. He also took an active part in music-making elsewhere in the city.

His letters from these early years in Venice reveal a complete change in his state of mind. He felt fulfilled, honoured, and was well (and regularly) paid, and as a result he seems to have been fairly prolific. He kept up his links with Mantua, largely because there was little chance of producing opera in Venice whereas opportunities came quite regularly from the Gonzaga court. From his correspondence with the Mantuan court councillor, Alessandro Striggio the younger, we see a philosophy of dramatic music emerging which was not only to mould Monteverdi's later work but was also to have an influence on the history of opera in general. Whereas the older type of opera had developed from the Renaissance *intermedio*, with its emphasis on the wishes of the gods, and from the pastoral play, with its paste-board shepherds and shepherdesses, Monteverdi became increasingly concerned with the expression of human emotions and the creation of recognizable human beings with their changes of mind and mood. In his Seventh Book of Madrigals (Venice, 1619) we see him experimenting with many new devices, mostly borrowed from the current practices of his younger contemporaries, but all endowed with greater power. There are the conversational 'musical letters', deliberately written in a severe recitative-like melody in an attempt to match the words, and on the other hand there is the ballet *Tirsi e Clori*, written for Mantua in 1616, which shows a complete acceptance of the simple tunefulness of the modern aria.

Monteverdi's attempt at creating a practical philosophy of music went on throughout the 1620s, leading to further stylistic innovations. Following ideas derived from Plato, he divided the emotions into three basic kinds—those of love, war, and calmness—which could each be expressed by matching rhythms and harmonies; at the same time we see a frank acceptance of realism in the imitation of the sounds of nature in various ways. His dramatic cantata *Il combattimento di Tancredi e Clorinda* (a setting of part of Tasso's *Gerusalemme liberata*) contains the result of these new ideas. It was first performed at the Palazzo Mocenigo, Venice, in 1624, and the rapid reiteration of single notes in strict rhythms combined with the use of *pizzicato* to express the clashing of swords marks an important step forward in the idiomatic use of stringed instruments. We know that these trends were continued in a comic opera, *La finta pazza Licori* (probably intended for the celebrations surrounding the accession of Duke Vincenzo II of Mantua in 1627), because although the score has been lost a sizeable correspondence between Monteverdi and Striggio on the subject survives.

In 1628 Monteverdi suffered further anxiety on the imprisonment of his eldest son, Massiliano, in Bologna for reading books banned by the Inquisition; it was some months before he was finally cleared of the charge. In the same year Monteverdi fulfilled a commission to write music (now lost) for the *intermedi* to Tasso's *Aminta* and for a *torneo* given in Parma to celebrate the marriage of Duke Odoardo Farnese to Margherita de' Medici. This was the last time Monteverdi was to receive a commission from the northern Italian courts, as the Mantuan wars of succession broke his link with the Gonzagas, who were ruined by them; and although it is possible that Monteverdi wrote an opera for performance in Venice in 1630, the plague which broke out in that year effectively stopped all musical activities in Venice and the provinces for about 18 months.

Monteverdi and his family seem to have emerged from the plague unscathed, and Monteverdi himself took holy orders during this period. He wrote a grand Mass for the thanksgiving service in St Mark's in November 1631, when the epidemic was officially declared over. The Gloria still survives, and shows him applying some of his theories concerning the diversity of mood suggested by the words, but both this and some other church music probably written about this time show a calm and majestic approach replacing the passion of his earlier years. A book of light-hearted songs and duets published in the following year is much the same, and there is a detached quality about much of the music in his final collection of madrigals. This anthology of *Madrigali guerrieri et amorosi* (Venice, 1638) contains much fine music, especially the *Lamento della ninfa*, another reworking of the mood of 1608 and of the *L'Arianna* lament in terms of the technical devices of 20 and 30 years later; the setting seems to indicate that the agony of the period when he lost his wife was never completely forgotten.

If this collection, put together when Monteverdi was over 70, might have seemed to mark the end of his composing life, chance played a part in inspiring him to an Indian summer of astonishing productivity. The first public opera houses opened in Venice in 1637, and as the one indigenous composer with real experience in the genre he was naturally involved almost from the beginning. *L'Arianna* was revived in 1640, and no fewer than four new operas were composed the following three years. Only two have survived in score—*Il ritorno d'Ulisse in patria* and *L'incoronazione di Poppea*—and both are masterpieces. Although they retain some elements of the Renaissance *intermedio* and pastoral play they can fairly be described as the first modern operas. Their interest lies in the portrayal of human beings in realistic situations, and sub-plots, especially in *Poppea*, allow for a greater range of character parts—the nobility and their servants, the evil, the misguided, the innocent, the good, and so on. Using all the means available to a composer of his time (the fashionable *arietta*, duets, ensembles), and combining them with the expressive recitative of the early part of the 17th century, Monteverdi showed how the philosophy of music he had developed during his early years in Venice could be put to use. The emphasis is always on the drama, and the musical units are rarely self-contained, but rather woven into a continual pattern so that the music remains a means rather than an end. There is also a sense of moving towards the grand climax of the drama, which inspires a grand *scena* for one of the main singers.

With these works Monteverdi confirmed his position as one of the greatest musical dramatists of all time. That he was held in highest esteem by his Venetian employers is shown by their gifts of money to him in these last years and by their granting him leave to travel to his native city in the last few months of his life. He died after a short illness, and the Venetian public showed its esteem at his funeral; a copy of their monument to him has been placed in the chapel of S. Ambrogio at the church of the Frari.

DENIS ARNOLD

FURTHER READING
Leo Schrade: *Monteverdi, Creator of Modern Music* (London, 1950); Hans F. Redlich: *Claudio Monteverdi: Life and Works* (London, 1952); Denis Arnold: *Monteverdi* (London, 1963); Denis Arnold, Nigel Fortune, eds: *The Monteverdi Companion* (London, 1968); Denis Stevens: *The Letters of Claudio Monteverdi* (London, 1980).

'Moonlight' Sonata. Nickname of Beethoven's Piano Sonata No. 14 in C♯ minor, Op. 27 No. 2, composed in 1801. It originated in a review by the poet Heinrich Rellstab (1799-1860) who wrote that the first movement reminded him of moonlight on Lake Lucerne—perhaps an eccentric approach to a movement with almost the character of a funeral march.

Moór, Emanuel (*b* Kecskemét, 19 Feb. 1863; *d* Chardonne, Switzerland, 20 Oct. 1931). Hungarian composer and inventor. He studied in Vienna and Budapest and was a prolific composer of concertos (for Casals among others). However, he is best remembered as the inventor in 1921 of a piano with two keyboards tuned an octave apart, so facilitating the performance of wide chords.

PAUL GRIFFITHS

FURTHER READING
Herbert A. Shead: *The History of the Emanuel Moór Double Keyboard Piano* (London, 1978).

Morales, Cristóbal de (*b* Seville, *c*.1500; *d* ? Málaga, Sept. or Oct. 1553). Spanish composer. He was probably a choirboy at Seville Cathedral, and would have come into contact with two important Spanish composers there, Francisco de Peñalosa and Pedro de Escobar. In 1526 he was appointed *maestro de capilla* at Ávila Cathedral, and two years later moved to a similar post at Plasencia. He resigned his post in 1531, and in the 1530s spent some time in Italy, much of it as a member of the papal choir. On his return to Spain in 1545 he took charge of music at Toledo Cathedral but had to resign two years later because of financial pressures, and went instead to the court of the Duke of Arcos at Marchena. He ended his days at Málaga Cathedral, but was unhappy there also, and shortly before his death applied to take up the post of *maestro* at Toledo again.

Morales composed very little secular music, and his importance in his lifetime and for the generation following him was as a composer of sacred music. He wrote many Masses (including *cantus firmus*, parody, and paraphrase types) and *Magnificat* settings, and his many motets show a special flair for conveying emotion while maintaining most of the strict principles of polyphonic music. Although somewhat old-fashioned in his adherence to modal melody, his flair for sonority is akin to that of his Venetian and Roman contemporaries.

DENIS ARNOLD

Moralities. See *Church Drama*, 2.

Moravian Music in America. Moravians (a small denomination established in 15th-century Bohemia) first came to North America as missionaries in 1735. In the next century they carried on an extraordinarily rich musical practice at their communities in Pennsylvania (Bethlehem, Nazareth, Lititz) and North Carolina (Salem, now Winston-Salem), composing and performing vocal and instrumental music for their love feasts, song hours, and other services. Instrumental *collegia musica*, church organists, highly organized choirs, and congregation members played and sang both imported and indigenous music. Important Moravian composers in 18th-century America include Johann Friedrich Peter (1746-1813), Jeremias Dencke (1725-95), Johannes Herbst (1735-1812) (all European-born), and John Antes (1740-1811). The American Moravians kept in touch with musical developments in Europe, but were isolated from American musical mainstreams. Perhaps this isolation was one of the reasons for the decline in their musical life after 1840. The Moravian Music Foundation (Winston-Salem), founded in 1956 by Donald McCorkle, sponsors performance and research in Moravian music through recordings and publications (musical editions, catalogues from the extensive Moravian Music Archives, historical studies, a semi-annual *Bulletin*) as well as biennial Early American Moravian Music Festivals.

NYM COOKE

Morbido, morbidezza (It.). 'Soft', 'gentle', 'softness', 'gentleness'. The term was originally used in connection with painting, where it is used to describe the delicate reproduction of flesh tints.

Morceau (Fr.). 'Piece'; *morceau symphonique*, 'symphonic piece'.

Morceaux en forme de poire, Trois ('Three Pear-Shaped Pieces'). Work for piano duet by Satie, composed between 1890 and 1903. In spite of the title it contains six pieces, which were later orchestrated by Roger Désormière.

Mordent (It.: *mordente*, from *mordere*, 'to bite'; Fr.: *mordant*; Ger.: *Mordent*). Ornament of the Baroque period, consisting of a rapid, often sharply rhythmic, alternation of main note, note below, and main note (Ex. 1).

There might be one or two repercussions (the latter, a double mordent, could be indicated by an elongation of the sign to ⋙). In modern terminology, chromatic alterations are marked as in Ex. 1(*b*), but Baroque composers often left this decision to the performer.

Contrary to popular opinion, the inverted mordent (using the note above) was not characteristic of the later Baroque period; the half trill fulfilled this function (see *Trill*). In the 19th century, however, the inverted mordent came into wide acceptance, indicated by the sign ⋘ which had formerly been used for the trill; often it was intended to be performed before the beat (see Ex. 2).

The terminology with regard to mordents is in some confusion: some modern writers have reversed the definitions of mordent and inverted

Ex. 2

mordent given above, while others prefer to speak instead of upper and lower mordents.

SIMON MCVEIGH

Morendo (It.). 'Dying' (away).

Moresca (It., Sp.), **moresque** (Fr.). A 15th- and 16th-century grotesque pantomime dance, in which the executants wore Moorish costumes, blacked their faces, and wore bells attached to their legs. It was the most popular dance of Renaissance ballets and mummeries, either as a solo dance or as a dance involving a mock sword fight between two groups, representing Christians and Moors. The latter type was also known as a *danse des bouffons*. The *moresca* still survives in Spain, Corsica, and Guatemala, and in England may be related to the *morris dance.

Lassus wrote some vocal pieces called *moresche* which resemble the *villanella*, but parody the speech of Africans living in Italy rather than the Neapolitan dialect.

Morgenblätter (Ger.). 'Morning leaves', or 'Morning papers'. Johann Strauss II (the 'Waltz King') wrote a piece with this title and dedicated it to the Vienna Journalists' Association; it is clearly intended to carry the second connotation.

Morgenlied (Ger.). 'Morning song'. See *Aubade*.

Morhange, Charles-Valentin. See *Alkan, Valentin*.

Mörike-Lieder ('Songs of Mörike'). Fifty-three songs for voice and piano by Wolf, all settings of poems by Eduard Friedrich Mörike (1804–75). Most of them were composed in 1888, and they include *Elfenlied*, *Gesang Weylas*, *Der Feuerreiter*, and *An die Geliebte*. Eleven of them were later orchestrated.

Morley, Thomas (*b* Norwich, *c*.1557; *d* London, in or after Oct. 1602). English composer, organist, writer, and publisher. He was the son

Ex. 1

of a Norwich brewer, and probably entered the choir of Norwich Cathedral as a boy. In 1574 he was promised the position of choirmaster (including the duties of organist) on the death of Edmund Inglott, taking up the post in 1583. Four years later he left Norwich. In 1588 he took the B.Mus. at Oxford, and by the following year he was in London, serving as organist at St Paul's Cathedral and, from 1592, as a Gentleman of the Chapel Royal. It is likely that Morley left Norwich because of his Roman Catholic sympathies, but there is evidence to show that in London he became an informer on those who followed the Roman faith. During the next few years he became known as a publisher, producing Italian works as well as his own.

Morley can be said to have founded the English madrigal school, for he chose such attractive Italian music (especially by composers such as the Roman Felice Anerio and the Venetian Giovanni Croce) that the vogue for madrigals, balletts, and canzonets became firmly established. His own work is often very Italianate, but he nearly always adds a personal touch and often improves on his models—for example, in copying the balletts of Gastoldi his contrapuntal skill gives new interest to what is really rather elementary music for dancing. Although less talented in a serious vein, there can be no doubt that he introduced the latest fashions to younger men such as Weelkes and Wilbye, and was highly respected by them.

He also wrote church music, to both Latin and English texts, and if he can hardly be considered one of the great masters, his funeral anthems are fine, expressive works. His virginal music includes some attractive dances and variations, but his masterpiece for instruments

Title-page of Morley's 'A Plaine and Easie Introduction to Practicall Musicke' (London, 1597).

is the *First Booke of Consort Lessons* (London, 1599), a set of arrangements for an ensemble of viols, flute, lute, cittern, and pandora. His delightful instruction book, *A Plaine and Easie Introduction to Practicall Musicke* (London, 1597, reprinted 1971), borrows freely from foreign treatises, but its down-to-earth attitudes in place of Renaissance abstractions frequently make matters much clearer; it is full of good common sense.

From 1598 until his death Morley had a monopoly of music publishing which he exercised through various printers, widening the scope of English publishing to include lute music (which had had short shrift under the previous owner of the monopoly, Byrd) and consort music. In 1601 he assembled and published an anthology in praise of Elizabeth I — *The Triumphes of Oriana*. He seems to have suffered from ill health in his later years, and resigned his position in the Chapel Royal in 1602.

DENIS ARNOLD

Mornington, Garret Wesley [the surname changed to Wellesley after his death], First Earl of (*b* Dublin, 19 July 1735; *d* Kensington, 22 May 1781). Irish composer of glees and catches. He may have been created Earl of Mornington by George III in 1760 because of his musical accomplishment. He studied at Trinity College in Dublin and was appointed professor of music there in 1764, remaining until the 1770s, when he moved to London. See also *Glee*.

Morris dance. A localized English country dance, probably a descendant of very old pagan rites, with the use of various accoutrements such as bells, handkerchiefs, swords, and sticks, originally intended to frighten away evil spirits. It is generally danced by groups of village men in costume — usually in groups of six and, in its purest form, to pipe and tabor accompaniment — as a public entertainment. It is likely that the name 'morris' is a corruption of 'Moorish', arising from the fact that the dancers often blackened their faces. An earlier theory that the Moors actually originated the custom is not generally accepted. Similar dances flourish all over Europe and in related forms worldwide. Many English villages have their own special dances used on occasions such as annual fairs or wakes, on May morning, or at Whitsuntide. Dancing round the maypole, supposed to bring good luck, is a specialized form of morris dancing. Often the dancers have their attendants, including a piper or a fiddler, a ragman who looks after their clothing, a Fool; sometimes a treasurer, a cake-and-sword bearer, a moll, or a king and queen. The Fool is generally the most important, acting as a sort of master of ceremonies and dance leader. Sometimes he is called the Squire or Rodney. A 20th-century development of these activities was the so-called 'jazz' band popular at village fêtes, with kazoo and tambourine bands also led by a 'fool', a sort of comical drum-major. The morris dance costume is usually a decorative silk or beaver hat, bowler, or cap; white linen shirt; black or white trousers or breeches with ribbons and bells round the calves; and light soft shoes. Sticks and handkerchiefs are often carried. The dress, the music, and the dance-steps are to be found in many local varieties. One of the first authoritative studies of the morris dance was *The Morris Book* (London, 1907) by Cecil J. Sharp, which included 95 discovered melodies.

PETER GAMMOND

Morris dancers

Morton, 'Jelly Roll' (Ferdinand Joseph) (*b* ?Gulfport, Mississippi, 20 Sept. 1885; *d* Los Angeles, 10 July 1941). Black American jazz musician. Starting his career as a pianist in New Orleans, he became one of the most talented of the early jazz writers and an unusually sensitive and distinctive player. The lack of appreciation in his lifetime led to bitterness and some exaggerated claims as to his part in the creation of jazz. He made many classic jazz recordings with a jazz group which he called his Red Hot Peppers, and achieved a level of organized jazz that was only equalled by Duke Ellington at the time. Many of his compositions have a ragtime flavour to them and the delicacy of his piano style owes much to the same source. His best-known compositions include *The Pearls*, *Grandpa's Spells*, *Kansas City Stomp*, *King Porter Stomp*, *Milneburg Joys*, *Shreveport Stomp*, and *Black Bottom Stomp*.   PETER GAMMOND

Morton, Robert (*b c.*1430; *d* 1476 or later). English composer. He worked at the Burgundian court from 1457 to 1476, under Philip the Good and his son Charles the Bold. Morton's surviving works are all secular, and they seem to have been widely known on the Continent; 'Le souvenir' and 'N'aray je jamais' were both used in works by other composers, including Josquin and Tinctoris.   DENIS ARNOLD

Mosaic type. See *Breitkopf & Härtel*; *Printing and Publishing of Music*, 2, 6.

Moscheles, Ignaz (*b* Prague, 30 May 1794; *d* Leipzig, 10 Mar. 1870). German pianist and composer of Czech birth. He studied first in Prague then in Vienna, where he arranged *Fidelio* for piano for the publisher Artaria. After concert tours as a pianist, he settled in London in 1826, where he was also active as a conductor (he directed the first English performance of Beethoven's Mass in D). He became friendly with Mendelssohn at whose invitation he became professor of piano at the Leipzig Conservatory in 1846. His technique was based on playing the classics and he never played the music of Chopin or Liszt. His own music is in the Mendelssohnian tradition and includes some charming songs.   DENIS ARNOLD

Mosè in Egitto ('Moses in Egypt'). Opera (*azione tragico-sacra*) in three acts by Rossini to a libretto by A. L. Tottola after F. Ringhieri's *L'Osiride* (1760). It was first performed in Naples in 1818, and the well-known 'Prayer' was added for the 1819 revival. Rossini revised the opera, as *Moïse et Pharaon, ou Le passage de la Mer Rouge*, with a new libretto by L. Balocchi and E. de Jouy; the new four-act version was first performed in Paris in 1827.

Moses und Aron. Opera in two acts (third uncompleted) by Schoenberg; text by the composer, after Exodus. Produced: Zurich, 6 June 1957; London, Covent Garden, 28 June 1965; Boston, Back Bay Theatre, 30 November

Scene from the first staged performance of Schoenberg's unfinished opera 'Moses und Aron' (Zurich Opera House, 1957).

1966. Moses (speaking role) receives the word of God, but lacks the gift of communication possessed by his less visionary brother Aron (ten.). While he is on Mount Sinai receiving the Ten Commandments, Aron encourages the Hebrews to erect a Golden Calf, as a tangible object they, as a simple people, can worship. The subsequent orgy is interrupted by Moses' return from Sinai: appalled, he shatters the tablets of stone and resolves to be released from his mission. The second act ends with him sinking to the ground mourning, 'O word, thou word, that I lack'. The (unset) third act was to show Moses triumphant in the desert.

Mosolov, Alexander (Vasilyevich) (*b* Kiev, 29 July 1900; *d* Moscow, 11 July 1973). Soviet composer. He studied composition with Glière, and later with Myaskovsky at the Moscow Conservatory. Although he composed operas, orchestral music, chamber works, and many songs and piano pieces, he is known in the West almost solely for his short orchestral piece *Zavod* (1926), usually translated as 'The Iron Foundry', though the word means simply 'factory' or 'works'. This was intended as a symphonic interlude for his ballet *Stal'* ('Steel', not completed, though a suite was compiled in 1927), and came to be regarded in its performances in the West—at Liège (1930) and the Hollywood Bowl (1932)—as a key example of modern, brutally realist Soviet music: the score incorporates a steel sheet, and other noises redolent of the workshop floor. But the work has long been neglected, and in the Soviet Union quickly earned the tag of *formalism.

GEOFFREY NORRIS

Mosso (It.). 'Moved'; *più mosso*, 'more moved', i.e. quicker; *meno mosso*, 'less moved', i.e. slower.

Motet. The most important form of polyphonic vocal music in the Middle Ages and Renaissance. Over its five centuries of existence there is no one definition that would apply throughout, but from the Renaissance onwards motets have normally had Latin sacred texts and have been designed to be sung during Catholic services.

The Medieval motet evolved during the 13th century, when words (Fr.: *mots*) were added to the upper parts of *clausulae*—hence the label *motetus* for such an upper part, a term that came to be applied to the entire piece. Whereas the lower part of such a composition (a tenor *cantus firmus*) moved in slower notes and was derived from a plainchant with Latin text, the upper part or parts might carry unrelated Latin or even French secular texts, and such parts were being freely invented by about 1250. During the

14th century, the structural principle of *isorhythm was applied to the tenors of motets (in the works of Machaut, for example), and, up to the early 15th century, sometimes to all voices, as in Dunstable's *Veni Sancte Spiritus* or Dufay's *Nuper rosarum flores*. The last-named was written for the consecration of Florence Cathedral in 1436; indeed, many Medieval motets were occasional in function, their several simultaneously sung texts 'glossing' upon one another.

Around the time of Dunstable and Dufay, however, a freely composed type of motet, often in simple style and with a single text, emerged, and by the late 15th century the motet had become a choral setting of sacred words in four or more parts. Its choral texture was more unified than before, the individual voices moving at the same sort of pace (though the tenor *cantus firmus* in long notes can still be found in some of Josquin's motets). The practice of imitation, whereby each voice entered in turn with the same distinctive musical idea, became fundamental to the motet as to other types of polyphonic music; at the same time composers reflected a new humanist spirit in their careful choice of motet texts and attention to the way the words were enunciated in the music. The motet, unlike the Mass, the psalm, the hymn, or the *Magnificat* setting, remained a form not strictly prescribed by the liturgy, but added (or substituted) at an appropriate place in the service on an appropriate day—in the same way as the English *anthem. The occasional 'ceremonial' type of motet survived too, and would be written or commissioned to mark any kind of event or honour any person, religious or otherwise.

The imitative motet style flowered with the generation after Josquin, and the device of 'pervading imitation', whereby successive phrases of the text are set to overlapping points of imitation, was developed by Gombert and refined by Palestrina and the other great late-Renaissance polyphonists—Lassus, Byrd, and Victoria. Palestrina wrote some 250 motets, Lassus twice that number (including a fair proportion of 'occasional' pieces), and Byrd published three collections of *Cantiones sacrae*—a Latin name often given to motets at that time. In Venice a polychoral type of motet developed with the Gabrielis, and Giovanni Gabrieli's later motets, which belong to the early years of the 17th century, are massive works scored for soloists, full choir, and instrumental ensemble (largely consisting of cornetts and sackbuts).

Although the old style (*stile antico*) of Palestrina was still sometimes cultivated in motets written during the Baroque, it was generally the motet that showed itself most adaptable to new

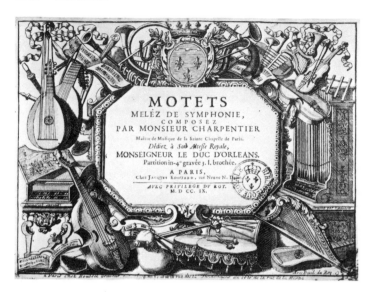

Title-page of Charpentier's 'Motets mêlez de symphonie' (Paris: Edouard, 1709).

styles for a wide variety of resources, including one or more voices with organ accompaniment and maybe also independent instrumental parts, often for strings. This was so especially in Italy. German composers such as Schütz adopted this 'affective' style in certain works but retained a contrapuntal, choral texture for others, a tradition that was continued in Bach's motets for choir and organ. In the France of Louis XIV the motet became an important sacred form, and Charpentier, Lalande, and Couperin wrote some impressive examples for both large and small resources.

Since the Baroque, motet composition has declined, though Mozart, Schumann, and Brahms all contributed to the genre. But motets of earlier centuries have constantly found their place in church services of many denominations, in particular as 'interlude' music at Mass.

JEROME ROCHE

Motetus. See *Motet*.

Mother, The (*Matka*). Opera in 10 scenes by Alois Hába to his own libretto. The first opera to use quarter-tones, it was first performed in Munich in 1931.

Motif [motive]. A melodic or rhythmic musical unit which reappears throughout a composition, either in its original form or at different pitches and perhaps with altered intervals. It is customarily much shorter and more fragmentary than a *theme (from which it may itself be derived). Many pieces of music are built up from such figures, but the technique is associated principally with Beethoven, who tended to use motifs rather than themes as unifying elements; the most famous instance is the four-note motif

which opens the Fifth Symphony (important throughout the work both rhythmically and melodically). Other notable 19th-century composers who consistently used motifs as a basis for their works were Brahms, Bruckner, and Liszt. The technique is especially important in the construction of sonatas and symphonies, where development sections are often largely based on motifs derived from the exposition.

The development of the motif was greatly expanded by Wagner in his use of *Leitmotiven* to identify characters and situations in his music dramas.

Motion. The linear pattern of a melody. Progression by step, ascending or descending, is described as 'conjunct' motion, by leap as 'disjunct' motion. In part-writing, simultaneous voice parts moving in the same direction are said to be in 'similar' motion; if, in addition, they move by the same intervals they are in 'parallel' motion. If they move in opposite directions the motion is described as 'contrary'. If one part is stationary (on the same pitch) while another moves away from it the motion is 'oblique'.

Motiv (Ger.). 'Motif'.

Moto (It.). 'Motion'; *con moto*, 'with motion', i.e. quickly; *moto precedente*, 'preceding motion', i.e. at the same speed as before.

Moto perpetuo (It.). See *Perpetuum mobile*.

Motto theme. A recurring theme, similar to Wagner's *Leitmotiv* and Berlioz's *idée fixe*. The term is often used in connection with earlier music, however, for example with those

15th- and 16th-century Masses that open each movement with an identical motif or motto (Ger.: *Hauptmotiv*, literally 'head-motif'). The 'motto arias' (Ger.: *Devisenarie*) of the 17th and 18th centuries, by such composers as Rossi, Legrenzi, and Cesti, worked on the same principle: a preliminary statement by the solo voice of the first motif of the melody would precede the instrumental introduction. Some of Bach's arias are of this type.

In later music the term can apply when a musical theme is given a symbolic significance, in much the same way as Berlioz's *idée fixe* symbolizes the 'loved one' in his *Symphonie fantastique*.

Motu proprio (Lat., literally 'of his own motion'). A decree issued by the Pope concerning the internal administrative affairs of the Church. The term is generally encountered in connection with church music on account of the *motu proprio* issued by Pope Pius X in 1903. This was of the nature of an Instruction upon Sacred Music, laying down general principles and placing emphasis upon the importance of traditional plainchant and of the 'classical polyphony' of Palestrina. Church music of a theatrical nature was strongly condemned and forbidden. Modern compositions were not prohibited but they were to be such as 'by their merit and gravity are not unworthy of the liturgical function'. Nothing was to be omitted from the liturgy 'except where the rubrics allow the use of the organ to replace several verses of the text whilst these are merely recited in the choir of the church' (see *Verset*). The Kyrie, Gloria, and Credo in composed Masses were not to be divided up into separate movements. Solo treatment of portions of the liturgy was not entirely forbidden but was to form but a small portion of the section in which they occurred. Boys, not women, should be used for the soprano parts. Instruments other than the organ were not to be employed without the bishop's special permission, and the organ was to play a modest role of accompaniment and not to be allowed to cover up the singing; long organ preludes or interludes were reprehended. The practice of the verset was not to be abused. The piano and instruments of percussion were not to be employed in the church. Wind bands were not to take part in church services, except in special cases recognized by the bishop, and then their music was to be of a grave style. In fine, music was to be at the service of the liturgy and not the liturgy at the service of the music.

To watch over all these things, each bishop was to appoint a special commission of competent people, well versed in sacred music. Theological students were to receive instruction in the music of the Church. The ancient *scholae cantorum* were to be revived and attached to the principal churches everywhere (see *Schola cantorum*).

About the same time as this *motu proprio* was issued the papal support was definitely given to the monks of Solesmes in their long-continued labours for the purity of plainchant (see *Antiphoner*; *Gradual*, 1).

See also *Cecilian Movement*.

PERCY SCHOLES

Mouret, Jean-Joseph (*b* Avignon, 11 Apr. 1682; *d* Charenton, 22 Dec. 1738). French composer. He was probably trained at the choir school of Avignon Cathedral but by 1707 he was in Paris. He began his career there as music master to the Marshal of Noailles, and in 1708 or 1709 was appointed *surintendant de la musique* to the Duchess of Maine, for whose celebrated Grandes Nuits de Sceaux he wrote much music. In 1714 his interests turned towards the theatre, and he conducted at the Paris Opéra; in 1717 he became appointed composer-director at the newly opened Théâtre Italien. In 1728 he became artistic director of the Concert Spirituel, writing many motets and cantatas for performance there. At the height of his career Mouret's fortune suddenly deserted him: between 1734 and 1737 he lost, in rapid succession, his posts at the Concert Spirituel, at Sceaux, and at the Théâtre Italien. Unemployed and reduced to living on the charity of friends, he suffered a nervous breakdown, and was committed to the asylum at Charenton.

Mouret, the 'musicien de graces' as he came to be called, was a typical regency composer: his works are elegant, charming, and essentially lightweight, although he was still one of the most important composers between Lully and Rameau. His best works are his *opéras-ballets* and *divertissements*, while his *Suites de symphonies* (1729) foreshadow the French symphony which developed in the second half of the 18th century.

WENDY THOMPSON

Mouth music. The same as **puirt a beul*. See also *Diddling*.

Mouth-organ. The familiar mouth-organ is now generally known as the harmonica and will be found under that name. The subject below is the far older series of oriental instruments commonly referred to in the West as 'mouth-organ' (Fr.: *orgue-à-bouche* etc.).

These likewise employ the free-reed (see *Reed*, 1), but in a quite different manner, although it is generally held that the Chinese variety, the *sheng*, first inspired the free-reed instruments of the West in the late 18th century (see *Harmonium*, 4). The Japanese equivalent is the *shō*. Southwards from China, similar but less sophisticated instruments are played in the Naga districts of Assam, the eastern highlands of Burma, in the former Indo-China (notably in Laos), and thence across the sea to northern parts of the island of Borneo.

The reeds are of brass, or of bamboo or palmwood, each cut integrally in a small, very thin rectangular plate of the same material and lying flat in the plane of that plate (i.e. not bent to one side as is the Western free-reed). Each plate is cemented or held with wax over an opening near the closed end of a pipe, usually of bamboo. The pipes are together held in a gourd or similar receptacle, which encloses the ends where the reeds are. A mouthpiece protrudes from the side. During playing, the pipes may either stand vertically or slant forward.

The reeds can speak equally whether the player exhales or inhales. In order to speak, a reed requires the co-operation of the air-column of its pipe, the pipes being graded in length accordingly. How, then, does the player prevent all the reeds sounding at once? For this, there is a small hole in each pipe just above where it emerges from the gourd and accessible to the finger. When open, the hole cuts out the pipe (save for a small bit at the bottom) and the reed will not speak. Immediately the hole is covered by the finger, the reed speaks, and thus, closing one hole after another (both hands are used in playing), melodies or, by closing a number of holes, chords are played. (To explain all this in scientific terms has so far not proved easy; no doubt differential air-pressures across the reeds are involved.)

The more primitive types of mouth-organ, from Assam southwards, typically have from six to nine pipes giving some form of pentatonic scale of vibrant, humming sounds in the alto-tenor voice register (or in Laos, where the longest pipe may reach 6′, baritone). Sometimes one of the pipes has no fingering hole, sounding continuously as a drone. The *sheng* and the *shō* are smaller, higher-sounding, with 17 pipes (of which four, or in Japan two, are dummy). How far before the Christian era the *sheng* dates is still disputed. The *shō*, its descendant, is today played in a tradition unbroken from the Middle Ages, notably in the gagaku and bugaku court music, in which it is one of three wind instruments (along with the transverse flute and the short cylindrical pipe *hichiriki* sounded with a bamboo double reed). The *shō*-player has beside him a small brazier over which he will now and then warm the instrument, to dispel condensed moisture. The scale of the *shō* is upwards from *a′* to *f♯‴* in A major, plus high G♮ and C♮. The notes are sounded in long-held six-note chord clusters, 10 in all, of which four are shown in Ex. 1 (sounding an octave higher).

Ex. 1

It will be seen that the notes *a″* and *b″* are present in all 10 of the chords, a kind of hidden two-note 'drone'. One can readily appreciate the effect that this oriental mouth-organ has had upon the ears of modern composers in the West, from Messiaen onwards.   ANTHONY BAINES

Mouton, Charles (*b* 1626; *d* after 1699). French lutenist and composer. He was a pupil of Denis Gaultier and wrote some charming lute pieces, mainly dances, which were grouped in suites and given descriptive titles in the manner of Couperin.   DENIS ARNOLD

Mouton, Jean (*b* Holluigue [now Haut-Wignes], nr Boulogne, *c*.1458; *d* St Quentin, 30 Oct. 1522). French composer, regarded during his lifetime as second in stature only to Josquin. His early life was spent at Notre Dame, Nesle, where he was made *maître de chapelle* in 1483. In 1500 he was in charge of the choirboys at Amiens Cathedral, and the following year he moved to Grenoble, where he was in charge of music at St André. Soon after that he became a member of the French royal chapel, serving under Louis XII and François I.

Mouton's music was highly popular in Italy, as well as in France, and remained in print for some 50 years after his death. More than 100 motets, 15 Masses, and some *chansons* survive. He was the teacher of Adrian Willaert, and thus forms an important link between the long line of Franco-Flemish polyphony and the Venetian school of composers.   JOHN MILSOM

Moussorgsky, Modest. See *Musorgsky, Modest.*

Mouvement (Fr.). 'Movement', either in the sense of motion, or in the derived sense of a section of a composition. It is often abbreviated to *mouvt*. Debussy and other composers sometimes used the term to imply a return to the original tempo after some deviation, such as a *rallentando*. *Mouvement perpétuel*, the same as **perpetuum mobile*.

Mouvementé (Fr.). 'Bustling', 'animated'.

Movable doh. See *Fixed doh.*

Movement (Fr.: *mouvement*; Ger.: *Satz*; It.: *movimento*). A term used in connection with musical forms (such as the sonata, symphony, concerto, etc.) that consist of a number of substantial sections, each one being called a 'movement'. The Classical symphony and sonata generally has four movements, and the concerto three, but later composers sometimes used unconventional formats, composing such works in one long movement (for example, Sibelius's Seventh Symphony), joining the movements together to be played continuously (Schumann's Fourth Symphony), and so on.

Mozarabic rite. See *Liturgy, 2a*.

Mozart. German family of musicians which moved to Austria, where its most important member was born. (Johann Georg) **Leopold Mozart** (*b* Augsburg, 14 Nov. 1719; *d* Salzburg, 28 May 1787) was a violinist and composer. He studied philosophy at the Benedictine University in Salzburg, but was expelled for poor attendance in 1739. He was valet and musician to the Count of Thurn-Valsassina and Taxis before becoming a violinist in the orchestra of the Archbishop of Salzburg in 1743; he remained in his service until his death, becoming deputy *Kapellmeister* in 1763. In 1747 he married Anna Maria Pertl. They had seven children, but only two survived: Maria Anna ('Nannerl') (1751-1829) and Wolfgang Amadeus. Leopold has sometimes been criticized for exploiting his famous son's talents, on the grounds that he was mainly interested in making money from his children's abilities, but it is more likely that he was just naturally proud and possessive, and there can be no doubt that if Wolfgang had not seen so much of the world his work would have been far less wide-ranging in style. Leopold was critical of his son's refusal to conform to social conventions, but had the good fortune to see Wolfgang flourishing in Vienna, and to hear those famous words of Joseph Haydn, 'Before God, and as an honest man, I tell you that your son is the greatest composer known to me', two years before he died.

Leopold's textbook on violin playing, the *Versuch einer gründlichen Violinschule* (Augsburg, 1756), soon became a standard work on the subject. He composed a considerable amount of music, including sacred music, symphonies, and keyboard sonatas, but his works are rarely performed today, and as a composer he is remembered mainly for including such 'instruments' as whistles and pistols in his 'Peasant Wedding' Divertimento and Sinfonia 'da caccia'.

The music of (Johann Chrysostom) **Wolfgang Amadeus Mozart** (*b* Salzburg, 27 Jan. 1756; *d* Vienna, 5 Dec. 1791), on the other hand, is perhaps more widely loved and respected than that of any other composer. This is due to the opposing sides of his nature: his inborn musical ability, which has scarcely been equalled and which enabled him to solve problems with enviable ease; and his sensitivity to the music of other men, which meant that wherever he travelled in Europe he was strongly affected by local taste. These two traits taken together gave him a unique mixture of individuality and universality. He wrote in virtually every genre known to him—expert in the composition of entertainment music, and yet also composing profound works which reveal a sombre, almost fatalistic, nature. Conversely, his lighter pieces often reveal a deeper element, while his most serious works rarely fail to delight as well as move the listener. Since he was strongly affected by his surroundings, it is worth recounting the facts of his life in some detail.

1. *The First Decade*. With his family background, it was natural that Mozart should have become acquainted with music at an early age, especially as his elder sister, Nannerl, had already developed some talent for playing the piano. Wolfgang was able to pick out chords at the age of three, and by his fifth year was improvising short minuets at the keyboard.

When Wolfgang was six, Leopold arranged for him and Nannerl to visit Munich and Vienna, where the children were duly admired for their precocity. This encouraged him to a more ambitious venture in 1763, when the three of them embarked on a tour taking in many of the principal cities of Germany, and finally Paris and London. The Mozarts were received at Versailles by the King and Queen and Madame de Pompadour, and the children were again thought to be marvels of talent. The London visit was equally successful socially, and quite satisfactory financially. But the main lasting effect was that Wolfgang was introduced to the music of two Germans settled in England, Abel and J. C. Bach. He copied some of their music, and not only the three symphonies composed for their concert series, but also many later works show their influence. Indeed, like J. C. Bach, Mozart attempted to adapt the fashionable Italian musical language of the day to more northern tastes. The family returned to Salzburg via the Low Countries—where the children were again a great success, though serious illness caused delays—and Paris. They finally arrived home in November 1766, after three and a half years away.

2. *A Period of Consolidation: 1767-77*. Mozart, like his sister, was now too old to be considered an infant prodigy, and Leopold began to take his education as a composer more seriously. Wolfgang received a number of commissions in

Salzburg, and arranged some sonatas by other composers as concertos for himself to play at concerts. The family made further visits to Vienna, where Maria Theresia and her son, Joseph II, commissioned an opera from Wolfgang; he composed an *opera buffa*, *La finta semplice*, but it was not produced because of court intrigues (it was given instead at Salzburg, in 1769). He also wrote a *Singspiel*, *Bastien und Bastienne*, in which he showed a knowledge of the French *opéra comique*.

Leopold was anxious for Mozart to make a concert tour to Italy. Accordingly the pair left in December 1769 and for the next two years travelled throughout that land, visiting virtually all the major cities. The most important events were a short stay in Bologna in 1770 to meet the principal theorist of the era, Padre Martini, for whom Mozart wrote some fugues; and a visit to Milan in October of that year, which resulted in an opera commission. This time, Mozart wrote an *opera seria*, *Mitridate, rè di Ponto*, which was received with great acclaim.

After a brief return home, a second commission, for a wedding serenata (*Ascanio in Alba*) to be given in Milan, took him back to Italy in 1771; and yet a third visit was arranged for 1772. The principal compositions of the third visit to Italy were an *opera seria*, *Lucia Silla*, and the famous motet *Exsultate, jubilate*. The opera was less successful than it might have been, probably because it was more elaborate than the audience expected (true also of Mozart's later operas), but his experience in Italy meant that at the age of 17 Mozart had virtually mastered all the genres most useful to a composer, and had the elements of a European reputation.

But no more opera commissions came, and the final return to Salzburg was therefore disappointing, especially since the old Archbishop, Count Schrattenbach, had died, and his successor, Count Colloredo, was by no means as accommodating to his employees. Mozart now became an active figure in Salzburg musical life. He composed mainly orchestral and chamber music, including four symphonies (K 184, K 199, K 162, and K 181) showing an original style, especially in orchestration. In 1775 he composed five violin concertos (K 207, K 211, K 216, K 218, and K 219), brilliant works, but of a more solid construction than those by Italian virtuosos which were then popular. He also produced some church music, though Colloredo's taste for brevity precluded these from the expansiveness found elsewhere in his Masses. None of these activities, however, led to an appointment at the Vienna court, in spite of the fact that his experience as an opera composer was increased by commissions from Munich (*La finta giardiniera*) and Salzburg (*Il rè pastore*).

3. *Another European Tour*. Since the expected progress in worldly success seemed to have eluded Mozart (though it is worth remembering that he was still only 20), Leopold planned yet another tour. On this occasion, he did not accompany his son, being unable to forfeit both salaries, so Mozart set out with his mother. This was to be the most important of his tours, firstly because it came at a time when he was mature enough to appreciate the various musical styles to be found in other cities, and secondly because it made him finally discontented with the provincialism of Salzburg. The first city of importance to be visited was Munich, familiar ground to Mozart. Next came Mannheim, which had then the most famous orchestra in Europe. Here Mozart learnt a great deal about orchestration, especially in the use of clarinets. He also met the Weber family, and fell in love with one of the daughters, Aloysia, an excellent soprano. Mozart thought of marriage, hoping that they might make a good living with their respective talents, but the uncertain prospect alarmed Leopold when he heard of it, and he wrote insisting that mother and son move quickly to Paris.

Musical life in Paris at that time was mainly taken up with the quarrel between Gluck and Piccinni, and Mozart was offered nothing more important than the post of organist at Versailles, which he refused. But he absorbed a great deal of the French style, notably the popular *concertante* manner—reflected in the Concerto for Flute and Harp, in the *Sinfonia concertante* for violin and viola (composed after his return to Salzburg, in 1779), and, unexpectedly, in the great aria 'Martern aller Arten' in *Die Entführung*—and the French orchestral sound, which Mozart mastered in the 'Paris' Symphony, K 297, a success at the Concert Spirituel. He also became acquainted with the music of Gluck.

While in Paris, Mozart's mother died, and Mozart was summoned home by Leopold; he went with reluctance, since he still had ideas of marriage and independence. His father had made a new arrangement with the Archbishop, whereby Mozart would be made court organist. Wolfgang came back via Mannheim, hoping to meet Aloysia, but she had moved to Munich, and when he met her at last he found that she no longer returned his affection. His hopes of a position with the German opera company at Munich came to nothing, and he finally arrived back in Salzburg in 1779.

4. *Final Years in Salzburg*. At the age of 23 Mozart had behind him, among other honours, successes at the principal concert series in Europe, won not as an infant prodigy but as a mature composer. As such tours had led to

considerable financial rewards for many other composers and performers, he had some right to expect the chance to move away from Salzburg. His disappointment was therefore understandable, the more so since the Archbishop was still not interested in elaborate music for the cathedral, and provided few opportunities for grand orchestral music. Thus Mozart's duties presented little challenge. The contacts he had established in the Munich circle, however, yielded fruit in the form of a commission to compose an opera, *Idomeneo*. In this work, Mozart showed his newly acquired knowledge of Gluck's 'reform' style, as well as a complete mastery of the Italian *opera seria*. *Idomeneo* was produced in January 1781, with apparent success.

Mozart's relationship with his employer now became very awkward. The Archbishop was already annoyed at the frequency with which Mozart was absent from his court, though it was difficult to refuse his requests for leave. He called Mozart to Vienna, where he and his retinue were staying, and did his best to humiliate him in various ways—making him dine with the servants and refusing him permission to give concerts. Eventually, in May 1781, there was a terrible row between them—Mozart was literally kicked out by the court chamberlain—and Mozart left the Archbishop's service for ever. This breach between employer and employee has sometimes been said to have heralded the new social position of the artist of the next century. Both sides have been blamed; and indeed neither came out of it with much credit.

Nevertheless, the conflict was less a sign of the times than a simple clash of personalities. In some ways Mozart got what he wanted, since he was convinced that he could be a major figure in the musical world if he left Salzburg, yet his ties to his father would not allow him to disobey that cautious man's wishes. In the event, his father was to prove right.

5. *Freelance in Vienna*. A freelance life was not as uncommon in the 18th century as is generally supposed, but it was, then as now, a precarious existence, dependent on continuous success, good health, and the ability to move from place to place as demand arose. The precariousness of the life was underlined by the fact that Mozart's only immediate form of income was from giving lessons—neither profitable nor to his taste. The first real sign that he might succeed was a commission for the Burgtheater, the *Singspiel Die Entführung aus dem Serail* (1782). Mozart followed the generally popular manner of Georg Benda, providing a mixed idiom, with elements of *opera buffa*, *opera seria*, and *opéra comique*. *Die Entführung* has a marvellously rich score, but this very richness meant that it was not practicable for every company, and even the Emperor, Joseph II, who liked Mozart's music, found it had 'very many notes'.

No similar commission followed, and Mozart had to rely instead on concerts to make his living. In the period 1782-4, he composed nine piano concertos (K 413-15, K 449-51, K 453, K 456, and K 459), some for himself to play at concerts, some for his pupils or for celebrated

Salzburg Cathedral (centre) *and the archbishop's palace* (right) *at the end of the 18th century.*

performers. He made his position still more uncertain in August 1782 by marrying Constanze Weber, sister of Aloysia, who turned out not to be a good manager of the family finances. Their first child, born the following year, died soon after birth, and it was not until the next year that a son survived to add to the financial burden. Thus, during the early years of marriage the Mozarts, though never well off, were not in severe difficulties, though it is noticeable that in this period Mozart had to compose a lot of small-scale works, rather than anything more substantial.

Mozart, unfinished portrait (1782–3) by Joseph Lange.

The major works of this period, apart from the piano concertos, were the six 'Haydn' Quartets, written under the influence of Haydn's Op. 33 quartets, and dedicated to that master, whom Mozart had got to know well and for whom he had great respect and love (reciprocated by the older man). But opera, the main source of income for the 18th-century composer, was closed to him for several years, since the failure of German opera had resulted in a new surge of interest in Italian opera. Mozart's next operatic commission came only in 1786, when he set a libretto based on Beaumarchais's *Le mariage de Figaro*, sequel to the play which had provided Paisiello with his success, *Il barbiere di Siviglia*, in 1782. Both plays had politically left-wing tendencies which were somewhat softened by the librettists, though Da Ponte's libretto for Mozart retains these undertones. *Le nozze di Figaro*, in spite of its extraordinary dramatic pace and the strength of the characterization,

was only a moderate success in Vienna, and Mozart seems to have had to supplement his income by composing more chamber works, some of which show a distinctly dark frame of mind.

This state was alleviated by a stroke of good fortune. Some months later, *Figaro* was given in Prague, and its great success led to a commission to write another opera for the theatre there. Mozart again persuaded Da Ponte to write the libretto, and *Don Giovanni* was chosen, then a popular subject with dramatists: four other operas on the legendary hero were produced that year, including a serenata called *Don Giovanni Tenorio*, by a little-known Italian composer, Giuseppe Gazzaniga, and in 1761 Gluck had composed music for a ballet called *Don Juan*. Mozart's masterpiece was conceived as an *opera buffa*, with ample ensembles and finales, but with *opera seria* characters. Situations were extremely important, and the overture, the murder of the Commendatore, and the dénouement all reflect the dramatic manner of Gluck and his followers, such as Salieri. *Don Giovanni* was extremely well received in Prague (as were various other compositions, including the famous 'Prague' Symphony, K 504), but the opera was given in Vienna only after a year had passed, and then had only modest success, apparently because the music was too 'advanced' and 'difficult' for the audience.

By this time, Mozart was in debt, borrowing money from fellow Freemasons (he had been a member of the Order for several years) which he seemed to have little prospect of repaying promptly. The three last symphonies (K 543, K 550, and K 551) were written in the summer of 1788, presumably for a concert series, though there is no record of one, and it seems likely that Mozart's main income at this time came from arranging Handel's oratorios for the private concerts of an enthusiastic musical antiquarian, Baron van Swieten. In 1789 Mozart went with Prince Karl Lichnowsky to Berlin, picking up various minor engagements and possibly a commission for some quartets from King Friedrich Wilhelm II. However, these scarcely relieved his financial state, especially as on his return Constanze was taken ill and needed an expensive cure at Baden. The journey was none the less of great value musically; on the way there he visited Leipzig, and both there and in Berlin he had the chance to study the works of J. S. Bach, which impressed him enormously and which were the cause of the increased contrapuntal interest in many of his own last works.

A new opera commission in 1789 renewed Mozart's hopes, and he again collaborated with Da Ponte. The result was *Così fan tutte*, produced with success in January 1790 and continuing with a series of ten performances,

Autograph MS of Mozart's opera 'Don Giovanni', the beginning of Donna Elvira's aria 'Ah fuggi il traditor', Act 1 scene 10.

interrupted only by court mourning for Joseph II. Mozart must have hoped for employment from the new Emperor, but was not immediately successful. The following year, however, opened with happier prospects, Mozart receiving commissions for two operas: an *opera seria* (*La clemenza di Tito*) for the crowning of the Emperor as King of Bohemia, and a *Singspiel*, *Die Zauberflöte*, for the impresario Emanuel Schikaneder. He also received a mysterious commission for a Requiem Mass, to be delivered secretly (the request came from a count, who wished to pass it off as his own work). *La clemenza di Tito* had some success, though *opera seria* was rapidly going out of fashion. *Die Zauberflöte*, planned as a kind of pantomime, inspired Mozart to write music which transformed it into an allegory of a quasi-religious kind, to be interpreted in the light of his most solemn Masonic beliefs. Its first performances were not overwhelmingly successful, probably because Mozart as usual had written music too elaborate for an audience seeking light diversion, but it soon became one of the most popular entertainments in Vienna. By this time, however, Mozart had fallen ill. He never finished the Requiem, which was completed by his pupil

Süssmayr, and after two months of decline he died, probably of rheumatic fever. Constanze was too distracted to make funeral arrangements, and Mozart was buried in a pauper's grave (though the horror with which this fact is often announced is misguided: such an arrangement was not at all unusual in Vienna at that time).

6. *Conclusion*. Mozart's life of poverty and his early death led to his 19th-century reputation as a Romantic artist born too soon, wishing to be independent of patrons and thus suffering to the point of anguish, as true artists should. The reality was different. While believing in the egalitarian ideas of the time, he did not suffer for them as, for instance, did Cimarosa, jailed in Naples, or Piccinni, dismissed from his job. It was not uncommon for composers to have financial difficulties, and Mozart's break with the Archbishop was as much a matter of ambition and temperament as of principle—after all, he spent the rest of his life in Vienna hoping for a place at court. His freelance existence could have been profitable if he had made the effort to please his audiences more, as did a host of Italian composers. Nor was it

purely his innate seriousness that denied him
great success; there were many popular composers at the time who were even more intense
in their attitudes—notably Gluck and his followers in France. Even less was Mozart the
sensitive, literate hero of the Romantic vision:
his letters had to be pruned of coarse expressions to satisfy 19th-century taste, and there are
few signs that he was really well read, though he
was obviously a shrewd judge of drama.

Mozart's value to posterity was in fact the
result of his extraordinary artistic gifts, not of
his symbolic position in history. He had a
remarkable ability to cross-fertilize one genre
with another: to the charm of the *galant*
symphony was added the dramatic power of
the Gluckian overture; Haydn's closely-argued
quartet style gained an Italian grace; and *opera
buffa* and *Singspiel* were enriched with the
serious qualities which would otherwise have
disappeared with the dying *opera seria*. This
breadth of artistic imagination was enhanced by
his keen interest in personality, which infects
his letters no less than his operas. His appreciation of the subtler shades of character and
mood makes him the theatre's most human
composer. For these reasons it was impossible
for the next generations of musicians to ignore
him. Beethoven owed a great deal to his
example, though he was in many ways less
subtle; the music of Haydn's last period was
affected deeply by Mozart's handling of instrumental music; and Rossini, surprisingly for an
Italian, achieved a better understanding of the
nature of *opera buffa* from Mozart. For the same
reasons, Mozart's music can stand a multiplicity
of interpretations, ranging from the slow and
solemn to the light and graceful. What it must
have is what it possesses in great measure—
humanity.

Mozart left two sons: Carl Thomas Maria
(1784-1858) and **Franz Xaver Wolfgang
Mozart** (*b* Vienna, 26 July 1791; *d* Carlsbad, 29
July 1844), who chose to call himself Wolfgang
Amadeus after his father. He studied piano with
Hummel, singing with Salieri, and composition
with the Abbé Vogler and Albrechtsberger. He
began his career as composer and teacher in
Vienna in 1805, later moving to Lemberg (now
Lvov). In 1819 he undertook an extensive European concert tour: his repertory as a pianist
included many of his father's works. His own
works include two piano concertos, some chamber music for piano and other instruments, a
symphony, and some cantatas and songs.

DENIS ARNOLD

FURTHER READING
Emily Anderson, ed.: *Letters of Mozart and his Family*
(London, 1938, 2nd edn (revised by Alec Hyatt King
and M. Carolan) 1966); Alfred Einstein: *Mozart: his
Character, his Work* (New York, 1945, 4th edn 1960);
Stanley Sadie: *Mozart* (London, 1966); Arthur
Hutchings: *Mozart: the Man, the Musician* (London,
1976); Ivor Keys: *Mozart: his Life in his Music*
(London, 1980).

Mozart and Salieri. Opera in one act by
Rimsky-Korsakov, a setting of Pushkin's poem
(1830). It was first performed in Moscow in
1898.

Mp. Abbreviation for *mezzo piano* (It.), 'half-
soft', i.e. not too soft.

M.S. Abbreviation for (1) *mano sinistra* (It.),
'left hand'; (2) manuscript.

Mudarra, Alonso (*b* c.1510; *d* Seville, 1 Apr.
1580). Spanish vihuelist and composer. From
1546 until he died he worked at Seville Cathedral. His *Tres libros de musica en cifras para
vihuela* (Seville, 1546) is an important collection
of music for vihuela and guitar, and includes
fantasias, *tientos*, dances, and transcriptions of
Franco-Flemish polyphonic music, as well as
some songs for solo voice and vihuela.

WENDY THOMPSON

Mudd, Thomas (*d* ? Durham, buried 2 Aug.
1667). English organist and composer. He
succeeded his father, John Mudd, as organist
of Peterborough Cathedral in 1631, but left
the following year. He was apparently an ill-
tempered alcoholic, unable to hold any post for
long although he managed to obtain work as
organist at several cathedrals including Exeter,
Lincoln, and York. His surviving works are
mostly anthems and services.

Mudd is sometimes confused with his uncle,
also called Thomas, who died c.1619. Only a few
of his works survive, including an *In nomine*
setting, anthems, and keyboard and viol pieces.

WENDY THOMPSON

Müde (Ger.). 'Tired', 'languid' in style.

Mudge, Richard (*b* Bideford, 1718; *d* ? Bedworth, Warwicks., Apr. 1763). English composer. He was known simply as 'Mr Mudge',
and studied at Oxford University from 1735 to
1741; he was then ordained. He became vicar at
Great Packington, near Birmingham, and in
1756 rector of Bedworth. He wrote an unusual
set of six concertos for two solo violins and
strings (London, 1749): in the first a solo
trumpet is added to the orchestra; the sixth
features a part for solo keyboard, and a short
Adagio which includes a passage for three voices
singing Byrd's canon 'Non nobis Domine'.

WENDY THOMPSON

Muette de Portici, La. See *Masaniello*.

Muffat, Georg (*b* Mégève, Savoy, May 1653; *d* Passau, 23 Feb. 1704). German composer of Scottish ancestry. He studied with Lully in Paris and then spent some time in the service of the Archbishop of Salzburg, who sent him to study in Rome for two years from 1680. There he became acquainted with the style of Corelli, and in his later years as *Kapellmeister* to the Bishop of Passau he produced works which combined French and Italian styles. The *concerti grossi* of his *Armonico tributo* (Salzburg, 1682) introduced Corelli's style into Germany, but he maintained a five-part texture and in the dances emulated Lully's 'natural and flowing style, rejecting all superfluous artifice, extravagant runs, frequent and awkward leaps . . .' (preface to his *Florilegium primum*, Augsburg, 1695). His prefaces to various publications are most informative about contemporary attitudes to bowing, tempo, and dynamics.

DENIS ARNOLD

Muffat, Gottlieb (*b* Passau, Apr. 1690; *d* Vienna, 9 Dec. 1770). German composer, the son of Georg Muffat. He was a pupil of Fux in Vienna and from 1717 worked as organist to the Viennese court. Among his duties was the tuition of Maria Theresia, who promoted him to the position of first organist in 1741 after becoming Empress. Unlike his father, he concentrated on keyboard music. His *ricercari* are in the old style of Frescobaldi, but he was also much influenced by French music, especially the ornamental style of Couperin's suites.

DENIS ARNOLD

Muineira [muñeira] (Sp.). A dance from the province of Galicia, in north-west Spain; it is characterized by 6/8 time and flowing motion.

Mulliner Book (London, British Library, Add. 30593). Collection of keyboard music copied by the organist Thomas Mulliner in the mid 16th century. It contains a wide variety of music, mostly intended for organ and including pleasing fantasias and transcriptions of anthems and secular songs. One of the most valuable sources for the keyboard repertory of its time, it has been published in the *Musica Britannica* series in an edition by Denis Stevens (1951, rev. edn 1954).

Multiphonics. See *Wind Instruments*, 6.

Multiple stopping. See *Stopping*.

Mundy, John (*b c.*1555; *d* Windsor, 29 June 1630). English composer. He was the son of William Mundy, and worked as an organist at St George's Chapel, Windsor, from *c.*1585 until his death. He was awarded the Oxford B.Mus.

in 1586 and the D.Mus. in 1624. He wrote songs and anthems, and his *Songs and Psalms* (London, 1594) recall the conservative idiom of Byrd rather than the newer madrigalian spirit of Morley. Of his few keyboard pieces, included in the *Fitzwilliam Virginal Book*, the fantasia *Faire Wether* is the best known today, mainly because of its descriptive portrayal of 'Lightning' and 'Thunder'.

JOHN MILSOM

Mundy, William (*b c.*1529; *d* ? London, 1591). English composer. He was the son of a sexton and musician of St Mary-at-Hill, London, and was head chorister at Westminster Abbey in 1543. He subsequently became a vicar-choral at St Paul's, and from 1564 was a Gentleman of the Chapel Royal. He composed a substantial quantity of sacred music, including anthems for the Anglican Church, and Latin antiphons for the Roman Catholic. He is best known today for a particularly beautiful anthem, 'O Lord, the maker of all things'.

DENIS ARNOLD

Muñeira (Sp.). See *Muineira*.

Muradeli, Vano (Ilyich) (*b* Gori, Georgia, 6 Apr. 1908; *d* Tomsk, 14 Aug. 1970). Soviet composer. He studied music in Georgia, then in Moscow with his fellow-Georgian Boris Shekhter (1900–61) and with Myaskovsky. He composed many songs, choruses, and some orchestral works (including two symphonies), but he is best known for his epic operas. In his first opera *Velikaya druzhba* ('The Great Friendship', 1947), featuring as the central character the real-life Komissar Sergo Ordzhonikidze, he sought to capture the prevailing mood of artistic *socialist realism, but the opera was swiftly withdrawn. The reason probably lay in Stalin's apparent antagonism towards Ordzhonikidze, who had died in suspicious circumstances in 1937: the conflicting evidence is laid out in Roy Medvedev's book *Let History Judge* (London and New York, 1971, pp. 193–6). The Party resolution condemning *The Great Friendship* (10 Feb. 1948) became a peg on which Andrey Zhdanov hung his purges of alleged *formalism in the music of Shostakovich, Prokofiev, Khachaturian, and others, and in the event the official dissatisfaction with *The Great Friendship* paled into insignificance alongside the wholesale attacks on music of far greater worth.

Muradeli picked up the threads of his career after Stalin's death in 1953 and composed at least one opera—*Oktyabr'* ('October', 1961)—which has remained in the Russian repertory. Here his tuneful, often folk-tinged musical style is sharply to the fore, and the score and subject (the October Revolution, with a sub-plot of love and divided loyalties) offer many opportunities for dramatic, if blatant, stage effects: crowd scenes, the arrival of Lenin's train at the Finland Station, pauses in the music for declamation of Lenin's speeches, and so on. *October* was also a landmark in Soviet music in being the first opera to give the character of Lenin a small singing role.   GEOFFREY NORRIS

Murciana (Sp.). A type of *fandango, named after Murcia, a town in southern Spain.

Murky bass. An 18th-century name for bass accompaniments in broken octaves. A well-known example of a murky bass occurs in the first movement of Beethoven's *Grande sonate pathétique*.

Murrill, Herbert (Henry John) (*b* London, 11 May 1909; *d* London, 25 July 1952). English composer. He studied with York Bowen, Stanley Marchant, and Alan Bush at the Royal Academy of Music (1925–8) and with W. H. Harris, Ernest Walker, and Sir Hugh Allen at Oxford (1928–31). In 1936 he joined the BBC, rising to become Head of Music in 1950. He also produced a number of compositions influenced by Stravinsky and Parisian neoclassicism; they include a string quartet (1939) and two cello concertos (1935, 1950), of which the second was based on a Catalan folk-song and dedicated to Casals.   PAUL GRIFFITHS

Muscadin. A dance occasionally encountered in English 16th- and 17th-century virginal music. It resembles the *allemande.

Muset, Colin (*fl. c.*1200–50). French *trouvère* poet and composer, thought to have worked in the region around Lorraine. Of humble birth, he became a *jongleur* by profession; several of his songs allude to his life as a wandering minstrel and to the instruments he played. Some 20 *chansons* have been attributed to him, but half of them survive without music.   JOHN MILSOM

Musette. 1. The bagpipe of 17th- and 18th-century French society, sometimes called 'musette de cour' (see *Bagpipe*, 9).
2. Also in France, in the 19th century, the musette was a small and simple oboe-like double reed instrument, with or without keys, pitched a fourth higher than the oboe and manufactured after the bagpipe musette had gone out of fashion. It is said to have served in the music for the *bal musette* in the towns or for country dances, but later to number more or less among the musical toys (the *bal musette* having adopted the *accordion). A 19th-century tutor, *Méthode de musette* by Cavaillé, states that the sound of the musette should be 'nasal' and close

in character to the Breton chalumeau (see *Bombarde*, 3).
3. A very popular dance at the court of Louis XIV and XV. It was a rustic form of the *gavotte, in a moderate 2/4, 3/4, or 6/8 time, the name deriving from the bagpipe-like bass drone. Musettes were also composed for keyboard, for example by François Couperin.

Musgrave, Thea (*b* Barnton, Midlothian, 27 May 1928). Scottish composer. She studied at Edinburgh University (1947–50) and with Nadia Boulanger in Paris (1950–4). Like many British composers of her generation she has sought a compromise between avant-garde and traditional methods, using serial and aleatory devices, for instance, in works of essentially conventional format. Her best pieces include a series of dramatic concertos from the late 1960s and early 1970s (for orchestra, clarinet, horn, viola), followed by a full-scale opera, *Mary, Queen of Scots* (1977).   PAUL GRIFFITHS

Musica alla Turca (It.). See *Turkish Music*.

Musica colorata (It.). See *Coloratura*; *Musica figurata*, 2.

Musica disciplina [originally *Journal of Renaissance and Baroque Music*]. An American yearly musicological journal founded in 1946; the new title dates from 1948.

Musica enchiriadis. Important 9th-century treatise and our earliest source of polyphony; see *Organum*. It was once thought to have been written by Hucbald.

Musica falsa (Lat.). 'False music'. See under *Musica ficta*.

Musica ficta (Lat., 'false music'). Before 1600 musical sources rarely indicated all the required accidentals, and so it was necessary for performers to add them. Nowadays, editors and performers of early music often insert what they consider to be the missing accidentals, and these additions are commonly called *musica ficta*. Actually the term should be used in a more restricted sense than this. It properly refers to any accidentals (or chromatic alterations by the performer) that lie outside the standard system of notes used in the Medieval and Renaissance periods. This standard system was based on three uniform interlocking scales, each of six notes, called *hexachords (see Ex. 1).

The resulting scale, in its original untransposed position, already includes a B♭. This B♭ is occasionally described as *fa fictum*, because there is no key signature, but in fact, as part of the standard scale, it is properly described as a *recta* ('aright', 'straight') note.

Ex. 1

ut re mi fa sol la
ut re mi fa sol la
ut re mi fa sol la

It will be noticed that these hexachords all have the same intervallic structure consisting of a series of tones with a semitone between *mi* and *fa*. The cautioning against the sounding of a *mi* note against a *fa* note (see Ex. 2a) was one of the few universally agreed rules of *musica ficta*—at least in the 14th to 16th centuries, the period of greatest consensus on these matters. This rule ensured that fifths and octaves would be perfect. Another oft-stated rule was that a perfect fifth, unison, or octave should be approached by the nearest imperfect interval. By this it was intended that one (but only one) of the voices would move by step up or down a semitone (see Ex. 2b).

Ex.2a

fa   fa

mi   mi

Ex.2b

(i)   (ii)   (iii)   (iv)   (v)

Most of the accidentals in this example (which has no key signature) are *ficta*, but 2b (v) employs the *recta* B♭ to move to the octave, and theorists say that whenever possible *recta* notes rather than *ficta* notes should be used to achieve these movements. The example 2b (ii) demonstrates another widespread application of *musica ficta*, the use of the sharpened leading note (C♯ in this case) to proceed to the octave. However, this is only one of the possible solutions to the rule about proceeding to perfect intervals, and the so-called 'leading-note principle' (i.e. sharpening the leading note) is rarely given the status of a rule in theoretical writings.

All of these rules are concerned with the

movement of two or more voices: they are harmonic rules. Only in this context is the use of the interval of the augmented fourth (the tritone or *diabolus in musica*) proscribed, and so the common view that *ficta* is designed to remove the *diabolus in musica* whenever it occurs is a misleading one. The melodic use of the tritone is almost never specifically banned by the theorists. Even in the 10th century a treatise of the monk Hucbald allowed the unaltered tritone a proper place in the chants *Iam corpus eius* and *Isti sunt dies quos*. Moreover, a melodic phrase bound by or containing the tritone is apparently acceptable in polyphonic music if the leading-note function is in operation (see Ex. 3a). In some writings (e.g. the *Tractatus de contrapunctu* by the 14th-century Italian, Prosdocimus) it is suggested that the leading note should be sharpened even if this then creates a melodic tritone with the preceding interval (see Ex. 3b), but this view is exceptional. Some writers do attempt rules for purely melodic application. In the 14th century Jean de Muris, for example, stated that lower returning notes should be raised (see Ex. 4a). Perhaps the mostly widely quoted melodic 'rule' in modern discussions of *ficta* is 'Una nota super *la*, semper est canendum *fa*' ('a note above *la* is always sung *fa*'); this is designed to avoid the melodic tritone (see Ex. 4b).

Ex. 4a   Ex. 4b

re mi fa sol la
ut re mi fa mi

Actually, this precise 'rule' is not found before the 17th century, when it appears in the writings of Praetorius. Whatever rules are given for *ficta* most writers agree that, in the case of polyphonic music, harmonic (vertical) considerations should take precedence over melodic (horizontal) ones.

A further complication in the application of *ficta* comes where, in music before 1600, the lower part (or parts) has one more flat in its key signature than the upper part (or parts). It seems that the function of these so-called 'partial signatures' was not to state a 'key' but to transpose the basic hexachord scheme (see Ex. 1) and thus include more notes within the *recta* system. For example, if the whole scheme is transposed up a fourth or down a fifth

Ex. 3a.
Dufay: 'Mille bonjours'   Ex. 3b

Ex. 5*a*   *b*

Ex. 6.

From Ockeghem: 'Mort, tu as navré de ton dart'

(requiring a 'key signature' of one flat) then it can be seen (Ex. 5*a*) that E♮ as well as B♮ becomes a *recta* note.

A 'key signature' of two flats will provide A♭, E♭, and B♭ as *recta* notes, and so on (Ex. 5*b*). (In the original sources of music before 1600 it is usual for only flat 'key signatures' to be found.) Thus, in the extract shown in Ex. 6 all the added accidentals are *recta* notes, not *ficta*.

Note that, in accordance with the rules, vertical relationships (see arrows) take precedence over horizontal ones (the leading C in the top voice is not sharpened); also, in applying accidentals *recta* notes have been preferred to *ficta* ones (the Bs in the top voice might have been natural, and the F in the middle voice sharpened). In the 16th century many experimental works were written (by Josquin, Willaert, Costeley, etc.) exploring chromatic writing by transposing the traditional hexachords to unusual positions. It is also possible that the many Baroque works which appear to have one less flat in the signature than their 'key' demands still follow the tradition in which an extra *recta* accidental must be added in performance.

ANTHONY PRYER

Musica figurata (It.). 1 Originally a term used to distinguish any type of polyphonic music from plainchant or other monophony. In the 15th and 16th centuries it was used to describe polyphony in which the voice parts are more florid and move more independently than in note-against-note counterpoint.

2. In a more specialist sense, *musica figurata* denotes the decorated, florid style found in the polyphony of some early Flemish composers (Ockeghem, Obrecht) as distinct from the generally more sober **musica reservata* of Josquin and later composers. In this sense too the less common *musica colorata* is used, which may also suggest any sort of florid decoration (see *Coloratura*).

See also *Figural*.

Musical Automatons. The history of musical automatons is a long and complex one. In pre-Christian times, it was not unknown to consider the manufacture of 'artificial' instrument players (see *Mechanical Musical Instruments*) and the work of Apollonius and Hero was extensive in this field.

Musical automatons can be broken down into two types: first the creation of an animated android made to perform, or appear to perform, on a musical instrument; and second, the production of animated figures or automated scenes to which music is an added embellishment.

1. In the first category must be included the extraordinarily complicated piece made by Henri-Louis Jaquet-Droz and preserved today in the Musée d'Art et d'Histoire in Neuchâtel, Switzerland. This piece, called *The Clavecin-player*, comprises a female figure seated before an 'organized clavecin', which is really a small pipe organ in the shape of a clavecin. This is provided with a keyboard arranged in two arcs corresponding to the radius of the forearms of the android figure. In motion, the fingers actually depress the organ keys as a powerful clockwork mechanism drives the arms to pre-set positions and operates the fingers in the correct manner. The figure itself moves the eyes, the head, and, in a lifelike way, the breast rises and falls as if in breathing.

Other fabricated performing musicians include Frederick Kaufmann's trumpeter and that of Leonard Maelzel, brother of Johann Maelzel, Beethoven's friend and developer of the metronome. This apparently saved the life of its inventor during the Vienna revolution of 1848, when Maelzel dressed it in the uniform of an imperial soldier and stood it in the window of his house where it played trumpet fanfares. The rebels who had surrounded his home retreated on hearing the trumpet-call, assuming there to be a battalion of loyalists entrenched therein. The Prague clockmaker, Peter Heinrich, built an automaton trumpeter on horseback which could ride at walking pace and play any of ten fanfares.

2. The second class of musical automatons is far larger and comprises, in its simplest form, automaton dolls and figures or animated scenes including pictures which have musical-box-type movements built in to them.

In these mechanisms, the music is usually an accompaniment to the display of ingenious mechanism. Both German and French makers were adept at this facet of musical automatons. Normally the musical movements employed would be of but average quality, although some of the early pieces, such as the Turkish tight-rope-walkers popular in the 1860s, used more sophisticated movements.

James Cox's celebrated museum was an early exhibition of musical automatons and one of the pieces seen there in the 1770s was a silver swan which preened itself and occasionally stopped to pluck a fish from the water in which it swam. The 'water' was simulated by rotating twisted glass rods, and all the while it was in motion a carillon driven by clockwork played one of several tunes.

Complex musical automatons of this type were very popular from the middle of the 18th century until the early part of the 19th. They were not intended to be musical interpreters, however, and the music which they played generally comprised popular airs and national songs as a light diversion.

FURTHER READING
Arthur W. J. G. Ord-Hume: *Clockwork Music* (London, 1973).

Musical comedy, Musical. Following the success of the Gilbert and Sullivan operettas or light operas, a more commercialized form of musical theatre arose at the end of the 19th century, in which there was an even greater emphasis on individual 'hit' songs and the allure of the female form. More loosely constructed and aimed at a mass audience, this kind of show enjoyed a great vogue at London theatres like Daly's and the Gaiety. Known as 'musical comedy', it cultivated its own stars like Gertie Millar and Lily Elsie, and also took in some of the comedy elements of the earlier *burlesque. *In Town* (1892) called itself a 'musical farce', while *Morocco Bound* in 1893 was called a 'musical farcical comedy'. The first to use the term 'musical comedy' specifically was *A Gaiety Girl*, staged at the Prince of Wales theatre in

1893, with music by Sidney Jones, who also wrote one of the best musical comedies, *The Geisha*, in 1896; other leading composers were Lionel Monckton, Ivan Caryll, and Leslie Stuart. This brand of musical comedy was imported to the USA, and shows were still termed musical comedies up to the Jerome Kern and George Gershwin period. Gradually the term was dropped as American productions showed more serious intent, integrating the score more with the story, and the term 'musical play' and just plain 'musical' came into common use.   PETER GAMMOND

Musical Competitions. See *Competitions in Music*.

Musical glasses. See *Glasses, Musical*.

Musical Joke, A (*Ein musikalischer Spass*). Divertimento in F major (K 522) by Mozart for two horns and strings, composed in 1787. It is a satire on composers and performers of popular music.

Musical Offering, The (*Das musikalische Opfer*). Collection of 13 works by J. S. Bach, consisting of ricercars and canons on a theme given to Bach for extemporization by Frederick the Great of Prussia in Potsdam in 1747. Some of the pieces are for keyboard, and others are for an ensemble of up to three instruments (flute and two violins). Many modern performing editions have been made, and various composers have orchestrated items from the work.

Musical Opinion [originally *Musical Opinion and Music Trade Review*]. An English monthly musical magazine founded in 1877; the new title dates from 1964.

Musical Quarterly [*MQ*]. An American musicological journal founded in 1915 and published by G. Schirmer.

Musical Sand. The phenomenon of sounds emitted by masses of sand (described in various different circumstances as a 'booming', a 'singing', or a 'wail like that of a trombone') is observable in the deserts of Arabia, in over 70 recorded places on the North American Atlantic coast, at Studland Bay, Dorset, on the west coast of the island of Eigg in the Hebrides, and elsewhere, and has often been discussed by scientists. It has been explained as due to the rubbing together of millions of clean and incoherent grains of quartz, free from angularities or roughness. Though the vibrations emitted by the friction of any two grains might be inaudible, those emitted from millions, approximately of the same size, would give an audible note. A small portion of such sand in a basin will emit the note when stirred, but moistening or the addition of flour immediately 'damps' the sound out of existence. (This is the traditional explanation of the phenomenon and it is apparently still accepted as correct.)

PERCY SCHOLES

Musical saw. See *Flexatone*.

Musical Times, The [originally *The Musical Times and Singing Class Circular*]. English monthly musical journal, the oldest musical journal to remain in continuous publication. It was founded by J. A. Novello in London in 1844 and continues to be published by Novello & Co. Editors have included William McNaught (father and son), Martin Cooper, Harold Rutland, Andrew Porter, and Stanley Sadie.

Music and Letters. English musical quarterly founded in 1920 by A. H. Fox Strangways, who was editor until 1937. His successors include Eric Blom (1937–50 and 1954–9), Richard Capell (1950–4), Jack Westrup (1959–76), Denis Arnold and Edward Olleson (1976–81), and Edward Olleson and Nigel Fortune (1981–).

Music and Musicians. English monthly musical magazine founded in 1952. Publication ceased in 1980 but was resumed in 1981.

Musica reservata (Lat.). A term used by theorists and writers in the latter half of the 16th century to describe a music 'conforming to the whole text and to each word, expressing every emotion and putting things before the imagination as if actually happening' (according to the German writer Samuel Quickelberg, writing about Lassus's penitential psalms *c*.1560). It thus implies a detailed musical expression of the words, which were themselves of serious intent. The means of expression often involved the newly-discovered chromaticisms attempted in imitation of Greek theories of pitch and intervallic relation. The music may have been described as 'reserved' because it was performed before a specially picked group of listeners. The earliest recorded use of the term is in Adrianus Petit Coclico's treatise *Compendium musices* (1552), where it is used to describe Josquin's music; Coclico also used it to describe his own.

DENIS ARNOLD

Musica transalpina. Title of two anthologies of Italian (i.e. transalpine) madrigals, with English words, edited and published in London by Nicholas Yonge. The first (1588) contains 57 madrigals, by Marenzio, Palestrina, Byrd, and Lassus, among others; the second (1597) contains 24, including examples by Ferrabosco, Marenzio, and Venturi. They were the first printed collections of Italian madrigals in England and had a great influence on English composers of the period.

Music Criticism. See *Criticism of Music*.

Music Drama. See *Gesamtkunstwerk*; *Opera, 12*; *Wagner*.

Music Educators National Conference (MENC). The largest and most important American organization of active and aspiring music teachers. It was founded in 1907 as the Music Supervisors National Conference. Today, with over 60,000 members (one-third of whom are college undergraduates), the MENC is a highly organized federation of state associations and various associated and auxiliary organizations. Its publications, journals (the monthly *Music Educators Journal* and the quarterly *Journal of Research in Music Education*), films, conferences, commissions, research groups, administered projects, and legislative activities have been valuable to music educators and music education alike.

NYM COOKE

Music for a While. Song by Purcell from the incidental music he wrote for Dryden and Lee's play *Oedipus* (?1692).

Music hall. The nature of music-hall entertainment is clearly indicated by an alternative name that was used throughout music-hall history—'variety'—an entertainment made up of a variety of comic, vocal, acrobatic, and miscellaneous acts. The heyday of music hall was from the 1850s to the First World War, when it became a distinct kind of entertainment with its own theatres, players, repertory, and subsidiary activities. The name 'music hall' was simply a description of the places where such entertainment took place in the formative days: in specially adapted or constructed halls added to public houses etc., to attract custom by providing entertainment while the customers ate and drank. At this stage the name 'variety' was frequently used, and also 'vaudeville' (which became more common in the USA); the first book on music hall, by C. D. Stuart and A. J. Park, was called *The Variety Stage* (London, 1895).

The kind of varied entertainment that music hall offered had existed well before the 19th century, for example with wandering minstrels, court entertainers, jesters and acrobats at inns and fairs (such as the famous Bartholomew Fair), and subsequently in cheap working-class theatres ('penny gaffs') and the flourishing pleasure gardens of the 18th and 19th centuries.

The success of music hall began when there was a sufficiently affluent working-class and lower-middle-class audience to support it, and it ended when it was supplanted by new popular entertainments such as the radio, gramophone, and cinema.

It was probably the success of the pleasure gardens and other places of entertainment that grew around the curative springs and 'wells' of London that suggested to the more enterprising publicans that they too ought to offer some organized family entertainment. Convivial song-and-supper rooms providing entertainment mainly for affluent male revellers were already established in London in the early 1800s (among them, Evans's at 43 King Street, Covent Garden, the Coal Hole in the Strand, and the Cyder Cellars in Maiden Lane), and these provided both entertainers, who could be lured by high fees to the new music halls, and the basis of the vocal entertainment, cleaned up for family ears, for music-hall fare. Among the better-known names were W. G. Ross, Sam Cowell (1820-64), Harry Clifton (1824-72), and Sam Collins (1827-65).

Once the first music halls had been established they proliferated with remarkable rapidity: the Mogul Saloon opened in 1847; the Grapes at Southwark built a Grand Harmonic Hall in 1848 (soon to be known as the Surrey Music Hall); and the Canterbury Hall was opened by Charles Morton in 1849. The Mogul Saloon became the Middlesex Music Hall in 1851. From 1860 there was a positive eruption of music-hall building: the South London Palace was opened in 1860 and some of the more specialized theatres included the Bedford in Camden Town (1861), the Metropolitan in the Edgware Road (1862), and Collins's in Islington (1862). By 1868 there were some 200 music halls in London and around 300 in the rest of the British Isles.

In relation to *popular music, music hall is important as the starting-point of the modern cult of linking songs and singers. No music hall entertainer was likely to achieve fame and subsequent demand for his services on the music-hall circuit without at least one familiar song connected with his name. In the days before the establishment of copyright around 1900, the music-hall stars would buy their songs outright from the hard-working professional composers and writers for extremely meagre amounts. Many a lasting favourite was originally sold for a guinea or so, and was then considered to be the singer's exclusive property. From that time on song writers have depended (with increased remuneration) on linking their creations with the name of some famous performer. Among the important early performers at the Canterbury and other halls were Alfred

Vance (1838-88), 'Jolly' John Nash (1830-1901), Arthur Lloyd (1839-1904), Harry Rickards (1843-1911), W. B. Fair (1841-1909), George Leybourne (1842-84), Harry Liston (1843-1929), Herbert Campbell (1844-1904), and G. H. McDermott (1845-1933).

As the halls grew in popularity their character changed and the larger Palaces and Empires arose—places like the famous Oxford Music Hall in Oxford Street. The music halls of the 1880s were enriched by such stars as Jenny Hill (1850-95), Arthur Roberts (1852-1933), James Fawn (1850-1923), Nelly Power (1853-87), G. H. Chirgwin (1854-1922), Charles Coborn (1852-1945), R. G. Knowles (1858-1919), Harry Randall (1860-1932), and Dan Leno (1860-1904). The term 'theatre of varieties' was a common billing and the music hall gradually developed from providing entertainment as an extra to the refreshments to being a place of theatrical entertainment. In 1914 the consumption of food and drink in the auditorium was forbidden, and this marked the end of the old music hall in its original form. Its stars were now accomplished and highly-paid professionals. Following the great star Dan Leno, came Eugene Stratton (1861-1918), Albert Chevalier (1861-1923), Tom Costello (1863-1943), Leo Dryden (1863-1939), Gus Elen (1863-1940), Vesta Tilley (1864-1952), Mark Sheridan (1867-1918), Little Tich (1868-1928), Harry Champion (1866-1942), George Robey (1869-1954), Bransby Williams (1870-1961), Nellie Wallace (1870-1948), Kate Carney (1870-1950), and two very notable stars, Marie Lloyd (1870-1922) and Harry Lauder (1870-1950). Many of these lived on into the new age of 'variety' shows and the dominance of radio and film entertainment. The last generation of true music hall artistes included Marie Kendall (1873-1964), Ada Reeve (1874-1966), Harry Tate (1873-1940), Vesta Victoria (1874-1951), Florrie Forde (1874-1941), Wilkie Bard (1874-1944), Billy Merson (1881-1947), G. H. Elliott (1884-1962), Will Fyffe (1885-1947), Randolph Sutton (1888-1969), and Clarice Mayne (1891-1966). Those who followed worked not in an old-fashioned music-hall atmosphere, but in the more lavish and less atmospheric world of the variety theatre (Max Miller, Billy Bennett, Gracie Fields, Billy Russell, Hetty King, and many others). The music-hall spirit has survived in many modern acts (e.g. Beryl Reid, Morecambe and Wise, Tommy Trinder), and in the working-men's clubs all over England, predominantly in the North with comedians like Les Dawson still performing very much in the old tradition.

The music-hall song was a mass-produced article, with perhaps a couple of hundred achieving immortality by virtue of an inspired tune or a good catch-phrase in the lyrics. Most were strophic, with several verses and repeated chorus; there were only rare ventures beyond this format, as in the fine songs, with their long rambling verses, that Leslie Stuart wrote for Eugene Stratton. The strength and vitality of the best music-hall songs arises from their origins in the folk-like songs of the early song-and-supper rooms: 'Vilikins and his Dinah', 'The Ratcatcher's Daughter', and 'Little Polly Perkins' take their tunes and ideas from established folk-songs, whatever credits were eventually attached to them. The music-hall song retained this spirit and earthiness and is the first corpus of commercially-inspired song to cater for the lowbrow, though discerning and decided, tastes of the working classes. The composers—men like Joseph Tabrar, who wrote literally thousands of songs—are only half remembered, their talents overshadowed by the well-loved stars who bought and sang their songs. The music-hall song set the wheels of Tin Pan Alley in motion, established the practice of song-plugging, and founded a new industry. Its surviving repertory is rich in good tunes and personal association and retains an atmosphere which a programme like 'The Good Old Days' fondly exploits on behalf of the modern world's nostalgia for the past. The songs are certainly good, even if we are left to doubt whether the days were as rosy as memory has painted them.   PETER GAMMOND

Musicians' Union. British trade union formed in 1921 by amalgamation of the National Orchestral Association of Professional Musicians and the Amalgamated Musicians' Union, both of which had existed since the 1890s under various titles. Its chief aim is to protect the interests of professional musicians (in the main instrumentalists), particularly in the areas of pay and working conditions.

Musick's Monument. Book written by Thomas Mace (and published in London in 1676), giving valuable information on English music around the middle of the 17th century. It includes several suites and pieces for viol.

Music Library Association (MLA). American organization founded in 1931 'to promote establishment, growth and use of music libraries'. The MLA sets standards of music librarianship, encourages the development of new systems of library organization, and works to improve services and collections of music libraries. Its efforts have facilitated scholarly research and brought a needed degree of specialization to the music librarian profession. Its publications include *Notes* (since 1943, a quarterly containing articles, reviews, and lists

of new music and recordings), *A Checklist of Thematic Catalogues*, and the 'MLA Index Series'.   MARK TUCKER

Music of the Spheres. See *Spheres, Music of the.*

Musicology. A word taken into English from the French (*musicologie*) in the second half of the 19th century. It is often used, sloppily, to mean almost any kind of writing about music, from chatty sleeve-notes for popular records to esoteric critical discussion, but it is best confined to the same meaning as the German *Musikwissenschaft*—the scientific or orderly investigation of musical phenomena. The word *Wissenschaft*, 'knowledge', implies the acquisition of facts, and this is the musicologist's primary duty, although he will inevitably have an interpretative function also. The kinds of facts required for any considered view on music are of a more than usually broad scope, and may be classified under various headings.

1. *Acoustical Information.* This is the oldest branch of musicology, dating back to the Ancient Greeks. It is concerned with the actual production of sound, and many of the experimental techniques of the natural sciences are appropriate to its study. As this volume has an ample article on acoustics, little need be said here, except that, surprisingly, these techniques have not yet been applied to discover many facts concerning another extremely important branch of musicology—

2. *Authenticity.* Before the invention of recording machines it was impossible to preserve sound. People had to rely on aural tradition, which was liable to change with the passing of time, or on notation, an imperfect method of storing facts which poses many difficulties of interpretation. Nevertheless, such interpretation must be attempted. It involves several skills which are discussed below, but it must be said that even after collating and assessing all the existing information on these aspects, there will remain a number of imponderables.

(a) *Discovery of the Composer's or Performer's Intentions.* This requires the study of original sources—manuscripts and printed books—and an interpretation of the notation. This is the task undertaken when making an edition (see *Editors, Editing*), and may be very difficult in the case of imperfect sources or complex notations.

(b) *Knowledge of Performing Practice.* Since notation has never been more than an approximation, to progress from it to the actual sound requires a knowledge of such matters as ornamentation, instrumentation, customary application of expression and *rubato*, realization of a continuo part, and a host of other matters. It must also include an idea of the situation for which the music was intended — whether it was a concert room or a church, roughly what size it was, and so on. See also *Performing Practice*.

(*c*) *Knowledge and Understanding of the Instruments Involved*. Some early instruments (such as the crumhorn) have fallen into disuse, so that their original sound is totally lost unless someone reconstructs and learns to play them. Alterations to other instruments which are still in common use (for example the flute and the French horn) mean that the sound to which we are accustomed is not that expected by the composer. It is a musicologist's task to unravel these facts, taking measurements and experimenting (with the help of expert players if need be) on surviving instruments, reading treatises on performance to elucidate original fingering and embouchure (which can make considerable differences in technique and sound), and investigating the important question of *pitch.

3. *The Human Factor*. Although sound may be held to exist even if no one can hear it (it can, after all, be perceived through scientific recording apparatus), music cannot: human perception is essential. The nature of this perception requires systematic investigation from various points of view.

(*a*) *The Physiology of Perception*. This is properly akin to acoustics and may be investigated by experimental methods.

(*b*) *The Psychology of Perception*. This can also be investigated by experimental methods, but to a lesser extent. Although tests have been devised to discover how people react to different aspects of music, they tend to isolate each phenomenon without being able to synthesize them, and the vaguer concepts of such a system as psychoanalysis are often more useful than the more precise techniques of the experimental psychologist. See also *Aesthetics of Music*.

(*c*) *The Process of Composition*. One of the earliest branches of musicological writing was the biographical study, and this seems an inevitable approach, given that music is usually the creative act of an individual. There is no doubt that the psychological make-up of the composer helps to shape his music. Yet it must always be remembered that biographical facts are relatively superficial—the composer is not usually available for Freudian investigation, and his documented emotional life is often not directly concerned with his music (the classic case of such dissociation may be found in Mozart's later years, where his letters indicate great misery while his music often seems to express the opposite). The most important biographical facts undoubtedly concern the

music with which the composer was acquainted. It can be argued that Mozart's relationship with his wife is less worth recording than his discovery of the works of Bach and Handel. To determine the indebtedness of a composer involves detailed stylistic analysis of his own music and of that which he probably knew. This can be achieved to some extent by taking each feature in turn —harmony, texture, orchestration, and so on—and comparing his 'input' with his 'output'. His development throughout life can be established by comparing his earlier with his later music (always taking into account that he was experiencing other men's works throughout). Here modern methods of analysis, sometimes using computer techniques, may result in a close knowledge of a composer's development and musical personality. See also *Analysis*; *Composition*.

(*d*) *Environment*. If consideration of the process of composition must begin with the individual, the fact that he lives in a community is of equal significance. One does not need to be a Marxist in order to appreciate that economic circumstances are very important. A composer usually depends on institutions for the realization of his product. The taste of his patrons, be they royalty or the general public, is often of crucial importance to him. The financial position of the patron is also important—whether he can afford an orchestra or not, for example. Thus both economic and social history may enter into musicology, although at the moment they have received enough attention to define their true importance only in the field of *ethnomusicology, where perforce they form a large part of the study. Of course, it is easy to make false assumptions. Composers create demands as well as fulfil them, just as musical institutions are shaped by, as well as shaping, their members. Similarly, it is easy to assume that a composer was affected by his literary or artistic surroundings, whereas in fact many musicians learn little, if anything, of the culture of their time outside music. Even inside music, the assumption that a composer has been affected by the 'spirit of the age' may be untrue. The 'spirit of the age' may be no more than a convenient fiction, built up by hindsight from surviving materials—or, worse, from what survives in the current repertory. It is more important for the musicologist to know what the composers of the epoch thought was important than what the later historian thinks was important. All but the simplest cultures are fragmented; it is for the musicologist to decide which fragments are significant for his purpose.

4. *The Purpose and Scope of Musicology*. In spite of these necessary imprecisions, writing the history of music, in detailed or in more general

studies, is an essential part of musicology, since it is in the ordering of material that insight is to be found. It has this in common with all historical study, and needs no defence or explanation. The purposes to which musicology may be put are capable of more debate. There can be no doubt that it is improper for it to be used to support social, religious, or political theories without considerable caveats. To propagate racial theories via musicological scholarship (as, for example, was done in Nazi Germany) is wrong. It is less dangerous to evolve purely musical theories—as for example Hugo Riemann's attempt at a 'universal rule' of phrasing—though the complexity of the material makes the formulation of general laws seem an impossible, even naïve, goal.

An obviously proper use of musicology is to help the performer formulate an approach to a work, or even an interpretation. Although there is some justification for the view that a great musical work is taken out of its epoch and becomes 'timeless', its corollary, that it must therefore be interpreted according to modern views, is open to the criticism that the composer did not think in notation but in sound. And it is certainly true that many of the difficulties of a modern performer come purely because of changed conditions. It is often easier to perform keyboard music of the 16th and 17th centuries using the original fingering than to try to adapt modern ones. It is always true that study of the original sound will increase insight. Nor is there any need for the result to be 'academic' or dry. Musicological preparation is not essentially different from technical preparation—the working out and practice of fingering or bowing. Both must be absorbed before the performance; both will improve it.

5. *The Profession of Musicology*. It is churlish and hair-splitting to deny the title of musicologist to the early historians, theorists, and antiquaries who sought out the material of the study in the 18th and early 19th centuries. Burney, Hawkins, Martini, and Forkel among the historians, Rameau among the theorists, Caffi and Köchel among antiquaries must be included in the list of founders of the discipline. Nevertheless, the attitudes of the modern musical scientist (to coin an equivalent of the social scientist) stem from the Germans, such as Winterfeld and Ambros, of the period 1820–60. These were amateurs—they made their living mainly as civil servants and lawyers—but by no means dilettantes. They were followed by the professionals, who, after a period following another profession (or other branch of music), became lecturers and professors of *Musikwissenschaft* in universities. Such men as Riemann and Adler had enormous influence on the next generation, and

the number of professors increased, especially in the early 20th century, until now virtually every major German university has a Faculty of Musicology. Scholars came from abroad to study if their countries did not offer similar facilities, the most distinguished American, Otto Kinkeldey, working at Berlin from 1902 until the First World War. Resistance in some countries, especially Britain, was more apparent, largely because their universities and institutes were already established on other lines. But Stainer and Parry, both Oxford professors (though amateur musicologists), did sterling musicological work, while Dent at Cambridge was one of the most respected scholars in the world. The great dispersion of the discipline came about through Nazi persecution in the 1930s, many German Jews seeking asylum in the USA, where eventually universities created the necessary posts. Notable among these was Alfred Einstein, of an older generation, and Manfred Bukofzer, of a younger one.

There is an *International Musicological Society, based in Switzerland, and most countries have their own national associations: see *American Musicological Society*; *Royal Musical Association*; *Società Italiana di Musicologia*; *Société Française de Musicologie*.

DENIS ARNOLD

Music Teachers National Association (MTNA). American organization dedicated to improving music education and setting standards for the music teaching profession. Theodore Presser founded MTNA in 1876. Among its accomplishments it has helped to set international pitch (1883); developed a national certification plan for music teachers (1967); and spawned other organizations concerned with music education (including the Music Educators National Conference and the National Association of Schools of Music). Although MTNA's activities are directed primarily towards the private music teacher, membership is open to anyone interested in the music teaching profession. Six times a year it publishes the *American Music Teacher*.   MARK TUCKER

Musique concrète (Fr.). A kind of *electronic music which uses natural sounds, not electronically-generated tones, as raw material. The recordings—of machinery, running water, musical instruments, or whatever—are transformed by electronic means and joined to form a composition. Pierre Schaeffer coined the term in 1948 to describe his first electronic studies.

Musique mesurée (Fr.). 'Measured music'. A French literary and musical experiment of the late 16th century. It began as an attempt to apply to contemporary French verse the principles of metrical accentuation found in classical poetry, and was devised by Jean-Antoine Baïf and a group of poets who called themselves the Pléiade. Baïf enlisted the help of contemporary musicians to transfer these poetic principles to vocal music—*musique mesurée à l'antique*. The process was simple: composers followed the metre of the verse, setting long, accented syllables as minims, and short, unaccented ones as crotchets. This resulted in irregular phrases and bar-lengths, with no regular pulse, and as a result much of this music has no time signature and is left unbarred. Baïf tried to further his project by founding an Académie de Poésie et de Musique (1570), but despite royal support it lasted only about three years. The prime importance of *musique mesurée* lies not in the music composed with it in mind, but in the transference of many of its characteristic features to the **air de cour*, which in turn influenced Lully's recitative style.

Musorgsky, Modest (Petrovich) (*b* Karevo, Pskov district, 21 Mar. 1839; *d* St Petersburg, 28 Mar. 1881). Russian composer. Like some other Russian musical pioneers (Glinka, Balakirev) he got much of his inspiration from folk music heard in childhood, and the folk tales he also heard gave him the literary basis for much of his composition. He came early in touch with Dargomyzhsky and all his life tried to apply his principles. In his works musical realism attains its culmination. His songs are very charac-

Musorgsky, drawing (1876) by Alexandrovsky.

teristic of him; they are sardonic, humorous, or tender, and 'go straight to the mark'.

His greatest works are operas, *Boris Godunov* (1869) and *Khovanshchina* (1886), now of

Autograph MS of the vocal score of Musorgsky's opera 'Boris Godunov', the opening of Act 1 scene 2.

world-reputation, though having no success during the lifetime of their composer. The version of *Boris* long used was one that had been (like other things of this composer) 'touched up' by Rimsky-Korsakov; the original version was published in 1928 and tends now to be adopted. (For the plot, etc., see *Boris Godunov*.)

In early manhood he was an officer in the guards; then he entered the civil service. His life was not admirable; he was slovenly and waged a long losing fight against the drink habit. His personal weaknesses were redeemed only by a great public purpose—to produce an art that should illuminate the life of many. In his determined nationalism he was the most typical member of 'The *Five' and he was not the least gifted of them.

See also *Opera*, 14; *Russia and the Soviet Union*, 4.　　　　　PERCY SCHOLES, rev.

FURTHER READING
M. D. Calvocoressi: *Mussorgsky* (London, 1974).

Muta (It.). 'Change'. It is applied to brass playing, meaning 'change the crook', and to kettledrum playing, meaning 'change the tuning'; thus *muta D in C* means 'change the tuning from D to C'.

Mutation. 1. See under *Hexachord*. 2. The change in the male voice which takes place at puberty. 3. The term can be used for the shift of position in violin playing, etc.

Mute (Fr.: *sourdine*; Ger.: *Dämpfer*; It.: *sordino*). A device which acoustically changes the customary sound of an instrument into one which is distinctively different, less resonant, more veiled, distant, or mysterious. Two groups of instruments are by far the most concerned: the violin family and, among wind, the brass.

1. *Violin Mute*. This is three-pronged, of wood (ebony), leather, or in various metal forms, clipped tightly to the bridge to dampen the full motion in transmitting string vibration to the sound-box. Similar mutes are made for viola, cello, and double bass (and are especially effective on the viola). The violin mute came in in the 17th century; Purcell uses it in Act 2 of *The Fairy Queen* where Night and Sleep sing, with two recorders accompanying Secrecy between their songs. The instruction to put on the mute, 'con sordino' (often abbreviated to 'con sord.'), is countermanded by 'senza sordino' ('without mute') or the equivalent in other languages. There are now also types of 'attached' mute (attached to the bridge, see Pl. 1) used in modern orchestral works where the mute may need to be applied or removed within the space of a bar's rest.

2. *Mutes for Brass Instruments*. These are placed

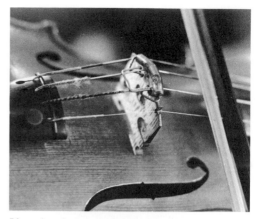

Pl. 1. A modern attached mute for violin.

in the bell, changing the tonal spectrum in ways by which the notes are heard mainly through their harmonics. An ancient form of trumpet mute (Fig. 2a) was in use probably before the violin mute was known. Others came in during the 19th century, since when many further types have been introduced through jazz. Among the chief now in use is the conical or 'straight' mute of cardboard, fibre, or synthetics, closed at the wide end (Fig. 1a); corks or ridges on the outside leave a narrow passage between mute and bell. It produces the thin, hissing quality often required with horn, trumpet, and trombone in the orchestra, and in orchestral parts 'con sord.' or 'muted' is normally understood to refer to this type. Its predecessor, as known to Richard Strauss and his generation, was similar in principle and effect but generally of wood or aluminium, often with a knob on the end for

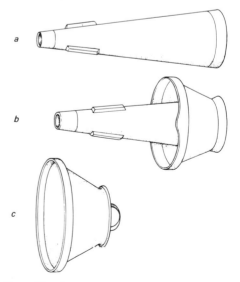

Fig. 1. Three brass instrument mutes: (a) 'straight' mute; (b) cup mute; (c) plunger mute.

attaching a string lest the mute should fall out (Fig. 2*b* and *c*).

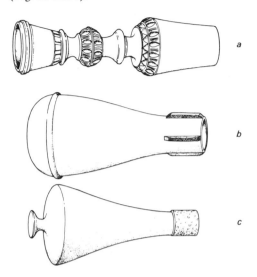

Fig. 2. (a) Wooden trumpet mute, 16th–17th century; (b) metal cornet mute, early form; (c) wooden horn mute, late 19th century (shown reduced).

The cup mute (Fig. 1*b*) is also conical, but instead of a plain closed end it carries a reflecting cup of width matching the bell rim and adjustable by a screw-thread to close the bell to a desired degree, giving different shades of clear crooning or 'blue' sound. The wa-wah mute is corked to fit the bell all round. Inside is a tube leading to a small open-ended cup, the air in this case passing through the mute; waving the hand over the cup gives the 'wa-wah' effects. A 'clear-tone' mute likewise fits the bell all round but has two cones, one projecting from the other and again open-ended. The plunger (Fig. 1*c*) is simply a cup with a handle by which it is held against the bell, to be moved in various ways while playing, e.g. outward and back as made famous on the trombones in Glenn Miller's 'Tuxedo Junction'. Jazz orchestrations have often called for 'in hat': an imitation bowler hat is held in the left hand, or fixed to the music stand for the trumpet or trombone bell to be brought close to it, for a kind of hollow sound.

Tuba mutes remain something of a problem, the very wide bell making it difficult to achieve an acoustically satisfactory result. They have often been home-made by trial and error, though latterly also manufactured in the USA.

The preceding mutes for the brass are all sometimes termed 'non-transposing' mutes, meaning that they do not alter the pitch of the instrument, whereas there are other mutes which do so, known as 'transposing mutes'. One of these is for the horn, giving the same effect as hand-muting and similarly raising the pitch, for which the player must compensate with the valves (see *Horn*, 3). Another is the ancient trumpet mute (mentioned above), of wood, raising the pitch by a whole tone. When used in the orchestra ('trombe sordinate' etc. in Baroque works, some of them funeral cantatas) the players compensated for the rise by inserting a crook, but Monteverdi, in the opening Toccata in *Orfeo*, tells the other instruments to transpose a tone higher if trumpet mutes are to be used.

3. *Other Instruments.* In the 18th century the oboe was sometimes muted with a pear-shaped wooden mute or screwed-up paper thrust into the bell (as in the *St Luke Passion* once ascribed to Bach). Berlioz thought of having the clarinet played inside a felt bag (*Lélio*, 1831), anticipating the low-register 'sub-tone' effect of playing inside a large cardboard 'megaphone' with slots for the hands. Some early pianos had a 'mute stop' or 'celeste': a leathered strip hinged to fall across the strings.

4. *Other Meanings.* 'Mute' also occurs in the name of certain instruments: mute cornett (see *Cornett*, 4); mute violin—a practice violin built in various forms with virtually no sound-box. *Sordino* once denoted the dancing-master's fiddle (see *Kit*), while 'sordone' is both an early organ stop and a wind instrument (see *Kortholt*).

ANTHONY BAINES

Müthel, Johann Gottfried (*b* Mölln, Lauenburg, 17 Jan. 1728; *d* Bienenhof, nr Riga, 14 Jan. 1788). German organist and composer. He studied at Lübeck and in 1747 became chamber musician and court organist at Mecklenburg-Schwerin. In 1750 he went to study with Bach, and lived with him during the last year of Bach's life; he was also a friend of C. P. E. Bach. In 1753 he was appointed organist at the Lutheran church in Riga, where he died.

Müthel was a fine keyboard player and an accomplished composer. His clavier sonatas were highly praised by Burney. Two of his harpsichord concertos were published at Riga in 1767.

WENDY THOMPSON

Myaskovsky, Nikolay (Yakovlevich) (*b* Novogeorgiyevsk, 20 Apr. 1881; *d* Moscow, 8 Aug. 1950). Soviet composer. He was born in a fortress, the son of a general in the Russian army, and himself trained for the army, in which he fought from 1914 to 1916. He had had a good musical education at the St Petersburg Conservatory under Rimsky-Korsakov and others, and on the conclusion of the War became a professor of composition at the Moscow Conservatory. He wrote 27 symphonies and some sonatas and other things. His musical style shows the influences of both Glazunov and Tchaikovsky, and emotionally he approaches the latter in his pessimistic and even neurasthenic outlook—his manner, however, being necessarily more progressive.

PERCY SCHOLES, rev.

My Country. See *Má Vlast*.

My Ladye Nevells Booke (privately owned). Manuscript collection of virginal music dating from 1591. It consists of 42 keyboard pieces by Byrd, who was probably Lady Nevell's teacher. She, however, must quickly have relinquished the manuscript, for 'Lord Abergavenny, called the Deafe, presented it to the Queene' (Elizabeth I). There is a modern edition by Hilda Andrews (1926, reprinted 1969).

Mysliveček [Mysliweczek, Mislivecek], **Josef** (*b* Horní Šárka, nr Prague, 9 Mar. 1737; *d* Rome, 4 Feb. 1781). Czech composer. After studying the organ and counterpoint in Prague, Mysliveček entered the family trade, becoming a master miller in 1761. On his father's death he abandoned this career for music, playing the violin in a church orchestra and in 1763 going to Venice where he studied composition with Giovanni Battista Pescetti. A year later his opera *Medea* was well received in Parma, and until the failure of *Armida* in Milan in 1779 Mysliveček remained popular throughout Italy. Neapolitan enthusiasm for the composer, coupled with local difficulties in pronouncing his name, led to the now famous appellation 'Il divino boemo'. Mysliveček was also well known in Vienna and

Munich where his opera *Ezio* (1775) and the oratorio *Abramo ed Isaaco* (1776) had considerable success in 1779. His last three years were dogged by operatic failures, poverty, and illness resulting from a dissolute life; he died alone and destitute in Rome. Mysliveček's many operas, almost all written for Italy, are marked by a pleasing if ingenuous lyricism, and observe without modification the conventions of *opera seria*. The oratorios show more inclination to experiment and generally display greater imagination. He was especially valued by singers for his attention to word-setting and considerate vocal lines. Burney recorded that his instrumental works—symphonies, concertos, octets, quartets, and trios—were as popular as his vocal music, and Mozart drew favourable attention to his keyboard sonatas. Certain features of his melodic style look back to his Bohemian origins, and despite the failure of his last operas Mysliveček's influence on contemporaries, not least Mozart, was significant.

JAN SMACZNY

Mystery plays. See *Church Drama*, 2.

Mystic chord [Promethean chord]. The name given to the chord c-$f\sharp$-$b\flat$-e'-a'-d'' by the Russian composer Skryabin. It forms the harmonic basis of his tone poem *Prométhée* (1911), from which work the chord takes its alternative name. See *Skryabin* for a discussion of its use in his works.

N

Nabucco (properly, 'Nabucodonsor'). Opera in four acts by Verdi; text by Solera, after the drama by Anicet-Bourgeois and Cornue *Nabucodonsor* (1836). Produced: Milan, La Scala, 9 March 1842; London, Her Majesty's, 3 March 1846 (as *Nino*); New York, Astor Opera House, 4 April 1848. The opera tells of the Babylonian captivity of the Hebrews and of Nabucco's (bar.) madness, recovery, and conversion to the faith of Jehovah, despite the opposition of his daughter Abigaille (sop.).

Nach (Ger.). 'After', 'in the manner of', 'towards', 'according to'; *nach und nach*, 'little by little'; *Nachahmung*, 'imitation'; *nach Es* etc., (tune) 'to E♭' etc. (a direction to timpani players); *Nachdruck*, 'emphasis', *nachdrücklich*, 'emphatic'; *nachgehend*, 'following'; *nachlassend*, 'loosening', 'slackening' (in speed); *Nachspiel*, 'after play', i.e. *postlude, or a concluding *voluntary.

Nachschlag (Ger.). 'After-stroke'. 1. In modern German terminology, the final two notes of the turn which normally concludes a *trill. 2. In 17th- and 18th-century music, the same as the English *springer.

Nachtmusik (Ger.). 'Night music'. A term applied in the late 18th century to a composition with the character of a *serenade. Mozart's *Eine kleine Nachtmusik* is the best-known example.

Nachtstück (Ger.). 'Night piece'. In the 19th century, the term was applied to pieces in a similar style to a *nocturne. In the 20th century it has been applied to instrumental pieces which evoke the sounds and the atmosphere of night, such as the third movement of Bartók's *Music for Strings, Percussion, and Celesta*, or the third movement ('Elegia') of his *Concerto for Orchestra*.

Nacht und Träume ('Night and Dreams'). Song for voice and piano by Schubert (D 827) to a poem by Matthäus von Collin (1779-1824). It was composed in 1823.

Naderman, François-Joseph (*b* Paris, 1781; *d* Paris, 3 Apr. 1835). French harpist, maker of stringed instruments, and composer. He studied the harp with Krumpholtz and in 1815 was appointed harpist to the royal chapel in Paris.

Ten years later he became the first harp professor at the Paris Conservatoire, where he taught the old-fashioned single-action harp. Naderman wrote a teaching method and his harp sonatas are still part of the repertory.

WENDY THOMPSON

Naenia (Lat.). 'Dirge'.

Nāgasvaram. A wind instrument, similar to a shawm, of South India. See *Indian Music*, 3*b*.

Nail violin, nail harmonica (Ger.: *Nagelgeige*). In a semicircular sounding-board nails are fastened around the curve, graduated in size so as to produce the different notes. This board is held in the left hand and the nails are made to vibrate by the use of a bow held in the right hand.

This instrument was invented in the 18th century and for a time was more or less popular—probably, however, generally rather as a 'stunt' than as a means of serious music-making. It was widespread in Europe, and in New York in 1786 we find Peter Van Hagen (formerly of Rotterdam) publicly performing 'a solo upon iron nails, called *Violin Harmonika*'.

Nakers. See *Timpani*, 5*a*.

Namensfeier ('Name Day'). Overture, Op. 115, by Beethoven, composed in 1814-15 for the name-day festivities of Emperor Francis II of Austria.

Nänie (Ger. from Lat. *naenia*, 'dirges'). Work, Op. 82, by Brahms for chorus and orchestra, composed in 1880-1. It is a setting of a text by Schiller.

Nanino, Giovanni Bernardino (*b* Vallerino, nr Viterbo, *c*.1560; *d* Rome, 1623). Italian composer. He lived and worked with his elder brother, Giovanni Maria, in Rome. His music reflects the transition from the polyphonic idiom (represented by his published collections of madrigals) towards the monodic style of the early Baroque, and much of his church music is dependent on the use of a figured bass.

JOHN MILSOM

Nanino, Giovanni Maria (*b* Tivoli, *c*.1545; *d* Rome, 11 Mar. 1607). Italian composer, the elder brother of Giovanni Bernardino Nanino. He worked at Rome from the early 1560s, perhaps studying with Palestrina, and spent the last 30 years of his life as a singer in the Sistine Chapel, taking his turn to act as *maestro di cappella* there. He was an important teacher (his pupils included Allegri and Felice Anerio), and his works were widely published in his lifetime. They include madrigals and *canzonette*, and sacred music which seems to have been closely modelled upon the technique and style of Palestrina, showing a preference for the conservative polyphonic idiom typical of Roman composers of the period. JOHN MILSOM

Napoleon, Ode to. See *Ode to Napoleon*.

Nápravník, Eduard (*b* Býšť, nr Hradec Králové, 24 Aug. 1839; *d* Petrograd, 23 Nov. 1916). Czech conductor and composer. He studied music in Prague, and later moved to St Petersburg, at first to direct the Yusupov family's private orchestra, then becoming assistant conductor (1867) and principal conductor (1869) at the Mariinsky Theatre. He identified himself so thoroughly with Russian life that his compositions took on a national character, and he counts as a Russian composer. In his day his operas—particularly *Dubrovsky* (1895)—enjoyed great success. He also composed some orchestral music and a good deal of chamber music, songs, and piano music, though his importance rests perhaps on his conducting activities, particularly of Russian opera.

PERCY SCHOLES, rev.

Nardini, Pietro (*b* Livorno, 12 Apr. 1722; *d* Florence, 7 May 1793). Italian composer and one of the best-known violinists of his day. He studied with Tartini in Padua and then, in the 1760s, worked in Stuttgart, as chamber musician and leader of the orchestra which, under Jommelli, was among the best in Europe. In 1769 he went to Padua to care for Tartini, who was dying, and then to Florence as director of music to Leopold I (later the Emperor Leopold II), Grand Duke of Tuscany. Admired as a player by Leopold Mozart and Burney, Nardini was noted for his sweetness of tone, rather than for virtuosity. He was one of the last to compose sonatas in the Baroque manner, with the slow-quick-quick order of movements and continuo accompaniments.

DENIS ARNOLD

Nares, James (*b* Stanwell, Middlesex, Apr. 1715; *d* London, 10 Feb. 1783). English organist and composer. He was a chorister in the Chapel Royal, and studied with Croft and Pepusch. In 1735 he was appointed organist of York Minster, and from the mid 1750s he held the posts of organist, composer, and Master of the Children to the Chapel Royal.

Nares published in London several sets of harpsichord lessons, two singing tutors, and *Il principio, or A Regular Introduction to Playing on the Harpsichord or Organ*. He also composed anthems, services, and other sacred vocal music, and six voluntaries and fugues for organ. His catches, canons, and glees were very popular.

WENDY THOMPSON

Narrator (It.: *testo*). Character who tells the story in a dramatic work, in musical works usually to recitative. The custom is derived from early Greek tragedy. The *testo* in Monteverdi's *Il combattimento di Tancredi e Clorinda* (1624) is given by far the most important part, describing the action, which is mimed by the protagonists to appropriate instrumental accompaniment. In Passion music the Evangelist is given the role of narrator. In the 20th century many works make use of such a part, for example Stravinsky's opera/oratorio *Oedipus rex* (which requires the Narrator to wear modern evening dress, to set him apart from the protagonists), Honegger's *Le roi David*, and Britten's *The Rape of Lucretia* (where the narrative and comment on the action are given by a tenor and a soprano, respectively the Male and Female Chorus).

Narváez, Luis de (*fl.* early 16th century). Spanish composer and vihuelist. Probably a native of Granada, he may have been in the service of Don Francisco de los Cobos (to whom he dedicated his *Los seys libros*) in Valladolid, before becoming music teacher at the royal chapel of the future Philip II.

Narváez was renowned as a vihuelist in his lifetime. Nearly all his music is contained in *Los seys libros del delphin* (Valladolid, 1538), one of the most important collections of vihuela music of the 16th century. The book includes fantasias, transcriptions of vocal music, and variations for vihuela solo, as well as *romances* and *villancicos* for voice and vihuela. WENDY THOMPSON

Nasco, Giovanni (*b* c.1510; *d* Treviso, 1561). Flemish composer. He worked at Vicenza before becoming the first *maestro di cappella* of the famous Accademia Filarmonica in Verona in 1547. In 1551 he left Verona to direct the music at Treviso Cathedral. He wrote some pleasing but unremarkable madrigals, and church music.

DENIS ARNOLD

National Anthems and Official Tunes. Taking the text of national anthems in general, it can hardly be said that they reach a high poetical, or indeed ethical, level. Those that are of the nature of prayers for a monarch, such as the old Austrian anthem and the British anthem, are, however admirable and however suitable for many occasions, hardly wide enough to merit the title 'national'. Eliza Flower's 'Now pray we for our country', Parry's 'Jerusalem', or Katharine Lee Bates's poem 'America the beautiful' is more fully national than 'God save the Queen', and some song like this might well be adopted as a secondary national anthem in those countries that possess one of the narrowly personal sort.

An equally faulty type is that of the song that arose out of some particular event of war or revolution, and that, while well worthy of being retained in the national repertory of song as a valuable historical relic, has lost its application and is, in any case, like the monarchical type too narrow for its purpose.

The tunes of national anthems vary greatly in merit. Sometimes a relatively poor tune, on being officially adopted, gains a permanency that it could not otherwise have won. In the main, however, the tunes have merit. Some of them have served other purposes before being allied with their present words. Few have been especially written, and of these the best is assuredly Haydn's *Emperor's Hymn*.

The following national anthems and quasi-official national songs are separately treated. See: *America the beautiful*; *Auferstanden aus Ruinen*; *Brabançonne, La*; *Einigkeit und Recht und Freiheit*; *Emperor's Hymn*; *Fratelli d'italia*; *Giovinezza, La*; *God save the Queen*; *Horst Wessel Song*; *Internationale*; *Marcha real*; *Marseillaise, La*; *Rule, Britannia*; *Star-spangled Banner, The*.

PERCY SCHOLES, rev.

National Centre for Orchestral Studies. A one-year course at Goldsmiths' College, University of London, designed to bridge the gap between study at a conservatory or university and a career as a professional orchestral player. An Advanced Orchestral Training Working Party was set up in 1977 with representatives from the Arts Council, the Association of British Orchestras, the BBC, Goldsmiths' College, and the Musicians' Union; the first intake of students was for the year 1979-80. The Director is Basil Tschaikov.

National Federation of Music Societies. British organization set up by the *Incorporated Society of Musicians in 1935 with financial aid from the Carnegie Trust. Now an independent society, its aims are to encourage and support choral societies, amateur operatic or orchestral societies, etc., and it is entrusted by the Arts Council with the administration of grants and subsidies.

Nationalism in Music. It is a generally accepted fact that the folk music of various races and nations (even when so near one another as those of Europe) differs in some more or less subtle way that can be accepted as expressing distinctions in national or racial feeling. This difference is inevitably carried into the work of the composers of those races and nations when they have not stultified their racial or national characteristics by adopting a mere cosmopolitan convention. There is a sense in which it may paradoxically be said that the most original composer is normally the most national, just as 'the greatest genius is the most indebted man'—for, instinctively keeping himself free from conventions, he allows free play to the feelings within him, and these are necessarily largely racial and national.

The more conscious expression of national feeling, and the deliberate adoption, to that end, of the melodic and rhythmic idiom of folk-song and folk-dance, dates from the middle of the 19th century, when composers of the northern nations, who (many of them trained at Leipzig) had for some time been under strong German influence, began to assert their right to express their own native temperament and the emotions of their own native life. A distinctively nationalist movement began, of which the motive may be said to have been dual, corresponding to the wave of national political feeling that went through Europe at this period and to the desire to get nearer to the primitive sources of life: it was, then, at one and the same time a 'my country' motive and a 'back to the land' motive.

The 'movement' was a branch of that larger one which we call the Romantic Movement (see *Romanticism*), the promoters of which sought vivid emotional expression rather than classic beauty, and which achieved at least this—the introduction into music of an immensely increased variety of rhythmic, melodic, and harmonic phraseology, so preparing the way for the apparently almost complete freedom from rule and convention of the period that has followed.

Among earlier composers of this period who may be called nationalists are Schumann, nurtured on German literature and music and expressing, intensely and naturally, the German spirit, and (with more sense of purpose, because actuated by conscious patriotism) Chopin, of mixed Polish and French origin, sometimes adopting Polish dance rhythms and forms and yet likewise exhibiting the French grace; in certain of Liszt's compositions there was, similarly, the attempt to express the Hungarian spirit.

But more decidedly and (perhaps one may use the term) *narrowly* nationalistic were a group of somewhat later birth—Smetana and

Dvořák in Bohemia, Grieg in Norway, Glinka, Balakirev, Borodin, Musorgsky, and Rimsky-Korsakov in Russia, and Albéniz, Granados, Falla, and Turina in Spain. All these adopted, of set purpose, idioms derived from the folk music of their native countries.

A British nationalistic trend began when Parry the Englishman, Mackenzie the Scot, and Stanford the Irishman showed in their work the characteristics of their countries—Parry expressing the bluff straightforwardness of his countrymen, and Mackenzie and Stanford, on occasion, basing their music on themes taken from the folk music repertories of the countries of their birth. In the opening years of the 20th century some of the younger contemporaries of these three composers were extremely nationalistic. Under the influence of the folk-song and folk-dance collecting movement of the day they frequently adopted folk melodies as the material of their composition. For a time this process was overdone, tended to become an affectation, and discouraged individuality, but nevertheless it served its purpose. The work of the Finnish composer, Sibelius, is, of course, very nationalistic—perhaps more obviously so in his earlier works.

Attempts have been made at nationalistic expression in American music by the use of Black American or American-Indian themes (which when used by White composers have no racial connection at all), and occasionally by the effort to represent in music a reaction to 'the American scene'. It would seem that there is some artificiality in all these expedients; but the American problem is very debatable and has been much discussed (see *United States of America*, 5).

Extreme views have been expressed by younger composers (those born, say, within the 20th century) as to the desirability or possibility of nationalism remaining an influence in artistic expression. So Constant Lambert wrote in 1931, 'The slogan of nationalism will die as soon as it is realized that each nation is aiming at the same ideal of mechanized civilization'. If during the 20th or 21st century national aspiration and ideals die out and racial differences of temperament disappear, and the world becomes one big family, Latin and Teuton and Celtic, black and yellow, then we may, indeed, expect national distinctions in art to vanish. But a period which has seen some great historic empires split into their racial constituents, and a jealous attempt to conserve their political and linguistic independence, seems hardly the period in which one can safely utter such prophecies.

PERCY SCHOLES

National Music Camp. American summer institute, located on a 1,400-acre lakeside campus at Interlochen, Michigan. It was founded in 1928 by Joseph Maddy, a Professor of Music at the University of Michigan. Although huge (over 1,700 students each year, with 175 faculty and 625 staff), the Camp seeks to maintain high musical standards in its training of young instrumentalists and vocalists. In addition to instrumental instruction and ensemble playing (several hundred concerts, some broadcast nationally, are presented in each eight-week session), courses are offered in music history, music theory, dance, drama, and some academic subjects.   NYM COOKE

National Opera Studio. Successor to the London Opera Centre, which was founded in 1963 to provide advanced training for student singers, répétiteurs, and stage managers. The Centre in its turn succeeded the National School of Opera, which started work in 1948 under the direction of Joan Cross and Anne Wood. The National Opera Studio opened in 1978 with the specific brief of providing advanced specialist training for 12 young professional singers and three répétiteurs recommended by opera companies and leading teaching institutions.

National School of Opera. See *National Opera Studio*.

National Training School for Music. British music college founded in 1873 to provide free musical training to the holders of scholarships awarded on a national basis. The idea was first mooted by Prince Albert in 1854, and revived after his death by the National Society of Arts. The School opened in 1876 with Arthur Sullivan as Principal; it was housed in purpose-built accommodation in Kensington, now occupied by the *Royal College of Organists. In 1882 the School was replaced by the *Royal College of Music.

National Youth Orchestra of Great Britain. Symphony orchestra for children aged between 13 and 19 founded in 1947 by Ruth Railton (now Dame Ruth King). It was assembled in Bath under the conductorship of Reginald Jacques. The players are selected by audition, the orchestra assembling during the school holiday for rehearsal and study under a guest conductor. A very high standard is achieved and many players have 'graduated' into leading symphony orchestras.

Nativité du Seigneur, La ('The Birth of the Saviour'). Organ work by Messiaen, composed in 1935. The nine pieces, or meditations, are: (1) *La vierge et l'enfant*; (2) *Les bergers*; (3) *Desseins éternels*; (4) *Le verbe*; (5) *Les enfants de Dieu*;

(6) *Les anges*; (7) *Jésus accepte la souffrance*; (8) *Les mages*; and (9) *Dieu parmi nous*.

Natural (Fr.: *bécarre*; Ger.: *Auflösungszeichen*, *Quadrat*; It.: *bequadro*). 1. A note which is neither raised (sharpened) nor lowered (flattened). 2. The sign (♮) which, after a note has been raised by a sharp or double sharp or lowered by a flat or double flat, restores a note to its natural pitch. After a double sharp or double flat, the reversion to a single accidental is notated either by the use of the single sharp or flat alone, or occasionally by ♮♯ or ♮♭. See *Accidental*; for the origins of the natural sign and its early use, see *Notation*, 2.

Natural harmonics. See *Acoustics*, 5.

Natural hexachord. See *Solmization*.

Natural notes. The notes available on brass instruments without the use of valves. See *Valves*.

Nature, Life, and Love (*Příroda, Život, a Láska*). Cycle of three overtures by Dvořák—*Amid Nature* (1891), *Carneval* (1891), and *Othello* (1892).

Naudot, Jacques-Christophe (*b* c.1690; *d* Paris, 26 Nov. 1762). Composer and one of the first French virtuoso flautists. From 1726 he taught the flute in Paris. His works include books of sonatas and other pieces for various instruments (among them the hurdy-gurdy, and usually featuring the flute) and six flute concertos (Op. 11, 1735-7), the second set, after Vivaldi's Op. 10, to be printed in Europe.

WENDY THOMPSON

Naumann, Johann Gottlieb (*b* Blasewitz, nr Dresden, 17 Apr. 1741; *d* Dresden, 23 Oct. 1801). German composer. He studied in Dresden and in 1757 went to Italy, where he took lessons from Tartini, Padre Martini, and Hasse. Hasse thought highly of him, and in 1764 obtained for him an appointment at the Dresden court chapel; he became *Kapellmeister* there in 1776. While he was at Dresden several of Naumann's operas, some to librettos by Metastasio, were performed in Italy. In 1777 Gustav III of Sweden invited him to take over the royal chapel at Stockholm and to develop a national opera. Under Naumann's direction the new Royal Opera House opened in 1782 with his own *Cora och Alonso*, and in 1786 his *Gustaf Wasa* was given there. Naumann's Swedish operas are noticeably different in style from the Italian ones he had written in Germany. In 1773 the Swedish opera had given Gluck's *Orphée et Euridice*, and Naumann shows an awareness of

Johann Gottlieb Naumann, engraving (1801) by G. G. Endner after Seydelmann.

Gluck's striving towards more 'natural' writing for the voice, and a corresponding move away from showy ornament and elaborate display.

After a brief appointment at Copenhagen, where he wrote a Danish opera on the Orpheus legend, Naumann returned to Dresden as *Kapellmeister* in 1786. His last years were increasingly occupied with writing sacred music, but he did compose an *opera buffa*, *Aci e Galatea*, in the last year of his life.

WENDY THOMPSON

Navarraise (Fr.). A dance from the former kingdom of Navarre.

Navarro, Juan (*b* ? Seville, c.1530; *d* Palencia, 25 Sept. 1580). Spanish composer. From 1553 to 1555 he sang in the choir of Málaga Cathedral, and in 1563 he became *maestro de capilla* at Ávila; three years later he took the same post at Salamanca. From 1573 he was choirmaster at Ciudad Rodrigo, and then *maestro* at Palencia, where he died. He wrote mainly sacred music, and virtually all his surviving output is contained in a posthumous publication, *Psalmi, hymni ac Magnificat totius anni* (Rome, 1590).

WENDY THOMPSON

Naylor, Bernard (*b* Cambridge, 22 Nov. 1907). English composer. The son of the organist and composer Edward Naylor (1867-1934), he studied with Holst and Vaughan Williams at the Royal College of Music. Since his first visit in 1932 he has spent much time in Canada as a teacher and conductor. His compositions consist mainly of choral and vocal works in a traditional style.

PAUL GRIFFITHS

NBC Symphony Orchestra. American orchestra. The existence of this ensemble, created specially for Toscanini by the National Broadcasting Company of New York in 1937, reflects not only Toscanini's supreme place among conductors but also the support given to art music by American radio broadcasting networks from the 1920s to the 1950s. The musicianship of its players, the genius and the tantrums of its conductor, its memorable weekly concerts (broadcast worldwide), and its influential recordings have endowed the NBC Symphony with a legendary quality since its dissolution in 1954 upon the 87-year-old Toscanini's retirement.   NYM COOKE

Neander, Joachim (*b* Bremen, 1650; *d* Bremen, 31 Mar. 1680). German poet and composer. He was educated in Bremen, and at the age of 20 was converted to Pietism. He then studied at Heidelberg University, and in 1674 was appointed headmaster of the Calvinist school in Düsseldorf. In 1677 he was sacked for his support of Pietist doctrines, and was unemployed for two years; he died shortly after finding a new post. He published a collection of psalms and hymns in Bremen, many of which were later used for community singing. His two most popular hymns, still sung today, are 'Lobe den Herren' and 'Wunderbarer König'.
                                    WENDY THOMPSON

Neapolitan sixth. Name given to one of the chromatic chords — the first inversion (i.e. the 'sixth' chord) of the triad built on the flattened supertonic. The following is an example in the key of C:

It is often used to replace the subdominant chord in the cadential progression IV–V–I. Although it was already an established feature in music (not only Italian) of the second half of the 17th century (it was used, for example, by Carissimi, Corelli, and Purcell), it appears to take its name from its use by composers of the 18th-century 'Neapolitan school', such as Alessandro Scarlatti, Porpora, Leo, Jommelli, and Pergolesi.

Neapolitan song (It.: *La canzone popolare Napoletana*). A romantic kind of song or ballad which obviously stems from the Italian opera of the early 19th century. The first *canzone* of the kind was perhaps Donizetti's 'Te voglio bene assaje', published in 1835, a typically graceful and tuneful piece. Neapolitan song, the Italian equivalent of the Victorian *drawing-room ballad, was melodic enough to have wide popularity, but written well enough to attract the attention of the celebrated classical singers. A number of talented writers and composers coincidentally combined at a certain period to provide sufficient songs in the vein to create a clear school of composition and a distinct Neapolitan style. The best pieces in the genre came at the end of the 19th century, e.g. Di Capua's 'O sole mio'. Other prominent composers were Costa, De Curtis, Denza, and Tosti. The Neapolitan song was popularized by performance of songs such as 'Santa Lucia' by singers like Caruso and Gigli and other leading opera singers since.   PETER GAMMOND

Nebenstimme (Ger.). 'Next voice'. A term introduced by Schoenberg for the second part in a polyphonic texture, indicated in the score by the symbol N. See *Hauptstimme*.
                                    PAUL GRIFFITHS

Neck. The projecting part of a stringed instrument; it carries the fingerboard and terminates in the peg-box.

Nedbal, Oskar (*b* Tábor, south Bohemia, 26 Mar. 1874; *d* Zagreb, 24 Dec. 1930). Czech composer, violist, and conductor. He studied the violin in his native Tábor and later in Prague with Bennewitz at the conservatory where he was also a pupil of Dvořák. As viola player of the Czech Quartet (1891-1906) he contributed significantly to the improving standards of Czech chamber music performance, and took part in several important premières including that of Dvořák's Quartet Op. 106. He was conductor of the Czech Philharmonic (1896-1906) and later of the Tonkünstlerorchester in Vienna (1906-18). After the First World War he returned to Prague and in 1921 went to Bratislava as head of opera at the newly founded Slovak National Theatre. Until his death he was a leading light in the city's musical life doing much to encourage the new generation of Slovakian composers. As a composer Nedbal was regarded as one of the most promising of Dvořák's pupils though he never showed the adventurousness of Suk or Novák. His operettas and some of his ballets were popular in Austria and Germany, but he had little success with his single opera *Sedlák Jakub* ('The Peasant James', 1920). Nedbal's music displays wit and imagination, but, though he made use of Polish and Yugoslav folk dances in addition to Czech, his style makes little advance on that of his master Dvořák.   JAN SMACZNY

Neefe, Christian Gottlob (*b* Chemnitz, now Karl-Marx-Stadt, nr Dresden, 5 Feb. 1748; *d* Dessau, 26 Jan. 1798). German composer. He began composing when he was 12, and although he entered Leipzig University to study law in 1769, he gave it up two years later in favour of music. He was taught by J. A. Hiller. In 1778 he married a singer, and a year later he went with a travelling theatrical troupe to Bonn, where he was until the French invasion of 1794. The last two years of his life were spent as conductor at the Dessau Theatre.

Neefe is chiefly remembered as one of Beethoven's teachers, but he was also a prolific composer. *Adelheit von Veltheim* (1780) was the most popular of his many dramatic works, and he also wrote numerous choral pieces, chamber and piano music, *Lieder* and ballads, all in a simple style derived from the *Singspiel*. He also made piano reductions of Mozart's operas, and contributed numerous articles to contemporary journals.   WENDY THOMPSON

Negri, Marc'Antonio (*b* Verona; *d*? Venice, in or after 1621). Italian composer. He was Monteverdi's assistant at St Mark's, Venice, from 1612 to 1619. He wrote some attractive instrumental sonatas and *sinfonie*, two books of *Affetti amorosi* (Venice, 1608, 1611) for voices and continuo, and a book of psalms for *cori spezzati* (Venice, 1613).   DENIS ARNOLD

Nell. Poem by Lecomte de Lisle, set for voice and piano by Fauré, as No. 1 of his Op. 18 (1878).

Nelson Mass (*Nelsonmesse*). Haydn's Mass No. 11 in D minor, composed in 1798. In his own catalogue of his works, Haydn headed it 'Missa in angustiis'. One story is that the work was written to celebrate Nelson's victory at Aboukir Bay; according to another, Nelson heard the Mass performed at Eisenstadt in 1800. It is sometimes referred to as the 'Imperial' Mass or 'Coronation' Mass.

Nenia (It.). 'Dirge'.

Nenna, Pomponio (*b* Bari, mid 16th century; *d*? Rome, *c*.1613). Italian composer. He may have been in Gesualdo's service in Naples at the end of the 16th century, and his madrigals show a similar interest in chromaticism. By 1608 he had moved to Rome, where his eighth book of madrigals was published posthumously. As well as his secular music (madrigals and *villanelle*) he wrote a small amount of church music.
                                        DENIS ARNOLD

Neo-classicism. In music, a style which, in a conscious and usually ironic manner, adopts techniques, gestures, or forms from an earlier period. It is associated particularly with the works of Stravinsky from the early 1920s to the early 1950s, a part of his output which includes

dislocated arrangements of earlier music (*Pulcinella*, after pieces attributed to Pergolesi, 1919-20), works which return to Bach's concerto forms ('Dumbarton Oaks' Concerto, 1938), others suggestive of the French Baroque (*Apollo*, 1927-8) or early Romanticism (Capriccio for piano and orchestra, 1928-9), and even a full-scale opera with numerous echoes of Mozart (*The Rake's Progress*, 1948-51).

The influence of Stravinsky's neo-classical scores was felt by many composers in Paris between the wars, among them Poulenc, Martinů, Honegger, Szymanowski, and Copland. Their works, like those of Stravinsky himself, use older procedures in a manner which is often ironic and occasionally humorous; there is the underlying suggestion that a decisive break has been made with the great musical tradition, and that, instead of basing his work organically on that of Bach, Beethoven, and Brahms, the composer can now view their music objectively and select what pleases him.

Neo-classicism in Austria and Germany tended to be less brisk and carefree, perhaps because composers there were working from within the great tradition. Some works from the first decade of the 20th century, such as Reger's variation sets and Schoenberg's Chamber Symphony No. 1 (1906), foreshadow neo-classical attitudes in using established formal methods to impose order on music of advanced harmony, but it was again at the beginning of the 1920s that neo-classicism took hold. Busoni, who propounded the notion of 'young classicity', argued for a return to the pure musicality of Mozart, and had some influence on such emerging composers as Kurt Weill, his pupil. However, the leading German neo-classicist, Paul Hindemith, was more impressed by Stravinsky, though his most neo-classical scores, which include a great many concertos and chamber pieces from the 1920s, have a boisterous vigour and a directness not shared by contemporary Parisian music.

Schoenberg regarded himself as the enemy of neo-classicism, whether Stravinsky's or Hindemith's, for he recognized the rupture with tradition which it implied. However, his own works from the 1920s and 1930s return to thematic development, metrical consistency, and old formal principles, all of which he had previously abandoned. As in the music produced at the same time by his pupils Berg and Webern, there is a distinct note of neo-classicism here. However, the mature instrumental and choral works of Webern, like the otherwise very different later works of Bartók, stand apart from other neo-classical music in their achievement of an integral relatedness without the irony of stylistic displacement.

                                        PAUL GRIFFITHS

Nera (It.). 'Black (note)', i.e. the crotchet or quarter-note (♩).

Netherlands. See *Low Countries*, 6.

Neu eröffnete musikalische Bibliothek. German musical magazine founded in Leipzig in 1736 by Lorenz Mizler; it ceased publication in 1754.

Neukomm, Sigismund (*b* Salzburg, 10 July 1778; *d* Paris, 3 Apr. 1858). Austrian composer and conductor. He seems to have spent most of his life travelling. A pupil of the Haydn brothers (Michael in Salzburg and Joseph in Vienna), he went to Stockholm in 1806, and then on to St Petersburg, where he became court musical director. He returned to Vienna for a short time, but in 1809 he settled in Paris. He was appointed pianist to Prince Talleyrand, whom he accompanied to the Congress of Vienna, and in 1816 he went with the Duke of Luxembourg to Rio de Janeiro, returning to Europe when fighting broke out in 1821. Eight years later he visited London, where he met Mendelssohn. He was enthusiastically received, and his oratorios *Mount Sinai* and *David* (1834) were given many performances, while his songs 'Napoleon's Midnight Review' and 'The Sea' became enormously popular. In all, Neukomm wrote about 1,000 works of all descriptions, including ten operas, 48 Masses, chamber music, and a Symphony in E♭ which was performed in 1831 by the London Philharmonic Society.

WENDY THOMPSON

Neuma. See *Pneuma*.

Neumark, Georg (*b* Langensalza, 7 Mar. 1621; *d* Weimar, 8 July 1681). German poet and musician. On his way to Königsberg University in 1640, to study law, he had the misfortune to be robbed of all he possessed, and as a result was forced to turn to teaching to earn a living. Between 1640 and 1650 he spent some time travelling in Germany and Poland, but finally, at the age of 30, he obtained a position as secretary and librarian to the Duke of Weimar.

Neumark's best-known work is the hymn 'Wer nur den lieben Gott lässt walten', which became a standard chorale tune in Germany and was the model for Bach's cantata of that name. In 1657 he published the *Fortgepflanzter musikalisch-poetischer Lustwald* in Jena, a collection of sacred and secular continuo songs with instrumental *ritornelli*.   WENDY THOMPSON

Neume (from Gk. *pneuma*, 'breath'). An early note form; see *Notation*, 2.

Neusidler. Family of German lutenists. **Hans Neusidler** (*b* Pressburg [now Bratislava], before 1510; *d* Nuremberg, 2 Feb. 1563) lived in Nuremberg from about 1530. He married twice (and had 17 children) and as well as teaching and publishing his music for the lute he was registered as a lute maker. His eight lute books contain arrangements of songs and motets, and some huge improvisatory preludes. His first book (1536) contains an introduction on lute playing, with exercises.

Title-page of the first edition of Neusidler's 'Teütsch Lautenbüch', designed by Tobias Stimmer (Strasbourg, 1574).

His son, **Melchior Neusidler** (*b* Nuremberg, 1531; *d* Augsburg, 1590), went to Augsburg soon after 1551, and was employed there by the city as leader of a group of musicians who provided music for special occasions. In 1565 he visited Italy and published some lute music there, and in 1580–1 was in the service of Archduke Ferdinand II at Innsbruck, but most of his life was spent in Augsburg, where his patron was Octavian II Fugger, the banker. Three books of lute music by him were published, two in Italy and one in Strasbourg (1574); they include Italian and German song and dance arrangements and some *ricercari*.

New England Conservatory of Music. One of the first independent music schools of its kind in the United States, the New England Conservatory (founded 1867) has enjoyed a succession of eminent presidents, including composers George Whitefield Chadwick, Quincy Porter, and Gunther Schuller. The Conservatory has long had a special relationship with the Boston Symphony Orchestra: many Orchestra players teach at the Conservatory, and the Conservatory Chorus often sings with the Orchestra.

NYM COOKE

New England Holidays. See *Holidays*.

Newman, Ernest (*b* Everton, Liverpool, 30 Nov. 1868; *d* Tadworth, Surrey, 7 July 1959). English music critic and scholar. His family name was Roberts, and he studied at Liverpool University before becoming a bank clerk. Self-taught in music but with a considerable grasp of foreign languages, he published books on Gluck (London, 1895, reprinted 1977) and Wagner (London, 1899, reprinted 1974) as the result of which he was appointed music critic of *The Manchester Guardian* in 1905. He spent the rest of his long life as a music journalist on newspapers in Birmingham and London, living up to his adopted pseudonym, an Earnest New Man, with penetrating, intellectual articles. His major work was the four-volume *Life of Richard Wagner* (London, 1933–47, reprinted 1977), which has not yet been superseded as a standard work; his other books on opera are among the most informative on individual works by the great 19th-century composers.

DENIS ARNOLD

New Music. A term which has recurred at intervals throughout the history of Western music to describe a period of radical change. The first known use was in France at the beginning of the 14th century—the time of the *Ars Nova, with Philippe de Vitry and his contemporaries. The second occurred some 300 years later, when Caccini used the term to describe the change from polyphonic to monodic music in his *Le *nuove musiche*. After 1850, the music of Wagner and of Liszt's late period was often referred to as the 'new music', or 'the music of the future'. In the 20th century the German term *Neue Musik* was applied *c*.1925 to the music which succeeded the breakdown of tonality, i.e. atonal or 12-note music.

Newport Jazz and Folk Festivals. George Wein produced the first Newport (Rhode Island) jazz festival in 1954. This annual event quickly became one of the world's major jazz festivals, featuring the best in jazz talent and styles, both old and new. In 1972 it moved to New York City, changed its name to the Newport Festival-New York, and expanded both its programmes

and its audience. The Newport Folk Festival has been a more modest affair. Wein began it in 1959, and in 1963 formed the non-profit Newport Folk Foundation which runs the annual summer festival.

MARK TUCKER

New World, From the (*Z nového světa*). Subtitle of Dvořák's Symphony No. 9 (No. 5 in the old numbering) in E minor, Op. 95, composed in 1893. Some of its themes are regarded as in the spirit of American Negro folk-tunes but none is quoted directly; the resemblance of one tune to 'Swing low, Sweet Chariot' is often mentioned. The main theme of the Largo has been made into a Negro spiritual to the words 'Goin' Home'. However, the Bohemian element is equally strong. Dvořák regarded the symphony as a sketch for a projected opera based on Longfellow's *The Song of Hiawatha*.

New York City Opera. The second largest opera company in America, the largest being the *Metropolitan. Founded in 1944, the company presents two annual 11-week seasons in the New York State Theater in Lincoln Center. Prominent directors have included Erich Leinsdorf, Julius Rudel, and Beverly Sills. In contrast to the Metropolitan, City Opera features younger, lesser-known, often American singers instead of all-star international casts, and explores a less familiar operatic repertory including works that are American, in English translation, contemporary, or simply obscure.

MARK TUCKER

New York Philharmonic Orchestra. American orchestra, which has enjoyed the longest continuous existence of any orchestra in the USA. It was founded in 1842, reorganized as a full-time professional orchestra in 1909, and amalgamated with various other local orchestras, including (in 1928) the Symphony Society. Something of the Philharmonic's stature is suggested by a partial list of its conductors: Mahler, Furtwängler, Toscanini, Walter, Barbirolli, Mitropoulos, Bernstein, Boulez, and Mehta. A special activity of the Orchestra since 1898 has been its Young People's Concerts.

NYM COOKE

New York Pro Musica. From 1952 until 1974 this group was a prime mover in the promotion of early music in the United States. Founded by Noah Greenberg, Pro Musica was both an ensemble of musicians and a focus for early music research in New York. Early successes were scored with productions of *The Play of Daniel* (1959) and *The Play of Herod* (1963). Combining informed scholarship with virtuosic musicianship and attractive programming, Pro Musica developed a wider audience for early music and served as a model for subsequent early music ensembles.　　MARK TUCKER

New York Public Library. Since its founding in 1924, the Music Division of the New York Public Library has become one of the finest research collections in the world, with over 500,000 titles. In 1963 it became part of the Performing Arts Research Center at Lincoln Center, along with the Rodgers and Hammerstein Archives of Recorded Sound (over 350,000 recordings), a Dance Collection, the Billy Rose Theatre Collection, and a circulating library. Elsewhere in the city are the Manuscripts and Archives Division and the Schomburg Center for Research in Black Culture.　　NYM COOKE

New Zealand

1. Introduction
2. Maori Music
3. The European Tradition
4. Music after the Second World War

1. *Introduction.* New Zealand's very distance from the musical centres of Europe and America has given its musical life an independence and vitality which, on the whole, have offset the disadvantages of remoteness. Before the arrival of the first Europeans and the first planned settlements of the 1840s, New Zealand was inhabited by the Maoris, who are thought to have reached New Zealand from Eastern Polynesia about a thousand years ago.

2. *Maori Music.* In pre-European days, Maori music was predominantly vocal. Monophonic chants were used ritually for all the major occasions of life, for children's games and lullabies, and for scaring demons away from the crops. This original Maori music has all but disappeared, though there are encouraging signs of revival. The process of acculturation began with the arrival of traders and missionaries. The Maori began to sing variants of 19th-century ballads and folk-songs, of popular operatic melodies, and missionary hymns. The older Maori music has been preserved in the Archive of Pacific Music at Auckland, directed by Dr Mervyn McLean.

The melody of Maori chant has very small steps, never larger than three semitones. The range seldom exceeds a fourth. Chants are built around one note, the *oro* (intoning note or tonic), which is in the middle of the range. Songs are often strophic, the end of each line being marked by a leader solo called the *hiianga*. Because the Maori consider it unlucky to break the flow of sound, the singers stagger their breathing.

Maori recited chants include the *karakia* (incantation which must be intoned word-perfect), the *paatere* (composed by women who have been slandered, often as a genealogical exercise to prove their own worthiness), and the more vitriolic *kaioraora* in which a woman might threaten to kill, cook, and eat her enemies, and

Pl. 1. One position of the haka shouted posture dance.

drink their brains. Most spectacular of all reciter forms is the *haka*, a shouted posture dance used in war and also for entertainment and welcoming, its forceful rhythmic movements being combined with a demonic jumping and shouting to terrify enemies.

Each chant has a different purpose. Of sung forms, *waiata tangi* lament the dead and are performed at the *tangi* (funeral ceremony). *Waiata aroha* and *waiata whaiaaipo* are love songs, tinged with the themes of unhappy or lost love. *Pao* are short songs about everyday life; *oriori* are sung to children, not only as lullabies, but also to pass on the history of the tribe. Most spectacular is the *poi*, a dance in which women swing *poi* (decorated flaxen balls) on strings. Alfred Hill's *Waiata Poi* (1907) became an

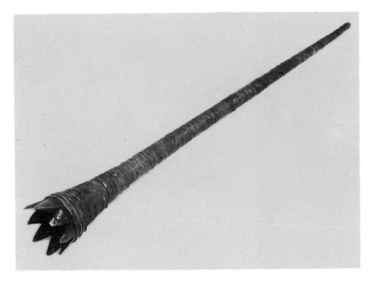

Pl. 2. Puukaaea (wooden war trumpet).

Pl. 3. Puutaatara (shell trumpet).

Edwardian hit and encouraged staid English prima donnas to attempt the *poi* dance on the stage of the Albert Hall in London.

The principal Maori instruments are aerophones. These included trumpets made of flax, shell, and wood, for example, the *puukaaea*, a long wooden war trumpet, and the *puutaatara* or *puu moana* shell trumpet. Flutes included the *koaauau*, a short end-blown flute, open at both ends and made from wood or bone, and the *nguru*, another end-blown flute made of wood, stone, or sometimes whale ivory. Most flutes have three finger-holes. Idiophones included a form of slit gong (called *pahuu*), clappers, and percussion sticks.

Although the Maori people are becoming increasingly integrated into New Zealand society, Maori culture retains its own identity with a number of fine writers, poets, and painters. The Maori language is taught in Maori schools and there are Maori broadcasts on Radio New Zealand. Visitors to New Zealand today may find the grace and rhythmic vitality of Westernized Maori music extremely attractive.

Pl. 4. Nguru (end-blown flute).

3. *The European Tradition.* In the 1840s, the New Zealand Company, founded by Edward Gibbon Wakefield, transplanted much of the culture of early Victorian England to the antipodes through its organized settlements at Wellington, Nelson, New Plymouth, and Wanganui. Many of these settlers (carefully chosen to retain the balance of English class structure) took with them the instruments, music, and skills of English musical life. Harpsichords and pianos, many of fine quality, were unloaded on to the beaches amid building materials, blankets, flour, and domestic utensils. 'The piano brought up and with much trouble got in at the drawing room window', wrote young Mrs Petre in Wellington in 1843. Many pianos made hazardous journeys into the back country on bullock drays, as did that of writer Samuel Butler, whose Canterbury sheep station was later immortalized in his novel *Erewhon* (1872). 'I have a piano at which I practise very regularly and fancy I am improving', he wrote. Jew's-harps and barrel organs had proved useful in bartering with the Maori in early land deals, along with blankets, beads, and muskets. Soon violins, cellos, flutes, fifes, guitars, harps, and accordions flowed in to be put to good use in the philharmonic societies, glee clubs, and sacred harmonic societies being re-created 12,000 miles away from their home.

British regimental bands played at balls and concerts. 'It is a very tolerable band', wrote Charlotte Godley, wife of one of the leaders of the Church of England settlement at Christchurch, of the 65th Regiment playing on Wellington's Thorndon Flat. 'And they play a great number of very pretty things, and altogether reminded me *too much* of home. There we met everyone, walking or sitting about in summer dresses, bonnets with feathers and flowers etc., and two or three big parties of natives, rolled in their blankets and *squatted* just behind the big drum.'

A musical life gradually evolved, nurtured in small communities who created a colonial variant of Victorian England. In 1864 an opera company was formed. When Meyerbeer's *L'Africaine* proved too ambitious a project for the Australian William Lyster to stage in Wellington, the company performed extracts from Bellini's *I Puritani*, the enthusiastic reception encouraging them to return. Harbinger of that remarkable 19th-century phenomenon, the touring opera company, Lyster was typical of a remarkable breed of Australian-born opera impresarios, usually from Melbourne, then enjoying an unprecedented boom as a result of the gold-rushes of the 1850s. Their names, including Simonsen, George Musgrove, and J. C. Williamson, conjure up casts of fine and resourceful singers several of whom later became great artists, a large, diverse repertory, and a passion for opera that has never quite been repeated. This era reached a climax in 1906-7 with the German opera season of George Musgrove. Opulent costumes and sets were made in Berlin and the singers, chosen by Musgrove himself, represented the best of German opera houses.

New Zealand's first composer, Melbourne-born Alfred Hill (1870–1960), grew up in this period of intense operatic activity. A fine violinist, he toured with the opera orchestras, playing everything from Weber's *Der Freischütz* to Wallace's *Maritana*. Later trained in Leipzig, he played in the Gewandhaus Orchestra, and eventually became a composer. His first important work, the cantata *Hinemoa* (1896), was based on a Maori legend and used Maori thematic material in an atmospheric rather than structural way. Its success coincided with a renewed artistic and scholarly concern with the Maori, then greatly demoralized after their defeat in the so-called Maori Wars of the 1860s. Hill's other works on Maori themes, including his *Maori Rhapsody*, helped re-awaken and widen interest in Maori traditions. Steeped in Maori mythology, greatly respected by the Maori people, an avid collector of *waiata* and its Westernized variants, Alfred Hill was a late 19th-century romantic with a genuine lyrical gift, at its best in smaller forms.

As conductor of the Wellington Orchestral Society, Hill instituted well-planned classical programmes, and later formed and conducted New Zealand's first fully professional orchestra for the Christchurch Exhibition of 1906–7. He wrote a number of successful romantic operas including *Tapu* and *A Moorish Maid*. In 1915, he became first professor of harmony and composition at the newly formed New South Wales State Conservatorium of Music. Hill's enduring contribution to the New Zealand and Australian traditions lies in his string quartets and Viola Concerto and in his fervent espousal of the works of composers of both countries.

The years following the First World War were generally bleak for musicians. New Zealand war casualties had been proportionately higher than those of Belgium and it took considerable time for cultural life to regain momentum. With the Depression of the 1930s, New Zealand's vulnerable agricultural economy, dependent wholly on overseas markets, became severely desiccated. Musicians earned precarious livelihoods in tearoom salon ensembles, on the trans-Tasman ships, or in the orchestras formed for the silent cinemas, which in the larger cities reached the proportions of full symphony orchestras and employed many of the country's best musicians. From the 1930s onwards, broadcasting provided increasing opportunities and the Broadcasting Service (partly modelled on the BBC) became music's principal patron. By 1940, the Service had established a string ensemble under the visiting English violinist, Maurice Clare, and in 1940, for the centennial celebrations, it formed a symphony orchestra which played for a national opera season. But the war eventually forced its disbandment and it was not until 1947 that the National Orchestra of the New Zealand Broadcasting Service (now the New Zealand Symphony Orchestra) gave its first concert in Wellington under Andersen Tyrer.

4. Music after the Second World War. During its first decade the National Orchestra tried to bring live music to every city and town. Based in Wellington, it often travelled over 10,000 miles a year until the formation of regional orchestras gradually relieved it of some of this burden. The National Orchestra was fortunate in some of its early conductors. After Andersen Tyrer, these included James Robertson and John Hopkins, with many notable guests, including Juan José Castro, Sir Eugene Goossens, Nikolay Malko, Karel Ančerl, Josef Krips, Alceo Galliera, Sir William Walton, and Igor Stravinsky.

After the touring opera companies of the Victorian and Edwardian eras, opera had been performed only sporadically, usually by specially formed Australian-based companies. In 1954, Donald Munro, a New Zealand singer, formed the New Zealand Opera Company, designed to play chamber opera to a wide audience. He introduced the chamber operas of Mozart, Menotti, Britten, and others. New Zealand has produced a number of outstanding singers, among them Rosina Buckman, Inia te Wiata, Kiri te Kanawa, Heather Begge, and Donald McIntyre.

Opera proved the most difficult of the musical arts to establish in a country with a widely scattered population of around three million. But chamber music is more manageable, and the Wellington Chamber Music Society, formed by exiles from Europe, became a national organization whose network extended to small towns. In 1972 the Society was re-formed as the Music Federation of New Zealand.

The university music departments have also played an important role in fostering music. Departments at Auckland, Wellington, Christchurch, and Dunedin have composers and performers on their staff and offer performance courses. The Mozart Fellowship (1969) at Otago University in Dunedin offers a resident scholarship to a composer. Each department has its own character, from the English atmosphere at Christchurch (the city was founded by a Church of England Society) to that of the avant-garde at Wellington and the reputation in musicology of Otago. Composers have found the annual Cambridge Summer School of Music (founded in 1946 by Owen Jensen) invaluable as well as the help and stimulus from the Government's Queen Elizabeth II Arts Council (1963) and the Australasian Performing Right Association with its subsidies for performance, recording, and publication.

Music historians find strange the gap between Alfred Hill and Douglas Lilburn (b 1915), though sociologists might point to economic and social conditions. Lilburn's first university studies were in journalism but he turned to music, a decisive factor being the prize, awarded by Percy Grainger, for his orchestral work *Forest* (1936). In 1940, while studying with Vaughan Williams and others at the Royal College of Music, London, he wrote *Aotearoa*, and its evocation of sea-drenched coasts, the clarity and intensity of light, and the character of the landscape has assured it of continued popularity. On returning to New Zealand in 1941, Lilburn wrote chamber works and theatre music for the productions of the writer of crime novels Ngaio Marsh. In 1942, Lilburn's *Landfall in Unknown Seas* for speaker and string orchestra, set to a poem by Alan Curnow, celebrated the discovery of New Zealand by the Dutch explorer Abel Tasman in 1642. Lilburn's sensitivity to words and the visual arts has resulted in several fine works, notably his setting of Alistair Campbell's sequence of poems, *Elegy* (1951), written in memory of a university student killed in a climbing fall in the Clutha Valley area in the South Island. *Sings Harry* (1953) is a setting of poems by Denis Glover; Harry is a wry lone figure who sings to an old guitar.

Having absorbed the influences of Sibelius and Vaughan Williams, Lilburn gradually forged a musical style of his own which reached fruition in the Second Symphony (1951). His Third Symphony (1961) is a one-movement work using serial technique, and was to prove virtually his last for traditional instruments. In 1963 he established the electronic music studio at Victoria University of Wellington, where he was awarded a special chair in 1970. His electronic works include the sound-poem *The Return* (1965), a setting of a poem by Alistair Campbell, *Carousel* (1976), and the *Three Inscapes* (1972) where Lilburn's preoccupation with landscape and its forms is intensely realized.

In the 1950s, composers tended to migrate towards the classes of Benjamin Frankel at the London Guildhall School of Music (Edwin Carr, Ronald Tremain, David Farquhar, and Larry Pruden, for instance). Edwin Carr (b 1926) is an eclectic, versatile musician with a natural flair for orchestral colour. Ronald Tremain (b 1923) has written sensitive string and vocal works. David Farquhar (b 1928) is

now professor of music at Victoria University of Wellington with a New Zealand classic to his credit (a deft period pastiche in his incidental music to Christopher Fry's play *Ring Round the Moon*). Larry Pruden (b 1925) is attracted by the atmosphere and history of a particular place (as in *Harbour Nocturne* of 1956 and *Taranaki: a Provincial Overture* of 1976). Ashley Heenan, John Ritchie, and David Sell have written effectively in a more traditional style.

By the 1960s, Darmstadt and the electronic music studios of Europe attracted young New Zealand composers. Anna Lockwood, doyenne of the extreme avant-garde, gave spectacular London concerts of glass music and piano burning. Jenny McLeod (b 1941) involved two entire New Zealand communities in *Earth and Sky*, which depicted the Maori creation myth, and *Under the Sun*, the evolution and running-down of the universe. Robin Maconie wrote the film score for the New Zealand full-length feature film *Runaway* (1964), and the book *Stockhausen* (Oxford, 1976).

Contemporary New Zealand composers working in Europe include Gillian Whitehead, Denis Smalley, Lyell Cresswell, and Robin Maconie. Whitehead (b 1941) studied with Peter Maxwell Davies in Sydney, worked with him in London, and has composed for his The Fires of London ensemble who have performed *Pakuru* and *Whakatau-ki*. Her one-act opera, *Tristan and Iseult*, used the 14th-century Italian estampie ('Lamento di Tristano') as a linking theme and was the outstanding event of the 1978 Auckland Festival with a subsequent BBC Radio 3 broadcast. Jack Body, first prizewinner at Bourges in 1976 with his *Musik dari Jalan*, based on Indonesian street sounds, is an inventive and vigorous composer with a sense of fantasy. John Rimmer (b 1939) has written impressions of a trans-Tasman air crossing, *Where Sea Meets Sky*, which won an honourable mention at Bourges and exists in both orchestral and electronic versions. Ross Harris (b 1945) has written works of charm and humour, including the electronic piece *Shadow Music*. Denis Smalley has been Fellow in Composition at the University of East Anglia since 1975. His *Gradual* for solo clarinet won the Fylkingen Competition in 1975 and the powerful *Darkness After Time's Colours* second prize at Bourges in 1977. Lyell Cresswell (b 1944) writes atmospheric, lean, and sometimes laconic pieces such as *A Feather of the Bird*, *Macpherson's Rant*, and the impressive orchestral work *Salm* (1977). Barry Anderson (b 1935) directs the West Square Electronic Music Workshop and has also written for traditional instruments. His works include *Sound Frames*, *Piano Pieces 1, 2 and 3*, and *Mask* for flutes, voice, two percussion groups, and five tape channels. Active composers of the younger generation include John Cousins, Ian McDonald, Noel Sanders, Gillian Bibby, Kit Powell, Christopher Norton, Jonathan Ladd, David Griffiths, and William Southgate.

In recent years New Zealand has not quite succeeded in retaining all of her many talented composers and performers, the latter especially needing a larger audience than a scattered three million people can provide. But greater opportunities are being created within the country and a recognition is growing that somehow Australia and New Zealand must cooperate culturally so that the musical life of the south Pacific can become richer and draw together the many strands of its challenging environment.

J. M. THOMSON

FURTHER READING
E. H. McCormick: *New Zealand Literature* (London, 1959); W. H. Oliver: *The Story of New Zealand* (London, 1959); Keith Sinclair: *A History of New Zealand* (London, 1959); Owen Jensen: *The NZBC Symphony Orchestra* (Wellington, 1960); Mervyn McLean and Margaret Orbell: *Traditional Songs of the Maori* (Wellington, 1975); J. M. Thomson: *A Distant Music: the Life and Times of Alfred Hill* (Wellington, 1980); J. M. Thomson: *A History of New Zealand Music* (Oxford, in preparation).

Nicene Creed. See *Creed.*

Nicholson, Richard (*d* Oxford, 1639). English organist and composer. He was choirmaster at Magdalen College, Oxford, in 1595, and graduated B.Mus. the following year; in 1626 he was appointed the first professor of music there. He composed some attractive songs, notably a madrigal cycle 'Joan, quoth John, when will it be', and some consort songs and anthems, including one which displays a certain academic skill by combining the 'Come Holy Ghost' psalm tune with the *In nomine* theme. He contributed a madrigal to *The Triumphes of Oriana*.

DENIS ARNOLD

Nicolai, (Carl) Otto (Ehrenfried) (*b* Königsberg, 9 June 1810; *d* Berlin, 11 May 1849). German composer. Son of a composer who was determined that his son should be an infant prodigy, he had a miserable childhood and finally ran away from home at the age of 16. He went to Berlin where he studied with Zelter and at the Royal Institute for Church Music, singing the part of Jesus in a performance of the *St Matthew Passion*; in 1831 he went to Rome as the organist to the Prussian Ambassador. There he studied the music of Palestrina and others but attracted attention by writing music on the death of Bellini—this eventually led to an appointment as singing teacher and conductor at the Vienna court opera. His year's contract there was not renewed and he successfully produced a number of operas at Italian theatres in the next few years, until he returned to Vienna in 1841 as musical director of the opera. Here he had a great success as a conductor, founding the Philharmonic concerts with the orchestra, but he had little opportunity to produce his own operas and in 1848 he left to take up the directorship of the cathedral choir in Berlin and conduct opera. His charming opera *Die lustigen Weiber von Windsor* ('The Merry Wives of Windsor') was given in 1849, and its mixture of delicate orchestral tone painting in the Mendelssohnian way, tunefulness, and Italianate skill in the ensembles has ensured its place in the repertory in Germany.

DENIS ARNOLD

Niederschlag (Ger.). 1. 'Down-beat' (the up-beat is *Aufschlag*). 2. In string playing, the 'down-stroke' of the bow, also called *Niederstrich*.

Niederstrich (Ger.). In string playing, the 'down-stroke' of the bow, also called *Niederschlag*.

Nielsen, Carl (August) (*b* Sortelung, nr Nørre Lyndelse, Fyn, 9 June 1865; *d* Copenhagen, 3 Oct. 1931). Danish composer. Born into a poor family, Nielsen played the fiddle as a boy in musical groups organized by his father. In 1880 he joined a military band as a bugler, and in 1884 he entered the Copenhagen Conservatory, where he studied with Niels Gade and others. He remained in the capital for the rest of his life, first as a second violinist in the Royal

Nielsen

Orchestra (1889-1905), then as a conductor at the Royal Theatre (1908-14) and with the Copenhagen Musical Society (1915-27). By the end of his life he was nationally and internationally esteemed as the greatest composer his country had produced.

Nielsen's reputation rests above all on his six symphonies: no. 1 in G minor (1890-2), no. 2 'The Four Temperaments' (1901-2), no. 3 'Sinfonia espansiva' (1910-11), no. 4 'The Inextinguishable' (1914-16), no. 5 (1921-2), and no. 6 'Sinfonia semplice' (1924-5). Clearly scored and forcefully argued, these have attracted attention for their tonal planning, and in particular for the 'progressive tonality' by which the music moves decisively from one key to another. This is also a feature of his other instrumental works, which include the half-hour organ piece *Commotio* (1931) and the Wind Quintet (1922). A performance of this latter work gave rise to his wish to compose a concerto designed to express the character of each player, but only those for flute (1926) and clarinet (1928) were written.

Unlike many of his contemporaries, Nielsen found a way to write symphonic tonal music without resorting to neoclassical artifice, though his opera *Maskarade* (1906) shows that he was capable of 18th-century pastiche. His other vocal works include the cantata *Hymnus amoris* (1896-7) and the highly-charged grand opera *Saul and David* (1902). PAUL GRIFFITHS

FURTHER READING
Robert Simpson: *Carl Nielsen, Symphonist* (London, 1952, 2nd edn 1979).

Niente (It.). 'Nothing'; *quasi niente*, 'almost nothing', i.e. fade the tone out gradually, or play as soft as possible.

Nightingale, The (*Solovey*; *Le rossignol*). Opera (musical fairy-tale) in three acts by Stravinsky to a libretto by the composer and S. Mitusov after a tale by Hans Andersen. It was first performed in Paris in 1914. *The Song of the Nightingale* (*Pesnya solov'ya*; *Le chant du rossignol*), a symphonic poem arranged from the opera, was first performed in Geneva in 1919 and staged as a ballet in Paris in 1920. The *Chants du rossignol et Marche chinoise* (1932), for violin and piano, were arranged from *The Nightingale* by Stravinsky and Dushkin.

Night on the Bare Mountain (*Ivanova noch' na Lysoy gore*: 'St John's Night on the Bare Mountain'). Orchestral work by Musorgsky, composed in 1867. It was inspired by the witches' sabbath in Gogol's story *St John's Eve*. It was revised as a choral piece for inclusion in the opera *Mlada* (1872), and again revised as a

choral introduction to Act 3 of *Sorochintsy Fair* (1874-80). This final version was freely revised and orchestrated by Rimsky-Korsakov (1886), and it is this version that is well known, but it is no longer really Musorgsky's.

Night Ride and Sunrise (*Öinen ratsastus ja auringonnousu*). Tone-poem, Op. 55, by Sibelius, composed in 1907.

Nilsson, Bo (*b* Skelleftehamn, 1 May 1937). Swedish composer. Though largely self-taught, he came to early prominence when his *Frequenzen* for eight instrumentalists was performed at Darmstadt in 1956. This and later works show the strong influence of Stockhausen. PAUL GRIFFITHS

Nimrod. The ninth of Elgar's '*Enigma*' *Variations*, so called because it is a portrait of Elgar's friend A. J. Jaeger (Jaeger is the German for 'hunter'; Nimrod was the 'mighty hunter' of the Old Testament). The piece enshrines a day when the two men discussed Beethoven slow movements, and it is often played separately as a commemorative item.

Ninna-nanna, ninnarella (It.). 'Cradle song'.

Ninth. See *Interval*.

Ninth chord. A chord with the seventh and ninth added. See *Diminished seventh*; *Dominant seventh*.

Ninth Symphony. Although several composers wrote nine symphonies, for example Mahler, Bruckner, Dvořák, and Vaughan Williams, this term, to the general music lover, means one work, Beethoven's Symphony No. 9 in D minor, the 'Choral', Op. 125, composed 1822-4.

Nivers, Guillaume Gabriel (*b* ? Paris, *c*.1632; *d* Paris, 30 Nov. 1714). French organist and composer. He was organist at St Sulpice, Paris, from the early 1650s until his death, and from 1678 was one of the organists of the royal chapel. From 1686 he was also in charge of the music at the convent school of St Louis at St Cyr. He composed some agreeable solo motets, but his most important music was for organ. His three *Livres d'orgue* (Paris, 1665-75) contain versets for performance in church, and the prefaces contain important information on performing practice of the time. DENIS ARNOLD

Nobile (It.). 'Noble'; *nobilmente*, 'nobly' (a favourite term of Elgar's); *nobiltà*, *noblezza*, 'nobility'.

Noblemen and Gentlemen's Catch Club. A London club founded in 1761 to encourage the composition of catches and glees. The Earl of Sandwich was among the founders, and the members included many professional musicians (Abel, Arne, J. C. Bach, Callcott). The minute-books go back to 1767: at that period every member had to sing a song at every meeting. It is reputed that anyone singing out of tune had to drink a glass of wine; sherry and Madeira were drunk, but coffee, tea, and other beverages were not permitted, and politics and religion were excluded from the conversation. From 1763 the club awarded prizes for compositions: for its centenary in 1861 it offered a silver goblet to the composer of the best commemorative four-part glee; and its bicentenary was celebrated with a part-song specially commissioned from Malcolm Arnold. The club is still in existence.

Noces, Les. See *Wedding, The*.

Noche (Sp.). 'Night'.

Noches en los jardines de España ('Nights in the Gardens of Spain'). Symphonic impressions by Falla for piano and orchestra, composed between 1911 and 1915. The movements are *En el Generalife, Danza lejana* ('Dance in the Distance'), and *En los jardines de la Sierra de Córdoba*.

Nocturn (Lat.: *horae nocturnae*). Part of the Office Hour of Matins. There are three nocturns in Matins, each comprising three psalms with antiphons and three Lessons, each followed by a *responsory (the last responsory may be replaced by the *Te Deum*).

Nocturne (Eng., Fr.; Ger.: *Nachtstück*; It.: *notturno*). 1. A name given to a composition which suggests a romantic view of night. In the 18th century, the name *notturno* was given to compositions similar to the *serenade, which were played as evening entertainments. Haydn wrote several *notturni*, with varying numbers of movements, for two *lire organizzate* (hurdy-gurdies), two clarinets, two horns, two violas, and bass (1790), and Mozart wrote one for strings and two horns (K 269*a*). The Bohemian composer Gyrowetz wrote 16 *notturni* for various combinations of instruments.

2. In the 19th century, 'nocturne' was specifically used as a title for Romantic piano pieces of a slow and dreamy nature, in which a graceful, highly-embellished melody in the right hand is accompanied by a broken-chord pattern in the left. This type of piece was first written by the Irish composer John Field, and was taken up with great success by Chopin, whose 19 examples were never surpassed.

See also *Nachtstück*.

Nocturne. Song-cycle, Op. 60, by Britten for tenor, seven *obbligato* instruments, and strings. It is a setting of eight poems about night by Shelley, Tennyson, Coleridge, Middleton, Wordsworth, Owen, Keats, and Shakespeare. The opening poem is accompanied by strings only; each succeeding setting is dominated by an *obbligato* instrument (bassoon, harp, horn, timpani, cor anglais, and flute and clarinet), and the finale is for the full complement. The work is dedicated to Mahler's widow and was first performed in Leeds in 1958.

Nocturnes. Orchestral triptych by Debussy, composed between 1897 and 1899. The movements are *Nuages* ('Clouds'), *Fêtes* ('Festivals'), and *Sirènes* ('Sirens'). The last piece includes a women's chorus. Ravel arranged the work for two pianos (1909).

Node. The point of rest between two wave motions of a vibrating string etc. Several nodes occur along the length of a string, and harmonics on a stringed instrument are produced by the player lightly touching the string at each of these points. In a vibrating air column, such as a pipe, nodes are the points of highest density, where the air particles do not move.

See *Acoustics*, 5.

Nō Drama. A Japanese theatrical entertainment involving music, dance, drama, and poetry. See *Japanese Music*, 6.

Noël (Fr.), **nowell** (Eng.). 'Christmas'. The word is used to mean a Christmas *carol, and often appears in the refrain of such pieces.

Noire (Fr.). 'Black (note)', i.e. the crotchet or quarter-note (♩).

Nola, Giovanni Domenico del Giovane da (*b* Nola, nr Naples, *c*.1510; *d* Naples, May 1592). Italian composer and organist. He was *maestro di cappella* at Ss. Annunziata, Naples, from 1563, and also taught singing there. He was famous as a composer of secular songs, especially *villanesche* and *napolitane*.

DENIS ARNOLD

Nomine, In (Lat.). See *In nomine*.

None. The sixth of the *Office Hours of the Roman Catholic Church.

Nonet (Fr.: *nonette*; Ger.: *Nonett*; It.: *nonetto*). Any combination of nine instruments or voices or a piece of music composed for such. Well-known examples include Spohr's Nonet, Op. 31, for string quartet, flute, oboe, clarinet, bassoon, and horn; Rheinberger's Op. 139, for violin, viola, cello, double bass, flute, oboe, clarinet, bassoon, and horn; and Webern's Concerto, Op. 24, for flute, oboe, clarinet, horn, trumpet, trombone, violin, viola, and piano.

Non nobis Domine. Celebrated vocal canon, attributed (without definite evidence) to Byrd. It is usually sung in three parts, the top voice entering first, the middle one a fourth below, and the lowest an octave below the top. However, a large number of solutions to the canon are possible, in various numbers of parts, and at varying pitch and time intervals, and even with the melody inverted. The opening phrase was very common in music from the 16th to the 18th centuries: Handel used it in his 'Hallelujah Chorus'. *Non nobis Domine* was traditionally sung at banquets, as a 'grace'.

Nono, Luigi (*b* Venice, 29 Jan. 1924). Italian composer. He studied law at the University of Padua and began composing under the influence of Malipiero. Then, between 1946 and 1950, he had lessons from Bruno Maderna and Hermann Scherchen, who introduced him to serial methods. With such works as *Polifonica—Monodia—Ritmica* for seven instrumentalists (1951) he established himself alongside Boulez and Stockhausen as a leader of the avant-garde, developing complex serial procedures in a style of impassioned rhetoric. The cantata *Il canto sospeso* (1955-6) placed that rhetoric at the service of anti-fascism, and in many subsequent works Nono has expressed his fierce commitment to revolutionary socialism. His opera

Luigi Nono

Intolleranza (1960-1, rev. 1970) concerns the plight of an immigrant in a hostile state; other pieces, such as *Non consumiamo Marx* (1969), are musical manifestos of a vehement and lyrical character, scored for voices and tape. Nono has also appeared as a lecturer, notably at the summer courses at Darmstadt and Dartington, and has organized concerts in factories.

PAUL GRIFFITHS

Nordqvist, Gustav (Lazarus) (*b* Stockholm, 12 Feb. 1886; *d* Stockholm, 28 Jan. 1949). Swedish composer. He studied composition with Ellberg and piano with Lundberg at the Stockholm Conservatory (1901-10), and was also a pupil of Hillner in Berlin (1913). While working in Stockholm as a teacher and organist, he composed around 200 songs and various other works in a late-Romantic idiom.

PAUL GRIFFITHS

Norfolk Rhapsody. Orchestral work by Vaughan Williams, composed 1905-6, based on three folk-songs collected in Norfolk in 1905 by the composer. Vaughan Williams wrote two other *Norfolk Rhapsodies* in 1906, the plan being a 'Norfolk Symphony', but they were later withdrawn.

Nørgård, Per (*b* Gentofte, 13 July 1932). Danish composer. He studied with Vagn Holmboe and Finn Høffding at the Royal Danish Conservatory in Copenhagen (1952-5) and has taught at conservatories in Fyn, Copenhagen, and Århus. His works, influenced by Sibelius, Ligeti, and the American minimalists, use repetitive material in glowing tonal harmony.

PAUL GRIFFITHS

Norma. Opera in two acts by Bellini; text by Felice Romani after Louis Soumet's tragedy (1831). Produced: Milan, La Scala, 26 December 1831; London, King's Theatre, 20 June 1833; New Orleans, 1 April 1836. Norma (sop.), a Druid priestess who has had two children by Pollione (ten.), a Roman pro-consul, finds that he has transferred his affections to another young priestess, her friend Adalgisa (sop. or mezzo). Norma tries to persuade him to renounce Adalgisa and return to her; when he refuses she confesses her own guilt publicly and is condemned to death. Pollione, moved by her action, asks to die with her.

North Country Sketches. Orchestral work by Delius, composed in 1913-14. Its four movements are 'Autumn' ('The wind soughs in the trees'), 'Winter Landscape', 'Dance', and 'The March of Spring' ('Woodlands, Meadows, and Silent Moors').

Domenico Dozelli (Pollione), Giulia Grisi (Adalgisa), and Giuditta Pasta (Norma) in the first production of Bellini's 'Norma' (La Scala, Milan, 1831).

Northern School of Music. See *Royal Northern College of Music*.

Norway. See *Scandinavia*, 1, 2, 5.

Nose, The (Russ.: *Nos*). Opera in three acts by Shostakovich; text by the composer, Alexander Preys, Georgy Ionin, and Evgeny Zamyatin, after Gogol's story (1835), with extracts from other works by Gogol and using Smerdyakov's song from Dostoyevsky's *The Brothers Karamazov*. Produced: Leningrad, Maly Theatre, 12 January 1930; London, Sadler's Wells by New Opera Company, 4 April 1973. *The Nose*

(composed 1927–8) was a product of the bold, experimentalist years immediately following the 1917 Revolution. Using as a catalyst Gogol's literary satire on the reign of Nicholas I, the opera in turn satirized the institutions and the very fabric of Soviet society in the 1920s, in music of wry wit and extreme harmonic and rhythmic complexity (and including, incidentally, one of the highest tenor roles in the repertory: the Police Inspector is required to sing up to e″). However, as firm ideological control came to be applied to the arts (see *Socialist Realism*) the opera fell from favour and eventually was attacked for its alleged adherence to *formalism. It had only 16 performances before being dropped from the repertory altogether. It was revived at the Moscow Chamber Music Theatre in 1974.

Major Platon Kovalyov (bar.), a minor civil official, loses his nose, which turns up in a breakfast roll being eaten by the barber Ivan Yakovlevich (bass), and then begins to lead a life of its own, even masquerading as a state councillor and treating its former owner with disdain. Finally it is arrested and returned to Kovalyov, who, now no longer disfigured, can resume his pleasantries with the leaders of St Petersburg society.

FURTHER READING
Geoffrey Norris: 'The Operas', *Shostakovich: the Man and his Music*, ed. Christopher Norris (London, 1982), pp. 115–24.

Nota cambiata (It.). 'Changing note'. An idiomatic melodic formula whose salient feature is the leap of a third away from an unessential note.

The *nota cambiata* should not be confused with the *cambiata* (see under *Échappée*).

Notation

1. Introduction
2. Neumatic Notation, 800–1200
3. The Rhythmic Modes, *c*.1200
4. Franconian and Petronian Notation, *c*.1260–*c*.1320

5. Italian and French Ars Nova Notation
6. Notation in the 15th and 16th Centuries
7. The 17th and 18th Centuries
8. From the 19th Century to the Present Day

1. *Introduction.* The term 'musical notation' can be applied to any formal indication of how sounds and silences intended as music should be reproduced. There are many varieties of notation and notational format. Major variations arise with dramatic changes of date or provenance, but decisive technical variations can also occur according to the performance medium (orchestral, electronic, keyboard, vocal, etc.),

the style or genre (cadenza, symphony, blues, etc.), the circumstances of the performer (braille notation, elementary didactic notations, etc.), and experiments in vocal and instrumental usage and technique (e.g. Cage's music for prepared piano, Bartók's expansions of string playing technique). This article will concentrate upon the origins and development of staff notation in the West, and upon music written for the standard ensembles and solo performers of art music.

Of course, notation is not the music itself and no notational system provides a totally unambiguous guide to the final musical experience. Some electronic notations, specifically designed to be 'interpretation resistant', control most of the factors of execution, but they rarely control the environment in which it takes place and cannot define its reception as music. Again, at various stages of music history almost all the parameters of music—exact pitch, instrumentation, rhythmic detail, pace, expression, and form—have been left to chance or convention. Most performers are aware of these variables in the performance practice of music. More difficult to appreciate is the role of modern editors, who, by their concern to clarify historical conventions and archaic notations, filter earlier music through a modern notational practice which is assumed to be more efficient and intelligible. In fact, the stylistic individuality of any period is closely linked with its notational devices. Renaissance music, for example, often requires conflicting time signatures in simultaneous voices or sudden switches from duple to triple metre in a single musical line. Renaissance notation had special means (mathematical signs, coloured notes, variable duple and triple values of each notational symbol, etc.) to accommodate these things; now they must be written down as makeshift and often misleading divisions of a basically duple system of notational relationships (two crotchets are equivalent to a minim, two minims to a semibreve, etc.). For these and other reasons there has been movement in

recent years towards performing earlier music from the notation in which it was written.

2. *Neumatic Notation, 800–1200: the Origins of the Staff, Clefs, and Accidentals.* The origins of our present notational system lie in the various plainchant sources and theoretical treatises of the 9th and 10th centuries. There had been earlier systems of notation (in Ancient Greece, for example) but they had fallen into disuse and, in the early 7th century, Archbishop Isidore of Seville wrote: 'unless sounds are remembered by man, they perish, for they cannot be written down' (*Etymologiarum*, chapter iii. 15).

Plainchant was first notated with 'neumes' written above the text. Neumes are small dots and squiggles probably derived in part from the accentual signs once used in the Latin language. Their various shapes (see Fig. 1) represent either single notes or groups of notes. Those that represent groups of notes strung together are sometimes called 'ligatures' (from Lat., *ligare*, 'to bind'), and this term continues to be used for all compound note forms found in various notations up to the 17th century. The basic plainchant neumes acted as a memory aid suggesting, but not precisely indicating, changes of pitch within the melody. There were also ornamental neumes which required special types of vocal delivery.

Several local families of neumatic notation existed including those from St Gall (Switzerland), Aquitaine, Benevento (used in much of southern and central Italy), and Lorraine (sometimes called 'Metz' neumes). The neumatic notational system is usually illustrated by

Fig. 1

BASIC NEUMES	St Gall	Modern plainchant	Approximate equivalent	SIGNIFICATIVE LETTERS (some examples from St Gall)
virga	/	⌐	♪	a = *altius*; chant rises higher in pitch.
tractulus/punctum	— ·	• •	♪ ♪	b = *bene*; 'very'—used with another letter.
pes/podatus	✓ ✓	•	♫	c = *cito* or *celeriter*; 'rapidly' or 'quickly'.
clivis/flexa	∩	▸	♫	e = *equaliter*; 'the same' (pitch).
scandicus	·/	♪ or ⌐	♫♪	k = *klenche*; with a ringing tone.
climacus	/··	⌐··	♫♫	t = *trahere* or *tenere*; 'drag out' or 'hold'.
torculus	∿	▴	♫♫	x = *expectare*; 'wait'.
porrectus	∿	N	♫♫	
ORNAMENTAL NEUMES				
oriscus	∾	؍	*Oriscus* (Gk) = 'limit' or 'little hill'; perhaps the pitch should rise to anticipate the following note. *Quilisma*: the theorist Aurelian of Réôme describes it as a trembling and rising sound.
quilisma	·ω/	◢	
LIQUESCENT NEUMES				
epiphonus (liq. *pes*)	✓	◢	Liquescence was used for singing certain consonants and dipthongs in the text; it resulted in semi-vocalization as the singer passed to the next note. This semi-vocalization occurred on the last note of each group; it was used particularly when words were sung containing the consonants l, m, n, r, d, t, and s followed by another consonant.
cephalicus (liq. *clivis*)	↗	⌐	
ancus (liq. *climacus*)	↗	⌐··	

those written or derived from the monastery of St Gall as they are both sophisticated and relatively early. Present-day Roman Catholic chant books use a form of square notation first evolved in North France.

The singers of plainchant in the 9th and 10th centuries were trained within an oral tradition; neumes were probably an attempt to describe graphically the hand signals a choirmaster might make to indicate a particular vocal contour or gesture. The only thing clearly indicated by the early neumes, though, was which groups of notes belonged to which syllables of text. However, by the end of the 10th century, some families of chant (e.g. the Aquitainian and Beneventan) arranged the neumes vertically on the page to show their relative pitch. These so-called 'heighted' or 'diastematic' neumes were further clarified by the addition of a faintly scratched line which usually represented the final note (or third above it) of the modal scale in which the chant was written.

Our modern association of vertical height or depth with stepwise pitch organization was first mooted in 9th-century treatises such as the *De harmonica institutione* by Hucbald (*c*.840-930), but it was Guido d'Arezzo (*c*.995-1050) who brought the various experiments brilliantly into focus. In his *Aliae regulae* (*c*.1030) he recom-

mended that a staff should be used with spaces as well as lines indicating pitches, and that at least one of the lines should be identified by a pitch letter (i.e. clef). In practice, he used a red line to indicate F and a yellow one for C, and, before long, a four-line staff was established for the writing down of plainchant. Guido also suggested that two different forms of the letter B be used to describe the pitches B♭ and B♮: he stipulates ♭ *rotundum* (Lat., 'round') for the former, and ♮ *quadratum* (Lat., 'square') for the latter. In fact, these shapes are found slightly earlier than Guido. They are the earliest known accidentals in Western music, and they developed into our modern flat (♭ → ♭) and natural (♭ → ♮ → ♮) signs, and thence to the sharp (♮ → ♯) sign. It is perhaps significant that this concern with precise pitch notation and chromatic inflexion coincided with the first written polyphonic music and its inevitable concern with vertical (harmonic) relationships. However, the new staff and clef arrangements had practical advantages for singers of plainchant too; Guido tells us that the repertory of chant could now be learnt in two years instead of ten.

The rhythmic interpretation of neumatic notation is still a matter of controversy. Some notations (e.g. St Gall) use small letters called

Ex. 1

Ex. 2

(a) Facsimile of the original

'significative letters' to indicate melodic pace as well as other factors such as vocal sonority (see Fig. 1 for a few examples). Furthermore, a number of theorists between the 9th and 11th centuries discuss plainchant rhythm making allusions to classical poetic metres. Unfortunately they illustrate their ideas only with syllabic chants and so it is difficult to apply their theories with certainty to any but the simplest types of chant (hymns, psalm intonations) or to those employing regular poetry (some tropes and sequences). Working from cases such as these, some scholars (e.g. Riemann, Jammers) have produced rhythmic transcriptions based on text accentuation. However, such 'accentualist' approaches have found little sympathy in the main Roman Catholic centre for chant study—the French Benedictine Abbey of Solesmes. The Solesmes monks prefer chants to be sung in notes of broadly equal length and their 'equalist' approach is the one usually followed today. A comparison of various chant notations can be seen in Ex. 1; part of the chant *Christus factus est pro nobis* now sung on Maundy Thursday is shown (a) in staff-less St Gall neumes; (b) in modern chant notation on a four-line staff with C clef and square neumes; and (c) in a modern 'equalist' transcription with the notes of any one ligature group encompassed under a slur sign.

Detailed work on the St Gall sources by Eugène Cardine (1968) revealed that there might well be rhythmic suggestions built into the presentation of the notation; the breaks between the groups of notes possibly indicate rhythmic phraseology and the ligatures frequently, but not invariably, seem to suggest patterns which begin with a short value and end with a long—that is, the phrases lead up to the most important stress, rather than begin emphatically like most later music. Some notes in the St Gall notation have specific stress or lengthening marks (small horizontal strokes) called *episemas* placed over them. If rhythmic patterning was a normal part of the St Gall

(b) Transcription

practice then this would be a clear anticipation of the more obviously organized rhythmic notation of the early 13th century (see below, 3).

3. *The Rhythmic Modes, c.1200.* By the beginning of the 13th century some pieces of music were so complex that they must have been at least partially conceived in writing. Pérotin's *Viderunt omnes* (?1199), for example, contains canonic sections, voice-exchange textures, hocket technique, and writing for four voices, all within the context of vertical 'harmonic' considerations. Ex. 2a shows a 13th-century source of Pérotin's work (Florence, *Bib. Laur.* Pluteo 29, 1); clearly the notation of pitch and the use of staff, clefs, and some accidentals (there is a B♭ 'key signature') had been more or less established. Five-line staves were usually employed, but the tenor part which is based on plainchant is written, like plainchant, on four lines. The top three voices have C clefs on their middle lines, and the lowest voice has a C clef on the top line.

A most important development c.1200 was the establishment of set ways of combining ligatures so as to clearly indicate the rhythmic patterns of the music. These set patterns were called 'rhythmic modes' and in the basic system there were six of them. Thus, if a composer wished to write the ♩♪♩♪ rhythm (first mode) he would use a three-note ligature followed by a two-note group, e.g. 𝄅 𝄅 . Just such a group can be seen in the top voice of Ex. 2a after the initial long note and rest. Note that, as was probably the case in plainchant, the second and subsequent ligatures start with a short note value and build up to the stressed note. The whole system is set out in Fig. 2. The smallest unit in each modal pattern (e.g.♩ ♪ in the first mode) was called an *ordo* (plural: *ordines*), and the ligature pattern which signalled the mode was sufficient for at least two *ordines*.

A glance at Ex. 2b will reveal that these patterns were not used relentlessly in any one part. The stereotyped rhythms could be broken up by the insertion of rests (*divisio modi*), the division of a long note into smaller ones (*fractio modi*), the occasional omission of a smaller note (*extensio modi*), the insertion of runs of smaller notes (*conjuncturae* or *currentes*), and other devices. These factors sometimes make the notation difficult to interpret and, in any case, recent work (by Roesner) has shown that modal rhythm existed alongside freer types of notation even in the same piece. During the 13th century modal rhythm was most common in the tenor parts of motets and in the discant sections of *organum*. Moreover, there appear to have been local dialects of modal notation with, for example, Scottish sources taking a stricter view of the modal system than the Parisians, and with the English employing their own version of mode 3 (♩. ♩♩ instead of ♩. ♪♪).

The origins of the rhythmic modes are rather obscure. Many Medieval hymns, for example, are written in the metres of the first or second modes (*Veni creator spiritus* is an instance of the second). Moreover, in the late 12th century Alexander de Villa Dei writing in Paris connected poetic metres with the word 'modes', and we have already seen that the St Gall neumatic notation seems to suggest rhythmic patterns which prefigure the modal system.

The fullest description of the rhythmic modes is given in *De mensurabili musicae* written by Johannes de Garlandia c.1240. He defines not only the rhythmic value of the ligatures and single notes, but also the rests. Until this point in time rests in musical notation had been rather imprecise in design if not in function.

4. *Franconian and Petronian Notation, c.1260–c.1320.* The trend towards greater definition of the individual components of modal rhythm

Fig. 2

RHYTHMIC MODES

Mode	Basic patterns (brackets ⌐─⌐ show ligature groups)			Examples of original notation	Grouping of notes	Greek poetic terms
			Phrase ends			
	Ordo 1	Ordo 2 etc.	thus			
I	♩♪	♩	♪|....|♩ ;	𝄅 𝄅	3 + 2	trochaic
II	♪♩	♪♩|....|♪ ;		𝄅 𝄅	2 + 3	iambic
III	♩	♪♩|♩	♪♩|....|♩ ;	𝄅 𝄅 𝄅	1 + 3 + 3	dactylic
IV	♪♩♩	|♪♩♩ | |....|♪♩ ;		𝄅 𝄅 𝄅	3 + 3 + 2	anapaestic
V	♩.	♩|♩. ♩|....|♩. ;		𝄅 𝄅 𝄅 𝄅	1 + 1 + 1 + 1 + 1	spondaic
VI	♬♬	♬♬ |....|♪ ;		𝄅 𝄅	4 + 3	tribrachic

NB. In any ligature with a slanting (oblique) section, such as 𝄅 or 𝄅, only the two ends of the slanting section represent notes. Thus in the ligature ▬𝄅 there are only three notes, viz: ▬▬

Fig. 3

<small>FRANCONIAN NOTATION</small>

(a) *Note values*

      ⌐ duplex long = two perfect longs   • ordinary breve = $\frac{1}{3}$ perfect long *or* $\frac{1}{2}$ imperfect long

      ▌ perfect long = three ordinary breves   • *altera* breve = $\frac{2}{3}$ perfect long

      ▌ imperfect long = two ordinary breves   • minor semibreve = $\frac{1}{3}$ ordinary breve

                                         • major semibreve = $\frac{2}{3}$ ordinary breve

(b) *Rests*

    1   2   3   4   5

    1. perfect long   2. imperfect long and *altera* breve   3. ordinary breve   4. major semibreve
    5. minor semibreve

(c) *Illustrations of note combinations*

    (i) perfect long and ordinary breve

    (ii) perfect long, ordinary and *altera* breves ordinary *altera*

    (iii) imperfect long, division sign (/) and ordinary breve

    (iv) breve and major and minor semibreves   minor sbs   major sb

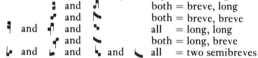

(d) *Examples of note values in ligatures defined according to the shape of the individual ligature*

          and   both = breve, long
          and   both = breve, breve
  and   and   all = long, long
          and   both = long, breve
  and   and   and   all = two semibreves

---

inevitably changed the very nature of the system itself. This gradual evolution was further encouraged by experiments in the motet; more small note values were needed in order to declaim the syllabically-set texts and so attention turned towards individual note values and rests. The new system that eventually emerged was first described *c.*1260 in *Ars cantus mensurabilis* by Franco of Cologne (hence the term 'Franconian notation'). Individual note forms and rests were codified, there was an attempt to define the value of ligatures according to their actual shapes rather than their contexts, and a hierarchical system was established giving particular attention to the distinct levels of operation between the ▌ long and the • breve on the one hand, and the • breve and • semibreve on the other (see Fig. 3).

(a) *Perfection, Imperfection, and Alteration.*
Basically, music still continued to be conceived in terms of the old rhythmic modes but the Franconian system attempted to translate the rhythms into individual note forms. The difficulty was that too few distinct note types were used, so that an element of context remained in

their interpretation. For example, the first rhythmic mode was expressed as ▌ • ▌ • (♩ ♪♩ ♪) with the breve one-half the length of the long, while mode three was expressed as ▌ • • (♩. ♪♩) with the first breve one-third of the long and the second breve two-thirds. This use of the breve with a variety of fractions of the long (one-third, one-half, two-thirds) led to the idea of seeing the breves as various subdivisions of a 'perfect' long worth three breves. If, as in the first mode, the long was worth only two breves it was looked upon as an 'imperfected' version of the note—an 'imperfect long' (see Fig. 4*a*). The perfect long, then, remained the ideal as it were; if only two breves were used together (as in the third mode ▌ • •, ♩. ♪♩) they still had to serve for the full equivalent of a perfect long. In this situation the second breve was 'altered' to fill up the full value of the perfect long—it was described not as an ordinary breve but as the 'other' (Lat. *altera*) kind. *Altera* or 'altered' breves were twice the length of ordinary ones (see Fig. 4*b*). In the 14th century and later the practices of imperfection and alteration were used extensively not only between the long and the breve, but also between the breve and semibreve and, eventually, between the semibreve and minim (see Fig. 4c). It even became the practice to curtail the length of a note by imperfecting it with a note several levels smaller as, for example, in the imperfection of a maxima by a following semibreve (see Fig. 4d). In reality this 'imperfection' by a remote note value became an *ad hoc* device for curtailing long notes, irrespective of whether they were originally perfect or imperfect, so as to introduce flexible rhythms. In Fig. 4d the 'imperfected' maxima was originally imperfect anyway, being equivalent to only two longs.

Franco of Cologne was the first theorist to recognize the semibreve as a distinct value but in his examples it always occurs in groups of two or more (as in Fig. 3c.iv). Units equivalent to three notes were sometimes marked off by dashes (/, a kind of barline) to indicate exactly where the 'perfections' began in ambiguous passages. In Fig. 3c.iii, for example, the first long is imperfected by the following breve, but the final long is imperfected by its preceding breve. If the dash were placed differently, e.g. ♩ ◆ ◆ ◗, then another reading would prevail: ♩. ♩ | ♩. ♩. | ♩ ♩. |

Very little music was written in pure Franconian notation, but Franco's description of individual notes and rests, the ideas of perfection, imperfection, and alteration, and his close definition of the ligature shapes opened the floodgates for later theorists. His work probably provided the common origin for the widely divergent Italian and French notational systems of the 14th century.

(*b*) *Petronian Notation.* A form of notation more obviously linked to the 14th-century Italian system was that devised by Petrus de Cruce *c.*1280. He introduced a method of subdividing the breve into as many as seven semibreves; to do this he simply placed the semibreves between two dots (*puncti divisioni*) which represented the length of a breve (see Ex. 3). This allowed for more complex syllabic settings of texts, a still greater movement away from the now archaic rhythmic modal patterns, and, in the hands of Petrus, a mellifluous and prominent vocal line in the top voice supported by slower moving accompanying parts. Moreover, the melodic top part, in spite of its greater activity, retained a clear and easy 'beat' since all small notes were dependent on the over-all length of the breve, and so there could be no syncopation across the regular breve stresses. This absence of 'across the bar' (in modern terms) syncopation remained a feature of 14th-century Italian notation, and perhaps signals the origin of the traditional Italian love of direct melodies with symmetrical phrasing. The nationality of Petrus is not known and even his writings only come down to us second hand in references from the English theorists Robert de Handlo and Hanboys.

5. *Italian and French Ars Nova Notation:* (*a*) *Italian.* The two principal theorists of Italian notation—Marchettus de Padua (*d c.*1330) and Prosdocimus de Beldamandis (*d* 1428)—predate and postdate respectively the surviving music written in Italian 14th-century notation. The exact way in which the notation was used can be gleaned only from the music itself as preserved in such sources as the Reina and Squarcialupi codices. The basic unit of Italian notation was the breve, which could be subdivided into triple or duple groups (see Fig. 5a). The particular subdivision of the breve chosen by the composer was equivalent in modern terms to choosing a

Fig. 4

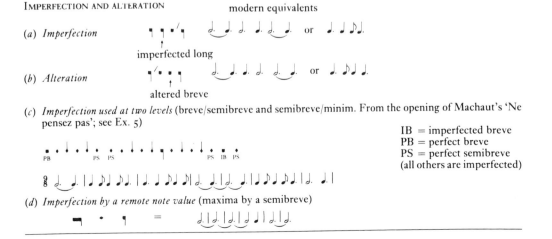

IMPERFECTION AND ALTERATION   modern equivalents

(*a*) *Imperfection*

imperfected long

(*b*) *Alteration*

altered breve

(*c*) *Imperfection used at two levels* (breve/semibreve and semibreve/minim. From the opening of Machaut's 'Ne pensez pas'; see Ex. 5)

IB = imperfected breve
PB = perfect breve
PS = perfect semibreve
(all others are imperfected)

(*d*) *Imperfection by a remote note value* (maxima by a semibreve)

Ex. 3

(a) Facsimile of Petrus de Cruce: 'Aucun ont trouvé' (Montpellier, Faculté des Médecins, MS H196, p. 278)

(b) Transcription

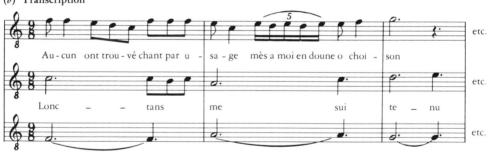

Fig. 5

ITALIAN ARS NOVA NOTATION

(a) Divisions of the breve

(b) Examples in octonaria

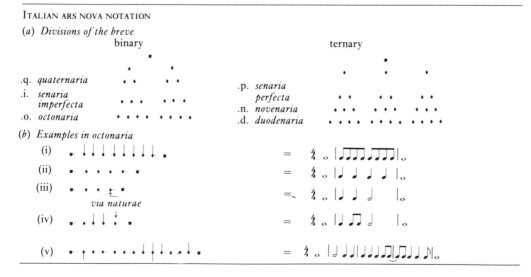

time signature. If, for example, *octonaria* were used, the maximum number of semibreves in a breve was eight; however, fewer than eight semibreves could still be used by simply stretching the value of the final semibreve to fill up the time left of the breve (see Fig. 5*b*). This device of placing the longest value at the end was known as the *via naturae* ('natural way') in contradistinction to the French preference for long–short rhythms (♩ ♪ ♩ ♪ etc.) which exemplified the *via artis* ('artificial way'). It was not impossible for a long semibreve to appear at the beginning of a group of notes in Italian notation, but if this occurred either a special note form with a downward stem ↑ was used, or specific mention was made in the score to the French (Gallic) practice of *via artis*. For example, the letters s.g. (*senaria gallica*) denoted the long–short rhythm ♩ ♩ ♪ ♩ ♪ .

A major contribution of the Italian music using the system was its total acceptance of duple metre. Furthermore, duple and triple metres were frequently used together in the same composition. Such things seem to have been established as early as Marchettus de Padua's treatise *Pomerium* (i.e. 'fruit tree' of musical knowledge) written *c*.1318–26. Later it became common to signal the minimum value of the semibreve in a given time (e.g. one-eighth of the breve in *octonaria*) with an up-stem, thus ↓ . The use of single letters to clarify the time signature (.o. for *octonaria*, .q. for *quaternaria*, etc.) was not sanctioned theoretically until Prosdocimus's *Tractatus* (1412). An example of basic Italian notation can be seen in the following extract from 'Io son un pellegrin' which is in *octonaria* (Ex. 4). It can be seen that Italian scribes used a six-line staff.

Ex. 4

(*a*) Facsimile of Anon: 'Io son un pellegrin' (Paris, Bibliothèque Nationale, MS ital. 568, folio 42 *verso*)

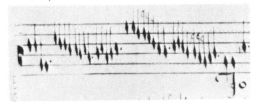

(*b*) Transcription

As the breve was the basic organizing unit it was impossible in the system to introduce any kind of extended syncopation that would transcend the length of a breve. In fact, the note shapes still depended for their value on their context within the over-all length of a single breve. In the later 14th century composers felt the need for greater flexibility and so devised note values that would be fixed by the shape of the note alone. Examples of such fixed values include the 'dragma' ↓ which was always equivalent to two minimum values of the semibreve, and a series of note values with stems out to the left (↗ , ↓) which acted as dotted versions (i.e. half the value again) of the basic shapes ♦ , ↓ (see Fig. 5*b*.v). After *c*.1360 many Italian composers (e.g. Landini) employed French notational features mixed in with the Italian system so as to achieve greater rhythmic variety.

(*b*) *French*. The term 'Ars Nova' ('new art') is taken from what is usually described as a treatise by Philippe de Vitry written *c*.1322. In fact, the writings might well be copies of notes taken at lectures given by de Vitry. Together with other discussions surviving from the 1320s (notably the *Ars nova musicae* of Jehan des Murs) they give a fairly clear account of the new notational system used by the French in the 14th century.

For the first time the minim is now fully accepted as a note value in its own right (an anonymous theorist hints that it was invented in the College of Navarre, Paris) rather than as a special (i.e. 'minimum') kind of semibreve. Moreover, the relationship between the semibreve and the minim is given exactly the same status as that previously accorded to both the long and breve, and the breve and semibreve (see Fig. 6*a*). A series of 'time signatures' (mensuration signs) eventually emerged which defined precisely the relationships between the various note values (see Fig. 6*b*). If there were three semibreves in the breve (i.e. perfect *tempus*) then this was shown by a perfect circle ○; imperfect *tempus* (two semibreves in the breve) was shown by the half circle ◡. Furthermore, a perfect or imperfect relationship between the semibreve and minim (prolation) was indicated by the presence or absence of a dot respectively. Thus, when both the *tempus* and prolation were imperfect, for example, the appropriate symbol was the half circle C on its own (incidentally, this is the origin of our present use of the C time signature for 2/4 and 4/4 time—it does not come from the initial letter of 'common time'!).

A brief illustration of the way in which the system worked can be seen from Machaut's *ballade* 'Ne pensez pas' in which both the *tempus* and prolation are perfect; this means that the piece is in ☉ time, but the time signature is not provided in the particular source shown (see Ex. 5). The practice of alteration and imperfection has already been discussed in relation to the breve and the long in the 13th century; but in the 14th century these operations were also extended to the semibreve/minim level (see Fig.

Ex. 5

(*a*) Facsimile of Machaut: 'Ne pensez pas' (Paris, Bibliothèque Nationale, MS frç. 1584)

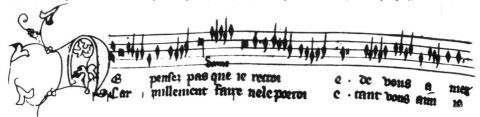

(*b*) Transcription

Fig. 6

FRENCH ARS NOVA NOTATION

(*a*) *Levels of operation*

(*b*) *Time signatures* (i = imperfect, p = perfect)

(*c*) *Coloration examples* (□ and ○ = red notes)

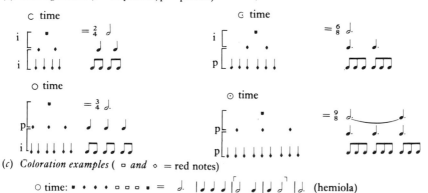

4c). For some time confusion existed between the preferred form for the semibreve and minim rests, both of which took up half a space on the staff. In the later 14th century the simple distinction arose of semibreve rests hanging ≡•≡ from the upper line, and minim rests standing ≡•≡ on the lower line; thus began the modern practice of 'semibreve suspends' ≡▪≡ and 'minim mounts' ≡▪≡ for these two rests.

Another innovation at this time was the use of red notes, or 'coloration' [sic], to indicate a reduction of one-third in the value of a note. Thus, a musical passage which would normally last for three bars in modern notation would, if written in coloration, fit into two bars (see Fig. 6c). If the red notes replace notes that are normally perfect then the result is 'across the bar' syncopation (hemiola). However, if they replace notes that are imperfect then triplets are produced. Modern editors usually indicate that a passage was originally written in coloration by enclosing the section in small brackets, thus ⌈ ⌉. Towards the end of the 14th century a highly complex form of notation and composition emerged known as *Ars subtilior* ('the more subtle art'). It involved the use of many kinds of colored notes, the simultaneous appearance of conflicting time signatures in different voices, extensive syncopation, and virtuoso canonic writing. The music itself was sometimes presented in a symbolic format such as a heart (for love-songs) or a circle (for canons). The subtle or 'mannered' style was mentioned by the theorists and composers Philipoctus de Caserta and Egidius de Murino. It was a fairly localized phenomenon found mostly in the music of composers associated with the papal court in Avignon, the court of Aragon in Spain, and the French colony of Cyprus. The *Ars subtilior* appeared alongside a more gradual evolution of the notational system; it had little lasting effect on the development of written music.

6. *Notation in the 15th and 16th Centuries*. A dramatic change in the appearance of notation came c.1420 when the solid black notes of earlier periods were replaced by void notes (compare Exx. 5 and 7). This was because paper replaced parchment as a writing surface about this time, and the concentration of ink needed for black notation tended to eat through the paper rather quickly; the solution was simply to put the notation in outline. Furthermore, it then became possible to show colored notes as solid black rather than in red which had required a change of ink. Black coloration can be seen in Ex. 6a which shows the tenor part of a 15th-century English Mass; it also contains an instance of imperfection by a remote value (see Fig. 4d) since the opening maxima is imperfected by a semibreve.

Some impression of the use of ligatures can be gleaned from Ex. 6; a summary explanation of their meaning is given in Fig. 7. Ligatures originated in plainchant notation (see above, 2) where a single ligature contained a group of notes sung to just one syllable of text. By the 15th century parts containing ligatures were not always texted, but when they were it was still

Ex. 6

(a) Facsimile of Anon: Gloria *Quem malignus spiritus* (Cambridge, University Library, MS I i. v. 18, folio 222)

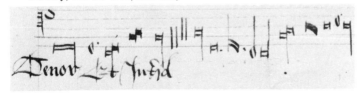

(b) Transcription

rare to find a ligature setting more than one syllable of text. In the 16th century it became common for several notes setting just one syllable to be written not as a ligature but as individual notes under a slur sign, just as we do today:

A ——— men   instead of   A—men

This practice, together with the proliferation of smaller note values (which had no equivalents in ligature form), the difficulty of using ligature forms in printed music (which became common after 1501), the unsuitability of ligatures for music written in score (which became the norm after c.1590), and the relative complexity of ligatures, led to their demise by c.1600. However, the ligature equivalent to two semibreves persisted for some time and is still found in Fux's works in the early 18th century. Modern editors indicate groups of notes originally written as a single ligature by enclosing them under a square bracket ⌐⌐ (see Ex. 6b).

By the early 16th century a complex system of special time signatures and numbers had evolved, called 'proportional notation', which indicated that notes could be sung at other than their normal speeds. Clever canons and intricate syncopations were written using augmented or diminished values of notes, but composers also exploited the system to write relatively fast music without using lots of small note values— they simply used semibreves and minims sung at twice their normal speeds. To indicate double-speed performance they modified the original time signature by putting a stroke through it; for example, four semibreves in C time, ◇ ◇ ◇ ◇ , would be sung in modern notation as ♩ ♩ ♩ ♩, but in ¢ time as ♫♫. When numbers were used as time signatures they indicated the relationship between the new and old (i.e. usual) value of a note. Thus, 4/3 meant that four notes (e.g. semibreves) at the new speed would be performed in the time of three at the usual speed (see Ex. 7). The system may seem to be a last vestige of Medieval complexity, but its concern with abstract numerical relationships stemmed rather from the neoplatonic movement of the Renaissance. Proportions played an important part in 'learned' music up to the time of Bach—they still have a shadowy existence in our use of C for *alla breve* music, and some other symbols.

Fig. 7

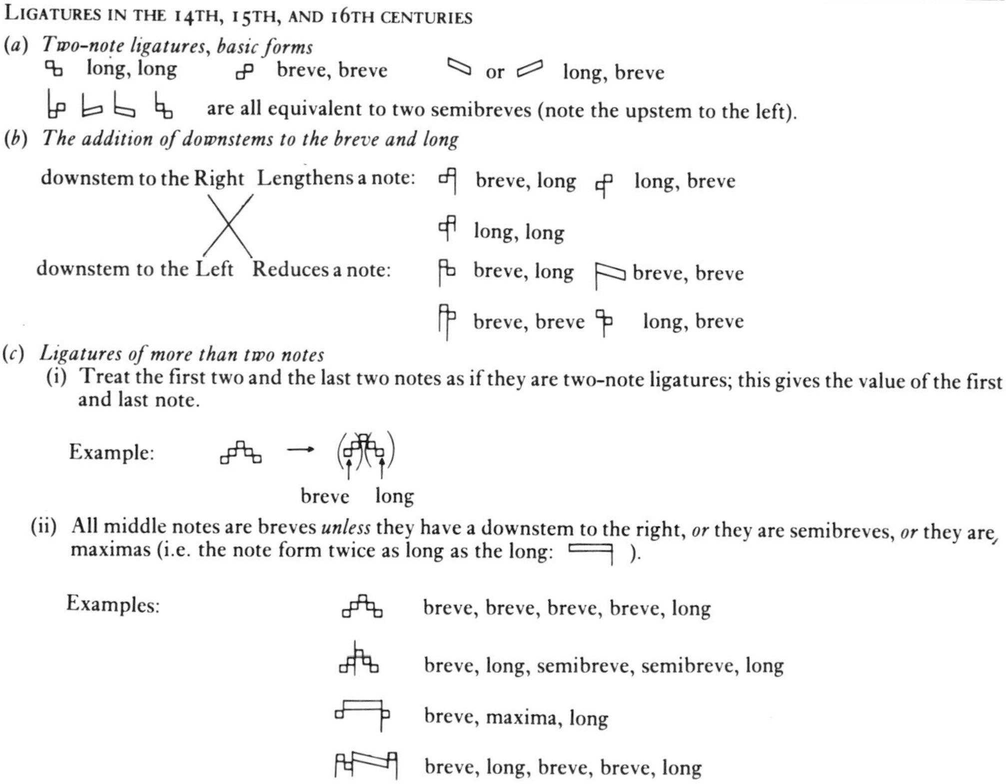

Ligatures in the 14th, 15th, and 16th centuries

(*a*) *Two-note ligatures, basic forms*

    ⌐ long, long   ⌐ breve, breve   ◣ or ◢ long, breve

    are all equivalent to two semibreves (note the upstem to the left).

(*b*) *The addition of downstems to the breve and long*

downstem to the Right Lengthens a note: breve, long   long, breve

    long, long

downstem to the Left Reduces a note: breve, long   breve, breve

    breve, breve   long, breve

(*c*) *Ligatures of more than two notes*

  (i) Treat the first two and the last two notes as if they are two-note ligatures; this gives the value of the first and last note.

    Example: → ( )

    breve   long

  (ii) All middle notes are breves *unless* they have a downstem to the right, *or* they are semibreves, *or* they are maximas (i.e. the note form twice as long as the long: ⌐⌐).

    Examples: breve, breve, breve, breve, long

                  breve, long, semibreve, semibreve, long

                  breve, maxima, long

                  breve, long, breve, breve, long

Ex. 7

(a) Facsimile of Gaffurius: *Practica musicae* (section on *sesquitertia* proportion; 1496)

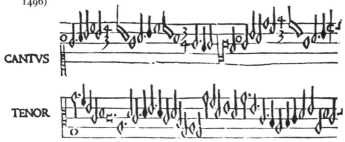

CANTVS

TENOR

(b) Transcription

etc.

etc.

Many of the details of present notational usage were established in instrumental music, particularly keyboard and lute compositions. The earliest extensive use of ties, slurs, and leger lines, for example, comes in Marco Antonio Cavazzoni's keyboard volume *Recerchari, motetti, canzoni* (*Venice*, 1523). Barlines, somewhat inconsistently used, occur as early as the 14th-century Faenza collection of keyboard music. In the 16th century we find Spanish lute composers (e.g. Narváez) barring their works regularly from 1538 onwards; however, each bar equalled only one semibreve (one crotchet in modern notation), and not until the mid 17th century do we find barlines arranged to coincide with regularly recurring accents in the music. It was also in the mid 17th century that accidentals became effective only for the bar in which they were found, though some attempt was made in the late 16th-century chromatic madrigals of Lassus and others to place accidentals consistently next to the note affected—a new practice. By the 15th century we find the natural sign ♮ used almost as frequently as the sharp ♯ and flat ♭ signs, and composers also began then regularly to use sharp 'key signatures' as well as the flat ones common in the Medieval period. The insertion of accidentals in the music by the performers (**musica ficta*) had been an important practice in the Medieval period but seems virtually to have disappeared by *c*.1600. It was quite common, however, for accidentals to apply to notes before the sign (i.e. to be retrospective) as well as to those immediately after.

Indications of pace are found as early as plainchant notation (see Fig. 1) but the consistent use of tempo markings began in the 16th century. In Luis de Milán's vihuela book *El maestro* (Valencia, 1536) each piece is prefaced by instructions which include tempo descriptions such as *apriessa* ('swift'), *espacio* ('slow'), and so on. The now standard Italian tempo markings (*allegro*, *largo*, etc.) did not become widespread until the mid 17th century, however, though they are found in the late 16th. This is also true of dynamic markings. Theoretical writers—e.g. Petrus de Canuntiis (1510)—discuss gradual dynamic shading fairly early on, but the earliest indication of volume in some actual music is found in the Capirola lute book of *c*.1517: the instruction *tocca pian' piano* ('play very softly') is given for one of the pieces. The *Sonata pian' e forte* (1597) by Giovanni Gabrieli is perhaps the most famous early example of specified dynamic contrast.

Score notation had been standard for the early Notre Dame sources of *c*.1200 (see Ex. 2), but in the late 13th-century motet the great difference in length between the upper texted parts and the tenor with its few long notes led to the separation of parts found in choirbook format (see Ex. 3). After the advent of music printing (1501) it became common for individual voices to be published separately in partbooks. It seems from remarks made by Pietro

Aaron (1523) and others that Josquin and Isaac adopted a way of writing their music in score format called *tabula compositoria*. Although keyboard works had appeared in a kind of score for at least two centuries, and although short vocal extracts appeared in theoretical works in score, it was only in England that score notation was used for some types of vocal music throughout the Medieval period. However, the earliest appearance of the modern score arrangement for vocal music complete with barlines came on the Continent with Cipriano de Rore's 1577 collection of four-voice madrigals published in Venice.

In 15th- and 16th-century vocal music standard clef combinations began to appear which probably indicated the usual voice ranges employed. In early printed sources, for example, soprano, alto, tenor, and bass were often signalled by three C clefs (on the lowest, and third and fourth lines up) and an F clef (on the fourth line up). Sometimes the standard combinations would appear transposed up or down a third (as in Palestrina's *Missa Papae Marcelli*) with the F clef on line 3, for example. This system is known as *chiavette* ('key code') and may have been used either to avoid leger lines or perhaps to signal transposition down a fourth or fifth. Our modern treble (or G) clef became fairly well established after c.1580; it is made up of two elements: 𝄞 for *signum* (sign) and the letter 𝑔 underneath: 𝄞–𝄞. The five-line staff was now standard except in English keyboard music which used six lines or more until c.1700.

From the 15th century on there was a progressive slowing down of the beat and shorter note values appeared, such as the semiquaver ♪, demisemiquaver ♫, and hemidemisemiquaver ♬. The English term 'crotchet' means 'crooked' and yet refers to a note without a crook, ♩ rather than ♪. This is because when

the change to void notation was made notes smaller than a minim were still shown black but with one less crook than previously. Thus the crotchet (Lat.: *crochata*) is the old semiminim which at one time did have a crook. The French, of course, use the term *croche* to refer to the modern note with a crook, the quaver; the crotchet is known to them as *noire*, the 'black' note. The Italians still sometimes refer to the crotchet as *semiminima*; the quaver they call *croma* (*cromatico* means 'coloured') because the quaver is a colored version of the old crooked semiminim. (See Fig. 8.) Towards the end of the 16th century, note forms became more rounded so that, for example, the semiminim ♩ came to look more like our modern crotchet ♩ .

7. *The 17th and 18th Centuries.* The Baroque period, like any other, was to some extent a time of transition. Archaic devices such as coloration, proportions, and ligatures are still found, though their use gradually became confined to certain genres or mannered effects. Coloration, for example, was frequently employed in the triple time sections of keyboard capriccios and courantes by Frescobaldi, Froberger, and others (see Ex. 8).

The black notes with stems in the second and subsequent bars of Ex. 8a look like crotchets but are actually colored minims with a value one-third of that of an ordinary minim (compare bar 1). This reduction of the minim value by two-thirds when colored was not usual in earlier centuries. We have already seen (section 5 and Fig. 6c) that the standard effect of coloration was to reduce a note by one-third of its value; this practice might well lie behind the Baroque device of the hemiola, or cross accent, approach to a cadence which is found frequently in Purcell and Handel (see Ex. 9).

The accents in the hemiola (3/2) bar come

Fig. 8

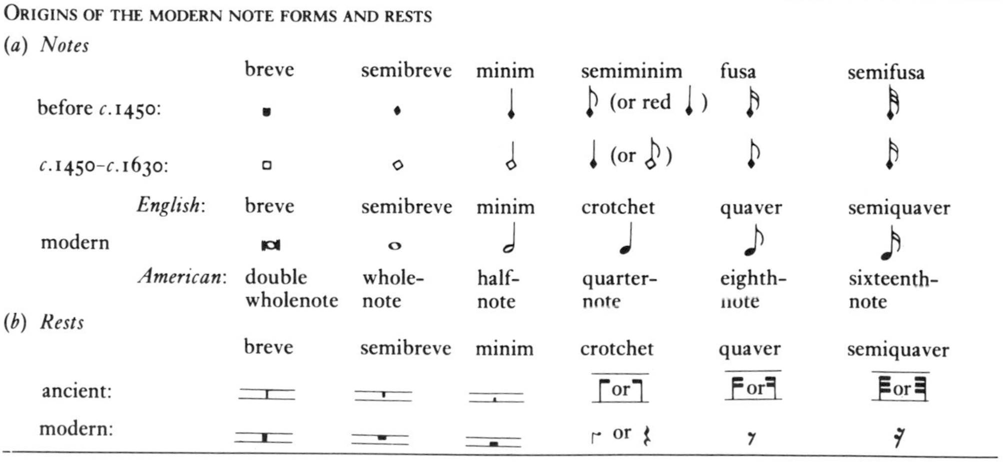

ORIGINS OF THE MODERN NOTE FORMS AND RESTS

(a) *Notes*

		breve	semibreve	minim	semiminim	fusa	semifusa
before c.1450:		▪	♦	♩	♪ (or red ♩)	♫	♬
c.1450–c.1630:		◻	◇	♩	♩ (or ♪)	♪	♪
modern	*English:*	breve	semibreve	minim	crotchet	quaver	semiquaver
		𝄺	𝅝	♩	♩	♪	♬
	American:	double wholenote	whole-note	half-note	quarter-note	eighth-note	sixteenth-note

(b) *Rests*

	breve	semibreve	minim	crotchet	quaver	semiquaver
ancient:	—	—	—	⌐ or ⌐	⌐ or ⌐	⌐ or ⌐
modern:	■	▬	▬	⌐ or 𝄽	𝄾	𝄿

every two beats whereas they had previously come every three, an effect which in earlier centuries had been produced by the use of coloration.

Proportional signs continued to be used, particularly by 'learned' composers writing in the *stile antico. The employment of numerical proportions (the use of 8/12 at the end of a passage in 12/8 to show a return to normal time, for example) was fairly straightforward. The use of proportional symbols, however, was frequently confused or inconsistent. For example, the sign ₵ traditionally indicated a quicker pace (diminution of note values) and was equivalent to 2/2 normally, but in the Credo of Bach's B Minor Mass it is used to mean 4/2 and by Schubert's time it is used for *adagio*.

Ex. 8

(*a*) Facsimile of Frescobaldi: *Il primo libro di capricci* (Venice, 1626)

(*b*) Transcription

[coloration section]

movements in the equivalent of 4/4. Such confusions are sometimes compounded by unscrupulous performers and publishers: for example, Mozart tells us (in a letter from Vienna, 7 June 1783) that Clementi may mark a sonata *prestissimo* and *alla breve* but play it only *allegro* and in 4/4 time. In general, Baroque and Classical music employed regular metres; there was a gradual acceptance of additive time signatures derived from such influences as the speech accents of *vers mesuré* (see *Musique mesurée*), though only rarely are such devices found in instrumental music—a famous example being the 5/8 'mad music' in Handel's *Orlando*.

With the growing interest in ornamentation and the greater use of smaller note values there was a gradual slowing up of the basic musical pulse. The minim was replaced by the crotchet as the main beat, but time signatures showing 4 rather than 2 as the denominator (3/4, 2/4) do not become common until the time of Corelli and Vivaldi. In any case, for duple time the old mensuration signs (C, ₵) were preferred, and straightforward numerical signatures (3, 3/2) were usually restricted to triple time for much of the 17th century. The notation and format of Baroque church music was often deliberately archaic, with its adherence to the old C clefs and the use of the minim rather than crotchet pulse. These 'antique' devices are found mostly in the works of Italians and of Germans who either worked in Italy or got to know the *stile antico* through anthologies of church music such as the one published in 1621 by Bodenschatz (Bach used Bodenschatz's work at Leipzig). Even today we still find hymn-books, psalters, Anglican chants, etc., written in archaic-looking

Ex. 9

Baroque use of hemiola, slurs, and beamed notes. Excerpt from Purcell: *Dido and Aeneas*, Act 3, 'Our next motion' (1689)

E – lis – sa   bleeds _____ to – night   and   Car –thage flames to – mor-row

Implied stress based on void and colored notes. Three colored notes are equivalent to two void ones (see Fig. 6c)

minims and semibreves—such is the pervasive influence of the *stile antico*.

In instrumental music and secular vocal music some far-reaching notational experiments took place. The G clef gained wide acceptance in French and English harpsichord music. In Italy and Germany the C clef was preferred for vocal and instrumental music alike; Mozart used it for many of his keyboard works, and it was not until Grétry published his *Memoires, ou Essai sur la musique* in 1789 that we find a real attempt to make G and F clefs standard for all music (Grétry was not entirely successful, of course). In spite of some early experiments with metronomes (Thomas Mace in 1676, Étienne Loulié in 1696, etc.) and notwithstanding the fact that many dance forms had their own conventions of pace, tempo was usually indicated by descriptive words. The terms *adagio*, *allegro*, and *presto* all appear in Banchieri's *Organo suonarino* of 1612, and in 1683 Purcell tells us (introduction to *Sonnata's of III Parts*) that Italian descriptions are in international use. Corelli is one of the earliest composers to provide descriptive tempo markings for everything he published, and a substantial list of such terms is included in Brossard's *Dictionaire de musique* (1703). In solo music the desire to translate into written notation the demands of ornamentation, free rhythm (in recitative, unmeasured harpsichord preludes by D'Anglebert and Louis Couperin, cadenzas in instrumental works, etc.), and performance experimentation (as in Heinrich Biber's *scordatura pieces) led to a wealth of new conventions.

In the Baroque, the use of the *basso continuo* and the growth of standard orchestral combinations led to a more uniform appearance in score format—particularly in some of the new genres such as the trio sonata and opera. When used, vocal parts were placed above the continuo part and in the string section violins appeared above the violas. Brass parts were placed at the top of the page. The function of the score remained ambiguous, however, and not until Purcell's *Diocletian* (1691) and Pepusch's edition of Corelli's sonatas (1732) do we find the idea of *Urtext study scores becoming established. Improved methods of engraving in the 18th century contributed to the great increase in the production of scores though it was still not absolutely standard practice to conduct from them. The French composer Habeneck, for example, was still conducting from the first violin part alone as late as the 1820s. Although bar-lines had been used in some keyboard music since at least the 14th century it was not until the late 1600s that they were carefully arranged to coincide with accents in the music. Additionally, a comparison of Exx. 8a and 10 reveals that only in the latter do notes appearing together vertically always sound together; the careful spacing of all parts horizontally even within the bar so as to cover the same musical time in the same distance was not really established until *c*.1650. Again, it was only in the late 17th century that bar-lines were finally understood to terminate the effect of accidentals and that the practice of applying accidentals retrospectively ceased. As for the accidentals themselves, the use of the symbols ♯, ♭, and ♮ for sharp, flat, and natural became universal and the modern form of the double flat (♭♭) and double sharp (×) became accepted—the latter makes an appearance as early as 1615 in Trabaci's *Il secondo libro de ricercare*.

Subtle changes also took place in some of the finer details of notation. Ex. 9 illustrates how slurs were now used to join together notes sung to the same syllable of text (a function previously carried out by ligatures) and that, within the same bar, notes sung to the same syllable were beamed together (♫) rather than written separately (♪ ♪). The beaming together of smaller note values is also found fairly early in instrumental music, though not until Beethoven's Rondo in Op. 10 No. 3 (1793) are notes beamed across a bar-line (♫♫). Clearly the beam came to have implications for accentuation and phrasing, as did the slur sign. The slur effect is described as early as Ortiz's *Trattado* of 1553, but signs indicating this became common only in the Baroque; later (in Bach, Mozart, etc.) the slur sign was occasionally used to indicate a *glissando*. An early example of careful phrase marking occurs in Cavalieri's *La rappresentatione di Anima e di Corpo* (1600) where a special sign (⸓) is placed above the final note of each phrase. The expressive importance of phrasing was increasingly recognized and in the 18th century was extensively discussed by writers such as Johann Mattheson.

The preoccupation with expression and articulation not only led to more dramatic styles of music and performance (*Empfindsamer Stil, *Sturm und Drang, the *Mannheim 'Rocket', etc.) but also to a host of ancillary symbols and instructions within the notation. We find bowing marks (e.g. in Corelli's *Follia*, Op. 5 No. 12, of 1700), fingering indications (as early as some sources of English virginal music), and, in the late 18th century, pedalling signs for the pianoforte (perhaps as in Haydn's Sonata in C, HXVI: 50, written *c*.1794–5, though it is possible that these were intended as *una corda* signs). Gradual changes of dynamic had been a desirable musical effect since at least the 16th century (they are described in treatises by Zarlino, Ganassi, etc.) and *crescendo*, *diminuendo*, and other markings were used extensively by Vivaldi and others in the Baroque period. It is certainly misleading to think that the Baroque was concerned only with terraced dynamics; the role of the relatively inflexible harpsichord, both soloistically and as part of the *basso continuo*, has probably over-influenced our resistance to dynamic shading in this music.

No aspect of Baroque notation is more contentious than the interpretation of dotted rhythms. A dot after a note ordinarily meant that it was half as long again as its normal value, but otherwise the dot simply signified that the notes on either side were irregular in some way. A dotted note might be used to assimilate duple to triple rhythms (Fig. 9*a*). The use of the dot was necessary here because the notational conventions of  did not exist until the 19th century. The only alternative was

to use such devices as introducing passages of 9/8 into music written in 3/4. It is by no means certain that the assimilation of dotted duplets in one part to triplets in another was always intended; Quantz (in his *Versuch einer Anweisung die Flöte traversiere zu spielen*, chapter 5, part 22) argues against it and, at a later date, Czerny in his account of Beethoven's playing of the 'Moonlight' Sonata felt it necessary to point out that the dotted and triplet rhythms were not synchronized. In some cases the meaning of dots is fairly clear as they are discussed unambiguously by theorists and/or appear in self-explanatory music examples. A dot might be used to increase the length of a note by more or less than the usual half (see Fig. 9*b*), or be used to show that a note is tied across a barline (Fig. 9*c*).

Fig. 9

IRREGULAR AND NOVEL USES OF THE DOT IN THE 17TH AND 18TH CENTURIES

(*a*) *Assimilation of duplet to triplet rhythm*

played

i.e.

(from C. P. E. Bach: *Versuch über die wahre Art das Clavier zu spielen* (1753), pt i, ch. iii, 27)

(*b*) *Dot used as a tie of irregular length*

(from C. P. E. Bach: *Versuch*, pt i, ch. iii, 23)

(NB. Dot increases quaver length by one-quarter, not one-half.)

meaning

(from F. Couperin: *Nouveaux Concerts* (1724), no. xiv, Prelude, bar 1)

(NB. Dot increases length of crotchet by nine-sixteenths.)

(*c*) *Dot used as a tie across the bar-line*

...an-xious care_____ and strife...

etc.

(from Purcell: *The Fairy Queen* (1692), 'Thrice Happy Lovers'; London, Royal Academy of Music, MS 1)

(*d*) *Double dot*

(from Chambonnières: *Pièces de Clavecin*, livre premier (1670), Courante, p. 51)

The possible application by the performer of dotted or unequal rhythms to undotted notes (*notes inégales*) creates problems best approached through the history of *performance practice since it is precisely the lack of notational guidance that leads to difficulties in resurrecting this practice. For the question of *over-dotting in the so-called 'French overture style' the notational evidence is a little more suggestive. It was Prout in his late 19th-century editions of Handel who first established the idea that rhythms written as ♩. ♪ and ♫ in French overture movements should be played as ♩.. ♪ and ♫ . However, Handel's copyist, John Smith the younger, when transcribing the overture to *Amadigi*, for example, made a careful distinction between the two rhythms ♩. ♪ and ♩. 𝄾 ♪ both in notation and spacing (see Ex. 10, last half of bar 10). The over-dotting of single dotted notes is clearly mentioned by writers such as Quantz (*Versuch*, chapter 5, part 21) but there is no reference to the French style and Quantz is speaking of soloistic rather than orchestral or ensemble music. Such references should probably be taken as a description of the new German *galant* style of soloistic playing rather than as retrospective references to a 'French overture style' convention. Incidentally, although double dots do appear in notation from the 17th century onward (see Fig. 9*d*), their use is not widespread until the very late 18th century—of Haydn's 60-odd keyboard sonatas, for example, only one (Hob. XVI: 52, written in 1794) employs the double dot.

8. *From the 19th Century to the Present Day.* Over the last 200 years the gradual separation of the role of composer and performer has contrived to increase the level of explicit instruction in music and the printed score has become the paramount intermediary between composer and public. Laws governing music copyright were set up at various times and places in the last century (see *Copyright*) but, as the quarrels between Verdi and his publisher Ricordi show, these did not guarantee that the printed score necessarily represented the composer's preferred version. The layout of the score was becoming more standard, though certain instruments such

as the harp and the bass clarinet never found a stable place and the horn was something of an anomaly (Wagner placed it between the clarinets and bassoons). The treatises on orchestration written by Berlioz, Rimsky-Korsakov, and others did not really solve all the problems of score layout, partly because they did not directly tackle the question of standardized formats.

Traditionally, transposing instruments were not written at sounding pitch, but with the highly chromatic music of the early 20th century there came a tendency to write all parts in C (as in, for example, Schoenberg's Variations for Orchestra, Op. 31, 1927–8). The same chromaticism led to the abandonment of key signatures by certain composers: Schoenberg (in the Second String Quartet), Busoni (in the *Sonata seconda*), and others simply prefaced each note with the required accidental. Experiments also took place with quartertones (e.g. in Alois Hába's Second String Quartet, 1920), which were written using such signs as ⧻ and ⧣ ; later on Hába and others employed sixth-tones and other microtones using a variety of *ad hoc* notational symbols. In jazz and popular music there have been simplifications of notational calligraphy, with sharp and flat signs, for example, being written as + and − respectively.

It is only in recent years that composers have shown an overwhelming preference for G and F clefs. C clefs are found in much music by Wagner, Brahms, and Schoenberg, in all kinds of Italian vocal music, and for certain instruments (e.g. violas, bassoons) or parts of their ranges. The use of semibreve rests to indicate a whole bar's rest in whatever time became common in the late 19th century. Compositions beginning with a bar's rest (or its equivalent) are known from as early as the 15th century (in works by Frye, Busnois, etc.), and from at least the 18th century we find pieces ending with a bar's rest (e.g. Mozart's Piano Sonata K 283)—perhaps intended as a silent completion of phrasing or as an imposed moment of repose. In the early 20th century the use of bar-lines simply to mark out a regular grid of time was abandoned and the performer was instead guided to the perhaps irregular points of stress;

Ex. 10

Facsimile of Handel: Overture to *Amadigi*, bars 10–11, transcribed for harpsichord by J. C. Smith (New York Public Library, Music Division: Astor, Lenox, and Tilden Foundation, MS Drexel 5856).

Stravinsky's Symphony of Psalms, for example, has bars of 1/4 for this purpose. Later in this century 'bar-lines' came to be used merely as reference points in time/space notation measured in seconds (see below, Ex. 13). They also show points of synchronization between passages of improvisation. Ties across the bar-line are usually indicated in the modern manner, though Brahms (or his publisher) occasionally uses a dot on the other side of the bar-line in the manner of Fig. 9c.

Partly as the result of a Romantic striving for individuality, the treatment of tempo and pulse became more erratic and extreme. In Beethoven's music any note from the semi-quaver to the minim is capable of functioning as the main beat. (It is even possible that the semibreve was intended to be the main beat in the original version of the Trio from his Ninth Symphony.) Dance movements no longer keep to traditional speeds (minuets became scherzos, and many Chopin waltzes are too quick for the feet to follow); however, genre tempo indications are still found convenient in some areas, a modern example being 'Tempo di Blues'. Nineteenth-century virtuosos such as Liszt and Paganini simply played some of their own music as fast as possible. The 20th-century composer Stockhausen actually gives the tempo indication 'fastest speed possible' in some sections of his *Zeitmasse* (1956); Schumann makes the same request in his Second Sonata Op. 22, and then directs 'faster and yet faster'! In the 19th century there are several instances where composers' metronomic markings seem too fast, or unplayable (e.g. in Beethoven, Schumann, and Reger).

The notation of rhythm still continued to harbour ambiguities. For example, there are undotted demisemiquavers in the Arietta of Beethoven's Sonata Op. 111 (bar 50), some of which are 'perfect' (i.e. worth three hemidemi-semiquavers) and some 'imperfect' (worth only two). Again, there is some evidence that the dotted rhythms in the accompaniment of Schubert's *Wasserflut* from *Winterreise* should be synchronized with the triplets in the vocal part (in the manner of Fig. 9a), and a similar problem arises in some of the chorus parts of Verdi's operas. Tody there are still certain genres where a conventional 'bending' of the rhythm is understood rather than notated (e.g. in the Viennese waltz, swing, jazz).

Conventions were still important in the execution of written ornamentation in the early 19th century, or even in the addition of unwritten ornamentation (e.g. in *bel canto* operas by Bellini and others, where the 'score' was really a conglomeration of set pieces and substitute arias lacking the fixed quality found, say, in the form of the German symphony); 19th-century treatises on the notation and interpretation of ornamentation survive by Clementi, Cramer, Hummel, Spohr, and many others. Later, ornamentation became absorbed into the style so that, in Chopin's Étude No. 13 (Op. 25 No. 1), for example, the main melody is picked out in larger notes with the ornamental decoration fully written out in smaller ones. In early Wagner scores we find *gruppetti* signs and the like, but later (as in Brünnhilde's main theme in the *Ring*) the 'ornamentation' is fully written out. With Mahler, ornamentation becomes completely absorbed into the style: the long appoggiatura, for example, is now recognized as an essential feature of his thematic identity. In the 20th century there has been some reintro-duction of the old ornamentation signs under the influence of neo-classicism, such as the upper and lower *mordent signs found in some works by Tippett.

The concern for virtuosity and expressive-ness in the 19th century naturally resulted in an increased concern for the notation of articula-tion, phrasing, and expressive nuance. *Staccato* marks (·), accents (>), and *tenuto* lines (–) had, of course, been available for some time, but they now became used much more frequently and in combinations which are not always unambiguous or even practicable. Bartók's *Mikrokosmos* piece No. 146, for example, has *vivacissimo* quavers, each of which is marked with an accent, a *tenuto*, and a *staccato* sign. Stravinsky has used a *tenuto* plus staccato sign (⁻) to mean 'sharp attack without accent'. Composers such as Stockhausen have invented further articulation signs such as ⸙ to mean 'hardest attack possible'.

The slur sign is particularly ambiguous as it can imply *legato* performance, breathing or bowing breaks, correct phrasing, and so on. Nineteenth-century editions by Czerny (of piano music), Ferdinand David (of string music), Riemann (of early music etc.), and others often sought to clarify matters of phrasing and expression with a welter of editorial markings. Composers, too, became more aware of the different levels of articulation within music, and we find in Reger and Mahler, among others, a proliferation of suggestive signs (see Ex. 11) which, in the last analysis, are often ambiguous to a greater or a lesser degree. As early as Beethoven we find the slur sign used to

Ex. 11

Mahler: 2nd Symphony; 4th movement, bb. 45-7

Slur signs indicating three levels of articulation.

mean both a slur and a tie at one and the same time (in the Adagio of the Piano Sonata Op. 110, or the Allegro of the *Grosse Fuge*, Op. 133); the indication ♩♩ suggests perhaps a sense of division within a single note or maybe a slight *decrescendo*. The great length of many musical phrases led Debussy to indicate their beginnings and endings separately with a broken slur sign, as in *La fille aux cheveux de lin* (incidentally, the score of this work contains the innovation of placing the title at the end). The articulation of the principal strand in a complex polyphonic texture preoccupied Schoenberg, who devised the two signs Ⓗ (*Hauptstimme* (Ger.), 'head voice') and Ⓝ (*Nebenstimme* (Ger.), 'subsidiary voice'); the former is the more frequently used, as can be seen in Schoenberg's Third String Quartet.

Dynamic levels have become more extreme in music since the 18th century. Romantic composers naturally used *fff* or *ppp* as one of several theatrically dramatic effects in their works (though Tchaikovsky's use of *pppppp* in his Sixth Symphony is perhaps a little absurd). Changes of dynamic have been used with increasing frequency even in short passages of music: in 20th-century works such as Stockhausen's *Kreuzspiel* and Xenakis's *Herma* many of the notes carry their own dynamic markings (in the latter the speed is so great that accurate performance seems impossible). Experiments have been made to indicate dynamics not by traditional methods (*ff*, *pp*, etc.) but by the size of note-head (e.g. in Stockhausen's *Zyklus*), numerical scales (e.g. in Cage's *Changes*), and other devices. Since the advent of total serialism dynamic levels have been used in a more schematic fashion as part of an integrated

control of the parameters of music within a work.

In the early 20th century the neo-classical composers (Stravinsky, Hindemith, etc.) had the intention, at least, of minimizing the element of personal expression in music. On the one hand, this led to the sparing but meticulous notation of dynamic and tempo changes (e.g. in works by Stravinsky) and, on the other, to non-subjective approaches such as the use of tape-recordings (e.g. by Stockhausen) or of chance rather than artistic choice to govern the direction and emphasis of a work (e.g. in pieces by Cage). Electronic scores are often, in part, instruction manuals showing precisely how sounds are to be reproduced. In Ex. 12, for instance, each block in the top half represents one sound made up of five frequencies (pitches) of which the highest and the lowest are defined. Overlapping mixtures of sounds are shown by darker shading. The frequency scale on the left-hand edge ranges from 100 to 17,200 cycles per second. The duration of each sound is shown by the centre line which is calibrated in centimetres allowing for a tape speed of 76.2 cm. per second. The lower half of the graph shows the intensity of sound (loudness and attack/decay elements) measured in decibels ranging from 0 to −30. This notation still bears some resemblance to conventional scores (duration moves from left to right, pitch is shown by height or depth, etc.) but some more recent *computer notations (e.g. MUSICOMP developed at the University of Illinois, MUSYS as used by the Electronic Music Studio in Putney, London) are highly sophisticated 'machine languages' for controlling and manipulating acoustical equipment; their visual appearance is no longer obviously analogous to

Ex. 12

Stockhausen: *Elektronische Studien II*, opening page

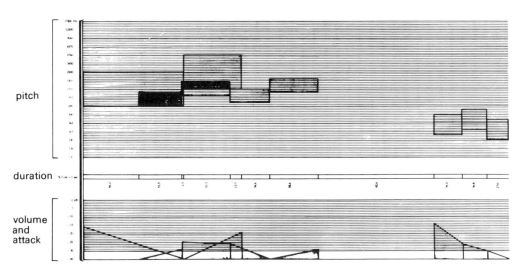

pitch

duration

volume and attack

the gestures in the resultant music. Not surprisingly, there has been an increased importance given to score prefaces in the 20th century, where notational problems and devices are explained.

Some types of aleatoric music allow random events outside the control of the performer to become part of the music (as in the 'silent' piano piece by Cage, *4'33"*), while others attempt to provoke the musician into a subjective response. This latter approach (often derived from Eastern mystical influences) frequently utilizes non-musical texts or pictures or musically suggestive shapes or graphs as its 'notation'. The 'score' of Earle Brown's *December 1952*, for example, consists of 13 black rectangles, and La Monte Young's *Piano Piece for David Tudor, No. 3* is comprised of the text, 'most of them were very old grasshoppers'. In the case of Cardew's *Treatise* (1963–7) we have a work which seems to have been constructed for its visual impact

Ex. 13

Penderecki: *Threnody*, sections 62 and 63

rather than its musical communicativeness. Less radical uses of aleatoric procedures are to be found in pieces by Stockhausen, Boulez, and others, where the performer is allowed some choice in the ordering of sections within a work (e.g. Stockhausen's *Klavierstücke XI*).

Apart from these avant-garde notations there has been a steady development of more traditional means, partly arising from new ways of using conventional instruments and the voice. The device of *Sprechgesang* first appeared in the first version of Humperdinck's *Königskinder* (1897), but it was developed mostly in the works of Schoenberg where it is indicated variously (in quavers for example) as ♪, ♪, or ♪. The expansion of string playing technique has been a particular interest of Eastern European composers. Bartók employed devices such as bowing with the wood of the bow (found at least as early as Berlioz's *Symphonie fantastique*) and a type of 'thwack' *pizzicato* which he indicated by the symbol ♪ . The Polish composer Penderecki has taken up and greatly expanded the use of such devices. Ex. 13 is from Penderecki's

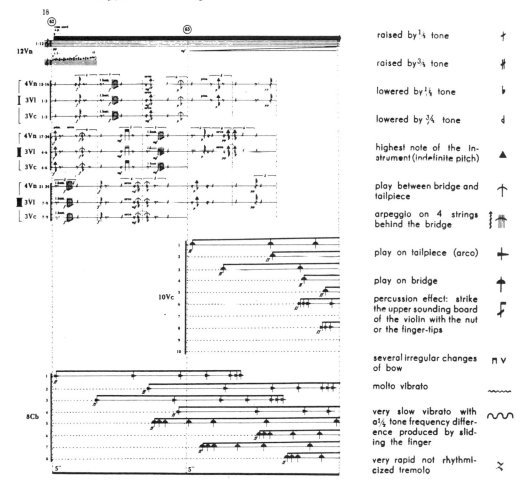

Threnody for 52 stringed instruments with an explanatory table (provided by the composer) showing the different techniques used. On the top staff there is the now common device of a note cluster (first developed in the USA by such composers as Ives and Cowell) in which, in this case, all the quartertones between two defined extremes are played together. Note also that duration is measured in seconds at the bottom, with the 'bar-lines' acting merely as points of reference.

Finally, the 20th century has spawned a number of didactic and academic notations. Of the former, one might mention the piano notation *Klavarscribo*, in which black and white notes are shown by black and void note-heads; *Equitone*, in which successive notes appear as black or void between two lines an octave apart; and 'shape notes', used by folk-singers and others. The disciplines of *ethnomusicology and musical *analysis have both developed their own notations, the former for recording non-Western musics, the latter for distinguishing between foreground and background materials and more or less significant harmonic events.

ANTHONY PRYER

FURTHER READING
Arnold Dolmetsch: *The Interpretation of the Music of the Seventeenth and Eighteenth Centuries* (London, 1915, rev. edn Washington, DC, 1969); Willi Apel: *The Notation of Polyphonic Music, 900-1600* (Cambridge, Massachusetts, 1942, rev. edn 1970); Carl Parrish: *The Notation of Medieval Music* (New York, 1957, 2nd edn 1959); Robert Donington: *The Interpretation of Early Music* (London, 1963, 3rd edn 1974); Erhard Karkoschka: *Das Schriftbild der neuen Musik* (Celle, 1966, Eng. trans. 1972); Hans Keller: *Phrasing and Articulation* (London, 1966); Hugo Cole: *Sounds and Signs: Aspects of Musical Notation* (Oxford, 1974).

Note. Written sign representing the pitch and/or duration of a musical sound. In English terminology the word has two further meanings: (1) the key of a keyboard instrument; and (2) the actual sound produced.

Notes inégales (Fr., 'unequal notes'). The rhythmic alteration of groups of notes which are written evenly, generally involving the lengthening of the first of a (generally) consecutive pair of notes and the corresponding shortening of the second; very occasionally the reverse happens, giving a rhythm like the *Scotch snap.

Inequality was rarely notated in French music, but was sometimes indicated by the written word *pointé* and cancelled by *égales*. Disjunct notes were rarely played as *inégales*, and when they were intended to be were usually written out.

In the 17th century, a general rule was that inequality was applied to the quickest prevailing notes in a given metre—usually semiquavers in 4/4 and 2/4 time, quavers in 2/2 and ₵ time, quavers in 3/4, 6/4, 9/4, and 12/4 time, and semiquavers in all metres with a denominator of eight. Some composers notated inequality by using dots, but generally they were wary of this since it implied strict dotted rhythm. True inequality varied from *louré*—a barely perceptible lilt in which the first of a pair of notes received slightly more time than the second—to *pointé*, which more nearly approached dotted rhythm. In between is a kind of triplet rhythm. Such nuances were left to the performer's discretion, and in vocal music he or she was expected to take the sense of the words into account when deciding how to apply *inégales*.

In most sources from outside France, inequality was notated by the composer; it occurs, for example, in music by Locke, Purcell, Clarke, and Handel. There is much controversy over its application to Italian music: some contemporary sources (e.g. Michel Corrette's flute Tutor, 1748) say that it was used in Italian music, others (e.g. Rousseau, 1768) that it was not. François Couperin seems undecided. It is therefore hardly surprising that 20th-century scholars argue endlessly on the subject and that no satisfactory compromise has been reached.

In Germany, pieces in the French style were treated as if they were French, i.e. with inequality. *Inégales* were clearly explained by Lully's pupil Georg Muffat in his *Florilegium primum* (1695), and other composers who employed the French style include Froberger, Buxtehude, Telemann, and Bach. However, only Quantz, in his celebrated treatise on flute playing (1752), actually states that the use of *inégales* was common in Germany, and even he does not clarify whether they should be used only in French-style German music. As with other unwritten musical conventions, the final decision as to when and whether to use *notes inégales* must be left to the performer.

See also *Dot*, 3.   WENDY THOMPSON

Notker (*b* nr St Gall, Switzerland, *c*.840; *d* St Gall, 912). Benedictine monk and scholar. He was the author of a book of Latin texts for the liturgical sequence, the *Liber hymnorum*, which appeared in 884, and is one of the few Medieval writers of liturgical texts known by name to whom specific texts can be ascribed. He is sometimes referred to as 'Balbulus' ('stammerer'). Notker's preface to the *Liber hymnorum* explains the nature and function of the sequence and describes how Notker originally came to write the verses. In all, he wrote texts for about 35 sequences, which are distinguished by their originality and an effective use of imagery. Where the *Liber hymnorum* links Notker's texts with specific melodies it has provided scholars with a reliable means of dating a large group of Medieval liturgical chants. See also *Sequence*, 2.

JUDITH NAGLEY

Notre Dame Mass. Mass by Machaut for four voices, a setting of six movements of the Mass Ordinary, including the 'Ite missa est'. It is the earliest four-part setting of the Mass Ordinary, dating from the mid 14th century.

Notturnino (It.). A miniature *nocturne.

Notturno (It.). See *Nocturne*.

Novák, Vítězslav (*b* Kamenice nad Lipou, 5 Dec. 1870; *d* Skuteč, 18 July 1949). Czech composer and teacher. Novák had a difficult childhood, dogged by illness and, after his father's death, poverty. He received some musical education at Jindřichův Hradec and then studied piano and composition at the Prague Conservatory while nominally pursuing a university course in law. A bad start with the harmony teacher Knittl led to a crisis in confidence which was only partly ameliorated by transferring to Dvořák's composition class. Though he often disagreed with Dvořák, he found his teaching stimulating and began to compose seriously. In an attempt to establish an artistic personality he made a study of Moravian and Slovakian folk melody, and was often to resort to these themes or their contours for compositional material rather than better-known Bohemian models. In 1909 Novák was appointed professor of composition at the Prague Conservatory, but after 1910 his popularity and more gradually his influence on younger composers declined, and in later life he was often accused of being reactionary. His preoccupation with nature and tendency to introspection led to some deeply felt programme works: the symphonic poems *V Tatrách* ('In the High Tatras', 1902) and *O věčné touze* ('Of Eternal Longing', 1905). His interest in monothematicism caused him to experiment with the metamorphosis of a single theme as in the piano suite *Pan* (1910) and cyclic structure as in the *Trio quasi una ballata* (1902) and the Second String Quartet Op. 35 (1905). In the 1920s Novák composed more for the stage, including two satirical ballet-pantomimes and the still popular *Lucerna* (1922). Novák's musical language owed much to his teacher Dvořák, though Strauss and Debussy were also important in forming his style. But despite the range of influence his music is both individual and original, particularly in his use of contrapuntal textures, and sets him apart as a major figure in 20th-century Czech music.

JAN SMACZNY

Novel, Music in the. Literary people—poets, philosophers, novelists—have frequently been suspicious of music. Its abstraction, its lack of morality, its connection with primal and charismatic forces, as well as its beauties, are all a challenge to the rationality of language and ideas of the ethical responsibility of art. Plato, Rousseau, and Tolstoy have all stood in this same adverse position, and vainly attempted to censor the expressive powers of music, leaving only its jolly and rousing capacities. Another tradition of thinkers has been troubled by music's failure to fit the theory of *mimesis*—art as imitation of nature, a holding-up of a mirror to life—and one of the first premonitions of *Romanticism is the acknowledgement in the middle of the 18th century that music evokes feelings rather than reflects realities. In Germany particularly, music was assigned to the realm of poetic inspiration and divine madness, embodying passion, yearning, melancholy, restlessness, and demonic energy. The startling harmonic and rhythmic innovations of works such as Mozart's *Don Giovanni* and Beethoven's Fifth Symphony fired and fuelled this new attitude towards the turn of the century, which culminates in Schopenhauer's belief in the mystical supremacy of music over all other art-forms.

Yet the first novelist to be seriously involved with music had no very exalted conceptions of it. Marie-Henri Beyle, alias Stendhal (1783–1842), had little technical knowledge and very lopsided tastes. He scarcely mentions Beethoven, and generally disliked instrumental music. His *Vies de Haydn, Mozart, et Metastasie* is a monument to plagiarism, while the *Vie de Rossini* and his largely musical travel-books are rambling, factually unreliable, and filled with records of the lost and forgotten. Yet Stendhal is one of the most entertaining and enthusiastic of musical littérateurs. His is music criticism for the common man, and a great part of its charm is that he associated music with happy sensual pleasure, brilliance, and wit. More than anything, he loved the music of Italy (from Pergolesi onwards) for its natural abundance of melody and vivacity, and regarded Rossini as 'the greatest living artist of our time'. This was an opinion deliberately designed to infuriate the complacent Parisian bourgeoisie which Stendhal so despised, but he does succeed in making a serious critical case for early operas like *Tancredi* and *La pietra del paragone* which are now little appreciated. He recognizes that 'it is desperately easy to hear too much of Rossini's music' and deplores its lack of 'true passion', yet he remains captivated not only by its extrovert and physical excitement, but also by the whole ambience of Italian opera—the personalities of the singers, the temperament of the audiences, and the high society of La Scala, with its '200 miniature salons which go by the name of boxes' and the foyer which served as 'a rendezvous for all the rakes and dandies in Milan'. It was all scarcely respectable, and for that alone Stendhal was infatuated.

Throughout the 19th-century novel, the Italian opera maintained its position as a place of intrigue, usually amorous. Stendhal's great successor Flaubert set one of the most pathetic scenes of *Madame Bovary* at a performance of *Lucia di Lammermoor* (a scene itself recalled by E. M. Forster in *Where Angels Fear to Tread*, where English ladies, attending a provincial Italian performance of *Lucia*, are appalled by the moral turpitude around them). Emma Bovary provides an example of the complete Romantic submission to music: it 'sent a vibration . . . through her whole being, as if the bows of the violins were being drawn across her own nerves', and Lucia becomes further food for poor Emma's fantasies. Tolstoy takes the moral dangers of music even further in *The Kreutzer Sonata*, where the erotic charge and tension in the first movement of Beethoven's violin sonata precipitates adultery between its players.

Music in the English novel is altogether a primmer affair. Jane Austen, touched with honest English philistinism, is not much interested in High Art. Music in her books is acceptable as a social accomplishment and an ornament to femininity (none of her heroes is susceptible to music): Emma Woodhouse claims, 'If I give up music, I shall take up carpet-work'—the two have an equal validity. An excessive attachment to music is generally the subject of mockery: Marianne in *Sense and Sensibility* 'spent whole hours at the piano-forte alternately singing and crying', while Mrs Elton in *Emma* coos 'I am dotingly fond of music—passionately fond . . . I absolutely cannot do without music: it is a necessary of life to me'. Yet the later novels do also show music as a comfort to the solitary: Emma's rival Jane Fairfax, a true musician, has nothing but her mysteriously donated piano to give solace, while it is remarked of Anne Elliot, the dignified heroine of *Persuasion*, that 'in music she had been always used to feel alone in the world'.

A generation later, in George Eliot's novels, we breathe a finer air, and music becomes something much more intimate and emotional, as well as serious. Philip Wakem, in *The Mill on the Floss*, is the Novel's first musical intellectual: he finds in Haydn's *Creation* 'a sort of sugared complacency and flattering make-believe . . . as if it were written for the birthday fête of a German Grand Duke'. The Vincys' musical evening in *Middlemarch* contains more sophisticated music than the inane country dances which make up Lady Catherine de Burgh's after-dinner recitals in *Pride and Prejudice*: Rosamund Vincy has been taught by 'one of those excellent musicians here and there to be found in our provinces, worthy to compare with many a noted *Kapellmeister*', and Lydgate senses 'a hidden soul . . . flowing forth' as she plays the piano. George Eliot was a first-class amateur herself, as well as being a regular concert-goer. She was in personal association with the contemporary musical *haut monde*, knew Liszt and Anton Rubinstein well, and entertained the Wagners on their visit to London in 1877 (although she admitted to being baffled by Wagner's music). This all bore fruit in the superb portrait of Klesmer in *Daniel Deronda*, the ferocious middle-European composer, dedicated to 'the music of the future', but stuck incongruously amidst the Midlands gentry and drawing-room singers like Gwendolen Harleth, who want to use music only as a ladder to fame and wealth. Klesmer would doubtless have been happier in the cultivated Schlegel household of Forster's *Howards End*, even if he would have detested the tiresome whimsy of Helen Schlegel's famous 'analysis' of Beethoven's Fifth Symphony—surely the nadir in the treatment of music by literature.

No composer has had such a profound effect on literature as Wagner. It was not just the idea of 'music drama' (the most obviously literary of musical forms) and the literary parallels to the *Leitmotiv* which excited writers; it was also the overwhelming and unabashed egocentricity of the man and his music, its uncompromising vastness and sensuality. Wagner was the apotheosis of the Romantic ideal of The Artist, and even a brief list of his disciples shows the breadth of his influence—Baudelaire, Verlaine, Mallarmé, Shaw, Oscar Wilde, Lawrence. Two novelists stand out for the degree to which they exploited the Wagnerian possibilities—Proust and Thomas Mann. Proust's wonderful novel *A la recherche du temps perdu* is full of musical insight and rare musical taste (he champions Debussy's *Pelléas* and Beethoven's Op. 131 Quartet, for example). *A la recherche* also contains a staggering gallery of music snobs, for whom, even more than for Jane Austen's equivalents, music is material for elegant and misinformed chatter. One thinks of Madame Verdurin, whose spirit was so seared by Wagner that it gave her a headache; or the moment when the violinist Charlie Morel, begged in a society drawing-room to play Debussy's *Fêtes*, slyly modulates into a march by Meyerbeer without anyone noticing. Wagner is a presence throughout, not just at the level of headaches or the comparison of the ringing of a telephone to the Shepherd's piping in *Tristan*, but inasmuch as he informs the whole conception of the book. It could be said that *A la recherche* is the *Ring* of the Parisian salons—both long, intricate, subtle, complex works of art built, in Proust's words, on 'the indefinite perception of motifs which now and then emerge, barely discernible, to plunge again and disappear and drown', an accumulation of small units or themes, repeated, developed, and transformed, drawing constantly on the faculties of memory and the unconscious. This is most evident in the way Proust uses the invention of the 'little phrase' from Vinteuil's violin sonata, introduced as the 'national anthem' of Swann's love for Odette, but heard again in every context of tragic love—the narrator's passion for Albertine, or the Baron de Charlus' for Morel (himself a player of the Vinteuil sonata).

After the delicacy of Proust's cork-lined world, Thomas Mann's fiction appears somewhat flat-footed. His attempts to take Wagner's ideas of musical structure into literature are overly self-conscious. Proust's Wagnerism is impressionistic, its effects subconscious: Mann has a point to prove and an axe to grind. He felt that 'Germany's innermost soul expresses itself in music', and that the music of Wagner, with its tendency towards tragic intensity and its scorn for the ordinary run of civilized life, heralded the tragic fate of Germany in the 20th century. Time and time again—in short stories like *Tristan*, *Blood of the Walsungs*, *Tonio Kroger*, or massive novels like *The Magic Mountain* and the *Ring*-inspired tetralogy, *Joseph and his Brothers*—Wagner moulds subject-matter, theme, plot, and form. Mann, it has been said, 'learnt the very nature of artistic effect and artistic formulation from Wagner', and he never lost his awe for the operas. Two other composers played a part in Mann's vision—Beethoven and Mahler. Beethoven's music represents a dangerous primitivism, the return to music of Dionysiac frenzy after the civilized restraints of polyphony (see Kretzschmar's lectures in the early part of *Doctor Faustus*); while Mahler's symphonies contained for Mann all the splendour and decadence of the period before the First World War. In *Buddenbrooks*, the history of a provincial German family, the symbolic figure of little Hanno, last of the Buddenbrooks line, touched with genius and fated to an early death, improvises on the piano. The suggestion of Mahler is impossible to miss:

...then came horns again, sounding the march; there was an assembling, a concentrating, firm, consolidated rhythm; and now a new figure began, a bold improvisation, a sort of lively, stormy hunting song. There was no joy in this hunting song: its note was one of defiant despair.

(Mahler's appearance was borrowed for the novelist Aschenbach in *Death in Venice*, a fact cleverly developed by Visconti in his famous film of the novella.)

The summit of Mann's devotion to music is found in *Doctor Faustus*, published in 1947. It is, in a sense, his history of German music, as well as his most powerful indictment of Germany. Adrian Leverkühn, the modern composer who sells his soul to the devil in exchange for artistic power, writes music that becomes progressively more barbarous, demonic, and horribly enthralling—music through which Mann tries to explain why Germany was the source of Nazism, and the logical end to the dissolution started by Wagner. Mann's command of musical history and technique is highly impressive—he even incorporates 12-note theory into Leverkühn's musical idiom—and the book is meticulously crafted: every sentence has its thematic relevance, every character its coherence. Finally, however, the novel is weighed down by the problems of 'composing' and then describing Leverkühn's music in purely literary terms—there should, one feels, be an accompanying cassette, cued in to the appropriate pages!

In *Doctor Faustus*, music triumphs over literature, reminding us of Schopenhauer's belief that all other art-forms aspired to the condition of music. It is also the culmination of what might be called the Wagnerian phase of European culture. When we move to literary modernism, the music we find there is lighter and clearer in texture: Ezra Pound used medieval music, Dowland, and Bartók in his verse, while James Joyce turns Wagner upside-down. Joyce's musicianship was not very sophisticated, although he did at one time consider schooling his tenor voice for a professional career. The music in his novel *Ulysses* is mostly vocal, therefore—from melodies and ballads (*Là ci darem la mano*, *M'appari*, *The Last Rose of Summer*) to what are politely called drinking songs (*The Night before Larry was Stretched*, and worse). Molly Bloom was a concert and oratorio singer, Stephen Daedalus confesses to a love of the English virginalists, but the music which really dominates *Ulysses* and becomes part of its great flow is the tinkle of daily life—whistled tunes, singing in the bath, favourite hymns. The rhythmic, allusive, incantatory qualities of Joyce's later prose, as well as his use of collage and randomness, have had a radical effect on composers since the war: Berio and Cage in particular have adapted Joyce's methods and practices to musical ends.

RUPERT CHRISTIANSEN

Novelette (Fr.; Ger.: *Novellette*). A title given by Schumann to the eight pieces of his Op. 21 for piano. They do not carry individual titles, but the composer said that each had its own character, and the set was the musical equivalent to a 'romantic story'. Schumann clarified this in two letters to his future wife, Clara Wieck, saying that in the pieces he called by this name she 'appeared in every possible attitude and situation'. He explained that he would have liked to embody her name in the title, but that, considerations of euphony intervening, he had come as near as possible by substituting the name of another musical Clara, Clara Novello, the famous singer, who was currently touring Germany with great success: 'I have called the whole *Novelletten* because your name is Clara and *Wiecketten* would not sound well'.

Several other composers, such as Gade, subsequently adopted the term, which carries no special connotation of form.

Novello. English family of musicians and music publishers. Vincent Novello (1781–1861), son of an Italian pastrycook, was a talented musician whose publishing activities led to the foundation of the firm Novello & Co. An active member of the Philharmonic Society, he was conductor and accompanist for a London opera company and was celebrated as the organist and choirmaster of the Portuguese Embassy chapel in London. His first publications, two folio volumes of *Sacred Music* (1811) and *Twelve Easy Masses* by Haydn and Mozart, were issued in vocal (rather than full) score with fully written-out piano and organ accompaniments (instead of figured bass) in an attempt to make the music more accessible to less skilful organist-choirmasters. His monumental editorial enterprises of the 1820s—five volumes of Purcell's sacred music, English music by Boyce, Greene, and Croft, oratorios by Handel and Haydn, and the music of Bach—permanently enriched music-making. The ready availability and cheapness of his scores had a profound influence on the development of English choral societies (then in their infancy), and for many years these works formed their basic repertory.

Vincent Novello's fourth daughter Clara (1818–1908) had a successful career as a singer. His eldest son Alfred (1810–96) set up as a publisher from his home in Frith Street, London, in 1829, and showed a zest and flair for publishing which distinguished the early years of Novello & Co. When he acquired Mendelssohn's oratorio *St Paul* in 1837, he began a lifelong association with the composer (*Elijah* eventually rivalled Handel's *Messiah* in popularity). Alfred Novello founded two journals—the *Musical World* (1836) and the *Musical Times* (1844). In 1847 he established his own printing office, issuing in a well-designed music type large numbers of choral pieces in the famed 'Octavo Editions' (which had originated in inserts in the *Musical Times*). These provided enormous impetus to choral societies. Cheap music, a primary aim of

both Vincent and Alfred Novello, became more of a reality in the 1860s when, thanks to Alfred's campaigning, paper and advertisement taxes were repealed.

Under Henry Littleton (1823–88) the firm continued to produce sacred music (anthems, and the first edition of *Hymns Ancient and Modern*), but also expanded into secular music (vocal scores of operas, Tonic Sol-fa editions, orchestral music) and began to promote concerts. Oratorios, however, remained their speciality. Henry Littleton's sons took over after his death, and Elgar became the most important English composer in their catalogue: his editor at Novello, A. J. Jaeger, was a close friend and is depicted as 'Nimrod' in the *Enigma Variations*. Later they published Holst, Bliss, and others of that generation, and began to issue school music, which has remained a continuing interest (they launched the journal *Music in Education* in 1944). They now publish a number of contemporary composers (Richard Rodney Bennett, Thea Musgrave, Jonathan Harvey), and have launched a new Elgar edition. Standard editions of choral works continue to figure largely in their catalogue. In 1970 they were absorbed by the Granada group of companies.

J. M. THOMSON

Novello, Ivor [Davies, David Ifor] (*b* Cardiff, 15 Jan. 1893; *d* London, 6 Mar. 1951). British composer. He was the son of Madame Novello Davies, well known in Wales and London as a teacher of singing. Coming from this musical background he was inclined to music at an early age, as a singer and pianist; and boyhood visits to the London theatre soon fixed his ambitions in that direction. He began to compose songs when he was about 15, and had an enormous success with the song 'Keep the Home Fires Burning' (more correctly 'Till the Boys Come Home'), which he wrote in 1914. His first complete score was *Theodore and Co.* (1916), the first of a number of revues and musical comedies in the vein of the period but not yet marked by the distinctive Novello style. By 1919 he had gradually established himself as a popular romantic actor and playwright. As a composer, he was to find his style and combine all his assets and talents in a series of operettas in an anglicized Viennese idiom starting with *Glamorous Night* (1935) and continuing with *Careless Rapture* (1936), *Crest of the Wave* (1937), *The Dancing Years* (1939), *Arc de Triomphe* (1943), *Perchance to Dream* (1945), *King's Rhapsody* (1949), and *Gay's the Word* (1950). He was still at the height of his powers and his popularity when he died shortly after a performance of *King's Rhapsody*.

PETER GAMMOND

Noverre, Jean-Georges (*b* Paris, 29 Apr. 1727; *d* St Germain-en-Laye, 19 Oct. 1810). French choreographer and innovator of the *ballet d'action*. He sought to replace convention and display with dramatically expressive dancing, using subjects mainly taken from mythology and history. He worked successively in Paris, London, Stuttgart, and Vienna, and defined his theories and principles in the celebrated *Lettres sur la danse et sur le ballet* (Lyons, Stuttgart, 1760), a widely influential treatise in ballet history.   NOËL GOODWIN

Nowell. See *Noël*.

Noye's Fludde. Children's opera in one act, Op. 59, by Britten. It is a setting of the Chester miracle play for adults' and children's voices, chamber ensemble, and children's chorus and orchestra, and it was first performed at the Aldeburgh Festival, in Orford Church, in 1958.

Nozze di Figaro, Le ('The Marriage of Figaro'). Opera in four acts by Mozart; text by Lorenzo da Ponte, after Beaumarchais's comedy *La folle journée, ou Le mariage de Figaro* (1778, produced 1784). Produced: Vienna, Burgtheater, 1 May 1786; London, Haymarket, 18 June 1812; New York, Park Theatre, 10 May 1824 (in Bishop's version of 1819). Figaro (bar.) is to marry Susanna (sop.) and is preparing the rooms allotted to them by the Count (bar.), whose roving eye has lit upon Susanna. Figaro is in further difficulties, having signed a contract promising to marry Marcellina (con.) if he cannot repay some money borrowed from her. She and Bartolo (bass) consider how he may be trapped, and there is naturally great tension between her and Susanna. The page Cherubino (sop.) is about to be banished for flirting; he sings about his susceptible nature, and hurriedly hides when the Count enters in search of Susanna. The arrival of the priest Basilio (ten.) sends the Count also into hiding, but they are both discovered. Cherubino is ordered off to the army.

The Countess laments the loss of her husband's love, and Figaro and Susanna plan to rearouse it by means of jealousy and ridicule. Cherubino enters with a love-song for the Countess, but has to hide in a neighbouring room when the Count enters. He emerges when the Count goes in search of tools to break the door, and escapes through the window while Susanna takes his place. She baffles the Count by blithely emerging; but the gardener has seen Cherubino's escape and disaster is only averted by Figaro's claiming that it was he who jumped from the window.

The Count tries to win Susanna by threatening to make Figaro marry Marcellina, and she pretends to yield. But Marcellina and Bartolo turn out to be Figaro's parents. The Countess, still mourning the loss of love, arranges a rendezvous between the Count and Susanna in which she will take Susanna's place. The marriage formalities of Figaro and Susanna are attended to.

In the garden, Susanna and the Countess appear in each other's clothes. Figaro, believing that Susanna is to yield to the Count, jealously hears a serenade actually meant for him. Cherubino has an appointment with Barbarina (sop.) but tries to kiss 'Susanna'. He is routed by the Count, who makes approaches to his own wife, as he then discovers to his horror and remorse. She forgives him, and all ends well.

Engraving by Jean-Baptiste Liénard from the first Paris edition (1784) of Beaumarchais's comedy 'Le mariage de Figaro', on which Mozart's opera was based.

FURTHER READING
Nicholas John, ed.: *The Marriage of Figaro*, English
National Opera Guides (in preparation).

Nuance. Adopted from the French word for a
difference, or 'shade', of meaning, feeling,
opinion, or colour. In a musical sense the word
is used to describe the delicate differences of
intensity and of speed which play a large part in
giving 'life' to music.

Nuits d'été, Les ('Summer Nights'). Song-
cycle, Op. 7, by Berlioz to poems by Théophile
Gautier. It was composed in 1840-1 and revised
in 1843 and 1856. The six songs are *Villanelle*,
Le spectre de la rose, *Sur les lagunes*, *Absence*, *Au
cimetière*, and *L'inconnue*. In the orchestral
version Berlioz specified a different voice for
each song; it is rare for one singer to be able to
encompass them all, and when orchestrating
them from the original version for mezzo-
soprano or tenor and piano, Berlioz transposed
the first three.

Nunc dimittis. *Canticle of Simeon in St
Luke's Gospel, 'Lord, now lettest Thou Thy
servant depart in peace'. It is sung at Compline
in the Roman Catholic Church, and was taken
over from that Office to be sung at Evensong in
the Anglican Church. Polyphonic settings were
fewer than of the *Magnificat*, but Anglican
composers frequently coupled the two, either on
their own or as a part of a Full Service.

Nuove musiche, Le (It., 'new music'). Term
referring to the monodic vocal style developed
in the early years of the 17th century. Caccini
published a volume entitled *Le nuove musiche*
and containing arias and madrigals in the
monodic style. See also *New Music*.

Nursery Suite. Orchestral suite by Elgar in
seven movements, composed and first performed in 1931. Elgar dedicated it to the
Duchess of York and her daughters Princess
Elizabeth (later Queen Elizabeth II) and Princess Margaret Rose. It was choreographed
by Ninette de Valois and given as a ballet in
London in 1932.

Nussbaum, Der ('The Nut Tree'). Song for
voice and piano by Schumann to a poem by
Julius Mosen (1803-67). It is the third song in
his cycle *Myrthen*, Op. 25 (1840).

Nut. 1. On a stringed instrument, the slightly
projecting ridge over which the strings pass on
leaving the pegs, their sounding length being
that which lies between the *bridge and the nut.

*A Swedish player of the
nyckelharpa.*

2. That end of the bow of a stringed instrument by which it is held, where there is a screw by which the tension of the hair may be adjusted. It is also known as the 'frog'.

Nutcracker (Russ.: *Shchelkunchik*; Fr.: *Casse-noisette*). Ballet in two acts and three scenes by Tchaikovsky to a libretto by M. Petipa after Alexandre Dumas *père*'s version of E. T. A. Hoffmann's *Der Nussknacker und der Maüsekönig* ('The Nutcracker and the King of the Mice'). It was choreographed by Ivanov and first performed in St Petersburg in 1892. It has since been choreographed by Balanchin, Cranko, and Nureyev, among others. Tchaikovsky arranged an orchestral suite (Op. 71a) of eight numbers from the ballet in 1892.

Nyckelharpa (keyed fiddle). Traditional and unique Swedish folk-instrument, revived today. It has the shape of an elongated fiddle body integral with the neck, and a key-box is fixed on top, the instrument being supported on a strap. The melody string is stopped by wooden blades pushed up by the left hand, held palm upwards (not palm downwards as on a *hurdy-gurdy).

The strings are sounded together by a short bow, and the hair is tightened by the thumb. There are also six to 11 steel sympathetic strings tuned to a chord or to part of the scale. Hundreds of polskas (the Scandinavian versions of the mazurka) and waltzes are preserved in *nyckelharpa* tune-books back to 1830 though the instrument is much older, a form of it already existing in the 15th century. It also appears in Denmark, and for a time in north Germany (*Schüsselfiedel*).   ANTHONY BAINES

Nymphs and Shepherds. Song by Purcell from the incidental music he wrote for Shadwell's play *The Libertine* (1692). It is often sung by a soprano but was made famous in a choral version recorded by Manchester schoolchildren's choirs, conducted by Harty, in 1929.

NZ Neue Zeitschrift für Musik [originally *Neue Leipziger Zeitschrift für Musik*]. German bi-monthly musical magazine founded in Leipzig in 1834 by Schumann (with Friedrich Wieck, Julius Knorr, and Ludwig Schunke). Schumann was editor until 1844 and was succeeded by Franz Brendel. The present title dates from 1979.

o. 1. In music for the violin etc., an indication that either an open string or a harmonic should be played. 2. In keyboard fingering of the 'English' type (as opposed to the 'German' system now in common use for the piano), an indication that the thumb should be used. See *Keyboard fingering*.

Obbligato (It.; Fr.: *obligé*; Ger.: *obligat*; sometimes incorrectly spelt *obligato*). 'Obligatory', 'necessary', i.e. a part which must not be omitted. A piece with 'violino obbligato' is one where the violin part is essential to the structure, or at least to the effect (an optional violin part would be marked 'violino ad libitum'). Unfortunately, in practice the term *obbligato* has come to mean the opposite, i.e. an accompanying part which may be omitted if so desired. Thus it has become necessary to decide in each case which meaning of the term should apply; in general, an *obbligato* part in music of the 18th century and earlier is an essential one, while in later, 19th-century, music *obbligato* can be taken to mean *ad libitum*.

Oberammergau. See *Passion Music*.

Oberek [*obertas*]. A Polish round dance for couples, similar in rhythm to the *mazurka*.

Oberon, or The Elf King's Oath. Opera in three acts by Weber to a libretto in English by J. R. Planché after W. Sotheby's translation of C. M. Wieland's poem *Oberon* (1780) which is based on *Huon de Bordeaux*, a 13th-century French *chanson de geste*. It was first performed in London in 1826.

Obligato, obligat, obligé. See *Obbligato*.

Oblique motion. See *Motion*.

Play-bill for the first performance of Weber's 'Oberon' (*Covent Garden, London, 1826*).

Oboe

1. Description
2. Mechanisms
3. Oboe-playing
4. History
5. Repertory
6. The Deeper Oboes
7. Oboe d'Amore
8. Cor Anglais
9. Bass Oboes

1. *Description.* The oboe (Fr.: *hautbois*; from which Ger.: *Hoboe*, *Oboe*, and It.: *oboe*—both pronounced as three syllables. The older Eng. form, hautboy, also derives phonetically from the Fr. and gave place to the It. in the early 19th century) is a double-reed, conical-bore wind

instrument and one of the four principal colours of the orchestral woodwind section. The oboe is, in fact, the instrument on which this section was founded, three full centuries ago, when its poignantly expressive sound stood alone as a regular wind complement to the violins. Many works of the 18th century name no other woodwind instrument, apart from the bassoon (its natural bass), and from that century comes an important section of the oboe's solo repertory. The *military band too had the oboe as its only treble instrument at first. Its sensitive character does not suit it to modern popular styles from jazz onwards, but in music for films and television the oboe is constantly needed for its unique emotive effect, which can never be truly matched when a similar tone-quality is produced without human breathing (electronically, for example).

The oboe is just under 2′ long. With the reed inserted it becomes as long as a clarinet, but in the orchestra it gives a visual impression of being smaller, partly through the more slender tube and partly because the player's hands come about 2″ closer to the face. It consists of two main joints plus a slightly flared bell, all normally made in African blackwood. The double reed, of which the player keeps a selection ready in a small reed-case, is usually made by the players themselves (see *Reed*, 3), or else reeds can be purchased, best in an unfinished state whereby the player can personally undertake the final thinning ('scraping') of the cane.

The compass is from $b\flat$ (a tone below Middle C) to g''' above the staff (see *Bassoon*, 2, where the ranges of the two instruments are compared); nowadays a high a''' is occasionally demanded in virtuoso works, but notes above f''' rarely appear before the 20th century. With the different schools of playing, and over details in the making of reeds, the sound, while always unmistakably the oboe's, can vary greatly from one player to another, and has always done so, from silvery to reedy, and from a pure instrumental sound to one which is produced with a remorseless *vibrato*. Mozart once wrote of the celebrated oboist Johann Christian Fischer (1733–1800) that 'his tone is entirely nasal, and his held notes like the tremulant of the organ', while in our own time Leon Goossens (*b* 1896), as he first rose to fame, captivated listeners in making the oboe sound, as many said, 'like a violin'. Goossens, it should be added, was one of the first great wind teachers to accept women without prejudice as professional pupils, leading the path to their present equal share in the most responsible orchestral positions not only on the oboe but on all other wind instruments also.

2. *Mechanisms*. The modern keywork has been evolved over the last 150 years by makers in Paris, and is of a delicate intricacy that makes the instrument rather more expensive to buy than a flute or clarinet of comparable workmanship. Many players continue to obtain their oboes from the specialist makers in Paris.

As used in Britain there is a distinction between two fingering systems: the 'Conservatoire system' (named from the Paris Conservatoire) in which the notes $b\flat'$ and c'' and their octaves are made by lowering the right-hand first finger; and the 'thumb-plate system' in which these notes are made by lifting the left thumb from a thumb-plate (indicated in Fig. 1, A) which is not present on the other system. British tradition has long favoured the thumb-plate, whereas other countries use only the Conservatoire.

Another choice concerns the two octave keys which the modern oboe has for producing the upper octave (second harmonics). These may be 'simple' (separate keys for thumb and first finger); 'semi-automatic' (without the need to

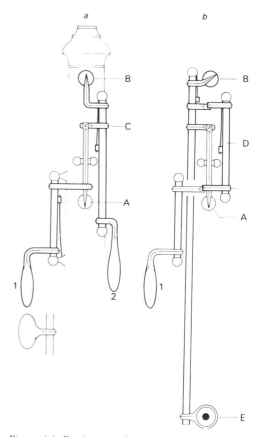

Fig. 1. (a) Semi-automatic octaves: pressing the key 1 (left thumb) allows A to open until key 2 (index finger) is pressed as well, which opens B and (via the arm, C) closes A. (b) Full automatic octaves: key 1 lifts the two arms fixed to the rod D, allowing A to rise while B is held down by the third finger on ring E; on raising this finger (still pressing 1) the ring rises to open B and close A.

the more up to date and provides for improvement of several trills, but has far from superseded the earlier models with rings, these being normal for example on the very satisfactory 'school' models that are obtainable.

3. *Oboe-playing*. In playing the oboe the lips are drawn over the teeth with the tip of the reed between them. All depends on the breathing and its control, for a considerable breath-pressure is required, and yet the aperture of the reed is extremely small and little air is actually expended. Hence the problem for the oboist is not so much one of running out of wind, as of getting rid of deoxygenated air pent up in the lungs. Thus in a long solo passage like the well-known tune in B minor in Tchaikovsky's *Swan Lake* ballet, the oboist could soar through the first eight bars or more in full *cantabile* in one breath, but will very likely break at some point, quickly to breathe *out* and take in fresh air; and similarly in the long *obbligato* passages that Bach wrote for oboe (far more than for any other wind instrument) as in 'I would beside my Lord' in the *St Matthew Passion*.

4. *History*. 'The present Hautbois not 40 years old' says James Talbot's account of *c*.1696, and 'an improvement' on the older Hautbois (see *Shawm*). The improvement is thought to have been effected in Paris by craftsmen-players in the Royal Music led by Jean Hotteterre (*d c*.1678, grandfather of the famous flute-player, Jacques Hotteterre), to produce an instrument which, though it could be played strongly in ceremonial duties taken over from the shawm, could also be sounded as softly as might be required ('with a good reed and skilful hand, as soft as the Flute' adds Talbot, 'Flute' here meaning the recorder). The shawm pirouette was abolished, for a more delicate reed to come under full control of the lips, while the instrument itself underwent reconstruction as broadly summarized in Fig. 2. This indicates internal profiles, with the widths

Pl. 1. Modern oboes: oboe d'amore (left), oboe, and cor anglais by Howarth of London.

release the first when using the second, and by and large the favourite arrangement); or 'fully automatic', needing the thumb key only (as on the saxophone), thanks to an automatic switch-over mechanism controlled by the ring for the third finger, left hand. Fig. 1 illustrates, diagrammatically, the principle of these last two, as an illustration of the 'articulated' type of mechanism which is employed on the oboe in many other places also. On some models the rings are replaced by padded plates ('plateaux') with, in most cases, a small perforation in the centre (Pl. 1, centre). The 'plateaux' system is

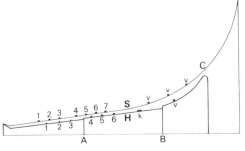

Fig. 2. Comparison on exaggerated scale of specimen bores of treble shawm (S) and Baroque oboe (H). The fingerholes are numbered; k, C-key; v, vent-holes (permanently open).

greatly exaggerated to about eight times the lengths in order to bring out the contrast. The upper line (S) shows the bore profile of a typical treble shawm, the whole instrument in one piece of wood ending in a trumpet-like flare with a series of 'vent holes' in the side. The line below (H) shows a Baroque oboe, with its three separate joints and the fingerholes lowered in position to give a basic scale of C (instead of D) while the balance in the hands is improved by

removing most of the end flare. In the first two joints the bores are more gently sloped than the bore in S, and they do not match at the junctions: first, a small abrupt 'step' (A) amounting to (on average) 1.3 mm. increase in bore, and then at the bell joint a larger step (B) of some 3.4 mm. Other Baroque woodwind quite often show small steps where joints meet, but not in this regular pattern, which remained normal in oboes everywhere until past Beethoven's time.

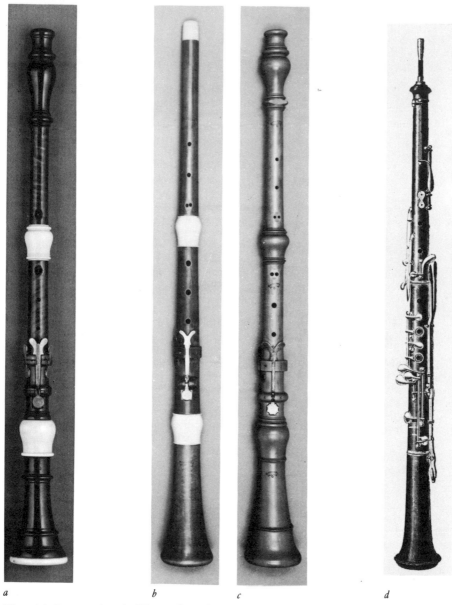

a   b   c   d

Pl. 2. (a) Baroque oboe: by Thomas Stanesby senior, London, early 18th century (3-keyed, the E♭ key—the smaller—being duplicated). (b) and (c) Two 2-keyed oboes of the late 18th century: by William Milhouse, Newark (illustrating the English 'straight-topped' design), and Thomas Collier, London (modelled on contemporary German design). (d) Simple-system oboe (Couesnon catalogue, 1930), with simple octave keys and bottom note B♮.

Next, the fingerholes in the upper joint (1, 2, 3) are greatly reduced in size from the corresponding three holes of the shawm and this joint has the more gentle gradient of the two: it marks the region where the shawm fails to overblow efficiently to the upper octave, while the oboe with these modifications avoids this defect. The lower joint required less drastic modification, while the two 'steps' compensate for the lighter gradients so that towards the end of the bell the bore may practically attain shawm width (just before it terminates in a small inwards flange).

The Baroque oboe has two keys, for the low C (giving $c\sharp''$ in the upper register) and for E♭— this last often duplicated for a 'left-handed' player, making three actual keys in all. Oboes of the Classical period mostly still have just the two keys; also the bore is further narrowed in both main joints, giving enhanced fluency at the top of the compass—nowhere better turned to effect than in Mozart's Quartet for oboe and strings, written in 1781 for the Mannheim oboist Friedrich Ramm (1744–after 1808), who must have been proud of his top f''', rare at that period, for the composer to write it for him so prominently.

The key of F was a favourite tonality for the old oboe although requiring cross-fingerings for the principal notes of the scale, F, B♭, and C. The instrument's expressive powers owe much to the player's skill in 'pressing' these basically weaker notes with the breathing and balancing the other notes to them. (Moreover, in sharp keys, F♯ has a flatness problem, and bottom C♯ is lacking.) Now that the Baroque/Classical oboe has been so extensively revived, listeners may have noticed how the sound compares with the modern sound very much as when the violin is restored to 18th-century condition and played in its old manner; also how the two instruments then closely match each other in quality and expressiveness. Many original instruments are again in use as well as careful copies. No French examples are known from the Hotteterre period, those by Denner of Nuremberg (see *Clarinet*, 4a) being among the earliest (c.1700). Great makers of the Handel/Bach period include Rottenburg (Brussels), Stanesby (London), and Bizey (Paris), while for the early Classical period the oboes of Milhouse, with the plain-turned upper joint then typical in England, are among the favourites for players in Britain. All these oboes require reeds made specially to suit them, on the whole a little wider than the modern.

By the time of Beethoven's last years makers were fitting six to nine further keys to provide alternatives to cross-fingerings. Without these keys the oboe parts in Berlioz's early works would have been hardly possible to render with correct observance of all the dynamic markings and accentuations demanded. A direct memory

of this late Classical phase is the oboe as today made in Vienna by Zuleger and played by the leading oboists there: still Classical in bore and sound, and externally recognizable by the Classical 'onion-shaped' top end. Meanwhile, back again in Paris makers commenced to evolve the modern instrument. In oboes of the late 1830s by Brod the steps in the bore and the flange at the bell are both eliminated, and by 1840 Triebert was making virtually the model which remained in manufacture up to the 1930s, often termed 'simple system' or 'military model', with 13 keys and the two rings which rectify F♯. By 1849 Triebert had brought in the thumb-plate (see above, 2), the Conservatoire system following in 1870 at the hands of his former foreman Lorée, who later (from 1906), in conjunction with the player Gillet, developed the more complicated 'plateaux' mechanism. Earlier, from the 1840s, Paris makers had also sought to redesign the oboe with fingering akin to that of Boehm's early flute mechanism (see *Flute*, 3), but players found the sound unsatisfactory and no subsequent 'Boehm-system' oboe can really be said to have caught on.

5. *Repertory*. The chief Baroque works include Handel's sonatas in B♭ and G minor and his concertos in G minor and B♭. There are many further concertos and sonatas by Italian composers, including Vivaldi, the Besozzis, and Sammartini; and also by Telemann and others. Bach's Concerto in D minor for two violins is also published for oboe and violin. The highlight of the Classical period is Mozart's Quartet (oboe and strings) K370 mentioned above. His Concerto in C, K314, is a version of the Flute Concerto in D. Other concertos are by Fischer, Krommer, and (doubtful) Haydn.

Romantic works include a light but charming concerto by Bellini, and Schumann's Three Romances for oboe or violin. Then (as with the flute) there is rather a gap until Saint-Saëns's Sonata, which was followed by a rush of concertos, by Richard Strauss, Eugene Goossens, Vaughan Williams, and others; sonatas by Poulenc and Hindemith; and, for unaccompanied oboe, Britten's *Metamorphoses after Ovid* and Berio's *Sequenza VII*. Some ultra-modern works have come from Heinz Holliger (b1939) and his school, some requiring 'multiphonics' (see *Wind Instruments*, 7), combination with transistor radio, a supplied tape (as in Holliger's *Cardiophonie*), or, in Globokar's *Tenstudie*, a throat contact-microphone.

6. *The Deeper Oboes.* Unlike the flute and clarinet families, the oboe family has not run to a regular species pitched higher than the normal instrument. An opportune moment for this to have occurred would have been during the great

expansion of military bands c. 1800 when, however, the oboe was being displaced from a major position by clarinets, and it was the smaller sizes of these that gained the interest of bandmasters and have continued to be made up to today. But the larger and deeper oboes, all of orchestral origin, number three types of which one, the cor anglais (see below, 8), is among the most important of the woodwind, while the oboe d'amore has special importance in the great choral works of Bach. The bass oboe and the heckelphone (a special form of it) are, however, heard rarely.

All of them end in a bulb-shaped bell. The original reason for this is unknown. Certainly it modifies the sound of the one or two notes that issue through it, to this extent contributing to these instruments' very distinctive tone-colours, though they owe more to the deeper pitches combined (save in the heckelphone) with a bore gradient more gentle than that of an oboe.

Each of the instruments requires a proportionately larger reed, and in all of them this is placed on a bent metal crook, thereby to incline the instrument downwards and bring the hands to a comfortable playing position. Practically every oboist possesses a cor anglais, even if only now and then asked to play it; many also own an oboe d'amore, but bass oboes are always a problem, save where a big opera house has managed to procure one for its own use.

7. *Oboe d'Amore* (Fr.: *hautbois d'amour*; Ger.: *Liebesoboe*). Built a minor third lower than the oboe, this measures some 25″ long plus 2¼″ for the crook (Pl. 1, left). The lowest note is the written *b*, sounding *g♯*, but in the 18th century, on the two- or three-keyed instrument, *c′* sounding *a*. The sound is veiled and intimate, as suggested by the name (compare viola d'amore, an older name by a few years). It is a German species, in existence by 1719, four years before Bach first scored for it in the *St John Passion*. In all he wrote for it in some 60 works, while no less than nine of the surviving original instruments were made in Leipzig during his time by Eichentopf, the city's chief wind-instrument

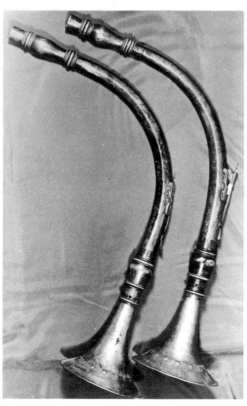

a   *b*

Pl. 3. (a) Oboe d'amore by J. H. Eichentopf, Leipzig, 18th century. (b) Oboe da caccia: a pair by Eichentopf, Leipzig, c.1726.

maker. Telemann and various minor German composers also wrote for it, but by the 1770s it was obsolete. Then, after 100 years, it was revived in modern form for Bach performances. (Without it the d'amore parts have to be played on oboe, or, if lying too low, on cor anglais.)

Debussy features the instrument in the solo melody, *doux et mélancolique*, in the third movement of *Images* (followed by the first reference to the 'Keel Row' on the bassoons). A few other composers have used it, up to Stockhausen in *Punkte*.

8. *Cor Anglais* (Amer.: English horn; Ger.: sometimes *Altoboe*; It.: *corno inglese*): (*a*) *Description*. The cor anglais is built a fifth lower than the oboe, and is in length 32″ plus about 3″ for the metal crook (Pl. 1, right). (For some general points see above, 6). The lowest note, written *b*, sounds *e*. Its rich dreamy sound is often heard in the orchestra in long solo melodies, always slow and often of a pastoral character: for example, in Rossini's *Guillaume Tell* Overture; Berlioz's *Symphonie fantastique*, slow movement; and Wagner's *Tristan und Isolde*, in the long off-stage call in Act 3. (The unusual way the part is written in *Guillaume Tell*, in the bass clef, must mean that the instrument was here first played by a bassoonist, reading the notes with bassoon fingering.) Among other great solos one probably thinks at once of Dvořák's 'New World' Symphony, slow movement; Franck's Symphony, again the slow movement; and Sibelius's *The Swan of Tuonela*, virtually a continuous solo recitative for the cor anglais.

(*b*) *History*. The first deep oboe at this pitch served the oboe as its tenor in four-part military music—a long straight oboe with an angled brass crook (see *Military Band*, 3; *Taille*). In England this tenor oboe continued to be made through the 18th century, sometimes named the 'vauxhumane' (i.e. *vox humana*), for church bands: many have been preserved in country churches along with other wind instruments, some no doubt at first played on by veterans from infantry bands of the early 18th century.

Distinct from this tenor oboe is the early cor anglais itself, which Bach writes for many times using the name 'hautbois da caccia' (in modern editions, oboe da caccia). Why 'da caccia' ('hunting') no one has truly discovered; nor has 'Englisches Horn', first met in a cantata of 1723 by Tobias Volckmar, been explained; one must presume both to signify the same instrument. We know it notably by two examples from Bach's time made by Eichentopf (see above, 7), built in a curve and ending in a flared brass bell. In other examples the bell is of wood, after 1750 always in the present bulbous shape. To form

the curve (which is one way of easing the stretch for the hands), the wooden tube, after piercing the bore, is generally found to be sawn almost right across in about 30 places along what is to become the inside of the curve, making cuts of ½mm. wide which allow the wood to be bent into a 120-degree arc. The inside of the curve is previously planed down to take a long wooden rib, now glued on to secure the curve. The tube is then covered with leather. Later on some instruments were made in two straight joints meeting in an obtuse angle (as commonly in basset horns, see *Clarinet*, 6), but the curved form remained a favourite, in France as well, and continued to be made well past the mid 19th century; the Rossini and Berlioz parts would have been played on this, and although Brod in Paris was building the instrument in the modern straight form by 1840, this took a long time to displace the curved, with its rather soft—indeed distantly horn-like—sound. It is said that *Tristan und Isolde* was first played on it, though in the *Ring* Wagner complains of its 'weak' sound and asks for a stronger-sounding *Alt-Hoboe*, in effect the modern instrument.

(*c*) *Repertory*. Outside the orchestra, the late 18th-century *Harmonie at the Austrian court of Schwarzenberg had a pair of cors anglais instead of the elsewhere customary clarinets. Beethoven's Trio, Op. 97, for two oboes and cor anglais is well known and there is evidence to suggest that it was written for the Schwarzenberg players, and perhaps likewise his Variations on Mozart's 'Là ci darem' for the same combination. A pleasant solo piece with orchestra by Donizetti has recently been discovered. Then there is little until such works as Tovey's Trio, with violin and piano; Honegger's *Concerto da camera*, with flute and strings; Warlock's *The Curlew*, for tenor voice with the same; Hindemith's Sonata; and, most recently, Stockhausen's *Zeitmasse*, for wind quintet with cor anglais replacing the horn.

9. *Bass Oboes*. These, an octave lower than the oboe, have been made experimentally since Denner's time (one by him exists). The French 'hautbois baryton' designed by Brod *c*.1825 has since remained in manufacture on demand (by Marigaux, for example). British oboists often call it 'bass oboe'. The bulb bell at first pointed upwards, later downwards. It is not clearly remembered whether in *The Planets* Holst envisaged this or the heckelphone, a more powerful instrument brought out in 1904 by the famous German bassoon-maker Heckel: 4′ long, lowest note the written *a*, sounding *A*, and a wide bore with gradient steeper than an oboe's. Richard Strauss has it in *Salome* and in *Elektra* (but absent in the reduced score sanctioned by

him), and Delius in the First Dance Rhapsody. Hindemith's Op. 47 is a Trio for viola, heckelphone, and piano (1929). The heckelphone is only made to order: in 1979 there were said to be only three heckelphones in the whole of Britain.

ANTHONY BAINES

FURTHER READING
Evelyn Rothwell: *Oboe Technique* (London, 1953); Philip Bate: *The Oboe* (2nd edn, London, 1975).

Obra (Sp.). 1. General term for a musical work. 2. In the early 18th century *obra* was sometimes used more specifically to refer to a **tiento*.

Obrecht, Jacob (*b* ? Bergen op Zoom, Brabant (now in Belgium), 22 Nov. *c*.1450; *d* Ferrara, 1505). Franco-Flemish composer. Obrecht was regarded by many of his contemporaries as second in stature only to Josquin. Unlike Josquin, however, he worked almost exclusively in the Low Countries, at Utrecht (where Erasmus, the humanist, sang as one of his choirboys), and later at Bergen op Zoom (1479–84), Cambrai (1484–5), Bruges (1486–7), and Antwerp (1494–6; 1498–1500). His career seems to have been an unsettled one, with a change in his place of work every year or two; he was in fact dismissed from Cambrai for financial irregularities and lack of interest in managing the choirboys. In 1487 he was granted leave of absence from Bruges to visit the court of Ercole d'Este in Ferrara, the only trip he is known to have made to Italy during his active career. By 1500 ill health had forced him into retirement; four years later he returned to Ferrara, but he succumbed to the plague and died there.

Obrecht was far less of an innovator than Josquin, and considerably less influential; his music never circulated widely, and mostly fell out of use early in the 16th century. Its value lies in its quality, which reveals an extraordinary creative talent, albeit one concerned more with musical and cerebral ideas than with the meaning and rhetoric of the texts. This is especially true of his 29 Masses, many of which are rich in number symbolism, ingenious *cantus firmus* presentations, and other intellectual devices which can sometimes seem a little inaccessible to modern listeners. A few of his technical achievements are more immediately impressive: each movement of the *Missa 'Sub tuum praesidium'*, for example, gains an extra voice, expanding from a three-part Kyrie to a seven-part Agnus Dei, in each case adding a new plainchant melody—thus in the Agnus Dei, four *cantus firmi* are sounding simultaneously. Much of the charm of Obrecht's Masses is provided by the freely-composed voices; less notable for their melodic grace than for their rhythmic energy, they often abound in lively syncopated

motivic ideas, repeated sequentially or passed between the voices in imitation.

More diverse in character are his 30 or so surviving motets, which vary in technique from complex canonic structures (e.g. *Haec Deum coeli*) to works of exquisitely transparent texture, in which the words are declaimed with a clarity unusual for Obrecht (as in *Factor orbis*, based on a miscellany of plainchant melodies for the Christmas period). His secular music is of rather less importance; although several of his Dutch songs and instrumental pieces were familiar throughout Europe, he cannot be said to rank with such *chanson* composers of the day as Josquin, Compère, and Hayne van Ghizeghem. Obrecht's musical personality may seem complex and a little impenetrable today; but to a north-European audience in the 1490s, with its world picture dominated by principles of divine order, the intellectual and symbolic content of his music must have been both familiar and satisfying.

JOHN MILSOM

O Canada! Canadian national song by Calixa Lavallée (1839–1920) to French words by A. B. Routhier. An English text was written in 1908 by R. S. Weir. It is used as a patriotic song, particularly by French Canadians, but has never officially been adopted as a national anthem.

Ocarina (from It., 'little goose'). Terracotta flute in torpedo shape with a projecting whistle mouthpiece and 10 holes for the fingers and thumbs. The instrument is a 'vessel flute', a form of cavity-resonator, giving practically pure tones without harmonics, while the pitches are determined, not by the length of an air-column as in most flutes, but by the sum area of the

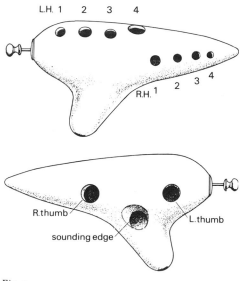

Fig. 1

holes uncovered divided by the internal volume, both expressed as a square root.

In practice, the holes are adjusted in size to be uncovered in a regular order as on a flageolet, starting by progressively opening the seven small holes beginning with the one at the pointed end. This gives one octave (accidentals being made by cross-fingering). Above this the scale is continued for three notes by opening the three large holes—for left little finger and the two thumbs—though the order of opening these varies with different designs. Some ocarinas have a tuning plunger in the wide end.

The instrument is always said to have been invented *c.*1863 by two young Italians of Budrio, near Bologna, as a musical development of the common earthenware bird whistle. Chiefly sold since as a toy, it has nevertheless been made in Germany in sets for playing in harmony, the largest size up to 12″ long. The fine porcelain ocarinas in Meissen ware are much prized pieces. The name may derive from an early shape of the instrument.

For another musical cavity-resonator, see *Gemshorn*, 2.   ANTHONY BAINES

Ochsenkuhn, Sebastian (*b* Nuremberg, 6 Feb. 1521; *d* Heidelberg, 20 Aug. 1574). German lutenist. He spent most of his professional life in the service of the Count Palatine, Ottheinrich, at Neuburg an der Donau and then at Heidelberg. His *Tabulaturbuch* (Heidelberg, 1558) contains transcriptions and arrangements of motets, German songs, madrigals, and *chansons* by Senfl, Josquin, Mouton, and other composers, including a charming one of 'Innsbruch, ich muss dich lassen'.   DENIS ARNOLD

Ockeghem [Okeghem], Johannes (*b c.*1410; *d* ? Tours, 6 Feb. 1497). Franco-Flemish composer. Nothing is known about his early career, except that during the mid 1440s he was a singer

Miniature depicting a performance of a motet by Ockeghem. The composer is presumed to be the elderly figure with glasses.

at Notre Dame in Antwerp. He may also have been connected with the musical circles at Cambrai Cathedral and Bruges. By 1446 he was a member of the chapel of Charles I, Duke of Bourbon, centred on the Burgundian town of Moulins (near Dijon). His talents were recognized by Charles VII, King of France, and by c.1452 Ockeghem had been attracted to the French court, where he remained for the rest of his life, serving three successive monarchs (Charles VII, Louis XI, and Charles VIII). He was handsomely rewarded, not least by being given the important post of treasurer of the church of St Martin-de-Tours in 1459. During his career at court, Ockeghem almost certainly travelled regularly outside France in the retinue of diplomatic missions, perhaps to Italy and certainly (1470) to Spain. After his death he was commemorated by some of the finest writers of the day: Erasmus, Guillaume Crétin, and Jean Molinet, whose lament 'Nymphes des bois' (set to music by Josquin) describes him as learned and handsome, and calls upon some of the leading composers of the day—Josquin, Pierre de la Rue, Brumel, and Compère—to weep for the passing of their 'bon père'.

Ockeghem was the leading composer of the generation between Dufay and Josquin. Unfortunately, little of his music has survived to the present day—14 Masses, fewer than 10 motets, and some 20 *chansons*, probably only a small fraction of his output—yet even this is sufficient to confirm his importance. His style is characterized by its rich contrapuntal texture, in which the various voices are of more or less equal importance. Imitation is not used extensively; instead, independent melismatic lines combine to produce an ever-changing effect, commended by the theorist Tinctoris as having the quality of 'varietas'.

Ockeghem is best known today for his Masses. These range in structure from the conventional (settings based on a *cantus firmus*, often the tenor voice of a *chanson*) to the bizarre: the *Missa prolationum* is constructed entirely out of canons, some of awesome complexity; and the *Missa cuiusvis toni* is without clefs and is capable of being sung in any of the church modes. Less spectacular but equally experimental is the *Missa 'Fors seulement'*, one of the earliest parody Masses, drawing freely upon the entire polyphonic fabric of its model, one of Ockeghem's own *chansons*. His *Missa pro defunctis* has the distinction of being the earliest surviving Requiem; Dufay is known to have composed one, but his setting is lost.

Too few of Ockeghem's motets survive to allow a fair assessment of his achievements in this field, although he appears to have been a pioneer of richly textured free works without *cantus firmus* (as in *Intemerata Dei mater*); he is

also reputed to have written a canonic motet for 36 voices, although the piece is lost. The *chansons*, by contrast, are less remarkable for their experimentation than for their quality: works such as 'Fors seulement l'attente' and 'Ma bouche rit' were justifiably among the most popular songs of their day.   JOHN MILSOM

O Come, all ye Faithful. See *Adeste fideles*.

Octave (Fr.: *octave*; Ger.: *Oktave*; It.: *ottava*). From Lat. *octavus*, 'eighth'. 1. The eighth note of the diatonic scale. 2. The interval of an octave (see *Interval*) is the most consonant interval of all, and one that gives the impression of duplicating the original note at a higher or lower pitch. Acoustically, the octave above a note is one with twice the frequency of the original (e.g. $a = 220$, $a' = 440$, $a'' = 880$). See *Acoustics*; *Harmonic series*. 3. In ecclesiastical terminology, the seventh day (exactly a week) after a feast day, or the period of eight days including the feast day and its octave. 4. The first eight lines of a sonnet.

Octave flute. See *Flute*, 6.

Octet (Fr.: *octette*, *octuor*; Ger.: *Oktett*; It.: *ottetto*). Any combination of eight instruments or voices, or a piece of music composed for such. The normal string octet is for four violins, two violas, and two cellos (i.e. a double string quartet): Mendelssohn (Op. 20), Spohr (four examples), and Shostakovich (Op. 11) were among those to write for this combination. Some composers, such as Beethoven (Op. 103) and Stravinsky, have written octets for various combinations of wind instruments; others, such as Haydn and Schubert (D 803), have combined wind and strings. Schubert's Octet is scored for clarinet, horn, bassoon, and string quintet (adding a double bass to the normal quartet arrangement), a combination which has been emulated in the 20th century by John Joubert.

Ode (from Gk *aoidē*, 'song'). Originally, a lyrical poem. In its musical sense, the term often means a ceremonial work, for example Purcell's 'Welcome' odes, his and Handel's odes for St Cecilia's Day, and Elgar's *Coronation Ode*. However, the term is sometimes used for works that have a particular significance for the composer, as in Elgar's *The Music Makers* or Stravinsky's *Elegiacal Chant*.

Ode for St Cecilia's Day. 1. Title of four choral works by Purcell, two composed in 1683, one in about 1685, and one in 1692. Three have English texts and the other is in Latin.

2. Choral work by Handel, a setting of Dryden's poem (1698). It was composed in 1739.

3. Cantata by Parry to words by Pope. It is for soprano, baritone, chorus, and orchestra and was composed in 1889.

Ode to Napoleon. Work, Op. 41, by Schoenberg for reciter, piano, and string quartet (later arranged for string orchestra). It is a setting of Byron's poem (1814), composed in 1942.

Odour and Music. The idea of a scale of perfumes was worked out in 1865 by S. Piesse, the Parisian manufacturer of them. In his book *Des odeurs*, he claimed, 'there is an octave of odours, as there is an octave of notes', and he set out in musical notation a range of six and a half octaves, every note of which had its own perfume, from patchouli on the lowest C of the piano to civet at its highest F. He said that bouquets ought to be grouped like the notes of a chord, and described the chord C–E–G–C as follows—geranium, acacia, orange-flower, and camphor. There was about as much science and sense in this as in some of the colour-scale theories mentioned in the article *Colour and Music*.

In 1891 there was given in Paris a public performance which combined music, colour, and odour. The work performed was *The Song of Solomon, a Symphony of Spiritual Love in Eight Mystical Devices and Three Paraphrases*, the 'book' being by Paul Roinard and the 'musical adaptations' by Flamen de Labrely. The programme set out the nature of each of the eight 'devices' in the following style—'First Device: orchestration of the word in I illuminated with O; orchestration of the music, D major; of the Colour bright orange; of the Perfume, white violet', and so forth. The meaning of this seems to be that in the recitation the vowels I and O predominated; that the music was in D major; that the stage decoration was of a bright orange colour; that a perfume of white violet was disseminated meanwhile.

The following year New York also experimented in a bold combination of appeals to the various senses in *A Trip to Japan in Sixteen Minutes conveyed to the Audience by a Succession of Odours*. This was claimed to be the 'First Experimental Perfume Concert in America', and also as 'A Melody in Odours (assisted by two Geishas and a Solo Dancer)'.

As explained in the article *Colour and Music*, the attempts at combination of appeal to the eye and the ear by a play of colours connected with simultaneous sounds have usually been based on analogies connected with the fact that both sound and light are vibratory stimuli conveyed by so-called 'waves': there is not even this basis for attempts to bring the sense of smell into the combination, as odours are conveyed by the dispersion of (infinitely tiny) particles of the material of the odoriferous substance.

PERCY SCHOLES

Oedipus Rex. Opera–oratorio in two acts by Stravinsky; text by Cocteau, after Sophocles' tragedy (*c*.430 BC), translated into Latin by Daniélou. Produced: Paris, Théâtre Sarah Bernhardt, 30 May 1927 (as oratorio); Vienna, 23 February 1928 (first stage performance); Boston, 24 February 1928 (concert), New York, 21 April 1931 (staged); London, Queen's Hall, 12 February 1936 (concert), Edinburgh, 21 August 1956 (staged). The Narrator describes how Oedipus was doomed from birth to the horror of killing his father and marrying his mother. Though Oedipus (ten.), Jocasta (sop.), Creon (bass-bar.), and Tiresias (bass) enact their roles, the chorus is static, and the dramatic metaphor is somewhere between opera and oratorio.

Oeuvre (Fr.). 'Work', 'composition'. See *Opus*.

Offenbach, Jacques [Jacob] (*b* Cologne, 20 June 1819; *d* Paris, 5 Oct. 1880). French composer. The career of 'the Mozart of the Champs-Élysées' was slow to take flight, and apart from a few composition lessons with Halévy (1836–7), Offenbach learnt his craft the hard way playing in the orchestra of the Opéra-Comique and performing in the 1840s as a cello virtuoso. His early commission for the vaudeville *Pascal et Chambord* (1839) was not followed by another performance in a Parisian theatre until 1853 (*Le trésor à Mathurin* and *Pépito*), even though he was appointed conductor at the Théâtre Français in 1850. But in

Offenbach

1855, encouraged by the success of *Oyayaie, ou La reine des îles* at Hervé's Folies-Nouvelles, he rented the tiny Théâtre Marigny in the Champs-Élysées for the Exhibition season (which he reopened as the Théâtre des Bouffes-Parisiens), and from then until the 1867 Exhibition he dominated the fashionable musical scene of Napoleon III's Second Empire: he satirized its politics and foibles and epitomized its developing cosmopolitanism and moral licence in light, entertaining operettas (a term he first invented for *La rose de Saint-Flour* in 1856). Initially, he was legally restricted to two or three stage performers, but the relaxation of this in 1858 allowed him to produce the two-act *opéra-bouffe, Orphée aux enfers* (with its famous Can-can), though, out of some 90 operettas, over 50 were in only one act. In the 1860s Offenbach broadened his horizons, composing works for Bad-Ems and the three-act opera *Die Rheinnixen* for Vienna in 1864 (containing the theme of what became the Barcarolle in *Les contes d'Hoffmann*). However, his greatest successes still remained in Paris (all with librettos by Meilhac and Ludovic Halévy): *La belle Hélène* (1864), *La vie parisienne* (1866), *La Grande-Duchesse de Gérolstein* (1867), and *La Périchole* (1868).

Offenbach's popularity declined after the war of 1870–1 and for the Third Republic he became the 'great corrupter', who was forced to make an American tour in 1876 to revive his ailing finances. He now turned largely to revisions of earlier successes or towards larger forms, and his consuming passion from 1877 onwards was the five-act opera *Les contes d'Hoffmann* in which he returned to the early 19th-century Germany of his birth and also sought to bridge the chasm between light and serious music which he had largely been instrumental in creating.

Like Diaghilev, Offenbach was an untiring impresario, low on financial acumen, but high on spotting and exploiting talent (like Halévy and Hortense Schneider). His musical parody consisted largely of quoting familiar themes in incongruous surroundings and the farcical element often lay more in the situations and texts he set, though he possessed an ability to heighten comic situations, to exploit rhythm and the stresses of the French language, and to build up excitement in his sparkling finales. Through the foreign success of his music, operetta became established as an international genre, and Offenbach's lead was followed by Johann Strauss, Sullivan, and Lehár, and ultimately led to the 20th-century musical.

ROBERT ORLEDGE

FURTHER READING
Siegfried Kracauer: *Offenbach and the Paris of his Time* (London, 1937); Alexander Faris: *Jacques*

Offenbach (London, 1980); Peter Gammond: *Offenbach: his Life and Times* (Tunbridge Wells, 1980); James Harding: *Jacques Offenbach: a Biography* (London, 1980); Tom Walsh: *Second Empire Opera* (London, 1980).

Offertory (Lat.: *offertorium*). Part of the Proper of the Roman Catholic *Mass, sung just after the Credo, while the priest is preparing the bread and wine and offering them upon the altar. (See also *Plainchant*, 2.) The plainchant is generally insufficient to occupy the time, so there may be interpolated a motet (sometimes repeating the words of the antiphon just heard) or an organ voluntary. Palestrina set the Offertory antiphons for the whole of the Church Year in order to provide for this need. In the Anglican Service the place of the Offertory is now usually taken by a hymn.

Office. In the Roman Catholic liturgy, the services of the Hours, as distinct from Mass, which is often called the 'Divine Office'. Until recent changes, this consisted of eight Latin services associated with a particular time of day: Matins (after midnight), Lauds (at dawn), Prime, Terce, Sext, and None (called the 'Little Hours' and sung respectively at 6 a.m., 9 a.m., midday, and 3 p.m.), Vespers (at sunset), and Compline (before retiring). In practice, Matins and Lauds were often combined and in a parochial context might be sung the previous evening; on the last three days of Holy Week this combined office was called Tenebrae.

The Hours all consisted of a combination of psalms and canticles with antiphons, lessons (readings) with responsories, hymns, and prayers; each ended with one of the four antiphons to the Blessed Virgin (this item was recently restricted to the end of Compline only). The format of the Office differed slightly as between the monastic and Roman rites, the latter applying in non-monastic cathedrals and parishes. In public worship the Office was normally sung to plainchant, but from the later Middle Ages onwards particular Hours came to be adorned with polyphonic settings. For example, pre-Reformation England, where the *Sarum Use was followed, saw a growth in ornate polyphonic settings of the hymn and *Magnificat* for Vespers, as well as of the responsories for Matins, Vespers, and Compline. These settings contained alternating sections of plainchant and polyphony based on it, according to a strict liturgical scheme; they include some of the finest choral works of Taverner, Tallis, Sheppard, and their contemporaries.

From the 16th century, continental composers tended to single out Vespers for settings in polyphony, which could range from the simplest *falsobordone* psalm chanting (similar to Anglican chant) to elaborate polychoral or (later) instrumentally-accompanied *Magnificat* settings. Monteverdi's Vespers of 1610 is an unusual case of a complete, specific Office—that of the Blessed Virgin—being set as a musical entity on the most sumptuous scale; the general practice in Italy at the time was to draw musical settings as required from functional compilations of Vespers music. Though Monteverdi still based his psalms on the ancient plainchant psalm tones, Baroque composers came to disregard plainchant as a means of musical construction. There was a general decline in composition for the Office by the later 18th century; Mozart's *Vesperae solennes de confessore*, however, is a well-known example of a self-contained Vespers setting from the period.   JEROME ROCHE

Offrandes oubliées, Les ('The Forgotten Offerings'). Orchestral work ('méditation symphonique') by Messiaen, composed in 1930.

Ogdon, John (Andrew Howard) (*b* Mansfield, 27 June 1937). English pianist and composer.He studied at the Royal Manchester College of Music and was joint winner with Vladimir Ashkenazy in 1962 of the Tchaikovsky Prize. Since then he has enjoyed an international career as a concert pianist. He is also the composer of a Piano Concerto (1968) and various solo pieces for piano.
                              PAUL GRIFFITHS

O God, our Help in Ages Past. Hymn of which the words, based on Psalm 90, are by Isaac Watts (1674-1748); it was first published in Watts's *Psalms of David* (1719) with the first words 'Our God, our help' altered to 'O God' by John Wesley in his *Collection of Psalms and Hymns* (1737). The tune is attributed to William Croft but first appeared anonymously, set to Psalm 42, in the 1708 supplement to Tate and Brady. The tune is known as 'St Anne', Croft being organist of St Anne's, Soho, in 1708. The first line is a stock 18th-century phrase found in J. S. Bach's organ fugue in E♭, which is therefore known in England as the 'St Anne Fugue'. It is perhaps the most popular of all hymns and is especially associated with Remembrance Day services.

Oioueae. 'Word' formed from the vowels of 'world without end, Amen' used as an abbreviation in Anglican liturgical books in a similar way to *aevia and *evovae.

Oiseaux exotiques ('Exotic Birds'). Work by Messiaen for piano, 11 wind instruments, xylophone, glockenspiel, and two percussionists, composed in 1955-6.

Okeghem, Johannes. See *Ockeghem, Johannes.*

Oktave (Ger.). 'Octave'; *Oktavflöte*, 'octave (above) flute', i.e. piccolo; *Oktavfagott*, 'octave (below) bassoon', i.e. contrabassoon; *Oktavkoppel*, 'octave coupler'.

Oktett (Ger.). 'Octet'.

Old Hall Manuscript (London, British Library, Add. 57950; formerly Old Hall, St Edmund's College, Ware, Herts.). The most important collection of English sacred music before the Eton Choirbook. Copied in the early 15th century, it contains a repertory of 147 works composed during the period *c*.1350-1420, written in a variety of styles. Some employ the chordal 'descant' idiom typical of English music while others are more linear or canonic in conception and may be based on isorhythmic principles, revealing some debt to continental music of the 14th century. Of the composers represented, many of whom belong to the generation before Dunstable, the most important is Leonel Power. A modern edition, prepared by Andrew Hughes and Margaret Bent, was published in the *Corpus mensurabilis musicae* series in 1969-73.

Old Hundredth (Amer.: 'Old Hundred'). Metrical psalm tune of uncertain origin. Its name indicates that it was set to the 100th psalm in the 'old' version of the metrical psalms (i.e. Sternhold and Hopkins as opposed to Tate and Brady). It first appeared in Daye's edition (1560-1) of Sternhold and Hopkins, where it was set to the words 'All people that on earth do dwell' by W. Kethe. However, the tune appeared in Marot and Béza's Genevan Psalter (1551), in which it is attached to Psalm 134, and an even earlier version of it appears in the Antwerp collection *Souter Liederkens* (1540). Vaughan Williams made a ceremonial arrangement of the tune, for choir, congregation, orchestra, organ, and 'all available trumpets', for the coronation of Elizabeth II in 1953.

Old Roman chant. See *Plainchant.*

O magnum mysterium ('O Great Mystery'). Cycle of four carols by Peter Maxwell Davies to Latin and Medieval English texts, composed in 1960. They are for mixed chorus, wind quintet, seven percussionists, viola, cello, and organ.

Ombra scene. In early opera, a scene set in the underworld, where a ghost, or 'shade' (*ombra*), is conjured up. Though originating in 17th-century opera, and a regular feature of Orpheus operas, the effect has proved tenacious; among the most celebrated *ombra* scenes are those in Berlioz's *Les Troyens*.

Ondes martenot. See *Electronic Musical Instruments*, 2f.

Ondine. 1. Ballet in three acts and five scenes by Henze, choreographed by Frederick Ashton. It was first performed at Covent Garden in 1958.
2. The first piece of Ravel's *Gaspard de la nuit*.

Ongarese (It.). 'Hungarian'; *all'ongarese*, 'in Hungarian style'. Music in the 'Hungarian' style, i.e. based on gypsy dances, became very popular in the early 19th century, and composers such as Beethoven and Schubert wrote piano pieces 'all'ongarese'. Later in the century, the Hungarian dances of Liszt, Joachim, and Brahms gave new impetus to the popularity of the Hungarian style.

On Hearing the First Cuckoo in Spring. Orchestral work by Delius, the first of his Two Pieces for Small Orchestra. Its main theme is based on *In Ola Valley*, No. 14 of Grieg's *Norwegian Folk Tunes*, Op. 66, and it was composed in 1912. The second of the Two Pieces is *Summer Night on the River*.

On this Island. Song cycle, Op. 11, by Britten to poems by W. H. Auden. The five songs are for soprano or tenor solo and piano and were first performed in 1937.

On Wenlock Edge. Song cycle by Vaughan Williams for tenor, string quartet, and piano, to six poems from A. E. Housman's *A Shropshire Lad* (1896), the first song being *On Wenlock Edge*. The cycle was composed in 1908–9 and Vaughan Williams arranged it for tenor and orchestra (*c*.1923).

Op. Abbreviation for *Opus.

Open harmony. See *Close harmony*.

Open notes. 1. Notes on the unstopped (or 'open') string of any bowed or plucked instrument. 2. On valved brass instruments, the notes of the harmonic series, which are produced without lowering (or closing) any valve. 3. In brass parts generally, the direction 'open', or 'ouvert', countermands 'muted' or 'stopped'.

Open string. A string of a bowed or plucked instrument not 'stopped' by the fingers.

Oper (Ger.). 'Opera', 'opèra house'.

Opera. English monthly musical magazine founded in 1950 by the Earl of Harewood, who was succeeded as editor in 1953 by Harold Rosenthal. The magazine gives news and reports of all matters concerning opera.

Opera

1. Introduction
2. The Origins of Opera
3. From the Florentines to the 1640s
4. From the Opening of the Public Opera Houses to the 1730s
5. Serious Opera in France until the Revolution
6. Rococo and Reform in opera seria, 1725–90
7. Comic Opera until the Time of Mozart
8. Mozart
9. Interlude
10. French Opera in the 19th Century
11. Italy during the 19th and Early 20th Centuries
12. German Opera from Mozart to Richard Strauss
13. Opera Elsewhere in Western Europe
14. Slavonic Opera
15. The 20th Century: Symbolism
16. Expressionism
17. Russian Fantasy
18. Naturalism Renewed
19. Myth and Allegory
20. Music Theatre
21. Return to Opera?

1. *Introduction.* Opera has probably aroused more passion and critical comment than any other musical genre. It has been condemned as irrational and nonsensical; on the other hand, it has been considered the supreme expression of the human spirit. It has helped to bankrupt kings; it has provoked revolutionary demonstrations; it has praised monarchs, encouraged populist movements, expounded philosophy, explored psychology; and, more often than any of these, it has simply provided entertainment. Such variety stems from the very mixture of elements in opera: music, drama, poetry, the visual arts, and (at times) dance. Although music is commonly thought to be the primary element, there have been times when the producer, ballet master, and performers have been more important than the composer. There has never been any formula for success, despite the polemics of critics and practitioners, but the very multifariousness of opera has ensured its survival for nearly four centuries.

2. *The Origins of Opera.* It is generally said that liturgical music drama and mystery plays (see *Church Drama*) and such pastoral plays as Adam

de la Halle's *Le jeu de Robin et de Marion* contain the seeds from which opera grew. While there is some truth in this, the form in which opera first appeared was a peculiarly Renaissance phenomenon, owing much to the cultural conditions of the late 16th century. It was the product of speculation by intellectuals, living mainly in Florence. Despairing of the triviality (as they saw it) of music in their own day, they were determined to revive the glories of the art of Ancient Greece (see *Camerata*). Lacking the music of the Greeks in any form they could understand, they had to rely on written accounts, from which they came to a number of conclusions. The most important was that Greek drama was sung, or said, in such a way that the words were emotionally heightened but were always clearly audible. They experimented with this principle in vocal chamber music (see *Monody*), developing a type of singing in which the words were sung syllabically with careful attention to their natural declamation in speech, modified by two features. First, emotive words could be embellished to underline their meaning; secondly, a lute or harpsichord provided an accompaniment, offering possibilities for expressive harmony (dissonance to express anguish, and so on), and also establishing a basic harmonic rhythm to control the embellishments of the singer. The result was far from the Greeks, but it was a fertile element in the evolution of opera.

The realization of this vocal principle within the context of 16th-century dramatic music can be observed in the pastoral play. Here the dramatic action was weak, the chief emphasis being on lyrical verse. Music was used when the action suggested it, one play, for example, having a temple scene where a priest and people sing incantations. By the end of the century such plays were given elaborate productions, as were the *intermedi* (interludes) performed between the acts of the play. These were usually light allegorical *tableaux*, such as *The Triumph of Time* or *The Harmony of the Spheres*; they used scenery (sometimes with machines to represent, for instance, clouds bringing the gods from the heavens) and music to provide a diverting interlude to the main drama. The music consisted of songs and madrigals, instrumental music, sometimes with dancing; the whole was often conceived for vast forces with an elaborate *mise-en-scène*, as in the *intermedi* separating the acts of Girolamo Bargagli's comedy *La pellegrina* (1589), performed during the celebrations for the wedding of the Grand Duke Ferdinand de' Medici and Christine of Lorraine. The instrumental ensembles were large and varied; the solo singers were virtuosos of the highest ability. Such interludes were therefore frequently attractive, and gradually came to assume more prominence than the play itself. With these developments in late 16th-century dramatic music the scene was set for the development of opera itself.

3. *From the Florentines to the 1640s.* Three composers involved in Florentine intellectual society at the end of the 16th century made attempts at a *dramma per musica* (literally a 'drama for, or in, music': the Italian word *opera* simply means 'work', and was coined for the genre by the English later in the 17th century). One of the composers, Emilio de' Cavalieri, was himself an intellectual; the other two, Jacopo Peri and Giulio Caccini, were singers. Paradoxically, it was the intellectual who produced the more conventional work: Cavalieri's *Rappresentatione di anima e di corpo* (1600) is in essence a mixture of the old religious mystery play and the techniques of the *intermedio*, belonging more properly to the early history of the *oratorio. Peri and Caccini, however, produced something new. As singers there was a tremendous rivalry between them, heightened by a difference in attitude: Peri was a dramatic singer, Caccini was more concerned with the lyrical art of *bel canto*. Peri wrote the first continuously sung pastoral, *Dafne* (1598), but the music is lost. Both composers then set the court poet Ottavio Rinuccini's version of the Orpheus legend, *Euridice*. Peri's work was given at the celebrations for the wedding of Maria de' Medici and King Henri IV of France (1600), though it was bedevilled with the jealousies so common in later operatic history, Caccini insisting on writing the parts which his own pupils were to sing.

In 1602 Caccini's own complete setting of *Euridice* was heard. Both operas contained traditional elements: the pastoral nature of the verse, the happy ending customary in the pastoral play, the use of choruses and songs, and, in Caccini's setting at least, the presumed use of an elegant *mise-en-scène*. But the new elements were significant: a simple, well-constructed plot, the use of a small group of instrumentalists in place of the vast assembly for the *intermedi*, and the continuous singing accompanied by such harmony instruments as harpsichord or lute—what was later to be called the *continuo group. There was also an essential difference between the two works: Peri had an imaginative harmonic sense and tended to break up the melodic line to match the dramatic action; Caccini, on the other hand, was content merely to enunciate the text accurately and to write attractive song-like passages. It has been said that these first operas are dull and dryly experimental; but, in the hands of expert singer-actors and performed before an audience which could follow the text in detail, there is no reason to doubt their effectiveness. Nor did they lack musical organization, since the concept of *strophic variation (a varied melody over a recurrent bass) helped to lend shape to the whole work. The absence of dramatic action was of little account to audiences used to the lyrical pastoral play. Possibly they missed rather more the sumptuousness and large scale of the old pastoral-with-*intermedi*, and it is noticeable that, while the *intermedio* retained its popularity, there were few operas to follow closely these early Florentine models.

Monteverdi's *Orfeo* (produced at Mantua, 1607) is significant both because of its masterly exploitation of the characteristics of early Florentine opera and because it also drew on the more spectacular features of the *intermedio*. The libretto, by Alessandro Striggio, uses in outline the same story as *Euridice*, retaining the happy ending (though either Striggio or Monteverdi tried in vain to break with 16th-century practice and revert to the tragic ending of the classical legend). Yet the opera is enriched by a greater sense of scale, atmosphere, and characterization. Monteverdi returned to the large orchestra typical of the *intermedio*, using it (as earlier composers had done) for the evocation of mood. His score also allowed for dancing and for the use of theatrical machines, re-creating the magnificence much loved by noble audiences and patrons. From the Florentines he took the concept of recitative (more closely from Peri than from Caccini), though his experience as a composer of expressive madrigals gave his style a more profound harmonic idiom, dissonance and chromaticism being integral elements. His particular gift, however, was his sense of timing and dramatic organization. Not only are the individual scenes carefully cast into musical patterns, but the whole opera works towards and from a grand climax, the *preghiera*, or plea of Orpheus to be allowed to enter Hades (see *Ornaments and Ornamentation*, 3, Ex. 2). Although the characters, with the exception of Orpheus, lack definition, the story is compellingly told and the music is nearly always interesting for its own sake. *Orfeo* can therefore claim to be the earliest opera to remain in the repertory on its artistic, rather than on its historical, merits.

The first performance was probably given before a select audience of nobles and intellectuals. By contrast his next opera, *Arianna*, was performed before a distinguished audience drawn to Mantua from all over northern Italy for the wedding of the Gonzaga heir and Margherita of Savoy (1608). With the exception of the famous 'Lamento d'Arianna' the score has been lost, but from contemporary accounts the opera seems to have followed the main trends of *Orfeo*. Evidently it represented a step

towards human, rather than mythological, drama: Ariadne's lament was clearly an expression of Monteverdi's grief at the death of his wife (1607), and the ladies in the audience seem to have identified with the character, weeping unashamedly at her plight.

Although *Arianna* undoubtedly revealed the potential of opera, the genre still did not become a common phenomenon. Monteverdi, as its most famous practitioner, would surely have received many commissions if it had, but he was more frequently asked for *intermedi* and ballet music, and had only one opportunity to compose an opera in the next 20 years. This commission came from Mantua in 1627, *Licori finta pazza* ('Licori who Feigned Madness'). The score is lost, but from correspondence it is clear that Monteverdi was now regarding opera as real human drama: the music depicted the sudden changes of mood of the characters, which were sung by performers of considerable acting skill. However, because of royal illness and death, the opera was apparently never staged, and Monteverdi had no chance of following this line of development for over 10 years.

The only city where opera had anything like a continuous development at this time was Rome, where the social life of the Papal court centred on such rich princes of the Church as Cardinal Barberini, whose palace had a huge theatre and whose taste for lavish entertainment was indulged regardless of expense. The choice of subjects for operas became broader, the pastoral persisting spasmodically, the mythological aspects being rendered less rarified and more down-to-earth in such works as Domenico Mazzocchi's *La catena d'Adone* ('The Chain of Adonis', 1626). There was also a taste for religious subjects, using the lives of the saints as a basis. Musically there was a mixture of conservative and forward-looking elements. The sumptuous *mise-en-scène* was marked by the frequent use of the chorus; the orchestra, though less varied in sonority than in the *intermedio* (it was now becoming a stabilized group of strings), had separate pieces including, sometimes, an overture on an ample scale. There was now a firm distinction between recitative and aria, the latter having a mobile bass which gave shape to the melody through regular changes of chord. By the 1640s there was a conscious effort to alleviate 'the tedium of the recitative' (Luigi Rossi's phrase), even though this entailed a final break with the high ideals of the 'play in music'. But even before the 1640s the combination of Monteverdi and the Roman operatic traditions had led to a new development.

4. From the Opening of the Public Opera Houses

to the 1730s. In 1636 two musicians, Benedetto Ferrari and Francesco Manelli, left Rome, fearing trouble after the apparently imminent death of Pope Urban VIII. They settled in Venice, which offered a more stable social life, and within a year decided to produce opera there. But Venice lacked patrons to support the venture, and they were forced to seek a new source of finance—the general public. The Teatro San Cassiano, the first public opera house, opened in 1637, admitting audiences either on a subscription basis (one hired a box for the season) or by the payment of a fee for a single performance. Consequently the audience represented a wider social spectrum than previously; moreover, the theatre had to entertain and satisfy its public patrons. The chief attraction was soon found to be a combination of virtuoso singing and spectacle. The former gave rise to a new type of artist—the 'star', particularly castratos and female singers (the earliest prima donna was Anna Renzi, on whose prowess sonnets were written). The latter created a demand for the skilled theatre designer and machinist, whose marvels now even surpassed those of earlier entertainments.

Such conditions resulted in a genre far removed from that envisaged by the Florentine intellectuals, though Monteverdi, as the one composer with operatic experience in Venice, was involved from the start and provided a link with the earlier period. His *Arianna* was revived, but he wrote several new works, the scores of two of which—*L'incoronazione di Poppea* (1642) and *Il ritorno d'Ulisse in patria* (1640)—have survived. From these it is clear that the unity and simplicity of Florentine opera had given way to diversity and discontinuity. Although both operas exhibit a strong dramatic instinct and a capacity to organize a story, they also contain scenes with no real connection with the plot, having comic characters and allegorical figures in addition to the main protagonists. Musically there was a similar diversity, with songs, duets, and occasional instrumental pieces interspersed among the recitative. However, the recitative was still used for the most dramatic scenes and expressions of emotion. There was little for the chorus to do, and the orchestra was small (though the actual size is open to debate). But Monteverdi's prime aim was to move his audience by displaying the human predicament. His comic scenes—which are never trivial—are essential to the formation of a rounded emotional picture.

During the 1640s opera became so successful that several theatres opened. Some were relatively small and lacked the resources for grand spectacle, others were larger and more lavishly equipped. The need to find new composers also tended to bring about a variety of attitudes. The

Monteverdian tradition was carried on by his pupil Cavalli, who wrote about 32 operas during the period 1639-73. Being conceived for different theatres, his operas displayed certain differences in detail, though in general he persisted with human drama in which the emotions of the characters were clearly expressed, particularly when they were placed in extreme situations, as in *Ormindo* (1644), where there is a prison scene which was to become a cliché in later librettos. In Cavalli's operas the main burden of the story-telling and the expression of emotion continued to be borne by the recitative; but it now moved seemingly effortlessly into *arioso* and short *arias, the latter shaped by bass patterns (as in the old strophic variation, though now usually more compact) or by repetitions of sections, sometimes resulting in a short *da capo* (ABA) aria. The operas contained many such arias, though they did not predominate.

The opposite is true of Cesti, whose interest in popular, tuneful set pieces was encouraged by the early success of *Orontea* (1649): this led to performances in Austria, where Cesti won commissions for large-scale spectacular operas, notably *Il pomo d'oro* (1668), written for the wedding of the Emperor Leopold I and Margherita of Spain. This called for 24 changes of scene and lasted eight hours (in addition, there were two hours of non-musical entertainment); it required 48 solo performers—not all singers—plus a ballet company and large orchestra. *Il pomo d'oro* created a fashion for festival operas, especially in Vienna where it lasted well into the 18th century. Writing for a foreign audience (which could not readily understand Italian) naturally put a premium on tuneful music, and, following Cesti's example, the melodious aria became the main concern of several composers whose initial successes had been in Venice: Marc'Antonio and Pietro Ziani (who worked in Austria and southern Germany), Carlo Pallavicino (Dresden), Antonio Sartorio (Venice), and Agostino Steffani (Munich, Hanover, and Düsseldorf). All these composers transferred the main emotional burden on to the aria, in which instrumental *ritornelli* assumed a more important role and so tended to lengthen the set pieces. The best composers writing from 1680 were capable of great variety of mood, and, if the librettos were sometimes too complex, the music is truly dramatic. They often contain comic elements (Legrenzi and Stradella were particularly good at these) and the operas are certainly not the product of mere formulas, as has been alleged of Baroque opera.

By the end of the 17th century opera was popular throughout Italy: Rome and Naples offered valuable alternatives to the theatres of Venice, though Venice continued to produce many more operas per season than anywhere

Set design by Fernando Tacca for the final scene of Cavalli's 'Ipermestra' (Florence, 1658).

else. The 'star' system was now well established, the public tending to favour the upper voices, particularly castratos. To satisfy public taste, the aria now became lengthier, with the reprise of the *da capo* aria allowing the singers to provide embellishments to the melody. As early as 1690 it was usual for the singer to leave the stage after his or her aria (though the rigid convention came later); there were therefore few opportunities for ensembles, and little chance for choral writing. However, the arias themselves covered a wide variety of moods and musical styles, from protracted pieces with extended instrumental *ritornelli* and *concertante* parts to simple songs based on dance rhythms. The orchestra assumed considerable importance, both in the overture (which could sometimes be a substantial piece) and in the accompaniment of the singers: indeed, in the later operas of Alessandro Scarlatti (the most influential opera composer of the period around 1700) arias are never accompanied solely by the continuo.

Numerous Italian composers wrote in this manner, which we may see as a forerunner of the more rigidly conventionalized *opera seria* of the early 18th century (see below, 6); chief among them were Antonio and Giovanni Bononcini, Francesco Gasparini, Antonio Lotti, Vivaldi,

and, above all, Handel. Although Handel's main activity as an opera composer spanned the 1720s and 1730s, his tastes were formed in the Italy of 20 years earlier. This is to some degree reflected in his varied choice of librettos: while most of his operas were on historical subjects (for example, *Giulio Cesare*, 1724), he also wrote on magical themes (*Alcina*, 1735), chose plots derived from French classical tragedy (*Rodelinda*, 1725, after Corneille's *Pertharite*), and even wrote the occasional comedy (*Serse*, 1738). Musically, the recitatives—relatively short, to suit English taste—convey each change of mood by means of modulation or by orchestral effects (his accompanied recitatives are often particularly fine). The arias are usually in *da capo* form and follow the 'exit' convention, but are richly varied in style. Far from being 'concerts in costume', as they were once considered, the operas show a tremendous flair for the theatre.

5. *Serious Opera in France until the Revolution.* Ideas not dissimilar to those which gave rise to the birth of opera in Florence were current at the same time in intellectual circles in France; but the stronger dramatic tradition and especially the popularity of elaborate court ballets meant that the concept of a drama sung throughout did not arrive until much later. Various attempts to

introduce opera were made around the middle of the 17th century, especially by Cardinal Mazarin, himself an Italian, whose enthusiasm had been aroused by seeing Landi's *Sant' Alessio* in Rome in 1632. Cavalli's *Egisto* was given in 1646 and the following year Luigi Rossi's *Orfeo*. From these and other performances it became clear that when there was a lavish *mise-en-scène*, preferably with machines, ballets, and even animals, the entertainment was a success; without such aids, the music tended to fall flat. This was confirmed by Cavalli's visit in 1660 for a production of his specially composed *Ercole amante*, which was delayed until 1662 because the machines were not ready: Cavalli's music was hardly noticed, while the ballets and scenery were enormously praised. There was a further period of little activity, although the so-called *comédies-ballets* (spoken plays with extended musical interludes) by Molière and Lully flourished from 1664 to 1670. In 1669 the poet and playwright Pierre Perrin (*c.*1620-75) began to establish 'académies d'opéra' in France, and together with the composer Robert Cambert inaugurated the Paris 'académie' with a pastoral in music, *Pomone* (1671), which has claims to be considered the first opera in the French language. The music for this has survived only incomplete, but it is clear that it was much more in tune with French taste, the use of the vernacular giving it a distinct advantage over Italian opera. Following intrigues, however, Perrin went bankrupt, was thrown into prison,

and his academy disbanded (1672). Lully seized his chance, and founded the Académie Royale de Musique, which was given a monopoly to produce completely sung drama. He produced first a pastoral in 1672, then in the following spring, a *tragédie héroïque*, *Cadmus et Hermione*. This was the first of a long series, Lully and his librettist Quinault writing one each year— including *Alceste* in 1674 and *Armide* in 1686— until Lully's death in 1687; and it was the style of these which governed French opera until the middle of the next century. Lully was a Florentine who had left his native city too early to gain a knowledge of contemporary Venetian opera. He had old-fashioned ideals, which, combined with the French taste for classical drama, produced an approach entirely independent from that current in Italy. Librettos were conceived as unified dramas, and although they took as themes the amorous adventures of mythological or legendary figures and scarcely merit the term 'heroic', they had the merit of lacking the incredible complexity of Italian plots. At the same time, there were simple *divertissements* to allow for the popular marvels of scenery and machines. The music was based on recitative rather than aria, though this recitative differed from Italian in that it was based on French prosody rather than on speech rhythms: it followed the regular accentuation of verse, imparting to the melody a more measured feeling. The *airs* were short, generally with a binary or rondo pattern, and were scarcely more

Designs by Boquet for La Haine in (left) *Lully's 'Armide' (revived 1761), and* (right) *Rameau's 'Zoroastre' (1769).*

melodious than the recitative. Several observers, accustomed to Italian opera, found the lack of differentiation between recitative and *air* disappointing, but, because the recitative style was based on the declamation of actors at the Comédie Française, its effect on the serious theatre-goer would have come close to the ideals of the Florentine founders of opera. The role of the chorus also looked back to earlier operas, notably those of the Roman school, Lully using it imaginatively as a participant in the drama, as well as for sonority in the *divertissements*. Lully's well-drilled orchestra provided ample ballets, the famous French overtures, and 'symphonies' to accompany action on the stage. Consequently French opera sounds very different from Italian opera; in addition, the absence of castratos, and the greater use of bass voices, gives a less brilliant effect, although some of the writing for high tenor is taxing enough. Lully's operas have been criticized for lacking a sense of drama. While the lack of adequate revivals makes it difficult to refute this, it is more likely that the lack of extended musical highlights would be more of an obstacle to the modern opera-goer, even though there is some fine music in them.

Lully's monopoly not only stamped out competition in his lifetime; it also meant that no other composers had the chance to gain experience in the genre. The consequences were immediately apparent. With few exceptions, the *tragédies héroïques* of the next generation were relatively unsuccessful, and although the works of Lully were revived for many seasons after his death, they gradually became unfashionable, even when alterations were made to bring them at least a little up to date. While the *tragédie héroïque* maintained its prestige, composers preferred the so-called *opéra-ballet* where conventions were less rigid. The *opéra-ballet* made no attempt at a continuous drama. Each act could be more or less independent, though sometimes there was an underlying theme. With this diminution in the role of the drama, it became possible to introduce Italian features, notably the extended *da capo* aria (called 'ariette' by the French to distinguish it from the shorter 'air'), with its more virtuoso singing and modern harmony. Campra's *opéra-ballet*, *Les fêtes venitiennes* (1710), includes a scene depicting the atmosphere and happenings at the Grimani theatre in Venice, while his *Le carnaval de Venise* (1699) actually contains a short Italian opera, *L'Orfeo nell'inferni*. Also more in tune with the times was the imaginative orchestration, to be found also in **tragédies lyriques* which often contain vivid storm scenes and other programme music.

In spite of the attractiveness of some of these works, the seriousness of French opera did not return until the 1730s, when Rameau's first

tragédie lyrique, *Hippolyte et Aricie* (1733), proved popular enough to encourage him to write theatrical pieces of various kinds for some 20 years (there was a gap from 1740 to 1745 when he seems to have disagreed with the management of the Opéra). His style might be described as 'Lully brought up to date', with the same basic forms of measured recitative (now more supple and embellished) and short arias (binary or ternary in form), to which are added the larger scale ariettas (virtuoso pieces after the Italian aria), choruses, and orchestral pieces, the last often programmatic depictions of psychological situations and such external features as storms. But this does scant justice to a real opera composer whose music is rich enough to stand on its own, enterprising in harmony and orchestration, expressive in melody, and conscious of dramatic considerations which are rarely impeded by the rigorous conventions of *opera seria*. Even the ballets are well integrated, while the overtures are frequently linked to the first scene, taking the place of the Lullian prologue. Rameau has been compared with Wagner in his flair for creating music drama: this is impossible to assess until his works have been seen on stage in good performances, but it would not be surprising to find his operas just as valid as those of Handel.

Rameau's operatic career finished in the 1750s (his final opera, *Les Boréades*, was written in 1764 but not performed). But by this time the *tragédie lyrique* was again under attack by the Italianate faction led by Rousseau, whose *opéra comique* was soon popular not only with the general public but with the intellectuals of the new Enlightenment (see below, 7). The older way was attempted by Boismortier and Mondonville with little success during the 1760s, but it was only with the arrival of Gluck in the following decade that the genre was truly revived (see below, 6). Thereafter, the Opéra was maintained until the political Revolution of 1789 by Italian Gluckists, Salieri, Sacchini, and Piccinni, the last brought to Paris in 1776 by yet another pro-Italian group especially to challenge Gluck. In fact, the result was opera on classical themes, though sometimes breaking away from classical attitudes: Salieri's *Les Danaides* (1784) includes a Hell scene in which Danaus is seen chained to a rock with his bleeding entrails being devoured by a vulture. The music is less florid than its Italian counterparts, but shares their harmonic idioms and general manner in many ways. However, choruses persist, the orchestration is fuller, and there is a penchant for ballet—all of which will continue until the 19th century.

6. *Rococo and Reform in opera seria, 1725-90*. Just as the French, perhaps unwittingly, had

stuck to the essential attitudes of the creators of opera, so the Italians, by 1725, were seeking to go back to at least some of them. The reformers were led at first by two librettists, Zeno and Metastasio. Both were court poets in Vienna, and wished to reassert the values of drama against the excesses of the star-based opera. For Zeno 'opera and reason are not necessarily incompatible'. The stories must be rid of comic elements and secondary plots and should show the opposition of love and duty in the rulers of state. The denouement must be brought about naturally and the climaxes should be built up in a planned manner. Metastasio developed this philosophy, adding elegance of poetry — verse full of conceits and similes — though not favouring the unities of time and place, as Zeno had tended to do. He worked in longer acts (three instead of five), placing an 'exit' aria at the end of each scene, the singer then leaving the stage. The recitatives were succinct, and the arias, expressing the character's state of mind or offering a reflection on the situation, were carefully arranged so that there should be the same number for each major character (to prevent quarrelling among the singers) and that no two arias of a similar type should be adjacent (to avoid monotony). This meant that the characters were limited to six or seven, three or four principal roles, the rest somewhat less important.

Into this logical and elegant mould dozens of composers poured their dramatic music for the next half century, changing the detail, but rarely the substance, of Metastasio's librettos to suit conditions. The arias were virtually all in the *da capo* pattern and were of three main types: *bravura* (to show off skill), used to express stress — emotional or real — and battle scenes; *cantabile*, for gentle zephyrs and more intimate aspects of love; *parlante* for less exalted moments. Ensembles were rare, although some beautiful duets (also in *da capo* form), expressing the grief of lovers, were written. An ensemble of the complete cast would sing a finale. This is sometimes marked 'chorus' but was not sung as such, though elsewhere in the operas there were crowd scenes. The *recitativo secco* is sometimes perfunctory, though at its best it effectively underlines the dramatic action, with changes of key to heighten changes of mood. It was only in the declining years of the *opera seria* that recitative could be relegated to insignificance: Mozart, in *La clemenza di Tito*, for example, held the composition of recitatives in such small regard that he entrusted them to his pupil Süssmayr. Accompanied recitative was scarce, reserved chiefly for moments of emotional climax.

The most famous composer of the Metastasian libretto was Hasse, who, as husband of the singer Faustina Bordoni, knew how to write expressively and effectively for the voice; and indeed, in spite of all the philosophizing, his operas, and those of many imitators, still favour vocal display. The melodic lines are decorated with appoggiaturas, which soften the rhythms; the harmony is simple and relatively slow moving. Some of the operas of this rococo style could perhaps be revived, especially those embodying grand spectacle: Hasse in one work, *Solimano* (1753), used a veritable zoo of horses, camels, and elephants, in a manner later to become familiar in performances of *Aida* at the Baths of Caracalla; but evidence suggests that they lack the strength of the pre-*galant* Baroque composers.

Certainly these operatic reforms were soon too mild to satisfy the really serious librettists and composers. Significantly, more far-reaching experiments came from two composers employed at courts where tastes were French: Jommelli at Stuttgart, Traetta at Parma. To these must be added Gluck at Vienna, who after thorough practice in the Metastasian *opere serie* in the 1740s, worked from 1756 for a monarch with French tastes, and then in the 1770s spent five years composing for the Paris Opéra. All these turned to the classical subjects typical of the *tragédie lyrique*, and all used the grand choruses characteristic of French opera, allotting an extensive role to the orchestra (Traetta especially having a penchant for pictorial effects after the manner of Rameau). The Italians replaced much of the *recitativo secco* with *recitativo accompagnato*, which often shows thematic development. The full *da capo* aria was used less often, only part of the first section being repeated. The influence of comic opera is apparent in the greater use of ensembles, and by the 1770s a two-part aria became popular. It was also common to interrupt arias with recitative, so enhancing the sense of dramatic continuity. Similarly, overtures set the mood of the drama, and sometimes ran straight into the first scene.

Gluck went further, having a librettist, Calzabigi, who became an anti-Metastasian and had the wisdom to see that opera did not depend solely on literary or musical values but was true spectacle and theatre. From *Orfeo ed Euridice* (1762), therefore, Gluck abandoned the *da capo* aria and *recitativo secco*, and wrote in a simple melodic style which seems consciously to have an 'antique' or classical flavour, paying attention to speech inflections: it is worth noting that the first excavations of Greek sites were being dug by Winckelmann at about this time. But in place of what might seem a Lullian attitude, his characters are human as opposed to symbolic, though the nature of these 'classical' librettos is to give them a moral tone.

Gluck's reforms (see also the separate entry

on Gluck) were exactly what was needed to keep French serious opera in being. As usual, Italy was less receptive and, in spite of his three 'French'-style but Italian operas of the 1760s, Metastasio settings continued as before. The inevitable result was that *opera seria* became increasingly old-fashioned, though its musical language was certainly affected by the more congenial style of *opera buffa*, to which we must now turn.

7. *Comic Opera until the Time of Mozart*. Comic scenes had been a successful feature of public opera from its beginnings. It was natural, therefore, that they should continue to be used in another form when the high-minded principles of composers and librettists led to their abolition. When the serious *tragédie héroïque* emerged in France, a species of comic opera was given by an Italian troupe acting improvised *commedia dell'arte* plays including songs. These dramas were given in Italian at first, but French scenes were gradually interwoven with them, and eventually they became entirely French. The songs, or *vaudevilles*, were popular tunes, sometimes with a folk-song flavour, but occasionally simple airs by Lully and others were used. There was usually an element of satire in the plot, and following a satirical attack on the King's mistress, Mme de Maintenon, such entertainments were abolished. The tradition, however, was continued at the annual Paris fairs, where acrobats and jugglers had performed for many years. The acting troupes were strictly supervised and were forbidden to use speech, a regulation they circumvented by displaying placards with the words written on them and by using *vaudevilles*. By 1714, pieces written completely *en vaudeville* were being called *opéras comiques*: these were so successful that five years later the official company for spoken drama, the Comédie Française, not liking the competition, had managed to have them banned. Yet an Italian company came back with their own entertainments, and *opéra comique* survived tenuously until the middle of the century, maintaining its tendency to satirize, to guy serious opera, and to use popular tunes, though the music was more often composed specially rather than being merely borrowed.

The French players brought *comédies en vaudevilles* to London in 1718 and it was probably this that gave the impetus for a similar kind of entertainment in English. John Gay's *The Beggar's Opera* (1728), the prototype for English *ballad opera, clearly borrowed some French attitudes: satire on politicians (the hero, Macheath, represented the Prime Minister Walpole in certain respects) and on *opera seria* (there is a mock prison scene which parodies a favourite operatic convention, of which the most recent

example had been in Handel's *Rodelinda* of 1725); the use of popular tunes and some folk-like material, and other melodies by Handel and other serious composers, harmonized simply and with additional material by Pepusch. As in France, the satirical element provoked censorship, and Gay's sequel, *Polly*, was banned from the stage by the Lord Chamberlain. *The Beggar's Opera*, dealing with low life in a jocular way, had an enormous public success and practically put *opera seria* out of business; it was also well received critically, Swift remarking that it exposed 'that unnatural taste for Italian music among us which is wholly unsuitable to our northern climate and the genius of the people'. It was the most promising step towards a popular, as opposed to a courtly, vernacular opera, and it was an English ballad opera, Charles Coffey's *The Devil to Pay* (1731), that sparked off the vogue for *Singspiel* ('plays in song') in Germany where it was widely given— as *Der Teufel ist los*—from 1743. In England itself, the fashion for ballad opera was at its height for about seven years, then faded until it finally disappeared about 30 years later. But it left a legacy of spoken drama with music, which was given greater coherence by composers such as Dibdin and Shield, who fully orchestrated the songs and provided ensembles and other Italianate elements.

More sophisticated comic opera, however, had been developed already in Italy. By the 1720s, it had become common to insert *intermezzi* between the acts of *opere serie*; at the same time a new type of opera—*opera buffa*— similar in style to these *intermezzi* was being given at some theatres in Naples. These *intermezzi* and *opere buffe* were in no sense related to the grand *intermedi* of the 16th century. At first, they were low dialect plays, but they soon developed into short social comedies, scenes from everyday life in which the wit of honest working girls and men triumphed over wealth and position. There were usually no more than three or four characters, who were played by singing actors rather than the virtuosos of *opera seria*. There were no castratos, and the bass voice came into its own. Unlike the French and English comedies, the Italian *opera buffa* was sung throughout, with recitatives and arias alternating; but the arias were much more varied in form and style than in serious opera. There were simple strophic songs, ariettas in two sections, rondo arias, with the occasional *da capo* aria used mainly for parody. The vocal style of all these was much simpler than in *opera seria*, using short phrases with strong rhythms rather than continuous long phrases needing great breath control. The words were mostly set syllabically and the gulf between recitative and aria is greatly reduced, the one seeming the

Painting by Giuseppe de Albertis of an intermezzo from an Italian opera, late 18th century. See Opera, 7.

extension of the other. So instead of a series of dramatic actions followed by contemplative static sections, the drama seems to be continuously in motion. This is especially true in the ensembles, the finales of acts being extensively developed so that there is a feeling of conversation and action. The orchestra is important in the ensembles, carrying the main melodic strand, while the voices chatter in short motivic phrases, a technique which again allows for a malleable relationship between action and music.

The most famous composer of the first phase of comic opera was Pergolesi, whose two-act *intermezzo*, *La serva padrona* (1733)—performed between the acts of Pergolesi's *opera seria*, *Il prigionier superbo*—achieved international renown for its tunefulness and vivacity. But by about 1750, a more sophisticated style was emerging, largely through the success of the joint efforts of the Venetians Goldoni and Galuppi. Goldoni, a first-class playwright of dialect comedies, provided more serious roles which Galuppi's music turned into quasi-sentimental characters. The purely farcical elements disappeared and a true social comedy began to cover a wide range of human emotions. Composers who understood the heroic idiom of *opera seria* turned to this more rewarding kind of comic opera, and from this time it became the most popular genre of the musical stage. Such a composer as Piccinni could take a plot based on Richardson's sentimental novel *Pamela*, and in *La buona figliuola* (1760) make a work rich in characters which transcend the normal stock types of the previous era. And although there was no great stylistic development after this, the form was pliable enough for Paisiello, Cimarosa, and others to explore the genre's possibilities and to provide it with a varying and extensive repertory until the end of the century.

The success of *opera buffa* had international repercussions. Pergolesi's *La serva padrona* was given in Paris in 1746, making apparently little impression; but when revived six years later it sparked a journalistic row, known as the Querelle des *Bouffons: here there were two opposing factions, one favouring Italian opera, the other defending native French traditions. One of the pro-Italian faction, Jean-Jacques Rousseau, produced a new kind of *opéra comique* in *Le devin du village* (1752), supposedly an *intermezzo* in the Italian style but in reality borrowing only the concept of recitative. Simple tunes, the rustic setting, and the dances are all entirely French in manner; but Rousseau's followers, including Gluck, employed more Italian means. However, the tendencies towards satire and the use of sometimes down-to-earth language persisted in the works of Favart, Monsigny, and Philidor.

Opera buffa also had its effect in Germany. After the introduction of ballad opera in the 1740s, there was a lull in the development of comic opera because of the Seven Years War. The resurgence came in 1766, when J. A. Hiller began composing *Singspiele*, writing catchy tunes as before (the borrowing of other composers' songs was abandoned), but also introducing numbers obviously owing their style to Italian comic opera. The next generation, including Benda, Neefe, and André, broadened this to the point of using *opera seria*-type arias, ensembles in a sentimental vein, and even *melodrama—in which speech was superimposed on 'dramatic' instrumental music. It was in this highly varied form that *Singspiel* achieved its popularity in Vienna, where the opening of the officially supported Burgtheater in 1778 gave it enormous impetus. Here was the chance to use really accomplished singers and a good orchestra. Moreover, this flowering of German opera happened to occur when an experienced operatic composer of genius—Mozart—was residing in Vienna.

8. *Mozart.* The complex state of opera during the latter part of the 18th century is encapsulated in the operas of Mozart, who worked in every theatrical genre of his age and had a genius for combining elements from each in such a way that, although his works are impossible to categorize exactly, opera became the kind of overwhelming experience desired and planned by its founders.

Mozart wrote five *opere serie*, the first (*Mitridate, rè di Ponto*) in 1770, the last (*La clemenza di Tito*) in 1791. All were commissioned, two for Milan and one each for Salzburg, Munich, and Prague. All but one of the librettos are either by Metastasio or in his style, and the music is based firmly on the aria: Metastasio's recitatives for *La clemenza di Tito* were shortened by Caterino Mazzolà, who recast the libretto for Mozart, at the same time rearranging the original three acts into two and adding eight ensemble pieces. The casts of Mozart's *opere serie* concentrate on high voices and include parts for castratos, the arias showing off their virtuosity; but the *da capo* aria is largely abandoned and the big *ritornelli* become shorter, particularly in the later works. The single exception to the purely Metastasian plan was, significantly, Mozart's undisputed masterpiece of Italian *opera seria*, *Idomeneo*, with a distinctive Gluckian flavour, including good choruses, and opportunities for orchestral pieces such as a chaconne, marches, and ballet

music. Mozart runs the overture into the first scene, uses trombones for the Oracle Scene, and writes extensive solo instrumental parts in the manner of the Parisian *sinfonie concertante*. Nevertheless, the style is predominantly Italian, especially the ensembles and one or two arias with *coloratura* (especially for the castrato).

There are seven *opere buffe* (including two which were unfinished) dating from 1768 to 1790. Of these, two had a pre-existing libretto which had been recently set by other composers; the rest were specially written, usually with active participation by the composer. Two were straightforward commissions, the others being intended for the general public and in some cases begun as speculative ventures (hence the unfinished pieces). As early as *La finta giardiniera* (1774) the characters are divided up between *parti serie* (serious characters) and *parti buffe* (comic characters), and the demands on some of the upper voices (and occasionally the basses) are as great as in *opera seria*. The plots are predominantly social comedy with distinctive groups of upper- and lower-class characters (as, for instance, in *Così fan tutte*, 1790), and although never overtly political or moralizing they make serious comments on manners. The musical organization put the emphasis on ensembles rather than arias. In *Le nozze di Figaro* (1786) arias and concerted pieces are equal in number. The latter, especially the finales, are longer and there is little chorus and no ballet, but in *Figaro* and *Don Giovanni* (1787) there is some less formal dancing. The finales are extended, continuous multi-sectional movements with a fast-moving conclusion in the major key. In these the orchestra has importance in maintaining the continuity in a symphonic style. Otherwise, it occasionally plays characteristic pieces; in *Don Giovanni* the overture leads into the first scene, and the Statue Scene uses trombones, both features reminiscent of Gluck. Thus, although certainly *buffa* in attitude and closer to life than the *opere serie*, these operas have serious elements.

Mozart wrote five large-scale works setting German, in the *Singspiel* manner, one being unfinished, another a sacred comedy with music; and also a one-act 'comedy' with musical numbers. Two childhood pieces have simple music in the *opéra comique* tradition. The mature works are comedies with exotic local colour (*Zaide*, 1779-80; and *Die Entführung aus dem Serail*, 1782) or magic elements (*Die Zauberflöte*, 1791). None can be considered purely humorous; indeed *Die Zauberflöte* is a masonic allegory in which elements of criticism of society and religious beliefs are intermixed. The social differentiation between nobility and lower classes is an equally integral part of the plot, expressed in music which ranges from simple songs for

Play-bill for the first performance of Mozart's 'Così fan tutte' (Burgtheater (Hoftheater), Vienna, 1790).

servants to elegant arias for princes and noble ladies. The variety of music is wider than even that of *opera buffa*. There are heroic arias (those of the Queen of Night in *Die Zauberflöte*), even with *concertante* instrumental parts (Constanze's 'Martern aller Arten' in *Die Entführung*), cavatinas, and *buffo* finales. In *Die Zauberflöte* there are unique elements: a Bachian choral prelude, the secular but religious-sounding march, and Sarastro's hymn-like aria 'O Isis und Osiris'. The overture does not lead into the first scene but the opening fanfares eventually occur in the body of the opera.

In Mozart's operas, we can see three different genres—*opera seria*, *opera buffa*, and *Singspiel*. All are capable of serious expression, using interchangeable elements. The Italian genres are more firmly based and will continue to dominate during much of the 19th century; but the vernacular genres are now much more than simple *Singspiele* and are capable of high seriousness (*Die Zauberflöte* can be held to be the starting-point for the German tradition of serious opera). These operas can embrace themes of religious and moral feeling, class structure, and heroic or domestic life. The music varies from the simple to the extraordinarily complex, and its established conventions are capable of the greatest fluidity according to the needs of the subject. Mozart thus achieved that aim of opera's Florentine founders 'to move the whole man'—though they would have been surprised at the means by which it had been effected. For this reason, Mozart's operas not only sum up previous achievement but also were highly influential in the future. Italian opera developed the *buffo* genre on his lines, through Paer and Rossini. In Germany, the moral Enlightenment in *Die Zauberflöte* encouraged a *Singspiel* of

much greater ambition. Only in France did his example have little impact, largely because of a chauvinism which was immediately extended by the Revolution.

9. *Interlude.* The year 1791, seeing the death of Mozart and the true beginning of Revolutionary institutions in France, presents a convenient dividing line in the history of opera. By this time, the genre was universal throughout Europe, from Russia to England. Although the French Revolution hastened the demise of its noble patronage, opera was far from perishing and the State (in various forms) took over the erstwhile role of princes. So widespread was the popularity of opera that it now lacks a central unified history (except perhaps for a short time in the 1880s to the 1890s when the vogue for Wagner was predominant). Nor can it truly be classified into 'serious' and 'comic', for the dividing line between the two is often blurred and they always interact on each other in the way we have seen with Mozart. The most convenient division is by nations, even though these also interact; and the most convenient batting order is (i) France, which became the Mecca of opera composers; (ii) Italy, which infiltrated virtually every country with both composers and performers; (iii) Germany, which had the most profound influence in the end with the works of Wagner; then (iv) other countries of western Europe, and (v) Slavonic opera.

10. *French Opera in the 19th Century.* One effect of the French Revolution (1789) was to increase the popularity of *opéra comique*. This now became more serious in story, with 'political' themes particularly common in the so-called *rescue operas, such as Gaveaux's *Léonore*

(1798)—the model for Beethoven's *Fidelio*—and Méhul's *La prise du pont de Lodi* (1797). The music maintained the division into numbers and the essential simplicity of melody and harmony, but Italian influence crept into the *airs*, now given roulades, while the finales acquired the characteristic speeding up, or *stretti*, of *opera buffa*. With first the Consulat and then the Imperial periods of Napoleon, the *tragédie lyrique* reasserted itself: the Gluckian repertory of the 1780s survived, and then in 1807 the Italian Spontini revived the style in *La Vestale*, preserving the classical attitudes and using short-breathed melody inherited from the 18th century, but giving weight to monumental spectacle and using a large orchestra imaginatively.

On the demise of Napoleon, therefore, there was substantial support for both serious and comic opera. The 1820s were fruitful chiefly in the field of *opéra comique*, with Auber and Boieldieu as its major exponents. Auber (who lived on and composed until 1871) established the main points of its 19th-century style. A tendency towards Romantic plots was highlighted by a vogue in the 1820s for Walter Scott and historical themes. The music itself was less Romantic, though brilliantly orchestrated. The forms of *air* and *romance* have an atmosphere of the salon, with regular phrases and inherent dance measures. The ensembles, though sometimes extended, lack contrapuntal interest, so there is little opportunity for individual characterization. But the result is always pleasing if rarely powerful, the repertory including such popular works as Rossini's *Le Comte Ory* (1823), a charming Frenchified *opera buffa* by Paer, *Le maître de chapelle* (1821), and eventually Donizetti's *La fille du régiment* (1840).

Rossini, by now a favourite in Paris, had been a major figure in the transformation of serious opera, first with a four-act reworking (1827) of his three-act opera-cum-oratorio *Mosè in Egitto* (1818), which had appealed through its large-scale choral scenes and opportunities for spectacle, and then with *Guillaume Tell* (1829), on a subject obviously in line with the Revolutionary traditions. The latter has elements of the *tragédie lyrique*, including ballets, choruses, and rich orchestral effects (including a truly original overture); it also has Italianate arias which appealed to the taste of an audience which could hear the latest foreign music at the Théâtre-Italien. Within a year one of the great exponents of *grand opera (as this must now be called, since it is no longer *tragédie lyrique*) had achieved prominence. Meyerbeer and his librettist Scribe in *Robert le diable* (1831) and then *Les Huguenots* (1836) created the archetype of a genre which was to fascinate all Europe and which in Meyerbeer's output was to reach its apogee in *L'Africaine* (1865). In *Les Huguenots* the story,

Scene from Act 3 of the first production of Meyerbeer's 'L'Africaine' (Paris Opéra, 1865).

although not badly worked out, is secondary to the scenic effect which is always extravagant and startling: Medieval settings, church scenes, a torrent, choruses of demons, crypts and grave-yards (some of these borrowed from Weber) abound. Such effects are matched in the music by mighty (and frequently very interesting) orchestral effects, ensembles with the soloists set against the chorus, both features which required a different and heavier type of voice from those developed for the florid Italian tradition. All that is lacking is memorable melody—and perhaps a sense of proportion, for verisimilitude does finally matter, at least in operas on historical themes.

Meyerbeer's work created a demand for grand opera which his slow method of working could not satisfy. Halévy, in *La juive* (1835), and Berlioz, in *Benvenuto Cellini* (1838), continued the tradition, though the latter was hissed off the Opéra stage despite some virile music and a splendidly dramatic scene as Cellini casts his statue. This fiasco in effect exiled Berlioz from the theatre for more than 20 years. His finest opera, *Les Troyens*, a huge work with a libretto after Virgil, was never given a complete per-formance in his lifetime, for it is a true *tragédie lyrique* written long after the taste for the genre had passed. The classical theme, the chaste music with a mixture of recitative, *arioso*, and aria that would not have seemed strange to Gluck, the use of recurrent themes rather than the symphonic *Leitmotive* of Wagner, the atmospheric interludes such as the Royal Hunt and Storm (reminiscent of Rameau's pictorial symphonies)—all make this a French work *par excellence*. But the lack of obvious excitements of grand opera was its downfall; only in the 20th century has it achieved its rightful place. Berlioz's other opera, a charming comedy *Béatrice et Bénédict* (1862), was first given in Germany; it conforms to no existing French genre, and its use of 'numbers' (some of them very attractive) looks back to the 1830s.

Barriers were nevertheless breaking down. *Opéra comique* was written by Meyerbeer him-self in the 1850s with *L'étoile du nord* (1854) and *Dinorah* (1859), though they were intended for great singers (such as Jenny Lind) and their 'numbers' are conceived on a large scale. They are best described as 'grand operas with spoken dialogue'. This helps to explain the strange fate of several famous operas of the 1860s and 1870s. For example, Gounod, a member of a generation turning away from the heroic and grand, composed *Faust* (1859) for the Théâtre-Lyrique with spoken dialogue; for its presenta-tion at Strasbourg the following year he added recitative; and when it finally arrived at the Opéra it had recitative and a ballet. Thus a work written in the tradition of *opéra comique*, with

separate numbers (some of which are related quite distinctly to salon music), was transformed into grand opera (which admittedly its subject might suggest). *Roméo et Juliette* (1867) was subjected to the same treatment. Bizet, who like all young French composers must have had ambitions to write for the Opéra, equally produced *Les pêcheurs de perles* (1863) for the Théâtre-Lyrique but with an oriental flavour then in fashion through the operas of Félicien David. His last opera *Carmen* was produced at the Opéra-Comique in 1875 with spoken dialogue, later being transferred to the Opéra with recitatives by Ernest Guiraud (1837–92). *Carmen* was more influential outside than inside France, certainly affecting the Italian verists (see below, 11) in its low life plot with a melodramatic ending. Its really French charac-teristics—the irony, the lack of sentimentality in portraying the heroine, the clarity of the pseudo-Spanish music—were not imitated, except perhaps by Chabrier.

By 1880 Wagner was all the rage, at least with the intellectuals (see *France*, 8); and while the Opéra was unwilling to produce any of his later works, the younger generation of composers knew of them either by going to experience them in Germany or by studying the scores. Most of them did not see their real significance. Operas on Nordic or Celtic (after *Tristan*) subjects were written, such as Reyer's *Sigurd* (1885, written after studying Wagner's writings on music drama, not the works themselves) and Lalo's *Le roi d'Ys* (1888); but although there are recurring themes and a 'through-composed' structure, the symphonic use of *Leitmotive* never penetrated French style. Instead, the taste of the public was for the Gounod-esque *opéra lyrique*, followed by Ambroise Thomas and Massenet on subjects frequently taken from novels (from *Werther* to *Manon*) or more am-bitiously Shakespeare or the Bible. Often attrac-tive in melody, well orchestrated and charming, they are at their best when not over-ambitious. This also applies to isolated works by other composers, notably Offenbach's *Les contes d'Hoffmann* (1881), an *opéra comique* with, as often, recitatives added later, its apparent *lyrique* quality spiced with an ironic tinge. At the turn of the century, a work in an entirely different manner appeared: Gustave Charpen-tier's *Louise* (1900), though generally seen as Wagnerian, is in fact nearer to Puccini in its story of the Bohemians and the sempstress, while its continuous structure with repeated themes is typically French. The next master-piece of French opera, *Pelléas et Mélisande* (1902), although more truly Wagnerian in technique shows a complete change of direction and must be treated as a 20th-century work (see below, 15).

11. *Italy during the 19th and Early 20th Centuries.* Although Italy's musical educational institutions were affected by the Napoleonic occupations, the opera houses continued little changed from pre-Revolutionary days. Larger cities had several theatres, usually under 'private' management, sometimes with a state subsidy; and most smaller towns had their own opera house. There were three seasons each year, and the larger houses produced at least one or two new operas in each. With composers paid for each work by the theatre and with no efficient copyright system, a successful composer could expect to write at least two and sometimes as many as four operas each year. This need in itself encouraged a fairly rigid framework for both serious and comic opera. The trend to conservatism was strengthened by the lack of a tradition of spoken drama on to which *Singspiel* or *opéra comique* could be grafted. Romantic literature, blossoming in northern Europe, had little immediate effect in Italy, there being no Italian equivalent of the novels of Scott, the lyric poetry of Goethe or Shelley, or the dramas of Schiller. The progressive Italian composers, such as Spontini or Cherubini, often settled abroad, perhaps in Paris or Berlin. Thus the considerable advances in matter and style found in France and Germany did not arrive in Italy until much later in the century. There were three main types of opera in the first 40 years of the 19th century. *Opera seria* changed its musical nature by tending to be organized by scene rather than by aria. It also differed from its 18th-century forebears by allowing a tragic ending in place of the conventional *lieto fine* (happy ending). *Opera buffa* continued much as it was, with patter songs, extended ensembles and finales, and ornamented arias for the sentimental roles. These sentimental parts are more prominent in the new *opera semiseria*, a hybrid which might be described as an *opera seria* with a happy ending (Bellini's *La sonnambula* of 1831 is the finest example, in which a tragic denouement expressed in very serious music is averted). As well as these there were curtain-raisers and shorter pieces called *farse*, almost harking back to the Neapolitan *intermezzo*.

Although composers now travelled so much that geographical divisions are only approximate, a rough division between the Neapolitan school (led by Zingarelli and culminating in the work of Bellini) and the north Italians (Mayr, Rossini, Donizetti, and ultimately Verdi) can be made. The work of the southerners adheres to the succession of arias and recitatives which can be fairly called 'numbers' opera. The melody is florid, the accompaniment and orchestration simple. The arias are no longer in the *da capo* form, but are often in two sections, a slower lyrical *cavatina* being followed by a faster more rhythmic *cabaletta*, thus allowing for the immediate expression of two contrasting emotions. The predominance of the upper voices continues. The operas of the northern school, on the other hand, are written in the knowledge of Mozart, adopting a more ensemble-based continuity, in which the orchestra plays a larger role, and in which the vigorous rhythms of *opera buffa* infect even serious arias, providing a much less flaccid ornamental melody. In *opera buffa* itself, the lower voices have a larger role, especially the comic bass (e.g. Don Basilio in Rossini's *Il barbiere di Siviglia*, 1816); but it is noticeable that Rossini also liked the *coloratura contralto* (as in *La cenerentola*, 1817). It is in this northern group that the gradual introduction of romantic subjects took place. Rossini turned to Scott (*La donna del lago*, 1819) and Shakespeare (*Otello*, 1816) and Donizetti not only to Scott again (*Il castello di Kenilworth*, 1829; and *Lucia di Lammermoor*, 1835) but also to tragic historical themes (*Anna Bolena*, 1830). These required more dramatic treatment, and although the 'numbers' concept does not actually disappear, it is much attenuated by turning the recitative into a grand, accompanied section of an aria (which it can interrupt as well as precede), by adding choral backing to the solo voice, breaking down the division between 'chorus' and 'aria', and by making the climax a splendid ensemble (such as in the sextet from *Lucia*). Composers such as Mercadante and Donizetti who had worked in Paris were keen by the later 1830s to make the forms more malleable, breaking away from the *cavatina–cabaletta* relationship and cutting out music superfluous to the dramatic situation.

It was at this point that Verdi transformed the situation. For a detailed account of his development the reader is referred to the biographical entry, but it can be said here that he appeared a giant in the field almost immediately and that the transformation of Italian opera was due almost entirely to him. Although his first success *Nabucco* (1842) was mainly in the Bellini tradition, the fame of its choruses gave importance to the role of 'the people' as had the German *Singspiel*. Verdi's interest in the supernatural aspects of psychology manifested itself as early as *Giovanna d'Arco* (1845); thereafter his international reputation took him to Paris where he came into contact with grand opera. His mature librettos were either taken from Shakespeare, Schiller, Hugo, and Spanish romantic drama, or were specially conceived as French 'historical' grand opera. His dramatic sense caused him to break away from traditional forms, the aria practically disappearing from some grand operas, and the orchestra given the job of providing continuity in a way that gave rise to charges of Wagnerism. Nevertheless,

Wagner's example played very little part in Verdi's development, for his interest was in character rather than symbol, in what happened on the stage rather than in the symphonic development of themes in the orchestra. His idiom remained fairly diatonic and clearly melodic, using chromaticism and counterpoint as decorative rather than structural features. Paradoxically, his very traditionalism made him a better dramatist than Wagner, because his interest in the vocal parts rather than the orchestra directed attention to the characters on stage rather than any supposed symbolic significance.

Wagner's influence remained slight. The first Italian performances of his music were of *Lohengrin* (1871) and *Tannhäuser* (1872) at Bologna; the *Ring* cycle was given only in 1882–3 by the German touring company of Angelo Neumann; native performances of these and the remaining music dramas only took place in the period around 1890, their complexities deterring the theatre managements. Lacking the devotion of French composers who experienced Wagner's operas in Munich (1870) and Bayreuth (1876), Italian composers knew of them only through written accounts and vocal scores. The sole composer to show any understanding was Boito, whose travels abroad had acquainted him with modern developments, his *Mefistofele* (1868), based on Goethe's *Faust*, showing attitudes and techniques similar to *Lohengrin*. He later translated Wagner's librettos and shows some Wagnerian traits in librettos he wrote for other composers; but his own musical development never came to pass (his *Nerone* was left incomplete) and Italian music continued on its non-German paths.

The next generation in fact followed up various Verdian ideas. Their style is generally known as *verismo*, or realism (not to be confused with Russian realism, with which it has little connection; see below, 14), though this is somewhat misleading. The sense of reality comes either in the determination to show the less agreeable side of life (in which it is not very different from middle-period Verdi) or in setting the scene among the bourgeois or lower classes—as in the case of *La traviata* (1853). The other main influences were Bizet's *Carmen* and Massenet, whose *Hérodiade* was even commissioned by Ricordi and whose supple melodic

Costume designs for the first production of Verdi's 'Rigoletto' (*La Fenice, Venice, 1851*).

style had a great effect on Puccini. The sources of librettos were frequently novels rather than plays, and the construction of the libretto accordingly episodic. The musical technique is also based on the malleable construction of Verdi's mature operas, the arias (now deprived of decorative figuration) using the upper ranges of the voice in a strong, rhythmic, syllabic melodic line. The results are often melodramatic as in the works of Ponchielli, Catalani, Giordano, Cilea, Mascagni, and Leoncavallo, the most concise examples being Mascagni's *Cavalleria rusticana* (1890) and Leoncavallo's *Pagliacci* (1892). Puccini's *Tosca* (1900) belongs to the same category; but his 'bourgeois' operas, notably *La bohème* (1896) and *Madama Butterfly* (1904), show a more delicate touch, and his musical style, taking in the novelties of Debussy and the new wave of orientalism, is more sophisticated than that of his contemporaries.

The enormous financial rewards made possible by modern copyright conventions and widespread international distribution, which Puccini (and his publisher Ricordi) reaped at an early age, stimulated a host of imitators, but since Puccini's death in 1924 no Italian opera has succeeded in holding the stage and most Italian composers of any worth have been trying to break away from what they consider a sterile tradition.

12. *German Opera from Mozart to Richard Strauss.* Mozart's *Die Zauberflöte*, though anything but a light *Singspiel*, was nevertheless produced at a theatre where pantomime and trivia were the basis of the repertory; his last *opera seria*, *La clemenza di Tito*, of distinctly lesser quality, was given at a state-supported theatre. This social superiority of Italian over German operas continued until the 1850s, when Wagner's polemic (rather than his operas) reversed this fashion. Thus the *Singspiel* continued as a domestic entertainment, comedies of little distinction being matched by similarly unambitious music for about 20 years after Mozart's death. But around the turn of the century, the plots of *Singspiele* began to show the influence of the German Romantic movement with its interest in the supernatural, while Beethoven's *Fidelio* (1805, 1806, 1814) reflected the internationalism of French Revolutionary music. The new spirit was seen in E. T. A. Hoffmann's *Undine* (1816), the composer-cum-poet-cum-producer taking up the challenge of *Die Zauberflöte* in an ambitious magic music drama, though the music fails to live up to the skill of the other elements. Nevertheless, this pointed the way for a more distinguished composer, Weber, whose experience in writing traditional *Singspiele* (of which *Abu Hassan* of 1811 is a fine example) was matched by his knowledge of the foreign repertory. The result was *Der Freischütz* (1821), a horror story of a highly romantic nature. The country (back to Nature) setting, the opposition of good and evil, and magic scenic effects are matched by music which fills the old moulds of *Singspiel* with a new spirit, containing original orchestral writing (including an overture which is a miniature symphonic poem), choral writing of a folk-song nature, and solo arias of real distinction. The popularity this achieved enabled Weber to compose *Euryanthe* (1823) as almost a German serious opera, cutting down the dialogue, and writing large-scale Italianate *coloratura* arias and extended ensembles; but probably because the Medieval chivalric plot was badly constructed this still did not overcome the feeling that really serious opera was an Italian prerogative.

Nor did various other operas of this so-called Biedermeier period, when comfortable middle-class audiences were not in tune with the heroics of grand opera or the ironies of social comedy. Spohr, with *Faust* (1816) and *Jessonda* (1823), did his best to infiltrate grand opera, displaying some skill in developing a continuous melody, advanced chromatic harmony, and delicate orchestration, with some immediate success. Others, such as Mendelssohn and Schumann, never acquired sufficient experience in the theatre. Of the well-known *Singspiel* composers of the 1830s and 1840s, Lortzing managed to make the genre more like *opera semiseria*, with ample ensembles, overtures better linked to the opera, but keeping the straightforward choruses and simple song arias. Marschner preferred the *Freischütz* type of horror plot (as in *Der Vampyr*, 1828). Nicolai, more Italian in taste, wrote something in the tradition of *opera buffa* in his delightful *Die lustigen Weiber von Windsor*, 1849.

It was in this condition that Wagner found German opera in the 1830s and it was almost entirely due to his efforts in the next decade that it was completely transformed. Since this change was brought about in a very personal way, readers must be referred to the article on Wagner for a discussion of how it came about. Here its various phases must be noted. In the 1830s, Wagner's operas show little sign of ambition to alter German opera. *Die Feen* (composed 1833–4) is a fairy opera little different from those of Weber and Marschner. *Das Liebesverbot* (1836) shows the influence of Italian and French opera, as though Donizetti and Auber were Wagner's models. *Rienzi* (1842) was an attempt at Parisian grand opera (Spontini's *Fernand Cortez* and Halévy's *La juive* were well known to Wagner).

The 1840s were years of assimilation and transformation of these influences. From

Wagner's writings it is clear that he regarded the musical theatre as one of the most important cultural manifestations, and that it must not be considered merely as entertainment. In *Der fliegende Holländer* (1843) the idea of man's redemption by a woman's love appears for the first time in his work, and his characters seem symbolic rather than human. The music is constructed with only a few recognizable set pieces, the most important of which is a 'ballad' for the heroine, Senta, which becomes a symbol of purity and love and the destiny to redeem. This recurs several times and attains symbolic significance, as does the storm music representing the Dutchman's fate (hence unredeemed mankind). Wagner's next two operas *Tannhäuser* (1845) and *Lohengrin* (1850) develop the style. The first has more elements of the grand opera (it is no coincidence that it was selected by the Paris Opéra for performance in 1860 rather than the more recent *Lohengrin*), including opportunities for grand choruses and more straightforward numbers. *Lohengrin*, though also a grand spectacular, is original in the way the symbols, expressed by thematic material stated in the overture, are used throughout the drama, coming together at the end in a kind of analogy to a symphonic recapitulation.

It was this analogy with symphonic style which gave Wagner the opportunity of creating a new kind of opera, which he called the 'music drama'. Because of his exile in Germany from 1848 he had less chance of having his work produced, and he took some time thinking about the nature of opera before resuming composition. His published theories were the basis for his concept of *Der Ring des Nibelungen*, and, although they underwent change over the years, they led him to a radically new style, the most important features of which can be summarized as follows. The subject-matter of the opera should be based on legend and deal with archetypal concepts applicable to mankind as a whole rather than to specific men (as historical subjects tend to do). The music should be constructed so as to follow the sense of the drama, and not impose its own pattern upon it. Hence recitative and aria (essentially a musical patterning) must be replaced by a continuous flow, halted by few cadences. This could be achieved by developing a number of themes associated generally with the archetypal concept (such a theme is called a 'leading motif'; Ger.: *Leitmotiv*) in the orchestra, the voices singing in an appropriately inflected *arioso*, generally with only one singing at a time so that the words could be heard.

The emphasis put on the individual components of these arguments varied from work to work, and it is true that the ideas were developments of those of previous composers. The symbolic nature of the drama harks back to Weber and even to Mozart's *Zauberflöte*. The continuity achieved by the use of the orchestra derives from the *opera buffa* finales of the 18th century and was a commonplace of Parisian grand opera, while the use of recurrent themes was quite common in Verdi's operas. Nevertheless the conscious logical application of these ideas led to a new and powerful kind of opera. The necessity for a continuous flow made Wagner develop a harmonic style with the capacity to modulate freely. The melody following the words now rarely fell into rigid phrase patterns. The emphasis on the orchestra encouraged more subtle effects. The net result was that dramatic continuity is preserved and the symbolism of the drama does reveal many traits of human psychology, especially those where logic is effected by man's fundamentally emotional nature. The most complete realization of the Wagnerian ideal was in *Tristan und Isolde* (1865), where the 'story' is essentially psychological, the musical means far removed from those of previous operas (the exception being the sailor's song in Act 3 which both in its own nature and in the way it is integrated into the musical texture goes back to *Der fliegende Holländer*). But both the *Ring* and *Tristan* were virtually inimitable. Probably more influential was *Die Meistersinger von Nürnberg* (1868) in which Wagner applies the musical means of 'music drama' to a comedy with elements of grand opera. The basic soundness of Wagner's thinking about music's relationship to text is revealed in this opera, where the plot involves 'real' people in almost conventional dramatic situations.

The musical power of these masterpieces, combined with their intellectual conceptions, virtually destroyed the hegemony of Italian music in Germany and led to a host of imitations, most of little worth. The composers of solid music dramas, setting Medieval or philosophic texts of the Wagnerian type, have generally sunk without trace, the exception being Pfitzner whose *Palestrina* (1917) is a Schopenhauerian philosophic drama using the full-scale apparatus of *Leitmotiv*. The composers who used Wagner's musical means for un-Wagnerian ends did better. Cornelius's *Der Barbier von Bagdad* (1858) looks back to the tradition of the 'serious-comic' operas of the 1840s; Humperdinck reverts to the German legendic themes in *Hänsel und Gretel* (1893) and *Königskinder* (1897), but, while using Wagnerian harmonic practices, modifies the scheme of music drama considerably. Wolf, on the contrary, followed Wagner all too closely in *Der Corregidor* (1896)—yet with some success since the model is *Die Meistersinger*.

In fact, Wagner's 'art-work of the future'

Adolphe Appia's design for the forest in Act 1 of Wagner's 'Parsifal' (1896).

never really materialized, as is shown by the major German opera composer of the 20th century, Richard Strauss, who, beginning as a close follower of Wagner in his first two operas, put the *Leitmotiv* and orchestral sophistication to expressionist non-philosophical use in *Salome* (1905) and *Elektra* (1909). He then turned to social comedy in *Der Rosenkavalier* (1911), deliberately interweaving 18th-century-type 'numbers' among music-drama orchestral continuity, a process taken further in the best of the later operas, notably *Arabella* (1933). Although his principal librettist, von Hofmannsthal, was of philosophic inclination, the delight of these operas lies in their characterizations, interpreted by Strauss with a sense of humour and compassionate understanding. Their weakness lies in their artificiality, a deliberate turning away from reality with an exquisite literary self-consciousness, which Strauss's extra-musical sophistication tends to inflate beyond its deserts.

13. *Opera Elsewhere in Western Europe.* Italy, France, and Germany have had continuous traditions of opera; elsewhere the development has been sporadic, interrupted by external circumstances or dominated by composers from the 'Big Three'. The main obstacles in the first instance were partly political (Protestant Europe

Scene from the first production of Strauss's 'Elektra' (Dresden, 1909), where Elektra offers to light Aegisthus' way into the palace.

being cut off from the humanist ideas of Florence and Rome), and partly the existence of a strong tradition of spoken drama (especially in England and Spain) which made some critics believe that opera was frankly ridiculous. Most European countries had had the same kind of entertainments that flourished in Italy in the 16th century. In Spain, plays were given with songs by such distinguished composers as Juan del Encina. England appreciated the *masque which was akin to the Italian *intermedio*. 'Recitative music' (as the English called it) crept into the masque as early as 1617, while Nicholas Lanier, after travelling in Italy, produced his *Hero and Leander* (1628) in which he tried to adapt Italian methods to English scansion.

But it was only after a number of travellers (among them the diarist John Evelyn) had seen the popularity of opera in Venice during the 1640s and 1650s that real attempts at transplanting it were made. In England, Cromwell's Commonwealth encouraged the growth of opera, since spoken drama was banned, while music was not. So the dramatist William Davenant (1606-68) wrote the text of *The Siege of Rhodes* in 1656; this was the first true English opera as far as we know (but the music by Locke and others is lost). After the Restoration, when drama was again permitted, he turned it into a spoken play with extensive music—what Roger North was shortly afterwards to call a 'semi-opera'. This kind of entertainment was popular until the 1690s, when Purcell was one of its

principal exponents, with such works as *The Fairy Queen* (1692) and *The Indian Queen* (1695).

There were 'real' operas too. In England Dryden's *Albion and Albanius* was set to undistinguished music by the Frenchman Louis Grabu (*fl.* 1665-94, after, but a long way behind, Lully), followed by Blow's entertaining and also French-influenced *Venus and Adonis* (*c*.1684, still called a masque) and Purcell's *Dido and Aeneas* (1689), a mixture of elements from France (dances and choruses), Italy (recitatives and Dido's Lament), and England (the songs). In Holland Carolus Hacquart (*c*.1640-?1701) produced *De triomfeerende min* (1678), which has been considered the first Dutch opera but which is in fact a Frenchified dramatic entertainment, or play with music.

But the most significant aspect of opera outside Italy, Germany, and France was the employment of Italian musicians. Pietro Ziani's *Le fatiche d'Ercole per Deianira* (1662) was heard in Amsterdam through the initiative of the former Dutch consul in Venice. The future King Sigismund III of Poland saw Francesca Caccini's *La liberazione di Ruggiero* on a visit to Florence in 1625 which led to a tradition of Italian opera productions in Warsaw. This process was to make attempts at creating national opera companies more difficult throughout the 18th century. The rival companies in London employing Handel, Bononcini, Ariosti, and others, from 1709 prevented serious opera in

The singers Senesino, Cuzzoni, and Berenstadt in Handel's 'Flavio', first performed at the Haymarket Theatre, London, 1723

English from coming into existence, at least for the time being. In Copenhagen the operas of Sarti were popular; in Sweden an Italian nonentity called Francesco Uttini (1723-95) held sway; Portugal was equally dominated by the Neapolitan Davide Perez (1711-78), and Spain was served by Italians setting Metastasio. In Russia, the arrival of an Italian company directed by Francesco Araia (*b* 1709) in the 1730s led to a stream of his fellow-countrymen— Galuppi, Traetta, and Paisiello among them— who were well paid for braving the northern climate. In Bohemia such young men as Mysliveček and František Míča (1746-1811) were sent south to study and then emulate the latest styles.

It was the increasing popularity of genres such as ballad opera and *opéra comique* which helped to break up this state of affairs, since the use of speech in the vernacular inevitably encouraged national styles. A distinctive manner was strong in Spain, where the *zarzuela flour-ished with two excellent composers, Sebastián Durón (1660-1716) and Antonio Literes (1673-1747): Literes wrote an *Accis y Galatea* (1708), and later in the century Rodrígues de Hita (*c*.1724-87) used guitars, mandolins, tam-bourines, and castanets for some spectacular dancing in *Las labradoras de Murcia* (1769). The *zarzuela* (in this sense) was eventually super-seded by a yet simpler entertainment, the *tonadilla escénica* (usually a down-to-earth story of everyday folk), but this too became increas-ingly sophisticated. However, in the 19th cen-tury there was a renewed interest in the *zarzuela* in Spain, just as in other countries an increasing national awareness gave rise to distinctive styles to combat the pervading influence of Italian, German, and French opera. England, for ex-ample, produced a species of ballad opera in the witty, often satirical operettas of Gilbert and Sullivan, and attempted opera on a grander scale in the operas of Wallace and Balfe, whose *Maritana* (1845) was enormously successful both in England and abroad. German influence persisted in the work of Delius, and in that of Ethel Smyth, several of whose operas were in fact given their premières in Germany: *Fantasio* (Weimar, 1898), *Der Wald* (Berlin, 1902), and *The Wreckers* (Leipzig, 1906). Similarly, Rutland Boughton's absorption with Wagner led him to plan a Celtic Bayreuth at Glastonbury, though at the height of the English folk-song revival both Holst (*At the Boar's Head*, 1925) and Vaughan Williams (*Hugh the Drover*, 1924; *Sir John in Love*, 1929) imbued their operas with national colour. However, nationalist sentiment was even more pronounced in the operas written in the countries of eastern Europe.

DENIS ARNOLD

14. *Slavonic Opera*. During the 19th century the emergence of local creative talent helped foster national operatic styles in Russia, Bohemia and Czechoslovakia, Poland, and Hungary, so curbing the dominance of Italy, France, and Germany which had persisted throughout much of the 18th century. As mentioned in section 13, Russia was largely overrun with Italian and French music from around the middle of the 18th century, a fact exemplified by such works as Bortnyansky's *Le faucon* (1786) and *Le fils rival* (1787), which combine Bortnyansky's own Italianate style with the conventions of *opéra comique*: both operas have spoken dialogue and both were written to French librettos by La-fermière, librarian to the (then) tsarevich Paul. Around the same time, however, an increasing interest in Russia's historical and artistic heri-tage, evident in the publication of the first folk-song collections, was reflected in Mikhail Sokolovsky's *The Miller-Magician, Cheat and Matchmaker* (1779), which, though in the tradi-tion of Rousseau's *Le devin du village*, achieves a certain local colour in its use of folk-tunes and in its folky plot. Similar tendencies are apparent in the operas of Fomin, Mikhail Matinsky (1750-*c*.1825), and Vasily Pashkevich (*c*.1742-*c*.1797), who again used folk-tunes (albeit with complete disregard for the melodies' modal character) and drew on subjects of peasant life and Russian history.

But it was left to Glinka to carry Russian opera on to a more professional plane. He possessed the natural skills, creative flair, and stylistic individuality which were distinctly lacking in earlier Russian composers, and these attributes combined to produce the first truly Russian operas, *Ivan Susanin* (or *A Life for the Tsar*, 1836) and *Ruslan and Lyudmila* (1842). Here the entire idiom—though still owing much to Italian *bel canto* and to French opera in the big scenes and dance sequences—exudes an unmistakeably Russian flavour, which was to have an impact on much later Russian opera: the heroic historical drama of *Ivan Susanin* had a successor in Borodin's *Prince Igor* (1890), just as the scintillating traits of magic and orientalism in *Ruslan and Lyudmila* were developed in several of Rimsky-Korsakov's operas—*The Tale of Tsar Saltan* (1900), *The Legend of the Invisible City of Kitezh* (1907), and *The Golden Cockerel* (1909). In turn these fantasy operas were to exert an influence on some Russian opera produced later in the 20th century (see below, 17).

Around the same time that Glinka was working in Russia, other eastern European countries were beginning to shake off the mantle of foreign opera and to explore their own cultural potential. In Poland, as in Russia, there had

Design by Benois for Rimsky-Korsakov's 'The Golden Cockerel' (Paris, 1927).

been attempts at native opera during the 18th and early 19th centuries by Maciej Kamieński (1734–1821), Józef Elsner (1769–1854), and Karol Kurpiński (1785–1857), though Poland's troubled history (see *Poland*, 3–4) impeded the consistent development of an operatic tradition and it was not until 1848 that Moniuszko produced his *Helen*, regarded nowadays as the first significant Polish opera. In Hungary Jószef Ruzitska (*c.*1775–after 1823) imbued his *Béla's Escape* (1822) with elements of Hungarian folk music, and so initiated a trend for Hungarian opera which was consolidated in the works of Ferenc Erkel (1810–93): his *Bánk bán* (1861), shot through with the traits of the traditional Hungarian *verbunkos*, was long popular. Similarly in Bohemia, František Škroup (1801–62) produced *The Tinker* (1826), a *Singspiel* which is credited as the first Czech opera, and nationalist operatic writing began to develop in earnest after 1859, when Italy's defeat of Austria released Bohemia from Austrian political (and by extension artistic) domination. Bohemia and Czechoslovakia have indeed enjoyed a particularly colourful operatic history since the mid 19th century: the chief exponents were Smetana, Dvořák, Foerster, Fibich, and Janáček (see below, 18), and a fuller discussion of their

contributions to the operatic repertory will be found in their individual articles.

In Russia, opera responded keenly to the spur which Glinka's music had given to the theatre, though it developed along several different paths. Tchaikovsky, for example, rightly dubbed Glinka the 'acorn' from which the oak of Russian music grew, but his own enthusiasm for opera—fired initially by Mozart's *Don Giovanni* and later coloured by Bizet's *Carmen*—was inextricably bound up with his own temperament. He chose a wide diversity of subjects for his operas, but almost invariably he produced his most successful works when the characters struck a sympathetic chord in his own personality. Such operas as *The Maid of Orleans* (1881) and *Mazeppa* (1884), impressive though they are in their dramatic organization, fail to impart the conviction, commitment, and emotional impact of *Eugene Onegin* (1879) and *The Queen of Spades* (1890): in the former the theme of unrequited, impetuous passion was specially fresh in his mind in the wake of his own disastrous marriage (1877), just as the fateful message of *The Queen of Spades*, composed between his last two 'Fate' symphonies (the Fifth and Sixth), was particularly significant to a composer who was himself so tortured by thoughts of Fate's inexorable power. Tchaikovsky's operas express an intensity of feeling and a breadth of experience which set them apart from Russian opera composed in the firmly nationalist Glinka tradition; and it is perhaps their very universality of expression which has lent them such wide international appeal. Anton Rubinstein, too, abjured a narrowly nationalist approach to his mature operatic writing, maintaining, after the failure of his early folk-tinged operas *Dmitry Donskoy* (1852) and *Tom the Fool* (1853), that nationalist opera was worthless. To some degree he contradicted himself in his *Kalashnikov the Merchant* (1880), but in the main he preferred to concentrate on serious biblical operas and on the melodramatic *Demon* (1875), substantially in debt to French grand opera, particularly Gounod's *Faust*.

However, there was a decisive break from foreign influence in the operas of Dargomyzhsky and Musorgsky. Dargomyzhsky, in common with the Realist philosophers of the day (Belinsky and Chernyshevsky), was concerned with questions of 'truth' in art, and in his songs he tended to pare down the vocal lines so that no melodic decoration should be allowed to cloud the meaning of the words. His opera *The Stone Guest* (1872) is an extension of this principle. Just as César Cui was advocating in the 1860s that opera should rid itself of gratuitous vocal display and that 'each note should reinforce the meaning of the text', so Dargomyzhsky wanted in *The Stone Guest* to cast off the fetters of operatic convention, rejecting arias and set pieces and formulating a style of continuous recitative. 'I want the note to express the word', he wrote in 1857, and he conceived *The Stone Guest* as a model of 'musical realism', in which the vocal lines, drifting in and out of pure melody as occasion demands, are guided by the inflections, the stresses, the emotional implications of the words. Tchaikovsky, whose own operas are couched in a firmly lyrical style, regarded this attempt to drag 'truth' into opera as utterly 'false', but other Russian composers were more enthusiastic about Dargomyzhsky's ideas: it is indeed the concept of musical realism which gives much of the finest 19th-century opera its thoroughly individual sound. Rimsky-Korsakov's *Mozart and Salieri* (1898), which, like *The Stone Guest*, is a word-for-word setting of one of Pushkin's 'little tragedies', is cast in much the same declamatory style, though, as he said, he tried to make the structure and the harmonic scheme rather less of a hit-and-miss affair than *The Stone Guest* had been. Cui's opera *William Ratcliff* (1869) mingles declamatory elements with the broader melodic writing for which he had a much more pronounced gift, and there is a comparable blend of lyricism and

realism in Rimsky-Korsakov's *The Maid of Pskov* (first version 1873; second version 1895).

But Musorgsky applied the principle of musical realism to its subtlest effect, harnessing it to his individual harmonic idiom, his ascetic, spare orchestration, and his keen perception of character to create operas of powerful dramatic impact. In the late 1860s he was himself at the height of his 'realist' phase, producing such starkly declamatory songs as 'Eryomushka's Lullaby' and 'With Nurse' (both 1868). At the same time he composed a word-for-word setting of Gogol's prose comedy *The Marriage*, in which he intended his 'music to be an artistic reproduction of human speech in all its finest shadings'. In the single act he managed to complete he succeeded in using continuous recitative, with recourse to the *Leitmotiv* principle, as a means to virile, sharply characterized vocal lines, but it was only later, when he tempered strict musical realism with warmer, lyrical music that he produced his two masterpieces: *Boris Godunov* (1874) and *Khovanshchina* (1886). Musorgsky's work had a lasting influence on later Russian music. His technique of continuous melodic recitative was echoed in such widely differing works as Rakhmaninov's *The Miserly Knight* (1906) and Shostakovich's *The Nose* (1930) and *The Lady Macbeth of the Mtsensk District* (1934); and the tableau-like construction, familiar enough from *Prince Igor*, became a formula for much Soviet opera, including Prokofiev's *War and Peace* (1946).

Boris Godunov and *Khovanshchina* stand as twin peaks of nationalist musical drama in 19th-century Russia: in the former the vivid portrayal of Boris's moral dilemma and his physical and mental decline is one of the most acute pieces of psychological perception in Russian opera (and indeed 19th-century opera in general); in the latter, while the characterization is less clearly defined, Musorgsky left a sensitive and richly coloured drama embracing themes of political instability and religious schism in the early reign of Peter the Great, impressing not only by its easy melodic flow and theatrical grandeur but also by its encapsulation of a true Russian spirit. In a sense these are the Russian equivalents of the naturalistic operas which, as we see in the next section, were part of the western European operatic picture at the beginning of the 20th century.

GEOFFREY NORRIS

15. *The 20th Century: Symbolism.* As at many other times in its history, opera in the early part of the 20th century was polarized between two extremes, which by analogy with contemporary literary movements can be called 'naturalism' and 'symbolism'. Naturalist composers, like

Puccini, Charpentier, and Bruneau, were concerned to give direct expression to the feelings of real people in an immediately recognizable world. Symbolist opera, on the other hand, made no such attempt to mirror observed reality. The immense influence of Wagner, still to be felt 20 or 30 years after his death, encouraged composers not only in their harmonic and orchestral daring but also in their approach to mythical subjects, where the characters are to be regarded as archetypes, as vehicles for philosophical debate or the examination of unspoken emotion. But there were other influences that pointed in the same direction: the work of playwrights of the time, notably Maeterlinck and Strindberg, and the insights of Freud in uncovering deep mental processes.

The first and greatest symbolist opera was a faithful setting of a Maeterlinck play which provided an abundance of classic Freudian situations of jealousy, guilt, and Oedipal conflict, all set in a subdued, dream-like atmosphere. In *Pelléas et Mélisande* (1902) Debussy's music takes on the responsibility, evaded in the original drama, of expressing the fluctuations of uncertain and vacillating emotion, so that inner feelings are exposed without words. Where the text does become explicit, in the Act 4 declaration of love, the music does not reinforce it at once but instead enters gradually to suggest the partners' growing confidence and assent. Indeed, only comparatively rarely does the music duplicate the text; it is much more concerned with expressing the characters' reactions to what they are saying. As a result, *Pelléas* is a work in which the naturalist functions of music—depicting events, outlining characters, and strengthening the message of the words – are to a great extent abandoned.

Debussy's achievement in *Pelléas*—which came after scores of sub-Wagnerian operas, particularly by French composers—was to show that Wagner's discoveries could be used to create something quite different. In matters of orchestral sound, seamless symphonic design, and even vocal treatment it is clear that Debussy learned much from *Parsifal*, yet his opera is entirely individual and new. At the same time, however, it closed more doors than it opened. Before the production of *Pelléas* Delius had been able to create his own gloss on *Tristan* in *A Village Romeo and Juliet* (1907), but afterwards it was necessary, as Satie recognized, to 'search elsewhere'. Debussy himself completed none of the many operatic projects he took up after *Pelléas*; other composers, like Webern and Ravel, were drawn to Maeterlinck but abandoned the attempt. Dukas's *Ariane et Barbebleue* (1907), based on a more colourful and fully stated Maeterlinck play, manages something

Lucienne Bréval and Maurice Raveau in the first Paris production of Fauré's 'Pénélope' (Théâtre des Champs-Élysées, 1913).

distinctive, however, by reintroducing definition of character, situation, and purpose, though still within a symbolist framework. Fauré's *Pénélope* (1913) is a different case. The single, late opera of an established master, it has a quality of understatement that may be compared with that of *Pelléas*, but the myth is presented with classical freshness, not as a symbolist drama of allusion. As for French composers of a younger generation, they went far away from *Pelléas* into brilliant farce (Ravel's *L'heure espagnole*, 1911) or exotic pageant (Roussel's *Padmâvatî*, 1923).

It was in Bartók's only opera *Duke Bluebeard's Castle* (1918) that the example of *Pelléas* was most fruitfully followed. This one-act piece uses the same Maeterlinck play as provided the basis of Dukas's opera, but in a drastically altered form which reduces the number of characters to two, Bluebeard and his new wife (now named Judith), and which virtually eliminates action. Like *Pelléas*, the opera concentrates on bringing forward the interior emotions of its characters, though in bolder terms: the text is more strongly shaped and heavier in its symbolism, and the music owes as much to Strauss's pictorialism as to Debussy's suggestion. Again like *Pelléas*, *Duke Bluebeard's Castle* was a success without a successor. In drawing on the Magyar folk ballad, poet and composer had invented what could have become a national operatic style, with a kind of recitative dictated by the nature of the Hungarian language (here again Bartók had followed Debussy in looking to Musorgsky for clues). But Bartók never attempted opera again, and his colleague Kodály achieved his only theatrical triumph with a comic fantasy, *Háry János* (1926).

16. *Expressionism*. In Germany and Austria the symbolists' charting of deep emotion by means of suggestion and imagery grew into naked exposure: it became expressionism. The subjects of expressionist opera were most usually sexuality and violence, as in Puccini, though treated without any sentimentality. Strauss's *Salome* (1905) and *Elektra* (1909) exemplify the unleashing of exultant, turbulent, or obsessive emotion that is characteristic of expressionism, here the product of a post-Wagnerian decadence, with all Wagner's resources—a large orchestra, chromatic harmony, and long, rich vocal phrases—pressed to the limits. If Strauss was a naturalist in his choice of precisely located situations, he was an expressionist, if only in these two operas, in his plumbing of extravagant emotion. His women are, like the otherwise very different Mélisande, natural beings who stand apart from their societies and indeed represent something presocial. Nor was this kind of subject-matter the property only of Strauss, for in its indulgent display of female sexuality Schreker's *Der ferne Klang* (1912) belongs to the same movement.

However, the purest, most intense kind of expressionism is to be found not in Strauss or Schreker but in Schoenberg. His *Erwartung* (composed 1909, produced 1924) goes even further than *Pelléas* or *Duke Bluebeard's Castle* in abandoning action in order to focus on volatile states of mind. Since there is only one character in this short 'monodrama' Schoenberg could ignore characterization and devote his attention to detailing at every moment the delirious anxieties, hopes, joys, and regrets of this woman searching a forest for her lover. In a second piece of similar dimensions, *Die glückliche Hand* (composed 1910-13, produced 1924), he turned to a subject more philosophical than psychological, and the style is more distanced and clear-cut. *Die glückliche Hand* also has some claims to being the nearest approach to the ideal of the *Gesamtkunstwerk*, for Schoenberg provided not only his own Strindbergian text but also abundant production memoranda, stage designs, and even the lighting schedule, which owes much to the theories and practice of Kandinsky.

With the outbreak of the First World War, pure symbolist and expressionist opera came to an end, though by no means did the devices of symbolism and expressionism fall immediately into disuse. Indeed, since 1950 expressionist shock has been the stock manner for such operas

as those of Ginastera (notably *Bomarzo*, 1966) and Penderecki (*The Devils of Loudun*, 1969), where the dramatic form is utterly conventional. And long before that Berg had drawn on the legacy of expressionism in what was to be the first work in a rebirth of naturalism, his *Wozzeck* (1925).

17. *Russian Fantasy*. The characters of symbolist and expressionist opera, though they may be located in no defined reality (Pelléas, Bluebeard, the Woman in *Erwartung*) or else only in a temporally distant one (Salome, Elektra), at least have recognizably human features. By contrast, other non-naturalist operas of the period, including many by Russian composers, are very much concerned with the bizarre, with characters as grotesque and stylized as those of a puppet show. Rimsky-Korsakov's last opera, *The Golden Cockerel* (1909), for example, is a satirical fantasy which shows a glittering, magic court ruled by a monarch as self-willed and obstinate as Nicholas II, with the music displaying all the composer's talent for opulent colour and bold harmonic contrast. It had a direct successor in Stravinsky's first and not very typical opera *The Nightingale* (1914), similarly alive with exotic incident and orchestral fireworks.

This Russian style was adapted to rather different purposes in Prokofiev's *The Love for Three Oranges* (1921), where the element of parody is uppermost and the plot is barely more than a framework for squibs directed at operatic and narrative conventions. Prokofiev followed this opera with a much more serious work influenced by the mystical Russian offshoot of symbolism, his *The Fiery Angel* (composed 1919-27, produced 1954), which concerns itself with demonic possession and religious-erotic hysteria. Meanwhile Shostakovich had followed *The Love for Three Oranges* with *The Nose* (1930), a similarly iconoclastic and even more comically grotesque piece, but opera of this kind was not long to be tolerated in the Soviet Union: Prokofiev turned to solidly naturalist subjects in the operas which followed his return to Russia in 1932, and Shostakovich's second opera, *The Lady Macbeth of the Mtsensk District* (1934), was also naturalist, though, as will appear, it certainly came nowhere near satisfying the authorities. Outside Russia, however, comic fantasy of a distantly Rimskyesque kind was able to flower in such quirky specimens of opera as Ravel's *L'enfant et les sortilèges* (1925), a work quite personal to its composer in its access to the world of the child and in its brittle depiction of inanimate malice.

In *The Love for Three Oranges* the fantastic element is determined largely by the Gozzi play, and there were other composers who found material for ironic and fantastic operas in 18th-century Italian drama and the *commedia dell'arte*. Gozzi's *Turandot* was used by both Puccini (1926) and Busoni (1917) in a pair of interestingly divergent works: where the naturalist composer strives to humanize the story, Busoni plays up that element of caricature which had already been important in his *Arlecchino* (1917) and *Die Brautwahl* (1912). Another Italian of partly German ancestry, Wolf-Ferrari, turned to Goldoni in creating his comic fantasies *Le donne curiose* (1903) and *I quattro rusteghi* (1906).

In going back to the 18th century for their subjects Busoni and Wolf-Ferrari were led to compose in a neo-classical spirit which quickly developed from pastiche into the serious reclamation of earlier styles and means. Nielsen's comedy *Maskarade* (1906) shows the same tendency. But in none of these works is the neo-classical return so delightedly or so ironically enacted as in Stravinsky's *Mavra* (1922), an opera which is a rather double-edged tribute to its artistic fathers and dedicatees Pushkin, Glinka, and Tchaikovsky (Rimsky has now been left far behind). In *Mavra* satire has evolved to the point where, even more insidiously than in *The Love for Three Oranges*, opera is blatantly and maliciously used against itself. Stravinsky gives the signal that the genre is becoming unworkable.

18. *Naturalism Renewed*. After the First World War there were changes which inevitably altered the climate of operatic composition. The fall of the German, Austrian, and Russian monarchies brought an end to court patronage, and so opera houses had to become more commercial in their dealings. Often this meant restricting the basic repertory to a group of two or three dozen acknowledged masterpieces—a group which still includes nothing later than *Wozzeck* (1925) and *Turandot* (1926). Moreover, the general movement in music in the 1920s towards clarity of form and straightforwardness of expression left many composers disinclined to write opera. For those who did, naturalism offered a more congenial frame than the pre-war vogues of symbolism and expressionism.

It is noteworthy, for example, that Janáček became an international figure only after the First World War, even though his first great opera, *Jenůfa* (1903), had been begun in the 1890s. As a portrayal of love and jealousy in a village setting, *Jenůfa* bears comparison with the contemporary *verismo* operas, but its hard-edged realism and its original musical style, intimately bound up with the language and the folk music of the Moravians, take it into a different world. The operas that followed, including *The Cunning Little Vixen* (1924) and *Kát'a Kabanová* (1921), showed the power that Janáček could achieve with his objective but involved treatment, his stark delineation of character and setting, and the swift emotional strokes of his vocal and orchestral writing. But the very individuality of Janáček's style made it difficult for other composers—except other Czechs—to follow him.

Though closer to the operatic mainstream, *Wozzeck* also shows a quite fresh approach. It was the first full-length opera to be composed

Survage's design for the first production, by the Diaghilev company, of Stravinsky's 'Mavra' (Paris, 1922).

Set design by Josef Gottlieb for the first Prague production of Janáček's 'Kát'a Kabanová' (1922).

without the resources of tonality, and Berg very skilfully solved the resulting problems of musical continuity by adapting abstract forms to his needs: the first act is a set of 'character pieces', the second a five-movement symphony, and the third a sequence of inventions. However, the opera-goer is likely to be less impressed by this than by Berg's binding of expressionism to naturalism. *Wozzeck* is the tragedy of credible characters (Wozzeck and Marie) in a credible environment, but with the heightening of expressionist devices such as the exaggeration of the inhumanity of other characters, the very deliberate placing of symbols (like the ominous red moon), and indeed the musical style. While using the innovations Schoenberg had made in such works as *Erwartung* and *Pierrot lunaire*, Berg also follows Mahler in his fierce contrasts of manner, switching at one point from a tortured chromatic outburst to the simplicity—horrifying simplicity in the context—of café music. In all these respects *Wozzeck* provided a very direct model for such later military operas as Zimmermann's *Die Soldaten* (1965) and Henze's *We Come to the River* (1976).

More immediately *Wozzeck* was followed by operas which set themselves to show particular features of contemporary life: Krenek's *Jonny spielt auf* (1927), which concerns the contrasted fortunes of a European intellectual musician and a natural American jazz player, was one of the first and, at the time, wildly successful. Many other composers followed Krenek in using modern scenic apparatus (telephones, motor cars, scenes in factories or railway stations) and in using the most conspicuously contemporary music: jazz. Sometimes, like Weill in *Die Dreigroschenoper* (1928) or Blitzstein in *The Cradle will Rock* (1936), they did so with the intention of making a clear political statement, but *Jonny* itself belongs to a different philosophical tradition, that of the opera which concerns the role of the artist, his duties to himself and to society. It is to this tradition that some of the century's most individual operas also belong, these including Pfitzner's *Palestrina* (1917), Hindemith's *Mathis der Maler* (1938), Schoenberg's *Moses und Aron* (composed 1930–2, produced 1954), and Davies's *Taverner* (1972). Hindemith and Schoenberg also wrote operas which emulate the contemporaneity of *Jonny*: Hindemith's *Neues vom Tage* (1930) is a story of newspaper rivalry, and Schoenberg's *Von heute auf morgen* (1930) characteristically mocks the genre through itself in a modern comedy of manners. As Schoenberg here so bitingly exposed, the 'Zeitoper', or 'opera of modern times', was an artificial and superficial solution to the evident problem of writing contemporary opera. Returning to the conventions of the number opera, as Krenek and Hindemith did (the latter most rigorously in

Cardillac, 1926), could not but produce music disquietingly at odds with its modern subject-matter.

This problem is not so acute for frankly conservative composers like Menotti and Britten, perhaps the most successful composers of opera since the Second World War. Menotti's talent is for passionate melodrama in the *verismo* tradition, as shown in his first great successes *The Medium* (1946) and *The Consul* (1950). Britten, a much more gifted and various musician, established his own distinctively English operatic style in *Peter Grimes* (1945), which takes some clues from *Wozzeck* but by no means abandons the forces of tonality as dramatic instruments. Curiously, those forces are most powerfully involved in a work which makes a tentative approach to 12-note serialism: the chamber opera *The Turn of the Screw* (1954). The key scheme of the scenes is organized to give a palindromic rise and fall in parallel with the events of the Henry James story, and the principal antagonists, the Governess and Quint, have their own opposed tonalities. Britten effectively demonstrates that narrative, naturalist opera depends on the forces of continuity and contrast generated by tonality, and it is noteworthy that his least tonal dramatic works, the trilogy of church parables *Curlew River* (1964), *The Burning Fiery Furnace* (1966), and *The Prodigal Son* (1968), are presented not as straightforward narratives but as ritual enactments. Influenced by the Japanese *nō* drama, the action in these works is even more stylized than it is in those operas, including *Billy Budd* (1951) and the chamber piece *The Rape of Lucretia* (1946), where Britten frames the drama with narration or commentary.

Britten's contemporaries in the Soviet Union were at this time bound to a more direct naturalism by the doctrine of *socialist realism, which directed that operas should extol the life of the worker or peasant, or else eulogize the fighter against fascism. Prokofiev provided examples of both kinds in his *Semyon Kotko* (1940) and *The Story of a Real Man* (1948), but very much superior to these is his *War and Peace* (1946), a dramatization of episodes from Tolstoy. Drawing on 19th-century Russian opera—the keen characterization and the grand choral scenes of Musorgsky, the romantic lyricism of Tchaikovsky—Prokofiev created a very backward-looking work which is still a stirring epic. Even so, Prokofiev encountered criticism for his operas, though never the vituperative rejection accorded Shostakovich's *The Lady Macbeth*. This work, at once a sharp satire and a moving melodramatic tragedy, was initially hailed in the Soviet press, but in 1936 it was condemned as modernist and not until 1962,

after Stalin's death, was the composer able to revive it as *Katerina Izmaylova*.

19. *Myth and Allegory*. Naturalism has had its antipole since the 1920s in operas of myth and allegory, dramatic forms particularly well suited to neo-classical music. One of the first examples was Honegger's 'dramatic psalm' *Le roi David* (1921), where the characters are stylized, the chorus has an important part, and the structure is clear-cut and severe. Stravinsky took up this style in his opera-oratorio *Oedipus rex* (1927), a work of similarly ritualistic splendour and one in which the use of Latin keeps the argument frozen at a distance from the spectator. The introduction of a narrator, speaking in the vernacular, only reinforces this separation. Indeed, so fixedly monumental is the work's form that Stravinsky could allow himself a Verdian effusion in the vocal writing without seeming at all indulgent. And by using similar techniques Milhaud was able to give a mythical aura to a contemporary subject in *Le pauvre matelot* (1926) or to a historical one in *Christophe Colomb* (1928), an operatic milestone in its use of film and of simultaneous action on different stages. The versatile Krenek, who had already responded to *Oedipus rex* with his jazzy, surrealist *Leben des Orest* (1930), followed *Christophe Colomb* with the similarly grandiose but 12-note *Karl V* (1933).

Other German composers, notably Hindemith, were influenced by the neo-classicism of Busoni as well as by that of Stravinsky and his French allies. Busoni's *Doktor Faust* (1925) is very much a sport in the history of opera, for in style it borrows equally from the late Romantics and from Bach, its characters are both given human fullness and manipulated like puppets, and it manages to combine deep, dark involvement with ironic distance. It is in all these ways a portrait of its many-sided creator.

In that respect, if in that respect alone, it can be compared with Schoenberg's *Moses und Aron*, which takes up the very personal problems of communication and truthfulness. The seer (Moses) does not have the means to express his vision; the articulate spokesman (Aron) has those means in abundance but can retail the message only at second hand and through the distortions of subterfuge and compromise. This problem enters into the opera in a very direct way, for Schoenberg was unable to compose his Act 3 text because, presumably, of the impossibility of giving adequate expression to Moses' final achievement of unity with God. It is, however, apt that the opera should have remained unfinished, and equally apt that it should end with Moses' cry of despair at his lack of command over the word.

The deep subjectivity of *Moses und Aron* contrasts markedly with the complex ironies of another allegorical opera, Stravinsky's Faustian *The Rake's Progress* (1951). In this, his only full-length stage work, Stravinsky reclaimed the conventions of the Mozart opera, complete with arias, ensembles, and dry recitative, creating a complete and knowing restitution on a scale no other neo-classical composer had attempted. Though Tippett also looks back to a Mozart work, *Die Zauberflöte*, in his *The Midsummer Marriage* (1955), the music is not at all Mozartian but cast rather in a rhapsodic style containing echoes reaching from the English madrigal to Wagner. And Tippett's later operas— *King Priam* (1962), *The Knot Garden* (1970), and *The Ice Break* (1977)—are also, though very different in style from *The Midsummer Marriage*, allegories which draw upon the most diverse literary and musical sources for appropriate resonances.

Henze is another eclectic of the post-1945 era. His two best operas, *Elegy for Young Lovers* (1961) and *The Bassarids* (1966), are both to librettos by Auden and Kallman, who had provided Stravinsky with the text for *The Rake's Progress*. Both are similarly formal in their dramatic planning, but Henze's treatment oscillates between romantic emphasis and parodistic charade (in the quasi-Baroque interlude of *The Bassarids*), and in the later work he consciously borrows from composers as different as Bach and Mahler: the piece is an immense choral symphony and a Passion at the same time. It is also a bold reworking of the *Bacchae* of Euripides, which Szymanowski had translated to 12th-century Sicily in his opulent and ornate *King Roger* (1924). Since *The Bassarids* Henze's allegories have been of an overtly political nature, following earlier committed operas by Dallapiccola (*Il prigionero*, 1949) and Nono (*Intolleranza*, 1961), of which the latter, demonstrating in strong yet closely defined terms the oppression of an immigrant, was the first opera produced by a member of the post-war avant-garde.

20. *Music Theatre.* In general avant-garde composers have preferred to work in the field of music theatre, which offers opportunities for music and drama to be brought together on a smaller scale and without the conventions of opera. The ancestors most commonly invoked have been Stravinsky's *L'histoire du soldat* (1918), a piece 'to be read, played, and danced' by a small ensemble of actors, dancer, and instrumentalists, and Schoenberg's *Pierrot lunaire* (1912), which has proved amenable to

Josef Svoboda's collage of slide and film projection for Luigi Nono's 'Intolleranza 1960' (La Fenice, Venice, 1961).

Scene from Act 1 of Stockhausen's 'Donnerstag aus Licht' (La Scala, Milan, 1980).

performance in costume with lighting effects. Among English composers, Birtwistle has shown his indebtedness to Stravinsky in the ritual outlines and the puppet-theatre manner of his *Down by the Greenwood Side* for soprano, actors, and band (1969) and his opera *Punch and Judy* (1967), while Davies has profited from *Pierrot* in several works scored for similar forces, most notably *Eight Songs for a Mad King* for male singer and sextet (1969).

Other composers, including such different artists as Berio and Kagel, have been so impressed by the theatrical possibilities of music-making that any categorization into concert and dramatic works becomes difficult. Berio has interested himself so much in the physical action of musical performance that most of his *Sequenza* series for solo performers (1958–79) are as theatrical as those works that fall more obviously into the genre of music theatre, such as his study of the disintegrating mind of a singer in *Recital I: for Cathy* for soloist and small orchestra (1972). In Kagel the distinctions are still less clear, for very nearly all his works use verbal or visual humour in taking an ironic look at the conventions and mechanics of musical performance.

The influence of Kagel in Germany and of Cage in the USA has encouraged composers to use all manner of resources—voices, instruments, electronics, visual displays of all kinds, miscellaneous objects, buildings, and natural features—in 'mixed-media shows', 'happenings', and other events which might take place in a theatre or might not. Here any continuing association with opera has quite disappeared, as it has also in the more structured music-theatre works produced by Stockhausen since the early 1970s. Typical of his grand, imaginative gestures is *Trans* for orchestra (1971), in which only the strings are visible, behind a magenta lit gauze, playing intense, still chords through which the more characterized music of other groups can be heard with greater or lesser clarity, and in which the dream-like vision is several times interrupted by worrying absurdities. If such works appear thoroughly untraditional, however, Stockhausen may be seen to be emulating an earlier master in planning a cycle of music-theatre works, *Licht* (begun 1977), to occupy the seven evenings of a week.

21. *Return to Opera?* Following Nono's example several avant-garde composers have made the return to opera, but in many cases their feelings of uncertainty are revealed in their self-regarding approach to the medium. They may not be as narcissistic as Bussotti, whose *Lorenzaccio* (1972) was created for himself as composer, librettist, producer, designer, and star, but their operas have tended to be as much concerned with the medium as with any outside subject-matter. Berio's *Opera* (1971) declares this in its title, and goes back to the origins of the genre, quoting from Monteverdi's *Orfeo* in an investigation of the triple decline of opera, western society, and the Titanic. In Kagel's *Staatstheater* (1971) the

observation of the genre is even more critical and utterly irreverent. All the resources of the modern opera house are turned against themselves in a mad sequence of skits: the costumed principals engage in a 16-voice ensemble; the ballet company is given a set of gymnastic exercises; the props of the repertory operas are trundled on and misused; and music drama is effected with the most unexpected and impoverished means.

Pousseur in his *Votre Faust* (1969) gives his attention not so much to opera *per se* as to the position of the contemporary opera composer, obliged for financial reasons to accept commissions in a genre which he may well find uncongenial if not irrelevant. Like Berio, Pousseur draws on the past, here on the musical and dramatic Faust tradition (Goethe, Marlowe, Liszt, etc.) and on bygone harmonic styles, in a complex labyrinth of quotation, allusion, and new invention. And in identifying himself with his composer hero, he follows the example of Berg in *Lulu* (1937, complete version 1979). Lulu herself is close kin to Salome and Elektra: she again is a pre-social being, one who cannot help but bring destruction to those she attracts. But she may also be read as a personification of opera, that medium to which composers have for nearly four centuries been drawn irresistibly, but which has so often proved recalcitrant, operable only through compromise. In that case Boulez may well have been right in his surmise that Berg knew he was bringing a tradition to its close.

PAUL GRIFFITHS

FURTHER READING
G. Kobbé: *Kobbé's Complete Opera Book* (London, 1922, rev. edn 1976 by the Earl of Harewood); Edward J. Dent: *Foundations of English Opera* (Cambridge, 1928, reprinted 1965); Ernest Newman: *Stories of the Great Operas and their Composers* (New York, 1929–31); Donald J. Grout: *A Short History of Opera* (New York and London, 1947, 2nd edn 1965); W. L. Crosten: *French Grand Opera: an Art and a Business* (New York, 1948, reprinted 1972); Martin Cooper: *Opéra-Comique* (London, 1949); M. Cooper: *French Music from the Death of Berlioz to the Death of Fauré* (London, 1951); M. Cooper: *Russian Opera* (London, 1951); Joseph Kerman: *Opera as Drama* (New York, 1956); Phyllis Hartnoll, ed.: *The Oxford Companion to the Theatre* (London, 1957, 4th edn 1983); P. Howard: *Gluck and the Birth of Modern Opera* (London, 1963); Harold Rosenthal and John Warrack: *The Concise Oxford Dictionary of Opera* (London, 1964, 2nd edn 1979); M. Robinson: *Naples and Neapolitan Opera* (Oxford, 1972); James R. Anthony: *French Baroque Music from Beaujoyeulx to Rameau* (London, 1973, rev. edn 1978); Roger Fiske: *English Theatre Music in the Eighteenth Century* (London, 1973); E. J. Dent, ed. Winton Dean: *The Rise of Romantic Opera* (Cambridge, 1976); Leslie Orrey, ed.: *The Encyclopaedia of Opera* (London, 1976); Robert Donington: *The Opera* (London, 1978); John D. Drummond: *Opera in Perspective* (London, 1980); R. Donington: *The Rise of Opera* (London, 1981); Nino Pirrotta: *Music and Theatre from Poliziano to Monteverdi* (Cambridge, 1982).

Opera buffa (It.; Fr.: *opéra bouffe*). 'Comic opera', the opposite of **opera seria*. It began as the use of a comic subject involving characters drawn from everyday life. Examples include Mozart's *Le nozze di Figaro*, Rossini's *Il barbiere di Siviglia*, and Donizetti's *Don Pasquale*. See *Opera*, 7, 8.

Opéra comique (Fr. 'comic opera'). Despite its literal meaning, 'comic opera' conveys a false impression of this vague but generally accepted term. The French themselves understand different things by it according to the date of its use. Beginning in the early 18th century with farces and satires using spoken dialogue with well-known airs (*vaudevilles*), the genre developed into the *comédie mêlée d'ariettes* (of which Rousseau's *Le devin du village* was one of the earliest examples). Thence, in the early 19th century, it drew closer to serious opera, handling serious or Romantic themes, as in Boieldieu's *La dame blanche*, Auber's *Fra Diavolo*, and others. Bizet's *Carmen* was a later example. By this stage the most marked difference between *opéra comique* and serious opera was the former's retention of spoken dialogue. See also *Opera*, 7.

JOHN WARRACK

Opera seria (It.). 'Serious opera'. In the 17th and 18th centuries the chief operatic genre, becoming very formal and complex with elaborate display arias. Mythological subjects were the norm, and Metastasio wrote many such librettos. The last and greatest examples of the form were Mozart's *Idomeneo* (1781) and *La clemenza di Tito* (1791). See *Opera*, 6, 8.

Operetta. Literally meaning a 'little opera', the term has become associated with a form of light opera, with spoken dialogue replacing recitative, following in the steps of the *opéra-comique* composers, and with a tendency to isolated musical numbers of a tuneful kind. The genre was to lead toward musical comedy and the modern musical. The first developments of the form are generally credited to France, and Adam's *Le chalet* in 1834 is often referred to as the first genuine operetta. Its chief propagator, however, was Jacques Offenbach, who wrote such classics as *Orphée aux Enfers*, *La belle Hélène*, *La grande duchesse de Gérolstein*, and *La Périchole*, among his hundred or so musical productions, and who led and influenced a thriving school of French operetta which included such composers as Hervé, Charles Lecocq, Robert Planquette, and André

Messager. Offenbach was also a source of inspiration to Franz von Suppé and Johann Strauss in Vienna: the latter wrote one of the supreme operettas in *Die Fledermaus* (1874), leading to the rich flowering of the Viennese operetta era and works by composers such as Heuberger, Kálmán, Fall, and Lehár—many of them of Hungarian origin. This in turn inspired a strong 20th-century school in America, mainly through immigrant composers like Romberg and Friml. The influence of Offenbach was directly felt in London, where his works were regularly produced, and inspired the works of Gilbert and Sullivan. Gradually the operatic nature of the pieces lessened and, as a formula of hit songs interspersed with dialogue became more custom-built for specific actors and for the demands of the gramophone, true operetta disappeared to be replaced by the less integrated forms of *musical comedy. PETER GAMMOND

Ophicleide. Brass instrument with keys down the side of the tube instead of valves and played with a cup mouthpiece resembling that of the trombone. About 3′ tall, it is held like a bassoon, the bell pointing to the left and the 11 keys worked with both hands, thumbs included. Invented in Paris in 1817, the ophicleide served through most of the 19th century to supply a bass in brass and military bands and in the brass section of the orchestra, though from the mid century onwards increasingly replaced in all these by the tuba.

The tubing is widely conical and doubled back on itself in a long narrow 'U'. The leather padded keys, stuffed with swan's-down or wool, are all sprung to be normally closed save for the key nearest the bell, this key (termed the first key) standing normally open. With all the keys at rest the instrument has the same pitch as the trombone or euphonium, 9′ B♭ (some, however, are built a tone higher, in C). Closing the first key lowers the harmonic series by a semitone to provide the notes of the harmonic series of A. Progressively opening the other keys shortens the tube-length to provide the other notes. Since the interval from the fundamental B♭′ below the bass staff (first key open) up to the A above (first key closed) comprises the 10 semitones from B♮ to A, 10 more keys are needed to fill this bottom octave chromatically in fundamentals. Hence the total of 11 keys. Above this point, as the intervals in the harmonic series become smaller, the chromatic scale needs only five of the keys (including the first), all of these situated on the ascending branch of the tube where the bore becomes widest and the width of the holes for the keys also widest, giving notes best matched in quality to those which issue through the bell mouth. The technique can be as agile as on a euphonium, and the sound has a crisp, 'open', almost vocal quality, though in *fortissimo* playing it can become rather hard, or, as orchestration books used to say, 'savage'.

Its inventor, Halary, having seen the British

Throne-room scenery by François Joseph Bélanger for first French production of Gluck's opera seria 'Alceste' (Paris, 1776).

Ophicleide, from Caussinus's 'Tutor' (c.1837). Note the open-standing key high on the bell; the player is opening the third key down (C key) with his left thumb.

keyed bugle (see *Bugle*, 4) in Paris at military reviews following Waterloo, devised the ophicleide as a bass version of this, coining the name from the Greek for 'serpent' and 'key', signifying an advance upon the old *serpent. France and England came to use it most, Germany and Italy less—Germany being the home of the early brass basses with valves (see *Tuba*, 3).

In the orchestra the ophicleide is best remembered for its parts (now played on the tuba) in the works of Berlioz, as in the *Symphonie fantastique* (with the *Dies irae* in the last movement on two ophicleides), and *Benvenuto Cellini* (a ribald solo). Well known too are the three deep notes far below the violins in Mendelssohn's *Midsummer Night's Dream* Overture, alluding to Bottom asleep wearing the ass's head, but in this case the ophicleide part may have been originally written for 'bass-horn', a more primitive wooden instrument of the serpent kind. Be that as it may, it will be noticed that the instances cited all relate to the fearsome or to the grotesque—though this tends anyhow to be the case wherever orchestral composers allot solos to deep wind instruments, for example the tuba in *Siegfried* (the dragon) and in Bartók's

Concerto for Orchestra (hectoring German troops).

The main trouble with the ophicleide lay in the easily-damaged keywork and the wearing out of the large key-pads. Also, the player had to master its special fingering (whereas valved instruments have a simpler fingering shared by all, making it quicker to teach to bandsmen and allowing them to change from one instrument to another). However, the ophicleide was still listed by Paris manufacturers up to the First World War. Well-preserved old instruments are by no means rare, and some enterprising players today have restored the ophicleide to the orchestral parts written for it.

ANTHONY BAINES

Opp. The abbreviated plural of *Opus.

Op. posth. See under *Opus*.

Opus (Lat., usually abbreviated to Op., plural *opera*, usually abbreviated to Opp.; Fr.: *œuvre*; Ger.: *Opus*; It.: *opera*). 'Work'. The custom of numbering a composer's works as they appear 'Opus 1' and so on is useful both as a means of identification and to show the place a particular work occupies in that composer's career. Unfortunately, the unsystematic application of the system has made it less helpful in practice than it is in theory.

The term appears in the late 15th and early 16th centuries, but was used systematically only from the early 17th, when it was applied by Venetian publishing houses issuing the works of prolific composers. 'Opus' customarily referred to a volume containing several pieces, so that, for example, the third sonata of a composer's fifth published volume would be numbered Op. 5 No. 3. This system was in general use by the time of Corelli, towards the end of the century, nearly all of whose works are neatly numbered in this way. Confusion can all too easily arise, however: a substantial part of a composer's output can remain unpublished; his works can be published, but not in the order they were written in; or more than one publisher can be involved, each applying a different sequence of opus numbers. For example, Handel's Op. 6 is a set of 12 *concerti grossi* published in 1739, but by that time he had composed many other works, including some 39 operas (it is rare, in fact, for large-scale dramatic works to be given opus numbers, partly because they were not normally published in the composer's lifetime, and partly because they were more easily identifiable by their title anyway). These kinds of confusion have persuaded some scholars to compile new systems of numbering (see, for example, *BWV*; *Deutsch*; *Hoboken*; *Kirkpatrick*; *Köchel*; *Ryom*).

In the 19th century, composers began to number each substantial individual work separately (though songs and short piano pieces, and in some cases quartets, were still numbered as sets), keeping the sequence of composition rather than of publication. This sequence was sometimes broken in the case of juvenilia published at a later date (e.g. Beethoven's Op. 79 sonatas), or when works were missed out of the sequence altogether (see, for example, *WoO*). If a work was published posthumously, it would be numbered 'Op. Posth.'. There are occasional eccentricities—Berlioz's treatise on orchestration is numbered Op. 10, and Massenet super-stitiously refused to have an Op. 13 (using Op. 12*b* instead)—but in general the 19th century sees the system at its most efficient.

Towards the end of the century, the increase in descriptive titles and the relative neglect of abstract forms such as sonata and string quartet made opus numbers less useful. Debussy jokingly numbered his String Quartet 'Op. 10', to show that he could behave as respectably as any German, but although some composers still assign opus numbers to keep track of their *œuvre*, it is no longer customary, and has become largely an historical usage.

DENIS ARNOLD

Oratorio

1. Introduction and Origins
2. The First Flowering
3. The Diffusion of Oratorio throughout Italy
4. The Oratorio outside Italy: the Roman Catholic Tradition
5. The Oratorio outside Italy: the Protestant Tradition
6. Handel
7. The Later 18th Century
8. The 19th and 20th Centuries

1. *Introduction and Origins*. The history of the oratorio is too varied to allow for an exact definition. The best that can be said is that it is a vocal piece using at least two solo singers, usually (but by no means always) on a religious theme which is treated by some narrative method (that is, it tells a story, however vaguely). It is often dramatic, even operatic, in approach, but it is not intended to be staged (though again there are exceptions). It may use a chorus and orchestra. It is not usually intended for performance as a part of the church ritual. The best way of making all this clear is to tell its history.

Among several religious orders which came into being in the 16th century, as part of the resurgence of the Roman Catholic Church under threat from Protestantism, was that of S. Filippo Neri. He was convinced that the spiritual health of the laiety would be helped by supplementing the Latin liturgy with meetings at which religious matters would be expounded in the vernacular and in which the congregation would take part. He therefore founded an 'oratory' (from Lat. *oratio*, 'prayer') in which it became the custom to hold an *oratorio vespertino* after Vespers; a sermon was given and motets and hymns sung. These hymns or **laude*, in a tradition going back to the hymns sung by the flagellant confraternities of the Middle Ages, sometimes told a story or had a framework of dialogue between, say, Mary and Joseph or the Pilgrim and his Guide. At about the same time, the Society of Jesus, in charge of the German College in Rome, sometimes gave plays in the vernacular on religious themes—stories based on the Bible or the lives of saints. These plays, designed to combat licentious carnival entertainments, were spoken but had some music.

From these two roots sprang the first musical oratorios. The most remarkable of these was the *Rappresentatione di Anima e di Corpo* (performed 1600) with music by Cavalieri, who had worked in Neri's Oratory at the Chiesa Nuova in the 1580s. The *Rappresentatione* was a lavish, fully staged entertainment with dancing; its allegorical story was in the tradition of Medieval mystery plays (see *Church Drama*, 2) and its spectacular elements after the manner of the *intermedio* (see *Opera*, 2). Because it was staged it has sometimes been denied the title of oratorio and called the first 'sacred opera'; nevertheless it was also supplied with short sermons for the intervals in the manner of the *oratorio vespertino* and some of the choruses are in effect *laude*. Whatever we may call it, it certainly pointed the oratorio in the direction of the sung drama — that is, opera. But at this stage in the development of oratorio there is no need to make so fine a distinction—the word 'oratorio' was used of the building, rather than the composition, until as late as 1640.

The *Rappresentatione* had no immediate successor, but in 1619 G. F. Anerio published some 'spiritual madrigals' under the title *Teatro armonico spirituale*. These had dialogue texts telling 'Stories from Sacred Scripture and Praises of all the Saints', as the dedication put it. Anerio set these with different voices taking the parts of the different protagonists, and with an ensemble or chorus to sing the words of a group of characters or to act as narrator. The voices are accompanied by a continuo part (probably an organ), and already such conventions are being established as the words of Jesus being sung by a bass. The madrigals were sung in pairs, one before and one after the sermon, but were not necessarily related to each other.

The 1620s and 1630s in Rome saw the

Pl. 1. Interior of the Oratorio del Ss. Crocifisso, Rome.

development of elaborate music at four oratories—S. Girolamo della Carità, the Chiesa Nuova, S. Maria dell' Orazione e Morte, and S. Maria della Rotonda—each for a slightly different audience of varying degrees of sophistication. Although the repertory has largely disappeared, we know that it used instrumental ensembles, choruses, and some first-rate solo singers. The composers involved included Mazzocchi, experienced in opera, and significantly there were several works which could be described as 'sacred operas', the subjects being the lives of the saints, the musical and dramatic treatment being in every respect like that of opera.

2. *The First Flowering*. By the late 1640s oratorios were attracting crowds in Rome, including foreigners, and two major (not to mention several minor) composers were employed in providing a substantial repertory. These were Carissimi, in charge of music at the German College, and Luigi Rossi. Rossi's two extant full-length oratorios, *Giuseppe* and the *Oratorio per la Settimana Santa* (both *c*.1641–5), are very operatic, telling stories largely by dialogue with a minimum of narrative. As in contemporary operas, there are short arias given shape by instrumental *ritornelli*; but unlike

opera, the role of the chorus is large, both as protagonist and as commentator (the latter function inspiring some huge and beautiful madrigals).

Carissimi is less operatic, using a narrator to tell the story and concentrating more on reflection than on action. His genius is shown at its height not in his oratorios setting Italian (the so-called *oratorio volgare*), but in those to Latin texts (the *oratorio latino*). These works were written for the more sophisticated audience of the Oratorio del Ss. Crocifisso and most were given on the Fridays during Lent, when two oratorios or 'dialogues', one on an Old Testament the other on a New Testament subject, were given either side of the sermon. Some were on a really large scale, using a number of singers and an instrumental ensemble. The texts were taken from the Vulgate and elaborated with original material, while the stories were essentially dramatic—Jonah and the Whale, Belshazzar, Jephtha, and so on. There is still a large amount of narration (not given consistently to a single singer, but divided among the ensemble), but the musical style is based on the manner of Monteverdi, with expressive *recitativo* and *arioso* breaking into arias or set pieces. The choruses range from grand, exciting double-choir pieces to elegiac madrigals. These works are truly a way of making the Bible come to life for an audience otherwise faced with a formal and complex liturgy.

3. *The Diffusion of Oratorio throughout Italy.* Carissimi's influence was large, since he had pupils throughout Europe. At the same time, the Filippine Order was spreading its wings and oratories were set up in many cities in Roman Catholic countries. In Italy Bologna, Florence, and Venice took to oratorios in the 1660s, and in Rome they began to be performed elsewhere than in the oratory churches, sometimes being given in the palaces of the cardinals, especially during Lent or when for some reason (a scandal or an act of penitence) the theatres were closed. In these circumstances scenery was possible, though usually restricted to a backcloth and drapes, but there was no acting. Since this was the period of the growth of opera companies it was natural for composers to write both operas and oratorios, and this meant that the two genres became even more similar. The role of narrator, common around 1660, had disappeared by the end of the century, and the popular subjects became hagiographical, the similarity of the lives of saints to those of operatic heroes and heroines providing the opportunity for love scenes in a genre nicknamed the *oratorio erotico*. There were usually about five main characters, and the texts were written in verse, while the conflict between good and evil offered opportunities for strong dramatic situations.

The history of oratorio music might be that of opera. In the period 1660–80 the flexible alternation of recitative (not the perfunctory *recitativo secco* of the later 18th century, but measured and expressive), *arioso*, and arias (most of them still rather short) inherited from Monteverdi and Cavalli still obtained. By 1700 a regular alternation of recitative and aria was usual, the arias being mainly extended and in *da capo* form. The chorus was virtually abolished, though all the characters often joined in a finale or *arietta allegra* to 'send away the audience with universal approval', to quote one commentator. The role of the orchestra — sometimes a large band of 30 or 40 players — increased, with grand overtures and full accompaniment in arias. It was in this form, of which Alessandro Scarlatti was the master, that Handel found the oratorio on his Roman visit.

4. *The Oratorio outside Italy: the Roman Catholic Tradition.* The proselytizing potential of the oratorio made it a favourite form outside Italy; but now national preferences began to show. In France, the period of its Italian expansion in the 1660s coincided with the beginnings of the chauvinistic monopoly of Lully, and only Charpentier, a pupil of Carissimi, exploited the genre. He favoured the Latin oratorio and his style resembles that of his master quite strongly, though he later gave the instrumental ensemble a larger part and wrote 'symphonies' with descriptive titles. Sometimes the influence of Lully is to be felt in the squarer tunes of the aria and the tie-up between aria and chorus. But Charpentier had no immediate followers until the early 18th century when Clérambault wrote *L'histoire de la femme adultère*.

The Italianate Viennese court proved more fruitful ground — ground, in fact, prepared by the Austrian love of theatrical effects in quasi-liturgical ceremonial. The so-called *sepolcro* was a dramatic enactment of the Passion drama, with scenery, costumes, and acting, developed from the Medieval liturgical dramas. These were very common in Vienna in the later 17th century, and encouraged the composition of oratorios, mainly by Italian composers such as Draghi and Caldara. The main differences between Viennese and native Italian traditions lie in the orchestration, which tends to be more colourful north of the Alps (this is especially true in the *sepolcri*, but also applies to the oratorios of Fux in the early 18th century). The court opera librettists, Zeno and his successor Metastasio, also wrote the texts for oratorios. Although they turned back to the Bible, the former actually imitating a biblical style, they kept to the five to seven characters of *opera seria*, and attempted to preserve the unities of time and place, with long recitatives to convey the action, and arias to express the moods of the protagonists. Metastasio's librettos are freer in style, but so excellent in characterization and dramatic action that they continued in use for many years (Mozart set *La Betulia liberata* in 1771 and Francesco Morlacchi *Isacco* in 1817).

5. *The Oratorio outside Italy: the Protestant Tradition.* Oratorio was late in arriving in Protestant lands, where it lacked the help of the Oratorian Order. The German Lutherans had in fact something similar in the more or less dramatic *Passion, but in the early 17th century this was unaffected by opera, which was virtually unknown in Germany. Some composers who had studied in Italy affected a compromise in the *historia* — Schütz's *historia* for Christmas, often known as his 'Christmas Oratorio', for example, shows a real dramatic sense, but the 'recitative' is more reminiscent of plainchant, in the manner of 16th-century Passion music. In the 1660s, the concept of the so-called *actus musicus* was developed, a form akin to the Italian oratorio in the telling of biblical stories with poetic interpolations. Although also without recitative, there were *arioso* pieces and instrumental symphonies, with choruses which included chorales. Some of the works performed

Pl. 2. Stage design by Juvarra for an oratorio performance in Cardinal Ottoboni's palace, the Cancelleria, early 18th century.

at Buxtehude's *Abendmusiken* seem to have approached oratorio, his own *Die Hochzeit des Lammes* (performed 1678) having a biblical text with allegorical interpolations (only the libretto survives).

Yet, predictably, it was only when a public opera house opened in Hamburg in the 1670s that anything really like oratorio developed in Protestant Germany. There were a number of operas on religious themes given in the theatre in the years between 1678 and 1695. Predictable also was the fact that the first German oratorio, in the Italian sense of the word, was by an opera composer, Keiser, whose *Der blutige und sterbende Jesus* (1704) was a Passion oratorio without a narrator and not using any biblical text, for which it was much criticized when first given in Hamburg Cathedral. Nevertheless, his example was followed—by Mattheson, who introduced women singers from the opera house into church performances, and by Telemann, whose mastery of both indigenous and foreign musical styles gave rise to some excellent works well worth reviving, notably *Der Tag des Gerichts* (1762). Passion music in oratorio form remained the most popular type, and the equivalent of the hagiographical Italian oratorio was rare. Such dramatic music as was composed went into the genre of the church cantata; and Bach's Christmas Oratorio is a set of six linked cantatas rather than a true oratorio.

6. *Handel.* An opera composer who worked in Hamburg and studied in Rome was ideally placed to become a great oratorio composer. How Handel came to the genre is explained in the article on the composer; what must be said here is how individual most of his oratorios are in both form and manner. His first oratorio was written for performance in the splendid Roman palace of a cardinal in 1707—*Il trionfo del Tempo e del Disinganno* sets an allegorical subject in the Italian manner, with virtuoso solo singers given a succession of recitatives and arias. The following year he composed *La resurrezione*, given in a theatre constructed in the Palazzo Ruspoli with scenery, a large orchestra, and some famous singers, including Durastanti, who sang Maddalena. His next work which could be called an oratorio is in fact Passion music, although the text of the poetaster Brockes is a complete rewriting of the biblical story, so that it is not unfair to think of it as an oratorio. The emphasis is still on the soloists in Handel's setting, made for Hamburg *c.*1715, though the chorus acts as the crowd, or *turba*, in the conventional way and there are several chorales. There are some very fine descriptive recitatives, which were to become a feature of his later oratorios. When he arrived in England there was no oratorio: the nearest musical equivalents were the grand charity concerts given on St Cecilia's Day in Westminster Abbey. The repertory consisted largely of choral anthems, services (especially settings of the *Te Deum*), and odes. Handel gained experience of this kind of music in 1720 in the various choral works written for the Peace of Utrecht and the King's coronation.

Handel's mature oratorios were thus created from these elements: the Italian operatic style with arias and recitatives; the German Passion with its choral protagonists; and the English anthem. To these should be added some influence of the French classical drama with its choral comments and tragic outcome (instead of the always happy endings of 18th-century *opera seria*). These elements are usually mixed up within a single work. In some works the anthem attitude predominates (*Messiah* is the cardinal example) and the drama is of minor importance. Others, notably *Susanna* and *Theodora*, are almost dramas in the tradition of the *oratorio erotico*. *Saul*, with its choral protagonists and tragic ending, is reminiscent of Passion music and French drama. In others the elements are more evenly balanced, as in *Belshazzar*, where the drama is strong and the chorus skilfully woven into it, yet anthem-like choruses resembling those of a St Cecilia's Day service occur.

The effectiveness of the dramatic elements has given rise to speculation that Handel would have liked to have staged his oratorios, especially as there are stage directions in some of the librettos; and indeed, the sense of drama is sometimes more pronounced than in his *opere serie*, since Handel felt no compulsion to retain the *da capo* aria convention which so often impeded the action of operas, and his sequence of recitatives, arias, and choruses is much more variable than in opera. In addition, his oratorios were mainly given first in theatres, not churches. Nevertheless, 20th-century efforts at staging even the more obviously theatrical oratorios have not proved fully satisfactory; maybe it is best to accept that the genre is a hybrid and is best performed 'in the oratorio way'—without acting, though not necessarily without scenery. This does not mean that they should be performed undramatically, or treated with great solemnity. It is worth remembering that Handel's choruses were frequently smaller than the orchestra, that his singers (even in his later works when he wrote for English rather than Italian soloists) were experienced in the opera house, and that he himself frequently added the sparkle of virtuosity by playing brilliant organ concertos in the intervals. The English helped to inspire these great masterpieces, believing that edification need not exclude entertainment. If they do not attempt the fervour of the Counter-Reformation oratorio, they still incline the listener to good—and have done now for over two centuries.

7. *The Later 18th Century.* The decline of the Italianate oratorio was bound up with the decline of the *opera seria* which had provided its idiom. The oratorio changed little in the 18th century, keeping the emphasis on the elaborately ornamented aria, often in *da capo* form. A few oratorios were staged, increasing their similarity to *opera seria*. Thus came a division between the up-to-date music of the modern *opera buffa* and the manner of the oratorio. In the end, the Italian oratorio virtually died out, in spite of the Viennese Tonkünstler-Sozietät's twice-yearly performances, at which Haydn's *Il ritorno di Tobia* (1775) and the arrangement of earlier music by Mozart to form *Davidde penitente* (1785) were given. The north German Protestants were provided with some dramatic oratorios by J. H. Rolle of Magdeburg, who added stage directions to his librettos, and whose *Der Tod Abels* (1769) and *Lazarus* (1778) might be worthy of revival; and by C. P. E. Bach, who continued the Hamburg oratorio tradition in *Die Israeliten in der Wüste* (1769), which certainly is. But the most popular work of the time was the Berlin composer Graun's *Der Tod Jesu* (1755), a devotional rather than a dramatic piece. Some oratorios were given at the Paris Concert Spirituel in the 1770s and 1780s, including interesting original pieces by Gossec,

Sacchini, and Lesueur, which showed the influence of Gluck, France's saviour from *opera buffa*. In England, Handel worship had already set in; his works were constantly performed, overwhelming even such worthy composers as Arne, whose *Judith* (1761) is charming in a lighter, less Baroque style.

Paradoxically, it was Handel who ensured the survival of the genre, although in a new form. A series of Handel commemorations were given in London, beginning (prematurely) in 1784 with the 'centenary' of his birth. His oratorios were performed by massive forces, which tipped the balance away from the dramatic and towards the monumental. The oratorio began to be seen as a largely choral work, and Haydn, who was inspired to compose *Die Schöpfung* ('The Creation', 1798) when he was at the 1791 festival was evidently influenced by this view. The libretto is said to have been written for Handel. There is little dramatic impulse, but, especially when sung in German, the solo music is reminiscent of Mozart's *Die Zauberflöte* (1791) in its simple direct melody and clear diatonic harmony. Yet the glories of *The Creation* are found in the choruses, modelled no doubt on those of Handel, but none the less characteristic of Haydn in sound. *Die Jahreszeiten* ('The Seasons', 1801) is more diffuse, the libretto providing descriptive scenes rather than continuous narrative, but it contains some extremely fine—and nowadays neglected—music.

8. *The 19th and 20th Centuries.* The religious and missionary spirit which had animated the oratorio for two centuries died away after the age of Napoleon, 19th-century composers increasingly expressing views which did not belong to orthodox Christianity. The oratorio was kept alive by the emergence of German choral societies, such as the Berlin Singakademie, and, somewhat later, by the English working-class choir. Their repertory was largely retrospective, with Bach in Germany and Handel and Haydn in England, and new compositions were naturally based on these models. But lacking both the initial impulse and an understanding of the dramatic nature of the originals, few succeeded, though many attempted. The two most successful Germans from a worldly point of view were Spohr and Mendelssohn. Spohr tackled transcendental subjects, such as *Die letzten Dinge* ('The Last Judgement', 1826) and *Calvary* (1835), in a style conservative and yet interesting in its chromatic harmony; he failed in his attempt to scale great heights, but succeeded in composing some pleasant music. Mendelssohn, knowing both German and English traditions, tried to set *Elias* ('Elijah', 1846) and *Paulus* ('St Paul', 1836) after the manner of the Bach Passions, using chorales

Pl. 3. A performance of Handel's 'Messiah' in the Festival Pavilion at Stratford-upon-Avon in 1864.

and dramatic choruses. Their weakness lies in the solo music which, though frequently melodious, lacks strength and drama—not surprisingly in view of Mendelssohn's almost completely non-operatic career.

The two great composers who added something more ambitious to the repertory were both interested in opera, and Liszt's hagiographical *Legende von der Heiligen Elisabeth* ('St Elizabeth', 1867) is a work almost possible to stage; *Christus* (1862-7), a massive piece, returns to an almost Counter-Reformation intensity of Catholic feeling. Berlioz, an opera composer denied access to the Opéra for years, wrote *La damnation de Faust* as an 'opéra de concert'; the subject must by 19th-century standards be accounted religious, and although its treatment is diffuse, it is a thrilling work. His *L'enfance du Christ* (1854), written with deliberate archaisms, may be accounted more respectable but less intense, though undoubtedly beautiful in its choruses. A clutch of works by Gounod, Massenet, and Saint-Saëns, favourites at the Birmingham Festivals, show a French penchant for charm rather than power—Franck's *Les Béatitudes* (1879) and Debussy's *Le martyre de St Sébastien* (1911) are worthier examples of French mysticism. In Italy, oratorio was little practised until the works of Lorenzo Perosi revived the genre briefly in the years between 1897 and 1904.

Most of the best oratorios of the 20th century

came from England. Elgar, a Roman Catholic cut off from the Anglican Establishment, and a Wagnerian in a country without a native operatic tradition, composed *The Dream of Gerontius* (1900), setting a poem by one of the leading Roman Catholic converts in England, Cardinal Newman. He used *leitmotiven* in a remarkably symphonic texture, put the emphasis on the drama, and imaginatively incorporated extended choruses in the narrative. *Gerontius*, and Elgar's other two oratorios, *The Apostles* (1903) and *The Kingdom* (1906), notably on New Testament subjects, represents a late achievement of the aims of the founders of the genre three centuries earlier. *Gerontius* at first proved difficult to perform well, a fact which underlines the increasing troubles of composers writing for the amateur choral society at a time when idioms have become less vocal and more complex. The next great success by an Englishman also taxes the chorus, but Walton's *Belshazzar's Feast* (1931) has proved popular because it re-creates the dramatic atmosphere of Handel in modern terms. Tippett's *A Child of Our Time* (1939-41) is retrospective in seeking to provide the equivalent of Bach chorales by incorporating Negro spirituals; and Britten's *War Requiem* (1961), which may count as oratorio with its interpolations of poems inspired by events, looks back in several ways to the choral music of Verdi.

The most interesting oratorio of the 1920s

was Stravinsky's highly dramatic *Oedipus rex* (1927), with a text sung in Latin, masked characters (the narrator in evening dress to emphasize his detachment from the action), and an important part for the chorus. This seems to grasp the essence of oratorio as a mixture of drama and comment. Stravinsky's late choral works are hard to classify but are scarcely oratorios as broadly defined in this article. Isolated but forward-looking works by Honegger (*Le roi David*, 1921), Martin (*Le vin herbé*, 1938–41), and Dallapiccola (*Job*, 1950, staged as a *sacra rappresentazione*) hardly constitute a tradition, and it may well be that the oratorio is near the end of its useful life. But musical history is unpredictable and it could be that the revival of the small, highly skilled choir for performances of early music in an 'authentic' manner may yet inspire a new repertory.

DENIS ARNOLD

FURTHER READING
Howard E. Smither: *A History of the Oratorio* (Chapel Hill, 1977–).

Orb and Sceptre. March by Walton, composed for the coronation of Elizabeth II in 1953.

Orchésographie. Manual on dancing by Thoinot Arbeau, written in French and published in Langres in 1588, with a second edition in 1589. It is an important source of information on dance types of the period and gives many clues about the performance of dance music. The text is in the form of a dialogue with Arbeau's pupil 'Capriol', hence the title of Warlock's *Capriol Suite* which uses dance tunes from the manual.

Orchestra. The word 'orchestra' comes from the Ancient Greek ὀρχήστρα (*orkhēstra*)—the semicircular area in front of the stage where the chorus sang and danced during the performance of a drama. Since the earliest operas came into existence partly through speculation about the nature of Greek drama, it was only natural that this term should be adopted to describe the instruments that accompanied them, since they too sat in front of the acting area. At first it was applied both to the instrumentalists and to the place where they sat (even in the 18th century the bandstands in the London Pleasure Gardens were called 'orchestras'), but gradually it came to be restricted to the performers themselves. By orchestra we therefore mean a number of instrumentalists playing together as an organized group, often with more than one player to a part. The matter of 'organization', however, is crucial. The mere haphazard coming together of players is not enough. The orchestra cannot truly be said to exist until the instruments began to be treated in specific groups or combinations, each making its own special contribution to a pre-conceived whole. That moment did not arrive until the beginning of the 18th century.

1. *To the 18th Century*. During the period of vocal polyphony such a concept was scarcely possible. Polyphony implies a texture wrought from independent melodic lines of equal importance. Even when the voice parts were supported (as they often must have been) by instruments, the nature of the music would not allow the effects of colour and contrast we associate with the true orchestra. But at the end of the 17th century the polyphonic style had all but given way to homophony—music conceived primarily as a dominant melodic line, supported on pillars of harmony rising from a firm bass line. It was these blocks of harmony that began to be thought of as having a colour of their own, and this, coupled with the fact that melodic lines could now be projected against a background of harmony, made possible what we now think of as a typical orchestral style.

Signs of the change can be seen in the church music of Giovanni Gabrieli. At first he explored the effect of combining and contrasting variously constituted groups of voices—a choir of high voices, say, interacting with one of low voices. And when, later on, he came to write purely instrumental works he adopted the same technique: exploring the different effects of light and shade, loud and soft, mass and individual line, to be obtained from different groups of instruments.

Even though Gabrieli's instrumental music treats the instruments as if they were voices (they play nothing that could not be sung), music conceived in this way inevitably made a greater impact than music written along purely contrapuntal lines. Its effect was outward-going and dramatic, rather than inward-looking and contemplative. It was designed as a series of events that could be listened to almost as a story, and therefore addressed itself to a new participant in the history of music—the audience.

Whereas earlier music had almost always been largely functional, serving the purposes of religion or accompanying such participation entertainments as dancing, the new attitude proposed a kind of music that was to be listened to for its own sake by a passive audience whose sole contribution was to enjoy and admire it as a work of art. The first important manifestation of this new approach was opera, an invention of the last years of the 16th century. Though initially confined to the salons of the nobility, it soon became generally popular. The first public opera house was opened in Venice in 1637 and within a very few years the rest of Italy had followed suit. From the very beginning, opera made use of instruments to accompany the voices, though

Pl. 1. Orchestra consisting of strings, continuo, ?oboes, and horns at a private house in Venice, painting by an unknown 18th-century artist.

it did not necessarily employ them in an organized way.

For example, the orchestra that Monteverdi used for the first great opera, *L'Orfeo*, consisted of such instruments as happened to be available at the court of Mantua in 1607. Although they can be divided into the groups we associate with later orchestras—strings, woodwind, and brass (plus a variety of plucked or keyboard instruments that do not appear in the standard orchestra)—Monteverdi does not appear to have treated them as such in any consistent way. The time for an orchestra of well-defined instrumental groups had not yet arrived.

Perhaps the decisive step came with the rise in popularity of the violin family. The violin triumphed over the viol precisely because it had those qualities the new, out-going, audience-orientated attitude to music demanded. Their tone was bright and forceful, the manner of their playing more suited to virtuoso display: they were, in short, more extrovert and commanding. Rapidly outgrowing their traditional role of instruments to accompany dancing, the violins became the mainstay of the orchestra.

While it is impossible to point to any one individual, or artistic centre, as being responsible for the creation and development of the orchestra, the practice of certain composers stands out as typical of general trends. The example of two

such men has already been noticed. A third can be found in Lully, working in France at the court of Louis XIV.

As part of the musical resources available to Lully two groups were of especial importance in the evolution of the orchestra. The first was the Grande Bande—the *Vingt-quatre Violons du Roi. This group normally played music in a five-part texture: six violins on the melody; six basses (probably the *basse de violon*, not the modern cello) on the lowest part; and four each of instruments tuned like the viola (each with a clef appropriate to the range assigned to it) on the three inner parts. To this self-sufficient group could be added, when necessary, instruments borrowed from the second important band—that of the 12 Grands Hautbois. This consisted of 10 members of the oboe family, plus two bassoons. Their main function was to perform music out of doors, and they were considered as part of the Musique de la Grande Écurie, which also included trumpets and drums. Oboes and bassoons could be called in to reinforce the top and bottom lines of the strings, providing a new colour in addition to the extra weight of sound. Lully's systematic use of such combinations in his opera and ballet scores did much to spread the custom among those courts that looked to the example of the Sun King.

The tendency, inherited from earlier times,

for the musicians attached to a court to be divided up according to their function as for indoor entertainment (strings), outdoor ceremonial (wind), military occasions (trumpets and drums), and the hunting field (horns), does indeed suggest the origin of all the component parts of the orchestra. It would be only natural for a composer wishing to add variety to his basic group of indoor musicians to borrow instruments from the other groupings. By the end of the 17th century all the instruments natural to the early Classical orchestra were available, but it was to be some time before they all found an equal acceptance. For the moment the centre of attention was the violin family.

Even so, at this early stage the strings were not always expected to function as a self-sufficient body capable of supplying all the notes of a harmony. The general practice was to give precedence to the melody and bass line, and leave the inner parts somewhat indeterminate. These inner parts were covered by the presence of the *continuo.

The continuo came into existence as part of the change of attitude that came over music during the late 16th century and which, as we have seen, shifted the emphasis from the weaving of independent parts to a single dominating melody, supported by a steady progression of vertical harmonies. The continuo comprises two instruments: one capable of supplying the necessary harmony as chords (harpsichord, organ, lute, etc.), and one able to supply the continuous bass line on which those harmonies are built (cello, bassoon, etc.). The harmonies themselves were indicated by means of figures placed beneath the notes of the bass line, as a shorthand to be interpreted by the player as he went along.

The practice of using the continuo in the orchestra remained widespread until well into the second half of the 18th century, even though (as the Lully example shows) it would have been perfectly possible to supply all the essential notes of the harmony from other instruments. Not all orchestras, however, could run to a sufficient number of instruments; moreover, it was helpful to the performance if a keyboard player (often the composer himself) was available to act as a unifying agent, since there were as yet no conductors.

2. *The Classical Orchestra*. By the beginning of the 18th century it was generally agreed that an orchestra should consist of strings (violins, violas, cellos, and basses), a continuo instrument (usually a harpsichord), with flutes, oboes, and bassoons as probable extras, and trumpets and horns as less frequent additions. Even so, there would be no guarantee that what passed for an orchestra in one part of the country would be identical with what would be found in another area. Orchestras might correspond in very general terms, but not in detail. A pattern was emerging, but it had not yet become standard.

To begin with this scarcely mattered. Communications were still restricted and few com-

Pl. 2. Orchestra of strings and continuo (including lute), flutes, oboes, and trumpets, at a private opera performance in the Royal Palace (Turin, 1722), engraving by A. Aveline after F. Juvarra.

posers expected that what they wrote for their local conditions would be in demand elsewhere. And if, like Handel, they chose to travel, they would certainly rescore their works to suit the orchestras as they found them, or, more often, simply write new works on the spot. The example of several orchestras at roughly the same date may serve to show the divergence possible at this period.

In 1728 the orchestra of the King's Theatre, London, consisted of 22 violins, two violas, three cellos, and two basses; two flutes, two oboes, and three bassoons; and two keyboard instruments and a harp. It was for this combination that many of Handel's operas were composed. Meanwhile, at Leipzig in 1730, Bach had to be content with six violins, four violas, two cellos, and one bass; three oboes and two bassoons; one set of kettledrums; and two keyboard instruments. At Dresden in 1734 the court orchestra could boast 12 violins, four violas, five cellos, and two basses; three flutes, three oboes, and two bassoons; two horns, two trumpets; and two keyboard instruments.

Little by little, however, the 18th-century orchestra began to take shape, until by the end of the century it was fairly generally established that it should consist of a balanced group of strings; two each of woodwind (flutes, oboes, bassoons, *and* clarinets); two horns and two trumpets; and a pair of kettledrums. By this time the continuo was no longer thought of as an essential binding agent.

Several factors helped to bring this situation about. One was undoubtedly the example of certain well-known orchestras—in particular that established in Mannheim at the court of Carl Theodore, Duke of Saxony and Elector Palatine, in 1742. He engaged the composer and violinist Johann Stamitz as his *Kapellmeister* and encouraged him to seek out the best musicians that money could buy. In consequence the

orchestra became famous throughout Europe, not only for the excellence of its playing, but also for its willingness to explore the possibilities of a truly orchestral style. Its carefully controlled dynamics came as a revelation—as did the delicacy of its phrasing. Many of its musicians were capable composers, and their efforts helped to establish the newly-emerging symphony as a viable form.

Another important influence was the example of certain great composers—Gluck, Haydn, and Mozart in particular. As the interest in their music spread beyond their immediate sphere of activity, it became necessary for orchestras elsewhere to provide the forces required for its performance. This in itself helped to impose a degree of uniformity, so that later composers, such as Beethoven, could take it for granted that orchestras everywhere would have the forces they had written for and which, by the very nature of the music, were now essential to its correct realization. For by the beginning of the 19th century the special characteristics of the different instruments, and the balance of sound between the different groups within the orchestra, had become vital ingredients in the art of composition. If the specified instruments were not available, then the new music would fail to make its proper effect.

3. *19th-century Developments*. The history of the orchestra in the 19th century is largely one of expansion and consolidation. Much of this was made possible by the improvement in the construction and playing mechanism of the woodwind and brass sections (the violin family had been mechanically perfect since its inception—only in the matter of playing technique was there room for fundamental improvement). In woodwind instruments the problem lay in the difficulty of cutting the holes that changed their sounding lengths (and hence their notes) in

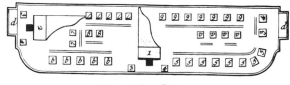

Renvois des Chiffres.

1. *Clavecin du Maître de Chapelle.*
2. *Clavecin d'accompagnement.*
3. *Violoncelles.*
4. *Contre-basses.*
5. *Premiers Violons.*
6. *Seconds Violons, ayant le dos tourné vers le Théâtre.*

7. *Hautbois, de même.*
8. *Flutes, de même.*
a. *Tailles, de même.*
b. *Bassons.*
c. *Cors de Chasse.*
d. *Une Tribune de chaque côté pour les Tymballes et Trompettes.*

Pl. 3. Plan of the orchestra at the Dresden opera under Hasse, from Rousseau's 'Dictionnaire de Musique' (1767).

Pl. 4. Orchestra accompanying an oratorio in St Mary's Church, Cambridge (6 July 1842), lithograph by Walker after Buss.

positions that could be controlled by the player's fingers, and yet were satisfactory from an acoustical point of view. Solutions came in the 1830s, when such players as Theobald Boehm extended and perfected the 18th-century idea of keys, controlled by levers and axles, which acted as an extension of the player's fingers. In 1847 he brought out an improved metal flute with 15 soundholes operated by 23 keys. The system was quickly adapted to the oboe, clarinet, and bassoon.

Early brass instruments also had their short-comings, for they could produce only the harmonic series appropriate to the length of metal tube involved in their construction. Notes outside this series could be introduced only by changing the length of the tube. The first solution was to equip each instrument with 'crooks'—extra lengths of tube, to be inserted by hand when required. This worked well enough, provided that the composer made allowance for the time involved in making the switch, and provided that the music did not modulate too often and too widely. But the harmonically more adventurous music of the 19th century demanded a less cumbersome method. For trumpets and horns the answer came c.1815 with the invention of valves. These enabled the player to switch over to extra lengths of tubing coiled permanently alongside the main body of the instrument. It is worth noting, however, that the trombone (which did not enter the orchestra on a permanent basis

until the early years of the 19th century) had always possessed a mechanism—the telescopic slide—whereby it could change its sounding length at will. But this method did not adapt well to trumpets and horns.

So far as expansion is concerned, we have noted already that clarinets (invented by Johann Christoph Denner c.1690) began to appear regularly in the orchestra from c.1780 onwards, thus improving the woodwind section by adding to its strength and increasing the range of tonal colour. Trombones, traditionally associated with solemn (church) music, had longer to wait before gaining an entry, but they too eventually helped to complete the brass choir. Their presence, however, added an extra weight of sound that required a complementary increase in the number of horns, and sometimes an additional trumpet. Thus by the mid century the standard symphony orchestra had come to consist of: double woodwind, with the optional addition of such instruments as the piccolo and double bassoon (both extending the range of existing instruments); four horns, three trumpets, and three trombones; and a sufficient number of strings to balance. By this time the percussion section had also begun to expand, now incorporating three timpani (tuned to different pitches and all capable of being adjusted by hand during the performance), side drum and bass drum, and a variety of exotica, such as tambourines, triangles, cymbals, and so forth. Instruments such as the harp made occasional appearances in music of a more colourful and deliberately descriptive nature.

It was this emphasis on the descriptive capabilities of music—all part and parcel of the Romantic movement—that accounted for the most striking developments in 19th-century orchestral writing, and thence of the orchestras themselves. The more expressive the music became, the greater the orchestral palette the composer required, and the more varied and numerous the instruments. Thus by the end of the century composers found themselves writing for orchestras of truly gigantic size. A typical symphonic poem of the 1890s by, say, Richard Strauss, might well call for an orchestra containing quadruple woodwind (three flutes and a piccolo, three oboes and a cor anglais, two clarinets, one soprano clarinet, and one bass clarinet, three bassoons and a double bassoon); brass to the tune of eight horns, five trumpets, three trombones, and tenor and bass tubas; a percussion section consisting of timpani, side drums, bass drum, military drum, cymbals, triangles, glockenspiel, tubular bells, and gong; two harps; and, of course, an enormous body of strings—probably 60 or more. This meant an orchestra of over 100 players—as compared to the 60 that Beethoven found desirable in 1824 for his largest-scale work, the Ninth Symphony, and the 40 or so that would have been average in the same period.

Long before orchestras reached this size it had become necessary to place performances under the control of one man: the conductor.

Pl. 5. Caricature of a Strauss orchestra by A. Schmidhammer.

The performance of earlier orchestras was directed either by the first violinist, or from the keyboard of the continuo. Often there was a degree of dual control (in opera, for example, the continuo player was responsible for the singers, while the first violin led the orchestra), but generally speaking the first violin took the lead, indicating by a quick gesture, or by the general movement of his bowing arm, or even by a change of facial expression the way the music should go. The method worked because at this stage the orchestra was small and intimate, the players sitting quite close together. But as orchestras grew, the leading violinist found himself having to use his bow more and more as a baton in order to communicate with the players furthest away, and then it was only a matter of time before an out-and-out conductor became a necessity.

The composer Louis Spohr, invited to London in 1820 to 'lead' a Philharmonic Society concert, recorded in his autobiography an account of the sensation he caused when he elected to 'conduct' them instead:

I . . . took my stand with the score at a separate music desk in front of the orchestra, drew my conducting stick from my pocket and gave the signal to begin. Quite alarmed at such a novel procedure, some of the directors would have protested against it; but when I sought them to grant me at least one trial, they became pacified. The symphonies and overtures to be rehearsed were well known to me, and in Germany I had already directed their performance. I could therefore not only give them the *tempi* in a very decisive manner, but also indicate to the wind instruments and horns all their entries, which ensured them a confidence such as hithertoo they had not known there. I also took the liberty when the execution did not satisfy me, to stop, and in a very polite but earnest manner to remark upon the manner of execution, which remarks Mr Ries (the first violin) interpreted to the orchestra. Incited thereby to more than usual attention, and conducted with certainty by the visible means of giving the time, they played with a spirit and correctness such as till then they had never been heard to play with. Surprised and inspired by this result the orchestra, immediately after the first part of the symphony, expressed aloud its collective assent to the new mode of conducting, and thereby over-ruled all further opposition on the part of the directors.

An account which, by implication, throws a very considerable light upon the standards likely to have been obtained from earlier methods!

By the middle of the century the conductor was an accepted part of orchestral life. Indeed, as orchestral scores became more and more complicated, his role changed from one of mere direction to one of detailed interpretation. It was up to him to decide exactly how loud or soft each passage need be to make its effect, and in exactly what proportions each section of the orchestra was to balance the others. He thus

Pl. 6. The hooded, deeply sunken orchestra pit of the Bayreuth Festival Theatre, designed by Wagner to throw the orchestral sound back towards the stage to blend with the voices before reaching the audience.

became, as it were, a performer—treating the orchestra as an instrument upon which he could play so as to interpret correctly the composer's intentions.

Needless to say, it was possible to abuse this privilege and allow personal 'interpretation' to override the composer's design—a danger perhaps more apparent in the 20th century, when the conductor has been elevated into a 'star' quite eclipsing orchestra, composer, and music!

4. *The Orchestra in the 20th Century*. The immense variety of music that 20th-century audiences are happy to listen to, and the variety of forces that contemporary composers often require for their music, has meant that the modern orchestra needs to be a very flexible instrument indeed. Its basic fare is still the classics of the 18th and 19th centuries, and this inevitably influences its general size and shape. The average 20th-century orchestra will consist of triple woodwind, four horns, three trumpets, and three trombones, a wide range of percussion, and strings to the tune of 16 first violins, 16 seconds, 12 violas, 10 cellos, and eight double basses—in all, about 100 players. Additional instruments will be engaged when required.

But it is by no means certain that all these players will be required to play throughout a concert. Unlike those of the 19th century, who tended to impose their own standards on music regardless of period or tradition, present-day interpreters like to make their performances as authentic as possible. Mozart's music will therefore not be played by an orchestra more suited in size to the music of Richard Strauss. Moreover, 20th-century composers seldom think of the standard (19th-century) orchestra as the only combination of instruments worth writing for. Indeed, the varied requirements of their scores hark back to the fluid orchestral situation of the late 17th century, and it is only the continued demand for routine classics that keeps the orchestra together as a consistent entity.

So far as the seating arrangements of an orchestra are concerned there has seldom been any agreement as to the best plan. In general terms the strings tend to be nearest the conductor, with woodwind next, and the brass and percussion furthest away. Strings, more often than not, are arranged fan-wise around the conductor's stand: first and second violins to his left, violas centre stage, with cellos and basses to his right. A few orchestras place the first and second violins on opposite sides of the stage—a practice that was quite common at the end of the 18th century. Various other arrangements have been tried—Leopold Stokowski in particular carrying out many experiments with his Philadelphia Symphony Orchestra—but the seating plan as detailed above seems to be the most generally acceptable. It is clearly sensible to place the loudest sounding instruments at the back of the stage, and bring the strings (on whom the greatest burdens in most scores fall) into close contact with the conductor. But on occasion there may well be excellent acoustic reasons why an unorthodox arrangement is preferable.

In recent years composers have begun actually to specify unorthodox layouts in order to emphasize particular features of their music— often conceived from the first with spatial effects in mind. Certain compositions even call for an element of theatre, in that the instru-

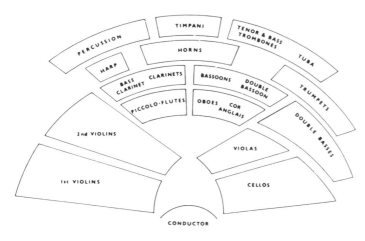

Pl. 7. Typical layout of a modern orchestra.

mentalists are required to move about, and sometimes indulge in non-playing activities. But these experiments do not affect the generality of orchestral dispositions. Only in the theatre pit (a relatively restricted space) do other arrangements obtain—the strings, for example, being often grouped on the left, with the wind and brass to the right of the conductor.

Finally, mention must be made of the development during the 20th century of chamber orchestras. These are usually cut along the lines of the late 18th-century orchestra, and as such are ideal for performing the music of that period. They have also been favoured by certain 20th-century composers (such as Stravinsky) who have turned away from the over-blown Romanticism of Mahler and Strauss to explore an astringent neo-classicism of their own. Similar specialist string orchestras also exist.

For further information on the different groups of instruments used in the orchestra, see *Brass Instruments*; *Percussion Instruments*; *Stringed Instruments*; *Woodwind*.

MICHAEL HURD

FURTHER READING
Charles Sanford Terry: *Bach's Orchestra* (London, 1932, 2nd edn 1958); Adam Carse: *The Orchestra in the XVIIIth Century* (Cambridge, 1940); A. Carse: *The Orchestra from Beethoven to Berlioz* (Cambridge, 1948); Robert Donington: 'Choirs and Orchestras', *The Interpretation of Early Music* (London, rev. edn 1974); Michael Hurd: *The Orchestra* (Oxford, 1981).

Orchestral Pieces, Five (*Fünf Orchesterstücke*). Orchestral work, Op. 16, by Schoenberg, composed in 1909. The pieces are scored for a very large orchestra but Schoenberg arranged them for a smaller one in 1949. They were arranged for chamber orchestra by Felix Greissle and for two pianos by Webern.

Orchestral score. See *Score*.

Orchestral Set. Title of two orchestral works

by Ives. The first set is usually known as *Three Places in New England*; the second has three movements: 1. *An Elegy to our Forefathers* (1909), 2. *The Rockstrewn Hills Join in the People's Outdoor Meeting* (1909), and 3. *From Hanover Square North, at the End of a Tragic Day, the Voice of the People Again Arose* (1915).

Orchestration. By 'orchestration' we mean the art of combining the sounds made by a large group of instruments. As tastes and fashions change, and as instruments can in fact be combined in an infinite variety of ways, it follows that the conventions of orchestration differ in different periods of musical history. The term 'instrumentation' is sometimes used as an alternative, but strictly speaking it means the study of the instruments themselves, and their individual characteristics. The student must necessarily study instrumentation before he can embark upon the practice of orchestration.

1. *The Early Years of Orchestration*. Although instruments have been played in combination almost since music first began, 'orchestration' only started to assume importance in the late 17th century with the rise of the orchestra itself. Even so, it was not until the late 18th century that it can be said to have begun to create for itself the conditions of an art. Composers before the 17th century seldom conceived their music for a specific combination of singers or instrumentalists. The range of each individual melodic line meant, of course, that only instruments or singers with the necessary notes could tackle them. Beyond that, the interpretation was very free. Pieces were played and sung by whatever forces happened to be to hand. For example, a motet for unaccompanied choir might be performed with instrumental support, or as a wholly instrumental piece for, say, recorders, viols, cornetts, and sackbuts. In

short, it was the performer and not necessarily the composer who decided how a piece was to be interpreted. But as music-making became more organized and more involved, with an audience paying to hear the results, the combination of instruments themselves began to become standardized. The orchestra was born, and with it the beginnings of a convention for exploiting its rich resources.

The first use of instruments combined in a body that can reasonably be called an orchestra belongs to the period of the early operas. Monteverdi's *L'Orfeo* (1607) was, we know, accompanied by a wide range of instruments—woodwind, strings, brass, and a whole battery of chord-playing instruments. But it was not yet the custom to publish complete scores that set down the precise use of these instruments, and therefore we can only guess at the 'orchestration' by observing the nature of the music itself—fanfare-like passages, for example, obviously calling for trumpets and drums. It is also evident that Monteverdi chose his orchestra largely from the instruments available at the court of Mantua at the time, and not because he had any strong notions as to what an orchestra should be.

As the orchestra began to assume a settled shape and size, so also did the conventions governing the use of its instruments start to fall into place. Until the second half of the 18th century the situation remained fluid, however. The orchestra of Bach and Handel consisted of a body of strings (supported by a keyboard continuo) to which oboes (or flutes) and bassoons were usually added, together with horns and trumpets on occasion. Inevitably the strings (at this period the most agile of the available instruments) did most of the work, and more often than not their individual lines (and usually only the melody and bass lines) were doubled by the woodwind. Occasionally, however, woodwind and brass groups were given short passages to themselves. Thus five colour combinations were possible: strings alone; strings doubled by woodwind; woodwind alone; strings and brass; brass (with drums) alone. Of these, the first two were the most frequently used.

Even so, there seems to have been no very strong desire to ensure that only certain instruments were used at any given moment. A movement that ostensibly called for oboes and strings could as effectively be played by flutes and strings if no oboes happened to be available. And judging by the widely differing constitution of orchestras at this period, this must very often have been the practice. It is fair to say that before 1800 scores were adjusted to fit the available orchestra. After 1800 the orchestra was adjusted to fit the score.

There is one exception to this *laissez faire* attitude, and in it lie the seeds of genuine orchestration as we know it today. In many early 18th-century scores there are clear indications of instruments being used for the sake of their particular characteristics and the associations these have for the listener. Thus, trumpets and drums belong to the battle-field, while flutes and oboes have pastoral connotations, and horns suggest the hunt. Used in this way, playing musical phrases that are typical of their natural style, they provided, in an abstract context, an imitation of something the listener was familiar with in daily life. Thus the foundations of a vocabulary of characteristic orchestral devices were laid.

Moreover, it is also clear that composers had begun to notice that instruments had personal characteristics that could be exploited. The cutting edge of the oboe's sound inclined it towards melancholy utterances that would elude the flute's softer tones. The high trumpet could add a brilliance and sparkle to a melodic line that had nothing to do with its military associations. It is hardly surprising that it was in the music written for the opera house (where musical scene-painting played a natural part) that the earliest and most far-reaching experiments were made in this direction.

2. Orchestration in the Classical Period. It was not until the end of the 18th century (the period of Haydn and Mozart's later works) that the orchestra itself settled into a standard grouping of woodwind, brass, and stringed instruments. And it is not until this happened that we can begin to talk of a consistent use of instruments and a system of orchestration. By this time the woodwind section had become a balanced group of flutes, oboes, clarinets, and bassoons, working in pairs and capable of supplying a complete harmony. Trumpets and horns also worked in pairs, but although capable of a fair degree of independent action were not yet expected to form a completely self-sufficient group. The strings, of course, formed the basis of all the action, and had by now freed themselves of the need for a supporting continuo. By the end of the 18th century composers were able to conceive their music in terms of specific instrumental colours. To change that colour, by using alternative instruments of a similar range, would be to change the nature of the music itself, for the colour was now an integral part of the composition. At this moment in musical history the true art of orchestration may be said to have been born.

What, then, are the basic methods of orchestration at this period? The strings, in earlier periods often restricted to a simple two-part texture (first and second violins in unison, with violas and cellos in octaves, and a continuo filling in between), are now deployed on a four-part basis: firsts, seconds, violas, and cellos corresponding roughly to an SATB vocal layout, with only the double basses pegged to the cello line as a means of enriching the lowest part. Not until Beethoven do the basses break away to find a life of their own. Woodwind instruments are used both to thicken the basic string texture, and as an independent sound— sometimes as a harmonically self-contained quartet, and sometimes as solo lines against a string background. Dialogues between the different wind instruments and between wind and strings are also a frequent occurrence. Horns and trumpets remain, for the most part, in a subsidiary role— the horns providing sustaining harmonies, and the trumpets a reinforcement at moments of climax. Both, at this period, were limited to the notes of the *harmonic series available from their sounding lengths, and therefore could not always make a more positive contribution. Moreover, the high 'clarino' style of playing popular in the earlier part of the century had fallen out of favour and neither instrument was expected to make much of a contribution to the melodic line. Nevertheless it is interesting to see how ingeniously composers were able to exploit the limitations of the brass, often incorporating melodic passages built on the available notes into the very fabric of their symphonic argument. Percussion instruments also make a modest contribution at this period— the timpani as a reinforcement to climaxes and as the natural partner of the trumpets, and side drum, bass drum, triangle, and cymbals as an occasional exotic colouring, borrowed from the fashionable Turkish Janissary bands of the period (see *Turkish Music*).

3. *The 19th Century*. The improvements made to all woodwind and brass instruments towards the end of the 18th century and in the first half of the 19th, released them from technical limitations and set them free to make as flexible and versatile a contribution as the basic string band. The change coincided with a change of emphasis in art: away from the restrained classicism of the 18th century and towards a new, poetic, emotionally charged romanticism. Without in any way wishing to suggest that Schubert and Weber were *better* orchestrators than Mozart and Beethoven, it is quite clear that they set greater store by the actual colour of each instrument's voice, and the colours to be obtained by mixing and blending the various tonal shades. And with this feeling for colour came a much stronger awareness of the individual personality of each instrument, and a determination to exploit its characteristics.

At the same time, composers began to treat the orchestra as if it were itself a single instrument. Great attention now began to be paid to the problems of internal balance—exactly how many violins might be needed to complement the woodwind and brass sections, and how they too were to be brought into effective balance with each other. Such composers as Berlioz went to great lengths in detailing precisely the number of instruments required to re-create the sound of his scores as he had imagined them—a far cry from the days of Bach and Handel when the composer was content to take pot luck. In short, this new attitude to music—the romantic spirit which required music to tell a story, conjure up an emotion, create an atmosphere— turned the composer into a painter in sound. The orchestra had become his palette.

Inevitably the orchestra increased in size, each department—woodwind, brass, and finally percussion—taking on board a complete complement of instruments covering the widest range of notes (from piccolo to double bassoon, trumpet to tuba). Throughout the century each instrument gradually acquired a comparable degree of virtuosity and technical assurance. All manner of subtle timbres were explored —the strings, for example, often being subdivided (*divisi*) or employing different bowing techniques (*col legno*, *sul ponticello*, etc.), in addition to the more usual plucked and multiple stopping effects of the previous century.

By a process of trial and error, those composers with the keenest ears and most far-reaching imaginations gradually built up a vocabulary of orchestral devices. Some passed on their knowledge in book form, providing manuals of instruction for the student. Berlioz's *Grand traité d'instrumentation* (1843) was one of the first in the field and remains to this day one of the finest. Others passed on their discoveries through the example of their music (as did Berlioz himself), for by now not only was music becoming more generally available through concerts, but also through the publication of scores and the consequent rapid dissemination of the latest achievements. By the end of the 19th century the scope and virtuosity of the standard orchestra had improved out of all recognition, and the vocabulary of proven orchestral combinations had expanded so as to cover virtually every expressive eventuality.

4. *The 20th Century*. With the rise of the *Impressionist composers at the end of the 19th century (Debussy etc.) the exploitation of orchestral colour in the purely painterly sense grew even more pronounced. Harmonic and orchestral colour became an integral part of composition, as did the matter of texture. Compared with the bold strokes and firm outlines of earlier music, the Impressionists

concerned themselves with subtle washes of sound, using a technique that has a parallel in water-colour painting itself.

A comparison of a late 19th-century score with one of, say, Beethoven's day will show an immense increase in the detail with which the composer directs precisely how each phrase and note is to be played, and the relationship of one instrument's utterance to the rest of the orchestra's. The late 19th-century score is a forest of carefully graded dynamics, directions as to exact timbre, and almost finickingly exact requirements of phrasing and interpretation. Instruments are treated, both individually and in their groups, almost as soloists—though with the understanding that the conductor (the real virtuoso of the period) will be there to guide and regulate the final outcome, like a great chef mixing and tending the ingredients of a culinary masterpiece.

In the 20th century the tendency has been to move away from the vast orchestral frescos of Mahler, Elgar, and Strauss. Economic circumstances alone would have forced the retreat, even if taste had not changed. But if the sounds and forces now favoured are cleaner and less bloated, and though a wider range of instruments is admitted into the orchestral fold (including some from the world of jazz, from non-European sources, and, most strikingly, from the world of electronics), the basic principles of subtle combination, careful balance, and effective contrast still apply in the manipulation of orchestral sound.   MICHAEL HURD

Ordinaire (Fr.), **ordinario** (It.). 'Ordinary', 'normal'. Used to rescind some direction to play in an unusual way, such as *col legno* on a stringed instrument. See also *Tempo ordinario*.

Ordinary of the Mass. The sections of the Mass whose texts do not vary; see *Mass*, 1; *Plainchant*, 2.

Ordo (Lat., pl.: *ordines*). The smallest unit forming part of one of the rhythmic modes. See *Notation*, 3.

Ordre (Fr.). See *Suite*.

Orfeo (Monteverdi). See *Favola d'Orfeo, L'*.

Orfeo ed Euridice. *Azione teatrale per musica* in three acts by Gluck; text by Calzabigi, after classical sources. Produced: Vienna, Burgtheater, 5 October 1762; London, King's Theatre, 7 April 1770; New York, Winter Garden, 25 May 1863. French version, with title-role transposed for tenor, produced: Paris, Opéra, 12 August 1774. The musician Orfeo (originally castrato, now mezzo or ten.) mourns his dead wife Euridice. Amor, God of Love

Kathleen Ferrier (Orfeo) in Gluck's 'Orfeo ed Euridice' (Covent Garden, London, 1953).

(sop.), appears and, with Jupiter's approval, urges Orfeo to seek Euridice in the underworld and to bring her back to earth, propitiating the God of the underworld with his music. The only condition is that Orfeo should not look at Euridice until they reach home. Orfeo gladly agrees, and sings his way past the initially implacable Furies and finds Euridice (sop.), but he cannot forbear to look at her. She dies again immediately. Following Orfeo's famous lament, 'Che farò senza Euridice' ('What shall I do without Euridice?'), Amor reappears and restores Euridice to life and to her husband. The opera ends with general rejoicing.

FURTHER READING
Patricia Howard, ed: *Orfeo*, Cambridge Opera Handbooks (Cambridge, 1982).

Orff, Carl (*b* Munich, 10 July 1895; *d* 29 Mar. 1982). German composer and educationist. He studied at the Munich Academy of Music and then worked as a *Kapellmeister* and choral conductor. In 1924, together with Dorothee Günther, he founded the Günther School for gymnastics, dance, and music, and for that school he developed a range of musical publications and percussion instruments which have been widely used in education (see *Education and Music*, 2). His first major work was the *Carmina Burana* for soloists, chorus, and orchestra (1935–6), a cantata of exultant, barbaric ostinatos based on Medieval poems. After its highly successful première he withdrew almost all his earlier works and devoted himself to composition for the stage, using the *Carmina*

Carl Orff (*1967*)

Burana style and principles from the Greek theatre.   PAUL GRIFFITHS

FURTHER READING
A. Liess: *Carl Orff: Idee und Werk* (Zurich, 1955); K. H. Ruppel: *Carl Orff: ein Bereicht in Wort und Bild* (Mainz, 1955); I. Kiekert: *Die musikalische Form in den Werken Carl Orffs* (Regensburg, 1957); U. Klement: *Vom Wesen des Alten in den Bühnenwerken Carl Orffs* (Leipzig, 1958).

Organ

1. The Pipes
2. Action
3. Blowing Machinery
4. Organ-playing
5. Early History

6. Classical European Traditions
7. The Romantic Organ
8. Repertory
9. Organ Stops
10. Foreign Terms Found in Organ Music

The organ (Fr.: *orgue*; Ger.: *Orgel*; It.: *organo*) is played from keyboards, the sound is produced by pipes, and the mechanism which runs between these is collectively termed the 'action'. In describing the instrument, probably the least confusing method is to start with the pipes, working back through the system to the keyboard. (For electronic organ, see *Electronic Musical Instruments*, 4.)

1. *The Pipes*. Although appearing in an almost infinite variety of shapes and sizes, the pipes belong broadly to two main types, flue and reed.

(*a*) *Flue Pipes*. The sound of flue-pipes is produced in the same way as in wind instru-

ments like the recorder. Wind enters through the toe of the pipe and passes a plate or 'languid', level with the lower lip of the 'mouth' (the oblong opening to the outside). The wind is then deflected by the upper lip causing vibrations to be set up in the air-column in the pipe (Fig. 1). In a 'stopped pipe' (see *Acoustics*, 5) the cap at the top is used as a reflector of the sound-wave, causing the pipe to act as though its length were doubled, thus producing a note of 8' pitch from a 4' pipe, though with a tone-quality that has less harmonic development (brightness) than in an 'open pipe', and most suitable for flute tones. An 8' stop of open pipes is so called because the pipe for its lowest note, *C*, is 8' in length from mouth to top. With an 8' stop the keys sound the notes at the written pitch as they do on the piano. With a 4′ stop the notes sound an octave higher; with a 2′, two octaves higher. The same principle holds good in the other direction, with 16′ and 32′ stops.

Sometimes a 2′ stop is named 'Fifteenth', the sounds being 15 white notes above the written pitch. Similarly various non-octave pitches are referred to as 'Twelfth', 'Nineteenth', etc., these being 'quints' (fifths) at various heights above the 8′. A Twelfth may further be designated by $2\frac{2}{3}$′ (sounding one octave plus a fifth higher than the 8′); or a Nineteenth by $1\frac{1}{3}$′ (for two octaves plus a fifth higher). Other harmonic intervals are also in use, some rather bizarre—e.g. the minor seventh, and the 'none' or major ninth—but historically the 'tierce' or Seventeenth is one of the most notable and widely used: $1\frac{3}{5}$′ (i.e. $\frac{1}{5}$ of 8′ length, two octaves and a major third higher). It is a constituent of the Cornet (five ranks sounding simultaneously, 8, 4, $2\frac{2}{3}$, 2, $1\frac{3}{5}$) as well as of the Sesquialtera ($2\frac{2}{3}$, $1\frac{3}{5}$) and of the various 'mixtures' which include the Seventeenth. Most mixture stops, however, are limited to quint and octave pitches which, being high in relation to the fundamental, make use of the builder's technique of 'breaking back' as the notes ascend, to avoid impossibly high pitches in the treble of the keyboard.

(i) Diameter and scaling: the diameter primarily affects tone-quality: a narrow pipe will produce a 'bright' and even 'stringy' sound rich in harmonics with a not very strong fundamental pitch, while a wide pipe will emphasize the fundamental pitch with relatively little in the way of overtones. The former type is represented by violes and other string stops, the wider by flutes. Diapasons, which provide the organ's 'basic' tone-quality, fall somewhere between.

In early organs, that is those from the 9th to the 12th century, all pipes had the same diameter, and the question of varying the width of a pipe in some proportion to its length was not crucial since the keyboard was of limited compass (not more than about two octaves) and avoided extremes of pitch. (An anonymous Medieval source from Berne gives the width of the pipes as equivalent to a dove's egg, 25-30 mm.) However, a rank of pipes of constant width would, over a considerable range, be too narrow in the bass and wide in the treble, and from the 14th century onwards many systems have been used to regulate the scale of a stop through its range.

(ii) Pipe shapes (flue pipes): the most common shape is cylindrical (open or stopped, wide or narrow). The most common cylindrical open pipes, starting with the widest, are: Hohlflöte, Nachthorn, Principal or Diapason, Salicional,

Viola da Gamba. Stopped cylindrical pipes are the Pommer, Gedackt, and Quintadena, while the Rohrflöte with an open chimney in the stopper is basically a stopped pipe although producing more overtones. A number of organ stops use conical open pipes with the names Blockflöte, Waldflöte, Gemshorn, and Spitzflöte. The Blockflöte is the widest, the Gemshorn a little narrower, both these having their upper diameters from a third to a half of the lower. The Waldflöte has a similar lower diameter to the Gemshorn, but less taper, while the Spitzflöte has more, the upper diameter being only a fifth to a third of the lower. There are also stopped conical pipes, not specially common and usually named Spitzgedackt. Occasionally some kind of combination-shape is used, as in the Koppel-flöte, a stop which begins by being cylindrical and then has a conical top.

(iii) Voicing: the most crucial operation in producing sound from an organ pipe lies in the mysterious and delicate technique of voicing, which is bound up with the treatment of the mouth of the pipe. G. A. Audsley admitted (in *The Art of Organ Building*, 1905) that it presents 'almost insuperable difficulties', remarking how almost every work on the subject known to him contained 'little if anything of value, or apparent value'. We are dealing essentially with the width and height of the mouth; generally, the larger the width of the mouth, the brighter the tone of the pipe, and the greater the height or 'cut-up', the duller the tone-quality. The mouth-width is expressed as a proportion of the circumference, and all pipes of a rank can have the same proportion (Fig. 1). Principal or Diapason

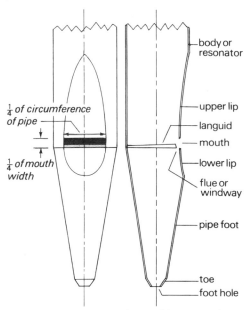

$\frac{1}{4}$ of circumference of pipe

$\frac{1}{4}$ of mouth width

body or resonator

upper lip

languid

mouth

lower lip

flue or windway

pipe foot

toe

foot hole

Fig. 1. Flue pipe, from the front and in cross-section.

mouths are usually given the width of a quarter of their circumference, with their cut-up a quarter of the width. For other open pipes, the Hohlflöte has a slightly wider mouth (up to the equivalent of three semitones wider) with normal cut-up; the Nachthorn has normal width but very low cut-up; the Salicional, a narrow mouth (six to 12 semitones narrower than normal) with normal cut-up; Viola da Gamba somewhat narrow mouth with low cut-up. For the stopped pipes, Gedackts can have narrow mouths (narrower, they become 'lieblicher') and not high cut-ups (to avoid edge-tones); Pommer a narrow mouth; Quintadena still narrower (as Salicional for width); Rohr-flöte has slightly narrow mouth with lowish cut-up; Rohrgedackt even narrower (three to five semitones below normal) but with high cut-up. Of the conical stops, Waldflöte has normal width and cut-up in the bass, becoming slightly wider in the treble; Blockflöte can be normal or slightly below for both width and cut-up; Gemshorn and Spitzflöte both have normal-width mouths, with low cut-up for Gemshorn but normal for Spitzflöte.

(b) *Reeds*. Despite their immense variety of appearance and sound, the reed stops fall into two main groups: those with resonators (pipes) of full or proportional length, and those with short resonators, making a group sometimes termed Regals. Stops of the first group may be called Trumpet, Trombone, Posaune, Fagott, Schalmei, Oboe, Dulzian, Cromorne, etc., the differences in tone and power being produced by the length, breadth, and thickness of the actual metal reed, the shape and size of the 'shallot', the design of the resonator, and the wind-pressure.

Regal resonator forms are numerous and bewildering; the most frequently met with are Trichter (funnel)-regal, Krummhorn, Rankett, Barpfeife, and Sordun. Tone-production in reeds is caused by the alternate closing and opening of the shallot by the reed pressing against it and then being released; the process continuing as long as wind enters the boot (see *Reed*, Fig. 2a).

The frequencies generated by the reed are amplified by the resonator which, in the case of large and full-length resonators, will greatly develop the fundamental frequency, which is relatively weak in reed tone. To tune the reed, the wire spring can be moved; shortening the vibrating length of the reed will raise the pitch, while lengthening lowers it. Concerning tone-quality in reeds, P. G. Andersen remarks that 'thin, broad, stiff tongued reeds generally provide more overtones than thick, narrow and soft tongues . . .' and that 'flat cylindrical shallots with a large throat-opening in relation to the

tongue promote the overtones, while deep, conical shallots, tapering upward and with a small thoat-opening, hinder the formation of overtones'. Andersen also gives width and thickness of reed for several builders' stops, among them these measurements for tenor *c*:

	Width (mm.)	Thickness (mm.)	Wind Pressure (mm.)
Schnitger Basun	16	0.41	*c*.60
Cahmann Trompet	10	0.25	*c*.60
Cavaillé-Coll (Trompette harmonique)	6.25	0.34	150 (possibly higher)

(c) *Wind-pressure*. The tone of a pipe is radically affected by the pressure of the wind going into it. Wind-pressure is measured by a gauge registering displacement of water level in an open glass U-tube, and is reckoned in these terms: an organ is said to be on, say, 60 mm. (approximately 2⅓″) pressure. Early organs were on very light wind-pressure (around 50 mm. or less than 2″), and in general the tendency towards pressures of 5″, 8″, 20″, and even 50″ was a special feature of the era 1850-1950 when power (generated by modern machinery) was the *sine qua non* of the organ. Historically, the organs of Spain and Italy are notable for their low wind-pressures, and hence their gentle *cantabile* quality; 40-50 mm. (rather less than 2″) is normal for these organs from the 16th century and 17th century, while in France and Germany pressures of 55-75 mm. (under 3″) are typical. The famous organ built by Christian Muller in 1735-8 in St Bavo, Haarlem (Nether-lands), has a pressure of *c*.75 mm.; the Waalse Kerk in Amsterdam (same builder, 1733-4), 84 mm.; Klosterneuberg, Austria (J. G. Freundt, 1636-42), 55-65 mm.; Weingarten (Gabler, 1737-50), now 70 mm.; St Maximin-en-Var (J. E. Isnard, 1772-3), 70 mm. The organs of Arp Schnitger tend to fall into the 65-70 mm. range, as do those of Gottfried Silbermann and Zacharias Hildebrandt, although Freiberg Cathedral organ (Silbermann, 1710-14) has considerably higher pressure (up to 94 mm.).

It is notable that often a single wind-pressure suffices for an entire instrument, even though there may be several divisions, and stops of varying pitch and power; large pedal pipes do not need high pressure any more than strong reeds do, and the tone and power of the pipes can be achieved through their voicing. Wind-pressures on modern organs often show great variation from one division to another.

(d) *Materials*. Much has been written about the material of organ pipes, and many claims of varying respectability have been made. At one time or another, organ pipes have been produced from just about anything solid: all kinds of metals and woods, paper, alabaster, clay, glass, various plastics, and even cement. The basic material, sometimes known as organ metal, is an alloy of approximately 30 per cent tin and 70 per cent lead (various trace elements, such as antimony, can be present in very small quantities). This metal can be used for just about every stop, whether it be flue or reed, open, conical, or stopped. Sometimes the proportions are altered, for example in the front pipes in the case, where the tin-content frequently rises to 70 per cent, but the limiting factor over choice of materials is very often cost. Tin is extremely expensive, and so organ-builders have tried to find cheaper materials which will produce equally good results. The metal must be malleable enough to work, yet hard enough not to collapse when set up as a vertical pipe. Zinc is sometimes used, on grounds of cheapness, but is hard to work, and on the whole the only practical alternative to organ metal is copper, which tends to be restricted to pedal bass pipes and other rather neutral-sounding stops. Many types of wood are usable for pipes, primarily for flute stops, although wooden principals are quite widespread, as are wooden resonators for reeds, whether they be short regals or large and 'gravitätisch' Posaunen. Wood, unless it is

thoroughly seasoned, can be problematical because it may move, and many organs have suffered tuning problems on account of this shifting; Baroque organ-builders, with the exception of the Compenius family, used wood only rarely. Oak is the most favoured, and among others used are boxwood, ebony, mahogany, pine, spruce, cypress, pear, and cherry.

2. *Action*. The parts of the organ which come between the keys and the pipes consist of a wind chest connected by pallets to the tracker, pneumatic, or electrical system which is eventually operated by the keys. Wind chests (Fig. 2) are of several types: spring chest; slider chest; cone-valve chest (mechanical or tubular pneumatic); membrane chest. Under the wind chest come, in the case of mechanical action organs, the trackers, rollerboards, etc., down to the keys (Fig. 3); in pneumatic action organs (Fig. 4) the pallet valves are connected to thin lead tubes containing wind which are joined on to 'touch boxes' directly controlled by the keys; electro-pneumatic and electric actions use magnets in place of pneumatic pouches close to the chest (Fig. 5).

In the standard arrangement on a chest, the pipes of each rank are mounted in a line, one rank behind another. Inside the chest there are airtight divisions which, depending on their

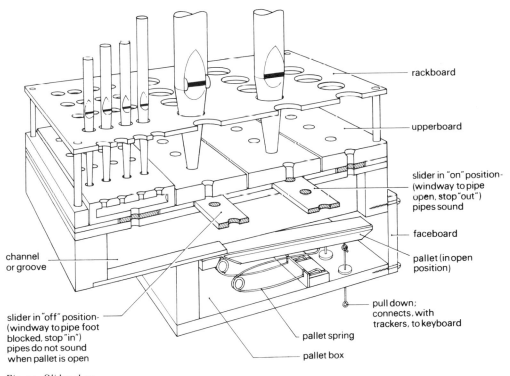

rackboard

upperboard

slider in "on" position·
(windway to pipe
open, stop "out")
pipes sound

faceboard

pallet (in open
position)

pull down;
connects, with
trackers, to keyboard

channel
or groove

slider in "off" position·
(windway to pipe foot
blocked, stop "in")
pipes do not sound
when pallet is open

pallet spring

pallet box

Fig. 2a. Slider chest.

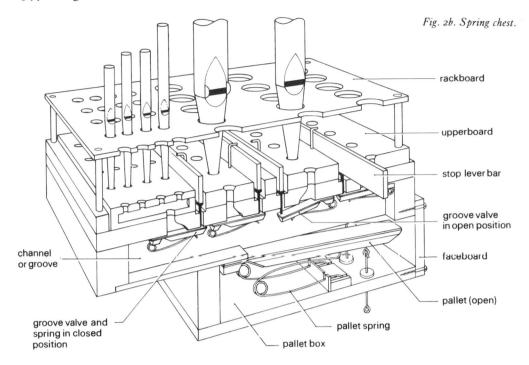

Fig. 2b. Spring chest.

rackboard

upperboard

stop lever bar

groove valve
in open position

channel
or groove

faceboard

pallet (open)

groove valve and
spring in closed
position

pallet spring

pallet box

direction, serve to separate either the ranks of pipes or the different notes of the keyboard; this latter type is sometimes called 'tone-channel chest' and is an essential constituent of the slider chest and the spring chest, which after more than 500 years of use remain the two best types. Its action is straightforward: when a key is played the corresponding pallet on the underside of the chest is pulled down, causing the wind under pressure in the pallet box to move

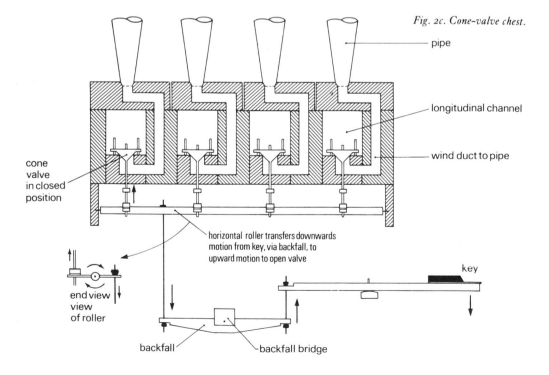

Fig. 2c. Cone-valve chest.

pipe

longitudinal channel

wind duct to pipe

cone
valve
in closed
position

horizontal roller transfers downwards
motion from key, via backfall, to
upward motion to open valve

key

end view
view
of roller

backfall

backfall bridge

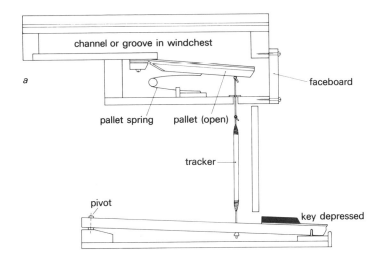

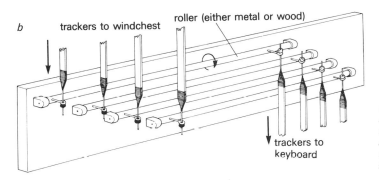

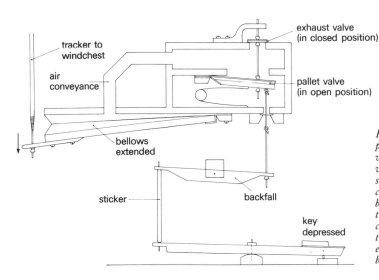

Fig. 3. Connections between key and chest: (a) suspended action; the keys are pivoted at the back and hang on the trackers from the pallet valve; (b) detail of the rollerboard.

into the chest and any pipes for which the stops are 'on'. With pneumatic action the pallet is connected to a small bellows which, when a key is depressed, has its wind supply cut off and collapses, pulling open the pallet in the process

(a magnet performs this function in electrical actions, where playing the key closes the circuit).

The technical problem with chests is more concerned with the control of stops than with the key mechanism, and the slider chest is so

Fig. 4. Pneumatic action: depressing the key opens the pallet valve and closes the exhaust valve allowing air, under pressure, to enter the bellows via the conveyancing. This expands the bellows which pull down the tracker connected to the windchest. Releasing the key closes the pallet valve and opens the exhaust valve; the air pressure is balanced and the bellows close.

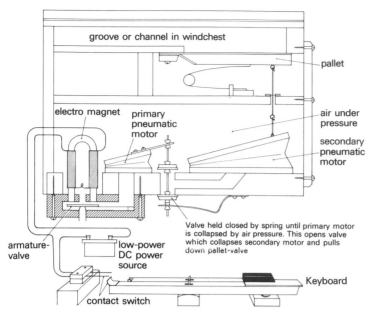

groove or channel in windchest

pallet

electro magnet

primary pneumatic motor

air under pressure

secondary pneumatic motor

armature-valve

low-power DC power source

Valve held closed by spring until primary motor is collapsed by air pressure. This opens valve which collapses secondary motor and pulls down pallet-valve

Keyboard

contact switch

Fig. 5. Electro-pneumatic action: electro magnet is activated when keyboard contact switch completes circuit, causing armature-valve to open and allowing pressurized air in primary pneumatic motor to escape. Air pressure within the chamber (maintained by armature-valve in its activated position) forces the primary motor closed (collapses it), activating the main valve which in turn collapses secondary motor, pulling down pallet-valve.

called because it includes a movable strip of some material (wood or plastic) which can be fitted below the top board, and in which there are holes to correspond exactly with the foot-holes of the rank of pipes concerned. With the slider in the 'off' position, the fitting would be perfectly airtight and no wind would reach the pipes, but with the stop pulled out the slider would move to the 'on' position with its holes immediately under the pipes. The spring chest is similar in construction to the slider chest, but the stop mechanism employs a beam (for each stop) to which are attached pieces of rigid wire (for all the notes). Under every pipe is a small pallet kept closed by a spring. When a stop is drawn (and secured in a notch, as it must be because of the tension) these small pallets are opened, and a similar condition to that of an opened slider is produced. Each type has its advantages: the spring chest does not suffer from the effects of shrinkage or warping of the wood, which can cause serious difficulties with the slider chest, but it is more complicated, takes up more space, and is relatively expensive. Spring chests are particularly associated with Italian organ-building, where they have been used from at least the 15th to the 19th century.

The essential difference in chest design between the traditional slider and spring types and some more modern systems (from the end of the 18th century) lies in the change in internal division from tone-channel to stop-channel design. The combination of the wind being available under each complete rank, and each pipe having its own pallet, makes sliders no longer of any significance. This is the basis of

'cone-chest' designs, and has obvious advantages where pneumatic or electrical aids can help to shift the mechanical load. Although in recent years there has been an almost universal return to slider-chest building, the problems of an effective mechanical system for organs in the 19th century should not be minimized: at that time both dimensions and power of the instrument were increasing strenuously, and traditional means of control were scarcely adequate. Possibly the most reputable and long-lasting invention was the Barker lever, dating from the 1830s, essentially a pneumatic bellows inserted along the course of otherwise tracker action; the tracker from a key would open a valve causing the bellows to inflate, while the next stage of the trackers would be activated by this bellows. Cavaillé-Coll (see below, 7) made use of the invention in all his organs of any size, sometimes for the Great only which was a big advantage when coupling the manuals together, although retaining mechanical (tracker) action throughout and slider chests.

3. *Blowing Machinery*. On small organs, as *portatives, it may be possible for one person to produce the wind-supply as well as play the instrument. But from earliest times the quantity and strength of wind required for all but the smallest organs have necessitated the use of somewhat cumbrous machinery involving the aid of one or more persons, whose sole job it is to blow the organ. Early organ-blowing machinery, until the 19th century, consisted of large wedge-shaped bellows, with one side fixed on the floor, the other moving up and down from a hinge at

one end and a multiple-fold piece of leather at the other. After levering the bellows into the 'up' position, the pressure is determined by the weight of the top of the bellows itself plus any additional weights put on. Large organs would need several bellows which would be operated in relay by the organ-blower.

This type of blower was superseded in the 19th century by a feeder bellows, which could be operated by hand in small instruments and by machinery in larger ones, sending wind into a reservoir. The feeder bellows was wedge-shaped, as the earlier type had been, but considerably smaller, and the advantage of the new system lay in improved steadiness of the wind, particularly when large numbers of stops were being used or sudden contrasts of dynamics (and hence of wind consumption) occurred.

At the present time almost all organ-blowers are electric, making it possible to achieve almost complete steadiness of wind together with economy of space. The system depends on an efficient electrical machine, together with the operation of 'Schwimmers', small wind chambers each having one end on springs; any variation in wind-pressure is immediately compensated for, by the expansion or contraction of the spring plate. Thus, from the same blower, different divisions of the organ can be easily set at different wind-pressures. The system has been described as perfect; it may well be too perfect, in that the elimination of slight unsteadiness and irregularities of old blowers has dehumanized the organ and caused it to become merely technological.

4. *Organ-playing.* Although the organ is sometimes thought to be an insensitive instrument on account of the player's inability to vary the tone or power directly through the keyboard touch, it possesses a large number of individual features which can be applied to achieve artistic results. Among these are: the various different manuals, which can be played simultaneously (each hand on a different manual) or in alternation, or even coupled together; the pedals, or keyboard for the feet, the music for which is normally the bass part, but which can produce high-pitched registrations if 4′ or 2′ stops are available; and the stops themselves and systems of managing and altering them, as in the interpretation of organ music the choice of and skill in controlling the stops is a crucial matter. Added to these points there is the one described by Percy Scholes as 'the wide differences between the resources and the mechanical apparatus of individual instruments, calling for a remarkable suppleness of adaptation'.

The touch of the organist is influenced by the fact that the pipes of any stops drawn will sound for the full length of time that any note is kept

down, but will stop immediately it is released. There is no sustaining effect as on the piano, nor any variation in strength depending on the touch. Until the late 19th century the action of the key was mechanical, or 'tracker', while most 20th-century organs have been made with electro-pneumatic action so that the touch can be light. Recent developments have achieved a return to mechanical action which, when well made, has much greater sensitivity than any other type. Systems of managing the stops have been much developed over the last 100 years, from mechanical 'combination pedals' to pneumatic pistons, adjustable electric setter systems and, most recently, computerized controls. The organist has not only to look after all these technical matters, but also to be able to play such pieces as fugues with an *obbligato* pedal part, solos on one manual with accompaniment on another, trios involving one part for the right hand, one for the left hand, and one for the feet, and sometimes even play on two manuals simultaneously with one hand.

5. *Early History.* For nearly a millennium the organ has been associated primarily, if by no means exclusively, with Europe and the Church, yet its origins are neither European nor ecclesiastical. Its invention is attributed to Ktesibios, an engineer in Alexandria, *c.*246 BC. He called the instrument *hydraulis* on account of using water (Gk *hydōr*) for pumping the bellows, and a row of reed pipes (**aulos*) for making the sound (Fig. 6). While Ktesibios and, three centuries later, Heron, also from Alexandria, apparently limited themselves to one rank of pipes, Vitruvius (*d c.*AD 26) expanded the specification by the addition of open and stopped flue-pipes to the reed rank, and also implemented some system, very much like that of

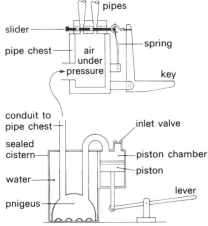

Fig. 6. Mechanism of the hydraulis: depressing key moves slider which allows air into the pipe(s); spring returns slider to 'off' position when key is released.

sliders in the modern organ, for bringing on and shutting off the separate ranks of pipes so that the performer could choose his registration. Information about the organ's popularity is scarce, though in Greece, an inscription at Delphi from 90 BC indicates that organ-playing could be accepted in a musical competition, and that the eventual winner, Antipatios from Crete, was allowed the privilege of taking precedence over others when he wished to consult the Oracle. In Rome, Nero acquired an enthusiasm for the instrument, which quickly became a symbol of wealth and flourished for possibly the next 300 years. The most remarkable survival from this period is the instrument constructed in AD 228 excavated in 1931 at Aquincum in Hungary. Although referred to as *hydra* on the inscription, this instrument evidently had its wind-supply produced by bellows and therefore counted as an 'organum pneumaticum' rather than 'organum hydraulicum'. The transition from water-power to bellows-blowing cannot be precisely dated, but by the 2nd century AD hand-blown bellows were being advocated for small organs, while the water machine was still thought to be most suitable for larger instruments which had to sound strong (organs were often used in the open air).

After about AD 300 the organ appears to be a spent force in Rome, to flourish next in the Eastern Empire, where, though it underwent no significant developments, a great deal of attention and money were spent on its adornment with gold and precious stones. Its use was still entirely secular, and still we have no idea of the nature of the music performed.

The reappearance of the organ in Western Europe came about through a very special and distinctive present from the Emperor Constantine V to King Pepin the Less in 757, while the first organ produced in the West was built for the palace at Aix-la-Chapelle in 826, with the work carried out by a priest from Venice, a city-state directly connected with Constantinople. From this point on, the organ is regarded almost exclusively as a church instrument. How this happened, and so quickly, remains obscure. The Church, up to then rigidly opposed to any kind of instrumental music in worship, revised its view and, from the middle of the 9th century, church organs and organists became increasingly accepted. The monster Winchester Cathedral organ of *c*.950 provides the most celebrated example from the period; said to have a compass of 40 notes with 10 ranks of pipes (which provided an enormous Mixture, as none of them could be shut off), it required two men to play it, but no less than 70 strong men to work the 26 bellows. The majority of Medieval organs were, however, small, and mostly came into one or other of the categories of positive, *portative,

and *regal. Positives are, as the name implies, too large and heavy to carry about, but contain no larger pipes than Stopped 8′ and Principal 4′.

With the rapid increase in the number of organs, and their introduction into churches and monasteries throughout Europe, came a commensurate development on the technical side—most of the features of the modern organ which do not rely on electricity had been invented by 1500, among them the two main types of chest design (slider and spring), wind supply and bellows design, mechanical key action, roller-boards, pedals, the arrangement and use of several manuals in one instrument, and various systems of scaling the pipes, to supersede the Medieval arrangement of having all pipes the same diameter as each other, whatever their length. The spring chest was a Netherlands invention of the 14th century (according to Michael Praetorius), and allowed for the separate stops on a division to be selected at will, rather than have them always sounding together; ironically, the Netherlands builders did not see fit to apply this invention to the Blokwerk (or Great Chorus) which remained an undivided Mixture until the time of Sweelinck, and this caused the organ to be expanded by the addition of a further division, the Bovenwerk ('upper work', above the Blokwerk), where such stops as would be used separately (e.g. flutes and reeds) could be found.

A particular innovation of the mid 15th century was the combination of two manual divisions in one organ. This came about through the organist's wish to have both organs of the church (the main organ on the wall; the Positive on the floor) under his control, and led to the Rugwerk or Rückpositiv, a division behind the organist's back, played from a manual below that of the main organ. An early example, from 1447, is recorded at Our Lady's Church in Zwolle in the Netherlands; a more famous one, where the case is preserved, can be seen at Strasbourg Cathedral (begun in 1498).

The incorporation of the roller-board into organ design enabled the pipes, instead of perforce being placed in sequence over their corresponding notes on the keyboard, to be set in any kind of arrangement over a sufficiently large area to house them. The effect of the roller-board, visually and functionally, can be appreciated by comparing the traditional Positive arrangement in the Van Eyck Ghent altar-piece with the 'swallow's nest' case at Sion (Valais, Switzerland, of *c*.1400, the world's oldest playable organ) where symmetry in the pipe fields is achieved through the use of roller-boards.

6. *Classical European Traditions.* The various countries of Europe have evolved differently in

organ-building, depending on their religious and political position and their economic prosperity. It is perilous to be too specific, but a general guide to distinctive national types through the 16th and 17th centuries could run as follows.

(a) *Italy*. The Renaissance organ here remained a one-manual instrument, a substantial enlargement of the Medieval organ employing the spring chest as a means of separating the ranks of the undivided Blokwerk. Several 15th- and 16th-century Italian organs still exist, carefully

Pl. 2. Organ (c.1400) with 'swallow's nest' case at Sion, Switzerland.

preserved and restored, among them the earlier organ at San Petronio, Bologna (da Prato, 1470–4), San Martino, Bologna (G. Cipri, 1556), and San Giuseppe, Brescia (G. Antegnati, 1581), of which the following is the specification:

Principal	16	Twenty-ninth	1
Octave	8	Thirty-third	$\frac{2}{3}$
Fifteenth	4	Octave flute	8
Nineteenth	$2\frac{2}{3}$	Flute at the 12th	$5\frac{1}{3}$
Twenty-second	2	Super-octave Flute (15th)	4
Twenty-sixth	$1\frac{1}{3}$	Fiffaro	16

Although this organ appears to be based on 16′ pitch, it is played, so to speak, 'up an octave' so that the Principal sounds at 8′ pitch and runs down to 16′ C, the remaining stops being correspondingly transposed. The higher pitches are subject to a general rule in Italian organ-building, that the pitch of a note never rises above c''''' (the top note of the piano); when exceeding this becomes imminent (c/c♯ for unison pitches, f/f♯ for quints) the rank 'breaks back' an octave and continues upwards at the lower pitch. This prevents the treble from becoming too shrill, while ensuring that the

Pl. 1. Positive organ, detail of a polyptique by van Eyck (early 15th century).

lower parts sound very bright. The pedal is a 'pull down' keyboard, almost solely for sustaining bass notes.

(*b*) *The Netherlands*. Just as Italian organ-building was more a Renaissance than a Baroque art—and likewise its organ music, which after Frescobaldi gives way to opera, concerto, and trio sonata—something of the same may be said of the Netherlands, where a chief characteristic is the long-lasting retention of the main Blokwerk (a chorus without stops for the separate ranks), and an upper or Bovenwerk for the stops which are to be used separately, as noticed earlier. All Netherlands builders, particularly the Brabanters who influenced France very decisively, used a large quantity and variety of reeds in their organs, while their pedals are used mainly for *cantus firmus* parts, as in French organ music. During the 17th century there was substantial German influence in the north, which may account for the more international

Pl. 4. Epistle organ (1746-7; rear view) by L. F. Dávila at Granada Cathedral, Spain.

character of the great organs of Gronongen, Zwolle, Alkmaar, and Haarlem.

(*c*) *Spain*. The organ does not here appear in full glory until rather late in the 16th century, when it was powerfully developed by the ubiquitous Netherlanders (Hans Brebos had built organs at El Escorial in *c*.1580), and the period of greatest activity, at least before decadence set in heavily, was the 17th century. Spain's lack of material prosperity in later centuries has had the fortunate result of leaving many historic organs unmodernized, even if left to become dilapidated. As with Italy, Spanish organs were mainly one-manual instruments, with pedals that sometimes had independent bass pipes for holding-notes. They did tend to have more varied and original registers than Italian organs, including a number of reeds of trumpet, cromhorne, and regal types, given Spanish names such as *chirimia* and *orlo*. The smaller members of these were sometimes mounted in horizontal position on the front of the case (not to be confused with the big trumpets and other stops of the similar-looking *lengueteria*, a late 17th/18th-century spectacular alteration or addition).

A feature of the Spanish organ which also appears to some extent elsewhere is the technique of dividing the stops into treble and bass halves, so that different registrations can be

Pl. 3. Organ (1735-8) by Christiaan Müller at St Bavokerk, Haarlem, Netherlands.

used in the upper and lower parts of the keyboard (as in a *harmonium).

A good (and surviving) 18th-century example is the Epistle organ of Granada Cathedral, built in 1746 by L. F. Dávila; Granada also exemplifies a system much practised in monastic churches in Spain and Italy, that of having two organs, one on each side of the choir, to be employed antiphonally in accompaniment and expressly in pieces composed for two organs (each organ has a decorated case-front facing into the choir, and another on to the side aisle, creating an impression of immense richness).

(d) *France*. The destruction of organs through wars and revolutions has been so thorough that it is only with the greatest difficulty that anything approaching a coherent picture can be established. The organs of Bordeaux (1510) and Toulouse (1531), for which contractual documents have survived, have been convincingly shown to be one-manual instruments with specifications of the Italian type, while Gisors, between Paris and Rouen, is strikingly Flemish in its constituents, which include Fourniture, Cymbale, Cornet, Trompette, Clairon, and Voix Humaine on the Grand Orgue, a Positif up to Cimbale and Cromorne, and Montre and Saqueboute (both 8′, with 'ravalement' (extension) down to 12′ F for the reed) on the Pedal. The Classical French Grand Orgue is already very nearly formed, and needs little more than a Positif Tierce, Cornet Séparé, and Echo Cornet to be complete.

The greatest French Classical organs date from the last years of the 17th century, and they are the instruments most fitted to the works of Boyvin, Couperin, and De Grigny, e.g. the specification for St Louis des Invalides, the organ built by Robert Clicquot (Table 1).

The Pedal is relatively undeveloped, seldom exceeding the provision of Flûte (= Principal) bass and Trompette 'plain chant'; it was with the 19th-century Bach revival and the war-horses of late Romantic composers that the Pedal became a generally heavier division.

(e) *England*. Beside the French organ, with its defined style and imposing stature, the English instrument of the pre-Reformation, Elizabethan, and Restoration times is on a comparatively small scale. For the oldest instruments, a case (but no pipes or action) survives from Old Radnor, and one built for New College, Oxford, in the early 17th century by Robert Dallam, provides a rare example of an early 'double organ' (i.e. with two manuals). After the Restoration, organ-building was again encouraged, and builders who were either foreign or had lived abroad during the Commonwealth, made organs incorporating some Flemish and French features. Chief among them were 'Father' Smith and Renatus Harris. Smith made instruments for the Banqueting House in Whitehall, Westminster Abbey, St Paul's Cathedral, the Temple Church, and Durham Cathedral among many others. The specification for Durham shows two particular features: first, the organ presumably had two fronts, therefore requiring one 8′ Principal in each (as in the Dallam case of 1605 for King's College, Cambridge); secondly, that well-known English characteristic, the absence of the Pedal. Many are the stories told of English organists' long-lasting reluctance to use the pedals; Percy Scholes cited the 75-year-old Sir George Smart at the Great Exhibition of 1851, on being invited to try one of the organs, replying 'My dear Sir, I never in my life played on a gridiron'. Harris was more unconventional than Smith in some of his features, such as

TABLE 1

Grand Orgue C–c'''		Positif C–c'''		Récit c'–c'''		Pédale AA–f		Écho c–c'''	
Montre	16	Montre	8	Cornet	V	Flûte	8	Bourdon	8
Bourdon	16	Bourdon	8	Trompette	8	Trompette	8	Flûte	4
Montre	8	Prestant	4					Nasard	2⅔
Bourdon	8	Flûte	4					Quarte	2
Prestant	4	Nasard	2⅔					Tierce	1⅗
Flûte	4	Doublette	2					Cymbale	II
Grosse Tierce	3⅕	Tierce	1⅗					Cromorne	8
Nasard	2⅔	Larigot	1⅓						
Doublette	2	Fourniture	III						
Quarte de Nasard	2	Cymbale	II						
Tierce	1⅗	Cromorne	8						
Fourniture	V	Voix Humaine	8						
Cymbale	IV								
Cornet	V								
Trompette	8								
Clairon	4								
Voix Humaine	8								

pioneering the Horn stop, and in his more frequent use of reeds generally; he also tried his hand at 'transmission', in order to make stops available separately on more than one manual. The first use of the Swell in England was probably by Abraham Jordan in the organ for St Magnus the Martyr, London Bridge. John Byfield, senior and junior, G. P. England, John Snetzler, and Samuel Green continued the 18th-century tradition which lasted well into the 19th century up to the time of Samuel Wesley and Mendelssohn.

(*f*) *Germany*. On the development of the organ in German, Scandinavian, and Slavonic countries, so much will have to be omitted as to produce but a very inadequate survey. Much of the impetus, particularly in the northern area, stemmed from the Netherlands.

The North German 15th-century Gothic organ is essentially a one-manual instrument with Pedal pull-downs. It would probably be elevated, on one of the walls of the church, and might be a large instrument based on 16′ Principal as in the Lübeck Jakobikirche. With the later addition of Rückpositiv, Brustwerk, and Pedal, the North German Baroque organ achieved wide currency, from North Holland to Scandinavia, and also produced a style which prevailed well into the middle of the 18th century. Many famous Baroque organs took their ultimate form in stages, a good example (and one in which this is visually evident) being that in the Johanneskirche in Lüneburg where the central sections, built in 1551–3 by Hendrik Niehoff of Brabant, are in quite a different style from the 32′ Pedal towers on the sides, which were added in the early 18th century by Matthias Dropa, a pupil of Arp Schnitger (the original Pedal consisted of Trompete 8′, Nachthorn 2′, and Bauerflöte 1′). The organ in the Jakobikirche in Hamburg is another which underwent profound alterations in various styles before it became the Arp Schnitger organ which

it is supposed to have remained. This organ was built in 1512–16, but was rebuilt twice by Dirk Hoyer, and then twice again by Hans Scherer the elder (the last time in 1605–7; Michael Praetorius gives the specification), and finally changed into a late Baroque organ by Schnitger in 1688 (Table 2).

This four-manual scheme seems to be the fulfilment of a counsel of perfection as far as modern concepts of the Baroque organ go:

(i) every division is contained in its own case and so located that it can speak directly out through the front of the organ without any impediments;

(ii) the visual design of the complete organ is heavily influenced by the individual divisions;

(iii) each division is tonally self-sufficient in that it has the stops to produce a chorus which will be approximately as powerful as that of another division, and therefore balance it. Couplers are not intended to be used, and indeed may well not exist in such an instrument;

(iv) in an organ of this type the proportions of the case may be influenced by the length of the Principal pipes, e.g. for the Pedal 32′, Hauptwerk 16′, Rückpositiv 8′, Oberwerk 8′, and Brustwerk 4′. This type of design is sometimes known as 'Werkprinzip';

(v) among other uses the organ would have the following: the Hauptwerk would be used for *pleno* (full organ) and other 'solid' work; the Rückpositiv has the second chorus (not so weighty as that on the Hauptwerk) and is the primary manual for solos; the Oberwerk is good for accompaniment and echoes; the Brustwerk is almost a second Rückpositiv, but has the freshest and lightest reeds in the organ, and besides is ideal for accompanying singers and instruments; the Pedal, which is very strong and always to be played uncoupled, would

TABLE 2

Hauptwerk		Rückpositiv		Brustwerk		Pedal		Oberwerk	
Principal	16	Principal	8	Principal	8	Gross Principal	32	Principal	8
Quintadena	16	Quintadena	8	Octave	4	Principal	16	Holzflöte	8
Octave	8	Gedackt	8	Hohlflöte	4	Subbass	16	Rohrflöte	8
Spitzflöte	8	Octave	4	Waldflöte	2	Octave	8	Octave	4
Gedackt	8	Flöte	4	Sesquialtera	II	Octave	4	Rohrflöte	4
Octave	4	Querflöte	4	Scharff	V	Nachthorn	2	Spitzflöte	4
Rohrflöte	4	Blockflöte	2	Dulcian	8	Rauschpfeife	II	Nasat	2⅔
Superoctav	2	Sifflet	1⅓	Trichter Regal	8	Mixtur	VI	Octave	2
Blockflöte	2	Sesquialtera	II			Posaune	32	Gemshorn	2
Rauschpfeife	II	Scharff	VI–VIII			Posaune	16	Mixtur	IV–VI
Mixtur	VI	Dulcian	16			Dulcian	16	Zimbel	
Trompete	16	Bärpfeife	8			Trompete	8	Trompete	8
		Schalmey	4			Trompete	4	Krummhorn	8
						Cornett	2	Trompete	4

provide not only matching bass registration for the manuals, but has its own solo stops, e.g. Krummhorn 8', Trompete 4', Cornett 2', Nachthorn 2', which could be used for playing a chorale in tenor, alto, or soprano, to be accompanied on the manual.

Moving southwards, through Silesia, Saxony, Bavaria, Czechoslovakia, and Austria there is a general change in the direction of a more singing, more Italianate style with correspondingly less emphasis on the strict arrangement and proportions of the instrument. An individual who stands apart is the German-born Eugen Casparini, whose wilful synthesis of styles was brought to fulfilment in Görlitz, SS. Peter and Paul (1697–1703); this was a large three-manual organ, with plenty of original registers such as Tubalflöt and compound Cornett mutations, but its special feature was the provision of visual effects and 'toy' stops. These have at various times appeared on organs (the Cymbelstern is the most widely known and 'approved'), but here Casparini fitted rotating suns, angels with sounding trumpets, bells, birds, and drums (produced by pedal pipes set slightly out of tune with each other, and still to be seen in the Casparini organ in Vilnius).

One builder of the next generation who probably learned much from Casparini was Andreas Silbermann, whose younger brother, Gottfried, from about 1709 up to his death in 1753, built some of the most distinguished organs that have ever been made (well over 20 still exist, many of them intact, almost all of them in Saxony). Though most celebrated for his big organs in Freiberg and Dresden, his general system can best be seen in his many smaller organs, which followed a remarkably uniform pattern as in the specification from Reinhardtsgrimma given in Table 3.

Silbermann's tendencies were in the 'pre-Romantic' direction, something his contemporaries and friends, J. S. Bach among them, were by no means blind to. He virtually eliminated reeds from his organs except in the Pedal; by his scaling methods he thickened the effect of the Principal chorus, causing it to lose

incisiveness; and through his system of often placing the second manual division behind the first, rather than above or below it, he weakened the concept of the Werkprinzip design. His instruments are exceptional for their quality, although they scarcely possess the characteristics demanded by J. S. Bach.

7. *The Romantic Organ.* Romanticism did not suit the organ; at any rate the organ did not suit Classical and Romantic musicians, who either avoided it or composed rather awkwardly and unresourcefully for it. Nevertheless, harnessing the developments of the Industrial Revolution, the organ responded fully, to become even larger, louder, more complicated, more scientific, and less trouble to play. Musically, the organ became an imitation orchestra, with stops of greatly contrasting power, expressive devices like swell-boxes, lots of couplers uniting different divisions, and so on. The builder who gave greatest impetus to 19th-century organ-building was undoubtedly Aristide Cavaillé-Coll (1811–98), who revolutionized the tonal design of the French Classical organ into an orchestral concept, and was the first to apply the Barker lever (see above, 2) to the playing mechanism. These developments took place very quickly and were first demonstrated in the organ for St Denis abbey, completed in 1840. It was fortunate that, a few years later, the concept should prove so perfect for the compositions of César Franck, for whose church, Ste Clothilde in Paris, Cavaillé-Coll built the organ in 1859–62.

Ste Clothilde, Paris (Cavaillé-Coll, 1859)

Pédale
Left: Contrebasse 16', Octave 4', **Bombarde 16'**, Trompette 8'.
Right: Clairon 4', **Basson 16'**, Basse 8', Sous-basse 32'.

Grande Orgue
Left: Montre 16', Viole de Gambe 8', Bourdon 16', Prestant 4', **Quinte 3'**, **Plein Jeu Harmonique**, Trompette 8'.
Right: **Clairon 4'**, **Bombarde 16'**, **Doublette 2'**, Octave 4', Flûte Harmonique 8', Bourdon 8', Montre 8'.

TABLE 3

Hauptwerk		Oberwerk		Pedal		
Principal	8	Gedackt	8	Subbass	16	(Manual and Pedal couplers added later)
Rohrflöte	8	Rohrflöte	4	Posaune	16	Tremulant
Quintaden	8	Nasat	3	Principal bass	8	
Octava	4	Octava	2			
Spitzflöte	4	Tertia	$(1\frac{3}{5})$			
Quinta	3	Quinta	$1\frac{1}{2}$			
Octava	2	Sifflot	1			
Mixtur	4 ranks	Cimbeln	2 ranks			
Cornett	3 ranks					

Positif

Left: Montre 8′, Flûte Harmonique 8′, Gambe 8′, Bourdon 8′, **Quinte 3′, Plein Jeu Cromorne 8′**.

Right: **Clairon 4′, Trompette 8′, Doublette 2′, Flûte Octaviante 4′**, Prestant 4′, Bourdon 16′, Unda Maris 8′.

Récit

Left: Voix Humaine 8′, Voix Céleste 8′, Viole de Gambe 8′, **Flûte Octaviante 4′, Trompette 8′**.

Right: (Sonette), **Clairon 4′, Octavin 2′**, Flûte Harmonique 8′, Bourdon 8′, **Basson-Hautbois 8′**.

Couplers and pistons from left to right: Tirasses GO, Pos., Réc./Anches Pédale/Octaves Graves GO, Pos., Réc./Anches GO, Pos., Réc./Accouplements Pos. to GO, Réc. to Pos./Expression Pedal Récit.

Compass of the manuals, *C–f‴*; compass of the Pedal, *C–d′*. The registers printed in bold face are printed in red on the console and belong to the ones which are brought into play by the *appel des anches*, for each manual and pedal separately.

Cavaillé-Coll's organs have risen above the adverse criticism levelled at almost every other 19th-century builder, partly through the ideas in their design, but chiefly because of the quality of the work. Cavaillé refused to work with other than slider chests, despite the superficial attraction of other types, and stuck firmly to mechanical action with only the Barker machine added. So in his structural system, he held very close to his Classical forerunners.

German organs, of Ladegast, Walcker, and Sauer, followed a similar path, becoming somewhat Wagnerian, with the manuals diminishing in strength from the Hauptwerk downwards. No longer were small organs miniatures of large ones—they were large ones with all the upperwork removed. An interesting instance appears in Töpfer and Allihn (*Die Theorie und Praxis des Orgelbauers* of 1888), where every detail of organ-building is scientifically defined; among descriptions of several large organs having around 100 stops and of course complete with a complement of reeds and mixtures, a specification for a small organ is given. This is practically confined to foundation stops (Table 4).

Pl. 5. Organ case (1686) by Bernard 'Father' Smith at St Katherine Cree, London.

In England, perhaps the first outstanding builder of the 19th century was Hill, who by 1840 had made the English equivalent of an 18th-century German organ, complete with independent Pedal chorus. He exported to Australia and other colonies, which are now possibly the best locations for study of English Victorian organs. Hill may later have become overshadowed by the dominating personality of Henry Willis who, after exhibiting at the Crystal Palace in 1851, achieved a virtual monopoly of English cathedral organ-building. Willis's work tended in the direction of Cavaillé-Coll, and he even developed the 'Willis' lever, on the lines of

TABLE 4

J. G. Töpfer's Design for a Two-manual Organ

Hauptwerk		Second Manual		Pedal	
Prinzipal	8	Quintaden	16	Subbass	16
Bordun	16	Geigenprinzipal	8	Violon	16
Viola di Gamba	8	Stillgedackt	8	Posaune	16
Rohrflöte	8	Dolce	8	Prinzipalbass	16
Trompete	8	Fagott und Clarinetto	8	Violonbass	8
Quintflöte	5	Flauto Amabile	4	Gedacktbass	8
Oktave	4	Oktave	4		
Rohrflöte	4				
Cornet	3fach				
Oktave	2				
Mixtur	4fach				

The second manual is to have only *sanfte und zarte* ('soft and sweet') stops.

Barker, as well as various systems of stop-combination action, eventually leading to the adjustable pistons of Hereford Cathedral in the 1890s. While he was undoubtedly a marvellous organ-builder, he tended to ride roughshod over much of the previous work in organs which he rebuilt, to the extent that pre-Willis characteristics in them are almost impossible to detect.

Console development and control seems to have had a special fascination for English builders, and it is largely from them that the American style of organ console derives. Scholes tentatively recorded the first one in the USA, at the Gloria Dei (Swedish) Church, Philadelphia, in 1694. Some organs were imported and constructed during the 18th century, the most famous builder being the Moravian, David Tannenberg, living in Pennsylvania. The 19th-century organs of Roosevelt are, like their brethren in Europe, obsessed with the engineering systems of the time and, with the coming of electricity, cheap materials, and easy communications the 20th-century history of the organ in the USA is witnessed chiefly in an interminable series of manufactured products, redeemed only by the determined attempts of builders such as Walter Holtkamp senior to produce musical instruments. The USA and Canada do now have some excellent organ-builders, both native and immigrant, as well as a large number of new organs imported from Europe, but this is a consequence of the organ-reform movement (*Orgelbewegung*), which must now be mentioned.

In the early years of the 20th century when electricity provided the power that previously had to be produced by hand, and when every new invention and discovery constituted progress over the previous order, it began to dawn on musicians that perhaps the works of early composers (e.g. J. S. Bach) did not invariably benefit from the use of the full battery of modern inventions. As it concerned the organ, this was not just a 'back to Bach' movement; it was both 'back beyond Bach' and 'to either side of Bach', and, being largely German-inspired, naturally focused primarily on German music. The Schnitger organ of the Jakobikirche, Hamburg, was revealed, not as an obsolete relic, but as an ideal medium for north European 17th-century organ music; a new 'Praetorius' organ, modelled on information in *Syntagma musicum*, was built in 1911 by the Walcker firm for the music school in Freiburg; various congresses were held; etc. Progress continued, if rather slowly, until, after the Second World War, there came a general move in the direction of returning to pre-19th-century principles in the making of organs. With much of Europe devastated, there was a need for new instruments and, so far as economic conditions allowed, new organs were made, often in a rigidly puritanical manner, in Germany, the Netherlands, and Scandinavia especially. Different concepts have applied at different times in the process: France, Britain, and the USA have largely tried to produce an eclectic (or compromise) organ, while the Germanic countries have stuck to a basically national Baroque style, with occasional additions. The present direction is to concentrate on one particular type of organ, e.g. French mid 18th-century, as in the Koenig instrument in Sarre Union, or North German mid 17th-century, to be seen at Edinburgh University (Ahrend, 1977). But it is inconceivable that for the organ, with its long history and great geographical diffusion, there will not be other solutions to the question.

Pl. 6. Organ (1732) by Andreas Silbermann at the Abbey church of Alsace, Ebersmunster.

Pl. 7. Organ (1977) by Jürgen Ahrend in the Reid Music School, Edinburgh University.

8. *Repertory:* (*a*) *Germany, Northern and Central Europe.* Ileborgh tablature (1448); *Fundamentum organisandi* (1452) by Conrad Paumann; the *Buxheimer Orgelbuch* (*c*.1460), containing more than 250 pieces, many of them 'coloured', or ornamented, keyboard arrangements of vocal pieces; among South Germans, works by Schlick (1512), Hofhaimer (*c*.1500), Buchner (*c*.1520), Erbach (*c*.1600), Kindermann (1645), Froberger and Kerll (both mid 17th century), Georg Muffat (1690), Johann Pachelbel (late 17th century); North and Middle Germans, Samuel Scheidt (1624), Tunder, Weckmann (both mid 17th century), Buxtehude and Böhm (both late 17th century); J. G. Walther (*d*1748), J. S. Bach. Classical, Romantic, and modern composers who have written for organ include Mozart, C. P. E. Bach, Mendelssohn, Schumann, Liszt, Reubke, Reger, Rheinberger, Carl Nielsen, Distler, Hindemith, Ligeti.

(*b*) *Netherlands and the Low Countries.* Sweelinck (16th–17th century); Cornet (early 17th century); Kerckhoven (late 17th century); 20th-century composers include Joseph Jongen and Peeters.

(*c*) *France.* Attaingnant (1531), liturgical organ music and 'coloured' motets; Titelouze (1623 and 1626), hymns and *Magnificats*; Lebègue (1676 etc.); François Couperin (1690); De Grigny (1699); Clérambault (*c*.1710); J.-F. and Pierre Dandrieu (18th century). More recent composers: César Franck, Saint-Saëns, Widor, Vierne, Dupré, Duruflé, Alain, Messiaen.

(*d*) *Italy.* Marc'Antonio and Girolamo Cavazzoni (early 16th century), liturgical organ music and 'coloured' motets, ricercars, canzonas; Andrea and Giovanni Gabrieli (late 16th century); Claudio Merulo (*c*.1600); Frescobaldi (early 17th century); M. A. Rossi (mid 17th century); Zipoli (*c*.1700); Martini (18th century). Very little Romantic or modern Italian organ music of good quality; Enrico Bossi (*c*.1900) an exception.

(*e*) *Spain and Portugal.* Spanish composers include: Antonio de Cabezón (*Obras de musica*, published 1578), liturgical organ music, *tientos*, *diferencias* (variations); Juan Bermudo (1555); Tomás de Santa María (1565); Aguilera de Heredia (early 17th century); Correa de Arauxo (1626); Cabanilles (late 17th century); Antonio Soler, mid 18th century. Among Portuguese composers: Manuel Coelho (1620); various composers (mostly anonymous) contained in manuscripts in Oporto, Braga, and Coimbra; Seixas (early 18th century). Very little Iberian organ music of good quality later than 1750.

(*f*) *Britain and the USA.* Compositions by Redford, Tallis, Preston, Blitheman, contained in 16th-century collections; Byrd, Bull, Gibbons, Tomkins (all late 16th–early 17th century); Blow, Purcell (late 17th century); John Stanley, Boyce, Greene (18th century). Later composers include Samuel Wesley (early 19th century); S. S. Wesley (mid 19th century); Elgar, Stanford, Parry (all late 19th–early 20th century); Vaughan Williams, Howells, Malcolm Williamson, Iain Hamilton, Sebastian Forbes, William Mathias (all 20th century). American composers include: J. K. Paine and Dudley Buck (late 19th century); Charles Ives (19th–20th century); Virgil Thomson, Piston, Copland, Sessions, Barber, Sowerby, Křenek, Schoenberg, Bloch, Creston, Persichetti, Albright (all 20th century).   JAMES DALTON

9. *Organ Stops.* No list of unarguable accuracy and completeness is possible, since not only are new names sometimes introduced by organbuilders but the older names vary in their significance with different periods, different countries, and different individual builders. It is hoped, however, that the following, which is the outcome of a good deal of time spent in the study of British and American organ specifications, old and new, and of consultation and comparison of a large number of authorities (often greatly at variance), may be found to provide for all ordinary requirements of readers. The classification adopted is, in the main, an artistic rather than a scientific one, i.e. it is often based less on the constructional principles of the pipes of the various stops than on their tonal

effect. It is in fact in some parts a player's classification rather than an organ-builder's classification. Doubtful cases have been decided according to a balance of experience, as, for instance, the classification of certain stops, the tone of which in some organs partakes more of a true diapason quality and in others more of a string or flute quality.

The length and pitch mentioned are (except when otherwise mentioned) those normal to the stops in question when found on the manuals; on the pedals they will usually be of double the length and an octave lower in pitch.

(a) Stops with Diapason Quality of Tone.

(i) *Open Diapason.* The characteristic stop of the organ; if an organ of only one stop can be imagined this would be the stop, and the organ would still sound like an organ, and like no other instrument whatever. As a manual stop it is generally of metal, but as a pedal stop often of wood. It is normally of 8′ length and pitch, but an organ may include additional examples of half or double the length, and thus an octave above or below the normal pitch. It is not uncommon to find more than one Open Diapason on the same manual, sometimes as many as four, of contrasting and complementary tone-quality.

Montre. An open diapason on a special raised soundboard of its own, generally so placed as to form the front of the organ case ('Montre' is French for 'shop window'; compare *Prestant*, later, in this connection).

(ii) *Double Open Diapason.* An open diapason of 16′ length and pitch. (For 'Double Diapason', see later.)

Major Bass. Generally a 16′ open diapason on the Pedals.

Horn Diapason. See under (c). 'String Quality of Tone'.

Violin Diapason. See under (c). 'String Quality of Tone'.

Geigen Principal. See under (c). 'String Quality of Tone'.

(iii) *Principal.* In British and American organ parlance this means an open diapason of 4′ length and pitch on the manuals or of 8′ length and pitch on the pedals. It is used to add brightness to the 8′ diapasons. In German parlance it normally (and quite properly) means the principal stop on the organ, i.e. the 8′ open diapason on the manuals (but the German organs have also 4′ and 16′ principals).

Prestant. Same as 'Principal' (i.e. the British–American principal, not the German; see above). The word comes from Latin *Praestare*, 'to stand before', and alludes to position in the organ case (compare *Montre* in this connection).

Octave. Same as 'Principal'.

(iv) *Fifteenth.* A diapason speaking two octaves (15 notes) above the normal, i.e. it is of 2′ length and pitch on the manuals and 4′ length and pitch on the pedals.

(v) *Bourdon.* The characteristic dull-toned, booming stop, especially on the pedals. If a small organ has only one pedal stop it is this. It is usually of wood, and has stopped pipes of 8′ length and 16′ pitch. (See 'Double Diapason' below.) It is of the Stopped Diapason

family (see below). 'Bourdon' in French is, among other things, a name for the bee, and also means the drone of a bagpipe. As regards the quality of sound thus fancifully attributed to the stop, note that the Bourdon of French organs suggests this less than that of English organs, being a clear-toned Stopped Diapason of either 16′ or 8′ pitch.

(vi) *Sub-bourdon.* A (pedal) Bourdon of 16′ length and 32′ pitch.

(vii) *Sub-bass.* Same as 'Bourdon'.

Untersatz (literally 'Under-position', i.e. lower than normal pitch). This is the German for a 'Sub-bourdon'.

(viii) *Double Diapason.* Sometimes this term is met with, applied to a 16′ manual bourdon (see above).

(ix) *Quintatön.* A bourdon (usually of metal) of which the scale and construction are such that the harmonic octave-fifth (i.e. the twelfth) is faintly heard with the normal sound. Occasionally a bourdon is unintentionally so made as to have something of this effect and it is then, in organist's slang, 'fifthy'.

Quintadena. Like the quintatön (see above), but with its tone more strongly tinged with the octave-fifth.

Cor de nuit (literally 'night horn', i.e. watchman's horn). A stop of 4′ length and 8′ pitch of the stopped flute or the quintatön class (see above), of large scale and thin metal and very individual tone-quality.

(x) *Dulciana.* In Britain a small-scaled, soft, open metal diapason; the most generally useful soft stop on the organ. Usually of 8′ length and pitch, but sometimes of 4′ or 16′. In the United States the dulciana belongs to the string quality type (see (c) below).

Dolce (literally 'sweet'). A small-scaled, soft-toned, 8′ metal stop, the pipes being of inverted conical shape. It tends, from this constructional feature, to be somewhat unsteady in tone.

Dolcan. Same as 'Dolce'.

Dulcet. A dulciana of 4′ length and pitch.

(xi) *Stopped Diapason.* A diapason of 4′ length and 8′ pitch. It may be argued that the quality of tone in many examples would rather justify the name 'Stopped Flute'.

(xii) *Gedact* or *Gedeckt* (literally 'covered', or 'roofed'). A soft-toned metal 'stopped' stop of small scale. It somewhat approaches flute quality (hence included in the list of flute-toned stops following).

Lieblich Gedact ('Lieblich' means 'lovely'). Same as above with a compliment added. See also (b).

Salicional. A quiet-toned 8′ metal stop of slightly reedy quality (Lat. *salix*, 'willow'). This stop often belongs to the string quality group.

Salicet. Same as 'Salicional' (see above), but 4′.

(xiii) *Voix céleste* or *Vox coelestis* (literally 'heavenly voice'). A stop with its pipes tuned slightly 'out', so as to 'beat' with one of the normal soft stops of the same manual (dulciana or salicional), which stop is automatically brought into action whenever the voix céleste stop is drawn. The slight 'wave' thus produced causes a pleasantly mysterious effect.

Vox angelica (literally 'angelic voice'). Usually much the same as voix céleste. Occasionally, however, the name is given to a single-rank stop of soft dulciana quality.

Unda maris (literally 'wave of the sea'). Much the same as voix céleste.

Diaphone. A loud type of diapason. Each pipe has a vibratory apparatus (of varying form), which gives the stop its characteristic quality—i.e. a peculiar lack of definiteness of timbre. It is of 32′, 16′, or 8′ length and tone.

(b)   Stops with Flute Quality of Tone.

(i) *Hohlflöte* (literally 'hollow flute', i.e. hollow-sounding). A metal or wood stop of 8′ length and pitch. Nearly the same as clarabella or claribel.

Clarabella. See above (Lat., *clarus*, 'bright', and *bellus*, 'beautiful').

Clarabel or *Claribel Flute.* As above.

(ii) *Suabe Flute* (Lat., *suavis*, 'sweet'). Very like Hohlflöte, but usually of 4′ length and pitch.

(iii) *Harmonic Flute.* A metal stop, of 8′ length but a 4′ pitch, the latter being the effect of a hole bored half-way up, which causes it to sound its octave harmonic, and gives it the characteristic silvery tone of harmonic sounds. (Sometimes of 16′ length and 8′ pitch.)

(iv) *Rohrflöte* or *Rohr Flute* (literally 'reed flute', but 'reed' here means a tube). Of metal stopped pipes, with a slender tube through the stopper (hence the name).

Flûte à cheminée (literally 'chimney flute'). The same.

Spitzflöte (literally 'pointed flute'). Of metal, with slightly conical shape (hence its name). It may be 8′, 4′, or 2′ in length and pitch.

Zauberflöte (literally 'magic flute', as Mozart's opera). A pleasant-sounding metal stop usually of 8′ pitch. It is really a kind of harmonic flute (see above), but has stopped pipes, not open ones, and the hole is pierced in such a place that the third harmonic (i.e. the twelfth) is the note heard, not the second harmonic (i.e. the octave)—the length of the pipe being adjusted accordingly.

Grossflöte (literally 'large flute'). The name is probably intended to distinguish it from 'Kleinflöte' (see below). A metal stop of 8′ length and pitch.

Fernflöte (literally 'far-flute' or 'distant flute'). A soft stop of metal of 8′ length and pitch.

Flauto traverso. Supposed to resemble the ordinary orchestral flute (the 'cross flute', as distinct from the old flageolet or recorder, i.e. from the end-played flute). Of 4′ length and pitch.

(v) *Waldflöte* (literally 'woodland flute'). Like the clarabella (see above), but often of 4′ length and pitch and with inverted mouth.

Clear Flute. Much like the above.

Flûte d'amour (literally 'love-flute'.) In Britain a soft stop of 8′ or 4′ length and pitch; in the United States of 2′ length and 4′ pitch and of small scale.

Flauto amabile. The same.

(vi) *Gedact* or *Gedeckt.* This stop sometimes approaches flute quality.

(vii) *Stopped Diapason.* The same may be said.

Lieblich Gedact (literally 'lovely and covered' or 'lovely and lidded'). A Gedact of 8′ or 4′ length and pitch. It has often a pretty pure flute quality.

Lieblich Flöte (literally 'lovely flute'). Same as above, but of 4′ length and pitch.

(viii) *Piccolo.* A metal or wooden flute stop of 2′ length.

Harmonic Piccolo. This stands to the piccolo as the harmonic flute does to the ordinary flute. Of 4′ length and 2′ pitch.

Kleinflöte (German for 'little flute'). Same as piccolo.

Flageolet. A soft piccolo.

(ix) *Gemshorn* (literally 'chamois horn'). A light-toned stop, with conical pipes of 8′, 4′, or 2′ length and pitch (generally of 4′).

Flautina. A gemshorn of 2′ length and pitch.

Doppelflöte (literally 'double flute'). A wooden stop, the stopped pipes having two mouths (hence the name). Of 8′ length and 4′ pitch as a rule.

Tibia. A large-scaled, loud type of stop, not brilliant, but full-toned. The tibia in anatomy is the shin-bone, and the shin-bone of birds was supposed by the ancients to have supplied the material for early flutes. The word 'Tibia' has been applied to stops in organs on the Continent for some centuries; in Britain and the United States it owes its use largely to Hope-Jones.

Tibia Major. A loud-toned flute of 8′ or 16′ length and pitch.

Tibia Minor. A name given to several rather different types of flute stop, generally open but sometimes stopped and of 8′ or 4′ pitch.

Clarinet Flute. A stop of 4′ length and 8′ pitch, having a hole through the stopper which gives it a slightly reedy quality.

Block Flute (Ger. *Blockflöte* = recorder; see *Recorder Family*). A metal stop of unusually large scale and of 2′ length and pitch, a sort of very robust piccolo.

Flûte à pavillon (literally 'tented flute'). A muted stop of which the pipes end in a sort of bell-tent structure. Of 8′ and 4′ shape and pitch.

Melodia. A stop popular in the United States, of 8′ length and pitch, of the same type as the Hohlflöte.

Major Flute. A loud flute of 8′ or 16′ length and pitch.

Bass Flute. A rather foolishly named 8′ flute on the pedal; should be named 'Flute 8'.

Concert Flute. The name is sometimes given to a harmonic or other flute, usually on the solo manual.

Corno dolce. A not very common type, of nonde-script soft flute colour ('Corno' is a misnomer as a rule).

Flauto dolce. Much the same as dolce (see (a) 'Diapason Quality'), but a little more fluty.

(c)   Stops with String Quality of Tone.

(i) *Gamba* (in full 'Viola da Gamba'). An agreeable and much-used stop with a very fair imitation of string tone. The pipes are of metal, often tapering somewhat towards the top, and then sometimes widening again into an inverted bell (thus sometimes called *Bell Gamba*). They are usually of 8′ length and pitch, but sometimes of 4′ or 16′. Some gambas have a small roller in front of the mouth of each pipe: these are called *Bearded Gambas.*

The Gamba of French organs has a much smoother tone than that of British organs, so that in registering French organ music some stop of the Violin Diapason type represents it better.

Viola da Gamba. See above.

Bell Gamba. See above.

Echo Gamba. A soft gamba.

Keraulophon (from three Greek words, meaning 'horn-pipe-voice'). Constructionally a sort of salicional (see (*a*) 'Diapason Quality'). It is almost obsolete.

(ii) *Violone.* A small-scaled stop of 8' length and pitch; or (much more usually and more properly, the instrument the 'Violone' being the double-bass) of 16' length and pitch.

Violoncello. Like the above; 8' length and pitch.

Contrabass. Much the same as 'Violone'.

Viola. A stop of 8' length and pitch.

(iii) *Geigen Principal* or *Geigen* (Ger. *Geige*, 'fiddle'). A sort of slightly string-toned diapason of 8' or 4' length and pitch—or sometimes 16'.

Horn Diapason. A stop of 8' length and pitch and of string-like tone, the word 'horn' being a little misleading.

Violin Diapason. A small-scaled diapason of 8' length and pitch.

Viole d'Amour. Much like the above. In the United States the pipes are usually tapered slightly.

Viole d'Orchestre. A small-scaled gamba of somewhat biting quality.

Aeolina or *Aeoline.* Of 8' length and pitch; a soft stop supposed to imitate the tone of the Aeolian harp. Sometimes it is tuned to 'beat' with another soft stop, like the céleste: other names are given it occasionally, always beginning with 'Aeol'. It is sometimes of gamba quality and sometimes of dulciana quality.

Erzähler. A soft stop of 8' length and pitch; the pipes are those of the gemshorn (see (*b*). 'Flute Quality'), tapered so that the top is only one-quarter or even one-fifth of the diameter of the pipe near the mouth. When properly voiced the first harmonic (i.e. the octave) is almost as strong as the fundamental. Two of them together make a good céleste. This stop was introduced by the Skinner firm and is a feature of many organs in the United States. (The word *Erzähler* is German for 'narrator'.)

Dulciana. See remark on this stop under (*a*) 'Diapason Quality'.

Salicional. See remark in section (*a*).

(*d*) *Mutation Stops* (i.e. Single Rank). All are open, metal stops.

Twelfth. It sounds an octave and a fifth above the normal, i.e. the interval of a twelfth. Length and pitch $2\frac{2}{3}'$.

Nazard. Same as above.

Seventeenth. It sounds two octaves and a third above the normal, i.e. the interval of a seventeenth. Length and pitch $1\frac{3}{5}'$.

Tierce. Same as above.

Nineteenth. It sounds two octaves and a fifth above the normal, i.e. the interval of a nineteenth. Length and pitch $1\frac{1}{3}'$.

Larigot (the old name for Flageolet). Same as above.

Septième. It sounds two octaves and a minor seventh above the normal, i.e. the interval of a minor twenty-first.

When these stops appear on the pedal their length and pitch are double (sometimes quadruple).

(*e*) *Mixture Stops* (i.e. Multiple Rank).

The following are old or modern names for various types of stops of this kind, from two ranks to five (occasionally more). Note that most of them 'break back' at certain points in their compass, i.e. their

various ranks, instead of continuing indefinitely up the scale and so arriving at last at very shrill notes, return (preferably not all the ranks of a stop at the same time) to a lower octave. Note too that it is a feature of the Cornet that its ranks do *not* 'break back'.

(i) *Mixture. Full Mixture.* A mixture of diapason scale.

Cornet. On this, as a solo stop, florid solo pieces, called 'Cornet Voluntaries', were much played in the 18th century (see *Voluntary*). It now usually has 4–5 ranks.

Mounted Cornet ('Mounted' = placed high on a sound-board of its own, so as to be well heard).

Echo Cornet. Of slight calibre and gentle tone.

Furniture, or *Fourniture.* A powerful mixture.

Cymbel. A brilliant loud mixture, resembling either 'Furniture' or 'Sharp Mixture' (see below). It 'breaks back', i.e. repeats itself, every octave.

Sesquialtera. Properly a two-rank mixture of a twelfth and tierce, but any kind of mixture came to be so called.

Dulciana Mixture. A soft mixture generally on swell or echo manual.

Harmonics. A type of mixture stop, usually of four ranks (seventeenth, nineteenth, flat twenty-first, twenty-second).

Quartane. A two-rank mixture (twelfth and fifteenth).

Sharp Mixture. A mixture of high-pitched pipes and bright tone.

Plein Jeu. A sort of mixture, including only the unison, octave, and fifth.

Ripieno maggiore and *Ripieno minore.* Types of mixture stops, respectively voiced louder and softer.

Carillon. A three-rank mixture (twelfth, seventeenth, twenty-second). It is chiefly found in the United States and is very piquant in its effect.

Stops of the mixture family can generally be used only against a good backing of normal pitched stops (whatever was done in earlier days), and their highest value is as an ingredient in the effect of 'Full Organ'.

(*f*) *Reed-Stops.* The pitch of a reed pipe depends on the length of the reed and not on the length of the pipe, which serves merely as a resonator—though generally made to scale. The pipes are mostly conical, not cylindrical.

(i) *Oboe.* A common and useful reed stop, and when avowedly imitative a very fair reflection of its instrumental counterpart. Of 8' pitch.

Hautboy. Same as above.

Cor Anglais. A type of oboe stop and, like it, of 8' pitch, or sometimes of 16'.

Bassoon. A 16' pitch oboe stop (usually in the pedal department).

Fagotto. Same as above.

(ii) *Clarinet.* Smoother toned than the oboe. Of 8' pitch (occasionally 16'). The pipes (cylindrical, not conical) are only half length.

Corno di bassetto. Much the same as clarinet but of broader tone, and, like it, of 8' pitch. The pipes sometimes have conical bells fitted to the top of the resonators.

Cremona. Much like the clarinet, and, like it, of 8' pitch (the name has nothing to do with the famous violin-making town, being a corruption of Cromorne).

(iii) '*Tromba*', *Trumpet.* A powerful stop of 8' pitch.

'Horn' and 'Cornopean' (see below) are practically synonymous with 'Trumpet'.

Clarion. Much the same as trumpet, but of 4′ pitch.

Cornopean. Much the same as trumpet, but generally softer, though smoother. Of 8′ pitch.

Horn. Much the same as trumpet, but fuller and smoother in tone. Of 8′ pitch.

Tuba. Something like the trumpet but on high pressure and very sonorous. Of 8′ or 16′ or 4′ pitch. The pipes are, for the most part, double the usual length. Usually the organ's loudest stop.

Tuba Major. A variety of the above.

Tuba Minor. A small smooth-toned tuba.

Tuba Mirabilis. A variety of the loud tuba.

Ophicleide. A variety of the loud tuba.

Bombarde, Bombardon. A powerful stop of 16′ pitch, often on the pedal; sometimes it is of 32′ pitch. Presumably originally an imitation of the instruments of the same name.

Trombone. A 16′ counterpart of the 8′ tromba or tuba—generally on the Pedal Organ.

Posaune. A broad 'splashy' kind of old-fashioned reed-stop, often on light wind pressure. (The word is German for trombone.) Of 16′ or 8′ pitch.

Harmonic Trumpet. A trumpet stop embodying (in its upper pipes, at any rate) the principle of the harmonic flute. Of 8′ pitch.

Vox Humana. A sort of clarinet stop with pipes of bigger bore and very short (usually only one-eighth the normal length). Of 8′ pitch.

10. *Foreign Terms Found in Organ Music* (alphabetically arranged). This list is a mere selection of a few of the most commonly used terms.

Buffet d'orgue. French for organ case.

Clavier de récit. French for swell organ keyboard. 'Récit' originally meant any sort of a composition for one voice, being the word invariably used until the Italian word 'solo' superseded it. (The word is *not* an abbreviation of 'recitative', as sometimes imagined.) Originally in French organs the manual which we call 'swell' was supplied with stops chiefly intended for melodic use accompanied by harmonies on another manual.

Clavier des bombardes (French). Keyboard of the Bombardes, i.e. the organ manual to which are attached the powerful trumpet and tuba stops (the French organs excelling in the reed department); in other words, the solo organ.

Echoklavier (literally, 'Echo Keyboard'). German for choir organ.

Grand Chœur. French for full organ.

G.O. or *G.* (= 'Grand Orgue') means 'Great'.

Grand Orgue. French for great organ.

G.P. (= 'Grand-Positif'), means 'Great and Choir coupled'.

G.R. (= 'Grand-Récit'), means 'Great and Swell coupled'.

Hauptwerk (literally, 'chief-work'), or *Hauptmanual.* German for great organ.

H.P.W. or *H.W.* = 'Hauptwerk'.

Oberwerk (Ger.; literally 'upper-work') means 'Swell'. It is sometimes abbreviated 'Obw.' or 'O.W.'.

P. (= 'Positif') means 'Choir'.

Pedalklavier (literally 'Pedal Keyboard'). German for pedal board.

Plein Jeu. French for 'Mixture' or for 'Full to Mixtures' (without reeds).

Positif. French for choir organ. The name perpetuates the idea of the old 'Positive' organ.

Principale. Italian for great organ, or diapason chorus.

Récit. See 'Clavier de récit', above.

Schwellwerk (literally 'swell-work'). German for swell organ.

Soloklavier (literally 'solo keyboard'). German for solo organ.

Unterwerk (literally 'under-work'). German for choir organ.

U.W. = 'Unterwerk'.

PERCY SCHOLES

FURTHER READING
W. Leslie Sumner: *The Organ* (London, 1952, rev. edn 1973); C. Clutton and A. Niland: *The British Organ* (London, 1963); Peter Williams: *The European Organ: 1450–1850* (London, 1966, 2nd edn 1968); P. G. Andersen: *Organ Building and Design* (Eng. trans. 1969); P. Williams: *A New History of the Organ* (London, 1980).

Organ chorale. A setting for organ of a *chorale. In the early Lutheran services chorales were sung in unison by the unaccompanied congregation, but it became the practice to relieve the monotony of texture by alternating strophes with the choir, or with a four-part organ setting. By the early 17th century, these organ settings were becoming quite elaborate, with such contrapuntal genres as the chorale *ricercar* (with the melody treated in strict fugal imitation), chorale variations (the melody forming the basis for a set of variations), and chorale fantasia (a free, idiomatic piece). Such pieces were composed especially by Sweelinck and his pupils Scheidemann and Scheidt.

Later in the 17th century, the forms of chorale fantasia and chorale variations were developed by north Germans such as Tunder (organist at St Mary's, Lübeck) and Matthias Weckmann (organist at St Jacob's, Hamburg). The most important settings, however, were those of Buxtehude, Tunder's successor at Lübeck, who cultivated many chorale forms. His variation set *Auf meinem lieben Gott* is unique, being cast in the form of a secular dance suite (allemande, courante, sarabande, and gigue). He was also the first important composer of *chorale preludes. Composers in central Germany concentrated on more strictly polyphonic genres, using the chorale melody as a *cantus firmus* or as a subject for fugues. Pachelbel was the great master of this school.

These two traditions, north and central German, were brought together in the first half of the 18th century, especially by J. S. Bach. He wrote over 150 organ chorales of all types: 45

short chorale preludes in the *Orgelbüchlein* (BWV 599-644); chorale partitas, including both early works (e.g. BWV 766-8) and the great set of canonic variations on *Vom Himmel hoch* which dates from the end of his life; chorale fugues, such as *Allein Gott in der Höh sei Ehr*; and chorales based on a *cantus firmus*, e.g. the Schübler chorales (1748-9).

The organ chorale was also cultivated by Bach's contemporaries, including Telemann, J. G. Walther, and G. F. Kauffmann, but the genre declined after the mid century, and revived only with the Bach renaissance of the mid 19th century. Notable 19th-century composers of organ chorales include Mendelssohn, Brahms, and Reger.

WENDY THOMPSON

Organ Mass. See under *Verset*.

Organ Solo Mass. Mozart's *Missa brevis* in C major (K 259), composed in 1776. It is so called because there is an important solo in the Benedictus.

Organ stops. See *Organ*, 9.

Organ tablature. See under *Tablature*.

Organum (Lat., from Gk. *organon*, 'tool', 'instrument', also 'system of logic'). The use of the original Greek word to mean an instrument of music did not occur until the 5th century AD. Since the use of instruments in Christian worship was forbidden, all instruments named in the Bible were interpreted in an allegorical way, and *organum* came to mean simply 'vocal music'. It did, however, acquire the special meaning of polyphonic vocal music at an early date; the earliest source of polyphony that we

have, *Musica enchiriadis* (north-eastern France, c.860), calls polyphony *organum*, and this terminology was to be standard up to the 13th century. Hence the term *vox organalis*, meaning the part added to a previous one (or *vox principalis*) to create polyphony. The choice of the word *organum* for polyphony should not be taken to mean that vocal polyphony was an imitation of, or was necessarily connected to, the organ (or any other instrument). Rather it indicates that the music was governed by measurable pitches and consonances, a symphonic system.

Four types of *organum* are known from between the 9th and 13th centuries, after which the term dropped out of use. All involve adding a part to a line of plainchant.

1. In parallel *organum* the added voice or voices begin, move, and end at the constant interval of a fourth, fifth, or octave (or an appropriate combination of these) from the main voice. Parallel *organum* is described in *Musica enchiriadis*; it was probably widely practised throughout the Middle Ages, though no other description is known.

2. The added voice begins in unison with the main voice. It repeats its opening note until the main voice has moved up and away to the distance of a fourth above it. It then moves in parallel fourths with the main voice. At cadences it repeats the sub-final while the main voice nears the final, then both voices merge in the final unison. Repeat notes are also frequently introduced in mid sentence if the main voice has a descending phrase; the added voice usually chooses to repeat the note to which the main voice is descending. This kind of *organum* is described briefly in *Musica enchiriadis*, and in great detail (with many other

Ex. 1

From *Alleluia. Video caelos*, Winchester Troper

(square brackets ⌐¬ = notes repeated during approach of main voice).

Ex. 2

Opening of *Alleluia. Vocavit Jesus* Codex Calixtinus

Vox organalis

Plainchant.

Al — — — le — — — — — lu — — ia.

alternative variant procedures) by Guido of Arezzo in *Micrologus* (*c.*1030). There are 174 compositions of this type in the Winchester Troper of *c.*990 (Ex. 1).

3. The added voice complements the given voice by contrary motion, one part going up while the other goes down, one moving in the top part of the available range, the other in the lower part. The term *discantus* came to be preferred to designate this style, known from *c.*1100 onward, and *organum*, while still carrying the general meaning of 'polyphony', was also used in a more special sense, to distinguish type 4 below from *discantus*.

4. The chant is drawn out into long held notes, while the added voice floats in faster motion above and around it. For this purpose the chant is usually split into two- or three-note segments, the two voices starting together and ending with a simultaneous movement on to their respective final notes (usually a unison). The earliest-known examples are from early 12th-century France (Ex. 2).

The last great repertory of polyphony termed *organum* was that of Notre Dame, Paris, in the late 12th and early 13th centuries. An anonymous theorist of the 1270s credited Léonin ('optimus organista') with the creation of a *Magnus liber organi* ('great book of *organum*') containing chant settings for the cycle of festival services of the Church Year. This was revised by Pérotin ('optimus discantor'). These chant settings are a mixture of held-note *organum* (i.e. *organum* in the special sense, type 4 above) and note-against-note discant (type 3), of a complexity and sophistication remarkable by any standards. Some of the polyphony is for three or four voices, but most of it, like that of previous centuries, is for two. The held-note type of polyphony seems to have gone out of favour in the 13th century, and with it the use of the term *organum* for any sort of polyphony.

DAVID HILEY

Orgel (Ger.). 'Organ'; *Orgeltabulatur*, 'organ tablature'; *Orgelwalze*, 'organ cylinder', i.e. a clockwork organ, functioning by means of a barrel (see *Mechanical Musical Instruments*, 3).

Orgelbüchlein ('Little Organ Book'). Collection of short chorale-preludes for organ by J. S. Bach. He intended to compose 164, for instruction and pedalling practice, but fewer than 50 were completed.

Oriscus. A type of ornamental neume; see *Notation*, 2.

Orlando. Opera in three acts by Handel to a libretto adapted from Capece after Ariosto's 16th-century poem *Orlando furioso* ('Mad Orlando'). It was first performed in London in 1733.

Ornaments and Ornamentation

<table>
<tr><td>1. Introduction</td><td>3. The Baroque Period</td></tr>
<tr><td>2. To 1600</td><td>4. Since 1760</td></tr>
</table>

1. *Introduction.* Ornamentation is the decoration of a pre-existent melody line. A desire to embellish in this way can be observed in all kinds of music, ranging from folk-song and jazz — both traditionally unnotated and assuming some creativity on the part of the performer — to notated Western art music, where the performer's invention has at times played almost as vital a role, although for reasons that will be seen this tradition is now lost.

The art of embellishment was at its zenith in the 16th to 18th centuries, when it was regarded as an essential part of virtuoso technique. C. P. E. Bach put the case in his *Versuch über die wahre Art das Clavier zu spielen*, part i (Berlin, 1753):

No one disputes the need for embellishments. They are, in fact, indispensable. They connect and enliven notes and impart stress and accent; they make music pleasing and awaken our close attention. Expression is heightened by them; let a piece be sad, joyful, or otherwise, and they will lend a fitting assistance. Embellishments provide opportunities for fine performance as well as much of its subject matter. They improve mediocre compositions. Without them the best melody is empty and ineffective, the clearest content clouded. [Yet] a prodigal use of embellishments must be avoided. Regard them as spices which may ruin the best dish . . .

Ornamentation could be applied on a first hearing, but it was most characteristically employed as a means of varying musical repeats, whether whole sections or short sequences. Two broad categories may be distinguished: the small-scale addition of ornaments, or 'graces', to single notes; and the more extensive, florid decoration of entire passages, in which the original melody might be submerged under torrents of fast runs. Naturally, the latter variety was the preserve of the virtuoso soloist, whether singer or instrumentalist. Cadences in particular invited elaboration, a practice that led eventually to the *cadenza. Choirs and instrumental ensembles, especially where there was more than one performer to each line, were necessarily more sparing, and might add only occasional graces where these could be co-ordinated.

In the 16th century, ornamentation was mainly left to the performer to improvise. Throughout the 17th and 18th centuries composers sought in varying degrees to limit this freedom, indicating embellishment more precisely by means of notation or with certain signs. Composers of the Romantic period made their intentions still more clear and neither expected nor tolerated ornamental departures from the printed text.

An important feature of these later developments was the adoption of signs to represent frequently used ornaments such as the appoggiatura, mordent, slide, trill, and turn. Such signs are found at an early date, for example in 15th-century German organ music, but they became especially prominent in the late 17th century. French composers in particular codified a large number of ornaments (known as *agréments*) with corresponding signs. Many of these signs outlived the Baroque period, and a few remain in use today.

Musical representations of these signs are found in writings of all periods. Two points regarding their interpretation are worth remembering. First, no single practice has been followed over several centuries or throughout Europe: a trill, for example, has been indicated by many different signs, and, conversely, a single sign may have had a number of different meanings. It is important therefore to consider both date and place of origin in the performance of a given ornament. Secondly, even where there

exists an apparently definitive explanation of a particular ornament, the performer must remain free to exercise his own taste in the adaptation of model to context. As Michel de Montéclair wrote in his *Principes de musique* (Paris, 1736): 'It is almost impossible to teach in writing how to execute well these ornaments since the live demonstration of an experienced master is hardly sufficient to do this'.

It is therefore difficult, even ill-advised, to be dogmatic about the performance of ornaments. Inconsistencies between contemporary sources and disagreements about their range of application have led to controversies about many aspects of ornamentation. Modern editors may offer well-considered advice, but ultimately the responsibility for the extent and the nature of ornamentation rests with the performer.

2. *To 1600.* Little information has survived about improvised ornamentation before the 16th century. It is possible that plainchant developed to some extent through the embellishment of simpler originals, these decorations later being incorporated in the earliest surviving manuscripts; the ecstatic *jubilus melismas of certain Alleluias are a likely example. There is some evidence that decoration played a part in the performance of the 12th-century *troubadours*, such as the ornamented doubling of the voice line by an instrument in *heterophony.

Ornamentation in polyphonic music was a more risky procedure, since harmonic factors came into play. Jerome of Moravia, however, writing in the late 13th century, implies that ornaments were applicable to all types of music. There are hints of embellishments being applied in certain circumstances to the music of Machaut, Dufay, Josquin, and others. It seems, therefore, that techniques of embellishment developed gradually, and by the later 16th century the practice had certainly reached heights of complexity verging on extravagance.

This latter period saw a flood of publications giving advice on embellishment, regarding both small graces and free ornamentation (sometimes called diminutions or *passaggi*). Among the graces, two stand out in importance: the *tremolo* (a type of half trill beginning on the main note); and the *groppo* (a full cadential trill ending with a turn). *Passaggi* were apparently extensively applied by soloists, and they became increasingly complex at the hands of late 16th-century virtuosos. The treatises of the period give innumerable models of figuration for practice, and occasionally complete examples.

Ornamentation seems to have been an essential technique for instrumentalists. Transcriptions of vocal pieces for keyboard, for example, display considerable embellishment, and this was presumably the style of improvisation by skilled performers. Single lines of polyphonic compositions also might be decorated by a virtuoso viol player over a keyboard accompaniment. The treatises are, as a whole, less concerned with singing, but there is no doubt that professional singers also ornamented their lines—in solos with lute, for example, and also in vocal polyphony. Referring to the latter, some authorities warned performers to avoid simultaneous *passaggi* in different voices. Ex. 1 shows a madrigal by Rore with diminutions by Girolamo dalla Casa (from his *Il vero modo di diminuir*, Venice, 1584). Similar decoration could be applied to sacred motets.

3. *The Baroque Period: (a) Italy.* The early opera composers theoretically rejected elaboration of the kind seen in Ex. 1 on the grounds that it espoused purely musical values at the expense of the meaning of the text. One triumphant exception, dramatically justified, is Orfeo's plea to enter Hades in Monteverdi's *Orfeo* (1607), for which the composer provided a virtuoso embellishment in early Baroque style (Ex. 2). But in general the early 17th century saw a reaction against the excesses of the previous age, and Caccini, in his famous study on Italian singing *Le nuove musiche* (Florence, 1602), was careful to decry the 'old way of composition', which destroyed the shape and sense of the verse, 'not a word of it being understood for the multitude of divisions made upon long and short syllables'.

With the late 17th century, however, emphasis began again to be placed on purely musical values and on vocal virtuosity for its own sake, and ornamentation returned with a vengeance. The stars of 18th-century *opera seria* hoped to dazzle their audiences with astonishing displays of improvised embellishment and extended cadences, especially on the return of the first section of a *da capo* aria. It is difficult to recapture this style of singing, but to judge from surviving transcriptions and from contemporary accounts, the technique and imagination shown in these ornamentations were brilliant indeed.

Ex. 1

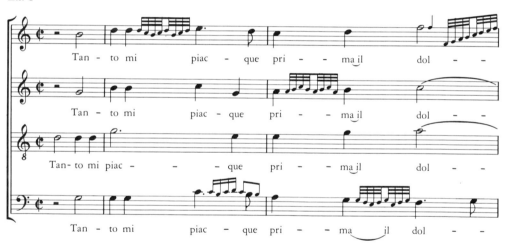

Ex. 2

The results from a dramatic point of view, however, were subject to criticism, then as now. Benedetto Marcello satirized the practice in his *Il teatro alla moda* (Venice, *c*.1720): 'If the modern composer should give lessons to some virtuosa of the opera house, let him have a care to charge her to enunciate badly, and with this object to teach her a great number of divisions and of graces, so that not a single word will be understood, and by this means the music will stand out better and be appreciated'. Other critics, however, praised Italian singers' ornamentation, stressing that it required moderation and sensitivity to the mood of the piece. Recitative was not embellished, but convention required the addition of appoggiaturas.

Italian instrumental music followed somewhat similar trends. In the late Baroque period soloists were expected to decorate skeletal slow movements with florid embellishment. In 1710 Corelli's violin sonatas Op. 5 were published by Estienne Roger in a new edition which included ornamented versions of the solo violin part in the slow movements from the six church sonatas. They were advertised as Corelli's own versions, and although their authorship has not been conclusively proved, they must represent general early 18th-century practice (Ex. 3).

Ex. 3

(+ here = trill)

Ornament signs are rarely found in Italian instrumental music of the 17th century. Shortly after the turn of the century it became more common for composers to indicate trills (though these still often have to be assumed at cadences), and small grace-notes were adopted from France to represent other ornaments. Thus musical sources begin to represent more exactly the composer's intentions, although additional ornamentation of slow movements was still expected, as is shown by some written-out examples in Tartini's autograph manuscripts.

(b) *France.* In his *Versuch einer Anweisung die Flöte traversiere zu spielen* (Berlin, 1752), the German flautist Quantz distinguished the French and Italian styles as follows: 'Pieces in the French style are for the most part *pièces caractérisées*, and are composed with appoggiaturas and shakes in such a fashion that almost nothing may be added to what the composer has already written. In music after the Italian style, however, much is left to the caprice, and to the ability, of the performer.' Although his comments were primarily directed towards the flautist, they may be extended to music of the late Baroque period generally. While the improvisation of embellishments remained an important element of the Italian art, French music was not open to elaboration, and even small ornaments were often indicated by signs whose meanings were explained in lengthy charts (one by D'Anglebert of 1689 lists no fewer than 29).

This had not been the case throughout the Baroque period. In the vocal field, the *air de cour* of the early 17th century was subject to considerable ornamentation on the repeat, but the practice declined in the later decades of the century under the influence of Lully, who in deference to the poetic sense condemned such embroidery as 'ridiculous'. Only the small graces (*agréments*) remained in general use.

On the instrumental side, the trend was also towards concentration on the *agréments*, which might be indicated by small notes or by signs. They are especially characteristic of French harpsichord music. François Couperin demanded that performers adhere strictly to the ornaments he marked; these he explained in his first book of harpsichord *ordres* (1713). Other writers were less rigid, and some composers left the selection of *agréments* to the performer. Typically French was the *double*, a second and more ornamented version of a dance.

(c) *England and Germany.* As both countries saw the influx of Italian and French music at different times, so the two trends of ornamentation were influential. In English harpsichord music of the later 17th century, for example, ornaments were indicated by signs independent from the French symbols but allied in practice. They are listed in Purcell's *A Choice Collection of Lessons* (3rd edn, published posthumously in 1699). The earlier signs of the virginalists' school have not been entirely elucidated. In the 18th century, Italians and their methods dominated English opera, as can be seen, for example, in the works of Handel. A certain modest ornamentation was even allowed in his oratorios, although surviving elaborations for *Messiah* (such as a cadenza for 'Ev'ry valley'), which were once thought to be contemporary, are now regarded as later additions.

Germany in the 17th century was closely allied to Italian practices, but with the increasing popularity of French music after 1700 many of the French signs for specific ornaments were taken over. Bach's unique synthesis of Italian and French styles with a native tradition makes the subject of ornamentation in his music particularly complex. In general, he leaves little room in his compositions—vocal or instrumental—for the addition of more than the smallest grace, preferring to write out complex ornamentation of the Italian type. His transcriptions of Italian compositions provide an illustration of his method (see Ex. 4), and it is demonstrated in an original form in the slow movement of his Italian Concerto. The two versions of the Sarabandes in the English Suites Nos. 2 and 3 display Bach's ornamentation technique in a different genre. Bach also made ample use of French ornament signs, which he explained briefly (on French models) in a manuscript of 1720; since they may be found in music outside the 'French style', however, they may be open to a variety of interpretations. Shortly after Bach's death in 1750, three major German treatises (Quantz's of 1752, C. P. E. Bach's of 1753, both mentioned above, and Leopold Mozart's *Versuch einer gründlichen Violinschule*, Augsburg, 1756) appeared. They include extensive information on ornaments for the mid-century musician, but how far this is applicable in Bach's older style continues to be a subject for dispute.

Valuable advice on free ornamentation is also to be found in these writings. C. P. E. Bach went further, and in a set of sonatas published in 1760 assisted the amateur with written-out variants for the repeats (Ex. 5). These provide an instructive comparison with the style of embellishment used by his father (Ex. 4).

4. *Since 1760.* With the trend towards the Classical style there began changes of attitude towards ornamentation. In part these represented the self-conscious desire of composers to notate their music in more detail, to preserve it more fully as they intended it; in part they reflected a growing need to provide guidance for

Ex. 4
From an arrangement for harpsichord by Bach of an oboe concerto by A. Marcello

amateur performers. More important, they paralleled changes in musical style, as a 'noble simplicity' and a more dramatic conception were sought.

Old habits lasted longest in Italian opera, where singers were wont to add embellishment well into the 19th century. But increasingly this practice went against the will of the composer. In his preface to the publication of *Alceste* (1769) Gluck made a famous tirade (if an ineffective one as far as Italian opera was concerned) against the vanities of singers. For the performance of an early opera, *Lucio Silla*, Mozart sketched out some elaborations in the current manner, but in the later operas any ornamentation needed is fully written into the

Ex. 5

score, and none should be added by the singer. Rossini, also, is credited with making a stand against the excessive embellishment still practised in the 1810s, by notating the ornamentation that he desired. It was a gradual process, but eventually, as a more naturalistic style of drama prevailed, added ornamentation became regarded as an affectation of a bygone age.

In the instrumental field, composers were quicker to exert control over ornamentation, as they did over tempo, dynamics, and phrasing. During the Classical period, at least in the works of the greatest composers, improvised embellishment became both unnecessary and undesirable, and the number of ornament signs in use also went into decline. While it is known that in performance Mozart and Beethoven did add

ornamentation, especially in slow movements, for publication they carefully wrote out any embellishment they required. Only some skeletal passages in those of Mozart's piano concertos that were not published in his lifetime need filling out; and Beethoven is said to have flared up in anger when Czerny added notes to the piano part in a performance of the Quintet Op. 16.

The Romantics perpetuated the view of the classic and definitive work of art representing the composer's ideal conception, the performer being relegated to the status of musical servant. Naturally they tended to write out most ornaments in full notation, thus avoiding the ambiguity of the traditional signs. Despite shifts in musical style, the same attitudes have largely prevailed in the 20th century. In a sense, special effects such as flutter-tonguing on the flute or *glissando* on the trombone represent a type of ornament; and some avant-garde composers have returned a share of musical creation to the performer. But improvised ornamentation, in the meaning used here of melodic decoration, is

The following Table gives the most commonly found ornament signs, and directs the reader to the articles covering the ornaments. It is by no means exhaustive, and the reader who wishes to pursue further the complex subject of ornamentation should refer to specialist books such as those listed in FURTHER READING.

Main articles	Description	Signs
Appoggiatura	appoggiatura	etc.
	short appoggiatura (often called acciaccatura)	
Mordent	(lower) mordent	
	double mordent	
	inverted (upper) mordent	
Slide	slide	also (
Tremolo	tremolo (17th–18th centuries)	
Trill	trill	*tr* (Baroque period also +)
	trill with various prefixes or with suffix (Baroque period)	
Turn	turn	
	inverted turn	

no longer a feature of Western art music. Twentieth-century composers have generally notated their music with a precision hitherto unknown. To add embellishment to a piece by Berg, for example, would be as unthinkable as to perform a Corelli sonata unembellished.

SIMON MCVEIGH

FURTHER READING
Walter Emery: *Bach's Ornaments* (London, 1953); Robert Donington: *The Interpretation of Early Music* (London, 1963, new version 1974); R. Donington: *A Performer's Guide to Baroque Music* (London, 1973); Frederick Neumann: *Ornamentation in Baroque and Post-Baroque Music* (Princeton, 1978).

Orpharion. Elizabethan and Jacobean stringed instrument, invented (it was said) by John Rose of London shortly after he had produced the *bandora. Like this, the orpharion is built with a wavy-sided body, though rather smaller, and is strung with wire. It differs in being tuned like a six-course *lute. The player could thus play

Orpharion, 16th–17th century.

from lute tablatures. There exist, however, some pieces written expressly for orpharion, some including notes higher up the string than normally found in lute music, the orpharion having a longer neck in relation to its size. At least two genuine orpharions are preserved: one by Rose himself, dated 1580; the second by another London maker, Francis Palmer, 1617, now in the museum in Copenhagen. The name is a fusion of 'Orpheus' and 'Arion'.

ANTHONY BAINES

Orphée aux enfers. See *Orpheus in the Underworld.*

Orphéon. The French name given to male-voice choral societies which were formed around 1835 in France in imitation of the German *Liedertafeln. From 1852 to 1860 Gounod was director of the Paris societies, and by 1880 there were 1,500 French societies with a total membership of 60,000.

Orpheus. 1. Symphonic poem by Liszt, composed as an introduction to his production of Gluck's *Orphée et Euridice* at Weimar in 1854.
2. Ballet in three scenes by Stravinsky. It was choreographed by Balanchine and given its first performance in New York in 1948.

Orpheus britannicus ('The British Orpheus'). Title given to two volumes of songs by Purcell (the 'British Orpheus') published posthumously (1698–1702) by Henry Playford, and to a volume of his songs published by John Walsh (1735). Britten and Pears realized and edited 18 of the solo songs for voice and piano and six duets for high and low voices and piano. They also made a suite of songs for soprano or tenor and orchestra and arranged three songs for soprano or tenor and orchestra.

Orpheus in the Underworld (*Orphée aux enfers*). Opera by Offenbach to a libretto by Crémieux and Halévy. It was composed in two acts and first performed in Paris in 1858; Offenbach revised it and expanded it into four acts, the new version being first performed in Paris in 1874.

Orr, Robin (Robert Kemsley) (*b* Brechin, 2 June 1909). Scottish composer. He studied at Cambridge, in Siena with Casella, and in Paris with Nadia Boulanger. In 1936 he embarked on a career as a university lecturer which culminated in his appointment to the chair of music at Cambridge (1965–75). His compositions, whose gritty harmony and rhythmic dynamism suggest influences as various as Hindemith and Shostakovich, include *Hermiston* (1975) and other operas, two symphonies, and church music.

PAUL GRIFFITHS

Lithograph poster by Jules Chéret for Offenbach's 'Orphée aux Enfers' (Théâtre de la Gaité, Paris, 1874).

Ortiz, Diego (*b* Toledo, *c*.1510; *d* ? Naples, *c*.1570). Spanish viol player and composer. He was *maestro de capilla* to the vice-regal chapel at Naples in the mid 16th century. His *Trattado de glosas* (Rome, 1553) is one of the earliest and most valuable treatises on playing the viol, and its advice on ornamentation and arranging a madrigal for solo viol is well worth study by players of 16th-century music. His ornaments in ensemble music are usually more modest than those of some later extremists.   DENIS ARNOLD

Orton, Richard (Henry) (*b* Derby, 1 Jan. 1940). English composer. He studied with Wilfrid Mellers at the Birmingham School of Music and with Alan Ridout at Cambridge. In 1967 he was appointed lecturer at York University, where he has directed the electronic music studio. His works include live electronic and taped pieces (*Sampling Afield*, 1968; *For the Time Being*, 1972; *Clock Farm*, 1973, among others) as well as essays in various other experimental techniques.   PAUL GRIFFITHS

Osanna (It.). See *Hosanna*.

Ossia (It.). 'Or'. The term is used to designate passages added (usually to piano or violin music) by the composer, or sometimes by an editor, as alternatives to the original. Such alternative passages are usually easier to execute than the originals, although Beethoven and Liszt, for example, frequently added alternative passages of equal or greater difficulty than those which they were intended to replace.

Ostinato (It.). Literally 'obstinate', 'persistent'. A *basso ostinato* is a form of *ground bass which is repeated many times unchanged and over which melodic variations occur.

Ostrčil, Otakar (*b* Prague, 25 Feb. 1879; *d* Prague, 20 Aug. 1935). Czech composer and conductor. Although he studied philology and taught languages at the start of his career, Ostrčil took composition lessons from Fibich and was influenced by the musical aesthetician Otakar Hostinský. He gained experience conducting choirs and the orchestra of the Vinohrady Theatre in Prague. In 1920 he succeeded Kovařovic as musical director of the National Theatre, a post which he occupied until his death. Here he encouraged and maintained high standards of performance, and in the 1930s he made formative recordings of Smetana's operas. As a member of the Society for Modern Music he encouraged young Czech composers and introduced many important foreign works including Debussy's *Pelléas* (1921) and Berg's *Wozzeck* (1926). Ostrčil's interest in modern music, his championing of Smetana's operas, and his work as a musical administrator were important in forming musical taste in Prague between the wars. His early compositions, especially the melodramas and the operas *Vlasty skon* ('Vlasta's Death', 1903) and *Kunálovy oči* ('Kunál's Eyes', 1908) show the influence of Fibich. Later stage works including *Poupě* ('The Bud', 1910) and *Honzovo království* ('Johnny's Kingdom', 1933) indicate a deliberate move away from excessive Romanticism. Ostrčil's orchestral works from the 1920s (*Summer*, 1926; *The Way of the Cross*, 1928) illustrate his absorption with counterpoint, and a flexible approach to tonality, though this never tipped over into atonality.   JAN SMACZNY

Otello. Opera in four acts by Verdi; text by Boito, after Shakespeare's tragedy (*c*.1605). Produced: Milan, La Scala, 5 February 1887; New York, Academy of Music, 16 April 1888; London, Lyceum, 5 July 1899. The plot of the opera follows Shakespeare closely, although the Venetian first act is omitted, with Otello (ten.), Desdemona (sop.), and Iago (bar.). Also an opera by Rossini (1816).

FURTHER READING
Nicholas John, ed.: *Otello*, English National Opera Guides (London, 1981).

Ôter (Fr.). 'To take off'; *ôtez*, 'take off'; *ôtez les sourdines*, 'take off the mutes'. In organ music it means to throw out of action a stop which had been in use up to that point.

Othello. Concert overture, Op. 93, by Dvořák, composed in 1892. With *Amid Nature* and *Carneval* it formed a cycle of overtures, *Nature, Life and Love*.

Othmayr, Caspar (*b* Amberg, nr Nuremberg, 12 Mar. 1515; *d* Nuremberg, 4 Feb. 1553). German composer. He studied at Heidelberg University and may have worked at the Palatine court there. In 1545 he became rector of the monastic school at Heilsbronn, and in 1547 a canon at the monastery of St Gumbertus, Ansbach. He was one of the earliest Lutheran composers, and his works include hymn settings and adaptations as well as some Latin motets. His most important works, however, are his German secular songs, including *Tenorlieder*, in four or five parts.   DENIS ARNOLD

Ottava (It.). 'Octave', sometimes abbreviated to *8va*. Sometimes in orchestral scores the term is used to show that one instrument should play in octaves with another; *coll'ottava*, 'with the octave'; *ottava alta, ottava sopra*, 'octave above'; *ottava bassa, ottava sotto*, 'octave below'. See also *All'ottava*.

Ottone (It.). 'Brass'; *stromenti d'ottone*, 'brass instruments'.

Our Father. See *Pater noster*.

Francesco Tamagno as the first Otello in Verdi's opera (La Scala, Milan, 1887).

Our Hunting Fathers. Symphonic song cycle, Op. 8, by Britten for soprano or tenor solo and orchestra. It is a setting of a text by W. H. Auden and was first performed at the Norwich Festival in 1936.

Our Man in Havana. Opera in three acts by Williamson to a libretto by Sidney Gilliat based on Graham Greene's novel. It was first performed in London in 1963.

Ouseley, (Sir) Frederick Arthur Gore (*b* London, 12 Aug. 1825; *d* Hereford, 6 Apr. 1889). English church musician and scholar. Son of a wealthy baronet who had travelled widely, he was one of the most foremost figures in the revival of English church music in the mid 19th century. As Professor of Music at Oxford from 1855 (a post he held simultaneously with that of Precentor of Hereford Cathedral) he was responsible for the organization of examinations on a modern basis. But his real claim to fame is his foundation (at his own expense) of St Michael's College, Tenbury, which became the model for cathedral choir schools, and which he provided with a magnificent collection of ancient manuscripts, now on permanent loan to the Bodleian Library, Oxford.   DENIS ARNOLD

Ouvert and clos (Fr., 'open' and 'closed'; It.: *aperto, chiuso*). In some 14th- and 15th-century vocal forms, e.g. the *ballade* and the *virelai*, repeated sections are given alternative endings, and these are labelled *ouvert* and *clos* or *aperto* and *chiuso* in the same way that we use *prima volta* and *seconda volta*, or first-time bar and second-time bar.

Ouverture (Fr.). 'Overture'.

Ouvrir (Fr.). 'To open'. The imperative, *ouvrez*, is often used in organ music in connection with the swell box, or as a direction to put into action some stop mentioned.

Over-dotting. See *Dot*, 3.

Overtones. See *Acoustics*, 5.

Overture. A piece of instrumental music composed as an introduction to an opera, oratorio, or other dramatic work, or intended for independent concert performance. In the Baroque period the title 'Ouvertüre' was sometimes applied to a keyboard or orchestral suite (Bach), or to its opening movement; and in 18th-century England 'Overture' could serve as an alternative title for a symphony (as in Haydn's 'London' symphonies).

1. *Dramatic Overture.* Dramatic entertainments in the 16th century, and the earliest operas and oratorios at the beginning of the 17th, either lacked any sort of introduction or began with a flourish of trumpets or other brief call to attention (as in the opening Toccata of Monteverdi's *Orfeo*, 1607). As opera and oratorio developed and became more organized, so did the introduction. Mid-17th-century operas often began with a slow, duple-metre orchestral movement followed by a faster triple-metre one; this was to form the basis of a standard overture-type which, through its later association with the operas of Lully and other composers of French opera, came to be known as the French overture. In its conventional form (such as Handel used for *Messiah*) it is characterized by a grave, sometimes pompous opening, with plentiful dotted rhythms and suspensions, leading straight into a fast, lively section in imitative, even fugal style, which often closes by echoing the mood of the first section. Later these closing chords, which originally amounted to little more than a decorated cadential phrase, were sometimes extended to form a moderately slow dance movement (as in the minuet in Handel's overture to *Samson*), or the entire first section might be repeated. The presence of this well-developed closing section has given rise to the mistaken assertion that the French overture is a tripartite (slow–fast–slow) structure, but that view overlooks the genre's essential binary-form features.

Later in the 17th century a real tripartite overture appeared in Naples, cast in short fast–slow–fast sections, which came to be known as the Italian overture. This type, sometimes entitled 'Sinfonia', was an important precursor of the Classical symphony. During the 18th century the overture's first section began to be regarded the most significant, the second and third sections were more or less discarded, and the overture thus diverged from the symphony, which by mid century had become an important orchestral form in its own right.

Until the mid 18th century there was little connection, beyond a general spiritual conformity, between an overture and what followed. In his famous preface to *Alceste*, however, Gluck sought a more intimate correspondence between the two: his overture to *Iphigenia in Tauris* traces closely the progress of a thunderstorm in an effort to set the mood for the first scene, with which the overture merges without a break. Haydn took this even further in *The Creation*, whose overture, with its vivid depiction of Chaos, actually sets in motion the whole drama which is then continued in the first vocal number.

It may well have been Mozart's experience with the symphony that persuaded him to cast his operatic overtures in moulds closely related to *sonata form, with a slow introduction but without a repeated exposition. Continuing to develop and perfect Gluck's ideas, he began the practice of anticipating in the overture some striking or significant passage from the opera, as for instance in the overture to *Don Giovanni*, which prepares us (by a brief reference) for the statue music of the last scene, and in those for *Die Zauberflöte* and *Così fan tutte*.

The general principle and style that Mozart established for the dramatic overture persisted into 19th-century early Romantic operas by Italian, French, and German composers. Wagner's early opera overtures conformed to this pattern, but in *Lohengrin*, the *Ring*, and *Tristan und Isolde* he preferred a fairly short, independent prelude ('Vorspiel'), as occasionally did Verdi, and some of the preludes he wrote for acts other than the first are as long and significant as any of his opening overtures.

An effective type of overture that served well for 19th-century comic or light opera and operetta was one put together from a medley or pot-pourri of tunes taken straight from the opera, with little or no linking material. This was particularly popular with Auber, Offenbach, and Sullivan, and its influence is clearly seen in a number of overtures for modern stage musicals.

2. *Concert Overture*. Although Mendelssohn is frequently hailed as the 'inventor' of the concert overture, its origins properly lie in the performance, as separate concert pieces, of Mozart's later opera overtures and of those that Beethoven wrote for stage plays by Goethe (*Egmont*) and Collin (*Coriolan*), and the rejected *Leonora* overtures.

Other early 19th-century concert overtures were 'occasional' (Beethoven's *Die Weihe des Hauses*) or abstract (Schubert's 'in the Italian style'), but it is the descriptive, poetic pieces such as Mendelssohn's *The Hebrides* and *A Midsummer Night's Dream* and Berlioz's *Carnaval romain* that typify the Romantic concert overture. Some of these pieces were written to commemorate events (Tchaikovsky's *1812*, Brahms's *Academic Festival Overture*); others were inspired by literature or art (Berlioz's *King Lear*, Liszt's *Hunnenschlacht*); still others, like Brahms's *Tragic Overture*, have no known extra-musical connections. A few overtures are narrative and programmatic, but more usually they are pure mood-pieces, cast in fairly traditional, Classical forms. But as the Romantics' attitude to form and expression grew ever more liberal as the 19th century advanced, the concert overture was all but usurped by the freer, more flexible, and more fashionable *symphonic poem advocated by progressive composers such as Richard Strauss, and there remained little purpose for the concert overture.

PERCY SCHOLES, rev. Judith Nagley

Overture, Scherzo, and Finale. Orchestral work, Op. 52, by Schumann, composed in 1841; the finale was revised in 1845.

Owen Wingrave. Opera in two acts, Op. 85, by Britten to a libretto by Myfanwy Piper based on Henry James's story. Written for BBC television, it was first broadcast in 1971 and received its stage première at Covent Garden in 1973.

Owl and the Pussy-Cat, The. 1. Setting by Searle of Edward Lear's poem (1870). It is for speaker, flute, cello, and guitar, and was composed in 1951.

2. Setting by Stravinsky of the same poem, for voice and piano, composed in 1966.

Oxford Elegy, An. Work by Vaughan Williams, composed 1947–9, for speaker, small mixed chorus, and small orchestra, to a text adapted from Matthew Arnold's poems *The Scholar Gipsy* (1853) and *Thyrsis* (1867). Some of the text is spoken and some sung by the chorus, and there is also a wordless choral part.

Oxford Movement. Religious movement (1833–45), based in Oxford, which aimed to restore the High Church ideals of the 17th century. Its leaders were John Keble, John Henry Newman, and Edward Bouverie Pusey. With regard to music, it encouraged fully sung services and did much to revive interest in plainchant and early polyphony. (See also *England*, 7.)

Oxford Psalter. See *Anglican Chant*, 5.

'Oxford' Symphony. Nickname of Haydn's Symphony No. 92 in G major, composed in 1789. It is so called because it was performed when Haydn received the honorary doctorate at Oxford University in 1791; when he composed it, however, Haydn did not have Oxford in mind.

Oxford University Press (OUP). English firm of publishers. A division of Oxford University, it is non-profit-making, without shareholders, and enjoys charitable status. In the 19th century sporadic but important music publications were issued by OUP from the Clarendon Press at Oxford and from the London house. These included Robert Bridges's *Yattendon Hymnal* (1899), an attempt to restore musical integrity to Victorian hymn-singing which used a music type cut at Oxford by Peter de Walpergen in 1694-5. This was followed by Percy Buck's *Oxford Song Book* of 1916, and in the early 1920s various sheet-music series such as Oxford Choral Songs and Oxford Church Music. Music books began to appear in 1901 with the first volume of the *Oxford History of Music*.

In 1925 Hubert Foss (1899-1953) created a separate music department. During his first decade an average of 200 works appeared each year, and his prodigious list soon included many important English composers, among them Vaughan Williams, William Walton, Alan Rawsthorne, Constant Lambert, Peter Warlock, and, briefly, Benjamin Britten. By 1931 Foss had over 1,750 titles. Famous anthologies, such as the *Oxford Book of Carols* and the *Oxford Song Book*, established themselves as the commercial core of the music department, while the important edition of *Tudor Church Music* (10 vols., 1922-9) increased its reputation. Foss's interests extended to every aspect of music, including the design of type. If the pace of his publishing aroused fears of bankruptcy among the Delegates, his energy and gifts put Oxford University Press Music Department at the centre of London musical life. His tea and sherry concerts at Amen House attracted the famous. When he resigned in 1941 he had established firm foundations for the future.

Foss was succeeded as music editor by Norman Peterkin (1941-7), Alan Frank (1948-54, who was head of department 1954-75), and Christopher Morris (from 1954, joint head of music publishing with Anthony Mulgan 1975-82, thereafter head). OUP have always remained dedicated to British composers and publish the music of William Walton, Lennox and Michael Berkeley, Gordon Crosse, Alun Hoddinott, and William Mathias among others. The firm's continuing interest in earlier music is seen in the series Musica da Camera, inaugurated by Robin Langley in 1973. They also publish educational music.

Oxford University Press have published a number of important music books, notably *Cobbett's Cyclopedic Survey of Chamber Music*, Tovey's *Essays in Musical Analysis*, and such standard reference works as *The Oxford History of Music*, *The New Oxford History of Music*, and Gerald Abraham's *Concise Oxford History of Music*. *The Oxford Companion to Music* was first published by Percy Scholes in 1938 and achieved its tenth edition in 1970 before being freshly conceived as the *New Oxford Companion to Music* (1983). The Press has also published a series of concise dictionaries of music, opera, and ballet, issued recordings, acquired *Music & Letters* in 1955, and became publishers of *Early Music* in 1973.   J. M. THOMSON

Ox Minuet (*Ochsenmenuett*). Minuet by Ignaz Xaver von Seyfried (1776-1841), a pupil of Haydn, who introduced it into his opera *Die Ochsenmenuett* (1823). The minuet has been misattributed to Haydn, the legend being that Haydn wrote it for a butcher who gave him an ox in return.

Oxyrhynchos Hymn. The earliest Christian hymn (*c*.AD 300) for which the music is preserved (in Greek vocal notation). It takes its name from the place in Egypt where the papyrus was discovered.

P

P, p. 1. An abbreviation for *piano* (It.), 'soft', always written in the italic form *p*. 2. An abbreviation for 'pedal' in keyboard music. 3. In French organ music, an abbreviation for *pédalier*, i.e. the pedal board, or for *Positif*, i.e. Choir Organ.

Pachelbel, Johann (*bapt.* Nuremberg, 1 Sept. 1653; *d* Nuremberg, Mar. 1706). German organist and composer. He came from a family of musicians, and was given his early music lessons in his home town. In 1669 he entered the University of Altdorf, where he was also parish organist, but could not afford to stay for more than a year. He then studied music and literature, with financial assistance from the school, at Regensburg, and in 1673 became organist at St Stephen's Cathedral, Vienna. In 1677 he was organist to the Eisenach court, and there became friendly with Bach's father. He left the following year, and worked at Erfurt (1678), where he lost his first wife and child in a plague epidemic, the Stuttgart court (1690), and Gotha (1692). Finally, in 1695, he returned home to Nuremberg as organist at St Sebald.

Pachelbel's importance as a composer lies mainly in his organ music which amalgamated the south and central German styles; it had a considerable influence on Bach. He also played a major role in the development of Protestant vocal music. Pachelbel wrote many fugues, toccatas, chaconnes, and organ chorales, but much of his output remained in manuscript; only two collections of organ music (*Acht Choräle*, Nuremberg, 1693; *Musicalische Sterbens-Gedancken*, Erfurt, 1683), one set of six harpsichord airs and variations (*Hexachordum Apollinis*, Nuremberg, 1699), and six trio sonatas (Nuremberg, 1695) were published in his lifetime. His vocal music includes nine German and two Latin motets with continuo and optional instruments, 13 *Magnificat* settings, two Masses, and several German sacred concertos.

WENDY THOMPSON

Pacific 231. Orchestral work by Honegger (*Mouvement symphonique No. 1*), composed in 1923. *Pacific 231* is a locomotive.

Pacific Islands

1. Introduction
2. Melanesia

3. Micronesia
4. Polynesia

1. *Introduction.* Following the convention set by European explorers and cartographers of the 18th and 19th centuries, the islands of the central and southern Pacific are usually divided into three regions, Melanesia, Micronesia, and Polynesia (from the Greek, *melanos*, 'black', *mikros*, 'small', *polys*, 'many', and *nēsos*, 'island'). Together, these regions cover a vast expanse of ocean (155 million sq. km., twenty times the size of the United States), yet their total combined land area (458,000 sq. km., excluding Papua New Guinea) is less than that of Spain. Melanesia lies north-east of Australia and includes New Guinea (largest island in the world), the Bismark archipelago, the Solomon Islands, Vanuatu (formerly New Hebrides), the Loyalty Islands, New Caledonia, and Fiji. Micronesia is to the north and incorporates the Mariana, Caroline, and Marshall archipelagos, and Kiribati (formerly the Gilberts). Polynesia lies to the east and is defined by a great triangle

with Hawaii at the northernmost point, New Zealand on the south, and Easter Island on the east.

The prehistory of the Pacific has been partly reconstructed from archaeological evidence. The earliest settlers probably travelled from mainland south-east Asia to New Guinea some 20,000 years ago. For the rest of Oceania, no record of settlement exists before the second millennium BC. By tracing the path of Lapita-ware pottery, we know that its makers had reached Fiji by 1000 BC and Tonga by 500 BC.

Inevitably, the sea shaped all aspects of early Oceanic culture. But for the people of the Pacific, with their highly developed navigational skills, the ocean proved more a highway than a barrier, and we do not find, even on remote islands, the cultural isolation one might anticipate. Before the arrival of Europeans, overpopulation was a continual incentive to migration, and also provoked fierce intra-island warfare, still enacted today in dynamic posturing dances such as the Maori *haka* (see *New Zealand*, 2).

European navigators who reached the Pacific during the 16th and 17th centuries encountered simple Neolithic cultures with technologies based on the use of stone, bone, and shell. Early accounts tell, with great clarity and detail, of local music and dance. In the journals of the great English north-countryman, Captain James Cook, we can, for example, read this careful description of the Tongan dance, the *me'elaufola*, which he witnessed in May, 1777:

The concert having continued about a quarter of an hour, twenty women entered the circle . . . and began by singing a soft air, to which responses were made by the chorus in the same tone; and these were repeated alternately. All this while, the women accompanied their song with several very graceful motions of their hands toward their faces, and in other directions at the same time, making constantly a step forward, and then back again, with one foot, while the other was fixed. They then turned their faces to the assembly, sung some time, and retreated slowly in a body, to that part of the circle which was opposite the hut where the principal spectators sat. After this, one of them advanced from each side, meeting and passing each other in the front, and continuing their progress round, till they came to rest . . .

Their manner of dancing was now changed to a quicker measure, in which they made a kind of half turn by leaping, and clapped their hands, and snapped their fingers, repeating some words in conjunction with the chorus. Toward the end, as the quickness of the music increased, their gestures and attitudes were varied with wonderful vigour and dexterity; and some of their motions, perhaps, would, with us, be reckoned rather indecent.

Other early travellers, less complimentary, found the songs of the Pacific monotonous, tuneless, and doleful, unaccustomed as they were to their *Engmelodik* style, typified by few notes and a narrow range.

During the early 19th century, parties of Congregational, Methodist, Anglican, and Roman Catholic missionaries began to frequent the Pacific. In the course of their ministries, they attacked and destroyed local customs, social organization, and values, which they found 'filled with all unrightousness' and threatening to their Western Christian outlook. By the 1890s the *me'elaufola* of Tonga, which Cook had so vividly described a century earlier, was condemned as a 'heathen dance' and prohibited upon pain of a five-dollar fine. As a substitute for native songs, the missionaries introduced Christian hymns (*himene*).

Other visitors, romantic in temperament— Melville, Somerset Maugham, Gauguin— perpetuated a myth of the South Seas as a primitive arcadia and Polynesian man as the noble savage. 'In the South Seas the Creator seems to have laid Himself out to show what He *can* do', wrote Rupert Brooke in 1914. 'Imagine an island with the most perfect climate in the world, tropical, yet almost always cooled by a breeze from the sea. No malaria or other fevers. No dangerous beasts, snakes, or insects. Fish for the catching, and fruits for the plucking. And an earth and sky and sea of immortal loveliness . . . And the things which civilisation has left behind or missed by the way are there, too, among the Polynesians: beauty and courtesy and mirth.' It is this myth of the South Seas, perpetuated by churchmen and romantics alike, of the licentious, carefree islander, that contemporary Pacific writers, artists, and composers are still struggling to dispel.

During the second half of the 19th century nearly all the islands of the Pacific came under the political domination of European countries and the United States. Since the Second World War, many have gained local autonomy and some have achieved independence. Throughout Pacific history the visual and performing arts have been moulded by the interplay of these many opposing forces: isolation and insularity, inter-cultural borrowing, migration, and, during the last few centuries, Westernization and modernization. Throughout, music has had a central role in ceremony, ritual, and daily life.

2. *Melanesia.* Melanesia is the most diversified region of the Pacific. Over 700 distinct languages are spoken, and its people vary greatly in the extent of their contact with the outside world and with other Melanesian groups. At one extreme, some interior mountain tribes of Papua New Guinea have lived in virtual isolation from European culture and even from the coastal dwellers until recent decades. At the other, the Trobriand Islanders have, for generations, engaged in wide-flung trade with other islands of the 'kula ring' (economic community of south-eastern Melanesia). This cultural diversity is reflected in musical style. Melodies, for example, may take many forms. Triadic and pentatonic structures are the most common, but other types have narrow ranges (less than a third) or are tiled (short, narrow phrases at descending tonal levels). In general, song texts have less intrinsic importance in Melanesia than in Micronesia or Polynesia, and melodic structure is usually influenced more by strictly musical, rather than textual, considerations. Often the words are in foreign languages or so ancient that they are not understood by the performers or the audience.

In Melanesia, and throughout the Pacific, music accompanies many everyday activities and is also used to highlight special occasions. In Vanuatu, for example, genres include lullabies, children's singing games, dance and story-narration accompaniment, secret magic songs to ensure a successful harvest, and songs to accompany all important ceremonies and rituals—some traditional, such as grade-taking and marriage, and some Westernized, such as church festivals and civic occasions.

In Papua New Guinea, great feasts with music and dance are called, in pidgin English, 'sing-sings'. They are usually held at night and often involve several groups performing simultaneously. In the past, sing-sings were held before and after battle; today, they are staged for pig feasts, initiation, garden fertility rites, and other ritual occasions.

The vocal music of New Guinea and western Melanesia (particularly the Bismarks) is predominantly monophonic, in unison or octaves. Group responsorial singing is the most characteristic style of Papua New Guinea. This 'call and response' form with alternation between leader (a strong singer who knows the song well) and chorus (presumably weaker singers less familiar with the material) is common throughout the world because it allows for the universal situation that any community has both good and bad singers. In theory, all that is required for a song in leader-chorus style to survive is one strong singer in a generation. In Vanuatu most traditional vocal music is also in a monophonic leader-chorus form, except in north Malekula, where polyphony, often with a drone, is more typical. There is no obvious explanation for this anomaly.

Vocal polyphony occurs in the Loyalty Islands, the Solomons, and Fiji. In Fiji, for example, the high voices are called *tagica* ('to cry' or 'to chime in') and *laga* ('to sing'), the bass voices are called *druku* and *vaqiqivatu*, and the descant *vakasalavoavoa*. Rudimentary musical theory of this nature is not unusual in the Pacific.

In Melanesia, it is common for songs to have known composers—evidence to dispel the misconception long held by Westerners that all folk and traditional music is communally composed. New songs are continually being produced, in both traditional and Westernized styles. Often songs are regarded as belonging to the composer, and other musicians must obtain permission or pay for the performance rights—a primitive form of copyright. New music may be composed in a variety of ways. In the Solomon Islands a political leader may commission songs for an important occasion, much as is done in the West. Sometimes, especially among the Siuai of the Solomons, new panpipes are constructed with tunings to suit newly composed music. In Fiji, creative inspiration is seen as a supernatural occurrence. Only the privileged *dau ni vucu* is allowed to compose or 'remember' music and poetry. Sometimes, it is believed, he is inspired by a god or *veli* (elf). Other *meke* (compositions) are thought to emanate from the souls of stillborn babies and to embody the cries they never made. Islanders believe that these special *meke* are 'found' at the child's grave, and that some lines may not be 'remembered', resulting sometimes in asymmetrical forms.

Instruments have a prominent role in Melanesian music. The most common are slit-drums, hourglass drum, panpipes, conch-shell trumpets, end-blown flutes, rattles, and bamboo concussion sticks and stamping tubes. Slit-drums (sometimes called slit-gongs because they are classified as idiophones, not membranophones) may be made from bamboo, or, more commonly, from hollowed-out logs. Usually, they are laid on the ground and played with one or two sticks, during ceremonies and for sending messages. Vertical slit-drums also are to be found, for example, in some regions of Vanuatu. The base is buried in the ground and often a human face is carved on the exposed section. The *garamut* slit-drum of Papua New Guinea comes in many shapes and sizes, the largest being over four metres long. They are usually carved with human figures, crocodiles, or birds.

Hourglass drum from the Sepik region of New Guinea, with elaborate carving of a bird and a human face.

Panpipes, played singly and in ensembles, are the most distinctive feature of musical life in the Solomon Islands. The 'Are'are people of Malaita, studied extensively by the French ethnomusicologist Hugo Zemp, have a well-developed technical vocabulary for panpipe music. *'Au* ('bamboo') is either *'au kia ka uuhi* ('bamboo which one blows')—flutes and pan-pipes—or *'au kia ka'ui* ('bamboo which one beats')—musical bows and stamping tubes. Panpipes are divided into solo instruments (*'au ta'a mane*, 'one-man bamboos') and ensembles (*'au rokoroko*, 'grouped bamboos'). Raft pan-pipes (*aapa ni 'au*, 'wing of bamboo') are distinguished from bundle panpipes (*hoko ni 'au*, 'bundles of bamboo'). Solo instruments have an 'irregular assemblage' of long and short tubes (*aara haisuri*) in contrast to the ensemble instruments, which have regular scale-wise 'decreasing assemblage' (*aara tahetahe*), with the shortest tube always held to the player's right. The technique for playing the panpipes is described as *uuhi rawariri* ('to blow quiver-ingly'), and is characterized by quick pulses of breath—some six or seven per second.

Ex. 1 is a transcription of an 'Are'are com-position played on a seven-tube panpipes. Simple harmonies are achieved as the player blows simultaneously on two adjacent holes. This technique is represented in the tablature above the conventional notation. The piece has a simple form (aabb/aabb/az).

3. *Micronesia*. Micronesia comprises some 2,000 small islands within an ocean area of nearly eight million sq. km. Its people speak some 15

Vertical slit-drums, with carved faces, of Malekula, Vanuatu (New Hebrides).

mutually unintelligible languages, although first Japanese and later English have become lingua franca. The high volcanic islands of the region, such as Palau, Yap, Truk, Ponapea, Nauru, and Kusaie, are culturally distinct from the low coral atolls, such as the Marshalls and Tuvalu, largely due to the different resources available. The volcanic islands, having richer soil and a greater variety of plant life, can therefore support larger populations. Consequently, widely separated low islands tend to have more in common with each other culturally than with their neigh-bouring high islands.

The traditional music of Micronesia is primarily vocal. Songs are usually monophonic and tend to have few notes (often only two or three) and a narrow range (a second or third—the *Engmelodik* style). Polyphony is usually restricted to drones or parallel movement (usually parallel fourths). In some regions, songs end with a *glissando*, sometimes spanning as much as an octave. The most striking feature of Micronesian music is its affinity with poetry and dance. Line dances and sitting dances are the most typical. Movement and music are beautifully integrated, as are music and text. Most dance movements are of the hands and arms and are intended to enhance the poetry they accompany. As summarized by the dance ethnologist Adrienne Kaeppler, Micronesian dance is a decoration of poetry, compared with Polynesian dance which serves as an illustration of poetry.

Micronesia has the smallest inventory of instruments in the Pacific region. Nose flutes (end-blown flutes sounded with nasal breath) are widespread but are not found in the

Ex. 1

'Are'are composition for seven-tube panpipes. (Recorded and transcribed by Hugo Zemp. From *Ethnomusicology*, xxv (1981), p. 400.)

ritardando

Marshalls and Kiribati. Hourglass drums are played in eastern Micronesia. Concussion sticks, conch-shell trumpets, and body percussion (slapping, foot-stamping, and clapping) are used throughout the region. Noticeably absent are instruments common in other parts of the Pacific—cylindrical drums, wooden trumpets, rolled mats used as idiophones, and stamping tubes.

4. *Polynesia*. Polynesia is the largest of the Pacific regions, covering an ocean area of some 30,000,000 sq. km. The islands are unified by cultural and ethnic similarities rather than by geology. There are four distinct island formations: low coral atolls (such as the Tuamotu archipelago), high volcanic islands (the Hawaiian Islands, Samoan Islands, and Tahiti), raised coral atolls (Makatea and Aitutaki), and an island of continental origin (New Zealand).

The Polynesian islands form one of the last regions of the globe to have been settled by man. The people are thought to have originated in mainland south-east Asia, to have migrated to Melanesia, and then to have sailed from the Fijian group first to Tonga, Samoa, and eastern Polynesia, and later to the outer points of the triangle—Hawaii, New Zealand, and Easter Island (Rapa Nui). These early voyages are still recalled in traditional dances and chants which have become a cherished feature of Polynesian cultural identity.

The early accounts of European navigators, such as those of Captain Cook, describe the Polynesians as an extremely musical people, and to the present day, they have maintained this reputation. Both traditional and modern music is primarily vocal. Songs from pre-European times included chant-like recitation, prayers, laments, love-songs, work-songs, game-songs, lullabies, and many other genres. Local history was passed on from generation to generation in sung genealogies. Some solo singing was reported, but most of these forms were sung by groups. Song texts had supreme importance in traditional Polynesian music, and the rhythm, and even the melody, of a piece was often determined by the poetry. This practice frequently resulted in asymmetrical rhythms and simple musical structures.

Traditional Polynesian music typically had a narrow melodic range and relatively uncomplicated tonality, as shown in Ex. 2, a portion of a Hawaiian hula chant recorded in the 1920s by the musicologist Helen Roberts. Pitch relationships were often variable, and the inflections of a tone or slides between tones were usually considered more important than the absolute pitches themselves. Techniques of inflection and sliding were carefully passed on from master to pupil. For this reason, conventional

analyses of Polynesian music, which stress interval counts, can be misleading as they single out for examination an aspect of style that is not particularly important to the tradition. A singing style with sliding pitches has, on many islands, been transferred to acculturated forms such as *hīmene*.

Christian missionaries, who began to reach Polynesia in numbers during the 19th century, discouraged local 'pagan' singing and introduced European *hīmene* (hymns). In modern times Polynesian music includes forms that are predominantly Western, forms that are traditional, and forms that are intermediate between these two extremes. For example, Catholic missionaries first arrived in Easter Island in 1864. Locals soon learned from them a form of European hymn-singing. Many islanders, however, died within a few years of smallpox and from the hardships of forced labour. By the 1870s, much traditional culture had already been lost. After the First World War, genres from other Polynesian islands, particularly

Hawaiian musician playing the pahu hula (dance drum) and the pūniu (knee drum).

Ex. 2

Hula 'ili'ili, chanted by Samuela Waiki, Kawainui, Hilo, Hawaii. (Recorded by Helen Roberts. From Roberts: *Ancient Hawaiian Music*, pp. 198-9.)

Tahiti, reached Easter Island, and by the 1950s, international pop styles, including the tango, waltz, foxtrot, and the Mexican *corrido*, had been introduced. All these styles have a place in the musical life of the 1980s.

Hīmene are popular today throughout Polynesia. The term has come to refer both to Christian hymns and to traditional island hymn-like choral songs. In Samoa, pre-contact polyphonic singing was in two or three parts. Missionaries introduced four-part polyphony with Western stereotyped harmonic progressions. New *hīmene* are continually being composed, especially for the Christmas and New Year holidays. Older songs are quickly replaced by new ones, and it is unusual for an item to survive in the repertory for more than 30 years. Ex. 3, the *hīmene*, *E Malama, Hoomaikai* ('The Lord bless and keep you'), was composed by Eliza K. Osorio (*b* 1898) from Paauhau on the island of Hawaii. Its harmonic and melodic form are typical of *hīmene* style.

Traditional Polynesian dance is intimately related to the poetry it accompanies. Graceful movements of the hands and arms are particularly important in expressing the meaning of the text. The Hawaiian hula, for example, requires great flexibility of the wrists and fingers. Dances performed while sitting are quite common in Hawaii and on other islands, and, in general, Polynesian forms are more stationary than those of Melanesia or Micronesia. With the growth of tourism in recent decades new dance styles have developed to fulfil the expectations of visitors. These dances often have wild undulating hip movements and sometimes are a distortion of traditional aesthetic norms. Some scholars of Polynesian culture call them 'airport art' since they have the same function and appeal as the inexpensive, mass-produced souvenirs available in practically every international airport today.

Although Polynesian music is essentially vocal, many types of instruments are played. These include tall *pahu* (cylindrical drums), often played in groups of twos or threes for ceremonial occasions, the *tini* (paraffin-tin drum), sticks and percussion tubes, stamping tubes, slit-drums, conch-shell trumpets, and nose flutes. Grass floor mats are sometimes used as musical instruments. They may be flicked to accompany dance-songs or they may be rolled and used as beaters. The *keho* is an unusual instrument of Easter Island. It consists of a pit in the ground covered by a flat stone with a gourd resonator attached. The performer stamps rhythmically on the stone to accompany dancing and singing.

Many Hawaiian instruments are specifically intended to accompany the hula. The *pahu hula* (dance drum) is a wooden cylindrical drum with a single head. The *pūniu* drum is made from half a coconut shell covered with skin. Both drums may be played at the same time by the same musician. Another accompanying instrument is the *ipu hula* (dance gourd), made from two gourds joined together. The player thumps the *ipu hula* on a mat, raises it up and strikes it briskly with the fingers, thumps it down again, and so forth. Hawaiian rattles include the *'uli'uli* (gourd rattle), the *pū'ili* (bamboo rattle), and the *'ūlili* (spinning rattle), made from three

Hawaiian musician playing the ipu hula (dance gourd).

Ex. 3

E Malama, Hoomaikai ('The Lord bless and keep you'). (From *Na Himeni Haipule Hawaii*, Sesquicentennial edition; Honolulu, 1972.)

gourds which are spun by twisting an attached string. *'Ili'ili* are clappers made of smooth stones or pieces of lava. Hawaiian aerophones include the *'ohe hano ihu* (bamboo nose flute) and the *ipu hōkiokio* (globular flute). Simple instruments, often played by children, include the *oeoe* (bull-roarer, named for the sound it produces), the *pū lā'ī* (leaf trumpet), and the *pū kani* (shell trumpet).

The ukulele (from the Hawaiian word meaning 'leaping flea') is a small four-string mandolin. It was introduced to Hawaii in the late 1870s by immigrants from Madeira. Although it has a Hawaiian name, the instrument is generally used to play Western chords to accompany melodies which have both Polynesian and Western elements. This mixture of Western and traditional forms is typical of all Polynesian musical life in the 1980s.   HELEN MYERS

FURTHER READING
J. Cook: *A Voyage to the Pacific Ocean . . . In the Years 1776, 1777, 1778, 1779, and 1780*, 3 vols (London, 1784); R. Brooke: 'Some Niggers', *New Statesman* (19 Sept. 1914), pp. 710-12; E. G. Burrows: *Songs of Uvea and Futuna* (Honolulu, 1945); J. Kunst: *Music in New Guinea* (The Hague, 1967); W. P. Malm: *Music Cultures of the Pacific, the Near East, and Asia* (Englewood Cliffs, N.J., 1967, 2nd edn 1977); A. L. Kaeppler: 'Tongan Dance: a Study in Cultural Change', *Ethnomusicology*, xiv (1970), 266; A. L. Kaeppler: 'Aesthetics of Tongan Dance', *Ethnomusicology*, xv (1971), 175; M. McLean: *An Annotated Bibliography of Oceanic Music and Dance* (Wellington, 1977); H. Zemp: ''Are'are Classification of Musical Types and Instruments', *Ethnomusicology*, xxii (1978), 37-67; M. McLean: 'Towards the Differentiation of Music Areas in Oceania', *Anthropos*, lxxiv (1979), 717-36; H. Zemp: 'Aspects of 'Are'are Musical Theory', *Ethnomusicology*, xxiii (1979), 5-48; *Ethnomusicology, Pacific Issue*, xxv/3 (1981).

Pacini, Giovanni (*b* Catania, Sicily, 17 Feb. 1796; *d* Pescia, nr Lucca, 6 Dec. 1867). Italian composer. Son of a famous operatic tenor, he studied singing and composition at the Bologna Conservatory, then at the Venetian one with Furlanetto. He produced his first opera in 1813 and had a series of successes in the period 1825-35 with works in a Rossinian style. After a failure in 1835 he retired to found and direct a music school in Viareggio, but after about five years he returned to active composition for the theatre, achieving renewed success with *Saffo* (Naples, 1842). He was known as the 'master of the cabaletta', and his music was extremely popular, Liszt writing a fantasia on one of his airs. His attractiveness to women was notorious, a Russian princess being enamoured of him and Napoleon's second sister, Princess Paolina Borghese, pursuing him with some determination.   DENIS ARNOLD

Paderewski, Ignacy [Jan] (*b* Kuryłówka, 6 Nov. 1860; *d* New York, 27 June 1941). Polish pianist and composer. He studied at the Warsaw Conservatory (1872-8), in Berlin (1881), and with Leschetizky in Vienna (1884), owing most to this last teacher. In 1887 he began his extraordinarily successful concert tours of Europe and the United States. He also received acclaim for his compositions, these including a Piano Concerto (1888), a Symphony (1903-7), and the opera *Manru* (1901), which had been presented in Lwów and several American cities within a year of its Dresden première. His fame, and the fervent Polish nationalism he had expressed in much of his music, made him a not unnatural choice as the first prime minister of a reconstituted Poland (1919), but he resigned after only 10 months in office and resumed his musical career.   PAUL GRIFFITHS

Padovana (It.). See *Pavan*.

Paduana (Ger.). See *Pavan*.

Paër, Ferdinando (*b* Parma, 1 June 1771; *d* Paris, 3 May 1839). Italian composer. In 1792 he became *maestro di cappella* at Parma, where his opera *Orphée et Euridice* had been staged the previous year. His first Italian opera, *Circe*, was given in Venice in 1792; it was followed by several others, including *L'Idomeneo* and *Griselda*. He spent some years in Vienna, where he heard Mozart's music, and then became *Kapellmeister* of the Dresden court chapel. It was in Dresden that his opera *Leonora ossia L'amore conjugale* was staged in 1804 (Beethoven adapted the libretto for his own *Fidelio* the following year). Napoleon greatly admired his music, and in 1806 took him to Warsaw; on their return to Paris. Paër was in charge of the imperial chapel.

Paër's success continued with his appointment, succeeding Spontini, as director of the Théâtre Italien in 1812, but from 1824 to 1827 he unwillingly shared the post with Rossini, and then resigned. He continued to be held in high esteem, however, and in 1832 became director of Louis Philippe's private chapel. He wrote over 50 operas, of which *Agnese* (1809) and *Le maître de chapelle ou Le souper imprévu* (1821) were the best known. His other works included instrumental music, cantatas, three oratorios, and some sacred music. His style shows the influence of Italian composers and of Mozart and Beethoven.   WENDY THOMPSON

Paganini, Niccolò (*b* Genoa, 27 Oct. 1782; *d* Nice, 27 May 1840). Italian violinist and composer. Born of a poor family, he was taught the elements of violin playing by his father, and soon developed into a virtuoso performer. He then studied with a notable teacher, Alessandro Rolla, at Parma and at the age of 15 went on his first concert tour, of northern Italy. For a time he was at the court of Napoleon's sister in Tuscany but after his Milan recital in 1813, he lived as a travelling virtuoso. He spent a great deal of time in northern Europe, and visited the British Isles in 1831 giving 59 concerts within six months. His fantastic appearance and extraordinary technique made him into a figure comparable with a modern 'pop' star: hats, shawls, etc., were named after him. Notorious for womanizing and gambling, he made considerable fortunes—and often lost them, as at the end of his life, in the Casino Paganini in Paris which went bankrupt. He suffered from venereal disease and various pulmonary afflictions but showed amazing energy to the end.

Paganini rarely played other men's music; his own was largely written to show off his extraordinary powers. If the concertos are mere showpieces, the famous *Capricci* (published by Ricordi in 1820) have a haunting quality which caused Liszt, Schumann, Brahms, and Rakhmaninov to transcribe and write variations on them. But his real achievement lies in his extension of violin technique, using the upper reaches of the instrument freely, incredible mixtures of *arco* and *pizzicato*, and multiple stoppings; also perhaps, in his art of publicity, which is not unknown to this day. See also *Concerto*, 6.   DENIS ARNOLD

Page, Frederick (Joseph) (*b* Lyttleton, New Zealand, 4 Dec. 1905). New Zealand pianist and writer on music. He studied piano with Ernest Empson, a notable Christchurch teacher, and composition with Vaughan Williams, R. O. Morris, and Gordon Jacob at the Royal College of Music in London (1935–7). He founded the Music Department of Victoria University College in Wellington in 1946, and from lecturer progressed to professor (1967–71). He created a department renowned for its espousal of contemporary music and engaged several composers, notably Douglas Lilburn and David Farquhar. He was founder and later president of the New Zealand branch of the ISCM. He became a frequent soloist and chamber music player and gave the first performances in New Zealand of the complete Schubert piano duets and Schoenberg's complete piano works. He is a polemical writer, with a characteristic freshness and vivacity, at his best in writings about the European avant garde and music in China.

J. M. THOMSON

Pagliacci ('Clowns'). Opera in two acts (originally one act) by Leoncavallo; text by the composer. Produced: Milan, Teatro dal Verme,

21 May 1892; London, Covent Garden, 19 May 1893; New York, Grand Opera House, 15 June 1893. In the Prologue, Tonio (bar.) tells the audience that the story they are about to see is a real one about real people. Canio (ten.), the leader of a travelling troupe of players, warns that if he were to find his wife Nedda (sop.) unfaithful, she would pay dearly for it. Tonio makes advances to Nedda but she repulses him; however, he overhears Nedda and her lover Silvio (bar.) planning to run away together, and he hurries to bring Canio back from the village inn. Canio gives vent to his grief; and in the play put on for the villagers (in which he takes the part of Pagliaccio, Nedda that of Colombine, and Beppe (ten.) that of Harlequin), he finds the situation so like reality that he stabs first Nedda, and then Silvio, who rushes to her aid.

Paisible, James (*d* London, Aug. 1721). French composer and instrumentalist. Little is known of his early life, but he probably grew up among the musicians of Louis XIV's court at Versailles, where he learnt to play wind instruments. By 1674 he was in England, and three years later he wrote the music for a French *comédie-ballet*, *Rare en tout*, performed at Whitehall for Charles II's birthday on 29 March. Apparently the production was 'most pitifully done, so ill that the King was aweary on't'. Although Charles is said to have been delighted with some of Paisible's later works he did not give him a court appointment, possibly because of Paisible's Catholic religion. In 1682 some of his pieces were beginning to appear in print, and on James's accession in 1685 he finally received a court appointment, in the band of the 24 Violins; he lost it only three years later, when James fled into exile. By this time Paisible had married the notorious Mary (Moll) Davis, Nell Gwynn's rival for the favours of Charles II. Despite scandalous rumours there is no evidence that Paisible was forced to act as a 'pimp and cuckold'.

Paisible may have been Queen Anne's official composer; he received a salary from her, and wrote the music for a dance performed annually on her birthday. He wrote a great deal of theatre music for Drury Lane, and his surviving music consists mainly of instrumental pieces written for plays by Shadwell, Cibber, Betterton, and others. By 1702–3 he had joined the Drury Lane orchestra as a 'bass violinist' (cellist) and oboist. He also appeared in concerts as a soloist, and the German traveller Conrad von Uffenbach wrote of a concert he attended in July: 'most notable of all was a most charming concerto played with Pepusch by a recorder and a viola da gamba. The person who plays the recorder is a Frenchman called Paisible, whose equal is not to be found'. Paisible is buried in the churchyard of St Martin-in-the-Fields.   WENDY THOMPSON

Paisiello, Giovanni (*b* Roccaforzata, nr Taranto, 9 May 1740; *d* Naples, 5 June 1816). Italian opera composer. He was the son of a veterinary surgeon and, after attending a Jesuit school at Taranto, spent nine years from 1754 at the Conservatorio di S. Onofrio in Naples; Durante was one of his teachers. Soon after leaving the conservatory he began composing operas, at first for theatres in northern Italy, but then also for Naples. His comic opera *L'idolo cinese* (1767) was especially successful, while Burney, on his visit to Naples in 1770, was much taken with *Le trame per amore*, attributing its popularity to its easily-remembered melodies and lively orchestral music. In 1776 Paisiello accepted a financially attractive offer from the Russian court to become *maestro di cappella* to Catherine the Great; he stayed in St Petersburg until 1784, producing many rather more concise operas—Catherine insisted operas should be short—with broad, clear characterization to keep the interest of a non-Italian speaking audience. On his way back from Russia, he produced *Il re Teodoro in Venezia* in Vienna (1784), and this, with *Il barbiere di Siviglia* (1782) which was also known in Vienna, had some influence on Mozart's style in *Le nozze di Figaro* and *Don Giovanni*.

On his return to Naples, Paisiello was made opera composer to Ferdinand IV, with the duty of composing at least one *opera seria* each year for the Teatro S. Carlo. He would probably have had a busy, undisturbed life if the Napoleonic Wars had not intervened, but when the French took Naples in 1799 he supported them—an unfortunate move, since the Bourbons returned to power later the same year. In 1801 he was finally pardoned and reinstated in his former posts, but he chose instead to go to Paris at the invitation of Napoleon, staying until 1804. In 1806 the French again ousted the Bourbons from Naples, and Paisiello became composer to the court of Joseph Buonaparte, subsequently of Joachim Murat; he was also made one of the directors of the new state conservatory. In 1815 the defeat of the French again left him in disfavour, and he was deprived of all but one of his posts.

Although Paisiello is now overshadowed by Mozart, and, indeed, similarities in style make comparison inevitable, his operas are often attractive. He was one of the generation of opera composers who turned *opera buffa* into a more serious entertainment, with sentimental roles added to the traditional *buffa* parts (a good example is *Il barbiere di Siviglia*). His aria melodies are frequently simple, and his use of the orchestra to maintain continuity in ensembles helps his comic operas to be dramatically effective. His church music includes a Christmas *Messa in pastorale* (1807) and some grand ceremonial works for his French patrons.
   DENIS ARNOLD

Palcoscenico (It.). 'Stage'; *banda palcoscenico*, 'on-stage band', a device used in many operas by Verdi (e.g. *Giovanna d'Arco*, *La traviata*) and his contemporaries.

Palestrina. Opera (musical legend) in three acts by Pfitzner to his own libretto. It is based on the legend that Palestrina composed his *Missa Papae Marcelli* to persuade the Council of Trent not to ban polyphonic church music, in which the words were unintelligible. It was first performed in Munich in 1917.

Palestrina, alla (It.). In the style of Palestrina. By the 17th century this had come to be termed the *stile antico*, or *stile osservato*. It was revived by the 19th-century *Cecilian Movement.

Palestrina, Giovanni Pierluigi da (*b* probably Palestrina, *c*.1525; *d* Rome, 2 Feb. 1594). Italian composer, most celebrated for his church music.

1. *Life and works.* Palestrina was the eldest of four children of reasonably well-off parents, and went at an early age to S. Maria Maggiore in Rome as a choirboy, remaining after his voice broke (tradition has it that he became a tenor). In 1544 he was organist and singing teacher at the Cathedral in Palestrina, a small town in the Sabine Hills about 25 miles from Rome. He married Lucrezia Gori in 1547, and they had

Paisiello, portrait (1791) by Louise Elisabeth Vigée-Lebrun.

Palestrina

two sons. Four years later the Bishop of Palestrina, Cardinal Giovanni Maria del Monte, was elected Pope Julius III, and he took the composer with him to be director of the Cappella Giulia.

Palestrina wrote the Mass *Ecce sacerdos magnus* in honour of his patron, and it was published in 1554 with a dedication to Julius; he was rewarded the following year with a place in the papal choir at the Cappella Sistina, in spite of the opposition of its members, who claimed the prerogative to appoint their own colleagues. This work (and others published in the same volume of Masses) reveals Palestrina's mastery of the Netherlands polyphonic style. Soon after this he published some other volumes, including one of competent but not very interesting madrigals to Petrarch's verse. In spite of their lack of sensuality he was to regret having set secular texts in later years.

Although Palestrina was thus gaining a substantial reputation, the next few months were difficult. Pope Julius died in 1555; Pope Marcellus II was elected, but died within three weeks; and Pope Paul IV, scandalized to find married men in his choir, turned Palestrina out, but gave him a pension. The following month Palestrina was made *maestro di cappella* at St John Lateran, where he found the musical arrangements in some disarray, even though Lassus had been in charge until the previous year. He built up the choir, but in 1560 resigned his post after a quarrel with the authorities about the allowance given him for the choir-

boys. He seems to have been without employment for some months, but in March 1561 returned as *maestro* to the other great Roman basilica, S. Maria Maggiore, where he had been a choirboy.

These years saw Palestrina's rise to fame, and also a change in style (in accordance with the requirements of the Council of Trent) towards a simpler way of writing so that the words could be clearly heard. The story that his *Missa Papae Marcelli* prevented the abolition of composed church music in favour of a return to plainsong is untrue; the Mass was probably written to satisfy Pope Marcellus II's demand that music for Holy Week should be suitably restrained and the text properly understood. As well as this Mass, his *Missa brevis* exemplifies this aspect of Palestrina's style, with a homophonic texture, clear presentation of the words, and a continual variety of choral sound.

Palestrina remained at S. Maria Maggiore for about six years, and then accepted an offer to direct the music of Cardinal Ippolito II d'Este at the Villa d'Este at Tivoli. This position was well paid and probably had a less demanding daily routine; it also had the advantage of summers at Tivoli, a delightfully cool place in the hills. It may have been here that he came into touch with more modern ideas, which came from the d'Este rulers of Ferrara in northern Italy; his motets over the next 20 years show more awareness of the vigorous rhythms and the word-painting of the madrigal composers, as well as of the grand manner of polychoral music developed in Venice. He refused a post at the imperial court in Vienna, and another to take charge of the new Gonzaga chapel in Mantua, S. Barbara (although he did write a series of Masses for use there). In 1571 Animuccia died, and Palestrina returned to the Cappella Giulia to succeed him as choirmaster; he remained there for the rest of his life.

In 1567 and 1570 his second and third books of Masses had been published in Rome, but the next ten years were not happy ones, a series of epidemics carrying off two sons, two brothers, and in 1580 his wife; he naturally published less, and the two books of motets of 1572 and 1575 may have been retrospective. Immediately after his wife's death he took minor orders as a step towards entering the priesthood, and was awarded a benefice. However, in February 1581 he suddenly married again. His second wife was a wealthy widow who had inherited her late husband's companies in leather and fur, and Palestrina took to running the business with remarkable aptitude. His new life is reflected in both the number and the nature of his works. The most remarkable is the cycle of settings of the Song of Songs (1584), where the imagery is similar enough to that of contemporary love

The Easter blessing at St Peter's, Rome, from an anonymous 16th-century engraving.

poetry to accommodate a madrigalian word-painting and a less strict style of writing. In view of this it is ironic that in the preface he apologizes for the sins of his youth, when he wrote of human rather than divine love. Some of the Masses from these years are composed in a splendid Counter-Reformation manner, among them the fine *Assumpta est Maria*, based on his own motet, where a rich effect is gained from a six-part choir with voices kept constantly in their upper registers. He also published some *madrigale spirituale* in 1581, and some secular madrigals in 1586.

Towards the end of his life an assistant did most of the routine work at the Cappella Giulia, although Palestrina continued to write for and attend the great festivals at St Peter's. In 1592 the new pope, Clement VIII, increased the pension granted Palestrina years before on his dismissal from the papal choir, and he also received a kind of musician's *Festschrift* in the form of a book of Vesper psalms contributed by several leading Italian composers (including Asola, Croce, and Gastoldi) and dedicated to him. He died both prosperous and honoured, and was buried in St Peter's (although the chapel has since been pulled down and the present whereabouts of his remains are unknown).

2. *Influence and Reputation*. Palestrina was one of the most influential composers of his day. For a time he taught at one of the principal seminaries, the Seminario Romano, and his pupils included the Anerio brothers, Soriano, and possibly Victoria. In 1577 Palestrina and a colleague were directed by Pope Gregory XIII to revise the plainsong of the Roman gradual and antiphoner (see *Plainchant*, 4), and as a result his music is naturally imbued with the traditional melodic style of the Catholic Church, a fact which undoubtedly endeared him to its ministers. The incentive, therefore, for other composers to continue in his ways was strong, and the Roman school continued to adopt his style long after new developments should have made it seem old-fashioned.

His music has been considered more genuinely 'religious' than any written in a more modern idiom, probably because secular—especially operatic—idioms have dominated music (including that for the church) since 1600. Thus a Neapolitan composer such as Francesco Durante could write a Mass 'alla Palestrina' in the 18th century without feeling that a contemporary idiom would be preferable for the purpose; a major theorist of that century, Fux, wrote the *Gradus ad Parnassum* in an attempt to codify the 'Palestrina style'; and the

Cecilian Movement in 19th-century Germany romanticized his works and made them appear the ultimately desirable in church music.

In this century Palestrina's style has been subjected to a closer scrutiny than that of any other composer (with the possible exception of Bach), and students of music are still expected to be able to write imitations of it, without much understanding of what the 'Palestrina style' really means. For there is no definitive set of rules which go to make up Palestrina's style, but, as with all great composers, rather a series of styles. In fact, Palestrina is at his best when he is at his most difficult to codify—in the grand works of his later years, where contrapuntal skill is less important than his ear for gorgeous sound.   DENIS ARNOLD

FURTHER READING
Jerome Roche: *Palestrina* (London, 1971); Malcolm Boyd: *Palestrina's Style: a Practical Introduction* (London, 1973).

Palm court music. An expression which has been adopted to identify a style of light orchestral playing and repertory that started in the 1870s, when many holiday resorts and spas supported groups ranging from a trio to a dozen or so players who performed in promenade bandstands, on piers, and in floral halls during the summer season. Some of the larger hotels also provided such entertainment, generally performed in rooms furnished with wicker furniture and potted palms (hence the name); perhaps the most famous was the Grand Hotel at Eastbourne from where the BBC broadcast a Sunday afternoon programme for many years. Before the Second World War the palm court group was frequently heard in the restaurants of famous stores, as, for example, in the Lyons Corner Houses and Lewis's department store in Manchester. Radio exploited the nostalgia of the music and publicized the 'palm court' image from the 1920s onwards, and such names as Albert Sandler and Max Jaffa became well known in the genre. The salon repertory was basically made up of the lighter classics, excerpts from opera and musical comedy, and music written by palm court specialists interspersed with instrumental solos and vocal items.
                                    PETER GAMMOND

Palmgren, Selim (*b* Pori, 16 Feb. 1878; *d* Helsinki, 13 Dec. 1951). Finnish composer. He studied in Helsinki (1895–9) with Martin Wegelius, and later in Germany and Italy with Busoni among others. He was an important figure in Finnish musical life between the wars, and an accomplished pianist. He toured the United States in the early 1920s and was for a time professor of composition at the then newly-founded Eastman School of Music. He wrote extensively for the piano and his output includes five concertos as well as a large number of miniatures, such as *Night in May*, which enjoyed great popularity during the 1940s. Among his best works, however, are his part-songs which have considerable eloquence. His idiom is neo-Romantic.   ROBERT LAYTON

Palotache [properly *palotás*]. A Hungarian type of instrumental piece in dance style (in duple or quadruple time) derived from the **verbunkos*.

Pammelia (From Gk, 'all honey'). First collection of vocal rounds, catches, and canons published in England. It contains 100 anonymous pieces, for three to 10 voices, and was published by Thomas Ravenscroft in 1609. A second part, *Deuteromelia*, was also published in 1609.

Pandean pipes. See *Panpipe*.

Pandiatonicism [pandiatonism]. Term coined by Nicolas Slonimsky, in his book *Music since 1900* (1938). He defined it as follows: 'Pandiatonicism is the technique of free use of all seven degrees of the diatonic scale, melodically, harmonically, or contrapuntally. Wide intervallic skips are employed, and component voices enjoy complete independence, while the sense of tonality is very strong due to the absence of chromatics. Visually, a page of pandiatonic music looks remarkably clean. C major is favoured by most composers writing in this style. The opening pages of Prokofiev's Third Piano Concerto, Casella's *Valse diatonique*, Stravinsky's *Pulcinella*, and certain pages of Malipiero are characteristic examples of pandiatonic writing. The added sixth and ninth, widely used in popular American music, are pandiatonic devices'.

Pange lingua. The title of two Latin hymns. 1. The Passiontide hymn *Pange lingua gloriosi proelium certaminis* by Venantius Fortunatus (*d* 610), often sung to a modification of J. M. Neale's translation, 'Sing, my tongue, the glorious battle'. 2. The Corpus Christi hymn *Pange lingua gloriosi corporis mysterium* by Thomas Aquinas (*d* 1274), often sung to a translation based on J. M. Neale and E. Caswell, 'Now, my tongue, the mystery telling'.

Panpipe [syrinx] (from Gk., Pan, the rustic god). A row of tubes of different lengths joined in a row side by side and sounded by blowing across the tops, each tube giving one note. There may be from three tubes up to more than

Pl. 1. Panpipe (syrinx), Roman period; cane pipes with leather or cloth covering.

40, in most cases made of cane and stopped at the lower ends by a knot in the cane or with wax. Being stopped pipes, each tube gives a deep note for its length (a 7″ pipe giving approximately *a'*). Other constructions are of a flat piece of wood with the tubes drilled down into it (from Ancient Rome to south-west Europe); pottery tubes cemented together in the firing (Ancient Peru); and, of course, moulded plastic.

There are many different arrangements of the tubes themselves. In the most common, found almost worldwide, the pipes are arranged in order from the longest to the shortest. Alternatively, the longest may be in the middle, as found from the Caucasus to Central Europe: the pipes on the left give the notes of a tonic chord and those on the right those of a dominant chord. Next, the pipes may zigzag up the scale, with any two adjacent tubes giving an interval of a third when sounded together, so that one is able to play tunes in consecutive thirds; this form is found in Ecuador. Or again, the pipes may be tied in a bundle, sometimes with a central tube filled with gunpowder for firing off as a musical rocket (for which the top ends of the sounding tubes are suitably bevelled to strike the air at a correct angle); this form is found in South-East Asia. Among the other varieties are pairs of panpipes, found chiefly in South America and Melanesia, one pipe giving notes that are not in the other, so that two players make tunes by blowing alternately; and examples

where the tubes are not stopped, serving for very quiet, solitary music.

Panpipes are important in ritual music, especially in the Solomon Islands and in Bolivia and Peru; the largest instruments may then contain tubes more than 2′ long. In Europe the panpipe is celebrated as a pastoral instrument ('syrinx') in the Idylls of Theocritus, though today one is most likely to hear it as the trade call of travelling tradesmen like knife-grinders. A notable exception is Romania, where country gypsy bands once used the instrument, since famous in the hands of Fanica Luca and after him Gheorg Zamfir. The Romanian panpipe (*nai*) characteristically has 20 tubes joined in a curve and giving a diatonic scale from *b'* up to *g''''*; accidentals are made by tilting the instrument towards the upper lip to flatten the note. Brilliant bird-song effects are favourite elements of the performances.

Though panpipes appear ethnologically among early neolithic cultures of the world, it is doubtful if they were known in the West much before the 6th century BC. The word 'syrinx' in Homer's *Iliad* may have denoted some other kind of flute. From a much earlier date some sets of small tubes of bone have been found in excavations near Kiev, but these were possibly for distribution individually among a group of performers blowing their notes in turn—a type of performance, with cane tubes, found up until recently in rural Lithuania. The well-known Greek legend tells how the nymph Syrinx, to escape the advances of Pan, was transformed into a reed which the frustrated god cut into

Pl. 2. The Romanian panpipe (nai) played by Radu Simion.

pieces; he then repented, kissing the pieces and, on hearing the sounds coming from them, devised the first panpipe.

There have also been in Europe panpipes for sounding on the recorder principle (duct flute) with block-and-window to each pipe, a form going back at least to the Middle Ages. (See *Instruments, Medieval*, Pl. 1.)

ANTHONY BAINES

Pantonality. Synonym for *atonality. Schoenberg preferred this term as indicating the combination of all keys rather than the absence of any, but it is rarely used.

Pantoum [*pantum*] (Fr.). A verse form of Malayan origin, adopted in the 19th century in France by Victor Hugo and others. Ravel called the second movement of his Piano Trio by this name, possibly in imitation of Debussy, whose song 'Harmonie du soir', a setting of Baudelaire, is a *pantoum*.

Panufnik, Andrzej (*b* Warsaw, 24 Sept. 1914). Polish, naturalized British, composer. He studied composition with Kazimierz Sikorski at the Warsaw Conservatory (1932-6) and worked during the war as a café pianist with Witold Lutosławski. In 1954 he moved to England, where he has worked as a conductor (notably with the City of Birmingham Symphony Orchestra, 1957-9) and composer. His works abound in tonal patterning based on cells of two, three, or four notes; they include eight symphonies and a small number of other pieces.

PAUL GRIFFITHS

FURTHER READING
Andrzej Panufnik: *Impulse and Design in my Music* (London, 1974).

Papillons ('Butterflies'). Work for solo piano, Op. 2, by Schumann, composed between 1829 and 1831. The 12 short dance pieces were inspired by the masked-ball scene at the end of Jean-Paul Richter's *Flegeljahre* ('Age of Discretion').

Parade. 'Ballet réaliste' in one act by Satie to a libretto by Cocteau. It was choreographed by Massine and first performed, with décor by Picasso, by Diaghilev's Ballets Russes in Paris in 1917.

Paradise and the Peri (*Das Paradies und die Peri*). Cantata, Op. 50, by Schumann to a text based on a translation and adaptation of T. Moore's poem *Lalla Rookh* (1817). It is for soloists, chorus, and orchestra, and was composed in 1843. In Persian mythology the Peri is a benign spirit seeking readmission to Paradise.

Paradise Lost. Opera in two acts by Penderecki to a libretto by Christopher Fry adapted from Milton's poem (published in 1667). It was first performed in Chicago in 1978.

Parallel motion. See *Motion*.

Parameter. Any compositional variable, e.g. pitch, note duration, instrumentation, loudness. The term, borrowed from physics, became current in the early 1950s, when Boulez, Stockhausen, and others were submitting each parameter to serial control.

Paraphrase. 1. In the 15th and 16th centuries, a contrapuntal technique involving the quotation in one or more voices of a plainchant melody. See *Cantus firmus*.

2. In the 19th century the term was applied to works based on existing melodies or pieces, often used as virtuoso showpieces. The supreme master of this type of recomposition was Liszt, who wrote numerous piano paraphrases of Italian operas, such as *Rigoletto*, and even of Wagner's operas.

Paraphrases. Collection of piano duets (24 variations and 14 other pieces) based on *Chopsticks*. They were composed by Borodin, Cui, Lyadov, Rimsky-Korsakov, and Liszt, and were published in 1880.

Paride ed Elena ('Paris and Helen'). Opera in five acts by Gluck to a libretto by Calzabigi. It was first performed in Vienna in 1770.

Parish Churches and Music. See *Anglican Parish Church Music*.

Parish Psalter. See *Anglican Chant, 5*.

Paris Symphonies. Haydn's six Symphonies Nos. 82-7. They were composed in 1785-6 for the Comte d'Ogny, who commissioned them for the Masonic concert society Le Concert de la Loge Olympique, and were first performed in Paris in 1787. Haydn's Symphonies Nos. 90-2 were also written for Paris.

'Paris' Symphony. Nickname of Mozart's Symphony No. 31 in D major, K 297, composed in 1778. It is so called because it was written in Paris and first performed at the Concert Spirituel.

Parker, Charlie ['Yardbird'; 'Bird'] (*b* Kansas City, 29 Aug. 1920; *d* New York, 12 Mar. 1955). Black alto-saxophonist. He was one of the dominant figures of the 'modern' or 'bebop' movement that changed the face of jazz in the

1940s. An early influence on his playing was altoist Buster Smith, with whose band he played in 1938. While with the Jay McShann band in 1940 he also showed a debt to the cool, questing playing of tenor-saxophonist Lester Young, and recordings made then had a strong influence on the future directions of jazz. Arriving in New York, he was able to play with musicians who were progressing along the same lines in clubs such as Minton's Playhouse and Monroes. These included trumpeter Dizzy Gillespie, pianist Thelonious Monk, guitarist Charlie Christian, and drummer Kenny Clarke. They broke away from the standard harmonies of traditional jazz, making use of the higher extended intervals of chords, introducing complicated harmonic changes, adding fresh life to old melodies, and producing sounds that were outrageous to older musicians but exciting to the young who were seeking a way out of the Dixieland patterns. There was also an avoidance of the old adherence to the regular beat. Parker contributed many new jazz themes to fit the new style, including *Confirmation*, *Yardbird Suite*, and *Anthropology*. He developed a distinctive, vibrato-less tone and showed an unlimited inventiveness in his solos which inspired many followers. He worked with Noble Sissle, Earl Hines, Cootie Williams, Andy Kirk, and Carroll Dickerson from 1942 to 1944, and in 1944 toured and made recordings with his own somewhat mixed group. In 1945 the Savoy recordings with Gillespie and Miles Davis proved to be the first definitive bebop sounds, endlessly subtle and exploring. In 1945 he went with Gillespie to California and helped to make Los Angeles a modern jazz centre, recording many of his classics for the Dial label. By 1946 he was suffering from drug addiction and spent several months in hospital. He returned to New York to work with Jazz at the Philharmonic, and visited Paris in 1949 and Scandinavia in 1950. Thereafter there were constant breakdowns of health and drug problems, and his work veered erratically between brilliance and chaos. Despite the modernity of his outlook he kept a deep feeling for the blues which gave his playing its lasting strength and depth. He died at the age of 34, already a jazz legend.

PETER GAMMOND

Parlando, parlante (It.). 'Speaking'. 1. Style of singing in which the voice must approximate to speech; it is found particularly in quick passages where there is a new syllable for each note. 2. In instrumental music, a request for expressive, 'eloquent' playing.

Parma, Nicola (*b* Mantua; *fl.* late 15th, early 16th centuries). North Italian composer. He worked at churches in Pavia, Lodi, and Novara and may have spent the years after 1613 at S. Barbara, Mantua. He wrote church music and some madrigals.   DENIS ARNOLD

Parody Mass. Polyphonic setting of the Ordinary of the Roman Catholic Mass based on a pre-existing polyphonic composition. See *Mass*, 2*d*.

Paroles tissées ('Woven Words'). Work for tenor and chamber orchestra by Lutosławski to a text by Jean-François Chabrun. It was composed in 1965.

Parry, (Sir) (Charles) **Hubert** (Hastings) (*b* Bournemouth, 27 Feb. 1848; *d* Rustington, Sussex, 7 Oct. 1918). English composer, teacher, and writer. He was one of the principal influences in the revival of English musical life in the last quarter of the 19th century. Born of a well-to-do family, he obtained his Mus.B. degree while still at Eton. At Oxford he studied composition with H. H. Pierson and then worked for Lloyd's Register of Shipping before having further lessons from Edward Dannreuther. He published songs, piano music, and chamber music in the 1870s but made a major advance in 1880 when his Piano Concerto was played at Crystal Palace and his *Scenes from Prometheus Unbound* was performed at the Gloucester Festival. The success of the latter led to several commissions for similar festival works, the oratorios *Judith* (1888), *Job* (1892), and *King Saul* (1894), and other choral works such as the *Ode on St Cecilia's Day* (1889), *The Soul's Ransom* (1906),

Hubert Parry

L'allegro ed il penseroso (1890), *The Pied Piper of Hamelin* (1905), *A Vision of Life* (1907), and *Ode on the Nativity* (1912). But he also composed five symphonies, the *Symphonic Variations* (1897), and works for strings.

Parry contributed to the first edition of Grove's *Dictionary of Music and Musicians* and helped Grove in its preparation. He joined the staff of the Royal College of Music in 1883, becoming director in 1894. He was Professor of Music at Oxford University from 1900 to 1908. Among his writings were *Studies of the Great Composers* (1886), *The Art of Music* (1893, revised and enlarged 1896), *Johann Sebastian Bach* (1909), and *Style in Musical Art* (1911). One of his pupils was Vaughan Williams. He was knighted in 1898 and created a baronet in 1903.

Time has dealt unkindly with Parry's choral works, with the exception of the short Milton ode, *Blest Pair of Sirens* (1887) and his superb Coronation anthem *I was Glad* (1902), but the orchestral *Variations* have been twice recorded by Boult. The *Ode on the Nativity*, a setting not of Milton but of William Dunbar, is well worth revival. The most enduring of his work would appear to be among his 74 song settings for voice and piano written between 1885 and 1918 and published under the generic title *English Lyrics*. His motets, too, are of high quality; and in his 1916 unison setting of Blake's *Jerusalem* he added to British life a national song as indispensable as Elgar's *Land of Hope and Glory*.

MICHAEL KENNEDY

FURTHER READING
C. L. Graves: *Hubert Parry* (London, 1926); Frank Howes: *The English Musical Renaissance* (London, 1966).

Parry, John (*b* Denbigh, Wales, 18 Feb. 1776; *d* London, 8 Apr. 1851). Welsh singer, instrumentalist, composer, and conductor. In 1807 he went to London, where he settled as a flageolet teacher. Between 1809 and 1829 he wrote and arranged the music for such entertainments at Vauxhall Gardens as *High Notions, or A Trip to Exmouth* (1819), and *My Uncle Gabriel* (1824). He also composed numerous songs, collected and arranged Welsh folk airs, and was music critic of *The Morning Post*, 1834-48.

His son **John Orlando Parry** (*b* London, 3 Jan. 1810; *d* East Molesey, 20 Feb. 1879) was a notable harpist and pianist. His talents as a comedian were much appreciated, and he took to giving entertainments such as his 'Buffo Trio Italiano', in which he imitated famous singers while accompanying himself on the piano. He composed numerous songs, to words by Albert Smith, which he sang himself. In later life, ill health forced his retirement from the stage and he became a music teacher and organist of St Jude's Church, Southsea.

WENDY THOMPSON

Parsifal. *Bühnenweihfestspiel* (sacred festival drama) in three acts by Wagner; text by the composer, principally after Wolfram von Eschenbach's poem *Parzival* (early 13th century). Produced: Bayreuth, 26 July 1882; New York, Metropolitan, 24 December 1903 (infringing the Bayreuth copyright, which did not expire until 31 December 1913); London, Covent Garden, 2 February 1914. The Bayreuth copyright was also broken by performances in English in Boston and elsewhere in the USA in 1904-5, in Amsterdam 1905, in Zurich 1903, and in Buenos Aires and Rio de Janeiro 1913.

In a forest near a lake at Monsalvat in the kingdom of the Grail, Gurnemanz (bass) and his two Esquires arouse themselves from sleep and offer up their morning prayers. They are interrupted by the wild entry of Kundry (sop.) who comes with balsam for the suffering Amfortas (bar.), who is carried in on a litter on his way to bathe his wounds. Gurnemanz relates to his Esquires how Amfortas, son of Titurel, who had entered the magic garden of the magician Klingsor armed with the Sacred Spear, had been seduced by Kundry and wounded by Klingsor, who had seized the Sacred Spear. The wound will only heal at the touch of the Spear, now in Klingsor's possession, and the only person who can gain possession of it is a 'Pure Fool made wise through pity'. Cries are now heard, and an unknown youth (Parsifal, ten.) is dragged in having killed a swan. In reply to Gurnemanz's questions it is clear that this youth may be the 'Pure Fool', and he is taken back to the castle to witness the unveiling of the Grail by Amfortas. Having failed to understand the ceremony, he is driven from the hall by the angry Gurnemanz.

Klingsor (bar.) summons Kundry and instructs her to seduce Parsifal, whom they have both recognized as the only possible redeemer of Amfortas and Kundry. In Klingsor's magic garden the Flower Maidens tempt Parsifal, but he remains indifferent. Kundry calls him by his name and recalls for him memories of his childhood and his mother. As she kisses him on the lips all is revealed to him: 'Amfortas! the wound!' he cries. Realizing the nature of Amfortas's temptation, he becomes 'wise through pity'; while Kundry changes from temptress to suppliant as she recognizes that her one chance of salvation is now at Parsifal's hands. Klingsor hurls the Sacred Spear at him, but it remains suspended in mid-air over his head. He seizes the Spear and, as he makes the sign of the cross, Klingsor's domain falls in ruins.

Many years have passed. Gurnemanz, now grown old, is a hermit, and the repentant Kundry comes to draw water for him. A knight in black armour approaches; it is Parsifal. He is recognized by Kundry but not by Gurnemanz, who chides him for coming armed on to holy ground on Good Friday. The knight kneels in prayer. Gurnemanz recognizes first the Sacred Spear, then Parsifal. After Kundry has bathed the knight's feet and dried them with her hair, Gurnemanz anoints Parsifal as the new King of the Holy Grail. His first task is to baptize Kundry. The three make their way to the Hall of the Grail, where the funeral of Titurel is about to take place. The knights call on Amfortas to uncover the Grail, but he is unable to do so. He tears open his tunic and, displaying his wound, asks the knights to kill him. Parsifal enters the hall and, touching the wound with the Spear, heals it. As the knights pay homage to their new King, Parsifal raises the Grail aloft; a white dove hovers over his head, and Kundry falls lifeless.

FURTHER READING
Lucy Beckett: *Richard Wagner: Parsifal* (Cambridge, 1981).

Parsley, Osbert (*b* 1511; *d* Norwich, early 1585). English composer of motets, services, and consort music. He worked as a lay clerk at Norwich Cathedral for 50 years, and is commemorated there by a memorial tablet in the north aisle of the nave. His works include a fine setting of verses from the Lamentations of Jeremiah and a piece for a five-part consort of viols, *Perslis clocke*, which is based on the notes of the hexachord.   JOHN MILSOM

Parsons, Robert (*b* Exeter, *c.*1530; *d* Newark-upon-Trent, 25 Jan. 1570). English composer. He became a Gentleman of the Chapel Royal on 17 October 1563, and he met his death by drowning in the River Trent. His works include a service, anthems, and motets, as well as some pieces for viol consort.   WENDY THOMPSON

Part [in vocal music, voice-part, voice] (Fr.: *partie, voix*; Ger.: *Part, Stimme*; It.: *parte, voce*). 1. In polyphonic vocal music, the designation for each individual line. In early polyphony the names for the voice-parts did not imply a precise range in the way that they do today: they were named according to their function and their place in the compositional scheme. The Table below gives the most common terms for the voice-parts in earlier vocal music (listed from the lowest upwards).

In choral music today the standard formation is (from the highest voice downwards, as is customary): soprano, alto, tenor, bass (usually abbreviated to SATB).

2. In instrumental music, the music for one particular instrument (e.g. oboe, first violin), as opposed to a score, which contains all the parts.

3. A section of a composition (binary form, for example, can be said to be in two parts, ternary form in three); a better word is section.

Part-books (Fr.: *parties séparées*; Ger.: *Stimm-bücher*). Manuscript or printed books containing the music for an individual part of a work,

9th to 12th century (*organum*)	Vox principalis/Cantus Vox organalis/Organum
12th century (*organum, conductus, clausula*, etc.)	Vox principalis/Cantus Duplum/Discantus Triplum Quadruplum
13th century (sacred music, including the motet)	Tenor Motetus/Duplum Triplum Quadruplum
14th century (secular music)	Tenor Contratenor Cantus/Discantus
14th to mid 15th century (all polyphonic forms)	Tenor Contratenor Superius/Cantus
15th century (England)	Tenor Meane Treble Quatreble
Mid 15th century to *c.*1600	Contratenor bassus/Bassus Tenor Contratenor altus/Altus Superius/Cantus

whether vocal or instrumental (see *Part*, 1, 2). One of the earliest known examples is the set of three part-books which makes up the *Glogauer Liederbuch* (*c*.1480).

Partch, Harry (*b* Oakland, Calif., 24 June 1901; *d* San Diego, Calif., 3 Sept. 1974). American composer, theoretician, instrument maker, and performer. Musically self-educated and influenced by a wide variety of world cultures, Partch by 1930 had developed his own philosophy of 'corporeal' music (personal, verbal, non-abstract, involving all the arts) and theoretical system, 'monophony', based on a 43-note scale with intervals derived from just rather than equal-tempered tuning. All his compositions and his many adapted or invented instruments conform to this system, described in his *Genesis of a Music* (Madison, 1949, reprinted 1974). Apart from six years as a hobo, Partch lived mainly in his native California and in the Midwest. He never taught, relying for support on grants and contributions, revenue from the concerts and recordings of his Gate 5 Ensemble, and odd jobs. Working on his own, Partch fashioned a unique creative world. His productive independence from musical and institutional systems distinguishes him from most 20th-century composers.   NYM COOKE

Parte, parti (It.). 'Part', 'parts'; *colla parte*, 'with the part', i.e. an indication to the accompanying forces to follow the solo line closely with regard to deviations in tempo etc.; *a tre parti*, 'in three parts', i.e. three vocal or instrumental lines.

Parthenia (Gk., 'virgin dances'). Choral dances of young girls in Ancient Greece. The name was given to a printed collection of 21 keyboard pieces by Byrd, Bull, and Gibbons, which was presented to Princess Elizabeth and Prince Frederick on the occasion of their marriage (1613), as 'Parthenia, or the Maydenhead of the First Musicke that ever was printed for the Virginalls' (all previous collections had existed only in manuscript). The pun in the title was reinforced in a companion volume, published around 1614, 'Parthenia In-Violata', which has a part for bass viol. 'Parthenia' was the first English music to be engraved on copper plates.

Partials. Constituents of the notes of the *harmonic series, the main (fundamental) note being the first partial and the remainder the upper partials.

Partial signature. See *Key signature*.

Parties de remplissage (Fr.). 'Filling-in parts'. It was the custom in France during the later Baroque for composers to write only the uppermost and lowest parts of music intended for a five-part texture, leaving the middle parts to be provided by assistants, or by the conductor directing a performance. In modern times, performers sometimes neglect to do this, although it is certainly necessary in works by Lully and De Lalande, for example. Some editors have added such parts to Italian opera scores of the 17th century, but evidence for this is not strong.
                                              DENIS ARNOLD

Partimento (It.). 17th- and 18th-century term for improvising melodies over a written bass.

Partita [*parte*, *Partia*, *Parthia*, etc.] (It.). 1. In the late 16th century and the 17th, one of a set of *variations, as in the titles of a number of volumes of instrumental (especially keyboard) music. Italian and, later, other composers customarily based sets of variations ('parti' or 'partite') on the bass lines of well-known tunes, like the *folia* or *romanesca* (Vincenzo Galilei's *Romanesca . . . con cento parti*, in a lute manuscript dated 1584, is the earliest known use of the term). It may have been from this usage that 'partita' came occasionally to be used to describe any sort of piece, variation or other, that was part of a larger collection (e.g. Froberger's *Diverse curiose e rare partite musicali*, 1696).

2. In late 17th-century Germany, an alternative title for a *suite, usually occurring in the form 'Partia' or 'Parthia'. In the 18th century it could be applied loosely to any sort of multi-movement instrumental piece of the suite or sonata type (e.g. Bach's partitas for solo violin and solo keyboard), which might include movements headed 'Largo', 'Allegro', etc., as well as the dance movements (allemande, courante, etc.) that traditionally make up the suite.

Partition (Fr.), **partitura, partizione** (It.), **Partitur** (Ger.). 'Score'.

Partito (It.). 'Divided'.

Part-song. In its broadest sense, any composition for two or more voices; more commonly, a vocal composition intended for choral rather than solo performance, tending more to homophony than to polyphony and usually without accompaniment. Although the term has sometimes been used in connection with 16th-century secular music for solo voices, like the *madrigal, and with the 18th-century *glee for men's choir, it is more usually and more correctly applied to 19th-century unaccompanied works for male, female, or mixed choruses, principally songs composed as a response to the growing interest in amateur choral singing in Britain, Germany, and the USA in the 19th century.

Among the earliest British composers of part-songs were Robert Pearsall (1795-1856), John Hatton (1808-86), the younger Henry Smart (1813-79), and George Macfarren (1813-87). The establishment and growth of competitive choral festivals later in the century prompted contributions from many other composers, including more significant figures such as Stanford, Parry, and most notably Elgar, who was responsible for a marked improvement in the literary and musical aspirations of the part-song. But it should be stressed that a large part of the repertory was supplied by composers of considerably lesser powers of invention and imagination. Their pieces were printed and circulated in vast numbers, and hence they bulk large in the libraries and repertories of the longer-established amateur choirs. Frequently performed favourites include Stanford's *The Blue Bird*, Parry's *Songs of Farewell*, Elgar's *My Love Dwelt in a Northern Land*, Delius's *To be Sung of a Summer Night on the Water*, and Vaughan Williams's *Three Shakespeare Songs*.

German composers of part-songs, encouraged by the establishment of institutions such as the Berlin Liedertafel, include Schubert, Schumann, Weber, and Mendelssohn, who wrote chiefly for male-voice choirs, and Brahms, whose part-songs for mixed choirs have remained firmly in the repertory of English as well as German choirs. Eastern European composers, notably Tchaikovsky, Kodály, and Bartók, have also contributed to the genre, but composers in Latin countries seem to have been attracted more to folk-song arrangements than to originally composed part-songs. At the same period in the USA choral singing was flourishing, encouraged by college glee clubs, and large numbers of part-songs were composed, notably by Horatio Parker (1863-1919) and Edward MacDowell (1860-1908).

In more recent years, the part-song tradition has largely lost its relevance, being diffused among, and thus barely distinguishable from, other complex styles of choral writing. A number of unaccompanied choral part-songs by Tippett and Britten successfully exemplify this merging of traditional and modern styles.

JUDITH NAGLEY

Part-writing (Amer.: voice-leading). The art of composing contrapuntal music; see *Counterpoint*.

Pas (Fr.). 1. 'Not', 'not any'. 2. A 'step' in ballet, e.g. *pas de basques*, 'Basque step', a step of three beats similar to the waltz movement; *pas de chat*, 'step of the cat', so called because of its similarity to the movement of a leaping cat; *pas*

coupé, 'cut step', a step which acts as a preparation for another, one foot 'cutting' the other away and taking its place. *Pas* also has a broader meaning in ballet, specifying a certain form or movement, e.g. *pas d'action*, a dramatic scene; *pas seul, pas de deux, pas de trois*, etc., a dance for that number of dancers.

Pas d'acier, Le (Prokofiev). See *Steel Step, The*.

Paso doble (Sp.). A dance which became popular, particularly in Latin America, in the 1920s. It is a one-step (i.e. quick) dance, rather than the slower 'two-step' its name would suggest, and is generally in 6/8 time. Walton included a 'tango-pasodoble' in his *Façade*, incorporating the music-hall tune 'I do like to be beside the seaside'.

Pasquini, Bernardo (*b* Massa da Valdinievole, nr Lucca, 7 Dec. 1637; *d* Rome, 21 Nov. 1710). Italian composer, harpsichordist, and organist. He may have been a pupil of Cesti before arriving in Rome *c*.1650. In 1663 he was appointed organist at S. Maria Maggiore, and the following year at S. Maria in Aracoeli, where he remained for the rest of his life. He was a celebrated keyboard player, and his patrons included princes and cardinals, as well as Queen Christina of Sweden. He composed operas and oratorios in a style similar to that of Alessandro Scarlatti, but is best known for his keyboard music, which includes suites, variations, toccatas, sonatas, and other pieces for one or other of his instruments. Among the distinguished musicians taught by him are Kerll, J. P. Krieger, Muffat, and possibly Domenico Scarlatti.

Passacaglia (It.; Fr.: *passacaille, passecaille*; Sp.: *pasacalle, passacalle*; from Sp. *pasar*, 'to walk', *calle*, 'street'). The Spanish *pasacalle* was originally a serenade performed in the street by dancing couples, but in the 17th century the term became attached only to the instrumental ritornellos which were performed between the verses of the song. Like the *chacona* (see *Chaconne*) refrains, these ritornellos were constructed over typical harmonic progressions (though the *passacaglia* nearly always used a version of the basic progression I–IV–V) which were to provide melodic formulas for instrumental variations. The *passacaglia* and *chaconne* were therefore very similar in construction, and this led to confusion after the Baroque period, when the forms themselves were no longer in use, but theorists and historians were making valiant attempts to define such terms in their dictionaries and histories of music. Similarities include the ways in which the melodic formulas were used (see under *Chaconne*) and the use of triple metre. The chief difference, and this was not a hard and fast rule, was that the *passacaglia* variations tended to be in the minor, and the *chaconne* in the major.

The *passacaglia* was popular in Italy throughout the Baroque period, and appeared in France in the mid 17th century, rather later than did the *chaconne*. Like the *chaconne*, it was given a place in the stage works of Lully and his contemporaries, as well as being used for individual solo, ensemble, and orchestral works. In Germany, the *passacaglia* appears most frequently as a keyboard piece, notably by such great composers for organ as Buxtehude and Bach.

In the 20th century the *passacaglia* has been revived by some composers, for example Webern (Passacaglia), Schoenberg (in *Pierrot lunaire*), and Britten (*Peter Grimes*, Act 2).

Passage work. A 'passage' in a musical composition is simply a section, but the term 'passage work' is generally applied to sections which have no intrinsic musical value, but rather serve as 'padding', often offering an opportunity for brilliant display on the part of the performer.

Passaggio (It.). 'Passage'. 1. Used in the plural (*passaggi*), a kind of ornamentation; see *Ornaments and Ornamentation*, 2.

2. Transition or modulation.

3. A passage of music intended to display the virtuosity of the performer.

Passamezzo [passemezzo, pass'e mezzo, etc.] (It.). An Italian dance of the 16th and 17th centuries, similar to, but quicker than, the *pavan (and sharing that dance's duple metre). Although the passamezzo was an Italian dance, it first appears in some lutebooks published by Hans Neusidler in Germany in 1536 and 1540, appearing in Italy shortly before the mid century, and in England and France soon after. Sir Toby Belch, in Shakespeare's *Twelfth Night* (Act 5 Scene 1), speaks of a 'passy-measures pavin'.

Most passamezzos were composed on one of two standard chordal basses, known respectively as the 'passamezzo antico' (Sir Toby's 'passy-measures pavin') and the 'passamezzo moderno' (known in England as the 'quadran pavan'); these basses were used also for other types of dances.

Passemezzo (It.). See *Passamezzo*.

Passepied (Fr.). A French dance of the 17th and 18th centuries, resembling a fast *minuet. It was usually in binary form, in 3/8 or 6/8 time, with continuous running movement in small note-values. The passepied first appeared as a

Breton court dance in the early 16th century, and is mentioned by Rabelais and Arbeau (who calls it a kind of *branle). It became popular at the court of Louis XIV, where it was danced to the steps of the minuet, usually by one couple.

Like other dances of rustic origin adopted by the court, the passepied was taken up by composers of stage music, including Lully, Campra, and Rameau. Passepieds were often performed in pairs to make a ternary structure, the first dance being repeated after the second. It also penetrated the 18th-century *suite as one of the optional dances. There is a pair of passepieds in Bach's orchestral Ouverture in C, BWV 1066, and Debussy gave the name to a piece in his early *Suite bergamasque* for piano.

Passereau, Pierre (*fl.* first half of the 16th century). French composer. Nothing is known for certain of his life, but many of his witty *chansons* were published by Pierre Attaingnant between 1529 and 1555. They are in the Parisian style of Janequin (one volume, published in 1536, is devoted to the two composers), and the most famous, 'Il est bel et bon', was sung as a popular song in the alleyways of Venice.

DENIS ARNOLD

Passing note. A note connecting two chords but belonging to neither of them, e.g.:

In the first beat of the above example (the opening of a chorale from Bach's *St Matthew Passion*), the second quaver in the bass is a passing note; other connecting notes occur (tenor and alto, bar 2, beat 1; alto, bar 2, beat 3), but they have the effect of creating a new chord, rather than simply connecting two chords but having no harmonic implication of their own.

Passion chorale. Protestant chorale associated with the Passion. The most famous example is 'O Haupt voll Blut und Wunden', an adaptation of a song by Hans Leo Hassler.

Passione, La. Nickname of Haydn's Symphony No. 49 in F minor, composed in 1768. It is so called because it begins with an Adagio suggestive of Passion music.

Passion Music. The idea of dramatizing the Passion of Christ is of great antiquity, and Passion plays for performance during Holy Week have been given from at least Medieval times. For example, in Rome in 1264 a Compagnia del Gonfalone was licensed with the purpose of enacting the sufferings of Christ during Passion Week; it was still active in 1554, when its statutes were printed. One at least of the old German Passion plays survives, that of Oberammergau in Bavaria, and is still enacted every 10 years. Though there may have been music in some of these plays it was not an essential ingredient.

1. *Origins and Development in the Roman Catholic Church.* During the liturgical observances of Holy Week, the story of the Crucifixion was read or sung by the priest from each of the gospels in turn: St Matthew on Palm Sunday; St Mark on Tuesday; St Luke on Wednesday; and St John on Good Friday. By the 12th century it seems probable that he declaimed the words of the narrator or Evangelist in his middle register, those of Christ on lower notes, and those of the other protagonists (including the crowd, known by the Latin word, *turba*) in an upper register, roughly corresponding to the tenor, bass, and alto ranges respectively. These may have been further distinguished by different tempos, the words of Christ being taken more slowly than those of the Evangelist, for example.

By the 13th century, the use of several singing clerks allowed an expansion of this principle. In one method, the complete ensemble sang all the words, the end of each section (Evangelist's words, words of Christ, those of the other protagonists) being marked by a cadence; not a very dramatic technique, but one which underlines the 'grammar' of the narration. Another, more dramatic, method used the responsorial technique common in plainchant—a clerk sings the narration, while the other protagonists are represented by the choir; in some cases the words of Christ on the Cross are sung by a special singer. From the 14th century the parts are usually taken by individual singers.

The introduction of polyphony into the Passion in the 15th century enabled a composer to make far more dramatic points. In the responsorial Passion all or part of the *turba* sections and the utterances of the minor characters were set polyphonically, and often in Italy from about the 1540s so were the words of Christ; the narration remained monophonic. Another type of Passion, sometimes called the 'motet' Passion or 'through-composed' Passion, was polyphonic throughout. A fine example of the responsorial type is the *St Matthew Passion* (*c.*1490) by the English composer John Davy, in the *Eton Choirbook*. Here the words of the Evangelist and Christ are taken by two clerks, while the rest of the music is composed in four parts, with a strong sense of personality and drama.

2. *The 16th and 17th Centuries.* Although there is a considerable amount of Passion music dating from before 1500, it was during the next 250 years that it became most popular with great composers. This was partly due to a general renewal of devotion and partly to the utility of setting biblical stories to music for Protestant church worship, particularly Lutheran. However, although Protestant settings in the vernacular have achieved most fame, setting the Passion story in Latin was also common for Roman Catholic churches, both in Italy and elsewhere.

Passion settings in both churches were similar in kind to those of the 15th century. In the through-composed Passion plainchant was sometimes used as a *cantus firmus* or as a basis for some of the thematic material, but sometimes the setting was completely free. In some works there is a certain amount of characterization, with the various combinations of voices associated with different protagonists. In one of the finest settings of this kind, the *St John Passion* (*c.*1630) of the German *Kantor* Demantius, the words of Christ are usually associated with various groupings of lower voices.

The practice of setting the words of Christ to polyphony in the responsorial Passion was probably introduced into Germany by the Italian Antonio Scandello. His *St John Passion* (composed before 1561) gives the words of Christ to a four-part choir, the music being in an expressively madrigalian style. The plainchant for the monophonic parts had to be adapted for singing in German, and this had been done by Johann Walter, Luther's principal musical adviser, *c.*1550. There were also additions to the narrative, notably an introduction and conclusion sung by the choir, which now therefore has the double function of comment and participation.

The finest examples, and the last, of the responsorial Passion are the three of Schütz (*St Matthew, St John*, and *St Luke*), dating probably from the 1660s and therefore the work of his old age. The 'chant', however, is composed by Schütz himself and is very expressive in effect. Schütz used melisma to paint individual words and also for realistic effects, such as the crowing of the cock in the scene of Peter's denial of Christ. The *turba* choruses are sometimes intensely dramatic, using the full resources of madrigalian counterpoint.

It is usually said that these Passions are austere in feeling, but this is true only if they are compared with later Passions in the oratorio manner. They represent an advanced and highly expressive phase of the older tradition. None the less, the influence of opera and oratorio did make itself felt in attempts to use a new dramatic style in Passion music. As early as 1627 a minor Italian composer, Michelangelo Capellini, had written a 'Lament of the Virgin Mary and Mary

Magdalene and St John on the death of Jesus Christ . . .' in the *stile recitativo*, and Luigi Rossi produced an 'oratorio for Holy Week' in the 1640s. While these are not strictly Passions, the idea of using operatic recitative and the associated *arioso* in religious dialogues-cum-oratorios such as those of Carissimi was to prove very influential. Several German composers began to set the biblical words to real recitative, with a continuo accompaniment, although the chorus was still employed for the *turba*. Some included an instrumental ensemble, to be deployed either for the interludes or to accompany the voices, with different timbres to represent the different personages. An early example of this style can be seen in Schütz's *Seven Last Words on the Cross* (1645), which takes its text from parts of all the Gospels; the words of Christ are sung by a tenor accompanied by a group of viols. This work has the by now traditional introductory and concluding choruses to non-biblical words and it also includes other words—sometimes verses from hymns, otherwise free glosses on the action or emotion—a practice that was to become steadily more popular in the later 17th century.

3. *1700–1750*. By the early 18th century there were two basic possibilities for the composer of Passion music. He could compose either an oratorio on the theme of the Passion, or a 'Passion oratorio'. In the first case he would set a libretto, of which the most popular were those of Brockes and, later, Metastasio. The story was given in recitative, with ample opportunity for contemplative arias in an operatic vein, and naturally the composers who favoured this type were often famous for their operas—such as Keiser of Hamburg, his pupil Handel, Italians at the Viennese court, such as Caldara, and, among Italians in Italy itself (where the genre was less popular), Alessandro Scarlatti. The role of the chorus was small. The 'Passion oratorio' differed from this in using the biblical text according to one or other of the Gospels (with arias and choruses added) and in making extensive use of a chorus as well as of soloists. Telemann composed no fewer than 44 such Passions, showing a distinct sense of drama, especially in the crowd choruses.

Bach's two surviving settings of the Passion are both of the second type. The *St John Passion* may have been written before he left Cöthen, but it was first performed in Leipzig in 1724; the *St Matthew Passion* was performed in 1727 and revised in 1736. They are complex in structure, using biblical narrative, insertions by local poets, and chorale melodies and verses. The narrative is treated as recitative (*secco* for the words of the Evangelist and the minor personages, but extremely expressive and full of realistic touches) and accompanied by a string

quartet 'halo' for the words of Jesus. The poetic insertions are mainly arias, set in the *da capo* convention of the time but surprisingly un-operatic in effect, partly because Bach writes out complex ornamentation of a kind unlikely to be improvised by singers and partly because of the frequent use of *obbligato* instruments, which take much of the attention from the singer. Recitative is not reserved for the biblical words but is also used to precede arias or choruses; and there are 'commenting' choruses in addition to the traditional introduction and conclusion. Finally there are chorales, harmonized with great richness by Bach, so that they seem less congregational hymns than comments on the story. The complexity of the mixture is such that a genre which began as simple story-telling, perhaps in order to make the meaning clear to an uneducated congregation, now becomes a meditation for men to whom every saying of Christ, every reaction to his life and teaching, has acquired an inner meaning.

4. *From the Mid 18th Century to the Present Day*. The vogue for Passion music, generally in the form of oratorio, continued for some time. C. H. Graun's *Der Tod Jesu* (1755) was immensely popular, providing what Gerald Abraham has called, unkindly but not unjustly, 'a sentimental tragedy of the Age of Enlightenment'. C. P. E. Bach produced 21 Passions, sometimes inter-spersing his own music with borrowings from his father, from Telemann, and from other composers. But the general climate of rational-ism in the later 18th century did not favour either drama or meditation on mysteries. As for the 19th century, the performance under Mendelssohn of J. S. Bach's *St Matthew Passion* in 1829 stimulated interest, but little emula-tion—the greatest 19th-century composers were on the whole not particularly concerned with writing for the church. Such composers of sacred music as Perosi (who composed a *St Mark Passion* in 1897) and Stainer (whose *Crucifixion* of 1887 was obviously an emulation of 18th-century Passion music) can hardly compare with the great men of the preceding centuries. Yet the continuing cruelty of man to man in the 20th century has meant that the Passion story has not yet lost its significance, a view expressed in contemporary unliturgical terms by Penderecki's *Passio et mors domini nostri Jesu Christi secundum Lucam* (1963–5).

DENIS ARNOLD

FURTHER READING
Basil Smallman: *The Background of Passion Music: J. S. Bach and his Predecessors* (London, 1957, 2nd edn 1970).

Pasticcio (It.). Literally 'pie' or 'pastry', though used also to mean 'mess', 'muddle', or 'imitation' (in a pejorative sense). In music it usually means a medley, especially an operatic medley in which favourite airs from many operas (not always by different composers) are taken and worked into a new scheme, with a new libretto. *Ballad opera may be considered a variety of this type of *pasticcio*.

The term may also refer to an opera in which each act is by a different composer, e.g. *Muzio Scevola* (1721) by Amadei, Bononcini, and Handel, or to an instrumental work containing different sections or items by different composers, e.g. Diabelli's *Vaterländischer Künstlerverein* (1823–4), containing variations by Beethoven and 50 other composers.

Pastiche (Fr.). 'Imitation', 'parody'. Not the same as *pasticcio*. A work written partly in the style of another period, such as Prokofiev's Classical Symphony (in the style of Haydn) or Stravinsky's *Pulcinella* (after Pergolesi). Many of Gilbert and Sullivan's operettas contain clever pastiches with numerous minuets and gavottes; there is a splendid mock-Handelian duet in *Princess Ida*.

Pastoral (Fr.: *pastourelle*; It.: *pastorale*). 1. In the 15th to 18th centuries, a type of stage work dealing with rural themes. Such subject-matter is also a feature of many madrigals of the late 16th and early 17th centuries, when imitation of Greek and Roman poetry resulted in such works as Tasso's *Aminta*, Guarini's *Il pastor fido*, and Sir Philip Sidney's *Arcadia*. Handel's *Acis and Galatea* (1718) is a pastoral.

2. A type of instrumental or vocal work resembling the *siciliano, generally in 6/8 or 12/8 and often suggesting a rustic or bucolic subject by the imitation of the drone of a shepherd's bagpipe or musette. Many countries associate pastoral music with the Christmas season, e.g. the 'Pastoral Symphony' in Bach's Christmas Oratorio, that in Handel's *Messiah*, the *pastorale* in Corelli's 'Christmas' Concerto, Op. 6 No. 8, and Tartini's Concerto Grosso Op. 8 No. 6, 'con un pastorale per il Santissimo Natale'.

'Pastoral' Sonata. Publisher's name for Beethoven's Piano Sonata No. 15 in D, Op. 28, composed in 1801. It was presumably so called because of the rustic rhythm in the finale.

'Pastoral' Symphony. 1. Symphony No. 6 in F major by Beethoven, Op. 68, composed in 1808. It is a programme symphony, in which bird-song and a storm are imitated, and its five movements have allusive titles, for example 'Awakening of happy feelings on arriving in the country', 'By the brook', and 'Shepherd's song: happy and thankful feelings after the storm'.

2. Symphony by Vaughan Williams, his

third, completed in 1921. It has a wordless solo for soprano (or clarinet) in the last movement.

3. Short orchestral movement in Handel's *Messiah* referring to the shepherds who were told of Christ's birth.

Pastor fido, Il ('The Faithful Shepherd'). Opera in three acts by Handel to a libretto by Rossi after Guarini's pastoral play (1585). It was first performed in London in 1712. Salieri wrote an opera with the same title (1789).

Pater noster (Lat., 'Our Father'). The Lord's Prayer, forming part of the Roman Catholic *Mass and given between the Sanctus and the Agnus Dei. It was retained as 'Our Father' in the Anglican liturgy (see *Common Prayer, Book of*).

Patet. Generic term for the melody types used in gamelan music. See *Indonesia, 2a, 3a, 4*.

'Pathetic' Symphony. Subtitle of Tchaikovsky's Symphony No. 6 in B minor, Op. 74 (1893). It was suggested as a title for this 'programme symphony' the day after its first performance by the composer's brother Modest, and Tchaikovsky authorized its use (the Russian word 'patetichesky' means 'passionate' or 'emotional' rather than 'pathetic'). There is no reason why the symphony should be referred to in England by its French title *Symphonie pathétique*.

Pathétique (Fr.). 'Pathetic', 'moving'; *pathétiquement*, 'pathetically', 'movingly'.

Pathétique Sonata ('Pathetic Sonata'). Beethoven's Piano Sonata No. 8 in C minor, Op. 13, probably completed in 1797–8. Beethoven called it 'Grande sonate pathétique'.

Patience. Comic opera in two acts by Gilbert and Sullivan. Produced: London, Opera-Comique, 23 April 1881; St Louis, 28 July 1881; Berlin, Kroll's Theatre, 30 April 1887. A satire on the contemporary cult of 'aestheticism', in which a chorus of ladies lavish their affection first on the 'fleshly' poet Bunthorne (bar.) and then on the 'idyllic' poet Grosvenor (bar.). Patience (sop.) is a simple milkmaid, impervious to poetry, and the plot also involves a regiment of heavy dragoons.

Patrick, Nathaniel (d Worcester, Mar. 1595). English composer. He was organist at Worcester Cathedral from 1590 until his death. Of his few surviving works, a short service is still regularly performed; it was published in the 18th century by Boyce in his collection of *Cathedral Music*. 　JOHN MILSOM

Patterson, Paul (*b* Chesterfield, 15 June 1947). English composer. He studied privately with Richard Rodney Bennett and at the Royal Academy of Music, where in 1970 he was appointed Manson Fellow. Influenced particularly by Penderecki, he is a ready and effective composer of works ranging from choral settings to television jingles, and from small vocal pieces to large-scale orchestral compositions, including concertos for trumpet (1968), horn (1971), and clarinet (1976), settings of the Kyrie (1972) and Gloria (1973), a Requiem (1975), and the five-movement *Voices of Sleep* (1979) for soprano, chorus, and chamber ensemble.

PAUL GRIFFITHS

Patter song. A type of song, usually found in opera, which depends for its comic effect on the speed of delivery on the part of the singer. Most patter songs are either in Italian or English, these being the most suitable languages. The *Largo al factotum* from Rossini's *Il barbiere di Siviglia* (Act 1 Scene 1) is a celebrated example. The comic operettas of Gilbert and Sullivan abound in such songs.

Pauer, Jiří (*b* Kladno-Libušín, Bohemia, 22 Feb. 1919). Czech composer. A major representative of Czech music, Pauer studied with Šín, Hába, and Bořkovec. Since the 1950s he has fulfilled many major official posts including that of secretary-general of the Union of Czech Composers, artistic director of the Czech Philharmonic, and now artistic director of the Czech National Theatre. His music, including several successful stage works, has managed to combine styles ranging from the romantic (*Zuzana Vojířová*, 1957) to the astringent (Bassoon Concerto, 1949) with the requirements of *socialist realism.

JAN SMACZNY

Paukenmesse ('Kettledrum' Mass). Haydn's Mass No. 9 in C major, composed in 1796. Haydn called it *Missa in tempore belli* ('Mass in Time of War'). It is sometimes referred to as *Kriegsmesse*.

Paukenwirbel Symphonie. See *'Drumroll' Symphony*.

Paul Bunyan. Opera in two acts with a prologue, Op. 17, by Britten to a libretto by W. H. Auden. It was first performed at Columbia University, New York, in 1941 and then withdrawn. After Britten had made some revisions, it was broadcast by the BBC in 1976 and received its stage première at Aldeburgh later that year.

Paumann, Conrad (*b* Nuremberg, *c*.1415; *d* Munich 24 Jan. 1473). German composer, lutenist, and virtuoso organist. He was born blind but by 1446 was organist at St Sebald, Nuremberg, and was appointed town organist in 1447. Three years later he accepted the post of court organist at Munich, and from there travelled widely in Germany, France, and Italy, where he was knighted. He was sought after as an adviser on organ building and was an important teacher, founding a school of organ composers whose products can be seen in many of the pieces in the *Buxheimer Orgelbuch*. Two works in that volume are ascribed to him, and his best-known work, a composition manual for the organ called *Fundamentum organisandi* (1452), includes works by him based on German *Lieder*. He is buried in the Frauenkirche, Munich, and an epitaph there shows him surrounded by his instruments.

DENIS ARNOLD

Pausa (It.), **pause** (Fr.), **Pause** (Ger.). 'Rest' (not *pause).

Pause (Fr.: *point d'orgue*; Ger.: *Fermate*; It.: *fermata*). A sign (⌒) indicating that the note, chord, or rest over which it appears is to be prolonged at the performer's pleasure. It is sometimes placed over a bar-line to indicate a short silence. It may also be used to indicate the end of a phrase, section, or composition. See also *GP*. The French word, *pause*, means 'rest', especially a semibreve (whole-note) rest (a *demi-pause* is a minim (half-note) rest).

Pavan [pavane, pavin] (It.: *pavana, padovana*; Fr.: *pavane*; Ger.: *Paduana*). A 16th- and 17th-century dance, probably originating in Italy and named after the town of Padua. The earliest known examples are in Dalza's lute-book of 1508. Arbeau, in his *Orchésographie* (1588), described the pavan as a processional dance in duple time, with two single steps and one double step forwards, followed by the same sequence in reverse.

Pavans appear in German, French, and Spanish sources of the 1520s and 1530s, but settings of the dance reached the height of perfection in the hands of the English virginal composers—Byrd, Bull, Gibbons, Morley, Farnaby, Philips, Dowland, and Tomkins. There are many examples in the *Fitzwilliam Virginal Book* and other collections of the period, such as Byrd's Pavan in *Parthenia* written as a memorial for the Earl of Salisbury (*d* 1612). Dowland wrote a famous example for five-part string consort, 'Lachrymae: Seven Teares Figured in Seven Passionate Pavans', which was transcribed for keyboard by several other composers of the time, including Byrd.

The pavan was generally coupled with another dance which was quicker, usually in triple time, and sometimes had thematic links with the pavan; in Italy the accompanying dance was a *saltarello, in France and England a *galliard.

After its brief flowering in the late 16th century, the pavan soon died out, though it survived for a while as the first movement ('Paduana') of the early 17th-century German suite and in pieces by Locke and Purcell. Several 20th-century composers have written pieces called 'pavan': the best known is Ravel's *Pavane pour une infante défunte*.

WENDY THOMPSON

Pavane pour une infante défunte ('Pavan for a Dead Infanta'). Work for solo piano by Ravel, composed in 1899. Ravel orchestrated it in 1910. It recalls the Spanish court custom of performing a solemn ceremonial dance at a time of royal mourning.

Pavillon (Fr.). 'Pavilion', or 'tent', hence (from the shape) the bell of a wind instrument. For 'Pavillon chinois', see *Turkish Music*, 'Jingling Johnny'.

Payne, Anthony (Edward) (*b* London, 2 Aug. 1936). English composer. He studied at Durham University but only emerged as a composer in the late 1960s, by which time he had made his name as a critic (his study *Schoenberg* appeared in 1968). His discovery of a personal voice, whose peculiarly English lyricism is not quashed by numerical procedures, is celebrated in the *Phoenix Mass* for chorus and brass (1965–72). His other works include chamber music (notably the String Quartet, 1978), vocal pieces, and orchestral compositions.　PAUL GRIFFITHS

Peacock Variations. Orchestral work by Kodály, composed in 1938–9. It is a set of variations on the Hungarian folk-song *Felszállott a páva* ('The Peacock').

Peasant Cantata (*Bauerncantate*). Nickname of J. S. Bach's cantata No. 212, *Mer hahn en neue Oberkeet*, to a libretto by Picander, composed in 1742.

Pêcheurs de perles, Les ('The Pearl Fishers'). Opera in three acts by Bizet to a libretto by M. Carré and E. Cormon. It was first performed in Paris in 1863.

Pedalgebrauch (Ger.). 'Pedal-use' (in piano playing).

Pedal point (Fr.: *point d'orgue*). The device of holding on a bass note (usually the tonic or dominant) through a passage including some chords of which it does not form a part (see Ex. 1, the closing bars of Bach's Prelude in C from

the *Well-tempered Clavier*). An inverted pedal follows the same principle, but the long held note is placed in the treble. If two different notes are held together (usually tonic and dominant) it is called a double pedal.

Ex. 1

Peebles, David (*fl.* mid 16th century; *d* before 1592). Scottish composer. He was a canon of the Augustinian Priory of St Andrews, and his music, which includes Latin motets as well as settings of English metrical psalms, led one contemporary to describe him as 'ane of the cheiff musitians into this land'.

JOHN MILSOM

Peer Gynt. Incidental music by Grieg for Ibsen's play, first performed in Oslo in 1876. Some of it was later arranged as two orchestral suites: No. 1 (Op. 46; 1874–5, rev. 1888)— *Morning, Death of Aase, Anitra's Dance*, and *In the Hall of the Mountain King*; No. 2 (Op. 55; 1874–5, rev. 1891 and 1892)—*Abduction of the Bride and Ingrid's Lament, Arabian Dance, Peer Gynt's Homecoming*, and *Solvejg's Song*. Additional items sometimes performed are *Wedding March, Solvejg's Cradle Song, Prelude*, and *Dance of the Mountain King's Daughter*. The suites were arranged for piano solo and duet, the first in 1888 and the second in 1893. Saeverud also composed incidental music for the play (1947) and Egk wrote an opera on the subject (1938).

Peerson, Martin (*b* ? March, Cambridgeshire, 1571–3; *d* London, *buried* 15 Jan. 1651). English composer. He took the B.Mus. at Oxford in 1613, and was choirmaster at St Paul's Cathedral from *c*.1624 until the Civil War (even after 1642 he received a salary from the authorities). He wrote some fine verse anthems and had a flair for expressing emotive words, but is known now mainly as one of the earliest English composers to use a figured bass in his attractive *Mottects or Grave Chamber Musique* (London, 1630), a volume of sacred songs in a madrigalian style which is by no means always 'grave'.

DENIS ARNOLD

Peeters, Flor (*b* Tielen, Belgium, 4 July 1903). Belgian composer and organist. He studied at the Lemmens Institute in Mechelen, where he has been cathedral organist since 1923; he has also been active as a recitalist throughout the world and as a teacher, directing the Royal Flemish Conservatory in Antwerp (1952–68). His enormous output includes organ music of all kinds, much of it reflecting his interest in Flemish masters of the Renaissance and Baroque periods. In addition he has composed Masses, other church music, piano works, and songs.

PAUL GRIFFITHS

Peinc (Fr.). The expression *à peine* means 'scarcely', 'hardly at all'; *à peine entendu*, 'barely audible'.

Pelléas et Mélisande. *Drame lyrique* in five acts, 12 *tableaux*, by Debussy; text a slight alteration of Maeterlinck's tragedy (1892). Produced: Paris, Opéra-Comique, 30 April 1902; New York, Manhattan Opera, 19 February 1908; London, Covent Garden, 21 May 1909. Golaud (bar.), grandson of King Arkel of Allemonde (bass), takes home a mysterious girl, Mélisande (sop.), he has found weeping in the forest. Geneviève (mezzo), mother of the half-brothers Pelléas (ten.) and Golaud, reads Arkel a letter from Golaud to Pelléas describing his meeting and marriage with Mélisande. Arkel accepts this marriage. Pelléas comes to tell of a summons he has had from a sick friend, but Arkel reminds him that he should stay with his own sick father, who lies upstairs. Mélisande and Geneviève are joined by Pelléas in the castle gardens and watch a ship departing.

Golaud (Hector Dufranne) meets Mélisande (Mary Garden) in a scene from the first production of Debussy's 'Pelléas et Mélisande' (Opéra-Comique, Paris, 1902).

Playing with her wedding ring, Mélisande loses it down a well; Pelléas advises her to tell Golaud the truth. Golaud, thrown from his horse at the moment the ring fell, is being tended by Mélisande. He notices the ring's absence, and tells her to go and search in the grotto by the seashore, where she says she lost it. Pelléas and Mélisande explore the grotto. Frightened by three sleeping beggars, they abandon their pretended search.

Mélisande drops her long hair from her window, and it is fondled by Pelléas. They are surprised by Golaud. Golaud shows Pelléas the stagnant castle vaults. Golaud warns Pelléas to leave Mélisande alone. Golaud questions little Yniold (sop.), son of his former marriage, about Pelléas and Mélisande and holds him up to the window to tell what he sees: they are sitting together.

Pelléas plans to leave, on his father's advice. Golaud enters and in jealous fury seizes Mélisande's hair and hurls her to and fro. In the park, Yniold is trying to lift a large stone. Pelléas comes to say good-bye to Mélisande, but they declare their love as the castle gates shut. Golaud appears and strikes down Pelléas; Mélisande flees, pursued by Golaud.

Arkel, Golaud, and the Physician wait by Mélisande's bed, where she is dying, having given birth to a child. Golaud, repentant but still jealous, questions her about her love for Pelléas—was it a 'forbidden' love? The castle servants enter, and fall on their knees as Mélisande dies without answering Golaud.

FURTHER READING
Nicholas John, ed.: *Pelléas et Mélisande*, English National Opera Guides (London, 1982).

Pelog. A tuning system used in gamelan music. See *Indonesia*, 2a, 3a, 4.

Peñalosa, Francisco de (*b* c.1470; *d* Seville, 1 Apr. 1528). One of the earliest known Spanish composers. Although primarily associated with Seville Cathedral he also served as chamberlain and singer in the chapel of Pope Leo X in Rome, and some of his Masses and motets may have been written for use there. His music shows clearly the influence of Josquin.

JOHN MILSOM

Penderecki, Krzysztof (*b* Dębica, Poland, 23 Nov. 1933). Polish composer. He studied composition with Artur Malawski and Stanisław Wiechowicz at the Kraków Music Academy, where he began teaching in 1959. His *Threnody to the Victims of Hiroshima* for string orchestra (1960) won international acclaim for its intensely expressive use of new sonorities, including massive glissandos and clusters, and in later works he has continued to exploit the drama of

Penderecki

the unexpected, usually with the help of large forces. In *Polymorphia* for string orchestra (1961) he tightened up the discoveries of his *Threnody*, and there were also similarly dynamic compositions with solo protagonist: the Sonata for cello and orchestra (1964) and the Capriccio for oboe and eleven strings (1965).

In other works of this period Penderecki was giving a definite expressive focus to the turmoil and sonic splendour of his music, usually choosing a religious theme. Here the chief example is his *St Luke Passion* (1963-5), a sharply theatrical piece followed up by a much more sombre and consistent treatment of Christ's burial and resurrection in *Utrenia* (1970-1): both works are scored for soloists, choruses, and orchestra, and both appeal to venerable exemplars—Bach's Passions and Orthodox chant respectively—as well as to the sound world of the avant-garde. They have been regularly followed by other sacred choral works: the *Canticum canticorum Salomonis* (1972), Magnificat (1974), and Te Deum (1979).

Fundamental religious truths are also central to Penderecki's two operas, *The Devils of Loudun* (1968) and *Paradise Lost* (1975-8), which can be seen as works of synthesis, the first concluding the expressionist drive of the early orchestral pieces and the *St Luke Passion*, the second drawing on the increasing thematic tendency in Penderecki's orchestral compositions of the 1970s. For while his First Symphony (1973) still holds to the brute energy he had exploited in the previous decade, his Second (1980) is a remarkable re-entry into the 19th century on the simplest possible terms.

PAUL GRIFFITHS

Pénélope. Opera in three acts by Fauré to a libretto by René Fauchois. It was first performed in Monte Carlo in 1913. Monteverdi's *Il ritorno d'Ulisse in patria* is also an opera on the legend of Penelope.

Penitential Psalms. Psalms 6, 32, 38, 51, 102, 130, and 143 (in the English numbering; all except Psalm 6 are numbered one digit lower in the Vulgate). In the Book of Common Prayer all seven are given as Proper psalms on Ash Wednesday, while in the Roman Catholic Church they are given after Lauds on Fridays in Lent. There are many settings of one or other of the Penitential Psalms, particularly of Psalm 51, 'Miserere', and Psalm 130, 'De profundis', but the most famous setting is Lassus's of all seven, in the *Psalmi Davidis poenitentiales* of 1560.

Pentachord. A five-note section of the scale, e.g. from C to G.

Pentatonic scale. See *Scale*, 6.

Pepping, Ernst (*b* Duisburg, 12 Dec. 1901). German composer. He studied composition with Walter Gmeindl at the Berlin Musikhochschule (1922-6) and has taught at the Berlin Kirchenmusikschule (1934) and also at the Musikhochschule (1953-). One of the leaders of the movement for reviving German church music between the wars, he has written a large body of music for the Lutheran liturgy, employing a style which combines Bachian polyphony with an expanded diatonic harmony suggestive of Hindemith.   PAUL GRIFFITHS

Pepusch, Johann Christoph (*b* Berlin, 1667; *d* London, 20 July 1752). German composer and theorist. He was the son of a Protestant clergyman and became organist at the Prussian court when he was only 14. He left Germany after seeing the public execution without trial of an officer and, after a short stay in Holland, arrived in London at the beginning of the 18th century. He spent much of his life in the service of the theatre, especially at Drury Lane, where he composed masques (including Cibber's *Venus and Adonis*, performed 1715), and became involved in ballad opera. He provided the overture and some basses for *The Beggar's Opera* (1728) and arranged the music for its sequel, *Polly* (1729). He was also active in the revival of older music, and was a founder and director of the Academy of Ancient Music and an influential figure in the forming of the Madrigal Society. He was awarded the D.Mus. at Oxford in 1713 and became a Fellow of the Royal Society in 1746, delivering a paper on Greek music. He married a wealthy opera singer, Signora Francesca Margherita de

Pepusch, portrait by an unknown artist.

L'Epine, with whom he lived in fashionable state.

As well as composing music for dramatic works, Pepusch wrote sonatas for the violin and for wind instruments, and edited Corelli's sonatas and concertos for publication in London. He was an influential teacher, his pupils including Boyce, and his collection of music and books contained the *Fitzwilliam Virginal Book*.
                                    DENIS ARNOLD

Percussion Instruments. In the conventional sense, instruments employed in the percussion section of an orchestra or band (Fr.: *batterie* or *percussion*; Ger.: *Schlagwerk.*; It.: *batteria*), or in a percussion band, or by the drummer of a jazz or rock group (see also *Drum set*). Their variety in kind and in range of sound and colour is, of course, enormous; vibraphone, bass drum, and castanets are all orchestral percussion instruments—what other group has such differently-sounding members?

In pure terms of sound, an immediate distinction among the instruments is between vibrating metal, wood, and membrane (drums). A summary list on these lines is given in 2, below. On the other hand, for composers and orchestrators a long-standing major concern has been over the matter of 'definiteness' of pitch.

1. *Definite and Indefinite Pitch.* An instrument of 'definite pitch' can play specified notes of the

musical scale, written as such in the music (unless, of course, this be of a kind which is not written down). Examples include the 'keyed percussion' (glockenspiel, vibraphone, xylophone, etc.; for a compass chart of these, see *Xylophone*), tubular bells, and, among drums, the timpani. For instruments of 'indefinite pitch' the sounds cannot be (or cannot easily be) expressed as notes of the scale. This group broadly speaking embraces the rest of the percussion, which before the modern era amounted to a limited number of instruments—e.g. side and bass drum, cymbals, triangle—all of which are by intention 'indefinite', approaching the point of real 'pitchlessness' as near as can be obtained, whereby they are sounded whatever the harmony of the rest of the orchestra may be, without having to harmonize with it themselves.

This classic division, however, has now often to be qualified in consequence of a parameter that has come much to the fore during the 20th century: a strong focus of attention upon relative impression of pitch among instruments of the 'indefinite' category. For example, a pair of percussionist's cowbells or temple blocks will give two perfectly distinct contrasting pitches, neither of them tuned to the musical scale (and so by definition 'indefinite') yet capable between them of two-note motifs ('tink-tonk' etc.) which can stick in the mind almost like melodic themes and be imitated vocally. So too with different-sized tom-toms or suspended cymbals softly struck (or, indeed, with two saucepans, odd pieces of wood, almost anything). One can easily understand how such distinctness of contrasted indefinite sounds among percussion instruments offers excellent material for atonal music. Since the pioneer concert works by Edgard Varèse (notably his *Ionisation* (1931) for percussion only), a composer will score for two, three, or more of such instruments designated as 'low', 'medium', 'high', etc., and combine them with other percussion instruments in such ways that, whereas a theme of traditional kind will run through notes of the scale, an atonal strand might rise through the 'indefinite' percussion from bass drum through different tom-toms, then temple blocks, to end at the top with the whip, and perhaps with a note on the marimba (an actual note of the scale) thrown in, dissociated from definite-pitch connotation by the over-all atonal context.

But there arises a complication. Since cowbells sound clearly different pitches, these can be adjusted by the maker to become 'definite', i.e. to give notes of the scale. Tuned sets have been made on these lines, and of sleigh bells and the small 'antique' cymbals (which Berlioz anyhow expected to be tuned to one or more notes of the scale), not to mention Puccini's gongs in *Turandot*; all these instruments thus become of definite pitch. But it is not every orchestra that can produce such tuned sets, nor every composer who wants the instruments to be so tuned, indeed most often requiring atonal 'indefiniteness' ('low', 'high', etc., as mentioned above). Thus we have to take into account a category of percussion instruments which are hard to define other than as 'usually of indefinite pitch', since to do otherwise would be to risk misinforming the student-orchestrator, which it is the whole object of the classic definition to avoid.

2. *The Instruments*. This list is provided as a guide to separate entries. It is by no means exhaustive; more and more instruments continue to creep into the percussionists' armoury with importation of folk and exotic species ('African drums' etc.) over and above those already established through earlier borrowings from folk and popular music and then from jazz and other dance music. (Numerous such novelties appear in the works of Orff.)

METAL: *Anvil*; bell plates (see *Bells*, 8); *Chains*; *Cowbell*; crotales (see *Cymbals*, 4); *Cymbals*; *Flexatone*; *Glockenspiel*; *Gong and Tam-tam*; *Lujon*; *Sistrum*; *Sleighbells* (pellet bells); *Triangle*; *Tubular bells*; *Vibraphone*.

WOOD: *Castanets*; *Claves*; *Guiro*; *Maracas* (with *chocolo, cabaza*); *Marimba*; *Rattle*; *Slit drum* (with log drum); *Temple blocks*; *Whip*; *Wood block*; *Xylophone*.

DRUMS: *Bongos* (with other Latin American drums, conga, timbales); *Boobams*; *Drum* (side drum, bass drum, tenor drum); *Friction drum*; *Rototom*; *Tambourine* (and tambour); *Timpani*; *Tom-tom*.

Occasional use is made of struck bottles or mugs (Britten), and imitative effects—thunder, wind, etc. (see below, 5).

3. *Sticks and Beaters*. While the true pitch of a percussion instrument is decided by its material, form, dimensions, and (with membranes) tension, there is another parameter, concerning high or low sound, which might be compared in a way with the 'registers' of a wind instrument: a percussion instrument's 'higher' sounds, arising from activation in a manner which particularly elicits high partials of the complex tone, and 'deeper' sounds, when lower modes of vibration predominate. The contrast may be effected by striking on different points or with differently directed strokes; but particularly by use of implements of different kinds.

It is quite instructive to tap a table top, first with the fingers (perhaps identifying the pitch one hears by humming in unison with it); and next with a pencil, when a higher pitch, previously only weakly audible, becomes the prominent one. Correspondingly with the percussion, a beater with a large, soft end will make contact with the vibrating surface (solid or

The Percussions de Strasbourg in performance. Among the instruments: (lower left) *bamboo or glass chime* (*clashed together*), *five-octave *marimba, *guiro* (*on tray of assorted beaters*), *2 suspended *cymbals;* (lower right) **tom-toms, conga drums and bongos* (*see Bongos*), *and* (beyond) **vibraphone;* (extreme right) **tubular bells, *timpani.*

membrane) over an appreciable area and thereby damp out shorter wave-length components to produce a booming or mellow sound; conversely a hard narrow stick produces the opposite effect, eliciting high partials while the fundamental or the lower modes are weakly aroused and producing a sound that is more hissing, brittle, or tinkling, as the case may be.

Through the Classical period we rarely hear of a percussion instrument deliberately sounded in any other than its traditional and expected manner. But from Berlioz onward, composers—and theatre and dance drummers—have increasingly introduced sounds made by using the 'wrong' sticks—as well as by hitting a cymbal ('suspended cymbal') instead of invariably clashing it against another. Any perusal of scores, especially from Bartók onwards—though with well-known prior instances in Elgar, Stravinsky, and others—reveals countless novel methods, too many to list.

4. *Notation.* In light music and band parts it is usual to write for the main percussion instruments together on a single staff; see *Brass band* for an example. Any further instruments are added higher on the staff, usually with the abbreviated form of the name, or, for suspended cymbal, a cross instead of a note head. Orchestral music allots a separate single line to each 'indefinite pitch' instrument; see Ex. 1. As lines

are provided only for instruments actually required at that moment in the music the player, who will probably have charge of several of them, requires to be told which these are. For this there are two methods: either to name them, as in Ex. 1 (a work involving six percussionists), or by graphic symbols, as in Ex. 2. These last are becoming pretty well standardized.

Most important in advanced percussion music is careful planning, both by the composer as he distributes the instruments among a stated number of players, and by the individual player so that everything is within reach. Stravinsky's *The Soldier's Tale* (produced in 1918) is still considered a model in both respects, including a diagram in the full score showing how to place the instruments.

5. *Effects.* For more than a century and a half it has been the percussionist's lot to be responsible for miscellaneous imitative and joke instruments now and then demanded, like the spurs (see *Sistrum*), whip-cracking, and pop-gun (for champagne polkas) of 19th-century Viennese light music, and many more from the music hall including wind instruments (siren, whistles, and bulb motor-horns) which are not entrusted to actual wind-players since it is not their job to watch events on the stage while playing. Some of the instruments have since gained the regular standing of symphonic percussion instruments

Ex. 1

Extract from Berio: *Circles*

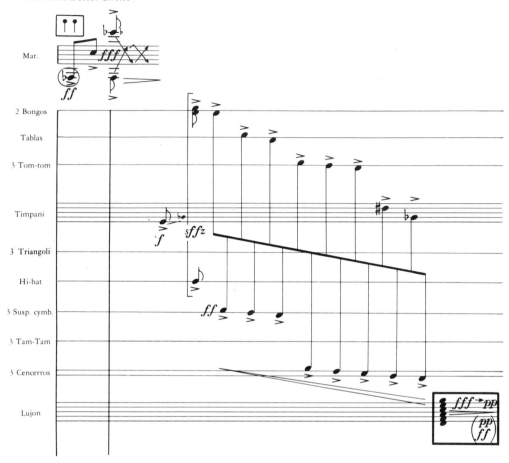

Ex. 2

Extract from Stockhausen: *Kontakte* (⊓ = bongos;   ⑴ = log drums;   △ = cowbells;   M▶ = marimba)

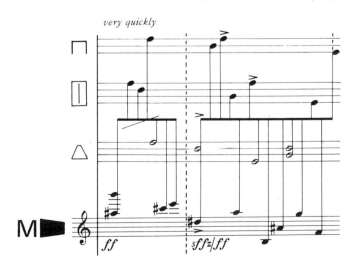

in their own right, for example anvil and slapstick (whip). Others are still counted as 'effects', including those which render dramatic manifestations of the weather. These include the rain machine (a rotating drum made of wire screen with pellets inside); wind machine (Fr.: *éoliphone*), a drum made of wooden slats, measuring some 30″ in diameter, and rotated under a sheet of light canvas (used e.g. by Richard Strauss in *Don Quixote*); thunder sheet (a tin sheet up to 12′ long, hung up and shaken or hit with a gong-mallet); another machine used for thunder is a rotating steel cylinder with stones or metal balls inside, or, nowadays more likely, amplified recordings of actual thunder. Of such 'instruments' Eric Blom wrote, in *Grove's Dictionary* (5th edn), that 'the objection to it [the wind machine] as an element in composition is that it produces by realistic means what music should suggest in its own terms'. ANTHONY BAINES

FURTHER READING
James Blades: *Orchestral Percussion Technique* (London, 1961); Reginald Smith Brindle: *Contem-* *porary Percussion* (London, 1970); J. Blades: *Percussion Instruments and their History* (London, 1971); J. Holland: *Percussion* (London, 1978).

Perdendo, perdendosi (It.; Fr.: *se perdant*). 'Losing', i.e. gradually dying away.

Peregrine tone (Lat.: *tonus peregrinus*). See *Tonus*, 3.

Perfect cadence. See *Cadence*, 2.

Perfect Fool, The. Comic opera in one act by Holst to his own libretto. It was first performed in London in 1923. There is an orchestral suite of the ballet music, which was first performed in 1920.

Perfect interval. See *Interval*.

Performance. English musical quarterly devoted to current musical events; it was founded in 1980.

Performance Practice

1. Introduction
2. Unwritten Notes
3. Sonority
4. Pitch
5. Tuning

6. Tempo
7. Rhythm
8. Phrasing and Articulation
9. Dynamics

1. *Introduction.* The term 'performance practice' is taken over from the German *Aufführungspraxis*, coined in the 19th century, and may be said to cover the mechanics of a performance that define its style. The serious study of performance practice belongs to the 20th century, pioneered in England by Arnold Dolmetsch but gathering real momentum only quite recently.

For better or for worse, the repertory of today's performing musician is probably wider than it ever has been. And as the repertory itself has expanded, so has interest in the study of performance practice. The extent to which a musician's choices should be dictated by such information is, of course, a matter of controversy. An informed performer has the options of working within the original conventions of a style or of modifying or even ignoring them in order to achieve equivalent results for his present-day audience. The wilfully ignorant performer merely uses somebody else's creation as a vehicle for self-expression.

The Western art music that we know from before the era of recorded sound survives simply in some notated form. This may be more or less intelligible as a record of relative pitches and rhythms (see *Notation*) but is almost inevitably a mere skeleton of the music, to be fleshed out by the unwritten and so often unnotatable conventions and nuances of performance. Notation has tended to become more explicit (compare a Handel *concerto grosso* with a Mahler symphony), but much remains unspecified. Will musicians in 200 years' time still assume equal temperament and a pitch standard of $a' = 440$ for today's music? Will a wide *vibrato* or no *vibrato* be in fashion? Will all the instruments of the orchestra (if there are orchestras) have retained their present character? Even with the music of our own contemporaries we may not always be clear when 'violin 1' means a single instrument and when a body of players, or when ♪ means ♫ and when an unmeasured *tremulando*.

The study of performance practice aims to pinpoint shifts in style, conventions, and conditions of playing and singing in order to give the performer the clearest possible view of a composer's original intentions and expectations. It should, of course, be understood that the most detailed historical knowledge of a performing style does not of itself produce a good performance. Conversely, it is clear that strong musical performances can emerge even when a composer's explicit intentions are ignored. Most musicians would in principle agree that the closer they are to a composer's thinking the better their performance is likely to be, that their highest aspiration is to give a performance which the composer would have considered ideal. However, there is general disagreement about which departures, if any, from the original style are desirable or necessary. The familiar argument that 'our ears have changed' and that the music must therefore change in order to achieve an equivalent effect ignores the obvious possibility that our mutable ears may be capable of re-education.

The first steps in the process of establishing the principles of performance practice belong to the editor, or those responsible for relaying the composer's written music (see *Editors, Editing*). With the work of a meticulous living composer there are clearly few problems, but, even with well-known 19th-century music, corrupt scores, perhaps incorporating the modifications made by particular performers, are quite common. With earlier music many larger questions tend to present themselves immediately. Should 16th-century church music be transposed, and if so by how much, to represent better its original sounding pitch in modern terms? Do we understand the rules of *musica ficta*? Should a *trouvère* song be performed metrically or not, and if so how, and if not how?

If the notation of music is so often ambiguous, where do we find the necessary supplementary information? The sources are bewilderingly diverse. Some folk traditions may perhaps retain some characteristics of earlier art traditions and, of course, certain elements of piano playing and teaching today may appear to go directly back to Liszt or Brahms. But the illusory nature of such 'traditions' is often exposed by the evidence of recorded sound. This 20th-century innovation has proved itself to be an invaluable adjunct to notation as a document of composers' intentions (there is also an enormous amount of music, notably pop music, which exists primarily in its recorded form). Stravinsky's own recordings are a fascinating legacy which we perhaps take for granted, while Elgar's reveal a significantly different style of orchestral playing from that of the 1980s.

For the music of earlier periods we are forced to rely on surviving instruments, visual representations of instruments and of music-making, and above all the written word—poor substitutes for actual music, each small clue often presenting its own intricate problem of interpretation. A gut-strung Stradivarius violin in its original condition will all too clearly reflect the character and preconceptions of its player, although an unaltered Baroque organ is rather less accommodating. A Medieval painting of angel-musicians does not prove that their rebecs, harps, and lutes had any place in church music but may in some way hint at the musical activities of their terrestrial counterparts. Among written sources, treatises often promise most but provide least: Morley's *Plaine and Easie Introduction to Practicall Musicke* (1597) teaches only notation and rudimentary composition; and sometimes the reader will be called upon to exercise undefined 'good taste', or perhaps be advised to observe some first-rate exponent. From the 16th century, however, a series of performing musicians have left us invaluable guides to their art: Ganassi on viol and recorder, Praetorius on almost everything, Mace on lute, Hotteterre on woodwind instruments, Geminiani and Leopold Mozart on violin, Quantz on flute and the string orchestra, François Couperin and C. P. E. Bach on keyboard instruments, Altenburg on trumpet, and so on through the 19th century to the present day. From the 17th century composers have occasionally added a practical preface to their published works (Caccini, Viadana, Frescobaldi, Schütz, Muffat), and since the 19th century it has not been uncommon for them to write publicly of their own music and its realization (Berlioz, Wagner, Stravinsky). The private letters of, for example, Monteverdi, Mozart, and Beethoven can sometimes throw light on contemporary practice, as can the observations of musical travellers (Burney and the Novellos), diarists (Pepys), dramatists (Shakespeare), poets (Chaucer), novelists (Hardy), critics (Shaw), and indeed anyone who sets pen to paper. In a rather different category are the archives of the thousands of cathedrals, courts, households, and public institutions that have employed musicians over the ages. A payroll may reveal the size and constitution of an orchestra or choir; there may be bills for new instruments, for repairs and strings for existing ones, contracts and specifications for a new organ, petitions and reports of disciplinary hearings concerning the exact duties of musicians. From all quarters come tell-tale details of the musical life of former ages, details which in isolation are perhaps of little consequence but which in conjunction with others may allow a clearer picture of particular performances to emerge.

2. *Unwritten Notes*. Before outlining the many intricate questions of the interpretation of written notes, let us briefly consider the matter of unwritten notes. Perhaps most speculative of all is the nature and desirability of adding accompaniments to Medieval monophonic

songs: we know little more than that such songs *were* often accompanied, usually by stringed instruments. The unwritten accompaniments to 16th-century polyphony were probably simple chordal intabulations of some sort, and may well have anticipated early Baroque continuo style. Seventeenth- and 18th-century styles of continuo playing are, by contrast, reasonably well documented, though each instrument, each ensemble, each performance requires its own realization. In particular, the accompaniment of recitative is a fluid art: it is not unlikely that the organ chords in J. S. Bach's cantatas were often played short (♩ when written ○), sometimes sustained, and sometimes with the left hand sustained and the right hand released (see *Continuo*). Signs indicating a specific ornament or any appropriate ornament on a particular note proliferated in the 17th century. Certainly until the end of the 18th century it was an essential part of the performer's art to be able to add ornaments and to embellish melodic lines tastefully (see *Ornaments and Ornamentation*). The *cadenza was simply a part of this improvisatory art.

3. *Sonority: (a) Vibrato.* While *vibrato* is an integral part of today's conventionally favoured sonorities, and there is evidence of its use from the 16th century and earlier, anything other than an occasional and discreet *vibrato* is probably out of place in pre-Classical music. Certainly there was no place for the powerful singing and playing that so often brings with it a large *vibrato*, nor for anything that might preclude subtlety of intonation. *Vibrato* was treated as an ornament and as such was rarely used continuously. In the 18th century it became more usual, and later (though even Wagner criticized a singer's 'sempiternal shake') it began to be considered more as a natural ingredient of good tone production.

(b) Voices. Qualities that were particularly prized in Renaissance and Baroque singing were clarity and agility (especially in the execution of ornaments). Distinctions were sometimes drawn between the manner of singing appropriate to churches and the soft, subtle style appropriate to chamber music. Later, even Berlioz considered the larger theatres damaging to the art of singing. Certainly the sheer vocal power required in such buildings often precludes agility and natural diction. This expansion of dynamic range parallels an increase in pitch range: most Medieval and Renaissance vocal music restricts itself to a 10th or so, and solo music would lie mostly in the middle of a singer's range.

Falsetto singing, much misunderstood and over-used in today's revivals, had an important role as the highest voice in much continental polyphony of the Renaissance and was only later associated with alto parts. Castratos dominated the 17th and 18th centuries with their combination of boys' voices and adult power and musicianship.

The flavour of, for example, spoken English has changed radically since Chaucer's time, and one may surmise that the palette of colours in accepted 'good singing' today has changed just as much. Also, the character of one's own language was probably more directly reflected in singing than today's wide repertory allows, and consequently national and regional styles were probably more clearly differentiated (Italian and French operatic traditions in the 18th century, for example, were evidently poles apart). Just as features of earlier 'courtly' language may survive in certain dialects, so may some characteristics of 'courtly' singing survive in folk traditions.

(c) Instruments. It is tempting to regard the evolution of instruments as a simple progression and process of perfection. But aesthetic values are continually shifting: a noble and courtly instrument, such as the Medieval bagpipe, may find itself relegated to the role of a folk instrument, while the violin is elevated from being merely a dance instrument.

Broadly speaking, the desire for more powerful instruments as music became a more public affair (see *Concert*) seems to have led to rounder sounds, and harmonically more chromatic music seems to have engendered safer, tonally smoother instruments. Thus, the brightness and directness of Medieval and Renaissance instruments may seem pungent and stark to our ears, attuned as they are to Wagnerian sonorities; or, conversely, a Brahmsian cello may seem oppressively thick and heavy in comparison to a light, ringing Baroque viol. Few improvements are without their drawbacks. In Wagner's opinion, the new valve-horn lacked some of the hand-horn's beauty, and Bach's natural trumpet had the delicacy to balance a recorder. The larger mouthpieces and widely-flared bells of modern trombones produce a powerful, velvety sound at the expense of their ancestors' natural brightness and clarity, and instruments constructed for high-tensioned strings (with their consequent possibilities of sheer power) similarly lose the natural, free resonances of lighter instruments. Electric- or pneumatic-action organs do not have the fine control of a tracker action, and the modern violin has much less flexibility than pre-Tourte models in playing triple- and quadruple-stopped chords. Some orchestral instruments (e.g. Mendelssohn's ophicleide, Verdi's valve-trombone) have been quietly replaced.

The influence of an outstanding musician can

quite quickly alter the course of a playing style. In our own time, while Viennese oboes are still distinctively mellower than the reedy Parisians, national styles are becoming less individual, as conductors (and players and students) adopt a more international life-style and as recorded music becomes available world-wide. Consequently, Tchaikovsky's symphonies may sound rather less Russian, Dvořák's less Czech, Berlioz's less French than they did originally.

(d) *Forces*. While the performance of an intimate Haydn quartet by a string orchestra, or Tchaikovsky's Serenade by a mere string quartet, would be unthinkable today, we are not always so discerning when it comes to the various sizes of performing body required for pre-Classical music. Although giant vocal and instrumental groups were occasionally assembled before the 19th century, Monteverdi's and Cavalli's orchestras were normally of single strings. At Leipzig, Bach's fullest orchestra was just over 20-strong and his optimum choir 12–16. (One cannot assume that Bach's Passion settings have any greater dramatic and emotional impact with larger forces.) Indeed, some of Bach's so-called choral music and much 17th-century church music (Monteverdi, Carissimi) may well have been written for vocal consorts (i.e. single voices) rather than choirs. Renaissance choirs of more than about 25 singers were rare and the vast majority of madrigals etc. are chamber music for single voices, the exact equivalent of string quartets.

But the scale of a performance is not all. The choir of King's College, Cambridge, may still have exactly the original number of singers, but its internal balance has changed—all the boys are trebles, whereas in the late 15th century they were both trebles and means. More significantly, a work such as Machaut's Mass, often sung with colourful support from an assortment of Medieval instruments, was almost certainly written for four unaccompanied solo voices, while a typical three-choir motet by Giovanni Gabrieli—apparently all-vocal and not specifying any instruments—was most probably intended for two instrumental groups (high and low), each with a solo singer, and one (small) choir. In Baroque music, the instruments of the continuo group are rarely named; the combination of harpsichord and cello is but one of several possibilities (on occasion even a chordal instrument may not be necessary). Also, the ever present 16′ string sound (double basses) of the modern orchestra was unknown to Lully and perhaps even to Purcell. (See also *Choir*; *Orchestra*.)

Sonority is also influenced by the placement of forces. The musicians of St Mark's, Venice, used much less separation (often vertical) of choirs than myth would have it (see *Cori spezzati*). In Classical music, the orchestral texture is often clarified by the common arrangement of first and second violins opposite each other. Wagner's sunken, 'hooded' orchestra pit at Bayreuth makes the balance with singers on stage easier than in almost any other opera house.

4. *Pitch*. Only recently has there been any successful international standardization of pitch (see *Pitch*, 1), but it is clear that a higher or lower pitch standard can colour music quite differently: a low-pitched French Baroque orchestra, playing almost a tone below $a' = 440$, must have sounded quite different from a Venetian one, playing at roughly $a' = 440$ or even higher. However, it is in vocal music that the matter is most crucial. For Dowland and Purcell a song must lie in the speech area of the voice, where the words are most naturally projected. In Bach and Beethoven we regularly create problems of stamina for the choral singer by pitching the music too high. With 16th-century polyphony we can easily misunderstand the intended scoring if our assumptions of pitch level are slightly wrong, and with Medieval polyphony, where our knowledge of pitch standards is almost non-existent, it may well be that our expectations are dramatically wrong.

5. *Tuning*. Today's musicians have grown up with the sound of equal temperament (see *Temperament*, 4)—in which all semitones are of exactly equal size—and this is appropriate for most 19th- and 20th-century music. But this would have sounded disturbingly out-of-tune to Renaissance ears as it is a compromise system in which no interval, except the octave, is pure—its advantage over other systems being that all keys are equally usable. Bach's *Well-tempered Clavier* was not a vindication of equal temperament but a brilliant demonstration of a system that approached it while retaining some individuality for all keys. To perform it on an equal-tempered instrument is to eliminate all these particular subtleties. The various characteristics of different keys is a vital ingredient of all Baroque music, especially dramatic music, and the dissonances of Medieval music become truly potent when Pythagorean intervals are used.

6. *Tempo*. Since its introduction in the early 19th century, the *metronome has been a mixed blessing. On the one hand, it offers the performer precise information of a type that was previously almost impossible; on the other, it can foster the belief that there is always just one correct tempo. Wagner abandoned metronome markings in favour of more general indications of tempo, and other composers (Stravinsky) have quite often in performance

departed from their own directions. Beethoven's metronome markings are often puzzling (was his metronome defective?) but are too often totally ignored, so that, for example, the *Marcia funebre* of his 'Eroica' Symphony is almost always heard at a substantially slower speed than the perfectly plausible (and more march-like) ♪ = 80.

Before Beethoven's day there were occasional attempts to measure tempos, but there is little precise information. Bach was said to have favoured 'brisk' tempos, and dance forms were, at least originally, closely associated with the natural speed of the dance steps. From the 17th century terms such as *allegro* and *adagio* began to be used, though their meaning has often shifted (not 'rather fast' and 'slow', respectively, but 'cheerful' and 'at ease'). A Schumann *andante* is slower and more introspective than a Handel one, with its implications of a moderate 'walking' pace. For Medieval, Renaissance, and even much Baroque music, the principal guide to tempo was simply the time signature; subsequent changes of tempo were governed by proportional signs. Just as music has steadily expanded its harmonic and dynamic palettes, so the normal range of tempos has probably grown. Greater flexibility of tempo within a movement may also be appropriate to much 19th-century music. However, the nature of *tempo* *rubato* seems to have changed: for Mozart (and probably still for Chopin) the pianist's right hand was given rhythmic freedom in an *adagio*, while the accompanying left hand kept strict time.

7. *Rhythm.* The notation of rhythms is almost always merely the most convenient approximation. Thus, even equal-note plainchant is capable of (and surely requires) endless minute rhythmic modifications. The practice of making pairs of notes (♫♫) unequal (♪.♫♪ or ♪.♫♪)—familiar to us in jazz—is first mentioned in the mid 16th century, and became a vital feature of Baroque music, especially, but not exclusively, of French music (see *Notes inégales*). Closely related is the principle of double-dotting (or over-dotting), where ♩. ♪♩ becomes more like ♩.. ♪♩ ; the written double dot is very rare in pre-Classical music. Discrepancies such as ♪♪♪ ♪♪♪ occur regularly in Baroque music and are often ambiguous: Bach evidently taught his pupils to observe such differences, others to accommodate one rhythm to the other. Even in the songs of Schubert, Schumann, and Brahms it is not always clear whether or not such rhythms should remain distinct.

8. *Phrasing and Articulation.* Even more impor-tant than tempo in establishing the character of a piece of music are the phrasing and articulation employed. It is therefore unfortunate that there is almost no evidence on these vital matters from the Middle Ages and early Renaissance, apart from a few notational features (such as the *plica). *Keyboard fingerings suggest that a rather detached manner of playing in the 16th century turned only slowly into the seamless *legato* of the 19th century. This shift is paralleled by the transition from the norm of one bow-stroke per note in 16th-century string playing to the general slurring and smooth bow-changing of the 19th century. Indeed, Baroque bows encourage a natural non-*legato*, while the Tourte bows in general use from *c*.1800 have quite different qualities. The deliberate un-evenness in passage-work of earlier keyboard fingerings also has its parallels in the tonguing syllables used by wind players. These syllables (such as 'le-re, le-re') are gentler than their later counterparts ('te-ke, te-ke'), just as bow-strokes rarely used the sharp attack—Leopold Mozart wrote that 'Every note . . . has a small . . . soft-ness at the start of a stroke'. With vocal matters one is forced to conjecture more, but it seems that Caccini's and Monteverdi's florid orna-ments were articulated in the throat and were consequently fast and light. Symbols for articu-lation (such as slurs) began to appear in the 17th century and proliferated with Romantic music. There are, however, occasional ambiguities: slurs and phrase-marks use the same symbol; Haydn's written ⌃ or printed ⌃ is usually a simple *staccato* (our ⌃) without implication of a sharp accent; and Verdi's ⌃ is probably a *tenuto* (our ⌃) rather than the heavy accent intended elsewhere.

9. *Dynamics.* Romantic orchestral and operatic music has accustomed us to a wide range of dynamics and their dramatic possibilities. These play no part in Medieval and Renaissance music, where the absence of indications reflects the fact that, apart from the subtle use of dynamic variety that is part of phrasing, a basic dynamic level is set by the choice of forces, and any obvious dynamic variation in an extended work (say, a Mass setting) is a natural result of a change of texture (for example, a reduction from five-part choir to solo trio) or, in organ music, of a change of registration between sections. The dynamic range of individual instruments was generally quite small. Some lute music of the 16th century contains indications of dynamic variety, but the rise of the violin family coincides with an interest in dynamics as a compositional tool, when the possibilities of sudden contrasts and echo-effects began to be exploited by early Baroque Italian composers, and the abbrevia-tions *f* (*forte*) and *p* (*piano*) gained common

currency. Increasingly large halls and theatres for public performance through the 18th century brought with them larger choruses and orchestras and a more common fascination with sheer volume. The greater the possible dynamic range, the more necessary and desirable it became for composers to specify their exact intentions.   ANDREW PARROTT

FURTHER READING
Thurston Dart: *The Interpretation of Music* (London, 1954, 4th edn 1967); Robert Donington: *The Interpretation of Early Music* (London, 1963, rev. edn 1974); Mark Lindley: 'Authentic Instruments, Authentic Playing', *The Musical Times* (April 1977); Michael Morrow: 'Musical Performance and Authenticity', *Early Music* (April 1978).

Performing Right. See *Copyright*.

Performing Right Society, The. See *Copyright*, 7.

Pergolesi, Giovanni Battista (*b* Iesi, nr Ancona, 4 Jan. 1710; *d* Pozzuoli, nr Naples, 16 Mar. 1736). Italian composer. The son of a surveyor, he seems to have been a sickly child and to have suffered from a tubercular disease all his life. He was educated at the Conservatorio dei Poveri di Gesù Cristo in Naples from *c*.1722, and was commissioned to write an *opera seria* by one of the Neapolitan theatres when he was only 21. In 1732 he was made *maestro di cappella* to the equerry to the Viceroy of Naples, and from then on he had a busy life writing both serious and comic operas (*Lo frate 'nnamorato*, performed 1732, was especially successful), as well as much church music. By 1735 his reputation extended beyond Naples, and he was commissioned to write an opera for Rome; the result, *L'Olimpiade*, was not immediately successful. Because of his deteriorating health Pergolesi moved back to live in the Franciscan monastery at Pozzuoli. He continued to compose, however, his *Stabat mater* and the C minor *Salve regina* belonging to this period.

When Pergolesi died at the age of 26 he was not particularly famous, but revivals of his music, especially of the *intermezzo*, *La serva padrona* (performed Naples, 1733), which was performed by travelling opera companies, were many over the two decades after his death. *La serva padrona* was given in Paris in 1746 and again in 1752; it triggered off the Querelle des *Bouffons and became a symbol of the Rousseau party. Many works have since been misattributed to him, including some of the music

Autograph MS of a page of Pergolesi's 'Questo e il piano' (1731) for alto and strings.

Pergolesi, caricature (c.1734) by Pier Leone Ghezzi.

recomposed by Stravinsky for his ballet *Pulcinella*. Today Pergolesi seems a minor figure, but *La serva padrona* is a little masterpiece, the characters well drawn, the plot well constructed, and the music the essence of *opera buffa*, with crisp rhythms and brief, vital themes. Neither should his church music be despised—the *Stabat mater* especially expresses delicately the emotions of the text, while the music for solo voice and orchestra is nearly always attractively melodious.   DENIS ARNOLD

Peri, Jacopo (di Antonio di Francesco) (*b* Rome, 20 Aug. 1561; *d* Florence, 12 Aug. 1633). Italian composer and singer. He came of a middle-class Florentine family (he called himself 'nobil fiorentino') and at the age of 12 was in Florence as a singer at the Servite monastery of Ss. Annunziata; over the following years he worked as singer and organist at various churches and monasteries in Florence. He studied music with Malvezzi, who gave him a sound contrapuntal training, and joined in the discussions of the Florentine *camerata* in the 1580s. His main talent as a composer was for the composition of dramatic music; in 1583 he contributed some music (now lost) to a set of *intermedi* given at the Medici court, and in 1589 he sang in and composed an aria for the famous *intermedi* for *La pellegrina* given at the celebrations surrounding Ferdinando I's marriage to Christine of Lorraine.

Peri is best remembered today for his collaboration with the composer Jacopo Corsi and the poet Ottavio Rinuccini to produce the first dramatic work with continuous music, *La Dafne* (1597–8). He composed the recitatives and Corsi the arias, but unfortunately little of the music survives. However, it was probably similar in style to the next Peri/Rinuccini collaboration, *Euridice* (1600; published 1601). Peri was again responsible for the recitatives, and Caccini insisted on re-composing the arias and choruses that were to be sung by his singers; the recitatives were less successful with the first audience, but today we can appreciate their dramatic effectiveness and expressiveness. (See also *Opera*, 2.)

Little of Peri's later music survives, and what does remain is rarely, if ever, heard. He continued to be active as a composer, however, cultivating connections with the Mantuan court and writing several dramatic works; publishing a song collection, *Le varie musiche*, in 1609; directing the Easter music at S. Nicola, Pisa; and writing *sacre rappresentazioni* for S. Maria Novella, Florence, in the 1620s. His health was not good in these years, and although he survived the plague epidemic which attacked Florence in 1630–3 he died soon after the city was declared free of the plague, at the age of nearly 72.   DENIS ARNOLD

FURTHER READING
Tim Carter: 'Jacopo Peri', *Music and Letters*, lxi (1980), pp. 121–35.

Peri in the role of Arion in the fifth intermedio for the comedy 'La pellegrina' by Bargagli, sketch by Buontalenti.

Périgourdine (Fr.). An old French dance originating from Périgord (now mostly in the Dordogne department). It was usually in 3/8 or 6/8 time, and the dancers sang the tune.

Perle, George (*b* Bayonne, New Jersey, 6 May 1915). American composer and writer. He studied composition with Wesley LaViolette at De Paul University (1934–8) and privately with Ernst Krenek during the 1940s. Since then he has taught at various institutions, and has produced a definitive study of serial music, *Serial Composition and Atonality: an Introduction to the Music of Schoenberg, Berg, and Webern* (Los Angeles and London, 1962, 4th edn 1977); he is also author of an authoritative study of Berg's *Wozzeck* (*The Operas of Alban Berg*, i: *Wozzeck*, Los Angeles and London, 1981). In his own music he has developed a system of 'twelve-tone modality', which combines features of tonality and serialism to create music which is lucid and coherent. Most of his works are for solo instruments or standard chamber ensembles, though he has also written some orchestral pieces and songs.

PAUL GRIFFITHS

Perosi, Lorenzo (*b* Tortona, nr Piacenza, 20 Dec. 1872; *d* Rome, 12 Oct. 1956). Italian composer. Son of the cathedral organist at Tortona, he studied in Rome and Milan before going to Regensburg in 1893, where he worked with the scholar F. X. Haberl. In 1894 he was appointed *maestro di cappella* at St Mark's, Venice, being ordained shortly afterwards by the future Pope Pius X. In 1898, he was made Director of the Sistine Chapel, and in this capacity was influential in drawing up the famous 'Motu proprio' of 1903, advocating the return to a 'pure' style of church music. Perosi's own compositions of this period, which include a St Mark Passion (1897), often performed in Italy, display the influences of both 16th-century polyphony and Wagner. In 1917 Perosi had a mental breakdown, but he recovered and had a second fruitful period of composition in the 1930s, producing some sacred works and also five piano quintets (1930–1). He was titular director of the Sistine Chapel until his death.

DENIS ARNOLD

Pérotin [Perotinus Magnus]. Composer who was active probably in the late 12th and early 13th centuries at the Cathedral of Notre Dame, Paris. Like the older Léonin, he is known from the remarks of the anonymous English theorist known as Anonymous IV (*fl. c.*1270), but his name appears also in a passage added at about the same time to a treatise by Johannes de Garlandia. Anonymous IV implies that Pérotin took Léonin's liturgical chant settings (*organa dupla*) as a starting-point, revising them and supplementing them with pieces in a more modern idiom. Léonin's 'magnus liber', he says, 'was used up to the time of Perotinus Magnus, who shortened it and made many better *clausulae* or *puncta* [i.e. sections of *discant*, as opposed to *organum*], for he was the best composer [or singer] of discant'. Anonymous IV goes on to name various compositions by Pérotin (he did not do this for Léonin); they include two chant settings for four voices (*organa quadrupla*)—the Graduals *Viderunt* and *Sederunt*—and two for three voices (*organa*

Ex. 1

tripla), as well as three *conductus*, for three, two, and one voice respectively.

Since there exist decrees of the Bishop of Paris of 1198 and 1199 allowing four-part settings specifically of *Viderunt* and *Sederunt*, it is likely that Pérotin's compositions date from around this time. We do not know whether they were early or late works—some scholars date his composing career as *c*.1170-1200, others *c*.1190-1220. If the latter dates are roughly correct it is likely that Pérotin would have composed motets, but Anonymous IV does not mention this.

Viderunt and *Sederunt* are among the crowning achievements of all Medieval music, and the other compositions, fine though they be, are hardly necessary to enhance Pérotin's standing. Both in large-scale tonal design—with massive pedal points sustaining majestic swings from one harmony to another—and in the detail of interplay between the three upper voices, they display a mastery amply justifying the adjective 'magnus' ('the great'). His contrapuntal style may be demonstrated in an extract from the three-part *conductus Salvatoris hodie* (Ex. 1)—particularly striking when one remembers that Léonin's known work consists simply of the addition of one part to plainchant tenors.

DAVID HILEY

Perpetual canon. See *Canon*.

Perpetuum mobile (Lat., 'perpetually in motion'; It.: *moto perpetuo*). A title sometimes attached to a rapid instrumental composition proceeding throughout in notes of equal value. Paganini (*Moto perpetuo*, Op. 11), Weber (Piano Sonata Op. 24, last movement), and Johann Strauss (*Perpetuum mobile*, Op. 257) were among composers to use the term.

Perrot, Jules Joseph (*b* Lyons, 18 Aug. 1810; *d* Paramé, 24 Aug. 1892). French choreographer. He collaborated with Coralli on *Giselle* (Adam, 1841) and then went on to make London a major ballet centre, with works including *Ondine* (1843), *La Esmeralda* (1844), *Pas de quatre* (1845), and *Lalla Rookh* (1846), all to music by Pugni. He was ballet master at St Petersburg between 1851 and 1858. NOËL GOODWIN

Perséphone. Melodrama in three scenes by Stravinsky to a libretto by André Gide. It is for narrator, tenor, chorus, children's chorus, and orchestra, and was choreographed by Jooss for its first performance in Paris in 1934. Stravinsky revised it in 1949. In the ballet version the person playing Persephone must recite and dance.

Persian Music. See *Middle Eastern Music*.

Persichetti, Vincent (*b* Philadelphia, 6 June 1915). American composer. He studied at the conservatory and the Curtis Institute in Philadelphia, and had composition lessons from Russell King Miller (1924-36) and Roy Harris (1943). He has taught composition at the Philadelphia Conservatory (1942-62) and the Juilliard School (1947-). A fluent and practical musician, he has produced a large output of orchestral, choral, chamber, and instrumental music, using various styles but normally keeping some relation to tonal centres. He is also author of the book *Twentieth Century Harmony* (New York, 1961). PAUL GRIFFITHS

Persimfans. See *Russia and the Soviet Union*, 5.

Perti, Giacomo Antonio (*b* Crevalcore, Bologna, 6 June 1661; *d* Bologna, 10 Apr. 1756). Italian composer. He studied with his uncle, a priest at the principal church in Bologna, S. Petronio, and then at the Jesuit College and possibly the university. He began to compose at an early age, and his first opera was produced when he was 18; the following year he directed a full-scale Mass at S. Sigismondo. Shortly after this he moved to Parma, where he continued to compose operas and sacred music; his operas were also produced at Rome and Venice. In 1690 he returned to Bologna as *maestro di cappella* at S. Pietro, and six years later was appointed *maestro* at S. Petronio, where he remained for the rest of his life.

Perti's operas and oratorios are rarely heard today, but his church music is well worth revival; his Masses, psalms, and motets are written both for full choir and soloists accompanied by orchestra (sometimes including trumpet or other *obbligato* instrumental parts) and *a cappella*, in the older 'Palestrina' style. He was also an extremely influential teacher and his pupils included Francesco and Vincenzo Manfredini, Torelli, and Padre Martini.

DENIS ARNOLD

Perugia, Matteo da. See *Matteo da Perugia*.

Pes (Lat.). 'Foot'. 1. Term used to describe the tenor part in some English manuscripts of the 13th century; in most cases the *pes* carries a melodic *ostinato* figure. The lowest two voices of the rota 'Sumer is icumen in' are called *pes* in the original manuscript. 2. Synonym for *podatus*, i.e. a neume comprising two notes. See *Notation*, 2.

Pesant (Fr.), **pesante** (It.). 'Heavy', 'weighty'; *pesamment* (Fr.), *pesantemente* (It.), 'heavily'.

Pescetti, Giovanni Battista (*b* Venice, *c.*1704; *d* Venice, 20 Mar. 1766). Italian composer. A pupil of Antonio Lotti, he devoted most of his career to the theatre, composing his first opera in 1725. In 1736 he went to London where he took over from Porpora as director of the Opera of the Nobility, returning to Venice about 10 years later. In 1762, a year after his last opera, *Zenobia*, was performed at Padua, he became second organist at St Mark's, Venice. As well as his dramatic works (the music of most of them is lost), Pescetti also wrote an oratorio, organ pieces, and a book of harpsichord sonatas (London, 1739).   WENDY THOMPSON

Pesenti, Michele (*b* *c.*1470; *d* after 1524). Italian composer, born in the region of Verona. He seems to have worked at the courts of Ferrara and Mantua as well as being *maestro* of the chamber music of Pope Leo X. He was an important composer of *frottole*, and his works appear in anthologies published by Petrucci in Venice between 1513 and 1521.   DENIS ARNOLD

Petenera (Sp.). A traditional Spanish song, named after a 19th-century singer. It is in brisk triple time, but vocal sections often alternate with passages for guitar alone in six-in-a-measure time.

Peter and the Wolf (*Petya i volk*). Symphonic fairy-tale, Op. 67, by Prokofiev to his own libretto. It is for narrator and orchestra and was composed in 1936. The boy Peter's tricking of a wolf is narrated and brilliantly illustrated by solo orchestral instruments, the characters in the story being represented by different instruments. The work was conceived as a way of instructing children in identifying orchestral instruments.

Peter Grimes. Opera in three acts by Britten; text by Montague Slater, after Crabbe's poem *The Borough* (1810). Produced: London, Sadler's Wells, 7 June 1945; Stockholm, 21 March 1946; Tanglewood, 6 August 1946.

In a little fishing village in Suffolk, Peter Grimes (ten.) has lost an apprentice at sea in suspicious circumstances. He is acquitted at the inquest, but warned not to take another apprentice. Ellen Orford (sop.), the schoolmistress, alone stands by him, and helps him to get another boy. Later she discovers that the boy has been ill-treated and she quarrels with Peter. He takes the boy to his hut on the cliff top, but they have been overheard, and popular feeling rises to such a pitch that the entire village sets out after him. Peter and his apprentice hear the mob coming, and as they descend by another route the boy falls to his death down the cliff. Three days later Grimes turns up in the village at dawn, exhausted. Balstrode (bar.), a retired sea captain, advises him that the only way to escape the village now is to sail his boat out to sea and sink in it. This Peter does as the village comes to life for another, ordinary day.

Peters. German firm of music publishers. It had its origins in the publishing house, printing

Peter Pears in the first performance of Britten's 'Peter Grimes' (Sadler's Wells Theatre, London, 1945).

works, and music shop opened by the composer F. A. Hoffmeister (1754–1812) in Leipzig in 1800. When it was bought in 1814 by the bookseller C. F. Peters (1779–1827), to whom the firm owes its present name, the catalogue included chamber and instrumental music by Bach, Haydn, Mozart, and Beethoven, as well as E. L. Gerber's famous biographical dictionary of musicians, and it then expanded to include Spohr, Weber, Hummel, and others. Max Abraham (1831–1900) became a partner, and in 1880 sole owner, and in collaboration with the Leipzig engraver C. G. Röder he built the firm's reputation on his Edition Peters, with its clear printing and distinctive covers (light green for works out of copyright, pink for original publications).

Abraham's nephew Henri Hinrichsen (1868–1942), an excellent businessman with artistic insight, joined the firm in 1894, and works by Grieg, Brahms, Bruch, Wagner, Wolf, Mahler, Schoenberg, and Richard Strauss entered the catalogue. His sons Max (1901–65) and Walter (1907–69) joined in 1931. After the Second World War the firm split, and each branch published parts of the original catalogue as well as promoting new music. The Leipzig branch became publicly owned in 1949–50 and promotes east European composers (e.g. Hanns Eisler). The London branch, set up by Max Hinrichsen in 1938 as Hinrichsen Edition (renamed Peters in 1975), publishes early English music as well as contemporary composers (e.g. Brian Ferneyhough). The New York branch, set up by Walter Hinrichsen in 1948, publishes composers such as Cage, Ives, Ligeti, and Schoenberg (under the Henmar imprint). The branch established in Frankfurt am Main in 1950 also concentrates on contemporary music.

J. M. THOMSON

Petipa, Marius (*b* Marseille, 11 Mar. 1818; *d* Gurzuf, Crimea, 14 July 1910). French choreographer, younger brother of the dancer Lucien Petipa (1815–98). After working as assistant to Perrot at St Petersburg, Marius became ballet master there in 1862. His 46 original ballets and *divertissements* were the basis of the Imperial Russian Ballet's success until his retirement in 1903. They include *Don Quixote* (Minkus, 1869), *Bayaderka* (Minkus, 1877), *The Sleeping Beauty* and the revised *Swan Lake*, *Raymonda* (Glazunov, 1898), *The Seasons* (Glazunov, 1900), and important sections of *Le Corsaire* (Adam and others, 1880) and *Paquita* (Deldevez and Minkus, 1881). NOËL GOODWIN

Petit détaché. See under *Détaché*.

Petite messe solennelle ('Little Solemn Mass'). Choral work by Rossini, a setting of the

Mass text composed in 1863. It is for soprano, mezzo-soprano, tenor, and baritone soloists, chorus, two pianos, and harmonium; Rossini arranged it in 1867 for full orchestra. The word 'petite' does not refer to the work's size, but to Rossini's too modest evaluation of its importance.

Petite Suite ('Little Suite'). Work by Debussy for piano duet, composed 1886–9. Its movements are *En bateau*, *Cortège*, *Menuet*, and *Ballet*. It was arranged for piano solo by Durand (1906), for orchestra by Büsser (1907), and for small orchestra by Mouton (1909).

Petrassi, Goffredo (*b* Zagarola, nr Palestrina, 16 July 1904). Italian composer. He studied at the Accademia di Santa Cecilia in Rome (1928–32), where he has taught since 1934. At first influenced by the neoclassicism of Stravinsky, Hindemith, and Casella, he moved on during the 1940s to a style of dense harmony and deep thought; the main works of this second period include his metaphysical opera *Morte dell'aria* (1949–50). In the early 1950s he began to use serial methods, and subsequent works avoid thematic working in favour of a vigorous, kaleidoscopic use of motifs. His development is best observed in the cycle of eight concertos for orchestra. PAUL GRIFFITHS

FURTHER READING
Fedele d'Amico: *Goffredo Petrassi* (Rome, 1942); John S. Weissmann: *Goffredo Petrassi* (Milan, 1957); Claudio Annibaldi, ed.: *Catalogo bibliografico delle opere di Goffredo Petrassi* (Milan, 1971).

Petrucci, Ottaviano (dei) (*b* Fossombrone, nr Urbino, 18 June 1466; *d* Venice, 7 May 1539). Italian music printer and publisher. He was the first to use movable type for printing polyphonic music. After an education in the humanities, probably at the court of Guidobaldo I, Duke of Urbino, he went to Venice, then an important centre for printing, in about 1490. In 1498 he obtained from the doge a 20-year exclusive privilege to print mensural music (i.e. everything but plainchant), and in 1501 he published his *Harmonice musices odhecaton A* (known as *Odhecaton* or 'Hundred Songs'), containing in fact 96 pieces, mostly *chansons* for three and four voices by Franco-Flemish composers. For this and subsequent volumes he designed and cast a music typeface of singular elegance which he combined with excellent press work; sometimes his method required three impressions, but more commonly he used only two.

Over the next eight years Petrucci made available for the first time a great deal of polyphonic music—*frottole*, Masses, motets, lute tablature—by the leading Franco-Flemish and Italian composers of the day (Josquin, Obrecht, Isaac, Brumel, Cara, Tromboncino). By 1511 he had returned to Fossombrone and continued printing there under a papal privilege until c.1520. When he returned to Venice in 1536 he concentrated on printing classical texts, leaving music to others who continued to develop his method. The success of his new printing technique and the elegance and reliability of his early publications brought him an unparalleled reputation and established him as the most significant music printer in the early 16th century.

See also *Printing and Publishing of Music*, 4.

J. M. THOMSON

Petrushka. Ballet (burlesque) in four scenes by Stravinsky to a libretto by Benois. It was choreographed by Fokine and given its first performance by Diaghilev's Ballets Russes in Paris in 1911. An orchestral suite from the ballet was first performed in Paris in 1914; it was re-orchestrated in 1947 as a suite in four parts with 15 movements. Stravinsky arranged three movements for piano (1921) and made a four-hand piano reduction of the score. Babin made a version for two pianos, and Szántó arranged five pieces into a piano suite (1922).

Petto (It.). 'Chest'; *voce di petto*, 'chest voice' (see *Voice*, 4).

Peuerl, Paul (*bapt*. Stuttgart, 13 June 1570; *d* after 1625). German composer. He worked as an organist and organ-builder in Steyr, Upper Austria, for most of his life, and from there published four volumes of instrumental suites (Nuremberg, 1611-25). The suites are made up of four dances in the pattern of a theme followed by three variations.

DENIS ARNOLD

Pezel, Johann Christoph (*b* Glatz, Silesia, 1639; *d* Bautzen, nr Glatz, 13 Oct. 1694). German composer. Between 1664 and 1681 he was a member of the Leipzig band of *Ratsmusiker*, or town musicians. He composed several works for wind and brass, mainly in the form of suites or sonatas, of which the best known are those scored for the typical town-band ensemble of cornetts and trombones.

DENIS ARNOLD

Pezzo, pezzi (It.). 'Piece', 'pieces', in the sense of a composition.

Pf., Pfte. Abbreviations for 'pianoforte'.

Pfeife (Ger.). 'Pipe'.

Pfitzner, Hans (Erich) (*b* Moscow, 5 May 1869; *d* Salzburg, 22 May 1949). German composer. Though born in Russia, he was of German parentage and was brought up and educated in Germany. The opera *Der arme Heinrich* (1895), one of his earliest works, contains hints of Wagner, but in looking back more particularly to Weber it shows his nostalgia for the midday of German romanticism. As time went on he felt increasingly that music was being undermined by the developments of Busoni, Schoenberg, and others, and he engaged in bitter polemics against modernism. His masterpiece was the opera *Palestrina* (1917), composed during his years as city music director in Strasbourg (1908-17). Through this elaborate and characterful work he argued for his view of the composer's duty to tradition, a view implicit in his Eichendorff cantata *Von deutscher Seele* (1921). During the 1920s and 1930s he taught composition at the Music Academy in Munich and received numerous honours, from the Weimar government and from the Nazis. However, he soon fell into disgrace, and he spent his last years in extreme poverty.

PAUL GRIFFITHS

FURTHER READING
Hans Pfitzner: *Gesammelte Schriften* (Augsburg, 1926-9); Walter Abendroth: *Hans Pfitzner* (Munich, 1935); Walter Abendroth, ed.: *Hans Pfitzner: Reden, Schriften, Briefe* (Berlin, 1955).

Phalèse. Flemish family of music printers and publishers. The elder Pierre Phalèse (c.1510-c.1576) became bookseller to the University of Louvain in 1542 and published scientific and scholarly books during the 1540s, as well as five books of *chanson* arrangements for lute. In 1551 he received a privilege to print ecclesiastical and secular music from movable type, and throughout the 1550s and 1560s he issued many volumes of *chansons*, dances, motets, lute intabulations, and other pieces (e.g. by Clemens non Papa, Guerrero, Lassus, and Rore). He was an accomplished printer and was the first in the Low Countries to issue parts in 'table-book' format, arranged so that performers sitting round a table could read from one copy. In 1570 he formed a partnership with the Antwerp printer Jean Bellère (1526-95), which his son Pierre Phalèse (c.1550-1629) continued, moving to Antwerp in 1581. The younger Pierre used his father's printing materials, and his extensive output includes many volumes of Italian madrigals, both anthologies and single-composer volumes (e.g. Lassus and Marenzio). His daughters Madeleine (1586-1652) and Marie (1589-c.1674) actively continued the family business in Antwerp until it finally lapsed in 1674.

J. M. THOMSON

Phantasie, Phantasy. See *Fantasia*.

Phantasiestücke (Ger.). See *Fantasiestücke*.

Philadelphia Orchestra. Founded in 1900 by Fritz Scheel, the Philadelphia Orchestra became one of America's major orchestras under Leopold Stokowski (conductor from 1912 to 1938). Stokowski experimented with orchestral sound, often performed contemporary music, and involved the Orchestra in pioneering stereo recording efforts. Under Stokowski's successor, Eugene Ormandy, the Orchestra toured and recorded extensively, reaping praise for its elegant style and opulent sonorities. In 1980 Ormandy became Conductor Laureate and Riccardo Muti was named Music Director.

MARK TUCKER

Philharmonia Orchestra. British symphony orchestra founded in 1945 by Walter Legge, primarily to make gramophone recordings. Among those who conducted the orchestra on records and in the concert hall were Karajan, Klemperer, Toscanini, Furtwängler, Strauss, and Giulini; Klemperer enjoyed a particularly close association, and was made 'conductor for life'. In 1964 the orchestra became a self-governing body under the title New Philharmonia; the 'new' was dropped in 1977. Riccardo Muti has been Principal Conductor since 1973.

Philharmonic Society. See *Concert*, 2.

Philidor. Adopted name of the Danicans, a French family of musicians. The first to use the name 'Philidor' was **Jean Danican** (*b* c.1620; *d* Versailles, 8 Sept. 1679), who played wind instruments in the *grande écurie* and was a virtuoso oboist. He had three musical sons. **André Danican Philidor** (*l'aîné*) (*b* Versailles, c.1647; *d* Dreux, 11 Aug. 1730) moved up through the hierarchy of the musical establishment to become a musician and composer in the royal chapel (he also helped to establish the Philidor Collection in Louis XIV's library at Versailles); **Jacques Danican Philidor** (*le cadet*) (*b* Paris, 5 May 1657; *d* Versailles, 27 May 1708) started like his father as a wind player in the *grande écurie* and by 1690 was a violinist in the *chambre du roi*; **Alexandre Danican Philidor** (*d* Paris, c.1700) played wind instruments in the *grande écurie*.

The third generation of musical Danicans comprised the four sons of André and four of Jacques'. The most important of them were two of André's sons. **Anne Danican Philidor** (*b* Paris, 11 Apr. 1681; *d* Paris, 8 Oct. 1728) was a flautist in the *grande écurie*, the royal chapel, and finally the *chambre*. He also held positions as *surintendant de la musique* to the Prince of Conti and director of concerts to the Duchess of Maine. He is remembered for his role as founder of the the first permanent public concert series, the Concert Spirituel.

His half-brother, **François-André** (*b* Dreux, 7 Sept. 1726; *d* London, 31 Aug. 1795), was the most illustrious member of the family. He was a page-boy in the royal chapel and studied music with Campra. At the same time he took up chess, and was to develop his skills as a player with considerable success, later becoming a professional and publishing a book, *L'analyze des échecs* (London, 1749). In 1744 he collaborated with Jean-Jacques Rousseau on a dramatic work, and subsequently began his career as a composer of stage music. His operas include *Blaise le savetier* (performed 1759), *Tom Jones* (based on Fielding's novel, performed 1765), and *L'amitié au village* (performed 1785). They range from simple *vaudevilles* to *tragédies lyriques*, and the development of the 18th-century *opéra comique* may be clearly traced in his examples of the genre (of which *Tom Jones* is the best known). F.-A. Philidor's sacred music is lost, but in 1755 he published a set of six quartets for violins, oboes, and continuo. In the troubled years preceding the Revolution, he found his musical career in France increasingly difficult, owing to his strong Royalist associations, and returned to chess. He died in London shortly after the Revolution.　　　WENDY THOMPSON

Philippe de Vitry. See *Vitry, Philippe de*.

Philippines. See *South-East Asian Music*.

Philips, Peter (*b* ? London, 1560–1; *d* Brussels, 1628). English composer. He was a choirboy at St Paul's Cathedral in 1574, but in 1582 left England because of his Roman Catholic faith. He went to the English College in Rome and entered the service of one of its patrons, Cardinal Alessandro Farnese, continuing to act as organist at the college. From 1585 he travelled for five years with the English Catholic Lord Thomas Paget, and on Paget's death in 1590 settled in Antwerp as a teacher of the virginals. In 1593 he was accused of plotting against the life of Elizabeth, and imprisoned in The Hague (while in prison he wrote his *Pavan and Galliard Dolorosa*); he was soon released, however, and allowed to return to Antwerp. His last position was in the Brussels household of Archduke Albert.

Philips was an Englishman in his keyboard music but a continental in his vocal works. Many of his virginal pieces were copied into the *Fitzwilliam Virginal Book*, and although his arrangements of Italian madrigals seem dry and over-ornate, his dances are superb, with unusual emotional power deriving from an imaginative use of chromaticism and ornament. His madrigals set Italian verse and are noted for their singability and delicate word-painting. He wrote some brilliant-sounding motets for double choir, as well as some (less successful) for solo, duet, and trio in the *concertato* manner. His neglect is probably due to the fact that 'he affected altogether the Italian vein' and has suffered the frequent fate of expatriots.

DENIS ARNOLD

Philosopher, The (*Der Philosoph*). Nickname of Haydn's Symphony No. 22 in E♭ major, composed in 1764. It was known by this name in Haydn's lifetime, in reference to the opening Adagio.

Phoebus and Pan (*Der Streit zwischen Phoebus und Pan: Geschwinde, ihr Wirbeln den Winde*: 'The Strife between Phoebus and Pan'). Cantata No. 201 by J. S. Bach to a libretto by Picander, after Ovid, satirizing a hostile music critic. It was probably composed in 1729 and is sometimes staged as an opera.

Phon. See *Acoustics*, 11.

Phrase. A short section of a work into which the music seems naturally to fall. The most frequently encountered phrase length is four bars (found regularly in folk and dance music), but shorter and longer phrases also occur. 'Phrase' is an inexact term: sometimes a phrase may be contained within one breath, and sometimes subdivisions may be marked. In notation, phrase-marks are the slurs placed over or under the notes as a hint of their proper punctuation in performance (Ex. 1; see *Slur*; *Tie* for the use of similar curved lines).

Ex. 1

A performer's phrasing, in a broader sense, is often instinctive and is one of the features by which a supreme artist may be distinguished from one of lesser inspiration.

Phrygian cadence. See *Cadence*.

Phrygian mode. The mode represented by the white notes of the piano beginning on E. See *Mode*, 2.

Phrygian tetrachord. A tetrachord (scale of four notes) made up of the first four notes of the Phrygian mode (the equivalent of the scale running from E on the white notes of the piano; see *Mode*, 2). The intervals of the Phrygian tetrachord are semitone-tone-tone (e.g. E–F–G–A), as opposed to the tone-tone-semitone of our major scale.

Piacere (It.). 'Pleasure'; *a piacere*, 'at pleasure', i.e. the same as *ad libitum*; *piacevole*, 'pleasing', 'agreeable'.

Piangendo, piangente (It). 'Weeping', 'plaintive'; *piangevole, piangevolmente*, 'plaintively'.

Pianissimo (It., often abbreviated to *pp*). Very soft indeed, the superlative of *piano*.

Piano

1. Introduction
2. The Invention of the Piano in Italy
3. Claims to German and French Invention
4. The German Development of the Instrument
5. The English Developments
6. The Three Shapes of Piano
7. The Viennese Action
8. The French Developments
9. An American Contribution—the Iron Frame
10. The Strings and Hammers
11. The Soundboard

12. The Pedals
13. The Compass of the Piano
14. 'Touch' in the Piano
15. Special and Experimental Instruments
16. Some Terms found in Makers' Catalogues
17. Early Public Appearances
18. Early Compositions for the Piano
19. Repertory
20. Four-hand Music, One-hand Music, Crossing-hand Music.
21. The Growth of Public Taste in Piano Music

1. *Introduction.* Although the piano (as it will be called throughout this article: strictly pianoforte, 'soft-loud'; often abbreviated to pf. or pfte.; Ger.: *klavier*; Fr. and It. as Eng.) has to be classed as a sophisticated form of percussion instrument (its mechanical ancestor being the dulcimer or the dulce melos), it first came into existence as a keyboard instrument under the guise of an improved harpsichord. At the opening of the 18th century the domestic keyed instruments were the *clavichord, which had high expressive qualities but was very faint in tone, and the *harpsichord, which was louder and more brilliant but was rather inflexible in tonal variety and nuance. Neither instrument produced a very long-lasting tone.

The natural desire seems to have grown up for a keyboard instrument combining the clavichord's power of accentuation, *crescendo*, *diminuendo*, and *cantabile* with the force and brilliance of the harpsichord. We find something distantly suggesting this desire expressed by the great French harpsichordist and composer François Couperin in 1713:

The Harpsichord is perfect as to its compass, and brilliant in itself, but as it is impossible to swell out or diminish the volume of its sound I shall always feel grateful to any who, by the exercise of infinite art supported by fine taste, contrive to render this instrument capable of expression.

2. *The Invention of the Piano in Italy.* As a matter of fact, unknown to Couperin, the physical means of swelling out or diminishing the volume of sound were already in existence when he wrote the above. Bartolomeo Cristofori (1665-1731) in Florence had already produced (*c.*1709) what he called a 'gravicembalo col piano e forte', i.e. a 'harpsichord with soft and loud'. For the plucking of quills of the harpsichord he had substituted hammers, and now, by greater or less force applied to the finger-keys, louder or softer sounds could be produced at will.

Cristofori's mechanism was ingenious. There was an 'escapement' by which immediately any hammer struck a string it returned, so leaving the string free to vibrate; and there were 'dampers' which, on finger-keys being released, fell at once upon the string and suppressed its vibration, bringing the sound to an immediate end (see Fig. 1).

Two, and only two, of Cristofori's instruments still remain: one (dated 1726) is at Leipzig, and the other (dated 1720) is in the Metropolitan Museum at New York. They are surviving ancestors of a progeny that has spread all over the world.

Although Cristofori is universally spoken of as the inventor of the piano there were apparently occasional experimental instruments of the piano type made before his day and then forgotten. One known example is dated 1610—a century before Cristofori. It is of Dutch origin. It has small hammers attached to the keys but no dampers. It seems to be an isolated example, resulting from a passing experimental fit on the part of some ingenious maker, and is said to have been made for a French nobleman. A manuscript of about 1440, by the Burgundian Arnault of Zwolle, mentions a similar instrument with strings and hammers but no dampers. However, it is only with Cristofori that the principle established itself.

3. *Claims to German and French Invention.* When any need is widely felt many minds set to work in the effort to find a means of meeting it, so it is a common thing to find priority of invention disputed. This priority as to the invention of the piano is now seen (apart from the isolated examples just mentioned) to belong undoubtedly to Italy, but at one time it was claimed for both France and Germany.

The French claim was based on the fact that in 1716 one Jean Marius submitted models of an instrument of the piano kind to the Académie at Paris, and the German claim on the fact that one Christoph Gottlieb Schroeter, in 1721, submitted such models (devised four years earlier) to the Court of Saxony. It will be seen that Cristofori has a priority of date to both of these, and moreover he actually made four instruments at that date, whereas Marius is not certainly known ever to have made an instrument, and Schroeter, an organist and general musical practitioner, decidedly never did.

Marius called his invention a *clavecin à maillets* ('mallet-harpsichord', or 'hammer-harpsichord'); Schroeter looked upon his rather as a developed dulcimer, having, as he said, been inspired with the idea of it by his experience of the performances of the renowned Pantaleon Hebenstreit upon the enlarged dulcimer called

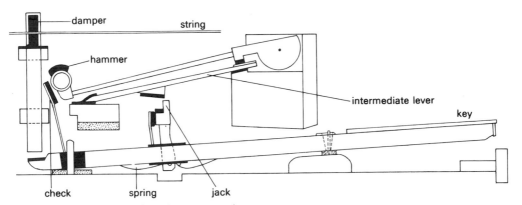

Fig. 1. Action of the Leipzig Cristofori piano, 1726.

Pl. 1. Grand piano by Bartolomeo Cristofori (Florence, 1726).

'pantaleon' (see *Dulcimer*, 2), of his invention. The relationship of the piano to the dulcimer was long kept in mind in Germany by the use of the name 'pantaleon' for certain kinds of piano.

In one respect the French and German inventions were very obviously inferior to the Italian. The French model, like the early Dutch one, possessed no dampers, so that once a string had been struck it remained sounding until the vibration had died away; and the German model had dampers which fell the moment the hammer had struck and had 'escaped', so making the sustaining of sound impossible and indeed compelling the use of a continuous *staccato*. Cristofori's hammers 'escaped' immediately they had struck their blow, but his dampers remained away from the strings until the player's finger allowed the key to rise: that has, of course, been the principle ever since. In every way, then, Cristofori is the true father of the piano as we know it.

4. *The German Development of the Instrument.* Schroeter's models seem to have led to nothing,

Pl. 2. Grand piano by Johann Andreas Stein (Augsburg, 1788).

and indeed they were not capable of leading to much. Cristofori's invention, however, was taken up in Germany and intelligently exploited by the famous organ-builder and clavichord-maker Gottfried Silbermann (1683-1753), who is thought to have first heard of it in 1725 through the appearance of a German translation of an Italian account of it. It is now considered probable that Silbermann later had access to a Cristofori instrument, since his own early piano bore such a close resemblance (e.g. that now in the Germanisches Nationalmuseum, Nuremberg).

In 1726 Silbermann made two pianos and a few years later he submitted them to Johann Sebastian Bach, who offended him by pointing out serious defects—heavy touch and weakness of the higher notes. Later instruments of his Bach was able to praise, and it is on record that when in 1747 Bach visited Frederick the Great at Potsdam he played upon Silbermann pianos, of which the king possessed a number.

All pianos up to this point were of the harpsichord shape—what we now call the 'grand', with the strings horizontal and in a line with the finger-keys.

5. *The English Developments.* The wars of the mid 18th century and especially the Seven Years' War (1756-63) drove many German workmen to England. Among these was one of Silbermann's pupils, Zumpe, who, on coming to London, at first worked for the great Swiss-born harpsichord-maker Tschudi (or Shudi) and then set up for himself and became famous all over Britain and France as the inventor and manufacturer of the so-called 'square' (really oblong) piano, which he introduced about 1760. The account given by Dr Burney connects the English development with the settling in London, in 1762, of J. C. Bach, who was famous as a pianist. He says:

After the arrival of John Chr. Bach in this country, and the establishment of his concert, in conjunction with Abel, all the harpsichord makers tried their mechanical powers at pianofortes; but the first attempts were always on the large size, till Zumpe, a German, who had long worked under Shudi, constructed small pianofortes of the shape and size of the virginals, of which the tone was very sweet, and the touch, with a little use, equal to any degree of rapidity. These, from their low price and the convenience of their form, as well as power of expression, suddenly grew into such favour, that there was scarcely a house in the kingdom where a keyed-instrument had ever had admission, but was supplied with one of Zumpe's pianofortes, for which there was nearly as great a call in France as in England. In short he could not make them fast enough to gratify the craving of the public. Pohlman, whose instruments were very inferior in tone, fabricated an almost infinite number for such as Zumpe was unable to supply. Large pianofortes afterwards receiving great improvement in the mechanism by Merlin and in the tone by Broadwood and Stoddard, the harsh scratching of the quills of a harpsichord can now no longer be borne.

Zumpe's square piano was later greatly improved by Shudi's son-in-law and former workman John Broadwood (1732-1812), who became his partner and then successor. At this period the London makers were among the finest in Europe.

Great numbers of English pianos were imported into the USA in the period following the revolution. The Shudi-Broadwood firm shipped quantities to John Bradford of Charleston, South Carolina. Early American makers were John Brent (*fl.*1774), Johann Behrent (1775; perhaps the same as the last-named), John Belmont (1775), Charles Jarvis (1785), and James Juhan (1786); all were in Philadelphia, which seems to have been the first great centre of the manufacture in the USA.

Fig. 2 shows an English grand action, *c.*1790.

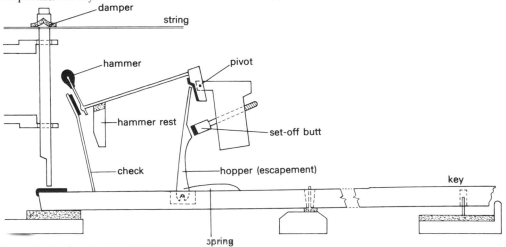

Fig. 2. Action of an English grand piano, c.1790.

6. *The Three Shapes of Piano:* (*a*) *The Square (or Table) Piano.* This conveniently shaped instrument (actually rectangular, not square) was the principal domestic keyboard instrument from the time of its invention (early 1740s) to about 1830 when it was gradually supplanted by the upright (see below, *b*). It is alleged to have been invented by an Italian pupil of Silbermann's, Christian Ernst Friederici, but the earliest known instrument extant today is one of four-and-a-half-octave compass by a south German maker, Johann Söcher, and is dated 1742. In appearance the square piano superficially resembles the clavichord, the recessed keyboard being set into one of the long sides of the rectangle, and the strings lying in a horizontal position down the length of the case, roughly at right angles to the keys. Mechanically, the early square was extremely simple, and even Zumpe's elegant models possessed neither a check to catch the rebounding hammers nor an escapement action, though some of them possessed the earliest known mechanism for raising the dampers *en bloc* (the forerunner, therefore, of the damper pedal of today). This device was worked by two handstops, the one operating the bass dampers up to the middle of the keyboard, and the other operating only the treble dampers. The curious effect caused by leaving these dampers off for a whole section of the music (or at least until one of the player's hands was free to bring them into action again) would have been far less offensive with the delicate resonances of the early square piano than it would be with any present-day instrument.

During the first quarter of the 19th century the square piano held a dignified place in the musical world. Fine examples by Broadwood, Tomkisson, and Clementi were made and sold all over the world. The English makers had the discernment to see that the instrument, though small, could be of very high quality. Their products were more sophisticated than Zumpe's and usually had a single (damper) pedal, normally operated by the left foot. It was customary to play the instrument with the lid closed.

After the middle of the century, the square piano became obsolete and was usually only to be found either in private ownership or in the salerooms of antique dealers, often minus strings and action, and reduced to menial functions, acting for instance as a sideboard, dressing-table, or, at a later date, a cocktail cabinet. During this ignominious period of its existence it frequently was further insulted by being described as a 'spinet'.

By the 1950s the square began to be evaluated at its true worth (indeed sometimes more than its true worth) and it is now greatly sought after by musicians, and by all those interested in the world of antiques.

(*b*) *The Upright Piano.* Another form of piano had been experimented with in Austria, Germany, and England—the upright piano, in which the strings ran perpendicularly. The necessary practical adjustments required by this form, for mechanical success, were made in 1800 by Isaac Hawkins of Philadelphia, and in the same year by the Viennese maker Matthias Müller. The idea of an upright keyboard instrument goes back to the 'clavicytherium' (see *Harpsichord*, 2) of the 15th century, and attempts at an upright piano had been made by several makers, notably Friederici, whose 1745 instrument can be seen today at the Musée du Conservatoire Royale de Musique, Brussels.

The Hawkins-type instrument was followed by various rival designs, the English maker Robert Wornum being the first to patent a small upright piano with strings reaching to the ground. This model appeared in 1811 and was perfected in 1829; it formed the basis for the whole future development of the instrument.

It was the perfecting of the upright type (called 'cottage piano', 'piccolo piano', 'pianino', etc.) that, after the middle of the 19th century, drove the once popular square piano from the field.

(*c*) *The Grand Piano.* This instrument, the earliest type of all, is the only one that not only persists today but seems to be unshakable; other types only maintain a domestic footing on the ground of smaller cost and smaller space required. Constructionally the 'grand' has certain definite advantages. The soundboard of the grand is in a better position for sonority, not being placed, as is usually the case with that of an upright, against a brick wall but parallel to a wooden floor and at an acoustically suitable distance from it; the dampers fall by gravity and not by spring and are hence more efficient.

It will be realized that the three shapes of piano mentioned all had their prototypes in the harpsichord family: the harpsichord proper supplied the model for the grand; the virginal for the square (though the latter has more in common with the clavichord); and the clavicytherium, or erect harpsichord, for the upright.

7. *The Viennese Action.* It should be noted that a distinct type of instrument became associated with Vienna (though it originated in south Germany), the makers Stein and Streicher (Stein's son-in-law) being prominent in its development. The action was different from the English and French types, the touch lighter and the tone less sonorous.

In the Viennese piano, the hammer was pivoted in a sheath (Ger.: *Kapsel*) fixed to the key, with the leather-covered hammerhead

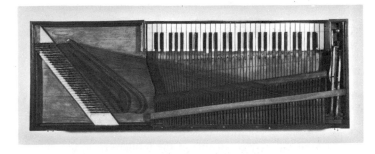

Pl. 3. Plan and general views of a square piano by Johannes Zumpe and Gabriel Buntebart (London, 1770).

pointing towards the front of the instrument. The butt end of the hammer, which was beak-shaped (Ger.: *Hammerschnabel*), slotted into a bouncing-rail (Ger.: *Prelleiste*) at the back of the case, and the hammer was freed and flung upwards as the 'beak' escaped from the bouncing rail. The strings and the soundboard were both thinner than their counterparts on the contemporary English model, and the tone was delicate but clear and distinctive. There was little resonance once the finger had left the key—in marked contrast to the English piano which produced a lingering 'halo' of resonance even when the damper pedal was not being employed. On the Viennese piano of Mozart's day the effect we describe today as the damper pedal was worked by a knee-lever, this being the intermediate stage between Zumpe's handstop and the present-day sustaining pedal.

Fig. 3 shows a south German and Viennese grand action.

8. *The French Developments.* As already stated, there is no evidence that Marius, claimed as one

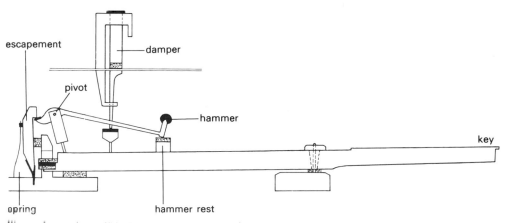

escapement

damper

pivot

hammer

key

spring

hammer rest

Fig. 3. Action of a south German/Viennese piano, 1700.

of the inventors of the piano, ever actually made anything more than models of his proposed action. It is usually considered that no piano was actually made in France for 60 years after this, i.e. until 1777, when Sébastien Érard (1752–1831) made a square piano in imitation of the English instruments. Érard worked for some time in London, where he established a branch in 1786; he adopted the 'English action' for his grand pianos, but soon introduced an action of his own, with means for easy and quick repetition: a 'double-escapement' which marked a definite step on the road towards the present-day action. (This important development was first tried out in 1808 but not fully patented until 1821.) The grand piano of today owes perhaps more to Érard than to any other single craftsman.

Pleyel (the composer, performer, and pupil of Haydn) was another important Paris maker of that period, and founded the firm which, long after (in 1931), was amalgamated with that of Érard. (The Érard and Pleyel pianos are now manufactured in Braunschweig by Wilhelm Schimmel.)

A characteristic of French pianos today is a markedly 'thinner' tone than that of German and British pianos. This is apparently a matter of national taste. The German and British makers have striven unceasingly for greater resonance, regarding 'fullness' or 'roundness' as one of the principal criteria of perfection, sacrificing both clarity and colourfulness in some degree as the inescapable acoustic price.

9. *An American Contribution—the Iron Frame.* Vital improvements subsequent to those already mentioned have largely depended on the strengthening of the framework of the instrument. How necessary strength is in this part of the instrument will be realized when it is stated that the strings of the very largest grands of today may have an aggregate 'pull' of as much as 20 tons, with the requisite weight of framework to stand it—times have changed since Zumpe's porter used to carry the instruments to the homes of London purchasers on his back.

A pioneer in the introduction of iron in piano construction was John Isaac Hawkins, an Englishman resident in Philadelphia, whose upright piano (see above, 6) had a full iron frame. Alpheus Babcock, also of Philadelphia, made further improvements in 1825, as did Conrad Meyer of that city in 1832 and Jonas Chickering, of Boston, in 1837; and in 1855

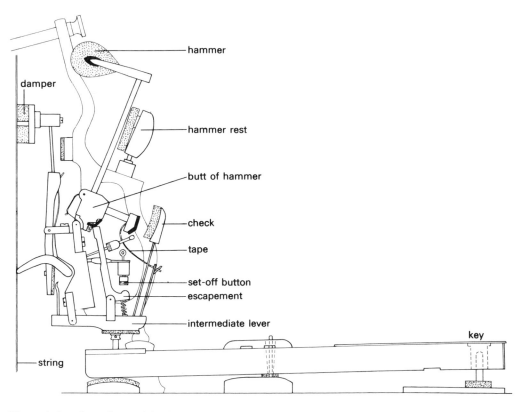

Fig. 4. Action of a modern upright piano.

Steinway & Sons of New York made such an advance as constituted one of the landmarks in the history of piano-making. Largely, then (but by no means completely), the successful application of iron to the framework of the piano is due to American invention and enterprise. The Steinway principle was first exemplified in a square instrument (1855), but the next year (1856) the firm made its first grand, incorporating the first full iron frame cast in one piece. Previously iron frames were cast in separate pieces then bolted together—some had just consisted of wooden frames with iron bars added. Iron is the best metal existing for the skeleton work of the piano since it shrinks least on cooling after casting (about one per cent); the fine adjustment of spaces and sizes in a piano is of the highest importance, and even this small shrinkage has to be very accurately allowed for in the design of an instrument. The casting of a piano-frame is, indeed, one of the most delicate operations in foundry practice. The fuller tone of the modern piano is largely due to the use of thicker wire, such as on the old tension would have given much too low a pitch. Brought up to the standard pitch of today, the tension would have laid the old wooden frame in ruins before all the strings were on.

Figs. 4 and 5 show modern grand and upright actions.

10. *The Strings and Hammers.* The pitch of a string depends upon its length, its diameter, the density of its metal, and the tension to which it is submitted. The tension of a single string today may be 180 to 200 lbs; the enormous total of tension sometimes reached has already been mentioned. The diameter varies from $\frac{1}{30}''$ to $\frac{1}{4}''$ (including the copper coiling on the bass strings). The stress on the frame can be distributed by 'overstringing', i.e. one large group of wires is made to cross another group more or less diagonally—a method introduced with the object of providing a requisite length of string and at the same time enabling instruments to be constructed of reasonable height (in the 'upright' shape) or length (in the 'grand' shape). Of even more importance is the fact that overstringing allows the bass bridge to be positioned nearer to the central, more resonant part of the soundboard, thus improving the quality of the bass notes. The principle seems to have been first adopted in the piano about 1835, but there had been occasional overstrung clavichords.

The harpsichords of the 18th century, with their different registers, had of course more than one string to a note, and Cristofori's piano had, like the average clavichord, two strings to each note throughout the compass. The piano of today has on average 26 bass notes with copper-wrapped strings, the lower 13 having one string to each note, the remainder two strings to each note. The remaining notes throughout the compass each have three unwrapped steel strings apiece. (The number of covered strings varies with each manufacturer, and with different sizes of instrument. On the larger concert grands, for instance, three covered strings are used for a certain number of notes in the covered string section.)

The general principle is obvious: the higher we proceed up the instrument the less resonance a string possesses, hence the increase in the number of strings towards the treble. Even with their three strings the very highest notes of all (ending with a mere 2″ of sounding length) have so little resonance that no dampers are provided.

There have been at different times examples of attempts to introduce pianos with four or even five strings to a note. Beethoven's last instrument, lent him by the Viennese firm of

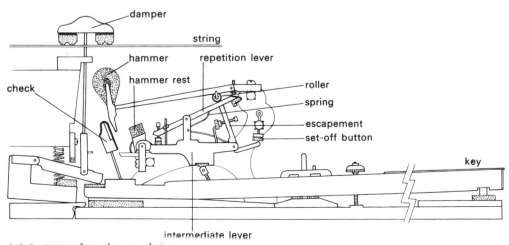

Fig. 5. Action of a modern grand piano.

Graf, was of this type. Many years later Broadwood & Sons made a number of grands with four strings to each note in the extreme treble, but the practice was discontinued, probably because four strings occupy so much more horizontal space than three that only very thin strings can be employed, and there is therefore no gain in tone-quality or quantity. A fourth string is still used by the firm of Blüthner (see below, 16, *Aliquot scaling*).

The length of the strings is not strictly proportioned to their pitch; if it were, the lowest bass strings would make the instrument far too long for any ordinary room. As above explained, length is only one of four factors controlling pitch and it is largely by an adjustment in the other three that the deeper pitches are obtained. The reason for the copper coiling just mentioned is to increase the mass of the string without too greatly reducing its flexibility.

The striking surface of the piano hammer is made of wool felt. It is the soundboard, string tension, quality of hammer felt, and the over-all design of the instrument that determines the quality of tone the piano will produce. In the final analysis, it is the hammer felts that are adjusted, either softened or hardened, to produce the correct and even level of sounds. The harder the felt, the harsher or louder the tone; the softer the felt, the more mellow the sound.

The making of piano hammers is an independent trade, the felting of them being a very special process. Piano manufacturers, in the main, do not make their own hammers, nor do they make their own actions, this also being a specialized trade. There are, however, some exceptions, two examples being the English firm of A. Knight, who make their own hammers, and the Japanese firm of Yamaha, who make both hammers and actions. One fact of present-day manufacture is that constant demands for brilliant concert grands with a tone able to fill vast concert halls has resulted, regrettably, in a much harder type of hammer felt being used than formerly.

11. *The Soundboard*. The strings would produce little tone were it not for the soundboard or belly—the broad expanse of wood which lies under them in a grand or behind them in an upright. It fulfils the same function as the body of a violin and is connected with the strings in the same way, i.e. they press upon a wooden bridge attached to the soundboard, which in turn presses upon them. The soundboard is strengthened by wooden bars, the position of which has been carefully calculated.

It seems curious that no application of the idea of a double soundboard, box-like as that of the bowed instruments, has ever proved successful. It was tried by Broadwood as early as 1783.

As everybody knows, a violin gains in beauty of tone with years, so that the oldest violin is (other things being equal) the most desirable. Pianos deteriorate with age. The difference comes, it is said, almost purely in the soundboard. The shape of the violin soundboard is permanent; time brings no loss of tone in that quarter. The shape of the piano soundboard, which is at first somewhat arched, tends to be bent back into flatness by the pressure of the strings, communicated (by the very long bridge) to its whole breadth. The board does not then bear against the body of strings as it should; the delicate adjustment of the two pressures, one to another, which has been a matter of elaborate care on the part of the designer of the instrument, is increasingly disturbed. As better means are discovered of strengthening the soundboard without adding to its rigidity, this defect should disappear. The strings, mechanism, felts, leathers, and wooden parts of the action also deteriorate with age.

12. *The Pedals*. The 18th-century harpsichord had made use of certain pedals for various purposes and it was natural to apply the device to the piano. Some applications have been mere gimmicks, as, for instance, that fairly common in the early 19th century which brought into action drum and cymbal effects, to be employed in playing Turkish marches and the like.

(*a*) *Sustaining Pedal*. Pianos today never have fewer than two pedals, frequently with a third. Of the two commonest pedals the more important is the right-hand, sustaining, or damper pedal, originally known in Viennese pianos as the 'forte stop'. (The term 'loud pedal' is now greatly discredited among piano teachers.) Originally worked by a handstop (see above, 6) and later by a knee-lever (mentioned in a letter of Mozart's dated October 1777), the device was redesigned as a foot-pedal by Broadwood in 1783. Its function is to remove the whole series of dampers from the strings, whereas depressing a finger-key removes the damper only from the strings of one note. The consequence of this complete removal are twofold: first, any note played is given longer duration, irrespective of whether the finger remains on the key (allowing beautiful effects such as two hands on a keyboard could not otherwise compass); and second, all the strings of the instrument are made available for sympathetic resonance on principles explained elsewhere (see *Stringed Instruments*, 6). The harmonics of a string are then enriched by the resonance of other strings in the harmonic series, and the tone becomes much fuller. A greatly increased power is obtained, when desired, by means of this pedal, but its effects are as much used in soft as in loud passages, and indeed a good modern player generally keeps his foot positioned over the right pedal as it is an essential part of his expressive equipment. It is, of course, important in most styles of music to release this pedal and depress it afresh at a change of harmony, so as to avoid the confusion of overlapping chords.

The sustaining pedal has naturally much greater influence over the lower notes of the instrument than over the higher, both because the longer strings, with their greater amplitude, are capable of a longer-lived tone, and because there are so many other strings higher up the compass which are capable of being awakened to sympathetic resonance.

When 'Ped.' or any similar sign occurs, this is the pedal intended: the sign to release it is usually printed as an asterisk. It does not always follow that the pedal is not to be lifted between the two signs; the player has to use his discretion, based on a sound knowledge of harmony and on constant and careful listening.

From the evidence of early printed editions of Mendelssohn and other composers, it seems possible that the early 19th-century pianists still regarded the pedal as a special effect (comparable to an exotic stop on the harpsichord) and used it only for certain 'romantic' passages. It was used more by players of English pianos (which had in any case a richer pedal resonance) than by the protagonists of the Viennese instruments—so much so that in 1830 Kalkbrenner, the composer and pianist, wrote: 'The use of the pedals is scarcely known in Germany'. It soon became an essential feature, however, in the music of Schumann, Chopin, and Brahms, and it achieved totally new dimensions under the French Impressionist composers.

(*b*) *Sostenuto Pedal.* It is obvious that the lower strings of a piano require more 'damping' than the higher, and if the pedal, after being lifted, be depressed again quickly it will be found that the lower strings are still sounding. This effect, known as 'half-pedalling' (or by some teachers as 'half-damping'), is facilitated by the sostenuto, or middle, pedal, which is attached to most pianos made in the USA and Canada, and to most of the larger grands made elsewhere. (It was perfected by Steinway in 1874.) This operates an apparatus which catches any dampers already raised (i.e. dampers of notes being temporarily held down by the fingers) and maintains those dampers only in their raised position until the sostenuto pedal is released. Thus one may sustain, for example, a long bass note (or chord) while changing harmonies at another pitch of the instrument. The device is

especially useful in Impressionist music, and may of course be used in conjunction with the normal damper pedal. Berio, in his *Sequenza IV* for piano, used the sostenuto pedal to create contrapuntal effects.

(*c*) *Soft Pedal.* This may act in one of several ways: (i) in 'grands', by moving keyboard and hammers sideways, so as to leave unstruck one string of each note; (ii) in 'uprights', by moving the whole set of hammers, in their position of rest, nearer to the strings, so that when any of them are brought into action they give a less powerful blow; or (iii) by interposing a piece of felt between the hammer and strings.

The last device, known variously as the Buff, Harp, *Jeu céleste*, Moderator, or Sordino, was very popular on early 19th-century Viennese pianos and is again in use today on reproductions of these instruments. However, method (i), the true *una corda*, was the one preferred by Beethoven, and became the standard model, as the printed signs for its use and disuse prove (*una corda* meaning 'one string' and *tre corde* 'three strings').

13. *The Compass of the Piano.* Of the two existing specimens of Cristofori's instruments, one has a compass of four octaves and the other of four-and-a-half. This compass was gradually increased. Mozart's concert grand piano, now in the Mozarteum at Salzburg, has five octaves. In 1790 Broadwood made the first piano with five-and-a-half octaves, and in 1794 the first with six octaves. Liszt in 1824 was still playing, in Paris, on an Érard with six octaves, and the works of Schumann and Chopin required nothing beyond six-and-a-half octaves. The present usual compass is seven-and-a-quarter octaves. Some small uprights are still made with only six or seven octaves. Extra notes are added to the bass of some large grands (notably Bösendorfers) to give a compass of seven-and-three-quarters or even eight octaves.

The inconvenience of the too-short compass of Beethoven's time can be seen in certain of his sonatas, where a long ascending passage will appear in two ways, according to its key (as, for instance, in the exposition of a movement and in its recapitulation), breaking back upon itself before its ascent is concluded when in the higher key, but ascending unbroken when in the lower key. In such instances it is surely permissible, on the modern piano, to play rather what Beethoven wished than what he wrote, and modern editors often observe this principle, which Liszt, with the increased compass of his later years, was the first to practise; however, the principle cannot be blindly carried out, as sometimes Beethoven, compelled to adopt an altered shape of passage, has introduced a new effect which should not be sacrificed.

Pl. 4. Liszt playing a piano by the Viennese maker Conrad Graf, painting (1840) by Joseph Danhauser; the other figures in the painting are (left to right) Alexandre Dumas, Victor Hugo, George Sand, Paganini, Rossini, and the Countess Marie d'Agoult.

14. *'Touch' in the Piano*. The word has two distinct meanings. As applied to the instrument it means the weight of the resistance of the finger-keys to the fingers, and as applied to the performer it means the manner in which he operates the finger-keys—a manner 'heavy' or 'light', varied or unvaried. Using the word in the first sense, it may be said that the touch of the piano from its earliest beginnings became gradually heavier as more power was sought. The better makes of instruments today have even graduated resistances from 53 g. for the lower bass notes to 45 g. for the higher treble notes (calculated without the weight of the dampers). The resistance of the dampers should in fact be slight as the key is already in motion when it encounters the resistance of the damper. Nevertheless, in some pianos the player senses a 'lightening' of the touch on the undamped notes at the top of the compass.

Piano manufacturers work with so many different action designs that to an expert each one could be said to have an individual 'feel' to it. Many professional pianists today like to work with a strong key resistance, and indeed have extra resistance added to the touch of the piano they habitually practise on.

15. *Special and Experimental Instruments*. The number of modifications of the piano that have been brought into existence without establishing themselves is enormous. Following the precedent of the harpsichord, pianos with more than one keyboard were early produced—Mozart played one, by Tschudi of London, in 1765. There have been many attempts to produce a piano with longer sounds or sounds of

unlimited duration. Most of these have involved the application of a revolving wheel or other imitation of a violin bow in place of hammers (see *Hurdy-gurdy*, 6), thus abandoning the real piano principle.

Sir Charles Wheatstone, the inventor of electric telegraphy, in 1836 attempted to secure duration by the device of a small aperture at the end of each string through which passed a current of air tending to keep the string in vibration after the hammer had left it.

An absurd invention of Daniel Hewitt, patented in 1854, provided for the saving of the expense of a piano framework by attaching the strings to the wall of a house.

A patent of the Pleyel firm provided for the performance of music for two pianos by building two grands as one, the two triangles fitting into one rectangle and players facing one another from opposite keyboards.

There have been many pianos made with tuning-forks or metal bars in place of stretched strings—these are sometimes known as mini-pianos (an imprecise term at the best of times), or dulcitones. They are in fact a kind of *celesta, with an excessively colourless tone (being grossly deficient in upper harmonics). But they have the advantage that they need no tuning!

It has also been common to combine other instruments with the piano, for instance percussion instruments (see above, 12). In 1722 the Paris organist Balbastre brought out a combined piano and flute; this probably meant the playing of a one-stop organ from the same keyboard. The poet Mason, in 1755, writes of buying in Hamburg a clever combination of harpsichord and piano. The London maker Merlin in 1774 introduced a two-keyboard combined harpsichord and piano, and a combination of clavichord and piano has also been attempted. Quarter-tone pianos have been made for the performance of contemporary music, and one such instrument, with three keyboards, was constructed in the 1920s by August Förster of Georgswald and is to be seen in the National Museum in Prague today.

An extremely robust type of instrument was in 1940 introduced by the London firm of Alfred Knight and brought into use in Army canteens during the Second World War. Some of its innovations were described as follows:

The lid has a double slope like a housetop so that no drinks can be stood on it. For a similar reason the lid of the piano has no level part. The woodwork above the pedals is reinforced with brass plates to receive kicks. The wood itself is solid oak with rounded corners for the mutual protection of heads, shins and the piano frame. Keyboard ends are made of copper to counteract smouldering butts. The ivory surfaces are bevelled so that they cannot be picked off. The instruments are also made to withstand tropical weather and danger in transit.

Various experiments have been made of late years in the production of piano tone from stringless instruments by electronic devices operated from a piano keyboard, and there are various types now in production. The totally electronic instrument produces piano tone by electronic circuits. This instrument is the shape of a small oblong box with a compass of about five octaves, and is easily portable. The keyboard is the only part of the mechanism that resembles a piano.

Another type of instrument retains the shape of a small upright piano. It has a keyboard, and a modified action with hammers that strike metal bars, the ensuing vibrations being amplified and heard through loudspeakers. There is no soundboard. The instrument is designed only for personal use, and the player uses earphones which are supplied with the instrument.

There have been, and still are, many 'pedal pianos'—pianos with playable pedals like those of an organ. Their chief use is for practising organ music, but Schumann, Alkan, Boëly, and others have written compositions for such instruments. (For the pianola and all forms of mechanically operated pianos, see *Mechanical Musical Instruments*, 8.)

16. *Some Terms found in Makers' Catalogues.*

Aliquot scaling: an arrangement whereby the weak upper notes of the instrument have each an extra free string, tuned to the octave above the proper pitch and acting, as 'sympathetic' strings on certain older bowed and plucked string instruments did, by mere resonance. In this way a fuller tone is obtained. (Compare *Duplex scaling*, below.) This device is the speciality of the Blüthner firm.

Baby grand: simply a grand piano on a small scale—normally under 5′ in length. The smaller the instrument the greater are the problems of design and durability. In this type of piano the soundboard is obviously smaller, the strings shorter and heavier. Some very small grands are not fitted with roller action but with a simplified type of action that requires much maintenance to keep it in correct condition. From the player's angle, the short keys on the baby grand have an adverse effect on the touch.

Barless: applied to the grand piano, iron frames made to be sufficiently strong and rigid without the usual strengthening bars believed to be inimical to tone (e.g. Broadwood).

Boudoir grand: a grand piano 6′ in length.

Cabinet piano: a tall type of upright piano invented by William Southwell in 1807 with an improved version of the English 'sticker action'. The strings were placed vertically and reached to the ground. The front was frequently filled in with pleated silk. (Now usually only to be found in the antique market.)

Concert grand: a grand piano of the largest size, 9′ long or over.

Console piano: this term is used by some American manufacturers for a type of miniature instrument.

Cottage piano: a term often loosely used to describe a small upright. Originally various attempts were made to create a smaller domestic upright than the cabinet or the giraffe piano, and these culminated in the so-called cottage piano (originally named the 'harmonic piano') first made by Robert Wornum in 1813. It was vertically strung, stood between 4′ and 5′ high, and proved very popular in English homes for many years. Later models saved further space by cross-stringing.

Double iron frame: an upright piano with a second iron frame at the rear of the upright instrument replacing the normal wooden beams. This design allows the piano to be made with a slimmer outline (e.g. Monington and Weston).

Diaphragmatic soundboard: a soundboard that is tapered gently from its centre, thickest part to its outer edges, producing a freer and more unified vibration (e.g. Steinway).

Duplex scaling: a system whereby those two portions of the strings that are normally dumb (i.e. on each side of the main or vibrating portion) are left free to vibrate also, and so arranged as to length that they correspond with, and thus (by sympathetic resonance) strengthen, some of the harmonics of the main portion. (See *Aliquot scaling*, above.)

Fully overstrung: maximum cross-stringing to secure the greatest string length possible, and therefore the greatest fullness of tone.

Full trichord (or tricord): three strings to each note (except the lowest ones).

Giraffe: the tall upright piano of Viennese origin, popular in the early 19th century, built in Empire style with the right-hand side following the ascending line of the lengthening strings and finally ending in a scroll at the top left-hand corner; the scroll obviously suggested the name. The piano attained a height of $7\frac{1}{2}$′–8′, was fitted with a down-striking action, and had at least four pedals, sometimes six. It is rarely found in England but is common in German and Austrian

Pl. 5. Giraffe piano by Van der Hoef, Amsterdam (early 19th century).

museums. One made by Van der Hoef can be seen at the Victoria and Albert Museum, London.

Hexagrip pinblock: this refers to the tuning-plank (or wrest block) made from laminated hardwoods, each lamination at a different angle, giving a better grip to the tuning-pin and thus making for more stability (e.g. Steinway).

Oblique: a term applied to upright pianos which have the strings running at an angle instead of perpendicularly, so as to secure greater length. The difference in fullness of tone as compared to the pianos with straight stringing is really very slight.

Overdamper: the term applies to uprights that have the dampers above the striking hammers, which results in poor damping. This design is no longer made.

Roller action: this is now considered the best type of

grand action, for control and for a generally sensitive touch, and is now used by all the leading makers.

Spinet: sometimes used misleadingly of a small upright or of a square piano.

Straight strung: old type of instrument with no cross-stringing. Over- (or cross-) stringing on grands was universally adopted by about 1870, but many upright models, normally the cheaper sort, continued to be manufactured with straight-stringing until as late as 1915.

Underdamper (i): upright models have dampers below the striking hammers, the design now used by all manufacturers.

Underdamper (ii): some French grands (e.g. Érard) were made with the dampers under the strings held against them by springs. The damping thereby acted at a point where the amplitude of vibration was great and therefore the damping was immediately effective.

Upright grand: this term has meant different things at different periods. The first patent for an upright of this type was Landreth's in 1787 (no surviving examples of this instrument). In 1785 William Stodart brought out his upright grand 'in the form of a bookcase', a model greatly praised by Haydn. In appearance it was like a rectangular cupboard set on a four-legged stand. It had two pedals, *una corda* and damper. The strings ran upwards vertically from keyboard level and the unoccupied space on the right, above the short treble strings, provided shelves for music storage. The model was copied by Clementi and others but became obsolete about 1825. The term 'upright grand' today usually means a large, over-strung upright with all improvements.

Yacht piano: a small upright with a fold-away keyboard.

17. *Early Public Appearances* . The first piano heard in Britain is said by Burney to have been made by an English monk in Rome, Father Wood, for Burney's friend Samuel Crisp, who brought it back with him. The date of his return does not seem to be known (probably *c*.1760 or earlier), and there seems to be some possible claim to priority on the part of another friend of Burney, the poet Mason (see above, 15).

The first public performance on the piano, so

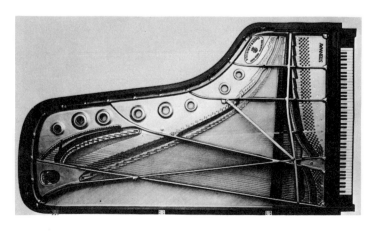

Pl. 6. Plan view of a modern concert grand piano by Steinway, New York.

far as is known, took place at Covent Garden Theatre a few years later, in 1767, when it was announced that Dibdin would use, in the accompaniment of a song, 'a new instrument called piano-forte'.

The following year, 1768, saw what are believed to be the first British appearances of the instrument in a public solo way, the performers being Henry Walsh, in Dublin, on 19 May 1768, and two weeks later, in London, J. C. Bach. The latter, who resided in London for the rest of his life (d 1782), contributed much to the popularization of the instrument (there is evidence in his banking account, which Dr Sanford Terry searched, of his buying a piano of Zumpe in the very month before this concert, the price being £50; we may suppose, then, that the instrument was a 'square').

Clementi set out from London for a European concert-tour (Paris, Strasbourg, Munich, Vienna) in 1781, and Messrs Broadwood's books show that they shipped to Paris for him both a harpsichord and a piano. In Vienna he met Mozart and, at the instigation of the Emperor Joseph II, competed with Mozart in performance; both played pianos and as a part of the entertainment they improvised on them in duet.

As already stated, the piano reached France via England. There is mention of the sale of a piano in Paris in 1759 (probably a solitary imported specimen), but the first recorded appearance does not seem to be until 1768, when a Mademoiselle Lechantre played at the Concert Spirituel a 'clavecin [i.e. harpsichord] forte-piano'. This was one year after the instrument's first public appearance in England. The next year (1769) a boy of nine, son of Virbès, organist of St Germain-l'Auxerrois, played under the same auspices a 'new instrument with hammers a sort of harpsichord in the form of those of England'. The father had made this instrument and it had been described in the press three years earlier (1766).

It is not known when the piano was first imported into the USA, but in 1771 Colonel Robert Carter, a Virginian landowner, purchased one to add to his instrument collection, and in the same year Thomas Jefferson countermanded an order for an English clavichord, demanding a piano instead.

In 1775 Behrent of Philadelphia (see above, 5) proclaimed that he had 'just finished an extraordinary instrument by the name of Pianoforte, made of mahogany, being of the nature of a Harpsichord, with hammers and several changes'. Philadelphia also figures as the venue for an early appearance of the piano on the concert platform. In 1786 the pianist Reinagle apparently played a 'Sonata Piano Forte' of his own, as well as one curiously described as being 'by Haydn and Reinagle'.

18. *Early Compositions for the Piano.* It took the piano just about a century (from its birth to *c.*1800) to oust the harpsichord and clavichord, for the piano was only slowly subject to improvements and the older instruments were in their full perfection. Enthusiasm for the piano in the 19th century did eventually succeed in wiping the harpsichord off the slate completely for a period of about 80 years. (The last Kirckman harpsichord is thought to have been made in 1809 and the first 'revival' harpsichord by Pleyel in 1888.)

The piano came to be considered as the final product in keyboard history and the most suitable medium for the entire repertory, and this point of view prevailed in most quarters until the 1960s, when a growing appreciation of the earlier instruments (harpsichord and clavichord) began to influence the selection of recital material and many pianists tended to leave the Baroque repertory to the instruments for which it was originally created.

The earliest-known compositions for the piano are the work of an Italian, Luigi Giustini di Pistoia, who published in Florence, in 1732, '12 Sonate da Cembalo di piano e forte detto volgaramente dei martellati' ('12 sonatas for the soft and loud harpsichord commonly called the one with hammers').

The growth of the popularity of the piano synchronized almost exactly with the growth of the new 'homophonic' school of keyboard composition. Bach and Handel, contrapuntists and heroes of the fugue and suite, used the harpsichord or clavichord, and though Bach (certainly) and Handel (possibly) played the piano on occasion, neither wrote a note for it; Bach's sons, and Haydn and Mozart, in the epoch of the Classical sonata, used the piano increasingly. Bach's ninth son, Johann Christoph Friedrich, wrote a sonata (*c.*1757) described on its title-page as 'for pianoforte or harpsichord', and this ambiguous labelling persisted in keyboard music until well into the 19th century. (Beethoven's sonatas, up to and including Op. 14, were described as being 'for harpsichord or pianoforte' and from Op. 22 to Op. 27 No. 2 (the so-called 'Moonlight' Sonata) they were advertised as being 'for pianoforte or harpsichord'.)

We may say, then, that for over 40 years composers seemed to take little account of the differing qualities and capabilities of the two instruments, but from the middle of the century we do find the distinctive powers of the piano increasingly recognized, first by the sons of Bach (and in particular the works of C. P. E. Bach whose style evolved from the expressive clavichord), and later by Clementi, whose sonatas were published in London from 1773 onwards.

Mozart was acquainted with the piano from his boyhood and his later sonatas (and Haydn's also) and above all his concertos obviously take account of its special powers. But it was Beethoven who really set the piano on a new path. His music from the first, however labelled, is obviously piano music (with the possible exception of the three early 'Bonn' sonatas in E♭, F minor, and D, written in 1783 in the composer's 14th year).

In Schumann and Chopin we have two composers who expressed themselves, the one largely and the other practically entirely, through the medium of the piano, and nobody looking at any page of their keyboard music could imagine that it was written for any other instrument.

It can be said of the history of the piano that the instrument really came before the world was ready for it, and that only towards the end of the 18th century did it become identified with current new styles—first with Classical sonata form and later with expressive Romantic music.

Another point worth noting is that many eminent players of the piano and composers for it have also been manufacturers (e.g. Clementi, Kalkbrenner, Pleyel, Herz): this cannot have been without effect in the simultaneous development of the three techniques of piano playing, piano composition, and piano manufacture, and the adapting of each of them to the suggestions of the other two.

19. *Repertory*. The repertory of the piano is larger than that of any other instrument and it is infinitely varied. Until recently it was considered to include all the music written for the clavichord and harpsichord family. Although these instruments are now part of the regular concert scene and in consequence many pianists leave the earlier repertory out of their recitals and begin their programmes with the Viennese classics, this does not alter the fact that for the purposes of general study young pianists are taught the clavichord and harpsichord repertory (e.g. the 48 Preludes and Fugues of Bach) as an integral part of their training.

The following list (which includes the repertory of the earlier instruments) gives the names of merely the outstanding composers of the repertory and barely enters on the difficult discrimination necessary when the names of living composers are introduced.

The English 16th- and Early 17th-century 'Virginal' Composers: Byrd, Bull, Gibbons, Farnaby, Tomkins, etc. developed the technique of keyboard composition and performance by writing variations (usually at that time described as 'divisions') on popular song and dance tunes. The linked pairs of dances (e.g. pavan and galliard, alman and coranto) produced some very brilliant keyboard writing, while the contrapuntal fantasias often based on a slow-moving central theme (*cantus firmus*) borrowed from plainchant, developed into a learned style suitable to players of serious tastes and of high intellectual ability.

The Late 17th-century and Earlier 18th-century Clavichord and Harpsichord Composers:

England: Blow, Purcell, Croft, and later Handel and Arne.

France: Chambonnières, Louis Couperin, François Couperin, Rameau, Duphly.

Italy: Frescobaldi, Cimarosa, Domenico Scarlatti.

Germany: Froberger, Buxtehude, J. S. Bach.

Most of the foregoing wrote suites, of various lengths and styles. Frescobaldi wrote sets of variations (called 'partite') and toccatas. Bach's harpsichord music included suites (sometimes called 'partitas'), toccatas, preludes and fugues, and sets of variations. Domenico Scarlatti wrote short single-movement compositions called sonatas but in no way resembling the later sonatas of the Classical period.

The Later 18th-century Composers: C. P. E. Bach, Mozart, Haydn. They developed the Classical form of the sonata, in several movements, with at least one in what we call sonata (or 'first movement') form. Their works span the transitional period from harpsichord/clavichord to piano.

Late 18th- and Early 19th-century Study and Sonata Composers: Hummel, Clementi, Cramer, Czerny, Dussek, Beethoven, Schubert, Weber, Field.

Clementi, Beethoven, and Schubert wrote many sonatas, the last two carrying the form and spirit of this type of music to their highest point. Clementi and Cramer wrote much technical practice material ('Studies'; Fr.: *Études*); Schubert many pieces in smaller one-movement forms (impromptus, *Moments musicaux*, waltzes, etc.); Field introduced the nocturne.

The Mid 19th-century Composers: Chopin, Schumann, Mendelssohn, Liszt, Franck, Alkan. These composers developed the Romantic qualities of the piano and its virtuosic side, the Études of Chopin and the *Transcendental Studies* of Liszt probably reaching the highest degree of technical brilliance ever achieved on the instrument. Though Chopin and Schumann each wrote three sonatas, Liszt one, and Mendelssohn four, they each made on the whole a greater contribution to the one-movement style of work, ranging from the four great Ballades of Chopin to the smaller miniatures of which Chopin's Préludes, Nocturnes, Polonaises, and Mazurkas, Schumann's *Noveletten*, and Mendelssohn's Songs without Words are examples. Schumann wrote strings of such pieces with a connected idea (*Carnaval*, *Papillons*, etc.); Liszt wrote Hungarian Rhapsodies and many fantasias on operatic arias and other popular music. Franck's rather solemn pianistic style is obviously transplanted from the organ, while Alkan wrote music of an exotic nature and of unparalleled technical difficulty.

The Late 19th-century Composers: Brahms, Grieg, Fauré, Saint-Saëns, Balakirev, Albéniz, Granados, Skryabin, Medtner, Reger. Essentially they wrote

Romantic music which followed logically on the music of the previous groups. A new feature was the strongly national element in the music, for instance, of Grieg (Norway), of Balakirev (Russia), and of Albéniz and Granados (Spain). Fauré's original but very French style led directly to the French Impressionists.

Early to Mid 20th-century Composers: Debussy, Ravel, Satie, Milhaud, Poulenc, Ireland, Bax, Berkeley, Tippett, Falla, Turina, Villa-Lobos, Dohnányi, Bartók, Webern, Berg, Hindemith, Szymanowski, Lutosławski, Rakhmaninov, Prokofiev, Shostakovich, Kabalevsky, Khachaturian, Cowell, Ives, Barber. With this period the character of piano music branched into many widely differing schools. Debussy and Ravel developed the delicate qualities of the instrument in the so-called Impressionistic style. Satie, Milhaud, and Poulenc in different ways exploited its witty and bizarre characteristics. All were to some extent influenced by American jazz. The English composers of this period wrote for the most part in a continuation of the Romantic style, mingled with other influences—English folk-song, for instance, and French Impressionism (the latter especially applies to the music of John Ireland). The Spanish national idiom was developed by composers like Falla and Turina, and the Brazilian Villa-Lobos. With Bartók national music took a new turn. He used both the percussive and expressive qualities of Hungarian music to create a sharply original style, in which irregular rhythmic patterns based on the Hungarian language and modal scale-foundations both played a significant part. The 'Bartók sound' is equally unmistakable whether in the many short pieces of his piano-teaching method *Mikrokosmos* or in the larger-scale works like the sonata for piano solo, the three piano concertos, or the sonata for two pianos and percussion.

A very different approach to piano music was taken by the Second Viennese School, represented mainly by Schoenberg and Webern (the two sonatas of Alban Berg being early works and post-Romantic in character). Schoenberg's incisive and angular style is built on serial techniques, though occasionally it makes a distant bow in the direction of the 18th-century Classical idiom. Webern's short serial pieces are full of learned devices—themes played backwards and forwards simultaneously, inverted into mirror images, etc. Among the academic works of this period, Hindemith's fugal *Ludus tonalis* also plays an important role. A very substantial addition to the repertory came out of Eastern Europe, from the Polish composers Szymanowski and Lutosławski, and the Russian school, of whom the most significant were Prokofiev, who wrote nine sonatas, and Shostakovich, who wrote two, besides 24 preludes and fugues, one for every key.

In the USA, as might be expected, there have been courteous acknowledgements to the jazz world (as in Barber's *Excursions*), but also more radical innovations, as in the works of Charles Ives and Henry Cowell, both of whom were early on the scene experimenting with aleatory techniques (i.e. allowing the player a certain degree of choice in what he plays, usually from a given set of alternatives). Ives was one of the earliest exponents of 'sound effects' on the piano, striking clusters of notes with the palm, fist, or forearm, and plucking, stopping, or stroking the strings with the fingers.

The Mid 20th Century: Messiaen, Boulez, Stockhausen, and on the American scene Aaron Copland, John Cage, Elliott Carter, and Roger Sessions. Olivier Messiaen's piano music stands apart from the main trends of the century. Infinitely colourful and often very virtuosic, his works are extremely precisely notated and annotated—the player is instructed to employ as many as 12 different 'touches' and seven different dynamic levels in a given work. The notation of pieces expressing birdsong is ornithologically very accurate and approaches as near to the actual sounds as is possible in musical terms. Though the style has some affinity with French Impressionists, it is far less evocative and more imitative than Debussy and is very far indeed from the aleatoric and 'chance' elements as exemplified by the music of Stockhausen, Cage, and others.

In 1938, Cage was the first to use the 'prepared piano', an instrument in which nuts, screws, bolts, felt and rubber pads, coins, or splinters of wood are variously inserted between certain strings. The result produced a new set of tonalities, some purely percussive, some microtonal. The influence of Zen Buddhism led him later (1951) to experiment with chance elements (tossing corn-stalks, etc., to determine choice between different alternatives) and to make a feature of silence, which, he stated, was never absolute, sound of some kind being always present.

Boulez and Stockhausen have both extended the piano repertory in new directions, evolving their own language and notation. Reaction against the strict serialism of their early works brought them both to use 'mobile forms' (movements and sections played in different order and sequence) and the practices of 'controlled chance' in performance. (Boulez's belief is that a work is never completed but remains open to continuous creation and alteration at every performance.) On a purely pianistic level, Stockhausen's *Klavierstücke* ('Piano Pieces') introduce many new effects, both with percussive techniques and with pedal sonorities. To sum up, it can be said that the piano after a brief period of temporary eclipse in the 1920s and 1930s has again resumed its role as the composer's instrument, and become an essential medium of much new music today.

20. *Four-hand Music, One-hand Music, Crossing-hand Music*: (a) *Four-hand Music*. The earliest known keyboard music for two players at one instrument is Nicholas Carlton's 'A Verse for Two to Play on one Virginal or Organ' (in the Tomkins manuscript in the British Library, dating probably from the late 16th century). In the same volume is 'A Fancy', also for two players, composed by Thomas Tomkins.

The earliest such music to be printed appears to be the single movements occurring in the 15th *ordre* of Couperin (1722) and apparently intended for three hands at one keyboard instrument (though the instrument has to be a two-manual harpsichord, the two upper parts overlapping to such an extent that they could not be executed on a single keyboard). The

MUSIC OF CHANGES

John Cage

THE RHYTHMIC STRUCTURE, 3·5·6⅜·6⅜·5·3⅜, IS EXPRESSED IN CHANGING TEMPI (INDICATED BY LARGE NUMBERS)(BEATS PER MINUTE). A NUMBER REPEATED AT THE SUCCEEDING STRUCTURAL POINT INDICATES A MAINTAINED TEMPO. ACCELERANDOS AND RITARDS ARE TO BE ASSOCIATED WITH THE RHYTHMIC STRUCTURE, RATHER THAN WITH THE SOUNDS THAT HAPPEN IN IT.

THE NOTATION OF DURATIONS IS IN SPACE. 2½ CM = ♩. A SOUND BEGINS AT THE POINT IN TIME CORRESPONDING TO THE POINT IN SPACE OF THE STEM OF THE NOTE (NOT THE NOTE-HEAD). IN THE CASE OF A SINGLE WHOLE NOTE THIS STEM-POINT IS IMAGINED BEFORE THE NOTE (AS), IN THE CASE OF ADJACENT-IN-PITCH WHOLE NOTES, BETWEEN THEM (AS), IN THE CASE OF A GLISSANDO, IN THE CENTER OF THE DURATION INDICATED. A STACCATO MARK INDICATES A SHORT DURATION OF NO SPECIFIC LENGTH. A CROSS (+) ABOVE AN ♪ OR AT THE END OF A PEDAL NOTATION INDICATES THE POINT OF STOPPING SOUND AND DOES NOT HAVE ANY DURATION VALUE. FRACTIONS ARE OF A ♩ OR OF 2½ CM.

PEDALS ARE INDICATED: ⌐___ = SUSTAINING; ⌐___ = AFTER THE ATTACK, SUSTAINING OVERTONES, ⌐___ = UNA CORDA; ⌐___⌐ = SOSTENUTO.

NOTE:

ACCIDENTALS APPLY ONLY TO THE TONES THEY DIRECTLY PRECEDE. ♦ (A DIAMOND) A KEY DEPRESSED BUT NOT SOUNDED. TONE-CLUSTERS ARE NOTATED AS IN THE WORK OF HENRY COWELL.

DYNAMICS ARE BETWEEN ffff AND pppp. ACCENTS ARE INDICATED BY A LOUDER DYNAMIC FOLLOWED BY A SOFTER ONE; E.G. ff>mf IS A ff SOUND ACCENTED LESS THAN ff>p.

IT WILL BE FOUND IN MANY PLACES THAT THE NOTATION IS IRRATIONAL; IN SUCH INSTANCES THE PERFORMER IS TO EMPLOY HIS OWN DISCRETION.

'Notations refer to what is to be done, not what is to be heard', John Cage. The first page of 'Music of Changes' by John Cage, and his instructions for performance.

sequenza IV

luciano berio

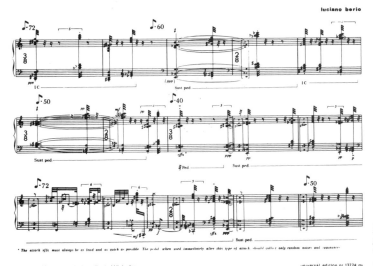

universal edition nr 13724 m

New resonances from the sustaining pedal. The opening of 'Sequenza IV' for piano by Luciano Berio.

3. The Banshee

Henry Cowell
(1925)

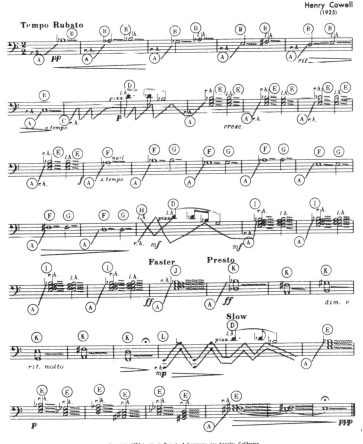

AMP-95611

'The Banshee' by Henry Cowell. 'The Banshee' is played by stroking the open strings of the piano with the fingers, hand, or nail, glissando fashion, the beginning and end of each 'stroke' being determined by the printed alphabetical letters. The sustaining pedal is depressed throughout 'third hand' may have been a part entrusted to a beginner, for it is usually a simple drone. (Bull's 'A Battle and No Battle—Phrygian Music', written about a century earlier, has a similar disposition.)

In England, the earliest printed example of keyboard duets seems to be Burney's 'Four Sonatas or Duets for two performers on one Pianoforte' (1777), while Theodore Smith's nine sonatas (Berlin) follow three years later. But before these composers published their work a good deal of duet music probably existed in manuscript.

Mozart and his sister, when in England in 1764–5, did much duet-playing in public (the early Sonata in C, K 19d is of this vintage), and the greatest period of piano duet compositions may be said to have begun with Mozart and ended with Schubert, some of whose works in this genre are of symphonic proportions. Duet-playing continued to be a popular domestic pastime throughout the 19th century and during the first two-thirds of the 20th, especially in France, and many composers, e.g. Chopin, Brahms, Schumann, Liszt, Weber, Grieg, Dvořák, Tchaikovsky, Rakhmaninov, Fauré, Bizet, Debussy, Ravel, Satie, Poulenc, Reger, Bax, Walton, and Rawsthorne, made felicitous additions to the repertory. The idea that this form of music-making was an amateurish, or even slightly juvenile, activity has been dispelled, over the 1960s and 1970s, by a real appreciation of this fine branch of chamber music, and by the playing of some first-rate professional teams.

Mention should also be made of the numerous arrangements, from Haydn's symphonies onwards, of orchestral works, either for two pianos or for piano duet—more frequently for the latter. Indeed, the piano duet in the 19th century was the main medium through which most amateurs became acquainted with symphonic music.

The earliest known composition for two keyboard instruments is Giles Farnaby's piece 'For two Virginals' from the Fitzwilliam Virginal Book. Pasquini, Le Roux, François Couperin, Dandrieu, J. S. Bach, Handel, W. F. Bach, and Padre Soler all left works for two harpsichords, and Bach, of course, both composed and arranged works for two, three, and four harpsichords and orchestra.

Mozart wrote two sonatas and a fugue for two pianos, and a double concerto for two pianos and orchestra.

During the whole of the 19th century and into the early years of the 20th much good music appeared for two pianos: Schumann, Brahms, Arensky, Reger, Rakhmaninov, Ives, Bartók, Milhaud, Hindemith, and Shostakovich were among those who contributed. The best-known works for the medium are perhaps Brahms's Variations on a Theme of Haydn, Schumann's Andante and Variations, Rakhmaninov's Suite No. 2 in C, Bartók's Sonata for two pianos and percussion, and Milhaud's popular suite *Scaramouche*.

The American George Crumb composed *Makrokosmos II* for two pianos and percussion and Charles Ives wrote three pieces for two pianos tuned a quarter of a tone apart.

Concertos for two pianos are rare: Mozart, Dussek, Liszt, Milhaud, Poulenc, Stravinsky, and Vaughan Williams have each contributed one.

(*b*) *One-hand Music.* A considerable amount of music has also been written for one hand: as practice material for pianists in general; as a *tour de force* of composition; or for the use of one-armed players, who have sometimes shown themselves capable of surprising execution. Some examples are the following:

Kalkbrenner: a Sonata for left hand. Skryabin: a Prelude and Nocturne for the same. Brahms: arrangement of the Bach Chaconne (from the D minor Violin Suite) for left-handed pianist. Janáček: a Capriccio for left hand and wind quintet. Ravel, Prokofiev, Franz Schmidt, and Erich Korngold: concertos for left-hand pianists. Richard Strauss: *Parergon*, a concerto-like treatment of themes from his *Sinfonia domestica*. Britten: Diversions on a Theme, for left-hand pianist and orchestra. Bax: Concertante for the same. Demuth: a Concerto and *Legend* for the same. Alkan wrote music for the right hand alone.

Some of these works were commissioned by the Austrian Paul Wittgenstein (1887–1961) who lost his right arm in the First World War.

Perhaps the most famous one-armed pianist was the Hungarian Count Zichy (1849–1924), a pupil of Liszt and an active recitalist and composer; his compositions include a book of studies for left hand alone, to which Liszt contributed a preface.

(*c*) *Crossing Hands.* The device of crossing hands was probably first used by John Bull in his 'Walsingham' Variations. It was introduced by Rameau in various movements from his book of harpsichord pieces of 1724, most dramatically in *Les cyclopes*. Domenico Scarlatti used the device frequently, as did Soler. In Bach it seldom occurs, though it appears in the Gigue from the Partita No. 1 in B♭, and in certain of the Goldberg Variations. In later piano music it is a common and convenient device. It should not be confused with the technique of the 'pièces croisées' written by Couperin and other French 18th-century composers, in which the hands remain crossed on the two manuals of a double harpsichord throughout a whole movement. The dazzling effect of hands crossing swiftly on the keyboard is undoubtedly partly visual.

21. *The Growth of Public Taste in Piano Music.* The courtly milieu of the harpsichord kept its repertory at a certain level of taste. The piano, being the first keyboard instrument to be mass-produced, became part of a much wider and shallower culture and, alongside its classical repertory, acquired a large selection of really worthless music. Some of this was easy meat technically (pot-pourris of popular operatic airs etc.) and intended for domestic consumption; some of it was virtuoso music of dubious value intended to dazzle an enthusiastic but undiscriminating public. Though concerts on the whole were rather longer in the 19th century than most audiences will endure today, it was thought wise to split up substantial works with lighter items between the movements—Clara Schumann, for instance, would sometimes interpolate short bravura pieces between the movements of a Beethoven sonata, while the greatest lion of the pianistic world, Franz Liszt, used to build his recital programmes out of an extraordinary jumble of components (song arrangements, operatic overtures, extemporizations on popular airs, etc., every one of them being either arranged or composed by himself).

By the early years of the 20th century a gradual change of taste had taken place; programmes tended to be more substantial, often consisting of a Bach work, a Viennese sonata, and a fairly comprehensive group of Chopin and/or Schumann and Liszt in the second half, with a handful of Debussy *préludes* thrown in for good measure. This change was due to many factors, one being the growing diversity of popular entertainment (music hall, cinema, etc.), which hived off much of the public and left a 'hardcore' of more serious music-lovers. (In Liszt's day the piano recital commanded a vast audience of 'fans', the like of which is found today only in the world of pop music or at football matches.) The trend towards 'serious' music was fostered by many far-seeing musicians—as random examples one could quote Sir Charles Hallé, who presented the first complete series of Beethoven sonatas in 1830, and Harold Samuel, who was the first to give a whole week of Bach recitals at the Wigmore Hall in the early 1920s. Centenary celebrations have helped—few Haydn sonatas were heard in piano recitals before 1932 (the bicentenary of Haydn's birth). But the greatest factor is probably the continuous progressive influence of radio and recording—two of the greatest educative forces in the modern musical world.

RUTH DYSON/GEORGE MENHENNICK

FURTHER READING
Rosamund Harding: *The Pianoforte: its History traced to the Great Exhibition of 1851* (Cambridge, 1933, rev. edn 1978), Arthur Loesser: *Men, Women and Pianos: a Social History* (New York, 1954); Rice Harris: *The

Piano: a Pictorial Account of its Ancestry and Development (Newton Abbot and London, 1975); Cyril Ehrlich: *The Piano: a History* (London, 1976); C. F. Colt: *The Early Piano* (London, 1981); Dominic Gill, ed.: *The Book of the Piano* (Oxford, 1981).

Piano (It., often abbreviated to *p*). 'Soft'.

Piano à queue (Fr.). Grand piano.

Pianola. See *Mechanical Musical Instruments*, 8c.

Piano quartet. An ensemble of four players, usually piano, violin, viola, and cello, or a work written for them to perform.

Piano quintet. An ensemble of five players, usually piano, two violins, viola, and cello, or a work written for them to perform. However, the most famous piano quintet, Schubert's 'Trout' Quintet, is scored for piano, violin, viola, cello, and double bass.

Piano score. See *Score*.

Piano trio. An ensemble of piano and two other instruments, usually violin and cello, or a work written for them to perform.

Pianto (It.). 'Lament', 'plaint'. Monteverdi's famous *Lamento d'Arianna* was subsequently set to sacred words as the *Pianto della Madonna*.

Piba. A Chinese four-stringed lute. See *Chinese Music*, 4e.

Picardy third. See *Tierce de picardie*.

Picchi, Giovanni (*fl.* early 17th century; *d* Venice, 1643). Italian composer and organist. Little is known of his life except that he was organist of S. Maria Gloriosa dei Frari, Venice, from before 1607 until his death. He composed lively dances for keyboard, using consecutive fifths quite freely, and he warned players that the dissonances, largely resulting from embellishments, were intentional. One of his toccatas was copied by Francis Tregian into the *Fitzwilliam Virginal Book*.   DENIS ARNOLD

Picchiettato, picchiettando (It.). 'Knocked', 'knocking'. Term used in connection with the bowing of string instruments to mean detaching the notes. See *Spiccato*.

Piccinni, Niccolò [Nicola] (*b* Bari, 16 Jan. 1728; *d* Passy, nr Paris, 7 May 1800). Italian opera composer. His father was a musician and his mother the sister of Gaetano Latilla. Piccinni is said to have been taught by Leo and

Piccinni

Durante at the Neapolitan Conservatorio di S. Onofrio, but the evidence for this is a little sketchy. However, he certainly composed an *opera buffa* for a Naples theatre in 1754, and he belongs to the circle of composers working there known as the Neapolitan school. In 1760 he composed his best-known opera, *La Cecchina, ossia La buona figliuola*, for Rome; the libretto, by Goldoni, was based on Richardson's novel *Pamela, or Virtue rewarded*, and the work was a great success. Thereafter, Piccinni had a prolific career, composing up to six operas a year; he combined this activity with appointments at Naples Cathedral and the royal chapel.

This success continued until Piccinni was invited to Paris in 1776. There the anti-Gluck faction engineered a silly quarrel by arranging matters so that both composers composed operas on the same subjects: Piccinni's *tragédie lyrique*, *Roland*, was begun before Gluck's, who abandoned his setting, and was produced to some public acclaim in 1778; on the other hand, Gluck brought out his *Iphigénie en Tauride* two years before Piccinni's opera on the subject, with the result that the latter was eclipsed (Piccinni was not helped by having an Iphigénie who drank, and the work was nicknamed *Iphigénie en champagne*). In general, however, Piccinni remained well liked in Paris.

He was forced to return to Naples by the outbreak of the Revolution, but there he was treated badly because his son-in-law was suspected of being a Jacobin, and he eventually returned to Paris in 1798. He was granted a pension by Napoleon, but none the less died in financial straits. The 'war' of the Piccinnists and the Gluckists has tended to obscure the fact that Piccinni was indeed a worthy composer of both comic and serious opera. *La buona figliuola* approaches Mozart's *opere buffe* in its lively ensembles and strong characterization, while *Didon* (1783) is by no means to be despised as serious opera after the manner of Traetta, rather than of Gluck. DENIS ARNOLD

Piccolo. An instrument pitched an octave above the flute. See *Flute, 6*.

Pictures from an Exhibition (*Kartinki s vystavki*). Suite for solo piano by Musorgsky, composed in 1874. It is a musical representation of 10 pictures at a memorial exhibition for the Russian artist Victor Hartmann (who died in 1873) with a 'promenade' as a linking passage. The pieces are *The Gnome*, *The Old Castle*, *Tuileries*, *Bydło* (Polish farm cart), *Unhatched Chickens*, *Samuel Goldenberg and Schmuyle*, *Market Place at Limoges*, *Catacombs*, *Baba-yaga* ('The Hut on Fowl's Legs'), and *The Great Gate of Kiev*. There are several orchestral versions, by Ravel, Henry Wood, Stokowski, and Elgar Howarth (brass and percussion) among others.

Pied (Fr.). 'Foot' (used in connection with organ stops). See *Organ, 1a*.

Pieno, piena (It.). 'Full'; *organo pieno*, 'full organ'; *coro pieno*, 'full choir' (as opposed to passages for soloists); *a voce piena*, 'with full voice'. See also *Ripieno*.

Pierné, (Henri Constant) **Gabriel** (*b* Metz, 16 Aug. 1863; *d* Ploujean, Finistère, 17 July 1937). French composer. He studied composition with Massenet and the organ with Franck at the Paris Conservatoire (1874–82), winning the Prix de Rome. He returned from Italy to succeed Franck as organist of Ste Clothilde in Paris (1890–8) but then concentrated on conducting and composition. As conductor of the Colonne concerts (1910–32) he was responsible for the first performance of Debussy's *Images*, among many other works. His own compositions range from light pieces to substantial oratorios, operas, and chamber works, and show a fertile imagination at work in a basically Franckian style. Apart from the appealing 'Marche des petits faunes' from his ballet *Cydalise et le chèvre-pied* (1923), however, his music has been largely forgotten. PAUL GRIFFITHS

Piero [Magister Piero] (*fl.* mid 14th century). Italian composer. He was active in Milan and Verona, and would have known Giovanni da Cascia and Jacopo da Bologna. His surviving works are written in the typical forms of the period, the two- and three-part madrigal and the pictorial, canonic *caccia*. JOHN MILSOM

Pierrot lunaire ('Moonstruck Pierrot'). Work, Op. 21, by Schoenberg for female voice, flute, piccolo, clarinet, bass clarinet, violin, viola, cello, and piano, composed in 1912. It is a cycle in three parts, each containing seven songs which are settings of poems by Albert Giraud translated from French into German by O. E. Hartleben. The singer has to use the technique of *Sprechgesang*, or 'speech song'.

Pijper, Willem (b Zeist, 8 Sept. 1894; d Leidschendam, 19 Mar. 1947). Dutch composer. He studied composition with Johan Wagenaar at the Utrecht Music School and then worked as a music critic. Subsequently he was co-editor of the magazine *De muziek* (1926–33), a teacher at the Amsterdam Conservatory (1925–30), and principal of the Rotterdam Music School. He had a notable influence on Dutch music as a teacher and also through his compositions, in which he favoured thick, polytonal harmonies, aggressive rhythms in rapidly changing metres, and the use of a 'germ cell' technique by which each piece was developed from a small melodic or harmonic unit. His works include two operas, three symphonies and many other orchestral works, songs, and a large body of chamber music.

PAUL GRIFFITHS

Pikieren (Ger.). To play *spiccato*.

Pilgrim's Progress, The. Opera (morality) in four acts by Vaughan Williams to his own libretto based on Bunyan's allegory (1674–9, 1684), but with Christian's name changed to Pilgrim. The work was completed in 1949, revised 1951–2, and first performed at Covent Garden in 1951. Act 4 scene 2 is *The Shepherds of the Delectable Mountains*, Vaughan Williams's pastoral episode performed in 1922. He also composed incidental music (some of it later incorporated into the opera) for a BBC production of *The Pilgrim's Progress* in 1942. His Fifth Symphony (1938–43) uses themes from the opera, which at that time he did not expect to finish.

Pilkington, Francis (b c.1565; d Chester, 1638). English composer. He took the Oxford B.Mus. in 1595, and spent his later life as a singer and minor canon of Chester Cathedral, becoming precentor in 1623. He published two books of competent, rather than highly individual, *Madrigals and Pastorals* (London, 1613, 1624), but is better known for a collection of exquisite lute-songs (London, 1605) which set some beautiful verse; 'Rest sweet nimphes' especially is a miniature masterpiece.

DENIS ARNOLD

Pincé (Fr.). 'Pinched'. 1. French term for *pizzicato*, but used only occasionally. 2. Old term for the *mordent*; *pincé renversé*, a *trill*; *pincé étouffé*, an *acciaccatura*. 3. Sometimes used to mean *vibrato*.

Pineapple Poll. Ballet in one act and three scenes to music by Sullivan arranged by Mackerras, to a libretto by John Cranko based on W. S. Gilbert's Bab Ballad *The Bumboat Woman's Story*. It was choreographed by Cranko and first performed in London in 1951. A concert suite has been arranged from the score.

Pini di Roma ('Pines of Rome'). Symphonic poem by Respighi, composed in 1923–4. Its four sections are entitled 'Villa Borghese', 'A Catacomb', 'Janiculum', and 'Appian Way'. The score includes a nightingale on a gramophone record.

Pinto, George Frederick (b London, 25 Sept. 1785; d London, 23 Mar. 1806). English composer and violinist. Taking his mother's name rather than that of his father, Saunders, Pinto was the grandson of Thomas and Charlotte Pinto, the latter of whom had, as Charlotte Brent, been a leading coloratura soprano and the mistress of Thomas Arne. Inheriting his grandfather's gifts (Thomas had been leader of the Drury Lane orchestra under Arne), Pinto soon became a pupil of Salomon and had played a violin concerto in public by 1796. Friendship with John Field drew him towards the piano and it is for these two instruments, alone or in combination, that all his surviving instrumental music was written. The music is astonishingly mature both emotionally and harmonically, the nearest parallel being with Schubert; but it appears to be the product of isolated genius, and, despite its unassailable merit, it exerted no discernible direct influence, for Pinto was dead—'a martyr to dissipation'—by the age of 21. His published music (carelessly engraved, doubtless in reflection of the original manuscripts) soon disappeared from general currency. Pianists will find much of interest in the three-movement sonatas in E♭ minor and A major of Op. 3, and that in C minor dedicated to Field (all 1803), and violinists in the unaccompanied duos in F and A major (Op. 5, 1805); of less interest are the violin and piano sonatas, the former often being cast in an archaically subordinate role. The songs (or canzonets), all for single voice and piano, are uneven, but at their best (e.g. *The Distressed Mother* and *A Shepherd Loved a Nymph*, from Six Canzonets, 1803) contain music both dramatic and lyrical, of considerable depth and melodic freshness.

ROBIN LANGLEY

Pipe and Tabor. A pipe and a drum played together by one person. The couple belongs chiefly to western Europe, played for folk dances from southern Spain and neighbouring parts of Portugal, up to the Basque regions, the Balearic Islands, Provence in France, and (up to about 1900) in southern England for the Morris dances in which it is now revived. In the Americas it is met in rural Mexico, having been introduced by the Spaniards.

1. *The Pipe.* This is a *flageolet with three holes, played by the left hand while the right beats the tabor, this being suspended from the left arm or shoulder. It is quite easy to play a scale on an ordinary tin whistle with one hand, using the lower three holes only (blocking up the rest) by starting on the overblown second harmonics, e.g. D to G, then repeating the sequence, blowing harder, for the third harmonics lying a fifth higher, A to D. A tabor pipe makes the scale in the same way except that the highest of the three holes is placed on the back for the thumb. The end of the pipe is then gripped between the third and the little fingers. Tunes may need a note or two more than the octave, obtainable as fourth harmonics; Ex. 1 shows the scale for the common 12″-long pipe in D, sounding two octaves higher than the notes shown.

Ex. 1

(1)   2   3   4

The English Morris pipe is of this pitch, 12″ in length with a cylindrical bore of *c*.8.5 mm. and made in two joints. Today there are efficient manufactured versions which are virtually tin whistles in D but with the tabor-pipe holes instead of the usual six. In some of the Oxfordshire villages it was considered important for the Morris to be played on pipe and tabor even if country dances were played on violin or concertina. Among the tunes for the Morris were 'Shepherd's Hey', 'Constant Billy', 'Three Meet', and 'Highland Mary'. The Provençal pipe, *galoubet*, resembles the English and is heard especially in the autumn *farandoles* danced through the vineyards; Bizet quotes one of the tunes (on piccolo) in his *L'Arlésienne* suite. In Catalonia the leader of the *sardana* bands plays a very small pipe, with a very small drum to match.

2. *The Tabor.* This traditionally resembles a side-drum in having two heads and a gut snare. Most are fairly small (the English 9″ in diameter), but the Provençal *tambourin* has a shell up to 30″ deep, and the snare lies across the upper drumskin; the player beats on the centre of this snare, giving to it a strong vibration which sustains the sound between one stroke of the stick and the next, almost as if it were a drone. In Medieval pictures, in England and Flanders also, one sees the player striking on the snare in this way. (For folk dancing nowadays other kinds of drum may serve for the tabor, e.g. a small-sized *tom-tom.)

It is interesting that, although one might think the pipe more difficult to play than the drum, it is the latter which occupies the right hand; and that from the Middle Ages (when the pipe and tabor were heard in all ranks of society) up to today in France the player is named from the drum—'taborer' (Fr.: *tambourinaire*)— while tunes in pipe-and-tabor style by Rameau and others are called *tambourins*. It is as though the drum beat, giving the time to the dancers,

Pipe and tabor with marion-ettes, in London, engraving (c.1835).

was felt to be the primary component of the music. Similarly, the earliest apparent mention of the instruments in the late 13th-century treatise of Aegidius of Zamora (Spain) tells how a *tympanum* ('drum') makes sweeter music when joined with a *fistula* ('pipe').

3. *History*. Through the earlier centuries the pipe and tabor were played all across western Europe. In the Renaissance period the pipe could be fairly large: a well-preserved example found in the wreck of the *Mary Rose* at Spithead (1545) measures 18″. Arbeau's *Orchésographie* (*c*.1588) illustrates such a large pipe along with simple tabor beatings for the various dances, among them (as a pavan) the well-known tune in Ex. 2, here set in four parts with the title 'Belle qui tiens ma vie'.

Ex. 2

Some of the French Basques use, instead of the drum, the *tambourin à cordes* or 'string drum' (locally *tun-tun*): a long wooden sound-box with five or six thick gut strings hit with a short thick stick. The strings are tuned to the keynote of the pipe and its dominant (compare the drones of the *hurdy-gurdy and *hagpipe).
ANTHONY BAINES

Piqué (Fr.). 'Pricked'. Term used in the bow-ing of string instruments to mean *spiccato*.

Pirates of Penzance, The. Comic opera in two acts by Gilbert and Sullivan. Produced: Paignton, Bijou Theatre, 30 December 1879; New York, New Fifth Avenue Theatre, 31 December 1879; London, Opera-Comique, 3 April 1880; Vienna, Theater an der Wien, 1 March 1889. Frederic (ten.) has been appren-ticed to a pirate crew, but at 21, is now freed from his indentures. Duty binds him to bring his former colleagues to justice—but it is revealed by his nurse Ruth (mezzo) that Frederic was born in a leap year, on 29 February, and his real age is thus only five and a half. Meanwhile, Frederic has fallen in love with Mabel (sop.), daughter of Major-General Stanley (bar.). A band of cowardly policemen attempt to overrun the pirates, but are them-selves captured. However, the police sergeant (bass) invokes loyalty to the Queen, and all the pirates yield. With the final revelation that the pirates are actually 'sons of noblemen who have gone wrong', Major-General Stanley is happy for them to marry among his many daughters, and Frederic gets his Mabel.

Piroye, Charles (*b* ? Paris, 1668-72; *d* ? Paris, 1717-30). French composer. He was a pupil of Lully and served as organist to several churches in Paris from the 1690s to 1717. His works include *airs*, organ pieces, and an oratorio, *Jephté* (1703), which is of some importance in the French history of that genre.   DENIS ARNOLD

Pisador, Diego (*b* Salamanca, 1509-10; *d* ? Salamanca, after 1557). Spanish vihuelist and composer. In 1552 he published an anthology of vihuela music which includes intabulations of sacred and secular music by Gombert, Josquin, Mouton, Willaert, and others, as well as his own music, which is mainly improvisatory in style but includes some attractive songs.
DENIS ARNOLD

Piston, Walter (Hamor) (*b* Rockland, Maine, 20 Jan. 1894; *d* Belmont, Mass., 12 Nov. 1976). American composer. After early art studies he turned to music and went to Harvard Univer-sity, graduating in 1924. He then spent two years in Paris as a pupil of Nadia Boulanger before returning to Harvard as a lecturer and later professor (1944-59). A disciplined crafts-man, he wrote influential textbooks on harmony, counterpoint, and orchestration, while in his music he consistently followed the neoclassical aims of the Boulanger school, preferring clear, sober musical argument to any kind of display. His output included eight symphonies, cham-ber pieces of various kinds, and a ballet, *The Incredible Flutist* (1938).   PAUL GRIFFITHS

Pitch. In music this term has a variety of meanings: it can be used in a relative sense, as when one sound is heard to be higher or lower in pitch than another (see *Ear and Hearing*), or when one instrument of a family is said to be 'pitched' higher or lower than another (e.g. the piccolo an octave above the flute; see *Trans-posing Instruments*). But we shall be concerned here with pitch in an absolute sense, as a norm to which instruments are built or tuned for playing with others. For this a note, usually 'A' (*a'*), is agreed to define a 'tuning', 'playing', 'per-forming', or 'concert' pitch (Fr.: *diapason*). The 'A' is carried about through the medium of a *tuning fork or *pitch-pipe, and in an orchestra is given out by the oboe (among wind instru-ments one of the least affected by temperature change), or, less frequently, by a metal tuning-bar struck with a beater, or by electronic means, though the last is apt to prove cloying and wearisome to musicians' ears. Since the 1830s there have been devices for accurately stating pitches in figures giving the vibration frequency of *a'* or any other note in cycles per second, or 'Hz' (see *Acoustics*, 4).

Widely used today are portable electronic

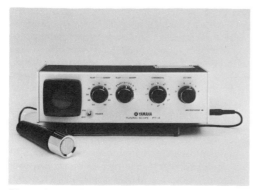

Electronic tuner by Yamaha, Japan.

'chromatic tuners' as made by Korg and other Japanese firms. Around $8'' \times 4''$ in size, they are battery- or mains-powered and have an earphone socket. A switch changes between 'meter' and 'sound'. On 'meter' the note from the instrument being tested is received through an incorporated microphone or input lead. The dial is set to the required note of the chromatic scale, in the relevant octave as selected by another switch. The dial shows deviations up to a semitone each way; if beyond this, the dial is reset to the next semitone. The dial shows deviations both in cents and in frequencies (Hz). On 'sound', to give out a pitch-signal, the note is set as before; it can be adjusted to other than standard pitch by a tuner button.

1. *Modern Pitch*. The present International Standard Pitch is $a' = 440$ Hz, agreed at a conference held in May 1939. Prior to that the general standard was $a' = 435$, a fifth of a semitone lower, except in Britain where it was $a' = 439$, virtually the same as the modern. One might have hoped that, once agreed, $a' = 440$ would have been strictly adhered to, and on the whole it has been against a tendency for pitch to rise. This 'sharpening' of pitch is due to a number of factors: a soloist may feel that an extra brightness of effect may be gained if the delivery be fractionally sharp to the accompaniment (within, of course, the tolerance of the ear's ability to identify pitch); or the strings of an orchestra may tune on the sharp side in anticipation of the wind becoming sharper as the performance proceeds. Thus it is said that in Berlin pianos for concert performance may be tuned as high as $a' = 450$, while some German manufacturers of wind instruments have been obliged to tune their instruments to $a' = 446$ (or above) to keep in step, thus reverting half-way up to the old 'sharp pitch' (see below, 3) which coexisted with standard pitch up to comparatively recent years in several countries, including Britain.

2. *Historical Pitches*. Over the last five centuries —so far as early values can be estimated from old forks, organs, and other wind instruments— tuning pitch has varied, in the main, over a range of about three semitones, a' varying from as low as our present g' up to the present $b\flat'$ or even above; this is not a great deal considering the length of time. Seldom has any pitch ruled completely for all places and in all circumstances; yet musicians, as they have travelled from country to country, tended to bring some measure of uniformity lasting in some cases over fairly long intervals between periods of instability and change.

The 18th century was, on the whole, one of the more stable periods. From roughly 1740 to 1820 concert pitches generally lay within the region of $a' = 420$-8 (that is, around a quarter-tone below the present $a' = 440$; for examples, see *Tuning fork*). This was the German *Cammerton* ('concert pitch') at which Mozart's music was performed, as well as most of Bach's, Handel's, and also Beethoven's. French pitch could be a trifle lower, and through the earlier part of the century definitely lower, spreading to England and Germany for a time chiefly through the powerful French influence on Baroque wind-instrument making. Thus recorders made in London by Bressan, who had come from France before 1700, can be nearly a whole tone below modern pitch. In Germany this low pitch was termed 'low *Cammerton*' (or 'French pitch') and often reckoned at about a semitone below the *Cammerton* just mentioned.

Today, performances of 18th-century music on original or replica instruments have very widely adopted a pitch of $a' = 415$, a semitone below modern pitch. This enables keyboard players to make a clean transposition of a semitone when an instrument tuned to modern pitch must be used, while it is also a pitch at which many original wind instruments can satisfactorily be played, and likewise stringed instruments when restored to their original condition (see *Violin*). Replica wind instruments are therefore commonly built to this pitch— though latterly there has begun a trend to specialize further, building alternatively, or on demand, to pitches around a quarter-tone below and above this.

There were also higher pitches in the 18th century, for example in Italy. Data here are more scarce, but performing pitches were said to be higher than the German *Cammerton*, with a Venetian pitch (from what Quantz tells us) nearly a tone higher. Still higher were the pitches among Baroque organs, not only in Germany but also among those built in England by makers from Germany. A German term for such pitches was *Chorton*. It is well known from J. S. Bach's orchestral parts how the continuo part for the organ might have to be written in a

TABLE I

$a' = 466$: reached in some historical pitch standards	(modern $b\flat'$)
$a' = 452$: former 'sharp pitch'	
$a' = 440$: modern standard pitch	(modern a')
$a' = 422$: Baroque/Classical pitch	
$a' = 415$: present usual 'historical' or 'Baroque pitch'	(modern $g\sharp'$)
$a' = 403$: higher Baroque French pitch	
$a' = 392$: Baroque French pitch	(modern g')

A rough indication of the approximate central areas of pitch back to the 1690s; the pitches are given at intervals of a quarter-tone apart.

key a tone (or even a tone and a half) lower than the key of the other instruments for all to agree.

For the 16th century and much of the 17th estimates of pitch have varied enormously. Michael Praetorius in Germany (1619) mentions two different pitches lying a tone apart. Many preserved wind instruments, particularly Italian but some German, seem to stand level with the Italian Baroque pitch region, up into the 460s for a', but the French were already lower. Stringed instruments played on their own would choose their own preferred pitch, as would voices, unless, of course, accompanied by the organ, in which case the compass of the voices, especially the upwards compass (where the severest limits lie), can give some indication of the pitches to which organs were tuned; much research is continuing along such lines.

3. *The 19th-century Rise in Pitch.* By 1820 European concert pitches had begun to shoot rapidly upwards, reaching before 1830, alike in Paris, London, and Vienna, the region of $a' = 434$, and often by that year 440, with further rises soon to follow. The possible causes are various: trends to sharpness among soloists, especially in the larger halls and before the more popular audiences; and certainly the vast expansion of military bands (players from which frequently manned the orchestras) with their tendency, especially out of doors, to play sharp for brilliant effect, in turn bearing influence on the instrument-makers. (This made it a difficult time for wind players: the principal horn of the Paris Opéra in 1829, having had his horn shortened to meet the rise in pitch, raised strong objection when a return to a lower pitch was mooted; and instruments like bassoons came for a time to be fitted with sliding tuning-devices, for a player to take engagements in this or that theatre or opera house.)

Already in 1834 J. H. Scheibler, a leading German scientist on pitch matters, recommended a standard of $a' = 440$ (our present pitch) arrived at by averaging out the tunings of grand pianos in Vienna. But further rises up to the 453 region through the 1850s brought directors of theatres and conservatories from all over Europe to co-operate, sending forks and comments to a commission in Paris which in 1859 decided upon $a' = 435$, the famous *diapason normal* ('standard pitch') already mentioned. It

came too late, however, for immediate universal acceptance. At Covent Garden in 1879 the organ had to be raised from 441 to 446 since it was impossible to get the woodwind to play any lower and singers too objected to any lowering. The general outcome was a polarization of pitch into 'low' and 'high', the 'low' being the *diapason normal* (confirmed by a conference in Vienna in 1885), the 'high' where circumstances or economics forbade a lowering, and in military bands. In Britain from the 1870s the 'high' or 'sharp' pitch lay at or near $a' = 452$, both for the Philharmonic concerts and for the British Army. The low pitch came only by degrees to replace it, from around 1890, and similarly in the USA. Up to 1930 many provincial British orchestras were still playing at sharp pitch, and a woodwind player taking an engagement outside his habitual orbit would require instruction as to which of his instruments to take, flat pitch or sharp, the wrong one being impossible to use. Many brass bands held to sharp pitch up to well after the Second World War, when eventually the expense of procuring flat-pitch instruments had to be faced in order for a band to take part in contests (involving massed bands) along with others which had already made the change. For choral societies the abolition of sharp pitch has been a considerable blessing—works like Beethoven's 'Choral' Symphony, with its long-sustained high As for the sopranos, proved extremely taxing at $a' = 452$; Beethoven, through the years preceding his deafness, would have heard this note up to a semitone lower by comparison.   ANTHONY BAINES

Pitch class. Property held in common by all pitches with the same name; thus middle C and every other C can be said to be a member of the pitch class C. It is particularly important in the discussion of serial music to distinguish between pitch and pitch class, since the classical 12-note series is a sequence of pitch classes, not of pitches.   PAUL GRIFFITHS

Pitch-pipe. 1. A small wooden pipe of square section, about 18″ long, with a whistle mouthpiece, much used during the 18th and 19th centuries. It has a leather-covered wooden stopper that can be pushed in to shorten the pipe and hence raise the pitch; on the stem of this stopper are marked the various notes. It was especially in starting psalm tunes in church, in the absence of any instrument, that the pitch-pipe was used in Britain, and the following from the *Scots Magazine* of 1755 will show the method:

As the tune must begin on a pitch neither too high for the tenor and other upper parts ascending to the highest notes the tune requires, nor too low for the bass, the leader must begin with striking such a sound as will answer this end . . . an instrument is used commonly called a pitch-pipe, which, by moving a slider properly divided, gives all the notes, with their subdivisions, which are proper for the tenor-part (i.e. the part with the tune itself). Upon this the leader gives one sound, acute or grave as the tune requires; with which all the performers immediately strike in; and the instrument is laid aside.

Tans'ur, in his *Elements of Music Displayed* (1772), tells us that before the introduction of a pitch-pipe a bell was used. It is said that the introduction of the pitch-pipe into American church life was due to the active choral promoter William Billings.

2. The reed pitch-pipe was popular in the 19th century as 'Eardsley's Patent Chromatic Pitchpipe'. It consists of a small cylindrical metal case (about 2″ long) enclosing a free reed, the vibrating length of which is adjustable by means of a cam on which are marked the names of the notes. Such instruments are today on sale. Sets of separate small metal free-reed tuners, each tuned to a different note, have also been made. The tuning-fork is, however, the most reliable pocket indicator of pitch that has yet been introduced.　　　　ANTHONY BAINES

Pitoni, Giuseppe Ottavio (*b* Rieti, 18 Mar. 1657; *d* Rome, 1 Feb. 1743). Italian composer. He was a choirboy at S. Giovanni dei Fiorentini and at SS. Apostoli, Rome. In 1676 he became *maestro di cappella* at Rieti, and then at the Collegio di S. Marco, Rome, a post he held until his death. He simultaneously held several other appointments at important Roman churches.

Pitoni was one of the best and most prolific composers of sacred music of his time. His output of sacred music, of which only one piece was published, included over 200 Masses and Mass movements for from four to eight voices, over 700 psalms (including one for 12 and one for 16 voices), *Magnificat* settings, motets, litanies, and Passions. He also wrote several composition treatises, and one of them, the first book of the *Guida armonica*, was published in Rome (*c*.1690).　　　　WENDY THOMPSON

Più (It.). 'More'; *più forte*, 'more loud'; etc.

Piva (It.). 'Pipe' or 'Bagpipe'.

Pizz. Abbreviation for *pizzicato.

Pizzetti, Ildebrando (*b* Borgo Strinato, nr Parma, 20 Sept. 1880; *d* Rome, 13 Feb. 1968). Italian composer. He studied at the Parma Musical Academy (1895–1901) and spent his life as a noted teacher of composition at conservatories in Parma (1907–8), Florence (1908–24), Milan (1924–36), and Rome (from 1936). In his music he reacted against the emotional extravagance of Puccini, being influenced by Debussy and the Italian renaissance. Opera, he felt, should give first place to the psychological portrayal of the characters, and he put this conviction to good effect in *Debora e Jaele* (1922), *Lo straniero* (1930), *Fra Gherardo* (1928), and *Assassinio nella cattedrale* (after Eliot, 1958). His other works include an intimate modal *Messa di Requiem* for small unaccompanied chorus (1922).　　　　PAUL GRIFFITHS

FURTHER READING
Guido Maria Gatti: *Ildebrando Pizzetti* (London, 1951).

Pizzicato (It., usually abbreviated to *pizz.*). 'Plucked'. A special effect obtained on bowed string instruments by plucking the strings with the fingers instead of bowing them. It was apparently first used in violin music by Monteverdi, in his *Il combattimento di Tancredi e Clorinda* (1624), where he requests 'Qui si lascia l'arco e si strappano le corde con duoi ditti' ('here the bow is laid aside and the strings are plucked with two fingers'). However, an earlier use of *pizzicato* (called 'thump') and other special effects occur in music by earlier composers of the English viol school, for example in Tobias Hume's *The First Part of Ayres* (1605).

Many different varieties of *pizzicato* are called for in later music, such as the left-hand *pizzicato*, used extensively by Paganini, which enables the player to bow one string while plucking another; the 'snap' *pizzicato*, indicated by the sign ↕ and used by Bartók in his string quartets (the string is pulled upwards and then allowed to snap back on to the fingerboard); and the *pizzicato* slide, also used by Bartók, where the left hand slides up or down the string that has been plucked to produce a range of notes sounding within the same *pizzicato* effect.

Pk. 1. An abbreviation for *Pauken* (Ger.), i.e. kettledrums. 2. In organ music, the abbreviation for *Pedalkoppel* (Ger.), i.e. Pedal Coupler (followed by an indication of the particular manual which is to be coupled to the pedal).

Placing of voice. See *Messa di voce*.

Placito (It.). 'Judgement'; *a bene placito*, 'at one's own judgement', i.e. *ad libitum*.

Plagal cadence. See *Cadence*, 2.

Plainchant

1. Function
2. History to the 8th Century
3. The 8th and 9th Centuries
4. Later Developments
5. Chant Books and Notation
6. Style

1. *Function.* Plainchant is the monophonic music of Christian worship, particularly that of the Roman Church. It is an essential element of some divine services; of others it is an adjunct serving to heighten the solemnity of the occasion. In the Office Hours, whose chief constituents are psalm-singing and the intoning of lessons, chant is in the very nature of the services. At Mass, the Eucharist is preceded by a preparation (the *synaxis*) where lessons and psalm-singing also alternate; but the chant which accompanies the entrance of the clergy, and, in the Eucharist, the chants sung during the offering of bread and wine and the Communion itself, are purely ceremonial adjuncts.

In more important churches, lessons were intoned rather than read; this was for acoustical reasons, to reduce the myriad and confusing tonal inflections of human speech in a resonant building. Chants for congregational singing—for example psalm tones and hymns—have retained a simple and direct character. But practically all other chants have come down to us in a form for trained choirs or solo singers, relatively ornate in style and rather remote or 'other-worldly' in character.

It is customary to refer to chants as either 'Proper' or 'Ordinary' (see *Mass*, 1)—a liturgical rather than a musical distinction. Two other terms used below are musical: 'antiphonal' and 'responsorial'. Some chants were performed by soloists and choir (or congregation) in alternation, the choir responding with a refrain to each of several soloists' verses; this is known as responsorial chant. When the performance is divided between two more or less equal groups of performers (say, the two halves of a choir), then the performance is said to be antiphonal. (See also *Alternatim*.) Items in the liturgical services at which chant is sung are discussed under *Mass*, 2, and *Office*.

2. *History to the 8th Century.* Of the music of Christian worship of the first three centuries little is known. Services were illegal and private and there was little scope for the development of elaborate ceremonial or music. The singing of hymns was popular. Some are cited in the New Testament and other writings, and the texts of others have survived in such collections as the Odes of Solomon (42 hymns from 2nd-century Alexandria). But very many are now lost because in the second half of the 3rd century there was a general suppression of non-biblical hymns, caused by the dangerous popularity of heretical compositions. Psalm-singing was

promoted instead. Solo and responsorial performance seem to have been widely practised at first. Then, in mid-4th-century Antioch, antiphonal psalmody became popular, and gradually spread throughout the Christian world. Refrain verses were often used in conjunction with antiphonal psalmody, just as in responsorial performance. (These verses are called, confusingly, *antiphons, but the adjective 'antiphonal' properly refers to the *alternatim* method of performance, as explained above, not to the use of refrain antiphons.) Hymn-singing did not, of course, cease entirely, but hymns always hovered on the margin of Roman liturgical use, and in the absence of central authority individual local traditions had room to develop.

Under Constantine the Great, persecution ceased and Christianity was declared the official religion of the Roman Empire (Edict of Milan, 313). The Church was now state supported, its worship public, and its congregations large, and there was an inevitable expansion of ceremonial detail in its services. A formal procession of celebrant and assistants from sacristy to altar was now accompanied by a solemn chant, the Introit; another chant, the Offertory, was sung while the bread and wine were brought in procession and laid upon the altar; and a third chant, the Communion, accompanied the distribution of the sacred elements to the congregation. All these consisted of psalms sung antiphonally, with antiphons, and all became a part of Roman worship between the later 4th and the 6th centuries. The antiphon and as many verses as required were sung; then at a signal from the celebrant the doxology and a final reprise of the antiphon terminated the chant.

Other musical items also entered the Roman Mass, some adopted after previous use in other parts of Christendom. After the entrance chant a litany whose response was the Greek phrase 'Kyrie eleison' ('Lord have mercy') was sung, probably from the 5th century. Even when Greek fell out of use in Roman worship (it had coexisted with Latin up to the 5th century, since the earliest Christian communities in Rome were Greek-speaking Levantines), the Greek refrain remained, although the invocations which followed it were Latin. This chant came to be succeeded by the hymn *Gloria in excelsis Deo*, which in a Greek version may have originated in the 1st century; it was used in Rome from c.500. The use of the Sanctus in the prefatory prayers of the Eucharist can be traced as far back as 3rd-century Alexandria; it had entered the Roman Mass by the time of Gregory the Great (590–604). The Agnus Dei was not introduced until c.700; it accompanied the breaking of the bread.

This expansion of the content of the Mass (we have mentioned only the musical accretions), most of it occurring in the 4th century, is but one aspect of a development affecting every feature of Christian worship. By the 4th century Communion regularly took place not simply on Sundays, but also on Wednesdays, Fridays, and Saturdays and on days commemorating saints. During the 4th century communities of people dedicated to a religious life attached themselves to major churches, and it was for them that further services throughout the day, beginning even before dawn, were organized. These consisted chiefly of psalm-singing and the reading of lessons; their classic form was established by St Benedict (c.480–c.547) and taken up by many monastic communities in the West.

Just as the day filled with worship, and the week with holy days, so a pattern was established for a year's cycle of commemorations—or rather, two interlocking cycles. On the one hand there were days commemorating events in Christ's life: Christmas, Easter, Whitsuntide, etc. Gradually it also became customary to honour early heroes of the Church—martyrs and others of special sanctity—each with services on his own particular day. Each of these commemorations had its own appropriate texts, lessons to be read and chants to be sung, eventually constituting 'Proper' cycles of liturgical material.

Not all Churches, even in the West, followed Roman custom. Of Churches whose music differed from that of Rome we have practically nothing from France, Germany, or Britain. We have complete manuscripts with musical notation from Spain, but we cannot read the notation. But we do have the music of the so-called Ambrosian liturgy of Milan. The history of the music of these non-Roman Churches probably resembles that of their lessons and prayers, about which we are better informed. There was a periodic but unsystematic circulation of Roman texts, and occasional borrowings from Rome did occur, but a distinct independence remained in much of the surface detail of worship.

3. *The 8th and 9th Centuries.* In the 8th century, however, the situation changed, with the reign of Pepin, King of the Franks from 751, and still more with that of Charlemagne (771–814), crowned Emperor in Rome on Christmas Day, 800. There was a deliberate attempt to bring church worship in Frankish lands into line with that in Rome. Charlemagne perhaps saw common forms of worship as a way of helping unite his vast empire; still more, he saw himself as a divinely appointed ruler of a chosen people, the new David of a new Israel, whose liturgical customs must approach the ideal, represented by papal usage.

The musical consequences of the importation of Roman Use were considerable. Uniformity was not easily achieved, and there arose tales that Frankish singers could not master the subtleties of Roman chant, and that Roman singing masters, jealous of their own special skills and repertory, deliberately confused their pupils. A question of fundamental importance for musicology hangs over the whole affair: exactly what chant was brought from Rome at this time? The surviving music manuscripts from Rome itself before the 13th century all show a type of chant quite different from that which we now call 'Gregorian'. Scholars are generally agreed that it represents a more archaic repertory, from which Gregorian chant evolved—hence its usual name 'Old Roman chant'. It has been argued that the revision of Old Roman to produce Gregorian chant was carried out by singers of the pope's own chapel (as opposed to the city basilicas), perhaps under Pope Vitalian (657–72), who was interested in Byzantine imperial liturgy. Others argue that the revision is Frankish work, the inevitable result of trying to import, learn, and eventually codify what was still an oral, not a written, repertory.

The situation is even more complicated than this, since the Old Roman repertory appears not to have been written down until the 11th century, and much of the surface detail of the chants as we know them is probably not what it was at the end of the 8th century, let alone during Vitalian's time. There is, among other things, clear evidence that the Gregorian repertory influenced some features of Old Roman chant. The same thing happened to the Ambrosian repertory of Milan, whose surviving sources are likewise very late (12th century onward).

Metz was the Frankish city which established itself as a musical model for other churches to follow in the late 8th and early 9th centuries. Unfortunately all its chant books are lost. The manuscripts we do have, from the end of the 9th century onward, are from many areas of Europe: Aquitaine and Brittany, Champagne and Picardy, St Gall, and Winchester. They are in different notational styles, and occasionally vary in small melodic details, so that it is uncertain whether they are all descended from a common exemplar, or whether cantors of several different churches each notated chant independently, from a common oral tradition.

What is clear is that we cannot recover the form of chant that St Gregory might have known. The association of his name with chant is unknown before the 8th century, and

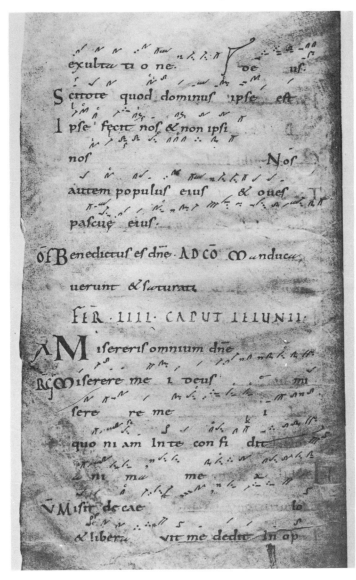

although he was responsible for putting the living arrangements for the singers of the Roman basilicas on a new footing, and for reorganizing some features of the liturgy and the role of chant within it, it is by no means certain that his dealings with chant amounted to 'composition'.

4. *Later Developments.* The energies of the cantors of the Frankish empire went far beyond learning and codifying the Gregorian repertory of plainchant. In three genres they made entirely individual contributions to the music of their day: *sequences, *tropes, and liturgical drama (see *Church Drama*, 1). And in all three, since a Roman tradition and authority did not exist, colourful local repertories were created.

In addition, many local musicians composed services for the patron saint of their church, some in verse (hexameters).

Our first evidence of liturgical polyphony comes from the 9th century, in the treatise *Musica enchiriadis* (see *Organum*). The 9th century also saw the beginnings of a great body of theoretical writing about chant, by such as Aurelian of Réomé (mid 9th century) and Hucbald of St Amand (*c*.840-930), which shows a fascinating attempt at the reconciliation of the non-traditional chant repertory with what had survived of Greek musical theory (transmitted through the individual medium of Boethius, *c*.480-*c*.524).

In the 11th century, new ideas again seem to

have become especially important. Exact notation of the pitches of melodies became practicable. Liturgical dramas first moved beyond the simple dialogues of the Marys at Christ's tomb and the shepherds at the manger. A new type of rhyming, rhythmic song, the *conductus*, came into fashion. Soon after this a completely new repertory of rhyming, rhythmic sequences began to develop, displacing the irregular prose of the previous type of sequence. Offices of the saints from the 12th century onward are commonly written in rhyme.

The Gregorian repertory, established with such care and skill in the 8th and 9th centuries, was not immune from attempts at reform by those who felt that important ideals were being betrayed. The Cistercian order of monks, reacting to over-elaboration of ritual, instituted reforms which included the rewriting of melodies to exclude notes outside the range of a tenth and to eliminate long melismas. The biggest revolution of this sort occurred after the Council of Trent (1542-63), which declared itself against tropes and sequences, and commissioned new chant books. Work was carried out first by Palestrina and Zoilo; later by Guidetti; and finally Felice Anerio and Soriano produced a gradual in 1614-15 (known as the *Editio medicaea*). The humanist ideals inspiring these 'compositions' eschewed even moderately long groups of notes on unaccented syllables, and the tonality of many chants was brought more into line with 16th-century sensibilities.

Another wave of liturgical reform swept France in the 17th and 18th centuries, chiefly because of anti-papal political feeling. But by the time opinion swung back in favour of conformity with Rome, it was realized by many French scholars that for plainchant, at least, this meant rejoining a tradition which was itself corrupt. In 1851, an 11th-century manuscript from Dijon was used as the basis for the new Rheims/Cambrai gradual, and in the same year Lambillotte published a pseudo-facsimile (somewhat 'edited') of a 10th-century St Gall manuscript. These were the first major steps of a journey now well known. Largely as a result of the work of Dom Pothier and the monks of Solesmes Abbey, chant books with melodies restored to their early Medieval forms were sanctioned by Pius X (*Motu proprio* of 22 November 1903) and published in 1905 (the Kyriale), 1908 (the gradual), and 1912 (the antiphoner).

5. *Chant Books and Notation*. The earliest chant manuscripts we have (of the late 8th and the 9th centuries) are simply copies of the texts to be sung—they contain no notation. When notation did appear, later in the 9th century, it indicated only the rise and fall of the melodies, sometimes with rhythmic indications, but without exact specification of pitches. Only in the 11th century were complete chant books written with exact pitch notation; one special case, the Dijon tonary, has parallel neumatic notation and alphabetic 'translation'. Also at this time came the first of hundreds of books employing staff-lines as recommended by Guido of Arezzo, c.1030 (see *Notation*, 2-3).

These facts, and the variations between the manuscripts, suggest that not all aspects of plainchant were regarded as of equal importance. Most important was the text to be sung, and soon after that the mode, the over-all design, and the formulas to be used within the design. Last of all came the detail of individual pitches (as opposed to over-all tonality), progressions from one structurally important point to another, and some surface ornament. Ex. 1 displays four Medieval notations of the Palm Sunday Gradual *Christus factus est* (first section), with a modern 'translation'. X marks places where the manuscripts differ from each other. (For the notation of this example, and a description of the conventions used in transcribing plainchant, see *Notation*, 2.)

Some early neumatic notations (particularly the sophisticated St Gall type) contain indications for lengthening and stressing certain notes. However, it is not known if these involved strictly proportional note lengths (equivalent to, say, modern crotchet and quaver), as their use is somewhat unsystematic and contemporary theoretical writing somewhat ambiguous; it is perhaps not surprising that they have been interpreted in contrary ways.

Different types of chant are contained in different books, usually according to the services for which they provided music. The Proper chants for Mass are contained in the *gradual, and Office chants in the *antiphoner. Some books include only soloists' chants: the *cantatorium*, containing those sections of Mass chants that were sung by soloists (verses of Graduals, Alleluias, and Offertories; and Tracts); and the troper, containing *tropes, often *sequences, perhaps liturgical dramas, and material from the *cantatorium* or processional. The processional has chants for processions. Most Ordinary of Mass chants first appear with tropes, in tropers. Later they were often transferred into graduals. Different areas of Europe liked to arrange material in different ways. In Italy, for instance, tropes and sequences were distributed in the appropriate liturgical places in graduals and *cantatoria*, and very few separate tropers appear to have been compiled.

From the 12th century it became common to include chants in the same book as prayers and lessons. These composite books are the missal

Ex. 1

St Gall,
10th century

Laon,
10th century

Aquitaine,
11th century

England,
13th c.

Chri - stus fact - us est pro no - - - - - bis

o - be - - - - di - ens us - - que ad mor - tem

Over [obe]-*di*-[ens] the St Gall MS has a four-note neume. Over *us*-[que] the St Gall and English MSS have ABCA, the others ACCA. The St Gall MS makes a distinction between dots (short?) and dashes (long?). Note also the alternative ways of notating two notes in descending order at 1 and 2. At 1 the St Gall MS has a letter 'c' (= *celeriter*, 'quickly'), the Laon MS a single stroke of the pen. At 2 the St Gall MS adds a bar across the top (to indicate lengthening?), while the Laon MS correspondingly splits the neume into two sickles.

(for Mass) and the breviary (for the Office). Some omit musical notation.

A book with a didactic function was the tonary. Since the mode of an antiphon governed the choice of psalm tone for singing psalms in the Office Hours, lists of antiphons according to their mode were drawn up in booklets called tonaries, at first without notation. Usually only the first few words of the antiphons were cited. The Dijon tonary mentioned above is almost unique in notating chants in full, and in containing Mass, not Office, chants.

It is unlikely that chant books were used by the choir during performance. The notation of most early ones is too small for even one person to read in the course of a service. They are reference books. Only after the 13th century do manuscripts become big enough for reading by more than one singer, and not until the 15th century would many choirmen have been musically literate.

6. *Style*. Since the plainchant repertory evolved orally, it is not surprising that it relies heavily on melodic formulas deployed in simple structures, all of which could be memorized. Each chant genre has its own structures and formulas, and with each genre there is a further subdivision of formulas according to mode. These principles hold good for descriptions of most of the basic Gregorian repertory, but not for compositions of the 9th century onward—i.e. not for many Alleluias, Ordinary of Mass chants, tropes, sequences, etc.

The Old Roman repertory relies even more heavily than the Gregorian on formulaic construction, and its modal system is more primitive. It is known that the Franks organized an eight-mode system for the chant repertory in emulation of Byzantine practice (see *Mode, 2a*), and it seems likely that what there is of the system in Old Roman chant has been adopted from Gregorian use.

Ex. 2

A further important factor affecting chant style is the number of performers involved. Office psalms chanted by a whole monastic community use very simple melodic formulas, and the accompanying antiphons are also restrained in style. Chants sung by soloists or a trained choir (as were practically all Mass chants) are far more ornate, their formulas intricate and subtle.

Different genres favoured different modes. Contrast the following figures, derived from counting chants in representative early manuscripts:

The use of formulas is most clearly demonstrated in psalmodic pieces. Choral Office psalms are intoned on one note (the *tenor*), usually approached from below and maintained until the end of a text phrase (i.e. the musical cadence). Ex. 2a gives the melodic scheme (or 'tone') for psalm verses sung with mode 1 antiphons (hence known as 'tone 1'). It provides one of several alternative cadences (*differentiae*) which could have been selected to lead smoothly back to the antiphon. In responsorial psalmody the verses were sung by a soloist, and the Office responsories have much more elaborate tones;

mode:	D(%)	E(%)	F(%)	G(%)
Gregorian Office antiphons (1235)	32	19	5	44
Gregorian Introits (147)	32	31	15	22
Old Roman Introits (148)	22	48	17	13
Gregorian Graduals (110)	32	12	43	13
Ambrosian *psalmelli* (Graduals; 104)	41	7	18	34

Ex. *2b* (from the responsory *Expurgate vetus fermentum*) gives the tone for the first mode. Most elaborate of all is the responsorial psalmody of Mass: for example in the Graduals, where phrase endings are prolonged melismatically and the *tenor* is submerged in floating roulades. In the verse of the mode 1 Gradual *Miserere mei* (Ex. *2c*), the *tenor* note is A, but could be thought of almost as a repeated oscillation A–C. The music for *Misit de caelo, in opprobrium, (conculcan)tes,* and *me* is all to be found in other mode 1 Graduals, but not all together in any other Gradual. However, the formulas will all be found at the same point in the verse: start, ends of first, second, third sections, etc. In structure and employment of formulas, the Old Roman version of the Gradual is designed similarly, but the actual formulas and surface detail are quite different, as Ex. *2d*

shows. The repeated Cs of the Gregorian version are absent from the Old Roman, and the *tenor* A is clearer, though often accompanied by auxiliary Bs.

For another example of solo Gregorian psalmody, see *Tract*, Ex. 1.

Antiphons, both antiphons of the Office and the Introit and Communion antiphons of Mass, are not developed from psalm intonations, but are free compositions. They do not, however, lack standard procedures. There are common openings and cadences for the antiphons of each mode (for an example, see *Antiphon*, Ex. 1, whose phrases are all to be found in other mode 1 antiphons). Communions and especially Introits are more elaborate than this (see *Antiphon*, Ex. 1) and, apart from a few common openings, standard phrases are not easily detected. (In Old Roman Introits they are much more clearly

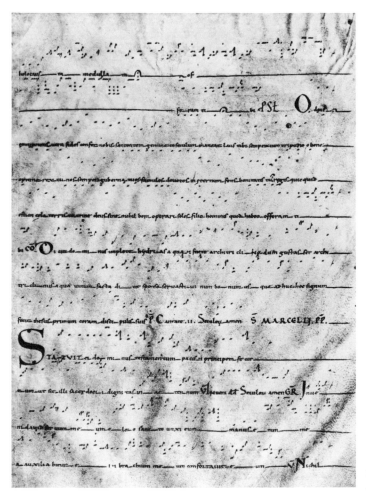

Pl. 2. *Part of a mid 11th-century gradual from St Yrieix, northern Aquitaine: (upper half) the Offertory 'Jubilate Deo' (see Ex. 3).*

visible.) With elaboration of style came the progressive loss of psalm verses. By the 11th century the Introit retained only one verse, while the Communion had completely lost its verses.

Although in ancient responsorial psalmody the choral refrains were probably simple, in the Gregorian repertory as it has come down to us they are no longer so. The first sections of responsories and Graduals, sung by the choir, are quite as elaborate as their verses—in the case of the responsories even more so; and again formulaic composition obtains. This elaboration of style presumably took place at the hands of the Roman Schola Cantorum. It also resulted in the loss of all psalm verses but one. Even more drastic was the transformation of the Offertory, originally an example of choral antiphonal psalmody. The antiphon section became an elaborate choir showpiece, and at some time in the 8th or 9th century the simple psalm intonations for the verses were replaced by brilliant solo melismatic music. Ex. 3 is a verse from the mode 1 Offertory *Jubilate Deo*. The melisma of 112 notes in this example is a rather shapeless fantasy. Melismas in many Alleluias

are ordered in an AAB or similar form, thus revealing the later date of their composition (many are known only from 10th- or 11th-century manuscripts, not earlier). Late additions to the Gregorian corpus, such as the later Alleluias, and tropes, sequences, and *conductus*, also show a move away from the predominantly pentatonic sound-world of earlier chant. The older corpus tended to treat E and B as notes of secondary importance; they were generally not repeated, and rarely approached or quitted by leap. But later chants frequently contain passages that use all notes of the gamut equally freely; they also appear to emphasize interlocking chains of thirds. The following melisma (Ex. 4), from the *Alleluia Justus ut palma*, is in AABB form, and moves from one set of thirds (C-E-G-(Bb)) to another (D-F-A). Leaps of a third are bracketed to make this clear.

The abandonment of old formulas and standard melodic procedures is nowhere more evident than in the new rhymed Offices of the 12th century and later. Our final example is from the festal Office of St James contained in the Codex Calixtinus of *c*.1160. One particularly 'modern' feature is the presence of a rhyme

Ex. 3

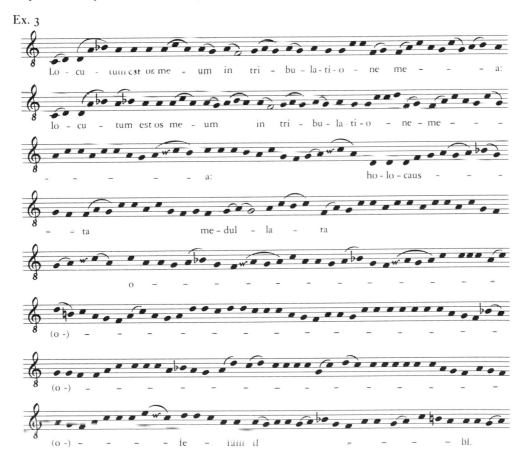

Ex. 4

Ex. 5

	Text rhyme	Music rhyme
Ja - co - be vir - gi - ne - i fra - ter	*a*	*a*
pre - ci - o - se Jo - han - nis,	*b*	*b*
qui pi - us Er - mo - ge - nem	*c*	*a*
re - vo - ca - sti cor-de fe - ro - cem,	*c*	*b*
ex mun - di vi - ci - is	*d (? b)*	*a'*
ad ho - no - rem cun - cti - po - ten -		
- - - - - - - tis.	*d (? b)*	*b* followed by *a* (at 'cunctipoten . . .'), then new ending

scheme for the text and the music. No trace of old mode 8 responsory formulas can be seen.

This wealth of stylistic variation makes the study of plainchant particularly rewarding. To those unfamiliar with it, chant can seem tedious and lacking in variety. But what seems uniform when contrasted with polyphony of the 13th to the 20th centuries breaks down on closer inspection into a fascinating mixture of genres and styles, clearly audible to the discerning listener. Quite apart from its intrinsic qualities, plainchant is by far the earliest and largest repertory of music to have been codified from oral traditions, and as such is of inestimable value for our understanding of human culture.

DAVID HILEY

FURTHER READING
Willi Apel: *Gregorian Chant* (Bloomington, Ind., 1958, 3rd edn 1966).

Plainchant Mass. Either the original plainchant for the Mass, or a polyphonic Mass composition in which each movement is based on the corresponding item of the plainchant. The term is sometimes broadened in its application to include a Mass based on any item of plainchant.

Plainte (Fr.). 'Complaint'. In music, a mournful piece lamenting someone's death or some other unhappy occurrence. The term was used in the 17th and 18th centuries, especially for keyboard works, by such composers as Rameau, Couperin, and Froberger (e.g. Froberger's *Plainte faite à Londres, pour passer le Mélancholie* from his Suite No. 30).

Plaisanterie (Fr.). A light movement (not a dance) in an 18th-century suite.

Planets, The. Orchestral suite, Op. 32, by Holst, composed between 1914 and 1916. Its seven movements reflect astrological associations: (1) Mars, the Bringer of War; (2) Venus, the Bringer of Peace; (3) Mercury, the Winged Messenger; (4) Jupiter, the Bringer of Jollity; (5) Saturn, the Bringer of Old Age; (6) Uranus, the Magician; (7) Neptune, the Mystic (with wordless female chorus). It was first performed privately in 1918; its first public performance was in 1919, without Nos. 2 and 7, and it was given complete in 1920.

Planh (Provençal), **planctus** (Lat.). A Medieval lament. The earliest *planctus* to survive with music are from a 10th-century manuscript, which includes one lament on the death of Charlemagne (814) and another on that of his son Hugo (844). Richard the Lionheart (*d* 1199) is mourned in a *planh* (with Provençal words) by Gaucelm Faidit, 'Fortz chausa es'. Another type of *planctus* took a biblical subject, such as David lamenting the death of Jonathan; six of this kind by Peter Abelard (1079-1142) survive with music.

Planquette, (Jean) **Robert** (*b* Paris, 31 July 1848; *d* Paris, 28 Jan. 1903). French composer. He was a student at the Paris Conservatoire who turned to writing witty songs for café concerts. He then graduated to the composition of operettas which won immense world-wide popularity. The best known of these is *Les cloches de Corneville* ('The Bells of Corneville', 1877) sometimes known in the USA as *The Chimes of Normandy* or *The Bells of Normandy*.
DENIS ARNOLD

Plantin, Christopher (*b* ?Tours, *c*.1520; *d* Antwerp, 1 July 1589). Flemish printer of French birth. A pious, modest, and deeply mystical man, he became the most important printer and publisher in Antwerp in the 16th century. His printing press, The Golden Compasses, established in Antwerp in 1555, issued scholarly books of every kind and became a renowned centre of humanist culture. At its peak it employed 160 men and operated 22 presses.

The basis of Plantin's economic success was the monopoly he acquired from Philip of Spain to print service books (missals, breviaries, etc.) for Spain and her territories. This was apparently the incidental cause of his turning to music printing: when Philip withheld a subsidy promised for a luxurious antiphoner, Plantin had to find a use for the 1,800 reams of royal format paper he had already ordered, and so he issued a volume of Masses by George de la Hèle in 1578, using the large woodcut initials designed for the antiphoner. During the following decade he published several other music editions, including works by Philippe de Monte, Andreas Pevernage, Jacob de Kerle, and Claude Le Jeune. Music was only a small part of his output, but his editions were of the highest quality and sold well, despite their high price. His printing house survives as the Plantin-Moretus Museum, which preserves most of the press's history through its remarkable collection of works of art, furnishings, and printing equipment (including the many typefaces that Plantin collected).

See also *Printing and Publishing of Music*, 4.
J. M. THOMSON

Plaqué (Fr.). 'Laid down'. Term applied to the playing of chords, indicating that all the notes are to be played simultaneously rather than as an arpeggio.

Platti, Giovanni Benedetto (*b* ? Venice, *c*.1700; *d* Würzburg, 11 Jan. 1763). Italian composer. From 1722 until at least 1761 he worked at the Würzburg court as an instrumentalist (he was a virtuoso oboist but played several other instruments as well), singing teacher, and composer. In 1742 he published a set of six harpsichord sonatas 'sur le goût italien', which are clearly influenced by C. P. E. Bach, and followed it up by a second set about four years later; he also published sonatas for flute, for violin, and for oboe, and several harpsichord concertos. WENDY THOMPSON

Playera (Sp.). A gypsy *seguidilla* which is sung and danced; another name is *seguidillas gitanas*.

Playford. English family of booksellers and music publishers. As publishers the Playfords showed remarkable flair: they were the first to cater for public taste on a large scale, and virtually dominated London music publishing in the second half of the 17th century. John Playford (1623-86), a musician, author, clerk to the Temple Church, and subject of Purcell's *Elegy on my Friend, Mr John Playford*, was the leading London music publisher from 1651 to 1684. He used Thomas Harper (successor to Thomas East) and William Godbid, Harper's successor, as his printers, and published engaging theory and instruction books, as well as many collections of instrumental pieces, songs, and arrangements of psalms. These included *A Musicall Banquet* (1651), *A Breefe Introduction to the Skill of Musick* (1654), and *The (English) Dancing Master* (1651), which went through numerous editions up until 1728. His catches, glees, and lessons for the cittern, viol, flageolet, virginals, etc., were also popular and were published in various permutations, amply supplied with dedications and prefaces which reflect Playford's preoccupations with commercial problems and his advocacy of English music in which divine service, under a restored monarchy, would have a proper place.

His younger son Henry (*c*.1657–*c*.1707) updated his father's editions, but was less prolific, concentrating on entertainment music. His best-known publications are *Wit and Mirth* (songs by Thomas D'Urfey set to popular tunes) and Purcell's song collection *Orpheus Britannicus*. From 1700 onwards his business declined, partly because he became more interested in concert promotion and in art dealing.

See also *Printing and Publishing of Music*, 5.

J. M. THOMSON

Play of Daniel, The. Medieval mystery play which exists in several versions. The only one to have survived with the music complete is the Beauvais version, composed between 1227 and 1234 for performance at Beauvais Cathedral, probably at Matins on 1 January. The play is in two parts, the first dealing with Daniel at Belshazzar's court and the second with Daniel's trials at the court of Darius. There are several modern editions of it, including one by David Wulstan.

Play of Robin and Marion, The. See *Jeu de Robin et de Marion, Le*.

Plectrum. 1. A plectrum or 'pick' is used with many kinds of stringed instrument, sometimes regularly, sometimes optionally, to sound the strings in place of using the bare fingers.

A plectrum (Fig. 1*a*) is held between finger and thumb, and is commonly termed a 'pick' by guitarists whose styles of music demand it (folk, jazz, rock, etc.) and by mandolin and many banjo players. For all these it is usually heart-shaped, of tortoiseshell, plastic, or other stiffly flexible material. Formerly, from the Middle Ages to the 18th century, it was characteristically of a quill (made from e.g. a goose feather). Many folk and oriental instruments use plectrums of leather, or of wood—including the vast axe-shaped wooden plectrums of the Japanese *shamisen* (see *Lute*, 4*a*), in size if not in shape recalling the large plectrum seen in use with the lyre in Greek vase paintings.

While a plectrum, from its normally hard material and pointed end, brings from the strings a bright and penetrating quality of sound (strong upper harmonics; compare the use of hard beaters for *percussion instruments), it brings a limitation in that, when sounding several strings at the same time, no two strings can be struck without also sounding the string between them.

The finger pick (Fig. 1*b*, *c*) is a slip of hard material attached to, or fitted into, a ring worn

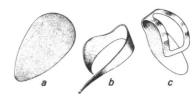

Fig. 1

on the individual finger or thumb (or a metal point integral with the ring). The other fingers can then sound other strings independently. (For an example, see *Zither*, 1.) Folk-guitarists often use such a pick, for instance to save wear on the thumb playing the bass notes, while beyond Europe there are instruments like the Near-Eastern *qanun* (see *Psaltery*) and the *koto* of Japan where one hand or both wear one or more such picks.

2. In a harpsichord the small leather or quill points carried by the 'jacks' to pluck the strings are named plectrums.

ANTHONY BAINES

Plenary Mass. An 'entire' Mass composition, i.e. one comprising both the Ordinary and the Proper of the Mass. Such a work is rarely composed, except in the case of the *Requiem, for reasons of economy since the Proper varies for particular festivals and occasions whereas the Ordinary remains the same.

Pleno (It.). 'Full'. See *Pieno, piena*.

Pleyel, Ignace Joseph [Ignaz Josef] (*b* Ruppersthal, Austria, 18 June 1757; *d* Paris, 14 Nov. 1831). Austrian composer, publisher, and piano manufacturer. From around 1722 he studied with Haydn at Eisenstadt, where he remained

Ignace Joseph Pleyel, engraving by Biosse after Guerin.

for about five years. Later he became *Kapellmeister* at Strasbourg Cathedral (succeeding F. X. Richter in 1789) and conducted concerts during a visit to London in 1791–2. In 1795 he set up as a music dealer in Paris, founding his piano factory in 1807. Pleyel's son Camille (1788–1855) became a partner in the firm in 1815, and they were joined by the pianist Friedrich Kalkbrenner in 1829. On Camille's death, the direction of the firm passed to Auguste Wolff (1821–87) and was renamed Pleyel, Wolff, et Cie. Ignace Pleyel was also a prolific composer, producing many symphonies, string quartets, and other orchestral and instrumental works.

Plica (Lat.). Literally, 'fold'. A term used in the Medieval period for liquescent neumes. See *Notation*, 2.

Pli selon pli ('Fold upon Fold'). Work by Boulez for soprano and orchestra, subtitled 'Portrait de Mallarmé'. It is in five movements and was composed between 1957 and 1962 but it has been subject to continuous revision.

Plugging. 20th-century term derived from the slang expression 'plugging away', meaning persistently working at something. It has come to be applied to the practice of incessantly playing a tune or song on the radio or television, in order to make it well known and thus commercially profitable.

Plummer, John (*b* c.1410; *d* c.1484). English composer. He served as a clerk at Henry VI's Chapel Royal from 1441, assuming the post of Master of the Children in 1444. His later life was spent at Windsor, where he was verger at St George's Chapel until his death; his name is still commemorated there four times a year. Some fine antiphons and motets by him have survived.
JOHN MILSOM

Pneuma [neuma] (Gk, 'breath'). Medieval term for passages sung to a single vowel at the end of certain passages of plainchant. The last vowel of 'Alleluia', in the traditional plainchant setting of this word, is an example (see *Jubilus*).

Pochette (Fr.). See *Kit*.

Poco (It.). 'A little', 'rather'; *poco lento*, 'rather slow'; *poco a poco*, 'little by little'; *poco a poco animando*, 'becoming lively by degrees'; *pochetto*, 'very little'; *pochissimo*, 'the least possible'.

Poèmes pour Mi ('Poems for Mi'). Song-cycle by Messiaen to his own poems, composed in 1936. It was written for soprano and piano, but

Messiaen made an orchestral version in 1937. 'Mi' was the composer's own name for his first wife, the violinist Claire Deslos.

Poème symphonique (Fr.), **poema sinfonica** (It.). 'Symphonic poem'.

Poem of Ecstasy (*Poema ekstasa*; *Le poème de l'extase*). Orchestral work, Op. 54, by Skryabin, composed 1905–8. It was inspired by the composer's theosophical ideas on love and art.

Poem of Fire. See *Prometheus, the Poem of Fire*.

Poglietti, Alessandro (*d* Vienna, July 1683). Austrian composer and organist of Italian birth. He worked at the Viennese court of Emperor Leopold I from 1661. His most important works are for keyboard, including sonatas, suites, *ricercari*, and so on; they are notable mainly for their extra-musical content, such as their imitations of national instruments (for example, the Bohemian bagpipe and the French flageolet). He died in the Siege of Vienna, and his six children were taken prisoner by the Turks.
DENIS ARNOLD

Pohjola's Daughter (*Pohjolan tytär*). Symphonic fantasia, Op. 49, by Sibelius, composed in 1906. It is based on a legend from the *Kalevala*.

Poi (It.). 'Then', e.g. (after some direction for the repetition of a passage) *poi la coda*, 'then the coda'.

Point. 1. The tip of the bow of a stringed instrument. 2. A 'point of imitation' is a melodic motif taken as a subject for imitation. 3. In early mensural notation, a 'point' (i.e. dot; Lat.: *punctum*) was used to group the rhythmic values of a group of notes; see *Notation*, 4.

Point d'orgue (Fr.). 1. The pause sign (⌒). 2. A harmonic pedal; see *Pedal point*. 3. A cadenza in a concerto, probably so called because cadenzas were generally indicated by pause signs.

Pointé (Fr.). 'Pointed', 'detached' (in articulation).

Pointillism. Compositional technique, named after Seurat's method of painting with tiny dots of colour, in which each note has a distinct quality of timbre, loudness, etc. Sometimes pointillism is a by-product of advanced *serial thought, as in certain works of Webern, Boulez, and Stockhausen. It may also appear in the work of other composers such as Xenakis, who aim to produce 'clouds' of musical points, and here the analogy with Seurat's method is closer.

Pointing. See *Anglican Chant*, 5.

Poisoned Kiss, The, or The Empress and the Necromancer. Opera (romantic extravaganza) in three acts by Vaughan Williams to a libretto by Evelyn Sharp after Richard Gar-

nett's *The Poison Maid* and Nathaniel Hawthorne's *Rapaccini's Daughter*. It was composed 1927-9 and first performed in Cambridge in 1936. Vaughan Williams revised the work, the last revision being in 1956-7. Ursula Vaughan Williams has revised the spoken dialogue.

Polacca (It.). See *Polonaise*.

Poland

1. Introduction
2. From the Middle Ages to the 16th Century
3. From the Baroque to the 18th Century

4. The Early 19th Century: Emergence of a National style
5. The 20th Century
6. Developments since 1956

1. *Introduction*. Poland's troubled political history has impinged powerfully upon the development of her musical life. The invasions and conflicts of the late 17th century, for example, dealt a blow to Polish music from which it had scarcely recovered a century later. Again in the early 19th century a gradually reviving musical life was all but stifled by the fierce repression and censorship which followed the 1830 uprising. In the 20th century, too, musical development has been inextricably tied to major political turning-points. The declaration of independence in 1918, the establishment of the socialist state in 1945, and the 'October Revolution' of 1956 have all evoked or demanded a response from Polish composers.

If political upheaval has influenced the development of Poland's music, it has also influenced our capacity to trace that development, for it has taken a cruel toll of essential documentation. The Second World War is the most recent chapter in a long history of destruction, in which valuable sources in libraries and private collections have disappeared. This has even inhibited the study of 20th-century music; and for earlier periods the source materials are at times so exiguous that historical reconstruction must depend on intelligent guesswork.

2. *From the Middle Ages to the 16th Century*. Medieval sources are particularly scanty and, as elsewhere in Europe, they are predominantly liturgical. Gregorian chant arrived in Poland with the acceptance of Christianity in the mid 10th century, and native elements were probably assimilated over the next two or three centuries. Only in the 12th and 13th centuries, however, do we find the earliest surviving Polish liturgical music—a handful of antiphons, rhymed Offices, and hymns connected with the cult of such national saints as St Wojciech, St Adalbert, and St Stanisław. Of

major symbolic significance is the earliest surviving setting of a Polish text *Bogurodzica* (Mother of God), a strophic song similar in type to some Italian *laude*. Its melody can be traced back to the 12th century, but its popularity survived well into the 15th century when, according to Jan Długosz's *Chronicle*, it was regularly sung by Polish knights in battle. By then the repertory of such vernacular songs had widened to include translations of Latin sequences, Marian hymns and Christmas carols, and songs for interpolation in the *Mysteries* which by the 15th century had moved from the churches to the courts and town squares.

There are ample records of a thriving and developing musical life in early 15th-century Poland, and not only in monasteries and bishoprics. Professional *igrcy* or minstrels and municipal instrumentalists had their own guilds and fraternities, and aristocratic courts prided themselves on their resident ensembles. The most flourishing centre was the capital Kraków, where the courts of Jadwiga and Władisław Jagiełło reflected in their pomp and ceremony the early stages of one of the most glorious periods in Polish history. Here, too, the Jagiellonian University, one of the oldest in Europe, offered lectures on the theory of music which laid the foundations for the later development of Polish scholarship in this field. Also in the early 15th century Mikołaj of Radom, the first Polish composer of significance, emerged. Before Mikołaj there are only isolated polyphonic sources. But the quality of Mikołaj's extant music, mainly Mass movements and a *Magnificat* in a Burgundian style loosely akin to Dufay, suggests that there may have been a thriving tradition of polyphonic composition closely in touch with progressive techniques in Western Europe. This may well have continued through into the later 15th century, but again extant sources are confined to a handful of compositions, including the earliest surviving polyphonic piece with words in Polish, a three-part song in honour of St Stanisław, *Chwała Tobie Gospodzinie* ('Glory be to God').

Kraków retained its position as the cultural and intellectual heart of Poland throughout the 16th century, with musical activities centred on the royal chapel. In 1543 King Sigismund I founded a Capella Rorantistarum for the study and practice of church music, and as the century progressed the Capella's repertory expanded to include works by leading European composers of the late Renaissance, including Gombert, Lassus, Victoria, and Palestrina. Polyphonic music was also cultivated outside Kraków in monasteries and in the chapels of the aristocracy; our knowledge of these repertories remains fragmentary, but it is unlikely that they could have matched the richness of music in Kraków.

Something of that richness can be gleaned from the organ tablatures of Jan of Lublin (compiled 1537–48) and the Cloister of the Holy Spirit (1548), the latter now surviving only in a copy. These tablatures contain a wealth of Polish and non-Polish music in a wide variety of forms and styles, sacred and secular, vocal and instrumental in origin. They include more than 20 pieces by the most distinguished Polish composer of the early 16th century, Mikołaj of Kraków. The tablatures also testify to a remarkable standard of organ playing in Poland in the 16th century. The organ was the most popular instrument of the time, but in the latter half of the century it was increasingly rivalled by the lute in its roles as an accompanying and solo instrument. The Hungarian lutenist Bálint Bakfark (at the royal court 1549–65) exerted a strong influence on later Polish lutenist-composers such as Wojciech Długoraj (*c.*1550–*c.*1619) and Jakub Reys (*c.*1545–*c.*1605) as well as on the Italian (naturalized Polish) Diomedes Cato (1570–*c.*1615); between them they left many vocal arrangements, preludes, fantasies, and dances (galliards and passamezzos).

The 16th century was an era of gathering strength in Polish music, and as our knowledge of the period increases the list of eminent composers grows. Two in particular, Wacław of Szamotuły (*c.*1526–*c.*1560) and Marcin Leopolita (*c.*1540–89), were recognized even in their own lifetimes as the greatest Polish masters of Renaissance polyphony, and the latter's five-part *Missa paschalis* is unparalleled in 16th-century Polish music for the ease and fluency of its counterpoint, the inventiveness of its *cantus firmus* treatment, and the freshness of its melodic style. A further high point was the publication in 1580 of Mikołaj Gomółka's *Melodie na Psałterz Polski* ('Melodies for the Polish

Psalter'), a collection of 150 Polish psalm settings whose predominantly 'note-against-note' idiom conceals remarkably sophisticated harmonic and contrapuntal procedures. They are also among the earliest Polish works to show pronounced national features. As the composer wrote in his introduction: 'They are not for Italians, but for the Poles, For the stay-at-home, simple souls'.

3. *From the Baroque to the 18th Century.* With the work of Mikołaj Zieleński, one of the finest Polish composers before Chopin, we are on the threshold of the Baroque. His main legacy consists of 113 compositions (Venice, 1611) in two collections, comprising his *Offertoria* and *Communiones totius anni.* The polychoral pieces of the *Offertoria* are fairly uniform in style, but the *Communiones* represent a wide diversity of forms. Motets for four, five, and six voices form the largest group, followed by compositions for one and two solo virtuoso voices with organ accompaniment, and finally three compositions for three voices with organ and three instrumental fantasies. The two collections offer us a cross-section of the styles and techniques found in European music in the late 16th century, with a particular leaning towards the 'progressive' Venetian school (see *Italy*, 3). Zieleński's part-writing is still based firmly on the principles of Renaissance polyphony, but already by the 1620s monody and figured bass had found their way to Poland and in 1628 opera arrived at the royal court (recently moved to Warsaw). In 1632 King Władysław IV established an opera theatre at the court (on the first floor of the royal castle), and for the next two decades there were regular performances there and at Kraków and Gdańsk by the royal musicians. The repertory was largely of Italian opera, including several by the king's *Kappelmeister* Marco Scacchi (*c.*1600 *c.*1685). The music of the first Polish opera *La fama reale* by Piotr Elert (*c.*1600–53) has not survived.

Instrumental music in the new Italian manner also flourished during the early 17th century, encouraged by the presence in Poland of Italian masters such as Tarquinio Merula. The leading Polish composers were Adam Jarzębski (*d* 1649), whose *Canzoni e Concerti* with *basso continuo* date from the 1620s, and Marcin Mielczewski (*d* 1651), who has left seven canzonas for two violins, again with *basso continuo*, probably dating from the 1640s. The new vocal-instrumental style also permeated church music, co-existing for some time with an earlier Renaissance idiom. Again Mielczewski was influential, composing Masses in the old style and church concertos for voices and instruments in Baroque *concertato* style. The greatest composer of church music, however, was Bartlomiej Pękiel (*d* 1670), who took over as royal *Kappelmeister* from Marco Scacchi in 1649, after many years in the king's service. His *Missa Concertata la Lombardesca* for 13 voices employs antiphonal choirs, accompanied solos, and purely instrumental sections in a powerful, colourful conception. He also composed a 'dialogo', *Audite mortales*, which can make some claim to be the first Polish oratorio.

The later years of Pękiel's life coincided with political storms which ultimately destroyed the stability of Poland's cultural life and left the country isolated from the mainstreams of Western art and thought. The Swedish invasions of the mid 17th century and the later conflicts with Russia and Turkey, together with growing political intrigues and disputes within Poland itself, resulted in a decline in the vitality of Polish music. Our picture of late 17th- and early 18th-century music is hazy and incomplete, but of the many composers active at the time the most talented were probably Stanisław Sylwester Szarzyński and Grzegorz Gerwazy Gorczycki (*c*.1667–1734). Even with their music, however, evaluation rests on only a small number of surviving works. There are only ten extant compositions by Szarzyński, including two church concertos, a *concertato* motet, and an impressive sonata for two violins and organ. Gorczycki, the last major composer of the Polish Baroque, has fared rather better and is remembered today by several Masses in contrapuntal manner as well as motets in *concertato* style.

The decline of Poland as a political power continued through the 18th century, culminating in the first of the three partitions in 1772. Recent research has revealed a considerable symphonic literature from the second half of the century, notably by Antoni Milwid, Wojciech Dankowski, and Franciszek Ścigalski, but little of lasting value has emerged; only towards the end of the century were there signs of new vitality in Polish music, the beginning of a renaissance which was to be smothered in the aftermath of 1830. A solid institutional framework for the teaching and performance of music was established in the pre-1830 years, with opera at the National Theatre, a Society for Religious and National Music, a music society organized by E. T. A. Hoffmann, and above all the foundation of the Warsaw Conservatory in 1821.

4. *The Early 19th Century: Emergence of a National Style.* Warsaw dominated musical life, and the music composed or performed there just before and during Chopin's years in the city (1810–30) reveals a heterogeneous range of styles and influences. There were High Baroque church cantatas by Jakub Gołąbek, character-

istic of the 'learned' manner often adopted by Polish composers for their devotional music even into the early 19th century. There were also Classical symphonies and chamber music by Józef Elsner (1769–1854) and Feliks Janiewicz (1762–1848); and especially popular with Polish audiences were the lightweight piano concertos and bravura solos by Franciszek Lessel (*c*.1780–1838) and Józef Deszczyński (1781–1844) and the piano miniatures by Maria Szymanowska (1789–1831), for the public 'benefit' concert and the fashionable salon were already beginning to shape musical tastes in Warsaw.

They could not rival the opera house, however. In the early 19th century opera in Warsaw was dominated by Italian styles and above all by Rossini. Several Italian composers made their home in the Polish capital, at least until the uprising, and one of them, Carlo Soliva, played a prominent part in its musical life as principal of the School of Singing and Declamation. From Maciej Kamieński's *Nędza uszczęśliwiona* ('Sorrow turned to Joy', 1778) onwards, Polish composers had made an increasing contribution to the operatic repertory of the National Theatre, excelling in comic operas on rustic themes, particularly in the form of *Singspiele* or 'vaudevilles'. Jan Stefani's *Cud mniemany* ('The Supposed Miracle', 1794) is generally regarded as a landmark in the period immediately preceding the more substantial operatic achievements of Elsner and in particular of Karol Kurpiński (1785–1857), the leading Polish composer of opera during the first half of the 19th century.

Despite this range of styles, the concept of a national Polish idiom was much in the air in the early 19th century. It was discussed at length in treatises by Wacław Sierakowski and Elsner, but in practice 'Polishness' in music had not progressed much further than an appropriate choice of subject matter and the introduction of modal and rhythmic characteristics derived from the krakowiak, mazurka, and polonaise. For the most part such characteristics were simply grafted on to familiar styles, so that Polish elements in Lessel and Elsner, for example, do not differ noticeably from Polish elements in Weber and Hummel. Nevertheless the ground for a more distinctive national style was being laid. Here the language factor was important, and in several of the *Historical Songs* of 1816 (by Kurpiński, Lessel, Szymanowska, and others) there were new approaches to Polish word-setting which were eventually to bear fruit in the songs and operas of Stanisław Moniuszko (1819–72). The many keyboard polonaises composed in the early 19th century were also significant. It was above all in the hands of Michał Kleofas Ogiński (1765–1833) that the polonaise was moulded into an independent miniature for harpsichord or piano, designed for the salon. Ogiński was one of a family of distinguished musicians who bore witness to the thriving tradition of successful amateur composers drawn from the Polish aristocracy, and his 20 or so polonaises were particularly influential. They have a simple, homespun character which is notably independent of Western influences, and they defined the basic framework of the form as a clear-cut 'da capo' type, usually with a short introduction. The large repertory of early 19th-century polonaises, including the earliest attempts by Chopin, owed a good deal to Ogiński's model, in both design and mood.

Chopin very soon looked beyond Poland for his inspiration, however, and the bulk of his mature music was composed in Paris, where he settled in 1831. Yet by integrating national characteristics with the most advanced achievements of European music, he did lay the foundations upon which a 'nationalist' tradition might have been built in Poland itself. That such a tradition failed to develop was due in large measure to the ruthless policies of denationalization carried out by the partitioning powers in the wake of the 1830 uprising. Musical life became increasingly insular and conservative, and the music which responded most directly to its needs was not Chopin's but Moniuszko's. In his *Home Song-books*, Moniuszko offered Polish music-lovers harmonically simple 'homely' ballads on Polish themes which successfully wooed them away from the German and Russian repertory. Moniuszko's major achievement was in the field of opera, however. His first opera, *Halka*, staged in Warsaw in 1858, fathered a national operatic style of admittedly conservative bent, colouring the Italian styles of an earlier generation with the rhythms of Polish national dances. This was the blend which was to dictate the musical formulation of 'Polishness' to later Polish composers. The songs and operas of Waładysław Żeleński (1837-1921) and the orchestral music of Zygmunt Noskowski (1846-1909) consolidated Moniuszko's achievement, but by contemporary European standards their musical languages were anachronistic. Only in a handful of works by Juliusz Zarębski (1854-85) was there any awareness of the more progressive tendencies of Chopin's music and of the innovations of Liszt and Wagner.

5. *The 20th Century*. Though the quality of Polish music was at a low ebb in the late 19th century, there were signs that the path was being cleared for a brighter future, notably in the revival of concert life and teaching. The Warsaw Conservatory was reconstituted, the Warsaw Music Society formed, and in 1901 the Warsaw Philharmonic Orchestra founded, with its inaugural concert including a work by Ignacy

Paderewski (1860-1941), Poland's most famous composer of the day. Within a short time of the orchestra's foundation, four young composition students, Apolinary Szeluto (1884-1966), Grzegorz Fitelberg (1879-1953), Ludomir Różycki (1884-1953), and Karol Szymanowski (1882-1937), had expressed their disappointment with its conservative programmes and organized themselves into a group known as 'Young Poland in Music', very soon to be joined by the slightly older composer Mieczysław Karłowicz (1876-1909). Karłowicz left some impressive Straussian orchestral music, but he died before his full promise could be realized and it was left to Szymanowski to achieve the group's original aim of up-dating Polish music. After a long apprenticeship in German late-Romantic styles, he found stylistic maturity in his music of the war years, responding in a highly individual way to the stimulus of Debussy, Ravel, and late Skryabin.

By couching folkloristic materials in lucid, tonally rooted structures, Szymanowski's later 'nationalist' works foreshadow to some extent Polish music of the 1930s and 1940s. But the younger generation of Polish composers looked more towards Paris—to the clear-cut forms and mannered charm of neo-classical styles, influenced by Stravinsky, Prokofiev, Milhaud, and Poulenc and owing much to the teaching of Nadia Boulanger. The Association des Jeunes Musiciens Polonais à Paris was established in 1926 with Szymanowski's pupil Piotr Perkowski as its first chairman, and the music composed by its members tended to adopt a moderately toned neo-classical idiom, often spiced with elements of Polish folk music. This is broadly true of Perkowski's own Sinfonietta, as well as the early music of Stanisław Wiechowicz (*Chmiel*, 'Hop Wine'), Michał Kondracki (Partita and Concerto for Orchestra), Antoni Szałowski (Overture), and Michał Spisak (Serenade for Orchestra). Neo-classical sympathies are also apparent in the Symphonic Variations by Witold Lutosławski (*b* 1913) and even in the surviving 12-note works by Józef Koffler (1896-1943/4), the only Polish composer at that time to take Schoenberg's path.

In the years after the Second World War and the creation of the new socialist state, Polish music was largely cut off from developments in Western music and composers were urged to cultivate 'concrete' genres—opera, oratorio, cantata, etc.—and to take their inspiration from folk music. The first major work to be condemned as *'formalist' was the First Symphony by Lutosławski, the work in which the composer's individual voice begins to emerge clearly from earlier influences. Predictably, Bartók was a major inspiration to Polish composers in pursuit of a progressive, folk-based music and his influence is clear enough on the major achievements of the post-war years, the Fourth String Quartet and Fourth Violin Concerto by Grażyna Bacewicz (1913–69) and the Concerto for Orchestra by Lutosławski.

6. *Developments since 1956.* The more liberal cultural policy which followed the October revolt of 1956 resulted in a dramatic stylistic change in Polish music as it responded to renewed contact with radical Western developments. Progressive trends were encouraged by the establishment in 1956 of the 'Warsaw Autumn' festival of contemporary music, by lavish state subsidies for music publishing and recording, and by the foundation of the Experimental Music Studio of Polish Radio. The result was a remarkable flowering of avant-garde composition which placed Poland firmly on the musical map of Europe. For many older composers the attempt to renovate their musical language had unhappy results, however, and it is notable that the best of them, including Bacewicz and Lutosławski, moved slowly and cautiously towards a brave new world. For Lutosławski the solution was the highly personal fusion of aleatory counterpoint and strongly directional harmonic schemes which has characterized all his recent music since *Jeux Vénitiens* of 1961.

Of middle generation composers the most talented were Kazimierz Serocki and Tadeusz Baird, both of whom died in 1981 while still in their 50s. Baird's lyrical, intensely expressive musical language always remained entirely unique, but Serocki's development mirrored to some extent the main lines of evolution in post-war Polish music, from the neo-classical world of his Sinfonietta, through a brief flirtation with post-Webern serialism in his *Musica concertante* to the exploration of new textural landscapes in his *Symphonic Frescoes.* The younger composers who have attracted most interest both at home and abroad are Krzysztof Penderecki, Henryk Górecki, and Wojciech Kilar. All three have entirely individual musical styles, yet there are common features which to some extent characterize the Polish contribution to modern European music. One is the sheer simplicity of their music, its preoccupation with textural surfaces at the expense of deeper structural levels. It was that very simplicity which led to the extraordinary impact of the 'Polish sound' on a wide musical public in the 1960s. It seemed at the time a refreshing, perhaps even a necessary, antidote to the structural complexities of much progressive European music since the war. In the late 1970s the music of all three composers changed dramatically, again reflecting a movement within Polish music as a whole. Yet their present commitment to a nostalgic world of tonality and romanticism is in a sense not so different from the 'texture music' of the 1960s, applying to melody and harmony the same big, simple gestures which had earlier been applied to texture and timbre. Certainly the effect is no less one-dimensional. This is the world inhabited by Penderecki's Violin Concerto, *Te Deum*, and Second Symphony, by Kilar's *Bogurodzica* ('Mother of God') and *Grey Mist*, and by Górecki's *Beatus vir.*

Despite the devastation of the Second World War and the economic pressures which have beset Poland since then, the reconstruction of an active and healthy musical life has been given major priority and has been achieved with remarkable success. There are seven conservatories and three university faculties of musicology, as well as the Institute of Musicology at the Warsaw Academy of Sciences. Two opera houses and seven concert halls have been built or re-built since the war and there are seven professional orchestras and eight opera companies. Apart from the 'Warsaw Autumn' there are major festivals and competitions at Wrocław, Bydgoszcz, Duszniki, and Słupsk. Most encouraging of all is the way in which contemporary music has become an integral part of the mainstreams of musical activity in Poland. In Warsaw and Kraków today the contemporary composer is part of the musical furniture, a familiar figure in the college and the concert hall. He has a direct contact with, and feedback from, his audience which might be the envy of many composers in the West.   JIM SAMSON

FURTHER READING
Józef Chomiński, ed.: *Słownik muzyków polskich* [Dictionary of Polish Musicians] (Kraków, 1967); S. Jarociński, ed.: *Polish Music* (Warsaw, 1965); Zofia Chechlińska and Jan Stęszewski, eds.: *Polish Musicological Studies*, i (Kraków, 1977).

'Polish' Symphony. Nickname of Tchaikovsky's Symphony No. 3 in D major, Op. 29, composed in 1875. It is so called because the finale is in *polonaise rhythm.

Polka. A Bohemian round dance which became one of the most popular ballroom dances of the 19th century. Originally a peasant dance, it was taken up in Prague in the late 1830s and soon spread all over Europe: it was danced in Paris in 1840 and in London four years later. The polka was a lively dance in 2/4 time, generally in ternary form with regular phrases. All the leading dance composers of the mid 19th century wrote polkas, especially the Strauss family and Adolphe Jullien. The polkas of the two Johann Strausses, such as the 'Thunder and Lightning Polka' and the 'Tritsch-Tratsch Polka', are still popular today in concerts of Viennese music.

Polly. Ballad opera in three acts by Gay with music arranged by Pepusch and Arnold. It is a sequel to *The Beggar's Opera* and was first performed in London in 1779. A revised version, with a text by Clifford Bax and music arranged by Frederic Austin, was performed in London in 1922; another modern version, by John Addison, was given at Aldeburgh in 1952.

Polo (Sp.). A folk-dance from Andalusia, in moderate triple time, heavily syncopated, and punctuated by vocal coloraturas sung to words such as 'Olé'.

Polonaise (Fr.; Ger.: *Polonäse*; It.: *polacca*). A Polish dance in triple time and of moderate speed. It has a processional and stately character, and seems to have originated in courtly 16th-century ceremonies. The early polonaise bears little resemblance to the 19th-century dance, which is characterized by triple time, phrases starting on the first beat of the bar, and the repetition of short, rhythmic motifs. The earliest examples to show any of these features were, strangely enough, by J. S. Bach, in his Sixth French Suite and his Second Orchestral Suite. The classic polonaise appeared around 1800, and was taken up by Beethoven (Op. 89), Mozart (*Rondeau en polonaise* from his sixth keyboard sonata, K 284), Schubert (Polonaises for four hands, Op. 61 and Op. 75), Weber, Liszt, Musorgsky (*Boris Godunov*), and Tchaikovsky (*Eugene Onegin*; the finale of his Third Symphony is marked 'Tempo di polacca'). But the composer chiefly associated with the polonaise is Chopin, whose 13 examples provided an outlet for his intensely patriotic feeling.

Polovtsian Dances. Sequence of choral and orchestral pieces forming a ballet scene in Act 2 of Borodin's opera *Prince Igor*. The Polovtsy were nomadic invaders of Russia who, in the opera, capture Igor.

Polska. A dance in triple time, probably of Polish origin and similar to the *mazurka. It has become one of Sweden's most popular folk dances, though it is also danced elsewhere.

Polymetric. Term used in the editing of early music for a piece where the barlines do not occur at regular intervals, but are placed according to the musical and textual requirements of the phrasing, resulting in irregular bar lengths.

Polyphony (from Gk *polyphonia*, 'of many sounds'; Ger.: *Mehrstimmigkeit*, *Vielstimmigkeit*). Musical texture in two or more, though usually at least three, relatively independent parts. In general, this term is applied to vocal music, but usages such as 'orchestral poly-phony' with reference, for instance, to the music of Mahler or Ives are to be found in discussions of 19th- and 20th-century instrumental styles. It refers to a fundamental category of musical possibilities, since all sound sources may be used on their own, in monophony, or with another or others, in polyphony. The usages are therefore many and varied in the history of Western art and folk music and in ethnomusicology. In the field of Western art music, a general and a particular meaning can be identified as the most important applications.

Polyphony, in the sense of vocal music in more than one part, as opposed to monophony, developed between roughly the 10th and the 13th century. The earliest manifestation was *organum*. The source of this parallel intoning of liturgical melody may be traced to the natural range of the human voice. Both boys and men (the female voice, and indeed the female, having had little part to play in the Medieval ecclesiastical world) tend to have one of two vocal ranges lying about a fifth apart, and the immature and mature versions of each tend to be an octave apart. The disposition of voices at a fifth, octave, and twelfth over the lowest part and the basis for this in acoustics—the octave, fifth, and fourth are the lowest overtones (see *Harmonic series*)—formed a remarkable natural foundation for early polyphony.

In the 14th century there was a rapid development of this rudimentary polyphony in the principle of mixed intervallic and rhythmic successions for parts sung simultaneously. Polyphonic independence was extreme, in comparison with both earlier and later styles. It involved, for instance, the vertical combination of different *isomelic and *isorhythmic constructions: indeed, in this early phase of vocal polyphony the three or four parts would often sing different texts together, in both Latin and the vernacular.

The combination of independent lines of music became a constant element of the Western tradition, and it is a means of comparing phases of musical language—from Medieval polyphony with its basically linear organization; through Renaissance and Baroque counterpoint, with its greater emphasis on the organization of the resulting vertical combination, and the conjunction of this with the evolution of major-minor tonality to produce the harmonic structures of Classical and Romantic music; to the new polyphony of the 20th century, where a multiplicity of independent strands is once more the shared ideal of many composers. In the simple meaning of 'multi-voiced', then, polyphony is to be found throughout the post-*organum* history of Western music.

The use of the term itself became common in theoretical and practical writings of the early

16th century. It replaced earlier terms such as *dia-*, *tri-*, and *tetraphonia* (which specified the number of parts) or *organica* (discant). The spread of a common meaning for polyphony coincided with the era of excellence in its practice discussed below. The great Classical theorist Heinrich Koch (1749–1816) established the two modern distinctions: monophony/polyphony, and polyphony/homophony. The first is a practical distinction, between single-voiced and multi-voiced composition, the latter being the predominant feature of Western art music. The second distinction is a stylistic one. It refers to the alternative approaches to musical continuity available for the post-Renaissance composer, one relying on counterpoint and the structural equality of voices, the other on a structural framework of melody supported by a bass-line with inner parts to provide harmonic, rhythmic, and textural expression. Although all homophonic music revealing harmonic differentiation is, logically, polyphonic or 'multi-voiced', stylistically the interplay of contrapuntal polyphony and harmonic homophony has been a crucial factor in the evolution of musical language, both vocal and instrumental, since the early 17th century.

A particular meaning of the term is reserved for 16th-century sacred music, the 'golden age' of polyphony. The milestones in its evolution are found in the music of Dunstable and of the 15th-century Franco-Flemish school. Their principal concern was to develop techniques for using one melodic idea in all parts by means of imitation. Hugo Riemann's concept *Durchimitieren*, or 'through-imitation', amply conveys the principle of distributing the main material of the polyphony—what was in earlier stages the *cantus firmus*—across every voice. The development of a more euphonious harmonic sense—especially in the treatment of the fourth as a dissonance requiring contrapuntal preparation and resolution—went hand in hand with increasing skill at complex polyphonic control. By the 16th century a coherent and consistent European imitative style had arisen. It was impelled by many historical forces, not least of which were the increase in the dissemination of music allowed by the printing of music from *c*.1500 onwards and the increasing focus of artistic control exercised by the Roman Catholic Church in reaction to the Reformation.

The high point of Renaissance polyphony was in the mid and late 16th century. Lassus, Victoria, and, in England, Byrd were and still are considered only the great among many giants. The peak of this activity came in the music of Palestrina, whose polyphony has been studied by most theorists and composers of the last three centuries, although the temporary reaction against vocal polyphony in the 17th century was as extreme as it was productive. Palestrina's compositions, his 'novum genus musicum' (preface to Second Book of Masses, 1567), had two outstanding features: the clear expression of the text, whether in three, four, or five parts, by means of formal articulation of the music according to the phrases of the text and by the matching of the cadence of melodic ideas, especially in their rhythmic proportions, to the words; and the independence and clarity of each line within the declamation structure, with an elegance of combination in dissonance treatment and textural flow that marks a pinnacle of Western art.   JONATHAN DUNSBY

Polyrhythm. Simultaneous use of different rhythms in separate parts of the musical texture. It is a characteristic feature of some 14th-century music, and also of some 20th-century pieces, by, for example, Hindemith and Stravinsky.

Polytextuality. Simultaneous use of different texts in the various parts of a vocal composition. It was particularly common in the early *motet.

Polytonality. Simultaneous use of two or more keys. If two keys are superposed the technique is known as *bitonality; more complex combinations are rare.

Pommer. Old German name for the larger sizes of *shawm, derived from *bombarde via an early form, *Pumhart*.

Pomp and Circumstance. Title given by Elgar (from Act 3 of Shakespeare's *Othello*) to a set of five marches for symphony orchestra, Op. 39: No. 1 in D major and No. 2 in A minor were first performed in Liverpool in 1901; No. 3 in C minor in London in 1904; No. 4 in G major in London in 1907; and No. 5 in C major in London in 1930. The trio section of No. 1, slightly altered and with words by A. C. Benson beginning 'Land of Hope and Glory', became the finale of Elgar's *Coronation Ode*.

Ponce, Manuel (Maria) (*b* Fresnillo, Mexico, 8 Dec. 1886; *d* Mexico City, 24 Apr. 1948). Mexican composer. He studied in Mexico City, Bologna, and Berlin, returning to Mexico in 1909 to take up a teaching post at the National Conservatory. Mexican folk music, which he was the first composer to study, had an important influence on his works, as did also the rhythms of Cuban music, which he studied during a stay in Havana (1915–17). However, most of his larger works date from after a period in Paris (1925–33), during which he had further lessons with Dukas. He produced numerous guitar and piano pieces as well as concertos for guitar (*Concierto del sur*, 1941) and violin (1943).

PAUL GRIFFITHS

Ponchielli, Amilcare (*b* Paderno Fasolaro, nr Cremona, 1 Aug. 1834; *d* Milan, 17 Jan. 1886). Italian composer. He studied at the Milan Conservatory, and had a provincial success with his first opera *I promessi sposi* (1856), which in a revised form brought him commissions to write several ballets for La Scala. His opera *La gioconda* (1876), to a libretto by Boito, which had an enormous vogue due to its vitality of style, shows its composer's knowledge of the sentimental manner of Meyerbeer and early Verdi.

DENIS ARNOLD

Ponticello (It.). Literally 'little bridge', i.e. the bridge of a stringed instrument. *Sul ponticello*, 'on the bridge', i.e. play with the bow as close to the bridge as possible; this greatly diminishes the intensity of the lower harmonics in favour of the higher, in order to produce a thin, ethereal quality.

Popper, David (*b* Prague, 16 June 1843; *d* Baden, nr Vienna, 7 Aug. 1913). Austrian cellist and composer. He spent much of his life touring Europe, being famed for his splendid tone and transcendental technique. He was latterly professor at the Brussels Conservatoire and his studies (published 1901–5) still provide the technical basis for cellists.

DENIS ARNOLD

Popular Music

1. Introduction
2. Popular Music and the Theatre
3. Orchestral Music
4. Popular Song
5. The Pop Revolution

1. *Introduction*. 'Popular' music can be said to comprise all the various kinds of music that might not be considered under the general heading of 'serious' or 'classical' music. The division between the two worlds has always been fairly clearly defined, with those active in one sphere rarely trespassing in the other, and never more so than today, when, instead of the distinction being based on fluctuating artistic 'taste', it is fairly firmly based on economic considerations. Popular music—music that is written for and sold to a wide audience who can enjoy it without being musically 'educated'—is, with such obvious exceptions as genuine folk music and some forms of jazz, written with the hope of financial gain. Much 'serious' music today is written in an experimental spirit and can be appreciated only by an audience which has a considerable awareness of the finer points of music; it therefore frequently requires financial support from the State and other benefactors and has no expectation of profit.

Paradoxically, as the dividing line between the two kinds of music becomes more clearly defined, the appreciation of both kinds becomes more general. There is now considerable academic interest in and study of popular music (there were virtually no books on the subject until the last decades of the 19th century, and very few until well into the 1920s), while classical music, at least of the traditional kind, now draws an appreciative audience from all classes. There have always been composers of popular music who have received the accolade of serious attention because of the craftsmanship and substance of their works (e.g. Johann Strauss for his waltzes and George Gershwin

because he wrote ambitious concert works and an opera), but today most musical reference works feel obliged to give all the various areas of popular music serious attention. Certainly the old snobbery that equated serious music with 'good' and popular music with 'bad' has largely disappeared.

The growth of popular music clearly coincided with the increasing wealth and purchasing power of the lower and middle classes in the mid 19th century, and with their demand for musical entertainment of an easily accessible nature. Other practical considerations were both created by and helped to create this demand: the development of cheaper methods of printing music; the extra mobility of both audience and performer brought about by the expansion of road and rail transport; the rapid growth of theatres and concert halls catering for popular taste; the general availability of cheaper instruments for home entertainment, beginning with the cottage piano; and, in the 20th century, the phenomenal spread of such entertainment media as the gramophone, cinema, radio, and television. In commercial terms, as measured by a modern yardstick like the sale of long-playing gramophone records, the average world sales of classical music now account for roughly 10 per cent of the output, and all forms of popular and light music for most of the remaining 90 per cent (this proportion varies from country to country).

2. *Popular Music and the Theatre:* (a) *Opera.* The gradual creation of a written tradition of popular music began in the late 18th century, with works like Gay's *The Beggar's Opera* (1728)

and its equivalents in Germany and elsewhere paving the way. These operas added words to already well-known traditional and composed melodies. Opera composers, as well as composers of other genres, were already aware of the particular satisfaction of writing blatant melodies that caught the popular imagination: Mozart recorded in his letters the pleasure of hearing tunes from *Le nozze di Figaro* whistled by the proverbial errand-boy and played on street corners, and Verdi established his fame with a chorus of Hebrew slaves in *Nabucco*, the chorus becoming an early 'hit song' (indeed, practically a national anthem), and continued to reveal his flair for what were sometimes contemptuously called 'barrel-organ' tunes in later works like *Rigoletto*.

The creation of operas of a light and tuneful nature full of material for commercial exploitation is epitomized by the entirely frivolous nature of a work like Donizetti's *La fille du régiment*, which was one of the vital sparks that led towards a popular musical theatre. The general public has neither the inclination nor the stamina to listen to lengthy and involved compositions, so popular music is almost invariably of shorter duration and less elaborate structure. The obvious way to avoid the potential tedium of grand opera was to break down the music into isolated and tuneful arias and ensembles, discarding the artificial practice of recitative and moving the music along more understandably by interspersed dialogue. The French, always

Jenny Lind in the first London production of Donizetti's 'Daughter of the Regiment', Her Majesty's Theatre (1847).

appreciative of elegance and lightness in music, were the prime movers in this direction, with a corpus of lighter operas, termed *opéra comique* and using spoken dialogue, by such composers as Boieldieu, Auber, Hérold, and Adam. The first firm step towards the establishment of a deliberately popular operatic convention was made by the German-born composer Offenbach who, after unfruitful studies at the Paris Conservatoire, settled in Paris and became very French in outlook. Finding the doors of the Opéra-Comique barred to his frivolities, he eventually acquired his own theatre, Les Bouffes-Parisiens, and during the hectic years of the Second Empire and the Great Exhibition of 1852 established a vogue for a saucy, tuneful, often bitingly satirical and highly comical form of light opera, variously termed 'opéra comique', 'opéra bouffe', and, finally, 'operette' (in the Italian form, *operetta). He wrote almost 100 of these works, with varying degrees of profitability, and his main and lasting successes were with such works as *Orphée aux enfers*, *La belle Hélène*, *La grande duchesse de Gérolstein*, *La vie Parisienne*, and *Les brigands*; he also had a final fling at grand opera in the posthumously performed *Les contes d'Hoffmann*.

With increasingly affluent audiences available and a rapid growth of theatres to be filled in all the principal cities of the world, the effervescent Offenbach operetta and the infectious naughtiness of the *can-can inspired a host of imitators. A contemporary rival was the then equally successful, but less lasting, Hervé (real name Florimond Ronger; 1825–92), whose greatest success was *Chilperic*; he was succeeded by a flourishing school of composers such as Charles Lecocq (1832–1918), Robert Planquette (1848–1903), and André Messager (1853–1929).

The Offenbach operettas made a great impact in other countries, especially in Vienna, where Franz von Suppé strove for similar light effects, eventually coaxing the famous Johann Strauss II into the theatre with such classics of the genre as *Die Fledermaus* and *Der Zigeunerbaron*. Vienna, with its inherent love of melody and romantic gaiety, very soon developed its own special brand of operetta, naturally dominated by the waltz, with Viennese-based composers like Karl Millöcker (1842–99), Richard Heuberger (1850–1914), Franz Lehár, Oscar Straus, and Leo Fall (1873–1925).

In London there was also a hungry host of theatres that imported and produced the latest French productions almost as soon as they were seen in Paris. Offenbach had a special success in London with *Geneviève de Brabant*, and the catchy Gendarmes' Duet was seen to put its imprint on much that was to follow. Most of his pieces had a London production in small theatres like the Opera-Comique and the Gaiety, or, on a more lavish scale, at the Empire and other manifestations of growing commercialism. A young Mr W. S. Gilbert was one of those employed to translate the French librettos, and when he and Arthur Sullivan embarked on the famous partnership that produced *Trial by Jury*, *HMS Pinafore*, and the other immortal Savoy operas, there was a strong flavour of Offenbach and 'gendarmery' in their strains. Because of Sullivan's strong and ever-demanding academic background, their pieces remained definably operatic.

Gilbert was also a key figure in a popular type of musical entertainment called *burlesque, which had a great vogue in the last half of the 19th century. This strongly satirical genre indulged in parody of grand opera and other highbrow entertainment (as is revealed in such titles as *Faust-up-to-Date* and *Little Christopher Columbus*), with the music generally taking second place. The true inheritors of the Gilbert and Sullivan tradition were a new brand of composers who, lacking Sullivan's capacity for sustained musical creation, many of them being musical directors bred in the theatre rather than the academy, took British operetta a step forward to a popular entertainment that was very much a dialogue sliced up by catchy songs—variety, later known as *musical comedy. The

moving spirit of this new form of entertainment was a worship of the female figure and other feminine charms, as epitomized by the famous Gaiety Girls. Its principal composers included Leslie Stuart (1856-1928); Ivan Caryll (1861-1921); Lionel Monckton (1862-1924); Howard Talbot (1865-1928); Sidney Jones (1869-1914); and Paul Rubens (1875-1917).

(*b*) *The American Musical.* The up-and-coming place for the future exploitation of the musical stage was to lie outside Europe, in the USA, where the growth of wealth and the means of commercial exploitation outpaced all other rivals. At first the American musical theatre imported its models: Gilbert and Sullivan had as great a vogue there as in London, and their works were pirated in every form until they found a means of stopping the robbery; and shows from the Gaiety and Daly's went over with the same automatic speed as the French shows had earlier come to London. French operetta also had its vogue in the USA, and Offenbach himself made a brief and unenjoyable visit. Like a monstrous tug-of-war the commercial battle went on, until gradually the British shows lost their popularity and shows written in the USA began to travel the other way; one of the first of these was *The Belle of New York*, which had had only a moderate

Gilbert and Sullivan's 'Trial by Jury' at the Royalty Theatre (1875).

success in New York but was hugely popular in London. In fact, the London domination of the American stage was soon to be pushed aside by two stronger currents. The USA had long been a haven for refugees from the uncertain political climate of Europe, and with the many composers and writers went a Viennese strain which had a strong influence, discernible particularly in the 20th-century musicals of such as Rodgers and Hammerstein. The American theatre now had its own school of composers, drawn from these immigrants, like Victor Herbert (1859-1924), Karl Hoschna (1877-1911), and Louis Hirsch (1887-1924), and the Viennese-flavoured tradition continued well into modern times in the works of Rudolf Friml (1870-1972) and Sigmund Romberg (1887-1951).

But the most compelling ingredient of American music—one that was to make the trade almost totally export in the coming years —was the native element of *ragtime and *jazz, a style that rapidly revolutionized the language of popular music in a couple of hectic decades roughly centred on 1900 (see 4 below). Early in the century a young composer called Jerome Kern had found himself stationed in London with the task of adding songs, correctly concocted to suit the new American tastes, to the imported British shows. A song like 'They didn't believe me' shines out like a beacon among the old-fashioned strains of a Sidney Jones-Paul Rubens score called *The Girl from Utah*. Kern's music formed a bridge between the old style and the new, his works being only lightly coloured by ragtime, and always keeping the gracefulness of the old operetta idiom. His music has lived on, divorced from a number of frivolous librettos—with the outstanding exception of *Show Boat* (1927), which was a leading work in the trend towards a new and stronger integration of music and plot.

More wholeheartedly in the new vein were the musical comedies of George Gershwin (the jazz element is most successfully integrated in his folk opera *Porgy and Bess*), Cole Porter, and Richard Rodgers (at least in the earlier works, written in collaboration with Lorenz Hart; the later pieces, with Oscar Hammerstein II, moved towards a more traditional style that took something from everything and produced true 'operas for the people' like *Oklahoma*, *South Pacific*, *The King and I*, and *The Sound of Music*).

With the coming of jazz, the American musical was to be the dominating force in the theatre. Britain would produce an isolated genius like Ivor Novello or Noël Coward, writing in an entirely personal Viennese idiom; and lesser figures like Noel Gay, Jack Strachey, and Vivian Ellis who continued to write in a British idiom mainly for British consumption.

The cover of the song 'Bess You is My Woman' from Gershwin's folk-opera 'Porgy and Bess' (1st edition).

One or two remarkable 1920s-flavoured revivals, for example Sandy Wilson's *The Boy Friend* and Julian Slade's *Salad Days*, had an exportable novelty element. The most successful British musical of the 1950s was Lionel Bart's *Oliver*, which surpassed all performance records set by such pieces as *Chu-Chin-Chow* in earlier days.

The early dominance of the Italian opera was never reflected by any such influence in operetta, while both French and Viennese operetta soon seemed to run out of steam and to meekly accept American leadership. The one influential European figure of the 1930s was to come from Germany, in the figure of Kurt Weill, who went back to *The Beggar's Opera* for his source of inspiration in *Die Dreigroschenoper*. He was exiled from his own country because of his Jewish blood, and ended up in the USA, writing still excellent and personal works, though much diluted by being in the American style.

3. *Orchestral Music.* The world of light orchestral music follows a path closely parallel to that of popular theatre music. Of course, many of the great classical composers themselves contributed to the popular musical repertory by writing in a light melodic vein, frequently in the course of longer works and notably, as in the case of Tchaikovsky, Delibes, and others, in ballet scores, where an essentially rhythmical idiom was essential. One of the outstanding 'serious' composers to write light music as to the manner born was Elgar (in pieces like *Salut*

A concert in the bandstand in Hyde Park, engraving (1895) by Arthur Hopkins.

d'amour and *Chanson de matin*), and he had an incalculable influence on the light composers, like Eric Coates, who maintained this British tradition. In the days before cinema there was a considerable demand for such light orchestral music, particularly for the orchestras which most spas and large seaside resorts maintained around the turn of the century, mixing light classics and genuine light music; this was the sort of fare that audiences were given at the early promenade concerts. With the end of live music in such places as the Lyons corner-houses and the restaurants of big stores, this kind of *palm court music died out except as an archaic revival on radio, and the chances of hearing such an orchestra today are remote. Where the light music tradition has been strongly continued is in the *brass and *military bands, which continue to commission works from composers, many from within their own ranks.

Another tradition that flourished in the 19th century and died out in the early 20th with the advent of cinema entertainment was that of dance music. The endless flood of waltzes and polkas, with quadrilles, lancers, and other set pieces basing their strains on the popular music of the day, was a highly commercial business, especially from the 1840s to the 1890s. The heart of this industry was, of course, in Vienna, with the famous Strauss family, Joseph Lanner, the Schrammel brothers, and a host of lesser lights. They were rivalled by such as Joseph Gung'l (1810–89), a Hungarian, and Emil Waldteufel (1837–1915), like Offenbach a German who settled in Paris; numerous hack writers, like Sidney Jones Senior and Charles d'Albert kept the British market well supplied.

4. *Popular Song: (a) Music Hall and Revue*. It is in turning to the popular song itself that we find a true intermingling of traditions. To begin with, there is the eternal question of where *folk music begins and ends. A true history of folk music, as opposed to the many shrewd and well-informed guesses at what is largely undocumented, is well-nigh impossible. With the

advantage of publication, many of the composers of our traditional songs would simply have been writers of popular song, rather than the many ghostly 'anons' whose music has acquired the fascinating wry flavour of folk music through being passed on by an unpredictable oral tradition which tends, as a general rule, to push all its music towards narrow intervals and minor keys. Similarly, if many of today's commercial songs were subjected to the same oral treatment they would become folksongs. Today, there is a flourishing trade in 'writing' folk-songs. The folk influence is to be felt mainly in the specialized arts of the music hall, in jazz, and, of course, in blues, which is now much more an element of the contemporary pop song than it ever was in the products of Tin Pan Alley.

In the early 19th century, with the advent of cheaper printing, there began to appear endless collections of popular songs, with titles like *The Minstrel's Companion*, and these show a clear tendency to polish up the tunes into symmetrical structures with clean lines that compare with their classical counterparts. The classical composers of this period made the folk-song into a polite art, as did, in coming years, many of the dedicated collectors who, with deference to strong Victorian traditions, minimized the

Title-page of the 1st edition of Balfe's 'Come into the garden, Maud'.

roughness of the folk tunes and the bawdiness of many of their lyrics. The popular song, produced as fodder for the obligatory parlour pianos and the amateur singers of Victorian family evenings, was related to folk music only through its rustic bias. Musically, it was a pale copy of the operatic aria, particularly the Italian aria, with naïve and not too virtuosic melody lines lyrically suited to the gentle melancholy of the verse-writers, with a simple Alberti bass or simple arpeggio accompaniment. This, the *drawing-room ballad, flourished, from the best-selling 'Ever of thee' (1852) by Foley Hall and George Linley and 'Come into the garden, Maud' (1858) by Michael Balfe and Alfred Tennyson to the last trite melodies that Arthur Sullivan wrote in the name of polite drawing-room song when he was not being coerced into writing sparkling melodies by the artful W. S. Gilbert.

Leaving aside, for the moment, the calculated vulgarities of music hall song—and all the best composers added a careful warning to their publications that they were not to be sung in the music hall—popular song seemed likely to continue in this somewhat insipid vein for ever. Samples from France, Italy, Germany, even the USA, are not discernibly different to the British brand. After 1900 the sentiments gradually changed. There was less of the 'pale and lonely loitering' lover material, and quite a flood of jovial and patriotic songs of the Wilfrid Sanderson type, such as 'Drake is going West' and 'Glorious Devon'. Such songs, of course, always spring up in and around warring periods: England, with the Boer War on its hands and the First World War sensed in the distance, was following a style that had produced such songs as 'The British Grenadiers' and 'Heart of Oak'. The ultimate result of all wars, from a narrowly artistic viewpoint, is to coarsen people's tastes. The First World War, apart from an isolated archaism like 'Keep the home fires burning', simply took society down a peg or two to the level of music hall: it was not permissible for members of all levels of society to sing a song like 'Mademoiselle from Armentieres'. In the theatre higher standards tend to prevail, because of the superior craftsmanship needed to contrive a lengthy score. A sideways glance at what the theatre is doing in any given year will usually throw light on the current fashionable trends in the wider areas of popular music.

The *music hall, at first a peculiarly British phenomenon, but quickly developed in France and on the American vaudeville stage, was itself a reflection of the economic elevation of the lower classes. Music hall entertainment was simply a miscellaneous collection of vocal and visual acts of a popular nature, with the items frequently given some coherence in the earlier

The Oxford Music Hall in 1861.

days by the presence of a jovial chairman who would exhort the patrons to sing and drink. 'Song-and-supper rooms' flourished in and around the Strand in London, with places like Evans's, the Cyder Cellars, and the Coal Hole. These were not in fact really intended for the poorer classes but were the haunts of the well-to-do, with good wine and brandies available. And it was only later that ladies were permitted to watch the proceedings, from a discreet balcony. The type of music heard here was still of a folk-like nature, with songs of the 'Vilikens and his Dinah' type sung by such earthy characters as Sam Cowell, Harry Clifton, W. G. Ross, Charles Sloman, and Jack Sharp.

The popular music hall grew out of and alongside such entertainments when the proprietors of some well-known taverns realized that they too might encourage custom by providing a 'music hall' where the audience could sit and enjoy their ales and stout, cheap wines, and homely food, while being entertained from the stage. One of the best known of these early music rooms was attached to the Eagle Tavern in the City Road, remembered in the song 'Pop goes the weasel'. All the large taverns followed suit. One of the most famous was the Canterbury, run by Charles Morton, an influential figure in music hall history. Here new stars like George Leybourne, the Great Vance, and Arthur Roberts built their reputations. It was not until 1914 that a law was passed confining the partaking of refreshments to separate bars, thus starting a decline in music hall tradition that was to be completed by the inroads of gramophone and radio entertainment, although variety theatres were still to be found in the 1950s. The old song-and-supper style of entertainment had a popular revival in the Players' Theatre and has remained a regular television favourite at the Leeds Palace of Varieties.

The music hall did not add much to the progress of popular music. It adapted itself to the current fashions for folk-song style, the ballad, and finally the ragtime and jazz idioms. What it added to our stock of popular music was a repertory of immortal songs easily remembered by their combination of a direct tune and earthy good humour.

French music hall followed a similar course, developing from the early café-concert, cabaret kind of entertainment to the grandeur of the big Parisian music halls like the Olympia. American vaudeville copied the British tradition in its own style and musical idioms.

Another form of intimate variety, in a far

more sophisticated form, was to be found in the legitimate theatre under the name of *revue. The entertainment is of French origin, but it had a forerunner in the British one-man entertainments organized by such writers as Charles Dibdin. The first British entertainment to consciously ape the French style was Planché's *Success* at the Adelphi in 1825. One of the first to style itself a 'revue' was *Pot-Pourri* in 1899. True intimate revue had something of the seaside pierrot show in its make-up, as seen in Pélissier's famous 'Follies' from 1897 onward, a style carried on by the 'Co-Optimists'. Revues on a lavish and spectacular scale were seen at larger theatres like the Empire from 1905. But it was the intimate revue that survived as an economical type of entertainment with a small cast, as epitomized by the Cochran revues of the 1920s and 1930s, in which the talents of Noël Coward, among others, were able to blossom. They led to the satirical revues of the 1960s, such as *Beyond the Fringe*. In the USA it was the spectacular revue that proved most popular, as represented by the famous Ziegfeld Follies and other shows of that nature. Revue provided an outlet for the talents of high-class songwriters, and was aimed mainly at the cultured middle classes.

(b) Black American Music. The nature of every kind of popular musical entertainment was to be deeply affected by the great musical revolution of the 1890s, when *ragtime, closely followed by *jazz, began to change the whole nature of popular song. The distinctive talents and styles of the Black American were submerged for some 300 years in the USA while slavery was still permitted. In the mid 19th century, before Black entertainers were generally allowed on the stage, something of the flavour of their songs and dances was caught in the popular black-faced minstrel shows. As the name implies, these were basically shows of a variety nature performed by White entertainers made up as Blacks. One of the most successful writers of such material was Stephen Foster (1826-64), whose great hit of 1851 was *Swanee River*, a song taken up by, and even published under the name of, Edwin Christy, leader of a popular American minstrel show: long after this such entertainments were nearly always popularly referred to as Christy minstrel shows. In fact, other minstrel leaders did more to popularize the genre, particularly in England. The Christy troupe never actually came to London but his name was frequently used by other organizers. Others, like the Moore and Burgess Minstrels and the Mohawk Minstrels, became immensely popular in London.

The music hall and the minstrel shows between them helped to establish the popular music publishing industry that was to become known collectively as 'Tin Pan Alley'. At first the average home found its domestic entertainment around the family piano and sales of sheet music began to reach the proportions that sales of gramophone records achieve today.

In the minstrel shows Black music was only being parodied. It was to be revealed to a wider public by the tours of the famous Jubilee Singers, a group of Black singers from the University of Fisk who made the *spiritual known all over the world. But it was to be revealed most tellingly in the strains of the cakewalk and ragtime, a music which utilized the syncopated rhythms of the banjo and which came with astonishing freshness to the ears of a public still fed on the four-square rhythms of the Victorian ballad. The first genuine Black rag was published in 1897, Tom Turpin's *Harlem Rag*; Scott Joplin published his *Original Rags* in 1899 and followed it with the phenomenally successful *Maple Leaf Rag* in the same year. The White composers of Tin Pan Alley, who had perhaps subconsciously suppressed the rise of Black music, now gave in to its infectious strains and the first ragtime boom was on. A new fillip came in 1911 with Irving Berlin's song 'Alexander's Ragtime Band', and the world went ragtime mad. The Ragtime Octet had brought the music to Britain and even serious composers like Debussy had heard the strains of the cakewalk on record and had indulged in the sincerest form of flattery.

The ragtime idiom was a comparatively

The cover of Scott Joplin's first published collection, 'Original Rags'.

simple thing for any composer to emulate—a mere matter of misplaced accents. Its form was that of the popular march as played by Sousa and his band; its melodies had their own distinction; but its harmonies were basically those of all Western music. A deeper strain of Black music was loosely covered by the name *'blues', which introduced an entirely new flexibility and dissonance to popular music. The syncopations were subtler, more a matter of feeling than of deliberation; the harmonies were more chromatic and fluid; and the rhythmic propulsion was something entirely new. In fact for many years the argument raged in jazz circles as to whether White musicians could ever produce jazz with the same authentic feel as Black musicians could. Probably they could not at first, at least until the idiom became absorbed into the natural language of popular music, but it was a White band, the Original Dixieland Jazz Band, who made the first jazz recording. They were also largely responsible for introducing jazz into England when they toured the country after the First World War. They played a jolly sort of jazz, loosely defined as *'Dixieland', which still had much of the ragtime strain in it. The real blues music was still very much confined to the Black market. But by the early 1920s new talents had emerged and, by dint of being entertainers as well as musicians, carried the jazz message all over the world—much of it by way of the gramophone, which was the new force in home entertainment. The talents of individuals like Louis Armstrong (who could produce a tone from a cornet or trumpet that no 'straight' musician had even dreamed of) and bands such as that led by the great composer/pianist Duke Ellington forced the strains of jazz into the world of music.

Within two decades the language of popular music had undergone a complete change. Only isolated pockets of polite music-making—the palm court orchestras, the brass and military bands (and even these have succumbed to some extent)—played popular music 'straight'. The musical theatre, still our yardstick of popular taste, also adopted the jazz idiom. A composer like Jerome Kern could still hover between the two worlds of music, but he was a pioneer in adding jazz-orientated tunes to popular London shows of the early 1900s so that they would export more easily to the USA. The new wave of theatre composers, like George Gershwin, was totally immersed in the new idiom. Even so, what was still dominantly White music written for a White audience was to retain an urbane, polite, restrained quality right through the inter-war years and well into the 1950s.

PETER GAMMOND

5. *The Pop Revolution*. It is ironic that it should have been a little-known hillbilly singer, Bill

Bill Haley and the Comets

Elvis Presley

Haley, who in 1954 sowed the seeds of a pop music revolution. For Haley was hardly a revolutionary figure, nor was he the stuff of which pop idols are made. None the less, the release of his recording of 'Shake, rattle, and roll' proved the first in a chain of events which ultimately transformed the world of pop.

The new music became known as *rock and roll, and subsequent releases by Haley and his band, The Comets, included 'Rock around the clock' and 'See you later, alligator'. However, Haley's success was soon eclipsed by that of Elvis Presley, whose uninhibited stage performances of songs such as 'Jailhouse rock' owed much to the example of Black rhythm and blues performers. Indeed, rock and roll was essentially a fusion of elements from Black urban rhythm and blues and White rural *country and western music. Rock and roll's blues form, electric instruments, and loud riffs (short, repeated tunes) stemmed from the former; the nasal vocal style, string bass, and straightforward melodies of rock and roll had their origins in country and western.

That elements of two previously segregated musics should be brought together in rock and roll was in itself revolutionary. That rock and roll releases came initially from small, independent record companies in the face of considerable opposition from the recording giants fighting to preserve the, for them, commercially successful status quo, was further evidence of deep-seated change within the pop music industry. Also revolutionary was the fact that, through rock and roll, Black performers were able to achieve commercial success comparable with that of Whites. And, as rhythm and blues performers such as Chuck Berry and Little Richard moved into rock and roll, they inspired young White musicians with their technique and fervour.

In Britain, many of these young musicians gained their first playing experience in the ad hoc 'skiffle' bands of the late 1950s. Skiffle also had links with earlier Black American music, being derived from the music of rural Blacks in the Mississippi delta. But it was urban rhythm and blues which became the dominant influence on such 60s' groups as The Rolling Stones and Cream. Indeed, the former took their name from a song by a rhythm and blues singer, Muddy Waters.

In the circumstances, Liverpool was a logical setting for the emergence of The Beatles. Imported rhythm and blues, country and western, and rock and roll records were readily available in this cosmopolitan sea-port, and, in linking these transatlantic influences with the modality of English folk music, Lennon and McCartney became dominant influences on the development of pop during the 1960s.

The emergence of The Beatles in England coincided with the beginning of Bob Dylan's career across the Atlantic. Dylan sang of contemporary issues, accompanying himself on acoustic guitar and abjuring melodic and harmonic complexity in order to express his themes of protest with maximum clarity. Dylan's

The Beatles at the Cavern in Liverpool (1962), Ringo's first appearance.

The Police

audiences consisted of young New York intellectuals, who contrasted sharply with the young teenagers dancing to the music of The Beatles at the Liverpool Cavern in England. Yet as Dylan and The Beatles matured, they grew closer together, exchanging influences and, as one critic put it, 'helping pop grow up'. Impressed by The Beatles' creative use of vocal harmonics and electric instruments, Dylan used a backing group and electric guitars on his album *Bringing it all Back Home* in 1965. In turn, The Beatles became influenced by Dylan's imaginative poetic imagery and social comment. The culmination of The Beatles' work is to be found on their album *Sergeant Pepper's Lonely Hearts Club Band* (1967).

By the end of the 1960s pop had matured enough for its various styles to coexist, rather than supersede one another. The many different styles represented on the programme of the 1967 Monterey Festival was an indication of this, ranging from the harmonious, folk-song influenced sound of Simon and Garfunkel to the aggressive, rhythm and blues influenced playing of The Who.

Pop during the 1970s and 1980s has continued to be characterized by such stylistic contrasts, ranging from the tuneful melodies of singer-songwriters such as Carole King to the complex and lengthy compositions of progressive groups such as Pink Floyd; from the Jamaican folk music derived *reggae of Bob Marley to the undemanding sophistication of ABBA. The development of punk rock during 1976 signified a rejection of such sophistication,

and, indeed, of what was seen by many younger people as the complacency of the pop music 'establishment' as a whole. Ironically called the 'new wave' despite its allegiance musically to the rock and roll of 20 years earlier, punk rock was short-lived, but its inherent simplicity of melody and harmony has proved a lasting influence in the music of Blondie, Depêche Mode, The Human League, and Dollar. It was no coincidence that reggae, and its antecedent ska, proved a vital influence on British pop during the late 1970s. For it, too, has a directness of style, albeit very different from that of punk, and a clarity of conception which fitted in well with the swing away from complacent sophistication. The Police's album *Reggatta da blanc* (1979) is evidence of the effectiveness of reggae's influence on British pop.

MICHAEL BURNETT

FURTHER READING
Charlie Gillett: *The Sound of the City* (London, 1971).

Pordon dantza (Basque; Ger.: *Lanzentanz, Stabtanz*). A dance of men with lances, formerly performed on the day of St John of Tolosa in commemoration of a military victory. It was accompanied by guitar or bandurria, often with the voice.

Porgy and Bess. Opera in three acts by Gershwin; text by Du Bose Heyward and Ira Gershwin, after the drama *Porgy* by Du Bose and Dorothy Heyward. Produced: Boston, Colonial Theatre, 30 September 1935; London, Stoll Theatre, 9 October 1952. The first American opera to achieve lasting international success. Set in South Carolina, the plot concerns Porgy (bar.), a cripple, and Crown (bass), a stevedore, who compete for the love of Bess (sop.). She is lured to New York by the gambler, Sportin' Life (ten.). Porgy kills Crown and follows Bess to New York.

Porpora, Nicola (Antonio) (*b* Naples, 17 Aug. 1686; *d* Naples, 3 Mar. 1768). Italian composer and singing teacher. He studied at the Neapolitan Conservatorio dei Poveri di Gesù Cristo, and achieved early fame as a composer—his opera *Agrippina* was produced in 1708 and may have been heard by Handel. The rest of his life was spent partly as teacher and *maestro* at various conservatories in Naples and Venice, and partly in the service of the Prince of Hessen-Darmstadt in Vienna and at the electoral court in Dresden. He was also employed in London as a resident composer to the Opera of the Nobility from 1733 to 1737, rivalling Handel in popularity for a short time.

Porpora was one of the most sought-after singing teachers of the age (his pupils included the famous castratos Farinelli and Caffarelli, as well as Haydn), and this interest in vocal skill shows in his operas, where virtuoso display is a more potent element than characterization. His church music for the girls of the two Venetian conservatories where he worked also makes use of vocal fireworks, though there are some pieces for choir and strings in a simpler style.

DENIS ARNOLD

Porta, Costanzo (*b* Cremona, *c.*1529; *d* Padua, 19 May 1601). Prolific Italian composer. He became a Minorite friar and in 1549 joined the monastic community at S. Maria Gloriosa dei Frari in Venice, where he studied with Willaert and became friends with his fellow pupil Merulo. He directed the music at Osimo Cathedral from 1552 to 1565, and then served as *maestro di cappella* at the Cappella Antoniana, Padua, at Ravenna, and at the Santa Casa, Loreto. He returned to the Cappella Antoniana in 1595, and remained there for the remaining six years of his life.

As a composer Porta had a considerable contrapuntal skill. He wrote mainly sacred works; some of the later motets are in the grand polychoral Venetian style, but others follow the instructions of the Council of Trent and are in a simpler style which allowed the words to be clearly heard. Viadana was among his many pupils.

DENIS ARNOLD

Port a beul. See *Puirt a beul*.

Portamento (It.). 'Carriage'. 1. When applied to the voice, trombone, or a bowed instrument, *portamento* means the gliding from one note to another (over an interval of more than a second) through the intermediate pitches, i.e. without any noticeable gaps. A *portamento* style of string playing was popular, for expressive purposes, in the 19th and early 20th centuries, especially with such violinists as Fritz Kreisler, but went out of fashion. See also *Slide*, 1; *Voice*, 8.

2. Sometimes used as a synonym for appoggiatura.

Portando, portato (It.). 'Carrying', 'carried'. A style of performance between *legato* and *staccato*. The term *portamento* is sometimes used, wrongly, to describe the technique. See also *Louré*.

Portative organ. A Medieval and early Renaissance type of organ (now often referred to simply as a 'portative'), small enough to be carried by a strap for playing while standing or walking. Only the right hand can play on the keys since the other has to pump the bellows from the opposite side, the organ being held with the line of pipes at right angles to the body. As first seen in 13th-century pictures, there are two parallel rows of pipes: open flue pipes, usually white or silver (of tin, no doubt) but sometimes yellow or gold. Each row has about eight pipes, and from their size we may conclude that they gave a compass of about two octaves upwards from Middle C (a wider compass later in the 14th century). No instrument survives, so details of the internal workings have to be conjectured. The notes of the scale are, however, evidently given from the front and back row of pipes alternately, keeping the over-all length of the instrument to a minimum. The keys, sometimes button-shaped, seem to be in two rows matching the two rows of pipes, and to be played with two or three fingers of the hand, suggesting a single line of melody only.

The pipes stand between two upright end-panels of Gothic woodwork with feet for standing the organ on a table when required. Frequently one also sees at one end (sometimes the treble end) a couple of pipes longer than the rest and partly encased in a model castle. One theory is that such pipes could be fed directly from the wind-chest to sound some kind of drone; how continuously this could sound will perhaps be discovered through reconstructions based on the pictures.

The portative, though obviously complex to make, was in fairly common use with other instruments, or on its own for private music and dancing among the wealthier classes, and also possibly in church processions. It went out of use during the 15th century.

ANTHONY BAINES

Portato (It.). See *Portando, portato*.

Port de voix (Fr.). 'Carrying of the voice'. A vocal *portamento*.

Porté, portée (Fr.). 'Carried', the same as *portamento*. As a noun, *portée* means staff.

Porter, Cole (Albert) (*b* Peru, Ind., 9 June 1891; *d* Santa Monica, Calif., 15 Oct. 1964). American song-writer. The grandson of a millionaire and son of a rich farmer, he was later cut off from the family fortune for following a musical career. He was educated at Yale and Harvard Law School, but transferred to the Department of Music and while there wrote his first Broadway show. Between 1910 and 1919 he managed to get songs included in various revues. During the war he joined the French Foreign Legion and wrote enough successful songs to make himself independent of the family. He married a wife with a private fortune, lived in Paris for a time, and began to have so much success with his music that he decided to take it more seriously, and wrote *Fifty Million Frenchmen* (1929), *Wake Up and Dream* (1929), *The New Yorkers* (1930), *Gay Divorce* (1932), *Nymph Errant* (1933), *Anything Goes* (1935), *Red Hot and Blue* (1936), and *Leave It to Me* (1938). In 1937 he had a serious riding accident and had to undergo a series of operations culminating in the amputation of a leg in 1958. Although constantly in pain he wrote *Du Barry Was a Lady* (1939), *Panama Hattie* (1940), *Let's Face It* (1941), *Something for the Boys* (1943), *Mexican Hayride* (1944), culminating with his best and most substantial shows *Kiss Me Kate* (1948), *Can-Can* (1953), and *Silk Stockings* (1955). He wrote his own very original and witty words as well as the music.   PETER GAMMOND

Porter la voix (Fr.). 'To carry the voice', i.e. to use the vocal *portamento*.

Portsmouth Point. Concert overture by Walton, composed in 1925. It was inspired by an etching by Rowlandson (1756–1827).

Portugal [Portogallo], **Marcos Antônio** (da Fonseca) (*b* Lisbon, 24 Mar. 1762; *d* Rio de Janeiro, 7 Feb. 1830). One of the first important Portuguese opera composers. He was a student at the Lisbon Seminário Patriarcal, and remained in the city as a conductor and opera composer until 1792. That year he went to study in Italy, although he seems to have spent more time composing operas than taking lessons; the most successful of the works he wrote in Italy was *Le confusioni nato della somiglianza* (1793). In 1800 he returned to Lisbon to take up the posts of royal chapel master and director of opera at the S. Carlos theatre. The court fled to Rio de Janeiro before the advancing French

Cole Porter (1933)

troops in 1807, but Portugal followed them only in 1811, in which year he opened the Teatro São João. He never returned to Europe, although the court moved back to Lisbon in 1821. Portugal wrote over 50 operas, both Portuguese and Italian, and over 100 sacred works. The finale of his cantata *La speranza* (1809) served as the Portuguese national anthem until 1834.   WENDY THOMPSON

Posaune (Ger.). 'Trombone'.

Position (Eng., Fr.; It.: *posizione*). 1. In the playing of string instruments the left hand is moved continually so that the fingers may fall on to a different set of places on the fingerboard, thus producing a different set of notes. Each of these locations is called a 'position' ('first position', 'second position', etc.). Shift (It.: *manica*) means the same thing.

2. Chords may be described as being in 'close' or 'open' position, depending on their layout. A chord of C major written thus:

would be described as being in 'close' position, while one notated thus:

would be in 'open' position.

Post-horn (Fr.: *cornet de poste*; Ger.: *Posthorn*; It.: *cornetta di postiglione*). A brass instrument formerly sounded on mail coaches to signal arrivals and departures. Music has frequently imitated its calls and post-horns are still made in Britain for performing solos in band concerts; also as non-functional decorations for country hotels, not only in Britain but also in Germany and Switzerland.

1. *English Post-horn*. This is perfectly straight, gently tapered, about 30″ long and pitched in A♭ (Fig. 1*a*). A cornet mouthpiece can be used and the harmonics normally sounded are the second, third, and fourth, *a*♭′, *e*♭″, and *a*♭″. The favourite band solo, the 'Post Horn Galop' of 1844 by Koening, cornet soloist in Jullien's orchestra, is based on genuine posting-calls of the day. The instrument developed in the early 19th century as a lengthened version of the straight-built English *hunting horn (Fig. 1*c*), though circular models were made as well up to *c*.1840. A later product of the same century is known as a 'coach horn', of copper, up to 4′ long, and once popular among coaching clubs, sounded in bugle-like tunes.

2. *Continental Post-horns*. These have normally been circular, in one or more coils (and today more familiar as an emblem on mail-cars). They date from the early 17th century, then typically made in a coil hardly more than 3″ across, wound with coloured cloth, held with the bell pointing upwards, and sounded in rapid calls on two notes an octave apart: the once-familiar sounds were imitated on strings or keyboard in many works of the first half of the 18th century, e.g. in Bach's 'Aria di Postiglione' (in *Capriccio sopra la lontanza del suo fratello*, BWV 992); Handel's *Belshazzar* (here taken from Telemann); and Vivaldi's *Il corneta da posta* (RV 363).

Later in the century German and Austrian post-horns were made with more coils, hence a longer tube and deeper pitch, allowing higher harmonics to be sounded. In Mozart's 'Sleigh Journey' (K 605), the two post-horns were originally to be played by the orchestra's horn players: one is in B♭, the other in F, this one probably to sound a fourth lower than written. Beethoven (German Dances of 1795) and Schubert ('Die Post', in *Die Winterreise*) both allude to calls of trumpet-like arpeggios, which remained the 19th-century German style (Fig. 1*b*). The post-horn was also made with valves, to enable it to sound ordinary tunes, and so appears in Mahler's Third Symphony. The *cornet itself was said to have originated (in Paris, late 1820s) as a valved version of the circular post-horn, which was then also a military instrument, *cornet de chasseurs* (corresponding to the bugle of the British Light Infantry) and, as *cornet ordinaire*, frequently added to the military band (see *Military Band*, Pl. 2).　　　　　ANTHONY BAINES

Post-Horn Galop. Solo for post-horn, with accompaniment, composed in 1844 by the cornet player Koening.

Postlude. The converse of *prelude, i.e. a composition played as an after-piece. In organ music, the 'postlude' is the concluding voluntary.

Songs by Schumann often end with an extended section of music for piano alone, often called a postlude, 'commenting' on the emotions conveyed by the words. Sometimes these postludes introduce new material, as in many of the settings in *Dichterliebe* (for example, 'Ich will meine Seele tauchen', 'Die alten, bösen Lieder').

Poston, Elizabeth (*b* nr Walkern, Hertfordshire, 24 Oct. 1905). English composer. She studied at the Royal Academy of Music and worked on the BBC music staff from 1940 to 1945. Her compositions include songs and incidental scores for radio; she has also edited various anthologies of songs and carols.

　　　　　PAUL GRIFFITHS

Potpourri (Fr.). Literally, 'rotten pot'. Originally the term meant a jar containing a mixture of rose petals, spices, etc. In music, it has come to mean a composition which consists of a string of favourite tunes, perhaps from an opera—in

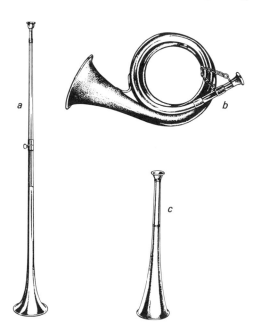

Fig. 1. (a) English post-horn in A♭; (b) German post-horn in E♭; (c) English hunting horn (see 'Hunting horn', 1).

other words, the same as *medley. The term has been in use since the early 18th century; it was introduced to England by J. B. Cramer.

Potter, (Philip) Cipriani (Hambly) (*b* London, 3 Oct. 1792; *d* London, 26 Sept. 1871). English pianist, teacher, editor, and composer. He was the first of a long line of English educationalists who prepared the way for the 'renaissance' of Parry, Stanford, and Elgar and the establishment of regular music colleges. He began his working life as a brilliant pianist and composer of lightweight concert pieces. After study under Attwood, Woelfl, and Crotch, his interest in Beethoven (by no means universally shared by his contemporaries) led him to Vienna and a period of study with Beethoven himself (1818-19). In 1822 he became principal piano professor at the Royal Academy of Music, where his most distinguished pupil was William Sterndale Bennett; he also appeared regularly as a pianist and conductor at the Philharmonic Concerts, performing his own music and particularly that of Mozart and Beethoven. The best of his music is to be found in the symphonies, especially the G minor (1819, rev. 1826). The piano concertos, even the best in E♭ (1833), and the solo piano works suffer from too great a dependence on prolixity of passage-work, though the chamber music—of which the Sonata for horn or bassoon and piano is typical —has period interest. Potter's editions of Mozart, in which a clean text is amplified only by instructive fingering, were in advance of their time.   ROBIN LANGLEY

Poule, La ('The Hen'). Nickname of Haydn's Symphony No. 83 in G minor, composed in 1785. The title is a 19th-century accretion, purporting to describe the 'clucking' second subject of the first movement.

Poulenc, Francis (Jean Marcel) (*b* Paris, 7 Jan. 1899; *d* Paris, 30 Jan. 1963). French composer. He had some piano lessons from Ricardo Viñes, but as a composer he was self-taught at the time when his witty and exotic *Rapsodie nègre* for voice and chamber ensemble (1917) won him a place in the circle around Satie and thus in Les *Six, the group which also included Milhaud and Honegger, and which was so christened in 1920. Several works of this time show him closely following Stravinsky: the sonatas for two clarinets (1918) and for brass trio (1922), in particular. Even so, the flippant, anti-conventional aesthetic seems to have held more attraction for him, and he remained a composer who relished the humorous jolt occasioned by the banal or unexpected.

In several early works, such as the *Trois mouvements perpétuels* (1918) for piano or the

Poulenc

ballet *Les biches* (1923), he used monotonous materials or popular-song styles in a spirit of snook-cocking, but he soon began to place such incongruities within music of smooth flow, melodic charm, and very French grace. This is the case in, for example, his keyboard concertos —for harpsichord (*Concert champêtre*, 1927-8), two pianos (1932), organ (1938), and piano (1949)—and also in his late sonatas for flute (1957), oboe (1962), and clarinet (1962).

Poulenc's gifts as a melodist, coupled with his literary friendships, led to a large output of songs, including cycles to poems by Apollinaire (*Le bestiaire*, 1919; *Quatre poèmes*, 1931; *Banalités*, 1940; *Calligrammes*, 1948), Cocteau (*Cocardes*, 1919), and Eluard (*Tel jour, telle nuit*, 1936-7; *Le fraîcheur et le feu*, 1950; *Le travail du peintre*, 1956). His sympathy with the surrealist poets is also displayed in his bizarre operatic treatment of Apollinaire's play *Les mamelles de Tirésias* (1947), while his solo opera *La voix humaine* (1959, text by Cocteau) shows his delicate sensitivity in underlining a scene from contemporary life, a woman speaking over the telephone to the lover who is abandoning her.

Between these came the opera *Dialogues des Carmélites* (1957), one of the works in which Poulenc expressed his religious faith after his return to the Catholic Church in 1936. The quiet depth of his spirituality is also to be felt in the unaccompanied Mass (1937) and other choral works, while the *Stabat mater* (1950) and the *Gloria* (1959), both scored for soprano, chorus, and orchestra, are more grandiose in their fervour.

PAUL GRIFFITHS

FURTHER READING
Henri Hell: *Francis Poulenc* (Paris, 1958, Eng. trans., 1959); Pierre Bernac: *Francis Poulenc* (Paris, 1977, Eng. trans., 1977).

Pound, Ezra. See *Novel, Music in the*.

Poussé (Fr.). 'Pushed'. In string playing, the up-bow; the down-bow is *tiré*.

Pousseur, Henri (León Marie Thérèse) (*b* Malmédy, nr Liège, 23 June 1929). Belgian composer. He studied with Pierre Froidebise and André Souris at the conservatories of Liège and Brussels (1947–53), and then quickly became associated with Boulez, Stockhausen, and Berio. In his first works, such as the Quintet in memory of Webern (1955), he used a complex serial style, modified by the addition of aleatory features in *Mobile* for two pianos (1956–8). His 'variable operatic fantasy' *Votre Faust* (1960–7, performed 1969) opened the way to an all-inclusive style in which the most varied harmonic materials could be coherently joined, and this style he has developed in subsequent works, sometimes emphasizing a parallel with egalitarian social organizations. *Couleurs croisées* for orchestra (1967), for instance, offers a progression from discord to concord based on the American human-rights song 'We shall overcome'. Pousseur was co-founder of the APELAC electronic music studio in Brussels (1958) and has taught at various institutions in Europe and America. He is also author of the books *Fragments théoriques* (2 vols., Brussels, 1970, 1972) and *Musique Sémantique Société* (Tournai, 1972).   PAUL GRIFFITHS

Henri Pousseur

Power, Leonel [Lionel] (*b c*.1370–85; *d* Canterbury, 5 June 1445). English composer and theorist. He was employed in the household of Thomas, Duke of Clarence, until 1421, and spent the remainder of his life at Canterbury Cathedral. Some 50 liturgical works by (or attributable to) him have survived, as well as a treatise on discant. Judging by the large quantity of his music which appears in the *Old Hall Manuscript*, it seems likely that he was in some way associated with its compilation. Power was a pioneer in the development of the cyclic Mass, in which the various sections of the Ordinary are thematically and structurally related to one another; his *Missa Alma redemptoris mater* is the earliest known example of the genre. Power's music, like Dunstable's, was advanced for its time in its use of full chordal sonority, and was both popular and highly influential on the Continent during the first half of the 15th century.   JOHN MILSOM

Pp, ppp. Abbreviations for *pianissimo* (It.), i.e. very soft indeed.

Prächtig,   prachtvoll (Ger.).   'Grand', 'pompous'.

Practical Cats. 1. Work by Rawsthorne for speaker and orchestra, a setting of six poems from T. S. Eliot's *Old Possum's Book of Practical Cats* (1939). It was composed in 1954.
   2. Musical, entitled *Cats*, by Andrew Lloyd Webber to a libretto by Tim Rice after Eliot. It was first performed in London in 1982.

Praeambulum (Lat.). 'Prelude'.

Praefatio (Lat.). See *Preface*.

Praeludium (Lat.). 'Prelude'.

Praetorius. Common name among German musicians in the 16th and 17th centuries. The Praetorius family which lived and worked mainly in Hamburg provided three composers whose names are still frequently encountered. **Jacob Praetorius (i)** (*b* Magdeburg, *c*.1530; *d* Hamburg, 1586), a composer and organist, worked for most of his life at St Jacobi and St Gertrud, Hamburg. Only one of his works survives, but he was an important teacher, and his pupils included his son, **Hieronymus Praetorius** (*b* Hamburg, 10 Aug. 1560; *d* Hamburg, 27 Jan. 1629). Hieronymus was an excellent composer of grand polychoral music in the Venetian tradition. From 1580 to 1582 he was town organist at Erfurt, taking over his father's job in 1586. His son, **Jacob Praetorius (ii)** (*b* Hamburg, 8 Feb. 1586; *d* Hamburg, 21–2 Oct. 1651), was also an organist. After studying in

Amsterdam with Sweelinck he worked at the Hamburg church of St Petri. He was well known for his organ music, especially for his chorale settings and for some so-called 'preludes', which comprised chordal preludes followed by monothematic fugues; they were direct precursors of Bach's preludes and fugues.

DENIS ARNOLD

Praetorius, Michael (*b* Creuzburg an der Werra, nr Eisenach, *c.* 1571; *d* Wolfenbüttel, 15 Feb. 1621). German composer and writer on music. He was not related to the Praetorius family discussed above, but was the son of a teacher and Lutheran pastor. He matriculated so early at the University of Frankfurt an der Oder that he had to wait a year before he could

be admitted to study philosophy and theology. He soon took to music, entering the service of Duke Heinrich Julius of Brunswick-Wolfenbüttel in 1595. Praetorius stayed in his service until the duke died in 1613, based in Wolfenbüttel but travelling around with his master. He spent his final years continuing to travel through Germany, and in Dresden he met Schütz, learning the latest Italian styles and fashions from him.

Praetorius was a prolific composer, producing especially a large number of sacred works. The bulk of these pieces were settings of Lutheran hymn tunes, in styles ranging from the Venetian polychoral manner to quite simple harmonizations. Of his equally popular dancing music only *Terpsichore* (1612) survives,

Title-page of Praetorius's 'Polyhymnia Caduceatrix Panegyrica' (1618).

containing over 300 tunes by Paris dancing masters. Although many of his compositions are interesting and of a high standard, he is best remembered for his treatise *Syntagma musicum* (1614–19), which explains to the German *Kapellmeister* how to perform works in various contemporary styles and also has a comprehensive section describing (with illustrations) the instruments then in use. This is one of the finest mines of information for today's performer, and an indispensable tool for the musicologist.

DENIS ARNOLD

'Prague' Symphony. Nickname of Mozart's Symphony No. 38 in D major, K 504, composed in 1786. It is so called because it was first performed during Mozart's visit to Prague in 1787.

Pralltriller (Ger.). 'Tight' or 'compact' trill. 1. In modern German terminology, the inverted *mordent. 2. Until *c*.1800, a rapid trill of four notes, beginning on the upper note of a descending second. It was usually indicated with the same sign as that now used for the inverted mordent (⁓). In quick passages, the two ornaments sound extremely similar, since there is not time to sound the first note of the *Pralltriller*, and it must be omitted, or tied to the preceding main note, e.g.:

Prayer Book. See *Common Prayer, Book of.*

Präzis (Ger.). 'Precise' (with regard to rhythm).

Precentor. Term (as old as the 4th century) meaning 'first singer'; it is attached to the official in charge of the singing in a cathedral or monastic establishment or a church. In the English cathedrals the dignity of the precentor varies.

The cathedral precentor sits opposite the dean—whence the name for the two sides of the choir: *decani* ('of the dean') and *cantoris* ('of the singer', i.e. the precentor).

In the Presbyterian churches of Scotland, which until the later 19th century had no organs, the precentor was a very important official (see *Hymns and Hymn Tunes*, 10). He was supplied with a pitch-pipe and gave out and led the metrical psalms. Sometimes he was called the 'Uptaker of the psalms'.

In the earlier settled parts of America the precentor has also had a place in the life of the religious community. As late as 1902 Professor Edward Dickinson, in his *Music in the History of the Western Church*, alluded to churches where

the congregation 'led by a precentor with voice or cornet assumes the whole burden of song' (see *Hymns and Hymn Tunes*, 11).

Preces (Lat.). 'Prayers'. In the Latin and Anglican Churches, a short series of petitions given on ferial days. They take the form of *versicles and *responses. In the Anglican Church the versicles leading up to the *Venite* in Morning Service and those leading up to the psalms at Evensong are sometimes referred to as *preces*, but strictly speaking the *preces* in the Anglican liturgy are the prayers given at those two services between the Creed and the Collects. Tallis made two settings of *Preces and Responses*.

Preface (Lat.: *prefatio*). Solemn declaration of praise introducing the central part of the Roman Catholic Mass and the Anglican Communion Service. It is preceded by the *Sursum corda* and followed by the Sanctus. There is a common form for the Preface, into which are interpolated words appropriate to special feasts. There are many of these 'Proper' Prefaces in the Roman Catholic Church, but they are provided only for Christmas, Easter, Ascensiontide, Whitsuntide, and Trinity Sunday in the Anglican. Traditional plainchants are used in both Churches.

Preghiera (It.). 'Prayer'. An aria or chorus in which the singer or singers make a prayer to God or to supernatural powers. The 'preghiera' scene became a feature of 19th-century opera, usually sung to poignant effect by the heroine (e.g. Desdemona's 'Ave Maria' in the last act of Verdi's *Otello*).

Prelude (Fr.: *prélude*; Ger.: *Vorspiel*; It.: *preludio*). A piece of music which is played as a preliminary to another or before any play, ceremony, etc. (Wagner's music dramas have *Vorspielen*, not overtures). The genre developed from the short improvisatory flourishes performed by a player to check the tuning or test the touch of his instrument, or, in liturgical use, to introduce the music of the service. Independent preludes are found in organ tablatures of the mid 15th century, in 16th-century French sources, such as the lute-books of Le Roy, and in late 16th-century sources such as the *Fitzwilliam Virginal Book*. In the 17th and 18th centuries the prelude was most commonly found at the beginning of a *suite, or preceding a *fugue (see also *Toccata*). Preludes as the opening movements of suites are found in German and English sources, e.g. Fischer's *Pièces de clavecin* (1696), Bach's English Suites, and Handel's keyboard suites. The pairing of prelude and fugue was cultivated by Scheidemann and Buxtehude, but especially by J. S.

Bach (as in the *Well-tempered Clavier*). In France, a unique kind of prelude appeared in the works of the harpsichord composers—the 'unmeasured' prelude, notated as a series of unbarred semibreves which were elaborated by the performer.

The prelude was little cultivated in the Classical period, but gained a new lease of life in the 19th century: Bach's preludes and fugues inspired similar works by Mendelssohn, Liszt, Brahms, and Franck, while the concept of the prelude as an independent piece was revived with Chopin's 24 Preludes (Op. 28). Thereafter the prelude was admitted to the genre of 'character' pieces, often exploring a particular mood. Sets of piano preludes were written by Rakhmaninov, Satie, Martinů, Alkan, and Busoni, each of whom wrote a set of 24 in all major and minor keys. In Debussy's 24, in two books, each is given an evocative title, such as *La fille aux cheveux de lin* ('The girl with the flaxen hair'), *La cathédrale engloutie* ('The submerged cathedral'), and *Voiles* ('Sails'). Orchestral preludes include Satie's prelude to his incidental music for *Le fils des étoiles* (later re-orchestrated by Ravel), Debussy's *Prélude à l'après-midi d'un faune*, Vaughan Williams's *Prelude on Three Welsh Hymn Tunes* for brass band, and Walton's 'Spitfire' Prelude and Fugue, inspired by the British fighter aeroplane used in the Battle of Britain.

WENDY THOMPSON

Préluder (Fr.). 'To prelude', often meaning 'to tune up', or to extemporize a few introductory chords.

Préludes. Piano pieces by Debussy, in two books of 12 pieces each. Book 1, composed in 1910: (1) *Danseuses de Delphes* ('Dancing Women of Delphi'), suggested by a pillar in the Louvre on which are sculptured three Bacchantes; (2) *Voiles* ('Sails'); (3) *Le vent dans la plaine* ('The Wind in the Plain'); (4) *Les sons et les parfums tournent dans l'air du soir* ('Sounds and Perfumes in the Evening Air'); (5) *Les collines d'Anacapri* ('The Hills of Anacapri'); (6) *Des pas sur la neige* ('Footsteps on the Snow'); (7) *Ce qu'a vu le vent d'Ouest* ('What the West Wind Saw'); (8) *La fille aux cheveux de lin* ('The Girl with the Flaxen Hair'), suggested by a poem of Lecomte de Lisle; (9) *La sérénade interrompue* ('The Interrupted Serenade'), using Spanish idioms; (10) *La cathédrale engloutie* ('The Submerged Cathedral'), based on the legend of the Cathedral of Ys with its tolling bells and chanting under the sea; (11) *La danse de Puck* ('Puck's Dance'); (12) *Minstrels*, reflecting negro or music hall styles.

Book 2, composed between 1912 and 1913:

(1) *Brouillards* ('Mists'); (2) *Feuilles mortes* ('Dead Leaves'); (3) *La Puerta del Vino*, the name of the famous gate of Alhambra; (4) '*Les fées sont d'exquises danseuses*' ('Fairies are Exquisite Dancers'); (5) *Bruyères* ('Heaths'); (6) *Général Lavine—excentric*, a wooden puppet who appeared in Paris music-hall performances; (7) *La terrasse des audiences du clair de lune* ('Terraces of Moonlight Audiences'); (8) *Ondine*, the water-spirit maiden of the early 19th-century story of de la Motte Fouqué; (9) *Hommage à S. Pickwick Esq, P.P.M.P.C.*, with a suggestion of the British national anthem; (10) *Canope* ('Canopic Vase'), an ancient Egyptian cinerary urn; (11) *Les tierces alternées* ('Alternating 3rds'); (12) *Feux d'artifice* ('Fireworks').

Préludes, Les ('The Preludes'). Symphonic poem by Liszt, the title being from one of Lamartine's *Nouvelles méditations poétiques*. The music was originally composed as the overture to *Les quatres élémens*, to a text by J. Autran, for male voices and piano (1844-5), orchestrated by Conradi (1848). *Les préludes* was composed in 1848 and revised in 1854; Liszt's preface to the revised score states that life is treated as a series of preludes to the unknown afterlife.

Premier coup d'archet (Fr.). See *Coup d'archet*.

Prepared piano. See *Piano, 19*.

Près (Fr.). 'Near', e.g. *près de la touche*, 'near the fingerboard' of a stringed instrument (referring to a style of bowing, or, in the case of the harp, of plucking).

Presser. American firm of music publishers. It was established in Philadelphia in 1883 by Theodore Presser (1848-1925), who earlier that year had founded *The Etude*, which was to become one of America's most successful music magazines. The Presser Company have acquired several other publishing houses and now have a large catalogue, many agencies, and a vast hire library. They publish many American composers, including Milton Babbitt, Elliott Carter, Henry Cowell, Charles Ives, and Walter Piston. The philanthropic activities of their founder included the establishment in 1906 of a home for retired music teachers and in 1916 of a foundation to provide financial support for needy musicians.

J. M. THOMSON

Presto (It.). 'Quick'; *prestamente*, 'quickly'; *prestissimo*, 'very quick'.

Previn, André (George) (*b* Berlin, 6 Apr.

1929). American composer. He studied at the Berlin Conservatory, at the Paris Conservatoire and with Castelnuovo-Tedesco in Los Angeles. At the age of 17 he began work as an arranger for films, at the same time establishing himself as a progressive jazz pianist. He has continued to compose scores for the cinema, though since the mid-1960s he has been more active as a conductor, notably with the London Symphony Orchestra (1968–75) and the Pittsburgh Symphony (from 1976). He has also produced a small output of serious compositions—a symphony (1962) and other orchestral and chamber works—most of them written for particular colleagues and reflecting his enthusiasms for American popular music and late Romantic gesture. He collaborated with Tom Stoppard on *Every Good Boy Deserves Favour* (1977), an unusual and effective fusion of spoken drama and orchestral music.

PAUL GRIFFITHS

Prez, Josquin des. See *Josquin des Prez*.

Pribautki ('Song Games'). Setting by Stravinsky of Russian traditional texts. The work is scored for male voice, flute, oboe, cor anglais, clarinet, bassoon, violin, viola, cello, and double bass, and was first performed in London in 1918.

Prick-song. 'To prick' is an obsolete English verb meaning 'to mark', and thus 'prick-song' came to be applied to music that was written down, or notated, as opposed to extemporized. In Shakespeare's day, the arms of the Parish Clerk's Company in London included, as a sign of their musical duties and skill, three prick-song books.

Prigioniero, Il ('The Prisoner'). Opera in a prologue and one act by Dallapiccola to his own libretto after Villiers de l'Isle Adam's *La torture par l'espérance* (1883) and Charles de Coster's *La légende d'Ulenspiegel et de Lamme Goedzak*. It was first performed on Italian radio in 1949 and staged in Florence the following year.

Prima donna (It.). 'First lady'. Originally she was the chief female singer in an opera cast, but the term has been generalized to mean a leading woman singer, alternatively known as a *diva*. Thus, for the original meaning, one has to use the term *prima donna assoluta*, 'the absolute first lady'. The same process has occurred in ballet with the *prima ballerina assoluta*.

Prima prattica, seconda prattica (It.). Terms used in the early 17th century to describe two different 'practices' in music. Monteverdi's style of composing secular vocal music, where irregular harmonies, intervals, and melodic progressions were used to express the meaning of the text, had been attacked by Giovanni Artusi in an essay called *L'Artusi, ovvero Delle imperfettioni della moderna musica* (1600), which quoted passages from two of Monteverdi's madrigals, 'Anima mia perdona' and 'Cruda Amarilli' (from the Fourth and Fifth books of madrigals respectively; 1603, 1605). A 'declaration' was printed with Monteverdi's first collection of *Scherzi musicali* (1607), defending the modern style, or 'seconda prattica', and declaring it to be as valid as the *prima prattica* as exemplified in the works of Josquin, Gombert, Willaert, etc.; in the *prima prattica* the perfection of the part-writing was more important than the expression of the words, whereas in the *seconda prattica* the words are made 'the mistress of the harmony, and not the servant'. Cipriano de Rore was said to have been the first master of the second practice, followed by Gesualdo, Cavalieri, Marenzio, de Wert, Peri, Caccini, and Luzzaschi. The declaration also quotes from Plato's *Republic* in defence of the *seconda prattica*.

Primary tones. An American term for the 'natural notes' (i.e. those available without the use of valves) of brass instruments. See *Valves*.

Prima volta (It.). 'First-time (bar)'; see *Double bar*.

Prime. 1. The third of the *Office Hours of the Roman Catholic Church. 2. The word has also some theoretical applications—to: (*a*) the lower of two notes forming an interval; (*b*) the generator of a series of harmonics (see *Acoustics*, 5); (*c*) the root of a chord; (*d*) a unison; (*e*) the first note of a scale; and (*f*) the interval formed by two notes written on the same line or space, e.g. F and F♯.

Primgeiger (Ger.). The leader of an orchestra (i.e. the principal first violin).

Prince Igor (*Knyaz' Igor'*). Opera in four acts and a prologue by Borodin to his own libretto after a scenario by Vladimir Stasov. Borodin worked on it in 1869–70 and from 1874 to 1887 but left it unfinished; Rimsky-Korsakov and Glazunov completed it and orchestrated much of it. The opera was first performed in St Petersburg in 1890.

Prince of the Pagodas, The. Ballet in three acts, Op. 57, by Britten, choreographed by John Cranko. It was inspired by a visit Britten made to the Far East and was first performed at Covent Garden in 1957. The 'Pas de Six' is published separately (Op. 57*a*), and Michael Lankaster has arranged an orchestral suite from the ballet score which was first performed in 1979.

Printemps ('Spring'). Symphonic suite by

Debussy for orchestra and female chorus, composed in 1887. The original score was lost and the work was reorchestrated in 1912 by Busser, under Debussy's supervision, from the piano version. This work is not to be confused with *Rondes de printemps*; see *Images*.

Printing and Publishing of Music

1. Introduction
2. Principal Techniques of Printing
3. Europe: Early History
4. Europe: 16th Century
5. Europe: 1600–*c*.1750

6. Europe: *c*.1750–*c*.1945
7. USA
8. Composers and Publishers
9. Publishing Today

1. *Introduction.* The history of music printing and publishing is technical, social, and artistic. The technical history encompasses the gradual solution of the difficult problems posed by music itself, with its complex visual symbolism. The social history shows how changing tastes, styles, and audiences have brought different genres to prominence, how publishers (as distinct from printers) arose and how their two roles have often been combined, and how publishing houses may build their fortunes on a single composer, school of composers, or popular craze. And the artistic history of musical typography highlights printed music in which the bounds of craftsmanship are transcended to produce exemplars of outstanding design.

It is not easy to become acquainted with these musical treasures of the past, and only rarely is it possible to handle them. Some are in libraries, friends or acquaintances may possess fine early editions, auction houses will permit one to see material waiting for a sale, and occasionally one may find a remarkable volume on the barrows of large cities. Much late 18th- and 19th-century music is still to be found thus; and a personal collection, however modest, provides that first-hand experience of the paper, binding, and texture of early editions which the facsimile can never quite provide.

2. *Principal Techniques of Printing.* Music printing has throughout its history employed three main techniques. First, printing from type, which is cast in the same way as that for the printed word. Secondly, engraving on a copper plate using a burin. Punches were used, subsequently, to stamp the fixed symbols on to a pewter plate, the variable signs such as slurs being cut in with the engraving tool. Thirdly, lithography, a method still at the heart of present-day music printing. These technical processes are difficult to describe in isolation, and readers are urged to view them by visiting collections in museums, institutions, and print-

ing houses. Although the techniques used today are likely to be almost entirely lithography and its associated photographic processes, some printers keep a small museum or archive that may illustrate music type-setting and engraving.

Music has never had the variety of typefaces available for use in books. An examination of music printed in this century shows a tendency to use several fairly standard designs, although gifted designers, punch-cutters, and artists have at times attempted to change this. A well-designed music type has a satisfying proportional relationship between the shape of the notehead and the other elements, such as the thickness and angle of the stem, and the shape of the tails and braces. The clefs, rests, and expression marks such as slurs and phrasing, even the thickness of the staves, make up a complex pictorial and typographical unity.

(*a*) *Music Type.* Music type is produced by the same technique as is used for the letters of the alphabet. The design for a note, rest, or clef is cut on to a punch, usually made of steel. A matrix is produced by striking the punch into a small metal bar, usually copper, which leaves the symbol recessed. The type is then cast in a mould, which opens to accommodate characters of varying widths and of a fixed height. The matrix is inserted at its base, the mould is adjusted to the desired width, molten lead is poured in to form a column, and the character is cast in the matrix at the bottom. The mould is taken apart, the metal broken off to the desired height, and the type remains. This process was used by Gutenberg, who is credited with the invention of printing in Mainz in the mid 15th century, and thereafter it has remained virtually unchanged. Symbols are run off as required, as are spaces of varying width so that the notes can be properly spaced. (The earliest surviving moulds for music type are in the Plantin-Moretus Museum, Antwerp.)

The notes and symbols are placed in a

wooden case ready for assembling by the compositor, who works from a manuscript marked up to show the ends of the musical lines and other relevant details. He assembles the music type in a composing-stick, from which it is transferred line by line to a chase and thence to the machine. Early music printers required relatively few 'sorts', or separate notes, managing with six or seven, plus rests. By the 19th century, however, a case of music type might contain more than 400 separate parts; three joined quavers, for example, might demand 16 pieces of type. The process was time-consuming, corrections proved costly, and musical knowledge was required of the compositor. In early music printing two or more impressions were sometimes required: notes and staves were printed separately, as were sections, texts, and initial letters requiring a different colour.

The first surviving example of music printed from type, and one of the finest, is the Constance Gradual (c.1473, in the British Library). Since the late 15th century printers and designers have continually sought improved methods of setting music, and several ingenious systems were developed, including those of Breitkopf (c.1755), the Parisian Eugène Duverger (1820), and the Londoner Edward Cooper (1827). An apotheosis was reached in the fount offered by V. & J. Figgins of London, which used 452 different sorts and specially cast spacing material. With these more complex methods, known as 'mosaic' systems, the type was set by the page, rather than line by line. During earlier periods music was printed directly from type, which eventually resulted in damage. This was avoided by the introduction early in the 20th century of stereo plates, suitable for fast contemporary printing methods.

Music type-setting flourished in London and other European cities, and in America, alongside engraving, but became obsolete in the mid 20th century (apart from its occasional use for music examples in books).

(b) *Woodblock*. By the late 15th century a tradition of cutting illustrative material in wood (or metal) had established itself, and it was natural to extend it to musical works that were short and relatively uncomplicated. Although much early woodcut music is of poor quality – the craftsman not yet having mastered the intricacies of the notation, the printer not having fully understood the problems of inking – there remains a quantity of good work, some of it superb. Woodblock printing was at its peak in the 16th century and continued, on a diminishing scale, until the 19th.

(c) *Engraving*. The engraving of music developed from techniques already successfully used by artists and map-makers. A fine burin was used to engrave the music on a copper plate, which was then etched with acid. This method was much more flexible than movable music type and could accommodate more complex notation. The art of the music engraver was highly prized: individual engravers showed recognizable artistic styles, and they often worked closely with the writing master, matching his calligraphic flourishes.

The earliest known example of music engraving seems to be *Intabolatura da leuto del divino Francesco da Milano*, published without indication of printer or date but probably issued before 1536. Copper-plate engraving by hand was a very common method of music printing in the 17th century. Towards the end of the period, however, it gave way to one that proved cheaper and quicker. Punches were used to stamp the fixed symbols such as notes and clefs on to a pewter plate, while the engraver continued to cut in the flexible signs, such as phrasing and note stems, with a hand tool. Pewter (or, in Austria, zinc) was adopted because it was easier to work and cheaper than copper, and the use of punches introduced a certain routine or craft element into what had previously been a skilled artist's preserve.

The manuscript is first 'cast off' to see how many pages it will make, page-turns are decided on, as is the size of the plate and punches. Working in mirror image, from right to left, the engraver 'lays out' the plate; with dividers he rapidly marks the points where the staves will go, draws in light lines, and then cuts the lines with a five-pronged tool called a score. He similarly draws in guide-lines for clefs, key signatures, barlines, and notes. The most skilled part follows, called 'writing in': again using dividers, he marks the spacing for the quavers and crotchets, and then sketches in the notes themselves, accidentals, rests—everything on the manuscript. All necessary information has now been transferred from the manuscript to the plate. With his punches he first stamps in any words, whether text or indications of tempo and expression. The 'heavy stuff' (clefs and braces) follows, along with key signatures, rests, accidentals, and minims. The other notes are left until last, as they can easily buckle the plate.

A cutting tool is then used to put in the barlines, stems, beams (or ties), leger lines, slurs, expression marks, etc. The plate is cleaned and tidied up, ready for proofing on a hand-press, traditionally in emerald or olive green ink. Mistakes are corrected by turning the plate over and punching the area around the error with a dot punch; the plate is turned over once more, the raised metal on the surface burnished, the plate gently tapped with a hammer over the same area, and when the surface is quite flat and

(a)

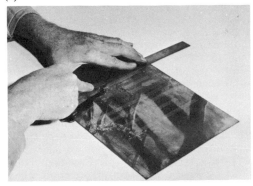

(b)

(c)

Pl. 1. Stages in the engraving of a pewter plate: (a) cutting the stave lines; (b) marking out the plate from the manuscript; (c) stamping the note heads on to the pewter plate.

smooth the corrections can be made. An extensive number of corrections usually necessitates a new plate. Although in the early 1800s a great deal of music was printed direct from the pewter plate, it later became general practice to transfer a proof taken from the engraved plate to a lithographic stone, and to print from that.

(d) *Lithography and Associated Photographic*

Processes. Alois Senefelder (1771–1834) experimented with a revolutionary method of printing which eventually became known as lithography. Senefelder, who left a detailed account of the development of his process, had sought to find a way of printing the plays he had written that was cheaper than copper engraving. He eventually discovered that if he wrote on the polished surface of Solnhofen stone in a special ink made of wax, soap, and lampblack he obtained a crisp impression. The remaining parts of the surface could be removed by etching, so that the method resembled that of wood engraving.

Further experiments, based on the principle that grease repels water, enabled him to develop true lithography. By 1825 he was using metal plates instead of stones, and the new process, known as 'lithographic transfer', rapidly spread throughout Europe. It was the cheapest, most efficient, and fastest method of printing music, and the principal publishers of the age, such as Schott of Mainz, Breitkopf of Leipzig, and Ricordi of Milan, took it up. In various forms it is still in use.

Lithographed music lacks the bite of engraved music; there is a marked tendency to softness, especially at the edges, but if the printer keeps the press well inked the image can be quite sharp. The process encourages freedom and variety of illustration, allowing a range of subtle and striking colours, which 19th-century publishers of popular songs were to exploit brilliantly. It also offered composers a convenient way to publication: in 1845 Wagner wrote out the 450 pages of his opera *Tannhäuser* on lithographic transfer paper in full score, ready for laying down on the stone.

The new method of lithography did not sweep away engraving or movable type; all three processes coexisted. Once the novelty of lithography had worn off it became a valuable adjunct to the other two. Combined with photographic methods it lies at the heart of most music printing today. The music can be written from left to right on lithographic transfer paper for direct transfer or on normal paper for photographing, and then transferred to stone or (more usually today) to a zinc plate, for printing. Vast quantities of music can be punched, proofed, transferred, and then printed by 'litho'. The process is widely used throughout Europe, and its basis is set out in many manuals.

A similar graphic process, dependent on an original technique using stencils, was devised and developed in 1919 by the brothers Harold and Stanley Smith. Known as the 'Halstan' process, and used at the Halstan firm at Amersham, England, it involves detailed drafting by a musician and subsequent working through by operators who use drawing instruments and stencils. The result is photographically reduced and printed on a lithographic zinc plate. Halstan have produced outstanding work for a number of music publishers, including Faber Music and Oxford University Press.

(e) *Recent Developments*. Dry-transfer techniques are in widespread use as an aid to designers, students, and the general public, and are marketed by Letraset, Notaset, and others. The music symbols on the master sheets are transferred directly on to paper by rubbing from the back; if necessary, the image can be touched up with a pen. The process, however, remains relatively slow.

Throughout the 19th century much effort went into the search for a practical music typewriter. A French patent of 1833 recognized the potential of such a device, but of the many types of machine that appeared in the 19th century relatively few established themselves. Among the successful ones were the Lily Pavey model marketed by the Imperial Typewriter Co. in England, the Robert H. Keaton typewriter made in San Francisco, and machines patented by Armando Dal Molin and Cecil Effinger which gained international recognition. In 1853 Dal Molin also developed a computer system later known as the Musicomp, which has operated with great success through Music Reprographics in New York. Cecil Effinger's Musicwriter also has computer applications and can be operated by the professional and amateur alike.

3. *Europe: Early History*. The early history of music printing relates closely to printing in general and to the ancillary arts of engraving, map-making, and die-cutting for coins and medals. Gutenberg is credited with the invention around 1440 of a method of casting type which enabled the printing press to develop. The famous 42-line Bible printed at Mainz about 1453–5, probably by Gutenberg, Fust, and Schoeffer, was followed by Fust and Schoeffer's Latin Psalter of 1457. Printing then spread along the Rhine and throughout Germany, and on to Italy and the rest of Europe.

The earliest examples of printing are known as 'incunabula', from the Latin *incunabulum* (cradle, or first beginnings), and this word is used by librarians and bibliographers to denote music and books printed before the end of the year 1500. Music manuscripts served as models for music-type design. This origin is clear from the Constance Gradual, the most notable example of the late 15th-century printer's art which survives in a unique copy in the British Library. It was printed in two impressions from music-type in 'Gothic' (diamond-shaped) notation, and the 'rubricated' (red-coloured) initials were added by hand. It bears no date or printer's name, but it is believed to have been

produced at Constance, in southern Germany, in about 1473. The 'registration' (alignment of notes on the staves) is excellent, the inking even and dark.

Other early examples of fine music printing include the Roman Missal of Ulrich Hahn (Rome, 1476), quite as distinguished as the Constance Gradual. Hahn's mastery of technique was to influence other European printers, including English ones: the fine Sarum Missal was printed in London by Pynson in 1500 (though many consider the 1520 edition superior).

Two styles of notation were in use at this time: the 'Gothic', or German, preferred in the German-speaking parts of Europe and used in the Constance Gradual; and the usually square 'Roman', preferred in Latin countries, England, and the Netherlands. Printers needed to stock only two kinds of note-shape (and some stocked only one). Few printers could afford to cast and use music type, which proved slow and expensive to print. Fortunately, the requirements for printing plainchant changed little, and the first printers did not attempt the more complex task of polyphony.

4. *Europe: 16th Century*. In the late 15th

Pl. 2. Page from the 'Constance Gradual', c.1473, the earliest known example of music printing from type. It survives in a unique copy in the British Library. The initial letters were added in red by hand and two impressions were required.

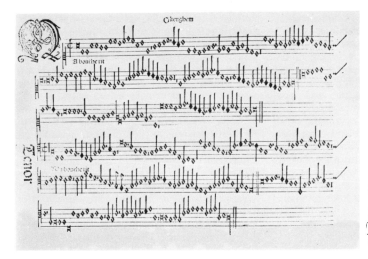

Pl. 3. A page from Petrucci's 'Harmonice musices odhecaton A' (Venice, 1501), one of the finest editions of music printed from type, requiring at least two impressions.

century Venice was at the centre of Italian printing. In 1498 a young printer named Ottaviano *Petrucci obtained from the seigniory of Venice an exclusive 20-year privilege to print 'canto figurato' (mensural, or measured music) and tablatures for the organ and lute. He believed that he had at last perfected a method of printing from movable type that could be used for polyphonic music, and on 15 May 1501 he published his *Harmonice musices odhecaton A* (known as *Odhecaton*) in the oblong quarto format he used for all his music books. It contains 96 pieces by French and Flemish composers arranged as part-songs, and the quality of the printing and type design made it outstanding. He had achieved accurate registration of the notes and masterly visual effects in the spacing of the parts; his initial letters, of singular beauty, did not unbalance the whole; and his ink was of a fine black.

Petrucci's innovations made available to the Venetian public an immense variety of polyphonic music that ranged from Masses, motets, and Lamentations to *frottole* and lute tablatures, in fine though admittedly expensive editions. In some books he used three impressions: one for staves, another for notes and other musical signs, and the third for the text. He subsequently simplified this to two impressions, again achieving extremely high standards. The

body of his publications, 61 of which are known, exerted a tremendous influence, not only on other music printers but on the musical life of his time.

The French were quick to follow Petrucci's lead. Pierre *Attaingnant established himself as a bookseller in Paris around 1514, when the city was pre-eminent in book production and publishing. After experimenting with music type for several years, he produced in 1527/8 an oblong quarto part-book of *Chansons nouvelles*, which showed the important technical advance of printing at one impression. Each note was cast as a separate unit, with the necessary staff lines attached to the note stem and head as part of the typographical unit. Attaingnant evolved a diamond-shaped note of clarity and style which fitted into the overall pattern of the staff, and his method of single-impression printing reduced production costs and time by at least half.

In 1537 Attaingnant became the King's Music Printer and, by making large quantities of music available at reasonable prices, he became in essence the first music publisher to operate on a large scale. He diffused the works of Parisian *chanson* composers (Claudin de Sermisy, Janequin, and Certon) and published breviaries, missals, and the first books of psalm settings. His press became a clearing-house for ideas and a moulder of taste. Attaingnant's

Pl. 4. The earliest dated mensural (measured) music with text and notes printed from type by one impression, an important technical advance pioneered by Pierre Attaingnant. This example from his 'Chansons nouvelles en musique' (Paris, 1527-8) shows the stylish diamond-shaped note he designed.

techniques were taken up by other French printers, such as Jacques *Moderne in Lyons, who based his note forms on those of Petrucci, and Robert Granjon. Granjon was an outstanding punch-cutter, whose contribution to typography, notably *civilité* type, is of great historical importance; his elegant music type reveals at once his calligraphic mastery.

After Attaingnant's death in 1551/2 the royal privilege passed to the lutenist and composer Robert *Ballard, whose descendants continued in business until 1825. The firm of Le Roy & Ballard developed a distinctive music type, cut by the notable Guillaume Le Bé, which was more rounded than the severe lozenge shape used by Attaingnant and others. In their heyday Le Roy & Ballard were a leading house, responsive to taste and defensive of their monopoly. They published *chansons*, motets, psalms, *chansons spirituelles*, and tablature for plucked string instruments, and they enjoyed warm relations with leading composers. In the 17th century they were the first to publish orchestral scores.

The earliest known specimen of musical notation printed in England occurs in Ranulphus Higden's *Polychronicon* (London, 1495, a summary of world history and scientific knowledge). The passage in which the notes appear concerns the consonances of Pythagoras. Wynkyn de Worde, the printer, set the musical notes by putting together quads (possibly reversed capitals) and rules and printed them with the text. At about the time when Attaingnant was experimenting with single-impression printing, an isolated example of it appeared in London, in John Rastell's *New Interlude and a Mery of the Nature of the iiii Elements* (c.1525). Rastell printed the first mensural music in Britain, the earliest broadside with music printed from type anywhere in Europe, and the earliest song printed in an English dramatic work; he was also the first in Britain to attempt to print a score, by any process.

The first known English printed vocal partbooks, *The Book of XX Songes* (1530), issued by an unnamed printer, shows craftsmanlike skill. The staves were printed from blocks at the first impression and the words and notes at a second impression. The result was excellent. Before the 1570s only about 60 volumes were printed in England, most of them sacred music, but in 1570 Thomas Vautrollier began to publish secular music, and the best of his work was equal in quality to that of his continental counterparts. In 1575 Tallis and Byrd received a royal patent from Queen Elizabeth I for 21 years for printing music and supplying paper, but it did not prove profitable and they had to petition the queen for assistance. The printer and publisher Thomas East acquired Vautrollier's music type and printed several part-book collections between 1588 and 1596. Other notable English publications include John Dowland's *First Booke of Songes or Aires* (London, 1597), which follows the continental 'table-book' format in which the parts are printed together in one volume but facing different ways on the page, so that performers seated round a table can read their parts from a single volume.

There were a number of skilled printers in northern Europe at this period, notably in Frankfurt (Christian Egenolff), Nuremberg (Hieronymus Formschneider, or 'Grapheus'), Wittenberg, and elsewhere. Venetian followers of Petrucci, such as Antonio Gardano and the Scotto family, kept Venice in the forefront of Italian endeavour. In the Low Countries, Tylman *Susato at Antwerp and the elder Pierre *Phalèse at Louvain established thriving businesses.

In 1555 Christopher *Plantin set up his press, The Golden Compasses, in Antwerp, then a centre for the publishing trade, and initiated a printing and publishing business that endured until the late 19th century. As the Plantin-Moretus Museum, it is now an unparalleled source of information, with its press room, the cases of type collected by Plantin himself, and all the documents and accessories of the past. These indicate that the well-organized workforce and constant production rates at the press, combined with Plantin's own strong commercial sense, contributed greatly to his success. Plantin usually decided the design, format, and print run of the editions himself, supplying specimen pages and proofs to authors and composers, who would compile lists of errata to be printed at the end if time did not allow for corrections before printing. Plantin's first volume of music, George de la Hèle's *Missae* (1578), sold for 18 florins, a high price, and he often financed his printing by asking composers to buy copies themselves, sometimes as many as 100 or 150. Although music was a small part of his publishing enterprise, he published the best composers available to him (e.g. Philippe de Monte, Andreas Pevernage, and Jacob de Kerle), many in lavishly designed editions; his press became a centre of humanist culture and, as official printer to King Philip of Spain, he was highly regarded by his contemporaries.

5. *Europe: 1600–c.1750.* The history of printing music by engraving begins properly in the 17th century, though the earliest examples of copper-plate engraving date from the 16th. Apart from the volume of Francesco da Milano's lute tablature of c.1536 (see section 2c), there are a number of devotional prints from the 1580s and 1590s that combine music with an artist's engraved illustration (e.g. Sadelar's *Virgin and Child* of 1584, which incorporates a motet by

Pl. 5. Philip Galle's superb engraving of a motet by Pevernage in his 'Encomium musices' (Antwerp, c.1590).

Verdonck, and Philippe Galle's *Encomium musices* of *c.*1590. Engraving became influential, however, through the work of Simone Verovio, a calligrapher and engraver, whose *Diletto spirituale* and *Primo libro delle melodie spirituali* were engraved in Rome in 1586. The technique spread gradually to other countries. William Hole (*fl.* London, 1612–18) engraved *Parthenia, or the Maydenhead of the First Musicke that ever was printed for the Virginalls* (*c.*1612), the first music to be produced by this method in England. It is a splendid volume, with free-flowing calligraphy (though it is somewhat tightly arranged for performance), famed for its title-page picture of a young lady at the keyboard. Other notable collections of engraved English music include *Parthenia in-violata* (1614), which is believed to be the work of several hands, Orlando Gibbons's beautifully engraved *Fantazies of III Parts* (*c.*1620), and Purcell's *Sonnatas of III Parts* (London, 1683), elegantly engraved by Thomas Cross.

Music engraving was adopted in the Netherlands in 1615, but not until *c.*1660 in France, and 1680 in Germany. Much later, in Diderot's *Encyclopédie* (1761–5), a Mme Delusse, a music engraver, gives a full account of the process, citing operas by Lully and Mouret, motets by Campra and Lalande, and cantatas by Bernier and Clérambault as early examples of French engraving. By the beginning of the 18th century music engraving had fully established itself, although it continued to coexist alongside music type, with a constant ebb and flow of one against the other and a continual search for improved techniques.

English music publishing from the mid 17th century to the mid 18th, in the hands of the Playfords and the Walshes, exemplifies that state of affairs, for their ideals and methods differed strikingly. John *Playford and his son Henry had most of their volumes printed from music type, while John *Walsh the elder began as an engraver and later turned to pewter plates and punches. The Playfords were cultured men who published music suitable for the tavern, the musical club, and the theatre, and for both amateurs and professionals. John Playford developed a racy style of publication, with attractive designs and lively illustrations. His distinct flair and personality show themselves in his first books, *The (English) Dancing Master*

(1651), *A Musicall Banquet* (1651), and *A Breefe Introduction to the Skill of Musick* (1654). To read his advertisements, exhortations to the purchaser and reader, and comments on the (unrecognized) qualities of English composers is to catch the zest and spirit of an engaging, shrewd publisher.

The Walshes were among the most influential publishers in Europe, but unlike the Playfords, whose hearts lay in music rather than commerce, they exploited their composers, notably Handel, and left posterity with many bibliographical tangles to unravel. The elder John Walsh developed new techniques in publishing, based principally on the cheap and speedy method of striking pewter plates with punches. He employed many apprentices and was wideranging in his enterprises, making arrangements with continental publishers such as the renowned Amsterdam engraver Estienne *Roger, pirating freely as was the custom, and publicizing his flood of editions through the newspapers and his own catalogues. He issued song-sheets and anthologies, instrumental music, and cheap instruction books, and was Handel's principal publisher. His unscrupulous editorial methods manifest themselves in the disarray of many Handel editions, especially the harpsichord music. He fell out with Handel over the publication of *Rinaldo* in 1711, and Handel returned to the firm only some 10 years later, when the younger John was in control.

John Heptinstall introduced improvements in the appearance and flexibility of music type in his *Vinculum Societatis, or The Tie of Good Company* (London, 1687), using round instead of lozenge-shaped noteheads and grouping quavers and semiquavers by beams, a procedure that became known as 'the new tied note'. In 1698 Peter de Walpergen printed a group of four songs in folio called *Musica Oxoniensis*, which showed for the first time a distinguished new type 'cut on steel and cast' with a stylishness and clarity that fully justify the high claims of its promoters.

A number of decorated title-pages of this period are justly admired, among them Walsh's edition of Daniel Purcell's *The Judgement of Paris* (1702), John Pine's striking title for J. E. Galliard's *The Morning Hymn of Adam and Eve* (1728), Walsh's frontispiece for John Weldon's *Divine Harmony* (c.1730), with its conjectural interior of the Chapel Royal, and John Cluer's and Walsh's title-pages for Handel's operas, several of which were later reused for other publications.

Many 18th-century music editions remain unequalled in grace and distinction. In England the collaboration between writing master and music engraver which had begun with William Hole's *Parthenia* flowered in a series of song-

books, of which the finest is George Bickham's splendid *The Musical Entertainer* (London, 1737–9); single sheets of it still appear in antiquarian shops. Also notable was Thomas Jeffery's collection of songs entitled *Amaryllis* (c.1750) and John Cluer's charming collection of opera airs, *A Pocket Companion for Gentlemen and Ladies* (1724–5).

French engraved music of the 18th century was generally of a very high standard. Couperin enjoyed the services of an excellent engraver for his *Pièces de clavecin* (1713), and his instruction book *L'art de toucher le clavecin* (1716–17) is at times like an engraver's notebook. The posthumous engraved editions of Lully's operas reached high levels, and among French songbooks, Laborde's *Choix de chansons* (1773) is outstanding. Music engraving attracted a number of extremely accomplished Frenchwomen, among whom were Mlle Vendôme (later Mme Moria), Mme Labassée, and Mme Lobry.

6. *Europe: c.1750–c.1945.* Between 1749 and 1755, in a pioneer attempt to overcome the problems still inherent in the use of music type, Jacques-François Rosart cut a series of punches which embodied an improved method of printing. He offered them first to Johannes Enschedé at Haarlem, who gave him no encouragement. Instead, the German typefounder and printer J. G. I. *Breitkopf, working on the same principles, began his own experiments in the mid 1740s which resulted in a superior fount of music type. He has been credited with the invention ever since. The sharp impression of the notes, the visual flow, and overall balance and elegance of the music characterized Breitkopf's type.

Instead of using a single type-unit made up of notehead, stem, and staff, Breitkopf used separate pieces for the head and stem attached to staff segments of varying lengths, and additional pieces for the notes of shorter value. This came to be known as the 'mosaic' system, and it

Pl. 6. John Heptinstall's improved and more flexible music type, as shown in his 'Vinculum Societatis, or the Tie of Good Company' (London, 1687), a pun on his invention of the 'new tied note', which grouped quavers and semiquavers by beams.

Pl. 7. A superb title-page from J. E. Galliard's 'The Morning Hymn of Adam and Eve' (London, 1728), designed by John Pine, outstanding amongst many English exemplars of this period.

reached its greatest level of complexity in the latter part of the 19th century. It required much careful and detailed work by the compositor and, usually, the ability to read music. Breitkopf's type was first properly demonstrated in *Il trionfo della fedeltà* (1756), a pastoral drama by the Electress Maria Anna Walpurgis of Bavaria, and it was subsequently used for many major publications of the Classical repertory.

In France, the distinguished typographer Pierre-Simon Fournier (1712–68) had been making similar successful experiments, the results of which appeared in his *Essai d'un nouveau caractère de fonte* (1756). His attractive type was used in Jean Monnet's *Anthologie françoise* (1765), and it is occasionally seen in pocket books of librettos with *airs*. However, Ballard's powerful monopoly in France prevented Fournier's design having an influence comparable to Breitkopf's. Breitkopf pioneered the printing of large numbers of copies, selling

Pl. 8. J. G. I. Breitkopf (1719–94) pioneered a superior fount of music type in the mid 1740s, with separate pieces for the stem and head of the type, attached to staff segments of varying lengths and additional pieces for the notes of another line. This came to be known as the 'mosaic system'.

them cheaply and distributing them widely. He also developed a market for manuscript copies of a wide repertory of works that did not justify a printed edition, and to publicize them he issued thematic catalogues. His own endeavours, and his heirs' successful partnership with G. C. Härtel, helped establish Leipzig as the centre of music publishing in Europe.

Following the rise of the great Viennese school of composers (Haydn, Mozart, Beethoven) and the growth of music-making among all sections of the community, new publishing houses were founded. Chief amongst them were *Schott (Mainz), Simrock (Bonn), and *Artaria (Vienna). From their presses flowed chamber music of every kind, parts for concertos and symphonies, arrangements, piano pieces, and songs. The widespread use of engraving brought down the costs, although the printing was of variable quality, and the development of lithography in the later 19th century helped meet the accelerating need for mass copies of music. The rise of public concerts and a demand for 'study scores' encouraged the publication of miniature scores, by Payne of Leipzig (the first to produce them on a large scale) and later by *Eulenburg.

Although Leipzig remained at the centre of music publishing throughout the century, houses in other cities were well established and productive (e.g. *Ricordi in Milan, Bote & Bock in Berlin, and *Novello and *Cramer in London). The enormous increase in output during the century can be seen by comparing the size of a major printing house (e.g. Röder of Leipzig) at the middle and end of the century.

Printing and publishing remained very much a German trade, however. In 1895 the London publisher Joseph Spedding Curwen inspected the printing works of Röder and Brandstetter in Leipzig and was impressed by its personal excellence and in particular by the skill and industry of the workmen, who earned less than their British counterparts. Until 1914 many Germans were employed in the engraving rooms of British firms such as *Augener, Novello, Curwen, and Lowe & Brydone, whose engraving department became one of the largest in the country, known in its heyday as 'the greatest music printing firm in the Empire'.

The 19th century also saw the growth of the pictorial title-page. Early in the century French publishers had included charming vignette engravings and lithographs on their title-pages, foreshadowing the later use of coloured drawings, portraits, and illustrations of domestic scenes, national occasions such as exhibitions, and so on, and several notable artists emerged (e.g. Nanteuil, Packer, Brandard, and Concanen). Editions of music by Louis Antoine Jullien (1812-60) showed exuberant, even spectacular, colour. Black and white title-pages and covers did not disappear: *The Musical Bouquet* (c.1846-8), which appeared in series and included over 5,000 pieces of music, epitomizes the best work of the English school.

Leipzig lost its pre-eminence as the centre of music printing and publishing after the Second World War. Bombing destroyed most of the great printing works, and the city's incorporation into the German Democratic Republic split many famous firms, some moving to the West, while others were taken over by the state. Leipzig's reputation had largely rested on engraving, which was by then restricted to selected and often prestige works. Printers throughout Europe were disbanding their engraving departments as lithographic techniques all but took over.

The pattern of musical life had also changed everywhere. Amateur music-making declined, as did sales of the piano, the ubiquitous domestic instrument of the 19th century. Much avant-garde music proved too difficult for amateurs and seemed at first inaccessible. New compositional techniques arose, such as electronic music, which required the publisher to find new marketing techniques. Publishers regrouped, rethought their roles, sought to develop new markets, and pruned, in order to survive.

7. *USA.* From the Puritan psalm-singing traditions of England there arose the first music to be printed in America, the *Bay Psalm Book*. Its early editions contained no music, but in the ninth (Boston, 1698) 13 psalm-tunes in two-part arrangements were crudely printed in diamond-shaped notes from woodblock, with basic instructions on performance. John Tuft's 12-page pamphlet containing 37 tunes in three parts, 'An Easy Method of Singing by Letters

instead of Notes', was followed by his *Very Plain and Easy Introduction to the Singing of Psalm Tunes* (3rd edn, Boston, 1723). Even more successful, however, was Thomas Walter's *Grounds and Rules of Musick Explained* (Boston, 1721), in which bar-lines appeared in American music printing for the first time.

From the mid 18th century onwards, several psalm collections broadened the repertory, some including tunes by native composers. Josiah Flagg's *Collection of the Best Psalm Tunes* (Boston, 1764) and *The New-England Psalm-Singer* (Boston, 1770) by William Billings, the colonial period's most rugged and energetic composer, had their plates or frontispieces engraved by Paul Revere, the leading goldsmith of New England. Nearly all the music of the colonial period was printed from polished copper plates engraved freehand by local engravers or silversmiths, most of whose names remain unknown, though Thomas Johnston, who also engraved maps, views, book-plates, certificates, and currency, was an exception.

The two earliest books to be printed from music type, not commonly used at this time, were *Geistreiche Lieder* (Germantown, 1752) and *Neu-vermehrt und vollstaendiges Gesang-Buch* (Germantown, 1757). The type was possibly cast by the publisher, a German immigrant named Christopher Sower (or Saur). They contained only a few short and simple melodies; the first full page of tunes appeared in William Dawson's *The Youth's Entertaining Amusement, or A Plain Guide to Psalmody* (Philadelphia, c.1754). Isaiah Thomas's *The Worcester Collection of Sacred Harmony* (Worcester, Mass., 1786), printed from Caslon foundry types purchased in London, set higher standards and also marked the first attempt to maintain a continuity of publications. After the Revolution, the flow of European immigrants increased, and American musical life broadened. Sacred and secular music widened in scope, and entertainments of every kind arose, all of which required music. Musicians and music teachers arrived in far greater numbers than ever before, among them many musician-engravers employing the technique of stamping notes on to pewter plates with punches. They provided the basis for a native publishing trade, which flourished first in Philadelphia.

Alexander Reinagle's *Selection of the Most Favourite Scots Tunes* (Philadelphia, 1787), engraved by John Aitken, was the first wholly secular music publication in the USA. Benjamin Carr, descended from a long line of English music publishers, became the most important and prolific figure in the 1790s. He was a leading composer too, and his influential *Musical Journal for the Piano Forte* of the late 1790s moulded taste for over 20 years. Philadelphia maintained its predominant position into the early 19th century, through the sheet-music business of Moller & Capron, and especially through the vigorous activities of George Willig and George E. Blake, publishing celebrities of their day. Other notable publishers include Gottlieb Graupner in Boston, Joseph Carr in Baltimore, and in New York, George Gilfert and James Hewitt, who established a music circulating library. New York soon became the chief centre of music publishing in the USA.

Music publishing spread west and south from the eastern seaboard, firms were set up in places such as Cincinnati, Louisville, Chicago (Root & Cady), and St Louis (Balmer & Weber), and the influence of London and European styles and tastes gradually declined. As the minstrel show emerged, American publishers sought to attract amateur musicians and provided a flow of spirituals, gospel songs, polkas, and schottisches, as well as innumerable sentimental ballads and salon pieces. Ballads were published to celebrate the completion of the Erie Canal in 1825, New York's first train, the first horse-drawn street cars, and so on. Many had lithographed pictorial covers original and vital enough to establish an American school. As immigrants continued to pour in, tune-books, hymnals, and chorus and anthem books were needed in greater numbers. Hundreds of sentimental songs by popular composers such as Stephen Foster were distributed by the New York publishers Firth, Pond, & Co. and reached an international audience.

In the latter half of the 19th century more immigrant Germans established music shops and firms which later grew into significant publishing houses. They included Gustav *Schirmer (New York, 1861), Joseph Fischer (Dayton, Ohio, 1864), Carl *Fischer (New York, 1872), Theodore *Presser (Philadelphia, 1884), and E. C. *Schirmer (Boston, 1891). Besides catering for popular needs, some pub-

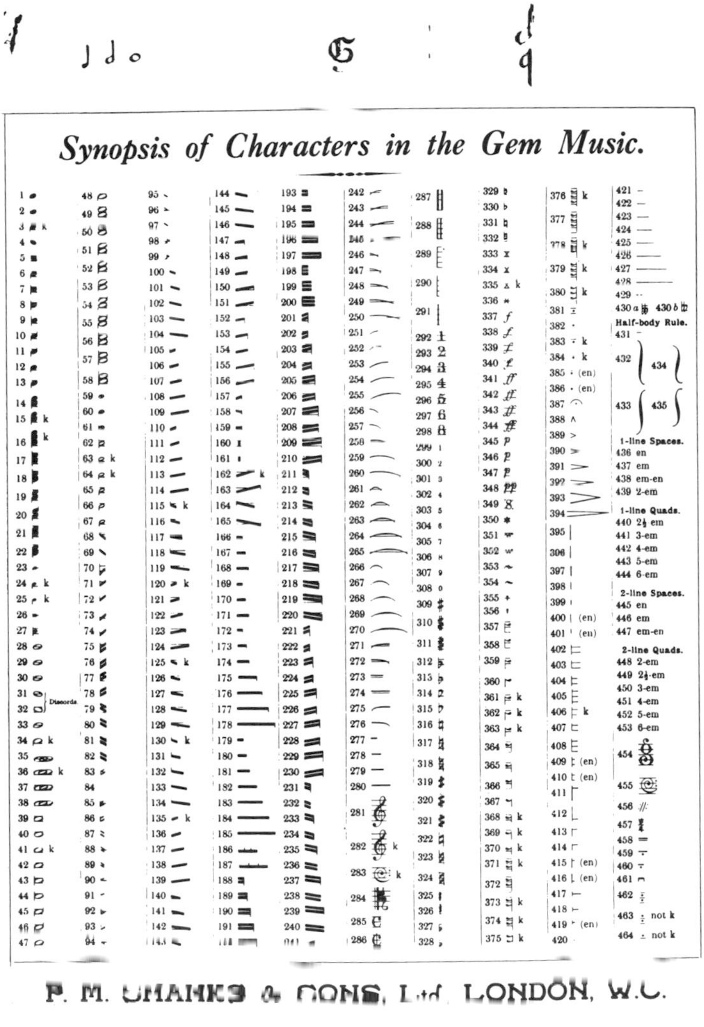

Pl. 9. A 'mosaic system' of 1922 showing the 464 characters offered in P. M. Shanks' synopsis of type characters for their Gem Music.

lished excellent editions of the classics and took financial risks with American composers, who by the end of the century had virtually established a 'school', with George Chadwick, Arthur Foote, Horatio Parker, and, best known of all, Edward MacDowell.

The growth of symphony orchestras, opera houses, and fine teaching institutions further stimulated national musical life and with it music publishing. But the phenomenon of ragtime, and subsequently the cake-walk, first indicated the growth of a new musical culture. John Stillwell Stark, a publisher in Sedalia, Missouri, published the piano rags of Scott Joplin. Meanwhile, *Tin Pan Alley (the name for New York's sheet-music publishers), notably firms such as Harms Inc. and Witmark, exploited vaudeville songs with new marketing methods, and by the time Irving Berlin's 'Alexander's Ragtime Band' appeared in 1911 ragtime was virtually dead and was succeeded by the blues and jazz.

American composers interested in folk and Indian music had been welcomed by Arthur Farwell's Wa-Wan Press (1901), fashionable at the time as a means of creating a truly American music. But most composers belonged to a more eclectic tradition, with Charles Ives at its head, which found plenty of American publishers ready to promote its works. Some firms took up the Broadway musical, still a living genre, and works of the 1930s such as George Gershwin's *Porgy and Bess*, an American classic, more than justified their faith and business instincts. American music publishing houses, some closely linked with those of Europe, continue today their distinctive role as vital links in the lively scene that is American music.

8. *Composers and Publishers*. The music publishing house first acted as a stimulus to musical life in the early 16th century, when Pierre Attaingnant gathered around him in Paris renowned composers, such as Claudin de Sermisy, Certon, and Janequin, and musicians and music-lovers of every kind. He could offer his composers little financial reward, but his fine printing and wide-ranging distribution could bring them honour and fame. Instead of payment the composer would accept an agreed number of printed copies, although if he had approached the publisher in the first place he would usually expect to finance the whole venture. With no legislation to guarantee copyright protection, and widespread piracy, some composers preferred to keep their works in manuscript and negotiate their own terms for performance.

An extant agreement of 2 January 1531 between the distinguished Avignon craftsman Jean de Channey and the composer Carpentras

illuminates publishing procedures of the time. Known as the Avignon Contracts (and discussed in detail in Daniel Heartz's study of Attaingnant, 1969), it sets forth the rights and obligations on both sides and shows the difficulties that faced de Channey when he attempted a monumental edition of Carpentras's works.

Handel's problems with the Walshes have already been outlined (see section 5). Without copyright protection composers had to bargain directly with publishers, securing the highest possible outright payment. Piracy had to be thwarted, as had the activities of unscrupulous copyists who passed around new works to the highest bidder. From the 18th century onwards composer–publisher relationships are well charted in correspondence. Haydn's letters from 1781 onwards to the Viennese house of Artaria have a predominantly friendly tone, but Haydn's shrewd business sense made him react sharply if he felt himself being taken advantage of, and he preferred to keep private his financial transactions with his publisher. Poorly engraved work angered him. In his later years he became dissatisfied with Artaria and began negotiations with Breitkopf & Härtel, who eventually became his principal publishers.

Mozart had little success with Breitkopf & Härtel. His father tried to interest them in his son's works early in his career, but this met with no response. Mozart's works were properly made known only after his death, when the publisher J. A. André of Offenbach purchased a quantity of manuscripts from Mozart's widow Constanze (although Breitkopf was subsequently to publish several important collected editions).

A large part of Beethoven's correspondence involves his publishers (Alan Tyson comments brilliantly on this in two chapters in *The Beethoven Companion*, ed. Denis Arnold and Nigel Fortune, London, 1971). Beethoven was determined to thwart piracy and unscrupulous copyists, and by 1801 he felt he was in a position to choose his own publisher from a possible six or seven and to state his own price for each work. Sometimes he kept back from publication works he might perform himself such as his finest concertos. He kept a number of copyists and proof-readers feverishly busy. He fretted over errors in his proofs, and had a sharp eye for a missing accidental or an omitted change of clef, but like most composers came to acknowledge that the work's creator was not the ideal proof-reader.

Verdi's relationships with *Ricordi are themselves an offstage drama, detailed in the correspondence. He quarrelled with the elder Tito Ricordi, son of Giovanni (founder of the firm), about printing errors in his operas, and even wanted the first edition of *La traviata* withdrawn; eventually Tito's son Giulio, who brought Verdi and his librettist Boito together for *Otello*, restored good relations.

The greatly differing personalities and needs of composers created constantly changing patterns with publishers. Elgar and his editor at Novello, August Jaeger ('Nimrod' of the *Enigma Variations*), established a unique artistic trust, a friendship vivacious and warm, so that the letters between them (1897-1908) mirror the composer's mercurial moods and feelings. When Jaeger died at the age of 49 in 1909, Elgar wrote: 'Despondent about himself, he was full of hope for others, and spent himself in smoothing their path to fame.'

Publishers on their side must be adaptable, diplomatic, experimental, businesslike, and above all sensitive to emerging gifts and talents and to the changing patterns of the musical scene. It is no profession for the fainthearted. Some German music publishers have still not forgiven Richard Strauss his mocking picture of them in his bizarre song cycle *Krämerspiegel* ('Shopkeepers' Mirror'). Schoenberg's clear imperative to Emil Hertzka, director of *Universal Edition in Vienna, in 1911, is one that all true composers might have made: 'I too have sung your praises. Now please print my work!!! I am certain it's good!!! . . . Well, you know what we musicians are like. And nobody so more than I.'

9. *Publishing Today*. Much of the commercial background to music publishing in the 20th century has been concerned with the changing nature of copyright and performing right, and with the growth of the recording industry, broadcasting, and television (see *Copyright*).

The music publisher's income is derived from performing right fees, mechanical reproduction fees, royalties, hire fees, and the sale of music (apart from any subsidiary interests and agency fees for overseas principals). The composer, on the other hand, shares the royalties on copies of his music that are sold and fees accruing from performances. The composer owns the copyright in his work during his lifetime and, in Britain, for 50 years after his death.

Hire fees follow a tariff set out by the Music Publishers' Association. Large orchestras may have on permanent loan a set of parts of a work they perform frequently, holding it in their library and paying the normal tariff. Conductors can make special arrangements to purchase a hire score.

From the sale of music the publisher will pay the composer a royalty of 10-12½ per cent. Such income in no way compares with the immense sums earned from sheet-music sales in the late 19th century and the early 20th. In 1898, for

instance, *The Soldiers of the Queen*, published during the Boer War, sold well over 250,000 copies, and in the 1920s *That Old-fashioned Mother of Mine* sold 704,000, bringing the composer Lawrence Wright £4,900. Recordings, broadcasting, and television are now principal income sources.

The typical print figures of a major publisher are eloquent. He will print 1,000 copies of the vocal score of a new opera, selling at £30, provided he has been able to arrange a subsidy. The hire library will absorb 500. He may then add 500 (or more) sets of parts and will prepare at least three full scores for conductors and for promotion. For an orchestral work, he will prepare sets of parts and full scores only for the hire library, as most concert-giving organizations prefer to hire rather than purchase outright, though he may later print miniature scores for reference and study which could yield reasonable but not spectacular profits. If the composer is under contract to the publisher, 25 or more promotional copies may be prepared instead of a miniature score. Contemporary chamber music (piano solos, small ensembles, etc.) sell more slowly and have small print runs (from 500 to 1,500), rising whenever a title is included in a teaching syllabus.

A gradual shrinkage of sales has led publishers to concentrate on the more profitable opera houses, international orchestras, and broadcasting companies, on the educational market, and on choral societies, brass bands, etc. For some time avant-garde music remained formidable to the amateur performer, but some composers and publishers have made a determined effort to win him back, at times with considerable success. In the 1970s several very small, specialist music publishers emerged, using the cheapest available methods and relying on direct sales. Some composers, notably Stockhausen, have formed their own publishing companies. Publishers' incomes have been seriously eroded by illegal photocopying, which a licensing system should help to control.

However, despite the formidable economic and artistic difficulties posed by present circumstances, many monumental publishing enterprises are in train, such as great scholarly editions covering an ever wider range of music and embodying research that is both meticulous and inspired. As new composers emerge, there will always be publishers responsive to their gifts, for the publishing of music is central to the Western musical tradition.

J. M. THOMSON

FURTHER READING

W. Gamble: *Music Engraving and Printing: Historical and Technical Treatise* (London, 1923, reprinted 1971); C. Humphries and W. C. Smith: *Music Publishing in the British Isles* (London, 1954, 2nd edn 1970); A. B.

Barksdale: *The Printed Note: 500 Years of Music Printing and Engraving* (Toledo, Ohio, 1957); Novello & Co. Ltd: *A Century and a Half in Soho* (London, 1961); Alec Hyatt King: *Four Hundred Years of Music Printing* (London, 1964, 2nd edn 1968); G. Fraenkel: *Decorative Music Title Pages 1500-1800* (New York, 1969); Daniel Heartz: *Pierre Attaingnant: Royal Printer of Music* (Berkeley, 1969); E. Roth: *The Business of Music: Reflections of a Music Publisher* (London, 1969); Doreen and Sidney Spellman: *Victorian Music Covers* (London, 1969); Leon Voet: *The Golden Compasses: a History and Evaluation of the Printing and Publishing Activities of the Officina Plantiniana* (2 vols., Amsterdam, 1969); Allen Huff: *Fournier: the Compleat Typographer* (London, 1972); Ronald Pearsall: *Victorian Sheet Music Covers* (Newton Abbot, 1972); Max Wilk: *Memory Lane 1890-1925: Ragtime, Jazz, Foxtrot, and Other Popular Music and Musicians* (London, 1973); D. W. Krummel: *English Music Printing 1553-1700* (London, 1975); Alan Peacock and Ronald Weir: *The Composer and the Market Place* (London, 1975); Richard J. Wolfe: *Early American Music Engraving and Printing: History of Music Publishing in America from 1787 to 1825* (Urbana, 1980).

Prise de Troie, La. See *Troyens, Les*.

Proceedings of the Royal Musical Association. See *Royal Musical Association*.

Processional (Lat.: *processionale*). A kind of chant book; see *Plainchant*, 4.

Prodigal Son, The. Several composers have written works on this subject, the best known being the following. 1. Church parable, Op. 81, by Britten to a text by William Plomer. It was first performed at the Aldeburgh Festival, in Orford Church, in 1968.

2. Oratorio by Sullivan, first performed at the Worcester Festival in 1869.

3. Ballet by Prokofiev, Op. 46, choreographed by Balanchine and first performed in Paris in 1929. Its Russian title is *Bludny syn* but it is often known by the French form *L'enfant prodigue*.

4. Cantata by Debussy; see *Enfant prodigue, L'*.

Profession of Music. The social and economic changes of the 20th century have had considerable effect upon music and musicians, as also has the rapid scientific and technological progress which largely brought about these changes; nevertheless composition, performance, and teaching have remained the principal occupations of the professional musician. The invention of radio and television, together with developments in the recording industry, have given ready access to music, just as the impact of the electronic age upon industry and commerce has allowed more leisure time. Ubiquitous music, on radio, disc, or tape in the home, the car, the supermarket, even on trains and buses, has had a polarizing effect; it has produced a knowledgeable and demanding public at the same time as it has encouraged the inattentive listener. The composer has wider opportunities and greater artistic freedom than ever before; contemporary composition ranges from the totally serial to the aleatory and from the abstruse to the unashamedly commercial. A small number of composers earn a highly successful living from satisfying the needs of television, films, and radio as do others in the ephemeral field of 'pop' music and the musical show of light theatre entertainment. There is also a small but continuing market for teaching material, both for school and private teaching purposes. However, the great majority of composers earn the bulk of their income in other ways than composition—a few from performance as conductors or instrumentalists, and many from teaching.

The growth of music as a subject in higher education has created more opportunities for composers to teach and work in universities, polytechnics, and colleges; such posts, in addition to providing some financial stability, afford the probability of at least local performance—the composer's principal obstacle to recognition remaining that of persuading concert organizers to perform his works. The Society for the Promotion of New Music is helpful and active in this connection, as are the Arts Council and Regional Arts Associations through bursaries and commissions, and the Contemporary Music Network. The Composers' Guild is a professional association promoting the interests of British composers, while the Performing Right Society and the Mechanical Copyright Protection Society collect and distribute royalties on behalf of their members (see *Copyright*).

Whereas there have always been performers of outstanding ability, the 20th century has seen a significant raising of technical standards generally. The present-day orchestral player takes in his stride works demanding a technique which his forerunners would have found, at the very least, daunting. In part this improvement stems from a recognition of the need for early identification of musical talent and the availability of suitable training. The post-1945 emphasis on instrumental work in schools and the formation of youth orchestras—particularly the National Youth Orchestra (1947)—have had an important influence; so also have the specialist schools catering for the musically gifted child, such as the Yehudi Menuhin School or Chetham's School of Music, Manchester. Most performing musicians receive their post-school age professional training at a music college, taking a three- or four-year course, often followed by post-graduate or further study. A smaller number proceed via university; one of the more recent developments in music departments at university has been a growing recognition of the importance of performance as part of an essentially academic course. Resident pianists or chamber music ensembles are now not uncommon, combining their professional performing career with a regular teaching commitment.

The Gulbenkian Report, *Training Musicians* (1978), noted the need for intending orchestral musicians to gain more experience before entering the profession than is practicable in an initial course at a music college. The establishment of postgraduate (or post-diploma) training orchestras at the Royal Northern College of Music, Manchester, and at Goldsmiths' College, London, is intended to provide such experience. The position in regard to opera in Great Britain has been steadily strengthened by the appearance of new companies, particularly outside London—Opera North, Scottish Opera, and Welsh National Opera, for example. This development, together with the opening or reopening of several provincial theatres, has given professional singers and instrumentalists additional scope for employment. Commercial sponsorship of music and indirect state patronage, through the Arts Council and local government subsidy, have become, in the later 20th century, increasingly vital to the professional performer, by offsetting the rising costs of concert and operatic production.

Almost all musicians teach, to some extent, during their career and the demand for instrumental and vocal tuition continues steadily. The schoolteacher in charge of music, particularly in secondary education, faces complex demands which reflect changes in society—a multi-ethnic school population, economic pressures, and the influence of jazz-derived and popular music of all kinds. The work of Carl Orff, notably, has affected class music-making, and the Suzuki method has produced remarkable results in the training of young string players.

Most professional performers, particularly those working in orchestras, belong to the Musicians' Union which negotiates rates of pay and conditions of employment. The Incorporated Society of Musicians is an association which caters solely for the professional musician, and incorporates specialist sections for solo performers, private teachers, and those working in education.

For discussion of the role of the musician at various times in history see *Composer*, *Concert*, *Conducting*, *Criticism of Music*, *Education and Music*, *Minstrels*, *Opera*, *Printing and Publishing of Music*, *Watt*, and the individual entries on countries.   PERCY WELTON

Profondo (It.). See *Basso profondo*.

Programme music. The term 'programme' was defined by Liszt as 'any preface in intelligible language added to a piece of instrumental music, by means of which the composer intends to guard the listener against a wrong poetical interpretation, and to direct his attention to the poetical idea of the whole or to a particular part of it'.

Berlioz's *Symphonie fantastique* is an example of this form of programme music. The programme of this five-movement symphony depicts an 'Episode in the life of an artist'. The programme is too long to reproduce here in its entirety, but it tells of an artist who sees, for the first time, a woman who embodies the ideal of beauty and fascination that his heart has been longing and seeking; he falls desperately in love with her. Every time the image of the loved one appears in the artist's imagination it is accompanied by a musical thought, the famous *idée fixe* of the symphony. The last two movements of the work present the image of the beloved through the eyes of the artist who in a fit of despair has taken opium. In the fourth movement, 'the March to the Scaffold', he imagines he has killed his beloved and has been condemned to death and witnesses his own execution. In the fifth movement, 'Dream of a Witches Sabbath', the artist sees himself surrounded by an assembly of sorcerers and devils come together to celebrate the sabbath. His beloved comes to join in the devilish orgy, which consists of a sabbath round-dance and burlesque parody of the 'Dies Irae'. Berlioz stated that the 'distribution of the programme to the audience at concerts where the symphony is to be performed is indispensable for a complete understanding of the dramatic outline of the work'.

Programme music in a more general sense, however, describes any musical composition which depicts an extra-musical idea. The programme itself is often restricted to merely a descriptive title, rather than an elaborate accompanying text as in the Berlioz example. Although programme music may be based on a conventional formal design (for example Mendelssohn's 'Hebrides Overture—Fingal's Cave' is a sonata form structure) it goes beyond 'absolute' music in its attempt to depict an extra-musical image or idea in sound.

                                        G. M. TUCKER

Progression. In harmonic theory, the movement of one note to another or of one chord to another. The term is frequently encountered as 'cadential progression', describing typical ways of leading up to a cadence.

Prokofiev, Sergey (Sergeyevich) (*b* Sontsovka, Ukraine, 27 Apr. 1891; *d* Moscow, 5 Mar. 1953). Russian composer. He was a true *enfant terrible*, reacting strongly to the heady atmosphere of Russian late Romanticism as soon as his own compositional style had acquired the strength and character to assert itself. During his late 20s and 30s he lived in the West, but he returned to the Soviet Union in the early 1930s and remained there for the rest of his life, producing some of his best-known works.

1. *The Early Years*. As a child he studied privately with Glière, and then entered the St Petersburg Conservatory where his principal teachers were Lyadov (harmony, counterpoint, and composition) and Rimsky-Korsakov (orchestration). Not unnaturally for a young man with such an iconoclastic spark, Prokofiev found the lessons restrictive, and preferred instead to ally himself with the avant-garde movement centred on the Evenings of Contemporary Music. He composed a number of exploratory solo piano pieces which spread alarm and incomprehension among the conservatives but which were hailed as fresh and progressive by the modernists: *Suggestion diabolique* (1908), *Sarcasms* (1912-14), and *Visions fugitives* (1915-17). He also made an impact on the wider St Petersburg public with his First Piano Concerto (1911-12), a work

Prokofiev

which echoes his own formidable pianistic skills and at the same time shows that even in his early works Prokofiev possessed a keen sense of orchestral colour, a firm grasp of structure, and a pronounced lyrical gift; there is, too, that touch of devilment which seems to underlie so much of Prokofiev's music. This last trait is even more prominent in the Second Piano Concerto (1912-13, revised 1923), which scandalized audiences and critics alike with its dissonant harmony, percussive, spiky piano writing, feverish activity, and its huge, 10-minute cadenza in the first movement. Around the same time he composed his crisp First Symphony (the 'Classical', 1916-17), and also became interested in ballet, largely under the influence of Diaghilev, whom he met in London in 1914. Diaghilev commissioned Prokofiev to write *Ala i Lolli* ('Ala and Lolli', 1914-15), and was later responsible for having *Chout* (or *The Tale of the Buffoon*, 1915, revised 1920) performed in Paris and London (1921).

The works of this period highlight those Prokofievan traits which we have come to call 'grotesque'—galumphing rhythms, growling basses, distorted melodic lines, and orchestral astringency. Prokofiev preferred to describe these facets as 'scherzo-like', with those implications of burlesque and laughter which are perhaps best exemplified by his opera *Lyubov' k tryom apel'sinam* ('The Love for Three Oranges'), based on the play by the 18th-century Italian playwright Carlo Gozzi.

2. *Years in the West*. Although *The Love for Three Oranges* sharply reflects the satirical atmosphere prevalent in Russia during the 1920s, the score was in fact written abroad, for, with the outbreak of the October Revolution in 1917, Prokofiev decided to emigrate, living first in America and then in Paris. The theatre director Vsevolod Meyerhold had introduced him to Gozzi's play *Amore delle tre melarance*, and Prokofiev read an adaptation of it as he sailed from Russia to America in 1918. The subject captivated him: the elements of the supernatural, the knock-about comedy, and the sheer absurdity of the story were ideally suited to Prokofiev's leg-pulling, snook-cocking mood of the moment, and they combined to inspire one of his most sparkling scores. He had already composed two substantial operas in Russia— *Maddalena* (1911-13, first performed on BBC Radio in 1979) and *Igrok* ('The Gambler', 1915-16, revised 1927-8, performed 1929); but neither had yet been staged, and it was *The Love for Three Oranges* (performed at Chicago in 1921) which established Prokofiev as a composer with a sure feel for the theatre.

In fact the theatre was to be a constant fascination throughout his life. Even while waiting for *The Three Oranges* to be produced, he began work on a very different project, *Ognennyy angel* ('The Fiery Angel', 1919–23, 1926–7), an opera about demonic possession and religious hysteria in 16th-century Germany; but it was not staged until 1954. It was entirely characteristic of Prokofiev that, with the score of *The Fiery Angel* lying unperformed on his desk, he should draw on material from it for his Third Symphony (1928); similarly the Fourth Symphony (1929–30) was derived from the ballet *Bludnyy syn* ('The Prodigal Son', 1928–9, performed in Paris in 1929). While in the West he also completed the Third Piano Concerto (1917–21), using themes he had collected over a number of years, and rounded off his set of five concertos with the Fourth, for the left hand (1931, commissioned but not performed by the pianist Paul Wittgenstein, who professed not to understand a single note of it), and the weaker, five-movement Fifth (1931–2). These three concertos exude the familiar vivacity of his earlier music, but the textures are smoother, the harmonies less acerbic, the lyricism more relaxed.

3. *The Later Years*. These were to be important aspects of Prokofiev's later music. In the late 1920s he revisited the Soviet Union and settled there in the early 1930s. He achieved an early success with his witty music for the film *Poruchik Kizhe* ('Lieutenant Kijé', 1933), a whimsical story which enabled Prokofiev to draw on his gifts for memorable melody, strong rhythms, and gently mocking turns of phrase, setting them in his highly individual harmonic idiom, succulent yet pungently spiced. The film was never completed, but Prokofiev extracted from the music a suite of five numbers, which has rightly become one of his most frequently performed works. Similarly a number of his other works of the 1930s and 1940s have gained a permanent place in the repertory: the ballets *Romeo and Juliet* (1935–6, performed 1938) and *Zolushka* ('Cinderella', 1940–4, performed 1945), the tale for children *Pyotr i volk* ('Peter and the Wolf', 1936), the cantata he based on his film score *Alexander Nevsky* (1939), and his comic opera *The Duenna* (or *Betrothal in a Monastery*, 1940–1, performed 1946). He also produced a number of firmly patriotic scores, and at the beginning of the Second World War began work on his epic opera *Voyna i mir* ('War and Peace', 1941–3, revised 1946–52), after Tolstoy's novel. The war also coloured his Seventh Piano Sonata (1939–42) and the Eighth Sonata (1939–44), and inspired the heroic Fifth Symphony (1944) and the broodingly pessimistic Sixth Symphony (1945–7).

The absence of jubilation in the Sixth Symphony undoubtedly contributed to the official feeling of dissatisfaction with Prokofiev's music, emphatically voiced during Zhdanov's purges of *formalism in 1948. However, unlike Shostakovich, Prokofiev no longer had the stamina to withstand Zhdanov's attacks: he had suffered a fall after conducting the première of the Fifth Symphony in 1945, and he never recovered. As a result his later works tend to show him relying on his old craftsmanship. Although such works as the ballet *Kamennyy tsvetok* ('The Stone Flower', 1948–53, performed 1954), the Seventh Symphony (1951–2), the choral suite *Zimniy koster* ('Winter Bonfire', 1949–50), and the 'festive poem' *Vstrecha Volgi s Donom* ('The Volga Meets the Don', 1951) reveal the natural skills of his earlier music, they perhaps show a creative weariness and lack the flair and conviction of his best music.

It was a sad irony that Prokofiev could not test the artistic climate after Stalin's death, for he died on the very same day as Stalin himself. None the less as a composer he stands at the very forefront of 20th-century Russian culture. In his early years he had set out purposefully to shock his public in music of flamboyance and hair-raising virtuosity, but in his 30s his musical style mellowed and he consolidated his reputation for ready tunefulness, rhythmic *élan*, instantly appealing charm, and alert humour, expressed with a zestful openness which has rendered much of his music enduringly popular.   GEOFFREY NORRIS

FURTHER READING
Semyon Shlifshteyn, ed.: *S. Prokofiev: Autobiography, Articles, Reminiscences* (Moscow, 1965); Victor Serott: *Sergei Prokofiev: a Soviet Tragedy* (New York, 1968; 2nd edn, London, 1969); Vladimir Blok, ed.: *Sergei Prokofiev: Materials, Articles, Interviews* (Moscow, 1978); *Prokofiev by Prokofiev: a Composer's Memoir* (London, 1979).

Promenade Concerts. See *Concert*, 2.

Promethean chord. See *Mystic chord*.

Prometheus. Symphonic poem by Liszt. It was originally composed (and orchestrated by Raff) as the prelude to a setting of choruses from Herder's *Prometheus Unbound*. It was revised and rescored by Liszt in 1855.

Prometheus, Die Geschöpfe des ('The Creatures of Prometheus'). Ballet (an overture, introduction, and 16 numbers) by Beethoven, choreographed by Salvatore Viganò and first performed in Vienna in 1801. Beethoven used two themes from the finale in other works: one in G major is No. 11 of his *12 Contredanses* for orchestra (1802); another in E♭ major is used as No. 7 of the *Contredanses*, as the theme of the 'Eroica' Variations, and in the 'Eroica' Symphony.

Prometheus, the Poem of Fire (*Prometey, poema ognya*; *Prométhée, le poème du feu*). Symphonic poem, Op. 60, by Skryabin, for orchestra with piano, optional chorus, and 'keyboard of light' (projecting colours on to a screen). It was composed between 1908 and 1910.

Proper of the Mass. The sections of the Mass whose texts change according to the Church calendar; see *Mass*, 1; *Plainchant*, 2.

Proprium missae (Lat.). The *Proper of the Mass.

Prosa (Lat.), **prose** (Fr.). Medieval name for the *sequence.

Proses lyriques ('Lyrics in Prose'). Four songs by Debussy to his own texts, composed in 1892–3. For voice and piano, they are *De rêve* ('Of a Dream'), *De grève* ('About the Shore'), *De fleurs* ('About Flowers'), and *De soir* ('About Evening').

Prosula. An insertion of new words into a pre-existing text at a point where there is a *melisma. See *Trope*, 2.

Protus. See *Mode*, 2.

Proust, Marcel. See *Novel, Music in the*.

Prozession ('Procession'). Work by Stockhausen for viola, tam-tam, electronium, piano, and two players operating microphones, filters, and potentiometers, composed in 1967. The score contains no new music, simply instructions for performing and adapting 'events' from some of the composer's earlier works—*Klavierstücke I–XI*, *Gesang der Jünglinge*, *Kontakte*, *Momente*, *Mikrophonie I*, *Telemusik*, and *Solo*.

'Prussian' Quartets. See *'King of Prussia' Quartets*.

Ps. Abbreviation for (1) (Ger.) *Posaunen*, i.e. trombones; (2) Psalm.

Psalm (from Gk., *psalmos*). Term denoting a Hebrew sacred song of the type found in the Old Testament *Book of Psalms*. The biblical psalms, which, as St Athanasius (*d* 313) declared, 'include the whole life of Man', have been a constant source of inspiration to composers, providing through the centuries the basis of much of the finest church music. For liturgical purposes the psalms are numbered according to two different systems, one for the Vulgate (the main Latin Bible) and the other, following the Hebrew, for all Protestant vernacular versions.

Psalms 9 and 10 in the Protestant versions are combined in the Vulgate to form psalm 9, while psalm 147 is divided to give the Latin psalms 146 and 147; as a consequence all the psalms between 10 and 146 are, in the Protestant numbering (used generally in this volume), one digit higher than in the Vulgate.

The word *Psalmos*, first applied to the ancient Hebrew verse by the translators responsible for the Septuagint (the Greek version of the Old Testament, dating from the 2nd century BC), means literally the striking or plucking of the strings of a musical instrument. It thus provides an indication, supported by numerous biblical and Talmudic references, that the ritual performance of the psalms involved, at least during the period of the second Temple (from *c*.514 BC onwards), an accompaniment of plucked-string instruments, specifically the *kinnor* (probably a small lyre or kithara) and the *nebel* (possibly a harp or psaltery).

In addition to daily Proper psalms, sung by Levites during the sacrifice, the Temple rites included on certain feast days two special categories of psalms: the Hallel (psalms 113–8), characterized by the refrain 'Praise ye the Lord',

King David, illumination from a late 12th-century English psalter.

and the 15 so-called 'psalms of ascent' (psalms 120–34), said to have been sung during the festival of booths, one psalm on each of the 15 steps which led to the inner courtyard of the Temple. The dating of the biblical psalms is the subject of much debate. Some may have originated as early as the reign of David, nearly 1,000 BC, while others, such as psalm 137 'By the waters of Babylon', clearly belong to the post-exilic era (after c.530 BC). The majority, however, almost certainly date from the second Temple period in their present form, and were the work of priests and Temple musicians.

Characteristic of the poetic form of the psalms is their parallelistic structure, whereby each verse is separated into two halves by means of a central strong or weak caesura, the second half-verse complementing the first in a variety of ways (for example, by stating the same idea in a different way, by opposing a contrasting idea, by completing a statement, or by building an utterance to a climax). Such a structure must from the earliest times have encouraged responsorial and antiphonal modes of musical performance (see *Alternatim*), and its influence is clearly felt in later methods of psalmody found in synagogue and early Christian worship, such as the use of congregational refrains in response to the solo delivery of a *cantor*.

Following the destruction of the Temple in AD 70, elaborate psalmody involving singers and instrumentalists was discontinued. Little is known about the musical element in Jewish and Christian ritual of Apostolic times, except that a prominent role was played by biblical recitation, delivered in unaccompanied cantillation (half speech, half song). With the full recognition of the Christian Church during the 4th century, liturgical observances were framed in which the psalms took a major part, psalmody having been introduced at Byzantium by St John Chrysostom (d 407) and at Milan by St Ambrose (d 397). As Gregorian chant developed, simple musical patterns were evolved for the singing of psalms, resulting in a series of eight 'psalm tones' related to each of the original church *modes, together with one extra tone called the *Tonus peregrinus* (see *Tonus*, 3). From the 6th century an important role began to be played by psalmody in the Divine Office, particularly at the services of Matins, Lauds, and Vespers. St Benedict's monastic rule required that the whole psalter be said or sung each week and the memorization of the entire book of psalms was an accepted part of the discipline imposed on monks.

Ever since, the psalms have continued to occupy a central place in Christian worship. In Latin they have provided the texts for numerous motets from the time of Josquin onwards, and in vernacular languages (of many countries) they have formed the basis of Protestant anthems, metrical settings, and chanted versions. Among the many concert works which have been based on psalm texts three notable 20th-century settings stand out—Kodály's *Psalmus hungaricus* (based on a Hungarian paraphrase of Psalm 55), Stravinsky's *Symphony of Psalms* (based on verses from the Vulgate psalms 38, 39, and 150), and Schoenberg's *De profundis* (based on the Hebrew Psalm 130). BASIL SMALLMAN

FURTHER READING
Peter Gradenwitz: *The Music of Israel* (New York, 1949); Eric Werner: *The Sacred Bridge* (London and New York, 1959).

Psalmody. The practice of singing not only psalms but also other forms of chant. With regard to the manner of performance, the term 'responsorial psalmody' refers to performance by congregation or choir in alternation, and 'antiphonal psalmody' to performance by two roughly equal groups, such as the two halves of a choir. Antiphonal psalmody is most commonly found in the singing of psalms and canticles, and responsorial psalmody in the great responsories of Matins and the lesser responsories of the daytime Hours, and in the Gradual and Alleluia at Mass. See also *Alternatim*; *Antiphon*; *Direct Psalmody*; *Responsory*.

Psalm tones. Plainchant recitation formulas for the psalms; see *Tonus*, 3.

Psalmus hungaricus. Work by Kodály to a text from the 16th-century Hungarian poet Mihály Kecskeméti Vég's paraphrase of Psalm 55. It is for tenor solo, chorus, children's chorus (ad lib), orchestra, and organ, and was composed in 1923 for the 50th anniversary of the union of Buda and Pest.

Psaltery. A plucked stringed instrument which existed in a multitude of forms during the Middle Ages and early Renaissance. Its only connection with 'psaltery' in the Old Testament is the name, which comes from the Greek *psaltērion*, a harp.

1. *True Psalteries.* The strings here run across a flat soundbox to be played on with both hands, the instrument usually being held more or less flat against the player's body. Shapes vary very much: square, or with one or both sides sloping. From the 13th century to the 15th the prettiest form and one of the commonest (Pl. 1) is that which gained in Italy the popular name *strumento di porco*, from the pig-snout appearance which comes about through grading the string-lengths approximately according to harmonic ratios (compare *Harp*, 1). The average compass would be around two and a half octaves. The instrument was generally played with a pair of quills,

Pl. 1. An initial E from a 13th-century psalter, showing (upper left) an early 'porco'-form psaltery (which in fact would be larger from top to bottom, with many more strings).

Pl. 2. 'Harp-psaltery', from the 'Cantigas de Santa Maria', Spain, late 13th century.

so the sound is likely to have been fairly soft, though there is evidence from the 14th century that the strings could be in double or triple courses of brass or silver. Such, probably, was the 'gay sautrie' of Chaucer's Clerk, in *The Canterbury Tales*.

2. *Harp-psaltery.* A modern historians' term for a form which is older than the above, shown in pictures of the 11th–13th centuries (Pl. 2). At first glance it can suggest a kind of harp: the tall right-angled triangle being held vertically edgeways to the body with the apex downwards; but a 'rose' soundhole and the obliteration of the

player's left arm reveal the presence of a flat soundboard behind the strings, which (numbering 21 in some pictures) are played with one hand while the other appears to grasp the instrument at the top. Though its name in Medieval Latin was *psalterium*, there is evidence that this 'harp-psaltery' had the vernacular name 'rote' or 'rotta' in Europe, in which case the rote which Chaucer's Friar could play in a manner mentioned later in the poem as 'harping' may have been of this kind also. However, the 'rotta' or 'chrotta', mentioned in earlier centuries back to the 6th AD, seems most likely to

Pl. 3. Near-eastern psaltery, qanun; note fingerpicks on index fingers, also small tuning jacks (beyond the 3 rows of wrest pins) for micro-intervals.

have been a form of *lyre (or in Anglo-Saxon, 'harp'), the name in this case leading to *crwth.

A much later type of 'harp-psaltery' is the German *Spitzharfe* or *Arpanetta*, a domestic instrument of the period 1650-1750, up to 3′ tall, placed upright on a table. It has strings (wire) on both sides of the soundbox, tuned at the bottom and played with the fingernails or finger-picks (see *Plectrum*, 1).

3. *Horizontal Psalteries*. It is, of course, possible that some of the square or trapezoid instruments mentioned above (1) were played flat on the lap but pictured in an upright position to comply with visual conventions. All the same, it is very rare to see a horizontally-played version before the 15th century, and then it is played not with plectrums but with beaters—the early 'hammered' *dulcimer, which in Italy and Spain continues to this day to bear the old name *salterio*, and is sometimes played with plectrums or finger-picks. These last are used also with the *qanun* of the Near East, another horizontal psaltery (Pl. 3) and a leading instrument of classical music from Egypt to Iraq. It yields a full, ringing sound from multiple courses of gut strings, played a great deal in 'broken octaves', often in Egypt by the leader of an ensemble with violin, lute, pot drum, tambourine, and the flute *nay*. There are usually small levers along one side for raising the strings by a half- or quarter-tone as required by the 'mode' (*maqam*) of the music. The *qanun* is said to date back to the 10th century; the name (deriving from Greek *kanōn*) appears now and then in Medieval French as *canon*, here denoting a psaltery of unspecified kind.

4. *Gusli*. There are yet other plucked instruments of the psaltery type, like the Russian folk instrument known as the 'Greek' or 'helmet' *gusli*, held against the body with the long side downwards.   ANTHONY BAINES

Psaume (Fr.). 'Psalm'.

Publishing. See *Printing and Publishing of Music*.

Puccini, Giacomo (Antonio Domenico Michele Secondo Maria) (*b* Lucca, Tuscany, 22 Dec. 1858; *d* Brussels, 29 Nov. 1924). Italian composer. He was the greatest of the 'giovane scuola' of the late 19th and early 20th centuries and the last of his countrymen to write operas which form the staple of the international repertory.

He was born of a long line of musicians who had lived in Lucca since the early 18th century. His father, Michele, was a respected figure in the community—organist and choirmaster of the Cathedral of S. Martino, director of the

Puccini

Istituto Pacini, the city's music school, and a prolific if undistinguished composer—who died in 1864 leaving a large family poorly provided for. His widow, Albina, was determined that Giacomo should continue the family's musical tradition. Accordingly, after lessons in singing and organ-playing from an uncle, he was enrolled in the Istituto Pacini whence he graduated in 1880 with a Mass known today as the *Messa di Gloria*. A grant from Queen Margherita combined with a generous subsidy from a wealthy cousin enabled him to proceed to the Milan Conservatory where his teachers were Ponchielli and Bazzini and his fellow students included Mascagni. By the time he left he had written two symphonic preludes, a number of liturgical settings, and a *Capriccio sinfonico*, his passing-out piece, which won high critical acclaim. But ever since seeing a performance of Verdi's *Aida* in Florence in 1876 he had determined that opera was his true *métier*. In 1883 he entered *Le Villi* for a competition for a one-act opera organized by the publisher Sonzogno. His score was rejected because of its illegibility; but a number of influential friends believed in its merit sufficiently to mount a performance at Milan's Teatro dal Verme. This brought the composer to the notice of Giulio Ricordi, the publisher, and convinced him that here at last was Verdi's true successor. His firm provided Puccini with a yearly retainer to enable him to compose in comfort; and after the comparative failure of his next opera *Edgar* (1889) Ricordi saw his confidence in the young

Autograph MS of Puccini's 'La bohème', from Act 2.

man justified by the triumph of *Manon Lescaut* at Turin in 1893. From then on Puccini's fortune was assured. He now settled at Torre del Lago where he built his own villa (now the Villa Puccini); here he could work undisturbed in between trips at home and abroad for premières or prestigious revivals of his operas. Only in his last few years did he move to nearby Viareggio.

Puccini was a slow worker, hard to please in the matter of subject and libretto, continually taking up projects only to abandon them. Ricordi found for him the accomplished team of Luigi Illica and Giuseppe Giacosa. The fruits of their collaboration were *La bohème* (1896), based on Murger's stories of impoverished Parisian artists; *Tosca* (1900), a version of Sardou's drama of that name; and *Madama Butterfly* (1904), taken from a play by Belasco; all would become world-wide

favourites, though the last was badly received at its première. That same year Puccini married the recently widowed Elvira Gemignani with whom he had lived since 1886 and who had already borne him a son. It was not a happy union. Puccini was an unfaithful husband; Elvira grew jealous and embittered, eventually driving to suicide a former maidservant of theirs, whose innocence was proved by a subsequent autopsy. The resultant legal proceedings and scandal, though followed by reconciliation, retarded the composition of *La fanciulla del West* (1910), another Belasco subject, given its première in New York. The years of the First World War were fruitful for Puccini, though he was criticized for showing insufficient patriotism—witness *La rondine* (1917), originally a Viennese commission and first performed in Monte Carlo. During this time he also worked on the trio of one-act operas

entitled *Il trittico*: *Il tabarro*, based on a *grand
guignol* story by Didier Gold; and *Suor Angelica*
and the comic *Gianni Schicchi*, both brain-
children of the librettist Giovanni Forzano. In
the aftermath of the war only New York
possessed the necessary resources for the
première, which took place in the composer's
absence in December 1918. Of his final opera
Turandot, based on a *fiaba* by Carlo Gozzi,
Puccini completed all but the final duet. He
died while undergoing treatment for cancer of
the throat in a Brussels clinic.

In style Puccini belongs to the generation of
veristi (see *Verismo*); nor was it mere chance
that he first found his individual voice after
Mascagni's *Cavalleria rusticana* had established
the new tradition. He alone, however, possessed
the power of self-renewal; alone, too, apart from
Catalani, he learned the Wagnerian lesson,
organizing his acts through a highly personal
use of motifs while not disdaining the finite,
self-contained melody. His interest in the
modern music of his day, especially Debussy's,
undoubtedly fertilized his mature style. His
limitations can be judged by his failure to finish
Turandot whose denouement required a sub-
limity that lay outside his range. Puccini's
operas symbolize the *Italietta* of his day, concerned as they are purely with personal emotions
and scene-painting, without any reference to
wider issues (all the political overtones of
Sardou's *Tosca* are played down in the opera).
But his supreme mastery of the operatic craft,
his melodic gift, and his emotional sincerity
combine to keep his operas as freshly alive today
as when they were written. The intense sadness
that permeates so much of his music reflects his
own temperament. For beneath the successful
composer with his penchant for blood sports,
fast cars, and women was a lonely and sensitive
man.   JULIAN BUDDEN

FURTHER READING
Giuseppe Adami, ed.: *Giacomo Puccini: epistolario*
(Milan, 1928; Eng. trans. 1931, 2nd edn 1974); V.
Seligman: *Puccini Among Friends* (London, 1938); L.
Marchetti, ed.: *Puccini nelle immagini* (Milan, 1949);
Mosco Carner: *Puccini* (London, 1958, 2nd edn 1974);
E. Gara, ed.: *Carteggi Pucciniani* (Milan, 1958);
William Ashbrook: *The Operas of Puccini* (London
and New York, 1968); William Weaver: *Puccini: the
Man and His Music* (New York, 1977); H. Greenfeld:
Puccini (New York, 1980; London, 1981).

Pugnani, (Giulio) **Gaetano** (Gerolamo) (*b*
Turin, 27 Nov. 1731; *d* Turin, 15 July 1798).
Italian violinist and composer. He played violin
in the Turin court orchestra from 1741 until
1767, although during this time he visited Rome
(1749–50) and Paris (1754). In 1767 he went to
London for two years as conductor at the King's
Theatre, and then returned to Turin, where he

held several important appointments. He made
further concert tours in the 1780s and 1790s.
Pugnani wrote some pleasant chamber music—
although the famous Praeludium and Allegro in
E minor for violin once attributed to him is
actually the work of its 'editor', Kreisler. Viotti
was one of Pugnani's pupils.   DENIS ARNOLD

Puirt a beul (Gaelic). In the folk music of the
Scottish Highlands, a type of vocal accompaniment for dancing, substituting for an instrumental one when none is available. The word
port (plural *puirt*) literally means 'a tune for
an instrument'. *Puirt a beul* often includes
sequences of improvised nonsense syllables and
words with personal or topical references, and it
may involve complex rhythmic patterns. It may
accompany many different types of Highland
dance, or can be sung on its own.

Pulcinella. Ballet and song in one act by Stravinsky to a libretto by Massine, who choreographed it for its first performance in Paris in
1920. For soprano, tenor, bass, and chamber
orchestra, the score is an adaptation of works
chiefly by Pergolesi. Stravinsky made a suite
from it for chamber orchestra (*c.*1922, revised
1947). His *Suite italienne* (1932) is also arranged
from *Pulcinella*: he collaborated with Piati-
gorsky in a five-movement version for cello and
piano, and with Dushkin in a six-movement one
for violin and piano.

Pulse. Term sometimes used as a synonym for
'beat', but a distinction is occasionally made—
e.g. 6/8 time may be said to have six 'pulses', but
only two 'beats'.

Pult, Pulte (Ger.). 'Desk', 'desks' (i.e. an
orchestral music stand generally shared between two string players). *Pultweise*, 'desk-
wise', i.e. in order of the players' desks (a
direction often given in connection with *divisi*
playing, or when the mutes should be put on or
removed gradually).

Punch and Judy. Opera in one act by Birtwistle
to a libretto by Stephen Pruslin. It was first
performed at Aldeburgh in 1968.

Punctum (Lat.). In some forms of early mensural notation a 'point' (i.e. dot) was used to
group the rhythmic values of a group of notes;
see *Notation*, 4.

Punk rock. See *Popular Music*, 5.

Punta, punto (It.). 'Point'; *a punta d'arco*, 'with the point of the bow'.

Purcell. English family of musicians which contained two composers of note—one, Henry, a genius; the other, Daniel, a journeyman. There is some dispute about exact parentage, but there can be no doubt that **Henry Purcell** (*b* 1659; *d* London, 21 Nov. 1695) was the second of four brothers. He proved from the start to be exceptionally gifted, composing songs at the age of eight. He was fortunate to be a chorister in the Chapel Royal at a time when Charles II, newly returned from exile in France, was in favour of elaborate church music; Blow and Humfrey were among his fellow choristers. Purcell left the choir when his voice broke in 1673. He was clearly favoured, because he was then made unpaid assistant in charge of the royal keyboard and wind instruments (such a position carrying the expectation of taking over in due course). During the next few years he tuned the organs and copied music for Westminster Abbey, until in 1677 he was appointed composer-in-ordinary for the violins. Two years later he succeeded John Blow as organist of Westminster Abbey.

Purcell's first mature compositions date from these years. In 1680 he wrote a set of viol fantasias which show a complete mastery of the old English polyphonic art, learnt perhaps from

Henry Purcell, drawing (1695) by Closterman.

studying the music of such masters as Byrd and Tallis. None the less, these fantasias are by no means mere academic exercises: they show a rich vein of imagination, contrasting polyphony with homophony, and simple diatonic with chromatic passages, so that the contrapuntal devices of imitation, diminution, and augmentation are little more than a backdrop to the expression of intimate, fluctuating emotions. The same depth of feeling and imagination can be found in the full anthems of this period, such works as 'Hear my Prayer, O Lord' and 'Remember not, Lord, our Offences' also stemming from Elizabethan polyphony, with its clashing harmonies and (to us) strange turns of phrase. There is also a trace of the influence of the late madrigal—Purcell is thought to have copied out music by Monteverdi. His theatre songs and official welcome odes for Charles II seem bluffly straightforward by comparison, but they also reveal something of his range and fluency.

Purcell married *c*.1681 and in 1682 was appointed one of the organists to the Chapel Royal. The following year a set of trio sonatas was published; according to the preface they were written after the manner of 'fam'd Italian masters'—meaning Cazzati and G. B. Vitali rather than Corelli. The format is indeed Italian, falling into several movements, as is the trio texture with continuo, in contrast with the equal-voiced fullness of the fantasias. The style, however, is by no means wholly Italianate: the second movements (sometimes marked 'canzona') especially show Purcell's gift for old-fashioned counterpoint.

Over the next few years, Purcell's energies were devoted to the verse anthem, those for the Chapel Royal using a string band to play overtures and ritornellos. The solo sections of these anthems contain *arioso* writing, with virtuoso decorations to highlight individual words or phrases (those composed for the bass John Gostling are especially spectacular). The choral writing tends to be sonorously homophonic rather than contrapuntal, reflecting the monarch's French tastes, but undeniably effective for the Chapel Royal.

Purcell also wrote many songs for publications by Playford and others. They vary from simple strophic tunes and straightforward rondo forms to dramatic cantatas of the kind known in England from the works of Rossi and Carissimi, which were then circulating in copies. He also used the ground bass, showing a marvellous flair for avoiding monotony and increasing tension by making the phrase ends of melody and bass overlap. Many of these songs are settings of trivial verse, but devotional pieces, such as the setting of Fuller's 'Now that the sun hath veiled

Autograph MS of Henry Purcell's Fantasia in four parts in B♮, 1680.

his light', match the seriousness of the verse in fine music.

Purcell was one of the composers of anthems for James II's coronation in 1685, but by the closing years of the decade he was beginning to be much involved in music for the theatre. In 1688 he contributed seven songs and a duet to D'Urfey's *A Fool's Preferment*, and the following year he wrote a short opera, *Dido and Aeneas*, for performance at Josias Priest's School for Young Ladies in Chelsea. England lacked an operatic tradition, Blow's masque *Venus and Adonis* providing the sole recent model, and, despite the limited circumstances of its performance, *Dido* was a unique contribution

to operatic history. There are elements in the French style which may stem from the performance in London of Lully's *Cadmus* in 1686, but there are also Italian elements—notably in the final lament, 'When I am laid in earth'. The restricted scale of the numbers may, as Jack Westrup suggested, give a feeling of breathlessness, but it must also be said that the work is a masterpiece, and its last scene one of the greatest in opera.

Thereafter, Purcell's taste was definitely for the theatre, and his last five years were spent largely in satisfying the demand for music in plays and 'semi-operas'. Between 1690 and 1695 he contributed to no fewer than 37 plays, the music varying from single numbers to lengthy suites of dances. His operatic ventures included four extensive works: *Dioclesian* (1690), *King Arthur* (1691), *The Fairy Queen* (1692), and *The Indian Queen* (1695); to these may be added *The Tempest* (*c*.1695), though the music may in fact be not by Purcell but by John Weldon. These works include all kinds of pieces—French overtures, dances, and songs, some forming long scenes in which Purcell shows a distinct sense of character and situation. The 'Cold' scene in *King Arthur*, with its descriptive music for chattering teeth, is a masterly evocation of atmosphere; the flirtation duet of Corydon and Mopsa in the *Fairy Queen* is delightfully humorous, the music never hindering the forward flow of the action; while popular tunes such as 'Fairest Isle' from *King Arthur* might well have led to a 'popular' vernacular operatic repertory.

The more austere attitudes of William III's reign (1689–1702) may account for the relative lack of church music from Purcell's last years. The *Te Deum* and *Jubilate* in D are bright rather than profound ceremonial pieces, with their use of trumpets and strings; they were composed for the St Cecilia's Day celebrations of 1694 and remained in favour for the annual festival for many years. On the other hand, he wrote nine odes for various occasions during the 1690s, among them two excellent works: 'Hail, bright Cecilia' (St Cecilia's Day, 1692), in which Purcell takes the opportunity to illustrate the musical references in Brady's text (the 'box and fir' turn out to be the recorder and the violin); and 'Come, ye sons of art' (1694, for Queen Mary's birthday), with its countertenor duet 'Sound the trumpet' set to one of those straightforward, memorable tunes typical of Purcell.

Purcell provided the music for Queen Mary's funeral in 1694. The following year he himself died, and at his funeral in Westminster Abbey, on 26 November, the music was sung by the choirs of the Abbey and the Chapel Royal. Several volumes of his music were published after his death, including a further set of trio sonatas in 1697 (composed *c*.1680) and some collections of songs.

Although Purcell was recognized as a genius in his own lifetime, his music was subsequently neglected and was not revived until the later 19th century, when a collected edition (completed in 1965) was begun in 1878. None the less, only a fraction of his music is widely known, and there are many riches to be found among the little-performed songs, odes, and church music. As with Mozart and Schubert, Purcell's early death was the greater tragedy because there are signs that he was still ripening as a composer.

His younger brother, **Daniel Purcell** (*d* London, *buried* 26 Nov. 1717), was also a chorister in the Chapel Royal. From 1688 to 1695 he was organist at Magdalen College, Oxford, but he then succeeded his brother as one of the principal composers of the London theatres, over the next 12 years writing music for about 40 plays. He wrote a masque to Congreve's words, *The Judgement of Paris* (London, 1700), and some odes, in the choruses of which his brother's contrapuntal skill is noticeably lacking, though the solos are competent enough. He also wrote some agreeable sonatas for violin and for flute.

DENIS ARNOLD

FURTHER READING
Jack A. Westrup: *Purcell* (London, 1937, 4th edn 1980); Ian Spink: *English Song: Dowland to Purcell* (London, 1974).

Purcell School. British specialist school for the musically gifted and others likely to benefit from the musical facilities—the first of its kind in Britain. It was founded in 1962 by Irene Forster and Rosemary Rapaport as the Central Tutorial School for Young Musicians; it was given its present title in 1973. The school was originally housed in Conway Hall, but as numbers increased it moved first to Morley College (1963) then to Heath House, Hampstead (1968), and finally to Oakhurst, Harrow (1975). Richard Taylor has been Principal since 1970.

Purcell Society. British society, founded in 1876, its main purpose being the preparation and publication of a modern edition of the composer's works. The final volume of the first edition appeared in 1959, and the whole series is now in the process of being re-edited, in accordance with modern techniques and standards of scholarship.

Puritani di Scozia, I (*I Puritani*; 'The Puritans of Scotland'). Opera in three acts by Bellini to a libretto by C. Pepoli after the play *Têtes rondes et cavaliers* by F. Ancelot and X. B. Saintine derived from Scott's *Old Mortality* (1816). It was first performed in Paris in 1835.

Putnam's Camp. Second movement of Ives's First Orchestral Set, *Three Places in New England*. It was composed in 1912 and is sometimes performed separately.

Puy (Fr.). A name given to Medieval French musical or literary societies, or guilds, which flourished in northern France up to the early 17th century. Their roots sprang from the *troubadour* tradition, and they held annual song or poetry competitions originally dedicated to the Virgin Mary (one at Évreux, founded *c*.1570, was held in honour of St *Cecilia). The contestants stood on a raised dais (Lat.: *podium*) to sing or recite, and it is thought that the name *puy* derives from this, rather than from the geographical formations of the Massif Central after which towns such as Le Puy are named. The winner of the competition was crowned 'Prince du Puy'. The song contest in Wagner's opera *Die Meistersinger* probably reflects the existence of a similar tradition among the German *Meistersinger*.

Q

Quadrat (Ger.). The natural sign (♮).

Quadrille. A dance for an equal number of couples which probably derived from displays of horsemanship and first appeared in the ballet. It came to the ballroom during the reign of Napoleon I in France and was brought to England around 1815. It consists of a group of five country dances of different rhythms and tempos, originally using folk-tunes. Its popularity led to arrangements being made of popular songs and operatic arias. The Strauss family were prolific providers of sets of quadrilles, but the vogue soon waned owing to the difficulty of the steps; it was then replaced by the *Lancers.

PETER GAMMOND

Quadruple concerto. A concerto for four solo instruments and orchestra, e.g. Vivaldi's for four violins and strings (arranged by Bach for four harpsichords and strings).

Quadruple-croche (Fr.). 'Quadruple-hook', i.e. the hemidemisemiquaver or 64th-note (♬).

Quadruplet. Term for four notes that are to be performed in the time of three; they are indicated by the figure '4' placed above or below the four notes, e.g.:

Quadruple time. See *Time signature*.

Quanto (It.). 'As much', 'so much'.

Quantz, Johann Joachim (*b* Oberscheden, nr Göttingen, 30 Jan. 1697; *d* Potsdam, 12 July 1773). German flautist, composer, and theorist. He was trained as a town musician and became proficient on all the usual wind instruments. From 1718, when he joined Augustus II's Polish chapel, he specialized in playing the transverse flute, and in 1727, after a three-year period of travel and study in France, England, and Italy, became a flautist in the Dresden chapel. In 1728 he was appointed flute teacher to Crown Prince Frederick of Prussia, and a year after Frederick became king (1740), he joined the royal band of musicians at Berlin and Potsdam. For the remainder of his life he

Quantz, drawing by Heinrich Frank.

enjoyed a privileged position as the most influential, and best paid, musician at court, greatly respected by the king.

Quantz's duties at court consisted of teaching, directing the king's regular chamber concerts at Sans-Souci, and composing flute music (over 200 sonatas, over 300 concertos, and some duets) for his royal pupil to play. His musical style is typical of the so-called 'Berlin school'—elegant and graceful, but not profound. Quantz's celebrated treatise *Versuch einer Anweisung die Flöte traversiere zu spielen* ('On playing the flute', Berlin, 1752) remains one of the major 18th-century sources of information on contemporary performing practice (not just of the flute), discussing details of dynamics, ornamentation, national styles, and so on.

WENDY THOMPSON

Quart. See *Quint*.

Quarter-note (Amer.). Crotchet (♩).

Quartertone. Interval of a quarter of a tone, i.e. half a semitone. See also *Microtone*.

Quartet (Fr.: *quatuor*; Ger.: *Quartett*; It.: *quartetto*). Any body of four performers, vocal or instrumental, or any piece of music composed for such. The most common vocal quartet consists of soprano, alto, tenor, and bass (SATB).

The most important instrumental quartet is the string quartet of two violins, viola, and cello, for which a huge body of music has been written (see *Chamber Music*, 4–6). A piano quartet (flute quartet, oboe quartet, etc.) is generally a combination of the first-named instrument plus a string trio (violin, viola, and cello).

Quartettsatz ('Quartet Movement'). Title given to a movement for string quartet in C minor by Schubert, D 703, composed in 1820. It was intended as the first movement of a whole quartet but only a fragment of the second movement was completed.

Quatreble. In Medieval vocal music, the name for a voice part pitched at a fixed interval above the treble. It derives from a confluence of the words 'quadruple' and 'treble', indicating a 'fourth' voice part added above the 'third' ('triplum' or treble). Some early theorists cited the prescribed interval between treble and quatreble as a fifth, others an octave. In 15th-century improvised *discant, a 'quatreble sight' is a part to be improvised above a plainchant tenor at a fixed interval (octave, or according to some theorists a twelfth, that is, a fifth above the treble).

Quatuor pour la fin du temps ('Quartet for the End of Time'). Work by Messiaen for clarinet, piano, violin, and cello, composed in 1940. It was written while Messiaen was in a Silesian prisoner-of-war camp and first performed there in 1941.

Quaver (♪). The eighth-note; i.e. an eighth of the time-value of the whole-note or semibreve.

Queen Mary's Funeral Music. Music composed by Purcell for the funeral in Westminster Abbey in March 1695 of Queen Mary, wife of William III. The music consisted of two of the sentences from the burial service, which he had set at least 12 years earlier; the anthem *Thou know'st, Lord, the secrets of our hearts*, specially composed; two canzonas for slide trumpets and trombones; and a march originally written for a scene in Shadwell's play *The Libertine* (?1692) for which Purcell had provided incidental music. Some of the music for Queen Mary was performed in Westminster Abbey for Purcell's own funeral in November 1695.

Queen of Spades, The (*Pikovaya dama*). Opera in three acts by Tchaikovsky; text by Modest Tchaikovsky, with contributions from the composer, after Pushkin's story (1834). Produced: St Petersburg, Mariinsky Theatre, 19 December 1890; New York, Metropolitan Opera, 5 March 1910; London, London Opera House, 29 May 1915. The opera tells of the love of Hermann (ten.), a young officer, for Lisa (sop.), granddaughter of the old Countess (mezzo), once a gambler known as the Queen of Spades, who is said to possess the secret of winning at cards. Hermann goes to the Countess's bedroom at night to obtain the secret from her so as to win enough money to marry, but so terrifies her that she dies without speaking. Her ghost appears to him and reveals the secret: 'Three, seven, ace.' As Hermann becomes obsessed with winning, Lisa drowns herself. He wins on the first two stakes he makes—3 and 7. He then stakes all on the third card, which he thinks will be the ace, but which is the Queen of Spades; at the same time the Countess's ghost appears, and Hermann, losing his reason, kills himself.

Quer (Ger.). 'Cross', 'transverse'; *Querflöte*, the transverse flute.

Querelle des Bouffons. See *Bouffons, Querelle des*.

Queue (Fr.). 'Tail'; *piano à queue*, 'grand piano'.

Quickstep. The most popular basic modern ballroom dance, probably because it is essentially the simplest. A direct descendant of the *charleston, although now totally dissimilar, its lineage was through the slightly more demanding *foxtrot, so that by 1924 it was known as the quick or quick-time foxtrot; the name was abbreviated to quickstep around 1927. It is danced to music in common time at about 48–50 bars a minute, each slow step occupying two beats and each quick step one beat.   PETER GAMMOND

Quilisma. A type of ornamental neume; see *Notation*, 2.

Quill. See *Harpsichord; Plectrum*.

Quilt canzona. A term derived from the mistaken translation of the German *Flickkanzone* ('patch canzona', not 'quilt'). The German term was applied by the theorist Hugo Riemann to a rare type of *canzona in which short, sharply contrasting sections follow each other in quick succession, as in a patched piece of fabric. Examples can be found in the music of Johann Schein.

Quilter, Roger (*b* Brighton, 1 Nov. 1877; *d* London, 21 Sept. 1953). English composer, one of the so-called Frankfurt group of Englishmen who studied at the Hoch Conservatory there under Iwan Knorr. His *Songs of the Sea*, four settings of his own words, were performed in London in 1900, and within a few years major singers such as Gervase Elwes were including in their recitals such songs as 'Now Sleeps the Crimson Petal' (1904), 'To Julia' (1906), and several memorable Shakespeare settings. The refined and sensitive melodic charm of these lyrics is also found in his *A Children's Overture* (1919). He wrote the incidental music to the once-popular children's play *Where the Rainbow Ends* (1911). An attempt at opera, *Julia* (1936), was a failure. Quilter endured illness and depression, but he was generous with his wealth and was a founder-member of the Musicians' Benevolent Fund. He was a gifted pianist and occasionally appeared as accompanist in his own songs.   MICHAEL KENNEDY

FURTHER READING
Trevor Hold: *The Walled-in Garden: a Study of the Songs of Roger Quilter* (Rickmansworth, 1978).

Quint, quart, terz. 1. Old prefixes, chiefly German, met from the 16th century to the 19th to denote instruments built or tuned respectively a perfect fifth, fourth, or third (major or minor) higher or lower than usual (in the 16th and 17th centuries, generally lower, but subsequently higher). In the earlier period the terms are found mostly in relation to wind instruments, as in the *Quint-posaune*, a trombone a fifth below the ordinary (and occasionally *Secund-*, a tone lower). In the later period we find *Quart-geige*, the violino piccolo, tuned a fourth higher than the violin, and the *Terz-flöte*, in English the 'F flute', a third above the ordinary.

2. Quint, or quinta, also very commonly denotes a fifth part in polyphonic music. In the French string orchestras of the 17th century it was one of three middle parts (see *Viola*, 4).

3. Quinton is the name of a late type of treble viol (see *Viol*, 5).

4. In organs, Quint is a register of flue pipes in which each pipe is combined with another of two-thirds the length (a fifth higher) for the two together to produce a 'difference tone' an octave below the first pipe. This achieves a 32′ result without the inconvenience of pipes of very great length.   ANTHONY BAINES

Quintern (Ger.). A 16th- and 17th-century name for the guitar and related instruments.

Quintet (Fr.: *quintette, quintuor*; Ger.: *Quintett*; It.: *quintetto*). Any body of five performers, vocal or instrumental, or the music composed for such. The normal vocal quintet consists of two sopranos, alto, tenor, and bass (SSATB), or soprano, alto, two tenors, and bass (SATTB). The normal instrumental quintet is the string quintet, which may consist of two violins, two violas, and cello (there is a considerable repertory of music by Boccherini, Mozart, Beethoven, Mendelssohn, Brahms, etc. for this combination), or of two violins, viola, and two cellos, a much less common arrangement, for which Schubert wrote his masterly Quintet in C. A piano (or clarinet etc.) quintet normally consists of the first-named instrument plus a string quartet (see *Quartet*), but other combinations (such as Schubert's 'Trout' Quintet for piano, violin, viola, cello, and double bass) are possible.

Quintuplet. Term for five notes that are to be performed in the time of four or of three; they are indicated by the figure '5' placed above or below the five notes, e.g.

Quintuple time. See *Time signature*.

Quodlibet (Lat., 'what you will'). A piece of music in which well-known tunes and/or texts are quoted, either simultaneously or in succession, generally for humorous effect. One 15th-century monophonic song, for example, has a text formed out of quotations from the opening words of 19 famous *chansons*; the music does not seem to be quoted, however.

R

Rachmaninoff, Serge. See *Rakhmaninov, Sergey*.

Racket (Ger., now adopted in English; Fr.: *cervelat*, 'sausage'; It.: *cortale*). A peculiar double-reed instrument first heard of in Germany in 1576 and now made again. It is a short, thick cylinder of wood or ivory 5″ to 14″ tall. Down this are drilled nine or so parallel cylindrical channels connected alternately at top and bottom to form a narrow bore (about 6 mm.) totalling 3′ or more in length. Eleven fingerholes open on the surface of the pillar for manipulation with both hands, thumbs included (the 11th hole being covered by the middle joint of one of the fingers). A short brass tube at the top takes the pirouette (see *Shawm*) and the reed. Rackets were made in various sizes (see *Instruments, Renaissance*, Fig. 1), each with the compass of a twelfth and producing a rather soft humming noise. It appears that the racket was most used singly among other instruments. As for the name, Germany on the whole favours derivation from a word *ranket*, 'to-and-fro', rather than from *Rackete*, a 'rocket'—though a Stuttgart court inventory of 1589, when the instrument was still fairly recent, has 'Zünd-

Ivory racket (?c.1580); height excluding (modern) reed, 7 inches.

fleschen, so Rageten' ('ignition flasks, i.e. rockets') listed with some other freak wind instruments.

In the late 17th century, when the racket was extinct in practice, it aroused the curiosity of several makers like Denner, who made a version with a coiled crook to take a bassoon reed and with a short bell on top instead of the original exit hole in the side of the cylinder itself.

ANTHONY BAINES

Raddoppiare (It.). 'To double'; *raddoppiato*, 'doubled'; *raddoppiamento*, 'doubling'.

Radetzky March. March, Op. 228, by Johann Strauss the elder, composed in 1848. Radetzky was an Austrian field marshal.

Radical cadence. See *Cadence*, 2.

Raff, (Joseph) Joachim (*b* Lachen, nr Zurich, 27 May 1822; *d* Frankfurt am Main, 24 or 25 June 1882). German composer. He came from a poor family and worked as a teacher before deciding, in about 1845, to devote himself to music. He worked for music-sellers and publishers in Cologne, Stuttgart, and Hamburg, was helped and encouraged by von Bülow, Mendelssohn, and Liszt, and in 1850 he became Liszt's personal assistant in Weimar. After six years he moved to Wiesbaden to teach the piano and compose, and in 1877 he became director of the Hoch Conservatory, Frankfurt, where his composition teaching influenced several younger composers, notably the American Edward MacDowell. He remained there until his death. Raff was an immensely prolific composer (his opus numbers exceed 200 and there are many unpublished works) who, like so many of his contemporaries, concentrated on piano music. But his contacts with Liszt and his circle persuaded him towards orchestral programme music, and he produced 11 symphonies, many with fanciful titles, as well as much incidental and chamber music. Although his piano music achieved great popularity in its day, some critics harshly condemned its attempts to synthesize traditional and progressive ideas, and its appeal was short-lived. Scarcely any of his music is heard today, though the *Cavatina*, composed originally in 1859 for violin and piano, is quite well known.

JUDITH NAGLEY

Rāga. Generic name for a system of Indian melody types. See *India*, 5, 6.

Ragtime. An offshoot of *jazz which first flourished in the late 19th century, when jazz itself was just emerging from three centuries of obscure germination. It followed the formal pattern of the typical march of the day with an introduction and several contrasting sections, its main characteristic being a syncopated melody whose shifts of accent lay within the bounds of existing notation over a regular accompaniment generally in 2/4 time. The emergence of this rather formal kind of jazz reflected not only the restraints of an entertainment world dominated by White Americans, but also the commercial need to publish it in a form that could be played by the amateur. It is quite probable that its original creators played it in a much freer style than the written score is able to suggest. The early ragtime is thought of mainly as piano music, but it was also used in orchestral form for dancing, ragtime being the music of the cakewalk vogue, and it is closely related to the jazz that became known as *Dixieland. The major composer of ragtime was and remains Scott Joplin (1868–1917), who wrote rags of considerable charm, ingenuity, and memorability and was ambitious enough to attempt a ragtime opera, *Treemonisha*, which was given only one trial performance in his lifetime. Successors of Joplin, in what is now considered the classic period of ragtime, were James Scott (1886–1938) and Joseph Lamb (1887–1960), but many others added isolated masterpieces to Joplin's solid achievement and generally advanced the genre in terms of complexity.

Alongside the piano ragtime the ragtime song was also developed to create a first really distinctive vein of American popular song. A new revival of ragtime interest came in the early 1900s, when Tin Pan Alley became fully aware of the new music and songs like Irving Berlin's 'Alexander's Ragtime Band' became best-sellers. Various later ragtime revivals occurred, but by now some of the original grace and charm had gone and it was generally played in a rather strident and comical vein. In the 1970s, however, the early ragtime was rediscovered, and Joplin's complete works were published by the New York Public Library and his *Treemonisha* publicly produced. Authentic ragtime was revived in properly styled performances and was successfully used as film background and ballet music. It is unlikely to be forgotten again, and will remain as a period music of considerable charm and strength — pioneering strains of the great jazz age.   PETER GAMMOND

Raimbaut de Vaqueiras (*b* Vaqueiras, Pro-

vence, mid 12th century). French *troubadour*. He spent much of his life at the court of Boniface II at Montferrat in northern Italy, and accompanied his patron in 1194 to the Sicilian war and in 1202 on a crusade to the Holy Land. 35 of his poems survive, seven of them with music; one of these, the celebrated 'Kalenda maya', is the oldest known example of an *estampie*.   WENDY THOMPSON

'Raindrop' Prelude. Nickname of Chopin's Prelude in D♭, Op. 28 No. 15 (1836–9), for piano. It is so called because it has been supposed that the repeated note A♭ suggests raindrops.

Rainier, Priaulx (*b* Howick, Natal, 3 Feb. 1903). South African-English composer. She settled in England in 1920 and studied at the Royal Academy of Music with McEwen. While working as a string player she also composed, and received encouragement from Bax, but it was not until after a period of study with Nadia Boulanger in Paris (1937) that she attained maturity as a composer: her First String Quartet (1939) is her first representative work. Her small output, concentrated in the fields of chamber and vocal music, is distinctively marked by vigorous motivic argument in a highly chromatic style, and by her penchant for working with unusual instrumental combinations, as in her Concertante for Two Winds (1980) for oboe, clarinet, and orchestra. She has also taught harmony and counterpoint at the Royal Academy of Music.   PAUL GRIFFITHS

Raison, André (*d* Paris, 1719). French organist and composer. He worked at the royal abbey of Ste Geneviève in the second half of the 17th century, and was Clérambault's teacher. His two published sets of organ Masses (Paris, 1688, 1714) give some interesting instructions on their performance and interpretation, advocating the selection of a tempo according to whether the piece is in the nature of a sarabande, gigue, or other dance.   DENIS ARNOLD

Rake's Progress, The. Opera in three acts and epilogue by Stravinsky; text by W. H. Auden and Chester Kallman, after Hogarth's engravings (1735). Produced: Venice, Fenice, 11 September 1951; New York, Metropolitan Opera, 14 February 1953; Edinburgh, 25 August 1953. Tom Rakewell (ten.) leaves Anne Trulove (sop.) to go to London when Nick Shadow (bar.) appears with news of sudden wealth. His physical pleasures palling, Tom is easily tempted by Shadow, now his servant, first to marry the fantastic bearded lady Baba the Turk (mezzo) and then to place his trust in a fake machine for turning stones into bread. He goes bankrupt, and all his effects are sold. The year and a day stipulated by Shadow for their association being at an end, Shadow reveals himself as the Devil and claims Tom's soul. But Shadow suggests a gamble for Tom's soul, and Tom wins; Nick sinks into the ground, but makes Tom mad. The final scene finds Tom in Bedlam, believing himself to be Adonis; Anne now takes her last leave of him. In the Epilogue the characters point the moral: 'For idle hearts and hands and minds the Devil finds a work to do.'

FURTHER READING
Paul Griffiths: *The Rake's Progress*, Cambridge Opera Handbooks (Cambridge, 1982).

Rakhmaninov, Sergey (Vasilyevich) (*b* Semyonovo, 1 Apr. 1873; *d* Beverly Hills, Calif., 28 Mar. 1943). Russian composer, pianist, and conductor. His family was comfortably affluent, but following his parents' separation and the consequent break-up of the home he had to rely on scholarships and goodwill to study music, first at the St Petersburg Conservatory, then at the conservatory in Moscow where his teachers were Nikolay Zverev and Alexander Ziloti (piano), Taneyev (counterpoint), and Arensky (harmony and composition). Although his main efforts at this time were channelled into practising for his piano finals (which he passed with honours in 1891), he became increasingly occupied with composition, writing a number of piano pieces, a little Mendelssohnian orchestral Scherzo (1887), and his First Piano Concerto (1890-1, revised 1917). For his graduation exercise in composition (1892) he also composed his one-act opera *Aleko*, warmly praised by Tchaikovsky whose influence it clearly shows.

Quite early on, however, Rakhmaninov forged his own distinctive musical style, marked by a sure gift for soaring melody and a taste for succulent harmony and rich textures, seen in such works as the famous Prelude in C♯ minor (1892), the *Fantaisie-tableaux* Op. 5 for two pianos (1893), and in his symphonic poems *Knyaz' Rostislav* ('Prince Rostislav', 1891) and *Utyos* ('The Rock', 1893). He also began to show his flair for vocal writing in two sets of songs, Op. 4 (1890-3) and Op. 8 (1893). In 1895 he began work on his first major orchestral

Autograph MS of Rakhmaninov's Third Piano Concerto, first movement cadenza.

composition, the First Symphony in D minor, an impassioned, defiant work which caused César Cui to liken it to 'a programme symphony on the Seven Plagues of Egypt' at its première in 1897. This poor critical reception (perhaps sparked more by the inadequate performance than by the music itself) plunged Rakhmaninov into a state of depression from which he could not emerge for about three years: composition was impossible, and only a conducting post in Moscow kept him musically active. He underwent medical treatment from Nikolay Dahl, a doctor who had been specializing in treatment by hypnosis, and gradually his confidence was restored to the extent that he was able to make headway with his Second Piano Concerto (1900–1), the success of which decisively launched him into international fame as a composer: together with Grieg's Piano Concerto and Tchaikovsky's First, it must surely rank as the most frequently performed concerto in the repertory.

Professional success was enhanced by the emotional security of his marriage in 1902, and for the next 15 years or so he was able to compose with a facility, assurance, and ever-increasing mastery of his art, producing many of his finest works: two sets of piano Preludes, Op. 23 (1901, 1903) and Op. 32 (1910), two piano sonatas (1907; 1913, revised 1931), two sets of Études-tableaux, Op. 33 (1911) and Op. 39 (1916–17), the Second Symphony (1906–7), the Third Piano Concerto (1909), and the symphonic poem Ostrov myortvykh ('The Isle of the Dead', 1909). Two forays into opera— Skupoy rytsar' ('The Miserly Knight', 1906) and Francesca da Rimini (1906)—were not specially happy, largely because of the unsuitability of the librettos, but they both contain some fine music and, like his songs of the period (Opp. 14, 21, 26, 34, and 38), reveal a sensitivity to Russian poetry which places him at the forefront of 19th-century and early 20th-century Russian vocal writing.

At the same time Rakhmaninov consolidated his career as a pianist, travelling widely in Russia and abroad: he made his American début in 1909 (giving the première of the Third Concerto there), an experience which stood him in good stead in later life. For, with the outbreak of the 1917 October Revolution, he decided to emigrate from Russia and make his home in America. With the necessity to provide for himself and his family (which now included two daughters), he had to concentrate on giving concerts and recitals. Almost every season from his arrival in America (1918) until 1942–3, he undertook an exhausting schedule of engagements, which all but precluded work on new compositions. Only rarely did he secure the necessary periods of relaxation; but when he did

Rakhmaninov (1924).

manage to get away from the concert platform—perhaps retreating to a rented house in the French countryside or Dresden, or from the early 1930s settling into his own Swiss villa on Lake Lucerne—he found the peace of mind to write music of extraordinary vitality, originality, and rhythmic zest. The element of nostalgia, familiar from the works composed in Russia, is still present but is now voiced not in the sumptuous style of the Second Symphony or the Second and Third Concertos but in a terser, more astringent tone utterly characteristic of his late works. The Fourth Piano Concerto (1926, revised 1941), the Three Russian Songs (1926), the 'Corelli' Variations for solo piano (1931), the Rhapsody on a Theme of Paganini (1934), the Third Symphony (1935–6, revised 1938), the Symphonic Dances (1940)—all were written during this creative Indian Summer. And all reveal a new, invigoratingly pungent bite to the harmonies, a new urgency in the rhythmic thrust, and (in the orchestral works) a spareness of scoring which contrasts sharply with his earlier music.

The Symphonic Dances were in fact his last major work. Having suffered bouts of ill health in his later years he decided that the 1942–3 concert season would be his last. Abnormal tiredness caused additional alarm, and in February 1943, after giving a concert in Knoxville, he had to be taken home to Beverly Hills. He died of cancer less than six weeks later, leaving a legacy of music which has proved enduringly popular and which has also shown itself to be of key importance in the late Romantic repertory. Moreover, during the last two decades of his life he had made many gramophone recordings, which happily preserve his pearly-toned, clearly articulated piano playing, with its unerring verve, refined *legato*, and sublime intensity of expression.

GEOFFREY NORRIS

FURTHER READING
Sergei Bertensson and Jay Leyda: *Sergei Rachmaninoff: a Lifetime in Music* (New York, 1956; 2nd edn, London, 1965); Geoffrey Norris: *Rakhmaninov* (London, 1976); Robert Threlfall and Geoffrey Norris: *A Catalogue of the Compositions of S. Rachmaninoff* (London, 1982).

Rákóczi March. This popular national Hungarian march was named after Prince Ferenc Rákóczi, who led the Hungarian revolt against Austria at the beginning of the 18th century. Berlioz used it (*Marche hongroise*) in scene 3 of his 'légende dramatique' *La damnation de Faust* (1846), although the piece was actually written as a separate march to be performed on a visit to Budapest in February 1846, where it roused the audience to transports of enthusiasm. Liszt also used the same piece as the basis of his 15th Hungarian Rhapsody for piano, published in 1852.

Ralentir (Fr.), **rallentare** (It.). 'To slow down'; *rallentando* (It.), 'becoming slower'. In the 18th century the term *lentando* was commonly used as a direction to slow down gradually.

Rallentando (It.). See *Ralentir, rallentare.*

Rambert, (Dame) **Marie** (*b* Warsaw, 20 Feb. 1888; *d* London, 12 June 1982). British dancer and teacher of Polish birth. She joined Diaghilev's Ballets Russes in 1913 as Nijinsky's rhythmic adviser for *The Rite of Spring*, and danced in the *corps de ballet*. In 1918 she settled in London; she opened her first ballet school in 1920 and formed her first company in 1926 (from 1935, the Ballet Rambert). She shares with Ninette de Valois the pioneering distinction in British ballet, and was responsible for discovering and developing original choreographic talent, notably Frederick Ashton and Antony Tudor, and later Norman Morrice and Christopher Bruce.

NOËL GOODWIN

Rameau, Jean-Philippe (*bapt.* Dijon, 25 Sept. 1683; *d* Paris, 12 Sept. 1764). French composer and theorist. The son of an organist, Rameau was sent to Italy at the age of 18 to study music. On his return to France he worked as organist in

Avignon, Clermont, and then (from 1706) in Paris. He returned to Dijon to succeed his father at Notre Dame for a short period, but in 1715 went as organist to Clermont Cathedral, where he stayed for eight years. Rameau's music from these years includes his first collection of harpsichord pieces (Paris, 1706), and in 1722 he published his first theoretical work, the *Traité de l'harmonie*.

At the end of 1722 Rameau returned to Paris, where he lived for the rest of his life. In 1726 he published another theoretical work, the *Nouveau système de musique*, but in 1723 he had begun to write music regularly for comic operas which were given at the Parisian Fair theatres in collaboration with the dramatist Piron. Rameau continued to play the organ for various churches in Paris, and he also began to take private composition pupils; he opened a school of composition in 1737. He was also introduced to a wealthy financier, Le Riche de la Pouplinière, who ran a private orchestra. In 1739 La Poupinière bought a large house in the rue de Richelieu, and from 1744 Rameau and his wife (he had married in 1726) occupied an apartment in the house. At La Poupinière's Rameau came into contact with the cream of Parisian musical and literary society, including several playwrights who were later to serve him as librettists. There, also, he met and alienated the young Jean-Jacques Rousseau: Rousseau submitted the score of his *Les muses galantes*

Rameau, portrait by Jacques Aved

to Rameau for approval, but the older man brusquely rejected it with stinging comments. In 1753 the Rameau family moved out of the rue de Richelieu and into their own flat in the rue des Bons Enfants.

Rameau is best remembered today as an opera composer, but this was a role he came to late in life. His first opera, the *tragédie lyrique Hippolyte et Aricie*, was composed in 1733 when he was 50. The last 30 years of his life were devoted to the composition of some 30 stage works, in all the contemporary genres—*tragédie lyrique*, *opéra-ballet*, ballet, *divertissement*, *pastorale*, *opéra comique*, and so on. Among the best of these are the first three *tragédies lyriques*: *Hippolyte et Aricie*, *Castor et Pollux* (1737), and *Dardanus* (1739, later extensively revised). They take up the tradition of French opera from where Lully had left it—indeed, Rameau paid

homage to Lully in *Hippolyte et Aricie*, modelling the mourning chorus at the end of Act 4 on that in Lully's *Alceste*, and even quoting a phrase from that work ('Hippolyte n'est plus') —and point the way forward to Gluck (the opening scene by Castor's tomb in the first version of *Castor et Pollux* itself provided the model for the opening tableau of Gluck's *Orfeo*).

Each act in Rameau's stage works contains a substantial *divertissement*, affording ample opportunity for many and varied dances. The element of *divertissement* is especially important in the *opéras-ballets*, of which the finest are *Les Indes galantes* (1735) and *Les fêtes d'Hébé* (1739)—again, both relatively early works. *Les Indes galantes* comprises a prologue and four *entrées*, each set in a different exotic surrounding, while *Les fêtes d'Hébé* has three *entrées* in a more pastoral vein. The *comédie lyrique*, *Platée*,

Prison de Dardanus.

The prison scene from Act 2 of Rameau's tragedy 'Dardanus', 1760 performance.

'La Lapoplinière' from Rameau's 'Pièces de clavecin en concerts' (1741).

and the comédie-ballet, La Princesse de Navarre, were both written for the wedding of the Dauphin in 1745, and several other pieces are connected with royal occasions.

Rameau's stage works were not universally appreciated. On the one hand he found himself under attack from the supporters of 'progressive' (i.e. Italian) music, led by Rousseau, and on the other from supporters of Lully, who considered Rameau's music extravagantly modern and almost incomprehensible. In the 1730s and 1740s a fierce polemical battle raged between the 'Lullistes' and the 'Ramistes'. One of the few balanced assessments of the differences between the respective styles of Lully and Rameau was provided by the writer Diderot in his satirical novel Les bijoux indiscrets (1748): 'Rameau . . . is excellent when he is good but he nods from time to time, and who does not? . . . Old Lully is simple, natural, even, too even sometimes, and this is a defect. Young Rameau is singular, brilliant, complex, learned, too learned sometimes . . . Nature has led Lully in the paths of tunefulness; study and experience have laid bare to Rameau the springs of harmony.'

Although Rameau was granted a court pension in the 1740s and held the title of compositeur du cabinet du Roy, the King's favourite, Madame de Pompadour, disliked him and his music, and in 1749 used her influence to prevent more than two of his operas being performed in any one year. In the early 1750s Rameau found himself an unwilling participant in the Querelle des *Bouffons, in which, ironically, his former detractors in the Lully camp began to promote his music as representative of the best French tradition, as opposed to the Italian opera buffa favoured by Rousseau and his supporters. In fact, Rameau admired Italian music, and confessed that if he had been younger he would have modelled his style on Pergolesi's. One result of the quarrel was that Rameau made enemies of the pro-Italian Encyclopédistes (see France, 5), including his former supporter Diderot.

Despite the popularity of his operas, Rameau himself considered his theoretical writings to be the most important part of his life's work. He treated music as a science, but related it to the aesthetics of composition, which he felt should always aim to please the ear, to be expressive.

and to move the emotions. His most important theoretical contribution was his emphasis on the importance of the root-position chord (or the 5-3 chord), to which inversions (the 6-3 and the 6-4 chords, respectively the first and second inversion) maintained a harmonic link. He formulated the concept of an imaginary bass line which was formed not out of the lowest notes present, but out of the roots of the chords employed—i.e. a *basse fondamentale* ('*funda-mental bass*'). For Rameau, the source of all musical consonance was the major or minor triad, while the seventh chord was the source of all dissonance. His writings on harmony had great influence on contemporary and subse-quent theorists, including Tartini, Marpurg, Helmholtz, Riemann, and Hindemith.

Apart from his operas and writings, Rameau left an important body of keyboard pieces, published in four collections (Paris, 1706, 1724, c.1728, 1741). Most are genre pieces with descriptive titles in the French tradition, and the rest are dances. He also published a volume of instrumental chamber music, the *Pièces de clavecin en concert* (Paris, 1741).

Rameau was not greatly liked: he was often accused of avarice and of insensitivity to his family, partly as a result of the malicious por-trait of him painted by Diderot in his *Le neveu de Rameau* (Paris, 1761; the nephew who was supposed to have given this description is Jean-François Rameau, the worthless son of Rameau's brother Claude). Rameau's extreme taciturnity on the one hand, and on the other his tendency to be outspoken and frank to the point of rudeness, alienated friends and enemies alike. One contemporary said of him 'His whole heart and soul were in his harpsichord; once he had shut it there was no one at home'.

WENDY THOMPSON

FURTHER READING
Cuthbert Girdlestone: *Jean-Philippe Rameau: his Life and Work* (London, 1957, 2nd edn 1969); James R. Anthony: *French Baroque Music from Beaujoyeulx to Rameau* (London, 1973, 2nd edn 1978).

Ramifications. Work by Ligeti for string orchestra or 12 solo strings, composed in 1968-9.

Ramsey, Robert (*fl.* Cambridge, first half of the 17th century). English composer of church music, consort and continuo songs, and madri-gals. He took the Cambridge degree in 1616, and from 1628 until 1644 worked at Trinity College, first as organist and later as Master of the Children. Like his contemporaries Deering and Philips, Ramsey's style is expressive and Italianate, and although most of his music is written in the polyphonic idiom of the *prima prattica*, his 'What tears, dear Prince' (probably written on the death of Prince Henry in 1612) is an early example of an English monodic song.

JOHN MILSOM

Randall, William (*b* London, *c.*1728; *d* Lon-don, ?Jan. 1776). English music-seller and music publisher. With his partner John Abell he published the first complete full-score edition of Handel's *Messiah* (1767). On the death of his cousin, the younger John Walsh, in 1766 he inherited (and subsequently reprinted) Walsh's publications, and issued his own collections of songs and dances, as well as a reprint of Morley's *Plaine and Easie Introduction* (1771). His widow carried on the business until it was sold in 1783.

Rands, Bernard (*b* Sheffield, 2 Mar. 1935). English composer. He studied composition with Reginald Smith Brindle at Bangor (1953-8) and with Roman Vlad, Dallapiccola, and Berio in Italy (1958-62). Since 1969 he has taught at the University of York. Following an early success with *Actions for Six* (1962-3), he has produced a large output of music for varied combinations, influenced by Berio in his view of music as a supple language of gesture and allusion.

PAUL GRIFFITHS

Rant. A dance which may have originated in the Scottish Lowlands or in northern England. It was popular in the 17th century, and John Playford included several in his publications (*The Dancing Master*, *Courtly Masquing-Ayres*, etc.).

Ranz des vaches (Fr.; Ger.: *Kuhreigen*, *Kuhreihen*). The name given to a type of Swiss mountain melody sung or played on the *alp-horn to call the cows for milking or for any other purpose. Every district has its own version, and over 50 have been said to exist, differing both in words and music. There are many variants in actual performance, as an element of improvisa-tion enters. The most celebrated version is that of the district of Gruyère, which bears the name (from its opening line) of 'Les Armaillis des Colombettes' ('Armaillis' are the men who spend the summer in the high mountains, taking charge of the cows sent there by the peasants of the neighbouring valleys). It is thought that the tune was originally for alphorn and that the words were a later addition, and the broken nature of the music, the intervals used, etc. support this view. In general style the tune in its various forms resembles that of the pipe of the shepherd boy in *Tristan*; a few short motifs are much reiterated, creating a slightly hypnotic effect.

There are many stories concerning the power

of the *ranz des vaches* to awaken an overwhelming feeling of homesickness in the Swiss peasants: Rousseau, in his dictionary of music (1767), alluding no doubt to the 18th-century employment of Swiss mercenaries in several of the armies of Europe, says that it was 'forbidden on pain of death to play it among the troops, because it caused those who heard it to burst into tears, to desert, or to die—so much did it arouse in them the longing to see their country again'.

The *ranz des vaches* has been introduced into various works: there are examples in the overtures to both Rossini's and Grétry's versions of *Guillaume Tell*, in the 'Scène aux champs' from Berlioz's *Symphonie fantastique*, and at the beginning of Act 3 of Wagner's *Tristan* (referred to above).   PERCY SCHOLES

Rape of Lucretia, The. Opera in two acts by Britten; text by Ronald Duncan, based on André Obey's play *Le viol de Lucrèce* (1931), in turn based on Shakespeare's poem *The Rape of Lucrece* (1594) and on Livy's history *Ab urbe condita libri*, i, 57-9 (*c.*26 BC–AD 17). Produced: Glyndebourne, 12 July 1946; Chicago, 1 June 1947. With a male (ten.) and female (sop.) Chorus commenting and eventually drawing a Christian moral, the opera relates the story of the proud, self-destroying Tarquinius (bar.). He rides from the camp where news has come of the Roman wives' infidelity to make an attempt on the virtue of the sole exception, Lucretia (mezzo), wife of Collatinus (bass). Claiming hospitality, he later enters her room and rapes her. Unable to bear the burden of her shame, she kills herself next day in the presence of her urgently summoned husband.

Rappresentatione di anima e di corpo, La ('The Representation of the Soul and the Body'). Staged oratorio by Cavalieri to a text by Manni, first performed in Rome in 1600. It is the first surviving play set to music and is therefore often described as the first opera.

Rapsodia (It.), **rapsodie** (Fr.). 'Rhapsody'.

Rapsodie espagnole ('Spanish rhapsody'). 1. Orchestral work by Ravel, composed in 1907-8. It is in four sections: *Prélude à la nuit*, *Malabueña*, *Habanera*, and *Feria*. The *Habanera* was originally a piece for two pianos, the first of the *Sites auriculaires* (1895-7).

2. Work for solo piano by Liszt, composed in about 1863. It was arranged for piano and orchestra by Busoni.

Rasch, rascher (Ger.). 'Quick', 'quicker'; *sehr rasch*, 'very quick'.

Rasgueado (Sp.). In guitar playing, the technique of strumming the strings, upwards with the fingertips, or downwards with the back of the fingernails.

Rasiermesserquartett. See *Razor Quartet*.

Rastell, John. See *Printing and Publishing of Music*, 4.

Rathgeber, Johann Valentin (*b* Oberelsbach, nr Meiningen, 3 Apr. 1682; *d* Banz Abbey, nr Coburg, 2 June 1750). German composer and Benedictine monk. He spent most of his adult life in the monastery of Banz, first as chamber musician, and after his ordination in 1711 as choirmaster. He wrote some popular songs which were published in three volumes of *Tafel-Confect* (1733, 1737, 1746) and include quodlibets, mock-folk-songs, and glee-like pieces for solo, duet, and chorus. Among his church music are some Masses with simple tunes, suitable for singing in parish churches—a style which was to become extremely popular.   DENIS ARNOLD

Ratsche (Ger.). 'Rattle'.

Rattenere, rattenendo, rattenuto (It.). 'To hold back', 'holding back', 'held back'.

Rattle. 1. The ratchet rattle (Fr.: *crécelle*; Ger.: *Ratsche*; It.: *raganella*) has a toothed wooden ratchet wheel and a flexible wooden blade. For outdoor use (as at football matches) the ratchet wheel is fixed tight to the handle; the frame, with the blade fixed in its other end, is swung round so that as each tooth of the wheel plucks the blade this snaps back against the following tooth with strong impact noise. If it is wished to dispense with swinging there can be a knob along the frame for turning while still holding the handle. There are also orchestral versions in which the frame is held still and the wheel is turned by a handle, sometimes preferred to the swung form should a more evenly continuous sound be required. Richard Strauss used the ratchet in *Till Eulenspiegel* and *Der Rosenkavalier* (Act 3), and before him Beethoven in *Wellington's Victory*, where it represents rifle fire. In history the ratchet rattle goes back to the Middle Ages, for night watchmen and lepers. Many will recall its function in Britain as the official gas warning during the Second World War. Some Spanish and Swiss church towers contain enormous rattles with blades 7' long and the ratchet wheel turned by ropes. These are for use during Holy Week when the bells are not rung from the Thursday to the Saturday.

2. *Shaken Rattles.* For rattles that produce sounds of a 'swishing' nature, see *Maracas*,

Sistrum and Jingles. Many different types of loud rattles are made in Catholic countries, again for use during Holy Week, sounded from the steps of the church: (*a*) a pair of wooden mallets pivoted in a frame to knock against a stationary mallet mounted between them; (*b*) a wooden hammer pivoted above a small board (also made with several small hammers worked by a miniature windmill, for a bird-scarer in fields and gardens); (*c*) one or two iron loops rather like door-knockers, pivoted over a stout board which is rapidly twisted to and fro in the hand.   ANTHONY BAINES

Rauschend (Ger.). 'Rushing', 'dashing'; or 'rustling'.

Ravel, (Joseph) **Maurice** (*b* Ciboure, Basses Pyrénées, 7 Mar. 1875; *d* Paris, 28 Dec. 1937). French composer of mixed Swiss–Basque parentage. He grew up in Paris and studied at the Conservatoire (1889–1904), notably with Fauré. His failure to gain the Prix de Rome, for which he competed four times between 1901 and 1905, caused a public scandal; meanwhile he associated with a group of artistic firebrands known as the 'apaches' and including the composer Florent Schmitt, the pianist Ricardo Viñes, and the poets Tristan Klingsor and León-Paul Fargue. Of these, Viñes was responsible for the first performances of many of Ravel's earlier piano works, including the *Pavane pour une infante défunte* (1899), *Jeux d'eau* (1901), and *Miroirs* (1904–5), while verses by Klingsor were set in the orchestral song cycle *Shéhérazade* (1903).

Several of these scores gave rise to accusations that Ravel was imitating Debussy, though

Ravel

the glittering cascades of *Jeux d'eau*, for example, stemmed rather from Liszt and in fact preceded Debussy's 'impressionist' piano pieces. *Shéhérazade* is more Debussyan in its vocal style and its use of whole-tone harmony, and yet this dream-picture of the east has a firmness which marks it as Ravel's. The ballet *Daphnis et Chloé* (1909–12), which benefits from Debussy's cool evocations of ancient Greece, is also utterly characteristic in the smoothness of its development; with some justice Ravel called it a 'choreographic symphony'. However, his gifts were not primarily for symphonic music. His musical ideas tend to be sharply defined and self-sufficient, his music to grow more by contrast and varied repetition than by continuous evolution. The classic instance of this is his orchestral *Boléro* (1928), in which a single melody is constantly repeated in a crescendo of colour, but the peculiarly objective nature of Ravel's genius is evident in most of his output (Stravinsky called him a 'Swiss watchmaker'). It is particularly to the fore in the clear-cut forms and often starker harmonies of his neoclassical period, which was ushered in by the piano suite *Le tombeau de Couperin* (1917) and which continued with the sonatas for violin and cello (1920–2) and violin and piano (1923–7).

The precision of Ravel's orchestration also reveals an artist for whom imagination had to be confirmed by calculation. One of the most inventive of orchestrators, he was able to make a version of Musorgsky's *Pictures from an Exhibition* (1922) which sounds like a fulfilment of the original, and he gave new, perfectly fitting orchestral dress to many of his own piano works, including the *Pavane* (orchestrated 1910), the suite *Ma mère l'oye* (1908/1911), the *Valses nobles et sentimentales* (1911/1912), and *Le tombeau de Couperin* (orchestrated 1919). Those he did not orchestrate, such as the three 'poems' of *Gaspard de la nuit* (1908), are those which Lisztian flourishes make unalterably pianistic. Besides orchestrating the music of others (Debussy and Schumann as well as Musorgsky), Ravel relished using pre-formed musical types in his own works. The conventions of 'Spanish' music, for instance, are reinterpreted with joyous *élan* in his orchestral *Rapsodie espagnole* (1907–8), his one-act comic opera *L'heure espagnole* (1911) and his song-cycle *Don Quichotte à Dulcinée* (1932–3), while the waltz and gypsy music, respectively, lie behind the dreamily macabre 'choreographic poem' *La valse* (1919–20) and the virtuoso *Tzigane* for violin with piano or orchestra (1924).

Suffering from a progressive disease, Ravel wrote comparatively little after completing his opera *L'enfant et les sortilèges* (1925, text by Colette), in which, with uncanny accuracy, he captured the mysterious, potentially malevolent world of a room at home as seen by a child. The only large-scale works of his last decade were two piano concertos, the dark left-hand work and the exultant, jazz-tinged G major, both written in 1931. PAUL GRIFFITHS

FURTHER READING
Arbie Orenstein: *Ravel* (New York, 1975); Roger Nichols: *Ravel* (London, 1977).

Ravenscroft, John (*d* before 1708). English composer who worked in Italy. In 1695 he published a set of 12 *sonate da chiesa* for two violins and continuo, and his Op. 2 was a volume of six *sonate da camera*, published posthumously in 1708. Both collections show him to have been a close disciple of Corelli.

Ravenscroft, Thomas (*b c.*1582; *d c.*1635). English composer, theorist, and music editor. He was a chorister at St Paul's Cathedral before taking the B.Mus. at Cambridge in 1605. His published works include a substantial revision of Thomas East's 1592 psalter (*The Whole Booke of Psalmes*, 1621) and three volumes of songs, canons, and catches, variously entitled *Pammelia*, *Deuteromelia*, and *Melismata*, illustrating the lighter side of Jacobean taste. His four fantasias for five viols give some indications as to the dynamics required. JOHN MILSOM

Rawsthorne, Alan (*b* Haslingden, Lancashire, 2 May 1905; *d* Cambridge, 24 July 1971). English composer. He studied at the Royal Manchester College of Music (1926–30) and had private piano lessons with Egon Petri (1930–1). After a brief period as music director of the school of dance and mime at Dartington Hall (1932–5) he worked as a freelance composer, producing numerous film scores. His serious output consists for the most part of abstract instrumental scores, including three symphonies, two concertos each for piano and violin, three string quartets, and a variety of other chamber works. In these he displayed a gift for athletic counterpoint in clear forms which depend on an enriched tonal harmony; the style is cosmopolitan, comparable more with Hindemith than with any English contemporaries. Among his few works of a more picturesque character are *The Creel* (1940), a suite of fish portraits for piano duet, and the brilliant overture *Street Corner* (1944).
PAUL GRIFFITHS

Ray. See *Re, ray*.

Razor Quartet (*Rasiermesserquartett*). Nickname of Haydn's String Quartet in F minor, Op. 55 No. 2, composed in the late 1780s. The story is that Haydn exclaimed when shaving, 'I'd give my best quartet for a new razor', and

was taken at his word by a visitor, the London music publisher Bland.

'Razumovsky' Quartets. Beethoven's String Quartets Op. 59 Nos. 1, 2, and 3 (in F major, E minor, and C major), composed in 1805–6. They are so called because they are dedicated to Count Andrey Razumovsky, Russian ambassador in Vienna, who was a keen quartet player.

Re, ray. The second degree of the scale in the *solmization system. In French (*ré*) and Italian usage it has, on the fixed-doh principle, become attached to the note D, in whatever scale it may occur. See *Tonic Sol-fa*.

Real answer. See *Fugue*.

Real sequence. See *Sequence*, 1.

Rebec. A fiddle of the Middle Ages and Renaissance. 1. The name first appears in the late 13th century in the form 'rubebe', and it appears in Chaucer's 'Miller's Tale', where the clerk could play songs on a 'small rubible'. The word points to some initial connection with the various Arab instruments named *rabab* (see *Bow*, 2)—in Morocco today, a small, stumpy, boat-shaped, two-stringed fiddle held on the knee like a viol. We see this in the Spanish *Cantigas de Santa Maria* manuscript (see *Instruments, Medieval*), while the contemporary treatise of Jerome of Moravia (see *Fiddle*, 2) describes the rubebe without saying what it looked like but noting the two strings, here also tuned to a fifth. Later, three strings are mentioned and the altered form of the name, 'rebec', appears; but it is not until the 15th century that one can define its form beyond the supposition that it was a small, carved-out, round-backed fiddle of one of the kinds seen in 14th-century pictures and carvings, held in the 'European' position up against the chest.

2. The rebec of the 15th and 16th centuries was of a slender 'pear shape', with integral neck and curving pegbox and (usually) a peculiar and characteristic fingerboard spreading out over the belly on a raised level. The pegbox curves back, with side pegs as on the violin. The three strings are tuned in fifths. There is nothing in the nature of a soundpost, and the tone (in reconstruction) tends to a rather hollow quality as compared with that of the violin. Reconstructions of the rebec in this form are now available for playing early music.

This rebec may have been the earliest bowed instrument to have been made in different sizes for playing together in parts: in Italy early in the 15th century the poem 'Il Saporetto' (by Prudenzani) mentions 'ribeche, rubechette, and rubecone as performing certain part songs (two titles named but neither of them have been traced). Such different-sized instruments are later described and illustrated by early 16th-century writers in Germany (Agricola, Gerle) under the name *kleine Geigen*: soprano, alto/tenor, and bass, with nominal tunings which give the lowest string as *g*, *c*, and *F* respectively, though such small instruments must in fact have been tuned considerably higher. The bass of the family was allowed a fourth string to go lower, and modern reproductions may be found to have this string. No actual rebecs have survived, apart from a couple or so of later date, perhaps from the 17th century, by which time the instrument had been almost wholly superseded by the violin, save for rare local survivals as a folk instrument up to the present century in Czechoslovakia and southern Poland. Even in the late 16th century, the name 'ribecchino', though still often met in Italy, had become a synonym for the violin.

ANTHONY BAINES

Rebel. French family of musicians. **Jean Rebel** (*d* Paris, before Feb. 1692) was from 1661 a singer in the royal chapel. Two of his children became distinguished musicians—**Anne-Renée Rebel** (*b* Paris, 1663; *d* Versailles, 5 May 1722), a singer who married de Lalande; and **Jean-Baptiste Féry Rebel** (*b* Paris, Apr. 1666; *d* Paris, 2 Jan. 1747). Jean-Baptiste studied with his father, and joined the orchestra of the Académie Royale de Musique as a

Jean-Baptiste Féry Rebel, portrait by Watteau.

violinist, later becoming its leader. From 1705 he also played in the royal band of Vingt-quatre Violons. He was a leading figure in the formation of the great 18th-century French school of violin playing. He wrote several stage works, including the ballet *Les élémens* (performed 1737) and a *tragédie lyrique*, *Ulysse* (1703), as well as several volumes of violin sonatas and other pieces, sacred music (some in collaboration with his brother-in-law, de Lalande), and some *chansons*.

His son, **François Rebel** (*b* Paris, 19 June 1701; *d* Paris, 7 Nov. 1775), succeeded him in the Violons before turning to the stage for a career. In collaboration with his great friend François Francœur he wrote a dozen or so popular dramatic pieces over a period of about 20 years. These include *Pirame et Thisbé* (performed 1726), *Scanderberg* (performed 1735), and *Le ballet de la paix* (performed 1738). In 1757 Rebel and Francœur became joint directors of the Paris Opéra, but the venture was doomed from the start: after the Opéra burnt down in April 1763 they were forced to resign. None the less, in 1772 Rebel was appointed *Administrateur général* of the Opéra.

WENDY THOMPSON

Rebop. See *Jazz*, 3.

Recapitulation. The final section of a *sonata form movement which resolves the tonal and thematic arguments set up in the exposition and development.

Recercar (It.). See *Ricercar*.

Rechants, Cinq. Five works by Messiaen for three sopranos, three altos, three tenors, and three basses, composed in 1949. The songs are to his own texts, and, like *Harawi* and *Turangalîla-symphonie*, were inspired by the legend of Tristan and Isolda.

Recit. Abbreviation for *recitative.

Recital. A concert given by one performer or a small group of performers. The term first gained currency when an advertisement appeared in London in 1840 stating that 'M. Liszt will give Recitals on the Pianoforte of the following pieces'. Formerly the term 'recital' was reserved for a solo performance (or accompanied solo), but in modern parlance it may be applied to various sorts of chamber or other small-scale concerts, which may be public or private.

See also *Concert*.

Recitando, recitante (It.), **récitant** (Fr.). 'Reciting', i.e. more like speech than song; *recitato*, 'recited'.

Recitative (from It. *recitativo*). Form of declamatory speech-like singing, used especially in opera and oratorio and free in rhythm. Recitative can serve for dialogue or narrative (as a means of advancing the plot), whereas the *aria is often static or reflective. In 17th- and 18th-century opera, especially *opera seria*, the distinction between recitative and aria is clear, but with Mozart's much more expressive and inventive use of recitative (as in *Don Giovanni*) the convention began to break up.

Recitativo accompagnato or *stromentato* (It., 'accompanied' or 'instrumental recitative'), in which the voice is accompanied by instruments other than the continuo ensemble, was introduced *c*.1663; in *recitativo secco* (It., 'dry recitative') the notes and metre of the singing followed the verbal accentuation, accompanied only by continuo instruments.

In some operatic genres the dialogue is spoken rather than sung, for example in the German *Singspiel*, the English *ballad opera, the French *opéra comique*, and the Spanish *zarzuela*. Conversely, in much opera of the late Romantic period, notably in Wagner, the aria disappears completely, the entire drama being borne along on a 'symphonic' recitative.

Recorder (Fr.: *flûte à bec*; Ger.: *Blockflöte*; It.: *flauto dolce*). The classic 'duct flute' (see *Flute*, 10) of Western music. Among the European names the German reminds us that a wooden block is inserted to form a windway to the 'window' where the tone is generated; the French, that the blowing end is shaped to a beak (or 'fipple') for the player to place comfortably in the lips; and the Italian, that the sound is sweet compared with that of other flutes of the Renaissance (fife and tabor pipe). The English name tells us that there was once held to be no better instrument with which to 'record' a tune in the old sense of recalling it to mind and repeating it: thus in Fairfax's *Tasso*, 'to hear the lark record her hymns and chant her carols blest'. After the 18th century the recorder passed out of use. Today, when everyone knows it again, it seems strange to remember that when Arnold Dolmetsch (1858-1940) first turned his attention to the instrument in 1919 most people knew the name only as a strange term met in Act 3 of *Hamlet*, while the recorder (*flauto*) parts in Handel and Bach were played as a matter of course on flutes (often they still are, though much less than formerly).

1. *Construction.* Dolmetsch revived the recorder in its 'Baroque' form (dating from *c*.1670), initially following originals by Bressan, the great early maker in London. This is the well-known form made in three pieces, of which the 'head' (with the oblong 'window') and the short 'foot'

Pl. 1. Treble (alto) recorder by Peter Bressan, London, early 18th century (Bressan, real name Pierre Jaillard, was born in 1663 in Bourg-en-Bresse, France).

are turned with decorative mouldings—often dispensed with, however, in low-priced 'school' models, where the small sizes may be made in two parts only. 'Renaissance' models are based on originals of the 16th century, turned all in one piece without mouldings; their bores on the whole taper downwards to a less marked degree and the window is generally wider; these produce a full, pure sound, rather 'vacant' on its own but ideal for playing early music in parts. The sound of a Baroque recorder is more colourful and expressive, suiting music of a solo or *obbligato* character as well as part music, and instruments of this type have come to be the 'general purpose' recorders.

The uniqueness of the recorder among other duct flutes (see *Flageolet*; *Pipe and Tabor*) stems from the 15th-century craftsman's achievement in integrating the many structural elements—bore, fingerholes, 'lip', 'windway'—to the best advantage for the instrument's participation in music of the highest class. Analysis of these elements, in separate terms or together, proves

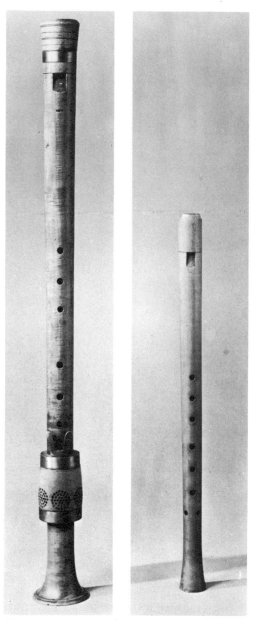

Pl. 2. Renaissance recorders: basset (right) *and tenor,*
late 16th century.

exceedingly difficult, but we may notice two main consequences for the technique. First, the recorder has an outstanding response to cross-fingered semitones, producing these notes with an even quality and excellent intonation equalled by no other wind instrument. The recorder commands every tonality through the finger-holes alone, and where keys beyond that for the lowest note are added to the larger recorders they are only to bring some hole within more comfortable reach.

Against this, the recorder is not one of the easiest 'overblowers'. To continue the scale above the fundamental register it is necessary, for a clean reliable attack, to half-uncover the thumb-hole by 'pinching' (bending the thumb for the nail to halve the opening); even then only four notes of the scale are made as simple overblown octaves (*e″* to *a″* on the descant recorder) and the highest of the four needs careful attack lest it 'breaks'. Three further notes are produced as higher harmonics, bringing the standard compass to two octaves plus one note, save for the semitone next to the top (high C♯ on the descant recorder), a very difficult note normally considered as absent. (It is interesting to compare duct flutes with thin walls and therefore holes of small or minimal depth—e.g. tin whistles and cane flageolets—which overblow easily but are practically hopeless for cross-fingered semitones. Very likely the greater prominence of partials in their sound has something to do with it.)

2. *The Block and Windway.* These take a similar form to that found in many wooden flageolets and tabor pipes (see *Flageolet*, 4), though with extreme attention to points of detail from which different makers or schools of making choose their options. For the general scheme, shown in longitudinal section with a cross-section of the block and windway, see *Flageolet*, Fig. 2c. The block is of cedar (e.g. pencil cedar, used also for harmonica bodies on account of its stability under moist conditions). For a treble recorder it is about 2″ long, made from a piece of nearly square section shaved down to fit the bore and leave the raised floor of the windway; the bore of the head may be cylindrical or it may slightly taper, the block, of course, shaped corresponding-ly. Great skill and experience go into the profiling and width of the windway, which may narrow towards the slit or be given a 'bow' (a kind of bulging profile), whichever is judged best to give a build-up of pressure behind the slit and project the air jet with energy across to the lip. Fine soloists like the masterly Frans Brüggen (*b* 1934) and his pupils in Holland know how to keep the windway always well filled with forward-moving air, to make the recorder strong and virile in its expression: a true woodwind instrument.

3. *The Recorder 'Consort'.* The recorders that most commonly make up a consort are descant, treble, tenor, and bass; in Germany and the USA the descant is termed 'soprano' and the treble 'alto'. The sopranino and great bass are rarer. Since the actual pitches have not always been the same in the past, the name of the bottom note is often appended to the title of the instrument, e.g. 'soprano in C'. With the standard instruments this bottom note is

Ex. 1

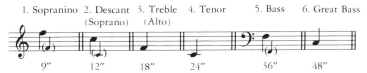

1. Sopranino 2. Descant 3. Treble 4. Tenor 5. Bass 6. Great Bass
(Soprano) (Alto)

9" 12" 18" 24" 36" 48"

alternately F and C (see Ex. 1). Nos. 5 and 6 are blown through a curving metal 'crook'. The small notes in brackets mark the instances where the music is written an octave lower than it sounds (No. 6, not a Baroque size, is generally played from the same part as the bass, adapting it at sight to make good use of the three deeper notes). The series of figures below the staff is a rough guide for quickly distinguishing the different sizes by their approximate over-all lengths (here in inches at modern pitch), the lengths fairly closely conforming directly with the pitch interval between one recorder and another, e.g. tenor twice the descant within an inch or so.

4. *History*. There is strangely little evidence of duct flutes through Antiquity, but from the earlier Middle Ages comes plentiful archaeological evidence of small flutes of sheep-bone, while references in literature point especially to the use of *fistulae* by bird-catchers, to which, we might imagine, could be added shepherds and children. A typical number of fingerholes for these bone relics is three, giving four notes; these (as change-ringers have calculated for us; see *Bells*, 5) can theoretically be arranged in 24 different sequences without allowing for repeated notes and varied rhythms: as a result, the entertainment-value of these little instruments could have been considerable.

If an old feeling had persisted that flute-playing among ordinary adults was in some way perilous to moral behaviour, this had been dispelled by the 13th century, when a few pictures show, along with other instruments, a duct flute with many holes, which could be claimed a forerunner of the recorder. Then, from the late 14th century—the time when the English name first appears, in a latinized form (*fistula in nomine ricordo*: 'flute called recorder') —comes the earliest actual example, the wooden instrument discovered under a ruined castle near Dordrecht in Holland. Now preserved in the Gemeentemuseum in The Hague, it is of descant (soprano) size, with the correct number of holes, though still not quite the complete recorder. It has no 'beak', the blowing end being squared off as often today among folk instruments of Central Europe, and the bore is a plain cylinder (11 mm.). And, again as common in folk instruments, the window is narrow and

almost square. The next example is believed to date from 100 years later, the end of the 15th century: an Italian instrument of tenor pitch in the Leipzig collection, bored cylindrically as far down as the fifth hole. Earlier in the same century one can see in Italian paintings two or three recorders down to tenor size being played together, and at a Burgundian wedding feast in 1468 a *chanson* was performed by four players of 'fleutes' disguised as wolves.

Details of the fully developed Renaissance instruments, fingering included, follow in the early 16th-century works of Agricola in Germany and Ganassi in Italy: treble in G (a tone higher than now), the next in C, and bass

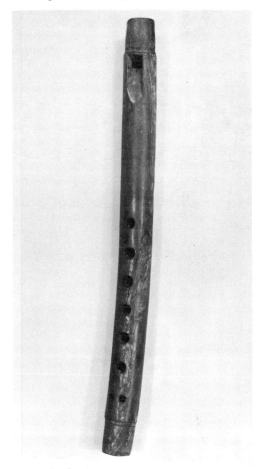

Pl. 3. The Dordrecht recorder, late 14th century.

in F, this last with the key for the bottom note partly concealed in a perforated wooden 'barrel'. By the mid century the smaller (now soprano) and larger sizes are named, the bass in F becoming termed in Germany 'basset', releasing the term 'bass' for the larger instrument in C (or B♭) below (No. 6 in Ex. 1). Lower still is the octave bass in low F, 6′ tall (see *Instruments, Renaissance*, Fig. 1). The basset is blown through a slot in the top of the head cap, but the larger instruments through a brass crook. The instruments were not necessarily confined to their nominal voices: a piece might be played on the larger ones only, with the tenor recorder playing the top part; the instruments are then in C (tenor), F (basset), C (or B♭), and low F, the whole sounding an octave lower than when played on modern recorders from descant to bass. Players today have demonstrated the beautiful effect of this, using original instruments (the richest collection is in Vienna) or reproductions.

The Baroque type of recorder may have been introduced first in France, by Hotteterre (see *Oboe*, 4), even though its earliest known description is in an Italian work compiled in 1677 by Bartolomeo Bismantova. This is immediately followed (1679) in England with John Hudgebut's *Vade mecum* for the 'Rechorder', a work particularly interesting for its information on ornamentation. After that the Tutors are for the 'flute' (as opposed to the 'German flute' or 'traversa', the flute itself). Among the surviving instruments, trebles, all but a few built in F as they are now, far outnumber the other sizes of recorder, demonstrating clearly how this was the central instrument and the great solo and orchestral member of the family. A number of pictures and engravings show its two players seated between the oboists and violinists in a chapel or opera theatre, though frequently one single pair of players would change from oboe to recorder as required during a work. The smaller sizes were at this time named by the interval above the treble: 'eighth flute' (today sopranino), 'sixth flute' (descant in D, presumably the 'flauto piccolo' in Bach's Cantata BWV 103), 'fifth' and 'fourth' flutes, the number often being inscribed on the instrument. The 'voice flute' in D below the treble was presumably so named because its range came closer to that of published vocal airs; several examples exist. A few solo pieces were published for the small sizes, and Purcell's last *Ode for St Cecilia's Day* has a part for the bass ('bass flute'). There are some unsolved problems, for example, the 'flauti di echo' (in modern scores, 'flauti') in Bach's Fourth Brandenburg Concerto: the parts cover the entire compass of the normal treble recorder, with echo effects in the Andante (difficult on a recorder without the echo repeat

sounding flat), but also make extensive use of the almost impossible high F♯. (Modern makers have found a way of making high F♯ possible by a key that closes the lower end of the instrument while fingering top G.)

Among the great recorder makers of the Baroque besides Bressan are Stanesby in London, Denner and Oberlander in Nuremberg, and many elsewhere. The instruments are of boxwood or maple, or else of ivory. Twin holes, for making the lowest semitones, very common today, were known but were less common than now.

5. *Revival.* By the late 18th century recorders were still being made, often showing influence of flute-making, as in a straight modelling of the foot-joint. Their purpose would have been solely for private entertainment and even in this they were superseded in the next century by the various *flageolets. Following Dolmetsch in England, Peter Harlan commenced recorder-making in Germany while, again in England, Edgar Hunt wrote the first modern recorder Tutor in 1935. The foundation of the Society of Recorder Players in Britain in 1937 by Max Champion and his wife, aided by Hunt and Carl Dolmetsch, led several British composers to write solo and chamber works for the instrument. The American Recorder Society was founded two years later by Suzanne Bloch, daughter of the well-known composer. Meanwhile school recorder classes in Britain depended mainly on the supply of cheap instruments from Germany, and when this was curtailed by the outbreak of war Edgar Hunt designed the first plastic recorder, a descant in bakelite.

Many of the makers in Germany through these times modified the fingering system ('German fingering') in order to make F♮ (on the descant) with the first four fingers (and thumb) only, instead of cross-fingering, and, though this complicates the fingering for F♯, some of their models continue to be made on this system. One can tell it at sight through the fifth hole in front being smaller than the fourth, whereas with instruments made to 'English' (i.e. Baroque) fingering it is of equal width or wider.

6. *Repertory.* The Baroque repertory is almost entirely for treble recorder. Among composers of solo sonatas or of trio sonatas with a second recorder or another instrument are Alessandro Scarlatti, Bononcini, Daniel Purcell, Hotteterre le Romain, Pepusch, Loeillet, Vivaldi (seven concertos), Woodcock (if the works are really his), Schickhardt, Telemann (a great deal, including eight solo sonatas, two solo concertos, and numerous trio sonatas), Christoph Graupner (concerto), Handel (Sonatas 2, 4, 7, and 11 of his early set, Op. 1), Babell (concertos for

descant recorder), Marcello, and Sammartini. Corelli's Sonata Op. 5 No. 3 was given an anonymous 18th-century arrangement for recorder.

Among modern works for recorder are Hindemith's Trio (ed. Walter Bergmann); Robin Milford's Three Airs (the second was originally an interlude, with harpsichord, in the oratorio *A Prophet in the Land* (1930), one of the first reappearances of a recorder on the orchestral platform); Rubbra's Sonatina (with harpsichord) and *Fantasia on a Theme by Machaut* (with harpsichord and string quartet); Lennox Berkeley's Sonatina; Hovhaness's Sextet (with strings, harpsichord); Francis Baines's Quartet for recorders and Fantasia for six recorders (descants and trebles); Antony Hopkins's Suite; and works by Walter Leigh, Rawsthorne, and Malcolm Arnold. Now to be added to these are some avant-garde compositions written for Frans Brüggen, among them Berio's *Gesti*.

ANTHONY BAINES

FURTHER READING
A. Rowland-Jones: *Recorder Technique* (London, 1959); Edgar Hunt: *The Recorder and its Music* (2nd edn, London, 1977); special 'Recorder' issue, *Early Music*, x, 1 (Jan. 1982).

Recording and Reproduction

1. Discs versus Cylinders
2. Electrical Recording
3. The Advance of High Fidelity
4. Magnetic Recording

5. Film Recording
6. Video and Digital Recording
7. Recording and the Musician

The ability to record musical performances and play them back at any time has accelerated the spread of music and its appreciation by a wider public than could ever be crowded into our concert halls. Even the development of music itself has been influenced, since performers and composers have easier access to the works and styles of their contemporaries world-wide than previously.

1. *Discs versus Cylinders*. The first hint of what technological developments were to follow was perhaps given by the Phonautograph invented by Leon Scott in 1857 as an aid to the study of sound-waves (see also *Acoustics*, 9). This recorded the vibrations of a sound-sensitive diaphragm as traces on the lamp-blacked surface of a revolving cylinder. Twenty years later, in 1877, the idea of imprinting such traces in some unyielding material so that they could be retraced and impart vibratory movement to a diaphragm, and so re-create the original sounds, occurred independently to researchers in France and the USA. The Frenchman, Charles Cros (1842–88), would appear to have conceived the idea first. He deposited a sealed paper with the French Academy of Sciences on 30 April 1877 outlining a scheme for photo-engraving the lamp-black traces to produce grooves on a flat disc of copper or steel. However, no working model ever appeared and the prolific American inventor, Thomas Alva Edison (1847–1931), was of a more practical turn of mind, and was able to demonstrate a prototype of his tinfoil cylinder phonograph in December 1877. He had already been busy with a telegraph relay which recorded signal impulses as indents on paper. When the paper was rerun at high speed and connected to a morse key, the signals could be dispatched with a saving in time of occupancy of the telegraph wire links. Edison observed that the chattering relay produced sounds resembling muffled human speech. This led him to experiment with indentations using a needle connected to a diaphragm into which he spoke, and later with a modified telephone receiver.

The original Edison Phonograph comprised a cylinder measuring 80 mm. long by 80 mm. in diameter with a helical groove at 10 turns per inch inscribed in its surface. A turning handle caused the cylinder to rotate and track along a shaft, threaded at the same pitch as the groove. Two diaphragms with crude mouthpiece horns and a steel needle at the centre were placed on either side of the cylinder which had a sheet of soft tinfoil wrapped around it to act as the recording medium. To record, the operator would first move the needle of the indenting diaphragm into contact with the foil at the start of the cylinder's traverse, begin to turn the handle at a steady, repeatable speed, and speak loudly. To replay the recording, the cylinder would be wound back to the beginning, the needle of the other (more sensitive) diaphragm would be rested on the foil, and the handle turned as before.

For all its crudeness, the phonograph impressed its first hearers and some 500 machines were produced during 1878. Edison, however, turned his attention to more pressing, and commercially viable, inventions leaving others to refine the process. At first the tinfoil was replaced by beeswax, and it is historically interesting that one of these wax cylinders was lodged in a sealed box in the Smithsonian

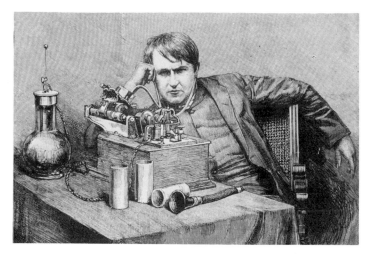

Edison in his laboratory; engraving from 'The Graphic' (18 August 1888).

Institute in 1881 and not opened or played until 1937. Then at a special ceremony the descendants of Alexander Graham Bell, the inventor of the telephone, heard the great man's voice intoning the words: 'There are more things in heaven and earth, Horatio, than are dreamt of in your philosophy. I am a Graphophone, and my mother was a phonograph.'

This Graphophone, the work of Bell and Tainter in Washington, made some progress as a dictating machine in 1885, sufficient to rouse Edison into developing his own 'perfected phonograph'. This used solid-cast waxes which could be shaved and reused, forming a marketable dictation machine taking about 400 words (two minutes) when driven at 120 revolutions per minute (rpm) by an electric motor. This was

the model used for many of our earliest-surviving recordings, including Brahms playing his Hungarian Dance No. 1 as a piano solo in Vienna in 1889. Development of the phonograph as a medium for music in the home depended on some viable method of duplicating recordings. At first the performers had to record an item over and over again, with the sound horn perhaps connected to a group of phonographs simultaneously. This gave way to a mechanical doubling (hence 'dubbing') system, and several moulding processes were also used until the demise of the cylinder phonograph around 1929.

The cylinder just could not compete, on this vital question of easy mass production, with the rival format—a flat disc. While Edison and

Edison's improved phonograph in use during the Handel festival at Crystal Palace (1888).

The Scott phonautograph

others had documented studies of a lateral disc-recording system, it was left to Emile Berliner, a German working in Washington, to carry out researches into what became the forerunner of the 'gramophone record' as we know it. At first Berliner made tracings on lamp-blacked glass discs, following the principle of Leon Scott's Phonautograph, and used a photo-engraving process to etch grooves into metal. Later he used zinc discs coated with beeswax and eventually, by about 1899, the technique of employing wax discs 50 mm. thick was introduced and remained the standard medium for more than 40 years. Berliner can be credited with many of the standard features of the disc record. The recording/cutting head was driven along a radial line towards the disc centre by a rotating threaded shaft, but the pivoted playback/pickup head simply relied on the force of the spiralling record groove on the needle to carry it into the centre. Also Berliner elected to drive the stylus laterally, producing a side-to-side waveform in the groove in preference to the vertical, 'hill-and-dale' stylus vibrations used on Edison's cylinders. This made for better reproduced sound quality and greater loudness.

Berliner's first discs had 50 grooves to the inch and measured only 125 mm. in diameter. Gradually the disc size increased to 7″ (1899), 10″ (1901), and 12″ (1903). Rotational speed varied from about 70 rpm up to 82 or 83 rpm, and was not standardized at 78 rpm until about 1918. The processes used for mass duplication of early gramophone records were remarkably similar to those still in use today. The surface of the newly cut wax master-disc was first metallized to make it electrically conducting, and then made to act as one of the electrodes in an

electroplating bath. The copper-plate 'negative' so formed was removed from the wax and then, in turn, used as the surface on which a 'positive' could be deposited capable of being played and checked. Yet another electroplating stage could yield any required number of negative 'stampers' or moulds to press out records in quantity. Even today, record companies are able to replay these old metal positives as a direct source of reissues on LP of vintage recordings by famous artists.

A modern record factory houses a number of presses each able to stamp out about 150 discs an hour. The two stampers, with their appropriate paper labels, for sides one and two, are carefully centred on each half or 'jaw' of the press and a measured quantity of the disc material is placed between. Then, in an automated cycle, the material is heated, the jaws close tight to press it out between the stampers, rapid cooling takes place, and the disc is removed and put into its sleeve.

2. *Electrical Recording*. The era of sound recording from Edison's first phonograph in 1877 (and Berliner's gramophone a decade later) up to around 1924 is referred to as the 'acoustic' age. During this period all the energy available to drive the stylus which etched out the recorded waveforms was 'acoustic energy'; that is, it came from the sound-waves themselves. The system was therefore very inefficient unless large collecting horns were used to funnel sound energy on to the diaphragm/needle assembly at the sharp end. This made balancing of singers and musical instruments an uncomfortable business at best, and ruled out the weaker instruments completely. A tuba might be used

instead of string basses, and the Stroh violin came briefly into vogue with a diaphragm and metal trumpet replacing the bridge to produce amplified sounds which could be directed towards the recording horn.

Things changed dramatically around 1925 when the acoustic horns were replaced by the new microphones and triode valve amplifiers introduced a few years earlier for radio broadcasting. These allowed the engineers to record even quiet voices or instruments effectively, and space the performers out more naturally. The microphone converted the acoustic energy into an electric current which could be amplified and sent along cables to any convenient point. Here, instead of relying on the horn diaphragm to drive the cutting stylus directly, an electromagnet cutterhead carried out a conversion in the reverse sense to change the electric current into a controllable driving force on the stylus.

Though the first electrically recorded discs were variable in sound quality, the best of them demonstrated the greater realism—wider frequency response and improved dynamic range—now possible. Initially these new records could be played only on the existing acoustic gramophones. However, electrical reproducers soon appeared. These replaced the acoustic soundbox with a pickup head containing a tiny electrical generator. Left/right motion of the needle (stylus) as it followed the waveform in the groove generated a proportionate alternating current which was amplified and fed to a loudspeaker. The latter behaves like a microphone in reverse. The alternating current causes vibrations in a lightweight diaphragm and the consequent emission of sound-waves. As many homes already possessed one of the new radio sets, electrical gramophones often consisted simply of a turntable and pickup which plugged into the radio's amplifier circuit—ironically, we might think, since radio broadcasting had been widely expected to make the gramophone obsolete.

3. *The Advance of High Fidelity.* The two decades leading up to the 1939-45 war witnessed small, but hardly spectacular, refinements in the quality and versatility of records and their reproducers. Then followed a period of accelerated technological progress and an unprecedented boom in record sales.

A major step forward was the introduction, by Columbia Records in June 1948, of Long Playing (LP) 'microgroove' records. These were the same size as the old 78 rpm discs, 12″ in diameter, but played for a full 25 minutes per side instead of only about four minutes. Thus many complete compositions could be heard without the irritation of frequently turning over or changing the record. The longer playing time

was brought about by two factors. First, the running speed was more than halved, to 33⅓ rpm in place of 78 rpm. Secondly, the grooves were made much narrower, to allow some 250 grooves per inch instead of only about 100. At the same time, the quality or 'fidelity' of the musical reproduction was soon found to be vastly superior. The change was made possible partly by improvements and miniaturization in the design of cutter heads and replay pickup cartridges, but the prime factor was the availability of new plastics, vinylite or polyethylene, from which the new LP records could be manufactured. The shellac used for 78 rpm records was coarse-grained and had abrasive powders added to withstand the considerable pressures of the early heavy pickups. The result was an obtrusive hissing noise as a continuous accompaniment to the music. The new plastics were very fine-grained and, provided lightweight pickups were used, no abrasive filler was needed. Background noise was therefore much reduced, allowing for more light and shade in the music itself. The new vinyl discs were also lighter, flexible, and unbreakable. However, they did need more careful handling as they scratched easily and retained static electrical charges which made them attract dust.

A parallel development to the 33⅓ rpm Long Playing record was a smaller 'singles' disc introduced by RCA Victor. This used the same vinyl material and groove dimensions as LPs, but was only 7″ in diameter and ran at 45 rpm. After a brief 'war of the speeds', both formats became accepted with record players geared to run at 33⅓, 45, and 78 rpm (with the last speed eventually falling into disuse). To complement the new records, home reproducing equipment was rapidly raised to 'high-fidelity' (hi-fi)

A master lacquer being examined by a disc-cutting engineer at EMI's Abbey Road studios.

standards. The resulting boost to record sales encouraged the record companies to re-record all the standard Classical and Romantic musical repertory and to explore rarities of Baroque and contemporary music not previously recorded.

A further excuse for re-recording familiar music was provided in 1957 by the introduction of stereophonic records. These put into practice the theories propounded more than 25 years earlier by the British engineer A. D. Blumlein. In essence, his ideas were to imitate the direction-finding mechanism of human binaural hearing (see *Ear and Hearing*, 6) by setting up a pair of left/right microphones. The twin signals remain in synchronism by being cut into a single record groove, but they maintain their discrete existence by being kept in separate electrical chains until they emerge from a pair of suitably spaced loudspeakers. The listener then hears the sounds of the individual musicians as if arranged in an arc between the loudspeakers. Given due care in the recording, and reasonable playback equipment, the sensation of listening to an actual performance takes on an added dimension compared with monophonic single-speaker reproduction.

At best, however, stereophonic reproduction leaves the listener sitting somewhat apart from the performance, as if the rear wall of his room had been dissolved away and the concert hall opened out just beyond it. Later experiments with 'surround sound' or 'quadraphony' have sought to re-create the sensation of sitting inside the concert hall, as if all four walls of the sitting-room had disappeared. Quadraphonic records were issued from about 1972 onwards, but the public were offered a number of competing and non-interchangeable systems simultaneously. Few people were therefore persuaded to buy the necessary four loudspeakers and associated decoding units and sales of four-channel discs were too small to justify their continuation.

4. *Magnetic Recording*. Edison had experimented with the magnetic reproduction of his mechanically indented recordings. However, the first practical demonstration of the feasibility of laying down a track of magnetic impressions and replaying these by electromagnetic conversion was given by the Danish engineer Valdemar Poulsen (1869-1942) in 1898. His Telegraphone somewhat resembled a cylinder phonograph but used 0.25 mm. steel piano-wire wrapped around a grooved brass cylinder. A single electromagnet tracked along the wire as its carriage was driven by an electric motor. During recording, the coil in the electromagnet carried the alternating currents produced by speech or music into a telephone microphone. The resulting fluctuations in magnetic field left a pattern of magnetization along the wire. Then,

to play back this signal, the electromagnet was lifted back to the start of the wire and connected to a telephone receiver. As the carriage moved, the electromagnet again tracked along the wire and the fields set up by the wire induced currents in the coil resembling those generated by the original sounds. For erasure, the wire was played through with the electromagnet simply connected to a battery, giving DC (direct current) and a state of uniform magnetization of the wire.

Though an original wire recording exists of Franz Josef I, the Emperor of Austria, praising the telegraphone at the World Exhibition in Vienna in 1898—proof of the permanence of magnetic recordings—it took until about 1912 to develop a reliable machine. The German Kurt Stille took up Poulsen's ideas and by 1928 produced improved wire devices, with finer wire to give longer playing time and DC bias which greatly improved the sound quality. Stille then described a steel-tape machine in 1930 and the film producer, Ludwig Blattner, went ahead with this system. The British Broadcasting Corporation acquired two of these Blattner-phones, which were highly suitable for repeat broadcasts beamed to different parts of the world several times during the 24 hours. They used steel tape 3 mm. wide and gave a playing time of 30 minutes.

A return to round wire took place during the 1939-45 war, when American companies produced numbers of small portable recorders for service use. Up to 60 minutes could be recorded on the 0.1 mm. stainless-steel wire running at 30″ per second, and quality was further improved by the introduction of high frequency AC bias and erase instead of DC.

However, the most important change in magnetic recording came with the development of coated tapes. The first attempt was by Fritz Pfleumer of Dresden around 1928 who coated soft iron powder in an organic binder on to tapes of paper or plastic film. By 1934, BASF (Badische Anilin und Soda Fabrik) were producing cellulose acetate base tapes coated with ferric oxide (Fe_2O_3). Within a year, AEG (Allgemeine Elektrizitäts Gesellschaft) had produced an advanced 'Magnetophon' recorder for the new tape and testimony to its qualities still exists in the recording of part of Mozart's E♭ Symphony performed by the London Philharmonic Orchestra under Sir Thomas Beecham at a concert in Germany in 1936.

These machines were further refined in Germany during the war, including the rediscovery of supersonic bias, and the post-war period saw magnetic tape-recording spreading throughout the world. Apart from numerous applications in industry and communications, tape soon replaced wire discs as the medium for master recording in the studios of both the record companies and the broadcasters. Long durations of uninterrupted recording were possible, there was no lengthy setting-up period as for waxes, and editing was a simple matter of cut and join.

When a sufficient number of home tape-recorders were in use, around 1954, the record companies began to issue pre-recorded tapes of selected items from their disc catalogues. However, though several formats were tried, including open-reels running at one of the popular speeds, $7\frac{1}{2}''$ or $3\frac{3}{4}''$ per second, and a variety of magazines or cartridges, sales were disappointingly small. Then in the late 1960s, a viable tape package came on to the market which was destined to compete with the gramophone record on almost equal terms. This was the Musicassette, and was based on a neat plastic box with the tape completely enclosed and anchored at each end to a pair of tiny spools or bobbins. The concept had been launched by Philips in a Compact Cassette portable recorder in 1963. In convenience and ease of operation it easily outstripped its competitors, the cassette being simply pushed into the machine without the need for laborious threading of the loose end of tape on to a second, empty reel.

An important reason for the inability of earlier tape formats to compete with the disc was their intrinsically higher cost of manufacture. The magnetic tape was basically more expensive than the small handful of vinyl needed for a disc, and, instead of a simple pressing operation lasting about 20 seconds, each duplicated tape had to be recorded along its whole length and given a tailpiece of non-magnetic leader tape. The Musicassette economized in raw tape by reducing the running speed to $1\frac{7}{8}''$ per second, cutting the tape width from the standard 6.35 mm. to only 3.81 mm., and recording four tracks across this narrow width — to give left and right stereo channels corresponding to sides one and two of the equivalent disc record. Manufacturing costs were also reduced by a high-speed duplicating procedure in which a specially prepared master tape was run at up to 64 times the normal speed, and the signals sent to 12 or more 'slave' recorders carrying large spools of cassette tape also running at high speed. This reduced the recording cycle for a complete cassette, all four tracks being recorded simultaneously, to less than 30 seconds, and was followed by an automated loading sequence to produce the final wrapped cassette.

Although the record companies made no special efforts to boost cassette sales — they did not, for instance, market any cassettes of performances not already available on disc — the medium flourished. Disc and cassette sales appeared to complement each other, rather than compete. Properly programmed cassettes were not restricted to the maximum of 30 minutes per side of discs, and so could give uninterrupted playing of the longer symphonies or opera acts. They were also convenient to use in cars and elsewhere, and easier to handle without damage. Discs, on the other hand, maintained their appeal to collectors of long-standing. The visible bands between movements or short items allowed immediate playing from a particular cue, and in any case the greater number of record players in use guaranteed higher numbers of disc sales compared with cassettes.

A worrying factor, from the record companies' point of view, was the illicit copying or pirating of records both by private individuals and commercially. Unlike a gramophone, which could only reproduce the music from discs, the cassette machine was also a recording device. It was tempting therefore for owners to borrow records, perhaps from a public library, and make illicit cassette copies. Blank tapes were comparatively inexpensive and could be erased and used over and over again. Unscrupulous traders even built up a business in supplying such pirated copies, and the record industry world-wide soon became engaged in a constant war against major purveyors of 'facsimile' or 'forged' recordings — both on disc and cassette — in which even the sleeves and labels were difficult to distinguish from the originals.

5. *Film Recording.* A desire to reproduce sounds in synchronism with moving pictures seems to have existed from the very beginning of cinematography. The name of Edison crops up yet again and, as early as 1889, we hear of him returning from a holiday in Europe to be greeted by a film of 12 seconds duration in which his English assistant William Kennedy Dickson could be dimly perceived raising his hat and saying: 'Good morning, Mr Edison. Glad to see you back. I hope you are satisfied with the Kineto-Phonograph.' This Edison research project relied on running a phonograph alongside first the camera and then the projector, with the operator somehow keeping the machines in step. This was to be the pattern for many years, with disc players coupled to projectors and elaborate cueing and speed correction facilities — and many occasions on which things got hopelessly out of step.

Plainly the way ahead was to record the sound-track on the film itself. Two methods of photographic sound recording had interested researchers from the beginning. In 'variable density' recording, the electric currents from the sound source were used to modulate an electric arc which shone through a slit on to the light-sensitive film. The second method, 'variable area' recording, depended on shining a constant light source on to a tiny mirror which was cemented on to a wire. When the sound signal current was passed through this wire, it would twist to and fro through an angle which varied with the strength of the current. The developed negative was opaque except where the light had exposed it, and the sound-track could be reproduced by passing the film between a light source and a photo-electric cell.

The 1930s were boom years for the film industry and saw the majority of the problems of synchronized sound-tracks being solved satisfactorily. There were, however, other problems that had to be tackled. For example, film cameras were bulky and noisy, so that the pictures came to be shot 'silent' or with only a rough guide sound-track. Later stages of laboriously showing the film and 'post-synchronizing' the actors' dialogue plus sound effects and music were necessary—adding greatly to the cost and time needed to make a feature film. Special filtering, to a frequency response graph known as the 'Academy Curve', was performed on the sound-tracks so that they would not sound 'boomy' when reproduced at higher volume in large cinemas.

This partly accounts for the indifferent sound quality when motion pictures are shown on television. But the change in speed, and consequently in musical pitch, is even more of a nuisance. Film systems are locked to a replay speed of 24 pictures or 'frames' per second. When shown on television, unfortunately, a speed of 25 frames per second is common in Europe (and 30 frames per second in the USA), so the action is speeded up and the pitch is raised slightly, unless special equipment is used at the television station.

There are technical limitations in optical recording, notably in respect of residual background noise, which can be overcome by recording magnetically. Therefore, as magnetic tape-recording advanced after the 1939–45 war, so it became practical to manufacture cinematograph film which carried a coating of magnetic material as one or more narrow tracks alongside the picture area. This brought advantages in terms of sound-film production and assembly, as well as in sound quality, and allowed as a bonus the preparation of stereophonic and other multi-track films. When reproduced in theatres having the necessary projection equipment and spaced loudspeaker arrays, these films gave a spectacular new dimension to sound in the cinema.

6. *Video and Digital Recording.* The recording of television programmes (see *Broadcasting*) was perfected by the Ampex Corporation of America in 1956. From the outset, video recording was a speedier and more flexible medium

than film. For example, the pictures taken by a film camera are captured on standard photographic film stock and overnight processing is necessary before trial prints or 'rushes' are available for viewing. By contrast, the signals from a television camera are already in the form of an electric current analogous with microphone signals. They can therefore be displayed on any number of monitor screens at the instant of shooting, and simultaneously recorded on a video recorder using ordinary magnetic tape. The producer therefore has an immediate check on his results, and editing can proceed as necessary, without the inevitable delays experienced in a film production.

On a domestic level, video recorders using cassettes of magnetic tape 25 or 12.5 mm. wide began to reach the market in 1972 and, despite a slow start due to the proliferation of models using different cassette shapes and running speeds, soon became a desirable acquisition for families already owning one or more colour TV sets. Mainly a home video recorder was purchased to allow later viewing of programmes transmitted while the owner was away or otherwise engaged. However, a small beginning was made in the marketing of pre-recorded video material including teach-yourself programmes and transcriptions of feature films.

The record companies conducted research into the viability of marketing a video equivalent of the sound-only gramophone record or musicassette. Costs of production would obviously be much higher, and artists' contracts would need revision to account for the longer and more arduous recording sessions. Another worrying question was the purely subjective one of what pictures should accompany the music? This aspect of music on television is discussed elsewhere (see *Broadcasting of Music*, 6) but is further complicated when considering the issue of video records, where repeated viewing is envisaged. It is generally acknowledged that, whereas a sound-only recording of, say, a Mozart symphony can be listened to over and over again with renewed and even increased enjoyment, the video equivalent soon loses its appeal. Perhaps because of greater retentiveness of optical impressions, it seems doubtful if large numbers of people could be persuaded to build up collections of relatively expensive video records, as they have done with gramophone records.

None the less, production plans are well advanced for music-with-pictures and the backroom technologists have not been idle. Aware that duplicating costs will always be high for a tape cassette medium, they have developed alternative video disc systems in which the disc can be pressed and packaged almost as easily and cheaply as an ordinary record. The combined video and sound signals are complex, of course, and need a recording medium capable of responding to frequencies up to several million cycles per second (Megahertz) compared with the mere 20,000 Hz required for sound only. Tape video systems get over the difficulty by running the tape past the magnetic heads at higher speeds, or using a spinning head system, or both. Video discs generally rotate at television-picture frame-speed (1,500 rpm in Europe, 1,800 rpm in the USA) and use either a mechanical or optical tracing system. The first mechanical system, demonstrated by Telefunken and Decca as early as 1966, used a thin flexible disc with 25 grooves in the space of a single LP groove. The signals were frequency modulated and hill-and-dale recorded. The pickup was a skid-shaped knife-edge which sensed the waveform as a change in pressure. Optical systems included that launched by Philips in 1978. This used a laser beam to trace a spiralling track of depressions or pits in the highly reflective aluminium layer on a vinyl disc. The reflected light spot activated a photodiode to produce an electrical signal which could be processed to reproduce colour pictures and sound on a standard TV set. With as many as six different video disc systems competing for public acceptance, alongside several video cassette formats, pre-recorded video programmes have not made much impression on the market so far.

There is, however, a good deal of interest in the application of video recording techniques to sound-only recording. It has been known for many years that most of the limitations of normal sound recording could be overcome if the signals were first of all converted into pulses or 'digits' as used in computers. In conventional recording, we inscribe a continuous pattern or wave-form which is an imitation or 'analogue' of the changing air-pressures in the original sound-waves. Unfortunately any discrepancies in the replay speed affect the musical pitch, and any graininess in the disc or tape material is reproduced as noise—as are scratches or particles of dust. At the same time, the recorded wavelengths at high sound frequencies are so tiny as to tax the capabilities of the stylus or tape head to trace them effectively.

Digital recording can side step these difficulties. As a first step, it samples the sound waveform at regular intervals—about 50,000 times per second—and compares the instantaneous amplitude with a set scale of values. Each amplitude sample has its value recorded as a series of pulses, using the so-called binary system of simple pulses and spaces. To replay a digital recording, the stream of pulses is again scanned and the original wave-form reconstructed with any desired degree of accuracy. A principal advantage of digital recording is that it ignores speed fluctuations on play-back and is almost totally protected against noise, interference, or degradation during storage or frequent playings. The individual pulses are all identical and recorded at the highest level that the medium will allow. The play-back system has only to identify the presence or absence of a pulse at each sampling point in time, not its level or shape. Therefore the pulses can be grossly interfered with during storage, and background noise can rise to many times the level that would be intolerable in an analogue system, with virtually no audible affect on the signal finally reproduced.

To provide a complete digital medium for music in the home means encapsulating the sounds in digital form from the studio right through to a domestic laser beam or other type of reproducer similar to the forms used for video (since a very wide frequency bandwidth is again needed). Such systems have been demonstrated successfully and were launched in Europe in March 1983. However, digital recording at the studios is already quite common. New digital tape recorders have largely replaced the conventional analogue ones for the preparation of master tapes. This gives an immediate benefit in eliminating tape noise and distortion at this important stage. Even when the traditional processes of transferring to an ordinary LP record are applied, overlaying the pristine qualities of the digital master tape with their own imperfections, the improved clarity and quiet background can still be detected. The record companies are thus building up stocks of digital masters against the day when home digital players spread to many households: they also find that they can edit these tapes and make any required number of identical copy masters for their agents in other countries.

7. *Recording and the Musician.* The attitude of the world of serious music to the earliest phonographs and gramophones was one of almost deafening lack of interest. Yet today musicians of all types must feel the influence of recording on every aspect of their lives, whether it be performing, composing, or even planning a career. The gradual metamorphosis of the gramophone from a mere toy or scientific curiosity to the powerful and ubiquitous music carrier which it is today may be outlined by mentioning just a few of the turning-points.

The first real boost came in March 1902 when the young impresario Fred Gaisberg (just at the start of a 50-year commitment to music recording) called on the Italian tenor Enrico Caruso (also, at 29, on the threshold of operatic stardom) and persuaded him to sing 10 songs and arias into a wax disc recorder set up in a Milan hotel room. The flat fee was reputedly an unprecedented £100 which Gaisberg is alleged to have paid over in defiance of head office instructions. His boldness was repaid in more senses than one. The recordings, for all their roughness, captured at least the flavour of Caruso's ringing tones and musicality. They demonstrated the pleasure-giving potentials of the gramophone to a wide public, who bought records and record players as never before. More important, they made other musicians interested in the medium, and their willingness to record was matched by a mushrooming of record companies anxious to build up substantial catalogues.

Another voice of terrific popular appeal was that of the soprano Adelina Patti. In 1905 she was finally persuaded to allow the Gramophone Company to install recording machinery in her Welsh castle Craig-y-Nos. The 14 records which these informal sessions produced caused a tremendous stir. They had a special 'Patti' label (to distinguish them from 'Melba' label records and others) and cost 21s. each. The primitive recording and reproducing machines somehow managed to contain the sounds of solo singing voices well enough, but were quite unable to capture the complexities of orchestral tones. Nevertheless, April 1909 saw the first large-scale orchestral work, Tchaikovsky's *Nutcracker Suite*, issued on four double-sided English Odeon discs. The following year, the Gramophone Company launched into the concerto repertory with part of the first movement of Grieg's Piano Concerto, played by Wilhelm Backhaus and the New Symphony Orchestra and issued on a pair of single-sided HMV discs. Arrangements for orchestral recording were curious indeed by today's standards, as this description of a 1919 session retold by Sir Adrian Boult confirms:

We trekked down to Hayes one morning and found ourselves in a studio, so small that it would hardly have held a full-size billiard table. Besides the essential chairs and music stands, there was an enormous gramophone horn, I should think three or four times the size of the one we know so well in the 'His Master's Voice' picture. Immediately in front of this sat the leader of the orchestra with his fiddle as nearly inside the mouth of the horn as he could hold it. He was surrounded by a few strings, but in those days, apparently, the low tones of the double-bass were an impossible proposition and the bass part was in the hands of a gentleman with a tuba who puffed away in the furthest corner of the studio with remarkable results. I was perched on a little seat high up on the wall near the great horn where I could certainly see everybody (including the cellos who were in rather lofty positions opposite). Other instruments were placed at various distances from the recording horn, and an original feature was a large looking-glass into which peered the four players of the orchestral horns

because, of course, the sound came out from the instruments behind them and therefore they turned their backs on us all.

But more comfortable, and less risky, recording conditions were on the way—made possible by the introduction of electrical recording and microphones sensitive enough to be placed at a reasonable distance from the performers. It also became possible to use the normal orchestral instrumentation and seating plan. The year 1925 saw feverish conversion to electrical recording by all the companies, and one disc in particular demonstrated the new medium's ability to deal both with large musical forces and the recording of live concerts. The 12″ Columbia disc featured 850 voices of the Associated Glee Clubs of America singing in the Metropolitan Opera House, New York. They sang 'John Peel' on one side of the disc and 'Adeste Fideles' on the other, in which they were joined by the 4,000-strong audience. The record was noticeably more brilliant and resonant than the previous acoustic recordings and made an enormous impact on gramophone sales. Conductors like Toscanini and Stokowski were won over to recording. By 1927, the latter was beginning his famous series of successful recordings with his Philadelphia Orchestra, helped by the acoustics of the Academy of Music Hall.

Though electrical recording freed musicians from the physical strait-jacket of acoustic horns and small, heavily curtained studios, several real restrictions remained, including the four minutes per side time-limit imposed by the 78

Francis Barraud at work on one of the many copies of his original painting 'His Master's Voice'.

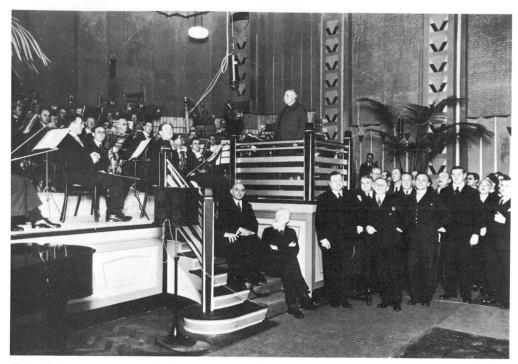

The opening ceremony (1931) at EMI's Abbey Road studios; among those present were Elgar (top centre), Bernard Shaw (bottom centre), and Landon Ronald (on Shaw's right).

rpm disc. At first the musicians had to chop up the score into recordable lengths. Later, the technicians became skilled in fading out one wax master as they lowered the cutting stylus on to another. If any slips or technical hitches occurred, it meant starting all over again on studio sessions and a missed recording at live concerts. The emergence of 33⅓ rpm Long Play records in 1948 (see above, 3) extended the length of continuous music to about 25 minutes. Recording equipment had also advanced in versatility to allow a certain speeding up of operations and limited copy-editing procedures to patch in retakes of fluffed passages.

Undreamed-of freedom for recording producers and musicians alike came a year or so later when tape recording of masters became the rule. Now any number of restarts or retakes could take place, with the touch of a button replacing the laborious setting-up and test cutting of wax discs which previously delayed such proceedings. On the other hand, if the performers wanted to record continuously for an hour or more, that was all right too. Pairs of tape machines could record non-stop. It became as easy to splice in a single re-recorded wrong note as a whole movement. One singer could interpolate difficult high notes in another's performance (as in a possibly apocryphal story connecting the names of Elisabeth Schwarzkopf and Kirsten Flagstad). With multi-track tapes,

one performer could record a duet—listening to the first recording on headphones while performing the second (one thinks of the famous Elisabeth Schumann duet from Humperdinck's *Hansel and Gretel*—actually a piece of pre-tape wizardry—and the Jascha Heifetz recording of Bach's Double Concerto). Geographical freedom allowed performances miles apart to be married together (as in the Saint-Saëns Symphony No. 3 with Daniel Barenboim conducting the Chicago Symphony Orchestra in Chicago and Gaston Litaize playing the important organ part in Chartres Cathedral). Time freedom was infinite, and perhaps most interestingly exemplified in a recording of George Gershwin's *Rhapsody in Blue* in which a modern jazz band conducted by Michael Tilson Thomas in 1977 was joined by the composer himself (though he had died 40 years earlier) performing on a piano-roll. It says much for the dedication of the recording producer that in fact the piano-roll had originally contained the composer's transcription of both the piano solo part and the orchestral accompaniment (an early example of a double recording!)—so that all the holes representing the orchestra had to be sealed with patches of paper before the reconstruction could begin.

As in all things, freedom implies responsibility and there is a clear danger of recording trickery being carried too far. In the transitory

The Concertgebouw Orchestra, Amsterdam, at a recording session, conducted by Bernard Haitink.

world of popular music it may not matter that on one record all the voices and instruments are contributed by a single multi-talented artist—while on another the sparse talents of a pop group are eked out by unnamed 'ghost' players or pieced together almost one note at a time. But in serious music we expect everything to be what it seems. It makes sense to retake a passage with an obvious wrong note, and edit this into place. After all, small blemishes which might go unnoticed at a live concert become distracting on repeated listening to a recording. Yet it remains important for the performance as a whole to constitute a single artistic interpretation, which a patchwork of short takes—with the 'difficult' bars perhaps played at half speed an octave lower, and then speeded up—could never be.

Many people assume that the aim of a recording of serious music should be to bring to the listener the same sounds as he would hear in the concert hall. Yet it is a mistake to suppose that this desirable result could be obtained, for example, by simply hanging a microphone over the best seat in the stalls. Home listening is a special sort of experience, and the best recordings are those which take this into account. To evoke the same conditions as we might ex-

perience in an ideal auditorium, it may be necessary to introduce subtle modifications to the resonance and perspectives so that they 'sound right' within the confines—and the inevitable constrictions—of a domestic room and its record-playing equipment.

Opera is perhaps a special case, and the producer John Culshaw was one of the first to demonstrate conclusively—for example, in his complete recording for Decca of Wagner's *Ring* cycle conducted by Sir Georg Solti—that it was possible to plan and direct a performance specifically for the gramophone. A brief extract from his notes in the booklet accompanying the 1959 *Das Rheingold* album may be contrasted with Sir Adrian Boult's description of a 1927 recording quoted earlier:

The idea was that of re-creating in the studio [actually the Sofiensaal in Vienna] an environment as close as possible to the theatre, with singers acting their parts in a production almost as elaborate as the real thing. Thus *Rheingold* demanded 25 piano rehearsals spread over a period of more than three weeks, during which the cast studied not only the conductor's musical requirements, but also the action through which we sought to impart theatrical reality to the performance. In planning this production for stereo sound we meticulously followed Wagner's original stage directions . . . just as Alberich can (and rarely gets) the

full amenities of the modern stage, we thought it legitimate to make full use of modern equipment in producing this work in an aural medium. On one effect only did we have to compromise: no Viennese bank would part with gold blocks for the piling of the hoard in Scene Four, so we had to make do with solid tin (under guard) . . . There would be little chance of assembling a cast of this calibre on the stage today, but there may be some point in trying to establish a standard on records, not only because the special conditions enable you to try for musical perfection, but because stereophonic recording is a medium in which great performances may be produced with dramatic impact.

There is perhaps a negative side to this striving for perfection and its encouragement of the 'star' system. When these star performances have been further enhanced in the production process, the result may surpass on a purely technical level that achievable at an ordinary performance. Fortunately for the continuing health of live music-making, however, even the best recordings cannot quite replace the special excitement of being present in the concert hall or opera house. To this extent, therefore, recording remains a servant to music and not a totally satisfactory substitute. There is plenty of evidence that listening to recordings increases rather than decreases the desire of music-lovers to participate in live music.   JOHN BORWICK

FURTHER READING
R. Gelatt: *The Fabulous Phonograph* (London, 1956); O. Read and W. Welch: *From Tin-Foil to Stereo* (New York, 1959); J. Culshaw: *Ring Resounding* (London, 1967); J. Borwick: *Sound Recording Practice* (London, 1976, 2nd edn 1980).

Redford, John (d London, 1547). English composer and organist. He was one of the vicars-choral at St Paul's Cathedral in the 1530s and 1540s. Nearly all his surviving works are for organ, many of them settings in two or three, sometimes four, parts using liturgical plain-songs as *cantus firmi*.   DENIS ARNOLD

Redoute (Fr.). See *Ridotto*, 2.

Redowa. A Czech dance in fairly quick triple time. It became popular in Paris around 1840, and resembles the *mazurka. See also *Rejdovák*.

Réduction (Fr.). 'Reduction', 'arrangement', e.g. *réduction pour le piano*, a piano arrangement.

Réduire (Fr.), **reduzieren** (Ger.). 'To reduce', 'to arrange'.

Reed. A vibrating device on which many different wind instruments depend. It is essentially a flexible tongue (or pair of tongues, face to face) made of metal, cane, wood, or plastic, fixed at one end and arranged so as to provide a narrow chink through which the blown air must flow. The high pressure on the blowing side will tend to bend the tongue inwards, but this would not result in vibration; briefly (to sum up the complexities of reed mechanics) it is the lower pressure beyond the reed that draws the tongue in the direction of the flow, reducing the chink, the flow, and the pressure difference. On this, the tongue springs back for the process to repeat and continue repeating so long as the flow is maintained. The term 'reed' may denote a tongue plus its holder, these together forming the chink; but with the clarinet, 'reed' denotes the tongue itself, the holder being here the 'mouthpiece'.

Broadly, reeds fall into the three main classes listed in Table 1. On the left are shown the types of chamber that seal the reed from the external air on the approach side of the flow ('mouth' = the cavity of the player's mouth); on the right are shown the types of tongue, plus its holder.

TABLE 1

1. FREE REED

(a) *Accordion, concertina, etc.*
Reed chamber   Tongue + frame

(b) *Oriental mouth-organs*
Gourd (etc.)   Tongue integral with frame

2. BEATING REED (single reed)

(a) *Organ, reed-horns*
'Boot', reed-cap   Tongue + 'shallot'

(b) *Reedpipes, bagpipes*
Mouth, reed-cap, bag   Tongue integral with holder

(c) *Clarinet, saxophone*
Mouth   Tongue ('reed') + mouthpiece

3. DOUBLE REED

(a) *Oboe, crumhorn, bagpipe*
Mouth, reed-cap, bag   Twin tongues ('blades') with or without 'staple'

(b) *Oriental shawm, etc.*
Mouth   As 3a, but differently constructed

With types 1 and 2a the pitch is normally that of the tongue itself (as if it were twanged with the finger) so that a separate reed is required for each note of the compass, as on the accordion and in organs; the holder may or may not communicate with a resonator, e.g. a pipe. With the others, one reed serves the entire compass in those cases where the notes are determined by a pipe with fingerholes (as with *woodwind instruments): the tongue complies with the pipe (a 'coupled system') so long as it is not asked to vibrate faster than its own high natural frequency.

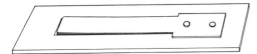

Fig. 1. *A harmonium reed.*

1. *Free Reed.* Each reed (Fig. 1) is riveted or clamped to a plate of stouter gauge, over a close-fitting slot in this; the reed is 'free' to move into the slot and back again. It vibrates when air is made to pass in the direction from the side on which the reed is attached. Air pressure can be applied on this side by blowing, or equally the air can be drawn through by suction from the other side. Should the direction of flow be reversed the reed will merely bend away from the slot without producing vibration, so normally a leather or plastic valve covers the opposite side of the slot to prevent wastage of wind in this way. Makers of free-reed instruments command considerable control over the tone-quality, according to the shape of the reed (e.g. parallel-sided or tapered) and its breadth, but particularly the shape and height of the 'tone-chamber' above the reed. Such considerations bear on the air-pressure fluctuations during the vibration, which lead to 'wave forms' containing harmonics of a regular series.

The oriental free reed (1*b* in the Table) differs in that it lies (at rest) flat in the plane of the frame. Air pressure initially deflects it from this plane and can be applied in either direction, after which the vibration is the same as with other free reeds but with a resonator pipe conjoined: see *Mouth-organ.*

2(*a*). *Beating Reed* (organ reed-stops etc.). Each metal tongue vibrates over a cavity formed by the metal 'shallot' (S, Fig. 2*a*), the edge of which the tongue overlaps and so cannot pass into the cavity. The shallot leads to a tone-controlling resonator, varying from a small perforated box (see *Regal*) to a full-sized pipe which emphasizes the harmonic overtones of an air-column. Each reed can be tuned from the outside by moving a stiff tuning-wire (T) which adjusts the vibrating length of the tongue.

This type of reed is also employed in one-note calling or signalling reed-horns, like the old bulb motor-horn and the horns (Fig. 2*b*) formerly sounded by European railway guards on departure from stations (see also *Hunting horn,* 1), and sometimes in *bagpipes (Czech and Northumbrian) as an alternative to 2*b* (below), with a tongue of brass or cane.

(*b*) *Idioglot Reed.* (See *Idiochord,* 2.) This is one of the oldest known reeds, with the tongue cut with a knife through the wall of a piece of cane, or of an elder shoot with the pith removed (Fig. 2*c*), one end being stopped up (often with

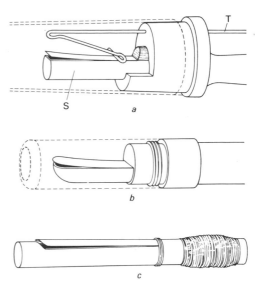

Fig. 2. (*a*) *Organ reed;* (*b*) *reed-horn, reed enclosed in cap (dotted);* (*c*) *idioglot reed, bagpipe drone. Wind direction from left to right.*

wax). The hollow tube of the piece serves in the manner of the shallot in the beating reed. The main use of the idioglot reed is in *bagpipes, *reedpipes, and also *hornpipes, in all of which it may serve for a one-note pipe (drone) or equally for a fingerhole pipe (chanter).

(*c*) *Single Reed.* This is a woodwind term corresponding to 'beating reed', which is primarily an organ-builder's expression. Single reeds for clarinets and saxophones (Fig. 3) are made from the tall cane (*arundo donax*) seen growing wild in warm climates and cultivated

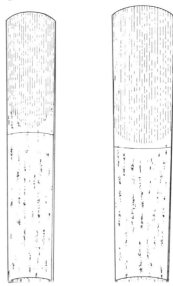

Fig. 3. *Left, clarinet; right, alto saxophone*

especially for reed-making in certain areas, notably the South of France around Fréjaus, and used likewise for the double reeds (see below, 3). Plastic reeds are also now available and have become popular for the saxophone. The cane single reeds are manufactured by first splitting a stick of cane into three or four slices. Each is pared down flat on the inner (concave) surface, and thinned on the outside for about half the length to form the vibrating part of the reed, thinnest at the tip. The reed is clamped, by a two-screw clip called a 'ligature', over the curving slot in the underside of the mouthpiece. Reeds are generally sold in boxes of 25 (though they can also be bought individually) graded in strength from 'soft' to 'hard', suiting players of different tone preferences or experience, the 'soft' demanding less strength in control from the mouth and also leading to a more 'reedy' kind of sound.

3. *Double Reed*. This has sometimes been termed by scientists a 'double beating reed', stressing a similarity in behaviour with the single reed described in 2c, above, with which for certain instruments it can be up to a point interchangeable (see *Bassoon*, 4b). Among the many double-reed instruments are, besides *oboe and bassoon, *crumhorn, *cornamuse, *kortholt, *racket, *shawm, *sarrusophone, and many of the *bagpipes.

The reed is made with a strip of cane of about twice the length of the finished reed. For the oboe reed the initial stick of cane (to be sliced into strips) may have an outside diameter of 11 mm. and for the bassoon 24 mm. The inner surface of the strip is gouged thin, by hand or on a gouging machine. The gouged strip is shaped to narrow towards the ends (Fig. 4a) and then, after soaking in water, folded right over at the mid-point, bark side outwards (Fig. 4b). The free ends are tightly bound to a short conical metal tube or 'staple' flattened to an oval at the smaller end (Fig. 4c; when an oboe reed is worn out, the staple is used for a new reed). The cane is then parted at the fold to separate the two blades of the double reed, which are then thinned down until the reed 'crows' correctly when blown in the mouth by itself (Fig. 4d). The oboe staple is mounted with cork (Fig. 4c, lower part) for airtight fit into the instrument. With a cor anglais reed the staple (just visible at the bottom in Fig. 4e) fits over the crook of the instrument. For a bassoon reed (Fig. 4f) the folded cane is bound with thread and wire over a steel mandrel, afterwards removed to leave a hollow rounded stem of cane for placing on to the crook.

Like single reeds, double reeds can also be made from synthetic materials (plastic) for many instruments, especially the crumhorn and

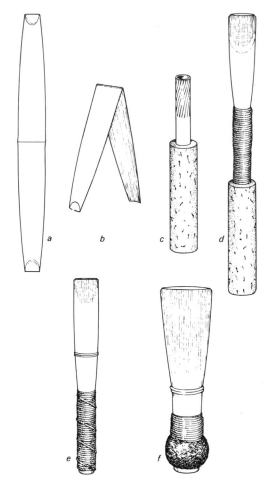

Fig. 4. (a)–(d) oboe reed; (e) cor anglais; (f) bassoon.

other Renaissance types. With skill it is possible to make a reed of practically anything (even a matchbox or yoghurt container), as bagpipers have long known.

In Antiquity (see *Aulos*) the double reed was made quite differently, by squashing flat one end of a fresh-cut material, very much as children all over Europe used to make one-note 'whit-horns' (or 'May horns') of green willow-bark coiled in a cone, secured by hawthorn spines, and given a willow-bark reed. The two faces of the flattened part, still joined along the sides, vibrate as a double reed. In Japan, the small cylindrical bamboo pipe (*hichiriki*; see *Japanese Music*, 3c), the only reed instrument of the ancient court music, employs a long, wide double reed of this type, as does the somewhat similar (though much deeper-sounding) pipe called in the east of Turkey *mey* and in the Caucasus *duduk*. The numerous shawm-like instruments played across Asia and North

Africa (see *Shawm*, 4) employ double reeds, similarly flattened out at the vibrating end, but made of material that is smaller in diameter, the narrow, tightly-bound stem placed on a metal tube resembling the oboe staple. And from Burma southwards reeds are found made from several superimposed strips of smoked palm leaf, bound to a staple so that two or more thicknesses of leaf lie on each side, acting as the blades of a double reed.

4. *The Grass Blade*. Among other vibrating devices sometimes classed as reeds is the grass blade, made to squeak when pressed between the thumbs and blown against. This could be said, however, to approach more nearly the tension-ruled behaviour of strings

ANTHONY BAINES

Reedpipe. 1. In literary tradition, any rustic pipe made of reed, or of several reeds, i.e. *panpipes (the 'mirlitons' of Tchaikovsky's *Casse-noisette* Suite).

2. In studies of folk and primitive instruments, the word has become a term to denote exclusively the pipes which are sounded by a reed (vibrating *reed), whether the pipe is made of reed or cane, cornstalk or straw, or wood, bone, quill, tinplate, etc. Shepherds or children almost everywhere in Europe and Asia make or have made such pipes, which give a strong humming sound. In Crete and elsewhere it is a winter occupation to make them in quantity for sale in gift shops through the summer. See also *Aulos*. ANTHONY BAINES

Reel. An ancient Scottish dance similar to Irish and Scandinavian dances and to the *strathspey, which is danced at a slower tempo. Couples dance face-to-face to music in 2/2, 2/4, or 6/8 time divided into clear eight-bar sections. A more exhilarating version is known as the Highland fling, while simplified versions came to English ballrooms at the beginning of the 19th century. PETER GAMMOND

Reformation. A radical change in religious thought, initiated during the early 16th century by Luther in Germany and by Zwingli and Calvin in Switzerland, which brought about a division of the Western Church and led to the growth of various forms of Protestantism. In addition to challenging many of the doctrines of the ancient faith, and seeking to break away from traditional church observances, the reformers held as a common aim the increased religious education of the people. To this end they encouraged the production of vernacular versions of the Bible (regarded as the sole foundation of true faith) and of new forms of public worship.

These changes had far-reaching consequences for church music. In countries (or separate areas within countries) where the teachings of Zwingli and Calvin were accepted, polyphony was entirely proscribed in church, since it was thought to be tainted by its traditional association with the Roman liturgy; the only music permitted was unaccompanied congregational singing of biblical texts, usually the psalms and canticles in metrical versions. The earliest Calvinist psalter (*Aucuns pseaumes et cantiques mis en chant*, Strasbourg, 1539) contained 19 metrical psalms and three canticles in new French translations, 13 of which were by Clément Marot and the remainder by Calvin; the music consisted of single-line melodies by Mathias Greiter and others. After Marot's death in 1544, his translation of the psalms was completed by Théodore de Bèze, and a finalized *Genevan Psalter*, with music, was published in 1562. At the same period there also appeared a large number of polyphonic settings of the psalms (often based on the familiar congregational melodies) by such composers as Bourgeois, Janequin, Le Jeune, and, particularly, Claude Goudimel. However, since polyphony was banned in Calvinist church worship, these settings were clearly intended solely for domestic use.

In Germany the influence of Luther ensured a more liberal approach towards the liturgy and its music. An Augustinian monk by training, and a traditionalist by nature, Luther sought to preserve as much as possible of the ceremonial of the ancient Church (including its plainchant and polyphony), prohibiting only those elements which were in direct conflict with his doctrinal reforms. Music he regarded as a 'beautiful and gracious gift of God', to be warmly encouraged, both in church and in the home, since it could 'drive away the devil and make people joyful'. In consequence, he not only provided amply for the congregation's needs through vernacular hymns (the so-called 'chorales') and with a German-texted Mass (the *Deutsche Messe und Ordnung Gottesdienst*, Wittenberg, 1526), but also readily supported the retention of an elaborate choral repertory, to both Latin and German texts, for the use of trained choirs in schools and churches. A prominent role in the development of Lutheran music was played by Johann Walter, who produced the first, and most famous, collection of polyphonic chorale settings; this *Geistliche Gesangbüchlein* (Wittenberg, 1524) passed through five editions up to 1551, and contained not only German hymn arrangements but also a wide range of Latin motets. An even more comprehensive contribution to the early Lutheran repertory was made by the composer and printer Georg Rhau, who between 1538 and 1545 published 16 volumes of

Latin and German liturgical settings, including Masses, Passions, *Magnificat* settings, motets, and responsories, by both Catholic and Protestant composers, all chosen for their suitability in Lutheran worship.

More protracted, but equally far-reaching in its effects, was the growth of the Reformation in England. Prompted initially by a new independence of thought characteristic of the period, particularly among the rising middle classes, the urge towards reform was eventually crystallized by the refusal of the Pope, in 1534, to sanction Henry VIII's divorce from Catharine of Aragon. After the resultant break with Rome, two events took place which profoundly affected the future of English church music: the dissolution of the monasteries, which deprived numerous church musicians of their livelihoods, and the adoption of the English Prayer Book (see *Common Prayer, Book of*), which confronted composers with the problem of providing music for entirely new forms of public worship in the vernacular. Following a period of unsettled conditions (not least those caused by the temporary reversion to Catholicism during the reign of Mary I, 1553–8), rapid progress was made towards an effective musical liturgy for the new Confession, involving English metrical psalms (from the publications of Sternhold and Hopkins) for the congregations, and a rich variety of polyphonic services and anthems for the use of trained cathedral and collegiate choirs. The earliest settings for the new Church, by such composers as Tye, Sheppard, Tallis, and William Mundy, were generally in a simple note-against-note style; however, these were followed, after 1565, by works of considerably greater elaboration, a notable innovation being the so-called 'verse' form, used in both anthems and services. During the Elizabethan and Jacobean periods major contributions to the Anglican repertory were made by Morley, Tomkins, Weelkes, and Gibbons. Byrd, the greatest English composer of the age, was a lifelong Catholic (possibly evading religious persecution through Elizabeth's special protection), but none the less produced works of superb quality for the Protestant as well as for the Roman rites.

BASIL SMALLMAN

FURTHER READING
Edmund H. Fellowes: *English Cathedral Music* (London, 1941, 5th edn rev. Jack Westrup, 1969); Paul Nettl: *Luther and Music* (Philadelphia, 1948); Peter Le Huray: *Music and the Reformation in England: 1549–1660* (London, 1967, 2nd edn 1978); Friedrich Blume: *Protestant Church Music: a History* (London, 1974).

Reformation Symphony. Mendelssohn's Symphony No. 5 in D major, Op. 107, composed in 1832. It was written for the tercen-tenary of the Augsburg Confession of 1530 but not performed until 1832 in Berlin. The first and last movements quote the 'Dresden Amen' and the Lutheran chorale *Ein' feste Burg*.

Refrapper (Fr.). 'To strike again'.

Regal. 1. This reed organ is the first known instrument to combine vibrating reeds with a keyboard—unless, as sometimes suggested, some organs of Antiquity did so. The regal dates from the mid 15th century and was made up to the end of the 17th as a continuo instrument transportable from room to room, or to different parts of a church.

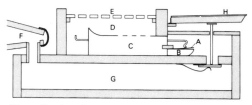

Fig. 1. Section of a regal.

About 30 original regals are known to exist. The reeds are brass tongues (Fig. 1, A), between about $\frac{1}{4}''$ and $2\frac{1}{2}''$ in length, each being wedged in place horizontally on top of a trough-like brass 'shallot' of matching size (B), as with organ reeds, and similarly tuned by a tuning-wire. As with the organ reed, the regal note is that of the vibrating tongue itself, though it is possible for three tongues to be cut to the same size and tuned by the wires to successive semitones. Each shallot leads straight into a small brass or tin resonator with air holes in the top (C). This stabilizes and mellows the sound without affecting the pitch. A long space (D) running parallel with the keyboard is covered by a grille (E) or by a sliding panel by which the volume may be controlled. Further from the player is a pair of horizontal bellows (F) worked by an assistant at the opposite end of the instrument (which either stands on legs or is placed on a table). The bellows feed air into a wind chest below the reeds (G). The keys (H) depress pallets located at the top of the wind chest near the front below the keyboard. The compass is from E to c''' or thereabouts. The sound is reedy, and can have tremendous effect, as in Monteverdi's *Orfeo* where it suddenly enters to accompany Charon's first recitative in Act 3.

Regals were also made to fold up, bellows and all, to look like a large book: the 'bible regal' is said to have been first made in Nuremberg near the end of the 16th century. 'Double regal' is a term not perfectly understood: it may denote a regal capable of sounding lower than the ordinary. Nor is the origin of the name 'regal' known.

2. 'Regal' has also been a term for an organ reed stop. ANTHONY BAINES

Regards sur l'enfant Jésus, Vingt ('20 Looks at the Child Jesus'). Work for piano solo by Messiaen, composed in 1944. The 20 pieces each have a title, for example 'Regard du Père', 'Regard des anges'.

Reger, (Johann Baptist Joseph) Max(imilian) (*b* Brand, Bavaria, 19 Mar. 1873; *d* Leipzig, 11 May 1916). German composer. His father, Joseph Reger, was a keen amateur musician who taught his son the organ and eagerly encouraged his early musical ability. Max's first formal teacher in Weiden, where he grew up, introduced him to the works of Bach and Beethoven, who were to be important influences; and by the age of 15 Reger had composed a number of his own instrumental works. In 1890 he was reckoned sufficiently talented to be sent to study with Hugo Riemann in Sondershausen and Wiesbaden, where he continued to compose chamber works, *Lieder*, and piano pieces. He later taught at the Wiesbaden Conservatory and did military service; at the same time he began to drink heavily.

In 1898 illness forced him to return home to Weiden, where he revived an earlier interest in the organ, composing for it several large-scale and elaborate works (e.g. chorale fantasias and the *Fantasia and Fugue on B-A-C-H* Op. 46) which both rely on and extend the traditions of Bach and Mendelssohn; these and other organ works were staunchly championed by the organist Karl Straube, a lifelong friend, who later was appointed to St Thomas's, Leipzig. Reger experienced a productive period in Munich from 1901, teaching, giving piano recitals, and composing; his works from this period include the Piano Quintet Op. 64, the piano *Variations and Fugue on a Theme of Bach* Op. 81, and the *Sinfonietta* Op. 90. But his bold ideas found little favour there with the 'New German School' of Liszt-Wagner supporters, and in 1907 he moved to Leipzig as professor of composition at the conservatory and university music director.

Reger made several concert tours throughout Europe which much enhanced his reputation. He received several honours, and in 1911 he was appointed music director of the court orchestra at Meiningen, where he conducted mainly Germanic symphonic works (Beethoven, Brahms, Bruckner) and increased his own output of orchestral music; it was here that he wrote the *Variations and Fugue on a Theme of Mozart* Op. 132. His duties were onerous; he grew ill in 1913 and, after the outbreak of war, moved in 1915 to a more restful situation at Jena. His sudden, early death was probably the result of a heart attack.

Reger's music has traditionally been much criticized and, apart from the organ works, is poorly appreciated outside his native Germany; but the stereotyped image of him as a drunkard and a turgid contrapuntist is now losing currency. His large, diverse *œuvre*, composed during a relatively short life, shows a sincerity and a consistency of approach: he attempted to combine contrapuntal disciplines (drawn from his familiarity with Bach) with a renewal of the Classical-Romantic traditions of Brahms and to strengthen that combination with his own bold harmonic and melodic ideas. With the help of a few close friends, he steadfastly promoted his works in the face of opposition from the staunch progressives and rampant Wagnerites in Germany at the turn of the century.

JUDITH NAGLEY

Reger (1913)

Reggae. A Jamaican popular song and dance form frequently associated with the Rastafarian religion (see under *West Indian Music*, 3). The lyrics of indigenous reggae songs are in Jamaican creole and are frequently concerned with social issues such as poverty and unemployment. Four basic musical elements combine to give reggae its characteristic style. The most obvious of these is a strong rhythmic emphasis on the second and fourth beats of the bar. This emphasis is accentuated in the playing of harmony instruments and by the occasional omission altogether of first or third beats. Complementary to this emphasis are the sophisticated rhythms of reggae's sung melodies, a result of the melodies' subservience to the complex accentuations of creole. Thirdly, the texture is dominated by the employment of a short, repeated tune in the bass, termed a 'riff'. A reggae band will contain five or more performers: vocalist, lead, rhythm, and bass guitarists, and percussionist. Larger bands will also contain backing vocal groups and additional instruments including conga drums, keyboards, saxophones, and trumpets.

The development of indigenous Jamaican reggae into a music of international repute was in no small measure due to the work of Bob Marley. Born in Kingston's Trenchtown area, Marley took a wider view of reggae than many of his Jamaican contemporaries and, using modern recording facilities, he succeeded in broadening the form's stylistic base without destroying its integrity. Famous Marley recordings include 'Duppy Conqueror' and 'No woman, no cry'. Bunny Wailer and Peter Tosh were at various times associated with Marley in his enterprise. The Third World Band is a potential successor to Bob Marley and the Wailers.

The history of the development of reggae dates back to the 1950s, when the proximity of Jamaica to the USA facilitated the importing of rhythm and blues records. The music of

Bob Marley

American urban Blacks proved of immense appeal in a country that was itself becoming increasingly urbanized. Of equal significance was the fact that rural musicians heard rhythm and blues in the urban setting of Kingston with ears attuned to the indigenous folk music of the island. This resulted in the creation of Jamaica's first amplified popular music, 'ska', early in the 1960s. In ska the riffs and raucous instrumentation of rhythm and blues were combined with the rhythms of 'mento' (see under *West Indian Music*), a national song and dance form which shares with the Trinidadian *calypso a bias towards social comment in its lyrics. Mento's banjo strum, which characteristically omitted the first beat of the bar, formed an important element in ska songs, the melodies of which, simple in the extreme, became a vehicle for lyrics in which mento's social comment was sharpened into protest. 'Rock steady', which succeeded ska in about 1965, was basically a slowed-down version of the latter. The slower speed gave opportunity for more elaborate vocal lines, while bass players were encouraged to support these with loud riffs. When reggae ultimately developed in Kingston in about 1969 it was essentially a combination of elements of rhythm and blues with the rhythms of mento, the lyrics of ska, and the speed and riffs of rock steady. Within a short time London became the second city of reggae with the arrival of records and musicians from Jamaica. Record companies were set up, reggae clubs opened, and new bands came into existence there. The London ska-revival of the late 1970s was a potent influence on British popular music as a whole, and today reggae is a flourishing aspect of Britain's musical life.

PEARLE CHRISTIAN, MICHAEL BURNETT

FURTHER READING
Stephen Davis and Peter Simon: *Reggae Bloodlines* (London, 1979); Sebastian Clarke: *Jah Music* (London, 1980).

Regina coeli laetare (Lat.). See *Antiphons of the Blessed Virgin Mary*.

Regis, Johannes (*b c*.1430; *d c*.1485). Flemish composer whose career was spent at Cambrai, Antwerp, and Soignies. Unlike his contemporaries Ockeghem and Busnois his output is dominated by motets, many of them large-scale festive works for five-part choir.   JOHN MILSOM

Regnart, Jacob (*b* ? Douai, *c*.1540; *d* Prague, 16 Oct. 1599). Netherlands composer. He was one of five brothers who all became musicians, and he spent most of his life in the service of the emperors Maximilian II and Rudolf II. From

1582 he was vice-*Kapellmeister* and then *Kapell-meister* to Archduke Ferdinand in Innsbruck, returning to Prague after Ferdinand's death to serve as vice-*Kapellmeister* under Philippe de Monte. He composed some charming songs in the style of the Italian *villanella*, and the three volumes published as *Teutsche Lieder* between 1576 and 1579 received several reprints, as well as being used in arrangements by other composers. DENIS ARNOLD

Reich, Steve [Stephen] (Michael) (*b* New York, 3 Oct. 1936). American composer. He studied philosophy at Cornell University (1953–7) and composition at the Juilliard School (1958–61) and Mills College, Oakland, California, with Berio and Milhaud (1962–3). More important, however, was his experience at the San Francisco Tape Music Center (1964–5) and his later acquaintance with the music of West Africa and Bali. From these sources he has created a style based on 'processes' of perpetual rhythmic transformation in a stable harmonic field. Since 1970 he has worked only with his own ensemble, Steve Reich and Musicians, in such works as *Drumming* for tuned percussion, voices, and piccolo (1971). PAUL GRIFFITHS

FURTHER READING
Steve Reich: *Writings about Music* (Halifax, Nova Scotia, and New York, 1974).

Reicha [Rejcha], **Antoine** [Antonín, Anton] (*b* Prague, 26 Feb. 1770; *d* Paris, 28 May 1836). Czech composer and theorist. Earliest instruction came from his uncle, the cellist and composer Josef Reicha (1752–95), with whom he is often confused. In 1785 he went to Bonn where he played the flute in the court orchestra and made friends with Beethoven and later Haydn. After a brief sojourn in Paris Reicha settled in Vienna where he renewed his friendships with Haydn and Beethoven. In 1808 Reicha returned to Paris where he remained for the rest of his life. While continuing to compose, he produced several treatises which were to mark him as a distinguished if controversial theorist. He was appointed professor of counterpoint and fugue at the Paris Conservatoire in 1818, and though his teaching was valued for precision and broad-mindedness by his pupils, he was often at loggerheads with his colleagues Cherubini and Fétis. His pupils included Liszt, Berlioz, and briefly but significantly César Franck. In 1829 Reicha became a French citizen and in 1831 was awarded the Légion d'Honneur. His preoccupation with contrapuntal experiment marked him as a genuine original. He also made interesting use of reminiscence motifs in his operas, and several of his orchestral and chamber works have thematic links between movements. Among his keyboard works the 36 Fugues (1803), dedicated to Haydn and widely known in his day, are notable for their experiments with tonality and irregular time-signatures. Reicha's idiomatic writing for wind distinguishes not only his numerous orchestral works but has ensured the popularity of his Wind Quintets. Although Reicha subjected most aspects of musical composition to theoretical scrutiny, his *Cours de composition musicale* (published 1816–18) followed by the *Traité de haute composition musicale* (1824–6) were most important in conditioning attitudes to composition and in fixing technical terms and processes in fugue and sonata composition. If they excited much contemporary criticism, his writings were sufficiently widely disseminated amongst 19th-century composers for Reicha to be of more than passing significance as a theorist. JAN SMACZNY

Reichardt, Johann Friedrich (*b* Königsberg, Prussia, now Kaliningrad, USSR, 25 Nov. 1752; *d* Giebichenstein, nr Halle, 27 Jan. 1814). German composer and writer. He was the son of a town musician and was an infant prodigy, playing violin, keyboard, and lute, and having a good singing voice. In 1771 he set out on the first of a series of tours that took him to Berlin, Leipzig, Dresden, and Prague and enabled him to meet such contemporary musicians as Franz Benda, J. A. Hiller, C. P. E. Bach, and J. A. P. Schulz. He was a friend of Goethe, who remarked on his 'Sansculottismus' or support of the French Revolution. An interesting writer on music, he was also a considerable composer of songs (he wrote about 1500), setting virtually all the lyrics of Goethe capable of musical treatment, and showing a fine understanding and respect for their mood and poetic structure. DENIS ARNOLD

Reiche, Johann Gottfried (*b* Weissenfels, 5 Feb. 1667; *d* Leipzig, 6 Oct. 1734). German composer and trumpeter. In 1700 he was engaged in Leipzig as a town musician. He became one of the foremost interpreters of Bach's trumpet parts. Twenty-four of his wind sonatas were published under the title *Neue Quatricinia* (Leipzig, 1696). WENDY THOMPSON

Reigen [reihen] (Ger.). 'Round dance', or just 'dance'. *Elfenreigen*, 'elf dance'; *Gnomenreigen*, 'gnome dance'.

Reincken, Johann Adam (*b* ? Wilshausen, Alsace, 27 Apr. 1623; *d* Hamburg, 24 Nov. 1722). Organist, possibly of Alsatian birth, who went to Hamburg to study with Heinrich Scheidemann and succeeded him at St Catherine's in 1663. His playing was so famous that Bach walked from Lüneburg to hear him. He wrote some virtuoso organ music as well as a set of sonatas in which the dance rhythms of the *sonata da camera* are used in a sequence of movements in the manner of the *sonata da chiesa*. DENIS ARNOLD

Reine, La ('The Queen'). Nickname of Haydn's Symphony No. 85 in B♭ major, probably composed in 1785. It is so called because, being the fourth of the Paris Symphonies, it was much admired by Marie Antoinette, 'La Reine de France'.

Reinecke, Carl (Heinrich Carsten) (*b* Altona, 23 June 1824; *d* Leipzig, 10 Mar. 1910). German composer. After early years as a concert pianist, in 1860 he became a teacher of piano and composition at the Leipzig Conservatory, and conductor of the famous Gewandhaus concerts, having earlier attracted the attention of Mendelssohn. One of the best-known exponents of the conservatory school of German composers, his pupils included Grieg, Svendsen, Sullivan, and Weingartner. He wrote some charming piano music and was a noted editor of the standard classics. DENIS ARNOLD

Reinhardt, Django (*b* Liberchies, 23 Jan. 1910; *d* Fontainebleau, 16 May 1953). Belgian jazz musician. The son of a gypsy violinist, he spent most of his early years in a caravan. He learned to play the violin, banjo, and guitar. A permanent injury to two of the fingers on his left hand in a caravan fire helped to shape his very individual guitar technique. He was soon a virtuoso player and his irregular association with various jazz groups in the early 1930s led to a strong grafting of the jazz idiom on to his inherent gypsy style. In 1934 he formed the famous Quintet of the Hot Club of France in association with the jazz violinist Stephane Grappelly. Their numerous recordings had a unique sound, a combination of driving guitar-based rhythms and the very individual improvisations of the two leaders. Grappelly went to England in 1939 and Reinhardt continued the Quintet with clarinettist Hubert Rostaing. He added the same drive and variety to various recordings with visiting American jazz musicians such as Dicky Wells and Bill Coleman in the last years of his life. In 1946 he had visited the USA to play with Duke Ellington and played in various New York clubs during 1947. His style was natural to the traditional guitar and experiments with amplified instruments were not successful. He remained an active musician until his death. PETER GAMMOND

Reizenstein, Franz (Theodor) (*b* Nuremberg, 7 June 1911; *d* London, 15 Oct. 1968). English composer of German birth. He studied with Hindemith in Berlin (1930–4) and with Vaughan Williams at the Royal College of Music (1934–6). Having settled in England he worked as a pianist and chamber musician. His smallish creative output consists of two sonatas for violin (1945, 1968) and one for viola (1967) and cello (1947) besides other chamber, orchestral, and vocal music, finely crafted in a style which departs from that of the later Hindemith. The same skill is shown in the comic pastiches he wrote for Hoffnung concerts, e.g. *Let's Fake an Opera* (1958). PAUL GRIFFITHS

Rejdovák. A Czech dance in triple time, a variant of the *redowa. It is followed by a rejdovačka, a dance in duple time similar to the *polka.

Rejoice in the Lord Alway. See '*Bell*' *Anthem*.

Réjouissance (Fr.). 'Rejoicing', 'merry-making'. Bach and Handel both used the word as the title of a lively movement (e.g. in Bach's Orchestral Suite No. 4).

Relâché (Fr.). 'Loosened', 'relaxed', for example with regard to the snare of a drum.

Related keys. In harmonic theory, keys seen in terms of their 'relationship' to the tonic. For example, in C major the closest related keys are the dominant major (G), the mediant minor (E), the subdominant major (F), the supertonic minor (D), and the relative minor (A). The first four of these keys have a difference in key signature from C major of only one sharp or flat, and the last has the same key signature as C major. See also *Circle of fifths*; *Modulation*.

Relative major, Relative minor. See *Key signature*.

Relish. English name for an ornament used in instrumental music of the 17th and early 18th centuries. A single relish (usually indicated thus: ∴) was simply a short *trill with a turn, but a double relish was more complex, consisting usually of a trill upon each of two successive notes, closing with a turn and an appoggiatura; it was indicated by a cluster of dots (e.g. ∴) or by two such clusters separated by two diagonal strokes (⟍), e.g.:

Remettre (Fr.). 'To put back'; *remettez*, in French organ music an indication that some stop which has been temporarily out of action should be replaced.

Renaissance

1. Introduction
2. The Spirit of the Age
3. Greek Theory and Modern Music
4. Conclusion

1. *Introduction*. In music, 'Renaissance' is nowadays used to refer to the 15th and 16th centuries. In general, however, the term denotes a movement of cultural and social attitudes which began in Italy *c*.1300 (some would date it earlier, others later) and spread to the rest of Europe during the next three centuries in varying degrees of strength. Some intellectuals were aware of such changes in attitude, especially with regard to the visual arts (Boccaccio in the *Decameron*, *c*.1350, could say that Giotto had revived a long-forgotten art), but it is only in retrospect that it becomes clear how greatly society and artistic creation were altered during this period.

'Renaissance' means literally 're-birth'— referring to the revival of interest in the pre-Christian world of the Ancient Greeks and Romans. The intervening years, or 'Middle Ages', had been concerned with establishing the authority of the Christian Church. The principal teachers and writers had been mainly interested in theology, and most of the long-established institutions were church-orientated—religious orders, confraternities, dioceses and parishes, the papacy, and the Holy Roman Empire. With the rediscovery of Ancient Greek literature and philosophy, however, secular thinking was encouraged: the individual, rather than the organization, was considered important; scientific experiment inspired more faith than did statements *ex cathedra*; ascertainable facts about the present world were more respected than were speculations about the world to come. Man's behaviour, and how it could be manipulated, became a central interest of those in positions of power (as Machiavelli's *Il principio* of 1513 reveals), while the concept of a lady and gentleman became more than purely a matter of birth, as the popularity of such 'courtesy' books as Castiglione's *Il cortegiano* (written 1508—published 1528) shows. Above all, the Greek love of and belief in the importance of the arts infected writers and influenced those members of the upper and middle classes with enough leisure to imitate the Ancients.

The results of the admiration of the Greeks were inevitably apparent in sculpture, in such works as Donatello's *David* (which stood originally in the courtyard of the Medici palace in Florence). In painting, a new realism reflects the interest in the human condition and replaces the mainly symbolic art of the Middle Ages. It is more difficult to see how the Renaissance can be said to have affected music, simply because no one had any firm knowledge of Ancient Greek music, and therefore no direct imitation could be attempted. Nevertheless, the word 'Renaissance' can be applied to music, because (*a*) the 'spirit of the age' undoubtedly had its effect; and (*b*) what the Greeks wrote about music (as distinct from Greek music itself) was studied in detail, and various ways of applying Greek theory to modern music were tried.

2. *The Spirit of the Age*. The most obvious musical manifestation of the spirit of the Renaissance was music's popularity. Rulers who would hitherto have had little interest in music established their own *cappella*—a 'chapel' which might comprise anything from one or two musicians to a considerable body of singers and players (the d'Este family in Ferrara had a *cappella* of at least ten singers in 1450, and the number was doubled by 1500). Some of its members would teach the children and ladies of the household, and among the nobility who could play and sing (and sometimes compose) were several members of the English royal family, notably Henry VIII and Elizabeth I, and, among the Italians, Guglielmo Gonzaga and Gesualdo, Prince of Venosa. The musical education of women led to ensembles which included female voices, and these became exceedingly skilled in the latter half of the 16th century; the Concerto delle Donne at Ferrara—

a group of three virtuoso women singers, one of whom was Tasso's mistress Tarquinia Molza—was especially famous.

This broadening of the audience made music publishing a profitable activity, and after 1500 the firms of Petrucci, Gardano, Attaingnant, and others produced editions of madrigals and *chansons* which sometimes ran from 500 to 2000 copies (and there was frequent reprinting of the most popular volumes). Noble houses also collected musical instruments, which were valued not just for their usefulness but also for their beauty. There was probably a greater variety of instruments being made in the late 15th and early 16th centuries than ever before, with recorders, transverse flutes, crumhorns, cornetts, shawms, bassoons, trombones, viols, and violins all being produced in various sizes, while organ building and the making of harpsichords, virginals, spinets, and clavichords prospered.

Church music also flourished, as can be seen from the large size of Roman choirs: the papal *cappella* under Sixtus IV (1471–84) had 20 singers, and a chapel (the Sistine Chapel) was built for its use; music at St Peter's was strengthened during the papacy of Julius II, by the establishment of a *cappella* and school (the Cappella Giulia); the basilica of St John Lateran acquired a *cappella* in 1535; and at about the same time so did S. Maria Maggiore. St Mark's in Venice followed the Roman example in 1527, when Willaert was brought in to organize the *cappella*. Music in the cathedrals of smaller cities is less well documented, but it is clear from the number of *maestri di cappelle* who published Masses and motets that during the 16th century there were choirs capable of singing polyphony in many of the larger churches.

If this adds up to a picture of exciting musical activity, it must be said that it had very little to do with a rebirth of Greek music. Nevertheless, from *c*.1540 our second application of 'Renaissance' becomes valid.

3. *Greek Theory and Modern Music*. In fact, the theorist Tinctoris was discussing Plato's writings on music as early as the 1470s. By 1500 Plato's works and the *Poetics* of Aristotle were generally available in Ficino's Latin translation, and by 1518 the Milanese theorist Franchinus Gaffurius (1451–1522) had studied the views of Ptolemy on acoustics. By the 1580s the whole corpus of Greek writing had been consulted by the most influential of all 16th-century theorists, Gioseffo Zarlino (1517–90). The fact that struck virtually all the readers of such literature was that music, for the Greeks, had the power to move man's spirit profoundly, and to affect his behaviour. David's cure of Saul's madness, the

arousal (and calming) of Alexander the Great's martial instincts by music, the magic power of Orpheus—all were constantly cited by 16th-century writers, with the equally constant question: 'Why could not modern music do the same?'

The attempts at an answer to this question were many and varied. Writers did not agree on a general solution, but their attempts to resolve the matter resulted in some interesting experiments.

The 1540s and 1550s saw many attempts at re-creating something like the sound of Greek music. The theorist Heinrich Glarean (1488–1563) tried to modify the Medieval system of modes according to the Greek scale system (see *Mode*, 2). More radical was Nicola Vicentino's (1511–*c*.1576) attempt to classify the Greek scales not only by reference to the modes, but also, and in more detail, by examining the different patterns of dividing the *tetrachord (roughly, a group of notes spanning a perfect fourth) into diatonic, chromatic, and enharmonic types; despite their origins in monophony, Vicentino proposed to apply them (slightly modified) to polyphony. To help him in this, he made a keyboard instrument which he called an arcicembalo, with additional keys to allow for the resulting microtones. As an acoustic experiment it failed, but many composers were interested in some of the strange new chord progressions made possible, and a crop of madrigals using chromatic harmonies appeared in the 1550s (see *Madrigal*, 3).

More fruitful than these acoustic explorations were the discussions about the relationship of words and music. It was generally agreed that the Greeks combined speech and music to create a more potent force than either was capable of alone. From about the 1530s this was interpreted to mean that music should match the words both in metre and in feeling. Zarlino, in his *Istituzione armoniche* (1558), expresses this view: 'In so far as he can, [the composer] must take care to accompany each word in such a way that, if it denotes harshness, hardness, cruelty, bitterness, and other things of this sort, the harmony will be similar, that is somewhat hard and harsh, but so that it does not offend. In the same way, if any word expresses complaint, grief, affliction, sighs, tears, and other things of this sort, the harmony will be full of sadness.'

This attitude was taken by many madrigal composers, and it had one significant effect. By paying attention musically to single words or phrases, contrasts of emotion could be closely juxtaposed, and music began to mirror the fluctuation of human feelings, rather than placing the emphasis on a thematic unity. Strophic forms—whereby different words are sung to music which is repeated for each verse or 'strophe'—became unfashionable for serious music, and were relegated to light genres, such as the *canzonetta* or the *villanella*. By the end of the 16th century, it was considered that no purely musical rules relating to either harmony or melody should stand in the way of the expression of the words. Monteverdi's formulation of a 'second practice' (see *Prima prattica, seconda prattica*), in which 'the words [are] the mistress of the harmony', is the essence of late Renaissance thinking in this respect.

Nevertheless, this means of expressing the words (or word-painting, as it is often called) was considered by some theorists of the 1570s and 1580s to be neither authentically Greek nor capable of re-creating their marvellous effects. The view of this group was that the words must be totally audible, as well as 'expressed'—something impossible in all but completely homophonic polyphony. The view had been mooted in a less extreme form as early as the 1520s (Castiglione recommended 'singing to the lute . . . for that gives such life and efficiency to the words'), and resulted in a tendency for musical textures to become simpler and more homophonic; in sacred music this was especially the case after the *Council of Trent had expressed its disapproval of verbal obscurity in 1562. But from the 1570s various experiments were made not only to make the words easily heard by using lutes, harpsichords, or other plucked strings as a light accompaniment to the voices, but also by developing a type of melody which used the rhythms and natural inflexions of speech—in other words, recitative. From this sprang the ultimate attempt at re-creating a Greek art form, and the attempt was to lead to the beginnings of *opera.

4. *Conclusion.* Of course, opera was really nothing like Greek drama, either in attitude or in technique. The Renaissance was a birth of new ideas, not a rebirth of old ones. Neither was it a universal phenomenon. It was largely an Italian movement, taken up by the leisured classes of the northern courts. It affected that part of Germany which remained Roman Catholic in religion—notably Bavaria, where the court had a *Hofkapelle* organized along Italian lines, with Lassus, a composer fully *au fait* with Renaissance thinking, as its *Kapellmeister*. But the important German vocal genres were little affected by humanist thought (though Hofhaimer and Senfl experimented with the metres of classical verse), and Medieval monophony was continued in the guilds of the *Meistersinger*. German music is therefore said to have gone straight from the Gothic (i.e. Medieval) to the Baroque.

France developed musically on lines akin to those of Italy only in the 16th century. It housed the first very active music printer outside Venice, Attaingnant, who from 1528 published a repertory of *chansons*, for what must have been a bourgeois audience, and church music. An individual working out of Renaissance ideas was developed in Baïf's attempt to revive Greek metrical accentuation, of which the musical result was *musique mesurée à l'antique*. This was no more successful in its aim than Italian interpretations of Greek theory had been. Nevertheless, the discussions held by his Académie de Poésie et de Musique helped to arouse interest in music at the court of Charles IX.

England was even later in coming to terms with Renaissance ideas. The Chapel Royal included some Italian musicians, some monarchs played instruments, and English courtesy books echoed Castiglione's precepts, but Henry VIII's break with Rome in the 1520s and 1530s virtually cut off England from Italian humanistic ideas. The finest English music of the early 16th century is for instruments, notably for viol consort and for keyboard. Little was known of either madrigal or *chanson* until the last quarter of the 16th century, when the Renaissance flowered in an astonishing way; a vogue for Italianate music swamped English musical life and madrigals and church music in which words and music were combined according to Zarlino's ideas were composed by native composers, as well as being imported 'transalpina' (see *Madrigal*, 4). Music printing flourished to cope with this vogue, and a bourgeois audience was clearly created, but the fashion had not put down deep roots and had disappeared by *c.*1625.

The Renaissance was the classic case of setting out for India and finding America. Greek music was never revived, but the paths along which the search was conducted proved equally as rewarding. There were two great achievements: the musicians of the time widened the audience for music, throwing it open to amateurs, who performed or listened; and they made music the servant of human psychology, replacing organized skill with the ability to express feeling. Music has never been the same again.

DENIS ARNOLD

FURTHER READING
Gustav Reese: *Music in the Renaissance* (New York, 1954, rev. edn 1959); Dom Anselm Hughes, Gerald Abraham, eds: *Ars Nova and the Renaissance: 1300–1540*, The New Oxford History of Music, iii (London, 1960); G. Abraham, ed.: *The Age of Humanism: 1540–1630*, The New Oxford History of Music, iv (London, 1968); Oliver Strunk: *The Renaissance*, Source Readings in Music History, iii (London, 1981).

Renard (*Bayka.* 'The Fox'). Burlesque in song and dance in one act by Stravinsky to his own libretto after Russian folk-tales. It was first performed in Paris in 1922.

Renversement (Fr.). 'Inversion' (of intervals, chords, subjects etc.).

Rè pastore, Il ('The Shepherd King'). *Dramma per musica* in two acts by Mozart to a libretto after Metastasio. It was first performed in Salzburg in 1775. The libretto was also used by Gluck and several other composers.

Repeat. The sign (:||) which appears at the end of a piece or section of music to indicate a return to the opening. If there is a reversed sign (||:) at the beginning of a section of music, the repeat sign at the end indicates a return to that sign only, not to the beginning of the piece. See also *Da capo*.

Répétiteur (Fr.), **repetitore** (It.), **Repetitor** (Ger.). Chorus-master of an opera house: one who coaches the singers. Répétiteur is the common English usage.

Replica (It.). 'Repeat'.

Reprendre (Fr.). 'To take up again' (e.g. an instrument which has been temporarily laid aside).

Reprise (Fr.). 'Repeat'. Return to a first section of music after an intervening and contrasting section, or a short refrain at the end of a movement which is intended to be repeated.

Reproaches. See *Improperia*.

Requiem Mass (Fr.: *Messe des morts*; Ger.: *Totenmesse*; It.: *Messa per i defunti*; Lat.: *Missa pro defunctis*). The Mass for the Dead, which begins with the Introit 'Requiem aeternam dona eis Domine' ('Give them eternal rest, O Lord'). The text is basically the same as that for the normal Latin *Mass, but with the more joyful parts (such as the Alleluia, which is replaced by the Tract) and the Credo omitted, and the long 13th-century sequence 'Dies irae' ('Day of wrath', attributed to Thomas of Celano) interpolated. In describing the musical settings of the normal Mass it was mentioned that certain parts were rarely set to music, because they vary their texts from day to day (i.e. the Proper of the Mass); in the Requiem Mass these passages are constant, and consequently were set (the opening Introit, which gives the Mass its name, is an example). Certain small changes occur in the text of some sections—for example, in the Agnus Dei the words 'Dona eis requiem' ('Give them rest') replace 'Miserere nobis' ('Have mercy upon us').

The traditional plainchant version of the Requiem Mass is very beautiful, and contrasts strangely with some of the dramatic, not to say operatic, settings of the 19th century. Although individual movements were set to polyphony before the 15th century, the first mention of a more or less complete setting (it is extremely rare for all the items to be included) comes in Dufay's will, where he requests that his own setting should be given the day after his funeral. Unfortunately, that setting is now lost, and the earliest known to us is Ockeghem's, from the late 15th century. Stylistically, settings of the Requiem Mass differed little from those of the normal Mass, the most important change being one of attitude. The more adventurous approach of 17th-century composers is exemplified in their settings of the 'Dies irae', to suitably dramatic music, where in the 16th century the original plainchant was nearly always retained. The 17th century also saw a considerable increase in the popularity of the Requiem Mass, the number known to us running into hundreds, whereas before *c.*1600 we know of under 50.

Of Requiem Masses setting the original liturgical texts the best-known before the 19th century are probably Palestrina's (printed 1591), Victoria's second (1605), Jommelli's (1756), and Mozart's (completed after his death by Süssmayr and with some additions by Eybler). In the 19th century two stand out for their highly dramatic treatment: Berlioz's (*Grande messe des morts*; 1837) and Verdi's (1874), which alters the order of the liturgical texts. Also notable are the settings by Bruckner (an early work; 1849), Saint-Saëns (1878), Fauré (1887-8), and Dvořák (1890). Brahms's *German Requiem* of 1868 took texts from the Lutheran Bible. Other Requiem Masses not intended for liturgical performance include Britten's *War Requiem* (written for the consecration of the new Coventry Cathedral in 1961, interpolating texts by Wilfred Owen deploring the violence of war) and Tavener's *Celtic Requiem* (a work for the stage in which children's games are linked to the idea of death; 1972).

Liturgically the Requiem Mass has its place at funerals and memorial services and on All Souls' Day (2 November), when it is celebrated in memory of the faithful departed.

Rescue Opera. The name given to an opera in which an essential part of the plot turns on the rescue of the hero or heroine from prison or some other threatening situation. Examples are to be found at various times in the 18th century, but it developed into a recognizable genre with the French Revolution (1789) and the closer involvement of opera with real-life situations, often highly dramatic. The first Revolutionary rescue opera was Berton's *Les rigueurs du cloître* (1790), concerning the repression of monasticism. Dalayrac's *Camille* (1791) involves the rescue of a girl from a haunted ruined castle; he also wrote *Léhéman, ou La tour de Neustadt* (1801). In Le Sueur's *La caverne* (1793) the heroine is held prisoner by brigands. Cherubini's *Les deux journées* (1800, to a libretto by Bouilly greatly prized by Beethoven) is set in the time of the Thirty Years War but has contemporary allusions in its theme of the rescue of innocent aristocrats from arrest. Bouilly's libretto *Léonore* (1798) concerns the rescue of the hero more exclusively in its first setting by Gaveaux than in Beethoven's *Fidelio* (1805), in which the genre is raised to the level of the ideal of freedom.   JOHN WARRACK

Reservata. See *Musica reservata*.

Resonance. See *Acoustics*, 7.

Resonanzsaiten (Ger.). Sympathetic strings.

Resonator. Any acoustical chamber, such as the hollow body of a stringed instrument, which serves to reinforce sounds by resonance.

Respighi, Ottorino (*b* Bologna, 9 July 1879; *d* Rome, 18 Apr. 1936). Italian composer. In 1891 he entered the Liceo Musicale, Bologna, to learn the violin, and went on to study composition there in 1898 with Luigi Torchi and later with Giuseppe Martucci. In 1900 and 1902 he visited Russia where he was taught by Rimsky-Korsakov, and in 1908–9 he attended Bruch's composition classes in Berlin. He played both the violin and viola and was for five years (1903–8) a member of Mugellini's quintet in Bologna. He was appointed professor of composition at the Accademia di S. Cecilia, Rome, in 1913 and director there in 1924, but he resigned the directorship in 1926 so that he could spend more time composing, teaching, accompanying his wife, the singer and composer Elsa Olivieri-Sangiacomo (*b* Rome, 24 Mar. 1894), and conducting his own works.

Respighi's earliest works were chamber and vocal—songs with piano or orchestra and a number of operas, including the highly successful marionette opera *La bella dormente nel bosco*. But it is for his orchestral music that he is best known, notably the descriptive suites *Fontane di Roma* (1914–16) and *Pini di Roma* (1923–4), with their picturesque, sparkling orchestration. In middle age he took a great interest in early music, more from the point of view of the arranger than of the scholar. His symphonic poem *Vetrate di chiesa* (1925) uses fragments of Gregorian chant, and several other works have titles with archaic references (e.g. the *Concerto gregoriano* for violin and orchestra, 1921). His most enduringly popular works are his arrange-

ments of music by Baroque and early Classical composers, such as the suite *Gli uccelli* ('The Birds', 1927), based on bird pieces by Rameau and others; and the ballet *La boutique fantasque* that he arranged for Diaghilev in 1919 from pieces by Rossini still retains its appeal. In his later years he returned to opera, but he never achieved more than ephemeral success in the field of dramatic music.   JUDITH NAGLEY

Respond (Lat.: *responsa*). 1. Alternative name for *responsory or *response. 2. More specifically, the section sung by the choir or congregation in responsorial chant (see *Responsory*). The responds, alternating with the verse or verses, are usually marked R or R̷.

Response. In Christian worship, the replies of the congregation or choir to the *versicles. The traditional Anglican responses used the original plainchant of the Roman Catholic Church, adapted to English words by Merbecke in the *Booke of Common Praier Noted* in 1550. In Elizabethan times various composers made choral settings of the responses, often taking Merbecke's plainchant adaptations as a *cantus firmus* in the tenor part. The best known of these settings are those by Byrd, Morley, and Tomkins, and two settings of *Preces and Responses* by Tallis. These are usually known as festal responses, ferial responses keeping the chant in the treble and being harmonized in a simple fashion.

Responsorial psalmody. See *Psalmody*.

Responsory (Lat.: *responsorium*). Type of liturgical chant, consisting in the responsories of the Roman Catholic Mass (now the Gradual and the Alleluia, but originally also the Offertory) of alternating *respond and *verse, and with the Lesser Doxology added in the great responsories (Lat.: *responsoria prolixa*) and lesser responsories (Lat.: *responsoria brevia*), given respectively at Matins and in the daytime Hours.

The verses of the responsory chants were originally sung by a cantor, with the congregation opening the responsory and replying to each verse with a respond, such as 'Alleluia' or 'Amen'. However, in Gregorian repertory the recitations for the verses became more and more elaborate (for an example of a highly melismatic Offertory verse, see *Plainchant*, 6), while the responds, once sung by the congregation, were instead sung by a trained choir, with the result that their music also became more sophisticated. To counter the inevitable increase in performing time, verses were gradually shed, in some cases only one remaining, and the repeat or repeats of the respond abbreviated. An addition to the Office responsories, however, was the Lesser Doxology, which took the place of a final verse.

Polyphonic settings of the responsories maintained the principle of alternation, until the 16th century setting to polyphony only the initial statement of the respond and the verses, but later in that century reversing the polyphonic and plainchant sections, so that only repeats of the respond were set to music. The latter tradition was developed especially in England, for example in Sheppard's setting of the Easter responsory for Matins, *Dum transisset Sabbatum*.

Rest. In musical notation, a sign indicating a momentary absence of sound. Every standard note value has a corresponding rest which, like the note itself, may be lengthened in value by the addition of a *dot or dots. Ex. 1 shows the common forms of rest.

Ex. 1

A whole bar's silence in any time signature is traditionally indicated by a semibreve rest (Ex. 1*b*). In individual instrumental parts two bars' rest may occasionally be indicated by a breve rest with a figure '2' above it (Ex. 2*a*), but in general more extensive periods of silence are normally represented by a horizontal line with a figure above it showing the number of bars' rest (Ex. 2*b*).

Ex. 2

See also *Notation*, Fig. 8; *General pause*; *Pause*; *Tacet*.

Restez (Fr.). 'Remain', i.e. linger on a note before leaving it, or (in string playing) play a particular passage in the same *position.

'Resurrection' Symphony. Mahler's Symphony No.2 in C minor, composed between 1888 and 1894. It is so called because the finale is a setting for soprano and alto soloists, chorus, and orchestra of the 'Resurrection' (*Aufersteh'n*) chorale by Klopstock (1724–1803).

Retardando (It.). The same as *ritardando*.

Retardation. The same as a *suspension, but resolved by rising a degree.

Retenant, retenu (Fr.). 'Holding back', 'held back', in the sense of slowing down, but immediately, like *ritenuto*, rather than gradually, like *rallentando*.

Retirada (It.). In 17th-century ballets and suites, a closing movement.

Retreat, Beating the. See *Military band and Corps of drums*, 4.

Retrograde [also *cancrizans* (Lat.), *Krebsgang* (Ger.), 'crablike' or 'crab motion']. The backwards version of a melody or, in *serial music, a series (i.e. the form obtained by reading the original from right to left). Since serial music allows any note in the series to be placed at any octave level, the retrograde form of a serial melody need not give rise to a reversal of melodic contour.

Retrograde canon. See *Canon*.

Retrograde inversion. A version of a melody or series that is both inverted and reversed (see *Inversion*, 3; *Retrograde*).

Reubke, Julius (*b* Hausniendorf, nr Quedlimburg, 23 Mar. 1834; *d* Pillnitz, 3 June 1858). German organist and composer. The son of an organ builder, he studied with Liszt. His few compositions, all published after his early death, include an Organ Sonata on the 94th Psalm which is one of the great Romantic works for the instrument. PAUL GRIFFITHS

Réunis (Fr.). 1. 'United', 'reunited' (e.g. in string playing, after *divisés*, 'divided'). 2. In organ music, 'coupled'. 3. In 18th-century French music, the term *les goûts réunis* ('reunion of tastes') was used to describe an ideal kind of music towards which composers should strive — the union of the best elements of French and Italian music, as opposed to the specifically French style adopted by the followers of Lully.

Composers of music in the *goûts réunis* include François Couperin and J. M. Leclair.

Reusner, Esaias (*b* Löwenberg, Silesia [now Lwówek Śląski, Poland], 29 Apr. 1636; *d* Berlin, 1 May 1679). German composer and lutenist. He studied with his father, and in 1651 entered the service of Princess Radziwiłł. From 1655 to 1672 he was lutenist to the Duke of Silesia, and he eventually became a chamber musician at the electoral court in Berlin. His lute pieces are French in style: they include 15 suites published at Breslau in 1668 as *Delitiae testudinis* and reissued in Leipzig as *Erfreuliche Lauten-Lust* (1697), and 13 more suites published at Berlin in 1676 as *Neue Lauten-Früchte*; he also published a collection of sacred songs (Berlin, 1676 or 1678).   WENDY THOMPSON

Reutter, Georg (von) (*b* Vienna, 1656; *d* Vienna, 29 Aug. 1738). Austrian organist and composer. He succeeded his teacher, Kerll, as organist at St Stephen's Cathedral, Vienna, in 1686. From 1696 to 1703 he was a theorbo player at the imperial court chapel, and from 1700 he was both court and chamber organist. In 1715 he became *Kapellmeister* at St Stephen's. He is known today only for his organ toccatas.

His son, (Johann Adam Joseph Karl) **Georg** (von) **Reutter** (*b* Vienna, 1708; *d* Vienna, 11 Mar. 1772), studied with his father and with Caldara. In 1731, he became court composer in Vienna, and in 1738 succeeded his father as *Kapellmeister* at St Stephen's. The boy Haydn was a chorister under Reutter, who is said to have treated him badly. In 1740 Reutter was ennobled by Empress Maria Theresia, and six years later became second court *Kapellmeister* (first *Kapellmeister* from 1751). His works include several operas and oratorios, and a great deal of church music (some 81 Masses, nearly 130 motets, and so on).   WENDY THOMPSON

Reveille. From *réveil* (Fr.), 'awakening'. The military signal which begins the day in the army (pronounced 'revelly' or 'revally' by the British).

Review of New Musical Publications, The. The first musical periodical to appear in England. It was founded in 1784 by T. Williams, but did not survive longer than a year.

'Revolutionary' Study. Nickname of Chopin's *Étude* in C minor, Op. 10 No. 12 (1830), for piano. It is so called because it has been supposed that it expresses Chopin's patriotic fury on hearing that Warsaw had been captured by the Russians.

Revue. A miscellaneous entertainment composed of a collection of songs and sketches, often of a satirical nature: more or less a variety show with an intellectual flavour. A revue is sometimes the work of one composer or writer, but is more often made up of contributions from many hands. The revue was of French origin, the name simply implying an end-of-the-year 'review' of events and caricatures of leading personalities, and its popularity began around 1840. A similar kind of entertainment flourished in England at a slightly later period. The modern revue followed two paths: the intimate revue with a small cast, generally with a satirical slant, which has been much cultivated in universities; and the lavish, spectacular revue, with more emphasis on dancing and song, which was established in England in the early 1900s with the Empire revues, and in the USA with such highly successful series as the Ziegfeld Follies.
                                  PETER GAMMOND

Rezniček, Emil (Nikolaus) **von** (*b* Vienna, 4 May 1860; *d* Berlin, 2 Aug. 1945). Austrian composer. He was sent to Graz to study law, but music was his first love and he soon moved on to Leipzig to study with Reinecke and Jadassohn. Later he held various posts as a theatre and opera conductor in Austria and Germany. His compositions include the opera *Donna Diana* (1894), whose overture has held a place in the light orchestral repertory, as well as other operas, four symphonies, and choral works. He wrote little after the First World War.
                                  PAUL GRIFFITHS

Rf, rfz. Abbreviations for **rinforzando*.

Rhapsody (Fr.: *rapsodie*; Ger.: *Rhapsodie*; It.: *rapsodia*). In Ancient Greece, the recitation of parts of an epic poem. In music it means a piece in one movement, often based on popular, national, or folk melodies. The term was first used in the 19th century by Tomášek, as a title for a set of six piano pieces published *c*.1803; thereafter it was applied to certain character pieces with no specific form. Rhapsodies may be passionate, nostalgic, or improvisatory in character. Nineteenth-century interest in Hungarian and gypsy violin playing led to the composition of pieces in that style, for example by Liszt (19 Hungarian Rhapsodies), Dvořák (Slavonic Rhapsodies), Dohnányi, and Bartók.

Brahms wrote three piano Rhapsodies (Op. 79, Op. 119) as well as the *Alto Rhapsody* Op. 53 for contralto, male chorus, and orchestra. The improvisatory element of the rhapsody inspired Debussy's two examples (one for alto saxophone, the other for clarinet), Gershwin's jazz-influenced *Rhapsody in Blue* for piano and orchestra, and Rakhmaninov's *Rhapsody on a Theme of Paganini* (variations on Paganini's Violin Caprice No. 2 in A minor). The influence of folk-song permeates many British examples, including Vaughan Williams's *Norfolk Rhapsody*, Butterworth's *A Shropshire Lad*, and Delius's *Brigg Fair* (subtitled 'An English Rhapsody'). WENDY THOMPSON

Rhapsody in Blue. Work by Gershwin for piano and orchestra, composed in 1924. It is among the first works to combine jazz with symphonic procedures, and was orchestrated by Ferdé Grofé.

Rhapsody on a Theme of Paganini. Rakhmaninov's Op. 43 for piano and orchestra, composed in 1934. It contains 24 variations on Paganini's Caprice No. 2 in A minor for violin.

Rhau, Georg (*b* Eisfeld an der Werre, nr Coburg, 1488; *d* Wittenberg, 6 Aug. 1548). One of the most important German music printers and Protestant musicians of his time. He studied at the University of Wittenberg, graduating in 1514, and in 1518 went to Leipzig, where he was Assessor for the arts faculty and one of Bach's predecessors as *Kantor* of the church and school of St Thomas's. He left Leipzig in 1520, having joined Luther's reform movement, and in 1523 returned to Wittenberg as a printer and publisher. In this capacity he provided the first basic musical literature for the Lutheran Church, publishing not only collections of hymn arrangements and other music to educate the young, but also Masses and Passion music. DENIS ARNOLD

Rheinberger, Josef (Gabriel) (*b* Vaduz, Liechtenstein, 17 Mar. 1839; *d* Munich, 25 Nov. 1901). German organist and composer. A professional organist from childhood, he studied at the Munich Conservatory (1850–4), where from 1859 he was a noted teacher of the organ and composition. He produced an enormous output of compositions in all genres, but is remembered almost exclusively for his 20 organ sonatas, solidly constructed in a Brahmsian style. PAUL GRIFFITHS

Rheingold, Das ('The Rhine Gold'). See *Ring des Nibelungen, Der*.

'Rhenish' Symphony. Schumann's Symphony No. 3 in E♭ major, Op. 97, composed in 1850 (the fourth in order of composition). The fourth of its five movements was inspired by the installation of a cardinal at Cologne on the Rhine.

Rhine Gold, The (Ger.: *Das Rheingold*). See *Ring des Nibelungen, Der*.

Rhosymedre ('Lovely'). Hymn-tune by J. D. Edwards (1808–85) on which Vaughan Williams based the second of his Three Preludes on Welsh Hymn Tunes (1920) for organ.

Rhumba. See *Rumba*.

Rhys, Philip ap. See *Ap Rhys, Philip*.

Rhythm

1. Introduction
2. The Components of Rhythm
3. History
4. Present-day Attitudes to Rhythm

1. *Introduction.* Rhythm in music is normally felt to embrace everything to do with both time and motion—with the organization of musical events in time, however flexible in metre and tempo, irregular in accent, or free in durational values. Much argument has been devoted to the question of whether rhythm or pitch is more fundamental to music. It is certainly the case that one is more likely to talk about rhythm without any mention of music, or 'time' without any mention of art, than one is to talk about pitch in a non-musical context. But this in itself merely serves to stress the fact that the connotations of rhythm are a good deal more complex than those of 'rhythmic' or 'rhythmical'. When people refer to the strongly rhythmic character of a march, or a typical piece of pop music, it is the recurrence of heavy, regular accentuation and the distinction between relatively strong and relatively weak accents which they have particularly in mind, no less than the presence of a constant pulse or tempo. 'Rhythmic' music tends to be that with the most predictable, least varied, rhythmic character.

2. *The Components of Rhythm.* The rhythmic character of the 'serious' music with which most people are most familiar—that of the late-Baroque, Classical, and Romantic periods—is often very different from that of both much earlier and more recent music. Obviously enough, regular accentuation and phrase-structure did not suddenly appear with Bach and Handel and vanish with Schoenberg and Stravinsky, but the rhythmic characteristics which prevailed in music between Bach and Schoenberg cannot always be used to describe the rhythmic qualities of music from other periods, or of other cultures. Ex. 1 reproduces a short piano piece by Schumann, from *Carnaval*

(1835), which has those features of regularity and equality which characterize musical rhythm between Bach and Schoenberg. This is a compound of various interdependent elements: (*a*) a metre, indicated by the time signature, which remains unchanged throughout, and which carries with it the implication that the strongest accent will normally fall on the first beat of the bar; (*b*) a pulse, or tempo, which also remains basically constant, and which relates to the time signature—it may be indicated by a metronome mark, a form of words, or, as here, by both; (*c*) the durations used for the various notes (crotchets, quavers, etc.), which combine to produce a rhythmic 'profile'; and (*d*) the phrases which result from the arrangement of musical material in groups of beats and bars—bars tending, as here, to be grouped in multiples of two and four. These features of regularity and equality—sometimes defined as 'isometric'—

will naturally be modified at times by the use of syncopation, cross-accents, or those 'irrational' durational values which temporarily override the units indicated in the time signature, as well as by modifications of tempo—*rubato, accelerando,* or *ritardando.* But such deviations make their effect precisely because the music has its basis in equality and regularity.

Ex. 2 presents eight bars of a Piano Piece by Stockhausen, composed in the early 1950s. The complete work is 16 bars long, but it subdivides rather less readily into units of equal length than does the Schumann. The music retains a regular quaver pulse, but the time signature changes frequently, and although the first beat of the bar is often marked with a relatively loud dynamic, the rhythmic profile of the music clearly reduces the structural significance of such accents as recurrent features. No tempo is indicated, though a note at the beginning of the complete

Ex. 1

Ex. 2

set of four pieces states that the speed is determined by playing the smallest note-value as fast as possible. Although no deviations from this basic pulse are indicated—no *accelerando* or *ritardando*—the avoidance of repeated rhythmic patterns prevents the emergence of any phrase-structure comparable to Schumann's.

Although the highly fragmented nature of the Stockhausen piece gives it a very specific rhythmic style, its essential irregularity and diversity link it in principle with a good deal of early music, in which a need for regular accents in all parts at once, a phrase structure and harmonic rhythm based on a four-bar norm, and constant time signatures had not yet evolved. What does connect the two examples, and a lot of earlier music too, is the presence of a constant pulse, and although the way in which such pulsation gradually evolved is still the subject of controversy—and research—it will be clear that it could not have been done so conclusively without a parallel evolution of musical notation. Music which was originally notated without the explicit provision of precise durations and a constant pulse (for example, early Christian hymns and *troubadour* songs) would not necessarily have been performed without such a pulse, however, and it is worth noting that when modern composers employ a notation in which rhythms and durations are left to the performer to improvise on the spur of the moment, they often feel it necessary to spell out in words the fact that they wish performers to avoid consistent pulsation.

3. *History*. It is in its emancipation from both speech and solo performance that music has developed its most characteristic and complex qualities. In ancient times, as for example with the Greek philosopher Aristoxenus (*c*.350 BC), musical rhythm and speech rhythm could be

discussed in the same terms, music and poetry differing only to the extent that music employed specific pitches and intervals. More than 1,000 years were to elapse before a form of musical notation evolved which showed time-values with any precision. But as music evolved from monophony to polyphony, and it became possible to create extended compositions involving large numbers of performers, so a notation which aimed at a high degree of precision with respect to duration as well as pitch emerged, as a means of co-ordinating and synchronizing the realization of the composer's intentions as expressed on paper. Such precision was certainly not to be found in neumes, however, and although by the late 12th century a system of six rhythmic modes was in use whose basic patterns of 'long' and 'short' durations were ultimately traceable to the 'feet' of Greek poetics, it was a 13th-century theorist whose work most clearly codified the fundamental change whereby a genuinely mensural form of notation became possible. Franco of Cologne, in his *Ars cantus mensurabilis* (*c*.1260), established the vital principle that the duration of a note should be indicated by its actual shape, and the four durational values he defined—duplex long (▬), long (▌), breve (▪), and semibreve (♦)—form the basis of all significant subsequent developments in rhythmic notation, and therefore in rhythmic organization. Another important early theorist, Philippe de Vitry, was the first to make a clear distinction between duple and triple metre in his treatise *Ars nova* (*c*.1323). However, although 14th-century music moved still closer to modern rhythmic practice, it was not until the 17th century that most of the complications and confusions of early rhythmic theory and procedures were finally eliminated.

It is particularly important not to confuse early and modern functions. For example, time signatures can be found in music from the 13th to the 16th century, but they do not imply the kind of regular, recurrent metrical accents in performance that are common in more recent music. It was the introduction of bar-lines, initially in 16th-century lute and keyboard music and then generally during the 17th century, which was ultimately the most crucial development, since through them modern metrical schemes became possible.

Such developments offer the strongest confirmation of the obvious point that music and poetry did not evolve in the same way. Verbal 'performance', whether on the stage or in everyday life, has remained essentially a monophonic rather than a polyphonic activity. And even when collective speech is required, as when a church congregation recites the Creed or the Lord's Prayer, a high degree of rhythmic unison—or 'homorhythm'—is aimed at. A large measure of metric regularity may indeed be achieved in the case of material which is spoken collectively week after week, year after year, in church, but it has never proved necessary to notate that material rhythmically and metrically —with precisely proportioned durations for every syllable of text—for the simple reason that no one has sought to combine other strands of text in counterpoint with it. By contrast, the polyphonic music which emerged in the late Middle Ages would not have made sense if there had been more than a slight degree of flexibility about the way in which the participating voices fitted together. Pitch relations could function only if they were notated rhythmically with reference to the same basic unit of value.

As, after 1600, music became more concerted, as instrumental styles emerged and the influence of the dance increased, the bar-line came into its own, and aesthetic and technical principles of unity and coherence came to govern rhythmic features. There was greater need for a regularity which applied as much to accent and the recurrence of metric units (bars and groups of bars) as it did to the repetition of rhythmic patterns and phrases in association with the melodic and harmonic organization of the composition. The climax of this process may be seen in the emergence of the conductor not just as someone indicating an unaccented *tactus* to a small choir, as in the 15th and 16th centuries, but as the controller of accent and phrasing as well as of pulse.

During the 18th century, the discussion of rhythm by theorists became more directly concerned with these new form-building features: for example, Joseph Riepel, in a treatise published in 1754, divided melodic lines into segments according to principles of pitch organization—an important stage in the working-out of analytical techniques which attempt to fuse hierarchic interpretations of tonal pitch function and rhythm. In the 19th century, Classical rhythmic characteristics began to break down, especially in the radically new form of music drama devised by Wagner. The two principal theorists of the time, Moritz Hauptmann (1792-1868) and Hugo Riemann (1849-1919), can both be seen as selective rather

than comprehensive in their work, and neither was primarily concerned with the most recent musical developments. Hauptmann was, indeed, essentially a theorist: he quoted no musical examples in his important study of metre, first published in 1864. Riemann's argument that musical structures have an ideal length based on multiples of four finds much support in the Classical music which was his principal source, but his exclusion of harmonic and tonal aspects from his analyses was a limitation for which many 20th-century theorists have sought to compensate.

Of course, the role of rhythm and metre in Classical and Romantic music is much more than the mere mechanical preservation of an inflexible beat with an unvaried emphasis at the beginning of every bar, or multiple of two, four, or eight bars. And in the 20th century a balance has been achieved in a certain kind of concerted music between the co-ordination of the parts at fixed points and the avoidance of exact synchronization between those points. In several works by Boulez and Lutosławski, for example, the conductor ceases to be a time-beater and phrase-shaper, and becomes the controller of large-scale formal and textural processes. Indeed, the 20th century may be seen to be reliving the entire history of musical rhythm to the extent that notations which avoid durational precision (and therefore reject the necessity for a constant pulse) can be found, while at the other extreme some composers— Messiaen, Babbitt, Maxwell Davies, etc.— employ rhythmic modes or series which extend the control of pre-determined duration patterns over entire structures.

4. *Present-day Attitudes to Rhythm.* While modern composers have been exploring various degrees of rhythmic freedom or strictness, 20th-century theorists have advanced most significantly towards the integration of rhythmic analysis with that of music's fundamental pitch processes. In particular, they have explored the possibility of an overall view of tonal structure in which rhythmic and durational factors participate more fully than they did in the pioneering harmonic and tonal analyses of Heinrich Schenker (see *Analysis*, 3).

Many analysts, even those who are basically sympathetic to Schenker's view of tonal organization, feel that he did not go far enough in exploring his perception that rhythm, like pitch, functions on distinct yet interacting levels in tonal music. For example, David Epstein, while noting that 'our perception of music seems strongly if not prevalently influenced by pitch and the structure of pitch . . . and less oriented towards purely rhythmic structures', seeks to proceed on the basis that 'in music time is primary', and that duration is 'the most fundamental and indispensable element of music'. Like Riemann, G. Cooper and L. B. Meyer (*The Rhythmic Structure of Music*, 1960), and many others, Epstein attempts an analysis based on the perception and indication of different stresses and accents (*Beyond Orpheus*, 1979). Like his predecessors, Epstein encounters the problem that such elements are not and cannot be notated with the precision of pitch and duration: 'If shape is easy to comprehend, emphasis is another matter indeed.' And it is so because accentuation is such a delicately variable entity, essential to the life of a performance, like tone quality and the infinite number of interpretative, expressive nuances that a performer employs, but not an aspect of music that can easily be subjected to analytical categorization and scrutiny.

As far as tonal music is concerned, the most penetrating analysis of rhythmic and metric structure is that which has been brought into the closest parallel with an interpretation of hierarchic pitch structure. Maury Yeston (*The Stratification of Musical Rhythm*, 1976) and Carl Schachter ('Rhythm and Linear Analysis', *The Music Forum*, Nos. 4 and 5, 1976 and 1980) have been the most significant pioneers in the complex and delicate art of relating the fundamental dimensions of pitch and duration, register and accent. In doing so, moreover, they bear out Epstein's claim that, in deeper levels of structural rhythm, Schenker was 'very much in tune with rhythmic reality'. But even such work as theirs has barely begun to explore the possibilities of fully worked-out rhythmic analyses of complete, large-scale tonal compositions. A pitch-and-rhythm analysis of compositional foundations is perhaps more immediately profitable in those composers, from Dunstable to Milton Babbitt, who have employed rhythmic modes, series, or mathematically-calculated proportions (like the Golden Section; see *Violin*, 3) as an essential part of their technique.

For most listeners, nevertheless, rhythm is likely to be most evident as an immediate succession of various durations and occasional accents, approached and quitted in ways which participate in the shaping processes of the entire musical fabric, and which may even, in certain very 'rhythmical' works, seem to dominate that fabric. As Schoenberg put it, in his *Fundamentals of Musical Composition*, 'rhythm is particularly important in moulding the phrase', which he regarded as the smallest structural unit of a composition. 'It contributes to interest and variety; it establishes character, and it is often the determining factor in establishing the unity of the phrase.' And it was Schoenberg who, in his *Theory of Harmony*, expressed with characteristic trenchancy the purpose, and

problem, of musical rhythm. 'If we ask ourselves why we measure music in time in the first place, we can only answer: because we would not otherwise bring it into being. We measure time to make it conform to ourselves, to give it boundaries. We can transmit or portray only that which has boundaries. The creative imagination, however, can envision the unbounded, or at least the apparently unbounded. Thus in art we always represent something unbounded by means of something with boundaries.' It is undoubtedly true that the boundaries of 'isometric' music, associated as they are with the rich but very specific relations pertaining to tonality, offer only one kind of musical rhythm. In the degree to which it moves beyond this, music seems to be rediscovering something more basic about itself, while possibly laying the foundations for a new kind of rhythmic richness.

See also *Metre*.   ARNOLD WHITTALL

Rhythm and blues. See *Blues*.

Rhythmic modes. See *Notation*, 3.

Ribible, rubible. See *Rebec*.

Ricciotti, Carlo (*b* c.1681; *d* The Hague, 13 July 1756). Italian musician. His name would be totally unknown today if six concertos ascribed to Pergolesi in his modern collected edition had not more recently been attributed to him. However, Ricciotti seems to have been only the editor of these *Concerti armonici*, published by him c.1730 at The Hague and later achieving three further editions in England; their composer remains unknown.

                                  DENIS ARNOLD

Ricercar [*ricercare, recercar*, etc.] (It., from *ricercare*, 'to seek'). A type of instrumental piece common during the 16th and 17th centuries. The earliest *ricercari* were improvisatory in style, often written for solo instruments such as the lute or bass viol. They consisted of highly embellished, unaccompanied melody, not very different from the *prelude of the early 16th century, having no distinct shape and seemingly designed as an exercise for the fingers. The composers of these pieces were usually themselves virtuoso players or teachers, and they include the first writers of treatises on individual instruments, such as Ganassi and Bassano. This kind of *ricercar* has little musical interest, and is artistically on a par with Czerny's duller technical studies.

Another type, which flourished later in the 16th century, was the duo, written for the instruction of beginners in part music. The instruments are rarely specified, but the frequent use of themes based on easily remembered *solmization syllables suggests that they were exercises in sight reading, perhaps for singers as well as instrumentalists. Some of these are much more attractive than solo *ricercari*, especially those of Lassus.

The best-known and most durable kind of *ricercar* was the instrumental equivalent of the vocal *motet. The earliest, dating from the mid 16th century, are obviously conceived in the same tradition as polyphonic church music, with flowing melodic lines organized by imitative points. The principal differences between the motet and the *ricercar* are that the instrumental pieces use a wider range of melody; they do not have to give frequent rests to each 'voice'; and, since there are no demands imposed by setting words, they can employ fewer themes, even in some cases being monothematic. At first they were mainly written in four parts, but Andrea Gabrieli wrote one for eight instruments and there were many keyboard transcriptions which added ornaments but preserved the basically polyphonic structure. The vogue for this kind of *ricercar* was at its height in the latter part of the 16th century, and by 1600 the genre was overtaken in popularity by the more tuneful *canzona francese. Some of the *ricercari* published about this time show the influence of the *canzona* in their sprightly rhythms, and it is sometimes difficult to distinguish between the two.

From c.1610, motet-like instrumental pieces are more often called 'sonata' (e.g. Giovanni Gabrieli's *Sonata pian'e forte*) and the term *ricercar* tends to be associated with works which display some form of contrapuntal learnedness. In this sense, the word persisted until the end of the Baroque period, the most notable examples being in Bach's *Musical Offering* (1747). There, as was almost traditional by this time, the two *ricercari* are placed among a set of canons and are fugal in style, written in old-fashioned note-values and conceived as a display of compositional skill. It is difficult by this stage to say how these differ from fugues, if in any way at all.

DENIS ARNOLD

Richafort, Jean (*b* c.1480; *d* ? Bruges, c.1547). One of the leading Franco-Flemish composers of the post-Josquin generation. His career was spent mainly in the Netherlands (although he was in Italy as a singer in the French royal chapel in the second decade of the 15th century) and he may have been in the service of Mary of Hungary, regent of the Netherlands, in the 1530s. He was *maître de chapelle* at St Gilles, Bruges, between 1542 and 1547. As well as *chansons* and church music, his output includes a fine Requiem Mass, which quotes some music

by Josquin and was perhaps written on the death of that master in 1521.   JOHN MILSOM

Richard Cœur-de-lion ('Richard the Lionheart'). Comic opera in three acts by Grétry to a libretto by Sedaine after La Curne de Sainte-Palaye. It was first performed in Paris in 1784.

Richettato (It.). The same as *spiccato.

Richter, Franz Xaver (*b* ?Holešov, 1 Dec. 1709; *d* Strasbourg, 12 Sept. 1789). German composer of Czech descent. Richter's origins are uncertain, but by 1740 he was assistant *Kapellmeister* at Allgäu. His musical education was gleaned from Fux's *Gradus ad Parnassum* which he may have studied with the author in Vienna. By 1747 he was working for the Elector Palatine Carl Theodor in Mannheim as composer and bass singer. He had become known as a composer in the 1740s with the publication of six symphonies, and was also valued as a teacher, counting some of the foremost representatives of the Mannheim school amongst his pupils including Carl Stamitz. It is from this period that Richter's large treatise on composition (*Harmonische Belehrungen*, published 1804), somewhat derivative of Fux, survives. His personal musical tastes, however, were not in tune with those of his contemporaries at Mannheim, and in 1768 he became *Kapellmeister* of Strasbourg Cathedral. Richter's compositions were largely conservative in style, favouring a greater use of counterpoint than was customary at Mannheim in the 1750s and 1760s, though the democratic part-writing in his string quartets looks forward to later Classical practices. Apart from chamber and orchestral music he was drawn increasingly to church music, composing at least two oratorios, some 39 Masses, and several cantatas and motets.   JAN SMACZNY

Richtig (Ger.). 'Right', 'precise'.

Ricochet (Fr.). 'Rebound'. A kind of bowing on a string instrument, in which the upper half of the bow is 'thrown' on to the string, causing it to bounce several times under its own weight and thus producing a series of rapid *staccato* notes. Paganini used the effect frequently. See also *Volante*.

Ricordi. Italian firm of music publishers. They established themselves as the predominant force in Italian music publishing in the 19th century chiefly through the initiative, enterprise, and individual personalities of the members of the Ricordi family. Indissolubly linked with both the publications and the careers of Verdi and Puccini, the firm was founded by Giovanni Ricordi (1785-1853), an imaginative, energetic violinist and copyist, who studied printing techniques in Leipzig with Breitkopf & Härtel and issued his first publication in Milan in 1808. His special association with La Scala, and his position as official copyist there, enabled him in 1825 to purchase their musical archives, and he was soon publishing more than 200 items a year. By 1853 his catalogue comprised over 25,000 works, including operas by Rossini, Bellini, and Donizetti, and, from 1837 onwards, Verdi—a publishing coup that brought his rivals to near-hysteria.

From the 1840s onwards Ricordi published nearly all of Verdi's operas, but his good relations with the composer were later imperilled by his son Tito (1811–88), whose extortionate attitudes temporarily alienated Verdi. Tito introduced new printing techniques, acquired several catalogues from other publishers, and opened branches within and outside Italy. His son Giulio (1840–1912), who succeeded him, was himself a composer and brought fresh lustre to the firm through his discovery of Puccini, with whom he developed a fruitful artistic relationship. He also greatly expanded the operatic and instrumental sections of the catalogue. The younger Tito (1865–1933), Giulio's son, was temperamentally less compatible with Puccini: he described *La Rondine* as 'bad Lehár'. He resigned from the firm in 1919.

After the First World War the Ricordi family was no longer associated with the business. The catalogue widened to include earlier Italian composers (Vivaldi, Scarlatti), editions of the classics, and, more recently, contemporary composers such as Pizzetti, Malipiero, and Petrassi. Critical editions of Rossini and Verdi are also in progress. Ricordi have maintained pre-eminence, however, largely through the foundations laid in the 19th century with the operas of Verdi and Puccini.   J. M. THOMSON

Rideau (Fr.). 'Curtain'. In opera or ballet scores, 'curtain rises (or falls)'. Satie's ballet *Parade* opens with a *Prélude du rideau rouge* (Prelude of the red curtain).

Riders to the Sea. Opera in one act by Vaughan Williams, an almost verbatim setting of Synge's play (1904). It was composed between 1925 and 1932 and first performed in London in 1937.

Ridotto (It.). 1. 'Reduced', 'arranged'.
2. An entertainment (Fr.: *redoute*) which was very popular in the 18th century, consisting of a mixture of music and dancing. Busby, in his *Concert Room and Orchestra Anecdotes* (1825), recalled that, in London, 'The year 1722 was distinguished by the introduction of a new species of entertainment called a *Ridotto*, con-

sisting of select songs, followed by a ball, in which the performers were joined by the company, who passed from the front of a house, over a bridge connecting the pit with the stage'. Other types of ridotto took place in the London pleasure gardens.

In Vienna, a great *Redoutensaal* (in fact two, one small and one large) was built on to the Hofburg palace. These rooms also served as concert halls, and Haydn, Mozart, Beethoven, and their contemporaries wrote dance music (*Redoutentänze*) for the ridottos held there.

Ridout, Alan (John) (*b* West Wickham, Kent, 9 Dec. 1934). English composer. He studied at the Royal College of Music with Gordon Jacob and Herbert Howells, and privately with Peter Racine Fricker and Michael Tippett. His works include five symphonies and several concertante pieces, but he is associated more with church music and children's operas produced in connection with his work as a teacher at the choir school of Canterbury Cathedral (1964–72) and subsequently at King's School, Canterbury.
PAUL GRIFFITHS

Riduzione (It.). 'Reduction', 'arrangement'.

Riegger, Wallingford (*b* Albany, Georgia, 29 Apr. 1885; *d* New York, 2 Apr. 1961). American composer. He studied at Cornell University (1904–5), at the Institute of Musical Art in New York (1905–7), and in Germany. There followed a period of 20 years during which he held various appointments as conductor, cellist, and teacher, composing in conventional late-Romantic and impressionist styles. In the late 1920s he settled in New York, and most of his important works date from after this move. Such pieces as *Study in Sonority* for ten violins (1926–7) and *Dichotomy* for chamber orchestra (1931–2), both in vigorous, almost atonal counterpoint, gave him a place in the avant-garde circle of Varèse, Cowell, and Ruggles. In later works, such as the three string quartets, the Third Symphony (1946–7), and Music for Brass Choir (1948–9), he pursued this dissonant contrapuntal style, sometimes on the basis of his own brand of 12-note serialism.
PAUL GRIFFITHS

Riemann, (Karl Wilhelm Julius) **Hugo** (*b* Gross-Mehlra, nr Erfurt, 18 July 1849; *d* Leipzig, 10 July 1919). German musicologist. After training as a pianist he spent most of his early life teaching music history at Leipzig University. He wrote an astonishing number of books and articles, of which his *Musik-Lexikon* (Leipzig, 1882) was (and remains in its latest revision) one of the best dictionaries of music, and his *Handbuch der Musikgeschichte* (Leipzig, 1904-13) one of the most stimulating of histories.   DENIS ARNOLD

Rienzi (*Cola Rienzi, der letzte der Tribunen*; 'Cola Rienzi, the Last of the Tribunes'). Opera in five acts by Wagner to his own libretto after E. Bulwer Lytton's novel (1835) and Mary Russell Mitford's play (1828). It was first performed in Dresden in 1842.

Ries, Ferdinand (*bapt*. Bonn, 28 Nov. 1784; *d* Frankfurt am Main, 13 Jan. 1838). German pianist, composer, and conductor. He was the son of Franz Anton Ries (1755-1846), a German violinist and the friend and teacher of Beethoven. Ferdinand studied with his father and Beethoven in Vienna and then toured Europe and Scandinavia as pianist. He settled in London for 11 years in 1813, then in Godesberg (1824-7), and finally in Frankfurt, where he conducted the Lower Rhine Festivals for the years 1825-7. He was also conductor of the municipal orchestra at Aachen. Ries was a successful composer, his works including eight symphonies, eight piano concertos, five operas, two oratorios, 20 violin sonatas, and several piano and chamber works. With Franz Gerhard Wegeler (1765-1848), he wrote the *Biographische Notizen über L. v. Beethoven* (Koblenz, 1838).

Rigaudon (Fr.). A 17th- and 18th-century dance in duple time, resembling the *bourrée. Like other French dances of folk origin, such as the *gavotte, it was originally rather crude and lively until taken up in courtly circles, when it became more elegant, though retaining its liveliness. Like other court dances it was used in French stage works, especially in the *opéra-ballets* of Campra and Rameau. In the mid 18th century it also appeared as an optional dance in the *suite.

The rigaudon became popular in England and Germany: one of the earliest English examples appears in a harpsichord suite by Purcell. After the mid 18th century it fell out of use, although it reappears occasionally in piano works of the late 19th century and the 20th, for example in Grieg's *Holberg Suite*, Ravel's *Le tombeau de Couperin*, and Prokofiev's Ten Pieces, Op. 12.

Rigoletto. Opera in three acts by Verdi; text by Piave, after Hugo's drama *Le roi s'amuse* (1832). Produced: Venice, La Fenice, 11 March 1851; London, Covent Garden, 14 May 1853; New York, Academy of Music, 19 February 1855. Also performed as *La maledizione*, *Viscardello*, *Clara di Perth*, and *Lionello*, owing to censorship restrictions. The licentious Duke of Man-

tua (ten.) has been paying court, disguised as a student, to Gilda (sop.), who unknown to him is the daughter of his court-jester Rigoletto (bar.). When Rigoletto, who has unwittingly helped in the abduction of Gilda, learns that she has been seduced by the Duke, he plans to have him killed by the professional assassin Sparafucile (bass). Sparafucile's sister Maddalena (mezzo) pleads that his life may be spared, and Gilda, who has overheard their conversation, sacrifices her own life in order to save the Duke.

FURTHER READING
Nicholas John, ed.: *Rigoletto*, English National Opera Guides (in preparation).

Rilasciando, rilasciante (It.). 'Releasing', 'relinquishing', i.e. getting gradually slower, the equivalent of *rallentando*.

Riley, Terry (Mitchell) (*b* Colfax, Calif., 24 June 1935). American composer. He studied composition with Robert Erickson at San Francisco State College (1955-7) and attended the University of California at Berkeley (1960-1). Since 1963 he has appeared internationally as a solo improviser on soprano saxophone or electronic keyboard instruments; he visited India in the early 1970s, and is much influenced by Indian musicians in his generation of music from a modal idea. His work is distinguished by obsessive repetition. Among his handful of notated pieces, *In C* (1964) provides merely a selection of figures on which any number of players may draw freely.   PAUL GRIFFITHS

FURTHER READING
Michael Nyman: *Experimental Music* (London, 1974).

Rimettendo, rimettendosi (It.). 'Putting back', 'replacing', a direction to resume the original tempo.

Rimmer, John (Francis) (*b* Auckland, 5 Feb. 1939). New Zealand composer. He studied composition and analysis with John Weinzweig, electronic music with Gustav Ciamaga, ethnomusicology with M. Kolinski at the University of Toronto (1967-8), and horn with Eugene Rittich. Since 1974 he has been a lecturer in music at the University of Auckland where he directs the electronic music studio and is musical director of the ensemble for new music, The Karlheinz Co. He has also worked with computer music at the Massachusetts Institute of Technology and in the electronic music studio of the University of East Anglia. A prolific and technically accomplished composer, he has written in most genres, being specially successful when depicting landscapes as in *White Island* (1974), an electronic music tape, and in *Where Sea Meets Sky* (1975), inspired by a trans-Tasman air crossing, existing in both orchestral and electronic versions. He has also written a dramatic *scena* for orchestra, *At the Appointed Time* (1973). His other works include a Viola Concerto (1980), *Sir Gawayne and the Green Knight* (1981) for music theatre, and *Tides* (1981) for solo horn.

J. M. THOMSON

Rimsky-Korsakov, Nikolay (Andreyevich) (*b* Tikhvin, Novgorod Government, 18 Mar. 1844; *d* Lyubensk, St Petersburg Government, 21 June 1908). Russian composer. Like others of the Russian nationalists (Glinka, Balakirev, Musorgsky) he was of 'gentle' birth and was reared in the country, so enjoying the early advantages of a soaking in folk-song.

His early manhood was spent as an officer in the navy, and his First Symphony (1861–5, rev. 1884) was partly written when on duty. The qualities of this work and of his symphonic poem, *Sadko* (an orchestral setting of a legend of the sea; 1867), led to his being offered the post of professor of composition at the St Petersburg Conservatory. He felt himself far from sufficiently equipped for such a post, but by dint of hard study he acquired the principles and the technique of his art and, indeed, made himself the best theorist of the whole group of 'The *Five'.

He was a strong nationalist and a devoted student of the folk music of his native country. He was urged by a powerful dramatic impulse,

Rimsky-Korsakov

with much rhythmic force and a vivid sense of orchestral colour. The last characteristic allies him with Berlioz, whose successor in this line he may almost be considered (as he may, likewise, be considered the predecessor of Stravinsky and others of the moderns); his own treatise on instrumentation is, like that of Berlioz, now a classic.

He composed freely and copiously. His operas include *Pskovityanka* ('The Maid of Pskov', original version 1872; third and last version 1892), *Snegurochka* ('The Snow Maiden', 1881), *Sadko* (1896; also the subject of a symphonic poem—see above), *Skazaniye o nevidimom grade Kitezhe* ('Legend of the Invincible City of Kitezh', 1907), and *Zolotoy petushok* ('The Golden Cockerel', 1908). He wrote three symphonies, the symphonic suite *Sheherazade* (1888), choral music, songs (especially important), and other things.

On the breakup of the group of 'The Five' he became the centre of another circle of similar aims, to which belonged Belyayev and Glazunov.

See also *Opera*, 14; *Russia and the Soviet Union*, 4.

PERCY SCHOLES, rev.

FURTHER READING
Gerald Abraham: *Rimsky-Korsakov* (London, 1945); Nikolay Rimsky-Korsakov: *My Musical Life* (London, 1974).

Rinaldo. Opera in three acts by Handel to a libretto by Rossi based on a scenario by Aaron Hill after Tasso's *La Gerusalemme liberata* ('Jerusalem Delivered'). It was first performed in London in 1711 and is Handel's first opera in English.

Rinforzando, rinforzato (It., often abbreviated to *rf*, *rfz*). 'Reinforcing', 'reinforced', a stress or accent applied to individual notes or chords; *rinforzo, rinforzamento*, 'reinforcement'.

Ring des Nibelungen, Der ('The Ring of the Nibelung'). A stage festival play for three days and a preliminary evening (*Ein Bühnenfestspiel für drei Tage und einen Vorabend*)—sometimes called a tetralogy—by Wagner; text by the composer, based on the Nibelung Saga. Produced: Bayreuth, Festspielhaus, 13, 14, 16, 17 August 1876. The separate operas were produced as follows:

Das Rheingold ('The Rhine Gold'). Prologue in one act to the trilogy *Der Ring des Nibelungen*. Produced: Munich, 22 September 1869; London, Her Majesty's, 5 May 1882; New York, Metropolitan, 4 January 1889.
Die Walküre ('The Valkyrie'). Music drama in three acts. Produced: Munich, Hofoper, 26 June 1870; New York, Academy of Music, 2

April 1877; London, Her Majesty's, 6 May 1882.

Siegfried. Music drama in three acts. Produced: Bayreuth, Festspielhaus, 16 August 1876; London, Her Majesty's, 8 May 1882; New York, Metropolitan, 9 November 1887.

Götterdämmerung ('The Twilight of the Gods'). Music drama in three acts. Produced: Bayreuth, Festspielhaus, 17 August 1876; London, Her Majesty's, 9 May 1882; New York, Metropolitan, 25 January 1888 (incomplete, without Norns or Waltraute scenes).

The *Ring* is an allegory, and tells of the struggle for power between the Nibelung dwarfs, the Giants, and the Gods.

In *Das Rheingold*, the Nibelung dwarf Alberich (bass-bar.) renounces love so that he may steal the Rhine Gold, guarded by the Rhine Maidens, and by forging himself a Ring from it become master of the world. Wotan (bass-bar.), ruler of the gods, has engaged the giants Fasolt and Fafner (basses) to build Valhalla for the gods; unable to pay for it he has promised them Freia (sop.), goddess of youth. Loge (ten.), the fire god, persuades Wotan to accompany him to Nibelheim where by a trick Wotan obtains the Ring and the Rhine Gold from Alberich; he intends to pay the giants with the gold and to keep the Ring himself. Alberich curses the Ring. The giants see the Ring on Wotan's finger and demand it as well as a magic helmet, the Tarnhelm. Wotan at first refuses, and the giants prepare to drag Freia away. Wotan's wife Fricka (mezzo) urges her husband to give the giants the Ring. Erda (con.), the earth goddess, warns Wotan of the consequences of retaining the Ring. He adds it to the gold, whereupon Fasolt and Fafner quarrel. Fafner kills Fasolt and takes away the gold, the Tarnhelm, and the Ring. The gods, watched cynically by Loge, enter Valhalla as the curtain falls.

[In order to defend Valhalla, Wotan begets with Erda nine warrior daughter Valkyries, who bear the bodies of dead heroes to Valhalla, where they are revived and help defend the castle. But in order to restore the Ring to the Rhine Maidens and rid the gods of the curse, Wotan has to beget human children. He descends to earth and begets Siegmund and Sieglinde, hoping that the former will one day kill Fafner and restore the Ring to the Rhine Maidens. The pair are separated, Sieglinde being married to Hunding (bass) and Siegmund driven to lead a wandering life of hardship.]

In *Die Walküre*, Siegmund (ten.) is forced to shelter in Hunding's hut. He and Sieglinde (sop.) feel a mysterious attraction. Sieglinde shows him the sword Nothung that Wotan had left embedded in the trunk of the tree growing in Hunding's hut to be withdrawn by a hero. He pulls the sword out and rushes off with Sieglinde. Fricka, the guardian of marriage vows, forces Wotan to side with Hunding in the

Sergey Eisenstein directing a scene from Act 1 of Wagner's 'Die Walküre' (Bolshoy Theatre, Moscow, 1940).

latter's coming combat with Siegmund. But Brünnhilde (sop.), Wotan's favourite Valkyrie, disobeys him and sides with Siegmund. Wotan intervenes and Siegmund is killed, the sword Nothung being shattered by Wotan's spear. Brünnhilde gathers the fragments and entrusts them to Sieglinde, who will soon bear Siegmund's child—the hero Siegfried. Brünnhilde is punished by being put to sleep on a fire-girt rock, through which one day a hero will come to claim her. The curtain falls on the magic fire.

[Sieglinde has died giving birth to Siegfried. The boy has been brought up by the dwarf Mime, brother of Alberich. Mime's cave is in the forest close to the cave where Fafner, who by means of the Tarnhelm has changed himself into a dragon, guards the treasure. Mime hopes to weld the fragments together so that Siegfried can kill Fafner: he means thereby to gain the Ring himself.]

In *Siegfried*, Wotan, disguised as a Wanderer, visits Mime (ten.) and prophesies that the sword will be forged by a hero. Mime recognizes Siegfried (ten.) as this hero and plans to kill him when it is done. Siegfried successfully forges the sword Nothung, and with Mime sets out to seek Fafner. After Siegfried has aroused and killed Fafner (bass), he burns his finger in the dragon's blood. Sucking it, he finds he can understand the language of the birds, one of which (sop.) warns him of Mime's treachery and then tells him of the sleeping Brünnhilde. Siegfried kills Mime, and with the Ring and Tarnhelm follows the bird to the Valkyrie's rock. The Wanderer, although he has told Erda that he longs only for the end, tries to bar his path, but Siegfried shatters his spear with Nothung and, making his way through the fire, awakens Brünnhilde and claims her as his bride.

In *Götterdämmerung*, the Three Norns (con., mezzo, sop.) prophesy the end of the gods. Siegfried gives Brünnhilde the Ring, and, leaving her, goes to seek adventure. He comes to the Hall of the Gibichungs, where Alberich's son Hagen (bass) lives with his half-brother Gunther (bar.) and his half-sister Gutrune (sop.). Hagen plans Siegfried's death, and by giving him a drug to make him forget Brünnhilde, arranges for him to marry Gutrune, and to fetch Brünnhilde as Gunther's bride; thus Hagen will have the Ring. To Brünnhilde comes her sister Waltraute (mezzo), who urges her to return the Ring to the Rhine Maidens. Brünnhilde refuses. Siegfried, wearing the Tarnhelm and in the guise of Gunther, penetrates the fire again, and, overcoming Brünnhilde, tears the Ring from

Scene from Act 1 of Patrice Chéreau's production of Wagner's 'Siegfried' (Bayreuth, 1976).

Joseph Hoffmann's design for the closing scene of Wagner's 'Götterdämmerung' in its first production (Bayreuth, 1876).

her finger and takes her back, an unwilling bride for Gunther. Hagen summons the Gibichungs for the double wedding ceremony. Gunther leads on Brünnhilde, unrecognized by the drugged Siegfried. Seeing the Ring on Siegfried's finger, she accuses him of treachery. With Gunther and Hagen she plans Siegfried's death.

Siegfried is resting on the banks of the Rhine, and the Rhine Maidens plead with him to return the Ring. Hagen, Gunther, and the huntsmen now arrive. Siegfried is asked to relate his adventures. Hagen gives him a second drug to restore his memory, and he speaks of his love for Brünnhilde. Hagen spears him in the back. Siegfried's body is carried back to the Gibichung Hall, and in a quarrel over the Ring, Gunther is killed by Hagen. When the latter approaches the dead Siegfried to remove the Ring, Siegfried's hand rises in the air. Brünnhilde orders a funeral pyre to be built for Siegfried, and taking the Ring from his finger places it on her own. On her horse, Grane, she plunges into the flames. The hall collapses, the Rhine overflows, and as Hagen tries to snatch the Ring from Brünnhilde, he is dragged below the waters by the Rhine Maidens. Valhalla rises in flames, and as the kingdom of the gods is destroyed, a new era of love dawns.

FURTHER READING
Deryck Cooke: *I Saw the World End: a Study of Wagner's 'Ring'* (London, 1979).

Rio Grande, The. Work by Lambert for solo piano, chorus, and orchestra. It is a setting of a poem by Sacheverell Sitwell and was composed in 1927.

Ripetizione (It.). 'Repetition'.

Ripiano. Erroneous spelling of *ripieno.

Ripieno (It.). 'Filled'. 1. Term used in Baroque music to denote the tutti (or *concerto grosso*) sections, as opposed to the solo (or *concertino*) group. In vocal music, the *concertino* string group generally accompanied the arias, while the *ripieno* joined in for choruses; the term is less usually applied to the vocal music itself, but Bach used it, for example for the boys' choir in the first chorus of the *St Matthew Passion*. *Senza ripieno*, all players except those at the leading desks should be silent; *ripienista*, an orchestral player who is not a leader or a soloist. Various corruptions of the term have arisen, such as *ripiano* or *repiano* in brass or military band music, to denote players not at the leading desk.

2. An organ stop.

Riprendere (It.). 'To take up again', i.e. resume the original tempo etc.

RISM. See *International Inventory of Musical Sources*.

Rispetto (It.). A type of Italian poetry, with eight 11-syllable lines to the stanza, set by *frottola* and madrigal composers. Wolf-Ferrari, Malipiero, and others have written music under this title.

Risposta (It.). 'Answer' in *fugues.

Ristringendo (It.). 'Drawing together', i.e. getting faster.

Risvegliato (It.). 'Awakened', i.e. animated.

Ritardando, ritardato, ritenendo, ritenente (It., often abbreviated to *rit.*). 'Holding back', 'held back', i.e. becoming gradually slower, the same as *rallentando*.

Rite (Ambrosian, Gallican, Mozarabic, Roman, etc.). See *Liturgy*.

Ritenuto (It.). 'Held back', i.e. slower. Properly, this means immediately, not gradually as with *ritardando* and *rallentando*.

Rite of Spring, The (*Vesna svyashchennaya*; *Le sacre du printemps*). Ballet (scenes of pagan Russia) in two parts by Stravinsky to a libretto by N. Roerich. It was choreographed by Nijinsky and given its first performance by Diaghilev's Ballets Russes in Paris in 1913, causing a celebrated riot. Stravinsky made a four-hand piano reduction of the score.

Ritmo (It.). 'Rhythm'; *ritmico*, 'rhythmic'.

Ritmo di tre battute (It.). See under *Battuta*.

Ritornello (It.; Eng.: ritornel; Fr.: *ritournelle*; Ger.: *Ritornell*). The Italian form of this word is the original and the most common. It means 'a little return'. 1. In the 14th-century *caccia and *madrigal, the *ritornello* was the concluding couplet at the end of the poem which was usually treated in musical settings as a separate section, often with a change of metre. It was not a refrain.

2. In 17th-century operas and cantatas, the term came to be applied to the short instrumental conclusion added to an aria or other type of song. Sometimes the *ritornello* also occurred at the beginning of the song. Apart from *sinfonie*, these *ritornelli* were the only instrumental portions of early operas. Eventually, by a logical process, the term came to be used as a synonym for *da capo.

3. '*Ritornello* form' is a term used to describe the first and often also the last movements of the Baroque concerto, especially the *concerto grosso*, in which the movements alternate between solo and tutti sections, the tuttis being based always on the same material. Thus these sections were equivalent to *ritornelli*.
See also *Form*, 7.

Ritorno di Ulisse in patria, Il ('The Return of Ulysses to his Homeland'). Opera in prologue and five acts by Monteverdi; text by Badoaro. Produced: Venice, Teatro San Cassiano, February 1641; London, St Pancras Town Hall, 16 March 1965; Washington DC, 18 January 1974. The opera relates the events of the closing books of Homer's *Odyssey*, with added comments from the gods and from allegorical figures (Human Fragility, Time, Fortune, and Love: these appear as a prologue, and are sometimes omitted). Penelope laments the continued absence of Ulisse to her nurse Ericlea. After a discussion of men's sins between Giove and Nettuno, Ulisse is put ashore on Ithaca and encouraged by Minerva to reclaim his palace, given over to the suitors of his wife Penelope. Eumete, his herdsman, is taunted by the jester Iro, and then welcomes the disguised Ulisse, who revives his hopes of his master's return. Eumete then welcomes Ulisse's son Telemaco, also returning home, and there is a joyful reunion, while Eumete tells Penelope that Ulisse may soon appear. The suitor Antinoo mocks Ulisse, disguised as a beggar, who first wins a contest with the suitors by being able to string his bow, and then turns it upon them. Penelope's fear that he may not truly be Ulisse is overcome by Ericlea, and they join in a love duet. The distribution of the voices varies in different editions.

Ritournelle (Fr.). 1. A 17th-century dance in quick triple time, found in the ballets of Lully.
2. See *Ritornello*.

Ritter, Christian (*b* *c*.1650; *d* after 1725). German organist and composer. He may have studied with Christoph Bernhard at Dresden, and in 1672 he was a court musician at Halle; he later became organist to the court. The rest of his life seems to have been divided between Dresden and the Swedish court at Stockholm, where Mattheson mentions him in 1725 as *Kappelmeister*. His works, which include motets, a sonatina for organ, and two keyboard suites, are rather old-fashioned in style.

WENDY THOMPSON

Ritual Dances from 'The Midsummer Marriage'. Orchestral work (with chorus ad lib) by Tippett, comprising four dances from his opera *The Midsummer Marriage*. The first three are from Act 2, and the fourth is from Act 3, and they were first performed in 1953. They are *The Earth in Autumn* ('The Hound Chases the Hare'), *The Waters in Winter* ('The Otter

Pursues the Fish'), *The Air in Spring* ('The Hawk Swoops on the Bird'), and *Fire in Summer* (a celebration of carnal love).

Ritual Fire Dance. Dance from Falla's ballet *El amor brujo*. It became popular in Falla's piano arrangement (played with exceptional brilliance by Arthur Rubinstein) and has also been arranged for other instruments, for example the cello.

Riverso, al (It.). 'Turned back', 'reversed'. The term is used both for inversion and for retrograde motion.

Robbins, Jerome (*b* New York, 11 Oct. 1918). American choreographer. His first ballet, *Fancy Free* (Bernstein, 1944), brought him success. He was associate artistic director of the New York City Ballet from 1949 to 1959, and ballet master, with Balanchine, from 1969. He draws on eclectic sources in numerous ballets, such as *Dances at a Gathering* (Chopin, 1969), *Goldberg Variations* (Bach, 1971), and *Requiem Canticles* (Stravinsky, 1972), and his musical productions include *The King and I* (1951), *West Side Story* (1957), and *Fiddler on the Roof* (1964).
NOËL GOODWIN

Roberday, François (*b* Paris, Mar. 1624; *d* Auffargis, nr Versailles, Oct. 1680). French composer and organist. He was the son of a goldsmith who also built organs. In 1659 he was *valet de chambre* to Anne of Austria and subsequently to Queen Marie-Thérèse of Spain. He published a set of fugues for organ (Paris, 1660) which lists the composers whose themes he used as subjects; they include the foreigners Froberger and Cavalli as well as contemporary French composers. He may have taught Lully composition. DENIS ARNOLD

Robert le diable ('Robert the Devil'). Opera in five acts by Meyerbeer to a libretto by A. E. Scribe and G. Delavigne. It was first performed in Paris in 1831.

Robin et Marion. See *Jeu de Robin et de Marion, Le*.

Robinson, Thomas (*fl.* early 17th century). English lutenist and composer. Little is known of his life, but from the dedications of his works it would seem that he worked at Elsinore in Denmark, and then served Thomas Cecil, Earl of Exeter. He wrote two instrumental Tutors which include his own compositions: the *Schoole of Musicke* (London, 1603), a tutor for lute, pandora, orpharion, and bass viol; and *New Citharen Lessons* (London, 1609) for the cittern.
WENDY THOMPSON

Robusto (It.). 'Robust' (e.g. *tenore robusto*, a powerful tenor voice); *robustamente*, 'in a robust manner'.

Rock and roll [rock 'n' roll, rock]. A commercial amalgam of the styles of American White country music and Black rhythm and blues, the forerunner and shaper of the popular music of the 1960s and 1970s that has simply become known as 'pop'. The all-important element is the beat, heavily emphasized and frenetic, and the music is generally full of energy, pace, and defiant themes. The tight-jeaned dress and attitudes of the singers emphasized the sexual nature of the music. Early pioneers of rock and roll were Amos Milburn, Matt Lucas, Curtis Ousley, Charlie Feathers, and Roy Brown, but the glory went to the more commercialized stars who became the first gods of the modern pop scene: Eddie Cochrane, Gene Vincent, Chuck Berry, Little Richard, and Jerry Lee Lewis. The first internationally-known pioneers of rock and roll were Bill Haley and his Comets, who set the world alight with their 'one o'clock, two o'clock, three o'clock rock'; the song provided an exciting beginning to the film *Blackboard Jungle* and owed something of its melody to Count Basie. The biggest star of rock and roll was Elvis Presley, who came to prominence in 1954 and later had a very successful film career. In Britain the style was pioneered by Tommy Steele, who has also become a successful star of stage and screen. Since Haley and his Comets put rock and roll on the map in the mid 1950s the style has gained historical respectability and has had several revivals. As the styles of pop music changed and rock and roll was absorbed into later developments, the word 'rock' was adopted for the higher forms of pop music, suggesting some sort of respectable jazz basis, but the word is now used without very much discrimination.
PETER GAMMOND

Rock of Ages, Cleft for Me. Hymn of which the words were written by the Revd Augustus Montague Toplady (1740–78), vicar of Broadhembury, Devon. It was first published in *Gospel Magazine* (1776, edited by Toplady). The tune is by Richard Redhead, from *Church Hymn Tunes, Ancient and Modern* (1853).

Rock steady. See under *Reggae*.

Rococo. See *Baroque*, 4.

Rodelinda. Opera in three acts by Handel to a libretto by Haym adapted from one by Antonio Salvi after Corneille's *Petharite*. It was first performed in London in 1725.

Rodeo. Ballet in one act by Copland to a libretto by Agnes de Mille, who also choreographed it. Subtitled 'The Courting at Burnt Ranch', it is set in the Wild West and uses traditional songs. It was first performed in 1942. Copland arranged four dance episodes for orchestra (1942) and arranged the work for piano (1962).

Rodgers, Richard (Charles) (*b* Hammels Station, Long Island, 28 June 1902; *d* New York, 30 Dec. 1979). American composer. He inherited his musical gift from his mother, who was a pianist, and at 14 had his first song published. At the age of 18, while studying at Columbia University, he met his first important collaborator Lorenz Hart with whom he worked on various college shows. Confident that they would conquer the professional theatre, they struggled without success for five years. On the point of giving up they were commissioned to write a revue for the Theater Guild called *Garrick Gaieties*, which ran for 18 months instead of the one evening that was planned; at the same time their show *Dearest Enemy* was produced. Rodgers and Hart continued to collaborate (until Hart's death in 1943) on such shows as *The Girl Friend* (1926), *Lido Lady* (1926), *A Connecticut Yankee* (1927), *Present Arms* (1928), *Heads Up!* (1929), *Evergreen* (1930), *America's Sweetheart* (1931), *On your Toes* (1936), *Babes in Arms* (1937), *The Boys from Syracuse* (1938), *Pal Joey* (1940), and *By Jupiter* (1942). Hart was one of the most brilliant, adept, and witty lyric-writers of the period, even if an unreliable partner through personal traits. It is the individual songs by Rodgers and Hart which tend to survive, the shows as a whole belonging to their times and not ideal for revival. The style and impact of

Rodgers' writing changed when Hart died and he had to find a new partner. He joined up with Oscar Hammerstein II, whom he had known at college and who was already the very successful writer of operetta-styled musicals like *Rose Marie*, *The Desert Song*, and *Showboat*. The Rodgers and Hammerstein musicals were substantial shows of lasting quality, each carefully tailored to its story with music operatically designed to fit. The Theater Guild were again the promoters, commissioning *Oklahoma!* (1943), which ran for over four years in New York. This was followed by *Carousel* (1945), *South Pacific* (1949), *The King and I* (1951), *The Sound of Music* (1959), etc. Hammerstein's death in 1960 left Rodgers without a suitable partner. He continued to write, often using his own librettos, but never achieved the same memorable productions as he had with Hammerstein. Rodgers was clearly a composer in the same class as Kern, Gershwin, and Cole Porter, but the quality of his later music and shows in the 1940s and 1950s suggests that he also had a greater awareness of the European tradition and was therefore able to write musicals of universal and lasting appeal. PETER GAMMOND

Rodrigo, Joaquin (*b* Sagunto, Valencia, 22 Nov. 1902). Spanish composer. Blind from an early age, he studied composition with Francisco Antich in Valencia (1920–3) and with Paul Dukas at the École Normale de Musique in Paris (1927–32), where he also met Falla. In 1944 he was appointed music adviser to Spanish Radio, and in 1946 he became professor of music history at the University of Madrid. His *Concierto de Aranjuez* (1939) quickly established itself as by far the most popular of guitar concertos, evoking old Spain in a colourful and nostalgic manner. Rodrigo has also composed

Richard Rodgers (right) *with Oscar Hammerstein.*

concertos in a similar style for piano, violin, cello, flute, etc.   PAUL GRIFFITHS

FURTHER READING
Federico Sopeña: *Joaquín Rodrigo* (Madrid, 1946).

Rodrigues Coelho, Manuel. See *Coelho, Manuel Rodrigues.*

Roger, Estienne (*b* Caen, 1665 or 1666; *d* Amsterdam, 7 July 1722). French music printer and publisher, based in Amsterdam. He moved from Normandy to Amsterdam in 1685 as a result of Protestant persecution, and in 1697 began publishing music and other books, which eventually totalled over 500 titles. He favoured the works of Italian composers and published first editions of Vivaldi, Corelli, Albinoni, Caldara, Marcello, Alessandro Scarlatti, and others. Under his own management and that of his successor, Michel-Charles Le Cène, his firm became the principal publisher and distributor of music in the first half of the 18th century.

Roger made full use of the prevailing freedom from copyright restrictions, copying much music of other publishers (notably *Ballard in Paris) and distributing his 'new' editions through agents in many European cities. He was one of the first printers to number his plates, and he also issued catalogues of his publications, both of which have facilitated study of his editions. After his death the business was carried on briefly by his elder daughter Jeanne, until in 1723 it was sold to his son-in-law Le Cène. Le Cène used many of Roger's plates, adapting them to include his own name, and he issued his own editions of music by Geminiani, Handel, Locatelli, Quantz, Tartini, Telemann, and others—over 100 titles by 1743, the year of his death. The reputation of both men was based on their scrupulous editing and splendid copperplate engraving.   J. M. THOMSON

Rogers, Benjamin (*b* Windsor, May 1614; *d* Oxford, June 1698). English organist and composer. The son of a lay clerk at St George's Chapel, Windsor, he was first a choirboy and later himself a lay clerk there. From 1639 to 1641 he was organist of Christ Church Cathedral, Dublin, and during the Commonwealth taught music in and around Windsor. At the Restoration, he became organist of Eton College, and in 1662 took up his former post as lay clerk at the reconstituted chapel of St George's. In 1664 he became organist of Magdalen College, Oxford, where he received the D.Mus. five years later.

Rogers's *Hymnus eucharisticus* is traditionally sung from the top of Magdalen Tower at dawn on May Day. Four of his services and some anthems were published in 18th-century collections, including Boyce's *Cathedral Music*

(London, 1760–73); others survive in manuscript. He also wrote several glees and some instrumental pieces which were published in Playford's *Courtly Masquing Ayres* (1662).
    WENDY THOMPSON

Rognoni Taeggio, Francesco. See *Taeggio, Francesco Rognoni.*

Roi David, Le ('King David'). Dramatic psalm in five parts (28 numbers) by Honegger to a text by R. Morax. It is scored for narrator, soprano, mezzo-soprano, tenor, chorus, and orchestra and was first performed at Mézières in 1921. Honegger revised and reorchestrated it in three parts (27 numbers) in 1923, and arranged an orchestral suite of four numbers.

Roi malgré lui, Le ('The King Despite Himself'). Comic opera in three acts by Chabrier to a libretto by E. de Najac and P. Burani (revised by J. Richepin) after A. and M. Ancelot. It was first performed in Paris in 1887.

Roman, Johan Helmich (*b* Stockholm, 26 Oct. 1694; *d* Haraldsmåla, nr Kalmar, 20 Nov. 1758). Swedish composer. He emerged at a time when Sweden had withdrawn from her role as a Great Power after the death of Charles XII, and had turned to the pursuit of the arts of peace. Roman showed such early talent as a violinist and oboist that the court took the then unprecedented step of paying for his studies abroad. He spent five years in England (1716–21), probably studying under Pepusch and certainly acquiring an admiration for Handel, and returned home to become in 1727 *Kapellmästare* to the court. He transformed the orchestra into a first-rate ensemble and together with a young player and composer, Per Brant (1713–67), started public concerts at the House of the Nobility in Stockholm, which became an important forum for new music. In 1735 he undertook a second journey abroad, which again brought him to England, where he met Handel, Bononcini, Geminiani, and others, as well as France and Italy. It would seem, however, that declining health and increasing deafness caused him to take a less active part in Stockholm's musical life after his return to Sweden in 1737.

In spite of the fact that Roman's earliest work was a cantata, *Festa musicale* (1725), the bulk of his output during the early part of his life was instrumental. The 12 flute sonatas were written in 1727, most of the concertos date from the early 1730s and it seems likely that the greater part of his (more than 20) *sinfonie* were composed during the decade following his second trip abroad. However, as his interest in instrumental music waned during the 1740s, he turned to vocal music, setting vernacular texts with increasing frequency. Among the most important of these are the *Andliga Sånger* ('Sacred Songs'), which occupied him up to the last years of his life.

Roman's music is a compound of various stylistic traits. He readily absorbed Italian and English influences, and his enthusiasm for Handel left an indelible imprint on his style. His earlier music showed him not unresponsive to the Lullian *ouverture*, but in his maturity the Neapolitan style constituted the most potent factor in his make-up. Although he never developed a pronounced personal idiom, he has many distinctive features, the two *sinfonie*, No. 16 in D and No. 20 in E minor, by which he is best known outside Scandinavia, revealing a crisp, fresh, and engaging melodic style. There is a keen awareness of proportion, and his invention in such works as the *sinfonie* and the *Drottningholmsmusik* never falls below a certain level of distinction.   ROBERT LAYTON

Roman Carnival, The. See *Carnaval romain, Le*.

Romance. 1. The Spanish *romances* are long epic ballads dating back to at least the 14th century, when they were sung for the entertainment of aristocratic patrons, usually by solo professional musicians. The subject-matter was normally legendary or historical. *Romance* tunes survived in the vihuela collections of Narváez, Milán, Daza, and Mudarra. In the Baroque era, the *romance* became virtually synonymous with the *villancico (i.e. a song with refrain, sung to guitar accompaniment), and in the 18th century it expanded into a miniature cantata. Thereafter it survived in folk music.

2. In France, the word acquired a musical connotation in the 18th century. Jean-Jacques Rousseau's definition of it in his musical dictionary (1767) indicates an unpretentious strophic verse of a simple kind: a short, often tragic, love poem, the melody simple and unaffected, with an unobtrusive instrumental support. Used extensively in France in the late 18th and early 19th centuries, it had ousted the *air, before yielding to the term *mélodie, which, however, bore a somewhat different meaning. The chief exponents of the French *romance* were lesser composers such as Boieldieu, Auguste Panseron (1795–1859), and Hippolyte Monpou (1804–41). It was inevitable that its essential artlessness, which linked it stylistically with the folk music of western Europe, should eventually become affected by the greater sophistication that was changing the whole character of song, and the term, which from the very first had been loose and ill-defined, gradu-

ally fragmented into subsidiary categories aimed at more precise definition.

The term soon spread beyond France. In Germany, for example, Reichardt in the 1790s published some Goethe songs as *Lieder, Oden, Balladen und Romanzen*. Schumann, perhaps borrowing the term from Heine (who classed some of his poetry including *Die Grenadiere* as 'Romanzen'), used it freely, for example in four collections of *Romanzen und Balladen* (Opp. 45, 49, which contains his setting of Heine's *Die beiden Grenadiere*, 53, and 64). We find it in Brahms too, for example *Lieder und Romanzen*, Op. 14; the *Romanzen und Lieder*, Op. 84; and his *Magelone* song-cycle, Op. 33, which he labels *Romanzen*. (It is not always easy to pinpoint the differences between 'Romanze', 'Ballade', 'Lied', and 'Gesang'.) The *romance* also spread to Russia (where it was first applied to songs with French words) and to Italy, for example Verdi's *Sei romanze* (1838) and *Album di sei romanze* (1845).

The typical *romance* of the *salon* or drawing-room made little demand on the performers, intellectually, emotionally, or technically. Never far from banality or sentimentality, it occasionally freed itself from the restraint of poetry to become the *romance sans paroles*, which was musically akin to the nocturne of John Field and Chopin. It is this nocturnal atmosphere which pervades Schumann's dreamy *Romanze* in F♯ major for piano (Op. 28) and the similarly labelled slow movement of his Fourth Symphony, in D minor. The first known use of the term for an instrumental movement occurs in Gossec's E♭ Symphony, Op. 4 No. 2 (1761 or 1762).   LESLIE ORREY

Romance sans paroles (Fr.). 'Song without words'. Mendelssohn wrote several piano pieces with this title.

Roman de Fauvel. Medieval poem by Gervais du Bus, which, in one of the manuscripts in which it survives, has been supplied with monophonic and polyphonic musical interpolations of many kinds. There are 167 of these musical items which provide a large and important repertory of early 14th-century French music.

Romanesca (It.). A type of *ground bass, using a specific bass pattern originating in Rome.

It was in use from around the middle of the 16th century to the middle of the 17th, being found in both instrumental and vocal music.

                                G. M. TUCKER

Romania. To the musical world at large, Romania is associated more with pianists such as Dinu Lipatti and Clara Haskil and conductors such as George Georgescu and Constantin Silvestri than with composers. Even George Enescu, the most prominent figure in Romanian music, gained his international reputation as much from teaching, conducting, and performing as from his compositions. Until recently he was known in the West through his least characteristic works, the two Romanian Rhapsodies (1901), while his greatest music, including the Octet for strings, the richly romantic Third Symphony, and the powerful opera *Oedipe*, remained largely unknown. Enescu's single-handed achievement was to draw Romania into the orbit of European music as a whole. He responded to many different stylistic influences, from Wagner and Reger to Fauré and Debussy. But whatever the model, his voice is recognizable, forging its individuality from a unique synthesis of Western European acquisitions and indigenous features drawn from the rich veins of Romanian church and folk musics.

1. *Folk Music and Early History*. Romanian folk music is as ancient and varied as the country's dramatic history, spanning over 2,000 years of continuity. With the defeat of the Dacian king Decebalus (AD 101-6) by Emperor Trajan, the country became a Roman colony and the many successive waves of foreign invasions by Goths, Tartars, Huns, and others did little to obliterate its Latin inheritance and character. Although it was influenced linguistically by invaders and neighbours (Turks and Greeks), Romanian has remained to this day a Romance language, with obvious implications for the character of its folk music. Incantations, laments, ritual dances, and songs have been transmitted from generation to generation, preserving a remarkable continuity in their detailed melodic and rhythmic characteristics. Even traditional instruments, including the *bucium*, *caval*, *naiu*, *fluier*, and *cobza* remain in constant use today. 19th-century Romanian composers drew upon this rich repertory of musical creativity in a fairly superficial way, but in the early 20th century it was tapped by Bartók, who published over a thousand folk-tunes and made creative use of them in his music, and by Enescu, who integrated it thoroughly and subtly into the substance of his musical thought. More recent composers such as Mihail Jora (1891-1971), Ion Dimitrescu (*b* 1913), Marţian Negrea (*b* 1893), and Sabin Drăgoi (1884-1968) have continued to draw extensively upon this folk inheritance.

Until the fall of Constantinople the Balkan peninsula, including old Dacia, was an important bulwark of Christianity against the fierce pagan attacks which took place continually from the 6th to the 12th century. As in Russia, Serbia, and Bulgaria, however, the early Christian rites in Romania were profoundly influenced by the Eastern traditions of the Byzantine empire, with its mixture of Roman, Greek, and Persian cultures. From Bishop Niceta of the 4th century onwards, the repertory of liturgical music of the Romanian Orthodox Church continued to expand and develop, and its richness and variety have been surveyed at length by the distinguished Romanian Byzantologist Ion Petrescu. More recently Romanian musicologists have demonstrated that Enescu's debt to this repertory is considerable (he himself referred to its importance), while the modality, microtonal inflections, and glissandos of the chant have further influenced younger composers such as Paul Constantinescu (1909-63), notably in his *Patimile şi Invierea Domnului* ('The Passion and Resurrection of Our Lord').

While the provinces of Moldavia and Wallachia remained faithful to old peasant traditions, Transylvania came into direct contact with Western harmonic developments, partly through the increasing tendency of Romanian musicians to travel to Italian and French courts during the 16th century. Psalms of Romanian origin were included in Italian and German collections at this time and other extant sources include an antiphonary of 1529 and an *Odae cum harmoniis* of 1562, the latter found at the Schola Coronensis in Braşov. Named composers also begin to appear in the 16th century with a handful of works by Nicolaus Olahus (1493-1568) and Ioan Căianu (1627-98) demonstrating stylistic affinities with Western European church music of the early Renaissance. The *Psaltires romaňească* by Filotei sin Agăi Jipei (1713) take another important step towards the notion of an indigenous music in their use of the vernacular, instigating a tradition in church music which was carried through into the 19th and 20th centuries in the music of composers such as Anton Pann and Dimitru Suceveanu (1816-98), followed by Gavriil Muzicescu (1847-1903) and D. G. Kiriac (1866-1928).

2. *Nationalism and Beyond*. In the early 19th century Romania responded to the growing wave of nationalist feeling which spread across Eastern Europe. Foreign ensembles were gradually replaced by indigenous Romanian players and an institutional framework for the teaching and performance of Western music was established. In 1833 the Philharmonic society began its activities in Bucharest, while three years later a Philharmonic school (later to become a state conservatory) was founded in

Iaşi, the Moldavian capital. Operas by Mozart and Rossini were frequently performed in the early part of the century, but the repertory gradually expanded to include Romanian comic operas or *vaudevilles* by Alexandru Flechtenmacher (1823–98), their subject-matter often reflecting stirring nationalist sentiments, and grand operas by Ion Andrei Wachmann (1807–63). One of these, *Mihai Bravul în ajunul bătăliei dela Călugăreni*, celebrating the brief union of the principalities under a single crown in 1600, became outstandingly popular. These activities culminated in 1877 with the establishment of the Romanian Opera in Bucharest and this in turn · stimulated a renewed enthusiasm for operatic composition. Mauriciu Cohen-Lînaru (1849–1928), a pupil of Bizet and César Franck, contributed a successful three-act opera *Meşterul Manole*, which, together with his five piano sonatas and song-cycles, earns him a place as one of the most important Romanian composers of the late Romantic era. He was rivalled only by Ciprian Porumbescu (1853–83), whose early death prevented him from realizing his full stature as a composer. Also prominent at this time were Chopin's pupil Carol Miculi (1821–97), whose compositions include a *Missa romena* for choirs and organ, and Eduard Caudella (1841–1924), whose greatest claim to fame was as the teacher of George Enescu.

Enescu himself proved of the utmost importance both as an inspiration to and a stylistic model for his contemporaries and successors, though the teaching of the Italian-born Alfonso Castaldi (1874–1942) at the Bucharest conservatory was hardly less important. Among Castaldi's most distinguished pupils were Alfred Alessandrescu (1890–1959), Mihai Andricu (1894–1971), who left 10 symphonies and eight sinfoniettas, Ion Nonna Ottescu (1888–1940), best known for his poem for violin and orchestra *Les enchantements d'Armide*, Robert Cremer (1889–1928), composer of the opera *Diane de Poitiers*, and Dimitrie Cuclin (1885–1975), who wrote 18 symphonies of almost Brucknerian proportions. The folkloristic synthesis which Enescu achieved and bequeathed was encouraged by official cultural policy in the years following the establishment of a socialist political system after the Second World War. As elsewhere in Eastern Europe, Romania saw a massive restructuring of its musical life during the early post-war years, with the formation of a composers' union (1920), of state philharmonic societies, opera houses, and academies. In general, the younger generation of composers today retains an allegiance to folkloristic elements as a compositional basis. At the same time, inspired by developments in Poland, many of them are beginning to respond to more progressive tendencies in post-war musical language. Among the most successful of these younger composers are Pascal Bentoiu (*b* 1927), whose opera *Hamlet* achieved recognition both in Romania and abroad, Anatol Vieru (*b* 1926), best known for his opera *The Whale*, Tiberiu Olah (*b* 1928), whose symphonic poem *The Endless Column* is an interpretation in sound of Brâncuşi's famous sculpture, and Cornel Ţăranu (*b* 1934), composer of *Incantations* and of a compelling and evocative *Sinfonia brevis*. Marcel Mihalovici (*b* 1898), a resident of Paris, by his considerable and original output of operas, ballets, and symphonies, contributed greatly to the prestige of Romanian music abroad.

MIRON GRINDEA/JIM SAMSON

Roman rite. See *Liturgy*, 2*b*.

Romanticism. In its original meaning, the word Romantic derived from Romance, the ancient language of France, and hence the term applied to the poems or tales, typical of its literature, that were characterized by imaginative adventurousness. 'Romantic' came, by the late 17th century, to mean something extravagantly fanciful, diverging from accepted norms. It was not until the 19th century that the term 'Romanticism' was needed to describe a new movement, which embraced the arts, philosophy, politics, and even the sciences. Romanticism grew in different countries at different times, taking different forms, and was never a coherent movement. However, the Age of Romanticism is now generally thought of as extending from the closing years of the 18th century to the early years of the 20th.

1. *The Spirit of Romanticism.* So lengthy a period, especially one associated with rapid political, social, and economic change, naturally embraced several phases and included a number of contradictory strains. However, in all its manifestations, Romanticism emphasized the apparent domination of emotion over reason, of feeling and impulse over form and order. This was often more apparent than real, since the disciplines of Romantic music needed to be no less secure than those of Classicism in order to express ideas effectively. But new value was set upon novelty and sensation, upon technical innovation and experiment, and upon the cross-fertilization of ideas from different disciplines, both within and without the arts.

In Germany the Romantic movement was primarily musical. Various poets conceded supremacy to the art of music, but their contribution, and that of painting, was welcomed in a Germany tending towards a synthesis of the arts—a trend initiated by Weber and crowned by Wagner. In Italy, the movement had stronger political overtones, both poets and composers associating themselves with the Risorgimento, the movement towards political independence and unity that claimed Verdi as its laureate. In France, the paintings in various salons and Victor Hugo's *Hernani* (1830) were at least as potent excitements in the Romantic movement as the largely misunderstood Berlioz. Britain, musically an outpost of Europe at this stage, made its greatest contribution to Romanticism with literary influences—the fake 'Ossian', then Scott and Byron, thrilled musical Europe.

It was largely in Rousseau, the philosopher adopted with special enthusiasm by the Romantics, that justification was found for the emphasis on emotion rather than intellect. From him, too, came delight in the country and admiration for the virtues to be found in simple, unspoilt people. There was also a turn from the rational (supreme principle in the Age of Reason) to the irrational, both mystic and merely spooky. Longings for things far away, an essential Romantic characteristic, could include dreams of remote lands (in a new liking for the exotic) and of the distant past (in the fascination for a past Romantic age of chivalry). The longing for freedom from restraints meant a passionate desire for national identity and independence, and comparably a search for individual identity and an admiration for the dominating, convention-scorning figure of the Hero.

It was in part the observation of some of these strains in Beethoven that led the writer and composer E. T. A. Hoffmann to claim him as a Romantic; but more crucially, Beethoven's music aroused in Hoffmann fear, suffering, and a longing for the infinite. The 'Pastoral' Symphony is clearly Romantic in its 'awakening of happy feelings on arrival in the country', its brook, its alarming storm, its Rousseauesque peasants. The Fifth Symphony is more intrinsically Romantic in its assertion of Man's defiant supremacy over his Fate; so is the 'Eroica', or Heroic Symphony, with its great Funeral March for the death of the hero, its triumphantly energetic scherzo, and its final variations on the theme Beethoven associated with Prometheus, the god who, by bringing fire from heaven, gave men independence from the gods. Beethoven delighted Rousseau's Romantic admirers with his demonstration of the moral force expressible in music.

However, Beethoven was not universally regarded as the most characteristic early Romantic, nor was the symphony to be the favoured Romantic medium. Opera assumed a new position of importance, finding new audiences and a new range of themes. In general, classical subjects were dropped in favour of settings remote in time or place; at the same time, the immediate dangers and horrors of revolution and war produced a genre, *Rescue Opera, of which Beethoven's *Fidelio* is the greatest example. Nature could play a crucial role in the plots, as with the avalanche in Cherubini's *Eliza*; others featured the supernatural, as with Weber's *Der Freischütz*; or contact between the supernatural and human worlds, as with Marschner's *Hans Heiling*; and in different countries of Europe composers began developing a consciously national tradition, drawing upon folk music, historical or legendary figures, or other devices to confer local colour and individuality.

2. *National Characteristics.* Russians have long claimed Glinka as the father of their national opera for his ability to absorb national ideas and folk music techniques into two major works, an heroic historical opera, *A Life for the Tsar* (1836), and a fantastic fairy-tale opera, *Ruslan and Lyudmila* (1842). Comparable father figures were, in Hungary, Ferenc Erkel with *Hunyadi Laszlo* (1844) and *Bank ban* (1861), in Poland, Stanisław Moniuszko with *Halka* (1848), and in Czechoslovakia, Smetana with *The Bartered Bride* (1866). In all these countries in the east of Europe, nationalist ideas tended to manifest themselves most vividly in opera, where local colour could be grafted on to the techniques of Italian opera, later French Revolutionary Opera and *Grand Opera, and German Romantic Opera. Among Glinka's other services to his country was the pioneering, in *Kamarinskaya*, of a technique of 'varied repetition' which Russian composers (including Tchaikovsky) found more instinctively sympathetic than sonata form. Composers who made particular efforts to define a national melodic idiom by drawing on the inflections of their spoken language include, in Russia, Dargomyzhsky and Musorgsky, and in Czechoslovakia, Janáček.

Except in Italy, where the voice continued to reign supreme, the orchestra assumed a more important role in opera, providing more sensational and descriptive elements in the drama: the development of *Leitmotiv provided not only graphic illustration but new dramatic coherence at a time when the old formal number opera was weakening. Orchestral music gave more attention to drama. Sonata form and the traditional layout of the symphony tended to give way to more dramatic, pictorial, or narrative methods of construction (another reflection of the Romantic tendency to find new connections between the arts). Though a major symphonist such as Schubert was content to work in traditional outlines, Schumann admitted a much stronger pictorial element (as in his 'Rhenish' Symphony), and it was still more characteristic to experiment with programme symphonies, as in Berlioz's *Symphonie fantastique*, or with new forms dictated by narrative or pictorial elements such as Liszt's symphonic poems. The enlargement of the standard orchestra was connected to the rise of the virtuoso conductor, initially composers such as Weber, Berlioz, Liszt, and Wagner.

Virtuosity, indeed, became a stronger musical element. The concept of the Artist as Hero, mastering sensational difficulties or having access by his special sensibility to heightened emotions, encouraged the success of Paganini, whose carefully cultivated sinister aura lent extra thrills to his virtuosity. His violin Caprices, and the concept behind them, strongly influenced Liszt, whose own brilliant virtuosity embraced novel compositional techniques as well as incomparable gifts as a pianist.

3. *The Orchestra and Opera*. If one of Romanticism's tendencies was to heighten and exaggerate, its intensification of the emotions also led to refinement and concentration. Romantic orchestration cultivated, in Wagner, a rich, smooth, sensuous blend, but, in Berlioz and Mahler, a liking for novel combinations of sound and chamber music textures within the full orchestra. The moment of exquisite sensibility—deriving from a mood, an image, or a nervous sensation, even the poetry to be found in a technical device—could give rise to Romantic miniatures, and to the short piano pieces by Schumann and Chopin. Schubert, first great master of the German *Lied*, found a new way of fusing poetry and music, with the piano often providing an illustrative background for the vocal narrative, and wrote the first great song-cycles in *Die schöne Müllerin* and *Winterreise*. His greatest successors, Schumann and Wolf, refined still further the expressive contact between poetry and music; none of the three, significantly, was at home in opera, despite repeated attempts by Schubert.

Opera retained, however, its dominant position throughout the century, combining as it did several arts in a dramatic context. Parisian Grand Opera stood somewhat to the side of the Romantic tradition, though the imposing resources of the Opéra attracted not only its own tradition of composers (Spontini, Auber, Halévy, Meyerbeer) but also interested Verdi, Tchaikovsky, and Wagner. The tradition of French Romantic opera really lay more with the somewhat sentimental vein cultivated by Massenet and Gounod: France studiously underrated her greatest Romantic, Berlioz, whose bold new forms and ideas proved disconcerting. Bellini's long, expressive melodies won admiration for Italian Romantic opera even

in Germany, as did the Romantic tragedies which Donizetti regarded as more important than his comedies.

But European opera in the middle and latter part of the century was dominated by Verdi and Wagner. The genius of each included the capacity to absorb into great art different strains from earlier phases in Romanticism, and bring them to culmination: this places them as late Romantics. Wagner, in particular, extended chromatic harmony (largely under the influence of Liszt) to the limits of tonality; Brahms's apparently more classical disciplines won him a following which set him in opposition to Wagner. However, Schoenberg regarded Brahms as a progressive, though he himself inherited much from Wagner, who indeed left few significant composers of the final stages of the Romantic movement unmarked in some way. Reaction against Wagner, or the difficulty in succeeding him, helped to hasten the emergence of ideas that moved away from Romanticism. Though the movement is conveniently held to have run its course by the outbreak of the First World War, it has bequeathed much to subsequent composers: to that extent, it is still with us.   JOHN WARRACK

FURTHER READING
Friedrich Blume: *Classic and Romantic Music* (New York, 1970); Carl Dahlhaus: *Between Romanticism and Modernism: Four Studies in the Music of the Later 19th Century* (Berkeley, Los Angeles, and London, 1980).

'Romantic' Symphony. Subtitle of Bruckner's Symphony No. 4 in E♭ major, composed in 1874 and revised in 1878–80 and 1886.

Romanze (Ger.). See *Romance, 2*.

Romberg, Sigmund (*b* Nagykanizsa, 29 July 1887; *d* New York, 9 Nov. 1951). American composer of Hungarian birth. He studied engineering at university and emigrated to America in 1909. He was unable to find work as an engineer; but, being also a proficient musician, he became a café pianist. He spent the next five years in this humble role before he was able to persuade the Shubert organization to let him write some music for one of their Winter Garden shows, *The Whirl of the World* (1913). His contributions were well received, and this led to his writing for a number of Shubert revues, including the *Passing Show* series. He was to write some 80 stage shows in all but really found his *métier* when he turned to a romantic operetta vein which obviously had its origins in his own Hungarian background and the Viennese school. There was *Maytime* in 1917 and *The Rose of Stamboul* (with Leo Fall) in 1922; but he found true success with this formula in *The Student Prince* (1924), *The Desert Song* (1926), and *The New Moon* (1928), which were also highly successful in London and elsewhere. At the same time he continued to write shows in a more American style, such as *Up in Central Park* (1945, filmed 1948) and *The Girl in Pink Tights* (1954), as well as music for films. The essence of Romberg is in the romantic songs from his operettas—'Deep in my Heart' and 'Serenade' (from *Student Prince*), 'One alone' (from *Desert Song*), and 'Lover Come Back to Me' (*New Moon*). He frequently worked in collaboration with other composers, such as Gershwin, Rodgers, Fall, Schwartz, and Straus. PETER GAMMOND

Romeo and Juliet. Several compositions have been based on Shakespeare's tragedy, among them: 1. *Roméo et Juliette*. Dramatic Symphony, Op. 17, by Berlioz to a text by E. Deschamps. It is for alto, tenor, and bass soloists, chorus, and orchestra, and was composed in 1839.

2. *Roméo et Juliette*. Opera in five acts by Gounod to a libretto by Barbier and Carré. It was first performed in Paris in 1867.

3. *Romeo i Dzhulyetta*. Fantasy overture by Tchaikovsky, composed in 1869, revised in 1870 and again in 1880.

4. *Romeo i Dzhulyetta*. Ballet in a prologue, three acts, and an epilogue by Prokofiev to a libretto by Lavrovsky, Prokofiev, and Radlov. It was choreographed by Psota and first performed in Brno in 1938. Prokofiev arranged three symphonic suites from the score: No. 1, Op. 64*b*, in seven movements (1936); No. 2, Op. 64*c*, in seven movements (1937); and No. 3, Op. 101, in six movements (1946).

Ronald, (Sir) Landon (*b* London, 7 June 1873; *d* London, 14 Aug. 1938). English conductor, pianist, and composer. His real name was Russell, for he was a son of Henry Russell, composer of ballads. He studied at the Royal College of Music and in 1891 became accompanist and coach at Covent Garden. In 1892 he conducted Augustus Harris's Italian Opera Company, and opera at Drury Lane. In 1894 he went as Melba's accompanist to the USA. He made his Covent Garden conducting début in *Faust* in 1896, but from 1898 to 1902 could obtain work only in musical comedy and at Blackpool summer concerts. From 1904, however, he worked as guest conductor of the London Symphony Orchestra, was conductor of the New Symphony Orchestra 1909-14, and of the Scottish Orchestra 1916-20. From 1910 to 1938 he was Principal of the Guildhall School of Music and was knighted in 1922. He was a friend and sensitive interpreter of Elgar, who dedicated *Falstaff* to him. He became musical

adviser to the Gramophone Company (HMV) and conducted several concerto recordings with his friend, the violinist Fritz Kreisler. Ronald's compositions are forgotten except for the song 'Down in the Forest'. MICHAEL KENNEDY

Roncalli, Conte Ludovico (*fl.* late 17th century). Italian guitarist and composer. A contemporary of the Bolognese guitarist G. B. Granata, Roncalli borrowed Granata's title *Capricci armonici* for his own publication of guitar music (Bergamo, 1692), a collection of nine suites in tablature for five-course guitar. WENDY THOMPSON

Ronde (Fr.). 'Round'. 1. The whole-note, or semibreve (𝅝). 2. See *Round*.

Rondeau (Fr.). One of the three standard poetic forms used for *chansons* of the 14th and 15th centuries (see also *Ballade*; *Virelai*). Unlike the other two, however, it was already well established in the 13th century.

The *rondeau* given below, by Adam de la Halle, shows its typical layout as a single stanza poem of four couplets. The first couplet, known as the refrain (indicated here by italics), is repeated at the end. In addition, the first line of the refrain is always used as the second line of the second couplet.

> *Tant con je vivrai*
> *N'aimerai autrui que vous*
>
> Ja n'en partirai
> *Tant con je vivrai*
>
> Ains vous servirai
> Loyaument mis m'i sui tous
>
> *Tant con je vivrai*
> *N'aimerai autrui que vous*

The musical setting of a *rondeau* is clearly divided into two sections (a and b), and each carries one of the refrain lines. The remaining lines of text are allocated to the two sections according to their rhyme, and this yields the characteristic musical form of the *rondeau* in performance: AB aA ab AB (capital letters indicate the position of the refrain).

This is the form of the *rondeau* as generally used by Guillaume de Machaut, the leading 14th-century *chanson* composer. Although his work established the long-term use of the *rondeau* in *chanson* writing, it was not until the 15th century that it became really popular, gaining complete ascendancy over the *ballade* and *virelai* as a medium for courtly love songs. These later *rondeaux* are generally longer, with refrains of either four lines (*rondeau quatrain*) or five (*rondeau cinquain*). In either case, they are set to music by the same method as before, and the resulting musical form is the same:

MUSIC

Ma belle dame souverainne *Faites cesser ma grief dolour*	} A
Que j'endure pour vostre amour *Nuit et jour, dont j'ay tres grant painne*	} B
Ou autrement, soies certainne, *Je finneray dedens brief jour.*	} a
Ma belle dame souverainne *Faites cesser ma grief dolour*	} A
Il n'i a jour de la sepmainne *Que je ne soye en grant tristour*	} a
Se me veullies par vo doulcour *Secourir, de volonte plaine*	} b
Ma belle dame souverainne *Faites cesser ma grief dolour*	} A
Que j'endure pour vostre amour *Nuit et jour, dont j'ay tres grant painne*	} B

PETER DAVIES

Rondeña (Sp.). A kind of *fandango of southern Spain; it takes its name from Ronda in Andalusia.

Rondo form. One of the fundamental forms in music. It is a structure comprising several sections, of which one, usually the first, recurs in the tonic key between thematically and tonally contrasting sections known as episodes: this produces a shape such as ABACA. The form is common in the final movements of sonatas, symphonies, concertos, and quartets.

Often the rondo element is combined with other forms which result in a more complex structure. It is not unusual, for example, to find each section of the rondo consisting of a small *binary structure. Mozart's famous 'Rondo alla turca', the last movement of the piano sonata K 331 in A major, combines binary, *ternary, and rondo elements:

Bar Nos.	Key	Section	
1–8	A minor—E minor	A:||	}
9–16	C major—V of A minor	B	} X
17–25	A minor	A:||	}
26–32	A major	C:||	C
33–41	F♯ minor—C♯ minor	D:||	}
42–48	A major	E	} Y
49–56	F♯ minor	D:||	}
57–64	A major	C:||	C
65–72	A minor—E minor	A:||	}
73–80	C major—V of A minor	B	} X
81–89	A minor	A:||	}
90–96	A major	C:||	C
97–127	A major	Coda	

As can be seen from this scheme, sections X and Y are each binary in construction, but also form part of a larger ternary design, XYX. Each section of this ternary structure, however, is separated from the next by the recurrence of an eight-bar rondo theme—C—in the tonic major.

See also *Form*, 4; *Sonata rondo form*.

G. M. TUCKER

Rontani, Raffaello (*d* Rome, 1622). Italian composer, probably born in Florence. He was in the service of the Medici from 1610, and subsequently moved to Rome, where he was *maestro di cappella* at S. Giovanni dei Fiorentini, as well as serving the Sforza family. His songs were mostly tuneful ariettas, which were very popular in their day.

DENIS ARNOLD

Root, root position (of a chord). The root of a chord is the note from which it takes its name. Thus, the C major chord has C as its root, even though the chord may be in *first or second inversion, with E or G respectively as its lowest note. If a chord is in root position, the lowest note is also the root. See also *Fundamental bass*; *Harmony*, 2, 3.

Rore, Cipriano de (*b c.*1516; *d* Parma, Sept. 1565). Flemish composer. He may have been a pupil of Willaert in Venice in the 1540s. By 1547 he was *maestro di cappella* to Duke Ercole II in Ferrara, but when his employer died in 1559 Rore was away visiting his parents and was not reappointed by Ercole's successor. He there-

Cipriano de Rore

upon entered the service of the Governor of the Netherlands, Margaret of Parma, and in 1561 returned to Italy to work for her husband in Parma. He was tempted away to Venice in 1563, to succeed Willaert as *maestro di cappella* at St Mark's, but found the burden of administration too heavy for him and returned to Parma, where he died.

Although he composed a good deal of church music, it is de Rore's madrigals that are remarkable for their quality and for their influence on other composers. His early madrigals are often settings of Petrarch in a serious style, but after leaving Ferrara he became interested in contemporary poets, concentrating on bringing out the meaning of the verse and using contrasts of rhythms and textures to match their accentuation. He was interested in the potential of chromaticism and unusual melodic intervals for expressing extreme emotions, and it was this trait that made Monteverdi recognize him as one of the fathers of the *seconda prattica* (see *Prima prattica, seconda prattica*).

DENIS ARNOLD

Rorem, Ned (*b* Richmond, Ind., 23 Oct. 1923). American composer. He studied at the American Conservatory in Chicago (1938-40), Northwestern University (1940-2), the Curtis Institute in Philadelphia (1943), and the Juilliard School (1946, 1948), and also had private lessons from Virgil Thomson and Aaron Copland. From 1951 to 1957 he lived in Paris under the patronage of the Vicomtesse Marie Laure de Noailles; he then returned to New York. Primarily a song composer, he has been influenced by his teachers and by the French musicians he came to know in Paris (Poulenc, Honegger, and others). His output also includes several operas, three symphonies and other orchestral works, and a variety of chamber pieces. He has also written the books *The Paris Diary* (New York, 1966), *The New York Diary* (New York, 1967), *Music from Inside Out* (New York, 1967), *Music and People* (New York, 1968), and *Critical Affairs: a Composer's Journal* (New York, 1970).

PAUL GRIFFITHS

Rosalia. A kind of sequence (see *Sequence*, 1).

Rosart, Jacques-François. See *Printing and Publishing of Music*, 6.

Rose. Soundhole cut to aid resonance in lute, guitar, mandolin, etc. The name derives from its flower-like shape.

Roseingrave, Thomas (*b* Winchester, 1688; *d* Dunleary, 23 June 1766). English composer. He was the son of an organist of possibly Irish origin, and studied music with his father, going with him to Dublin at the age of 10. In 1709 he went to Italy to study music, and in Venice he met Domenico Scarlatti, who made a great impression on him. He followed Scarlatti to Rome and Naples, and on his return to England in 1714 set about promoting Scarlatti's music, publishing an edition of keyboard sonatas by him in 1739. His own harpsichord music, curiously enough, shows little of Scarlatti's influence.

In 1725 Roseingrave successfully competed for the post of organist at St George's, Hanover Square. He was now at the height of his career as an organist, teacher, and outstanding improviser, though Hawkins, never one to mince words, thought his compositions 'harsh and disgusting, manifesting great learning, but devoid of eloquence and variety'. But before long Roseingrave fell hopelessly in love with a young pupil whose father forbade their marriage. Thereafter Roseingrave neglected his teaching and his post as organist and eked out a miserable existence; he was apparently able to converse rationally on any subject except that of his blighted hopes, the mention of which would reduce him to a state of acute depression. He eventually retired to Dublin, where his opera *Phaedra and Hippolitus* was produced in 1753, emerging occasionally from his seclusion to give harpsichord recitals. He died at the age of 78 and was buried in St Patrick's Cathedral.

WENDY THOMPSON

Rosenkavalier, Der ('The Knight of the Rose'). Opera in three acts by Richard Strauss; text by Hofmannsthal. Produced: Dresden, Hofoper, 26 January 1911; London, Covent Garden, 29 January 1913; New York, Metropolitan Opera, 9 December 1913. The Princess of Werdenberg, known as the Feldmarschallin (sop.), has been having an affair with the young Count Octavian (sop. or mezzo). The Princess's cousin, Baron Ochs (bass), arrives to announce his marriage to the much younger Sophie von Faninal (sop.), and to ask for a young Cavalier to take the traditional Silver Rose to her. Octavian, who has spent the night with the Marschallin, is forced, in order to prevent discovery, to dress himself up as a young maid, whom Ochs immediately pursues. In his normal guise, Octavian acts as the Rose Cavalier, and he and Sophie fall in love at first sight; Sophie is repelled by the manners and age of Ochs and tells her father, Faninal (bar.), that she will not marry him. Octavian hatches a plot to discredit Ochs and, disguising himself again as the Marschallin's maid ('Mariandl'), arranges a rendezvous with Ochs at a disreputable inn. The Marschallin arrives, reminds Ochs of his

Alfred Roller's Act 1 set for the première of Richard Strauss's 'Der Rosenkavalier' (Dresden, 1911).

rank, gives the young couple her blessing, and Octavian walks out of her life with Sophie.

FURTHER READING
Nicholas John, ed.: *Der Rosenkavalier*, English National Opera Guides (London, 1981).

Rosenmüller, Johann (*b* Oelsnitz, nr Zwickau, *c.*1619; *d* Wolfenbüttel, Sept. 1684). German composer. He studied theology at Leipzig University, matriculating in 1640, and then became assistant to the *Kantor* of St Thomas's; in 1651 he was organist of the Nicolaikirche. Four years later he was forced to leave Leipzig on account of his homosexual activities, and from 1658 to 1682 he lived in Venice. The last two years of his life were spent as *Kapellmeister* in Wolfenbüttel.

Despite his unsettled life Rosenmüller found time to compose a huge quantity of music, including suites and sonatas (*Studentmusik*, 1654; *Sonate da camera*, 1670; *Sonate*, 1682) and a great deal of church music, of which two sets of sacred concertos were published (*Kern-Sprüche*, Leipzig, 1648; *Andere Kern-Sprüche*, Leipzig, 1652–3).   WENDY THOMPSON

Roses from the South (*Rosen aus dem Süden*). Waltz, Op. 388, by Johann Strauss II. It is from the score of his three-act operetta *Das Spitzentuch der Königin* ('The Queen's Lace Handkerchief'), composed in 1880.

Rosetti, Francesco Antonio. See *Rössler, Franz Anton*.

Rosin, resin. A substance made from gum of turpentine which is rubbed on the hair of a string player's bow to give it a grip on the strings, and so produce vibration.

Roslavets, Nikolay (Andreyevich) (*b* Dushatino, Chernigov district, Ukraine, 5 Jan. 1881; *d* Moscow, 23 Aug. 1944). Russian composer. He studied at the Moscow Conservatory (1902–12) and swiftly earned a reputation as an avant-garde composer, developing, independently of Schoenberg, theories of 12-note serialism, evident in such works as the Third String Quartet (1920) and the Violin Concerto (1925). Although his name has been deleted from most Soviet music dictionaries, he is listed in the recent directory *Kto pisal o muzyke* ('Writers on Music'), vol. 3 (Moscow, 1979), where, significantly enough, we find that he contributed articles on Webern's Op. 7 and on Schoenberg's *Pierrot lunaire* to the contemporary music journal *K novym beregam* ('Towards New Shores', 1923).   GEOFFREY NORRIS

Rosseter, Philip (*b c.*1568; *d* London, 5 May 1623). English composer. In 1601 he published a book of ayres with lute accompaniment, half his own, half by Thomas Campion. His own are delicious trifles setting elegant anacreontic verse, with simple accompaniments since he disliked a style 'intricate, bated with fuge'. In 1603 he was appointed lutenist to James I, in which post he remained for the rest of his life. His book of *Lessons* for broken consort, which has unfortunately survived incomplete, was published in 1609, and at about this time he became associated with a company of boy actors known as the Children of Whitefriars (after performing at court in the winter 1609-10 they were allowed to call themselves the Children of the Queen's Revels); in 1615 he was one of a consortium to build a new theatre at Blackfriars for the use of the company. After various protests, however, this was closed by the King in 1617.

DENIS ARNOLD

Rossi, Luigi (*b* Torremaggiore, nr Foggia, 1597-8; *d* Rome, 19-20 Feb. 1653). Italian composer. He was a pupil of the famous madrigal composer Giovanni de Macque, and entered the service of the Borghese family in Rome in the 1620s. In 1633 he became organist of S. Luigi dei Francesi, a position he held for the rest of his life. He became famous for his cantatas and was a favourite of Cardinal Antonio Barberini, whose service he entered in 1641;

Barberini was a notable patron of opera, and for him Rossi wrote *Il palazzo incantato* (performed 1642), as well as some oratorios. After the death of Pope Urban VIII in 1644 the Barberinis lost favour in Rome and went to Paris, where they were responsible for the introduction of opera. At the invitation of Cardinal Mazarin, Rossi was engaged, with a group of Italian singers, to produce his second opera in Paris. *Orfeo* (performed 1647) was a marked success, but the sumptuousness of its production was much criticized and a second visit the following year did not result in the production of a similar work. He returned to Rome and died there a remarkably wealthy man, his possessions including paintings by Leonardo and Raphael. His tombstone is at S. Maria in Via Lata.

Rossi's influence on European music in general was considerable, and about 300 of his cantatas survive. In his own words, he introduced tuneful arias to 'relieve the tedium of the recitatives' (although in truth his recitatives

Luigi Rossi's autograph copy of a piece by his teacher, de Macque.

were as skilful a part of the cantatas as any other), and his melodious style became popular beyond the confines of Italy—French opera especially benefited from his example. His music was also well known in England, aided by the fact that the royalists were in exile in Paris when he was at the height of his popularity there; he composed a cantata on the death of Charles I.   DENIS ARNOLD

Rossi, Michelangelo (del Violino) (*b* Genoa, 1601–2; *d* Rome, 1656). Italian composer. His early life was spent in Genoa, but by 1624 he was in Rome, where, apart from visits to various important centres of music, he remained for the rest of his life. He was taught by Frescobaldi and in the 1630s was involved with the Barberini family; his opera *Erminia sul Giordano* was performed with sets by Bernini at the Palazzo Barberini in 1633. The music includes some splendid arias and ensembles.

Rossi's most important music is for keyboard, although in his lifetime he was best known for his playing on the violin. In *c*.1640 he published a volume of keyboard music which includes toccatas in a style similar to that of Frescobaldi.

Rossi, Salamone (*b* ? Mantua, 1570; *d* ? Mantua, after 1628). Italian violinist and composer. He was associated with the Gonzaga court in Mantua from at least 1587 until 1628, mainly as a virtuoso violinist, and in this capacity may have played in the first performance of Monteverdi's *Orfeo*. His good reputation earned him exemption from wearing the yellow badge which was compulsory for the other members of the Jewish ghetto in Mantua. Rossi composed a number of attractive madrigals, including the earliest published continuo madrigal, but his fame as a composer is for the *Hashirim asher liSh'lomo* ('The Songs of Solomon', a reference to his first name rather than to the source of the texts), settings of Hebrew psalms, hymns, and so on in a contemporary Italian style, a rare attempt at non-traditional Hebrew music.
                                           DENIS ARNOLD

Rossignol, Le. See *Nightingale, The*.

Rossini, Gioachino (Antonio) (*b* Pesaro, 29 Feb. 1792; *d* Passy, 13 Nov. 1868). Italian composer. As the most influential Italian composer of his generation, he not only raised *opera buffa* to new and unsurpassed heights but also laid the foundations for the Italian Romantic opera of the mid century.

1. *The Early Years*. His father was a trumpeter and horn-player, his mother a singer. Both toured the theatres of the Romagna, leaving Gioachino in the care of grandparents. In 1802

the family moved to Lugo, then Bologna, where under private tuition the boy made rapid progress on the horn, the keyboard, and especially as a singer (in 1805 he made a public appearance as the boy Adolfo in Paër's opera *Camilla*). In 1804 he was admitted to membership of the Accademia Filarmonica of Bologna at an earlier age even than the young Mozart. To the same year belong the six 'sonate a quattro', deftly written if not markedly original works which are in the repertory of every string orchestra of today. In 1806 Rossini entered the Liceo of Bologna and the famous counterpoint class of Padre Mattei; here two years later a cantata on the *Lament of Harmony on the Death of Orpheus* won him a prize. His first opera, *Demetrio e Polibio*, was composed probably in 1807 for the Mombelli family but not performed until 1812. His professional career began with a one-act 'farsa' commissioned for the Teatro San Moisè in Venice, *La cambiale di matrimonio*; it proved so successful that it was followed over the next three years by several others, including *La scala di seta* and *Il Signor Bruschino* which are remembered mostly for their overtures. With the oratorio *Ciro in Babilonia* (Ferrara, 1812) he ventured into the serious genre; but as yet his talent was mainly for comedy. *La pietra del paragone* (Milan, 1812) earned him exemption from military service.

In 1813 he achieved a double triumph in Venice with the heroic *Tancredi* and the comic *L'italiana in Algeri*, both of which carried his name far beyond Italy. With these his style was fully formed and his strong musical personality

Rossini, lithograph (1827) by G. Bozza.

Autograph MS from Rossini's opera 'Guillaume Tell'.

carried all before it. Failures were few and mostly temporary (e.g. *Il turco in Italia*, Milan, 1814). In 1815 he signed a long-term contract with Barbaja, impresario of the Neapolitan San Carlo and Fondo theatres, to assume the musical directorship of both, with the obligation to produce annually a new opera at each.

2. *Years of Maturity*. This effectively placed him in the same position as Haydn at Eszterháza with a captive audience before whom he could experiment; at the same time it left him free to accept commissions elsewhere. The important operas of this period are *Elisabetta Regina d'Inghilterra* (Naples, 1815), the first in which Rossini dispensed with *recitativo secco*, using full strings instead of keyboard; *Il barbiere di Siviglia* (Rome, 1816), which survived a disastrous first night to become a universal favourite; *Otello* (Rome, 1816), which broke fresh ground by ending with a murder on stage; *La Cenerentola* (Rome, 1817), *La gazza ladra* (Milan, 1817), *Armida* (Naples, 1817), *Mosè in Egitto* (Naples, 1818), *La donna del lago* (Naples, 1819), and

Maometto II (Naples, 1820). By now Rossini had married the prima donna Isabella Colbran with whom he was to make triumphal tours to Vienna (1822), Paris, and London (1824). His last opera for Italy was *Semiramide* (Venice, 1823). The following year he was appointed musical director of the Théâtre des Italiens in Paris, where he wrote the cantata *Il viaggio a Rheims* for the coronation of Charles X, followed by four works for the Paris Opéra: *Le siège de Corinth* (1826) and *Moïse et Pharaon* (revised French versions of *Maometto II* and *Mosè in Egitto* respectively), the comedy *Le comte Ory* (1828), and the grand opera *Guillaume Tell* (1829), his final work for the stage. Rossini was now at the zenith of his fame and influence. He left Paris for Bologna where he had built himself a villa, intending to return next year for a new opera on the subject of *Faust*. But meanwhile the Bourbon monarchy had been overthrown, the Opéra had changed hands, and former commitments were disowned; Rossini's main concern was to fight in the law courts for the continuance of the annuity that he had been granted by Charles X. The case dragged on for six years before being settled in Rossini's favour. During this time he published a set of salon pieces under the title *Soirées musicales* (1835). Meanwhile in 1831 he obliged Varela, a Spanish state counsellor, by agreeing to compose a *Stabat Mater* on condition that it was never published. When in due course Varela's heirs did attempt to sell the work, Rossini revealed that only half of it was by him, and hastened to complete the remainder, which was performed with great success in 1842, first at the Théâtre des Italiens, then at the Liceo Musicale of Bologna of which Rossini was now honorary director. He had already parted from his first wife, who died in 1845, leaving him free to marry Olimpe Pélissier, former mistress of the painter Horace Vernet, who had nursed him through bouts of ill health that were becoming increasingly frequent. A demonstration against him by the patriots of 1848 who had not forgotten the pro-Austrian texts he had set for the Congress of Verona in 1822 at the instance of Metternich, induced him to leave Bologna for Florence, where his inertia and depression reached a crisis. At last in 1855 he left for Paris to enjoy for the next 13 years an Indian summer of health and composition. A visit either to his villa in Passy or to his town quarters in the Rue de la Chaussée d'Antin was obligatory for every eminent musician who was passing through the French capital—whether Verdi, Wagner, Boito, or even Balfe. All were entertained by his wit and good cooking. The most substantial composition of these years is the *Petite messe solennelle* (1863); but he also left a collection of pieces for piano with and without voices which he called *Péchés de vieillesse*. Mostly humorous, always musicianly, and curiously modern in their sound, their publication began only in the 1950s.

Rossini used to describe himself as 'the last of the classicists'. In the Romantic age his serious works—with their formalism, their avoidance of expressive harmony, and their vocal virtuosity—soon fell into disfavour, while his comic operas have always remained fresh. Yet though he never fully entered the world of Italian Romanticism he was in a sense its architect. The plan of cantabiles, cabalettas, three-movement duets, and multi-movement finales that served Bellini, Donizetti, and the young Verdi had been defined by him. To the modern listener, for whom Wagner's way with opera is not the only one, Rossini has much to offer: melodic vitality, an unerring sense of proportion, and in the case of *Moïse* and *Guillaume Tell* moments of unforced grandeur worthy of a late Haydn Mass. His mastery of form derives from his mastery of rhythm—a quality which gives his musical personality its force, enabling him, for instance,

to stamp his patent on the famous 'crescendo', not in itself an especially novel device. The strength of his comedy, like that of P. G. Wodehouse, depends in great measure on a faultless command of style. JULIAN BUDDEN

FURTHER READING
G. Radiciotti: *Gioacchino Rossini: vita documentata, opere, ed influenza su l'arte* (Tivoli, 1927); G. Roncaglia: *Rossini l'Olimpico* (Milan, 1953); Francis Toye: *Rossini: a Study in Tragi-comedy* (London, 1963); Herbert Wienstock: *Rossini: a Biography* (New York, 1968); Stendhal: *Life of Rossini* (Eng. trans., London, 1970) [not for accurate information]; L. Rognoni: *Rossini* (Parma, 1977).

Rössler, Franz Anton [Rosetti, Francesco Antonio] (*bapt.* Leitmeritz (now Litoměřice), 26 Oct. 1746; *d* Ludwigslust, 30 June 1792). Bohemian composer. He studied theology, but in 1773 entered the service of the Prince of Oettingen-Wallenstein, soon becoming *Kapellmeister* to the court chapel. In the 1780s he visited Paris, leaving on the outbreak of the Revolution to become *Kapellmeister* to the Duke of Mecklenburg-Schwerin at Ludwigslust. Rössler's numerous instrumental works, which show the influence of both Haydn and Stamitz, include nearly 30 symphonies, many concertos for flute, oboe, horn, violin, keyboard, etc., and much chamber music for wind and strings. He also composed a cantata, *Das Winterfest des Hirten* (1789), and two oratorios (the second of which, *Jesus in Gethsemane* (1790), was revised to form *Der Tod Jesu*).

WENDY THOMPSON

Rota (Lat.). See *Round*, 1.

Rote. See *Psaltery*, 2.

Rototom. A remarkable tunable drum invented in the USA in the 1960s by the percussionist-composer Michael Colgrass. It has no shell and is tuned on the mechanical principle of rotary timpani (see *Timpani*, 3). The flesh hoop, with plastic head (Fig. 1, A), is borne on a star-shaped metal frame (B), which turns freely on a vertical central stem. The counterhoop (C) is joined by the tension rods to a lower frame (D) which engages a screw-thread in the stem. The stem is square at the base, to be held firm without

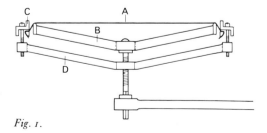

Fig. 1.

rotation in a stand or drum bracket below. On turning the drum with one hand both of the hoops rotate together but D moves up or down on the thread to change the tension on the head. When played with soft-ended beaters the roto-tom can give absolutely clear musical notes of a range of up to an octave (if of the smallest, 6″ size, upwards from around *d*′). It was first used in television background music and the like and has since spread to rock music and other fields. There are now also pedal-tuned models, leaving both hands free while playing.

ANTHONY BAINES

Rotulus (Lat.). Medieval name for a manuscript in the form of a parchment roll (from *rota* (Lat.), 'round').

Rouget de Lisle, Claude-Joseph (*b* Lons-le-Saunier, 10 May 1760; *d* Choisy-le-Roi, 26 June 1836). French composer. He was an officer in the French army, and in 1791 was sent to Strasbourg. There, when war was declared in April 1792, he wrote the stirring patriotic song *Chant de guerre pour l'armée du Rhin*, which was taken up by a battalion of volunteers from Marseilles and renamed the *Marseillaise*. Rouget de Lisle's other music, which includes patriotic songs and cantatas, is almost totally unknown. He was the author of several opera librettos.

Roulade (Fr.). A vocal *melisma. In Germany, the term is used pejoratively to describe inessential vocal coloraturas inserted for mere display in the performance of arias. It originally meant an ornament of quick passing notes connecting two melodic notes.

Roulant, roulante (Fr.). 'Rolling'; *caisse roulante*, a tenor drum.

Round. 1. A short, circular *canon at the unison or octave, normally for three or more unaccompanied voices. In its simplest form, the round consists of a short melody divided into sections of equal length which serve as the points of entry for each voice. As each singer reaches the end of the melody he begins again, so that the round is self-perpetuating and can be repeated as many times as desired. 'Three Blind Mice', which dates from the the 16th century, is a well-known example.

The word 'round' derives from the Latin *rota* ('wheel'), the title that appears on the 13th-century 'Sumer is icumen in', which however combines elements of the round, *ostinato*, and finite canon. The heyday of the round in England was the late 16th century and the 17th, and it was a particularly popular form of amateur music-making for convivial social gatherings. Several collections of rounds were

published, the earliest Thomas Ravenscroft's *Pammelia* (1609), followed by his *Deuteromelia* of the same year (which includes 'Three Blind Mice') and *Melismata* (1611), which also includes madrigals. Later collections were made by John Playford, notably *A Musicall Banquet* (3rd vol., 1651) and *Catch as Catch Can* (1652).

At various times from the Restoration period onwards the term *catch has been used as an alternative to 'round', although the catches sung in the later 17th century and the 18th were customarily distinguished by humorous or bawdy puns and other verbal devices. In the 19th century round-singing declined as a social recreation, but it has survived through school singing-classes, where the round is still often used to teach and develop an awareness of independent contrapuntal lines.

2. A country dance in which the dancers form a circle of men and women alternately. Tunes for such dances, such as 'Cheshire Rounds', survive in later editions of John Playford's *English Dancing Master* and in other 17th- and 18th-century collections. One of the earliest is 'Sellinger's Round', which Byrd used as the basis for a set of keyboard variations.

JUDITH NAGLEY

Round, Catch, and Canon Club. A London club for music-making founded in 1843 to encourage the composition and performance of rounds, catches, and canons. When it was dissolved in 1911 its membership had reached about 70.

Round O. A 17th- and 18th-century anglicization of the French word *rondeau* (see *Rondo*), used by Matthew Locke, Purcell, Jeremiah Clarke, and others. A 'Round O' by Purcell, composed as incidental music for the play *Abdelazer, or The Moor's Revenge*, was used by Britten as the theme for his *Young Person's Guide to the Orchestra*.

Rousseau, Jean-Jacques (*b* Geneva, 28 June 1712; *d* Ermenonville, 2 July 1778). Swiss philosopher, playwright, and composer. He was the son of a Geneva watch-maker and dancing-master. Deserted by his father, he embarked on a musical career, undertaking his own musical education and teaching at Neuchâtel and Lausanne. In 1743 he submitted to the Académie des Sciences a new system of musical notation, only to be told that it was 'neither new nor useful' (despite this, his idea was later taken up in the *Galin-Paris-Chevé System). After a visit to Venice in 1743 he composed and produced an *opéra-ballet*, *Les muses galantes* (1744), and in 1752 his most successful opera, the little *intermède*, *Le devin du village*, was performed both before the court of Louis XV at Fontainebleau

Rousseau, engraving after Devosge.

and, more publicly, in Paris. The combination of a pastoral plot with Italianate recitatives, simple *airs*, and dances proved so successful that 12 years later Burney translated it for the English stage, while it became a regular feature at the Paris Opéra for the next 75 years. His only other stage work, the experimental melodrama *Pygmalion* (in one act, one scene, and with only one character), was given at Lyons in 1770 (some of the instrumental music is by one Horace Coignet).

Rousseau took the Italian side in the Querelle des *Bouffons and attacked French music in his *Lettre sur la musique française* (1753), the trend of which is sufficiently indicated by the fact that its author was hanged in effigy by the musicians of the Opéra. He consorted with Diderot and d'Alembert and supplied articles on music and on political economy for the famous *Encyclopédie* (see *France*, 4): Rameau published three pamphlets on the errors of this publication. Rousseau's own *Dictionnaire de musique* (Paris, 1768), although containing errors and prejudices, is a valuable source of information on 18th-century French and Italian music.

Rousseau's ideas on social justice were the foundation of a new humanism, and as such were a huge contributing force to the art of Beethoven and to *Romanticism in general. He shattered in fragments notions of the rights of kings and aristocrats and so cleared the way for the French Revolution, which broke out a decade or so after his death. And with the old regime in politics went the old formal rules in art. 'Back to Nature' is the best brief statement of a creed that needed volumes to express.

PERCY SCHOLES, rev.

Roussel, Albert (Charles Paul Marie) (*b* Tourcoing, N. France, 5 Apr. 1869; *d* Royan,

Côte d'Azur, 23 Aug. 1937). French composer. Born into a prosperous family, he lost both parents while he was still a small child, and was brought up by his paternal grandfather, then Mayor of Tourcoing. He was sent away to school in Paris, where his first love was mathematics, though he also had some musical education. He entered the French Navy as a cadet in 1887, but after a short time as a sub-lieutenant he resigned his commission in 1894 in order to take up music professionally. For about four years he studied with a distinguished organist, Gigout, in Paris, and in 1898 enrolled at the Schola Cantorum to work under d'Indy, where he remained for ten years, finally graduating in 1908 at the age of almost 40. The same year he married, and went on a honeymoon cruise to India, which proved to be the inspiration for his *Evocations* (1912), his first work to receive major critical and public acclaim, and which was succeeded by the still more successful ballet, *Le festin de l'araignée* (1913). He had been teaching counterpoint at the Schola Cantorum since 1902, but resigned in 1914 owing to lack of sympathy with the rigid doctrines of d'Indy, though he was a good teacher, whose pupils included Satie (at the Schola) and later Martinů, Riisager and Jean Martinon (privately). At the outbreak of the First World War he tried to re-enter the navy but was not allowed to, for health reasons. He eventually enlisted in the Artillery and was a transport officer until the spring of 1918, when his health again gave way.

Roussel (1937)

The remainder of his life was spent in the country. In 1921 he bought a house on the Normandy coast at Vasterival, and except for visits to Paris and abroad, he remained there, composing regularly almost every day. The work of this post-war period included several major orchestral pieces such as his Second Symphony (1919-21), the Suite in F (1926), songs, and chamber music. His 60th birthday was marked by a Roussel festival in Paris, and in 1930 his Third Symphony was given its first performance in Boston, conducted by Koussevitzky in the composer's presence. His best-known work, the ballet *Bacchus et Ariane*, was given the following year in Paris and a steady stream of compositions, including a Fourth Symphony (1934), continued until his death. Roussel's music is agreeable, refined, full of *sensibilité*. His idiom is basically diatonic, though he was interested in polytonality and there is some chromaticism to enrich the harmonic style. His crisp rhythmic interest owes a little to Stravinsky, but in general his music has a highly individual flavour, a pleasing clarity, and wit.

DENIS ARNOLD

FURTHER READING
Norman Demuth: *Albert Roussel* (London, 1947).

Rovescio, Al (It.). 'In reverse'. The term can mean either *retrograde motion or *inversion.

Row. Synonym for *series. The latter term is preferred in this book.

Rowley, Alec (*b* London, 13 Mar. 1892; *d* London, 11 Jan. 1958). English composer. He studied with Frederick Corder at the Royal Academy of Music and taught at Trinity College from 1920. His compositions include many piano pieces, written especially for children.

PAUL GRIFFITHS

Roxolane, La. Haydn's Symphony No. 63 in C major, probably composed in 1779. The second movement uses material from the incidental music for the play *Soliman II*, in which the heroine was Roxolane.

Royal Academy of Music (i). An association founded in London in 1718-19 for the promotion of performances of Italian opera. It was organized by members of the nobility in the wake of Handel's earlier successes with Italian opera in London, notably *Rinaldo* (1711), and its seasons at the King's Theatre, Haymarket, from 1720 to 1728, were financed entirely by private subscription. Handel was the musical director, J. J. Heidegger the manager. As well as giving the first performances of several Handel operas, the company also mounted operas by

Bononcini and Ariosti, bringing before the London public some of the finest singers in Europe. In a relatively short time the Royal Academy greatly enriched London's musical life. Its last seasons were dogged by quarrels with rival companies and notorious internal squabbles between its own composers and leading singers.

Royal Academy of Music (ii). British music college; one of the oldest institutes of advanced musical training in Europe. It was founded in 1822 by John Fane, Lord Burghersh (later 11th Earl of Westmorland), began its public work in 1823 under the patronage of George IV, and received its royal charter in 1830. In 1853 a board of professors was appointed to advise the management committee, one of its first recommendations being that students should no longer be resident. The Academy left its original premises in Tenterden Street, Hanover Square, in 1912 and moved to Marylebone Road, where the buildings have been enlarged in recent years. The extensive library includes Sir Henry Wood's collection of orchestral scores and parts, presented to the Academy in 1938. The Academy's courses prepare students for careers as performers and teachers, and the Licentiate diploma (LRAM) may be taken externally; students may also read for the music degree (B.Mus.) of London University. David Lumsden succeeded Anthony Lewis as Principal in 1982.

Royal Ballet. Name bestowed by royal charter in 1956 on the former *Sadler's Wells Ballet, Sadler's Wells Theatre Ballet, and Sadler's Wells Ballet School. In 1931 the Academy of Choreographic Art, formed by Ninette de Valois in 1926, moved to the newly-built Sadler's Wells Theatre under the direction of Lilian Baylis to become the Vic-Wells Ballet, directed by Constant Lambert and with Ashton and de Valois as leading choreographers. This became the resident company at Covent Garden in 1946, opening with its famous production of *The Sleeping Beauty*. A second company (originally the Sadler's Wells Opera Ballet) was formed in 1946. Norman Morrice has been Artistic Director since 1977.

Royal College of Music. British music college, founded by royal charter under the presidency of the Prince of Wales (later Edward VII) in 1883 as successor to the *National Training School of Music. In 1894 the College moved from its premises in Kensington Gore to Prince Consort Road; here the buildings have been substantially enlarged, notably by extensions built in 1964 and 1973. Among the College's archival materials are a valuable collection of historical musical instruments and a department of musical portraits. Courses are open to students who intend to pursue a career in music as performers, composers, or teachers. The Associate diploma (ARCM) may be taken externally. Sir David Willcocks has been Director since 1974.

Royal College of Organists. British music college, founded in 1864 by Richard Davidge Limpus with the primary aim of promoting the art of organ playing and choir training, and to advance musical education. In 1904 the College moved to its present building in Kensington Gore (previously the home of the *National Training School for Music and the *Royal College of Music), facing the west side of the Royal Albert Hall. The College was incorporated by royal charter in 1893. It offers examinations for Associateship, Fellowship, and Choir-training diplomas. Membership of the College is open to all those who take an interest in the work and profession of the organist and in organ music. George Guest has been Principal since 1976.

Royal Hunt of the Sun, The. Opera in two acts by Hamilton to his own libretto after a play by Peter Shaffer. It was first performed in London in 1977.

Royal Manchester College of Music. See *Royal Northern College of Music*.

Royal Military School of Music. British music college, formed in 1957 by Field Marshal HRH the Duke of Cambridge. Two courses run concurrently at Kneller Hall: one for promising young army musicians, mainly instrumental in content, and a Student Bandmasters' course, which caters for experienced army musicians who have been recommended as future bandmasters of one of the army's regimental bands. The school aims to give a comprehensive musical education. Training is the responsibility of the Director of Music, assisted by military and civilian tutors.

Royal Musical Association. A society founded in London in 1874 as the Musical Association 'for the investigation and discussion of subjects connected with the art and science of music'. Its founder members included William Chappell, George Grove, George Macfarren, Frederick Gore Ouseley (President, 1874-89), and John Stainer. It holds regular meetings at which papers are read and discussed, and these are subsequently published in the annual *Proceedings*. Past presidents have included Stainer (1889-1901), Parry (1901-8, 1915-18), Edward Dent (1928-35), E. H. Fellowes (1942-7), Frank

Howes (1947-58), Jack Westrup (1958-63), Anthony Lewis (1963-9), Gerald Abraham (1969-74), Alec Hyatt King (1974-8), and Denis Arnold (from 1978). Its membership stands at around 800.

In addition to the *Proceedings* the association continues to publish the series *Musica Britannica* (1951-), an important collected edition of British music of all periods, and the *RMA Research Chronicle* (1961-), as well as a number of occasional and commemorative facsimiles. It also awards annually the Dent Medal for an outstanding contribution to international musicology.

Royal Northern College of Music. British music college, formed by the amalgamation of the Royal Manchester College of Music and the Northern School of Music. The College was opened in 1973. Courses are provided for prospective performers and teachers, at undergraduate and postgraduate levels, and are planned within the framework of the College's six schools of study, comprising academic studies, composition and performance, keyboard, strings, vocal, and wind and percussion. The Principal is John Manduell.

Royal Opera House, Covent Garden. London theatre, situated in Bow Street. The site was originally church property—a convent garden. The first theatre was built there in 1732 and used mainly for plays, though three of Handel's operas were given there for the first time. After this was destroyed by fire, in 1808, a second theatre opened in 1809, still mixing plays and opera; this became the Royal Italian Opera in 1847, retaining the title until 1892. This theatre was also destroyed by fire, in 1856, and the third and present building opened in 1858. During the Second World War it was used as a dance-hall, but it reopened in 1946 with its own resident opera and ballet companies, which were renamed the *Royal Ballet (1957) and the Royal Opera (1969). Between 1924 and 1939 the principal opera conductors at Covent Garden were Bruno Walter and Thomas Beecham. Musical directors from after the Second World War have included Karl Rankl (1946-51), Rafael Kubelik (1955-8), Georg Solti (1961-71), and Colin Davis (from 1971). The General Administrator from 1944 to 1970 was Sir David Webster, who was succeeded by Sir John Tooley.

Royal Philharmonic Orchestra. British symphony orchestra, founded in 1946 by Sir Thomas Beecham, who remained Principal Conductor until his death in 1961. Rudolf Kempe was appointed Assistant Conductor in 1960, Principal Conductor in 1961, and Artistic

Director in 1964 ('conductor for life' from 1970). Antal Dorati was Conductor-in-chief from 1975 to 1978, Walter Weller from 1980.

Royal Philharmonic Society. See *Concert*, 2.

Royal School of Church Music. British music college, founded by Sydney Nicholson in 1927 as the School of English Church Music. Its purpose was to provide a centre for work in the interests of church music, and to arrange for trained church musicians to visit different parts of the country giving practical advice and help. The School was initially controlled by a provisional council with an advisory committee of members of the Church Music Society. The first training college, Buller's Wood, Chislehurst, was dedicated to St Nicolas, the patron saint of choirboys. During the war Kent County Council requisitioned Chislehurst, and in 1946 the College of St Nicolas resumed work at Canterbury. In 1954 the permanent headquarters of the school and the college became Addington Palace, Croydon. The School of English Church Music was renamed the Royal School of Church Music in 1945 by command of George VI. By that time the activities of the School included regular visits by the Director and appointed commissioners to advise church choirs in Britain and abroad, the organization of resident courses for choristers and of combined choir festivals, the publication of church music, and the administration (with the *Royal College of Organists) of the examinations for the Archbishop of Canterbury's Diploma in Church Music (ADCM). Lionel Dakers has been Director since 1973.

Royal Scottish Academy of Music and Drama. Scottish college, situated in Glasgow. It was established in 1890 as the Glasgow Atheneum School of Music. A plan to combine a faculty of music at the University of Glasgow with a Scottish National Academy of Music was put forward in 1928, and a Principal was appointed to hold the joint headship; in 1953 the posts were separated, and the principal is now concerned solely with the direction of the Academy. A royal charter was granted in 1944 by George VI; the Academy received its present title in 1968, the College of Dramatic Art having been established in 1950 as an integral part of the institution. Emphasis is placed on preparation for the teaching profession, though students may take a performer's diploma as further study or as an alternative to the teacher's diploma. Philip Ledger succeeded David Lumsden as Principal in 1982.

Rubato, Tempo rubato (It.). Literally 'robbed', 'robbed time'. A feature of performance in which strict time is for a while disregarded, what is 'robbed' from some note or notes being paid back later. When this is done with genuine artistry and instinctive musical sensibility an effect of freedom and spontaneity is imparted. Performed badly, *rubato* can ruin the over-all shape and structure of a piece. The question of *rubato* in Chopin is contentious, since its frequently implied use in his music may be dangerously open to abuse. Accounts of his playing (and of Mozart's) suggest that he kept the left hand in strict time, allowing the right to 'bend' its time over a steady accompaniment.

Rubbra, (Charles) **Edmund** (*b* Northampton, 23 May 1901). English composer. He studied at Reading University (1920-1) and the Royal College of Music (1921-5), his composition teachers including Holst and R. O. Morris. He then worked as a pianist and as senior lecturer in music at Oxford University (1947-68). Influenced by 16th- and 17th-century English composers, he develops long, lyrical themes in tireless polyphony, eschewing anything merely decorative. His major contribution is a cycle of 11 symphonies, begun in 1938, but his output also includes concertos, chamber music, and sacred choral pieces. He has also written the books *Holst: a Monograph* (Monaco, 1947) and *Counterpoint: a Survey* (London, 1960).

PAUL GRIFFITHS

FURTHER READING
R. Murray Schafer: *British Composers in Interview* (London, 1963), pp. 64-72.

Rubinstein, Anton (Grigoryevich) (*b* Vikhvatinets, Podolsk district, 28 Nov. 1829; *d* Peterhof, nr St Petersburg, 20 Nov. 1894). Russian composer and pianist. As a pianist he was a child prodigy, travelling widely throughout Europe before being appointed, at the age of 19, pianist to the Grand Duchess Elena Pavlovna. Under the Grand Duchess's patronage Rubinstein founded the Russian Musical Society in 1859, and then in 1862 the St Petersburg Conservatory, of which he was director until 1867, and again from 1887 to 1891. Like his brother Nikolay, Anton was a stimulating and often exacting teacher, and he was revered by Tchaikovsky who had studied under him at the conservatory. He had a less easy relationship with the composers of the St Petersburg school— the *moguchaya kuchka* (see *Five, The*)—who despised his German-Jewish origins and were temperamentally opposed to the academicism of conservatory teaching: in 1889 Balakirev refused to attend Rubinstein's jubilee celebrations, and wrote a letter accusing Rubinstein of having had a harmful influence on Russian music. And the members of the *kuchka* resorted to calling him names: Tupinstein (derived from the Russian for 'dimwit') and Dubinstein, which could be freely translated as Blockheadinstein. Rubinstein countered these thrusts with an accusation of 'amateurishness' in the *kuchka*'s music, which so infuriated Musorgsky that he in turn condemned Rubinstein for producing 'quantity instead of quality', dubbing Rubinstein's huge 'Ocean' Symphony (the Symphony No. 2, 1851, rev. 1863 and 1880) a 'puddle'.

Such artistic bickering has tended to obscure Rubinstein's own worth as a composer. True, he was inclined to dash off undemanding trifles like the popular Melody in F (1852), but some of his large-scale works are worth a second glance, notably the Fifth Symphony (1880), the often colourfully nationalistic opera *Kupets Kalashnikov* ('The Merchant Kalashnikov', 1880), and above all his melodramatic *The Demon* (1875)— the first Russian opera to be performed in Russian on the London stage (1888). This last, strongly influenced by French grand opera, reveals Rubinstein's lyrical gifts (particularly in the well-known Act 2 aria 'In the Ocean of the Air'), though in the main his characters are little more than cardboard cut-outs (see also *Opera*, 14). In all he wrote 20 operas (of which a number are sacred operas—really oratorios in costume), and composed a good deal of piano and chamber music, songs, and orchestral works, including five piano concertos. Yet he is perhaps remembered chiefly for his work in music education, and during his time at the St Petersburg Conservatory he did much to raise standards of performance in Russia.

GEOFFREY NORRIS

Rubinstein, Nikolay (Grigoryevich) (*b* Moscow, 14 June 1835; *d* Paris, 23 Mar. 1881). Russian pianist and composer. Like his brother Anton, he achieved early recognition as a pianist of outstanding qualities. He also became a key figure in Moscow's musical life, founding the Moscow branch of the Russian Musical Society in 1860: six years later the RMS's music classes blossomed into the Moscow Conservatory, of which Rubinstein was director until his death. He was a close friend of Tchaikovsky, but his name has endured in musical history for his condemnation of the First Piano Concerto as 'worthless and unplayable'. However, he conducted the first Moscow performance of the concerto (later becoming a noted exponent of the solo part), and also gave the premières of several of Tchaikovsky's other large-scale works, including *Eugene Onegin* (1879). He also championed the music of the St Petersburg *moguchaya kuchka* (see *Five, The*), in particular giving the première of Balakirev's fantasy *Islamey*. He had a more extrovert personality than his brother: Tchaikovsky found him at Wiesbaden in 1870, 'losing his last ruble at

roulette', and it was entirely in character that he should consume a dozen oysters on his deathbed in Paris. Tchaikovsky wrote his Piano Trio in Rubinstein's memory, dedicating it 'to the memory of a great artist'.

GEOFFREY NORRIS

Ruddigore. Comic opera in two acts by Gilbert and Sullivan. Produced: London, Savoy Theatre, 22 January 1887; New York, 21 February 1887. This satire on the supernatural hinges on the curse hanging over the Murgatroyd family, whose heirs are doomed to commit a crime a day or die in agony. With a characteristic Gilbertian twist, the curse is broken when it is discovered that to refuse to commit this daily crime would be tantamount to suicide, itself a criminal offence. The operetta includes Mad Margaret (mezzo), whose music guys the Italian operatic tradition of 'mad scenes'.

Rueda (Sp.). A Spanish round dance in quintuple time, popular in Castile.

Ruffo, Vincenzo (*b* Verona, *c*.1510; *d* Sacile, nr Venice, 9 Feb. 1587). One of the most prolific and important Italian composers before Palestrina. His early career was spent largely at Verona Cathedral, and it was in this period that the bulk of his considerable output of madrigals was written. In 1563 he became *maestro di cappella* at Milan Cathedral, a post from which he retired 10 years later, spending his last years in less demanding employment at Pistoia, Verona, and Sacile. Ruffo's church music reflects the spirit of the Counter-Reformation in its attention to intelligibility of the texts and freedom from profane influences.

JOHN MILSOM

Ruggiero (It.). A characteristic harmonic bass line popular in Italy in the late 16th century and the 17th, chiefly as the basis of sets of instrumental variations (Ex. 1).

Ex. 1

It may originally have served as a harmonic pattern over which a singer could improvise a melody for chanting poetry: this connection tends to support the theory that the name derives from the first word of a stanza of Ariosto's epic poem *Orlando furioso*, 'Ruggier, qual sempre fui'. The *ruggiero* eventually became standardized as a sort of *ground bass for songs and dances. Frescobaldi was one of several composers to write keyboard variations on it; later in the 17th century it also appeared in vocal music, both solo and ensemble.

Ruggles, Carl [Charles] (Sprague) (*b* East Marion, Mass., 11 Mar. 1876; *d* Bennington, Vermont, 24 Oct. 1971). American composer. He played in theatre orchestras during his teens and also had private lessons with John Knowles Paine. In 1907 he went to Winona, Minnesota, to teach and conduct, and it was not until about 1912 that he began to compose seriously. From 1917 onwards he divided his time between New York, where he associated with Varèse among others, and Vermont. He worked slowly on a small number of compositions, all atonal and often containing a visionary intensity within a short span. His two major orchestral works, *Men and Mountains* (1924) and *Sun-treader* (1931-2), both have striding, masculine themes balanced by flowing tendrils of polyphony; equally characteristic is the radiance of *Angels* for brass ensemble (1921). Ruggles composed no new piece after 1947, devoting his creative energies to painting.   PAUL GRIFFITHS

Carl Ruggles

FURTHER READING
Henry Cowell, ed.: *American Composers on American Music* (New York, 1961).

Ruhe (Ger.). 'Peace'; *ruhig*, 'peaceful'; *ruhelos*, 'restless'.

Ruhepunkt, Ruhezeichen (Ger.). 'Rest-point', 'rest-sign', i.e. the pause sign (⌢).

Rührung (Ger.). 'Feeling', 'emotion'.

Ruinen von Athen, Die ('The Ruins of Athens'). Overture and incidental music, Op. 113, by Beethoven, composed in 1811. It was written for A. von Kotzebue's epilogue given at the first night of the German theatre in Budapest (1812). See also *König Stephan*. Strauss and Hofmannsthal edited and arranged *Die Ruinen von Athen* and included parts of *Die Geschöpfe des Prometheus* (1922-4).

Rule, Britannia! Song written by Arne for inclusion in his masque *Alfred* (1740, words by James Thomson and David Mallet). The song was published in 1740, a few months after its first performance, in an appendix to Arne's music for Congreve's masque *The Judgment of Paris*, which was performed at Cliveden on the same night as *Alfred*. Six years later Handel introduced the opening strain of the song in his *Occasional Oratorio*. Another composer who took advantage of its enduring popularity was Beethoven, who wrote a set of piano variations on it (1803, WoO 79), and also introduced it into his Battle Symphony (*Wellington's Victory at the Battle of Vitoria*, 1813). It also appears in Attwood's anthem *O Lord, grant the King a long life*. Both Wagner and Alexander MacKenzie wrote overtures based on it, and it has been convincingly put forward as a candidate for the 'enigmatic' tune in Elgar's *Enigma Variations*.

Rumba [rhumba]. A Latin American dance with a strongly African character; it is basically in 2/4 metre, with syncopated and broken rhythms played with strong percussive effect. Emanating mainly from Cuba, it became known as the Cuban rumba or El Son. The Cubans tamed the original African dance into a ballroom dance called the danzon, and with the general outflow of Latin American music to North America and Europe, the modern rumba came into vogue in New York about 1931, the most popular and typical composition to which it was danced being 'The Peanut Vendor'. It is a complicated dance, performed more or less on the spot, and its difficult steps are generally only tackled by professionals, among whom it is still very popular.   PETER GAMMOND

Running set. An English folk-dance still practised in the Appalachian mountain region of North America. It is in fast duple or quadruple time with a constant and invariable refrain: the figures, however, may differ in many ways. It is danced to any appropriate tunes, usually played on the fiddle.

Ruslan and Lyudmila. Opera in five acts by Glinka to a libretto by V. F. Shirkov and V. A. Bakhturin after a poem by Pushkin (1820). It was first performed in St Petersburg in 1842.

Russia and the Soviet Union

1. Introduction
2. Before Glinka
3. The Prospering of Russian Music
4. Years of Consolidation
5. The Soviet Era

1. *Introduction.* If we read the musical histories of Italy, France, Germany and Austria, Spain, or England, it immediately becomes clear that by the early 1700s they had all enjoyed centuries of more or less continuous musical development. Set in this wide European context, the state of Russian music in the 1720s, as recorded by the foreign diplomat Friedrich Christian Weber, seems conspicuously unsophisticated:

They are taught musick . . . by the help of the batogs [cudgels], without which discipline nothing goes down with them . . . If a general pitches upon some spare fellow in a regiment, whom he will have to learn musick, notwithstanding he has not the least notion of it, nor any talent that way, he is put out to a master, who gives him a certain time for learning his task . . . If the scholar has not learnt his lesson during the term prefixed, the batogs are applied, and repeated till such time as he is master of the tune.

So, while Bach was writing his Brandenburg Concertos, Couperin his *pièces de clavecin*, and Handel his *Giulio Cesare*, Russians were being hit over the head to awaken their musical potential. The country possessed no composers of international standing; instrumental playing was evidently in its infancy.

There are several linked reasons why this should be so, but at the heart of the matter lies the Russian Orthodox Church's attitude to music. Russia had adopted Byzantine Christianity late in the 10th century, and over the years had developed an individual style of ecclesiastical singing, at first monophonic, then from the mid 16th century polyphonic, and from the late 17th century polychoral, influenced (somewhat indirectly, via Poland) by the kind of music which the Gabrielis had been composing in Venice many decades earlier. During the second half of the 17th century Russia had also cultivated the three-part vocal genre known as the *kant, which flourished for a century or so. But all this music was unaccompanied: the Russian Church forbade (and continues to forbid) the use of instruments. True, there were folk instruments (though the Russian folk tradition is chiefly a vocal one), and instrumental playing was practised by travelling players, or *skomorokhi*; but the Church successfully had the

skomorokhi barred from playing in the most powerful cultural centres, so their influence was severely limited, perhaps negligible.

With the Church's proscription of instruments, Russia had no opportunity to develop any independent instrumental 'art' music from its vocal liturgical repertory. As a result no foreign composers had the incentive to work in Russia—even if anybody in Russia had been interested enough to invite them—and so the kind of cultural interchange which Western countries had experienced simply did not occur. For centuries Russia had remained musically insular.

2. *Before Glinka.* Things began to change during the reign of Peter the Great (1682-1725), that far-sighted monarch who, through his foreign travels and enlightened policies, opened his well-known 'window on Europe'. In 1711 he invited musicians from Germany to train his military bands. The court also maintained a choir which in 1763 was to become the illustrious Imperial Court Chapel Choir. And there was instrumental music at court—fanfares for state occasions, background music for banquets, and dance music for the tsar's ambitious social *assemblées*, an institution which he had imitated from France in an effort (not wholly successful) to impose decorum on unruly Russian society.

If during Peter's time music was little more than a starkly utilitarian commodity, the Empress Anna's reign (1730-40) brought to the arts a greater degree of glamour. On her initiative an envoy, Johann Hübner, was sent to Italy to persuade musicians to brave the northern climate, and one of them, the Venetian violinist Luigi Madonis (c.1690-c.1770), composed some of the earliest instrumental music in Russia: these 12 so-called 'symphonies' (in fact violin sonatas with a bass, each comprising a slow introduction and a sequence of dance movements) were published in St Petersburg in 1738, around the same time as 12 more violin sonatas by Giovanni Verocai (c.1700-45), another Venetian in the service of the Russian court. With the opening of theatres in Moscow and St Petersburg, Anna also encouraged opera companies to visit Russia: the opera *Calandro* (1726) by Giovanni Ristori (1692–1753), performed by a troupe headed by Ristori's father Tommaso, was the first Italian comic opera given in Russia (1731); the first *opera seria*, staged in 1736, was *La forza dell'amore e dell'odio* (1734) by Francesco Araja, whom Anna had created *maestro di cappella* in 1735. He remained in St Petersburg until 1759, thriving on the court's taste for Italian opera and composing (in 1755) the first opera to a Russian text, *Tsefal i Prokris* ('Cephalus and Procris'), with a libretto by Alexander Sumarokov (1718–77). Araja's appointment heralded the arrival of a host of other foreign musicians (chiefly Italian) who were to help mould Russian musical life for most of the century. For instance, Galuppi (in Russia from 1765 to 1768) was director of the Court Chapel Choir, and as such had a potent influence on Russian sacred music: he taught two of the key 18th-century ecclesiastical composers, Maxim Berezovsky (1745–77) and Dmitry Bortnyansky. Sarti, who also worked in Russia (1784–1802), numbered among his pupils the opera composer Stepan Davydov (1777–1825) and two other composers of church music, Stepan Degtyaryov (1766–1813)—who wrote the first Russian oratorio, *Minin i Pozharsky, ili Osvobozhdeniye Moskvy* ('Minin and Pozharsky, or The Liberation of Moscow', 1811)—and Artemy Vedel (1767–1806).

From around the 1730s, then, Russia began to enjoy a number of 'firsts': its first instrumental music, its first experience of foreign opera, its first opera in the vernacular. Music printing, too, got under way, significantly enough with a laudatory hymn composed for Anna's coronation in 1730, and it flourished in the later years of the century when such firms as Gerstenberg and Dittmar began to engrave and publish music in earnest (their plate numbers had reached 1260 by 1808, the firm having been founded only in 1795). At the same time music education began to be organized along more formal lines than the forceful methods recorded in the 1720s. The Academy of Arts, established in 1757 by the Empress Elizabeth (reigned 1741–62), had music on its curriculum: the violinist Ivan Khandoshkin (1747–1804) taught there, and Evstigney Fomin, the most important Russian opera composer of the later 18th century, studied there (though when he graduated in 1782 he was awarded only 50 rubles instead of the gold or silver medals reserved for students of other, more highly regarded arts). Fomin's career is specially interesting, because, while Italian musicians flocked to Russia, some young Russians were being sent to Italy to complete their education: Fomin was one of these (he studied at Bologna) and others included Berezovsky and Bortnyansky.

During Elizabeth's reign Italian opera retained its popularity (notably when Locatelli was in Russia from 1757 to 1762), but with the accession of Catherine II (1762–96) the court's taste shifted towards French *opéra comique*, which, with its characteristic spoken dialogue, possibly influenced the emerging native Russian opera—usually simple domestic plots with interpolated musical numbers, often based on folktunes (see *Opera*, 14). In fact it was during Catherine's reign that the earliest collections of Russian folk-songs appeared: the four-volume *Sobraniye russkikh prostykh pesen s notami* ('Collection of Simple Russian Songs with Music') by Vasily Trutovsky (*c*.1740-1810) appeared in 1776-95, and the *Sobraniye narodnykh russkikh pesen s ikh golosami* ('Collection of Russian Folk-songs with Vocal Parts') by Johann Pratsch (or Ivan Prach as he was known in Russia, *c*.1750-*c*.1818) was published in 1790, with larger editions in 1806 and 1815. These songs, crammed into Western harmonizations which disguised the modal nature of the melodies, were taken up by many composers (Russian and foreign) for sets of instrumental variations, and, even more importantly, found their way into Russia's earliest known symphonies. These three 'sinfonies nationales à grand orchestre' were composed by 'Mr le Baron de Wanczura'—the Bohemian composer and pianist Arnošt Vančura (*c*.1750-?1801),

Title-page of the orchestral parts of Vančura's three 'national symphonies', published in 1798—the earliest known Russian symphonies.

First page of Vančura's Ukrainian Symphony, as published in his keyboard 'Journal', 1785.

who was on the staff of the Imperial Theatres in St Petersburg and played in a court chamber ensemble. Two of the symphonies—the 'Ukrainian' and the 'Russian'—had appeared in keyboard versions in Vančura's *Journal de musique dédié aux dames* of 1785-6, a collection (typical of its time) containing keyboard pieces and arrangements, opera tunes, variations, and trifles. The orchestral parts of all three symphonies (including a 'Polish') were published in 1798.

By this time orchestral music had advanced out of all recognition from the barren years earlier in the century. Catherine herself had no ear for music, but she employed a large number of musicians, in which she was emulated by leading members of the aristocracy. Towards the end of the 1780s the Sheremetev family had an orchestra of 43 musicians, and the Vorontsov family one of 38 musicians and 16 'apprentice musicians', who played music by Pleyel, Stamitz, Dalayrac, Haydn, and others. Catherine (herself a competent librettist) had also done much to lay the foundations for the future development of opera performance: during her reign the Petrovsky Theatre (which, though burned down twice, is now the Bolshoy) was built in Moscow in 1780, and adjacent to the Winter Palace in St Petersburg she built a Hermitage (1764-7) and a Hermitage Theatre

(1783-7), centres of cultural activity. So, in little over 50 years Russia had grown from a country all but devoid of music into one of artistic enthusiasm and musical verve. It was left to the next generation to raise Russian music to international stature.

3. *The Prospering of Russian Music.* To say the stage was now set for the future development of Russian music is particularly apt, for it was in the field of opera that the country was to assert its individuality in the first instance. However fascinated we may be to examine the countless instrumental polonaises of Josef Kozłowski (1757-1831) who was never at a loss to produce one for important (and unimportant) state occasions, or however enchanted we may be to hear the graceful string quartets of Alyabyev, they are pale compared with the colourful activity in the opera theatre. Again it was a Venetian composer who showed Russia what could be achieved: Catterino Cavos (1776-1840) probably arrived in Russia in 1798, and quickly carved out a career for himself both as an opera conductor and as a composer. Beginning with some additional numbers for an adaptation of Kauer's *Singspiel, Das Donauweibchen* (translated into Russian as *Rusalka*, 1804), he continued to produce operas in a deliberately Russian vein, most notably his four-act *Ilya bogatyr* ('Ilya the Bogatyr', 1807) and the two-act *Ivan Susanin* (composed 1815, performed 1822). Like his ballet *Opolcheniye, ili Lyubov k otechestvu* ('The National Guard, or Love of the Motherland', 1812), *Ivan Susanin* was written in the patriotic atmosphere generated by the victory over Napoleon in 1812, and uses the same story as Glinka's *Life for the Tsar* (the première of which Cavos conducted in 1836), though in Cavos's opera Susanin does not in fact give his 'life for the tsar' but is rescued from the Poles by the Russian army. Cavos gave an added spur to Russian opera by producing a son, Alberto (1801-63) who, as an architect, was responsible for redesigning the Bolshoy Theatre in Moscow when it burned down for the second time in 1853, and in 1860 for rebuilding the Mariinsky Theatre (now the Kirov) and in 1859 the Mikhaylovsky (now the Maly) in St Petersburg.

Throughout the 19th century Russia was to continue exploring lively, often innovatory ideas in opera, ideas which were realized in the music of Glinka, Verstovsky, Dargomyzhsky, Musorgsky, Rimsky-Korsakov, and others (see *Opera*, 14). Concert life, too, was beginning to prosper. In 1802 the St Petersburg Philharmonic Society was founded by a group of well-to-do amateurs, including the father of the two brothers Wielhorski, Michal (1788-1856) and Mateusz (1794-1866), who in turn were instrumental in arranging for performances of much Western music in Russia. From 1826 they made their house in St Petersburg a centre of musical culture, encouraging such composers as Liszt, Schumann, and Berlioz to visit Russia; and in 1850 they established a Concert Society to co-ordinate their activities. Russia was also beginning to produce performers who could travel abroad and be received with acclaim: for instance, the violinist Alexey Lvov (composer of the Russian national anthem) was in Leipzig in 1840, where he was praised by Schumann and played Mendelssohn's Violin Concerto at the Gewandhaus, with the composer conducting.

Although it was Russian opera which seemed to be taking the most exciting steps forward at this time, Russian composers were beginning to investigate other areas as well. Besides Alyabyev's instrumental works, Michal Wielhorski (himself an accomplished musician) produced a number of symphonies and chamber works, and such composers as Iosif Genishta (1795-1853), Alexander Gurilyov (1803-58), and Ivan Laskovsky (1799-1855) began to expand the Russian piano repertory, partially under the influence of Chopin and John Field. Laskovsky in particular composed a number of works—notably a Nocturne in B♭ and a Ballade in F♯ minor—which show themselves to be the precursors of piano works by Tchaikovsky and Balakirev. Such music, confined these days to historical anthologies, deserves to be revived, not simply for scholarly interest but also because of its artistic worth, its appeal, and its wide-ranging exploration of piano sonority. In addition, the first half of the 19th century saw the flowering of Russian song—the *romans*—particularly in the works of Alexander Varlamov (1800-48), Andrey Esaulov (*c*.1800-*c*.1850), and Nikolay Alexeyevich Titov (1800-75). Titov, one of a family of musicians, composed about 60 songs, earning the nickname 'the father of Russian song', and his works, together with songs by other composers, were published in the musical 'albums' which proliferated from around the 1820s onwards.

Alongside this creative activity and the performances of newish Western music came the earliest serious Russian writing on music. Two names are specially prominent. Alexander Ulybyshev (1794-1858) had received his music education in Germany (his father was Russian ambassador to Dresden), and wrote the first Russian studies of Mozart (Moscow, 1843) and Beethoven (Leipzig and Paris, 1857), though at the same time he was a keen champion of Balakirev. Prince Vladimir Odoyevsky (1804-69), for some time deputy director of the Imperial Public Library, was known chiefly for his stories and for his philosophical studies published under the title *Russkiye nochi*

('Russian Nights', 1844), but he also did much in his critical writings on music to promote interest in the works of Haydn, Mozart, Weber, Berlioz, and Wagner. It was also Odoyevsky who encouraged Glinka to write his *Life for the Tsar*, which he later greeted as 'a new element in art', opening up 'the period of Russian music'.

4. *Years of Consolidation*. By the 1850s the 'period of Russian music' had indeed opened: the second half of the 19th century produced the bulk of the Russian music with which we are most familiar today—the works of Tchaikovsky, Balakirev, Borodin, Musorgsky, Rimsky-Korsakov, among others. Russian musical life was now being organized more systematically than before; music was beginning to play a more prominent role; and as a result composers could, to a greater or lesser degree, rely on income from their works (or sponsorship from wealthy industrialists and impresarios) to earn a living. No longer was music primarily the province of the aristocratic amateur, though the composers of the *Five offer interesting examples of prominent musicians who combined musical activity with work in other, largely unrelated fields.

Without doubt the two factors which contributed most to the raising of music to a professional standard in Russia were the founding of the Russian Musical Society in 1859 and the establishment of the St Petersburg Conservatory in 1862: both were instigated by Anton Rubinstein, whose brother Nikolay directed the conservatory in the (then) comparatively provincial Moscow when that institution was inaugurated in 1866. In fact the conservatories grew out of the Russian Musical Society, since one of its aims had been to give music classes, not only in St Petersburg and Moscow (where they were eventually developed into the conservatories) but also in far-flung cities of the empire. Another aim of the society was to give concerts. A similar dual purpose characterized the Free Music School, founded in St Petersburg in 1862 by Balakirev and the choral director Gavriil Lomakin (1812-85) and offering musical training and imaginatively programmed public concerts.

Although there has often been a tendency to see these two St Petersburg institutions—the Conservatory and the Free Music School—as implacably opposed factions, the one academic and reactionary, the other progressive, this is a gross over-simplification and distortion of the facts. True, there was often violent antagonism. The group of nationalist composers centred on Balakirev and the critic Vladimir Stasov—the so-called *moguchaya kuchka* (see *Five, The*)—had themselves received little musical training save that which they could glean from discussion and mutual criticism of their works. Moreover, they were dedicated to the ideal of producing distinctively 'Russian' music. At the conservatory the first members of the teaching staff were, in the main, brought in from abroad; the teaching methods were borrowed from German conservatories; and there can be no doubt that Balakirev and his circle harboured resentment at Anton Rubinstein's own German origins and also at his success. There were fierce exchanges in the press, and the correspondence between members of the *kuchka* is peppered with bitter comments about Rubinstein. But musically there were links. Rubinstein, though in general looking to German models, composed a fairly colourful nationalist symphony in his Fifth, and a folky opera in *The Merchant Kalashnikov* (even though he had denigrated nationalist opera when two of his own early attempts had flopped). Rimsky-Korsakov, conversely, found himself working within German symphonic patterns when he composed his First and Third Symphonies.

Even less tenable is the assertion that there was no creative link between the Moscow school (Nikolay Rubinstein, Tchaikovsky, Taneyev, Arensky) and that of St Petersburg (Balakirev, Rimsky-Korsakov, Borodin). In fact, to choose just two examples, Balakirev's music was championed by Nikolay Rubinstein (who gave the première of Balakirev's *Islamey*); and it was Stasov, doyen of the St Petersburg group, who gave Tchaikovsky the idea (and a synopsis) for his orchestral fantasy *The Tempest*. And there is good reason to regard Tchaikovsky's music as being as 'Russian' as anybody else's. Indeed, instead of looking for clear-cut groups in 19th-century Russian music, we should perhaps be

remarking on the development of individual compositional styles. Whereas in music from earlier in the century we might be hard pressed to identify an overture by Alyabyev, a song by Titov, a piano piece by Genishta, we can now with certainty tell that a piece is by Tchaikovsky, Rimsky-Korsakov, Borodin, Musorgsky, or almost any other leading Russian composer. This is not simply because we are more familiar with their music, but also because Russian music had largely shaken off the generalized foreign influences which had helped to get it off the ground in the first place, and composers now had the confidence, the knowledge, the essential sparks of individuality to assert their own musical personalities. Any factional battles, such as they were, were perhaps carried on more in the polemical articles of the critics. Cui assiduously (though not always predictably) promoted the cause of his St Petersburg colleagues, the critics of Moscow (notably Laroche) supported Tchaikovsky and hit out at the St Petersburg group. Straddling all camps was Alexander Serov, who managed in his time to upset practically everybody.

With the development and consolidation of music education (in the realm of performance as well as in composition), and with the expansion of publishing by such firms as Jürgenson, Belyayev, Gutheil, Bessel, and Koussevitzky's Éditions Russes de Musique, Russian music continued to prosper, and the conservatories produced many of the composers who were to retain a permanent place in the repertory: Rakhmaninov, Skryabin (not to mention lesser 19th-century figures like Lyadov and Lyapunov), Prokofiev, Myaskovsky, and Shostakovich. But with these last three names

The Moscow Conservatory, inaugurated in 1866.

we are on the threshold of a new era of Russian music, heralded by the October Revolution of 1917.

5. *The Soviet Era.* Revolutionary sentiments had been brewing in Russia for many years, and had already affected musical life to a certain degree when Rimsky-Korsakov resigned from the St Petersburg Conservatory in sympathy with the students supporting the 1905 uprising. In 1917 the decisive October Revolution took place; the 300-year-old Romanov dynasty had been deposed; communism had asserted itself.

There were several immediate implications for the country's musical life. First of all, a number of composers emigrated: Rakhmaninov left in 1917, Prokofiev in 1918 (though he was to return later); Stravinsky, already abroad at the time, decided to remain in the West; and at various times over the next few years such figures as Lyapunov, Glazunov, and the Tcherepnins made their way out of the country. Within Russia itself there were also important changes. Various institutions in private hands or under imperial patronage—publishing houses, conservatories, opera houses—were nationalized, and, in view of the value placed on opera by the communist regime, new 'opera studios' were established. Konstantin Stanislavsky (1863-1938) founded a studio at the Bolshoy Theatre in 1918; Vladimir Nemirovich-Danchenko (1858-1943) opened one at the Moscow Art Theatre in 1919; and in 1941 both institutions merged to form the Stanislavsky/Nemirovich-Danchenko Music Theatre, scene of many important opera premières, notably the revised version of Shostakovich's *The Lady Macbeth of the Mtsensk District* (as *Katerina Izmaylova*) in 1962. In the realm of orchestral performance, too, there were new developments: in 1922 the collective symphony orchestra Persimfans (an acronym for the 'First Symphony Ensemble of the Moscow Soviet') was formed in Moscow, and survived until 1932 on its policy of playing without a conductor.

With the change in political climate there had to be a comparable overhaul of Russia's artistic outlook, but Lenin realized that he could not alter a composer's way of thinking overnight. In a speech outlining his New Economic Policy on 17 October 1921, he declared:

. . . a cultural problem cannot be solved as quickly as political or military problems . . . It is possible to achieve political victory during an acute crisis in a few weeks. In war it is possible to achieve victory in a few months, but it is impossible to achieve cultural victory in such a short time. For that we must adapt ourselves to a longer period, plan our work, and display the greatest persistence, perseverance, and systematism.

In other words composers were being given time to find their feet, and were being encour-

aged to explore modes of expression compatible with the prevailing revolutionary mood. Composers of the older generation, of course, could not be expected to change their ways drastically. It is inconceivable that Glazunov could pull up his Romantic roots and write a 'Hymn to Lenin', or that a 19th-century epigone like Lyapunov could compose a programmatic symphony on the problems of the steel industry. But these were two of the areas which the new generation of Russian composers—Kabalevsky, Shaporin, Shebalin, Myaskovsky, Shostakovich, and many lesser figures—were beginning to investigate.

There were two principal strands of thought as to how the Revolution could best be expressed in musical terms. On the one hand, there was the hard-line socialist group known as the Russian Association of Proletarian Musicians (RAPM), founded in 1923. The RAPM advocated that Soviet music, in its effort to appeal to a mass audience, ought to be couched in a direct language, harmonically traditional, melodically lyrical, texturally clear, rhythmically stirring. In the atmosphere generated by this organization one of the most extraordinary experiments of the immediately post-Revolution years was perpetrated—the renaming (and recasting with fresh librettos) of well-known operas: so *Tosca* (with the action shifted to the Paris of 1871) became *The Battle for the Commune, Les Huguenots* became *The Decembrists* (after the early 19th-century revolutionary movement), and Glinka's *Life for the Tsar* was reworked as *Hammer and Sickle*. Happily, though, these crass meddlings with the classics failed to find many sympathetic ears; and the enlightened commissar for education and the arts, Anatoly Lunacharsky, quipped that *Tosca* had been turned into *toská*, the Russian word for boredom.

On the other hand, there was the more forward-looking, open-minded Association for Contemporary Music (ASM), also founded in 1923. Under the ASM's auspices fairly new works by Schoenberg, Berg, Webern, and Stravinsky were heard in the Soviet Union, discussed, and written about in the musical press. The leading spokesman of the ASM, the composer and critic Boris Asafyev (1884-1949), was convinced of the positive value of the ASM's aims. 'Acquaintance with the best examples of contemporary Western music', he wrote in 1927,

will help the development of Soviet music, will free it from amateurishness and profiteering on 'revolutionism', and will lead to the invention of new forms and new means of artistic musical expression; by showing the masses the musical art of the West we will provide criteria for the evaluation of the works of Soviet musical creativity.

Asafyev wanted Soviet composers to widen

their artistic horizons, to free themselves from the dull conservatism which had dogged so much early Soviet music. And in the wake of his comments we find such composers as Nikolay Roslavets exploring 12-note serialism, and Shostakovich working with highly complex textures and extreme dissonance in his opera *The Nose* (1930) and using polytonality and polyrhythm in his Second Symphony (1927), dedicated 'To October'. Moreover, by making this symphony a musical picture of the Revolution, Shostakovich was responding to another idea prevalent at the time, that orchestral music should reflect aspects of contemporary life—that it should *mean* something. This notion also gave rise to such works as the 'Agricultural' Symphony (1923) by Alexander Kastalsky (1856–1926) and to the once-popular orchestral fragment *Zavod* ('The Iron Foundry', 1926) by Alexander Mosolov.

The 1920s, then, were years of comparative freedom in Soviet music: composers were fired with enthusiasm to create something genuinely new which broke with the old imperial order. The 1930s, by contrast, were years of restraint. By the early 1930s both the ASM and the RAPM had outlived their usefulness, and in any case the arguments between the two groups were often so bitter that their work tended to be counter-productive. In 1932 the diverse strands were gathered together, for on 23 April that year the Communist Party passed a resolution bringing all musical activity under the control of the Party-dominated Composers' Union; during the next decade similar unions were established in the other republics constituting the Soviet Union. Most important, the concept of socialist realism was formulated. At this point the reader is directed to the separate article on socialist realism for a more thorough discussion of its meaning and implications, but suffice it to say here that it signified, in Isaiah Berlin's words, that there was to be 'no more argument; no more disturbance of men's minds. A dead level of state-controlled orthodoxy followed.'

Socialist realism remains to this day the chief guideline for Soviet composers, and, although its definition is hazy, its 'merits' were to be emphatically asserted in two famous incidents. First, in 1936, the *Pravda* editorial 'Sumbur vmesto muzyki' ('Chaos instead of Music') showed decisively that Shostakovich's *The Lady Macbeth of the Mtsensk District*, though originally hailed as 'a work of genius' (Samuil Samosud) and 'the result of the general success of socialist construction' (Alexander Ostretsov), was *not* now considered to be in the socialist realist tradition: this at least gave Soviet composers a fair idea of the kind of music they should *not* be writing. Then, in 1948, shortly after the 30th anniversary of the Revolution, Stalin's adviser on the arts, Andrey Zhdanov, attacked almost every Soviet composer for allegedly straying from the path of socialist realism and leaning towards formalism (again, see the separate entry on formalism, and also the articles on Muradeli, Khrennikov, and Shostakovich for some incidental facts).

After the death of Stalin in 1953 the artistic climate became less oppressive. By November

СУМБУР ВМЕСТО МУЗЫКИ

Об опере «Леди Макбет Мценского уезда»

The article 'Sumbur vmesto muzyki' ('Chaos instead of Music'), published in 'Pravda' (28 Jan. 1936). In its condemnation of Shostakovich this was a key document in Soviet music history.

of that year *Pravda* was asserting the composer's right to 'independence, courage, and experimentation', a right which many composers of the younger generation have on occasion boldly exercised: the Russian concert-goer of recent years has been able to hear, amid standard repertory works, such pieces as the *Concerto-buffo* (1965) by Sergey Slonimsky (*b* 1932), using 12-note material and incorporating an aleatory section; he has also had a taste of atonalism in the later works of Rodion Shchedrin (*b* 1932), and pointillism in Andrey Volkonsky (*b* 1933), as well as other avant-garde music. These works are played and published. Indeed, Russian music publishing has flourished in the hands of the State Publishing House, even though its cautious print-runs often leave maddeningly few copies for the enthusiastic Westerner. Nevertheless, in addition to sheet music and miniature scores, the publishing house has issued commendable complete editions (sometimes not quite complete) of the music of Rimsky-Korsakov, Musorgsky, and Tchaikovsky, among others; an edition of the complete works of Shostakovich, one of the best Soviet music publications in recent years, is now under way. Music book publishing, too, is a flourishing business, and in particular the publication of the letters of such composers as Tchaikovsky, Musorgsky, Rimsky-Korsakov, Rakhmaninov, and Medtner (generally well produced and cheaply priced) have been invaluable to the student of Russian music, provided he is aware that the State occasionally puts obstacles in the way of a full understanding of a subject: the 'complete' edition of Tchaikovsky's letters, for instance, replaces all references to his homosexuality (which the Soviet Union refuses to acknowledge) by that favourite device for concealing the undesirable, '[. . .]'.

For the Western observer the interference of the State in artistic matters—particularly in the realm of composition—is difficult to comprehend; the notion of an officially prescribed doctrine of socialist realism is alien to our way of thinking. Despite cultural exchanges the country remains musically insular (though hardly as insular as it was in the early 18th century), and, perhaps as a result, comparatively little Soviet music has travelled to the West: we are, after all, most familiar with the music of Shostakovich, Khachaturian, Prokofiev, perhaps Kabalevsky, leaving a mass of music from the Russian republic—not to mention the music of the flourishing compositional schools of the Georgian, Armenian, Ukrainian, Azerbaijanian, and other republics of the Union—largely unexplored by Western musicians. But there is one area in which the Soviet Union has contributed immeasurably to international musical life: the area of performance. The conservatories founded by the Rubinsteins in Moscow and what was then St Petersburg (now Leningrad) continue to thrive, and have produced artists of the calibre of Gilels, Richter, Ashkenazy, and Alexeyev, Kogan and Oystrakh, Rostropovich, Obraztsova, and Nesterenko. In that respect the tables have turned. Peter the Great may have imported musicians from Germany, but we are certainly now reaping the benefits.

GEOFFREY NORRIS

FURTHER READING
Gerald Abraham: *Studies in Russian Music* (London, 1935); M. D. Calvocoressi and Gerald Abraham: *Masters of Russian Music* (London, 1936); Gerald Abraham: *On Russian Music* (London, 1939); Gerald Abraham: *Eight Soviet Composers* (London, 1943); Gerald R. Seaman: *History of Russian Music: From its Origins to Dargomyzhsky* (Oxford, 1967); Stanley Dale Krebs: *Soviet Composers and the Development of Soviet Music* (London, 1970); Boris Schwarz: *Music and Musical Life in Soviet Russia 1917–1970* (London, 1972); Gerald Abraham: *The Tradition of Western Music* (London, 1974); Robert C. Ridenour: *Nationalism, Modernism, and Personal Rivalry in 19th-century Russian Music* (Ann Arbor, 1981); Richard Taruskin: *Opera and Drama in Russia as Preached and Practiced in the 1860s* (Ann Arbor, 1981).

Russian Easter Festival (*Svetly prazdnik*). Overture by Rimsky-Korsakov, composed in 1888. It is based on Russian Orthodox Church melodies.

'Russian' Quartets. Name given to Haydn's six string quartets Op. 33, composed in 1781. They are so called because they are dedicated to Grand Duke Paul of Russia. They are also known as *Gli scherzi* (from the character of their minuets) and as *Jungfernquartette* ('Maiden' Quartets).

Russo, russa (It.). 'Russian'; *alla russa*, 'in the Russian style'.

Russo, William (*b* Chicago, 25 June 1928). American composer. He studied English at Roosevelt University, Chicago (1951–5), and had private composition lessons from John J. Becker (1953–5) and Karel Jirák (1955–7). Since 1947 he has been involved with various jazz orchestras (including the London Jazz Orchestra, 1962–5) as trombonist, conductor, and composer. His output includes numerous works for jazz orchestra, rock cantatas, several operas, and two symphonies. He has also written the books *Composing for the Jazz Orchestra* (Chicago, 1961) and *Jazz: Composition and Orchestration* (Chicago, 1968).   PAUL GRIFFITHS

Rustle of Spring (*Frühlingsrauschen*). Piano piece by Sinding, the third of his Six Pieces Op. 32 (1896). It is extremely popular and exists in many arrangements.

Rute [Ruthe] (Ger.). A switch (like a small besom) or a thin cane, formerly and still sometimes required instead of a drumstick when playing the bass drum. See *Drum*, 4*d*.

Ruy Blas. Overture, Op. 95, by Mendelssohn, composed in 1839. It was written for a German performance of Victor Hugo's play of that name (1838).

RV. See *Ryom*.

Ryba [Poisson, Peace, Ryballandini, Rybaville], **Jakub Jan** (*b* Přeštice, nr Klatovy, 26 Oct. 1765; *d* Rožmitál pod Třemšinem, 8 Apr. 1815). Czech composer, teacher, choirmaster, and writer. After learning a range of musical skills with his father, Ryba studied the organ, cello, and theory in Prague. He curtailed his studies to help his ailing father in his teaching duties and in 1788 became assistant teacher and choirmaster at Rožmitál. With wide-ranging interests and liberal ideas Ryba tried to make alterations to broaden the school curriculum and cultivate a more enlightened attitude among the townsfolk. The resistance he met and the stifling atmosphere of a provincial town led to frustration and eventual suicide. The most significant of his writings was a treatise (published 1817) on *The First and General Principles of the Entire Art of Music* which attempted to fix a system of Czech musical terms. His vast output, much of which was written under fanciful pseudonyms, includes symphonies, concertos, and chamber and vocal music though only his sacred works survive in any quantity. In style he made little advance on his Czech contemporaries Kozeluch and Vanhal, and owed much to Haydn and Mozart, but he had the added distinction of being among the first to set his native tongue rather than German in solo songs. His Czech Christmas Mass, a compilation of folk-like texts coinciding with the movements of the Ordinary of the Roman Catholic Mass, shows Ryba making effective use of Czech folk-song (Christmas pastorellas) while doing little to avoid cliché. The work's energy and simplicity, however, has made it one of the most frequently performed Czech settings of the period.   JAN SMACZNY

Ryom. Abbreviation for the standard thematic catalogue of the works of Vivaldi drawn up by Peter Ryom (Leipzig, 1974, supplement Poitiers, 1979). Vivaldi's works are often referred to by Ryom number (often further abbreviated to RV, standing for Ryom *Verzeichnis*, 'Ryom catalogue').

Ryūteki. The 'dragon flute' used in Japanese *tōgaku* music. See *Japanese Music*, 3*c*.

S

S. 1. Abbreviation for *segno* (see *Al segno*), *subito*, or *sinistra*. 2. Abbreviation for *soprano* (e.g. SATB: soprano, alto, tenor, bass) or *superius*. 3. Abbreviation for Schmieder in his catalogue of works by Bach; see *BWV*.

Saccadé (Fr.). 'Jerked', i.e. sharply accented.

Sacchini, Antonio (Maria Gaspare Gioacchino) (*b* Florence, 14 June 1730; *d* Paris, 6 Oct. 1786). Italian composer. After being a pupil at the Conservatorio S. Maria di Loreto in Naples, he embarked on a career writing operas for various theatres in Venice, Rome, Florence, and Naples. In 1769 he was elected director of the Venetian Conservatorio dell'Ospedaletto, and in 1770 he travelled around Germany, commanding high fees for his works. For ten years from 1772 Sacchini was in London, where he was highly praised by Burney and others but fell into dire financial trouble because of his luxurious tastes. He then moved to Paris, where he was a favourite of Marie Antoinette. There he composed operas in the style of Gluck—ironically, since Italian composers were being held up precisely in opposition to Gluck by members of the Piccinni faction—and was a serious rival to Piccinni himself. His *tragédie lyrique Oedipe à Colone* was an enormous success on its second performance at the Opéra in 1787, and maintained its place in the repertory until the 1840s; it is all the more unfortunate that he was not alive to appreciate this success because the previous year it had been forced out of its promised position as the first opera to be performed at Fontainebleau by political intrigues. Altogether, Sacchini wrote more than 40 operas, but they are rarely heard today.

DENIS ARNOLD

Sachs, Curt (*b* Berlin, 29 June 1881; *d* New York, 5 Feb. 1959). American musicologist of German birth. A member of an ancient Jewish family, he turned to musicology after studying art history at Berlin University. He was director of the State Instrument Collection in Berlin from 1919 and professor at various institutions until 1933, when he emigrated first to France, then to the USA where he became professor at New York and subsequently Columbia University. He was one of the greatest scholars and most stimulating teachers of his age, and his writings on instruments and ethnomusicological subjects are standard works.

DENIS ARNOLD

Sachs, Hans (*b* Nuremberg, 5 Nov. 1494; *d* Nuremberg, 19 Jan. 1576). German poet and the most famous of the *Meistersinger*, commemorated especially in Wagner's opera *Die Meistersinger von Nürnberg*. He was educated at the Latin school of his native city until in 1509 he took up the trade of cobbler. For some years he wandered around Germany, but finally settled in Nuremberg in 1516, becoming a highly influential and honoured member of the *Meistersinger* guild; he acted as 'marker' or judge of the competitions on many occasions. He wrote a large number of poems and *Lieder*, as well as verse dramas based on Latin models and Shrovetide plays, or moralizing dramas, to educate the populace. He was a staunch supporter of Luther, whom he called 'the nightingale of Wittenberg', and did much to advance the Reformation in Nuremberg and, through the guild's influence, elsewhere in Germany.

DENIS ARNOLD

Sackbut. See under *Trombone*.

Sacrati, Francesco (*b* Parma, 1605; *d* ? Modena, 20 May 1650). One of the earliest Italian composers for the public opera houses in Venice in the 1640s. Of his music only isolated arias and madrigals survive, but he was highly thought of by his contemporaries, and his *La finta pazza*, taken to Paris by Torelli in 1645, was one of the first Italian operas to be given in France.

DENIS ARNOLD

Sacred and Profane. Eight songs, Op. 91, by Britten for five unaccompanied voices. They are settings of Medieval lyrics—*St Godric's Hymn, I mon waxe wod, Lenten is come, The long night, Yif ic of luve can, Carol, Ye that pasen by*, and *A death*—and were first performed at Snape in 1975.

Sacre du printemps. See *Rite of Spring, The*.

Sadler's Wells. Theatre in north London (Rosebery Avenue). In 1683 a Mr Sadler discovered a well in his garden with supposedly medicinal properties, and enlarged his buildings and grounds to accommodate customers, for whom he also provided entertainments. In 1765 a theatre was built on the site, and various entertainments were given there before it fell into disuse. In 1925 a public appeal raised £70,000 in five years to restore the theatre as a home for opera and drama. It opened with a capacity of 1,650 in January 1931 under the management of Lilian Baylis. Opera and ballet alternated with Shakespeare productions between Sadler's Wells and the Old Vic, but from 1934 to 1935 the opera was based at Sadler's Wells. During the war the company concentrated on touring, but it was built up again under the directorship of Joan Cross. For the return to its London home in June 1945 the company produced a new opera by Benjamin Britten, *Peter Grimes*.

In 1948 Norman Tucker became Director, and post-war musical directors include James Robertson (1946-54), Alexander Gibson (1957-9), Colin Davis (1961-5), Charles Mackerras (1970-8), Charles Groves (1978-9), and Mark Elder (from 1979). Stephen Arlen was Director from 1966 to 1972, and pioneered the company's move from the Rosebery Avenue theatre to the London Coliseum; in 1974, under the directorship of the Earl of Harewood, the company's name was changed from Sadler's Wells Opera to English National Opera. A separate company, English National Opera North, based in Leeds, was founded in November 1978, with David Lloyd-Jones as Musical Director.

For the Sadler's Wells Ballet, see *Royal Ballet*.

Sainete (Sp.). A type of late 18th-century Spanish comic opera in one act. It is the Spanish equivalent of *opera buffa*, but has at times approximated more closely to farce. Major composers in the genre included Antonio Soler and Blas de Laserna.

St Anne. Hymn-tune, probably by William Croft. It has always been ascribed to him, although it was first published in an anonymous collection (1708), and is usually sung to the words 'O God, our help in ages past'. J. S. Bach's Fugue in E♭ for organ, the last item in the *Klavierübung* book 3, is known as the 'St Anne Fugue' because it begins with the same notes as the hymn-tune.

'St Anthony' Variations. See *Variations on a Theme by Haydn*.

Saint Cecilia. See *Cecilia, Saint*.

St John Passion (*Passio secundum Johannem*; *Johannespassion*: 'The Passion according to St John'). Setting by J. S. Bach of the Passion of Christ narrated in St John's Gospel, with interpolations, based in part on B. H. Brockes's poem. It is for soloists, chorus, and orchestra, and was first performed in Leipzig on Good Friday 1724. There are also *St John Passion* settings by Selle (1623), Schütz (1666), and Telemann (several).

St John's Night on the Bare Mountain. See *Night on the Bare Mountain*.

St Luke Passion (*Passio et mors domini nostri Jesu Christi secundum Lucam*). Oratorio by Penderecki for soprano, baritone, and bass soloists, narrator, boys' chorus, three mixed choruses, and orchestra. It was first performed in Münster Cathedral in 1966.

St Matthew Passion (*Passio secundum Matthaeum*; *Matthäuspassion*: 'The Passion according to St Matthew'). Setting by J. S. Bach of the Passion of Christ narrated in St Matthew's Gospel, with interpolations by Picander. It is for soloists, chorus, and orchestra, and was first performed in Leipzig on Good Friday 1727 and/or Good Friday 1729. There are also *St Matthew Passion* settings by Richard Davy (late 15th century) and Schütz (1666).

St Paul (*Paulus*). Oratorio, Op. 36, by Mendelssohn to a text by Julius Schubring after the *Acts of the Apostles*. It is for soprano, alto, tenor, and bass soloists, chorus, and orchestra, and was composed between 1834 and 1836.

St Paul's Cathedral Psalter. See *Anglican Chant*, 5.

St Paul's Suite. Suite for string orchestra, Op. 29 No. 2, by Holst, composed in 1912-13. It was written for the string orchestra of St Paul's Girls' School, Hammersmith, where Holst was director of music from 1905. Its four movements are Jig, Ostinato, Intermezzo, and Finale: the Dargason (an English folk-tune to which the tune *Greensleeves* is used as a counterpoint).

Saint-Saëns, (Charles) Camille (*b* Paris, 9 Oct. 1835; *d* Algiers, 16 Dec. 1921). French composer. His father died shortly after his birth, and he was brought up by a musical mother and a highly intelligent, well-educated great aunt, who discovered his musical talents and his keen intelligence in other subjects at a very early age. He started to give piano recitals when still a young boy, entering the Paris Conservatoire at the age of 13, where he studied composition with Halévy as well as piano and organ. He failed to gain the Prix de Rome in 1852, but the following year had a symphony publicly performed, which was much praised by Gounod.

Saint-Saëns

Soon he became highly popular as a concert pianist and composer, and in December 1857 was appointed organist at the Madeleine, one of the most important of Parisian churches.

The 1860s saw him fully established as a composer. His concertos were performed by such leading virtuosos as Sarasate and Anton Rubinstein, while in Germany he was considered to be one of the most progressive of French musicians. He was largely responsible for the introduction of the symphonic poem to France, and of his own works *Le rouet d'Omphale* and *Danse macabre* were highly successful. He was also concerned with the establishment of a more healthy concert life in Paris, was a champion of Mozart's piano concertos at a time when they were still thoroughly undervalued, and encouraged various young French composers. In part this activity was the result of his lack of success in the opera house, although his *Samson et Dalila* (produced at Weimar in 1877) became immediately popular.

An unhappy marriage and the tragic death of his two young sons clouded his middle years, but from the age of about 45 the remarkable fact of Saint-Saëns's career lies in the contrast between his extremely successful public life and his failure to consolidate his achievements as a composer. Elected a member of the French Académie, popular in England where he wrote works for the Birmingham Festival and was received by Queen Victoria, and latterly even moderately successful with operas which were generally produced at Monte Carlo rather than Paris (where his rival Massenet was in full sway), he survived into the 20th century as a 'grand old man'. But the younger generation, under the influence successively of Wagner, Franck, and Debussy, were estranged from him. His failure was probably caused by the fact that he was born into an age which encouraged the great Romantic gesture, while his essential tastes were for clarity and wit. It is no coincidence that his most generally accepted work is the witty *Carnival of the Animals* (1886), full of delightful humour and a refusal to take himself too seriously, rather than the grand oratorios and operas over which he had spent much time and trouble.   DENIS ARNOLD

Saite, Saiten (Ger.). 'String', 'strings'. *Saiteninstrumente*, 'stringed instruments'.

Salieri, Antonio (*b* Legnago, nr Verona, 18 Aug. 1750; *d* Vienna, 7 May 1825). Italian opera composer. The son of a wealthy merchant, he was orphaned when he was 15, and taken up by a Venetian nobleman, Mocenigo, who took him to Venice and introduced him to the principal opera composer of Vienna, Gassmann. Gassmann was responsible for *Salieri* settling in Vienna in 1766, where he was appointed court composer on his teacher's death in 1774, and later court *Kapellmeister*. From *c*.1780 onwards he was the favourite opera composer in Vienna, and it was his success as much as anything else which caused Mozart's difficulties in obtaining commissions. He set both German and Italian texts, but his *succès de scandale* was the horrific *Les Danaïdes*, produced in Paris in 1784, which had not only a murder scene but also a vivid portrayal of the torments of Hades. In later life Salieri gave up opera

Salieri, engraving by J. J. Neidl after a drawing by G. Stainhauser.

composition, devoting himself to church music and directing the concerts of the famous Tonkünstler-Sozietät. Although there was certainly rivalry between him and Mozart, Salieri attended and praised *Die Zauberflöte* and there is no reason to believe he poisoned Mozart as legend and Rimsky-Korsakov's opera *Mozart and Salieri* proclaimed.   DENIS ARNOLD

Sallinen, Aulis (*b* Salmi, 9 Apr. 1935). Finnish composer. He is generally regarded as the leading Finnish composer of his generation. After studies in Helsinki at the Sibelius Academy (1955-60) with Aare Merikanto and Joonas Kokkonen, Sallinen joined the staff of the Finnish Radio (1960-70) and also taught harmony and counterpoint at the Academy (1963-76). In recent years he has devoted himself entirely to composition. His early output is largely chamber and instrumental music but he attracted wide attention in the early 1960s with his *Mauermusik* for orchestra (1962), a response to the inhumanity of the Berlin wall. Although he showed an early interest in serial technique, his mature style is predominantly tonal, and in the 1970s he had been increasingly drawn to traditional forms: the symphony and opera. His First Symphony (1971) experiments successfully with a one-movement structure and is accessible in idiom and distinctive in character. A Second (1972) is also in one movement. The Third (1975) is a dark, powerful, and evocative work in three movements with some roots in late Sibelius and the sound world of Benjamin Britten, yet bearing a thoroughly individual stamp. His opera, *The Horseman* (1973-4) to a libretto by Paavo Haavikko, was a key work in the renaissance of Finnish opera in the 1970s, and showed Sallinen to possess both dramatic flair and a command of atmosphere. He has written four symphonies, a Cello Concerto, four string quartets, an opera *The Red Line* (1978), and a quantity of instrumental and vocal music.   ROBERT LAYTON

Salmo (It.). 'Psalm'.

Salome. Opera in one act by Richard Strauss; text, Oscar Wilde's drama (1893) in the German translation of Hedwig Lachmann. Produced: Dresden, Court Theatre, 9 December 1905; New York, Metropolitan Opera, 22 January 1907; London, Covent Garden, 8 December 1910. During a banquet Jochanaan (John the Baptist) (bar.) proclaims—from the cistern where he is imprisoned—the coming of the Messiah. He is brought out for Salome (sop.) to see, and repels her fascinated advances: he urges her not to follow the ways of her mother Herodias (mezzo). He is taken back to the cistern. Herod (ten.) asks Salome to dance; she

agrees on condition that he will grant her a wish. After her Dance of the Seven Veils she demands the head of Jochanaan, which Herod is forced to have brought to her. She fondles and kisses it until the revolted Herod orders his soldiers to crush her with their shields.

Saltando, saltato (It.). 'Leaping', 'leapt'. Term used in the bowing of stringed instruments to mean the same as **sautillé*.

Saltarello (modern It.: *salterello*). A lively dance of Spanish and Italian provenance. It is characterized by triple metre and the jumping movements that form part of the steps to the dance. In the 16th century it often occurred as the 'after dance' (Ger.: *Nachtanz*) to a **pavan* or **passamezzo*, the music often being indistinguishable from that of a **galliard*. Mendelssohn called the finale of his 'Italian' Symphony 'Saltarello'.

Salvation Army bands. See *Brass band*, 1.

Salve regina (Lat.). See *Antiphons of the Blessed Virgin Mary*.

Salzedo, Leonard (Lopès) (*b* London, 24 Sept. 1921). English composer of Portuguese origin. He studied with Howells at the Royal College of Music (1940-4), since when he has been active as composer, conductor, and violinist. Much of his work has been for the ballet: he was musical director of Ballet Rambert (1966-72) and principal conductor for Scottish Theatre Ballet (1972-4), and he has composed scores for *The Witch Boy* and other ballets. His other works include a cycle of string quartets and various essays in jazz-classical fusion.
                                        PAUL GRIFFITHS

Samba. A dance from Brazil which comes in two distinct forms: the rural samba, which has African influences and a complicated rhythmic structure; and the urban samba, known as the 'samba-carioca', a more popularized form developed from the **maxixe* in the dance-halls of Rio de Janeiro. It has a simple step, and combines easily with other dances, as in the samba-tango and samba-rumba. There is also a distinct song form. The samba has been taken up by modern Brazilian composers, and the modern dance form, closer to the maxixe than the original rural samba, has a simple emphatic rhythm in 2/4 time; it was made very popular in Britain in the 1940s by Edmundo Ros.
                                        PETER GAMMOND

Sammartini. Italian family of musicians which produced two composers and performers of distinction; their works have often been con-

Sammartini, copy (1778) by D. Riccardi of a lost portrait by an unknown artist.

fused with each other's. **Giuseppe** (Francesco Gaspare Melchiorre Baldassare) **Sammartini** (*b* Milan, 6 Jan. 1695; *d* London, Nov. 1750) was a virtuoso oboist. He played in the opera orchestra in Milan in the 1720s, where he was heard and praised by Quantz. He visited London *c.*1728, becoming oboist at the King's Theatre and taking a very active part in the concert life of the city. He was later received into the service of the Prince of Wales. Burney describes his tone as superb, and near to that of the human voice (showing that wind playing in the 18th century was not always coarse and out of tune). He composed some interesting *concerti grossi*, after the Handelian model but with a distinctly more up-to-date idiom. However, he was overshadowed as a composer by his brother, **Giovanni Battista Sammartini** (*b* ? Milan, *c.*1700; *d* Milan, 15 Jan. 1775), who worked for most of his life in various churches in Milan. He was one of the most influential figures in the early development of the symphony, beginning in something like the Baroque manner of Vivaldi, but going on to develop a style which is the apotheosis of the grace and elegance of the *galant* style. He may have taught, and he certainly influenced, Gluck, and Mozart learnt a great deal from him during his stay in Milan in 1770. Prince Esterházy possessed copies of two of his symphonies, and although Haydn called him a 'scribbler' there is a distinct similarity of style between the two composers.

DENIS ARNOLD

Sammlung (Ger.). 'Collection', 'anthology'; *Sammelwerke*, an edition of the 'collected works' of a composer.

Samson. Oratorio by Handel to a text adapted by Hamilton from Milton's *Samson Agonistes* and other poems. It was first performed in London in 1743.

Samson et Dalila. Opera in three acts by Saint-Saëns; text by Lemaire, after Judges 14–16. Produced: Weimar, 2 December 1877 (in German); New York, 25 March 1892 (concert); New Orleans, 4 January 1893; London, Covent Garden, 25 September 1893 (concert), 26 April 1909. Samson (ten.), the Hebrew warrior, leads a revolt against the Philistines. Delilah (mezzo), the Philistine temptress, is urged by the High Priest of Dagon (bar.) to seduce Samson and discover the secret of his strength. Samson reveals to her that it lies in his hair, which Delilah cuts off, thus rendering him powerless. He is taken prisoner by the Philistines, and his eyes are put out. Brought to the Temple of Dagon, where he is mocked by his captors, he prays to God for the return of his strength and brings down the Temple, thus killing himself and his enemies.

Sämtlich (Ger.). 'Complete', 'collected'. Used, for instance, for an edition of the works of a particular composer, or for the body of stops on an organ.

Sanctorale. In the Roman Catholic liturgy, the feasts of Saints.

Sanctus (Lat., 'Holy'). Part of the Ordinary of the Roman Catholic *Mass, sung between the Preface and the *Pater noster*. It usually falls into five main sections: 'Sanctus . . . Pleni . . . Hosanna . . . Benedictus . . . Hosanna'. See also *Plainchant*, 2. The Sanctus was retained in the Anglican liturgy, occurring in the Communion Service (see *Common Prayer, Book of*).

Sandrin, Pierre (*d* ? Italy, after 1561). French composer. He held various ecclesiastical appointments in France and in the 1540s entered the service of the royal court, but in the following decade he spent some years in charge of the music of Cardinal Ippolito d'Este in Rome; he is last heard of there in 1561. Sandrin was one of the best-known 16th-century composers of *chansons*. His most famous *chanson*, 'Doulce memoire', is a highly attractive piece in the vein of a melancholy pavan and was arranged countless times for lute and other instruments, as well as being used as the basis for Masses by Rore and Lassus.

DENIS ARNOLD

Sanft, sanftmütig (Ger.). 'Soft', 'gentle', 'gently'.

Sanglot (Fr.). 'Sob'. Eighteenth-century name

for a descending *appoggiatura, usually sung to plaintive words.

Sanguine Fan, The. Ballet, Op. 81, by Elgar to a scenario by Ina Lowther based on a fan design, drawn in sanguine (blood-red crayon) by Charles Conder, showing Pan and Echo with 18th-century figures in the background. It was composed in 1917 and first performed that year in Chelsea at a matinée to raise money for war charities.

Sansa. African musical instrument with iron tongues placed side by side on a wooden base and plucked with the two thumbs. Other names for this very popular instrument are *mbira* and *likembe* (see *African Music*, 4).

In Pl. 1 the base is a thick piece of hardwood 7″ long; but more frequently the base forms the top of some kind of box which acts as a resonator. The tongues, of wrought iron (but sometimes wood or hard bark), may number from three to 16 or more, and are about 1 mm. thick, hammered thinner towards the free end. They are held in place by iron rods, both to hold them down and to act as a bridge, and also to allow a tongue to be tuned by pushing it further inwards or outwards. The instrument is held in the two hands with the tongues pointing towards the player; the longest tongues are generally in the middle, as suits the natural arc of sideways motion of the thumbs as they pluck the tongues one after another. Tuning is mostly of a pentatonic kind, and the players improvise fast motifs, reiterated with great agility and a sound somewhat recalling a musical box (which likewise has metal tongues, though smaller and plucked by mechanism).

The *sansa* seems to be a wholly original product of African iron technology. Its age is unknown, but it was first reported by European

travellers in 1586. Its main range is from Nigeria, through the Congo, and down as far as Mozambique in the south.   ANTHONY BAINES

Santa María, Tomás de (*b* Madrid, 1510–20; *d* Ribadavia, 1570). Spanish composer and theorist. He was a Dominican friar and served as organist at the monastery of S. Pablo, Valladolid. His most important work was the *Libro llamado Arte de tañer fantasía* (Valladolid, 1565), which deals with aspects of music theory, practice, and composition and includes several short keyboard pieces.   WENDY THOMPSON

Santini, Fortunato (*b* Rome, 5 Jan. 1778; *d* Rome, 14 Sept. 1861). Italian priest, who spent much of his life collecting and copying music of the Renaissance and Baroque eras. He became a major figure in the 'old music' revival by Mendelssohn and others. His collection is largely housed in Münster.   DENIS ARNOLD

Sanxian. A Chinese three-stringed lute. See *Chinese Music*, 4e.

Sanz, Gaspar (*b* Calanda, Aragon, *c*.1640; *d* ? Madrid, *c*.1710). Spanish guitarist and composer. He studied theology and philosophy at the University of Salamanca before going on to Italy to pursue musical studies. There he learnt the guitar, soon becoming a skilled player. On his return to Spain he wrote the celebrated *Instrucción de música sobre la guitarra española* (Saragossa, 1674). This treatise includes popular Spanish song-tunes and dances transcribed for guitar.   WENDY THOMPSON

Sapphische Ode ('Sapphic Ode'). Song for voice and piano by Brahms, the fourth of his set of five, Op. 94 (1884). It is a setting of a poem by Hans Schmidt.

Sarabande (Sp.: *zarabanda*). A 17th- and 18th-century dance form. It originated in Latin America and appeared in Spain in the early 16th century. In view of the staid dignity of many of the sarabandes known to us today, it is interesting that Father Mariana (1536-1624), in his *Treatise against Public Amusements*, speaks of it as: 'A dance and song so loose in its words and so ugly in its motions that it is enough to excite bad emotions in even very decent people.' In 1583 Philip II suppressed the dance in Spain, but it managed still to flourish. It seems to have been quick and lively in character, alternating between 3/4 and 6/8 metre.

It was introduced to France and England at the beginning of the 17th century, and it was at that time, particularly in France, that preference was given to the graceful and stately version of the dance, in slow triple time, that we

Pl. 1. Sansa player, Cameroons.

associate with the sarabande today. That the more lively type continued in existence, however, is revealed by a passage from Thomas Mace's *Musick's Monument* (1676): 'Serabands, are of the shortest triple time, but are more toyish and light than corantes; and commonly of Two Strains.'

The sarabande became a standard movement of the *suite. Purcell often placed it last, but Bach, Handel, and others generally followed it with the lively gigue. There is a particularly beautiful example in Bach's English Suite No. 2 in A minor, for which Bach provided a second, ornamented version.

The sarabande has been revived in the 20th century, for instance by Debussy (in the suite *Pour le piano*), Satie (*Trois sarabandes*), and Vaughan Williams (in the 'masque for dancing', *Job*).

Sarasate, Pablo de [Martín Melitón Sarasate y Navascués] (*b* Pamplona, 10 Mar. 1844; *d* Biarritz, 20 Sept. 1908). Spanish violinist and composer. He gave his first concert at the age of seven, and studied at Madrid with Rodriguez before entering the Paris Conservatoire on 1 January 1856 to study with Alard. He subsequently embarked on a highly successful career as a concert violinist, travelling widely in Europe and North and South America. He owned two Stradivarius violins, and founded his own quartet in Paris in the 1860s. Sarasate was famed for the classic purity of his style, beauty of tone, and facility of execution. His repertory included the major works of the German, French, and Belgian schools. He inspired several famous pieces, including Lalo's *Symphonie espagnole*, Bruch's Second Violin Concerto and Scottish Fantasy, and Saint-Saëns's *Rondo capriccioso* and Violin Concertos Nos. 1 and 3. His own works, inspired by the folk music of his native country, include fantasias, romances, and transcriptions, of which the *Zigeunerweisen*, *Jota aragonesa*, and four books of Spanish dances are still among the most popular violin solos. WENDY THOMPSON

Sardana (Sp.). The national dance of Catalonia, which acquired its present form in the mid 19th century. It is danced in a circle to the Spanish equivalents of the pipe and tabor, and resembles the Provençal *farandole. It is normally in 6/8 time.

Sarrusophone. In 1856, 10 years after Sax patented the *saxophones, another Paris wind-instrument maker, Gautrot (later Couesnon), put into production a corresponding family of double-reed instruments, likewise built of brass and with similar keywork and fingering and the same notation and transpositions. He generously

Bass sarrusophone in B♭ (c.1912).

named them after Bandmaster Sarrus of the 13th Infantry regiment, who had first suggested the idea. The soprano looks like a brass oboe; from alto to contrabass the tube is doubled back from one to five times. Over the years a fair number of bands in France, Italy, and Spain came to employ them, chiefly as outdoor substitutes for oboe and bassoon. In Italy the deeper sizes, E♭ baritone and B♭ bass, may still be heard in use in the largest municipal bands. Their sound is not as full as a saxophone's, since with a double reed the conical bore must start narrower and continue narrower all through.

Some orchestral works include a part for contrabass sarrusophone (Stravinsky's *Threni* is a late example). This, from the days of Saint-Saëns, was often used in France and Spain for contrabassoon parts. It has also been manufactured in the USA (for bands), while in literature it is immortalized in Sir Thomas Beecham's account, in *A Mingled Chime*, of his 1908 production of Holbrooke's *Apollo and the Seaman*.

The contrabass sarrusophone is not to be confused with another deep double-reed instrument of brass, *contrebasse-à-anche*, formerly made for bands by Mahillon (Brussels): in this, all keys (except one) rest normally closed, one key only being opened for each note. They are so arranged that the scale runs upwards from the key for the left little finger to that for the right, in this respect matching the piano.

ANTHONY BAINES

Sarti, Giuseppe (*bapt.* Faenza, 1 Dec. 1729; *d* Berlin, 28 July 1802). Italian opera composer. He was appointed organist of Faenza Cathedral as a young man, and became well known after his opera *Il re pastore* was produced in Venice in 1753. Later that year he visited Denmark with a touring opera company, and was invited to stay in Copenhagen as *Kapellmeister* to the court; he later became director of the Italian Opera there, remaining until it closed in 1763. However, after only three years back in Venice Sarti returned to Copenhagen in 1768, writing operas (both Danish and Italian) for the court theatre until 1775, when court intrigues brought about his dismissal. On his return to Venice he was immediately made director of the Conservatorio dell'Ospedaletto. In 1779 he became *maestro di cappella* of Milan Cathedral, but an invitation took him to St Petersburg in 1784, and there he directed the Italian Opera and was highly successful, in spite of vicissitudes caused (again) by court intrigues—at one point he was exiled to the Ukraine, but there he founded a music school which was so successful that Catherine the Great called him back to St Petersburg to direct the conservatory, which was modelled on Italian lines. He died visiting his daughter in Berlin.

Sarti's success as an opera composer owes more to his melodiousness and charm than to his dramatic sense. However, it is worth noting that his *Fra due litiganti* (1782)—from which Mozart quoted a tune in Act 2, scene 5 of *Don Giovanni*—kept the Italian Opera in Vienna prosperous when Mozart's operas were relatively unsuccessful. DENIS ARNOLD

Sarum Use. The liturgy, ritual, and manner of performing the plainchant in the cathedral church of Salisbury (the cathedral and city of old Salisbury have been destroyed, and the new town constructed on another site; the present cathedral was completed in 1266) from Medieval times up until the Reformation. In the later Middle Ages the Sarum Use was increasingly followed by other dioceses, such as York, Lincoln, Hereford, and Bangor, which until then had followed their own local Uses. This fact was ignored in the preface to the first Book of *Common Prayer of 1549, which condemned the 'diversity in saying and singing in Churches within this Realm; some following Salisbury Use, some Hereford Use, some the Uses of Bangor, some of York, some of Lincoln'. The books of the Sarum Use furnished the reformers with their main material for the Prayer Book, despite their condemnation of the 'number and hardness' of its rules, and English settings of liturgical music continued to use Sarum versions of the plainchant in such works as votive antiphons, hymns, and settings of the Lamentations of Jeremiah and the *Magnificat*.

'Satchmo'. See *Armstrong, Louis*.

Satie, Erik (Alfred Leslie) (*b* Honfleur, 17 May 1866; *d* Paris, 1 July 1925). French composer. Of mixed French-Scots parentage, Satie spent his formative years, between the ages of four and 12, living with grandparents and an eccentric uncle in Honfleur, where he had his first piano lessons. He then moved to Paris to join his father, and studied at the Conservatoire (1879–86) without much success. Among his earliest compositions were sets of three *Gymnopédies* (1888) and *Gnossiennes* (1890) for piano, evoking the ancient world by means of pure simplicity, monotonous repetition, and highly original modal harmonies; they had an influence on his friend Debussy. A similar manner was used to serve the exotic Rosicrucian sect, whose mysteries were austerely celebrated in, for example, the 'Christian ballet' *Uspud* (1892) and the *Danses gothiques* for piano (1893). The *Messe des pauvres* for organ or piano (1895) is more orthodox in subject-matter if not in style.

Satie

During this period Satie was earning his living as a café pianist in Montmartre; he also contributed to the café repertory with songs and little waltzes. In 1898, however, he retired to the industrial suburb of Arcueil-Cachan, where he lived in self-imposed poverty for the rest of his life. He began to compose works with bizarre titles, such as the *Trois pièces en forme de poire* for two pianos (1903), in fact a set of six pieces, still childlike in their simplicity and utterly unassuming. Spurred by the charge of naïvety, he studied with Roussel and d'Indy at the Schola Cantorum (1905–8), but there was little effect on his style. In 1911 Debussy and Ravel gave performances of Satie's piano pieces and brought him to wider attention. He now began to compose more abundantly, continuing to produce sets of small instrumental pieces with absurd titles: *Embryons déssechés* for piano (1913) and *Choses vues à droite et à gauche (sans lunettes)* for violin and piano (1914) are typical. Often, as in the piano set *Sports et divertissements* (1914), the performer is confronted by instructions which are also absurd or else ironically humorous.

Satie's modest, mocking art endeared him to a new generation of French composers around the time of the First World War. In 1915 he was discovered by Cocteau, who eulogized him in his manifesto *Le coq et l'arlequin* (1918) and ensured that his influence spread to Les Six. Cocteau and Satie collaborated on the ballet *Parade* (1917), whose score is flatly anti-conventional in its discontinuous form, its repetitive material, and its inclusion in the orchestra of a typewriter, a revolver, and other unusual instruments. This was followed by the cantata *Socrate* (1919), which takes creative humility almost to its limits; but not quite, for the next year Satie provided an art exhibition with 'furniture music' which was designed to be ignored. His last major work was a deliberately inconsequential score for the Dadaist ballet *Relâche* (1924).   PAUL GRIFFITHS

FURTHER READING
Jean Cocteau: *Le coq et l'arlequin* (Eng. trans., London, 1921); Rollo Myers: *Erik Satie* (London, 1948); Pierre Daniel Templier: *Erik Satie* (London, 1971).

Satz (Ger.). This word has several meanings. It is most commonly found meaning 'movement', in the sense of first movement, slow movement, etc. It can also mean 'theme' or 'subject', 'composition' or 'piece', 'texture', and 'style'. *Hauptsatz* (literally 'head-subject') means 'first subject', and *Seitensatz* or *Nebensatz* 'second subject'. A *Schlusssatz* is a finale or a coda.

Saudades (Port.). Milhaud wrote a set of short tango-like dances with the title *Saudades do*

Brazil, and Peter Warlock a set of songs with this title. It 'expresses the haunting sense of sadness and regret for days gone by'.

Sauguet, Henri [Poupard, Jean-Pierre] (*b* Bordeaux, 8 May 1901). French composer. He studied with Marie-Joseph Canteloube and then, after his move to Paris in 1922, with Charles Koechlin. More important, however, was his association with Erik Satie: he was a member of the École d'Arcueil, a group of Satie's disciples, and he accepted his master's aesthetic of unpretentiousness. Taking the name 'Henri Sauguet' he earned his living as a composer for the cinema, theatre, and radio. His more serious works include ballets, notably *La chatte* (1927) and *Les forains* (1945), operas, and a variety of orchestral works, all marked by simple charm.   PAUL GRIFFITHS

Sautillé (Fr.; Ger.: *Springbogen*; It.: *saltando, saltato*). A short bow-stroke played with the middle of the bow so that it bounces slightly off the string, producing a brilliant effect capable of great dynamic variation. A separate wrist movement is needed to produce each note, unlike the *jeté* or *ricochet* strokes, where the bow bounces of its own volition. Sometimes the *sautillé* is indicated by dots placed above or below the notes, or by arrowhead strokes, but often its use is left to the performer's discretion.

Savoy Operas. Name by which the operettas of Gilbert and Sullivan are known, because from *Iolanthe* (1882) onwards they were first produced at the Savoy Theatre, London, built specially for them. The performers were known as 'Savoyards'.

Saw, Singing. See *Flexatone*.

Sax, Adolphe [Antoine Joseph] (*b* Dinant, nr Brussels, 4 Nov. 1814; *d* Paris, 1894). Belgian inventor of the *saxophone and the *saxhorn. He was the son of the leading maker of wind instruments in Brussels, Charles Sax. While working with his father he studied the clarinet at the Brussels Conservatoire and produced designs for improvements to the clarinet and for a bass clarinet which heralded the modern form of this instrument. In Brussels he also first built saxophones. He moved to Paris in 1842; in 1845 he patented the saxhorn (at once imported into England by Henry Distin, founder of the firm later to become Boosey & Co.) and the following year the saxophone. The rapid adoption of saxhorns by French army bands aroused intense antagonism among established Paris makers who banded together to contest his claims to originality in a series of lawsuits that nearly ruined him. He nevertheless continued to improve his instruments and to invent others (like the bowl-less timpani, 1859). Sax was one of the great personalities of the instrument world, with Berlioz among his close supporters. His firm continued for some time after his death, and many saxophones made up to the 1930s still bear his name, though built by other makers.

For the possible saxhorn origin of Wagner's tubas for the *Ring*, see *Tuba*, 5.

ANTHONY BAINES

Saxhorn. Over half of the brass instruments which make up the *brass band in Britain and France are descended from the saxhorns patented in Paris in 1845 by Adolphe Sax, who had already invented the *saxophone and patented it a year later. Makers in most countries were by that time producing new valved instruments for bands, but Sax was the first seriously to conceive them as the single family of saxhorns, unified in technique and homogeneous in musical effect from highest to lowest, pitched alternately in B♭ and E♭ (or sometimes F). He seems to have originally built the small members of the family in trumpet shape, then adopted the tuba shape for all of them, though with less wide bores than in the later and present models, and rather less fullness of sound.

The family—which at once began to be imported into England by the firm of Distin (later absorbed by Boosey)—runs as follows:

E♭ soprano (today the soprano cornet)
B♭ contralto (this later disappeared, players preferring the ordinary cornet)
E♭ alto, also called tenor (now in Britain, the tenor horn)
B♭ baryton (baritone)
B♭ basse (euphonium)
E♭ contrebasse (E♭ bass)

To these the B♭ contrebasse (BB♭ bass) was added by 1851. Two further afterthoughts were: B♭ *suraigu* (i.e. sopranino), with the pitch of the present piccolo trumpet and used for a time in some bands; and an E♭ *bourdon* (sub-bass) which remained little more than experimental, though several examples by Sax and later makers have been preserved as curiosities in Europe and the USA.

Sax also produced a similar family, very slightly different and intended by him for mounted bands, named saxo-tromba, since forgotten.

In the USA, after the saxhorns were first imported, makers began to show a characteristic independence, especially in making models in which the bell points back over the shoulder. These were very popular through the time of the Civil War. Normal models were then re-adopted for use in brass bands as long as these lasted in that country, though the baritone and tuba, needed in every military band, are often made with the bell bent round to face forwards.

In the orchestra, saxhorns other than tubas have rarely appeared. Berlioz, having allotted a fine solo to E♭ tenor saxhorn in *The Trojans* ('The Royal Hunt and Storm'), later transferred it to the horn. Yet it seems clear from Wagner's own words that it was Sax's instruments (saxhorns presumably) which at least partly suggested to him the quartet of special tubas for the *Ring* (see *Tuba*, 5).

ANTHONY BAINES

'Saxhorn Baryton en Sib' (baritone saxhorn in B♭), one of the early models by Adolphe Sax, Paris.

Saxophone. Patented by Adolphe *Sax in Paris in 1846, the instruments of this family combine a wide conical brass tube (plated or lacquered) with a single reed and mouthpiece broadly similar to those of the clarinet (see *Reed*, 2c). Their first regular place was in the *military band, in which saxophones of several sizes remain in nearly every country as essential as ever. Their impact on orchestral music has been relatively limited, counterbalanced by their towering success in jazz. It is curious to read in

Saxophones, soprano, alto, tenor, and baritone (descending to low A) by Yamaha of Japan.

Kling's *Modern Orchestration* (1902 edn) that 'the peculiar tone-quality of the Saxophone does not fit it for use in dance music', but jazz changed dance music, and here the instrument scored from the effortless volume of sound of which it is capable, having a tube that starts wide at the mouthpiece end and expands at an angle around three times as great as in other conical reed instruments so that the mass of vibrating air inside a saxophone is very large indeed.

1. *Compass and Mechanism.* Thanks to the conical tube, the saxophone overblows at the octave: the fundamental scale is repeated throughout from *d″* (at written pitch) in second harmonics, giving the instrument its most beautiful, pure-sounding register. For this an octave key pressed by the tip of the thumb permits two small octave vents to open while a connection from the third-finger key controls which shall do so, the higher-placed vent acting from *a″* upwards (as on many oboes). No higher harmonics are easily obtainable, so that the higher notes of the standard compass (up to *f‴*)

are made with four keys situated high up on the instrument, three of them worked with the bottom joints of the first and second left-hand fingers (these notes being in fact second harmonics of non-used fundamentals). Soloists have found it possible to add up to another octave using special fingerings, and there are published Tutors detailing such fingerings. But the standard compass continues to be two and a half octaves, from *b♭* to *f‴* (written pitch); the actual pitch of these notes depends on which member of the family is being played, all saxophones being *transposing instruments (see also below, 2). The keywork looks complex, but the fingering is quite straightforward, very much like that of the flute.

2. *The Saxophone Family.* There are seven members in the family, pitched alternately in E♭ and B♭ (that is, the written scale of C will sound in E♭ or B♭ respectively; see Ex. 1). The two high saxophones are the E♭ sopranino and the B♭ soprano, both normally built as a perfectly straight cone (whence in France their nickname, 'carrot'). The soprano (also available

Ex. 1

in a rarer 'bent' model shaped like the alto) has figured comparatively little in jazz but is important as the top voice in a saxophone quartet (see below, 3c); it is also fairly popular for casual music (busking etc.), as is, to a lesser degree, the sopranino. Both are in current production.

The main three instruments of the family all have the typical saxophone shape with the bell rising upwards and a curved crook (or 'neck') to take the mouthpiece; they are the E♭ alto, the B♭ tenor (with a dip in the crook), and the E♭ baritone (considerably larger, with a loop in the top of the main tube, the crook inserted into this). The baritone has for some years been regularly extended with a longer bell and an extra key to reach the written low A, sounding the useful note C (bottom note of the cello). Some designs of tenor, alto, and soprano saxophone have an extra key for making a high F♯ (on tenor sounding *e''*). There used also to be a tenor in C ('C melody saxophone'), handy for playing from song copies without need for transposition.

The deeper sizes are the B♭ bass (like the baritone but over 4′ tall) and the huge E♭ contrabass (made only to order). The bass saxophone featured in jazz for a time, notably in the hands of Adrian Rollini, but its main place is in large European military bands.

The reeds differ in length, since the frequency of vibration of a bar (which the reed is, basically) varies inversely in proportion to the square of the length. Should it be necessary to make a reed for a soprano saxophone in a hurry and with nothing to copy from, an alto reed may be cut down in the proportion $\sqrt{(2/3)}$ (approx. 0.82, i.e. to about 30 mm.), these two instruments being a fifth apart. The width (in theory immaterial) would be reduced

to match the narrower mouthpiece, and the tip of the reed thinned appropriately.

3. *History*: (*a*) *The Invention*. Adolphe Sax produced a viable bass clarinet, and this formed the subject of his first patent, in 1838. Like so many great instrument inventors, he left no personal account of his work, but it seems that with the same object of improving the resources of the bass register of the woodwind (and probably thinking not only of the military band) he may have experimentally tried the mouthpiece of his bass clarinet on the *ophicleide, a regular product of the Sax workshop, and thus, substituting 'open' keys for the ophicleide's 'closed' keys, found his way to the first saxophones—as a bass instrument. Thus Berlioz reported it in the *Journal des débats* in June 1842, a few months before Sax left Brussels to set up business in Paris: 'a brass instrument . . . rather like an ophicleide in shape but with a mouthpiece like that of the bass clarinet', adding 'there is not a bass instrument to compare with it'. The early deep-pitched saxophones in fact show widths of tube much the same as those of the average ophicleide if one measures at points where the same actual note issues from the two instruments.

Well into the 20th century the saxophones, used by far the most in military bands, including the celebrated American bands from Dodworth to Sousa (though rarely British bands before the 1890s), retained early features: separate octave keys, lowest note B♮, etc. One may also bear in mind when thinking of, say, the alto saxophone solo in Bizet's *L'Arlésienne* that with the older rather narrower tubing and especially the old form of mouthpiece (more roomy internally than now) the tone was more closed and velvety, less ringing than it has been since the present more constricted mouthpiece was developed for more penetrating sound in large jazz orchestras.

(b) *Use in the Orchestra*. Most frequently and characteristically up to recently, the saxophone appeared singly in the orchestra, at first usually the alto, and including, before Bizet, a virtuoso *obbligato* in Ambroise Thomas's *Hamlet* (1868) which lies perfectly for the instrument although it is in five sharps. The alto is again prominent in works of the 1920s and 1930s, e.g. Walton's *Belshazzar's Feast*; Kodály's *Háry János* suite; and Vaughan Williams's *Job* (the saxophone here for the hypocritical Comforter). The tenor comes next, as in Vaughan Williams's Fourth Symphony and Prokofiev's *Romeo and Juliet* (especially the second suite). Naturally, to demand a single saxophone is only practical; an orchestra may well have in its clarinet section a player who is expert on saxophone, or have a saxophonist regularly brought in from outside; but to have to engage three or more players for a single work is, of course, a different matter. All the same, works have often been written that demand several, particularly recently. Among composers to use more than one saxophone in orchestral works are d'Indy (who is also said to have liked saxophones for supporting the voices in his choral works) and Stockhausen (who scored for alto, tenor, and baritone in *Carré*; 1960). Perhaps particularly worth noticing is Honegger's use of three alto saxophones replacing the horns of the orchestra in *Saint Joan at the Stake*, produced in 1936.

(c) *Solo and Quartet*. There have been prominent soloists since Lefèbre of Sousa's band and the American Elise Hall, who commissioned works from d'Indy and Debussy; they since include Marcel Mule, founder of the Quatuor de Saxophones de Paris (started in 1928 as the quartet of the Garde Républicaine); Sigurd Rascher, who went to the USA from Germany; and Cecil Leeson, of the USA. It has been said that most of the serious compositions for the saxophone up to 1950 were written for either Mule, Rascher, or Leeson.

Of earlier ensembles, Tom Brown's Saxophone Sextet was well known in the USA at the time of the First World War—also a peak period for the saxophone soloist on the variety stage. Latterly the London Saxophone Quartet led by Paul Harvey has been rated on a par with Mule's. The normal quartet is for soprano, alto, tenor, and baritone, giving a range sounding from low C to about *d'''* in the treble. So well do they blend together that one excuses a repertory largely, though by no means entirely, composed of arrangements.

Solo works for alto saxophone include Debussy's *Rhapsodie* (published in 1919, the orchestration completed by Roger-Ducasse), which, scarcely written with enthusiasm, does not show off the instrument as do Glazunov's Concerto and Ibert's *Concertino da camera* (1934, dedicated to Rascher), both fine works. On the same high level are some of the compositions written for Mule's Quartet. A gem among these is Jean Françaix's *Scherzo humoresque* (1935).

(d) *Jazz and Dance Music*. The saxophone is said to have already been heard in the famous Basin Street, New Orleans, around 1915. Not all leaders of bands came to welcome it, regarding it as a fashionable intrusion urged upon them by record companies. Nevertheless, increasing use through the 1920s led to the basic saxophone section of three players—first alto, second alto, and tenor, all doubling on clarinet—playing mostly in 'block harmony' of 6-3 and 6-4 chords, and still a normal requirement in commercial ten-piece dance-band orchestrations (usually with *ad libitum* parts for second tenor and baritone). For jazz solos the tenor, husky and virile, was an early favourite; on this Coleman Hawkins rose to be acclaimed as the greatest of all jazz saxophonists, rivalled only by Lester Young from the early 1940s. A fine soloist on the more mellifluous alto was Johnny Hodges of Duke Ellington's orchestra, with his partner Harry Carney excelling on the throbbing baritone. But the alto really came to the fore as a solo instrument with the 'bop' style of Charlie Parker (d 1955), semiquavers and all. Rock music for a time brought the tenor back to first place (played without the traditional *vibrato*), but in this area the saxophone cannot be said to have regained the place it won in jazz, even with the aid of a contact pick-up slipped between reed and mouthpiece and wired to an amplifier/loudspeaker system.

ANTHONY BAINES

FURTHER READING
Wally Horwood: *Adolphe Sax, his Life and Legacy* (London, 1979).

Sbalzato (It., often abbreviated to *sbalz.*). 'Dashed', i.e. with a sense of impetuosity.

Scala enigmatica (It.). See *Scale*, 7.

Scale (Fr.: *gamme*; Ger.: *Tonleiter*; It.: *gamma*, *scala*). A schematic arrangement, chiefly for theoretical purposes, of the notes in ascending or descending order of pitch which in practice are regularly used in the music of a particular period or culture. The materials of music may comprise any number of pitches; thus the number and variety of scales are enormous and for all practical purposes incalculable.

1. *Origins*. The processes by which scales have originated and have been adopted are various and may involve intuition, scientific reasoning, chance, contrivance, or any combination of those factors. A number of scales from early times (e.g. Greek church modes) are constructed along lines which later scientific discoveries have endorsed as being in accordance with natural mathematical (and hence acoustical) principles. Other scales were categorized by scientists (e.g. Pythagoras) as a combined result of theoretical reasoning and practical experimentation, and these form the basis of a whole musical culture. Still others have been developed by musicians in an attempt to meet some specific compositional demand (e.g. Skryabin), though few of these have subsequently been accepted into standard musical language.

Probably the ultimate origin of scales lies in speech inflexions (see *Melody*). In theory the total number of available speech inflexions is infinite, that is, anyone may develop his own and maintain it as a personal characteristic; but in practice whole nations or regions adopt a particular type of inflexion (e.g. when ending a sentence) which may distinguish them from others. Similarly, in their music, whole groups of people have often adopted characteristic idioms and inflexions that may be expressible in terms of scale patterns.

The fact that some scales are particularly familiar throughout Western music should not urge their superiority, for in world terms their number is relatively small. All scales—diatonic, chromatic, modal, whole-tone, pentatonic, microtonal, etc.—have equal authority if they can be shown to represent a viable basis for music of any kind.

2. *Intervals in Scales*. The precise definition of notes used in music can be expressed only in terms of frequency vibration (see *Acoustics*, 4). The octave, fifth, and fourth were the first intervals to be thus categorized by early scientists such as Pythagoras (see *Monochord*). Experimenting with vibrating strings, they found that a division of the string at the mid-point raised the pitch of each half to an octave above that of the full length, and they took this ratio of 2:1 as the most basic relationship in musical acoustics. A division at a point two thirds of the way along the string's length raised the pitch a fifth, and at three quarters a fourth. Smaller intervals were derived on the same principles, so that the octave could eventually be marked out into tones and semitones which could be combined to form other intervals (see *Temperament*).

In comparing scales of different musical cultures, there is no guarantee that, for example, the equal-tempered major third of the Western diatonic scale is exactly the same size as the interval conventionally notated as a major third in a Chinese pentatonic scale; for non-Western music is frequently notated in accordance with conventions familiar to Western transcribers, and may not therefore accurately represent the intervals concerned.

Although there appears to be no one interval common to all known scales, one or two are found in many. The octave is the most important of these, not surprisingly, as the acoustic relationship of the two notes of an octave is so close. In many different cultures men and women (or men and children) singing the same tune do so naturally at the interval of an octave without consciously choosing to do so. The perfect fifth and, to a lesser extent, the perfect fourth are also common to many scales. These too are intervals with close acoustic relationships.

3. *Diatonic Scales*. The establishment of the diatonic scale as the basic scale of Western art music was a slow process deriving from the development of the *mode. Two authentic modes, the Ionian (equivalent to a scale of white notes on the piano beginning on C) and the Aeolian (beginning on A), have survived as the modern major and minor scales respectively. A scale is described as diatonic, then, if it consists of an arrangement of tones and semitones within the octave that corresponds to either of those two modes (Ex. 1).

Major and minor scales may be transposed to begin on any of the 12 degrees of the octave, but the characteristic order of tones and semitones in the scale is always preserved (Ex. 2). Thus 12 major and 12 minor scales are available, one in each key.

The minor scale exists in several forms: the natural minor (Exx. 1*b*, 2); the harmonic minor, with the characteristic interval of an augmented second (Ex. 3*a*); and the melodic minor, in ascending form with sharpened sixth and seventh degrees avoiding the augmented second and 'leading' to the tonic (Ex. 3*b*), and in descending form equivalent to the natural minor. All three forms have in common the flattened mediant, producing a characteristic minor third with the keynote.

4. *Chromatic Scales*. The chromatic scale consists of a succession of all 12 semitones of the octave and, like the diatonic scale, may begin on any degree. It is normally conceived in terms of tonality, that is, viewed as a diatonic scale with added 'chromatic' notes which are properly extraneous to the key but serve to 'colour' it. In theory there are two standard ways of notating the chromatic scale. In 'harmonic' notation

Ex. 1
(a) Ionian/major   (b) Aeolian/minor

Ex. 2
(a) D minor   (b) F♯ minor

Ex. 3
(a) Harmonic minor   (b) Melodic minor

Ex. 4
(a) Chromatic scale: harmonic notation

(b) Chromatic scale: melodic notation

Ex. 5 Whole-tone scale
(a)   (b)

Ex. 6 Pentatonic scales
(a)   (b)

(Ex. 4a) the notes of the prevailing key are notated in the context of that key's major and minor scales, with the addition of a minor second and an augmented fourth from the keynote. The 'melodic' notation (Ex. 4b) uses raised notes ascending and lowered ones descending, thus economizing on accidentals (though in any other key but C major or A minor the key signature will anyway account for some accidentals). In practice, however, composers rarely observe these theoretical systems, notating chromatic scales as is convenient for the performer and appropriate to the context.

In the context of 12-note music, where there is no 'keynote' and all 12 notes of the octave are considered points of equal reference, the chromatic scale is sometimes termed the 'dodecaphonic' scale.

5. *Whole-tone Scale.* This scale consists of six notes within the octave, a whole tone apart. In conventional equal temperament, it exists in only two forms (Ex. 5). Its lack of semitones (particularly leading-note to tonic) and perfect fifths, both basic materials of tonal music, gives it an impression of tonal vagueness, which has made it particularly attractive to Impressionists and other 20th-century composers seeking to avoid tonal centres. Debussy exploited the whole-tone scale in much of his music (*Pelléas,*

La mer, and several of the piano preludes) as a means of rebelling against the traditional tonal system of the 19th century.

6. *Pentatonic Scales*. These scales consist of five notes within the octave and exist in several forms. They are sometimes misleadingly termed 'gapped' scales, by comparison with seven-note diatonic scales (which however are themselves 'gapped' in terms of microtonal scales); but the pentatonic scale is no less complete than any other scale, and the term 'gapped' is best avoided.

The most familiar form is the tonal pentatonic, the order of its intervals corresponding to that of the black notes of the piano keyboard (Ex. 6a). It can begin on any degree of the octave, and is specially common on C (Ex. 6b). The pentatonic scale is the basic scale of music in many non-Western cultures, notably *China, *Japan, and parts of *Africa, and it is also a feature of American Indian music, some plainchant, and much European folk music, especially Scottish and Celtic.

The octave may be divided into numerous other pentatonic scales, with different arrangements of intervals (tones, semitones, thirds, etc.); a great many are found in non-Western repertories, many of which use intervals that fall outside European musical traditions (e.g. the Javanese *slendro*, which divides the octave into five nearly equal intervals; see *Indonesia*, 2a, 3a). The pentatonic scale, like the whole-tone scale, has attracted some Western composers (Stravinsky, Bartók, Debussy) as a means of echoing nationalist or folk traditions or for creating special effects.

7. *Other Scales*. In recent times composers have grown increasingly dissatisfied with conventional scales. Some have experimented with unfamiliar, non-Western, or other systems; others have devised their own scales to suit their special needs. Microtonal scales, formed by the division of the octave into intervals of less than a semitone, have long been used in Eastern cultures (e.g. in Hindu ragas), and they have also been adopted by a number of Western composers (e.g. Hába, Julián Carrillo (1875-1965), John Foulds (1880-1939); see *Microtone*). Some composers, particularly Russian ones, have sought to develop new scales by combining elements of pre-existing ones. Skryabin, for example, derived an original six-note scale from the notes of his 'mystic chord'; Verdi used what he called a 'scala enigmatica' in the 'Ave Maria' of his *Quattro pezzi sacri*; and less familiar figures such as Oscar Esplá (1886-1976) and Nikolay Obukhov (1892-1954) have contrived other scales of their own invention.

The number of scales used in music throughout the world is incalculable: the music of many non-Western peoples has not yet been sufficiently studied for all their scale patterns to be properly categorized. And throughout both non-Western and Western cultures, wherever and whenever scales are felt to be a significant element in music, it seems inevitable that new ones will continue to evolve.

PERCY SCHOLES, rev. Judith Nagley

Scandinavia

1. Introduction
2. Music in the Late Renaissance
3. Sweden in the 17th Century
4. The Age of Roman
5. Song and the Rise of Nationalism
6. Sweden after Berwald
7. Denmark after Nielsen
8. Finland before Sibelius
9. After Sibelius

1. *Introduction*. Civilization in the West began round the Mediterranean basin with its gentle climate and was slow in spreading outwards to the more hostile latitudes of the North. Music flourished in Rome and Vienna long before it did in Stockholm and Helsinki, and most musiclovers are scarcely conscious of any Scandinavian composer before the middle of the 19th century, when an upsurge of national feeling created the climate in which a Grieg could emerge. In recent years, however, there has been a revival of interest in Johan Roman and an awareness that Buxtehude belongs as much to the Scandinavian as to the north German tradition. Yet considering the extent of Scandinavian power in the 10th century, it would be surprising if their musical procedures had not had some influence, however modest, on those parts of northern Europe with which they came in contact. They certainly played some part at least in the development of polyphony. The practice of *gymel* (two-part singing based partly on parallel thirds), prevalent in England in the late 12th and 13th centuries, may well be Scandinavian in origin. The two-part hymn *Nobilis, humilis* preserves traces of skaldic chant, and Giraldus Cambrensis ascribed the partsinging practised in the northern part of Britain to the influence of the invading Vikings. There are some interesting survivals of the chanting

of ballads (*kvaedir*) in the Faeroes and in Iceland where the practice of *organum* is still encountered.

2. *Music in the Late Renaissance.* As a vital force, however, the Scandinavian countries were comparatively dormant in the Renaissance, and although many of the famous Flemish and Italian masters were heard in the northern courts, no great indigenous composer appeared. The Swedish court was musical: King Eric XIV attempted an eight-part polyphonic work and his father, Gustav Vasa, had played the lute. Johan III, who succeeded Eric XIV in 1568, encouraged the performance of works by Lassus, Hassler, Giovanni Gabrieli, and Isaac in the royal chapel. The Danish court maintained a large musical establishment of singers and instrumentalists and reached the height of its importance at the time of King Christian IV (1588–1648), one of the greatest of the late Renaissance princes. He was an accomplished amateur musician and attracted to his court such figures as Dowland and Schütz, and extended his patronage to many others, including Michael Praetorius and Vecchi. Not content with that, however, the King sent a number of his most promising young musicians to study in Italy, including Møgens Pederson (*c.*1585–1623), then a boy of 14 or thereabouts, and Hans Nielsen (*c.*1585–?1626). Pederson studied with Giovanni Gabrieli on a later visit (1605–9) and was subsequently sent to England (1611–14). Both composers wrote madrigals in the Italian style and to Italian texts, Nielsen even going so far as publishing them under an Italian name, Giovanni Fonteijo. Pederson also published madrigals in Venice showing a good command of the techniques perfected by Marenzio. His most important work was the *Pratum spirituale* (1620) which includes a Latin Mass, albeit in the shortened form favoured in the Lutheran Church (Kyrie, Gloria, a shortened Credo, and Sanctus) as well as motets and psalm settings in Danish. Yet no distinctive Danish voice can be discerned in Pederson's finely crafted music and the chorale settings of Jacob Årn (*d c.*1653) do not strongly differ from the north German Protestant tradition, even if they speak with a slight Scandinavian inflection. The lavish musical resources of the court, which had enticed Schütz to come to Copenhagen, were dispersed after Christian's death.

3. *Sweden in the 17th Century.* Unlike King Christian IV, the Vasas had made little effort to foster native talent but were content to import foreign musicians. Prominent among them was the Düben family, who came from Leipzig and whose members dominated Swedish musical life throughout the 17th century. Andreas Düben

(*c.*1590–1662) studied in Amsterdam with Sweelinck before settling in Stockholm where he became organist of the German Church and subsequently (1640) *Hofkapellmästare*, a position that he and his descendants occupied well into the 18th century. Queen Christina evinced a lively interest in music both before and after her abdication, maintaining three diverse stylistic ensembles, including the French. She had invited Vincenzo Abrici (1631–96) to her court, and was the patron and admirer of such composers as Carissimi, Alessandro Scarlatti, and Corelli who dedicated his Trio Sonatas, Op. 1, to her. Abrici composed a setting in Swedish of the Lord's Prayer, the first known polyphonic setting in the language. The most important member of the Düben dynasty was Andreas's son, Gustaf (*c.*1628–90), whose output includes some eloquent Latin settings as well as a number of monodic songs to both sacred and secular texts, in which he shows considerable imagination in his approach to the Swedish language. However, the first composer of any real note belongs to the late Baroque.

4. *The Age of Roman.* Johan Helmich Roman (1694–1758) emerged at a time when Sweden had withdrawn from her role as a Great Power after the death of Charles XII, and had turned to the pursuit of the arts of peace. Roman showed such early talent as a violinist and oboist that the court took the then unprecedented step of paying for his studies abroad. He spent five years in England (1716–21), probably studying under Pepusch and certainly acquiring a love of Handel, and returned home to become in 1727 *Kapellmästare* to the court. He transformed the orchestra into a first rate ensemble and together with a young player and composer, Per Brant (1713–67), started public concerts at the House of the Nobility in Stockholm, which became an important forum for new music. Roman's pupil, Johan Agrell (1701–65), settled in Munich, but for the most part movement was in the other direction and not always to the main centres. Johan Daniel Berlin (born in Memel, 1714) settled in Trondheim, but, for all his expertise, did not possess as distinctive a musical profile as did Roman; he was also outshone by his son, Johan Henrik (1714–1808), who succeeded him in Trondheim Cathedral where he was one of the founder members of the Musical Society. However, the first orchestral society to be founded was the Bergen *Harmonien* in 1765.

The most important figures in Sweden were also German. Johann Gottlieb Naumann (1741–1801), a native of Dresden, spent much of his time in Copenhagen and Stockholm, and composed the first Swedish opera on a national theme, *Gustaf Vasa* (1786), to a libretto by the poet Kellgren on a prose sketch by King

Stage design by Louis-Jean Desprez for Naumann's opera 'Gustaf Vasa', first performed at the New Opera House, Stockholm, in 1786.

Gustav III himself. The arts generally, and music in particular, flourished during the Gustavian Era (1772–92), for he founded not only the Royal Opera but also the Royal Swedish Academy of Music. Yet though opera flourished, the talent remained imported. *Gustaf Vasa* was followed by a nationalist *Singspiel* called *Gustaf Adolf och Ebba Brahe* by Georg Joseph Vogler. But the most interesting and worthwhile symphonic figure to emerge after Roman was Joseph Martin Kraus (1756–92), an exact contemporary of Mozart. Kraus came from Miltenberg in south Germany and settled in Sweden in his early 20s, eventually becoming *Hovkapellmästare* to Gustav III. His Symphony in C minor has the unmistakable flavour of the *Sturm und Drang* epoch, and his finest music has a dark intensity that recalls Gluck and C. P. E. Bach. His *Funeral Cantata for Gustav III of Sweden*, written in the last months of his life, reveals a powerful and original mind, and it is small wonder that his music earned him the admiration of Haydn. Among his pupils was Johan Wikmanson (1752–1800) whose quartets show the extent of Haydn's influence throughout Europe. Mention must also be made of a special

phenomenon of the Gustavian era, Carl Michael Bellman (1740–95), whose songs are unique in their skill in adapting words of high poetic distinction to melodies from the *opéra comique* and other sources.

5. *Song and the Rise of Nationalism*. The turn of the century saw an upsurge of interest in song which flourished in both Denmark and Sweden. Perhaps the greatest figure (certainly underrated outside Scandinavia) is Christoph Ernst Friedrich Weyse (1774–1842), who settled in Copenhagen in 1789. His songs have even been compared with Schubert's, and both he and his successor, Peter Heise (1830–79), possess spontaneity and inventiveness. In Sweden, Adolf Lindblad (1801–76) possessed a rich fund of melody and purity of style, but despite such talented poets and composers as Erik Gustaf Geijer (1783–1847) and C. L. J. Almqvist (1793–1866) Sweden produced no really great master of the *romans* (the equivalent of the German *Lied* or the French *mélodie*) commensurate with the quality of its singers such as Jenny Lind and Christine Nilsson. In Norway, Ludvig Mathias Lindemann (1812–87) drew

the attention of his countrymen to the riches of their folk music by the publication of his *Aeldre og nyere Fjeldmelodier* (1853–67), which did much to stimulate the growth of Norwegian art song during the latter half of the century. The foundations were laid by Halfdan Kjerulf (1815–68) and Rikard Nordraak (1842–66) who played a formative part in Grieg's development. Throughout the 19th century, the upsurge of national self-consciousness went hand in hand with liberal movements; it was natural, therefore, that when Norway came under the sway of Sweden in 1809, as compensation for the loss of Finland, Norwegian national feeling grew and its artists looked to their own cultural roots.

Gade in Denmark and Berwald in Sweden were relatively indifferent to folk music, which took strongest hold in Norway, partly because of the strength and richness of the folk music itself. Few composers after the generation of Grieg and Svendsen remain untouched by its inspiration: Johan Halvorsen (1864–1935), Arne Eggen (1881–1955), and Ludvig Irgens Jensen (1894–1969) are three instances. Jensen makes most effective and original use of it in his *Partita sinfonica* (1937). Perhaps the boldest and certainly the most individual of all is Harald Saeverud (*b* 1897) whose wartime symphonies and post-war incidental music to *Peer Gynt* brought him recognition outside Norway. His melodic style is simple, aphoristic, and vital, rhythms are robust, and harmonies diatonic yet often astringent. Reacting against the folk heritage, Fartein Valen (1887–1952) evolved a 12-note style all his own in the 1920s. His achievement is all the more remarkable for his isolation, and his textures in works like *Le cimetière marin* (1933) and the Violin Concerto (1940) have an almost luminous quality, with something of Delius and Berg about them, and show a distinctly individual poetry. Younger composers have continued with folk-inspired material, including Eivind Groven (*b* 1901) and Geirr Tveitt (*b* 1908), both from Telemark; but the post-war years have witnessed developments not dissimilar from those in the neighbouring Scandinavian countries. Almost every modern school has its adherents, though perhaps the most widely recognized figure to emerge is Arne Nordheim (*b* 1931), an eclectic and imaginative composer.

6. *Sweden after Berwald.* Most Swedish composers writing in the second half of the 19th century were relatively pale figures reflecting either the ideals of Leipzig, as did Ludvig Norman (1831–85), or of Wagner, as did Andreas Hallén (1846–1925). By far the strongest figure to emerge in Berwald's wake was Wilhelm Stenhammar (1871–1927). An impressive pianist (and, in later years, conductor),

Stenhammar was strongly drawn to Brahms, of whom he was a noted interpreter, and, among his contemporaries, to Nielsen and Sibelius. He was of a quiet, aristocratic cast of mind, and the finest of his music has a quiet-spoken quality with something of Fauré's gentleness and Elgar's sense of nostalgia, though in idiom he resembles neither. His fine craftsmanship, lively fantasy, and sense of poetry shine through such works as the Serenade for Orchestra, Op. 31, and the Second Symphony, Op. 34, and he possesses much the same keen feeling for nature as did his great Nordic contemporaries, and the same awareness of the evanescence of experience that distinguishes such late Romantics as Mahler, Elgar, and Delius. The pale short-lived summer is central to the Swedish sensibility, and few can express its gentle melancholy with greater eloquence. Yet Stenhammar possesses a command of the sonata process and a sense of momentum that leaves no doubt that Sibelius's example was not lost on him. His art is not so overtly national or as folk-inspired as that of Hugo Alfvén (1872–1960) or Wilhelm Peterson-Berger (1867–1942) and, paradoxically, seems far more attuned to the Swedish spirit. Alfvén is best remembered for his rhapsody, *A Midsummer Watch*—a brilliant repertory piece and in a sense the Swedish equivalent of Svendsen's *Norwegian Rhapsodies*—rather than as a symphonist. Both Ture Rangström (1884–1947) and Kurt Atterberg (1887–1974) were symphonists, though Rangström was more at ease as a miniaturist. His best songs have an affecting simplicity and directness of appeal that have won them a place in the international repertory.

The generation that followed reacted against the lush orchestral opulence and folk-derived inspiration of Alfvén and Atterberg and turned to the Continent for stimulus. The most influential figure to emerge between the wars was Hilding Rosenberg (*b* 1892). Apart from Sibelius and Nielsen he was influenced in the 1920s by Honegger, Milhaud, Hindemith, and the Schoenberg of the First Chamber Symphony. An enormously prolific figure, he has composed a large-scale opera-oratorio, *Joseph and his Brethren*, eight symphonies, two of them choral, and 12 quartets. Rosenberg's achievement was not merely to open the doors to the outside world but to do so without any loss of identity. However cosmopolitan his sympathies, he remained recognizably Swedish and his work is enriched as a result.

Rosenberg's eclecticism has been reflected not only by Lars-Erik Larsson (*b* 1908) but by his pupils, Karl-Birger Blomdahl (1916–68), Sven-Erik Bäck (*b* 1919), and Ingvar Lidholm (*b* 1921). Dag Wirén (*b* 1905), whose delightful *Serenade* has attained world-wide currency, is perhaps the least outward-looking; his roots remain in Sibelius and Nielsen, yet his work has an individual colouring and is refreshingly Nordic. Blomdahl, Bäck, and Lidholm proved the dominant figures in the 1950s, Blomdahl assimilating the diverse influences of Hindemith, Bartók, Schoenberg, Webern, and the post-serial school. At its best his music shows a dark, powerful imagination as in his Symphony No. 3 (*Facets*), though his much-acclaimed space-opera *Aniara* (1959) has failed to hold the stage. A more conservative tradition was upheld by Allan Pettersson (1911–80), whose symphonies are stronger in atmosphere than they are in real substance. Younger composers include Lars-Johan Werle (*b* 1926) whose operas, *Drömmen om Therèse* and *Tintomara*, show a strong sense of theatre, and Sven-David Sandström (*b* 1942) who has written effectively for voices. Sweden has the strongest operatic and vocal tradition of all the Scandinavian countries, producing voices of the order of Björling, Nilsson, and Söderström as well as superb choirs.

7. *Denmark after Nielsen.* Copenhagen was a thriving musical centre in the 19th century and produced a number of composers besides Niels Gade. Both C. F. E. Horneman (1841–1906) and Peter Lange-Müller (1850–1926) possessed melodic facility and charm, the former exerting, along with Svendsen, some influence on Carl Nielsen. But like Sibelius in Finland, Nielsen loomed so large on the horizon that younger Danish composers could not escape his magnetism. This is certainly the case with both Knud Jeppesen (1890–1974) and Finn Høffding (*b* 1899). The former's *Intonazione boreale* continues where Nielsen's *Commotio* left off. Others such as Knudaage Riisager (1897–1974) and Jørgen Jersild (*b*1913) turned to French models, as did Uuno Klami (1900–61) in Finland and Gösta Nystroem (1890–1966) in Sweden. Denmark also produced its 'outsider' in Rued Langgaard (1893–1952), who composed 16 symphonies and an iconoclastic work, *Music of the Spheres* (1918), which blends traditional expressive means with cluster-like sounds, and a piano part played directly on the strings.

It is in the music of Herman D. Koppel (*b* 1904), Vagn Holmboe (*b* 1909), and Niels Viggo Bentzon (*b* 1919) that Nielsen's influence is assimilated alongside neo-classical figures such as Hindemith and Stravinsky. Holmboe has proved the most consistent stylistically. His world of feeling is as disciplined as the expressive means he chooses. There is an inexorable sense of forward movement in his symphonies and an organic coherence that place him in the tradition of Sibelius, yet there is no trace of Sibelius's influence in his sound world. The best of his 11 symphonies and 15 string quartets

have an impressive clarity and distinction of mind, while his scoring is of comparable translucence. Neither the five symphonies of Herman D. Koppel nor the 13 of Niels Viggo Bentzon have quite the same concentration. Bentzon, who is descended from the composer J. P. E. Hartmann (1805–1900), has not shown the same consistency of style, yet the Third, Fourth, and Seventh Symphonies (like Holmboe's symphonies 7–10) are remarkably imaginative and possess real vision. Both Holmboe and Bentzon were fascinated in the post-war years by thematic metamorphosis and both show remarkable resource. Holmboe has also enriched the repertory of choral music, as has his younger contemporary, Bernhard Lewkovitch (*b* 1927).

Of the younger composers to come to the fore, two Holmboe pupils must be mentioned: Per Nørgaard (*b* 1932) and Ib Nørholm (*b* 1931). Nørgaard is eclectic and accomplished, and his early music, including a Piano Sonata and *Constellations*, leaves no doubt as to his technical finesse; subsequent works, including the ballet *Le jeune homme à marier* and some symphonies show the wide extent of his sympathies.

8. *Finland before Sibelius.* For more than two centuries (1582–1809) Finland had been a Grand Duchy of Sweden, and its musical life was, broadly speaking, Swedish in outlook. The main cultural centre during the late Renaissance was Åbo (Turku), where Didrik Peter of Nyland compiled the famous song collection, *Piae cantiones* (1582), a Finnish version of which appeared in Stockholm in 1616. Åbo was the seat of the Finnish University until 1827 and had a flourishing musical life. Yet composers such as Bernhard Crusell (1775–1838), best known for his clarinet concertos, and Erik Tulindberg (1761–1814), who composed a number of string quartets, were essentially Swedish in culture. When, in 1809, Finland became a Grand Duchy of the Tsarist Empire, the stage was set for the growth of national self-consciousness, which soon gathered momentum in literature—with Elias Lönnrot's publication of folk-poetry *Kantele* (1831) and the *Kalevala* (1835)—and much later in the century in music. The so-called 'Father of Finnish music', however, was Fredrik Pacius (1809–91), a German-born composer, a pupil of Spohr who spent some years in the Stockholm Opera Orchestra before settling in Helsinki in 1834. He and Martin Wegelius (1846–1906), Sibelius's teacher, set in motion a more active musical life in Helsinki, though it was not until 1882 that Robert Kajanus (1856–1933) put the Helsinki Orchestra on a permanent footing, and not until early in the present century that the Finnish national opera was founded. The extent of Sibelius's achievement can be measured against

this provincial background and the relatively pale, wholly conventional work of such predecessors as Filip von Schantz (1835–65), Axel Gabriel Ingelius (1822–68), and Pacius himself.

9. *After Sibelius*. Such was the strength of Sibelius's personality that only the hardiest plant could survive in his shadow. Many of the composers writing in his immediate wake reflect some measure of intoxication with his idiom: Leevi Madetoja (1887–1947) and Erkki Melartin (1875–1937) did not escape his magnetic pull. Indeed, the attractions of the idiom spread far beyond Finland's borders: only one of his younger contemporaries, Yrjö Kilpinen (1892–1959), has carved himself a special place in Finnish music and the history of song, and few have matched his skill in distilling a powerful atmosphere with such economy of means. Aare Merikanto (1893–1959) is another independent figure: his opera *Juha* reveals a striking and vivid personality that offers some curious parallels with Janáček, while one of his violin concertos almost suggests Szymanowski. *Juha* serves as a reminder that, although Sibelius chose not to pursue an operatic path, there is a lively native tradition: Madetoja's *Pohjalaisia* ('The Ostrobothnians', 1924) was a vigorous, pioneering work and has borne fruit in the resurgence of interest in opera in the 1970s.

Among the middle and younger generation of composers one encounters as broad a spectrum of sympathies and as wide a variety of styles as one could find in any big Western country. Joonas Kokkonen (*b* 1921) is among the most highly regarded. His alert and intelligent scores with their refined craftsmanship and well-calculated textures combine cosmopolitan neo-classicism with an inward-looking Nordic intensity. He has inherited something of Sibelius's feeling for form, and has written four powerful symphonies and an opera, *The Last Temptations*. But the very existence of such diverse musical personalities as Erik Bergman (*b* 1911), Einar Englund (*b* 1916), Einojuhani Rautavaara (*b* 1928), who attracted attention in the 1950s with his *Requiem in our Time* for wind, Aulis Sallinen (*b* 1935), Paavo Heininen (*b* 1938), Bengt Johansson (*b* 1914), and others points to a vitality out of all proportion to the country's size. ROBERT LAYTON

FURTHER READING
Kristian Lange and Arne Östvedt: *Norwegian Music: a Brief Survey* (London, 1958); John Horton: *Scandinavian Music: a Short History* (London, 1963); Timo Mäkinen and Seppo Nummi: *Musica Fennica* (Helsinki, 1965); Humphrey Searle and Robert Layton: *Britain, Scandinavia, and The Netherlands*, Twentieth-Century Composers, iii, ed. Nicholas Nabokov and Anna Kallin (London, 1972); Nils Grinde: *Contemporary Norwegian Music 1920–80* (Oslo, 1981).

Scaramouche. Suite for two pianos by Milhaud, composed in 1937. It is based on the incidental music he wrote for Molière's *Le médecin volant* ('The Flying Doctor') for a production in 1937 at the Théâtre Scaramouche, Paris, hence the title.

Scarbo. Piano piece by Ravel, the third of his set *Gaspard de la nuit* (1908).

Scarlatti. Italian family of musicians. (Pietro) **Alessandro** (Gaspare) **Scarlatti** (*b* Palermo, 2 May 1660; *d* Naples, 22 Oct. 1725) was born into a poor family and was sent to Rome when he was 12 to be brought up by relatives. Virtually nothing is known of his early education. His first known opera, *Gli equivoci nel sembiante*, was given in Rome in 1679; it was a success and received many performances all over Italy. Although Scarlatti was resident in Rome (his patrons included Queen Christina of Sweden and two powerful cardinals, Pietro Ottoboni and Benedette Pamphili), he seems also to have visited Austria and Germany in the early 1680s.

Scarlatti left Rome for Naples in 1684. His appointment as *maestro di cappella* to the Viceroy, and that of his brother, Francesco (1666–

Alessandro Scarlatti, portrait by Lorenzo Vaccaro.

c.1741), as first violinist of the chapel was a controversial one, leading to much malicious gossip. The Scarlattis kept their posts, however, and Alessandro stayed in Naples for 18 years, composing many operas (some of which were performed elsewhere in Europe as well as in Naples) as well as serenatas, oratorios, and numerous cantatas. By 1700 he was beginning to feel overworked and underpaid, and in 1702 he left Naples for Florence, where a hoped-for appointment at the Medici court failed to materialize. He then returned to Rome and his former patron Cardinal Ottoboni. He was also assistant music director at S. Maria Maggiore, and from 1707 *maestro di cappella*. Since few operas were performed in the Vatican-dominated city, Scarlatti concentrated instead on composing cantatas, serenatas, and oratorios. However, a couple of his operas were produced in Venice, including what many consider to be his finest work, *Il Mitridate Eupatore* (1707).

Scarlatti was still beset by financial worries, and at the end of 1708 he returned to his old job in Naples. He stayed there for ten years, composing some 12 operas (including *Il Tigrane*, 1715, *Il Cambise*, 1719, and the comedy *Il trionfo d'amore*, 1718), and his first instrumental pieces. From 1718 to 1721 he again visited Rome, where three new operas (*Telemaco*, 1718, *Marco Attilio Regolo*, 1719, and *La Griselda*, 1721) failed to achieve the success of his earlier works. His last years were spent in Naples.

Scarlatti was held in high esteem at the end of his life, but regarded as somewhat old-fashioned, even by such staunch admirers as Hasse and Quantz. His music was neglected after his death, and only in the 20th century has his importance as an opera composer been recognized. His surviving output includes around 70 operas (and many are lost), some of them incomplete, and they must be accounted his most important works. In them he established the three-movement Italian *sinfonia* form for the overture and the *da capo* aria, as well as expanding the orchestra from a basic string group to include trumpets, oboes, flutes, and horns. He also wrote over 600 chamber cantatas, mostly for solo voice and continuo. Scarlatti was one of the last and most important contributors to this Baroque genre.

Alessandro married when he was 18, but only five of his 10 children survived. He probably taught his sixth child, (Giuseppe) **Domenico Scarlatti** (*b* Naples, 26 Oct. 1685; *d* Madrid, 23 July 1757), to begin with. At the age of 15, Domenico was appointed organist and composer to the Neapolitan royal chapel, under his father, and he accompanied Alessandro to Florence in 1702, although instead of going on with him to Rome he returned to Naples. In

The beginning of Sonata XXIX from Domenico Scarlatti's 'Essercizi per gravicembalo' (London, 1738).

1705 Alessandro sent him to Venice, saying that neither Naples nor Rome offered sufficient scope for his 'young eagle whose wings are grown'. However, four years later Domenico rebelled against his father's authority and entered the service of the exiled Polish Queen Maria Casimira in Rome. In 1713 he was made *maestro di cappella* at the Basilica Giulia, and then of the chapel of the Portuguese ambassador to the Vatican. While in Rome he met the young English composer Thomas Roseingrave, who did much to promote Scarlatti's music in England. He is also said to have taken part in a keyboard-playing contest with Handel. But, although he was now in his late 20s, he continued to suffer from his father's overbearing attitude, and this may have influenced his decision to leave Rome for Portugal in 1719. His works up to this time—14 or so operas, numerous cantatas, and sacred music—are little more than pale imitations of his father's.

In Lisbon, Scarlatti became *maestro* of the Seminario Patriarcal, at the same time teaching the harpsichord to the Infanta Maria Barbara, daughter of John V. In 1728 she married the Spanish Crown Prince Fernando and Scarlatti went to Madrid with her. He remained in Spain for the rest of his life, except for a visit to Italy in 1728 when he married. Scarlatti was created a Knight of the Order of Santiago in 1738, but his years in Spain were on the whole uneventful.

Scarlatti's move to Portugal coincided with the development of his independent musical personality, which can be seen most clearly in the harpsichord works on which his reputation rests. Over 500 of these attractive one-movement, binary-form 'sonatas' for harpsichord or piano survive—Scarlatti himself called his first published collection (London, 1738) 'Essercizi'. They were written for his royal pupil, Maria Barbara, and some may have been conceived in pairs, related by key though not by thematic material. Many show traces of Spanish and Portuguese influence, probably derived from guitar technique, and they in turn left their mark on the works of his Spanish contemporary Antonio Soler, as well as on the music of several 18th-century English composers. Despite the attempts of scholars to impose a chronology on the sonatas (that by Ralph Kirkpatrick is the best known, and Scarlatti's works are usually given 'K' numbers), the order in which these works were composed is not entirely clear.

Giuseppe Scarlatti (*b* Naples, *c*.1718 or 1723; *d* Vienna, 17 Aug. 1777) was a nephew of Domenico Scarlatti (he was probably the son of Domenico's brother Tommaso). From 1739 he lived in Rome, Florence, and Lucca, where several of his operas were performed. In 1747 he seems to have left for Vienna, but he failed to find suitable employment there, and returned to Italy. His opera *Adriano in Siria* was given at the Venice Carnival in 1752, and three years later he returned to Naples. He spent his later life, from 1757, in Vienna, where he was befriended by Gluck. There he composed several comic intermezzos and comic operas in a somewhat old-fashioned style.   WENDY THOMPSON

FURTHER READING
Ralph Kirkpatrick: *Domenico Scarlatti* (Princeton, 1953, 3rd edn 1968); Giorgio Pestelli: *Le sonate di Domenico Scarlatti: proposta di un ordinamento cronologico* (Turin, 1967); Donald J. Grout: *Alessandro Scarlatti: an Introduction to his Operas* (Berkeley, 1979).

Scat singing. In jazz, the use of nonsense syllables and other vocal effects, introduced by Louis Armstrong and others. The British group of Swingle Singers use the technique in their vocal performances of instrumental tunes.

Scemando (It.). 'Diminishing' (in volume of tone), i.e. *diminuendo*.

Scena (It.). In opera, an extended episode consisting of a loosely constructed sequence of related sections (e.g. introduction, recitative, arioso, one or more arias), often for a solo singer and principally dramatic in intent. In the 18th and 19th centuries the title was given to specially composed dramatic episodes intended for concert performance by a solo singer, rather in the style of a cantata. These were normally settings either of an extract from an opera libretto or of some other dramatic text (e.g. Beethoven's *Ah, perfido!*).

Scenario. An outline libretto of a play or opera, which indicates the characters, the number of scenes, the places where the chief dramatic and musical climaxes will occur, etc.

Scenes from Childhood. See *Kinderscenen*.

Scenes from Comus. Work by Hugh Wood for soprano, tenor, and orchestra to a text from Milton's masque *Comus* (1634). It was commissioned for the 1965 Promenade Concerts.

Scenes from Goethe's Faust. See *Faust, Scenes from Goethe's*.

Scenes from the Bavarian Highlands. See *From the Bavarian Highlands*.

Schafe können sicher weiden ('Sheep may safely graze'). Recitative and air by J. S. Bach, with an *obbligato* for two recorders, from his Cantata No. 208, *Was mir behagt, ist nur die muntre Jagd!*, composed in the early 1740s. Several arrangements of it have been made, among them one by Walton, as the seventh number of his ballet *The Wise Virgins* (No. 5 in the orchestral suite), and one by Barbirolli for cor anglais and strings.

Schafer, R(aymond) **Murray** (*b* Sarnia, Ont., 18 July 1933). Canadian composer. He studied composition with John Weinzweig at the Royal Conservatory in Toronto (1945–55) and then moved to Europe, where he worked as a journalist. In 1961 he returned to Canada, and in 1965 he was appointed resident in music at Simon Fraser University, British Columbia. His very varied output, including large-scale dramatic works, orchestral pieces, and choral music, reveals deep concerns with the languages and mythologies of ancient peoples. He has also been influential as a campaigner against noise pollution and as an originator of new ideas in music education. His writings include *The Composer in the Classroom* (Toronto, 1965; London, 1972), *Ear Cleaning* (Toronto, 1967; London, 1972), *The New Soundscape* (Toronto, 1969; London, 1972), *When Words Sing* (Toronto, 1970; London, 1972), and *The Book of Noise* (Vancouver, 1970).

PAUL GRIFFITHS

Schalkhaft (Ger.). 'Roguish'.

Scharf (Ger.). 'Sharply'; e.g. *scharf betont*, 'sharply accented'.

Schauerig, schauerlich (Ger.). 'Ghastly', 'gruesome'.

Schauspieldirektor, Der ('The Impresario'). Opera in one act by Mozart to a libretto by G. Stephanie. It was first performed in Vienna in 1786.

Scheherazade. See *Sheherazade*.

Scheidemann, Heinrich (*b* Wöhrden, nr Hamburg, *c.*1596; *d* Hamburg, 1663). German organist and composer. He was the son of an organist who sent him to study for three years with Sweelinck in Amsterdam. He took his father's post at the Catharinenkirche, Hamburg, *c.*1625, and was a much sought-after adviser on organ building.

Scheidemann was a major composer of organ music. His best works are the chorale arrangements, in which the tune is treated in a variety of ways—simply as a *cantus firmus*, as a subject for harmonization and embellishment, or occasionally as the basis for a lengthy fantasia. His idiomatic writing for the Baroque organ was an important influence on younger composers, such as his pupil Reincken.

DENIS ARNOLD

Scheidt, Samuel (*bapt*. Halle, 3 Nov. 1587; *d* Halle, 24 Mar. 1654). German composer. Scheidt was to serve Halle throughout his life in various musical capacities—as court organist, principal *Kapellmeister*, and, at one period, *director musices*. At an early age (possibly when only 16) he was appointed organist to the Moritzkirche, and in 1607 or 1608 he went to Amsterdam to study with Sweelinck, from whom he absorbed technical skills which were to be of crucial importance to his later development. In 1618 he collaborated with Schütz and Michael Praetorius in introducing church music in the new *concertato* style at Magdeburg Cathedral, and the following year, with the same colleagues, he performed as organist 'before princes and nobles in the splendid courts of Bayreuth' (preface to *Concertus sacri*). In the later part of his career, life in Halle was severely disrupted by the Thirty Years War, and Scheidt was able only with great difficulty to maintain his customary high standards of music-making.

The work for which Scheidt is chiefly renowned is the three-volume *Tabulatura nova* (Hamburg, 1624), a collection of keyboard (mainly organ) pieces; the title refers to the layout of the music in open score, instead of the more usual organ tablature. The first two volumes contain a wide selection of pieces, including canons, dances, fantasias, fugues, and, particularly, sets of variations on chorales and secular themes where the principal melody is accompanied by a remarkable variety of

Samuel Scheidt, engraving from 'Tabulatura Nova I' (*Hamburg, 1624*).

intricate contrapuntal patterns. The style is often virtuosic, owing not a little to the example of Sweelinck, Frescobaldi, and the English virginalists, and the organ writing is strikingly idiomatic for the period. The third volume consists of organ pieces based on plainchant, suitable for substitution (in place of the choir) at Mass and Vespers in the 'high' Lutheran worship characteristic of Halle, Leipzig, and other large centres. Only one other major organ work by Scheidt has survived, a collection of 100 'sacred songs and psalms' (i.e. chorales) arranged for organ solo, known as the *Görlitz Chorale Book* because of its dedication to officials of that town. The chorales are straightforwardly set, though not without some contrapuntal elaboration in the lower parts. Some of the simpler settings may have been intended for accompanying the congregation, but the majority were probably designed for *alternatim* performance between hymn verses sung unaccompanied by the choir or congregation. Interestingly enough, all but 13 of the chorales correspond with those found in Schein's *Cantional* (Leipzig, 1627) and are placed in virtually the same order.

In the sphere of sacred vocal music Scheidt contributed profusely (though somewhat less adventurously than his famous contemporaries, Schütz and Schein) to the Italianate repertory which evolved in Lutheran Germany during the early Baroque period. His output comprises three principal collections, representative of the main church styles of the time: the *Cantiones sacrae* (Hamburg, 1620), double-choir motets without continuo; the *Concertus sacri* (Hamburg, 1622), grand *concertato* settings for solo voices, *a cappella* chorus, and instruments; and the four-volume *Geistliche Concerte* (Halle, 1631–40), small *concertato* settings, mainly of chorales, for from two to six voices with continuo. Scheidt's preface to the second volume of the *Geistliche Concerte* implies that several of these works were originally composed for much grander vocal and instrumental forces, but that their publication in this form was prevented by the exigencies of war. The *Geistliche Concerte* are none the less the most characteristic, and forward-looking, of Scheidt's sacred vocal compositions. Several of the later concertos (such as 'Christ, der du bist der helle Tag') use a system of variation, involving contrasts of scoring, vocal layout, texture, and rhythm between successive chorale verses, that not only recalls the organ variation techniques of the *Tablatura nova* but also points interestingly forward to the chorale cantata structure of later times.

BASIL SMALLMAN

FURTHER READING
Friedrich Blume: *Protestant Church Music: a History* (London, 1974).

Schein, Johann Hermann (*b* Grünhaim, nr Annaberg, 20 Jan. 1586; *d* Leipzig, 19 Nov. 1630). German composer. He played a prominent part, together with his contemporaries Schütz and Scheidt, in introducing into Germany the new Italian styles of Monteverdi's *seconda prattica* (see *Prima prattica, seconda prattica*)—in particular the free treatment of dissonance and melodic leaps and the expressive use of solo voices and instruments with continuo support.

Schein, woodcut from the title-page of 'Venuskrantzlein' (Wittenberg, 1609).

Despite ill health and personal tragedy (the early death of his first wife and the death in infancy of seven of the nine children of his two marriages), Schein's life was richly productive. Following his school years at Schulpforta he studied law at the University of Leipzig, and subsequently undertook private music-teaching in Weissenfels, where he met Schütz and probably also Scheidt, developing lasting friendships with both composers. In 1615 he was appointed *Kapellmeister* to the ducal court at Weimar, but he relinquished this position after only 15 months on his election to the post of *Kantor* at St Thomas's, Leipzig. His tenure of this prestigious post (later held by Kuhnau and Bach) continued until his death at the age of 44.

Although instrumental music represents only a small proportion of Schein's output, particular importance attaches to his early *Banchetto musicale* (Leipzig, 1617), a collection of 20 groups of dances organized, possibly for the first time in musical history, into unified suites, with

Title-page of Schein's 'Fontana d'Israel', or 'Israelsbrünnlein' (Leipzig, 1623).

common thematic ideas providing a relationship between the individual movements.

Schein's sacred vocal works reveal a considerable variety of styles. In the modestly titled *Opella nova* ('A new little work', two volumes, Leipzig, 1618, 1626), the few-voiced *concertato* style is deployed in 62 settings for varying vocal and instrumental forces, composed 'in the Italian manner customary nowadays'. The first volume contains mainly small-scale chorale settings for from two to four voices and continuo, and may well have been modelled to some extent on Viadana's famous *Cento concerti ecclesiastici* of 1602. The pieces in the second set, on the other hand, are larger in structure and concerned more with biblical texts. Especially noteworthy are the richly scored settings of the Lord's Prayer, the Beatitudes, and the Annunciation. Equally rewarding, though quite different in style, is the fancifully named *Israelsbrünnlein* ('Little streams of Israel', Leipzig, 1623), a collection of 26 sacred madrigals based on texts from the Old and New Testaments. Particularly impressive is the setting of 'Die mit Tränen säen' from Psalm 126, in which the extremes of emotion are painted with vivid musical effect—'tears' by rising chromatic motifs and dissonant harmony, and 'joy' by lively diatonic descending scale passages.

Madrigal writing and the small-scale *concertato* style are evident also in two important secular compositions by Schein, respectively the *Diletti pastorale* (Leipzig, 1624) and the *Musica boscareccia* (three volumes, Leipzig 1621, 1626, 1628). As with all Schein's secular vocal works, these settings are based on his own German texts—in this case somewhat artificial verses in the Italian pastoral manner. In his preface to *Musica boscareccia* he provides an interesting indication of the flexibility of performance methods acceptable at this period, suggesting a surprisingly wide range of possibilities, from a full vocal ensemble at one extreme to solo voice and continuo at the other.

Prominent among Schein's last works is his *Cantional* (Leipzig, 1627), a large-scale Lutheran chorale book. Several of the melodies are traditional, dating from the earliest Reformation period, and Schein retains their original free-rhythm form while providing them with up-to-date diatonic harmonizations. Other chorale melodies, and a not inconsiderable number of the hymn verses, are of Schein's own composition, and of these many were to retain their place in Lutheran worship in later times.

BASIL SMALLMAN

FURTHER READING
Friedrich Blume: *Protestant Church Music: a History* (London, 1974).

Schelle, Johann (*b* Geising, Thuringia, Sept. 1648; *d* Leipzig, 10 Mar. 1701). German composer. After singing as a boy in the Dresden court chapel, he became *Kantor* first at the small town of Eilenburg and then, in 1677, at the Thomasschule in Leipzig. He composed some interesting *concertato* pieces on hymn-tunes which are precursors of Bach's cantatas.

DENIS ARNOLD

Schelmisch (Ger.). 'Roguish'.

Schemelli Hymn Book. English title generally given to the *Musikalisches Gesang-Buch* (1736), containing 954 sacred poems, compiled by a German cantor, Georg Christian Schemelli (*c.*1676-1762). He employed Bach as musical editor of the 69 tunes included, some of which were by Bach himself. Many are sacred songs rather than congregational hymns.

Schenker, Heinrich. See *Analysis*, 3*a*.

Scherz (Ger.). 'Fun', 'joke'; *scherzend*, 'humorously'.

Scherzando, scherzante, scherzevole, scherzevolmente (It.). 'Jokingly', 'playfully'.

Scherzetto, scherzino (It.). A short *scherzo.

Scherzi musicali ('Musical Jokes'). Two sets of madrigal-like songs by Monteverdi, influenced by the French style. The first set, 15 songs for three voices, was published in Venice in 1607; the second set, 10 for one or two voices with continuo, was published in Venice in 1632.

Scherzo (It.). 'Joke', 'game'. A quick, light movement or piece, often in triple time. Like the *minuet, which it replaced in the late 18th century as the traditional third movement of large-scale forms such as the symphony and string quartet, it is generally in ternary form, with a contrasting middle section, or *trio. The term was first applied, in the 17th century, to vocal music, as in Monteverdi's *Scherzi musicali* (1607). From the later Baroque onwards, however, it was used mainly for instrumental music.

Haydn was the first composer to use a movement marked 'Scherzo' instead of a minuet, in his string quartets (the Op. 33 set are known as 'Gli scherzi' for this reason), but it was Beethoven who firmly established the scherzo as a genuine alternative to the minuet: all his symphonies except the First and the Eighth have scherzos rather than minuets. They often incorporate rhythmic effects, such as cross-rhythms, often investing the movement with a rough, almost savage, humour. Schumann, Schubert, and Brahms followed Beethoven's example in their symphonies, while the scherzos of Mendelssohn (e.g. in the Octet, the incidental music to *A Midsummer Night's Dream*, the string quartets) and Berlioz (Queen Mab Scherzo from *Roméo et Juliette*) are delicate and almost ethereal in orchestration and tone. Some late 19th-century composers, such as Dvořák and Tchaikovsky, used national dance forms, such as the furiant, in their scherzos, while some of Mahler's draw on Austrian dances and others use grotesque elements.

Chopin's four piano scherzos are all in quick triple time. Examples of independent orchestral scherzos include Saint-Saëns' tone-poem *Danse macabre*, Dukas' *L'apprenti sorcier*, and Stravinsky's *Scherzo fantastique*.

WENDY THOMPSON

Scherzoso, scherzosamente (It.). 'Playful', 'playfully'.

Schickalslied ('Song of Destiny'). Work, Op. 54, by Brahms for chorus and orchestra, composed between 1868 and 1871. It is a setting of a poem by Hölderlin.

Schirmer. American firm of music publishers, known as G. Schirmer, Inc., not to be confused with the firm of E. C. *Schirmer. Gustav Schirmer (1829-93) emigrated from Germany to New York in 1837, and in 1854 became manager (in 1866 owner) of the Kerksieg & Bruesing Company, which he renamed G. Schirmer. The Schirmer family remained active in the business, which continued to flourish, establishing a large engraving and printing plant in 1891 and building up a national network of affiliated companies, one of the most important of which is Associated Music Publishers. G. Schirmer, Inc., is now one of the largest and most influential of American publishing houses. The Schirmer Library of Musical Classics, whose distinctive yellow covers and clear typography are known worldwide, is perhaps the best-known section of a catalogue that also includes opera librettos, a wide range of vocal and instrumental works, and the music of many leading American composers (including Harris, Barber, Schuman, Menotti, and Bernstein). Since 1915 Schirmer have published the

Musical Quarterly, a leading American musicological journal; they also publish *Baker's Biographical Dictionary of Musicians*. Crowell-Collier-Macmillan are now the proprietors.

J. M. THOMSON

Schirmer, E. C. American firm of music publishers, not to be confused with G. *Schirmer. Ernest Charles Schirmer (1865–1958) founded the firm in Boston in 1921. They began by publishing the choral repertory of university glee clubs, but soon expanded into music books, the standard Classical and Romantic repertory, American music, and electronic music. The composers they publish include Copland, Piston, Rorem, and Randall Thompson.

J. M. THOMSON

Schlag (Ger.). 1. 'Stroke', 'blow'; *Schlaginstrumente*, percussion instruments. 2. 'Beat' (in the sense of 'three beats to the bar' etc.); see *Beat*, 1.

Schlägel (Ger.). 'Drumstick'.

Schleifer (Ger.). See *Slide*, 2.

Schleppend (Ger.). 'Dragging' (generally used in the negative—*nicht schleppend*).

Schlick, Arnolt (*b* ? Heidelberg, before 1460; *d* ? Heidelberg, after 1521). German composer and one of the earliest virtuoso organists. Blind for most, perhaps all, of his life, he was organist at the Heidelberg court chapel, played at the coronation of Maximilian I in 1486 and for various meetings of the Reichstag, and toured the Netherlands and Germany as organ adviser and performer. His *Spiegel der Orgelmacher und Organisten* (Speyer, 1511) is full of useful information about organ building, and includes a statement which indicates that organ pitch may have been lower than it is today (at $a' = 377$).

DENIS ARNOLD

Schlick, Johann Conrad (*b* nr Münster, *c*.1748; *d* Gotha, 1825). German composer and cellist. He worked at the Münster court and, from 1777 until his death, at Gotha. He was a virtuoso cellist and made several European concert tours, many with his wife, the violinist Regina Strinasacchi (1764–1839). He composed a cello concerto, a double concerto for violin and cello, and other instrumental music.

Schlummerlied (Ger.). 'Slumber song'.

Schluss (Ger.). 1. 'End', 'conclusion'; *Schlusssatz*, 'last movement', 'finale'; *Schlusszeichen*, the signal to end a piece, i.e. the double bar. 2. 'Cadence'.

Schlüssel (Ger.). 'Clef'.

Schmachtend (Ger.). 'Languishing'.

Schmeichelnd (Ger.). 'Coaxingly'.

Schmelzend (Ger.). 'Melting', i.e. dying away.

Schmelzer, Johann Heinrich (*b* Scheibbs, Austria, *c*.1623; *d* Prague, 1680). Austrian violinist and composer. He was a scholar at the Vienna court and later became the leader of the court chapel orchestra. In 1665 he was made one of the official composers of dance music, his duties including the provision of ballets for operatic entertainments (he composed the dances for Cesti's *Il pomo d'oro*). He was promoted to the post of court *Kapellmeister* in 1679, following the court to Prague where it had moved to avoid an outbreak of the plague; he none the less died of the plague a few months later. He left a considerable sum of money and three sons (by two wives) who also became musicians.

Schmelzer's dance suites herald the beginning of the tuneful Viennese style, and his sonatas, written in the sectional manner of the Italian *'quilt' canzona, are also highly attractive. Some of his church music is in a grand style, using *cori spezzati*.

DENIS ARNOLD

Schmerz (Ger.). 'Pain', 'sorrow'; *schmerzlich*, *schmerzvoll*, 'painful', 'sorrowful'.

Schmetternd (Ger.). 'Blared out' in horn-playing, i.e. stopped notes produced with the hand in the bell, combined with hard blowing. British composers indicate the effect by the sign + combined with *ff*.

Schmidt, Franz (*b* Pressburg, now Bratislava, 22 Dec. 1874; *d* Perchtoldsdorf, nr Vienna, 11 Feb. 1939). Austrian composer and cellist. After early piano lessons in Pressburg, he studied privately with Leschetizky in Vienna and from 1890 with Bruckner, Fuchs, and Hellmesberger at the Vienna Conservatory. He played the cello in the court opera orchestra (1896–1911) and also taught it at the Gesellschaft der Musikfreunde (1901–8). He taught piano (from 1914) and composition (from 1922) at the Vienna Staatsakademie, becoming its director in 1925; he was also director of the Musikhochschule (1927–31). Much of his time was thus taken up with teaching and administration, but he none the less managed to find time to compose, and he produced two operas, an oratorio, some chamber music, and works for piano and organ, as well as the orchestral music which brought him to public notice. Apart from his four symphonies, his *Variations on a Theme of*

Beethoven (1923) and Piano Concerto (1934), both for piano left hand and orchestra and written for Paul Wittgenstein, are well known. With its masterly variation technique and rich Romantic style his orchestral music owes something to both Brahms and Reger and yet its roots are firmly anchored in Classical traditions. Schmidt was awarded the Beethoven Prize by the Prussian Academy in Berlin, which indicates the high regard in which his contemporaries held him.

JUDITH NAGLEY

Schmitt, Florent (*b* Blamont, Meurthe-et-Moselle, 28 Sept. 1870; *d* Neuilly-sur-Seine, 17 Aug. 1958). French composer. He studied with Massenet, Fauré, and others at the Paris Conservatoire from 1889 to 1900, in which year he won the Prix de Rome. During the next decade he produced many of his most important works, including a bold setting of Psalm 47 for soprano, chorus, orchestra, and organ (1904), a massive Piano Quintet (1902–8), and the ballet *La tragédie de Salomé* (1907), whose pounding rhythms foreshadow to some degree *The Rite of Spring*. In later years he continued to compose prolifically, particularly for the orchestra, while also working as a pianist and music critic.

PAUL GRIFFITHS

Schnell, schneller (Ger.). 'Quick', 'quicker'; *Schnelligkeit*, 'speed'. *Schneller* is also the German name for the inverted *mordent.

Schnyder zu Wartensee, Xaver (*b* Lucerne, 18 Apr. 1786; *d* Frankfurt am Main, 27 Aug. 1868). Swiss composer. He taught himself to play many different instruments, but his main studies were piano and composition. He became a highly regarded teacher, and in 1847 he created the Schnyder zu Wartensee Foundation for the publication of scientific and artistic literature. His compositions included several dramatic works, vocal music, four symphonies, a concerto for two pianos, and piano music.

WENDY THOMPSON

Schobert, Johann (*b* c.1735; *d* Paris, 28 Aug. 1767). Composer, probably German. In the early 1760s he settled in Paris, where he worked for the Prince of Conti and became a celebrated keyboard player. Although he died young (from eating poisonous mushrooms), Schobert was a respected and much-liked figure, whose original compositions exercised considerable influence on contemporary musical life. Both Mozart and Beethoven admired his music, which includes several sets of keyboard sonatas with violin accompaniment, five keyboard concertos, and other instrumental works.

Schoeck, Othmar (*b* Brunnen, Switzerland, 1 Sept. 1886; *d* Zurich, 10 Mar. 1957). Swiss composer. He studied at the Zurich Conservatory (1905–7) and with Reger at the Leipzig Conservatory (1907–8). Thereafter he worked as an accompanist, choral conductor in Zurich (1909–17), and director of the St Gallen Symphony Concerts (1917–44). He composed a large quantity of *Lieder* to poems by Goethe, Eichendorff, Lenau, and others, following Hugo Wolf in style. His other works include several operas, concertos, and a few chamber pieces. Though he was not a teacher, his example proved important to the next generation of German Swiss composers.

PAUL GRIFFITHS

Schoenberg, Arnold (Franz Walter) (*b* Vienna, 13 Sept. 1874; *d* Los Angeles, 13 July 1951). Austro-Hungarian composer. One of the greatest and most influential figures of 20th-century music, Schoenberg was a reluctant revolutionary, and his pioneering work in *atonality and *serialism has to be understood within the context of a lifelong commitment to the Austro-German tradition, particularly to the music of Mozart, Beethoven, and Brahms. This commitment was not the product of education, for Schoenberg had no formal training in theory or composition; only when he was in his 20s did he benefit from some instruction from his friend

Schoenberg

and later brother-in-law Alexander Zemlinsky. His feeling for tradition was, rather, the
natural allegiance of a man who had grown up
playing violin and cello in string quartets, and
who always strove to emulate the quality of
musical thought he found in the chamber music
of the past.

1. *The Early Years*. Schoenberg's earliest compositional efforts date from his boyhood, but not
until he was in his mid-20s did he consider his
works worthy of publication. Even the String
Quartet in D major (1897), an engagingly relaxed piece reminiscent of Dvořák and Smetana,
was printed only after his death, for he could
never be content with anything slight, second-
hand, or unworthy. According to his high moral
view of his own responsibilities, the artist's gifts
and insights carried with them the obligation of
utter truthfulness and discipline; it was his duty
to reveal his inner self and to create something
which did not betray the achievements of his
predecessors. Those achievements he saw as
being undermined by the casual approach to
harmony common in the late 19th century, and
in two of his earliest published works, *Verklärte
Nacht* for string sextet (1899) and *Pelléas
und Mélisande* for orchestra (1902–3), he
brought the harmonic innovations of Wagner
and Richard Strauss into thoroughly worked
forms. Both are narrative symphonic poems,
but both are also consistent musical arguments.
In the case of *Pelléas*, which tells the story of
Debussy's roughly contemporary opera, the
music takes the form of a single-movement
symphony, rich in thematic connection and
contrapuntal development, deriving as much
from Brahms and Reger as from Strauss.

From this point Schoenberg's style developed swiftly. His First String Quartet
(1904–5) and First Chamber Symphony (1906)
both weld four symphonic movements into a
continuous whole, and both strain to accommodate a more chromatic harmony by means of
prodigious motivic and polyphonic working; the
music struggles against the disintegration
and incoherence threatened by its dissonant
material.

2. *The Atonal Works*. This process could not go
on indefinitely, and in 1908 Schoenberg made
the break into atonality, abandoning the attempt
to fit atonal harmonies into tonal forms. In this
he may have been encouraged by the two gifted
young pupils he had recently acquired, Alban
Berg and Anton Webern, though it is important
to note that he rarely based his teaching on his
own new compositional ideas. For him teaching
was as much a vocation as composing, even if at
times it must also have been a financial necessity, and like composing it carried heavy re-

sponsibilities: to provide the student with a solid
knowledge of his musical heritage and to help
him find his own personality.

It was this inner search, conducted on himself, which drove Schoenberg towards atonality,
as well as his feeling that musical history was
pressing him in that direction. His early atonal
works, particularly the Five Orchestral Pieces
(1909) and the 'monodrama' *Erwartung* (also
1909), sound like products of the subconscious.
They use a fantastic variety of harmony, rhythm,
and colour, and they take place at an intense
emotional level which justifies the term 'expressionist' (see *Expressionism*). *Erwartung*, for instance, is a one-act opera with a single soprano
role which explores the innermost sensations of
terror, regret, and hope felt by a woman
searching a dark forest for the lover who has
abandoned her. And *Pierrot lunaire* (1912),
whose theatrical use of a reciter with small
ensemble makes it one of Schoenberg's most
accessible works, inhabits a nocturnal world
of the macabre and ironic, its strangeness
heightened by the reciter's use of *Sprechgesang*, which is a kind of vocal production lying
between speech and song. The ruthless introspection of these works could not have been
achieved without atonality, but it would be
wrong to suppose that atonality necessarily
presupposed tortured expression. Many of
Schoenberg's atonal songs and piano pieces are
more rarefied in tone, and his most ambitious
work of this period was a religious oratorio, *Die
Jakobsleiter* (1917), which deals with the characteristic theme of moral steadfastness as the stony
but unavoidable route to perfection of the soul.
Its composition was interrupted when Schoenberg was called up for war service and, like
many later projects, it was never completed.

During the next few years Schoenberg began
to work out the technique of serial composition
as a means of bringing order into atonality. The
lack of any coherent harmonic framework had,
since 1908, prevented him from writing fully
developed music; his atonal works are either
short (the Six Little Piano Pieces of 1911
particularly so) or else rely on a text to provide
continuity. But with serialism he was able to
return to thematic forms in the old manner, as in
the Piano Suite (1921–3), which looks back to
keyboard suites of the Baroque, or the Wind
Quintet (1923–4), which has the usual four
movements of a classical chamber work. The
possibilities of the technique were extended in
a succession of major abstract works: the Variations for orchestra (1926–8), the Third and
Fourth String Quartets (1927, 1936), the concertos for violin (1935–6) and piano (1942). In
these Schoenberg found, with increasing flexibility and resource, serial analogues for the
devices of modulation and development which

Autograph MS of a page from Schoenberg's 'Ode to Napoleon', for reciter, piano, and strings.

had sustained tonal forms. Though he was working within the tradition rather than, like Stravinsky or Poulenc, from outside, there is something here of *neo-classicism; certainly the control of these serial works contrasts markedly with the emotional and technical extravagance of the atonal music.

3. *Serialism and the Return to Tonality.* One may readily understand how Schoenberg could not sustain the unreserved self-disclosure of such works as the Five Orchestral Pieces. It may be, too, that he felt a need to re-establish contact with the audience which had violently rejected his atonal works—hence his return to the old formal models and also his essaying of lighter modes of expression. Among his earliest serial compositions are two divertimento-like pieces, the Serenade (1920–3, not totally serial) and the Suite for instrumental septet (1924–6), as well as the comic opera *Von heute auf morgen* (1928–9). Another opera, *Moses und Aron* (1930–2), found him returning to a religious subject: the problem of communicating a vision of God. Moses, the seer, lacks the means to do this, while Aaron can speak the message, but only by recourse to compromise and subterfuge,

as when he takes a complaisant attitude to the construction of the Golden Calf. This was very much Schoenberg's own problem—how to express his vision with perfect integrity—and significantly the opera remained unfinished.

In 1933, with the rise of the Nazis to power, Schoenberg left the teaching post he had held since 1926 at the Prussian Academy in Berlin, and he made a formal return to the Jewish faith of his birth, a return which had already taken place in *Moses und Aron* and other works (he had converted to Protestantism in his youth). He emigrated to the USA and took a teaching post at the University of California at Los Angeles, where he lived for the rest of his life. During these last years he made intermittent returns to tonal composition, as in the Theme and Variations for concert band (1943). He also achieved a rapprochement between serialism and tonality in the *Ode to Napoleon Buonaparte* for reciter and piano quintet (1942), which turns Byron's spite against Hitler. *A Survivor from Warsaw* for reciter, male chorus, and orchestra (1947) was another impassioned response to contemporary events. By this time, however, Schoenberg's thought was turning increasingly inward. His last instrumental pieces, the String

Trio (1946) and the Phantasy for violin and piano (1949), make some return to the wild nervosity of the atonal period, and his final project was a set of *Modern Psalms* (1950) on the subject of the search for God. Only one of them was set, and that incompletely, breaking off appropriately at the words: 'And still I pray'.

PAUL GRIFFITHS

FURTHER READING
Egon Wellesz: *Arnold Schoenberg* (London, 1925, reprinted 1971); Rene Leibowitz: *Schoenberg and his School* (New York, 1949, reprinted 1975); George Perle: *Serial Composition and Atonality* (London, 1962, 4/1978); Josef Rufer: *The Works of Arnold Schoenberg* (New York, 1963); Karl H. Wörner: *Schoenberg's 'Moses und Aron'* (New York, 1964); Anthony Payne: *Schoenberg* (London, 1968); Charles Rosen: *Schoenberg* (London, 1975); Arnold Schoenberg: *Style and Idea*, ed. Leo Black (London, 1975); H. H. Stuckenschmidt: *Arnold Schoenberg* (London, 1977).

Schola Cantorum (Lat., 'school of singers'). 1. School for the church singers in Rome, said to have been given its final organization by Gregory the Great (590–604). The choir of the school provided the music for papal ceremonies and services, and the school also trained boys in singing and other musical skills. Some of the singers travelled from Rome to instruct singers in other countries, and some schools modelled on the Roman were set up, for example in York. The Roman Schola Cantorum gradually declined, however, and in 1370, while the papal seat was temporarily in Avignon, was suppressed by Pope Urban V.

The term is now frequently used to describe the choral body of a choir school, but in its true, broader, sense it refers to places of study as well as of choral training. Perhaps the most famous today is the school of the monks of Solesmes, whose special work is the study of plainchant; see *Antiphoner*; *Gradual*, 1; *Plainchant*, 4.

2. An educational institution founded in Paris in 1896 by Vincent d'Indy, Charles Bordes (choirmaster at the church of St Gervais), and the organist Alexandre Guilmant. At first it was intended as a society for the performance of sacred music, and then as a school for the continuation of the church music tradition. The founders' chief objective was 'a return to the Gregorian tradition of performing plainsong'. The curriculum had a strong antiquarian and musicological bias, encouraging the study of works by Monteverdi, Bach, Rameau, and Gluck, Gregorian chant, and Renaissance polyphony. A solid grounding in technique was encouraged, rather than originality, and the only Schola graduates who were able to stand comparison with the best Conservatoire students were Albert Roussel, Déodat de Séverac, Albéric Magnard, and Pierre de Bréville.

Scholes, Percy A(lfred) (*b* Headingley, Leeds, 24 July 1877; *d* Vevey, Switzerland, 31 July 1958). English musicologist and first editor of this *Companion*. Largely because of ill-health he was educated privately; he became an organist and schoolteacher, at the same time being active as a journalist and lecturer, gaining prominence in the 'Music Appreciation' movement. In 1908 he founded *The Music Student* (later *The Music Teacher*). He wrote for the London *Evening Standard*, and later was appointed chief music critic of *The Observer* (1920–7, in succession to Ernest Newman) and *Radio Times* (1923–9).

An advantageous contract to write annotations for pianola rolls enabled him to withdraw to Switzerland and tackle single-handed the task of writing *The Oxford Companion to Music*, which appeared in 1938 and by which he is best known. But his major work of scholarship was his doctoral thesis, published as the book *The Puritans and Music* (London, 1934), in which he shows that 17th-century dissenters (to whose traditions Scholes as a Methodist belonged) were by no means against music as was so often believed. He lived in Britain during the war, at the end of it in Oxford, where he was involved in the appointment of the first full-time professor of music, J. A. Westrup, in 1947. To these post-war years belong excellent studies of the music historians Burney (London, 1948) and Hawkins (London, 1953). He eventually returned to Switzerland where he died.

DENIS ARNOLD

Schöne Müllerin, Die ('The Fair Maid of the Mill'). Song-cycle for male voice and piano by Schubert, D 795, composed in 1823. The songs are settings of 20 poems by Wilhelm Müller (1794–1827) from his *Gedichte aus den hinterlassenen Papieren eines reisenden Waldhornisten* (1821). They are: *Das Wandern* ('Wandering'), *Wohin?* ('Where to'), *Halt!*, *Danksagung an den Bach* ('Grateful Address to the Millstream'), *Am Feierabend* ('After the Day's Work'), *Der Neugierige* ('Curiosity'), *Ungeduld* ('Impatience'), *Morgengruss* ('Morning Greeting'), *Des Müllers Blumen* ('The Miller's Flowers'), *Tränenregen* ('Rain of Tears'), *Mein!* ('Mine'), *Pause*, *Mit dem grünen Lautenbande* ('With the Lute's Green Ribbon'), *Der Jäger* ('The Huntsman'), *Eifersucht und Stolz* ('Jealousy and Pride'), *Die liebe Farbe* ('The Beloved Colour'), *Die böse Farbe* ('The Hated Colour'), *Trockne Blumen* ('Dry Flowers'), *Der Müller und der Bach* ('The Miller and the Millstream'), *Des Baches Wiegenlied* ('The Millstream's Lullaby').

Schoolmaster, The (*Der Schulmeister*). Nickname of Haydn's Symphony No. 55 in E♭ major, composed in 1774. It is so called because it has been thought that the dotted figure in the slow movement suggests the admonishing finger of a schoolmaster.

Schools of Music. The earliest formal schools of music were those organized by the Medieval Church in connection with training singers in the correct performance of plainchant (see *Schola Cantorum*). Specialist schools of music, where students could receive a thorough professional training in several branches of music, originated in the orphanages and other institutions of Medieval foundation which cared for needy children ('conservatorio'). In the late 16th century and the early 17th, those in Naples and Venice began to concentrate on teaching music, partly as a means of raising money through having their pupils sing at weddings and in public performances. Institutions for boys in Naples (e.g. Conservatorio di S. Onofrio, Conservatorio dei Poveri de Gesù Cristo) and those for girls in Venice (e.g. Ospedale della Pietà, Ospedale degli Incurabili) gained wide recognition and an enviable reputation for their music teaching, and soon began to admit fee-paying pupils as well as children in need. Each institution had a *maestro* in charge of specific parts of the music curriculum, and there were specialist teachers for singing and instrumental tuition. The conservatories aimed to include on their staff a number of notable composers (e.g. Vivaldi, at the Pietà in Venice).

In the later 18th century the idea of music conservatories began to spread. After visiting Italy, Burney produced in 1774 a plan for a music school, but neither this nor an earlier plan devised by John Potter in 1762 bore fruit in England. In Leipzig a private singing school was founded in 1771 and other similarly limited schools sprang up, but a larger-scale project was the first French conservatory, founded in 1783 as the École Royale de Chant (and closely associated with the Opéra), which taught singing, theoretical subjects, and performance. In 1795, however, it was superseded by the Conservatoire National de Musique et de Déclamation, which expanded rapidly and, despite its reputation for a certain conservatism, was distinguished throughout the 19th century; its teaching staff included Gossec, Méhul, and Cherubini.

After the decline of the charitable institutions in Italy in the late 18th century and the upheavals of the Napoleonic wars, Italy was slow to develop new schools of music. The surviving Naples conservatories eventually merged in the early 19th century to form the Real Collegio di Musica; a part-time college of music was established in Bologna in 1806 and one in Milan in 1807; but it was only in 1824 that Milan had its first large-scale school of music,

the Regio Conservatorio di Musica, and other Italian cities eventually followed suit (Genoa, 1829; Florence, 1861; Turin, 1867; and Rome, 1877).

Central and northern Europe have many notable conservatories, the oldest of which are Prague (1811) and Vienna (1817). The Leipzig conservatory, founded by Mendelssohn in 1843, also included among its teachers Schumann, Moscheles, and Joachim; with its broadly based curriculum in all theoretical and practical areas of music, it attracted young students from all over Europe and the USA. The Munich conservatory was established along similar lines in 1846 and was closely followed by Berlin (1850), Dresden (1856), Frankfurt am Main (1861), Moscow (1862), St Petersburg (1866), Weimar (1872), Budapest (1875), and many others. Brussels has had a conservatory since 1813 (reconstituted in 1832 as the Conservatoire Royal and headed for many years by Fétis), and Geneva since 1835.

In Britain it was almost 50 years after Burney's plan before the first academy of music was founded (1822) and opened (1823) in London. It was soon granted a royal charter, and in 1830 it became the Royal Academy of Music. Pupils were admitted at an early age and many boarded on the premises until 1853, after which a series of government grants enabled the Academy to survive and flourish up to the present day in a much enlarged and diversified form.

Other London schools of music included the Church Choral Society and College of Church Music, which specialized in sacred music; it was founded in 1872 and was renamed Trinity College of Music in 1875. The National Training School of Music was established in 1876 to train performers for the profession; in 1883 it became the Royal College of Music, with Sir George Grove as its first director. The Guildhall School of Music was established by the City of London in 1880 as a municipal institution for training musicians.

Among important British schools of music outside London are the Birmingham School of Music (founded 1859), the Royal Scottish Academy of Music and Drama in Glasgow (founded in 1890 as the Athenaeum School of Music), and the Royal Northern College of Music in Manchester, which was formed in 1972 from an amalgamation of the Royal Manchester College of Music (founded in 1893 by Sir Charles Hallé) with the Northern School of Music (founded in 1942). As the Associated Board of the Royal Schools of Music, those schools of music with royal charter (as well as Trinity College) have long exerted influence throughout Britain and in English-speaking countries abroad by administering series of local graded examinations in instrumental playing, singing, and the theory of music.

Specialist schools of music in Britain include the Royal Military School of Music, Kneller Hall, Twickenham (founded in 1857 as the Military School of Music), the Royal College of Organists in London (founded in 1864 as the College of Organists), and the Royal School of Church Music at Addington Palace, Croydon (founded in 1927 as the School of English Church Music).

The USA has an immense number of conservatories, some independent and some attached to universities and colleges. They first appeared in the 1860s (Oberlin, Ohio, 1865; Peabody Conservatory, Baltimore, 1866; New England Conservatory, Boston, 1867), but the early 20th century saw the establishment of the greatest numbers (Juilliard School of Music, New York, 1905; Eastman School of Music, Rochester, 1921; Curtis Institute of Music, Philadelphia, 1924). The close association between American conservatories and university departments allows generous provision for talented young musicians, who can often combine training in musicology with developing practical skills in solo and ensemble playing (as is also possible at several British conservatories).

While schools of music in the USA were much influenced by those in Europe, particularly Germany, conservatories in other English-speaking countries naturally tended to follow the lead of the London institutions. The first Australian conservatories independent of university music departments were established in Melbourne (1895) and Adelaide (1898), and Sydney followed in 1916 with the New South Wales State Conservatorium. In New Zealand, however, professional training in music has traditionally remained the responsibility of the university music departments. In Canada, as in the USA, schools of music more often take the form of university music departments than of independent conservatories, but some of the older schools (Royal Conservatory of Toronto, 1886; McGill School of Music, Montreal, 1904) continue to play an important role in teaching and examining students preparing for performing careers.

See also *Education and Music*.

PERCY SCHOLES, rev. Judith Nagley

Schopenhauer, Arthur. See *Aesthetics of Music*, 3.

Schöpfung, Die. See *Creation, The*.

Schott. German firm of music publishers. Bernhard Schott (1748–1809), a clarinettist who had a thorough knowledge of music engraving on both copper and pewter, founded the firm in Mainz in 1780. Besides publishing works by composers associated with the Mainz court, he issued piano scores and arrangements of popular operas, notably the first piano scores of Mozart's *Die Entführung* (1785) and *Don Giovanni* (1791). His sons Johann Andreas (1781–1840) and Johann Joseph (1782–1855) developed the catalogue and absorbed various other firms, and 'B. Schott's Söhne', as it came to be known, flourished throughout the 19th century. They formed important associations with leading composers, such as Beethoven (from 1824, publishing his *Missa solemnis*, Ninth Symphony, and some late string quartets) and Wagner (from 1859, publishing *Der Ring des Nibelungen*, *Die Meistersinger*, and *Parsifal*).

Schott's present interest in contemporary music began with Stravinsky's *Fireworks*, published in 1910, and they now publish many notable German composers, including Hindemith, Orff, Weill, and Henze. They have issued important musicological works, including the twelfth edition of Riemann's *Musik Lexikon* and Anthony van Hoboken's thematic catalogue of Haydn; their music journals include *Melos/ Neue Zeitschrift für Musik*, *Musik und Bildung*, and *Das Orchester*. Unlike many other German publishing houses, Schott survived the Second World War virtually untouched. Their archives, containing valuable letters from Beethoven and others, are now in the Mainz Stadtbibliothek.

Schott of London became independent in 1914, but in 1980 Schott of Mainz resumed control. Since the Second World War Schott of London have published several leading British composers, such as Tippett, Humphrey Searle, Peter Racine Fricker, Alexander Goehr, and Peter Maxwell Davies. They have played a leading role in the recorder revival, supported by their own recorder manufacturer, issuing hundreds of recorder editions and founding *Recorder and Music Magazine* in 1963.

J. M. THOMSON

Schottische (Ger.). 'Scottish'. A round dance similar to, but slower than, the *polka. It is sometimes coupled with the *écossaise but, despite the similarity of name, bears no resemblance to that dance beyond the fact that both are in duple time. The Schottische was called the 'German polka' when it first appeared in England, in the mid 19th century.

Schrammel. Family of musicians active in Vienna in the latter half of the 19th century. They helped to create the repertory and style of music that was popular in the *Heurigen* (where the Viennese gathered to drink the new wines) and in other Viennese places of entertainment. The real founder of the family tradition was Kaspar Schrammel (*d* 1870), but his sons

Johann (*b* Neulerchenfeld, nr Vienna, 22 May 1850; *d* Vienna, 17 June 1893) and Joseph (*b* Ottakring, nr Vienna, 3 Mar. 1852; *d* Vienna, 24 Nov. 1895) were the ones who popularized the music. They both played the violin and formed a quartet with the help of two friends, Georg Dänzer on clarinet and Anton Strohmeyer on guitar: this became the traditional Schrammel quartet make-up. Subsequently the piano accordion became an integral part of the music, generally replacing the clarinet. The brothers also started a half-sung, half-spoken style of singing and began to write much of their own music, such as *Wien bleibt Wien*, which has become a classic of the genre. Their music was a strong influence on that written by Lanner and the Strauss family. The Schrammels' fame spread beyond Austria and they played at the World Exhibition in America in 1890. The tradition they set was carried on by others and still survives. There was a dedicated revival of the original styling and music in the 1960s, when their scores were rediscovered.

PETER GAMMOND

Schrittmässig, schrittweise (Ger.). 'Stepwise', i.e. at a walking pace (the equivalent of *andante*).

Schubert, Franz (Peter) (*b* Vienna, 31 Jan. 1797; *d* Vienna, 19 Nov. 1828). Austrian composer. The only one of the great composers to be born in Vienna, he was also the only one who failed to win international recognition in his own lifetime. For this his untimely death is only a partial explanation. The reasons for the world's neglect of his genius are to be sought rather in his own nature, shy of the limelight, and totally indifferent to the arts of self-assertion. He had neither the talent nor the inclination for the role of virtuoso performer, and he disliked the regular routine imposed by continuous employment. Moreover, the democratization of taste, and the development of commercial publishing, not to mention the illiberal political climate of his day, made life difficult for a freelance composer, a species of which Schubert was perhaps the first thorough-going example. He was dependent throughout his life on the fees he could earn from patrons and dedicatees, from the publication of his songs and keyboard compositions (which did not begin till he was 24), and occasional teaching or performing. He never achieved financial security, except for a year or two; on the other hand, the idea that he lived in feckless bohemian poverty is a popular myth.

1. *The Early Years*. Schubert was the fourth surviving son of a school assistant from Moravia and a domestic servant from Silesia, who met and married in the suburb of Lichtental. Franz learnt to play the piano and the violin from his father and brothers, and later the viola. He had a few lessons in counterpoint from the local church organist, Michael Holzer. But his serious musical education began at the age of 11, when he won a choral scholarship to the Imperial College (the Konvikt, or religious seminary). Here under the supervision of the court organist Wenzel Ruzicka and the *Kapellmeister* Anton Salieri his gifts soon revealed themselves. From Salieri he inherited conservative notational habits and a reverence for the music of Gluck, and a coolness towards that of Mozart and Beethoven which Schubert was later to grow out of. The most impressive achievement of these years is the series of string quartets which he wrote in 1812. Even earlier, in 1811, came his first attempt at opera, but the setting of Kotzebue's *Die Spiegelritter* ('The Looking-Glass Knight') was abandoned after the first act. Even earlier still were the first songs, ambitiously modelled on the cantata-like settings of Schiller by Zumsteeg.

Schubert left the Konvikt in 1813, declining the offer of an endowment which would have enabled him to continue his education. Instead, he spent a year training as a teacher, and then returned home to teach in his father's school. There followed a period of sustained creativity which strains credulity. In the space of three years his compositions include five symphonies, four Masses, three string quartets, three piano sonatas, six operas, and some 300 or more songs. This torrent of music, none of it publicly performed or paid for, laid the foundation for his future greatness. The early symphonies, for instance, particularly No. 2 in B♭ and No. 3 in D major, anticipate the first-movement form and the rhythmic drive of the Great C major Symphony, though the idiom is still 18th-century. There are lyrical digressions in the string quartets which foreshadow the mature Schubert. But the major achievement of these years was an outburst of text-inspired song which laid the foundation for the Romantic *Lied*. The discovery of Goethe's *Faust* in October 1814 led to the first unassailable masterpiece, *Gretchen am Spinnrade* ('Gretchen at the Spinning Wheel'), soon to be followed by others, *Nähe des Geliebten* ('Nearness of the Beloved'), *Heidenröslein* ('The Wild Rose'), and *Erlkönig*; and the poetic sensibility which Goethe had evoked in the composer was carried over into his exploration of the work of Hölty, Claudius, Uz, Jacobi, and many others. The claim that Schubert 'invented' the *Lied* can hardly be sustained, but there is no question that he made of it a new art form, and went on to reveal its full potential.

In 1816 this first phase of his work seems to

reach a plateau; his music displays a stable mastery, but not of a kind that can be called fully Schubertian. Instead, such music as the three Sonatinas for violin and piano (D 384, 385, and 408), the Symphony No. 5 in B♭, and the concerto movements for piano and strings (Adagio and Rondo, D 487) and for violin and strings (Rondo in A, D 438) have a Mozartian grace and lucidity. The identity of form and utterance is complete. Much the same is true of songs like *Ins stille Land* ('The Land of Peace'), *Litanei* ('Litany'), and *Orpheus*. About this time Schubert's first love affair, with Therese Grob, drifted to its unhappy end. Deep feelings were involved, at any rate for the composer, but there was no foreseeable future in it, and they went their separate ways.

2. *The Path to Independence.* By the autumn of 1816 the urge to escape from the drudgery of the schoolroom had become irresistible. After an unsuccessful attempt to obtain a teaching post at Laibach (Ljubljana), he decided to throw in his lot with Franz von Schober, a young man with artistic connections and hedonistic tendencies, and went to live in the inner city. For the next six years his reputation steadily grew in Vienna, and in provincial centres like Linz, Steyr, and Graz. Early in 1817 he was introduced to J. M. Vogl, the leading baritone of the Court Theatre, who became an enthusiast for the songs, and did much to spread his fame. In 1818 his orchestral compositions began to make occasional appearances at public concerts. Wider horizons and new opportunities opened up. The second half of 1818 was spent at Zseliz in Hungary, where Schubert acted as music tutor in the family of Johann Karl, Count Esterházy, in a rural, semi-feudal environment far removed from the schoolroom. In 1819 he accompanied Michael Vogl on his annual holiday at Steyr (Vogl's birthplace), and this first glimpse of the mountains of Upper Austria proved a powerful stimulus. The liberating effect of these experiences can be traced in his music. The songs of 1817 range from the lyrical perfection of *An die Musik* ('To Music') and *Die Forelle* ('The Trout') to the dramatic power of *Memnon*, *Ganymede*, and *Gruppe aus dem Tartarus* ('Scene out of Hades'). The philosophical insight and vivid pictorialism of these and other songs owe much to his friend Johann Mayrhofer, a poet whose vision of life as a kind of antechamber to the 'happy land' strongly influenced Schubert, and inspired many of his finest songs. A new interest in Beethoven is also plainly to be felt in 1817, especially in a series of piano sonatas (several left incomplete), of which the best known are the ones in A minor (D 537), E♭ (D 568), and B

Autograph MS of Schubert's Piano Sonata in A minor (1817), D537, the opening of the second movement.

major (D 575), and in the violin and piano Duo in A major Op. 162. The Symphony No. 6 in C major pays its tribute both to Beethoven and to Rossini, whose operas had impressed Schubert on their first appearance in Vienna by their vigour and musicality, and who was an important secondary influence on his mature style. The Piano Quintet in A major (the 'Trout'), finished in the autumn of 1819, is the first instrumental work which can be called thoroughly Schubertian in spirit and in idiom. It was clearly inspired by the beauty of the Styrian countryside, a work full of high spirits and dancing rhythms, yet at the same time guarding at its heart a kind of enchanted stillness; so that the pulse is constantly slowed in a meditative dance. It is the first full statement of Schubert's natural mysticism.

3. *The Years of Maturity*. On his return from Zseliz Schubert was commissioned to write a one-act comic *Singspiel* for the Kärntnertor Theater. *Die Zwillingsbrüder* ('The Twin Brothers') reached the stage in June 1820, and had a modest *succès d'estime*. Two months later *Die Zauberharfe* ('The Magic Harp'), a magic play with music, ran at the rival Theater an der Wien for eight consecutive performances. The champions of German opera began to form themselves into a kind of Schubert lobby as a counterblast to the all-conquering Italians, and he and Schober started work on a full-length all-sung opera, *Alfonso und Estrella*. But before it was finished, the management of the court theatres had been taken over by the Italian impresario Antonio Barbaja, and Schober had retired from the stage. *Alfonso* was set aside, and efforts to produce it elsewhere failed. In 1823, however, Schubert was commissioned to write *Fierabras*, a tale of love and war during the Crusades, with Josef Kupelwieser, the manager of the theatre, as librettist. This time the project foundered because of intrigues within the theatre, which led to Kupelwieser's resignation. As a compensation, Kupelwieser arranged for Schubert to write the musical interludes in *Rosamunde*, a 'grand Romantic drama' by Helmina von Chezy. In December 1823 this actually reached the stage. The delightful music was warmly received, but the silly plot doomed the piece, which was withdrawn after two performances.

The years 1820-3 were thus largely taken up with a fruitless pursuit of operatic success. Those years were also marked, however, by a series of vocal and instrumental works of striking brilliance and originality. The settings of poems by Goethe, Friedrich von Schlegel, Matthäus von Collin, and Rückert reveal a new dramatic power and poetic insight. The part-songs include the ever popular setting of the 23rd Psalm, and the setting of Goethe's 'Song of the Spirits over the Waters' for male voices and orchestra. The Mass in A♭ completed in 1822 is the most idiomatic of his six settings. Characteristically, however, his most original work was left unfinished. The Quartet Movement of December 1820 is an enormous advance on the string quartets of his adolescence, but it breaks off in the middle of the sketch for the slow movement. The dramatic oratorio *Lazarus* (February 1820), an astonishingly forward-looking work which replaces the usual alternation of recitative and aria with a continuous flow of orchestrally accompanied *arioso*, is a tantalizingly brilliant fragment. Even more enigmatic is the case of the Unfinished Symphony itself. The two surviving movements are the most dramatic and personal statement of the *lacrimae rerum* in symphonic literature. There are sketches for the Scherzo, and competent judges believe that the symphony was in fact finished. Yet it seems clear that Schubert disowned the work. In September 1823 he handed over the first two movements to Josef Hüttenbrenner, and thereafter never referred to it again, so far as we know.

4. *The Late Years*. If, as seems probable, the work was occasioned by some emotional crisis in the composer's life, it may well have some connection with his illness. Towards the end of 1822, or early the next year, he began to show the symptoms of venereal disease, almost certainly syphilis. His condition deteriorated rapidly in the first half of 1823, and then began to improve slowly. In 1824 he resumed a more or less normal life, but the evidence suggests that the bouts of sickness and headaches by which he was plagued for the rest of his life were induced by his chronic complaint. The winter of 1822-3 thus marks a crisis in Schubert's affairs, when his reputation was at its highest. The sensational success of *Erlkönig* at a public concert in March 1821 had led to the publication of his songs, and to financial independence. But the failure of his operatic hopes, and the collapse of his health, marked the end of his short-lived success. In the remaining years his life, never outwardly eventful, recedes into the half-world of Metternich's Vienna. At this time too his aspirations change direction. Abandoning his hopes of a stage success, he resolved to concentrate on the prestigious—but no longer fashionable—forms of sonata, string quartet, and symphony. To the last five years of his life belong the Great C major Symphony, the three great string quartets, the two piano trios, the two song-cycles, the Heine and Rellstab songs, the greatest of his keyboard works both for solo piano and piano duet, and the most ambitious of his settings of the Mass.

Comparatively minor events serve as landmarks because of their association with these masterpieces. The meeting with Schuppanzigh early in 1824 encouraged him to plan the series of the three mature quartets. If on his return visit to Zseliz in 1824 a kind of *amitié amoureuse* sprang up between him and the young Countess Karoline Esterházy, this seems important mainly because it motivated his finest works for piano duet, including the finest of all, the Fantasie in F minor of January–April 1828, which was dedicated to her. The long summer holiday of 1825, during which he and Vogl once again toured the mountains, was a halcyon interlude, well documented except in the most important particular, the identity of the symphony which Schubert sketched in Gmunden and Gastein, once thought to have disappeared, but now generally acknowledged to be the work we know as the Great C major Symphony. This is Schubert's greatest 'public' work, comparable in scale and conception with Beethoven's symphonies, but lyrical in content, the first expression in symphonic literature of the Romantic doctrine of the unity of man and nature. It remained entirely neglected until 1839, when Mendelssohn rescued it from oblivion. Only in this century, however, has it become a regular part of the repertory.

The supreme achievements of the song writer also belong to these years. The greatness of the song-cycles, *Die schöne Müllerin* (1823) and *Winterreise* (1827), owes something to the Dresden poet and publicist Wilhelm Müller, whose essays in the folk-song tradition so exactly met Schubert's needs. Their strong rhythms and evocative language embody the Romantic love-affair with death which rests at the heart of so much of Schubert's best work, though with him it never ceases to be life-enhancing. The two groups of songs to texts by Heine and Rellstab, though they do not constitute a cycle in the true sense, take even further the dramatic and impressionist qualities inherent in the *Lied*.

The compositions of his last year, especially the F minor Fantasie, the three last piano sonatas, and the incomparable String Quintet in C, are 'private' works which seem to embody the personal vision of a composer whom Liszt called 'le plus poète que jamais'. His final illness was diagnosed as 'typhus abdominalis', which seems to have been equivalent to typhoid fever. But it may well have been hastened, even caused, by the disease which he knew to be incurable. If so, the clairvoyant quality of these last works, their vision and authority, reflects the fate of a man who knew himself to be doomed.

Schubert, watercolour (1825) by W. A. Rieder.

Franz Lachner, Schubert (centre) and Eduard von Bauernfeld, drawing by Moritz von Schwind.

The spontaneity and clarity of Schubert's music appeal equally to the expert and to the layman. He had many styles—it has been fairly said, indeed, that he had a different style for every poet he set—and his music often sounds like that of other composers. Yet the adjective 'Schubertian' is indispensable. He gave some impetus to the development of monothematic forms by the example of his 'Wanderer' Fantasy; but in general he was no innovator, content to adapt classical forms and the classical language to his own purposes. His poetic sensibility enabled him to give an entirely new emotional weight to familiar formulas like the major/minor alternation, the enharmonic shift, and the tonic/German sixth/tonic sequence, introducing new harmonic tensions between the tonic and its more remote relations. This process made possible the development of the *Lied* as an independent art form, and led him further to adapt the symphony, the quartet, and the sonata to the emotional world of the new poetry.

JOHN REED

FURTHER READING
Richard Capell: *Schubert Songs* (London, 1928, rev. edn 1973); Alfred Einstein: *Schubert* (London, 1951, reprinted 1971); Maurice J. E. Brown: *Schubert. a Critical Biography* (London, 1958); M. J. E. Brown: *Schubert Songs* (London, 1967); Philip Radcliffe: *Schubert Piano Sonatas* (London, 1967); Jack A. Westrup: *Schubert Chamber Music* (London, 1969); M. J. E. Brown: *Schubert Symphonies* (London, 1970); John Reed: *Schubert: the Final Years* (London, 1972); Hans Gál: *Franz Schubert and the Essence of Melody* (Eng. trans. London, 1974).

Schuhplattler (Ger.). 'Clog dance'. A jolly Bavarian dance in which the dancers slap their knees and the soles of their feet with their hands.

Schuller, Gunther (*b* New York, 22 Nov. 1925). American composer. Largely self-taught, he has worked as a horn player at the Metropolitan Opera (1944–59) and as a teacher at various institutions. In 1966 he was appointed president of the New England Conservatory. His music draws on various influences, including those of Schoenberg, Babbitt, and the European avant-garde, and often seeks what he has called a 'third stream' between jazz and classical music. *Seven Studies on Themes of Paul Klee* (1959), one of his many orchestral scores, shows his vivid invention for instruments. He has written the books *Horn Technique* (New York, 1962) and *Early Jazz: its Roots and Musical Development* (New York, 1968).

PAUL GRIFFITHS

Schulmeister, Der. See *Schoolmaster, The.*

Schultz, Johannes (*bapt.* Lüneburg, 26 June 1582; *d* Dannenberg, Feb. 1653). German composer. From 1605 until he died he was organist at Dannenberg. His music includes a set of *40 . . . neuwe Paduanen, Intraden und Galliard* for four-part instrumental ensemble (Hamburg, 1617), several motets, and the *Musicalischer Lustgärte* (Lüneburg, 1622), a mixture of instrumental and vocal music.

WENDY THOMPSON

Schulz, Johann Abraham Peter (*b* Lüneburg, 31 Mar. 1747; *d* Schwedt an der Oder, 10 June 1800). German composer. He showed an early interest in music, and went at the age of 18 to Berlin, where he studied with Kirnberger and made the acquaintance of C. P. E. Bach. In 1768 he entered the service of Princess Sapieha Woiwodin von Smolensk of Poland and travelled in Europe with her; in Danzig (now Gdańsk) he met and became good friends with Reichardt. He returned to Berlin in 1773 and worked producing operas at local theatres, from 1780 working also in Rheinsberg as court composer. He spent five years from 1790 in Copenhagen as director to the Royal Court Theatre and in charge of the *Hofkapelle*, but then returned to work again in Berlin and Rheinsberg.

Schulz is best known for his songs; with Reichardt and Zelter he was a member of the so-called second Berlin school, setting the verse of such poets as Goethe and Klopstock to simple folk-like music. This kind of song is sometimes known as the *volkstümliches Lied*.

Schuman, William (Howard) (*b* New York, 4 Aug. 1910). American composer. He studied at Columbia University and privately with Roy Harris (1936–8), whose foremost disciple he is. His cycle of ten symphonies shows a bold and forceful imagination, developing typically American themes in strong diatonic forms. From 1945 to 1962 he was president of the Juilliard School.

PAUL GRIFFITHS

Schumann, Clara (Josephine) (*b* Leipzig, 13 Sept. 1819; *d* Frankfurt am Main, 20 May 1896). German pianist and composer; the wife of Robert. She was the daughter of a fine piano teacher, Friedrich Wieck, and his wife Marianna who was also a good pianist but who left her husband when Clara was about five. She was taught by her father, gave recitals in the Leipzig Gewandhaus at a young age, and began to tour in her early teens; but she was given a good general education and her taste for Beethoven and the classics was well formed. By the age of 20 she was well known and had been given the title of *Kaiserlich-Königliche Kammervirtuosin* by the Viennese court. Schumann had by this time fallen in love with her but was not considered a suitable match by her father, and it was only on the eve of her 21st birthday that they married without parental consent. She continued to play in public, though she committed herself totally to Robert's interests (for her life therefore, see his), and had no fewer than eight children.

On her husband's final madness and subsequent death, she had to earn her living, and took to mammoth concert tours, being one of the earliest artists to do so on a regular basis, helped by the newly created railway network. Although Brahms, a life-long friend, tried to dissuade her, she clearly enjoyed this kind of life, especially her visits to England where she had enormous success, until illness, seemingly some kind of arthritis, forced her to curtail her playing activities. She lived at various times in Berlin, Baden-Baden, and from 1878 at Frankfurt, there becoming one of the most valued teachers at the conservatory. She edited the collected works of Robert, was composer of some charming piano music and songs (though these were mainly written before his death), and received the Gold Medal for Art from Kaiser Wilhelm in 1889.

DENIS ARNOLD

Clara Schumann (1888)

Schumann, Robert (Alexander) (*b* Zwickau, Saxony, 8 June 1810; *d* Endenich, nr Bonn, 29 July 1856). German composer. Youngest of five children of a notable citizen, who made his living as a bookseller but also wrote novels and translated the works of Byron, Robert was educated first at a private school and then at the Zwickau Lyceum, or Grammar School. His father died in 1826, his sister thereupon committed suicide, and he was then somewhat spoiled by his mother, being allowed to indulge in such expensive tastes as champagne and cigars while still at school. He enrolled to study law at Leipzig University in 1828, continuing to live the good life rather than studying. He began to take piano lessons from a notable teacher, Wieck, whose daughter Clara, his future wife, he met when she was only nine years old. After a year he transferred to Heidelberg University, did a customary Grand Tour in Italy, and was finally told by the Professor of Law that he had no talent for the subject.

He began studying the piano seriously on advice from Wieck in whose house he lived; but was left in no doubt that while he might become a piano virtuoso, he was more likely to become a teacher—a profitable occupation none the less. In the event, his ambitions as a player were ruined by damage to his hand caused by a device to strengthen the fingers. Fortunately even by this time he had begun to show talent as a composer, writing mainly for the piano, and immediately finding an imaginative idiom. He used cyphers to invent themes (e.g. ABEGG = A B♭ E G, the name of a friend, provides the motto for the theme of a set of variations Op. 1) and then developed them into delicate mood pictures, often based on literary allusions and rarely of any great length. His piano writing is extremely individual, using the sustaining pedal and the middle range of the instrument to make a sensuous, rather brilliant sound. Nearly all the works of the 1830s are masterly, especially *Carnaval*, a suite of pieces expressing various aspects of his character, notably the contrasting introvert and extrovert sides; the C major Fantasie, conceived as a sonata but in a very free style with both beautiful lyrical melody and delicious piano textures; and the *Études symphoniques* (1834, published 1837), a set of free variations with a grand finale.

By this time, he was thoroughly in love with Clara, after various indecisive affairs with several women. He was also deeply involved in musical journalism as editor of the *Neue Zeitschrift für Musik*. Of a musician capable of making a serious career there was as yet little sign, which probably explains the refusal of Wieck to let his daughter marry Schumann on the latter's proposal in 1837 (Clara's career,

although she was only 18, must have seemed far more promising). Nor was Robert particularly robust in health, having had a nervous breakdown in 1834 following the deaths of one of his brothers and his sister-in-law. Nevertheless, Schumann, still often in debt, went to view the prospects of working in Vienna in 1839 and found some Schubert manuscripts, including the C major Symphony; and by this time his own compositions were selling well. He decided to take legal steps to break Wieck's veto, and married Clara in 1840, one day before her 21st birthday.

The result of this passionate love affair—and rarely are the connections between exterior events and individual pieces of music so clear—was what is known as Schumann's 'song year'. In 1840 he composed a great many songs, including the two great cycles *Dichterliebe* and *Frauenliebe und -leben*. The verse is mainly subjective and so easy to relate to his or Clara's feelings that the songs are extraordinarily personal. Technically, his transference of his new piano idiom to the accompaniments allows still greater expressiveness, especially in preludes and postludes where the piano comments on and expands the sentiments of the verse.

The year 1840 also saw the beginning of his first successful symphony (there had been an abortive attempt in the 1830s) which was given under Mendelssohn at the Gewandhaus concerts the following year; this encouraged him to begin another (the D minor, known now as No. 4) and what was in effect another, the Overture, Scherzo, and Finale. Clara was also having some success as a performer and played what was to become the first movement of the Piano Concerto in A minor. A daughter was born to them in September 1841 but this hardly interrupted her career; and on a concert tour in northern Germany in 1842 she received greater applause for her playing than did Robert for his compositions.

The same year (1842) was taken up mainly with the composition of chamber music, three string quartets and the masterly Piano Quintet and Quartet being the main results. But the strains of maintaining a professional career in music, accentuated by the birth of another daughter which cut down Clara's musical activities, began to show, and from 1843 breakdowns or near breakdowns were a commonplace of his life. That some part of his mental instability was inherited seems probable from the family history. The circumstances of his lack of early musical training and living in a musical environment meant that he was unsuited to the composition of the money-spinners of the era—the festival cantatas, operas, salon pieces, and the like which came so naturally to Mendelssohn and Spohr. He was no performer and though an

Schumann's 'Kinderscenen', Op. 15 No. 1; autograph manuscript of the copy Schumann made for his sister-in-law, Marie Wieck.

excellent critic and writer could not maintain his family from this source. That he felt the pain of being outshone by Clara added to his difficulties, and when she went away on concert tours he found it hard to concentrate on composition.

In the event, he obtained various official positions which he held with mixed success. First was the professorship of composition in the newly founded Leipzig Conservatory in 1842. About the same time he began conducting choirs. In 1845 they settled in Dresden where he completed his Piano Concerto with two more movements; and he managed to write the Symphony in C major (No. 2 in modern numeration). A miniature concert tour with Clara took in Vienna, where his music was not received with great enthusiasm, so that plans for moving there were abandoned in favour of staying in Dresden where in 1847 Robert took up the conductorship of the *Liedertafel* or male voice choir. He founded a Choral Union in the following year, escaping the Revolution in which Wagner was much involved by staying in the country. He now composed an opera *Genoveva* which was not a great success when produced in Leipzig in 1850, the year in which he moved to Düsseldorf as conductor of the local choral society and orchestral subscription concerts. For a time all went well and he was happy and productive, composing the 'Rhenish'

Schumann, daguerreotype (1850).

Symphony, typically inspired by outside circumstances. But his inadequacies as a conductor, not so much a matter of technique as the inability to communicate to ordinary musicians, led to some strong criticism in the local paper, and in 1852 he had another breakdown. In 1853 he conducted at the Lower Rhine Festival, where the players found him very poor in comparison with his predecessor Hiller who returned for the season, and after a disgraceful concert in Düsseldorf in October he retired from conducting. He made new friends in Joachim and Brahms and went on a concert tour of Holland with Clara, both achieving successes. He composed some conventional overtures, incidental music, and cantatas but in February 1854 he began to show signs of serious mental trouble, attempting suicide by throwing himself in the Rhine but being rescued by fishermen. He was then taken to a private asylum near Bonn, where he spent the remainder of his days, visited by Clara who now had to keep their family of seven children entirely by her own efforts. She was eventually responsible for the issue of a collected edition of her husband's works.   DENIS ARNOLD

FURTHER READING
Joan Chissell: *Schumann* (London, 1948, 2nd edn 1967); Alan Walker, ed.: *Robert Schumann: the Man and his Music* (London, 1972, 2nd edn 1976).

Schurmann, (Edward) Gerard (*b* Kertosono, Indonesia, 19 Jan. 1928). British composer of Dutch origin. He has spent most of his life in London, where he studied with Alan Rawsthorne and where he was Netherlands Cultural Attaché. Though he has written scores for numerous plays and films, his serious output is relatively small, its conservative style intensified by his introspective rhetoric. His chief works include concertos for violin and piano, other orchestral pieces, *Chuench'i* for soprano and orchestra (1966), and piano compositions.
                                    PAUL GRIFFITHS

Schusterfleck (Ger., 'cobbler's patch'). A kind of sequence (see *Sequence*, 1).

Schütz, Heinrich (*b* Köstritz, now Bad Köstritz, nr Gera, Oct. 1585; *d* Dresden, 6 Nov. 1672). German composer. The leading figure in 17th-century German music, Schütz was productive in virtually every branch of composition except independent instrumental music. His extant secular music is not unimportant, but it is mainly on his output of sacred vocal works that his reputation as the first German composer of truly international stature is based. In association with Michael Praetorius, and with his immediate contemporaries, Johann Schein and Samuel Scheidt, he played a major role in

introducing into his native country the new Italian styles of the period, thus providing much of the initial impetus for the musical Baroque in Germany.

At the age of six Schütz moved to Weissenfels, where his parents had inherited a substantial property. Some seven years later he gained the attention of the Landgrave Moritz of Hessen-Kassel, who accepted him as a choirboy into his chapel and provided for his education at the *Gymnasium* in Kassel. Schütz's academic progress led him, in accordance with his parents' wishes, towards law studies at the University of Marburg, but a further intervention by the Landgrave enabled him to travel to Venice in 1609 for a prolonged period of study with Giovanni Gabrieli. On his return in 1613 he resumed (probably more dutifully than eagerly) his legal studies, this time at Leipzig. But shortly afterwards, on a visit with his patron to Dresden, his musical abilities caught the attention of Elector Johann Georg I of Saxony who, after prolonged wrangles with the Landgrave, eventually won his services permanently, appointing him principal *Kapellmeister* to the royal chapel in Dresden, a post he was to occupy for the remainder of his career. In 1619 he married Magdalena Wildeck, but she died after only six years of marriage, leaving the composer with two daughters to rear. A few years later Schütz returned to Venice, where he learnt, possibly from Monteverdi in person, the new techniques of composition which had developed there since his previous visit. On returning again from Italy he brought with him several Italian musicians with whose help he hoped to revitalize the work of the Dresden chapel; however, his plans were frequently frustrated, as were those of many German musicians of the period, by the effects of the Thirty Years War. Between 1633 and 1642, partly to escape from his problems at Dresden, Schütz paid three visits to Copenhagen, where he accepted the post of director of music to Christian II of Denmark. During his last years the composer returned to Weissenfels in semi-retirement, but finally moved again to Dresden so that he might be buried there beside his wife.

A large proportion of Schütz's output is contained in 13 printed collections, published, most of them under his personal supervision, during his lifetime. The first comprises 19 Italian madrigals which Schütz composed as a type of graduation 'exercise' on the completion of his studies with Gabrieli. Clearly rejoicing in his newly won technical mastery, the young composer employs daring harmonic effects and dramatic vocal figuration to express the emotional and pictorial qualities of his texts, recalling the techniques of Monteverdi in his fourth and fifth books of madrigals.

The remaining collections are devoted to sacred music, and contain examples of all the principal church forms cultivated by Schütz: the large- and small-scale *concertato* setting, the motet and the sacred madrigal with continuo, the monody, the dialogue, and the biblical *historia* (a dramatic piece anticipating the development of the oratorio). Most of the texts were drawn from Luther's translation of the Bible; Latin, though not uncommon, is used exclusively in only two of the major collections: the *Cantiones sacrae* (Freiberg, 1625) and the first set of *Symphoniae sacrae* (Venice, 1629). In his choice of texts, and in his musical treatment of them, Schütz frequently adopts a markedly didactic approach, imparting doctrine through the scriptural medium in a clear-cut and unequivocally Protestant manner. However, in conformity with a growing tendency of the period, he uses chorales comparatively rarely.

Gabrieli's influence is apparent in Schütz's first church publication, the *Psalmen Davids* of 1619, a collection of 26 German-text settings laid out in the grand Venetian manner for eight or more vocal and instrumental parts. In his preface to the work, Schütz indicates the nature of the various performance resources he expects and the flexibility with which they can be deployed: solo singers (the *cori favoriti*), whose contribution is obligatory; choruses of less-skilled singers or of instruments (the *cappella*), which may be introduced 'for the sake of sonority and splendour', or may be omitted; and

the continuo, either single, or one for each participating group. Only in one later collection did Schütz employ forces on such a lavish scale, the third set of *Symphoniae sacrae* (Dresden, 1650), in which vivid vocal and instrumental effects serve to enhance such notable 'biblical-story' settings as the parable of the tribute money from St Matthew's gospel and the even more famous account of St Paul's conversion on the road to Damascus.

The *Cantiones sacrae* is a marvellously rich collection of Latin motets. Schütz's fervent and imaginative settings, apparently designed for private worship, are laid out mainly for four voices supported by a continuo part which is only strictly necessary in some of the final items. The somewhat strange mixture of styles, from old-style choral polyphony at one extreme to the latest monodic and *concertato* styles at the other, is explained in the preface, which reveals that several of the pieces were composed at an earlier date. A companion volume to these sacred madrigals is the *Geistliche Chormusik* (Dresden, 1648) containing 29 German motets which demonstrate Schütz's mastery of the contrapuntal style, absorbed into the German musical mainstream through the pupils of Lassus. Much of the intensely German, and particularly Lutheran, character of these settings results from the intimate relation between the musical style and the rhythms, cadences, and inflections of the German language. In his preface Schütz encourages young German composers not to

Schütz in the Dresden Hofkapelle, with his choir.

The castle at Dresden in Schütz's time, engraving from 'Wechschen Chronik' (Nuremberg, 1679).

neglect the study of pure vocal counterpoint in favour of the facile, continuo-based Italian styles cultivated at the period.

Of special interest for its text-structure is the *Musikalische Exequien*, composed in 1636 for the funeral of Prince Heinrich Posthumus of Reuss. Although Schütz normally avoided texts compiled from diverse biblical and other sources, the special circumstances underlying this funeral composition led him to produce a complex and deeply affecting text-arrangement. Three units are involved: an amalgamation of the scriptural texts and chorale verses inscribed on the prince's coffin, thus producing a short German burial Mass, for solo voices and chorus; the text selected for the funeral oration, set for double choir; and an extraordinarily impressive juxtaposition of the *Nunc dimittis*, sung by a *chorus primus* marked 'near the organ', with passages from *Revelation* and the *Wisdom of Solomon*, presented by a *chorus secundus* marked 'in the distance'.

Monodies and small-scale *concertato* works are represented in the two sets of *Kleine geistliche Konzerte* (1636, 1639) and in the first two volumes of the *Symphoniae sacrae* (1629, 1647). In their modest performance requirements, the sacred concertos may well reflect the economies made at Dresden because of the war. However, Schütz shows himself fully able to profit from any restrictions imposed, for example in the striking monody for soprano 'Eile, mich, Gott, zu erreten' which stands at the beginning of the first set. The *Symphoniae sacrae*, as their title suggests, display richer instrumental resources and a greater diversity of scoring. In the second set Schütz pays his most significant homage to Monteverdi, not only by including words of tribute to him in the preface, but also by repeatedly using the *stile concitato*, and by adopting two of his madrigals as the basis for one of his own settings.

Only one of Schütz's miniature oratorios was published complete during his lifetime, the *Resurrection History* (Dresden, 1623), a setting of an Easter text compiled from all four gospels. For the part of the Evangelist Schütz employs a mock plainsong commonly used in Germany for the Easter Story, providing for it an accompaniment for four viols, notated in held chords but

Schütz, miniature in oils (1670) by an unknown artist.

designed (as the composer reveals in his preface) to be decorated by improvised *passaggi*—ornamental scales and flourishes. The principal characters in the story are each represented by two solo voices and continuo, though Schütz makes it clear that one of the voices may be omitted or a voice replaced by an instrument. The *Christmas History* (Dresden, 1664) was published incomplete, while the *Seven Last Words from the Cross* (*c*.1645) and the three Passions (*c*.1664–6) remained in manuscript until modern times.

In the *Seven Last Words*, a compact and beautifully-structured work, Christ is represented by a tenor soloist, accompanied always by two unspecified *obbligato* instruments (probably viols) with continuo, while the part of the Evangelist is taken by various solo voices and at times by four voices in polyphony. With its intensely subjective character this work points significantly forward to the meditative oratorio of later times. The *Christmas History*, probably composed some 20 years later, is notable for its overtly popular style, which makes it exceptional among Schütz's late works. The Christmas scenes are presented as a series of lively musical *tableaux*, characterized instrumentally and bound together by recitative in a fluent narrative style. By contrast the Passions are markedly austere and withdrawn, shunning all

instrumental accompaniment, even the organ, and achieving effects of astonishing beauty by the simplest of means. These works of Schütz's last phase, and others such as the *Zwölff geistliche Gesänge* (Dresden, 1657) and the German *Magnificat* (1671), his last completed composition, show clearly the changes which had taken place in the composer's musical language during his long career. The bold experimentation and daring effects of his earlier style are here supplanted by a new moderation, a new philosophical calm, a new leaning towards objectivity and detachment, revealing modes of thought comparable to those of Bach and Beethoven in their final creative periods.

BASIL SMALLMAN

FURTHER READING

Basil Smallman: *The Background of Passion Music: J. S. Bach and his Predecessors* (London, 1957, 2nd edn 1970); Hans Joachim Moser: *Heinrich Schütz: a Short Account of his Life and Works* (trans. from the German by D. McCulloch) (London, 1967); Friedrich Blume: *Protestant Church Music: a History* (London, 1974).

Schwach, schwächer (Ger.). 'Weak' (i.e. soft), 'weaker'.

Schwanendreher, Der ('The Swan-turner'). Concerto for viola and small orchestra by Hindemith, composed in 1935. It is based on German folk-songs, the soloist being (in the composer's words) one who 'comes among merry company and plays the music he has brought from afar: songs grave and gay and, to conclude, a dance'.

Schwanengesang ('Swan Song'). Collection of songs for voice and piano by Schubert, D 957, composed in 1828 and issued after his death as a 'cycle' by the publisher Haslinger. The 14 songs are settings of poems by Heine, Rellstab, and Seidl. In published order, they are: Book 1, *Liebesbotschaft* ('Love-message'), *Kriegers Ahnung* ('Warrior's Presentiment'), *Frühlingssehnsucht* ('Longing for Spring'), *Ständchen* ('Serenade'), *Aufenthalt* ('Staging-post'), *In der Ferne* ('In the Distance'); Book 2, *Abschied* ('Farewell'), *Der Atlas* ('Atlas'), *Ihr Bild* ('Her Portrait'), *Das Fischermädchen* ('The Fisher Girl'), *Die Stadt* ('The Town'), *Am Meer* ('By the Sea'), *Der Doppelgänger* ('The Ghostly Double'), *Die Taubenpost* ('The Pigeon-post').

Schwankend (Ger.). 'Swaying'.

Schwebungen (Ger.). 'Beats', in the acoustical sense; see *Acoustics*, 8.

Schweigen (Ger.). 'Silence', or 'to be silent'; *schweigt* means the same as *tacet*; *Schweigezeichen*, a rest.

Schweigsame Frau, Die ('The Silent Woman'). Opera in three acts by Richard Strauss to a libretto by Stefan Zweig after Ben Jonson's *Epicoene* (1609). It was first performed in Dresden in 1935.

Schwellen (Ger.). 'To swell', i.e. to increase in tone (*crescendo*); *Schweller*, the 'swell' of an organ; *Schwellwerk*, the swell organ; *Schwellkasten*, 'swell box'.

Schwer (Ger.). 1. 'Heavy' (in style); *schwermütig*, *schwermutsvoll*, 'heavy-hearted'. 2. 'Difficult'.

Schwindend (Ger.). 'Diminishing' (in tone), i.e. *diminuendo*.

Schwung (Ger.). 'Swing'; *schwungvoll*, 'full of go', 'vigorous'.

Scintillante (It.). 'Sparkling', 'scintillating'.

Sciolto, scioltamente (It.). 'Loosely', 'easy', 'unconstrained'.

Scivolando (It.). 'Sliding', i.e. *glissando*.

Scoop. In singing, an exaggerated sliding (see *Portamento*) from one note to another. It is much used in pop singing.

Scordato (It.). 'Out of tune'. See *Scordatura*.

Scordatura (It.; Fr.: *discordé, discordable, discordant*; Ger.: *Umstimmung, Verstimmung*). From *scordare*, 'to mistune'. The alteration of the normal tuning of the strings of a bowed or plucked string instrument for certain pieces or for certain passages. The main reasons for using it are (*a*) to make certain passages easier to play, especially those requiring multiple stopping; (*b*) to vary the tone colour of the instrument, making it brighter either by using a higher tuning or sometimes by allowing more use of open strings; and (*c*) to extend the range of the instrument, usually downwards.

Scordatura was frequently used in lute music of the late Renaissance and early Baroque, and in violin music from the early days of that instrument. Biagio Marini was one of the first to use *scordatura* for violin music: in his *Sonata seconda per il violino d'inventione* (Op. 8, 1626–9) he demanded that the E string should be lowered a third and then retuned to the original pitch in the middle of the work.

The required *scordatura* is shown by a preliminary 'accord', as in the following example from Bach's Fifth Suite for solo cello. He indicates that the top string is to be tuned to G rather than A; since the player will use the same fingering as he would if the top string were tuned to A, the notes are written at the pitch they would sound on that string, so as not to confuse the performer by presenting him with notes that he would associate with different fingerings. Ex. 1*a* gives the opening bars of the movement as they appear, and Ex. 1*b* transposes the notes that need to be played on the highest string to their actual pitch (these notes are marked with an asterisk; the F in the top line of bar 2 is played on the D string, and thus is not affected by the *scordatura*). This example is fairly clear in its intentions, but more complex ones, which seem to offer a variety of possible interpretations, do occur, for example in the works of Biber.

Score. A printed or manuscript copy of a piece of music which shows the parts for all the performers arranged on separate staves, as distinct from a 'part', which shows only the music for one performer (or for one group of performers).

A 'full' score has each instrumental or vocal part separately displayed, with full performance details, and is the type of score normally used by a conductor.

An 'orchestral' score is an alternative term for the full score of an orchestral work.

A 'vocal' score shows all the vocal parts of a

Ex. 1

(*a*)

(*b*)

Presto capriccioso ♩=152±

William Walton

FLUTES

OBOES

COR ANG.

CLARINETS IN A

BASSOONS

HORNS IN F

TRUMPETS IN B♭

TROMBONES

TUBA

TIMPANI

PERCUSSION

HARP

VIOLIN 1

VIOLIN 2

VIOLA

VIOLONCELLO

BASS

The first page of Walton's 'Johannesburg Festival Overture' showing the standard vertical arrangement of the instrumental parts.

work on separate staves, with the orchestral parts reduced to a keyboard arrangement.

A 'piano' score is a full score reduced to form an arrangement for piano; a 'short' score is a similar reduction of a full score to a smaller number of staves, but not necessarily arranged for piano.

A 'miniature' score is a printed score of pocket size.

The act of 'scoring' is to decide on and write down the orchestration or instrumentation of a work that is already conceived for another medium (e.g. for piano), or to assemble in score form the individual instrumental or vocal parts of a work (e.g. as with 16th-century partbooks, where no score exists).

The standard vertical arrangement of instrumental parts in a full score of a work for standard orchestra is, from top to bottom:

woodwind (piccolo, flutes, oboes, clarinets, bassoons); brass (horns, trumpets, trombones, tuba); percussion (timpani, side drum, bass drum, triangle, etc.); strings (first violins, second violins, violas, cellos, double basses). A cor anglais part is normally placed below the oboes, bass clarinet below clarinets, and double bassoon below bassoons. A harp or celesta part is placed between the percussion and string sections, and any solo part in a concerto immediately above the first violins. Voice parts, if any, are placed above the string section, with soloists above the chorus, which is arranged in descending order of voices.

Deviations from these standard conventions may be required by, for example, the introduction of unusual instruments or a desire to group together certain instruments. In particular, scores of contemporary music may vary a great deal from standard patterns, especially where a degree of improvisation or indeterminacy is involved. In scores of aleatory music, verbal directions may well predominate over conventional musical notation. Some modern scores reject traditional mensural notation and adopt instead a sort of measured space-time system or indicate only the relative positions of the conductor's downbeat. A few composers have abandoned traditional staff notation in favour of graphic notation, where words, pictures, abstract patterns, and symbols are used to suggest to the performer both what to play and how to play it. Exponents of graphic and other modern notations include Feldman, Stockhausen, Cage, Ligeti, Cardew, Kagel, and Boulez, some of whom have combined graphic notation with conventional staff notation, sometimes in the same work. Scores of electronic music may consist of precise mathematical symbols and calculations, or of pictures, colours, or graphics, or they may combine any of those elements with standard staff notation.

See also *Notation*, 8.

PERCY SCHOLES, rev. Judith Nagley

Scorrendo, scorrevole (It.). 'Scouring'. 1. A gliding from note to note, i.e. *glissando*. 2. In a flowing style.

Scotch snap, Scotch catch. A rhythmic feature in which a dotted note is preceded, rather than followed, by a note of shorter value (e.g. ♪♩. as opposed to ♩. ♪). It is a characteristic feature of the Scottish *strathspey, and is also found in some Scottish song-tunes as well as in the pseudo-Scottish melodies which were such a popular feature of 18th-century London pleasure gardens. However, no Scottish song earlier than the 18th century seems to display the feature.

The 'Scotch snap' appears in French songs of the late 16th century as a feature of *musique mesurée*, and it was apparently just as commonly used in the performance of 17th-century *notes inégales* (see *Inégales*). It was also common in Italian music of the early 17th century, where it was known as the *stile lombardo* (Lombardy style); Sammartini and J. C. Bach, who both worked in the capital of Lombardy, Milan, used it in their music. Inverted dotting was also used by some 17th-century English composers, such as Purcell, where it suits the accentuation of the English language.

Scotland

1. Folk-song
2. Instrumental Traditions
3. Church Music

4. Court and Concert Music
5. Music in Education and Performance

1. *Folk-song*. Scottish folk-song embraces two traditions, each with its own language: the Gaelic music of the Highlands and Hebrides, and the music of the Lowlands and eastern (English- or Lallans-speaking) areas. Orkney and Shetland have distinct styles of their own.

(a) *The Gaelic Tradition*. Gaelic song owes its individuality to language, geography, and politics. Tunes have survived from an era of musical pre-history, partly because of the great tenacity of the Gaelic folk memory, and partly because most Gaelic verse was intended to be sung. Interchange of Gaelic and Lowland culture was minimal, and cross-currents were largely confined to literature and linguistics. For example, Burns (1759-96) borrowed Gaelic tunes for some Lowland verses, and certain Lowland names and terms have Gaelic roots. Gaelic song has some features in common with all Scottish music, including a fondness for pentatonic scales and for the *Scotch snap rhythm. Gaelic song also has source links with Ireland, notably in the art of the Celtic bards.

The *òran mòr* ('great song') comprises the Heroic Lays, the Ossianic Ballads, and songs linked with pipe music—laments and 'pibroch songs' (see 2 below). Gaelic labour songs are of great variety—songs for tasks such as waulking (shrinking the newly-woven cloth), reaping, rowing, spinning, churning, etc.—and there are also lullabies, fairy songs, love songs, mourning songs (the 'coronach'), and so on. *Puirt-a-beul* ('mouth music') is a popular form of vocal dance music, often with humorous words.

Important collectors and scholars of Gaelic music include Frances Tolmie (1840-1926), Father Allan McDonald (1859-1905), John Lorne Campbell (*b* 1906) and his wife Margaret Fay Shaw, and Francis Collinson (*b* 1898). The work of Marjory Kennedy-Fraser (1857-1930) in collecting and popularizing Hebridean tunes is better known, but her arrangements are too free and fanciful. An Comunn Gaidhealach (the Highland Society) has stimulated interest in Gaelic culture over the last century, through publications and competitions (the annual Mod).

(b) *Lowland Songs and Ballads*. More than 160 years before Gaelic tunes were printed, Lowland airs were written down (for example in the

Skene Manuscript of c.1615, which is in the National Library of Scotland, Edinburgh), and there are countless published editions of Lowland tunes, from Playford's *English Dancing Master* (1651) onwards. This is one essential difference, together with that of language, between the two traditions. Language and availability have made Lowland songs far more widely known than Gaelic ones. Many songs generally considered 'Scottish' are not folksongs, however, but may be old tunes arranged to new words, or even purely drawing-room creations. Printed editions preserved and sustained Lowland song, as well as corrupting it in some instances.

Lowland ballads (longer narrative songs) exist in many collections of words and tunes, notably those of Francis James Child (1825–96), Gavin Greig (1856–1915), and Bertrand Bronson (b 1902). 'Bothy Ballads' are associated with farm life, and many have been collected in Aberdeenshire and surrounding counties.

(c) *Orkney and Shetland.* The music of these areas is of Scandinavian origin, and the Norn language was indigenous until the late 17th and mid 18th century in Orkney and Shetland respectively. Little of the native music of Orkney has survived, although interesting finds have been published by Otto Andersson (1879–1969) of Finland. Shetland song has fared better through the work of the Shetland Folk Society and the collections of Patrick Shuldham-Shaw (d 1977).

2. *Instrumental Traditions.* The most ancient of Scotland's three national instruments is the harp, or *clàrsach*, stone carvings of which exist from the early 9th century. Only two original examples (of the 15th or 16th century) survive, and these are preserved in the National Museum of Antiquities of Scotland, Edinburgh. Accounts of harpists abound until the early 18th century (when the *clàrsach* fell from fashion), but few actual names are known. A notable exception is Roderick Morison (c.1656–c.1714), called Rory Dall ('Blind Rory'), the only known example of a minstrel bard in Gaelic Scotland. Born in Lewis, Rory Dall studied the *clàrsach* in Ireland, and on his return to Edinburgh met the Chief of MacLeod, whose harper at Dunvegan on Skye he then became. No example of his music, indeed none of the ancient harp music of Scotland, has survived in its original form.

It is clear that the harp tradition came from Ireland and that the instrument enjoyed a vogue in both the Highlands and the Lowlands. Less clear is the nature of its music, but it would seem that it was passed on to other instruments as they gained popular ascendancy—the fiddle,

'The Queen Mary', one of the West Highland Harps preserved in the Museum of Antiquities, Edinburgh.

the lute, and the flute. It is also possible that the tunes and the style of *clàrsach* music passed to the bagpipe, and that *piobaireachd* (see below) found its origins there.

The modern revival of the instrument dates from 1892, when Lord Archibald Campbell instituted a competition in *clàrsach* playing at the first Gaelic Mod. Marjory Kennedy-Fraser's daughter Patuffa helped to popularize the instrument in the early 20th century. In 1931 a Clàrsach Society (Comunn na Clàrsach) was founded, and today there are several *clàrsach* makers.

No other country is so much associated with

the bagpipe as Scotland, where it is depicted in sculpture from the early 15th century. The great Highland bagpipe has survived for many reasons, and against huge political odds: it is pre-eminently an instrument for the great outdoors; its players have always strictly preserved their repertory and traditional style of playing; its finest and classical music—*piobaireachd*—by its very nature disposes of the myth that bagpipe music is 'barbaric'; and its survival after the defeat of Culloden (1746), when its playing was outlawed, testifies to its resilience and its essential place in Gaelic culture.

The Highland bagpipe scale is highly idiosyncratic; its approximate notation is shown in Ex. 1.

Ex. 1

Sometimes pipe music is notated with a key signature of one or two sharps, the two notes marked * being roughly a quartertone sharp. The drone notes shown in parentheses are harmonics.

'Pibroch' (Gaelic: *piobaireachd*) is the *ceòl mòr* ('great music') of the Highland pipe, comprising a very highly developed form of theme (or ground, *urlar*) and variations (involving intricate grace-note patterns). Its development is unique to the Scottish Highlands, and indeed it was the earliest European instrumental variation form to be perfected. From *c.*1500 to 1825 the art of *piobaireachd* was developed and disseminated throughout the Highlands by the MacCrimmon family, hereditary pipers to the MacLeods of Dunvegan, where there was a college of piping in the 18th century. Another notable piping family were the Mackays of Raasay (until 1858).

The ancient notation of pipe music is *canntaireachd*, a representation in vocalized syllables of the notes and figurations of *piobaireachd*. Staff notation (as far as such metrically free music can be notated) began to be used in the early 19th century. Ex. 2 shows the opening of an *urlar* which has been hailed as one of the finest single-line melodies in European music— the 'Lament for the Children' by Patrick Mòr MacCrimmon (*c.*1595–*c.*1670).

The lighter types of bagpipe music, broadly classed as *ceòl beag* (the 'small music'), embrace marches, airs, and dances such as the *strathspey and *reel.

The Lowland or Border bagpipe passed out of fashion by the mid 19th century. Unlike the Highland instrument, which is blown through the mouth, it is bellows-blown. Many Lowland pipe tunes survive, but its more ancient music and manner of performance are matters for speculation.

There are references in the 13th century to three bowed string instruments in Scotland: the fiddle, the rebec, and the *croud* (Welsh: *crwth*). Of these, the fiddle came to predominate, and today, notably in Strathspey and Shetland, fiddle-playing in both solo and concerted forms is a lively and popular art; both districts possess distinctive features. The dance form strathspey, although also played on the pipes, is essentially fiddle music, with a characteristic up-bow stroke and marked use of the Scotch snap rhythm. Shetland fiddle music shows Scandinavian features and a fondness for resonant open-string sounds.

Countless fiddlers are chronicled from the 15th century onwards, and the list of those whose music survives is a long one. Mention must be made of James MacPherson (whose impending execution in 1700 inspired his famous 'Rant'); Niel Gow (1727–97) and his family of players, composers, and publishers; John Bowie of Perth (1759–1815), whose collection of 1789 contains a number of airs adapted from the old harp music of Scotland; and the prolific James Scott Skinner (1843–1927). Many printed collections and manuscripts exist from the late 17th century onward, by which time instruments of fine Italian

Ex. 2

A pianistic version of this *urlar* may be seen in Ronald Stevenson's *Passacaglia on DSCH* (1967).

'Geordy Sime, lowland Scots Bagpiper' from John Kay's portraits and caricatures.

craftsmanship were influencing Scottish violin makers.

3. *Church Music*. The earliest evidence of indigenous sacred music survives in a manuscript (Wolfenbüttel 677) compiled at St Andrews *c*.1250; the Scottish music appears alongside music of the Notre Dame school, and it is known that the Scottish theorist Simon Tailler (*fl.* ?1320–40) studied in Paris. Of earlier music, only written accounts survive, for example by Giraldus Cambrensis in the late 12th century: 'in the opinion of many, Scotland has not just equalled Ireland, her teacher in music, but has . . . surpassed her'. A wedding hymn for Margaret of Scotland and Eric II of Norway (1281) and the roughly contemporary Orkney Hymn to St Magnus, *Nobilis, humilis*, are preserved. The history of Scottish church music is fragmentary, disrupted by wars with England and internal power struggles, and affected by the Reformation (1560) and abortive attempts to restore Episcopacy or Roman Catholicism during the 17th century, which ultimately left Presbyterianism triumphant.

From the 13th century, ecclesiastical centres such as Aberdeen, Elgin, Abernethy, and Lincluden possessed sizeable musical resources. The great period of sacred music dates from the reign of James IV (1488–1513), who had a flourishing Chapel Royal at Stirling, to the establishment of the Reformation. Robert Carver (*b c*.1490) is known by five surviving Masses (including one on 'L'homme armé') and two motets (one, remarkably, for 19 voices). This flowering of music coincided tragically with the struggle towards Reformation: of three notable composers, Patrick Hamilton was

Autograph copy of a song by Robert Burns that appeared in Johnson's 'The Scots Musical Museum'.

executed for heresy in 1528, Robert Johnson (*c*.1500–*c*.1560) fled to England shortly after, and David Peebles (*d* before 1592) found himself arranging psalm tunes for the Protestants and composing Latin church music for the court of Mary Queen of Scots.

Most sizeable towns had active song schools and sustained high standards of education and performance until, as a result of the Reformation, their revenues were directed elsewhere and their influence declined. The Aberdeen song school outlived the others and was still active in the later 17th century.

Niel Gow, portrait by Sir Henry Raeburn.

The only provision made by Calvinist reformers for music in worship was simple metrical psalm settings; the first Scottish psalter appeared in 1564. The anthems of John Black (*c*.1520–87) and Andrew Blackhall (1536–1609) elaborated the severe chordal style with some imitative counterpoint, but polyphonic music became confined to privileged circles. The Chapel Royal at Edinburgh lingered on fitfully after the departure of James VI in 1603, and as the century progressed examples of that 'popish instrument' the organ were everywhere destroyed—indeed the organ was not restored to established worship in Scotland until the late 19th century. With such attitudes prevailing, it is not surprising that no more church music of merit was composed until the 20th century.

One important and independent development must be mentioned—the remarkable Gaelic 'long psalms', still sung today and, like *piobaireachd*, unique to Celtic Scotland. The unaccompanied congregation profusely ornament the Precentor's psalm melody with melismatic phrases akin to elaborate Celtic knot patterns.

4. *Court and Concert Music.* The first notated secular music to be preserved is of the 16th century: part-songs much influenced by French models. Two poet-musicians were Alexander Scott (?1525–?1584) and John Fethy (*fl. c*.1530–68). There are also some examples of instrumental music, including some viol music by James Lauder (1535–95) and keyboard music by William Kinloch (*fl*. 1600) and Duncan Burnett (*d* 1652). Madrigals are conspicuously lacking.

The removal of James VI's court to London in 1603 and the hostile attitude to music of the Church combined to leave composition in the hands of amateurs, often associated with northern castles, who turned their interest more and more to folk-songs, arranging them for stringed instruments and keyboard. Thus Scotland became the first nation consciously to collect, arrange, and publish her musical heritage. Certain song schools still flourished in the earlier 17th century, where professional composers taught vocal and instrumental music. Although the Baroque period can be said to have passed Scotland by, her own traditional music was greatly in vogue in London by 1700.

A new impetus in music centred on the Edinburgh Musical Society concerts, founded in 1720 and housed in St Cecilia's Hall from 1762. There was an influx of foreign composers, mostly Italian, and also a move among native composers to study abroad. Sir John Clerk (1676–1755) studied with Corelli and composed some solo cantatas, and Thomas Alexander Erskine, Sixth Earl of Kelly (1732–81), studied with Stamitz and wrote symphonies and chamber music. The chamber works of William McGibbon (*c*.1690–1756) and the violin sonatas of David Foulis (1710–73) are also worthy of note.

The interest in national song continued unabated throughout the century, with many editions of tunes with old and new verses. Allan Ramsay (?1685–1758) played his part in this, but all other collections are overshadowed by Johnson's *The Scots Musical Museum* (1787–1803), and Robert Burns overshadows all other contributors to it. Burns provided texts for over 300 tunes (thus helping to ensure their survival) and collected many tunes himself. Another publisher, George Thomson, enlisted Haydn, Beethoven, Weber, and other Europeans to arrange tunes, but as these distinguished collaborators had no understanding of Scots idioms, their efforts belong to the realm of the comic and curious.

'*Cock of the North*', *painting by Keith Henderson.*

Generally, the 19th century saw Scotland's music at one of its lowest ebbs, despite the nation's European fame engendered by 'Ossian' and Walter Scott and the visits of such composers as Mendelssohn and Chopin. One composer, John Thomson (1805–41), is noteworthy, if only because he wrote the first analytical programme notes.

In the last decades of the century new opportunities were provided by the emerging choral and orchestral societies, the Church's changing attitude, and the musical homage paid to his native Scotland by Sir Alexander Campbell Mackenzie (1847–1935). A conscious, if only colouristic, evocation of Scotland also pervades the music of Mackenzie's younger contemporaries: Learmont Drysdale (1866–1909), Hamish MacCunn (1868–1916), J. B. McEwan (1868–1948), and William Wallace (1860–1940).

These composers embraced many aesthetics and were mainly eclectic in style. Twentieth-century figures who have deliberately adopted Scottish idioms have mostly worked in isolation, and there has been no concerted nationalism in Scottish music, unlike her literature and painting. Both Ian Whyte (1901–60) and Erik Chisholm (1904–65) drew on folk sources, including pipe music; Cedric Thorpe Davie (*b* 1913) adopted a consciously Scottish idiom in his film and theatre music; and a prize-winning orchestral *Salm* (1978) by Lyell Cresswell (*b* 1944) was based on the long tunes. Two Aberdeenshire composers of characteristically independent minds are Ronald Center (1913–73) and Martin Dalby (*b* 1942). Like Dalby, David Dorward (*b* 1933) is on the staff of BBC Scotland.

Two outstanding composers have firmly rooted their work in Celtic culture: the song composer Francis George Scott (1880–1958) who, together with his pupil Hugh MacDiarmid (1892–1978), spearheaded the musico-literary movement, the 'Scottish Renaissance', in the 1920s; and Ronald Stevenson (*b* 1928) in his many songs, piano works, and concertos.

5. *Music in Education and Performance.* A Chair of Music was founded at Edinburgh University in 1839 with a bequest from General Reid (1721–1807), an amateur composer; full academic recognition came, however, only in 1893, when degree courses were established. Reid professors of music have included Friedrich Niecks (1845–1924); Donald Tovey (1875–1940), who founded the Reid Orchestra in 1916 and greatly awakened popular musical consciousness; Sidney Newman (1906–71), who expanded the faculty, helped restore St Cecilia's Hall, and housed the Russell Collection of Keyboard Instruments there; and the composer Kenneth Leighton (*b* 1929); two other composers on the staff are Leon Coates (*b* 1937) and Edward Harper (*b* 1941). Edinburgh University also has a School of Scottish Studies which has achieved tremendous success in collecting music of the oral tradition.

In Glasgow, the Athenaeum School of Music was founded in 1890; today it is the Royal Scottish Academy of Music and Drama, and contains an opera department. A Chair of Music was founded at Glasgow University in 1929: the department has an electronic studio, and the Scottish Music Archive, for documentation and study of Scottish music, is housed there. Aberdeen and St Andrews have more recent music departments. In 1972 St Mary's Music School for specially gifted children was established in Edinburgh.

Among Scottish artists who achieved worldwide recognition are the pianist Frederic Lamond (1868–1948), the singers Mary Garden (1874–1967) and Joseph Hislop (1884–1977), and the choral conductor Hugh S. Roberton (1874–1952).

The Scottish Orchestra (founded in 1893) became the Scottish National Orchestra in 1950. Its conductor since 1959, Sir Alexander Gibson (b 1926), founded *Scottish Opera in 1962 and introduced the series now called 'Musica Nova', promoting contemporary music at Glasgow University. Scottish Opera is based in Glasgow, tours widely, and has performed several operas by Scots—Robin Orr (b 1909), Iain Hamilton (b 1922), Thomas Wilson (b 1927), and Thea Musgrave (b 1928).

The BBC in Scotland has encouraged composers and performers; the BBC Scottish Symphony Orchestra was founded by Ian Whyte in 1935. There is a Scottish branch of the Composers' Guild of Great Britain, established largely by William Wordsworth (b 1908) Another group commissioning and performing new music is the Saltire Society. Recent professional ensembles include the Scottish Baroque Ensemble (founded by Leonard Friedman in 1969), from which grew an additional group, the Scottish Chamber Orchestra. Since 1975 the composer Edward Harper has directed the New Music Group of Scotland.

The annual Edinburgh International Festival (founded in 1947) has greatly enhanced the life of the capital, but has given very limited opportunities to Scottish composers. Its magnificent Festival Chorus was first conducted by Arthur Oldham (b 1926).   DEREK WATSON

FURTHER READING
H. G. Farmer: *A History of Music in Scotland* (London, 1947, rev. edn 1970); F. Collinson: *The Traditional and National Music of Scotland* (London, 1966, rev. edn 1970); H. M. Shire: *Song, Dance and Poetry of the Court of Scotland under King James VI* (Cambridge, 1969); David Johnson: *Music and Society in Lowland Scotland in the 18th Century* (London, 1972).

Scott, Cyril (Meir) (b Oxton, Cheshire, 27 Sept. 1879; d Eastbourne, 31 Dec. 1970).

English composer, pianist, and writer. At the age of 12 he went to the Hoch Conservatory in Frankfurt to study under Humperdinck for 18 months. In 1895 he returned there as a pupil of Iwan Knorr, where he was one of the Frankfurt group. He returned to Liverpool to teach in 1898. Richter conducted his *Heroic Suite* in Manchester and Liverpool in 1900 and his First Symphony was performed in Darmstadt; Henry Wood conducted the Second Symphony at a London Promenade Concert in 1903. The harmonic richness and sinuous lines of his music led to his being dubbed 'the English Debussy', an impression confirmed by the 160 short piano pieces he wrote to fulfil a publisher's contract, and of which *Lotus Land* is the most popular. In 1915 Beecham conducted his Piano Concerto.

Scott's one-act opera *The Alchemist* (1917) was performed in Essen in 1925 and he composed choral works for the Norwich Festival (1936) and the Leeds Festival (1937). Thereafter, interest in his music declined and although he contemplated giving up composing, he wrote an opera *Maureen O'Mara* and an oboe concerto in 1946, and an oratorio in 1947. No large-scale revival of interest in his work yet seems likely. If one occurs, its target may well be the chamber music.

Scott also had a large literary output. He translated the work of his friend the poet Stefan George, and when he became interested in Indian philosophy this led to a study of occultism. He wrote about it, and also about medical topics such as naturopathy, osteopathy, and homoeopathy. He published several volumes of poetry and wrote his autobiography, *My Years of Indiscretion* (1924).   MICHAEL KENNEDY

Scottish Fantasy (*Schottische Fantasie*). Fantasia on Scottish folk-tunes by Bruch for violin and orchestra, composed in 1879–80. A Scottish tune is featured in each of its four movements: *Auld Rob Morris, The Dusty Miller, I'm a doun for lack of Johnnie,* and *Scots wha hae wi' Wallace bled* (an Allegro guerriero: 'warlike Allegro').

Scottish Opera. Opera company based in Glasgow but giving seasons in Aberdeen, Edinburgh, and elsewhere in Scotland and also paying regular visits to English provinces. It was founded in 1962 by Alexander Gibson and, with Peter Hemmings as Administrator from 1963, the company began to build a reputation for striking productions with excellent sets and lighting; the singers are mainly British, but several international artists have worked with the company for long spells. In 1975 the company moved into the re-equipped and refurbished Theatre Royal, Glasgow, as its permanent headquarters, setting the seal on the finest and most important operatic development in Britain since the foundation of *Glyndebourne. In 1976 Hemmings was succeeded by Peter Ebert. In addition to the Scottish National Orchestra, orchestras playing regularly for the company are the BBC Scottish Symphony Orchestra, the Scottish Chamber Ensemble, and the Scottish Philharmonia. With the Edinburgh Festival and the expanded life of the Scottish National Orchestra, Scottish Opera is a remarkable example of the flowering of Scottish musical life since 1945, especially under the aegis of Sir Alexander Gibson.

Scottish Symphony. Mendelssohn's Symphony No. 3 in A minor, Op. 56, composed between 1830 and 1842. It was inspired by a visit to Holyrood, Edinburgh, and dedicated to Queen Victoria.

Scozzese (It.). 'Scottish'.

Scriabin. See *Skryabin*.

Sculthorpe, Peter (Joshua) (*b* Launceston, Tasmania, 29 Apr. 1929). Australian composer. He studied at the University of Melbourne (1947–50) and with Edmund Rubbra and Egon Wellesz at Oxford (1958–60). In 1963 he was appointed to teach at the University of Sydney. His output includes many orchestral and chamber works, most of them markedly influenced by Balinese and other east Asian music.

PAUL GRIFFITHS

FURTHER READING
James Murdoch: *Australia's Contemporary Composers* (Melbourne, 1972), pp. 163–73.

Sdegno (It.). 'Disdain'; *sdegnante*, 'disdaining'; *sdegnoso*, 'disdainful', *sdegnamente*, 'disdainfully'.

Sdrucciolando (It.). 'Sliding', i.e. *glissando*.

Sea Drift. Work by Delius for baritone, chorus, and orchestra, composed in 1903–4. It is a setting of an extract from Whitman's *Out of the Cradle Endlessly Rocking*.

Sea Fever. Song by Ireland for voice and piano, composed in 1913. It is a setting of John Masefield's poem beginning 'I must down to the seas again', but Ireland's song begins 'I must go down . . .'.

Sea Interludes, Four. Concert work, Op. 33*a*, by Britten, first performed in Cheltenham in 1945. It consists of the descriptive orchestral music from his opera *Peter Grimes* (1945). The movements are 'Dawn' (Act 1), 'Sunday Morn-

ing' (Act 2), 'Moonlight' (Act 3), and 'Storm' (Act 1). The passacaglia from Act 2, Op. 33*b*, is often performed with the interludes.

Sea Pictures. Song cycle, Op. 37, by Elgar for alto solo and orchestra, composed 1897–9. The five poems set are by Noel, C. A. Elgar, E. B. Browning, R. Garnett, and A. Lindsay Gordon.

Searle, Humphrey (*b* Oxford, 26 Aug. 1915). English composer and writer on music. He studied at Oxford University (1933–7), with John Ireland, R. O. Morris, and Gordon Jacob at the Royal College of Music (1937), and with Webern in Vienna (1937–8). His music is classically serial, though closer to Schoenberg than to his teacher and often imbued with a romantic rhetoric that stems from his interest in Liszt. Among his works are three operas (including *Hamlet*, 1964–8), five symphonies, and various choral pieces. He has composed music for films and plays, besides working as a BBC producer (1938–40, 1946–8) and teaching at the Royal College of Music (1965–). He is also author of the books *Twentieth-Century Counterpoint* (London, 1954), *Ballet Music: an Introduction* (London, 1958), and *The Music of Liszt* (New York, 1966).   PAUL GRIFFITHS

FURTHER READING
R. Murray Schafer: *British Composers in Interview* (London, 1963).

Sea shanty. See *Shanty*.

Seasons, The (*Die Jahreszeiten*). 1. Oratorio by Haydn to a text by Baron Gottfried van Swieten after an English poem by James Thomson (1700–48), translated into German by B. H. Brockes. It is for soprano, tenor, and bass soloists, chorus, and orchestra, and was composed between 1799 and 1801.

2. Ballet in one act by Glazunov, composed in 1899.

Sea Symphony, A. Symphony by Vaughan Williams, his first, for soprano and baritone soloists, chorus, and orchestra, to a text taken from poems by Walt Whitman. It was composed 1903–9 and later revised, the last revision being in 1923.

Šebor, Karel [Schebor, Carl] (*b* Brandýs, 13 Aug. 1843; *d* Prague, 17 May 1903). Czech composer and conductor. After showing early promise, he was sent to the Prague Conservatory at the age of 11 where he studied the violin, and composition with J. B. Kittl. From 1861 to 1863 he taught music in Poland followed by a short spell conducting at the theatre in Erfurt. In 1865 he had considerable success with his first opera *Templáři na Moravě* ('The Templars in Moravia'), the first opera to an original Czech text to be given in the Provisional Theatre after Škroup's *Dratenik*. As a result, Šebor became assistant conductor of the Theatre. Both his succeeding operas *Drahomíra* (1867) and *Husitská nevěsta* ('The Hussite Bride', 1868) were well received, and in the same year as the latter work he composed a cantata for the celebrations attendant on laying the foundation-stone of the National Theatre in 1868. The failure of his 'fantastic-romantic' opera *Blanka* (1870) marked the beginning of a decline in his fortunes and morale. After a brief appointment at the theatre in Lvov he took up a commission as a military conductor in 1873 which he held for 20 years before returning to Prague in 1894 and a number of minor conducting jobs and teaching.

His work included chamber music, overtures, songs, choral music, some theatre music, and two symphonies, but his major contribution was his five operas (the last of which was the *Zmařená svatba* ('The Frustrated Wedding') given in Prague in 1879). The first three make effective use of elements from Italian and French grand opera enhanced by efficient craftsmanship and attractive if short-breathed lyricism. His later two operas hardly measure up in quality to his early successes. Although he was largely forgotten after his death, interest is now being shown in his role in the development of national opera in Czechoslovakia which may be described as formative.   JAN SMACZNY

Sec, sèche (Fr.). 'Dry', 'crisp'; *sécheresse*, 'dryness'. Term used by French composers, especially Debussy, to indicate that a note or chord should be struck and then quickly released.

Secco (It.). 'Dry', i.e. *staccato*. See also *Recitative*.

Sechzehntel, Sechzehntelnote (Ger.). '16th', '16th-note' or semiquaver (♪).

Second. See *Interval*.

Seconda prattica (It.). See *Prima prattica, seconda prattica*.

Seconda volta (It.). 'Second-time (bar)'; see *Double bar*.

Second inversion. See under *First inversion*.

Second subject. The first or principal theme of the second group of a *sonata form movement.

Second-time bar. See *Double bar*.

Secret Marriage, The. See *Matrimonio segreto, Il*.

Seele (Ger.). 'Soul' (i.e. feeling); also used to mean the sound-post of a bowed stringed instrument, which may be considered fancifully as the 'soul' of the instrument. *Seelenvoll*, 'soulful'.

Segno (It.). 'Sign'. See *Dal segno; Al segno*.

Segovia, Andrés (*b* Linares, Granada, 21 Feb. 1893). Spanish guitarist. He had to overcome parental opposition to his following a musical career and as a player was virtually self-taught. After giving a number of successful early recitals in Spain and Latin America he toured further afield, to Paris (1924) and the USA (1928), in an attempt to gain widespread recognition for the guitar as a serious recital instrument. His world-wide tours did much to free his instrument from the limitations of the popular and nationalist Hispanic repertory to which it had largely been relegated in the 19th century, and he created an enormously wide audience for guitar music in general. Segovia's desire to increase the extent and improve the quality of the repertory urged him to make guitar transcriptions of early music originally composed for the lute or vihuela. In addition, he made arrangements of a wide variety of instrumental works by some of the greatest composers (Bach, Handel, Mozart, Brahms); and composers of his own day (Falla, Ponce, Turina, Villa-Lobos, Rodrigo) were in turn encouraged by his undisputed technical and expressive virtuosity to write substantial original works for him. In later years his teaching was a profound influence on younger players (e.g. John Williams), who while developing their own individual playing styles have continued his work on behalf of their instrument. In his late 80s Segovia was still giving occasional recitals and holding regular master classes in Spain, the USA, and elsewhere.   JUDITH NAGLEY

Segue (It.). 'Follows', i.e. an instruction to the performer to play the following movement without a break; *segue la coda*, 'here follows the coda'; *seguente, seguendo*, 'following'. It may also mean to continue in the same way, e.g. with a repeated accompaniment pattern (in order to save writing it out).

Seguidilla (Sp.). A dance from southern Spain, possibly of Moorish origin. It is in quick triple time and alternates *coplas* (passages sung by the dancers) with passages played on guitar and castanets. The *coplas* are generally of four lines, alternately of seven and five syllables, which have assonance (agreement of vowel) rather than rhyme.

The dance is still performed today, especially in Andalusia, although each province has its own variety. Albéniz used the dance form in his piano music, and there is an example in Act 1 of Bizet's *Carmen* which has been much criticized because it is untypical.

Sehnsucht (Ger.). 'Longing'; *sehnsüchtig*, *sehnsuchtsvoll*, 'longingly'.

Seiber, Mátyás (György) (*b* Budapest, 4 May 1905; *d* Capetown, 24 Sept. 1960). British composer of Hungarian birth. He was a pupil of Kodály at the Budapest Music Academy, and after the First World War settled in Germany as an orchestral player, conductor, and teacher of composition and jazz at the Hoch Conservatory, Frankfurt. His works from this period include the Bartókian *Sonata da camera* for violin and cello (1925) and the Second String Quartet (1934–5), in which he used Schoenberg's serial technique (see also *Serialism*). After his move to England, in 1935, his use of serialism became more individual, allowing the reintroduction of triads in a style of fluent musicality and keen rhythmic inventiveness. His finest works of this period include the Third Quartet, or *Quartetto lirico* (1948–51), and cantatas to texts by Joyce (*Ulysses*, 1946–7), Goethe (*Faust*, 1949), and Virgil (*Cantata secularis*, 1949–51).

Seiber earned his living in England by writing functional music and teaching composition, privately and at Morley College. As a teacher, and as co-founder of the Committee (later Society) for the Promotion of New Music, he had a notable influence on younger English composers.

PAUL GRIFFITHS

Seises (Sp.). The name for choirboys of the great cathedrals of the Spanish-speaking world from the 16th to the 19th century. They were so called because there were generally six (Sp. *seis*) of them. On festival days and at processions the boys would also dance to the accompaniment of various instruments, including castanets.

Seite (Ger.). 'Side', e.g. a page of a book, or one skin of a drum; *Seitenthema*, the second theme, e.g. of a sonata-form movement.

Seixas, (José António) **Carlos de** (*b* Coimbra, 11 June 1704; *d* Lisbon, 24 Aug. 1742). Portuguese composer, harpsichordist, and organist. He was organist at Coimbra Cathedral in 1718, and from 1720 at the Portuguese royal chapel in Lisbon. Like his colleague, Domenico Scarlatti, Seixas wrote highly original harpsichord sonatas, but he retained the multi-movement format, although some are in single movements. He also composed organ, orchestral, and sacred music.

WENDY THOMPSON

Sellinger's Round, Variations on an Elizabethan Theme. Work for string orchestra by Oldham, Tippett, Lennox Berkeley, Britten, Searle, and Walton, composed to celebrate the coronation of Elizabeth II in 1953. It consists of six variations on the Elizabethan tune *Sellinger's Round*. Tippett expanded his contribution into his *Divertimento on Sellinger's Round* (1953–4), the tune appearing in all five movements.

Semel. See *Gymel*.

Semele. Masque or musical drama in three acts by Handel; text a version of Congreve's drama (1710), itself based on classical sources. Produced: London, Covent Garden, 10 February 1744; Evanston, Ill., Northwestern University, ?January 1959. Jupiter (ten.) is in love with, and loved by, the mortal Semele (sop.), to whom he appears in disguise. Through the trickery of Jupiter's wife Juno (mezzo), Jupiter is thwarted and Semele is scorched to death at the sight of the god in his true immortal state.

Semibiscroma (It.). The semidemisemiquaver or 64th-note (♬).

Semibreve (o). The whole-note, half the value of the breve and double the value of the minim.

Semicroma (It.). The semiquaver or 16th-note (♪).

Semidemisemiquaver [hemidemisemiquaver]. The 64th-note (♬), i.e. 1/64 the time value of the whole-note or semibreve.

Semifusa (Lat.). An early note-value (♪ before *c*.1450, ♪ from then until *c*.1630) from which derives the modern *semiquaver. See also *Notation*, 6.

Semihemidemisemiquaver. The 128th-note (♬), i.e. 1/128 the value of the whole-note or semibreve.

Semiminima (Lat.). An early note-value (♪ before *c*.1450, ♩ or ♪ from then until *c*.1630), from which derives the modern *crotchet. See also *Notation*, 6.

Semiquaver (♪). The 16th-note, i.e. 1/16 the time value of the whole-note or semibreve.

Semiramide. Opera in two acts by Rossini to a libretto by Rossi after Voltaire's *Sémiramis* (1748). It was first performed in Venice in 1823. It is the subject of about 40 other operas, including those by Porpora, Vivaldi, Hasse, Gluck, Galuppi, Paisiello, Salieri, Cimarosa, Meyerbeer, and Respighi.

Semitone. The smallest interval in common use in Western music, covering half a tone.

Semplice, semplicità (It.). 'Simple', 'simplicity'; *semplicemente*, 'simply'.

Sempre (It.). 'Always', e.g. *sempre legato*, the whole passage or composition is to be played smoothly.

Senaillé, Jean Baptiste (*b* Paris, *c*.1688; *d* Paris, 15 Oct. 1730). French composer. He was the son of one of the Vingt-quatre Violons du Roi and studied violin with a pupil of Corelli. In 1717 he visited Italy, where he may have met Tomaso Vitali, and from his experiences there gained a virtuosity unknown in Paris at that time; he returned to Paris in 1720 to become one of the best-known composers of sonatas. It is a pity that a movement from his fourth book of violin sonatas (Paris, 1721) has become famous in humorous arrangements for bassoon and euphonium, since his work is attractive on its own merits.   DENIS ARNOLD

Senfl, Ludwig (*b* ?Basle, *c*.1486; *d* Munich, 1542–3). Swiss composer. He was a singer and copyist at Maximilian I's court in Vienna from 1496, and travelled around Europe with his patron for many years; in 1497 Heinrich Isaac was made court composer, and Senfl probably studied with him. He was given a living in Verona by the emperor in 1510, and may have stayed in Italy with Isaac for a few years. In 1517 he succeeded Isaac as court composer in Vienna, but the following year he lost a toe in a hunting accident and did not recover fully for a year. Maximilian died in 1519 and the musical establishment was disbanded soon after; it took Senfl four years to obtain another post, as a member of the Bavarian court chapel in Munich, and after regaining his security he took care not to lose it again, remaining in Duke Wilhelm's service for the rest of his life.

Senfl was a prolific and talented composer of all kinds of music. He is best known today for his polyphonic *Lieder*, which range from popular tunes arranged in the manner of a quodlibet, to more sophisticated four-part settings in the Netherlands style. Although himself a Catholic, he corresponded with Luther and wrote two motets for him, and some of his sacred songs appear in Georg Rhau's publications. His sacred music is nearly all to Latin texts, and shows the influence of Isaac and Josquin.

Senleches, Jacob de (*fl.* late 14th century). French composer active in France and Italy. His surviving *chansons* illustrate the extreme rhythmic complexity of the post-Machaut generation.   JOHN MILSOM

Sennet. A stage direction in Elizabethan plays to indicate a type of fanfare before players entered or left the stage, performed with cornetts or trumpets. See also *Trumpet, 6b*; *Tucket*.

Sensibile (It.), **sensible** (Fr.). 'Leading note'.

Sentito (It.). 'Felt', i.e. with expression.

Senza (It.). 'Without'; e.g. *senza sordini*, 'without mutes' (in string playing), or 'without dampers' (in piano playing, i.e. *with* the right-hand pedal, which throws the dampers out of action).

Séparé (Fr.). 'Separated' (in French organ music, 'uncoupled').

Septet (Fr.: *septette, septuor*; Ger.: *Septett*; It.: *settimino, septetto*). Any combination of seven singers, or, more commonly, players, or any piece of music composed for such a combination. Beethoven's Op. 20 for violin, viola, cello, double bass, clarinet, bassoon, and horn is the most famous example; others exist by Spohr, Hummel, and Saint-Saëns, and Ravel's *Introduction et Allegro* for harp, flute, clarinet, and string quartet may be classed as a septet.

Septuplet [septimole, septolet]. Term for seven notes that are to be performed in the time of four or of six; they are indicated by the figure '7' placed above or below the seven notes, e.g.

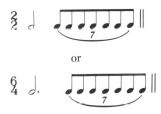

Sequence. 1. Term applied to the more or less exact repetition of a melody at another level, higher or lower. If the repetition is only in the melody, with changed harmony, it is called a 'melodic sequence', and if the repetition is followed in the harmony also, a 'harmonic sequence'. If the repetition is made without leaving the original key, which necessarily means that some of the intervals come out larger or smaller by a semitone, then it is called a 'tonal sequence'. If, in order to preserve the exact intervals, the key is changed, then the name given is 'real sequence' (see *Fugue* for a corresponding use of the words 'tonal' and 'real'). Some sequences are 'real' in some of their repetitions, and 'tonal' in others (in some instances to avoid carrying the modulation too far); these are called 'mixed sequences'.

When a sequence is in the nature of an exact repetition in another key (i.e. when it is a 'harmonic real sequence') it is sometimes called a *rosalia*, after an Italian popular song, 'Rosalia, mia cara', which begins with this device. A condition sometimes laid down as a qualification for the designation is that the passage shall be repeated one degree higher, e.g. from C to D to E, and so on—a very mechanical method of composing and an uncomfortable scheme of modulation through unrelated keys. In any case, the term is usually used contemptuously, as is its German equivalent *Schusterfleck* ('cobbler's patch'). Another German term for this kind of sequence is *Vetter Michel*, again from a popular song which opens with a rising sequence:

PERCY SCHOLES

2. Type of Latin hymn, usually in couplets with the music repeating in the pattern AA BB CC DD, and so on. From the 9th to the 16th centuries sequences were sung on feast-days after the Alleluia at Mass in the Roman Church, but after censure during the *Council of Trent (1542–63) their use declined rapidly.

The origins of the genre are uncertain. It is not clear whether the earliest melodies were originally sung without words, or were texted from the beginning, or if the earliest melodies were originally part of the festal Alleluias of their time, or were connected with the Alleluia at a later stage.

A typical sequence up to the 11th century has some six to twelve pairs of lines, each pair of a different length. The melodies differ markedly from those of Gregorian chant, with strong cadences often approached from the note below the final, and a tendency for each line to have its own individual tessitura. Several lines may cadence at the upper fifth, and even strive towards the upper octave. There is a clarity and strong sense of direction in the sequence, whereas Gregorian chant tends to dwell on ornamental figures. Ex. 1, the first four lines of a popular sequence for the Blessed Virgin Mary, illustrates these features.

A few sequences, however, do not exhibit these characteristics, lacking the typical verse structure and resembling rather lengthy Alleluia *jubili* (see *Jubilus*). This is in fact what they are, their connection with Alleluias being attested as early as the end of the 8th century. They were originally *jubili* to be sung when the Alleluia was repeated after its verse, as follows: Alleluia with 'normal' *jubilus*–*Verse*–*Alleluia* with extended *jubilus*. In this they resemble several Alleluias of the Old Roman chant repertory, which have survived in just this form. Later they were given texts, on the principle of one syllable per note.

It is possible, but not provable, that long sequences with paired verses are likewise 'second Alleluias'. Their non-Gregorian character argues against this, but the fact that as far back as our evidence goes (late 9th century) they were sung after the Alleluia argues for it. The Ambrosian Alleluia repertory of Milan has extremely long 'second' and 'third' Alleluias, with repeat structure, which may be analogous to the sequence, but unfortunately manuscripts of Ambrosian chant survive only from the 12th century onward.

Similarities have been noted between the sequence and the secular *lai* and *estampie*. But our sources for the latter two genres are too late for us to be certain of any real connection. Many

Ex. 1

sequence melodies bear titles in early manuscripts, some of them distinctly non-sacred, and it is thought that some of these may be the last traces of a secular origin for the melodies. Unfortunately definite proof is again lacking.

Our first witness to the long paired-verse sequence shows them already texted. Notker, a monk of St Gall in Switzerland, reported that a monk of Jumièges (on the Seine, north of Paris), fleeing from the devastations of the Northmen, brought to St Gall a book containing some texted sequences. These inspired Notker to compose his own texts, and his 'hymnbook', as he called the finished collection, was completed c.880. The first surviving copies of sequences date from shortly afterwards.

Some 150 melodies and nearly 400 texts are known from the period up to the end of the 10th century, from all areas of Europe. The most important surviving early collections are those from German lands (9th to 10th centuries, centred on Notker's texts), Aquitaine (10th century), and Winchester (late 10th century). Because sequences were not part of the Gregorian corpus of chant established in the late 8th century, different churches had very different collections. For example, only 35 melodies are common to both France and Germany in the early centuries (which may mean they were in circulation before the partition of Charlemagne's Empire at the Treaty of Verdun in 843). However, almost no texts were common to both areas. The texts display great variety of style: Notker's are in sophisticated Latin, with a strong theological content, and not particularly mellifluous; French texts are frequently in a less elevated style, full of laudatory exclamations and references (allegorical?) to musical instruments; Winchester texts are replete with arcane and learned-sounding words.

During the 11th and 12th centuries there was a gradual change in the style of texts, and thus of the music too. Texts in regularly accented verse, with verse pairs of the same length, became fashionable, and regular rhyme became usual. The opening of a sequence for St Thomas of Canterbury (d 1170) shows what a revolution had been accomplished by the 12th century (Ex. 2).

Texts in the new style first appeared in northern France, and many early examples are attributed to Adam, monk of St Victor in Paris (fl. 1160–70). The eventual production was immense. It is estimated that over 5,000 sequences had been composed by the end of the Middle Ages, of which many have never been edited in modern times.

DAVID HILEY

Serenade (Fr.: *sérénade*; Ger.: *Serenade, Ständchen*; It.: *serenata*). A word deriving from *sereno* (It., 'calm'), although serenades were generally played or sung in the evening, and this has led to some writers imagining that the word derived from *sera* (It., 'evening'). Serenades were originally played or sung by a lover at his lady's window, or as a greeting to an important personage, frequently featuring the use of a guitar or other plucked instrument. By the 18th century a serenade was a piece of instrumental music of up to 10 movements, scored for small instrumental ensemble, usually with a predominance of wind instruments. There are reminiscences of the original connotations of serenade and a plucked instrument in the serenade arias of some operas, e.g. 'Deh, vieni alla finestra' (*Don Giovanni*, Act 2).

Instrumental serenades were written by composers such as Boccherini, Michael Haydn, and Dittersdorf. Mozart's 13 examples (also called *Finalmusiken, notturni*, or cassations) were generally commissioned for specific occasions, such as the one he wrote in 1776 for a wedding in the Haffner family (the 'Haffner' Serenade, K 250). Most of his serenades begin and/or close with a march-like movement, framing a large-scale sonata form piece, two slow movements alternating with minuets, often a quicker movement such as a rondo, and a very quick finale. They are scored for a variety of combinations: strings and wind (e.g. the 'Haffner' Serenade), winds alone (e.g. K 361, K 365, K 388), string quartet (*Eine kleine Nachtmusik*), and even double or quadruple orchestra (*Serenata notturna*, K 239, and *Notturno*, No. 8). Beethoven's only serenades are chamber pieces, for string trio (Op. 8) and for flute, violin, and viola (Op. 25).

Ex. 2

Spe mer-ce-dis et co-ro-ne ste-tit Tho-mas in a-go-ne ad mor-tem o-be-di-ens.
Mor-te Chris-tum i-mi-ta-tus fi-de fir-mus et fir-ma-tus fir-mo gres-su gra-di-ens.

Fu-rit fu-ror mi-li-ta-ris ut vir sa-cer sa-cis a-ris im-mo-le-tur hos-ti-a.
Quem oc-ci-dunt ut sci-en-tes in-tro-du-cunt ne-sci-en-tes ad e-ter-na gau-di-a.

In the 19th century orchestral serenades were composed by Brahms, Dvořák, Tchaikovsky, Elgar (*Serenade for Strings*), and Strauss, among others. Vaughan Williams scored his *Serenade to Music* for 16 solo voices and orchestra. Other 20th-century examples include Schoenberg's Op. 24 and Britten's *Serenade for Tenor, Horn, and Strings*.

Serenade for Tenor, Horn, and Strings. Song cycle, Op. 31, by Britten. A prologue and epilogue for solo horn enclose settings of six poems on the theme of evening by Cotton, Tennyson, Blake, an anonymous one (*The Lyke-Wake Dirge*), Jonson, and Keats. It was written for Peter Pears and Dennis Brain, who first performed it in London in 1943.

Serenade to Music. Work by Vaughan Williams for 16 solo voices (four sopranos, four altos, four tenors, and four basses) and orchestra, a setting of a passage from Shakespeare's *The Merchant of Venice*. It was composed for Sir Henry Wood's golden jubilee as a conductor, and was first performed in London in 1938. Vaughan Williams also arranged it for four soloists and orchestra, for chorus and orchestra, and for orchestra alone.

Serenata (It.). 1. See *Serenade*.

2. A large-scale, cantata-like work for performance at court or at the home of an aristocratic family on a special occasion. A typical *serenata* had a pastoral, allegorical, or mythological subject, which involved at least two characters. In length somewhere between a cantata and an opera, it was often divided into sections, each consisting of recitatives and arias, and was given in an elaborate setting with costumes but without dramatic action. Handel's *Acis and Galatea* is a well-known example. Alessandro Scarlatti wrote 25 for his various patrons, and the form was extensively cultivated by 17th- and 18th-century Italian composers, and at the imperial court in Vienna (e.g. by Fux and Caldara).

Serenata notturna ('Nocturnal Serenade'). Title of Mozart's Serenade No. 6 in D, K 239, composed in 1776. It is scored for two small groups of strings.

Serenatella (It.). Diminutive of *serenata.

Sereno, serenità (It.). 'Serene', 'serenity'.

Serialism. Compositional technique in which the 12 notes of the chromatic scale are arranged in a fixed order, the 'series', which can be used to generate melodies and harmonies, and which normally remains binding for a whole work.

The series is thus a sort of hidden theme: it need not be presented as a theme (though, of course, it may be), but it is a fount of ideas and a basic reference. It may be manipulated in a composition in a variety of ways: the individual notes of the series may be changed in register by one or more octaves; the whole series may be uniformly transposed by any interval; it may be inverted; it may be reversed; and it may be both inverted and reversed.

By these means the composer is provided with a whole range of forms of the series, all related by the same sequence of intervals, and he may use these forms in any way he chooses. It is not necessary for themes to contain 12 notes, nor for the series to be used in melodies; it may be employed to construct both a theme and its accompaniment, or several forms of the series may be combined in a sequence of chords or a stretch of polyphony. The possibilities are vast, but the serial principle can be a guarantee of harmonic coherence, since the fundamental interval pattern is the same. Such coherence is not necessarily vitiated by the fact that, in most cases, the workings of serialism in a piece of music are not audible, nor meant to be.

Serialism originated as a technique to bring back some degree of order into the universe of *atonality, which had first been glimpsed by Schoenberg in 1908. Tentative movements towards the new method may be discerned in the 12-note themes of Berg's *Altenberglieder* (1912) and Schoenberg's *Die Jakobsleiter* (1917), and also in the 'trope' technique evolved by Hauer at the same time (see *Trope*, 4). The first fully serial movements appeared in three works which Schoenberg completed in 1923: the Five Piano Pieces, the Serenade, and the Piano Suite. Thereafter Schoenberg used serial methods in most of his major works, and they were adopted

Ex. 1

Prime

Inversion

Retrograde

Retrograde Inversion

Ex. 2

also by many of his pupils, including Berg and Webern.

The application of serialism in Webern's later music is clearer and more rigorous than any to be found in Schoenberg's works, so an example from one of his pieces may most readily demonstrate the serial principle in action. His Second Cantata (1941–3) is based on the series shown in Ex. 1 in its prime (or original), inverted, retrograde, and retrograde-inverted forms.

Ex. 2 is taken from the opening of the first movement, a recitative for the solo bass, and demonstrates the use of the series in melodic and harmonic units. Notice how, for instance, the initial wind chord announces the first six notes of the inversion, which is completed by the flute. The final flute note, F♯, then starts the retrograde form, which is continued by solo violin and clarinet and completed by the voice's entry on C, which also begins the prime form.

Works of this kind are apt to prompt the accusation that serial composition is somehow mathematical or mechanical, but the effect here is to produce a very natural homogeneity between harmonic character and melodic shape. And indeed, the ground rules of serialism are in many ways less restrictive than those of diatonic harmony or fugal composition: certainly they do not impose any kind of stylistic uniformity.

Developments of the serial method began rapidly after the Second World War. Before the war the technique had been adopted by few composers outside Schoenberg's circle: Ernst Krenek and Frank Martin were the notable exceptions. After the war, however, several younger composers began to seek ways not only of establishing independent serial styles, but also of extending serial methods to other aspects—of rhythm, dynamics, instrumentation, and so on. In the USA, Milton Babbitt elaborated procedures for creating music of unprecedented structural complexity and cogency, extrapolating from Schoenberg's technique until he quickly arrived at a view of serialism as a quasi-mathematical system.

Advances in Europe were more empirical and diverse. Messiaen and Boulez evolved methods by which rhythm could be subjected to serial control; to take one example, the composer could choose a number of different note values (say, made up of from one to 12 demisemiquavers) and arrange them in a 'series of durations' which could then be used in the composition of rhythms. Boulez's *Structures I* for two pianos (1951-2) is the classic work of 'total serialism', involving the serial manipulation not only of pitches and durations, but also of dynamics and nuances of touch.

The apotheosis of serialism in such works was short-lived, and since the early 1950s composers have often sought their means of integration, if any, elsewhere. However, the serial idea remains highly important in much of the music of Boulez, Stockhausen, Babbitt, and others.

PAUL GRIFFITHS

FURTHER READING
Josef Rufer: *Composition with Twelve Notes* (London, 1954); George Perle: *Serial Composition and Atonality* (Berkeley, California, 1962, 4th edn 1978).

Series. Basic musical idea, usually a sequential

ordering of the 12 notes of the chromatic scale, which is used as a starting point in the composition of serial music. See also *Serialism*.

Serio, seria (It.). 'Serious'; *serioso, seriosa, seriosamente*, 'seriously'. See also *Opera seria*.

Sermisy, Claudin de (*b* c.1490; *d* Paris, 13 Oct. 1562). French composer. He spent much of his life in the service of the French royal household, and from 1532 until at least 1554 was virtually in charge of the music—though theoretically only *sous-maître*. He may well have been present at the meeting of Francis I and Henry VIII in 1520 at the Field of the Cloth of Gold. He composed a substantial amount of church music (including a polyphonic setting of the St Matthew Passion, one of only two to survive from 16th-century France), but his main achievement lies in his *chansons*, which are short, tuneful, homophonic, gently sentimental, and distinctly singable. They were among the most popular of their time.

DENIS ARNOLD

Serov, Alexander (Nikolayevich) (*b* St Petersburg, 23 Jan. 1820; *d* St Petersburg, 1 Feb. 1871). Russian composer and music critic. In the latter capacity he was in many senses a pioneer, though his tastes were narrow, his views bigoted, and he managed to antagonize most of his Russian contemporaries at one time or another, cultivating (in Gerald Abraham's words) the 'gentle art of making enemies'. When writing about the music of composers outside his immediate circle, however, he could display reasoned argument and discernment, as in his enthusiastic comments on Liszt and Wagner. Like many Russian musicians of the time, Serov had followed a career in the civil service, having to regard music as little more than a pastime, until the extraordinary success of his first opera, the grand Meyerbeerian *Judith* (1863), and his second, *Rogneda* (1865), allowed him to devote all his time to composition and writing. He also began work on the five-act *Vrazh'ya sila* ('The Power of Evil'), completed after his death by his widow and by the composer Nikolay Solovyov (1846-1916) and performed in 1871. Despite these operas' popularity in their day (and their considerable influence on Tchaikovsky, Musorgsky, Rimsky-Korsakov, and Borodin), none has stood the test of time. They have never been staged complete in the West, though Act 4 of *Judith* was given in Paris during Diaghilev's 1909 opera season.

GEOFFREY NORRIS

Serpent. Wind instrument of former times, with a wooden tube in serpentine shape pierced with six fingerholes and sounded with a cup mouthpiece of roughly trombone proportions

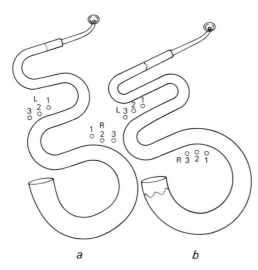

Fig. 1. Serpent, views from the back (as if playing), the six holes therefore on the other side in the positions shown by the small circles. The fingers are numbered 1 (index), 2, 3 for each hand. (a) Old form, both hands above tube, finger sequence: L, 1 2 3; R, 1 2 3. (b) Later form, right hand below tube, finger sequence: L, 1 2 3; R, 3 2 1.

and commonly of ivory. Fig. 1 shows the unmistakeable shape, with the brass crook inserted in the narrow end to bring the mouthpiece to the player's lips. The body (for which some recommended walnut) is constructed by hollowing out the wood in two halves which are then glued together and covered first with canvas and then with black leather. The two pieces may be cut from a single plank or built up in shorter pieces. The bore is conical and wide, and the sound is unique, somewhere between those of the tuba and the bassoon. The compass runs from the bottom C of the cello up to well into the tenor register when needed. As with the *cornett, good intonation and equality of the notes need very practised control by ear and lips.

The serpent was known first in France, shortly before 1600 (reputedly the invention of a canon of Auxerre). Its function there was to support the singing of plainchant (for which the organ was for a long time not used): the French Royal Chapel had its *joueur de serpent* up to at least the 1720s, and still in the early 20th century the serpent (or replaced by ophicleide) is said to have been performing the same duty in some French parish churches. There are 19th-century accounts of how some players would improvise a bass to the chant, or insert scale-like cadenzas between the lines. Neighbouring countries knew of the serpent by the 1660s: in Italy it was played, for example, in San Petronio, Bologna, along with trombones up to 1700; in England it was sometimes used in outdoor

secular music, and Handel calls for it in the *Fireworks Music* to add weight to the bass part.

A rich chapter in the serpent's history came with its addition to military music to strengthen the bass in the lower octave. Late 18th-century bandmasters, many from Germany, thus established the serpent in British bands, where it lasted for some 70 years. Three or more brass keys were added to it and, instead of holding the instrument in the old way with both hands above the tube (palm downwards) — which gives the same fingering order as other wind instruments (Fig. 1a) — the newer instrument was designed for playing with the right hand palm-upwards (giving better support, and holding the serpent more tilted) with the result that the fingering order for this hand becomes reversed (Fig. 1b), the opposite to the old way and to all other instruments, and at first rather confusing. The note with all holes uncovered is B♭; the key nearest the mouthpiece is opened for B♮. Technique could be brilliant: Mr André, of George IV's Household Band, is said to have performed one of Dragonetti's double bass concertos on the serpent.

Pl. 1. Serpent player, Band of the 17th Regiment (1830).

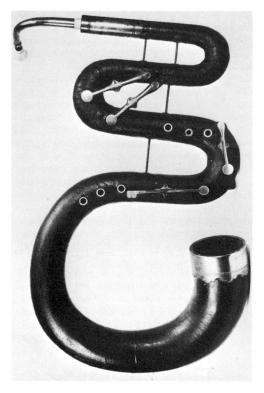

Pl. 2. Serpent, 7-key, by Thos. Key, London, allegedly played at Waterloo with the 23rd Regiment (later the Royal Welch Fusiliers).

Hardy's reference to the serpent in a village band is well known (*Under the Greenwood Tree*). There was indeed said still to be a village serpent-player in Czechoslovakia in 1950, i.e. just before the instrument's revival elsewhere for historical performances of the *Fireworks Music* and late 18th-century military pieces.

2. *Bass Horn*. In Europe from the 1790s the serpent was by degrees redesigned in various bassoon-like shapes, with the bell upwards. These were still called 'serpent', or else 'basson russe', 'bass-horn', or 'serpent Forveille' (see *Military band*, Pl. 2), and though primarily band instruments were frequently used in the orchestra. Hence 'serpent' in 19th-century scores (e.g. Wagner's *Rienzi*) can be taken to refer to one of these newer 'upright' models. In England, however, 'bass horn' denoted an all-metal version invented before 1800 by a French refugee serpentist, L. A. Frichot: two conical brass or copper tubes rise from a short connecting 'butt' in a tall V, in height about 40″. The bell has a pronounced flare and a swan-necked crook takes the mouthpiece. With a sound more resonant than the serpent's, it was regularly present in British bands until replaced by the ophicleide. Some English military band scores name it in Italian, 'corno basso'.

ANTHONY BAINES

Serrando, serrato (It.), **serrant, serré** (Fr.). 'Pressing', 'pressed', i.e. getting quicker. The French term was much used by Debussy.

Serse ('Xerxes'). Opera in three acts by Handel; text from a libretto by Minato, written for Cavalli (1654) and revised for Bononcini (1694). Produced: London, Haymarket, 15 April 1738; Vienna, Schönbrunn, 30 May 1925; Northampton, Mass., Smith College, 12 May 1928. Handel's only comic opera, in which Xerxes (ten.)—a purely imaginary picture of the historical King of Persia—is involved in various simultaneous amorous escapades. What has come to be popularly known as Handel's 'Largo' occurs in this opera—in fact, a *larghetto* aria 'Ombra mai fu', 'Never was there shade'.

Serva padrona, La ('The Maid as Mistress'). Intermezzo (to *Il prigionier superbo*) in two parts by Pergolesi to a libretto by Federico. It was first performed in Naples in 1733. See also *Opera*, 7.

Service. In the Anglican Church, a more or less elaborate and continuous setting of the canticles for Morning Prayer or Evensong, or of certain parts of the Communion Service. A choir member in conversation will distinguish between a 'service setting' of these passages and the singing of them to a traditional chant. Strictly the use of such service settings (unless very simple) is proper only in cathedrals, college chapels, and the like, as in the parish church it is frequently desirable to give every member of the congregation the opportunity to participate audibly in the more important choral items.

The effect of the Reformation on the composition of service music was mainly twofold: (*a*) the canticles had now to be set in the vernacular, and (*b*) they had to be set without lengthening with repetition of phrases, and as much as possible on the principle of a syllable to a note. This last point was apparently found impracticable by composers and, with a few exceptions such as Tallis and Merbecke, was totally disregarded from the beginning. Some 16th-century Communion services exist in two forms: that of the Latin Mass and that of an adaptation, in English, to the new conditions. The terms 'short service' and 'great service' were often used by 16th- and early 17th-century composers to distinguish between settings that faithfully followed the new regulations and those composed for festal occasions, scored for a large choir and falling into something like the old length and complexity. During the 18th century almost all services were composed on the 'short' principle; this was, however, in all ways a period of poverty in service composition.

Antiphonal treatment (by the *decani* and *cantoris* sides of the choir) is a frequent feature in service music, and, on the same principle, 'verse' and 'full' passages are also used, alternating a soloist accompanied by an independent organ part with full choir and organ doubling.

In the 19th century S. S. Wesley exercised a great influence on the composition of service music. The publication of his Service in B♭ in 1879 marked the beginning of a more economical and consistent use of material in service composition, a whole movement (and indeed the whole service) being bound together by motivic development, and with the organ taking a large share in this treatment.

The successive styles and composers of service music, being, on the whole, the same as those discussed under *Anthem*, need not be set out here, but it may be said that as with the anthem so with the service a great deal of purely conventional music has been brought into temporary existence. A common technical fault of such music is faulty accentuation of the words, probably resulting largely from the need for concision, which does not allow much 'elbow room'. From this last-mentioned condition effective composition in service music is perhaps more difficult to attain than in any other form. It is easy to set the words phrase by phrase, but flexibility, balance, and unity are harder to achieve. PERCY SCHOLES

Sessions, Roger (Huntington) (*b* Brooklyn, New York, 28 Dec. 1896). American composer. He studied at Harvard University (1910-15) and with Horatio Parker at Yale (1915-17). Then he had private lessons with Ernest Bloch, whom he assisted at the Cleveland Institute of Music (1921-5). After a period in Europe (1925-33) he taught at various American institutions, notably Princeton University (1935-45, 1953-65). A superlative musical craftsman, he has shown throughout a long and varied creative career the power to create purely musical discourses, subsuming detail to large-scale design. His early works, though influenced by Stravinskyan neoclassicism, are sober and without irony; since 1953 he has used Schoenbergian *serialism with the same skill and seriousness. His output includes two operas, *The Trial of Lucullus* (1947) and *Montezuma* (1941-63), eight symphonies, and various chamber pieces. He has also written the books *The Musical Experience of Composer, Performer, and Listener* (Princeton, New Jersey, 1950), *Harmonic Practice* (New York, 1951), and *Questions about Music* (Cambridge, Mass. 1970).

PAUL GRIFFITHS

Sestetto (It.). 'Sextet'.

Set. Musical unit, usually a small group of notes, which the analyst or composer determines to have significance in a work. For example, the C major triad could be described as an important set in Mozart's 'Jupiter' Symphony. However, the term is normally reserved for *atonal music.

Ex. 1 shows the opening bars from the fourth of Webern's Five Movements for string quartet (1909), in which one may detect several appearances of a set which, in its closest configuration, contains the intervals of a semitone and a perfect fourth (e.g. B–C–F, F–F♯–B, etc.). Some of these appearances are ringed in the example.

In the case of *serial music (this Webern example is not serial) the series or a part thereof may be regarded as a set. PAUL GRIFFITHS

Seufzend (Ger.). 'Sighing'.

Seul (Fr.). 'Alone', e.g. *violons seuls*, 'violins alone'.

Seven Deadly Sins, The (*Die sieben Todsünden der Kleinbürger*). Ballet in a prologue, seven scenes, and an epilogue by Weill to a libretto by Brecht. It includes songs for soprano, male chorus, and orchestra, and was choreographed by Balanchine for its first performance in Paris in 1933.

Seven Last Words. The final utterances of Christ on the Cross, drawn from the four

Ex. 1

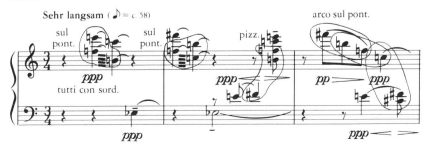

Gospels. The texts of *Passion music have sometimes been based on them, for example in Schütz's *Die sieben Worte* (*c*.1645). Haydn's instrumental setting was commissioned for the Cathedral of Cádiz for use on Good Friday; it was published in Vienna as *7 sonate, con un' introduzione, ed al fine un terremoto* ('7 sonatas, with an introduction, and at the end an earthquake'). It appeared in three versions: as Op. 47 for orchestra, as Op. 48 for string quartet, and as Op. 49 for piano. The choral version of the work, in the form of a cantata, may have been arranged by Haydn's brother, Michael.

Another well-known setting is Gounod's *Les sept paroles du Christ sur la croix* (1855).

Seven Penitential Psalms. See *Penitential Psalms*.

Seven Sonnets of Michelangelo. Song cycle, Op. 22, by Britten for tenor and piano. The sonnets set are Nos. 16, 31, 30, 55, 38, 32, and 24, and the work was first performed in London in 1942.

Seventh. See *Interval*.

Seventh chord. A chord consisting of a triad plus a seventh. See *Dominant seventh*; *Diminished seventh*.

Sevillana (Sp.). A Spanish dance originating in Seville.

Sext. The fifth of the *Office Hours of the Roman Catholic Church.

Sextet (Fr.: *sextette*, *sextuor*; Ger.: *Sextett*; It.: *sestetto*). Any group of six performers, vocal or instrumental, or a composition written for such a group. A string sextet normally comprises two violins, two violas, and two cellos (e.g. Brahms's Op. 18 and Op. 36, Dvořák's Op. 48), but other combinations may occur. Beethoven's Wind Sextet, Op. 71, is for two clarinets, two horns, and two bassoons. Other types of sextet may involve mixtures of wind and string instruments, such as two horns and string quartet, a combination found in many divertimentos by Haydn and Mozart and in Beethoven's Op. 81*b*; piano with string instruments (e.g. Mendelssohn's Op. 110); or piano with wind instruments (e.g. Poulenc's Piano Sextet).

Sextuor (Fr.). 'Sextet'.

Sextuplet [sextolet]. Term for six notes that are to be performed in the time of four, either as two groups of three or as three groups of two. It may be notated either

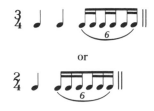

or

Seyffarth[Seiffart, Seyfart], **Johann Gabriel** (*b* Reisdorf, nr Weimar, 1711; *d* Berlin, 6 Apr. 1796). German composer and violinist. He studied piano in Weimar with J. G. Walther, and later went to Zerbst, where he studied violin and composition. He became a chamber musician at the court of Prince Heinrich of Prussia *c*.1741. Seyffarth's surviving works include symphonies, cantatas, concertos, and some keyboard pieces and songs.

Sf. Abbreviation for *sforzando* or *sforzato*; *sff.* abbreviation for *sforzatissimo*.

Sfogato (It.). Light and easy in style. Used as an expression mark it is usually qualified by an adjective, e.g. *sfogato dolce*. A *soprano sfogato* is a light soprano voice.

Sforzando, sforzato (It., often abbreviated to *sf.* or *sfz.*). 'Forcing', 'forced'. A strong accent. In the 19th century it was generally used to mark an accent within the prevailing dynamic, not necessarily loud, but it has now acquired the connotation of sudden loudness.

Sfp. Abbreviation for a *sforzato* followed immediately by a *piano*, i.e. a strongly accented note followed by a quiet note or passage.

Sfz. Abbreviation for *sforzando*.

Sgambati, Giovanni (*b* Rome, 28 May 1841; *d* Rome, 14 Dec. 1914). Italian composer. Son of an Italian lawyer and an English mother, he showed promise as a pianist at an early age and achieved a reputation in the 1860s for his playing of the German classics. He studied with Liszt while the latter was in Rome, and began conducting, introducing the 'Eroica' Symphony to the Roman public for the first time. In 1869 he went to Munich and heard music by Wagner with whom he later became friendly. He thus became one of the leading exponents of German music in Italy when it was still unfashionable. His later life was spent in giving concert tours and teaching. He composed some charming songs and piano pieces, his deft arrangement of Gluck's 'Dance of the Blessed Spirits' being very popular at one time.　　DENIS ARNOLD

Shake. Early English name for the *trill.

Shakuhachi. A Japanese end-blown bamboo flute. See *Japanese Music*, 3*c*.

Shamisen. The most frequently heard of the traditional Japanese lutes. See *Japanese Music*, 3*b*; *Lute*, 4*a*.

Shanty [chanty, sea shanty]. A term possibly derived from the French verb *chanter*, 'to sing'. The term has become especially attached to sailors' work-songs (as opposed to songs which sailors sang simply for enjoyment, which would probably have been much the same as those sung by landsmen); these, like the Black work-songs of the USA, were sung to aid and encourage arduous work—hauling in the halliards, pulling on ropes, pushing capstan and windlass, etc.—each task having its special type of song and repertory. In the days of the sailing ship, a special shanty man was frequently employed to lead the singing (he was excused other heavy labour). Many shanties have gone into the archives of folk-song and have become very well known (e.g. 'Whisky Johnnie', 'Blow the man down', 'Rio Grande'). With the advent of steam the shanty tradition came to an end.

PETER GAMMOND

Shapero, Harold (Samuel) (*b* Lynn, Mass., 29 Apr. 1920). American composer. He studied composition with Walter Piston and Ernst Krenek at Harvard University (1937–41) and with Nadia Boulanger in Cambridge, Massachusetts. In 1952 he was appointed professor at Brandeis University. His music, which includes a Symphony (1947), several sonatas, and other chamber works, is in a neoclassical style influenced by Stravinsky and Copland.

PAUL GRIFFITHS

Shaporin, Yury (Alexandrovich) (*b* Glukhov, 8 Nov. 1887; *d* Moscow, 9 Dec. 1966). Soviet composer. Although he did not at first intend to become a professional musician, he pursued musical activities in his native Ukraine, then moved to St Petersburg where, after reading law, he entered the conservatory to study composition with Nikolay Sokolov (1859–1922), orchestration with Maximilian Shteynberg (1883–1946), and score-reading with Nikolay Tcherepnin. During the 1920s he became closely associated with the leading artistic figures of the day (including the poet Alexander Blok, the writer Alexey Tolstoy, and the artist Alexander Benois), and he was, with Boris Asafyev (1884–1949), a key figure in the Association for Contemporary Music. His own music, however, is firmly rooted in the traditions he inherited at the St Petersburg Conservatory, and, although he composed some instrumental music, a choral symphony (1928–32), other choral works, and

much incidental music, he has retained prominence chiefly through his four-act lyric opera *Dekabristy* ('The Decembrists'), a work which occupied him on and off for more than 30 years, from the early 1920s to 1953 when it was given its première at the Bolshoy Theatre, Moscow.

GEOFFREY NORRIS

Sharp (Fr.: *dièse*; Ger.: *Kreuz*; It.: *diesis*). The sign (♯) which when placed before a note raises it in pitch by a semitone. See *Accidentals*; for the origins of the sharp sign and its early use, see *Notation*, 2.

In the 18th century, the 'key of E sharp' meant the key of E which has a major third, i.e. E major (Beethoven, for example, described his first Leonore Overture, in C major, as 'Ouverture in C♯').

As an adjective applied to vocal or instrumental performance, 'sharp' means inexact intonation on the high side.

Sharp, Cecil (James) (*b* London, 22 Nov. 1859; *d* London, 28 June 1924). English collector of folk music. After completing his education at Cambridge he went to Australia. Returning to England he became head of the Hampstead Conservatory, occupying this position for nine years. He then gave himself to the collection, publication, and performance of the folk-song and folk-dance of his native land, and he, far more than any other single person, is responsible for the salvaging of this national heritage. Towards the end of his life he enjoyed a small pension from the government. In his memory has been built, in London, Cecil Sharp House—as headquarters for the English Folk Dance and Song Society.

PERCY SCHOLES

FURTHER READING
Maud Karpeles: *Cecil Sharp: his Life and Work* (London, 1967).

Shaw, (George) **Bernard** (*b* Dublin, 26 July 1856; *d* Ayot St Lawrence, Herts., 2 Nov. 1950). Irish dramatist and music critic. He came from a musical family (his father was a trombonist, his mother a singer), and later confessed that Mozart, especially *Don Giovanni*, was an early and important influence on his musical thinking. In London he first wrote music criticism for *The Hornet* (from 1876), and joined *The Star* in 1888, becoming its music critic, with the penname 'Corno di Bassetto', in 1889. He moved to *The World* in 1890 and wrote weekly criticism for it until 1894. His knowledge and love of music, combined with his skill with language, enabled him to produce hundreds of well-informed and colourful reviews of music in London in the 1890s. His writing could be unashamedly subjective and strongly (at times outrageously) expressed, and his turn of phrase memorable for its perspicacity and trenchant wit. He was persuasive, if sometimes controversial, in his persistent championship of Wagner's music; his study of the *Ring*, *The Perfect Wagnerite* (London, 1898, 4th edn, 1923, reprinted 1972), is a highly personal interpretation of Wagner's music drama in terms of Shaw's own socialist attitude to the capitalist society in which he lived. He was also a supporter of Richard Strauss and a close friend of Elgar, and was always eager to help young contemporary composers if he thought them talented. His plays have inspired music by several composers, including Oscar Straus (*The Chocolate Soldier*, 1908, based on *Arms and the Man*), Walton (film music for *Major Barbara*, 1941), and, of course, Frederick Loewe, whose musical *My Fair Lady* (1956) is based on *Pygmalion*.

JUDITH NAGLEY

Shaw, Geoffrey (Turton) (*b* London, 14 Nov. 1879; *d* London, 14 Apr. 1943). English composer and educationist. He studied with Stanford and Charles Wood at Cambridge, and worked as inspector of music for the board of education while also composing music for the church and for children. His brother Martin Shaw (1875–1958) was a composer and church musician. PAUL GRIFFITHS

Shawm (formerly in Eng. also 'shalme', 'hautboy', 'hoboy'; Fr.: *hautbois* or, before 1500, *chalemie*; Ger.: *Schalmey*, *Pommer*; It.: *pifaro* (though this can also mean 'fife'); Sp.: *chirimia*). Wind instrument with conical bore and double reed, the predecessor of the oboe (as the name 'hautbois' for both commemorates) and more powerful in sound. Through its main period, from the 14th century to the 17th, its duties lay in professional music for ceremonial or festive occasions performed outdoors or in large buildings; still in this tradition, shawms modernized in construction lead the music for the sardana dances in Catalonia (see below, 3). The old shawm has now been revived for early music along with certain variant species (*Rauschpfeifen* etc.) noticed below (5).

1. *The Shawm Family*. Original 16th- and 17th-century examples of each member are preserved in museums in Europe (notably Brussels and Berlin). The smallest size (Ger.: *Exilent* or *Klein-Diskant Schalmey*), 18″ long, is very rare and seems to have been little used, so it is best to begin with the normal treble of the family. The major reference source for the instruments is German (Praetorius, 1619: see *Instruments, Renaissance*, Fig. 1). The lowest notes for each size are given in Ex. 1 (the notes given with seven fingers down are shown as minims).

Highest notes are not standard but depend on both the instrument and the player.

Ex. 1

The treble shawm (Ger.: *Diskant-Schalmey*) is a plain thick-walled pipe, 25″ long, with a spreading bell, turned all in one piece of wood, usually box or maple. Seven fingerholes in front (none behind) give the lowest note, *d′* or *c′* according to the model, and the usual compass is an octave and a fifth, or a note or two more with an effort. Below these holes are a number of permanently open 'vent holes' in the bell. The bore expands at a greater angle than with an oboe (see *Oboe*, Fig. 2), making for a naturally loud sound, strongly coloured by the vibration of the reed, which is set in a 'pirouette'. Fig. 1 shows (*a*) the brass staple, its lower part to be wound with thread for inserting into the instrument, and on it the wooden pirouette (*b*), recessed to make room for the base of the reed (*c*). The lips are pressed to the pirouette, allowing the reed to vibrate fairly freely inside the mouth, while being tongued as on an oboe.

The alto shawm (in Eng. originally 'tenor'; Ger.: *Altpommer*) is 30″, with lowest note *g* or *f*. The little finger has a brass key for the lowest note, acting inside a removable wooden protecting 'barrel' with small holes to let the sound out (and often described by the French term *fontanelle*). The pirouette is as above but longer.

The tenor shawm (Ger.: *Tenorpommer* or *Nicolo*, an unexplained name) is 43″. The

Fig. 1

would lead one to expect up to 20″ for each group.

2. *History*. The shawm, broadly speaking, took over the musical functions of the ancient reed instruments of the *aulos kind. Where and when it first evolved is still very uncertain, but there is evidence pointing to the Middle East during the early centuries of Islam. It was apparently brought to Europe following the third Crusade—a quite small instrument no doubt with a piercing treble compass such as one still hears from similar small instruments played in Asia and North Africa (see below, 4), sounding at a distance rather like a Scottish bagpipe. It was played chiefly at royal events and on military campaigns along with long trumpets and a drum. By the 15th century it had been lengthened to the treble size and joined by the alto shawm, then named *bombarde. With a trumpet (a slide trumpet possibly) they made a three-part group known in French as the *haut*

Pl. 1. Angel with a tenor shawm (bombarde), detail from a Flemish painting, 'Mary, Queen of Heaven', by the Master of the St Lucy Legend (active 1480-9).

pirouette is placed on an angled brass crook, the instrument being too long to be held straight out forwards. The shawm which was recovered in 1980 from the *Mary Rose*, Henry VIII's flagship, has the dimensions of this tenor size.

A variant of the tenor shawm is known as the basset shawm: it varies from the preceding only in that it is extended down to low G by three more brass keys, two of them on the back for the right thumb.

The bass shawm (Ger.: *Basspommer*) is pitched a fifth below the basset and also has the extra keys. It is a massive instrument, 6′ tall, and is played standing with the bell on the ground; an S-shaped crook brings the reed within reach and it seems that no pirouette was used. The sound at the bottom is like that of a powerful bassoon, but becomes less resonant, more strained, higher up.

The great bass shawm (Ger.: *Grossbasspommer*) is a fifth lower still, over 9′ tall. Despite being awkward to manœuvre, with the 9″ wide bell resting on the ground 5′ astern of the player, it gave good, true notes: the old makers knew well how to cope with the matter of a group of fingerholes necessarily bunched within the span of the hand, although theoretical proportions

Pl. 2. Burgundian haut musique in the 15th century, detail from 'The Hunt of Philip the Good' (destroyed 1608) in a copy by a follower of Jan van Eyck; the musicians play slide trumpet, bombarde, and shawm (the length of the last apparently exaggerated).

('loud') *menestrels* whose duties included playing at state balls, as in Italy also. Their method
seems to have been for the bombarde to take the
cantus firmus or tenor, the shawm to extemporize above, and the trumpet—or later in the
century, trombone—to make up some kind of
contratenor part.

The larger shawms were being made by the
mid 16th century, after which it became a
regular practice to play stately music in up to six
parts on the shawms augmented by a cornett
(for the second treble part) and retaining the
trombone for the part next above the bass; for
processions, the non-portable bass shawm was
replaced by a dulcian (see *Bassoon*, 4a). A few
items of their special repertory are known,
including some solemn *pavanes pour les hautbois*
(among the Philidor manuscripts in Paris)
played by the French royal band up to the time
when the old instruments were abolished under
Lully's regime.

In England these instruments were played
together by town *waits up to the end of the
17th century. Shakespeare's 'hoboys without'
shows them hired for theatrical spectacles. But
for more cultivated music such players played
other instruments, not shawms. Nor did the
shawms enter into the music of the Italian
academies, the great Venetian ensembles, or, in
Germany, the serious music of Schütz and his
contemporaries. In some of the Leipzig cantatas
of Knüpfer, however, there are parts for 'bom-
bardi' in three parts, presumably shawms of the
town musicians.

3. *Other European Forms*. The present Catalan
shawms have long dropped the Spanish shawm
name *chirimia* (or *xeremia*), being known simply
as the *tiple* ('treble') and the *tenora*. They keep

Pl. 3. Tiple and tenora players, Barcelona.

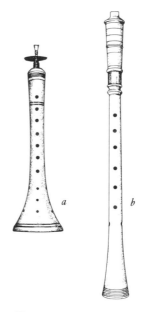

Fig. 2 (a) *Zurla, Macedonia.*
(b) *Rauschpfeife, modern reproduction.*

the pirouette and the old steep bore-gradient,
but are otherwise brought up to date with
keywork of the 19th-century type. Both are
transposing instruments: the *tiple* is pitched in F
(a fourth above the oboe); and the *tenora* is a
fifth lower, in B♭, with a long metal bell for the
second *tenora* player to be able to reach low
notes, down to $f\sharp$ (sounding e). Their penetrating but very expressive sounds are backed by
five brass instruments and a double bass, while
the leader of the band makes introductory
flourishes on a small *pipe and tabor—a memory
of times early in the 19th century when this,
with shawm and bagpipe, alone provided the
music for the dance.

The Spanish-derived *chirimias* of Central
America are cylindrically bored and played
without a pirouette.

4. *Oriental 'Shawms'*. The word 'shawm' has
today become a convenient over-all term for
related oriental double-reed instruments
(though some prefer 'oboes'). Most have some
form of metal disc for the lips to press against,
and are played without pausing for breath,
inhaling through the nose to store air in the
cheeks—though this method is not confined to
such instruments, being practised over the
world in various kinds of instrument (see
Didjeridu). As air is rapidly inhaled through the
nose (lowering the soft palate) the inflated
cheeks are drawn in to propel the air held in
them into the instrument before the soft palate
is raised for resumption of normal blowing.

Among these oriental 'shawms' are the Turkish *zurna*, in Egypt called *zamr*, and well known in the southern Balkans as the gipsy *zurla* (Fig. 2*a*), played at feasts and weddings, always with a large drum. Among many varieties further east are the Indian *shanāī*, the country's principal reed instrument, and the Chinese *sona* (both names related to 'surna') which has a brass bell and is much used in the theatre (see *Chinese Music*, 4*g*).

5. *Rauschpfeifen and Schreierpfeifen.* These are German names for a variant of shawm played with a cap over the reed (like a crumhorn) and mentioned in many court and town inventories, evidently found useful in music where the shawm would be inappropriate. Some 12 examples of various pitches are known (in Berlin, Prague, and a small one in Vienna): the bore is conical but at a smaller angle than a shawm, and the bell is scarcely flared. The name *Rauschpfeife* occurs early in the 16th century after which, up to the mid 17th century, it is with one exception always *Schreierpfeife* or some other form of this word (*Schryari* etc.). The reconstructions manufactured today (Fig. 2*b*) usually go under the 'Rausch-' name, which Curt Sachs, who knew the Berlin examples well, thought to be the correct one. This is largely because Praetorius (who mentions no *Rauschpfeifen*) illustrates the 'Schreier-' in a strange and possibly not wholly correct way. The Berlin instruments came from the church at Naumburg, Saxony, which has preserved old inventories in which these same instruments are clearly included under the name 'Schreiarien'.

There was in those times yet another family of double-reed instruments called *bassanelli*, or in an Italian manuscript work (by Virgiliano) *armilloni*. Praetorius describes them briefly, but nothing has been found to match them, so we really know next to nothing about them.

ANTHONY BAINES

Shebalin, Vissarion (Yakovlevich) (*b* Omsk, 11 June 1902; *d* Moscow, 28 May 1963). Soviet composer. He studied music at the Moscow Conservatory, of which he was later director (1942–8). He composed five symphonies, the two-hour choral symphony *Lenin* (1931, rev. 1959), the opera *The Taming of the Shrew* (composed 1946–56), and a completion of Musorgsky's *Sorochintsy Fair* (1931).

PERCY SCHOLES, rev.

Sheherazade. 1. Symphonic suite, Op. 35, by Rimsky-Korsakov, composed in 1888. It is 'after the Thousand and One Nights'.

2. Overture for orchestra by Ravel, composed in 1898.

3. Song-cycle for mezzo-soprano and orchestra by Ravel to poems by Tristan Klingsor

(pseudonym of Léon Leclère), composed in 1903. The three songs are *Asie* ('Asia'), *La flûte enchantée* ('The Magic Flute'), and *L'indifférent* ('The Indifferent One').

Sheng. A Chinese mouth-organ. See *Chinese Music*, 4*h*.

Shepherd, John. See *Sheppard, John.*

Shepherd on the Rock. See *Hirt auf dem Felsen, Der.*

Shepherds of the Delectable Mountains, The. Pastoral episode in one act by Vaughan Williams to his own libretto based on Bunyan's *The Pilgrim's Progress* (1674–9, 1684). It was first performed in London in 1922. Vaughan Williams later used the work (without its final section) as the second scene of Act 4 of his morality *The Pilgrim's Progress.*

Sheppard [Shepherd], John (*b* c.1515; *d* 1559 or 1560). English composer. Little is known about his life, except that he served as *informator choristarum* at Magdalen College, Oxford, from 1543 to 1548, and then joined the Chapel Royal as a Gentleman, a position which he appears to have retained until his death.

Sheppard was one of the foremost composers of church music of his time, and more music survives by him than by any of his English contemporaries. With the exception of several part-songs and carols, his output is exclusively liturgical, and reflects the religious upheavals of his time by containing both Latin-texted works for the Catholic rite (as celebrated during the reigns of Henry VIII and Mary), and English church music written during the formative years of Protestant worship under Edward VI and Elizabeth. Although several works belong to the tradition of florid polyphony practised by the composers of the *Eton Choirbook* and by Taverner, much of Sheppard's Latin music tends towards a declamatory and largely imitative style, although one in which word-painting is virtually absent and textures sometimes unvaried over long spans. Especially characteristic are his many works for Vespers and Matins—hymns, responds, and antiphons —which may have been written in collaboration with Tallis as part of a comprehensive cycle for the entire Church Year. These works are constructed on plainchant *cantus firmi*, with notes of equal length, around which the remaining voices weave an abstract polyphonic web, often continuously peaking on particular notes to give rise to an effect which has been aptly described as 'perpendicular'. By contrast, Sheppard's works on English texts are mostly modest in scope, following the directives of the church reformers for settings which appealed more to the intellect than to the senses. JOHN MILSOM

Shield, William (*b* Swalwell, Co. Durham, 5 Mar. 1748; *d* London, 25 Jan. 1829). English violinist and composer. His father, a singing teacher, died when William was nine, but he continued to study music with Charles Avison in Newcastle and eventually decided to become a musician. After a period as first violin of an orchestra in Scarborough he went to London and *c*.1773 was appointed a second violin at the King's Theatre and shortly afterwards a principal viola. He was composer to Covent Garden 1778-91 and 1792-7, and in 1817 was made Master of the King's Music. Shield composed over 40 light operas, pantomimes, and ballad operas, six string quartets (London, *c*.1782), six string trios (London, 1796), and other instrumental pieces. However, he was best known for his tuneful songs, which are the only parts of his stage works to survive. Of these, 'Auld Lang Syne' from *Rosina* (1782) is the most famous, though hardly representative of Shield at his best. WENDY THOMPSON

Shift. See *Position*.

Shimmy. An all-embracing name for a type of Black American, African-based dancing, involving much movement of the body and generally of a provocatively sexual nature; the type has been formalized in dances ranging from the *black bottom to modern *rock and roll. The name, like many jazz terms, is of obscure origin: it has been credited to the pianist Tony Jackson, *c*.1900, but probably has earlier, folk beginnings. Various songs popularizing the word (e.g. 'I wish I could shimmy like my sister Kate') brought about a 'shimmy' craze in North America, and the shimmy featured in the show *Sometime*, danced by Mae West, and in *The Ziegfeld Follies* of 1922, danced by Gilda Grey. PETER GAMMOND

Shirley, James (*bapt.* London, 7 Sept. 1596; *buried* London, 29 Oct. 1666). English dramatist. He wrote numerous plays and the texts of several masques, including *The Triumph of Peace* (1634, music by William Lawes and Simon Ives), *The Triumph of Beautie* (1646, music partly by Lawes), and, by far the most important, *Cupid and Death* (1653, music by Matthew Locke and Christopher Gibbons). See also *Masque*.

Shivaree. An American corruption of *charivari.

Shō. A Japanese mouth-organ. See *Japanese Music*, 3*c*.

Shofar. The traditional ramshorn of the Jewish synagogue, sounded on certain feasts of the year. It is ritually made, the horn being straightened, the wider end bent upwards, and the whole partly flattened. Two notes are sounded, usually a fifth apart.

In the Old Testament, 'shofar' in the Hebrew is in most places translated in the Latin Bible by 'tuba' and in the English by 'trumpet', as in Psalm 150. Psalm 98 also names the 'hazozerah', the ancient short metal trumpet (the silver trumpets described in Numbers 10), this and shofar being correctly translated in the Latin: 'Psallite Domino . . . in tubis ductilibus, et voce tubae corneae', and by Wycliffe (who began his translation in 1378): 'in trumpis betun out with hamer, in vois of a trumpe of horn'.

ANTHONY BAINES

Short octave [broken octave]. Systems once used in the organ and other keyboard instruments whereby the keys of the lowest octave on the keyboard produce notes other than their apparent ones. In keyboard music written before *c*.1700 (i.e. before equal temperament became common), some chromatic notes were hardly ever needed in the bass register and so were omitted from the bottom of the keyboard. In one common type of short-octave keyboard the keys for the notes F, G, A, B♭, and B were as normal, but those for C♯ and D♯ were omitted and those for E, F♯, and G♯ were made to sound C, D, and E. In another common arrangement the lowest octave was complete from C to C, but the normal C♯ and D♯ keys sounded the more useful notes of low A and B, and an additional key for low G was placed immediately to the left of the C key.

One particular advantage of using short-octave tuning on the organ was the avoidance of the cost of large, heavy metal pipes for bass notes which were rarely required. On keyboard instruments without a pedal-board (e.g. harpsichord, spinet, virginals) a short-octave system allowed the left hand to span certain widely-

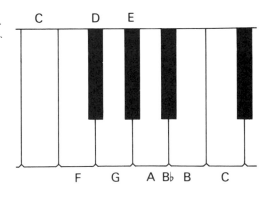

spaced chords that might otherwise be beyond its stretch.

The term 'broken octave' is sometimes used to describe certain types of short-octave tuning. In addition, it describes a tuning system for some stringed keyboard instruments that was common in the 17th century in which the lowest 'sharp' keys were split in two, the front half sounding one pitch, the back another. Thus the instrument's compass was extended while its external dimensions remained unchanged.

PERCY SCHOLES, rev. Judith Nagley

Short service. See under *Service*.

Shostakovich, Dmitry (Dmitriyevich) (*b* St Petersburg, 25 Sept. 1906; *d* Moscow, 9 Aug. 1975). Soviet composer. He was born at a crucial time in Russian history. Revolutionary fervour and dissatisfaction with the tsar and government had led to the bloody January uprising of 1905, and Shostakovich was just 11 when the decisive October Revolution occurred in 1917. His career as a musician ran parallel with the history of the new Soviet state. Nevertheless he was often at odds with official artistic doctrines, and, although he appeared at times to bend with the fluctuating Soviet attitudes to music, he maintained to the last an integrity and individuality which have marked him as the most important composer in the Soviet Union.

1. *Early Years.* At first he was destined to become a pianist. He studied piano at home with his mother and then at the Petrograd Conservatory with Leonid Nikolayev. He also studied composition with Maximilian Shteynberg and formed a close association with the conservatory's principal, Glazunov, whose influence is discernible in the crisp scoring of Shostakovich's First Symphony (1925). But Shostakovich swiftly outgrew the conservatory teaching, and Shteynberg was later to express incomprehension of some of his dissonant early piano works, notably the First Piano Sonata (1926) and the *Aphorisms* (1927). At this time Shostakovich had allied himself with the forward-looking principles of the Association for Contemporary Music (ASM), which actively promoted the study and performance of contemporary Western music by such composers as Hindemith, Berg, and Schoenberg. The fruits of this phase are seen not only in Shostakovich's astringent piano works but also in the incidental music which he wrote for Vladimir Mayakovsky's play *Klop* ('The Bedbug', 1929), the ballets *Bolt* ('The Bolt', 1930-1) and *Zolotoy vek* ('The Age of Gold', 1929-32), and the music for the silent film *Novyy Vavilon* ('New Babylon', 1929): this last (though it was rejected by most cinema orchestras as being too difficult) revealed an alertness to dramatic situation and characterization which manifested itself in later film scores and in his two completed operas, *Nos* ('The Nose', 1930) and *Ledi Makbet Mtsenskovo uyezda* ('The Lady Macbeth of the Mtsensk District', 1934).

The Nose is a vivid sign of its times, reflecting Russia's satirical mood of the 1920s and also emphasizing—in its extremely complex harmonies and rhythms—the modernism of Shostakovich's style of the moment. It also reveals Shostakovich's keen sense of theatre and a highly original treatment of the voice. As his close friend Ivan Sollertinsky remarked, Shostakovich was 'perhaps the first among Russian composers to make his heroes speak not in conventional arias and cantilenas but in living language, setting everyday speech to music'. Such a notion of 'musical realism'—of vocal lines closely moulded to the inflections and rhythms of spoken Russian—had been a feature of much Russian vocal writing (particularly in Musorgsky's music) since its advocacy by Dargomyzhsky in his opera *The Stone Guest*. In *The Nose* Shostakovich applied a similar technique, but injected into it a new vitality, producing potent, virile vocal lines which the composer Sergey Slonimsky has aptly described as 'brilliantly eccentric'.

But brilliant eccentricity was soon to fall into disfavour. As the Soviet authorities, with Stalin in power, sought to invest the arts with a purpose directed towards the welfare of the state (see *Russia and the Soviet Union*, 5), so the atmosphere of musical experimentation which had been allowed to thrive in the 1920s was firmly dispelled. At the time of the 1932 decree bringing all musical activity under state control Shostakovich was nearing completion of his four-act opera *The Lady Macbeth of the Mtsensk District*, intended as the first part of a trilogy of operas dealing with Russian womanhood. After its Leningrad première in 1934 the opera was hailed as a model of the new concept of *socialist realism; but only two years later—just after Stalin himself had seen the opera—it was condemned in the notorious *Pravda* editorial 'Sumbur vmesto muzyki' (Chaos instead of Music) for its explicitness and dissonance. It was dropped from the repertory, and was not seen again in Russia until its revival—as *Katerina Izmaylova*—in 1962.

2. *The Years of Maturity.* The condemnation of *Lady Macbeth* had far-reaching consequences not only for Soviet opera but for Soviet music in general. At the time Shostakovich was working on his Fourth Symphony (1935-6). Although its complexity was certainly not so pronounced as the polytonality, polyrhythm, and frenetic

activity of the Second Symphony (1927), Shostakovich realized that it was stylistically a companion piece to *Lady Macbeth* in its bold gestures and grim power, its harnessing of lavish orchestral resources, and its huge, unorthodox symphonic structure. In the prevailing cultural climate it was the wrong work at the wrong time. He withdrew it, and it was not in fact performed until 1961. Instead he produced his Fifth Symphony (1937)—dubbed 'a Soviet artist's reply to just criticism'—which is couched in a clearer, more direct manner than the Fourth Symphony: its essential euphony, its sense of grandeur and nobility, conformed more closely to the ideals of socialist realism. But this is not to suggest that Shostakovich's artistic principles were compromised: the path of ultra-modernism suggested by his music of the late 1920s was arguably a cul-de-sac. The Fifth Symphony revealed a maturing personality which had already been evident in such works as the First Piano Concerto (1933) and the Cello Sonata (1934), and which Shostakovich was to assert in such works as the First String Quartet (1938), the Sixth Symphony (1939), and the Piano Quintet (1940). He also confirmed his talent as a cinema composer in a number of film scores, and re-scored Musorgsky's *Boris Godunov* (1939–40). This last was of particular significance. Later on he was to prepare an edition of *Khovanshchina* (1959) and orchestrate the *Songs and Dances of Death* (1962): his own vocal music has a clear affinity with the stark realism of Musorgsky's writing, and Musorgsky's influence on the Thirteenth and Fourteenth Symphonies, and on the bleak song-cycles of Shostakovich's last years, is particularly prominent.

At the heart of this period of Shostakovich's career lies the music he wrote during the Second World War. The Soviet Union entered the war in 1941, the year in which Leningrad was surrounded by German forces. The siege was to last for two-and-a-half years, a period of incredible deprivation and suffering but also one in which the people displayed a remarkable degree of heroism. Shostakovich captured the mood of these years in his Seventh Symphony (1941): he described it as 'a symphony about our epoch, about our people, about our sacred war, about our victory', and he dedicated it 'to the city of Leningrad'. It is a demonstrative work, graphically depicting human life and human tragedy, the resilience of Soviet mankind, and (in the finale) its strength and ability to survive. The mood of the Seventh contrasts sharply with that of the Eighth Symphony (1943), written at the height of the war and couched in the bitter, pessimistic terms which also imbue the Piano Trio (1944) written in memory of Ivan Sollertinsky. Only in his projected opera *Igroki* ('The

Dmitry Shostakovich (1943)

Gamblers', 1941) could Shostakovich find a lighter touch, though he abandoned it at the end of scene 8 and the surviving music was not performed in public until 1978.

To mark the end of the war Shostakovich wrote his Ninth Symphony (1945), dominated, as the composer said, 'by a transparent, clear mood'. The jauntiness and air of trouble-free serenity dashed official expectations of a defiant, heroic celebration of victory, a fact which clearly contributed to the criticism the symphony attracted during the cultural purges carried out in 1948 by Stalin's right-hand man Andrey Zhdanov. Along with every other composer of note, Shostakovich was condemned for alleged *formalism in his music, and was urged forcefully to find his way back to the path of socialist realism.

3. *The Late Years.* As in the crisis of 1936 Shostakovich once again had to take stock in the wake of Zhdanov's criticisms. He withheld a few potentially controversial works which were either completed or planned: the First Violin Concerto (1947–8), the song-cycle *Iz evreyskoy narodnoy poezii* ('From Jewish Folk Poetry', 1948), and the Fourth String Quartet (1949). Instead he offered to the public a few more film scores and such choral works as the oratorio *Pesn' o lesakh* ('Song of the Forests', 1949), the Ten Poems on Texts by Revolutionary Poets (1951), and the cantata *Nad Rodinoy nashey solntse siyayet* ('The Sun Shines over our Motherland', 1952).

With the death of Stalin in 1953 the cultural climate thawed to the extent that Shostakovich's works of the late 1940s could be given their delayed premières. He also began work on his Tenth Symphony (1953), in which the undercurrents of melancholy and dark soul-searching flowing beneath much of his earlier music came powerfully to the surface. The Tenth Symphony is a deeply personal work—making overt use of his musical monogram *DSCH—and as such was the subject of a vigorous three-day debate at the Moscow branch of the Union of Soviet Composers (29 and 30 March and 5 April 1954). Some commentators felt that the symphony was 'non-realistic' and attacked its pessimism; others stressed that the Soviet composer ought now to be guided by his own artistic instincts, particularly since the process of de-Stalinization was now allowing for 'independence, courage, and experimentation' in music. From this time onwards Shostakovich's own music became gradually more inward-looking, more concerned to express openly those concerns which he had so far kept largely suppressed. To a greater extent he withdrew into the intimate medium of the chamber ensemble: he composed seven of his 15 quartets in his last decade or so, and wrote the brooding Viola Sonata (1975) in his very last year. He also composed a number of song-cycles which reflect the preoccupations with irony, terror, and death which coloured his later life: *Satiry* ('Satires', 1960) to words by Sasha Chorny, Seven Romances on Poems by Alexander Blok (1967), Six Poems of Marina Tsvetayeva (1973), and the Suite on Verses of Michelangelo

Dmitry Shostakovich, drawing (1973) by his son Maxim Shostakovich.

Buonarroti (1974). His last symphonies, culminating in the enigmatic Fifteenth (1971), reveal comparable traits. In the Thirteenth Symphony (1962), for bass solo, male chorus, and orchestra, he painted a savage, terrifying picture of Stalinist oppression; and in the Fourteenth Symphony (1969), a song-cycle (to poems by Rilke, Garcia Lorca, Apollinaire, and Küchelbecker) scored for soprano and bass soloists with a small orchestra of strings and percussion, the deep introspection of his last years is achingly asserted in music of sinister drama, heart-rending lyricism, chill gloom, and martial brutality, combining to create a work of harrowing intensity.

Much has been written about Shostakovich's position in the Soviet political scheme, about the wide gap which separates his apparently 'public' works from his more 'personal' ones like the late symphonies and quartets. He was indeed capable of the profound and the banal. On the surface it may seem odd that in a single year (1953) he could write the Tenth Symphony together with an entirely untroubled Ballet Suite and a sprightly Concertino for two pianos, and that in another year (1957) he could conceive the massive Eleventh Symphony and the jaunty, limpidly lyrical Second Piano Concerto. Similarly, at the very time he was working on the massive Fourth Symphony (1934–5) he was able to turn his mind to the lightweight 'cartoon opera' *Skazka o pope i rabotnike evo Balde* ('The Tale of the Priest and his Workman Balda', 1933–6). But this diversity should not be attributed to political pressure, more to his multi-faceted personality, which was able to create music of (usually) high artistic merit for all manner of audiences. True, he had little time for the musical bureaucracy which sought to restrain compositional flair through blanket decrees. His relationship with officials within the Union of Soviet Composers is vividly described in *Testimony: the Memoirs of Shostakovich*, a book which, if almost certainly owing much to the editor Solomon Volkov's own interpretative mind, none the less seems to voice in words the sentiments which are so strongly expressed in Shostakovich's music. And, more than any amount of writing, it is the music which should occupy our time, for, as Shostakovich said, 'by studying my music you will find the whole truth about me as a man and as an artist'.

GEOFFREY NORRIS

FURTHER READING
Norman Kay: *Shostakovich* (London, 1971); Boris Schwarz: *Music and Musical Life in Soviet Russia 1917–1970* (London, 1972); Hugh Ottaway: *Shostakovich Symphonies* (London, 1978); Solomon Volkov, ed.: *Testimony: the Memoirs of Dmitri Shostakovich* (London and New York, 1979); L. Grigoryev and

Yakov Platek, eds.: *Dmitry Shostakovich: About Himself and his Times* (Moscow, 1981); Eric Roseberry: *Shostakovich: his Life and Times* (London and New York, 1981); Derek C. Hulme: *Dmitri Shostakovich: Catalogue, Bibliography, and Discography* (Muir of Ord, 1982); Christopher Norris, ed.: *Shostakovich: the Man and his Music* (London, 1982).

Si. The seventh degree of the major scale, according to the *solmization system. In tonic sol-fa it has been changed to *te*. In French and Italian usage it has, on the fixed-doh principle, become attached to the note B, in whatever scale it may occur. See *Tonic Sol-fa*.

Sibelius, Jean [Johan] (Julius Christian) (*b* Hämeenlinna, 8 Dec. 1865; *d* Järvenpää, 20 Sept. 1957). Finnish composer and symphonist. He was unquestionably the greatest composer Finland has ever produced, and the most powerful symphonist to have emerged in Scandinavia. He was born in Hämeenlinna, a Russian garrison town in south central Finland, into a Swedish-speaking family. He was educated, however, in the first Finnish-speaking grammar school ever founded in Finland, which brought him into contact with

the world of Finnish mythology through the *Kalevala*. He showed considerable aptitude for the violin and for composition, and adopted the name, Jean, by which he is generally known, when he went to Helsinki (1885). At first, he studied law but soon abandoned it for music, becoming a pupil of Martin Wegelius (1846-1906). After further studies in Berlin and Vienna (1889-91), he returned to Finland and scored a great success with his *Kullervo Symphony* (1892), based like so much of his music on the *Kalevala*. This is a five-movement work for soloists, male chorus, and orchestra, and established him overnight as the leading Finnish composer of the day. A number of other orchestral works followed (*En Saga*, *Karelia*, and the *Four Legends*, which include *The Swan of Tuonela*, originally intended as the prelude to his opera, *The Building of the Boat*) before he composed his first purely instrumental symphony.

During the first years of the 20th century he became closely identified with the cause of Finnish national self-determination, and such works as *Finlandia* (1899, rev. 1900) and *Valse triste* carried his name all over the world, even

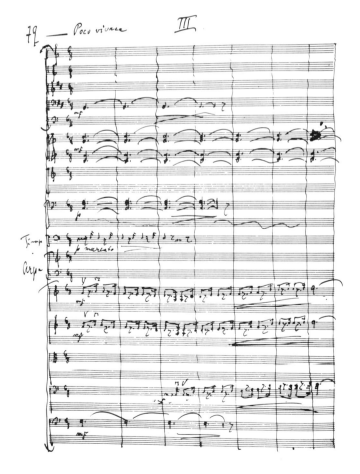

Autograph MS of Sibelius's Sixth Symphony, the beginning of the third movement.

for a time masking his achievement in other fields. If his early music shows the influence of the Viennese classics, Grieg, and Tchaikovsky, his style sheds its neo-romantic nationalist aura after the Second Symphony (1902) and the Violin Concerto (1903, rev. 1905). While retaining a strong national profile, his music assumes a more classical direction in the Third Symphony (1904–7) and *Pohjola's Daughter* (1906), in marked contrast to such contemporaries as Richard Strauss, Skryabin, Mahler, and Ravel. Indeed, this severity of style was taken a stage further in the years immediately following, in the Fourth Symphony (1909–11) and the tone-poem, *The Bard*, though this was in no small measure due to the suspected throat cancer that seemed at the time (1908) to threaten his life.

During this period his music made headway both in Germany, thanks to his publisher, Breitkopf & Härtel, and in England and America, and he travelled widely conducting his own works. The First World War cut him off from his income from Breitkopf and his concert activities outside Scandinavia, and apart from the Fifth Symphony (1915–19) he concentrated on smaller pieces. The post-war musical scene was wholly transformed. His later works and in particular his Sixth and Seventh Symphonies (1923–4) are completely out of step with the musical climate of the times. Indeed, Sibelius spoke of the Sixth Symphony as 'offering pure spring water' at a time when others were mixing cocktails of various hues. After the incidental music to *The Tempest* and the tone-poem *Tapiola* (1926), he spent the remaining three decades of his life in seclusion at Järvenpää, publishing little of note, though it would seem that an Eighth Symphony was nearing completion in 1929. During the 1930s and 1940s, his music enjoyed enormous popularity in England and America and was championed by such conductors as Koussevitzky, Beecham, and Barbirolli as well as influential writers like Newman and Cecil Gray.

The primary sources of his inspiration were Finnish national mythology as enshrined in the *Kalevala*, which was the basis of many of his tone-poems (*Pohjola's Daughter*, *Luonnotar*, and *Tapiola*), and the nordic landscape whose power he so strikingly conveys in almost all his orchestral output. Few composers identified themselves more strongly with nature than did Sibelius. The seven symphonies lie at the heart of his achievement and span his creative career like an Alpine chain. It is impossible (at least after the Second Symphony) from the vantage point of one to predict the character of the next, for their approach to musical form is never the same. Sibelius possessed a highly developed sense of form and feeling for organic growth. He was also a master of the orchestra who created a

Sibelius (1923)

sound world that is completely individual in its handling of colour and layout. His output also includes more than a hundred songs, mainly settings of lyric poets such as Runeberg and Rydberg, writing in Swedish, the finest of which possess as original an atmosphere as his orchestral music. He also wrote extensively for the theatre and his music to *Pelléas et Mélisande* and *Belshazzar's Feast* as well as *The Tempest* shows mastery of smaller forms, hardly less developed than the symphonic music. He wrote more than a hundred piano pieces but these are much less characteristic and many are less than distinguished. Apart from an early preoccupation (1881–90), there is little chamber music of note from his later years save for the String Quartet in D minor (*Voces intimae*, 1909).

ROBERT LAYTON

FURTHER READING
Cecil Gray: *Jean Sibelius* (London, 1931); Gerald Abraham, ed.: *Jean Sibelius: a Symposium* (London, 1947); Robert Layton: *Sibelius* (London, 1965); Erik Tawaststjerna: *Sibelius*, i (Eng. trans., London, 1976).

Siciliana [siciliano] (It.; Fr.: *sicilienne*). 1. 'Sicilian'; *alla siciliana*, 'in the Sicilian style', or 'in the style of the *siciliana*' (see 2 below).

2. A 17th- and 18th-century dance and aria form, probably of Sicilian origin. It was generally in ternary form (ABA), with fairly slow tempo, and in 6/8 or 12/8 metre. It is often in a minor key; other characteristic features include a flowing accompaniment, a gentle lyrical melody, often with a dotted rhythm, and the use of a Neapolitan sixth at cadence points.

In the 18th century, the *siciliana* was popular

as a slow movement in suites and sonatas (e.g. by Corelli and Bach); according to Quantz, the melody should not be embellished, in order to preserve the rhythm. In vocal music (operas and cantatas) it was frequently used in pastoral scenes.

Sieg (Ger.). 'Victory'; *Siegesmarsch*, a march in commemoration of a victory. Beethoven's 'Battle Symphony' is entitled *Wellingtons Sieg* ('Wellington's Victory').

Siège de Corinthe, Le ('The Siege of Corinth'). Opera in three acts by Rossini to a French libretto by Balocchi and A. Soumet. It was first performed in Paris in 1826. The opera is a revision of an earlier opera, *Il Maometto II*, to an Italian libretto by C. della Valle, first performed in Naples in 1820.

Siege of Rhodes, The. Opera with music by Matthew Locke, Henry Lawes, Henry Cooke, Charles Coleman, and George Hudson to a libretto by W. Davenant. It was first performed in London in 1656. The music is now lost, but it is said to be the first English opera.

Siegfried. See *Ring des Nibelungen, Der*.

Siegfried Idyll. Orchestral work by Wagner, composed in 1870 as a birthday gift for his wife Cosima and first performed on Christmas morning 1870, her 33rd birthday. It was played by about 15 musicians, conducted by Wagner, outside Cosima's bedroom in their villa at Lake Tribschen; it was never intended for public performance, but financial hardship forced Wagner to sell it for publication (1878), and he expanded the original scoring. The material is based on themes from an unfinished string quartet, composed in 1864 when Wagner met Cosima, motifs from the opera *Siegfried*, on which he was working when their son Siegfried was born, and a lullaby he had noted (or composed) in 1869.

Siegfrieds Tod ('Siegfried's Death'). Proposed opera by Wagner, the libretto of which he wrote in 1848. From it developed the idea of a four-opera cycle on the legend of Siegfried and the Nibelung's ring. *Siegfrieds Tod*, much revised, eventually became *Götterdämmerung*.

Siegmeister, Elie (*b* New York, 15 Jan. 1909). American composer and writer on music. He studied composition at Columbia University with Seth Bingham (1924-7), privately with Wallingford Riegger (1926) and in Paris with Nadia Boulanger (1927-32). He was then active in New York as a composer, conductor, pianist, and teacher, and in 1949 he was appointed to teach at Hofstra University, near New York. His large output, covering most genres, often shows the use of American material, whether jazz or folk-song. He has also written the books *Harmony and Melody* (Belmont, California, 1965-6) and *The New Music Lover's Handbook* (New York, 1972).   PAUL GRIFFITHS

Sighting. A 15th-century term for a technique used to facilitate the singing of parallel lines of music to the written plainchant. See under *Faburden*.

Sight-singing. The process of converting written or printed musical symbols into the sounds they represent without having previously made a study of the passage in question. Just as, having read and understood the printed word in his script, an actor is able to declaim it, so should the trained musician be able to make the conversion from symbol to sound. (An interesting and significant difference between the two types of symbol is that notes, unlike words, tells us not only the pitch of the sounds but also their length and rhythm.)

Most arts and sciences have methods by which instructions and information can be permanently recorded on paper (probably the most recent development of this has been in the field of choreography, where dancers' steps and movements can now be plotted precisely via the written language of choreology; see *Dance Notation*). Over the centuries the notation of music evolved until it became possible to represent almost any pitch audible to the human ear by means of various staves, each consisting of five lines and four spaces. Another, but rather limited, system of representing pitches is that of *Tonic Sol-fa*.

Sight-singing is an essential part of musical training: its practice develops the student's ability to read and understand the language of music, and its study serves to emphasize to the student the importance in Western tonal music of key structure. Once a key had been established, each of its pitches will have a permanent and immutable relationship to the fundamental note, or tonic, of that key. The second note in the scale of that key will be exactly a tone above the tonic, and the other steps of the scale will also have their own measured distance from it and from one another. The would-be sight-singer must, then, in addition to his grasp of time and rhythm, be able to relate every note to the tonic, mentally hearing, for example, the note B in the key of C as the leading note.

Often students of sight-singing make the mistake of attempting to identify individual notes simply as a certain interval higher or lower than the previous one. This is unhelpful musically, as it does nothing to enhance the student's awareness of key or harmonic structure, and is dangerous because one wrongly judged interval may cause all subsequent pitches to be inaccurate by the same degree as the original error. The correct procedure by which a pitch is related to the key's tonic is the same for every key once the tonic has been established. (This rule applies also to chromatic notes—i.e. pitches which are not normally considered to be in the key in question but which are imported from other keys.)

Sight-singers who will seldom be troubled at the prospect of singing a correct pitch are those who possess 'perfect', or 'absolute', pitch. However, even this gift of being able simply to remember a pitch is often variable. For some musicians perfect pitch is here one day and gone the next, while others seem to possess the ability to recognize a pitch without being able to reproduce it, or even vice versa.

A single pitch heard in isolation is unlikely to carry with it any sort of emotional message, but for many musicians different keys make widely differing emotional impacts, and can even be related to different colours (see *Colour and Music*). While this is purely subjective, one cannot fail to notice how often great composers have used a certain key for a certain mood: one thinks of Beethoven's tragically heroic utterances in C minor, for example, or, perhaps even more significant, the especially expressive and often darkly romantic and chromatic music for which Mozart chose the key of G minor. Is it only a coincidence that works such as the 40th Symphony, the String Quartet K 516, and, perhaps most revealing of all, Pamina's tragic aria in *Die Zauberflöte* are all in this key?

In discussing sight-singing, or in a broader sense the ability to understand intellectually and musically the significance of the printed note, we are dealing with the very grammar of music. It follows that only those musicians who have mastered the technique can be looked upon as being musically literate.   CHRISTOPHER FRY

Signature. Sign placed at the beginning of a composition or movement, and sometimes within it, to indicate the key or change of key (*key signature) or the metre or change of metre (*time signature).

Signature tune. Originally any popular song or dance tune which a performer adopted as a means of identifying himself. In the 1920s and 1930s it was particularly common for dance bands and light orchestras to use a signature tune when broadcasting; it would frequently be played at the end of a programme and sometimes at the beginning, as a sort of signal to listeners. A signature tune was also commonly used to herald the entrance of an individual performer.

Since the 1940s and 1950s signature tunes and 'theme music' have become increasingly associated with regular or long-standing radio and television programmes (e.g. *The Archers, Desert Island Discs, Coronation Street*) and with films, rather than with individual performers. They frequently consist of well-known popular tunes, or of arrangements and reorchestrations of classical themes, or they may be specially composed. As a result of exposure to mass audiences some tunes gain a wider familiarity and appeal than they would otherwise ever be likely to achieve, and they often become popular in their own right, independently of the programmes with which they were first associated.

Significative letters. Early indications of performance instructions concerning such features as tempo, dynamics, etc. See *Notation*, 2.

Silence (Fr.). 'Rest'.

Silent keyboard. A dummy keyboard, with standard layout of keys (though often reduced in compass), which has no sound-producing mechanism of strings, hammers, soundboard, etc. The action of its keys produces a dull but rhythmic clatter, which makes it useful for practice and exercise purposes in environments where a sounding instrument might cause annoyance to others. Silent keyboards have sometimes been used for class-instruction in piano playing.

Silenzio(It.). 'Silence'.

Sillet (Fr.). The nut of the violin.

Silver band. A *brass band in which all the instruments are silver-plated.

Similar motion. See *Motion*.

Simile, simili (It.). 'Similar'. This direction indicates that the player is to continue with some particular effect (such as an accompaniment figure) or technique (such as a kind of bow-stroke). See also under *Segue*.

Simone Boccanegra. Opera in a prologue and three acts by Verdi to a libretto by F. M. Piave and G. Montanelli after Gutiérrez's play *Simón Boccanegra* (1843). It was first performed in Venice in 1857. Arigo Boito revised the libretto and Verdi revised the score, composing a new council chamber scene (Act 1, Scene 2); the new version was first performed in Milan in 1881.

Simonelli, Matteo (*b* Rome, *c*.1618; *d* Rome,

20 Sept. 1696). Italian composer. He spent his life in Rome, at first as a choirboy at the Cappella Giulia, then as *maestro di cappella* at S. Giovanni de Fiorentini, and from 1662 to 1687 as a countertenor at the Cappella Sistina. The old-fashioned, *a cappella* style of his vocal music (three Masses and about 36 motets) earned him the title of the 'Palestrina of the 17th century'.

WENDY THOMPSON

Simple Symphony. Work for string orchestra (or quartet), Op. 4, by Britten, based on tunes he wrote when he was 12 (1925). Its four movements are 'Boisterous Bourrée', 'Playful Pizzicato', 'Sentimental Saraband', and 'Frolicsome Finale', and it was first performed in Norwich in 1934.

Simple time. See *Time signature*.

Simpson, Christopher (*b* c.1605; *d* ? London, 1669). English composer and theorist. He was a virtuoso player of the bass viol and entered the service of a Lincolnshire family after the Civil War (when he fought for the royalists). In his lifetime he was much sought after as a viol teacher, and he is now known principally for his treatises on playing that instrument and on the art of ornamentation; the most important is *The Division-violist* (London, 1659). He also composed some effective chamber music for his instrument.

DENIS ARNOLD

Simpson, Robert (Wilfred Levick) (*b* Leamington Spa, 2 Mar. 1921). English composer. He studied at Durham University and in 1951 joined the BBC music staff. Influenced by the 'developing tonality' of Nielsen, he has maintained an adherence to solidly worked-out forms impelled by diatonic harmony, his works including seven symphonies and eight string quartets. He is also the author of *Carl Nielsen, Symphonist* (London, 1952), *The Essence of Bruckner* (London, 1966), and shorter studies of the symphonies of Sibelius and Beethoven.

PAUL GRIFFITHS

Simpson, Thomas (*bapt.* Milton-next-Sittingbourne [now Milton Regis], Kent, 1 Apr. 1582; *d* ? after 1630). English composer and viol player. Like Dowland, Brade, and other instrumentalists at that time he spent most of his life on the Continent. In 1608 he was in the service of the Heidelberg court (where he married a German woman), and in 1616 of the court of Holstein-Schaumburg; from 1622 until 1625 he was at the Danish court, after which he may have returned to England. He wrote some simple, attractive dance music which influenced Peuerl, Schein, and other German composers of instrumental music.

DENIS ARNOLD

Simultaneity. Group of notes played at the same time. Some writers on atonal music have preferred this term to the more usual 'chord', seeking to avoid the latter's implications of harmonic function.

Sin' (It.). Abbreviation of **sino*, 'until'.

Sincopa (It.). 'Syncopation'.

Sincopas. See *Cinque pas*.

Sinding, Christian (*b* Kongsberg, 11 Jan. 1856; *d* Oslo, 3 Dec. 1941). Norwegian composer. He was the leading Norwegian composer of the generation after Grieg and Svendsen. After studying the violin in Leipzig (1874-8), he turned his energies to composition, attracting attention with a Piano Quartet (1882). He enjoyed early success in the 1880s and 1890s with a Piano Concerto (1889) and his First Symphony (1890). His Piano Quintet (1882-4), written while he was studying composition in Munich, established him as a serious force both at home and abroad, and enjoyed the advocacy of Busoni and the Brodsky quartet. The Norwegian Government gave him an annual grant from 1889 onwards, and later in life he became professor of composition at the newly-founded Eastman School of Music, USA (1921-2). His musical language is frankly Romantic and has its roots in Wagner, Liszt, and Richard Strauss. Although his idiom bears a Scandinavian stamp, there is scant evidence of interest in Norwegian folk music. His output is extensive and comprises 132 opus numbers: there are four symphonies, the last of which was written in his late 70s and first performed on his 80th birthday in 1936; three violin concertos; a string quartet; three piano trios; a host of piano miniatures including his best-known work, *The Rustle of Spring*; and more than 250 songs. It is arguably in the songs that he has made his most distinctive contribution to Norwegian music, for there is a more subtle command of atmosphere and mood than in his larger-scale works. Sinding remained unresponsive to the changing musical climate of his day, and his musical language underwent little change throughout the course of his life.

ROBERT LAYTON

Sinfonia Antartica ('Antarctic Symphony'). Title given by Vaughan Williams to his seventh symphony, for soprano solo, women's chorus, and orchestra, composed 1949-52. It is based on music he wrote for the film *Scott of the Antarctic* (1948) and contains a part for wind-machine.

Sinfonia concertante (It.). See *Symphonie concertante*.

Sinfonia da requiem. Orchestral work, Op. 20, by Britten composed in 1940 in memory of his parents. It was commissioned by the Japanese government to celebrate the (spurious) 2600th anniversary of Mikado's dynasty (1940) but was forcefully rejected because the programmatic titles of the three movements ('Lacrymosa', 'Dies irae', 'Requiem aeternam') refer to the Roman Catholic liturgy. The symphony was first performed in New York in 1941.

Sinfonia espansiva ('Expansive Symphony'). Subtitle of Nielsen's Symphony No. 3, Op. 27, composed in 1910-11. The score includes parts for soprano and baritone soloists.

Sinfonia semplice ('Simple Symphony'). Subtitle of Nielsen's Symphony No. 6, Op. posth., composed in 1924-5.

Sinfonietta (Fr.: *symphoniette*). A small-scale symphony, either in terms of length, or of the size of the orchestra. Janáček's Sinfonietta employs a large orchestra, but the movements are shorter than those of the average symphony, and the work could be described as an orchestral suite. The term has in recent years been used to describe a chamber ensemble, such as the London Sinfonietta.

Sinfonische Dichtung (Ger.). 'Symphonic poem'.

Singbar (Ger.). 'Singable', or 'in a singing style'.

Singend (Ger.). 'Singing', in a singing style, similar to *cantabile*.

Singhiozzando (It.). 'Sobbingly'.

Singing Mice. Wide interest in these performers was aroused in 1937 by a series of competitions held by radio in the United States, followed by an international competition, also by radio, in which eminent mouse vocalists of the United States, Canada, and Britain were heard in friendly artistic rivalry. A scientist's description of a prima donna examined by him ran:

Its voice ranged through two octaves, the notes partly resembling the high tones of the lark, partly the long-drawn flute-like tones of the nightingale, and partly the deep, liquid trilling of a canary.

Post-mortem examination of such performers has disclosed the disappointing fact that they do not, like the birds and the humans, sing out of the joy or sorrow of their heart, but merely out of an inflammation of their respiratory organs, their song being, in fact, merely an accidentally artistic wheeze.   PERCY SCHOLES

Singing saw. See *Flexatone*.

Single-tonguing. See under *Tonguing*.

Singspiel (Ger., 'sing-play'). Although the term was in use before the 1700s, it acquired its most commonly accepted meaning—an opera in which musical numbers are interspersed with spoken dialogue—in the early 18th century. From around the 1750s the influence of French *opéra comique* and English *ballad opera helped to polarize usage of the word to mean a comic opera with spoken dialogue (though it should be noted that when Mozart's *opere buffe* were given in Germany they were referred to as *Singspiele*). The operas of Benda and Hiller conform to the accepted pattern of comic works with spoken dialogue, the genre reaching its zenith in such operas as Mozart's *Die Entführung aus dem Serail* (1782) and *Die Zauberflöte*, and in Beethoven's *Fidelio*—though this last, with its essentially heroic, serious plot, should more properly be regarded as an early German Romantic work. See also *Opera, 7, 8*.

Sinistro, sinistra (It., sometimes abbreviated to *S*.). 'Left'; *sinistra mano*, 'left hand'.

Sink-a-pace (from Fr. *Cinque pas*). Name by which the original five-step form of the *galliard was known.

Sino, sin' (It.). 'Until'; e.g. *sin' al segno*, go on 'until the sign'. See *Al segno*.

Sir John in Love. Opera in four acts by Vaughan Williams to his own libretto after Shakespeare's *The Merry Wives of Windsor* (1600-1) with interpolations from other Elizabethan dramatists. The score quotes several folk-songs, including *Greensleeves*. The work was first performed in London in 1929. See also *In Windsor Forest*.

Sir Roger de Coverley. English country dance to a tune of uncertain origin, being a variant of *The Maltman*, a Scottish tune sometimes called *Roger the Cavalier*. It was first printed by Playford in 1685. Arrangements have been made of it by several 20th-century composers, among them Bridge and Grainger.

Sirventes, sirventois. A type of song composed by the *troubadours* and *trouvères*, where the subject-matter is concerned with morality, political events, etc. The 13th-century *trouvère* Thibaut de Navarre wrote a *sirventois* called 'Dex est ausi comme li pellicans' ('God is like the pelican').

Sistrum and Jingles. 1. The sistrum was originally a cult instrument of Ancient Egypt sacred to the goddess Hathor, later taking part in other rites, and in Rome associated with the Isis cult. It was most commonly made (Fig. 1a) of a flat bronze strip bent in a loop with a handle. Through holes in the strip two or three thin rods pass loosely from side to side, their ends bent to stop them falling out. Since it gives a soft jingle when waved it was listed by the Ancients among musical instruments (the word 'sistrum' itself is Greek). Some late examples have metal rings or discs on the rods, increasing the jingle. Today such a sistrum, with discs, numbers among orchestral percussion instruments sometimes demanded.

2. The name 'sistrum' has also been given to other instruments: in the Renaissance period to the triangle, xylophone, and even the cittern (through confusion with French *cistre*). And there is another orchestral 'sistrum' in use, also known as 'Chinese bell-tree': a set of small cup-shaped bells (Fig. 1b) tuned to a scale, mounted one above the other on a metal stem, the largest on top so that their edges can overlap. They are struck with a small beater; a separate set can provide the accidentals. This type has been known for a century or more: some believe that the *sistro* in Rossini's *Barber of Seville* was something of the kind. A keyboard version also exists, named 'celestette'.

3. Common jingling devices include the jingle ring or 'Brazilian tambourine' (Fig. 1c)—an instrument resembling a tambourine but without the membrane, it is an old traditional dance instrument from Sicily to the Azores, and is today also in use by rock singers and in percussion bands.

Many folk versions have jingle discs—or metal bottle tops—loosely nailed in groups in a row along a wooden holder, or on wires fixed in slots in the same (Fig. 1d). The holder may be notched for scraping with a stick to set the jingles going (for instance in Naples in the Piedigrotta procession). A larger type, with bottle tops nailed in pairs to a broomstick, is the 'lagerphone' featured in Australian 'bush music': the stick is notched, or else 'bowed' with a notched stick (compare *Bumbass*).

For 'jingle bells', see *Sleigh bells*.

4. The jingle of spurs as a horseman entered the scene on foot gave rise to imitation of the sound in operetta (as in Johann Strauss's *Die Fledermaus*) by means of some device such as that shown in Fig. 1e, often found in old theatre-drummers' kits: the steel discs, slightly dished and strung loose on the rod, clink together as the instrument is moved vigorously up and down. The discs are checked by a felt washer at each end of the rod.

ANTHONY BAINES

Sitār. Indian lute, one of the major instruments of Indian classical music. It is large in size, the top leaning well above the head of the player as he sits cross-legged on a carpet.

The body, onion-shaped, is of a dried gourd up to 16″ wide, with portions cut away (i) to make the opening for the wooden block to which the neck is attached, and (ii) for the wooden belly, fig-shaped in outline, slightly convex and without soundhole. The broad neck, 3″ wide, is of a hollow construction. Often a smaller gourd is bolted to it below the region of the main tuning-pegs. Some 21 brass frets are tied to the neck, arching above it to leave room below for sympathetic strings (see *Stringed Instruments*, 6).

The strings, of metal, form three groups. (i) Four principal playing strings usually tuned (taking the tonic of the music as C) *f*, *c*, *G*, *C*. (ii) Three thin strings on the bass side (the player's right), *g*, *c′*, *c″*, the last two of these with their pegs in the side of the neck (Fig. 1, A, B) and with upright nuts further down (indicated by the black dots at C, D); these are the *chikari* strings, not stopped but struck together as a kind of rhythmic drone. (iii) Eleven sympathetic strings with their pegs also on the side of the neck and tuned to the scale of the *rāga* in which the player is to perform. The bridge of the *sitār* (as of the *vīṇā, from which this bridge is derived) is of a unique kind, being a broad plate of bone or horn (E) with the top surface very carefully sloped down in the direction of the frets, with the effect of filling the sound with high partials, giving a nasal ringing. The sympathetic strings have a smaller, lower bridge placed just above.

The *sitār* is played with a finger-pick (see

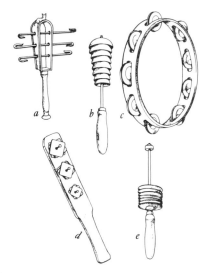

Fig. 1

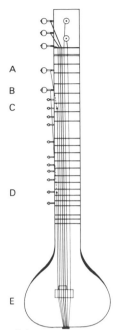

Fig. 1. Plan view of sitar.

Plectrum, 1) made of a loop of fine wire and worn on the right index. The fingering of the strings is with the left middle and index fingers, pressing behind the frets and frequently using that essential expressive device by which a string is pulled sideways by the left hand after striking with the right, to raise the pitch by up to a fifth. For this reason the strings are seen to lie to one side of the neck, allowing room for this sideways deflection over a fret.

In performance the repeated tonic or 'drone' essential to Indian music is very often supplied by another type of lute, the *tambūrā,* with four strings (no frets) tuned to the tonic and the dominant, and sounded open, always in the same order. For fine tuning each string of the *tambūrā* is threaded, beyond the bridge, with a bone bead which, if shifted downwards, presses on the belly like a wedge to tighten the string.

An essential partner to the *sitār*-player is the drummer, with *tablā.* It would exceed the scope of this article to try to summarize the form and subtlety of their combined, improvised performance.

The *sitār* was developed through the Muslim period from one of the Persian 'long lutes' (compare *Lute,* 4*a*), by degrees absorbing technical features of the *vīṇā* as demanded by the nature of Indian music. The *sarod* is another Indian lute, of an Afghan type, with very deep wooden body and skin belly. Yet others are 19th-century or modern elaborations based upon the *sitār.*

See also *Indian Music,* 3*a.*

ANTHONY BAINES

Six, Les. Name applied in 1920 by the critic Henri Collet (by analogy with the Russian *Five) to Georges Auric, Louis Durey, Arthur Honegger, Darius Milhaud, Francis Poulenc, and Germaine Tailleferre. The group were briefly united by their adherence to the flip anti-romanticism put forward in Cocteau's manifesto *Le coq et l'arlequin* (1918), but they soon took quite different paths. Honegger, who had never shared the others' idolization of Satie, became a serious-minded composer of symphonies, while Milhaud pursued the technique of *poly-tonality in his enormous output; Durey became a committed socialist and Tailleferre faded into obscurity. Only Poulenc and Auric retained some loyalty to the group's original ideal that music should be spare, witty, and up-to-date.

PAUL GRIFFITHS

FURTHER READING
Martin Cooper: *French Music* (London, 1951); Rollo Myers: *Modern French Music* (Oxford, 1971).

Six épigraphes antiques ('Six Ancient Inscriptions'). Work for piano duet by Debussy, composed in 1914 (incorporating music from his *Chansons de Bilitis*). The pieces are *Pour invoquer Pan* ('To Invoke Pan'), *Pour un tombeau sans nom* ('For a Nameless Tomb'), *Pour que la nuit soit propice* ('That Night may be Propitious'), *Pour la danseuse aux crotales* ('For the Dancing Girl with Castanets'), *Pour l'égyptienne* ('For the Egyptian Girl'), and *Pour remercier la pluie du matin* ('To Thank the Morning Rain').

Six-four chord. See under *First inversion.*

Sixteenth-note (Amer.). Semiquaver (♪).

Sixth. See *Interval.*

Sixth, Added. See *Added sixth.*

Six-three chord. See *First inversion.*

Sixty-fourth-note (Amer.). Hemidemisemiquaver (♬).

Ska. See under *Reggae.*

Skalkottas, Nikos (*b* Halkis, Eubea, 21 Mar. 1904; *d* Athens, 20 Sept. 1949). Greek composer. He studied the violin at the Athens Conservatory (1914-20) and with Willy Hess at the Berlin Musikhochschule (1921-3). Remaining in Berlin, he had composition lessons from Weill (1924-5), Jarnach (1925-7), and Schoenberg (1927-31). In 1933 he returned to Athens, where he earned his living as a back-desk violinist and composed an enormous quantity of music. Very little of this was played during his lifetime, and it was not until the 1960s that

Skalkottas's stature began to be recognized. He developed his own serial techniques in music which is often densely elaborated and of long duration: the Third Piano Concerto (1938–9), lasting for an hour, is not untypical. Among other works of this character are four string quartets, four piano suites, two symphonic suites and the single-movement symphony *The Return of Ulysses* (1942–3). Skalkottas's output of serial music is probably greater than that of any other composer, but he also produced a large number of tonal works at the same time. These include a colourful collection of 36 Greek Dances for orchestra (1931–6) as well as large-scale abstract pieces. PAUL GRIFFITHS

Skolion (Gk.; Ger.: *Skolie*). A drinking song. The title was used by Schubert for two of his *Lieder*, 'Lasst im Morgenstrahl des Mai'n' (1815) and 'Mädchen entsiegelten' (1816).

Škroup, František (Jan) (*b* Osice, East Bohemia, 3 June 1801; *d* Rotterdam, 7 Feb. 1862). Czech composer and conductor. Born into a musical family, Škroup received with his brothers Ignác (1807–89) and Jan Nepomuk (1811–92) a thorough introduction to the skills of music from their father, the composer Dominik Josef Škroup (1766–1830). František's achievement surpassed those of his brothers though Jan Nepomuk had some success with his opera *Švédové v Praze* ('A Swedish Girl in Prague', 1844). After studying law in Prague, Škroup turned his attention to the cultivation of opera in Czech, an interest probably dating from a stay in Hradec Králové (1814–19), a rising centre of nationalism. In 1823 he organized a performance of Weigl's *Die Schweizerfamilie* in a Czech translation, the first such production in Prague in the 19th century. This was followed in 1826 by a *Singspiel*, *Dráteník* ('The Tinker') to a libretto by Chmelenský, the first Czech opera. It seemed that he would consolidate the enormous success of *Dráteník* when in 1827 he was appointed assistant *Kapellmeister* of the Estates Theatre and in 1837 first *Kapellmeister*, a post held until 1857. But his operas *Oldřich and Božena* (1828) and *Libušin sňatek* ('Libuse's Wedding', 1835) met with little public interest, and in later years Škroup resorted to German librettos. His music for J. K. Tyl's play *Fidlovačka* (1834) was one of his few successes in these years, mainly for the emotive song 'Kde domov můj?' ('Where is my home?') which was adopted as the Czech part of the Czechoslovakian national anthem in 1918. In 1857 Škroup left Prague to become conductor of the Opera in Rotterdam where he died. He also contributed to the national revival by compiling six volumes of 'Patriotic Songs' by Czech composers, but the naïvety and frequent unoriginality of Škroup's musical idiom limited the effectiveness of his pioneering achievements for Czech music. JAN SMACZNY

Skryabin, Alexander (Nikolayevich) (*b* Moscow, 6 Jan. 1872; *d* Moscow, 27 Apr. 1915). Russian composer. He inherited his musical instinct from his mother, who was a fine pianist.

He early showed a remarkable musical gift, being able, from the age of six onwards, to play on the piano almost anything he heard once performed. His education was received in the school for training military officers, but latterly he also attended the Moscow Conservatory, where he studied under Taneyev and Arensky. Then Belyayev, the patron-publisher of Russian music, took him up, planned recital tours for him, and published his compositions as they were finished. He taught in his old conservatory, but the claims of recital-travelling (in Europe and America) and of composition caused the relinquishment of this activity; for a time he lived in Brussels. He owed much to the help of the conductor Koussevitzky, who brought about many performances of his works. In 1914 he was in London, giving piano recitals. He was then suffering from a tumour of the lip and within about a year died.

His strange mystical theory, uniting aesthetics with religion and cosmogony, had much in common with theosophy, and some of the

Skryabin (1914)

works devoted to its musical exposition may be described as a sort of philosophical programme music. Among works so to be classified are the big orchestral compositions, including *The Divine Poem* and *The Poem of Fire* (or 'Prometheus', 1913); this last has a line in its score for a keyboard of light, throwing a play of colour on to a screen.

The piano writing of Skryabin is very able; he set out as a close student, admirer, and imitator (yet with great originality) of Chopin. Gradually his harmonic idiom changed, until at last he was making much use of a chord of his own, a chord of superposed fourths (see *Mystic chord*). His melodic idiom also became very distinctive particularly in the characteristic use of many upward leaps; his rhythms became extremely complex; the powerful expression of the most passionate moods became a notable feature of his works, and his climaxes are often overwhelming.

He did not use native idiom or attempt to express national thought or feeling, yet in the temperament that shows through his music he is essentially Russian.

See also *Colour and Music*, 4.

PERCY SCHOLES, rev.

FURTHER READING
Hugh Macdonald: *Skryabin* (London, 1978).

Skye Boat Song. Popular 19th-century Scottish song which, contrary to popular belief, has no connection with the flight of Bonnie Prince Charlie to the island of Skye. In fact, the tune is partly a sea-shanty heard in 1879 by Miss Annie MacLeod (later Lady Wilson), who completed the tune herself. The words were by Sir Harold Boulton, and date from 1884. Later Robert Louis Stevenson supplied another set of words to the tune, which he mistakenly believed to be a genuine folk-tune. Both texts include the phrase 'Over the sea to Skye'.

Slade, Julian (Penkivil) (*b* London, 28 May 1930). English composer. He studied at Eton and Cambridge and composed two musicals while still at university. He joined the Bristol Old Vic and composed incidental music for various productions, including a complete new score for Sheridan's *The Duenna* (1953). He had an enormous success with the musical *Salad Days* composed for Bristol in 1953; it transferred to the Vaudeville Theatre, London, enjoying a run of 2,283 performances. His subsequent musicals have included *Free as Air* (1957), *Follow that Girl* (1960), *Vanity Fair* (1962), and *Trelawney* (1972).

PETER GAMMOND

Slancio (It.). 'Impetus', 'outburst'; *con slancio*, 'with impetus', 'with dash'.

Slargando, slargandosi (It.). 'Slowing down', i.e. *rallentando*.

Slavonic Dances. Two sets of dances by Dvořák, composed for piano duet but often heard in the orchestral versions made by the composer. The first set (Nos. 1–8), Op. 46, dates from 1878; the second set (Nos. 9–16), Op. 72, dates from 1886. The dances are in the style of folk music but the melodies are original.

Slavonic Rhapsodies. Three orchestral works, Op. 45, by Dvořák, composed in 1878. The first is in D major, the second in G minor, and the third in A♭ major. They are strongly reminiscent of folk music idioms but the melodies are original.

Sleeping Beauty, The (*Spyashchaya krasavitsa*). Ballet in a prologue and three acts by Tchaikovsky to a libretto by M. Petipa and I. Vsevolozhsky after Perrault's *La belle au bois dormant*. It was choreographed by Petipa and first performed in St Petersburg in 1890. In London in 1921 Diaghilev staged it as *The Sleeping Princess*; the last act is sometimes performed separately as *Aurora's Wedding*.

Sleigh bells. Today the usual orchestral and trade term for the well-known spherical shaken objects popularly known as 'jingle bells' or to musicologists as 'pellet bells' (Fr.: *grelots*; Ger.: *Schellen*; It.: *sonagli*). Each bell has a slit-like mouth and a metal or clay pellet inside. They were once cast in bronze, the pellet embedded in the core prior to casting. Now they are forged or pressed, and sewn in a row on a leather strap (Fig. 1*a*) or a long handle. Since the Middle Ages they have hung from the collars of horses and dogs or been sewn to straps tied round

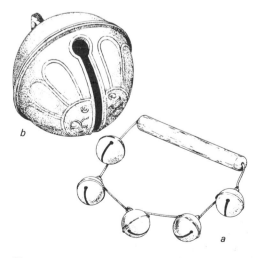

b

a

Fig. 1

dancers' legs, or to jesters' caps; also attached to tambourines (along with or in place of jingle discs) and to the bow-sticks of folk-fiddles (often in Greece).

The term 'sleigh bells' derives from light music, beginning with Mozart's German Dances K 605 (see also *Post-horn*). In this work they are intended to sound chords, needing tuned sets. There have been in Britain, in the past, amateur groups playing tunes on such tuned pellet bells, the bells for each note sewn to an individual leather strap. Orchestrally the size, irrespective of tuning, can be important. The old carriage and harness bells were often large, 4″ or more across (Fig. 1*b*), and of thicker metal than the bells which one ordinarily buys nowadays, and produced a more powerful and deeper sound—with the result that the largest were known as 'rumblers'. They are needed in works like Elgar's *Cockaigne* Overture (1902), where they are shaken *fff* under a long *tremolo* sign, supported by the triangle.

ANTHONY BAINES

Slendro. A tuning system used in gamelan music. See *Indonesia, 2a, 3a, 4.*

Slentando (It.). 'Slowing down', i.e. the same as *rallentando.*

Slide. 1. (Fr.: *glissade, port de voix*; It.: *portamento*). In string playing, a method of changing position between two notes (not adjacent). It was much used for expressive effect in the late 19th and early 20th centuries, and often considerably abused. Ex. 1 shows its usual indication;

Ex. 1

but Bach notated it as shown in Ex. 2.

Ex. 2

Paganini introduced a virtuoso version by executing chromatic scale passages, often in thirds, with the same finger or fingers.

2. (Fr.: *coulé, flatté*; Ger.: *Schleifer*). An ornament common to the Baroque period, consisting of two short notes rising by step to the main note. It may be indicated by a sign or by small notes (see Ex. 3), and is found as late as Beethoven's String Quartet Op. 135.

Ex. 3

On keyboard instruments, the first note may be required to be sustained (Ex. 4).

Ex. 4

Baroque   19th century

3. The telescopic joint of the trombone and of the slide trumpet; see *Trombone, 1; Trumpet, 1.*

Slide flute (Fr.: *flûte à coulisse*) [also known as 'Swanee whistle' or 'lotus flute']. An instrument resembling a *flageolet but with a plunger pushed in and out from the lower end by one hand (and with no fingerholes). In India slide flutes of bamboo are made as toys. As commercially made in the West, now usually in synthetic resin, the flute is about a foot long and allows a 7″ movement of the plunger, giving a musical range approaching two octaves upwards from about middle E♭ (*e♭′*). The slide flute is particularly suited to *glissandi* and Ravel thus introduces it in his *L'enfant et les sortilèges* (1925).

ANTHONY BAINES

Slit drum. Wooden percussion instrument native to many tropical peoples. It has no drumskin or membrane, so the term 'slit gong' has also been proposed, but one has become used to 'slit drum' (in Germany it is similarly *Holztrommel*). It varies greatly in size, from a tree trunk three times a man's height to a small portable block, hollowed out through a length-

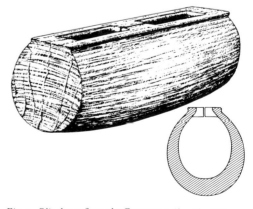

Fig. 1. Slit drum from the Cameroons (length 18″).

ways slit. The two sides of the slit are usually of different thickness, so when struck (with a stout club) the thinner side gives a lower sound than the thicker (the fundamental frequency of a vibrating plate rises with thickness). Many instruments are made as shown, the slit being cut to leave two projecting sounding surfaces in the middle. Slit drums may be strictly bound to ritual, or be used for sending messages in drum language based on speech tones—one form of 'talking drum'.

Some modern compositions have incorporated slit drums: Stockhausen in *Gruppen* calls for six giving contrasted pitches, borrowing them from an ethnological museum for the first performance. Some more easily-made substitutes for the real thing have become available from percussion manufacturers.

ANTHONY BAINES

Slur. A curved line used in musical notation to group notes for various purposes. It commonly indicates that the notes it affects are to be played or sung *legato*, or smoothly (Ex. 1). On string instruments this normally implies that the notes should be taken in one bow-stroke or, if this is physically impossible, that a change of bow-stroke should be imperceptible. In music for wind instruments, and in vocal music, the slur normally implies that the affected notes should be taken in one breath. If notes within a slur have dots above or below them (Ex. 2), they are to be played slightly detached (i.e. *mezzo-*

staccato, but not as detached as *staccato*). Additionally in vocal music the slur is used to call attention to the fact that a single syllable is to be sung to several notes (Ex. 3). A slur over an extended group of notes may indicate the limits of a *phrase and may encompass smaller groups of slurred notes (Ex. 4).

A curved line similar to the slur may be used to indicate a *portamento effect; the same sign between two adjacent notes of the same pitch serves as a *tie.

See also *Performance Practice*, 8.

Smalley, Denis (*b* Nelson, New Zealand, 16 May 1946). New Zealand composer. He studied at the University of Canterbury and at Victoria University of Wellington. In 1971 he studied in Messiaen's composition classes in Paris, and then at the University of York (1972–5). From 1972 to 1975 he was northern music critic for *The Guardian*. In 1975 his *Gradual* (1974) for tape and clarinettist playing amplified bass clarinet and trombaphone (trombone with a sax mouthpiece) won the international prize for electronic music composition sponsored by 'Fylkingen', the Swedish Composers' Organization. In 1977 his *Darkness After Time's Colours* (1976) won second prize in the Bourges Electro-acoustic awards. From 1975 to 1976 he was composition fellow at the University of East Anglia, where he became lecturer in music and director of the Electronic and Recording Studio. He was a member of the Advisory Panel of the Arts Council of Great Britain (1978–82) and chairman of the British section of the ISCM (1979–82). His other important works include *Pentes* ('Slopes', 1974, an electronic piece), *Pneum* (1976, revised 1982) for five amplified vocalists and percussionists with five talking drums, five tuning forks, two Chinese gongs, and tam-tam, *Chanson de Geste* (1978) for amplified voice and clavichord, *The Pulses of Time* (1979), *Word Within* (1981), and *Vortex* (1982). His accomplished use of the electro-acoustic medium shows a keen intelligence, an original approach to sounds, and a dramatically convincing way of using them.

J. M. THOMSON

Ex. 1

Ex. 2

Ex. 3

Long to— reign— o - ver us

Ex. 4

Smalley, Roger (*b* Swinton, Manchester, 26 July 1943). English composer. He studied with Peter Racine Fricker and John White at the Royal College of Music (1961–5), with Alexander Goehr at Morley College (1962) and with Stockhausen in Cologne (1965–6). His early works, including the *Missa brevis* for 16 voices (1966–7), use English Renaissance material and advanced serial methods in a manner close to Maxwell Davies. Later, in such pieces as *Pulses* for brass, percussion, and electronics (1969), the influence of Stockhausen became paramount.

In imitation of Stockhausen, Smalley founded a live electronic ensemble, Intermodulation, in 1969; he has also appeared as a pianist. In 1976 he took a post at the University of Perth, Australia.   PAUL GRIFFITHS

Smetana, Bedřich (Friedrich) (*b* Litomyšl, Bohemia, 2 Mar. 1824; *d* Prague, 12 May 1884). Czech composer. Regarded in his country as the major Czech national composer of the 19th century he was decisively influential at a formative stage, and established virtually single-handed a style of national opera.

1. *The Early Years.* Born into a reasonably prosperous family—his father was a brewer—Smetana exhibited a prodigious musical talent and quickly outgrew any teaching available locally. He attended school in Německý Brod and Prague but neglected his studies in favour of the capital's cultural life and was sent to study in Plzeň in 1840. He had composed and arranged for string quartet in Prague and continued to write for the piano, considering the Three Impromptus (1841) as the start of his composing career. In 1843 he began studying composition with Joseph Proksch (1794-1864) in Prague, sustaining himself by teaching the piano. Although a fine pianist, he had to abandon a concert tour in 1847 because of poor attendance. More encouraging was Liszt's acceptance of the dedication of Smetana's Op. 1

Smetana

(*Six morceaux caractéristiques*, 1848) and later publication by Kistner (1851). A music institute he opened in 1848 was not a financial success, but with continued teaching Smetana was able to support a wife, marrying Kateřina Kolářová in 1849. He supplemented his income by playing to the deposed Emperor Ferdinand, but the next years were marked by economic difficulties and personal tragedy with the death of his daughters, in memory of the oldest of whom he wrote the G minor Piano Trio (1855). Orchestral works composed at the time included the *Triumph-Symphonie* (1854) written in the hope of a national revival after the Prague revolt of 1848; no reforms were forthcoming, and, hearing of a post in Göteborg, Smetana left for Sweden in October 1856.

The favourable impression of his first few months in Sweden led Smetana to think of settling permanently. However, the ill health of his wife and his feelings of artistic isolation brought a return to Prague in the spring of 1859. Kateřina died on the journey, and Smetana went back to Göteborg. In 1860 he brought his second wife Bettina Ferdinandová to Sweden, but he was ready to make a final return to Prague and needed no encouragement when the opening of the Provisional Theatre for the performance of Czech plays and opera was announced in February 1861. Apart from piano music, Smetana's work in Sweden—principally the symphonic poems *Richard III* (1858), *Wallenstein's Camp* (1859), and *Hakon Jarl* (1861)—confirmed his interest in the music of Liszt and attracted much adverse criticism.

2. *Years of Maturity.* His years in Prague were devoted to composing national operas, the first of which, *Braniboři v Čechách* ('The Brandenburgers in Bohemia', 1862-3), was a huge success when premièred in 1866. The same year saw the less successful first performance of the *Prodaná nevěsta* ('The Bartered Bride'), though it began to make its way in a revised version later in 1866. Apart from the directorship of the choral society Hlahol, Smetana failed to gain any major appointments until in autumn 1866 against much conservative opposition he realized a major ambition by becoming conductor of the Provisional Theatre. He did much to expand the foreign repertory and encourage Czech works during his tenure, though his own operas *Dalibor* (1868) and *Dvě vdovy* ('The Two Widows', 1874) were the most substantial national contributions. Smetana's time in office was marked by controversy, but despite vicissitude he completed *Libuše* in 1872 and began planning the cycle of Symphonic Poems *Má vlast* ('My Country', 1874-9). Before finishing the first of these in 1874 symptoms of syphilis became apparent, the most alarming being

increasing deafness. Extended leave from the theatre was followed by resignation and financial difficulty. The depression experienced by the composer found expression in the programmatic String Quartet in E minor, 'From my Life' (1876). In the same year he completed the comedy *Hubička* ('The Kiss') and despite increasing difficulty in working composed *Tajemství* ('The Secret', 1878) and completed *Má vlast*. The performance of the festival opera *Libuše* at the opening of the National Theatre in 1881 was a personal triumph although Smetana, now totally deaf, appeared to be shunned by the theatre authorities. The performance of his last opera *Čertova stěna* ('The Devil's Wall', 1882) was poorly prepared and by comparison fell rather flat. Against a background of growing disability he completed his second String Quartet (D minor, 1883) and an introduction and polonaise for an orchestral suite entitled *Prague Carnival*; he also made sketches for an opera based on *Twelfth Night* called *Viola*. The distressing final stages of his illness ended with his death in a Prague lunatic asylum in 1884.

3. *Smetana's Style.* The sources of Smetana's musical style range widely: Schumann may be detected as an influence on his early piano music; Mendelssohn and in particular Liszt in the orchestral works and the use of thematic transformation in the Piano Trio and later the operas. On returning from Sweden, Smetana gave himself almost entirely to the creation of a national style of opera composition which provided a model and stimulus for a generation of Czech composers. Smetana's patriotic feelings had been well to the fore in 1848, and though a German speaker Smetana took pains to improve his command of Czech in the 1860s. He drew surprisingly little on folk models in constructing his national style, making only occasional use of folk-song. Folk-dance rhythms occurred more frequently and the polka in particular gave a suitably Bohemian accent to his musical vernacular. In the opera Italian influence and that of German early Romanticism is felt in *The Brandenburgers in Bohemia*, Wagner in *Libuše*, and Meyerbeer as late as *The Devil's Wall*. Smetana's personal imprint was always apparent and his well-developed feeling for dramatic pacing far outstripped the efforts of his Czech predecessors. The cycle of symphonic poems *Má vlast* celebrating the history, mythology, and landscape of Bohemia is still an important point of musical reference for his nation though the handful of chamber works embody utterances of a more personal nature reflecting a less optimistic view of fate. Outside Czechoslovakia his choral works are largely neglected: they represent a small but significant contribution to

a form which played a major part in the country's musical revival. If Smetana has never acquired the international standing of his younger contemporary Dvořák, his achievement is regarded in Czechoslovakia as the more fundamental.   JAN SMACZNY

FURTHER READING
Brian Large: *Smetana* (London, 1970); John Clapham: *Smetana* (London, 1972).

Smith, John Christopher (i) [Schmidt, Johann Christoph] (*b* Kitzingen, 17 Mar. 1683; *d* London, Jan. 1763). German music publisher and editor. He met Handel in Halle, and in 1716 was invited to join him in London, where he set up as a music editor and publisher and acted as agent for the sale of Handel's works. He remained with Handel, acting as copyist and general amanuensis, until that master's death. His son, **John Christopher Smith (ii)** (*b* Ansbach, 1712; *d* Bath, 3 Dec. 1795), was a composer. He studied with Handel, Roseingrave, and Pepusch, and in 1733 made his début as an opera composer with *Ulysses*. He was organist of the Foundling Hospital chapel from 1754, where he directed the annual performance of Handel's *Messiah*, and in 1762 he entered the royal service as music master to the dowager Princess of Wales.

The younger Smith's compositions include Italian and English operas (two of them, *The Fairies*, 1755, and *The Tempest*, 1756, were based on Shakespeare), oratorios (including *Paradise Lost*, after Milton, 1760), and other vocal and instrumental pieces. Handel bequeathed his manuscripts to John Christopher Smith (i), and the younger Smith presented them to George III; they now form part of the Royal Music Library at the British Museum.
                                    WENDY THOMPSON

Smith, John Stafford (*bapt.* Gloucester, 30 Mar. 1750; *d* London, 21 Sept. 1836). English composer and scholar. He studied with Boyce and entered the Chapel Royal as a choirboy; he was to stay in its employ until 1817, becoming a Gentleman in 1784, one of the organists in 1802, and Master of the Children in 1805. He is remembered for his vocal music (see *Glee*), and his song 'To Anacreon in Heaven' provided the tune for the American national anthem 'The Star-spangled Banner'. However, he was also important for his work as an editor and writer, and John Hawkins acknowledged his debt to Smith in the preface to his *General History of the Science and Practice of Music* (1776–89). Among Smith's collection of manuscripts were such valuable sources as the *Old Hall Manuscript* and the *Mulliner Book*.

Smith Brindle, Reginald (*b* Bamber Bridge,

Lancaster, 5 Jan. 1917). He studied at the University College of North Wales, Bangor (1946–9), with Pizzetti at the Accademia di Santa Cecilia, Rome (1949–52), and with Dallapiccola privately in Florence (1949, 1952–3). He has retained contacts with Italy (he worked for Italian radio from 1956 to 1961) and has been influenced by Berio, Maderna, Donatoni, and others in his compositions. In 1967 he was appointed lecturer at his alma mater, now Bangor University, and from 1970 to 1980 was professor of music at the University of Surrey. He has written the books *Serial Composition* (London, 1966), *Contemporary Percussion* (London, 1970), and *The New Music* (London, 1975).

PAUL GRIFFITHS

Smorendo (It.). Becoming gradually softer and slower.

Smorzando (It., sometimes abbreviated to *smorz.*). 'Extinguishing', i.e. toning down, dying away to nothing.

Smyth, (Dame) **Ethel** (Mary) (*b* Marylebone, 22 Apr. 1858; *d* Woking, 9 May 1944). English composer, conductor, and suffragette. One of the most courageous and unconventional women of her time, she came of a military family and developed the capacity to out-general her opponents. In 1877 she went to Leipzig Conservatory, studying first with Reinecke, later with Herzogenberg. In Germany she was en-

Ethel Smyth (1943)

couraged by Brahms, Grieg, Dvořák, Joachim, and Clara Schumann. She wrote an interesting account of Mahler's operatic period in Leipzig in the 1880s. Her Mass in D, performed in London in 1893, surprised the chauvinistic world of that day by its power and scope, but England offered no opportunities to her in the way of productions of her operas. Her first, *Fantasio*, was produced in Weimar (1898), *Der Wald* in Berlin (1902, and Covent Garden the same year), and *The Wreckers* at Leipzig (1906, conducted by Nikisch). Remarkably, she wrote her own libretto for *Fantasio* in German and that for *The Wreckers* in French (a French production seemed to be likely).

The Wreckers, a tale set in an 18th-century Cornish village, was conducted by Beecham at Covent Garden in 1909. About this time Smyth enlisted in Mrs Pankhurst's army of campaigners for women's suffrage, writing the *March of the Women* in 1911. She was imprisoned for a spell in Holloway. In 1916 she conducted her comic opera *The Boatswain's Mate*. She was created DBE in 1922. Her last stage works were two one-act operas, *Fête galante* (Birmingham 1923) and *Entente cordiale* (London 1925). Other post-war works were the concerto for violin, horn, and orchestra (1927) and the 'choral symphony' *The Prison* (1930).

In the last 15 years of her life Dame Ethel wrote little music but added four volumes to her two-volume autobiography, *Impressions that Remained*, published in 1919. Her music is generally considered to have been too eclectic for its own durability. There is certainly a disconcertingly sharp variation between originality and conventionality, and between experiment and conservatism, but parts of the Mass have a compelling authority and intensity, and *The Wreckers* brought an entirely new and strong sense of style and purpose into English opera at a time when its grip on life was tenuous.

MICHAEL KENNEDY

FURTHER READING
Ethel Smyth: *Impressions that Remained* (London, 1919); Christopher St John: *Ethel Smyth* (London, 1959).

Snap. See *Scotch snap*.

Snello, snella, snellamente (It.). 'Nimble', 'nimbly'.

Snow Maiden, The (*Snegurochka*). Opera in a prologue and four acts by Rimsky-Korsakov to his own libretto after Ostrovsky's play (1873). It was first performed in St Petersburg in 1882. Rimsky-Korsakov revised the opera in the mid 1890s.

Soap opera. A term applied not to opera but to

a broadcast serial story of a sentimental nature that is principally concerned with the emotional involvement of its characters. Some of the first such serials were sponsored by American soap manufacturers in a bid to sell their products.

Soave (It.). 'Sweet', 'soft', 'gentle'; *con soavità*, 'with gentleness' etc.; *soavemente*, 'gently' etc.

Sociable Songs. Title given by Warlock to three of his settings of anonymous poems. They are *The Toper's Song* (1924) for voice and piano, *One More River* (1925), and *The Lady's Birthday* (1925), both for baritone, four-part men's chorus, and piano.

Socialist Realism. The officially prescribed artistic doctrine in the Soviet Union. The term was coined in 1932, at a time when the Soviet authorities were drawing together the diverse creative elements that had been allowed to flourish during the 1920s in an attempt to establish a centralized, unified structure for the arts, guided by the dictates of socialism and governed in effect by the Communist Party. With the founding of Party-dominated unions for the arts (see *Russia and the Soviet Union*, 5), composers, writers, playwrights, and film-makers were steered away from any experimentalist notions they may have entertained in the years immediately after the 1917 Revolution and were directed instead towards the single goal of socialist realism, which, according to the statutes of the Union of Writers (1934), 'demands from the artist a truthful, historically concrete depiction of reality in its revolutionary development'. Taken up by the Union of Composers, the term was said to 'demand an uncompromising struggle against the anti-people, modernistic tendencies which manifest themselves in the decline and demoralization of contemporary bourgeois art'. 'The chief attention of the Soviet composer', the statutes maintain, 'must be directed towards the conquering, progressive principles of reality, towards those heroic, bright, and beautiful traits which distinguish the spiritual world of Soviet mankind and which must be embodied in musical images full of beauty and life-affirming strength.'

Dogged from the start by such hazy definition, socialist realism has continued to cause confusion and disagreement: for example, Shostakovich's *The Lady Macbeth of the Mtsensk District*, praised as a model of socialist realism after its first performance (1934), was bitterly condemned only two years later. Moreover, the problems of adhering to the tenets of socialist realism were exacerbated during the Stalinist era, when composers were expected to depict the 'reality' of Party-mindedness, patriotism, and optimism rather than the reality of the prison camps, unexplained disappearances, and political murders.

Notwithstanding the volte-face over Shostakovich's *Lady Macbeth*, opera has proved the most amenable vehicle for socialist realism, containing as it does the elements of drama and spectacle which can be used as powerful conveyers of the socialist message. The official praise in 1936 of Ivan Dzerzhinsky's tuneful, undemanding, but stirringly patriotic *Tikhiy Don* ('The Quiet Don') gave clear indications of the type of opera preferred by the Soviet musical establishment, and *The Quiet Don* proved to be a model for many more so-called 'song' operas, among them Kabalevsky's *Colas Breugnon* (1938), Khrennikov's *V buryu* ('Into the Storm', 1939), Muradeli's *October* (1964), and Dzerzhinsky's own *Sud'ba cheloveka* ('The Fate of a Man', 1961). Prokofiev's *Voyna i mir* ('War and Peace', 1946), itself in the socialist realist tradition, serves to indicate that even in Stalinist times the concept did not necessarily preclude music of high artistic worth.

Ballet and such large-scale vocal forms as cantatas and oratorios can also embrace the principles of socialist realism, but it is more difficult to apply them to such abstract forms as symphonies, quartets, and sonatas. Nevertheless, composers have tackled the problem in a variety of ways since 1932—by combining voices and instruments in topical or fervently patriotic 'song' symphonies, by dedicating their works to such national institutions as the Red Army or Lenin, by drawing on the folk music of the Soviet republics, or simply by ensuring that their works are couched in the accessible, melodious, euphonious, invigorating idiom that the authorities have believed to be the most accurate musical expression of the Soviet ideal.

The principles of socialist realism have been reaffirmed throughout the Soviet period, most notably during the cultural purges of 1948 when its merits over *formalism were decisively and indiscriminately asserted. But after the death of Stalin (1953) the concept was broadened to allow for the creative independence of the composer, provided that such independence did not reject the general ideals of Communism. The fact that Shostakovich could write (and be praised for) such introspective works as the Fourteenth Symphony, the late string quartets, and the dark, brooding song-cycles indicates that socialist realism is now more tolerant of personal expression. It remains, however, a subjective, ambiguous concept, and we can continue to sympathize with a former secretary of the Union of Writers, the author Alexander Fadeyev, who once remarked: 'If anyone should ask me what socialist realism is, I should have to answer that the devil alone knows.'

GEOFFREY NORRIS

Società Italiana di Musicologia. Italian society, founded in 1964 to encourage musicology and general musical culture in Italy. It has held several conferences, publishes the periodical *Rivista italiana di musicologia* (from 1966), and initiated the series *Monumenti musicali italiani* (from 1975), which began with the complete keyboard works of Frescobaldi.

Société Belge de Musicologie (Belgische Vereniging voor Musikwetenschap). Organization formed in 1946 to promote musicology in Belgium. Its founder-members included Charles van den Borren and Suzanne Clercx-Lejeune. In 1946 it began the publication of the periodical *Revue belge de musicologie*.

Société des Concerts du Conservatoire. See *Concert*, 4.

Société des Jeunes Artistes du Conservatoire. See *Concert*, 4.

Société Française de Musicologie. Organization founded by Lionel de la Laurencie in Paris in 1917 to encourage French musicology. It publishes a journal, *Revue de musicologie*, which until 1922 was called *Bulletin de la société française de musicologie*. Since 1925 it has also published editions of early French music, studies, documents, and catalogues.

Société Internationale de Musicologie (Fr.). See *International Musicological Society*.

Société Internationale pour la Musique Contemporaine (Fr.). See *International Society for Contemporary Music*.

Société Nationale de Musique. Parisian concert society founded in 1871 after the Franco-Prussian War in order to encourage and promote contemporary French music. It was founded by Saint-Saëns and his circle. See *France*, 8.

Society for Ethnomusicology (SEM). Founded in 1955, SEM has emphasized the study of world musics other than the Western art tradition, and places special importance on the study of music in its cultural context. The SEM has held annual meetings since 1956, and its four regional chapters in the USA also meet regularly. An international membership of about 2,100 receives the triannual journal *Ethnomusicology* and the *SEM Newsletter*. The Society also publishes a monograph series and offers prizes for outstanding papers by graduate students.   NYM COOKE

Society for the Promotion of New Music

(SPNM). British organization, founded in 1942 (active from 1943) to promote and perform music by younger composers. Vaughan Williams was its first president.

Society for the Publication of American Music (SPAM). American organization, founded in 1919 with the aim of publishing new American chamber music. It survived until 1969, issuing around 85 works by American composers; it was then taken over by the Theodore Presser publishing house.

Society of Women Musicians. British organization, formed in 1911 at a time when the male domination of musical life was beginning to be challenged. Its aims were the promotion of music by women composers (Ethel Smyth was a vice-president) and the protection and furthering of the interests of women musicians. It was dissolved in 1972, having made considerable headway in sexual equality, notably in the employment of women in British orchestras.

Socrate ('Socrates'). Symphonic drama by Satie to texts by Plato, translated by V. Cousin, composed in 1918. It is for one or more voices, with piano or chamber orchestra, and is in three parts: *Portrait de Socrate*, *Les bords d'Ilussus*, and *Mort de Socrate*.

Sofort (Ger.). 'Immediately'.

Soft hexachord. See *Solmization*.

Soft pedal. See *Piano*, 12c.

Soggetto (It.). 'Subject', or 'theme'. In 18th-century theory, a fugue subject of a traditional nature, similar to the subjects of the earlier *ricercar.

Soggetto cavato (It.). 'Extracted subject'; see *Cantus firmus*.

Sogleich (Ger.). 'Immediately'.

Soh. See *Sol*.

Soir (et la tempête), Le ('The Evening (and the Storm)'). Haydn's Symphony No. 8 in G major, probably composed in 1761. The last movement is 'La tempête'. Haydn's Symphonies Nos. 6 and 7 are nicknamed *Le matin* ('Morning') and *Le midi* ('Noon').

Soirées musicales ('Musical evenings'). Collection of songs and duets by Rossini, published in 1835. Britten orchestrated five of them under the same title (Op. 9, 1936) and the rest were orchestrated by Respighi for his ballet *La boutique fantasque*.

Sol. The fifth degree of the scale in the *solmization system. In French and Italian usage it has become attached, on the fixed-doh principle, to the note G, in whatever scale it may occur. See *Tonic Sol-fa*.

Solage (*fl.* late 14th century). French composer. He was a younger contemporary of Machaut, and was associated with Jean Duc de Berry. Among his few surviving *chansons* is the satirical 'Fumeux fume par fumee', which explores eccentric chromatic harmonies as an exercise in intellectual absurdity.

JOHN MILSOM

Soldier's Tale, The. See *Histoire du soldat, L'*.

Soleá (Sp.). A Spanish folk-song from Andalusia. It is arranged in three lines of eight syllables each, with assonance (agreement of vowels, not rhyme) on the last syllables of lines one and three. It often has a plaintive character.

Soler, Antonio (*bapt.* Olot, Gerona, 3 Dec. 1729; *d* El Escorial, 20 Dec. 1783). Spanish composer. He showed early musical promise at the Montserrat choir school, and when he was about 30 he was appointed *maestro de capilla* at Lérida. In 1752 he became a monk at the monastery of the Escorial, and a year later was admitted to Holy Orders. He spent the rest of his life there, as *maestro*, organist, and a highly respected teacher: his pupils included the royal children.

Much of Soler's music was destroyed in 1808 when the Escorial was ransacked by French troops. The influence of Domenico Scarlatti, with whom he studied, is apparent in the *c.*120 keyboard sonatas which survive together with organ works, six concertos for two organs, six quintets for strings and organ, dramatic works, sacred vocal music, and a celebrated treatise, *Llave de la modulación y antigüedades de la música* (Madrid, 1762).

WENDY THOMPSON

Solesmes, Monks of. In Solesmes, a village in France near Le Mans, a Benedictine abbey houses the monks of Solesmes, famous for their work on plainchant. Their aims and, later, their revisions of liturgical books and their music were adopted by the Roman Catholic Church in the early years of the 20th century (see *Motu proprio*), while their interpretation of the neumatic notation used in plainchant is generally followed in performances today (see *Notation*, 2).

Among those particularly associated with this work are Dom Prosper Guéranger (1805–75), Canon Augustin Gontier (1802–81), Dom Paul Jausions (1834–70), Dom Joseph Pothier (1835–

1923), Dom André Mocquereau (1849–1930), and Dom Joseph Gajard (*b* 1885). Dom Mocquereau was responsible for, among other things, the founding of *Paléographie musicale*, a series of publications containing facsimiles of original manuscripts in neumatic notation. From 1911 to 1964 a periodical, the *Revue grégorienne*, was published bi-monthly.

Sol-fa. See *Tonic Sol-fa*.

Solfeggietto (It.). 'Little study'. A term used by some composers (e.g. C. P. E. Bach) as the title of a short keyboard piece.

Solfeggio (It.; Fr.: *solfège*). 1. A type of vocal exercise sung either to a vowel (in which case it should properly be called a *vocalise*) or to the *solmization syllables (the term is derived from 'sol-fa'). The exercise serves a dual purpose: as basic voice-training; and as practice in sight-reading, since the student learns to recognize the intervals and notes.

2. The term has also been applied to instruction in the rudiments of music: sight-singing, aural-training, study of notation, etc. Extensive courses in *solfège* were first introduced at the Brussels and Paris conservatories, and have been adopted by some American institutions.

Solito (It.). 'Usual'; *al solito*, 'as usual'.

Sollecitando (It.). 'Pushing forward', 'hurrying'; *sollecito*, 'eager'.

Solmization. The use of syllables in association with pitches in the oral teaching of melodies. The name is derived from the most common set of such syllables known in Europe: ut, re, MI, fa, SOL, la. This set was invented by Guido of Arezzo (*c.*991–*c.*1033), and is described in his *Epistola de ignotu cantu* ('Letter about unknown chant'), written to his friend and fellow-monk Michael *c.*1030. It is made up of the first syllable of each of the first six lines of a hymn to St John (Ex. 1). Although the text is older than Guido, the melody is not and he may have composed it himself.

By 1100 the six syllables were used not only for the six notes C–D–E–F–G–A, but also for F–G–A–B♭–C–D and for G–A–B–C–D–E, which have the same interval pattern (tone–tone–semitone–tone–tone). These three sets of six notes are known as hexachords. The hexachord on C has no B and was known as the 'natural' (*naturale*) hexachord; that on G has a B♮ and was known as 'hard' (*durum*—from the way of writing the natural B, ♮, with four corners); and that on F needed a B♭ and was known as 'soft' (*molle*—with a rounded shape, ♭). The complete range of notes as usually given

Ex. 1

Ut que - ant la - xis,

re - so - na - re fi - bris,

Mi ra ges - to - rum,

fa - mu - li tu - o - rum,

Sol - ve pol - lu - ti,

la - bi - i re - a - tum,

Sanc - te Jo - han - nes.

by Medieval theorists, and the hexachords which could be fitted to them, are shown in Ex. 2 (note the system used at that time for indicating the pitch of the note; the system used throughout the *Companion* is laid out to the left of the table).

These syllables were frequently depicted on the so-called *Guidonian Hand, a visual aid to learning solmization.

The whole purpose of the system was to facilitate the memorization of unfamiliar melodies. The pupil had in mind the six syllables, and knew their pitch relationships—he would have been especially aware of the semitone *mi-fa* in the middle of the hexachord. He probably did not readily associate the syllables with letters of the alphabet; the choirmaster would translate the melody to be learnt into solmization syllables, which the pupil could then sing and learn.

Melodies that went beyond the range of one hexachord presented problems. For the second phrase of the Kyrie shown in Ex. 3, a change (or 'mutation') would have to be made to the lower hexachord, either immediately or within five or six notes.

The availability of B♭ and B♮ in the soft and hard hexachords respectively may have meant that those responsible for copying music did not feel the need to be as exact in writing these accidentals as were later musicians. In the later

Ex. 2

Ex. 3

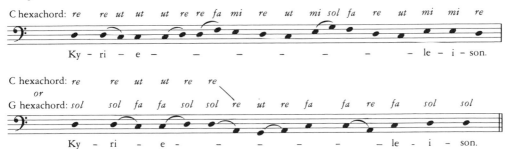

Ex. 4

Middle Ages, hexachords on other degrees came to be used: on D, needing F♯; on A, needing C♯; on B♭, needing E♭; and on E♭, needing A♭. In these cases, too, performers could easily learn with the aid of solmization accidentals not always copied into a score. Ex. 4 is the opening of an anonymous *ballade* of the early 15th century, 'Se vrai secours'. The contratenor part could be solmized in the hexachord on F, or in G mutating to E.

There are many examples of sets of solmization syllables (not necessarily six in number) in non-European musical cultures, from the Middle East to the Far East, and they were also known in Ancient Greece. Guido's six syllables were not the only ones known in his time in Europe, but no others gained wide currency. Renaissance attempts to extend the series to cover an octave, or to simplify mutation and reduce the number of hexachords, show dissatisfaction with the system; most theorists of the 16th century onward display little interest in it. That such systems can still aid the teaching of music is amply demonstrated by the success of the *Tonic Sol-fa system.   DAVID HILEY

Solo (It.). 'Alone', e.g. *violino solo*, 'solo violin'; the plural is *soli*.

Solomon. Oratorio by Handel to a biblical text by an unknown author. It was first performed in London in 1749.

Solo pitch. Pitch slightly higher than normal, sometimes used for its extra brilliance of sound. See *Pitch*.

Sombrero de tres picos, El. See *Three-cornered Hat, The*.

Somervell, (Sir) Arthur (*b* Windermere, 5 June 1863; *d* London, 2 May 1937). English composer and educationist. At Cambridge he studied composition under Stanford. He went to Berlin from 1883 to 1885 and then to the Royal College of Music for two years. Later he studied privately with Parry and joined the college staff in 1894. Although his Leeds Festival cantata *The Forsaken Merman* (1895) made his name, his song-cycles are more likely to ensure that he is remembered. His *Maud* (1898) is among the finest settings of Tennyson, and he was among the first composers to set the *Shropshire Lad* poems of Housman (1904). Tovey thought highly of his Violin Concerto (1932) and of the '*Normandy*' *Symphonic Variations* for piano and orchestra (1912). Somervell's knighthood in 1929 was not, however, for composition but for his work from 1901 to 1928 as Inspector of Music to the Board of Education. More than anyone, he helped to bring about the recognition of music as a school subject. He composed several operettas for children.   MICHAEL KENNEDY

Somis, Giovanni Battista (*b* Turin, 25 Dec. 1686; *d* Turin, 14 Aug. 1763). Italian violinist and composer. He was one of the chief mentors of the French ('Piedmont') school of violin-playing. His pupils included Guignon, Leclair, and Guillemain (probably the greatest French violinists of the century), as well as Pugnani and Giardini. After studying in Rome with Corelli, Somis returned to his native Turin and was appointed *maestro di cappella* there.

His works are all instrumental, including sonatas (all of the *da camera* type, but without dance titles) for violin and continuo and for cello and continuo, trio sonatas, and a book of *Ideali trattenimenti* for two melody instruments without continuo, a combination adopted by his pupil Leclair.

WENDY THOMPSON

Sommesso (It.). 'Subdued', 'soft'.

Son, sons (Fr.). 'Sound', 'sounds', or 'note', 'notes'; *son bouché*, in horn playing, a 'stopped note'.

Sonare (It.). 'To sound', 'to play', 'to blow'; *sonante, sonevole*, 'resonant', 'sounding'.

Sonata

1. Introduction
2. The Sonata to the Time of Corelli
3. Corelli and his Contemporaries
4. Corelli's Influence
5. The Pre-Classical Sonata
6. The Classical Keyboard Sonata
7. Beethoven's Contemporaries
8. The Romantics
9. The Post-Romantics
10. Conclusion

1. *Introduction.* The term has undergone considerable changes in meaning since its emergence around 1600, but it has been used by many composers to denote their most serious essays in solo (or duo) instrumental music. In Italian the word simply means 'played' (as opposed to *cantata*, or 'sung'), and it was first used by such composers as Giovanni Gabrieli to warn performers that a piece was intended for instruments rather than voices, at a time when madrigals and *chansons* could be performed by a group of voices, a mixture of voices and instruments, or even by a purely instrumental ensemble.

2. *The Sonata to the Time of Corelli.* It took about 80 years for the sonata to acquire a distinctive shape and form. In the first instance, Gabrieli and others mainly used the word for pieces which were too solemn to be called *canzona, yet not learnedly contrapuntal enough to merit the title *ricercar. These pieces were often intended as an emotional high point of the Mass, such as the Elevation of the Host, and were composed for a quite large ensemble of such instruments as cornetts and trombones. Although impossible to sing (some use low C and B♭ constantly), they nevertheless sound like motets written for *cori spezzati*, relatively slow-moving and often with much use of counterpoint to build up the climaxes. Such a piece as Gabrieli's famous *Sonata pian e forte* (1597) is of this type.

The new music which came with the emergence of the *basso continuo* around 1600 placed emphasis on accompanied melody rather than polyphony, in which all members of the ensemble had the thematic material. Although intended mainly for vocal music, the new style quickly affected instrumental forms and it became clear that the violin, with its capacity for expressive and sustained melody, could take the role of the human voice. Thus, during the first half of the 17th century, a school of composers arose who wrote either for a single violin or for two, with accompaniment by a continuo group (a minimum of a keyboard player, who was sometimes augmented by a cello, bass viol, bassoon, or even of several of these together). The publications for such combinations usually implied a mixture of genres: a typical example is Marco Uccellini's *Sonate, sinfonie, et correnti a 2, 3, & 4, lib. secondo* (Venice, 1639). Other sonatas appeared in books of religious music, showing that they were still intended for performance during Mass or Vespers. Very occasionally there is a liturgical link, as in Monteverdi's 'Sonata sopra Sancta Maria' published among his Vespers music in 1610, where a voice sings a separated plainsong prayer to the Virgin Mary while the instruments play their sonata. This piece has many elements of the canzona, including its division into sections with different material and the repetition of the opening section at the end. Variations over a ground bass proved equally attractive (Salamone Rossi, for example, wrote a *Sonata sopra l'aria della* *romanesca). By the middle of the century, sonatas were thus commonly sectional to the point that they seem to be a succession of short movements in different tempos (Legrenzi and Buonamente were masters of the technique whereby similar themes for each section helped to hold the piece together). Also significant was the tendency for sonata books to include dances, grouped together into rudimentary suites in a manner which suggests independent movements.

3. *Corelli and his Contemporaries.* The first climax and most crucial phase in the establishment of the sonata came in the last 30 years of the 17th century, notably in the hands of a group of composers born and working in and around Bologna and Modena. Many of them played in the orchestra of the basilica of S. Petronio in Bologna, where an excellent school of trumpeters inspired such composers as Colonna, Cazzatti, and Jacchini to write for that instrument; at the same time the Este court at Modena encouraged string-players such as Giovanni Maria Bononcini (1642–78) and Tomaso Antonio Vitali (1663–1745) to compose dances often grouped together under the title 'sonata da camera' (chamber sonata).

The composer who drew all these developments together and popularized the genre throughout Europe was Corelli, 60 of whose violin sonatas were published in five sets from 1681 to 1700. Of these, four sets were of 'trios', the remaining one of solo sonatas. Corelli organized his works for church ('sonate da chiesa') in alternating slow and fast movements, the main fast movement often being contrapuntal. His 'sonate da camera' were suites of dances in no fixed order. Nevertheless, this division by function is too rigid to describe the style, for many movements in his church sonatas are in dance rhythms (his gigues are particularly infectious). In his slow movements, especially in the solo sonatas, the melody was freely embellished to show off the player's skill, and his writing for the violin is always grateful and effective. Most of all, his ability to move from one key to another gave new possibilities for the construction of extended movements. Corelli's attractiveness lies in his sense of emotional balance. His phrase lengths and changes of harmony tend to regularity; his modulations never seem forced, since they are worked out from sequential repetitions (he avoids a purple patch or once-and-for-all key changes); imitation between the violins in a trio sonata generally occur at expected places and use closely related intervals (such as the fifth or fourth). Corelli is rarely extreme, and, if after hearing several of his works he may seem predictable, his works also possess a nobility and calm elegance which endeared him to his contemporaries and succeeding generations.

4. *Corelli's Influence.* Corelli's popularity spread rapidly throughout Europe, and his music was widely imitated, though adapted to local circumstances. Some imitations seem quite close: in Italy the music of Caldara, Tomaso Vitali, and Albinoni is distinctly Corellian; in England, so is that of Handel (though in Handel the emotional balance is upset by a greater unexpectedness in both harmony and melody) and that of the *émigré* Geminiani. In France, in spite of the usual opposition to Italian music, Corelli's music was appreciated to the extent that Couperin wrote *Le Parnasse, ou L'apothéose de Corelli, grande sonade en trio* (Paris, 1724), which is superficially Corellian (in the trio texture and some of the harmonies) but sounds extremely French in the nature of the ornaments and in a tendency for greater irregularity in harmonic movement. In Germany, the popularity of wind instruments meant that the specifically violinistic idioms of Corelli tended to disappear in a kind of generalized melodic style; but Telemann wrote a set of *Sonates Corellisantes* (1735). Purcell was largely unaffected by Corelli; his works may have been written as 'a just imitation of the most fam'd Italian Masters' but were nevertheless 'clog'd with somewhat of an English vein'—by which Roger North probably meant intricate counterpoint in the faster movements; but they also reflected such pre-Corellian composers as Cazzati and G. B. Vitali.

A move away from Corelli was evident by the 1720s, with the encroachment of the newer *galant style. The influence of the Neapolitan opera overture gave a new order of movements, fast-slow-fast, to which a minuet was sometimes added, often immediately preceding the last movement. Weaker rhythmic patterns and slower-moving harmonies associated with the operatic aria, coupled with the increase in pure display in sonatas by such composers as Veracini, resulted in what might be called a 'concert' sonata, as opposed to that intended for performance in church.

5. *The Pre-Classical Sonata.* Before 1730 the sonata was largely the province of the violinist or woodwind player accompanied by a continuo team. J. S. Bach gave his keyboard player a greater role in some sonatas where the right hand was allowed a melody line to match the flute in a trio sonata texture; but this was unusual. Among the earliest sonatas to break away from this tradition are those for keyboard alone by Domenico Scarlatti; but these were less sonatas than *essercizi* or 'studies'. They

were single movements in binary form and were of importance because Scarlatti was original in several ways. His thematic material was not melodious after the manner of the violinists but consisted of shortish developed figures coming from keyboard technique; and he appreciated that sudden changes from one key to another could maintain interest and even (if unconventional enough) add a touch of drama. Isolated as he was in Spain, Scarlatti had little influence on the further development of the sonata (though there was a pocket of English 'Scarlatti-ists', of whom John Roseingrave was the most important); but the use of tonality and of keyboard figuration presages the sonata of the Classical era.

6. *The Classical Keyboard Sonata*. Compared with Scarlatti's, the keyboard sonatas of the Italians working around 1750 seem insipid. The sonata style of Galuppi, Alberti, and Rutini shows little flair for inventing memorable themes and developing them. There is no fixed number of movements: sonatas of two or three movements are common, but there are sometimes as many as five. Some of these are in dance rhythms (finales are frequently minuets). If these Italian composers were largely concerned to charm, the north Germans, especially C. P. E. Bach, found in the sonata a medium for music in the 'empfindsamer Stil' (see *Empfindsamkeit*). Their favourite instrument was the clavichord which allowed rapid changes of mood, expressed in sudden changes of key, strange alterations of direction in the melody, and the exploitation of dynamics. C. P. E. Bach also tended to change the theme in its successive statements, so that the principal subject of a rondo would never appear the same twice. In the large-scale movements, with the opening subject returning (see *Sonata form*) in the concluding section, he made a point of altering the original on its return (the title of a set of sonatas published in 1760 is *Sechs Sonaten . . . mit veränderten Reprisen*). He also developed thematic material throughout a movement (not just in a separate development section), a technique which Haydn also enjoyed.

By the 1770s sonatas were vying with orchestral music in their emotional capacity. It is interesting that many opera overtures (or 'symphonies') were arranged for keyboard and that Mozart made a number of J. C. Bach's sonatas into concertos. Thus the formal techniques of symphonic and concerto movements were transferred to sonatas. Themes became more motivic, the melody less decorated; sonorities became weightier (many sonatas include octave passages after the manner of orchestral doublings), and simple Alberti figurations (see *Alberti bass*) occurred less often. Such devices are

Title-page of Mozart's 'Fantaisie et Sonate' K 457 (Vienna: Artaria, 1785).

common in the sonatas of composers working in Paris, notably Schobert; but they are also to be found in the sonatas written by Mozart for his tour of 1777-8, of which the Sonata in C major, K 309, was written to Mannheim taste (the contrasting dynamics being a feature of music written for the famous orchestra there) and that in A minor, K 310, for Paris (the broken octave figurations in the first movement are obviously derived from string *tremolandi*). Such sonatas were played at recitals in the houses of noblemen. If most of them contain a large-scale movement in sonata form, it is also noticeable that this movement did not always conform to the textbook pattern described by later theorists, and that the number of movements had not been stabilized as it had been to a large extent in the symphony. The fact that keyboard composers played their own works, and did not need to follow the letter of the written notes, led to a work such as Mozart's Fantasia (K 475) and Sonata in C minor (K 457), in which, while the lengthy improvisatory fantasia need not be played with the sonata, it clearly belongs to it and adds both scale and emotional variety — facts not lost on Beethoven in his Op. 27 sonatas.

The 'symphonic' sonata (as it might be called) flourished in the hands of Clementi and Beethoven in this period. The former had produced over 70 sonatas by 1790, the earliest dating from the 1770s and deriving from the Italianate sonatas using Alberti figurations; he later progressed to sonatas, written in Vienna and London in the 1780s, which are in three movements and seem to presage Beethoven's keyboard style of the following decade. Of his sonatas composed in the 1790s, one was an arrangement of a concerto, another was conceived as a symphony.

The earliest of Beethoven's 36 piano sonatas date from the 1790s, and 25 of them were written by 1802, after which his deafness (and the giving up of his pianistic activities) and his preoccupation with orchestral music made sonata composition a rarer activity for him. The sonatas of his early years in Vienna were large-scale works written to display his magnificent piano technique. They are mainly in four movements, including a scherzo; his first movements, in sonata form, use much thematic material which is developed at length. The Sonata in C, Op. 2 No. 3, often sounds like a concerto, even to the extent of having a written-out cadenza in the first movement. But when he is writing in a serious, extended symphonic manner, as, for example, in the sonatas Op. 10, his piano figuration (unlike that of Mozart) does not sound in the least like a reduction of an orchestral score. By 1800 Beethoven was writing more orchestral music, and the sonatas began to break away from the symphonic mould. Op. 27 consists of two sonatas, each marked 'quasi una fantasia' and with an unexpected order of movements. The second sonata, the so-called 'Moonlight', begins with a movement in an improvisatory, pianistically conceived style; the second movement is a skittish minuet or scherzo; and the last movement is in sonata form with themes based on piano figuration. Further fruits of this break from conventional symphonic order are seen in Beethoven's later sonatas, such as the 'Waldstein' Op. 53, which has a slow movement conceived simply as a link between a huge opening movement and an expansive rondo. Even more remarkable are the five sonatas written from 1816 to 1822. No two are alike, either in order of movements or proportions. The earliest of these, Op. 101, opens as though it were to be 'quasi una fantasia'; it has a fierce march in place of a scherzo, and then a short link in an intricate, ruminating style before a fugal finale. Op. 106, the 'Hammerklavier', is one of the longest sonatas ever written, not only in time (it lasts around 50 minutes) but also in emotional intensity, ending with a colossal fugue. The last sonata, Op. 111, has only two movements, the first a titanic piece in sonata form, the second a set of sublime variations, which Gerald Abraham has aptly described as the equivalent of the 'Heiliger Dankgesang' of the String Quartet Op. 132. It is difficult to convey in words the effect of these sonatas. They have the emotional scale of a symphony but are more intimate and frequently more profound. They are virtuoso pieces, yet they are not written to show off the player's skill. Each is unique in form and emotional content. In the wake of these works, composers found a sonata a major undertaking.

7. *Beethoven's Contemporaries.* Beethoven's lifetime saw the rise of the travelling virtuoso who used the sonata as an extended *pièce de résistance*, while filling in the remainder of his recital with improvisations, variations set on popular operatic airs, and small genre pieces. The application of 'symphonic' techniques in Beethoven's manner is rare, though Dussek wrote sonatas of similar emotional scope, of which the two-movement *Élégie harmonique sur la mort du Prince Louis Ferdinand de Prusse* (1806-7) and *L'invocation* (1812) in F minor show a remarkable variety of mood and exploration of keyboard textures. Another famous pianist was Hummel, a pupil of Mozart, whose sonatas show little interest in the development of themes, and whose early works especially hark back to the Italian tradition of elegant decorative melody in the right hand (exploiting the upper reaches of the piano) accompanied by simple chordal figuration. Among his pupils, Voříšek was capable of a Beethovenian strength, developing short, rhythmic motifs in his Sonata in Bb minor Op. 20. The finest of all this Mozart-Hummel line of sonata composers was Schubert, from whom over 20 piano sonatas and another 10 for ensemble survive, not all of them complete. The usual criticism of these is that they tend to use beautiful melodies which are either unsuitable for development or are left undeveloped; but the quality of their melodies is their strength, and Schubert's capacity for harmonic juxtaposition of distant keys succeeds in maintaining interest, even in the marvellous (but exceedingly long) piano sonatas in A and Bb major, published posthumously. His works for more than one player include a large-scale sonata or 'Grand Duo' in C, for piano, four hands (1824), a sonata for the arpeggione and piano (1824), and three sonatinas for violin and piano (1836). These last restored the violin to something like the dominant position it had lost in the mid 18th century, not surprisingly in view of Schubert's interest in lyrical melody. But more significant still is the fact that two of Schubert's major works are called 'fantasy': one, the famous *Wanderer* Fantasy (1822), is an important, four-movement example of *cyclic form; the other, a four-handed piece, is the Fantasie in F minor (1828). The idea of the sonata was going out of fashion.

8. *The Romantics.* The sonata was going out of fashion because composers were seeking the continuous intensity possible only in short lyric forms—Schubert's failure to finish several of his sonatas was another symptom of the trend which becomes especially apparent in the 1830s, when piano composers took to dance music, often with a nationalist flavour, or wrote pieces entitled 'scherzo' or 'ballade'. Sometimes these were grouped together to form a larger work

such as Schumann's *Carnaval*; when composers did attempt a more extended yet unified work, they were still influenced by his fashion, even if they used the sonata mould of three or four matched movements, one or more in sonata form. Another symptom of the new mood is the frequent use of the term 'sonatina', which implies the basic form without arousing the expectations of a weighty musical statement. Many teaching pieces were so called, especially by the major pedagogues such as Czerny, Riemann, and Gurlitt. The sonata was often used by young composers to master the techniques of sonata form, and several composers such as Wagner and Richard Strauss (who were to have no further interest in such traditional forms) tried their hand. Rossini's 12 sonatas for strings really belong to an 18th-century tradition, while the virtuoso works of Paganini for both violin and guitar are equally retrospective in attitude. In France, in spite of some influence of Beethoven on such composers of the Revolution as Méhul, old-fashioned charm predominated in the works of Boieldieu and the German-born Steibelt.

The serious sonata was in fact a mainly German preserve, with Beethoven's ghost hovering near. The difficulties which even great Romantic composers experienced with the genre are illustrated in Schumann's piano sonatas, which have what one critic has called 'pseudo-development sections' of considerable length. It is a trait not unknown in the young Brahms, whose early piano sonatas are surrogate symphonies, with some fat chordal piano writing seemingly crying out for orchestration but in fact satisfying to play. The best movements of these sonatas are usually not those in sonata form, but slow movements which can use lyrical themes (Brahms actually borrowed song melodies). Significantly the really successful piano sonatas of the mid 19th century are those which break away from the traditional form to encompass the genre piece, as does Chopin in both his mature sonatas, that in B♭ minor (1839) having the well-known Funeral March as a third movement and also a finale which resembles one of his preludes in its exploitation of piano tone rather than themes. Liszt avoids 'pseudo-development' in his sonatas, either by conceiving them as programmatic works (*Après une lecture de Dante, fantasia quasi sonata*, final version 1849) or, as in the B minor Sonata (1852-3), using the methods of thematic transformation developed from Schubert's *Wanderer* Fantasy. While this might seem even more artificial in approach than the 'development' sections of sonata form, the very malleability of proportion avoids thematic working out for working out's sake, and the B minor Sonata remains one of the most exciting of piano

sonatas, not merely for the virtuosity which tempts nearly all concert pianists to attempt it.

The real gems of the later part of the 19th century belong to the ensemble sonata, perhaps because the possible contrasts of colour soften the apparent necessity to overdevelop themes. Schumann's violin sonatas contain interesting effects of sonority and some delicate weaving together of movements with common thematic material. Brahms's three violin sonatas are even more beautiful, as are his later sonatas for clarinet and cello (both with piano), because of a similar approach. Finest of all, perhaps, is the Violin Sonata (1886) by Franck, which applies a post-Lisztian attitude in harmony and free thematic reminiscence, though its finale uses canon in a way possible only to an organist of that period, well schooled to the point where the strictest form comes naturally.

9. *The Post-Romantics.* It was the Wagnerian revolution which dealt the final blow to the sonata. After *Tristan*, the moderns felt they had to explore the paths of extreme chromaticism, the death-knell to sonata form which depends on recognition of tonal relationships. After the *Ring*, Wagner (with his theories of the *Gesamtkunstwerk*) replaced Beethoven as a god for even progressive rather than revolutionary composers. The only sonatas which can be said to show a Wagnerian approach are the last five (Nos. 6-10) of Skryabin, which are offshoots of Skryabin's desire to create the ultimate sensual experience or 'mystery'; but his early sonatas reveal more clearly that he belonged to the line of fine Russian pianist-composers, including Balakirev and Rakhmaninov, both of whom wrote sonatas. To the Liszt-type sonata using the transformation of themes belongs the unique example of Berg's Piano Sonata (performed in Vienna, 1911).

For the most part, sonatas have been written in the last century by those who either wished to get away from the later Romantic tradition or to add to the repertory of specific virtuosos. Of the first type, the French desire to break away from Germanic influence manifested itself early in the works of Saint-Saëns (back to Mozart and even Rameau) and then in the music of Fauré (back to plainsong and Palestrina), whose violin sonatas show a nice judgement of sound (especially in the piano writing) and a classical sense of clear structure. The 18th-century spirit was consciously evoked by Debussy (whose last works were a set of sonatas, planned to be six in all—as in the publications of the Baroque composers—though he completed only three). Ravel's Sonatine (1903-5) for piano is even more clearly in that tradition (two of its three movements being a minuet and a toccata). The neo-classical movement of the 1920s and 1930s naturally turned composers' minds to such a traditional genre, both Poulenc and Hindemith composing sonatas which clearly follow the forms of the later 18th century (among the best works being piano sonatas for four hands by each). In the USSR the most notable examples are the piano sonatas of Prokofiev, and Shostakovich's five sonatas, including a work for violin and piano (composed for Oistrakh and Richter) which combines serial melodic material with a feeling for sonata pattern.

10. *Conclusion.* This survey has mentioned only the most important landmarks in the history of a genre which must surely be accounted one of the greatest in Western music. In the classical sense of the term, it must now be accounted dead. Sonatas by Tippett, Henze, Maxwell Davies, and Boulez have little connection with the past history of the genre, except perhaps that the word is reserved for an ample and seriously emotional statement. If, as Schoenberg said, there is still much music to be written in C major, it may be said that it is unlikely to be in sonata form. But the principle of a 'played piece' is very much alive, as electronic music, which has no need to follow vocal patterns, shows. If the term survives, it will probably be in this sense: sonata, a piece to be played, as opposed to cantata, a piece for singing.

DENIS ARNOLD

FURTHER READING
Donald Tovey: *A Companion to Beethoven's Piano Sonatas* (London, 1948); William S. Newman: *A History of the Sonata Idea*, 3 vols (Chapel Hill, 1959-69); Charles Rosen: *The Classical Style: Haydn, Mozart, Beethoven* (New York, 1971).

Sonata a tre (It.). 'Trio sonata'; see *Sonata*, 2-5.

Sonata da camera, Sonata da chiesa (It.). 'Chamber sonata', 'church sonata'; see *Sonata*, 3.

Sonata form. Sonata form is one of the basic forms in music. It most often occurs in the first movement of a sonata, piano trio or quartet, string trio, quartet, or quintet, and a symphony. Hence it is sometimes known as first movement form. It may, however, also be used as the form of an independent movement such as an overture or tone poem.

Sonata form comprises a two-part tonal structure in three main sections. Section 1, the 'exposition', presents all the thematic material of the movement, opening with one theme, or group of themes, in the tonic key. The first (or principal) theme of the first group is known as the 'first subject'. The exposition then moves, often by means of a modulatory section called a transition or bridge passage, to a second theme or group of themes in a contrasting key. The first (or principal) theme of the second group is known as the 'second subject'. The key of the second subject is usually the dominant for movements in the major and the relative major for movements in the minor, although other keys may be used. For example, in the 19th

TABLE 1

Bar Nos.	Thematic Function	Key Progressions
EXPOSITION		
1-8 (Ex. 1)	First Subject	G major
9-25 (Ex. 2)	Transition (Bridge)	G major—D major
26-32 (Ex. 3)	Second Group—1st theme	D major
33-46 (Ex. 3)	Second Group—2nd theme	D major
47-56 (Ex. 3)	Second Group—3rd theme	D major
58-63 (Ex. 4)	Codetta	D major
DEVELOPMENT		
64-73	First Subject (motivic components)	G minor—V of B♭ major
74-80	Second Group—1st theme	B♭ major
81-98	First Subject (motivic components) with new two-bar continuation	A♭ major—G minor—F minor—V of E♭ major
99-106	First Subject extended	E♭ major
107-124	Eighteen bars of dominant preparation for the return; includes motivic components of First Subject	Dominant pedal
RECAPITULATION		
125-132	First Subject	G major
133-152 (Ex. 5)	Transition. Three inserted bars (137-9) adjust the tonality so as to lead to chord V of the tonic	G major—V of G major
153-186	Unaltered recapitulation of Second Group brought to a slightly adjusted cadence (compare 56 and 183) (Codetta omitted)	G major
187-200 (Ex. 6)	Coda based on the First Subject	G major

century it became quite common to employ the mediant as the second main key area. The exposition generally closes with a codetta, a short and sometimes reiterated cadential figure in the key of the second group. A double bar, most usually with repeat marks, signifies the close of the first main section.

The second section, the 'development', exploits the thematic material of the exposition, although new thematic material may be presented. These themes are often broken down into their motivic components, which are freely juxtaposed and developed. This section is tonally unstable, exploring a wide variety of keys by means of harmonic sequence and other modulatory devices. It leads, most usually, to the dominant chord in preparation for the 'recapitulation', the third section.

This final section marks the return to the tonic key and also a return to the thematic material of the exposition. The recapitulation essentially repeats all the thematic material of the exposition in its original order, but here the second group remains in the tonic key. This means that if there was a transition between the first and second groups it must now be tonally adjusted so that the modulation of the exposition is not effected. After all the material of the exposition has been recapitulated, a 'coda' often concludes the movement. The codas vary in length from a few bars to a large section.

The first movement of Beethoven's Piano Sonata in G major, Op. 14 No. 2, provides an example of the form (Table 1; Exx. 1-6).

Although many sonata form movements follow the above plan, it must be stressed that it is by no means a rigid compositional formula. Thematic and tonal elements may become separated so that, for example, a recapitulation could start with the 'right' theme in the 'wrong'

Ex. 1
First subject

Ex. 2
Transition

key (Mozart's Piano Sonata K 545 recapitulates the first subject in the subdominant); conversely it may start with the 'wrong' theme in the 'right' key (Mozart's Piano Sonata K 311 recapitulates the second group material before the reappear-ance of the first subject). The exposition is sometimes preceded by an introduction which is often in a slower tempo than the rest of the movement.

See also *Form*, 6.

G. M. TUCKER

Ex. 3

Ex. 4

Ex. 5
Transition

Ex. 6
Coda

Sonata pian e forte (alla quarta bassa).
Work by Giovanni Gabrieli for eight instruments. It was written for St Mark's, Venice, and, as the title suggests, exploits contrast and dialogue between the brass instruments. It was published in Gabrieli's *Sacrae symphoniae* (1597).

Sonata rondo form. As the name implies, the sonata rondo is a hybrid design incorporating elements from both *sonata form and *rondo form. It may be represented by the letter-scheme ABACABA. B denotes not, as in rondo form, an episode but rather a second subject; C denotes the development or, if new material is introduced, an episode; and the final A is the coda based on the rondo theme, i.e. first subject.

The scheme may thus be more clearly expressed as:

Section	Function	Key
A	1st Subject	Tonic
B	2nd Subject	Dominant or relative major
A	1st Subject	Tonic
C	Development/Episode	Related key or keys
A	1st Subject	Tonic
B	2nd Subject	Tonic
A	Coda	Tonic

Thus a sonata rondo is differentiated from sonata form by the additional appearance of the first subject in the tonic key after the second subject and before the development; it is differentiated from rondo form because the second subject—B—returns in the tonic key. The form was often used for the final movement of multi-movement works by Haydn, Mozart, and Beethoven. Like sonata form it is not a rigid formula and therefore the above scheme can be taken as only a rough guide to its general features.

See also *Form*, 6.   G. M. TUCKER

Sonate (Fr., Ger.). 'Sonata'.

Sonatina (It., diminutive of *sonata*). A short, relatively undemanding type of *sonata, often for piano. Several composers of the later Classical period (e.g. Clementi, Kuhlau) wrote large numbers of keyboard sonatinas for didactic purposes, and these are still used as teaching material. Although sonatinas generally follow the sonata-form principle, their development sections are frequently less extended and they may have fewer movements (e.g. Clementi's Sonatinas Op. 36). In the 20th century, however, the term has been applied more loosely to lightweight (though not necessarily easy) sonata-type instrumental works, often of the less serious kind (e.g. those for piano by Busoni, Ravel, and Prokofiev).

Sonatine (Fr.). 'Sonatina'.

Sondheim, Stephen (Joshua) (*b* New York, 22 Mar. 1930). American composer and lyric-writer. A graduate in music at Williams College, he wrote words and music for student productions and won the Hutchinson Prize which allowed him to study for two years with Milton Babbitt. After writing various scripts for radio and television he made his name on Broadway by writing the lyrics for Leonard Bernstein's *West Side Story* (1957), then for Jule Styne's *Gypsy* (1959) and Richard Rodgers's *Do I Hear a Waltz?* (1965). In 1962 he had a big success as composer and lyric-writer of *A Funny Thing Happened on the Way to the Forum*. This was followed by *Anyone Can Whistle* (1964), *Company* (1970), *Follies* (1971), *A Little Night Music* (1973), *Pacific Overtures* (1976), and *Sweeney Todd* (1979). In 1975 a show called *Side by Side by Sondheim* gave a cross-section of his works so far.

PETER GAMMOND

Sonetti di Petrarcha, Tre ('Three Petrarch Sonnets'). Three songs for voice and piano by Liszt, composed in 1838-9. He transcribed them for piano (?1839-46) and incorporated revised versions as Nos. 4-6 of Book 2 of *Années de pèlerinage*.

Song

1. Introduction
2. Monophonic Song
3. Polyphonic Song
4. Madrigal and Monody

5. The 17th and 18th Centuries
6. The 19th Century
7. The 20th Century

1. *Introduction.* Singing is an instinctive activity of the human species, a natural means of self-expression common to all races of mankind. Its origins can be traced back into prehistory, most obviously to the human fascination for rhythm (which in turn evolved from patterns of body movement) and the inflections of speech; song still retains a close association with dance and recitation in the cultures of many of the world's less developed countries. Although by definition a vocal activity, whether solo or choral, monodic or polyphonic, many types of song involve the use of instruments, played either by the singers themselves or by accompanists.

2. *Monophonic Song.* Before musical notation evolved, song-repertories could be preserved only by being committed to memory and passed down through an oral tradition. Because of this, few songs dating from before the 12th century survive to the present day, except perhaps in the form of folk-song. Although the Bible contains

the texts of many religious songs of the Jewish people (such as psalms and canticles) and makes frequent reference to their performance, we know virtually nothing about their musical substance or style. Singing occupied an important place in the cultures of ancient Egypt and Greece; but while the words of some lyric and epic songs are still extant, all but a few scattered remains of the music itself has been irretrievably lost.

As the repertory of plainchant (the liturgical chant of the church) expanded during the first thousand years of the Christian era, it became necessary to devise a system of musical notation which would preserve the melodies and allow them to disseminate more widely and accurately than was possible using memory alone. Early notation was thus the preserve of a church-educated élite, and the few secular songs which they chose to write down reflect the culture of only a small (though powerful and influential) element of society. With the development of

Pl. 1. A page from the 'Carmina Burana' (13th century).

musical notation, the distinction between 'folk-song' and 'art-song' grew rapidly, the former repertory comprising songs passed down orally through succeeding generations and changing substantially during the process, the latter consisting of songs of ever-increasing sophistication and complexity, often composed for specific occasions or at the request of a patron or employer.

Many of the earliest surviving songs of the Medieval world are settings of Latin lyrics. Particularly famous is the *Carmina Burana*, a 13th-century anthology of religious, amorous, and bawdy songs compiled by goliards (educated clerics who adopted the life of wandering poet-musicians). Also typical of the period are processional songs in Latin known as *conductus, whose subjects range from matters of politics and topical events to religious devotion, moral preaching, and satire. With their strong metrical

rhythms, limited voice-ranges, and short, regular phrases, the idiom of these songs often comes closer to folk-song than to the luxuriance of liturgical plainchant (see Ex. 1).

The earliest extant repertory of songs written in a language other than Latin is that of the *troubadours, an aristocratic class of poet-musicians which flourished in southern France during the 12th and 13th centuries. This period saw the evolution of an elaborate convention of behaviour among the courts of the nobility, in which the status of women was idealized and attributes such as chivalry, refinement, and education commended in their suitors. Song occupied an important place in this 'game of love': a nobleman would solicit the attention of his lady through verse and melodies of his own composition, performing them personally, often to the accompaniment of professional minstrels. As well as the *canso* (or courtly love-song), *troubadours* wrote songs on a wide variety of themes, including satirical, moral, and political topics (the *sirventes*), debate-like dialogues (the *tenso*), laments (the *planh*), and crusade-songs. The musical style of these songs varies considerably, from simple, syllabic melodies to elaborately flowing compositions fashioned after melismatic plainchant. It is impossible to be sure how *troubadour* songs sounded in performance; few are notated with a precise indication of rhythm, and we know little about the style of instrumental accompaniment they received.

The art of the *troubadours* provided a model for secular song throughout Western Europe during the 12th century, spread by the intermarriage of the nobility and by the crusades. Similar movements evolved in northern France (the **trouvères*) and Germany (the **Minnesinger*), while religious song fashioned after *troubadour* models flourished in Spain (**cantigas*) and in Italy (**laude*). By the end of the 13th century, the vogue for composing and performing courtly song had spread to educated members of the merchant class and bourgeoisie such as Adam de la Halle and Jehan de L'Escurel. During the 14th and 15th centuries,

monophonic song gradually fell into decline, although a few isolated movements (such as the **Meistersinger*) survived until much later.

3. *Polyphonic Song.* The 13th century also witnessed the first flowering of songs for two or more voices. Extra parts were added to (or improvised around) *conductus* and *trouvère* melodies, converting them into simple part-songs. The principal form of secular polyphonic song at this time, however, was the **motet*, a genre of French origin which grew out of *organum* (the plainchant-based polyphony of the church), and was initially cultivated within ecclesiastical circles for secular entertainment. Most 13th-century motets are anonymous, preserved in fine manuscripts such as the Montpellier and Bamberg codices. Generally for three voices, of which the lowest sings a fragment of plainchant, motets frequently set more than one text simultaneously, sometimes even mixing French and Latin, although texts are normally closely related to one another in subject-matter; most are concerned with themes of political, topical, satirical, or amorous nature. In the hands of 14th-century composers such as

Ex. 1

Mors vite propitia (anon., French, 13th-century).

Pl. 2. King Arthur and his courtiers listening to a knight singing to the gittern, miniature from the 'Roman du Roi Meliadus de Leonnoys', 1352–62.

Philippe de Vitry and Machaut, the motet became a lengthy, intellectual, and sometimes formidably complex form of song, usually constructed on the principle of *isorhythm.

Other forms of secular polyphonic song, mostly treating the subject of courtly love, evolved at the very end of the 13th century. Outstanding among these were three poetical and musical structures known collectively as the *formes fixes*: the *ballade (an equivalent form, the madrigal, existed in Italy; see *Madrigal, 2*), *rondeau, and *virelai (in Italy, known as the *ballata). These song-forms differed from the motet in being freely composed, without any plainchant basis; instead, the composer would first write a principal melodic line, then add between one and three subordinate parts in counterpoint against it. One of the earliest—and shortest—examples of a polyphonic *chanson* is Adam de la Halle's *rondeau* 'Bonne amourette' (Ex. 2); typically, the entire text—whether refrain (shown in capital letters) or verse (in lower-case letters)—is sung to only two musical phrases, repeated in the order ABaAabAB.

1	*Bonne amourete*	A
2	*Me tient gai;*	B
3	Ma compaignete,	a
4	*Bonne amourete,*	A
5	Ma cançonete	a
6	Vous dirai:	b
7	*Bonne amourete*	A
8	*Me tient gai.*	B

Polyphonic songs of this type, setting conventionally artificial love poetry in one or other of the *formes fixes*, soon became a characteristic ingredient of entertainment at the principal courts of both France and Italy, remaining popular among aristocratic *cognoscenti* and their circles for almost 200 years, from the early 14th century to the end of the 15th. At first, songs from different regions contrasted in style, for French composers such as Machaut favoured a busy, often dissonant effect with angular melodic lines full of syncopations and recurrent rhythmic motifs, while contemporary Italians such as Giovanni da Cascia, Magister Piero, and later Landini preferred a more flowing, harmonious style and graceful melodies moving largely by step in dance-like rhythms. By the late 14th century, however, these two idioms had essentially merged into a more 'international' style, discernible in the songs of Matteo da Perugia and Ciconia. In the hands of their 15th-century successors—Dufay, Binchois, Ockeghem, and Busnois—courtly songs became longer and more lyrical, often dominated by expansive melodies of haunting charm, accompanied by two subordinate parts (Ex. 3). Composers never stipulated any precise performance medium; most songs were presumably intended for a soloist supported by lutes, harps, or bowed instruments, although many are also suitable for an entirely vocal ensemble. The refined quality of these songs, with their under-stated texts and subtly intricate polyphonic texture, admirably reflects the sophisticated cultural life of the leading courts of the time—Burgundy, Savoy, Naples, etc.—as do the exquisite manuscripts into which they were copied, such as the Dijon, Mellon, and Cordiforme ('heart-shaped') *chansonniers*.

Ex. 2

1, 4, 7. *Bonne a - mour - e - te* 2, 8. *Me tient___ gai.*
3. *Ma com - paign - e - te,*
5. *Ma can - çon - ne - te* 6. *Vous di - rai:*

4. Madrigal and Monody. Towards the end of the 15th century, a new type of song began to emerge at certain principal north Italian courts, including Florence, Mantua, and Ferrara. It grew from a tradition, apparently native to Italy, of adding music to poetry in an extempore fashion, using simple, stylized melodic formulas supported by stock patterns of chords played on the lute or a similar instrument. The resulting idiom—tuneful with homophonic accompaniment, the rhythm of the text mirrored in the music—could hardly have stood in greater contrast to the skilful and increasingly imitative polyphony which northern composers such as Ockeghem and Josquin were developing. By 1500, two distinct repertories of declamatory Italian song had emerged: the Florentine *canti carnascialeschi* ('carnival songs') and the more widespread *frottola*. Although usually scored for three or four voices, songs of these types were often performed by a soloist supported chordally by a lute or keyboard instrument, producing a texture equivalent to the solo song of later centuries.

While the *frottola* and related forms of declamatory Italian song enjoyed only relatively short-lived popularity, their impact on the general development of European song was far-reaching. The idiom of Italian song, with its emphasis on melody, bass, and harmony, clear-cut phrases rounded off by strong cadences, and above all syllabic word-setting, offered itself as a radical alternative to the polyphonically-minded composers of the Low Countries; and as elements from these two stylistic extremes gradually merged, polyphonic song entered one of its richest and most complex phases. In the hands of Josquin, Compère, Mouton, and their contemporaries—northern composers whose careers were partly spent south of the Alps—the polyphonic *chanson* began to change in character: lighter forms of verse, often bawdy or narrative, gradually replaced the courtly *formes fixes*, and were set to music in a more syllabic, *parlando*

Ex. 3

Binchois: *rondeau* 'Adieu, mon joieulx souvenir'.

A - dieu, a - dieu mon___ joi - eulx sou - - ve - nir,

Le plus hault bien qui___ me puist___ ad - ve - nir, etc.

fashion than before, although still within a contrapuntal framework. Transplanted back into the north, this revitalized form of *chanson* was propagated with great success by composers such as Claudin de Sermisy, Janequin, and Crécquillon. At the same time, the *frottola* gradually absorbed polyphonic elements from the *chanson*, giving rise during the 1520s to a new and equally popular form of ensemble song in Italian, the madrigal (see *Madrigal*, 3).

The extraordinary vogue for polyphonic song which existed during the 16th century can partly be explained by the rise of a new class of performer, the educated amateur. As the ability to sing and read music came increasingly to be regarded as a desirable social accomplishment, the demand for new songs in the latest fashion grew, a demand which the newly-invented printing press was able to satisfy at a price which the public could afford. Songs composed in a wide variety of idioms thus became more readily available than ever before, stimulating not only the exchange of ideas between Italian, French, and Flemish composers but also the rapid development of vernacular song in more peripheral countries. Influenced by the styles of *chanson* and madrigal, forms such as the Spanish *villancico, German *Lied, and English *part-song flourished as never before.

During the 16th century, a polyphonic texture was normal in most leading genres of song, suiting an ensemble of voices or instruments in which each line contributed a roughly equal part to the effect of the whole. But changes were on the way; with the development of instruments capable of accompanying a solo voice, such as lute, vihuela, and harpsichord, the rise both of the virtuoso singer and of the art of embellishing vocal lines, and new theories about the expressive advantages of solo song over a contrapuntal texture, existing forms of polyphonic song gradually fell into decline. In their place, new types of lyric or declamatory song such as Italian *monody, the French *air de cour, and the English *ayre came into fashion. With their rise, we enter the era of modern song.

JOHN MILSOM

5. *The 17th and 18th Centuries*. By the beginning of the 17th century, the solo art-song was already fully fledged. In Italy, Caccini's *Le nuove musiche* (1601–2) marks the beginning of the popularity of *monody, the *aria, and, from the 1630s, the secular *cantata. Germany had its own tradition of monophonic song in the *Meistergesang*, but otherwise German composers remained firmly committed to the idea of equal-voiced polyphonic song until the 1620s, when the continuo *Lied* began to take over in importance. The French had developed declamatory solo singing since the late 1560s

(see *Musique mesurée*), and the first *airs de cour* were published in the 1570s; this became an extremely popular genre in the 17th and 18th centuries, together with its less sophisticated cousins the *air à boire and the *brunette.

In England, the solo song with instrumental accompaniment had its own tradition in the *consort song and the slightly later *lute-song, but these faded out almost as quickly as did the English madrigal, their light, delicate, polyphonic accompaniments giving way to the ubiquitous continuo part. In the hands of such composers as Henry Lawes and John Wilson, the solo song settles down into a basically strophic form, and the words are frequently set in a natural, declamatory style (contemporaries described it as 'recitative music'). This trait was developed by Pelham Humfrey and John Blow, and reaches its finest expression in the songs of Henry Purcell.

During the 17th and 18th centuries, the musical presses of Germany, England, and France turned out hundreds of song books for solo voice and continuo—requiring only two staves, they were conveniently small and cheap to produce. In Germany, they were important in the early history of the *Lied*; their contents were both sacred and secular, so that they also played their part in the development of Protestant church music, which culminated in the sacred cantatas of J. S. Bach. In 18th-century England, vast numbers of songs were written for the fashionable entertainments at Vauxhall and Ranelagh Pleasure Gardens and elsewhere by Thomas Arne, William Boyce, Charles Dibdin, James Hook, and many others. French composers were equally prolific in writing *airs*. Few from either country have survived, but songs written in this form did not die out until the 19th century.

6. *The 19th Century*. The dominant country for song in the 19th century was undoubtedly Germany. The remarkable amalgam of word and tone in the great *Lied* composers Schubert, Schumann, and Brahms set a standard by which song in other countries tends to be judged. France, with a long and distinguished poetic heritage to draw upon, stands next in importance; her typical *mélodie is as far removed from the *Lied* as the French language is from the German. France's finest 19th-century song composer was Gabriel Fauré, who in such masterpieces as 'Clair de lune' (Verlaine), 'Le parfum impérissable' (Leconte de Lisle), and 'Les roses d'Ispahan' (Leconte de Lisle) brought an exquisite musical subtlety to these essentially French texts. The same is true of Henri Duparc, whose 'L'invitation au voyage' (Baudelaire) ranks very high in the literature of song. Debussy, 'musicien français' as he styled him-

Pl. 3. Schubertabend at the home of Joseph von Spaun, drawing by Moritz von Schwind; Schubert is at the piano, with Vogl on his right and Spaun on his left.

self, was also attracted by the Wattcau-esque nostalgia of Verlaine (*Fêtes galantes*), and also found a stimulus in the other Symbolists, Baudelaire (*Cinq poèmes*) and Mallarmé (*Trois poèmes*). Spanning the whole of his creative life, his songs embody his quintessential style, his harmonic and colouristic explorations paving the way for 20th-century emancipation.

In the British Isles, 19th-century song produced little of lasting value. The level was uneven, and unfortunately the peaks of achievement were hardly exalted enough to compensate for the humdrum general standard of both words and music. The noticeable improvement towards the end of the century is less significant than it at one time appeared: the several sets of *English Lyrics* by Hubert Parry, for instance, now seem well made rather than inspired. The Irish composer Charles Villiers Stanford possessed more of the divine spark; a song such as 'The Fairy Lough' has an other-worldly quality that endears it to all singers, and the imaginative 'Middle Watch' stands out refreshingly above the 'breezy and unmistakeably English atmosphere' of the remaining *Songs of the Fleet*.

19th-century Russia was rich in song. Songs were composed by all the important composers (and many minor ones) from Dargomyzhsky and Glinka to Musorgsky, Tchaikovsky, and Rakhmaninov. Typically, their approach was direct, close to the speech of the people and avoiding the learned devices of the music schools. Musorgsky wrote about 60 songs, setting not only the Russian classics (Lermontov, Pushkin) but also Heine and Goethe, in a personal style which preferred vigour to polish and owed much to Russian folk music. *The Song of the Flea* (from Goethe's *Faust*) and the two cycles *The Nursery* and *Songs and Dances of Death* are characteristic. Compared with Musorgsky, Tchaikovsky was elegant and cosmopolitan; happiest, like Richard Strauss, with big orchestral canvases, he was less at ease in the intimate world of song. A few of his *c.*90 songs have become popular, particularly 'None but the lonely heart' and *Don Juan's Serenade*; there are others, for example the *Sixteen Songs for Children*, Op. 54, which ought not to be forgotten.

In Norway, Grieg, ill equipped by temperament to cope with the large 19th-century musical forms, in some of his *c.*140 songs displayed a charm and freshness that many greater composers might envy. His best and most characteristic songs are to Norwegian words, such as the well-known *Solvejg's Song* (from Ibsen's *Peer Gynt*); others, perhaps less familiar, are *En svane* ('A swan', Op. 25 No. 2) and the set of children's songs Op. 61. Sibelius, who was at home in the symphonic world, also cultivated the solo song, and wrote about 90, but perhaps the most outstanding song composer of Finland is Yrjö Kilpinen, with a fecundity challenging that of Schubert—he wrote over

700 songs, to Finnish, Swedish, and German words.

7. *The 20th Century*. Despite the fact that he died in 1958, Vaughan Williams as a song-writer belongs more to the 19th century than to the 20th. His many songs include some of the most rewarding in the English language, for instance 'Silent Noon' (from Rossetti's *House of Life* cycle) and 'The Watermill'. He worked closely with Cecil Sharp in the collecting of folk-songs; he made several arrangements of them for voice and piano, but his actual song-writing is in a quite different style, even though his musical idiom was strongly influenced by the English folk-song tradition. In Vaughan Williams's generation a number of other composers contributed richly to the repertory of English song: Ireland, Quilter, Warlock, Finzi, Butterworth, and Gurney are known especially for their settings of English verse (Gurney set to music a number of his own poems), while Delius's more cosmopolitan outlook led him to look further afield to the poetry of Verlaine, Ibsen, and other Norwegian poets. Other song-writers of the present century whose work, though 'modern', has not broken the mould of accompanied song, include Hindemith, Poulenc, and Britten, whose eclectic choice of poets has ranged from John Donne to Michelangelo and Hölderlin. Tippett, a less prolific composer of solo songs than Britten, has tended to extend the bounds of vocal technique in his operas, which in turn have inspired his *Songs for Achilles*, *Songs for Ariel*, and *Songs for Dov*, and Peter Maxwell Davies has further explored the flexibility of the voice in such works as *Eight Songs for a Mad King*.

Other composers, particularly Schoenberg, Berg, and Webern, moved so far away from previous norms that it would be misleading to describe them as for 'voice and accompaniment'. In their songs vocal and instrumental lines are interwoven to form an integrated polyphony differing substantially from previous song textures. The wide, awkward leaps can, it is true, be seen as extensions of the vocal techniques of Wagner, Richard Strauss, and Wolf, and atonality as a logical continuation of late 19th-century chromaticism, but now the whole is subject to an *a priori* intellectual control, rather than springing directly from the demands of the words: such an 'intellectual' approach is even more prominent in recent works by such composers as Pousseur and Berio, calling for a so-called 'extended vocal technique' which makes ever-increasing demands on the voice's capabilities. Yet the words, often esoteric, mystical, recondite, remain as always the springboard for the composer, and in the hands of Schoenberg, Berg, and Webern the angularities

of the vocal line were central to the expressiveness of their songs, which constitute a small but significant portion of their total output.

LESLIE ORREY

FURTHER READING
Denis Stevens, ed.: *A History of Song* (London, 1960); R. Hinton Thomas: *Poetry and Song in the German Baroque* (Oxford, 1963); Wilfrid Mellers: *Harmonious Meeting* (London, 1965); Sydney Northcote: *Byrd to Britten: a Survey of English Song* (London, 1966); Peter Dronke: *The Medieval Lyric* (London, 1968); Pierre Bernac: *The Interpretation of French Song* (London, 1970, 2nd edn 1976); Frits Noske: *French Song from Berlioz to Duparc* (London, 1970); Ian Spink: *English Song: Dowland to Purcell* (London, 1974).

Song-cycle (Ger.: *Liederkreis*, *Liederzyklus*). A group of songs with a common theme, the poems usually, but not necessarily, by one poet. The music may or may not reveal an over-all coherence, of key schemes, form, and so on; or it may present little more than a unity of mood; or it may simply follow the dictates of the poems, with little or no attempt at organic unity.

The song-cycle is a 19th-century phenomenon. The first important example was Beethoven's *An die ferne Geliebte* ('To the distant beloved'), written and published in 1816: six songs make up the cycle, composed to a coherent, systematic key-scheme, with each song linked musically to the next, and the poetic theme—distant, unattainable love—running through all six. The last song recapitulates the first. Schubert followed a few years later with two cycles, both considerably larger: *Die schöne Müllerin* (1823), 20 songs; and *Die Winterreise* (1828), 24 songs, both to words by Wilhelm Müller.

Thereafter there were song-cycles from every quarter; we can mention only a few of the most notable. Schumann, not always comfortable with abstract instrumental forms, found it particularly congenial; two of the several he wrote are outstanding—*Dichterliebe* (Heine) and *Frauenliebe und -leben* (Chamisso), both dating from 1840.

An early French song-cycle was Berlioz's *Nuits d'été* (Gautier). Written originally with piano accompaniment (*c*.1834), the songs are best known in his own orchestral version. The finest of Fauré's several cycles is *La bonne chanson* (1892–4), setting nine poems by Verlaine, on whom Debussy drew for his *Fêtes galantes* (1892 and 1904). The genre has appealed strongly to Vaughan Williams (for example, his superb *On Wenlock Edge*, A. E. Housman; 1908–9) and Benjamin Britten (*Les illuminations*, Rimbaud; 1939), among many others. Two interesting cycles by Musorgsky should be noted: *The Nursery* (to his own words; 1868–72) and the *Songs and Dances of Death*

(Golenishchev-Kutuzov; 1875–7). Modern German examples include Hindemith's *Das Marienleben* (Rilke; 1922–3) and, in a very different idiom, Schoenberg's *Pierrot lunaire* (Albert Giraud; 1912) and *Das Buch der Hängenden Gärten* (Stefan George; 1908); Mahler's *Lieder eines fahrenden Gesellen* (1883–5), *Kindertotenlieder* (1901–4), and *Das Lied von der Erde* (1908–9), each for voice and orchestra, are in a way the apotheosis, the final summing up, of the spirit of the *Lied*.   LESLIE ORREY

Song for the Lord Mayor's Table, A. Song-cycle by Walton for soprano and piano. The six songs are settings of words collected by Christopher Hassall from poems by Blake, Thomas Jordan, Charles Morris, Wordsworth, and two anonymous 18th-century poets. It was written for the 1962 City of London Festival and also given in a version for soprano and orchestra at the 1970 festival.

Song of the Flea (*Pesnya Mefistofelya o blokhe*). Song by Musorgsky for voice and piano, composed in 1879. It is a setting of Mephistopheles's song in Goethe's *Faust*.

Song of the High Hills, A. Work by Delius for orchestra and chorus (wordless), with solo parts for soprano and tenor, composed in 1911.

Songs and Dances of Death (*Pesni i plyaski smerti*). Song-cycle by Musorgsky for voice and piano, composed between 1875 and 1877. The four songs are settings of poems by Golenishchev-Kutuzov.

Songs for a Mad King, Eight. Theatre piece by Peter Maxwell Davies to a text by Randolph Stow and King George III. In eight movements, it is scored for a male actor/singer and ensemble (including railway whistle, didjeridu, and chains) and was first performed in 1969 in London.

Songs for Dov. Song-cycle by Tippett for tenor and small orchestra (including six percussionists), to his own texts. They are based on songs for the character Dov in Tippett's opera *The Knot Garden*, and they were composed in 1969–70.

Songs of Farewell. 1. Six unaccompanied secular motets by Parry to texts by Vaughan, J. Davies, Campion, Lockhart, Donne, and from the Bible. They were composed 1916–18.
    2. Five songs by Delius, settings of poems by Whitman for chorus and orchestra. They were composed in 1930, one of them notated with Eric Fenby's help, and were first performed in 1932.

Songs of the Sea. Five songs, Op. 91, by Stanford to poems by Henry Newbolt (1862–1938). They are for baritone, male chorus, and orchestra and were first performed in Leeds in 1904.

Songs of Travel. Song cycle by Vaughan Williams for voice and piano to nine poems by Robert Louis Stevenson from his *Songs of Travel*. Eight of them were composed in 1904 but the seventh song was written in 1901. Some are sung separately, including *The Vagabond*, *The Roadside Fire*, *Whither must I wander?*, and *Bright is the Ring of Words*.

Song without Words (Ger.: *Lied ohne Worte*; Fr.: *chanson sans paroles*). Title given by Mendelssohn to his 48 piano pieces published in eight groups of six (1830–45), each written in the style of a song, i.e. with a distinctive melody and accompaniment. It was essentially a Romantic conception, foreshadowed by Schubert's Impromptu in G, Op. 90 No. 3, and by some of the slow movements of Beethoven's piano sonatas. The piano nocturnes of Field and Chopin are similar in style, and some of Field's pieces are even called 'Song without Words' (but the name may have been added later by the editor, Liszt). Of Mendelssohn's 48 examples, only five have individual titles: the three 'Venetian Gondola Songs' (Nos. 6, 12, and 29); the *Duetto*, No. 18; and the *Volkslied* ('Folk-song'), No. 23.

Sonnambula, La ('The Sleepwalking Girl'). Opera in two acts by Bellini to a libretto by Romani. It was first performed in Milan in 1831.

Sonore (Fr.), **sonoro, sonora** (It.). 'Sonorous'; *sonorité* (Fr.), *sonorità* (It.), 'sonority'; *sonoramente* (It.), 'sonorously'; *onde sonore* (Fr.), 'sound-wave', 'acoustic wave'.

Sons bouchés (Fr.). In horn playing, 'stopped notes'.

Sopra (It.). 'On', 'above'; *sopra una corda*, in string playing, 'on one string' (for its meaning with regard to piano playing, see *Una corda*); *come sopra*, 'as above'; *mano sinistra* (*ms*) *sopra*, in piano playing, with the left hand above the right.

Sopran (Ger.). 'Soprano'.

Sopranino (It.). 'Little soprano'. A name given to the size of instrument higher than a soprano, e.g. sopranino recorder, sopranino saxophone.

Soprano (From It. *sopra*, 'above'). 1. The highest female (or artificial male) voice, with a range of roughly *b* to *c′′′* (in high sopranos often *f′′′*). There are several types of soprano, of which the commonest in general use are the 'coloratura soprano', a light, high voice of great agility (e.g. the Queen of the Night in Mozart's *Die Zauberflöte*); 'lyric soprano', the most common, with a warmer tone-quality and a slightly lower range; 'dramatic soprano', with a heavier production throughout the range (e.g. Tosca); and 'soprano spinto', or 'soprano lirico spinto', basically a lyric voice that is capable of more dramatic quality and a cutting edge at climaxes (e.g. Desdemona in Verdi's *Otello*).

2. The term is also used for high instrumental registers, e.g. soprano cornet, soprano saxophone. See also *Sopranino*.

Soprano clef. A clef which places Middle C on the bottom line of the staff; it is now obsolete.

Sor, Fernando (*bapt.* Barcelona, 14 Feb. 1778; *d* Paris, 10 July 1839). Spanish composer. He studied at the choir school of Montserrat 1790–5, and in 1797 his opera *Telemaco* was staged in Barcelona. He stayed in Spain during the Peninsular War, but in 1813, having collaborated with the occupying French, found it expedient to leave the country. He went first to Paris, where his talent was recognized by Méhul and Cherubini, and then to London, where his compositions were much admired. He then went on to Russia for three years, and there he composed his masterpiece, the ballet *Hercules y Onfalia* (1826), for the coronation of Tsar Nicholas I. Sor is remembered today for his guitar pieces, which form part of the standard repertory, and for his important tutor, *Gran Método de Guitarra* (Bonn, 1830).

WENDY THOMPSON

Sorda, sordo, sordamente (It.). 'Subdued', 'muffled'.

Sordino (It.). 'Mute'; *sordini alzati* (*levati*), 'mutes raised', i.e. taken off. Applied to the piano, *sordini* means dampers; see under *Senza*.

Sordun. An uncommon double-reed wind instrument of the late Renaissance. See *Kortholt*.

Soriano, Francesco (*b* Soriano, nr Viterbo, 1548–9; *d* Rome, 1621). Italian composer. He was a pupil of Palestrina and, having been a choirboy in St John Lateran, became *maestro di cappella* at several notable churches in Rome, finally at St Peter's. He wrote madrigals, motets, and Masses, and with Anerio was responsible for completing the *Edito medicaea* (see *Plainchant*, 4), the revision of chant books begun by Palestrina and Zoilo. He also arranged Palestrina's *Missa Papae Marcelli* for eight voices in double choir, probably to give a more resonant effect in the vastness of the new nave in St Peter's.   DENIS ARNOLD

Sorochintsy Fair (*Sorochinskaya yarmarka*). Unfinished opera in three acts by Musorgsky to his own libretto after the story by Gogol. He worked on it between 1874 and 1880 but it was completed and orchestrated by Lyadov, V. G. Karatigin, and others, and first performed in Moscow in 1913. A completion by Cui was performed in St Petersburg in 1917, and one by Tcherepnin in Monte Carlo in 1923. Another completion, by Shebalin, was published in 1933.

Sortie (Fr.). 'Exit', 'departure', hence a postlude or a concluding voluntary.

Sospirando, sospirante, sospirevole, sospiroso (It.). 'Sighing', i.e. plaintive in style.

Sostenendo, sostenente (It.). 'Sustaining'; *sostenuto*, 'sustained'; *andante sostenuto*, a 'sustained', i.e. rather slow, *andante*; *pedale sostenuto*, the *sustaining pedal.

Sostenuto pedal. The middle pedal which is fitted to some grand pianos. It sustains some, but not all, of the notes of a chord. See *Piano*, 12*b*.

Sotto voce (It.). 'In a low voice', 'in an undertone', i.e. barely audible. The term may be applied to both vocal and instrumental performance.

Soubrette (Fr.). A secondary female role in comic opera, often a lively and coquettish lady's maid such as Despina in *Così fan tutte* or Adèle in *Die Fledermaus*.

Soudainement (Fr.). 'Suddenly'.

Soul. A term which more or less encompasses all the popular music of North America that has arisen from Black sources, deriving from the *blues, and including rhythm and blues and *rock. It implies a somewhat deeper and more spiritual character than is found in the Tin Pan Alley rooted music of White Americans, just as Black jazz (rightly or wrongly) is considered to possess greater depth than White jazz.

Soundboard. See *Piano*, 11.

Soundholes. The *f*-shaped holes cut in the belly (i.e. the upper surface) of a stringed instrument of the violin family.

Soundpost (Fr.: *âme*; Ger.: *Seele*, *Stimme*, *Stimmstock*; It.: *anima*). The piece of pine fixed between the back and belly (i.e. inside the instrument) of a violin etc., which counters the downward pressure of the bridge. It should be set just behind the right foot of the bridge.

Sound-waves. See *Acoustics*.

Soupirant (Fr.). 'Sighing'; i.e. plaintively.

Souple (Fr.). 'Supple', 'flexible'.

Sourd, sourde (Fr.).'Muffled', 'muted'; *pédale sourde*, the soft pedal; see *Piano*, 12*c*.

Sourdine (Fr.). 1. 'Mute'. 2. See *Kortholt*.

Sousa, John Philip (*b* Washington, DC, 6 Nov. 1854; *d* Reading, Penn., 6 Mar. 1932). American composer and bandmaster. He grew up studying music, became a competent violinist, and played mostly in theatre orchestras as a young man. Appointed director of the US Marine Band in 1880, he resigned that post in 1892 to form a band of his own. Sousa's Band successfully toured the USA over the next four decades, also making several European tours and one around the world. Sousa's creed as a conductor was to 'entertain' his audience and to 'educate' them at the same time. His pro-gramme mixed popular favourites with excerpts from the classics, often featuring virtuoso solos by band members. Through its concert appearances and its many recordings, Sousa's Band introduced polished ensemble music-making to an unusually wide audience. Sousa's marches, which number more than 130, show his special strengths as a composer: melodic inventiveness, rhythmic vigour, an ear for harmonic surprise, and an understanding of a wind band's sound capabilities. Emphasizing changes of theme, colour, texture, dynamics, and even key, Sousa's marches are in effect miniatures for large ensemble whose brief time span is animated by sharp, bold contrasts.

RICHARD CRAWFORD

Sousaphone. See *Tuba*, 3.

Souster, Tim(othy Andrew James) (*b* Bletchley, 29 Jan. 1943). English composer. He studied at Oxford University (1961-5), at the Darmstadt courses with Stockhausen and Berio (1963), and in London with Richard Rodney Bennett (1965). Closely associated with Stockhausen as performer and assistant, he has been a founder-member of the live electronic ensembles Intermodulation (1969-76) and odB (1976-). His works show the influences of Stockhausen, the American avant-garde, and rock.

PAUL GRIFFITHS

South-East Asian Music

1. Introduction
2. Instrumental and Vocal Forms

3. Music and Theatre

1. *Introduction*. The South-East Asian culture area includes the island republics of *Indonesia and the Philippines, Borneo (politically divided between Malaysia, Indonesia, and the independent state of Brunei), as well as the mainland countries of Burma, Thailand, Kampuchea (formerly Khmer, then Cambodia), Laos, Vietnam, and Malaysia. The region is vast and diverse, extending approximately 3,750 miles from the hills of northern Burma to the eastern border of Irian Jaya (Indonesia) on the island of New Guinea. The mainland countries, particularly Vietnam, have been greatly influenced by Chinese culture, and the predominant religion is Buddhism. Indonesia has been influenced both by Hinduism and Islam, and the Philippines by both Islam and Christianity. Even the high civilizations of the mainland are isolated from each other by jungle and mountain terrain, all factors which have encouraged independent cultural development in each region. Nevertheless, South-East Asian peoples are surprisingly unified by their musical preferences: first, for gapped scales (with intervals greater than a whole tone); secondly, for compositional processes (such as the Thai *thâw* and the Javanese *irama*) whereby recurring melodies are expanded, contracted, and varied; thirdly, for melodic (rather than harmonic) organization of musical forms; fourthly, for stratified orchestration (labelled 'colotomic structure' by Jaap Kunst), whereby each instrumental (or vocal) part in a polyphonic composition has a characteristic and idiomatic density (some active, for example xylophones, and others with a slower, punctuating role, for example large gongs); and finally, for melodic percussion instruments, especially xylophones, metallophones, tuned drum-chimes (such as the Burmese *hsaing-waing*), and tuned bronze gongs and gong-chimes, often played in orchestras such as the well-known Indonesian gamelan, the Filipino *kulintang*, and the Thai *pī phāt*.

2. *Instrumental and Vocal Forms*. South-East Asian countries are sometimes referred to by

Thai musician playing the khǭng mǭn (bossed gong-chime).

musicologists as 'gong-chime cultures' because of the variety of gongs and gong-chime ensembles played throughout the area. Each orchestra consists of gongs, one or more drums, xylophones, and sometimes metallophones (xylophones with metal keys), flutes, and occasionally chordophones (stringed instruments). The combination of instruments and the size of the ensemble varies from country to country; the largest Javanese gamelan have up to 75 instruments, whereas simple village groups have only a few. Gongs are made of bronze, brass, or iron, and an instrument may consist of a single gong or a tuned set which is called a gong-chime. Gongs may be suspended from a frame or placed on a rack. Sets may be arranged horizontally in a row, on a wooden case, in a frame, or suspended. The cases and frames may be ornately carved and painted, often in brilliant colours, and individual instruments especially prized for their beauty may be given proper names, have magical powers attributed to them, and receive ritual offerings. Gongs often have a central knob called a 'boss', and they are tuned to fit into one or another local scale (many with equidistantly-spaced intervals)—usually pentatonic (five note) or heptatonic (seven note).

In Thailand, the principal gong-chime ensemble is the *pī phāt*. A large outdoor *pī phāt* ensemble usually includes at least one pair of each of the main instrument types: gong-chimes (*khǭng wong yai, khǭng wong lek*), xylophones (*ranāt ēk* and *ranāt thum*), metallophones (*ranāt ēk lek, ranāt thum lek*), barrel drums (*taphōn, klǭng that*), cymbals (*ching, chāp lek, chāp yai*), a gong (*mōng*), and shawms (*pī nai, pī nǭk*), which

lend the ensemble their name. Smaller indoor groups have fewer melodic percussion instruments.

The sound of the *pī phāt* is distinctive. The instruments, by their very nature, have a limited dynamic range, so that the relative loudness may best be adjusted by the listeners, who can move closer to, or further from, the group. The repertory is generally typified by regular, repeating rhythmic figures (usually in duple metre). The colotomic structure (phrase organization punctuated by gong or cymbal strokes), while akin to that of the Javanese and Balinese repertories, is much less elaborate. Three basic tempos are used: slow, medium (twice as fast), and fast (twice as fast again). The pace is marked by the *ching* (cymbals): one stroke per bar in the slow tempo, two in the medium, and four in the fast. Consequently, Thai instrumental music, with its metric regularity and unchanging dynamics, may seem to the Western ear somewhat monotonous on first hearing.

The *pī phāt* is one of the loudest of the Thai ensembles. Other quieter groups include the *mahōrī* (with gong-chimes, xylophones, fiddles and spike-fiddles, zithers, flutes, goblet and frame drums, and cymbals) and the *khrǔang saī*, softer still (with fiddles, zithers, flutes, goblet and frame drums, cymbals, and gong).

The *pin peat* orchestra of Kampuchea is similar to its Thai counterpart, the *pī phāt*. It consists of two xylophones (*roneat ek, roneat thung*), gong-chimes (*kong touch, kong thom*), shawms (*sralai*) or flutes (*khloi*), a cylindrical double-headed drum (*samphor*), a large drum pair (*skor thom*), and cymbals (*ching*). The ensemble accompanies shadow plays and dance-dramas, and performs for religious celebrations. The *phleng khmer* ensemble plays in more traditional folk contexts such as weddings and ceremonies of magic. It comprises a long-necked lute (*cha pei*), fiddle (*tro khmer*), shawm (*pey âr*), and drums (*skor arak*).

The *kulintang* is the gong-chime orchestra of the southern Philippines and northern Borneo. The main instrument, from which the ensemble takes its name, is the *kulintang*, a gong-chime with from seven to twelve (most commonly eight) bossed gongs. This instrument, generally played only by men, always carries the main melody. Orchestras may also include other gongs (*agung, gandingan, tunggalan,* and *dua-han*), and drums (*dabakan, gandang*). The size of the ensemble and the exact instrumentation varies from region to region. In the northern Philippines, ensembles of flat gongs (*gangsa*) are more common. *Gangsa* are made of bronze or brass, and are slapped or tapped with the hands, or beaten on the top or underside with a stick. A variety of timbres, mostly clangy and without specific pitches, results, depending on the playing technique used. *Gangsa* ensembles may sometimes also include barrel, conical, or cylindrical drums, and iron clappers.

The most characteristic Burmese orchestra is the *hsaing-waing*, which takes its name from the main instrument, a chime of 21 tuned wooden drums suspended from a circular wooden frame. The performer sits inside the circle and strikes the drums with the sticks. This unusual and beautiful instrument has a range of more than three octaves, and it therefore is capable of playing melodies. In large urban groups, the *hsaing-waing* drum-chime is accompanied by the *kyì-waing* (a gong-chime with 21 bossed gongs arranged on a circular frame), the *maùng-zaing* (a gong-chime with 18 or 19 bossed gongs,

arranged in rows), the *hnè* (shawm), *chauk-lòn-bat* (set of six drums), *byauk* (slit-drum), *walet-hkok* (clappers), *yagwìn* (cymbals), *sì* (hand cymbals), and *maùng* (gong). Village groups might include only the *hsaing-waing* drum-chime, the *kyì-waing* gong-chime, shawm, barrel drum, and hand cymbals. Both large and small orchestras accompany traditional Burmese theatrical forms and also religious rites and festivals.

Gong-chime ensembles are conspicuously absent in Vietnam, where strong Chinese influence has perhaps swayed the balance more towards orchestras of chordophones and aerophones. The *dai nhac* court orchestra, for example, includes four shawms (*kèn*), fiddle (*dan nhi*), flat drum (*tamâmla*), barrel-shaped 'rice drum' (*trông com*), clappers (*sinh tiên*), hourglass drum (*bông*), slit-drum (*mo sung trâu*), cymbals (*châp choa*), and gong.

Many South-East Asian instruments are intended for solo rather than ensemble performance. The *khaen* is a popular free-reed bamboo mouth-organ of South-East Asia, akin to the Chinese *sheng* and the Japanese *shō*. It consists of a carved wooden wind-chest and a set of clustered bamboo pipes (as many as 18), each with a copper or silver reed. *Khaen* are made in various sizes; some for children have only a few pipes, while large versions measuring two to three metres in length have been noted. The instrument is extremely versatile, and can produce chords, drone, and melody simultaneously and continuously (as the performer practises nasal breathing, constantly replenishing the air supply in the wind-chest). The *khaen* may be played solo or in ensembles.

One of the loveliest solo instruments is the 14-string Burmese arched harp (*saùng-gauk*), elegant both in the graceful curve of its neck and in the subtle refinement of its repertory. Some

Mahōrī ensemble of Thailand: front row (left to right) *small hand cymbals, sǭ sām saī* (*spike fiddle*); *centre row, jakhē* (*zither*), *ranāt ēk lek* (*metallophone*), *ranāt ēk, ranāt thum* (*xylophones*), *ranāt thum lek* (*metallophone*); *back row, khlui* (*flute*), *khǭng wong yai, khǭng wong lek* (*gong-chimes*), *rammanā* (*frame drum*), *thōn* (*goblet drum*).

Burmese hsaìng-waìng ensemble, with hsaìng-waìng (tuned drum chime, centre), hnè (conical shawm with flared metal bell, centre right), kwì-waìng (bossed gong-chime, right), pat-má (large barrel drum suspended from a pole frame, centre left), yagwìn (cymbals, left), accompanying a marionette play (above).

scholars maintain that the *saùng-gauk* derives from the arched harps of ancient India, but the Sanskrit term for the instrument (*vīṇā*) does not occur in Burma, leaving this question open pending further research. The student of the modern *saùng-gauk* must master complex theories of modes and tunings, as well as intricate playing techniques. Various types of finger-strokes are used: upwards strokes of the index finger (*let-kat*), outwards and upwards strokes with a hooked finger (*kaw*), and strokes of the hooked index finger and thumb together (*zon-hswè-gyìn*). The basic repertory of the

Burmese saùng-gauk (classical arched harp).

instrument comprises 13 *kyò* ('string') songs which date from the 18th and 19th centuries. They are composed in the oldest of the four harp tunings (*hnyìn-lòn*), and are usually accompanied by hand cymbals (*sì*) and clappers (*wà*).

These *kyò* form an important part of the Burmese classical vocal tradition. The basic repertory consists of several hundred songs, whose texts are recorded in two great anthologies, the *Maha Gi-tá* and the *Gi-tá Wi-thàw-dani*. The tunes are not written down but are passed from teacher to pupil in oral tradition. Most of the items fall into the categories of old Burmese court songs, songs reputedly of Thai origin, songs for spirit worship, or laments. These two large collections are known in their entirety by more professional Burmese singers.

The folk music of Thailand and Burma provides a sharp contrast to the classical repertories such as those of the gong-chime ensembles and the *saùng-gauk*. Judith Becker reports that the music of the Pwo Karen people of northern Thailand, for example, is intimately linked to poetry; *mae-tae*, the local term referring to music, literally means 'poeming', indicating that the words are the most important feature of a song, and most songs have a specific function, be they for drinking, courting, funerals, or lullabies. The only local Pwo Karen instrument is a side-blown buffalo horn. Cymbals, drums, and gongs are played in Buddhist ceremonies, but these instruments are of Thai origin. Bossed gongs are played by the hill peoples of northern Burma, often to accompany dances; the gong patterns generally consist of short phrases, repeated many times. Dances of the Kachin and Shan peoples are accompanied with a free-reed mouth-organ (*hnyìn*) and bamboo panpipes.

3. *Music and Theatre*. Throughout South-East Asia, music is intimately linked to the theatrical arts—plays, mask plays, puppet shows, shadow-dramas, dance-dramas, and operas—often held in the open air and lasting many hours into the night (and sometimes for several days). Many of these genres date back to the local animistic rites of ancient times, intended to placate the spirits of nature. Later dramatic texts are often based on foreign sources, especially the Hindu epics, the *Rāmāyaṇa* and the *Mahābhārata* (introduced during the first millennium AD), and also on the *Jātaka* stories from the life of the Buddha. From 1200 to 1750, Chinese theatrical forms were introduced to the northern mainland, and during approximately the same period, extensive Arabic influence reached the southern mainland and the islands.

Most dramatic forms are accompanied by singing and by instrumental ensembles. The best known of South-East Asian dramatic arts is the *wayang kulit* shadow-puppet play of Java. Most of the immense repertory of *wayang kulit* plays are based on the Hindu *Mahābhārata* epic. Stylized flat leather puppets (showing the character in profile) are manipulated behind a white cotton screen by a single puppeteer (*ḍalang*). The audience may sit in front of the screen, watching the subtle shadow effects, or behind the screen, watching the *ḍalang* manipulate the colourfully decorated puppets.

Shan musician of Central Burma playing a free-reed mouth organ with five pipes.

Wayang kulit performances are accompanied by a full gamelan orchestra, and last for many hours. Other Indonesian dramatic forms accompanied by music include the *sĕndratari* ('art-dance-drama'), the *kĕtoprak* (prose dialogue drama), the Sunda (West Java) *wayang golek* (doll theatre), and the Balinese *barong* (trance dance-drama) and *arja* (sung drama).

In Burma, *zat-kyì* (classical court dance-drama, largely based on the Hindu *Rāmāyaṇa* epic) flourished during the 18th and 19th centuries. It is still performed in the second half of the 20th century in the state music academies in Rangoon and Mandalay. *Zat-kyì* dancers may be masked or unmasked, and masked performers may lift their disguise during passages of dialogue. The play is accompanied by the *hsaìng-waìng* drum-chime ensemble. Other Burmese dramatic forms include the *nat-pwè* (spirit-invocation dance) and the *yok-theì-pwè* (marionette drama).

Laotian dramatic forms, both folk and classical, are performed by the Royal Lao Ballet (the only surviving royal troupe of South-East Asia) as well as by professional itinerant companies. *Mawlum lüang* is a popular commercial form which developed in the early 20th century. It derived from the traditional *mawlum* genre, which combines tales from the *Rāmāyaṇa* with Lao folk stories and local news. *Mawlum* is performed by a vocalist (*maw lum*) and *khaen* player (*maw khaen*).

The classical dance-drama of Thailand dates from the 15th century. The two principal forms, *lakhọn nai* (for women) and *khon* (masked mime for men), are accompanied by the *pī phāt* orchestra, often with an additional *khọ̄ng wong* (gong-chime) and gongs, cymbals, and split-stick clappers. The ancient *lakhọn jatri* folk drama of southern Thailand was traditionally danced by shamans as part of an animistic rite. The most important play of this repertory is *Manora*, based on the *Jātaka* stories. It lasts for 12 nights (or longer) and is accompanied by the *pī* (shawm), *khọ̄ng khu* (double gong), two *thab* (single-headed drums), *klọ̄ng* (barrel drum), and *ching* (small cymbals). Other dramatic genres of South-East Asia include the Malaysian *wayang siam* (shadow play), *ma'yong* (dance-drama), and the Vietnamese *hat bôi* (classical opera).

During the 19th century, Western-influenced popular commercial genres, aimed at urban audiences, took hold in many regions, and in recent years 'pop' music is disseminated even to remote areas through films, cassettes, radio, and television. None the less, South-East Asian drama and music of the 20th century retain a local flavour, particularly in rural areas, where village troupes still enact the animistic rituals that are the true origin of their art.

HELEN MYERS

FURTHER READING
J. Kunst: *Music in Java* (The Hague, 1949); M. Hood: *The Nuclear Theme as a Determinant of Paṭet in Javanese Music* (Groningen and Jakarta, 1954, reprinted 1977); Trân van Khê: *La musique vietnamienne traditionnelle* (Paris, 1962); C. McPhee: *Music in Bali* (New Haven, 1966); W. P. Malm: *Music Cultures of the Pacific, the Near East, and Asia* (Englewood Cliffs, NJ, 1967, reprinted 1977); J. Becker: 'Percussive Patterns in the Music of Mainland Southeast Asia', *Ethnomusicology*, xii (1968), pp. 173-9; J. Becker: 'The Anatomy of a Mode', *Ethnomusicology*, xiii (1969), pp. 267-79; U. H. Cadar: 'The Role of *Kulintang* in Maranao Society', *Selected Reports in Ethnomusicology*, ii/2 (1975), pp. 49-62; M. Harrell: 'Some Aspects of Sundanese Music', ibid., pp. 81-101; D. Morton: 'Instruments and Instrumental Functions in the Ensembles of Southeast Asia: a Cross-Cultural Comparison', ibid., pp. 7-15; M. C. Williamson: 'Aspects of Traditional Style Maintained in Burma's First 13 Kyò Songs', ibid., pp. 117-63; D. Morton: *The Traditional Music of Thailand* (Berkeley, 1976).

Spacing. The arrangement of the notes of a chord, according to the requirements of the individual voices. If the upper voices are close together, the spacing is described as close position, or close harmony; if not, the arrangement is called open position, or open harmony. See *Position*.

Spain and Portugal

1. The Middle Ages to 1450
2. 1450-1530
3. The Late Renaissance: 1530-1600
4. The Baroque Era
5. Music under the Bourbons
6. The 19th Century
7. The 20th Century

1. *The Middle Ages to 1450.* The history of Spain up to 1450 was one of repeated invasions, each bringing a new kind of culture which exercised strong and lasting influence over Spanish life and art. In the first millennium BC the peninsula was conquered by the Romans, who introduced musical instruments such as the trumpet and organ (*hydraulos*), used to accompany singing and dancing. They also brought six centuries of political stability, during which Christianity was introduced and spread rapidly despite repression: it was officially recognized by Constantine the Great in 312, though the peninsula did not become wholly Christian until the late 15th century. Around AD 500 the Roman Empire disintegrated and Roman rule was replaced in Spain by a series of barbarian kingdoms, in particular the Visigoth Empire, which flourished in the south with Toledo as its capital. The years 562 to 681 saw the flowering of Visigoth culture and with it the growth of a liturgy—Spanish Christians were still permitted to practise their religion, on payment of taxes. The Visigothic Church developed liturgical chant, known as Mozarabic chant (see *Liturgy*, 2a), which remained in use until abolished in the 11th century.

In 711 the peninsula was invaded again, this time by Muslims from north Africa. Within a few years they had conquered most of Spain and were pushing northwards into France, held back only by a bulwark of Christian states in the extreme north. The Moors exercised enormous influence on Spanish culture, imparting to it an exotic oriental aspect, until their final expulsion in the 15th century: the famous Arab court at Seville was praised by a 12th-century writer for the opulence of its buildings, the splendour of its palaces and gardens, the excellence of

its music, and the variety of musical instruments kept there. These included tambourines, drums, nakers, castanets, psalteries, flutes, lutes, rebecs, and trumpets. Many are depicted in the most important Medieval Spanish manuscript of secular music, the *Cantigas de Santa Maria*, a collection of 402 songs compiled in the 13th century by King Alfonso X 'the Wise' of Castile and León. Moorish instrumentalists were hired at Christian courts in the north, and even worked in churches, until barred from participating in Christian ceremonies by the Valladolid Council in 1322. Arab poets cultivated such literary forms akin to European models as the *virelai*. In general, the two cultures coexisted fairly peacefully in a climate of relative religious tolerance.

However, by the 11th century the Christian monarchs in the northern states had begun to organize campaigns to drive out the Moors. In 1085 the capture of Toledo by the Christian King Alfonso VI initiated a gradual process of repossession of the peninsula which, with the exception of Granada, was virtually complete by the mid 13th century. The modern peninsular states began to emerge as a result of alliances and the inter-marriages of their rulers. Unlike their Moorish counterparts, the Christian monarchs were in general not noted as patrons of the arts: they were too busy fighting to concern themselves with culture (a philistine attitude which persisted among Spanish monarchs and aristocrats up to the late Renaissance). This attitude, combined with Spain's relative geographical isolation, the absence of a middle class, and a spirit of strong religious zeal which characterized Spain up to the 17th century, prevented the early spread of humanist ideas, and had important repercussions on

The first page of the section on practical music-making from St Isidore's 'Etymologiae'.

Alfonso X and his musicians and scribes, miniature from the 'Cantigas de Santa Maria'.

Spanish art, literature, and music. Scholarship and culture were the prerogative of the monastic communities, such as Ripoll, Gerona, and Tarragona in the north, which were particularly receptive to the influence of French orders such as the Benedictines and Cistercians. This influence is evident in art by the rapid spread of the Gothic style of architecture in northern Spain, in literature by the introduction of Carolingian script, and in music by the introduction of 'Gregorian' chant. Toledo, after initial resistance, became one of the most important European schools of plainchant, while the Benedictine abbey of Ripoll produced one of the earliest theoretical works on polyphony, Abbot Oliva's *Breviarum de musica* (*c*.1050). Three important sources of Medieval Spanish polyphony survive: the 12th-century *Codex Calixtinus*, intended to publicize the shrine of St James of Compostela; the early 14th-century Huelgas Manuscript from the convent of Las Huelgas, near Burgos; and the mid 14th-century *Llibre Vermell* (Red Book—so-called from the colour of its binding), found in 1806 at the Montserrat Monastery. The shrine there drew pilgrims from all over Europe, who sang and danced in front of the church. Nearly all the songs in the manuscript are dedicated to the Virgin, and one is the earliest known version of the Dance of Death.

In the later Middle Ages, the Spanish language began to emerge, and with it secular lyric poetry, intended for the amusement of the aristocracy. This poetry, at first written in Galician-Portuguese dialect, was of two main types—the epic ballad, and the courtly love-song (*cantiga de amor*), influenced by Provençal *troubadours*. It was performed by a minstrel who accompanied himself on a stringed instrument. In the 14th century such pieces tended to be of a deeply pessimistic nature, reflecting the low expectation of life and general misery of existence in a land constantly ravaged by political strife and the Black Death. By the early 15th century, these forms had largely been replaced by the ballad and *romance, mainly in the Castilian tongue.

2. *1450-1530.* By the mid 15th century, the two most powerful Spanish states were Castile and Aragon, ruled respectively from Toledo and Seville. Their rulers had begun to think in terms of expansionism—the Castilian monarchy maintained strong links with France and the Netherlands, while in 1442 Alfonso V of Aragon annexed Naples and Sicily. He was the patron of one of the earliest known Spanish composers, Juan Cornago. In 1469 Ferdinand (King of Aragon 1479-1516) married Isabella (Queen of Castile 1474-1504). They then ruled jointly as 'The Catholic Monarchs' in both kingdoms,

paving the way for the unification of Spain with the recapture of Granada (the last remaining Moorish stronghold) in 1492. From then onwards, Spain was regarded by the rest of Europe as an entity. Ferdinand and Isabella restored the power of the crown, built up the economy, and, like Louis XIV of France some two centuries later, curtailed the power of troublesome nobles by encouraging them to live at court, while excluding them from central positions of power. They also encouraged education through the establishment of universities and theological colleges, and with it the spread of printing. But their reign was also characterized by a new mood of religious zeal amounting to fanaticism. They destroyed thriving Jewish and Moorish communities, and in 1478 the notorious Holy Inquisition began its campaign to stamp out heresy—a factor which influenced the character of Spanish culture for the next two centuries.

Unlike earlier Spanish monarchs, Ferdinand and Isabella were themselves important patrons of music. They maintained separate musical 'chapels', which did not merge until after Isabella's death. Ferdinand's chapel numbered 41 adult musicians, singers, minstrels, and trumpeters, some drawn from abroad. Isabella employed up to 20 singers, three organists, and about 25 choirboys. Their son, the Crown Prince Juan, also had (until his early death) his own chapel, under the *maestro de capilla* Juan Anchieta (1462-1523). The Catholic Monarchs employed some of the best musicians of the time: Francisco de Peñalosa, Francisco de Millán, Pedro Díaz, Juan Fernández de Madrid, Juan Ponce, and Francisco de la Torre. Isabella was particularly fond of the vihuela—which, rather than the lute, was the typical Spanish Renaissance stringed instrument, and she kept three or four vihuelists at court, including Lope de Baena (*fl. c*.1475-*c*.1508).

The great Spanish cathedrals also provided training and employment for many important Renaissance musicians, including the Portuguese Pedro de Escobar, *maestro* at Seville 1507-14, Martín de Rivafrecha (at Palencia), Juan de Triana (*fl.* 1478-83, at Seville and Toledo), and Juan de León (*fl.* 1480-1514, at Santiago de Compostela and Málaga). A typical cathedral chapel in the early 16th century supported about 20 choirboys, trained by the *maestro de capilla*, who was responsible also for their welfare, and was in addition required to conduct the cathedral music at week-ends and feast-days. Chapelmasters in the time of Ferdinand and Isabella were generally much better paid than later masters. Their appointments, together with those of top singers and organists, were normally decided by open competition, for which any reasonably qualified musician might apply. Vacancies were widely advertised, and the result decided by secret ballot—a system which ensured the frequent migration of staff between cathedrals. In addition to the permanent music staff, large cathedrals also employed a few instrumentalists, usually wind players, and the use of wind instruments became a distinctive feature of Spanish sacred vocal music.

During the Renaissance Spain began to extend the boundaries of her empire to become the most powerful nation in Europe. In 1492 Columbus made his epic voyage to the New World, leading to the Spanish acquisition of most of Central and South America, while Naples, Milan, Sicily, Burgundy, Portugal, and the Netherlands were all annexed. This inevitably led to cultural interchange between Spain and her new colonies: Italian Renaissance ideas were transmitted via the Spanish viceregal court at Naples, while Flemish humanism arrived around 1515 with the accession of Charles V (Holy Roman Emperor from 1519), who was brought up at the Burgundian court under the influence of Erasmus. As a result, Italian and Flemish artistic influence began to make headway in the peninsula, a notable example being the Italianate architecture of the royal palace and cathedral at Granada. Many Spanish composers worked abroad, especially in Italy, where in 1503 the papal choir in Rome had six Spaniards out of a total of 21 singers. At the same time foreign composers began to exercise strong influence on Spanish music, notably the Netherlands polyphonic masters Ockeghem, Agricola, La Rue, and especially Josquin, whose music was widely disseminated and copied. But it is significant that Spain only opened her cultural frontiers to Renaissance values when the Renaissance was virtually over in Italy: this, together with the censorship exercised by the Inquisition, may explain why foreign secular genres such as the madrigal made little headway in Spain. Instead, Spanish composers tended to cultivate the *villancico. About 400 villancicos (mostly secular), together with other types of vocal music, are found in the greatest secular collection of the period, the Cancionero musical de palacio (Palace Song-book), which contains music by all the major contemporary composers.

3. *The Late Renaissance: 1530-1600.* During the reigns of Charles V (1516-56) and his son Philip II (1556-98) Spain nurtured some of the finest writers, painters, and musicians of the time—men of the calibre of Cervantes, El Greco, Morales, and Victoria. This was the 'golden age' of Spanish culture. Charles V was the first truly cosmopolitan Spanish monarch. On his accession he established a chapel of musicians drawn from his native Flanders (capilla flamenca), which travelled about with him. His Portuguese wife maintained a similar chapel of Spanish musicians (capilla española), and this dual tradition continued throughout the reign of their son, Philip. The two chapels each cultivated independent repertories until they merged as the royal chapel in 1636. However, during the last years of Charles's reign the growing influence of Lutheranism provoked the backlash of the Counter-Reformation, and under Philip II the Inquisition exercised an iron grip on the country's culture. Many musicans, finding themselves working in increasing isolation, chose to work for the churches, and secular music other than the purely instrumental declined. Very little music was printed in Spain: despite the growing demand for Spanish sacred music for use in New World cathedrals and universities, most circulated only in manuscript copies, and a great deal was lost.

The principal schools of music in the 16th century were the Andalusian (based on Seville), Castilian (centred on Toledo and Salamanca), and Catalan (the abbeys of Ripoll and Montserrat). Valencia and Aragon were also important, to a lesser degree. Seville, centre of the Andalusian school, was the richest city in Spain, owing to its monopoly of trade with the New World. The cathedral had a choir school attached to the archbishop's palace, where the boys were trained in religion, music, and letters. They then entered cathedral service, assisting at the daily rituals, and especially on feast-days. The Seville school produced a number of the most famous late Renaissance Spanish composers—Cristóbal de Morales, whom the theorist Juan Bermudo called 'the light of Spain', and his pupil and successor Francisco Guerrero, who was assisted in his capacity as chapelmaster at Seville by several distinguished organists, including Francisco de Peraza, Jerónimo de Peraza, and Diego del Castillo. Morales's output is almost exclusively sacred, and most was written in Italy where he sang in the papal choir. Another Morales pupil, Juan Navarro, was educated at Seville and subsequently worked at other Spanish cathedrals, as did Rodrigo de Ceballos, who later became the royal chapelmaster.

The Castilian school was centred on Toledo Cathedral, described in 1549 as 'the most illustrious, the richest, the most splendid, the best and most completely staffed of any in all the Spanish dominions', surpassed only by St Peter's in Rome. The Archbishop of Toledo was one of the richest men in Spain, with an annual salary of over three times that of the Archbishop of Seville. Many Castilian-trained musicians worked in the papal choir in Rome, and in the royal chapels of Spain and Italy. Among those who followed such careers were Diego Ortiz, Luys de Narváez (Philip II's vihuelist), Bernardo Clavijo del Castillo (c.1549-1626), Juan Esquivel de Barahona (c.1563-after 1613), Sebastián de Vivanco (c.1551-1622), and Sebastián López de Velasco (d after 1648). But the most celebrated Castilian musician of all was Tomás Luis de Victoria, most of whose extensive output of sacred music was published during his years in Italy. Together with his teacher Palestrina, Victoria was regarded as one of the greatest polyphonists of his age, and his music has an individual colour and dramatic vigour.

After Ferdinand's death in 1516 few Aragonese composers (of the Catalan school) were able to find noble patrons, and most worked for the cathedrals at Barcelona, Tarragona, Lérida, and Urgel. Few travelled abroad, and little of their music was published. Among the best Catalan composers of the time were the two Mateo Flechas (the uncle was chapelmaster at Lérida, and the nephew worked at Vienna until 1599—both were famous for cultivating a particular Spanish form of quodlibet called *ensalada*), Pedro Alberto Vila (1517-82), the finest Catalan organist of his day, Joan Brudieu (c.1520-91), and Juan Pujol (c.1573-1626). Catalan composers favoured secular rather than sacred music in the late 16th century: collections of madrigals and *villancicos* were issued by Brudieu, Vila, Flecha the elder, and others. Aragon also nurtured the famous organist Sebastián Aguilera de Heredia, while the best Valencian composers of the time were Juan Ginés Pérez (1548-1612) and the *villancico* composer Juan Bautista Comes (1568-1643).

As in Italy the beginnings of Spanish musical drama are found in Renaissance dialogues and pastorals with music, notably those by Juan del Encina, written for his patron the Duke of Alba, and in the stage works written by the dramatist Gil Vicente (c.1465-1537) for performance at the Portuguese court. Sixteenth-century Spanish instrumental music is represented mostly by music for vihuela and organ. Seven important vihuela publications appeared in the course of the century, by Luis de Milán, Luys de Narváez, Alonso Mudarra, Enríquez de Valderrábano, Diego Pisador, Miguel de Fuenllana, and Estéban Daza. These contain music for voice with vihuela accompaniment, and for solo vihuela (fantasias, *tientos*, variations on a ground, *ciaconas*, dances, and intabulations of sacred and secular pieces). But the greatest instrumental composer of the period was undoubtedly the blind organist Antonio de Cabezón, favourite of Philip II, who was among the first composers of genuinely idiomatic keyboard music. Among his best pieces are his *tientos*, which show great structural variety,

glosas (intabulations of foreign works), and *diferencias* (variation cycles mostly based on Spanish secular tunes). Cabezón travelled widely abroad in the king's entourage, and his influence may be seen in the keyboard works of his European contemporaries. Many 16th-century treatises dealt with aspects of vihuela or keyboard technique, such as Diego Ortiz's *Tratado de glosas* (1553), Tomás de Santa María's *Arte de tañer fantasía* (1565), and Luis Venegas de Henestrosa's *Libro de cifra nueva para tecla, harpa y vihuela* (1557). Others, by Juan Bermudo and Francisco Salinas, cover a wide variety of musical topics.

Portugal was ruled from 1580 to 1640 by Spanish kings, but managed to maintain an independent musical tradition. Portuguese composers tended to be conservative, because of strong Jesuit influence: one of the first to achieve distinction was the humanist scholar Damião de Gois (1502-74), a friend of Erasmus. The composer-king John IV wrote music and treatises, and founded one of the world's great music libraries (later destroyed in the Lisbon earthquake of 1755). Musicians were trained at Évora Cathedral under Manuel Mendès (d 1605); his pupils included Duarte Lobo (c. 1565-1646), one of the few Portuguese musicians to achieve a European reputation, Manuel Cardoso, and Filipe de Magalhães (c.1571-1652), chapelmaster to the King from 1623 to 1641. Musical activity also took place at the palace of the dukes of Bragança at Vila Vicosa, and at the Santa Cruz monastery at Coimbra.

4. *The Baroque Era*. The defeat of the Armada in 1588 caused a crisis of national confidence. Spain's influence as a world power began to decline as she lost her overseas colonies, while famine and plague in the early years of the 17th century were followed by a disastrous war with France and rebellions in Catalonia, the Italian possessions, and Portugal. This decline was mirrored musically by a shift of emphasis from sacred to secular genres, with a corresponding decrease in the quality and quantity of sacred music. One of the best and most prolific composers of sacred music to work for Philip III was Mateo Romero (1575-1637), who was head of the king's chapel. The Montserrat choir school continued to produce a few outstanding figures such as Juan Cererols, who excelled in sacred music for double chorus and in vernacular *villancicos*, while organ music thrived under Aguilera de Heredia and the Portuguese Manuel Rodrigues Coelho, court organist to Philip III. His *Flores de música* of 1620 was followed six years later by Francisco Correa de Arauxo's important collection *Facultad orgánica*, containing 62 *tientos* and three sets of variations; but the major figure in Spanish

Baroque organ music was Juan Cabanilles, organist at Valencia, whose *tientos* and variations represent a continuation of the great Spanish Renaissance tradition.

Culturally and intellectually, Spain in the 17th century was dominated by the Jesuits, who established schools and colleges all over the country. They proved surprisingly receptive to Baroque styles, especially to the development of literary genres sympathetic to musical setting: most court poetry of the period was written to be sung. The first Spanish drama to be set to music in its entirety was *La selva sin amor* (1629) of Lope de Vega, a dramatist in the Italian classical tradition. Italian professional actors were active in Spain from the mid 16th century onwards, and by 1600 municipal theatres (*corrales*) had been established in all major Spanish cities. In 1632 Philip IV built a court theatre at his palace of Buen Retiro, where in 1660 two musical dramas by the playwright Pedro Calderón de la Barca were performed, with music by the harpist-composer Juan Hidalgo (*c*.1600–85). The Buen Retiro court theatre was one of the first in Spain to make use of spectacular stage machinery, and works written for performance there included music and dancing on a grand scale, along the lines of French or Italian opera. In addition to over 120 *comedias*, Calderón created the religious dramatic genre known as the *auto sacramental*, while his *El golfo de las sirenas* (1657, composer unknown) was the first important example of the **zarzuela*, a lighter type of musical entertainment with spoken dialogue, similar to the Italian *intermezzo*, which took root during the second half of the century.

In instrumental music, the five-course guitar replaced the vihuela in the 17th century, and was thereafter regarded as the typical Spanish instrument: its characteristic sound and idiomatic techniques have permeated music by Spanish composers up to the present day. Luis de Briceño's guitar method (Paris, 1626) introduced a new kind of tablature adapted to dances and songs while the most important guitar manual of the period, Gaspar Sanz's *Instrucción* (Saragossa, 1674) was a compendium of popular dances.

In Portugal during the Baroque era the *vilhancico* was regularly used in church services. The finest composer of such pieces, the Carmelite monk Francisco de Santiago (*d* 1646), spent most of his life as choirmaster at Seville rather than in his native land, and other Portuguese musicians followed the same course. Two pupils of Duarte Lobo became noted theorists: João Álvares Frouvo (1608–82), librarian and chaplain to John IV, and António Fernandes, whose *Arte de musica* (1626) was the first treatise in Portuguese.

5. *Music under the Bourbons.* In the 18th century Spain was ruled by the Bourbon dynasty, and as happened in England, with the arrival of the Hanoverians, native culture quickly succumbed to a flood of imported art and artists. The French-born king Philip V (ruled 1701–46) set up a number of national institutions on French lines, such as the National Library (1712) and the Royal Spanish Academy (1713), while stocking his music library with French cantatas and Italian operas. The increasing secularization of musical life, especially the decline in sacred music, was attacked by Padre Benito Feijóo (the first influential Spanish critic). In his essay *La música en los templos* (1726) Feijóo deplored the growing taste for theatrical church music with instrumental accompaniment, exemplified in the works of Sebastián Durón, whose religious *villancicos* were performed as far afield as South America. On the other hand, Feijóo had nothing but praise for the 'pure' church music of Durón's contemporary, Antonio Literes, whose *a cappella* Masses continued the Renaissance tradition. Under Philip V the direction of the palace orchestra at Buen Retiro was shared by three men, one Italian and two Spaniards, one of the latter being José de Nebra (1702–68) who wrote much sacred music for the royal chapel. The orchestra was led by José Herrando, whose *Arte de tocar el violin* (1756) was among the earliest Spanish violin treatises.

Ferdinand VI (reigned 1746–59) and his Portuguese consort Maria Bárbara of Bragança were thoroughly Italianate in sympathies, and Italian musicians, such as Bárbara's music-master Domenico Scarlatti, quickly occupied important court posts. Scarlatti evidently found the atmosphere at the Spanish court less restricting than in his native Italy: in Spain he was free to experiment, and several commentators have noted certain distinctly 'Spanish' idioms in his keyboard sonatas, such as thrummed accompanimental figures suggestive of the guitar, or 'trompe de chasse' hunting calls. Together with Scarlatti, the castrato singer Farinelli served the Spanish court for nearly 25 years, enjoying a position of prestige and power, until he was pensioned off in 1759 by Ferdinand's philistine successor, Charles III. A period of musical stagnation at court ended in 1788 with the accession of Charles IV. A competent violinist, the king built up a large collection of chamber music including many pieces by his Italian music-master, Gaetano Brunetti. From 1768 to 1785 another famous Italian musician, Boccherini, lived in Spain under the patronage of the king's uncle, Prince Luis. However, the king's brother, Prince Gabriel, chose a Spaniard as his teacher — the composer-monk Antonio Soler — who is best remembered for his harpsichord sonatas, which rival Scarlatti's in originality.

Durón, Nebra, and Literes were the outstanding early 18th-century composers of stage music, especially of *zarzuelas*. For nearly 30 years José de Cañizares (1676–1750) supplied composers with *zarzuela* texts, but in general Italian opera reigned supreme throughout the century. Philip V encouraged Italian troupes of female singers (according to Spanish custom) to perform Italian operas in Spanish translation in the rebuilt Caños del Peral theatre in Madrid, where other important theatres opened, including the Cruz (1743) and the Principe (1745). Only Italian operas were performed in Spain in the 1750s, while the native-born composer Domingo Terradellas (1713–51), unable to be heard in Spain, spent his life writing operas in Italian for Rome, Florence, Venice, and London. On Charles III's accession in 1759 operatic performances were confined to private palaces and to the Caños del Peral theatre: by 1777 the Italian troupe had returned to Italy, and opera languished for a decade. One of the few 18th-century operatic masterpieces by a Spanish composer was Vicente Martín y Soler's *Una cosa rara*, written for Vienna, where Soler was regarded as Mozart's greatest rival in the operatic field.

The late 18th-century *zarzuela* was dominated by the librettist Ramón de la Cruz (1731–94) who collaborated chiefly with the composer Antonio Rodriguez de Hita (1704–87): their burlesque *zarzuela*, *Las segadoras de Vallecas* (1768), was the first such work to incorporate a contemporary setting with working-class characters, instead of heroic or mythical characters in the distant past. The late development of such genres in Spain has something to do with the ingrained attitude of Spanish upper and middle classes towards the peasants, who were regarded as a group to be ignored or exploited, rather than idealized. *Las segadoras de Vallecas* breathed new life into the *zarzuela*: in the same year Pablo Esteve (*d* 1794) produced his *Los jardineros de Aranjuez* along similar lines; but later in the century the two-act *zarzuela* declined, overtaken in popularity by smaller dramatic forms such as the *zarzuelita*, *sainete*, and *tonadilla escénica* (a short musical play with a cast of two to four, on a comic subject). The outstanding composers of *tonadillas* were the Catalan flautist Luis Misón (*d* 1766), who wrote over 100, and Blas de Laserna, who wrote over 700. The genre gave way to Italian *opera buffa* in the early 19th century.

As in Spain, the Portuguese king John V imported Italian musicians and sent native composers such as Francisco António de Almeida (the first Portuguese opera composer) to study in Italy. In the field of instrumental music, the rococo keyboard sonatas of Carlos de Seixas and Frei Jacinto rivalled those of Scarlatti. John's successor, Don José, also encouraged musical activity. He also sent musicians to study in Italy, including João de Sousa Carvalho and his pupils Marcos Antônio Portugal, the greatest Portuguese opera composer of the century, and J. D. Bomtempo, founder of a National Conservatory of Music and the first Portuguese symphony orchestra. In April 1755 the Teatro de Ribeira opened in Lisbon. Burney thought that it 'surpassed in magnitude and decoration all that modern times can boast', but only seven months later it was destroyed in the earthquake that consumed much of Lisbon's cultural heritage.

6. *The 19th Century*. Like other liberal intellectual movements, Enlightenment ideas came late to Spain, which in the late 18th century was still a deeply conservative country with a rigid social hierarchy strongly resistant to change. But the French Revolution and the subsequent Napoleonic invasion had a profoundly unsettling effect on Spanish life: after Napoleon's expulsion in the Peninsular War the country was subjected to a series of civil wars and revolutions which disrupted and virtually destroyed her social and cultural development. Indeed, the only artistic genius of the early 19th century could be said to be the painter Goya, whose works capture the pessimistic spirit of his age. The restoration of the unpopular monarch Ferdinand VII caused an intellectual 'brain-drain', and from a musical point of view the early 19th century was entirely dominated by Italian imports. Ferdinand's fourth wife, Maria Cristina of Naples, was a great admirer of Rossini, and when the Madrid Conservatory was founded in 1830 it had as director an Italian singer rather than a Spaniard. Only two names are outstanding in the music of the period: Manuel Garcia (1775–1832) and Fernando Sor. Garcia, his son Manuel (1805–1906), and his daughters Pauline Viardot-García and Maria Malibran revitalized Spanish singing, while Sor, known as 'the Beethoven of the guitar', is considered to be the founder of the modern Spanish guitar school, together with his friend and rival Dionisio Aguado. Spanish instrumental music suffered a severe loss with the early death of Juan Crisostomo de Arriaga, who by the age of 16 was proving equally competent in the fields of symphonic, operatic, and chamber music.

The decline in church music in the 18th century accelerated in the 19th. A government act of 1835 caused the closure of religious institutions all over Spain, and in 1851 the Concordat made matters worse by reducing the musical personnel of churches to a *maestro* and an organist, one tenor singer, and a handful of

'*La Copla*', *oil painting by Cabral Bejarano (1827-91)*.

choirboys. The loss of morale among church musicians was not halted until 1896, when a congress examined the penurious state of sacred music and recommended changes, including the publication of early Spanish masterpieces. Such work had been undertaken earlier in the century by Hilarión Eslava (1807-78), editor of *Lira Sacro-Hispana*, but his work fell victim to financial cutbacks.

In operatic music, the *zarzuela* disappeared after 1782, and was supplanted by the *tonadilla* and by Italian opera; by 1830 native Spanish works were practically extinct. However, the first composition professor at the Madrid Conservatory, Ramón Carnicer (1789-1855), influenced a generation of young composers by his use of Spanish themes in his own stage works, such as *Don Giovanni Tenorio*: this stimulated a revival of interest in the *zarzuela* as a native art-form among composers such as Joaquín Gaztambide, Emilio Arrieta, Cristóbal Oudrid, and especially Francisco Asenjo Barbieri, composer of the first three-act *zarzuela grande*, *Pan y Toros* (1864), and founder of a concert society which developed into the Sociedad de Conciertas de Madrid. Later 19th-century Spanish opera was dominated by Tomás Bretón, whose *Los amantes de Teruel* and *La verbena de la paloma* achieved international success. His rivals included Ruperto Chapí (whose works are still in the repertory), Federico Chueca, Fernandez Caballero, and Amadeo

Vives. Many new theatres opened in Madrid during the century, including the Real Palacio (1849), the Real (1850), the Liceo, Circo, and Variedades, the Circo del Principe Alfonso (renamed the Rivas in 1863 and used as an opera house), and the Teatro de la Zarzuela.

The Romantic movement in Spain was always weaker than in Germany, England, or France. It arrived only after the death of Ferdinand VII (1833), when many intellectuals returned from self-imposed exile, bringing with them the novels of Hugo, Dumas, and Byron. With Romanticism came a cult of local colour in art-forms, so important in Spanish music of the late 19th and early 20th centuries, together with a growth of nationalism and a renewed sense of regional identity, especially in the Catalan areas. These movements coincided with a liberalization of the political climate, the growth of a powerful urban middle class, and the introduction of left-wing ideas, leading to the establishment first of a constitutional monarchy, and then of the short-lived First Republic (1873-5). The nationalist movement is reflected in the use of idioms and dances derived from regional folk music, such as the *jota*, *habanera*, *fandango*, and *seguidillas*. Such idioms, which owe much to gypsy music, contribute to the essential 'Spanish' flavour of music by Pablo de Sarasate, Isaac Albéniz, Enrique Granados, Manuel de Falla, and Joaquin Turina. Albéniz and Granados immortalized their native land

A scene from Tomás Breton's zarzuela, 'La verbena de la paloma' (1897).

in their piano works, such as *Iberia* and the *Goyescas*, while Falla, the finest Spanish composer of the late 19th and early 20th centuries, is best known for his stage and orchestral music, imbued with the spirit of Andalusian folk music. Turina's major orchestral work is probably the colourful *Sinfonia sevillana* (1920), a celebration of his native city. All these composers had strong links with Paris, where many studied, and a reciprocal influence may be seen in the large number of French works of the same period which make use of Spanish idioms and local colour—works such as Bizet's *Carmen* (the famous *Habanera* was borrowed from a popular song by the 19th-century Spanish composer Sebastián Iradier), Lalo's *Symphonie espagnole* (1875), dedicated to Sarasate, Chabrier's *España* (1883), and numerous pieces by Debussy (*Ibéria, Soirées dans Grenade*, etc.) and Ravel, who was of Basque origin (*Boléro, L'heure espagnole, Rapsodie espagnole, Alborada del gracioso*, etc.). Spanish idioms held a similar fascination for several Russian 'nationalist' composers, including Glinka (*Jota aragonese, Summer Night in Madrid*), Balakirev (*Overture on Spanish Themes*), and Rimsky-Korsakov (*Spanish Caprice*).

As in other countries, this nationalist spirit produced a desire to rediscover the great national masterpieces of the past, and Felipe Pedrell (1841-1932) championed the nationalist cause in his capacities as writer, lecturer, editor, musicologist, and teacher (his pupils included Albéniz, Granados, and Falla). Similarly in Portugal, a progressive, nationalist spirit is evident in the works of the Paris-trained August Machado (1845-1924), director of the National Conservatory, and of Alfredo Keil (1850-1907), composer of the Portuguese national anthem, though Italian influence was still to be felt in the works of Xavier Migone (1811-61), Joaquím Casimiro (1808-63), Francisco Sá da Navonha (1820-81), and the Viscount of Arneiro (1838-1903).

7. *The 20th Century.* A brief period of relative political stability and economic prosperity in the last two decades of the 19th century came abruptly to a halt when Spain lost her last colonies on the American continent, and the early years of the present century, up to the establishment of the Second Republic in 1930, were characterized by political upheaval, the growing agitation of Basque separatists, and

industrial unrest. However, the arts flourished in a more liberal, cosmopolitan climate, and by 1900 Barcelona rivalled Paris as a centre of intellectual activity. As in Paris, this centred on a café—Els Quatre Gats—whose habitués included Pablo Picasso, the architect Gaudí, the poet/artist Mestres, and musicians such as Albéniz and Granados. The Catalans were concerned with the preservation of their language, and in 1891 the Basque choir Orfeo Catalá was founded to perform Catalan folk music and early Spanish music: in 1908 it moved into its own concert hall in Barcelona. The early 20th century produced a number of talented Catalan composers and musicians, including the violinist Joan Manén, author of an influential violin treatise, the cellist Pablo Casals, who throughout his long life tirelessly promoted the music of his native region, and the opera composers Jaime Pahissa (1880–1969), Jesús Guridi (1886–1961), and José Maria Usandizaga, who died in 1915 at the early age of 27, having written his masterpiece *Las golondrinas* (1914). Two other Catalan composers, Federico Mompou (*b* 1893) and Manuel Blancafort (*b* 1897) maintained strong links with Paris, where they both studied, while still cultivating native Catalan subjects.

Besides this important group of musicians united by their common heritage, other 20th-century Spanish composers have shown a tendency to group themselves together to promote a common cause. One of the most significant was the so-called 'Madrid Group', established during the Second Republic and characterized by liberal or left-wing political views. It included the poets Guillén and Federico García Lorca (one of the most prominent victims of the Civil War), the musicologists Jesús Bal y Gay (*b* 1905) and Adolfo Salazar (*d* 1958), and composers such as Joaquín Nin-Culmell (*b* 1908) and the Halffter brothers (Ernesto, *b* 1905, and Rodolpho, *b* 1900), all pupils of Falla, who cultivated national Spanish music in a modern idiom; Oscar Esplá (1886–1976), a director of the Madrid Conservatory, and Roberto Gerhard, another Catalan and a pupil of Granados and Pedrell. All these musicians were forced into exile when Franco came to power after the Civil War—Ernesto Halffter settled in Lisbon and his brother in Mexico, Nin-Culmell went to the USA, Esplá to Belgium, and Gerhard to England, where much of his best music was written. Such a drain of talent inevitably left Spanish music greatly impoverished. The post-war dictatorship re-imposed artistic censorship, clamped down on regional separatism, and generally discouraged innovation: it is not surprising that the most successful 20th-century Spanish composers should be those who continued in the nationalist style using traditional techniques. Such is Joaquín

Interior of the Palau de la Música Catalana, Barcelona, the concert hall of the Basque choir 'Orfeo Catalá'.

Rodrigo, who in 1939 scored an international success with his popular guitar concerto (*Concierto de Aranjuez*). He has since written piano and cello concertos, including one for the British cellist Julian Lloyd Webber. Xavier Montsalvatge's *Cinco canciones negras* of 1946 established him as a major composer of songs in an evocative Spanish idiom, and he is also known for his chamber music; while the leading opera composer of the century was Conrado del Campo (1878-1953), whose 15 operas are in a post-Romantic idiom. More cosmopolitan, avant-garde trends have been represented in Spain by Joaquín Homs (*b* 1906), a pupil of Gerhard and an exponent of serialism, though his music still retains an essential Spanish flavour. This is no longer true of the works of a generation of younger composers belonging to the group Música Abierta, who have looked to mainstream European developments for their inspiration—composers such as Luis de Pablo (*b* 1930), Cristobal Halffter (*b* 1930), Alberto Blancafort, and García Avril (*b* 1933). Their music is influenced more by Webern and Stockhausen than by Spanish folk music.

Spain has produced many notable performers in various fields: guitarists such as Yepes and Segovia; cellists such as Casals (who founded the first symphony orchestra in Barcelona) and Gaspar Cassádo; pianists such as Ricardo Viñes, José Iturbi, and Alicia de Larrocha; and singers such as Julián Gayarre, Conchita Supervia, Victoria de los Angeles, Montserrat Caballé, and Teresa Berganza. The principal centres of musical activity are Madrid (home of two symphony and three chamber orchestras, and of the state-controlled radio network—Radio Nacional de España, which devotes about 20 per cent of its air-time to serious music) and Barcelona, the theatrical centre of Spain: its Liceo Theatre is the largest and best-equipped in the country. The Spanish Institute of Musicology, founded by Pedrell and Anglès, is based in Barcelona, as is the music printing industry. In Portugal, early 20th-century neo-classicism was represented by Luís de Freitas Branco (1890-1955) and his pupil Jorge de Vasconcellos; while a Portuguese nationalist group included José Vianna da Motta (1868-1948), pianist, scholar, author, and director of the Lisbon Conservatory. Two notable Portuguese composers, Ruy Coelho and Fernando Lopez-Graça, studied with Schoenberg. Lisbon supports two symphony orchestras and two choral societies, while Oporto maintains a conservatory and the country's oldest choral society. There is an important music faculty at Coimbra University.

WENDY THOMPSON

FURTHER READING
J. B. Trend: *The Music of Spanish History to 1600*

(London, 1926); Gilbert Chase: *The Music of Spain* (New York, 1941, 2nd edn 1959); Robert Stevenson: *Spanish Music in the Age of Columbus* (The Hague, 1960, 2nd edn 1964); Robert Stevenson: *Spanish Cathedral Music in the Golden Age* (Berkeley and Los Angeles, 1961); A. Livermore: *A Short History of Spanish Music* (London, 1972).

SPAM. See *Society for the Publication of American Music*.

Spanisches Liederbuch ('Spanish Songbook'). Forty-four songs for voice and piano by Wolf, all settings of Spanish poems translated by Paul von Heyse (1830-1914) and Emanuel Giebel (1815-84) and published in 1852 under the title *Spanisches Liederbuch*.

Spartacus (*Spartak*). Ballet in four acts by Khachaturian to a libretto by N. Volkov. It was choreographed by Jacobson and first performed in Leningrad in 1956. Khachaturian revised the score in 1968.

Spartito (It.). 'Score' (also called *partitura*).

Spass, spasshaft (Ger.). 'Joke', 'jocular' (e.g. Mozart's *Ein musikalischer Spass*, 'A Musical Joke').

Spassapensieri (It.). 'Jew's-harp'.

Später (Ger.). 'Later'.

Species counterpoint. Sometimes known as 'strict counterpoint', species counterpoint was a method of learning, by easy stages, the technique of 16th-century vocal counterpoint. The method is usually associated with the treatise *Gradus ad parnassum* (1725) by the Austrian composer Johann Joseph Fux, although the idea can be traced further back. Given a *cantus firmus* (a set theme in long notes), the student first learns to add one note against each note of the theme ('first species'), then two against each note ('second species'), and so forth, until the more complex rhythms are mastered. The method, formerly used in university teaching, unfortunately became overlaid with superfluous and anachronistic rules, and does not now meet with much favour, 16th-century technique being today more usually taught by a direct approach to the music itself.

ROGER BULLIVANT

Spectre de la rose, Le. Ballet in one act to the music of Weber's *Invitation to the Dance* (1819). It was choreographed by Fokine and staged in Monte Carlo in 1911 by Diaghilev's Ballets Russes, danced by Nijinsky and Karsavina.

Speer, Daniel (*b* Breslau, 2 July 1636; *d* Göppingen, 5 Oct. 1707). German writer and composer. He studied at Breslau and then led a bohemian existence, wandering around Europe. From 1673 onwards he was organist and music master at Göppingen. His political activities caused his imprisonment and temporary exile in 1689. Speer wrote an important treatise, the *Grund-richtiger . . . Unterricht der musicalischen Kunst* (Ulm, 1687), which includes sections on the direction of church music, instrumental technique, especially keyboard, and composition. His own compositions included sacred music and some collections of quodlibets.

WENDY THOMPSON

Spem in alium numquam habui. Motet by Tallis in 40 parts, for eight five-voice choirs, dating from the mid 16th century.

Sperdendosi (It.). 'Fading out', 'dying away'.

Speth, Johann (*b* Speinshart, Upper Palatine, 9 Nov. 1664; *d* Augsburg, *c*.1720). German organist and composer. He was organist at Augsburg Cathedral and published in 1693 a collection of keyboard pieces, the *Ars magna consoni et dissoni*. WENDY THOMPSON

Spezzato (It.). See *Cori spezzati*.

Spheres, Music [Harmony] **of the.** An Ancient Greek theory of harmonious relationships among the heavenly bodies of the universe. Pythagoras and his followers believed in a correlation between the direct numerical proportions of musical consonance and those that govern the ordering of the universe. Each planet was thought to produce a musical sound (fixed mathematically in accordance with its velocity and distance from the earth) which harmonized with those produced by other planets and was audible, though unrecognized, on earth. Later upheld by Plato and other philosophers, these ideas had considerable influence on Renaissance theorist-musicians, such as Vincenzo Galilei (father of the astronomer, Galileo) and Gioseffo Zarlino, and they have continued to interest scholars even in modern times.

Spianato, spianata (It.). 'Levelled', 'smooth'. Chopin used the direction in the Andante which precedes his E♭ Polonaise, Op. 22, to indicate a smooth, level-toned style of performance.

Spiccato (It., from *spiccare*, 'to detach'). In string playing, a term sometimes used synonymously with *sautillé*, i.e. a fast, detached stroke produced by the wrist, generally in the middle of the bow where it will bounce naturally. Before 1750 the term was generally taken to mean simply *staccato*.

Spiegando (It.). 'Unfolding', i.e. becoming louder.

Spiel, spielen (Ger.). 'Play', 'to play', 'to perform'; *spielend*, 'playing', 'playful'; *volle Spiel*, 'full organ'; *Spieler*, 'player'; *Spielfigur*, a short, playful figure or motif (the term is used mainly in connection with keyboard music, for example by Bull, Sweelinck, or Scheidemann).

Spieloper (Ger.). 'Opera-play'. A type of 19th-century light opera, resembling *Singspiel* in that it uses spoken dialogue. Examples include Lortzing's *Zar und Zimmermann*.

Spinacino, Francesco (*fl.* early 16th century). Italian lutenist and composer from Fossombrone. His two collections of improvisatory *ricercari* and over-elaborate arrangements of *chansons* were published in 1507 by his fellow townsman, Petrucci; they were the first examples of lutebooks printed in tablature.

DENIS ARNOLD

Spinet (Fr.: *épinette*; Ger.: *Spinett*; It.: *spinetta*). Small early keyboard instrument of the *harpsichord* family.

Spinnen des Tons (Ger.). The same as *filar la voce*.

Spinnerlied (Ger.). 'Spinner's song'; *Spinnlied*, 'spinning song'.

Spirante (It.). 'Expiring', 'dying away'.

Spirito (It.). 'Spirit', 'vigour'; *spiritoso*, 'spirited'; *spiritosamente*, 'in a spirited manner'; *con spirito*, 'with spirit'.

Spirit of England, The. Settings, Op. 80, by Elgar of three poems by Binyon: *The Fourth of August*, *To Women*, and *For the Fallen*. The work is scored for soprano or tenor soloist, chorus, and orchestra, and was given its first complete performance in London in 1917.

Spiritual. A religious song usually associated with the Black people of the southern states of the USA. Many authorities give the spiritual a White origin, an adaptation by the White settlers of the USA of Wesleyan and other Methodist hymns to their own needs. There followed further adaptations by the Black slaves during the first half of the 19th century, when missionary zeal was offering a strong line of 'pie-in-the-sky' as a reward for putting up with the unbearable conditions of life on earth. The themes of death, release, and escape which run through the spirituals have a double meaning: first, a literal and practical longing for a better life after death; second, a symbolic identification with the Israelites who, in their passage from Egypt, symbolize the escape of the Black races from White domination. David and Goliath, the collapse of the walls of Jericho, the removal of many apparently invincible obstacles in the Bible are favourite spiritual themes summing up the aspirations of the singers. The knowledge and recognition of the Black spiritual as a powerful form of religious singing came about in the 1860s, with such publications as *Slave Songs of the United States* (New York, 1867), and with the tours of the famous Fisk University Jubilee Singers, who brought the Black songs of the South first to North America and then to Britain and Europe. Even so, the polite renderings of organized choral groups probably gave little impression of the fervour and rhythm of the singing in the plantations and other working areas and in the Black churches. The spiritual was one of the elements of Black music that went into the make-up of *jazz. The early spirituals have now been almost entirely superseded by a style of singing which has, in turn and as far as its musical conventions are concerned, come back from the jazz world—the gospel song, an amalgamation of blues and popular song with religious import.

PETER GAMMOND

Spitta, Julius August Philipp (*b* Wechold, nr Bremen, 7 Dec. 1841; *d* Berlin, 13 Apr. 1894). German musicologist. After graduating in classics at Göttingen University, his friendship with Brahms resulted in his following a natural inclination to study music. He wrote the first standard life of J. S. Bach (Leipzig, 1873–80, Eng. trans. reprinted 1951), and as professor of music history at Berlin University taught a host of distinguished pupils before his early death from a heart attack. DENIS ARNOLD

Spitze (Ger.). 'Point'; *an der Spitze*, 'at the point' (of the bow) in string-playing.

Spleen. Poem by Verlaine set for voice and piano by Debussy, as No. 6 of his *Ariettes oubliées* (1885–8), and by Fauré, as No. 3 of his Op. 51 (1888).

SPNM. See *Society for the Promotion of New Music*.

Spohr, Louis (*b* Brunswick, 5 Apr. 1784; *d* Kassel, 22 Oct. 1859). German composer and violinist. The eldest son of a doctor who was an amateur flautist, Spohr spent the early part of his life as a virtuoso violinist, touring throughout Europe with immense success. He became specially popular in England, where in 1820 he directed a concert of the London Philharmonic Society, causing something of a sensation by

Spohr

conducting with a baton, though he was not the first to use this method (see *Conducting*). He had had a short period as director of the orchestra at the Theater an der Wien in Vienna in 1813, and in 1822 was appointed to the same post at the court theatre at Kassel, where he remained for the rest of his life. Although he quarrelled with his patron, the Elector, from time to time, the security of the post persuaded him to remain: he was one of the last composers of any prominence to be a court musician.

As a violinist, Spohr was noted for the agility and strength of his left hand and the delicacy of his tone, though the brilliance of Paganini eclipsed his style from the 1830s. His earliest compositions were mainly for his own concert use, being violin concertos and chamber music in which the violin was accompanied by the harp (his first wife was an excellent harpist). Later he turned to the composition of operas and oratorios, including the opera *Jessonda* (1823). He often had interesting basic ideas, notably in the Eighth Violin Concerto (1816) written in the form of a huge operatic *scena* and in his double quartets for strings (one quartet being contrasted with the other). However, his music reveals little personality, though his Nonet (in F, for violin, viola, cello, bass, flute, oboe, clarinet, bassoon, and horn) is attractive in a quasi-Schubertian way. His autobiography is full of information about the musical life of Germany and England in the early 19th century. DENIS ARNOLD

Spontini, Gaspare (Luigi Pacifico) (*b* Maiolati, nr Ancona, 14 Nov. 1774; *d* Maiolati, 24 Jan. 1851). Italian composer. Son of peasants, he was at first destined for the Church but eventually his parents were persuaded to allow him to study at one of the Neapolitan conservatories, where after about three years he absconded to escape punishment for some misdemeanour. In 1796 he had success in Rome with a comic opera, following it up with several others in Palermo, where the Naples court had fled to avoid the French invasion. In 1803 Spontini went to Paris where his operas became popular at the Théâtre-Italien, but he was not well received in *opéra comique*. He learned a great deal from the operas of Gluck, and *La vestale* (first produced at the Opéra in 1807, but composed two years earlier) combined that peculiarly French taste in classical drama and emotional romantic attitudes to such effect that it was one of the greatest successes of its time. He was immediately taken up by the Empress Josephine and after a second opera in the same manner, *Fernand Cortez* (1809), he was the major figure in French music, conducting the official Italian opera and composing various political *pièces d'occasion*. In 1814 he came to the notice of King Frederick William III of Prussia who eventually tempted him to become chief *Kapellmeister* in Berlin with an enormous salary. By this time he found composition was difficult and produced comparatively little, but again achieved a reputation as a conductor. Although his last finished work, *Agnes von Hohenstaufen* (first version 1827, revised versions 1829 and 1837), was an attempt to come to terms with modern taste, his career was virtually over by the time his patron died in 1840 and he was pensioned off to retire, first to Paris, later to his native village. The formidable list of his decorations (among them the Légion d'Honneur) seems strangely at odds with his reputation today, as his operas are almost completely forgotten. The esteem of his contemporaries was, however, by no means just official, and his dramatic flair and gifts for orchestration were admired—and imitated—by many composers, not least Wagner and Berlioz.   DENIS ARNOLD

Sprechchor (Ger.). 'Speech-choir', i.e. *Sprechgesang* applied to a choir rather than a solo voice.

Sprechend (Ger.). 'Speaking'.

Sprechgesang (Ger.). 'Speech-song'. A kind of vocal production, midway between speech and song, used in Schoenberg's *Pierrot lunaire* and other works.

Sprechstimme (Ger.). 'Speaking voice'. Term sometimes used in its literal sense to mean a speaking part (e.g. in a straightforward recitation with musical accompaniment), but more often as a synonym for *Sprechgesang*.   PAUL GRIFFITHS

Springar. A popular Norwegian dance from the Telemark district for two people.

Springbogen (Ger.). A kind of bow-stroke. See *Sautillé*.

Springdans. 'Leaping dance' (as distinct from the *gangar*, or 'walking dance'). A Norwegian dance in triple time. Grieg wrote several.

Springend (Ger.). 'Springing'; e.g. *mit springendem Bogen*, 'with a springing bow'.

Springer [acute, sigh] (Fr.: *accent*, *aspiration*, *plainte*; Ger.: *Nachschlag*). Ornament used in 17th- and 18th-century music; it consists of a short auxiliary note inserted after the main note and taking part of its time-value, i.e. the opposite of an *appoggiatura*, being an anticipation, rather than a delaying, of the following note. It was generally indicated with a diagonal line or with a small note (Ex. 1).

Ex. 1

Spontini, engraving (1830) by P. Grevedon.

'Spring' Sonata (*Frühlingssonate*). Nickname of Beethoven's Violin Sonata in F, Op. 24 (1801).

Spring Song (*Frühlingslied*). Mendelssohn's *Lied ohne Wörte* No. 30 (Op. 62) in A major (Book 5, 1844) for piano solo.

Spring Symphony, A. Choral work, Op. 44, by Britten for soprano, alto, and tenor soloists, boys' choir, chorus, and orchestra. It is a setting of poems by Herrick, Auden, Barnefield, Peele, Blake, Beaumont, Fletcher, Nashe, Vaughan, Spenser, Clare, Milton, and an anonymous one, and it was first performed in Amsterdam in 1949.

'Spring' Symphony. Schumann's Symphony No. 1 in B♭ major, Op. 38, composed in 1841.

Square dance. An American folk dance, popular in rural areas, which is performed by four couples in a square formation. It is derived from the French *quadrille, and the dance movements have French names such as 'chassez'. The music, based on popular songs, is lively and rhythmic in character, usually in duple time, and in regular phrases. It is played on any combination of wind instruments, piano, fiddle, guitar or banjo, double bass, and accordion.

Squillante (It.). 'Shrill', 'pealing'. When applied to cymbals it means that they should be suspended and struck with drumsticks, not clashed together; as an expression mark it means 'harshly'.

Staatskapelle (Ger.). State orchestra. See *Chapel*.

Stabat mater dolorosa (Lat., 'Sorrowfully his mother stood'). Poem forming part of the Roman Catholic liturgy, appointed as a sequence for the Feast of the Seven Dolours on 15 September and as an Office hymn for the Friday of Passion Week. Its authorship is unknown, but it is often attributed to Jacopone da Todi (*d* 1306), an Italian Franciscan monk. He is said to have been the author not only of the *Stabat mater dolorosa*, describing the Mother at the foot of the Cross, but also of a *Stabat mater speciosa* (no longer used), which describes her at the cradle.

Apart from its traditional plainchant, the *Stabat mater* has had many composed settings, by composers including Josquin, Palestrina, Lassus, Pergolesi, Haydn, Schubert, Rossini, Liszt, Dvořák, Verdi, and Stanford. Many of the settings are given at concert performances.

Stabreim (Ger.). An early versification style based on alliteration, common in German and other northern-European poetry. It was adopted by Wagner when writing his own librettos for *Tristan und Isolde* and *Der Ring des Nibelungen* as a means of heightening textual expression with strong alliterative syllables, as in the lines 'Winterstürme wichen dem Wonnemond, in mildem Lichte leuchtet der Lenz' ('Winter's storms have vanished at Spring's command; in gentle radiance sparkles the Spring'; *Die Walküre*, Act 1, Scene 3, trans. Andrew Porter).

Staccato (It.). A term meaning 'detached' or 'separated', the opposite of *legato* ('smoothly'), and indicated in musical notation in several ways (Ex. 1).

Ex. 1

The degree of separation required in each case varies according to the type of instrument being played, the manner of bowing, tonguing, touch, or attack being used, and the general style and period of the music itself. In general though, a *staccato* dot (Ex. 1*a*) implies a reduction of the note value by at least half (e.g. a crotchet would become a quaver followed by a quaver rest); and other *staccato* markings such as the vertical stroke (Ex. 1*b*), small wedge or arrowhead (Ex. 1*c*), and horizontal dash (Ex. 1*d*) may indicate greater degrees of separation. *Staccato* dots within a slur imply a *mezzo-staccato* ('half-staccato') effect (Ex. 1*e*); the combination of dot and horizontal dash, indicating a combination of pressure and slight separation (Ex. 1*f*), is also roughly equivalent to a *mezzo-staccato* effect.

Until comparatively recent times there has in practice been little consistency of usage among composers; modern notation however generally prefers to use the dot for a standard *staccato* effect and the horizontal dash for a more pronounced one.

See also *Martelé*; *Portando*; *Sautillé*; *Spiccato*.

Staden, Johann (*bapt.* Nuremberg, 2 July 1581; *d* Nuremberg, Nov. 1634). German organist and composer. He spent a few years at the Bayreuth court, moving with the margrave to Kulmbach in 1605, and from 1611 was organist at various churches in his home town; his last and most prestigious appointment was at St Sebald. His reputation as an organist and composer was widespread, and he established the so-called Nuremberg school of composers. Johann Kindermann was one of his pupils.

Staden composed some attractive songs in a popular style to both sacred and secular German texts. The earlier ones are usually in four parts, but in 1630 he published a collection which contained some early German examples of the continuo song. He also composed church music, some in the new *concertato* style, and a great deal of dance music. Of his six children three became quite well-known musicians—Johann (1606-27), Sigmund Theophil (1607-55), and Adam (1614-59).   DENIS ARNOLD

Staff (plural, staves). In musical notation, a number of horizontal lines on and between which musical notes are placed. A *clef placed on the staff indicates the pitch of one line (and, by extension, of all the lines) and thus defines the pitch of each note written on the staff. Notes outside the pitch range of the staff are normally given *ledger lines. Since the late Middle Ages a five-line staff has been preferred for most music. Staves may be bracketed together on the left (as in piano music) to form a 'system'.

See also *Notation*, 2.

Stainer, (Sir) **John** (*b* London, 6 June 1840; *d* Verona, 31 Mar. 1901). English composer and scholar. He was a choirboy at St Paul's Cathedral, and in 1872 returned there as organist, after studying at Oxford and having been an undergraduate at St Edmund Hall. He revived the standard of music at St Paul's considerably and was an influential educationalist through his textbooks and by being an Inspector of Schools. In 1888 bad eyesight forced him to resign his posts, but he was knighted and in the following year became Professor of Music at Oxford. He wrote a considerable amount of church music (including hymn-tunes) and an oratorio, *The Crucifixion* (1887), which achieved enormous popularity. If its style, largely based on Mendelssohn and Spohr, is nowadays generally out of favour, his scholarly work producing editions of some of the early music surviving in manuscripts held by the Bodleian Library in Oxford remains extremely valuable.

DENIS ARNOLD

Stainer & Bell. English firm of music publishers. The group of young composers who founded Stainer & Bell in 1907 as specialist publishers of British music invented the name for its euphony (there being neither a Mr Stainer nor a Mr Bell). They began publishing the later works of Stanford, but soon promoted music by British composers then attracting attention—Holst's *Hymn of Jesus*, Vaughan Williams's *A Sea Symphony* and *London Symphony*, and works by Granville Bantock and Rutland Boughton. The Carnegie Trust appointed them publishers of the Carnegie Collection of British Music in 1917, and several outstanding historical series subsequently appeared under the editorship of the distinguished pioneer scholar E. H. Fellowes (English Madrigal School, 1913-24; Complete Works of William Byrd, 1937-50; English School of Lutenist Song Writers, 1920-31). From 1953 to 1971 Thurston Dart, a brilliant musician and scholar, was music adviser and supervised revised editions of these series. The firm began the Musica Britannica series for the Royal Musical Association in 1951 (Festival of Britain year) and the Early English Church Music series for the British Academy in 1963. Stainer & Bell purchased the firm of Galliard (with *Augener) in 1973 and have incorporated titles from Joseph *Williams and Joseph Weekes into the catalogue.

J. M. THOMSON

Stamitz, Carl (Philipp) (*b* Mannheim, *bapt.* 8 May 1745; *d* Jena, 9 Nov. 1801). Composer and violin, viola, and viola d'amore virtuoso, of Bohemian origin. He was brought up at the court of Mannheim, and had his first musical instruction from his father, Johann. Although this was curtailed by his early death, the influence of the elder Stamitz was doubtless embodied in the teaching of his successors Cannabich, Holzbauer, and F. X. Richter. In 1762 he became a second violinist in the court orchestra where he remained until his departure for Paris in 1770. From 1771 he was composer and conductor for the Duke de Noailles, a post which did not preclude successful appearances at the Concert Spirituel and trips to Vienna, Frankfurt am Main, Augsburg, and Strasbourg. In 1771 he began to pursue a somewhat perilous career as an itinerant virtuoso. His travels took him to London and the Hague, and in the 1780s he travelled widely in Germany without securing any permanent posts until 1789, when he was in charge of a concert series in Kassel for a year. After settling in Grietz for a few years he moved with his family to Jena in 1795, where he had a post as *Kapellmeister* and music teacher. Neither permanent employment nor continued commissions and the sale of compositions were sufficient to keep Stamitz out of debt, and his effects had to be auctioned at his death.

With his training at Mannheim the younger Stamitz was well qualified to continue the work of his father. Many of the stylistic features of the Mannheim orchestral style are to be found in his symphonies, and he was specially successful in consolidating the tonal and instrumental contrast of second themes. Like his Italian contemporary Toeschi he favoured the more old-fashioned three-movement symphony above the increasingly common four-movement type. Less conservative was his interest in slow introductions motivically related to the first movements they preceded, and in several symphonies he made use of programmatic elements. Along with other Mannheim contemporaries Stamitz cultivated the *symphonie concertante*, composing over 30 works in the genre mostly for two stringed instruments. He enriched the repertory of one of his chosen instruments, the viola d'amore, with numerous solo works. If Stamitz's contribution to the development of the symphony was less fundamental than that of his father, the contemporary popularity of his music—much admired for its lyrical qualities—is evident from the wide publication of chamber and orchestral works.　JAN SMACZNY

Stamitz, Johann (Wenzel Anton) [Jan Waczlaw Antonin] (*b* Německý Brod, now Havlíčkův Brod, *bapt.* 19 June 1717; *d* Mannheim, ?27 Mar., *buried* 30 Mar. 1757). Czech composer and violinist. He was the most prominent member of a Bohemian family of musicians and father of the two composers Carl Philipp and Anton Stamitz (1750–89/1809). His first musical instruction came from his father Antonín Ignác, an organist and choirmaster. From 1728 to 1734 he studied at the Jesuit Gymnasium in Jihlava followed by a year at university in Prague. It seems likely that the next few years were spent pursuing a career as an itinerant violin virtuoso until he settled at the court of the Elector Palatine at Mannheim probably in 1741 or 1742. Stamitz's progress went in tandem with the rapid growth in size and proficiency of the Elector Carl Theodor's orchestra. Graduating from first violinist (1743) to *Konzertmeister* (1745 or 1746), his pre-eminence in the musical life of the court was recognized when he was made director of instrumental music in 1750, although since 1745 he had been the best paid of the orchestra's violinists. From 1754 to 1755 Stamitz spent a year in Paris performing and propagating his compositions. These activities saw the start of links between Mannheim and the French capital which later composers including Stamitz's sons did much to exploit. His successes led to the publication of the six orchestral trios Op. 1 (1755) and later issues of symphonies in Paris.

In his capacity as *Konzertmeister* and director of instrumental music at Mannheim, Stamitz's training fostered the high standards of performance later observed by numerous commentators. His influence on pupils and subordinates was vital in laying the foundation of an orchestral technique which for its tonal qualities and unanimity was the envy of Europe. Stamitz's output comprised orchestral, chamber, and a small amount of church music including a Mass in D which was widely performed in his day. Interest in his work focuses on the symphonies although he wrote several violin concertos (presumably for his own performance) and a smaller number for wind including probably the first solo clarinet concerto. The symphonies on which Stamitz's modern reputation rests show a development away from the three-movement Italian *sinfonia* to a standard four-movement type. They reveal a strong musical personality with occasional reminiscences of his Czech origins (*Sinfonia pastorale* in D, Op. 4 No. 2). The more spectacular features of his style—the *crescendos* (probably influenced by Jommelli), bold dynamic effects, and light ornamental figures which so delighted contemporary audiences—often obscure his more lasting contributions to symphonic style. Of greater importance was his extension of phrase lengths, greater contrast of material within movements, an interest in thematic development, and the expansion of finales, innovations which lend justification to Burney's description of the elder Stamitz as 'another Shakespeare . . .[who] without quitting nature pushed art further than anyone had done before him'.　JAN SMACZNY

Ständchen (Ger.). 'Serenade'.

Stanford, (Sir) Charles Villiers (*b* Dublin, 30 Sept. 1852; *d* London, 29 Mar. 1924). British composer. Son of an Irish Protestant lawyer who was also a talented amateur singer and cellist, he studied music with various local Dublin musicians before leaving to become choral scholar at Queens' College, Cambridge, in 1870. While there he conducted the Cambridge University Music Society and then in 1873 became organist at Trinity College (a post he held until 1892). He also studied in Leipzig and Berlin and then began to achieve success as a composer, winning a prize in London with a symphony and having his first opera *The Veiled Prophet of Khorassan* performed at Hanover in 1881. With Parry, he was professor of composition at the foundation of the Royal College of Music (1883), continuing in this for the rest of his life and teaching virtually all the English composers of the next 40 years. In 1885 he became conductor of the Bach Choir in London and two years later was appointed Professor of Music at Cambridge. Several operas were produced in the next decades—one, *Shamus O'Brien* (1896), with considerable success—and his Anglican church music rapidly became very popular. He was knighted in 1902 and also conducted the Leeds Festivals from 1901 to 1910. His church music and such songs as his 'A Song of the Sea', 'Songs of the Fleet', and his setting of Tennyson's *The Revenge*, have ensured his fame. He is buried next to Purcell in Westminster Abbey. DENIS ARNOLD

Stanley, John (*b* London, 17 Jan. 1712; *d* London, 19 May 1786). English organist and composer. The son of a mason and minor official, he was accidentally blinded at the age of two, which did not, however, deter him from pursuing a musical career. He was a pupil of Maurice Greene, with whom, according to Burney, 'he studied with great diligence and a success that was astonishing'. By the age of nine he was apparently deputizing as organist at All Hallows, Bread Street, and in 1723 he succeeded William Babell as organist there. A contemporary newspaper report described him as one who 'is become the surprise of the Town for his ingenious performance on the Harpsichord and Organ'. Three years later Stanley became organist of St Andrew's, Holborn, and in 1734 of the Inner Temple. He took the degree of B.Mus. at Oxford when he was 17—the youngest Oxford music graduate ever to do so—and in 1738 he married. When Handel died, Stanley and J. C. Smith (ii) directed the annual oratorio concerts at Covent Garden and Drury Lane. Seven years before his death Stanley succeeded Boyce as Master of the King's Band of Musicians.

According to Burney, Stanley was 'a neat,

John Stanley

pleasing, and accurate performer, a natural and agreeable composer, and an intelligent instructor'. He composed the music for several dramatic pieces, including the pastoral *Arcadia, or The Shepherd's Wedding* (1761) for the marriage of George III and Queen Charlotte, the opera *Teraminta*, and three oratorios. He published three sets of organ voluntaries (London, 1748, 1752, 1754), which are still frequently performed, and other instrumental music. WENDY THOMPSON

Stark (Ger.). 'Strong', 'loud'; *stärker*, 'stronger', 'louder'; *stark anblasen*, *stark blasend*, 'strongly blown' (in the playing of wind instruments).

Starlight Express, The. Incidental music by Elgar, Op. 78, for Violet Pearn's play based on Algernon Blackwood's *A Prisoner in Fairyland*, produced in London in 1915. It contains songs for soprano and bass soloists, and the score calls for cowbells and a wind-machine. Some of the themes are from Elgar's suites *The Wand of Youth* (1907–8).

Star-spangled Banner, The. National anthem of the USA, officially adopted in 1931. Francis Scott Key (1779–1843) wrote the poem in 1814, and it was printed in the *Baltimore Patriot* on 20 September of that year, together with an account of the circumstances from which Key received his inspiration:

A gentleman [Key] had left Baltimore in a flag of truce for the purpose of getting released from the British fleet a friend of his [Dr Beanes] who had been captured at Marlborough. He went as far as the mouth of the Patuxent, and was not permitted to return lest the intended attack on Baltimore should be disclosed. He was therefore brought up the bay to the mouth of the Patapsco, where the flag vessel was kept under the guns of a frigate, and he was compelled to witness the bombardment of Fort McHenry, which the admiral had boasted that he would carry in a few hours, and that the city must fall. He watched the flag at the fort through the whole day with an anxiety that can be better felt than described, until the night prevented him from seeing it. In the night he watched the bombshells, and at early dawn his eye was again greeted by the proudly waving flag of his country.

The words of the song begin 'O say, can you see by the dawn's early light / What so proudly we hailed at the twilight's last gleaming'. The words were evidently intended for, and have always been sung to, the tune of John Stafford Smith's song 'To Anacreon in Heaven', composed for the Anacreontic Society of London and very popular in America at that time. The adoption of the song as national anthem was strongly opposed by the Music Supervisors' Conference of America, on the grounds that 'the text of the song is largely the reflection of a single war-time event which cannot fully represent the spirit of a nation committed to "peace and goodwill"'.

Stasov, Vladimir (Vasilyevich) (*b* St Petersburg, 14 Jan. 1824; *d* St Petersburg, 23 Oct. 1906). Russian music and art critic. Although his interests were wide, he was also a passionate nationalist, and as such it was natural that he should be regarded as a father-figure by the 19th-century Russian nationalist composers, for whom he coined the tag *moguchaya kuchka*, or 'Mighty Handful' (see *Five, The*). He was closely involved in the composition of many important Russian works: for example he carried on a lengthy correspondence with Musorgsky about his great historical opera *Khovanshchina*, Musorgsky pouring out his sometimes erratic ideas to Stasov, who then offered encouragement and perceptive criticism; he helped Balakirev with his incidental music to *King Lear* by rooting out suitable English tunes which were incorporated into the score; and he gave Tchaikovsky the idea (and a detailed plan) for his orchestral fantasia *The Tempest*. He also wrote extensively on music, and some of his more substantial writings have been translated and published in the collection *Vladimir Stasov: Selected Essays on Music* (London, 1968), prefaced by a valuable assessment of Stasov's work by Gerald Abraham.   GEOFFREY NORRIS

Stave. Alternative spelling of *staff.

Steel band. A band consisting mainly of instruments which have been fashioned from 55-gallon oil drums and are termed 'pans'. The process of making a pan is a complex and lengthy one. First, the top of the drum is beaten into a concave shape (sinking) and marked off into sections, each of which is hammered so that it corresponds to a specific pitch (grooving). The top is then usually cut off the drum at a depth which will define the instrument's over-all pitch: 'tenor' pans are about 20 cm. deep; 'guitar' pans about 45 cm.; and the entire drum is used for 'bass' pans. Burning and then cooling in water help give the pan a good tone, and it is ultimately fine-tuned with a small hammer. Pans are played with pairs of sticks tipped in rubber. Long notes are sustained by a fast alternation of sticks which produces a characteristic *tremolo* effect. There may be 10 or more pans in a steel band, with tenor instruments playing the melody, guitars the harmony, and bass instruments the lowest notes. The rhythm section of a band consists of such percussion instruments as conga drums, maracas, and tambourines. Repertory includes both dance and classical music, and the art of arranging for steel band is a skilled one.

The home of the steel band is Trinidad and Tobago where, as in the case of a number of other islands in the eastern Caribbean, bands provide an important focus for the cultural and social lives of local communities. Steel bands may also be found elsewhere in the Caribbean, in the USA, and in Britain, where there have been moves to incorporate steel band work in the curriculum of some schools. The origin of the steel band lies in the Trinidadian *tamboo bamboo* bands which were formed to circumvent the banning of African drums under the Peace Preservation Act of 1884. Members of such bands took bamboo tubes of various lengths and banged them together, struck them with other objects, or beat them on the ground. No doubt such activities proved as much of a breach of the peace as drumming. However, since the Peace Preservation Act was aimed principally at the use of drums in Afro-Christian cult ritual (see *West Indian Music*, 3), which the government saw as being a challenge to colonial authority, *tamboo bamboo* bands survived into the 20th century, when they grew larger with the addition of dustbin lids, bottles, and pieces of scrap metal. When, during the 1940s, bandsmen discovered the oil drum's properties as a tuned idiophone the steel band was born. The early steel bands in Port of Spain gained notoriety because of street fighting between supporters of rival bands, and subsequently membership of a band often coincided with political views of an anti-establishment nature. Today, however, the steel band movement is officially recognized, and individual bands are sponsored by local businesses and given government support. Such bands participate in the festivals and competitions which take place regularly in Trinidad and Tobago; however, the most important annual event in the Republic's steel band calendar is undoubtedly Carnival week, for performances by the country's many steel bands provide the musical stimulus for the lively celebrations associated with this famous event.

PEARLE CHRISTIAN, MICHAEL BURNETT

Steele, (Hubert) John (*b* Wellington, 13 Apr. 1929). New Zealand musicologist. He graduated from Victoria University College and the University of Otago (1953) and gained the first New Zealand government bursary in musicology to study under Thurston Dart at Cambridge. He was appointed lecturer in music at the University of Sydney in 1959 where he stimulated the performance of early music, producing an edition of Monteverdi's *Beatus vir* which has since had wide currency. His interest in early English keyboard music, the motets and madrigals of Peter Philips and Marenzio, and in Italian Baroque church music has resulted in editions of John Bull and Peter Philips for *Musica britannica* and elsewhere of Alessandro

Scarlatti and Marenzio. He holds a chair in the music department of the University of Otago, which is a centre of musicological research in New Zealand.   J. M. THOMSON

Steel Step, The (*Stal'noy skok*; *Le pas d'acier*). Ballet in two scenes, Op. 41, by Prokofiev to a libretto by the composer and G. Yakulov. It was choreographed by Massine and first performed in Paris in 1927. Prokofiev arranged an orchestral suite from the score (1926).

Steffani, Agostino (*b* Castelfranco, Veneto, 25 July 1654; *d* Frankfurt am Main, 12 Feb. 1728). Italian composer. Born of poor parents, he was educated at Padua and at the age of 13 his voice earned him a position with Elector Ferdinand Maria of Bavaria, who took him back to Munich. There Steffani was provided with a thorough musical training and placed in the custody of Kerll, who was *Kapellmeister* at the court. He went to Rome in 1672 to study with Ercole Bernabei, who became *Kapellmeister* to the Munich court in 1674, taking Steffani with him. Steffani was appointed court organist and in 1680 was ordained as a priest, but his main occupation in these years was the composition of operas, in a style that shows the influence of Legrenzi and other Venetians. In 1688 he was disappointed in his expectation of succeeding Bernabei (Bernabei's son was appointed) and left Munich for Hanover, where he was *Kapellmeister* to the newly opened Italian opera theatre.

Although he continued to compose operas and other works, Steffani spent much of his later life as a diplomat and ambassador, travelling around Europe. During a period in Rome (1708–9) he met Handel, who was much influenced by Steffani's attractive chamber duets to Italian texts. His work was also known in England and in 1727 he was made honorary president of the Academy of Vocal Music (the future Academy of Ancient Music). One of the best-known opera composers in Germany, he was capable of real emotional power in both recitative and aria; however, his best works are the chamber duets. Some of his church music, which includes an excellent setting of the *Stabat mater* for six voices, strings, and continuo, is also attractive.   DENIS ARNOLD

Steg (Ger.). 'Bridge' (of a violin etc.); *am Steg*, the same as *sul ponticello* (It.), i.e. bow on the bridge.

Steibelt, Daniel (*b* Berlin, 22 Oct. 1765; *d* St Petersburg, 20 Sept. 1823). German composer. He was the son of a piano and harpsichord maker and had a successful career as a pianist in Paris and London—though he had to leave both cities at various times because of his shady business dealings. He married an Englishwoman and in 1808 settled in St Petersburg at the invitation of Alexander I, directing the French Opéra and from 1810 acting as *maître de chapelle*, as Boieldieu's successor. He met and became friendly with John Field. Steibelt composed a number of operas, most of which are now lost, and a great deal of rather showy piano music. His innovations include the use of a double orchestra in his 'Grand Military Concerto' for piano (*c*.1816) and that of a chorus in his Eighth Piano Concerto (1820).
                          DENIS ARNOLD

Steinmetz, Johann Erhard (*fl.* mid 18th century). German composer. Little is known of this shadowy figure: he seems to have been an oboist in the Dresden hunting-band. The symphonies (now lost) attributed to him in the Breitkopf Catalogue of 1762 were probably works by Johann Stamitz.

Autograph MS of the opening of Steffani's chamber duet 'Occhi perche piangete'.

Stendhal. See *Novel, Music in the*.

Stentare (It.). 'To strive', i.e. to play in a laborious way; *stentando*, 'labouring', 'holding back'; *stentamento*, 'laboriously', 'slowly'; *stentato*, 'laboured', i.e. held back and every note stressed.

Štěpán [Steffan, Steffani, Stephan, Staphani], **Josef Antonín** (*b* Kopidlno, Bohemia, *bapt.* 14 Mar. 1726; *d* Vienna, 12 Apr. 1797). Czech composer, keyboard teacher, and virtuoso. He studied with Hammel and Wagenseil in Vienna, but his first musical tuition probably came from his father who was organist and schoolmaster at Kopidlno. In Vienna where he settled in 1741 after fleeing from the invading Prussian army, he had a distinguished reputation as a keyboard virtuoso and teacher, counting royalty amongst his pupils. Štěpán's output includes a small amount of church music and some four collections of *Lieder*, of which *Sammlung deutscher Lieder*, vol. 1 (1778) was the first Viennese publication of its kind. But his solo keyboard works and harpsichord concertos represent his most significant contribution to the music of the period. The early sonatas, composed in the mid 1750s, show an advance on current models in the Italian style. His later sonatas and capriccios (1770s-90s), in their figuration and use of dynamics composed for the piano rather than the harpsichord, stand out from those of his contemporaries and did much to further the development of the Classical solo sonata. Notable features of these works are several effective minor-key introductions, a practice he also adopted for some of his concertos. Štěpán's occasional use of programmatic elements and thematic integration between movements indicate a more than passing interest in formal experiment.   JAN SMACZNY

Sterbend (Ger.). 'Dying away'.

Sterndale Bennett, (Sir) **William** (*b* Sheffield, 13 Apr. 1816; *d* London, 1 Feb. 1875). English composer, who for a brief period in the 1830s enjoyed a high reputation in the Germany of Mendelssohn and Schumann. He was the son of the organist of Sheffield parish church but was orphaned when three years old and was brought up in Cambridge, where he was a King's chorister. In 1826 he was admitted 'as a prodigy' to the Royal Academy of Music, studying violin, piano, and composition (under Crotch). Soon his brilliance as a pianist became well known, and a piano concerto he wrote in 1832, when Cipriani Potter had become his teacher, earned him an invitation to Germany from Mendelssohn. In the next six years he composed three more concertos, several symphonies, and songs and piano pieces; Schumann expressed intense admiration for his work. But after about 1840 he found it hard to complete his compositions and concentrated on conducting, playing, and teaching. He became professor of music at Cambridge University in 1856, instituting examinations (instead of 'exercises') for the music degrees, and principal of the RAM in 1866. In 1871 he was knighted. In his last years he regained his flair for composing, writing a cantata *The May Queen* (1858), *The Woman of Samaria* (1867), and a new symphony (1864). He also edited works by Bach and Handel.

MICHAEL KENNEDY

Steso (It.). 'Extended', 'spread out', i.e. 'slow'.

Stesso, stessa (It.). 'Same'; *lo stesso tempo*, *l'istesso tempo*, 'the same tempo', usually meaning that although the nominal value of the beat has changed (in Ex. 1 below, from crotchet to dotted crotchet) its duration is to remain the same (often expressed as ♩ = ♩.).

Stevens, Bernard (George) (*b* London, 2 Mar. 1916). English composer. He studied with Edward Dent and Cyril Rootham at Cambridge (1935-7) and with R. O. Morris and Gordon Jacob at the Royal College of Music (1937-40). After service in the war he joined the Workers' Musical Association (1946), impelled by his socialist principles. His compositions draw on the European mainstream tradition represented by such composers as Hindemith, and include orchestral works, choral music, and songs.

PAUL GRIFFITHS

Ex. 1. Grieg: Piano Sonata, Op. 7, second movement

[Andante molto]

L'istesso tempo

etc.

Stevens, Halsey (*b* Scott, New York, 3 Dec. 1908). American composer amd musicologist. He studied composition with William H. Berwald at Syracuse University (1926-31, 1935-7) and with Ernest Bloch at the University of California at Berkeley (1944). In 1946 he was appointed to teach composition at the University of South California. His large output, including numerous instrumental sonatas and sonatinas, shows the influence of Bartók, on whose music he has written an authoritative study: *The Life and Music of Béla Bartók* (New York, 1953, 2nd edn 1964). PAUL GRIFFITHS

Stevens, Richard John Samuel (*b* London, 27 Mar. 1757; *d* London, 23 Sept. 1837). English composer. He sang at St Paul's Cathedral as a boy, and then worked in various London churches as organist. He became Gresham Professor of Music in 1801 and music master at Christ's Hospital in 1808. He is remembered for his songs (see *Glee*).

Stevenson, Ronald (*b* Blackburn, 6 Mar. 1928). Scottish composer and writer on music. He studied at the Royal Manchester College of Music (1945-8) and with Guido Guerrini at the Accademia di Santa Cecilia in Rome (1955). His scholarly interest in Busoni, however, has had more influence on his musical thinking, and he has emulated not only Busoni's preference for elaborate forms (*Passacaglia on DSCH* for piano, 1960-2) but also his use of alien folk elements. Stevenson has also been active as a pianist and writer on music, and is author of the book *Western Music: an Introduction* (London, 1971). PAUL GRIFFITHS

Stierhorn. See *Horn, 9d.*

Stile antico (It.). 'Old style', one of the terms frequently applied to 17th-century church music written in the style of Palestrina, with smooth, flowing polyphony and scored *a cappella*, rather than in *stile moderno*, for a few voices with continuo accompaniment. It became fashionable for composers to write certain kinds of church music in the *stile antico*, even though they might use the *stile moderno* in other works; Mass music, for example, was frequently unaccompanied and less directly expressive than were motets. See also *Palestrina, 2.*

Stile concitato (It.). 'Agitated style'. A term used by Monteverdi when explaining his interpretation of Plato's three categories of music— 'anger, moderation, and humility or supplication'—in the preface to the *Madrigali guerrieri ed amorosi* (1638). In this context it implied military rhythms to 'stir people to war', and in the *Combattimento di Tancredi e Clorinda* (1624)

Monteverdi first worked out this idea, by making a semibreve correspond to a spondaic beat (chosen by the Greek philosophers as suitable for calm dances), and then dividing it into 16 equal parts (i.e. semiquavers) to achieve an equivalent of a pyrrhic beat (used for lively and warlike dances). Today the term is sometimes used to mean simply 'vigorous' or 'very lively'; because of its vagueness it is better avoided.

Stile moderno (It.). 'Modern style'; see *Stile antico.*

Stile rappresentativo (It.). 'Representative style', 'dramatic style'. Term first used by Caccini in the dedication (to Giovanni de' Bardi) of his opera *Euridice* (1600). It refers to the new dramatic style of writing for the voice which was developed by the Florentine *camerata* as an attempt to match in emotional power the music of the Ancient Greeks; Caccini wrote more fully about the style in his collection of monodic songs *Le nuove musiche* (1601-2). Some music written in the style survives from Peri's opera *Dafne* (1594, performed 1598), and Cavalieri adopted it in his *Rappresentatione di Anima e di Corpo* (1600). Music in *stile rappresentativo* is characteristically free in rhythm and phrasing, with frequent pauses and the use of unusual intervals for emotional effect. In the foreword to his version of *Euridice* (to which Caccini contributed some arias and choruses), Peri wrote that 'having in mind those inflections and actions that serve us in our grief, in our joy, and in similar states, I caused the bass to move in time to these, either more or less, following the passions'. See also *Monody.*

Still (Ger.). 'Quiet', 'calm'.

Still, William Grant (*b* Woodville, Mississippi, 11 May 1895; *d* Los Angeles, 3 Dec. 1978). Black American composer. Still was educated at Wilberforce College and Oberlin Conservatory, and later studied composition with Varèse and George W. Chadwick. In the 1920s he settled in New York and played in dance and theatre orchestras, worked for W. C. Handy's publishing firm and the Black Swan Phonograph Company, and arranged and composed for radio. At the same time he began writing large-scale compositions. The first of these to win Still recognition (and still his best-known work) was the *Afro-American Symphony*, premièred by the Rochester Philharmonic under Howard Hanson in 1931. During the next 40 years or so a steady stream of compositions and nearly as many prizes, awards, and honorary degrees earned him the sobriquet 'Dean of Negro Composers'.

Still's music tends towards a conservative, tonal style; it is often attractive, well-constructed, lyrical, and readily accessible. Besides his operas, symphonies, sacred music, and many instrumental works, Still also composed popular songs, arranged spirituals, wrote for films and television, and conducted. Still's work in art music helped break new ground for other Black composers, but his contribution to American musical life is better gauged by considering his sustained involvement in a wide range of musical styles and contexts.   MARK TUCKER

Stilt, The. The name given in Hart's Psalter (1615) to the well-known common metre tune now called *York*. It moves by large steps, and doubtless thus suggested the striding of a walker on stilts. Hawkins, in his *History of Music* (1776), says that the tune is 'so well known that within memory half the nurses of England were used to sing it by way of lullaby; and the chimes of many country churches have played it six or eight times in 24 hours from time immemorial'. Vaughan Williams introduces it as a village church clock tune in his opera *Hugh the Drover* (first performed in 1924).

Stimme (Ger.). 'Voice', including the sense of a vocal or instrumental part; also used to mean organ stop, and sound-post (in a string instrument); the plural is *Stimmen*. The verb *stimmen* means 'to tune'.

Stimmgabel (Ger.). 'Tuning-fork'.

Stimmhorn (Ger.). 1. 'Pitch-pipe'. 2. A tool used for tuning organ-pipes.

Stimmstock (Ger.). The soundpost of a string instrument.

Stimmung (Ger.). 1. 'Mood'; hence *Stimmungsbild*, a piece of music expressing a particular mood, and *Stimmungsmusik*, 'background' or 'mood' music.
   2. 'Tuning'.

Stimmung ('Tuning'). Work by Stockhausen for two sopranos, mezzo-soprano, tenor, baritone, and bass, composed in 1968. The six unaccompanied singers, each with a microphone, vocalize without words for 75 minutes.

Sting. 17th-century English term used for the normal vibrato in lute playing, i.e. that produced by the motion of one finger alone.

Stinguendo (It.). 'Extinguishing', i.e. fading out.

Stirando, stirato, stiracchiando, stirac-

chiato (It.). 'Stretching', 'stretched', i.e. expanding the music by means of a *ritardando*.

Stochastic music (from Gk, *stokhos*, 'aim'). Originally a mathematical term, a 'stochastic process' being one whose goal can be described but whose individual details are unpredictable. In music, it refers to composition by the use of the laws of probability. By contrast with *indeterminate music, stochastic music is fully composed: chance enters only into the process of composition, the composer perhaps allowing the distribution of pitches, for example, to be determined by some concept from the mathematics of probability. Stochastic techniques, which often depend on the use of a computer to calculate distributions, can be useful in the creation of sound masses where the details are less important than the large-scale effect. The word was introduced into the musical vocabulary by Xenakis, much of whose music is stochastic.   PAUL GRIFFITHS

Stockend (Ger.). 'Coming to a standstill', i.e. slowing down.

Stockhausen, Karlheinz (*b* Burg Mödrath, nr Cologne, 22 Aug. 1928). German composer. He studied at the Cologne Musikhochschule (1947–51) with Hans Otto Schmidt-Neuhaus for piano, Hermann Schroeder for harmony and counterpoint, and Frank Martin for composition. In 1951 he attended the Darmstadt sum-

Stockhausen

mer courses, where he was impressed by Karel Goeyvaerts's essays in applying serial methods to rhythm and also by Messiaen's *Mode de valeurs et d'intensités* (1949), which uses scales of rhythmic values and dynamic levels. Drawing his own conclusions from these examples, he quickly wrote *Kreuzspiel* for oboe, bass clarinet, piano, and percussion, and *Formel* for orchestra (both 1951). In 1952 he went to Paris, where he studied with Messiaen and worked in Pierre Schaeffer's *musique concrète* studio. He then returned to Cologne, where he completed *Kontra-Punkte* for ten instruments (1952–3), the first work which he acknowledges as mature.

Within a short period Stockhausen had thus established himself, along with Pierre Boulez, as a leader in the attempt to create a new musical language along strictly serial lines (see *Serialism*), and to each new work he brought a fresh view of musical possibilities. In the two electronic *Studien* (1953–4), composed at the newly founded studio in Cologne, he tried to synthesize timbres from pure tones; in *Zeitmasse* for five woodwind (1955–6) he integrated strict with variable tempos; in *Gruppen* for three orchestras (1955–7) he added acoustic space to the composer's repertory of means; and in *Gesang der Jünglinge* on tape (1955–6) he achieved a full union of music and language.

In his next electronic work, the four-channel *Kontakte* (1958–60), Stockhausen chose to tackle complex sounds which did not lend themselves to the serial methods and the complex formal schemes of earlier works, and accordingly he introduced more empirical techniques; the heard quality of a sound, rather than its symbolic representation, became the prime consideration. Stockhausen had always been an acute judge of acoustic effectiveness, but now the composition and relation of timbres became increasingly important. This is the case in *Momente* for soprano, chorus, and instruments (1961–72) and in various works in which Stockhausen applied electronic transformation to musical performance: *Mixtur* for modulated orchestra (1964), *Mikrophonie I* for tam-tam and microphones (1964), and *Mikrophonie II* for modulated chorus, Hammond organ, and tape (1965). There followed two tape pieces, *Telemusik* (1966) and *Hymnen* (1966–7), in which he integrated recordings of music from around the world, as well as several works, including *Prozession* (1967) and *Kurzwellen* (1968), for his own ensemble of musicians using natural and electronic instruments. His experience with this group led to his allowing a large degree of freedom to the performer, especially in *Aus den sieben Tagen* (1968), a set of prose poems intended to stimulate the musician's intuition.

With *Mantra* for two pianos and electronics (1970) Stockhausen entered on a new phase, basing each work on one or more haunting melodies. Sometimes, as in *Mantra* or *Inori* for dancer and orchestra (1973–4), the result is a massive, continuous development; in other works, such as *Musik im Bauch* for six percussionists (1975), the emphasis is on the ritual enactment of a musical fable. The orchestral *Trans* (1971) combines musical strength with dramatic effectiveness, having the strings alone visible, placed behind a gauze and bathed in violet light, while the other sections are heard from behind. Similar combinations of music and theatre are intended for *Licht* (1977–), a cycle of scenes planned to be performed during the evenings of a week. Through all the phases of his development Stockhausen has had an enormous influence. Since 1957 he has taught frequently at Darmstadt, and he has given lectures all over the world. He has also appeared widely as a conductor and performer of his own music.   PAUL GRIFFITHS

FURTHER READING
Karlheinz Stockhausen: *Texte* (4 vols., Cologne, 1963, 1964, 1971, 1978); Karl H. Wörner: *Stockhausen: Life and Work* (London, 1973); Jonathan Cott: *Stockhausen: Conversations with the Composer* (London, 1974); Jonathan Harvey: *The Music of Stockhausen* (London, 1975); Robin Maconie: *The Works of Karlheinz Stockhausen* (London, 1976, reprinted 1981).

Stolle (Ger.). The first strophe, which is then repeated, of **Bar* form.

Stoltzer, Thomas (*b* Schweidnitz, Silesia, 1480s; *d* Moravia, 1526). German composer. He was a priest in Breslau in 1519, and became *magister capellae* to the Hungarian court in Ofen (now Budapest) three years later. Like some English composers he was torn between the Protestant and Catholic churches, writing four splendid psalm motets in translations by Luther as well as more conventional Latin church music, in a style akin to Isaac's.   DENIS ARNOLD

Stölzel, Gottfried Heinrich (*b* Grünstädtel, Harz Mountains, 13 Jan. 1690; *d* Gotha, 27 Nov. 1749). German composer. The son of an organist, he was taught singing and clavier by his father before going to Leipzig University in 1707 to study theology. He soon turned to music for a career, and in his early 20s was teacher to various noble families in Breslau. In 1713 he made an extended tour of Italy (where he met Vivaldi), going to Prague in 1715. After three years in Prague and a further period of teaching, he became *Kapellmeister* to the Saxe-Gotha court in 1720; he remained in this post for the rest of his life.

Stölzel was one of the best-known composers of his time, but a great deal of his music has been lost, including his works for the stage. However, his splendid concerto for '4 chori' (two of trumpets and drums, one each of wind and strings) reveals his considerable talent; Bach transcribed one movement for Wilhelm Friedemann to play on the clavier. He was also interested in the experimental tunings that produced the '48', writing an *Enharmonische Sonata*, and his theoretical works include an interesting treatise on recitative. The famous song 'Bist du bei mir' is ascribed to him, rather than to J. S. Bach, by some scholars.

DENIS ARNOLD

Stone, Robert (*b* Alphington, Devon, 1516; *d* London, 2 July 1613). English composer. Following an early association with Exeter Cathedral, he entered the service of the Chapel Royal *c*.1543, remaining there until his death. His setting of the Lord's Prayer (*c*.1550) is still very popular.   JOHN MILSOM

Stone Guest, The (*Kamenny gost*). Opera in three acts by Dargomyzhsky, a setting of Pushkin's play (1830) on the same story as *Don Giovanni*. It was begun in the 1860s and left almost finished; Rimsky-Korsakov orchestrated it and Cui provided an overture. It was first performed in St Petersburg in 1872.

Stopped notes. See *Horn*; *Trumpet*.

Stopping. On string instruments, the placing of the fingertips of the left hand on the strings, so that their vibrating length is shortened and different notes can be obtained. Double stopping is the stopping of and playing on two strings at a time; it is also used, however, when one or both of the strings in use is not stopped, simply indicating that two strings are being bowed simultaneously. Multiple stopping is the playing of more than two strings simultaneously.

Stops. See *Organ*, 9; *Harpsichord*.

Storace, Stephen (John Seymour) (*b* London, 4 Apr. 1762; *d* London, 19 Mar. 1796). English composer. The son of a Neapolitan double bass player working in Dublin, he was sent back to Italy for his early musical training (from 1776). Six years later he published one of the first collections of canzonets (or chamber songs) with an independent piano accompaniment to the voice part (London, 1782). His sister Nancy was in Vienna by the later summer of 1783. She was one of the finest sopranos of her day (Mozart wrote the part of Susanna in *Le nozze di Figaro* for her), and she and Stephen benefited greatly from Mozart's friendship, which continued after Storace's return to England in February 1787. From the mass of manuscripts gathered together

during his travels, he published during the next two years *Storace's Collection of Harpsichord Music*, which included solo works, chamber pieces, and concertos, among them the first English printing of Mozart's E♭ Piano Quartet and the first ever of the Trio K 564. Three of Storace's own trios appeared in the collection; all are good, and that in D is masterly in its Mozartian independence of writing for all three instruments.

Storace's natural bent was towards opera. In 1785 he was commissioned to write for Vienna *Gli sposi malcontenti*, possibly through his sister's friendship with the Emperor. In the next year he produced one of his most successful works, *Gli equivoci*, to a libretto by da Ponte, in which he shows an impressive command of late Classical Italian operatic procedures. Back in England, he plunged into a ceaseless round of theatrical activity, the most remarkable products of which were the dialogue operas *The Haunted Tower* (1789), *No Song, No Supper* (1790), and *The Pirates* (1792). However, because of the lax English operatic traditions, in which most operas were a patchwork of several composers' work, and the destruction of manuscript scores and performing material in the two fires at Covent Garden (1808) and Drury Lane (1809), Storace's undoubted gifts did not achieve the recognition they deserved.   ROBIN LANGLEY

Stornello (It.). A traditional type of Tuscan folk-song, improvised by a male singer (*stornellatore*) or a female (*stornellatrice*). The poem has only three lines of text.

Strad, The. English monthly musical magazine dealing with all aspects of the world of bowed string instruments, their makers, and performers. It was founded in 1890 by Eugene Polonaski and was for many years associated with the Lavender family; it is published by Novello & Co.

Stradella, Alessandro (*b* ? Nepi, nr Viterbo, 1638/9; *d* Genoa, 25 Feb. 1682). Italian composer. Stradella was a *gentiluomo*, the son of a knight of the Order of S. Stefano of Pisa. Nothing is known of his early life except that he seems to have studied in Bologna. He became a favourite of Queen Christina of Sweden, then a Catholic convert living in great state in Rome, and *c*.1664 was appointed her *servitore di camera*. He composed motets and cantatas for various nobles but was increasingly involved in scandals concerning women and money, and in 1677 had to leave Rome. He went to Venice where he was employed as music master to Alvise Contarini's mistress, but after only a few months ran off with her to Turin, followed by Contarini and then by two assassins. Stradella survived this attempt on his life, and in 1678 left Turin (alone) to live in Genoa, where he remained for the rest of his life.

Stradella was an extremely versatile composer. His operas include *Il Trespolo tutore* (performed Genoa, *c.*1677), an *opera buffa* with a plot similar to that of Donizetti's *Don Pasquale* and music which sends up the conventional operatic style. But his finest music comes in the dramatic oratorios, especially *S. Giovanni Battista* (performed Rome, 1675), with their vividly drawn characters and situations— some of them perhaps drawn from personal experience. The most important feature of his instrumental music is his use of *concerto grosso* solo/tutti contrasts.

He was murdered by a soldier—the trouble being, as usual, a woman. In Flotow's opera *Alessandro Stradella* (1844) his life is spared when the hired assassins repent their purpose on hearing the composer's new motet in praise of the Blessed Virgin Mary.   DENIS ARNOLD

Stradivari, Antonio (*b* Cremona, ?1644; *d* Cremona, 18 Dec. 1737). This greatest of violin-makers first worked, up to the mid 1660s, with Nicolò Amati (1596–1684). On this account he is often named as one of Amati's many celebrated pupils, among these Andrea Guarneri, great uncle of Giuseppe [Joseph] Guarneri 'del Gesù', rated closest rival to Stradivari. Through his long life Stradivari has been estimated to have produced over 1,100 instruments of which some 400 are believed to exist today in the hands of players or collectors – mainly violins, with perhaps 16 violas and 50 cellos, and a few instruments of other kinds including bass viols and a guitar. (All these amount, of course, to but a minute fraction of the immeasurable quantity of violins etc. that bear non-genuine 'Stradivarius' labels.)

Stradivari developed his designs through stages recognizable to the connoisseur, achieving his classic form by *c.*1700. Many of his instruments are known by the names of past owners, for example, among the violins, the 'Hellier' (1679), the 'Betts' (1704), and the 'Sarasate' (1724). The 'Messie' ('Messiah', 1716)—preserved, having virtually never been played, in the Ashmolean Museum, Oxford— had its sobriquet conferred by the French violinist Alard (1815–88) on being shown 'what one waits for always but never appears'.

Why do his violins excel? Modern wave-analyses of his and of other fine old Italian violins have certainly exhibited optimum characteristics for tone and response. Age is not a major factor: Stradivari's reputation was of international stature in his lifetime. His selection of materials is not exceptional. A craftsman's genius, self-critically applied through the

years, can best account for his pre-eminence. It has, however, been proposed that historical fortune has been on his side, inasmuch as he arched the violin body less than was common at the time, and that when the instruments later came to be altered (new necks etc.: see *Violin*, 6*c*), the 'Strads' answered to the process particularly well. The great soloists of past and present have largely chosen a Stradivarius, or if not this, most likely a Guarnerius. Prices (sterling) have latterly run high into five figures.

No authenticated portrait of Stradivari is known (he was described as tall and spare). Among his children, two sons, Francesco and Omobono, continued together in the craft to their deaths six or so years after their father's. Many of his tools, drawings, letters, etc. are now to be seen in the Museo Stradivariano in Cremona.

                    ANTHONY BAINES

Straff, straffer (Ger.). 'Strict', 'stricter', or 'tight', 'tighter'; *straffen*, 'tighten' (a drum-head etc.).

Strambotto (It.). A type of poem much set in the years around 1500 by composers of *frottole* and madrigals. Each verse usually had eight lines of 11 syllables, with a rhyme scheme abababcc.

Straniera, La ('The Foreigner'). Opera in two acts by Bellini to a libretto by Romani. It was first performed in Milan in 1829.

Strascicando, strascicato (It.). 'Dragging', 'dragged'. The same as *strascinando*.

Strascinando, strascinato (It.). 'Dragging', 'dragged'. A direction to play a passage with heavily slurred notes.

Strathspey. A national dance of Scotland, a slower version of the *reel, which takes its name from the *strath* ('valley') of the River Spey. The strathspey is characterized by 4/4 time and an abundance of dotted rhythms, often in the inverted pattern of the *Scotch snap. The strathspey is essentially fiddle music, but is also played on the pipes. Several collections of strathspeys and reels were published in Scotland in the 18th century.

Straus, Oscar (*b* Vienna, 6 Mar. 1870; *d* Bad Ischl, 11 Jan. 1954). Austrian composer. He studied music in Vienna and Berlin with Max Bruch as one of his teachers. Early in his career he wrote orchestral and instrumental music but from 1895 he became active as musical director of various theatres in Germany, turning his attention to cabaret and writing operettas in the

Offenbach mould. Gradually his Viennese heritage asserted itself and he moved into the Strauss–Lehár tradition with works richly endowed with waltzes, the first success in this style being *Ein Walzertraum* (1907). The following year he wrote *Der tapfere Soldat* ('The Chocolate Soldier'), unofficially based on Shaw's *Arms and the Man*: one of the numbers, the waltz-song 'My Hero', became one of Straus's best-known songs. He wrote a steady stream of musicals until the 1930s, having further outstanding successes with *Der letzte Walzer* (1920) and *Drei Walzer* (1935). In 1950 he branched out into film music and wrote a popular hit, 'La ronde de l'amour', for the film *La ronde*.

PETER GAMMOND

Strauss. A family of Viennese composers and conductors who were responsible, in the 19th century, for establishing high professional standards in ballroom music, raising it to a level, particularly in their exploitation of the *waltz, which has rarely been equalled. The founder of the dynasty was Johann Strauss (*b* Vienna, 14 Mar. 1804; *d* Vienna, 25 Sept. 1849), the son of a Viennese innkeeper who was drowned in the Danube, probably committing suicide, soon after his son's birth. His mother remarried and his stepfather did all he could to encourage the child's obvious musical talents but, believing music to be a perilous occupation, apprenticed him to a bookbinder. Strauss eventually followed his own bent and at 15 joined the well-known

Johann Strauss (1894)

orchestra of Michael Pamer as a viola player. In the same orchestra was violinist Josef Lanner who left to form his own trio and in 1819 invited Strauss to join him. This became an orchestra which grew popular by virtue of the excellent music that both Lanner and Strauss wrote for it. In 1825 they quarrelled and the following year Strauss formed his own orchestra which became so popular that at one time he was employing around 100 players. He played at the Sperl, Vienna's most famous dance hall, and in 1833 began to travel abroad with his orchestra. His music was graceful and full of rhythmic vitality but not always distinctive. His most lasting pieces were the waltz *Lorelei-Rheinklänge* and the opportune *Radetzky March*. His wife Anna bore him six children the eldest of whom was also christened Johann and showed the same musical talents. Father Strauss was strongly opposed to his eldest son following in his footsteps, but in 1844 Johann (*b* Vienna, 25 Oct. 1825; *d* Vienna, 3 June 1899) started his own orchestra, with his mother's secret encouragement, and it became a successful rival to his father's. Eventually they were reconciled and when the elder Strauss died the two orchestras were amalgamated under Johann who likewise gained a universal reputation through many tours abroad. The younger Johann was a far more distinctive composer than his father and his waltzes such as *The Blue Danube* and *Tales from the Vienna Woods* are acknowledged masterpieces that are as much at home in the concert hall played by the Vienna Philharmonic and other famous orchestras as they were in the ballroom. Waltzes, polkas, and marches flowed from his pen in inspired profusion. Following the success in Vienna of the Offenbach operettas, Strauss, encouraged by his wife, tried his hand in the theatre, at first without success, but when the right librettos came along he wrote two perfect operetta masterpieces in *Die Fledermaus* (1874) and *Der Zigeunerbaron* (1885) as well as many lesser pieces. The next son Josef (*b* Vienna, 22 Aug. 1827; *d* Vienna, 21 July 1870) had great musical talent but was happy to pursue a career as an engineer. However, when Johann was too preoccupied with composing and suffering ill health, he was persuaded to take over the family orchestra and from then on continued a musical career. He was a quieter character than his brother and this is reflected in his own fine waltzes and polkas which lack the power of Johann's but have great beauty and craftsmanship. The brothers jointly wrote the famous *Pizzicato Polka*. A third son Eduard (*b* Vienna, 15 Mar. 1835; *d* Vienna, 28 Dec. 1916) received the best musical education, played in the orchestra and became a popular conductor and a competent but less inspired composer. He took over the family orchestra after Johann's death. Various descendants of the Strauss brothers continued the Strauss tradition into the 20th century.   PETER GAMMOND

Strauss, Richard (Georg) (*b* Munich, 11 June 1864; *d* Garmisch-Partenkirchen, Bavaria, 8 Sept. 1949). German composer. He was the son of an excellent horn player in the Court Orchestra in Munich; his mother came from a well-off family of brewers. It was the independence allowed by her money which permitted Strauss to publish a number of his schoolboy compositions, and his father's connections assured their performance, so that by the age of 18 he was a composer of some accomplishment. Most of this early music is written in classical forms, probably due to the conservative views of his father (a strong anti-Wagnerian), and the main influences are those of Brahms, Schumann, and Mendelssohn. The reputation engendered by these works led to the invitation by Hans von Bülow to become assistant conductor of the Meiningen Court Orchestra in 1885, and until about 1924 Strauss made his living mainly by conducting, being successively conductor at the Munich Opera (1886-9), the Weimar Opera, returning to Munich as associate conductor in 1894, and eventually becoming director of the Berlin Philharmonic Concerts in 1898 and conductor (later director) of the Court Opera there.

As a composer, Strauss's development changed radically about the time he was at Meiningen, where he came into contact with more progressive musicians than those he could meet at home. He followed the Lisztian-Wagnerian paths initially by writing a number of symphonic poems, beginning with *Macbeth* (1886-8), continuing with two comparatively short works, *Don Juan* (1888-9) and *Till Eulenspiegels lustige Streiche* (1894-5), and some longer ones, *Also sprach Zarathustra* (1895-6), *Tod und Verklärung* (1888-9), *Don Quixote* (1896-7), *Ein Heldenleben* (1897-8), and finishing with a programmatic symphony *Symphonia domestica* (1902-3). Although these take as their starting-point literary or philosophical concepts, and in some cases embody realistic imagery in sound (such as the description of sheep in *Don Quixote*), some of them are remarkable for their adherence to classical

A page from the autograph score of Strauss's 'Tod und Verklärung' (1888-9).

forms, *Macbeth* and *Don Juan* being basically
sonata movements, *Till Eulenspiegel* a rondo,
and *Don Quixote* a set of variations. It is because
of this, together with his superb mastery of
orchestral resources, rather than the at times
mawkish programmatic content, that these
works are so successful, and in the best of
them there is a humour and sense of slightly
ironic detachment which shows Strauss moving
away from the romantic seriousness of his
predecessors.

His next major works were the one-act operas
Salome (1905) and *Elektra* (1909). Although he
had earlier written two full-length stage works
in a strongly Wagnerian style, these had not
achieved wide popularity. In these two shorter
works, both subjects break away from the
legendic traditions to become studies in
abnormal psychology. Musically, they are
remarkable for their elaborate orchestral
scores, very subtle in tone quality and complex
chromatic counterpoint, and for the compression of their thematic development, which
results in an extraordinary emotional tension.
Both works achieved some notoriety when they
were first produced, and *Salome* had difficulties
with the censorship in various cities, but they
set the seal on Strauss's reputation and the
financial rewards, of *Salome* especially, allowed
him to build a substantial villa at Garmisch in
Bavaria where he lived the rest of his life.

During the period immediately following,
Strauss's main interest remained in the composition of operas, but he felt it impossible to

'*Die Elektrische Hinrichtung*', *caricature (1909) of
Richard Strauss by F. Jüttner.*

continue in the same vein. He was fortunate that
the author of *Elektra*, Hugo von Hofmannsthal,
was willing to write him a libretto for a comedy
with a 'period' theme, which eventually was
staged as *Der Rosenkavalier* (1911). Though
composed in the continuous manner of the
Wagnerian music drama, with the same
emphasis on a large orchestra, this work
represents a distinct move away from the
nervous intensity of his recent music, and, by
the inclusion of arias and a certain tendency
towards pastiche, Strauss matches the comic
subject with both charm and humanity. The
complexity of the contrapuntal texture and of
the chromaticism is much reduced, and while
Hofmannsthal's libretto places a certain
emphasis on the symbolic it is the composer's
mastery of characterization which gives the
opera its place as a major masterpiece in the
repertoire. *Ariadne auf Naxos* (1912, in its first
version) attempted to exploit the same manner,
starting as an operatic postlude to Hofmannsthal's version of Molière's *Le bourgeois gentilhomme*, written for a small orchestra and with
still greater emphasis on pastiche idioms. It
proved unwieldy for its original purpose, however, and later Strauss added a prologue to
replace the spoken drama and make the work
viable in the opera house. The final result lacks a
natural unity, but both the prologue and the
quasi-*opera seria* contain fine music: the
disparity between the former (which is less
pastiche-based) and the latter (with its
deliberate chamber orchestra manner) is less
than might be imagined, for Strauss's rich
counterpoint gives a fullness to the sound of
even the smaller ensemble which removes it far
from the neo-classicism of the 1920s.

The years after the first production of
Ariadne saw the composing of a ballet on the
biblical subject of Joseph for Diaghilev, which
was not a success, and the grandiose *Alpensinfonie* (1911-15), which demands such a large
orchestra that, in spite of its intrinsic merits, it is
rarely given. The next venture with Hofmannsthal was *Die Frau ohne Schatten* (1919), an opera
on a highly symbolic theme, suggested in part
by *The Magic Flute*, partly by complex philosophic concepts. Again, this work proved
relatively unsuccessful, and though Strauss
thought well of it, he also admitted that the
mythological basis was less appropriate to his
genius than the flesh-and-blood characters of
his earlier operas, and for a few years there was
no further collaboration between poet and
musician. Strauss had a substantial sum of
money in British securities confiscated by the
British Government during the war, and to
restore his financial situation he was active as a
conductor, at times taking engagements which
received considerable criticism. He and Hof-

Richard Strauss

mannsthal were also deeply involved in the foundation of the Salzburg Festival in 1920, and until 1924 Strauss directed the Vienna State Opera which had replaced the old Court Opera. It was during this period that Strauss began to feel out of touch with contemporary developments, and his next opera, *Intermezzo* (1924), an autobiographical, down-to-earth anecdote set to music, represents an attempt to break away from the elevated manner in which Hofmannsthal had encouraged him. But eventually he returned to his former librettist with *Arabella* (1933), in which the element of symbolism was much reduced. In 1929 Hofmannsthal died before *Arabella* was completed, and Strauss's remaining operas were never to achieve the same success. *Die schweigsame Frau* ('The Silent Woman', 1935), an adaptation by Stefan Zweig of a play by Ben Jonson, was the most interesting of those composed in the Nazi era, during which Strauss found himself accused of co-operating with the regime, though the evidence suggests that he was simply apolitical, and that he did attempt to help his Jewish friends. But after about 25 years without a creative triumph equal to that of his older music, in the 1940s he wrote a number of masterpieces, in which a mood of nostalgia predominates. *Capriccio* (1942), a one-act discussion-type opera on the old theme of words versus music, *Metamorphosen* (1945), a piece for 23 strings using themes from Beethoven's 'Eroica' Symphony written in memory of the destruction of the Dresden Opera House where Strauss's greatest triumphs had taken place, a delicious

Oboe Concerto (1945–8) and finally four songs (1948) with orchestra, all demonstrate a return of genius. At the end of the Second World War he again found himself in financial difficulties, but his fortunes were somewhat restored by a festival of his music organized by Sir Thomas Beecham in London in 1947.

Strauss's posthumous reputation has suffered the usual fluctuations. He was somewhat despised by a generation which did not see why he should not have followed the paths of Stravinsky and kept pace with the musical changes of the 1920s and 1930s; and his association with the Nazis led to a distaste for his music in some quarters. He had a curious detached quality as a man and as a conductor, seemingly being more interested in money than in his dignity as an artist (though it is worth noting he turned down a considerable sum for the film rights of *Der Rosenkavalier* because he insisted on an uncut version). A quarter of a century after his death, however, it must be acknowledged that he was one of the great masters of his time. His limitations were that he lacked the power of philosophical expression in his music, which tends to appear merely bombastic instead of exalted. As a realistic artist (in the best sense of the term, i.e. capable of conveying the complexities of everyday human feeling) few can surpass him.　　DENIS ARNOLD

FURTHER READING
Norman Del Mar: *Richard Strauss: A Critical Commentary on his Life and Works* (1962–72); William Mann: *Richard Strauss: A Critical Study of the Operas* (London, 1964); Michael Kennedy: *Richard Strauss* (London, 1976).

Stravaganza, La ('The Extraordinary'). Title of Vivaldi's Op. 4, 12 violin concertos published in two books in Amsterdam, *c*.1712–13.

Stravinsky, Igor (Fyodorovich) (*b* Oranienbaum, now Lomonosov, 17 June 1882; *d* New York, 6 Apr. 1971). Russian composer. Stravinsky's unleashing of new rhythmic force in *The Rite of Spring* was one of the great musical revolutions of the years before the First World War; but it was only the most striking innovation by a composer who never tired of setting himself new problems. Often these took the form of giving his own unmistakable imprint to manners and materials he drew from music of the past. Little, from Machaut to Stockhausen, escaped his critical, inventive regard, and few later composers have escaped his influence.

The son of a renowned bass at the Imperial Opera, Stravinsky studied the piano and composition from boyhood, and from 1903 to 1906 he was a private composition pupil of Rimsky-Korsakov. His early works show the influence of Rimsky, but they show too that the young composer was learning from Skryabin, Tchaikovsky, Debussy, and Dukas. This period of eclectic preparation came to an end in 1910, when Stravinsky went to Paris with the ballet company of Sergey Diaghilev, who commissioned from him a series of scores beginning with *The Firebird* (1909-10). Though still indebted to the opulent fantasy of Rimsky's *Golden Cockerel*, *The Firebird* gives some hint of the brilliant, stylized sonorities and the almost mechanical rhythmic drive of its successor, *Petrushka* (1910-11), yet nobody could have expected that Stravinsky would so quickly go on to produce such a startlingly novel work as *The Rite of Spring* (1911-13).

Certainly the first-night audience was taken by surprise, excited to uproar by the violent rhythms of Stravinsky's music and Nijinsky's choreography. By means of syncopation and rapid changes of metre Stravinsky did away with the regular pulse which had governed almost all Western music since the Renaissance: the rhythm now is angular and propulsive, the music's main motivating force. And it makes the score a perfect counterpart to scenes of pagan ritual in ancient Russia.

Cut off from his homeland by the First World War, Stravinsky returned again and again during the next few years to the folk-tales of a later Russia. There were several cycles of little songs, the farmyard ballet *Renard* (1915-16), and another ballet, *Les noces* (1914-23), for which he took some years to find the appropriate scoring: eventually this intricate rhythmic machine was given the monochrome colouring of chorus, percussion ensemble, and four pianos. The last of these folk-tale pieces, *Histoire du soldat* (1918), can be counted an early example of music theatre, requiring as it does a narrator, two actors, a dancer, and seven instrumentalists.

Like several shorter works of this period, *Histoire du soldat* finds Stravinsky taking an ironic look at different musical conventions: there is a ragtime number, and also a chorale. In his next theatrical work, the ballet *Pulcinella* (1919-20), he took this a step further by basing the music entirely on pieces then thought to be by Pergolesi, adding the zest of his own rhythmic, harmonic, and orchestral imagination to the originals. After this there came a final, abstract return to the 'Russian' manner, in the Symphonies of Wind Instruments (1920), before he gave himself wholeheartedly to re-investigating the musical past.

Stravinsky's *neo-classicism takes the form of borrowing forms, ideas, and styles from throughout Western music, not just (in fact, least of all) from the Classical period. For instance, his *Oedipus rex* (1926-7), which can be

Stravinsky (seated) with Massine, Goncharova, Larionov, and Bakst at the Villa Belle Rive, Ouchy, 1915.

Stravinsky (1924)

given as an opera or as an oratorio, looks back to Handel in its general shaping and in its massive choruses; the arias have something of Verdi's passion, while the 'Dumbarton Oaks' Concerto (1937-8) is a modern Brandenburg. There are reminiscences of Bach again in the Concerto for piano and wind (1923-4), while the Capriccio for piano and orchestra (1928-9) sprinkles Weber-like playfulness on a *concerto grosso* format. During this period Stravinsky was living in France, no longer able, since the revolution of 1917, to draw on funds from Russia. He was therefore obliged to earn his living as a performing musician: the two *concertante* piano works were written for himself to play, and he began to conduct his own works, especially at first performances and for recordings.

As before, ballet scores continued to form an important part of his output. *Apollo* (1927-8), with its euphonious music for strings, was one of the last presentations by the Diaghilev company before the impresario's death; other ballets included the Tchaikovsky-based *Le baiser de la fée* (1928), the coolly classical *Perséphone* (1933-4), the witty *Jeu de cartes* (1936), and even a *Circus Polka* for a young elephant (1942). All these show Stravinsky's gift for creating musical gestures which call forth physical ones, and it is a gift that is not restricted to his music explicitly composed for dancing: the spirited vitality of such works as the Violin Concerto in D (1931) has led to many successful ballet productions of Stravinsky's concert music.

The Violin Concerto, which is written 'against' the great 19th-century works in the same key (by Beethoven, Brahms, and Tchaikovsky), exemplifies the anti-Romantic tendency in Stravinsky's neo-classical music. As he wrote in his *Chroniques de ma vie* of 1935:

'I consider that music is, by its very nature, essentially powerless to *express* anything at all. . . . The phenomenon of music is given to us with the sole purpose of establishing an order in things.' This statement is belied by everything Stravinsky wrote, in that his music is always strikingly expressive, but in eulogizing order it gives an important clue to understanding his neo-classical works.

Increasingly it was to divine order that he gave his attention. His first important religious work was the Symphony of Psalms for chorus and orchestra (1930), succeeded by the optimistic Symphony in C (1938-40), 'composed to the Glory of God'. During the composition of this work, and following the outbreak of the Second World War, Stravinsky moved from Paris to Los Angeles, which was his home for the rest of his life. Proximity to Hollywood brought requests for film music, but these projects foundered and Stravinsky put his material to use in the *Four Norwegian Moods* (1942) and *Ode* (1943). The major work of his early American years, however, was another symphony, the tough and dynamic Symphony in Three Movements (1942-5).

The output of religious works continued with the cantata *Babel* (1944) and the Mass for chorus and double wind quintet (1944-8), which was designed for use in church. There was then a final and exultant neo-classical essay, the full-length opera *The Rake's Progress* (1948-51), which takes *Don Giovanni* as its point of departure, before Stravinsky started out on a gradual process of exploring serialism. The ground was prepared by his use of Medieval and Renaissance practices in the Mass and in the Cantata on English texts of the 15th and 16th centuries (1951-2), as also by the strict contrapuntal writing of the latter work and the Septet (1952-3). Then, in his works from the Three Shakespeare Songs (1953) to the cantata *Threni* (1957-8), he came to a full adoption of 12-note serial methods.

Stravinsky's turn to serialism, surprising to those who had seen him as rival pope to Schoenberg, was perhaps helped by Schoenberg's death in 1951, releasing him from a position he had not sought. At the same time he was stimulated by what his younger contemporaries were achieving in extrapolating beyond Webern: his *Movements* for piano and orchestra (1958-9) suggests, in its lean scoring and rhythmic complexity, that he had learned something from Stockhausen's *Kontra-Punkte*. His ability, at this late stage in his career, to remain open to new ideas is astonishing, yet no more so than the distinctive individuality of his own serial works. As in his neo-classical music, he took complete ownership of the means offered to him.

*Autograph MS of Stravinsky's
'Capriccio' for piano and orchestra, a page from the revised
version (1949).*

Many of Stravinsky's late works are short epitaphs, such as the 'dirge-canons and song' *In memoriam Dylan Thomas* (1954) and the *Elegy for J.F.K.* (1964), or else sacred cantatas. Among these, the *Canticum sacrum* (1955) was designed expressly, in subject, form, and style, for the Basilica of St Mark in Venice, and the *Requiem Canticles* (1965-6), Stravinsky's last major work, is what he described as a 'pocket Requiem' in nine short, stark movements.

PAUL GRIFFITHS

FURTHER READING
I. Stravinsky: *Chroniques de ma vie* (Paris, 1935-6; Eng. trans., London, 1936, 2nd edn 1975); I. Stravinsky: *Poetique musicale* (Cambridge, Mass., 1942; Eng. trans., Cambridge, Mass., 1947; bilingual edn, Cambridge, Mass., 1970); I. Stravinsky and R. Craft: *Conversations with Igor Stravinsky* (London, 1959); I. Stravinsky: *Memories and Commentaries* (London, 1960); R. Vlad: *Stravinsky* (London, 1960); I. Stravinsky: *Expositions and Developments* (London, 1962); E. Walter White: *Stravinsky: the Composer and his Works* (London, 1966); I. Stravinsky: *Themes and Conclusions* (London, 1972).

Street Music

1. Introduction
2. Street Cries
3. The Waits
4. Street Performances in Italy

5. Street Performances in Germany
6. Attempts to Control or Suppress Street Music
7. Street Music in Decline

1. *Introduction.* This article is designed to call attention to the fact, often overlooked, that a great part of the musical life of the populations of European countries has been lived not in the

concert hall, opera house, or church, but in the streets, where all, whatever their social position or wealth or poverty, could participate in its enjoyment.

It will be noted that the music of the streets has covered a very wide range—from the traditional melodic 'cries' of the hawker (a branch of folk music) to four-part choral music and four-movement symphonies.

2. *Street Cries.* These constitute an interesting (and too little investigated) branch of folk music and have supplied the basis of a certain amount of composed music by musicians of repute.

The large trade done for centuries in the streets of all great cities by itinerant vendors and workers, all of whom cried their wares or services, led to the evolution of an accepted code of 'cries', most or all of which in time, moulded by the natural rhythms of the words and the natural cadence of the language, fell into different little tunes, these becoming so accepted that, very usefully, the distant approach of the vendor would be known even to those who only heard the music and could not catch the words.

An early record of the words of many of the London Cries is found in the poem *London Lackpenny* (by John Lydgate, *c.*1370–*c.*1450). Each verse embodies different cries, as:

Then met I one cryed *Hot shepe's feete*;
One cryde *Mackerell*; *rushes grene* another gan grete;
One bade me by a hood to cover my head;
But for want of money, I might not be sped.

Just as the cries are here worked up into a poem, so they have been worked up into several ingenious musical compositions, these using not only the traditional words of each cry but also its traditional music.

Italy, from the late 14th century, had simple songs made up from such cries. A 13th-century French motet, *On parole | A Paris | Frese nouvele*, makes use of the street cry 'fresh strawberries, wild blackberries' ('Frese nouvele, Muere france'), presumably as sung in Paris, and the 16th-century composer Janequin has left a well-known *quodlibet* which brings in the cries of Paris (*Les cris de Paris*, 1550). In the 19th century Louis Clapisson in his opera *La fanchonnette* (1856), Charpentier in *Louise*, and Puccini in *La bohème* made use of Paris cries.

Ravenscroft's *Pammelia* and *Melismata*, at the beginning of the 17th century, have a number of cries cleverly arranged as choral rounds, and there are pieces of the same period of the character of fancies (see *Fantasia*) for viols with vocal parts added, and respectively by Weelkes, Orlando Gibbons, and Deering, which introduce the cries. In these last-named compositions there are 150 different cries represented, and as when the words are duplicated in the different compositions the same music is always associated with them in each, it is clear that the traditional music is thus preserved. The cries include those offering fruit, vegetables, and fish, etc., and services—'Bellows to mend', 'Wood to cleave', 'Have you any work for a Tinker', and the like: civic officials like the Town Crier and the Watchman have their place in the chorus and so have beggars, the dentist, and the chiropodist. Deering also wrote one of these compositions on 'Country Cries'. That of Weelkes ends, 'Now let us sing and so we will make an end with Alleluia'; that of Gibbons is in the form of an *In nomine* and is for viols and voices.

Handel introduced street cries of his day into one of the movements of his opera *Serse* ('Xerxes', 1738). Moreover, Lady Luxborough, writing to the poet Shenstone in 1748 (i.e. during Handel's lifetime), states, 'The great Handel has told me that the hints of his best songs, have several of them been owing to the sounds in his ears of cries in the street'.

In English literature there are a good many allusions to the London street cries showing the delight their melody and variety gave to all sorts of cultivated people. Leigh Hunt in his biography, in telling of the removal of his family to Chelsea about 1833, speaks of the abundance, 'quaintness and melodiousness' of the cries there as a great attraction, and tells us (strangely!) that they had 'the reputation of being composed by Purcell and others'. He adds, 'Nor is this unlikely when it is considered how fond those masters were of sporting with their art and setting the most trivial words to music in their glees and catches'. Nollekens, the once-famous sculptor (1737–1823), 'loved to imitate the cries of the itinerant vendors' as they were passing by while he was 'measuring the stone in the yard for a bust or figure' or 'improving the attitudes of his Venuses'. This led his biographer, John Thomas Smith, to devote several pages to the subject of these cries, and to set out words and music of some of them. He gave one or two of a fairly elaborate nature.

Besides the musical cries mentioned above, about sixty years back [i.e. about 1770], there were also two others yet more singular, which, however, were probably better known in the villages round London than in the metropolis itself. The first of these was used by an itinerant dealer in corks, sometimes called 'Old Corks', who rode upon an ass, and carried his wares in paniers on each side of him. He sat with much dignity, and wore upon his head a velvet cap; and his attractive cry, which was partly spoken and partly sung, but all in metre, was something like the following fragment:

Spoken. Corks for sack
I have at my back;
Sung. All handy, all handy;
Some for wine and some for brandy.

Spoken.   Corks for cholic-water,
          Cut 'em a little shorter;
          Corks for gin,
          Very thin;
          Corks for rum,
          As big as my thumb;
          Corks for ale,
          Long and pale:
Sung.   They're all handy, all handy.
          Some for wine and some for brandy.

The other cry, which was much more musical, was that of two persons, father and son, who sold lines. The father, in a strong, clear tenor, would begin the strain in the major key, and when he had finished his son, who followed at a short distance behind him, in a shrill falsetto, would repeat it in the minor, and their call consisted of the following words:

    Buy a white-line,
    Or, a jack-line,
    Or, a clock-line,
    Or, a hair-line,
        Or, a line for your clothes here.

A famous series of colour prints, *The London Cries* by Francis Wheatley, RA (1747–1801), preserves for us the figures of the unconscious artists who performed these tiny vocal melodies, as they were to be seen in the late 18th century. An earlier set, and a much larger one, is that of engravings after drawings of Laroon, issued by the London printseller, Pierce Tempest, in 1711, which gives us the figures of about 60 of the singing vendors.

In France, chair-menders, scissor-grinders, rag-and-bone dealers, etc. were known by tunes which they played on the mirliton (see *Kazoo*), each trade having its distinctive tune.

3. *The Waits.* Street playing was one of the duties of the *waits. When London came under Puritan control at the beginning of the Civil War the authorities decided (1642) to do away with Sunday street playing:

That the City Waits shall cease to play at the Royal Exchange on the Sundays as heretofore hath been accustomed, but shall perform the said service every holiday hereafter and for the time accustomed.

And after the Restoration (when Sabbatarianism was little, if at all, relaxed) the famous Norwich waits were also restricted in the same way:

To playe att the Crosses, but not upon the Lord's dayes.

In 1648, at Newcastle, we find the waits playing outside the Mayor's door to entertain Cromwell, who was visiting the city on his journey from Scotland.

In the 18th century the Bath waits, as soon as they got wind of the arrival of a visitor, would play outside the house in which he was lodging.

The same customs, of course, obtained in other parts of England and in many continental countries.

4. *Street Performances in Italy.* Burney in Italy, in 1770, found street music everywhere. Thus at Turin a band of two girl vocalists, two violins, a guitar, and 'base' (probably a cello) performed on a stage in the public square and sold ballads, while in another part of the square a man and woman sang Venetian ballads (Burney says that the Italian street musicians were mostly Venetians), accompanied on a dulcimer. At Milan the same customs obtained.

At Brescia he heard outside his inn a band of two violins, a mandolin, a French horn, a trumpet, and a cello.

And, though in the dark, they played long concertos, with solo parts for the mandolin. I was surprised at the memory of these performers; in short it was excellent *street* music, and such as we are not accustomed to; but ours is not a climate for serenades.

At Vicenza he heard

A psalm, in three parts, performed by boys of different ages, who were proceeding from their school to the cathedral, in procession, with their master, a priest, at their head, who sung the base. There was more melody than usual in this kind of music; and although they marched through the street very fast, yet they sung well in time and tune. These boys are a kind of religious *press-gang* who seize all other boys they can find in their way to the church, in order to be catechised.

In Venice he heard a group of two violins, a cello, and a voice who, 'though unnoticed here as small-coalmen or oyster-women in England, performed so well that in any other country in Europe they would not only have excited attention, but have acquired applause, which they justly merited'. From a barge on the Grand Canal (and the canals are, of course, the main streets of Venice) he heard 'an excellent band of music, consisting of violins, flutes, horns, bases, and a kettledrum'. It was 'a piece of gallantry, at the expense of an inamorato, in order to serenade his mistress'. He was charmed with the singing of the gondoliers. Their superior performances he put down to the fact that they had free admission to the opera-houses.

At Bologna he found less street music and less good than at Venice, but nevertheless he was saluted on arrival at his inn, 'as every stranger is', with a duet, very well played by a violin and a mandolin, and later 'an itinerant band played under my windows several symphonies and single movements, extremely well, in four parts'.

In Florence, Burney heard the long-celebrated *laudisti* (see *Lauda spirituale*) 'in grand procession, dressed in a whitish uniform with burning tapers in their hands'. Outside the cathedral they sang 'a cheerful hymn in three parts, which they executed very well'.

In this manner, on Sunday and holidays, the

trades-people and artizans form themselves into distinct companies, and sing through the streets on their way to church. Those of the parish of S. Benedetto, we are informed by Crescimbeni, were famous all over Italy; and at the great Jubilee, in the beginning of this century, marched through the streets of Rome, singing in such a manner as pleased and astonished everybody.

In Burney's experience this Italy of the late 18th century was *par excellence* the country of street music of all kinds. 'It is not to be wondered at that the street music here is generally neglected, as people are almost stunned with it at every corner.'

The Spanish have always been great devotees of music and dancing in the street, and still are.

5. *Street Performances in Germany*. The street was long the popular concert room of Germany. It will be remembered how Luther and his fellow choirboys used at Eisenach to go from door to door collecting small doles by singing hymns and 'quartets at Christmas-time in the villages, carols on the birth of the Holy Child at Bethlehem'. This was apparently long a universal student and choirboy custom in north Germany, both before and after the Reformation, and it continued into the late 18th, and even the 19th century. In 1782 Moritz (*Travels in England*) observes in the streets of London the Christ's Hospital boys in their blue cloaks, and expresses surprise that they are not heard singing in the streets, as the boys of such an institution would be in Germany.

Burney, in Munich in 1772, found 'a very good concert in the street' at his inn door, and was told that they were 'poor scholars'. Next day he discovered that they were students of the music school and that their performance was intended as a compliment to him because he had been to the school to 'inform himself concerning the institution'. Next evening he heard the same performers elsewhere in the streets of the city. They had violins, a cello, 'hautboys', French horns, and a bassoon; 'I was informed that they were obliged frequently to perform thus in the streets, to convince the public, at whose expence they are maintained, of the proficiency they make'.

In Frankfurt, too, he heard good street music, young theological students singing 'hymns in three or four parts attended by a chaplain . . . who in this manner excite the benevolence of passengers that contribute towards their cloathing'. He also heard a band of street musicians who played several symphonies 'reasonably well, in four parts'. Passing into Austria, he heard music students from the Jesuit college at Vienna singing before the inn vocal duets and 'a kind of glees in three and four parts'.

Instrumental street music was for centuries of German town life supplied regularly by the municipal musicians, or 'Stadtpfeiferei' (presided over by the 'Stadtmusiker'), corresponding very closely to the British waits. It will be recalled that many of Bach's ancestors and relatives were employed in this capacity.

6. *Attempts to Control or Suppress Street Music*. Street musicians (other than the authorized waits) were suppressed by two Acts of Parliament of the reign of Queen Elizabeth I, they being declared rogues and vagabonds. And there were laws enacted against ballad singing and ballad hawking, in various reigns. The fact that such Acts were enacted during the Commonwealth has led thoughtless historians to put them down to Puritan feeling, but any Commonwealth laws on the point were only re-enactments or modifications of laws already existing. The suppression of ballad singers and hawkers was due to the frequently political nature of the ballads and the suppression (or attempted suppression) of other street musicians largely to that dislike of all wanderers and 'masterless men' that persisted through many centuries. (It will be remembered that under Elizabeth and the early Stuarts no bodies of actors could exist unless attached to the household of some nobleman.)

In the 18th century Hogarth's well-known picture *The Enraged Musician* showed that room for a little useful legislation still remained. More recently there have been many attempts to restrain street music by law. Thus an English Act of Parliament early in Queen Victoria's reign gave London householders power to require street musicians to withdraw, on grounds of 'illness or other reasonable cause'. In 1864 Mr Michael T. Bass, MP (the brewer), led a campaign against street musicians, publishing a book entitled *Street Music in the Metropolis*, and introducing a Bill into Parliament. Members of the various professions presented petitions in favour of this Bill, including 'the leading composers and professors of music of the metropolis, who sent one with 200 signatures headed "The Street Organ Nuisance"', and complaining of the way in which 'our professional duties are seriously interrupted'. The main point of Mr Bass's Bill was the removal of the clause about 'illness or reasonable cause', which latter phrase left far too much to the interpretation of the magistrate. Carlyle, Tennyson, Millais, Holman Hunt, and a great number of other distinguished intellectual and artistic workers supported Mr Bass by signing a document in favour of his Bill. Professor Babbage, the eminent mathematician and inventor of the calculating machine, considered that 'one-fourth of his entire working power had been destroyed by audible nuisances, to which his highly strung nerves rendered him peculiarly sensitive'. He had often prosecuted offenders in the police courts, under the existing unsàtisfactory Act, spending on this attempt at defence during the first six months of 1861 alone the sum of £103. He sent Mr Bass a list of 165 interruptions to his work in 90 days, including six brass bands and 96 street pianos and organs.

As a result of this well-justified agitation was passed the Metropolitan Police Act, 1864, which is still in force, but of which the relevant provisions do not operate as effectively as was hoped—owing partly to the provision which requires any householder complaining to 'accompany the constable who shall take into custody any person offending as aforesaid to the nearest police station house and there sign the charge-sheet'. Apparently many persons prefer to suffer rather than to make part of this interesting little group moving through the public streets, and, indeed, not every one can spare the time to carry through a prosecution.

Apart from the metropolis it is competent for local authority to enact a by-law against street music under Section 23 of the Municipal Corporations Act of 1882: the reason London was left out of this Act is that the 1864 Metropolitan Police Act was supposed to provide adequately for that city.

7. *Street Music in Decline*. The itinerant 'German Bands', formerly so common everywhere in Britain, were not heard after 1914. They numbered from six to 15 performers—all Bavarians working at their trade at home in winter and migrating to various countries every summer. The 'one-man-band', playing simultaneously some sort of a wind instrument and (with elbows, feet, and head) a variety of percussion, was also at one time a feature of street life.

The unemployed in London and the provincial cities in England, in the 1930s, with their Welsh choirs, bagpipes, and scratch bands, caused a temporary revival of street music in England, and the occasional accordionist or violinist can still be heard.

In the early 1930s some Parisians were deploring the rapid disappearance from their streets and courtyards of the singers formerly so common there.

Si la chanson française ne doit pas mourir ce sont les chanteurs des rues qui doivent la perpétuer en apportant de la musique à ceux qui sont trop occupés ou trop indifférents pour aller à sa recherche. Mainte chanson qu'on entendait récemment par tout Paris aurait subi une mort prématurée ne fût-ce que pour les musiciens de la rue.

Occasional street pianos and organs could still be heard in London in the 1950s but soon became a dwindling phenomenon. At least one manifestation of lively street music was to be found in a band of disabled persons who called themselves the Happy Wanderers and frequented the Oxford Street area playing a brand of revivalist jazz. They achieved sufficient fame to be asked to make recordings of their atmospheric music. The surviving street music is now in the hands of the busker. The busker, according to Partridge's *Dictionary of Historical Slang*, was one who sang or performed in a public house, and part of busking was to sell obscene songs and books in these venues. Ejected from the public houses by the laws controlling music on such premises, the busker became very much a street entertainer and one or two regulars who entertained the theatre queues around Leicester Square became well-known personalities. The majority of modern buskers appear to be out-of-work music students and 'folk-singers' who station themselves in various underground passageways where they are least likely to be moved on by the police. Otherwise street music appears to be virtually extinct.

PERCY SCHOLES, PETER GAMMOND

Streich (Ger.). 'Stroke', in the sense of bow-stroke; *Streichinstrumente*, 'bowed instruments'; *Streichquartett*, 'string quartet'; etc.

Strepito, strepitoso, strepitosamente (It.). 'Noise', 'noisy', 'noisily', i.e. in a boisterous manner.

Stretto (It., 'squeezed together'). A fugal device in which subject entries follow closely in succession, each subject overlapping with the next. See *Fugue*.

Strict counterpoint. See *Counterpoint*.

String drum (Fr.: *tambourin à cordes*). See *Pipe and Tabor*, 3; for Fr.: *tambour à cordes*, see *Friction drum*, 2.

Stringed Instruments

1. The Strings
2. The Soundboard
3. Terminology

4. Keyboard Instruments
5. Striking-point
6. Sympathetic Strings

1. *The Strings*. A clear fact of music history is that, from Antiquity to today in every major civilization, it is almost invariably stringed instruments (Fr.: *instruments à cordes*; Ger.:

Saiteninstrumente—also *Streichinstrumente*, 'bowed instruments'; It.: *cordi*) that have held the highest place among instruments: mainly because the vibrating stretched string uniquely combines a clear fundamental pitch (the note heard) with rapid and accurate tunability and re-tunability (repeated tightening, slackening, and re-tightening). Not that the string is capable of music by itself: it is too thin to communicate appreciable vibration to the air directly in contact; it merely cuts through the air without forcing it into periodic vibration. But once the string is made, via a bridge, to bear upon a soundboard—a plate of wood or a stretched membrane—causing this to vibrate as well, the air, trapped against this larger surface, is forced to take up the vibration and dispatch sound waves for the ears to receive.

Among the materials used for the strings, vegetable matter (spun hemp, flax, etc.) has figured little. Animal materials have always predominated (that is, before metal): sinew; horsehair (especially across the north from Central Asia to, formerly, Wales); silk (the classic string material in the Far East); and above all gut, normally sheep-gut ('catgut' being merely a joke term). Fragments of strings judged to be of sheep-gut and 1 mm. thick have been found with an Ancient Egyptian lute of 1500 BC (see *Lute*, 4a).

A chief centre for manufacture of gut strings has long been Italy, particularly Rome. The small intestines of sheep of under a year old are taken warm from the slaughterhouse immediately to commence the long and repeated processes of scouring, washing, slicing into strips for twisting into threads on a frame, and bleaching and polishing. The former violin E string (now replaced by steel) was spun from some five threads of the thinnest width; a double bass D string from up to 85 threads. Though now so extensively superseded by nylon, plain gut strings remain normal for the harp and are obtainable for most other instruments, for some of their strings at least. Nylon, dating from 1938, provides filament strings having much the same density and thickness as gut but being free from inequalities of the kind that could make the selection of gut strings a trying business in older days; it is, of course, also less prone to break or become rough to the fingers with wear.

Metal strings go back historically to the 13th century in the Arab countries for certain instruments of the 'long lute' kind (see *Lute*, 4a) but were rare in the west before German advances in commercial wire-drawing from the late 14th century. Thicknesses of metal strings are specified in thousandths of an inch or in millimetres; or usually for keyboard instruments in 'Music Wire Gauge' numbers. These run from No. 1 (0.2 mm. diameter) up to No. 32 (2.2 mm.); a

grand piano may use Nos. 14 (0.81 mm.) to 32.

A problem arose in the 16th century over deep tunings from gut strings of restricted length, as when adding extra bass strings to the lute. These would have to be thick enough to deliver the low frequencies and even then, although it set string-makers developing special methods of twisting, tended to be too stiff to sound really well. The solution of loading a gut string with an overwinding of fine wire, preserving full flexibility, has been so far traced to the mid 17th century, since which the deeper-tuned strings in all instruments, gut or metal, have come to be overwound; thus, for instance, the Austrian *zither sounds the low A below the bass staff (A') with an overwound metal string a mere 18″ in length, albeit at modest tension. Today the overwinding is often with metal 'ribbon' (or 'tape'), an American innovation of the late 1930s which gives a very smooth surface.

The 'string equation' interrelates length, tension, thickness, and material to the note produced. The frequency (f) follows from the general law: $f = c/\lambda$, where c is the wave-velocity, given in its turn by the square root of: tension (T) divided by unit mass or $\pi r^2 \rho$ (radius r, density ρ); λ is the wavelength, of which the vibrating length of the string (l) represents half. Using conventional units—f (Hz), l (cm.), T (kg., in the equation qualified by 981, gravity, since tension is being expressed as a weight), r, or more conveniently d (diameter; this time in mm.), and ρ (CGS, water = 1)—the equation can be reduced to: $f = \dfrac{5588}{l \times d} \sqrt{\dfrac{T}{\rho}}$.

The average density of steel (7.8) being about six times that of gut or nylon, a steel string will be thinner than a gut string of the same length and at the same tension by $1:\sqrt{6}$ (or approximately $1:2\frac{1}{2}$). But strings are normally tensioned to near breaking-point to sound their best, and this involves a rather higher tension for the steel string. Average tension per string is quoted at around $6\frac{1}{2}$–7 kg. for classical guitar (increasing slightly towards the sixth string); much the same for the violin (but lessening towards the lowest string); about twice for cello; three times for double bass; and 10 times or more for piano. Steel strings tend to give a brighter sound than gut from the slower damping of high harmonics. Yet the replacing of gut with steel (see, e.g., *Guitar*, 2) is obviously not of immense musical consequence or it would hardly have been possible to make the change (see *Violin*, 5a). Rather curiously, Praetorius in 1619 remarked on the softer, more *lieblich* ('lovely') tone that he had heard violinists produce with strings of brass and steel, then very unusual.

2. *The Soundboard* ['top', 'belly', or, after the

Fr., 'table']. We do not find the names of string-makers celebrated in the history books, even though developments in their craft, like over-winding, have had no small bearing on the developing forms of many instruments. The names we do find are of the instrument-makers—such as Ruckers, Stradivari, Torres—great names because they were in the first place makers and mounters of those precious sound-boards which above all distinguish a fine instrument from an indifferent one. Yet the action of a soundboard—how it answers so readily to every frequency fed to it from the strings—remains partly a mystery, even though modern laboratory aids are continually enabling more to be discovered.

The classic material is low-density wood from the conifers, chiefly the pine family, such as silver fir (*genus Abies*) or, more particularly, close-grained spruce (*genus Picea*). Thicknesses vary from barely over 2 mm. in lutes to 1 cm. in a grand piano, balanced to the thickness and tension of the individual strings. Were the wood either too thick or too thin—or, to use the useful expression introduced by American acousticians, were its 'wave impedance' too different from that of the string—then most of the string energy would be reflected back, little passing to the soundboard.

The soundboard is attached round the edges (or on three sides) to the body of the instrument, as with a diaphragm, but unlike this it is 'non-isotropic' owing to the grain: vibrations travel four times faster in the direction of the grain than across it. Usually the soundboard is 'barred' in some way, with one or several softwood bars glued to the underside, often in positions crosswise or askew to the grain so that, besides offering some support, their stiffness accelerates wave transmission along the 'slower' direction. Plywood may be mentioned in this connection, having a middle layer with the grain at right angles to the rest; as it is also strong it has latterly won considerable successes with key-board instruments and harps, and up to a point with guitars and double basses.

The completed soundboard will have its own natural vibration frequencies; a violin-maker will often test the fundamental by ear, tapping the plate or bowing it on the edge. Since 1970 plates of different instruments have been experimentally excited by electrical means, and the swirling nodal patterns that appear at particular frequencies are made visible photographically by 'laser holograms', examples of which are now often reproduced in books on instruments. But it is clear that in the completed instrument the plate has the ability to respond under forced vibration from the strings over frequencies with ranges that extend to both sides of each natural

peak, sufficiently to take up all frequencies passed to it via the bridge. It may be noted too that the shape of the plate can in many cases be drastically changed without very noticeably, if at all, impairing musical quality. There have been guitars and violins in every conceivable shape (waistless, three-cornered, etc.; see *Violin*, 8d) produced during the 19th century with apparently most satisfactory results by some of the finest craftsmen in Paris and Vienna; but musicians do not feel happy playing on an unconventional-looking instrument, nor are audiences happy to see them do so.

Fig. 1 illustrates some basic assemblies of string and soundboard, especially to indicate where solid blocks of wood form main structural centres, fixed to the body which completes the soundbox, or with keyboard instruments to the surrounding case. As for the soundbox, it is possible to play a guitar which has the sound-board only, but the sound, while clear, is weak and 'tinny'. The sides alone improve it, and then, with the back as well, the air inside boosts the sound from the deeper fundamentals. These lie rather low for the wood alone to resonate efficiently, for the air resonance is normally well below the lowest wood resonance, even though raised very considerably by the soundhole or soundholes, in which air oscillates in and out under the pumping action of the table. Some soundboxes perform their duty without any such hole at all (e.g. *sitār*); but soundholes further divide up a soundboard into distinct areas, influencing the vibration patterns, and some hold that their major function lies in this.

3. *Terminology: Fingerboard Instruments* (i.e. those on which the left hand stops the strings while the right hand sounds them—guitars, violin, etc.). (*a*) The string placed on the side nearest the web of the left hand, being basically the most convenient to play on, is the one on which it is most natural to play the tune—or, at any rate, so it was through the formative stages in most instruments' development. Hence it is almost invariably the highest-tuned and termed the 'first string'. Does one describe it as being on the left side or the right? This depends on how the instrument is held—on the violin the first string is to the player's right but on the cello it is to the left. So, to avoid ambiguity (which can be extremely tiresome in literature on instruments), it is safer to speak of the 'treble side' as being where the first string lies and of the 'bass side' for the other; this is now a fairly standard usage.

(*b*) *String Length.* Just below the tuning-pegs or -pins the strings bear on the 'nut' (Fig. 1, N), a short transverse bar traditionally of ebony

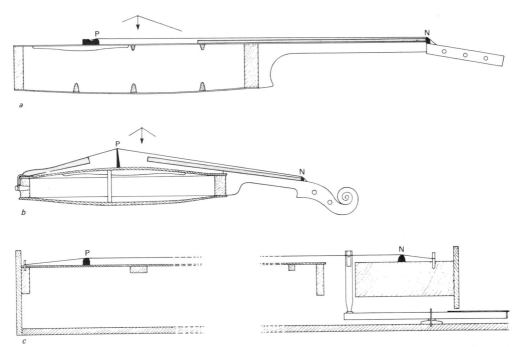

Fig. 1. (a) Guitar; (b) viola; (c) harpsichord: P, bridge; N, nut. The arrows in (a) and (b) indicate the striking (bowing) point with limits of variation for tonal effect.

with the grain at right angles to the strings. The length of string from this to the bridge (P) is termed the 'string length' and is the most important single dimension in the whole instrument. It not only decides the finger-stretch on going from note to note up the string, but also the highest pitch to which the strings can safely be tuned in circumstances where the player has a choice, as when playing a lute on its own. The tension at which a string breaks is proportional to the tensile strength of the material divided by the diameter of the string. The frequency at which it breaks is the same, however, for a thick string as for a thin, the thicker requiring (to reach that frequency) a tension greater to exactly the same degree that it is thicker.

(c) *Courses.* By 'string' one is frequently referring not to one single string but to a pair tuned to the same note and sounded as one, producing a stronger, more ringing sound. An example is the mandolin, with four pairs. The most apt expression to use here is the historical term 'course': a 'four-course mandolin', strung in four double courses. In many instances one of a pair is a thinner string tuned an octave higher, so that every note played on that pair of strings sounds in octaves—an 'octave course'. The thinner string is with some instruments put on the treble side, with others on the bass side: Fig. 2 shows some examples diagrammatically, look-

ing at the instrument from the front, the nut along the top. Fig. 2a shows the '12-string' guitar now often seen (see *Guitar*, 3b), which is a 'six-course' guitar with each course double and the three lower of them octave courses. Fig. 2b shows a lute with typical 16th-century tuning and 11 actual strings, the first course single, the rest double. Fig. 2c shows a cittern (old French tuning) with two 'octave triple courses'; the fourth course is tuned higher than the third (as also in the ukulele, though this is normally single-strung); when such a departure from a straight pitch sequence occurs the tuning is often now described as 're-entrant'.

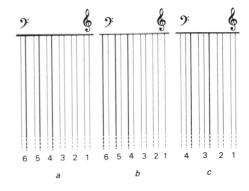

Fig. 2.

4. *Keyboard Instruments* (i.e., with rare exceptions, instruments with a keyboard that is played on with both hands: the hurdy-gurdy, with keys for one hand only, is usually grouped with the fingerboard instruments, to which it is more closely allied). The tuning-pins are termed 'wrest-pins'. Next to them, the strings again bear on the nut (a long low wood bar) running thence to the bridge (another bar), beyond which they are attached to 'hitch-pins'. The term 'nut' is, however, not invariably employed, some terming this likewise a 'bridge', distinguishing between the two bridges by position: 'wrest plank bridge' and 'soundboard bridge'.

Where there are two or more strings to a note, the terms 'bichord' and 'trichord' are commonly used. Harpsichords differ, having up to four strings per note which are brought into action independently or together as required, so the terms 'registers' or 'stops' are used, as with the organ. Also borrowed from the organ, the harpsichord uses the term '8″' (8-foot) for a register in which the strings sound the notes corresponding to the keyboard; '4″' for a register of shorter strings sounding an octave higher; and sometimes '16″', for longer strings sounding an octave lower than the notes on the keyboard. (The double bass is sometimes described as an instrument of '16′ tone', through normally sounding an octave lower than written.)

5. *Striking-point.* Naturally, strings are normally excited (plucked, hit, bowed) at the point along their vibrating length where they give the best sound. The piano-maker fixes it at or close to one-seventh of the length, this being a point where the discordant seventh harmonic has a node and will therefore be only weakly excited by the wide felt hammer.

On the fingerboard instruments, on which the place can be varied at will, the normal point may be departed from for different tonal effects (see *Acoustics*, 6) obtained by subduing the intensity of upper harmonics (sombre tone) or exciting them more while weakening the lower (metallic tone). A late 18th-century French mandolin Tutor puts it nicely: further from the bridge (over the end of the fingerboard) for *son fluté*; close to the bridge for *argentin* ('silvery'). One hears the contrast a great deal in guitar recitals.

6. *Sympathetic (or Resonance) Strings.* These are additional strings, always of wire, included in certain stringed instruments to provide special background resonance (see *Acoustics*, 7). The oldest instruments known to possess them seem to be Indian and Central Asian (e.g. the Indian fiddle *sarangi* and lute *sitār*). In Europe they appeared in the 17th century, the chief instruments using them including the *viola d'amore;

the *baryton (a rather special case since here the wires can also be plucked); the Harding fiddle of Norway; and sometimes the *tromba marina. See also *Viol*, 4. Sympathetic strings are usually tuned to a scale in the key in which the instrument is going to be played.

It may be added that with ordinary stringed instruments (lacking sympathetic strings) the sympathetic resonance of strings which are not being played at a particular moment can be an important ingredient in the sound, notably with the piano.   ANTHONY BAINES

Stringendo (It.). 'Squeezing', i.e. progressively quickening the time.

String quartet. See under *Quartet*.

String quintet. See under *Quintet*.

String trio. See *Trio*, 1.

Strisciando, strisciato (It.). 'Trailing', 'trailed', i.e. smooth, slurred, or *glissando*.

Stroh violin. See *Violin*, 8e.

Strophic. The word comes from the terminology of Ancient Greek literature, a Greek ode consisting of 'strophe', 'antistrophe', and 'epode', the first two corresponding in length and metre. In music the term is used to describe any structure founded on a repeated pattern, AAAA etc. It is most commonly found in songs where each stanza of the poem is set to the same music.

See also *Form*, 2.   G. M. TUCKER

Strophic variations. A vocal form found, for example, in *monodies of the early 17th century. A strophic text is set so that each stanza retains the same bass, while the melody or solo part is varied at each repetition of the bass pattern. The bass is not necessarily strictly identical in every repetition, but the essential outline is maintained so that the same succession of harmonies occurs in every strophe. A famous example is 'Possente spirto' from the third act of Monteverdi's *Orfeo*.

See also *Form*, 2   G. M. TUCKER

Strumento (It.). 'Instrument'; *strumentato*, 'instrumented' (e.g. *recitativo strumentato*, 'accompanied recitative'); *strumenti a corde*, 'stringed instruments'; *strumenti d'acciaio*, see *Glockenspiel*, 2; *strumenti d'arco*, 'bowed instruments'; *strumenti di legno*, 'wood(wind) instruments'; *strumenti d'ottone*, 'brass instruments'; *strumenti a percossa*, 'percussion instruments'; *strumenti da tasto*, 'keyboard instruments'; *strumenti a fiato*, 'wind instruments'.

Stuart, Leslie [Barrett, Thomas Augustine] (*b* Southport, 15 Mar. 1864; *d* Richmond, Surrey, 27 Mar. 1928). English composer. He started his professional musical life as organist of the Roman Catholic cathedral at Salford. He held this post for seven years then went to London in 1895 to attempt a career in theatre music. He had quick success with *Florodora* in 1899, followed by *The Silver Slipper* (1901), *The School Girl* (1903), *The Belle of Mayfair* (1906), *Havana* (1908), *Peggy* (1911), and *The Slim Princess* (1910). Another profitable outlet was found in writing songs for the music-hall, notably those he wrote for black-faced dancer-singer Eugene Stratton, such as 'Little Dolly Daydream', 'Lily of Laguna', and 'My little Octoroon', and many for other stars of the halls. He frittered away his fortune in gambling and drinking and ended in poverty and obscurity.

PETER GAMMOND

Stück (Ger.). 'Piece', 'composition'; *Klavierstück*, 'keyboard piece', usually 'piano piece'.

Study. See *Étude*.

Stürmend, stürmisch (Ger.). 'Stormy', 'passionate'.

Sturm und Drang (Ger.). Literally 'storm and stress'. The name given to a German literary movement of the mid to late 18th century. It was to some extent a reaction against the extreme sensibility of *Empfindsamkeit*, and aimed to portray violent emotions in the most dramatic way possible. The chief literary exponents of *Sturm und Drang* were Schiller (in his play *Die Räuber*, *c*.1780) and Goethe, but the expression was actually coined by Christoph Kaffmann, who persuaded the playwright Maximilian Klinger to change the title of his play *Der Wirrwarr* to *Sturm und Drang* (1776).

The *Sturm und Drang* style is most evident in the musical portrayal of dramatic or tragic subjects, as a comparison of the respective scenes at the gates of Hell in Rameau's *Castor et Pollux* (1737) and Gluck's *Orfeo* (1762) will show. Gluck had already attempted to infuse new life into supernatural horror scenes in his ballet *Don Juan* (1761), which influenced Mozart (the storm scene and flight in *Idomeneo* and, especially, the end of *Don Giovanni*).

However, *Sturm und Drang* also had an effect on instrumental music. The period *c*.1766–1772 have been called Haydn's 'Sturm und Drang' years, because his symphonies and quartets seem to aim at the portrayal of an inner turmoil, and other Austrian symphonists and composers working at Mannheim and Stuttgart were receptive to the style, especially the Abbé Vogler; his pupils Weber and Meyerbeer were also influenced.

WENDY THOMPSON

Style brisé (Fr.). 'Broken style'. The characteristic style of 17th-century lute music, in which the notes of a chord were not plucked simultaneously but arpeggiated. The style had considerable influence on composers of keyboard music of the late 17th and early 18th centuries, especially on French composers such as the Couperins, d'Anglebert, and Chambonnières, but also on J. S. Bach.

Style galant (Ger.). See *Galant*.

Style luthé (Fr.). Term used by François Couperin for the *style brisé*.

Su (It.). 1. 'On', 'near'; e.g. in violin playing, *sul G*, 'on the G (string)'. 2. 'Up'; e.g. *arcata in su*, 'up-bowed'.

Subdominant. Fourth degree of the major or minor scale. The prefix, 'sub', refers to the position of the subdominant five degrees *below* the tonic, whereas the dominant is five degrees above the tonic.

Subito (It.). 'Suddenly', 'immediately'; *attacca subito*, 'begin immediately', placed at the end of a movement to show that the next one should follow without a break.

Subject. A structurally important theme or melodic fragment. 'Subject' has two specific, technical meanings. 1. In the study of *fugue*, a subject is 'the theme announced in the first instance by any one part or voice without harmony on which the whole composition is founded' (Ebenezer Prout: *Fugue*, 1891). The fugal subject was derived from the 'point' and *cantus firmus* of Renaissance imitative technique and is a common identifiable feature of contrapuntal structures from the Baroque onwards.

2. 'Subject' has also been used in the terminology of thematic accounts of *sonata form*. Thus a sonata exposition, which in Mozart or Beethoven may often have two contrasting themes, is said to have a 'first subject' and a 'second subject'. This usage appears even in the descriptions of expositions with only one theme ('monothematic'), where 'subject' refers to the entire tonic and dominant passages of the typical harmonic structure, just as it may be used in more elaborate sonata forms to refer to groups of themes, usually in the same harmonic region.

3. In a more general sense, 'subject' is occasionally used to name the sections of dance forms, the *Leitmotive* of Wagner's music dramas, or the contrasting themes of *atonal* music structures, but its application has traditionally been restricted to the two forms of fugue and sonata.

JONATHAN DUNSBY

Submediant. Sixth degree of the major or minor scale. The prefix, 'sub', refers to the fact that the submediant is a third *below* the tonic, whereas the mediant is a third above it.

Succentor. In a cathedral church of the Old Foundation, the title usually given to the deputy of the *precentor; the succentor is generally a *minor canon.

Successive counterpoint. See *Species counterpoint*.

Suchoň, Eugen (*b* Pezinok, West Slovakia, 25 Sept. 1908). Slovak composer. He studied composition at the Academy in Bratislava and from 1931 to 1933 with Novák at the Prague Conservatory. He has held various academic and official posts including head of the Slovak Composers' Union. After studying with Kafenda he made considerable use of Slovakian folk-song in his work, culminating in his successful national opera *Krútňava* ('The Whirlpool', 1949). Since then he has experimented with serial techniques allied to modality. Suchoň's influence on his native contemporaries has been considerable and he is regarded as a major representative of Slovak music.   JAN SMACZNY

Suite. An instrumental genre consisting of a succession of fairly short, congruous movements. During the Baroque period, when the suite was a principal instrumental form, each movement took on the more or less stylized character of a particular dance; the dances were normally in the same key and were sometimes linked thematically. Other terms used in different countries and at different periods to describe pieces conforming to the suite principle include *ordre* (France), *sonata da camera* (Italy; see *Sonata*, 3), *partita* or *Partie* (Italy, Germany), and *Ouvertüre* or *overture* (Germany, England).

1. *Origins*. Although the term 'suite' did not appear until the mid 16th century, the form's origins lie in the pairing of dances, which dates back to the late 14th and the 15th centuries. A common pattern was for a relatively slow, duple-metre dance such as the *pavan (England, France) or the *passamezzo (Italy) to be followed by a faster, triple-metre dance such as the *galliard or *saltarello, which might use the same thematic material or at least begin with a similar melodic or rhythmic motif. The earliest such pieces were for lute or keyboard.

A number of early 16th-century lute-books went on to include sets of dances grouped in threes, such as pavan-saltarello-piva (arranged by J. A. Dalza in a lute-book of 1508 printed by Petrucci) or passamezzo-gagliarda-padovana (arranged by Andrea Rotta, 1546). In Germany in particular dances could be grouped in sets of four or five (e.g. in Johann Schein's *Banchetto musicale*, 1617), and a few standard patterns of arrangement (e.g. Paduana-Intrada-Dantz-Galliarda) began to emerge, as in Paul Peuerl's collection of 1611.

Composers and compilers of keyboard music also began to group dances in this way. *Parthenia* (1612-13), the first collection of keyboard music printed in England, has a number of linked pavans and galliards by Byrd, Bull, and Gibbons, some prefaced with a 'Preludio' to form a set of three movements; and there are similar examples in the *Fitzwilliam Virginal Book* (a substantial manuscript of keyboard music compiled about 1609-19) and in other contemporary collections.

2. *Growth of the Classical Suite*. As courtly French dances like the *allemande and *courante eventually overtook the pavan and galliard in popularity, so they were assimilated into the suite. J. J. Froberger is customarily credited with establishing the standardized sequence of movements in the classical suite: two pairs of slow and fast dances originating in four different countries, the allemande (Germany) and courante (Italy) followed by the *sarabande (Spain) and *gigue (England). This standard order was not finally achieved, however, until after Froberger's death; in his own suites the sarabande was the last piece, the gigue being inserted earlier in the sequence.

Other dances might either be substituted for any of those four or included additionally (e.g. minuet, gavotte, bourrée). Later a prefatory prelude, not in dance rhythm, became common and was often elaborately ornamented and improvisatory in character; such opening movements went under a variety of titles, including 'fantasia', 'préambule', and 'overture'.

Froberger's successors in Germany include Johann Rosenmüller, J. E. Kindermann, and Georg Muffat, all of whom composed keyboard suites under various titles (usually 'sonata') which conformed to the established scheme. But as the 17th century progressed the number and order of dances in the suite varied increasingly, particularly among French composers. They frequently combined traditional dance movements with less formal, fancifully titled pieces to form larger-scale, loosely connected suites, and introduced other dances such as the *rigaudon, *loure, and *musette. Some of the *ordres* of François Couperin, for example, include up to 20 movements, normally all in the same key: his third *ordre*, in C, from the first book of *Pièces de clavecin* (1713), comprises the following pieces: *La ténébreuse* (allemande),

Première courante, Seconde courante, La lugubre (sarabande), *Gavotte, Menuet, Les pélérines, Les laurentines, L'espagnolète, Les regrets, Les matelotes provençales, La favorite* (chaconne), and *La lutine*. Other French composers such as Chambonnières, Jean Henri d'Anglebert, and Nicolas Lebègue achieved an extraordinary variety of invention in their suites, many of which are in a distinctive, elaborately embellished style that is typical of French Baroque harpsichord music.

Outside Germany and France the suite was slower to develop during the 17th century. In Italy the most important composer of keyboard music was Frescobaldi; he wrote no suites as such, but some of the dances for harpsichord in his later publications (e.g. *Toccate*, 1637) are grouped in twos and threes, suggesting the beginnings of the suite idea. In England, Matthew Locke's *Melothesia* (1673), an anthology of keyboard music by various composers including Locke himself, contains a number of fairly simple suites based on the allemande–courante–sarabande pattern, a line of development that was continued by Blow and by Purcell, whose short, uncomplicated three- and four-movement suites published in the 1680s and 1690s were often entitled 'Lessons'.

3. *18th Century.* Like so many genres of the Baroque period the suite reached its peak with Handel and Bach; through their keyboard and orchestral suites we are able to complete the picture of the suite's development up to the end of the most important phase of its history. Nearly all suites up to and including Handel's and Bach's have a unity of key: changes of key between movements are limited to the major-minor (tonic or relative) type. Most of the dances are in simple *binary form, that is, falling into two roughly equal sections, the first moving to the key of the dominant (or if in a minor key to the relative major), the second returning to the original key, and both halves are repeated. Melodic or rhythmic figures introduced in the opening bars of each movement are normally referred to, developed, and repeated in the course of the movement and may even be used to link two or more movements of the same suite.

Handel's keyboard suites (eight were published together in 1720) are mainly conventional in form (allemande–courante–sarabande–gigue) though some include a chaconne, an 'abstract' fugue, or a set of variations on an air. For some of these pieces Handel typically re-used material from earlier works, and several of the movements are linked thematically. Better known than the keyboard suites are the orchestral *Water Music* (actually three separate suites, in F, D, and G) and *Music for the Royal Fireworks*;

like the keyboard suites their value lies more in their invention and vitality than in any formal originality they may display.

Bach's contribution is typically wide-ranging —six cello suites, four orchestral suites, six 'French' and six 'English' keyboard suites, six keyboard partitas, and several individual partitas and sonatas for various instruments (suites in all but name). All his keyboard suites follow the standard pattern of allemande–courante–sarabande–gigue; some have an opening prelude, which may be quite extensive, and all have at least one (usually several) additional dance movement (bourrée, menuet, gavotte, etc.). Though they embody few significant formal or technical innovations, Bach's suites provide a brilliant and masterly synthesis of the entire history and development of the Baroque suite.

4. *The Later Suite.* The characteristic use in the later Baroque suite of contrasting keys at the start of each section and occasionally of contrasting thematic material, the increasing emphasis on development followed by repetition or recapitulation—these features all hint at the chief elements of the *sonata, which in the second half of the 18th century replaced the suite as the standard instrumental genre. Sonata-form concepts dominated music throughout the later 18th century and for much of the 19th, to the extent that the sonata, symphony, concerto, and related genres all but banished the suite from the repertory. Traces of the suite principle remain, however, in chamber-orchestral works such as the *serenade, *cassation, and *divertimento (forms used by Haydn, Mozart, Beethoven, and Brahms) and even in some song-cycles and piano music (e.g. by Schumann). But conscious attempts to reassert the suite over symphonic forms were not made until the later 19th century (e.g. Raff's and Lachner's orchestral suites of the 1860s and 1870s, and Grieg's *Holberg Suite* of 1884); and some of these resulted only from a romantic desire to evoke a bygone era.

In general, the instrumental suite of the late 19th century and the early 20th had little to do with its Baroque predecessor. By the 1880s traditional dance movements were being supplanted by a free succession of national or folk dances, sometimes with a programmatic background (e.g. Dvořák's orchestral suites), or by numbers extracted from a ballet, opera, or other dramatic work and rearranged for concert performance (e.g. Bizet's *L'arlésienne*, Grieg's *Peer Gynt Suite*). In the early 20th century the programmatic and extract suite (e.g. Holst's *The Planets*, Richard Strauss's *Rosenkavalier* suites) existed alongside a new and deliberate attempt to re-create the Baroque suite, which was prompted by an interest in neo-classicism

(Debussy's *Suite pour le piano*, Ravel's *Le tombeau de Couperin*, Stravinsky's *Pulcinella*). Among later 20th-century works the title 'suite' occurs only occasionally (Schoenberg's *Piano Suite*, Berg's *Lyric Suite*), doubtless because the need for musical unification to which the suite has traditionally catered has been met more successfully through the more abstract compositional techniques of contemporary music.

JUDITH NAGLEY

Suite bergamasque. Work by Debussy for piano, composed in 1890 and revised in 1905. Its four movements are *Prélude*, *Menuet*, *Clair de lune*, and *Passepied*. The first, second, and fourth movements were orchestrated by G. Cloez, the third by André Caplet.

Suivez (Fr.). 'Follow'. 1. A direction that the next movement or section is to follow immediately, i.e. the same as *attacca*. 2. A direction that an accompanying part or parts should follow the solo with regard to rhythm or tempo, i.e. the same as *colla parte, colla voce*.

Suk, Josef (*b* Křečovice u Neveklova, 4 Jan. 1874; *d* Benešov, 29 May 1935). Czech composer and violinist. He studied at the Prague Conservatory (1885–92) with Antonín Bennewitz for violin and with Dvořák (whose daughter Otilie he married) for composition. Dvořák's was the strongest influence on his earlier works, which include the Serenade in E♭ for strings (1892) and the String Quartet in B♭ (1896). Later, as in the expansive symphony *Asrael* (1905–6), he moved in the direction of Strauss, but his rate of composition now grew slower and he produced little after the First World War. He was also second violinist in the Bohemian Quartet (1891–1933) and a composition teacher at the Prague Conservatory (1922–35).

PAUL GRIFFITHS

FURTHER READING
Jiří Berkovec: *Josef Suk* (Prague, Eng. edn, 1969).

Sul, sull', sulla, sui, sugli (It.). (1) 'On the'; e.g. in violin playing, *sul G*, *sul IV*, 'on the G (string)', 'on the fourth (string)'; in string playing, *sulla tastiera*, *sul tasto*, '(bow) on the fingerboard'. (2) 'Near the'; e.g. in string playing, *sul ponticello*, '(bow) near the bridge'.

Sullivan, (Sir) Arthur (Seymour) (*b* Lambeth, 13 May 1842; *d* London, 22 Nov. 1900). English composer and conductor. In collaboration with the librettist W. S. Gilbert (1836–1911) he contributed to English music a distinctive style of light opera, a mixture of parody, burlesque, and satire, which has achieved immense popularity in Britain and the USA. The marriage of

Arthur Sullivan (c.1875)

words and music in these 'Savoy operas' (so called because several were first performed at the Savoy Theatre, London) is so close that 'Gilbert and Sullivan' is sufficient description of the genre.

Son of an Irish bandmaster, Sullivan entered the Chapel Royal as a chorister in 1854 and had a sacred song published by Novello in 1855. He studied at the Royal Academy of Music under Sterndale Bennett in 1856 and went to Leipzig Conservatory from 1858 to 1861. His first success as a composer was in 1861 when his incidental music to *The Tempest* was performed in Leipzig. There followed a Symphony and Cello Concerto in 1866, the oratorio *The Prodigal Son* at the Worcester Festival of 1869, and the *Overture di ballo* at the Birmingham Festival of 1870. He was organist of St Michael's, Chester Square, London, 1861–7, and at St Peter's, Cranley Gardens, 1867–72. He composed a ballet for Covent Garden in 1864. In 1867 he accompanied his friend George Grove to Vienna where they discovered Schubert's lost *Rosamunde* music.

Sullivan's first success in comic opera was with the one-act *Cox and Box* (1867). During its run he met Gilbert and their first collaboration was in 1871 in *Thespis* (now lost). *Trial by Jury* (1875) was more successful and stimulated the impresario Richard D'Oyly Carte to form a company specially to perform works by Gilbert and Sullivan. *The Sorcerer* (1877) led to the great success of *HMS Pinafore* (1878) and *The Pirates of Penzance* (1879). During the run of *Patience* (1881) the company moved into the new Savoy Theatre. Works produced there were *Iolanthe* (1882), *Princess Ida* (1884), *The Mikado*

(1885), *Ruddigore* (1887), *The Yeomen of the Guard* (1888), and *The Gondoliers* (1889). In 1886 the cantata *The Golden Legend* was performed at the Leeds Festival, of which Sullivan was chief conductor from 1880 to 1898. He also conducted for many other organizations and was principal of the National Training School (forerunner of the Royal College of Music) from 1876 to 1881. He was knighted in 1883. In 1891 his romantic opera *Ivanhoe* ran for 150 performances. A quarrel with Gilbert in 1890, though later resolved, ended their run of success, though *Utopia Limited* (1893) and *The Grand Duke* (1896) are prized by some devotees.

Of Sullivan's other works only the *Overture di ballo*, the hymn-tune *Onward, Christian Soldiers* (1871), and the song *The Lost Chord* (1877) are still often heard. His fertile eclecticism was the root cause of the success of the Savoy operas. He could draw on elements from a variety of styles, and his brilliant parodies of Handel, Bellini, Purcell, Donizetti, Verdi, and Mendelssohn, added to a natural gift for melody and the rhythmical basis of his word-settings, resulted in music which is both witty and accomplished. His orchestration is always apt, often inspired, and such pieces as 'When the Night Wind Howls' from *Ruddigore* and 'The Sun whose Rays' (*The Mikado*) are inspired inventions.   MICHAEL KENNEDY

FURTHER READING
Herbert Sullivan and Newman Flower: *Sir Arthur Sullivan: his Life, Letters, and Diaries* (London, 1927, 2nd edn 1950); L. Baily: *Gilbert & Sullivan and their World* (London, 1973); J. Wolfson: *Sir Arthur Sullivan* (New York, 1976).

Sumer is icumen in. This piece, one of the earliest surviving secular works, is an infinite canon at the unison, a round or rota (from Lat. *rota*, 'wheel'), written around 1250, probably in Reading, and therefore known as the 'Reading Rota'. It is also known as the 'Summer Canon' (from its text, which celebrates the coming of summer). It has been ascribed, probably erroneously, to the monk John of Fornsete. It has two alternative texts, one in English (*Sumer is icumen in*), and the other a sacred Latin text (*Perspice christicola*), supported by a *pes*, or five-note ground bass, with words related to the English text (*Sing cuccu nu*). A note in the manuscript, in Latin, describes the proper method of performance, using four tenor voices with two basses singing the *pes*.

Summend (Ger.). 'Humming'.

Summer Night on the River. Orchestral work by Delius, the second of his Two Pieces for Small Orchestra, composed in 1911. It is not to be confused with Delius's *Two Songs to be*

Sung of a Summer Night on the Water, textless works for chorus, composed in 1917. The first of the Two Pieces is *On Hearing the First Cuckoo in Spring*.

Sung Mass. See *Mass*.

Suonare (It.). See *Sonare*.

Suono (It.). 'Sound', 'note'.

Suor Angelica ('Sister Angelica'). Opera in one act by Puccini; text by Forzano. The second part of Puccini's *Il trittico*. Produced: New York, Metropolitan Opera, 14 December 1918; Rome, Teatro Costanzi, 11 January 1919; London, Covent Garden, 18 June 1920. Sister Angelica (sop.) has taken the veil in expiation of a love affair that has produced a child. News comes to her from her aunt (con.) of its death. Praying for forgiveness, she commits suicide, but this second sin is forgiven when the Virgin and Child appear to her in a vision.

Superius (Lat.). In early vocal music, the name given to the highest voice-part in an ensemble and to the part-book that contains its music. The terms 'cantus' and 'discantus' may also be used.

Supertonic. Second degree of the major or minor scale, i.e. the degree that lies one step *above* the tonic.

Supertonic seventh chord. See *Added sixth*.

Suppé, Franz (von) (*b* Spalato, Dalmatia, now Split, Yugoslavia, 18 Apr. 1819; *d* Vienna, 21 May 1895). Austrian composer. Son of an Austrian official in Dalmatia, he was sent to study law at Padua University but spent much of his time seeing operas in Milan. His father died in 1835, and the family returned to Vienna, where he studied with Sechter (Bruckner's teacher) and became conductor at various theatres. He was one of the first Viennese composers of operetta in the Offenbach manner and had a string of successes, including *Die schöne Galatea* ('The Beautiful Galatea', 1865) and *Boccaccio* (1879). His overtures *Dichter und Bauer* ('Poet and Peasant') and *Die Leichte Kavallerie* ('Light Cavalry') were long popular, arranged for innumerable combinations including two flutes.   DENIS ARNOLD

Suppliant (Fr.), **supplicando, supplichevole** (It.). 'Supplicating', 'pleading'.

Supprimez (Fr.). 'Suppress', 'withhold'. In French organ music, a direction to put out of action the stops in question.

Sur la touche (Fr.). In string playing, '(bow) on the fingerboard'; *sur le chevalet*, '(bow) near the bridge'.

Surprise cadence. See *Cadence, 2*.

'Surprise' Symphony. Nickname of Haydn's Symphony No. 94 in G major, composed in 1791. It is so called because of a sudden *forte* drumbeat in the slow movement. In Germany the symphony is known as 'mit dem Pauken-schlag' ('with the drumstroke').

Sursum corda (Lat., 'Lift up your hearts'). The words addressed by the celebrant to the congregation immediately before the Preface. They are included in all known Christian liturgies of all ages.

Susato, Tylman (*b* ?*c*.1500; *d* ?Antwerp, 1561–4). Composer and music publisher, possibly Flemish. His several talents included those of professional calligrapher and trumpeter at Antwerp Cathedral. From 1543 to 1561 he concentrated on music publishing in Antwerp, forming various partnerships and establishing the first significant press in the Low Countries. A skilful and resourceful publisher, he was one of Lassus's first publishers (issuing his *chansons* in 1555), and he also encouraged local Flemish composers to send him songs with Flemish words, though few materialized. During his career he issued 25 books of *chansons*, three of Masses, 19 of motets, and 11 volumes entitled *Musyck boexken*, which contain Flemish songs, dances based on popular tunes arranged by himself, and *Souterliedekens* (metrical psalm settings in Dutch). Apart from his well-known dance tunes, his own compositions include sacred vocal music and two books of *cantus-firmus chansons*, written to help young singers gain experience. The music he issued found special favour in the early music revival of the 1960s, notably Janequin's stirring *chanson*, *La bataille* (printed in 1545), which was a special favourite of David Munrow's.

J. M. THOMSON

Suspended cadence. See *Cadence, 2*.

Suspension. A form of discord arising from the holding over of a note in one chord as a momentary part of the chord which follows, it then resolving by falling a degree to a note which forms a real part of the second chord:

When two notes are held over in this way, it is called a double suspension.

Süss (Ger.). 'Sweet'.

Süssmayr, Franz Xaver (*b* Schwanenstadt, 1766; *d* Vienna, 17 Sept. 1803). Austrian composer. He was educated at the monastery of Kremsmünster until in 1788 he settled in Vienna, becoming a pupil of Salieri and Mozart. He was Mozart's assistant during 1791 and may have composed some of the *secco* recitatives for *La clemenza di Tito*. He himself composed a number of successful operas and *Singspiele* for theatres in Prague and Vienna, as well as some church music. After Mozart's death Constanze Mozart asked Süssmayr to complete the Requiem. Debate has surrounded exactly how much of the Requiem is by him and how much was done according to Mozart's detailed sketches, and it is not known how much of his letter on the subject to the publishers Breitkopf & Härtel was true: he stated that he had filled in and orchestrated the early movements, and then composed the Sanctus, Benedictus, and Agnus Dei. However, there seems little reason to doubt his account, especially if he was acquainted with Mozart's intentions, and in any case, it is hardly likely that a better version could be reconstructed today.

DENIS ARNOLD

Sustaining pedal. The right-hand pedal on the piano. It sustains the notes by lifting the dampers from the strings. See *Piano, 12a*.

Susurrando, susurrante (It.). 'Whispering', 'murmuring'.

Svegliando, svegliato (It.). 'Awakening', 'awakened', i.e. brisk, alert.

Svelto (It.). 'Smart', 'quick'.

Svendsen, Johan (Severin) (*b* Christiania, now Oslo, 30 Sept. 1840; *d* Copenhagen, 14 June 1911). Norwegian composer and conductor. Born three years earlier than Grieg, whom he outlived by four years, Svendsen was the leading Norwegian symphonic composer of his day, and a master of the orchestra. His achievement has been overshadowed by his great contemporary, who remained creative throughout his career, while Svendsen's distinction as a conductor drew him away from composition during the last 25 years of his life. Svendsen showed early musical promise, studying first with his father who was a military bandsman. He rapidly became proficient on the flute, clarinet, and violin, and joined the Christiania Theatre Orchestra. After studies in Christiania, he went to Leipzig but was soon forced to abandon his ambitions as a violinist owing to problems with his left hand, and concentrate on composition. A String Quartet, Op. 1, an Octet for strings, Op. 3, and his First Symphony, Op. 4, date from this period (1863–7). He presented the last in Christiania on his return from a long journey to Scotland, Iceland, and the Faeroes in 1867. After the première of the symphony, which made a great impression on Grieg, he went to Paris (1868–70), earning a living as an orchestral player. There he began a Violin Concerto, Op. 6, completed on his return to Leipzig (1870–2) where he composed a Cello Concerto, Op. 7 (1870), and other works. His best-known piece, *Carnival in Paris* (1872), was written, somewhat incongruously, in Bayreuth, where he made the acquaintance of Wagner. During the 1870s Svendsen returned to Norway to conduct the Christiania Orchestra and to teach at the conservatory. From this period come the famous *Fest-Polonaise* and *Norwegian Artists' Carnival* as well as the Second Symphony (1876) and his *Norwegian Rhapsodies* Nos. 1–3. The fourth was composed in Italy (1877–8). A further two years in Paris (1878–80) yielded two sets of songs, Opp. 23 and 34, but, apart from the famous Romance for violin and orchestra, Op. 26 (1881), the remainder of his energies went into conducting. He directed the Royal Orchestra, Copenhagen, from 1883 until his retirement through ill health in 1908.

While Grieg's interest in Norwegian folk music resulted in his cultivation of the miniature, Svendsen excelled where Grieg did not: in larger forms. He succeeded in fusing the Viennese classical legacy with his keen awareness of the Norwegian folk tradition in both the symphonies and the *Norwegian Rhapsodies*, which are expertly laid out for the orchestra. His invention blends a liveliness and exuberance with a vein of poetic fantasy not unworthy of Grieg himself. His two symphonies, together with Berwald's four, are the finest to have appeared in Scandinavia before Sibelius.

ROBERT LAYTON

Swan Lake (Russ.: *Lebedinoye ozero*; Fr.: *Le lac des cygnes*). Ballet in four acts by Tchaikovsky to a libretto by V. Begichev and V. Heltser. It was choreographed by Reisinger and first performed in Moscow in 1877. It was later choreographed by Petipa and Ivanov for the St Petersburg production in 1895.

Swan of Tuonela, The (*Tuonelan joutsen*). Symphonic legend, Op. 22 No. 3, by Sibelius, composed in 1893 and revised in 1897 and 1900. It was composed as a prelude to an unfinished opera but was published as the third movement of Sibelius's *Lemminkänen Suite*. A cor anglais represents the swan; Tuonela is the Finnish Hades.

Sweden. See *Scandinavia*, 1, 2, 3, 4, 5, 6.

Sweelinck [Swelinck, Zwelinck, etc.], **Jan Pieterszoon** (*b* Deventer, ?May 1562; *d* Amsterdam, 16 Oct. 1621). Dutch composer and organist. He learnt music from his father, Pieter Swybbertszoon (Jan Sweelinck adopted his mother's maiden name), and he may also have studied in Haarlem. By 1580 he had been appointed to the important position of organist at the Oude Kerk, Amsterdam, where he remained for the rest of his life; the post was previously held by his father, later by his son, and was thus retained by the family almost uninterrupted for nearly a century. Sweelinck never left the Netherlands, and left Amsterdam only rarely—to visit other Dutch towns to inspect new organs or to advise on restoring old ones. His official duties at the Oude Kerk lay chiefly in providing music for the church services, but he was widely known for his virtuoso improvisations before and after the services which doubtless helped to attract large congregations.

Sweelinck's surviving compositions—over 250 vocal works and about 70 for keyboard—represent a peak in late Renaissance composition in northern Europe. His polyphonic setting of the entire Psalter, using the French metrical

M. Joannes Petri Swelingus Amstelo-batavus,
Muficus et Organifta toto orbe celeberrimus,
vir fingulari modeftia ac pietate, cum in vita,
tum in morte omnibus fufpiciendus.
Obijt M·DC·XXI·XVI·Octob·Æt·Ix.
Joan Müller sculp. 1624.

Sweelinck, engraving (1624) by Müller.

psalm texts of Clément Marot and Théodore de Bèze, is an impressive achievement which fills four published volumes and which occupied him throughout his working life. Though rooted firmly in the traditions of earlier Protestant psalm settings, it surpasses them in invention and spiritual expression. His Latin motets, French *chansons* (his earliest published works), and Italian madrigals are in a less severe, more frankly popular style than the psalms.

The keyboard works—contrapuntal fantasias, brilliant toccatas, and sets of elaborate variations—summarize the technique and spirit of late 16th-century keyboard music, and, with the marked independence of their contrapuntal lines, exploit fully the tonal potential of the organ of the day. The variation sets in particular demonstrate Sweelinck's knowledge of the music of his English contemporaries (especially John Bull, possibly a close friend, and Peter Philips), while the fantasias hint at Italian and Spanish predecessors (Andrea Gabrieli, Cabezón). The keyboard works were never published, but they circulated in manuscript copies and were widely known until at least the mid 17th century.

Sweelinck was celebrated throughout the Netherlands and Germany as a teacher. Aspiring composer-organists were sent to him from all parts, and he had a profound influence on a long line of pupils (including Samuel Scheidt and Heinrich Scheidemann) who came to be regarded as members of the north German school, culminating at the end of the 17th century in J. S. Bach.   JUDITH NAGLEY

Swing. A kind of jazz generally played by those bigger bands that clearly base their style on the jazz idiom as distinct from the more commercial styles of dance music. The term can also apply to smaller groups playing a light, 'swinging' style of jazz. The essence of swing is the ensemble playing of the various sections of the band, frequently employing riffs (repeated phrases) and having a solid, driving rhythmic basis, the whole engendering a controlled excitement. The movement towards arranged jazz began in the 1920s, and the first important swing bands to establish themselves were the Black groups headed by Duke Ellington, Fletcher Henderson, and McKinney's Cotton Pickers. Ellington, Henderson, and McKinney's Don Redman were all brilliant arrangers and they gave their bands much of the freedom of the small jazz groups. They were followed by the bands of Bennie Moten (later taken over by its pianist, Count Basie), Jimmie Lunceford, and Chick Webb. White musicians gradually took over the style and by 1935 the band of Benny Goodman had achieved world-wide success and Goodman had styled himself 'the King of Swing'. Other well-known band-leaders in the heyday of swing were Jimmy and Tommy Dorsey, Woody Herman, Artie Shaw, Glenn Miller, Charlie Barnet, Harry James, Les Brown, and Gene Krupa.

PETER GAMMOND

Switzerland. Mountainous countries, where conditions are not conducive to the creation of surplus wealth, are not usually great musical centres, and Switzerland is no exception; none the less, its musical history is not without interest.

In the Middle Ages, Switzerland was notable for several great monasteries, mainly in the north, for example at St Gall, Einsiedeln, and Engelberg. Some of these have preserved manuscripts of plainchant which reveal that the standard 'Gregorian' chant was not in use throughout the area, Ambrosian forms persisting in Italian-speaking regions until recent times. In the later Middle Ages there were song schools in various towns, and by the later 15th century a group of organists and composers seemed to be coming into existence.

The *Reformation affected the progress of music in Switzerland deeply, largely because the two major religious leaders, Ulrich Zwingli (1484-1531) and Jean Calvin (1509-64), did not approve of any kind of elaboration in church music (though Calvin had no objection to devotional music sung domestically). Organs were destroyed or removed from churches (the cathedral organ of Berne was sold to the more tolerant church at Sion), and only monophonic psalm singing was allowed at first. In the mid 16th century, four-part singing was permitted, but organs began to reappear only in the 17th. The Renaissance organists had created a strong enough tradition for there to be chamber organs in many private houses, and a number of tablature books survive from these. None the less, lacking firm patronage from either court or church, music was at a low ebb until after 1800. There were *collegia musica* in certain university towns and a number of concert societies came into being, but native composers, from Senfl in the 16th century to Albicastro in the 18th, tended to move to more important musical centres, and no great figure was drawn to Switzerland from elsewhere.

The ideas of two Swiss-born educationalists, Jean-Jaques Rousseau and Johann Heinrich Pestalozzi (1746-1827), encouraged choral singing, and a number of male-voice choirs were formed in the early 19th century. Other forms of musical activity were slow to enter Swiss life. Travelling companies brought opera sporadically, and theatres were built in Geneva (1738), Zurich (1833), Basle (1834), and, later, Berne (1903). When Wagner settled in Zurich

'Concerto a Cembalo obligato con Stromenti', engraving by J. R. Holzhalb, which was distributed to members of the Swiss 'Musicroom Society' as a New Year's greeting in 1777.

in the 1850s he found a very provincial musical life, which he did a certain amount to improve.

Swiss wealth in the 20th century, based on banking and light industry, has put the country on a level with its neighbours. The major cities have orchestras, theatres, and radio stations. Two famous orchestras are the Orchestre de la Suisse Romande, founded in 1918 by Ernst Ansermet, and the more specialized Basle Chamber Orchestra, under Paul Sacher. A group of Swiss-born composers has emerged, including Bloch, Schoeck, Martin, Honegger, Conrad Beck (*b* 1901), and Robert Suter (*b* 1919), but Switzerland has never had a nationalist school of composers.   DENIS ARNOLD

Sylphides, Les ('The Sylphs'). Ballet in one act, originally called *Chopiniana*, to music by Chopin. It was choreographed by Fokine and first performed in St Petersburg in 1907, with Pavlova among the dancers. The first version of the score used five piano pieces, orchestrated by Glazunov; subsequent performances have included additional pieces, scored by Keller and, for Diaghilev's 1909 Paris production, by Tcherepnin, Lyadov, and Stravinsky. It is one of the most popular ballets in the repertory. English versions have used Chopin arrangements by Roy Douglas, Malcolm Sargent, and Gordon Jacob, among others.

Symphonia domestica ('Domestic Symphony'). Orchestral work, Op. 53, by Richard Strauss, composed in 1902–3. It depicts a day in the life of the Strauss family, with themes representing the composer, his wife Pauline, and their baby son; but it is also a one-movement sectional symphony, not dependent on a programme for its musical effectiveness.

Symphonic Dances. Orchestral work, Op. 45, by Rakhmaninov, composed in 1940.

Symphonic Metamorphosis of Themes of Carl Maria von Weber. Orchestral work by Hindemith, composed in 1943. It originated in sketches (1940) for a ballet for Massine on Weber themes, using the *Turandot* overture (the second movement is called '*Turandot* Scherzo').

Symphonic poem. A piece of orchestral music, usually in one movement, based on a literary, poetic, or other extra-musical idea. It began in the mid 19th century with Liszt and, as a direct product of a Romantic movement which encouraged literary, pictorial, and dramatic associations in music, it developed into an important form of *programme music in the second half of the 19th century. The term 'tone poem' has largely been used interchangeably with 'symphonic poem', but a few composers, notably Richard Strauss and Sibelius, have preferred 'tone poem' for pieces that are less 'symphonic' in design, where there is no special emphasis on thematic or tonal contrast.

The symphonic poem has its ancestry in the concert *overture of the earlier 19th century, such as Beethoven's *Coriolan* and Mendelssohn's *Midsummer Night's Dream* (which also serve as musical illustrations of literary subjects), as well as in the symphony itself in the much expanded and expressive form that it had attained by mid century. Liszt attempted to combine features of the overture and symphony with descriptive elements, and produced a number of narrative, one-movement orchestral works that approach a symphonic first movement in form and scale (e.g. *Ce qu'on entend sur la montagne*, after Victor Hugo, 1848; *Mazeppa*, after Hugo, 1851; *Hunnenschlacht* ('The Slaughter of the Huns'), after a painting by Kaulbach, 1857; and *Hamlet*, 1858). Some follow a detailed narrative programme; others paint a more general picture in the mind's eye by outlining the features of a literary character or creating a scene or atmosphere.

Other composers seized on the symphonic poem as a suitable vehicle for expressing nationalism in music. Notable among them was Smetana, whose cycle of six symphonic poems entitled *Má vlast* ('My Fatherland', *c*.1872-9) describes scenes from the history and everyday life of his beloved Bohemia; and this began a fashion, as countless other composers were moved to attempt to illustrate their homeland through the symphonic poem. Russian nationalist composers were particularly attracted by the form (e.g. Musorgsky, *Night on the Bare Mountain*, 1867; Borodin, *In the Steppes of Central Asia*, 1880), as was Tchaikovsky, whose 'fantasy overture' *Romeo and Juliet* (1869) is a symphonic poem in all but name. Later Russian contributions to the form are numerous (e.g. Skryabin, *Poem of Ecstasy*, 1905-8; Rakhmaninov, *The Isle of the Dead*, 1909), though they are now rarely heard in the West.

France was less concerned with nationalism than many other countries, but her well-established tradition of narrative and illustrative music, reaching back to Berlioz, meant that composers were attracted to the poetic elements of the form. Saint-Saëns's *Le rouet d'Omphale* (1872) was the first of a long line of symphonic poems, mainly by lesser composers, notwithstanding a handful of better-known, more significant ones (e.g. Debussy, *Prélude à l'après-midi d'un faune*, 1892-4, and *La mer*, 1903-5; Dukas, *L'apprenti-sorcier*, 1897; Ravel, *La valse*, 1920).

The symphonic poem reached its apogee in the work of Richard Strauss. A pupil of Alexander Ritter, who encouraged him towards the form, he vastly increased both its scale and its depth of expression, through a bold choice of subjects, brilliant orchestration, vivid realism, and supremely skilful compositional crafts (such as thematic transformation). Strauss's symphonic poems include *Don Juan* (1888-9), *Tod und Verklärung* (1888-9), *Till Eulenspiegel* (1894-5), *Also sprach Zarathustra* (1895-6), *Don Quixote* (1896-7), *Ein Heldenleben* (1897-8), and *Sinfonia domestica* (1902-3); probably more than any other works in the form, they have retained their place and popularity in the standard concert repertory.

During the late 19th century and the early 20th innumerable other composers contributed to the form to some degree, though few of their works remain in the current repertory. Of those that do, Sibelius's tone poems (e.g. *The Swan of Tuonela*, 1893; *Finlandia*, 1899; *Tapiola*, 1926) are the most significant, and Respighi's *Fontane di Roma* (1914-16) and *Pini di Roma* (1923-4) have always been popular. Elgar's 'symphonic study' *Falstaff* (1913) is perhaps the only British contribution of any real significance, though several composers, including Vaughan Williams and Delius, wrote a number of single-movement orchestral works describing scenes or landscapes which come close to the symphonic poem idea.

The form's decline in the second decade of the 20th century naturally followed on the decline of Romantic ideals in general. It was an inevitable result of a decreasing interest in music that was primarily descriptive, in favour of more abstract forms. During its heyday, however, the symphonic poem was a most important independent orchestral genre, and an especially appropriate vehicle for the intense Romantic and nationalist expression that characterized its time.

PERCY SCHOLES, rev. Judith Nagley

Symphonic prologue. See *Overture*.

Symphonic concertante (Fr.; It.: *sinfonia concertante*). A hybrid instrumental form with elements of both symphony and concerto which flourished in the late 18th century. It was essentially a concerto for more than one solo instrument (usually between two and seven), generally of a light-hearted character, in which the role of the orchestra was to accompany the solo parts. The *symphonie concertante* was especially popular in Paris: almost half of all known Classical examples were written either by French composers, or for performance at the celebrated Concert Spirituel. The combination of soloists ranged from the usual two violins to more unusual groups (e.g. Leopold Kozeluch's Concerto for piano, mandolin, trumpet, and double bass).

The form first appeared in the 1760s, and the earliest, though not the best known, examples were written by Parisian composers such as Devienne, Gossec, and Pleyel, and in Mannheim by Cannabich, Holzbauer, Anton and Carl Stamitz, and Danzi. The Italians Boccherini and Brunetti each wrote five, while in London J. C. Bach wrote about 15, both for his own concerts and for Paris (most are scored for at least three solo instruments). The form was also cultivated by Austrian and Bohemian composers—e.g. Wagenseil, Vanhal, and Dittersdorf—but the most enduring examples of the genre are inevitably by composers of the stature of Haydn and Mozart. Only one piece by Haydn, his *Symphonie concertante* for violin, cello, oboe, and bassoon (Op. 84), composed for the Salomon concerts in London, actually bears the title, but his six *divertimenti concertanti* (Op. 31) are of the type. Mozart completed four examples for Paris: one for four wind instruments (K 297b) which subsequently disappeared; one for violin and viola, K 364; one for two pianos, K 365; and one for flute and harp, K 299. He also wrote an early *Concertone* in C for two violins, K 190. In Germany the double keyboard concerto was cultivated especially by the Bach sons, and by C. H. Graun.

The importance in the 19th century of the star solo performer caused the decline of the *symphonie concertante* in favour of the virtuoso solo concerto, although it lingered on in such pieces as Beethoven's Triple Concerto, Mendelssohn's early double piano concertos,

Schumann's *Konzertstück* for four horns, and Brahms's Double Concerto. The 20th century has seen a revival of interest in the form, by such composers as Martinů (many of whose works are based on the *concertante* principle, including a *sinfonia concertante* for the same combination of instruments as the Haydn piece, on which it is modelled, and a Concerto for piano, strings, and timpani), Frank Martin (*Petite symphonie concertante* for piano, harpsichord, harp, and strings), and Poulenc (Concerto for organ, timpani, and strings). Some 20th-century composers, such as Walton (*Sinfonia concertante* for piano and orchestra), have used the term even when only one solo instrument is involved, to imply the close integration of soloist and orchestra.   WENDY THOMPSON

Symphonie fantastique (épisode de la vie d'un artiste) ('Fantastic Symphony: Episode in the Life of an Artist'). Symphony, Op. 14, by Berlioz, composed in 1830. One of the most remarkable Romantic compositions, it is the forerunner of the programme symphonies and symphonic poems of Liszt, Mahler, Strauss, Tchaikovsky, and others. Its five movements are *Rêveries, passions* ('Dreams, Passions'), *Un bal* ('A Ball'), *Scène aux champs* ('Scene in the Fields'), *Marche au supplice* ('March to the Scaffold'), and *Songe d'une nuit du Sabbat* ('Witches' Sabbath'). The work was inspired by Berlioz's unrequited love for the Irish actress Harriet Smithson (whom he later married) and this is symbolized in the music by a melody (*idée fixe*) which acts as a motto theme and recurs in different guises, like a Wagnerian *Leitmotiv*. See also *Lélio*.

Symphonie sur un chant montagnard français ('Symphony on a French Mountain Song'). Work for piano and orchestra, Op. 25, by d'Indy, composed in 1886. It is subtitled 'Symphonie cévenole' because the theme comes from the Cévennes region.

Symphony

1. The Origins and Early History to c.1730
2. Symphonies for the Concert Room, c.1730–1800
3. Beethoven

4. The Symphony after Beethoven
5. The Symphony from 1920
6. Conclusion

1. *The Origins and Early History to c.1730.* The word 'symphony' emerged in the late 16th century. At this time, however, it denoted nothing more specific than 'music for ensemble' —from the Greek *syn* ('together') and *phone* ('sounding'). For instance, Giovanni Gabrieli's *Sacrae symphoniae* ('Sacred Symphonies', 1597) were simply motets, canzonas, and other works for an ensemble of voices and/or instruments. In

this respect, symphony was interchangeable with the word *concerto. There were as yet none of the structural or stylistic implications which the symphony was to acquire during the 18th century.

By the 1620s a symphony (or *sinfonia*) could be an instrumental piece placed at the beginning or in the middle of a vocal piece such as a motet, madrigal, or cantata, much in the manner of a *ritornello*, though the *sinfonia* was not as a rule repeated as a refrain throughout the piece. When the public opera houses opened in Venice during the 1630s (see *Opera*, 4), the new-style operas often had a 'sinfonia avanti l'opera', or *overture, and some operas included a *sinfonia* as a purely instrumental interlude: the 'sinfonia infernale' in Cavalli's *Le nozze di Teti e di Peleo* (1639) is one example. Some of these opera *sinfonie*, notably that of Monteverdi's *L'incoronazione di Poppea* (1642), were divided into two linked sections, an idea which possibly spawned the French overture developed by Lully later in the 17th century. Towards the end of the century overtures to Italian operas similarly acquired distinctive structural characteristics, Alessandro Scarlatti using a three-movement pattern (fast–slow–fast) for some of his opera overtures.

This trend was consolidated from around the 1720s by opera composers of the Neapolitan school working throughout Europe (see *Opera*, 6). Such composers as Leonardo Vinci and Leonardo Leo wrote 'sinfonie avanti l'opera' which generally had a fast–slow–fast sequence of three movements, with the central movement brief and ornamented and the third movement couched in a light dance idiom. The first movement tended to be constructed of short themes with strong rhythmic shapes, underpinned with simple harmonies emphasizing the prevailing tonality. Momentum was maintained less by thematic development than by bustling, non-thematic passage-work, and interest was generated by a sharp contrast of thematic ideas and by the composers' feel for orchestral effects, with prominent use of the string *tremolando*, held wind notes, the implied *crescendo*, and so on. Such a style of writing was perhaps elementary when set beside the more refined manner of the concerto, but it was just the thing for beginning an evening at the opera. It was also the seed from which developed the symphony as we know it today.

2. *Symphonies for the Concert Room, c.1730–1800.* With the increasing popularity of series of concerts, particularly in Paris (see *Concert*, 4), large-scale pieces were required to show off the large and efficient orchestras assembled by impresarios. Similarly, at the Electoral Court at Mannheim (see *Concert*, 5) the prince took pride in his ensemble ('an army of generals', it was called by Burney). Although the concerto continued to be popular, the new emphasis on orchestral music favoured the symphony which became the major orchestral genre, especially in Central Europe. The libraries of many of the large Austrian and south German monasteries show that symphonies were much performed there also, while those of some minor noblemen

reveal their emulation of Mannheim. An enormous repertory developed to satisfy the courts' needs, with at least 7,000 symphonies written in the half century from c.1740. It was a cosmopolitan repertory with works by Italians, Bohemians, Austrians, Germans, French, and English, the works of the major composers being widely known (the Central European composers were especially valued in Paris).

It has so far proved beyond the capacity of scholars adequately to classify this vast repertory, the more especially since much of it survives only in the form of orchestral parts, without scores. However, certain general observations can be made, and a number of less certain generalizations about style must be hazarded if any order is to emerge. In the early years of the 'symphonic' period, symphonies remained mainly in three movements after the Italian manner. Isolated examples of the addition of a minuet occurred around 1740, as did slow introductions to first movements (puzzlingly, rarer with French composers accustomed to the traditions of the French overture than with some Austrians, such as Hoffmann). The basic ideas of *sonata form were used for first movements—though with many variants and variable understanding of its potential.

There were three mainstreams of symphonic writing in this period. The earliest and most tenuous was the Italian represented by Sammartini, whose *galant* style, with its elegant slow movements, light scoring, and *buffa*-esque finales, was very popular in the middle of the century. It was a manner which came to London via J. C. Bach and which influenced Mozart, some of whose early symphonies were written in this style in preparation for his Italian tours. There were more substantial symphonies by C. P. E. Bach, composed for Berlin. These were often more heavily scored, but above all they showed a capacity for thematic development and a use of tonality as an important element in their structure. But the most popular and widespread manner was that of the Mannheim school led by Johann Stamitz, who influenced a host of composers—F. X. Richter, Falk, Karl Stamitz, Eichner, Benda, and others. The 'Mannheim' symphony used all known tricks to show off orchestral skill: sudden changes in dynamics and expression, the imaginative use of wind instruments including the new clarinets, and above all the famous *crescendo* (sometimes known as the Mannheim Steam Roller). The Concert Spirituel in Paris added to these effects the sonorous opening tutti, known as the 'premier coup d'archet'. All these traits gave composers the chance to expand the actual size of movements by maintaining interest during the non-thematic passage-work derived from

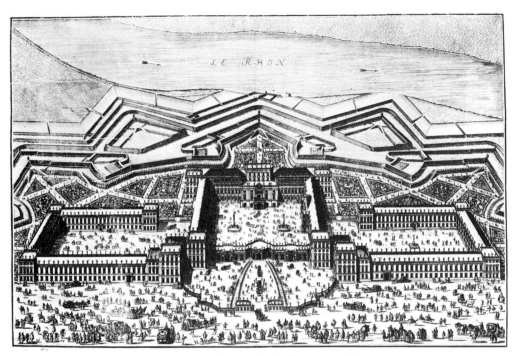

Pl. 1. The Electoral Palace at Mannheim (1725), engraving by Ostertag and Coentgen.

the Italian overture style. Thus first movements expanded and finales could be more ample and powerful; the slow movements remained decorative in melody with a comparatively simple accompaniment, but they also became longer and more emotionally ambitious.

This new type of music at Mannheim resulted in an attractive and worthwhile repertory, especially when taken in collaboration with the Viennese school, which, though prone to greater Italian influence and therefore showing more sentimental expression and less sheer force in rhythm and orchestral sound, was essentially an offshoot of it. Such composers as Gassmann and Vanhal wrote more tuneful themes, and the former tended to recapitulate his subjects in the subdominant or (in a minor key) the submediant, so eliminating the surprise effects made necessary when the bridge passage had to be altered to accommodate the new key relationship. If there is much note-spinning of no particular value in many 18th-century symphonies, it is also true that the best composers (Richter, Dittersdorf, Vanhal, d'Ordonez) wrote works worthy of revival today; perhaps their neglect is caused mainly by the fact that they are akin to, yet just lack the subtlety of, the symphonies by the two great masters of the 18th century.

These two masters, Haydn and Mozart, transformed less the structures than the emotional scope of the symphony. Both began in the Italian tradition, but Haydn early revealed

a seriousness similar to that of C. P. E. Bach: his interest in thematic development and experiments in formal design show his knowledge of the older Baroque traditions of the *sonata da chiesa* as well as of more recent ideas. His themes were more rhythmic, less *galant*. A major turning-point for both composers seemingly came in the early 1770s, when, during the period known as *Sturm und Drang*, music became more intense. Mozart's symphonies of the time show his increasingly dramatic power (e.g. No. 25 in G minor, K 183, 1773) and contrapuntal dexterity (No. 29 in A major, K 201, 1774). Haydn wrote several symphonies in minor keys, all of them serious; but it was the grandness of scale, the refusal to accept rococo clichés, and the contrapuntal writing constantly permeating the texture which transformed the works of this period from entertainment music into something more ambitious.

The most notable results of this new thinking on the nature of the symphony came in the 1780s, when Mozart, after visiting Paris and composing a symphony (No. 31, K 297, 1778) in the traditional manner of the Concert Spirituel, settled in Vienna: taking for granted a skilled orchestra, he began to exploit the orchestral tone palette of the Mannheimers. His experience in chamber music, gained from Haydn, now was transferred to the symphony, more especially in his last three symphonies, of which No. 40 in G minor (K 550, 1788) is orchestrally broader

Pl. 2. Title-page of a set of three symphonies by Haydn, dedicated to Prince Nikolaus Esterházy, and published in Vienna in 1784.

but just as emotional a work as his String Quintet (K 516) in the same key; similarly, No. 41, the 'Jupiter' (K 551, 1788) has an intricate fugal finale, elaborating the art of the G major String Quartet (K 387). His other interest, opera, thoroughly permeates the 'Prague' Symphony (No. 38, K 504, 1786), the ultimate Italian overture (in effect to *Don Giovanni*) transmuted into a concert symphony.

Haydn, who by the 1780s was very famous, was writing for Paris, also using the Mannheim orchestral technique to the full, but with greater subtlety and an imaginative exploitation of sonata form. First movements now became very large, often with expansive slow introductions; slow movements could be written in variation and other extended forms; minuets were no longer dances but were intricately worked movements, suggesting miniature sonata form; finales were often grand, witty, and climactic. The throw-away 3/8 dances of the Italian symphony had been entirely superseded. Haydn's 'London' symphonies, written after Mozart's death, took these traits still further. All but one of the 12 have slow introductions, some prolonged and by no means concerned just to prepare for the movement to follow. The slow movements were entirely un-*galant*, often based on simple hymn-like melodies which have an almost religious solemnity. The length and wit of the finales reveal an inventiveness which has

rarely been matched, never simply 'effective' or 'brilliant' but tightly constructed with elements of rondo and sonata form: they are always entirely satisfying. Haydn's influence can be detected in a whole generation of symphonists working in the 1790s, especially in such men as Rosetti and Reicha.

3. *Beethoven*. First Haydn, then Beethoven, transformed the symphony for all other composers. If Beethoven's First Symphony (1800) is very close to Haydn's grand C major manner (compare it with his No. 97), the Second (1801–2) is extremely original, a new kind of pleasurable or entertainment symphony with straightforward lyrical tunes in place of the courtly graces of the 18th century: it was to lead to Schubert's symphonic style. Both symphonies put aside any relic of the *galant*, the minuets having been replaced by a vigorous scherzo.

The great transformation came with the Third Symphony, the 'Eroica' (1803), its political overtones evident not only from the title-page (with its first dedication to Napoleon) but also in the increased use of wind instruments after the manner of the Revolutionary wind bands in Paris, the funeral-march slow movement, and the use of a theme from his *Prometheus* ballet in the finale, suggesting some elements of Titanic struggle. The symphony is enormously long, at some 50 minutes almost twice the length of even the grandest 18th-century symphonies. With the 'Eroica' the symphony became the equivalent of the great religious genres—Mass, cantata, motet—of the Baroque: a public statement of belief and feeling of the highest order. It had the advantage over vocal genres in not being tied to words: it could therefore deal with segments of experience, sensuous pleasure, and moods evoked by places or literature, rather than attempt a complete or stereotyped expression of belief. It was a human rather than a religious genre (though religion need not be excluded). In his later symphonies Beethoven refined and developed this new concept. The Fifth (1807–8) and Seventh (1811–12) Symphonies are simpler in aim but built on a similar scale, the one clearly heroic, the other a supreme expression of joy; the subtle mixtures of the Third, let alone its element of tragedy, are not equalled. More original was the Sixth Symphony, the 'Pastoral' (1808), an expression of feelings aroused by exterior surroundings, i.e. the countryside. Its five movements were given titles in the manner of much 18th-century programme music. But the storm music is impressionistic in a novel way, with no thematically significant content nor any real 'form': it relies entirely on imitations of nature for its effect. Two technical innovations were significant in the post-'Eroica' symphony. Movements were now sometimes joined together, either by fully developed links (as between the last three movements of the 'Pastoral') or by the use of recurring themes (as in the last two movements of the Fifth). Scherzos were often amplified into a scherzo-trio-scherzo-trio-scherzo-coda pattern, this allowing some deceptive effects (in the Seventh Symphony, for example, the coda suggests yet another repetition of the trio, before it is abruptly chased away). All four movements were now of considerable weight.

The climax of this transformation of the genre came in Beethoven's Ninth Symphony (1822–4), a mixture of symphony and French Revolutionary cantata. The first three movements expanded the traditional forms almost to breaking-point. There is a huge sonata-form first movement with tight thematic development throughout, and a dramatic coup at the recapitulation, with major harmony now replacing the exposition's minor third; the scherzo has a fugal texture, sketchy themes, a pastoral trio in duple time, and a 'dismissive' ending after the manner of the Seventh Symphony; and the long slow movement is a set of variations on a double theme, using the filigree ornamental melody found in the final quartets. The choral last movement does not fit into any symphonic pattern any more than that of the 'Eroica' had done, though a set of variations is the nearest succinct description. It is in fact a cantata on the theme of liberty (it bears distinct resemblances to Beethoven's early *Cantata on the Accession of Emperor Leopold II*, 1790), using soloists and choir to their limits.

4. *The Symphony after Beethoven*. After this, writing a symphony became a major undertaking. If the number of symphonies composed from 1750 to 1800 can be counted in the many thousands, those written from 1825 to 1875 can only be numbered in the dozens. Brahms said (admittedly prematurely), when he was a mature and famous composer aged 38, 'I shall never compose a symphony! You have no idea what a man such as I am feels like when he hears a giant like [Beethoven] marching behind him'. This was an extreme but not uncommon reaction to Beethoven's symphonies, which only the most insensitive composers could ignore.

Relics of the 18th-century concert symphony in the Viennese tradition are to be found in the earlier works of Schubert, whose first six symphonies were written before 1820 for amateur or unskilled orchestras. The 'entertainment' quality is based on Haydn and Mozart, though in the Sixth Symphony (1817–18) he brought it up to date to a certain extent by a knowledge of Rossini's overture style, which preferred tunes

instead of pregnant motifs for the thematic material. Three out of the six reverted to a minuet for the third movement, while the slow movements were in the hedonistic 'Andante' manner of the late 18th century. Schubert's final two symphonies, the Eighth ('Unfinished', 1822) and Ninth ('Great', ?1825–8), written in the full knowledge of Beethoven's Seventh, were more ambitious, using a larger orchestra very imaginatively. There was less concentration on sheer thematic development, the 18th-century 'passage-work' between themes now becoming 'orchestral effect'; the themes themselves are given fresh orchestral colourings (the development sections of the first movement of the 'Unfinished' with its *tremolando* strings, and the noble statements of one theme of the 'Great C major' by the trombones in its first movement are fine examples). The result might be described as 'anti-heroic', and it is a pity that these symphonies were not known at the time of their composition (being performed only in 1839 (Great C major) and 1865 (Unfinished)), since they might have released composers' inhibitions and inspired a new kind of pleasurable yet by no means unambitious symphony.

In the event, Beethoven provided the example for those who wanted to make some grand public statement. These may be divided into two groups: those who borrowed his techniques, and those who saw him as an inspiration to the spirit. The first group included the German conservatives Mendelssohn and Schumann. Mendelssohn wrote some youthful 18th-century-style symphonies (rather as sonata composers still composed sonatinas), but his later symphonies of the later 1820s and 1830s followed Beethoven's model, though without his power. The 'Reformation' (the Fifth Symphony, 1832) is a 'religious' piece, using the chorale 'Ein' feste Burg' in its finale; the Second Symphony, 'Lobegesang' (1840), contains a choral finale; the Third ('Scottish', 1842) and Fourth ('Italian', 1833) Symphonies are obvious offshoots of the tone-painting of Beethoven's 'Pastoral'. The basic trouble with all is that techniques evolved by Haydn and Beethoven to break away from entertainment music were here applied to works which do no more than charm. The romantic trait of short-windedness meant that thematic material more suited to a short 'characteristic' piece had to be moulded into sonata form—and the seams show. Even Mendelssohn's shortish first movements seem too long. Schumann, who revealed similar tendencies in his sonatas, coped more successfully in his symphonies. Here his principal preoccupation was with linking movements together (after the manner of Beethoven's Fifth). In this he succeeded very well in his Fourth Symphony (1841, rev. 1851), an ambitious piece in which virtually all the material is given out in the slow introduction and exposition of the first movement. As Gerald Abraham has pointed out, the Third Symphony, the 'Rhenish' (1850), is more like a suite than a symphony, with a scherzo which is an evocation of 'Morning on the Rhine' and a slow movement inspired by a ceremony in Cologne Cathedral.

But the real achievements of the 1830s and 1840s lay with those who emulated Beethoven's spirit. Of these, Berlioz was first on the scene. Paris was one of the cities where Beethoven's symphonies were efficiently performed from the 1820s, and Berlioz's *Symphonie fantastique* was composed in 1830, clearly inspired by their grandeur. This was not an organically conceived work: rather was it compiled from fragments of abortive operas and overtures. These achieve an acceptable unity only when Berlioz's programme (after de Quincey's opium dreams and the composer's contemporaneous love affair) is taken into account. The five-movement plan was modelled on Beethoven's 'Pastoral' and the linking of the movements with an *idée fixe* on his Fifth Symphony; the slow introduction to the first movement derived from the Seventh Symphony. None the less, the result is entirely un-Beethovenian, being nearer to opera or cantata than to the traditional symphony. Berlioz followed this up by *Harold en Italie* (1834), a kind of *symphonie concertante* with a solo part for viola, using the same programmatic links as before. In *Roméo et Juliette* (1839), a choral symphony with seven movements, it is possible to see a conventional orchestral work embedded among the choral movements; but again this was not really in the symphonic tradition, but was conceived more in terms of operatic scenes.

Berlioz's music was itself not well enough known to have any real influence on other composers: the programmatic idea, on the other hand, was a stimulating alternative to the abstract symphony. Spohr was one of the first to follow it up, with his Fourth Symphony, 'Die Weihe der Töne' (1832), an attempt at evoking the creation and development of the world. He wrote several other symphonies, among them his Sixth, the 'Historic' (1840), conveyed through various pastiches of Bach, Haydn, etc.; the Seventh, 'The Earthly and Divine Elements in Human Life' (1841), using a double orchestra, a large one for 'earth' and an ensemble of 11 solo instruments for the 'divine'; and the Ninth, 'Seasons', Symphony (1850) of more conventional imagery expressed in two contrasting movements. In the 1840s the concept of the programme was so strongly established that even a composer writing Classical-type instrumental symphonies, such as Berwald, gave them titles such as 'Sérieuse' (1842), 'Capricieuse' (1842), and 'Singulière' (1845). The giant who

really did succeed with the programme symphony was Liszt, whose *Faust-Symphonie* (1854-7), consisting of three movements depicting the main protagonists of the story (Faust, Marguerite, and Mephistopheles), used the technique of distorting the Faust themes to depict Mephistopheles, surely a traditional symphonic process: Liszt, however, applied it differently, and his technique of 'thematic metamorphosis' was to have a considerable influence on later composers. Beethoven's example was also perhaps in mind when Liszt added, three years after its original composition, a choral finale, using the material to express Goethe's idea of the 'Eternal Feminine'.

By this time, the ideas of Wagner, exiled and pamphleteering in Switzerland, were beginning to make headway among the progressives: he put forward the notion that the symphony was really an impossible genre after Beethoven's Ninth, and that the great music of the future lay in the music drama. Those who were happier out of the opera house chose the next best thing—the *symphonic poem—which was taken up in the 1850s and 1860s by composers who previously might have taken to symphonies. It was in 1860 that the manifesto of the young Brahms, under the influence of Clara Schumann, polarized views, resulting in the foundation of a deliberately conservative school, committed to traditional forms.

The symphony therefore came back into fashion in the period around 1870. Brahms was the finest, though not the most fecund, of the new symphonists. His four symphonies at first sight seem traditional works in four movements, the major differences from Beethoven being their gently melodious third movements which take the place of Beethoven's vigorous scherzos. Like Beethoven's, the last movements are the most difficult to categorize: the finale of the First Symphony (1855-76) has a slow introduction followed by a full-scale sonata movement which incorporates the material of the introduction (it was immediately compared with Beethoven's Ninth, but in fact is nearer to some of Haydn's late sonata-form movements in technique); in the Fourth Symphony (1884-5) the finale is a passacaglia (shades perhaps of the 'Eroica'). These last movements are all weighty, the slow movements profound in feeling (Adagio rather than Andante in attitude). If this, and Brahms's tendency to think in terms of thematic development, continued the Beethovenian line, it is also true that the Romantics had left their mark on Brahms's style. In the Second Symphony (1877) most of the themes in each movement are related in some way to the first bar of the symphony; in the Third (1883) the opening bars are brought back in the concluding pages to give a typically romantic nostalgic glow. Themes, even in Brahms's sonata-form movements, are lyrical rather than germinal, a tendency which can occasionally lead to contrived rather than natural bridge passages. The third movements are more in the manner of a Schumann *intermezzo* than of Beethoven. However, Brahms's symphonies were almost the last to be conceived as important public statements, not of politics or ideas but of the power of musical thinking, the ability of men to express and put into order intense feeling.

The other symphonist who emerged around 1870 was Bruckner. His symphonies are often said to be Wagnerian, but such influence is superficial, mainly confined to orchestral effects and an occasional thematic resemblance. Beethoven's Ninth is the more immediate model, Bruckner often starting with the same kind of theme and orchestral sound. He was not principally a thinker in thematic development; he bothered less about links between sections, frequently simply leaving a gap and abruptly beginning again. His orchestration owes something to the stop-changing techniques of the organ, something also to Austrian Catholic church music with its brass instruments supporting the choir.

The most interesting symphonies of the period were, in fact, being written by composers outside the Austrian-Viennese circle, though many of them had connections with it. Closest to this centre was Dvořák, whose symphonies are based on Classical procedures though the melodic material is more tuneful and less easy to develop, a fact disguised to some extent by the attractiveness of his orchestration; the scherzo movement is sometimes derived from a Czech folk dance. His greatest symphony, the Seventh in D minor (1884–5), was clearly modelled on Brahms's Third; his last one, 'From the New World' (1893), uses a kind of *idée fixe* to unite the work. Of all the nationalist composers, Dvořák showed that folk-like material could be moulded into symphonic forms. The result is not unlike Schubert in its blend of pleasurable melody and occasional dramatic effect, taking the place of close thematic argument.

Tchaikovsky was less affected by conservative Viennese ideals: his last three symphonies (Nos. 4–6) are guided by programmatic ideas, each being a highly personal expression of the inexorable power of Fate. It is often said that Tchaikovsky was not a real symphonist — he himself admitted that 'the seams show' — but thematic development is not the only criterion for success, and, judged by the standards of musical and emotional interest, the Fourth (1877–8) and Sixth (1893), by juxtaposing powerful themes projected in vivid orchestral colour, convey varied moods in a logical and convincing way. In this respect, they are more successful than Borodin's symphonies, though these are also highly attractive works, the themes transformed and combined in ways seemingly close to those of Liszt. And it was certainly Liszt's methods which were followed by those French composers of the 1880s who took to the Symphony: Saint-Saëns, whose Third Symphony (1886) with organ was dedicated to Liszt; d'Indy's attractive *Symphonie sur un chant montagnard français* (1886), with an *obbligato* part for piano which makes it almost a concerto; and especially Franck, whose chromatic symphony in D minor (1886–8) is the finest of 'theme transformation' symphonies. Another notable French symphony, written somewhat earlier (1855), was a student piece by Bizet, an almost 18th-century 'pleasure' symphony — on a Haydnesque scale yet showing a lightness of touch which is typical of Bizet and is not in the least archaic.

Symphonies continued to be composed in some number until the First World War. At the turn of the century, Mahler was the greatest composer involved (for a fuller discussion of his symphonies and aesthetic principles see the separate entry on Mahler). A song composer rather than a developer of themes, his First Symphony (completed 1888 and rev. 1893–6) was inspired by a novel of J. P. Richter (Schumann's favourite author) called *Titan*, and is really a series of scenes or impressions. His Second Symphony (1888–94, rev. 1903) is also programmatic, based on the 'Wunderhorn' songs and with a choral finale setting a 'moral' ode by Klopstock. And although for his middle symphonies (Nos. 5–9 excluding No. 8) he reverted to purely orchestral forces, they still seem subjective and programmatic, even when there is no programme. His idea that the symphony should 'be like the world — it must embrace everything' is exemplified at its most colossal in the Eighth Symphony (1906), which consists almost of two cantatas, one setting the 'Veni Creator Spiritus', the other the last scene from Goethe's *Faust*. It is possible to analyse such works from the point of view of the Classical symphony, with groups of themes taking the place of first and second subjects, and sections within a movement seen as scherzo, slow movement, and finale — but this approach is not very useful. They are grand public statements of belief and feeling which, unlike Beethoven's from which they ultimately derive, are not argued in musical terms.

Programme symphonies continued to be popular with composers brought up in the late 19th-century traditions. Skryabin's *Le poème de l'extase* (1905–8) and *Prométhée* (1908–10) belong to this category as much as Richard Strauss's *Symphonia domestica* (1902–3) and

Alpensinfonie (1911–15); while Vaughan Williams's *Sea Symphony* (1903–9, rev. 1923) belongs to the cantata-cum-symphony category, replacing Goethe and Klopstock with Whitman. But there were composers who saw that the non-programmatic symphony had not yet exhausted its possibilities. Of these, Elgar's two symphonies are rhapsodic, grandly orchestrated works, the First (1907–8) using Lisztian-type links between movements. Sibelius, after a First Symphony (1899) which followed the general attitudes of Tchaikovsky, turned to a style in which the development of small germinal themes was the guiding principle: they are emotionally taut, gradually progressing towards the ideal condition of a single, continuously argued movement (as in the Seventh Symphony of 1924).

5. *The Symphony from 1920.* Economic circumstances after the First World War made the Mahlerian symphony impractical (and it may be significant that Mahler's symphonies only achieved universal popularity when the resources of gramophone companies made their performances possible in the 1960s and 1970s). Nor was the mood of the times favourable to grand moral statements. The neo-classical composers naturally turned to earlier ideals. Stravinsky's *Symphonies of Wind Instruments* (1920) are nearer to the Baroque in approach than to Mozart; and although his later Symphony in C (1939–40) and Symphony in Three Movements (1942–5) do follow the sonata-form symphonic style, they give a distinct impression of irony—as does the Classical Symphony (1916–17) of Prokofiev.

The Romantic symphony carried on largely in circumstances where this new anti-emotional style arrived late, and especially where nationalism was still a force. In England Vaughan Williams's use of a lightly modalized tonal harmony allowed him to continue using quasi-Classical forms, as did Walton, whose First Symphony is a fine example of the adaptation of Sibelius's style. Bax, however, continued to write 'atmospheric' symphonies, which often sound as though they have a programmatic content, albeit of a not very precise nature. In America, this quasi-programmatic tradition is carried on, for instance in the symphonies of Ray Harris, who (besides writing abstract symphonies) based his Fourth (1941) on folksongs and his Sixth (1944) on Lincoln's Gettysburg Address, in the hope of inspiring an American musical consciousness. But in America, the arrival of the *émigré* composers from Europe, and the tendency of Americans to study with Nadia Boulanger in Paris, encouraged a return to Classical ideals and, in many cases, Classical methods.

The one country where the symphony has continued to be produced in quantity is the most nationalist, Russia, [and in the years since the 1917 October Revolution symphonic writing has acquired special significance in the general musical development of the Soviet Union. As the critic and composer Boris Asafyev once wrote, 'Soviet symphonism is our pride, for only in our great land has symphonic music not lost itself, . . . has not squandered itself . . . in eccentric experiments'. The term 'Soviet symphonism' is important, implying as it does that the symphony was now vested with the purpose of expressing the Soviet ideal. The heady subjectivism of Skryabin was to be left behind (though in the 1920s Skryabin was described as 'the supreme expression of musical Romanticism of the Revolution'), and symphonic music was to reflect aspects of Soviet life. To be sure, abstract symphonies were composed in the 1920s—the early symphonies of Myaskovsky, Shostakovich's First (1924–5), Prokofiev's Second (1924–5)—but at the same time programmatic content was being earnestly encouraged. Symphonies should 'mean' something; they should be topical; they should have something to say to contemporary Soviet society. These ideas gave birth to such works as the 'Agricultural' Symphony (1923) by Alexander Kastalsky (1856–1926), Kirillov's symphony *To Lenin: by his Graveside* (1924), the *Hymn to Labour* (1927) by Ippolitov-Ivanov, and the once well-known constructivist orchestral fragment *The Iron Foundry* (1926) by Alexander Mosolov (1900–73). More important, these notions of symphonic writing also spawned Shostakovich's Second ('October') Symphony of 1927 and Third ('1 May') Symphony of 1929, both conforming to the desirable pattern of having choral endings based on verses by Soviet poets.

With the onset of *socialist realism in the early 1930s, the symphony came under closer scrutiny, particularly during a three-day debate held at the Composers' Union in 1935, when composers discussed plans for the realization of a true Soviet symphonism. And the subsequent history of the Soviet symphony has to be seen against the background of these efforts. Readily accessible 'song' symphonies (generally with patriotic sentiments reinforced by vocal parts), symphonies dedicated to Lenin, symphonies using the national music of the Soviet republics – all became part of the quest for the key to Soviet symphonism, often applying the word 'symphony' extraordinarily loosely and carrying it well beyond its conventional meaning. Yet the greatest and most enduring works—Shostakovich's muscularly argued Fifth Symphony (1937) and Myaskovsky's Sixteenth (1935–6)—indicate that the concept of socialist realism need not be insular but instead could embrace less specific, more generalized themes: humanity, hope, heroism, and so on.

It was indeed the theme of heroism which imbued much of the symphonic writing of the war years, as in Shostakovich's Seventh ('Leningrad', 1941), Prokofiev's Fifth (1945), and Myaskovsky's 'war' symphonies (Nos. 22 and 23) composed in 1941 (the Twenty-second coloured with traits of Caucasian folk music which Myaskovsky heard while evacuated to the south). But some of the searching, pessimistic works composed at the height of the war (notably Shostakovich's Eighth of 1943) and some others composed just when war had been concluded (Shostakovich's Ninth, 1945; Prokofiev's Sixth, 1945–7) attracted severe criticism during the Zhdanov purges of 1948, as did such attempted celebratory works as Khachaturian's Third (1947), written for the 30th anniversary of the Revolution. The nature of the Soviet symphony again had to be rethought. After Stalin's death (1953) and after the première of Shostakovich's Tenth Symphony in the autumn of that year, there was a further Composers' Union debate (1954), when the Tenth Symphony was volubly discussed, some objecting to its pessimism, others acknowledging that the Soviet composer ought now to be guided by his own artistic instincts. In the aftermath, the symphonic tradition has been upheld, explored, and widened by such composers as Kara Karayev (b 1919), Moysey Vaynberg (b 1919), Eduard Mirzoyan (b 1921), Andrey Eshpay (b 1925), Boris Tchaikovsky (b 1925), Alexey Nikolayev (b 1931), Rodion Shchedrin (b 1932), Sergey Slonimsky (b 1932), and Boris Tishchenko (b 1939), among others. Moreover, many of their works have been widely praised within the Soviet Union, but it remained for Shostakovich himself to place the Soviet symphony before a permanent international audience. Following the abstract Tenth Symphony, he again reverted to programmatic writing for the Eleventh ('The Year 1905', 1957), Twelfth ('The Year 1917', 1961), and Thirteenth ('Baby Yar', 1962), before attaching the term 'symphony' to his most unconventional piece, the Fourteenth Symphony (1969), a bleak song-cycle which strenuously works the themes of death which so preoccupied him in his last years. It is perhaps Shostakovich's symphonies which most powerfully reveal that, though conceived in the Soviet tradition, the Soviet symphony can, in the hands of a composer of humanity, depth of feeling, and breadth of experience, transcend national boundaries and exercise a profound impact on a wide general public.]

6. *Conclusion* Works called 'symphony' continue to be written, by Tippett, Peter Maxwell Davies, Henze, and others, but it is difficult to find a common link between them. Perhaps the meaning of the term has reverted to its 16th-century vagueness. In this it is unlike the concerto, which embodies a distinctive principle still much valued by composers. Whether the genre, therefore, has a real future must remain uncertain. Of its great past there is no doubt; nor can it be doubted that, by offering composers the chance to speak in a large-scale, public form, it surely changed the course of Western music.   DENIS ARNOLD

FURTHER READING
Donald Tovey: *Essays in Musical Analysis* (London, 1935, reprinted 1982); Adam Carse: *18th Century Symphonists: a Short History* (London, 1951); Jan LaRue: 'Major and Minor Mysteries of Identification in the 18th-century Symphony', *Journal of the American Musicological Society*, xiii (1960); Barry S. Brook: *La symphonie française dans la seconde moitié du XVIIIe siècle* (Paris, 1962); Robert Simpson, ed.: *The Symphony*, 2 vols (Harmondsworth, 1966–7); Gerald Abraham: 'Some Eighteenth-century Polish Symphonies', *Studies in Eighteenth-century Music: a Tribute to Karl Geiringer* (New York and London, 1970); Louise Cuyler: *The Symphony* (New York, 1973).

Symphony in Three Movements. Orchestral work by Stravinsky, composed 1942–5 and first performed in 1946. The first movement incorporates Stravinsky's sketches for an unfinished piano concerto, the second includes some abortive film music, and the third is a response to wartime newsreels.

'Symphony of a Thousand'. Nickname of Mahler's Symphony No. 8 in E♭ major (1906). It became known, somewhat misleadingly, by this name because of the huge vocal and orchestral forces required to perform it. More than 1,000 people took part in the first performance (at Munich in 1910) but it is not necessary to use so many performers and Mahler did not approve of the symphony's nickname.

Symphony of Psalms. Work for chorus and orchestra by Stravinsky to a Latin text from Psalms 38, 39, and 150. It is in three movements and was first performed in Brussels in 1930.

Syncopation. The displacement of the normal musical accent from a strong beat to a weak one. In mensural music beats fall naturally into groups of two or three with a recurring accent on the first of each group. Any irregularity, either brief or extended, introduced into this pattern, which has the effect of rhythmic contradiction may be termed syncopation.

Some common methods of creating syncopation are shown in Ex. 1. In Ex. 1a notes on

Ex. 1

(a)

Beethoven: Symphony No. 6, 3rd movement

(b)

Haydn: String Quartet, Op. 74 No. 3, finale

(c)

Mozart: Symphony No. 38, finale

(d)

Brahms: Variations and Fugue on a Theme of Handel, Var. 1

normally weak beats are held over to normally strong ones, effectively shifting the accent; in Ex. 1*b* rests have displaced the notes from strong beats to weak ones; in Ex. 1*c* notes are placed between beats and are held over each beat; and in Ex. 1*d* stresses are marked on the weak beats. Two or more of these methods may be used in combination.

Syncopation commonly occurs in only one part or voice (or a small group of parts) at one time, while the other parts adhere to normal accentuation. Some composers however, notably Beethoven, Brahms, and Schumann, have used syncopation in all the parts over extended passages to create a restless effect, which in extreme cases may also result in the listener's rhythmic disorientation (Ex. 2).

Syncopation in various forms is a common device in all periods of Western music, from the 13th century to modern times. It is also a characteristic feature of some non-Western musics, particularly African and Black American, hence its importance to ragtime, jazz, and other popular music cultures.

See also *Cross accent*; *Rhythm*, 1.

PERCY SCHOLES, rev. Judith Nagley

Synnet. See *Sennet*.

Synthesizer. The term 'synthesizer' may be

Ex. 2

Beethoven: String Quartet, Op. 135, 2nd movement

used to describe any grouping of electronic devices for the purposes of sound synthesis. It is more usual, however, to reserve this label for complete systems of an integral construction, purpose-built by a single manufacturer. The early electronic music studios of the 1950s were assembled from individual items of equipment, in many instances originally designed for quite different applications such as circuit-testing in the laboratory. Each of these devices had to be adjusted by hand, placing a considerable onus on the practical skills of the composer. The production of complex sound material usually demanded several stages of preparation, building up layers of recordings from simple components. The search for more efficient methods of working led in due course to the introduction of improved facilities for the control of the various functions.

In 1956 the RCA Victor company presented a specially designed synthesizer to the public. This consisted of a bank of tone generators, capable of producing an eight-octave range of tempered pitches, and an array of processing devices to shape and modify the nature of the sound material thus produced. The synthesizer was controlled by a row of brush sensors and an associated decoding system, responding to patterns of holes pre-punched in a moving roll of paper. The composer was thus able to programme his requirements in advance. A second, improved version of the RCA synthesizer was installed at the Columbia-Princeton

Electronic Music Center, New York, in 1959, and provided a major stimulus not only for composers but also for electronic designers, who were quick to appreciate the commercial potential of electronic music facilities.

The RCA synthesizers were both very large machines based on valve technology. The key to more compact machines with a marketing potential was provided by the transistor, which opened up a new world of microtechnology towards the end of the 1950s. Two Americans, Robert Moog and Donald Buchla, formed separate companies for the manufacture of synthesizers in 1966, and others quickly followed suit: for example the American firm Tonus, which produced the ARP range of synthesizers, and EMS London, which was founded by Peter Zinovieff. These systems, commonly known as voltage-controlled synthesizers, are modular in design and usually portable, allowing their use both as studio facilities for the production of works on tape and also as live performance instruments. Each of the constituent devices may be operated directly by hand in the manner of their antecedents, or indirectly via a range of performance aids such as keyboards or joysticks. The latter facilities generate control voltages which may be routed to one or a number of devices, allowing several characteristics to be altered simultaneously. In addition, the devices themselves may be connected to interact with each other, in the case of tone generators providing a rich source of timbres. Most syn-

The RCA synthesizer. It is shown here in operation at the David Sarnoff Research Centre of RCA Laboratories in Princeton, NJ.

Keith Emerson playing a Moog synthesizer.

thesizers are designed to offer a wide range of sound production facilities suitable for many different applications. A few have been specifically engineered to generate a particular family of sounds, for example the keyboard-operated string synthesizer, which will produce realistic imitations of the violin family (see *Electronic Musical Instruments*).

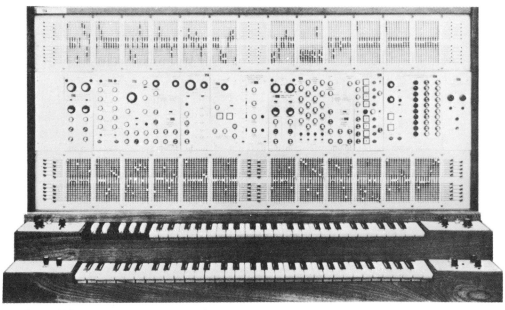

The Tonus ARP 2000 synthesizer, featuring the matrix switch patching system and two control keyboards.

The operation of these synthesizers has been further enhanced by the addition of sequencers. These units generate voltage patterns which may be used to control devices in a manner similar in effect to that described for the RCA synthesizers. A number of different methods of specifying these patterns are used, depending on the design. Some versions require the voltage steps to be set via an array of knobs or sliders. Others, known as memory sequencers, register the voltages generated by a control device within the synthesizer, for example a keyboard. Simple sequencers generate single voltage patterns of a relatively short duration. More elaborate designs allow several different patterns of a significant length to be generated simultaneously, allowing individual control of a number of functions. One pattern may control the pitch of a sound, for example, while another controls its amplitude.

The continuing advance of microtechnology during the 1970s led to a more sophisticated method of device control in the form of the microcomputer. The calculative and logical capabilities of this facility allow the use of powerful programs of instructions instead of step by step voltage values. Further developments towards the end of the decade have led to the construction of synthesizers which employ digital techniques not only for the preparation of control information but also for the synthesis of the sounds themselves.

See also *Computer*.   PETER MANNING

Syrinx. Work by Debussy for solo flute, composed in 1913 for Louis Fleury.

System. In musical notation, two or more staves bracketed together on the left, indicating that the music on them is to be played or sung at the same time.

Szymanowski, Karol (Maciej) (*b* Tymoszówka, Ukraine, 6 Oct. 1882; *d* Lausanne, 28 Mar. 1937). Polish composer. He had piano lessons from childhood and studied composition with Noskowski (1901–5). In 1901, together with several other emerging Polish musicians, he founded the Young Poland movement with the aim of bringing Polish music into the international arena. Brahms, Strauss, and Reger were the main influences on such ambitious works as the Second Symphony (1909–10) and the Second Piano Sonata (1910–11), both composed during a period when he was spending much of his time in Berlin and Vienna.

In 1915 there came a change, marked by the *Métopes* for piano, the *Mythes* for violin and piano, and the *Songs of a Fairy-Tale Princess*. All these works suggest the influences of Debussy and Ravel, but more particularly that of

Szymanowski

late Skryabin: tonality is obscured by extreme chromaticism, and the piano writing is highly ornate. Equally characteristic is the exotic subject-matter, classical in the instrumental pieces, eastern in the songs and again in the Third Symphony, 'Song in the Night', for tenor, chorus, and orchestra (1914–16). The voluptuous orchestral manner developed for this work was also put to effect in the opera *King Roger* (1924), which sets the story of Euripides' *Bacchae* in the Byzantine court of 12th-century Sicily.

Most of these 'impressionist' works had been written at Szymanowski's family home in the Ukraine. When he returned to Poland in 1920 he found that the newly independent country required a simpler and specifically national music, and so he began to draw on folk sources in such works as the ballet *Harnasie* (1923–31), the *Stabat mater* for soloists, chorus, and orchestra (1925–6) and various smaller works. Stravinsky's use of Russian material was the model here, to be followed by Bartók in the big abstract works of Szymanowski's last few years: the Second Quartet (1927), the *Symphonie concertante* for piano and orchestra (1932), and the Second Violin Concerto (1932–3).

                              PAUL GRIFFITHS

FURTHER READING
B. M. Maciejewski: *Karol Szymanowsky* (London, 1967); Jim Samson: *The Music of Szymanowski* (London, 1980); Christopher Palmer: *Szymanowski*, BBC Music Guides (London, 1983).

T

T. Abbreviation for *tenor (e.g. SATB: soprano, alto, tenor, bass).

Tabarro, Il ('The Cloak'). Opera in one act by Puccini; text by Adami, after Didier Gold's Tragedy *La houppelande* (1910). The first part of Puccini's *Il trittico*. Produced: New York, Metropolitan Opera, 14 December 1918; Rome, Teatro Costanzi, 11 January 1919; London, Covent Garden, 18 June 1920. The Seine bargee Michele (bar.) suspects his wife Giorgetta (sop.) is unfaithful, but tries to win her back by reminding her of how she used to shelter under his cloak. She has arranged a meeting with her lover, the bargehand Luigi (ten.), who mistakes Michele's lighting of his pipe for the signal that the coast is clear. Michele kills him and covers the body with his cloak. When Giorgetta appears, Michele tells her to come under the cloak again; then he reveals Luigi's body and flings her down on top of her dead lover.

Tablā. A type of drum found in North India. See *Indian Music, 3c*.

Tablature (Fr.: *tablature*; Ger.: *Tabulatur*; It.: *intavolatura*). Musical notation based on figures, letters, and/or graphic symbols used in tabular form instead of, or in addition to, conventional staff notation. Most tablatures are used for chordal or part-music and are based on the playing technique of a particular type of instrument, using one set of symbols showing pitch (which fret to stop, which key to depress, or which hole to cover) and another indicating rhythm.

1. *Lute, Vihuela, Guitar, etc.* Grid systems for fretted strings emerged in the late 15th century, using the intersection of fret and string (or course) to indicate specific notes. One of the earliest of these, a system for five-course lute, appears in Virdung's *Musica getutscht* (Basle, 1511), where it is ascribed to the blind musician Conrad Paumann. In rising order, it uses numbers (1–5) to represent the courses, and letters to show the frets, with a b c d e for the first fret of each course, f g h i k for the second, etc.; double letters indicate the upper frets. (See Pl. 1.) This system was later adapted for the six-course lute in a variety of ways.

Simpler and more successful lute tablatures based on a visual representation of the finger-board were introduced in Italy and France. The Italian system showed each course as a horizontal line, the highest line representing the lowest-pitched string. Numbers (1–9) represented the frets, and o indicated an open string. Flagged stems above the numbers showed the duration of the notes; they were repeated for each note in early sources published by Petrucci (see Pl. 2), but later full staff notes were used for the first note of a group, the duration remaining valid until contradicted by another sign. The French system used a five- or six-line grid, the top line (or the space above it) representing the highest string or course, with letters indicating the frets (a for open string, b for first fret, etc.). The signs for the duration of the notes followed the same pattern as the Italian system. Diapasons (extra low courses) were indicated by letters or numbers—below the grid in the French system, above in the Italian.

English sources generally followed the French

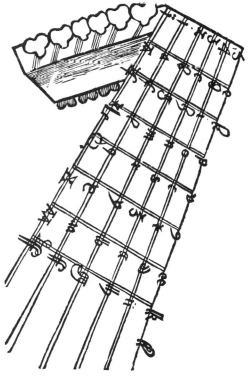

Pl. 1. Grid system for five-course lute, from Virdung's 'Musica getutscht' (1511).

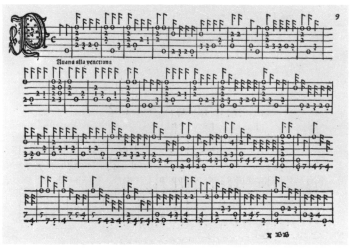

Pl. 2. 'Pavana alla Venetiana' from Dalza's 'Intabulatura de lauto', libro quarto (Petrucci, Venice, 1508).

system (see Pl. 3), some later examples indicating a seventh string tuned a fourth lower in the space below a six-line grid. The Italian system was occasionally used in Germany, Poland, and, for the vihuela, Spain. Luis Milán's vihuela book *El maestro* (Valencia, 1536) was exceptional in that it used numbers, as in the Italian system, with the French grid (highest line for the highest string).

French lute tablature was modified in the 17th century when the new tuning (*nouveau ton*: *A–d–f–a′–d′–f′*) was introduced by Denis Gaultier (*c*.1650). Reduced variants of the French or Italian systems were used for the four- or five-course cittern, gittern, and guitar. A new scheme, introduced in J. C. Amat's *Guitara española* (Barcelona, 1586), indicated the most common left-hand positions for chords by numbers, and a shorthand system (*alphabeto*) for *rasgueado* ('strumming') appeared in G. Montesardo's *Nuova inventione d'intavolatura* (Florence, 1606), with the most common chords

being shown by letters above or below a horizontal line, according to whether the chord was to be strummed upwards or downwards. Later 17th-century guitarists improved and modified the system, and some, like Foscarini and Corbetta, combined it with conventional tablature.

Other plucked instruments (e.g. chitarrone, mandolin, orpharion, theorbo) used reduced or expanded versions of French or Italian lute tablature. Bowed instruments, such as the lyra viol, lirone, and baryton, often used modified French lute tablature in the Baroque period; some viol and early violin music used an Italian or German lute system. Other numerical systems were later employed for accordion, autoharp, balalaika, guitar, and zither, and ukulele tablature (sometimes adapted for the guitar) uses dots to mark the left-hand finger positions on an intersecting grid of vertical and horizontal lines, representing strings and frets respectively.

2. *Keyboard.* In the early 14th century a com-

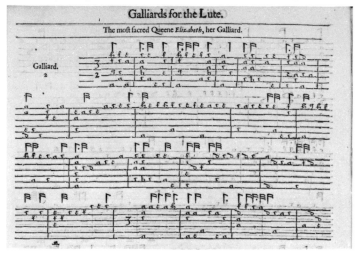

Pl. 3. 'The most sacred Queen Elizabeth, her Galliard' by John Dowland, from 'Varietie of Lute-Lessons' edited by Robert Dowland (1610).

Pl. 4. Anon.: keyboard Estampie (c.1325) from the Roberts-bridge Codex.

bination of tablature and staff notation is found for keyboard music, for example in the Robertsbridge Codex (see Pl. 4), which has the top part notated on a five-line staff and the lower parts aligned below in letter notation, with rests indicated by the letter 's' (for Lat. *sine*, 'without'); sharps are indicated by a wavy line after the letter. This system was used in a developed form in 15th- and 16th-century German sources, including Conrad Paumann's *Fundamentum organisandi* (1452). The top part was notated on a staff of six, seven, or eight lines, and the lower parts were shown by rows of letters—lower case (a, b, etc.), doubled (aa) or with dashes placed above (ā), and capital (A), according to pitch (middle, high, and low octaves, respectively). Rhythm signs were placed above each letter and rests were indicated by their staff notation equivalents.

In the later 16th century letter notation was introduced for all parts, and the rhythm signs,

which had hitherto tended to vary from source to source, became standardized (| = ◦ , ⌐ = ↓ , ⌐ = ↓ , etc.; for the names of these notes and their modern equivalents, see *Notation*, Fig. 8). This 'new' German keyboard tablature was introduced in publications by Nikolaus Ammerbach and his contemporaries, and was still used, as a means of saving space, by J. S. Bach in the *Orgel-Büchlein*. Scheidt's so-called *Tabulatura nova* (1624) was new to Germany in that it adopted the Italian *partitura* system, each part using a five-line staff. Open score systems were used in Italy from the early 16th century, while French and Italian keyboard sources tended to use short scores with staves of from five to eight lines.

Spanish keyboard music of the 16th century developed different forms of tablature, with a horizontal line representing each part and numbers indicating the notes. These systems had the advantage of being cheaper to print than

Pl. 5. 'Susana un jur' from Cabezón's 'Obras de musica' (1578).

those employing staves, but could not easily accommodate rhythmically complicated music.

Juan Bermudo's *Declaración de instrumentos musicales* (Ossuna, 1555) introduced the first two of these numerical schemes. One used numbers (1–42) to represent the keys, beginning with the diatonic notes of a short octave (CFDGEA) and then proceeding chromatically. The other used numbers (1–23) for the white keys, with a cross above the number to indicate a sharp. In the second scheme, the single horizontal line did not represent an individual part, but separated left and right hands. In the first system rhythm was represented simply by the position of the number within the bar; in the second, flagged stems were shown above the figures, remaining valid until contradicted by another sign.

A more successful scheme for Spanish keyboard (or harp or vihuela) tablature was that introduced in Venegas de Henestrosa's *Libro de cifra nueva* (Alcalá, 1557) and used in Cabezón's *Obras de musica* (Madrid, 1578) (see Pl. 5), among other sources. Again, each part was allocated a single horizontal line, on which the numbers 1 to 7 represented the notes *f* to *e'* (a key signature would be given at the beginning of the work to indicate whether 4 represented B♭ or B♮); sharps (and B♮, where appropriate) were shown by a cross, and flats by a rounded 'b' sign. One or two dashes through the number indicated the lower octaves, superscript dots or commas the upper octaves. Derivations of this

system survived for psaltery and dulcimer music in Spain until the mid 18th century.

3. *Wind Instruments.* Diagrams relating fingering to notes have occasionally been used for such wind instruments as the recorder, flageolet, oboe, and clarinet in instrumental Tutors since the 16th century. 'Dot way' notation, used in the 17th and 18th centuries for English flageolet music, had dashes on a six-line staff to show the fingerholes, with the durations indicated above as in lute tablature.   FRANK DOBBINS

FURTHER READING
Johannes Wolf: *Handbuch der Notationskunde*, ii (Leipzig, 1919); Willi Apel: *The Notation of Polyphonic Music, 900–1600* (Cambridge, Massachusetts, 1942, rev. edn 1961).

Table (of bowed instruments). See *Belly*.

Tacet (Lat.). 'Is silent', used in the imperative sense to direct a player to remain silent; *tacet al fine*, the player is silent, i.e. has no part, until the end of the piece or movement.

Tactus (Lat.). A 15th- and 16th-century term for 'beat'.

Taeggio, Francesco Rognoni (*d* c.1626). Italian composer and theorist. He was in the service of the Polish court in his youth, later living in Milan as director of the instrumental music to the city's governor and *maestro di cappella* at S. Ambrogio. His important treatise on ornamentation, the *Selva di varii passaggi* (Milan, 1620), contains interesting information on the bowing of stringed instruments. He composed church and instrumental music.

DENIS ARNOLD

Tagelied (Ger.). 'Day song'. See *Alba*.

Taglioni, Filippo (*b* Milan, 5 Nov. 1777; *d* Como, 11 Feb. 1871). Italian choreographer, the father of Marie Taglioni, whom he schooled to become the new type of Romantic ballerina; he created for her the first version of *La sylphide* (Schneitzhoeffer, 1832). This followed her appearance in his ballet of the spectral nuns in Meyerbeer's opera *Robert le diable* (Paris, 1831), which virtually initiated the Romantic style of ballet.

NOËL GOODWIN

Taille. 1. French term used from the 16th century to the 18th to denote the part that other languages call 'tenor'; hence 'taille de violons' for the viola, 'taille d'hautbois' for the tenor shawm or, from 1660, the tenor oboe, etc.

2. The term was taken over by German musicians of the Baroque along with other French terms and 'Taille' occurs as the heading for a part for tenor oboe in five of Bach's cantatas; these parts are now usually played on the cor anglais (see *Oboe*, 8).

Tailleferre, Germaine (*b* Parc-St-Maur, Seine, 19 Apr. 1892). French composer. She studied at the Paris Conservatoire and with Ravel. Though she was a member of Les *Six, her adherence to the iconoclastic ideals of the group was short-lived, and she emerged as a composer of graceful music very much in the French tradition. Her output includes operas, many film scores, and concertos for unusual combinations, including one for baritone, piano, and orchestra. She has also been active as a pianist and teacher.

PAUL GRIFFITHS

Takahashi, Yuji (*b* Tokyo, 21 Sept. 1938). Japanese composer and pianist. He studied with Minao Shibata and Roh Ogura at the Toho School of Music (1954–8) and privately with Xenakis. A brilliant interpreter of the most demanding modern piano scores, he has composed a few works under the influence of Xenakis's *stochastic methods.

PAUL GRIFFITHS

Takemitsu, Tōru (*b* Tokyo, 8 Oct. 1930). Japanese composer. He studied with Yasuji Kiyose (1948–50) but is essentially self-taught in composition. Influenced by a number of 20th-century European composers (Schoenberg, Messiaen, Webern, Boulez) he has developed a style of fragile sound poetry sug-

gesting a specifically Japanese sensibility. His works, mostly instrumental or electronic, include *November Steps* for two Japanese instruments and orchestra (1967), but in most cases he has used only western media.

PAUL GRIFFITHS

Takt (Ger.). The word has three basic meanings. 1. 'Time', or 'metre'; *Taktzeichen*, 'time signature'; *3/4 Takt*, '3/4 time'; *im Takt*, 'in time' (i.e. *a tempo*); *Taktfest*, 'in steady time'.

2. 'Beat'; *ein Takt wie vorher zwei*, 'one beat as previously two' (i.e. one beat should be allowed as much time as two beats were previously).

3. 'Bar'; *Taktnote* (literally 'bar-note'), the semibreve; *Taktpause*, a bar's rest; *Taktstrich*, 'bar-line'; *dreitaktig*, literally 'three bar-ish', i.e. in three-bar phrases.

Tāla. Generic name for a system of Indian rhythmic patterns. See *Indian Music*, 7.

Talbot, James (*b* London, 1665; *d* Cambridge, 1708). Regius Professor of Hebrew at Cambridge University and of major importance in musical instrument history for his recording of the particulars (notably measurements) of instruments of all kinds as used by musicians in London during his time. They are contained in his manuscript preserved in Christ Church Library, Oxford, Music MS 1187 (written *c*.1695). For many instruments Talbot's are the first known detailed particulars since Mersenne (1636), and they have continually been cited since their publication in the *Galpin Society Journal*, 1948–68 *passim*.

ANTHONY BAINES

Tales from the Vienna Woods (*Geschichten aus dem Wienerwald*). Waltz, Op. 325, by Johann Strauss II, composed in 1868.

Tales of Hoffmann. See *Contes d'Hoffmann, Les*.

Tallis, Thomas (*b c*.1505; *d* Greenwich, 23 Nov. 1585). English composer. His first known employment was as an organist in Dover in 1532. By 1537 he was in London, but the following year he went to Waltham Abbey in Essex. On the dissolution of the abbey in 1540 Tallis became a lay clerk at Canterbury Cathedral until 1543, when he was appointed a Gentleman of the Chapel Royal. He remained in the royal service for the rest of his life, receiving from Queen Mary in 1557 a 21-year lease on the manor of Minster, Isle of Thanet, which he held jointly with the Master of the Children. In 1575 he and Byrd were granted a monopoly in music printing and later that year they produced the volume of Latin motets called *Cantiones sacrae*. The venture was not successful financially,

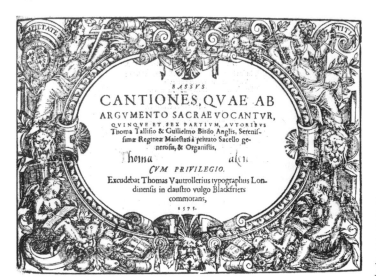

Title-page of 'Cantiones quae ab argumento sacrae vocantur' (1575), the first publication by William Byrd and Thomas Tallis after they received a 25-year music printing monopoly from Queen Elizabeth.

however, and Elizabeth granted them a further lease worth £30 to replace the expected income from it in 1577. Tallis married c.1552 but seems to have had no children. He is buried in the parish church of St Alphege, Greenwich.

Tallis was brought up in the Catholic tradition, and his earlier music includes several Latin liturgical settings, often on a grand scale and evidently intended for major church festivals. One of his larger works, the Mass *Puer natus est nobis*, may have been written on the occasion of the marriage of Mary to Philip of Spain in 1554. After the accession of Elizabeth he continued to set Latin texts, but in a more restrained style, showing the influence of the syllabic settings required by the Anglican church. For the Anglican church Tallis composed some excellent English anthems, not only for Elizabeth but also previously, under Edward VI. His masterpieces are settings of the Lamentations of Jeremiah—dark-hued, harmonically rich, and extraordinarily emotional works which can compare with the finest music ever written for Holy Week. Little of Tallis's organ music survives, but the *Mulliner Book* does contain some of his keyboard works, as well as some arrangements of part-songs by him.

DENIS ARNOLD

FURTHER READING
Paul Doe: *Tallis* (London, 1968, 2nd edn 1976).

Tallis's Canon. The eighth of nine tunes composed for Archbishop Parker's *The Whole Psalter translated into English Metre* (1567). The canon is formed by the tenor and treble voices, originally with the tenor leading (all the tunes for the psalter were placed in the tenor part), but now frequently given with the treble leading. It was originally attached to the 67th Psalm, but since the early 18th century has been

associated with Bishop Ken's evening hymn for the Winchester College boys, 'Glory to Thee, my God, this night' (1692). Most of the tunes in the psalter are in current use as hymn-tunes, and the third of Tallis's was made famous by Vaughan Williams in his *Fantasia on a Theme by Thomas Tallis*.

Talon (Fr.). 'Heel', i.e. the nut of the violin bow; *au talon*, 'at the heel' (a direction in violin bowing).

Tamboritsa. See *Lute*, 4a.

Tambour (Fr.). 'Drum'.

Tambourin (Fr.). An old Provençal dance, in lively duple time and accompanied by pipe (*galoubet*) and tabor. In the 18th century, French composers often wrote tambourins, imitating the regular drum beats by throbbing bass notes, usually on the tonic and dominant. Rameau was particularly fond of the dance, which he used in his operas and ballets: there is a famous example in *Les fêtes d'Hébé* which also appears in the second of his harpsichord books.

Tambourine (Fr.: *tambour de Basque*; Ger.: *Tamburin*, *Schellentrommel*; It.: *tamburino* or, in popular language, *cembalo*; Sp.: *pandereta*). A shallow drum with pairs of thin metal jingle plates mounted in slots in a wooden hoop, leaving a space for one hand to hold the hoop. The tambour, as sold today (a name borrowed from the French word for 'drum'), is a similar instrument, but without the jingles and made chiefly for educational music. (For the form which, on the contrary, has the jingles but no drumskin, see *Sistrum and Jingles*, 3.)

1. *Construction and Playing Technique.* The single head, vellum or plastic, is normally nailed or glued to the hoop; screw-tensioning, though some models have this, makes the instrument heavy and also can obstruct some of the playing techniques. (The nailed head, if too slack, may be tightened by wetting and leaving to dry.) The average diameter for an orchestral tambourine is 10″, though many sizes are available.

Fig. 1. (a) tambourine; (b) tambour

The natural or 'folk' way of playing the tambourine, as in the popular music of Italy and Spain, is to hold it up in one hand and strike it with the other, shaking it between-times. When introduced in the orchestra for 'local colour' this manner of playing is sometimes indicated with a single note followed or preceded by a trill or *tremolo* sign. When struck with the hand (or on the knee for a strong abrupt sound) all three components of the instrument contribute to the sound—wood, membrane, and jingles. For soft, delicate rhythms played with the fingers the tambourine may be held horizontally; the jingles then gently colour the sound. A roll in which the jingles contribute most of the sound is achieved either by shaking, or by rubbing the moistened thumb round the edge of the membrane, the friction causing vibration which produces a hissing sound from the jingles. Since with this last method the thumb must soon come to a stop, a roll cannot last for more than perhaps eight seconds even in *pianissimo*, when the thumb moves at slowest speed. Among many unusual effects the most celebrated must be Stravinsky's where Petrushka expires to the tambourine dropped from a small height on to the floor (or a cushion).

2. *History.* In *instrument classification both

tambourine and tambour come under the designation 'frame drum'. The only drum in common use throughout Western Antiquity (Lat.: *tympanum*) was of such kind, normally without jingle plates (like the tambour); many historians think that it had, or generally had, a skin on both sides (and perhaps rattling objects inside) —a point very hard to determine from representations in art, no complete actual *tympanum* having survived. Mostly the drum was played by women on festive occasions—thus in the Old Testament ('timbrel', Hebrew *toph*) by Miriam the sister of Aaron (Exodus 15: 20), and by Jephthah's daughter (Judges 11: 34). In the rural Middle East women still wave and play tambourines in processions of all kinds, but men play it extensively too, especially in ensemble music (see *Psaltery*, 3). The instrument is generally made by sieve-makers, but there are also square kinds, always with two skins: in Portugal country-women make them of four small softwood slats 2″ wide joined by cross-wires, and stitch the skins over these, without forgetting to put rattling beans inside. They play deft rhythms using the fingers of both hands.

Jingle plates appear in Medieval Islamic art (five pairs) and in 13th-century Europe; often the skin is seen to be traversed by a snare. The instrument was played in popular dancing—in England, for folk dances up to the 20th century in some parts of Sussex. For the upper classes some very beautiful 18th-century French tambourines exist, made for ladies, some quite large, 18″ across, with scenes painted on the skin. Tambourines manufactured for the military *Turkish music from around 1790 are heavier instruments, tensioned with iron screws. A London firm's price-list of 1839

Pl. 1. Square tambourine (adufe), Portugal.

Pl. 2. Irish bodhran.

(D'Almaine & Co.) lists 12″ to 16″ tambourines for each of the categories mentioned—'common', 'ladies best', and (the most expensive) 'military'.

3. *Bodhran* (pronounced 'borán'). Irish frame drum, some 2′ in diameter, with a single skin, and sticks or ropes across the interior for grasping with one hand. The other hand, back to the skin, holds the stick ('pin'), striking alternately with the knob at each end, making a deep sound traditionally used in 'hunting the wren' customs, but now in folk music generally.

ANTHONY BAINES

Tambūrā. A plucked string instrument of India. See *Indian Music*, 3a.

Tam-tam. See *Gong and Tam-tam*.

Tancredi. Opera ('melodramma eroico') in two acts by Rossini to a libretto by Rossi after Tasso's *Gerusalemme liberata* (1575) and Voltaire's *Tancrède* (1760). It was first performed in Venice in 1813.

Tändeln (Ger.). 'Dally', 'trifle', 'dawdle'.

Taneyev, Sergey (Ivanovich) (*b* Vladimir-na-Klyazme, 25 Nov. 1856; *d* Dyudkovo, 111 Moscow, 19 June 1915). Russian composer. At the Moscow Conservatory he studied piano with Nikolay Rubinstein and composition with Tchaikovsky, and with the latter formed a lasting and fruitful friendship: in fact Taneyev played the solo parts in the premières of all Tchaikovsky's works for piano and orchestra. After Tchaikovsky's resignation from the conservatory, Taneyev joined the staff to teach harmony and orchestration (1878); after Rubinstein's death he took over the piano class (1881), then taught composition (1883), and finally was appointed director (1885). Taneyev wrote four symphonies, marked more by rigorous craftsmanship and cogency than by melodic charm, though the finale of the Second Symphony (1877–8) has spontaneity and lyrical warmth. He also composed six string quartets, a Piano Quintet (1906), a Piano Trio (1907), various other chamber works, choral music, many songs, and some piano music. His most ambitious work, however, was the remarkable 'trilogy' (in fact a three-act opera) *Oresteia*, composed 1887–94 and performed in 1895. In view of Taneyev's reputation as an academic and theorist—he wrote important books on invertible counterpoint (1909) and on canon (published posthumously in 1929)—we have perhaps tended to think of Taneyev as a pedant, forever busying himself with problems of counterpoint. But this feeling is immediately dispelled by *Oresteia*. As Rimsky-Korsakov remarked in his autobiography, Taneyev's obsession with fugues, canons, and other contrapuntal devices 'ought to have resulted in a dry and academic work, lacking even a vestige of inspiration, but in the case of *Oresteia* it proved to be the opposite . . . the opera was striking in its wealth of beauty and expressiveness'. The score is also one of great originality, not only in its choice (unusual in 19th-century Russian opera) of a non-Russian subject (Aeschylus' tragedy) but also in the musical treatment of it. To be sure there are occasional (and understandable) echoes of Tchaikovsky, but for the most part the music has an individual voice and shows genuine dramatic skill.

GEOFFREY NORRIS

Tanglewood. See *Berkshire Music Festival*.

Tango. A Latin American dance in duple metre which resembles the *habanera. It has a characteristic repeated rhythmic figure (♫♪♫) in the accompaniment, and consists of two sections of equal length, the second usually in the dominant or relative minor. It is danced by couples. There is a stylized tango in Stravinsky's *L'histoire du soldat*, and the dance has found its way into works by English composers, including Walton ('Tango-Pasodoble' in *Façade*). The dance was very popular in Argentina in the early 20th century.

Tannhäuser (properly, *Tannhäuser und der Sängerkrieg auf dem Wartburg*; 'Tannhäuser and the Song Contest at the Wartburg'). Opera

The tango (1914).

in three acts by Wagner; text by the composer. Produced: Dresden, 19 October 1845; New York, Stadt Theatre, 4 April 1859; London, Covent Garden, 6 May 1876. Revision (dictated by the Paris Opéra's rule that foreign works must be presented in French, and the absolute requirement for a ballet in the second act), known as the 'Paris' version, produced: Paris, Opéra, 13 March 1861; New York, Metropolitan Opera, 30 January 1889; London, Covent Garden, 15 July 1895. In the Venusberg, Tannhäuser (ten.) sings in praise of the pleasures offered him by Venus (mezzo). But he longs to return to the world, and when he names the Virgin, the Venusberg disappears and he finds himself in the valley of the Wartburg where a young shepherd (sop.) is singing. A group of pilgrims pass on their way to Rome, and then horns herald the Landgrave Hermann (bass), Wolfram (bar.) (Tannhäuser's close friend), and other knights. They welcome Tannhäuser after his year's absence, and he decides to return with them on hearing how sad Elisabeth, the Landgrave's niece, has been since his departure.

Elisabeth (sop.), happy at Tannhäuser's return, greets the Hall of Song in the Wartburg Castle. Tannhäuser will not tell her where he has been. The knights and guests enter for the contest of song. The landgrave announces the theme as love. Wolfram sings of a pure selfless love. Tannhäuser follows with an outburst in praise of Venus. The knights threaten Tannhäuser, but Elisabeth intervenes. Tannhäuser promises atonement; he is banished to seek absolution from the Pope and joins the pilgrims.

Several months later Elisabeth is praying in the valley of the Wartburg that Tannhäuser may be forgiven. When she sadly returns home, Wolfram prays to the evening star to guide and protect her. Tannhäuser staggers in, distraught at the Pope's refusal of absolution: he can now only return to Venus. A funeral procession approaches: Elisabeth has died of a broken heart. Tannhäuser sinks beside her bier, and he too dies. Pilgrims arrive from Rome bearing the Pope's staff, which has sprouted leaves in token that God has forgiven Tannhäuser.

Tansman, Alexandre (*b* Łódź, 12 June 1897). French composer of Polish birth. He studied composition with Adalbert Gawroński and Piotr Rytel at Warsaw University (1915-19) and then moved permanently to Paris. There he was deeply influenced by Stravinskyan neoclassicism, which he combines in his music with Polish and Jewish elements. His output includes eight symphonies and other orchestral pieces, ballets, operas, and choral works. He has toured widely as a conductor and pianist, and is author of the book *Igor Stravinsky* (New York, 1949).

PAUL GRIFFITHS

FURTHER READING
Irving Schwerke: *Alexandre Tansman: compositeur polonais* (Paris, 1931).

Tant (Fr.), **tanto** (It.). 'As much', 'so much'; *allegro, ma non tanto*, '*allegro*, but not too much'.

Tanz, Tänze (Ger.). 'Dance', 'dances'.

Tap-dancing. A stage dance characterized by rhythmic taps made on the floor by the toes and heels of the dancer. Also known as step-dancing, it developed during the 19th century in England and the USA from popular dances such as the jig and clog dance, although lighter shoes than clogs were worn, with toes and heels modified to sound out the taps clearly. Tap-dancing was popular as music-hall and vaudeville entertainment up to the 1920s and later in stage shows and films. Virtuoso tap-dance routines, as devised by Fred Astaire in films such as *Top Hat* and later by Gene Kelly in *Singin' in the Rain*, did much to popularize it as a stage and competitive dance for both solo dancers and chorus lines.

Tapiola. Tone-poem, Op. 112, by Sibelius, composed in 1926. Tapio was the god of Finnish forests.

Tapissier, Johannes (*d* before Aug. 1410). French poet and composer. His career from *c.*1391 until his death was spent in the service of two successive dukes of Burgundy, Philip the Bold and John the Fearless, and he also seems to have maintained a music school in Paris. To-gether with Carmen and Cesaris his music was described by Martin le Franc, in *Le champion des dames* (*c*.1440), as having 'astounded all Paris' in the years before Binchois and Dufay. Only three works by him survive, a Credo, a Sanctus, and a motet.   JOHN MILSOM

Tarantella (It.; Fr.: *tarantelle*). A dance which takes its name from the southern Italian seaport of Taranto. The bite of the tarantula spider (found in the surrounding countryside and also named after the town) was popularly supposed to cause a disease which would prove fatal unless the victim performed a lively dance, or which itself caused 'tarantism' or dancing mania. It has long been known that the spider's bite is comparatively harmless, and that any disease subsequently contracted was more likely to be hysterical in origin. In 1662 Pepys records a meeting with a gentleman who 'is a great traveller, and, speaking of the tarantula, he says that all the harvest long . . . fiddlers go up and down the fields everywhere, in expectation of being hired by those that are stung'. From the 17th to the 20th century there were apparently great communal outbreaks of tarantism, in which whole towns would suddenly give themselves over to outbreaks of wild dancing, and the musicians had a profitable time.

By the 19th century, however, musicians made more money out of tarantellas by their popularity as compositions. Chopin, Liszt, Heller, Auber, Weber, Thalberg, Balakirev, Cui, and Dargomyzhsky, among others, wrote tarantellas, all in rapid 6/8 time and often involving *perpetuum mobile* (proceeding throughout in notes of the same value). The *saltarello is a similar type of piece, and the finale of Mendelssohn's 'Italian' Symphony, though called a saltarello, is actually a combination of that dance with a tarantella melody.

Taras Bulba. Rhapsody for orchestra by Janáček after Gogol's story about Bulba, the Ukrainian Cossack leader. Composed between 1915 and 1918, it has three movements: (1) 'Death of Andrea' (*Smrt Andrijova*); (2) 'Death of Ostap' (*Smrt Ostapova*); (3) 'Prophecy and Death of Taras Bulba' (*Proroctví a smrt Tarase Bulby*).

Tardo, tarda (It.). 'Slow'; *tardamente*, 'slowly'; *tardando*, *tardante*, 'slowing down' (gradually).

Tarogato. This wind instrument looks rather like (and sounds very like) a soprano *saxophone but is made in wood, with plain fingerholes and keywork based on that of the clarinet. It was invented in Budapest *c*.1890 by the maker Schunda (who had seen the soprano saxophone),

Tarogato by Schunda, Budapest, late 19th century.

to restore in modern guise an old *shawm of Turkish origin called tarogato, then still played by some town watchmen. (In the same spirit of nationalism Schunda produced the big cimbalom: see *Dulcimer*, 1.) The tarogato is still made, especially in Romania where it is a great favourite in folk music. See also *Alphorn* for its use in *Tristan und Isolde*.   ANTHONY BAINES

Tárrega, Francisco (*b* Villareal, Castellón, 21 Nov. 1852; *d* Barcelona, 15 Dec. 1909). Spanish guitarist and composer. Known as 'the Sarasate of the guitar', he studied the then neglected classical guitar as a child, and also piano and composition at the Madrid Conservatory. He subsequently devoted himself to the guitar, giving numerous recitals in Spain and elsewhere, and doing much to promote it as a popular instrument. In 1880 he made a triumphant début in Paris and London. Tárrega added many of his own compositions to the guitar repertory, as well as over 100 transcriptions of music for other instruments.

WENDY THOMPSON

Tartini, Giuseppe (*b* Pirano, Istria, 8 Apr. 1692; *d* Padua, 26 Feb. 1770). Italian composer, theorist, and violinist. The son of a minor public official, he was intended for the priesthood, but defied his parents to follow a musical career. In 1708 he went to Padua, where he enrolled as a law student at the University and in 1710 contracted a secret marriage. As he was still officially destined for the ecclesiastical life, his marriage incurred the wrath of the Bishop of Padua, and Tartini was forced to take refuge in the Minorite monastery in Assisi. There, over the next few years, he studied music, probably with Černohorský. In 1714 he was offered a part as a violinist in the opera orchestra at Ancona, and the following year he was pardoned. However, he chose to leave his wife again and to go into self-imposed exile for four years, in order to improve his violin-playing.

In 1721 Tartini became first violinist at the Basilica S. Antonio in Padua, where he stayed until his retirement in 1765. However, over the next 20 years he frequently took time off for visits abroad, including a period spent at Prague in the mid 1720s. After 1740 he appeared less often in public. He founded his own violin school in Padua, and among his pupils were such distinguished violinists and composers as J. G. Graun, Nardini, and J. G. Naumann. He also worked on musical and acoustical theory, carrying on a 40-year correspondence on the subject with Padre Martini. His death at the age of 77 was caused, like Lully's, by gangrene resulting from an abscess on the foot.

Tartini's published works include over 60 violin sonatas (though some are of doubtful authenticity), some 24 trio sonatas, 24 *concerti grossi*, and the famous *L'arte del arco* (a set of 38 variations on a gavotte by Corelli). A great deal of music survives in manuscript, including about 135 violin sonatas, the same number of concertos, and about 40 trio sonatas. His sonatas follow a three-movement slow–quick–quick pattern, while the concertos are in the Vivaldi mould, quick–slow–quick. The most famous of the sonatas is the 'Devil's Trill' in G minor (*c*.1745), supposedly written as the result of a dream in which the Devil seized Tartini's violin and played a piece which had a 'fiendishly' difficult trill in the last movement.

WENDY THOMPSON

G. TARTINI

Né en 1692, Mort en 1770.

Gravé par Lambert d'après le Dessin Original de P. Guérin appartenant à Mr. Cartier.

Giuseppe Tartini, engraving by Lambert after a drawing by Guérin.

Taste, Tasten (Ger.), **tasto, tasti, tasticra** (It.). 1. 'Key', 'keys', 'keyboard', in the sense of the finger-keys of a keyboard instrument. Hence, the expression *tasto solo* in early music with a figured bass means 'play the key (note) alone', i.e. do not add other chords above the bass line. In other words, the bass momentarily becomes itself a melodic part, rather than the basis for harmony.

2. *Tasto* (It.) also means the fingerboard of a stringed instrument. Thus *sul tasto, sulla tastiera*, 'on the fingerboard', means bow over the fingerboard. For Skryabin's *tastiera per luce* (keyboard of light), see *Colour and Music*.

Tastiera (It.). The same as **tasto*.

Tasto (It.). 1. The 'key' of a keyboard instrument. In music with a figured bass accompaniment, *tasto solo* means that only the bass notes should be played, rather than the filled-in harmonies.

2. The 'fingerboard' of a bowed instrument; *sul tasto*, 'on the fingerboard', i.e. bow well up the strings.

Tate, Phyllis (Margaret Duncan) (*b* Gerrards Cross, 6 Apr. 1911). English composer. She studied at the Royal Academy of Music but was relatively slow to make her reputation as a composer. Since the 1950s, however, she has won success with works for chamber groupings, choir, and children, all in a neat tonal style which does not forswear humour. Her output also includes a Saxophone Concerto (1944), the opera *The Lodger* (1960), and the television opera *Dark Pilgrimage* (1963).   PAUL GRIFFITHS

Tattoo. The music of bugles and drums which recalls soldiers to their barracks at night. In the British Army it lasts for 20 minutes, beginning with the fanfare called the First Post and ending with the Last Post (which is also played at military funerals). The word is also used to describe military musical festivals, such as the Edinburgh Tattoo.

Tauber, Richard [Seiffert, Ernst] (*b* Linz, 16 May 1892; *d* London, 8 Jan. 1948). Austrian, naturalized British, tenor. He studied music in Frankfurt and became a professional conductor at 18. He then studied singing and made his first operatic appearance at Dresden in 1912 in *The Magic Flute*. He won instant acclaim and became the leading tenor at Dresden until 1920. He appeared in Berlin in 1915 and was frequently heard in Munich, Vienna, and Salzburg. His good looks and sympathetic voice led his career away from opera to the operetta stage, where he became closely associated with Franz Lehár, reviving the composer's waning fortunes with his appearance in such shows as *Frasquita* (1922), *Paganini* (1925), *Frederika* (1928), and *The Land of Smiles* (1929); from the last, 'You Are My Heart's Delight' became inextricably associated with Tauber. He first appeared in London in this show in 1931 and was naturalized in 1940, thereafter becoming very active as a conductor in the London theatre where he produced one of his own operettas, *Old Chelsea*, in 1943.   PETER GAMMOND

Tavener, John (Kenneth) (*b* London, 28 Jan. 1944). English composer. He studied composition at the Royal Academy of Music with Lennox Berkeley (1962–8) and privately with David Lumsdaine (1965–7). In 1960 he was appointed organist of St John's, Kensington, and in 1969 he began teaching at Trinity College, London. His music makes effective use of simple materials and procedures derived from Stravinsky, Messiaen, and Stockhausen. He has composed the dramatic cantata *The Whale* (1969) and the opera *Thérèse* (1979), but most of his music is sacred, e.g. the imposing *Ultimos ritos* for soloists, choirs, and orchestra (1969–74). His large-scale *Akhmatova: Requiem* (1979–80), a setting in Russian of Anna Akhmatova's cycle of poems, incorporates chants of the Russian Orthodox Church, into which he was received in 1978.

PAUL GRIFFITHS

John Tavener

Taverner. Opera in two acts by Peter Maxwell Davies to his own libretto drawn from 16th-century letters and documents concerning the life of the composer John Taverner. It was composed 1962–8, partly revised in 1970, and first performed at Covent Garden in 1972.

Taverner, John (*b* Lincs., *c.*1490; *d* Boston, Lincs., 18 Oct. 1545). English composer. Little is known of his early life, though he may have spent some time in London *c.*1514, when there is a record of a member of the Guild of Parish Clerks bearing his (not uncommon) name. In 1524 he was at Tattershall College, Lincolnshire, a collegiate church which had sufficiently skilled forces to sing the Office to elaborate music. The following year he was appointed *Informator choristorum* at Wolsey's newly founded Cardinal College (the future Christ Church), Oxford, where choral music on a grand scale was encouraged. In 1527–8 he was apparently accused of heretical (Lutheran) activities, avoiding prosecution because he 'was but a musician'. Two years later he resigned, probably because the college's future was uncertain after the political down fall of Wolsey. His whereabouts for the next few years are unknown, but he seems to have returned to Lincolnshire and served as a lay clerk at St Botolph, Boston. From 1538 to 1540 he was

'Et in terra pax' from Taverner's Missa 'Gloria tibi Trinitas', with a reputed portrait of the composer.

responsible for the purging of the church ritual there, and he died a respected alderman, and prospective mayor, of Boston.

John Foxe's picture in the 1560s of a composer who felt the need to 'repent him very much that he had made songs to popish ditties in the time of his blindness', and who persecuted Catholics, is almost certainly wide of the mark. His 'popish ditties' are in fact a glorious contribution to English sacred music, and he wrote a number of very fine Masses, some, such as the six-part *Corona spinea* and *Gloria tibi Trinitas*, in a large-scale festal manner, not only showing great contrapuntal skill but also making a splendid sound. His smaller-scale Masses, including the well-known one on the 'Western Wynde' melody, point the way to the simpler style of church music which was to become common later in the century. Best of all are the three antiphons to the Blessed Virgin Mary—vast polyphonic edifices worthy of the Oxford Lady Chapel they were probably intended for.

DENIS ARNOLD

FURTHER READING
Colin Hand: *John Taverner: his Life and Music* (London, 1978).

Taylor, Silas (*b* Harley, Shropshire, 16 July 1624; *d* Harwich, 4 Nov. 1678). English antiquarian and composer. He fought on Cromwell's side in the Civil War, and after the Restoration became a customs officer. As well as contributing vocal music to Hilton's *Catch that catch can* and two dance suites to Playford's *Court-Ayres*, he wrote sacred music and an essay on the *Collection of Rules in Musicke*.

WENDY THOMPSON

Tchaikovsky, Pyotr (Ilyich) (*b* Kamsko-Votkinsk, Vyatka Province, 7 May 1840; *d* St Petersburg, 6 Nov. 1893). Russian composer. He once wrote that his whole life was spent 'regretting the past and hoping for the future, never being satisfied with the present'. This feeling of unease and dissatisfaction with life imbued much of his music, particularly in his later years, when the disasters of his personal life found expression in music of extraordinary emotional anguish and tragic drama. In these forceful, highly individual works, couched in an intensely lyrical idiom and scored in rich orchestral colours, Tchaikovsky laid bare his personality with vivid immediacy, bequeathing to the repertory a range of symphonies, concertos, and operas which have remained enduringly popular and affecting.

1. *The Early Years.* As a child he had piano lessons, but in 1850 he entered the St Petersburg School of Jurisprudence. He remained there until 1859, then, after working for a while in the civil service, began to study music seriously with the theorist Nikolay Zaremba (1821–79) in the classes of the newly formed Russian Musical Society. When the classes blossomed into the St Petersburg Conservatory in 1862 Tchaikovsky continued working there with Zaremba and also had lessons in composition (1863–5) from Anton Rubinstein, a composer whom Tchaikovsky held in lasting respect.

Tchaikovsky, c.1864

In 1866, on the invitation of Rubinstein's brother, Nikolay, Tchaikovsky moved to Moscow to teach harmony at the conservatory there: he held the post until 1878, and in connection with his academic work produced a number of textbooks, among them the *Rukovodstvo k prakticheskomu izucheniyu garmoniy* ('Guide to the Practical Study of Harmony'), written in 1871, published in the following year, and translated into English in 1976. Even as a student Tchaikovsky had shown facility for composition, producing such works as his exuberant yet warmly lyrical overture to Ostrovsky's play *Groza* ('The Storm', 1864), and in his early years in Moscow he consolidated his reputation with his First Symphony, 'Winter Daydreams' (composed and revised 1866, and reaching its final form in a third version of 1874), and the First String Quartet (1871). He achieved less success with his first opera, *Voyevoda* ('The Voyevoda', 1869) and eventually destroyed the score, incorporating some of the music into another opera, *Oprichnik* ('The Oprichnik', 1874).

In 1868 Tchaikovsky met the composers of the nationalist group centred on Stasov and Balakirev in St Petersburg (see *Five, The*). Balakirev conducted the first St Petersburg performance of Tchaikovsky's symphonic poem *Fatum* ('Fate', 1868) at a concert of the Russian Musical Society in 1869, and later the same year Balakirev helped Tchaikovsky formulate his ideas for one of his most popular works, the fantasy overture *Romeo and Juliet* (1869, rev. 1870 and 1880). We can perhaps look to Tchaikovsky's association with the nationalist composers at this time for an explanation of the overt nationalism in such works as the Second Symphony, 'Little Russian' or 'Ukrainian' (1872, rev. 1880), the opera *Kuznets Vakula* ('Vakula the Smith', 1876, rev. as *Cherevichki*, 'The Slippers', 1887), and his incidental music to Ostrovsky's *Snegurochka* ('The Snow Maiden', 1873), though in fact Tchaikovsky's interest in Russian folk music stretched back to his earliest years. As he recorded in his autobiography, he grew up in a remote place, Votkinsk, 'and from my earliest childhood I was immersed in Russian folk music and the indescribable beauty of its characteristic features'.

2. *The Years of Maturity.* From 1872 Tchaikovsky began to appear in print as a music critic for the newspaper *Russkiye vedomosti*, and in 1876 he was sent to Bayreuth to cover the *Ring*. However, he reported that food was the prime concern of Bayreuth patrons ('there was much more talk of beefsteaks, cutlets, and roast potatoes than of Wagner's music') and he summed up his opinion of Wagner, glimpsed only from an upstairs window, as 'a sprightly little old man with an aquiline nose and thin, supercilious lips—the characteristic trait of the initiator of this entire cosmopolitan festival'. Tchaikovsky remained unaffected by Wagner's style, and instead his own music of this period shows a developing of that open, emotionally charged idiom which was to become so familiar in his mature music: the First Piano Concerto (1874–5)—harshly criticized by Nikolay Rubinstein—the symphonic fantasia *Francesca da Rimini* (1876), and his first ballet *Lebedinoye ozero* ('Swan Lake', 1877) forged a highly individual style, marked by flair and brilliance yet often tinged with that brooding fatalism which was to dominate his later years. In addition several of his works began to hint clearly at his fascination for 18th-century music, in particular that of Mozart, who, Tchaikovsky said, 'captivates, delights, and warms me'. He had already harked back to Classical models in the little minuet in *Vakula the Smith*; he now affirmed his love of the cool, clear lines of Classical music in his Variations on a Rococo Theme for cello and orchestra (1876), and was to reassert it in such works as the opera *Pikovaya dama* ('The Queen of Spades', 1890), set in the time of Catherine II and incorporating 18th-century pastiche as well as music by 18th-century Russian composers.

In the late 1870s Tchaikovsky's personal life and his creative career reached a watershed. Tchaikovsky had long yearned for a settled domestic life; he was also haunted by feelings of guilt about his homosexuality, to which he had been giving covert expression in his letters and writings; and as a result he longed to free his family from any shame and embarrassment at the prevailing rumours about his proclivities. By chance, in the spring of 1877 he received a letter from a yound admirer, Antonina Milyukova. At the time he was fired with enthusiasm for his opera *Evgeny Onegin* ('Eugene Onegin'), and thoughts of the famous 'Letter Scene' urged him to follow up Antonina's protestations of love. They were married in July 1877, but within days of the wedding he was finding his wife 'absolutely repugnant' and living a life of torment. He swiftly found that marriage required a commitment into which he was quite unable to enter, and he was to be plagued with problems of separation and divorce proceedings for many years to come.

3. *The Final Years.* It is tempting to see Tchaikovsky's disastrous marriage as a direct inspiration for *Eugene Onegin* and the Fourth Symphony (1877–8, the first of his three so-called 'Fate' symphonies), yet the idea of writing the opera, or at least setting the Letter Scene, had occurred to him long before he had even heard of Antonina, and much of the Fourth Symphony had been written before his marriage. Yet the consequences of this incautious step served to strengthen his belief that life was directed by some implacable, unconquerable force—a theme running through much of the music of his later years: the Fifth Symphony (1888), *Manfred* (1885), and the opera *The Queen of Spades*. Other works like the Violin Concerto (1878), the four orchestral suites (No. 1, 1879; No. 2, 1883; No. 3, 1884; No. 4, 'Mozartiana', 1887), and the overture *1812* (1880) show him in happier vein, though a number of other works with which he felt out of tune—the operas *Orleanskaya deva* ('The Maid of Orleans', 1881), *Mazeppa* (1884), and *Charodeyka* ('The Sorceress', 1887)—were conspicuously unsuccessful. Tchaikovsky described *The Sorceress* as 'a pearl' while he was working on it, but he changed his mind after its first performance and dubbed it 'a fiasco'; and in *Mazeppa* he declared he was 'not much drawn to the characters'. Indeed, neither opera displays the sharp perception of character of either *Eugene Onegin* or *The Queen of Spades*, though he did achieve greater lasting success with his two other ballets, *Spyashchaya krasavitsa* ('The Sleeping Beauty', 1890) and *Shchelkunchik* ('The Nutcracker', 1892).

Around the time of his marriage Tchaikovsky entered into his curious epistolary relationship with Nadezhda von Meck, who had written him an admiring letter in 1876. Although (or perhaps because) they never met, Tchaikovsky poured out his innermost feelings to Mme von Meck in hundreds of letters, which have become an invaluable guide both to his creative processes and to his state of mind. Aside from

Autograph MS of Tchaikovsky's Sixth Symphony, part of the second movement.

Tchaikovsky photographed in the last year of his life.

providing him with an outlet for his thoughts, Mme von Meck also gave him a degree of financial security by settling on him a substantial allowance, though this was terminated in 1890 when she wrote to him declaring that she was bankrupt; as this was apparently untrue, Tchaikovsky was plunged into increasing depression at the abrupt breach in their distant friendship, and, whether as a direct result or no, his last years were tinged with gloom, highlighted in such works as the oppressive Sixth Symphony, 'Pathétique' (1893). Until recently it was generally accepted that, a few days after the première of the Sixth Symphony on 28 October 1893, Tchaikovsky drank a glass of unboiled water and contracted cholera, from which he died. Yet this can hardly be true. Even Rimsky-Korsakov remarked in his autobiography that it was strange that mourners should be allowed to troop through Tchaikovsky's apartment after his death: the regulations stipulated that cholera cases should immediately be isolated, in view of the possibility of contagion. It has been suggested by the Soviet scholar Alexandra Orlova that, rather more plausibly, Tchaikovsky committed suicide by poison (possibly arsenic) at the behest of a court of honour, which had met to assess the implications of Tchaikovsky's alleged relationship with a male member of the imperial family. The supporting evidence has the ring of probability, and it is almost uncanny that the emotional state which had caused him so much remorse throughout his mature life should eventually result in his death.

FURTHER READING
Gerald Abraham: *Tchaikovsky* (London, 1944); Gerald Abraham, ed.: *Tchaikovsky: a Symposium* (London, 1945); John Warrack: *Tchaikovsky Symphonies and Concertos* (London, 1969, 2nd edn 1974); Edward Garden: *Tchaikovsky* (London, 1973); John Warrack: *Tchaikovsky* (London, 1973); David Brown: *Tchaikovsky: a Biographical and Critical Study* (London, 1978–); John Warrack: *Tchaikovsky Ballet Music* (London, 1979).

Tcherepnin, Alexander (Nikolayevich) (*b* St Petersburg, 21 Jan. 1899; *d* Paris, 29 Sept. 1977). Russian composer, conductor, and pianist; son of Nikolay Tcherepnin. With his father he settled in Paris. He composed four symphonies, concertos, sonatas, and other works. In some of his later compositions he made use of a nine-note scale, consisting of three progressions of a semitone, tone, and semitone. He also toured extensively as a piano recitalist. In 1949 he became instructor in theory at De Paul University, Chicago.

PERCY SCHOLES, rev.

Tcherepnin, Nikolay (Nikolayevich) (*b* St Petersburg, 15 May 1873; *d* Paris, 26 June 1945). Russian conductor and composer. He was prominent as conductor in St Petersburg and Paris, in which latter city he was attached to the Diaghilev Ballet, then touring with them (1909–14). In 1918 he became head of the Tiflis (now Tbilisi) Conservatory, and then from 1921 lived in Paris. He composed ballets, operas, symphonies, symphonic poems, and other works, and in 1923 conducted at Monte Carlo his own completed version of Musorgsky's opera *Sorochintsy Fair*.

PERCY SCHOLES, rev.

Tecla (Sp.). A 16th- and 17th-century name for 'key', or 'keyboard'; *musica para tecla*, 'music for keyboard (instruments)'.

Tedesca (It.). 'German'; *alla tedesca*, 'in the German style'. This can be taken to mean 'in the style of the most characteristic German dance' of the period, for example the allemande in the 17th century or, from about 1800, the Ländler (or other similar dance in triple time). Beethoven used the term in the first movement of his Piano Sonata, Op. 79, and the fourth movement of his String Quartet, Op. 130 (marked 'Allemande Allegro').

Te Deum laudamus (Lat., 'We praise Thee, O God'). The long hymn which constitutes the supreme expression of rejoicing in the Roman Catholic, Anglican, and other Christian Churches. The Roman Catholic breviary calls it the canticle of Ambrose and Augustine, from the legend that at the baptism of Augustine by Ambrose it was sung antiphonally, extempore, by the two saints. Actually it may have originated in the Gallican or Mozarabic liturgy (see

Liturgy, 2a), and its authorship has been put down to both Hilary, Bishop of Poitiers, in the 4th century and Hilary of Arles in the 5th; in either case it seems as though portions of an older hymn were incorporated. Another ascription, now very generally accepted, is to Nicetas of Remesiana, a Dacian bishop of the early 5th century. However, the content and arrangement of the *Te Deum* clearly indicate that it is not a unity, and probably the minds and hearts of a number of writers of different places and periods express themselves in it.

In the liturgy of the Roman Catholic Church the *Te Deum* finds a place as the outpouring of praise at the moment of climax of the service of Matins on Sundays and festivals; in the Anglican Church the English version is a part of the service of Morning Prayer, except when replaced by the *Benedicite*.

The traditional plainchant to the Latin hymn is of a very magnificent character. In Anglican cathedrals and larger churches elaborate 'service' settings are used (see *Service*), and in smaller churches series of Anglican chants or, nowadays frequently, simple 'service' settings. The most popular *Te Deum* ever in use in England was that of William Jackson of Exeter (1730–1803), in the service 'Jackson in F', which was for a century sung from every village choir loft; any musician of taste must call it trivial, yet there was something in the simplicity of its means and the broad effects obtained by them that carried it into the hearts of the whole church going population of the nation.

Naturally, the hymn has inspired innumerable composers of all periods, and many of their settings, from the late 17th century onwards, have been on extended lines, with solos, choruses, and orchestral accompaniment. The earliest known polyphonic setting is in the 9th-century *Musica enchiriadis*, but there are few settings by important composers before the 16th century, when many English composers, such as Taverner, Sheppard, Redford, and Blitheman, chose it. Important settings have been made by Purcell (for St Cecilia's Day, 1694), Handel (for the Peace of Utrecht, 1713, and for the Victory of Dettingen, 1743), Graun (written after the Battle of Prague, 1757), Berlioz (for the Paris Exhibition of 1855, and composed on a huge scale, with three choirs and large instrumental forces), Bruckner (1885), Dvořák (1896), Verdi (1898), Stanford (using the Latin words, 1898), Parry (Latin original, 1900, English adaptation, 1913; also another for the coronation of George V in 1911), Kodály (for the 250th anniversary of the end of the Turkish occupation of Buda, 1936), Britten (1934), and Walton (for the coronation of Elizabeth II, 1953).

A solemn *Te Deum* is ordered on all occasions of rejoicing in Christian countries, so that throughout history nations opposed in war have used the same hymn to thank God for their victories over one another.   PERCY SCHOLES

Teil [*Theil*] (Ger.). 'Part', or 'portion', 'section'; *teilen* [*theilen*], 'to divide'.

Telemann, Georg Philipp (*b* Magdeburg, 14 Mar. 1681; *d* Hamburg, 25 June 1767). German composer and organist. He came of a family of Lutheran pastors and taught himself the art of composing while still at school, studying the scores of Lully, Campra, and others. He wrote his first opera when he was 12, and several years later composed some songs for school plays by the rector of Hildesheim, J. C. Losius (Telemann may also have been the composer of the music to Losius's *Singende Geographie*). He went on to study law at Leipzig University but soon transferred to music, writing sacred cantatas for St Thomas's and in 1702 forming a *collegium musicum* (a student society which gave public concerts). By 1704, when he was appointed organist and director of the Neukirche in Leipzig, he had several operas to his credit, composed for the Leipzig Opera, of which he was musical director from 1702. In 1705 he left Leipzig to become *Kapellmeister* at the court of Sorau [now Żary, Poland], where he became further acquainted with the French style; the vitality of the folk music of the region also made an impression. By 1707 he was in Eisenach, as *Konzertmeister* and then *Kapellmeister*, and in 1712 he went to Frankfurt am Main as municipal director of music and *Kapellmeister* at the Barfüsserkirche. In Frankfurt he organized further concert series, including performances of his own instrumental music, and,

Telemann, engraving by G. Lichtensteger.

in 1716, of his first oratorio, the Brockes Passion (named after B. S. Brockes, who wrote the text). In 1721 Telemann was preferred to Bach for the vacant position of *Kantor* at St Thomas's, Leipzig, but he went instead (at a higher salary) to Hamburg, where he remained, as musical director and *Kantor*, for the rest of his life. He married twice, and left 11 children.

Telemann's duties at Hamburg included the composition of several cycles of cantatas for the town's five principal churches, an annual Passion setting, and occasional works for municipal events. He also reorganized the Hamburg *collegium musicum* which had been founded in 1660. From 1722 he combined these duties with the post of musical director of the Hamburg Opera, but on his return from a visit to Paris in 1737 the Opera closed, and his last years brought forth a series of great oratorios, including *Der Tod Jesu* (1755), *Donnerode* (1756–60), a setting of two parts of Klopstock's *Messias* (1759), *Das befreite Israel* (1759), *Die Auferstehung und Himmelfahrt Jesu* (1760), and *Der Tag des Gerichts* (1762). He also wrote some theoretical works.

During his lifetime Telemann was considered Germany's leading composer, his reputation far exceeding that of Bach. His music was truly cosmopolitan (in 1729 he confessed to the influence of Polish, French, and Italian styles), and he was a supreme exponent of the new *galant* style, writing music designed to meet the needs not only of professional musicians and his various patrons but also of the growing numbers

Autograph MS of the opening of Telemann's church cantata 'Articulus secundus de Redemptione'.

Gänsemarkt opera house, Hamburg, built in 1677 by G. Sartorio; drawing by P. Heineken.

of middle-class amateur musicians. His awareness of the changing social function of music reflected in his efforts to establish musical societies in each of the major cities where he worked.

None the less, like many other composers whose aim was the satisfaction of contemporary demand, Telemann's posthumous reputation declined rapidly, and by the turn of the century his music had been largely forgotten. With the rise of interest in earlier music in the second half of the 19th century some of his huge output was re-examined but was compared unfavourably with Bach's music, and it is only fairly recently that he has been recognized as an individual and original composer. He is probably the most prolific composer in the history of music (Handel said he could write a motet in eight parts as easily as anyone else could write a letter), and it is not surprising that he has been accused of a 'fatal facility naturally inclined to superficiality'. Unlike Bach he worked in every major genre, including opera.

Of his many operas fewer than ten survive complete. They none the less supply a wide variety of styles, from the comic *Der geduldige Socrates* (1721) and the satirical *Der neumodische Liebhaber Damon* (1724) to the more serious *Flavius Bertaridus* (1729); perhaps the best known of all is the *intermezzo, Pimpinone* (1725). His other vocal music includes secular cantatas, such as *Die Tageszeiten* (1759), serenades, *Kapitänsmusiken* (sacred oratorios and secular serenades performed at Hamburg between 1728

and 1763), oratorios, Passions (the St John is perhaps the best known), sacred cantatas (including six complete annual cycles such as *Der harmonische Gottes-Dienst*, 1725-6), odes and *Lieder*, chorales, sacred canons, and innumerable Masses, psalms, and motets.

The catalogue of instrumental works is almost as overwhelming. His orchestral works included around 1,000 suites (only 125 or so are extant) and 120 concertos, and his chamber music numerous solo sonatas (mainly for flute or violin), duos, trio sonatas, quartets, quintets, and a considerable amount of keyboard music. Some of this music was published in three collections of entertainment music called *Musique de table* (Hamburg, 1733) and some in a volume called *Essercizii musici* (containing trio sonatas, solo sonatas, and two keyboard suites; 1739-40).

WENDY THOMPSON

Tel jour, telle nuit ('Such a Day, Such a Night'). Song-cycle by Poulenc to poems by Paul Éluard, composed in 1937. The nine songs are *Bonne journée, Une ruine coquille vide, Le front comme un drapeau perdu, Une roulotte couverte en tuiles, A toutes brides, Une herbe pauvre, Je n'ai envie que de t'aimer, Figure de force brûlante et farouche,* and *Nous avons fait la nuit.*

Tema (It.). 'Theme', 'subject'. *Tema con variazioni,* 'theme with variations'. See *Variation form.*

Temperament. Term for the adjustment of intervals involved in the various systems used in tuning the notes of the octave, required particularly with keyboard instruments, on which chords as well as melody lines are played but on which the notes cannot be adjusted for tuning during performance. We now use equal temperament (see below, 4), by which the octave is made up of 12 equal semitones. We take it for granted that an interval is always the same, whatever note you start from, and that every note of the keyboard, white or black, will be able to act equally well as a keynote. Formerly this was not so. Prior to equal temperament (known in theory from c.1600 but not in general use until some 200 years later) the scale was built up on a basis of natural ('pure', 'untempered') intervals, the chief among them being (apart from the octave, 2:1, which is always observed) the perfect fifth (ratio 3:2) and the major third (5:4), each in itself making a pure-sounding interval (with no 'beats'; see *Acoustics*, 8). But combinations with the octave and with themselves lead to incompatibilities: for example, semitones are not equal, and common chords are not properly available in every key.

1. *The Basic Problem.* In what follows it must be remembered that in adding intervals the ratios are multiplied, and in subtracting they are divided; also, the pure octave is always assumed, so that 'up an octave' equals '× 2', and 'down an octave' equals '× $\frac{1}{2}$', etc.

A first stage in the problem can be illustrated by the interval C–E. In Ex. 1a the E is arrived at by tuning through four pure fifths of 3:2, making $(3/2)^4$; from this we may deduct two octaves (dividing by four), with the result 81:64. But this is not the E reached (Ex. 1b) as a pure major third above C (5:4). The difference (81/64 × 4/5, or 81/80) is the small ratio famous throughout the history of music theory as the 'Didymian comma', amounting to approximately 21.5 *cents, or more than a fifth of a semitone, and readily appreciable to a good ear. Yet harmony ideally asks for E in both capacities (both as a true fifth to A and as a true third to C). Similarly with other notes: A, for example, needs to be a pure fifth in chords of D (major or minor) but a pure third in the chord of F major. Since the keyboard cannot supply both, what is to be done? At first the problem was seen, at least in theory, as a choice between the two, giving priority, from c.1500, not to so-called Pythagorean temperament, based on the pure fifth (as when tuning a violin), but to the pure major third. This gave rise to 'mean-tone temperament'.

2. *Mean-tone Temperament.* Cherishing the pure third as essential to proper harmony means taking a comma off the four perfect fifths (Ex.

1a) to match the E to that of the pure major third C–E (Ex. 1b). The single fifth, e.g. C–G, thus shrinks by a quarter of a comma (i.e. 3:2 is divided by the fourth root of 81:80, which works out at $\sqrt[4]{5}$), to approximately 697 cents, which is flat to the pure fifth (702 cents) by a trifling amount which the ear will comfortably tolerate and which the tuner will set through experience.

A convenient byproduct of this manœuvre is that two of these perfect fifths add up to the square of $\sqrt[4]{5}$ (i.e. to $\sqrt{5}$); or, taking off an octave to get the whole tone C–D, $\sqrt{5}:2$, which, being the square root of 5:4, exactly bisects the major third to give the 'mean tone' (in cents 193, while the major third is 386) which eliminates the natural distinction (see *Harmonic Series*) between C–D (9:8) and the smaller D–E (10.9), and gives the system its name; the scales of C and D now both start with the same whole-tone interval.

Ex. 1

But beyond this looms a second stage to the problem, namely where a note is required to serve in two capacities, enharmonically, which, in the Renaissance period, means the black notes of the keyboard. Take for instance the note between G and A (Ex. 2): in (a) it serves as G♯, the major third to E, and thus two major thirds up from C—(5/4)² or 25:16; but in (b) the note is A♭, the major third below the upper C— two divided by 5:4, making 8:5. The difference, 128:125, amounts to 41 cents, getting on for a quarter-tone. If tuned to G♯ a chord of F minor (with A♭) is out of the question (unless, as one writer suggested, heavily disguised by trilling or some other means). In short, three pure major thirds simply do not add up to an octave. Mean-tone tuning therefore involved enharmonic choices over the black notes, most typically C♯, E♭, F♯, G♯ (for the important chord of E), and, of course, B♭.

Ex. 2

A comparatively rare expedient for providing at least some of the enharmonic pairs was to complicate the keyboard by divided black keys acting on separate strings (or pipes) for the sharp and the flat. But the main developments were as follows.

3. *Modifications of Mean-tone.* Before the end of the 16th century it had begun to be recognized that, while many musicians and organ-builders would prefer the above system, the ear would tolerate, or even perhaps react favourably to, small departures from the strict major third such as could be made with the object of bringing each enharmonic sharp and flat closer together, thus offering wider scope in tonality and modulation. The simplest method was to reduce the perfect fifth not by a quarter of a comma but by one-sixth, i.e. by the sixth root of 81:80, making (in theory) a fifth of some 698 cents. This stretches the major third to 394 cents, but it reduces the enharmonic discrepancy to 19 cents—less than half what it had been. Again, it yields a 'mean-tone', now half of 394 cents.

Other important methods through the 17th and particularly the 18th centuries were to modify the above 'regular' mean-tone systems by 'irregular' systems, in which some of the fifths are reduced by less than others in order to tamper less with the most important thirds. J. S. Bach was probably most familiar with tunings of such kinds (rather than with equal temperament), allowing free modulation from key to key with good effect, as in his 48 Preludes and Fugues (*Das wohltemperierte Klavier*—'The Well-tempered Keyboard'). A name often associated with these developments is that of the German organist Andreas Werckmeister (1645–1706), though in fact he was a prominent advocate and exponent rather than a discoverer. In fact, one of the earliest accounts of mean-tone tuning (in Pietro Aron: *Toscanello in musica*, Venice 1523) could already be called 'irregular' in that after first tuning C–E pure and the fifths C–G, G–D 'a little flat', the A is made so that D–A and A–E sound equal (and thus smaller fifths than C–G).

4. *Equal Temperament.* This radical solution to the foregoing problems was accurately propounded by Mersenne (1636). It starts afresh, side-stepping the natural intervals (save for the octave) by dividing the octave logarithmically into 12 parts. Each semitone step then has the ratio of one to the 12th root of two (or 1:1.05946; equal to 100 cents, the complete octave being 1,200 cents). The Table below shows how some of the intervals discussed above work out in cents, alongside corresponding values at the 'regular' mean-tone. (With cents, intervals are added or subtracted simply by adding or subtracting the figures.) Enharmonic differences have vanished. Double sharps and flats can enter, each exactly a whole tone away from the named note. The fifth lies imperceptibly below perfect (then beating at just below one per second), and though the major third, 400 cents,

is 14 cents (or one-seventh of a semitone) sharp to the pure third, ears have grown so accustomed to it that the pure third of mean-tone temperament, when heard in an historical performance using this tuning, can be at first pronounced to be flat. Among the last to adopt equal temperament were (it is said) British organ-builders up to the Exhibition of 1851. The design and tuning of many non-keyboard instruments, too, as among wind instruments (see *Flute*, 2), has long been regulated by equal temperament, and the positioning of *frets on guitars and other fixed-fret instruments for longer still.

	Mean-tone (¼-comma)	Mean-tone (⅙-comma)	Equal Temperament
E	386	394	400
G	697	698	700
G♯	772 ⎱	787 ⎱	800
A♭	813 ⎰	806 ⎰	
A	890	895	900

5. *Expressive Intonation.* It should perhaps be noticed that temperament has nothing to do with the flexibilities in melodic intonation that often occur naturally and, with non-keyboard instruments and in singing, are often taught, such as what are known in French as *notes sensibles*—sharpened leading-notes—and their complement, the flattened semitone above the tonic. In each case the direct opposite to the tuning of mean-tone temperament applies, in that the sharp is higher than the flat, and (as Berlioz put it, perhaps unnecessarily strongly, in his treatise on instrumentation under 'Concertina') mark 'the practice of musicians' as opposed to 'the doctrine of acousticians' (i.e., of course, those up to his time). ANTHONY BAINES

FURTHER READING
J. Murray Barbour: *Tuning and Temperament* (East Lansing, Michigan, 1953).

Tempestoso, tempestosamente (It.). 'Tempestuous', 'tempestuously'.

Temple blocks (Chinese or Korean). Hollow wooden percussion instruments carved in a skull-like shape, properly of camphor-wood, with wide slit-like mouth. Their traditional carving and lacquering in red and gold imitate their Chinese prototype, named 'wooden fish' (*mu-yu*). From two to five of different sizes, sounding from high to low (not tuned to specific notes), are clamped to a stand and struck with a soft or hard stick according to the sound desired. They became added to dance drummers' kits in the 1920s and orchestral percussion sections have them available for the parts that Walton (three blocks in *Façade*), Britten, and others have written for them.

Temple block: an example of the oriental prototype.

The term 'temple' comes from their former use in Confucian ceremonies, along with a wooden 'trough' in the form of a grain-measure struck on the inside, and the wooden 'tiger' scraped along its notched back with a bamboo.

The *mokubio* is a Japanese version that has become known to percussionists since the 1960s; it may be cylindrical in shape.

ANTHONY BAINES

Tempo (It.). The performance speed of a piece of music. Tempo is traditionally indicated in two ways: by *metronome marks (e.g. ♩ = 70, prescribing a tempo of 70 crotchet beats per minute); and, less precisely, by verbal instructions, conventionally (but not invariably) in Italian (e.g. *adagio*, slow; *accelerando*, quickening; *allegro*, fast). Music before about 1600 (and the music of most non-Western repertories) rarely contains any indication of tempo, this being inferred from the notation and style of the music, or even from its title, if any. Some contemporary, notably aleatory, music demands a more scientifically precise (or differently defined) measurement of tempo than traditional methods provide.

Theoretically, every piece of music with a tempo indication has a 'correct' tempo. In practice, however, such indications vary in usefulness. To begin with, *metronome marks in 19th-century music cannot always be reckoned reliable, for many composers (e.g. Brahms) are known to have disapproved of the rigidity they impose, some (e.g. Beethoven) prescribed different tempos on different copies of the same piece, and some metronome marks are so unreasonably fast as to suggest either that a composer's metronome was faulty or that he had not actually tried the music with the metronome.

Moreover, verbal directions such as *allegro*, *andante*, etc. are imprecise terms, subject to various implications by composers and various inferences by performers. In early (notably Baroque) music they may indicate a 'mood' or 'manner' of performance rather than a speed (e.g. *allegro*, literally 'cheerful'); or they may be used in a purely relative sense in the context of other tempo designations in the same piece; or their meanings and associations for musicians may have changed over the years. In addition, it is not always clear in a music edition whether metronome marks or verbal instructions have the composer's authority or are editorial additions.

Tempo may also be subject to variation through a number of external factors: the size and reverberation time of a hall (e.g. a large or particularly reverberant hall may require a slower tempo if the music is to sound clearly); differing sonorities of instruments, especially keyboard ones; the size of an orchestra; and, above all, the interpretation of the performer. This last factor accounts to the greatest degree for the widely differing tempos encountered in different performances of the same work, all of which may be equally valid. For example, one performer may prefer a slower tempo in order to stress the music's detail or to voice its expressive qualities, while another may consider a faster tempo better suited to its mood or style. Either may overrule the composer's metronome mark or tempo instruction, if any, if he judges it less effective than another; for example, when conducting the Funeral March of Beethoven's 'Eroica' Symphony, Toscanini took about half and Beecham about a third as long again as Beethoven's metronome mark indicates.

The importance of tempo to composers' thinking is reflected in their letters and other writings. Berlioz, for example, related in his *Memoirs* that Mendelssohn maintained that the metronome was unnecessary, since a good musician could judge for himself the proper tempo for a composition; yet the next day, when trying out a piece of Berlioz's at the piano, he asked him what its tempo should be. Wagner complained in his essay on conducting of the wildly incorrect tempos at which some conductors took his *Tannhäuser* overture. And Brahms advised Clara Schumann when publishing her late husband's works not to add metronome marks, as she might well want to change them later and performers would in any case probably ignore them. That attitude was perhaps more common in the 19th century and the early 20th than it is today, when an increasing concern with authenticity has led to greater respect for composers' tempo markings.

See also *Performance Practice*, 6.

PERCY SCHOLES, rev. Judith Nagley

Tempo: A Quarterly Review of Modern

Music [originally *Tempo: The Boosey & Hawkes News Letter*]. English musical magazine founded in 1939.

Tempo alla breve (It.). See *Breve*.

Tempo comodo [*commodo*] (It.). At a convenient, or comfortable, speed.

Tempo di ballo (It.). In the time, or style, of a dance; also the name given to a movement of that type.

Tempo giusto (It.). 1. In strict time. A direction to the performer to keep strictly to time after a departure away from it.
2. At the right, or appropriate, speed.

Tempo maggiore (It.). An equivalent term to *alla breve*; see *Breve*.

Tempo minore (It.). An equivalent term to *Tempo ordinario*, 2.

Tempo ordinario (It.). 1. At an ordinary speed, neither fast nor slow.
2. Common time (4/4), with four beats in the bar (as opposed to two, as in *tempo alla breve*).

Tempo primo (It.; Ger.: *Tempo wie vorher*). In the first time. A direction to the performer to resume the original speed after a change of speed; where there has been more than one such change, 'tempo primo' refers to the first-mentioned speed.

Temporale. In the Roman Catholic liturgy, the feasts of the Lord.

Tempo rubato (It.). See *Rubato*.

Tempo wie vorher (Ger.). 'Tempo as before', i.e. the same as *tempo primo*.

Temps (Fr.). 'Time', usually in the sense of 'beat'; see *Beat*, 1.

Temps fort (Fr.). The first, 'strong', beat of the bar; see *Beat*, 1.

Ten. Abbreviation for *tenuto* (It.), 'held'.

Tenebrae (Lat., 'darkness'). In the Roman Catholic Church, the name for the services of Matins and Lauds sung during the afternoon or evening preceding Thursday, Friday, and Saturday of Holy Week. All the lights are extinguished, one by one, as the psalms are sung, the final candle going out after the *Benedictus*, and Psalm 51 (Psalm 50 in the Vulgate), the 'Miserere', is given in complete darkness. This commemorates the darkness which is said to have enveloped the earth at the time of the Crucifixion.

Tenebroso (It.). 'Dark', 'gloomy'.

Tenendo (It.). 'Holding', 'sustaining'; *tenendo il canto*, 'sustaining the melody'.

Tenor (from Lat. *tenere*, 'to hold'). 1. The term has had various meanings in connection with plainchant, of which the most common were (*a*) a psalm tone (see *Plainchant*, 6); (*b*) the final or key note of a mode; and (*c*) a kind of reciting tone.
2. From the mid 13th to the 16th century, 'tenor' denoted the fundamental voice-part of a polyphonic composition, usually in the form of a pre-existing *cantus firmus*; the other parts were composed 'against' this (hence the term *contratenor*), and at first were named in the order they were composed in after the tenor (*duplum*, *triplum*, etc.). 'Tenor' did not imply any particular range until the 15th century, when well-known singers of tenor parts were sometimes known as 'tenoriste' or 'tenorista'.
3. The tenor voice is the highest male voice using normal voice production, with a range of roughly *c* (known as 'tenor C') to *b′*, or, in fine voices with good training, even high *c″* or *d♭″*. According to the vocal quality, a tenor can be divided into three broad types: light, lyric, and dramatic ('spinto'). The *Heldentenor* (Ger., literally 'hero tenor') is a heavy tenor with much of the quality of a baritone. See also *Counter-tenor*.
4. The name is given to certain instruments deemed to be equivalent in range etc. to the tenor voice, e.g. tenor saxophone, tenor tuba.
5. In the 18th century, an occasional name for 'viola'.

Tenor clef. See under *Clef*.

Tenor cor. Valved brass instrument. See *Horn*, 8.

Tenor horn (Amer.: alto horn; Fr.: *saxhorn alto*, *alto*; Ger.: *Althorn*; It.: usually *genis*). A valved brass instrument. It has the bell pointing upwards and three valves; the pitch is E♭, a fifth below the cornet. See *Brass band*; *Saxhorn*. For the German *Tenorhorn*, a deeper-pitched instrument in B♭, see *Tuba*, 6.

Tenorlied (Ger.). The basic form of German secular song from the 15th to the mid 16th century. The word 'Tenor' refers not to the voice-part of that name, but to the borrowed tune, or *cantus firmus*, which was the only part to be underlaid with the complete text. This

'Tenor' was at first usually sung by the top voice of a three-part ensemble and accompanied by instruments, but later, when four-part writing became the norm, moved down to the tenor voice proper and frequently received vocal accompaniment. However, there was no fixed rule regarding the position of the borrowed tune.

Tenor Mass. The most common type of Mass based on a *cantus firmus, i.e. with the *cantus firmus* placed in the tenor part.

Tenor violin. See *Viola*, 4 and 6.

Tenso. A type of *troubadour* or *trouvère* poetry cast in the form of a dialogue about politics or morality, or some other important social question.

Tenth. See *Interval*.

Tenu, tenue (Fr.). 'Held'.

Tenuto (It., sometimes abbreviated to *ten*.). 'Held', i.e. sustained to the end of its full value, or, sometimes in opera, to be sustained beyond its full value for dramatic effect.

Terana. A sensuous oriental-style dance introduced by Delibes in his opera *Lakmé*. It is in 6/8 time, occasionally lapsing into 3/4.

Terce. The fourth of the *Office Hours of the Roman Catholic Church.

Ternary form. A three-part structure which may be represented by the letter scheme ABA, the final section being a repeat of the first. Each section is usually, though not always, self-contained: i.e. it closes in its own key, and the middle section often provides a strong contrast to the outer two, both in terms of tonality and theme.

Pieces in ternary form may be quite long, because the sections, being self-contained, will often have a formal shape of their own. For example, each of the three sections may itself be *binary in structure. This is particularly true of the *minuet and trio. Here the ternary structure arises from the repeat of the minuet after the trio, though each section may be itself in either binary or ternary form. There are numerous examples of the form, but next to minuet and trio perhaps the most clear is that of the *da capo aria, a stereotyped vocal form most prevalent in the late 17th and early 18th centuries. Here, after a contrasting middle section, the first section of the aria is repeated, often with elaborate embellishments. Ternary form was also used frequently as the basic structure of many 19th-century piano works, particularly

the shorter ones. There are, for instance, numerous examples in Chopin's mazurkas and nocturnes.

See also *Form*, 4.   G. M. TUCKER

Terpsichore. The Greek Muse of dance.

Ter Sanctus (Lat., 'thrice holy'). Properly the same as *Trisagion, but sometimes applied to the Sanctus ('Holy, Holy, Holy') as found in the Roman Catholic Mass or the Anglican Communion Service.

Terz. See *Quint*.

Terzet, terzetto (It.). 'Trio'; *terzettina*, 'triplet'.

Terzi, Giovanni Antonio (*fl*. late 16th, early 17th centuries). Italian lutenist and composer. He published two collections of lute music in Venice (1593, 1599) containing transcriptions of madrigals and motets with some attractive dances and other purely instrumental works, a few by Terzi himself. Some of the works are for several lutes.   DENIS ARNOLD

Terzina (It.). 'Triplet'.

Tessarini, Carlo (*b* Rimini, *c*.1690; *d* after 15 Dec. 1766). Italian violinist and composer. He was a violinist in the orchestra of St Mark's, Venice, until *c*.1733 when he moved to Urbino. He went on several concert tours in the Netherlands, settling there in 1761. His music includes some attractive concertos and sonatas, mainly for strings.   DENIS ARNOLD

Testa (It.). 'Head'; *voce di testa*, 'head voice'. See *Voice*.

Testo (It.). 1. 'Text'. 2. 'Narrator', as in, for example, Monteverdi's *Il combattimento di Tancredi e Clorinda* (1624).

Tetley, Glen (*b* Cleveland, 3 Feb. 1926). American choreographer. He worked with the Netherlands Dance Theatre from 1962. In 1974 he succeeded John Cranko as director of the Stuttgart Ballet; from 1976 he went freelance. He is trained in both classical and modern dance, and his works were at first uncompromisingly modern, for example *Pierrot lunaire* (Schoenberg, 1962); later works have a distinctive blend of classical and modern styles, notably *The Tempest* (Nordheim, 1979) and *Dances of Albion* (Britten, 1980).   NOËL GOODWIN

Tetrachord. A succession of four notes contained within the compass of a perfect fourth. In Ancient Greek theory, tetrachords with the descending order tone–tone–semitone (e.g. A–G–F–E) were joined together to form a series of eight-note *modes, which served, like the modern *scale, as the basis of melodic composition. Medieval theorists likewise adopted several ascending tetrachords, with different arrangements of tones and semitones within the perfect fourth, to act as a melodic basis (see also *Hexachord*). The modern diatonic scale may also be considered divisible into two tetrachords (e.g. C–D–E–F, G–A–B–C).

Tetrardus. See *Mode*, 2.

Thailand. See *South-East Asian Music*.

Theater (Ger.). 'Theatre', but often used to man specifically 'stage'.

Theme. A term most commonly used to denote the principal melodic passages of tonal music, and of non-tonal music which retains the feature of melodic continuity. 'Theme' usually refers to complete phrases or periods, in contrast to the terms 'idea' or 'motive', and is used typically of the more important melodic passages. Thus the first and second themes (or 'subjects') of a sonata-form movement may expose most of the melodic material of the piece and carry the greatest structural weight. Such a view of tonal forms in general is often called 'thematicism', especially when it attempts to show that apparently heterogeneous themes have one common source in a movement or work.

The thematic nature of music from the last 300 years is so conspicuous that it is possible and useful to make thematic catalogues, which record the first theme of a piece. Among the earliest to survive are Haydn's and Mozart's thematic catalogues of their own works. In the 19th century, especially in Liszt's symphonic poems, one theme of an extended composition could represent the central character of a literary programme, and the variation, or 'metamorphosis', of this theme would convey the changing action. Berlioz's *Symphonie fantastique* (1828), with its recurring principal theme or *idée fixe*, is an early, seminal example. See also *Variation form*.

JONATHAN DUNSBY

Theme and Variations. See *Variation form*.

Theme song [theme tune, theme music]. A recurring song or tune which is introduced into a film or television series and which contributes greatly to its success. The first such song seems to have been 'Sonny Boy' from a film called *The Singing Fool* (1928; music by Lew Brown, Ray Henderson, and B. G. de Sylva). Notable examples of the use of theme songs or tunes in

well-known films include the 'Harry Lime' theme from *The Third Man* (Anton Karas) and 'Lara's theme' from *Dr Zhivago* (Maurice Jarre). Each film in the series of James Bond films has its own theme song, such as 'Diamonds are forever' and 'You only live twice', while Henry Mancini's theme tune to the Pink Panther films has already attained immortality.

Some films have used extracts from classical music in the same way, notably *Death in Venice*, which uses the Adagietto from Mahler's Fifth Symphony (as well as other music by Mahler), *Elvira Madigan*, which takes as its theme tune the slow movement of Mozart's C major Piano Concerto, K 467, and *Sunday, Bloody Sunday*, which borrows the Act 1 trio from Mozart's *Così fan tutte*.

Theodora. Oratorio by Handel to a text by Thomas Morell after R. Boyle's *The Martyrdom of Theodora and Didymus*. It was first performed in London in 1750.

Theorbo. See *Lute*, 3.

Theory of Music. Music theory comprises a study of the structure of music, its nature, and its *notation. It is concerned, therefore, with the rudiments of music—essentially the basic terminology of pitch and time—as well as with such subjects as *harmony, *counterpoint, *form, *analysis, and *acoustics.

Theorists of the past have not only provided valuable evidence of contemporary musical thought, but have also helped us re-create, to a surprising degree, the musical sounds of their day. Theorists have also attempted to relate music to *aesthetics and philosophy, and here purely theoretical studies overlap wider areas of *history and *criticism. Among many who have contributed to various aspects of the theory of music are Pythagoras (5th century BC), who linked a mathematical theory of consonance with a conjectured cosmic harmony (see *Ancient Greek Music*, 6d); Gioseffo Zarlino (1517–90), who summarized Renaissance theoretical views (see *Renaissance*, 3); Hermann von Helmholtz (1821–94), a scientist who laid the foundations for modern research into the physiological basis of music theory (see *Acoustics*, 6); and Heinrich Schenker (1868–1935), who developed a system of musical analysis (see *Analysis*, 3a). Others of importance include Guido of Arezzo (c.995–1050; see *Guidonian Hand*; *Hexachord*; *Notation*, 2), Philippe de *Vitry, Johannes *Tinctoris, Heinrich Glarean (see *Mode*, 2c), Thomas *Morley, Jean Philippe *Rameau, Arnold *Schoenberg, and Paul *Hindemith.

Some understanding of theory is indispensable to most musicians, although it is quite feasible to play or sing entirely by ear or through learning by rote without having any technical knowledge of music. Theory and practice need to grow side by side, from the beginner's clefs, note names, and time values, through the music student's study of stylistic composition, orchestration, and authenticity in performance, to the specialized interests of the musicologist.

PERCY WELTON

Theresienmesse ('Theresa Mass'). Haydn's Mass No. 12 in B♭ major, composed in 1799. It refers to the consort of Emperor Francis II of Austria.

Thesis. See *Arsis and thesis*.

Thibaut IV (*b* Troyes, 30 May 1201; *d* Pamplona, 7 July 1253). Count of Champagne and Brie; crowned King of Navarre, 7 or 8 May 1234. Despite his royal descent and involvement with matters of state, warfare, and the crusades, Thibaut IV was one of the leading and most versatile *trouvères* of his day; more songs and verses by him have survived than by any other *trouvère*. His varied output, which was mentioned by Dante and served as a model for many younger poet-musicians, includes courtly love-songs, *jeux-partis* (debates or dialogues in verse form), religious pieces, and crusade songs; most are set syllabically and they are often cast in *Bar form (AAB).

JOHN MILSOM

Third. See *Interval*.

Third inversion. Only chords with four notes (e.g. the *diminished and *dominant sevenths) or more can be placed in third inversion, i.e. with the fourth note of the chord as the lowest:

root position   third inversion

Third stream music. Term introduced by Gunther Schuller in the 1950s to denote music which borrows both from jazz and from 'classical' traditions. Examples include Stravinsky's *Ebony Concerto* (1946), Milhaud's *La création du monde* (1923), and works by Schuller himself.

PAUL GRIFFITHS

Thirty-second note (Amer.). Demisemiquaver (♪).

This Day. See *Hodie*.

This Have I Done for my True Love. Work for unaccompanied chorus, Op. 34 No. 1, by Holst. It is a setting of a traditional carol and was composed in 1916.

Thomas, Charles Louis Ambroise (*b* Metz, 5 Aug. 1811; *d* Paris, 12 Feb. 1896). French composer. He came of a musical family, and studied at the Paris Conservatoire, bringing his studies to a triumphant close by winning the Premier Grand Prix de Rome in 1832. On his return from Rome he turned to the stage for a living and composed a steady stream of *opéras comiques*. His first real success was *Le Caïd* (1849), but his talent was confined to light opera, and his attempts to deal with more serious subject-matter lacked scope and imagination. His successes were the ever-popular *Mignon* (Opéra-Comique, 1866), on a subject from Goethe's *Wilhelm Meisters Lehrjahre*, which achieved 1,000 performances in under 30 years; and, strangely enough, *Hamlet* (after Shakespeare, Opéra, 1868), which remained in the repertory for 70 years. His last three stage works—the operas *Gille et Gillotin*, *Françoise de Rimini*, and the 'fantastic ballet' *La tempête*—were coolly received, owing to Thomas's failure to adapt to changing tastes after the Franco-Prussian War.

Thomas found himself showered with academic honours: in 1851 he was elected to the Académie des Beaux-Arts in the place of Spontini; in 1894 he became the first musician to be awarded the Grand Cross of the Légion d'Honnneur; and having taught at the Conservatoire from 1852 onwards he was finally appointed its director. His tenure of that exalted position (1871–96) was marked by rigid conservatism, against which independent and adventurous students, such as the young Debussy, rebelled; he was also implacably opposed to the younger generation of French composers, such as Bizet, Franck, and Fauré.

WENDY THOMPSON

Ambroise Thomas

Thomson, Virgil (*b* Kansas City, 25 Nov. 1896). American composer. He studied at Harvard University, with Nadia Boulanger in Paris (1921-2) and with Rosario Scalero in New York (1923-4). From 1925 to 1932 he lived mostly in Paris, where he associated with Les *Six and with Gertrude Stein, later the librettist of his operas *Four Saints in Three Acts* (1934) and *The Mother of us All* (1947). In 1940 he settled definitively in New York and became music critic of the *Herald Tribune*, retaining that post until 1954. His style, influenced by Satie, is cool and unpretentious, avoiding anything complex or rhetorical. Songs, piano music and orchestral pieces form the bulk of his large output. He has also written the books *The State of Music* (New York, 1939), *The Musical Scene* (New York, 1945), *The Art of Judging Music* (New York, 1948), *Music, Right and Left* (New York, 1951), *Virgil Thomson* (New York, 1966), and *American Music since 1910* (New York, 1971).

PAUL GRIFFITHS

FURTHER READING
Kathleen Hoover and John Cage: *Virgil Thomson* (New York, 1959).

Thorough bass. See *Continuo*.

Three Blind Mice. Children's round, among the best known in the world. It appears in the *Deuteromelia* (1609) of Ravenscroft, but in the minor, in a shorter form, and with different words.

Three Choirs Festival. See *Festivals, 2*.

Three-cornered Hat, The (*El sombrero de tres picos*; *Le tricorne*). Ballet in two scenes with music by Falla to a scenario by Martinez Sierra based on P. A. de Alarcón's story *El sombrero de tres picos* (1874). It was choreographed by Massine and first performed by Diaghilev's Ballets Russes in London in 1919. It is an expanded and revised version of the pantomime *El corrigedor y la molinera* by Sierra and Falla, performed in Madrid in 1917. Falla arranged two orchestral suites from the score (1919). The work has the same plot as Wolf's *Die Corregidor*.

Threepenny Opera, The. See *Dreigroschenoper, Die*.

Three Places in New England. Orchestral work by Ives, also known as the First Orchestral Set (or *A New England Symphony*). Its three movements are: 1. *The Saint-Gaudens in Boston Common* (1911-12), 2. *Putnam's Camp, Redding, Connecticut* (1912), and 3. *The Housatonic at Stockbridge* (1908-?14).

Threni: id est Lamentationes Jeremiae

Prophetae ('That is to say, the Lamentations of the Prophet Jeremiah'). Choral work by Stravinsky to a biblical text. It is scored for soprano, alto, two tenor and two bass soloists, chorus, and orchestra, and was first performed in Venice in 1958.

Threnody (from Gk *thrēnos*, 'wailing', *ōidē*, 'ode'). A song of lamentation, especially on a person's death. Penderecki's *Threnody for the Victims of Hiroshima* is a 20th-century example.

Through-composed (Ger.: *Durchkomponiert*). Any composition which does not rely on repeating sections for its formal design may be described as through-composed. However, the term is most usually applied to a song in which the music for each stanza is different.
See also *Form, 10*.

G. M. TUCKER

Thule the Period of Cosmographie. Madrigal for six voices by Weelkes, published in 1600. It is one of the most remarkable examples of musical settings of ostensibly unmusical words.

Thunder sheet. See *Percussion Instruments, 5*.

Thunderstick. See *Bull-roarer*.

Tie [bind]. In musical notation, a curved line joining two successive notes of the same pitch, showing that they should form one sound lasting for the duration of their combined values. It is used to join notes either side of a bar-line (Ex. 1*a*) or to make up a total note value that is not available in single notes (e.g. five crotchets, seven quavers; Ex. 1*b*). A tie is also occasionally used to indicate the subtle repetition of the second note.

Ex. 1

(*a*)

(*b*)

See also *Slur*.

Tief (Ger.). 'Deep', 'low'; *tiefgespannt*, 'deep-stretched', i.e. (of a drum-head) loosely fastened, in order to give a low-pitched sound.

Tiento (Sp.), **tento** (Port.). 'Touch'. The Iberian equivalent of the Italian *ricercar*. The term first appeared in vihuela music to denote a free study specially designed for that instrument, and it was later transferred to organ music, where it denoted a contrapuntal piece. Most 17th-century Spanish organists, including Cabanilles and Correa de Arauxo, wrote *tientos*.

Tierce (Fr.). 1. The interval of a third. 2. An organ stop. See *Organ*.

Tierce de Picardie (Fr.). 'Picardy third'. A major third in a tonic chord at the end of a composition which is otherwise in a minor key, thus converting the expected minor chord into a major one (e.g. in the key of C minor the expected closing chord C-E♭-G becomes C-E♮-G). The origin of the name is unknown. It seems to have been introduced by Rousseau in his *Dictionnaire de la musique* (1767), but his derivation is implausible: ' "Picardy third" because this way of ending survived longest in church music, and thus in Picardy, where there is music in a great number of cathedrals and other churches.'

The use of the *tierce de Picardie* was common in the 16th century and throughout the Baroque period.

Till Eulenspiegel. Tone poem, Op. 28, by Richard Strauss, the full title being *Till Eulenspiegels lustige Streiche, nach alter Schelmenweise—in Rondeauform* ('Till Eulenspiegel's Merry Pranks, after an Old Rogue's Tune—in Rondo Form'). Strauss composed it in 1894-5 and abandoned the idea of an opera on the subject of Till's adventures, which are told in a 15th-century source and which have become part of German folklore. Strauss's score has been the basis of several ballets, including one by Nijinsky (1916). Other composers who have written works on the subject include Alpaerts, Blockx, Jeremiáš, Rezniček, and Maximilian Shteynberg.

Timbales (Fr.), **timpani** (It.). In English today used as short for *timbales créoles*: see *Bongos*, 3.

Timbrer (Fr.). 'To stamp'; Debussy's *doucement timbré* means 'softly accented'.

Time. See *Metre*; *Rhythm*; *Tempo*.

Time signature. A sign placed at the start of a piece of music (after the clef and key signature) or during the course of it, indicating the time, or *metre, of the music. It normally consists of two numbers, one above the other, the lower one defining the unit of measurement in relation to the semibreve, the upper one indicating the number of those units in each bar. So a time signature of 3/4 indicates that there are three

crotchets ('quarter-notes', or notes worth one quarter of a semibreve) to the bar, one of 6/8 that there are six quavers ('eighth-notes', worth one-eighth of a semibreve) to the bar.

The table below shows the time signatures commonly found in Western mensural music since about 1700. Some signs, such as C and 𝄴, are relics of Medieval proportional notation, which had a complex system of time signatures of its own (see *Notation*, 6). The sign C now indicates 4/4 (common time); 𝄵 indicates 2/2 and implies a quick duple time (or *alla *breve*).

'Simple' times have a binary subdivision of the unit (e.g. into two, four, eight, etc.); 'compound' times have a ternary one (e.g. into three, six, nine, etc.). The grouping together, or 'beaming', of smaller note values within the unit in each time signature is conventionally arranged in twos or threes in accordance with these principles. It will be seen that the basic unit of measurement in compound time is always a dotted unit, which cannot be shown in the signature as a fraction of a semibreve; signatures for compound time, then, use the next smallest unit as point of reference (e.g. two dotted crotchets to the bar has to be shown as six quavers, 6/8). Although bars under different time signatures may have the same total duration in terms of beats, there is a difference in rhythmic effect, as between, for example, a bar of 3/2 (dividing into three minims) and one of 6/4 (dividing into two dotted minims: see Table 1, facing page).

Signatures other than those illustrated here are occasionally found (e.g. 24/16 in Bach's Prelude No. 15 in the first volume of the *Well-tempered Clavier*). Quintuple time (usually 5/4, subdividing into either 2 + 3 or 3 + 2) has been used for complete pieces or movements from the 16th century onwards, though only rarely and chiefly for special effect; among the better-known examples are the second movement of Tchaikovsky's Sixth Symphony and the movement entitled 'Mars' from Holst's suite *The Planets*. Quintuple time and other 'irregular' metres such as 7/4 and 11/4 are common in some folk musics, particularly east-European, and have thence entered the works of some folk-influenced 20th-century composers, such as Bartók. Composers of contemporary music, if they use time signatures at all, tend to adopt whatever symbols, conventional or otherwise, best express the metre of their music.

PERCY SCHOLES, rev. Judith Nagley

Timore (It.). 'Fear'; *timoroso*, 'fearful'; *timorosamente*, 'fearfully'.

Timpani [kettledrums] (Fr.: *timbales*; Ger.: *Pauken*; It.: *timpani*). The large cauldron-like instruments tunable to different notes, and,

TABLE 1

	BASIC UNIT / TIME	♩ (half)	♩ (quarter)	♪ (eighth)
DUPLE	SIMPLE	$\frac{2}{2}$ or ¢	$\frac{2}{4}$	$\frac{2}{8}$
DUPLE	COMPOUND	$\frac{6}{4}$	$\frac{6}{8}$	$\frac{6}{16}$
TRIPLE	SIMPLE	$\frac{3}{2}$	$\frac{3}{4}$	$\frac{3}{8}$
TRIPLE	COMPOUND	$\frac{9}{4}$	$\frac{9}{8}$	$\frac{9}{16}$
QUADRUPLE	SIMPLE	$\frac{4}{2}$	$\frac{4}{4}$ or C	$\frac{4}{8}$
QUADRUPLE	COMPOUND	$\frac{12}{4}$	$\frac{12}{8}$	$\frac{12}{16}$

though not historically the oldest drums of the West, the oldest in the orchestra and without question the classic drums of our symphonic music. Normally of copper, two, three, or more timpani of differing sizes are played by one performer, each drum tunable over the range of a fifth by changing the tension of the head (calfskin, or nowadays of plastic, which can give very clear notes).

1. *Hand-tuned Timpani.* The traditional timpani, tuned by six or eight T-handled screws which draw down the metal counterhoop (see *Drum*), remained in professional use longest in British orchestras, up to the 1950s, and many amateur societies rely on them still. Otherwise they have been almost entirely replaced by the more expensive, and heavier to transport, pedal timpani or other 'machine' drums (see below, 2, 3), which enable the player to re-tune instantly to different notes.

Most music up to the mid 19th century and much since is scored for two timpani, normally tuned to the tonic and dominant of the movement or piece. The central notes of their respective tuning-ranges lie a fourth apart, *d* and *A*. This makes the compass B♭ to *f* for the

smaller and low *F* to *c* for the larger. It allows eight tonalities, from *F* down to B♭, to have the tonic on the small drum, the ancient choice; these are likewise the keys of the classical *trumpet with which the timpani were intimately allied. Changes in tuning are mostly demanded between movements or, if during a movement, allowing sufficient bars' rest for re-tuning with the handles. The average diameters for a set of two drums are 25″ and 28″.

Works of the Romantic period increasingly call for three drums, as Brahms in some of his major works and Tchaikovsky in most. With the third drum of an intermediate size, the other two became separated more widely in size to add a whole tone at each end of the total compass, the lowest useful note of each drum now usually considered to be, from the smallest downward, *c*, *G*, and E♭; typical diameters are 24″, 26″, and $29\frac{1}{2}$″. (According to the laws of physics, the pitch given by circular stretched membranes of the same thickness varies inversely with the radius and directly with the square root of the tension. From this, two drums of diameters 25″ and 28″, when tuned a fourth apart, frequency ratio 4:3, would show tensions in the ratio 1:0.7, i.e. with the larger drum at about 30 per cent

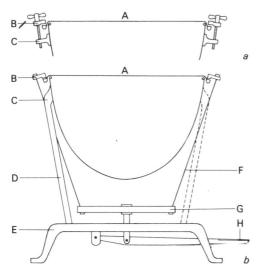

Fig. 1. (a) section of top part of hand-tuned drum;
(b) section of a pedal drum, showing the basic principle.

lower tension. Yet there seems to be some mystery: recent work by Herbert Tobischek lists experimentally-determined pressures of shell against head in which, at D and A tuning for example, both drums show the same tension of approximately 1,000 lbs. By one view, the effects of the air masses within the shells may have some bearing on the apparent discrepancy from simple theory.)

2. *Pedal Timpani.* The basic principle of these is illustrated diagrammatically in Fig. 1. The head (A) is to be tightened from below by the pedal while keeping the main stress on the shell within the top region (B–C) as on a plain hand-tuned drum (upper diagram). The shell is supported on four metal struts (D) rising from the heavy base (E). The tension rods, one of them shown (F), lead down to a disc- or star-shaped frame (G) which is moved up or down by the pedal (H). The classic system is that designed in Dresden by Pittrich, from 1872. Later designs include lighter-weight American models, some with fibreglass shell, and with the tension rods passing inside the shell, emerging near the top to engage the counterhoop.

Pedal actions are very sophisticated, with balanced movement that can be held in any position and an adjustable pitch indicator placed up beside the rim. On one single pedal drum different notes can be played quickly one after another, but never to the point of replacing the need for two or more separate timpani.

There are also 'single handle' machine drums, with one large handle instead of the pedal, allowing a drum to be quickly tuned to a different note with one hand, leaving the other hand free to strike the notes. These appeared in

Germany *c.*1850 and are the timpani that Wagner wrote for in the *Ring.* In Act 1, scene 3, of *Götterdämmerung,* the second of the two timpanists plays seven different notes on two drums within the space of 28 bars, including Hunding's sinister rhythm, absolutely solo.

3. *Rotary Timpani.* These are mounted on a central column which rises from a base and for one part of its length has a screw-thread. The tension-rods lead down to a frame which engages the thread, while another frame, supporting the shell, turns freely on the column. Hence, when the player rotates the drum one way or the other by one hand, both frames rotate together but the tensioning frame moves up or down the screw-thread. The mechanism is usually concealed inside the shell, but may lie outside it. Also, the action is in some cases reversed, the shell engaging the screw and the tensioning turning free, so that in this instance the shell is moved up against the head to increase the tension. These drums do not, of course, leave both hands free from tuning as the pedal does, and the rotation can move the player's favourite striking spot out of reach. But a timpanist has only two feet, and if he must quickly change the note of a third drum, then a rotary drum or one of the old hand-tuned drums can offer the solution.

4. *Timpani-playing.* The two sticks are of cane or wood with ends of felt, or of felt discs pressed together, and of various degrees of softness to suit the music. Each stick is held between thumb and index, the wrist held low. The drums are struck fairly near the rim and if necessary the sound is damped with the fingers.

Pl. 1. Pedal timpani (model by Premier, Leicester).

Ex. 3

Orch.

The timpani roll is also made with hand-to-hand strokes. Among special effects many composers have specified hard or side-drum sticks, giving a more brittle sound. With pedal timpani, the *glissando* with the pedal, upwards or downwards, first became familiar to audiences in works by Bartók.

5. *History: (a) Nakers* (from Arabic *naqqara*). Early kettledrums were of this small kind, beaten with thick sticks, and introduced in Europe after the later crusades from the Middle East (Pl. 3). There they are still played in instrumental ensembles of various kinds: small bowls, often of wood or pottery rather than metal, the larger around 9″ diameter and the other a little smaller. The players may distinguish their sounds as 'tum' and 'tak' (as again where contrasting sounds are made on other drums, struck by the hand in different manners). Medieval European pictures may show little visible difference in size between the two nakers but a remark of Gerson of Paris, soon after 1400, strongly points to sounds of the 'tum-tak' kind.

(*b*) *Large Kettledrums.* These were made in the Middle East from the 12th century as royal instruments. With this status they spread to India and in Africa to Uganda, where they are splendid-sounding drums hollowed in wood and played in carefully tuned sets. The large drums reached Europe in the 15th century as brass horse-drums accompanying trumpets, and these together began to appear in the orchestra during the 17th century, the drums struck with heavy sticks or often in later periods with sticks with disc-shaped wooden ends about 2″ across giving a very crisp sound. In France, Kastner still illustrates these in his *Méthode des timbales* of 1845, though by then Berlioz had been insisting on the choice of soft-ended sticks ('sponge sticks' he terms them) for orchestral use. The 18th-century kettledrums were usually smaller in diameter than later (often around 20″), with the two of a pair differing by only $1″-1\frac{1}{2}″$; this may point to a very considerable difference in tension, giving a markedly brighter sound from the smaller drum whose duty it was

Pl. 2. 'Jubilee', drum horse of the 7th Dragoon Guards, in Edinburgh, 1938; note the smaller drum to the kettledrummer's left.

The two hands are used as far as possible alternately ('hand to hand'), which frequently leads to crossing one hand over the other from drum to drum. Ex. 1 is a timpani flourish in Purcell's *The Fairy Queen* (Symphony to Act 4), one of the earliest solo passages for the drums and in this instance lying naturally for alternate hands starting with the left—as one can test for oneself in dumb-show, the small drum tuned to D being placed on the right (though on the Continent often the other way round). Ex. 2 on the other hand shows a simple group of notes yet calling for cross-beating in either of the two ways indicated (cross-beats here shown bracketed) and executed with a rhythmic swing and a fine visual effect recalling the timpanist's historical parent, the cavalry kettledrummer with the drums slung on either side of the drumhorse. In complete contrast, Ex. 3 is from one of the first major composers to write for pedal drums, Richard Strauss, in *Till Eulenspiegel*: the part is simply headed 'Pauken', without stating initial tunings in the old manner. After a few pages in the score the drums give out five notes of the principal theme (this indicated in Ex. 3 by small notes): the first two notes on the middle drum of three and the last two on the large drum, ending with a roll.

Ex. 1   Ex. 2

L R L R L   L R L R L R L R
                         R L R L R L R L

Pl. 3. Nakers carried on the back of a boy (right), *and a fiddle accompanying dance, miniatures from 'The Romance of Alexander' (early 14th century).*

to sound the tonic. Cavalry kettledrums in Europe today will often be seen to preserve such small dimensions.

The major orchestral breakaway from the formal trumpet-bound, tonic-and-dominant tradition is due to Beethoven: timpani entrusted on their own to principal themes, as at the start of the Violin Concerto and in the Scherzo of the Ninth Symphony, in the latter case exploiting the full tuning-range of the octave Fs—one of his several novel tunings for the two drums. One could say that nothing has really measured up to

Pl. 4. Timpanist from Weigel's 'Musikalisches Theatrum' (c.1720), showing sticks with wooden disc ends.

this since, even with addition of a third drum, which Weber, in the *Peter Schmoll* overture (1804), was early in trying (although he used it merely to continue the old formula when the music moves into the dominant key). There had, in fact, been some enterprising use of the timpani before those times, but in works little known today; Christoph Graupner in a Sinfonia of 1747 gives six timpani a melody on the notes from low *F* up to *d*—very much like Holst in *The Planets* though far exceeded by Berlioz with his 16 drums (10 players) in the *Grande Messe des Morts* (1837).

(*c*) *Pedal Drums.* The first attempt at a 'machine drum' tunable by a single movement is, needless to say, credited to Leonardo da Vinci. Little more was done before a spate of inventions in every country, from a rotary drum by Stumpff, a German living in Amsterdam, in 1821, to the Dresden pedal drum noticed already. Some pedal drums built to earlier specifications back to the 1840s are said still to have been in use in the opera house at Munich in the 1960s.

6. *Solo Repertory.* The written solo repertory of the timpani would not be expected to be large. One might begin it with the Baroque kettle-drummers' improvised flourishes. Kastner (1845) tells how a Berlin timpanist had recently performed a concerto on six drums, running from one to another on a sort of gallery, throwing the sticks in the air and going through the most extraordinary motions without his execution suffering in the least, all accompanied by eight trumpets and full orchestra. There are timpani concertos by P. Pieranzorina, a timpanist born in 1814, and Julius Tausch. There is a sonata for two timpanists by Tcherepnin.

ANTHONY BAINES

Tinctoris, Johannes (*b* Braine l'Alleud, nr Nivelles, *c.*1434; *d* ? 1511). Franco-Flemish theorist and composer. His early career was spent at Orléans, Chartres, and perhaps also as a singer at Cambrai under Dufay. By 1472 he had moved into the service of Ferdinand I of Naples, acting as tutor to the King's daughter, Beatrice. In 1487 he was sent abroad to recruit singers for the Neapolitan chapel; it is not known whether or not he returned to Naples for the remaining years of his life. Only a small quantity of Tinctoris's music has survived, including five settings of the Mass. His theoretical writings, on the other hand, are numerous; they include a dictionary of musical terms (the *Terminorum musicae diffinitorium*, *c*.1473) —the first ever to appear in print (Treviso, 1495)—and at least 11 other treatises variously concerned with notation, contrapuntal technique, and philosophical matters. Popular and influential in Tinctoris's own time, these books are important today for the information they provide about the craft of composition and methods of music education in the late 15th century. JOHN MILSOM

Tin Pan Alley. Originally the name given to a district in New York (28th St., between 5th Ave. and Broadway) where many songwriters, arrangers, and music publishers were located, Tin Pan Alley became synonymous with the American popular music industry from the late 1880s until the middle of the 20th century. During the heyday of Tin Pan Alley, composers like Charles K. Harris, Paul Dresser, Harry von Tilzer, Irving Berlin, Jerome Kern, George Gershwin, Cole Porter, and Richard Rodgers dominated the scene, developing a type of popular song notable for its melodic appeal, well-constructed form, fresh lyrics, and immediate accessibility. MARK TUCKER

Tinto (It.). 'Colour'; *con tinto*, 'colourfully'.

Tin whistle. See *Flageolet*, 1.

Tiomkin, Dmitry (*b* St Petersburg, 10 May 1894; *d* London, 12 Nov. 1979). American composer of Russian birth. The family moved to St Petersburg in 1912 where he studied at the conservatory, played the piano for silent films, and began to compose. He moved to Berlin after the Revolution, studied with Busoni, played with the Berlin Philharmonic, and had some dance music published. He then went to Paris as part of a two-piano act, which toured America in 1925. He appeared at the Carnegie Hall as duettist and soloist and composed the *Mars Ballet* for his ballerina wife Albertina Rasch. He was asked to write for films, which he did reluctantly at first but soon found a fascinating activity; he was to be one of Hollywood's busiest composers and conductors. He wrote a steady stream of film-scores, many of them winning Academy Awards. Some of the best-known are *Duel in the Sun* (1946), *High Noon* (1952), *Return to Paradise* (1953), *The High and the Mighty* (1954), *Friendly Persuasion* (1956), *The Alamo* (1960), and *The Guns of Navarone* (1961). PETER GAMMOND

Tiple (Sp., literally 'treble'). 1. A species of small guitar, see *Guitar*, 5*a*
2. The smaller of the two shawms of the sardana bands in Catalonia; see *Shawm*, 3.

Tipperary. This song, which begins 'It's a long way to Tipperary', was written in 1912 and became a great hit with the British troops during the Great War, and also with the civilian population. It was composed jointly by a crippled man called Harry J. Williams, of the Plough Inn, Temple Balsall, Warwickshire, and a music-hall entertainer called Jack Judge, of Oldbury. In 1928 Judge (who died in 1938) wrote a sequel called 'It's a long way no longer'. The first line of *Tipperary* is inscribed on Williams's tombstone.

Tippett, (Sir) Michael (Kemp) (*b* London, 2 Jan. 1905). English composer. He studied composition with Charles Wood and C. H. Kitson at the Royal College of Music (1923–8) and then worked as a schoolteacher. Feeling, however, that his compositional technique was still immature, he took further lessons with R. O. Morris (1930–2), and even after this it was

Michael Tippett

some years before he was writing music he considered adequate: the Concerto for double string orchestra (1938-9), a piece of strong melodic appeal, is the earliest work which he has published without revision. Here, as in the first three string quartets (1934-46), he was developing a quite individual style comparable with nothing else in English music at the time, the emphasis being on bounding polyphonic lines, luminous textures, and an enriched tonal harmony reminiscent on occasion of Hindemith or Fauré. Sprung, dancing rhythms, which have remained a hallmark of his style, testified to his admiration for the English madrigalists and Purcell, whose music he was bringing to performance through his work with amateur musicians at Morley College in London.

In 1940 Tippett became director of music at Morley College, and the next year performed with musicians there his oratorio *A Child of our Time* (1939-41), the first of several public works in which he has addressed himself to subjects of the deepest current interest. The oratorio is a reaction to a particular Nazi atrocity, but the message it conveys, with reference to a Bach Passion in which Negro spirituals replace the chorales, is not a simple one. Tippett asks not for a condemnation of hatred and oppression but for a recognition of the darkness and light mixed in every human personality, an awareness of division as the prerequisite for healing and wholeness. This is, he has written, 'the only truth I shall ever say', and in different forms it is the theme of the four operas which succeeded the oratorio: *The Midsummer Marriage* (1955), *King Priam* (1962), *The Knot Garden* (1970), and *The Ice Break* (1977).

For all of these works Tippett has written his own texts, curiously combining everyday idiom with philosophizing and a range of imagery stretching from the Bible to contemporary technology, guided by his reading of Jung. He has also developed for each opera a distinctive style. *The Midsummer Marriage*, in which two young people are conducted through self-knowledge before they can join in union, is a great sweep of lyrical melody, rich harmony, and brilliant colour, and its exuberance and

Autograph MS of Tippett's Fourth Symphony, the opening Andante.

vitality brimmed over into other works of the period, including the song-cycle *The Heart's Assurance* (1950-1), the Fantasia concertante on a theme of Corelli for strings (1953), and the Piano Concerto (1953-5).

However, with his Second Symphony (1956-7) Tippett began to be more compact in his musical development and less thoroughly embedded in diatonic harmony. Then, in *King Priam*, he achieved a style, influenced by the most recent music of Stravinsky and Messiaen, in which abrupt juxtaposition was the rule, with ideas strongly marked off from each other by contrasts of harmony, speed, character, and instrumental colour. The fresh vigour of Tippett's style remains, but it is now contained and enclosed in starker images, and the vocal delivery is similarly much more declamatory than in the earlier works—fittingly for an opera of heroes, though heroes of doubt and choice rather than war.

Again there was a group of works exploring the stylistic possibilities opened up by the new opera: the Second Piano Sonata (1962), the Concerto for Orchestra (1962-3), and the cantata *The Vision of St Augustine* (1963-5). And indeed the concision of *King Priam* has continued, even when there has been some return of Tippett's earlier luxuriance, as in *The Knot Garden* and the Fourth Symphony (1976-7). Typically the works of this period are concerned with short, pregnant ideas, and even though these may be fused into something like continuous development—notably in works where Tippett very consciously uses Beethoven as his model, these including the Third Symphony (1970-2) and the Third Piano Sonata (1972-3)—the impression is still of a restless imagination returning again and again to the same preoccupations.

This impression is reinforced by Tippett's choice of subjects for his later works, where again he states the need for an all-encompassing understanding, of different character types in *The Knot Garden*, of different social, racial, and age groups in *The Ice Break*. Moreover, he looks back in both these works to *A Child of Our Time*, as he does too in his Third Symphony and the *Songs for Dov* (1969-70) that came as a pendant to *The Knot Garden*, in finding the promise of redemption and comfort in the blues and jazz of American Blacks. And though since his retirement from Morley College in 1951 he has published his ideas in broadcasts, lectures, and books, it is no doubt in his music that his claims as a modern prophet most powerfully reside.

PAUL GRIFFITHS

FURTHER READING
Michael Tippett: *Moving into Aquarius* (London, 1958, 2nd edn 1974); Ian Kemp, ed.: *Michael Tippett: a Symposium* (London, 1965); David Matthews:

Michael Tippett: an Introductory Study (London, 1979); Michael Tippett, ed. Meirion Bowen: *Music of the Angels* (London, 1980); Eric Walter White: *Tippett and his Operas* (London, 1980); Meirion Bowen: *Michael Tippett* (London, 1982).

Tirade [*coulade*] (Fr.), **tirata** (It.). A Baroque ornament consisting of a quick succession, or 'run', of more than three passing notes, usually but not always consecutive, connecting two principal melody notes separated by a large interval. It was occasionally indicated by a sign ( ), but frequently written out or improvised.

Tirana (Sp.). An Andalusian dance-song, usually in 6/8 time with syncopated rhythms. It was popular in Spain in the 18th century, and the *Tirana del tripili*, thought to be by Blas de Laserna (*c*.1751-1816), became well known in the 19th from its use in Mercadante's opera *I due Figaro*.

Tirare (It.), **tirer** (Fr.). 'To draw', 'to pull out'; *tirando* (It.), *tirant* (Fr.), 'drawing'; *tirato* (It.), *tiré* (Fr.), 'drawn'. The term is used in connection with string playing to mean the down-bow. See also *Poussé*.

Tirata (It.). See *Tirade*.

Titelouze, Jehan (*b* St Omer, *c*.1563; *d* Rouen, 24 Oct. 1633). French organist and composer. In 1585 he went to Rouen and worked as organist at St Jean until 1588, when he became organist at Rouen Cathedral. He was much in demand as an organ restorer and adviser. Comparatively few of his works have survived—mainly skilled polyphonic settings for organ of hymns and the *Magnificat*, designed for performance during Mass. They use old-fashioned contrapuntal techniques based on plainsong but some are enlivened by emotional dissonances and chromaticism. He was also noted as a theorist and literary man, and the prefaces to his organ publications are interesting for the light they shed on contemporary styles of performance. DENIS ARNOLD

Toccata (It.). The past participle of the verb *toccare*, 'to touch'. A toccata is a piece in a free and idiomatic style, usually for keyboard and often in several sections and incorporating virtuoso elements designed to show off the player's 'touch'. The term first appeared in the early 16th century, but the first important collections date from the last decade of the century; they include publications by Andrea Gabrieli and Claudio Merulo. The fanfare preceding Monteverdi's *Orfeo* (1607) is headed 'toccata'. The first great master of the keyboard toccata was Frescobaldi, whose first book appeared in 1615. He was followed by other Italians, such as Rossi, Pasquini, Zipoli, and Alessandro Scarlatti, and by Germans, including his pupil, Froberger, who wrote 24 toccatas. The Baroque toccata in Austria reached its peak in the works of Georg Muffat and Pachelbel; in the Netherlands the form was cultivated by Sweelinck, who modelled his toccatas on those of the Gabrielis, while in north Germany composers such as Buxtehude developed a large-scale rhapsodic type of toccata. Buxtehude's long, sectional pieces, alternating free and fugal sections, are almost indistinguishable from his organ preludes and fugues. Bach wrote six harpsichord toccatas (BWV 912-15 and 910-11) and several for organ, probably modelled on Buxtehude's. Some are coupled with a fugue, in the manner of a prelude. Handel wrote no toccatas.

The form was little used in the early 19th century, but was revived in France by organ composers such as Vierne and Widor, who often concluded their massive organ symphonies with a toccata (Widor's example from his Fifth Organ Symphony is now a popular choice at weddings). Debussy (*Pour le piano*) and Ravel (*Le tombeau de Couperin*) both used toccatas as finales, as did John McCabe in his Concertante for harpsichord and chamber ensemble. Other 20th-century composers, such as Honegger, Martinů, and Prokofiev, have written toccatas in the style of a *perpetuum mobile*, following the example of Schumann (Toccata in C, Op. 7).

Toccatina, toccatino (It.). A miniature *toccata. In the 19th century, Rheinberger and Henselt wrote toccatinas, while Widor included an example in one of his organ symphonies.

Toch, Ernst (*b* Vienna, 7 Dec. 1887; *d* Santa Monica, 1 Oct. 1964). He studied medicine at the University of Vienna, philosophy at the University of Heidelberg (PhD 1921), and piano with Willy Rehberg at the Hoch Conservatory, Frankfurt (1910-13). In composition he was self-taught. He taught composition at the Mannheim Musikhochschule (1913-29) and privately in Berlin (1929-32) before emigrating to the United States in 1934. There he taught at the New School for Social Research in New York (1934-6) and the University of California, Los Angeles (1940-8), and had a notable influence in disseminating the standards and principles of the Austro-German tradition. His works include six symphonies, 13 string quartets, and a variety of vocal pieces. He has also written the book *The Shaping Forces in Music* (New York, 1948).   PAUL GRIFFITHS

Tod Jesu, Der ('The Death of Jesus'). Passion cantata by Graun to a text by Ramler after

Princess Amalia, composed in 1755. Until the mid 20th century it was performed annually in Berlin.

Todt (Ger.). 'Dead'; *Todtenmesse*, 'Mass for the Dead', i.e. *Requiem; Todtenmarsch*, 'Dead March'.

Tod und das Mädchen, Der ('Death and the Maiden'). Song for voice and piano by Schubert (D 531) to a poem by Claudius. It was composed in 1817. Schubert used the theme for variations in the second movement of his String Quartet No. 14 in D minor, D 810, composed in 1824, which is known by the title of the song.

Tod und Verklärung ('Death and Transfiguration'). Tone-poem, Op. 24, by Richard Strauss. It depicts a man's death-bed visions and was composed in 1888-9.

Tōgaku. Literally 'Tang music', a Japanese music imported from China. See *Japanese Music*, 5.

Togli (It.). 'Take away'. A direction used in organ music for the shutting off of any stop etc.

Tolstoy, Lev. See *Novel, Music in the*.

Tomášek, Václav (Jan Křtitel) [Tomaschek, Wenzel Johann] (*b* Skuteč, 17 Apr. 1774; *d* Prague, 3 Apr. 1850). Czech composer and teacher. He received some musical tuition at an early age, but as a composer was largely self-taught. After pursuing a miscellany of disciplines at Prague University he began to study law in 1797, although he already had a reputation as a music teacher. In 1806 he took a position as music teacher and composer to the family of Count George Buquoy where he stayed some 16 years. By the early 1820s he was well known enough to continue as a teacher and freelance composer, and in 1824 he set up a private music school to which many of the composers and performers of the younger generation were attracted, such as Voříšek, Kittl, Měchura, and the critic Hanslick. Tomášek rose to a position of pre-eminence in artistic circles in Prague and was considered important enough for many visiting musicians including Clementi, Wagner, Clara Schumann, and Paganini to pay their respects. Thus his memoirs give a fascinating view of Prague's musical life and many illustrious contemporaries. His attitudes and many of his compositions show Tomášek to have been a committed Mozartian though by no means a slavish imitator. In addition to numerous rhapsodies and seven sonatas for the piano he supported his dislike of current virtuoso showpieces by composing some 42 technically undemanding eclogues. These light, uncomplicated pieces served as models for a variety of composers including Voříšek and Schubert. Apart from a small but distinguished collection of church music and some less successful stage works, Tomášek composed several groups of songs including settings of Goethe (*Erlkönig*), Schiller, Gellert, and some Czech texts.   JAN SMACZNY

Tombeau (Fr.). 'Tomb', 'tombstone'. A name given to compositions written in memory of someone, e.g. Froberger's *Tombeau fait à Paris sur la mort de Monsieur Blancheroche* (Monsieur Blancheroche was a Parisian lutenist who died after falling down the stairs of his home). A 20th-century example is Ravel's *Le tombeau de Couperin*.

Tombeau de Couperin, Le ('The Tomb of Couperin'). Suite for solo piano by Ravel, composed between 1914 and 1917. It is in six movements, each dedicated to the memory of friends who died in the First World War: (1) *Prélude*; (2) *Fugue*; (3) *Forlane*; (4) *Rigaudon*; (5) *Menuet*; and (6) *Toccata*. Ravel orchestrated Nos. 1, 3, 5, and 4 (in that order) in 1919. The score, without No. 1, was used for a ballet, choreographed by Berlin and first performed in Paris in 1920.

Tomkins, Thomas (*b* St Davids, Pembroke-

shire, 1572; buried Martin Hussingtree, Worcs., 9 June 1656). English composer and organist. The third child of a vicar-choral at St Davids Cathedral, he was one of a notable musical family which included several church musicians of some distinction. He was probably a choirboy at St Davids, and at some stage in his career studied with Byrd. In 1596 he was appointed organist in charge of the music at Worcester, and in 1607 he took the B.Mus. at Magdalen College, Oxford. By 1620 he was a Gentleman of the Chapel Royal, succeeding Edmund Hooper as one of the organists the following year; one of his colleagues was Orlando Gibbons. This position worked on a rota system which allowed him to keep his Worcester post. After the death of Gibbons in 1625 Tomkins was one of the principal royal composers, providing much of the music for the coronation of Charles I. The king granted him an annual income of £40 as 'composer of our music in ordinary', but promptly revoked the award on discovering the position had already been promised to Alfonso Ferrabosco (ii). During the Civil War the large organ at Worcester was virtually destroyed, and in 1646 organs were forbidden. Tomkins's home was damaged in the fighting, and he spent the last few years of his life in debt, moving to his son's home in Martin Hussingtree in 1654.

Autograph MS of Tomkins's 'Pretty Wayes for Young Beginners to Looke on', variations on a plainsong.

Tomkins was one of the finest composers of the English school. The bulk of his music was composed for use in church, and while his verse anthems are enterprising, giving the organ some idiomatic keyboard writing in contrast to the solid vocal-based counterpoint of his contemporaries, it is some of the full anthems, such as the superb laments 'When David heard' and 'Then David mourned', which show his emotional power. His book of madrigals (*Songs of 3. 4. 5. & 6. parts*, London, 1622) is one of the most consistently good of its kind by an English composer, its tone predominantly serious even when there are outward signs of gaiety (for example, setting 'fa-la' refrains to complicated rhythms and wistful harmonies). His keyboard works are equally inviting, from the sorrowful pavans (including one 'for these distracted times' written on the death of his royal patron in 1649) to complicated pieces employing a ground bass or plainsong.

Tom-tom. A drum first adopted by jazz drummers of the 1920s, subsequently to become one of the most important of drums both in rock music (see *Drum set*) and in the modern percussion section.

1. In early jazz the tom-tom was a two-headed Chinese drum: fairly shallow, with somewhat bulging shell painted with dragons and flowers, and the heads secured with wide brass nails as customary with drums in China. This is now known as a 'Chinese tom-tom' but has become little used.

2. A modern tom-tom has a deeper cylindrical shell (laminated or acrylic) with screw-tensioning for the two heads. Diameters are from 10″ to 18″, and depths about the same; there may be an internal felt damper to reduce 'thud' noise. A drum set will include from one tom-tom to three or more of different sizes to sound higher or lower. They have brackets for

Chinese tom-tom.

attachment to the bass drum or to a separate metal stand. A 'floor tom-tom' is a large one standing on its own three legs.

Among modern composers who have included tom-toms, Stravinsky has three in *Agon* and suggested their use in *The Soldier's Tale* in place of his original side-drums with the snares silenced. There are also single-headed tom-toms, and these can be tuned to specific notes (like *timpani) by turning the tuning-screws with a coin. For educational music there are versions of these known as 'timp-toms'.

ANTHONY BAINES

Ton. 1. (Fr.). Term with several meanings: (*a*) 'pitch'; *donner le ton*, 'to give the pitch'; (*b*) 'key', 'mode'; *ton d'ut*, 'key of C'; *ton majeur*, 'major key'; *ton d'eglise*, 'church mode'; (*c*) 'tone', in the sense of Gregorian tone (see *Tonus*, 3); (*d*) 'crook'; *ton de trompette*, 'trumpet crook'; *ton de rechange*, 'spare crook' (or simply 'crook'); (*e*) the interval of a whole tone, as distinct from *demiton*, 'semitone'; (*f*) 'sound', 'note', etc.; *ton aigre*, 'shrill sound'; *ton bouché*, 'stopped note' (of horn); *ton doux*, 'sweet tone'.

2. (Ger.). Again, there are several meanings: (*a*) 'pitch'; *den Ton angeben*, 'to give the pitch'; (*b*) 'key', 'mode'; *Tongeschlecht*, 'tone-gender' (i.e. major or minor etc.); (*c*) 'note'; *den Ton halten*, 'to hold the note'; *Tonabstand*, 'interval'; *Tonfarbe*, 'tone colour', i.e. timbre; *Tonfolge*, 'melody'; *Tonfülle*, 'volume of tone'; *Tonhöhe*, 'pitch'; *Tonlage*, 'pitch', 'compass', 'register', etc.; *Tonleiter*, 'scale'; *Tonreihe*, 'note row'; *Tonmass*, 'time' (i.e. length of a beat etc.); *Tonschlüssel*, 'keynote'; *Tonsetzer*, 'composer'; (*d*) 'sound', 'music'; *Tonkunst*, 'knowledge (etc.) of music'; *Tonkünstler*, 'musician'; *Tonlehre*, 'acoustics'; *Tonbühne*, 'orchestra'; *Tonbild*, 'tone picture'; *Tonmalerei*, 'programme music'; *Tondichtung*, 'tone poem'.

Tonadilla (Sp.). The diminutive of *tonada*, 'song'. The word came to be applied to a short Spanish comic opera, with from one to four characters, made up mostly of vocal solos and a few choruses. Like the Italian *opera buffa*, it began as short interludes performed between the acts of a play or opera, but later became an independent piece. The *tonadilla* flourished from the mid 18th century to the early 19th: notable composers of *tonadillas* include Luis Misón, Antonio Guerrero, Esteve y Grimau, and Blas de Laserna. Granados composed some *tonadillas* for voice and piano.

See also *Zarzuela*.

Tonal answer. See *Fugue*.

Tonality. The organization of pitch material

whereby more and less important elements allow music to be articulated in time. All systems of tonality have in common the idea that music progresses away from and towards fundamental pitches, which control the relative importance of all the notes available within a work. Thus in major–minor tonality from the period 1600–1900 the tonal centre is fixed for a passage, movement, or piece; the note a perfect fifth above is the next most important, the fifth below the next, and so on (in C major, these notes would be the tonic C, the dominant G, the subdominant F, and so on).

The tonality of melody in the period of Western music before the 17th century is still the subject of debate. Various modal systems were described by Medieval theorists to account for compositional practice (see *Mode*). Around 1600, a more unified chordal language in European music served to iron out the differences between the modes and to emphasize the concept of *transposition. Two modes (the Ionian on C and the Aeolian on A) became the most common for use at any pitch level, an historical process which combined with the practice of tuning at equal temperament (see *Scale*, 3; *Temperament*, 4).

Major–minor tonality has been described from three points of view. In the 18th century, Rameau codified the principle of inversion: for any key, tonality could be defined in terms of a progression of root notes and their associated triads, whether or not the root note actually sounds in the bass (see *Fundamental bass*). In the 19th century, Hugo Riemann proposed that tonic, dominant, and subdominant roots are of first importance in expressing a tonality. These two theories of the harmonic basis of tonality, called 'fundamental' and 'functional' respectively, suggested that music expresses various tonalities, moving from one to another by means of *modulation. In the early 20th century, both Schoenberg and Schenker proposed that a piece of music can express only one tonality, the less important 'keys' which articulate its structure being only 'regions' or 'prolongations' of tonality (see *Analysis*, 3). This final phase of tonal theory argues in favour of a natural basis for major–minor tonality in the overtones of the *harmonic series. Riemann even suggested that an imaginary 'undertone' series may explain minor tonality (since the major tonality of the overtone series becomes minor if it is inverted 'below' the fundamental), and Schenker believed that all tonality was an unfolding in time and elaboration of the 'chord of nature'—the notes of the major triad.

The increasing chromatic richness of 19th-century music heralded a breakdown of the major–minor system, most famously in Wagner's *Tristan* (1865). In the 1880s and 1890s Debussy was already experimenting with new tonal relationships, using the whole-tone scale to produce symmetrical divisions of the octave. The most radical development of these trends was Schoenberg's *twelve-note style (not to be confused with 'serialism'). Although historians consider this style to have marked the final dissolution of tonality in the 1920s, Schoenberg believed that all music must express tonality in some form, and objected to the term 'atonal'. The concept of a 12-note tonality has recently been investigated, notably by George Perle (*b* 1915). Other developments of tonality, using new kinds of mode (Messiaen), bitonality and polytonality (Milhaud, Ives), and an axis system based on keys related by the tritone (Bartók), reveal the variety of modern concepts of tonality. Schoenberg described music which maintains a remote sense of traditional tonal functions in a chromatic context as using 'extended' tonality. This practice has found its way into some modern jazz and popular music, most of which, however, remains aggressively loyal to the tonal language devised by 17th-century composers.

JONATHAN DUNSBY

Tonal sequence. See *Sequence*, 1.

Tonart (Ger.). 'Key' (in the sense of the key of C major etc.).

Tonary (Lat.: *tonarium, tonarius, tonale*). A kind of chant book; see *Plainchant*, 4.

Tondichtung (Ger.). 'Symphonic poem'.

Tondo (It.). 'Round', i.e. full-toned.

Tone (Fr.: *ton*; Ger.: *Ton*; It.: *tono*). 1. The quality of a musical sound; for example a violinist may be said to have a 'powerful', or a 'full-bodied' tone, a singer to have 'good' tone, etc. 2. In American usage the word 'tone' is synonymous with the English 'note'. The interval of two semitones, i.e. a major second (but see *Temperament*); also known as the 'whole tone'. 4. The recitation formulas in plainchant. 5. For the use of various types of tone in acoustical terms, see *Acoustics*.

Tone poem. See *Symphonic poem*.

Tonguing. In the playing of wind instruments, the interruption of the flow of wind by a motion of the tongue. Single tonguing is effected by a motion equivalent to that required for the enunciation of the letter 'T'; double tonguing by one equivalent to that of 'TK'; and triple tonguing by one equivalent to that of 'TTK' or some such group (see also *Performance practice*, 8). Double and triple tonguing allow of more rapid performance of passages or of repeated notes.

Flutter tonguing (Ger.: *Flatterzunge*) is a special variety introduced by Richard Strauss (chiefly on the flute but possible also on the clarinet and some brass): it consists of a trilling of the letter 'R'.

Tonic. First degree of the major or minor scale.

Tonic accent. The effect of an accent, produced not by emphasis but simply by a note falling on a higher pitch than those following or preceding it. See *Accent*.

Tonic Sol-fa

1. Introduction
2. Early History
3. Letter Notation

4. Later Developments
5. The *New Curwen Method*

1. *Introduction.* Tonic Sol-fa is a method of teaching sight-singing devised by John Curwen, in which the degrees of the scale in any major key are given the *solmization syllables *doh, ray, me, fah, soh, lah, te, doh'* (notes above the compass of the first seven degrees of the scale are marked thus; the *doh* below would be marked *doh,*). The name Tonic Sol-fa emphasizes the fact that the major key note (or 'tonic') is always to be called *doh.*

Curwen's aim was to ensure that a note should be 'heard' mentally before it is uttered. He thus introduced pupils first to the notes of the common chord (*doh-me-soh*), patterning the sounds with the voice and exercising the intervals involved until sound and symbol were firmly associated in the pupil's mind. The rest of the scale was taught in stages in the same deliberate way. Only then was the whole octave attempted. To help the beginner, *sol-fa* initials were employed as a simple form of notation.

Tonic Sol-fa is, in fact, an ingenious system of aural training, not just an alternative way of writing down music, as later developments tended to suggest (see 3 below). Its current revival as the *New Curwen Method* preserves Curwen's teaching principles while introducing further refinements in the light of more recent experience. The obsolete letter notation has been abandoned, and notes are related to the staff from the outset.

Once the beginner has become familiar with the seven *sol-fa* syllables, he should be able to pitch the notes of a simple diatonic tune. With more elaborate melodies, further resources are required. Chromatic degrees are named by changing the vowels of the syllables: sharpened notes use *e* (pronounced 'ee'), and flattened notes *a* (pronounced 'aw'). For the full chromatic scale in the key of F, see Ex. 1.

These chromatic note names are used only for incidental sharpening or flattening. When a tune changes key (or 'modulates'), the new key note is named *doh,* the transition being expressed by a 'bridge note' with a double name. In the following example, the fourth note, *soh* of D major, becomes the new *doh,* of A major, and is therefore given both names (sung as *s'doh*):

Ex. 2.

doh   me   soh   soh/doh   te   doh   soh   doh

To avoid unnecessary chromaticism, scales other than the major are based on different *sol-fa* notes. The minor scale begins on *lah,* the characteristic sharpened sixth of the ascending melodic form being named *bay*:

Ex. 3.

lah,   te,   doh   ray   me   bay   se   lah

lah   soh   fah   me   ray   doh   te,   lah,

Ex. 1.

de   re   fe   se   le

doh   ray   me   fah   soh   lah   te doh'

ta   la   fe   ma   ra

doh' te   lah   soh   fah me   ray   doh

Similarly, the Dorian mode (see *Mode*, 2) runs from *ray*, and the Aeolian from *lah*.

These additional features are introduced only as the need arises. The learner is thus able gradually to build up a vocabulary of musical sounds, each associated with other sounds and in conjunction with the mental stimulus of the familiar *sol-fa* names. Tonic Sol-fa depends upon 'association of ideas' in a musical context. Particularly where children are concerned, this mental process is furthered by consistent use of the hand signs which Curwen devised in 1870 to represent the degrees of the scale. Adopted (and slightly adapted) by Kodály when he made Curwen's Tonic Sol-fa the basis of the method designed for use in Hungarian schools, the hand signs are familiar today in the schools of many lands.

After his discovery of the time names used in the French *Galin-Paris-Chevé system, Curwen adopted them in Anglicized form to simplify the teaching of rhythm. These names are pronounced rhythmically so as to represent the sound of the notes themselves, e.g.:

$\quad$ ♩ = taa $\quad$ 𝅗𝅥 = taa-aa $\quad$ ♫ = taa-tai $\quad$ ♬ = ta-fa-te-fe

2. *Early History.* The circumstances which led Curwen to frame his Tonic Sol-fa method help to explain its character. As a young man he was a gifted teacher and a pioneer in this country of the educational reforms inspired by Pestalozzi (see *Education and Music*, 2). His natural ability coupled with his wide study of teaching methods gave him a remarkable instinct for analysing the processes of the learner's mind. While in his 20s, he was often invited to lecture on general teaching methods in various parts of the country, and it was on an occasion of this kind, in 1841, that he was first called upon to investigate and recommend the most suitable way of teaching children and church-goers to sing.

In the course of that inquiry, Curwen examined and rejected the method outlined in the government-sponsored textbook prepared by John Hullah for use in elementary schools. *Hullah's Manual*, a translation of a French 'method' by Guillaume Wilhem (Paris, 1836), was published in London in 1841; it employed the continental, or 'fixed-*doh*', system, where *doh* is always C. While progress was fairly easy in the early stages, keys other than C major caused difficulties which baffled and discouraged both child and teacher. Curwen was much more impressed by the 'Norwich Sol-fa' system, described by Sarah Glover (1786–1867) in her *Scheme for Rendering Psalmody Congregational* (London and Norwich, 1835) and used by her to train a celebrated children's choir which sang at St Lawrence's Church, Norwich.

Sarah Glover used a 'movable-*doh*' system,

equally applicable in any key, and Anglicized the syllables as *do, ra, me, fah, sole, lah, te*. Her pupils were first trained to pitch intervals pointed out on a vertical chart showing the rising scale; next they sang simple tunes written in her *sol-fa* notation; and finally they sang in parts. Only then were they introduced to staff notation.

After studying and trying out Sarah Glover's system, Curwen was convinced that it was 'the most easy to teach, and the most easy to learn'. He nevertheless subjected Norwich Sol-fa to careful analysis; and though always anxious to acknowledge later the debt which his own system owed to Sarah Glover, Curwen's insight into the beginner's problems enabled him to refine and considerably augment her work. Many of his modifications were the result of his wide study of teaching methods adopted elsewhere, and the source of such incorporated ideas was always meticulously acknowledged in his writings. Tonic Sol-fa was to evolve through that process of analysis and synthesis throughout Curwen's lifetime.

Lacking the government sponsorship accorded to Hullah's method, Curwen was obliged to rely upon meetings of Sunday School teachers, the clergy, mission and temperance workers, evening classes, and his own publications to promote Tonic Sol-fa. Yet, after 20 years' effort, by 1863 it was widely used in Britain, encouraging Curwen to set up his own printing press to publish Tonic Sol-fa scores. Following the Education Act of 1870, Tonic Sol-fa was adopted in the nation's elementary schools. At Curwen's death in 1880 it was in use in schools and amateur choral circles throughout the English-speaking world.

3. *Letter Notation.* The opposition of professional musicians to Tonic Sol-fa centred on the 'peculiar' form of letter notation adopted by Curwen's followers. As we have seen, this notation was originally intended only as an approach device. In his early teaching, Curwen had always firmly related *sol-fa* to staff notation. The position of *doh* on the staff was indicated by a square notehead enabling the pupil to calculate the remaining notes of the scale visually. Both adult and child pupils were expected to learn the *sol-fa* and the staff notation. As time went on, many of his adult pupils were content to rely on letter notation alone to meet their simple needs. And Curwen, anxious to bring music to the poor, insisted less and less on the use of staff notation—a score or a hymnal could be printed in letter notation far more cheaply than in staff notation. After 1863, by which time the publication of an extended repertory in *sol-fa* seemed attainable, Curwen abandoned teaching staff notation. This decision to promote a

rival form of musical notation now seems a rare error of judgement on Curwen's part. For while the Tonic Sol-fa movement was to flourish for at least half a century after Curwen's death, its eventual decline was due to the inability of most of its devotees to read from standard notation.

The brief account of the original form of letter notation that follows should therefore be regarded as a historical document, rather than a guide to current practice, except in a few developing countries where letter notation, first introduced by English missionaries during the 19th century, is still employed.

Pitch. The notes of the rising major scale were notated as *d, r, m, f, s, l, t, d'* (notes in the octave above or below were indicated by an upper or lower index mark). Chromatic note names were written in full, e.g. *d, de, r, re,* etc. The key of a piece was stated at the beginning, and when extended modulation occurred the new key note was named in the score at the point of transition.

Rhythm. The basic symbols were the bar-line and the colon. Bar-lines were equally spaced across the page, no matter how many notes occupied a bar; the weak beats were marked by equally spaced colons; and any subsidiary beat was marked by a shortened bar-line. A dot between two notes divided a beat into half-beats; a comma between two notes divided a half-beat into quarter-beats; and triplets were shown by placing two inverted commas between the notes. Prolongation of a note was shown by a dash. Rests were not given symbols—silence was represented by an empty space. Time signatures were not used. The melodies given in Ex. 4 show the main features of letter notation.

4. *Later Developments.* By the turn of the century, Tonic Sol-fa had not only been adopted throughout the British colonies and in the mission fields, but had also been introduced in adaptations in German-speaking Switzerland, Flemish-speaking Belgium, and in Poland—all areas where the 'fixed-*doh*' system was not traditionally employed. Soon after their introduction in 1870, Curwen's hand signs were adopted in Switzerland by Thomas Wiget to augment J. R. Weber's *do–re–mi* system of 1849. In Germany, Agnes Hundoegger published a version known as *Tonika Do* in 1897. Her work

was continued by Dore Gotzmann, Fritz Jöde, and Elisabeth Noack in the present century. Kodály's choice of Tonic Sol-fa as the basis of a Hungarian method has already been mentioned.

During the last decade of his life, John Curwen had founded the Tonic Sol-fa College 'to preserve and develop' his work. Sadly, as it now seems, preservation received more energy than did development. Curwen's own policy of constantly revising his methods was not followed—even in the 1930s when Tonic Sol-fa began to appear outmoded. By mid-century the institution had adopted a purely defensive role. Tonic Sol-fa had been allowed to petrify. Ironically enough, at that very time the lasting worth of Curwen's principles was being demonstrated afresh in the schools of Hungary.

A chart showing Curwen's and Kodály's hand signals.

To remedy that situation, a working party of experienced teachers was set up at the London University Institute of Education during 1970–1 to re-examine Tonic Sol-fa with the present needs of schools in mind. They found that the outmoded letter notation could indeed be dispensed with, leaving Curwen's main

Ex. 4.

Key Bb .s₁ | d :d |d ,r .m ,f :s .d | r   :r .m ,f |m ||

Key D :l | s :– |– .f ,m :f ,m ,r | d :– | ||

teaching principles intact; that *sol-fa* and staff notation could readily be integrated; and that sight-singing could be seen as a means of sharpening children's aural awareness rather than as an end in itself. Those recommendations were forwarded to the Tonic Sol-fa College, and after due debate a collateral institution, the Curwen Institute, was founded in 1974 to promote a revised form of Tonic Sol-fa on the lines recommended.

5. *The New Curwen Method*. As a result of these deliberations, the *New Curwen Method* was prepared by Dr W. H. Swinburne and published, after two years' experimental use in schools, in 1980. It follows Curwen by concentrating upon training the ear, by introducing the notes of the scale in careful stages, and by using hand signs. But instead of letter notation, the hand signs are themselves used as a preliminary form of notation—the hand being moved up and down against a blackboard staff so as to represent accurately the rise and fall of pitch. Other innovations include devices to develop the inner ear and the musical memory; a creative element is provided by regular call for individual extemporization of balancing phrases; and part-singing is introduced at an early stage. The intention is not to teach sight-singing as an end in itself, but to develop those aural concepts and skills upon which all musical response depends, and without which attempts to teach sight-singing invariably disappoint. Once this has been achieved—with obvious benefit to all aspects of music-making, in and out of the classroom—reading from staff notation follows effortlessly.   BERNARR RAINBOW

FURTHER READING
Bernarr Rainbow: *John Curwen: a Short Critical Biography* (London, 1980).

Tonkünstlersozietät. See *Concert*, 5.

Tonlos (Ger.). 'Toneless', or 'soundless', 'unaccented'.

Tono. 1. (Sp.). In general, any type of Spanish song, sacred or secular; more specifically in the 17th century, a short song originally for solo voice, later for two or three voices, used to introduce a play or other stage performance.
  2. (It.). 'Tone', in any general sense; specifically 'whole tone' (see *Tone*, 3).
  3. (It.). 'Key' or 'mode'; specifically a church mode, or the recitation formula belonging to it (see *Tonus*).

Tonreihe (Ger.). 'Note-row'.

Tonus (Lat., from Gk. *tonos*, 'tone'). Term used in three senses in the Middle Ages. 1. The

interval of a major second. 2. *Mode. 3. A plainchant recitation formula. There were numerous chant recitation tones in the Middle Ages, mostly for the singing of psalms and canticles and the intoning of prayers and lessons. For psalms there were more than a dozen, one for each of the eight modes and several others—the best-known irregular one was the *tonus peregrinus*, or 'wandering tone', so called because its main reciting note changed half-way through. Tones for prayers are usually extremely simple, but those for some important lessons, such as the reading of the Genealogies of Christ at Christmas, are more ornate. Usually most of an intonation takes place on one note, the *tenor*, repeated over and over again for as much of the text as is necessary. The first few notes usually lead on to the *tenor* through rising steps; a cadence at the end of each line falls away from the *tenor*. There are usually subordinate cadences half-way through a verse (*mediatio*; sometimes also at other points (*flexa*) in long verses). This same procedure is repeated for each verse of the psalm or other text.
(For illustration see *Plainchant*, Ex. 2.)
                                    DAVID HILEY

Torch dance. A dance which accompanies a torch-lit procession. See *Fackeltanz*.

Torch song. A term used occasionally in the late 1920s and the 1930s to classify a blues-orientated ballad of lost, unrequited, or otherwise unsuccessful love. Generally in the jazz idiom, it was the Tin Pan Alley equivalent of the blues, and would usually be sung by a female singer in cabaret or revue, such as Libby Holman (1906–71); she was considered the leading torch singer of her day with songs such as 'Moanin' low' and 'Body and soul'. The first use of the term and its origins are difficult to pinpoint, but it was probably simply a slang abbreviation of 'carrying the torch' with its implication of suffering. Published songs that used the title included *The Torch Song* by Harry Warren in *The Laugh Parade* (1931), *Torch Song* by Irving Berlin in *Face the Music* (1932), and *The Torch Singer* by Henry Sullivan in *Thumbs Up* (1934).

Tordion [tourdion] (Fr.). A 16th-century dance, described in Arbeau's *Orchésographie* (1588) as being similar to the *galliard, but lighter and quicker. The dance has the basic step pattern of the *cinque pas*, is in triple time, and was usually performed after a *basse danse.

Torelli, Giuseppe (*b* Verona, 22 Apr. 1658; *d* Bologna, 8 Feb. 1709). Italian violinist and composer. He was a member of the Bolognese school of composers, playing in the orchestra of the Accademia Filarmonica there from 1684 and two years later becoming one of the string players at the civic church of S. Petronio. He remained there until the orchestra was temporarily disbanded in 1696, when he became leader of the orchestra of the Margrave of Brandenburg at Ansbach. He visited Vienna in 1699, but returned to Bologna in 1701 on the revival of the S. Petronio orchestra, remaining in its service until his death.

Torelli was one of the major figures in the early history of the concerto (see *Concerto*, 4). Although a contemporary of Corelli, he represents a more progressive attitude to the *concerto grosso*. Among the works from his early years in Bologna are several unpublished pieces for trumpets and strings, and it was probably the experience of writing bright, simple melodies for the trumpets that gave him a penchant for incisive, rhythmic themes. In place of Corelli's rich counterpoint there is an emphasis on the top line, and an early leaning towards the solo concerto (to be realized in his Op. 8) is apparent in some movements, where quickly moving passages are marked 'solo', in order 'to avoid confusion'. He was one of the first to use the *ritornello* principle, and the *concerti grossi* and solo concertos of his Op. 8 (Bologna, 1709) use the three-movement quick–slow–quick order of the Italian opera overture, as opposed to the previously more usual slow–quick–slow–quick scheme of the *sonata da chiesa*. Torelli's music was influential and widely known in his lifetime, and eight volumes of sonatas and concertos were published in Bologna between 1686 and 1709, although a considerable amount remains in manuscript.   DENIS ARNOLD

Tornare, tornando (It.). 'To return', 'returning'.

Tosca. Opera in three acts by Puccini; text by Giacosa and Illica, after Sardou's drama *La Tosca* (1887). Produced: Rome, Teatro Costanzi, 14 January 1900; London, Covent Garden, 12 July 1900; New York, Metropolitan Opera, 4 February 1901. Cavaradossi (ten.), a painter and republican, aids Angelotti (bass), the consul of the former Roman Republic, who has escaped from prison. Tosca (sop.), a singer and Cavaradossi's lover, jealously believes that Cavaradossi is having an affair with the beautiful Marchese Attavanti. The cruel and lustful police chief, Baron Scarpia (bar.), plays on Tosca's jealousy and also her love for Cavaradossi, whom he has had arrested and tortured. The cries of her lover break down Tosca's resistance and she reveals Angelotti's hiding place. Scarpia tells her she can save her lover's life only by giving herself to him, and in exchange he will arrange a mock execution for Cavaradossi. Tosca agrees, but seeing a knife on Scarpia's supper table, seizes it and kills him. She hurries to join Cavaradossi to tell him of the mock execution he must go through. The shots ring out and Cavaradossi falls dead; Scarpia has tricked Tosca. But his murder has been discovered, and, distraught, she jumps from the battlements of the Castel Sant'Angelo.

FURTHER READING
Nicholas John, ed.: *Tosca*, English National Opera Guides (in preparation).

Toselli, Enrico (*b* Florence, 13 Mar. 1883; *d* Florence, 15 Jan. 1926). Italian composer of operas and operettas. A pupil of Sgambati and Martucci, he was a successful concert pianist in his early years, until his sensational marriage in 1907 to Archduchess Louise of Austria-Tuscany led to the neglect of his keyboard technique. He is still known by his popular song *Serenata* (1900).   DENIS ARNOLD

Tosti, (Sir) (Francesco) Paolo (*b* Ortona sul Mare, 9 Apr. 1846; *d* Rome, 2 Dec. 1916). Italian composer and singing teacher. He was educated in Naples where he taught until 1869. He was soon a prolific writer of ballads and light songs and settled in Rome where he became singing-master to Queen Margherita of Italy. He made many visits to London from 1875, and finally settled there in 1880, becoming singing-master to the Royal Family, for which services he was knighted in 1908. He wrote a vast number of songs to Italian, French, and English texts, many of which had a great vogue in Victorian times—such as 'Goodbye' (*Addio*), 'Ideale', 'La Serenata', and 'Mattinata'.

PETER GAMMOND

Tosto (It.). 'Rapid'; *più tosto*, 'quicker' (not to be confused with *piuttosto*, 'rather'—either meaning 'rather than' or 'somewhat'); *più che tosto*, 'as soon as'.

Tost Quartets. Name given to 12 string quartets by Haydn, Op. 54 Nos. 1–3, Op. 55 Nos. 1–3, and Op. 64 Nos. 1–6, all composed between 1788 and 1790. They are so called because they are dedicated to the Viennese violinist Johann Tost.

Totentanz ('Dance of Death'). Work for piano and orchestra by Liszt, composed in 1849 and revised in 1853 and 1859. It comprises variations on the *Dies irae*. Busoni made an arrangement of it.

Touch (on piano etc.). See *Piano*, 14; *Organ*, 4.

Touche (Fr.). 1. 'Fingerboard', of a stringed instrument such as the violin; *sur la touche*, 'bow over the fingerboard'. 2. 'Key', e.g. of a piano. 3. 16th-century name for a fret (of a lute, guitar, etc.).

Toujours (Fr.). 'Always', 'still'; e.g. *toujours lent*, 'still (remain) slow'.

Tous (Fr.). 'All'; see *Tutti*.

Tovey, (Sir) Donald (Francis) (*b* Eton, 17 July 1875; *d* Edinburgh, 10 July 1940). English pianist and writer on music. He was the son of a master at Eton College; he trained privately as a pianist, and then went to Oxford to study classics. On graduation in 1898 he spent some years as a pianist and composer. In 1914 he was appointed professor of music at Edinburgh University, in which post he remained for the rest of his life. It was there that he wrote his famous programme notes for the Reid concerts (which he also conducted), although they were only collected together in his later years and published as the seven-volume *Essays in Musical Analysis* (London, 1935-44, cut and reprinted in two volumes, 1981). These, together with a slight book on Beethoven (London, 1944) and some miscellaneous essays, are nowadays unfashionable among musical scholars because their general descriptive analysis has been displaced by the more thorough thematic analysis of Schenker and his followers. Nevertheless, they are models of their kind and helpful guides to the general reader, especially for Tovey's insight into the effects of tonality on musical structures.   DENIS ARNOLD

Toye. A name given in the Elizabethan and Jacobean periods to a short, light-hearted composition for keyboard or lute, e.g. John Bull's *The Duchess of Brunswick's Toye*, from the Fitzwilliam Virginal Book.

Toy Symphony (Ger.: *Kindersymphonie*; Fr.: *La foire des enfants* or *Symphonie burlesque*). Name originally given to the little symphony, once thought to be by Haydn, scored for first and second violins, double bass, keyboard instrument, and a series of toy instruments, including cuckoo, quail, nightingale (bird warbler), trumpet, drum, rattle, and triangle.

The piece is now thought to be by Leopold Mozart (1719-87), or possibly by Haydn's brother, Michael. It is still popular with school orchestras. A similar, but more elaborate, composition was written by Andreas Romberg (1767-1821), and other composers have followed suit. Mendelssohn wrote two, but they are lost.

Tpt. Abbreviation for trumpet.

Tr. Abbreviation for trumpet, trill, or treble.

Trabaci, Giovanni Maria (*b* Monte Pelusio [now Irsina], nr Potenza, *c*.1575; *d* Naples, 31 Dec. 1647). Italian composer and organist. He was in the service of the royal chapel at Naples for much of his life, succeeding Giovanni de Macque as *maestro di cappella* in 1614. He composed a considerable amount of keyboard music, including two pieces intended for chromatic harpsichord, remarkable for their strange harmonies; some of his toccatas demand a virtuoso technique and are reminiscent of Frescobaldi's style. He also wrote over 150 sacred works.   DENIS ARNOLD

Tract. Latin chant of the Roman Mass, usually sung before the Gospel at Lent and on other penitential days. A small group of chants for the procession to the font at the Easter vigil service were also given Tract melodies. Tracts have texts comprising several psalm verses.

It has been the traditional belief that Tracts are among the oldest of all Gregorian melodies, because: *a*) they were sung by a soloist throughout, without any antiphon or response, a type of psalm-singing known to date back to the 4th century; and *b*) they rely heavily on ornamental melodic formulas arranged according to a plan akin to simple psalmodic recitation, perhaps the outcome of ancient oral tradition. However, recent research inclines to the opposite view. The argument is bound up with the problem of Old Roman chant (see *Plainchant*, 3), that is, the version of Roman chant used in Rome itself, modified during its adoption in the Empire of Charlemagne to produce what we now know as Gregorian chant. Contrary to the usual pattern of events, it appears that several tracts, perhaps the majority, were composed in Frankish lands

Ex. 1

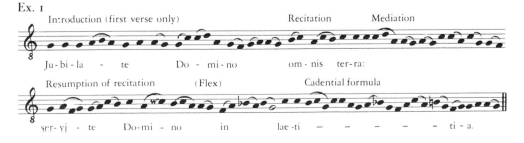

and later adopted in Rome. Thus they may be no older than the 8th century. This also agrees with the fact that the oldest manuscripts (of the late 8th century) appear to have caught the Tract in mid-development, as it were, while new Tracts were still being composed and before they had all found a fixed place in the liturgy. The oldest sources contain only 21 Tracts between them, but new ones were composed throughout the Middle Ages; the modern Vatican *Graduale romanum* has 70.

All Tracts are in either the 2nd or the 8th mode (see *Mode*, 2). Ex. 1 gives an analysis of one verse of a Tract in mode 8 (for an explanation of the terms used, see *Tonus*, 3).

DAVID HILEY

Traduction (Fr.), **traduzione** (It.). 1. 'Translation' (of a libretto etc.). 2. An 'arrangement'. 3. 'Transposition'.

Traetta, Tommaso (*b* Bitonto, nr Bari, 30 Mar. 1727; *d* Venice, 6 Apr. 1779). Italian composer. He studied in Naples under Porpora and Durante, and then produced operas there from 1751. In 1758 he was taken up by the Duke of Parma, whose French theatre intendant introduced Traetta to the music of Rameau and the conception of the *tragédie lyrique*. Traetta thereupon wrote several works on classical themes, including *Armida* (1761), *Ifigenia in Tauride* (1763)—both for Vienna—*Sofonisba* (1762), and *Antigone* (1772). *Ifigenia* and *Antigone* show the ideals of Gluck at work in an Italian style. Traetta was director of music at the Venetian Conservatorio dell'Ospedaletto in 1765, and in 1768 went to Russia, where he succeeded Galuppi as composer to Catherine the Great; he left in 1775 because of ill health and after a season in London returned to Venice. Traetta was one of the most remarkable opera composers of the 18th century, and study of his scores reveals a strong sense of drama in his music; there is clearly a case for occasional revival of his 'reform' operas.   DENIS ARNOLD

Tragédie lyrique. Term coined by the librettist Philippe Quinault (1635–88) and by Lully—and first used by them for *Cadmus et Hermione* (1673)—for a genre of opera which would make use of tragic mythological or epic subjects, with great attention to clarity of declamation and naturalness of action. It was nevertheless much criticized, even in its heyday, for the high-flown and exaggerated treatment of its subjects in its reflection of the *gloire* essential to Louis XIV's court entertainment. It became a stilted convention, anticipating many of the rigid features of *opera seria* and laying itself open to vigorous parody by the librettist Charles-Simon

Favart (1710–92). The term fell into disuse in the early 19th century; it had long been applied in a much more general way by Lully's successors from Rameau to Gluck and then Grétry, Gossec, and others. See also *Opera*, 5.

JOHN WARRACK

Tragic Overture (*Tragische-ouvertüre*). Concert overture, Op. 81, by Brahms, composed in 1880 and revised in 1881.

'Tragic' Symphony. Schubert's Symphony No. 4 in C minor, D 417, composed in 1816. The title is Schubert's own.

Traîné (Fr.). 'Dragged'.

Tranquillo (It.). 'Tranquil'; *tranquillamente*, 'tranquilly'; *tranquillità, tranquillezza*, 'tranquillity'.

Transfiguration de notre Seigneur Jésus-Christ, La ('The Transfiguration of our Lord Jesus Christ'). Work by Messiaen to texts from the Bible, the Missal, and by St Thomas Aquinas, for 100 voices, piano, cello, flute, clarinet, vibraphone, marimba, xylorimba, and orchestra. It is in 14 sections and was composed between 1965 and 1969.

Transposing Instruments. Instruments for which the music is written higher or lower than it sounds by a known or stated interval. (Should the interval always be an octave—as an octave higher with guitar and double bass—then the instrument need not be considered a transposing one.)

Stringed instruments are rarely transposing (an exception is the violino piccolo: see *Violin*, 8*b*). Practically all the regular transposers are wind instruments. With these the operative interval is in most cases stated in the instrument's designation, e.g. 'B♭ clarinet' or 'clarinets in B♭'. The rule is that the named note, in this example B♭, is that which the instrument will sound when the player reads or composer writes the note C. All the other written notes correspondingly sound a tone lower. There are, however, some cases where knowledge of the transposing interval is assumed, as with the cor anglais (English horn), the interval (a fifth lower than written) here being always the same, whereas on clarinet, horn, trumpet, saxophone, etc. this is far from being the case.

These transpositions are for the benefit of the performer, in that they allow a woodwind player, for example, to react to any given note written on paper always with the same fingering when required to change to a deeper or higher

TABLE 1

WOODWIND TRANSPOSITIONS	
Parts as written	Actual sound
Alto flute (in G)	Fourth lower
Oboe d'amore (in A)	Minor third lower
Cor anglais (in F)	Fifth lower
Bass oboe or Heckelphone (in C)	Octave lower
Clarinet in E♭	Minor third higher
Clarinet in D	Tone higher
Clarinet in C	As written
Clarinet in B♭	Tone lower
Clarinet in A	Minor third lower
Basset horn (in F)	Fifth lower (see Note 1 below for notes written in bass clef)
Alto clarinet in E♭	Major sixth lower
Bass clarinet (normally assumed to be in B♭)	Here two notations: (i) normal, in treble clef: a ninth lower; (ii) Wagner and some others: a tone lower, using bass clef freely. The part then looks more 'bass' but infringes the purpose of transposing since it makes the player 'rethink' while fingering
Bass clarinet in A	Similarly two notations: (i) tenth lower; (ii) minor third lower
Saxophone, B♭ soprano	Tone lower
Saxophone, E♭ alto	Major sixth lower
Saxophone, B♭ tenor	Ninth lower
Saxophone, E♭ baritone	Octave and a sixth lower (so that by imagining bass clef instead of treble, one can read the actual sounds, but remembering to add three flats to the key signature)

TABLE 2

BRASS TRANSPOSITIONS		
Designation	Sounds above/below the written notes	
	HORN	TRUMPET
In B♭	'B♭ alto': tone lower 'B♭ basso': ninth lower (see Note 1)	Tone lower
In A	Minor third lower	Minor third lower
In A♭	Major third lower	Minor sixth higher (see Note 3)
In G	Fourth lower	Fifth higher
In F	Fifth lower	Fourth higher (see Note 4)
In E or E♭	Sixth lower (minor or major)	Third higher (major or minor)
In D or D♭	Seventh lower (similarly)	Tone or semitone higher
In C	Octave lower (see Note 2)	As written

Notes to Table 2

1. Horn in B♭. Parts in older music frequently fail to specify 'alto' or 'basso', in which case the matter has to be decided as best one can by context (if with many high notes, 'basso'). 'Horn in A', or 'A♭', is occasionally 'basso' in later music, e.g. Verdi, then sounding a tenth lower.

2. 'In C'. Occasionally in the earlier Viennese classics this is 'C alto', sounding as written.

3. The octave difference between 'in A' and 'in A♭': in early 19th-century music, usually 'in A' means trumpets crooked down to A; 'in A♭', crooked up to A♭. Should in either case the transposition listed above make nonsense of the music, then try the other! In the same period 'in B♭' occasionally reads a seventh higher.

4. 'Tromba contralta' in F in Russian works, e.g. Rimsky-Korsakov, sounds a fifth lower than written.

instrument of the same kind, irrespective of the different sounds produced; and correspondingly with brass instruments. The composer or arranger obligingly arranges for this with the appropriate transposition, to which he is so accustomed that when writing a part for cor anglais or for horn in F, and wanting the sound of F, he writes the C above, without having to stop to think. A conductor or other experienced score-reader then does the opposite, seeing (in this example) C but mentally 'hearing' the F below, having quickly noted the various different designations at the beginning of the score. Only in more complex instances like that quoted in Ex. 2a might he have to pause for an instant on a first reading of the score, to see what the harmony of the wind instruments actually amounts to. Schoenberg held that these transpositions should be abolished, in full scores at least, but they are so ingrained among musicians that to write all wind parts at sounding pitch has been found to make things harder, not easier.

Tables 1 and 2 below are laid out from the score-reading point of view. In Table 1, wherever the key is stated in parentheses, it is, or can be, omitted from the designation of the instrument in score and part. A part 'in C' (sounding as written or an octave lower) needs to be specified as such in cases where (as with clarinet, trumpet, etc.) the instrument can be in other keys also. With the brass in Table 2, the note headings do not necessarily refer to different actual instruments as they do in Table 1, for in older times a horn or trumpet was put in different keys by inserting crooks (see *Horn*, 6b) and the heading tells which crook to insert; players today, no longer using crooks, make as needed their own transpositions at sight, but this is no concern of the score-reader.

For some transpositions especially concerning band music, see *Brass band*, and for flute band, *Flute*, 9.

Note also: bass clef when used for low notes of horn (also basset horn, Table 1) and occasionally trumpet; the older practice is to write the notes an octave lower than they would be if in the treble clef (Ex. 1a). The preferred modern practice is to continue into the bass clef logically (Ex. 1b). The context usually makes it quite clear which method is adopted.

Cornet transpositions: as horn from 'in B♭' (alto) downwards; but 'in C' sounds as written.

Bass trumpet: as horn in E♭, D, C, and B♭ 'basso'.

Wagner tubas: Wagner himself changed his method for these in the full scores of the *Ring*.

(i) In the Prelude to *Götterdämmerung*: tenor tubas in B♭, sounding a ninth

Ex. 1

(a)

Sounds on Horn in F

(b)

lower; bass tubas in F, sounding an octave and a fifth lower. Bruckner follows this method in his Seventh Symphony, but in the Eighth partly the next (ii).

(ii) *Das Rheingold*: sounding respectively a tone and a fifth lower than written.

(iii) For the rest of the cycle the scores have (tenor) 'in E♭', sounding a sixth lower (but in bass clef a third higher); and (bass) 'in B♭', sounding a ninth lower (but when in bass clef, a tone lower).

ANTHONY BAINES

Transposition. Performance or notation of music at a pitch different from the original by raising or lowering all notes by the same interval.

For certain instruments music is usually notated in transposition (see *Transposing Instruments*). Many 20th-century composers, led by Schoenberg, have preferred to write scores entirely 'in C', that is, with all parts written as they sound. Transposing keyboard instruments, where the keyboard may be shifted in relation to the strings, date from at least as early as 1537, but fell into disuse in the 19th century.

Transposition of the notated music in the performance of Medieval vocal works was probably common, but by the early 16th century the use of soprano, alto, tenor, and bass clefs at pitch—that is, non-transposing notation—was becoming standard. The printing of vocal music at various transpositions to suit different vocal ranges (high, middle, and low voice) is still widespread: for some Romantic song cycles where the tonal relationships between numbers ought to be preserved (e.g. Schumann's *Frauenliebe und -leben*) it is questionable. Being able to transpose from one key to another at sight is an important skill for the church organist, and was considered an indispensable way of practising by the great 19th- and early 20th-century piano teachers. Brahms noted at the beginning of his *51 Exercises for Piano*, 'these and similar exercises are also to be practised in other keys'.

Ex. 2

(a) Orchestral score
of Bruckner:
Symphony No. 7,
Adagio

(b) Short score with
transposing
instruments
written at sounding
pitch

The concept of transposition is central to theories of *twelve-note composition and of the set structure of *atonal music. Messiaen codified 'modes of limited transposition', where certain transpositions produce the same scalic segments as appear in other transpositions: that is, a mode can be transposed at only a limited number of intervals, so that a specific, coherent pitch vocabulary is available for any mode. Webern in his later works often used twelve-note sets which similarly permit of only a limited transpositional variety.　JONATHAN DUNSBY

Traps. A name given to the percussion ensemble of the jazz and dance orchestras. Once the jazz band had ceased to be a marching band, which sometimes employed more than one drummer, the percussion unit became a one-man affair, with the bass drum operated by a foot-pedal (an invention credited to a Black drummer called Dee Dee Chandler *c*.1895), side-drum, hi-hat or sock cymbal (introduced by Vic Berton but given its ultimate 'high' form by Kaiser Marshall *c*.1926), woodblocks, cowbells, and so on (see *Drum set*). These became popularly known as the 'traps', presumably an adaptation of the English abbreviation of the word 'trappings' which was in common vogue from early in the 19th century. The term is no longer in fashionable use.　PETER GAMMOND

Traquenard (Fr.). Literally, 'ambush' or 'trap'. A late 17th-century German dance found in the orchestral suites of Georg Muffat, Johann Fischer, and J. P. Krieger. The origin of the name is unknown.

Trascinando (It.). 'Dragging', i.e. holding back, *rallentando*; *tratto*, 'dragged' (usually used in the negative, *non tratto*).

Trascrizione (It.). 'Transcription', 'copy'.

Trattenuto (It.). (1) 'Held back'. (2) 'Sustained'.

Trauer (Ger.). 'Mourning', 'sorrow'; *trauerig*, 'mournfully'; *Trauermarsch*, 'funeral march'; *Trauermusik*, 'funeral music'; *trauervoll*, 'sorrowful'.

Trauermusik ('Mourning Music'). Work by Hindemith for viola (or violin or cello) and orchestra, composed in 1936. He wrote it in a few hours, after he heard of the death of King George V, for performance at a concert the next day. The last of its four short movements uses the chorale *Vor deinen Thron tret ich hiermit* ('Old Hundredth').

Traum (Ger.). 'Dream'; *Traumbild*, 'dream-picture'; *träumend*, 'dreaming'; *Träumerei*, 'reverie'; *träumerisch*, 'dreamy'; *Liebesträume*, 'love-dreams'.

Träumerei ('Reverie'). Piece for solo piano by Schumann, No. 7 of his *Kinderscenen*, Op. 15 (1838).

Travers, John (*b c*.1703; *d* London, June 1758). English composer and organist. A chorister at St George's Chapel, Windsor, he studied with Maurice Greene and with Pepusch, who bequeathed him part of his valuable library. He pursued a career as an organist, and was appointed to the Chapel Royal in that capacity in 1737.

Travers wrote a great deal of sacred music, including a collection entitled *The Whole Book of Psalms* for one to five voices and harpsichord (London, *c*.1750) and a Service in F, a *Te Deum*, and several anthems included in Samuel Arnold's volume of *Cathedral Music* (London, 1790). His *18 Canzonets* were very popular.
　WENDY THOMPSON

Traversa, traverso (It.), **traversière** (Fr.), **Traversflöte** (Ger.). See *Flute*.

Traviata, La ('The Wayward One'). Opera in three acts by Verdi; text by Piave, after the drama (1852) and novel (1848) *La dame aux camélias* by Alexandre Dumas fils, based on his own experiences. Produced: Venice, Fenice, 6 March 1853; London, Her Majesty's, 24 May 1856; New York, Academy of Music, 3 December 1856. Alfredo Germont (ten.) falls in love with the beautiful courtesan, Violetta Valery (sop.), known as the Lady of the Camelias. She is aware that she is dying from consumption. Finding a man she can truly love for the first time in her life, she leaves her *demi-monde* life and goes to live with Alfredo in the country. There she is visited by Alfredo's father, Giorgio Germont (bar.), who has come to ask her to give up Alfredo: his daughter's engagement is threatened by the scandal of the association. She agrees to make the sacrifice and returns to her former protector, the Baron Douphol (bar.). Alfredo publicly insults Violetta at a party given by Flora Bervoix (mezzo); he is challenged to a duel by the Baron and is also disowned by his father. He eventually learns the truth about Violetta's sacrifice and returns to find her dying.

FURTHER READING
Nicholas John, ed.: *La traviata*, English National Opera Guides (London, 1981).

Treble. A high voice (particularly of a child), or a high instrument in a family of instruments (e.g. recorder, viol); hence the appropriate vocal or instrumental part. In early music it was the

Adelina Patti as Violetta in Verdi's 'La traviata' (Covent Garden, London, 1880s).

name given to the highest (or occasionally second highest) part in a vocal ensemble and was thus equivalent to 'superius', 'cantus', and 'discantus'. Later the voice was more usually referred to as 'soprano', except for children's voices.

Treble clef. The G clef (not to be confused with the *soprano clef). See under *Clef*.

Tre corde (It.). In piano music, an indication to depress the sustaining pedal. See *Piano*, 12.

Tregian, Francis (*b* 1574; *d* London, 1619). English amateur musician. The son of a Catholic who was imprisoned and exiled for his faith, Francis Tregian was sent to study at Douai and subsequently became chamberlain to Cardinal Allen of the English College in Rome. He returned to England in 1605 to reclaim his father's estate in Cornwall, but four years later was himself convicted of recusancy and incarcerated in the Fleet Prison, where he remained until his death.

It was during his period of imprisonment that Tregian copied three large anthologies of music. They included vocal and instrumental works by the principal Italian composers of the time as well as keyboard pieces by his fellow countrymen, especially by those with sympathy for the Catholic cause. The most famous of these volumes is the *Fitzwilliam Virginal Book*.

DENIS ARNOLD

Tregian's Anthology. This term is loosely used to describe two of the three manuscript collections of keyboard music compiled by Francis Tregian during his 10-year period of incarceration in the Fleet Prison, London, as a Catholic recusant. The other manuscript is the *Fitzwilliam Virginal Book*. The two manuscripts comprising Tregian's Anthology are now MS Egerton 3665 in the British Library (containing over 1,000 villanellas, madrigals, fancies, dances, and motets), and the 'Sambrooke MS', now in the New York Public Library, which is a continuation of the first, containing motets, a pavan, and madrigals for five to eight voices. These three manuscripts together (comprising over 2,000 pieces) are among the most important early 17th-century collections of English and Italian music. Several pieces by Tregian himself are included: Egerton 3665 includes a five-part instrumental *Balla d'amore* and two Italian polyphonic madrigals. The collection is biased towards Catholic composers, such as Byrd, but nearly one-fifth of the total is devoted to the works of the Protestant Giles Farnaby.

Treibend (Ger.). 'Driving', i.e. hurrying.

Tremain, (Albert) **Ronald** (*b* Feilding, New Zealand, 9 Oct. 1923). New Zealand composer. He studied at Canterbury University College and at the Royal College of Music in London. He attended Petrassi's summer masterclass in Rome and a conducting course in Siena, and was appointed senior lecturer in music at the University of Auckland in 1957, a position he held until 1967, when he became Visiting Professor of Theory and Composition at the State University of New York, Buffalo. He was senior lecturer in music at Goldsmith's College, London (1969–70), then professor and chairman of the Department of Music at Brock University, Ontario, Canada. He has won a variety of awards and prizes for his music, which is characterized by a sensitivity to words and a lyrical feeling, as in his *Three Mystical Songs* for mezzo and string orchestra (1951, settings of Vaughan, Traherne, and Herrick) and his later *Four Medieval Lyrics* (1964) for mezzo and string trio which employ an extended chromatic tonality. His settings of New Zealand poets include M. K. Joseph's 'Boy, Girl, Flower, Bicycle', and 'Three Poems' by A. R. D. Fairburn. His *Allegro for Strings* and *Five Epigrams for Strings* show accomplished writing with transparent textures. His latest works exhibit a creative eclecticism.

J. M. THOMSON

Tremando, tremante, tremolando (It.). To be played or sung with *tremolo.

Tremblement (Fr.). In the 17th and 18th centuries, an alternative name for the *trill; *tremblement mineur*, alternative name for *vibrato.

Tremolando (It.). See under *Tremolo*, 1.

Tremolo (It.). 'Trembling', 'quivering'. Confusion of terminology surrounds the terms *tremolo* and *vibrato. The simplest solution would seem to be to use *tremolo* for change of intensity on or repetition of one note, and *vibrato* for a wavering of pitch; but some writers on the voice reverse this distinction. *Tremolo* in the first sense describes a number of related effects.

1. On stringed and other instruments, the fast repetition of a single note, or, by extension, the alternation of two notes. It may be regular in rhythm (as in Ex. 1), or unmeasured (the latter is sometimes distinguished as *tremolando*). The measured repetition has been used to create tension and excitement in music since the early Baroque period; it was generally superseded by the unmeasured variety in the later 19th century. The piano can simulate these effects by an alternation of notes an octave apart.

Ex. 1

(a)

(b)

2. More specifically, an ornament used by string players of the 17th and 18th centuries. The note is lightly repeated within a single bow-stroke, the separations being scarcely noticeable. The sign is a wavy line above a long note, or above a series of repeated notes.

3. A vocal ornament of the 17th century, consisting of a fast reiteration of one note (but without the exaggerated separations sometimes perpetrated today). Confusingly, the contemporary Italian term was *trillo*, while *tremolo* at the time meant a type of trill (see *Ornaments and Ornamentation*, 2). For an example of the vocal *tremolo*, see Ex. 2 in the latter article.

SIMON MCVEIGH

Tremulo. The same as *tremolo.

Trenchmore. An English country dance of the 16th and 17th centuries. It was in lively triple time, with dotted rhythms. The dance became very popular during the Restoration period; one writer complained in 1689: 'in King Charles's time there has been nothing but Trenchmore and the Cushion-Dance, *omnium gatherum*, tolly-polly, hoite come toite'.

Trenodia (It.). 'Threnody'.

Trepak. A Cossack dance in rapid duple time. There is an example in Tchaikovsky's *Nutcracker* suite.

Trescone (It.). A lively Italian folk dance in duple time which originated in the district around Florence. The dancers indicate their chosen partners by dropping a handkerchief before them.

Trg., Trge. Abbreviation for triangle.

Triad. A chord of three notes, consisting in its most basic form of a 'root' and the notes a third and fifth above it, forming two superimposed thirds (Ex. 1a). If the lower third is major and the upper one minor, the triad is described as major (Ex. 1a); if the lower is minor and the upper major, the triad is minor (Ex. 1b); if both are major, the triad is augmented (Ex. 1c); if both are minor the triad is diminished (Ex. 1d). In practice, triads frequently occur in inversions (Ex. 2a) and in open positions (Ex. 2b). See also *Harmony*, 2, 3.

Ex. 1.

Ex. 2

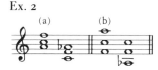

Trial by Jury. Operetta in one act by Sullivan to a libretto by W. S. Gilbert. It is styled a 'dramatic cantata' and is the only one of their works which is sung throughout with no spoken dialogue. It was first performed in London in 1875.

Triangle. A percussion instrument made of a steel rod, usually around a centimetre thick and long enough to be bent into a triangle measuring from 4″ to 10″ along each side and open at one corner. It is best suspended by a fine gut, held in the hand or by a paper-clip attached to the music stand. The beater is a steel rod, thinner than that of the triangle and up to 6″ long. For single strokes the triangle is struck on the outside, choosing the place where the sound will best suit the musical context. The trill is made on the inside from side to side: for a *crescendo* one begins near the top corner, gradually coming downwards where more force can be given with the beater. Sometimes special effects are demanded, as using a wooden or soft-ended beater, giving a more bell-like sound (bringing out lower harmonics of the vibration).

The triangle shape suggests that the instrument was evolved primarily for trills or quick rhythms (a square, or rather a lozenge, hung by one corner, would, with the 90-degree angle, make quick side-to-side playing far more difficult). In folk music the triangle is used chiefly in those southern parts of Europe where the castanets are played, and in similar quick rhythms. Its widest non-orchestral use has, however, been as an easily made and far-carrying calling instrument, often very large, hung up outside farmhouses—in the USA as in Europe—or to serve as a fire alarm, the large size and great thickness of the rod giving a far-carrying, clanging trill.

In many old forms (the triangle is seen from the 14th century) there are five or six loose iron rings on the lowest side, apparently to jingle in fast rhythms; some village-bands in Bohemia are said still to have had such rings on their triangle at the beginning of the 20th century. In the Renaissance period the instrument was also made in a trapeze-shape with a holding-ring at the top and called, from its appearance, a 'stirrup'; this had no open corner and must have sounded more like a little bell.

The triangle entered the orchestra first in opera. A Hamburg opera of 1710 has it in a 'folk' scene. Grétry, and Gluck (*Iphigénie en Tauride*, 1779), used it for exotic colour, and it became added to the military *Turkish music. Berlioz, in Act 1 of *The Trojans*, calls for a whole *jeu de triangles* to accompany a group of the antique *sistrums shaken on the stage, and modern works may call for four or so different triangles, contrasting in sound from high to low.

ANTHONY BAINES

Tricinium (Lat.). A composition for three voices or instruments. The term was most often used in Germany in the 16th century.

Trihoris [trihory] (Fr.). A kind of *branle danced in Brittany in the 15th and 16th centuries. Arbeau describes it in his *Orchésographie* (1588) and provides the only surviving example of the music.

Trill [shake] (Fr.: *cadence, tremblement, trille*; Ger.: *Triller*; It.: *trillo*). An ornament consisting of a rapid alternation of the main note and the note above, normally slurred, and particularly, though not uniquely, associated with cadences. More natural to instruments, and very characteristic of earlier keyboard music, a good trill has nevertheless long been regarded as part of a virtuoso vocal technique.

Both sign and method of performance have varied over many centuries of use. Among the signs used are *tr*, ⁀, and +, all appearing over the note. The first of these has been standard since the late 18th century. A flat, natural, or sharp sign can be placed above *tr*, to indicate a chromatic inflexion of the upper note; a wavy line may define the extent of the trill (see Ex. 1).

Ex. 1

The method of performance is variable in a number of ways. In the first place, written-out interpretations have normally been couched in carefully measured rhythm. But there is evidence of a more flexible practice in performance throughout the trill's period of use—for example, the possibility of gradually and imperceptibly speeding up the repercussions.

Further, the beginning and ending of the trill have been differently treated over the ages. The modern trill simply begins on the main note and ends without suffix, unless otherwise indicated (see Ex. 2; note that Ex. 2*d* approximates to a turn; see *Turn*, Ex. 2*c*).

The late Baroque trill, however, begins with the upper note. This may be extended into an *appoggiatura (sometimes notated ⁀), and more complex openings are possible (see Ex. 3; both *b* and *c* may be indicated by small notes).

It will be noted that the upper-note start gives this trill a harmonic colouring quite unlike that of the modern type. Two types of ending are typical: the single note of anticipation (separated from the trill; see Ex. 4*a*); and the turn (incorporated into the rhythm of the trill; see Ex. 4*b*). The sign ⁀ also indicates the turned ending.

One of these endings should be provided even when not notated (and, conversely, if the suffix is notated a trill should be added). However, in fast passages a half trill will suffice (Ex. 5; there may be more repercussions).

Although Baroque composers may use the extended sign (⁀) to indicate a trill of some length, the short sign (⁀) does not generally imply only a half trill.

Ex.2

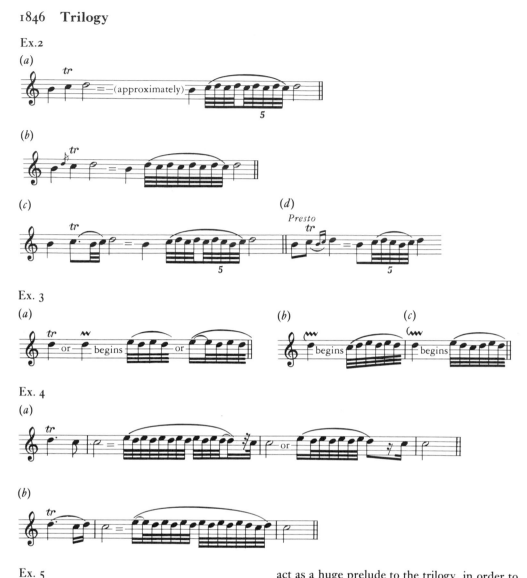

(a)

(b)

(c)   (d)

Ex. 3

(a)   (b)   (c)

Ex. 4

(a)

(b)

Ex. 5

In music of the Classical period (to Beethoven) an upper-note start is still expected. Increasingly the suffix (usually a turn) was notated in full-size or grace-notes. The present conception of the trill, starting on the main note, dates from *c*.1830.   SIMON MCVEIGH

Trilogy (Fr., Ger.: *Trilogie*; It.: *trilogia*). In music, a set of three compositions on a common theme. Wagner described his *Ring* cycle of operas as a trilogy (*Die Walküre*, *Siegfried*, and *Götterdämmerung*), since these deal with the conception, birth and manhood, and death of the hero, Siegfried. *Das Rheingold* is intended to

act as a huge prelude to the trilogy, in order to explain why the Rhine Gold was stolen in the first place, and the resulting curse. The conductor and composer Felix Weingartner wrote an operatic trilogy based on the *Orestes* plays of Euripides. See also *Trittico*.

Trinity College of Music, London. British music college, founded by H. G. Bonavia Hunt in 1872 as a School for the Study and Practice of Music for the Church, but from 1876 extending its activities to cover all fields of music. The College was incorporated with the title Trinity College in 1875, and renamed Trinity College of Music in 1904. In 1880 the present buildings in Mandeville Place, Wigmore Street, were opened. The founders and successive generations of musicians and administrators were pioneers in many areas of education, and in 1874 the College instituted a system of Local Centre

Examinations in Music and Speech which now covers 1,000 local and school centres. In 1902 the College endowed the King Edward VII Professorship after a petition to the University of London urging the establishment of a chair of music; the College is recognized as a teaching school of the University. Courses are for performers and teachers, and the College continued its pioneering work by inaugurating a scheme of Junior Exhibitions in 1906, which was subsequently taken up by other music colleges, and by establishing a department of 16th- and 17th-century music in 1936. Meredith Davies has been Principal since 1979.

Trinklied (Ger.). 'Drinking song'.

Trio (Ger.: *Terzett*; It.: *terzetto*). 1. Any group of three performers, singers or instrumentalists, or any music written for such a combination. A vocal trio may or may not have an accompaniment: examples of unaccompanied trios include the three-voiced canzonets of Morley and his contemporaries, while many 16th-century madrigals associated with the court of Ferrara included trio sections inspired by the voices of the three famous 'ladies of Ferrara' (three virtuoso sopranos). Famous operatic trios include that for three sopranos in the last act of *Der Rosenkavalier*, and there are several trios for different vocal combinations in Mozart's *Così fan tutte*. The normal string trio is for two violins and cello (Haydn wrote 20 such trios), but the most important type is the piano trio (piano, violin, and cello), for which Mozart, Beethoven, Schubert, Schumann, Mendelssohn, Brahms, Dvořák, and Ravel, among others, have written fine works. Another fairly common type is the horn trio, of which Brahms's Op. 40 is perhaps the best known. An instrumental trio usually has three movements.

2. The central part of a *minuet or *scherzo (in a sonata, symphony, or similar work). In the 17th century it was usual, especially in France, to compose two dances to be performed in alternation: they would frequently be scored to provide contrast, with, for example, a minuet for strings in four or five parts being followed by one for wind in three parts (hence the name 'trio' for this second dance). This practice led to the common 18th-century arrangement of minuet–minuet 'en trio'–minuet (repeat of the first), as in Bach's First Brandenburg Concerto. In 18th- and 19th-century sonatas and symphonies the trio, which formed part of the third movement (originally a minuet, later a scherzo), retained the lighter contrasting texture, in orchestral works often involving prominent woodwind. In late 19th-century orchestral works (e.g. the symphonies of Dvořák, Bruckner, and Mahler), trio sections are often in dance rhythms and styles. A trio section is normally followed by a repeat of the first part of the movement, usually modified in some way or with a coda. In some pieces, e.g. Beethoven's Seventh Symphony, the trio section may be briefly recapitulated.

The central section of a march is also known as a trio, on the same principle of contrast: it, too, is generally more melodious. The trio section of Elgar's *Pomp and Circumstance* March No. 1 in D contains the famous tune which was adapted to be sung as 'Land of Hope and Glory'.

3. In organ music, a piece (or section thereof) to be played on manuals and pedals, each in a different registration for contrast.

WENDY THOMPSON

Trionfi ('Triumphs'). Theatrical triptych by Orff, comprising *Carmina Burana*, *Catulli Carmina*, and *Trionfo di Afrodite*. It was first performed in Salzburg in 1953.

Trionfo di Afrodite ('Triumph of Aphrodite'). Scenic concerto (*concerto scenico*) by Orff for soloists, chorus, and orchestra. It is a setting of Latin and Greek texts by Catullus, Sappho, and Euripides and was first performed in Milan in 1953. It is the third part of Orff's trilogy *Trionfi*.

Trio sonata. The most important form of Baroque chamber music, usually scored for two violins (or other melody instruments) and cello or bass viol with keyboard continuo. See *Sonata, 3*.

Triple concerto. A concerto for three solo instruments and orchestra or other instrumental ensemble. Bach wrote two triple concertos for three harpsichords and strings, but probably the best known today is Beethoven's Triple Concerto in C, Op. 56, for piano, violin, and cello with orchestra.

Triple counterpoint. See *Invertible counterpoint*.

Triple-croche (Fr.). 'Triple-hook', i.e. the demisemiquaver or 32nd-note (♬).

Triplet. Three notes that are to be performed in the time of two; they are indicated by the figure '3' placed above or below the three notes, e.g.

Triple time. See *Time signature*.

Triple-tonguing. See under *Tonguing*.

Triplum (Lat.). 1. In three parts; used in Medieval polyphony to describe a composition for three voices, e.g. 'organum triplum'.

2. In 13th- and 14th-century polyphony, the 'third' voice-part in *organum* or a motet, that is, the voice immediately above the *duplum and next but one above the tenor. In later music the equivalent voice was termed 'cantus', 'superius', or similar. The term 'triplex' is also found. See also *Part*, 1.

Triptych (Eng.), **triptyque** (Fr.). See *Trittico*.

Trisagion or **Trishagion** (from Gk, *tris*, 'thrice', *hagios*, 'holy'). The chant 'Holy God, Holy and mighty, Holy and immortal, Have mercy upon us', found in all the ancient Eastern liturgies, the Gallican liturgy, and thence the Roman Catholic liturgy, where it is sung as part of the *Improperia on Good Friday. It is sung antiphonally by phrase, the Greek 'Hagios o Theos ...' being answered by the Latin 'Sanctus Deus ...' to the same melody.

Tristan und Isolde. Opera in three acts by Wagner; text by the composer, after Gottfried von Strassburg's *Tristan* (*c*.1210). Produced: Munich, Court Theatre, 10 June 1865; London, Drury Lane, 20 June 1882; New York, Metropolitan Opera, 1 December 1882. Tristan (ten.)

Lauritz Melchior and Frieda Leider, celebrated interpreters of Wagner's 'Tristan und Isolde' during the 1930s.

is taking Isolde (sop.) to be King Mark's bride. He refuses through his squire Kurwenal (bar.) to see her on the ship. She describes to Brangäne how he was wounded in winning her from her betrothed, but healed by her (she will not admit love). She orders Brangäne to prepare poison for her and Tristan, but Brangäne substitutes a love potion. They drink it and become aware of their love.

Isolde takes advantage of her husband Mark's absence hunting with Melot (ten.) to meet Tristan. In the great love duet they sing of their passion and how it can only flourish in night. Melot causes them to be surprised, but the king is too grief-stricken to show anger at Tristan's betrayal. Isolde answers Tristan that she will follow wherever he goes; he is attacked by Melot and allows himself to be wounded.

In Tristan's castle in Brittany, Kurwenal tries to cheer his sick master, who thinks only of Isolde. The repeated sad strain of a shepherd's pipe tells that Isolde, sent for by Kurwenal, is not in sight. When the shepherd's joyful tune announces Isolde's ship, Tristan excitedly tears off his bandages and dies in her arms. A second ship brings Mark and Melot, and Kurwenal dies in killing Melot, unaware that they have come to pardon Tristan. Isolde sings of the love which she can only now fulfil in the deeper night of death.

FURTHER READING
Nicholas John, ed.: *Tristan and Isolde*, English National Opera Guides (London, 1981).

Triste (Fr., It.). 'Sad'; *tristesse* (Fr.), *tristezza* (It.), 'sadness'.

Tritone (Lat.: *tritonus*). An interval of three whole tones, i.e. the augmented fourth (C–F♯) or diminished fifth (C–G♭). In the early Medieval period the tritone required no special treatment: it occurs in some plainchant melodies, and the Lydian and Hypolydian modes span an augmented fourth with their first four notes (F–B). It seems first to have been designated a 'dangerous' interval when Guido of Arezzo developed his system of hexachords, and with the introduction of B♭ as a diatonic note (see *Solmization*), at much the same time acquiring its nickname of 'diabolus in musica' ('the devil in music'). However, as the little rhyme 'mi contra fa/Diabolus est in musica' indicates (it is the sound of *mi* 'against' *fa*, not juxtaposed with it, that is forbidden), the tritone was considered dangerous only in a vertical sense; melodically it continued to be used fairly freely (see *Musica ficta*).

In traditional harmonic thinking the tritone forms a part both of the diminished and of the dominant seventh; it is therefore important in the first instance for weakening the tonality of a passage and thus assisting modulation, and in the second for affirming the tonality, particularly at cadences (see *Harmony*, 3). The tritone has continued to be associated with evil, especially in 19th-century opera (e.g. Scarpia in *Tosca*). It also occurs in the whole-tone scale (see *Scale*, 5).

Trittico (It.). 'Triptych', i.e. a series of paintings on three panels, such as is commonly found over an altar, where the two side panels close over the central one. Puccini gave the name *Il trittico* to his group of three one-act operas (*Il tabarro*, *Suor Angelica*, *Gianni Schicchi*), which are not connected in subject-matter, but were intended to be performed together as one evening's entertainment: thus, his use of the term distinguishes it from *trilogy.

Tritus. See *Mode*, 2.

Triumphes of Oriana, The. Collection of English madrigals, generally assumed to be in praise of Queen Elizabeth I. Thomas Morley gained the idea from an Italian anthology called *Il Trionfo di Dori* written on the occasion of the wedding of a Venetian nobleman. He commissioned most of the better-known English composers to contribute and intended to publish it in 1601, but because of delays it came out two years later, and the queen had already died. Each madrigal ends, ironically in these circumstances, with the refrain 'Long live fair Oriana'.

Triumphlied ('Song of Triumph') Work, Op. 55, by Brahms for baritone, chorus, and orchestra, composed in 1870-1 to celebrate Prussia's defeat of France. It is a setting of a text from Revelation 19.

Triumph of Neptune, The. Pantomime in 10 scenes to music by Berners with a libretto by Sacheverell Sitwell. It was choreographed by Balanchine and first performed in London in 1926. Some of the music was scored by Walton; an orchestral suite was arranged by Berners (1926-7) and a longer one by Roy Douglas.

Trochaic. See under *Metre*.

Trochee. A poetic foot of two syllables, strong–weak (– ◡). The adjective is 'trochaic'. For its equivalent in the rhythmic modes, see *Notation*, 3.

Troilus and Cressida. Opera in three acts by Walton to a libretto by Christopher Hassall based on Chaucer and other sources (but not Shakespeare). It was first performed at Covent Garden in 1954, in a revised form in 1963, and with further revisions in 1976.

Trois (Fr.). 'Three'; like *à deux*, *à trois* has two opposing meanings: either 'in three parts', or a direction that what have been three instrumental parts (e.g. three violins) should now join to play the same line of music.

Troisième (Fr.). 'Third'; *troisième position*, in string playing, 'third position'. See *Position*.

Tromba marina [trumpet marine] (Fr.: *trompette marine*; Ger.: *Trumscheit*). A bowed stringed instrument of the past which existed in an early form now known only from pictures and descriptions of the 15th and 16th centuries; of the later form many examples have survived in collections, mostly from the 18th century.

Scene from the première of Walton's 'Troilus and Cressida' (Covent Garden, London, 1954).

1. *The Early Form.* This consists of a narrow tapered soundbox from 3′ to 4′ long, triangular in section and open at the wider end. Along it runs a single gut string tuned by a peg at the narrow end. The instrument was generally held up in the left hand, pointing forwards and upwards, with the narrow end against the chest (Pl. 1), while the thumb (or forefinger) of the same hand touched the string at points where it would produce natural harmonics of the note it was tuned to. The other hand bows the string, normally between the nut and the fingering hand, to make tunes on these harmonics. An important feature, possessed also by the later type (see below, 2), is the 'buzzing bridge' with a central foot and sideways extension which the lateral vibration of the string causes to drum on the soundboard (or on an ebony, ivory, or metal plate fixed upon this). The jarring quality so imparted (compare the 'trompette' drone of a *hurdy-gurdy), coupled with the limitation of the melodies to natural harmonics, recalls a trumpet, whence no doubt the first part of the name (the second remains unexplained despite numerous guesses).

The tromba marina was known, especially in the 15th century, from Italy to England, but the German name 'Trumscheit' is the only one definitely recorded for that period. The best description is by Glareanus (1547), who says it was played in the streets (a later German court inventory lists it among carnival instruments). A shorter second string was sometimes added, apparently to sound the octave keynote or the dominant as a drone; or there might be three shorter strings for a drone on the keynote in octaves plus the dominant in between (compare *Bagpipe*, 2).

2. *The Later Form.* In the early 17th century the instrument was made larger and played with the wide end resting on the floor (Pl. 2). Later

Pl. 2. Tromba marina, with bow, by Claude Pierray (Paris, c.1700).

on, Lully connected 'marine' with sailors, and in 1660 wrote a part for it in a 'Divertissement pour les matelots' for Cavalli's *Xerxes* (see also *Crumhorn*, 2). By that time the instrument was sometimes given wire sympathetic strings (see *Stringed Instruments*, 6), as when Pepys heard solos played on the trumpet marine in London. Many of the extant specimens were obtained

Pl. 1. 15th-century Trumscheit, detail from the painting 'The Birth of Christ' by B. S. Bramantino (c. 1466-1536).

from monasteries and convents in Germany, where the instrument also had the name *Nonnengeige* ('nun's fiddle'). Unfortunately no musical details of its use in those institutions seem to be preserved. ANTHONY BAINES

Tromboncino, Bartolomeo (*b* in or nr Verona, *c*.1470; *d* ? Venice, after 1535). Italian composer. The son of a Venetian player of wind instruments, he spent much of his life in the service of the Gonzaga court at Mantua. He is said to have murdered his wife in a fit of jealousy in 1499, and he left Mantua two years later, according to Francesco Gonzaga 'in a deplor-

able manner . . . he will be well advised not to leave the territory of St Mark'. At some point in the first decade of the 16th century Tromboncino served Lucrezia Borgia in Ferrara, but in 1521 he asked to be repatriated as a Venetian citizen.

Tromboncino was famous in his lifetime for his over 150 *frottole*, which show a more sophisticated literary taste than was usual at the time and which may be considered the immediate precursors of the madrigal. He also wrote *laude* and a setting of the Lamentations of Jeremiah.

DENIS ARNOLD

Trombone

1. Description
2. Slide Positions
3. The Trio of Trombones
4. Bass Trombone

5. Contrabass Trombone
6. Valved Trombones
7. History
8. Repertory

1. *Description*. The trombone (Eng. and Fr. formerly sackbut, *sacqueboute* before both languages adopted It.: *trombone* in the late 18th century; Ger.: *Posaune*) is the brass instrument immediately distinguished by the forward-pointing extendable slide, 2′ long as it stands and as long again when fully extended. The slide (Fr.: *coulisse*; Ger.: *Zug*; It.: *tiro*) corresponds in function to the valves of other brass instruments, though it is historically the older device by nearly four centuries and so makes the trombone the eldest, by a long way, of our brass instruments to possess a full chromatic compass.

A trombone takes to pieces in two parts, the slide and the bell. Put together, they are grasped in the left hand, leaving the right hand perfectly free to move the slide, while the part of the bell which reaches back over the left shoulder provides a counterbalance for the slide to be moved quickly with the minimum effort. The slide comprises two parallel stationary tubes (the 'inner slide') over which run the two moving tubes ('outer slide') connected at the bottom by a U-bend. These tubes, necessarily of cylindrical form, commit the trombone for a great part of its length to a cylindrical bore (see *Brass Instruments*, Fig. 1), though containing two dimensions: the outer slide has a wider bore by up to $1\frac{1}{2}$ mm. The further the slide is pushed outwards the more the greater diameter comes into effect, bringing, however, a good result in that it balances the freedom and weight of the sound as the whole trombone grows longer.

2. *Slide Positions*. The trombone is built in B♭, giving the harmonic series of '9″ B♭ when the slide is closed (the 'first position'). From this the slide is extended through chromatic positions

until at full extension (seventh position) the instrument gives the series of low E a diminished fifth below. The distance along the slide from first position to second is just over $3\frac{1}{4}$″, then increasing to nearly $4\frac{1}{2}$″ from sixth to seventh. These are considerable amounts—from F to E in the bass staff, roughly two and a half times the corresponding distance on the cello—and mean 7″ or more for a whole tone. But one can readily appreciate how such large 'shifts' are well adapted to physical movements made chiefly from the elbow (the cross-stay of the slide being lightly grasped between thumb and one finger or two).

The positions have, of course, to be made by 'feel'; and with $\frac{1}{2}$″ 'out' amounting to up to one-seventh of a semitone in pitch, the trombonist possesses the power in a very positive way to adjust intonation to circumstance, for example to make brass chords perfectly pure and satisfying. Naturally, good slide lubrication is essential: there are special preparations in spray form; or, older and simpler, application of cold cream to the 'stockings'—the bearing surfaces at the lower ends of the inner slide—and diluting it with the warm water condensed from the breath (otherwise expelled through the 'water key' mounted on the U-bend).

The normal compass is up to the C (*c*″) above Middle C, with higher notes up to F now and then required or featured in solos (e.g. in modern jazz). It will suffice here, in the Table, to illustrate the central range only, up to the tenor F. The harmonics are numbered on the left. The basic positions are shown to the left of the stepped line, those to the right being alternatives, those most constantly used being ringed.

Harmonic	1st	2nd	3rd	4th	5th	6th	7th
6	f′	e′	eb′	(d′)	db′	c′	b
5	d′	c#′	c′	b	(bb)	a	g#
4	bb	a	ab	g	gb	(f	e)
3	f	e	eb	d	db	c	B
2	Bb	A	Ab	G	Gb	F	E
1 (pedals)	Bb′	A′	Ab′	G′	Gb′	(F′	E′)

Ex. 1 illustrates how alternatives may be used for two purposes: numbers above show the basic positions and those below when substituting an alternative. In (a) the sixth-position F avoids a long shift (sixth to first) immediately followed by another (first to seventh). Ex. 1b is more subtle. The *legato* phrase may be played in the basic way with the D in first position, and probably tonguing very lightly to avoid the suspicion of a *glissando* down to the B; but if D is taken in fourth position, not only is the tendency to flatness of the D in first position avoided, but the process of rising to and falling from the next harmonic above (the sixth), making the slur 'with the lip' instead of on the slide, completely changes the expressive character of the slur. In a multitude of such ways the trombonist commands a power of choice analogous, in a way, to that of a string-player.

Ex. 1

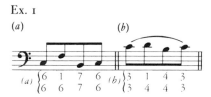

A by-product of the slide is the ability to make deliberate *glissandi*, for which the alternative positions are often needed (and are sometimes specified by a composer to ensure that he gets the maximum result, as Stravinsky in *The Firebird*, 'Danse infernale').

3. *The Trio of Trombones*. By ancient tradition the trombonists of an orchestra, and in most bands, form a team of three who before the 19th century played trombones of three different sizes termed alto, tenor, and bass after the choral parts they matched (the soprano having been played on the *cornett as long as this instrument continued to be played anywhere). The ordinary trombone of the present time perpetuates the tenor of the group; often in band parts it is still called so (see *Brass Band*).

Now all three parts are played on instruments of the tenor pitch. Nevertheless, the old alto remains in manufacture in Germany. Built in Eb a fourth higher than the tenor, there are some orchestral first trombonists who find it useful in classical works where the first part is meant for alto trombone (and then usually written in the alto clef, and sometimes reaching up to f″) to make a better-balanced effect where the part lies high, especially with small orchestras or when the part supports the altos of a chorus. A few recent composers have written specifically for it, for example Berg (Three Orchestral Pieces) and Britten (*The Burning Fiery Furnace*).

4. *Bass Trombone*. Trombones will often be seen to have a coil of tubing incorporated in the bell behind the player's head. This was an invention of a Leipzig maker, Sattler, in 1839, with the principal object of enabling low notes that occur in bass trombone parts, like low D and C, to be played on the tenor-pitched instrument, on which such notes, lying as they do in the gap above the fundamentals or 'pedals' (shown at the bottom of the Table) are otherwise possible, up to a point, only by using a special embouchure. A sprung rotary-valve for the left thumb instantly admits this coil (or 'attachment' as the whole device is often called) to add 3′ of tubing to lower the pitch by a fourth, to '12″ F. The low D and C then no longer fall in a gap. The addition can also greatly reduce long shifts in the low register generally (as where low Bb comes rapidly next to the C or Bh immediately above). On this account many trombonists who normally play the first or second part have adopted this 'Bb/F' system.

For use as a bass trombone the instrument is built with a wider bore for a fuller sound in its lower registers. American firms have been their greatest developers and the first to deal with a problem on the lowest notes: when the attachment is switched in the instrument becomes longer by 4:3 and the slide shifts correspondingly, to an extent that the standard length of slide is 1½″ too short for a true sixth position for the bottom C (thereby weakening the note by

Pl. 1. Modern American trombone ('tenor' in B♭), Vincent Bach model, by Selmer.

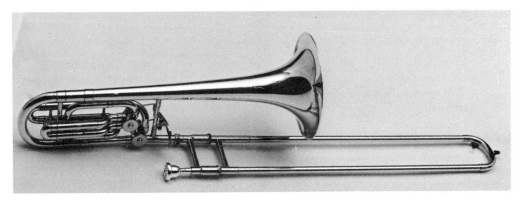

Pl. 2. Modern American bass trombone in B♭/F/E♭ (with two thumb valves, see Pl. 3), Vincent Bach model, by Selmer.

obliging the player to 'lip it down') and 8″ short for a B♮. To lengthen the slide would make it too heavy, so a second thumb-valve is placed beside the first (Pl. 2, 3) and, for these notes, pressed with it, to make up the shortfall by means of a small extra coil in the bell; the two together lower the instrument to a little above E♭, or to E♭ itself. The technical description is B♭/F/E (or B♭/F/E♭) bass trombone.

In Britain up to the 1950s bass trombone parts were always played on the 'G bass

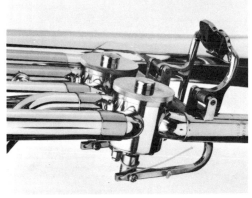

Pl. 3. Close-up view of two thumb valves as now fitted on many bass trombones; one valve lowers the instrument to F, both together to E♭ (or just above).

trombone', pitched a minor third below the ordinary. One may still see it in brass bands: large, with a long slide provided with a handle for reaching the lowest positions, otherwise out of arm's reach. See *Brass Band*, Pl. 1 and 2.

5. *Contrabass Trombone.* This is needed primarily for the *Ring*, in which Wagner takes it down to the bottom E of the double bass. It is built an octave below the B♭ trombone, with a 'double slide' (four legs instead of two, needing two bows at the bottom and one at the top). This halves the length of the otherwise impossibly long shifts. The part can also be managed on the above B♭/F/E bass trombone, using the pedal notes for bottom F and E; or on a special German F bass trombone invented in 1963 in which two thumb-valves are employed in a quite different manner.

6. *Valved Trombones.* These have been much used in bands and theatre orchestras in the Latin countries and still are to some extent, both tenor in B♭ (some in C) and bass in F, and occasionally contrabass in B♭. They have three valves (some four) and no slide, yet retain a recognizably trombone-like over-all format (Pl. 4). Their technique is very agile, and the sound has a certain character in its own right, trombone-like but in a rather nondescript sort of way. Verdi is among those who wrote with

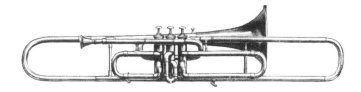

Pl. 4. A valved trombone, French model, from a Couesnon catalogue (c.1930).

valve trombones in mind, and some of his operas contain passages (Ex. 2) which were very difficult or impossible on the slide instrument before the F attachment came into use outside Germany, e.g. the long trill on low B♭ near the beginning of *Otello*, under the thunder and lightning on the stage. This is now possible by trilling with the thumb-valve, holding the slide stationary.

Ex. 2

(*ff*)

7. *History: (a) Renaissance and Baroque.* The trombone evolved during the years round 1460, very likely first in Italy, with its parent the Renaissance type of slide trumpet (see *Trumpet,* 7) played by court musicians in conjunction with *shawms. With this slide trumpet the left hand steadies the mouthpiece against the lips; the right hand pushes the whole instrument outwards along a telescopic tube. With the early trombone the moving part is now a two-leg slide, reducing needed extensions by a half, but requiring that the rest of the instrument be kept perfectly stationary: the left hand grasps a cross-stay which holds the bell to the mouthpiece socket, and the right hand moves the slide. Next, the bell is brought backwards over the shoulder for balance, while the bell and the slide are lengthened to give the instrument a deeper pitch, that of the 'ordinary' (in German, *gemeine*) trombone, later 'tenor' (Pl. 5). Its average bore of 10 mm. is about that of a contemporary trumpet and is likewise maintained until past the bend in the bell, though after that point the bell starts to funnel out sooner. The manner of playing strongly distinguished the two instruments—Mersenne (1636) stresses how wrong it was to blow the 'saqueboute' strongly like a trumpet (there was then no such thing as a 'brass section'). The mouthpieces, however, were very much alike, with a width that the trombone (but not the trumpet) has retained since.

The instrument rose early in the 16th century to become by far the most highly regarded of deeper-pitched wind instruments. It produced trombone sound on a Renaissance level of intensity, less ample than today's, and heard in instrumental and part-vocal groups of all kinds. One early piece known to have been performed by a choir of trombones is Corteccia's five-part madrigal 'Vientene almo riposo' in Florence in 1539 (see *Crumhorn*), with a male voice singing the top part. A culmination is in the works of Andrea and Giovanni Gabrieli in Venice; one *canzone* by the latter requires 12 trombones along with two cornetts and a violin. All 12 would certainly have been obtained from the celebrated Nuremberg trumpet-makers, who supplied Italy as well as Germany. Over 50 of their trombones exist from the period 1550–1650, most of them tenors, with a fair number of basses but rather fewer altos. The basses are built either a fourth or a fifth below the tenor (see *Quint*) and the altos similarly above, that is in D or E, for the nominal pitch (first position)

Pl. 5. German trombone (sackbut) player, engraving (1538) by H. Aldegrever; note the small bell, and the trombonist's old-style grasp of the slide (the other two instruments are probably slide trumpets, Zugtrompeten).

of the tenor in those countries was 'A', though at such high tuning standards that this A can in fact lie even above modern B♭ (the present trombone pitch of B♭ was probably first recognized in 18th-century Austria). One could also adapt a trombone to deeper pitches, e.g. a fourth lower, by inserting a crook between slide and bell. (Fine replica trombones have now for some years been manufactured in Germany by Meinl and Lauber, but are expensive, so that it may be worth even now having a crook by which the tenor can up to a point be played as a bass, a practice several times referred to in the old sources.)

For the cornett-trombone combination through the Baroque period, see *Cornett*, 3. This apart, we hear relatively little of the trombone. France lost it when Lully took command of the royal music; all that a leading French musician (the flautist De la Barre) could remember in 1740 was 'le cacbouc' (*saqueboute*), 'a kind of cornemuse [see *Bagpipe*] but a good deal bigger'. In England Handel's splendid trombone parts in *Saul* and *Israel in Egypt* were rarities (possibly played by Germans from the King's Band). But in Austria the instrument maintained its old status throughout the 18th century: Fux, Caldara, and others, in music for the imperial chapel, write *obbligato* passages for trombone, often the alto; in the same tradition are Mozart's parts for trombones including the solo in the 'Tuba mirum' of the Requiem, and the solemn associations where he brings them into opera (the appearance of the Commendatore in *Don Giovanni*, for example). The 18th-century instruments keep the old narrow dimensions, but the bell had developed a more abrupt flare, nearer to the modern.

(*b*) *To the Present Day*. The second phase of trombone history, leading directly to modern times, began around the time of the French Revolution, on a quite new footing: the trombone as a strong bass voice in military music. Cavalry bands adopted the old bass trombone to give a diatonic bass to the natural trumpets; infantry bands would have a bass part marked 'trombone or serpent', for whichever was available.

Germany early in the next century found two different ways of making such parts easier to play when mounted or marching on foot. One was to fit the old bass trombone (in F) with a double slide to reduce the shifts (as later with contrabass trombones; see above, 5); the other, which set the trombone on its modern course, was to use the tenor trombone instead. The French did simply this. The Germans, however, built a wide-bore tenor for the purpose, calling it 'bass trombone'. Next the alto was dropped from regular use, leaving a trio composed basically of tenors throughout: in France a general-purpose tenor trombone was used, keeping the bore fairly narrow but widening the bell somewhat to help the lower register. This was taken over in Britain to remain the normal instrument up to the 1930s (but with G trombone for the bass; see above, 4). In French works, also those of Elgar, old ears may sometimes miss the team's bright, crisp sound, decidedly nasal in *ff*. Elgar played the instrument himself, and so did Holst: their silver-plated narrow-bore trombones are preserved side by side at the Royal College of Music, London. German makers meanwhile developed wider bores throughout the section, the second and third players having the thumb-valve (see above, 4). Both types went to the USA, the French later to be developed with wider dimensions for the jazz orchestras of the 1930s. No summary of trombone history can understate what the instrument has owed to jazz, bringing it to the fore as it had rarely been since the 17th century. So successful were these American models that they rapidly became the normal trombones for all purposes in Britain and eventually in Italy, France, and Russia too, played in orchestras and bands alongside the wider thumb-valve type for the bass part.

8. *Repertory*. Among the older concertos are those by Albrechtsberger (for alto), Wagenseil, Reicha, and the player F. A. Belcke (1832). David's Concertino, Op. 4, has long been a favourite, along with Rimsky-Korsakov's Concerto (originally for trombone with military band). In the later repertory one finds works by several composers well known for having written solo works for practically every orchestral instrument: Saint-Saëns (Cavatina), Hindemith (Sonata), Tcherepnin (Andante), Gordon Jacob (Concerto), Milhaud (*Concerto d'hiver*), Frank Martin (Ballade); also Bernstein, 'Elegy for Mippy II', and Bloch, *Symphony for Trombone and Orchestra*.

The modern school is of special interest and promise, the trombone being capable of the most varied novel sound-effects, as in Berio's *Sequenza V*, and above all in works from 1962 by Vinko Globokar, himself a remarkable trombonist, combining the instrument with the voice (spoken into it) and electronics, e.g. *Discours II* (with tape).

ANTHONY BAINES

FURTHER READING

Philip Bate: *The Trumpet and Trombone* (London, 1966); Denis Wick: *Trombone Technique* (London, 1971); Anthony Baines: *Brass Instruments: their History and Development* (London, 1976).

Trompette à clef (Fr.). See *Bugle*, 4; *Trumpet*, 8.

Trope (Lat.: *tropus*, from Gk *tropos*, 'turn (of phrase)'). From the time of Martianus Capella (*c*.400) and Boethius (*d* 524), the word was used by Medieval music theorists to mean 'octave species' (see *Mode*, 3). But its more important meaning was a textual and/or musical addition to plainchant. There were three basic types which all probably originated in the third quarter of the 9th century. Most tropes did not remain in use after the 12th century; the longest lasting were Kyrie tropes (if they are indeed tropes; see 2 below), which in some churches were still sung in the 16th century.

The production of tropes was spectacularly large, particularly from the 10th to the 12th century, and their study enables one to 'feel the pulse' of their times in a remarkable way. Each church created its own repertory, and the transmission of tropes from one place to another is a valuable indication of Medieval cultural contacts.

1. *Supplementary Phrases of Words and Music*. These were provided for three of the Proper chants of the Mass (the Introit, Offertory, and Communion) and for the Kyrie, Gloria, Sanctus, and Agnus Dei chants from the Ordinary. Some examples of tropes for Lessons are also known (sometimes called 'farsed Lessons'). Most common of all these were Introit tropes. The technique for the Proper chants was to introduce the main chant with a phrase pointing to the message or significance of the main text. The main chant was also frequently split into phrases, and introductions provided for each of these. Ex. 1 gives the opening of a Christmas Introit trope. The full text reads in translation (main text in capitals):

God the Father sent his Son into the world today, wherefore rejoicing let us sing with the prophet: UNTO US A CHILD IS BORN, UNTO US A SON IS GIVEN, who shall sit upon the throne of David and shall reign for ever, AND THE GOVERNMENT SHALL BE UPON HIS SHOULDER. Behold there comes God and man from the house of David to sit upon the throne, AND HIS NAME SHALL BE CALLED—he whom the seer foretold—ANGEL OF MIGHTY COUNSEL.

It will be noticed that the music of the trope uses turns of phrase from the original chant, although not many tropes make such explicit reference as this.

Ordinary of Mass texts, which had no particular connection with any one festival day, could be made 'Proper' by means of tropes, although many of these are simply neutral expressions of invocation or praise. Gloria tropes, where over a dozen lines were often provided for dispersal throughout the original chant, are the largest of all sets of tropes. They, like most others, fell out of favour during the 12th century, although one Gloria trope, *Spiritus et alme* for the Blessed Virgin Mary

Ex. 1

Trope, sung by soloist, in lower-case letters
Main chant, sung by choir, in small capital letters
⌐‾‾⌐ = *melismatic trope; see 3 below*

(composed probably in Normandy, late 11th century), remained popular throughout the Middle Ages, even being set in polyphony.

2. *Texting of Melismas*, according to the principle of one syllable per note. The added text was often called *prosa* or *prosula*. This happened to the Alleluia, to the melismas of Offertory verses and Office responsories, and also to the 'Hosanna' of some Sanctus chants. The usual technique was to 'gloss' the text of the main chant, if possible, referring to the theme of the festival day.

It has been the traditional belief that many melismatic Kyries were given tropic Latin texts in this way; later in the Middle Ages, when tropes went out of fashion, these Kyries were usually copied without the Latin texts, and they also appear without them in the modern Vatican chant books, thus regaining their supposed original form. But since the earliest manuscripts (10th century) already have the Latin texts, these Kyries may have been so conceived from the beginning, as special festal compositions in their own right. While Kyrie tropes of type 1 passed from use fairly early, Kyries with Latin text were still used in some churches (including those following the *Sarum Use) up to the 16th century.

3. *Addition of Melismas*. A tiny handful of early manuscripts show melismatic extensions of Introit phrases (see the final phrase of Ex. 1 above). One pair of manuscripts (from St Gall, Switzerland) has added texts for some of their melismas. A small number of other manuscripts are witness to a rather limited fashion for *responsory melismas—they have old melismas redeployed several times over in different responsories, some newly composed melismas, and melismas borrowed from Offertory verses to be inserted in responsories. Some of these melismas were then texted as in type 2 above.

All the above are additions of one sort or another to the main corpus of Gregorian chant established at the end of the 8th century. Some other additions, never so called in the Middle Ages, have also been called tropes by modern scholars: *a*) sequences, according to the theory that at least some of the early ones are texted Alleluia *jubili* (see *Sequence*); *b*) 'Benedicamus' songs (see *Conductus*); and *c*) *organum*, now sometimes regarded as a sort of 'vertical troping' of plainchant.   DAVID HILEY

4. *20th-century Meaning*. In the 1920s a quite different meaning of 'trope' was introduced by the Austrian composer and theorist Josef Matthias Hauer (1883 1959). He devised a system of 12-note composition based not on the series, as in Schoenberg, but on a division of the 12 notes of the chromatic scale into two groups of six, e.g. (C, C♯, E, F♯, B♭, B) + (D, E♭, F, G, A♭, A). Within each group the order may vary freely, but in principle the two groups will be kept apart: such an arrangement Hauer called a 'trope', and though his own music is rarely encountered, the term has survived in descriptions of other works using this system, such as Schoenberg's *Ode to Napoleon Buonaparte*.
                                  PAUL GRIFFITHS

Troppo (It.). 'Too much'. It is generally used with a negative, and as a warning, e.g. *allegro ma non troppo*, 'quick, but not too quick'.

Troubadours (Fr.). Poet-musicians, often of noble birth, of 12th- and 13th-century southern France. *Troubadour* verse, written in Provençal (the 'langue d'oc'), dwells largely on the theme of courtly love, reflecting the growing importance of women in society during a period of political stability and prosperity. Much of this verse was set to music, and would have been sung by the *troubadours* themselves, sometimes with instrumental accompaniment provided by professional minstrels known as *jongleurs*. The melodies of

these songs were mostly passed down orally, committed to memory rather than to paper. Those that do survive to the present day are written in an imprecise notation which indicates neither their rhythm nor the nature of their accompaniment.

During the 12th century, the art of the *troubadours* spread throughout Europe, with similar movements becoming established, particularly in northern France (the *trouvères) and in Germany (the *Minnesinger), but also in Italy and Spain. Among the most important *troubadours* were Guillaume IX, Duke of Aquitaine (1071-1127), and Bernart de Ventadorn (*c*.1130-90). The Provençal culture, of which the *troubadours* were a part, was destroyed by the Albigensian crusades at the beginning of the 13th century, but the songs of Jaufre Rudel and Guiraut Riquier, two of the last *troubadours*, were written towards the end of that century. See also *Minstrel; Song, 2*.   JOHN MILSOM

FURTHER READING
H. van der Werf: *The Chansons of the Troubadours and Trouvères: a Study of the Melodies and their Relation to the Poems* (Utrecht, 1972); Jack Lindsay: *The Troubadours and their World* (London, 1976).

Trout, The. See *Forelle, Die*.

'Trout' Quintet. Nickname of Schubert's Piano Quintet in A major, D 667, composed in 1819. It is so called because the fourth of its five movements, an Andantino, is a set of variations on the tune of his song *Die Forelle* ('The Trout').

Trouvères (Fr.). Poet-musicians of the late 12th and 13th centuries, active in northern France, especially in the region around Arras. Like the somewhat earlier *troubadours, trouvères* were largely of aristocratic birth, sophisticated in their tastes, and often well educated. Much of their verse was written within the conventions of courtly love, sometimes taking the form of amorous complaints expressed as dialogues, and used an early form of French known as the 'langue d'oïl'. *Trouvère* melodies were often notated with greater precision than were those of the *troubadours*; some 2000 survive to the present day, although none gives any indication of how the songs would have been accompanied. Prominent composers of the movement included the Chastelain de Couci (*d* 1203), Thibaut IV, King of Navarre (1201-53), Adam de la Halle (*c*. 1250-88), and Jehan Erart (*c*.1200-59). Important connections exist between the art of the *trouvères* and the songs of Guillaume de Machaut, the leading French composer of the 14th century. See also *Minstrel; Song, 2*.
                                  JOHN MILSOM

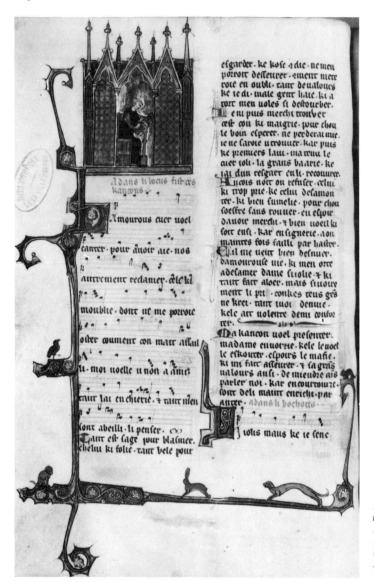

Page from the Arras Chansonnier of trouvère songs, with the song 'D'amourous cuer' by Adam de la Halle, and a miniature showing the composer seated at a writing-desk, late 13th century.

Trovatore, Il ('The Troubadour'). Opera in four acts by Verdi; text by Cammarano, after the drama *El Trovador* by Gutiérrez. Produced: Rome, Teatro Apollo, 19 January 1853; New York, Academy of Music, 2 May 1855; London, Covent Garden, 10 May 1855. The notoriously confused action takes place in 15th-century Spain, during the civil war caused by the rebellion of the Count of Urgel against the King of Aragon. The leader of the King's army is the Count di Luna. *Act 1, Scene 1.* Ferrando (bass), an old retainer of di Luna, tells the soldiers how, many years previously, the Count's young brother had been kidnapped by a gipsy whose mother had been burned as a witch by the Count's father. It was believed that the stolen child was burned by the gipsy.

Scene 2. In the palace garden that night Leonora (sop.), lady-in-waiting to the Queen of Aragon, tells her companion Inez (sop.) of her love for the troubador Manrico, who nightly serenades her, and who is the leader of the rebel army. Di Luna (bar.), himself in love with Leonora, enters the garden. Leonora, hearing the voice of Manrico (ten.), rushes out, but mistakes di Luna for her lover. Manrico now enters, and the two men prepare to fight.

Act 2, Scene 1. Several months later in the gipsy camp, Manrico, who was wounded by di Luna, is being nursed by Azucena (mezzo), whom he believes to be his mother. She relates how her mother had been burned at the stake, and how in her madness she had thrown the wrong child into the flames (she had in fact killed her own child, and Manrico is di Luna's brother, though no one but Azucena knows this). A messenger brings news that Leonora, believing her lover dead, is to enter a convent. Manrico hurries off to prevent this.

Scene 2. Di Luna and his followers assemble outside the Jerusalem Convent to abduct Leonora. They are thwarted by Manrico, who takes Leonora to the castle of Castellor.

Act 3, Scene 1. A military encampment. Di Luna and his men are besieging Castellor. Azucena is found lingering near the camp. Ferrando recognizes her; she says she is Manrico's mother. Di Luna condemns her to be burned.

Scene 2. Preparations are being made in the castle for Manrico's marriage to Leonora. Learning from his retainer Ruiz (ten.) that Azucena is to die, Manrico hurries off to rescue her.

Act 4, Scene 1. Manrico has been captured trying to rescue Azucena. Leonora comes to the palace hoping to see him and prays that her love will ease his suffering. Monks chant a Miserere and Manrico sings of his longing for death. Leonora pleads with di Luna for Manrico's life. He agrees to spare Manrico on condition that Leonora gives herself to him. She consents, di Luna goes to order Manrico's release, and Leonora drinks poison from a ring.

Scene 2. Manrico tries to comfort Azucena, reminding her of their home in the mountains. Leonora arrives to tell Manrico that he is free. When he learns the price of his freedom he curses her. But already the poison is working, and di Luna enters to see Leonora die in her lover's arms. He orders Manrico's execution—and as Manrico dies, Azucena tells him triumphantly that he has killed his own brother. 'Mother, you are avenged!' she cries as the curtain falls.

FURTHER READING

Nicholas John, ed.: *Il trovatore*, English National Opera Guides (in preparation).

Troyens, Les ('The Trojans'). Opera in five acts by Berlioz; text by the composer after Virgil's *Aeneid* (*c*.27-19 BC). Composed 1856-8. To achieve a performance Berlioz was obliged in 1863 to divide the work into two parts: acts 1 and 2 into *La prise de Troie* ('The Capture of Troy') (three acts), produced at Karlsruhe, 6 December 1890; acts 3, 4, and 5 into *Les Troyens à Carthage* ('The Trojans at Carthage') (five acts, with added prologue), produced at Paris, Théâtre-Lyrique, 4 November 1863. The complete work was first produced at Karlsruhe, 6-7 December 1890; Glasgow, 18-19 March 1935; Boston, Opera House, 27 March 1955 (much shortened); San Francisco, Opera House, 1966 (shortened); New York, Metropolitan, 1973.

In the following synopsis, the original arrangement is preserved, with the act divisions of the second version given in parentheses.

Act 1 (Troy, 1). The Greeks have abandoned their camp, leaving behind the wooden horse. The forebodings of Cassandra (sop. or mezzo), daughter of Priam (bass), are disbelieved even by her lover Choroebus (bar.). (*Troy, 2*) The celebrations of peace are interrupted by Aeneas (ten.), who brings news that the priest Laocöon,

Set design by Philippe Chapéron for the first (incomplete) performance of Berlioz's 'Les Troyens' (Théâtre-Lyrique, Paris, 1863).

who mistrusted the horse, has been devoured by serpents: the horse is thereupon dragged into the city to propitiate Athene.

Act 2 (*Troy*, 3). Hector's ghost (bass) tells Aeneas to flee from Troy and found a new city in Italy. The priest Pantheus (bass) describes the burning of Troy by Greeks who have hidden in the horse. In the Temple of Vesta, Cassandra tells the women of Choroebus' death and Aeneas' escape. As the Greeks rush in, the women stab themselves.

Act 3 (*Carthage*, 1). At Carthage, festivities are in progress. Queen Dido (sop. or mezzo) states her intention of remaining single in devotion to her dead husband: her sister Anna (con.) tries to shake this resolve. The poet Iopas (ten.) reports the arrival by sea of strangers. Aeneas' son Ascanius (sop.) successfully begs Dido for hospitality. When her minister Narbal (bass) brings news of invasion, Aeneas, hitherto disguised, steps forward and offers help. (*Carthage*, 2) In a symphonic interlude (Royal Hunt and Storm), Dido and Aeneas are driven into a cave, where they make love.

Act 4 (*Carthage*, 3). Aeneas is fêted in Dido's gardens. Narbal's apprehensions over Aeneas' impending conflict between love and duty are seen to be justified as Dido allows her firm resolve to weaken. Mercury exhorts Aeneas to voyage on to Italy.

Act 5 (*Carthage*, 4). The ghosts of Trojan heroes add their exhortations to depart, and Aeneas, now deaf to Dido's pleas, sets sail. (*Carthage*, 5) On hearing this, Dido, distraught with grief, decides to die; prophesying the glory of Rome, she kills herself on Aeneas' sword.

Trump. See *Jew's-harp*.

Trumpet

1. Introduction
2. B♭ and C Trumpets
3. Smaller Trumpets
4. Natural Trumpets
5. Bass Trumpet
6. History
7. Slide Trumpets
8. Keyed Trumpet
9. Repertory

1. *Introduction*. The trumpet (Fr.: *trompette*; Ger.: *Trompete*; It.: *tromba*) was originally the instrument of command in battle, herald of authority, proclaimer of the destiny of man ('The Trumpet Shall Sound'). The great trumpet music of the Baroque harks back constantly to these themes, uttered within the restricted scope of the old 'natural' instrument before *valves existed. Valves then rendered the trumpet chromatic, capable of the same melodies as other instruments, by degrees to submerge old memories and finally, greatly helped by jazz, free it from its ancient ties and establish it as the popular instrument we now know.

For a general description of the trumpet in relation to other brass instruments, and for the mouthpiece, see *Brass Instruments*. The central instrument of the last 100 years has been the B♭ trumpet, which one sees in every music shop. Besides this are other modern trumpets built in higher tonalities, from C upwards, the higher of them having been introduced in the first place for performing the Baroque repertory on the valved trumpet. On top of this the natural trumpet has itself been experiencing a considerable revival for playing old works in an authentic way. Hence 'trumpet' has come to cover a good number of different forms of the

Fig. 1.

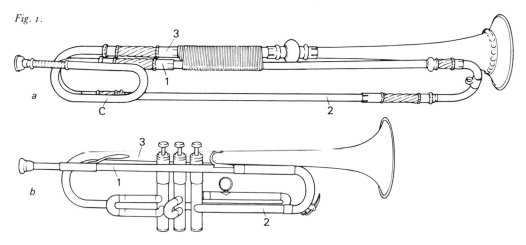

Pl. 1a. B♮ trumpet by Vincent Bach, Elkhart, Indiana; note ring and hook for adjusting the valves while playing.

instrument, of which an orchestral trumpeter today may have at least two, very likely more, ready to meet all contingencies.

All are built (with a few exceptions) in the traditional trumpet shape of one long loop. Fig. 1a illustrates the format of a natural trumpet, with three parallel 'branches': (1) mouthpipe, (2) lower branch, and (3) bell, connected by two 'bows'. A crook (C) is seen inserted into the mouthpipe. Fig. 1b shows a modern trumpet, with the three valves mounted on the lower branch. The outer bow (right) incorporates the main tuning-slide; the near bow (left) is formed integrally with the bell. The modern mouthpipe generally embodies a small taper back to the mouthpiece socket up to 8" long in a B♭ trumpet. The tuning-slide of the third valve (third finger, right hand) usually carries a ring (as shown) by which the left hand can extend the slide while playing, to take the onus off the lips in correcting the sharpness of notes like the low D when they occur in very exposed passages. Less common is a corre-

sponding device for the first valve in the form of a thumb lever called a 'trigger'.

2. *B♭ and C Trumpets.* The ordinary B♭ trumpet is approximately 50" long if unwound. It sounds a whole tone lower than written, and is the trumpet played in jazz, in military bands (in which it now often replaces the cornet), and in the orchestra, though here there is increasing preference for the C trumpet, following the French orchestral tradition. The C trumpet looks a little smaller or, as is often the case, the main loop is shorter which makes the bell seem to stick out further. Its higher pitch by a whole tone can make for extra brilliance in the high register and also make playing less tiring in long heavily-scored works.

3. *Smaller Trumpets.* These began to be made in 1885 (the bicentenary year of Bach's birth) for coping with the arduous high-lying parts that Bach wrote in major works now constantly performed, as in the B Minor Mass, and the Second Brandenburg Concerto (in which the solo trumpet part reaches the high g''' above the staff).

(a) *Trumpets from D to G.* Fifty years ago practically every symphony trumpeter owned a D trumpet for these purposes and for the works of Handel too; and possibly also an F trumpet for the Second Brandenburg. Since then, the D trumpet has been very largely replaced by the E♭ trumpet. This can be provided with a longer set of slides to lower it to D; but the player is just as likely to perform the Baroque D parts on the E♭ trumpet as it stands, transposing the part a semitone lower into B major, which may seem unnecessarily complicated but in fact is not, as will be seen from the comparison shown below of the valving for the eight notes of the opening passage of the great *obbligato* in Handel's

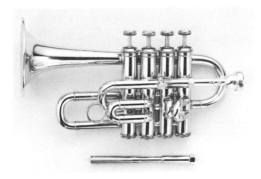

Pl. 1b. Piccolo trumpet (Vincent Bach) with four valves and (below) shank to lower the instrument from B♮ to A.

Pl. 1c. Bass trumpet in B♭ (Vincent Bach).

Messiah: the top line as on the D trumpet, five (or four) of the notes being 'open' (i.e. no valves); the lower line as on E♭ trumpet, seven notes (or all eight) made while holding the second valve down, and in a way more comfortable. (It is customary to show the use of two valves together by placing one valve number above the other.)

C	E	G	C	D	E	F	G
o	1 2	o	o	1	o $\binom{1}{2}$	1	o

B	D♯	F♯	B	C♯	D♯	E	F♯
2	2 3	2	2	1 2	2	o $\binom{1}{2}$	2

(*b*) *Piccolo Trumpet*. This has now widely supplanted those above. Built in high B♭ an octave above the B♭ trumpet, its tube is but 2′ long (about that of an oboe) yet it is possible to make it in traditional trumpet format, while its musical effect to all but very critical connoisseurs in the audience is a most satisfactory trumpet sound. It needs a fourth valve to reach down to the sounding middle *d'* (below which *a* is obtainable as second valve fundamental). Many players also employ the piccolo trumpet for high-lying parts in Classical and later works, such as Haydn's Concerto in E♭, and for parts which Stravinsky (in several works from *Petrushka* onwards), Britten (*Peter Grimes*), and others have written for the D trumpet. This means for the player constant different transpositions at sight, but such, for the experienced orchestral trumpeter, are part of his normal way of life.

(*c*) *Reasons for Using Small Trumpets*. Seeking the aid of these small trumpets is not purely a matter of altitude: lips can vibrate as fast today as they could in Bach's time; and notes sounding as high as any written by Bach are frequently reached by jazz players on B♭ trumpet. All the same, this trumpet, with a bell expansion and width that secures a rich flexible sound over the main compass down to the low notes, was not evolved for the very high notes; moreover, in the concert hall, the utmost accuracy is essential in striking them. So it was in the 18th century, but the players then gave their whole lives to the one technique only, not having to play Richard Strauss and Tchaikovsky as well. Ex. 1 shows how the small trumpets meet the circumstances: all notes are given at sounding pitch, each instrument's keynote being shown in semibreves; numbers refer to the harmonic series (seventh not shown). (*a*) Baroque D trumpet: the available notes, harmonics of the 7′ tube-length, offer a scale from the eighth harmonic to the sixteenth (written by Bach a tone lower). (*b*) B♭ trumpet: the series has risen by a sixth; the scale region is covered by five harmonics (filling the gaps with the valves) but takes the instrument above its normal compass, valved. (*c*) D trumpet (i.e. modern, valved): the series is now an octave above that in (*a*)—the tubing is half as long—making the lower keynote of the scale, *d''*, a fourth harmonic instead of the eighth; four well-separated harmonics provide the scale, greatly reducing chances of a mis-hit and making performance relatively secure. (*d*) Piccolo trumpet: only three and still better separated harmonics for the scale—and also with no unwanted seventh harmonic to get in the way.

Ex. 1

Incidentally, if (*a*) were put a third lower we would have the sounds of the natural trumpet crooked in B♭, as in Beethoven's off-stage call in the *Leonora* No. 3 Overture (low harmonics only, in military style, fourth to eighth). Thus there are altogether three B♭ trumpets to be reckoned with in music, each with half the tube-length of the other, the notes written sounding a tone lower in all three cases.

4. *Natural Trumpets* (in addition to the Baroque trumpet): (*a*) *The Cavalry Trumpet*. This is, in European countries, built in E♭ (a fifth below B♭ trumpet and bugle) normally in a double loop, save for state trumpets (such as those of the British Household Cavalry) and 'fanfare trumpets' (see *Fanfare*), which retain the old long format in a single loop (better for carrying a banner). Military duty calls range from the third harmonic to the eighth; fanfares may rise to the tenth (sounding *g″*) or higher.

(*b*) *American Field Trumpet*. This is often termed by infantrymen 'bugle'; see *Bugle*, 1.

(*c*) *Bass Natural Trumpets*. Variously manufactured to accompany either of the foregoing in band music, these date back to the times of the Napoleonic wars and are now, in Europe, called 'bass-fanfare' (or in France, 'trompette de basse de cavalerie'). The usual pitch is low E♭, an octave below the cavalry trumpet (thus with the 13′ tube-length of an E♭ tuba), formed in three

loops, with wide bell and the general appearance of a very large brass bugle.

(*d*) *Herald's Trumpet*. In a 'Medieval' straight format, this is supplied by some manufacturers for pageants and the like.

(*e*) *Clarino*. The spirally wound 'clarino trumpet' in D has often been seen since 1960 in performances of Baroque music. It was invented in Germany on the basis of a coiled silver trumpet seen in the 1727 portrait of the Leipzig trumpeter Gottfried Reiche (see *Cornett*). The modern version has two small holes (and there may be others), normally covered by the fingers. The chief of these holes when uncovered causes the trumpet to sound the harmonic series of G, a fourth above its normal D series; the bell, beyond the hole, continues to radiate the sound. The object is to produce the notes G and B (Ex. 1*a*), which are problematic eleventh and thirteenth harmonics on a D trumpet, by the unproblematic eighth and tenth harmonics of the G series. Such a hole is now often provided on replica Baroque trumpets of conventional Baroque format.

5. *Bass Trumpet* (orchestral). Of the bass natural trumpets, there were early valved versions, made in Germany in the 1820s for cavalry music. Some large military bands still employ them, as in Italy. Wagner would have known such instruments when he thought of a bass

Pl. 2. Trumpeters at a wedding, miniature from a 15th-century Burgundian manuscript.

trumpet for the *Ring*, in which it plays an important and thrilling role. It is still uncertain exactly what pitch he expected it to be built in, but he writes for it, as he does for the trumpets too, in various transpositions (see *Transposing Instruments*). When 'in C' it sounds an octave lower than a C trumpet. It is now normally made in C (8′) and often it is given to a trombonist to play owing to the fairly large mouthpiece required. Stravinsky is one who subsequently requires it, as in *The Rite of Spring*.

6. *History:* (*a*) *Ancient and Medieval.* The oldest existing trumpets are the two from the tomb of Tutankhamun, preserved in the Cairo Museum: short and straight, around 18″ long, exactly as seen in Egyptian art in the hands of soldiers. Probably they sounded one note, perhaps two. The Israelites adopted the same instrument; see under *Shofar*. The next important trumpet is the Roman (and later Byzantine) bronze *tuba*, 4′–5′ long; we have no idea what notes it sounded (see also *Ancient Greek Music*, 4, 6*b*). Next is the Medieval brass trumpet, modelled at least in part on Islamic trumpets seen and heard during the Crusades: again

straight, but around 5′ long, with ornamental brass 'pommels'. One sees pairs of these instruments in countless pictures of warfare, tournaments, triumphs, and banquets, but still we have no precise knowledge of the sounds. Its most usual French name is *buysine*, but in England usually 'trompe' (an older Anglo-Saxon word, *beme*, may have denoted some more primitive instrument of wood).

(*b*) *To the 18th Century.* By the end of the 14th century, trumpet-makers had begun to bend the tube to form the since characteristic three branches, but often positioned one above the other—an S shape. From this period we can begin to form an idea of the military sounds through allusions in vocal part-music. Dufay's Gloria *Et in terra ad modum tubae* ('in the manner of trumpets') seems to point to cavalry calls not dissimilar to many that were heard up to the 19th century or even today: largely on deep harmonics and ending with a flourish to the eighth. There are a few late 16th-century instruction manuscripts which write out such calls along with short fanfares (It.: *toccata*, whence Eng.: 'tucket') and longer flourishes (It.: *sonata*, whence 'sennet'). The most inform-

Pl. 3. Trumpets and drummers with (right) *a shawm, Manali, North India.*

ative of these works is by the Italian trumpeter Cesare Bendinelli; in 1614 he left the manuscript along with his best trumpet (by Schnitzer of Nuremberg) to the Accademia Filarmonica in Verona, where both remain. Ex. 2 gives the start of the first of the toccatas (the oblique stroke denotes a kind of slur). After these he goes on briefly to describe the clarino register, serving as a decorative part above the rest when a corps of trumpets played on ceremonial occasions. Monteverdi gives us a complete written example of this in the Toccata that opens *Orfeo*: the lowest parts make a kind of drone; above them is a typical tucket (marked *alto e basso*); above this (*quinta*) the fragment of a ducal sennet; and on top, a free *clarino* (see also *Mute*).

Ex. 2

Bendinelli: Toccata

Some 100 instruments survive from 1578 onwards, the majority built in Nuremberg up to the late 18th century by makers of the Ehe, Haas, and other families. There are also fine English trumpets from after the Restoration, especially by William Bull of London. Musically, the great development lay in singling out the clarino register to combine with voices and other instruments, from early in the 17th century in Praetorius's setting of 'In dulci jubilo' up to its peak with Bach and Handel. The technicalities are fully set out in the expert

book of J. E. Altenburg, 1795 (now translated by Edward Tarr, who has also edited Bendinelli with translations and commentary). By many accounts it seems that these high parts were normally played quite softly, when one could do most to humour the eleventh and thirteenth harmonics, as well as produce occasional quick passing notes outside the harmonic series, like the leading note below the scale, met now and then in Bach.

There are problems in German music over terms like 'tromba di caccia' (as in Telemann's Violin Concerto in F) and 'tromba selvatica' (in the same composer's *Tafelmusik* of 1735), in each case rising to the eighteenth harmonic. Bach writes this note also, for his ordinary trumpets. It is an unsolved question whether these terms refer not to a trumpet of some kind but to the horn (equating 'tromba' with Fr. *trompe*, Sp. *trompa*, meaning 'horn'). The parts are nowadays usually played on horns.

(*c*) *Later Developments*. The later 18th century produced some of the most difficult high-register writing of all, reaching to the twenty-fourth harmonic in a Clarino Concerto in D by Michael Haydn. But by that time orchestral music called no longer for the old clarino idiom, and the trumpets came to serve in the more restricted and formal way that one hears through the classics. At the same time, in order to play in a wide selection of tonalities, the instrument was shortened to give the key of F (rare before), with crooks for all important keys down to B♭ or even A. We also know that by this period some players would place the hand in or across the bell to

Pl. 4. Baroque trumpets with kettledrummer, from Sandford's 'History of the Coronation . . . of James II and Queen Mary' (1687); the trumpets (with large 'pommels') are held by the right hand only.

flatten notes up to a semitone in hand-horn fashion: special 'curved' trumpets were made in France to facilitate this, mainly for bands, but there seems little doubt that Mendelssohn, for instance, was aware of the technique when he wrote the held leading note for the trumpets at the start of the *Ruy Blas* Overture.

Then came valves, on the trumpet from about 1820, and almost from the start bringing in the trumpet built in the then new key of high B♭ (our present B♭ trumpet). Within 50 years this was becoming the usual instrument for the orchestra in Germany and France, even though

Pl. 5. English 19th-century slide trumpet, held by its master player, Thomas Harper jr. (b 1816) in full dress as Sergeant Trumpeter to the Royal Household of Queen Victoria. Part of the slide is visible in the central spring-rod; note also the angled position of the mouthpiece, for the backwards-moving slide to avoid the chin.

most composers—Wagner, Verdi, and Richard Strauss among them—continued to write their trumpet parts in F, E♭, D, etc., in the Classical tradition. In England and the USA the progress of the valved trumpet was delayed chiefly through orchestral use of the cornet, and only towards the end of the century did leading players start to adopt it.

7. *Slide Trumpets.* With these we first return to the 15th century, when pictures make it quite clear (though no contemporary instrument has survived to prove it) that there were then special trumpets which could be pushed to and fro along a telescopic mouth-pipe to make a diatonic scale below the eighth harmonic: see *Trombone, 7a*. Such trumpets were (Burgundian court records tell us) 'for the minstrels', as opposed to 'war', and were used with the *shawm and also, apparently, sometimes with voices in church music, as in Masses by Arnold de Lantins and Estienne de Grossim. Reconstructions have recently been made, based on the pictures.

Pictures of the 16th century continue to show such trumpets, particularly in Germany and Central Europe, where they were much played along with voices and other instruments and lasted into the 18th century: *Zugtrompete*, or in some of Bach's cantatas, 'tromba da tirarsi' (Ger. *Zug* and It. *tiro* both now denote the slide of a trombone). The only extant example, dated 1651, is preserved in Berlin. By Bach's time such trumpets were mainly used by the town trumpeter to play chorale melodies from the tower, but Bach shows us that the Leipzig players were far more expert than this.

A quite different slide trumpet arose in post-Restoration England, probably of French origin: the 'flat trumpet', i.e. playable in 'flat', that is minor, keys. Purcell wrote for it so in his music for Queen Mary's funeral. The slide comprises the near bow, which draws back towards the player's face. The system went out of use but was not forgotten, for late in the 18th century, when critics were losing patience with the wayward eleventh and thirteenth harmonics of the ordinary trumpet, it was revived as the English slide trumpet, much used in orchestras and bands alike through half the 19th century, and almost to its end for *obbligato* passages in Handel. Examples now often come up at sales: built in F with crooks for the lower keys, the slide, though primarily intended for correction of such harmonics, made diatonic playing in the lower register up to a point possible and popular soloists made use of this.

8. *Keyed Trumpet.* An Austrian invention of the 1790s. Haydn and Hummel wrote their trumpet concertos for it, the original soloist in each case having been Anton Weidinger. Four

or five leather-padded keys opened with the fingers made the instrument chromatic from the written Middle C upwards. Weidinger was reported to have played it very beautifully, when soft, sounding 'like a clarinet'. But it never caught on beyond Austria and Italy: in French opera scores of the time 'trompettes à clef' can generally be assumed to mean valved trumpets.

9. *Repertory*. The trumpet can be said to possess the oldest individual solo repertory of any wind instrument (except the organ). It is, of course, for the natural trumpet and begins with the sonatas with *basso continuo* in Fantini's great Tutor of 1638. It continues with sonatas with solo trumpet written for Bologna Cathedral by Cazzati, Corelli (one sonata), Torelli (very many, and a *Concerto con tromba*), and D. Gabrielli (a composer also known in connection with the *cello). Then, among the better-known composers, we have Purcell (sonata), Vivaldi (concerto for two trumpets), Telemann (six concertos), Reutter the younger (two concertos), Molter (five), Mudge (one), Leopold Mozart (one, 1762), Hertel (four), Albrechtsberger (concertino; see *Jew's-harp*), and Michael Haydn (a concerto and part of a serenade). Next come the concertos for keyed trumpet of Joseph Haydn and Hummel, but very little of note for the valved trumpet. Among some more recent works are Hindemith's Sonata; Poulenc's Sonata with horn and trombone; and several works for trumpet, piano, and strings, from Saint-Saëns (Septet, Op. 65) to Jolivet (Introduction) and Shostakovich (Concerto, Op. 35).

ANTHONY BAINES

FURTHER READING
Philip Bate: *The Trumpet and Trombone* (London, 1966); Anthony Baines: *Brass Instruments: their History and Development* (London, 1976).

Trumscheit (Ger.). See *Tromba marina*.

T.s. Abbreviation for *tasto solo*.

Tsigane, tzigane (Fr.). 'Gipsy'. Ravel gave this name to his concert rhapsody for violin and piano, later orchestrated (1924).

Tuba (in brass and military bands termed 'bass'; for *tuba* in the original Lat. sense, see *Trumpet*, 6a; *Ancient Greek Music*, 4, 6b). Valved brass instrument, the largest of them all. In the orchestra the player sits with the three trombones, making a fourth member of the team and extending its compass down to the bottom D of the piano.

1. *Description*. The instrument varies a good deal. In Britain and France the valves are ordinary upright piston-valves. To finger them,

the right hand rests under the top bend of the tubing and the bell therefore points to the player's right. In the USA a frequent alternative is to mount the piston-valves obliquely or at right angles to the main tubing, or to use rotary-valves as on the German instruments; then the right hand passes over the instrument and the bell necessarily points to the left. (A British military band used sometimes to have one of its basses made with these slanting valves, for the fine visual effect of a tuba bell pointing outwards at each end of the front rank on the march.)

Pitch also varies with the different types. For bands, the instrument is always built in two sizes: E♭ (approximately 13′ if uncoiled); and low B♭ (18′), also called 'Double B♭' (BB♭). They play the bass part in octaves where appropriate. The ordinary 'tuba-shaped' basses of the brass band look very different from the American-invented *sousaphone (see also below, 3), with a 2′-wide bell pointing forwards above the player's head, but both are built in these same two keys.

For the orchestra either of the above pitches may be chosen, or alternatively, at a tone higher, F and low C ('CC'), these being more central

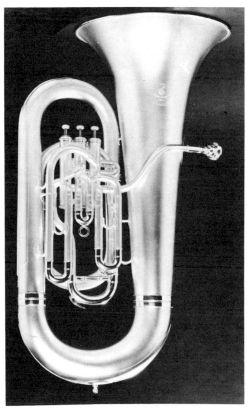

Pl. 1. E♭ tuba (modern wide-bore or 'double E♭' type, with compensating third valve) by Boosey & Hawkes, London.

Pl. 2. BB♭ tuba (with four rotary valves) by Yamaha, Japan.

tonalities in symphonic music generally. The choice goes largely by countries. In Britain tubas are normally in E♭, but from the 1950s usually fitted with a bell of the width of that of the BB♭ bass to produce a fuller sound; it is then commonly called a 'double E♭' tuba. In the USA and Italy the deeper pitches, BB♭ or CC, are preferred; they make a very sonorous tuba. In Germany the tuba generally keeps its first historical pitch of F (see below, 3), with the deeper tubas mainly reserved for special duties like the contrabass tuba part in the *Ring*, in which it is given the boldest, deepest, and most memorable solo passages for tuba in the whole of the regular repertory—as at the beginning of *Siegfried* where it represents the dragon. In France, the orchestral tuba has up to recently always been quite different: in C, a tone above the *euphonium. It reaches the lowest notes with the aid of six pistons (three for each hand), while of course it can easily reach notes well above the practical range of the largest tubas. No tuba really likes to be taken above its eighth harmonic, as Wagner well knew: the high *e'* in

the famous tune in the *Meistersinger* Overture lies just within this limit for the F tuba. But where correspondingly high notes are written for the French tuba (the most quoted example is 'Bydlo' in Ravel's orchestration of Musorgsky's *Pictures from an Exhibition*) players elsewhere may have to change to a smaller instrument to perform the part.

2. *Valve Systems:* (*a*) *Four Valves.* Orchestral tubas always have at least four valves, the fourth lowering the instrument by a perfect fourth in order to fill the gap above the fundamentals (see *Valves*, 3) and so give the instrument a continuous range of deep notes below the staff down to bottom D, or lower if asked for. British and French makers give this valve to the left hand (first finger); American and German usually to the right little finger. But the problems of sharpness inherent in the valve-system when valves are used in combination become acute in many combinations with the fourth valve. The player will adjust the tuning-slides to help matters as far as possible, but there will still be notes that demand conscious lowering by ear and lip, enough so to impair strong, positive attack in *ff* while keeping strictly in tune.

To mitigate these troubles (though in no case wholly to remove them) two chief modifications of the system are in current use.

(*b*) *Five Valves.* This began with the famous Berlin bandmaster Wieprecht's new bass tuba in F, of 1839 (the name 'tuba' in the modern sense here making its first appearance). Wieprecht's scheme is ingeniously simple. He provided (Ex. 1*a*) whole-tone (1) and semitone (2) valves for the F tuba, worked by the left hand; and for the other hand, longer whole-tone (T) and semitone (S) valves as required for the low C tuba, which the instrument becomes if at the same time the valve (4) is lowered for the perfect fourth. The bottom octave is played as shown in Ex. 1*a*, giving well-tuned notes down to low G, the lowest string of the contemporary three-stringed double bass and the lowest note for tuba in Tchaikovsky's three last symphonies (save in one place only in the Fifth Symphony).

In many ways, no better system has ever been devised; but, for bandsmen (bands are always the biggest buyers of tubas, and in former times every tuba-player was also a bandsman), it was too unconventional. So it soon became modified to match other valved instruments by providing a standard third valve (3, Ex. 1*b*; in fact this often in Europe lowers by two tones instead of one-and-a-half tones but without much gain from the point of view of intonation). The valve for the perfect fourth now follows (4) and, if retaining a fifth valve (5), it is a close equivalent to S in Ex. 1*a*, adding approximately one-eleventh of the open tube-length, equivalent to

Ex. 1

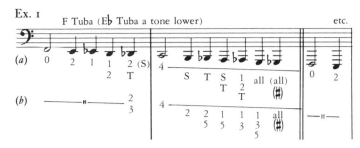

a three-quarter tone. Ex. 1*b* indicates how it may be used for improving notes from B♭ downwards (A♭ downwards on E♭ tuba). Such is the customary five-valve tuba in Germany and the USA, where it correspondingly helps with the CC tuba from the bottom F downward.

Some tubas add a sixth valve tuned in various ways to offer useful alternative fingerings (or on the small French tuba to reach the lowest notes).

(*c*) *Other Systems.* In Britain, Blaikley's 'compensating pistons' (1874) are employed, frequently on band basses and the euphonium also. The principle is virtually the same as that of the 'compensating' double horn (see *Horn*, 2), though using piston-valves not rotary. Fig. 1, purely schematic, indicates how the loop of the fourth valve (shown lying horizontally on the right) is led through the tops of the other three valves, which are made tall enough to contain it. Each of these three carries a small 'increment' loop situated above the main loop. While the fourth valve is not in use these small loops remain idle, nothing passing through them. If the fourth valve is lowered when one or more of the other valves are lowered too their increment

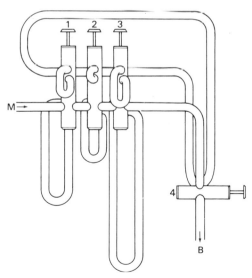

Fig. 1. Schematic illustration of Blaikley's compensating fourth valve (employed in most British tubas): M, lead from mouthpipe; B, exit to bell.

loops join the circuit, automatically supplying the extra length needed now that the instrument is lowered a perfect fourth by the fourth valve. But the deepest of the valved notes still have to be watched against sharpness.

There have certainly been inventions for valves which free the tuba from all these difficulties, for it to give the whole compass with no problem (the most radical was made by Martin Vogel in 1961), but such inventions introduce mechanical complications as well as uprooting the traditional basis of fingering. So tuba-players have preferred to be left with their problems and, thanks partly to modern advances in the matter of breathing, listeners will grant that they produce vast, booming deep notes both impressively and accurately.

3. *History.* The first valved basses were made in Germany and Austria in the late 1820s, mostly with the name 'bombardon'. In general they follow the shape of the then 10-year-old *ophicleide, and are built in F in order to reach the low notes of that instrument with the aid of three valves. With their fairly narrow dimensions the sound is warm and pleasant but without the power reserve of the later instruments (see also *Cimbasso*).

Adolphe Sax knew of Wieprecht's tuba (see above, 2*b*) when developing the E♭ bass of his *saxhorn family of 1845, from which the British tuba is ultimately derived. The first BB♭ bass appeared in Austria about the same time, and four years later, again in Austria, the first 'circular bass' or 'helicon'. This is often seen in military bands in Europe and was used in many British regimental bands up to the First World War. It is placed over the head to rest upon the left shoulder, the bell pointing more or less forwards level with the head. From this, Conn in the USA devised the sousaphone (1898), named in honour of the great bandmaster John Philip Sousa (1854–1932). At first it was built with the huge bell pointing straight upwards like an enormous flower vase. Not all American bands insist on it, many using basses of ordinary tuba-shaped format, or these with the bell bent round to face forwards. This last feature was introduced when music was recorded into a horn, and a tuba, preferably of this 'recording bass' type, was called in to help the double basses: one often hears it in early recordings, thumping out the bass part below a singer or violin soloist of international fame.

4. *Repertory*. One work is well known in the concert hall, Vaughan Williams's Tuba Concerto written for the F tuba at a time (1955) when some leading players in London, including Philip Catelinet (by whom the work was first performed), were still using this instrument, following the older British tradition. With piano, there is a Sonata by Hindemith and a Suite by Gordon Jacob, and later works by Edward Gregson (*b* 1945) and others.

5. *Wagner Tuba* (in Ger. often *Ring-Tuba*). This was made for performance of the *Ring*, in which four are required: two *Tenortuben* in B♭ (with the pitch of the euphonium) and two *Basstuben* in F (with the pitch of an F tuba or F horn). For their notation, see *Transposing Instruments*.

It appears that soon after starting work on *Das Rheingold* in 1853 the composer was shown the instruments recently produced in Paris by Sax and that these suggested to him this masterly addition to his orchestral palette, with an effect which arrests the listener from their first entry (the opening of Scene 2 of *Das Rheingold*), where they solemnly announce no less than the 'Valhalla' theme itself.

Pl. 4. Wagner tuba (tenor in B♭) by Demusa, Markneukirchen.

The four instruments are built in the oval format common among German band instruments, with fairly wide bores and rotary-valves. The mouth-pipe tapers to a narrow dimension in order to receive a horn mouthpiece, for the instruments are to be played by four of the eight horn players, who change between horn and tuba as the parts instruct. After Wagner, Bruckner uses the instruments in a similar manner in his last three symphonies, and Richard Strauss in *Elektra*.

6. *Tenor Tuba*. Where a score has a part with this name—as in Richard Strauss's *Don Quixote* and *Ein Heldenleben*, Stravinsky's *The Rite of Spring*, and Holst's *The Planets*—it is normally played on the euphonium (in Amer.: baritone), though it seems possible that Strauss may have had, at least at first, the tenor Wagner tuba in mind.   ANTHONY BAINES

Pl. 3. Sousaphone by Boosey & Hawkes, London.

FURTHER READING
Clifford Bevan: *The Tuba Family* (London, 1978).

Tubular bells [orchestral chimes] (Fr.: *cloches, cloches tubulaires*; Ger.: *Röhrenglocken*; It.: *campanelli, campanelli tubolari*). Plated brass tubes, with closed upper ends, hung by cords from a tall frame and struck against the top with a rawhide or plastic mallet. There are 18 tubes in a normal set, graded in length but of the same diameter (from 1″ to 1½″). The sharps are hung behind the naturals, with their upper ends at a higher level so that they can be reached by the mallet. The normal range is written *c′-f″* (sounding an octave higher). A horizontal felted damper is provided, worked by a cord or, more usually, a pedal. For some works, such as Berlioz's *Symphonie fantastique* (last movement) and Puccini's *Tosca* (Act 3), special, extra-large tubes are needed, unless some different bell substitute is to be used (see *Bells*, 8).

The first mention of tubular bells is found in Paris, *c*.1867; next, in England, in a patent by John Harrington of Coventry, upon which Sullivan is said to have tried them out in *The Golden Legend* (1886). Invented as substitutes for church bells, they became for a long time familiar in small orchestras and bands in diatonic sets, usually in the key of E♭. They have also been incorporated into organs and, from the 1920s, electrically amplified, in carillons. In modern writing for percussion, however, the tubular bells have gained an important place in their own right (not as church bells), even playing chords, tremolos, and glissandos, as well as single notes.

ANTHONY BAINES

Tucket. A term mostly found in stage directions from the late 16th century to the 17th, and particularly in the works of Shakespeare and his contemporaries. The word appears to be an anglicization of *toccata, and describes a flourish of trumpets or drums. See also *Sennet*; *Trumpet*, 6*b*.

Tudor, Antony (*b* London, 4 Apr. 1908). British dancer and choreographer. He helped to lay the foundations of British ballet in the 1930s, with the Ballet Rambert, creating *Lilac Garden* (Chausson, 1936) and the first ballet to music by Mahler, *Dark Elegies* (1937). He settled in New York in 1940, becoming resident choreographer at the formation of the American Ballet Theatre. Works from this period include *Pillar of Fire* (Schoenberg, 1942), and *Undertow* (Schuman, 1945). Later came *Shadowplay* (Koechlin, 1967) for the Royal Ballet and *The Leaves are Fading* (Dvořák, 1975). He became associate director of the American Ballet Theatre in 1974.

NOËL GOODWIN

Tůma, František (Ignác Antonín) (*b* Kostelec nad Orlicí, Bohemia, 2 Oct. 1704; *d* Vienna,

30 Jan. 1774). Czech composer. He studied first with his father and later in Prague. In the early 1720s he went to Vienna where he pursued a successful career as a church musician and later as *Kapellmeister* to Count Franz Ferdinand Kinsky, and in 1741 to the Dowager Empress. After her death in 1750, Tůma remained in Vienna and seems to have been in demand as an instrumentalist as well as a composer. He was admired both for his numerous *a cappella* settings of the Mass in which he followed the model of Fux, and for his accompanied church music. Contrapuntal expertise is also to the fore in his instrumental sonatas and sinfonias. Though largely conservative in approach, there are sometimes indications that Tůma was prepared to make use of the less rigorous *Stil galant*.

JAN SMACZNY

Tunder, Franz (*b* Bannesdorf, nr Burg, island of Fehmarn, 1614; *d* Lübeck, 5 Nov. 1667). German composer. He began his career as organist to the Schleswig court and in 1621 was appointed organist to the Marienkirche in Lübeck. He is chiefly remembered as the founder of the series of *Abendmusiken* (evening concerts comprising a mixture of sacred vocal and organ music) which was later taken over by Buxtehude.

Only 17 of Tunder's vocal works survive: they include solo motets, some in the Italian style, others (e.g. *Ein kleines Kinderlein*) based on German songs; and early examples of the kind of chorale cantata later developed by Bach (e.g. *Wachet auf, An Wasserflüssen Babylons, Ein' feste Burg*). His organ music includes four important preludes, which were the first examples in North Germany of the prelude in three parts (toccata-fugue-prelude), and seven chorale fantasias in antiphonal style. His importance lies in his contribution to the various types of Lutheran church music later cultivated by Bach.

WENDY THOMPSON

Tuners, Electronic. See *Pitch*.

Tuning-fork. A two-pronged device, of tempered steel, obtainable from music dealers and in a wide selection of notes and pitches from suppliers of scientific instruments. The note and pitch (Hz) are stamped on the fork, the most used being the fork for the tuning A (*a′*) at standard pitch (*a′* = 440), but for historical performances other values such as *a′* = 415 or 422 may be needed (see *Pitch*). Metals used are such that there is virtually no variation of pitch with temperature. One prong is struck, e.g. on the knee, and the stem is pressed to a resonant surface; or the fork can be bowed with a violin bow or kept in vibration electromagnetically.

Tuning-forks from the past are naturally of

immense value as evidence of former playing pitches, the great study in English from this aspect being by A. J. Ellis (see *Pitch*) who lists some 150 forks from the 18th century onwards and from all over Europe. One fork ($a' = 409$) was owned by Taskin, the great harpsichord-maker in Paris; another ($a' = 421.6$) by Stein of Vienna, whose pianos Mozart played; others are official forks for the standard pitches like the French *diapason normal* of 1859 ($a' = 435$). One of the most celebrated forks in this list was preserved in its box inscribed 'This Pitchfork was the property of the Immortal Handel, and left by him at the Foundling Hospital, when the Messiah was Performed in 1751: . . . Invented by M. [John] Shore, Serj. Trumpeter, time of Purcell'. Shore was also lutenist to the Chapel Royal, and an old fork in the list ($a' = 419.9$ as measured by Ellis) was thought to have possibly been made by him; he is said to have invented it in 1711. The old forks were made by welding a stem to the centre of a metal bar which was then bent round in a long horseshoe shape; the present form was developed in the 19th century, notably by Rudolf Koenig in Germany.

ANTHONY BAINES

Turandot. Opera in three acts by Puccini, completed by Alfano; text by Adami and Simoni, after Gozzi's drama (1762), itself possibly derived from the *1,001 Nights*. Produced: Milan, La Scala, 25 April 1926; New York, Metropolitan Opera, 16 November 1926; London, Covent Garden, 7 June 1927. An opera

Brunelleschi's costume design for the princess in the first performance of Puccini's 'Turandot' (La Scala, Milan, 1926).

of the same name by Busoni (1917) is also still occasionally performed. The cruel Princess Turandot (sop.) poses three riddles for her suitors to answer; if they fail they will be beheaded. The unknown Prince Calaf (ten.) succeeds in answering them and challenges her to discover his name by morning, in which case he will forfeit his life. Turandot tortures the slave-girl Liù (sop.), Calaf's faithful companion, in an attempt to discover the name of the Prince; but Liù, rather than reveal it, kills herself. Turandot, realizing what true love really is, accepts Calaf's hand.

Turangalîla-symphonie. Symphony by Messiaen for large orchestra including ondes martenot, piano, and a section of pitched and unpitched percussion, composed between 1946 and 1948. Its title comes from the Sanskrit *Turanga* ('the passage of time, movement, rhythm'), and *lîla* ('play in the sense of divine action on the cosmos, also the play of creation, destruction, life and death, also love'). It is the largest of the three works by Messiaen inspired by the legend of Tristan and Isolda (the others are *Cinq Rechants* and *Harawi*). Its 10 movements are *Introduction, Chant d'amour I, Turangalîla I, Chant d'amour II, Joie du sang des étoiles, Jardin du sommeil d'amour, Turangalîla II, Développement de l'amour, Turangalîla III, Final*. It has been the basis of a ballet choreographed by Petit and performed in Paris in 1968, and one choreographed by Vesak and performed in San Francisco in 1971; three movements were used for a ballet choreographed by Van Dyk and performed in Hamburg in 1960.

Turba (Lat., 'crowd'). In a *Passion, the name given to the crowd.

Turca, alla (It.) 'In the Turkish style'. See *Turkish music*.

Turco in Italia, Il ('The Turk in Italy'). Opera in two acts by Rossini to a libretto by Romani. It was first performed in Milan in 1814.

Turina, Joaquín (*b* Seville, 9 Dec. 1882; *d* Madrid, 14 Jan. 1949). Spanish composer. He studied at Seville and Madrid, and then in Paris, where he was a pupil of d'Indy at the Schola Cantorum. From 1931 he was a professor at the Madrid Conservatory. His works are infused with the colour and atmosphere of his native Andalusia. Several, such as the orchestral *Sinfonia sevillana* (1920) and *Sevilla* for piano (1909), were inspired by his native city. His *Procesión del Rocío* (1913) for orchestra was praised by Debussy. Turina compiled a two-volume *Enciclopedia abreviada de música*

(Madrid, 1917) and also wrote a treatise on composition (Madrid, 1946).

WENDY THOMPSON

Turini, Francesco (*b* Prague, *c.*1589; *d* Brescia, 1656). Italian organist and composer. The son of a musician in the service of Emperor Rudolf II, he was sent at an early age to study music in Venice and Rome. He eventually became organist at Brescia Cathedral where he remained until his death. He composed attractive madrigals, solo motets, and some sonatas for two violins and continuo, early instances of the trio sonata (published in his first book of *Madrigali*, Venice, 1621).

DENIS ARNOLD

Turkey, Music of. See *Middle Eastern Music*.

Turkish crescent. See *Turkish Music*.

Turkish music (Fr.; *bande turque*; Ger.: *Janitscharmusik*; It.: *musica alla turca*). A term covering additional percussion instruments—mainly bass drum, cymbals, triangle—that now and again appear in music of the Classical period, e.g. in Mozart (*Die Entführung aus dem Serail*), Haydn ('Military' Symphony), and Beethoven (in the *alla marcia* section of the finale of the Ninth Symphony). It was through 'Turkish music' that these instruments first gained a place in both orchestra and military band.

The first signs date from the 1720s, when the Turks had been pushed back beyond Hungary and Western powers responsible for their ejection were able to procure a genuine set of the Turkish Janissary music whose magnificent display and ferocious sounds had left a strong impression. The Janissaries, crack troops of the Turkish forces, had since the 14th century been recruited as boys from Christian subjects, some to be trained to man these military bands. Visitors to modern Istanbul may have witnessed the music in progress as now revived in 17th-century costume (the Janissaries having been disbanded in 1826) and based as far as possible on original sources. One sees bass drums played with stick and cane (see *Drum*, 4), pairs of small kettledrums held on the left arm (see *Timpani*, 5), cymbals, and *surnas* (see *Shawm*, 4) for the melodies, doubled by ordinary Western valved trumpets (since no record survives as to what the original natural trumpets did). In front are singers, each with a 'Turkish crescent'—a staff surmounted by a brass crescent and hung with horsetails—raised up and down in time with the music; the director has his own staff and a whistle that calls the band to commence.

The 18th-century West rejected the small kettledrums and the wind instruments while picturesquely adding the triangle, played in bands by a boy. Gluck has it in the Turkish music for the Scythian storm in *Iphigénie en Tauride*. Next was added a tambourine, played in bands in a spectacular manner by a black man. In Ex. 1, from the manuscript of a late 18th-century opera *La constanza alla fine premiata*, by the obscure composer Orodaet, 'tamburo ord' possibly means the tambourine. With the bass drum ('tamburo grosso') the lower Cs are struck with the heavy stick (right hand) and the upper Cs with the cane (or a switch) on the other side of the drum. A marching band might include the Turkish crescent, then hung with small bells and named in England 'jingling Johnny', predecessor of the present lyra glockenspiel (see *Glockenspiel*, 4). It

A passage for Turkish instruments from Orodeat's 'La constanza alla fine premiata'.

Ex. 1

can be seen (somewhat roughly drawn) in *Military band*, Pl. 2.

ANTHONY BAINES

Turmmusik (Ger.). 'Tower music', i.e. music played from the towers of churches, town halls, etc. by town musicians (*Stadtpfeifer*) in Germany, chiefly in the 17th century. See *Wait*.

Turn (Fr.: *doublé*; Ger.: *Doppelschlag*; It.: *gruppetto*). An ornament found in music from the 17th century to the 19th. It consists essentially of four notes—note above, main note, note below, main note—but the rhythmic configurations are numerous. The graphic sign is ∾; in modern practice chromatic inflexions of the upper or lower notes are indicated above or below the sign respectively (see Ex. 2*d*).

The sign may be found above a note, as was usual in the Baroque period (Ex. 1), or (especially from the Classical era onwards) it may be written, and the turn played, between two notes (Ex. 2).

Ex. 1

Ex. 2 (*a*)   (*b*)   (*c*)

Ex. 2(*c*) may also be found suitable in music of this period when the sign is placed above the note. Turns are sometimes indicated in small notes, but composers of the later 19th century tended to write them in full notation, to remove any rhythmic ambiguity.

An inverted turn, indicated by ∾ , ⌇ or ⌐, simply reverses the direction (Ex. 3).

Ex. 3

SIMON McVEIGH

Turn of the Screw, The. Opera in prologue and two acts by Britten; text by Myfanwy Piper, after Henry James's story (1898). Produced: Venice, La Fenice, 14 September 1954 by English Opera Group; London, Sadler's Wells, 6 October 1954; New York, College of Music (Kaufmann Concert Hall), 19 March 1958. The Governess (sop.), sent to look after two children in a country house run only by an old housekeeper, Mrs Grose (sop.), comes to realize that they are visited by the evil ghosts of two former servants, Miss Jessel (sop.) and Peter Quint (ten.); more, that the children cherish the relationship. In fighting this she has first to convince the housekeeper, and having persuaded her to take the girl away, battles with the ghost who haunts the boy, and wins—only to find him dead in her arms. The 'screw' of the title is represented by a theme that 'turns' through 15 variations, interludes between the eight scenes of each act.

Turque (Fr.). 'Turkish'. See *Turkish music*.

Tusch (Ger.). A 'fanfare' played on brass instruments.

Tutta, tutto (It.). 'All'; *tutte le corde*, 'all the strings', i.e. (in piano music), remove the *una corda* pedal.

Tutti (It., pl. of *tutto*). 'All'. In orchestral scores and parts, *tutti* is used to indicate that all the performers should take part after a passage in which only certain of them were required. In the 18th-century *concerti grossi*, *tutti* was the equivalent of *ripieno* (the whole body of performers) as opposed to *concertante* (the solo group). A '*tutti* passage' is a passage for the whole orchestral force.

Twelfth. See *Interval*.

Twelve-note music. Music in which all 12 notes of the chromatic scale have equal importance; i.e. music which is not in any key or mode and which may be described as 'atonal'. The term has also been used for all serial music, or alternatively for serial music which follows the principles established by Schoenberg rather than those of later composers such as Boulez or Babbitt. See *Atonality*; *Serialism*.

There are occasional examples in 18th- and 19th-century music of themes which contain all 12 chromatic notes: that of Bach's *Musical Offering* is one such, and Liszt's *Faust Symphony* provides at its opening a striking instance of a theme using each of the 12 notes once only. However, these works should not be described as '12-note music', since the context in both cases is tonal. A few of Liszt's last piano pieces show him coming very close to atonality, but the first true 12-note compositions were probably the 15 songs of Schoenberg's *Das Buch der hängenden Gärten* (1908-9). Charles Ives came to atonality at about the same time quite independently. Schoenberg, Berg, and Webern continued to write 12-note music from 1908 onwards, though Schoenberg made some

returns to diatonic composition. After his development of serialism in the early 1920s, the three composers concentrated on that compositional method.

Much of the 12-note music produced by later composers has also been serial, at least in some manner. However, many of the works of Henze, Penderecki, Lutosławski, and others are atonal and not serial.   PAUL GRIFFITHS

FURTHER READING
George Perle: *Serial Composition and Atonality* (Berkeley, California, 1962, 4th edn 1978).

Twelve-note scale (Eng.; Amer.: 12-tone scale). The chromatic scale of 12 equal notes, as used in *twelve-note music. See also *Scale*, 4.

Twenty-four violins. See *Vingt-quatre Violons du Roi*.

Twilight of the Gods, The (Ger.: *Götterdämmerung*). See *Ring des Nibelungen, Der*.

Tye, Christopher (*b* c.1505; *d* ? Doddington, Isle of Ely, ? 1572). English composer. He was a choirboy and subsequently a lay clerk at King's College, Cambridge, taking the B.Mus. there in 1536. He became choirmaster at Ely Cathedral in 1543, with a stipend of £10 a year, and probably remained there, or was at least based there, until he was offered the living at Doddington in 1561. In 1545 he was awarded the Cambridge D.Mus. He was apparently also a member of the Chapel Royal, probably on a part-time or visiting basis.

Tye was a composer of splendid music for the Latin rite—the sonorous Mass *Euge bone* especially shows a mastery of new continental imitative techniques—and it is a pity that he is known now mainly for his less important, albeit attractive, music for the Anglican church. The possibly apocryphal but none the less amusing story told by Anthony Wood is worth repeating as something many a musician would like to say to an unappreciative audience: 'Dr Tye was a peevish and humoursome man, especially in his latter days, and sometimes playing on the organ in the chapel of Queen Elizabeth which contained much music but little delight to the ear, she would send the verger to tell him that he played out of tune; whereupon he sent word that her ears were out of tune'.   DENIS ARNOLD

FURTHER READING
John Langdon: 'Tye and his Church Music', *The Musical Times*, cxiii (1972).

Tzigane (Fr.). 'Gipsy'. See *Tsigane*.

U

Über (Ger.). 'Over', 'above', 'across', etc.; *überblasen*, 'to overblow'; *Übergang*, 'transition'; *übergreifen*, 'to cross the hands' (in piano playing); *Überleitung*, 'transition'.

Übung (Ger.). 'Exercise'.

U.c. Abbreviation for **una corda*.

Uguale (It.). 'Equal'; *ugualmente*, 'equally'; *ugualità, uguaglianza*, 'equality'.

Uillean pipe. Irish bagpipe. See *Bagpipe*, 11.

Ukulele. One of the smallest of the guitar family, with four single strings and 12 frets, meant for strumming accompaniment to the voice. The strings can be violin A and E strings or be obtained specially. The tuning follows the pattern of the first four strings of the guitar save that the fourth string is raised by an octave. Also, the pitch of the whole tuning is higher, often by a fourth (*a'*, *e'*, *c'*, *g'*). The strings are typically struck downwards with the nails and upwards with the fingertips. Chord diagrams often placed above the vocal line in sheet-music show with black dots where to place the fingers (the top line of the diagram representing the nut).

The ukulele (in Hawaiian, 'flea') arose apparently after seamen, during the 1870s, acquainted the Hawaiians (then under their own rulers) with small guitars of Portuguese types. For the ukulele-banjo, see *Banjo*, 4.

ANTHONY BAINES

Ultimos ritos ('Last Rites'). Work by Tavener to a text by St John of the Cross and the Crucifixus from the Nicene Creed. It is for soprano, alto, tenor, and bass soloists, five male speakers, chorus, large brass ensemble, and orchestra, and was composed 1969-72.

Umfang (Ger.). 'Compass', 'range' (of a voice, instrument etc.).

Umkehrung (Ger.). 'Turning round', 'reversal'. *Kanon in der Umkehrung*, 'canon by inversion'. See *Canon*.

Umlauf, Ignaz (*b* Vienna, 1746; *d* Meidling, nr Vienna, 8 June 1796). Austrian composer. He began his career in 1772 as a violist in the Vienna court orchestra. In 1778 he was commissioned to compose a *Singspiel, Die Bergknappen*, to inaugurate the National Singspiel at the Burgtheater. Four years later he was appointed deputy to Salieri as director of the Italian Opera; he subsequently became music teacher at the court. Umlauf's *Singspiele* are typically Viennese in spirit in their fusion of Italian and German features.

His son, **Michael Umlauf** (*b* Vienna, 9 Aug. 1781; *d* Baden, 20 June 1842), was a conductor and composer. He studied with his father before becoming a violinist in the Vienna court orchestra; he was later one of the directors of the Vienna court theatres. Beethoven and he shared the conducting of the first performance of *Fidelio* in 1814 and of the Ninth Symphony in 1824—in fact, Beethoven's deafness restricted his useful contribution to setting the tempos. Umlauf composed three *Singspiele*, several ballets, and some piano and sacred music.

WENDY THOMPSON

Umstimmen (Ger.). 'To tune to another pitch' (*e g* the strings of a violin).

Una corda (It.). In piano music, an indication to depress the 'soft' pedal. See *Piano*, 12.

Unanswered Question, The. Work for small orchestra by Ives, composed in 1906. It is the first of *Two Contemplations*, the other being *Central Park in the Dark* (1906).

Undine. See *Ondine*.

Unequal voices. A term given to a mixture of male and female voices; see also *Equal voices*.

Unessential notes. See *Essential note*.

'Unfinished' Symphony. Schubert's Symphony No. 8 in B minor, D 759, composed in 1822. There are many unfinished symphonies, for example by Tchaikovsky, Mahler, Elgar, and Shostakovich, but the title is generally taken to refer only to Schubert's. His seventh (in E major) was also left incomplete. No one knows why Schubert only wrote two movements and sketches for a scherzo of the 'Unfinished'; many romantic answers have been suggested, but it seems that Schubert either forgot the symphony or abandoned it because he could not find comparable inspiration for the third and fourth movements.

Ungebunden (Ger.). 1. 'Free', 'unconstrained'. 2. Of keyboard and stringed instruments, 'unfretted'.

Ungezwungen (Ger.). 'Unforced', 'easygoing', 'natural'.

Ungrader Takt (Ger.). 'Uneven (triple) time'.

Uniment (Fr.). 'Smoothly', i.e. slurred together.

Unison (Fr.: *unisson*; Ger.: *Prime*; It.: *prima*). 1. Simultaneous performance of the same line of music by various instruments or voices, or by the whole choir or orchestra. This can be at exactly the same pitch, or in a different octave. The direction is sometimes given as *all'unisono* (It.). 2. The 'interval' formed between the same two notes. See *Interval*.

United States of America

1. Introduction
2. Musical Life in Early America
3. The 19th Century

4. Folk Music
5. The 20th Century
6. Popular Music

1. *Introduction.* Developing free from the nurturing presence of either an established, liturgically-minded Church or an aristocratic court, music in the United States has evolved without the securely defined functions and continuous patronage that such powerful institutions have provided during much of Western European history. In Western Europe, many different kinds of music-making have existed, but at the top of the hierarchy has always stood fine-art music, an extension of the power and splendour of church, aristocracy, or state. Musicians working in that realm have been bred to a musical practice of continuity and high prestige. Employed by the leaders of society, and responsible only to them and to Almighty God, such musicians have been given little reason to doubt the worthiness of their chosen careers. Their music has undisputedly been their society's most important music. They are considered, and they consider themselves in some sense, partners in the collective enterprise of making their country's culture.

In the democratic United States things have worked out differently. In the absence of powerful institutions' continuous need for it, music as a fine art has never held the place of favoured dominance that it has enjoyed in Europe. There simply has been no corresponding role for it. Consequently, musical life in the United States has been shaped less by the preferences of society's leaders than by the tastes and needs of humbler folk. Foremost among them have been musicians themselves, working to satisfy the needs of various social groups—for artistic expression, worship, instruction, entertainment, or participatory recreation. Most American musicians have worked as individuals in a commercial society.

That society has generally been less concerned that they develop the highest artistry than that they find proper niches for their skills, adapting those skills to the tasks at hand. More than in any particular style, genre, or school of composers, the vitality of American music is to be found in the range and diversity of the American musician's responses to the musical tasks he or she has accepted and in the artistry that some have summoned in the course of doing a day's work.

2. *Musical Life in Early America.* It is surely wrong to assert, as have some earlier commentators, that the first settlers of the English-speaking American colonies were opposed to music. The idea of the Puritans as music-haters has been laid to rest by scholars, who found ample evidence that, as well as the psalmody of the congregational meeting-house, early New Englanders practised social singing and dancing and played instruments as well. It is one thing, however, to tolerate and even encourage people to make music on their own, and another to foster the growth of musical skill. The first can crop up among individuals in any circumstance. The second requires institutional support. Much of the story of music in America, especially before 1800, is to be found in the development of institutions to support the making of music.

Except for the Quakers, all the religious groups that settled in early America called for music in their worship. However, it took many generations for them to begin to pay much attention to the musical skills of their worshippers. Liturgical denominations like the Anglicans and Lutherans commonly hired from the Old Country the organists they required.

Pl. 1. Singing and dancing at a Shaker religious ceremony.

Even less promising for the art of music were the activities of the Reformed Calvinists, including the Puritans who settled New England. Believing the theatre immoral, they successfully opposed its firm establishment in the colonies until near the end of the 18th century. As for sacred music, they mistrusted the motives of those who wanted to expand its role in worship, and they discouraged such expansion. Following the practice begun by John Calvin, they assigned music-making during public worship entirely to the congregation. Not until the 18th century, and then only very gradually, did the unaccompanied, monophonic psalm singing of the Calvinist worship begin to be elaborated.

The elaboration began in Massachussetts around 1720. Its origin lay in ministers' complaints that congregational psalm singing, left to its own devices, had grown into a free-for-all in which each singer embellished the melody according to his own fancy, rendering the words of the metrical psalms unintelligible. Reform of this 'usual way' of singing was recommended, and singing schools were established. These schools, instructional sessions run by a singing master, sought to teach the scholars how to sing congregational tunes in a co-ordinated way, as they were written down in musical notation. Instructional tune-books like John Tufts's *An Introduction to the Singing of Psalm-tunes* and Thomas Walter's *The Grounds and Rules of Musick* (both Boston, 1721) were published, condensing the rudiments of music and offering a supply of harmonized tunes for singing schools or public worship. The transforming of congregational singing from a traditional custom to a prescriptive practice was a critical event in American Calvinist sacred music. As 'regular singing' was adopted in New England communities—usually by vote of the whole congregation, and often not without strong

opposition—the first step towards a richer sacred music was taken.

The first reform of American sacred music had been effected by an alliance of clergymen and musicians. Beginning in the 1750s and 1760s, musicians began to take over sacred music-making from both clergy and congregation. Singers banded together to form choirs, at first to lead singing in public worship. Soon, however, in some places, choirs began to sing pieces that other members of the congregation did not know, or that were too complicated for them to learn. More and more American tune-books were published. Most, like Lyon's *Urania* (Philadelphia, 1761) and Bayley's *The American Harmony* (Newburyport, 1769), carried choir music—'fuging' psalm tunes, through-composed 'set-pieces', and prose anthems—together with standard congregational fare. By the 1780s a modest hierarchy of music-making organizations had grown up around the Calvinist meeting-house. Singing schools, designed for beginners, usually ended with a public exhibition of the singers' skill. Choirs performed in public worship. And some of the more dedicated singers formed musical societies to sing the choir music they most admired. Indications are that the clergy played little or no role in the establishment of this structure, and that congregations were generally indifferent or opposed to it.

Crowning the new sacred musical life of New England was the appearance of the American composer. Beginning with the Boston tanner William Billings's *The New-England Psalm-Singer* (Boston, 1770), American-born musicians, including storekeeper Daniel Read of New Haven, hatter Timothy Swan of Suffield, carpenter Oliver Holden of Charlestown, and dozens more, taught singing schools, composed their own sacred pieces, compiled tune-books, and, as these and other tune-books were sold,

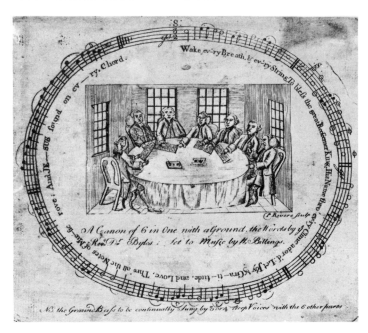

Pl. 2. Frontispiece to William Billings's 'New-England Psalm-Singer' (Boston, 1770), with a canon of six in one with a ground.

saw their compositions circulate in print. Their music, generally set for unaccompanied four-voice chorus, lacks the melodic and harmonic suavity of European music of the time. Nevertheless, written by self-taught musicians who composed for their neighbours or for singers of similar background and skill, New England sacred music of the 18th century showed considerable vitality and staying power. As the frontier pushed westward after 1800, evangelical religious groups that settled the west and south established a practice of sacred music-making that in some ways resembled that of William Billings's New England. Tune-books compiled by 19th- and 20th-century southern singing masters, like *The Sacred Harp* (compiled in Hamilton, Georgia, 1844; latest edition still in print), usually contained both newer local compositions and a selection of favourites by the New Englanders.

Secular music-making in early America organized itself along lines very different from sacred. Here the chief presence was not the native-born yeoman with a taste for music, but the immigrant musician from Europe, the professional in search of an audience. Ranging through the cities of the eastern seaboard, he began presenting public concerts as early as 1729 in Boston and 1731 in Charleston. Shortly after mid century, with the arrival of Hallam's theatre company, which toured widely and long and was soon joined by rival companies, the musical theatre began to make its first real impact, the players performing the best-known English ballad operas. By the time of the Revolutionary War, European-born music

masters were teaching young American harpsi-chordists, flautists, and violinists in cities and towns, and also on the plantations of the South. These activities were sporadic, however, compared with what happened after the war. As residents of the cities along the Atlantic seaboard enjoyed increased wealth and leisure time, European professionals like Gottlieb Graupner (1767-1836) and Benjamin Carr (1768-1831) found more reason to settle in the New World. By the mid 1790s, each of the major Atlantic coastal cities—Boston, New York, Philadelphia, Baltimore, Charleston—had its own musical theatre. Concerts of vocal and instrumental music were given regularly. Music lessons were available to those who could afford them. And a domestic music trade was beginning to flourish: publishers brought out songs and pieces from the Anglo-American musical theatre in sheet-music form, and both imported and American-made instruments were widely for sale.

Although sacred and secular musical life in early America differed in structure, function, and leadership, they held one fundamental trait in common. Both were shaped by musicians working to satisfy a particular public and dependent in the long run upon some measure of commercial success. One remarkable group of religious dissenters made music entirely apart from commercial considerations—the Moravians who had settled in North Carolina and Pennsylvania by the 1750s, and whose high level of performance and composition centred on sacred music and instrumental chamber music as well (see *Moravian Music in America*).

Another musician to whom commercial success was unimportant was the 'gentleman amateur' Francis Hopkinson, whose *Seven Songs* (Philadelphia, 1788) are among the earliest American-composed art songs. But the Moravians and the aristocratic Hopkinson are exceptions: few of their music-minded contemporaries were in a position to follow their example. Thus, in the 18th century the foundations for the support of American musicians were laid, not in salons and cathedrals, but in the market-place.

3. *The 19th Century*. The volume of all aspects of organized music-making increased greatly during the 19th century. The rapid growth of the country's population and settled territory helped to bring about a corresponding growth in the size of the American middle class, whose needs and tastes did a great deal to shape 19th-century American musical life. Musicians who first learned how to address middle-class musical needs, and who set up means for doing so, wielded an influence beyond what their purely musical talents might seem to warrant. Lowell Mason (1792–1872), Patrick Sarsfield Gilmore (1829–92), and George Frederick Root (1820–95) were three such musicians.

The Massachusetts-born Mason, who compiled more than 50 musical publications, is said to have made a fortune as an editor. One of the leading reformers of American sacred music, Mason composed many hymn tunes in a simple 'devotional' style that was widely imitated. Committed to the ideal of American musical 'progress' through the dissemination of musical learning, Mason recognized that children could be the key to such progress. Late in the 1830s, he began to teach music in the Boston public schools, and within a short time other communities hired other music teachers to do the same. As the 'father' of public school music in America, Mason can hardly be held responsible for its subsequent history, during which it has absorbed widely diverse musical practices. Nevertheless, by being the first to see the public school system as a focus for the teaching of music, Mason began the building of a structure that has proved, for better or worse, to be one of the chief continuing sources of musical patronage in the United States.

Gilmore, who emigrated to America from Ireland as a young man, made his mark in the realm of the public concert. The wind band was his medium, the mass audience his quarry. Having led bands of his own before and during the Civil War, he subsequently organized two 'Peace Jubilees' in Boston (1869, 1872), the second of which brought 10 days of musical

Pl. 3. Opening concert of Gilmore's second Peace Jubilee, held in Boston, 17 June 1872, engraving.

events to a climactic conclusion with a performance by some 22,000 singers and players, supplemented by occasional cannon fire. In later years Gilmore formed a professional band which made successful concert tours in both the Unites States and Europe. In the hands of Gilmore and later John Philip Sousa, the wind band came to be the medium most successful in drawing a concert audience virtually anywhere in the world. Much of the band's broad appeal lay in its eclectic programming—a musical mixed bag of marches, patriotic airs, popular songs and dances, and excerpts from classics. Taken up by orchestras in their 'promenade' or 'pops' concerts, this programming principle, which seeks to meet the general public on its own ground, has persisted to the present day.

Root's career reflects a third strain in 19th-century American musical life: the development of the home as a centre of music-making. Born in Massachusetts, Root trained as a music teacher under Mason, helped in the 1850s to found a Normal Musical Institute to train teachers in Mason's methods, and then gave up teaching and turned his energies elsewhere. As a partner in the Chicago publishing house of Root & Cady (1860-71), he brought out music by many composers, including the talented song-writer, Henry Clay Work (1832-84). He also composed 'people's songs' and cantatas himself —works whose studied avoidance of musical complication was supposed to fit them for the broadest possible market. Many hit the mark, in fact, and especially Root's Civil War songs, which had a wide and lasting appeal. By that time, the availability of low-priced pianos had prompted thousands of Americans to install pianos in their parlours. Together with dozens of other music publishers, Root & Cady stood ready to supply vocal and instrumental music to fit all tastes. Pieces like Root's own songs, or the flood of piano pieces written expressly for the amateur performer, formed only two of the many species of 19th-century American sheet music. Arrangements and adaptations abounded: opera arias, variations on favourite melodies, battle pieces, overtures, even symphonies. In a career which blended composing, teaching, and publishing, Root made a handsome living by addressing himself to the needs

Pl. 4. Title-page of the Civil War song 'Glory! Glory!' by Root (Chicago: Root & Cady, 1866).

Pl. 5. 'Ethiopian' minstrels playing bones, banjos, accordion and tambourine, lithograph from the title-page of 'Music of the Ethiopian Serenaders' (New York: Firth Pond & Co., 1847).

of the amateur making music in his own house.

Mason, Gilmore, and Root all worked in circumstances that offered some promise of commercial success. Yet none of the three was involved with the popular musical theatre, which continued under English domination through much of the first half of the 19th century. The American presence on American musical stages was first forcibly felt in the 1840s, when the Ohio-born musical entertainer Dan Emmett and three cohorts blackened their faces with burnt cork, dressed in rag-tag costumes, affected the heavy dialect and loose-jointed motions associated with the American Negro, and as 'The Virginia Minstrels' put on the first full-length blackface minstrel show. The idea caught on like wildfire; 'Ethiopian' troupes multiplied with amazing speed and found audiences wherever they went.

The minstrel show drew much of its vitality from the source it parodied—the music, dance, and speech of Black Americans. How 'authentic' the music was has been the subject of debate. While the original minstrels, most of whom were White, surely did not reproduce indigenous Black folk music—that would have been as foreign to most of them as to their audiences— the traits they did borrow from folk sources, both Anglo- and Afro-American, flavoured their music distinctively. The instrumentation of the original minstrel band gave it its own sound of crackling dryness: fiddle, tambourine, banjo, and bones. The repetitive melodic simplicity of many of the songs helped make them catchy and easy to recall. And the ensemble's free-wheeling rhythm, spiced with syncopation, made its sound infectious.

The minstrel show, a loose arrangement of songs, dances, skits, and speeches, has been condemned by many recent commentators as a racist institution. Yet its broad appeal derives from more than simply a disdain for Negroes set to toe-tapping music. Perhaps the chief attraction of the minstrel show was its irreverence. Using the black face as a comic mask, it gave entertainers a chance to take pot-shots at literally everyone: sanctimonious preachers and politicians, self-important opera singers, country bumpkins, city slickers, ignorant people

Pl. 6. Playbill for a performance by Christy's Minstrels at Mechanics' Hall (New York, 1849).

of all races—to the obvious delight of their audiences. The songs and dances of minstrelsy circulated through sheet music publication and were widely performed in American homes. Of special significance is that after emancipation in 1863, minstrelsy was taken over increasingly by Black performers. Touring Black minstrel troupes flourished from the 1860s into the early years of this century, providing an avenue by which Black Americans could make a living as musicians. Song-writer James Bland (1854–1911) spent his career performing in minstrelsy; and blues singers Gertrude 'Ma' Rainey (1886–1939) and Bessie Smith (1894–1937) and composer-publisher W. C. Handy (1873–1958) all got their start as members of Black minstrel troupes.

Sustained partly by the minstrel stage and partly by the home music market was the career of Stephen C. Foster, whose songs, sung widely in his own day, have endured to form part of the cultural experience of almost every American since. Born to a relatively prosperous family in a small town outside Pittsburgh, Foster struggled with his choice of career even after some of his songs for the minstrel stage ('Oh Susannah!') had become hits, for in his social circle, song-

writing was not considered a proper career. By the early 1850s, however, he was actively engaged in writing songs, mostly to texts of his own, and by 1860 he had settled in New York. As well as snappy, rhythmic minstrel numbers ('Camptown Races') he composed vaporous love ballads ('I Dream of Jeannie with the Light Brown Hair') and, also for the minstrel stage, 'Home' songs which focused nostalgically on the plantation of the irretrievable past. Reaching behind the comic blackface mask, these latter songs imbued the Negro stage character with an emotional range that went far beyond the minstrel-show stereotype ('Old Folks at Home', 'My Old Kentucky Home'). Although Foster's songs could have earned him a handsome sum in performance fees and publication royalties, he managed his financial affairs badly and died in straitened circumstances without reaping the full benefit of his labours. His legacy, however, remains secure. As well as any other American, he struck the note Longfellow's weary traveller calls for in 'When Day is Done', when he arrives home on a rainy night, wishing to hear

> Not from the bards sublime
> . . . [But] from some humbler poet,
> Whose songs gushed from his heart.

Although the differences in the careers of musicians like Mason, Gilmore, Root, Emmett, Bland, and Foster are great, the circumstances in which they worked held important elements in common. All co-operated or competed with other musicians who were trying to reach substantially the same audience. All depended for their livelihood on reaching and pleasing that audience. All in their composing worked within a set of extremely limited stylistic and formal conventions, which they shared with their competitors, their creative goal being to find that telling dash of fresh invention that might recommend their work to public attention. All, in a nutshell, worked in a commercial tradition shaped by themselves and their audiences—a collective, stylistically conservative process in which creators and consumers were linked interdependently.

Practitioners of art music in 19th-century America struggled to build a tradition of their own, for none had been part of their inheritance. Their initial success is best measured by the gradual increase in the number of American institutions devoted to teaching, performing, and promoting European art music. One kind of performing organization is typified by the Handel and Haydn Society of Boston (founded 1815), in which local citizens, encouraged perhaps at least as much by religious as by artistic motives, formed a chorus with regularly scheduled meetings. Accompanied by an or-

Pl. 7. Title-page of Stephen Foster's ballad 'Jeanie with the Light Brown Hair' (New York: Firth Pond & Co., 1854).

chestra of professionals and available amateurs, and joined by solo singers, they gave public concerts of sacred music, sometimes including full oratorios, seeking to cover expenses by selling tickets. Choral societies similarly drawn from the community at large grew up throughout the country in the 19th century and continued to flourish in the 20th.

At the other end of the spectrum from oratorio, the art music of the God-fearing Protestant, stands grand opera, which, with its exotic spectacle and temperamental virtuoso performers, had its own strong appeal to a certain kind of audience. Opera first took root in the New World in New Orleans, which had its own resident company through much of the century (1859-1919). Elsewhere, most Americans had to depend on touring companies. Relying on publicity to drum up audiences and hence promoted as a branch of show business, troupes such as the one managed by Max Maretzek performed operas by Mozart, Rossini, Donizetti, and other European masters, sometimes in versions that the composers themselves might not have approved of. New York, fitted for the role by its concentration of wealth and high proportion of foreign-born residents, has been the chief centre of operatic performance in America since the late 19th century. Its Metropolitan Opera (founded in 1883) holds a place as one of the great international houses, although in the 20th century a number of other American cities have established companies of their own, including San Francisco, Chicago, Boston, Seattle, Santa Fe, and Houston.

Somewhere between the steady respectability of the choral society and the emotional *brio* of the opera company stands the orchestra, a medium indispensable to both, and one that also has its own history and repertory. Throughout most of the 19th century American orchestras tended to be groups assembled from among available musicians on an *ad hoc* basis. The maintenance of a standing ensemble as large as a symphony orchestra was simply more expensive than the need for its services would warrant. The oldest such continuing ensemble in America, the New York Philharmonic Society, began in 1842 as a 'co-operative', with the musicians themselves running the orchestra, whose concerts were open only to other members of the Society. The conductor, Theodore Thomas (1835-1905), perhaps the dominant figure in American concert-life during the second half of the century, himself established and managed the Thomas Orchestra, which toured for years from a base in New York. In general, however, standing ensembles were organized wherever musicians succeeded in tapping a community's wealthy people for support. This was usually done through sub-scription, with a number of patrons agreeing to commit funds to cover the ensemble's expenses. Thus, through the patronage of some of their affluent citizens, cities like Philadelphia, Chicago, Cincinnati, Pittsburgh, San Francisco, and New York managed to maintain professional orchestras and to build halls acoustically suited to their playing. The founding in 1881 of the Boston Symphony Orchestra by a single patron, Henry Lee Higginson, who maintained the ensemble out of his own pocket for nearly 40 years, is unique in American musical history.

In the 19th century the musical leadership of opera companies, symphony orchestras, and even most choral societies was assumed from the beginning by Europeans, and the repertory they performed was almost entirely European as well. Thus it is not surprising that American composers of art music found themselves in the role of outsiders. Anthony Philip Heinrich (1781-1861), self-described as 'the log-house composer from Kentucky', emigrated to the United States from Bohemia in 1810, taught himself to compose, and wrote eclectically original songs, piano pieces, chamber music, and scores for huge orchestra. Both technically demanding and unusual in style, 'Father' Heinrich's music found no place in any continuing repertory, and Heinrich earned his own modest living as a teacher. Two more composers, both active in New York City from mid century, complained publicly that American music, including their own, was being overlooked by the city's performers. William Henry Fry (1813-64), music critic of a New York daily newspaper, and George Frederick Bristow (1825-98), violinist with the New York Philharmonic Society and music teacher in the city's public schools, thus raised an issue of fundamental and continuing importance to American musical life, though with little noticeable effect on concert programming. The one 19th-century American composer of art music who consistently found an audience was the New Orleans-born Louis Moreau Gottschalk, pianist *par excellence*. Trained in France, Gottschalk returned to the United States in 1853 and spent most of the rest of his life touring as a virtuoso concert artist. His recitals emphasized his own music, much of which shows a freshness of invention and a lively vernacular flavour. It was more as a brilliant, crowd-pleasing recitalist than as a composer that Gottschalk found an audience for his music.

Only by ignoring the extreme diversity of the music of Heinrich, Fry, Bristow, and Gottschalk could anyone perceive them collectively as a 'school' of American composers. Rather do they seem like four isolated figures, each pursuing his own aesthetic goals in his own way, and none fully accepted as a composer by the

Europeans who led America's established musical institutions.

Beginning around the time of the Civil War, the first real 'school' of American-born composers began to come of age. Sharing an Anglo-Saxon heritage, east-coast birth, and a strong leaning towards the musical style of German Romanticism—most, in fact, studied in Germany—composers like John Knowles Paine (1839-1906), Horatio Parker (1863-1919), George Whitefield Chadwick (1854-1931), Arthur Foote (1853-1937), Amy Cheney Beach (1867-1944), and others gained for American composers a foothold in the country's institutional structure. Most were organists who for all or part of their lives held posts in large urban churches. All except Mrs Beach were also teachers of music. American universities began towards the end of the century to include musical study in their liberal arts curriculum—chiefly composition, harmony, counterpoint, and history. Paine was named the first professor of music at Harvard College (1875), and some years later Parker earned the same distinction at Yale (1894). American conservatories, devoted to the study of practical music-making, also began to open up in the 1860s; Chadwick held the presidency of the New England Conservatory in Boston for more than three decades. All members of the group were competent composers, most holding positions that guaranteed performances of their works. The most famous American composer of the time, and one who stood apart from the New England group, was Edward MacDowell, who held the chair in music at Columbia University from 1896 to 1904. With a keen ear for novel harmonies, MacDowell applied his special feeling for nature to such piano miniatures as *Woodland Sketches* (1896) and *New England Idylls* (1902), which, together with his Piano Concerto in D minor, Op. 23, are the works of his generation that are the most likely to be performed today. MacDowell and the so-called 'New England Classicists', with more craftsmanship than original inspiration, stood for music-making of high seriousness and 'good taste', removed from the hurly-burly of everyday American life.

4. *Folk Music*. Beneath the busy surface of the organized musical world of 19th-century America, there existed folk music brought to the New World by different groups of settlers. In this sphere the shaping agent was not the professional tunesmith working in the musical market-place. Rather was it the community as a whole. Consensus among community members selected the music that linked past with present and determined the forms in which oral transmission would carry it, both over time to the next generation, and across space to other communities.

Anglo-American folk music offers some ready examples of two complementary traits of oral transmission: continuity and variation. When Cecil Sharp, the noted English folk-song collector, travelled to Appalachia early in this century, singers there performed for him versions of English and Scottish songs that had changed remarkably little in their long journey over time and space. Not only could many songs that Sharp heard be traced to British sources; the care with which the tunes and words had been orally transmitted suggested that their carriers set a high value on preservation. At the same time, many songs in the same repertory reflected transmission as a more complex process than merely rote transfer. As singers learned songs, they made them their own, changing details or events here and there, preserving some core of the 'original', but making their own creative variations as well. Ballads brought to America often underwent considerable sea change, as, for example, in two versions of 'Barbara Allen', the first collected in Scotland and the second in Kentucky:

> It fell about a Martimas time,
> When the green leaves were a-fallin',
> That Sir John Grahame
>   from the west countrie
> Fell in love wi' Bawbie Allan.

> 'Twas early in the month of May
> The flowers were a-blooming,
> Sweet Williams came
>   from a Western State
> And courted Barbara Ellen.

Anglo-American folk music, and the folk music of other ethnic groups, was preserved with the least change in communities, chiefly rural, where Old World customs and social structures were strongest. There it could serve the roles of traditional music in traditional society: confirming community values, providing entertainment, performing ritual functions. It is a peculiarity of American musical history that when, early in the 19th century, scholars and artists in many European countries began to explore their unwritten cultural traditions and to draw inspiration and materials from them, American musicians experienced no corresponding rediscovery of their own 'folk'. Instead, most professional musicians and music teachers reacted to folk music with indifference or 'hostility', to use Charles Seeger's word, apparently believing that its untutored roughness placed it beneath their own serious attention. In retrospect, it is easy to see the irony of their position. For most of the popular musical forms that circulated in writing during the 19th century—forms from which they made their own livelihood—had roots in Anglo-American folk music: psalmody, hymnody, and a good deal of secular song, inspired by the rhyme schemes, narrative techniques, and strophic forms of the oral ballad; the 'broadside' and the 'songster', which printed strophic texts to be sung to tunes people knew by heart; and printed dance music, reflecting the characteristic rhythmic patterns and the multi-strain musical forms of folk-dance.

Anglo-American folk music has been so widely studied, and its influence on written practice has been so evident, that its place as a central element in the making of American music is seldom questioned. The traditional folk musics of other European groups, however, are usually considered as regional phenomena, tied to places where such groups settled and maintained cultural separateness. Thus, Hispanic-American folk music seems to belong to the south-west and to California, French-American to the Cajuns in Louisiana, German-American to the 'Pennsylvania Dutch', and eastern European musics—Greek, Russian, Balkan—to ethnic communities in large American cities like New York, Chicago, and Detroit. Also restricted to circulation within culturally distinct, isolated groups are the musics of the many *American Indian tribes, aboriginal settlers of the North American continent.

No folk music has enjoyed a more complex history in the New World than that of the Afro-Americans, who were brought there against their will. Most Blacks in the 18th- and 19th-century United States were slaves; hence, most Afro-American communities existed under some degree of White control, which discouraged the survival of such elements as drums, Old World languages, and African religious beliefs. Living in proximity to Whites, Afro-Americans gradually adopted certain White musical genres without abandoning their own indigenous performing styles—much more aggressive in rhythm and freer in pitch than any Euro-American singing or playing. Perhaps the most famous example of an acculturated vocal music is the so-called Negro spiritual, the Afro-American version of the Protestant hymn. First set down by White amateur musicians in the landmark collection, *Slave Songs of the United States* (1867), then sung in harmonized choral versions by the Fisk Jubilee Singers and other groups of young Blacks under White direction, and much later turned by trained Black musicians into art songs for solo voice and piano, the spirituals illustrate how the folk music of a people considered 'half-barbarous' by its first White collectors could be adapted without losing its distinctive, haunting beauty.

The rhythmic complexity that early White collectors of spirituals found hard to capture in notation also pervaded Afro-American instrumental folk music, much of it tied up with dance. Black musicians' fondness for off-beat accents within a steady metre was expressed through all available means: vocables, body-slapping, and foot-stomping; African-derived instruments like the bones and the banjo; and eventually European instruments, especially the fiddle and the piano. By the end of the 19th century, Black American performers had fashioned an entertainment and dance music called 'ragtime', in which square cut, syncopated melodies were played in a series of contrasting, march-like strains. Published as piano music around the turn of the century, ragtime achieved special elegance in the works of composer-pianist Scott Joplin—as far removed from folk tradition as H. T. Burleigh's settings of spirituals, but just as unmistakably marked by it.

The ability of Afro-Americans to assimilate European-based forms and bend them to their own purposes, as in the spiritual and ragtime, and to provide the inspiration for some of the most lively White music-making of the age, as in the minstrel show, suggests that in 19th-century America cultural power did not necessarily depend upon social position. That fact was to become even clearer in the 20th century, when Afro-American musical traditions made a decisive impact on virtually all American popular music.

5. *The 20th Century*. Charles Ives, one of the most original of all 20th-century composers, stood almost entirely apart from the musical world that his American predecessors had struggled to build. Composition studies with Parker at Yale helped him to recognize that his own radically independent view of music was irreconcilable with that of most musicians. Carrying on a highly successful business career in New York City, he composed in his spare time, isolated almost entirely from contact with other musicians and composers. Ives's music fuses the most commonplace materials—quotations from familiar songs, hymn tunes, and dance tunes—with musical techniques unprecedented for their time: bitonality, dissonant canonic writing, and atonality. Written in part as an act of reconstructing life in the New England of his boyhood, and also to celebrate his belief in the innate goodness of that society's earth-taught men and women, Ives's music was hardly performed until long after he stopped composing. Landmark performances include John Kirkpatrick's of the 'Concord' Piano Sonata (1939) and Leopold Stokowski's of the Symphony No. 4 (1965). These and other performances, recordings, and publications have won champions for Ives's music, especially

for its unmistakable 'made in America' stamp and its technical innovations. The composer's own hope, however, that at some time in the future music like his would be understood and perhaps even composed by 'the majority' in whose taste he so firmly believed is still a long way from being realized.

By 1920 the institutions supporting art music in the United States—symphony orchestras, opera companies, choral societies, conservatories and schools, and, a newer agency, phonograph recording companies—formed a superstructure of some permanence. Shaped by musicians and musically active citizens, that superstructure was a major part of the 20th-century composer's legacy. Although the American composer who came of age in the 1920s had no stylistically unified tradition to carry on, he at least inherited a tradition of professionalism in art music. Another part of his inheritance, however, conspired to exclude him from that tradition. In the years before the First World War the European avant-garde attacked artistic institutions and conventional aesthetic values, asserting that bourgeois society was the enemy of meaningful art. Such an attack carried certain penalties, especially in the United States, where musical institutions and composers depended upon the support of the very citizens whom the avant-garde attacked. American composers who carried avant-garde influences to the New World found most musicians and audiences indifferent or hostile in their responses. It therefore fell to them to find or organize their own forum.

Edgard Varèse, who had made his home in New York since 1915, had by the 1920s already begun to think of music as an 'art-science', and was composing works like *Hyperprism* (1922–3) that can now be seen as direct precursors of *electronic music. In 1921 Varèse helped to found in New York the short-lived International Composers' Guild, dedicated to performing contemporary music. Aaron Copland returned to New York from study in Paris writing a lean-textured music alive with jazz-derived rhythms (*Music for the Theatre*, 1925; Piano Concerto, 1927). However 'American' the origins of Copland's music, it was too harsh for the ears of most American concert audiences of the time. As one of the founding members of the League of Composers (1923), Copland began his career as a tireless worker on behalf of the cause of new music—a career that has encompassed organizing, promoting, lecturing, writing, and performing, as well as teaching and composing. California-born Henry Cowell had discovered some of the beauties that lay unrealized in the piano; at a Carnegie Hall recital in 1924 he unveiled pieces that called for many unconventional techniques, including tone-clusters played with fists and forearms and

strumming on the strings of the open instrument. In 1927 Cowell, with the financial backing of his new friend, Charles Ives, founded the New Music Edition, which for the next quarter of a century published modern works by a whole range of composers, most of them American. The International Composers' Guild, the League of Composers, and the New Music Edition all signal the building of a framework in which the 'advanced' American composer of the 1920s could pursue his calling.

The economic depression of the 1930s touched almost every facet of American life, including music. In a social atmosphere of deprivation and misery, some composers reached a new understanding of their role in society. Rather than an embattled minority of artists in a hostile environment, they began to think of themselves as citizens with special talents that could be tapped for the general improvement of other Americans' lives. Simultaneously, institutional changes brought more Americans than ever before into contact with art music. The government's *Federal Music Project, begun as a relief measure, put the resources of the state in the service of art music for the first time. Radio networks began to broadcast performances of symphony orchestras and opera companies, giving a large audience virtually free access to professional performances of art music. The commercial film industry hired established American composers to provide scores for its productions. With composers standing ready to meet audiences half-way, hopes ran high during the years 1930–45 that, by addressing a broader audience in an idiom that it understood, they could strengthen their presently rather tenuous place in American society.

In line with its new agenda, American art music of that period shows a greater tendency than ever before to celebrate American history, American heroes, and the American 'folk'. Oklahoma-born Roy Harris, writing in an idiom shaped by his lifelong acquaintance with folk music, was a symphonist whose career blossomed in the 1930s. Virgil Thomson was another who plainly welcomed American subject-matter. A native of Kansas City, Thomson returned from years in Paris to work as a composer and later (1940–54) as a music critic. Working on commission, Thomson composed film scores and a ballet on vernacular subjects in the late 1930s. His opera on the suffragette Susan B. Anthony, *The Mother of Us All* (1947; libretto by Gertrude Stein), features in its cast an august, if anachronistic procession of notable Americans. Copland himself modified his style and focused on rural Americana during the period, producing *Appalachian Spring* (1944) and other ballet scores that have sealed his popular reputation as *the* American composer of the 20th century. The fourth movement of Copland's Symphony No. 3 (1946) begins with a flourish whose separate title can be taken as a byword of the age: 'Fanfare for the Common Man'.

In the years immediately after the Second World War, American composers of art music were generally more interested in exploring new technical dimensions of their art than in broadening their audience. Many began to assimilate Schoenberg's serial technique, which had earlier seemed mathematical and artistically confining. One institutional change that supported such exploration, and encouraged the notion that composers were intellectuals, was the rapid post-war expansion of college and university departments and schools of music, many of which hired composers as teachers. A faculty position required the composer to do more than just compose; yet it freed him to compose as he wished. Moreover, by assigning talented young musicians to his instruction, it affirmed his importance in the perpetuation of American music. Composer-teachers like Walter Piston at Harvard and Howard Hanson at the Eastman School carried on the traditional, academic posture of the earlier New England Classicists. Others, like Roger Sessions at Princeton and the University of California, Milton Babbitt at Princeton, and Ross Lee Finney (*b* 1906) at the University of Michigan, have emphasized the importance of the university as a place to work freely—especially for young composers who need the support of a creative community as they declare and confirm their vocation. With its concentration of resources and performers, and its mandate to remain open to new ideas, the American university in the second half of the 20th century has often been a patron of innovation. It has seemed natural, for example, that electronic music, with its need for expensive equipment and its stylistic novelty, has found university sponsorship in places like New York's Columbia-Princeton Electronic Music Center (since 1951) and the Massachusetts Institute of Technology in Cambridge. By employing composers and encouraging performances of music by them, their colleagues, and their students, the university has created a public forum separate from that of the other established institutions of art music.

For all the importance of academic institutions, many musicians have managed to exist outside them as composers of commissioned pieces, performers, or writers on music. Copland, Thomson, Samuel Barber, and others, aided by royalty fees and payments from licensing agencies like *ASCAP and *BMI, have sought to build their careers on contact with a general musical audience rather than the more specialized one for new music. California native John Cage, a conspicuous avant-garde figure since his first New York concerts in the early 1940s, has succeeded in finding another kind of audience. Working in collaboration with dancers, painters, sculptors, and poets, Cage has appeared in many theatrical-style events, often with the Merce Cunningham Dance Troupe, for which he was longtime musical director. When Robert Frost wrote of listening to the sound of the trees

> Till we lose all measure of pace,
> And fixity in our joys,
> And acquire a listening air,

he struck a note concordant with Cage's musical philosophy. Influenced deeply by his study of Japanese Zen Buddhism, Cage has said that the chance methods he employs in his compositions are merely a reflection of nature itself, whose processes are ruled by randomness. Thus Cage, in effect, sets the environment on stage, and through that radical twist seeks to redefine music—not simply as a man-made art of sound but as an attitude towards experience.

In view of the past history of art music in America, it is remarkable that not even thorough-going, anti-establishment radicalism could inhibit the growth since the mid 1960s of musical philanthropy. Private foundations, some of which had long supported musicians, stepped up their giving. Various states, most notably New York, established arts councils to disburse money financing worthy projects. The involvement of universities continued. And in 1965 the federal government established the National Endowment for the Arts, a funding agency whose budget grew quickly in the following years. Only a small part of this money went to American composers and their activities. Nevertheless, American public policy by the 1970s held that the creative and performing arts could flourish better when partially subsidized than in a free commercial market. 'Grant' became a common word in the artist's vocabulary.

American art music entered the 1980s in an atmosphere of resolute pluralism. Earlier hopes that such a thing as an 'American music' might accompany national maturity seemed naïve as the outline of a mature American culture began to appear. For, rather than pulling it towards a single, national style, the passing of time had seemed to diversify American art music more and more. It is thus entirely to be expected that, for example, three leading American composers at this time—Elliott Carter, George Crumb, and Steve Reich—should e l be inventing music with aesthetic goals and sound surfaces that have little in common. With such wide diversity established as a normal state of affairs, it is doubtful that any unifying centripetal movement will occur without some transforming cultural crisis.

6. *Popular Music*. With economic stakes so much higher than in art music, American musicians working in vernacular genres in the 20th century have worked within a group of highly competitive institutions: the theatrical circuit, the night-club circuit, a network of music publishers and distributors, and the recording, film, and broadcasting industries. By the end of the 19th century theatrical entertainments involving music included both musical theatre (operettas and other shows with an integrated plot and many musical numbers) and the variety show or review in which a series of different acts, some musical, shared the stage. Control of both was centred in New York City, where dozens of theatres flourished. Some operettas and musical shows toured, and the 'vaudeville' circuit sent variety shows through the whole country in a network of theatres. Songs from the musical theatre represented one of the staples of the music-publishing industry, which was now also centred on New York in the so-called *'Tin Pan Alley' district. The industry also served vaudeville performers, competing to sell them their songs and pieces because theatrical performances helped to popularize the pieces and boost the sales of sheet music.

This process represents a refinement of earlier 19th-century practice, in which music publishing and musical theatre were much less centralized. Subsequently it grew more complex, as the phonograph recording, the sound film, and radio and television broadcasting entered the picture. Yet its fundamentals have remained the same: a large public that enjoys singing and dancing, whether as spectators or participants; a group of professional composers, lyricists, singers, players, and dancers dedicated to pleasing them; and a network of entrepreneurs and agents who settle the terms on which audience and artist meet, dictating the economics of the whole enterprise by insisting that a song, a dance, or even a performance be treated as private property. The forum has not changed since the 19th century either; now, as then, the industry's products are made for both the stage and the home.

The American popular song of the 20th century, somewhat like the industry that has supported it, presents a constantly changing surface whose fundamental subject-matter has altered little. Most popular songs are love songs. The strain of high romantic rhetoric that pervaded the Viennese operetta is reflected in its early 20th-century counterpart in songs by Victor Herbert (1859–1924) and Sigmund Romberg (1887–1951). The impact of Afro-American music helped to bring a new rhythmic

Pl. 8. *Title-page of 'Alexander's Ragtime Band' by Irving Berlin (New York: Ted Snyder Co., 1911).*

vitality and an informality of expression to shows of the 1910s and 1920s and their songs, as suggested by Irving Berlin's 'Alexander's Ragtime Band' and 'I Got Rhythm' by the Gershwin brothers. This new 'hot' style of song was rooted in dance—especially in new ways of moving like the fox trot and the Charleston, which reflected the syncopated dance music increasingly referred to as *'jazz'. A widening range of harmonic possibilities enriched the song-writer's expressive resources, as shown in songs by Jerome Kern and Harold Arlen (*b* 1905). Formally, the 32-bar chorus was almost universal, which made a song with a 48-bar chorus like Cole Porter's 'Night and Day' remarkable. But the song-writer's craft calls on him to hide rather than flaunt his technique, working for something both natural-sounding and catchy. A song like 'My Funny Valentine' from Rodgers and Hart's *Babes in Arms* (1937) shows the creators' special gift for compression and sophisticated intimacy, crystallizing a lover's perspective in a few phrases, and making a fleeting glimpse into a permanent reflection.

The songs of Tin Pan Alley and Broadway, expressing only one kind of sensibility, did not appeal to all Americans. One of the most important discoveries in 20th-century American music, however, was that people of all backgrounds and walks of life would pay for a chance to hear music they felt at home with. This discovery brought a whole range of traditional musics into the commercial realm, giving a new richness and diversity to American popular music.

Afro-American *blues was among the first indigenous musics to penetrate a commercial market. Observing the powerful response of rural southern Black audiences to traditional folk music performed by members of their own community, the bandleader W. C. Handy began around 1915 to publish blues in sheet-music form. Recordings of blues were made by Black singers as early as 1920, and the unexpectedly strong reception they received from record buyers—mostly Black, since the records were issued on 'race' labels that circulated chiefly where Blacks lived—helped to create a new branch of the popular-music industry. The same kind of process took place among rural and small-town Whites in the south-eastern USA. As early as the 1920s, performers like 'Fiddlin' John' Carson and the Carter Family were recording their own kind of music, leading to the establishment of the *"country music' industry, with headquarters in Nashville, Tennessee. Traditional folk musics of other kinds also found their way outside the context in which they originated. Beginning in the 1920s, immigrant musicians from many different European ethnic groups made commercial recordings in their indigenous Old World styles. Anglo-American folk-tunes, together with their instrumentation and singing style, served as both a source and a model for performers linked with political causes—from Woody Guthrie's labour-union songs of the 1930s to Pete Seeger's and Bob Dylan's anti-war songs of the 1960s. Arranged for a wider commercial audience, folk music also contributed a fresh repertory in the 1950s and 1960s for such entertainers as the Kingston Trio and Harry Belafonte. At the same time, musicians like Mike Seeger, performing in coffee houses and folk festivals, dedicated themselves to preserving the 'authenticity' of traditional Anglo-American folk styles.

The predominant popular style since the 1960s, *rock and roll, was also conceived for a particular social group, American teenagers. Unlike blues, country music, and folk music—upon all of which it has drawn—rock and roll originated as a strictly commercial music. Beginning in the late 1950s, it addressed the tastes of youngsters who were not much drawn to the music of Tin Pan Alley and Broadway—written for performers like Bing Crosby, Frank Sinatra, and Peggy Lee, who sang primarily to other adults. Promoted at first by independent record producers and disc jockeys on off-beat radio stations, and sold cheaply in single-disc form, rock music soon became big business as the economic power of the youth market and the vitality of the new musical style revealed themselves. Talented and successful performers including Elvis Presley, The Beatles, Jimi Hendrix, and many others, have contributed to the maturing of rock music. Through various style changes, two elements have remained more or less constant as well-springs of the music: an aggressive, driving beat implying sexuality, and a posture of rebellion against the values of conventional society, expressed both in song lyrics and in the dress and behaviour of the musicians, often calculated to offend non-aficionados.

Of all commercially based American musics, jazz is the one that has most consistently fostered musical artistry on a high level. Developing first among Black musicians, notably in New Orleans, jazz originated not as a new genre but as a style of performing dance music in places of popular entertainment. Through most of the music's subsequent history, performers whose articulation, phrasing, and time-sense have generated an infectious, 'swinging' quality, and whose playing and singing have carried a feeling of spontaneous invention—whether or not they were being improvised—have been said to be making music in jazz style.

Black jazz performers began to record early in the 1920s. Composer-pianists like New Orleans-born Ferdinand 'Jelly Roll' Morton played pieces from the repertory of *ragtime and blues, as well as originals. The same kinds of pieces were also played by instrumental ensembles of seven or eight performers. The characteristic sound of a cornet, a clarinet, and a trombone weaving strands of free-wheeling counterpoint over a supporting rhythm section marks the New Orleans ensemble as one in which collective collaboration outweighs the purely personal statement. Nevertheless, the New Orleans-style ensemble provided the framework for the career of cornettist-trumpeter Louis Armstrong, perhaps the most powerful and poetic soloist in jazz history.

Larger dance orchestras of the 1920s were influenced by the new jazz style, and some, like the New York-based Black band of Edward Kennedy 'Duke' Ellington, were organized especially to play it. By the 1930s a 'swing' style had evolved for 'big bands' of some 12 to 14 players. Sacrificing some spontaneity for increased sonority and rhythmic drive, composer-arrangers like Ellington and Fletcher Henderson still left ample room in their music for their outstanding soloists to improvise. The jazz-influenced big band won a wide audience. White dance bands of the 1930s and 1940s, like the group led by Chicago-born clarinettist Benny Goodman, gained great commercial success through touring, record sales, and radio broadcasts, playing a repertory that included both jazz numbers and Tin Pan Alley songs.

The appearance of *'be-bop' in the 1940s added a new style to the field of jazz—one in a self-consciously 'advanced' musical idiom perceived from the first as a radical departure from earlier jazz. Be-bop also helped to introduce to jazz an aggressively anti-commercial orientation. The performer now considered himself more an artist than an entertainer. His worth was to be judged chiefly by his skill as an improviser; the highest calling of the jazzman's vocation was to forge a distinctive personal style of improvisation, preferably on the exploratory edge of the idiom, and then to keep on 'growing' or changing, as the case may be. Be-bop shifted the focus in jazz from the ensemble to the soloist, from the dance-hall to the jazz club, from the dancing participant to the rapt listener, perhaps in his own room in front of the phonograph. While performers like Armstrong, Ellington, and Goodman continued to hold their audiences by playing the kind of music that had won them a following in the first place, be-boppers like saxophonist Charlie Parker, trumpeter John Birks 'Dizzy' Gillespie, and pianist-composer Thelonious Monk worked in a smaller, more specialized sphere with its own institutions—clubs, record companies, publications, and critics—and its own devoted audience.

Not the least of be-bop's achievements was that it helped to stimulate critical, historical interest in jazz. How had a music of be-bop's artistic complexity grown from such unlikely commercial soil? Investigation and careful listening confirmed that the potential for artistic complexity had been there all along: that in the hands of musicians as gifted as Armstrong and Ellington, earlier jazz idioms had and could sustain musical statements of such convincing eloquence that virtually any audience could recognize and respond to them. In the meantime, younger performers like Ornette Coleman, John Coltrane, and Cecil Taylor contributed to an avant-garde movement that extended the jazz idiom further and further away from its original roots. By the 1960s the jazz avant-garde was beginning to be recognized by the academic-philanthropic establishment as a special kind of art music whose future required institutional support beyond what the commercial market could provide. Many of its practitioners were conservatory-trained, and their sources of support resembled those of many composers of art music: teaching, concert-giving, and grants. At the same time, the persistent appetite for earlier jazz, manifested in club dates, concert-hall appearances, and recordings, is shared by a public small enough to remind the observer that most professional jazz performers have found their vocation economically precarious.

It is no surprise that in a musical culture like that of the USA, one that has developed without a single powerful centre, music of high artistic integrity and durability has appeared, like wild flowers, all over the landscape. Since jazz has been a uniquely American music of international impact—one clearcut example of influence moving eastward rather than westward—perhaps it is fitting to take a jazz performance as a paradigm of American musical vitality. In October 1947 the 27-year-old Black alto saxophonist from Kansas City, Charlie Parker, played Gershwin's song 'Embraceable You' in the course of a recording session. That brief recorded moment preserves an uncanny balance: the fantasy of improvisatory inspiration within the restraint of a Tin Pan Alley love ballad's formal and harmonic structure; the decorative profusion of the virtuoso controlled by a disciplined, cohesive command of newly invented materials; a statement in a thoroughly personal idiom, delivered with the communicative power of a performer who seems to be speaking or singing through his instrument. Here is a fusion that testifies to artistic maturity; here is an American artist at work in a tradition.

RICHARD CRAWFORD

FURTHER READING
Oscar Sonneck: *Early Concert Life in America* (Leipzig, 1907, reprinted 1969); Oscar Sonneck: *Early Opera in America* (New York, 1915, reprinted 1963); Cecil Sharp and Maud Karpeles: *English Folk Songs from the Southern Appalachians* (London, 1932); Henry Cowell, ed.: *American Composers on American Music* (Stanford, 1933, reprinted 1962); Percy Scholes: *The Puritans and Music in England and New England* (New York, 1934); Gilbert Chase: *America's Music: from the Pilgrims to the Present* (New York, 1955, 3rd edn 1977); C. Keil: *Urban Blues* (Chicago, 1966); R. Abrahams and G. Foss: *Anglo-American Folksong Style* (Englewood Cliffs, NJ, 1968); Gunther Schuller: *Early Jazz: its Roots and Musical Development* (New York, 1968); H. Wiley Hitchcock: *Music in the United States* (Englewood Cliffs, NJ, 1969, 2nd edn 1974); Eileen Southern: *The Music of Black Americans: a History* (New York, 1971); Bruno Nettl and Helen Myers: *Folk Music in the United States: an Introduction*, 3rd rev. edn (Detroit, 1976).

Uniti (It.). 'United'. Usually used to revoke a direction such as *divisi*.

Universal Edition. Austrian firm of music publishers. They have come to be known for their special association with contemporary music, their championship of successive generations of avant-garde composers, and their adoption of distinctive designs and musical typography. Founded in Vienna in 1901, the firm incorporated several other houses and quickly acquired a substantial catalogue, which included the major works of Richard Strauss. Their move towards modern music came during the directorship (1907–32) of Emil Hertzka, when Schoenberg and his pupils were attracted to the firm. Universal Edition's catalogue is like a roll-call of 20th-century music: hardly any composer of significance is omitted, and many experimental composers whose reputations have not survived are included. Bartók, Weill, and Janáček rub shoulders with Zemlinsky and Martinů. The generation of Messiaen, Stockhausen, and Boulez, which found expression particularly through the annual courses at Darmstadt, has been strongly supported by Universal. They have not neglected musical scholarship: they have published major historical anthology series, complete editions of Monteverdi and Gabrieli, and, more recently, an avant-garde journal, *Die Reihe* (1955–62, with an English edition). They are also active in educational publishing.

Alfred Kalmus (1889–1972), a member of the Viennese firm from 1909, founded the London branch in 1937, and during the Second World War worked in association with *Boosey & Hawkes, forming the Anglo-Soviet Press to promote Soviet composers. After the London branch of Universal became independent in 1949 they strongly supported avant-garde composers like Berio, Boulez, and Stockhausen, and they now publish many English composers (David Bedford, Richard Rodney Bennett, Harrison Birtwistle, Hugh Wood).

J. M. THOMSON

Unmerklich (Ger.). 'Imperceptible'.

Unruhe (Ger.). 'Disquiet', 'lack of peace'; *unruhig*, 'restless'.

Upbeat [anacrusis] (Fr.: *anacruse*; Ger.: *Auftakt*). The 'weak' beat of the bar which anticipates the first, 'strong' beat of the following bar, or *down-beat, e.g.

See *Conducting*.

Upper mordent. See under *Mordent*.

Upper partials. See *Acoustics*, 5.

Urtext (Ger.). 'Original text'. The term is used to describe a modern edition of music which embodies the composer's original intent with minimal editorial interference.

Ut. The first note of the scale according to the *solmization system. Since the 17th century, *ut* has been replaced by the more singable *do* (in French and Italian usage), or *doh* (in the tonic sol-fa system). The French retain *ut* and the Italians use *do* to refer, on the fixed-doh principle, to the note C, in whatever scale it may occur. See also *Tonic Sol-fa*; *Hexachord*.

Ut queant laxis. See *Solmization*.

Utrecht Te Deum and Jubilate. Liturgical settings by Handel composed to celebrate the Peace of Utrecht. They were first performed in St Paul's Cathedral, London, in 1713.

Utrenia. Work by Penderecki for five vocal soloists, two choruses, boys' chorus, and orchestra. The first part, *The Entombment*, was first performed in Altenberg Cathedral in 1970; the second part, *The Resurrection*, was first performed in Münster Cathedral in 1971. *Utrenia* is the Russian Orthodox Matins.

V

V. Abbreviation for (1) violin (also found as V°); (2) *voci* (It.), 'voices'.

Va (It.). 1. 'Go on', 'goes on', i.e. continue, continues; e.g. *va diminuendo*, 'it goes on getting softer'. 2. Abbreviation for viola (also *vla*).

Vaccai, Nicola (*b* Tolentino, 15 Mar. 1790; *d* Pesaro, 5 or 6 Aug. 1848). Italian composer. He studied with Paisiello in Naples and, after trying his hand at writing operas, worked as a singing teacher there from 1815. Vaccai was more successful with later operas, two of which (*Zadig ed Astartea* and *Giulietta e Romeo*) were staged in 1825. In 1830 he went to Paris, where he again taught singing, and in the same year moved on to London for three more years before returning to Italy. He was appointed professor of composition at the Milan conservatory in 1838. Vaccai wrote a total of 17 operas, as well as church music, cantatas, songs, and four ballets, but he is best known for his singing Tutor, the *Metodo pratico di canto italiano per camera* (London, 1832). His singing exercises still form a part of the standard repertory.

WENDY THOMPSON

Vacillant (Fr.), **vacillando** (It.). 'Wavering', i.e. the string instrument's vibrato.

Vaet, Jacobus (*b* Courtrai, *c*.1529; *d* Vienna, 8 Jan. 1567). Flemish composer. He spent some years in the service of Charles V before becoming *Kapellmeister* to the imperial chapel in Vienna. His surviving music is virtually all sacred, and he was best known for his motets. The earlier works are similar in style to those of Gombert, but later works show the influence of Lassus, for example in their use of polychoral techniques.

DENIS ARNOLD

Vaghezza (It.). 1. 'Longing'. 2. 'Grace', 'charm'.

Valderrábano, Enríquez de (*fl.* mid 16th century). Spanish composer and vihuelist. He was in the service of the Duke of Miranda in 1547, in which year he published a seven-volume anthology of music for the vihuela, the *Silva de sirenas*. As well as arrangements of works by many famous composers there are several highly skilful fantasias and variations (including 120 variations on *Guárdame las*

vacas). The anthology is one of the earliest printed sources to give tempo indications to the performer.

DENIS ARNOLD

Valente, Antonio (*fl.* late 16th century). Italian organist and composer. Although blind from an early age, he held the post of organist at S. Angelo a Nilo, Naples, from 1565 to 1580. He published two volumes of music at Naples, the *Intavolatura de cimbalo* (1576), including a fantasia, *ricercari*, dances, and variations, and some *Versi spirituali sopra tutti le note* (1580).

WENDY THOMPSON

Valentini, Giuseppe (*b* Florence, *c*.1680; *d* ? Florence, after 1746). Italian composer and violinist. He was a pupil of Corelli and soon became well known as a virtuoso violinist. From *c*.1708 he was in the service of Prince Francesco Maria Ruspoli in Rome, and he may also have worked for the Prince of Caserta there. He is thought to have returned to Florence in 1735. He was best known in his lifetime for his *concerti grossi* (Op. 7, Bologna, 1710), which were popular in England and in much of Europe, but he also wrote some sonatas in a style similar to Corelli's, and operas, oratorios, and cantatas.

DENIS ARNOLD

Valeur (Fr.), **valore** (It.). 'Value'; e.g. as used by Debussy, *La m.g. un peu en valeur sur la m.d.*, 'the left hand to have a little more value (i.e. importance) than the right hand'. The word also means 'valour', 'courage'.

Valkyrie, The (Ger.: '*Die Walküre*'). See *Ring des Nibelungen, Der*.

Vallée d'Obermann ('Obermann Valley'). Work for solo piano by Liszt, No. 6 of Book 1 of *Années de pèlerinage*.

Valois, (Dame) Ninette de [Stannus, Edris] (*b* Baltiboys, Ireland, 6 June 1898). British dancer and choreographer. Her association with Lilian Baylis at the Old Vic and Sadler's Wells theatres led in 1931 to the forming of the company which in 1956 became the Royal Ballet, of which she was officially named founder. A member of Diaghilev's Ballets Russes in the 1920s, she applied his artistic principles to a repertory of British ballet, and herself choreographed several successful works, notably *Job*

(Vaughan Williams, 1931), *The Rake's Progress* (Gordon, 1935), and *Checkmate* (Bliss, 1937).

NOËL GOODWIN

Valse (Fr.). 'Waltz'.

Valse, La ('The Waltz'). Orchestral work ('poème chorégraphique') by Ravel, composed in 1919–20. The score was used for a one-act ballet, choreographed by Nijinskaya and first performed in Paris in 1928. It has since been choreographed by Balanchine (1951) and Ashton (1958). Ravel arranged the work for two pianos (1921) and L. Garban arranged it for piano duet.

Valses nobles et sentimentales ('Noble and Sentimental Waltzes'). Work for solo piano by Ravel, composed in 1911. Ravel orchestrated it in 1912 and the score was used for the ballet *Adélaide, ou Le langage des fleurs*, to his own libretto; it was choreographed by Clustine and first performed in Paris in 1912. It has since been choreographed by Lifar (1938), Ashton (1947), MacMillan (1966), and Hynd (1975).

Valse triste ('Sad Waltz'). Waltz, Op. 44, by Sibelius, composed in 1903 as part of the incidental music for A. Järnefelt's play *Kuolema* ('Death'). It was originally for strings but Sibelius revised the orchestration in 1904 and also arranged it for piano.

Valves (Fr.: *pistons*; Ger.: *Ventile*; It.: *chiavi*). The means by which the majority of present *brass instruments gain their chromatic compass.

1. *How Valves Work.* The basic provision is three valves. Each, lowered by the finger against its own spring, admits a short extra length of tube into the whole (Fig. 1). When 'up' (at rest) the tube circuit from 1 crosses through the valve, by means of the passage marked 2, to emerge at 3. When 'down' (on right), 2 is cut out of the circuit, which is now diverted to 4, through the valve loop (indicated in broken line) and so to 5 to emerge again at 3. The lengths of the loops can be calculated in the traditional way by simple fractions, or by proportions in equal temperament (see *Temperament*, 4). The fractions are the easier to consider. The first valve

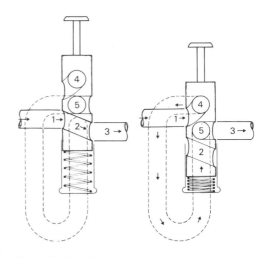

Fig. 1. Section of piston valve: left, *valve at rest;* right, *valve lowered.*

(index finger) adds one-eighth to the instrument's tube-length to lower the harmonic series by a whole tone—see Ex. 1, the notes marked 1. The second valve adds one-fifteenth, to lower by a semitone, and the two together (marked ½) lower by a minor third. To complete the chromatic scale several notes require the third valve. This again lowers by a minor third (adding one-fifth to the total), but is normally reserved for making these further notes by combination with the others as shown. Note that the seventh harmonic is omitted, being skipped over by the player since its pitch lies a third of a semitone below B♭, disqualifying it from normal musical use. The written compass shown, up to 'top C', is usually regarded as the safe range for general purposes, although players often go considerably higher.

The fingering in Ex. 1 applies in parts for cornet, brass band instruments (see *Brass Band*), and trumpet (on which, however, transposition is often needed). In horn parts the series is placed an octave lower (the top C now the sixteenth harmonic), and this modifies the fingering shown in one or two places, and more so when playing on B♭ horn.

2. *Types of Valve.* Valves were first patented in Berlin in 1818, by two Silesian wind players, Stoelzel (a horn-player) and Bluhmel. Their original form of valve remains uncertain. The

Ex. 1

piston-valves now in widest use (Fig. 1) are basically a Paris design of 1839 (Périnet). The horn, however, now uses rotary valves, patented in Vienna about eight years earlier and in Germany used on trumpets, tubas, etc., as well. Each valve here contains a rotating cylinder (rotor) which is turned through 90 degrees to divert the tube circuit through the valve loop (Fig. 2).

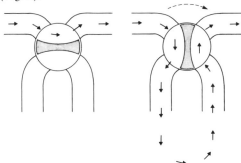

Fig. 2. Diagram of rotary valve: left, *at rest;* right, *valve pressed (i.e. rotor turned through* 90°).

In Vienna many horn-players remain true to another early type of valve: the 'double piston' or 'Vienna' valve, with two parallel pistons, moving together, for each of the three valves.

Among types no longer made but often found with 19th-century cornets and other instruments is the so-called Stoelzel valve (possibly owing something of its design to Stoelzel), a piston-valve distinguishable at sight from the ordinary in that one of the entry tubes leads from the bottom of the casing, not both from the side.

3. *Problems.* With valves of any normal sort a problem arises when two or more valves are lowered together. Thus the low D (Ex. 1) theoretically needs four-thirds the tube-length of the G a fourth above, or an addition of 33.3 per cent. But the first valve adds 12.5 per cent (one-eighth) and the third adds 20 per cent (one-fifth), together making 32.5 per cent only. The shortfall amounts on the B♭ trumpet to approximately 1cm. or, on a large tuba, 4 cm.: the note comes too sharp and the player must drag it down with his lips, though he gets accustomed to doing this almost unconsciously. However, the problem is often mitigated by pulling out the tuning-slide of the third valve a little, to make up the difference (each valve loop incorporates its own tuning-slide).

To take the compass below the lowest note in Ex. 1, as often necessary with bass instruments like the *tuba, there is a gap to be filled down to the fundamental C a diminished fifth below. The simple method is to provide a fourth valve which lowers the instrument by a perfect fourth (see *Tuba, 2a*)   ANTHONY BAINES

Vamping. Improvising an accompaniment which consists of a series of simple chords, generally the tonic, dominant, and subdominant. A 'Vamping Tutor' is a book of instruction in ·his type of accompaniment.

Vampyr, Der ('The Vampire'). Opera in two acts by Marschner to a libretto by W. A. Wohlbrück. It was first performed in Leipzig in 1828.

Van den Gheyn, Matthias (*b* Tirlemont, Brabant, 7 Apr. 1721; *d* Louvain, 22 June 1785). Flemish organist and composer. In 1741 he became organist, and in 1745 'carillonneur' (he came from a family of bell-founders), at St Peter's, Louvain. He wrote six *divertissements* for harpsichord, published in London, a thoroughbass tutor, published in Louvain, and an unpublished treatise on harmony and composition.

Vanhal, Johann Baptist [Wanhal] (*b* Nové Nechanice, Bohemia, 12 May 1739; *d* Vienna, 20 Aug. 1813). Czech composer and teacher. Of humble origins, Vanhal received his first instruction from the organist of a nearby village, later learning the organ in his home town. His first compositions and his abilities on the violin attracted the attention of his superiors, and in 1761 he was taken to Vienna by Countess Schaffgotsch. Here he studied with Dittersdorf and began establishing a reputation as a composer and teacher, counting Pleyel among his pupils. In 1769 he travelled widely in Italy returning to Austria in 1771. He refused a *Kapellmeister* post in Dresden owing to mental illness and after further travel and convalescence he settled permanently in Vienna around 1780, where he supported himself independently by teaching and composing. Vanhal was well acquainted with the major musical figures of the day in Vienna; according to the Irish tenor Michael Kelly he took the cello part in a quartet with Mozart, Haydn, and his master Dittersdorf. His music was popular and widely distributed in manuscript and printed form. In his numerous symphonies, mostly written between 1767 and 1785, Vanhal made early use of sonata styles contributing significantly, and largely without the influence of Haydn, to the development of the Classical symphony. After 1785 he turned to less weighty genres aimed at the amateur solo player, producing keyboard sonatas, sonatinas, and capriccios, programme works, and towards the end of his life some contrapuntal teaching pieces. Apart from published quartets, quintets, trios, and duos, 60 Masses remained in manuscript. If his melodic style lacked the variety of his more illustrious colleagues, it was quite adequate to his needs, and possesses the virtue of being enlivened on occasion by the use of Czech folk traits.

JAN SMACZNY

Varèse, Edgard (Victor Achille Charles) (*b* Paris, 22 Dec. 1883; *d* New York, 6 Nov. 1965). American composer of French birth. He spent much of his childhood with his mother's family in Burgundy, where the massive architecture of the Romanesque churches affected him deeply. His father intended he should train as an engineer, but he was determined to become a composer, and in 1903 he left home (then in Turin) to study in Paris. He was a pupil of d'Indy, Roussel, and Bordes at the Schola Cantorum; he also attended Widor's classes at the conservatoire. Between 1908 and 1915 he divided his time between Paris and Berlin, gaining acquaintance with Busoni, Strauss, and the music of Schoenberg. He then emigrated to America.

With the exception of a single song, *Un grand sommeil noir* (1906), all the music Varèse wrote before his emigration has been lost. His output effectively begins with *Amériques* (1918–22), scored for an enormous orchestra and celebrating not only a new homeland but also new worlds of the imagination. Though influenced by Debussy, Stravinsky, and Schoenberg, the work is quite original in its perpetually evolving form, its rhythmic complexity and its massive eruptions of sound; it is also marked by Varèse's love for the speed and sounds of modern city life. In all these respects *Amériques* contained

Varèse (1910)

the seeds for the more polished works which followed: *Hyperprism* for a small orchestra of wind and percussion (1922–3), *Intégrales* for a similar ensemble (1924–5), *Octandre* for seven wind and double bass (1923–4), *Arcana* for orchestra (1925–7), and *Ionisation* for 13 percussionists (1930–3). The quasi-scientific titles signify a calculating approach to form and sonority, but he also saw himself, perhaps romantically, as comparable with the scientists in grappling with the unknown. His feeling for the primitive and magical is uppermost in *Ecuatorial* (1933–4), setting a Maya imprecation for bass voice and small orchestra.

Ever since his arrival in New York Varèse had been pressing for new electronic means as necessary to the music of the future. He included two of Theremin's electronic instruments in *Ecuatorial*, but, lacking the resources he required, he completed only a short flute piece, *Density 21.5* (1936), during the next 15 years. The availability of the tape recorder enabled him to continue with *Déserts* (1949–54), which interleaves orchestral with electronic sections, and then with the *Poème électronique* (1957–8). However, his last work, the unfinished *Nocturnal* (1960–1), was for voices and instruments without electronics.

PAUL GRIFFITHS

FURTHER READING
Fernand Ouellette: *Edgard Varèse* (New York, 1968; London, 1973); Louise Varèse: *Varèse: a Looking-Glass Diary* (New York, 1972).

Variation form. Many musical forms are based on the variation principle, but in its strict sense variation form may be described as a *strophic structure, $AA^1A^2A^3$ etc.: the first section A presents a 'theme' or 'air', which is then repeated many times with various changes. These changes, which do not conceal the theme's identity, may be harmonic, melodic, rhythmic, and timbral. The form is sometimes referred to as 'Air and Variations' or 'Theme and Variations'. The first movement of Beethoven's Piano Sonata Op. 26 provides an illustration (Ex. 1, facing page).
See also *Form*, 3.   G. M. TUCKER

Variations. Six works by Cage in which indeterminacy is taken to remarkable limits. The score of Variations I (1958) for example, consists of transparent plastic sheets inscribed with lines and dots which the performer or performers superimpose in any way and play on any instrument or instruments. Variations II (1961), III (1963), and IV (1963) are similarly for any number of players using any means. Variations V (1965) is for audio-visual performance, the score consisting only of a description

Ex. 1

of previous performances. Variations VI (1966) is for several sound systems. Variations VII (1966) is written 'for various means', and Variations VIII (1978) is for 'no music or recordings'.

Variations and Fugue on a Theme of Purcell. See *Young Person's Guide to the Orchestra, The*.

Variations on 'America'. Work for organ by Ives, probably composed in 1891. It was arranged for orchestra by William Schuman in 1964 and for concert band by Schuman and W. Rhoads.

Variations on a Theme by Haydn. Orchestral work, Op. 56a, by Brahms, composed in 1873. It is often called the 'St Anthony' Variations because the theme is called the 'St Anthony Chorale'; Brahms took it from a suite in B♭ major for military band (*Feld-partita*) by Haydn, who had in fact, as research has shown, borrowed the theme himself. Brahms arranged the work for two pianos (Op. 56b).

Variations on a Theme of Frank Bridge. Britten's Op. 10 for string orchestra using a theme from Bridge's *Idyll* No. 2 for string quartet. It was first performed at the Salzburg Festival in 1937.

Variato, variata (It.). 'Varied'.

Variazione, variazioni (It.). 'Variation', 'variations'.

Varsovienne (Fr.). A French version of the Polish *mazurka, named after the Polish city of Warsaw (Fr.: *Varsovie*). It was popular as a ballroom dance from the 1850s to the 1870s, and differs from the mazurka in being slower and in taking some characteristics of the *waltz.

Vasquez, Juan (*b* Badajoz, SW Spain, *c.*1500; *d* ? Seville, *c.*1560). Spanish composer. He was a singer at Palencia Cathedral and spent five years in charge of the music at Badajoz Cathedral before moving to Seville in 1551. In 1560 he published an anthology of his secular vocal works, the *Recopilacion de sonetos y villancicos*, for which he was famous in his lifetime. His *Agenda defunctorum* (Seville, 1556) is a huge collection of music for the dead, including a polyphonic Requiem Mass.   DENIS ARNOLD

Vater unser (Ger., 'Our Father'). The German translation, by Luther, of the *Pater noster*, i.e. the Lord's Prayer. It is sung as a hymn to a tune that may also have been written by Luther.

Vaudeville. 1. Two types of French song of the 16th century bear names which could have been corrupted to form 'vaudeville': the 'val' (or 'vau') 'de vire', a popular song concerning love, drinking, and satire on topical matters from the valley of the Vire River in Normandy; and the 'voix de ville', a courtly song which may have developed in response to the popular *vau de vire*. In the 17th and 18th centuries, vaudevilles were usually concerned with satire on political and courtly matters. See *Opera*, 7.

2. In the USA the name is synonymous with 'variety', a term much preferred by one of its pioneers, Tony Pastor, who opened his variety theatre in Tammany Hall, New York, in 1881. The American entertainment was similar in nature to the British *music hall, which had developed considerably earlier.

Vaughan Williams, Ralph (*b* Down Ampney, Glos., 12 Oct. 1872; *d* London, 26 Aug. 1958). English composer. He was a leading figure in the so-called renaissance of English musical life—creative, executive, and musicological—which began in the last years of the 19th century coincident with the rise to fame of Elgar.

1. *The Early Years*. Descended from Darwins and Wedgwoods, he had a conventional upper-middle-class education in which music played a surprisingly prominent part. He had violin and piano lessons at preparatory school, and played in the school orchestra at Charterhouse. He began to compose when he was six and continued until the day of his death. From Charterhouse in 1890 he went, unconventionally, direct to the Royal College of Music as a composition pupil of Parry. In 1892 he entered Trinity College, Cambridge, to read history and for his Bachelor of Music degree, continuing weekly lessons at the RCM and studying composition at Cambridge with Charles Wood. In 1895 he re-entered the RCM as a Stanford pupil. During this briefer spell there he formed a mutually enriching friendship with Gustav Holst. In 1897, after his marriage to Adeline Fisher, he went to Berlin, where he had lessons and encouragement from Max Bruch.

His compositions at the turn of the century were mainly chamber music (later withdrawn) and songs, including *Linden Lea* (1901). He edited the *Welcome Odes* for the Purcell Society, wrote articles for periodicals, and contributed to the second edition (1904) of Grove's *Dictionary of Music and Musicians*. In 1904 his *Songs of Travel*, settings of R. L. Stevenson, were sung in London. A significant event in 1902 was his introduction by Lucy Broadwood to the systematic collecting of folk-songs; further impetus was given to this activity in December 1903 when he heard 'Bushes and Briars' sung by an old shepherd in Essex. In the course of the next nine years he collected tunes in Norfolk, Hereford, Surrey, and Sussex, publishing many of them in various arrangements. In 1904 he accepted an invitation to be music editor of a new hymn-book, *The English Hymnal* (1906).

2. *The Years of Maturity*. His principal composition around the turn of the century was a short choral setting of Whitman, *Toward the Unknown Region* (1905). Although this was a success at the 1907 Leeds Festival, Vaughan Williams was dissatisfied with his compositions generally and early in 1908 went to Paris for three months of intensive study with Ravel. This released creative energies which had been dammed up. He rapidly produced the String Quartet No. 1 in G minor (1908), the Housman song-cycle *On Wenlock Edge* for tenor, piano, and string quartet (of which Gervase Elwes gave the first performance in 1909), and incidental music for the 1909 Cambridge Greek Play, *The Wasps*. In the same year he completed a choral symphony on which he had been at work since

1903: as *A Sea Symphony* (also to a Whitman text) it had an enthusiastic reception at the 1910 Leeds Festival and established Vaughan Williams in the front rank of English composers. The *Fantasia on a Theme by Thomas Tallis* for strings (Gloucester, 1910) eventually became one of his best-known works. It was followed by the *Five Mystical Songs* (Worcester, 1911) and *A London Symphony*, first performed in London in March 1914. From 1910 to 1914 he was also at work on a ballad-opera set in Napoleonic days, *Hugh the Drover*. This was completed in August 1914, whereupon it was shelved while its composer, although in his 42nd year, joined the army and spent most of the next four years in France.

In 1919 he joined the staff of the RCM and in 1921 became conductor of the Bach Choir. His experience as a choral conductor dated chiefly from 1905 when he had become conductor of the Leith Hill Festival at Dorking, near his family home. His Bach performances, highly idiosyncratic but artistically compelling, were the festival's major attraction until 1958. From

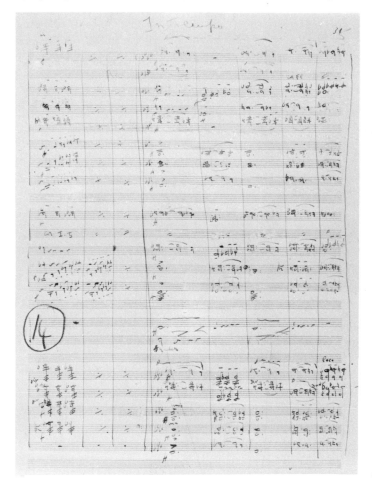

Autograph MS of Vaughan Williams's Fourth Symphony, a page from the first movement.

Vaughan Williams at a rehearsal by the Covent Garden Orchestra of his opera 'The Pilgrim's Progress' (1951).

1922 he produced ambitious and enterprising works in several genres. These included *A Pastoral Symphony* (London, 1922), the Mass in G minor (Birmingham, 1922), *Hugh the Drover* (London, 1924), *Flos Campi*, a suite for solo viola, small chorus, and orchestra (London, 1925), the oratorio *Sancta Civitas* (Oxford, 1926), and a Violin Concerto (London, 1925). His Falstaff opera, *Sir John in Love*, was produced in London in 1929, the masque for dancing, *Job* (based on Blake's illustrations), was first performed as an orchestral work at Norwich in 1930 and reached the stage in London in 1931, the Piano Concerto was played by Harriet Cohen in London in 1933, and in 1935 his violent Fourth Symphony was introduced by Adrian Boult at a BBC concert in London. A few weeks later he was appointed to the Order of Merit.

3. *The Final Years*. The last 22 years of Vaughan Williams's life showed no diminution in his activities, either as a conductor and member of numerous musical committees or as a composer. Five more symphonies followed (No. 5, London, 1943; No. 6, London, 1948; No. 7, the 'Antarctic', Manchester, 1953; No. 8, Manchester, 1956; No. 9, London, 1958), he wrote his first film score in 1940, his Second String Quartet in 1942–4, completed an opera, *The Pilgrim's Progress*, on which he had been working for many years (Covent Garden, 1951), and produced several choral works, notably *Hodie* (Worcester, 1954), and many smaller works.

Vaughan Williams drew his inspiration from many sources—folk-song and the English 16th-century school chief among them—and the influence of Ravel is frequently discernible. A lyrical melodic gift is at the heart of his work, but besides modality, there is a gritty harmonic toughness, such as occurs in *Job* and the Fourth Symphony, which places him firmly within the 20th century. His nationalist creed was that a composer must reach his fellow countrymen before he can hope to reach a universal audience. His symphonies, choral works, and songs are the central core of his output, but the operas, particularly *Riders to the Sea* (London, 1936), contain fine music which overcomes the dramatic problems they pose. The nobility, integrity, and visionary qualities of the man are reflected in his music.   MICHAEL KENNEDY

FURTHER READING
Frank Howes: *The Music of Ralph Vaughan Williams* (London, 1954); Ursula Vaughan Williams and Imogen Holst, eds.: *Heirs and Rebels: Letters between Vaughan Williams and Holst* (London, 1959); James Day: *Vaughan Williams* (London, 1961, revised edn 1974); Ralph Vaughan Williams: *National Music and Other Essays* (London, 1963); Michael Kennedy: *The Works of Ralph Vaughan Williams* (London, 1964, revised edn in 2 vols, 1980, 1982); Hugh Ottaway: *Vaughan Williams Symphonies* (London, 1972).

Vautor, Thomas (*fl.* early 17th century). English composer. He was in the household of the Duke of Buckingham, George Villiers, in Leicestershire, and dedicated his book of madrigals to the duke's son, George Villiers the younger. He received the Oxford B.Mus. in 1616. His madrigals, 'Apt for Vyols and Voyces', are attractive and pleasant to sing, and show a gift for comedy as well as for portraying the more sorrowful side of life.   DENIS ARNOLD

Vc. Abbreviation for violoncello.

Vecchi, Orazio (Tiberio) (*b* Modena, 5 Dec.

1550; *d* Modena, 19 Feb. 1605). Italian composer. The third of six children, he became a priest early in life and then took up music as a profession. He was *maestro di cappella* at Salò Cathedral (Lake Garda) from 1581 to 1584, and then at Modena Cathedral. However, he seems to have found it hard to settle down, and only two years later moved first to Reggio Emilia and then, in the same year, to Correggio. He remained there until 1598, when he returned to Modena, resuming his old position in the cathedral and taking charge of the court music for the Este family.

Vecchi composed some excellent church music, but his fame rests on his light madrigals and *canzonette*, written in an eminently singable and attractive style. His best-known work is the madrigal-comedy *L'Amfiparnaso* (1597), a *commedia dell'arte* set to music, with amusing character studies using Italian dialects.

DENIS ARNOLD

Vejvanovský, Pavel (Josef) (*b* Hukvaldy or Hlučín, *c*.1633; *d* Kroměříž, buried 24 Sept. 1693). Moravian composer and trumpeter. His family circumstances, place, and date of birth are uncertain, but by his death in 1693 Vejvanovský was among the most respected and without doubt one of the best paid Czech musicians of the day. It is possible that he studied in Vienna, and certain that from 1656 to 1660 he attended the Jesuit School in Opáva, northern Moravia. A year later he entered the service of Castelle, the administrator of the court of the Prince-Bishop of Olomouc at Kroměříž. In 1664 he was appointed first trumpeter and director of the court orchestra in which position he remained until his death. In addition to his work at the court he was director of the choir of the church of St Mořice where several of his works were performed, probably including his dozen Mass settings. Apart from accompanied church music Vejvanovský's output consists of multi-movement sonatas in the manner of Schmelzer, and suite-like serenades, scored mostly for strings, continuo, and a combination of brass instruments. His style has much in common with that of his younger contemporary Heinrich Biber with whom he worked at Kroměříž, suggesting a degree of mutual influence. Vejvanovský had a distinctive if limited melodic repertory, and made imaginative use of Moravian folk-song, but it is his use of sonority which commands attention, in particular his treatment of the various types of trumpet he himself played. JAN SMACZNY

Velato, velata (It.). 'Veiled', 'misty'.

Veloce, velocemente (It.). 'Fast', 'quickly'; *con velocità*, 'with speed'.

Velouté (Fr.). 'Velvety'.

Venetian Games (Pol.: *Gry weneckie*; Fr.: *Jeux vénitiens*). Work for chamber orchestra by Lutosławski, composed in 1961. It is the first work in which he used aleatory procedures.

Veni Creator Spiritus (Lat., 'Come, Creator Spirit'). A 9th- or 10th-century Whitsuntide hymn, of which translations exist in most languages (by Luther, Dryden, etc.). The English translation generally used is the 17th-century one by Bishop Cosin ('Come, Holy Ghost, our souls inspire'). This is one of only two metrical hymns included in the English Common Prayer, and thus officially authorized; the other is an alternative translation given in the same place (the Ordering of Priests). The tune usually sung to Cosin's translation is a harmonized adaptation of the plainchant. Bach made several choral arrangements of the plainchant, and wrote a fine organ chorale prelude based on it.

'Veni Creator Spiritus' is also sung at the creation of a pope, the consecration of a bishop, the elevation or translation of a saint, the coronation of a monarch, and on many other occasions.

Veni Sancte Spiritus (Lat., 'Come, Holy Ghost'). A sequence of the Roman Catholic liturgy, appointed for Whitsunday and the following six days. In Medieval times it was called the Golden Sequence. The words date from the 13th century. It is one of the four sequences that were allowed to remain when the rest were abolished by the *Council of Trent (1542-63). The words are now attributed by some good authorities to Stephen Langton, Archbishop of Canterbury (*d* 1228).

E. Caswell's translation ('Come, Thou Holy Spirit, come') is used in some hymn-books, and J. M. Neale's ('Come, Thou Holy Paraclete') in others.

Dunstable wrote a four-voice isorhythmic motet in which the text is sung in the top voice, but the melody he borrowed as a *cantus firmus* is from the hymn 'Veni Creator Spiritus'.

Venite (Lat., 'Come'). Psalm 95 (Psalm 94 in the Vulgate), called the *Invitatorium* or Invitatory Psalm, or, in Henry VIII's Primer, 'A song stirring to the Praise of God'. In the Roman liturgy it is the opening chant of Mattins, and in the Common Prayer of the Anglican Church it is sung as a prelude to the morning psalms, and is, even where there is a good choir, chanted, not (except by some Elizabethan composers and a few others) set with the rest of the service. Some elaborate settings of this psalm, not intended for liturgical use, do exist, for example that by Mendelssohn.

Vent (Fr.). 'Wind'; *instruments à vent*, 'wind instruments'.

Ventadorn, Bernart de. See *Bernart de Ventadorn*.

Ventil (Ger.), **ventile** (It.). 'Valve'.

Venus and Adonis. Opera in a prologue and three acts by Blow to a libretto by an unknown author. Described by the composer as a masque for the king, it was first performed in London *c*.1684.

Vêpres siciliennes, Les ('The Sicilian Vespers'). Opera in five acts by Verdi to a libretto in French by E. Scribe and C. Duveyrier from the libretto for Donizetti's *Le duc d'Albe* (1839). It was first performed in Paris in 1855.

Veracini, Francesco Maria (*b* Florence, 1 Feb. 1690; *d* Florence, 31 Oct. 1768). Italian violinist and composer. Born of a musical family, he studied with his uncle, Antonio Veracini (1659-1733), also a distinguished violinist, and in 1711 embarked on the first of a series of concert tours. He played at St Mark's, Venice, and went to Florence for a performance of his first oratorio (all his oratorios are now lost). In 1714 he went to London and then, in 1717, became 'guest' violinist at the Saxon court at Dresden, his high salary causing much ill feeling among resident musicians such as Pisendel and Zelenka. Mattheson wrote that he tried to commit suicide in 1722, but Veracini led an active life until at least 1750, returning to London in 1733 and playing for the Opera of the Nobility, the rival company to Handel's Royal

Veracini, engraving from 'Sonata Accademiche a violino' (1744).

Academy; his own operas were put on in 1735, 1737, and 1738. He continued to travel widely in Europe until 1755, when he became *maestro di cappella* to S. Pancrazio, Florence. He died an extremely wealthy man, according to his obituary in the *Gazzetta toscana*, 'more perhaps than any previous instrumentalist'.

Veracini's temperament can be gauged by the story that he once said 'there is but one God and one Veracini', and in fact he does seem to have been quite extraordinary as a performer. His music shows his interest in various kinds of special effects, such as *spiccato* and bowed *tremolo*, and he marked up- and down-bows in certain works with great care. His sonatas have been sadly and inexplicably neglected in modern times. Though he followed Corelli in style at first (later paying homage to that master by rewriting the Op. 5 sonatas to conform to up-to-date violin technique), he had an almost romantic streak; this shows especially in his Op. 2 sonatas (London, Florence, 1744), their movements bearing such titles as *cotilla*, *scozzese*, and *aria schiavonna* and containing impressive fugal writing and interesting harmonic quirks.   DENIS ARNOLD

Veränderungen (Ger.). A term sometimes used instead of *Variationen* for 'variations', as in Beethoven's Diabelli Variations, Op. 120, which were issued as *Veränderungen über einen Walzer von Anton Diabelli*.

Verbunkos. A Hungarian soldiers' dance, used from around 1780 to attract recruits into the army (the name is a corruption of Ger. *Werbung*, 'enlistment'). It was danced to the music of gypsy bands by hussars in uniform. It lost its purpose when the Austrian government imposed conscription in 1849, but survived as a ceremonial dance. The verbunkos consisted of two or more sections, similar to those of the *csárdás, some in the style of a slow introduction (*lassu*), others fast and wild (*friss*). Many collections were published during the 19th century.

The dance form has been used by Hungarian composers such as Liszt (Second Hungarian Rhapsody), Bartók (rhapsodies for piano and violin with orchestra), and Kodály (Intermezzo from *Háry János*).

Verdelot, Philippe (*b* Verdelot, Orange, ? 1470-80; *d* before 1552). French composer who spent much of his life in Italy. He was in Venice in the early years of the 16th century, but the first known fact about his life is that in 1522 he was in Florence, where for the next few years he was *maestro di cappella* at the Baptistery and the Cathedral. In 1523 he visited Rome. He wrote a good deal of church music, but is famous for his madrigals, which have been shown to belong to the years before the first madrigal publications c.1530. See *Madrigal*, 3.   DENIS ARNOLD

Verdi, Giuseppe (Fortunino Francesco) (*b* Le Roncole, nr Parma, 10 Oct. 1813; *d* Milan, 27 Jan. 1901). Italian composer. He was one of the greatest opera composers of all time.

1. *Background and Early Years.* Verdi was the son of illiterate peasants who ran the *osteria* (tavern-cum-shop) in a small village in the then French-governed state of Parma (it shortly afterwards became Austrian). It is not known when exactly his musical talent was discovered, but he learned the organ from the village organist, whom he succeeded at the age of 10. This led to his removal to the nearest town, Busseto, to attend school, although he kept up the organist's post at Le Roncole to pay his way. In Busseto he was taken up by a shop owner, Antonio Barezzi, who in 1832 arranged for a scholarship to be awarded by a local charitable foundation to allow Verdi to study in Milan. There he was rejected by the conservatory, largely because he had not had a conventional music education (also because he was over age and a foreigner), and had to study privately, the additional expense for which was provided by Barezzi. His teacher, Lavigna, gave him a good grounding in composition, but his principal education probably came from his constant attendance at the theatres where he heard the works of Mercadente, Donizetti, and Luigi Ricci. He also directed a performance of Haydn's *Creation*.

In 1834 the combined post of cathedral organist and director of the Philharmonic Society at Busseto fell vacant and since at this stage there was no sign of his future fame, he was expected to take this up. In the event, there seems to have been some reluctance on his part (he had anticipated a longer period in Milan); and while the Philharmonic Society appointed him, the cathedral's provost preferred someone else, a situation causing a row of incredible proportions: Verdi harboured a bitterness towards the citizens of Busseto to his last years. However, in 1836 he returned to the town, married Barezzi's daughter, and composed an opera *Rocester*, intended for the opera house at Parma. This was turned down, Verdi perhaps using some of the material in *Oberto*, which he persuaded a Milan impresario, Merelli, to take; it was eventually produced at La Scala in 1839. By this time, Verdi had had two children; a daughter, born in 1837, died in the following year, and a son, born in 1838, died during the rehearsals for *Oberto*. On the modest but distinct success of this piece, Merelli commissioned more works, the first of which was to be an *opera buffa*, *Un giorno di regno* (1840). During its composition, tragedy struck again: Verdi's wife died, and it is usually said that the opera's failure was due to his personal circumstances. However, it is more than likely that Verdi did not fully understand the genre, though, as he himself said later, the piece is neither better nor worse than many others of the period. But the private tragedy and the public failure together led to a period of intense depression, and it is to Merelli's credit that he managed to tempt Verdi back to composing by showing him a libretto with distinct possibilities. This was *Nabucco*, a biblical drama on the theme of the Jewish exile in Babylon. Verdi's music owes a great deal to fashionable models of the time, notably Bellini, though it is less enterprising in form than the best operas of the 1830s. Its real glory is the vitality of its characterization (especially of the two villains, Nebuchadnezzar and his daughter Abigaille) and of its choruses, probably influenced by Rossini's similar biblical opera-cum-oratorio *Mosè*. It is one of these choruses, 'Va pensiero', the prayer of the Jews in exile, which was taken up for its political significance (the fight against the Austrians was especially vigorous at this period) and caused the opera's incredible success, gaining not only eight performances in the spring season, but no fewer than 57 in the autumn of 1842. Thereafter Verdi was the best-known Italian composer of his time, and a period of distinct poverty, from which he was saved only by Barezzi's generosity, was replaced by prosperity and even riches.

2. *The Years in the Galleys.* This was Verdi's own expression for the period which followed. After real poverty in his youth, he was determined to make his fortune while the opportunity lasted, perhaps in the hope that, like Rossini, he could retire early and lead a quiet existence (significantly he bought a farm and a house at S. Agata, near his birthplace, in 1848). To achieve this, he was willing to write two operas each year at considerable cost of energy and, at times, health. This was a much more difficult task in the conditions of the 1840s than it had been for Rossini 20 years earlier, since both the musical forms and the treatment of the drama were less stereotyped and Verdi took considerable trouble over the librettos. Given the success of *Nabucco*, there was a strong demand for operas with political themes, which Verdi satisfied with *I Lombardi* (1843), *Attila* (1846)— this notable for the words 'You can have the universe, if Italy is left to me'—and *La battaglia di Legnano* (1849), written as an overt statement of Italian nationalism after the abortive revolution of the previous year. These are notable for their memorable, highly rhythmic melodies and strong (at times even vulgar) orchestration. But

in other works, while the political content remains to attract the crowds, it is turned to more positive use as Verdi's interest in character developed. *Ernani* (1844), *I due Foscari* (1844), *Giovanna d'Arco* (1845), and especially *Macbeth* (1847) all attempt character studies, usually of people in unusual circumstances, sometimes affected by supernatural forces (a late manifestation in Italian opera of a romantic trend), rarely of conventional heroic cast. To give dramatic power to these, Verdi dispenses with the traditional forces, reducing the role of the aria and increasing that of the ensemble, using reminiscence motifs (not in the *Leitmotiv* symphonic manner of Wagner but with great effect) and refining his orchestration. Even where quasi-conventional arias occur, they are given new twists, as in the famous sleep-walking scene in *Macbeth*, which is an obvious example of the grand soprano *scena* but which ends mysteriously as an extended orchestral postlude precluding the opportunity for applause. Moreover, as the most sought-after composer of the time, Verdi became a virtual tyrant in matters of production, insisting on singers who could act, and instructing them in new ways of singing, less *bel canto* than dramatically effective.

These trends increased as Verdi moved on to the international scene. His operas were early in demand in Paris where they were first given at the Théâtre-Italien and an invitation to London resulted in *I masnadieri* (Her Majesty's Theatre, June 1847) and an invitation to direct the future seasons at that theatre, tempting because it required Verdi to write only one opera a year, in addition to a very high fee; but he eventually turned it down. A commission to produce a work for the Opéra resulted in a stay in Paris in this year while he reworked *I Lombardi* for the special tastes of that institution, the result being *Jérusalem*. While he was there he re-met a soprano who had sung in *Nabucco* in 1842, Giuseppina Strepponi, fell in love with her, and began an affair which lasted 12 years until he finally married her. She proved a remarkable companion to whom Verdi owed a great deal. Verdi spent considerable periods away from Italy at this very difficult time for the Austrian provinces, and after *La battaglia di Legnano* his operas become markedly less political. *Luisa Miller* (1849) is a turning-point towards a still more flexible style and away from the heroic grand manner, and although the following year saw one of his few total failures, *Stiffelio*, Verdi was preparing for three works of new dramatic import.

The first of these was *Rigoletto* (1851) based on a then notorious play, Hugo's *Le roi s'amuse*, which included a rape and was considered generally outrageous. It has no hero, both Rigoletto and the Duke cast in the mould of

Verdi in the 1850s.

anti-hero, and little love interest or alleviating local colour. Verdi's by now extraordinary capacity to bring the characters to life and projection of the drama is achieved by tremendous plasticity of forms, there being only two real arias (Gilda's 'Caro nome' being one of the few infelicities in dramatic content); rather is there a succession of ensembles, especially duets, the grand climax being the famous quartet (one of the greatest examples of a genre developed by Donizetti) with its simultaneous portrayal of character equalled only by Mozart. The orchestra is used in a highly imaginative way, partly to carry much thematic material, as in the opening scene, partly to conjure mood (the duet between Rigoletto and the assassin Sparafucile is a remarkable example with its muted cello and double bass solo). *Rigoletto* was a great success and was followed by *Il trovatore* (1853), a more conventional piece in mood and musical construction but again strong in its portrayal of character, notably that of the gypsy nurse Azucena, another anti-hero conception. The third of the group, *La traviata*, was produced in Venice within two months of *Il trovatore*, a fact which probably helps to explain its initial failure (the usual explanation that it was because it was given in 'modern' dress is untrue) since Verdi had little time to take part in the rehearsals—and its unusual style needed this more than ever. An intimate piece, its plot drawn from real life via Dumas's play *La dame aux camélias*, it has no direct predecessors (many later works are its debtors), though it has main characters in a more obviously heroic (if bourgeois) frame. Slightly less original in form than *Rigoletto*, its orchestration is extraordinarily delicate, the divided strings of the Prelude reminiscent of Wagner's *Lohengrin*, an opera Verdi cannot have known at this time; and the capacity to illuminate emotional detail without disturbing the musical flow is remarkable.

3. *After 'La traviata'*. These three operas were the last in which Verdi worked at the pace which had made his fortune. In the next 20 years the offers had to be sufficiently tempting (significantly they mainly came from outside Italy) or the project interesting in its own right. His next contract was with the Paris Opéra in which he had about two years to compose *Les vêpres siciliennes* to a libretto by Scribe following the usual French Meyerbeerian pattern with a religious theme, and opportunities for spectacle and ballet. Although the production in 1855 was successful, these peculiar conditions did not please him and his next work *Simon Boccanegra* was written for Venice, following his earlier pattern of historical operas. At this juncture the work pleased neither him nor the public, although in its later revision it proved more successful. A commission from Naples produced a much better libretto, *Un ballo in maschera*, although troubles with the censorship which forced a change of scene from 18th-century Sweden to colonial Boston did the piece no good; but the music is admirably inventive, better orchestrated after his Parisian experiences, and putting traditional forms to good use. It was at the period of its production in 1859 that the acrostic VIVA VERDI—Viva Vittorio Emanuele Re d'Italia ('Long live Victor Emanuel, King of Italy')—was heard. The King of Savoy was almost certain to head the first united Italy; and Verdi was constrained by Cavour to become Deputy for Busseto in the new Italian parliament at Turin; he held the post until 1865, even though he had little interest in politics as such. Probably to avoid embarrassment at becoming a public figure of this kind, he married Giuseppina, quietly, away from Busseto (her presence at S. Agata had been a constant sore point in his relationship with both his family and the neighbouring population). These distractions caused a lull in composition, and he accepted a profitable commission from St

Petersburg to compose an opera for 1861, possibly needing the money to pay for alterations to his house and farms. A first trip to Russia in that year proved abortive, since one of his singers fell ill, and he returned to London where his *Hymn to the Nations* for a Great Exhibition was given. A second visit to Russia in the following year brought *La forza del destino* to a successful production, in spite of an episodic libretto which nevertheless inspired some splendid music again in traditional form. *La forza* was given almost immediately afterwards in Madrid under his direction, and was followed by a revival of *Les vêpres* at the Paris Opéra, at which he walked out after a dispute at rehearsals.

After this he went almost into retirement, content to live as a farmer, revising operas for new productions from time to time, and it was only another profitable commission, from the Opéra for the Paris Exhibition of 1867, that tempted him to new work. This was *Don Carlos*, to another historic-religious libretto with the usual scenic grandeur of the Opéra (as in the *auto-da-fé* scene), but this time resulting in a splendidly integrated work with several excellent character studies, especially that of King Philip, one of Verdi's noblest quasi-heroes. Although it is possibly the finest of all French grand operas (and best heard in that language) it had an indifferent reception and Verdi's technique of placing much thematic material in the orchestra gave rise to the first charges of Wagnerism against his music, although he had used this technique extravagantly since at least *Rigoletto* and it was derived, if from anywhere, from Meyerbeer. The Italian version of the piece had a better reception at La Scala in 1868. Again there was another lull in productivity, an attempt to organize a 'co-operative' Mass (involving all the leading Italian composers) to honour Rossini (who had died in 1868) proving fruitless, except for Verdi's own 'Libera me' which was later used in his own Requiem. This was broken by yet another well-paid commission, this time from Cairo (but via Paris) for a work to be given *post facto* in honour of the opening of the Suez Canal—which took place in 1869—the scenery to be built in France, the music to be Verdi's property everywhere except Egypt. After delays due to the Franco-Prussian War, *Aida* was eventually given on Christmas Eve 1871 and February 1872 at La Scala. Obviously modelled on French grand opera, the libretto is much more compact and cohesive than its models, and although the grand march and ballet of Act 2 are in the best Parisian tradition, the building up of character, with a conflict of emotions which makes it difficult to find a true hero or heroine, is typically Verdian. Beautifully orchestrated, with the conventional aria and ensemble forms expanded and modified but still recognizable, it achieved the total success which it has enjoyed ever since. A String Quartet, slight but attractive, written in 1873 while in Naples with the production of *Aida* held up because of the illness of a prima donna, was the only new work of the next three years. The silence was broken this time on the death of Manzoni, the famous novelist and patriot who occupied much the same position in letters that Verdi did in music. Verdi knew and revered him, and proposed to the city of Milan a grand Requiem Mass to be performed in the church of S. Marco on the anniversary of Manzoni's death. Composed within the year, it was first so given on 22 May 1874, followed by several performances at La Scala and a European tour. Criticisms, notably by Wagner's disciple Hans von Bülow, that it was really just an opera were muted by the sheer power of the music which ensured its fame and popularity, and are anyway beside the point, for although it is composed in Verdi's natural idiom (there are obvious links with *Aida*) it is sincerely felt and belongs to a well-established tradition in which Rossini's

sacred music was also written. However, Verdi's interpolations in the text (the repetitions of the words of the 'Dies irae' in un-liturgical contexts) show that it was no conventional statement of belief, rather a prayer for deliverance by a man who had suffered much in a turbulent era and life, and was probably at the time of writing something very like an agnostic (there is evidence that he returned to the Roman Catholic faith in his last years).

4. *The Final Period.* When Verdi finished the Requiem he was only 60 and still possessed of great vigour. Yet he showed no signs of wishing to compose, and devoted his time to improving his home and farms. He agreed to supervise performances in various places, and was indeed enamoured of (though not to the point of having an affair with) one of his principal interpreters, the soprano Teresa Stoltz. He quarrelled with his publisher, Ricordi, on the grounds of various inefficiencies and gained a huge sum in back royalties; he also became a 'grandfather' by his adopted daughter. But his view that he need no longer compose ('That account is settled') was

Autograph MS of Verdi's 'Otello', a page from Act 1.

disturbed only by various plots by Ricordi and Giuseppina who found a replacement for his favourite librettist, who had died in 1861, in Arrigo Boito. The Shakespearian subject of *Otello* was broached as early as 1874, but nothing came of it immediately, and their first collaboration was a full-scale revision of *Simon Boccanegra* resulting in a much more satisfactory version, somewhat disturbed by the disparity of his earlier and later styles, but none the less successful at its Milan production in 1881 and holding the stage ever since. Verdi also revived *Don Carlos* for the Italian market in 1883, cutting the ballet and various other sections written originally with Parisian tastes in mind, although the original remains in many ways the better. Only after this did he take up *Otello* and Boito, proving his best librettist ever, with a fruitful, resourceful manner, it was finished and produced at La Scala in 1887. This is the finest of all Italian Romantic operas, the libretto taut, the music not completely ignoring traditional forms but making them infinitely serviceable in projecting the drama. The technique of using the orchestra to maintain the continuity does not diminish the importance of the voice, and there were no accusations of Wagnerism. The first Verdi opera for 16 years, it was received in an enthusiastic way from the beginning.

It clearly stimulated Verdi's inclination to compose, but it was again a lengthy period before *Falstaff* was finally conceived. Verdi began work on it when he was over 75, but he worked steadily for about two hours a day, the first act coming easily, the latter ones slightly delayed by Boito's own operatic ventures; it was completed in 1893, when it was produced at La Scala as a tremendous social and musical event. Concise, to a masterly libretto which is rather better than Shakespeare's *Merry Wives of Windsor*, this breaks new ground by virtually cutting out traditional formal designs, following the meaning of the words in astonishing detail and in a conversational manner; masterly in orchestration, *Falstaff* is one of the great comedies, funny but compassionate in characterization, and yet showing a detachment only possible to the old in the final fugue 'All the world's a comedy'.

This might well have seemed the fitting end to a career; none the less Verdi still had a lively mind, writing ballet music of all things to satisfy the Opéra's requirements in producing *Otello*. His major interest about this time, however, was in establishing his Home for Old Musicians (Casa di Riposo) in Milan, to look after indigent musicians left without means of support. Old age finally overtook him in 1897, when he had a minor stroke, and then Giuseppina died, which upset him very much. His way of overcoming this was, astonishingly, to compose two large-scale pieces of church music, a Te Deum and a Stabat Mater more restrained than the grand dramatic manner of the Requiem, although both shot through with human emotion. Together with a setting of some words by Dante, 'Laudi alla Vergine Maria', composed for female voices in 1888, they were given as a group in 1898 in Paris; a further piece, an Ave Maria on a puzzle scale written as an intellectual exercise in 1889 (see *Scale*, 7), was added at later performances. This really was the end of his composing career. After a stroke, he died in the Grand Hotel in Milan, where he had spent the Christmas of 1900, and was buried, next to Giuseppina, at the Casa di Riposo. His influence on his Italian followers was generalized rather than particular, proving more that the Wagnerian way was not the only one rather than yielding material for stylistic imitation. In general underestimated by non-Italian historians for many years, his music had long fulfilled his own test: it enraptures the public by its understanding and expression of the human psyche. The force of his personality is still to be felt at his house at S. Agata, kept more or less as it was, revealing his peasant stock and his complex simplicity even in its present form as a museum; while his generosity continues in the Casa di Riposo.   DENIS ARNOLD

FURTHER READING
F. Toye: *Giuseppe Verdi: his Life and Works* (London, 1931); F. Walker: *The Man Verdi* (London, 1962); J. Budden: *The Operas of Verdi*, 3 vols (London, 1973–81); D. Kimbell: *Verdi in the Age of Italian Romanticism* (Cambridge, 1981).

Verdoppeln (Ger.). 'To double'; *verdoppelt*, 'doubled'; *Verdoppelung*, 'doubling', 'duplication'.

Vergebliches Ständchen ('Vain Serenade'). Song for voice and piano by Brahms, the fourth of his set of five, Op. 84 (1882). It is a setting of traditional words.

Vergrösserung (Ger.). 'Augmentation'.

Verhallend (Ger.). 'Dying away'.

Verismo (It., 'realism'). The term applied to the type of Italian opera dealing with 'real-life' (and in general low-life) subjects. Mascagni (*Cavalleria rusticana*) and Leoncavallo (*Pagliacci*) are undisputed examples of *veristi*, or realists, but certain works by Giordano, Puccini, Verdi, and others could be said to be in the *verismo* spirit. See *Opera*, 11.

Verklärte Nacht ('Transfigured Night'). Work, Op. 4, by Schoenberg for two violins, two violas, and two cellos, composed in 1899. It is based on a poem by Richard Dehmel (from *Weib und Welt*). Schoenberg arranged the work for string orchestra in 1917 and made a second version in 1943.

Verkleinerung, Verkürzung (Ger.). 'Diminution'.

Verlierend, verlöschend (Ger.). 'Dying away', 'extinguishing'.

Vermeulen, Matthijs (*b* Helmond, 8 Feb. 1888; *d* Laren, 26 July 1967). Dutch composer and writer. He was largely self-taught, and his output included seven symphonies, other orchestral pieces such as *The Flying Dutchman*, chamber music, and songs. From 1907 onwards he worked as a music critic (he was music editor of *De groene Amsterdammer* from 1947 to 1956).
WENDY THOMPSON

Verovio, Simone. See *Printing and Publishing of Music*, 5.

Verschwindend (Ger.). 'Disappearing', 'fading away'.

Verse (Fr.: *vers*; Ger.: *Vers*; It.: *verso*; Lat.: *versus*). 1. In poetry, a metrical line, or a group of a definite number of such lines. 2. In plainchant, a verse of a psalm or canticle or a short scriptural sentence sung by a soloist in alternation with the choir or congregation. The verses are usually marked V or V̌. See *Psalmody*. A continuation of the practice of alternation can be found in polyphonic music, in the verse anthem.

Verse anthem. Anthem with verses for solo voices accompanied by independent instrumental parts alternating with those for chorus doubled by instruments. See *Anthem*, 1.

Verset. The word simply means 'verse' but has also a special application in the Roman Catholic Church to a verse of a hymn, psalm, or other liturgical item which would usually be sung by the choir but is instead repeated by them silently to themselves while the organist plays. A large repertory of organ music intended for such performance exists but frequently the organist either simply plays the music which would have been sung or extemporizes.

A similar practice is sometimes followed in connection with the performance of parts of the Ordinary and, less frequently, the Proper of the Mass, the organ 'supplying' alternate phrases to the choir's setting, which is usually plainchant. Similarly, the antiphons at Vespers may be supplied on their repetition after the psalm.

There are five Mass movements set in this fashion in the Faenza Codex (*c.*1400), and in 1531 Pierre Attaingnant published two books of organ versets; the genre reached a peak in Italy and France in the 17th century, with fine examples by Frescobaldi (e.g. *Fiori musicali*)

and François Couperin (e.g. *Pièces d'orgue consistantes en deux messes*). The popularity of *messes en noëls* (see *Carol*, 2) in the 18th and 19th centuries ensured the survival of the 'organ Mass' in France: the organist would base his versets upon popular Christmas carols. In his *motu proprio* of 1903, however, Pope Pius X directed that the clergy were 'not to omit the prescribed texts in cases where the rubrics do not permit of replacing verses by the organ whilst they are simply recited in the choir'.

Versetzung (Ger.). 'Transposition'; *Versetzungszeichen*, 'accidental'.

Versicle (from Lat.: *versiculus*, 'small verse'). Short sentence, often taken from the psalms, which is said or sung antiphonally in Christian worship. It is followed by a response from the congregation or choir. A typical versicle and response in the Roman Catholic liturgy is 'Dominus vobiscum' ('The Lord be with you') answered by 'Et cum spiritu tuo' ('And with thy spirit'). See also *Preces*.

Verstärken (Ger.). 'To strengthen'; *verstärkt*, 'strengthened', i.e. *rinforzando*.

Verstovsky, Alexey (Nikolayevich) (*b* Seliverstovo estate, Tambov Government, 1 Mar. 1799; *d* Moscow, 17 Nov. 1862). Russian composer. Like all Russian musicians of his generation, he was essentially a dilettante, having at first studied engineering before taking to music (he had lessons from Steibelt and Field). He was appointed inspector (1824) and then director (1842) of the Moscow theatres, and for the rest of his life his work centred on the stage, both as administrator and as composer. He is known chiefly for his opera *Askol'dovaya mogila* ('Askold's Tomb', 1835), which effects a fragile compromise between overt 'Russianisms' and German Romantic traits clearly imitative of Weber's *Der Freischütz* (which had been seen in Russia in 1824). The opera enjoyed huge success in its time, though by the late 19th century something of Verstovsky's declining reputation can be judged from the attitude of one conductor (Rakhmaninov) who, when asked to conduct *Askold's Tomb* and the later *Gromoboy* (1858) in 1897, remarked, 'Now please tell me what artistic and commercial sense [is there] in doing these blasted operas?'. Earlier in his career Verstovsky had written *Pan Twardowski* (1828), and he followed up the success of *Askold's Tomb* with *Toska po rodine* ('Longing for the Homeland', 1839) and *Churova Dolina, ili Son nayavu* ('Chur Valley, or The Waking Dream', 1841). He also composed about 30 vaudevilles, and wrote a number of songs, which continue to be published in the

Soviet Union and reveal not only a melodic facility but also, especially in such extended pieces as *Chornaya shal'* ('The Black Shawl', a Pushkin setting), a keen dramatic sense.

GEOFFREY NORRIS

Verteilt [*vertheilt*] (Ger.). 'Divided'.

Verweilend (Ger.). 'Delaying', i.e. *rallentando*.

Verzierungen (Ger.). 'Ornaments'.

Vesalii icones ('Images of Vesalius'). Theatre piece by Peter Maxwell Davies for male dancer, solo cello, and ensemble (including out of tune piano, knife grinder, and saucepan). It was first performed in 1969 in London.

Vesperae solennes de confessore ('Solemn Vespers of the Confessor'). Work by Mozart (K 339) for soprano, alto, tenor, and bass, chorus, organ, and orchestra, composed in 1780.

Vesperal. A Roman Catholic service book containing the liturgy and music for *Vespers, and often also for some of the other Office Hours. It is an extract from the *antiphoner.

Vespers. The seventh of the Office Hours of the Roman Catholic Church. It is also known as Evensong. This service has always been a favourite with composers, and many have provided elaborate settings (see *Office*).

Vespers of 1610. See *Vespro della Beata Vergine*.

Vespro della Beata Vergine ('Vespers of the Holy Virgin'). Collection of motets by Monteverdi, composed in 1610 for performance at Mantua. They are *Domine ad adiuvandum* (six voices, three trombones, two cornetts, and six strings), *Dixit Dominus* (six voices and six instruments), *Nigra sum* (solo voice), *Laudate pueri* (eight voices and organ), *Pulchra es, amica mea* (two voices), *Laetatus sum* (six voices), *Duo seraphim clamabant* (three voices), *Nisi Dominus* (ten voices), *Audi coelum* (solo voice and six-voice chorus), *Lauda, Jerusalem* (seven voices), *Sonata sopra 'Sancta Maria'* (solo voice, two cornetts, three trombones, two violins, and cello), *Ave maris stella* (two voices, eight-voice chorus, and five instruments), *Magnificat* (seven voices, two flutes, two recorders, three cornetts, two trombones, two violins, and cello), and *Magnificat* (six voices and organ). The *Sonata sopra 'Sancta Maria'* is sometimes performed separately. There are many modern editions of the Vespers, including those by Harnoncourt, Redlich, and Norrington.

Vestris. French family of musicians and dancers. **Gaetano Vestris** (*b* Florence, 18 Apr. 1729; *d* Paris, 27 Sept. 1808) was a dancer and choreographer. He was a pupil of the great French dancer Louis Dupré and made his début in Paris in 1748; within three years he had succeeded his teacher as *premier danseur* at the Opéra, a post he held for over 30 years. He also worked for the French court and made many tours abroad, and during the Revolution he was obliged to flee with his family to London. Vestris played a major part in the ballet reforms of the mid 18th century (see *Ballet and Theatrical Dance*, 1).

His illegitimate son, **Auguste Vestris** (*b* Paris, 27 Mar. 1760; *d* Paris, 5 Dec. 1842), made his début at the Opéra in 1772. On retiring in 1816 he taught at the Opéra dance school, where his pupils included Taglioni.

WENDY THOMPSON

Via (It.). 'Away'; *via sordini*, a direction to remove the mutes.

Viadana, Lodovico (*b* Viadana, nr Mantua, *c*.1560; *d* Gualtieri, nr Mantua, 2 May 1627). Italian composer and friar. He was *maestro di cappella* at a number of less important Italian churches, including Mantua Cathedral (late 1590s), the convent of S. Luca, Cremona (1602), and the cathedrals of Concordia (1608-9) and Fano (1610-12). A prolific composer of everything from light *canzonette* and madrigals to massive polychoral psalm settings, he is best known for his *Cento concerti ecclesiastici* (Venice, 1602). This is the earliest publication of church music to use a true *basso *continuo, which Viadana used as a means of avoiding some of the problems of composing for the sparse resources of small churches. Whereas earlier *a cappella* works were often performed with some of the voice parts omitted, Viadana avoided the resulting gaps in the music by providing a melody which could be sung by one voice or spread among several, at the same time providing a continuous accompaniment for the organ. This convenient procedure became immediately popular, and was to form the basis for most sacred music for the next 150 years.

DENIS ARNOLD

Vibraphone [vibraharp]. Percussion instrument of tuned metal bars, constructed in the same general shape as a xylophone. The bars are of aluminium alloy, about 12 mm. thick, suspended on spring-tensioned cords. The two rows, for the naturals and the sharps, are placed on the same level since this makes possible the use of two beaters (soft-ended) in each hand for playing four-note chords, very characteristic with this instrument (as with the *marimba also).

Tubular resonators are suspended vertically

below the bars, but the special feature of the vibraphone is the long axle passing along the top of each row of resonators and bearing small circular metal or plastic fans, one for each resonator, rotated together by an electric (originally clockwork) motor to make the tremulant or *vibrato* which gives the instrument its name. The motor may have certain set speeds, or be variable-speed to make from three to eight pulsations per second. Very important is the damper, consisting of a long felted strip for each row of bars and moved against their ends by a pedal. Its use demands much skill, as in half-damping fast passages for the notes to be distinct yet without losing vibraphone quality. Damping with the fingers may also be needed, for instance where certain notes are to have shorter duration than the others in a chord played with the dampers lifted. The normal compass is *f* to *f'''* (see *Xylophone* for a comparative compass chart).

In the early design by the Leedy Drum Co. in the USA, 1916, the *vibrato* was obtained by moving the resonators up and down. The rotating fans followed about 1921, after which variety soloists made the instrument well known, as later the advanced jazz of Lionel Hampton. In the orchestra, Berg has it in *Lulu* (1934) and Milhaud wrote a Concerto (1947) for vibraphone and marimba. Two British works of around 1950—Britten's *Spring Symphony* and Vaughan Williams's *Sinfonia antartica*—link vibraphone chords with frostiness and freezing (as in Walt Disney's famous cartoons). But mainly the instrument has become an essential member of orchestral percussion for 'abstract' colour in its own right.

More recently from the USA comes the 'electravibe', in which the resonators and fans are replaced by a pick-up under each bar, to convert the acoustic vibration into electrical for amplification, and with *vibrato* control by a pulsator and optional 'fuzz' and 'wah' units as used with electric guitars.   ANTHONY BAINES

Vibration. See *Acoustics*, 4.

Vibrato (It., from Lat. *vibrare*, 'to shake'). The slight wavering of pitch used to enrich and intensify the tone of the voice and of many instruments, especially stringed. *Vibrato* on notes of reasonable length is now taken for granted, and a composer must direct *senza vibrato* if he wishes a straight sound.

This has not always been the case. Violinists, for example, from the Baroque period until Kreisler, have generally regarded *vibrato* as an ornament to be used for particularly expressive moments. Admittedly Geminiani in 1751 advised its use 'as often as possible', but modera-

tion in the application and width of *vibrato* in earlier music, especially of the 17th and 18th centuries, is to be encouraged.

The terms *vibrato* and **tremolo* have often been interchanged, especially in writings about the voice. (See also *Voice*, 6.)

Vicar choral. Term peculiar to the Anglican Church, used to designate a cathedral singing man. The position varies in the details of its conditions in different cathedrals, and at some the term 'lay clerk', or 'lay vicar', is used. The word vicar indicates that the duties are really those of the canons, done vicariously. At one time every canon had a vicar choral or a minor canon (the latter being in orders) attached to him. The office came into being at the time of the Reformation; formerly all these various 'clerks' and 'vicars' had been in holy orders.

Vicentino, Nicola (*b* Vicenza, 1511; *d* Milan, *c*.1576). Italian theorist and composer who had a considerable influence on music in the late 16th century. A pupil of Willaert in Venice, he began his studies of Ancient Greek music in about 1534, eventually evolving a theory that the scale system of the Greeks could be used in modern music. This theory, which he developed when music master to the family of Duke Ercole II d'Este at Ferrara, involved the use of microtones, and in *c*.1561 he had a harpsichord, or *arcicembalo*, built with additional keys to accommodate these extra notes; he also developed an expanded system of notation using dots. The theory, discussed in his book *L'antica musica ridotta alla moderna prattica* (Rome, 1555), was to prove unsound, and the use of microtones impractical, but it did result in the relatively free use of such notes as D♯, A♭, G♭, and D♭, which had previously been very rare; his ideas also did much to inspire the chromatic madrigal style of Gesualdo and Monteverdi.   DENIS ARNOLD

Victimae paschali laudes (Lat., 'praises to the Paschal victim'). A **sequence of the Roman Catholic liturgy, appointed for Easter Day. It dates from the 11th century and was one of the four sequences allowed to remain after most sequences and tropes were abolished by the **Council of Trent.

Victoria, Tomás Luis de (*b* Ávila, 1548; *d* Madrid, 20 Aug. 1611). Spanish composer. He was a choirboy at Ávila Cathedral, and when his voice broke was sent to the Jesuit Collegio Germanico in Rome; he may also have taken some lessons from Palestrina, who was *maestro di cappella* at the nearby Seminario Romano. In 1569 Victoria became a singer and organist at S. Maria di Monserrato, Rome, from 1571 also teaching at the Collegio Germanico; he was appointed *maestro* there in 1575. During these seven years he published five volumes of sacred music (hymns, *Magnificat* settings, Masses, an Office for Holy Week, and motets). He dedicated his second book of Masses (1583) to Philip II of Spain, and indicated in the preface that he now wished to return home. Philip recalled him and made him chaplain to his sister, the Dowager Empress Maria, at the Descalzas Reales de S. Clara convent in Madrid. Victoria served her from at least 1587 until her death in 1603, thereafter remaining as organist at the convent until his own death eight years later. From 1582 to 1585 he again visited Rome, where he published another book of Masses.

Victoria was the greatest Spanish composer of the Renaissance, and also one of the finest European composers of the time, even though his total output is much smaller than that of, say, Palestrina or Lassus. He was one of the few Spanish composers to have his complete output issued in print during his lifetime. In 1600, a magnificent collection of his Masses, *Magnificat* settings, motets, and psalms was issued in a limited edition of 300 part-books. It contained three of his most popular Masses, the *Missa pro Victoria* (a battle Mass based on Janequin's chanson 'La guerre') and the *Missa Ave regina coelorum* and *Missa Alma Redemptoris mater* (based on his own antiphons). Now, however, Victoria's reputation rests mainly on a handful of motets, such as *Jesu dulci memoria*, *Vexilla regis*, *O magnum mysterium*, *O vos omnes*, and *O quam gloriosum*, and on the *Officium defunctorum*, which he wrote after the death of his patroness. Although he wrote no secular music, a certain amount of madrigalian word-painting can be seen in some of his works—for example in *Vere languores nostros*, with the minor seconds at the word 'dolores', and in *Cum beatus Ignatius*, with its vivid imagery depicting the wild beasts tearing the martyr to pieces.

WENDY THOMPSON

FURTHER READING
Robert Stevenson: *Spanish Cathedral Music in the Golden Age* (Berkeley and Los Angeles, 1961).

Victory, Gerard (*b* Dublin, 24 Dec. 1921). Irish composer. He studied in Dublin at University College and Trinity College. In 1953 he began work as a producer for Radio Telefís Éireann, of which he was appointed music director in 1967. His compositional style was at first based on Irish folk music, but in 1961 he turned to serial methods. Among his works are several operas (to librettos in Erse and in English), a variety of orchestral and chamber pieces, and music for the stage, radio, and films.

PAUL GRIFFITHS

Vidal, Paul Antonin (*b* Toulouse, 16 June 1863; *d* Paris, 9 Apr. 1931). French composer, conductor, and teacher. He studied at the conservatories of Toulouse and Paris, where he was a pupil of Massenet. He was a brilliant student, and won the Prix de Rome in 1883 with his cantata *Le gladiateur*, beating Debussy into second place. Debussy won the prize in the following year, and in Rome he and Vidal became great friends. In 1906 Vidal was appointed conductor at the Paris Opéra: over the years he gave the premières of works by several notable French composers. During the First World War he was musical director of the Opéra-Comique, and for many years taught composition at the Paris Conservatoire. His works include operas and ballets (including the successful *La maladette* of 1893); orchestral, incidental, and chamber music; songs; and cantatas. He also wrote keyboard and theoretical works.

WENDY THOMPSON

Viel (Ger.). 'Much', 'many'; *vielstimmig*, 'many-voiced', i.e. polyphonic.

Vier (Ger.). 'Four'; *vierfach*, 'quadruple'; *viergesang*, 'four-part' (song etc.); *vierhändig*, 'four-handed', i.e. a piano duet; *vierhändiges Tonstück*, a piece arranged for four hands.

Vier ernste Gesänge. See *Ernste Gesänge, Vier*.

Vier letzte Lieder ('Four Last Songs'). Songs by Richard Strauss for soprano or tenor solo and orchestra to poems by Hesse and Eichendorff. Composed in 1948, they are Strauss's last works and a fifth song is unfinished; the title of the cycle was given by the publisher. In order of composition, the songs are: 1. *Im Abendrot* ('In the Sunset'), 2. *Frühling* ('Spring'), 3. *Beim Schlafengehen* ('Falling Asleep'), 4. *September*; Strauss favoured the order 3, 4, 2, 1. The songs were first performed by Flagstad and the Philharmonia Orchestra, conducted by Furtwängler, in London in 1950.

Vierne, Louis (*b* Poitiers, 8 Oct. 1870; *d* Paris, 2 June 1937). French organist and composer. Virtually blind from childhood, he studied organ with Franck and at the Paris Conservatoire. He went on to further studies with Widor, whom he succeeded as organist at St-Sulpice, and as organ professor at the Conservatoire. He also taught at the Schola Cantorum. In 1900 he was appointed organist of Notre Dame, and he died while playing there. His skill at improvisation was legendary. Vierne's pupils included Joseph Bonnet, Marcel Dupré, Duruflé, Albert Schweitzer, and Nadia Boulanger: through them he exercised enormous influence on 20th-century French organ playing.

Vierne's compositions are conservative in nature: they include six organ symphonies (published 1898-1930), *Quatre suites de pièces de fantaisie* for organ (1926-7), two organ Masses, piano pieces, a string quartet, an unpublished symphony, two works for violin and orchestra, and the symphonic poem *Les Djinns* (1912). His brother René (1876-1918) was also an organist and composer.

WENDY THOMPSON

Viertel, Viertel-note (Ger.). 'Quarter', 'quarter-note' or crotchet (♩).

Viertelton (Ger.). 'Quartertone'.

Vierundsechzigstel-note. (Ger.). '64th note' or hemidemisemiquaver (♬).

Vietnam. See *South-East Asian Music.*

Vieuxtemps, Henri (*b* Verviers, 17 Feb. 1820; *d* Mustapha, nr Algiers, 6 June 1881). Belgian violinist and composer. He made his public début at the age of six in Rode's Violin Concerto No. 5. One year later, he became a pupil of Charles de Bériot, who introduced him to the Parisian public and then encouraged him to undertake a German tour, which was a great success. Vieuxtemps also visited the USA, and from 1846 to 1851 taught at St Petersburg. In 1871 he became professor at the Brussels Conservatoire and director of the Concerts Populaires there. Vieuxtemps wrote six violin concertos, as well as concertinos, fantasies, and caprices for violin and orchestra, and the ever-popular *Rêverie*, Op. 22. He was one of the greatest 19th-century violinists, whose powerful tone, flawless technique, and superb bow-control have rarely been surpassed. Eugène Ysaÿe was one of his pupils.

WENDY THOMPSON

Vif, vive (Fr.). 'Lively'; *vivement*, 'briskly'.

Vihuela. Spanish stringed instrument of the Renaissance period. The name (pronounced 'vi-wha*i*la') is the Spanish equivalent of 'viola', but whereas this in most countries denotes a bowed instrument, 'vihuela' has the principal meaning of 'one that is plucked'. The Renaissance vihuela is shaped much like a guitar, with six courses of strings which are tuned in the manner of a lute, i.e. with the major third between the third and fourth courses, not between the second and third as on a guitar. The instrument held a place in Spanish courtly music through the 16th century corresponding to that of the lute in Italy and elsewhere, and has similarly left a large musical repertory written in tablature. Early collections include those by Luis de Milán (1535) and Fuenllana (1554). A technical description is in Bermudo (1555). Guitarists today play this repertory from the tablature, tuning the third string a semitone lower.

The appearance of the vihuela is known from pictures, and by a single example surviving in Paris (Musée Jacquemart-André). Its photograph has often been reproduced: a large example (like the lute, the vihuela varied in size), with a body some 4″ longer than the present Spanish guitar, shallower sides, and five small roses placed in a quincunx instead of one large rose.

The vihuela was frequently termed 'vihuela de mano' ('played with the hand') to distinguish it from its derivative the 'vihuela de arco' ('bowed'), i.e. the *viol.

ANTHONY BAINES

Village Romeo and Juliet, A (*Romeo und Julia auf dem Dorfe*). Opera in a prologue and three acts by Delius to a German libretto by C. F. Keary based on a story by Gottfried Keller. It was first performed in Berlin in 1907. The intermezzo before the final scene (added at Beecham's request to cover a scene change in the 1910 Covent Garden production) is the *Walk to the Paradise Garden*. Fenby arranged an orchestral suite (1948) from the score of the opera.

Villa-Lobos, Heitor (*b* Rio de Janeiro, 5 Mar. 1887; *d* Rio de Janeiro, 17 Nov. 1959). Brazilian composer. The details of his early life are obscure, but it seems that, after his father's death in 1899, he travelled around Brazil and grew to know the country's folk music. He was discovered in 1919 by Artur Rubinstein, who took his music all over the world, and in 1923 he was sent to Europe by the Brazilian government. After a long stay in Paris he returned to Brazil in 1930. He held various official positions in music education and was responsible in 1945 for the foundation of the Brazilian Academy of Music.

He produced a vast number of works, a stream of music diverse in style and in worth. Among his best pieces are the 12 symphonies and the 16 string quartets, as well as the more familiar series of *Chôros* and *Bachianas brasileiras*. These last, in which he achieved an evocative synthesis of Bachian mannerisms with Brazilian folk music, are scored for various combinations, ranging from woodwind duo (No. 6) through an ensemble of soprano and cellos (No. 5) to full orchestra (Nos. 2, 3, 7, and 8); the 16 *Chôros* are similarly various, the name here coming from that for bands of folk musicians in turn-of-the-century Brazil.

PAUL GRIFFITHS

FURTHER READING
Carleton Sprague Smith: *Heitor Villa-Lobos* (Washington, 1960); Vasco Mariz: *Heitor Villa-Lobos, Brazilian Composer* (Gainesville, Florida, 1963).

Villancico (Sp.). In the 15th century, a variety of Spanish secular poetry, generally of a pastoral or amorous nature and often set to music as a popular dance-song. The poetic form was closely related to that of the Italian *ballata* and the French *virelai*: several stanzas (*coplas*) connected by a refrain (*estribillo*), each *copla* being divided into two sections, *mudanza* and *vuelta*. Many of the songs in the late 13th-century *Cantigas de Santa Maria*, though based on religious subjects, are *villancicos* in all but name. Many three- and four-part *villancicos* are found in the great Spanish song-books of the 15th and 16th centuries, such as the *Cancionero musical de Palacio* (*c*.1490–*c*.1520); some are simple and chordal, others contrapuntal in style. Most are love-songs, but some have a religious theme, intended for use at Christmas and other church festivals. The most important early composer of *villancicos* was Juan del Encina, who wrote them for the little dialogues and pastorals with which he entertained his employers.

After 1500 the *villancico* developed along two different lines: as solo songs with vihuela accompaniment, by such composers as Luis de Milán, Miguel de Fuenllana, and Alonso Mudarra; and as unaccompanied part-songs, a type cultivated by Morales, among others. By the mid century the polyphonic *villancico* had absorbed various elements from the Italian madrigal, but during the late 16th century the sacred *villancico* had begun to predominate.

The 17th-century *villancico* developed into a large-scale composition resembling the cantata: the *estribillo* now took the form of an elaborate choral movement with instrumental accompaniment, while the *coplas* were short solo songs accompanied by organ. Important composers of this type of *villancico* were José de Nebra, Cabanilles, and Sebastián Durón, who was criticized by the theorist Benito Feijóo for introducing such instruments as violins and operatic arias into sacred music. Indeed, by the early 18th century the sacred *villancico* had become so unashamedly secular in idiom that it lost its devotional context, and the form died out.

The Baroque *villancico* was cultivated in Latin America, especially Mexico. Such works resembled the cantata, with arias and choruses, and also began to incorporate folk-songs and to develop stylized offshoots such as the *aguinaldo* and the *adoración*.

Villanella (It.). Also known as *villanesca alla napolitana*, *canzon napolitana*, and a host of other synonyms, the *villanella* emerged *c*.1535 as a three-voiced part-song setting 'low' verse in the Neapolitan dialect. Musically it was characterized by its 'ungrammatical' use of consecutive fifths, deliberately guying the elegant harmony of the madrigal. The principal composers of the *villanella* in this form were G. T. di Maio and G. D. da Nola. By *c*.1545 the genre had reached northern Italy, where such composers as Willaert and Donato set Venetian dialect but made the music more respectable by removing the consecutive fifths and satirical content, though it often had lively rhythms and a close relationship with dances. Lassus was the finest composer in this vein, writing sometimes bawdy but always witty *villanelle*. From the 1570s, in the hands of such composers as Ferretti, Marenzio, and de Wert it became still more respectable, losing both dialect and bawdiness and becoming virtually a small-scale madrigal with its own distinctive structure (AABCC).

In this form the *villanella* achieved popularity in Germany and England. Morley was one of its best exponents and described it in his *Plaine and Easie Introduction to Practicall Musicke* (1597) as 'a counterfeit to the madrigal, wherein little art can be shown, it being made in strains, every one repeated except the middle'.

The *villanella* gave way to the aria in the early 17th century, although more recently the term has occasionally been used in a general way to evoke 'olden' times, as in Fauré's well-known song *Villanella*.

DENIS ARNOLD

Villotta (It.). A form of popular vocal music, akin to the *villanella*, which flourished in the period 1520–40. The *villotta* often used folk-songs arranged for three or four voices, and set poetry of an earthy kind, frequently in the dialects of Naples, Venice, Bergamo, or Mantua. It seems to have had connections with dances, sometimes having a 'fa la' refrain which makes it the immediate predecessor of the *balletto*.

DENIS ARNOLD

Vīṇā (Hind.). Stringed instrument of classical Indian music. There are two kinds, that of the North and that of the South. The northern form, by far the older, is composed of a wide bamboo tube about a yard long, to which are attached towards each end two gourds, about 15″ in diameter and open below. The upper gourd rests above the player's left shoulder and the other on the right knee. Along the tube are some 22 high brass frets, the first fret over 1″

tall. These, and the broad sloping bridge, resemble those of the *sitār*, which took them from the *vīṇā*. The arrangement of the steel and brass strings is also similar, but in reverse order. The four main playing strings have a typical tuning of *f'*, *c'*, *g*, *c* (taking the tonic as C), the first of these, the chief melody string, being to the player's right. They are sounded by the right thumb and index, with wire finger-picks. The *meend* (pulling the string sideways on a fret to sharpen the note) is executed towards the left, as on the *sitār*. Of the three unstopped *chikari* strings, softly struck in accompaniment, the highest is placed to the left and struck with the left little finger; the other two, on the other side, are struck upwards with the nail of the right little finger; these are tuned *c'* and *c''*, but the high string varies (*e'*, *a*) according to the *rāga*. There may also be nine or so sympathetic strings (see *Stringed Instruments*, 6) passing under the frets and tuned by pegs along one side.

In Western instrument classification the *vīṇā* is put among 'zithers', having neither separate neck nor built-in body, and also in being evidently derived (it appears first during the early centuries AD) from the simple one-stringed popular instrument which still exists under the name *toila* (see *Instruments, Classification of*).

The southern *vīṇā* looks more like a *sitār*, with large rounded wooden body, the three *chikari* strings all on one side, and different tunings.

See also *Indian Music*, 3a.

ANTHONY BAINES

Vinci, Leonardo (*b* Strongoli, Calabria, *c*.1690; *d* Naples, 27–8 May 1730). Italian opera composer. He studied in Naples, at the Conservatorio dei Poveri di Gesù Cristo, and remained there to become *maestro di cappella* to a nobleman and, from 1725, *pro-vicemaestro* to the royal chapel. From *c*.1722 he received regular commissions for three or more operas a year. Some are attractive comedies in the Neapolitan dialect, while others are *opere serie*, often setting librettos by Metastasio. Vinci was one of the first to add serious elements to comic opera, his longer arias and more subtle treatment of the orchestra starting a line that was to lead to Mozart; his ornamental melody lines over simple harmonic accompaniments give his arias a *galant* flavour. Among his followers were Pergolesi and Hasse. Probably his best-known opera today is *Didone abbandonata* (performed Rome, 1726), his first *opera seria* to a libretto by Metastasio. DENIS ARNOLD

Viñes, Ricardo (*b* Lérida, 5 Feb. 1875; *d* Barcelona, 29 Apr. 1943). Spanish pianist. He studied in Barcelona, but settled in Paris in 1887. He was a close friend not only of his fellow-countrymen Granados and Albéniz, but also of the most notable French composers of the time, especially Ravel and Debussy. He also associated with painters, writers, and intellectuals such as Colette, Cocteau, Max Jacob, and Picasso. Viñes premièred many important French piano works, among them Ravel's *Jeux d'eau* and *Miroirs* and Debussy's *Images*. He also specialized in Russian music, giving the French première of Musorgsky's *Pictures at an Exhibition*, among other works.

WENDY THOMPSON

Vingt-quatre Violons du Roi. Name given to the select band of 24 stringed instruments of the violin family in the service of the French court in the 17th and 18th centuries. The group was officially recognized by Louis XIII in 1626 and was often referred to as the Grande Bande. Often reinforced by 12 wind instruments (the Grands Hautbois), the 24 Violons could claim to be Europe's first regular orchestra. According to French custom there were five string parts: six first violins (*dessus*), four each of the three middle parts (*haut-contre*, *taille*, *quinte*), and six basses (bass violins). In 1656 Lully founded a smaller and even more select band of 16 string players, the Petite Bande.

Viol (rhymes with 'dial'; Fr.: *viole*; Ger. as It., or *Gamba*, plural *Gamben*; It.: *viola da gamba*). Bowed instrument of the Renaissance and Baroque periods, with six strings and with seven gut frets tied round the neck. It has a large and varied solo repertory, but its special pride is the music composed for the family of viols, treble, tenor, and bass, in England from the reign of Elizabeth I up to the Restoration, and constituting without question the most distinguished corpus of purely instrumental chamber music written prior to the 18th century. Few instruments are more perfectly suited to domestic music-making than the viols, for with the frets they should be easy to play in tune; and if able to play one viol it becomes a simple matter to play the others, all being held downwards, the smaller on the legs ('da gamba') and the bass viol between the knees, and all being fingered and bowed in the same way—unlike, say, the violin and the cello, which are fingered quite differently from each other.

1. *Description*. Viols differ in many ways from the instruments of the violin family, the two having been evolved for different musical purposes. Among distinguishing features one notices at once the wider neck of the viol to take the six strings and the proportionately greater length of the neck, giving plenty of room for tying on the seventh fret (one-third of the distance from nut to bridge). One notices also how the shoulders

of the body slope up to the neck; the viol back is flat, bent inwards towards the neck, and the sides are deep, in a treble viol quite twice as deep as in a violin. The body construction is generally kept rather light; belly and back end are flush with the sides instead of overlapping them as in the violin family, and outward points at the centre bouts are lacking, making a plainer outline. The purfling or inlay can, however, be very ornate, often with interlaced trellis designs on sides and back and a floral design on the belly. The internal reinforcement of the body is normally kept light, matched by strings that are fairly thin and low-tensioned. Through all these things the sound of a viol is less strong and the tone more nasal than in the violin family, while the frets (now often of nylon) impart the ring of an open string to every note. But it is the peculiar ability of a set of viols to integrate their sounds, and this is what gives such a pleasing effect when the instruments are played together.

Among further details, the tailpiece is hooked to a wooden post at the base of the body; the soundholes are usually C-shaped; and at the top of the long pegbox a human or animal head is often carved instead of a scroll, or the scroll may take the very beautiful form of an 'open scroll', carved right through from side to side.

2. *Strings and Tuning.* The next great difference from the violins is in the tuning of the strings. This (Ex. 1) follows the scheme of the Renaissance lute. Though the smaller viols rarely need to play on the lower strings, these can add sympathetic resonance. The strings were normally gut, the lowest three overwound, but nowadays nylon (perlon) or steel-core strings also serve quite well. The bow is slightly outcurved and held palm-upwards, inclined with the bow stick nearer the bridge. The second finger is placed between stick and hair with the third finger below the hair, to produce subtle differences in hair tension as the wrist is flexed with each stroke. The stronger stroke is the 'push' stroke (Fr.: *pousser*), the opposite to the down-bow of the violin.

The sizes of original viols vary considerably. Today a treble viol has an average body length of around 15″ (Arnold Dolmetsch, who revived the viol consort in England, used himself to play the treble). The bass viol has double the body length of the treble, around 30″. The tenor varies more (and in former times might be tuned

a tone higher than shown in Ex. 1), but averages some 21″ in the body.

Most of the old viols played today have survived through having at some time been converted into violas or cellos. By so keeping them in use, they have been saved from the ravages of woodworm. Now they have been converted back, while new instruments are much in demand and are all hand-made.

3. *History:* (*a*) *Origins.* It appears that musicians of Spain, in the courts of Aragon in the late 15th century, had sought ways of employing the bow on the guitar-like but lute-tuned and normally plucked *vihuela. How this was effective with the flat bridge of that instrument (as some paintings of the time seem to show) is a mystery. But the idea reached the courts of northern Italy, and it was no doubt there, in the years just before 1500, that the true viol first took shape. An early name for it there is 'viola grande', or, after the Spanish manner, 'viola da arco' (from 'vihuela de arco'). Six of them were being played together by musicians of the d'Este court in Ferrara in 1502. From Italy the instruments reached Germany and France, and then, under the patronage of Henry VIII, England, the players having been brought from Italy; one of his inventories includes 'xix Vialles great and small with iii cases of wood covered with black leather'.

(*b*) *Early Italian Viols.* Nearly all the earliest existing viols are Italian, from the period around 1560 or just after. In shape they are variable, some like a deep-bodied guitar much elongated and sloping to the neck. Others are instantly recognizable as viols if not yet quite of the classic form: the finest examples are Venetian, by the Linarol and Ciciliano families. Much research has been undertaken in recent years to trace early technological trends: a change from arching the belly by bending a plate to a fully carved plate; from side-linings of linen or parchment to wooden strips; from support of the belly by transverse bars as in a guitar to the bass-bar and soundpost principle by the end of the century or later. Further questions relate to early tunings. Two of the earliest accounts, by Ganassi in Venice (1543) and Gerle in Nuremberg (1532), both say that players might use five strings, not six, i.e. like the present tunings minus the first string, or tuning a fourth deeper and omitting the bottom string. Ganassi also

Ex. 1

Treble   Tenor   Bass

refers to playing pitch. Makers built the instruments without standard sizes to go by; should the treble and tenor be on the large size, requiring a lower tuning-pitch, it might be necessary (he says) to match the bass viol to them by moving the bridge downwards to make a longer string-length or to choose thicker strings (methods unheard of since); or, if the treble were too small, to reverse the process.

(c) *Ensemble Playing*. In Europe ensemble viol-playing was largely from part-books of vocal or dance music. Ganassi, referring to the former, stresses how the players should convey the sense of the text through the strength of bowing emphasized by appropriate motions of the head and expressions of the eyes: one can witness good viol-players doing the same today, no doubt unconsciously.

To this playing from vocal part-books England became the great exception, with intricate compositions specifically for viols, first in works of the *In nomine type built upon the *cantus firmus* of this name. To these became added fantasies and pavans in anything from three to seven parts by composers including Tye, Byrd, Tomkins, Coprario, Gibbons, Jenkins, William Lawes, and Locke—a magnificent list. None of it was printed, the demand for this sensitive and elaborate music having been no doubt too limited for printed editions.

A 'chest of viols' would consist of two each of treble, tenor ('mean'), and bass, supplied by the great makers in London such as John Rose, up to 1600; Henry Jaye who worked up to past 1660; and Henry Smith. One of the surviving viols by Rose, a full-sized 'consort bass', has the festooned (scalloped) outline which became favoured by some makers in Germany. The London viol-making tradition came near its end with Barak Norman (d 1740), who also made violins and cellos; his handsome viols (and those in Europe from the same period) show a certain stylized perfection which new-made viols now often tend to follow rather than the more free and vigorous models of Rose and Jaye.

4. *Division and Lyra Viol*. The bass viol had already become important in the 16th century for playing the bass part below varied ensembles of other instruments and voices; or with voice and lute alone, for which music was published. An example is Philip Rosseter's *Booke of Ayres . . . to be song to the Lute, Orpharion, and Base Violl* (1601), with the viol part printed upside down at the top of each page for the player sitting at the opposite side of the table.

Another province of the bass viol lay in the art of playing 'divisions'—variations improvised (or learnt from a book) over a given bass or 'ground', and already given great attention in

Pl. 1. *Viol, from Christopher Simpson, 'The Division Violist'* (1659).

early works on the viol, like Ortiz's *Tratado de glosas* (Rome, 1553). Rather than the full-sized bass viol of the 'chest', a rather smaller instrument was preferred for this and became termed in 17th-century England a 'division viol'—for example, in the title of Christopher Simpson's important work in this field *The Division Violist* (1659). The player might begin by 'breaking the ground' with increasingly fast and elaborate runs and figures, then 'descant' upon it on the higher strings, and finally proceed to do both virtually at once, with wide leaps, while yet aiming for artistic unity over the whole performance.

A different way of solo playing was from tablature, largely using special tunings which, though different from the ordinary, were easily read from tablature (see *Tablature*, 1). Again a smallish bass viol was customary. In Italy and Germany from the 1580s 'viola bastarda' was a term for it, the music amounting mainly to divisions on one part after another of a known composition. The English on the other hand, from the first years of the 17th century (as in Hume's *Ayres* of 1605 and Ferrabosco's *Lessons* of 1609), spoke of playing the viol 'lyra way', and by the mid century the term 'lyra viol' was sometimes used for an instrument coming in size between a bass and a tenor—even though being played alone the instrument could be of any size and the tunings set to any pitch in actual sound. The English tablatures differ considerably from the European, demanding many chords (Ex. 2), some plucking of the strings, and eventually as many as 22 different tunings, mainly to bring open strings on principal notes of the tonality of the music, to vibrate sympathetically while not bowed. Two examples of these tunings are given in Ex. 3: (a) 'The Bandora set', and (b) 'The Harp way sharp', this latter being the one prescribed for Ex. 2.

Playford's *Musicke's Recreation* (1661) tells us that 'lyra viol' had originally, around 1600, meant a viol with wire sympathetic strings (see *Stringed Instruments*, 6): a viol with 12 such strings does exist, by Francis Baker, 1697 (preserved at Brussels; see also *Viola d'amore*).

5. *Other Viol Music*. English 17th-century composers for viols also wrote fantasias and suites for violin with bass viol (one to two of each) with continuo for organ or virginals. German answers to this include sonatas by Buxtehude and others. The bass viol was also extensively employed as a solo continuo instru-

Ex. 3

(a)   (b)

ment, for instance in France by Lully. Marin Marais (1656–1728), a pupil of Lully, rose to be one of the greatest of solo viol players. He composed countless 'pièces de viole' for one, two, or three bass viols with continuo; one solo piece amusingly expresses the apprehensions and agonies of undergoing an operation for gout, with running commentary text beneath the music: short extracts are shown in Ex. 4. For this repertory a seventh string was frequently included in France, tuned to low A. Louis and François Couperin also wrote pieces for viols, and there are three sonatas for bass viol (viola da gamba) by Bach.

There was also about that time a vogue among court ladies in France for the treble viol, especially the new 'pardessus de viole' (i.e. sopranino), with a 13″-long body, tuned a fourth higher and omitting the bottom string: Guerson of Paris is its best-known maker. (Another French instrument, *quinton*, was a kind of five-stringed hybrid with the violin.)

The bass viol continued after this to retain a

Ex. 2

Extract from *Narcissus Marsh's Lyra Viol Book* (c.1660)

(Tuning:)

Pl. 2. A consort of viols, detail from the portrait of 'Herzog August the Younger and his Family' (c.1645) by A. Freyse.

Ex. 4

certain popularity. The famous player and composer Abel gave his last concert in London just before he died, buried with his viol. There, one might say, the viol rested until its revival at the end of the 19th century.

FRANCIS BAINES/ANTHONY BAINES

FURTHER READING

Sylvestro di Ganassi: *Regola Rubertina* (Venice, 1542, Eng. trans. by D. and S. Silvester, 1977); Natalie Dolmetsch: *The Viola da Gamba* (London, 1968); special 'viol' issues, *Early Music*, vi, 1 and 4 (Jan. and Oct., 1978).

Viola (in Eng., formerly 'tenor'; Fr.: *alto*; Ger.: *Bratsche* (derived from the older It. *viola da braccio); It.: *viola*. Also in Ger. Baroque scores often *violetta*). Held like a violin but a little bigger, the viola is the essential middle member of the violin family, both in the orchestral sequence of parts—first violin, second violin, viola, cello, and bass—and in chamber music, most notably in that pinnacle of the genre, the string quartet.

1. *Description.* The viola is made in the same way as a violin but tuned a fifth lower, a', d', g, c, thus having no high E string but instead a low C string. Hence the larger dimensions, also the notation in alto clef, which suits the deeper range (Ex. 1), though where a part rises high a change is usually made to the treble clef. The difference in size from the violin is not very great. Many people would be unable to tell them apart at a quick glance: a difference in body-length of about $2\frac{1}{2}''$—that is, on average, for the viola is not completely standardized in size and can vary by an inch either way.

Ex. 1

To the ear, on the other hand, the viola is at once distinguished, as for instance when in orchestral works the violas emerge from their customary supporting role to announce a theme, as in the Andante of Beethoven's Seventh Symphony, and the furious lead to the recapitulation of the first movement of the 'Emperor' Concerto; or again the slow opening and following Allegro of Tchaikovsky's Sixth Symphony. Equally it is heard as a solo instrument: one could then liken it to the solo contralto voice, warm and moving, though one instinctively feels the soprano voice to be the more sensational and dramatic, and the violin similarly; while next in dramatic power comes the solo tenor voice, with its string counterpart the cello. The viola, of the three, is the least prominent in a concerto; and in symphonies one notices how Brahms will allot a subject to the cellos with the violas supporting in thirds below—but all the better for not being cellos themselves. Time and time again, in music of all kinds, the viola amidst its two brilliant companions controls the hue of the texture, maintaining interest and staving off any risk of monotony.

2. *Dimensions.* The viola's distinctive quality comes not only from the pitch a fifth below the violin, but from the dimensions in relation to that pitch. A geometric analysis based on the Golden Section (as suggested in *Cello*, 1) would put the viola body-length at 1.309 times the

violin (arithmetic mean of 1 and 1.618), making 46.6 cm. or just over $18\frac{1}{4}''$, which, plus the neck, would make a very large instrument for holding like a violin. There have indeed been violas of this size and greater (see below, 4). If also of fine quality, they are able to sound very full and bright on all strings, yet remain open to criticism not only in being too big to manage but also in matching the other instruments too well in tone-quality, i.e. losing the viola sound which generations of musicians have expected and written for.

Equally there have been protests against use of violas that are too small, then tending to sound rather weak on the lower strings. Nevertheless, Mozart, who liked to play the viola in quartets, possessed an instrument said to have had a size of $15\frac{3}{4}''$, fairly typical of his period (see below, 4) though verging on what would now be considered small. Bach also, according to C. P. E. Bach, liked best to play viola in instrumental works since from this position no doubt he could particularly well hear what the others were doing. Like Mozart he, of course, played the violin also. Violinists have seldom found any difficulty (unless at first in reading the alto clef) in playing the viola when they wish to. The distance apart of the left-hand fingers is anyhow changing all the time as the hand moves up and down the string, and the increased distances in the low positions on the viola come quite easily.

3. *Strings.* Viola strings are usually of gut overwound with silver or aluminium, or the top string may be plain gut. Steel strings too are occasionally used. Thicknesses are much as for the violin strings for the same notes, or may be a fraction thicker, but owing to the greater string-length come under rather higher tension. The bow is if anything shorter than a violin bow and around 10 per cent heavier, with a distinctly wider band of hair.

4. *History.* There are no strong reasons for supposing that the viola (rather than the violin) represents the initial germ of the family; previous fiddles had been both large and small, while the viola bears the plain family name only because the Italian suffixes '-ino', and for the bass '-one', leave nothing special for the one in the middle.

Important through the viola's first 150 years was a distinction of function between 'alto' and 'tenor'. A general early 16th-century practice with families of instruments—viols, flutes, etc. —was to supply an instrument of one single pitch between the soprano and the bass for performing both the middle parts. With a wind instrument 'one pitch' necessarily means 'one size', but, of course, with a stringed instrument it need not: it can be made larger for a low tenor resonance while tuned to the same notes as when made smaller for playing alto. Violas were so distinguished up to 1700. Stradivari's patterns and moulds are for the 'contralto viola' (alto) and for the 'tenore viola', and he supplied both to order. Of the contralto, the instruments by him and before him by the brothers Amati and Andrea Guarneri measure around $16\frac{1}{2}''$, the average today. The tenor, as made from Andrea Amati and Gasparo da Salò up to Stradivari, could be 2″ longer in the body, though generally built with a proportionately short neck, bringing a string-length little longer than on the alto and rendering the instrument not too awkward to play in the relatively simple parts written for it.

The distinction is mirrored in much 17th-century writing for five-part strings with two viola parts each in a different C clef: an example is Monteverdi's *Il ritorno d'Ulisse* (1641). Often the alto viola part scarcely goes below violin compass, though sounding 'alto' from the viola dimensions. The tenor meanwhile would go down to the bottom C. How rigorously musicians observed the distinction in the actual instruments might be another matter, but they evidently did so in the French royal orchestra. Here, in the works of Lully and others for the full string band, there is no second violin part, but the viola parts number three—named *haut-contre* (i.e. contralto), *taille* (tenor), and *quinte*, together termed 'les parties' ('de remplissage', 'filling in', these parts being said often to have been written by the composer's assistants)—and these were officially to be performed on violas of three sizes. In England, too, copying the French, the King's Violins in 1634 had two players of low tenor violin, three of tenor, and two countertenor (i.e. *haut-contre*).

With the four-part string writing that afterwards became normal, players continued with the more manageable alto viola, while the magnificent tenors were either 'cut down' in size (see *Cello*, 4a) or preserved as curiosities. New instruments, especially those made in Germany and England, tended to be rather small, even down to $15\frac{1}{4}''$, but the viola is anyhow a fairly powerful instrument and Quantz (1752) noticed that one alone could be a match for six violins (as in a small touring orchestra today). Also in Germany the viola began to emerge as a soloist and the overwound C string had by then come in to help the small size. A solo in a dramatic work by F. T. Richter has been mentioned as perhaps the earliest of the Baroque; then Bach, notably in the Sixth Brandenburg Concerto, where the violas play the lead; many parts for solo viola in the works of Telemann; and an increasing quantity of concertos, culminating in Mozart's *Sinfonia concertante*, K 364, with violin—in which the solo viola is tuned up a semitone to sound brighter (and again in a concerto by Carl Stamitz).

England also contributed, if in a minor way. William Flackton published (1770) a work including 'Solos for a Tenor Violin', 'intended to shew that Instrument in a more conspicuous Manner, than it has hitherto been accustomed; the Part generally allotted to it being little more than a dull Ripiano, an Accessory or Auxiliary, to fill up or compleat the Harmony in Full Pieces of MUSIC'. And before him, the astronomer Herschel had written three viola concertos among his numerous compositions. France wins credit for the earliest Tutor specifically for viola, one of Corette's *Méthodes* for various instruments (this one published in 1782); and later for the full-scale *Méthodes* by Bruni, and by Martinn, of the years 1805-15 and both still in use. Again in France, Paganini, having acquired (from an English dealer) a splendid large Stradivari viola, today preserved in Washington, DC, asked Berlioz for something to play on it. Thus began *Harold in Italy*. The great virtuoso, however, failed to approve, finding too many bars' rest in the solo part, and the finished work was first performed by the Paris player Urhan (see *Viola d'amore*).

Nearly a century later, Lionel Tertis (1876-1975), though for a quite different reason (finding the work too strange), declined the first performance of Walton's Concerto, which many would place among the finest written for the instruments of the violin family. The soloist on that occasion (in 1929) was, in fact, Paul Hindemith, in his day no less celebrated as a viola virtuoso than he became as a composer. The next international celebrity, the Scottish player William Primrose (1904-82), gave in the USA the performance of the Walton which decided Bartók to go ahead with his own concerto for the instrument. He left it, on his death, far from completed, but as afterwards assembled from the composer's sketches, by Tibór Sérly, it now has its place in the standard repertory.

5. *Repertory*. From the 18th century come Telemann's Viola Concerto, concerto for two violas, and many trio sonatas for viola with violin or other instrument; J. G. Graun's sonatas and a concerto; Georg Benda's four concertos; Dittersdorf's Viola Concerto and a concerto for viola and double bass; Vanhal's Concerto; Carl Stamitz's at least three concertos and four *sinfonie concertante* with viola solo; Anton Stamitz's four concertos; and Mozart's *Sinfonia concertante*, K 364 (see above, 4), Trio,

K 498 (with clarinet), and duets with violin, K 423.

The 19th-century repertory includes: Beethoven's Notturno, Op. 42 (arr. from Trio, Op. 8); Hummel's Sonata; Spohr's Duo with violin, Op. 3; Weber's Andante and Hungarian Rondo (for his brother, subsequently published by Weber for bassoon); Berlioz's *Harold in Italy* (see above, 4); Mendelssohn's youthful Sonata; Schumann's *Märchenbilder*, Op. 131 (viola and piano); Anton Rubinstein's Sonata, Op. 49; Brahms's two clarinet sonatas adapted for the viola by the composer, and two *Lieder* for contralto voice, viola, and piano, Op. 91 (intended for Joachim and his wife); and Max Bruch's *Romance* and some works with clarinet.

Among later works are Hindemith's sonatas Op. 11 and Op. 25, his *Trauermusik*, and *Der Schwanendreher*, both for viola and orchestra; Walton's Concerto (see above, 4); and numerous works by British composers written for Lionel Tertis (see above, 4), including Holst's Lyric Movement and Vaughan Williams's Suite for Viola (with orchestra). Among interesting more recent works may be mentioned Britten's *Lachrymae on a Song by Dowland* (with piano) and Stockhausen's *Kurzwellen*, with, among six players, viola with contact microphone. Berio's Sequenza VI also has a solo viola. ·

6. *Experimental Developments*. Before coming to these we may notice that in early times, from the years round 1600, there are several references to an instrument of the family intermediate in pitch between viola and cello, with bottom string *G* or *F* (giving a first-position compass up to about *a'*). In some instances it served apparently in place of the cello (then 'bass violin'), but in others as a tenor, replacing or joining with the viola. In Hizler's singing manual of 1628 a tuning down to *F* is given for the *Tenorgeige*, alongside viola tuning for the *Altgeige*; perhaps the deeper and presumably larger instrument, even if its part never went below viola *c*, could give fine effect in the harmonies of the period. No corresponding instrument seems to have survived—one might expect a body-length approaching 2'—but the well-known painting by Mielich of Lassus with his musicians in Munich shows one player, partly obscured, apparently holding such an instrument, playing it somehow across the knees (see *Instruments, Renaissance*, Pl. 1).

We hear of this pitch again later. In the 1830s a French maker and double bass player, Dubois, made a 'violon-ténor' as a curiosity. But later in Germany, from 1870, some instruments invented by Hermann Ritter became rather more than curiosities: first a large 19″ viola (he was

himself a large man). He called it 'viola alta' and, having impressed Wagner with its resonant sound, led the violas with it at the first full performance of the *Ring*. He had many made, some said to be still in use. Next (1905) he proceeded to the deeper pitch mentioned above: a 'viola tenore' tuned an octave below the violin and literally twice its size, held between the knees; also a 'viola bassa', cello-tuned but twice the size of his viola alta. They were all played together in a quartet, the first violin part remaining on the violin.

In the USA, from the 1920s, F. L. Dautrich resumed such experiments with a 20″ viola played downwards like a viol, a 'tenor' a fourth deeper and looking like a small cello, and a small bass an octave lower, also tuned in fifths. And now, starting from around 1960, again in the USA, a most interesting redesigning of the entire violin family has been in progress under the leadership of Carleen M. Hutchins. Her main precept, more scientific than simple proportional measurement, rests on accurate confirmation by electronic methods of the known fact that with fine violins the main wood resonance-frequency (of the belly) and the main air-frequency (of the contained air) come, respectively, near to the open A and D of the strings. With a viola or cello they normally come higher than the corresponding open strings, with consequences for the tone which have often in the past prompted the view that these two instruments are 'too small' for their pitch. Very briefly, Mrs Hutchins accordingly set about enlarging and adjusting them to bring the resonances down to the second and third open strings as in a good violin, which the instruments should then fully match in richness and quality of sound. So promising were the results that she proceeded to augment the family with other instruments designed on the same principle, keeping the violin as the focal point: thus (naming the bottom string) the enlarged viola ('vertical viola', played downwards, *c*); tenor (body 26″, *G*); baritone (34″ body, 4″ bigger than a cello, *C*); and two basses tuned in fourths (*A'* and *E'*). And above the violin, a soprano (*c'*) and a treble (body under 11″, like a quarter-size violin but tuned an octave above the violin, *g'*). The actual string-lengths of the instruments are not necessarily in strict proportion to body-length but are adjusted to playing demands. The total effect of the instruments in music arranged for them is said to be stupendous, offering immense possibilities for string music of the future—and perhaps even of the past: a cellist is reported to have said, after testing the new baritone, that here at last was something which he could pit against the piano in a trio, provided that he could manage so large an instrument. (The enterprise was first described by Mrs Hutchins in the *Scientific American*, Nov. 1962.) ANTHONY BAINES

FURTHER READING
Sheila M. Nelson: *The Violin and Viola* (London, 1972); Maurice W. Riley: *The History of the Viola* (Ann Arbor, Michigan, 1980).

Viola da braccio, Viola da gamba (It., literally 'arm viola', 'leg viola'). Terms that came into use in Italy in the 16th century to distinguish between the violin family (*da braccio*) and the viols (*da gamba*). Musicians knew, of course, that the bass violin (later the cello) was not played on the arm and that some musicians might hold the smallest viol upwards like a violin. In each group the instruments were defined as soprano, tenore, basso, plus sometimes sottobasso ('sub' or contrabass). After 'violino' became the accepted name for the 'soprano di viole da braccio', the family name became identified with the viola. After the 17th century, when viols were no longer regularly played together as a family, 'viola da gamba' came to be understood specifically as the bass viol. ANTHONY BAINES

Viola d'amore. Instrument of the 18th century made by many of the best luthiers, mainly in Germany, for musicians wishing to play solos on something out of the ordinary. Though now of small musical significance, it is much prized by collectors. It is roughly of viola size, often with wavy outline and wavy soundholes, and played on the arm, without frets. There are six or seven strings generally tuned to a common chord such as D major (or, in Vivaldi's Concerto for viola d'amore, in D minor) to facilitate chord-playing in the key of the piece. Beneath these strings run an equal number of wire sympathetic strings (see *Stringed Instruments*, 6) passing under the fingerboard and tuned as one pleases, for instance to the scale of the music.

The composer Attilio Ariosti published a volume of pieces for viola d'amore in London, 1728. Some think, however, that they may be for a slightly earlier instrument of the same name, apparently a kind of violin with five strings—four metal and one gut—likewise tuned to a common chord. No surviving specimen answers to this description, though a rather later instrument recalls it: the 'cither' viol (or 'sultana') of the Dublin violin-maker Thomas Perry from about the 1760s, with six metal strings tuned similarly to a common chord (compare the lyra viol of the previous century—see *Viol*, 4*b*—and also the English guitar; see *Cittern*, 6). This was outlived by the true viola d'amore, which Leopold Mozart had said sounded especially charming in the stillness of

Viola d'amore by Johann Paul Schorn (Salzburg, 1712) (the type with 14 sympathetic strings).

the evening. Berlioz commended its effect in the part Meyerbeer wrote for it in Act 1 of *Les Huguenots*, played by Chrétien Urham (see *Viola*, 4*b*). The score of *Madama Butterfly* has a 'viola d'amor' offstage at the end of Act 2, playing the long melody in unison with the hidden voices. ANTHONY BAINES

Viola pomposa. An early 18th-century name

met in Germany and apparently borne by two kinds of instrument, both with five strings. One (the larger) was like a large viola with deep sides (a good $2\frac{1}{2}''$ deep in an example of 1720 by Hoffmann of Leipzig) and, with the aid of overspun strings, tuned like a cello plus a high e' string. It was once mistakenly said to have been 'invented by Bach' (compare the violoncello piccolo described in *Cello*, 6*b*). The other (smaller) was like a smallish viola, tuned as a viola plus a high e'' string (thus an octave above the other kind); known equally as *violino pomposo*, it has a part in two works by Telemann and one by J. C. Graun, in each case beside a flute. No actual example of this latter type seems to be known.   ANTHONY BAINES

Violin

1. Description
2. Mechanics
3. Geometrical Foundations
4. Violin-makers
5. Violin-playing
6. History
7. Repertory
8. Some Violin Variants

1. *Description.* The violin (Fr.: *violon*; Ger.: *Violine, Geige*; It.: *violino*; in Eng. the familiar name 'fiddle' is frequently used by violinists and connoisseurs when speaking of the instrument) has for four centuries excelled in practically everything, from solo and chamber music at its greatest heights to playing for folk dances. And beside its supreme qualities as a solo instrument, it has the rare capacity to be combined in large numbers to produce sounds equally captivating, without which the orchestra would never have come into being. Yet, familiar as it is, the violin remains to a great degree acoustically inexplicable. No one really understands completely how it works; it may well for ever hold its mystery as a marvel of the wood-carver's art.

Its essence is the bulging soundbox, $14''$ long, which converts the bowed string vibration into violin sound via a bridge. For this purpose it is lightly constructed yet strong enough to support the downwards force (today around 17 lbs.) created by the tension of the four strings. As with many other stringed instruments, the front, or 'belly', is made from two pieces of spruce joined together, and for the violin these are from a single thick wedge hewn from the tree in such a way that the grain will match identically on either side. After carving and planing the arching, the thickness of the belly will be some 3 mm. in the middle area, diminishing towards the sides. The back is carved from maple, joined in the same fashion, or sometimes from one piece (which can be handsome but does not in itself necessarily add to the value). The thin sides or ribs, of maple bent by heat, are shaped round a wooden mould (a number of such moulds for assembling violins, violas, and cellos are preserved from workshops of the old Italian makers including Stradivari; see below, 4). Strength is gained from the top and bottom blocks inside the body (see *Stringed Instruments*, 2) and from a small block at each of the four corners, and by lining the ribs with narrow strips (side linings) for the belly and back to be glued to them.

The neck and the scroll, this last a form of Ionian volute, are carved from maple, the neck being mortised (or in older days nailed) to the top block. The little semicircle at the root of the neck, visible from the back, is the 'button'. Fingerboard, tailpiece, and pegs are now usually of ebony. The tailpiece is held to the tailpin at the base of the instrument by a loop of black gut. The bridge, of maple, is placed between the nicks of the soundholes, or *f*-holes, and presents a sloping face, slightly curved, on the fingerboard side but perpendicular on the tailpiece side. Fingerboard and bridge are often referred to in playing instructions ('sur la touche' etc.; see below, 5*c*), so it may be useful to give their names in other languages: fingerboard—Fr.: *touche*, Ger.: *Griffbrett*, It.: *tastiera* or *tasto*; bridge—Fr.: *chevalet*, Ger.: *Steg*, It.: *ponticello*.

The purfling round the edges of the violin is usually of black-dyed pear with white poplar between (or in cheap instruments it is inked). The suggestion has been offered that where tone improves with age, one cause is that the glue in the purfling has disintegrated through desiccation to a degree that brings added flexibility of the belly towards the edges. The effect of the varnish upon tone is, however, usually very much overrated. Oil varnish gains in becoming integrated with the wood, while it dries very slowly, whereas spirit varnish dries immediately but has the defect that it shows up every scratch.

2. *Mechanics.* The mechanics of the instrument concern first the bridge, which, unlike that of a lute or guitar, rises high above the soundboard, as it must do for the bow to clear the waist when playing on the outer strings. Then, at some early time in the violin's development—not apparently in the beginning but perhaps nearer the mid 16th century—makers came to incorporate a principle which is encountered in cruder forms (but whether older one cannot say) in flat-topped instruments like the folk fiddles of Eastern Europe and the *crwth, namely a bridge which bears on the soundboard in an

asymmetric manner. This, with the violin, is achieved firstly by the soundpost, a round stick of pine wedged between belly and back just to the tailpiece side of the treble (E-string side) foot of the bridge, its exact position and tightness being very critical. The belly at this point, partially deprived of vibration by the soundpost, then forms a kind of fulcrum for the bridge to rock upon, making the other foot of the bridge do most of the work in communicating vibration. It also exerts a damping effect which eradicates any hollow 'echoing' sound when the strings are bowed—though at the same time reducing the sound when they are plucked to the dry snap of the *pizzicato*.

For the vibration from the bowed strings to be distributed in an optimum manner, also to increase strength under the string pressure, the bass-bar, also of pine, is glued lengthwise beneath the other (G-string side) foot of the bridge.

3. *Geometrical Foundations*. The outline of the violin soundbox is formed by a combination of 12 or more arcs (on each side) of different radii, meeting imperceptibly to make the flowing curves. It may be that scarcely any two violins are exactly alike; yet in an instrument that first took shape in the period of the Renaissance one might expect to find signs of some underlying initial plan involving numerical bases of proportions. The average widths of the body—lower, upper, and middle—follow the proportion of or close to 15, 12, 8, with the lower width coming just under 3:5 to the body-length (this approximately 3:5 to the instrument's original total length). As for the arcs of curvature, to take the lower part of the body for illustration, the flat arc at the base will be centred perhaps half-way up the centre-line, or perhaps at the golden-section ($\frac{1}{2}(\sqrt{5}\pm 1)$) division higher up. The rounded arcs which continue up from this on each side are likely to have a radius of one-fifth of the body-length, their centres at some chosen distance apart. The 'eyes' of the *f*-holes are geometrically placed (at least by Stradivari). Other instruments, like guitars, have arisen from design features evolved from similar geometrical foundations, subsequently changing as time and genius both edged their way ahead.

4. *Violin-makers*. Below is a list of some of the major Italian makers through the greatest period, in order of the year, or approximate year, of their deaths. Some, like the Rugeris and Montagnana, are noted especially for cellos, or for double basses as well. The Italian cities where they worked were appropriate not only because

Pl. 1. Violin ('The Gillott') by Joseph Guarneri del Gesù (Cremona, 1734).

of their favourable climate for seasoning wood and their proximity to the southern slopes of the Alps whence came the slow-growing spruce so essential to the craft, but also because of the trade they did with the East, whence came the gums for making varnish. Cremona figures the most prominently: three generations of the Amati family worked there, Andrea (born early in the 16th century), whom many believe to have first achieved the basic form of the violin; the 'brothers' Antonio and Girolamo; and the latter's son Nicolò; from Nicolò's workshop came Andreas Guarneri, great-uncle of the celebrated Giuseppe Guarneri 'del Gesù'; and other Cremonese makers include Rugeri, Rogeri, Stradivari, and Serafin. Space precludes mention of makers in other countries— such as Stainer (Tyrol), Lupot (France), and Banks (England), to name just three—and of the continuation of the great Italian school in the first half of the 19th century by Pressenda and Rocca, both in Turin.

Instruments by such makers, above all Stradivari and Giuseppe Guarneri del Gesù, have been copiously copied in violins advertised as 'copy of' or 'after' while sent out with a label inside bearing the name of the master with no qualification. No old violin seriously suspected of being a genuine original can pass without certification by a firm of recognized experts, and such instruments are becoming few on the market since the best (some 500 by Stradivari exist) often continue like other great works of art to fall into the hands of collectors, and at a price; one famous 'Strad' sold for £25 in 1794, went for £12,000 in 1954, and might fetch ten times that today.

The great demand for Italian violins of the 18th century as playing instruments has no doubt been because they proved to be best adaptable (see below, 6c) for use in large halls.

Death date		Place of work
1684	Nicolò Amati	Cremona
c.1695	Francesco Rugeri	Cremona
1698	Andrea Guarneri	Cremona
c.1705	Giovanni-Battista Rogeri	Brescia
1710	Giovanni-Battista Grancino (i)	Milan
1720	Pietro Giovanni Guarneri	Cremona
c.1720	Carlo Giuseppe Testore	Milan
c.1730	Giacinto Rugeri	Cremona
1735	Giovanni-Battista Grancino (ii)	Milan
c.1735	Alessandro Gagliano	Naples
1737	Antonio Stradivari	Cremona
c.1739	Giuseppe Giovanni Guarneri (son of Andrea)	Cremona
1742	Matteo Goffriller	Venice
1744	Giuseppe Guarneri ('del Gesù')	Cremona
1747	Carlo Bergonzi	Cremona
1748	Lorenzo Guadagnini	Piacenza
1750	Domenico Montagnana	Venice
c.1758	Santo Serafin	Venice
1762	Pietro Guarneri	Venice
c.1775	Carlo Ferdinando Landolfi	Milan
c.1780	Gennaro Gagliano	Naples
c.1780	Nicolò Gagliano	Naples
1786	Giovanni-Battista Guadagnini	mainly Turin
c.1800	Lorenzo Storioni	Cremona
c.1818	Giovanni-Battista Ceruti	Cremona

The earlier instruments tend to sound softer and sweeter, which is why, at the beginning of the 19th century, the high-arched models of Nicolò Amati fetched the highest prices of all. To meet the huge demand for violins, cheaper instruments have long been produced on the lines of cottage industry—'outworkers' each specializing in some particular component—as in Mirecourt in the Vosges, Mittenwald in Bavaria, and Markneukirchen in Saxony; also (from about the 1860s) in factories inferior violins numbering up to tens of thousands a year

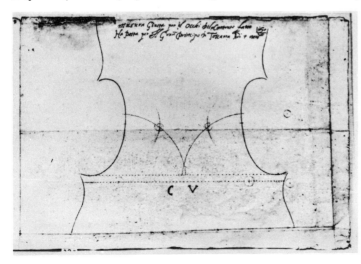

Pl. 2. One of Stradivari's drawings for placing the upper 'eyes' of the f-holes, in this case for a viola (CV, 'contralto viola'). Several 'golden sections' can be detected among the radii and distances.

are assembled with the front and back pressed out by machine, the grain no longer looking the same as when they are carved.

Yet violin-making on the highest plane is far from being in decline: a violinist-cum-connoisseur would continue the above summary list through the 19th century and into the 20th with names that are now very highly thought of. Modern makers will spend three years at one of the violin-making schools that exist in many countries, Britain included, and become capable of producing exact and worthy copies of the old masters. Violins are also made in smaller sizes for children, down to 'quarter size' (with body-length up to 1′), and even smaller for the Japanese Suzuki method of teaching, in which children are taught from the age of two, with fiddles down to 'sixteenth' size and bows to match.

5. *Violin-playing: (a) Strings.* The four strings are tuned in fifths: e'' (first string), a', d', and g (fourth string). In Stradivari's day, and up to the end of the 19th century, they were of gut, with a metal-overwound G string. Today one is most likely to find a steel E string, and the A and D of gut wound with aluminium and the G overwound with silver wire. But strings with a roped steel or nylon core covered with steel ribbon are also in use. Steel strings, higher tensioned than gut, are not successfully tuned by the pegs alone, so require screw attachments ('fine tuners' or 'adjusters') on the tailpiece. (See also *Mute*.) On the relative merits of gut and steel opinions vary. Gut can be ideal when playing the earlier music, especially using the older types of bow, whereas in later music, requiring the most movement of the left hand, gut can become rough on the fingers and, with the modern bow, give less carrying power.

The violin is placed against the collarbone or shoulder and gripped there by the chin against the chin rest (a device which much surprised French audiences when Spohr first introduced it—then a very small one—in 1819). It is supported from below by anything from a small pad to a large wooden frame (shoulder rest). This is to prevent the fiddle drooping towards the floor and to leave the left hand free from supporting it.

(b) Fingering. The fingering is basically diatonic, e.g. on the G string, index finger for A and the little finger D, the same note as the next open string above. For semitones the appropriate finger is shifted up or down the fingerboard. For notes higher than b'' (little finger on the E string in first position) the whole hand must be shifted to a higher position, such as the third (index finger on A) and so on. This, and the return shifts, make one reason for securing the instrument with the chin for the hand to move

freely. Needless to say, since the distances between fingers diminish as the string is shortened, the difficulties of learning to play in tune are formidable, the violin, unlike most other kinds of musical instrument, offering no ready-made guide to the fingers. Higher positions concern the lower strings too, whether to bring a passage better under the fingers, or for the sake of the different sounds produced by the different strings: hence, for example, the instruction 'sul G' or 'sulla 4ᵃ', meaning the whole passage should be played on this string, not proceeding to the next as might be the normal thing to do. Vibrato too is easier if the hand is free—a movement of the left hand or forearm, causing the stopping finger to roll without moving from its place, but causing a fluctuation in pitch which may amount to an eighth of a tone each way. Double-stopping is possible in intervals up to a tenth, or more if the lower note be an open string. In chords played across more than two strings no more than two of the notes can be properly sustained with the bow, and this applies with the polyphonic lines implied in Bach's sonatas for solo violin (Ex. 1).

Ex. 1
Bach: Partita II, Chaconne, bars 88–9

Chords on three or four strings can also be held by the left-hand fingers while the notes are sounded one after another in broken chords (*arpeggiando*), detached or slurred.

(c) Bowing. It is in no sense derogatory to the violin's musical powers to recall, or imagine, how in times before recording and broadcasting the audience at a solo performance was held perpetually alert through eyes riveted upon the movements of the violinist's bow. In sound, the immense variety in tone and effect comes through combination of bow speed and interruption of the speed through the pressure of the right first finger on the stick, and the distance of the bow from the bridge.

The *bow is drawn across the strings with the stick leaning slightly away from the bridge (i.e. further from the bridge than the hair). Where there is reason to indicate the direction of the bow, ⊓ marks a 'down bow' (to the player's right) and ∨ an 'up bow'. 'In the same bow' means notes are played in the same stroke; 'separate bows' means that they are played up and down (or vice versa). 'On the string' means that the bow is not lifted between notes; 'off the string' that it is. The following are among the principal bowings.

legato (It.): slurred notes, played smoothly, on the string (and including the most difficult of all strokes to perfect, where a note is to be continued through a change of bow).

detaché (Fr.): non-*legato* 'on the string'.

martelé (Fr.; It.: *martellato*, the 'hammered' stroke): for *staccato* (in separate bows or, if the music has dots under a slur, in one bow); made by pressure and quick release of the first finger on the stick at the beginning of each stroke, and done in the upper half of the bow.

sautillé (Fr.; It.: *saltato*, *saltellato*): a very fast *staccato* that comes when playing on the string at the middle of the bow, at a point where the spring of the stick causes the bow to bounce without being lifted by the hand.

spiccato (It.): a bouncing *staccato* 'off the string', nearer to the nut and lifting the bow between notes.

portato (It.; used especially where there are lines under a slur over the notes): a light articulation by pressure and release of the first finger without halting the bow; also used for notes repeated in one bow, and occasionally in scale passages (Ex. 2).

Ex. 2

(a)

(b)

All the violin music up to the Classical period can be played with the above uses of the bow, and within a compass of somewhat over four octaves. Then, in the 19th century, virtuoso performers from Paganini onwards brought in a number of tricks.

'Flying *staccato*' (Fr.: *jeté*): notes played many to a bow using its natural bounce (therefore not at the heel).

Ricochet bowings: the bow dropped on to the string and allowed to rebound slowly or fast—often used in *arpeggiando* figures or up and down arpeggios.

Left-hand *pizzicato* in descending passages: plucking with the finger next above the stopping one (marked if necessary by +).

Combination of *pizzicato* and *glissando* where the left-hand finger slides up or down from the stopped note to rest on another note before the sound dies away (marked by *pizz.* under a slur, and since used with great effect by Bartók).

Tremolo (*tremolando*): a very fast shaking at the point of the bow, effected in several ways.

Sul ponticello (It.): playing close to the bridge, for a thinner quality of sound, or *sul tasto* (It.; Fr.: *sur la touche*) over the fingerboard, for a dulled quality.

(*d*) *Harmonics.* Harmonics are rarely met in violin music before the 19th century, but then occur increasingly frequently in solo music and, later, in orchestral writing also. In 'natural harmonics' the finger, instead of stopping the string, lightly touches its surface at some nodal point (see *Acoustics*, 5), whereupon the whole length of the string vibrates at one of its harmonic frequencies. Thus a limited number of high notes are available with a quality which the German term 'flageolet tone' expresses fairly well. Touching at exactly mid point gives the octave harmonic (second of the *harmonic series). Other points lie at one-third, one-quarter, etc., from either end of the string. From the nut end all are obtainable in the first position: the little finger for the twelfth above the open-string note, the third finger for the double-octave, and the second for the next harmonic lying a major third higher still. Alternatively, if playing in high positions, the same harmonics can be obtained at corresponding distances back from the bridge (the whole string vibrating as before). To notate octave and double-octave harmonics one need only write the note (the sound of the harmonic) with a small circle over it (Ex. 3*a*). For other harmonics the diamond (Ex. 3*b*) indicates where to lay the finger on the string in terms of ordinary fingering, and the small note above in brackets may be included to show the actual sound (the string here being the A string).

'Artificial harmonics' enable any note to be played as a harmonic. The first finger stops the string in the normal way for another finger (usually the little) to touch it for a harmonic of the stopped (shortened) string. In Ex. 3*c* the lower note is the stopped note, in this example *d″* on the A string, and the diamond above shows where to touch it, here at the point where the little finger would normally make *g″*, a fourth higher. The resulting harmonic is the double octave (*d″″*) of the stopped note *d″*. Other harmonics are similarly obtainable, writing the diamond a note higher or lower, for the touching finger to divide the string differently.

Ex. 3

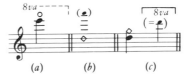

(a)   (b)   (c)

6. *History:* (*a*) *Early Violins.* (For a note on violin predecessors, see *Fiddle*.) One of the earliest pictures—before the instrument assumed the classic form of an Amati or a Gasparo da Salò—is in a wall-painting at Ferrara dated as early as 1505-8, about the time when Andrea Amati was born. The corners do not yet stick out, the bridge is placed far below the *f*-holes (so not yet a soundpost), and there are probably (as one might expect at that time) three strings; the great Italian collector Count Salabue (*d.* 1840) left a rather vague account of an Amati dated 1546 still with three strings. Four strings are first described 10 years later than this, in France (see *Cello*, 4*a*), with particular reference to the violin band of the French court, Europe's first regular string orchestra, playing for dances and ballets. The English court also had one, first manned by Italians (see *Viola*, 4). At Munich a smaller team of seven *viole da braccio* played during dinner, their leader performing on the violin florid divisions 'with such sweetness and clarity that all who hear give pride of place to that instrument' (Trojano, 1569). Later, in operas such as Monteverdi's *Orfeo*, the 10 *viole da braccio* do the greater part of the work on the instrumental side.

A humble illustration of the popularity quickly won by the violin as an instrument for day-to-day music is a manuscript of *c.*1600, at Nuremberg, giving a collection of well-known tunes written out in a four-line tablature, with numbers for the left-hand fingers. Dance music had meanwhile been virtually commandeered by the violin. The Tudor 'country dances', whatever

their origins may have been, by the time of Playford's collection *The English Dancing Master* in the mid 17th century are purely violin music, not at all comfortable for any other instrument to play. The tunes travelled round the country, with corresponding tunes (some the same) in the Low Countries and Scandinavia until every community across northern Europe had its fiddler (in France, 'violonneux') playing at feasts and weddings, eventually to leave a corpus of violin-inspired folk music almost comparable in bulk to that of the concert hall (see, for example, *Scotland*, 2).

(*b*) *Violinist-composers of the Baroque.* Nearly all from Italy, a few of the early names are of 'stunt' men, Farina, and Biagio Marini, both also playing in Germany and (with published works from 1617 onwards) entertaining audiences like successions of double-stops, hitting the strings with the bow-stick ('col legno', revived by Berlioz in the Witches' Sabbath towards the end of the *Symphonie fantastique*), and 'programme' effects like bird and animal imitations (ever since a stock-in-trade encore of popular fiddlers everywhere—trivial no doubt, yet what other musical instrument has the power to do it?).

On the serious level, the great Italian school of composing for the violin rose after the mid century with Corelli to become its most renowned and in his day successful figure. He and his compatriots played with a bow, now sometimes referred to as a 'sonata' bow, as suited to *cantabile* expression as the contemporary

Pl. 3. *Violinist with harpsichordist and singer, painting* 'Florentine Court Musicians' *by A. D. Gabbiani (1652-1726).*

French bow, up to several inches shorter and held differently (thumb under the hair), was to music in dance forms. The English too had been playing in the French way until, as Roger North tells us, the Italian, Matteis, taught them 'to hold the bow by the wood only and not to touch the hair which was no small reformation'. Some 'folk' fiddling, however, has escaped this reform; in Ireland a player may still be seen playing with the violin held low against the chest in the early manner and the bow held in this old way.

A great bonus for performance study are some ornamented versions of slow movements from Corelli's sonatas Op. 5, published by Estienne Roger in Amsterdam near the end of Corelli's life: not personally by Corelli, but 'as he played them'. One notices most the very fast slurred runs of many notes, decorating the plain melody of the original. Two well-known Corelli pupils are Geminiani, who settled in London where he wrote *The Art of Playing on the Violin* (1751, five years before Leopold Mozart's even more informative *Versuch*), and Locatelli, who settled in Amsterdam and is noted for the extreme technical fireworks in his music published as *L'arte del violino* (1733). Tartini in Padua left another notable contribution from this period in his *Arte dell'arco* (1758).

(c) Developments from the Classical Period. Through the revival of Baroque performance everyone has come to know that from the latter part of the 18th century the violin and other instruments of the family began to undergo certain modifications and to be played with a bow of the present kind (see *Bow*, 2), making possible stronger attacks and strokes that depend on elasticity of the stick in a different way from previously (e.g. *martelé*; see above 5c). For stronger string resistance to bow pressure, the bridge height was increased by a good 5 mm., and the angle of the strings over it by up to eight degrees. With the original form of the neck, lying in a straight line with the soundbox (Pl. 5, upper), the fingerboard was canted up by an inserted wedge. To avoid need for a thicker wedge to match a higher bridge (which would make the neck-plus-fingerboard awkwardly thick, hampering fingering, especially on the lower strings) the new form of neck—not entirely new, since one meets it on older bass viols—slopes backward, needing no wedge for the fingerboard, and brings the level of the nut just below that of the belly. The neck is also a little longer. Then, to support the greater down-bearing, and the more so when playing-pitches had started to rise, the old bass-bar was replaced by a longer and deeper one. Practically every older violin has undergone the alteration, first apparently in France, perhaps even as early as the 1770s. Modern reconstruction on original

Pl. 4. Jascha Heifetz.

lines commenced around 1930 in Germany, and now and then an unaltered violin comes to light—though its value for performance will naturally depend on whether it is anyhow a good instrument or not. (Pl. 5 shows such a violin, an unremarkable example but a good one.) Some feel today that when restored to its original lightness of stringing and played with a bow equally light, of the older kind, then learning the violin becomes a pleasure from the very beginning, a harsh sound well-nigh impossible. It gives its best sound more naturally, and in this connection we may remember that 18th-century violinists normally played without *vibrato*, keeping this in reserve as a special nuance, and that some great 19th-century soloists, like Joachim, did much the same.

Contemporary with the onset of these developments (though not specifically a spokesman for them) was Viotti, 'the father of modern violin-playing'. He advanced teaching principles which met increasingly difficult expectations without losing the best in the old Italian tradition. He occupies a place of extraordinary importance in the master-pupil chains of great soloists up to the present time. Himself a great-grand-pupil (as it were) of Corelli, via Pugnani, he taught, to name but one, Rode of France, from whom the line continues to no less than Joachim (for whom Brahms wrote his Violin Concerto), Auer (founder of the great Russian school), Heifetz, and Menuhin, each of whom has in turn unfolded fresh aspects of style, technique, and repertory. A recording by Joachim, perhaps the oldest in existence of past great players, of a Brahms Hungarian dance strikes one not only with its small use of *vibrato* but with its considerable amount of *portamento* (*glissando*), common enough until (it has been said) soloists developed a distaste for it as they increasingly heard themselves on records. But this is also partly fashion. Connoisseurs of solo violin-playing on records and in the memory say

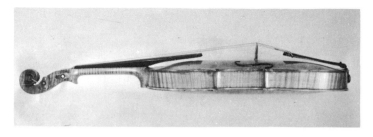

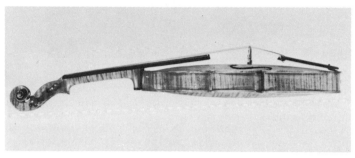

Pl. 5. Above: *an anonymous early 18th-century English (or Scottish) violin in its original condition; note surface of neck in straight line with edge of body (the short fingerboard elevated by a wedge).* Below: *violin by the brothers Amati (1618), an older violin but refitted with modern neck and fingerboard.*

that there have been at least five recognizable changes in style during the 20th century.

As always, difficult things that a great player can do are likely to appear in a contemporary concerto. Beethoven's Violin Concerto abounds with passages that can be found in solo pieces by Viotti, Rode, and their contemporary Kreutzer—for example the very opening two bars of the solo part. The concerto was, in fact, first performed by Franz Clement, who had been a child prodigy and gave Beethoven advice on the part. It is touching—and in a way in keeping with the violin's demon versatility—that having given his fine performance of one of the greatest musical works of all time, with improvised cadenzas included, he should have entertained the audience in the second half of the concert by playing a piece with his violin held upside down.

7. *Repertory:* (a) *Baroque.* From Italy come four sets of trio sonatas and one set with cello by Corelli; some sonatas and the famous but doubtfully attributed Chaconne of T. A. Vitali; numerous solo violin concertos from Vivaldi, of which Op. 8, *Il cimento dell'armonia*, contains the *Four Seasons*, and also concertos for two, three, and four violins and sonatas for one or two. Other sonatas include those by Geminiani, F. M. Veracini, and, especially, Locatelli and Tartini (two books, including the 'Devil's Trill' Sonata).

From other countries come, among other works, Purcell's Sonata in G minor and his two sets of sonatas with two violins (including No. 9 in F, the 'Golden Sonata'); Bach's two concertos for solo violin, in A minor and E major respectively, and his Double Violin Concerto in D minor, six solo sonatas (partitas), two with

continuo, and six sonatas with klavier; some sets of sonatas for one or two violins (or other instruments) by Handel; Telemann's sonatas and sonatinas; and Leclair's sonatas.

(b) *Classical.* Haydn wrote violin concertos in G and in C and a sonata in G; Mozart six concertos, the Rondo K 373, a *Sinfonia concertante* in E♭ (with viola), and 34 sonatas; Beethoven the Violin Concerto, Op. 61, two Romances, Op. 40 and Op. 50, the Triple Concerto, and sonatas including Op. 23 in A minor, Op. 24 in F (the 'Spring' Sonata), the three sonatas of Op. 30, Op. 47 in A minor (the 'Kreutzer' Sonata), and Op. 96 in G. Paganini's 24 Caprices are well known for their display of violin technique. Schubert wrote four sonatas and the *Rondo brillante*, Mendelssohn the Violin Concerto in E minor and four sonatas, and C. de Bériot some 10 violin concertos.

(c) *Romantic and 20th-century.* The following list gives some of the best-known works from this period, proceeding in order of composers' births. Vieuxtemps, concertos etc.; Franck, Violin Sonata in A; Lalo, *Concerto russe* and *Symphonie espagnole*; Brahms, Violin Concerto, Double Concerto, three sonatas, Op. 78, Op. 100, Op. 108; Saint-Saëns, concertos and sonatas; H. Wieniawski, Violin Concerto in D minor, fantasies, etc.; Bruch, three concertos, including the well-known one in G minor; Tchaikovsky, Violin Concerto in D; Dvořák, Violin Concerto in A minor, Sonata in F; Grieg, three sonatas; Fauré, Violin Sonata in E minor Op. 108; Janáček, sonatas; Chausson, *Poème*; Elgar, Violin Concerto in B minor, Sonata in E minor; Debussy, Violin Sonata in G minor; Delius, sonatas; Glazunov, two concertos;

Sibelius, Violin Concerto in D minor; Vaughan Williams, *The Lark Ascending*; Schoenberg, Fantasia, Op. 47; Kreisler, many works; Ireland, two sonatas; Bartók, Violin Sonata for unaccompanied violin, several duos, two sonatas with piano; Enesco, sonatas; Stravinsky, Violin Concerto in D; Szymanowski, two concertos, sonatas; Webern, Four Pieces, Op. 7; Berg, Violin Concerto; Prokofiev, two concertos, two sonatas; Hindemith, Violin Concerto, sonatas; Walton, Violin Concerto; Messiaen, Theme and Variations, *Fantaisie*.

8. *Some Violin Variants:* (*a*) *Kit* (Fr.: *pochette*). The dancing-master's fiddle; see *Kit* for details.

(*b*) *Violino piccolo.* Occasionally named in German Baroque works. A cantata by J. Michael Bach, an older cousin of J. S. Bach, names a 'Quart Violino, non di grosso grande' ('not of big size') tuned, as the transposition of the part shows, a fourth above the violin. Bach himself writes for violino piccolo in the First Brandenburg Concerto, here tuned a minor third above the violin. Nowadays a three-quarter size violin is often used.

(*c*) *Norwegian Harding Fiddle* (Norwegian: *Hardangerfela*). A violin of 17th-century model, usually decorated with much inlay, and carrying four or more metal sympathetic strings (see *Stringed Instruments*, 6). These may be tuned to the tonic chord of the music, which consists mainly of dance tunes, played with much double-stopping and 'drone' notes. Grieg knew it well.

(*d*) *Experimental Models.* From early in the 19th century, at first mainly in Paris, there have been experimental designs of violin quite different in shape from the normal, yet claimed to produce good violin sound. Among them a more or less triangular design by the French acoustician Savart (1791-1841) is not forgotten, inasmuch as the model has had a limited revival for the making of fiddles by school children.

(*e*) *Stroh Violin.* With a metal diaphragm and horn, named after its inventor, Augustus Stroh (1828-1914), an acoustician and electrical engineer originally from Frankfurt but becoming a naturalized British subject and colleague of Sir Charles Wheatstone (see *Concertina*). Patented in London in 1899, it is a violin in which the body is replaced by a shallow, circular wood soundbox, the top of which is formed by a corrugated aluminium diaphragm. The motion of the bridge is communicated to this by a rocking lever. From the bottom of the soundbox issues a metal horn, to direct the sound forwards, and often a smaller horn points backwards for the player to hear the notes better. *The Strad* magazine in 1902 describes it as sounding 'as

loud as four ordinary violins. The G string is a dream. It possesses the deep rich quality of a fine cello A.'

It was used for recording purposes by violinists as celebrated as Jan Kubelík, and also in dance orchestras and by street musicians. Today there are fiddlers who prefer it for playing folk dances. Stroh also designed one-string fiddles with diaphragm and horn, later copied by others as 'phonofiddle'. (This should not be confused with *Strohfiedel*, i.e. 'straw fiddle', an ancient German name for the *xylophone, with the bars laid on straw bundles.)

(*f*) *Mute Violin.* Made in former centuries for practising the violin without disturbing other people in the house: usually like a violin but without the back, and with no sides save for a small portion to support the neck.

ANTHONY BAINES

FURTHER READING
Leopold Mozart: *Versuch einer gründlichen Violinschule* (Augsburg, 1756), trans. by Edith Knocker as *Treatise on the Fundamental Principles of Violinplaying* (London, 2nd edn, 1951); David D. Boyden: *The History of Violin-playing from its Origins to 1761* (London, 1965); Sheila M. Nelson: *The Violin and Viola* (London, 1972); Margaret Campbell: *The Great Violinists* (London, 1980).

Violone. 1. A name used today chiefly for a double-bass viol, with six strings tuned upwards from low *G'*, a fifth deeper than the bass viol. A few fine original instruments of this description are preserved, the earliest of 1585, by Linarol of Padua, with a body length of 39″. In its day it would have been called in full 'sottobasso di viola da gamba'. The 'Great Dooble Bass' in one of Orlando Gibbons's fantasias for viols was perhaps something similar.

2. In the 16th and 17th centuries, 'violone' was used more broadly, sometimes in the plural for the violin family, then often in Italy for the early cello. In German Baroque scores, including those of J. S. Bach, it refers to the double bass (of the violin orchestra).

ANTHONY BAINES

Virdung, Sebastian (*b* Amberg, 19-20 Jan. *c.*1465; *d* after 1511). German theorist and composer. The son of an innkeeper, he studied at Heidelberg University and took music lessons from the *Kapellmeister* to the Palatine court there. Until about 1505 he sang alto at the Heidelberg chapel, and he seems to have become *Kapellmeister* there some time after 1495. In 1507 he was appointed a succentor at Konstanz Cathedral, but he was dismissed a year later and moved to Basle. It was there that his celebrated treatise *Musica getutscht* was published in 1511. This is the oldest printed manual on musical instruments, the first part dealing with the classification of the different families, and the second with their notation in tablature (for keyboard, strings, and wind). *Musica getutscht* provides much valuable information (despite some irregularities in the engravings) on instruments and their use in the late 15th and early 16th centuries.

WENDY THOMPSON

Virelai (Fr.). One of the three standard poetic forms used for *chansons* of the 14th and 15th centuries (see also *Ballade*; *Rondeau*). It received definitive expression in the works of Guillaume de Machaut, of which 'Plus dure qu'un diamant' is a typical example:

> *Plus dure qu'un dÿamant* ⎫ MUSIC
> *Ne que pierre d'aÿmant*
> *Est vo durté,*
> *Dame, qui n'avez pité* ⎬ A
> *De vostre amant*
> *Qu'ocies en desirant*
> *Vostre amitié.* ⎭
>
> Dame, vo pure biauté ⎫
> Qui toutes passe, à mon gré, ⎬ b
> Et vo samblant ⎭
> Simple et plein d'umilité ⎫
> De douceur fine paré, ⎬ b
> En sousriant. ⎭
>
> Par un acqueil attraiant, ⎫
> M'ont au cuer en regardant
> Si fort navré
> Que ja mais joie n'avré, ⎬ a
> Jusques à tant
> Que vo grace qu'il atent
> M'arez donné. ⎭
>
> *Plus dure* etc. ⎬ A

A musical setting in two clear sections (a and b) is used for the *virelai*. To the first section is allocated the refrain (the opening and closing group of lines, shown in italics) and the third group which has the same structure. The second musical section, heard twice, carries the second group of lines. The resulting musical form is AbbaA (capitals indicate the refrain). In fact Machaut's *virelais* have three stanzas, so the full form is Abba, Abba, AbbaA.

Although some later 14th-century *virelais* employed three stanzas (for example Solage's 'Tres gentil cuer'), most apparently have only one or two. Many are examples of the 'realistic *virelai*', in which reserved expressions of courtly love, the normal subject for *chanson* texts in whatever form, are replaced by more lively and dramatic imagery, such as the urgent appeals for rescue from the fire of love in the anonymous 'Rescoes rescoes'. Many such pieces are concerned with a lover's feelings at the approach of Spring (for example, the anonymous 'Contre le

temps' or 'Je voy le bon tens venir') and several include imitations of bird-song, as in Vaillant's 'Par maintes foys' or Senleches 'En ce gracieux temps' (Ex. 1).

Ex. 1

Jacob Senleches, virelai *En ce gracieux temps*, bb 41–45

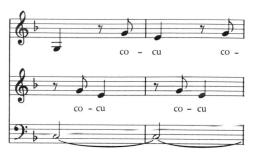

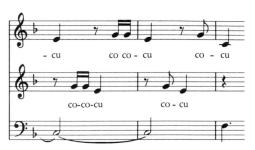

The *virelai* was almost completely neglected by early 15th-century composers, but later enjoyed a revival, particularly in the works of Antoine Busnois, as a single form known as the **bergerette*.

PETER DAVIES

Virginal(s). An early plucked keyboard instrument. See under *Harpsichord*.

Virtuoso. Generally, a person who has a special knowledge of or interest in the fine arts; more specifically, one who excels in the technical skills of an art, especially music. Before the 18th century, the term 'virtuoso' was used of musicians in the former, more general sense as well as the latter, and with reference to composers and theorists as well as to performers. Throughout the 16th and 17th centuries Italian composers used it when commending each other (or themselves) for court or ecclesiastical appointments. The finest instrumentalists and singers were summoned to perform at all the courts of Europe, and though comparatively few reports of such occasions survive, the music that they are known to have performed attests to their considerable virtuoso skills. The Italian Renaissance courts constantly vied with one another over the excellence of their resident instrumentalists and, particularly, singers (e.g.

the brilliant Concerto delle Donne of Ferrara, whose virtuosity prompted court composers to write pieces specifically to demonstrate their talents; see *Renaissance*, 2). Moreover, the rise of opera and oratorio in the early 17th century led to an increasing regard for virtuosity in a solo singer. Instrumentalists who were renowned as virtuosos later in the 17th century include the violinists Carlo Farina and Heinrich Biber, and the keyboard composers Buxtehude and Froberger in Germany, Frescobaldi in Italy, and Bull in England.

With the growing importance of operatic and concerto soloists in the 18th century, the virtuosity of individual performers was highlighted still more. Italian opera proved to be a fine vehicle for virtuoso solo singers. Handel's Italian opera seasons in London attracted the best singers in Europe, who endeared themselves to the public with brilliant displays of technique in arias written specially for that purpose; among them were the castratos Farinelli (1705-82) and Senesino (*d c.*1759), and the rival sopranos Francesca Cuzzoni (*c.*1698-1770) and Faustina Bordoni (1700-81).

With the rise of public concerts, virtuoso instrumentalists were much in demand; violinists like Giuseppe Tartini and Francesco Veracini wrote a good deal of brilliant solo music principally to demonstrate their skills as executants, as did Domenico Scarlatti, renowned for his harpsichord playing throughout Europe. Mozart, who from the age of six was taken by his father round the courts of Europe to display his musical virtuosity, is the most notable example of innumerable child prodigies whose performing skills were recognized and exploited from an early age; often they failed to make successful professional careers later in life.

In the early 19th century, solo performers were prized more for sheer technical mastery than for qualities of musicianship: anyone who could play the most demanding music with apparent ease and rapidity was hailed as a virtuoso, whether or not he had interpretative gifts. That attitude soon sparked off a reaction against virtuosity for its own sake among serious Romantic musicians and critics, like Liszt and Schumann.

Nevertheless, the 19th century, perhaps more than any other, was to be the true age of the virtuoso. Liszt himself held his audience's rapt attention as he amazed them with his brilliant piano technique; Chopin was another child prodigy who entranced his public throughout his life; Paganini dazzled and delighted concert-goers with his pyrotechnics on the violin. Later in the century, performers (and their concert agents) were able to amass considerable wealth from making concert tours and guest appearances, especially after the USA became part of the standard recital circuit and businessmen were ready to exploit the public's love for artistic personalities. Among the more successful of countless 19th-century virtuosos were the violinists Joseph Joachim (1831-1907), Henry Vieuxtemps (1820-81), Pablo de Sarasate (1844-1908), Henryk Wieniawski (1835-80), and Eugène Ysaÿe (1858-1931); the pianists Anton Rubinstein (1829-94), Theodor Leschetizky (1830-1915), Moscheles, and Isaac Albéniz (1860-1909); and the singers Jenny Lind (1820-87), Adelina Patti (1843-1919), Nellie Melba (1861-1931), Jean de Reszke (1850-1925), and Mattia Battistini (1856-1928).

The early 20th century saw a continuation of the virtuoso phenomenon with such performers as Fritz Kreisler (1875-1962), Jascha Heifetz (*b* 1901), Pablo Casals (1876-1973), Ignacy Jan Paderewski (1860-1941), Rakhmaninov, Josef Lhévinne (1874-1944), Dohnányi, Artur Rubinstein (*b* 1887), Vladimir Horowitz (*b* 1904), Amelita Galli-Curci (?1882-1963), Enrico Caruso (1873-1921), and Fyodor Ivanovich Chaliapin (1873-1938) commanding the same sort of public adulation as had their predecessors. More recently, however, the term 'virtuoso', perhaps suffering from over use, has acquired somewhat patronizing and even disparaging overtones. It is sometimes used to describe popularizing performers who stress exhibitionism and showmanship in order to reach a wider audience, or to describe compositions of shallow invention that demand technical brilliance but little else. Nevertheless, although the term itself may be devalued, the greatest performers of the day, combining technical mastery with interpretative powers of the highest order, are no less 'virtuoso' than were their predecessors.   JUDITH NAGLEY

Visigoth Rite. See *Liturgy*, 2a.

Vision of Aeroplanes. Motet by Vaughan Williams for mixed chorus and organ to a text from Ezekiel 1. It was composed in 1956.

Vision of St Augustine, The. Work by Tippett for baritone, chorus, and orchestra. It is a setting of texts from St Augustine's *Confessions* and from the Bible, and was composed between 1963 and 1965.

Visions de l'Amen. Suite for two pianos by Messiaen, composed in 1943. The seven movements each have a title, for example 'Amen de la création', 'Amen du désir'.

Visions fugitives (*Mimolyotnosti*; 'Fleeting Visions'). Twenty pieces for solo piano, Op. 22, by Prokofiev, composed between 1915 and 1917.

Vitali. Italian family which produced at least three generations of musicians in the 17th and 18th centuries. The most important composers were Giovanni Battista and his son, Tomaso Antonio.

Giovanni Battista Vitali (*b* Bologna, 18 Feb. 1632; *d* Bologna, 12 Oct. 1692) was a singer and string player at the famous church of S. Petronio, Bologna, in 1658 and soon after became a member of the Accademia Filarmonica. He became *vicemaestro di cappella* at the Modena court of Duke Francesco II d'Este in 1674 and remained there until his death. His instrumental works are both attractive and important in the history of the trio sonata, especially of the *da camera* type with its emphasis on dances and idiomatic writing for the violin. His oratorios are also worthy of revival.

Tomaso Antonio Vitali (*b* Bologna, 7 Mar. 1663; *d* Modena, 9 May 1745) was a member of the court orchestra at Modena when he was only 12, and later became its leader, spending all his life in the court's service. He was more of a virtuoso violinist than his father and his works, in the style of Corelli, are all instrumental. The attribution to him of the famous and popular Chaconne for solo violin and continuo has recently been cast in doubt.   DENIS ARNOLD

Vitali, Filippo (*b* Florence, *c.*1590; *d* ? Florence, after 1 Apr. 1653). Italian composer. He seems to have remained in Florence, apart from visits, until around 1631, when he was nominated for a place in the papal choir. He sang there from 1633 to 1642, when he was appointed *maestro di cappella* at S. Lorenzo, Florence.

Vitali wrote the first opera to be staged in Rome, *Aretusa* (performed 1620), which was influenced (as he himself admitted) by the Florentine opera composers. His most important works, despite their basically old-fashioned style, are probably the cycle of 34 *Hymni* (Rome, 1636), using the revised Latin texts commissioned by Pope Urban VIII. In contrast, his secular vocal music, which includes five volumes of *Musiche*, three of *Arie*, and one called *Concerto*, is in the new monodic style of the Baroque.   WENDY THOMPSON

Vite, vitement (Fr.). 'Quick', 'quickly'.

Vitry, Philippe de (*b* Paris, 31 Oct. 1291; *d* Paris, 9 June 1361). French composer, and one of the leading intellectuals and music theorists of his time. He studied at the Sorbonne, and subsequently worked at the French court as a diplomat and political adviser, before being created Bishop of Meaux in 1351. Vitry is mentioned by many of the leading writers of the period, and Petrarch paid homage to his skill as a poet and philosopher, while most 14th-century music theorists readily acknowledged their debt to his writings. His outstanding achievement, the treatise *Ars nova* (*c.*1323), introduced important new concepts to the method of notating rhythm, allowing for greater accuracy and sophistication. His system ranks as one of the landmarks in the early development of mensural notation, which remained in use until *c.*1600 (see *Notation*, 5). Little of Vitry's music survives today; although some 14 motets have been attributed to him, all but four are of questionable authenticity. Most are pioneer works in the development of *isorhythm, one of the characteristic technical procedures in use in France during the period of the *Ars Nova.

JOHN MILSOM

Vivace (It.). 'Vivacious', 'lively'; *vivacetto*, 'rather lively'; *vivacissimo*, 'very lively'.

Vivaldi, Antonio (Lucio) (*b* Venice, 4 Mar. 1678; *d* Vienna, 28 July 1741). Italian violinist and composer.

1. *Life*. Apart from the fact that he was the first of six children of a violinist in the orchestra at St Mark's, Venice, little is known of Vivaldi's early life. He was tonsured in 1693, and thereafter proceeded to the full priesthood in 1703; he was known as the 'red priest' because of the colour of his hair. Also in 1703 he was absolved from saying Mass on the grounds of suffering from an illness which he described as a 'strettezza di petto' and which seems to have persisted throughout his life. Later that year he entered the service of the Conservatorio della Pietà, an orphanage for girls in Venice which placed special emphasis on a musical education and which had an excellent choir and orchestra. His first duties were those of a violin teacher, but he was also to compose a great deal of music for the Pietà, including some oratorios which were usually given during Lent. At this stage he was evidently well liked by the governors of the orphanage, who gave him various sums of money in addition to his regular salary; they also granted him leave of absence in 1713, probably to compose and produce his first opera, *Ottone in Villa*, in Vicenza.

It was at this time that Vivaldi's fame began to spread considerably, mainly as a result of the publication of his Op. 3, *L'estro armonico*, by Estienne Roger (Amsterdam, 1711). These 12 concertos for one, two, and four solo violins were greatly admired, not least in Germany, where Bach copied and arranged several of them. Vivaldi now seems to have devoted much of his energy to writing operas and travelling throughout Italy to produce them. From 1718 he was in the service of the governor of Mantua; he spent several years in Rome; while he often

Canaletto, Venice: La Riva degli Schiavoni ove sorgeva l'Ospedale della Pietà, at the time of Vivaldi.

returned to Venice to produce operas (and act as impresario) at the Teatro S. Angelo. He was closely associated with an outstanding singer, Anna Girò (who may well have been his mistress), writing parts especially for her. Naturally this peripatetic activity did not please the governors of the Pietà, who, however, came to terms with it, in 1723 signing a contract for him to provide them with two concertos a month, rehearsing them if and when he was in Venice. Finally, in 1735, Vivaldi was appointed *maestro de' concerti* to the conservatory, and this time his contract stated, somewhat optimistically, that he no longer had 'ideas of going away as he had done in the past'. This was probably a final attempt to keep Vivaldi on a full-time basis, and three years later, when his habits showed no sign of changing, the contract was not renewed; he did, however, continue to supply the Pietà with music.

A major event in Vivaldi's final years was a visit to Amsterdam, where he was considered a notable attraction in the celebrations of the centenary of the Schouwburg Theatre. He went back to Venice in 1739, and composed some music for a grand festival which took place in March 1740 in honour of a visit from the son of the King of Poland. The reason for his presence in Vienna the following year is not known, but this celebrated composer was buried there in a pauper's grave on 28 July 1741. As a contemporary wrote, 'Vivaldi had earned at one time more than 50,000 ducats, but his inordinate extravagance caused him to die poor in Vienna'.

2. *Music*. Vivaldi was of enormous importance in the development of violin playing and in the history of the concerto. He was the prototype of the modern virtuoso, capable of bewitching an audience with his skill as a performer. To quote one observer, 'Vivaldi performed a solo accompaniment [to an aria] admirably, and at the end he improvised a fantasy [i.e. cadenza] which

Vivaldi, caricature (1723) by Pier Leone Ghezzi.

quite confounded me, for such playing has not been heard before and can never be equalled; he played his fingers but a hair's breadth from the bridge, so that there was hardly room for the bow. He played thus on all four strings, with imitations and at unbelievable speed'. This report is confirmed to some extent by Vivaldi's compositions, which include high passages, cross-string writing, and a great variety of bowing techniques. He was fascinated by the range of possibilities of the sound of the violin— as can be seen in the slow movement of his B minor concerto for four violins from *L'estro armonico*, where the effect lies solely in the different methods of spreading a chord and bowing it.

This interest in sound and technique is reflected in all his concertos. Those using a group of soloists stem from the *concerto grosso* but are nearly always treated as solo works, each player in turn having a significant solo passage, while the solo concertos exploit to the full the contrast between the virtuoso and the orchestra. Though his starting-point was the older four-movement *sonata da chiesa*, Vivaldi heralded the three-movement plan of the Classical concerto, reducing Corelli's slow first movement to the role of a slow introduction on the few occasions it is used at all. The true 'first movement' is nearly always in *ritornello* form, and Vivaldi is notable for the rhythmic drive of his opening themes and for his imaginative use of the opening themes later in the movement. The second movements are usually slow, and in place of the brief and inexpressive bridge passage of most of his predecessors Vivaldi brings to them the art of the opera composer, writing what are in effect passionate arias which show off the sweet *cantabile* of the violin, the orchestra providing little more than an introduction and postlude and harmonic support. Finales are usually light, fairly quick movements, sometimes with a hint of dance rhythms, which presage the last movements of the Classical symphony.

Although his concertos were and remain the foundation of his fame—especially the enormously popular *Four Seasons*—Vivaldi was also an opera composer of some distinction. While it would take staged revivals to be able to judge the dramatic merit of his surviving 21 operas, individual arias often display the virtues of his instrumental music, with strong rhythms, interesting phrase structure, and virtuosic writing. Of the music he wrote for the girls of the Pietà much is for solo voices, including an astonishing series of motets for either soprano or alto in which the 18th-century *penchant* for vocal fireworks is indulged to the full (the pupils of the conservatory sometimes went on to become opera singers). Some of these works use the well-

drilled orchestra to good effect, placing important thematic material in the violin rather than the choral parts. This music is well worthy of revival.

Vivaldi has been described by Dallapiccola as a composer of 'a single concerto 600 times' (in fact Vivaldi's concertos number around 500), and it is true that some of his music is rather perfunctory. But much is unpredictable in phrasing and in sonorities, passionately romantic in slow movements, and vigorous and spare in the best of the *ritornello* movements. Bach transcribed and copied an ample selection of his works, and his own concerto style as seen in the solo works and the Brandenburg Concertos shows signs of Vivaldi's influence. Indeed, few instrumental composers of the early 18th century could avoid it.   DENIS ARNOLD

FURTHER READING
Michael Talbot: *Vivaldi* (London, 1979).

Vive, vif (Fr.), **vivo, vivido** (It.). 'Lively'.

Viviani, Giovanni Buonaventura (*b* Florence, 15 July 1638; *d* ? Pistoia, after Dec. 1692). Italian composer. He was director of music at the Innsbruck court between 1672 and 1676, and the following year returned to Italy as musical director and harpsichordist at theatres in Venice and Rome; he was responsible for a revival of Cavalli's *Scipione affricano* as well as for performances of his own operas. From 1678 he also spent some time in Naples, again producing operas. He is last heard of as *maestro di cappella* of Pistoia Cathedral in 1692. As well as operas he composed oratorios and cantatas, and two of his sonatas (Op. 4, 1678) belong to the slender repertory of works for trumpet and continuo.   DENIS ARNOLD

Vl. Abbreviation for 'violin'.

Vlad, Roman (*b* Cernăuţi, Romania, now Chernovtsy, Ukraine, 29 Dec. 1919). Italian composer and writer on music, of Romanian birth. He studied at the Cernăuţi Conservatory and with Casella at the Accademia di Santa Cecilia, Rome (1938-41). Since then he has been active in Italy as a composer, pianist, critic, teacher, and promoter of new music. His works make rather conservative use of serial techniques and include operas, ballets, cantatas, and orchestral pieces. He is author of the book *Stravinsky* (London, 1960, 3rd edn 1978).
          PAUL GRIFFITHS

Vocalise (Fr.; Ger.: *Vokalise*; It.: *vocalizzo*). A melody sung without text, i.e. on a vowel sound. The term embraces vocal technical exercises (see *Solfeggio*) and is also used disparagingly to imply technical display for its own sake.

Vocalized passages were an important element in Medieval composition, e.g. the untexted melismas of plainchant.

In later music composers have used vocalized passages as a special effect, e.g. Debussy in *Sirènes* (the third movement of his orchestral *Nocturnes*), Holst in the 'Neptune' movement from *The Planets*, Ravel (*Vocalises en forme d'Habanera*), Rakhmaninov (*Vocalise*), Medtner (*Sonata-Vocalise* and *Suite-Vocalise*), and Janáček (in the scene of the Vixen's Wedding from Act 2 of his opera *The Cunning Little Vixen*).

Vocal score. See under *Score*.

Voce, voci (It.). 'Voice', 'voices'; *colla voce*, 'with the voice', i.e. the accompanist should take the tempo from the soloist and follow him or her closely.

Voce di petto, Voce di testo (It.). 'Chest voice', 'head voice'; see *Voice*, 4.

Voces aequales (Lat.), **voci eguali** (It.). See *Equal voices*.

Voces intimae ('Friendly Voices'). Subtitle of Sibelius's String Quartet in D minor, Op. 56, composed in 1909.

Vodorinski, Anton. See *Ketèlbey, Albert*.

Vogel, Wladimir (Rudolfovich) (*b* Moscow, 29 Feb. 1896). Swiss composer of German-Russian parentage. He studied in Berlin with Heinz Tiessen and Ferruccio Busoni, and then taught at the Klindworth-Scharwenka Conservatory (1929–33). He moved to Switzerland, and in 1954 took Swiss citizenship. His most notable contribution to music has been in the use of speaking voices, solo and choral; he has also drawn on Schoenbergian *serialism and a Busoni-like classicism.   PAUL GRIFFITHS

FURTHER READING
Hans Oesch: *Wladimir Vogel* (Berne and Munich, 1967).

Vogelweide, Walther von der. See *Walther von der Vogelweide*.

Vogler, Georg Joseph [Abbé Vogler] *b* Pleichach, nr Würzburg, 15 June 1749; *d* Darmstadt, 6 May 1814). German theorist, organist, and composer. He studied theology and law at Würzburg University and then at Bamberg. In 1772 he became chaplain to the Elector Palatine at Mannheim, who allowed him to study music in Bologna, with Padre Martini, and in Padua. He returned to Mannheim in 1775 as adviser and vice-*Kapellmeister* to the Elector, but chose not to move with the court to Munich in 1778, staying in Mannheim where he had founded the influential Mannheim Tonschule, a proving ground for his unorthodox musical theories. He spent some time in Paris and then, in 1784, finally went to Munich as *Kapellmeister* to the electoral court. Two years later he was appointed to the same position at the Stockholm court, where he stayed for some 13 years. During this time he undertook a research trip studying folk music in Portugal, North Africa, and Greece.

On leaving Sweden in 1799 Vogler turned his talents to organ building, and invented a portable organ called the 'Orchestrion'. He settled temporarily in Mannheim again in 1805, but two years later Louis I of Hessen-Darmstadt offered him the post of *Hofkapellmeister* to the Darmstadt court. His last years were spent mainly teaching and writing, and it is in these areas that his historical importance lies, rather than in his compositions, which include several dramatic works, instrumental music, and a great deal of church music. Weber and Meyerbeer were among his pupils.

WENDY THOMPSON

Voice

1. Introduction
2. Breathing
3. The Mechanism of the Larynx
4. Registers
5. Resonance
6. Vowels
7. Vibrato
8. Diction
9. Refinements of Vocal Production

1. *Introduction.* The voice in its undeveloped state is the oldest of all musical instruments. Although the earliest singing could not have been very refined, man must have realized that this instrument within himself had a considerable effect on his listeners. It is not necessary for a singer to develop his vocal technique in order for his voice to be affecting; it is rather the quality of emotional expression that is the most important factor, as any consideration of famous popular and folk singers will verify. However, in order to sing the vast repertory of Western art music the voice must be trained in a particular way so as to enable it to sing over a wide range,

at different dynamic levels without artificial amplification, and in both slow and florid music. Artistic singing cannot therefore be described as natural, although some singers have intrinsically better voices or a more intuitive understanding of vocal technique. It is important to remember that no matter how developed a technique becomes it should sound natural and allow the direct communication of whatever emotions are being portrayed.

From the earliest times man has combined an empirical approach to training the voice with scientific investigation. The first example of any thorough investigation is that of Galen (AD 130–200), after which there was very little advance until the 16th century. By the end of the 16th century, with the developments in vocal music and the emergence of opera, interest in vocal science flourished. Those singers who dislike the intrusion of science into their profession should remember that one of the greatest vocal teachers, Manuel García (1805–1906), carried out much scientific research into the workings of the voice. It should be stated, however, that although most of the theories of vocal physiology before this century were incomplete and in many cases wrong, great singing still flourished, even when the technique was based on a mistaken scientific concept. Clearly the traditional teaching methods worked and continue to do so.

It will be useful therefore, in discussing how to 'build a vocal instrument' capable of interpreting the vast range of vocal music from 1600 to the present day, to examine both the science of vocal production and the traditional methods. It will be seen that the two complement rather than oppose each other.

2. *Breathing*. Any musical instrument consists of a power supply, tone producer, and resonators. The power supply in the case of the human voice is the breath. Every healthy individual knows how to breathe in order to speak. However, to sing one has to sustain vocal tone for relatively long periods. It is therefore not surprising that for many singers breathing is the single most important aspect of technique. Many singers quote the old masters of the past, claiming that the secret of great singing is the 'breath', and many teachers have devised elaborate systems of breathing and breath control. In fact, breathing efficiently for singing is a very straightforward function. The difficulties arise in co-ordinating the breath with the act of vocalizing in such a way as to have both freedom and control.

Because the singer is using his body as a musical instrument, some attention must be called to posture. As with breathing itself it is easy to place too much importance on this. A visit to the opera will show that once a vocal production has become secure one can sing in almost any position.

The head should be erect, not stiffly but imagining that it hangs from a string suspended from the ceiling. The chest should be kept reasonably high, with shoulders relaxed and arms hanging. The back of the neck should be lengthened. The pelvis should be tipped so that the frontal part is moved inwards and upwards and the rear part moves downwards. The singer should feel the weight on the balls of his feet. He should feel 'ready for action', perhaps imagining he is about to draw a sword, although not too aggressively. Some amount of pulling in may be felt in the lower abdomen but the muscles should not be consciously tensed. If the abdomen is tensed, especially at the region of the epigastrium (the part of the abdomen immediately over the stomach), the diaphragm will be prevented from descending sufficiently. The singer should breathe silently and deeply, experiencing expansion around the lower ribs. The diaphragm descends and flattens somewhat allowing the thorax to enlarge (see Fig. 1). On exhalation (as required for vocalization) the sternum should not be dropped. The abdominal muscles contract and are resisted by the intercostals and diaphragm. If the singer takes a good breath and exhales on an 'f' sound he will feel

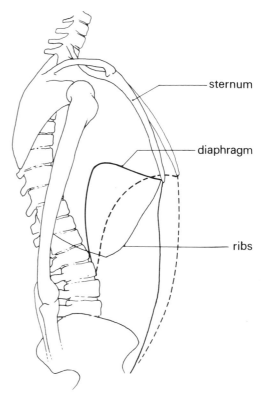

Fig. 1. An ideal posture for singing.

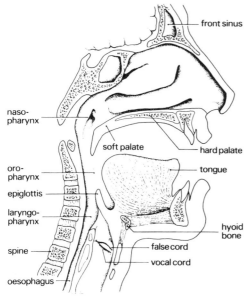

Fig. 2. The mouth and vocal cavity.

- naso-pharynx
- soft palate
- oro-pharynx
- epiglottis
- laryngo-pharynx
- spine
- oesophagus
- front sinus
- hard palate
- tongue
- hyoid bone
- false cord
- vocal cord

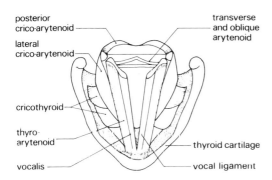

Fig. 3. The muscles of the larynx.

- posterior crico-arytenoid
- lateral crico-arytenoid
- cricothyroid
- thyro-arytenoid
- vocalis
- transverse and oblique arytenoid
- thyroid cartilage
- vocal ligament

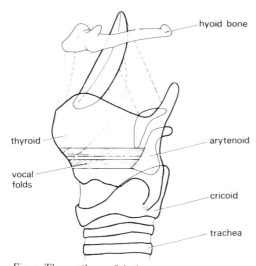

Fig. 4. The cartilages of the larynx.

- thyroid
- vocal folds
- hyoid bone
- arytenoid
- cricoid
- trachea

the gradual upward and inward movement balanced by internal pressures.

Of course, any physical activity that improves the singer's health and fitness will benefit his breathing and therefore singing, but it is not necessary for breathing to become a fetish. It is a good idea for breathing to be practised as a reaction to some imagined stimulus, such as pleasant surprise, horror, etc., thus making the whole process more spontaneous.

3. *The Mechanism of the Larynx.* Vocal tone is produced in the larynx. The main function of this complicated organ is that of a valve to hold breath and to prevent foreign bodies entering the lungs. It is situated at the top of the trachea or windpipe, a tube made up of rings of cartilage.

The larynx consists of a cartilaginous framework joined together with a complicated system of muscles and ligaments (see Figs. 2–4). There are two large cartilages: at the base of the larynx is the cricoid cartilage, which is shaped rather like a signet ring; and above the cricoid is the thyroid cartilage, consisting of two surfaces which are fused at the front. The bulge in the neck known as the Adam's apple is the front of this cartilage. The back of the thyroid cartilage extends upward and downward in horn-like projections. The upper horns (or superior *cornua*) meet the back of the hyoid bone, while the inferior *cornua* are attached to the side of the cricoid, forming a pivotal joint.

On the top edge of the cricoid are the two small arytenoid cartilages. Each arytenoid narrows upwards, and attached to the apex are the corniculate cartilages. At the base of each arytenoid is the vocal process (a process is a protuberance or outgrowth). The vocal cord is attached to this process.

The larynx is connected at the top to the hyoid bone, which lies in the upper part of the neck. The epiglottis is a flap-like cartilage connected to the thyroid cartilage.

The vocal cords themselves consist of a pair of muscular folds that converge towards the centre at the level of the arytenoids. During breathing the vocal folds open up and lie parallel to the sides of the larynx. Above the true cords are false cords that have no influence on tone-production.

Below the vocal folds is a ligament called the *conus elasticus* which is joined to the upper edge of the cricoid at the bottom and at the top blends into the edges of the glottis.

The vocal folds themselves are formed by the thyro-arytenoid muscles. They extend from the notch of the thyroid to the arytenoids. This pair of muscles is really quite complicated. They form two folds on each side. The upper folds are the ventricular bands or false vocal cords. The internal thyro-arytenoids form the body of the two vocal cords and are also called the *vocalis*. The edges of the folds are the vocal ligaments. Thus the thyro-arytenoids are a very complicated structure of various muscle fibres.

Before considering actual tone production, mention should also be made of the external muscular network that is necessary to the efficient functioning of the voice. The larynx is suspended in what might be described as an 'elastic scaffolding' of muscles which is even more complex than the internal structure of the larynx. Some of the muscles hold the larynx downward and backward. The cricoid cartilage is kept stationary and against the spine. The muscles joining the hyoid bone to the jaw should be relaxed as the larynx would then be pulled forward and upwards. Another set of muscles provides connections between the larynx, shoulder blades, and sternum, thus helping to balance the muscles that pull the larynx upwards towards the tongue, palate, and cranium. The downward-pulling muscles cannot function if the chest is not kept high and wide as described in section 2. There is a limit to the extent that the external muscular structure can be controlled, and certainly the internal muscular structure can be controlled only indirectly. It should be the aim of the teacher to find images that correspond to the correct functions and to maintain a balance between all the various muscular forces.

In order to produce tone the vocal folds must be brought together (adducted) and air allowed to flow. First the singer imagines the pitch at which he is going to sing. The crico-thyroid muscle contracts and causes the distance from the thyroid and cricoid to increase, thus stretching the vocal folds to the correct length. An increase in length causes the folds to vibrate more quickly. The vocal folds are brought together by the action of the transverse arytenoid muscle, helped by the oblique inter-arytenoid muscles. The lateral crico-arytenoids also co-ordinate with the inter-arytenoids in adducting the vocal folds perfectly.

When phonation is required to take place the folds are brought almost parallel. Because of what is known as the Bernoulli effect there is a lowering of pressure along the edges of the vocal folds which sucks them together. Then the difference in air pressure across the glottis throws the folds apart. Thus the air travels through the cords in a rapid series of puffs. The Bernoulli effect is explained by the fact that moving air exerts less pressure than stationary air. Thus if one holds two parallel sheets of paper in front of the lips, about half an inch apart, and blows through them, the reduction of pressure between them will cause them to be brought together. During phonation the tension

and density of the vocal folds change in relation to the breath pressure to achieve the tonal quality that is imagined by the singer.

The attack of a vowel tone is a combination of muscular adjustment and the action of breath. It should be noted that the vocal attack initiated by suction is different to that in which air is forced through vocal folds that are completely closed. In this case the sound begins with what is really a slight cough, or 'glottal plosive' (represented by ? in the International Phonetic Alphabet). This attack is what is usually meant by the term 'coup de glotte' and should be avoided, as most laryngologists agree that it is potentially harmful, especially on high notes, where the increased tension causes the vocal cords to strike against each other.

It is often advisable in practising an attack on a high note to allow some breath to escape in order to relax the valvular mechanism. Ideally one should aim for the closure of the folds and the breath flow to be simultaneous, thus producing a clean attack that is neither breathy nor violent. It is often helpful for the singer to imagine that the sound does not begin in the throat at all, concentrating instead on the focus of the sound in the front of the face while relaxing the throat (see section 5). Of course, this is total fiction, but as the muscles of the larynx are not under conscious control the singer must find the sensations that are produced by the correct mechanism.

In some pedagogies a 'soft attack' is actually encouraged, allowing the sound to be accompanied by a certain amount of breath. It may be broadly stated that the Germans tend to encourage a soft attack, while the Italians favour a clean attack, often featuring a 'coup de glotte'. A perfectly clean attack is to be preferred, however, if the singer wishes to develop a vocal production that deserves the name 'bel canto'.

4. *Registers.* It has been suggested that the existence of registers is caused by purely acoustical phenomena, namely the relationship between the larynx and its resonators. While the resonators are involved in changes of vocal registers, and indeed the names of the registers derive from concepts of resonance, it is generally accepted that the changes are within the larynx. It has already been mentioned that the vocal folds consist of a complex web of different muscle fibres. Thus the tension and density of vocal folds can vary considerably. On the lowest notes the thyro-arytenoid muscles are relatively relaxed and vibration takes place in the main body of the vocal fold. There is a limit to the tension that can be placed on the whole of the *vocalis* muscle, and at a certain pitch the muscle will give way, causing a 'break' in the voice. With the *vocalis* muscle thus relaxed the vocal

ligaments can be tensed independently and one then sings 'falsetto'.

Thus we have a heavy mechanism and a light mechanism. Vocal pedagogies have always disagreed over the number of registers. Johann Friedrich Agricola (1720–74) talked of three registers, whereas Giambattista Mancini (1714–1800) described two. In fact both ideas can be justified. The singer has to learn to go smoothly from one mechanism to the other. At the bottom of the voice one can use just the heavy mechanism and gradually lighten as the pitch ascends, 'combining' the two in the middle voice. At the top one uses purely the light mechanism. Thus in a woman we have chest, middle, and head registers, and in a man chest, head, and falsetto. The man's head voice corresponds to the woman's middle, and the man's falsetto to the woman's head voice. A man will not normally use falsetto except for special effect or if he sings alto. A useful analogy is to think of the different qualities as colours: if one thinks of the heavy quality as dark blue and the light as yellow, then the middle voice could be imagined as varying shades of green. Continuing the analogy, it is clear that the singer can use different shades according to the requirements of the music. The chest voice should not be carried up too high, as this will result in forcing, and no matter how heavy or dramatic a voice becomes as a singer matures, he or she should not neglect the light mechanism if high notes are to be retained throughout a long career.

A soprano will often at first sing in light mechanism or falsetto throughout the voice. The middle register must therefore develop a heavier quality. Similarly a contralto will often have to find how to use her head register.

Generally speaking, in the Baroque and early Classical repertories light quality should be favoured. With the developments of Wagner, Verdi, and the later *verismo* composers, singers gradually began to use a heavier quality. The early singers certainly used the chest voice, but in the upper range favoured a light bright sound. It is a lamentable fact that many singers today try to make their voices so big and heavy that they distort much of the music they sing.

5. *Resonance.* Like every other musical instrument, the voice has resonators as well as a tone-producer. One of the most important skills to be learnt is the production of different vocal tone-colours, according to the mood and emotional content of a song or aria. Much time is spent by singers in learning to adjust the resonators to achieve this. It is important to remember that most resonator adjustments also affect the larynx itself. As much of the muscular activity of the larynx is subconscious and not completely understood, one cannot be totally clear as to the relative importance of resonance and actual adjustments in the larynx itself. In fact even the most scientific teachers use the sorts of imagery that have been used for centuries. Many of them concern sensations of resonance in various parts of the face, chest, and head.

It is certain that the most important resonator is the pharynx. Almost every singer agrees that the throat must be kept 'open'. Pedagogical concepts—such as holding a ball of air in the pharynx, or imagining that the tone travels backwards instead of forwards—are common (the latter sensation is reported to have been experienced by Caruso). Another common idea is to induce a feeling of yawning. The enlarged pharynx reinforces the lower overtones, and gives the voice a mellow or rich quality. The pitch of the pharynx has been estimated variously at 350 Hz to 750 Hz. Thus the singer adjusts the resonator according to the pitch at which he is singing, and for whatever tone-colour he requires. Also important in acquiring an open throat is the role of the tongue. It should be kept low and forward in the mouth, thus not only leaving the pharynx unconstricted but also enlarging the mouth, which works together with the pharynx to add further resonance. It is desirable that the larynx should be kept fairly low (it will rise a certain amount on high notes and follow the tongue in producing certain vowels). If one breathes deeply and silently the larynx will drop naturally and the tongue will relax. In addition to the deep, open throat most teachers ask for the soft palate to be stretched high. When this upward stretch is co-ordinated correctly with a downward stretch there is a strengthening of high overtones. There is an important high overtone in the voice which lies around 2,800 Hz in men's voices and slightly higher in women's. This is the frequency which gives a voice 'ring', brilliance, or focus. Once discovered the singer should maintain this resonance during singing, whether loud or quiet. The resonator for this frequency is believed to be in the 'collar of the larynx', between the epiglottis and the ary-epiglottic folds. Singers often feel this 'ring' or 'focus' in frontal areas of the face and nasal cavities. If the singer opens up these cavities ('as if smelling a rose' is a term often used) this ring can be intensified. In singers' terminology this is known variously as 'forward resonance', 'singing in the mask', or 'impostazione della voce' ('voice placement'). It is therefore surprising for singers to find that the nasal cavities or head sinuses do not add anything significant to the vocal tone as heard by an audience. The same is true of so-called 'chest resonance', although there is some resonance in the trachea on low notes. This is not to deny, however, that the sensations as experienced by the singer are useful. One must aim to get the right balance between 'forward brilliance' and 'open-throated richness'. Careful practice of attack, co-ordinating it with a free breath-flow, will help to achieve this.

6. *Vowels.* Although there are slight differences within the larynx when different vowels are sung, a consideration of vowels belongs to the discussion of resonance. Every sound produced in the larynx consists of a fundamental and a series of overtones. The relative strength of the overtones gives a voice its particular timbre. However, one must also take into account the existence of 'formants'—that is, of the characteristic pitch-constituents of the different vowel sounds. We have already seen the existence of the high formant of 2,800–3,000 Hz. Now to be considered are the two main lower formants which characterize each vowel sound. The approximate frequencies for the vowels are as follows:

oo: 400 Hz, 800 Hz
oh: 500 Hz, 850 Hz
ah: 825 Hz, 1,200 Hz
ă ('as in 'pat'): 750 Hz, 1,800 Hz
ĕ (as in 'pet'): 550 Hz, 1,900 Hz
ā (as in 'cage'): 550 Hz, 2,100 Hz
ee: 375 Hz, 2,400 Hz

It is interesting that the vowel 'ee' contains a formant close to the high 'ring' formant. Hence the common practice of relating the other vowels to 'ee'.

The existence of the formants explains the difficulty of pronouncing certain vowels such as 'ee' or 'oo' on high notes. Both these vowels contain a low formant which will not sound on high notes. If the singer makes the rest of his diction clear the listener will modify the vowel in his own mind.

It can readily be seen that a modification of the resonators will cause a change of vowel sound. One can learn to mix the characteristics of different vowels just as one mixes the different qualities of registration. Thus to darken a whole phrase one can practise it on 'oo', and when singing the actual words keep something of the 'oo' quality. Many teachers link concepts of registers to resonance. For example, the low formant vowel 'oo' corresponds to chest voice, 'ah' to middle voice, and a light 'ah' or 'ü' to head voice. Although this is not strictly scientific it is helpful, and difficult transitions of register can often be solved by different vowels and resonance adjustments. Certainly, by a combined utilization of registration and resonance the singer has an instrument capable of more variety of colour than any other.

7. *Vibrato.* A *vibrato* is a pulsation in pitch, accompanied by fluctuations in intensity and timbre. The pitch fluctuation is quite wide—about a semitone, increasing at particularly loud moments to as much as a tone. Unless the *vibrato* is particularly excessive, intonation is not affected, as the listener hears an average of the two outer limits. In tests using singers with and without *vibrato* there has been found to be no connection between *vibrato* and intonation. At the same time, the intensity varies slightly and some high overtones come and go. In a well-trained voice the frequency of the *vibrato* is about seven per second (this will vary slightly according to the music). As a rule, opera singers have a quicker *vibrato* rate than concert singers. Also, in more dramatic and intensely emotional music the rate will increase. All this, of course, is heard by the listener as variations in colour. The *vibrato* gives the voice its emotionally affecting quality. In fact it is directly related to the emotional state of the singer. Each tiny muscle of the larynx is balanced by another. In maintaining the balance when vocalization takes place there is a fluctuation in the energy of the muscles themselves. The speed of the fluctuation is dependent on the speed of the nerve impulses. If there is too much uncontrolled emotional stimulation the frequency of nerve impulses will be faster. If the *vibrato* is too fast the listener will hear a 'flutter'; if too slow, a wobble.

Some vocal pedagogies favour a slow, rather wide, *vibrato*. What one could call a 'German sound'—the very rich but often overweighted vocal production especially common in Wagnerian singers—possesses a *vibrato* rate which is often as slow as five per second. Such a sound may be suitable for German Romantic music but it is not really the right sound for Italian music, which requires a very concentrated sound. Many opera singers, in an effort to produce more sound, over-weight their voices. It is this type of vocal production that has caused the extreme reaction of some 'early music' specialists. They claim that 17th- and 18th-century music should be sung with a totally 'straight' tone. A straight tone can be produced only by a lack of activity of the muscles involved, as well as by a lack of energy in the breath supply. Such a voice has little flexibility, and hardly any emotional impact. Apart from such technical considerations, there is much source material which acknowledges the existence of *vibrato* as a necessary feature of good singing: Michael Praetorius and Mozart are two notable examples.

8. *Diction.* The voice does not merely produce musical tone but is also required to pronounce words, and consonants have to be co-ordinated with the vowel sounds to make them intelligible.

Consonants can be categorized in different

ways. When resonance continues through the consonant, for example, they are called 'voiced', and when the tone is interrupted, 'unvoiced'; more technical terms are 'sonant' and 'surd'. The sonants include w, m, v, z, b, th, zh, n, l, r, g, ng, and y; the surds include f, p, t, s, sh, k, h, and th.

Another classification is that of 'stops' and 'continuants'. The stops (p, b, t, k, g) are sounds that cannot be prolonged; they are called 'plosives' if they occur at the beginning of a word. The continuants (w, f, v, m, s, sh, z, zh, th, n, l, r, ng) can be prolonged; some are 'fricative' (i.e. they are produced by the friction of the breath in a narrow opening, e.g. th). Vowels are also continuants.

In another classification, the one most commonly met with in singing, the consonants are described according to how they are produced:

labials (lips): p, b, w
labio-dentals (lips to teeth): f, v
linguo-dentals (tongue to teeth): th
alveolars (tongue touching the ridge of the gum): t, d, n, l, r
sibilants (anterior tongue raised towards the gum ridge): s, z, sh, zh, ch, j
velars (back of the tongue moves towards the soft palate): k, g, ng
aspirates (breathing): h

The nasals may be regarded as vowels, and are sometimes called 'semi-vowels', as are l and r. All these sounds can be sung. Also very much like vowels are w and y, which 'glide' quickly from one sound to another: w begins like 'oo', and y like 'ee'. One should also consider the glottal plosive used when one says the German word 'Arbeit'. In singing one should be careful not to make the glottal attack too harshly. If one acquires a perfect attack as described in section 3, then the hard glottal plosive can be avoided.

The singer should clarify just where every different consonant is formed, so it can be produced with the utmost speed and precision. In any discussion of singing the question arises of how much one should concentrate on the music and how much on the words—the answer is on both! In a well-composed song or aria the rhythm and articulation provided by the words always adds to purely musical rhythm. Double consonants (tr, pl, etc.), for example, take a certain time to pronounce clearly. Providing the vowel tone does not lose resonance, the taking of time will result in rhythmical flexibility. It is important that consonants are not accompanied by an escape of breath that forms another vowel —for example, 'sleep' can become 'sleepuh'. It is also often a good idea to practise the attack of a vowel tone before adding a preceding consonant. Care should also be taken to maintain the resonance during the pronunciation of

different words. If this is achieved the result is a good 'line'. A good 'line' may be spoilt by diphthongs. In attempting to sing such a word as 'might' the tone is often shallow and lacking in colour. To correct this, the first of the two sounds that constitute the diphthong ('ah') should be prolonged for as long as possible, and the second sound ('ee') added at the end. Having practised all diphthongs in a similar manner and acquired a resonant sound, it may be necessary to modify the tone slightly in order that the pronunciation will sound more natural. The singer should regard the acquisition of good diction as being of the greatest importance. The suggestive power of language should be exploited, as regards both the onomatopoeic effect of the consonants (as in *Lüftchen* (Ger.), 'breeze') and the emotional colouring of vowels (as in *dunkel* (Ger.), 'dark', and *Tod* (Ger.), 'death'). Wagner intended his music to be sung exactly as written, in a *legato* style, with clearly articulated consonants, and with vowel sounds that are coloured so that they express the emotion suggested by the word itself. In Italian 'bel canto', good diction is just as important. The rhythm of the language must be allowed to bring flexibility to the vocal line.

Every vowel sound, although being equally resonant, should be quite distinct: as Tosi wrote in 1723, 'Let him take care that the words be uttered in such a manner, without any affectation that they be distinctly understood, and no one syllable be lost . . . for [if not] . . . there will be no great difference between a human voice and a hautboy'.

9. *Refinements of Vocal Production.* It is not enough for the singer merely to produce the same sound for every type of music. From the basic elements of voice-production it is possible to build very different types of vocal instrument. Today, the singer is expected to sing music of all periods. Although some compromise is necessary, it is possible to use one's voice differently according to the music to be sung. A consideration of some of the traditional methods of voice-training will be of lasting value to the singer, as much of the repertory can be regarded as within the tradition that developed in Italy in the 17th century and continued unchanged until the mid 19th.

First to be considered is the idea of 'singing on the breath', or *portamento* style. *Portamento* here is not used in the narrow sense of slurring between two notes. It is rather the idea of the voice being carried on the breath, so that every note melts smoothly into the next. The feeling is a physical one, and the sound is felt to pour out of the body with no feeling of pushing. The physical feeling is inextricably linked to the rhythm of the music, and so the *portamento* is felt to continue throughout a piece, and is implied even through rests. As well as being a matter of breathing, this is also a matter of attack. The correct feeling cannot be acquired if the 'coup de glotte' is used; the clean attack as described in section 3 is required. Another important aspect of voice-training as described in sources of the 18th and early 19th centuries is the development of the registers. The different registers were developed fully but joined smoothly. Certainly in Baroque music the chest voice was fully exploited, a fact rather ignored in today's performances. A vocal device which trained the singer's attack, breath control, and registration was the *messa di voce* (It., 'placing of the voice'). This simply means allowing a long note to swell from soft to loud and then to die away. To practise this one must begin with a perfectly clean attack, very quietly. This will be almost falsetto but will have enough heavy quality to enable the singer to *crescendo* smoothly. As the singer increases the volume the quality becomes heavier and there is an increase of resonance. This process is reversed in the *diminuendo*. It will be seen that this is training the muscles of the larynx, as well as their co-ordination with the breath.

The singer should practise swell-tones throughout the range, with different proportions of light and heavy registration, and different amounts of 'focus' and 'open throat' resonance. After regular practice of the *messa di voce*, the singer will automatically shape his phrases more imaginatively. Long notes will have varying colours and a sense of musical flow. The feeling of co-ordination between the breathing and tone-production will give a rhythmical flexibility. One can declaim words or sing *marcato* without losing the feeling of line.

It is important also that the singer practises *coloratura*. Florid passages are not sung as *legato* phrases speeded up (although slow practice may be helpful in securing a mental picture of the shape of a run and to check intonation). The key to singing *coloratura* stylishly is the meaning of the word itself, 'colouring'. One does not sing it with the full voice, but lightly, so that it emerges out of the line, supported by a strong bodily rhythm. Ornaments such as the trill (which is really an exaggerated *vibrato*), turn, and mordent should also be sung with a light quality 'extracted' from the main tone without disturbing the line. The *coloratura* as required for Handel, Mozart, and later composers is often felt to be controlled in the face. The very quick *coloratura* common in Monteverdi and Caccini is usually felt to be in the throat itself and is like a quick trembling of the larynx. It is consequently much drier than the melodic passage-work in Mozart and Handel.

The voice can be seen as a balance between certain extremes. The actual physical mechanism depends on a delicate balance of opposing muscular forces. One also has extremes of light and heavy registration and of brilliant and dark resonance (or 'focus' and depth). While accepting the intrinsic quality of his voice, the singer must get the right balance for the music. Generally speaking, lightness and brilliance are required for Baroque and Classical music, and the low and high registers will be very different in quality (as in early pianos). In later, more dramatic music there will be more emphasis on a heavier production throughout the whole range.

However, in the training of a young singer the emphasis should be on a light or lyric production. If the voice has the potential, it will develop more dramatic quality as it matures.

DAVID MASON

FURTHER READING
Giambattista Mancini: *Practical Reflections on Figured Singing* (Vienna, 1774, Eng. trans. by Edward Foreman, Illinois, 1967); Manuel García; *Traité complet de l'art du chant* (Paris, 1840, part ii trans. as *Complete Treatise on the Art of Singing* and ed. by Donald Paschke, New York, 1975); Philip Duey: *Bel Canto in its Golden Age* (New York, 1957); Frederick Husler and Yvonne Rodd-Marling: *Singing: the Physical Nature of the Vocal Organ* (London, 1965); William Vennard: *Singing: the Mechanism and the Technique* (New York, 1967); R. Miller: *Singing Techniques* (Metuchen, NJ, 1977).

Voice exchange. From the German, *Stimmtausch*. In polyphonic music, the alternation of phrases between two voices of equal range, a feature found frequently in music of the 12th and 13th centuries.

Voice-leading (Amer.). See *Part-writing*.

Voice-part. See *Part*, 1.

Voile (Fr.). 'Veil', the cloth used for muffling a drum; *voilé*, 'muffled'.

Voix (Fr.). 'Voice'.

Voix humaine, La ('The Human Voice'). Opera ('tragédie lyrique') in one act by Poulenc to a libretto by Cocteau. A monodrama for soprano and orchestra, it was first performed in Paris in 1959.

Volante (It.). 1. 'Flying', i.e. swift and light. 2. In string playing, a kind of bow-stroke where the bow bounces on the string to produce an effect similar to that of the *ricochet*.

Volkmann, Friedrich Robert (b Lommatzsch, Saxony, 6 Apr. 1815; d Budapest, 29 Oct. 1883). German composer. He studied music at

Freiberg, and then at Leipzig (1836–9). In 1839 he was teaching singing in Prague, and two years later he settled in Budapest. From 1875 until his death he was professor of composition at the Budapest Academy of Music. His music is in the German style, with occasionally glimpses of Hungarian elements, and his works include much piano and chamber music (including six string quartets, two symphonies, overtures, a Violin Concerto, incidental music to Shakespeare's *Richard III*, and vocal music.

WENDY THOMPSON

Volkslied (Ger.). 'Folk-song'.

Volkston (Ger.). 'Folk style'.

Volkstümliches Lied (Ger.). 'Popular' or 'folk-like' song. In the mid 18th century an amateur musician, Christian Gottfried Krause (1719–70), began a movement towards *Lieder* in a folk-like manner, with simple accompaniments and an unembellished vocal line. His lead was followed especially by J. A. Hiller and J. A. P. Schulz, and their music in turn had an influence on the songs of Schubert. Schubert's folk-like songs, such as *Heidenröslein*, give an impression of artless simplicity but in fact use highly sophisticated and subtle means to achieve this effect.

Voll (Ger.). 'Full'; *vollstimmig*, for full orchestra or full chorus; *volltönend*, *volltönig*, 'full sounding', 'sonorous'.

Volles Werk (Ger.). 'Full organ'.

Volonté (Fr.). 'Will'; *à volonté*, 'at pleasure', i.e. *ad libitum*.

Volta (It.). 1 (from *voltare*, 'to turn', 'to turn round') [lavolta, levalto]. A quick dance which was popular in France from the 1550s; it was usually in triple time, and resembled the *gal-liard. The name derives from one of the movements of the dance, in which the lady is lifted by her partner, who uses his thigh to assist him, while turning round. The dance became popular in England and Germany towards the beginning of the 17th century, but in France Louis XIII (1610–13) banned it from his court because of its lack of decorum. As with most courtly dances, it became a popular instrumental form in its own right, and English virginal and lute pieces are found with the title 'Lavolta'. See also *Waltz*.

2. For *prima volta* and *seconda volta*, see *Double bar*; see also *Ouvert and clos*.

Volti (It.). 'Turn', 'turn over'; *volti subito* (often abbreviated to *v.s.*), 'turn over quickly', often found at the bottom of pages in orchestral parts.

Volubile, volubilmente (It.). 'Voluble', i.e. flowing easily, 'volubly'.

Voluntary. Nowadays the term is used to describe a piece, written or improvised, played by the organist after (and sometimes before) a church service. The word is found in a musical application as early as the mid 16th century, at first, apparently, meaning an instrumental composition in which, instead of the composer adding parts to a plainchant theme, as was still common, he left himself free to fashion all his parts as he liked. We see an example of this application of the word in Morley's *Plaine and Easie Introduction* (1597), where he says that 'to make two parts upon a plaine song is more hard than to make three parts into voluntarie'.

In the Mulliner Book (*c*.1560) the term is applied in this way, and voluntaries there are seen to be a sort of contrapuntal fantasia or ricercare without any *cantus firmus*.

But the idea of freedom implicit in the word allowed it to be applied in another way. Thus from the same date or a little later we find voluntary used as meaning what we now call 'extemporization' or 'improvisation', and this use of the word persists well into the 19th century, and for any extempore performance on any instrument. Thus we find in the 16th century the expression 'a voluntary before the song'.

Samuel Butler applies the same idea metaphorically (*c*.1667) in one of his 'Characters', describing a person who in light conversation is sparkling but in considered discussion dull, 'He is excellent at voluntary and prelude, but has no skill in composition'.

Burney (*c*.1805) in Rees's *Cyclopaedia* defines voluntary as 'a piece played by a musician extempore, according to his fancy', and says that such a piece is often used before the musician 'begins to set himself to play any particular composition, to try the instrument and lead him into the key of the piece he intends to perform'. 'In these performances', he says, 'we have frequently heard great players produce passages and effects in fits of enthusiasm and inspiration that have never appeared on paper', and he magnanimously defends the liberties taken— 'In these happy moments', he says (dropping into verse):

> Such sounds escape the daring artist's hand
> As meditation never could command;
> And though the slaves to rigid rule may start,
> They penetrate and charm the feeling heart.

He then, very naturally, goes on to call attention to a machine for automatically recording organ voluntaries (described in the *Philosophical Transactions* of the Royal Society, No. 483, section 2).

As late as Thackeray's *Vanity Fair* (1848) we see this use—'Sitting down to the piano she rattled a triumphant voluntary on the keys.' And Leigh Hunt (1850) talks of 'modulating sweet voluntaries on the pianoforte'.

Because of the habit of 'voluntarizing' (as we may call it) before a song or the set performance of a piece, the word early came to have as one of its senses (perhaps a less common one) that of 'prelude'. So we find a warrant of Charles I which lays down the rhythm to be used by army drummers including one as a 'Voluntary before the March'.

Almost from the beginning of the introduction of the word 'voluntary' into musical parlance it had still another application. Just as later Schubert, Chopin, and Schumann applied the word 'impromptu' to a written piece for which they had no other name handy, and which they wished to suggest was more or less in the style of an extemporization, so composers from at least Purcell onwards (see his *Voluntary on the 100th Psalm Tune*) have used this word 'voluntary' for written and printed music. It was thus applied even to string music, as in a collection of *Select Preludes and Voluntarys for the Violin* published by Walsh of London in 1705.

Organists have always been active extemporizers and the service in the cathedrals and such churches as possessed organs allowed them scope for the exercise of their skill in voluntary playing. Thus 'voluntary' has come in time to collect round it a special flavour of the ecclesiastical and to signify much what was referred to in the opening lines of this article—organ playing before, during, or after a service, whether extempore or not. In the 18th century three voluntaries, at least, were commonly played—at the beginning and end of the Anglican service (as now) and also after the first lesson (or before the sermon, while the clergyman was changing from his surplice to his preaching gown). The *Spectator* mentions another place for the voluntary: 'By a voluntary before the first lesson, we are prepared for admission of those divine truths, which we are shortly to receive.'

There were several distinct types of voluntary in use in the English Church during the 18th century, of which the principal were, perhaps, the solid *Diapason Voluntary* and the showy *Cornet Voluntary*. The Cornet was a powerful sort of mixture stop, and these voluntaries provided for it (in the right-hand part) a very florid runabout line of single notes, with (in the left-hand part) an accompaniment to be played on another manual. (Often the left-hand part was a line of mere single notes also.) If in addition to its loud cornet the organ had an 'Echo Cornet' (a soft stop), passages for the two alternated in the right-hand part. Dr Burney's *Six Cornet Pieces . . . proper for young Organists*

would perhaps hardly be considered 'proper' for any one today—even on the gayest ecclesiastical occasion. More than half a century before these were written, Addison (in the *Spectator* for 28 Mar. 1712) had made this protest against their kind:

When the Preacher has often, with great Piety and Art enough, handled his subject, and the judicious Clerk has with the utmost diligence culled out two Staves proper to the discourse, and I have found in my self and in the rest of the Pew good Thoughts and Dispositions, they have been all in a moment dissipated by a merry jig from the organ loft.

(The Clerk's 'culling out of two staves' here seems to refer to his psalm.) Similarly Bedford's *Great Abuse of Musick* (1711) complains of organists dismissing the congregation 'as if they play'd them out of a tavern, or out of an Alehouse, or, rather, out of a Play-house'.

Nowadays a great variety of music is brought into use for 'voluntary' purposes, much of it originally written for the organ, and some of it of the nature of 'arrangement'. Many of the older English organ voluntaries of the more sober kind have been republished. Mendelssohn's Organ Sonatas (1845) were the result of a commission given him when in England to write some voluntaries for English use, and the decision to call them 'Sonatas' instead of 'Voluntaries' was an afterthought (they would, as wholes, hardly serve the usual purpose of voluntaries, and this may be the reason for the change of title).   PERCY SCHOLES

Vom (Ger.). 'From the'; e.g. *vom Anfang*, 'from the beginning'.

Von ewiger Liebe ('Eternal Love'). Song for voice and piano by Brahms, the first of his set of four, Op. 43 (1868). It is a setting of a poem by Hoffmann von Fallersleben.

Von Heute auf Morgen ('From One Day to the Next'). Opera in one act by Schoenberg to a libretto by Max Blonda (pseudonym of Gertrud Schoenberg). It was first performed in Frankfurt in 1930.

Voraus (Ger.). 'Beforehand'; *im voraus*, in organ music, a direction that the stops in question are to be 'prepared'.

Vorbehalten (Ger.). See under *Aufführen*.

Vorbereiten (Ger.). 'To prepare'; the term is used in organ music, often in the form *bereite vor*, mentioning a particular stop.

Vorhalt (Ger.). 1. A suspension (*vorbereiteter Vorhalt*). 2. An appoggiatura (*freier Vorhalt*).

Voříšek, Jan Václav [Worzischek, Johann Hugo] (*b* Vamberk, 11 May 1791; *d* Vienna, 19 Nov. 1825). Bohemian composer and keyboard player. Early tuition came from his father, a choirmaster and organist, but his remarkable abilities as a keyboard player led to a brief career as a child prodigy touring Bohemia. While pursuing a course in law at the university in Prague he continued his musical studies with Tomášek, whose high regard for contrapuntal excellence had a considerable effect on Voříšek's church music, and on the texture of his piano works. But in the Prague of the 1810s Mozartian elegance was cultivated at the expense of experimentation, and Voříšek had little opportunity to indulge in newer musical trends. Thus in 1814 he moved to Vienna to observe in particular the music of Beethoven at closer quarters. Here he was active as composer, pianist, and (from 1818) conductor of the Gesellschaft der Musikfreunde. Highly regarded as an organist, he succeeded his fellow Czech Růžička as court organist in 1823. Voříšek's early death occasioned numerous tributes from Vienna's musical community. Beethoven had spoken well of his Rhapsodies Op. 1, and Schubert, with whom Voříšek was friendly, seems to have been influenced by the piano writing in the Impromptus Op. 7. His style owed virtually nothing to his Czech origins: melodically he showed an interest in motivic thematic material akin to Beethoven's, harmonically an absorption with diminished chords which sometimes anticipates Schumann and Mendelssohn. Voříšek's shorter piano compositions (impromptus, rhapsodies, eclogues) made a significant contribution to the infancy of the Romantic piano piece and his single Symphony (in D, Op. 24, 1821) indicates a dynamic (in the slow movement almost theatrical) talent quite justifying contemporary regret at his untimely demise. JAN SMACZNY

Vorschlag (Ger.). An *appoggiatura; *kurzer Vorschlag*, 'short appoggiatura'; *langer Vorschlag*, 'long appoggiatura'.

Vorspiel (Ger.). 'Prelude'. Wagner called the introductions to his operas *Vorspielen*, and described *Das Rheingold* as a *Vorspiel* to the *Ring* trilogy.

Vortrag (Ger.). 'Performance', 'execution', or 'recital'; *Vortragsstück*, a virtuoso show-piece, designed to show off technique; *Vortragzeichen*, expression marks; *vortragen*, *vorzutragen*, 'to perform', or 'to bring into prominence', 'to emphasize'.

Vorwärts (Ger.). 'Forwards'; *Vorwärts gehend*, 'progress', 'move on', i.e. faster.

Vorzeichnung (Ger.). 'Signature'; sometimes time signature and key signature are specified as *Taktvorzeichnung* and *Tonartvorzeichnung*, respectively.

Vox principalis, Vox organalis (Lat.). In *organum, the 'principal voice' (i.e. the preexistent part used as a basis for polyphony) and the composed second voice.

V.s. Abbreviation for *volti subito, 'turn over quickly'.

Vuoto, vuota (It.). 'Empty'; *corda vuota*, 'open string'.

W

Wachet auf ('Awake!'). Cantata No. 140 by J. S. Bach based on a Lutheran chorale and composed in 1731. It is also the title of a chorale-prelude for organ by Bach. 'Wach' auf' is the chorus in Act 3 of Wagner's *Die Meistersinger*, sung to words by Hans Sachs. *Wachet auf* is often translated as 'Sleepers, Awake'.

Wachsend (Ger.). 'Growing', i.e. *crescendo*.

Wachtel (Ger.). 'Quail'. Beethoven used the term in the oboe part of the 'Pastoral' Symphony, where it imitates the cry of the bird. The same name is given to an instrument used in the 'Toy' Symphony by Leopold Mozart (formerly attributed to Haydn), which makes the same noise (sometimes called a *Wachtelpfeife*, i.e. 'quail-pipe'). See *Whistle*, 1.

Waelrant, Hubert (*b* Antwerp, *c*.1517; *d* Antwerp, 19 Nov. 1595). Flemish composer, teacher, theorist, and music publisher. His printing house, set up jointly with Jean de Laet in Antwerp in 1554, issued important collections of music by Lassus, as well as *chansons* and Protestant psalm settings in French.

JOHN MILSOM

Wagenaar, Johan (*b* Utrecht, 1 Nov. 1862; *d* The Hague, 17 June 1941). Dutch composer and teacher. After studying in Utrecht and Berlin he became a teacher at the Utrecht Music School, and its director in 1887. From 1919 to 1937 he was director of The Hague Conservatory. His best-known work is probably the overture *Cyrano de Bergerac* (1905), but he also wrote operas, cantatas, and the symphonic poem *Saul en David* (1906). His son **Bernard Wagenaar** (*b* Arnhem, 18 July 1894; *d* York, Maine, 19 May 1971) studied with his father and at Utrecht University, and became a conductor and music teacher. In 1920 he emigrated to the USA, becoming an American citizen in 1927. From 1925 to 1968 he taught at the Institute of Musical Art in New York. His works include four symphonies, vocal music, and a chamber opera. His *Song of Mourning* (1944) was commissioned by the Netherlands American Foundation to commemorate Dutch war victims.

WENDY THOMPSON

Wagenseil, Georg Christoph (*b* Vienna, 29 Jan. 1715; *d* Vienna, 1 Mar. 1777). Austrian composer. He was born into a middle-class family, and became a pupil of Fux, who recommended him to the Viennese court. There he was made court composer in 1739, organist to the Dowager Empress Elisabeth Christine in 1741, and music master to the Archduchess Maria Theresia and her daughter in 1749. In 1745 he made a journey to Venice to produce his opera *Ariodante*, and over the next 15 years he made his reputation as an opera composer. In 1765 he was pensioned off, and in his later years he suffered badly from sciatica and gout. Although he managed to teach some distinguished pupils, he was in financial straits at this time, but Burney found him still active in 1770. A composer of church music and popular keyboard music, his main fame in history rests on his symphonies, which in their exploitation of the potentialities of sonata form probably influenced Haydn, and on his concertos, which were well known to Mozart.

DENIS ARNOLD

Wagner, (Wilhelm) Richard (*b* Leipzig, 22 May 1813; *d* Venice, 13 Feb. 1883). German composer. From his very earliest days, Wagner was absorbed by a simultaneous interest in music and the theatre. This was to take him from obscure beginnings, as a provincial *Kapellmeister* and the composer of operas in the German Romantic manner, to world fame as the founder of Bayreuth as the ideal theatre in which could be staged the music dramas he based on a new expressive synthesis of words and music. He formed his artistic aims early in life, and pursued them to realization with ruthless determination.

1. *The Early Years*. Whether Wagner was the son of the police actuary Friedrich Wagner or the painter, poet, and actor Ludwig Geyer can never be determined, for by the time of Friedrich's death from typhus in 1813, Johanna Wagner was already Geyer's mistress. On her marriage to Geyer, the family moved to Dresden, where Wagner studied at the Kreuzschule and had his love of music first kindled by the example of Weber. Returning to Leipzig, he became absorbed in the theatre and made his first attempt at dramatic writing, also making efforts to teach himself music. However, what by his own account roused him to his sense of vocation as a dramatic composer was seeing Wilhelmine Schröder-Devrient, the greatest

singing actress of the day, in *Fidelio*; in the following year, 1830, his admiration for Beethoven was to take practical form in a piano arrangement he made of the Ninth Symphony, and in later life his story *Eine Pilgerfahrt zu Beethoven* ('A Pilgrimage to Beethoven', 1840) declares in fictional form his belief that after this symphony—'music crying out for redemption by poetry'—the true consequence was music drama.

In June 1830 Wagner enrolled at Leipzig University, where he studied music under Theodor Weinlig. Surviving compositions from this period include piano sonatas and a symphony: the latter is strongly coloured by Beethoven, to some extent by Mozart and Weber, but contains suggestions of Wagner's own emerging voice. In Prague in 1832 he wrote the libretto for an opera, *Die Hochzeit*, which he partly composed, then beginning work on *Die Feen* ('The Fairies'; composed 1833-4, produced 1888). This is a Romantic opera (after Gozzi), in the line of Weber though closer in manner to Marschner, especially in its treatment of the interaction of the human and spirit worlds and in the nature of some of its idiom and scoring. As chorus master at Würzburg (1833-4) Wagner came to widen his knowledge of opera to include Cherubini, Auber, and Meyerbeer, all to be influential on his music. But it was the Italian music he also admired, Bellini in particular, which most influenced his next opera, *Das Liebesverbot* (1836, after Shakespeare's *Measure for Measure*). Though he later regarded the work as a deviation from his ideals, it strengthened his understanding of vocal melody, the importance of which he always impressed upon his countrymen.

Moving to Magdeburg as conductor in 1834, Wagner conducted operas by Bellini and Rossini as well as German works (Weigl, Spohr, Weber, Marschner) and the French *opéra-comique* repertory that had played an important part in the evolution of German Romantic opera. He also married the actress Wilhelmine (Minna) Planer; their stormy and erratic marriage lasted until her death in 1866, though he was not by then living with her. Partly so as to provide distraction from his unhappy private life, he began work on *Rienzi*. In Riga as conductor in 1837-9 he extended his range of activities with symphony concerts and with the first of many articles outlining his ideas; he also conducted operas by Mozart and Méhul. However, he was forced to flee Riga to escape his creditors, and took ship for London. Driven into a Norwegian fjord by a storm, the crew stirred his imagination with their singing and with stories of the Flying Dutchman. From London, he and Minna went on to Paris, where he hoped to conquer the Opéra, then the most

influential theatre in Europe, with *Rienzi* (1840). He was disappointed of this hope, though the work was well matched to the demands of the Opéra. It is to some extent influenced by Meyerbeer, but more significantly by the style of Grand Opera which had been developed for Paris by Spontini, Halévy, Auber, and Rossini, all of whom he deeply admired; in Spontini, moreover, he found a conductor whose magisterial control was to inspire his own manner.

In Paris, where he endured considerable hardship, Wagner completed *Rienzi*, wrote his *Faust Overture*, came to know and admire Berlioz, was introduced to the legends of Tannhäuser and Lohengrin, and wrote the text and music of *Der fliegende Holländer* ('The Flying Dutchman', 1841). The first of Wagner's operas to retain its place in the regular repertory, it includes much inherited from Weber, though this is absorbed into a work of new individuality and strength. Among the ideas that were growing in Wagner's mind was the Romantic theme of Redemption through Love that was to absorb him throughout his life: the treatment of the story of the girl sacrificing herself for the legendary Dutchman far transcends the immediate example in Marschner's operas about contacts between the human and supernatural worlds.

Leaving Paris in 1842, Wagner arrived in Dresden to his first triumph with *Rienzi*. When this was followed by a more modest success for *Der fliegende Holländer*, Wagner took the work to Berlin, only to encounter his first taste of the critical hostility that was thereafter to divide musical Germany into Wagnerians and anti-Wagnerians. He had meanwhile begun work on *Tannhäuser*, completing it in the spring of 1845; its doubtful reception strengthened his feeling of isolation, but also his determination to insist on his aims being understood. *Tannhäuser* is in fact a transitional work on the way to realization of these aims, and retains features from Parisian Grand Opera as well as German Romantic opera: to a considerable extent, and despite some lapses into banality and some *longueurs*, it transcends both genres with a new imaginative strength and a richer quality of musical invention.

2. *Years of Maturity.* Wagner had meanwhile accepted a post as conductor at Dresden in 1843, also beginning work on *Lohengrin* (1848). Elements of earlier strains of Romantic opera remain in the work, together with some concessions to singers' demands; but if Act 1 still reflects Spontini and Auber, and the handling of Ortrud and Telramund as 'black' pair against Lohengrin and Elsa derives from Weber's *Euryanthe*, the 'Grail' prelude and the whole of Act 2 look forward from *Tannhäuser* to

much larger creative achievements. But pursuit of these was temporarily interrupted by the political events of 1848.

Fired with revolutionary zeal, and convinced that some social realignment was necessary if his artistic ideals were to be realized, Wagner threw in his lot with the insurrectionists in Dresden in 1849. A warrant was issued for his arrest, and he fled to Switzerland. Here he sketched various plans for operas and dramas (including one on *Jesus of Nazareth*, based on Feuerbach's ideas of Christianity as an expression of myth), and began work on *Siegfrieds Tod*. It was also a period of taking stock: he wrote a number of essays on his theories of art, among them *Das Kunstwerk der Zukunft* ('The Art-work of the Future', 1849) and *Oper und Drama* (1851). These outlined ideas of opera as a 'total work of art' (*Gesamtkunstwerk*) in which poetry should directly give rise to music in a form of opera making use of all the theatrical resources, one that should, moreover, be given in ideal conditions as a social ritual involving both performers and audience. Though some of these ideas were modified or abandoned, they formed the starting-point for his mature work.

In 1850 Liszt conducted the first performance of *Lohengrin* in Weimar, and Wagner was encouraged to proceed with work on *Siegfrieds Tod*. As the idea grew in his mind (together with the ambition to found a special festival theatre), he added to the original concept texts for first *Der junge Siegfried* ('Young Siegfried'), then *Die Walküre* and *Das Rheingold*. Thus the works that were to form *Der Ring des Nibelungen* ('The Ring of the Nibelung') came to be written in reverse order. The text was completed at the end of 1852, and despite considerable financial difficulties Wagner began work on *Das Rheingold*, completing it in September 1854. At the same time, under the influence of his love for the wife of a Swiss benefactor, Mathilde Wesendonk, he conceived the idea for *Tristan und Isolde* and revived an earlier interest in the story of *Parsifal*. Having completed *Die Walküre* and begun work on *Siegfried* (as the third *Ring* opera was now called), he broke off to devote himself to *Tristan* in August 1857. At this time he also wrote the *Wesendonk-Lieder*; two of these are preliminary studies for *Tristan*, which he eventually finished in 1859.

Hitherto, Wagner's operas had been in different ways extensions of the older Romantic opera, each representing a significant creative advance. *Der fliegende Holländer* was the first to make use of construction by scenes rather than numbers; and in it Wagner later discovered glimmerings of his technique of *Leitmotiv*, the association of a musical idea with a dramatic ingredient. The full implications of the device, a development of the old Reminiscence Motive

(which was hardly more than a simple piece of identification), are not realized in this work, only partially in *Tannhäuser*, with its stylistic unevennesses, and *Lohengrin*. However, in the latter work Wagner did make considerable advances in allowing the demands of musical structure to guide the text: this necessitated repudiation of some of the theories in *Oper und Drama*, and there is evidence that in *Tristan* the essential concept, though as always in mature Wagner a simultaneous process between text and music, was dominantly musical.

The motivic technique in *Tristan*, though not so far-reaching as in the still-uncompleted *Ring*, does provide Wagner with a cohesive basis for music that is now freed from numbers or scenes as structural guides; and a further characteristic is the use in the verse of *Stabreim*, a technique of rhyme by alliteration rather than by similar word-endings which Wagner revived from earlier models. The absence of periodicity leads in turn to a freely moving chromatic harmony in a style that was unprecedented in music. These methods, implying in turn orchestration of new intensity, suppleness, and richness, were ideally matched to a story in which doomed love finds realization only by turning away from the light of day towards darkness and ultimately death. Wagner's ideas were here much imbued with his philosophical reading, in particular with the renunciatory philosophy of Schopenhauer.

Forced to leave Zurich over his liaison with Mathilde Wesendonk, Wagner went first to Venice and then to Paris, where his new (1861)

Wagner (1860)

version of *Tannhäuser* (with an opening Bacchanale composed out of the experience of *Tristan*) met with violent demonstrations but won him new admirers, among them Baudelaire. A projected performance of *Tristan* drew him to Munich, but when this was postponed he resumed his travels, beginning work on *Die Meistersinger von Nürnberg*. At the moment when his financial affairs, always precarious, seemed finally about to overwhelm him, an offer came from Ludwig II of Bavaria: the outcome was generous support and the promise of performances. Though differences were to intervene, Wagner was rescued, and in his turn provided the lonely, idealistic young king with the artistic joy of his unhappy life.

Thanks to the king, *Tristan* was performed in 1865 under Hans von Bülow, with whose young wife Cosima, Liszt's daughter, Wagner had fallen in love. But plans for a Festival Theatre fell through owing to opposition in Munich to Wagner and his plans, and he left Bavaria to set up house in Tribschen, on the Lake of Lucerne. Here he completed *Die Meistersinger* in the autumn of 1867; Bülow conducted the first performance in Munich in June 1868, and four

months later Cosima moved to Tribschen to live with Wagner. She had already borne Wagner two daughters; the birth of their son Siegfried in 1869 prompted the *Siegfried Idyll* on themes from the *Ring*. As Cosima's diaries reveal, their domestic life, which included an inner circle of loyal admirers, was marked by unswerving devotion on her part, and on his by an autocracy that was tempered by much greater kindness, tolerance, and humour than has often been suggested.

By contrast with *Tristan*, *Die Meistersinger* can seem a robust assertion of bourgeois normality. It is in fact deeply coloured by its predecessor, not least by Wagner's assertion that, 'Great is the power of love, but greater still is the power of its renunciation'. The chromaticism is latent, but none the less essential to a style in which the diatonicism associated with the burghers of Nuremberg and their ordered lives is not only 'reconstructed' against the chromaticism but thereby serves to express at once a nostalgically distant view of Medieval Germany and the precarious achievement of Sachs, by his renunciation of Eva, in preserving order. As always with mature Wagner, *Die*

Autograph sketch for Wagner's 'Siegfried', the beginning of Act 2.

Caricature by Daumier on the music of Wagner.

Meistersinger is about many things at once. They include Walther, the pioneering young instinctive artist Wagner associated with himself, overcoming the opposition of the entrenched Mastersingers, seen at their most pedantic in the person of Beckmesser, whom Wagner identified, originally even by name, with his hostile critic Hanslick. But by insisting on the virtues of the Mastersingers, Wagner is declaring that tradition must not be overthrown but refreshed. It was appropriate to this most open and warming of Wagner's works that melody and even identifiable numbers should return to his style within the framework of a continuous web in which an important part is played by *Leitmotive*: these are, understandably, exceptionally fluent and melodic in character.

3. *Bayreuth and the 'Ring'.* Wagner now turned his attention to the foundation of the ideal opera house that had so long eluded him; and after many difficulties he opened the new Festspielhaus in Bayreuth, supported by Ludwig and an army of subscribers and loyal workers, in 1876 with the completed *Ring*, now consisting of *Das Rheingold*, *Die Walküre*, *Siegfried*, and *Götterdämmerung* ('The Twilight of the Gods'). The Festival was attended by an array of luminaries from all over Europe: Wagner was by now the most famous artist of the day, though still one

capable of arousing violent feelings, as was shown by the continued hostility of Hanslick, the incomprehension of rival composers such as Brahms and Tchaikovsky, and the violent break that now occurred with his former admirer Nietzsche. Ruler of the artistic kingdom he had created, he settled into the Bayreuth house built for him by Ludwig, which he named Wahnfried (meaning peace achieved out of turmoil).

In the *Ring*, Wagner created the last great epic cycle that has been written. He was conscious that this must be achieved through the medium of music, though his ideas grew out of the love of Greek epic he had acquired as a student together with readings on myth under the influence of Feuerbach and his own careful reading of early German epic. The expansion from one opera to four reflects not only the scale of the drama but his compositional needs; for the subtlety and complexity of his *Leitmotiv* technique here demands the largest possible canvas if it is to work freely and expressively. The technique itself develops, for the comparatively simple methods of identification that mark *Das Rheingold* evolve by *Götterdämmerung* into a dense network of allusive music that achieves the condition of a conceptual language. *Leitmotiv*, as a method, was much misunderstood, including by those most admiring of Wagner: he resisted the facile labelling that ensued, with reason, since (for instance) the so-called Spear motive really represents not a physical spear (despite its thrusting, energetic nature) but the treaties graven on it by which Wotan rules, and whose infraction leads to the downfall of the gods. The *Ring* is essentially a myth of power, love, and renunciation, expressed in a dramatic conflict fought out between gods, giants, humans, dwarfs, and other beings. Its text makes full use of *Stabreim*, less for reasons of musical assonance than for the invocation of an archaic diction and still more for the symphonic freedom, within a verse structure, which it provided.

The success of the Festival by no means assured the future of Bayreuth, not least since the king had lost some faith in Wagner over his elopement with Cosima and eventual marriage to her in 1870. But the Festival, which he attended, helped to reconcile him to Wagner, and further support was forthcoming while Wagner turned his attention to what, apart from projected symphonies, he intended to be his last work, *Parsifal*. Aging and tired, he paid frequent visits to Italy for his health (he suffered from erysipelas and from angina pectoris), drawing ideas for the staging of *Parsifal* from gardens at Ravello and from Siena Cathedral. He completed the score in Palermo early in 1882; the first performance took place in Bayreuth, which long reserved exclusive rights to the work, in July and August under Hermann Levi.

Parsifal, like the *Ring*, draws on myth, in this case a much closer and more complex set of sources. Various versions of the Grail legend, particularly that in Wolfram von Eschenbach's Medieval German poem, provide the framework for the plot, which also enshrines Wagner's subtlest and most penetrating ideas about belief, about human structures, and not least about feminine psychology, since Kundry—his most remarkable character—is at once the temptress and the agent of Parsifal's redemption, he in turn bringing about her redemption. The correlation between text and music is more detailed and far-reaching than in previous works, though the use of motive is freer than in the *Ring*, and *Stabreim* is abandoned in favour of a limited use of end-rhyme. Because of its static nature, *Parsifal* has often been underrated in the range and density of its psychological action, which includes new insight into the themes of redemption and renunciation which had so long absorbed Wagner. He gave the work the description *Bühnenweihfestspiel*, or 'stage dedication festival play': its difficult synthesis of so many different strands of experience continues to arouse more resistance and incomprehension than any other of his works.

In September 1882 Wagner travelled with his family to Venice. He planned now only to write some one-movement symphonies making use of the motivic techniques he had evolved. On 13 February 1883 he had a fatal heart attack. His body was conveyed back to Bayreuth and buried in the garden of Wahnfried. Cosima survived him, at first reluctantly, to become the dominating figure at Bayreuth Festivals until her death, shortly before that of her son Siegfried, in 1930.

JOHN WARRACK

FURTHER READING
Ernest Newman: *The Life of Richard Wagner* (London, 1933–47); C. von Westernhagen, trans. M. Whittall: *Wagner: a Biography* (Cambridge, 1978); C. Dahlhaus, trans. M. Whittall: *Richard Wagner's Music Dramas* (Cambridge, 1979); M. Gregor-Dellin and D. Mack, ed., trans. G. Skelton: *Cosima Wagner's Diaries* (London, 1978–80).

Wagner-Régeny, Rudolf (*b* Szász-Régen, 28 Aug. 1903; *d* East Berlin, 18 Sept. 1969). German composer, conductor, and pianist, of Romanian birth. He studied at the Leipzig Conservatory and then at the Berlin Hochschule für Musik. From 1923 to 1925 he was chorusmaster at the Berlin Volksoper, and in 1930 became a German citizen. In 1935 Karl Böhm conducted the première of his opera *Der Günstling* at Dresden. It was an immediate success, praised in Nazi circles, but his subsequent works were less to the Party's taste (the operas *Die Bürger von Calais* and *Johanna Balk*, were influenced by Weill and Brecht). Wagner-Régeny survived the war to become director of the Rostock Hochschule up to 1950, and then composition professor at the East Berlin Academy of Arts until his retirement in 1968. His later works employ 12-note techniques.

WENDY THOMPSON

Wagon. A Japanese six-stringed zither. See *Japanese Music*, 3*b*.

Wait [wayte]. Originally, a watchman; later, a civic minstrel. In the 13th and 14th centuries watchmen employed by a town or noble household guarded the gates and patrolled the streets during the night, sounding the hours and watching for fire and other dangers (like the Night Watchman in Wagner's *Die Meistersinger von Nürnberg*). The instrument they used to show they were on duty was a type of shawm, also known as a wait or wayte-pipe (see *Shawm*, 2).

In the 15th and 16th centuries civic minstrels were also called waits, probably by association with the instrument they played, though they had no watchmen's duties. Many were good musicians who could play a variety of 'outdoor', loud-toned instruments (shawm, slide trumpet, sackbut, etc.); later they also sang and used

English City Waits of the 17th century, wash drawing attributed to Marcellus Laroon (c.1649–1702).

quieter instruments (recorder, cornett, viol). They were well thought of by the municipal authorities and were given handsome uniforms, often with chains and badges. They customarily attended on the mayor at civic functions and ceremonial occasions, and sometimes played in the street at night. From the 16th century onwards it was customary for town waits to attend at inns and taverns for the arrival of any notable guest who might recompense them for a musical welcome, to play during mealtimes, and, in some towns, to give public street concerts on Sundays and at Christmas and other holidays (though Sunday playing was somewhat curtailed under the Puritan regime of Cromwell's time).

The numerous British towns and cities that have records of employing waits include London, Aberdeen, Bath, Cambridge, Chester, Edinburgh, Exeter, Newcastle, Norwich, Nottingham, Oxford, and York. The London waits were established by Henry III in 1253 and, like those at Chester and a few other towns, they later had a 'signature' tune associated with them, which became known as 'London Waits'. The Norwich waits seem to have been particularly renowned and are known to have existed in 1288. They have a more or less continuous history, well documented up to the end of the 18th century: in the 16th century they participated in the Norwich mystery plays, and Sir Francis Drake requested five or six of them to go with him on a voyage to Lisbon.

Membership of the waits was often a family tradition. Orlando Gibbons's father, William, was a city wait in Oxford and later in Cambridge, and his brother Ferdinand also became a Cambridge wait. Many of the Bach family too were town musicians in Thuringia in Germany, where the equivalent term was *Stadtpfeifer*, though the tradition survived longer there and the duties were wider-ranging. They included playing dances, chorales, and signal-pieces (a considerable body of *Turmmusik*, or 'tower music', was composed for *Stadtpfeifer* to play from the towers of the churches and town halls), as well as instrumental teaching. Several well-known musicians were first trained as town musicians (e.g. Telemann and J. J. Quantz).

The tradition of city waits in Britain continued until the late 18th or even early 19th century, long after most other minstrel traditions had died out. The term 'wait', however, survived well into the 19th century to describe street musicians who serenaded the public at Christmas time with seasonal songs and music.

See also *Minstrel*; *Street Music*, 3.

PERCY SCHOLES, rev. Judith Nagley

Waldscenen ('Woodland Scenes'). Nine pieces for solo piano, Op. 82, by Schumann, composed in 1848–9.

'Waldstein' Sonata. Beethoven's Piano Sonata No. 21 in C Op. 53, composed in 1803–4. It is so called because Beethoven dedicated it to his patron, Count Ferdinand von Waldstein (1762–1823).

Waldteufel, (Charles) **Émile** (*b* Strasbourg, 9 Dec. 1837; *d* Paris, 12 Feb. 1915). French composer. Born into a musical family, he studied at the Paris Conservatoire, and proceeded to devote himself to composition. In 1865 he became pianist to the French court. His waltzes and other dances, composed for state balls, were enormously popular in France and abroad. They include such gems as *Manolo*, *Estudiantina*, and *España*.   WENDY THOMPSON

Wales

1. The Welsh Tradition
2. Art Music
3. Festivals and Concert Life

4. Opera
5. Education, Libraries, and Publishers

1. *The Welsh Tradition.* The importance of music in ancient Welsh culture is attested by its prominence in pre-Christian myth and the part it played in the services of the early Celtic Church, and also by the esteem enjoyed by the bards in the households of the Welsh princes before the country came under English rule in 1282. The bards were poets and musicians who rhymed and sang the exploits of Welsh heroes or fashioned elegies for them. No doubt they also entertained their princes with lighter songs, as did the *troubadours* and *trouvères* in France, but unfortunately nothing of their music has survived. Regulations governing the conduct and remuneration of the bards were laid down in the mid-10th-century Laws of Hywel Dda ('Howell the Good'), and their professional status and duties were reviewed in several convocations which resemble, in many important respects, the *eisteddfod* of more recent times (see 3 below).

The Laws of Hywel Dda point to the harp and the crwth as the main bardic instruments; they also mention *pybeu* ('pipes'; possibly bagpipes or hornpipes), but these were evidently held in lower esteem. The crwth was a bowed lyre, an ancestor of the violin, with three or four strings; crwth players were among those present at the historic festival held by Lord Rhys at Cardigan in 1176 (see 3 below). Still more important among the bards was the harp, which has long been recognized as Wales's national instrument. While the Medieval repertory of the crwth has disappeared, along with the original instruments themselves, some vestige of early bardic harp music is perhaps preserved in the famous Robert ap Huw manuscript, the most ancient source of Welsh music of any kind, now in the British Library (Add. 14905). This dates from about 1613 but it was copied, in part at least, from another manuscript belonging to the 16th-century harpist William Penllyn, and there are reasons for thinking that it may represent the practice of some 300 years previous to this. It contains pieces for harp, including some evidently used to accompany singing or poetic recitations, written in a letter tablature some-

A page from the Robert ap Huw manuscript.

what resembling that of German organists of the period (see *Tablature*,   ). Attempts to transcribe the manuscript into modern notation have so far been thwarted by uncertainties about ap Huw's directions for tuning the instrument, with the result that the nature of the repertory is still imperfectly understood.

The Welsh cleric Giraldus Cambrensis, Archdeacon of Brecon from 1175 to 1204, also referred in his writings to the popularity of the harp, crwth, and pipes among the Welsh in Medieval times, and he mentioned as well the playing of 'very long straight trumpets'. But the best-known passage in Giraldus's *Descriptio Cambriae* (1194) is the controversial one describing part-singing in Wales: 'When they make music together, they sing their songs not in unison, as is done elsewhere, but in parts, with many modes and phrases, so that in a crowd of singers . . . you would hear as many songs and differentiations of voices as you could see heads'. Giraldus's Latin is open to various interpretations, and opinions differ as to the precise nature of the singing he is here describing, but the Welsh love of part-singing is deeply ingrained, and their feeling for sonorous harmony can still be experienced among remote communities in the principality, and for that matter in public houses during the National Eisteddfod meetings or at Cardiff Arms Park before an international rugby match.

Singing and harp-playing come together in the peculiarly Welsh form of music-making called *penillion* (literally 'stanzas'), another branch of the bardic tradition which flourished particularly in the north of the country. The intricate art of improvising vocal stanzas to a traditional tune played on the harp has been revived at modern *eisteddfodau*, but the airs used have become increasingly standardized and the improvisatory element correspondingly weakened. Choral *penillion*, necessarily rehearsed, is apparently a recent development, and in the opinion of many a degenerate one.

Although of Welsh descent, the Tudors in England were hostile to the existence of an independent Welsh culture and did what they could to anglicize the language and customs of the principality. The role of the bard consequently declined in Wales, and bardic traditions were kept alive during the succeeding centuries only in lowly and sometimes wretched conditions. Recovery was slow. In the 17th century popular ballads were sung to the traditional airs, and these were published in great numbers during the 18th century. Volumes of harp airs also began to appear, compiled for the most part by expatriates such as John Parry of Ruabon (*c.*1710-82) and Edward Jones (Bardd y Brenin, 1752-1824) and published in London. Jones's *Musical and Poetical Relicks of the Welsh Bards* (1784) contained about 60 such airs (the number was increased to over 100 in the second edition of 1794), as well as examples of *penillion* and a valuable if not altogether trustworthy account of Welsh minstrelsy from the earliest times. It was not until the 19th century that collections of folk-tunes, including songs, carols, and dances, began to appear in print. Maria Jane Williams's *Ancient National Airs of Gwent and Morganwg* (1844) was the first, and it was soon followed by others, including John Thomas's *Y Caniedydd Cymreig* ('The Cambrian Minstrel', 1845) and John Owain's *Gems of Welsh Melody* (1860-4), in which the Welsh national anthem *Hen wlad fy nhadau* ('The Land of my Fathers') was first published. But the systematic collecting and printing of Welsh folk-song began with the founding in 1906 of the Welsh Folk Song Society and the inauguration of its journal, edited by J. Lloyd Williams and from 1951 by W. S. Gwynn Williams. The latter's *Welsh National Music and Dance* (1932) remains the standard general work on traditional Welsh music. A centre for the study of Welsh folk music was established at the Welsh Folk Museum, St Fagan's (Cardiff), in 1976, and in 1979 a research post in the subject was created at University College, Bangor.

2. *Art Music*. If, despite its long traditions and the innate musicality of its people, Wales has yet to produce a composer of the first importance, the reason may be traced in part to the social and economic consequences of the Tudor dynasty in England. With the accession of Henry VII in 1485 and the decline in the role of the native bard, there began that long exodus of composers and performers from Wales into England, a migration which, as far as singers and instrumentalists are concerned, continues today. The vigorous flowering of English music in the 16th and early 17th centuries had no parallel in Wales, and the most outstanding Welsh composer of the period, Thomas Tomkins (1572-1656), found employment across the border, like many of his compatriots. During the later 17th and 18th centuries the rise of Nonconformism and the absence of any strong theatrical

John Parry, the blind Welsh harpist, engraving (1776) by his son William Parry. The engraving was done as a ticket of admittance to a morning concert for John Parry's benefit.

tradition ensured that the new musical styles of the Baroque left the principality virtually untouched. The main contributions to art music at this time were made by harpist-composers such as John Parry (Barrd Alaw, 1776-1851), who as well as writing for his own instrument composed music for Vauxhall Gardens and for operatic farces and other stage entertainments in London.

During the 19th century, the Nonconformist movement, which had at first done much to stifle any ambitious music-making, began to bear its own musical fruit. William Williams (Pantecelyn) had already established himself as Wales's leading hymn writer with printed collections in 1744 and 1787, but it was not until the 19th century that the hymn began to replace the folk-song as an expression of a collective musical, social, and religious awareness, and the *cymanfa ganu* ('hymn-singing festival') began to enjoy the popularity it has retained to this day. From hymn to oratorio chorus was a small step for those schooled in *Tonic Sol-fa, and the choirs that began to form up and down the country were soon engaged in rehearsing items from the better-known oratorios of Handel, Haydn, and Mendelssohn. (The first two names soon became as familiar in baptismal registers as they were in concert programmes.) At the same time, industrialization encouraged the formation of brass bands and male choirs, and in both these activities the pre-eminence of the Welsh is still acknowledged.

It was the vigorous choral tradition that stimulated composers in the late 19th century to turn to the composition of more ambitious works which might employ professional orchestras and soloists as well. At first they took the German Romantics and prominent figures of the so-called English Renaissance as models, and there is little in the cantatas and oratorios of such composers as Joseph Parry (1841-1903), David Evans (1843-1913), and David Jenkins (1849-1915) to distinguish them from those of Cowen and Mackenzie, from whom works were commissioned for the Cardiff Festival. A more distinctively national voice can be heard in the music of the next generation of composers, notably David Vaughan Thomas (1873-1934) and David de Lloyd (1883-1948). Their works were again primarily vocal, but with David Wynne (*b* 1900), Grace Williams (1906-77), and Arwel Hughes (*b* 1909) we find composers who begin to match their achievements in choral music and song with a fresh interest in instrumental and orchestral writing, stimulated by new developments in the musical life of the principality (see 3 and 5 below). Daniel Jones (*b* 1912) has been Wales's most prolific symphonist so far, with 10 such works to his credit.

Most of these composers, if not all, have drawn upon their Welsh background and upon Welsh folk-song in their music. This is true also, though to a lesser extent, of Alun Hoddinott (*b* 1929) and William Mathias (*b* 1934), whose music, influenced by Bartók, Hindemith, Stravinsky, and more recent composers, belongs to a more progressive Western European tradition. Hoddinott and Mathias have been the most successful of Welsh composers in terms of performances and publication, and their works are quite widely known outside Wales. Both have been active as teachers and have helped to train and encourage a new generation of composers even more cosmopolitan in outlook. Among members of the younger generation who have remained to work in the principality are Jeffrey Lewis (*b* 1942) and John Metcalf (*b* 1946).

3. *Festivals and Concert Life.* The *eisteddfod* (literally 'session'), one of the most ancient of competitive festivals, is devoted mainly to music and poetry. The National Eisteddfod, which takes place in August and lasts for one week, has been held annually since 1880, alternately in the north and south of Wales, but its origins may be traced to gatherings held irregularly by the Medieval bards. The earliest about which documentary evidence exists was that summoned by Lord Rhys at Cardigan in 1176, and others are recorded from the 14th century to the 16th. An important meeting was held at Caerwys, Flintshire, in 1567 (or 1568) under commission from Elizabeth I to rid Wales of numerous 'vagraunt and idle persons naming theim selfes mynstrelles Rithmers and Barthes'. With the decline of the bards the *eisteddfod* also declined, but its traditions were recalled in the 'tavern' *eisteddfodau* of the 18th century (so called because of the places in which they were held) and in a famous meeting at Corwen in 1789 which started the movement towards establishing a permanent festival. The Gorsedd of Bards, which became linked with the National Eisteddfod in 1880, was a fabrication of Iolo Morganwg in 1819, but its activities are now indissociable from the Eisteddfod and admission to the Gorsedd is looked upon as a high honour. The main changes during the 20th century have been the establishing of Welsh as the only language for Eisteddfod proceedings and the placing of a greater emphasis than formerly on professional concerts in the evenings. The National Eisteddfod remains a main focal point for the expression of Welsh nationhood and for the renewal of cultural traditions, while at the International Eisteddfod, an important offshoot held annually since 1947 at Llangollen, competitors from many countries exhibit their native songs and dances.

Non-competitive festivals, fostered by the 19th-century choral movement and modelled

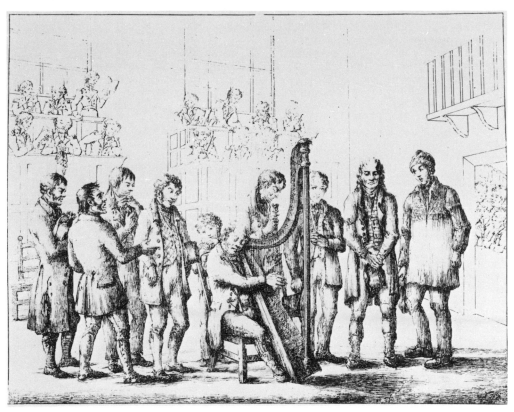

Engraving of the Powys Eisteddfod of 1824.

on the triennial festivals of Birmingham and Leeds, were held at Harlech (1867–1934), Cardiff (1892–1910), and other centres. In 1948 the Swansea Festival was inaugurated, and this remains the most important Welsh festival as far as its size and its capacity to attract the finest orchestras and soloists from Britain and abroad are concerned. It was soon joined by many others, including those at Llandaff, Cardiff, the Vale of Glamorgan, Fishguard, and St Asaph. The BBC in Cardiff organizes a St David's Festival each March, with concerts and recitals in various Welsh towns, and the Extra-mural Department of University College, Swansea, holds an annual Bach Week at which lectures and seminars are supplemented by public concerts devoted to the music of J. S. Bach and his contemporaries.

Since the Second World War festivals such as these have helped to reinvigorate concert life in Wales, which had previously suffered more than the English provinces from a lack of professionalism and the poor provision of concert halls. At the same time the Welsh Arts Council, with its headquarters in Cardiff, arranged tours by visiting artists and orchestras which set new standards for Welsh musicians. (The Council has also been the main patron of all the Welsh festivals and has financed the commissioning of Welsh composers and the recording of their work.) Several unsuccessful attempts have been made to form a national symphony orchestra, but the only professional orchestra in Wales, apart from that of the *Welsh National Opera, remains the BBC Welsh Symphony Orchestra. This was founded in 1936, reconstituted in 1946, and brought up to full symphonic strength by 1977. Welsh towns are now quite well endowed with small concert halls and this has facilitated the promotion of chamber music, in which ensembles resident at the university colleges of Aberystwyth, Bangor, and Cardiff have played an important role. But except for the Brangwyn Hall in Swansea (capacity 1,500), Wales had no large hall specifically designed for orchestral concerts until the completion in 1982 of the St David's Hall in Cardiff (capacity 2,000).

4. *Opera.* For a long time opera was cultivated even less than concert-giving in Wales. The first Welsh opera was probably *Blodwen*, composed by Joseph Parry to a libretto by Richard Davies and produced at Aberdare in 1878. Others were written by Parry's son, Joseph Haydn Parry (1864–94), David de Lloyd, Haydn Morris

The auditorium of St David's Hall, Cardiff, the national concert and conference hall of Wales (completed August 1982).

(1891–1965), and others, but they received only isolated and mainly amateur performances, and it was not until the formation of the Welsh National Opera in 1946 that opera in Wales was placed on a regular and eventually a fully professional basis. The company first attracted wide notice in the 1950s with its productions of early, neglected operas by Verdi and of other works which brought into prominence its excellent chorus, still one of its main strengths. Since then the repertory has been extended in every direction, but particularly into the 20th century, with cycles of Britten and Janáček operas and notable productions of Strauss's *Elektra* and *Die Frau ohne Schatten* and of Tippett's *The Midsummer Marriage*. In 1971 the company staged the first British production of Berg's *Lulu* and in 1981 it did a similar service for Martinů's *The Greek Passion*. New operas have been commissioned from Arwel Hughes, Grace Williams, Alun Hoddinott, William Mathias, and John Metcalf. Several singers of international repute, including Gwyneth Jones, Margaret Price, and Stuart Burrows, made or consolidated their early reputations with the Welsh National Opera, and the company continues to provide a training ground for young Welsh singers, as well as attracting guest singers, producers, and conductors from the major European houses.

Amateur societies have continued to exist alongside Wales's professional company. Among the most worthwhile productions have been those of the Neath Operatic Society, some of which have been given in the small theatre constructed at Craig-y-Nos for the famous Italian soprano Adelina Patti after her retirement from the public stage.

5. *Education, Libraries, and Publishers.* Of the four main constituent colleges in the University of Wales, all except that at Swansea have music departments offering honours and post-graduate degrees. The first Chair of Music was established at Aberystwyth in 1874, with Joseph Parry as Professor; it was followed by those at Cardiff (1910) and Bangor (1920). Walford Davies (1869–1941) did a great deal to promote music education at every level, not only as Professor at Aberystwyth from 1919 to 1926 but also as lecturer and adjudicator throughout the principality and through his work with the National Council of Music, a university body set up in 1919 to improve and extend music education in schools, colleges, and adult centres. Among its activities was the running of summer schools at Coleg Harlech and Howell's School, Denbigh. It was disbanded in 1961. In 1949 the National College of Music (later the Welsh College of Music and Drama) was founded at Cardiff to provide professional training for performers and teachers. At first situated in Cardiff Castle, it moved to purpose-built premises nearby in 1973.

As well as the Welsh Arts Council and the BBC, there are three important organizations devoted to education in a wider sense and to promoting Welsh music, particularly recent art music. The Guild for the Promotion of Welsh Music, founded in 1954, has organized discussions and performances and commissioned new works from Welsh composers. Its valuable journal, *Welsh Music*, appears about three times a year. The Welsh Amateur Music Federation has existed since 1968 to help to provide facilities for non-professional choirs and orchestras and to assist them in engaging professional soloists for their performances. And the Welsh Music Archive, established at University College, Cardiff, in 1976, aims to provide for Welsh composers the same kind of support given to their English and Scottish colleagues by similar but older institutions in London and Glasgow.

The Welsh Music Archive houses a useful and growing library of scores, records, and tapes, mainly of 20th-century Welsh music; these are available for general use. Other important repositories are the university departmental libraries and the National Library of Wales, Aberystwyth. Wales is not rich in collections of older music, but the Mackworth and Aylward collections of mainly 18th-century material at Cardiff Central Library contain some interesting and unique items.

Most modern Welsh composers and writers on music look to England for publication of their works, but a good deal of music (particularly short vocal pieces) has been published by D. J. Snell of Swansea and by the Gwynn Publishing Co., Llangollen. The principal publisher of music and of literature on music in Wales today is the University of Wales Press, Cardiff.   MALCOLM BOYD

FURTHER READING
J. Graham: *A Century of Welsh Music* (London, 1923); W. S. Gwynn Williams: *Welsh National Music and Dance* (London, 1932, 4th edn 1971); P. Crossley-Holland, ed.: *Music in Wales* (London, 1948); T. Parry: *The Story of the Eisteddfod* (Denbigh, *c*.1950); D. Jones: *Music in Wales* (Cardiff, 1961); G. Thomas: *The Caerwys Eisteddfodau* (Cardiff, 1968); K. A. Wright: *Gentle are its Songs* (London, 1973); M. Stephens, ed.: *The Arts in Wales 1950-75* (Cardiff, 1979).

Walker, Ernest (*b* Bombay, 15 July 1870; *d* Oxford, 21 Feb. 1949). English writer on music, teacher, and composer. He spent most of his life at Oxford where he had immense influence on a whole generation of musicians. His compositions include some interesting songs and chamber music, influenced by Brahms; but his major work was his *A History of Music in England* (Oxford, 1907, 3rd edn, rev. and enlarged by Jack Westrup, 1952), an excellent study not yet superseded.   DENIS ARNOLD

Walk to the Paradise Garden, The. Intermezzo for orchestra before the last scene of Delius's opera *A Village Romeo and Juliet*. The 'Paradise Garden' was the village inn. It was not in the original score, but was added in 1910 at Beecham's request to cover a scene change in the Covent Garden production. It is now frequently played as a concert item.

Walküre, Die ('The Valkyrie'). See *Ring des Nibelungen, Der*.

Waller, 'Fats' (Thomas Wright) (*b* Waverley, New York, 21 May 1904; *d* on board the Santa Fe Chief express to Kansas City, 15 Dec. 1943). Black American jazz musician and composer. He was the son of the Rev. Edward Martin Waller, in whose Baptist Church in Harlem he learned to play the organ. His first professional job was as organist at the Lincoln Theater, New York. Later he worked as pianist in a silent movie theatre in Washington. He became known there as an exuberant entertainer and jazz pianist, and he started composing songs in the 1920s, writing the music for the revues *Keep Shufflin'* (1928) and *Hot Chocolates* (1929). During the Depression he was a staff pianist on radio; he then returned to the stage in the 1930s with an established reputation as the composer of such songs as 'Ain't misbehavin'' and 'Honeysuckle rose'. He reached the height of his fame in the mid-1930s as a prolific recording artist with his Rhythm group, noted for a slyly humorous interpretation of sentimental songs and for his talent as a jazz pianist. He appeared in various films, notably *Stormy Weather* (1943), and went to Europe and London to appear in the theatre and to record. A too hectic life and heavy drinking ended his life at the age of 39.
                                    PETER GAMMOND

Walmisley. English family of musicians. **Thomas Walmisley** (*b* London, 22 May 1783; *d* London, 23 July 1866) was an organist, teacher, and composer. He began to study music at the age of 14 with Attwood, and became a well-known teacher and a composer of glees. From 1814 to 1854 he was organist at St Martin-in-the-Fields. His son **Thomas** (Attwood) **Walmisley** (*b* London, 21 Jan. 1814; *d* Hastings, 17 Jan. 1856) showed great musical precocity as a child. He also studied with Attwood, and at the age of 16 became organist of Croydon Church. He then went to Cambridge, where he became organist of Trinity and St John's Colleges. In 1835 he wrote an ode for the installation of the Marquis of Camden as Chancellor of the University, and in the following year he became Professor of Music. He took the degree of Mus.D. in 1848, was one of the finest English organists of his day, and wrote a number of extremely competent anthems and services, as well as songs and duets for oboe and piano.

                                    WENDY THOMPSON

Walsh. English family of music-sellers, music publishers, and instrument makers. They built up the most extensive business of the early 18th century, based largely on pewter-plate engraving, and were particularly influential through their mass methods of publishing. The elder John Walsh (?1665 or 1666–1736) set himself up in London around 1690 and two years later was appointed Musical-Instrument-Maker-in-Ordinary to William III at 'The Golden Harp and Hoboy', the trade sign of his predecessor, John Shaw. He began publishing in 1695, using pewter plates and punches, and issued a great range of publications (single songs, anthologies, instrumental music, and instruction books). Most of those issued before about 1730 also carry the name of Hare, Walsh's associate in the City.

Many of Walsh's editions were pirated, some in collaboration with other houses such as Estienne *Roger of Amsterdam. He frequently bought up stock from other publishers, sorting out sheets to make up his own editions, and issued many of Handel's works without the composer's knowledge or authority. He published the first of Handel's operas to be performed in England, *Rinaldo* (1711), but his relationship with Handel was predominantly stormy and led Paul Henry Lang, Handel's biographer, to describe Walsh as 'a hardbitten, ruthless, piratical businessman'. Handel was reconciled only when the younger John Walsh (1709–66) took over the firm in the 1730s; in 1739 he was granted a 14-year monopoly of Handel's music. Both father and son at their deaths left considerable fortunes. The firm eventually inherited by the younger Walsh's cousin William *Randall.

See also *Printing and Publishing of Music*, 5.

J. M. THOMSON

Walter, Johann (*b* Kahla, nr Jena, 1496; *d* Torgau, nr Leipzig, 25 Mar. 1570). German composer. He studied at Leipzig University, at the same time singing in the court chapel of the Elector of Saxony. Apart from six years spent as musical director at the Dresden chapel he lived in Torgau from 1526. He collaborated with Luther to produce the first hymn book of the Reformation (Wittenberg, 1524), and advised Luther on the form the new German liturgy should take.   DENIS ARNOLD

Walther, Johann Gottfried (*b* Erfurt, 18 Sept. 1684; *d* Weimar, 23 Mar. 1748). German composer and organist. He was a cousin and close friend of Bach and studied with Johann Bernhard Bach, Johann Sebastian's uncle, in Erfurt. In 1703 he travelled around Germany, meeting musicians and gaining experience as an organist, and in 1707 he became organist at the town church of Weimar, where he remained until his death. He was an excellent composer of organ music, especially of chorale preludes, but is probably better known today for his dictionary of music, the *Musicalisches Lexicon* (Leipzig, 1732).   DENIS ARNOLD

Walther, Johann Jakob (*b* Witterda, nr Erfurt, *c*.1650; *d* Mainz, 2 Nov. 1717). German violinist and composer. He travelled to Italy *c*.1670, gaining experience of the virtuoso school of violin playing, and then entered the service of the Dresden court. He had moved to Mainz by 1681. His surviving music is for the violin, and although he wrote some rather silly pieces imitating birdsong he was important for the development of violin technique in Germany.

DENIS ARNOLD

Walther von der Vogelweide (*b c*.1170; *d c*.1230). German *Minnesinger*. He spent his early life in the service of noble patrons in Vienna until 1198, when he began a period of about 20 years wandering through Europe. He was at the court of Emperor Otto IV in 1212, and was granted a fief near Würzburg by Emperor Frederick II *c*.1220, as a reward for his support of the Hohenstaufen family in their various political manoeuvres.

Vogelweide's poetry has been fairly well preserved, but his music was written down only long after his death, so that it is unlikely that much of it survives in its original form. His early *Lieder* deal mainly with courtly love, in an attractive, unstilted way, but at the end of the 12th century he turned to writing *Sprüche*—songs dealing with political and topical matters—and became a master of that genre.

DENIS ARNOLD

Walton, (Sir) William (Turner) (*b* Oldham, Lancs., 29 Mar. 1902; *d* Ischia, Bay of Naples, 8 Mar. 1983). English composer. He was a chorister at Christ Church, Oxford, and the admiration won by his already emerging creative gifts made it possible for him to be accepted as an undergraduate there in 1918. However, he left in 1920 without taking a degree and was then unofficially adopted by the Sitwells. The first fruit of this association was music for a recitation of poems by Edith Sitwell, *Façade* (1921–2), and Walton's score for instrumental sextet soon won him a reputation as a musical wit and iconoclast. Variously influenced by Les Six, Stravinsky, and, in an ironic fashion, Schoenberg, the work combines rhythmic zest, allusions to popular music, and plangent harmony in a highly polished manner.

Walton's next major work, the overture *Portsmouth Point* (1925), was the first of several bustling orchestral capriccios, while the deeply

William Walton

of pagan opulence and pageantry, flamboyantly scored for a large orchestra with separate brass ensembles. But when Walton turned from this to a more personal statement, his First Symphony (1932–5), he experienced difficulties: the completion of the work was long delayed, and despite the force with which the composer wields a Sibelian technique, his problems with the work remain evident beneath the surface.

During the next two decades most of Walton's music was on a smaller scale or of an occasional nature—though his coronation marches *Crown Imperial* (1937) and *Orb and Sceptre* (1953) have long outlived the occasions for which they were written, and his contributions to Olivier's Shakespeare trilogy, *Henry V* (1942–3), *Hamlet* (1947), and *Richard III* (1955), still demand admiration as among the most skilful scores ever written for the cinema. This was the period too of his only important chamber works, the String Quartet (1945–7) and the Violin Sonata (1949), both of which outshine his major orchestral works of the time: the Violin Concerto (1938–9), which was a more brilliant successor to that for viola, and the ballet *The Quest* (1943).

Walton's next work for the theatre was his three-act opera *Troilus and Cressida* (1950–4), an adaptation of Chaucer in which he was able to display all his facility for sumptuous atmosphere or steely drama, though the work has been criticized for its slow pace and its lack of incisive characterization, as well as for its 'grand opera' rhetoric. Only after a gap of more than a decade did Walton return to the theatre, and only then with a one-act comedy, *The Bear*

serious Viola Concerto (1928–9) established a characteristic union of this vivacity, influenced by Prokofiev and by jazz of the period, with Elgar's romantic longing. It was followed by another surprise, *Belshazzar's Feast* (1930–1), which exposed the English oratorio to a parade

Autograph MS of the piano score of Walton's Cello Concerto, part of the third movement.

(1965-7). Otherwise he contented himself after *Troilus* with a further sequence of superbly conceived orchestral works—the Cello Concerto (1956), the Partita (1957), the Second Symphony (1959-60), the Variations on a Theme by Hindemith (1962-3), and the Improvisations on an Impromptu of Benjamin Britten (1969)—and, more suprisingly, with a variety of smaller choral works, among which the anthem *The Twelve* (1965), to words by Auden, is outstanding.

The comparative smallness of Walton's output after the Second World War, coupled with his emphasis on professionalism and accomplishment, have often led to charges of 'relaxation', and indeed the three string concertos, for instance, show a steady decrease in emotional unrest and structural boldness, a steady increase in ease. It may be, however, that Walton's serenity was as valuable as his disquiet.

PAUL GRIFFITHS

FURTHER READING
Frank Howes: *The Music of William Walton* (London, 1965, 2nd edn, 1974); Stuart R. Craggs: *William Walton: a Thematic Catalogue* (London, 1977).

Waltz (Fr.: *valse*; Ger.: *Walzer*). A dance in 3/4 time, whose origins remain obscure in spite of many attempts to clarify the matter. The 3/4 rhythm is rare in early dances, almost totally absent in some folk music, and not in common use in classical music until the end of the 18th century, at least with the particular emphasis given to it in waltz form. Earlier dances in 3/4 time such as the *allemande and the *minuet bear little relation to the waltz, because the three beats are given equal and unemphasized stress. There is little doubt that the dance form of the waltz, with its heavy accent on the first beat of the bar, came about through the influence of the *Ländler, a dance basic to the folk music of Austria, southern Germany, and the Alpine regions, whose discovery by polite society probably caused as much surprised delight as jazz rhythms did at the end of the 19th century. The derivation of the word 'waltz' has caused some confusion with regard to musical origins, as most European languages had some word of similar nature describing a rotating or turning motion, the basic movement of the waltz: the French dance the *volta came to England as 'lavolta' and in German this became 'volter', from which 'walzer' probably derived.

The early German folk dances, like the Drehtanz and the Ländler, were active, springing dances full of lively steps and the throwing into the air of the lady partner, but all had the revolving characteristics. As these dances came into urban life and the ballroom, the steps became smoother and a gliding motion replaced the boisterous movements of the folk dance.

'La valse' by Philopon.

But polite society still saw it as conducive to lasciviousness and immorality, and Dr Burney shuddered to think what an English mother would have thought if her daughter were subjected to the familiar treatment that he had witnessed abroad.

The waltz did not grow out of the minuet, as some historians have suggested, but simply replaced it; the minuet remained stately and artificial until the waltz invaded European music around 1770 or 1780. One of its first appearances in piano music was in a sonatina by Haydn where the normal minuet was replaced by a 'mouvement de Walze', and its first use in opera is generally credited to Martín y Soler's *Una cosa rara* in 1786. It caused a sensation, and was quickly and avidly taken up by composers of dance music, particularly in Vienna. A pioneer in this respect was Michael Pamer (1782-1827), who wrote many waltzes and Ländlers, followed with relentless profusion by Joseph Lanner and Johann Strauss the elder, both of whom started their careers in his orchestra. The greatest exponent of the waltz was unquestionably the younger Johann Strauss, who took over from his father in writing richly melodic extended works that have since flourished as much in the concert hall as in the ballroom. The Viennese waltz developed the characteristic of a slight anticipation of the second beat of the bar, a device known as the *Atempause* (literally, 'breathing space'), which gives a delightful and distinctive lilt to the playing. In the hands of composers of other nationalities it took on a slightly different character: Emil Waldteufel in France returned the emphasis to the first beat, while the 'English' or 'Boston' waltz went back to a more even emphasis on all three beats, as found in the works of a 20th-century composer like Eric Coates.

The classical composers have exploited the waltz in every possible way. Schubert, who often spent his evenings listening to Pamer and Lanner, wrote numerous sets of waltzes for the piano, exploring its formal possibilities, while Weber crystallized the orchestral form in his *Aufforderung zum Tanz* ('Invitation to the Dance'). Notable examples of symphonic movements in waltz time are to be found in Berlioz's *Symphonie fantastique* and Tchaikovsky's Serenade for Strings. The waltz was taken to sophisticated extremes in Ravel's *La valse* and to the heights of romantic sumptuousness in Richard Strauss's *Der Rosenkavalier*.

PETER GAMMOND

Walze (Ger.). 1. *Crescendo* organ pedal. 2. 18th-century term for conventional musical figures, such as the *Alberti bass.

'Wanderer' Fantasia. Nickname of Schubert's Fantasia in C major for piano, D 760, composed in 1822. It is so called because the Adagio section is a set of variations on a passage from his song *Der Wanderer*, D 489 (1816). Liszt arranged it for piano and orchestra (*c*.1851).

Wand of Youth, The. Two orchestral suites by Elgar, Opp. 1*a* and 1*b*, arranged and orchestrated in 1907 and 1908 respectively from material Elgar wrote for a family play when he was 12. He used some of the themes again in his music for *The Starlight Express*

Wankend (Ger.). 'Wavering', 'shaking'.

War and Peace. Opera in five acts by Prokofiev; text by the composer and M. Mendelson-Prokofieva, after Tolstoy's novel (1869). First version, 13 scenes with choral prologue, produced: Leningrad, Maly Theatre, 12 June 1946; second version, Leningrad, Maly Theatre, 31 March 1955; London, Coliseum, 11 October 1972; Boston, 8 May 1974. Chosen to open the Sydney Opera House 5 August 1974. The long, episodic score has undergone various revisions, but was finally cast in 13 scenes, the first seven concentrating on Peace, the last six on War. Choosing dramatic key moments from Tolstoy with great skill, Prokofiev follows the tragic course of the love of Natasha Rostova and Prince Andrey, setting it against the epic struggle of the Russian people against the Napoleonic invader.

Ward, John (*bapt.* Canterbury, 8 Sept. 1571; *d* before 31 Aug. 1638). English composer. He may have been a choirboy at Canterbury Cathedral before serving as a domestic musician in the household of Sir Henry Fanshawe, Remembrancer of the Exchequer during the early years of the 17th century. Ward himself was described as a 'Gentleman', but he was also a considerable composer, especially of madrigals. His *First Set of English Madrigals* (London, 1613) contains some of the finest elegiac music of the time. He also composed fantasias and *In nomine* settings for viols, and services and verse anthems.

DENIS ARNOLD

Warlock, Peter [Heseltine, Philip Arnold] (*b* London, 30 Oct. 1894; *d* London, 17 Dec. 1930). English composer, critic, and author. He devised the pseudonym 'Peter Warlock' in 1916, using it for his compositions only from 1918. He had no formal musical education, but his interest in music was apparent from preparatory school years and was further fostered at Eton. An uncle who lived near Grez-sur-Loing introduced him to Delius in 1910. Warlock's lifelong devotion to Delius's music resulted in a warm friendship and in a book on the composer published in 1923. He also made piano arrangements of some Delius scores. For a year Warlock studied in Germany, then read classics at Oxford up to the outbreak of the First World War. In 1916 he met Bernard van Dieren, whose encouragement and influence led to a more mature individual style than was apparent in songs written when Warlock was 17. In 1920 he founded and was co-editor of the magazine *The Sackbut*.

Warlock's compositions are mainly vocal and choral. The solo songs are in many cases settings of Elizabethan poets with whom he had a natural affinity, while the best of his part-songs have a skill and sensitivity which entitle them to be ranked among the finest written by Englishmen. The two contrasted moods of his music—an extrovert, rumbustious joviality, and a refined, meditative lyricism, epitomized by such songs as, on the one hand, 'Captain Stratton's Fancy' (1920) and, on the other, 'The Frostbound Wood' (1929)—reflect the duality of his personality. He was found dead in a gas-filled room in Chelsea and an open verdict was returned. His best-known instrumental work is the charming collection of dances, the *Capriol Suite* (1926), and there is a *Serenade* for strings (1921-2), composed as a tribute to Delius on his 60th birthday.

MICHAEL KENNEDY

FURTHER READING
Cecil Gray: *Peter Warlock: a Memoir of Philip Heseltine* (London, 1934); Ian Copley: *The Music of Peter Warlock: a Critical Survey* (London, 1979).

Wärme (Ger.). 'Warmth'.

War of the Bouffons. See *Bouffons, Querelle des*.

War Requiem. Choral work, Op. 66, by Britten for soprano, tenor, and baritone soloists, boys' choir, chorus, organ, and orchestra. Settings of nine poems by Wilfred Owen (1893–1918), accompanied only by a chamber orchestra, are interpolated into Britten's setting of the Requiem Mass. The work was first performed in the new Coventry Cathedral in 1962.

Warsaw Concerto. See under *Addinsell, Richard.*

Wasps, The. Incidental music by Vaughan Williams for tenor and baritone soloists, male chorus, and orchestra composed for the 1909 Cambridge University production of Aristophanes' play. The composer arranged a five-movement orchestral suite with an overture (1909) from the score.

Wassail. A festive occasion which involves drinking. The word is associated particularly with the Christmas season, and occurs in many English Christmas carols. It derives from the Old Norse greeting *ves heill*, 'be in good health'.

Wassmuth, Johann Georg Franz (*d* Würzburg, 1766). German composer. In 1729 he was appointed a violinist in the archbishop's chapel in Würzburg, and the following year he became court organist and choirmaster. In 1731 he was made court composer, and finally, in 1737, *Kapellmeister.* Wassmuth's compositions include 16 serenatas, eight burlesques, Masses, concertos, suites, and symphonies.
                                    WENDY THOMPSON

Water Carrier, The. See *Deux journées, Les.*

Water Music. 1. Instrumental suites by Handel of pieces written for a royal procession on the River Thames. The well-known story that Handel wrote the music in 1715 for a royal water party to restore himself to favour with King George I (whose employment he had left to settle in England when the king was Elector of Hanover) is unsubstantiated. However, Handel did provide music for a royal water party on the Thames in 1717. Dating the suites is impossible, largely because no complete autograph score survives. The 20 pieces are scored for trumpets, horns, oboes, bassoons, flutes, recorders, and strings. Six of them have become well known as a suite orchestrated by Hamilton Harty (1922).

2. Work by Cage composed in 1952 for a pianist. Visual interest is a feature of its performance: the pianist is required to pour water from pots, play cards, blow whistles under water, use a radio, etc., while the score is displayed like a poster.

Weaver, John (*b* Shrewsbury, 21 July 1673; *d* Shrewsbury, 24 Sept. 1760). English dancer and choreographer. The son of a dancing master, he was associated with the Drury Lane and Lincoln's Inn theatres for many years. He is important for having evolved the *ballet d'action*, a dramatic work without dialogue in which the story is conveyed through mime. Two works of this kind were given at Drury Lane, *The Tavern Bilkers* (1702) and *The Loves of Mars and Venus* (1717). They were followed by similar pieces before Weaver retired to Shrewsbury in 1736. He also wrote theoretical works, including *Anatomical and Mechanical Lectures upon Dancing* (London, 1721), and translated Feuillet's *Chorégraphie* as *Orchesography* (London, 1706).   WENDY THOMPSON

Webbe, Samuel (i) (*b* ? London, 1740; *d* London, 25 May 1816). English organist and composer. He began his career as a music copyist and started to compose vocal music when he was in his 20s. In 1766 he was awarded a medal by the Catch Club for his canon 'O that I had wings', and in 1794 he became secretary to the Club. He was also organist to the chapel of the Sardinian Embassy in London and possibly to the Portuguese Embassy. He published two collections of sacred music (1792) but is best remembered for his numerous catches, canons, and glees. 'Glorious Apollo', written in 1787 on the foundation of the Glee Club, was sung at every meeting of the Club.

His son, **Samuel Webbe (ii)** (*b* London, *c*.1770; *d* London, 25 Nov. 1843), studied with his father and became a competent organist and pianist. He was also a notable composer of glees, songs, and motets.   WENDY THOMPSON

Weber, Bernhard Anselm (*b* Mannheim, 18 Apr. 1764; *d* Berlin, 23 Mar. 1821). German pianist and composer. He studied music with the Abbé Vogler and with Holzbauer. In 1787 he became music director of an opera troupe based in Hanover, and three years later went to Stockholm. In 1792 he was conductor at the National Theatre in Berlin, where he introduced the operas of Gluck, as well as producing some of his own. He also wrote a number of songs.   WENDY THOMPSON

Weber, Bernhard Christian (*b* Wolferschwenda, 1 Dec. 1712; *d* Tennstedt, nr Erfurt, 5 Feb. 1758). German organist and composer. He settled in Tennstedt as town organist in 1732. His only distinction as a composer seems to be that he wrote a collection of 24 preludes and fugues entitled *Das wohltemperierte Clavier* in emulation of Bach.
                                    WENDY THOMPSON

Weber, Carl Maria (Friedrich Ernst) **von** (*b* Eutin, nr Lübeck, 18/19 Nov. 1786; *d* London, 5 June 1826).German composer and critic. Son of a musician who was *Kapellmeister* to the Prince Bishop of Lübeck, Weber spent his early years travelling around with a theatre company which his father directed. He was therefore conversant with the repertory of *Singspiel* and opera from an early age, but gained little systematic musical training until, when he was about 11, he had lessons from Michael Haydn in Salzburg (where the Weber family were temporarily held up during the Napoleonic Wars). His first opera *Das Waldmädchen* was given in 1800, and a year later he composed a delightful *Singspiel, Peter Schmoll*, produced in Augsburg where his brother was director of a theatre. In 1803 he stayed for some time in Vienna studying with the Abbé Vogler on whose recommendation he was appointed in the following year musical director of the opera house at Breslau, where his extreme youth and ambitious reorganization of the repertory caused him some trouble. He remained there until 1806 when, during a period recuperating from an accidental dose of engraver's acid, he saw all his reforms set aside, and resigned.

He spent the next few years travelling around Germany, staying for a time at the Württemberg court at Stuttgart, from where he was eventually expelled due to a combination of intrigue and debt, and then in Mannheim and Darmstadt. In 1811 he wrote *Abu Hassan*, a witty one-act *Singspiel* much in the manner of Mozart's 'oriental' music, which was given in Munich with some success. About this period he met a virtuoso clarinettist, Heinrich Bärmann, with whom he went on tour (providing some excellent works for the instrument), visiting such important centres as Prague, Leipzig, and Berlin. By this time he was feeling the necessity to settle down, and he accepted the directorship of the Prague theatre where he took the opportunity to put into practice his anti-Italian views on repertory, concentrating principally on French and German works. The paucity and relative unpopularity of this repertory meant that he was continually giving new productions and he eventually resigned from here also, possibly in the hope of finding work in Berlin, where he was by now well known.

After a short time, the next offer of employment came from Dresden, where he accepted a job as director of the German repertory of the theatre (Morlacchi was in charge of the Italian repertory) in 1817. The divided control of the opera house caused difficulties, but Weber married a girl he had known in Prague, and held his post for the rest of his life. By this time he was beginning to suffer from tuberculosis, contracted about 1812, but again he showed immense energy in promoting German works, including the major operas of Mozart. At first he composed mainly instrumental music, and it was a commission for a work to open the new Schauspielhaus in Berlin which made him return to opera with *Der Freischütz*, a romantic *Singspiel* on a folk legend. The popularity of this work depended partly on its excellent tunes for the chorus, which were based on folk melodies, and partly on the famous 'Wolf's Glen Scene', the music for which is a *melodrama, the scenic effects being made possible by new methods of stage lighting which Weber had been instrumental in installing at his own theatre. While in Berlin for the first production in 1821, he composed another successful work, the *Konzertstück* for piano and orchestra, one of the rare concertos to belong to the field of programme music, and showing considerable novelty in its form.

Der Freischütz was an immediate success throughout Europe, although its fantastic story sometimes led to unscrupulous rewriting and rearrangement for other theatres (especially in Paris and London). In spite of the resultant fame, Weber was annoyed by criticism that he could do no more than write *Singspiele*, and so he was happy to accept a commission from Vienna for an opera on a grander scale, even though this meant putting aside a comedy already half written, *Die drei Pintos* (he never finished this, although it was completed and re-orchestrated by Mahler in 1888). The greater facilities of the Kärntnertor Theatre allowed him to write the ambitious *Euryanthe*, a work without immediate predecessors and difficult to

Carl Maria von Weber, portrait by Caroline Bardua.

Autograph MS of Huon's 'Prayer' from Act 2 of Weber's opera 'Oberon'.

classify, it best being described as a German grand opera. As in certain French models, the originality lies in its breaking down of the division between recitative and aria, with an upgrading of the importance of the orchestra, which uses *Leitmotive* and generally anticipates many Wagnerian devices. This novelty of form caused some puzzlement to the critics and the work has never achieved the popularity of *Der Freischütz*.

After its first performance in October 1823, Weber returned to Dresden in increasingly bad health which taking the cure at Marienbad did little to alleviate. He soon received an invitation to come to England to direct *Der Freischütz*, then appearing in travestial arrangements in London, and to produce a new opera at Covent Garden. Although advised to take a rest in Italy, he felt that he must accept the commission and he began work on *Oberon*, an opera based not on Shakespeare so much as German legend popularized by the poet Wieland. He found the libretto distinctly unsatisfactory, as English taste was rather for scenic marvels than for elaborate music, but he set off for London in January 1826, visiting Paris on the way where he met—and was honoured by—many musicians including Cherubini and Rossini. Desperately ill on arrival, he yet fulfilled his engagements, including several 'oratorio concerts' and drawing-room recitals. He was widely ap-

plauded, but he died, after several opera performances, in the home of Sir George Smart in Great Portland Street. He was buried in London, his body being exhumed and reinterred in Dresden, where in 1844 Wagner gave an oration over the grave.

Wagner's tribute seems particularly appropriate, since his early operas owe a great deal to the example of Weber. Nevertheless it is an injustice to consider the latter mainly as an influence rather than as an artist in his own right. It is a misfortune of history that the taste for the supernatural evident in *Der Freischütz* has disappeared and that the librettos of both *Euryanthe* and *Oberon* were deficient. Weber's music is impressive and original and some of his instrumental music well deserves revival, as does *Abu Hassan*. His position as a major composer, which has always been maintained in his homeland, is apparent to those who have experienced his principal works done well.

DENIS ARNOLD

FURTHER READING
J. Warrack: *Carl Maria von Weber* (London, 1968).

Webern, Anton (Friedrich Wilhelm von) (*b* Vienna, 3 Dec. 1883; *d* Mittersill, 15 Sept. 1945). Austrian composer. He began piano lessons with his mother and then studied the piano and theory with Edwin Komauer while at school in Klagenfurt. In 1902 he became a student at the University of Vienna, where he studied musicology under Guido Adler, receiving a doctorate in 1906 for his edition of the second part of Isaac's *Choralis Constantinus*. Much more decisive, however, were the private studies with Schoenberg which he began in 1904, at the same time as Berg. The two pupils benefited greatly from Schoenberg's challenging instruction: Webern graduated quickly from the mediocrity of his early pieces to the confidence of his single-movement Quartet (1905) and Five Dehmel Songs (1906–8). The Quartet, though influenced by his teacher's *Verklärte Nacht*, is already individual in its development from a small motif and in its spirituality, while his mastery of chromatic counterpoint is evident in the songs and the orchestral Passacaglia (1908). His first essays in atonality came, like Schoenberg's, in songs to poems by Stefan George, 14 settings dating from 1907–9.

In 1908, his studies over, Webern began a period of conducting operettas and light music in summer theatres. He disliked this work, but it did give him the opportunity to develop his technique as a conductor: later he directed the Vienna Workers' Symphony Concerts (1922–34) and was conductor and musical adviser for Austrian Radio (1927–34); he also appeared several times in London to perform music by Schoenberg, Berg, and himself. Meanwhile he continued to compose. The George songs were followed by several sets of instrumental pieces, all atonal and increasingly concise. The some-

what Mahlerian Six Orchestral Pieces of 1909, for instance, were succeeded by a group of Five Pieces for smaller forces (1911–13), the shortest of which lasts for 14 seconds. Yet these are perfectly finished compositions, typically developed from small cells and delicately variegated in colour. Their brevity, however, allowed no room for continuation along the same path, and for the next decade Webern concentrated on songs, usually with accompaniment for instrumental ensemble. Perhaps the finest are the Six Trakl Songs for voice, two clarinets, violin, and cello (1917–21).

Webern's adoption of *serialism in 1924 at first brought little change to his style, but in his Symphony for small orchestra (1928) he realized the potentialities of the technique for creating music in strictly symmetrical forms: the first of the two movements is a double canon in sonata form, the second a palindromic set of variations. All his later instrumental works—the Quartet for violin, clarinet, tenor saxophone, and piano (1930), the Concerto for nine instruments (1931–4), the Piano Variations (1936), the String Quartet (1937–8) and the Orchestral Variations (1940)—are similarly tightly structured. Often the series itself is symmetrical, most extremely so in the Concerto, where a single three-note idea is perpetually shown in new lights. This delight in all-pervasive unity reflected Webern's aim to emulate the perfection of the natural world; the flowers and mineral crystals of the alps were a particular joy

Autograph MS of the opening of Webern's Five Pieces for small orchestra, Op. 10.

Webern (1932)

to him. In the poetess Hildegard Jone he found a kindred spirit, and it was her verse that he set exclusively in his vocal works after the Symphony: two sets of songs with piano (1933–4), *Das Augenlicht* for chorus and orchestra (1935), and two cantatas (1938–9 and 1941–3). A third cantata was germinating in his mind when he was accidentally shot by an American soldier during the postwar occupation of Austria.

A reserved man, Webern had passed his last years in relative obscurity, supporting himself and his family by taking on menial jobs for his publisher after he had been obliged by the Nazis to relinquish his appointments. Within a few years of his death, however, young composers had proclaimed him 'THE threshold' (Boulez) to the new music.   PAUL GRIFFITHS

FURTHER READING
Demar Irvine, ed.: *Anton von Webern: Perspectives* (Seattle, 1966); Friedrich Wildgans: *Anton Webern* (London, 1966); Walter Kolneder: *Anton Webern* (London, 1968); Hans Moldenhauer: *Anton von Webern: Chronicle of his Life and Works* (New York and London, 1978).

Weckerlin, Jean-Baptiste (Théodore) (*b* Guebwiller, Haut-Rhin, 9 Nov. 1821; *d* Trottberg, nr Guebwiller, 20 May 1910). French bibliographer. He was librarian of the Paris Conservatoire for many years, and a notable scholar and collector of folk-songs.

Weckmann, Matthias (*b* Niederdorla,

Thuringia, *c.*1619; *d* Hamburg, 24 Feb. 1674). German composer. He was a choirboy at the Dresden chapel under Schütz, and then a pupil of Praetorius and Scheidemann at Hamburg. Around 1642 he went to Denmark to join Schütz, remaining as organist until 1647. Eight years later he became organist at St Jacobi in Hamburg, where he founded a *collegium musicum*.

About 13 sacred vocal works by Weckmann have survived, many of them in the Protestant chorale *concertato* tradition of Schütz and his successors. His instrumental works include eight sets of chorale variations for organ, keyboard pieces, and some four- or five-part ensemble sonatas for cornetts, violin(s), trombone, and bassoon, which bear a strong resemblance to Giovanni Gabrieli's instrumental canzonas.   WENDY THOMPSON

We Come to the River. Opera in two parts by Henze; text by Edward Bond. Produced: London, Covent Garden, 12 July 1976; Berlin, Staatsoper, 18 September 1976. A victorious general (bar.) is told that he will soon go blind— a revelation that gives him compassion for the victims of war. When he publicly renounces violence, he is confined to a madhouse. He gives no encouragement to a revolt of the oppressed, and refuses to support the Emperor (mezzo) faced with civil war. The Emperor blinds the general. The inmates of the madhouse smother the general under sheets they take for river water, as the ghosts of war victims sing of their hope for a better future.

Wedding, The (*Svadebka*; *Les noces*). Choreographic scenes by Stravinsky to words adapted by the composer from Russian traditional sources. The four scenes are for soprano, mezzo-soprano, tenor, and bass soloists, chorus, four pianos, and percussion ensemble. The work was composed 1914–17, scored 1921–3, and given its first performance in Paris in 1923.

Wedding Day at Troldhaugen (*Bryllupsdag på Troldhaugen*). Piano piece by Grieg, No. 6 of his *Lyric Pieces* (Book 8), Op. 65 (1897). It was later orchestrated. Troldhaugen was the name of Grieg's villa, built in 1885 outside Bergen.

Wedding March. The traditional music for the entry of the bride in British church weddings has since the mid 19th century been an organ arrangement of the bridal chorus from Wagner's opera *Lohengrin*, and for the exit of the married couple, the wedding march which is the sixth number of Mendelssohn's incidental music to *A Midsummer Night's Dream*. The vogue for Mendelssohn's piece began in 1847 and was boosted in 1858 when Queen Victoria's daughter, the Princess Royal, used it at Windsor. In 1960 the Duchess of Kent left York Minster to the strains of the Toccata from Widor's Fifth Organ Symphony, an example which was subsequently widely copied. Many court composers have written marches and other pieces for the weddings of royal and aristocratic brides.

'Wedge' Fugue. Nickname of a fugue in E minor for organ by J. S. Bach, composed between 1727 and 1731. It is so called because of the shape of the subject, which proceeds in gradually widening intervals.

Weelkes, Thomas (? *bapt*. Elsted, Sussex, 25 Oct. 1576; *buried* 1 Dec. 1623). English composer. In 1598 he was organist at Winchester College, receiving a miserly stipend of 13*s*. 4*d*. a quarter with board and lodging. He was awarded the B.Mus. degree from New College, Oxford, in 1602 and the following year married Elizabeth Sandham (who was apparently already pregnant), a member of a wealthy Chichester family. He had probably moved to Chichester a couple of years earlier, serving as organist and instructor of the choristers at the cathedral, and although his life there was at times stormy, the Chapter disapproving of his drinking habits and in 1617 temporarily dismissing him, he remained there for the rest of his life. He died in London at the home of a friend, and his will,

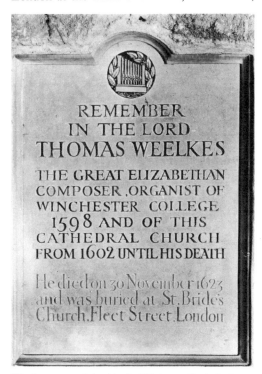

Weelkes, memorial tablet in Chichester Cathedral.

dividing his goods between his three children, suggests that in spite of his handsome marriage he was a poor man.

Weelkes was one of the best composers of madrigals to work in England, with a flair for finding a lively musical equivalent to the texts he set. He occasionally used a chromatic and dissonant idiom to gain emotional effects, but he also wrote some delightful light music, notably balletts. His church music was more traditional, although he experimented with new ways of gaining sonority in his Service *In medio chori*. He also produced some fine anthems, especially those employing soloists accompanied by organ.

DENIS ARNOLD

FURTHER READING
David Brown: *Thomas Weelkes: a Biographical and Critical Study* (London, 1969).

Weerbeke, Gaspar van. See *Gaspar van Weerbeke*.

Weg (Ger.). 'Away', 'off'.

Wegelius, Martin (*b* Helsinki, 10 Nov. 1846; *d* Helsinki, 22 Mar. 1906). Finnish composer. He studied in Helsinki, Germany, and Vienna, and then returned to Helsinki as pianist, critic, and conductor of the Finnish Opera. A composer of orchestral, chamber, and choral music, his primary importance was as a teacher: in 1882 he founded the Helsinki Music College (now the Sibelius Academy). His most famous pupils were Palmgren and Sibelius.

WENDY THOMPSON

Wehmut [*Wehmuth*] (Ger.). 'Sorrow', 'melancholy'; *wehmütig, wehmütsvoll*, 'sorrowful'.

Weich (Ger.). 'Soft', 'tender', 'light'.

Weihnachtslied (Ger.). 'Christmas song', i.e. **carol.

Weill, Kurt (Julian) (*b* Dessau, 2 Mar. 1900; *d* New York, 3 Apr. 1950). German composer. He studied at the Berlin Musikhochschule with Humperdinck (1918–19) and privately with Busoni (1921–4). Busoni's influence is apparent in the thoroughly calculated neoclassical aspects of such early works as the String Quartet (1923), but more important here is the bitter **expressionism and the near **atonality which Weill developed from Schoenberg's example. These are features also of his first opera, the one-act *Der Protagonist* (1926, libretto by Georg Kaiser), and of the Concerto for violin and wind (1924).

Weill's music took a new direction when he became Brecht's collaborator in 1927. He now evolved a cabaret style, using popular clichés and an acid tonality to point up the corruption

Weill (left) *with Busoni, c.1923.*

of capitalism which Brecht was exposing in such works as *Aufstieg und Fall der Stadt Mahagonny* (1930), *Die Dreigroschenoper* (1928), and *Die sieben Todsünden* (1933). In 1933, soon after Hitler's takeover, he was obliged to leave Berlin, and in 1935 he settled permanently in the United States. There he concerned himself almost exclusively with the Broadway musical theatre, for which he composed *Johnny Johnson* (1936), *Knickerbocker Holiday* (1938), *Lost in the Stars* (1949), and others. Such numbers as 'Mack the Knife' (from *Die Dreigroschenoper*) and 'September Song' (from *Knickerbocker Holiday*) have become standards of the popular song repertory.   PAUL GRIFFITHS

Weinberger, Jaromír (*b* Prague, 8 Jan. 1896; *d* St Petersburg, Florida, 8 Aug. 1967). American composer of Czech origin. He studied at Prague and Leipzig, and after visiting the USA was employed at the Slovak National Theatre in Bratislava. There the work for which he is chiefly remembered, the opera based on Czech folk idioms *Švanda Dudák* ('Shvanda the Bagpiper'), scored a great success in 1927. From 1932 onwards Weinberger lived in Prague and Austria. His last opera, *Valdštejn* (*Wallenstein*, after Schiller), was performed at Vienna in 1937, just before the Nazi threat forced its composer to leave Europe for the USA, where he committed suicide at the age of 71.
               WENDY THOMPSON

Weinberger, Josef. Austrian firm of music publishers. Josef Weinberger (1855–1928) founded the firm in Vienna in 1885. They first specialized in central European opera composers (Smetana, Goldmark) and promoted the music of Wolf-Ferrari. They acquired the rights to large numbers of operettas (Johann Strauss, Suppé, Lehár, etc.) and also issued instrumental music by Austrian composers. The London branch of the firm publishes the music of Malcolm Williamson.

Weinend (Ger.). 'Weeping', 'wailing'.

Weingartner, (Paul) Felix (*b* Zara, Dalmatia, 2 June 1863; *d* Winterthur, 7 May 1942). Austrian composer and conductor. He studied composition at Graz and philosophy at Leipzig. A protégé of Liszt, his first opera *Sakuntala* was produced at Weimar in 1884, and Weingartner then began his career as a conductor. He was *Kapellmeister* of the Berlin Opera (1891–8), then conductor of the royal orchestral concerts. In 1908 he took over from Mahler as conductor at the Vienna Court Opera, and also conducted the Vienna Philharmonic. His subsequent career took him to the Hamburg Opera, Darmstadt, the Vienna Volksoper, and finally, in 1927, to Basle, where he conducted concerts and became director of the Conservatory. Weingartner was married five times, but found time to write nine operas (all to his own librettos), seven symphonies, and other orchestral and chamber works.   WENDY THOMPSON

Weinlied (Ger.). 'Drinking song'.

Weiss, Silvius Leopold (*b* Breslau, 12 Oct. 1686; *d* Dresden, 16 Oct. 1750). German lutenist and composer. He studied with his father, also a lutenist, and around 1706 entered the service of the Count Palatine Carl Philipp. From 1708 to 1714 he lived in Italy. On his return to Germany he spent the rest of his life in the service of the electoral court at Dresden.

Weiss was one of the last great lute virtuosos at a time when the lute was rapidly going out of fashion. He wrote many fine lute suites which are available in a modern edition.

WENDY THOMPSON

Weissenburg, Heinrich. See *Albicastro, Henrico.*

Weldon, John (*b* Chichester, 19 Jan. 1676; *d* London, 7 May 1736). English composer. He was a chorister at Eton and then a pupil of Purcell, afterwards becoming organist of New College, Oxford (1694), Gentleman of the Chapel Royal (1701), and finally organist of the Chapel Royal, succeeding Blow, and from 1714 of St Bride's, Fleet Street, and St Martin-in-the-Fields. From 1715 to his death he was second composer to the Chapel Royal, under Croft. In 1700 he won first prize in a competition for a setting of Congreve's masque *The Judgement of Paris* (beating John Eccles, Daniel Purcell, and Gottfried Finger), and he later wrote some incidental music for a performance of *The Tempest*; the score has never been traced, and it has been suggested that what we know as Purcell's music may in fact be by Weldon. He seems to have composed little in later life.

Weldon's operatic and other secular music is now forgotten, but some of his church music remains in use, notably, perhaps, the anthem 'Hear my crying'.

PERCY SCHOLES, rev. Wendy Thompson

Wellesz, Egon (Joseph) (*b* Vienna, 21 Oct. 1885; *d* Oxford, 9 Nov. 1974). Austrian composer and musicologist. He studied at the University of Vienna (1895–1908), where under Guido Adler he did research into Cavalli's operas, and he had private composition lessons with Schoenberg (1905–6). He remained a member of Schoenberg's circle, published the first book on the composer (1925, reprinted 1971), and adopted serial methods in his music. However, the influence of Strauss was also important, especially in the several stage works he wrote during the 1920s, these including the opera *Alkestis* (1924), with a libretto by Hofmannsthal. He also taught at the University of Vienna (1913–38), his musicological interests now turning to Byzantine chant.

In 1939 he left Vienna for Oxford, where he was appointed reader in Byzantine music. He stayed in Oxford for the rest of his life, and wrote an opera in English, *Incognita* (1951), for the university opera club. In England he also composed a set of nine symphonies and a Violin Concerto (1961), re-examining tonality by way of Mahler and Bruckner. Other important works include nine string quartets and an Octet (1948–9) for the same combination as

Schubert's. Besides his study of Schoenberg, he was also the author of the books *Eastern Elements in Western Chant* (Boston, 1947) and *A History of Byzantine Music and Hymnography* (London, 1963).

PAUL GRIFFITHS

FURTHER READING
Robert Schollum: *Egon Wellesz* (Vienna, 1963).

Well-Tempered Clavier. See *Wohltemperierte Klavier, Das.*

Welsh College of Music and Drama. Welsh music college, founded in 1949 as the Cardiff College of Music and Drama (it was housed in Cardiff Castle); it received its present title in 1970, and in 1975 moved to new, purpose-built accommodation in the Castle grounds at Cathays Park. Full-time and part-time courses are available for prospective performers and teachers. Raymond Edwards has been Principal since 1959.

Welsh National Opera. Opera company based in Cardiff and founded in 1946. It has a semi-professional choir and a professional orchestra, and tours widely, giving seasons in Birmingham, Manchester, Liverpool, Leeds, etc. Musical directors have included Charles Groves (1961–3), Bryan Balkwill (1963–7), James Lockhart (1968–73), and Richard Armstrong (from 1973).

See also *Wales*, 4.

Wenig (Ger.). 'Little'; *ein wenig*, 'a little'; *weniger*, 'less'.

Werner, Gregor Joseph (*b* Ybbs an der Donau, 28 Jan. 1693; *d* Eisenstadt, 3 Mar. 1766). Austrian composer. In 1728 he became *Kapellmeister* to Prince Esterházy at Eisenstadt, where he stayed until his death. From 1761 his assistant there was Joseph Haydn, who arranged for string quartet six of Werner's introductions and fugues. Werner's other works include sacred music, some suites for two violins and continuo published as *Neuer und sehr curioser musicalischer Instrumental-Calender* (Augsburg, 1748), and a set of six sonatas (Augsburg, 1735).

Werner, Johann Gottlob (*b* Grossenhain, 1777; *d* Chemnitz, 19 July 1822). German organist and composer. He was organist in various provincial German towns until 1819, when he was finally appointed cathedral organist and music director at Merseburg; he died three years later. His compositions, which were principally intended for teaching purposes, include several organ methods, of which the *Orgelschule* was widely used. He also wrote chorale preludes and other organ pieces.

Wert, Giaches de (*b* 1535; *d* Mantua, 6 May 1596). Flemish composer. Brought to Italy at a very early age, he served at several minor courts before being appointed *maestro di cappella* at the newly built ducal chapel of S. Barbara at Mantua in 1565. He remained in the service of the Gonzaga family for the rest of his life, but was also a frequent visitor at the d'Este court at Ferrara, where he fell in love with a famous singer, Tarquinia Molza. Unfortunately he was already married, although separated from his wife who had committed adultery with a rival musician at the Gonzaga court, and the affair was doomed to failure.

Wert was primarily a madrigal composer, and he was an important forerunner of the chromatic and dissonant style of Monteverdi's *seconda prattica* (see *Prima prattica, seconda prattica*) in his concentration on the creation of expressive melody; at the same time he employed homophony as a means towards the accurate declamation of the words. 16 volumes of madrigals by him were published between 1558 and 1608, and he was evidently extremely well known, not only to those who were directly influenced by him but also to composers of quite a different character, such as Palestrina, who described him as a 'virtuoso raro'.

DENIS ARNOLD

FURTHER READING
Iain Fenlon: *Music and Patronage in Sixteenth-century Mantua*, i (Cambridge, 1980).

Werther. Opera in four acts by Massenet; text by Blau, Millet, and Hartmann, after Goethe's novel *Die Leiden des jungen Werthers* ('The Sorrows of Young Werther', 1774). Produced: Vienna, Staatsoper, 16 February 1892 (in a German version); Chicago, 29 March 1894; London, Covent Garden, 11 June 1894. Werther (ten.) loves Charlotte (mezzo), who returns his love although betrothed to his friend Albert (bar.). He leaves her, returning to find Charlotte married. She urges him to leave her again, but on hearing that he has asked Albert for his pistols rushes to him through a snowstorm to find that he has shot himself.

Wesendonk Songs, Five (*Fünf Gedichte für eine Frauenstimme*) (*Wesendonk-Lieder*). Five songs by Wagner for voice and piano to poems by his mistress Mathilde Wesendonk, composed in 1857-8. They are (1) *Der Engel* ('The Angel'), (2) *Stehe still* ('Stand Still'), (3) *Im Treibhaus* ('In the Greenhouse'), (4) *Schmerzen* ('Agonies'), and (5) *Träume* ('Dreams'); themes from *Tristan und Isolde* occur in Nos. 3 and 5, which are 'studies for *Tristan*'. The songs were orchestrated by Mottl under Wagner's supervision; they have been arranged for violin and piano (1872)

Frontispiece of score of Massenet's 'Werther' (1892).

by H. Léonard, and for high voice and chamber orchestra (1979) by Henze.

Wesley, Charles (*b* Bristol, 11 Dec. 1757; *d* London, 23 May 1834). English harpsichordist and composer; nephew of John Wesley (1703-91, the founder of Methodism), eldest son of Charles Wesley (1707-88, the hymn writer). In his youth he showed immense musical promise, and became a pupil of William Boyce from 1774 when the family moved to London. He took part with his younger brother Samuel Wesley in a remarkable series of concerts (1779-85) in their Marylebone house (programme details survive in the British Library). Of his works from this period, the 14 organ concertos (1775-81) and six string quartets (1776) all contain music in the mixed Handelian/Classical vein. However, having learnt his craft and established set working principles, his imagination ceased to function, his talents withered, and with his appointment as official harpsichordist to George III (who would hear only Handel) in 1794, his increasing absorption in the past prevented any further creative development.

ROBIN LANGLEY

Wesley, Samuel (*b* Bristol, 24 Feb. 1766; *d* London, 11 Oct. 1837). English organist, violinist, teacher, and the most important English composer of his generation. Nearly as precocious as his elder brother, Charles Wesley, he completed an oratorio, *Ruth*, at the age of eight. He was educated musically 'second-hand' through his brother's teachers, and the two even collaborated on some compositions. Boyce declared that Samuel 'unites by nature as true a bass as I can do by rule and study', and his early works show an imagination (if not sense of construction) already in advance of his brother's: compare their contemporaneous string quartets. From 1784 Samuel's contact with particularly the Portuguese Embassy Chapel widened his knowledge of European music, not only for the church, and mitigated beneficially the traditional English and increasingly stifling reverence for Handel. A large-scale and uneven Mass dedicated to Pope Pius VI dates from that year,

The young Samuel Wesley.

and within two years Samuel had produced his first masterpiece, the *Ave Maris stella* (1786) for two upper voices and strings. From this time too came the violin concertos, written for himself to play in his brother's series of concerts in Marylebone, and a substantial collection of symphonies and overtures of which that in D

(1784) for two horns and strings equals those of J. C. Bach.

Samuel's independence of thought and character (tellingly revealed through a large correspondence) prevented a conventionally successful career in terms of lucrative appointments. Though he was the finest English organist of his day, he held only minor positions in the Church of England, and his sporadic appearances as director of especially the Lenten Oratorio concerts were supplemented by teaching and lecturing. He continued to compose prolifically in all forms; much is uneven and for financial reasons directed towards no more than fashionable use, but throughout his long career he produced a number of works of European stature: among these were the large-scale setting of *Confitebor tibi Domine* (1791), the B♭ Symphony (1802)—in an age of great symphonies it compares favourably with those of Arriaga and Voříšek—the 12 Voluntaries (1805-17, containing some of the most important organ music between Bach and Mendelssohn), and the Concert Overture in E (1834). A leader of the Bach revival in England, he was responsible for the first publication there of the '48' (1810-13); he was also the selfless editor of the music of two of his shorter-lived contemporaries, G. F. Pinto and William Russell. As a composer he possessed an individual style encompassing contrapuntal ingenuity, harmonic daring, and melodic freshness.   ROBIN LANGLEY

Wesley, Samuel Sebastian (*b* London, 14 Aug. 1810; *d* Gloucester, 19 Apr. 1876). English composer and organist; son of Samuel Wesley. Of supreme importance in the improvement and development of English church music as performer, composer, and vituperative pamphleteer, Wesley was educated at the Chapel Royal from 1820, though his father gave him his earliest lessons in composition. After apprenticeship as organist and conductor in London, he was appointed organist of Hereford Cathedral in 1832, there dedicating himself almost exclusively to the revivification of an Anglican tradition which had deteriorated since Handel's day. To the best of his own music he brought a strength of harmony, apt melodic illustration to the setting of texts more freely and imaginatively chosen than before, and a theatrical flair free of the mawkishness of the majority of his contemporaries. He brought a determined zeal to the reform of lax administration and tolerance of low standards of instruments and performers, and campaigned for the recognition of music within the church hierarchy. From Hereford Wesley moved to Exeter Cathedral (1835), Leeds Parish Church (1842), Winchester (1849), and finally Gloucester (1865), where he revised most of his important compositions. At the centre of his compositions are his anthems: often these are of considerable length and power and are accompanied by elaborate organ parts (ably orchestrated for festival use). *Blessed Be the God and Father*, *The Wilderness*, *Wash Me Throughly*, and *Ascribe Unto the Lord* are the most notable. Wesley's brilliant command of the organ is reflected particularly in the large-scale F major Andante which forms the second of the three pieces for chamber organ (Set II, 1842–3). ROBIN LANGLEY

Western Wynde. English 16th-century secular tune. It was used as a cantus firmus in masses by Taverner, Tye, and John Sheppard (see '*Western Wynde*' *Mass*). The use of such secular tunes in sacred music was eventually banned by the Roman Catholic Church, not surprisingly when one considers that the anonymous and beautiful words to which congregations usually heard the tune sung were:

> Western wynde, when wilt thou blow,
> The small raine down can raine.
> Christ, if my love were in my armes
> And I in my bedde again!

'Western Wynde' Mass. Title given to Mass settings by Taverner, Tye, and Sheppard that use the secular tune *Western Wynde* as a cantus firmus. Each is a set of contrapuntal variations on the tune, for four voices, and they were probably composed in the late 1530s or early 1540s.

West Indian Music

1. Introduction
2. Instruments

3. Music for Ritual, Work, and Play

1. *Introduction.* English-speaking islands of the Caribbean which constitute the West Indies include, from north to south, the Bahamas, Jamaica, St Kitts and Nevis, Antigua, Dominica, St Lucia, Barbados, St Vincent, Grenada, and Trinidad and Tobago. Mainland Belize and Guyana are also considered a part of the West Indies as they share a common history with the islands. Fundamental to this history are the cruel facts of colonization and slavery, and the resultant emergence of a population as fascinatingly diverse in ethnic background as anywhere on earth.

The first inhabitants of the West Indies were the peace-loving Arawak Indians whose journey northwards through the Caribbean islands from the South American mainland had, by AD 700, brought them to Jamaica. The Arawaks were followed by the more war-like Carib Indians who settled in the small islands to the south. A few descendants of the Caribs survive in Dominica and St Vincent. Little is known of the music of the Amerindians, although Columbus noted the use of large and small drums and wooden trumpets among the Arawaks in Jamaica in 1494. It seems likely that the Indians used bamboo flutes as well, and probably tambourines made with sea shells. Pieces of pottery found in Jamaica suggest that the Arawaks also had earthenware drums. Some 19th-century Trinidadian sources refer to the survival of an Arawak dance called the *arectoe* which was accompanied by drums and conch shells.

With the arrival of the Spanish colonists the Arawaks were decimated by European diseases and ill treatment. The Spanish soon began importing slave labour from Africa and their lead was followed by Dutch, French, and English colonists, with the result that when slavery was ultimately abolished in the 19th century the majority of the West Indian population was of African descent. As a result, African cultural attitudes have been fundamental to the development of music in the West Indies. The African conception of music as functional—as having a role to play in all human activity, be it social, religious, or ritualistic—is a dominant one in West Indian music. The importance of drums in African music is mirrored in that of the West Indies, while the call and response patterning of much West Indian folk music is also essentially African derived.

Forms of music which today are seen as characteristically West Indian (*reggae and *calypso, for example) are the result of a creative synthesis of these African elements with aspects of the music of the European colonizers. Predominant here was the music of English Protestantism, but, of course, many Caribbean countries changed colonial hands several times. Indeed, before being ceded to the British Crown in 1802, Trinidad was a Spanish colony with a predominantly French or French-speaking population. It is no accident that the African–Catholic–Protestant fusion found in the music of the Shouters, a small group of Baptist converts in the north-east of the island, has remarkable affinities with the shouting spiritual, an important influence on the development of jazz in the USA.

Subsequent to the emancipation of the slaves large numbers of East Indian indentured labourers were brought to the West Indies.

Descendants of these immigrants today form a high proportion of the populations of Trinidad and Tobago and of Guyana, and a vital musical life exists within the Hindu and Muslim communities there. The East Indian musical tradition has, however, always been quite separate and distinct from other forms of music in the West Indies.

2. *Instruments.* Drums proliferate in West Indian music. They are frequently played in pairs, when one instrument (the Jamaican *kbandu* and the *boolay* of Trinidad and Tobago) sustains a basic rhythmic pattern while complex, syncopated rhythms are improvised in counterpoint on the other (the Jamaican 'playing cast' and the 'cutter' of Trinidad and Tobago). Many different sizes and shapes of drum are in use, ranging from the large bass drum associated with Rastafarian ritual to the East Indian *tassa* drum, a goatskin-covered clay or metal bowl. The drums are played with fingers, palms, and sticks of all kinds.

Other instruments commonly found in the West Indies include a number fashioned from bamboo. The bamboo violin may be heard in some isolated areas and the bamboo flute is common throughout the region. 'Boom pipes' are also found, consisting of pieces of bamboo about a metre in length and 6 cm. in diameter.

A bamboo fife.

The pipes are blown into energetically to produce the low booming sound which characterizes the instrument. Rattles are often made from gourds, and a variety of improvised guitars and banjos are to be found. The small, four-string *cuatro* guitar has made its way from the Spanish Caribbean to a number of West Indian countries. In Jamaica, the *abeng* is played by the Maroons, descendants of slaves who escaped from the Spanish during the 17th century. The

abeng is a cow's horn, the pitch of which is altered by movement of the lips and by covering a thumb-hole near the pointed end of the horn. The home of the *steel band is Trinidad, but the pans which constitute these bands can be found throughout the West Indies. Other than in the eastern Caribbean, however, steel bands are most often to be discovered in tourist hotels.

3. *Music for Ritual, Work, and Play.* It is in the ritual music of the various West Indian cult groups that the most significant African retentions are to be found. By means of such music members of cults communicate with the supernatural and naturally a great deal of secrecy is involved. Cult music is essentially speech-derived, and chanting and vocal improvisation dominate ceremonies, in conjunction usually with clapping and stamping. Rhythmic breathing is used to induce a trance-like state among participants, and drumming usually plays a leading role in assisting spirit communication. A particularly striking example of an African retention is the use of Congolese words in the improvised songs of the Jamaican Kumina cult. The Trinidadian Shango cult combines Nigerian Yoruba religious practices with Catholic and Baptist beliefs. Each of the various African and Christian deities of Shango is identified with specific songs and rhythms, and the double-headed *bemba* and *congo* drums used in Shango ritual are believed to speak directly to Catholic identifications of the Yoruban Ogun (St Michael) and Shango (St John the Baptist) respectively. Other Africanisms found in Shango include rhythmic body-swaying, antiphonal singing, and polyrhythmic textures. The Jamaican Afro-Christian revivalist cults of Zion and Pukkumina take European hymn-tunes as the basis of much of their music, and cultists often sing in unknown tongues. The development of Rastafarianism in Jamaica during the 1940s, and the subsequent spread of ideas associated with this cult throughout the West Indies, has proved a significant new departure, and has had an often considerable effect on the cultural and social lives of many. Rastafarians identify Ethiopia as their homeland, and the chanting and drumming which form the basis of their ritual is consciously African. Reggae music is closely associated with Rastafarianism and the words of many reggae songs discuss the return of members of the cult to their homeland.

Of social song and dance forms the work-song is today principally of historical interest. The origins of these songs lie in slavery, when it was forbidden for members of work-gangs to speak to each other. However, well aware that it could assist in the efficient performance of collective tasks, overseers permitted rhythmic singing. This was led by a slave appointed as the

The Rastafarian bass drum is played with a heavy padded stick. These large drums often have religious texts painted on them.

singer-man, or *bomma*. There were collective songs of this type for agricultural and other tasks, and many of the old songs survive in the repertory of today's folk-groups, such as the Kingstown Chorale of St Vincent and the Jamaican Folk-singers.

A number of contemporary dance forms date back to slavery. Limbo dancing, which is found throughout the region, is said to have originated in a competition between slaves. Whoever danced lowest under the horizontal bar would, so it was said, win his freedom. The quadrille consists of a number of dances of European derivation and is again found throughout the West Indies. Its origins lie in the imitation by slaves of the formal steps of 19th-century settlers as they danced the mazurka, polka, and jig. Today the dances are accompanied by a band which includes a saxophone, trumpet, harmonica, *cuatros*, banjos, drums, and a string bass.

Social comment dominates the lyrics in the Jamaican mento and Trinidadian calypso song and dance forms, both of which again have a long history. Mento is characterized by strong syncopation on the last beat of each bar, and the banjo strum which dominates the sound of a mento band has found its way into reggae. Eastern Caribbean *bèlè* dance-songs, sung in English or French creole, make use of characteristically African call and response patterning. They are performed at festivals, at public events, and occasionally at wakes.

Hoosay is an East Indian festival. Bamboo models of mosques and stick puppets are carried by men who dance to the sound of Indian drums. A great deal of East Indian musical activity in Trinidad centres on the many orchestras that play commercial Indian film music. These orchestras are large and include electric organs and guitars as well as bongo drums. They perform a function within the Asian community roughly equivalent to that performed by calypso and steel bands in the Black and creole community. In like fashion, membership of an orchestra carries prestige, the orchestras are locally sponsored, and weekly rehearsals provide a focus for community life. The incorporation of *bhajan* chants in East Indian films has also helped popularize these forms which are now taught in Trinidad's Hindu primary schools.

Annual independence celebrations provide a focus for the musical life of most West Indian countries. In addition, a number of eastern Caribbean countries including Dominica and Trinidad have annual carnivals. These perform a similar function in providing an opportunity for the mounting, on a national scale, of activities which demonstrate the artistic traditions and achievements of each country. At an international level, the rich fabric of West Indian musical life is demonstrated in the bi-annual Caribbean festival of the arts, Carifesta. This month-long festival is hosted in turn by one of the countries of the region, most of which send musicians and ensembles which were often originally chosen at national independence and carnival celebrations. In recent years Carifesta has been hosted by Guyana, Jamaica, Cuba, and Barbados.

PEARLE CHRISTIAN, MICHAEL BURNETT

FURTHER READING
John Storm Roberts: *Black Music of Two Worlds* (London, 1973).

Westminster Chimes. See *Crotch, William*.

Westrup, (Sir) **Jack** (Allan) (*b* London, 26 July 1904; *d* Headley, nr Guildford, 21 Apr. 1975). English musicologist. He read classics at Oxford University (1923–6) where he was active in founding the University Opera Club, its first production being his edition of Monteverdi's *Orfeo* in 1925. After a period of schoolmastering, he became a music critic in London, eventually becoming lecturer at King's College, Newcastle upon Tyne (1941), professor of music at Birmingham University (1944), and Heather Professor at Oxford (1947–71). He conducted many productions of the University Opera Club, many of them virtually unknown works (including Berlioz's *The Trojans*). His scholarly work included a definitive book on Purcell (London, 1937, 4th edn 1980) and many essays on subjects ranging from Medieval song to Elgar's '*Enigma*' *Variations*, his writing being notable for its good sense and its impish cutting of pretentiousness down to size.

DENIS ARNOLD

Wetterharfe (Ger.). See *Aeolian harp*.

Whale, The. Dramatic cantata by Tavener to his own text compiled from *Collins' Encyclopaedia* and the Vulgate. It is for narrator, mezzo-soprano, baritone, chorus, and orchestra and was composed in 1965–6.

Whip. Percussion instrument, formerly the slapstick of the theatre drummer. It is composed of two flat pieces of hardwood. One piece is the longer, to form a handle; the other is hinged upon it with a strong spring. A deft shake makes it strike on the other with a sound like the crack of a whip. It appears in Mahler's Sixth Symphony and in many works since. It was probably first introduced in Vienna for comedy polkas (in which a real whip could be dangerous). Actual whip-cracking takes place in rural festivals in Central Europe, chiefly around the New Year, 'to drive winter away' with whips up to six yards long. See *Instruments, Classification of* (4.*a*).

ANTHONY BAINES

Whistle. 1. In the 13th century Jean de Grocheo remarked how, while horses reacted to trumpets and drums, hounds got their pleasure from horns and whistles (*fistulae*); both may be used today by Africans when hunting. In Europe a great variety of whistles have served bird-catchers as 'bird-calls', to lure wild birds by imitating their sounds, though less so today when the practice of taking birds live has become increasingly frowned upon. Fig. 1 shows a selection of whistles, some familiar as signalling instruments, several of them bird-calls as well and long manufactured in Britain by the Acme firm. Most are related to flutes in that they employ the principle of the 'edge'-generated tone, though where a rasping or squeaking sound is required, the principle of the reed may be used.

Fig. 1*a* is a two-disc whistle, until recently a familiar object in a Christmas cracker: two small metal plates with a space between, each plate with a hole and usually dished inwards. Placed in front of the teeth, and either blowing or sucking, the pitch changes with the air speed. Fowlers used it for larks and linnets. Steam-operated, it is used in whistling kettles. As a lure or toy it is also widely made of a plum stone, with a hole bored in each face.

Spherical whistles include the Boatswain's Pipe (Fig. 1*b*), described in the 18th century as also for larks; and (Fig. 1*c*) the Referee's whistle, with a cork pellet blown about inside to make the sound chirrup. The scout's whistle, or police

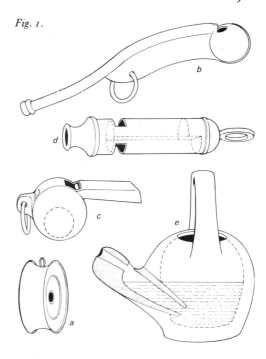

Fig. 1.

whistle, is a divided tubular whistle (Fig. 1*d*), containing a metal plate down the centre to make two semicircular tubes, stopped at the ends, one tube shorter than the other, for sounding two notes simultaneously a tone apart, giving a powerful beating trill.

Clay whistles, widely sold over Europe as toys and gifts, are of two main types, both having a small duct-flute component of clay forming the tail of a bird or the spout of a little jug. The bird has a fingerhole in the breast for making a second note (and may be the parent of the *ocarina). The jug, on the other hand, is partly filled with water, enough to cover the inside end of the spout (Fig. 1*e*). On blowing, water is pushed down the spout, which adds to the length of its small air-column, lowering the note. Air then bubbles out through the water, reducing pressure, so that the water flows back and the note rises again, and so on, with the total effect of a sustained chirrup. This is the nightingale of the 'Toy' Symphony, along with the cuckoo and the quail. The quail here imitates the male bird, but all over Europe and the Near East quails are lured imitating the hushed call of the female with a small pipe of cane or bone to which the air is fed from a soft purse-like skin bag, lightly and rapidly tapped with the fingers, which can make a faster reiteration than is possible by 'tonguing'.

For the tin whistle, see *Flageolet* 1.

2. The technique of whistling with the mouth has sometimes been developed to the point of virtuosity. In the late 19th century the American

Mrs Alice Shaw was a famous whistler, known as 'La Belle Siffleuse'. As one of her countrymen wrote of her in the New York *Musical Courier* in 1931, 'No jazz or cheap crooning stuff had a place in her repertoire and her performances were equally sensational in the drawing-rooms of kings, czars, emperors, and maharajahs and the homes of the intelligentsia of the world's capitals'. (Incidentally, those performances were among the first to be circulated by Edison as records for his Phonograph in 1887 and the following years.)

Whistling, however, can be dangerous. Over much of the world, from Iceland to South Africa, it is believed to lure the spirit away or to attract an evil one. An Arab whistler's mouth, it is said, stays unclean for 40 days. It is bad luck to whistle in a theatre, and on British merchant ships whistling is, or certainly was up to the Second World War, strictly forbidden, felt to bring ill luck, no doubt a relic from days of sail when it was feared to raise a gale.

ANTHONY BAINES, PERCY SCHOLES

White, Robert (*b* 1530–5; *d* London, Nov. 1574). English composer. His name is common enough to cause some confusion, but it seems likely that he was the son of an organ builder, and was himself organist at St Andrew's, Holborn, in the 1550s. He took his Mus.B. at Cambridge in 1560, became Master of the Choristers at Ely Cathedral in 1562, and married Christopher Tye's daughter in 1565. He then seems to have spent some years as Master of the Choristers at Chester Cathedral before taking up a similar position at Westminster Abbey in 1570. He died of the plague, leaving his widow comfortably off.

White was a fine composer, particularly of Latin church music; his psalms and settings of the Lamentations of Jeremiah are especially good. His instrumental works include fantasias and *In nomine* settings for viols.

DENIS ARNOLD

Whitehead, Gillian (*b* Whangarei, New Zealand, 23 Apr. 1941). New Zealand composer. She studied music at the Universities of Auckland, Wellington, and Sydney, and after attending Peter Maxwell Davies's composition class at Adelaide University in 1966 she continued working with him in London, where several of her works were performed by the Pierrot Players, later renamed The Fires of London. In 1971 her String Quartet won the NZBC/APRA Chamber Music Federation prize. From 1978 to 1980 she was composer-in-residence for Northern Arts at Newcastle University, where she began working with the poet Fleur Adcock: settings include *Inner Harbour* (1979) for choir and chamber orchestra, and *Hotspur* (1980) for

soprano and instrumental ensemble; an opera *Eleanor of Aquitaine* is in preparation.

She is attracted by Maori subjects dealing with mythology and the ritual of the seasons, as in *Pakuru* (1967), *Whakatau-ki* (1970), and *Te Tangi a Apakura* (1975) for string orchestra, among others. Her chamber opera *Tristan and Iseult* (1975) employed the 14th-century Italian *estampie* 'Lamento di Tristano', with its rhythmic and melodic variant the *rotta*, along with plainsong and ballad styles, and was a highlight of the Auckland Festival in 1978. Her immensely concentrated music can resemble musical sculpture or architecture, with its emphasis on a mathematical basis, but underneath lies a highly refined musical sensitivity.

J. M. THOMSON

Whitlock, Percy (William) (*b* Chatham, 1 June 1903; *d* Bournemouth, 1 May 1946). English composer. He studied at the Royal College of Music and the Guildhall School, then held various posts as church and municipal organist in the south of England. He also broadcast frequently, and composed practical church and organ music. PAUL GRIFFITHS

Whole-note (Amer.). Semibreve (o).

Whole tone. An interval of two semitones. See *Interval*.

Whole-tone scale (Ger.: *Ganztonleiter*). A scale of six whole tones. See *Scale*, 5.

Whythorne, Thomas (*b* Ilminster, 1528; *d* London, July 1596). English composer. The son of a Somerset gentleman, he was educated at Magdalen College School, Oxford. He spent most of his life in the service of various English noblemen, teaching music and in one case looking after his patron's business affairs. In the early 1550s he travelled to Italy via the Netherlands and Germany. His most important position was as Master of Music in the Archbishop of Canterbury's chapel at Lambeth Palace between 1571 and 1575.

Whythorne was the first English composer to publish his secular music—a set of *Songes for Three, Fower and Five Voyces* (London, 1571) which foreshadow Byrd's vocal writing rather than the Italian style of Morley and his school. He also published some attractive duets in 1590, but his principal claim to fame is his fascinating autobiography, which describes the uncertainties of a musician's life in the 16th century.

FURTHER READING
James M. Osborn, ed.: *The Autobiography of Thomas Whythorne* (Oxford, 1961).

Widmann, Erasmus (*bapt.* Schwäbisch Hall,

nr Stuttgart, 15 Sept. 1572; *d* Rothenburg ob der Tauber, 31 Oct. 1634). German composer. He was educated at the University of Tübingen and then worked as organist in Styria and Graz, before returning to Schwäbisch Hall because of his Lutheran sympathies. His next post was as organist to the Weikersheim court, and in 1613 he went to Rothenburg ob der Tauber as *Kantor* and organist. He remained there until he died, with his wife and daughter, of the plague. Widmann wrote sacred music to Latin as well as German texts, but he is best known for his secular works—balletts and *Lieder* which show the Italian influence. He also published a volume of dance music for instrumental ensemble, the *Gantz neue Cantzon, Intraden, Balletten und Courranten* (Nuremberg, 1618).

DENIS ARNOLD

Widor, Charles-Marie (-Jean-Albert) (*b* Lyons, 21 February 1845; *d* Paris, 12 Mar. 1937). French composer and organist. He studied with his organist father and then in Brussels with Lemmens for the organ and Fétis for composition. In 1870 he was appointed organist of St Sulpice in Paris. He succeeded Franck as professor of organ at the Paris Conservatoire, where he also taught composition. Though he wrote three operas and a great variety of other works, he is best known for his organ works, and in particular for his ten symphonies for the instrument, these combining vital Bachian counterpoint with grand Romantic gesture. The Toccata from his Fifth Symphony has become one of the most popular of organ pieces.

PAUL GRIFFITHS

Wieder (Ger.). 'Again'; *Wiederholung*, 'repetition'.

Wiegenlied (Ger.). 'Lullaby', 'cradle-song'.

Wienerisch (Ger.). 'Viennese'.

Wigthorp, William (*fl.* late 16th, early 17th centuries). English composer. He was a choirboy at Winchester Cathedral before studying music at New College, Oxford, where he graduated B.Mus. in 1605. Little of his music survives, but four consort songs are contained in a manuscript in the British Library and two anthems in the Batten Organ Book.

WENDY THOMPSON

Wikmanson, Johan (*b* Stockholm, 28 Dec. 1753; *d* Stockholm, 16 Jan. 1800). Swedish musician and composer. He studied music as a child and was sent to Copenhagen to pursue further studies in mathematics and instrument-making. The life did not suit him, however, and he returned to Stockholm in 1772. There he

worked as a civil servant and organist, also studying composition with the Abbé Vogler. In 1796 he was appointed to the staff of the Stockholm Royal Academy of Music. He was a fine organist and pianist, and also played stringed instruments. Three of his string quartets, composed in the mid 1780s, were posthumously published and dedicated to Haydn.

WENDY THOMPSON

Wilbye, John (*bapt.* Diss, Norfolk, 7 Mar. 1574; *d* Colchester, autumn 1638). English composer. The son of a tanner, he entered the service of the Kytsons before 1598, living as part of their household at Hengrave Hall, near Bury St Edmunds, and remaining there until the death of Lady Kytson in 1628. He then moved to the house of Lady Kytson's daughter, Lady Rivers, at Colchester, staying with her until his death. He inherited a substantial amount of furniture from his first employer, and his will shows that at the end of his life he was quite well off—his 'best vyall' was left to the Prince of Wales, the future Charles II.

Wilbye's reputation as a composer rests on about 60 madrigals published in two volumes (London, 1598, 1609). This slim output contains a number of masterpieces, in which a gift for finding the right music to express the mood of the text is matched with the ability to write highly singable melodies. His preference is for a sombre atmosphere, sometimes with an ironic tinge as he considers the cruelty of the beloved in the popular anacreontic verse of the age. His best works are on a large scale, using grand sonorities and making effective use of the juxtaposition of major and minor chords. One of his most successful works is the well-known pair 'Sweet honey-sucking bees' / 'Yet sweet, take heed' from the 1609 collection.

DENIS ARNOLD

FURTHER READING
David Brown: *John Wilbye* (London, 1974).

Wilder, Philippe van (*d* London, 24 Feb. 1553). Flemish composer resident in London from *c.*1520 until his death. He served as lutenist and keeper of instruments to Henry VIII. His music, mostly *chansons*, appears to have been better known in England than that of his more famous contemporaries, such as Gombert and Willaert.

JOHN MILSOM

Wilhelmj, August (*b* Usingen, 21 Sept. 1845; *d* London, 22 Jan. 1908). German violinist and composer. The child of musical parents, he made his début, aged eight, in 1854, and was sent to Liszt, who in turn passed him on to the great violinist Ferdinand David, recommending him as 'the future Paganini'. He studied at the Leipzig Conservatory and in Frankfurt before embarking on a virtuoso career. From 1878 to 1882 he made a grand world tour of the Americas, Australia, and Asia, and on his return he tried unsuccessfully to run a violin school. In 1894 he wet to London, where he became professor of violin at the Guildhall School of Music. Wilhelmj was renowned for his secure technique and powerful tone, and for his intelligent interpretation. As a composer, he is remembered only for his arrangement of the Air from Bach's D major Suite as 'Air on the G string'.   WENDY THOMPSON

Willaert, Adrian (*b* ? Bruges, *c*.1490; *d* Venice, 17 Dec. 1562). Flemish composer. He studied law at Paris University, giving it up to study music with Mouton. In about 1515 he went to Italy, where he spent some years at the d'Este court in Ferrara and then went to Milan in the service of Cardinal Ippolito II d'Este, the Archbishop of Milan. In 1527 he became *maestro di cappella* at St Mark's, Venice, remaining in that position until his death. He taught several important composers of the next generation, including Andrea Gabrieli, Cipriano de Rore, and Costanzo Porta as well as the theorist Gioseffo Zarlino, and was responsible for making Venice a leading musical centre.

Willaert was a many-sided composer, especially famous for his church music which developed from a style close to that of Josquin to a highly individual, sonorous manner, eminently

Willaert, woodcut from 'Musica nova' (1559).

suitable for grand, solemn occasions. His vesper psalms (Venice, 1550) were important for establishing the practice of writing for double choir (known as *cori spezzati) which was to become a special feature of Venetian sacred music. He was equally skilled at writing madrigals, and was one of the first to compose an extended poem in sections to form a madrigal cycle; although a little too serious to equal Lassus in the composition of comic songs he was also a tuneful and lively composer of *villanelle*. Monteverdi described his music as the crowning achievement of the *prima prattica* (see *Prima prattica, seconda prattica*).   DENIS ARNOLD

Willan, (James) Healey (*b* Balham, 12 Oct. 1880; *d* Toronto, 16 Feb. 1968). Canadian composer. He studied in London with William S. Hoyte and Evelyn Howard-Jones, and emigrated to Toronto in 1913. There he held posts as precentor of St Mary Magdalene (1921–68), teacher of theory at the conservatory (1913–36), and lecturer at the university (1914, 1936–50). Though he composed in all genres he is remembered as the leading Canadian church musician of his time; his output includes 11 settings of the *Missa brevis*.   PAUL GRIFFITHS

Will Forster's Virginal Book (London, British Library, R.M.24.D.3). One of the four great collections of Elizabethan and Jacobean virginal music (the others being the *Fitzwilliam Virginal Book*, *My Ladye Nevelles Book*, and *Benjamin Cosyn's Virginal Book*). It contains 78 pieces of keyboard music by Byrd, Morley, Bull, John Ward, etc., and some anonymous pieces. It was compiled by William Forster, and the table of contents is dated '31 Januarie 1624'. At one time the volume was owned by the music historian Sir John Hawkins.

Williams, Alberto (*b* Buenos Aires, 23 Nov. 1862; *d* Buenos Aires, 17 June 1952). Argentinian composer and pianist. He studied in Buenos Aires, and in 1882 won a scholarship to the Paris Conservatoire, where he studied composition with Franck and piano with Bériot. On his return to Argentina in 1889 he earned his living as a concert pianist, while also taking an interest in the music of his native land and incorporating folk-tunes into his own works. During his long life he played a major part in Argentinian musical life, founding the Conservatorio Williams in 1893 and several concert societies in Buenos Aires. His own works include nine symphonies.   WENDY THOMPSON

Williams, Grace (Mary) (*b* Barry, Glamorgan 19 Feb. 1906; *d* Barry, 10 Feb. 1977). Welsh composer. She studied with Vaughan Williams at the Royal College of Music and with Egon

Wellesz in Vienna. Her brand of Romantic nationalism paralleled, rather than was influenced by, Vaughan Williams and Sibelius; she was also impressed by Britten. Her output includes a comic opera, *The Parlour* (1961), two symphonies (1943 and 1956), and a large body of choral and vocal music, some of it to texts in Welsh, but her sensitivity to atmosphere and colour is best shown in her smaller orchestral pieces, such as the *Sea Sketches* for strings (1944) and *Penillion* (1955).   PAUL GRIFFITHS

FURTHER READING
Malcolm Boyd: *Grace Williams* (Cardiff, 1980).

Williams, Joseph. English firm of music printers and publishers. Lucy Williams, a music printer, founded the firm in 1808 and in 1843 was joined by her son Joseph William Williams. The firm's success was based on their holding the British rights of Robert Planquette's extremely popular operetta *Les cloches de Corneville* (1877). They also published works by Elgar, Vaughan Williams, and other English composers, as well as much educational music. The firm remained in the Williams family until 1961, when they were taken over by *Augener. They are now part of *Stainer & Bell.

J. M. THOMSON

Williamson, Malcolm (Benjamin Graham Christopher) (*b* Sydney, 21 Nov. 1931). Australian composer. He studied at the Sydney Conservatory (1944–52) and privately in London with Elisabeth Lutyens and Erwin Stein (1950–5). Remaining in England, he has produced a large quantity of music and has also appeared as a pianist and organist, usually in his own works. In 1975 he was appointed Master of the Queen's Music. His output includes full-scale operas, notably *Our Man in Havana* (1963) and *The Violins of St Jacques* (1966), three piano concertos, and many other orchestral pieces, chamber works, church music and 'cassations' involving audience participation. He ranges freely through the gamut of mid-20th-century styles, though with a liking for rich, sweet harmony which sometimes leads him close to Richard Strauss, Messiaen, or Poulenc.

PAUL GRIFFITHS

Willis, Henry (*b* London, 27 Apr. 1821; *d* London, 11 Feb. 1901). English organ-builder, known in the last three years of his life and ever since as 'Father Willis'. One of the greatest English organ-builders of the 19th century, he set up business in Gray's Inn Road, London, in 1848, and in the course of his long career built well over 2,000 organs, including those at St Paul's (London), Canterbury, and Truro Cathedrals and those for the 1851 Great Exhibition and the International Exhibition (rebuilt in Alexandra Palace and damaged in the 1980 fire there).   WENDY THOMPSON

Wilson, John (*b* Faversham, Kent, 5 Apr. 1595; *d* London, 22 Feb. 1674). English composer of songs and lute music. He wrote music for the London theatres in the early part of the 17th century, possibly including some for Shakespeare's company, and in 1622 joined the waits of the City of London. He was a favourite of Charles I and joined the King's Musick in 1635, following the royal household to Oxford on the outbreak of the Civil War. He gained the Oxford D.Mus. in 1644, and after a period as house musician to Sir William Walter in Sarsden, Oxfordshire, became Heather Professor of Music at Oxford in 1656. He felt deeply the loss of the king, composing some laments on his death, and although he returned to London after the Restoration to become a Gentleman of the Chapel Royal he seems to have composed little more music. He gave a volume of his songs and lute music to the Bodleian Library, Oxford, in 1656. His music reveals a fondness for harmonic experiments, a set of lute fantasias being arranged to show the potential of all the major and minor keys. He seem to have been a jovial man and a worthy, active professor.

DENIS ARNOLD

Wilson, Sandy [Alexander] (Galbraith) (*b* Sale, Cheshire, 19 May 1924). British composer. He was educated at Harrow and Oriel College, Oxford, where he made a name writing for and appearing in university revues. He contributed to various London revues in the 1940s and made his name with the highly successful pastiche of the 1920s, *The Boy Friend*, which became one of London's longest-running shows after its initial presentation at the Players' Theatre in 1953, followed by two Broadway productions in 1954 and 1958 and a film version in 1972. This was followed by several less successful productions such as *Valmouth* (1958, probably his best work), *Divorce me, Darling* (1964), and further contributions to revue. He has also pursued a career as an author and novelist.

PETER GAMMOND

Wilson, Thomas (Brendan) (*b* Trinidad, Colorado, 10 Oct. 1927). Scottish composer. He studied at the Royal College of Music and at Glasgow University, where in 1957 he was appointed lecturer and in 1972 reader in music. His compositions include two operas, a variety of orchestral pieces, chamber works, and choral music, usually showing a blending of diverse mainstream modernist traits in a vigorous discourse.

PAUL GRIFFITHS

Wind Instruments. To be considered here are some general aspects of wind instruments in the ordinary sense of those which are tubular in form and blown from the player's mouth; and particularly the ones that are played with fingerholes or keys—in the orchestra grouped together as *woodwind—as distinct from *brass instruments, which with few exceptions are not.

1. *The Different Families.* All depend on some arrangement by which the air-flow of the breath is interrupted to form a succession of pulses which initiates and maintains 'standing wave' oscillation of the air in the tube whence comes an instrument's sound. The arrangement takes three main forms.

(*a*) *Flutes* (including those of the 'duct flute' type like the recorder). When a jet of air meets a solid, fixed edge (as provided by the mouth-hole of a flute or the 'lip' of a recorder) it will, if the direction, distance, and speed be correctly adjusted, divide, not into smooth streams to either side, but into spiralling eddies forming alternately to either side, inwards to the flute and outwards from it. The fixed edge being open to the outer air, there is no significant pressure change, but a fast alternation of motion at the head of the air-column sets up the standing wave in the instrument. For individual articles, see *Flageolet*; *Flute*; *Panpipe*; *Pipe and Tabor*; *Recorder*. Also, though not tubular but 'cavity resonators', *Gemshorn*; *Ocarina*. See also *Whistle*.

(*b*) *Reed Instruments.* The flexible *reed is sealed from the outer air by the player's mouth, to vibrate like a kind of valve as the breath escapes past it. Alternation in pressures here gives rise to the standing wave. Reed instruments need further subdivision, for not only may the reed be double (e.g. oboe, crumhorn) or single (clarinet, saxophone), but also, cutting across this division, is the important distinction between conical bore and cylindrical, as illustrated below, taking as examples the four instruments just named.

	double reed	single reed
conical	1. Oboe	4. Saxophone
cylindrical	2. Crumhorn	3. Clarinet

Thus arranged, articles include:
1. *Bassoon*; *Bombarde*; *Dulcian*; *Oboe*; *Sarrusophone*; *Shawm* (with *Rauschpfeife*).
2. *Aulos*; *Cornamuse*; *Crumhorn*; *Kortholt* (*Sordun*); *Racket*.
3. *Clarinet*; *Hornpipe*; *Reedpipe*.
4. *Saxophone*; *Tarogato*.

(In *bagpipes, two of the above categories are often combined in one instrument.)

(*c*) *Brass Instruments.* In brass instruments, and certain non-brass instruments like the Renaissance *cornett, the player's lips, placed against a cup-like mouthpiece, vibrate in a manner analogous to that of a reed, from which comes a term sometimes used for this group (brass included) in instrument literature: 'lip-reed' instruments. Articles include: non-brass (with fingerholes): Bass horn (see *Serpent*); *Cornett*; *Serpent*; and (without fingerholes): *Alphorn*; *Didjeridu*; *Shofar*; *Horn*; *Hunting horn*; brass: *Baritone*; *Brass band*; *Bugle*; *Cornet*; *Euphonium*; *Flugel horn*; *Horn*; *Hunting horn*; *Lituus*; *Ophicleide*; *Post-horn*; *Saxhorn*; *Tenor horn*; *Trombone*; *Trumpet*; *Tuba*. See also *Valves*.

2. *Fingerholes and Overblowing.* Fingerhole instruments have a natural basis in that (*a*) the speed of sound-waves in air is such that an open-ended pipe of convenient length to handle, say from 6″ to 2′, will sound a note lying in the musically congenial range of the soprano octaves (e.g. 6″, approximately c''', the C above the staff in the treble clef; 12″, the octave below); (*b*) holes placed according to the natural span of the fingers and successively uncovered automatically lead to at least some recognizable approach to a melodic scale (whether diatonic, pentatonic, or other). In practice no more than nine digits can cover holes since one thumb must support the pipe. This (through times prior to key mechanisms) restricts the fundamental scale to nine plus one notes, the 'one' being when all holes are uncovered. But the range is in most cases increased upwards by what is collectively termed 'overblowing'—sounding harmonics of the fundamentals, and indeed so constantly that with an average orchestral woodwind part the player may well be sounding harmonics for 90 per cent of the time.

On the flute overblowing is by a slight change in the blowing (see *Embouchure*), aided in the third octave by special fingerings; and similarly on bassoon (also Baroque oboe) by barely conscious pressure on the reed. Other instruments require the uncovering of some small aperture with the left thumb, directly (recorder) or by a key (clarinet, saxophone). Flutes are open pipes, producing a regular series of harmonics (see *Flute*, 2, compass chart). The clarinet acts as a stopped pipe (see *Acoustics*, 5, 6) producing odd-numbered harmonics only (see *Clarinet*, 2, compass), and each fundamental lies an octave lower than with an open pipe of the same length: this is easily tested by 'playing' the clarinet by smacking the fingers down on the holes without putting it to the mouth, the faint sounds all being an octave higher than when the instrument is actually being played.

The hardest behaviour to understand is that of the conical bore reed instruments, which overblow to both even- and odd-numbered harmonics as the flute does. This has nothing to do with the kind of reed (a double reed can be exchanged for single; see *Bassoon*, 4). Physics explains it on the basis of a 'spherical' wave-front, emanating in theory from the apex of the cone, which is in practice non-existent (with the oboe it would lie over 3″ beyond the reed). But to express it in simple graphic terms is not so easy. Here Charles Taylor in *Sounds and Music* (London, 1975, p. 69) is helpful: a wave returning to the narrow end of a conical pipe loses velocity and no real reflection takes place there; the wave is damped out, so that one need consider only one wave-journey outwards and back, and equally so whether the narrow end be open or (as on oboe) in effect closed, the possible harmonics being the same in either case.

3. *Keywork and Cross-fingering.* Keys are of two principal kinds. An open key is one that is sprung to keep open when at rest. Usually it is named after the note it gives when closed by the finger. The key for the little finger on large recorders is a typical open key. A closed key keeps normally closed by its spring (a stronger spring than for an open key since no finger pressure in this case assists airtightness). It is named after the note it gives when opened. The single key of the Baroque flute is a typical closed key. A ring, as seen on clarinet and most oboes encircling a fingerhole, is connected to a key placed somewhere else along the instrument; when the finger is lowered it lowers the ring also. On the modern flute and the saxophone, where the holes, being exceptionally wide, are covered by padded plates, these also where necessary perform the function of rings. Many other mechanical interconnections are used in keywork. For an example, see *Oboe*, Fig. 1, an 'articulated' mechanism by which two different fingers control the same key, one to open it, the other to close it.

Keys, especially closed keys, provide the semitones outside the basic scale. Before they came into use all such semitones were made by cross-fingering as follows.

Fingerholes are usually small, so that they can easily be covered and made airtight with the fingertips. A small hole acts as though it were a larger one situated further down: the wave-length of the note is greater than would correspond with the distance to the hole from the blowing end. If the hole beyond the opened hole be closed, the wavelength is further increased, in very many cases sufficiently to lower the note by a semitone, e.g. on recorder and Baroque

oboe: all front holes open, C♯; with the second hole closed (the first still open) C♮. But on Baroque flute, closing the second hole is not enough and the third has to be closed as well. So expert were 18th-century musicians at cross-fingering—both with the fingers themselves and with the breath in controlling the tuning and the equality of cross-fingered notes—that when, in the late 18th century, closed keys began to be introduced for semitones many players for a long time spurned them, or avoided them as (in those days of primitive leather key-pads) liable to leak air and ruin the instrument's performance.

A less common way of lowering the note emitted by a hole is to half close the hole; with small holes this is difficult to control accurately at speed. There are, however, instances where a hole is replaced by a pair of still smaller holes placed side by side (known as a 'twin hole'), uncovering one of them then giving the semitone, e.g. on Baroque oboe for G♯, and for the lowest semitones on recorder.

4. *Manufacture.* The materials most used before the 18th century were the yellow boxwood (native or imported from the Near East) and maple, with ivory a luxury alternative for the smaller instruments, or now and then ebony. Then, in the course of the 18th century, these came to be rivalled, and in the next century surpassed, by imported woods of the family *Leguminosae*, first rosewood and cocuswood and finally, today standard for oboes and clarinets, African blackwood (or grenadilla). Ebonite was once highly thought of for clarinets and various synthetics have proved satisfactory since. The making of the instruments is primarily lathe work, turning the wood roughly to shape, boring it with augurs and reamers, then finishing the exterior. Next, the fingerholes, which in some instruments with small holes are 'undercut', i.e. to be wider where they meet the bore, for freer emission of the notes. This is done with a kind of inverted countersink, introduced inside and turned from the outside. Keys, which often used to be made by specialist key-makers, are forged or finished from castings. The steel springs, needle or flat, are mounted and the skin-covered pads are cemented in the key-cups (replacement springs and pads of graded widths are obtainable from instrument suppliers). The instrument is finally checked for tuning, minute corrections being possible to the holes and the bore.

5. *Breathing and Tonguing.* With wind instruments, the blowing is always referred to as the 'breathing'. While the hands find the different notes, the breathing could be said to correspond to the motion of the string-player's bow, the

expression of the music likewise depending on a variety of speeds and pressures. Tuition nowadays gives it meticulous attention, with every instrument from flute to tuba, to ensure that breath is taken in deeply in the natural manner (swelling the abdomen, not contracting it) followed by fully controlled outflow (contracting the abdomen).

Tonguing is the principal means of articulation. In written music it is normally assumed that every note will be tongued unless joined to the preceding note by a slur. On the flute and on brass instruments this is achieved by a flick of the tongue against the teeth, and on reed instruments against the tip of the reed. Where the music has dots under a slur, the notes are lightly separated by tonguing, matching the effect produced on the violin when notes are written in this way.

In very fast passages 'double tonguing' is often used: the player tongues with a 'tu ku' possible even on reed instruments although here the 'ku' makes no contact with the reed. There have also been other ways of tonguing, in use from the 16th century to the mid 18th when playing runs of quick notes, and generally described as 'te re', or 'di ri'; the 're' apparently something like a very soft 'de' and usually falling on the second quaver of a pair to give the music a lilt. How it arose is unknown, but great importance was attached to it. French players of the Baroque period came to change the consonants round, placing the 're' (or 'ru') on the first of the pair, save for the first note of the passage: a group of six quavers would then be tongued 'tu tu, ru tu, ru tu', possibly lengthening the first of each pair. Many players of early music have studied such methods very thoroughly in the quest to do full justice to the period.

Flutter-tonguing is effected by trilling 'r', making a whirring effect. It belongs almost entirely to the 20th century. In Richard Strauss's *Don Quixote* all the wind instruments do it (clarinets and brass in Variation 2, for the sheep). Schoenberg and Webern demand it mainly from the brass, but Britten has all the wind flutter-tonguing in the second movement of his *Sinfonia da Requiem*.

6. *Complex Sounds and 'Multiphonics'.* An ancient practice widespread over the world is to hum a kind of drone while playing a flute. The chords which Weber wrote for the horn in the Concertino, Op. 45, are made by playing one note, humming the next, and hoping that the third will become audible as a 'difference tone' (see *Acoustics*, 8). Vocal processes have also been used to alter the natural sound of an instrument, as in jazz the trumpet growl of Louis Armstrong, the 'talking' trombone of Ellington's Sam

Nanton, and by subsequent jazz players of the flute.

'Multiphonics' is a recently introduced term for producing on a wind instrument several sounds at once. From a long time ago students of the bassoon have known that one can sound an approximate common chord of six notes or so by means of 'trick' pressures on the reed. Then 1967 saw the publication of Bruno Bartolozzi's *New Sounds for Woodwind*, in which are codified all the compound sounds that could be discovered by woodwind members of the orchestra of La Scala, Milan, using trick embouchures and trick fingering, and often demanded in music of advanced kinds. They are seldom chords, even atonal chords, but superposed pitches, some of them impossible to write down in notation, so various signs and symbols may be used to guide the player as to what to do.

Ex. 1 is from Heinz Holliger's Wind Quintet 'h' of 1969; the holes in the diagrams run downwards from the first to the sixth, black signifying 'closed', white 'open' (the standard practice in fingering charts for instruments, as also are the numbers for the keys).

Ex. 1

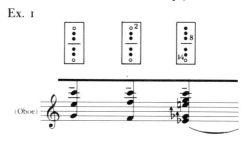

ANTHONY BAINES

Wind machine. See *Percussion Instruments*, 5.

Windpipe. See *Voice*, 3.

Wind quintet (Fr.: *quintette à vent*; Ger.: *Blasquintette*; It.: *quintetto a fiato*). A chamber-music combination consisting of four woodwind instruments, flute, oboe, clarinet, bassoon, and one brass instrument, the horn. Its repertory really starts in the early 19th century, with works by Danzi and Reicha, and leads on to numerous works from later in the century up to the present time, for example Stockhausen's *Zeitmasse* of 1956 (in which, very unusually, a cor anglais replaces the horn); see also *Wind Instruments*, 6. It must be granted that the past level of the repertory falls infinitely below that of the string quartet and also below the quintets for piano and wind by Mozart and Beethoven, neither of whom, like the vast majority of great composers, wrote a wind quintet. Yet the wind quintet can offer unceasing pleasure to the amateur wind player, while there are many professional quintets formed from among the finest orchestral players, whose recitals can grip the audience with the brilliance and finesse of their renderings.   ANTHONY BAINES

Winter, Peter von (*bapt*. Mannheim, 28 Aug. 1754; *d* Munich, 17 Oct. 1825). German composer. At the age of 10 he entered the Mannheim court orchestra as a violinist. He studied for a while with the Abbé Vogler, and when the electoral court moved to Munich in 1778 Winter became conductor of the orchestra. In 1780–1 he visted Vienna, where he studied with Salieri and met Mozart. From 1798 he was *Kapellmeister* at the Munich court, and over the next decade or so his stage works (over 40 ballets and operas including the *Singspiel, Das Labyrinth* (1798), a sequel to Mozart's *Die Zauberflöte*) were produced in Munich, Vienna, London, and elsewhere. Winter's later years were devoted mainly to teaching and writing sacred music. He also composed cantatas and symphonies.
                                    WENDY THOMPSON

Winterreise ('Winter Journey'). Song-cycle for male voice and piano by Schubert, D 911, composed in 1827. The songs are settings of 24 poems by Wilhelm Müller (published in 1823–4). They are: Book 1, *Gute Nacht* ('Good Night'), *Die Wetterfahne* ('The Weathervane'), *Gefrorne Tränen* ('Frozen Tears'), *Erstarrung* ('Frozen Rigidity'), *Der Lindenbaum* ('The Lime Tree'), *Wasserflut* ('Flood'), *Auf dem Flusse* ('On the River'), *Rückblick* ('Backward Glance'), *Irrlicht* ('Will-o'-the-Wisp'), *Rast* ('Rest'), *Frühlingstraum* ('Dream of Spring'), *Einsamkeit* ('Loneliness'); Book 2, *Die Post* ('The Post'), *Der greise Kopf* ('The Hoary Head'), *Die Krähe* ('The Crow'), *Letzte Hoffnung* ('Last Hope'), *Im Dorfe* ('In the Village'), *Der stürmische Morgen* ('The Stormy Morning'), *Täuschung* ('Delusion'), *Der Wegweiser* ('The Signpost'), *Das Wirthaus* ('The Inn'), *Mut* ('Courage'), *Die Nebensonnen* ('Phantom Suns'), *Der Leiermann* ('The Hurdy-gurdy Man').

Winter Words. Song cycle, Op. 52, by Britten for soprano or tenor and piano. The title is taken from Thomas Hardy's last published volume of poetry (1928), from which Britten set eight poems. It was first performed at the Leeds Festival in 1953.

Wirbel (Ger.). 1. 'Drum roll'. 2. The 'peg' of a violin.

Wirén, Dag (Ivar) (*b* Striberg, Närke, 15 Oct. 1905). Swedish composer. He studied at the Royal Conservatory in Stockholm (1926–31) and in Paris (1932–4), where he was influenced by Honegger. He then returned to Sweden,

where for a time he worked as a librarian and music critic. In his Third Symphony (1943–4) he established a 'metamorphosis technique' by which whole works could be generated from small units, paralleling the precedures of such contemporaries as Holmboe. His output includes five symphonies, five string quartets, and a variety of other large-scale instrumental works, but he is best known for his light Serenade for strings (1937).
                                    PAUL GRIFFITHS

Wise, Michael (*b* Wiltshire, *c*.1648; *d* Salisbury, 24 Aug. 1687). English composer. At the Restoration he was a Child of the Chapel Royal, and from 1666 a countertenor in St George's Chapel, Windsor. He became organist and choirmaster at Salisbury Cathedral in 1668 and was made a Gentleman of the Chapel Royal in 1676. In 1687, the year of his death, he was appointed Master of the Children at St Paul's Cathedral. He was killed in a violent scuffle with the Salisbury night watch following a domestic dispute. His works include some fine anthems (such as 'Awake up my glory' and 'How are the mighty fallen') and services.
                                    WENDY THOMPSON

Wishart, Peter (Charles Arthur) (*b* Crowborough, 25 June 1921). English composer. He studied at Birmingham University and in Paris with Nadia Boulanger, from whom he inherited a taste for that Stravinskyan neoclassicism which is at the root of his music, modified in later works by a simpler, more direct approach. His output includes four operas, two symphonies (1953 and 1973) and various other orchestral works, choral music, chamber pieces, and songs. As a teacher he has worked at various institutions, and in 1977 was appointed professor of music at Reading University. He is also the author of *Harmony* (London, 1956) and *Key to Music* (London, 1971).
                                    PAUL GRIFFITHS

Wöchentliche Nachrichten. German weekly musical magazine, the first to address itself to the musical amateur. It was founded by J. A. Hiller in Leipzig in 1766 but ceased publication in 1770.

Wohlgefällig (Ger.). 'Pleasant', 'pleasantly'.

Wohltemperierte Klavier, Das ('The Well-Tempered Clavier'). A name given by J. S. Bach to his collection of 48 Preludes and Fugues for keyboard in all the major and minor keys. The first 24 were written in Cöthen in 1722, and the second set in Leipzig, around 1744. The two sets are often known simply as 'the 48'. The collection was not published until 1800–1.

Wolf, Hugo (Filipp Jakob) (*b* Windischgraz, Styria, now Slovenj Gradec, Yugoslavia, 13 Mar. 1860; *d* Vienna, 22 Feb. 1903). Austrian composer. His father was a leather-merchant and an able instrumentalist who taught him the piano and violin. After some generally unsatisfactory schooling he entered the Vienna Conservatory in 1875 to study the piano, harmony, and composition, and it was there that he first became obsessed with Wagner's music. He was dismissed for disciplinary reasons in 1877 and, after a short visit home, attempted to make a living in Vienna as a teacher. He was always subject to bouts of deep depression and melancholia, unable to compose for long periods, then suddenly overtaken by a hectic flood of inspiration. His efforts were encouraged by a number of established musicians (the composer Adalbert von Goldschmidt and the conductor Felix Mottl), and he was befriended—for much of his life materially supported—by various well-to-do families.

In 1881 he was appointed second conductor at Salzburg under Karl Muck, but he was temperamentally unsuited and left after only a few months. From 1884 to 1887 he wrote criticism for the *Wiener Salonblatt*: his writings were often provocative, and his pro-Wagner, anti-Brahms views hindered his advancement in Viennese circles. The late 1880s were a particularly productive period for his songwriting, but by 1897 his mental health had severely deteriorated (the inevitable outcome of an earlier syphilitic condition) and he was admitted to a sanatorium. He was discharged as cured in 1898 but later that year had to enter an asylum, where he spent the last few unhappy years of his life.

In a comparatively short career Wolf made an individual and significant contribution to the *Lied* repertory, in which he has been reckoned a natural successor to Schubert. In his settings of poetry by Mörike, Eichendorff, and Goethe, written mainly in a feverish burst in the late 1880s, he allowed the verses to trigger the release of mental tensions and established a highly personalized mode of musical expression, which often sets dramatic declamation in the voice against strikingly original harmonic ideas in the piano. In the *Spanisches Liederbuch* (1889-90) and the two volumes of the *Italienisches Liederbuch* (1890-1, 1896), translations into German by Heyse and Geibel of Spanish and Italian verse, he responded to the texts' directness of expression with deft, colourful musical characterizations.

In addition to his output of some 300 songs (more than a third remained unpublished in his lifetime), he struggled doggedly with instrumental composition: a string quartet in D minor (begun in 1878), the symphonic poem *Penthesilea*

Hugo Wolf (1895)

(1883-5), and the *Italienische Serenade* for string quartet (1887; arranged for orchestra in 1892) had some success. A desire to explore larger forms and his obsession with Wagner caused him to labour long with opera. The only opera he completed, *Der Corregidor* (1895), on a Spanish theme, has been criticized as lacking dramatic continuity; his hypersensitive, egocentric disposition seemed to respond more naturally to the stimulus of short, concentrated song texts with their scope for a more personal musical expression.

JUDITH NAGLEY

FURTHER READING
Eric Sams: *The Songs of Hugo Wolf* (London, 1961, rev. edn 1981); Mosco Carner: *The Songs of Hugo Wolf* (London, 1982).

Wolff, Christian (*b* Nice, 8 Mar. 1934). American composer of French birth. He took American citizenship in 1947 and studied classics at Harvard University (1951-63). Though influenced by his association with John Cage in the early 1950s, he is self-taught as a composer. He has been particularly concerned to encourage performers to contribute creatively in his music, allowing them to choose, improvise and react to each other. Since 1968 he has endeavoured also to awaken sympathy for revolutionary political ideals through his music. He has taught classics at Harvard (1962-71) and at Dartmouth College (1971-   ).

PAUL GRIFFITHS

Wölfl, Joseph (*b* Salzburg, 24 Dec. 1773; *d* London, 21 May 1812). Austrian pianist and composer. A chorister at Salzburg Cathedral, he was taught by Leopold Mozart and Michael Haydn. He was a gifted child, making his début as a violinist at the age of seven; his first compositions also date from the 1780s. In 1790 he met Mozart in Vienna and through him obtained a post as composer in Warsaw. He returned to Vienna in 1795, working as a pianist and composer in competition with Beethoven. He then spent some time travelling and giving concerts, and at the turn of the century he moved first to Paris, and then to London, where his works met with great success. His early death at the age of 38 was mourned by many London concert-goers. His piano sonatas remained in the repertory until the mid 19th century.   WENDY THOMPSON

Wolf-Ferrari, Ermanno (*b* Venice, 12 Jan. 1876; *d* Venice, 21 Jan. 1948). Italian composer. Son of a German father and an Italian mother, he had little formal tuition in music until 1892 when he went to Munich to study with Rheinberger. He returned to Venice, became a friend of Perosi, and composed a certain amount of religious music before having his first operatic success, *Le donne curiose*, given in Munich in 1903. He was then made director of the Liceo Musicale Benedetto Marcello in Venice, composed another two operas for Munich, the second of which—*Il segreto di Susanna* ('Susanna's Secret', 1909), a witty conversation piece—has had a continuing place in the repertory. He resigned his post in Venice in the same year, and composed a serious opera, *I gioielli della Madonna* ('The Jewels of the Madonna', 1911), in the *verismo* style of Mascagni, which was also successful. During the First World War a spiritual crisis made him give up composition, but from 1925 he wrote several other comic operas. From 1939 he was professor of composition at the Mozarteum in Salzburg for some years. His operas have rarely achieved the success their wittiness seems to deserve, but Wolf-Ferrari was one of the first anti-Romantic Italian composers, returning to Goldoni and the *commedia dell'arte* for inspiration, and as such he was the precursor of Malipiero and the younger Italian school.   DENIS ARNOLD

Wolkenstein, Oswald von (*b* Schöneck in Pustertal, South Tyrol, *c*.1377; *d* Merano, 2 Aug. 1445). Austrian poet and composer. Born of a noble family, he spent much of his life travelling in the service of various noblemen, and later as a diplomat for Emperor Sigismund. These travels took him to the Middle East and Africa as well as to Italy and other parts of Europe. In 1417 he married Margarete von Schwangau, but continued to make references in his poetry to an earlier love, Anna Hausmann. She was a member of the family with which Oswald was in dispute over the apportioning of his lands, and the dispute led to several sentences of imprisonment, also mentioned in his verse. He was a notable *Minnesinger*, but his works include not only monodic love- and sacred songs, but also more elaborate polyphonic *Lieder*.   DENIS ARNOLD

Wolpe, Stefan (*b* Berlin, 25 Aug. 1902; *d* New York, 4 Apr. 1972). American composer of German birth. He studied at the Berlin Musikhochschule (1919-24) but was more influenced by informal lessons at this time with Busoni and with Hermann Scherchen. Also important was his association with Klee and others at the Bauhaus (1923). His works from the 1920s often show a vein of sharp political satire, but the arrival of Hitler in power forced a change of direction. Wolpe left for Vienna, where he had lessons with Webern (1933-4), and then settled in Palestine. There he wrote specifically Jewish music, using Hebrew texts and certain Semitic musical characteristics. In 1938 he moved to the United States, where for three decades he was an influential teacher and where he devoted his creative attention principally to abstract pieces for instrumental combinations. Often having such austere titles as *Piece for Two Instrumental Units*, these works have novel forms which grow with unerring sureness, driven by the constant variation of keenly defined atonal motifs.
                    PAUL GRIFFITHS

WoO. Abbreviation of *Werk ohne Opuszahl* (Ger.), 'work without opus number'. The term is especially common in references to Beethoven's music, since a number of his works were not published in his lifetime. See *Opus*.

Wood, Anthony (*b* Oxford, 17 Dec. 1632; *d* Oxford, 29 Nov. 1695). English amateur musician. The son of a landed gentleman, he was educated at Merton College, Oxford, graduating in 1652. He was a skilled amateur player on both the viol and the violin, and during the Commonwealth played regularly in chamber music groups with visiting professionals who had temporarily abandoned London. Wood seems to have given up music in favour of antiquarian studies after the Restoration. His informative, if perhaps less than reliable, manuscript notes on the lives of contemporary musicians are now in the Bodleian Library, Oxford   WENDY THOMPSON

Wood, Charles (*b* Armagh, 15 June 1866; *d* Cambridge, 12 July 1926). Irish composer and teacher. He studied with Stanford at the Royal

College of Music (1883–7), where in 1888 he was appointed to the teaching staff. Also in 1888 he began teaching at Cambridge, eventually becoming university lecturer (1897) and professor of music (1924). His compositions include three string quartets and a large quantity of church music, some of which has entered common use.

PAUL GRIFFITHS

Wood, Haydn (*b* Slaithwaite, Yorks., 25 Mar. 1882; *d* London, 11 Mar. 1959). English composer and violinist. A child prodigy, he won a scholarship to the Royal College of Music, where he studied composition with Stanford. A period of study in Brussels was followed by a world tour. He is best remembered for his 200 or so ballads, which include the evergreen favourites *Love's Garden of Roses* (1914) and *Roses of Picardy* (1916). His other music, including concertos for piano and violin, is largely forgotten.

WENDY THOMPSON

Wood, (Sir) Henry J(oseph) (*b* London, 3 Mar. 1869; *d* Hitchin, 19 Aug. 1944). English conductor. After a period as an organist and two years of study at the Royal Academy of Music, he began conducting with various opera companies, including some performances of *Eugene Onegin* in 1892. This led to his engagement as conductor of some summer Promenade Concerts in 1895. Starting with deliberately popular programmes, he soon acquired a reputation for introducing the most important novelties to his audiences (including works by contemporary composers as varied as Schoenberg and Shostakovich), and he was largely responsible for the popularity in England of Richard Strauss and most Russian music in the early years of this century. A man of great energy, he conducted many provincial choral and orchestral societies including those at Hull, Liverpool, and Nottingham, as well as symphony concerts during the London season. He can be considered the founder of modern orchestral playing in England, training many of his players at the Royal Academy of Music, helping to get rid of the deputy system in rehearsal, bowing and phrasing all his own parts, and in general imposing a better standard of discipline. Appreciated by the wider public, he was somewhat denigrated by critics for lacking a sense of style (he enjoyed playing Bach with huge orchestras) and by others for superficiality. Nevertheless, his music making was often exciting and alive, and the over-all musical life of the country would be much poorer without the radical changes he brought about.

DENIS ARNOLD

Wood, Hugh (Bradshaw) (*b* Parbold, Lancs., 27 June 1932). English composer. He studied

at Oxford and privately with Lloyd Webber (1954–6), Iain Hamilton (1956–8), Anthony Milner (1957–60), and Mátyás Seiber (1958–60). Consistently in his music he has used twelve-note serial methods to create forms of continuous and purposeful development, drawing strength from the examples of Beethoven and Schoenberg in particular, though his abundant lyricism and his alert, dancing rhythms are peculiarly English. His chief works include three string quartets (1962, 1969–70, and 1978), concertos for cello (1965–9) and violin (1970–2), *Scenes from Comus* for soprano, tenor, and orchestra (1962–5), and several sets of songs. He has also taught at various institutions, including the universities of Glasgow (1966–70), Liverpool (1971–3), and Cambridge (from 1977), and is a thought-provoking writer and broadcaster on music.

PAUL GRIFFITHS

Wood block, Wood drum. The wood block is a percussion instrument, of a rectangular hardwood block about 8″ long, partly hollowed out to form a deep slot along each side, the slots facing in opposite directions. The block (Fig. 1*a*) is struck with a drumstick or some other beater, to give a high, hollow, and abrupt sound. It came in with jazz, since when many composers have used it, as Walton in *Belshazzar's Feast*, where the God of Wood follows the God of Iron (anvil) and the God of Stone (whip). It is also made in different sizes to give contrasted sounds, high and low, and Stockhausen and Berio have so used it.

There is also a tubular type (Fig. 1*b*), with a slit cut down each end, one end being hollowed deeper than the other, so that contrasted sounds may be produced. This form is much used in school percussion groups.

The wood drum, or wood-plate drum, is a recent addition to the percussion, virtually a *tom-tom with wood replacing the drum-skin.

Fig. 1.

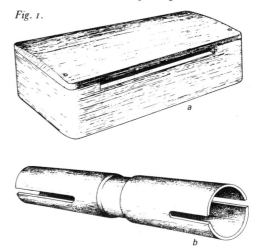

'Wood-plate' drum is the preferable term since 'wood drum' can be muddled with German *Holztrommel*, which normally means a *slit drum. ANTHONY BAINES

Woodcock, Robert (*b* ? 1691; *d* 10 Apr. 1728). English composer and recorder player. Little is known of his life, except that he was apparently born of a good family and held a government post which he resigned some time after 1723 to become a professional artist. One authority says that Woodcock 'died of gout, in his 37th year, April 10, 1728, and was buried at Chelsea'; another reports that he committed suicide. He evidently possessed a talent for music as well as for painting. Hawkins described him as a celebrated player who 'composed twelve concertos so contrived, as that flutes of various sizes, having the parts transposed, might play in concert with the other instruments'; they were the earliest solo concertos for wind instruments to be published in England (London, 1727–30). His music was apparently popular, judging from the frequent appearance of his name in concert announcements of the 1720s and 1730s. WENDY THOMPSON

Wooden Prince, The (*A fából faragott királyfi*) Ballet in one act by Bartók to a scenario by Béla Balázs. It was first performed in Budapest in 1917. Bartók arranged an orchestral suite from the score (?1921–4).

Woodwind. Collective orchestral term for flute, oboe, clarinet, bassoon, and their sub-species (piccolo etc.). The orchestral woodwind section has a classic basis of two players of each of the four above-named main instruments, known as the 'first' (or 'principal') and the 'second'. A full-sized symphony orchestra will also have at least a third player of each, who has special responsibility for piccolo, cor anglais, bass clarinet, and contrabassoon. Frequently a fourth player is needed, and may be on the permanent strength, bringing the section up to 16 all told. The third and fourth players may then take their turn in relieving the principal pair on occasions when works in the programme do not otherwise require them.

Many works of the early 20th century, when composers were writing for very large orchestras, demand even more woodwind players. Richard Strauss's *Elektra* includes no fewer than eight clarinet parts (E♭ clarinet, four ordinary and two basset horns, and bass clarinet). Stravinsky's *Rite of Spring* needs five of each woodwind (the equal sign '=' denotes 'interchanging with'):

piccolo; 3 flutes (3rd = piccolo 2), alto flute
2 oboes, 2 cors anglais (2nd = oboe 4)
E♭ clarinet, 2 clarinets, 2 bass clarinets (2nd = clarinet 4)
3 bassoons, 2 contrabassoons (2nd = bassoon 4)

The saxophone, when used in the orchestra, is also counted among the woodwind (even though, like the modern flute, it is not made of wood), being played by one who normally also plays the clarinet.

'Woodwind' is clearly a term with strong overtones of the Romantic period. The older expression was simply 'wind instruments' or 'the wind', whether or not including the brass, and this is now often preferred by groups specializing in Baroque music, in which the 'wind' may include a pre-Romantic instrument like the recorder; and still more so with earlier music which may call for shawms etc., and particularly the cornett, which cannot be properly described as either woodwind or brass. ANTHONY BAINES
FURTHER READING
Anthony Baines: *Woodwind Instruments and their History* (2nd edn, London, 1963).

Wordsworth, William (Brocklesby) (*b* London, 17 Dec. 1908). English composer. A descendant of the poet's brother, he studied in Edinburgh with Tovey (1934–6), whose ideas have had a continuing influence on his music. His works include five symphonies, six string quartets, and songs. PAUL GRIFFITHS

Worshipful Company of Musicians. English music society based in London. It developed from the 15th-century London Fellowship of Minstrels, and now encourages many aspects of music-making, chiefly by awarding prizes, scholarships, and medals, such as the Collard Fellowship for composers (established 1931), the Cobbett chamber music prize, the Santley medal for singers, and various other prizes and medals at the schools and colleges of music. A new charter was drawn up in 1950.

Wotquenne (-Plattel), **Alfred** (Camille) (*b* Lobbes, Hainault, 25 Jan. 1867; *d* Antibes, 25 Sept. 1939). Belgian bibliographer. He was librarian at the Brussels Conservatoire from 1894 to 1918, and his catalogue of that library is a standard work of reference. His best-known contribution to scholarship is his thematic catalogue of the music of C. P. E. Bach (Leipzig, 1905), whose works are (by analogy with Köchel's numbers for Mozart's) assigned 'Wq' numbers. DENIS ARNOLD

Wozzeck. Opera in three acts by Berg; text by the composer, after Georg Büchner's play (1836). Produced: Berlin, Staatsoper, 14 December 1925; Philadelphia, 19 March 1931; London, Covent Garden, 22 January 1952.

Design by Pavos Aravantinos for Act 1, scene 4 of the first production of Berg's 'Wozzeck' (Staatsoper, Berlin, 1925).

Wozzeck (bar.), an ordinary soldier, is lectured by the Captain (ten.), who despises him. Gathering sticks with his friend Andres (ten.), Wozzeck is alarmed by strange sounds and visions. Wozzeck's mistress Marie (sop.) flirts from her window with a passing Drum Major. Wozzeck is examined by a half-crazed Doctor (bass) who is using him for experiments. The Drum Major (ten.) seduces Marie.

Wozzeck becomes suspicious of Marie. The Captain taunts him with suggestions of her infidelity and Wozzeck accuses her. He finds her dancing with the Drum Major. The Drum Major boasts of his success, and, when Wozzeck refuses to drink with him, beats him.

The repentant Marie is reading the Bible. As they walk by a pond, the distraught Wozzeck stabs her. Later, drinking in a tavern, he is seen to have blood on his hands, and rushes away. Wading into the pond to find the knife, he drowns. Their child is playing with his hobby-horse, and does not understand when the other children tell him that his mother is dead.

FURTHER READING
George Perle: *The Operas of Alban Berg, i: Wozzeck* (Berkeley, Los Angeles, and London, 1981).

Wq. Abbreviated prefix to numbers in the *Wotquenne catalogue of C. P. E. Bach's works.

Wranitzky, Paul [Vranický, Pavel] (*b* Nová Říše, Moravia, 30 Dec. 1756; *d* Vienna, 26 Sept. 1808). Czech composer and conductor; the brother of Anton Wranitzky (1761–1820), the composer, violinist, and founder of the Vienna

violin school. After studying music and theology in his native Moravia he left for Vienna at the age of 20, where he studied briefly with Haydn. During the 1790s he was chief director ('from the violin') of the orchestras of the Vienna court theatres, and later took a lead in Vienna's concert life as secretary of the Tonkünstler-Sozietät and director of the Cavalier-Konzerte. Wranitzky maintained friendly relations with Haydn and Beethoven, and won the approval of both composers as a conductor of their works, premièring the latter's First Symphony in 1800. Popular as a composer of stage and instrumental music, his *Singspiel*, *Oberon*, written for the coronation celebrations of Leopold II in 1790, was particularly successful and remained in the repertory until the 1820s. His symphonies and string quartets were admired for their lyrical qualities, and in the former, in common with his master Haydn, Wranitzky made use of folk melodies.   JAN SMACZNY

Wunderhorn, Des Knaben. See *Knaben Wunderhorn, Des*.

Wunsch (Ger.). 'Wish'; *nach Wunsch*, 'according to one's wish', i.e. *ad libitum*.

Wuorinen, Charles (*b* New York, 9 June 1938). American composer. He studied with Otto Luening, Jack Beeson, and Vladimir Ussachevsky at Columbia University, where he was appointed to the staff in 1964. Active as a pianist and conductor, he has payed particular attention to the articulating function of the performer, and this concern has marked not only his large output of concert music but also his few electronic works, of which *Time's Encomium* (1969) is among the most impressive achievements in the medium. Most of his music uses complex serial methods derived from Babbitt.   PAUL GRIFFITHS

Wut [*Wuth*] (Ger.). 'Rage'; *wütend*, *wütig*, 'furious', 'raging'.

Wylkinson, Robert (*fl.* late 15th, early 16th centuries). English composer. He worked at Eton College, first as parish clerk and later as Master of the Choristers, from 1496 to 1515. His music survives in the Eton Choirbook and includes a monumental nine-part *Salve regina* and a curious setting of the Apostles' Creed in the form of a 13-part canon.

JOHN MILSOM

X

Xabo (Sp.). See *Jabo*.

Xácara (Sp., Port.). See *Jácara*.

Xaleo (Sp.). See *Jaleo*.

Xenakis, Iannis (*b* Brăila, Romania, 29 May 1922). French composer of Romanian birth. Born to Greek parents, he moved with his family to Greece in 1932. There he began musical studies two years later under Aristotle Kundurov and took a degree in engineering at the Athens Polytechnic. In 1947 he moved to Paris, where he had lessons from Honegger, Milhaud, and Messiaen, and where he served as assistant to the architect Le Corbusier (1948–59). He became a French citizen in 1965 and the next year set up the School of Mathematical and Automated Music in Paris. In 1967 he began teaching also at the University of Indiana.

Xenakis's works are examples of a new and individual kind of musical thinking, based on models drawn from architecture, physics, and mathematics. Specially important has been the mathematics of probability, which Xenakis has used to calculate the mass effects he favours: complexes of soaring glissandos in a string orchestra, for instance, or nebulous passages of sound on tape. He introduced the term '*sto-chastic music*' for music using probabilistic processes, and he has sometimes used computers to assist in the elaborate calculations demanded. His output includes several orchestral works, among them *Metastaseis* (1953–4) and *Terretektorh* (1965-6), a variety of extraordinarily difficult solo pieces, such as *Herma* for piano (1960-4) and *Nomos alpha* for cello (1965), and music on tape, including *Orient-Occident* (1960). In his *Polytope* series he has combined electronic sound with laser beams and other visual effects.   PAUL GRIFFITHS

FURTHER READING
Iannis Xenakis: *Formalized Music* (Bloomington and London, 1971).

Xiao. A Chinese end-blown flute. See *Chinese Music*, 4*g*.

Xuan. A Chinese globular flute or clay-whistle. See *Chinese Music*, 4*f*.

Xylophone. Percussion instruments of tuned wooden bars. The bars (or 'keys') of rosewood lie in two rows like piano keys, with tubular metal (or plastic) resonators suspended vertically beneath them, and are played with appropriate beaters with round ends of wood, hard rubber, or plastic. The *marimba has a deeper compass. Fig. 1 shows the customary ranges,

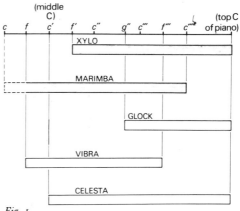

Fig. 1.

Xenakis

including for comparison those of the three main instruments that have metal bars. Xylophone parts are written an octave lower than the (sounding) compass shown.

1. *Construction and Technique.* The bars, about $1\frac{1}{2}''$ wide and $1''$ thick, are supported on cords or pads towards the two ends, where there are vibration nodes, and are normally struck in the middle, where there is a fundamental vibration antinode (see *Glockenspiel*, 5, which notices also the relative lengths of bars over the compass). The row of sharps is placed on a higher level than the naturals for their ends to overlap a little, which brings the striking points closer together. There are, however, models with the rows level.

Each resonator tube is tuned to the bar above it, for sympathetic vibration of the air inside as a 'stopped pipe' (see *Acoustics*, 5). For this each resonator is closed at or towards its lower end. Externally, however, the tubes can be of any length required for visual effect, e.g. for their bottom ends to form an arch.

The basic technique is to strike with the two beaters alternately (if playing a scale, moving the hands together along the keys). 'Double' beats (two consecutive notes with the same beater) and 'cross over' beats are, however, frequently needed (as with *timpani) for fluent rendering of a passage. A player will often work out beforehand how to beat a passage of any

difficulty, and at least partly memorize it in order not to have to look at the music as well as the instrument and the conductor.

2. *Trough Xylophones.* Now well known in school music, these have the bars laid over an open-topped box or 'trough' with a sloping floor to make it deeper towards the bass end, and thus acts as a combined resonator for the whole compass. This follows ancient practice for xylophones in Burma and Indonesia, borrowed by Carl Orff for his educational music (*Schulwerk*) and put into production from the 1930s by Maendler. As on the school metallophones (see *Glockenspiel*, 3) the bars are quickly removable and different sizes (alto, bass, etc.) are available.

3. *History and the Four-row Xylophone.* The above trough form goes back to before the 9th century AD in Java, where a general name is 'gambang' (see *Indonesia*, 2-5). The West, however, produced a quite different type, known in Central Europe as a popular instrument from the 15th century. The bars are here placed in a row, not from right to left but with the longest bar crosswise to the player's body and the smallest furthest away. The bars, threaded on cords, are laid upon long tied bundles of straw about three-quarters of an inch thick, whence in Germany the name *Strohfiedel* ('straw fiddle'). When in the early 19th century folk instruments came to be exploited by touring soloists (the

A three-and-a-half octave xylophone by Deagan, Chicago.

*zither being one), this xylophone was improved in scope by adding from one to three further rows of bars beside the original one, their ends overlapping to save over-all breadth. With four rows, the main scale zigzags through the two middle rows and the outer rows provide the sharps in duplicate, making these available to either hand. On such an instrument one player, M. J. Gusikov (1806-37), greatly impressed everyone including Mendelssohn. It became the standard concert xylophone in Europe until the introduction of the present form from the USA, and many Russian orchestras retain it still. There are no resonators: when not in use the instrument can be folded up, with the straw bundles (or later, solid rails) inside, and transported in a compact box. The beaters are wood with narrow spoon-shaped beaters recalling the shape of dulcimer beaters. The first celebrated orchestral xylophone part, in Saint-Saëns's *Danse macabre*, was for this type. The score quotes the poem by Cazalis: 'the winter wind blows, the night is cold . . . the white skeletons race and leap under their great shrouds', to which the publisher has added, 'Le Xilophone est un instrument de bois et paille analogue à l'Harmonica [i.e. glockenspiel], on le trouve chez MM. Durand et Fils'.

Xylophones with the bars arranged in the now familiar way were also known in Europe in earlier times: there is an 18th-century drawing of a street busker 'playing the sticks', apparently a sort of 'trough' pattern. The arrangement has, of course, the advantage of being easier for musicians brought up with a knowledge of the piano. ANTHONY BAINES

Y

Yale University. Founded in 1701, Yale waited over 200 years before emerging as an important force in America's musical life. Starting in 1904 with Horatio Parker's tenure as Dean, the Yale School of Music (founded 1894) became known particularly for its composition department, a reputation upheld in later years by such composers on the faculty as Hindemith, Gunther Schuller, Penderecki, and Yehudi Wyner. Yale University boasts strong academic programmes in music. Its library contains the manuscripts of Charles Ives and many books collected by Lowell Mason.　　　　　　MARK TUCKER

Yankee Doodle. Burlesque song, to a jolly tune, which was first used by the British troops during the American War of Independence, to deride the American colonial revolutionaries, and was subsequently adopted by the Americans and turned to their own advantage. A version of the tune first appeared in print around 1778 in Aird's collection *A Selection of Scottish, English, Irish and Foreign Airs*, published in Glasgow (this contains several American airs). Other versions appeared shortly afterwards. The first American publication to include it is believed to be the *Federal Overture* of Benjamin Carr (1795), while two American manuscript versions exist, dated 1775 and 1790. The history of the tune, so far as it is known, is printed in Sonneck's *Report on the Star-Spangled Banner, Hail Columbia!, America, and Yankee Doodle*, published by the Library of Congress in 1909. Anton Rubinstein wrote variations on this tune, which he dedicated to the American pianist William Mason and played at his farewell concert in New York. A modified version of the tune appears in the last movement of Dvořák's Symphony No. 9 ('From the New World').

'Yardbird'. See *Parker, Charlie.*

Yardumian, Richard (*b* Philadelphia, 5 Apr. 1917). American composer. Not until he was 22 did he begin formal musical studies; as a composer he is self-taught. While working as a piano teacher and church music director in Pennsylvania he has composed a number of large-scale works in a Romantic style influenced by the modes of Armenian music. Among these are two symphonies (1961 and 1964), concertos for violin (1949) and piano (1957), the Mass 'Come, Creator Spirit' for chorus and orchestra

(1966), and the oratorio *The Story of Abraham* (1969–71).　　　　　　PAUL GRIFFITHS

Yehudi Menuhin School. British specialist school for the musically gifted, founded by Yehudi Menuhin in 1963 and situated in Stoke d'Abernon, Surrey. In 1973 the school was accorded special status as a centre of education for the performing arts, and was awarded a government grant. Peter Norris has been Director of Music since 1980.

Yeomen of the Guard, The. Operetta in two acts by Gilbert and Sullivan. Produced: London, Savoy Theatre, 3 October 1888; New York, Casino Theatre, 17 October 1888; Vienna, Carl Theater, 2 February 1889. Set in the Tower of London in the 16th century, this stands as the most 'serious' of Gilbert and Sullivan's collaborations. It deals with Colonel Fairfax (ten.), who, under sentence of death on a trumped-up charge, marries a strolling player Elsie Maynard (sop.) so as to preserve his estate. With the help of the yeoman of the guard's daughter Phoebe (mezzo), he escapes from gaol in disguise, and when his reprieve comes he and Elsie are truly in love. The pathos of the piece is concentrated in Elsie's companion, Jack Point (bar.), who had hoped to marry her himself.

Yodel. See *Jodel.*

Yonge, Nicholas (*b* ? Lewes, Sussex; *d* London, Oct. 1619). English music editor. He sang in the choir of St Paul's Cathedral between 1594 and 1618. His main claim to musical fame is his compilation of the famous anthology of Italian madrigals called *Musica transalpina*, published in two volumes (London, 1588, 1597). The first was especially important for setting off the vogue for madrigals in England; it was the earliest to provide translations of the original poetry, and may have prompted composers to use their native verse rather than set Italian.　　　　　　DENIS ARNOLD

York. Psalm tune. See *Stilt, The.*

Youll, Henry (*fl.* early 17th century). English composer, probably from Newark. From being a pauper he became, after apprenticeship in 1590 to a 'song school master', household musician to an English gentleman called Edward

Bacon. He wrote some charming light canzonets and balletts which were published in his *Canzonets to Three Voyces* (London, 1608).

DENIS ARNOLD

Young, La Monte (*b* Bern, Idaho, 14 Oct. 1935). American composer. He studied at the University of California (1957-60), with Stockhausen at Darmstadt (1959) and with Richard Maxfield at the New School for Social Research, New York (1960-1). His early works, such as the String Trio of 1958, exploit sounds held for a very long time, and he has continued to concern himself with sustained, slowly evolving tones. In 1960-1, however, he produced a number of text compositions which are more theatrical than musical: *Composition 1960 No. 5*, for instance, requires the performers to release butterflies into the auditorium. He returned to his main interest in 1962 with the foundation of his own ensemble, the Theatre of Eternal Music, who perform extended improvisations on static pure harmonies.   PAUL GRIFFITHS

FURTHER READING
Richard Kostelanetz: *The Theatre of Mixed Means* (New York, 1967); Michael Nyman: *Experimental Music* (London, 1974); La Monte Young: *Selected Writings* (Munich, 1970).

Young, William (*d* Innsbruck, 23 Apr. 1662). English composer. Nothing is known of his early life, but he left England during the Commonwealth to seek a post abroad. By 1652 he was in the service of Ferdinand Karl, Archduke of the Netherlands, accompanying him on a tour of northern Italy. By the mid 1650s, when Young played for the recently abdicated Christina of Sweden at Innsbruck, he was reckoned to be one of the best viol players in Europe. He died in Innsbruck not long after returning from a visit to England.

Young wrote some works for the viol played 'lyra-way' (see *Viol*, 4) and he apparently developed an eight-string viol to be played in this fashion while he was in Innsbruck. A few of his compositions were published, and his 11 *Sonate à 3, 4 e 5 con alcune allemand, correnti e balletti à 3* (Innsbruck, 1653) were the first English pieces to be called 'sonata'.

WENDY THOMPSON

Young Person's Guide to the Orchestra, The. Orchestral work (with speaker), Op. 34, by Britten. It was written for a documentary film, *The Instruments of the Orchestra* (1946); a narrator (using a text by Eric Crozier) describes the uses and characteristics of the instruments and sections of the orchestra which are then illustrated by Britten's variations on a theme from Purcell's incidental music to the play *Abdelazer* (1695). The first performance of the orchestral version was in Liverpool in 1946. The work is sometimes known (against the composer's wishes) by its subtitle 'Variations and Fugue on a Theme of Purcell'.

Ysaÿe, Eugène (*b* Liège, 16 July 1858; *d* Brussels, 12 May 1931). Belgian violinist and composer. He studied the violin first with his father, then at the Liège Conservatory, and finally with Wieniawski briefly in Paris (1873) and with Vieuxtemps in Brussels (1876-9). One of the outstanding virtuosos of his day, he toured widely as a soloist, quartet leader, and conductor. He made a particular feature of new works, including Franck's sonata and Debussy's quartet, and himself composed six violin concertos, an opera, and numerous smaller pieces for the violin.   PAUL GRIFFITHS

Yugoslavia. Various regions of southern Central Europe and the western Balkan Peninsula, united as the state of Yugoslavia in 1918, were previously subjected to a variety of cultural influences. In the Middle Ages this part of Europe was the meeting ground of Western and Eastern Christianity: Western influence extended to Slovenia, Croatia, the Dalmatian coast, and parts of Bosnia, whereas Serbia, Montenegro, and Macedonia experienced a strong Byzantine influence. The Turkish thrust into the Balkans which occurred in the 15th century, and the presence of Turkish administration in Bosnia, Serbia, and Macedonia throughout several centuries, meant that in these areas cultural development was halted: art music and musical institutions started to develop only in the 19th century. Elsewhere the development has been uninterrupted since the Middle Ages. Frequent wars and clashes of administrative and cultural interests in which Hungary, Austria, Venice, and Turkey all sought to establish their supremacy in this part of the world, meant that the area lacked long-established aristocratic courts or strong political and administrative centres which could act as sources of patronage. Periods of lively activity, reflecting the presence of patrons and creative personalities, were interspersed with periods of stagnation.

1. *The Middle Ages to the 17th Century.* In the Middle Ages monasteries and churches in Dubrovnik, Split, Trogir, Osor, and Zadar were the main centres of musical activity, and the first records of organs date from the 13th century. Inland Croatia and the city of Zagreb reflected some Hungarian influence, inevitable after the union of the two kingdoms in 1102, although a separate 'Zagreb rite' evolved in the 14th century. German influence, including the presence of *Minnesinger*, was evident in Slovenia.

There are few records of music in Medieval Serbia and Macedonia before the Turkish invasions. Musical instruments depicted on the frescoes of the period offer indirect evidence of musical activity, and the sources of liturgical music, dating mainly from the late Middle Ages, show some individual trends within the frame of the Orthodox liturgy. Dalmatia and inland Croatia found themselves in the 15th century in close proximity to the advancing Turks and cultural life went through a period of stagnation.

The ideas of Italian humanism were evident in Dalmatia in the 16th century, resulting in a rich flowering of the native Slavonic literature, architecture, and painting. Dubrovnik began to develop as a musical centre and towards the end of the century attracted several musicians from the Courtoys family. Giulio Schiavetto, composer of some fine five- and six-part motets, was active in the service of the Bishop of Šibenik. Various literary sources contain ample evidence of the practice of secular music; even so, gifted composers sought recognition in larger European centres: Franciscus Bossinensis was active in Venice, Vincenz Jelić in Alsace, and the Slovene Jacob Handl (Gallus) in Vienna, Prague, and Olomouc. The cathedral churches of Split and Hvar gained importance as musical centres towards the end of the 16th century and early in the 17th century fostered an active local school of composers (Lukačić, ?1587–1648; Cecchino, c.1580–1644; Romano, c.1552–1636) whose music reflected all the significant characteristics of the early Baroque monody and the Venetian style of the time. The new genre of opera did not pass unnoticed and P. Primović's translation of Rinuccini's *Euridice* (dating from 1617) is probably the earliest translation into any language of an Italian operatic libretto.

2. *The 18th and 19th Centuries*. The Jesuit Gymnasiums in Ljubljana and Zagreb were the main centres of activity in inland areas throughout the 17th century. After 1660 visiting operatic companies performed intermittently in Ljubljana, their performances becoming more regular after 1740. The absence of significant aristocratic patrons encouraged the urbanized nobility and richer commoners to form musical societies which often extended their activities into the fields of education and publishing. Academia Philharmonicorum was formed in Ljubljana in 1701 and its activity was continued in 1794 by the Philharmonische Gesellschaft. A similar model was followed in Zagreb in the 19th century: the Musikverein, founded in 1827, later gave up its German title and is active to this day as the 'Croatian Musical Institute' (Hrvatski Glazbeni Zavod).

With the fall of the Republics of Venice and Dubrovnik, Dalmatia became a neglected peripheral part of the Austro-Hungarian monarchy and all the artistic activity of Croatia was centred on Zagreb. The 'Illyrian Movement' for national emancipation was cultural in character with the aim of resisting German and Hungarian dominance. It encouraged the formation of choral societies and the production of suitable vocal music, using the elements of the rich popular tradition. The first Croatian national opera, Vatroslav Lisinski's *Ljubav i zloba* ('Love and Malice') was produced in 1846, but in general the operatic life was dominated by the visiting Italian companies until 1870, when the opera of the Croatian National Theatre was formed. This coincided with the arrival in Zagreb of Ivan Zajc (1832–1914), a native of Rijeka, who had established a solid reputation in Vienna as a composer of operettas. Under Zajc's directorship the repertory of the Opera showed a remarkable awareness of the new developments in operatic production abroad and included nearly all the major works soon after their premières in the big European opera houses. The singing class at the Music School of the Croatian Musical Institute (later the Academy of Music) and the Opera produced a number of excellent singers, some of whom (Milka Ternina, later Zinka Milanov and Sena Jurinac) achieved world fame.

The proximity of Slovenia to the major musical centres of Central Europe gave a particular flavour to Slovene nationalism. It too relied on vocal music to advance the national cause but the composers were more acutely aware of the need for solid workmanship and followed more closely the developments in German and Czech music. The presence of strong German cultural communities in major Slovenian towns divided the performing forces and the attention of audiences. At one time the German Philharmonische Gesellschaft and the Slovene Glasbena Matica maintained separate orchestras in Ljubljana and a similar division was evident in the opera. (Mahler was engaged as a conductor in the German theatre during the 1881–2 season.)

Musical life in Serbia started to develop only in the second half of the 19th century, after the newly-won independence from Turkey. There too the accent was on vocal, particularly choral, music, and the choral societies which came into existence at the time nearly always had the task of also providing liturgical music in churches. The Belgrade Choral Society (Beogradsko Pevačko Društvo) was formed in 1853 and maintained a high standard of choral singing until it was disbanded at the beginning of the German occupation in the Second World War. One of its conductors, Stevan Mokranjac (1856–1914), created in his choral compositions the foundation for a national Serbian style and his influence was still evident in Serbian music in the 1920s. Opera had a slow start as the audiences seemed to prefer a form of Serbian *Singspiel* of which Davorin Jenko (1835-1914), a Slovene by birth, was a notable exponent. The first Serbian opera was Stanislav Binički's *Na uranku* ('At Dawn', 1903). The permanent opera company was established in 1920 and soon acquired a reputation particularly for the performances of the Russian 19th-century repertory.

It was mostly the Austrian regimental bands that after 1878 brought organized musical activity to the former Turkish province of Bosnia and Herzegovina. The first opera was performed in Sarajevo in 1882, the first local choral society was formed in 1879, and the Austrian-inspired Männergesangverein in 1886.

3. *The 20th Century*. After the formation of the independent state at the end of the First World War the demand for choral music became less urgent with the corresponding flourishing of symphonic and chamber music. In the pre-1918 period, following the Viennese pattern, symphonic music was performed mainly by the operatic orchestras, but now the new independent orchestral bodies were established: the Zagreb Philharmonic in 1920 and the Belgrade and Sarajevo Philharmonic Orchestras in 1923. The impact of the European avant-garde was felt during the 1920s and 1930s most strongly among the Slovene musicians (Marij Kogoj and Slavko Osterc), partly because the Slovene Romanticism had been broader in outlook than the similar movements in Croatia or Serbia and imposed fewer limitations on the members of the younger generation. Among the Croatians Josip Slavenski (1896-1955) came closest to the style and outlook of Bartók, and combined a feeling for the Yugoslav folk tradition with an awareness of the avant-garde spirit of the time. In Serbia time was needed to shake off the mannerisms of the school of Mokranjac and Binički. In the 1930s the ideas of Alois Hába and the Prague school gained a short-lived prominence among Belgrade composers.

After the Second World War music received support from the state on a hitherto unprecedented level resulting in the foundation of new opera houses, orchestras, and schools. However, the period of state intervention in the matters of artistic policy was short and with none of the stifling of creative freedom character-istic of some east European countries. The fact that the ideas of the post-war avant-garde were accepted on a wider scale only in the late 1950s had more to do with the general historical condition than with any political intervention. The Zagreb Biennale of Contemporary Music, founded in 1961, has been acting as an important focus for younger composers, but has also inspired some members of the older generation to re-examine thoroughly their stylistic orientation and has helped them to free themselves from the less relevant aspects of folkloristic eclecticism and neo-classicism. Music being written now by Yugoslav composers reflects all the major tendencies in European music of the last 30 years. Zagreb and Ljubljana, with their rich musical past, continue to be the musical centres of the country and the attractions of Belgrade as the capital have helped it to overcome the lack of a longer established tradition. The coastal cities of Dubrovnik, Split, and Zadar count on their heritage to maintain summer music festivals that are more than a convenient tourist attraction. Yugoslav Radio-Television has emerged as a significant patron, maintaining some of the country's best orchestras. There are now ten permanent opera companies (in Belgrade, Ljubljana, Maribor, Novi Sad, Osijek, Rijeka, Sarajevo, Split, and Zagreb) and eight conservatories.

The rich folk tradition of the country is on the one hand kept alive by a number of excellent folk dance and music groups, and on the other hand exploited commercially. A phenomenon characteristic of the areas where the tradition of art music is more recent is the so-called 'new folk music', a mixture of Slavonic, Greek, and Oriental elements which seldom, if ever, raises itself above the level of kitsch. Pop music has enjoyed immense popularity with the younger generation. Indeed, the dividing line between classical and pop music in the taste of younger people is much more clearly marked than in the West: music education in secondary schools is still poorly organized, so that 'serious' music is sometimes suspected of élitism. This, however, may be nothing but a passing phase.

Like Portugal, Sweden, or Bulgaria, Yugoslavia has not produced any composers of international stature. It may be that its music, like some of its wines, does not travel well, but the works of Yugoslav composers, as well as the concert life of the country's major cities, offer plenty of rewards.   BOJAN BUJIĆ

Z

Zacconi, Lodovico (*b* Pesaro, 11 June 1555; *d* Firenzuola di Focara, nr Pesaro, 23 Mar. 1627). Italian theorist. In 1575 he was ordained priest at Pesaro. While pursuing literary studies in the convent of S. Stefano, Venice, he studied with Andrea Gabrieli. In 1585 he became a singer in the chapel of the Austrian Archduke Karl in Graz. From 1590 he served the Bavarian ducal chapel in Munich, under Lassus, and in 1596 returned to Pesaro as a prior in his old order.

Zacconi's most important theoretical work was the *Prattica di musica*, published in two parts (Venice, 1592, 1622). Though the work is marred by errors and deficiencies it does cover a wide range of topics. Part i deals with notation, embellishments, mood, time and prolation, proportions, and modes, and part ii with improvised counterpoint.　　WENDY THOMPSON

Zachow, Friedrich Wilhelm (*bapt.* Leipzig, 14 Nov. 1663; *d* Halle, 7 Aug. 1712). German organist and composer. He learnt to play the organ at Leipzig, and from 1684 until his death was organist and musical director at the Marienkirche in Halle. There he taught Handel. About 32 of his church cantatas have survived. He excelled in chorale variations and in the so-called 'reform cantata', of which *Das ist das ewige Leben* is a fine example, anticipating the structure and content of many Bach cantatas.

　　WENDY THOMPSON

Zadok the Priest. Anthem by Handel, the first of four composed for the coronation of George II in 1727. It has been performed at every English coronation since.

Zádor, Jenő (Eugene) (*b* Bátaszék, 5 Nov. 1894; *d* Hollywood, 4 Apr. 1977). American composer, born in Hungary. He studied at the Vienna Conservatory and at Leipzig with Reger, and in 1921 became a teacher at the New Vienna Conservatory, and then at the Budapest Academy of Music. On the outbreak of the Second World War he emigrated to the USA, where he became a successful composer of film scores for Hollywood. He also wrote orchestral pieces, including concertos for unusual instruments such as accordion (1971) and cimbalom (1969).　　WENDY THOMPSON

Zahlzeit (Ger.). 'Beat' (in the sense of 'three beats to the bar' etc.); see *Beat*, 1.

Zaide. Unfinished opera in two acts by Mozart to a libretto by Schachtner after F. J. Sebastiani's *Das Serail*. The work lacks an overture and a final chorus but was performed in Salzburg in 1779–80. Mozart did not give the work its title.

Zamba (Sp.). An Argentine dance of Peruvian origin; it is in 6/8 time, and is based on a repeated four-bar theme with guitar introduction.

Zampa, ou La fiancée de marbre ('Zampa, or The Marble Bride'). Opera in three acts by Hérold to a libretto by Mélesville. It was first performed in Paris in 1831.

Zampogna (It.). See *Bagpipe*, 4.

Zandonai, Riccardo (*b* Sacco, Trento, 28 May 1883; *d* Pesaro, 12 June 1944). Italian composer. He studied with Mascagni at the Pesaro Liceo Musicale, of which he was director for the last five years of his life. Regarded as a possible successor to Puccini, he combined a gift for lyrical melody with a love of colourful pageantry; *Francesca da Rimini* (1914) was the most successful of his operas. His other works include several orchestral pieces, choral music, and songs.　　PAUL GRIFFITHS

Zapateado (Sp.). A Spanish solo clog dance in triple time, with a strongly accented rhythm marked by stamping the heels. It makes much use of syncopation.

Zapfenstreich (Ger.). A military 'tattoo', or more elaborate military musical performance.

Zarlino, Gioseffo (*b* Chioggia, nr Venice, ?31 Jan. 1517; *d* Venice, 4 Feb. 1590). The leading Italian theorist of the 16th century. He entered the Franciscan Order, and after completing his novitiate he moved to Venice, where he turned to his real love, music, studying with Willaert. He became *maestro di cappella* at St Mark's in 1565 and remained in that post until his death (in spite of his election as Bishop of Chioggia in 1583, succumbing to the pleas of Doge and Senate to stay). Not a very interesting composer, he became famous for a series of large treatises, in which he tried to elucidate Greek music theories, as well as teach practical matters such as counterpoint. Among his most influential ideas were the concept of word-painting as used in later madrigals; the different emotional qualities of major and minor chords; and the suggestion of dividing the scale into equal intervals, as later developed into equal temperament (see *Temperament*, 4).

DENIS ARNOLD

Zart (Ger.). 'Tender'; *Zartheit*, 'tenderness'; *zärtlich*, 'tenderly'.

Zar und Zimmermann ('Tsar and Carpenter'). Comic opera in three acts by Lortzing to his own libretto after a play (1818) by A. H. J. Mélesville, J. T. Merle, and E. Cantiran de Boirie. It was first performed in Leipzig in 1837. Lortzing gave the opera the alternative title *Die zwei Peter*; it was first performed in London in 1871 as *Peter the Shipwright*.

Zarzuela (Sp.). An idiomatic Spanish form of opera, with spoken dialogue. The name derives from the Palace of Zarzuela, near Madrid, where festive entertainmen.s known as *Fiestas de zarzuela* were given in the 17th century. The earliest known composer was Juan Hidalgo (*c*.1612–85), who wrote the music for *zarzuelas* by the important Spanish dramatist Pedro Calderón de la Barca. At this stage the *zarzuela*

was similar in character and form to the French *ballet de cour*. In the 18th century the popularity of the genre was challenged on the one hand by Italian opera, and on the other by the lighter and slighter *tonadilla*, and, despite a brief revival, the *zarzuela* languished until the first half of the 19th century, when a desire to create a Spanish national opera led to the composition of *zarzuelas* by such composers as Francisco Barbieri (1823–94), Tomás Bretón (1850–1923), and Amadeo Vives (1871–1932). Some were in three acts, with serious subjects, and the form, always flexible, has been expanded to embrace features from operetta and jazz.

See also *Opera*, 13.

Zauberflöte, Die ('The Magic Flute'). Opera in two acts by Mozart; text by Emanuel Schikaneder, after the story 'Lulu' in Wieland's collection of Oriental fairy-tales *Dschinnistan* (1786). Produced: Vienna, Theater auf der Wieden, 30 September 1791; London, Haymarket, 6 June 1811; New York, Palmo's Opera House, 17 April 1833. Tamino (ten.) is saved from a serpent by three attendants of the Queen of Night, but having fainted believes his rescuer to be the bird-catcher Papageno (bar.). For not admitting the truth, Papageno is punished by the attendants, who produce a picture of Pamina with which Tamino falls in love. Her mother, the Queen of Night (sop.), arrives to tell Tamino

Karl Friedrich Schinkel's design for the Fire and Water Scene in Mozart's 'Die Zauberflöte' (*Berlin Schauspielhaus, 1816*).

of Pamina's capture by Sarastro. For their rescue mission, Tamino is provided with a magic flute, Papageno with magic bells (played on the glockenspiel). Pamina (sop.) is guarded in Sarastro's palace by the evil Moor, Monostatos (ten.), who flees, mistaking Papageno for the Devil. Tamino learns that Sarastro is a wise priest, and that it is the Queen who is evil. Papageno and Pamina are caught trying to escape by Monostatos and his slaves, but the magic bells set the capturers dancing helplessly. Tamino and Pamina meet and fall in love; they are made ready for initiation ordeals.

Sarastro (bass) obtains the consent of the priests for Tamino to undergo initiation to their brotherhood. In the vaults, Tamino and Papageno are under a vow of silence which the latter finds intolerable. Tamino refuses to flee when urged by the Queen's attendants. Monostatos tries to kiss Pamina, who is told by the Queen to kill Sarastro; she asks mercy for her mother and is told by Sarastro that in a holy place there is no hatred. Papageno is provided with a feast, and Tamino resists the temptation to speak to a hurt and bewildered Pamina, who thereupon longs for death. Sarastro reassures the lovers. Papageno wishes for a wife, and an old woman (sop.) who had previously brought him water presents herself. As Papageno reluctantly accepts, she turns into a beautiful girl, Papagena, but disappears immediately. Pamina's suicide is forestalled by three boys. The lovers pass together through fire and water, protected by the flute. The dejected Papageno tries to hang himself but on the boys' advice he uses the magic bells to bring Papagena back. The Queen, her attendants, and Monostatos make a last attempt to destroy Sarastro and rescue Pamina, but flee before the noise of thunder. Tamino and Pamina are united, and all join in praise of Isis and Osiris.

FURTHER READING
Nicholas John, ed.: *The Magic Flute*, English National Opera Guides (London, 1980).

Zehn (Ger.) 'Ten'.

Zeichen (Ger.). 'Sign'.

Zeitmass (Ger.). 'Tempo'.

Zeitmesser (Ger.). 'Metronome'.

Zelenka, Jan Dismas (*b* Lounovice, Bohemia, 16 Oct. 1679; *d* Dresden, 22 Dec. 1745). Czech composer. He began his career as a double bass player at Prague and in 1710 joined the Dresden royal chapel. After studying with Lotti and Fux in Italy he became vice-*Kapellmeister* at Dresden in 1721. His output includes about 20 Masses and Mass fragments, responsories,

two *Magnificat* settings, psalms, and three oratorios. His highly original instrumental music includes six chamber sonatas, five orchestral capriccios, and a chamber concerto. He also wrote an opera in Latin. Zelenka has only fairly recently been recognized as a composer of considerable stature.   WENDY THOMPSON

Zeller, Carl (Johann Adam) (*b* St Peter in der Au, 19 June 1842; *d* Baden, nr Vienna, 17 Aug. 1898). Austrian composer. After being a member of what is now known as the Vienna Boys' Choir, he studied law and became a senior official in the Austrian Ministry of Education. He was taught music by Bruckner's teacher, Sechter, and was an excellent pianist. His light opera *Der Vogelhändler* (1891), one of his half dozen operettas in the tradition of Suppé and Offenbach, is a tuneful work still given in Germany.   DENIS ARNOLD

Zelo, zeloso, zelosamente (It.). 'Zeal', 'zealous', 'zealously'.

Zelter, Carl Friedrich (*b* Berlin, 11 Dec. 1758; *d* Berlin, 15 May 1832). German composer and musical educationalist. The son of a stonemason, he himself served an apprenticeship in the craft, eventually becoming a master mason and having a successful business as a builder. However, he was also a good violinist, and led the orchestra at the first Berlin performance of Handel's *Messiah* (1786). He spent the later part of his life much occupied with music, directing the Berlin Singakademie from 1800 (the Singakademie was at the time much involved with the revival of Bach's music), and acting as an inspector for schools in Prussia. In 1809 he established the Liedertafel, the first of a series of societies encouraging performance of choral music for male voices. He was a friend of Goethe, whose verses he set in some pleasant and sensitive folk-like songs. Among his many pupils were Mendelssohn, Meyerbeer, and Loewe. He was appointed Professor of Music at the newly-founded University of Berlin in 1809.   DENIS ARNOLD

Zémire et Azore. Comic opera in four acts by Grétry to a libretto by Marmontel after M. Le Prince de Beaumont's *La belle et la bête*. It was first performed at Fontainebleau in 1771. Tozzi, Spohr, and Garcia have also written operas on this subject (Beauty and the Beast).

Zemlinsky, Alexander (von) (*b* Vienna, 14 Oct. 1872; *d* Larchmont, New York, 15 Mar. 1942). Austrian composer. He studied composition with J. N. Fuchs at the Vienna Conservatory (1884–90) and began to make a career as a conductor. During the 1890s he gave some instruction to Schoenberg, who married his sister and wrote the libretto for his opera *Sarema* (1897). He admired Schoenberg's later development but felt himself unable to follow, pursuing instead a post-Mahlerian style often marked by wistful melancholy. His small output includes five later operas, three string quartets, a set of Six Maeterlinck Songs with orchestra (1910–13), and the *Lyric Symphony* to poems by Tagore (1923), quoted in Berg's *Lyric Suite*. He was also music director of the Prague Opera (1911–27) and of the Kroll Opera in Berlin (1927–32).   PAUL GRIFFITHS

Zheng. A Chinese zither. See *Chinese Music, 4e*.

Ziehen (Ger.). 'To draw out'.

Ziemlich (Ger.). 'Rather'; e.g. *ziemlich schnell*, 'rather fast'.

Zigeuner (Ger.). 'Gipsy'; *Zigeunerlied*, 'gipsy song'.

Zigeunerbaron, Der ('The Gypsy Baron'). Operetta in three acts by Johann Strauss II to a libretto by Ignaz Schnitzer after M. Jókai's libretto on his story *Saffi*. It was first performed in Vienna in 1885.

Zilcher, Hermann (*b* Frankfurt, 18 Aug. 1881; *d* Würzburg, 1 Jan. 1948). German composer, pianist, and conductor. He studied at the Frankfurt Hoch Conservatory, and then began a career as a concert pianist. A teacher at the Munich Academy of Music 1908–20, he was principal of the Würzburg Conservatory 1920–44. His own works, in the German Romantic tradition, include operas, symphonies, violin concertos, and piano concertos.
                    WENDY THOMPSON

Zimmermann, Bernd Alois (*b* Bliesheim, nr Cologne, 20 Mar. 1918; *d* Königsdort, nr Cologne, 10 Aug. 1970). German composer. He studied philology at the universities of Bonn, Cologne, and Berlin, and was a composition pupil during the 1940s and early '50s of Heinrich Lemacher, Philipp Jarnach, Wolfgang Fortner, and Rene Leibowitz. His first important works, including the Symphony in One Movement (1947) and *Canto di speranza* for cello and chamber orchestra (1953, rev. 1957), strike a balance between Schoenberg and Stravinsky; the music is urgently expressive and serially composed but also lithe in movement, having a balletic quality characteristic of Zimmermann's instrumental scores.

After completing his post-*Wozzeck* opera *Die*

Soldaten (1958–60, rev. 1963–4) Zimmermann began to evolve a style in which musical quotations are introduced, often to disturbing effect. Works of this kind include the piano trio *Présence* (1961), the orchestral prelude *Photoptosis* (1968), and the *Requiem für einen jungen Dichter* (1967–9), where a literary collage is set to music for solo voices, choruses, orchestra, jazz group, and tape. Zimmermann committed suicide shortly after completing his 'ecclesiastical action' *Ich wandte mich und sah an alles Unrecht, das geschah unter der Sonne* for voices and orchestra.   PAUL GRIFFITHS

Zingarelli, Niccolò Antonio (*b* Naples, 4 Apr. 1752; *d* Torre del Greco, nr Naples, 5 May 1837). Italian composer. He studied at the Conservatorio di S. Maria de Loreto and began his career as an organist and violin teacher before turning to the stage in 1781. In 1794 he was appointed *maestro di cappella* at Santa Casa di Loreto. While there he turned out a series of nearly 550 sacred pieces for the Church Year, called *Annuale di Loreto*. He became *maestro* at St Peter's, Rome, in 1804, but in 1813 he returned to Naples as head of the newly-founded Conservatory. His pupils there included Mercadante and Bellini. He succeeded Paisiello as director of Naples Cathedral in 1816, but continued his teaching duties.

Zingarelli was conservative in his attitudes towards teaching and composition. His 40 or so operas reveal his old-fashioned approach: most are *opere serie*, and many include castrato roles, by then virtually obsolete. He also obeyed the 18th-century convention of the happy ending, even in his best-known opera, *Giulietta e Romeo*. He also wrote many sacred works, cantatas, songs, and symphonies (nearly all in one movement).   WENDY THOMPSON

Zither. A stringed instrument native to Austria and Bavaria, developed during the 19th century from earlier and simpler forms (see below, 2), many of them also played today, the Appalachian dulcimer of America being one (see *Dulcimer, 3*).

1. *Construction*. The zither has a shallow soundbox around 2′ long, typically of pine veneered with rosewood. It bulges on the far side, and has spiked ball-feet to keep it still while placed on a table for playing. Along the near side runs a series of some 29 metal frets. There may be in all 34 strings, the highest-tuned of steel, the others overwound on metal or silk. They run from hitch-pins on the right to tuning pins or machines (geared pins) on the left.

Five strings pass over the frets. These are melody strings, stopped with the left thumb and first three fingers, and plucked by a metal pick

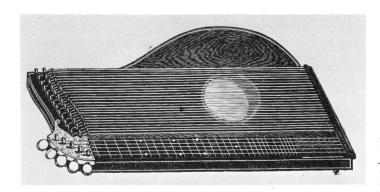

Pl. 1. Austrian zither from a German catalogue (c.1900); the five melody strings in front (over the frets), the chord and bass strings beyond.

or 'zither ring' (see *Plectrum*, 1) worn on the right thumb. Strings one, two, four, and five are tuned to the same notes as the viola, namely *a'*, *d'*, *g*, *c*. String three is tuned to *g'* and is mostly reserved for playing in thirds with notes on the *d'* string, stopping with the first two fingers.

The remaining strings form two groups. First, 13 chord strings, plucked by the first and second fingers of the right hand. Their tuning follows the cycle of fourths: *ab'*, *eb'*, *bb'* . . . *c♯'*, *g♯'*, all within this one octave, and providing for every tonality a three-note major or minor chord in which two adjacent strings are plucked by one finger while the other strikes the third note. Beyond are the bass strings, also tuned cyclically *Eb*, *Bb*, *F* . . . *C♯*, *G♯* (much as in a piano *accordion) bringing together the tonic, dominant, and subdominant in each key. Further bass strings may be added chromatically below. Through both these two sets of accompaniment strings, those for *F*, *A*, and *C♯* may be coloured red (thus every fourth string being a red one). The zither is played in its homelands in music of local character, often with a distinctive *vibrato* on the longer melody notes. It is also extensively exported for domestic music-making. Little used in the orchestra, being not as loud as the harp or piano, it nevertheless appears solo in the introduction to Johann Strauss's *Tales from the Vienna Woods* (1868), cued in small notes in the string parts for the sad occasions when no zither is available (Ex. 1).

2. *Older Zithers*. These are played, or were played up to the end of the 19th century, in many European regions, from the Alps and the Carpathians northwards to Scandinavia: mainly farmhouse instruments for dancing and accompanying old songs. Today they may be heard particularly in Hungary (*citera*), Norway (*langeleik*), Belgium (*vlier*, also other names), and Alsace (*buche*, or *épinette des Vosges*, the smallest zither); the old Alpine *Scheitholt* is now rare, replaced by the more advanced zither described above.

The basic provision is a long narrow soundbox (Pl. 3) placed across the knees or on a table with the frets nearest the player. These are usually diatonic, and over them run two or more wire melody strings tuned in unison and characteristically stopped by pressing to the frets with a short metal or wooden rod held in the left hand (compare *Dulcimer*, 3), but in some cases with the fingers. The other hand sweeps a plectrum (of bone, horn, etc.) back and forth across these strings and, in the same movement, the accompaniment strings which lie beyond and are tuned to sound a 'dronc' on the keynote in different octaves and its dominant (compare *Bagpipe*). The effect can be strong and rhythmic (the instrument seems always to be played alone), with plectrum strokes fitted to the rhythm of a dance: e.g. in Norway, if the tune is in 3/4 time, two beats struck outwards and the third backwards (but if a waltz, once outwards, twice backwards), while quavers in the melody are made by short strokes in between.

Some of these instruments have been traced in pictures back to the 15th century. The Medieval *monochord of monastic music

Ex. 1

J. Strauss 'Tales from Vienna Woods'

Pl. 2. The old Austrian 'Kratz-zither' played in a Tyrolean farmhouse, painting (1876) by F. Defregger; note the left hand pressing the melody strings and the right plucking these and the bass strings together.

Pl. 3. Épinette des Vosges.

teachers has been suggested as their source, though on morphological grounds only.

For 'Zither' in the present ethnomusicological sense, covering a far wider range of instruments, see *Idiochord; Instruments, Classification of*. There have also been made, by late-19th-century German zither-makers, versions for playing with a bow. Another of their products is the well-known *autoharp.

ANTHONY BAINES

Zitternd (Ger.). 'Trembling', i.e. *tremolando*.

Zoppa, alla (It.). 'Lame', 'limping'. 1. A term used in the 17th century to describe dance movements in syncopated rhythm. 2. A term used more specifically to describe a rhythm where the second quaver of a 2/4 bar is accentuated, e.g.

Zortzico [zortziko] (Sp.). A Basque folk-dance in quick 5/8 time, featuring dotted rhythms on the weak beats of each bar.

Zuerst (Ger.). 'First', 'at first'.

Zug (Ger.). 1. 'Slide'; e.g. *Zugtrompete*, 'slide trumpet'. 2. A stop, usually an organ stop.

Zugeeignet (Ger.). 'Dedicated'; *Zueignung*, 'a dedication'.

Zumsteeg, Johann Rudolph (*b* Sachsenflur, nr Stuttgart, 10 Jan. 1760; *d* Stuttgart, 27 Jan. 1802). German composer. He was the son of a soldier and was taught at the military academy in Stuttgart, where he showed his talent for music at an early age. The first of a long series of successful *Singspiele* by him, *Das tartarische*

Gesetz, was produced in 1780. He held various posts at the Württemberg court in Stuttgart. Although he is mainly thought of as an opera composer, Zumsteeg's best work lay in his songs, and especially in the vivid realism of his ballads, which point the way forward to Loewe and Schubert; the latter told a friend that he could 'revel in these songs for days on end'.

Zunge (Ger.). 'Tongue' or 'reed'.

Zurückgehend (Ger.). 'Returning' (to the original tempo after a change); *Zurückhaltend*, 'Holding back', i.e. *rallentando*.

Zusammenschlag (Ger.). 'Together-stroke', i.e. the *acciaccatura.

Zwei, zwo (Ger.). 'Two'; *zweimal*, 'twice'; *zweit*, *zwot*, 'second'; *zweihändig*, 'for two hands'; *zweistimmig*, 'for two voices'; *zweistimmiger Gesang*, 'vocal duet'.

Zweiunddreissigstel-note (Ger.). '32nd-note' or demisemiquaver (♪).

Zwingli, Ulrich (*b* Wildhaus, Toggenburg, 1 Jan. 1484; *d* Cappel, 11 Oct. 1531). Swiss theologian. After meeting Erasmus and other religious humanists he became one of the most influential figures in the Reformed Church. He is important for the history of music because he did much to promote the abolition of music in church services, although like the later English Puritans he enjoyed private music-making and was himself a composer in a modest way. He died on the battlefield at Cappel, fighting for the Protestant cause. DENIS ARNOLD

Zwischenspiel (Ger.). 'Interlude', or 'entr'acte' (between the acts of an opera etc.). The term is particularly used to describe the instrumental interludes between the stanzas of a vocal piece or the solo portions between the *tutti* sections of a concerto. It is also used to denote the episodes in fugue or rondo form, and the organ interludes between the stanzas of a congregational hymn.

Zyklisch (Ger.). 'Cyclic'. See *Cyclic form*.

Zyklus ('Cycle'). Work by Stockhausen for percussionist, composed in 1959. The work may be begun on any page of the spiral-bound score, in which graphic signs represent instruments and dynamics.

ACKNOWLEDGEMENTS

Thanks are due to the following for permission to reproduce photographs and musical examples on the pages indicated. Every effort has been made to contact copyright holders; we apologize to anyone who may have been omitted.

ACL, Brussels: 831; photo Marianne Adelmann Olsen, Zurich: 1113, 1246; Tiberiu Alexandru: 1388 (Pl.2); Alinari, Florence: 173, 402 (Pl.2), 1388 (Pl.1), 1850 (Pl.1), 1930; Allen Organ Studios (London) Ltd: 620; American Folklore Society, Washington: 57; Archiv für Kunst und Geschichte, Berlin: 277, 278, 1277, 1308 *bottom*, 1551, 1637, 1644, 1756, 1969, 1970; Archivio di Stato Bologna: 958; Ashmolean Museum, Oxford: 401 (Pl.1), 403 (Pl.3), 1932 (Pl.5 *below*); Associated Music Publishers Inc., New York: 510 *right*, 1437 *bottom*; Lizzie Auerbach, London (photo Erich Auerbach): 217, 528; Australian Information Service, London: 558.

Photo Mick Baines, London: 1226; J. R. Granville Bantock: 170 *top*; U. Bär Verlag, Zurich: 972 (photo Fred Mayer; from F. Mayer/T. Immoos, *Japanisches Theater*, 1974); Clive Barda, London: 246, 333 (Pl.4), 485, 540, 668, 1068, 1402, 1482, 1804, 1825; Barnes & Mullins Ltd, London: 122 (Pl.1), 168 (Pl.1), 248 *left*, 1124; Bartók Archives, Budapest: 178 *bottom*; Bartók Estate, New York: 179; Bate Collection, Oxford: 408 (Pl.2 *right*), 411, 1616, 1672; Bayerisches Nationalmuseum, Munich: 753; Bayerische Staatsbibliothek, Munich: 941, 1236, 1714; Bayreuther Festspiele: 1156, 1335, 1572; BBC Copyright, London: 269, 271, 272; BBC Hulton Picture Library: 226 *right*, 283 *top*, 1479, 1522, 1696, 1698, 1902; Belmont Music, New York: 650; Belwin Mills Music Ltd, Croydon: 1267 (Ex.13); Benesh Institute of Choreology, London: 536; Bernice P. Bishop Museum, Honolulu: 1379, 1381; Bettmann Archive, New York: 169 *top*, 1808; Deben Bhattacharya, Paris: 909 *top*, 1506 (Pl.3); Biblioteca Apostolica Vaticana: 1413 *top*, 1937 *bottom*; Biblioteca Medicea-Laurenziana, Florence: 953, 1041, 1250 (Ex.2*a*); Biblioteca Nazionale, Florence: 1413 *bottom*; Biblioteca Nazionale, Turin: 1326; Biblioteca Nazionale Marciana, Venice: 674 (Pl.1), 1628; Biblioteka Narodowa, Warsaw: 378; Bibliothèque Interuniversitaire, Section Médecine, Montpellier: 1254 (Ex.3*a*); Bibliothèque Municipale d'Arras: 1858; Bibliothèque Nationale, Paris: 24, 40, 41, 45, 46, 129, 194, 214, 221, 223, 224, 238 *top*, 357, 358, 387, 393, 473 (Pl.6), 544, 564, 584, 589, 658, 711 (Pl.1), 714, 715, 716, 717, 718, 723, 727, 771, 776, 777, 782, 1072, 1091 *bottom*, 1111, 1195, 1206, 1213, 1255 (Ex.4*a*), 1256, 1285, 1287, 1295, 1311, 1313, 1315, 1321, 1370, 1440, 1454, 1458 *bottom*, 1493, 1524, 1530, 1584, 1586, 1589, 1609 *top*, 1630, 1642, 1740, 1757, 1854 (Pl.5), 1863; Bibliothèque Royale, Brussels: 531 (Pl.1), 712; Bildarchiv Preussischer Kulturbesitz, Berlin: 391, 691; Lady Bliss: 226 *left*; Bodleian Library, Oxford: 361, 456 (photo Thomson-Photos, Oxford), 1470 (Harding Collection, Box 542), 1805 (Bodl. MSS Mus.Sch.e.377, f.4*r*), 1824 (MS Bodley 264, f.172), 1882 (Harding Collection, Box 457), 1884 (Harding Collection, Box 406); Bolshoy Theatre Museum, Moscow: 648, 1571; Boosey & Hawkes Ltd, London: 179, 255, 266, 496 (Pl.1), 502 (Ex.3), 649, 769, 820 (Ex.11), 950 (photo Allan Chappelow), 1521, 1867, 1870 (Pl.3), 1997 (photo G. Rancy); photo Max Yves Brandîly, Paris: 832; Braunschweiges Landesmuseum für Geschichte und Volkstum: 1920 (Pl.2); John F. Brennan, Oxford: 1350, 1354, 1355, 1356; Brera Gallery, Milan: 1070; British Library, London: 21, 131, 228, 266, 289, 299, 341, 344, 351, 355, 470, 471, 573, 625, 629, 630, 632, 633, 675 (Pl.3), 689 (Pl.2), 805, 830 (Pl.4), 847, 852, 883, 888 (Pl.1), 889, 967, 997 (Pl.4), 1005, 1044, 1078, 1116, 1128, 1146, 1147, 1202, 1261 (Ex.8*a*), 1412, 1483, 1490, 1494, 1506 (Pl.1), 1511, 1521, 1525, 1587, 1599,

1632, 1650, 1658 bottom, 1706, 1716, 1747, 1760, 1793, 1794 (Pl.3), 1795, 1796, 1798, 1810, 1826, 1829, 1865 (Pl.4), 1873, 1901, 1904, 1958, 1984; Trustees of the British Museum, London: 74, 552, 1658 top, 1959; Trustees of the Britten-Pears Library, Aldeburgh: 266; Alexandr Buchner, Prague: 138; photo Christina Burton, London: 275, 1965 top.

Syndics of Cambridge University Library: 907, 1257 (Ex.6a); Camera Press, London: 910 top; Carnegie Hall, New York: 100; CEDRI, Paris: 6 (Pl.3); Trustees of the Chatsworth Settlement (Devonshire Collection): 1134 (photo Courtauld Institute of Art); J. & W. Chester/Edition Wilhelm Hansen London Ltd: 212 (photo Camilla Jessel), 1104, 1521, 1804 (photo Clive Barda); Christie's South Kensington: 1149, 1937 top; Civici Musei (Archivio Fotografico), Milan (Raccolta della Stampe Achille Bertarelli): 960, 1112; Civico Museo Bibliografico Musicale, Bologna: 494, 958, 1611; Civico Museo Correr, Venice: 738, 957; Conservatoire Royale de Musique (Museum of instruments), Brussels: 140; Conservatorio di Musica Pietro a Majella, Naples: 1627; Madame Françoise de Cossette: 193; photo Fin Costello, London: 1477; Courtauld Institute of Art, London: 1102 top; Covent Garden Archives, London: 230, 243 top, 317, 623, 1843, 1848; Creative Dance Artists Trust: 529 (photo Anthony Crickmay); Culver Pictures Inc., New York: 758, 1576; Curwen Institute, London: 1834 right.

Deutsche Fotothek Dresden: 726, 1651; Deutsche Grammophon Gesellschaft, Hamburg: 918 (Ex.4b); Deutsches Museum, Munich: 415, 416; Deutsche Staatsbibliothek, Berlin: 286, 1515, 1652, 1974; Deutsches Theatermuseum, Munich: 750, 902; photo Douglas Dickins, London: 933, 1864; Dienst Verspreide Rijkscollecties, The Hague: 1088; Dover Publications Inc., New York: 709 (from J. Camner, ed., Great Composers in Historic Photographs, 1981), 1089 (from G. S. Fraenkel, Decorative Music Title Pages, 1968); Lucy Durán, London: 1191 top; Durand S.A./ UMP, Paris: 502 (Ex.2).

Edward Elgar Will Trust: 625; Raymond Elgar, St Leonard's-on-Sea: 571; EMI, London: 921 (Ex.5), 1537, 1538, 1543, 1544; Brian Etheridge Collection, London: 137.

Faber Music Ltd, London (on behalf of J. Curwen & Sons Ltd, © Goodwin & Tabb, 1921): 823 (Ex.18); Fairlight Instruments Pty, Australia: 450; Famous Music Corp. (1961): 824 (Ex.22); Folkways Records, New York: 917 (Ex.4a, original notation by Dr B. R. Deodbar); Fürstlich-Oettingen-Wallerstein'sche Bibliothek, Schloss Harburg: 752.

Galleria e Museo di Palazzo Ducale, Mantua: 1198 (photo Giovetti); John Gay, London: 871, 1203; Gemäldegalerie, Dresden: 1098 (photo Deutsche Fotothek Dresden); Gemeentemuseum, The Hague: 877 (Pl.4), 1097, 1148 (Pl.4), 1533 (Pl.3); Germanisches Nationalmuseum, Nuremberg: 309, 1100, 1422 (Pl.2), 1924; Gesellschaft der Musikfreunde, Vienna: 252, 253; Giraudon, Paris: 1349 (Pl.1); Glasgow University Library: 1504; photo Ian Graham: 265; Graphics International, Washington (collection of Harry Lunn): 364; Greater London Council as Trustees of the Iveagh Bequest, Kenwood: 793; Malcolm Green, London: 34 top left, 1800; William Green, London: 7 bottom, 143 top, 586 (Pl.3), 1274; Gulbenkian Foundation, Lisbon: 404 (Pl.4; from E. V. de Oliveira, Musicais Populares Portugeses), 1799 (Pl.1).

Robert Hale Ltd: 202 (Pl.3); Hamburg State Opera: 114 (photo Fritz Peyer); Hamlyn Group Picture Library, London: 316, 458, 713, 1053, 1056, 1081, 1973; The Rev. J. A. Harper: 1866; Harvard University Press: 479 (Ex.2, from Davison and Apel, Historical Anthology of Music, ii, © 1950, President and Fellows of Harvard College; © 1978, W. Apel and Mrs A. D. Humez), 502 and 503 (Exx.1, 5, from Davison and Apel, Historical Anthology of Music, i, © 1946, 1949, President and Fellows of Harvard College; © 1974, W. Apel and Mrs A. D. Humez); Hawaii Conference United Church of Christ: 1381 (Ex.3); Haydn-Museum, Eisenstadt: 644; Heidelberg University Library: 1180; photo Ernst Heins, Amsterdam: 932 top; Her Majesty the Queen (Crown copyright): 1135 top; David Hiley: 789; Historisches Museum der Stadt Wien:

457, 846, 849, 1719; Victor Hochhauser, London: 1683; Hohner Ltd, London: 5, 7 *top*, 811 (Pl.2); Harold Holt Ltd, London: 794 (Pl.2, photo Sophie Baker); Horniman Museum, London: 1814; T. W. Howarth & Co. Ltd, London: 1279 (Pl.1); Ursula Howells: 397.

Illustrated London News: 636; Imperial War Museum, London: 135 (Pl.1), 169 (Pl.3), 280 (Pl.1); Institute of Jamaica: 1979, 1980; International Institute for Comparative Music Studies and Documentation, Berlin: 909 *bottom* (photo Jacques Cloarac); International Museum of Photography at George Eastman House, Rochester, NY: 1906; Israel Department of Antiquities and Museums, Jerusalem: 995.

Japan Foundation, Tokyo: 979; Jean Jenkins, London: 1172; Max Jones, London: 987, 988, 989.

Karl-Marx-Universität, Musikinstrumenten-Museum, Leipzig: 107, 418, 498 (Pl. 1, *right*), 1422 (Pl.1), 1519; Kaye Photographs, Liverpool: 1476; Keystone Press Agency Ltd, London: 462 (*right*), 810 (Pl.1), 1145; Anthony King, London: 37 *right*; Kobal Collection, London: 1754; Kongelige Bibliotek, Copenhagen: 1243; Koninklijk Muziekconservatorium (Instrumentemuseum), Brussels: 140; Kunsthistorisches Museum, Vienna: 136, 186 (Pl.2a), 1532; Kunstsammlungen Veste Coburg: 166 (Pl.1), 741 *top*, 955; Kurpfälzisches Museum der Stadt Heidelberg: 755.

H. C. Robbins Landon: 1139; Editions Alphonse Leduc, Paris: 1167 (photo Mali); Martin Lessen, Rochester, NY: 280 (Pl.2, photo Smithsonian Institution); Bill Lewington Ltd, London: 185 (Pl.1*b* and *c*), 406 (Pl.1, except extreme right), 688, 1169, 1444, 1617, 1853 (Pl.3), 1868, 1870 (Pl.4, photo Foto Jobst); Library of Congress, Washington: 1782; Longman Inc., New York: 63 (Exx.2a and *b*; © 1979; ed. and Eng. trans. by E. Oster); Nigel Luckhurst, Cambridge: 542; Lyon & Healy, Chicago: 827.

The Master and Fellows, Magdalene College, Cambridge: 1957; Manchester Art Gallery: 1660; Mander & Mitchenson, London: 637, 659, 1309, 1468, 1469, 1472, 1473, 1772; Mansell Collection, London: 84, 116, 593, 725, 737, 806, 1106

(Pl.1), 1125 (Pl.3), 1162, 1170, 1328, 1570, 2010 (Pl.2); Märkisches Museum, Berlin: 1071; The Marquess of Bath: 1135 *bottom*; Mary Evans Picture Library, London: 305, 473 (Pl.7), 561, 591, 677, 719, 756, 1133, 1181, 1333, 1471, 1536 *bottom*, 1646, 1801, 1966; MAS, Barcelona: 940, 1735, 1736, 1737; Massachusetts Institute of Technology: 448 (photo Jim Harrison); Metropolitan Museum of Art, New York: 956 (Pl.4; Harris Brisbane Dick Fund, 1931), 1106 (Pl.2; Fletcher Fund, 1956); Mondadori, Milan: 171; Moravské Museum, Brno: 966; Barbara Morgan, New York: 158; Roderick Conway Morris: 1191; Marion and Tony Morrison, London: 54 *bottom*; Movement Notation Society, Holan, Israel: 535; Mozart-Museum der Internationalen Stiftung Mozarteum, Salzburg: 1212; Musée de l'Homme, Paris: 1378 *top*; Musée Instrumental du Conservatoire, Brussels: 1282 (Pl.3a); Musée des Beaux-Arts, Dijon: 1523; Musées Nationaux, Documentation Photographique, Paris: 694 (Pl.6), 1099 (Pl.5), 1677 (Pl.2), 2010 (Pl.3); Museo Bardini, Florence: 1095 (Pl.2); Museo di Roma: 1386; Museo Teatrale alla Scala, Milan: 238 *bottom*, 420, 565, 961, 1247, 1299, 1305, 1371, 1872; Museum für Geschichte der Stadt Leipzig: 128; Museum für Völkerkunde, Munich: 1048, 1726 *top*; Museum of London: 155 *bottom*; Museum of the American Indian, New York: 56 *left*.

National Army Museum, London: 1178 (Pl.1), 1671 (Pl.1), 1823 (Pl.2); National Gallery, London: 1094 (Pl.1); National Gallery of Art, Washington (Samuel H. Kress Collection): 1677 (Pl.1); National Gallery of Ireland, Dublin: 143 *bottom*; National Library of Wales, Aberystwyth: 520; National museum, Stockholm: 345, 1624; National Museum of Antiquities of Scotland, Edinburgh: 1656; National Museum of Finland, Helsinki: 1011; National Museum of History, Taipei: 367 *bottom*; National Museum of Wales (Welsh Folk Museum), Cardiff: 1961; National Portrait Gallery, London: 105, 804, 1510; New York Public Library at Lincoln Center (Music Division), Aston, Lenox and Tilden Foundations: 1109, 1264; New Zealand House, London: 1238; Novello & Co. Ltd, Borough Green: 208, 482 (Ex.6a; ed. Atkins), 483 (Ex.6b; ed. Elgar/Atkins), 822 (Ex.15), 881 (photo Reg Wilson); Novosti Press Agency, London: 153, 1019, 1225 *bottom*, 1602, 1682, 1692.

Opera Rara, London: 86, 198, 566, 1084 *top*, 1588; Orbis Press Agency, Prague: 1132; Österreichische Nationalbibliothek, Vienna: 209, 210, 360, 472 (Pl.5), 735, 754, 1063, 1065, 1119, 1137, 1301, 1430, 1609 *bottom*, 1794 (Pl.2), 1881, 1972, 1990; Oxford University Press: 480, 506 (Ex.10), 823 (Ex.19), 824 (Ex.21), 906 (Ex.1, from A. L. Basham (ed.), *A Cultural History of India*, 1975), 1336 (from M. Kennedy, *The Concise Oxford Dictionary of Music*, 3rd edn, 1980); 1654, 1715 (Ex.1, from W. T. Marrocco and N. Sandon (ed.), *Medieval Music*, 1977).

Robert Pacey, Oxford: 814; Patrimonial Nacional, Madrid: 1506 (Pl.2), 1729 *bottom*; Keith Pattison, Gateshead: 934, 1028 (Pl.3); Paxman Ltd, London: 875, 876; John Paynter, York: 608; Peabody Museum of Archaeology and Ethnology, Harvard University, Cambridge, Mass.: 54 (Ex.2; from Peabody Museum Papers, vol. 41 no. 3, 1954); Performing Artservices Inc., New York: 296 (photo Alex Kayser); Peter Newark's Western Americana, Bath: 578, 1536 *top*, 1879, 1883 (Pl.6), 1890; Peters Edition, London: 823 (Ex.17), 1436 (© 1961, Henmar Press Inc.); Photo-News, Brussels: 204, 205; Pierpont Morgan Library, New York: 1120, 1164, 1755; Pinacoteca Ambrosiana, Milan: 1850 (Pl.1); Pitt Rivers Museum, Oxford: 406 (Pl. 1, *extreme right*); Gwendolen Plumley, Cambridge: 1105; photo Barry Plummer, Ascot: 1552; Popperfoto, London: 27, 34 *right*, 35, 37 *top* and *bottom left*, 258, 339, 1724, 1725, 1726 *bottom*, 1727; Prague National Opera: 993, 1316; Premier Drum Co., Leicester: 581, 1822 (Pl.1); private collection: 1600.

Radio Times, London: 270; Rarepic, London: 1475, 1476 *top*; RCA, New York: 1789; RCA Records, London: 1931; Real Academia de la Historia, Madrid: 1729 *top*; photo David Redfern, London: 990; Reiss-Museum, Mannheim: 1781; Richard-Wagner-Museum, Bayreuth: 1573, 1954; Ricordi, Milan: 1508, 1908; Rijksmuseum, Amsterdam: 417 (Pl.3), 1775; Robert-Schumann-Haus, Zwickau: 1648; Rosetti Ltd, London: 618; photo Alec Roth: 926, 928; Royal Albert Hall, London: 98 (photo Lauri Tjurin); Royal College of Music, London: 190, 264, 328 (Pl.2), 333 (Pl.3), 397, 419, 423, 460 *top*

right, 546, 575, 745, 780 *top* (from photo Baron de Meyer), 785, 843, 1091 *top left*, 1101, 1233, 1390, 1507, 1592 *top*, 1685, 1745, 1803; Royal Philharmonic Society, London: 847; Royal Tropical Institute, Amsterdam: 908, 912 *top*, 913, 1377; Roy Thomson Hall, Toronto: 304; Russell Collection of Early Keyboard Instruments, Edinburgh University: 839.

Sächsische Landesbibliothek, Dresden: 1809; Sadler's Wells Theatre, London: 163 (photo Martha Swope); St Bride Institute, London: 1495 (Pl.8), 1497; St David's Hall, Cardiff: 1962; Salzburger Museum Carolino Augusteum: 1211; G. Schirmer Ltd, London: 170 *bottom*, 319; School of Oriental and African Studies, London: 30–33 (Ex.2), 912 *bottom* (photo A. A. Bake); Schools Council, London (photo Robert Fromer): 610; Schott & Co. Ltd, London: 853 (photo Misha Donat), 1150, 1340, 1826, 1988; photo Harald Schultz: 55 *top*; Schweizerisches Theatersammlung, Berne: 1308 *top*; Scope, Paris: 886 *top*; Scottish National Portrait Gallery, Edinburgh: 1659; Edward G. Seidensticker, Tokyo: 968 (from Murasaki Shikibu, ed.: *Tale of Genji*, trans. E. G. Seidensticker, 1976); Sibeliusmuseum, Turku: 1684; Smetana Museum, Prague: 177; Smithsonian Institution, Washington: 56 *right*, 1425 (Pl.3); Society for Cultural Relations with the USSR, London: 142 *left*, 335, 336, 337, 338, 340, 766, 767, 1084 *bottom*; Society for Ethnomusicology Inc., Ann Arbor: 36, 1378 (Ex.1); Sotheby Parke Burnet, London: 331, 408 (Pl.2, *left*), 497, 585 (Pl.2), 811 (Pl.3), 840, 841, 1280 (Pl.2*a*, *b*, *c*), 1531, 1866, 1926; Sotheby Publications, London: 910 *bottom* and 916 (from F. S. Aijazuddin: *Pahari Paintings and Sikh Portraits in the Lahore Museum*); Sovfoto, New York: 1225; Staatliche Graphische Sammlung, Munich: 726 (photo Deutsche Fotothek Dresden); Staatliche Kunstsammlungen, Kupferstichkabinett, Dresden: 1331, 1651; Staatliche Museen, Kupferstichkabinett, Berlin: 2006; Staatliche Museen Preussischer Kulturbesitz, Kupferstichkabinett, Berlin: 1021 (photo Jörg P. Anders); Staatliches Institut für Musikforschung Preussischer Kulturbesitz, Musik-Instrumenten-Sammlung, Berlin: 519; Staatsarchiv, Hamburg: 1811; Staatsbibliothek Preussischer Kulturbesitz, Berlin: 748; Staats- und Universitätsbibliothek, Hamburg:

1631; Städelsches Kunstinstitut, Frankfurt: 690 (Pl.3); Stadtbildstelle, Augsburg: 749; Städtische Galerie, Munich: 1645; Städtisches Museum, Braunschweig: 1369; Steinway, New York: 1432 (Pl.6); Stiftsbibliothek, St Gall: 1449 (Pl.1); Streetly Electronics Ltd, Sutton Coldfield: 622; Studio Camera, Sion: 1349 (Pl.2); Studio Klein, Strasbourg: 1405; Supraphon, Prague: 232; Josef Svoboda, Prague: 1318; Swiss National Tourist Office, Zurich: 48.

Tameside Local Studies Library, Stalybridge: 257; Tate Gallery, London: 197; photo Eric Taylor, Durham: 925, 932 *bottom*; Teatermuseet, Copenhagen: 151; Teatro alla Scala, Milan: 1319; Theater-Museum, Munich: 233; John M. Thomson: 1489; Tiroler Landesmuseum Ferdinandeum, Innsbruck: 1197.

Uffizi Gallery, Gabinetto Disegni e Stampe, Florence: 877 (Pl.3); Universal Edition (Alfred A. Kalmus Ltd), London: 505 (Ex.9), 1266, 1669, 1673; Universal Edition (London) Ltd: 178 *top*, 179, 211, 222 (photo J. F. Munro), 1009, 1131, 1176, 1406, 1437 *top*, 1564, 1597, 1750, 1791, 1994; Universal Edition, Vienna: 210, 1635, 1971; Universitetsbiblioteket, Lund: 287; University of Auckland, Department of Anthropology: 1239 and 1240 (photo Creative Photography, Auckland); University of Michigan, Ann Arbor (William L. Clements Library): 1880; University of Oxford, Faculty of Music: 281, 284, 493, 516, 761, 1052, 1080, 1403.

VAAP, Moscow: 166 (Pl.2); Ursula Vaughan Williams: 1901; Victoria and Albert Museum, London (Crown Copyright): 181, 330, 410, 635, 829, 835, 911, 1432, Theatre Museum: 147, 149, 150, 157, 634, 1091 *right*, 1339 and 1416 (photo Houston Rogers); Victoria Art Gallery, Bath: 452; Vincent Bach International Division of the Selmer Co., Elkhart: 1853 (Pls. 1, 2), 1861 (Pl.1a and b, photo Rich LaMar & Associates), 1862 (Pl.1c, photo Knepp Studio); H. Roger Viollet, Paris: 113, 154, 243 *bottom*, 342, 525, 543, 664, 665, 722, 770, 780 *bottom*, 784, 799, 854, 857, 872, 884, 1039, 1092, 1155, 1178 (Pl.2), 1302, 1401, 1481, 1502, 1528, 1592 *bottom*, 1614, 1741, 1759, 1818, 1955, 1976; Vision International, London: 123.

Alan Walker, Hamilton, Ontario: 61; Wallace Collection, London; 174; Wallraf-Richartz-Museum, Cologne: 830 (Pl.5), 838; Warner Bros. Inc., Los Angeles (© 1954, renewed): 534; Whitechapel Bell Foundry, London: 200 (Pl.1); William Ransom Hogan Jazz Archive, Tulane University Library, New Orleans: 986; photo Reg Wilson, London: 881, 1849; Michael and Veronica Wright, Newton Abbot: 802.

Zentralbibliothek, Zurich: 1777; Peter Zinovieff, Swaffham Prior: 449; Ziolo, Paris: 43 *right*, 155 *top*, 398, 521, 657, 741 *bottom*, 1003, 1141, 1384, 1385, 1953; Zurich Opera House: 1204 (photo Susann Schimert-Ramme).

NOTES

NOTES

NOTES

NOTES

NOTES

NOTES